A
Dictionary of Christ
and the Gospels

A
Dictionary of Christ
and the Gospels

EDITED BY

JAMES HASTINGS, D.D.

WITH THE ASSISTANCE OF

JOHN A. SELBIE, D.D.

AND (IN THE READING OF THE PROOFS) OF

JOHN C. LAMBERT, D.D.

VOLUME II
LABOUR—ZION
WITH
APPENDIX AND .INDEXES

NEW YORK: CHARLES SCRIBNER'S SONS
EDINBURGH: T. & T. CLARK
1917

TO

SAMUEL ROLLES DRIVER
WILLIAM SANDAY
HENRY BARCLAY SWETE

PREFACE

In issuing the second volume of the DICTIONARY OF CHRIST AND THE GOSPELS, the Editor desires, first of all, to thank his colleagues and contributors for the interest that they have taken in the work. He desires, further, to express his gratitude for the reception which the first volume has met with. All concerned in it are ready to confess that the task of producing a Dictionary which could be spoken of as really worthy of its subject has been beyond them. And they have felt this only the more as the work has proceeded. But reviewers have generously recognized the fact that no trouble has been spared to make the Dictionary as worthy as possible; and the public everywhere, but especially preachers of the Gospel, have responded. It is hoped that the second volume will be found to be not inferior to the first.

The Appendix belongs to the original idea. It was felt from the beginning that the articles which it contains should be placed in a group, apart from the general alphabetical order.

LIST OF ABBREVIATIONS

I. General

Alex. = Alexandrian.
Apoc. = Apocalypse, Apocalyptic.
Apocr. = Apocrypha, Apocryphal.
Aq. = Aquila.
Arab. = Arabic.
Aram. = Aramaic.
Assyr. = Assyrian.
Bab. = Babylonian.
c. = *circa*, about.
Can. = Canaanite.
cf. = compare.
ct. = contrast.
D = Deuteronomist.
E = Elohist.
edd. = editions or editors.
Egyp. = Egyptian.
Eng. = English.
Eth. = Ethiopic.
f. = and following verse or page : as Ac $10^{34f.}$.
ff. = and following verses or pages : as Mt $11^{28ff.}$.
Gr. = Greek.
H = Law of Holiness.
Heb. = Hebrew.
Hel. = Hellenistic.
Hex. = Hexateuch.
Isr. = Israelite.
J = Jahwist.
J" = Jehovah.
Jerus. = Jerusalem.
Jos. = Josephus.

LXX = Septuagint.
MSS = Manuscripts.
MT = Massoretic Text.
n. = note.
NT = New Testament.
Onḳ. = Onḳelos.
OT = Old Testament.
P = Priestly Narrative.
Pal. = Palestine, Palestinian.
Pent. = Pentateuch.
Pers. = Persian.
Phil. = Philistine.
Phœn. = Phœnician.
Pr. Bk. = Prayer Book.
R = Redactor.
Rom. = Roman.
Sam. = Samaritan.
Sem. = Semitic.
Sept. = Septuagint.
Sin. = Sinaitic.
Symm. = Symmachus.
Syr. = Syriac.
Talm. = Talmud.
Targ. = Targum.
Theod. = Theodotion.
TR = Textus Receptus.
tr. = translate or translation.
VSS = Versions.
Vulg. = Vulgate.
WH = Westcott and Hort's text.

II. Books of the Bible

Old Testament.

Gn = Genesis.
Ex = Exodus.
Lv = Leviticus.
Nu = Numbers.
Dt = Deuteronomy.
Jos = Joshua.
Jg = Judges.
Ru = Ruth.
1 S, 2 S = 1 and 2 Samuel.
1 K, 2 K = 1 and 2 Kings.
1 Ch, 2 Ch = 1 and 2 Chronicles.
Ezr = Ezra.
Neh = Nehemiah.
Est = Esther.
Job.
Ps = Psalms.
Pr = Proverbs.
Ec = Ecclesiastes.

Ca = Canticles.
Is = Isaiah.
Jer = Jeremiah.
La = Lamentations.
Ezk = Ezekiel.
Dn = Daniel.
Hos = Hosea.
Jl = Joel.
Am = Amos.
Ob = Obadiah.
Jon = Jonah.
Mic = Micah.
Nah = Nahum.
Hab = Habakkuk.
Zeph = Zephaniah.
Hag = Haggai.
Zec = Zechariah.
Mal = Malachi.

Apocrypha.

1 Es, 2 Es = 1 and 2 Esdras.
To = Tobit.
Jth = Judith.

Ad. Est = Additions to Esther.
Wis = Wisdom.
Sir = Sirach or Ecclesiasticus.
Bar = Baruch.
Three = Song of the Three Children.

Sus = Susanna.
Bel = Bel and the Dragon.
Pr. Man = Prayer of Manasses.
1 Mac, 2 Mac = 1 and 2 Maccabees.

New Testament.

Mt = Matthew.
Mk = Mark.
Lk = Luke.
Jn = John.
Ac = Acts.
Ro = Romans.
1 Co, 2 Co = 1 and 2 Corinthians.
Gal = Galatians.
Eph = Ephesians.
Ph = Philippians.
Col = Colossians.

1 Th, 2 Th = 1 and 2 Thessalonians.
1 Ti, 2 Ti = 1 and 2 Timothy.
Tit = Titus.
Philem = Philemon.
He = Hebrews.
Ja = James.
1 P, 2 P = 1 and 2 Peter.
1 Jn, 2 Jn, 3 Jn = 1, 2, and 3 John.
Jude.
Rev = Revelation.

III. English Versions

Wyc. = Wyclif's Bible (NT *c.* 1380, OT *c.* 1382, Purvey's Revision *c.* 1388).
Tind. = Tindale's NT 1526 and 1534, Pent. 1530.
Cov. = Coverdale's Bible 1535.
Matt. or Rog. = Matthew's (*i.e.* prob. Rogers') Bible 1537.
Cran. or Great = Cranmer's 'Great' Bible 1539.
Tav. = Taverner's Bible 1539.
Gen. = Geneva NT 1557, Bible 1560.

Bish. = Bishops' Bible 1568.
Tom. = Tomson's NT 1576.
Rhem. = Rhemish NT 1582.
Dou. = Douay OT 1609.
AV = Authorized Version 1611.
AVm = Authorized Version margin.
RV = Revised Version NT 1881, OT 1885.
RVm = Revised Version margin.
EV = Auth. and Rev. Versions.

IV. For the Literature

AHT = Ancient Hebrew Tradition.
AJSL = American Journal of Sem. Lang. and Literature.
AJTh = American Journal of Theology.
AT = Altes Testament.
BL = Bampton Lecture.
BM = British Museum.
BRP = Biblical Researches in Palestine.
CIG = Corpus Inscriptionum Græcarum.
CIL = Corpus Inscriptionum Latinarum.
CIS = Corpus Inscriptionum Semiticarum.
COT = Cuneiform Inscriptions and the OT.
DB = Dictionary of the Bible.
DCA = Dictionary of Christian Antiquities.
EBi = Encyclopædia Biblica.
EBr = Encyclopædia Britannica.
EGT = Expositor's Greek Testament.
EHH = Early History of the Hebrews.
ERE = Encyclopædia of Religion and Ethics.
ExpT = Expository Times.
GAP = Geographie des alten Palästina.
GGA = Göttingische Gelehrte Anzeigen.
GGN = Nachrichten der königl. Gesellschaft der Wissenschaften zu Göttingen.
GJV = Geschichte des Jüdischen Volkes.
GVI = Geschichte des Volkes Israel.
HBA = Handwörterbuch des biblischen Altertums.
HCM = Higher Criticism and the Monuments.
HE = Historia Ecclesiastica.
HGHL = Historical Geog. of Holy Land.
HI = History of Israel.
HJP = History of the Jewish People.
HPM = History, Prophecy, and the Monuments.
HPN = Hebrew Proper Names.
HWB = Handwörterbuch.
ICC = International Critical Commentary.
IJG = Israelitische und Jüdische Geschichte.
JBL = Journal of Biblical Literature.
JDTh = Jahrbücher für deutsche Theologie.
JE = Jewish Encyclopedia.
JQR = Jewish Quarterly Review.
JRAS = Journal of the Royal Asiatic Society.
JSL = Journal of Sacred Literature.
JThSt = Journal of Theological Studies.
KAT = Die Keilinschriften und das Alte Test.
KGF = Keilinschriften u. Geschichtsforschung.
KIB = Keilinschriftliche Bibliothek.
LB = The Land and the Book.
LCBl = Literarisches Centralblatt.

LOT = Introd. to the Literature of the Old Test.
LT = Life and Times of Jesus the Messiah [Edersheim].
MNDPV = Mittheilungen u. Nachrichten d. deutschen Pal.-Vereins.
NHWB = Neuhebräisches Wörterbuch.
NKZ = Neue kirchliche Zeitschrift.
NTZG = Neutestamentliche Zeitgeschichte.
ON = Otium Norvicense.
OP = Origin of the Psalter.
OTJC = The Old Test. in the Jewish Church.
PB = Polychrome Bible.
PEF = Palestine Exploration Fund.
PEFSt = Quarterly Statement of the same.
PSBA = Proceedings of Soc. of Bibl. Archæology.
PRE = Real-Encyklopädie für protest. Theologie und Kirche.
QPB = Queen's Printers' Bible.
RB = Revue Biblique.
RE = Realencyklopädie.
REJ = Revue des Études Juives.
RP = Records of the Past.
RS = Religion of the Semites.
RWB = Realwörterbuch.
SBE = Sacred Books of the East.
SBOT = Sacred Books of Old Test.
SK or *TSK* = Theol. Studien und Kritiken.
SP = Sinai and Palestine.
SWP = Memoirs of the Survey of W. Palestine.
ThL or *ThLZ* = Theol. Literaturzeitung.
ThT = Theol. Tijdschrift.
TS = Texts and Studies.
TSBA = Transactions of Soc. of Bibl. Archæology.
TU = Texte und Untersuchungen.
WAI = Western Asiatic Inscriptions.
WZKM = Wiener Zeitschrift für Kunde des Morgenlandes.
ZA = Zeitschrift für Assyriologie.
ZAW or *ZATW* = Zeitschrift für die Alttest. Wissenschaft.
ZDMG = Zeitschrift der Deutschen Morgenländischen Gesellschaft.
ZDPV = Zeitschrift des Deutschen Palästina-Vereins.
ZKSF = Zeitschrift für Keilschriftforschung.
ZKW or *ZKWL* = Zeitschrift für kirchliche Wissenschaft und kirchl. Leben.
ZNTW = Zeitschrift für die Neutest. Wissenschaft.
ZThK = Zeitschrift f. Theologie u. Kirche.

A small superior number designates the particular edition of the work referred to: as *KAT*², *LOT*⁶.

AUTHORS OF ARTICLES IN VOL. II

Rev. ROBERT M. ADAMSON, M.A., Ardrossan.

Rev. WALTER FREDERICK ADENEY, D.D., Professor of Theology and Principal of the Lancashire College, Manchester.

Rev. GROSS ALEXANDER, S.T.D., late Professor of New Testament Greek and Exegesis in Vanderbilt University, Nashville.

Rev. WILLOUGHBY C. ALLEN, M.A., Chaplain, Fellow, and Lecturer in Theology and Hebrew, Exeter College, Oxford.

Rev. FREDERICK LINCOLN ANDERSON, M.A., D.D., Professor of New Testament Interpretation, Newton Theological Institution, Mass.

Rev. BENJAMIN WISNER BACON, D.D., LL.D., Lit.D., Professor of New Testament Criticism and Exegesis in Yale University, New Haven.

Rev. P. MORDAUNT BARNARD, B.D., late Rector of Headley, Epsom.

Rev. J. VERNON BARTLET, M.A., D.D., Professor of Church History in Mansfield College, Oxford.

Late Rev. FRANCIS R. BEATTIE, Ph.D., D.D., LL.D., Professor of Apologetics and Systematic Theology in the Presbyterian Theological Seminary of Kentucky.

Very Rev. JOHN HENRY BERNARD, D.D., D.C.L., Dean of St. Patrick's and Archbishop King's Professor of Divinity in the University of Dublin.

Rev. HARRY BISSEKER, M.A., The Leysian Mission, London.

Rev. ANDREW BOGLE, M.A., Leith.

Rev. ALBERT BONUS, M.A., Alphington, Exeter.

Rev. GEORGE H. BOX, M.A., late Hebrew Master, Merchant Taylors' School, London, Rector of Linton, Ross.

Rev. E. P. BOYS-SMITH, M.A., Vicar of Hordle, Brockenhurst.

Rev. J. B. BRISTOW, B.D., Rector of Clondalkin, Co. Dublin.

Rev. MORISON BRYCE, Baldernock, Milngavie.

Rev. A. E. BURN, D.D., Rector of Handsworth, Birmingham, and Prebendary of Lichfield.

Rev. ADAM G. CAMPBELL, M.A., Afton, New Cumnock.

Rev. R. J. CAMPBELL, M.A., City Temple, London.

Rev. WILLIAM M. CHRISTIE, Aleppo.

Rev. DUGALD CLARK, B.D., Glassary, Lochgilphead.

Rev. JOHN S. CLEMENS, B.A., B.D., Principal of Ranmoor College, Sheffield.

Rev. CAMDEN M. COBERN, Ph.D., D.D., Professor of the English Bible and the Philosophy of Religion in Allegheny College, Meadville, Pa.

Rev. ARTHUR W. COOKE, M.A., Newcastle-on-Tyne.

Rev. JAMES COOPER, D.D., Professor of Ecclesiastical History in the University of Glasgow.

Rev. HENRY COWAN, D.D., Professor of Church History in the University of Aberdeen.

Rev. HUGH H. CURRIE, B.D., Keig, Aberdeenshire.

Rev. EDGAR DAPLYN, Child's Hill, London.

Right Rev. CHARLES FREDERICK D'ARCY, D.D., Bishop of Clogher.

Rev. EDWARD CHARLES DARGAN, D.D., LL.D., formerly Professor of Homiletics and Ecclesiology in the Southern Baptist Theological Seminary, Louisville, Ky.

Rev. PERCY DEARMER, M.A., Vicar of St. Mary's the Virgin, Primrose Hill, London.

Rev. FRANCIS BRIGHAM DENIO, D.D., Professor of Old Testament Languages and Literature in Bangor Theological Seminary, Maine.

Rev. JAMES DENNEY, D.D., Professor of New Testament Language, Literature, and Theology in the United Free Church College, Glasgow.

Rev. MARCUS DODS, D.D., Principal and Professor of Exegetical Theology in the New College, Edinburgh.

Rev. JAMES DONALD, D.D., Keithhall, Inverurie.

Rev. HENRY E. DOSKER, D.D., LL.D., Professor of Ecclesiastical History in the Presbyterian Theological Seminary of Kentucky.

Rev. F. HOMES DUDDEN, D.D., Fellow of Lincoln College, Oxford.

Rev. ALEXANDER A. DUNCAN, B.D., Auchterless, Aberdeenshire.

Rev. HUGH DUNCAN, B.D., Garturk, Coatbridge.

Rev. W. H. DUNDAS, B.D., Rector of Magheragall, Lisburn.

Rev. WILLIAM HENRY DYSON, Edgerton, Huddersfield.

Rev. GEORGE BOARDMAN EAGER, D.D., LL.D., Professor of Biblical Introduction and Pastoral Theology in the Southern Baptist Theological Seminary, Louisville, Ky.

Right Rev. ROWLAND ELLIS, D.D., Bishop of Aberdeen and Orkney.

Rev. CYRIL W. EMMET, M.A., Vicar of West Hendred, Berks.

Rev. W. EWING, M.A., Edinburgh.

Rev. R. A. FALCONER, D.Litt., D.D., President of the University of Toronto, Canada

Rev. J. H. FARMER, B.A., LL.D., Dean in Theology and Professor of New Testament and Patristic Greek in M'Master University, Toronto.

Rev. C. L. FELTOE, D.D., Rector of Duxford, Cambridge.

Rev. ADAM FYFE FINDLAY, M.A., Arbroath.

Rev. J. DICK FLEMING, B.D., Professor of Systematic Theology and Ethics in Manitoba College, Winnipeg.

Rev. FRANK HUGH FOSTER, Ph.D., D.D., Professor of History in Olivet College, Michigan.

Rev. WILLIAM BARRETT FRANKLAND, M.A., late Fellow of Clare College, Cambridge, and Assistant-Chaplain at Giggleswick School.

Rev. ROBERT SLEIGHTHOLME FRANKS, M.A., B.Litt., Birmingham.

Rev. NORMAN FRASER, B.D., Edinburgh.

Rev. HENRY WILLIAM FULFORD, M.A., Fellow of Clare College, Cambridge.

Rev. ALFRED ERNEST GARVIE, D.D., Principal of New College and Professor of Ethics, Theism, and Comparative Religion in New and Hackney Colleges, London.

Rev. OWEN H. GATES, Ph.D., Librarian and Instructor in Hebrew in Andover Theological Seminary, Mass.

Rev. LUCIEN GAUTIER, D.D., Ph.D., Honorary Professor of Old Testament Exegesis and History, Geneva.

Rev. ALFRED S. GEDEN, M.A., Professor of Biblical Literature and Exegesis in Richmond College, Surrey.

Rev. RICHARD GLAISTER, B.D., Kirkcudbright.

Rev. CALVIN GOODSPEED, D.D., LL.D., Professor of Systematic Theology in Baylor University, Waco, Texas.

Rev. GEORGE PEARCE GOULD, M.A., Principal of Regent's Park College, London.

Rev. THOMAS GREGORY, M.A., Kilmalcolm.

Rev. Canon CHARLES T. P. GRIERSON, B.D., Rector of Seapatrick, Banbridge, Co. Down.

Rev. G. H. GWILLIAM, B.D., Rector of Remenham, Henley-on-Thames.

Rev. JAMES O. HANNAY, M.A., Rector of Aughaval, Westport, Co. Mayo.

Rev. J. M. HARDEN, B.D., Headmaster, Kilkenny College.

Rev. CHARLES HARRIS, D.D., Vicar of Claverley, Wolverhampton, late Lecturer in Theology in St. David's College, Lampeter.

Rev. D. A. HAYES, Ph.D., S.T.D., LL.D., Professor of New Testament Exegesis in Garrett Biblical Institute, Evanston, Ill.

Rev. W. J. HENDERSON, B.A., Principal of the Baptist College, Bristol.

Rev. R. TRAVERS HERFORD, B.A., Stand, Whitefield, Manchester.

Rev. JOHN HERKLESS, D.D., Professor of Church History in the University of St. Andrews.

Rev. W. W. HOLDSWORTH, M.A., Professor of New Testament Language and Literature in Handsworth College, Birmingham.

Rev. A. MITCHELL HUNTER, M.A., Cardross, Dumbartonshire.

Rev. H. L. JACKSON, M.A., Vicar of St. Mary's, Huntingdon.

Rev. ARTHUR JENKINSON, Innellan, Greenock.

A. J. JENKINSON, M.A., Fellow of Brasenose College, Oxford.

Rev. M. P. JOHNSTONE, B.D., Fraserburgh.

Rev. E. GRIFFITH-JONES, B.A., Principal and Professor of Theology in the Yorkshire United College, Bradford.

FRIEDRICH WILHELM FERDINAND KATTENBUSCH, D.D., Ph.D., Ord. Professor of Dogmatics in the University of Halle.

Rev. JOHN KELMAN, D.D., Edinburgh.

Rev. W. S. KERR, B.D., Vicar of Ballywalter, Co. Down.

Rev. DAVID M. W. LAIRD, M.A., Edinburgh.

Rev. J. C. LAMBERT, D.D., Fenwick, Kilmarnock.

Rev. HARRINGTON C. LEES, M.A., St. John's Vicarage, Kenilworth.

Rev. ROBERT LEGGAT, Berwick-on-Tweed.

Rev. JOHN ROBERT LEGGE, M.A., Buckhurst Hill, Essex.

Rev. THOMAS M. LINDSAY, D.D., Principal and Professor of Church History in the United Free Church College, Glasgow.

Rev. WILLIAM F. LOFTHOUSE, M.A., Professor of Old Testament Languages and Literature in the Theological College, Handsworth, Birmingham.

Rev. CHARLES SCOTT MACALPINE, B.D., Manchester.

Rev. A. B. MACAULAY, M.A., Dundee.

Rev. C. A. M'DONALD, B.D., Arrochar, Dumbartonshire.

Rev. JOHN EDGAR M'FADYEN, M.A. (Glas.), B.A. (Oxon.), Professor of Old Testament Literature and Exegesis in Knox College, Toronto.

Rev. GEORGE M'HARDY, D.D., Kirkcaldy.

Rev. GEORGE M. MACKIE, D.D., Chaplain to the Church of Scotland at Beyrout, Syria.

Rev. DUNCAN A. MACKINNON, M.A., Marykirk, Kincardineshire.

Rev. ROBERT MACKINTOSH, D.D., Professor of Christian Ethics, Apologetics, and Sociology in the Lancashire Independent College, Manchester.

Right Rev. ARTHUR J. MACLEAN, D.D., Bishop of Moray.

Rev. A. H. M'NEILE, B.D., Fellow and Dean of Sidney Sussex College, Cambridge.

Rev. JAMES EDMOND M'OUAT, B.D., Logiealmond, Perthshire.

Rev. ROBERT MACPHERSON, D.D., Elgin.

Rev. JOSEPH T. L. MAGGS, D.D., Leeds.

Rev. DAVID SAMUEL MARGOLIOUTH, M.A., D.Litt., Laudian Professor of Arabic in the University of Oxford.

Rev. JOHN TURNER MARSHALL, D.D., Principal of the Baptist College, Manchester.

Rev. NEWTON HERBERT MARSHALL, M.A., Ph.D., Hampstead, London.

Rev. A. STUART MARTIN, B.D., Scone, Perth.

Rev. G. CURRIE MARTIN, B.D., Professor of New Testament Theology and Patristics in the United College, Bradford.

E. W. GURNEY MASTERMAN, M.D., F.R.C.S., F.R.G.S., D.P.H., Jerusalem, Syria.

Rev. SHAILER MATHEWS, D.D., Professor of Historical and Comparative Theology and Dean of the Divinity School in the Unversity of Chicago.

Rev. ANDREW MILLER, M.A., Glasgow.

Rev. W. J. S. MILLER, B.D., Houndwood, Reston.

Rev. GEORGE MILLIGAN, D.D., Caputh, Murthly.

Rev. JOSEPH MITCHELL, B.D., Mauchline.

Rev. JAMES MOFFATT, D.D., Broughty Ferry.

Rev. W. S. MONTGOMERY, B.D., Abbeyleix, Queen's County.

Rev. R. W. MOSS, D.D., Professor of Systematic Theology in the Didsbury College, Manchester.

Rev. WARREN JOSEPH MOULTON, M.A., B.D., Ph.D., Associate Professor of New Testament Language and Literature in Bangor Theological Seminary.

Rev. T. ALLEN MOXON, MA., Vicar of Alfreton, Derbyshire.

Rev. JOHN MUIR, B.D., Kirkcowan, Wigtownshire.

Rev. GEORGE MURRAY, B.D., Sauchie, Alloa.

Rev. JAMES ROSS MURRAY, M.A., Manchester.

Rev. JAMES MURSELL, M.A., Adelaide, South Australia.

EBERHARD NESTLE, Ph.D., D.D., Professor at Maulbronn.

Rev. M. R. NEWBOLT, B.A., Vicar of Iffley, Oxford.

Rev. ALBERT HENRY NEWMAN, D.D., LL.D., Professor of Church History in Baylor University, Waco, Texas.

Rev. THOMAS NICOL, D.D., Professor of Biblical Criticism in the University of Aberdeen.

Rev. W. O. E. OESTERLEY, B.D., Organizing Secretary of the Parochial Missions to the Jews.

Rev. JAMES ORR, D.D., Professor of Systematic Theology and Apologetics in the United Free Church College, Glasgow.

Rev. JAMES PATRICK, B.D., B.Sc., Burntisland.

Rev. WILLIAM PATRICK, D.D., Principal of Manitoba College, Winnipeg.

ARTHUR S. PEAKE, D.D., Professor of Biblical Exegesis and Dean of the Faculty of Theology, Victoria University, Manchester.

Rev. JOHN ROBERT VAN PELT, Ph.D., Methodist Episcopal Church, Lewisburg, Pa.

Rev. SAMUEL PLANTZ, Ph.D., D.D., LL.D., President of Lawrence University, Appleton, Wis.

Rev. ALFRED PLUMMER, D.D., late Master of University College, Durham.

Rev. EDWARD B. POLLARD, D.D., Professor in Crozer Theological Seminary, Chester, Pa.

Rev. WILLIAM LOUIS POTEAT, M.A., LL.D., President of Wake Forest College, N.C.

Rev. CYRIL HENRY PRICHARD, M.A., Rector of Wiston, Steyning, Sussex.

Rev. LEIGHTON PULLAN, M.A., Fellow and Lecturer of St. John Baptist College, Oxford.

Rev. FREDERICK J. RAE, M.A., Aberdeen.

Rev. F. S. RANKEN, M.A., Rector of South Walsham, Norwich.

Rev. W. H. RANKINE, B.D., Glasgow.

Rev. JOHN REID, M.A., Inverness.

FRANK RICHARDS, M.A., Kingswood School, Bath.

Rev. CHARLES WESLEY RISHELL, Ph.D., Professor of Historical Theology and Assistant Dean in Boston University, Mass.

Rev. JOHN EDWARD ROBERTS, B.D., Manchester.

Rev. FRANK EDWARD ROBINSON, B.A., Professor of Hebrew and Church History in the Baptist College, Bristol.

Rev. GEORGE LIVINGSTONE ROBINSON, Ph.D., D.D., Professor of Old Testament Literature and Exegesis in the M'Cormick Theological Seminary, Chicago.

Rev. ARTHUR E. ROSS, B.D., Rector of Portrush, Co. Antrim.

Rev. ALFRED NORMAN ROWLAND, M.A., London.

Rev. JOHN RICHARD SAMPEY, D.D., LL.D., Professor of Interpretation of the Old Testament in the Southern Baptist Theological Seminary, Louisville, Ky.

Rev. WILLIAM SANDAY, D.D., LL.D., Litt.D., Lady Margaret Professor of Divinity, and Canon of Christ Church, Oxford, Chaplain in Ordinary to H.M. the King.

Rev. CHARLES ANDERSON SCOTT, M.A., Professor of the Language, Literature, and Theology of the New Testament at Westminster College, Cambridge.

Rev. ERNEST F. SCOTT, B.A., Prestwick.

Rev. HUGH M'DONALD SCOTT, D.D., Professor of Ecclesiastical History in the Theological Seminary, Chicago.

Rev. ROBERT SCOTT, D.D., Professor in Wilson College, Bombay.

Rev. EDWARD SELL, D.D., M.R.A.S., Fellow of the University of Madras and Hon. Canon of St. George's Cathedral, Madras.

Rev. HENRY CLAY SHELDON, D.D., Professor of Systematic Theology in Boston University.

Rev. EDWARD SHILLITO, M.A., London.

Rev. S. J. RAMSAY SIBBALD, B.D., Crathie, Ballater.

Rev. J. G. SIMPSON, M.A., Principal of the Clergy School, Leeds.

Rev. W. J. SPARROW SIMPSON, M.A., Chaplain, St. Mary's Hospital, Ilford.

Rev. JOHN W. SLATER, B.D., Scone, Perth.

Rev. DAVID SMITH, M.A., Blairgowrie.

Rev. HAROLD SMITH, M.A., Rector of Grimley, Worcester.

Rev. J. CROMARTY SMITH, B.D., Coatdyke, Coatbridge.

W. TAYLOR SMITH, B.A., Sevenoaks, Kent.

Late Rev. J. SOUTAR, M.A., Tiberias, Palestine.

ALEXANDER SOUTER, M.A., D.Litt., Yates Professor of New Testament Greek and Exegesis in Mansfield College, Oxford.

Rev. JAMES STALKER, D.D., Professor of Church History and Christian Ethics in the United Free Church College, Aberdeen.

Rev. WILBUR FLETCHER STEELE, M.A., S.T.D., Professor in the Department of Biblical Science of Denver University, Colorado.

Rev. ROBERT STEVENSON, B.D., Gargunnock.

Rev. G. WAUCHOPE STEWART, B.D., Fyvie, Aberdeenshire.

Rev. ROBERT LAIRD STEWART, D.D., Professor of Biblical Archæology in the Theological Seminary of Lincoln University, Pa.

Rev. DARWELL STONE, M.A., Pusey Librarian, Oxford.

Rev. G. GORDON STOTT, D.D., Musselburgh.

Very Rev. THOMAS B. STRONG, D.D., Dean of Christ Church, Oxford.

Rev. A. POLLOK SYM, B.D., Lilliesleaf.

Rev. JOHN G. TASKER, D.D., Professor of Biblical Literature and Exegesis in Handsworth College, Birmingham.

Rev. R. BRUCE TAYLOR, M.A., London.

Rev. W. H. GRIFFITH THOMAS, D.D., Principal of Wycliffe Hall, Oxford.

Rev. CHARLES H. THOMSON, M.A., Constantinople.

Rev. WILLIAM D. THOMSON, M.A., Edinburgh.

Rev. EDWARD HARPER TITCHMARSH, M.A., Sheffield.

Rev. GEERHARDUS VOS, Ph.D., D.D., Professor of Biblical Theology in the Theological Seminary, Princeton, N.J.

Rev. Canon G. H. S. WALPOLE, D.D., Rector of Lambeth.

Rev. BENJAMIN BRECKINRIDGE WARFIELD, D.D., LL.D., Charles Hodge Professor of Didactic and Polemic Theology in the Theological Seminary of the Presbyterian Church at Princeton, N.J.

Rev. GEORGE C. WATT, B.D., Edinkillie.

Rev. THOMAS H. WEIR, B.D., M.R.A.S., Lecturer in Hebrew and Arabic in the University of Glasgow.

JOHANNES WEISS, D.D., Professor of Theology in the University of Marburg.

Rev. E. WHEELER, M.A., Canning Town, London.

Rev. B. WHITEFOORD, D.D., Prebendary of Salisbury Cathedral and Principal of the Theological College, Salisbury.

Rev. OWEN C. WHITEHOUSE, D.D., Senior Tutor in Cheshunt College, Cambridge.

Rev. A. R. WHITHAM, M.A., Principal of the Culham Training College, Abingdon.

Rev. J. R. WILLIS, B.D., Rector of Preban and Moyne, Rathdrum, Co. Wicklow.

Rev. CHARLES TRAVERS WOOD, M.A., Fellow and Lecturer in Hebrew in Queens' College, Cambridge.

Rev. H. J. WOTHERSPOON, M.A., Edinburgh.

Rev. ARTHUR WRIGHT, D.D., Fellow, Tutor, and Vice-President of Queens' College, Cambridge.

Rev T. H. WRIGHT, Edinburgh.

Rev D. G YOUNG, B.D., Moneydie, Perth.

Rev. J YOUNG, B.D., Paisley.

Rev. ANDREW C. ZENOS, D.D., Professor of Ecclesiastical History in the M'Cormick Theological Seminary, Chicago.

Dictionary of Christ

and the Gospels

VOL. II.

DICTIONARY OF CHRIST
AND THE GOSPELS

———◆———

L

LABOUR.—The verb κοπιᾶν in NT Greek signifies not only the weariness produced by constant toil (see Jn 4⁶ κεκοπιακώς), which is the idea attaching to the word in classical writings (cf. Liddell and Scott's *Lex. s.v.*) ; it also has reference to the toil itself (cf. Mt 6²⁸ 11²⁸, Lk 5⁵ 12²⁷, Jn 4³⁸), and sometimes to its result in the field of operations (ὃ οὐχ ὑμεῖς κεκοπιάκατε=τὸν κόπον in Jn 4³⁸). This extension in the use of the word is not confined, however, to the NT, and it is probable that it is borrowed from the LXX. We find it employed, for instance, in Joshua (24¹³). Nor is it unlikely that Jesus had in His mind this passage and was even conscious of a parallel between Himself and the warlike leader of Israel's armies, who brought the nation into a land on the development of which they spent no wearisome toil (ἐφ᾽ ἣν οὐκ ἐκοπιάσατε, κ.τ.λ.). The perfection of Christ's human nature is emphasized by the use of this word in the Johannine narrative of the woman of Samaria (Jn 4⁶), and it is worthy of note that the record of this incident is peculiar to that writing (see Westcott's *Gospel of St. John, ad loc.*).

Closely allied to this word is ἐργάζεσθαι and its cognates, ἐργάτης which occurs frequently in the Gospels, and ἐργασία almost peculiar to the Lukan writings. The last mentioned word not only implies the business or trade by which men gain their livelihood (Ac 19²⁴), but includes in its meaning the resultant gain or profit accruing (see Ac 16¹⁶. ¹⁹), and sometimes the trouble or toil involved in the pursuit of an object (Lk 12⁵⁸). An ethical content is imported into the word by St. Paul (Eph 4¹⁹), just as is done in St. Luke's Gospel where a Latinism (δὸς ἐργασίαν) is employed to emphasize the warning of Jesus with respect to the conciliation of an adversary. 'In medical language it was used for the making of some mixture, the mixture itself —the work of digestion and that of the lungs,' etc. (Hobart, *The Medical Language of St. Luke*, p. 243). At the same time it must not be forgotten that this word is found in the LXX (cf. *e.g.* Wis 13¹⁹), where St. Luke may have become familiar with its uses. A similar spiritual significance frequently attaches to the words κοπιᾶν, κόπος, and ἐργάτης in the Gospel narratives (cf. Jn 4³⁸, Mt 9³⁷ᶠ· =Lk 10², Mt 10¹⁰=Lk 10⁷ 13²⁷).

Considerations like these show us clearly in what spirit Jesus claimed the active support of His followers. Theirs was to be no half-hearted

allegiance. They were expected to work in His cause ceaselessly and in spite of weariness, for the field of operations was large and the toilers few (οἱ ἐργάται ὀλίγοι, ὁ θερισμὸς πολύς, Mt 9³⁷=Lk 10²). The conditions as to remuneration which obtained in the case of the ordinary field-labourer held good in the case of those who preached the Gospel (ἄξιος γὰρ ὁ ἐργάτης τῆς τροφῆς αὐτοῦ, Mt 10¹⁰, cf. Lk 10⁷). His disciples were reminded that they were the successors of a long line of toilers who sowed the seed, of which they were about to reap the fruit (ἄλλοι κεκοπιάκασιν, καὶ ὑμεῖς εἰς τὸν κόπον αὐτῶν εἰσεληλύθατε, Jn 4³⁸).

This is a thought which has a large place in the Pauline conception of Christian work, and the Christology of St. Paul enhances the dignity of, as it supplies the motive power which guides and strengthens, the toiler (cf. πολλὰ ἐκοπίασεν ἐν Κυρίῳ, Ro 16¹²; see also 1 Co 15¹⁰, Gal 4¹¹, Ph 2¹⁶, Col 1²⁹, 1 Th 5¹²). With this conception of laborious effort as the norm of Christian life we may compare what is told of Rabbi Judah in the Midrash on Genesis, who sat labouring ' in the law' before the Babylonish synagogue in Zippor (*Bereshith Rabba*, § 33). We are reminded of the exhortation respecting those ' who labour (οἱ κοπιῶντες) in the word and in teaching' (1 Ti 5¹⁷). It may not be out of place to call attention here to those incidental statements which picture for us the Apostle of the Gentiles and his companions working day by day to supply their physical necessities (1 Co 4¹² κοπιῶμεν, cf. 9⁶, 1 Th 2⁹, 2 Th 3⁸).

Not only does the life of Jesus exhibit the great example of self-sacrificing labour for the sake of the souls of men ; it furnishes, moreover, the principle that human life in all its phases is, at its best, a life of service. In its earliest stages obedience to parental authority (καὶ ἦν ὑποτασσόμενος αὐτοῖς, Lk 2⁵¹) leads the way to willing obedience to a primal and fundamental law which conditions man's living to the full his present life (see Gn 3¹⁹ ἐν ἱδρῶτι τοῦ προσώπου σου φάγῃ τὸν ἄρτον σου, κ.τ.λ.). The question of His Galilæan neighbours who were familiar with the circumstances of Jesus' early life, 'Is not this the worker in wood?' (ὁ τέκτων, Mk 6³), shows clearly how fully He adopted this principle as regulating the preparatory discipline of His young manhood. Nor must we forget that it was amongst that class which is dependent for its livelihood upon its capacity for physical labour and endurance that Jesus gained His most thoughtful, whole-hearted adherents (cf. Mk 1¹⁶⁻²⁰=Mt 4¹⁸⁻²², Lk 5⁵ᶠ·), while many of His most beautiful and effective similes are taken from the surroundings of the busy life (cf. Jn 4³⁵ᶠᶠ·, Lk 10²ᶠ·, Mt 9³⁷ᶠ· 20¹⁻¹⁵ etc.). On the other hand, He reserved His profoundest commiseration for those upon whom superfluous wealth had imposed a selfish idleness (see Mt 19[23ff.] = Mk 10[23ff.], Lk 16[19ff.]), and perhaps the most caustic remark in connexion with the life led by the unjust steward was that in which he confessed his inability for honest physical work (σκάπτειν οὐκ ἰσχύω, Lk 16[3]).

The remarkable apocryphal addition to Lk 6[4] found in Codex Bezæ (D), while primarily having reference to the Sabbath controversy, may not be without its bearing on this question. This passage relates that Jesus ' seeing a certain man working on the Sabbath day said to him, "O, man, if thou indeed knowest what thou art doing, thou art blessed; but if thou knowest not, thou art cursed, and art a transgressor of the law."' Westcott believes that this saying ' rests on some real incident' (see his *Introduction to the Study of the Gospels*, App. C); and, indeed, the spirit underlying these words is not out of harmony with the general tenor of Christ's known attitude towards the active life of busy service. Whether any man's labour is a blessing or not to himself depends, of course, on whether he knows what he does and recognizes its bearing upon his whole life and character (cf. εἰ οἶδας in the passage just quoted, where there is evidently a reference to the relation between the work done and the doer of that work [see Cremer's *Biblico-Theol. Lexicon of NT Greek*, p. 229]).

A charge, which has been brought again and again against the Christian religion, is that it is too exclusive in its other - worldliness to be of practical value in the midst of life's stern realities. Enough has been already said to show that such an accusation misinterprets completely the moving spirit of Christianity. At the same time, we must not forget that at a very early period of the Church's history there was a grave danger of professing Christians degenerating into idle dreamers and useless busybodies (περίεργοι, 1 Ti 5[13], cf. 2 Th 3[11]). Against this abuse St. Paul felt compelled repeatedly to contend (cf. Eph 4[28], 1 Th 4[11]), while he set the example in his own life of unflagging industry (see Ac 18[3] etc.). There can be no doubt that in his restatement of the law of social economics (' if any will not work, neither let him eat,' 2 Th 3[10]) St. Paul was profoundly influenced by the life as well as by the teaching of Jesus.

No thoughtful student of modern problems can fail to note how completely the future of the Christian Church is bound up with her attitude towards the labour question. Year by year that question assumes graver proportions as the danger of a complete breach between employer and employed becomes more formidable. Nor can there be any serious doubt in the mind of a loyal subject of ' the Kingdom of the Incarnation,' that in the true interests of Christian development and progress a real active harmony of aims and aspirations between capital and labour must be established. Representatives of both must be taught that the only solution of problems which seem to baffle them lies in the recognition of the truth that at bottom all human life is true and sacred according as it may be measured in terms of service. Jesus, who employed labourers in fields of activity selected by Himself (cf. Mt 10[5]), points out distinctly the complete identification of employer and employed as being the root idea underlying all vital progress (ὃς ἂν θέλῃ ἐν ὑμῖν εἶναι πρῶτος ἔσται ὑμῶν δοῦλος, Mt 20[27], cf. Mk 10[43]). Nor is the Incarnation above the sphere of this universal law. The Son of Man Himself (ὥσπερ) came not to be served but to serve (διακονῆσαι), yielding up even His life for the sake of His fellow-men (λύτρον ἀντὶ πολλῶν, Mk 10[45] = Mt 20[28]; cf. Lk 22[26f.]).

'The labourer is worthy of his hire' (Lk 10[7]) is a basal principle both broad and deep. It does not mean either that the employer's liability to his servant is discharged when he has paid him his stipulated wage, or that the latter's duty to his master ends with the outward fulfilment of a set task. Personal relationship involving mutual responsibility forms an essential part in the Christian solution of this economic problem. For the labourer is no longer in the position of a bond-servant but of a friend, and is to be recognized as such (οὐκέτι λέγω ὑμᾶς δούλους . . . ὑμᾶς δὲ εἴρηκα φίλους, Jn 15[15]).

LITERATURE.—See three remarkable addresses on social service by Westcott in his *Christian Aspects of Life*, especially that on 'The Christian Law,' in which he quotes from Bishop Tucker of Uganda the salutation ordinarily addressed in that country to a man engaged in manual labour, 'Many thanks; well done.' Consult also Westcott, *Social Aspects of Christianity*; W. H. M. H. Aitken, *Temptation and Toil*, p. 209; E. Griffith-Jones, *Economics of Jesus* (1905); and *The Citizen of To-morrow* (ed. S. E. Keeble), esp. ch. vi. with the bibliography on p. 123.

                  J. R. WILLIS.

LAKE OF GENNESARET.—See SEA OF GALILEE.

LAMB.—See ANIMALS (vol. i. p. 64[a]), NAMES AND TITLES OF CHRIST, and SHEEP.

LAME.—This word, perhaps originally meaning *bruised*, signifies a crippled or disabled condition caused by injury to or defect of a limb or limbs; specifically walking with difficulty, inefficient from injury or defect, unsound or impaired in strength. It is applied metaphorically to all kinds of inefficiency, such as inadequate excuses, or verses which offend against the laws of versification. The term embraces all varieties of defect in walking arising from various causes, and includes *halting* and *maimed* (see artt.), which are separate and distinct species of lameness.

The Greek word is χωλός, from obsolete χάω or χαλάω (*to loosen, slacken*), which is tr. ' lame' in Mt 11[5] 15[30]. 31 21[14], Lk 7[22] 14[13]; but in other passages for no apparent reason the same word is translated ' halt.' In Jn 5[3] χωλῶν is rendered ' halt' without any indication that a special species of lameness is intended, where the description is quite general as in the above passages. In Mk 9[43-45] it is used synonymously with κυλλός, where ἀνάπηρος might have been expected in both cases, seeing that the injury referred to is the definite cutting off of the hand or foot. κυλλός is, however, most commonly associated with the hand, while χωλός more specifically has to do with lameness in the foot or feet. In Mt 18[8] we have χωλὸν ἢ κυλλόν—transposed in the authorities followed by RV, making the correspondence between χείρ and κυλλόν, and πούς and χωλόν.

Healing of the lame was a characteristic work of Christ. Among the multitudes that gathered round Him seeking restoration for various ailments were probably sufferers from many different kinds of lameness (as Mt 15[30], Lk 7[22]). Jn 5[3] gives a comprehensive list of such sick persons, including the feeble, the blind, the lame, and the withered (πλῆθος τῶν ἀσθενούντων, τυφλῶν, χωλῶν, ξηρῶν). Probably these miscellaneous cases would include those suffering from chronic rheumatism and from infirmities having a nervous origin, many of which resulted in a withering of the limbs and of the bodily frame. It is significant that Jesus is never said to have restored the ἀνάπηροι, the badly mutilated — deprived of their limbs (see MAIMED).   T. H. WRIGHT.

LAMECH.—Father of Noah, mentioned in our Lord's genealogy, Lk 3[36].

LAMENTATION (θρῆνος, θρηνεῖν).—An expression of sorrow accompanied by wailing and other demonstrations of grief. It is associated in Jn 16[20] with weeping, and also in Lk 23[27], in the case of the women accompanying the Saviour to the Crucifixion. It is applied equally to sorrow for the dead and to grief for approaching disaster (Mt 2[18], Jn 16[20], Lk 23[27]), and it is referred to by the Lord as one of the common games of children.

When a death occurred, it was intimated at once by a loud wail which is described (Mk 5[38]) as accompanied by a ' tumult,' and this lamentation was renewed at the grave of the deceased. Oriental demonstrations of grief are very vivid. Mourners hang over the lifeless form and beg for a response from its lips. When a young person dies unmarried, part of the ceremony of mourning is a form of marriage (see art. MOURNING). Lamentation for the dead was also accompanied by beating the breast and tearing the hair, as well as by rending the garments (see RENDING OF GARMENTS) and fasting.   W. H. RANKINE.

LAMP.—There are two words in the Gospels translated 'lamp,' λύχνος and λαμπάς. The former (RV 'lamp,' AV 'candle') is used Mt 5[15], Mk 4[21], Lk 8[16] of the usual means of lighting a house. In Mt 6[22] the eye, as the source of light, the organ by which light is appreciated, is called the lamp (RV; AV 'light') of the body. In Jn 5[35] the same word is applied to John the Baptist, who is not the eternal light (φῶς, Jn 1[8]), but the burning and shining lamp kindled by it and bearing witness to it.

The word λαμπάς occurs in Jn 18[3], where it is rendered 'torch.' It is also used in the parable of the Ten Virgins, Mt 25, where it would be better translated 'torch.' In Eastern countries the torch, like the lamp, is fed with oil, which is carried in small vessels constructed for the purpose (ἀγγεῖον, Mt 25[4]). See CANDLE, LIGHT, TORCH.

LITERATURE.—Trench, *Synonyms*, xlvi.; Hastings' *DB*, artt. 'Lamp' and 'Lantern'; Edersheim, *Life and Times*, ii. 455 ff.; H. J. van Lennep, *Bible Lands and Customs*, p. 132; W. M. Thomson, *Land and Book*, iii. 472.

          C. H. PRICHARD.

LANE.—See STREET.

LANGUAGE OF CHRIST.— Recent historical and critical research has narrowed the ground which it is necessary to cover in the discussion of the question as to the language spoken by Christ. It has ruled Hebrew out of court. The practically unanimous verdict of recent scholars is that, considerably before the time of Christ, though when is uncertain, Hebrew had ceased to be spoken in Palestine, and its place as the vernacular had been taken by Aramaic, the language represented in OT by Ezr 4[8-16] 7[12-26], Jer 10[11], and Dn 2[4]-7[28], and mistakenly named 'Chaldee.'

The transition from Hebrew to Aramaic involved no great linguistic revolution, as it was simply a transition from one Semitic language to another, and that a closely cognate one. It was, however, only very gradually effected, and was chiefly due to the predominance to which Aramaic attained in Western Asia during the Persian period, coming, as it did, to be, with dialectical differences, the *lingua communis* from the Euphrates to the Mediterranean. While, however, Aramaic thus gradually superseded Hebrew as the living tongue of Palestine, and by the time of Alexander the Great had probably reached a position of ascendency, if it had not gained entire possession of the field, yet Hebrew remained, though with some loss of its ancient purity, the language of sacred literature, the language in which Prophet and Psalmist wrote, and as the language of the books ultimately embraced in the OT Canon, continued to be read, with an accompanying translation into Aramaic, in the synagogues, and to be diligently studied by the professional interpreters of the Scriptures. It is, therefore, quite possible that Christ possessed a knowledge of Hebrew, and had thus access to the Scriptures in the original.

With Alexander the Great, however, there came a fresh disturbance of the linguistic situation. Thenceforward Greek entered into competition with Aramaic. And though, as a non-Semitic language, the adoption of Greek could not come so readily to the Jews as Aramaic, yet the circumstances were such as to tend in no small degree to counterbalance the disadvantage under which Greek thus lay. For not only was it the official language alike of the Lagid, Seleucid, and, after the Maccabæan interregnum, of the Idumæan-Roman rulers to whom the Jews were successively subject; but its cause was furthered by the Hellenizing policy which these rulers generally followed, and by the existence, more or less, all through of a party among the Jews themselves favourable to that policy. The result on the linguistic situation of the political conditions thus obtaining cannot be certainly determined from the historical data bearing directly thereon. It is, however, clear that whatever headway Greek may have made before the Maccabæan revolt,—which was a revolt against the Hellenizing policy referred to, as pushed to extremes by Antiochus Epiphanes, —it suffered a decided set-back, and was practically expelled the country during the Maccabæan régime. And though it had again made considerable progress by the time of Christ, and especially through the influence of Herod the Great, who particularly affected Greek culture, there is nothing to show that the political conditions were such as to secure for it the ascendency claimed by some scholars, and notably by Dr. Roberts in his book, *Greek the Language of Christ and His Apostles*.

At the time of Christ, then, Palestine was bilingual, Greek as well as Aramaic being, to some extent at least, spoken. The question, therefore, to be answered is, Which of these languages did Christ speak, or, if He knew and spoke both, which of them did He mainly, if not exclusively, employ as the vehicle of His teaching? Consideration need be given to the question only in its latter form. For, as undoubtedly spoken by some of the Palestinian Jews, as the language of perhaps the great majority of His countrymen scattered throughout the Roman world, as the predominant language of the representatives of the Gentile world in Palestine and of that Gentile world itself, which, though wide, was not yet wider than He conceived the scope of His mission to be, and as, besides, the language of the Septuagint Version of the OT, which had no doubt acquired considerable popularity, it may reasonably be assumed that Christ would acquire some knowledge of Greek, and be able, in some measure at least, to speak it. Was it, then, Aramaic or Greek that Christ habitually employed in His public ministry? The question resolves itself into that of the relative prevalence of the two languages in the country at the time, so far as that can be determined by such evidence, direct and indirect, as is available. And this evidence, though somewhat meagre, is decisive for Aramaic. That furnished by the reported words of Christ Himself does not go very far, but yet goes some length towards that conclusion. All that it certainly establishes is that Christ knew Aramaic, and, apart from His employment of Aramaic terms and proper names, on which perhaps little stress is to be laid, as these terms and proper names may have formed part of the ordinary vocabulary of Greek-speaking Jews, expressed Himself in Aramaic on three different occasions. The *three expressions* are: (1) ταλειθὰ κούμ, the Gr. transliteration of the Aram. טְלִיתָא or טְלִיתָא קוּם Mk 5[41]; (2) ἐφφαθά, euphonic for the Aram. אתפתח Mk 7[34]; and (3) ἠλεὶ ἠλεὶ λαμὰ σαβαχθανεί (Mt 27[46]), or according to Mk 15[34] ἐλωί, ἐλωί, λεμὰ σαβαχθανεί, the Aram. אֵלִי אֵלִי לְמָא אֵלָהִי שְׁבַקְתָּנִי or אֱלָהִי. How these three Aramaic expressions alone came to be preserved is matter of conjecture. An obvious explanation is that they alone were preserved because they were exceptional, Greek being the language for the most part used by Christ. That, however, is not the only possible explanation. More probable is it that they alone were preserved because associated with moments of exceptional emotion on Christ's part, and therefore felt to be exceptionally precious. The cry upon the cross was peculiarly a cry *de profundis*. In the case of the deaf and dumb man, Christ, for some reason or other, was unwontedly moved, for it is said that 'he looked up to heaven and sighed.' And, though it is not stated, the spectacle of Jairus' child-daughter lying cold yet beautiful in death, was calculated to touch profoundly the heart of the great Child-Lover.

The two main sources of direct evidence conclusively proving the predominance of Aramaic as the popular language, are the *Book of Acts* and the *Works of Josephus*.

1. In Ac 1^{19} it is said with reference to the suicide of Judas in the field which he had purchased 'with the reward of iniquity,' 'And it was known unto all the dwellers at Jerusalem; insomuch as that field is called *in their own tongue* (τῇ διαλέκτῳ αὐτῶν) Akeldama.' Now *Akeldama* is the Aram. קְבֵל דָּם, and points not only to the fact that Aramaic had superseded Hebrew as the vernacular, but that at the time of Christ it was the popular language, even of the inhabitants of Jerusalem. Equally conclusive on the latter point are two other passages in the Acts. In describing his conversion to Agrippa, St. Paul said, 'And when we were all fallen to the earth, I heard a voice speaking unto me, and saying, *in the Hebrew tongue*' (τῇ Ἑβραΐδι διαλέκτῳ), Ac 26^{14}. By 'Hebrew' St. Paul undoubtedly meant Aramaic. The terms Ἑβραΐδι and Ἑβραϊστί, as is generally admitted, are used both in the NT and by Josephus when not Hebrew but Aramaic is meant. Thus in Jn 19^{13} it is said that 'Pilate sat down in the judgment-seat in a place that is called the Pavement, but in the Hebrew Gabbatha' (Ἑβραϊστὶ δὲ Γαββαθά); and Γαββαθά is not Hebrew, but Aramaic. That the ascended Christ should have spoken to Saul in Aramaic is unintelligible except on the supposition that that had been the language which He had spoken when on earth, and that it was the prevailing language of Palestine.

Quite as significant is the circumstance mentioned in Ac 22^2 that Paul addressed the infuriated Jerusalemites in Aramaic, and that when they ascertained from his opening words that he was to speak to them in that language, 'they kept the more silence' (μᾶλλον παρέσχον ἡσυχίαν), the reference being to the fact that Paul had not attempted to speak until by a gesture indicative of his desire to be heard he had stilled the uproar, and, as it is said, 'there was made a great silence.' It does not necessarily follow, as has been maintained, that the people expected Paul to address them in Greek, and that the fact that they were prepared to give him a hearing when they expected him to speak in that language, proves that they were familiar with it. The simple fact that, as his gesture indicated, Paul was going to address them was in itself sufficient to secure their quiet attention. And in any case, even though they had expected to be addressed in Greek, the deeper silence into which they settled when they found that they were to be addressed in Aramaic, proves that they were more familiar with the latter language than the former, and that the latter was the language generally spoken by them.

2. The evidence of *Josephus* is as direct and conclusive as that furnished by the Acts of the predominance of Aramaic. In *BJ* v. vi. 3, Josephus records how during the siege of Jerusalem the Jewish watchmen warned their compatriots of the discharge of the Roman missiles by crying out *in their native tongue* (τῇ πατρίῳ γλώσσῃ), ὁ ἰὸς ἔρχεται. In the same work, VI. ii. 1, he tells how in his capacity of intermediary during the same siege he communicated the proposals of Titus to the besieged *in their native tongue* (τῇ πατρίῳ γλώσσῃ). In the preface to *BJ* he records how that work was at first written in Aramaic and afterwards translated into Greek.

The passage runs : 'I have proposed to myself, for the sake of such as live under the government of the Romans, to translate these books into the Greek tongue, which I formerly composed in *the language of our own country*, and sent to the Upper Barbarians,' *i.e.* to the Aramaic-speaking peoples, whom he describes in the following paragraph as 'the Parthians, Babylonians, the remotest Arabians, and those of our nation beyond Euphrates, with the Adiabeni.'

That a Palestinian Jew such as Josephus, who was of a distinguished priestly family, who received a careful rabbinic education and studied in the various schools of the Pharisees, Sadducees, and Essenes, should not only characterize Aramaic as 'the language of our own country,' but should write his first book in that language, is in itself conclusive proof that Aramaic had not then been materially driven from its position as the vernacular of Palestine. Suggestive also in this connexion, and giving added weight to the case for Aramaic, is Josephus' own confession of the difficulty he experienced in acquiring such mastery of Greek as that which he ultimately attained. In the preface to his *Antiquities* he tells how he found the writing of that work a hard and wearisome task, 'it being,' as he says, 'a large subject, and a difficult thing to translate our history into a foreign and to us unaccustomed language' (εἰς ἀλλοδαπὴν ἡμῖν καὶ ξένην διαλέκτου συνήθειαν), and how he was able to continue and accomplish the task only by the encouragement and help of a friend, Epaphroditus. To the same difficulty he refers in the closing paragraphs of the *Antiquities*:

'I am so bold as to say, now that I have completed the task set before me, that no other person, either Jew or Greek, with whatever good intentions, would have been able to set forth this history to the Greeks as accurately as I have done; for I am acknowledged by my countrymen to excel them far in our national learning. I also did my best to obtain a knowledge of Greek by practising myself in the grammar, though native habit prevented me from attaining accuracy in its use.'

Josephus' difficulty with Greek is very significant. For if that difficulty obtained with him, what of his countrymen generally? Stress has been laid, as, *e.g.*, by Dr. Roberts, upon the attainments in Greek of such men as Peter and James and John, as shown in the speeches or writings attributed to them, and it has been argued therefrom that a knowledge of Greek must have been common among the rank and file. But even though Peter and James and John were the authors of the speeches and writings referred to, and did speak or write such Greek as is found therein, which is open to question, they cannot fairly be regarded as representative of the people generally in this respect. The very fact of their not only being of the number of the Twelve, but forming the inner group of that favoured circle, differentiates them from the crowd. 'Unlearned and ignorant men,' the Council at Jerusalem dubbed them (Ac 4^{13}); but the contemptuous epithets were but the expression of a twofold prejudice, the prejudice of antagonism and the prejudice of the Schools. In virtue of their discipleship, Peter and James and John have to be placed in a different category from the mass of the people of their social rank, who, as compared with them, must have been 'unlearned and ignorant' in the broader sense of the terms.

3. The case for Aramaic as the prevailing language of Palestine in the time of Christ, and the language, therefore, which Christ must necessarily have employed generally in His teaching, is thus incontestably established by the direct evidence of the Acts and of Josephus. And though less direct and certain, there is other evidence to the same effect to which reference may be made, and specially that furnished by the *Targums* and what is known as *The Aramaic Gospel*.

(*a*) The Targums are Aramaic translations or paraphrases of the OT books, and cover the whole of those books with the exception of Daniel, Ezra, and Nehemiah. The two principal Targums are (1) that on the Pentateuch, known as the Targum of Onḳelos, which is characterized by its almost slavish literalism; and (2) that of Jonathan ben-Uzziel on the Prophets, *i.e.* the Historical books and the Prophets properly so called, which is largely paraphrastic. The dates of these Targums are uncertain, and by scholars they have been made to range from the end of the 1st to that of the 4th cent. A.D. The important point, however, is that they undoubtedly embody material from a much earlier time, and were the outcome of the practice, originating in the gradual disuse of Hebrew as the vernacular, of translating the synagogue readings of the OT into Aramaic for the benefit of the people generally. Written Targums were at first forbidden. The translation was required to be oral, the translator (מְתֻרְגְּמָן) giving his translation after each verse of the Pentateuch and every three verses of the Prophets. Whether the rule which forbade written Targums had fallen into desuetude by the time of Christ cannot be definitely determined. Probably it had. But even though it had not, and there were no written Targums till a later date, yet the existence of written Targums at that later date points conclusively to the prevalence of the practice of the oral translation of the synagogue lessons into Aramaic, and therefore to the prevalence of that language as the vernacular.

As against this, the supporters of Greek hold that the Septuagint version was in such general use that it may be described as the 'People's Bible.' The special arguments in favour of this theory are: (1) that copies of the Septuagint could be had at a much smaller cost than Hebrew or Aramaic MSS, that indeed the price of the latter was prohibitive so far as the people generally were concerned; and (2) that the OT quotations in the NT point to a very general familiarity with the Septuagint, inasmuch as the majority of them are verbatim or practically verbatim, or show unmistakable traces of the Septuagint, and particularly as in some cases the Septuagint is followed when it differs from the Hebrew. The *price* argument scarcely deserves notice, and very little weight is to be attached to the *quotation* argument. For while it must be admitted that those who were responsible for the quotations were familiar with the Septuagint, it by no means follows that such familiarity obtained with the people generally. And while it was to be expected that the writers of the NT books would not only be familiar with the Septuagint, but in quoting from the OT would take advantage of a translation ready to hand, it is yet a significant fact that that translation was not always taken advantage of, not a few of the quotations showing an entire independence of the Septuagint.

(*b*) The question of an Aramaic Gospel (*Ur-Evangelium*), while important chiefly in connexion with the Synoptic problem, bears closely upon that of the language spoken by Christ. If Christ spoke Aramaic, such a Gospel was to be expected, and at the same time its existence would furnish weighty proof at once of the prevalence of Aramaic and of the use of that language by our Lord. And the labours of recent critical scholars, if they have not conclusively established the existence of an Aramaic *Ur-Evangelium*, have at least made it much less open to question. Of special interest in this connexion is the series of articles in the *Expositor* (Ser. IV.), by Professor Marshall, on 'The Aramaic Gospel.' The theory which Professor Marshall in these articles works out with great ability and skill is that the variant Greek words in parallel passages of the Synoptic Gospels can be traced to one original Aramaic word; and the

result of the application of his theory is that the Aramaic Gospel contained, speaking generally, the ministry of Christ in Galilee. That Professor Marshall's theory will ever find anything like general acceptance is perhaps unlikely. But whether or not it may be possible by his or any other method to recover with certainty and to any extent the precise Aramaic words used by our Lord, there can be no doubt that Aramaic had the supreme honour of being the language in which He gave expression to His imperishable thoughts.

LITERATURE. — Pfannkuche, *Language of Palestine*, Clark's Cabinet Library, vol. ii.; Roberts, *Greek the Language of Christ and His Apostles*, 1888; W. H. Simcox, *Language of the NT*, 1889; T. K. Abbott, *Essays chiefly on the Original Texts of OT and NT*, 1891, p. 129; A. Meyer, *Jesu Muttersprache*, 1896; Dalman, *The Words of Jesus*, Eng. tr. 1902; Schultze, *Gram. der Aram. Muttersprache Jesu*, 1899; Marshall, *Expositor*, Ser. IV. ii. 69 ff., iii. 1 ff., 109 ff., 205 ff., 275 ff., 375 ff., 452 ff., iv. 208 ff., 373 ff., 435 ff., vi. 81 ff., viii. 176 ff.; *Exp. Times*, iv. 260; Schürer, *HJP* I. i., II. ii.   JAMES YOUNG.

LANTERN (φανός) occurs in Jn 18[3], where the band of soldiers accompanying Judas is described as provided with lanterns and torches (see LAMP).

LAST DAY.—See DAY OF JUDGMENT.

LAST SUPPER.—Although the relation of the Last Supper to the Jewish Passover is treated with more or less fulness elsewhere (see DATES, vol. i. p. 413 ff., and LORD'S SUPPER (I.)), it appears advisable to handle the whole subject in a special article.

The Paschal controversy, which agitated the first ages of Christianity (see CALENDAR), has only a general connexion with the inquiry on which we are entering. We note [*] that the trend of opinion at first was towards the view that Christ was crucified on the 14th day of the Jewish month Nisan, and therefore on the day on which the Paschal lamb was killed; from which it follows that the Last Supper (whatever was its nature) preceded the Jewish Passover by several hours. In the 3rd cent. the view that our Lord kept the Passover with the Jews on the 14th, and was crucified on the 15th, began to come into favour. When we approach the sacred records, we find that the first three Evangelists so express themselves, that, in the opinion of some, they represent our Lord as eating the Paschal Supper with His disciples on the night of His betrayal. It is certain that St. John (18[28]) represents some of the Jews as not having eaten the Passover several hours later. On these premises, there appears to be a discrepancy between the accounts in the sacred narratives. When an honest attempt is made to arrive at a conclusion, a great authority on the history of Christ's ministry is compelled to confess his inability to solve the enigma.[†] By some it has been thought that Christ anticipated the day of the Paschal Supper, in order to eat it with His disciples; [‡] by others, that the heads of the Jewish people deferred their Passover in order to have time to apprehend and condemn Jesus.[§] The object of this article is to show that the first three Gospels preclude the notion that the

---

[*] See art. 'Chronology' (Turner) in Hastings' *DB* i. 411 f.

[†] See Sanday, art. 'Jesus Christ' in *DB* ii. 634[b].

[‡] This seems to be the view which Dr. Sanday, on the whole, favours; see art. quoted in preceding note. For the view that the Last Supper was an anticipated Passover meal, resembling the ordinary Passover in form and order, and held before the statutory date, see artt. 'Jesus Christus' (Zöckler) in *PRE*[3], ix. p. 32; 'Eucharist' (J. Armitage Robinson) in *EBi*, col. 1419. A good summary of arguments and opinions is given by Ellicott in *Lectures on the Life of our Lord*, pp. 322, 323, nn.

[§] The Passover might be deferred for a month for those who were legally debarred from observing it on the proper day (Nu 9[9-12]), but there is no provision in the Law for postponing it for one day: this explanation of the action of the rulers is improbable in itself, and contrary to their expressed intention (Mt 26[5]); further notice of it is superfluous.

Last Supper was a Passover, and therefore, as St. John certainly seems to represent the Passover as still to come while the Supper was proceeding,[*] that there is no discrepancy in the accounts.[†]

1. In examining the evidence afforded by the four accounts, we find, with satisfaction, that they have been handed down to us intact, and that no attempt was made to harmonize the records, as by the omission of the words τὸ πάσχα from Lk 22[15], which seem at variance with the statements in St. John. There is one critical problem in St. Luke—the retention, or omission, of the mention of a second cup, and the order of the Bread and the Cup in the Institution ; [‡] but the solution of this problem will not affect the chief thesis in our position. Herein is another proof, if proof be needed, of the honesty and faithfulness of the ancient scribes, who, in the midst of one of the greatest controversies of the early Church, resisted the temptation to accommodate the records to particular views of the event.

2. The five following indications of time may be collected from the several accounts :

(1) When Jesus had finished His great eschatological discourse, and the rulers were forming a plan for His apprehension and condemnation, it wanted two days to the commencement of the Paschal Feast — μετὰ δύο ἡμέρας τὸ πάσχα γίνεται (Mt 26[2], Mk 14[1], Lk 22[1]). 'After two days' must be interpreted according to the reckoning which makes 'after three days' equivalent to 'on the third day.' This Jewish usage is well known, and is found, e.g., in Mt 20[19] parallel with Mk 10[34] and Lk 18[33], where τῇ τρίτῃ ἡμέρᾳ in the First and Third corresponds to μετὰ τρεῖς ἡμέρας in the Second Evangelist.[§] Now the Passover was slain late in the afternoon of the 14th Nisan, and some hours earlier leaven was put out of the houses, in preparation for the 'days of unleavened bread,' which, strictly speaking, began with the eating of the lamb in the early hours of 15th Nisan.[‖] The *terminus ad quem* of the 'two days' must be the last hours of 14th Nisan. The *terminus a quo* may be any hour after 12th Nisan had been succeeded by the 13th.

(2) In arranging for the apprehension of Jesus, the rulers decided that it should not be attempted on the Feast Day (Mt 26[5], Mk 14[2]). If they carried out their intention, it follows that the night of the apprehension and trial was before the slaying of the Passover ; and that the Last Supper, whatever it was, did not coincide with the Paschal Feast.

The hurried proceedings of the night suggest an attempt to secure a condemnation within a limited time. This is intelligible if the Feast had not begun ; otherwise it is hard to see why men who were, in that case, willing to try a prisoner on the first day should have scrupled about extending the proceedings to any necessary length.

(3) The third indication of time presents some difficulty. On a day called 'the first day of *Azuma*' preparations were made for the Feast, according to Mt. (26[17]) and Mk. (14[12]), at the suggestion of the Twelve ; according to all three (Mt 26[18. 19], Mk 14[13-16], Lk 22[7-13]), with the consent and at the command of the Master. Strictly speaking, the πρώτη τῶν ἀζύμων would indicate the 15th Nisan, for the period during which leaven was prohibited commenced with the Paschal meal, following the slaying of the Paschal lamb in the closing hours of 14th Nisan. So late a date for the πρώτη is precluded by the circumstances of the narrative ; but it is incredible that Mt. could make an erroneous statement in a matter connected with the greatest solemnity of the whole of the Jewish sacred year. The reasonable conclusion is, that, in a popular way of speaking, a day before the legal day had acquired the name of 'First day of *Azuma*,' and not unfitly, if on that day early arrangements were commenced for the complete exclusion of leaven from the houses.[*] Mk., bearing in mind, as often, the needs of non-Jewish readers, adds, ὅτε τὸ πάσχα ἔθυον. The point of time need not be pressed too strictly ; the gloss is no more than an explanation that the season of *Azuma* was the time of the offering of the Passover. The expression in Lk. is more difficult. In 22[7] we read, ἦλθεν δὲ ἡ ἡμέρα τῶν ἀζύμων, ἐν [†] ᾗ ἔδει θύεσθαι τὸ πάσχα. But there was more than one day of *Azuma*. In v.[1] he had written ἤγγιζεν δὲ ἡ ἑορτὴ τ. ἀζ. It looks as if ἡμέρα below was equivalent to ἑορτή above — not 24 hours, but a period ; [‡] or else there is some little inexactitude in a mere reference to an observance which it was unnecessary for the purpose of the narrative to describe precisely.

(4) The fourth note of time is given by the ὀψίας γενομένης of Mt 26[20] and Mk 14[17].[§] These verses immediately follow the statement that the disciples 'made ready the Passover.' The natural interpretation is to take them as indicative of the evening of the day when the Upper Room was engaged. We have therefore another date, from which we may argue backwards to the limitations of the πρώτη τ. ἀζ. It ended with sunset on the night of the Betrayal. It began with the preceding sunset. At any time during those 24 hours

---

[*] Jn 13[29]. Edersheim (*Life and Times*, ii. 566 ff.) explains the φαγεῖν τὸ πάσχα of Jn 18[28] as referring to sacrifices of the Paschal season. The opinion of such a writer demands respectful consideration, and a similar explanation is adopted by many. From 2 Ch 35 we learn that other sacrifices were offered at the Paschal season besides the lambs ; see vv.[7. 8. 13].

[†] The position maintained in this article is identical with the explanation given by the late G. Wildon Peiritz in *The Gospels from the Rabbinical point of view*, 1873. By birth a Jew, of German nationality, a Cambridge graduate, and an Anglican priest, of wide reading and profound learning, Peiritz had, to an exceptional extent, the ability to form a correct opinion on the problem before us.

[‡] The Received Text of Lk 22[19. 20] is read in 'codd. Græc. et verss. fere omn.' (*Nov. Test.*, Lloyd-Sanday, Append. p. 121)—*i.e.* it has the very highest diplomatic attestation, including the old uncials. It can be rejected only on *a priori* grounds. The case illustrates the difference between two schools of criticism—those who follow the testimony of ancient MSS, and those who are influenced by subjective considerations. Dr. Sanday (*l.c.* 636[b]) says : 'We cannot doubt that both these types of text existed early in the 2nd cent. Either may be original. And this is just one of those cases where internal evidence is strongly in favour of the text which we call Western. The temptation to expand was much stronger than to contract ; and the double mention of the Cup raises real difficulties of the kind which suggest interpolation.' See also a full discussion of the Lukan account of the Institution by Mr. Blakiston, in *JThSt*, July 1903, p. 548 f. Dr. Lambert (*ib.* Jan. 1903) well sums up the arguments and authorities for adhering to the Received Text.

[§] As there is a *v.l.* harmonizing the text of Mk. with that of Mt. and Lk., we may compare Mt 27[63], where the text is certain.

[‖] So Chwolson in *Das letzte Passamahl Christi und der Tag seines Todes*, quoted by Mr. Box and Dr. Lambert ; see note [*], p. 8[b] below. Cf. Turner, *l.c.*

[*] Wieseler, quoting from the Talmudical tract *Pesachim*, that the search for leaven in houses must be made in the night preceding 14th Nisan, in order that it might be put away by midday, and nothing leavened eaten afterwards, argues that the day before the Passover was made ready was reckoned as belonging to the Feast of Unleavened Bread. See *Chronological Synopsis of the Four Gospels*, tr. Venables, pp. 334, 335, and art PASSOVER in Hastings' *DB* (W. J. Moulton), vol. iii. p. 690. Peiritz (*op. cit.* pp. 28, 29, 33, 34) describes the arrangements made by Jews on *the day before* the legal Preparation day, and adds : 'There is a very intelligible reason why that Thursday should, in a subordinate sense, — loosely, we may allow, — be called *the first day of unleavened bread*.'

[†] ἐν is omitted by some authorities ; but the attestation is insufficient, nor would the omission affect the translation—'*when* it behoved,' or '*in which*'; see Winer's *Grammar*, iii. § xxxi. 9, *a*.

[‡] Many examples occur of the use of ἡμέρα for a period of long duration ; but it is then regarded in contrast to conditions which may be described as 'night,'—*e.g.* Ro 13[12] ; or as the time when certain conditions are realized,—*e.g.* 2 Co 6[2], to which latter sense belongs the oft-recurring expression 'day of the Lord,' or 'my day' (Jn 8[56]) ; but there seems no exact parallel to the use we have supposed of ἡμέρα as equivalent to ἡμέραι. Yet, if we limit the term to the 'first day,' the remainder of the sentence is inexact, the lamb being slain before the legal 'first day' began. It seems impossible to treat the sentence as rigidly and historically accurate, in the terms in which the text has come to us.

[§] Of the 'two evenings,' it is better to take this as the *second*, rather than the *first*, which would be our 'late afternoon.'

it is permissible to place the commencement by the disciples of preparations for a Passover which would be kept in circumstances they never anticipated. According to our present argument, the Master had passed into Paradise before the Passover was eaten. That would not prevent the disciples complying with the requirements of the Law, except in so far as some might have contracted ceremonial defilement during the events of Good Friday. But this would not apply to all; and here may be found the explanation of the preparations. The Master permitted the disciples to make ready for what was legally requisite; but He made this the occasion of suitable provision for the new Passover which He designed to provide, but of which they, as yet, knew nothing.

Parallel with the ὀψία of the first two Evangelists is an interesting expression in Lk 22[14] ὅτε ἐγένετο ἡ ὥρα. While in itself absolutely vague, in connexion with the preceding words, 'they made ready the Passover,' it would naturally indicate the commencement of 15th Nisan, when the lamb was eaten; but in view of considerations already stated, we must reject such interpretation, and read the term in connexion with what follows, and is peculiar to Lk., 'with desire I have desired to eat this Passover with you before I suffer.' The ὥρα was the Master's time for one of the great acts of His incarnate life, not a particular division of a particular day in the Jewish calendar. So it is used in v.[53] below—αὕτη ὑμῶν ἐστιν ἡ ὥρα, 'your time,' 'opportunity.' *

(5) The appellation *paraskeuē* affords yet another mark of time. There were *paraskeuai* before various days. In connexion with our present inquiry we note the Preparation of the Sabbath (Mk 15[42], Lk 23[54]), and the Preparation of the Passover (Jn 19[14]). On this latter *paraskeuē* our Lord stood before Pilate, and was condemned (Jn. *l.c.*). Therefore the Passover had not yet been eaten; much less could the day before have been the Day of the Passover. But the day of the condemnation and crucifixion was also the *pro-sabbaton* (Lk 23[54. 56], cf. Mk 15[42]). In that year the two *paraskeuai* coincided, and the *first day of unleavened bread* was also the Sabbath; hence St. John calls that Sabbath 'an high day' (19[31]). The *paraskeuē* was our Friday,† Nisan 14, and the day of the crucifixion.

3. (i.) St. John was one of the two disciples who were specially charged with the Paschal preparations. It is recognized that the evidence afforded by his narrative is absolutely plain and consistent. It has been said that he silently corrects the others.‡ From our point of view, as we hold that they preclude the notion that the Last Supper was a Passover, St. John adds the emphatic testimony of an eye-witness to our conclusion. The Supper was *before the feast of the Passover* (13[1]); it was supposed that it might be necessary to buy what there was *need of against the feast* (13[29]); several hours later some of the rulers had not yet eaten the Passover (18[28]); § the following

day, when Jesus was crucified, was *the preparation of the Passover* (19[14]). Language could hardly be more distinct; and some evidence, which seems to support a different view, can be explained. Taking St. John's words in their natural sense, and reading them without prejudice, no one would gather from them that the Supper described by him was the Passover. It seems reasonable to demand that the less distinct and somewhat inexact language of the other three should be interpreted in the light of the last account.

(ii.) It has been claimed by some that the account of the meal in the three Evangelists agrees with the ritual of a Passover; by others, that no trace of a Passover can be found in it. To us, we confess, it seems that the details of a Paschal celebration have been discovered after the importation of ideas which are not on the surface of the narrative. The initial statement that Jesus *sat down* with the Twelve (ἀνέκειτο, Mt 26[20]; ἀνέπεσεν, Lk 22[14]) is against the usual interpretation of the directions given in Ex 12[11]: it is supposed that a change of posture had been admitted in later times. The two cups of wine are regarded as two of the four or five which were handed round at the feast; but in view of the serious difference of opinion amongst critics as to the genuineness of the reading in Lk., which gives the notice of a second cup, it seems unfair to press this identification. The dish in which the sop was dipped is identified with the dish of *ḥaroseth*, a kind of sauce,* which was an adjunct of the Paschal meal; but this is an assumption, rather than a deduction from evidence. The *hymn* sung on leaving the upper chamber is identified with the *Hallel* (Pss. 115–118) sung at the conclusion of the Passover ritual; but ὑμνεῖν (Mt 26[30], Mk 14[26]) does not necessarily denote the use of a particular composition, and in Eph 5[19], Col 3[16], ὕμνοι are distinguished from ψαλμοί.

(iii.) Those who fail to discover traces of a Passover meal in the accounts of the Last Supper, who point to the absence of allusion to a lamb, and generally to the weakness of the evidence adduced, may reasonably claim an argument *e silentio* for what that is worth. It may be added that the supposition of the disciples, that the preparations for the feast were not complete (Jn 13[29]), seems strange indeed if they were already keeping the feast. Preparation for the Passover was so important in the eyes of the Jews, that the day preceding had derived its appellation of *paraskeuē* from their scrupulous care; see Mt 27[62].

4. We can now tabulate the order of the sacred days in accordance with the conclusions at which we have arrived. It will be convenient to use the modern names for the days. In the early morning of Sunday our Lord rose. This tradition is universally accepted, and further discussion would be superfluous. The Saturday was the 'first day of unleavened bread' (for the eating of unleavened bread began legally with the Paschal meal),† and was Nisan 15. Friday, Nisan 14, was the official Preparation Day. Between it and the commencement of Nisan 15 the lamb was slain and eaten. Thursday evening was the beginning of the *paraskeuē*, and some hours before that the exclusion of leaven commenced, from which custom, as we have suggested, the day had acquired the popular appellation of 'first day of *Azuma*.' This was the 13th

---

* Cf. the same use of ὥρα by Christ at Cana (Jn 2[4]), and a similar sense in 1 Jn 2[18].

† *Paraskeuē* is rendered in the Pesh. by 'arubhta, which is from a root meaning *to set* (of the sun). It became the name of *Friday* in the use of the Syrians, 'because on that day the sun set and darkness reigned' (see Payne-Smith, *Thes. Syr.* col. 2984). Herein is preserved a tradition of the day of the Crucifixion, accepted with such confidence that from it the sixth day derived its name, as the first day has been known from earliest times as the Lord's day, because it was the day of the Resurrection. Cf. Mr. Turner's remarks, *l.c.* p. 411 f.

‡ So Mr. Turner in art. quoted above.

§ The Passover, which was slain 'between the evenings' of Nisan 14, was usually eaten in the early hours of the night following, for time must be allowed for taking the lamb to the house and roasting it. This would be the commencement of Nisan 15 (see Ex 12[8]). But Ex 12[10], Nu 9[12], and Dt 16[4] suggest the possibility of extending the time of eating, provided all was

consumed before morning light. But it was already morning (Mt 27[1. 2]) when the Jews objected to enter the Judgment Hall (Jn 19[28]) lest they should be debarred from eating the Passover. Therefore they could not have contemplated eating of a lamb slain the afternoon before. They must have anticipated a Passover in the hours to follow. Every scrap of evidence tends to confirm the view for which we contend.

* Its nature is described in Buxtorf, *Lex. Talmud.* col. 831.

† Ex 12[18]; but in later practice, for greater strictness, leaven was excluded earlier. See note *, p. 6[b] above.

of Nisan, and began with sunset on Wednesday evening. During the 24 hours which followed Wednesday afternoon, the disciples began to make ready for the Passover. On Thursday evening (Mt 26[20], Mk 14[17]) Jesus sat down with them for the Last Supper; and this, according to St. John (13[1]), was *before* the Passover.

5. But our Lord called that Thursday evening meal a 'passover'—τοῦτο τὸ πάσχα, Lk 22[15]. As we have shown that the meal preceded the legal Passover by some 24 hours, there are but two explanations of the words recorded by St. Luke— (i.) an anticipatory celebration was held, or (ii.) πάσχα is used in a mystical sense.

(i.) An anticipation of the Passover might have been either (*a*) from a desire to keep with the disciples a rite which, on the legal and customary day, would be precluded by the crucifixion; or (*b*) with the intention of reverting to a more exact date, and correcting an error in time which had crept into the Jewish calculations.[*] The impossibility of procuring the sacrifice of a lamb except on the day commonly observed, would have been fatal to any such plan. (1) Our Lord was not a householder, but a guest. It would be usual, perhaps, in such a case, to share in the lamb offered by the householder. This would require the assent of the householder to an abnormal, and apparently illegal, arrangement. Or if (2) we suppose that the thirteen were to constitute a family, and have their lamb to themselves, there would still be, as there would be in the former case also, the insuperable difficulty of getting the lamb killed by the priests before the legal day. (3) It has been supposed that there was a difference of opinion between Jewish schools as to the date of the Passover; but this argument, if it has, which is doubtful, any foundation, is of no value in the present inquiry. One party only was paramount at a time: there is no proof that there was a choice of dates for the celebration.[†] If, however, by an 'anticipatory Passover' is meant an imitative meal, with herbs and unleavened bread and wine, but without a lamb,[‡] this is not forbidden by the second explanation of our Lord's words; yet we doubt whether such an imitation of the reality would have been contemplated. It seems so utterly alien to Jewish sentiment,[§] as to be inconceivable for the deliberate act of One who held the Law in honour. Moreover, the act could hardly have been kept secret, even if the 'goodman of the house' had respectfully submitted to what would have greatly shocked his religious sentiments. Some rumour must have reached the ears of those who were willing to bear witness against Jesus. On such evidence a most damaging charge could have been founded; yet not a word of such charge is found in the records of the trial.[*]

(ii.) Seeing then that a literal interpretation of πάσχα in our Lord's words to the Twelve is precluded by the conditions of the occasion, we adopt the alternative, and understand 'passover' to be here used in a mystical sense.[†] In such sense undoubtedly He spoke when He called the bread His body, and the wine His blood. Whatever opinion may be held of the nature of the presence in the Eucharist, the bread and the wine were then before His sacrifice, as they are now after His resurrection, His body and His blood in a mystical and spiritual sense. His promise to drink wine with them in the Kingdom of God (Mt 26[29], Mk 14[25], Lk 22[18]) was conveyed in the same terms of mystery; for in the kingdom of redemption there is no place for the Jewish Passover,—that has waxed old and vanished,—and still less can a literal fulfilment be conceived as having hereafter a place in the kingdom of glory. Yet in that kingdom there will be a feast, the mystical and spiritual supper of the Lamb, where the host will be the real Passover, of which the annual victims were the figures; He who is therefore called by St. Paul, 'Christ our passover.'[‡]

6. It has been thought that the Last Supper, while not an imitation, was celebrated with some outward features which connected it with the annual Passover, although the chief characteristic, the lamb, was absent.[§] It may have been so. Perhaps there was unleavened bread, and the dish of bitter herbs; but the narratives contain not a word to favour such a supposition. They seem to describe an ordinary Eastern meal, ‖ with the one dish in the centre, into which all the guests put their hands. The usual custom of giving the complimentary sop was observed, and wine was passed round. We believe that the Last Supper was in form only an ordinary repast, but that it was attended by the exceptional circumstances of the washing of the feet by the host, the mystic acts with bread and wine, and the strange, prophetic, and spiritual utterances of a long discourse. As we attempt to portray the scene, the outlines

---

[*] The Rev. Matthew Power, S.J., in his learned and elaborate essay, *Anglo-Jewish Calendar for every day in the Gospels*, says, 'Our Lord, keeping to the lunar-legal computation, partook of His last supper on Thursday evening, Nisan 14. . . . The Jews, in obedience to the popular reckoning, had their Paschal Supper on Friday evening. . . . The Synoptists adopt, like our Lord, the strict lunar-legal mode of reckoning; the Fourth Gospel elects to follow the popular style.' Even if the rule of *Badhu* was already in force, as Father Matthew supposes, there remains the difficulty, which writers shirk, of any one obtaining the sacrifice of the lamb before the hour appointed by the priests. Stapfer is one of the few who recognize the difficulty; but he overcomes it by rejecting the Johannine account and accepting the others. See *Palestine in the time of Christ*, p. 323 f. Cf. *JE* ix. 553.

[†] Mt 26[2] and parallels compared with Jn 13[1. 2] do not suggest any difference of practice as to the date of observing the anniversary.

[‡] Caspari (*Chron. Geogr. Einleit.*), referring to *Pesachim* x., supposes the Supper to have been a *Mazzoth* meal, of which the essential element was unleavened cakes (*mazzoth*), with or without a lamb, eaten everywhere, and by all—for *all* were required to eat unleavened bread, though only the ceremonially clean were permitted to partake of the lamb—such meals being still observed in the present age.

[§] 'Jews . . . would consider it a shocking piece of profanation to enact anything resembling the great Paschal meal the evening before its time.' Peiritz (himself a Jew), *op. cit.* p. 30.

[*] The Rev. G. H. Box has contended with much ability in an article in *JThSt*, April 1902, that not the Passover, but the weekly *Ḳiddush*, which preceded the meal on the eve of the Sabbath, is the antecedent of the Eucharist. In this case our Lord must have celebrated it 24 hours earlier; but Mr. Box supposes that He often celebrated *Ḳiddush*; there was *Ḳiddush* of Passover and of Pentecost, and other occasions, besides the weekly Sanctification. In the January number of *JThSt* the Rev. Dr. Lambert, replying to Mr. Box's argument, that the evidence of the first three Evangelists is self-contradictory, follows Chwolson by supposing an error in the text. We make no supposition, but offer an explanation of the traditional evidence.

Dr. J. Armitage Robinson expresses himself in harmony with our view: 'The Eucharist had, in its earliest form, an element in common with the ordinary Jewish meal, which was sanctified by thanksgivings uttered over the bread and over the cup. . . . Our conception of the original institution must not be dominated by the consideration of the elaborate ceremonial of the Passover celebration. Such a consideration belongs rather to the subsequent development of the Eucharist as a Christian rite' (art. 'Eucharist' in *Encyc. Bibl.* coll. 1419, 1420).

[†] Our Lord was pleased to veil the meaning of His words in many ways. Besides prophecies of His death, which were misunderstood (Mk 9[32]), and parables, which were not explained to all (Mt 13[11]), and figures, as sleep for death (Jn 11[11]), He spoke in mystery of His body as a temple (Jn 2[19]), of birth by water and the Spirit (3[5]), of eating His flesh and drinking His blood (6[53]). So, we believe, He called the Supper 'this Passover,' not in the literal, but in a mystical sense.

[‡] This title of the Saviour, although of such frequent occurrence in ecclesiastical and theological language, occurs in the NT only at 1 Co 5[7], the writer being St. Paul, who was intimately associated with the only Evangelist who records (Lk 22[15]) that our Lord spoke of His Last Supper as τοῦτο τὸ πάσχα.

[§] See note [‡] on preced. column.

‖ See the account, from personal experience, of an Eastern supper, given by Peiritz, *op. cit.* pp. 13-15 and note, and the similar account by Thomson in *The Land and the Book*, pp. 126-128.

are simple, homely, ordinary; but the whole is pervaded by an air of mystery. It was not the Passover of Moses, but it was the initiation of the Passover of Christ.* But see PASSOVER (II.).

7. When we pass from the sacred narratives to Patristic tradition, we encounter controversy about the date of Easter which lasted for several generations, but produced no decision as to the nature of the Last Supper. The early separation of the Church from the Synagogue, although inevitable, was a loss to the former. Gentile converts found themselves the inhe.itors of rites and Scriptures derived from Jewish believers whose language and ideas they understood but imperfectly; hence the opinion obtained some credence, that Christ celebrated an anticipatory Passover; for they overlooked the insuperable hindrances to such an act which the Jewish customs would present. But one tradition has an important bearing on our inquiry. The Primitive Church had no scruple about the use of leavened bread in the Eucharist. Such has been the immemorial custom of the unchanging East; while in the West (as few would now deny), the use of unleavened wafers was brought in during the Middle Ages. If our Lord instituted the Sacrament at a Paschal Supper, He used, of necessity, unleavened bread. The desire to imitate His acts would, surely, if He had consecrated in unleavened, have found expression in an opinion that ordinary bread was inadmissible. There is no ancient tradition, of universal acceptance, that the sacramental bread must be unleavened. The use of ordinary bread is an unconscious admission that the Last Supper was not a Passover.†

8. The discussion of this question is not merely academical. The practice of some Christians has been affected by the views entertained of the nature of the Last Supper. On the supposition that it was a Passover, it has been contended that the use of unleavened bread is obligatory in the Eucharist. The teetotaller extends the exclusion of leaven to the chalice, and demands the use of unfermented wine. Many love to think that they can find the words sung after the Supper in the Psalms of the Paschal *Hallel*. But the conclusions at which we have arrived lend no authority to the exclusion of leaven from the Lord's Table, and are inconsistent with many expressions in well-known Communion Hymns, and in books of Sacramental devotion.‡ There may be practical reasons for the use of wafers in preference to cubes of ordinary bread. As to what is called 'unfermented wine,' a previous question arises, whether mere grape juice is true wine. But whatever may be deemed most suitable for the sacramental elements in present-day use, our contention is that the Holy Mysteries were first administered at an ordinary meal, and with ordinary bread and wine for their outward and visible form.

LITERATURE.—See under DATES and LORD'S SUPPER.

G. H. GWILLIAM.

LATCHET (ἱμάς, Lk 3¹⁶, Mk 1⁷, Jn 1²⁷).—The leathern strap attached to the sandal, which, passing several times across the foot, was secured round the ankle, thus fixing the sandal securely. See artt. SANDAL and SHOE. The most menial service which can be exacted from an Oriental is to remove o. carry his master's shoes. Hence, too, the greatest honour a host can show to his guest is to stoop down and remove his shoes. John the Baptist counted himself unworthy to perform this service for Christ. J. SOUTAR.

LATIN.—See TITLE ON CROSS.

LAUGHTER.

The two words found in NT for 'laughter' correspond almost exactly in significance with the two commonly occurring in OT. καταγελάω (Mt 9²⁴ ‖ Mk 5⁴⁰ and Lk 8⁵³) = לָעַג, which always means *scornful, derisive laughter* (e.g. Pr 17⁵, Is 37²², Ps 2⁴). On the other hand, γελάω (Lk 6²¹) = שָׂחַק, which is the more general term, and while sometimes implying derision (as in Job 30¹, Pr 1²⁶), is more usually found in the sense of *merry laughter*, as opposed to the gloom of sadness (e.g. Pr 29⁹, Ec 3⁴ 2² 10¹⁹, Pr 14¹³). But, while in OT these words and others denoting mirth and gleefulness are often found, their parallels are very rare in NT. Beyond the two passages already mentioned, there is only one (Ja 4⁹) in which laughter is referred to, —and this is obviously a reminiscence of Christ's sayings as reported in Lk 6²¹·²⁵,—and one other in which jesting (εὐτραπελία)* is forbidden to the Christian by St. Paul (Eph 5⁴). The word which does occur in NT, and which is characteristic of it, is χαρά (53 times), χαίρω (6 times); but this is almost always a restrained and chastened joy rather than one which breaks out into laughter—describing the condition of the mind rather than the expression of the emotions. A stronger word, implying more emotional demonstration, is ἀγαλλιάω; see esp. Lk 10²¹, where it seems to be implied that Jesus manifested His joy by outward signs; the word in 14¹·⁴⁴ 6²³ (σκιρτάω) is stronger still, and can hardly be used except where almost extravagant demonstrations of pleasure are intended.

It has been too readily inferred from the comparative absence in NT of allusions to mirth, that Jesus was characterized by a certain sobriety of demeanour which precludes us from thinking of Him as ever laughing or even smiling, and that Christianity from the first discouraged anything in the form of laughter-provoking mirth. Thus the statements—'We are never told that (Jesus) laughed, while we are once told that He wept' (Farrar, *Life of Christ*, p. 242); 'we never read that Jesus laughed, and but once that He rejoiced in spirit' (Jer. Taylor), and similar statements are based on nothing more than a dim and untrustworthy tradition,† and convey an impression which is far from being warranted by the general tenor of the Gospel narrative. The common use of the title 'Man of Sorrows,' dictated no doubt by the deepest motives, and the conventional portraits of Christ, showing Him always pensive and often sorrowful, have been responsible for fostering the thought of a Christ who was constantly grave, if not sad. A writer like Renan goes to the opposite extreme; but there is at least as much support for his representation of a teacher whose 'sweet gaiety constantly found expression in lively reflexions and kindly pleasantries.'‡ What evidence there is, indeed, is on the whole against the traditional view. Jesus definitely dissociated Himself from the austerer school of His time (Lk 5³³ff·, Mt 9¹⁴, Mk 2¹⁸); He made it a habit to enter convivial assemblies, and was a guest at feasts where laughter, jest, and song were a part of the order of the day;§ He watched, if He did not join in, the merry games of children (Lk 7³²), and loved their company. He chose, as an analogy for the joy of God over a redeemed soul, the exuberant merry-

---

* Compare the remarks of Isaac Williams in *The Holy Week*, pt. iv. § ii. It is interesting to note that two writers so widely separated by antecedents and education, and to some extent by sympathies, as were he and Peiritz, arrive from different points at the same conclusion. In one case it is the opinion of a mind steeped in Patristic lore, in the other of a very learned Rabbinical scholar.

† See full account of the Eucharistic bread in art. 'Elements' in *Dict. of Christ. Antiq.* (Smith and Cheetham), i. p. 601 f.; cf. Bingham's *Antiquities*, bk. xv. ch. ii. § 5. Some heretics of early days, the Aquarians, Encratites, and Hydroparastatæ, who were teetotallers, consecrated in water; see Bingham, *ib.* § 7.

‡ The Anglican Liturgy in the Proper Preface for Easter recognizes Christ as 'the very Paschal Lamb,' but throughout the Service there is not an expression or allusion which implies a particular view of the nature of the Last Supper.

---

* See Trench, *Synonyms*, *s.v.*; and cf. 'the pleasantries of fools' (χάριτες μωρῶν), Sir 20¹³.

† The alleged Ep. of P. Lentulus, Procons. of Judæa, to the Roman Senate.

‡ *Vie de Jésus*, 1879, p. 196.

§ Edersheim, describing marriage-feasts, says, 'Not a few instances of riotous merriment and even dubious jokes on the part of the greatest Rabbis are mentioned' (*Life and Times of Jesus the Messiah*, i. p. 355).

making (Lk 15[23. 25]) of a father to whom his son was restored,* and in bidding His disciples rejoice in their very tribulations, uses a word which suggests vehement demonstrations of joy (Lk 6[23]). There is nothing in the Gospels to encourage the supposition that He frowned upon innocent mirth or checked its exhibition in His followers. On the contrary, on one occasion at least, He declined to interfere with a spontaneous outburst of exhilaration on their part (Lk 19[37]). He bade them, even when they fasted, not be of a sad countenance (Mt 6[16]), and His chief concern was not so much to regulate the manner of their joy as to purify its motive (Lk 10[20]).

Against the *a priori* view that Jesus never laughed, a view which is based upon a misdirected reverence and a one-sided conception of His nature, has to be set the consideration that such a view tends to dehumanize the 'Son of Man.' The faculty for laughter, as recent psychologists have shown, is eminently human, and its absence is a defect.† There may be saintly men to whom anything like boisterous hilarity is impossible, but he whose face is never lit with a smile, and whose voice never has the infectious ring of joy, is lacking in full-orbed humanity (cf. Carlyle, *Sartor, ad init.*). If Jesus showed the natural emotions of sorrow, there is every reason to suppose that He showed those of joy.

There is as little support for the view that the NT encourages a religion in which laughter finds no legitimate place. The first disciples of Jesus, like those of St. Francis, who became known as *joculatores Domini*, appear to have shown a vivacity and cheerfulness in complete contrast to the rigid and frigid demeanour engendered by Pharisaism ; and this attitude was encouraged by their Master, who did not expect 'the sons of the bride-chamber' to mourn so long as the 'bridegroom' was with them (Mt 9[15], cf. 15[1. 2]).

But there is more to be said. Nearly all the world's greatest teachers have employed laughter, in one or other of its subtler forms, as a means of gaining a hearing for the truth they had to deliver. Was Jesus an exception to this rule? Is there any real reason for refusing to apply to His case the saying, *Ridentem dicere verum quid vetat?* Can it be said that He never used the Socratic method of proving the reasonableness of His teaching by showing the incongruous and even ridiculous position in which those who rejected it involved themselves? It has been very generally assumed that such a method was beneath the dignity, or foreign to the nature of the Son of God. Thus it is said, 'He brought peace wherever He came, but He never awakened mirth . . . The inquiry whether Jesus had the sense of humour is not simply trivial and irreverent ; it betrays a fundamental misconception of that holy life of redeeming love.' ‡ The question, however, cannot be so easily disposed of. In the Gospels there are sayings of Jesus which a rational exegesis finds it almost impossible to explain apart from the assumption that they show a vein of humour. Indeed, the writer just quoted admits that Jesus 'deigned to make use of the quaint and often humorous maxims so dear to the common folk.' It is allowed by writers of the most orthodox school that irony and satire were used by Jesus upon occasion ; if He saw fit to employ these sterner weapons, the gentler one of humour would not be beneath Him. When Jesus says to the Jews, 'Many good works have I showed you

from my Father ; for which of these works do ye stone me?' the touch of irony is unmistakable (Jn 19[32]),* as it is also in the expression 'everlasting tents' (Lk 16[9]). When He says to His disciples, 'Sleep on now' (Mk 14[41]), it is in a tone of gentle raillery ; † and His conversation with the Syrophœnician woman is in the same tone (7[25ff.]). His answer to the lawyer, 'This do and thou shalt live,' seems to be most naturally interpreted as ironical (Lk 10[28]). The reply to His critics, 'I came not to call the righteous, but sinners' (Mk 2[17]), is in the same vein, as is the passage, 'Full well (καλῶς) do ye reject the commandment of God' (7[9]). In Mt 6[2], literalists have sought in vain to prove that it was a practice among Pharisaic almsgivers to 'sound a trumpet' ; obviously the passage is satirical. The element of satire runs through the scathing denunciations of the Pharisees and scribes (23, etc.). But the crucial instance is the parable of the Unjust Steward (Lk 16[1-9]). Commentators have exhausted their ingenuity in devising all possible and impossible explanations of Christ's commendation of the steward, through failing to see that the whole passage is sarcastic, pouring laughter upon the futile trust that men put in the power of mammon ; v.[9] in particular is 'a sudden turn of the sublimest and most crushing irony.' ‡

But if it was in keeping with the mission of Jesus that He should use irony, still more natural was it that humour (wh. see) should enter into His speech. Humour is in its nature both human and humane. The greatest humorists have been the best lovers of men and the most endowed with sympathy (*e.g.* 'gentle' Shakspeare and Charles Lamb). The foremost religious teachers have almost invariably been possessed of humour, and have proved the truth of Milton's dictum (Preface to *Animadversions upon the Remonstrant*) that 'the vein of laughing hath ofttimes a strong and sinewy force in teaching and confuting.' It is probable that the reluctance, which has existed from early times, to admit any tone of raillery or playfulness in Christ's teaching, has been responsible for the loss of the original force of some of His sayings. Jesus has suffered from His reporters. Yet enough passages remain to show that this element was often present. The pictures of a man endeavouring to serve two masters at once (Mt 6[24]), of another who feeds swine with pearls (7[6]), of a camel trying to get through a needle's eye (19[24]), of a light being put under a bushel (5[15]), of him who sees a splinter in his brother's eye, but fails to notice the beam in his own (7[3]), of Beelzebub at variance with Beelzebub (12[24ff.]), of men who have eyes but do not see (Mk 8[18]), of one blind man guiding another (Mt 15[14]), of a father who should give his son a stone instead of a loaf (7[9])—these are all instances of that perception of the incongruous which is the soul of humour.§ We know that Jesus sometimes used words with a play upon their meaning (Lk 5[10], Mt 4[19], Lk 9[60]). The ready way in which He answers a question by propounding another which at first seems irrelevant (Mt 20[22] 21[24]), His unexpected manner of turning the tables upon a critic (Lk 7[36ff.]), His use of illustrations which would cause, by their homely aptness, an involuntary smile (Mk 2[21], Lk 11[6]), His epigrammatic way of putting a truth so as to give a sudden satisfaction (Mk 2[27]), and His use of daring hyperbole (Lk 19[40]),||

---

* εὐφραίνεσθαι in Lk. is specially used of convivial mirth (see 12[19] 15[23]).

† See James Sully, *Essay on Laughter.*

‡ See art. 'Our Lord's Use of Common Proverbs,' *Expositor,* Dec. 1902.

* Westcott, *in loc.*

† Cf. F. W. Robertson, *Serm.* (2nd ser.) xx. 'The Irreparable Past.'

‡ See *Expositor,* Dec. 1895 ; *Good Words,* Oct. 1867.

§ Cf. the *Logion* of Grenfell and Hunt : 'Thou hearest with one ear (but the other thou hast closed).'

|| Cf. the obscure saying, reported by Papias and quoted by Irenæus (*adv. Hær.* v. 33. 3), of the vine with ten thousand

are indications that Jesus thought it not beneath Him to laugh with those that laugh.

On this whole subject nothing can be more just than the words of A. B. Bruce (*Parabolic Teaching of Christ*, p. 149):

'With pathos often goes humour, and so it is in the parables. . . . The spirit of Jesus was too earnest to indulge in idle mirth; but just because He was so earnest and so sympathetic, He expressed Himself at times in a manner which provokes a smile; laughter and tears, as it were, mingling in His eyes as He spake. It were a false propriety which took for granted that an expositor was necessarily off the track, because in his interpretation of these parables an element of holy playfulness appears blended with the deep seriousness which pervades them throughout.'

LITERATURE.—Martensen, *Chr. Ethics*, i. 186 ff.; D. Smith in *Exp. Times*, xii. [1901] 546; *Expositor*, II. viii. [1884] 92 ff.; Welldon, *Fire Upon the Altar*, 105; G. H. Morrison, *Sun-rise*, p. 43.

J. ROSS MURRAY.

LAW.—The question of Christ's relation to the Jewish law is one of fundamental importance for the origin of Christianity, but at the same time one of peculiar difficulty. The difficulty arises, to some extent, from the fact that His own teaching marks a period of transition, when the old was already antiquated, while the new was still unborn. A further difficulty is created by the relation in which the actual conduct of Jesus stood to the principles which He laid down. Moreover, the question arises whether His attitude remained the same through the whole course of His ministry, or whether He came to realize that His fundamental principles carried Him further than He had at first anticipated. Lastly, when we remember how bitter was the strife which this very question aroused in the primitive Church, the misgiving is certainly not unreasonable, that this may have been reflected back into the life of the Founder, and sayings placed in His mouth endorsing one of the later partisan views. Our present subject is that of the **Ceremonial Law.**

It must be clearly recognized that the distinction between *moral* and *ceremonial* law is not one sanctioned in the Law itself. All its parts alike were the command of God. The distinction has maintained its vitality in virtue of a praiseworthy ethical interest. The antinomianism of St. Paul seemed to endanger morality, and those who could not rise to his point of view, that it was precisely in this way that morality was secured, turned Christianity into a new legalism, and explained his doctrine that the Law was abolished to mean that Christians were no longer compelled to practise Jewish ceremonies. This was, of course, to reduce much that he said to the unmeaning. It is precisely the moral law that St. Paul had chiefly in mind. The Decalogue is described as 'the ministration of death written and engraven on stones' (2 Co 3⁷ RV); and, to illustrate the sin-producing effects of the Law, St. Paul quotes one of the Ten Commandments (Ro 7⁷). His doctrine was unquestionably that the Law as a whole was done away for all who were in Christ, inasmuch as they had crucified the flesh, which was the home of sin, and thus had lost everything to which the Law could appeal as provocation to sin, while they had escaped into the freedom of the Spirit, and could therefore no longer be under the constraint of the Law. But even St. Paul was forced to recognize that his magnificent idealism was not milk for babes, hence moral exhortation found a large place in his Epistles, side by side with the loftiest assertions of a Christian's freedom from sin, flesh, and the Law. But St. Paul is quite explicit that this freedom is to be strenuously maintained in the sphere of Jewish ceremonies, especially circumcision, and sacred days and seasons. On the other hand, a party in the Early Church insisted passionately on the permanent validity of the Law, and especially of circumcision, as essential to salvation. It lies beyond our limits to trace the history of this controversy, but a reference to it is necessary for the reason already indicated.

Jesus was Himself born into a Jewish home, and the rites prescribed by the Jewish law were scrupulously fulfilled in His case. His parents did not belong to the ranks of the Pharisees, hence His early training was healthier than that of St. Paul; but He, like His great Apostle, was born under the Law (Gal 4⁴), and initiated by circumcision into the Covenant on the eighth day (Lk 2²¹). His mother presented Him as her firstborn male child to the Lord in the Temple, and offered the

stems. In its exuberant playfulness of fancy it exceeds anything in the Gospels; it is probably based on an actual saying of Christ (see Westcott, *Introd.* p. 433).

sacrifice of purification prescribed in the Law (Lk 2²²⁻²⁴), and thus 'accomplished all things that were according to the law of the Lord' (Lk 2³⁹). Joseph and Mary went up each year to the feast of the Passover at Jerusalem (Lk 2⁴¹). So far as we can see, Jesus Himself was a strict observer of the Law. Whatever His attitude towards it during His ministry, we may assume without question that, till He was conscious of His Messianic vocation, His obedience to the Law was scrupulously and heartily rendered. It lay in the nature of the case, however, that the old bottles of Judaism should be unfit to receive the new wine of the Kingdom with which He knew Himself to be intrusted. The question whether this was clear to Him from the first, or whether it became clear only in the course of His controversy with the scribes, cannot be answered with certainty, in view of the doubt which hangs over the chronology of the ministry. And His conduct here was regulated by much the same need for reserve as He practised in reference to His self-revelation as Messiah. A premature declaration would have created an extremely difficult situation. All He could do was to utter His principles and leave the practical inferences to be drawn, when the time was ripe, by those who shared His spirit.

On one great branch of this question, however, Jesus expressed Himself clearly and without compromise. The morbid anxiety of the scribes to make a hedge about the Law so that all possible approaches to its violation might be blocked, added to the hair-splitting casuistry in which moralists of their type delighted, and the lawyer's instinct for precise and exhaustive definition, had led to the elaboration of the precepts in the Law into a vast system of tradition. Moreover, the heavier the burden grew, the greater grew the temptation to find a literal fulfilment which should be an escape from the spirit. All this apparatus of piety demanded leisure to master and perform, such leisure as no man with his daily bread to earn could command; hence arose a morality unfitted for the normal human life. Against all this tradition Jesus entered an emphatic protest. His attitude towards it was wholly different from that which He assumed towards the written Law. The scribes made void by their tradition the word of God, and every plant which His heavenly Father had not planted He said should be rooted up. Nevertheless, in vindicating the Law against the tradition, He enunciated principles which pointed forward to the abolition of both. The points on which He came into conflict with Jewish ceremonialism were Fasting, the law of Uncleanness, the Temple service, and the cancelling of primary human duties by feigned respect for duties to God.

1. If the order of incidents in the Gospel of St. Mark could be accepted as chronological, the first collision of Jesus with the representatives of the tradition was occasioned by His eating with publicans and sinners at the house of Levi (Mk 2¹⁵ᶠᶠ·). Although stress cannot be laid on the order in which the incidents are narrated, this furnishes us with an excellent illustration of the way in which the fundamental ideas of Jesus brought Him into conflict with the religious prejudices of His time. His doctrine of the Fatherhood of God and of the incomparable value of the human soul were fundamental convictions. To this was added the consciousness of His own mission to restore the lost children to their Father. Hence He met the criticism of His conduct in associating with the degraded by the explanation that He was a physician, and where was the physician's place but in the midst of the sick? There is indeed a terrible irony in the words, for there were none whose moral and religious health was, to the eyes of Jesus, in a more desperate condition than that of His critics. But scandalized as they might be by conduct so unprofessional on the part of a teacher, there was an obvious conclusiveness in the reply of Jesus which could have been evaded only by the assertion that the salvation of such people was not desirable. The two types of holiness emerge in clear contradiction—the type which seeks to avoid all contact with the contaminating in order that personal purity may not be compromised, and the type that is entirely forgetful of self in its zeal for the regeneration of others. It is in connexion with a similar accusation that St. Luke relates the parables of the Lost Sheep, the Lost Drachma, and the Lost Son (Lk 15). Similarly Christ's lodging with Zacchæus the publican gave rise to criticism; and here again Jesus explained His action by His mission: 'The Son of Man came to seek and to save that which was lost' (Lk 19[10]).

2. The second point in which the new type displayed a contrast with the old was in the matter of **Fasting**. Wonder was excited that, while the Pharisees and the disciples of the Baptist fasted, the disciples of Jesus neglected this religious exercise. The Pharisees fasted twice in the week, on Monday and Thursday. What fasts were observed by the disciples of John we do not know. But the distinction was not one simply between disciples, it went back to the leaders. The Baptist was an ascetic, clothed in camel's hair and a leathern girdle, with locusts and wild honey for his food; his congenial home was the desert, his message one of judgment to come, the axe already lying at the root of the tree. He came neither eating nor drinking, and this unsociable disposition called forth the charge that he had a devil. Jesus, on the other hand, was no ascetic; so little of an ascetic, in fact, that His enemies taxed Him with over-indulgence: 'The Son of Man came eating and drinking, and they say, Behold a gluttonous man and a winebibber, a friend of publicans and sinners' (Mt 11[19]). Jesus defends His disciples against the criticism implied in the question, 'Why do John's disciples and the disciples of the Pharisees fast, but thy disciples fast not?' (Mk 2[18]) by the answer, 'Can the sons of the bride-chamber fast while the bridegroom is with them? as long as they have the bridegroom with them they cannot fast.' The principle underlying this is that the external practice must be a spontaneous expression of the inward feeling. Fasting is out of place in their present circumstances, they have the bridegroom with them, therefore all is joy and festivity. It would be a piece of unreality to introduce into their present religious life an element so incongruous. But He proceeds: 'The days will come, when the bridegroom shall be taken away from them, and then will they fast in that day.' The reference is to His own death; and possibly the foreboding expressed should lead us to assign this incident to His later ministry, after the declaration of Messiahship had been made and the prediction of death had been uttered. On the other hand, the veiled allusion makes it possible that those who heard it would not catch His meaning, and we can, in that case, assign it to a late date only if we are clear that Jesus Himself became conscious at a comparatively late period in His ministry of the death that awaited Him. The incident itself rather makes the impression that it belongs to the earlier period of Christ's activity. This was one of the respects in which failure to conform to conventional piety would early attract attention.

Wellhausen regards the incident as unauthentic. He points to the curious fact that the question is one between the disciples of the Baptist and of Jesus, and draws the inference that it is a justification for the deviation of the later practice of Christ's followers from that of Jesus Himself, who in practice conformed strictly to the Judaism of His time. He confirms this by pointing out that as a matter of fact the bridegroom is not taken away from wedding festivities, and here therefore the choice of expression has been determined by the actual fact of Christ's removal by death. However plausible this suggestion may be, the sayings bear rather the stamp of Jesus than of the early Apostolic Church. The criticism of the disciples rather than of Jesus has its parallel in the incident of the plucking of the ears of corn on the Sabbath and the disciples eating with unwashed hands, and the temper of the Master was much freer than that of the timidly legalistic disciples.

In the Sermon on the Mount fasting is recognized as a fitting religious exercise; but, as in the case of prayer and almsgiving, it is essential, for its true religious quality to be preserved, that it should be practised without ostentation. The religious self-advertisement which characterized the Pharisees eviscerated these exercises of all their value. They were to be a secret between a man and his God. In the most rigorous fasts washing and anointing were forbidden (*Taanith*, i. 6), while they were allowed in the less severe (*ib.* i. 4 f.). Jesus bids His followers anoint the head and wash the face when they fast, that no one may be able to detect that they are fasting (Mt 6[16-18]). See FASTING.

Immediately following the defence of the disciples for not fasting, we have in all the Synoptics (Mt 9[16f.], Mk 2[21f.], Lk 5[36f.]) the sayings about the undressed cloth and the new wine in the old wine-skins. The parables are difficult; the lesson taught is clearly the incompatibility of the new with the old, and the disaster that will inevitably follow any attempt to combine them. But it is by no means clear with what 'old' and 'new' should be identified, nor again can we assume that both parables express the same truth. It is possible, though improbable, that Jesus may intend by 'the old' the ancient piety of the Old Testament, and by 'the new' the new-fangled regulations of the scribes, His sense being that the old Divinely-given mode of life is being ruined by the tradition of men. But it is more likely that the usual view is right, according to which 'the old' is Judaism and 'the new' is the gospel. Even so, however, various interpretations are possible. Usually it has been thought that in both sayings Jesus is defending the attitude of His disciples: you cannot expect the new spirit of the gospel to be cast in the old moulds of Judaism; the new spirit must create new forms for itself. Weiss, however, considers that both parables constitute a defence of the attitude of John's disciples, they cannot be expected to combine the spirit of the Gospel with their legalist and ascetic habit of life (*Bibl. Theol. of NT*, i. 112). It is possible, however, that Beyschlag is correct in thinking that the parable of the undressed cloth on the old garment is a justification of John's disciples in fasting, while the parable of the new wine in the old bottles is a justification of the disciples of Jesus for refusing to follow their example (*NT Theol.* i. 114). The two sayings are connected by 'and,' it is true, but this conjunction has in the Synoptics a wider range of meaning than in English. Wellhausen finds the sayings difficult. He is not disposed to question their authenticity, though, as already mentioned, he strikes out the sayings immediately preceding.

3. Another point in which Jesus came into conflict with the tradition was that of **Ablutions** (Mk 7[1ff.] ||). To secure that nothing ceremonially unclean should be eaten, the Jews were very scrupulous in washing the hands before meals. The laws of cleanness and uncleanness touch life so much more closely than any others, that the casuistry of the scribes naturally finds in this matter a large field of exercise. The largest of the six books of the Mishna is given up to this topic. The purification of vessels alone occupies thirty chapters of this book. The Pentateuch itself exhibits more than the usual tendency to casuistry in this matter, but the tradition left the Law out of sight in the elaborateness of its regulations. In the time of Jesus tradition had become very strict with reference to the washing of the hands. The practice originated with the Pharisees, but was adopted by almost all the Jews. Even when the hands were ceremonially clean it was necessary to wash them, no doubt to guard against the possibility of unconscious defilement. If they were known to be unclean, they had to be washed twice before a meal; they were also washed after food; and some Pharisees washed even between the courses. The hands were held with the fingers up, so that the uncleanness might be washed down from them; and for the ceremony to be effectual it was necessary that the water should run down to the wrist (though we should probably not translate $\pi\upsilon\gamma\mu\hat{\eta}$, Mk 7^3, 'to the wrist'; see Swete, *ad loc.*). In Jn 2^6 we read of the six stone water-pots for the water of purification at the marriage in Cana; and the same Gospel tells us how the Jews purified themselves for the Passover (11^{55}), or took precautions against defilement which would disqualify them from eating it (18^{28}).

It was therefore natural that the neglect of some of the disciples should evoke criticism; and this criticism was uttered by officials from Jerusalem who had come down to watch the new movement (Mk 7^1). No mention is made here of any violation of the tradition on the part of Jesus Himself; though in Lk 11^{38} we are told that the Pharisee, at whose house Jesus was eating, was surprised that He neglected this ceremony. Jesus defended His disciples by a complete repudiation of the tradition. He pointed out that its effect was to nullify the Law rather than to establish it; and He illustrated this from the practice of dedicating to God that which ought to have been used by a man for the support of his parents. To this point it will be necessary to return. But in connexion with the question of hand-washing Jesus enunciated a principle of far-reaching importance which not only set aside the tradition, but even abrogated a large section of the Law. He asserted that not that which is without a man can, by going into him, defile him, but the things which proceed out of the man. The heart is the essential thing, food cannot come into contact with that; but it is in it that evil thoughts, words, or actions have their rise, and it is these that make a man unclean. Not what a man eats, but what he is, determines the question of his purity. Thus Jesus lifted the whole conception of cleanness and uncleanness out of the ceremonial into the ethical domain. But it is plain that this carried with it revolutionary conclusions, not only as to the tradition, but as to the Law; for much of the Law was occupied precisely with the uncleanness created by external things, and it is not improbable that St. Mark has definitely drawn this inference in his Gospel.

It is possible that the usual view taken of the passage, according to which the words 'making all meats clean' (Mk 7^{19}) are the concluding words of Jesus, should be accepted. This involves, however, a grammatical irregularity, and we ought perhaps to adopt the view taken by Origen, Gregory Thaumaturgus, and Chrysostom, ably defended by Field (*Notes on the Translation of the NT*, pp. 31, 32) and adopted by RV, Weizsäcker, Swete, Gould, Salmond, that they are the comment of the Evangelist, and that we should translate '*this he said*, making all meats clean.' On the other hand, the notes of Menzies and Wellhausen on the passage may be consulted.

The evasion of the Law by the Tradition here asserted by Jesus has been affirmed by some Jewish scholars not to have existed. (The reader may consult an appendix on 'Legal Evasions of the Law,' by Dr. Schechter in Montefiore's *Hibbert Lectures*, pp. 557-563; an article by Montefiore on 'Jewish Scholarship and Christian Silence' in the *Hibbert Journal* for Jan. 1903; the rejoinder to this by Menzies in July 1903, with a further rejoinder by Montefiore in Oct. 1903.) It is urged that the reference in the Jewish treatise *Nedarim* does not confirm the statement in St. Mark about Corban. Dr. Menzies accepts this; but when that is said, the matter is by no means ended. To the present writer it seems that the evidence of St. Mark is quite good evidence for the contemporary Judaism. If the assertion about Corban is untrue, of course it cannot be ascribed to Jesus, who could not have quoted, as a conclusive proof that the Jews cancelled the Law by their tradition, an example which His hearers would know to have no existence. Accordingly, if the statement is mistaken, it would have to be put down to the account of the Evangelist, though how he should have hit upon it unless such a custom was actually in vogue would be difficult to understand. In forming our judgment on a question of this kind certain leading principles must be kept in mind. The contemporary Judaism is most imperfectly known to us, and the documents which we have to use as our sources of information are, in many instances, centuries later than the rise of Christianity. Further, the stereotyping of Judaism must not be blindly accepted as if it guaranteed that doctrines or practices for which we have only late literary attestation were already developed in the time of Christ. We must remember that Judaism did not live in an intellectual vacuum, but in an atmosphere saturated with Christian germs. Especially, we cannot forget that controversy went on between Jews and Christians; and under its pressure it is by no means unreasonable to believe that Judaism may have undergone a considerable modification, above all, in the elimination of matter which proved susceptible to criticism. In the light of these principles the present writer has no hesitation in regarding the statement in St. Mark as good evidence for the existence of the practice of Corban in the time of Christ.

4. The next question touches Christ's relation to the **Temple**. His personal attitude towards it was that of a loyal Jew. Not only did He as a boy of twelve years recognize it as His Father's house (Lk 2^{49}), but, after He had entered on His ministry, He cleansed it by driving out the money-changers, and overturning the stalls of the traders (Mt $21^{12\text{ff.}}$ ||). According to the Fourth Gospel, His visits to Jerusalem were largely connected with the feasts. In His Sermon on the Mount He assumes that His disciples will offer sacrifice, and only requires that, before he offers, a man shall be reconciled to his brother (Mt $5^{23\text{f.}}$). In His great indictment of the scribes and Pharisees He rebukes them for their ruling that an oath by the temple or by the altar counts for nothing, while an oath by the gold of the temple, or a gift at the altar, is binding. The temple is greater than its gold, and makes it holy; and similarly it is by the altar that the gift is sanctified. To swear by the altar is to swear not only by it, but by the offering placed upon it; while to swear by the temple is to swear not only by it and all that it contains, but by Him who dwells therein (Mt $23^{16\text{ff.}}$ ||). But all this loyal recognition of the place filled by the temple and the honour due to it was combined with an inward detachment from it, which was a presage of the ultimate deliverance of Christianity from its connexion with it. This comes out very clearly in the story of the stater in the fish's mouth (Mt $17^{24\text{ff.}}$). The very doubt which was implied in the question whether Jesus paid the half-shekel which was levied as a temple-tax is most significant as to the drift towards freedom, which was already detected in His teaching. That He had not repudiated the toll, Peter is aware; but the reason for His obedience comes out plainly in the conversation He has with Peter on the subject. Taxes are taken by monarchs not from their sons, but from strangers. Therefore, since Jesus knows that He and His disciples are not aliens to God, but His children, the inference is that no payment of the tax can be legitimately expected from the children of the Kingdom. Jesus, however, bids Peter pay the tax for both, to avoid giving offence. In other words, Jesus regarded Himself and members of His Kingdom as released from every obligation to pay the half-shekel for the service of the temple, even if, in tender concession to the feelings of others, they did not avail themselves of their liberty. The temple-due in question was not definitely commanded in the Law, though it was a not unnatural deduction from Ex 30^{13}, which was itself a development of the rule of

Nehemiah that there should be an annual payment of a third of a shekel for the temple service (Neh 10[32, 33]). The temple itself, Christ predicted, would be destroyed. However we may explain the saying, 'Destroy this temple, and I will build it up in three days' (Jn 2[19]), He certainly foretold in His eschatological discourse (Mt 24[2]) the overthrow of the literal temple, and therewith naturally the cessation of the Jewish cultus.

It is not improbable that the saying, 'Destroy this temple,' should be similarly interpreted. The authenticity of the utterance is guaranteed by the use made of it in the trial of Jesus (Mk 14[58]), and the similar accusation at the trial of Stephen (Ac 6[14]), as well as the taunt addressed to Jesus on the cross (Mk 15[29]). It is true that the author of the Fourth Gospel interprets the saying as a reference to the body of Christ, fulfilled in the death and the resurrection. But this interpretation did not at the time occur either to the Jews or to the disciples. The retort of the former showed that they understood the reference to be to the literal temple, while the Evangelist expressly says that the interpretation he adopts occurred to the disciples only after the resurrection. It is, in fact, very difficult to believe that the saying referred to the death and resurrection of Jesus. In its connexion with the desecration and cleansing of the actual temple the allusion could naturally be nothing less than to its destruction, unless Jesus made His meaning clear by pointing to His body. But in that case the misunderstanding on the part of the Jews and the disciples would have been impossible, even if we leave aside the objection that so unveiled an allusion to His death and resurrection at this early period is most unlikely. Moreover, the contrast with the temple made with hands (Mk 14[58]) does not at all suit the human body. A difficulty, however, is raised by the Johannine version of the saying. We may, perhaps, assume that the latter is to be preferred to the version of the witnesses at the trial, in that it refers the work of destruction not to Jesus Himself, but to the Jews. Their present course of desecration, if they persist in it, will lead to the destruction of the temple. But it is not easy to believe that Jesus can have said that He would rebuild the temple that had been destroyed. Here the version of the witnesses is intrinsically the more credible, that He would build another temple in its place. And the contrast between the temple made with hands and the temple made without hands bears also the stamp of authenticity; the new is not simply to be a reproduction of the old, it is to be not a material, but a spiritual, structure. We may therefore conclude with some confidence that Jesus definitely anticipated the destruction of the centre of Jewish worship and the substitution of a spiritual temple in its place.

In the conversation with the woman of Samaria (Jn 4), Jesus is represented as dealing specifically with the question of the legitimate sanctuary as against the Samaritan temple (vv.[20-24]). He gives His verdict in favour of the temple at Jerusalem, but He asserts that the hour has already come for both sanctuaries to lose whatever exclusive legitimacy they may possess. The true worship of God transcends all local limitations; for God is spirit, and as such cannot be localized; and the worship He desires is a worship in spirit and in truth. There is no reason whatever for supposing that here the Evangelist is putting his own doctrine into the mouth of Jesus. The pregnant aphoristic form and penetrating insight of the saying stamp it as authentic. Moreover, it is quite in the line of the other teachings of Jesus with reference to the temple. He recognizes that the temple is His Father's house, and yet looks forward to its destruction; and similarly here He asserts the legitimacy of the Jewish as against the Samaritan temple, and yet looks forward to the speedy termination of worship in it.

5. It is certainly a very striking fact, in view of the immense importance attached in Judaism to the rite, that Jesus nowhere raises the question of the permanence of **Circumcision.** Had He pronounced upon it, the bitter controversy excited by the question in the primitive Church could hardly have arisen. But, naturally, occasion for discussing it did not so readily arise, and it was part of the method of Jesus to leave questions of practice to be settled by His disciples under the guidance of the Spirit and in the light of principles with which He had imbued them. There can be no reasonable doubt that St. Paul drew the true Christian inference. The great principle, that the external was unimportant in comparison with the inward, expressed in the abolition by Jesus of the Levitical laws as to unclean food, and in His doctrine that for worship in the material temple there was to be substituted worship in spirit and in truth, carried with it the conclusion that as a purely external rite circumcision could have no place in the religion of the spirit. Moreover, it was the sign of the Old Covenant; but Jesus knew that His blood consecrated a New Covenant. This implied the abolition of the Old Covenant, and naturally the abolition of circumcision, which was its sign. Indeed, the Old Testament itself was on the way to this, not simply in Jeremiah's prediction (31[31ff.]) of the New Covenant, but in the prophetic demand for a circumcision of the heart (Jer 4[4] 9[26]; cf. Ezk 44[7], Lv 26[41]). Here, as elsewhere, the attitude of Jesus linked itself closely to that previously taken by the prophets. Nor must we forget that Jesus contemplated that His religion would become universal. This in itself suggested the abolition of a rite which possessed no spiritual value, and was at the same time an almost insuperable barrier to the wide acceptance among the cultured of a religion that required it for full membership. See, further, art. CIRCUMCISION.

6. We have left till the last the much-debated passage Mt 5[17-20], since it is helpful in our interpretation of it to have before us the application of the principle in detail. The opening words of the passage, 'Think not that I am come to destroy the law or the prophets,' show clearly that Jesus was conscious that His teaching might not unjustifiably seem to carry this implication with it. There was an element which suggested a revolutionary attitude, but it was a mistaken inference that He meant to destroy the Law or the Prophets; it was His intention to fulfil them. It is important to observe here and elsewhere the way in which Jesus combines the Prophets with the Law. Unlike the current theology of His time, His teaching brought the Prophets into equal prominence with the Law; and it is of the OT system as a whole that He is thinking, and not simply of the legal enactments which constituted for the Rabbis almost the whole of religion. Yet it would be a mistake to infer that the Levitical requirements are here left out of sight. It is true that both the Rabbis and Jesus recognized degrees of importance among the laws, though their emphasis was very differently placed. Yet the Levitical laws were equally with others regarded by Jesus as laws of God, so that, in a comprehensive statement of the relation of His teaching to the religion of the OT, He could not leave them out of account. Now, we have already seen that the teaching of Jesus came into conflict not simply with the Tradition of the Elders, but with the Levitical laws of purity; that He explicitly abolished the laws of clean and unclean food, and looked forward to the cessation of the temple worship. Accordingly, we must give such a sense to His words as will harmonize the explanation of His intention not to destroy the Law with the fact that He did abolish some of its precepts, and contemplate the impossibility, through the destruction of the temple, of a large part of its injunctions. The unifying conception is contained in the word 'fulfil' ($\pi\lambda\eta\rho\tilde{\omega}\sigma\alpha\iota$). Jesus does not mean that He came to render a perfect obedience to the Law and the Prophets in His own life. The fulfilment forms an antithesis to the destruction. The destruction was such as would be accomplished by His teaching, not by His action, and similarly the fulfilment is something effected by His teaching. Besides, it is very difficult to believe that with the freedom of His principles, Jesus should have attached any importance to the perfect carrying out in action of the Law and the Prophets. What is meant is that, to use a familiar illustration, the gospel fulfils the Law as the flower fulfils the bud. Jesus sees in the Law a Divinely ordained system, but He is conscious that it is stamped with immaturity and defect. His function is to bring out its intrinsic significance by disengaging and carrying to perfection the principles entangled in it. Thus He does not abrogate the Law, but He transcends it, and, in doing so, antiquates it. In Beyschlag's words, it is 'confirmed and transformed in one breath.' What this means is admirably explained by Stevens in the following words: 'Jesus fulfils the OT system by rounding out into entire completeness what is incomplete in that system. In this process of fulfilment all that is imperfect, provisional, temporary, or, for any reason, needless to the perfect religion, falls away of its own accord, and all that is essential and permanent is conserved and embodied in Christianity' (*The Theology of the New Testament*, p. 19).

The two following verses (Mt 5$^{18.\ 19}$) create much difficulty. They seem to assert a permanence of the Law and its minutest details, and to affirm the insignificant place assigned in the Kingdom to any who should set aside one of the minor commandments. In view of the attitude adopted by Jesus towards the law of uncleanness, the Sabbath, and divorce, it is not surprising that doubts have been expressed as to the genuineness of the saying. It is out of the question to argue with Wendt that 'the law' is not a written law but an ideal law, for the reference to the jot and tittle implies a written law, and there is nothing to indicate that 'the law' is used here in two different senses. Beyschlag argues for the genuineness of the saying, which is also attested by Lk 16^{17} 'It is easier for heaven and earth to pass away, than for one tittle of the law to fail.' If it is genuine, the best explanation is that given by Beyschlag, that we must explain here of spiritual fulfilments. No commandment, even the most trifling, is a mere empty husk; each has a Divine thought which must come to its rights before the husk of the letter is allowed to perish (*NT Theol.* i. 110 f.). It is, however, very difficult to believe that this interpretation is correct, inasmuch as it would be hard to understand what Divine idea Jesus could think was latent in innumerable trifling details of the Law. The immediate impression made by the words is surely that the Law, to its minutest details, was to be regarded as permanent. When we remember how bitter was the controversy created by the question of the Law in the Early Church, it is not easy to avoid the conclusion that here we have an expression from a Jewish-Christian point of view, according to which Jesus is made explicitly to disavow the movement led by St. Paul, not indeed that St. Paul is regarded as outside the Kingdom, but as one of the least in it. It would, however, be perhaps too far-fetched to connect the words 'least in the kingdom of heaven' with St. Paul's designation of himself as the 'least of the apostles.'

LITERATURE.—The subject is discussed in the New Testament Theologies, the treatises on the Teaching of Jesus, and in the Lives of Christ and the commentaries. A very able monograph by R. Mackintosh, *Christ and the Jewish Law*, is devoted to the subject. Other works that may be mentioned are: Schürer, *Die Predigt Jesu in ihrem Verhältniss zum alten Testament und zum Judenthum* (1882); Bousset, *Jesu Predigt in ihrem Gegensatz zum Judenthum* (1892); Jacob, *Jesu Stellung zum mosaischen Gesetz* (1893); also the section 'Christus und das mosaische Gesetz' in Ritschl's *Die Entstehung der altkatholischen Kirche* [2] (1857); cf. also Hastings' *DB* iii. 73–76, and Extra Vol. p. 22 ff.

See also following article.

                     A. S. PEAKE.

LAW OF GOD.—We are not entitled to gather from the teaching of Jesus in the Gospels that He made any formal distinction between the Law of Moses and the Law of God. His mission being not to destroy but to fulfil the Law and the Prophets (Mt 5^{17}), so far from saying anything in disparagement of the Law of Moses or from encouraging His disciples to assume an attitude of independence with regard to it, He expressly recognized the authority of the Law of Moses as such, and of the Pharisees as its official interpreters (Mt 23$^{1-3}$).

One great aim of His teaching being, however, to counteract the influence of the Pharisaism of the time, under which zeal for the Law had degenerated into a pedantic legalism, which made outward conformity to the letter all-important and caused the true interests of religion and morality to be lost sight of amid the Shibboleths of national ritualism, He sought to concentrate the attention of His hearers upon the true meaning of the Law. In doing this He practically ignored the distinctions of the scribes between greater and lesser commandments of the Law, and between the Law, the Prophets, and the Psalms (or 'the Writings'), and insisted upon the authority of Scripture as the word of God. What God says in Scripture, the inspired record of Revelation, is for Jesus the final court of appeal. 'The Scripture cannot be broken' (Jn 10^{35}) is a principle never once lost sight of in any controversy.

At the same time, as Jesus Himself taught as One who had authority (Mt 7^{29} ‖ Mk 1^{22}), quietly but none the less emphatically asserting His right to explain the spirit and meaning of the Divine word, He did distinguish and teach His disciples to distinguish between letter and spirit, that which was permanent and universal in the Law and that which was partial and temporary. It is therefore possible, and even almost necessary, with a view to a clear understanding of Christ's attitude towards the Law, to distinguish between the Law of God, meaning by the term that which is of universal validity, and those elements in the Law of Moses which are merely associated with a particular dispensation, a temporary manifestation of God's will.

1. A typical illustration of the propriety of such a distinction is found in that passage in which Jesus, dealing with the question of marriage and divorce, treats the Mosaic law on the subject as an instance of accommodation to an imperfect state of society (Mt 19$^{3-8}$ ‖ Mk 10$^{2-9}$). 'For the hardness of your heart he wrote you this precept. But from the beginning of the creation God made them male and female,' etc. (Mk 10$^{5-6\text{ff.}}$). Here we see at once a distinction made between the Mosaic precept and the Divine law. The former allowed divorce upon certain well-understood grounds. The Pharisees put their own lax interpretation upon this precept, and multiplied the causes of divorce to an extent far beyond what the precept actually justified. Christ's reply to the question of His adversaries on this point was simply to remind them of the original Divine ordinance, according to which the marriage bond was made indissoluble. The Law of Moses permitted divorce, but the Law of God maintained the sanctity of the marriage bond, and this represented the point of view from which the whole question ought to be regarded. 'They twain shall be one flesh. What therefore God hath joined together let not man put asunder.' In this connexion the Law of God and the Law of Moses are to one another in the relation of the spirit to the letter. This typical instance illustrates the principle upon which Jesus proceeded in His interpretation of the Divine law. His aim throughout was to call at-

tention to the true spirit and purpose of the Law, to that in it which was of essential and permanent value. That the spirit of the Law, of which the letter is but the necessarily inadequate expression, is the Law of God, the manifestation of the Father's will for the moral and spiritual good of His children.

2. The attitude which Jesus adopted towards the whole question of the Law, considered as the Law of God, is well exemplified in the Sermon on the Mount, and in particular in those words which may be fitly taken as the motto of His teaching : 'Think not that I am come to destroy the law or the prophets. I am not come to destroy, but to fulfil' (Mt 5[17]; see preced. art.). In the contrast between what 'was said by them of old time' and His own emphatic 'But I say unto you,' we find the distinction between the Law of Moses and the Law of God. In the latter case He clearly speaks as God's representative, and we are reminded of John the Baptist's illustration of the difference between Christ and himself, the last of the Prophets : 'He whom God hath sent speaketh the words of God ; for God giveth not the Spirit by measure [unto him]' (Jn 3[34]). In the one case, the statute which Jesus *quotes*, we have to do with the letter of the Law, that with which alone the scribes occupied themselves and upon which they founded their casuistical refinements. In the other case, the words 'But I say unto you' bid us go behind the letter and get at the root of the matter, 'for the letter killeth, but the Spirit giveth life' (2 Co 3[6]). Thus, in proceeding to apply the principle which He has just laid down (Mt 5[17]), Jesus starts with the comprehensive statement of v.[20] 'For I say unto you, That except your righteousness shall exceed the righteousness of the scribes and Pharisees, ye shall in no case enter into the kingdom of heaven.'

From this point He goes on to deal with typical instances of the difference between letter and spirit in the Law. He begins with a commandment of the Decalogue, the Sixth, coupled with a corresponding passage from the Mosaic legislation, 'and whosoever shall kill, shall be in danger of the judgment' (5[21]). He says in effect, 'The spirit of the commandment is this : Anger is murder. I say unto you, That whosoever is angry with his brother . . . shall be in danger of the judgment' (v.[22]). And then, as if still further to emphasize the point that the Law is not satisfied by negative or formal obedience, Jesus shows that brethren at variance must give effect to the positive law of love before they can render acceptable worship at God's altar (Mt 5[23-26]). Nor is this enough. At a later point in His discourse, in connexion with the law of retaliation, He returns to the subject and insists upon the Divine principle of love, showing that the aim of God's Law is to make man resemble God Himself. The law of love leaves no room for enemies. A Christian has no enemies ; for by loving and praying for them he makes them friends (vv.[38-45]).

So again, in another place, Jesus shows that the neighbour to whom the Law of God refers is any one in need whom one can help (Lk 10[29-37]). Again Jesus takes up the Seventh Commandment. According to the letter it forbids the sin of unchastity, unchaste actions, unlawful intercourse between the sexes. The spirit of the commandment has a far higher aim. It is only one aspect of the grand law of purity. It demands purity of heart. Every impure thought, every unchaste look, are transgressions of this law of God (Mt 5[27-32]). Jesus deals with the Ninth Commandment upon the same principle. According to the letter, it forbids false swearing. According to the spirit, it is just a form of the law of sincerity and truthful-

ness. Its real meaning is that God desireth truth in the inward parts (vv.[33-37]).

Proceeding (Mt 6[1ff.]) to the subject of religious exercises, Jesus shows that questions of ritual and outward form, upon which the Pharisees founded their ideas of 'righteousness' (δικαιοσύνην . . . ποιεῖν, v.[1]) and meritorious service, are of trifling importance in comparison with the question of the heart's approach to God. Religion is not a performance, to be judged by what men can see and pronounce their opinions upon, and involving such trivial points as ritual, excellency of speech, propriety of form, reverence and decorum of posture. It is a matter of communion of spirit with spirit, needy souls, humbly conscious of their needs, confessing their wants and desires to One who seeth in secret, the poor in spirit hungering and thirsting after righteousness, and so convinced of their entire dependence upon the forgiveness and compassion of the All-Merciful as to feel that for them to claim the mercy and grace of God is to bind themselves by the law of love to the duty of forgiving as they would themselves be forgiven. From this point of view the essence of worship is prayer,—not sacrifice and offering— the humble, fervent outpouring of contrite hearts (cf. Lk 18[10-14]), and cordial surrender to the will of God—not questions of posture or of such material things as rich gifts (Lk 21[3. 4], Jn 4[23. 24]). Prayer is the kernel ; all external ordinances, whole burnt-offerings, sacrifices and the like, are but the husk (Mt 6[1-18]). So the prayers even of the Gentiles are of infinitely more consequence than the temple offerings, and God's house is a house of prayer for all people (Mt 21[12ff.] ‖ Mk 11[17] ‖ Lk 19[45. 46], cf. Jn 2[14-16]).

In connexion with Christ's teaching on the subject of heart religion and morality, and the true meaning of the Law considered as the Law of God, an interesting case suggests itself, in which Jesus seems to anticipate the abrogation of the Old Covenant with its laws and ordinances. It is that of His controversy with the Pharisees with reference to the ceremonial ablutions which the disciples were accused of neglecting (Mt 15[1-20] ‖ Mk 7[1-23]). Jesus defends His disciples by turning the tables upon the Pharisees, whom He taxes with setting their traditions above the express commandments of God Himself, and with neglecting in the interest of mere technicalities the weightier matters of the Law (cf. His denunciation of Pharisaic scrupulosity in Mt 23[4-30] ‖ Lk 11[37-47]), and cites as an instance their treatment of the Fifth Commandment and the law of filial affection. But what calls for notice is, in particular, the circumstance that what specially offended the Pharisees, and startled even Christ's own disciples, was His pronouncement upon the point immediately in dispute, the question of ceremonial ablutions, and the whole Levitical legislation on the subject of the clean and the unclean. In view of the fact that a large portion of the Mosaic law is taken up with and deals minutely with these very points, in view also of the fact that the controversies in the Early Church itself between Jewish and Gentile Christians turned upon these things, our Lord's treatment of the question is very remarkable, and illustrates clearly the nature of the distinction which, in His revision of the Law, He emphasized between letter and spirit. He practically teaches that the principle of those Levitical precepts is simply the Divine law of holiness. Rightly understood, they only restate in another form the command, 'Be holy, as the Lord your God is holy'; and they are truly obeyed only by those whose hearts are renewed in every thought by the Spirit of God. The scribes who, forgetting the teaching of the prophets (for here Jesus made no essential addition to Jeremiah's doctrine of the New Covenant or Ezekiel's doctrine of the renewed heart and the washing of regeneration, Jer 31[31ff.], Ezk 36[25-27]), made the external ritual everything, and took no account of heart-religion, were on that account compared to those who should cleanse the outside of the cup and the platter, and be utterly careless as to the condition of the inside. If, on the other hand, the heart were purged from evil thoughts and wicked inclinations, then the life would correspond, as the tree is known by its fruit, and God's law would be fulfilled in the spirit of it. The Law of God appeared thus as the perfect law of liberty, the worship of God in spirit and in truth. In a word, true religion and true morality, the teaching of which in all their particulars is the grand purpose of the Law of God, are from first to last a matter of the heart. Let the heart be pure. Let it be truly turned to God, in simple faith casting aside every care and anxious thought of the world and things of time, and trusting that God will deny His children no good thing, temporal or spiritual, of which, as their Father, He knows them to stand in need, and there is the secret of the fulfilling of the Law. All else follows from that. The pure in heart see God, the poor in spirit are already inheritors of the Kingdom of heaven (Mt 6[19-34] 7[15-27]).

Jesus taught essentially the same truth when, in controversy with the Pharisees, He summarized the teaching of the Law and the Prophets. So far from repudiating as a mere matter of Pharisaic casuistry the question often agitated among the scribes as to whether there were any commandments which in themselves summed up the teaching of the whole Law, He was ready to discuss such questions with them; and when, in response to His definition of love to God and one's neighbour as the essential commandment of the Law, a scribe commended His answer, and said that such love was 'more than all whole burnt-offerings and sacrifices,' He declared that he was not far from the Kingdom of God (Mk 12[28-34]).

On the same principle, Jesus at once defended His disciples against the charge of Sabbath-breaking, and vindicated His right to perform works of beneficence on the Sabbath day, by appealing to the spirit of the ordinance. Like other parts of the Law, He showed that this was only an expression of God's beneficent will for the good of man, a provision for his temporal and spiritual welfare. Therefore in the case of the cripple at Bethesda, He declared that, as God's providential government of the world recognized no distinction between the Sabbath and other days, so Christ Himself, as Son of God, must, like the Father, seek man's benefit even on the Sabbath. Again, as Son of Man, He no less emphatically asserted His right to interpret the Sabbath law in the interest of man, for whose benefit it was framed (Jn 5[17ff.], Mt 12[1-8] || Mk 2[23-28] || Lk 6[1-5]). See also artt. ACCOMMODATION, AUTHORITY OF CHRIST, LAW, etc.

LITERATURE.—Cremer, *Bib.-Theol. Lex. s.v. νόμος*; Grimm, *Lex. Novi Testamenti, s.v. νόμος*; Comm. of Meyer and Alford; Wendt, *The Teaching of Jesus*, i. 261-313, ii. 3-26; H. J. Holtzmann. *Lehrbuch der NT Theol.* i. 29-45, 116-146; Beyschlag, *NT Theology*, i. 37-40, 97-129; Weiss, *Bibl. Theol. of NT*, i. 107-120; Briggs, *Ethical Teaching of Christ*, 143; Gore, *Sermon on Mount*; Bruce, *Kingdom of God*, 63-84; Dykes, *Manifesto of the King* [ed. 1887], 203-329; cf. also Literature at end of preceding article.   HUGH H. CURRIE.

LAWLESSNESS.—The service of God becomes perfect freedom through the work of the Holy Spirit restoring the Divine image more and more in the heart of man. This liberty cannot therefore be a licence for lawlessness. St. Augustine's maxim, 'Love, and do as you like,' derives its truth from the principle that love is not the

abolition but the recapitulation of all the Divine law for mankind. The love of God and the love of man constitute the essence of the Law's demands and the Prophets' promises (Mt 22[40]). It is not the Law which Christ denounces, but traditional excrescences and empty forms (Mk 7[13]). These traditional excrescences gave opportunities for hypocrisy, a condition detested by the Lord (Mt 15[7-9]). The empty forms distracted attention from vital concerns (Mk 7[4]). The scribes and Pharisees were losing all sense of proportion in the duties of the religious life (Mt 23[24], Lk 11[42]). The exponents of the Law were erring, yet the Law itself stood as a Divine ordinance (Mt 23[3], Lk 16[17]). The commandments are necessary to eternal life (Lk 18[20]). Nay, not one tittle can pass away from the Law (Mt 5[18]). Perfect and complete obedience will be demanded of men (Mt 5[19]). Not less but more will be expected of the disciples of Christ (Mt 5). And yet Christ's yoke is to be easy (Mt 11[30]). So there is a paradox, the solution of which lies in the recapitulation of the entire Law as consisting in the love of God and the love of one's fellow-man. The revelation of the guiding principle summing up the Law renders light a burden which the Pharisees made heavy (Lk 11[46]). Mechanical conformity to a legal code is thus avoided. The conscience of man finds exercise and discipline. This point is emphasized in the Western addition to Lk 6[4] 'O man, blessed art thou if thou knowest what thou doest.' In His technical breaches of the Sabbath the Lord knew what He did (Lk 14[5]). Yet the legalists took advantage of these to charge Him with lawlessness (Jn 9[16]). Nevertheless, He came fulfilling all righteousness (Mt 3[15]), and appealing to the Law in the face of temptation (Mt 4[4-10]). When He cleansed the Temple, He vindicated His action from Scripture (Lk 19[46]). There was no lawlessness in His pattern life of perfect obedience to God (Jn 15[10]). Lawless efforts at good, however strenuous, are not acceptable (Jn 10[1]). Indeed, St. John sums up the matter in the words, 'Sin is lawlessness' (1 Jn 3[4]).

LITERATURE.—Hastings' *DB*, art. 'Law (in NT)'; Bruce, *Training of the Twelve*, pp. 67-95; *Kingdom of God*, pp. 63-84; Wendt, *Teaching of Jesus*, ii. 1-48; Dykes, *Manifesto of the King*, pp. 203-220; Dale, *Christian Doctrine*, 198; Hobhouse, *Spiritual Standard*, iii.   W. B. FRANKLAND.

LAWYER (νομικός) or 'teacher (doctor) of the law' (νομοδιδάσκαλος) is found occasionally, almost exclusively in Lk., for the more usual 'scribe' (γραμματεύς). The identity of these terms is shown by the following passages. **1.** Lk 5[17], Pharisees and *doctors of the law* are sitting by; but (v.[21]) the *scribes* and Pharisees begin to reason (so || Mt., Mk.). **2.** Lk 11[37ff.] is a denunciation first of Pharisees, then of *lawyers*; this is parallel to Mt 23 against *scribes* and Pharisees; and at its close (v.[53]) 'the *scribes* and Pharisees began to urge him vehemently.' The TR reading (v.[44]) 'scribes and Pharisees, hypocrites,' which, when compared with the next verse, might imply a difference between 'scribes' and 'lawyers,' is omitted by critical editors on the authority of אBCL Vulg. etc.; and is obviously an assimilation to Mt 23[27]. **3.** Mt 22[35], a *lawyer* questions Jesus as to the greatest commandment; in Mk 12[28] it is 'one of the *scribes*'; cf. also Lk 10[25] 'a certain *lawyer*.' **4.** The martyr Eleazar is called in 2 Mac 6[18] 'one of the principal *scribes*,' in 4 Mac 5[4] he is a *lawyer*. Thus these titles are equivalent. γραμματεύς ('scribe') is a literal translation of the Heb. סֹפֵר (a literary man or a student of Scripture), while νομικός ('lawyer,' 'jurist,' a regular term for Roman lawyers, Vulg. *legis peritus*), and, still better, νομοδιδάσκαλος, are more distinct descriptions of this class, explaining to Gentile readers their character and office. Hence their comparative frequency in Luke. 'Rabbi,' the title by which they were addressed, is perhaps for us their best designation.

Mt. has γραμματεύς 23 times, νομικός once only (22³⁵, where Syr-Sin omits). Mk. has γραμματεύς only, 21 times. Lk. has γραμματεύς 14 times, besides (of Jewish scribes) twice in Acts; νομικός 6 times (7³⁰ 10²⁵ 1145. 46. 52 143), νομοδιδάσκαλος once (5¹⁷, and in Ac 5³⁴ of Gamaliel). Josephus also, while once using ἱερογραμματεύς (BJ VI. v. 3), commonly uses phrases with more definite meaning for Gentile readers: σοφιστής (BJ I. xxxiii. 2, II. xvii. 8) or ἐξηγητής τῶν πατρίων νόμων (Ant. XVII. vi. 2).

These titles show that the great sphere of their activity was the Law, whether contained in Scripture or handed down traditionally. They studied, of course, the other books of Scripture besides the Pentateuch, but these were regarded as merely supplementary to the Law of Moses, and as themselves presenting a revealed rule of life and conduct; so that the term 'Law' is applied sometimes in the NT to the whole of the OT (Jn 10³⁴ 15²⁵, 1 Co 14²¹). So also in the Mishna (see Buhl, *Canon*, § 3).

Their work, in all its departments, is sketched in the saying ascribed to the 'Men of the Great Synagogue,' their traditional predecessors: 'Be careful in judgment, raise up many disciples, and set a hedge about the Law' (*Pirḳe Aboth*, I. i.). They acted as judges; they gave instruction in the Law, and trained disciples; and they interpreted and developed the Law. Though anyone might be a judge, the office was naturally most commonly held by those learned in the Law; and we find the leaders of the Scribes an integral part of the Sanhedrin (Mk 15¹ etc.). Their leaders gathered disciples round them, and taught them the traditional law, instructing them by discussing real or imagined legal cases; and they developed the Law, applying it to all actual and possible cases, and laying down rules to secure against its being broken. See SCRIBES.

LITERATURE.—Schürer, *HJP* II. i. p. 312 ff., and literature there mentioned; Edersheim, *Life and Times*, etc., i. 93; artt. 'Lawyer' and 'Scribe' (by Eaton) in Hastings' *DB*, and literature there.   HAROLD SMITH.

LAZARUS.—A common Jewish name, meaning 'God hath helped'; a colloquial abbreviation of *Eleazar* (cf. *Liezer* for *Eliezer*).*

1. Lazarus the beggar, who, in our Lord's parable (Lk 16¹⁹⁻³¹), lay, a mass of loathsome sores, at the gateway of the rich man, named traditionally Nineuis (Euth. Zig.) or Phinees (Clem. *Recogn.*). The notion that he was a leper (whence *lazar-house*, *lazzaretto*) is impossible, since he must then have kept afar off, and durst not have lain at the rich man's gateway.

This has been pronounced no authentic parable of Jesus, but an 'evangelic discourse upon His words—"that which is exalted among men is an abomination in the sight of God"' (Lk 16¹⁵),† on the following grounds: (1) *Its introduction of a proper name.* Nowhere else in the Gospels is a parabolic personage named, and the idea prevailed in early times that this is not a parable but a story from real life (cf. Tert. *de Anim.* § 7; Iren. *adv. Hær.* iv. 3. 2).

(2) *Its alleged Ebionism.* The contrast between the two men on earth is not moral or religious. It is not said that the rich man got his wealth unrighteously, or that he treated Lazarus cruelly. The difference was merely that the one was rich and the other poor, and their dooms are a reversal of their earthly conditions. 'In this parable,' says Strauss, 'the measure of future recompense is not the amount of good done

or wickedness perpetrated, but of evil endured and fortune enjoyed.'

(3) *Its Jewish imagery.* (*a*) 'The beggar died, and he was carried away by the angels.' It was a Jewish idea that the souls of the righteous were carried by angels to paradise (cf. Targ. on Ca 4² 'Non possunt ingredi Paradisum nisi justi, quorum animæ eo feruntur per angelos.' (*b*) The Jews called the unseen world Sheol; and so closely identical was their conception thereof with that of the Greeks, that Sheol is rendered by the LXX Hades.* It was the common abode of all souls, good and bad alike, where they received the due reward of their deeds; and it was an aggravation of the misery of the wicked that they continually beheld the felicity of the righteous, knowing all the while that they were excluded from it. See Lightfoot and Wetstein on Lk 16²³; cf. Rev 14¹⁰. So in the parable 'the rich man in Hades lifts up his eyes, being in torments, and seeth Abraham from afar, and Lazarus in his bosom.' (*c*) There were three Jewish phrases descriptive of the state of the righteous after death: 'in the Garden of Eden' or 'Paradise'; 'under the throne of glory' (cf. Rev 6⁹ 7⁹. ¹⁵); 'in Abraham's bosom.' The last appears in the parable (vv.²². ²³). The meaning is that Lazarus was a guest at the heavenly feast. Cf. Lk 14¹⁵ and the saying of R. Jacob: 'This world is like a vestibule before the world to come: prepare thyself at the vestibule, that thou mayest be admitted into the festal-chamber.' Lazarus occupied the place of honour, reclining on Abraham's breast, even as the beloved disciple at the Last Supper reclined on the Master's (Jn 13²³).

These objections, however, are by no means insurmountable. The name *Lazarus* is perhaps introduced significantly, defining the beggar's character. He was one who had found his help in God. It was not because he was poor, but because God had helped him, that the beggar was carried away into Abraham's bosom; and the rich man was doomed not simply because he had been rich, but because he had made a selfish use of his riches. The parable is an illustration and enforcement of the moral which Jesus deduces from the preceding parable of the Shrewd Factor: 'Make to yourselves friends by means of the mammon of unrighteousness (*i.e.* earthly riches, unsatisfying and unenduring†), that, when it faileth, they may receive you into the eternal tents' (v.⁹). Had the rich man befriended the beggar, he would have laid up for himself treasure in heaven. He would have bound Lazarus to himself, and would have been welcomed by him on the threshold of the unseen world.

As for the Jewish imagery, it constitutes no argument against the authenticity of the parable. Jesus was accustomed to speak the language of His hearers in order to reach their understandings and hearts. He often spoke of the heavenly feast: cf. Mt 8¹¹. ¹² (Lk 13²⁸. ²⁹), Lk 13²⁵⁻²⁷ (Mt 7²². ²³), Mt 22¹⁻¹⁴ (Lk 14¹⁶⁻²⁴), Mt 25¹⁻¹³, Lk 22¹⁸ = Mt 26²⁹ = Mk 14²⁵. And it is noteworthy how, when He employed Jewish imagery, He was wont to invest it with new significance. Thus, the Rabbis taught that the abodes of the righteous and the wicked in Hades were nigh tó each other; according to one, there was only a span between them; according to another, the boundary was a wall (Midr. *Ḳohel.* 103. 2: 'Deus statuit hoc juxta illud (Ec 7¹⁴), id est, Gehennam et Paradisum. Quantum distant? Palmo. R. Jochanan dicit: Paries interponitur.') But what says Jesus? 'In all this region betwixt us and you a great chasm has been fixed, that they that wish to pass over

---

* *Juchasin*, 81. 1: 'In Talmude Hierosolymitano unusquisque R. Eleazar scribitur, absque Aleph, R. Lazar.'
† E. A. Abbott in *Encycl. Bibl.* art. 'Lazarus,' § 2.

* Cf. Schultz, *OT Theol.* ii. p. 321 ff.
† Cf. Ps 23³ מַעְגְּלֵי־צֶדֶק, τρίβους δικαιοσύνης, in contrast to 'delusive tracks which lead nowhere' (Cheyne).

from this side unto you may not be able, nor those on that side cross over unto us.' The sentence, He would indicate, is final, the separation eternal. See GULF.

2. Lazarus of Bethany, brother of Martha and Mary. There was a close and tender intimacy between Jesus and this household (cf. Jn 11[3. 11. 36]). From the Feast of Tabernacles (October) until the Feast of Dedication (December) Jesus sojourned in Jerusalem, making His appeal to her rulers and people. The former proved obdurate, and finally proceeded to violence (Jn 10[31. 39]). It was unsafe for Him to remain among them, and He retired to Bethany beyond Jordan (v.[40], cf. 1[28] RV). A crowd followed Him thither, and, undisturbed by His adversaries, He exercised a ministry which recalled, while it surpassed, the work of John the Baptist on the same spot three years earlier. All the while He was thinking of Jerusalem. He would fain win her even yet, and He prayed that God would bring about some crisis which might persuade her of His Messiahship or at least leave her without excuse (cf. Jn 11[41. 42]). He saw not the way, but He was waiting for God to open it up ; and suddenly a message reached Him from the other Bethany that Lazarus was sick (Jn 11[3]). He recognized in this turn of events God's answer to His prayer. It afforded Him just such an opportunity as He had craved. 'This sickness,' He said, 'is not unto death, but for the glory of God, that the Son of God (*i.e.* the Messiah) may be glorified thereby.' He did not hasten to Bethany and lay His hand upon the sick man, nor did He, abiding where He was, 'send forth His word and heal him,' as He had done to the courtier's son (Jn 4[46-54]) and the Syrophœnician woman's daughter (Mt 15[21-28] = Mk 7[24-30]). He deliberately remained where He was for two days, and then set out for Judæa. On His arrival at Bethany, Lazarus was dead and buried, and a large company, including many of the rulers from the adjacent capital (v.[19]), had gathered, in accordance with Jewish custom, to testify their esteem for the good Lazarus and condole with his sisters. The situation favoured the Lord's design. He repaired to the sepulchre, which lay at least 2000 cubits outside the town,* and in presence of the assemblage recalled the dead man to life and summoned him forth in his cerements.

It was an indubitable miracle. In the sultry East it was necessary that the dead should be buried immediately (cf. Ac 5[5. 6]), and it sometimes happened that a swoon was mistaken for death, and the man awoke. The Jewish fancy was that for three days after death the soul hovered about the sepulchre, fain to re-enter and reanimate its tenement of clay ; and the bereaved were wont to visit the sepulchre to see if haply their dead had come to life. After three days decomposition set in, and when they saw its ghastly disfigurement on the face, they abandoned hope.† Had Jesus arrived within three days after Lazarus' death, it might have been pronounced no miracle ; but He arrived on the fourth day, when decomposition would have already set in (v.[39]).

If anything could have conquered the unbelief of the rulers, this miracle must have done it ; but they hardened their hearts, and all the more that the people were profoundly impressed. The Sanhedrin met under the presidency of Caiaphas the high priest, and resolved to put Jesus to death, at the same time publishing an order that, if any knew where He was, they should give information for His arrest. He did not venture into the city, but retired northward to Ephraim, near the Samaritan frontier. There He remained until the Passover was nigh, and then He went up to keep the Feast

* Lightfoot, ii. p. 424.   † Lightfoot on Jn 11[39].

and to die. Six days before the Feast began, He reached Bethany, and in defiance of the Sanhedrin's order received an ovation from the townsfolk. They honoured Him with a banquet in the house of Simon, one of their leading men, who had been a leper, and had perhaps been healed by Jesus (see art. ANOINTING, I. 2.). Lazarus of course was present. The news that Jesus was at Bethany reached Jerusalem, and next day a great multitude thronged out to meet Him and escorted Him with Messianic honours into the city. It was the raising of Lazarus that had convinced them of the claims of Jesus (Jn 12[17. 18]). The Triumphal Entry is a powerful evidence of the miracle. Without it such an outburst of enthusiasm is unaccountable.

It might be expected that Lazarus of all men should have stood by Jesus during the last dread ordeal ; but he never appears after the banquet in Simon's house. His name is nowhere mentioned in the story of the Lord's Passion. What is the explanation? Enraged by the impression which the miracle made and the support which it brought to Jesus, the high priests plotted the death of Lazarus (Jn 12[10. 11]) ; and it is probable that, ere the final crisis, he had been compelled to withdraw from the vicinity of Jerusalem.

It was a stupendous miracle, the greatest which Jesus ever wrought ; yet it is not the supreme miracle of the Gospel - story. The Lord's own Resurrection holds that place, and one who is persuaded of His claims will hardly hesitate to believe in the raising of Lazarus. 'He raised the man,' says St. Augustine,* 'who made the man ; for He is Himself the Father's only Son, through whom, as ye know, all things were made. If, therefore, all things were made through Him, what wonder if one rose from the dead through Him, when so many are daily born through Him? It is a greater thing to create men than to raise them.'

Naturalistic criticism, however, has assailed the miracle. Much has been made of the silence of the Synoptists, who must, it is alleged, have recorded it had they known of it, and must have known of it had it occurred. Their silence in this instance, however, is merely part of a larger problem —their silence regarding the Lord's Judæan ministry generally, and their peculiar reticence regarding the family of Bethany.

It is no exaggeration to affirm that the desperateness of the assaults which have been directed against it constitute a powerful apologetic for the miracle. (1) The earlier rationalists (Paulus, Venturini), in spite of the Evangelist's specific testimony to the contrary, supposed that Lazarus had not really died but only fallen into a trance. He had been buried alive, and he awoke to consciousness through the combined influences of the coolness of the cave, the pungent odour of the burial spices (cf. Jn 19[40]), and the stream of warm air which rushed in when the stone was removed. Jesus, looking in, perceived that he was alive, and bade him come forth.

(2) According to Strauss, the story, like the two earlier stories of resuscitation (Mt 9[18. 19. 23-26] = Mk 5[21-24. 35-43] = Lk 8[40-42. 49-56] ; 7[11-17]), is a myth, originating in the desire of the primitive Church that the Messiah should not only rival but surpass His great prototypes in the OT. Elijah and Elisha had wrought miracles of resuscitation (1 K 17[17ff.], 2 K 4[8ff.]), and Jesus must do the like in a more wonderful manner.

(3) Renan regarded the miracle as an imposture. 'Tired of the cold reception which the Kingdom of God found in the capital, the friends of Jesus wished for a great miracle which should strike powerfully the incredulity of the Jerusalemites.'

* *In Joan. Ev.* Tract. xlix. § 1.

And the sick Lazarus lent himself to their design. Pallid with disease, he let himself be wrapped in grave-clothes and shut up in the sepulchre ; and when Jesus, believing that he was dead, came to take a last look at his friend's remains, Lazarus came forth in his bandages, his head covered with a winding-sheet. Jesus acquiesced in the fraud. 'Not by any fault of his own, but by that of others, his conscience had lost something of its original purity. Desperate and driven to extremity, he was no longer his own master. His mission overwhelmed him, and he yielded to the torrent. . . . He was no more able than St. Bernard or St. Francis to moderate the avidity for the marvellous displayed by the multitude, and even by his own disciples.'

(4) Later criticism is still more destructive. Not only was the miracle never wrought, but there was never such a man as Lazarus. The story is 'nonhistorical, like the History of the Creation in Genesis, and like the records of the other miracles in the Fourth Gospel ; all of which are poetic developments.' * Keim finds the germ of the story in the Ebionite parable of the Rich Man and the Beggar (Lk 16¹⁹⁻³¹). 'If,' says Abraham in the parable, 'to Moses and the prophets they do not hearken, not even if one rise from the dead will they be persuaded'; and the Johannine narrative is this saying converted into a history : a man rose from the dead, and the Jews did not believe. Lazarus full of corruption corresponds to the beggar full of sores. The story is thus doubly divorced from reality, being an unhistorical development of an unauthentic parable.

Literature.—1. Hastings' *DB*, art. 'Lazarus and Dives'; Trench, Bruce, Orelli, and Dods on the *Parables* ; Plummer, 'St. Luke' (*ICC*), *in loc.* ; Bersier, *Gospel in Paris*, p. 448 f.

2. Hastings' *DB*, art. 'Lazarus of Bethany' ; the standard *Lives of Christ* ; Elmslie, *Expository Lectures and Sermons*, p. 92 ff. ; Maclaren, *Unchanging Christ*, p. 282 ff. On the rationalistic objections to the miracle see the chapter on 'The Later Miracles' in Fairbairn's *Studies in the Life of Christ* (or in *Expositor*, 1st Ser. ix. [1879] p. 178 ff.), where the theories of Paulus, Strauss, Baur, and Renan are fully dealt with.

D. SMITH.

LEADING.—'Lead' is used in the Gospels in its ordinary senses : intransitively in the description of the ways that lead to life or destruction (Mt 7¹³· ¹⁴), and transitively often. The OT metaphor of Jehovah as a Shepherd leading His people like a flock (Ps 23¹ 80¹) is repeated in the parables representing Christ as a Shepherd whose sheep recognize and obey Him (Jn 10³· ⁴· ²⁷). The general conception of God's leading His people, so frequent is in the Psalms and in Deutero-Isaiah and elsewhere, is assumed in the petition 'Lead us not into temptation' (Mt 6¹³, Lk 11⁴) ; for the true life is along a right path wherein God leads His children.

The leadership of religious authorities is referred to in the description of scribes and Pharisees as 'blind guides' or 'blind leaders of the blind' (Mt 23¹⁶ 15¹⁴) ; the metaphor being based on the sight, familiar in Eastern cities, of rows or files of blind persons each holding by the one in front. But, as this saying is placed by St. Luke (6³⁹) in immediate connexion with the appointment of the Twelve, it may be presumed that Jesus pressed on His disciples the necessity of their recognizing and qualifying for the duties of true leadership. They are required to have light and to let it shine, to be, in short, 'men of light and leading.'

The position of Jesus as a Leader is most frequently expressed in terms of following. The imperative 'Follow me' is addressed to individuals, as Peter and Andrew, James and John (Mt 4¹⁹· ²¹), Matthew (Mt 9⁹), and Philip (Jn 1⁴³) ; and to unnamed disciples or listeners (Mt 8²² 19²¹). It is repeated in the fundamental law of the Kingdom, where self-denial or cross-bearing is enjoined (Mt 16²⁴, Mk 8³⁴, Lk 9²³, Jn 12²⁶) ; but here the refer-

* E. A. Abbott, art. 'Lazarus,' § 4, in *Encyc. Biblica*.

ence is to Jesus as a supreme example rather than a present guide, and the instruction is primarily spiritual. It may be said that during His whole public ministry Jesus was leading and training disciples to carry on His work ; while the risen Christ is the Head of the Church and the Leader of the Christian army (Mt 28¹⁸⁻²⁰).

Four times the term 'Leader' (ἀρχηγός) is applied to Christ : in the EV phrases 'Prince of life,' 'Prince,' 'Captain (RV 'Author') of salvation,' 'Author of faith' (Ac 3¹⁵ 5³¹, He 2¹⁰ 12²) ; and a similar meaning is expressed by πρόδρομος, 'Forerunner' (He 6²⁰). In these passages the leadership is through death from life on earth to life in heaven.

Literature.—H. Bushnell, *The New Life*, p. 74 ; Phillips Brooks, *Mystery of Iniquity*, p. 171 ; B. B. Warfield, *Power of God unto Salvation*, p. 151.   R. SCOTT.

LEARNING.—To what extent did learning prevail in Palestine in the time of Christ ? and is it correct to say that He Himself and His Apostles and disciples were illiterate ?

Higher education existed at least in the collegiate institutions of the capital. From the restoration following the epoch of the Exile there was a class of men who are known to us as 'scribes' (sŏphĕrîm). Their point of union was their knowledge of the Law, and Scriptures, and Traditions. So far they are parallel to the *shastris*, who are the authorities on Hindu literature. Ezra, the second founder of the theocracy and a man of priestly birth, is designated a scribe (Ezr 7⁶). From his date measures were taken, directed to the establishment and maintenance of the sacred authority of the Law. The scribe was an interpreter to the people. The period of higher inspiration was giving place to an age of didactic literature. And a succession of able scribes arose who expounded the sacred books, cherished and enlarged tradition, determined the details of religious observance, and wrote the Law in its exclusiveness on the minds of the people. They were at their best in the 4th or 3rd cent. B.C. ; but they continued for many centuries. Pharisaism was a development of them, and they are also connected with the later books of Wisdom, while in the post-Christian period their chief men are the Rabbis. Part of their work consisted in the training of young scribes, and for this end schools or colleges were formed. In these the Scriptures formed a literary and theological basis, the Law, traditions, and national history were expounded, and judgment was given on the problems and practical questions of the time. This education was professional, and contained no secular culture ; and it was intensely national or Jewish. Yet here as elsewhere there were varieties of opinion and diverging tendencies. The schools of Hillel and Shammai were rival institutions in the years preceding the birth of our Lord. A generation later Hillel was succeeded by his perhaps more liberal grandson, Gamaliel, to whose classroom St. Paul came from Asia Minor to be trained in the Law.

Other schools less exclusively religious, more akin to Greek institutions, are known to have existed in Jerusalem and other towns, where especially the sons of men not opposed to the Roman occupation might be trained for public life. Jews of the Dispersion were at home in the Greek language, and had more immediate access to Greek literature. About the time of Christ several of the later apocryphal books were written. Culture was widespread, and at least two Jews belong to general literature : Philo the philosopher of Alexandria, who endeavoured to reconcile Hellenism and Judaism ; and Josephus the historian, who was brought up in Jerusalem.

But the work of the scribes was not confined to

'higher education.' In every village they had planted a synagogue, and in connexion with every synagogue an elementary school was ultimately opened. For many centuries the training of the young was a duty enjoined upon parents. About B.C. 75, Simon ben Shetach, a scribe and Pharisee, is said to have carried a law requiring boys to attend 'the elementary school.' Probably before that date a lower school system (such as was known to exist in the Greek world) was tentatively tried in all leading centres. Now education was made compulsory. The schoolroom, known as the 'house of the book,' was either part of the synagogue or of the teacher's house. The teacher, or ḥazzan, belonged to a humble rank of the fraternity of scribes. Lk (5[7]) refers to a gathering of teachers of the law (νομοδιδάσκαλοι) from every city and village of the land. Whether or not schoolmasters are included, the reference implies a wide diffusion of education.

The instruction given in these schools is considered by Ramsay (*Education of Christ*) superior to that of Greece or any other ancient land. The subjects of study and methods of teaching were calculated to call forth and develop the best mental faculties of the boys. In the choice of subjects the theoretical and practical were successfully combined; and pupils were taught both to think and to act, while maxims of duty were graven on their memories. The standard of average intelligence was therefore high. And while in most cases no regular secondary education followed, it is to be remembered that the synagogue remained a place of instruction rather than of formal worship, and also that talented young men could carry reading and study farther than public provision was made for. Whether any of the leading disciples were educated in Jerusalem cannot be definitely known. But they were not ignorant. On the contrary, they were men of keen intelligence and ardent spirit, who had been cherishing the Messianic hope and found in Jesus the realization of their dreams.

Ancient literature was mainly religious; and learning is founded on literature. But though the circle of learning had religion as its centre, it included some study of all the obvious phenomena of nature. Modern discovery is proving that not only famous countries such as Egypt or Babylonia, but also peoples whose very names were formerly unknown, had a developed civilization and system of thought. Amongst the Israelites Moses and Solomon are credited (Ac 7[22], 1 K 4[29-34]) with all the knowledge the world then possessed; and to the latter are attributed not only poetry and philosophy, but also an exhaustive knowledge of Natural History. The people were skilled in music and in works of architecture. But while Israel was producing its prophets, the imaginative genius of Greece was creating a secular literature and founding sciences. Gradually Greek influence extended to all lands. It was felt in Jerusalem even in the days of greatest exclusiveness. Greek was the language of the Hellenistic Jews, and the Septuagint was their Bible. Greek ideas were thus diffused over the surface of Hebraic religion, and helped to enrich the thought and life of the planters of Christianity. Of the NT writings it may confidently be said that they are not the work of unlearned men. St. Paul was probably much more learned than his letters show (Ac 26[3. 24]). The Johannine writings are artistically conceived, and studded with gems of thought and expression. The Epistles to the Hebrews and Ephesians show an imaginative scope and a rhetorical power scarcely surpassed. St. Luke had a literary faculty rare amongst physicians. It is true that Peter and John are styled 'unlearned'

(Ac 4[13]); yet this is but the technical description (ἀγράμματοι καὶ ἰδιῶται) of men who had not graduated in the colleges of the scribes. If not many noble were called (1 Co 1[26]), there were at least some who combined spiritual insight with literary culture, and who were able to express the new ideas in forms whose beauty is partially hidden by their Divineness.

Of Jesus Himself His enemies asked (Jn 7[15]), 'How knoweth this man letters (γράμματα), having never learned?' No doubt it was true that He had never studied Jewish theology at any of the great Rabbinical schools. But not only did He have a thorough knowledge of the letter of the OT, as He repeatedly showed (see, *e.g.*, Mt 5[21-43] 12[3ff. 40ff.] 13[14f.] 15[4. 7f.] 19[4ff. 17ff.] 21[13. 16. 42] 22[32. 37ff. 43ff.] 24[15. 37ff.] 26[54] 27[46]), but He revealed an insight into Scripture and an expository skill (and this was what the Jews specially meant by His 'knowing letters') at which they were compelled to marvel (Jn 7[15a]). This 'learning' of Jesus, for γράμματα in Gr. (like Lat. *literæ*, Eng. 'letters') is synonymous with 'learning,' had its human side without doubt. His education in Scripture would begin in the family circle, and most probably be continued in a synagogue school. In early youth He showed His interest in the synagogal instruction (Lk 2[46]), and ever afterwards it was His 'custom' to frequent those services of the synagogue at which Moses and the Prophets were read and explained (Lk 4[15]). But His 'learning' and consequent 'teaching,' on the spiritual side, as He Himself declared, came from an inward and Divine spring (Jn 7[16. 17]), a saying which helps to explain the statement of two of the Synoptists (Mt 7[29] ‖ Mk 1[22]), 'He taught them as one having authority, and not as the scribes' (γραμματεῖς). See also art. EDUCATION.

LITERATURE.—Hastings' *DB*, art. 'Education'; Schürer, *HJP* II. i. 323–350, ii. 47–52; Edersheim, *Life and Times*, i. 228–234; Stalker, *Imago Christi*, pp. 147–164.   R. SCOTT.

LEAVEN.—The effect of leaven upon dough to which it is added is due to minute living organisms disseminated through it in great numbers. These organisms are one or more species of yeast-fungi. They are the most important agents of the alcoholic fermentation, which they produce in dough as well as in solutions of sugar. Whether lodged in sour dough (leaven) or collected free out of fermenting vats (compressed yeast), they cause the same effect when introduced into bread sponge. At the present time leaven is not so much used for the lightening of bread as yeast, because it is apt to impart to bread a sour taste and a disagreeable odour.

Yeast-fungi were first recognized (1680) by the Dutch naturalist Leuwenhöck in the scum floating on the surface of fermenting beer. With his imperfect lenses he was able to observe little of their structure beyond the fact that they were very small globules. They are now known to be single-celled plants, having for the most part an oval or ellipsoidal shape. The individual yeast-cell consists of a mass of protoplasm enclosed in a delicate wall of cellulose. The protoplasm, as in the case of all the fungi, contains no chlorophyll, and is, accordingly, dependent upon organic matter for its nourishment. It is granular, and usually shows one large non-contractile vacuole or several small vacuoles containing water. It has also a nucleus, which, however, can be brought into view only after special treatment. The size of the yeast-cell varies from 1·5 microns to 15 microns in diameter. (The micron equals $\frac{1}{25000}$ inch). During the inactive stage the cells are isolated, but in an actively fermenting medium they occur in groups or families, organically united and consisting of from two to six or eight members in varying stages of development. When the members reach maturity, they separate from one another, each one having the capacity to produce a new group. This is the method by which the plant propagates itself. An isolated cell sends out a little pimple or bud on the surface. The bud is destined to become an independent cell of the same size as the cell which produced it; but, before it is mature, it may itself form a bud which in turn may form another bud of its own, the mother-cell in the meantime forming a second bud at a different point. A sort of chain of sprouts, usually curved, is formed as the result of this process of *budding* or *gemmation*. The successive buds round up and finally separate themselves as independent individuals. Pasteur, to whose elaborate investigations we are deeply indebted for our knowledge of the agents and the process of fermentation, found that two cells produced eight in two hours at a temperature of 13 degrees C. The multiplication is more rapid at a higher temperature.

Yeast-fungi secure their food for the most part from weak solutions of grape-sugar. They convert grape-sugar into alcohol and carbon dioxide. This conversion is known as the alcoholic fermentation. The same action takes place in moistened wheat-flour when yeast is mixed with it. The wheat grain contains a ferment, *diastase*, whose function is the conversion of the insoluble starch of the grain into soluble grape-sugar for the nourishment of the embryo when the grain germinates. Diastase is present, of course, in wheat-flour, and when the conditions of moisture and temperature are supplied, as in a gently heated bread sponge, it effects the same conversion as under natural conditions in the germinating grain. Some of the flour starch is changed into grape-sugar, in which the yeast-cells excite the alcoholic fermentation. The bubbles of the gas carbon dioxide produced in the fermentation are entangled in the glutinous sponge, and, expanded by heat, puff it up or lighten it. If, now, more flour is thoroughly mixed with this sponge so as to scatter the yeast-cells of the sponge throughout the mass, the whole will shortly be leavened by the gas which continues to be given off by the agency of the rapidly multiplying cells. A practically indefinite quantity of flour so treated can be leavened by 'a little leaven.'

The week which began with the Passover is called 'the days of unleavened bread' (Mt 26[17], Mk 14[1. 12], Lk 22[1. 7]), from the practice enjoined in Ex 23[15], Lv 23[6], Dt 16[3. 4. 8].

The effect of leaven in raising a mass of dough (see above) is the basis of our Lord's parable of the Leaven (Mt 13[33], Lk 13[20. 21]), which sets forth the gradual and pervasive influence of the Kingdom of God upon the whole of human society.

The fermentation produced by leaven was regarded as a species of putrefaction, and this, together with the tendency of leaven to spread, explains the figure in which 'the leaven of the Pharisees and Sadducees' stands for their corrupt teaching (Mt 16[6. 11], Mk 8[15]), or, as St. Luke puts it more specifically in the case of the Pharisees, their hypocrisy (Lk 12[1]). 'The leaven of Herod' (Mk 8[15]) similarly denotes the policy of the Herodian party.

LITERATURE.—Trench, Dods, Bruce, Orelli on the Parables; Winterbotham, *Kingdom of Heaven*, 70; Drummond, *Stones Rolled Away*, 144; Scott-Holland, *God's City*, 143; Macmillan, *Two Worlds are Ours*, 153; R. Flint, *Christ's Kingdom*, 170.

W. L. POTEAT and JAMES PATRICK.

LEAVES.—The tree is often used in NT as a symbol of the life of a man. Leaves are the indication of the existence of life in the tree. The barren fig-tree was cursed by our Lord because it had leaves only (Mt 21[19], Mk 11[13]) and no fruit. See FIG-TREE. We have here a type of religious profession unaccompanied by practice, a spiritual condition which always drew from our Lord the strongest condemnation.

The putting forth of leaves by the fig-tree is referred to by our Lord as one of the indications that summer is nigh (Mt 24[32], Mk 13[28]). See Robertson Nicoll, *Ten Minute Sermons*, 59.

C. H. PRICHARD.

LEBBÆUS.—The name 'Lebbæus' has completely disappeared from the RV; in the AV it occurs (Mt 10[3]) in the list of the Apostles: 'Lebbeus, whose surname was Thaddeus.' [On this spelling see Scrivener's *Paragraph Bible*, p. lxxxi, note 3]. This is the reading of the Received Text, which is still maintained in the Patriarchal Edition of the Greek Testament (Constantinople, 1904), and supported by most of the Greek MSS, to which was added lately the Palimpsest of Cairo. The modern critical editions are unanimous in the omission of 'whose surname was,' but are divided about the name itself, reading either 'Thaddæus,' as Lachmann, Tregelles, WH, RV, or 'Lebbæus,' as Alford, Tischendorf, and WH in the margin. The question of reading is here of singular importance; for the name is one of the test passages of textual criticism in the NT. WH (§ 304) adduce the reading 'Thaddæus' found only in אB as proof of the

unique excellence of these MSS, and are inclined to attribute the name 'Lebbæus' to an attempt to bring Levi (Mk 2[14]) within the number of the Twelve. But if so, why was this attempt not made in Mk 3[18]? There 'Lebbæus' is attested only by D and the Old Latin MSS *a b d ff i q r*, whereas in Mt. D has the support of at least one Greek minuscule (122), of *k*—the oldest Latin witness, spelt *iebbæus* [the others, *a b g h gat*, read in Mt. 'Judas Zelotes']—and of all witnesses for the TR. The reading of the latter is apparently a conflation of the name Lebbæus (Mt.) with the name Thaddæus (Mk.); while D, as is its custom, assimilated Mk. to Mt. Allen (*EBi* 5032) sees in 'Lebbæus' the 'Western' gloss of a copyist, who connected the name Thaddæus with *thĕdā = mamma*, and wished to substitute a not dissimilar name, which should be more appropriate to an Apostle and less undignified.

A trace of the name 'Lebbæus' is also found in the list of the Apostles as given in Tatian's *Diatessaron* according to Ishodad; but here 'Lebbæus' is inserted between 'James' and 'son of Alphai,' and Judas Jacobi is added afterwards (see Zahn's *Com. on Mt.*, and Burkitt, *Evangelion da-Mepharreshe*, ii. 270). The Syriac lexicographer Bar Bahlul explained that Judas Thomas was called *Lebbæus* and *Thaddæus* on account of his wisdom. Very curious is the testimony of the MSS of the *Evangeliarium Hierosolymitanum*. The MSS AB give ליביום הרין דאתקרי תאדי סימון ק'
C has וליידם הרין דתקרי סימון ק'
Here וליידם seems to be a combination of 'Lebbæus' and 'Judas,' and תקרי a confusion of 'Thaddæus' with 'was surnamed.' In the *Ap. Const.* vi. 14, cod. *h* spells Λεναιος, viii. 25, cod. *d* Λεβαιος; it is a pity that the new edition of Funk does not contain the lists of the Apostles given by de Lagarde, p. 282 f. In *Ap. Const.* vii. 46, Judas Jacobi is mentioned as third bishop of Jerusalem. The list of Lag. p. 283, distinguishes Judas Jacobi as the tenth Apostle from Θαδδαῖος ὁ Λεβαῖος καὶ Ἰούδας as the eleventh. In the Synaxaries of the Greek Church (1) Judas (in Lk.), 'who is called by Mt. and Mk. Thaddæus and Lebbæus,' the brother of Jesus after the flesh, is celebrated on the 19th June, and, together with the other Apostles, on 30th June, as the last of them. From him is distinguished (2) the Apostle Thaddæus, who is also Lebbæus, one of the Seventy, celebrated on the 21st August; and (3) Judas Zelotes on the 22nd May.

As supplement to the art. JUDAS (i. 906), it may be stated that this strange combination 'Judas Zelotes,' mentioned above as the reading of the Old Latin MSS in Mt 10[3], is attested for Rome by the chronographer of the year 334, by the list of the canonical books of the year 382; and for Ravenna by the mosaics of the great Baptistry (5th cent.). From the oldest MSS of the *Martyrologium Hieronymianum* it would appear that also in the name of the 28th Oct. 'SS. Simon and Jude App. MM.' the latter name is not an abbreviation of *Judas Jacobi*, but of *Judas Zelotes*.

The meaning of the name 'Lebbæus' is equally doubtful. The explanation *corculum* by Jerome (after the surname of Scipio Nasica) is not proved. For relationship with *Levi* the spelling Λεναιος and Λαβιδ might be adduced, against it the double *bb*. A *l* at the beginning of a name may have the same origin as the *L* in Lulianus = Julianus, Lestus = Justus, etc. J. Lightfoot (*Hor. Heb.* 325) derived 'Lebbæus' from the home of the man, and so already Ishodad. Josephus (*Ant.* xiii. § 97) mentions a town *Lemba* in Moab, which he calls *Libba* (xiv. 17 [*v.l. Libias*]). Dalman (*Words of Jesus*, 50, *Grammatik*[2], 178) compares Phœn. לבא (*CIS* i. 147), and Sinaitic לבאי (Euting, *Sin. Inschriften*, 421) and denies affinity with *Levi*. Finally, the name Labbu (= Nebo) may be compared in the Syriac *Doctrine of Addai*.

That there was another Judas besides the traitor among the Twelve is attested by Jn 14[22], and it is possible that later his name was less used to avoid remembrance of the traitor and confusion with him, and that his original name 'Judas' was replaced by 'Thaddæus' in Mk. and by 'Lebbæus' in Mt. (if this be the true reading for Mt.). In Ac 1[13] we have three names—Joseph, Barsabbas, Justus ; in a similar way we should get here three or even four — Judas, son of James, Lebbæus, Thaddæus. The testimony of Origen (c. Cels. i. 62 [Berlin ed. i. 113]) is rather confused. Against Celsus, who mentioned 'publicans and sailors' in the plural among the ten or eleven followers of Jesus, Origen says that by the sailors Celsus may mean the sons of Zebedee ; but of publicans there was only Matthew among the Twelve. Even if the publican Λευής (so cod. A, Λευΐς P) followed Jesus, yet he was not of the number of the Twelve, ΄εἰ μὴ κατά τινα τῶν ἀντιγράφων τοῦ κατὰ Μάρκον εὐαγγελίου. Did Origen know the reading of D and its Latin allies in Mk., and identify Lebbæus with Levi ? *

LITERATURE.—See vol. i. pp. 103, 457, 906 ; and below at end of art. THADDÆUS.   EB. NESTLE.

LEGION (λεγιών [λεγεών], a loan-word from the Latin legio, which meant originally a 'gathering' of the citizen army of Rome).—The word 'legion' occurs in two contexts in the Gospels. One is in the scene at Gethsemane, when Peter cut off the ear of the high priest's slave (Mt 26[53]) ; the other occurs in the narrative about the man with the unclean spirit in the country of the Gerasenes (Mk 5[9, 15], Lk 8[30] ; but not in Matthew's account, which gives two men). In both cases the reference is to the large number of persons who compose a legion : in the one case the legions of angels are at the disposal of Jesus, if He asks for them ; in the other the great number of evil spirits can be described only by the name 'legion.' The present writer cannot recall any such use of the word 'legion' in non-Christian authors. It seems certain also that in the NT the word is not a translation of any Aramaic word. The conclusion is that, if Aramaic is behind the passages where the word occurs, the expression was imported into that language from Greek, and reveals the great impression made on the minds of Orientals by the vast organized unity of the Roman army, with which they had become acquainted since the Roman occupation of Syria by Pompey (B.C. 64–63). At least three and often more (see Hardy's Studies in Roman History, 181 ff.) legions were quartered in that province during the whole of the 1st cent. A.D., and the sight of these magnificent troops, as they marched in column along the great roads of the country, must have powerfully impressed the natives with the numbers and power of the Roman people. An innumerable number of persons came to be spoken of as a legion.

The full strength of a Roman legion was about 6000 men, or about that of a modern infantry division, but the subdivision was different. Instead of brigades, battalions, companies, and sections, there were 10 cohortes, each commanded by a tribunus militum, 3 manipuli in each cohors, and 2 centuriæ in each manipulus. The uniform of all ordinary legionaries was the same. The legion was commanded by a legatus legionis (lieutenant-general). See also BAND.

LITERATURE.—W. Ramsay, A Manual of Roman Antiquities, revised and partly rewritten by R. Lanciani, 15th ed. (London, 1894) ch. xii. (on p. 459 f. there are references to other literature).   ALEX. SOUTER.

* On the reading Θαδδαῖος ὁ ἐπικληθεὶς Λεββαῖος for Mt. see v. Soden, 1. p. 1074, and ib. p. 1313 for the reading of D in Mk. What, according to v. Soden, the true reading in Mt. is we have not been able to discover. The MSS אB represent, according to him (and others), the recension of Hesychius.

LEGS (Jn 19[31f.]).—The breaking of the legs with a heavy club or bar (σκελοκοπία, crurifragium) was inflicted as a capital punishment on slaves and others who incurred the anger of irresponsible masters (for reff. see Westcott's note). The victim, with legs broken, hands cut off, and otherwise mutilated, was thrown still alive into a pit ; often the deathblow was given in some other way ('fractis cruribus occiduntur,' Ammian Marcell. Hist. xiv. 9). Crurifragium formed no part of crucifixion itself, but was perhaps usually added in Judæa to secure a speedy death, as otherwise those crucified might linger for several days (cf. Lactantius, iv. 26, 'His executioners did not think it necessary to break His bones, as was their prevailing custom'). Death would then ensue in one of the following ways—(1) From shock ; in which case it would be immediate. (2) From hæmorrhage ; such blows given by a heavy bar might cause complete tearing of the skin, producing what is known as 'a compound fracture,' which would speedily result in bleeding to death owing to the tearing of the blood-vessels. This would be especially likely to occur from the upright position in which the victim was suspended. (3) From gangrene, which would ensue if neither shock nor hæmorrhage were fatal, and would make recovery impossible. Thus the bodies might be removed. Edersheim says (Life and Times, ii. 613) : 'The breaking of the bones was always followed by a coup de grâce by sword, lance, or stroke (the perforatio or percussio sub alas), which immediately put an end to what remained of life. Thus the "breaking of the bones" was a sort of increase of punishment by way of compensation for its shortening by the final stroke that followed.' Cf. Quintilian, 'cruces succiduntur: percussos sepeliri carnifex non vetat.' But Meyer is of opinion that the addition of a finishing blow by which (and therefore not by crurifragium in itself) death was brought about, cannot be shown, and least of all from Jn 19[34]. Crurifragium, as well as crucifixion, was abolished by Constantine, the first Christian emperor. The Jews did not make their request to Pilate with the desire to intensify the sufferings of Jesus and the robbers, but because only in this way could they have the bodies taken down. They had in view Dt 21[23] (though this law did not refer to crucifixion, a punishment unknown to the Israelites), more especially as they feared the pollution of the coming Sabbath, which was a high day (v.[31]).

Jesus being crucified 'in the midst,' the soldiers would naturally begin with the robbers who were on either side, and so come last to Him. This is better than Bengel's explanation ('cui destinatum crurifragium distulerant, diuturnioris doloris causa'). His legs were not broken as He was already dead, but a soldier gave the spear-thrust to make sure. Thus the type of the Paschal lamb (Ex 12[46], Nu 9[12]), and the declaration of God's protection of the righteous (Ps 34[20]), were remarkably fulfilled (Jn 19[36]) ; and the sacred body of Christ, which had previously been subjected to insult and abuse, was preserved from the last indignity when once His work was finished. The omission of the crurifragium is very important, showing that the executioners were convinced of the reality of the death of Jesus. The Synoptists make no mention of the incident, probably (as Godet) because Jesus Himself was not affected by it and His Person alone was of consequence to them, not those of the two malefactors. Neither would St. John have mentioned it but for the relation of the fact to the prophecy which struck him so forcibly. 'To understand what John felt at the moment which he here recalls, we must suppose a believing Jew, familiar with the OT, seeing the soldiers approach who are to break the legs of the three victims. He asks himself anxiously what is to be done to the body of the Messiah, which is still more sacred than the Paschal lamb. And lo, simultaneously and in the most unexpected manner, this body is rescued from the brutal operation which threatened it, and receives the spear-thrust, thereby realizing the spectacle which repentant Israel is one day to behold.'

The so-called *Gospel according to Peter* has a curious perversion of the account, representing the *crurifragium* as omitted not in the case of Jesus, but in that of the penitent robber. 'One of the malefactors reproached them, saying, We have suffered this for the evils that we have done, but this man having become the Saviour of men, what wrong hath He done to you? And they, being angered at him, commanded that his legs should not be broken, that he might die in torment' (see Robinson and James, *Gospel and Revelation of Peter*; also the edd. by Swete (p. 7) and by the author of *Supern. Rel.* (p. 63)).

LITERATURE.—Neander, *Life of Christ*; Edersheim, *Life and Times of Jesus the Messiah*; Godet, *St. John*; Keim, *Jesus of Nazara*, vi. 253; Lipsius, *de Cruce*, ii. 14, iii. 14; Hastings' *DB* iii. 94ᵃ.

W. H. DUNDAS.

LEPROSY (λέπρα, Mk 1⁴², Lk 5¹²; and λεπρός, [leper] Mt 8² 10⁸ 11⁵ 26⁶, Mk 1⁴⁰ 14³, Lk 4²⁷ 7²² 17¹²).— The name of a disease common in Palestine in the time of Christ, for the cleansing of which many mighty works were performed. The great difficulty in knowing the exact nature of the disease from which the leper suffered lies in the fact that the word 'leprosy' is used as the English equivalent of three different foreign words—the Heb. צָרַעַת (zāra'ath), the Gr. λέπρα, and the Gr. ἐλέφας and ἐλεφαντίασις. And the subject is further complicated by the fact that the term last mentioned, *elephantiasis*, is used to-day for a disease of quite another nature from that described under that name by the early Greek medical writers.

(1) צָרַעַת (zāra'ath) is the word tr. in EV 'leprosy'; the root meaning is *to smite*. The symptoms of *zāra'ath* are fully described in Lv 13, and we have other scattered references to the disease in the OT. To enter into a full examination of OT leprosy would be out of place here, but it may be said that neither true leprosy (in the modern sense) nor any other known disease answers to all the signs described. We must either suppose, as is conceivable but not highly probable, that the disease described in Lv 13 has disappeared or greatly changed its character from new environment, or that the term *zāra'ath* included a great variety of skin diseases, some infectious in the modern sense, but all of them regarded in ancient times as rendering their victims ceremonially impure. Of these diseases, to take a few examples, we seem to be able to recognize *psoriasis* in the expression 'a leper white as snow'; *favus* (a common disease among Eastern Jews to-day) and perhaps 'ringworm' in the description of the 'plague of the head and the beard' (vv.²⁹⁻³⁰); and the disease *vitiligo* in the symptom termed 'freckled spot' (בֹּהַק,. v.³⁹), the exactly equivalent word بَهَق (bohak) being used for this condition in Palestine and Arabia to-day. On the other hand, there are in the references to *zāra'ath* an extraordinary absence of the symptoms of true leprosy which will be mentioned lower down; the extremely slow process of this latter disease, and its practically hopeless outlook, ill tallies with either the frequent examinations—at intervals of seven days—or the elaborate directions, evidently meant for use, for restoration of a cured person to the community.

The history of medicine shows that in the undeveloped state of medical science many diseases which a later age learns to differentiate are classed as one disease; of no department has this been truer than of diseases affecting the skin. In the Middle Ages many persons affected with syphilis were put in the lazar hospitals of Northern Europe through the mistaken idea that they were lepers.

(2) λέπρα (meaning 'rough' or 'scaly') was the name given by the Greek physicians to a disease known to-day as *psoriasis*. It is a non-contagious, irritating, but by no means fatal disease, in which white scales form on various parts of, and occasionally all over, the body. In such cases the expression 'a leper white as snow' might be not inappropriate. The disease is not hereditary nor in any marked degree repulsive, unless, as is unusual, the face is attacked; in this respect it is the very opposite of true leprosy, with which, moreover, it cannot be confused.

In the LXX λέπρα is used as the equivalent of *zāra'ath*; and as the former was well known, the translators apparently regarded this disease as the nearest equivalent to that described in the OT. In the same way the Synoptists, and among them Luke, the 'beloved physician,' in using λέπρα and λεπρός, were using words which had a definite meaning to the outside world.

(3) True leprosy—the ἐλεφαντίασις of the Greeks —is certainly no new disease, and references to it are found in Egyptian inscriptions many centuries before the Israelites left Egypt. It is also said that it was known in India at an equally primitive period. Hippocrates appears to refer to it under the name of the 'Phœnician disease,' and Galen under the name 'elephantiasis.' It is stated by Pliny that it was brought to Europe from Syria by the army of Ptolemy (61 B.C.). From this time references to it are common, but always under the name *elephantiasis*.

It is evident, therefore, that at the time of the Gospels, λέπρα—in the classical medical sense—was primarily the well-known skin disease *psoriasis*. At the same time it is highly probable that the disease *elephantiasis*—true leprosy—together with other skin affections, *e.g. vitiligo, favus*, etc., were, from the point of view of ceremonial uncleanness, included in the term *lepra*, the word having, as is usual with medical terms, a much wider signification among the lay public than among the medical authors. The fact that tradition has from the earliest period pointed to true leprosy as the disease of the Bible, certainly makes it probable that it at least was one of the diseases recognized by the Rabbis as *zāra'ath*; and doubtless its specially horrible and fatal character has caused it to gradually displace all others in the popular mind.

It might be thought that Rabbinical commentaries or existing Jewish custom might help to throw a light on the subject, but neither of these is any real help. The Talmud teaches that *zāra'ath* refers to any disease with cutaneous eruptions or sores, and indeed some references appear to demonstrate that the writers considered the disease non-contagious; as, for example, the rule that a bridegroom, suspecting himself affected, might wait till seven days after his marriage before reporting his condition. The Rabbinical comments, instead of correlating the Levitical description with known medical facts, are rather engaged in impressing the importance of a literal adherence to the text of the Mosaic law.

Modern custom among the Jews in the East does not seem to view true leprosy with the aversion of even Moslems and Christians. Of six cases of well-marked leprosy among the Jews of Jerusalem which the present writer can recall, only one of them, a stranger from India, was in any way isolated, and he only after he had been in the English Hospital for some days among all the other patients; when he could no longer be kept he was sent to the Leper Hospital, where he died. The other cases, a Russian Jewess, three Spanish Jewesses, and a Spanish Jewish boy, all lived at home and mixed freely with their friends; the boy, indeed, long after he had marked symptoms of anæsthetic leprosy, continued to attend a large Jewish boys' school without any sign of opposition or trouble. The Eastern

Jews, on the other hand, manifest at times great fear of the contagiousness of tuberculous, or as they would popularly be called, 'scrofulous' affections of the skin and of the lymphatic glands. These seem by tradition to be recognized as contagious.

When it is remembered that it is only in very recent years, in the life of the present generation of medical men, that the true nature both of leprosy (*elephantiasis*) and of 'scrofula' has been discovered, it is difficult to believe that the Jews of Palestine, even in NT times, recognized the sharply-defined varieties of disease we do to-day. It is therefore probable that, while the leprosy of the NT certainly included some developments of the disease we now know as *psoriasis* and allied affections with a scaly eruption, and almost certainly a proportion of cases of 'true leprosy,' it may also have included cases of 'lupus,' 'scrofulous' (*i.e.* tuberculous) glands, and varieties of parasitic skin affections, such as 'ringworm' and *favus*, both of which are very common among the Jews of the East to-day.

True leprosy (*elephantiasis*) has for so many centuries been identified with the disease now called by that name, and, indeed, is likely to be for so many generations, that some description of this disease, especially as it occurs to-day in the Holy Land, is here not out of place. It is a disease of world-wide distribution, though apparently dying out of most European lands, where, as in England and France, it was once rampant. India, China, South Africa, and the Sandwich Islands are to-day the great habitats of leprosy. Climate appears to have no real effect on it. It is not hereditary; the children of lepers, if removed to healthy surroundings at an early age, seldom take the disease, while advance of the disease usually produces sterility. There is no doubt that it is contagious, but only by close personal contact; attendants on lepers run very little risk if they are careful; and they cannot, as was once supposed, carry the contagion to others. Although the almost world-wide custom of isolating lepers is founded upon the doubtful tradition of this being the special and peculiar disease described in the Mosaic law, yet from every point of view this is desirable both for the poor victims themselves, who are always to some degree incapacitated and suffering, and for the sake of their healthy neighbours. Although a leper in the street is no danger to the passer-by, he must in his home be a danger to his family, and no other disease reduces a human being for so many years to such a hideous wreck.

With respect to the ultimate cause of leprosy, Hansen has demonstrated (1871) that it is due to a special micro-organism, the *bacillus lepræ*, similar in appearance, and to some extent in the action on the human tissues, to the tubercle *bacillus*. How the poison enters the body is not known. The disease occurs so sporadically that there must be some cause other than contagion; but what this may be has never been proved. The theory recently revived by Mr. Jonathan Hutchinson, F.R.C.S., that the disease is due to a diet of fish, is not borne out by the facts. In Palestine, in particular, the great majority of the lepers have never eaten fish at all, as they come from inland villages: fish is very seldom eaten by the Moslems in Palestine, and the only people who eat it—the Jews regularly, and the Christians at their fasts when living in the cities—suffer least from this disease.

Leprosy manifests itself in three forms: (1) the tubercular or nodular, (2) the anæsthetic, and (3) the mixed. Chronic cases, however they begin, tend to assume in the later stages the third or mixed type.

(1) In the *tubercular* form, after a prodromal period of indefinite duration during which there is a gradual loss of power and vivacity, obscure pains in the limbs and joints, feverish attacks and loss of appetite, the first definite signs to appear are symmetrical discoloured blotches, especially over the back. These blotches are at the first most marked during feverish attacks. Soon afterwards, definite tubercles, at first pink but later brownish, arise; the skin in these places is thickened and found to be infiltrated. The tubercles have a special tendency to form on the folds of the cheek, the nose, the lips, and the forehead. At this time some amount of ulceration about the soft palate often assists the diagnosis. The nodules enlarge and from time to time ulcerate and become encrusted with discharge. In cases where the face is particularly attacked the expression is entirely altered, and a most characteristic 'lion-like' or 'satyr-like' expression is developed. The *leontiasis* of Aretæus and the *satyrias* (=*satyriasis*) of Aristotle (*de Gen. Animal.* IV. iii. 22) are both supposed on these grounds to have been true leprosy. As a rule the eyebrows fall out, and the eyes, in addition to suffering from *keratitis*, become staring in appearance through scarring about the eyelids. The voice is often hoarse, and the breathing loud and wheezing through ulceration of the vocal chords. The hands and feet, sometimes the first to suffer, always in time become ulcerated, though the most severe changes in them are probably secondary to nerve lesions. The disease from first to last has an average duration of nine years; if it runs its full course and is not terminated, as is usual, by the onset of tuberculosis, it leads to gradual mental decay, coma, and death.

(2) The *anæsthetic* variety, if not complicated, is not nearly so horrible nor so fatal. Here the incidence of the disease falls on the nerve trunks, which may quite early in the disease be felt thickened from inflammation due to bacterial infection. The prodromal symptoms are similar to those described, but the onset of the disease is often not remarked until the patient finds that certain parts of the body are without sensation. Thus it is narrated of Father Damien that, although he had vague symptoms which made him suspicious, he was not convinced that he was a leper until he found he had placed his feet in scalding water without feeling the heat. As the disease progresses, the nerve lesions cause various discoloured patches and blisters on the skin, wasting of muscles and contraction of the tendons, a peculiar claw-like appearance of the hands,—the result of partial paralysis,—disfigurement of the nails, deep chronic ulceration of the foot, and finally progressive loss of various fingers and toes, and even of the feet and occasionally of the hands. Many of these later changes also occur in the tubercular form as the nerves become affected. An anæsthetic case which keeps to this type may last 20, 30, or even more years, and some such cases become 'cured,' that is, the disease actually ceases to progress, though the results of its work can never be remedied.

(3) In Palestine, as has been already suggested, the great majority of cases are of the *mixed* form; cases of pure anæsthetic type are exceptional.

Leprosy in modern Palestine is not a common disease, but is prominently to the front from three causes: firstly, because of the interest excited in Christians of all Churches, and the special appeal made to their charitable feelings from the traditional view that these sufferers are the veritable lepers of the OT and NT; secondly, because its results are so manifest and repulsive, and its progress so slow, that a comparatively small number of cases are very much in evidence; and, lastly, because practically all the lepers in the land are segregated together by order of the Government in a few chief towns, all resorted to by travellers. There the lepers, being unable to work for a living, sit in groups in prominent places, and endeavour by an exhibition of the miseries of their condition to touch the sympathy of the passer-by. In Jerusalem, at any rate, they collect in this way large sums for their community. They live in huts provided by the Government at Silwân (near Jerusalem), Ramleh, and Nâblus. At Damascus also there is a community, some members of which are also drawn from Palestine, but the majority from Syria and around Damascus; the traditional 'House of Naaman' is their home. In addition to these, there is the voluntary community—now numbering nearly 60—at the excellent Moravian Hospital in Jerusalem; the patients there are not allowed to go begging, and are employed in various ways on the premises. Including these last, there must be between 100 and 120 lepers in Jerusalem, some 25 at Ramleh, about 40 at Nâblus; altogether, allowing for some Palestine lepers in the Damascus community, there are not more than 200 known victims of this disease in the country. It is quite possible that sometimes cases may be hidden away, as with the Jewish cases above mentioned, by their relatives; but this cannot often happen in the villages, as the village sheikhs are very prompt in detecting early signs of the disease, and a suspected case is soon expelled from the community. Sometimes the heads of the village make mistakes; cases of this sort have come to the medical officer of the Leper Hospital in Jerusalem, and their friends learning that they have been mistaken, they have been restored to their rights.

It has been mentioned that one of the striking things about leprosy is that it occurs so sporadically. It is not the rule in Palestine, at any rate, that whole villages or families become leprous, but a case arises here and there. To illustrate this, we give a list of villages from which came some 60 cases that were in the Moravian Hospital during 1903. They are as follows:—From Ramallah and 'Ain Arîk, 3 cases each; from Zeta, Bait Ammar, Nahalîn, Saidna Ali, ed-Dîr, Deir Diwân, and Nazareth, 2 cases each; from Abu Dîs, 'Ain Kairem, Bîr Zait, Bait Ummar, Bait Jebrîn, Bettîr, Beita, Biddu, Bait Hanîna, Bait Jala, Bait Safafa, 'Asîreh, Dûra, Jerusalem, Feddar, Yasîneh, 'Allâr, Mesar'a, Fara'un, Marassa, Kefrenji, Kefr Akâb, Kefr Hâris, Shafât, es-Salt, and Jummain, 1 each. In addition there were 3 Bedawîn from scattered tribes, one gipsy, one case from Mosul, and two from Greece. Any one who will consult a map of modern Palestine will appreciate from how wide an area, both W. and E. of the Jordan, these cases come. Probably there is no district that does not furnish cases at some time.

The only kind of treatment that can alleviate the disease is a well-managed Leper Home. In the Jerusalem Leper Hospital (founded in 1867 and formally taken over by the Moravian Brethren in 1881) all that medical science and Christian kindness can accomplish is done.

LEPROSY IN THE GOSPELS.—It has been often pointed out that, whereas the cure of disease in general is called 'healing' (ἰᾶσθαι), that of the lepers is called 'cleansing' (καθαρίζειν). This was, no doubt, appropriate on account of the very evident restoration of cleanness of skin, but primarily because the miracle enabled the leper to become ceremonially clean. Doubtless the lepers drifting about the land had intractable skin diseases, and as they were shut out from the temple, the synagogues, certainly in all the towns, and to a large extent from the social life of their fellow-beings, their lot was truly pitiable. Their 'cleansing' meant much more than getting rid of

a disagreeable and often, doubtless, painful disease, repulsive to all their fellow-men; it meant restoration to the worship and service of God.

Of lepers mentioned in the NT we have but one named, Simon of Bethany (Mt 26[6], Mk 14[3]), probably a grateful recipient of the Saviour's mercy. Tradition has made the Lazarus of the parable a leper, and the terms *lazzaro* for leper and *lazarhouse* for leper hospital were a result of this. Also the order of the Knights of Lazarus, founded during the Crusades, made the care of lepers one of their special duties, and they had always a leper as their Grand Master. But though Lazarus was 'full of sores,' the very account in the parable that he lay in such intimate contact with passers-by would, apart from the express omission of the statement in the parable, make his being a leper highly improbable.

In spite of the great prominence given to the cleansing of lepers both in Jesus' account of His own works (Mt 11[5], Lk 7[22]) and in His directions to His disciples (Mt 10[8]), we have only two actual incidents described. (1) The incident of the man whom Jesus touched, with the words, 'I will, be thou clean,' and whose grateful excess of zeal prevented Jesus from entering that 'certain city,' and drove Him to seek seclusion in the wilderness (Mt 8[2] ‖ Mk 1[42] ‖ Lk 5[12]). (2) The story of the nine thankless lepers and the grateful tenth, who was a Samaritan (Lk 17[11ff.]). It is noticeable that he turned back because he was healed (ἰᾶσθαι); but he was not yet finally cleansed (καθαρίζειν), because he had not yet been to the priest; unless, indeed, it is because he was a Samaritan that he is spoken of as healed rather than cleansed.

LITERATURE.—This is enormous. Here only a selection of modern articles in English is given, which will furnish all necessary information and references for following up the subject:— P. S. Abraham, art. 'Leprosy' in Allbutt's *System of Medicine*, ii. 41; J. R. Bennett, *Diseases of the Bible*, R.T.S. 1887; T. Chaplin, 'Diseases of the Bible,' *Proceedings of Victoria Institute*, vol. xxxiv.; C. V. Carter, *Leprosy and Elephantiasis*, 1874; Hansen and Looft, *Leprosy in its Clinical and Pathological Aspects*, 1895; A. Macalister, art. 'Leprosy' in Hastings' *DB*; do. by C. Creighton in *EBi*; Report of the Leprosy Commission to India, 1893; A. S. Waldstein, art. 'Leprosy' in *Jewish Encyclopedia*. On the moral aspects of leprosy in NT, see Edersheim, *Life and Times*, i. 491 ff.; *Expositor*, IV. vi. [1892] 443 ff.

E. W. G. MASTERMAN.

LETTERS.—The word γράμματα (Jn 7[15]) may be intended to indicate literature in general, as it might do in Ac 26[24]. But to the ordinary Jew γρ. were practically constituted exclusively by the Sacred Scriptures, certain esteemed Apocryphal books, and the Rabbinical commentaries upon them. The surprise of the question recorded in the reference suggests consideration of the amount of human learning Jesus possessed.

With the rudiments of the Law every Jew was made thoroughly and intimately conversant from his earliest intelligent years (see EDUCATION). The education of the Jewish child had the primary purpose of enabling him to read the passages which it was essential for him to know for the proper discharge of his religious duties. Beyond this elementary knowledge comparatively few carried their studies. It was, indeed, the ideal of Judaism that every Israelite should have a professional acquaintance with the Law in its details. But only a small fraction attended the schools of the scribes at which advanced instruction was given in its more recondite matters and the commentaries upon them contained in the Midrash and other Rabbinic books. It would seem from the surprise expressed in this question that Jesus had not prosecuted such studies, at least in the recognized schools, whether from disinclination or from poverty which prevented Him from paying the fees exacted in spite of the understanding that such instruction should be gratuitous. There are convincing indications, however, that Jesus was to some extent familiar with the literature studied in the schools, both from His direct reference to passages contained in it, and from striking parallelisms in language and thought between various sayings of His and maxims of uncanonical books such as Sirach and the Wisdom of Solomon.* He is also evidently acquainted with the kind of teaching supplied by the scribes. In the apocryphal Gospel of the Infancy, Jesus is credited with an intimate and astounding acquaintance with 'learning,' partly derived from the reading of books. The bestowal of the title 'Rabbi' upon Him implies that, though not having studied after the usual manner, He was recognized to possess learning. But He Himself in His reply accepts the implication of the question that His teaching was not derived from any human source, but was the immediate communication from His heavenly Father. See also LEARNING.

A. MITCHELL HUNTER.

LEVELLING.—1. In mountainous countries like Palestine landslips are not uncommon, and in this way roads are blocked, or obstructed by falling *débris*. The drenching rains loosen the stones on the hillsides and send them rolling down to the plains, and the swollen burns and torrents cut new channels for themselves, and dam up old ones, so that familiar paths not infrequently become obliterated. Besides that, the farmers in some places are in the habit of gathering the stones from the fields and throwing them out on the highway, thus making the roads both dangerous and uncomfortable for travellers. It was needful, therefore, to have the roads restored by removing the obstacles and filling up the inequalities. When a sovereign rode forth, a company always went before him to clear the way : hence, 'Prepare ye the way of the people : cast up, cast up the highway : gather out the stones' (Is 62[10]), and, 'A voice crying in the wilderness, Prepare ye the way of the Lord, make his paths straight' (Mt 3[3], adapted from Is 40[3]). When Ibrahim Pasha proposed to visit certain places in Lebanon, the emirs and sheikhs sent out a general proclamation commanding the people to prepare the way. The same took place in 1845 when the Sultan visited Brusa. 2. Of the Temple, Jesus said, 'There shall not be left one stone upon another, that shall not be thrown down' (Mt 24[2], Mk 13[2], Lk 21[6]). This prophecy was fulfilled when the Temple was destroyed in 70 A.D. With the levelling of the sacred building to the ground there came an end to the Ceremonial Law so long cherished by the Jews, and this paved the way for a wider acceptance of the gospel of Christ (Ro 5[12], 1 Co 3[23]).

R. LEGGAT.

LEVI.—1. The name occurs twice in our Lord's genealogy (Lk 3[24. 29]). 2. See LEVITES and PRIEST. 3. See MATTHEW.

LEVIRATE LAW (Lat. *levir*, 'a husband's brother') regulated the marriage of a man with his dead brother's widow. In the story of Tamar and Judah (Gn 38) there is record of a marriage of this type, and at certain stages of civilization the Levirate marriage was a widespread custom.[†] Among the Jews the law was laid down that 'if brethren dwell together, and one of them die, and have no child (son), the wife of the dead shall not marry without unto a stranger : her husband's brother . . . shall take her to him to wife' (Dt 25[5]). It almost seems, however, that the Levirate custom was not permitted by later legislation (Lv

18[16] 20[21]) ; but it has been suggested (1) that the forbidden marriage of that legislation was one between a man and the wife of his living brother ;* and (2) that the custom consecrated in Dt. was the exception to the general law set forth in Leviticus.[†] The object of the Levirate marriage (Dt 25[6]) was to secure that the firstborn of the new union should succeed in the name of the dead brother, whose name thereby might not be blotted out from Israel. In the earlier ages of Judaism there was no clear conception of personal immortality ; and the Levirate law was doubtless framed so that there might be the survival through posterity of the name of the representative of a family.

For the statement of a problem regarding the resurrection, propounded to Jesus (Mt 22[23-33], Mk 12[18-27], Lk 20[27-38]), the Levirate law was used by the Sadducees, who are described by the Synoptists as saying that there is no resurrection, and by Josephus (*Ant.* XVIII. i. 4) as holding 'that souls die with the bodies.' Regarding as obligatory only those observances which are found in the written word, they rejected those derived from the traditions of their forefathers. The Pharisees, on the other hand, accepted such traditions, and with them a belief in the doctrine of the resurrection (cf. Jos. *Ant.* XIII. x. 6). This doctrine, taught clearly in Dn 12, was made popular in Jewish theological discussions by the Book of Enoch,[‡] and suggested the problem set forth by the Sadducees, who evidently sought by the authority of Moses to discredit a doctrine held by the Pharisees and taught by Jesus. In stating their problem they brought forward a case of seven brothers who one after the other married the same woman. It is not necessary to take the case as one of actual fact, since the phrase παρ' ἡμῖν in Mt. may have been used merely for literary effect.

In each of the Synoptics the setting forth of the problem is prefaced by a statement of the Levirate law as spoken or written by Moses (Mt. has Μωϋσῆς εἶπε, but in Mk. and Lk. it is Μωϋσῆς ἔγραψεν ἡμῖν). In none of the three statements are the *ipsissima verba* of Dt 25[5] used, and Mt. borrows the words ἐπιγαμβρεύσει καὶ ἀναστήσει σπέρμα from the LXX version of Gn 38[8].

The problem propounded by the Sadducees may be thus stated :—The Levirate law was enacted by Moses, and there was a case of seven brothers who in obedience to it married, one after the other, the same woman, who herself died after the death of the last of the seven. In the resurrection, since they all had her, whose wife shall she be of the seven? Jesus in His answer to the Sadducees did not discuss the justice or injustice of the Levirate law, or examine the purpose of Moses in decreeing it ; but, asserting that they had erred, not knowing the Scriptures or the power of God, He showed them that in the resurrection men neither marry nor are given in marriage, but are as the angels of God in heaven ; and then He proceeded to declare that belief in immortality is involved in our consciousness of the being of God. J. HERKLESS.

LEVITES.—According to one line of tradition, the Levites were appointed to assist the priests (Nu 3[9] 8[19] 18[1-6]), but were not themselves, like Aaron and his sons, to approach unto the most holy things (4[19]) ; yet according to another representation the priesthood belonged to them as an inheritance (Dt 33[8-11], Jos 18[7]). Whatever may have been the origin and date of the distinction between priest and Levite, it existed in the post-

---

* With Mt 6[7], cf. Sir 7[14] ; Mt 6[14] (Mk 11[26]), cf. Sir 28[2-4] ; Mt 6[20], cf. Sir 29[11] ; Mt 7[1. 2], cf. Sir 31[15] ; Mt 19[12], cf. Wis 3[14] ; Mt 27[43. 55], cf. Wis 2[16-18. 20] ; Mk 9[44], cf. Sir 7[17] ; Lk 11[41], cf. Sir 3[30] ; Lk 12[16. 20], cf. Sir 5[1] 11[18. 19] ; Jn 17[19], cf. Sir 36[4].

† Westermarck, *The History of Human Marriage*, London, 1891, pp. 510–514.

* Note to Dt 25[5ff.] in Steuernagel, 'Deuteronomium und Josua' (Nowack's *Hdkom. zum AT*, Göttingen, 1900).

† Driver, *Deuteronomy*, p. 285 ; note to Lv 18[16] in Dillmann, *Exodus und Leviticus*, Leipzig, 1897.

‡ Charles, *The Book of Enoch*, p. 52 (Oxford, 1893).

exilic period, since it was recognized in NT times. The Levites are to be classed among the Temple officials, and to their office with its specific duties (Nu 1⁵⁰· ⁵¹ 3⁸) they were formally set apart (8⁶· ⁷). Among their duties was the instruction of the people * (Neh 8⁹, 2 Ch 30²² 35³) and 'the killing of the passovers for every one that was not clean,' as also the handing of the blood to the priests to be sprinkled by them according to the Law † (2 Ch 30¹⁶· ¹⁷).

The relation of assistantship which associated the Levites with the priests was similar to that which connected deacons with bishops in the Christian Church; and it is not improbable that that connexion was suggested by the arrangement of the functions of the Temple officers with which the Jewish converts to Christianity were familiar.‡

In the Gospels there are only two places where the word 'Levite' is found. In the first of these, the parable of the Good Samaritan (Lk 10³⁰⁻³⁵), a priest and a Levite, representatives of the religion of Israel and at the same time examples of Jewish traditionalism, are unfavourably contrasted with a Samaritan, one of a people with whom the Jews had no dealings. The parable is the answer of Jesus to the lawyer who asked, 'Who is my neighbour?' and it seems evident that the Levite, described by Jesus, when he looked on the wounded man and passed by on the other side, recognized that he was not a Jew, and therefore not a neighbour to be humanely treated according to the commandment, 'Thou shalt love thy neighbour as thyself' (Lv 19¹⁸). The Levite, it may be concluded, accepted a Jewish traditional conception of 'neighbour' which excluded all those who were not of Israel. Clement of Alexandria wrote that Jesus, 'on His interlocutor inquiring, "Who is my neighbour?" did not, in the same way with the Jews, specify the blood-relation, or the fellow-citizen, or the proselyte, or him that had been similarly circumcised, or the man who uses one and the same law.' §

In the Fourth Gospel (1¹⁹) the distinction between priest and Levite is made by naming together the representatives of these classes, who were sent from Jerusalem to ask John the question, 'Who art thou?' The Levites, as teachers of the people, would be deemed qualified to judge of claims of Messiahship (so Hengstenberg and Godet, but see B. Weiss, *ad loc.*); but it is significant that the mission to John of priests and Levites, who were officially connected with the Passover ceremonies, is recorded, and in it alone, in the Gospel which, according to the theory held by many critics, identifies Christ with the Paschal lamb. They were told by John that he was not the Christ; and immediately after the account of their interview with him there is the statement that he, seeing Jesus, said, 'Behold the Lamb of God, which taketh away the sin of the world' (Jn 1²⁹).

LITERATURE.—Schürer, *HJP* II. i. 223 ff., 265 ff.; Milman, *Hist. of the Jews*, ii. 408; Kautzsch, *Lit. of the OT*, 90, 117; Schultz, *OT Theology*, i. 337; K. Budde, *Rel. of Israel to the Exile*, 80; and the art. 'Priests and Levites' by Baudissin in Hastings' *DB*.　　　　　　　　　　J. HERKLESS.

LIBERALITY.—1. This may be considered to begin when the requirements of the Law have been fulfilled. Thus the payment of tithe, which in our Lord's time was evidently regarded as an ideal (cf. Lk 18¹²), cannot be described as liberality, though it seems certain that many of the wealthier among the 'dispersed' regarded it as a duty to

* Cf. Schürer, *HJP* II. i. 306 ff.
† Cf. Keim, *Jesus of Nazara*, v. 276.
‡ Cf. Hatch, *The Organization of the Early Christian Churches*, 52.
§ *Ante-Nicene Christian Library*, xxii. 205.

send, by way of Temple tribute, generous and even munificent contributions, far in excess of the legal requirement. These were collected at different centres abroad, and then sent by certain specially appointed 'ambassadors' to Jerusalem, where they were placed in three large chests within the Temple, which were opened with great solemnity at certain seasons of the year. Apart from the Temple tribute, the treasury was enriched by voluntary offerings of different kinds; and out of this grew the abuse which our Lord denounces in Mt 15⁵· ⁶. It seems probable that the faithful rarely visited the Temple, at least on Sabbaths and feasts, without making some contribution to its revenues. Though votive offerings cannot be regarded, strictly speaking, as instances of liberality, and led to abuses against which the more devout Rabbis protested, the motives which prompted them may not infrequently have been generous and sincere.

In the Court of the Women, within the Temple, were the *shopharoth*, or 'trumpets,' vessels whose shape is indicated by their name, in which contributions for religious purposes and for charitable objects might be placed. The contents of these were at fixed times placed in the treasury; and in addition to these there was a chamber where donations to be applied to the maintenance and education of poor children might be given. There is reason to believe that, whatever the motives in individual cases might be, there was a constant flow of liberality through these channels (cf. Mk 12⁴¹, Lk 21¹). On the wealth of the Temple treasury and the pious purposes for which it was partly intended, cf. 2 Mac 3. ⁶· ¹⁰. Whatever may have been the greedy and grasping spirit of the Pharisees, whose extortions our Lord denounces (Mt 23¹⁴), it is probable that the Deuteronomic precept (Dt 15⁷⁻¹¹) received a generous fulfilment among all classes.

2. *Christ's teaching as to liberality.*—(*a*) Of mind. The whole life and teaching of Christ may be regarded as a protest against prejudice and narrow-mindedness, and therefore as an appeal for liberality. His injunctions to love enemies (Mt 5⁴⁴· ⁴⁵· ⁴⁶, Lk 6²⁷· ²⁸), to refrain from passing judgment on others (Mt 7¹⁻⁵, Lk 6³⁷), and indirectly, the parable of the Good Samaritan, afford instances in which He condemns the spirit of prejudice and inculcates an open mind and generous bearing towards others.

(*b*) In the use of wealth, etc. The claim to which no follower of Christ is to turn a deaf ear is that of *need*. Need, as evidenced by asking, is a sufficient ground for giving (Mt 5⁴²). The *measure* of our giving is to be in proportion to the extent of our own blessing (Lk 11⁴¹ 12³³), and although the command 'Freely ye have received, freely give' (Mt 10⁸) was spoken with reference to the use of the miraculous powers given to the disciples, we cannot doubt that it extends also to all endowments of wealth or talents wherewith God has blessed us. Liberality in the form of almsgiving is to be *without ostentation* (Mt 6¹· ²· ⁴); its *reward* is the heavenly treasure 'that faileth not' (Lk 12³³), and a generous return, here or hereafter, for the right use of wealth (Lk 6³⁸ 16⁹). The complete bestowal of earthly possessions on the poor, accompanied by 'taking up the cross' and following Christ, which is required of the rich young ruler in addition to the observance of the commandments (Mt 19²¹, Mk 10²¹, Lk 18²²), is not necessarily a rule of universal obligation, but evidently intended to meet this special case; underlying it is the idea, never absent from our Lord's teaching as to the use of wealth, that wealth is a trust from God, and to be renounced when it becomes a hindrance to spiritual life. While liberality is assured of a reward, the reward, or even return, is not to be the object of the giver (Lk 6³⁵, where μηδὲν ἀπελπίζοντες may be 'hoping for nothing again,' as in AV; or 'never despairing,' as in RV; or, if read μηδένα, 'driving no one to despair,' or 'despairing of no man,' as in RVm).*

There are three utterances of our Lord with reference to liberality to the Temple and the purposes connected therewith. The gift is to be brought to the altar only after reconciliation to an offended brother (Mt 5²³·²⁴); outward liberality being thus shown to be unacceptable to God unless the heart be filled with the spirit of love. Natural duties are not to be set aside by a liberality which becomes sinful (Mt 15⁵) in devoting to the Temple what ought to be given to the support of parents. The teaching of the incident of the widow's two mites is best summed up in the words of Ambrose: 'It is not considered how much is given, but how much remains behind.' The answer of John the Baptist (Lk 3¹¹) may be quoted as in accordance with the teaching of our Lord: liberality is here shown to be an evidence of repentance, and a practical testimony to a change of heart. See also artt. ALMSGIVING, GIVING.

LITERATURE.—J. O. Dykes, *Manifesto of the King*, 351; J. Ll. Davies, *Spiritual Apprehension*, 244; S. Cox, *Biblical Expositions*, 195; W. M. Sinclair, *Christ and our Times*, 279; W. Dickie, *Culture of the Spiritual Life*, 183; Edersheim, *The Temple: Its Ministry and Services*; works on Jewish Antiqq.; the Comm. *in loc.*

S. J. RAMSAY SIBBALD.

LIBERTY.—Christ and His first disciples clearly regarded liberty as an essential of the highest religious life. He begins His mission at Nazareth with the words of Isaiah that His work was 'to set at liberty them that are bruised' (Lk 4¹⁸). By His contrast of the Mosaic law with His own 'I say unto you' of Mt 5²²·²⁸·³⁹, He declares His disciples to be free of the ancient law; their worship no longer fettered by place (Jn 4²¹); their very Sabbath, which had held them together in the Captivity, an institution to be sanely used for any kind of good work and any sinless pleasure (Mk 2²⁷, Mt 12⁸, Lk 5¹⁻⁵). New wine-skins must be made for the new wine (Mk 2²², Lk 6³⁸). The disciple must hold himself entirely at liberty from the things of the world for the world's sake; he must stand 'with loins girded about and lamp burning' (Lk 12³⁵), unhindered by multitudinous possessions (Lk 12¹⁵), not anxious as to the lesser matters of clothing, food, and shelter (Mt 6²⁵, Lk 12²²), taking 'no bread, no wallet, no money,' whereon he may come to depend too much (Lk 9³ 10¹, Mt 10⁹, Mk 6⁸). If the rich young man would be perfect, he must learn to be the free master of his riches, not their slave, even though he may have entirely to disperse them in order to assure himself of his spiritual liberty (Mt 19²¹, Lk 18²²). In all things the disciple must be absolutely free for his mission, and 'leave the dead to bury their own dead' (Mt 8²², Lk 9⁶⁰). His utterance itself must partake of the same liberty, not crippled by the slow movement of the intellectual faculties, but made vivid by immediate contact with the Holy Spirit: 'Settle it therefore in your hearts not to meditate beforehand how to answer' (Lk 21¹⁴, Mk 13¹¹, Mt 10¹⁹). Christ promises that the disciple who prizes His word shall come to know the greater fulness of truth, and that revelation shall liberate him; he shall no longer be a bond-servant of sin (it would be impossible, having once seen the light); he shall be free with all the liberties of sonship (Jn 8³²·³⁴⁻³⁶).

Jesus Himself exhibits the surprises which the 'law of liberty' (Ja 1²⁵) has within it. He tells of the master who, finding his servants alert and faithful, flings conventionality to the winds, 'girds

* One of the few sayings of our Lord quoted outside the Gospels commends liberality (Ac 20³⁵).

himself, makes them sit down to meat, and himself serves them' (Lk 12³⁷). He tells His host that it were a higher thing to dare to invite, not his relatives and wealthy friends, but the poor, the lame, the blind, who could never recompense him (Lk 14¹²). In dealing with the woman taken in sin,* He takes the course of the moment, as novel as it is searching in its free way (Jn 8¹⁻¹¹). The cruse of precious ointment is looked at as the symbol of an affectionate impulse, more to be valued than a calculated act of philanthropy—selling and giving to the poor (Mk 14⁵, Mt 26⁶⁻¹², Jn 12⁵). Pharisees are startled at His frank intercourse with publicans and sinners (Mk 2¹⁶, Lk 5³⁰ 15²). In vain He likens the liberty of the Spirit to the wind 'that bloweth where it listeth' (Jn 3⁸); few can understand the variety of the workings of the Divine Spirit in man, Wisdom only being justified by 'all her children' (Mk 11¹⁹, Lk 7³⁵), to the confusion often of those who cannot comprehend a John the Baptist abstaining and the Son of man 'eating and drinking.' There are times when Christ seems deliberately to lead His hearers, and especially the formalists among them, into problems that find no solution in 'the Law,' but that compel an exercise of liberty of judgment, as in the 'Render unto Cæsar the things that are Cæsar's' (Lk 20²⁵, Mt 22²¹), 'the baptism of John, was it from heaven, or of men?' (Lk 20⁴), and the question, 'Is it lawful to heal on the Sabbath day, or not?' (Mk 3⁴, Lk 6⁹ 14³). The principle of true liberty, as our Lord taught and lived it, would go far in encouraging the believers in 'the reunion of Christendom,' especially such a command as 'Forbid him not: for he that is not against you is for you' (Lk 9⁵⁰).

That the Apostles so understood Christ can hardly be questioned. Throughout the NT liberty (ἐλευθερία, and its even more confident form ἐξουσία) runs as a golden thread, distinguishing the New Dispensation from the Old. There is the same joyous exercise of the power of a new life that Christ foretold. The writers have met one of the deepest problems of philosophy (man's freedom of will), and have boldly pronounced upon it. St. Paul has no hesitation in asserting man's natural liberty in the light of the spiritual liberty now made known through Jesus Christ. He claims the right (ἐξουσία) of free action in the common affairs of life, in food, in marriage, in the pastor not necessarily labouring manually, but sharing in material provision in return for his spiritual toiling (1 Co 9⁴⁻⁶·¹² *bis*), just as St. John will claim for the purified soul the same liberty (ἐξουσία) of approach to the tree of life and entry by the portals of the eternal city (Rev 22¹⁴). Perhaps this particular word is most suggestively used in 1 Co 8⁹ 'Take heed lest by any means this liberty of yours become a stumbling-block to the weak,' *i.e.* lest the very strength and assurance of the new-found liberty may lead you to flourish it boastfully, thus courting temptation yourself, and perhaps ruining the weaker brethren, who, seeing you able to join in certain practices unharmed, will be tempted to copy you, to their own hurt. It is clear that in the first days liberty was fundamental with the Christian. Each man has to 'work out his own salvation' (Ph 2¹²), to be 'fully assured in his own mind,' to 'give account of himself to God' (Ro 14⁵·¹²). Christians are the free citizens of the heavenly Jerusalem, children of liberty (Gal 4²⁶). For abiding freedom did Christ set them free (5¹), calling them into liberty (v.¹³). Henceforth no Mosaic veil of past traditions, laws, rites, can bind them. When Moses is read, it shall be with no hindering timidities (2 Co 3¹⁵ff.) of the letter, but in the reverent freedom of the spirit (vv.⁶⁻⁸). The disciple feels himself freed from that yoke 'which neither we nor our fathers were able to bear' (Ac 15¹⁰). The Law has but led into a larger world, in which is prized 'the liberty which we have in Christ Jesus' (Gal 3²⁴ 2⁴). The escape has been from the bondage of a religion of fear into the liberty of a faith that discerns in God the Eternal Fatherhood (Ro 8¹⁵). So St. Paul prays that the word may have 'free course,' may run (RV) (τρέχῃ), spreading the gospel abroad with a free unhindered spirit (2 Th 3¹), and leaving each worker to develop his own methods (1 Co 9¹) and rules of conduct—'Why is my liberty judged by another man's conscience?' (10²⁹). But this does not imply licence. That his liberty is Christian implies a limitation. He is to be 'as free, yet not using his liberty for a cloak of maliciousness, but as the bond-servant of God' (1 P 2¹⁶), having no part with those worldly ones so ready in 'promising liberty while they themselves are bond-servants of corruption' (2 P 2¹⁹). He knows that he will be judged in his speech and

* Although no part of the correct text of Jn 8, the *Pericope Adulteræ* probably embodies a true reminiscence of an incident in our Lord's ministry.

conduct by the law of liberty which has taken the place of the ancient law (Ja 2¹²). Being made free from sin he is still a servant, but of righteousness, a ˙servant to God' (Ro 6¹⁸·²⁰·²²), and from the 'bondage of corruption' has entered into the 'liberty of the glory of the children of God' (Ro 8²¹). This liberty has been the exchange of a hateful for a precious bondage. If you were actually a slave, you are now 'the Lord's freedman,' if you were free, you are now 'Christ's bond-servant' (1 Co 7²¹·²²), and that service is the ministry of the brethren, a bondage into which St. Paul boasts and glories that he had brought himself (1 Co 9¹⁹). He has found a new law in place of the ancient prohibitory 'law of sin and of death,' and this 'law of the spirit of life in Christ Jesus' has made him free (Ro 8²). The practical comment of the Apostles upon this doctrine of the Gospels indicates also the immeasurable indebtedness of Christianity to that principle of liberty with which Christ inspired His disciples.*

See also artt. FREE WILL and NECESSITY.

EDGAR DAPLYN.

LIE, LYING.—See DECEIT.

LIFE (ζωή).—The term applied by Jesus, alike in the Synoptic and the Johannine records of His teaching, to the supreme blessing mediated by Him to men. Certain elements in the conception are common to the two records, but their differences are so marked that it will be necessary to consider them separately.

1. *The idea of Life in the Synoptic teaching* is substantially that of the OT, unfolded in all its potential wealth of meaning. Hebrew thought, averse to metaphysical speculation, conceived of life as the sum of energies which make up man's actual existence. The soul separated from the body did not cease to be, but it forfeited its portion in the true life. It either departed to the shadowy world of Sheol, or, according to the later view of Ecclesiastes, was reabsorbed (?) into the Divine Being,—'returned to God who gave it' (Ec 12⁷). Thus the highest good was simply 'length of days,'—the continuance of the bodily existence right on to its natural term. Two factors, however, were latent in the OT conception from the beginning, and became more and more prominent in the course of the after-development. (1) The radical element in life is activity. Mere physical being is distinguished from that essential 'life' which consists in the unrestricted play of all the energies, especially of the higher and more characteristic. In the loftier passages of the Psalms, more particularly, the idea of 'life' has almost always a pregnant sense. It is associated with joy, peace, prosperity, wisdom, righteousness; man 'lives' according as he has free scope for the activities which are distinctive of his spiritual nature. God Himself is emphatically the 'living One,' as contrasted with men in their limitation and helplessness. ·(2) Since God alone possesses life in the highest sense, fellowship with Him is the one condition on which men can obtain it. 'By every word of God doth man live' (Dt 8³). 'With thee is the fountain of life' (Ps 36⁹). In the higher regions of OT thought, life and communion with God are interchangeable ideas. The belief in immortality is never expressly stated, but, as Jesus Himself indicates, it was implicit in this conception of a God who was not the God of the dead but of the living. See art. LIVING.

Jesus accepted the idea of life as it had come to Him through the OT. To Him also life is primarily the physical existence (cf. Mt 6²⁵ 'Take no thought for your life, what ye shall eat and drink,' etc.), and He advances on this conception along ethical and religious lines, in the same manner as the Psalmists and Prophets. (1) He distinguishes between the essential 'life' and the outward subsidiary things with which it is so easily confused. 'The life is more than meat'

* The various terms used, and the many English equivalents, will be found fully treated in Hastings' *DB*, artt. 'Free,' 'Freedom,' etc.

(Lk 12²³). 'A man's life consisteth not in the abundance of the things which he possesseth' (v.¹⁵). 'What shall it profit a man if he gain the whole world and lose his life?' (Mk 8³⁶). (2) Thus He arrives at the idea of something central and inalienable which constitutes the reality of life. This He discovers in the moral activity. The body with its manifold faculties is only the organ by which man accomplishes his true task of obedience to God. Meat, raiment, and all the rest are necessary, 'but seek first the kingdom of God and his righteousness.' (3) In this way He is led to the conception of a higher, spiritual life, gained through the sacrifice of the lower. 'If a man hate not his own life, he cannot be my disciple' (Lk 14²⁶). 'He that findeth his life shall lose it, and he that loseth his life for my sake shall find it' (Mt 10³⁹ 16²⁵).

Here, however, we become aware of the difficulty which meets us under different forms throughout our Lord's teaching. In His account of the supreme blessing for which lower things must be sacrificed, He seems to pass abruptly from ethical to eschatological ideas. 'Life' is a reward laid up for the righteous in the world to come. It is regarded sometimes as a new state of being (Mt 25⁴⁶), sometimes as a sort of prize that can be bestowed in the same manner as houses and goods and lands (Mk 10³⁰). The precise meaning to be attached to 'the world to come' in which this 'life' will be imparted, depends on our interpretation of the general conception of the Kingdom of God. Our Lord would appear to waver between the idea of a world beyond death and that of a Messianic age or æon, apocalyptically revealed on earth. In either case, however, He thinks of 'life' as of something still in the future, the peculiar blessing of the realized Kingdom of God.

This future possession is defined more particularly in several passages as '**eternal life**,' and the epithet might appear at first sight to imply a distinction. We find, however, on closer examination that the term 'life' itself usually involves the emphatic meaning. 'This do and thou shalt live' (Lk 10²⁸) is our Lord's reply to the inquiry concerning 'eternal life.' So when He says, 'It is better to enter into life halt or maimed' (Mt 18⁸, Mk 9⁴³), or 'Narrow is the way that leadeth unto life' (Mt 7¹⁴), it is evidently the future blessing that is in His mind. There is good ground for the conjecture that Jesus Himself never used the expression 'eternal life.'

Since the ethical and eschatological ideas are denoted by the same word, we are justified in assuming that in the mind of Jesus they were bound up with one another. The 'life' which is projected into the future and described figuratively as a gift bestowed from without, is in the last resort the life of moral activity. This becomes more apparent when we take account of certain further elements in our Lord's teaching.

(*a*) The condition on which the future reward is given is faithful performance of the moral task in the present. Those shall 'live' who keep the commandments. The narrow way that leads to life is the way of obedience and sacrifice. By voluntary loss of earthly things in the cause of Christ, the disciples will gain 'life' (Mk 10³⁰). The apocalyptic imagery does not conceal from us the essential thought of Jesus, that the promised 'life' is nothing but the outcome and fulfilment of a moral obedience begun on earth.

(*b*) Life is not only a future fulfilment, but has a real beginning in the present. Thus in the saying, 'Follow me, and let the dead bury their dead' (Mt 8²² = Lk 9⁶⁰), Jesus implies that the disciples even now enter into possession of a new and higher life. They are the 'living' as opposed to the children of this world, who are spiritually dead. The same thought appears in the parable of the Prodigal Son: 'he was dead and is alive again' (Lk 15³²). Life in its full reality is the blessing of the world to come, but it will be different in degree, not in kind, from the present life of true discipleship.

(c) One element is common to the two types of 'life,' and marks their ultimate identity. The future consummation, described by Jesus in vivid pictorial language, is in its substance a closer fellowship with God. In the Kingdom which He anticipated, the pure in heart were to see God (Mt 5[8]); those who hungered and thirsted after righteousness were to be satisfied with God's presence (v.[6]). This perfect communion with God is the supreme reward laid up for the believer. It constitutes the inner meaning and content of the future Life. In like manner the present life of moral obedience is in its essence a life of fellowship with God. The aim of Jesus is to bring His disciples even now into such a harmony with the Divine will that they may be children of their Father who is in heaven, resembling Him and holding real communion with Him. The eschatological idea of life thus resolves itself at its centre into the purely ethical and religious. The Kingdom is already come when God's will is done on earth as it is in heaven.

Jesus is Himself the Mediator of the new life. He imparts to His disciples His own consciousness of God's presence and Fatherhood. He inspires in them a faith and obedience which without Him would have been for ever impossible. Through knowledge of Him and participation in His spirit, they enter into that fellowship with God which is eternal life. See MEDIATOR.

2. *In the Fourth Gospel* the idea of Life is much more prominent than in the Synoptics. The Evangelist expressly states (20[31]) that he has 'written these things that believing ye may have life,' and this statement of his main intention is fully borne out by the detailed study of the Gospel. The teaching of Jesus, as he records it, centres wholly on the subject of Life.

This in itself need not be regarded as a breach with the authentic tradition. We have seen that in the Synoptics also the idea of Life lies at the heart of our Lord's teaching, since life is the peculiar blessing of the Kingdom of God. St. John, after his manner, detaches the essential thought from the eschatological framework. The future 'kingdom' becomes simply 'life.'

The idea of Life as a present possession (already implicit in the Synoptic teaching) becomes in the Fourth Gospel central and determinative. 'He that believeth on the Son hath (even now) everlasting life' (3[36]). 'He that heareth my word . . . is passed out of death into life' (5[24]). The whole purpose of the work of Christ, as conceived by the Evangelist, was to communicate to His disciples, here and now, the eternal life. To those who have received His gift the death of the body is only a physical incident, a 'falling asleep' (11[11]). The true death is the state of sin and privation, out of which they have been delivered, once and for all, in the act of surrender to Christ.

Isolated passages in the Gospel might seem to conflict with this, the characteristic and prevailing view. In the 6th chapter more especially, the conception of Life as a spiritual possession in the present appears side by side with repeated allusions to a resurrection 'at the last day' (6[39. 44. 54]). These allusions are partly to be explained as reminiscences of an earlier type of doctrine, not completely in harmony with the writer's own; such 'concessions' to a traditional belief meet us continually in this Gospel. At the same time, they serve to emphasize a real, though secondary, aspect of John's own teaching. He anticipates in the future world a full manifestation of the Life which under earthly conditions is necessarily hidden. For the believer, as for Christ Himself, the escape from this world and its limitations marks the entrance into a larger activity and 'glory' (cf. 14[2. 3]).

The Evangelist nowhere attempts to define his conception of Life. The great saying, 'This is life eternal,' etc. (17[3]), cannot be construed as a definition. It only declares that the knowledge of God through Jesus Christ carries with it the assurance of life (cf. 'His commandment is life everlasting' [12[50]]). The nature of the life is indicated only in vague and half-figurative terms. It is indestructible (6[58] 11[26]), satisfies all spiritual thirst and hunger (6[35] 4[14]), is the source of light (1[4] 8[12]). But, while little is said by way of express definition, the general import of the Johannine conception is sufficiently clear. The Life which Christ communicates is the absolute, Divine Life. 'As the Father has life in himself, so he hath given the Son to have life in himself' (5[26], cf. 1[4]). It is assumed that in God and in the Logos, who is one with Him, a life resides which is different in kind from that of men, and is the real, the 'eternal' Life.

The conception arises from the blending in the Fourth Gospel of Hebrew and early Christian with Greek-philosophical influences. Hebrew thought did not concern itself with questions regarding the ultimate nature of God. He was the 'living' God, who could be known only through His activity in the creation and moral government of the world. The Greek thinkers, on the other hand, tried to get behind His activity to His essential Being. He was the absolute and self-existent, over against the world of phenomena. His Life, so far as Life could be predicated of Him, was an energy of pure thought, abstracted from every form of sensible manifestation (cf. Arist. *Metaph*. xii. 7). The Fourth Evangelist, carrying out more fully the suggestion of Philo, combines the Hebrew and Greek ideas. He thinks of God as the 'only true' (17[3]), the absolute Being who is eternally separate from the world which He has created. Nevertheless He is a living and personal God. The Life which He possesses is analogous to the life in man, but of a higher order, spiritual instead of earthly.

It follows from this attempt to combine Hebrew with Greek ideas, that the ethical moment falls largely out of sight. The difference between the human and the Divine Life is one of essence. Till man has undergone a radical change, not in heart merely but in the very constitution of his being, there can be no thought of his participating in the life of God. St. John thus involves himself in a conception which may be described as semi-physical. The Divine life is regarded as a sort of higher substance inherent in the nature of God. How can man, who is 'born of flesh' (3[6]), become partaker in this substance, and so experience a new birth as a child of God? This is the religious problem as it presents itself to St. John.

The solution is afforded by the doctrine of the Incarnate Word. Jesus Christ, as the eternal Logos, possessed 'life in himself,' and yet assumed humanity and entered into our lower world. He therefore became the vehicle through which the life of God is imparted to men, or at least to those elect natures who are predisposed to receive it. He not only possesses, but is Himself the Life. To impart His gift He must also impart Himself, since life is inalienable from the living Person. This idea, which lies at the very centre of St. John's thinking, determines his theory of the communication of Life through Christ.

The subjective condition, apart from which the gift cannot be bestowed, is belief in Jesus as the Son of God. This belief is primarily an act of intellectual assent to the claim of Christ; but such an act implies a religious experience which has led up to it and gives it value. It runs back in the last resort to the 'drawing by the Father' (6[44]), the work of God's Spirit in the heart. Through the act of belief a man is brought into such a relation to Christ that His power as Life-giver becomes operative.

Three means are indicated by which Christ imparts the gift to those who have believed. (1) It is conveyed through His word, regarded not simply as the medium of His message, but in the Hebrew sense as active and creative. The words spoken by Jesus are of the same nature as the quickening word of God. They are 'spirit and life,' carrying with them some portion of His own being. He can say indifferently, 'My word shall abide in you' and 'I shall abide in you' (15⁷). It is this imparting of Himself through His words that renders them 'words of eternal life.' (2) The gift is conveyed likewise in the Sacraments, more especially in the Lord's Supper. The Eucharistic reference in the 6th chapter appears to the present writer unmistakable, and, while the Supper is interpreted in a spiritual sense, its real validity is also emphasized. Ignatius, writing in the same age, describes the Eucharist as the φάρμακον ἀθανασίας (*Ephes.* 20), and St. John accepts this current belief, and harmonizes it with his own doctrine of Life: 'Except ye eat the flesh of the Son of Man and drink his blood, ye have no life in you' (6⁵³). Since Jesus in His own Person is the Life, it can be given only through an actual incorporation of His 'flesh and blood,' and this is offered in the mystery of the Eucharist. The idea of Life as a semi-physical essence here comes to its sharpest expression. (3) In this same chapter, however, we have the indication of another and still more mysterious means by which the Life is imparted. The Eucharist, while it possesses in itself a real validity, is typical of an abiding union of the believer with Christ. He is like the vine (15¹ff.), out of which the several branches draw their nourishment. He is united with His disciples in a relation so profound and intimate that they feel themselves to be one with Him. They abide in Him and He in them, and the life which He possesses becomes their life, springing up within them like a perennial well (4¹⁴). This doctrine of a mystical union with Christ in which He imparts His Divine life to the believer, contains the central and characteristic thought of the Fourth Gospel.

Thus far we have considered the Johannine idea of Life as it is determined by the Logos theory. It becomes apparent, however, the more we study the Gospel, that the writer is working throughout with two conceptions, essentially different from each other and never completely reconciled. The incarnate Logos is at the same time the historical Jesus, who revealed God and drew all men to Himself by the moral grandeur of His personality and life. Doctrines which are presented theologically on the lines of the Logos hypothesis are also capable of a purely religious interpretation. They require to be so interpreted if we are not to miss their underlying and vital import.

Life regarded from this other side bears a meaning substantially the same as in the Synoptic Gospels. Jesus was the Living One, inasmuch as He realized in His own Person the love and goodness and holiness which constitute the inmost nature of God. The life He sought to communicate was nothing else than His own Spirit, as it was revealed in the scene of the feet-washing (Jn 13), and in the subsequent discourse with His disciples. Even in the Eucharistic chapter in which the theological view of Life is expressed most forcibly, we can discern this other view in the background. To partake of Christ's flesh and blood is to become wholly conformed to Him, absorbing into oneself the very spirit by which He lived. We cannot read the chapter attentively without feeling that St. John is always passing from the metaphysical conception to this moral and religious one. Both are present in his mind, and he endeavours to fuse them, though such a fusion is in the nature of things impossible. The cardinal doctrine of union with Christ assumes a new meaning in the light of this other

aspect of St. John's thought. What is elsewhere described as a mystical indwelling becomes a moral fellowship. 'Henceforth I call you not servants, but friends; for the servant knoweth not what his lord doeth; but I have called you friends' (15¹⁵). The disciples are to enter into a perfect harmony of mind and will with their Master. His spirit is not to act on them from the outside, through set commandments, but inwardly and spontaneously. The relation of discipleship thus passes into one of 'friendship,'—a friendship so close that they lose all sense of separateness between themselves and Christ. He 'abides in them,' and replaces their will with His own.

To the Synoptic teaching St. John adds one element of priceless value. He perceives that the new Life proclaimed by Jesus was bound up indissolubly with His living Person. 'In him was life' (Jn 1⁴), and it is not enough to render some vague obedience to His teaching. There must be a real and personal communion with Christ, so that He may impart His very self to His disciple. In his presentation of this truth, John avails himself of metaphysical modes of thinking which are not wholly adequate to the Christian message. The conception of Christ as Logos obscures the true significance of His Person and of the higher life imparted through Him. But the essential thought of the Gospel is independent of the form, borrowed from an alien philosophy, in which it is expressed. Jesus Christ is not only the Life-giver, but is Himself the Life. He imparts His gift to those who know Him by an inward fellowship, and become one with Him in heart and will. See also LIVING.

LITERATURE.—H. Holtzmann, *NT Theol.* i. 293 ff. (1897), Schrenck, *Die johan. Anschauung vom 'Leben'* (1898); Titius, *Die NT Lehre von der Seligkeit* (esp. the Johannine section, 1900); Grill, *Untersuchungen über die Entstehung des vierten Evang.* 206–327 (1902); G. Dalman, *Words of Jesus*, 156; G. B. Stevens, *Johannine Theology*, 241, 312; P. Brooks, *More Abundant Life*; B. F. Westcott, *Historic Faith*, 142; F. J. A. Hort, *The Way, the Truth, the Life* (1893); E. Hatch, *Memorials*, 181; J. G. Hoare, *Life in St. John's Gospel*, (1901).

E. F. SCOTT.

LIGHT.—Apart from the ordinary use of this word to denote outward light (as in Lk 11³⁶, Mt 17² 24²⁹ etc.), there are three applications of the metaphor of light in the Synoptic Gospels which demand attention.

1. The first occurs in the figurative and somewhat enigmatic saying preserved in Mt 6²². ²³ = Lk 11³⁴. ³⁵, where the eye is called the lamp of the body, the symbolism pointing to *sincerity of soul* as the decisive feature of life. Each Evangelist gives the saying a different setting. In Mt.'s version of the Sermon on the Mount it occurs in a context laying stress upon the supreme need of the heavenly mind in religion; and as the main rival to God in man's affections is the world, in the shape of material wealth, the pursuit of the single mind is naturally correlated with the avoidance of covetousness. This shade of meaning is reflected from vv.¹⁹⁻²¹ and ²⁴. ²⁵ (see MAMMON) upon the intervening *logion*. The soul is to human life what the eye is to the body (so Philo, *de Opif. Mundi*, 17, 'reason [νοῦς] is to the soul what the eye is to the body'); it is a lamp, by means of which the way and work of life are illuminated. As the functions of the physical life depend largely upon the soundness of the organs of vision, by means of which men move safely and freely in the outside world, so the mental and moral health of man is bound up with the condition of his inner life. The inward disposition (cf. Jn 11¹⁰) is the key to all (cf. Ruskin's *Queen of the Air*, § 93; *Eagle's Nest*, §§ 106–110). The employment of 'light' in this connexion is thus one illustration of the inwardness of the teaching of Jesus. He brought men from the circumference to the centre, laid supreme stress on motive, and sought to emphasize—as in this saying—the vital importance of the inner spirit for conduct. The symbolism turns on the ethical meaning implied in 'single' (ἀπλοῦς) and 'evil' (πονηρός), the former suggesting 'liberality,' the latter 'niggardliness' in the moral sphere. Hence 'light' means that condition of life which is void of covetousness and the grasping spirit. Such a spirit confuses life by diverting it from the supreme inward and heavenly aim which is its true pursuit. The hoarding temper, which absorbs men in outward possessions, is pronounced by Jesus to be a flaw in the moral vision, a speck that blurs 'the light that is in thee,' i.e. the inner light of conscience, the heart, or the soul. When the latter is darkened by the intrusion of a divided affection, especially in the form of some appetite such as covetousness or worldliness, then 'how great is the darkness'! For religion, as Christ taught it, is not admitting God into life. It is putting Him first in life. Faith is not thinking Him good, but hailing Him as best. And nothing can be more ominous than when the soul, which is man's delicate faculty for seeing and choosing God, is diverted to double-mindedness or to an attempt to reconcile the competing interests of God and of the world. The outcome is compromise and its inevitable product, hypocrisy—that sin which a Frenchman once called the firstfruits of English society—ripening under the very breath of conventional religion.—The *logion* may be, as Brandt suggests, a Jewish aphorism based on Pr 20²⁷, which Jesus here quotes and applies.

The introduction of the saying in Lk 11³³⁻³⁶ is due to the key-word λύχνος. Here, as often, Lk. groups sayings together less from their internal correspondence than from some verbal common element. He sharpens the point of the saying by introducing v.³⁵. As eyes may become injured by the blinding glare and dust which make ophthalmia a prevalent complaint in the East, so, it is implied, the inner disposition lies exposed to risk and disease, against which it is a man's duty to guard. For if the heart rules the life, the life, on the other hand, can stain and spoil the heart. Yet the stress of the saying falls on attention to the inward life as determining the course and value of the outer. '"Take care of the little things of life, and the great things will take care of themselves," is the maxim of the trader, which is sometimes, and with a certain degree of truth, applied to the service of God. But much more true is it in religion, that we should take care of the great things, and the trifles of life will take care of themselves. "If thine eye be single, thy whole body will be full of light." Christianity is not acquired, as an art, by long practice; it does not carve and polish human nature with a graving tool; it makes the whole man; first pouring out his soul before God, and then casting him in a mould' (Jowett's *Paul*, ii. 117).—The point of v.³⁶ is not easy to grasp. It seems a somewhat tautological expansion of v.³⁴ᵇ (so Blass). D, Syrᶜᵘʳ etc., omit it, while Syrˢⁱⁿ has a different form of it; yet, as Wellhausen observes, it does not read like an interpolation, and probably we must be content to suspect, with Westcott and Hort, *e.g.*, and J. Weiss (in Meyer⁸, pp. 476–477), some primitive corruption of the text.

2. The connexion of v.³³ with the saying is not immediate. Lk 11³³ is simply an equivalent of Mk 5¹⁴⁻¹⁶, which is incorporated here under the rubric of 'light,' and Luke has already more appropriately used it in 8¹⁶ (= Mk 4²¹) in the second phase of the light-symbolism in the Gospels, viz. that of *influence*. The disciples are cautioned against the tendency, whether due to modesty or to cowardice, to refrain from letting their faith tell

upon the world. In Lk 11³³ it is impossible to trace any very obvious connexion between this and what precedes, any more than between it and what follows, unless the idea of the editor is that Solomon's wisdom and Jonah's preaching were frank and open to the world (hence v.³³), while no sign (v.²⁹) is needed if the inner heart be pure and true (vv.³⁴⁻³⁶). The context in Mt 5 is much more congenial. Jesus is warning His disciples that while their relation to the outside world is often full of annoyance and suffering, yet this bitter experience (v.¹⁰ᶠ) must not drive them into a parochial and secluded attitude of negative protest. 'You are the light of the world,' He urges. You owe it a duty. Your faith lays you under an obligation to let your life tell upon your environment (cf. *EBi*, 4377, 4384–4385), instead of weakly relapsing into some esoteric or Essene-like seclusion. The allusion to *good works* is peculiar to Matthew. It emphasizes that frankness of spirit and necessity of good conduct which the saying upon light advocates as the sole reasonable position for Christian disciples to assume. The vocation of a Christian is to be visible. And visibility means influence. The reference is not to Apostles but to Christians in general, nor is preaching in view. What Jesus inculcates is an attitude of consistent goodness, void of monasticism and ostentation alike, as corresponding to the nature of His Kingdom, whose property and destiny it is to become manifest to the world (cf. Mozley's *Parochial and Occasional Sermons*, p. 212 f.).

This latter idea, without the moral counsel, is reproduced by Mk 4²¹ (= Lk 8¹⁶) as a sequel to the interpretation of the parable of the Seeds, as if to suggest that such knowledge as had just been imparted to the disciples was not to be kept to themselves but to be diffused like light (cf. Menzies, *Earliest Gospel*, pp. 112–114), the placing of the lamp in its proper position perhaps corresponding (so Jülicher) to the fruitful and useful qualities of the good seed in the good soil (v.²⁰). Others, like Wrede (*das Messiasgeheimnis*, p. 68 f.), prefer to read the saying in the light of the Apostolic age, as if it meant that after the Resurrection all reserve upon the Christian mysteries was to be thrown aside (v.¹¹). This, however, cannot be the original sense of the saying, and there is no reason why one should give up the interpretation which makes the lamp here equivalent to the teaching of Jesus or the knowledge of the gospel (see *Expos.* Nov. 1900, on 'The Peril and the Comfort of Exposure'). The point is less general than in Mt 5¹⁴⁻¹⁶. But the essential bearing of the saying is the same, viz. that as the function of light is to radiate, so Christian privileges imply the duty of propaganda. Similarly, Mt 10²⁷ = Lk 12³ (cf. Jülicher's *Gleichnisreden*, ii. 86 f.). In the fourth of the New Oxyrhynchus Logia, we have the words: 'for there is nothing hidden which shall not be made manifest, nor buried which shall not be raised.'

3. If Christians, however, are to arise and shine, it must be because their light has come. Consequently *revelation* is also embraced under the light-symbolism of the Gospels, in Mt 4¹⁶, Lk 1⁷⁹ [Is 9²] 2³², where the reference, based on OT quotations, is to the redeeming life of Christ. This semi-mystical application, which associates light with the Divine effluence, runs far back into human history. 'Heaven means both the world of light above us and the world of hope within us, and the earliest name of the Divine beings is simply "the bright ones." Such names are more than metaphors. But if they were simply metaphors, they would show how closely the world without is adapted to express and render definite the yearnings and the fears of the world within' (J. Wedgwood, *The*

Moral Ideal, pp. 6, 7). It is needless to illustrate from ancient thought how light was almost invariably, if variously, allied to the conception of heaven and the Divine nature, the latter being conceived as radiant and glorious. The gradual evolution of the religious idea slowly purified the symbolism, especially in the deeper reaches of faith within the later Judaism (notably in the Book of Enoch). The semi-physical element, though not entirely excluded even from the NT idea of glory and spiritual phenomena, came to be subordinated to the moral and mystical. The purity, the noiseless energy, the streaming rays of light, all suggested religious qualities to the mind, until the light of God came to be an expression for the healing influence and vitalizing power exercised by Him over human life. The light of Christ, the Messiah, was thus His ministry (see Bruce's *Galilean Gospel*, p. 13 f.). His person formed the creative power in the life of the human soul. Through work and word alike, His being operated with quickening effect upon the responsive hearts of His own people.

This application of the metaphor of light to the Divine revelation in Jesus is developed especially in the Fourth Gospel, where 'light' is reserved almost exclusively for this purpose. John the Baptist is indeed described once as 'the burning and shining lamp,' in whose light (cf. 1[7. 8]) the Jews were 'willing to rejoice for a season' (5[35], cf. Sir 48[1]), with all a shallow nature's delight in transient impressions (see Martensen's *Individual Ethics*, p. 385). And Christians are incidentally called 'sons of light' (12[36], cf. Lk 16[8]). But, if John the Baptist is *the lamp*, Jesus is *the Light*; if Christians become *sons of light*, it is by *believing on the Light*. It is not Christians but Christ, the incarnate Logos, who is *the Light of the world* (1[4] 8[12] 9[5] 12[46]). Already in the ancient mind the supreme God had been frequently defined as the God of light, and the later Judaism had expressed its profounder consciousness of this truth in the collocation of life and light (*e.g.* Ps 36[9], En 58[3]) and in the employment of 'light' as a summary expression not only for cosmic vitality, but for the bliss of mankind, chiefly, though not solely, in the future (cf. Volz, *Jüdische Eschatologie*, 328 f.). In the Fourth Gospel, however, this idea is developed with singular precision and breadth. The Logos-Christ is defined in the Prologue not only as Logos but as Life and Light, the former category being confined to Christ's being as a Divine factor in the creation and in the essence of God (1[1-3]), as well as to His incarnation (1[14-18]), after which it is dropped. The intervening paragraph (1[4-13]), dealing with the Logos-Christ as a historical phenomenon, is subsumed under the category of Light and Life, which afterwards dominates the entire Gospel, except (curiously enough) the closing speeches (14–17), where the symbolism of Light is entirely absent. 'In him was life, and the life was the light of men.' This profound sentence really gives the keynote to the Gospel, in which Christ as the Light represents the essential Truth of God as revealed to human knowledge. The Messiah (*e.g.* En 48[4]) and the Logos (as in Philo) had already been hailed as Light. But here the metaphor of light denotes much more than the self-revelation of God in the person of Jesus (Weiss); it describes the transcendent life streaming out on men, the absolute nature of God as truth, as the supreme reality for man to believe in, and by his belief to share. In sharp antithesis to this Light is the Darkness, by which the writer symbolizes all that is contrary to God in human life, whether unbelief or disobedience, all that resists the true Life which it is the function of the Light to produce in humanity, all the ignorance and wilful rejection of Christ which issue in

practical consequences of confusion and rebellion. Historically, this opposition emerged during Christ's lifetime in the Jews' rejection of His mission. But, as the present tense φαίνει seems to imply, the truth is general; the same enmity pervades every age—a conception to which there is a remarkable parallel in the Logos-teaching of Heraclitus (cf. Pfleiderer's *Urchrist.*[2] ii. 339). This antithesis means more, however, than a metaphysical dualism running through the world. The hostility of men to the Light is described as their own choice and fault (3[19. 20]), and this conception naturally permeates the entire Gospel. The determinism is apparent rather than real. Whether positive or negative, the attitude of men to God in Christ is run back to their own wills, although the writer makes no attempt to correlate this strictly with Divine prescience. Nor, again, is the conception purely intellectual, though the terminology would seem occasionally to suggest this view. Light and darkness represent moral good and evil as these are presented in the spiritual order introduced by Christ. To love the light (3[19-21]) is not a theoretical attitude, but a practical, equivalent to *doing the truth*. The light has to be followed (8[12], cf. 12[35f.]); Christ's revelation is an appeal to the reason and conscience of mankind as the controlling principle of conduct; 'the light of life' is the light which brings life, and life is more than mere intellectualism (17[3]). To walk in or by the light is to have one's character and conduct determined by the influence of Christ, the latter being as indispensable to vitality in the moral and religious sphere as light is to physical growth (cf. 2 S 23[4], Ps 49[19] 56[13] etc.). See, further, art. TRUTH.

These and other applications of this metaphor throughout the Fourth Gospel are all suggested in the somewhat abstract language of the Prologue. Three further points may be selected as typical of this mode of thought.

(*a*) The function of Christ as the Light is described as bearing not only upon the creation of the Universe, but on the spiritual and moral life of men (vv.[3. 4]). In this sphere it encounters an obstacle in the error and evil of man's nature, but encounters it successfully. This is proleptically described in v.[5] (cf. 1 Jn 2[8]), where οὐ κατέλαβεν probably means 'failed to overpower, or extinguish' (cf. 12[35], Sir 15[7]); despite the opposition of man's ignorance and corruption, the true Light makes its way. The climax of this triumph in history is then described. It was heralded by the prophetic mission of John the Baptist, the allusion to whom is, like 5[35], carefully phrased in order to bring out the transient and subordinate character of his ministry (cf. Lightfoot's *Colossians*, p. 401); whereupon the historic functions of the real Light are resumed in v.[9f.]. 'The true light, which lightens every man, was coming into the world'; *i.e.* had arrived, even when the Baptist was preaching (cf. v.[26]). Later on, this is frankly stated by Jesus Himself at the feast of Tabernacles, when brilliant illuminations were held every night—a symbolism which may have suggested the cry, 'I am the light of the world' (8[12]; cf. Is 60[1]). The description in 1[9] is probably an echo of Test. Levi 13[4] ('the light of the Lord was given to lighten every man').

(*b*) While the Light is the Christian revelation, it is implied that already (3[21]), not merely in Judaism but throughout humanity (cf. 11[52] 12[21f.]), there were individuals whose honesty and sincerity had prepared them to receive the truth of God (1[11. 12]) mentally and morally. When the light fell on those who sat in darkness, some were content to sit still. But others rose to welcome the fuller knowledge of God in the perfect revelation of Christ's person, men like Nathanael and the Greeks. For it is characteristic of the Fourth

Gospel that good people, rather than sinners (as in the Synoptic narratives), flock to Christ. The Logos, as Hausrath puts it, draws God's children to the light as a magnet attracts metals, while mere stones are left unmoved by its presence. And God's children are those who respond to Christ by the exercise of their moral instincts and religious affections. Unlike Philo, the author refuses to trace back this lack of susceptibility towards God to any source in the material constitution of mankind (cf. 8⁴⁴) ; but the semi-Gnostic idea of a special class remains.

(c) Upon the other hand, Christ, the Light, came to His own people ; and there are repeated allusions to the brief opportunity of the Jews (9⁴ 11⁹. ¹⁰ 12³⁵. ³⁶), in sayings which warn the nation against trifling with its privilege,—a privilege soon to be taken from its unworthy keeping. Here the author is reflecting the period in which he writes, when the Jews' day of grace had passed, with tragic consequences to themselves. 'Light, accept the blessed light, if you will have it when Heaven vouchsafes. You refuse ? Very well : the "light" is more and more withdrawn, . . . and furthermore, by due sequence, infallible as the foundations of the universe and Nature's oldest law, the light *returns* on you, this time, with *lightning*' (Carlyle's *Latter-Day Pamphlets*, iii. *ad fin.*).

LITERATURE.—In addition to the references already given, see Norris, the Cambridge Platonist, *Reason and Religion*, p. 222 f.; Berkeley, *Siris*, § 210 ; and, for the use of the idea in morals and religion, Fiske, *Myths and Myth-Making*, p. 104 f., and D. G. Brinton, *Religion of Primitive Peoples*, p. 73 f. The use of the symbol in the Gospels is analyzed by Titius, *die Johan. Anschauung d. Seligkeit* (1900), p. 119 f.; Holtzmann, *Neutest. Theologie*, ii. 304 f., 399 f. ; and especially Grill, *Untersuchungen über die Entstehung des vierten Evang.* (1902), pp. 1–31, 217–225, 259–271, 308 f. See also Dalman, *Worte Jesu*, i. (Eng. tr.) iv. § 3 ; and Drummond, *Philo Judæus*, i. 217 f. For the moral uses of the word see Phillips Brooks, *Candle of the Lord*, 305, *Light of the World*, 1 ; R. W. Church, *Village Sermons*, i. 296, iii. 46 ; B. F. Westcott, *Revelation of the Father*, 45 ; F. Temple, *Rugby Sermons*, 3rd series, 149 ; G. Macdonald, *Unspoken Sermons*, iii. 163 ; G. A. Smith, *Forgiveness of Sins*, 89 ; R. Rainy, *Sojourning with God*, 64.   J. MOFFATT.

LIGHTNING (ἀστραπή).—There are 3 references to lightning in the Gospels, one of these being duplicated (in Mt. and Lk.).

1. Lk 10¹⁸ 'I beheld Satan fallen as lightning from heaven.' The word 'beheld' (ἐθεώρουν), being in the impf., indicates a continuous contemplation. Taken in conjunction with the aorist participle 'fallen' (so RV, not 'fall' as in AV, the Gr. being πεσόντα), this cannot mean that in a pre-existent state Jesus beheld the fall of Satan taking place, *i.e.* when the devil was cast out of heaven, as described in *Paradise Lost*. The meaning of the expression should be arrived at through the context, where we read of the Seventy returning to Jesus with joy, and exclaiming, 'Lord, even the demons are subject unto us in thy name' (v.¹⁷), in reference to their successful exorcism. This meaning seems to be that the news brought to Jesus by His disciples did not take Him by surprise, because at the very time when they were carrying on their successful work He was looking at the prince of the demons lying fallen (so Holtzmann, Plummer, etc.),—a highly figurative expression which need not point to an actual vision. Jesus had the intuitive assurance that His arch-enemy was defeated already. Therefore the disciples were able to cast out the demons. The situation may be illustrated by the parable of the strong man bound by a stronger so that his house can be robbed (Mk 3²⁷), Satan being the strong man, Christ the stronger, the demons the vessels that are taken from the house, which may be either the world or the possessed victims. There is no indication when Satan fell (as perhaps at the Temptation of Jesus). He is contemplated as fallen. Still the aorist points to a definite action, and the comparison with lightning empha-

sizes this point. Possibly our Lord was alluding to Is 14¹². A similar idea appears in Rev 12⁹. Wellhausen regards the verse in Lk. as apocryphal ; but Jesus frequently used apocalyptic imagery. In the *Koran* (Sura 72) the demons are cast out of heaven at the coming of Mohammed, the angels bombarding them with stars.

2. Mt 24²⁷ 'For as the lightning cometh forth from the east, and is seen even unto the west ; so shall be the coming of the Son of Man' (cf. Lk 17²⁴). The idea seems to be that of widespread and unmistakable evidence. The coming of the Son of Man will be seen everywhere, and that very manifestly (so Plummer, Wellhausen, etc.). A second thought, the suddenness of the flash (Plummer), is not so apparent, if it is even present at all, in this application of the idea of lightning to the Parousia. For the apparent contradiction between this thought and that in Lk 17²⁰ see OBSERVATION.

3. The one other Gospel reference to lightning is in the description of the angel of the Resurrection (Mt 28³), whose appearance is 'as lightning,' the idea being dazzling brightness.

W. F. ADENEY.

LILY.—The lily (שׁוּשַׁן, שׁוֹשַׁנָּה, κρίνον) is mentioned by various OT writers (1 K 7¹⁹, 2 Ch 4⁵, Ca 2¹ etc., Hos 14⁵). In the NT there is but one reference (Mt 6²⁸ and ‖ Lk 12²⁷). From the expression 'lilies of the field,' we gather that they were wild flowers, while the comparison of them with the regal robes of Solomon (Mt 6²⁹) implies that they were not white, but coloured (cf. Ca 5¹³). The plant that best accords with these conditions is the scarlet anemone (*A. coronaria*), with which, in the spring of the year, the Galilæan hillsides are clothed. (See Tristram, *Fauna and Flora of Palestine*, p. 208 ; *Nat. Hist. of Bible*, p. 462). The nature of the reference might, however, favour the supposition that our Lord used the term 'lilies' in a very general way, and that it should be taken as comprising a variety of flowers, such as anemones, poppies, and tulips.   HUGH DUNCAN.

LINEN (βύσσος, σινδών).—Cloth of various kinds prepared from the fibre of flax was largely used in Egypt and Palestine for under-garments. It was preferred to cotton or wool, as being cleaner and cooler in the hot climate. It formed an important element in priestly dress, and in the Temple hangings. Worn together with purple it constituted the characteristic clothing of the wealthy (Est 8¹⁵, Lk 16¹⁹), and probably of royalty (Gn 41⁴²). Linen was used in Egypt to prepare the bodies of both men and animals for burial, and in Palestine it was the common wrapping of the dead. Wool was avoided, the belief being that it tended to breed worms. To this day linen is used for these purposes in Palestine by all who can afford it. Coarser cloth was made in the country, but the finer sorts were imported, the products of Egypt being held in high esteem. As an article of merchandise, linen ranked with gold, silver, precious stones, silk, etc. (Rev 18¹²).

σινδών (Mk 14⁵¹. ⁵²) probably corresponds to the Rabbinic *sadin* or *sedina*, a linen cloth, or loose linen wrapper ; although possibly it may also mean a night-dress (Edersheim, *Life and Times of Jesus*, 1900, ii. 545). In this garment the body of Jesus is wrapped when taken from the cross (Mt 27⁵⁹). It may have been torn into strips to form the ὀθόνια in which, with the spices, the body was bound (Jn 19⁴⁰ 20⁵ᶠᶠ.). Probably, however, these were the bandages fastening the σινδών.

W. EWING.

LIP.—This word, in the plural, is found in the Gospels only in Mt 15⁸ ‖ Mk 7⁶, where it stands for χείλεσιν in a free quotation from the LXX. It is rendered by AV, 'This people honoureth me *with* *their lips,* but their heart is far from me' (cf. Is 29[13]). St. Matthew, who quotes oftenest from the LXX, does so here (v.[8f.]), even though it departs considerably from the Hebrew. But he modifies its phraseology so as to improve it, and to bring out the prophet's thought more clearly than would be done by a literal translation of the Hebrew. (See Toy, *NT Quotations from the OT*). The expression 'honoureth me with their lips' is explained by some as an allusion to the Jewish custom of putting the tassel of the *tallith* to the lips during worship, as a sign that the Law was accepted, not as of duty only, but as the enthusiastic preference of the heart (cf. Job 31[27], where putting the hand to the lips is an act of astral worship; and the Oriental salutations in which putting the hand to the lips is supposed to have been originally a sign and assurance of sincerity; see *Jewish Encyc.* art. 'Lip'). Others explain this clause, in relation to the entire passage, as intended to put in sharp contrast a worship of God, or a form of religion, that is taught of men (cf. 'teaching teachings which are precepts of men,' v.[9]), and a worship that is really according to the teachings of God's word, *i.e.* which springs from a devout and trusting heart (cf. 'But *their heart is far from me,* v.[8], with the suggestion of emptiness in v.[9] '*In vain* do they worship me,' etc.).

It would seem from the OT that the lips had come to be regarded as a sort of originating centre of life and morals. We read of 'lying lips' (Ps 31[18]), of 'the lip of truth' (Pr 12[19]), of 'unclean lips' (Is 6[5]), and of 'the poison of asps' as 'under the lips' (quoted in Ro 3[13]); and in the NT also, of 'the fruit of the lips' (He 13[15]), and of 'lips that speak no guile' (1 P 3[10]), etc.

But whatever be the implied allusion or exact meaning of the words here, this much is certain, that our Lord in speaking to His own contemporaries said, 'This prophecy of Isaiah was *concerning you*'—language that would seem to require us to interpret the passage so as to make it include and describe the unbelieving Jews of His day, and, probably, all people of all times who were, or are, or will yet be, guilty of offering to God a worship in which they do not draw near to Him in heart.

GEO. B. EAGER.

LITTLE ONES.—The phrase 'one of these little ones' occurs in the records of our Lord's discourses in the Synoptic Gospels six times (Mt 10[42] 18[6. 10. 14], Mk 9[42], Lk 17[2]), although, to satisfy these references, it need not have been employed by our Lord on more than two or three different occasions. It seems to have been used with marked solemnity and to be charged with high emotion. To understand its implications, we shall need to inquire whom our Lord designates as 'little ones,' whence the designation was derived, and what its significance is.

1. It seems to be quite generally assumed that at least in some of the instances of its occurrence the phrase designates, quite simply, actual *children*. Thus, multitudes of Christians appear to be accustomed to read Mt 18[10] as a declaration that the 'angels of children' (whatever these 'angels' may be) hold a particularly exalted place in heaven. The connexion of this whole passage with the opening verses of the chapter, where a 'little child' is presented as a type of the children of the Kingdom, seems to many to require this interpretation, and the parallel passages, Mk 9[37. 42], Lk 9[48] 17[2] to add their support to it. A careful scrutiny of the passages in which the phrase occurs, however, will show that its reference is never to actual children, but in every case to *our Lord's disciples*.

The earliest recorded employment of the phrase is reported in Mt 10[40-42]. Our Lord is here bringing to a close His instructions to His Apostles as He sent them forth on their first, their trial, evangelistic tour. His words are words of highest encouragement. 'He that receiveth you,' He says, 'receiveth me; and he that receiveth me, receiveth him that sent me.' Our Lord makes common cause with His messengers: that is the general declaration. Then comes the enforcement by illustration. It was a matter of common understanding that 'he that receiveth a prophet in the name of a prophet'—that is, not in the name of another prophet, but on this sole ground, that he is a prophet, or, as we should say in our English idiom, as a prophet—'shall receive a prophet's reward; and he that receiveth a righteous man in the name of a righteous man'—that is, again, merely because he is a righteous man—'shall receive a righteous man's reward.' The broad principle, then, is that the receiver shall be put, in the matter of reward, on the level of the received; by his reception of the prophet or righteous man, he takes his place by his side and becomes sharer in his reward. Now comes the application, marked as such (and not the continuation of the examples) by a change of construction. 'And, whosoever'—perhaps we might paraphrase 'Likewise whosoever'—'shall give to drink unto one of these little ones a cup of cold water only. in the name of a disciple, verily I say unto you, he shall in no wise lose his reward.' The parallelism of the clauses here with those in the preceding sentences compels us to read 'one of these little ones' as a synonym of 'a disciple.' The sense is, as the receiver of the prophet shall share the prophet's reward, and the receiver of the righteous man the righteous man's reward, so the receiver of the disciple shall share the disciple's reward. The general purport of the declaration, moreover, demands this sense. Its object was to hearten and encourage the Apostles on their mission. For that, they needed assurance, not that goodness to children would be marked and rewarded, but that they, the Apostles, were under Divine care. The very variations from the phraseology of the earlier sentences which are introduced into the application have their part to play in emphasizing this needed lesson. These variations are five in number. In the first place, instead of the simple 'he ·that' receiveth, we have here the emphasized universal 'whosoever'; there is no danger of failure here. Next, instead of the simple, comprehensive 'receiveth,' the least conceivable benefit is here specified—'shall give to drink a cup of cold water only': the slightest goodness to the disciples shall be noted and rewarded. Next, instead of the simple statement that the benefiter shall share the reward of the benefited, we have a solemn asseveration that in no case will a due reward be missed: the nature of the reward is left in large vagueness, and it is hinted only that it shall be appropriate, treated as of obligation, and surely given. Lastly, instead of the cold 'disciple,' we have the tender 'one of these little ones.' The disciples our Lord has in mind are *His own* disciples: His own disciples He cherishes with a devoted love; and this love is pledged to their protection. The effect of these variations from the formally exact parallel is to raise the saying to its emotional climax. The lesson conveyed is that Christ's disciples are under the watchful care of His jealous love.

The case is similar with that in the paragraph Mt 18[5-14]. It is important that the relation of this paragraph to the preceding one (18[1-4]), and the nature of the transition made at v.[5] be correctly apprehended. The Apostles had been disputing about their relative claims to greatness in the Kingdom of heaven; and the Lord teaches them a much needed lesson in humility by the example of a little child. Setting a little child in their midst, He exhorts them to see in it a type of the children of the Kingdom, and to seek to become like it if they would be greatest in that Kingdom (cf. art. CHILDREN, vol. i. p. 304). With v.[4], however, this incident closes, and the lesson from it is concluded. The discussion that follows in the succeeding verses is no longer an inculcation of humility. It is an exhilarating pledge of the whole Divine power to the sustaining, protection, and glorification of Christ's disciples. The connexion between the two paragraphs seems to turn on the idea that, though men enter the Kingdom like helpless infants, they are not therefore abandoned to the adverse forces of the world : the power of God is outstretched for their salvation. 'Such little children' (v.[5]) God takes under His own protection, rewarding those who do them benefits, and visiting with the severest punishment those who evil-entreat them ; their angels ever behold the Father's face in heaven ; if they go astray everything is left that they may be recovered ; the Father's will is pledged that no one of them shall perish. The force of these great assurances is indefinitely enhanced by the individual note that is thrown into them. Throughout, the stress is laid upon the individual, as distinguished from the class, as the object of the Divine love (vv.[5. 6. 10. 12. 14]) : not a single one of them shall be without the Father's care, no single one of them shall perish. The passage is in effect just the Synoptic parallel of the seventeenth chapter of John, or the Evangelic parallel of the eighth chapter of Romans. Christ's 'little ones' in it are, in short, just 'those that believe on him,' of whom 'it is not the will of the Father that one should perish,' whose 'angels in heaven do always behold the face of the Father which is in heaven.'

The declaration of Mk 9[42] is parallel with that of Mt 18[6], and is immediately preceded by a verse the thought of which is parallel with that of Mt 10[42]. This passage gives us thus afresh in a single context the two primary statements we have met with in Matthew. The variations of the phraseology in v.[41] from what we have seen in Mt 10[42] supply commentaries on the meaning of the phrases in the latter. 'Little ones' in the one becomes 'you,' that is, Christ's disciples, in the other : 'in the name of a disciple' in the one, 'in the name that ye are Christ's' in the other. Thus the interpretation suggested of the passage in Matthew is confirmed by the very language of the passage in Mark. But this language in v.[41] settles the meaning also of the phrases in the succeeding verse. The 'you,' i.e. the disciples, of v.[41] is replaced in v.[42] by 'these little ones that believe,' which must, therefore, mean the same thing. This indeed would be independently true, since these 'little ones' are specifically defined here not as 'little ones' simply, but as those 'little ones' 'that have faith.' It is quite clear, therefore, that 'these little ones' in this passage means not children, but believers.

The only other passage in which the phrase occurs, Lk 17[2], is parallel in its assertion with Mt 18[6] and Mk 9[42], and repeats in effect their language. There is no allusion to children in the entire context, in which our Lord simply warns His 'disciples' against sins against their brethren. In this and the parallel passage 'in Mk., in other words, we have merely renewed manifestations of the Saviour's concern for those He calls 'these little ones.' He pronounces the sin of causing those for whom His love was thus pledged to stumble, almost too great to be expressed in words.

On every occasion of its occurrence, therefore, the phrase 'these little ones' evinces itself independently a designation, not of children, but of the disciples of Christ. In these circumstances, we cannot permit doubt to be thrown on its meaning in the palmary passage, Mt 18[5f], by the circumstance that certain passages in Mark (9[33-37]) and Luke (9[46-48]) which are parallel to Mt 18[1-5] might easily be so read as to make literal children the subject of their declarations (Mk 9[37], Lk 9[48]) parallel to Mt 18[5]. The account in Matthew is the fuller, and permits the connexion of the clauses to be more exactly estimated. It seems as if it were merely the compression of Mark's and Luke's reports which tempts to the identification of the 'little child' of the earlier verses with the 'one of such little children' (Mk.), or 'this little child' (Lk.) of the closing verse : and the pressing of this language literally is not free from difficulties of its own. In any event, we cannot permit any difficulties that we may feel in explaining Mk 9[37], Lk 9[48] to affect the determination of the meaning of a phrase which does not occur in them, when we meet it in other passages where its sense seems clearly indicated.

We may take it as established, then, that the phrase 'these little ones' on the Master's lips means not 'children,' but distinctly and always 'my disciples.' The question still remains open, however, whether our Lord means by it all His disciples, or only a specially designated class of them. The latter has been quite commonly supposed, and interpreters have busied themselves defining the characteristic qualities of the particularly designated class. Hahn, for example, argues strenuously that the disciples at large cannot be meant ; but that the designation presupposes gradations among the disciples (cf. Lk 7[28]), and the essence of the exhortation in Lk 17[2] at least is that the greater must not despise the lesser. Godet similarly supposes that the 'little ones' are 'beginners in the faith,' 'those yet weak in the faith.' Surely, however, such distinctions are foreign to the contexts in which these phrases occur, and even inconsistent with them. In Mt 10[42], for example, the broad identification of 'one of these little ones' with 'a disciple' excludes from thought all divisions within the body of disciples ; and the definition of 'these' as the disciples to whom our Lord was speaking, as He spoke of them as 'these little ones,' looks in the same direction. In Mk 9[42], again, the phrase 'these little ones' takes up broadly the 'you' of the preceding verse, and therefore designates just the disciples at large. 'These little ones' are, moreover, defined here as 'these that believe,' that is to say, as 'believers,' in their essential characteristics as such. Much the same may be said of Lk 17[2], in the context of which there is a distinction between brother and brother but no discrimination between greater and lesser, while the whole drift of Mt 18[5-14] is to exalt the 'little ones' and to identify them with that body of chosen ones to whose salvation the will of the Father is pledged. It may be taken as exegetically certain, then, that by 'these little ones' our Lord does not intend to single out a certain section of His disciples,—whether the weakest in faith or the more advanced in that humility of spirit which is the fruit of a great faith,—but means the whole body of His disciples. This is therefore just one of the somewhat numerous general designations which He gives to His disciples by which to express His conception of their character and estate, and the nature of His feelings towards them.

2. Whence this particular designation of His disciples was derived by our Lord remains indeed somewhat obscure. It used to be quite generally supposed that in it He had simply adopted and applied to His own disciples an ordinary designation for their pupils current in the Rabbinical schools. This idea seems traceable to J. J. Wetstein, who illustrates the phrase on its first occurrence (Mt 10⁴²) by the following quotation from the *Bereshith Rabba* (xlii. 4):

'Where there are no little ones, there are no disciples; where there are no disciples, there are no sages; where there are no sages, there are no elders; where there are no elders, there are no prophets; where there is no prophet, there is no God.'

Following this suggestion, commentators like Bolten, Kuinoel, Bloomfield, Fritzsche have accordingly explained the phrase as simply a Hebraism for 'disciples.'

It was early pointed out, however (*e.g.* by Meyer, ed. 2, p. 215 note; Bruno Bauer, ii. 241), that the currency in the Rabbinical schools of such an employment of 'little ones' as a designation for 'disciples' is neither shown by the citation from the *Bereshith Rabba* nor supported by any other evidence. Accordingly this notion has quite generally died out (cf. Meyer-Weiss, ed. 8, 1890). Its place has been largely taken by the very natural supposition that our Lord has done for Himself what the Rabbis had been supposed to have done for Him,—applied affectionately to His disciples a designation appropriate literally only to children. The difficulty of this supposition, otherwise most satisfactory, is that the particular designation in question—'little ones' —is not a Biblical designation of children, and not one which would readily suggest itself as a term of affection. Neither the Hebrew (קטן) nor the Greek (μικρός) lent itself readily to adoption as a term of tenderness; and accordingly neither in the Hebrew nor in the Greek Bible does the term 'little ones' (הקטנים, οἱ μικροί) ever occur as a periphrasis for children. Where we read of 'little ones' in the English Bible in the sense of children, this is an imposition of an English idea upon a totally divergent Hebrew conception (טַף Gn 34²⁹ 43⁸ 46⁵ etc.). It is quite true that in Rabbinical Hebrew קטנים has become a standing term for children; but not as a term of affectionate feeling so much as with the simple implication of immaturity. The *ḳaṭan* and *ḳĕṭanna* were to the Rabbis merely the 'boy' and 'girl' as undeveloped and unripe, in opposition to the mature man and woman. And although this term was occasionally transferred by them metaphorically to their pupils, it was not, if we can trust the lexicographers, in a very pleasant sense. The 'little one' among the disciples was just an 'abortion'—one who disregarded his teacher and set his immaturity against his master's ripe learning; or one who, while yet fit only to be a learner, wished to set himself up prematurely as a teacher (cf. Levy or Jastrow, *sub voce* קטן, quoting the tract *Sota 22a*; but consult *Sota 24b*, where we are told that Samuel was surnamed הקטן 'the Little,'—cf. 'James the Little' in the NT, and 'Kleigenes the Little' in Xenophon,—because he made himself little, that is, bore himself humbly; here a good sense seems to be attached to the metaphorical use of the word). It was assuredly not from this circle of ideas that our Lord derived His use of the phrase, even if we may suppose that this Rabbinical use of it was already developed in His day.

Only two OT passages suggest themselves as offering natural points of departure for the framing of such a phrase as our Lord employs. The one of these is Is 60²² and the other Zec 13⁷. In the former, the terms employed, from which our Lord's phrase may have been derived, are הקטן in the first clause and הצעיר in the second. In the latter the Hebrew term employed is הצערים, translated in the LXX οἱ μικροί. Both passages are Messianic, though only Zec 13⁷ is adduced in the NT and given explicit application to Christ (Mt 26³¹, Mk 14²⁷). In neither is there any allusion to children; but in both the reference of the diminutive term is to the smallness of the beginnings out of which the Lord in the days of the coming blessing shall recreate His Church. If we may believe that the Master had these passages in mind when He called His disciples 'these little ones,' then the application of the term to them obviously meant to point them out as those 'little ones' who, Zechariah had promised, should be refined as silver and tried as gold, only that they might for ever become the Lord's people; who, Isaiah had promised, should be the unassuming nucleus out of which by gracious expansion should be developed the newly created city of God which should be to Him an everlasting possession. The consonance of this implication of the term with all the allusions of the contexts in which it occurs, and with all the declarations concerning His 'little ones' which our Lord makes, lies on the face of things. And on its assumption all the peculiarities of the form and use of the phrase at once find an adequate explanation.

3. If, now, we ask why and with what meaning our Lord designated His disciples 'these little ones,' a twofold answer seems indicated. It is on the one side His chief Messianic designation of His followers: it is on the other side the chief of His hypocoristic designations of them. Other designations of each order exist. When Jesus speaks of His followers as 'children of the kingdom,' for example, He is applying to them a Messianic designation; or, to confine ourselves to the circle of ideas most closely related to the passages of the Old Testament supposed to be in His mind in the instance holding our attention, when He calls them His 'sheep' (Mt 26³¹) or more pointedly His 'little flock' (Lk 12³²), these are Messianic designations which He is applying to them. Similarly His language with reference to them was full of hypocoristics. They were not merely His 'children' (Mk 10²⁴, Jn 21⁵), but His 'little children' (Jn 13³³). They were not merely His 'flock' (Mt 26³¹, Jn 10¹⁶), but His 'little flock' (Lk 12³²). They were not merely His 'sheep' (Mt 10⁶), but His 'little sheep' (Jn 10⁷·¹⁶); not merely His 'lambs' (Lk 10³), but His 'little lambs' (Jn 21¹⁵). In the designation 'little ones' both these lines of expression reach their height. In calling His disciples the 'little ones' of Is 60²², Zec 13⁷, He points to them as the true seed of the Kingdom, the branch of God's planting, the work of His hands in which He shall be glorified (cf. Schwartzkopff, *The Prophecies of Jesus Christ*, pp. 199–202). In calling them 'little ones,' (οἱ μικροί) He applies to them the hypocoristic by way of eminence,—so pure a hypocoristic that the very substantive is lacking, and nothing persists but the bare endearing diminutive. There is combined, therefore, in this designation the expression of our Lord's deep-reaching tenderness for His disciples and the declaration of His protecting care over them as 'the remnant of Jacob.' The ordinary suggestions of the meaning of the phrase as applied to the disciples may doubtless be neglected as artificial. Reuss, for example, thinks they were called 'little ones' because they were drawn from the most humble, the least distinguished section of society; de Wette, because they were despised and meanly esteemed for Christ's sake; Dr Riddle, in recognition of their weakness in themselves in the midst of the persecution of the world. These are all secondary ideas. Primarily our Lord's disciples were called by Him 'little ones' because this was the natural utterance of the tenderness of Jesus' love for them, and the strongest mode of expressing the glorious destiny that was in store for them. The passages in which the epithet occurs are full of the note of pledged protection, and they run up into that marvellous declaration that no man and no thing can snatch them out of the Father's hand. We shall not go far wrong, then, if we say simply that our Saviour calls His disciples 'these little ones' because He thinks of them as the peculiar objects of His protecting care, and sees in them already of the travail of His soul that He may be satisfied. The greatness of His love for them, the greatness of their significance as the seed of the Kingdom,—these are the two ideas that combine in this designation.

BENJAMIN B. WARFIELD.

LIVING.—1. βίος = 'livelihood,' 'means of living.' It is often used in this sense in class. Gr., e.g. τὸν βίον κτᾶσθαι, ποιεῖσθαι, etc.; Plato, Gorg. 486 D, (men) οἷς ἔστι καὶ βίος καὶ δόξα καὶ ἄλλα πολλὰ ἀγαθά; Phocylides, Frag. 10, ed. Bergk, δίζησθαι βιοτήν, ἀρετὴν δ' ὅταν ᾖ βίος ἤδη (like Hor. Ep. I. i. 53, 'quærenda pecunia primum est, virtus post nummos'). It is rendered 'living' in four passages in the Gospels. (1) Mk 12⁴⁴ (‖ Lk 21⁴) ἔβαλεν ὅλον τὸν βίον αὐτῆς, Vulg. totum victum suum = 'all that she had to live upon until more should be earned' (Swete). Jesus knew that this was the case, and that she might have retained one of the λεπτά when she cast in both (Nestle, Expos. Times, xiii. 562, who adds that 2 Co 8¹² looks like the moral drawn from this passage; cf. Holtzmann, Hand-Commentar, 256). Compare the praise of the virtuous woman, Pr 31¹⁴ (LXX συνάγει δὲ αὕτη τὸν βίον). (2) Lk 8⁴³ ἰατροῖς προσαναλώσασα ὅλον τὸν βίον, Vulg. omnem substantiam suam: the πρός implying that besides what she had suffered, she had expended all her means of subsistence (cf. Plummer, 234; Holtzmann, 157; Hastings' DB iii. 322ᵃ). Ca 8⁷ LXX, ἐὰν δῷ ἀνὴρ πάντα τὸν βίον αὐτοῦ ἐν τῇ ἀγάπῃ, ἐξουδενώσει ἐξουδενώσουσιν αὐτόν, forms a suggestive parallel. (3) Lk 15¹² διεῖλεν αὐτοῖς τὸν βίον, Vulg. divisit illis substantiam: ὁ βίος being equivalent to ἡ οὐσία ('his estate'). Such a division of property in the father's lifetime was perhaps not uncommon. What precise rights the father retained after the division is not clear. The words πάντα τὰ ἐμὰ σά ἐστιν (v.³¹) are not spoken in a legal sense, but are an expression of fatherly affection (cf. Plummer, 372; Simcox, Expositor, 1889, ii. 124, 127). τὸ ἐπιβάλλον μέρος was a technical formula, as appears from the papyri (Deissmann, Bible Studies, 230). The share of the younger son would be a third (Dt 21¹⁷, cf. Jülicher, Gleichnisreden, 338). (4) Lk 15³⁰ ὁ καταφαγών σου τὸν βίον. Plummer thinks there may be bitterness in the σου, when αὐτοῦ might have been more fairly used. But the σου τὸν βίον may have been due to correct feeling; the elder son not regarding the share which he himself had received as being absolutely his own as long as his father lived (cf. Jülicher, Gleichnisreden, 337). βίος is used in the same sense : 1 Jn 3¹⁷ ὃς δ' ἂν ἔχῃ τὸν βίον τοῦ κόσμου, where it is rendered 'this world's good' (AV), 'goods' (RV), and includes 'all the endowments which make up our earthly riches, wealth, station, intellect' (Westcott, in loc.). For the distinction between ζωή and βίος, in NT and in the writings of the Apostolic Fathers (ζωή the principle of life, vita qua vivimus; βίος the process, the circumstances, the accidents of life, in its social relations, vita quam vivimus; cf. Lk 8¹⁴), see the valuable note of Lightfoot, Ignat. ad Rom. vii. 3 (Apostolic Fathers, second part, ii. 1, 225–226); and cf. Haupt on 1 Jn 2¹⁶, and Trench, Synon. xxvii.

2. Ζῶν.—(1) as applied to God: by St. Peter, Mt 16¹⁶ ὁ υἱὸς τοῦ θεοῦ τοῦ ζῶντος; by the high priest, Mt 26⁶³ ἐξορκίζω σε κατὰ τοῦ θ. τ. ζ.; by Christ Himself, Jn 6⁵⁷ ὁ ζῶν πατήρ.

The title 'the living God' occurs in OT in the following passages : אֱלֹהִים חַיִּים Dt 5²³ (26), 1 S 17²⁶⁻³⁶, Jer 10¹⁰ 23³⁶; אֱלֹהִים חַי 2 K 19⁴·¹⁶ (‖ Is 37⁴·¹⁷); אֵל חַי Jos 3¹⁰, Hos 2¹ (1¹⁰), Ps 42³ (2) 84³ (2); אֱלֹהָא חַיָּא Dn 6²¹ (20)· ²⁷ (26). It is found besides (in LXX) Dt 4³³, To 13¹, Est 6¹³, Dn 4¹⁹ 5²³ 127, Bel 5, 3 Mac 6²⁸. A

study of the OT passages shows that God is called 'the living God,' not only as contrasted with the dead idols of the heathen, but also as the God of active Providence, as Israel's Protector and Helper, as He who is Life, and the never-failing Source of spiritual life to men. It is perhaps the title of God that comes nearest in significance to Jahweh, and it seems to have been used at times of great emotion as a substitute for it, particularly when the name Jahweh had disappeared from popular use (cf. Dalman, Words of Jesus, 195). Sanday (BL, 1893, p. 153, cf. 124) justly calls attention to the richness and depth of this prophetic title as compared with modern terminology : 'the Absolute, the Infinite, the Unconditioned, the First Cause, the Moral Governor,' and so on (cf. Flint, Sermons and Addresses, 170).*

'The living God' occurs often in NT, and the writer of Hebrews uses it with special force and emphasis (see A. B. Davidson, note on He 3¹²). On the lips of St. Peter (Mt 16¹⁶) it amounts to a confession that the living God is now revealed in Christ, who thus becomes the Source of eternal life to His followers (Jn 6⁶⁸; cf. Hastings' DB iv. 574ᵇ). The high priest's use of the title adds a certain dignity to his adjuration; and Jesus answered on being thus solemnly appealed to. 'The living Father' (Jn 6⁵⁷) is a remarkable expression, combining as it does all that was signified by 'the living God' in the OT with Christ's revelation of God as the Father who sent His Son (or, of God as the Source of life on the side of love). The meaning of this verse may be briefly stated as follows: our Lord's words, 'I live by (διά, RV 'because of') the Father' are to be referred to the personal life of human weakness and suffering now in progress. In living this life Jesus is dependent upon the support and sustenance which He is receiving at every moment from the Father who sent Him. A like dependence exists in our case upon Jesus Himself. Being Himself strengthened, He becomes the source of strength to us. It is the very fact of His coming and living this life of human weakness and suffering on earth that puts it within our power to take Him for our spiritual support and sustenance. When we take home the truth of His self-humbling love for our sake, and assimilate it to ourselves as the bread we eat, we receive into our souls the true life that cannot die (cf. Beyschlag, NT Theol. i. 272; and for a similar profound saying as to the relation between the Father and the Son and believers, see Jn 10¹⁴·¹⁵).

(2) As applied to the Risen Lord : Lk 24⁵ τί ζητεῖτε τὸν ζῶντα μετὰ τῶν νεκρῶν ; the angels' question conveyed a reproof to the women who were come to the place where the dead was laid, bringing the spices which they had prepared : it was like asking them, 'Where is your faith ?' They had heard the announcement Christ made to the circle of His followers before leaving Galilee, that He would rise again the third day (vv.⁶·⁷). At the same time, the question was spoken sympathetically, and conveyed to them the first intimation of the astonishing truth, οὐκ ἔστιν ὧδε, ἀλλὰ ἠγέρθη. Here ὁ ζῶν simply implies that Jesus lives, and is not now to be sought in the place where the dead are, i.e. continues no longer under the power of death (cf. v.²³ ἀγγέλων . . . οἳ λέγουσιν αὐτὸν ζῆν). But as spoken at the empty sepulchre, it undoubtedly has something of the exaltation of meaning with which it was afterwards used by our Lord in His glorified state (Rev 1¹⁸ ἐγώ εἰμι . . . ὁ ζῶν 'the Living one,' RV). There is comprehended in it the completeness of that triumph over death which was afterwards so richly unfolded to the mind of the Church by the Holy Spirit, as, for example, when St. Paul used the exultant language of Ro 6⁹·¹⁰, or spoke of Christ as a πνεῦμα ζωοποιοῦν (1 Co 15⁴⁵).

(3) As applied to Water and Bread in the Fourth

* 'O Thou Infinite, Amen,' was the form of prayer Tennyson used in times of trouble and sorrow (Memoir by his Son, i. 324). The language of the founder of the Gifford Lectureship may also be recalled.

Gospel : Jn 4¹⁰. ¹¹ ὕδωρ ζῶν ; 7³⁸ ποταμοὶ ὕδατος ζῶντος ; 6⁵¹ ἐγώ εἰμι ὁ ἄρτος ὁ ζῶν.—ā. Jn 4¹⁰. ¹¹. 'Living water' is spring water, as contrasted with that collected in a well or cistern. It is the מַיִם חַיִּים of the OT (Gn 26¹⁹ [see Driver's note], Lv 14⁵. ⁶. ⁵⁰⁻⁵², Ca 4¹⁵, Jer 2¹³ 17¹³, Zec 14⁸ ; also LXX Gn 21¹⁹, Nu 5¹⁷). The woman of Samaria was familiar with the expression, and her question was quite natural and appropriate, ' Art thou greater than our father Jacob?' 'Here is an ordinary man offering to supply better water, spring water, in the place where the patriarch Jacob had been obliged to content himself with building a cistern and drinking cistern water' (Wendt, *St. John's Gospel*, 124). The water in Jacobs Well (wh. see) is believed to be due to 'percolation and rainfall' (cf. Hastings' *DB* ii. 536, *Encyc. Bibl.* iv. 4829, Smith's *DB*² ii. 1503). Jer 2¹³ especially illustrates the difference between the spring or fountain, gushing forth with its unstinted and unfailing supply, 'overflowing, ever-flowing,' and the cistern, so liable to be destroyed by cracking (*Land and Book*, 287), which at the best cannot afford a refreshing draught like that of the bubbling spring, and which cannot permanently retain the water collected in it. Christ does not call Himself 'the Living water,' as He calls Himself 'the Living bread.' What He means by ' the living water' is the word of salvation which He preaches (cf. vv.⁴¹. ⁴²). This word, He says (v.¹⁴), enters into the inner personal life, and becomes there a gushing spring, a perennial fountain (πηγὴ ὕδατος), 'springing up into eternal life,' *i.e.* persisting to flow upwards till we reach our end of full communion with God. C. Wesley's 'Spring Thou up within my heart, Rise to all eternity,' is quite in harmony with Israel's water-drawing song, in which the spring is addressed as a living being (Nu 21¹⁷, cf. *Encyc. Bibl.* i. 515, iv. 4778).

b. Jn 7³⁸.—' Pouring out water before the Lord' was a primitive ritual practice, of which the origin is uncertain. It was 'in all probability a survival from a time when water (in the desert) was considered an article of value' (Kautzsch in Hastings' *DB*, Ext. Vol. 620ª). It is mentioned as a prayer-offering, 1 S 7⁶ ; as a thank-offering, 2 S 23¹⁶. There are no traces of it beyond the time of David (a reference to it in 1 K 18³³ is not probable) ; but the practice of pouring out water as a drink-offering continued to be observed, or was revived, in connexion with the Feast of Tabernacles. Every morning during the seven days of the feast water was drawn from the spring of Siloam in a golden pitcher, and was poured into a basin at the top of the altar (*Encyc. Bibl.* iv. 4213). The libation of water was probably a prayer-offering for abundant rain for the new seed-time (*ib.* iv. 4880, cf. iii. 3354). Rain was an emblem of Messianic blessings (2 S 23⁴, Ps 72⁶, cf. Hos 6³) ; and we may well believe that the symbolical act of pouring out water gave occasion to our Lord's looking forward to the abundant showers with which He was soon to water the earth. — Further, this joyous festival brought to our Lord's mind the Rock at Horeb (Ex 17⁶, Nu 20¹¹, cf. 1 Co 10⁴), and perhaps more especially those OT sayings in which it had been predicted that living water should flow out from Jerusalem, or from the House of the Lord (Ezk 47¹. ¹², Zec 14⁸, Jl 3¹⁸, cf. Ps 87⁷). What was the precise connecting link of thought between these predictions and the phrase ἐκ τῆς κοιλίας αὐτοῦ, it is difficult to say. But may it not be the case that, in our Lord's view, what had been spoken concerning Jerusalem and the Temple was now to be applied to the inner personal life of the believer, enriched by the entrance of His word, and renewed by His Holy Spirit ? This sanctified personal life was what now answered to the sanctuary from

which it had been foretold that living waters should flow out. Our Lord's application of the term κοιλία to it was in keeping with the use of בֶּטֶן in certain passages of the OT, where it denotes the whole of man's emotional nature and sympathetic affections (Pr 20²⁷. ³⁰, Hab 3¹⁶, cf. Sir 19¹² 51²¹ ; cf. also the expression 'his bowels yearned,' Gn 43³⁰, 1 K 3²⁶). The words καθὼς εἶπεν ἡ γραφή, κ.τ.λ., are thus a terse and eloquent paraphrase of the scope of the passages above referred to. It need hardly be said that the clause καθὼς εἶπεν ἡ γραφή cannot possibly be connected with the preceding ὁ πιστεύων εἰς ἐμέ (' there are not different ways of believing,' Principal Campbell, *The Four Gospels, in loc.*). This saying of our Lord supplements and extends that of 4¹⁴. The word of salvation which becomes a gushing spring when received into the inner personal life of the believer, and rises up there unto eternal life, Jesus now announces, is to become a rushing stream, and is to flow out from the believer in rivers of blessing to others (ποταμοὺς ἐκάλεσεν, οὐχ ἕνα ποταμὸν, ἀλλὰ ἀφάτους, Chrys. *in loc.*). The limitations to its diffusion that at present exist will be removed when Christ shall have entered into His glory. His sending His Holy Spirit upon the company of believers will enable them to proclaim His word with full power, and will make their holy lives a means of spiritual replenishment to all mankind. The saying was fulfilled after Pentecost, when ' rivers of living water' flowed out from the Lord's witnesses ' unto the uttermost part of the earth,' ' beginning at Jerusalem ' * (cf. Dykes, *Expositor*, 1890 (i.) p. 127 ff.). When the water from Siloam was brought to the Temple, priests and people sang the words, 'Therefore with joy shall ye draw water out of the wells of salvation' (Is 12³). But in the verses following (vv.⁴⁻⁶), it was implied that the water so drawn was not to be Israel's exclusive possession, but that the salvation which it symbolized was to be communicated to other nations (v.⁵ ' let this be known in all the earth,' RV). With the leading thought of Jn 7³⁸ may be compared what St. Paul says about Christians first receiving and then giving forth ' the light of the knowledge of the glory of God in the face of Jesus Christ' (2 Co 4⁶).

c. Jn 6⁵¹.—Two things—the manna and the bread of the miracle which He had just wrought— were present to our Lord's mind when He preached at Capernaum, and also to the minds of His hearers. They had said, after His feeding the five thousand, 'This is of a truth the Prophet that cometh into the world' (v.¹⁴). But the earthly and material good which they expected to follow not being immediately forthcoming, and the first favourable impression produced by the miracle having worn off, they began to criticise and find fault. 'After all, His multiplying the loaves is not anything so very wonderful. Can He "rain down manna upon us to eat, and give us of the corn of heaven" (Ps 78²⁴), that we may see and believe Him (v.³⁰)? The manna,' said they, 'supplied the wants of all the hosts of Israel for forty years, but He has furnished us with no more than one meal.' This led Jesus to set forth the difference between the manna and 'the true bread from heaven' (v.³²). Inasmuch as the manna was sent down from above, and was continually renewed, it was a type of the true bread. But *that* bread it was not, being simply a provision which was made for a special purpose, and which lasted only until that purpose had been fulfilled (cf. Jos 5¹²) ; nor

* The Patristic expositors applied the saying mainly to the effusion of the miraculous gifts of the Holy Spirit (Hare, *Mission of the Comforter*, Note H, where a passage is quoted from a sermon preached by Luther in 1531, in which he states the right sense with his usual vigour).

had their fathers' having eaten it eventually delivered them from the power of death (v.[49]). Jesus also showed that His hearers had failed to perceive the true purpose of the miracle He had wrought. The bread of the miracle was intended for 'a sign' (v.[26]), which they had not had faith to discern (v.[36]), that He could supply them with the true bread of the soul. Inasmuch as the multiplying of the loaves was due to His love, and involved the repeated action of that love in the gift of a satisfying meal to each of them severally (cf. Swete, *St. Mark*, 127[b]), it was 'a sign' that should have led them to believe that He could give them the true bread. But they had sought Him at Capernaum, not hungering for this bread, but hankering after more earthly good, like that which they had already received. Accordingly, Jesus spoke of the bread of the miracle as 'the meat which perisheth,' and contrasted it with 'the meat which endureth unto eternal life' (v.[27]). These distinctions of the bread of the miracle as well as the manna from the true bread of the soul are important and vital, and they assist us to lay hold of our Lord's meaning when He said, 'I am the living bread.' This expression has no parallel in the OT, but it is in close affinity with the 'living water' in ch. 4. As 'living water' is water that never ceases to gush forth, so 'living bread' is bread that Jesus never ceases to multiply for the supply of our spiritual wants,—bread, therefore, by which our spiritual sustenance is perpetually renewed (cf. Dods, *Expositor's Bible, in loc.*). It is bread in ever-multiplying, unmeasured store, that can never be exhausted by the famishing. As Jesus speaks of 'giving' this bread (v.[27]), it must mean, in the first instance, the same thing as the better water which He also spoke of 'giving,' namely, His word. This view is in agreement with the teaching of vv.[63.68], and is also supported by our Lord's use of Dt 8[3] (Mt 4[4], Lk 4[4]). But He not only speaks of 'giving' bread, He also says, 'I am the living bread.' The key to His meaning is found in the Prologue. Jesus not only utters the word of God, but is 'from eternity the very *Word of God*, by which God manifests Himself. He is not one who leads to the way, but Himself the Way ; not one who preaches truth, but Himself the Truth' (1[1] 14[6] ; *Hibbert Journal*, Oct. 1905, p. 6). So here Jesus not only gives the bread, but is Himself 'the living bread,'—'the actual source of nutrition.' He 'speaks of Himself not as resembling, but as being the veritable vine, the veritable bread, the veritable light of the world ; implying that He is the absolute truth of all these things ; the supreme reality which they partially manifest in their several spheres' (Illingworth, *Divine Immanence* [2], 135, cf. 137). Jesus adds, 'which came down from heaven.' As in the physical realm, so, too, in the spiritual, the food that sustains us comes down from heaven, and to procure it is beyond the reach of our own powers (Is 55[10. 11]). As the heaven-given bread which feeds our bodies ultimately assumes the humble form of the baked loaf, which, inasmuch as it nourishes life, retains the life of the living wheat, and can impart it, so Jesus, in order to feed our souls, must humble Himself and 'be found in fashion as a man,' be born, and that in a low condition (v.[42]), undergo the miseries of this life, and at the end of His earthly course even 'give his flesh for the life of the world.' The power of this truth of His self-humbling love for our sake enters into our inner personal life, and we are enabled to assimilate it to ourselves as the food we eat, by means of His word. His word is the 'bread which strengtheneth man's heart' (Ps 104[15]), because it is the embodiment of Him who, having humbled Himself to death, now for ever lives. Through it the repeated action of His love still ministers the gift to each hungering soul. The Bread of heaven, in heaven itself, will be the word which Jesus speaks to His people.—It is the same truth respecting Christ as our Living Food and Strength that is 'represented, sealed, and applied' to us in the Lord's Supper.

(4) *As applied to the Patriarchs* : Mk 12[27] (‖ Mt 22[32], Lk 20[38]) οὐκ ἔστιν θεὸς νεκρῶν, ἀλλὰ ζώντων. — In expounding this cardinal saying, we have first to inquire what doctrine our Lord is here vindicating. Religious minds among the Jews had already arrived at the clearly defined hope of a future life (Driver, *Sermons on OT*, 92), which life they conceived of as comprehending 'the deliverance of an existent personality from Sheol, and its re-endowment with life in all its powers and activities' (Hastings' *DB* iv. 232[a]). Sadduceeism, which represented the old Jewish standpoint, rejected these doctrines. The Sadducees were hostile to our Lord's whole teaching respecting 'the kingdom of God,' which carried the consummation of the Kingdom into a future life, and accordingly implied that there would be a resurrection of the dead. It was with reference to the resurrection that they chose their line of attack on His teaching. In His discussion with them, it was our Lord's object not only to maintain that there is a life after death, but also to reveal what deliverance from death really implied. Had He made use of Ex 3 simply to prove the continued existence of men after death, He would not have met the objections of His opponents. It was their attack on the resurrection that He successfully repelled (cf. Wendt, *Teaching of Jesus*, i. 222). The Sadducees, although not actually rejecting the other books of the OT, considered them as being very inferior in value to the five books of Moses (cf. *Encyc. Bibl.* iv. 4240). It was from the latter, accordingly, that they drew their objection to the resurrection. Founding on the law of the Levirate marriage (see LEVIRATE LAW), they thought to put our Lord in an embarrassing position by propounding the case of seven brethren, who, after having married the same wife in succession, had all died childless, and then asking, 'In the resurrection, when they shall rise, whose wife shall she be of the seven?' The story of Glaphyra (Jos. *Ant.* XVII. xiii. 4 ; cf. Addison, *Spectator*, No. 110) was probably much canvassed about that time (Holtzmann, *Hand-Commentar*, 245) ; and in it the marriage-relation was conceived of as still standing in the world beyond death. Our Lord took the opportunity afforded Him by the disputation which had arisen to set free the doctrine of the resurrection from such grossly materialistic notions as these, and to show that the resurrection life is not a continuation of the present life of the body, or of human relations as they now exist (v.[25]). As to the main point at issue, He met the Sadducees on their own ground. He directed their attention to a passage which they had overlooked in one of their revered books, and prefacing the quotation with the words, 'As touching the dead that they rise,'—thus showing that it was the resurrection He was vindicating,—He asked them, 'Have you considered the bearing of this passage upon the doctrine in question?' As to our Lord's use of this passage of the OT, all that need be said here is that the revelation given to Moses at Horeb, and made by him the ground of his appeal to the Hebrew tribes,—the revelation, namely, of Jahweh as the God of their fathers,—lies at the very root of Israel's religion (cf. W. R. Smith, *Proph.*[1] 32, *OTJC*[2] 303 ; Kautzsch in Hastings' *DB*, Ext. Vol. 624, 625[a]). Our Lord's argument, based on the passage quoted, may be stated as follows :—The words of Ex 3[6. 13. 15. 16] spoke of the relation of the patriarchs to God as a still

existing relation, and set forth a fellowship with God in which they, being dead, yet lived. But their fellowship with God contained in itself the promise and the pledge of a more complete life and more perfect fellowship which should hereafter be granted them by God. It followed, by an inner principle of necessity, from their being united to Him who is 'the God of the living,' that He would not leave any part of their being for ever under the destructive power of death, but would in the end awaken them to a heavenly life with Himself (Wendt, *l.c.* i. 223 ; cf. Bengel, note on Mt 22³² ; Salmond, *Chr. Doctr. of Immortality* ³, 366 ; Swete, *St. Mark*, 266). Or, to state the argument in a more compact form :—God is Life. The patriarchs are in God, therefore they partake of life. But life cannot die, therefore they must continue living for ever. But a purely incorporeal existence does not give the full conception of life in man's case. Each patriarch is soul plus body. Therefore the body, as well as the soul, is secured in an ever-lasting life. Compare the remarkable treatise on the Resurrection by the apologist Athenagoras (*c.* A.D. 177), especially chs. 14–17 (Donaldson, *A Critical History of Chr. Lit. and Doctr.* iii. 116, 136 ff.). The ground of the resurrection-hope which our Lord found in this passage was beyond question contained in it, seeing that *He* found it there and set it forth. He could see all that God meant when He called Himself 'the God of Abraham, and the God of Isaac, and the God of Jacob.' He could discern the full witness borne by this title to the certainty of the hope which He defended. 'He who spoke in the OT was God, and from the first that which He spoke about was the consummation which filled His thought' (A. B. Davidson, *Expositor*, 1900 (i.), 15 ; cf. *OT Prophecy*, 14). Further, in the Resurrection of Christ Himself we have the conclusive proof that communion with God involves the restitution of the whole of our personal being. What the proper view of the resurrection body is we find later on from St. Paul, whose doctrine of a σῶμα πνευματικόν as contrasted with a σῶμα ψυχικόν (1 Co 15⁴⁴), and of a σῶμα τῆς δόξης αὐτοῦ as contrasted with a σῶμα τῆς ταπεινώσεως ἡμῶν (Ph 3²¹), was no doubt evolved from our Lord's saying.

(5) *As applied to the manner or course of life* : Lk 15¹³ ζῶν ἀσώτως, 'with riotous living' (cf. Jos. *Ant.* XII. iv. 8, ἀσώτως ζῆν). Contrast 'holy living.' From this phrase is derived the title ὁ ἄσωτος υἱός, *filius prodigus*, by which this parable is generally known (Trench, *Par.*⁸ 393 ; Jülicher, *Gleichnisr.* 337, 341).* See also art. LIFE.

LITERATURE.—In addition to the reff. in this art., see Dale, *The Living Christ and the Four Gospels* ; Forsyth, *The Holy Father and the Living Christ* ; van Dyke, *The Reality of Religion*, p. 121 ; Liddon, *Passiontide Sermons*, p. 244.

　　　　　　　　　　　　JAMES DONALD.

LOAF (ἄρτος).—The Eastern loaf is not at all like the bread in use among ourselves. The Passover loaf—a large round thin cake—probably preserves the shape of the loaf in use among the Jews of our Lord's time. The same shape of loaf is found to-day among the Bedawîn and *fellahîn* as well as in many villages and towns. The loaves are of considerable size,—18 in. or more in diameter, —and are of an extreme tenuity and of a peculiar but not unpleasant toughness. They are baked usually on a convex girdle, very often on the implement which is used for roasting coffee—hence the name 'girdle bread.' They may also be baked on heated stones or on the outside of a jar within which a fire has been kindled. Such without doubt would be the kind of bread baked by the

* Chrys. (*de Pœnitentia*, Hom. i. 4) calls the younger son ὁ ἄσωτος, but the sermon εἰς τοῦ ἀσώτον υἱόν referred to by Jülicher is omitted as spurious, ed. Montfauçon (Paris, 1839).

children of Israel in their desert wanderings. And at the present time one may see this loaf in almost every part of Palestine. Even where other kinds of bread are used, this is still highly relished. If there is a guest in a native house, the loaves are often folded up in quarter size and laid beside his plate, and more than one European traveller has mistaken them, when so placed, for table napkins !

In all probability the loaves in Mk 6³⁸ 8⁶, etc., were of this kind, inasmuch as such bread is almost always carried on a journey, and by workmen, because of its keeping properties. The loaf is never cut ; it is broken or torn asunder. Small scoops are made of the portions, with which the meat, rice, or *leben* (curdled milk) is scooped up—spoon and contents being eaten together. A man will eat three or four of these loaves at a meal (Lk 11⁵).

Another loaf in common use at the present day is smaller in circumference and considerably thicker, and very much resembles in appearance the 'scones,' baked on a girdle, so common in some parts of Scotland. Bread of this kind is found only in towns where there are public ovens. See also art. BREAD.　　　　J. SOUTAR.

LOANS.—There are frequent references to money, and many illustrations suggested by financial obligations, in the teaching of Jesus. These have been gathered together as indications of 'the economic background of the Evangelical history' (Hausrath, *NT Times*, i. p. 188 f., quoted also in full by Bruce in *Parabolic Teaching*, p. 243 f.). We learn from Tacitus that the year 17 was marked by great discontent in Judæa and throughout Syria, on account of the burdensome taxation, and that the year 33 was one of financial crisis throughout the Empire. There is thus full justification for the numerous Gospel intimations of hardship and debt, and impoverishment generally. See DEBT.

But the relation of debtor and creditor is so obviously adaptable to moral obligations, that under any social condition the use of this figure is to be expected. The very terms for financial obligations are freely used to express the obligations of moral life. Thus the same Gr. verb (ὀφείλω) is variously rendered in the RV 'owed,' 'owest,' 'that was due' (Mt 18²⁸. ³⁰. ³⁴, Lk 7⁴¹ 16⁵. ⁷ of financial obligation) ; 'debtor' (Mt 23¹⁶. ¹⁸ [AV 'guilty']), 'duty' (Lk 17¹⁰), 'ought' (Jn 13¹⁴ 19⁷), 'indebted' (Lk 11⁴ ; all of moral obligation) ; and the noun (ὀφειλέτης) is translated 'owed' (Mt 18²⁴ of money debt), 'debtors' (Mt 6¹² of moral debts), 'offenders' (Lk 13⁴ [AV 'sinners'] of guilt before God). Financial obligations afford also a ready measure of moral indebtedness ; our sins against one another are as debts of £50 or £5 (Lk 7⁴¹), but our sin against God runs into 'millions sterling' (Mt 18²⁴).

The very naturalness of these illustrative uses of money values and financial relations makes it obviously wrong to press them into the support of economic theories, *e.g.* the justification of commercial loans from 'Thou oughtest therefore to have put my money to the bankers, and then at my coming I should have received back mine own with interest' (Mt 25²⁷ = Lk 19²³). In parables any relations may hold which the story demands. In Christian economics only moral relations are to be tolerated. Because then, in the Gospel narratives, debtors and creditors, borrowers and lenders figure largely, we are not able to say that the teaching of Jesus either supports or condemns modern commercial arrangements. The true basis of Christian economics must be found in the ethical teaching of the Gospels as a whole.

Apart from incidental references in parables, there is one saying of Jesus which calls for fuller notice. 'If ye lend (δανείζω, *lend upon interest* ;

contrast κίχρημι, of *a friendly loan*, Lk 11⁵ only) to them of whom ye hope to receive, what thank have ye? even sinners lend to sinners, to receive again as much. But love your enemies, and do them good, and lend, never despairing; and your reward shall be great, and ye shall be sons of the Most High : for he is kind toward the unthankful and evil' (Lk 6³⁴ᶠ·, cf. Mt 5⁴²). The difficulty, in part one of textual reading, but mainly of interpretation, finds adequate representation in 'hoping for nothing again' (AV), 'never despairing' (RV), 'despairing of no man' (RVm). This uncertainty cannot, however, affect the meaning, which is determined by the preceding verses, and though the rendering of the AV must be rejected on critical grounds, it may well stand as an adequate gloss. On the authority of this saying the unlawfulness for Christians of receiving interest on loans has been based ; and, rightly understood and applied, the inference is just. The commandment is one of benevolence. Christian charity is not to be by way of loans at interest. It is the duty of giving Jesus teaches, as if He said, 'Let *your* lending be giving'—a rule of charity which experience justifies, and which, from the would-be borrower's side, receives support in St. Paul's saying, 'Owe no man anything, save to love one another' (Ro 13⁸).

W. H. DYSON.

LOCUST.—1. *Zoological description.* — Locusts belong to the natural order Orthoptera. The members of this order are insects which undergo only a partial metamorphosis ; the larva is scarcely distinguishable from the adult, unless by its smaller form and by the atrophy of its wings, which develop only gradually in proportion to its growth. Excepting this difference, it has the same form and the same habits as the adult. In its perfect state, the first pair of wings, though remaining supple, have a certain consistency. They cover the hind wings, which are membranous and transparent, and folded under the upper wings in the form of a fan. The mouth is of shape suitable for mastication, and the jaws act like a pair of scissors. Formerly the Orthoptera were divided into *runners* and *leapers*, but this division has been abandoned. Locusts were classed among the leapers. According to the present nomenclature, we must class them among the *Orthoptera genuina*. Among these appear among others (*a*) the family of *Locustodeæ*, to which the European grasshoppers (the subfamily of the *Locustidæ*) belong ; and also (*b*) the family of *Acridiodeæ*, which includes in its various sub-families the principal locusts of Palestine. It is of the highest importance to avoid the confusion which may arise from this misleading terminology, according to which the 'locusts' of the Bible do not belong to the scientific family *Locustodeæ*.

We are, then, to treat of the family *Acridiodeæ*. Their antennæ are relatively short, scarcely exceeding the length of the head, whereas the antennæ of the *Locustodeæ* are very long, as long as their bodies. Their hind legs, adapted for leaping, have very strong thighs furnished with indentations, which are easily seen if slightly magnified. The head is vertical. The first pair of wings are more leathery than the second, but both present the same reticulated appearance. The rapid brushing of the thighs of the hind legs, furnished with indentations, against the nervures of the front wings produces, when the insect is at rest, a stridulation, the tone and height of which vary according to the species. The *Acridiodeæ* are generally diurnal, and their food is essentially herbaceous. In the females the abdomen ends in a pair of short pincers, whereas in the *Locustodeæ* this appendage is greatly prolonged like the blade of a sabre. These pincers serve to bury in the earth, one by one, the

eggs, which are disposed in cylindrical masses and held together by a frothy secretion.

The insect moults six times, but the principal stages of its development are only two—*larva* and *imago* (perfect state). The intermediate state (*pupa*) which we find in other orders of insects is imperceptible in the Orthoptera. In their state of larvæ, locusts, having no wings, or more correctly, merely the rudiments of wings, *hop* on the ground ; even at this stage they are extremely destructive. Later, with the succeeding moultings, the wings develop, but remain enclosed in a membranous case ; the insects now advance *walking*. At last, at their sixth moulting, which takes place from six to seven weeks after their coming out of the egg, locusts attain to their perfect state, and, unfolding their wings, *fly* through the air, producing what travellers describe as 'a hissing or a buzzing noise.'

In Palestine as many as forty different species of *Acridiodeæ* have been noted. The most important of these belong to the sub-families of the *Tryxalidæ*, the *Œdipodidæ*, and the *Acridiidæ* properly so called. The commonest species, those which are rightly associated with the locusts mentioned in the Bible, are the *Pachytylus migratorius* (formerly called *Œdipoda migratoria*) and the *Schistocerca peregrina* (formerly called *Acridium peregrinum*). The colour of these insects is generally brown bordering on green, but with a bluish tint round the mouth, and with black spots on the body and green spots on the wings. The males are coloured differently from the females. In regard to their dimensions, locusts are as much as three or even four inches long when they are full grown.

Locusts are migratory insects, as the qualifying words, *migratoria*, *peregrina*, applied to them denote. They are produced chiefly in desert regions on the lofty plateaux of the East, and, carried by their wings and driven on by the east wind, they invade western Palestine in compact bodies.

2. *Biblical names.*—The OT mentions locusts under at least nine different names. These are (1) אַרְבֶּה *'arbeh*, Ex 10⁴· ¹²⁻¹⁴· ¹⁹, Lv 11²², Dt 28³⁸, Jg 6⁵ 7¹², 1 K 8³⁷, 2 Ch 6²⁸, Job 39²⁰, Ps 78⁴⁶ 105³⁴ 109²³, Pr 30²⁷, Jer 46²³, Jl 1⁴ 2²⁵, Nah 3¹⁵· ¹⁷. (2) חָגָב *ḥāgāb*, Lv 11²², Nu 13³³, 2 Ch 7¹³, Ec 12⁵, Is 40²². (3) סָלְעָם *ṣolʿām*, Lv 11²². (4) חַרְגֹּל *ḥargōl*, Lv 11²². (5) יֶלֶק *yeleḳ*, Ps 105³⁴, Jer 51¹⁴· ²⁷, Jl 1⁴ 2²⁵, Nah 3¹⁵ᶠ·. (6) חָסִיל *ḥāṣīl*, 1 K 8³⁷, 2 Ch 6²⁸, Ps 78⁴⁶, Is 33⁴, Jl 1⁴ 2²⁵. (7) גָּזָם *gāzām*, Jl 1⁴ 2²⁵, Am 4⁹. (8) גֵּב, גּוֹב *gēb*, *gōb*, *gōbai*, Is 33⁴, Am 7¹, Nah 3¹⁷. (9) צְלָצַל *ẓělāẓal*, Dt 28⁴².

It would naturally be a matter of the greatest interest to know if these various names correspond with as many different species. But before replying to this question, (*a*) we should have to be certain that the ancients, the Easterns, the Hebrews in particular, were capable of making a distinction similar to that of genus and species used by modern scholars ; (*b*) we should have to be equally certain that Biblical writers employed the terms in their language in a strict and rigorous fashion (a thing which even modern writers do not always do) ; and (*c*) we should require sufficient data to enable us to assign such and such a Hebrew name to such and such a particular species. Now these three conditions cannot be fulfilled, and in such a case it may well seem chimerical to demand a systematic classification, in accordance with present zoological principles, of the various locusts mentioned in the Bible. We must remember that Oriental languages, such as Hebrew and Arabic, possess a considerable choice of synonyms to denote one and the same animal. We note that the LXX proceeds on no regular system. It translates the Hebrew by using the terms ἀκρίς, βροῦχος, κάμπη, ἀττέλαβος (ἀττέλεβος), ἐρυσίβη (ἐρισύβη), ἀττάκης, ὀφιομάχης, etc., in a purely arbitrary and, it would appear, conjectural manner, without taking the least care always to translate the same Hebrew by the same Greek word. The same is true of the version of Jerome and of translations into modern languages. The EV has had no better success with its varying use of 'locust,' 'grasshopper,' 'canker-worm,' 'palmer-worm,' 'caterpillar,' and even 'beetle' (for ḥāgāb, manifestly a false translation).

We must also avoid the error of thinking that the various terms employed, for example, by Joel and Nahum refer to locusts at various stages in their development. The fact that the order of the four terms gāzām, 'arbeh, yeleḳ, ḥāṣīl in Jl 1⁴ is followed in 2²⁵ by the order 'arbeh, yeleḳ, ḥāṣīl, gāzām, in itself disproves this theory. Besides, it would be difficult to perceive in the development of the Orthopterous insect four stages easily distinguishable by every observer, since, as we have seen, the insect changes very little from moulting to moulting.* We must add to the passages of the canonical OT cited above Jth 2²⁰, Wis 16⁹, Sir 43¹⁷. The term used in these three texts is ἀκρίς; the Hebrew Sirach has 'arbeh.

The names that the Hebrew language gives to locusts prove that these insects were peculiarly feared (a) on account of their great numbers, and (b) on account of their voracity and their power of destruction. In fact, 'arbeh probably goes back to a root meaning to be numerous, to multiply. On the other hand, gāzām, ḥāṣīl, yeleḳ, and ṣol'ām all have the sense of destruction (literally to clip, to cut, to devour, to swallow).† The sense of gēb (gōb, gōbai) and of ḥāgāb is a problem. Ḥargōl appears to signify one who gallops, and ẓělāẓal is a more harmless term, referring to the humming of the locust's wings, or rather to the stridulation it makes when it is at rest (a word akin to this is used to denote cymbals).

3. *Locusts in the OT.*—In the books of the OT the locust is sometimes used figuratively to denote smallness (Nu 13³³, Is 40²²), lightness (Ec 12⁵, but the passage is obscure and in dispute), and great numbers (Jg 6⁵ 7¹², Jer 46²³). But, as a rule, when locusts are mentioned, it is usually as an instrument of destruction or as food.

The former of these two usages is much the more frequent in the OT. Particularly forcible, vivid, and picturesque descriptions of the *destructive power* of the locust are given in the passages quoted above from Exodus, Joel, Amos, and Nahum. The fear-inspiring character of these insect invaders, as they advance in regular companies (Pr 30²⁷), is in no way exaggerated. Locusts are a veritable plague. We find graphic descriptions in the writings of travellers or residents in the Holy Land, such as Wilson, Tristram, Thomson, Van-Lennep, as well as of other writers in various countries. Their accounts have, among others, been collected by Driver (*loc. cit. inf.*). Van-Lennep even says of locusts (p. 314) that 'their voracity is such that in the neighbourhood of Broosa, in the year 1856, an infant having been left asleep in its cradle under some shady trees, was found not long after partly devoured by the locusts.' See also the singularly graphic passage in which Thomson relates

<hr>

* Perhaps one might instance, to prove that the Hebrews had noticed the successive stages of development in the locust, the fact that in Jer 51²⁷ yeleḳ is qualified by סָמָר ṣāmar (EV 'rough'): this might be understood to apply to the state of the insect before it has the use of its wings (?).

† It is striking to note, in view of these names of serious and even terrible import, that similar insects in Europe (the *Locustidæ*) are tricked out with such innocent names as 'grasshopper' (German, *Heuschrecke*, from *Heu*, 'hay,' and the old word *scricchan*, 'to leap'; in French *sauterelle*); note also the German *Heupferd* and the Italian *cavaletta*, due to the resemblance of the grasshopper's head to a horse's.

his personal experiences (*LB* ii. p. 296 f.). On a sculptured stone found at Babylon is an exact representation (reproduced in Van-Lennep, *l.c.*) of two locusts devouring a bush. The present writer has seen on both sides of the Dead Sea, and also in the neighbourhood of Jericho and Gadara, locusts at the various stages of development devastating the country and making all verdure disappear in an instant. He has also been a witness of the efforts of the *fellaḥīn*, under the direction of the officials of the Turkish Government, to check the advance of the insects by lighting along their track fires fed with petroleum. Another device is to compel the Bedawîn, proportionally to the number of members of each family, to bring in a fixed weight of the eggs or larvæ of locusts. The wind, which brings the swarms of locusts, also drives them hither and thither (cf. Ps 109²³), and sometimes carries them into the sea (Ex 10¹⁹, Jl 2²⁰). One who has read, for example, Jl 1–2, or has seen with his own eyes the ravages of the locusts, is not surprised to find in Rev 9³⁻¹¹ this insect playing an apocalyptical part and accomplishing a mission of destruction.

4. *Locusts in the Gospels.*—But in the Gospels—with which this Dictionary is principally concerned—locusts are never mentioned as devastating insects. In Mt 3⁴ and in the parallel passage Mk 1⁶ they appear only as an article of *food*. It is in this character, then, that we have chiefly to study them here. The word used is ἀκρίς; it is said that John the Baptist fed on 'locusts and wild honey' (see art. HONEY). An ancient tradition of the Christian Church held that the locusts eaten by the Baptist were not insects, but the pods or husks of a tree, the **carob** or locust tree (*Ceratonia siliqua*, Arab. *kharrûb*). Curiously enough, this old interpretation has been resuscitated in our own times by Cheyne (*Encyc. Bibl.* ii. cols. 2136, 2499), who sees in the locusts of John the Baptist 'carob-beans,' but for reasons which do not seem to us convincing. In fact, locusts are a well-known food in Eastern countries. Herodotus mentions this (iv. 172); Thomson says (*LB* ii. p. 301): 'Locusts are not eaten in Syria by any but the Bedawîn on the extreme frontier. By the natives, locusts are always spoken of as a very inferior article of food, and regarded by most with disgust—to be eaten only by the very poorest people. John the Baptist, however, was of that class . . . he also dwelt in "the wilderness" or desert, where such food was and is still used.' There are, according to travellers, several ways of preparing locusts for food. 'The Bedouins eat locusts,' says Burckhardt (p. 239), 'which are collected in great quantities in the beginning of April. After having been roasted a little upon the iron plate on which bread is baked, they are dried in the sun, and then put into large sacks, with the mixture of a little salt. They are never served up as a dish, but everyone takes a handful of them when hungry. The peasants of Syria do not eat locusts. . . . There are a few poor fellahs in the Haouran, however, who sometimes, pressed by hunger, make a meal of them; but they break off the head and take out the entrails before they dry them in the sun. The Bedouins swallow them entire.' 'The wings and legs are lopped off the body,' says Wilson (p. 330), 'and fried with salt and pepper.' 'They are roasted and eaten as butter upon loaves of bread,' says Van-Lennep (p. 319), 'resembling shrimps in taste, or they are boiled in water with a little salt, dried in the sun, and, being deprived of their wings and legs, are packed in bags for use. They are beaten to a powder, which is mixed with flour and water, made into little cakes, and used as a substitute for bread when flour is scarce. Dried locusts are generally exposed for sale in the markets of Medina, Bagdad, and even Damascus.

Palgrave goes so far as to say (p. 346), 'Locusts are here an article of food, nay, a dainty, and a good swarm of them is begged of Heaven in Arabia no less fervently than it would be deprecated in India or in Syria. . . . When boiled or fried they are said to be delicious, and boiled and fried accordingly they are to an incredible extent.' It would appear likewise, to judge from Thomson (*l.c.*), that occasionally dried, boiled, or fried locusts are eaten with honey. Even horses (Blunt, ii. p. 79) and camels (Daumas, p. 258) are fed on locusts.

The Law of Israel, which strictly forbade the eating of creeping things, insects, etc., made an exception in the case of locusts, which are mentioned under four different names, two of which (*ṣol'ām* and *ḥargōl*) are found only in this one passage (Lv 11[22]). The Law characterizes them in this sentence: 'Yet these may ye eat of all winged creeping things that go upon all four, which have legs above their feet, to leap withal upon the earth.'

LITERATURE.—Bochart, *Hierozoicon*, i. pp. 34–36, ii. pp. 441–496; Burckhardt, *Travels in Syria*, 1822, p. 238 f., *Notes on the Bedouins*, 1830, p. 269; William Rae Wilson, *Travels in Egypt and the Holy Land*[2], 1824, pp. 329–331; Berggrèn, *Guide français-arabe*, 1844, p. 702 f.; Général E. Daumas, *Le Grand Désert*, 1856, pp. 257–265; Robinson, *BRP*[3], 1867, ii. pp. 205, 340; Wood, *Bible Animals*, 1869, pp. 596–604; Van-Lennep, *Bible Lands*, 1875, pp. 313–319; Franz Delitzsch, *Hoheslied und Koheleth*, 1875, Excursus by Wetzstein, pp. 445–455; Lady Anne Blunt, *A Pilgrimage to Nejd*[2], 1881, i. p. 94, ii. pp. 57 f., 79; Palgrave, *Central and Eastern Arabia*, 1883, pp. 345–347; Tristram, *Natural History of the Bible*, 1885, pp. 306–318; Thomson, *The Land and the Book*, ii. [1883] pp. 295–302, iii. [1886] p. 130 f.; Morris, *Bible Natural History*, 1896, pp. 211 f., 269 f.; Driver, *Joel and Amos* (Cambr. Bible for Schools), 1897, Excursus on Locusts, pp. 82–91; Tümpel, *Die Geradflügler Mitteleuropas*, 1901; F. H. Fabre, *Souvenirs entomologiques*, vi. pp. 196–212, 248–297.   LUCIEN GAUTIER.

LOGIA.—

1. Ancient use of the term.
2. Modern use of the term : (*a*) of Jesus' Sayings ; (*b*) of compilations.
3. Tradition on transmission of the Sayings.
4. Criticism of the tradition : (*a*) Internal evidence of the tradition : (*b*) Internal evidence of the Gospels.
5. Conjectural reconstructions of the source.
6. Conclusions.
      Literature.

1. *Ancient use of the term.*—The Gr. λόγια is the plural of λόγιον 'a brief utterance,' 'apothegm,' 'saying' (so Schol. *ad* Aristoph. *Ran.* 969. 973). According to Liddell-Scott (*Lex.*) and Meyer (on Ro 3[2]), λόγιον is the neuter of λόγιος = 'learned,' 'rational,' and hence means 'a wise saying.' More correctly, according to Grimm-Thayer and others. it is a diminutive of λόγος 'word,' like βιβλίον from βίβλος 'book,' plur. τὰ βιβλία 'the (sacred) books,' Eng. 'Bible.' In secular writers (Herodotus, Thucyd., Aristoph., *et al.*) it is applied to the Divine oracles (because brief utterances), as those of the Sibyl of Dodona, of Delphi, etc. The same connotation of *sacred* utterances attaches to the use of the word as applied to the Hebrew Scriptures, as by Philo and Josephus. Thus the contents of the OT, as *Divine* utterances, are called τὰ λόγια τοῦ θεοῦ. In particular the Ten Words (Eng. 'Ten Commandments') are called by Philo τὰ δέκα λόγια (ed. Mangey ii. p. 180ff). By NT writers the term is applied to the Scriptures generally, as 'oracles' of God, or to individual inspired utterances of prophets, pre-Christian or Christian (Ac 7[38], Ro 3[2], He 5[12], 1 P 4[11]). In Ecclesiastical writers of the sub-Apostolic age τὰ λόγια τοῦ θεοῦ is used of the admonitions of God in Scripture (Clem. Rom. *ad Cor.* liii. 1, in parallel with αἱ ἱεραὶ γραφαί), and τὰ λόγια τοῦ κυρίου, or simply τὰ λόγια, of the precepts of Jesus, *not including* embodying narrative. So especially Polycarp *ad Phil.* vii. 1, denouncing heretics, who 'pervert the precepts of the Lord (τὰ λόγια τοῦ κυρίου) to their own lusts, denying that there is either (bodily) resurrection or (day of) judgment' (cf. Hegesippus *ap.* Eus. *HE* ii. xxiii. 9); and Papias (*ap.* Euseb. *HE* iii. 39), who interpreted 'the oracles of the Lord' (λόγια κυριακά) in accordance with the tradition of elders who had been followers of the Apostles. In Papias the λόγια are made equivalent to 'the commandments (ἐντολαί) delivered by the Lord to the faith,' and stand in contrast with 'alien commandments' (ἀλλότριαι ἐντολαί) of heretical teachers, and the 'loquacity sought by the multitude' (οὐχ ὥσπερ οἱ τὰ πολλὰ τοῖς τὰ πολλὰ λέγουσιν ἐχαίρον). The true interpretation of these *logia* is matter of tradition transmitted through (1) the Apostles, (2) the Elders 'the disciples of these' (lege οἱ τούτων—sc. τῶν τοῦ κυρίου μαθητῶν—μαθηταί [see ARISTION-ARISTO], Iren. *Hær.* v. v. 1 : οἱ πρεσβύτεροι [οἱ] τῶν ἀποστόλων μαθηταί, Origen *ap.* Eus. : οἱ διάδοχοι τῶν ἀποστόλων). Compare Polycarp (*l.c.*), 'Wherefore leaving the vain talk (ματαιότητα) of the multitude and the false teachings (ψευδοδιδασκαλίας), let us

turn to *the word handed down by tradition from the beginning*' (τὸν ἐξ ἀρχῆς ἡμῖν παραδοθέντα λόγον).

At a much later time the term τὰ λόγια is applied to NT Scripture generally in the same sense as to the OT (Ignatius, *ad Smyrn.* iii. [longer form in the interpolated matter]). See in general Grimm-Thayer, *Lexicon*, *s.v.* λόγιον, and Lightfoot, *Contemp. Rev.* for Aug. 1875, p. 399 ff. On Papias' use see Hall, *Papias*, 1899, p. 242.

2. The *modern use* of the term 'logia' is partly (*a*) conformed to the Patristic application to the precepts of Jesus conceived as 'brief and pithy apothegms' (Justin M. *Apol.* xiv.) of sacred authority ; partly (*b*) designates a compilation, or compilations, antecedent to or parallel with the canonical Gospels, supposed to have been entitled or called τὰ λόγια ; cf. the use of 'Bible' (Lat. *Biblia* = τὰ βιβλία), to mean 'the (sacred) books' of the Canon.

(*a*) Of the former (correct) use it is enough to say that science has no better designation for the apothegms of Jesus in the form wherein tradition has transmitted them, whether in the Synoptic Gospels or as uncanonical *agrapha*. The connotation of sacredness in the designation *logion*, if we have regard to the later period of transmission, is not inappropriate. The cherished utterances of Jesus soon obtained such currency independently of our Gospels (Ac 20[35], Clem. Rom. *ad Cor.* xiii. 1, xlvii. 7, Polyc. *ad Phil.* vii. 2) as rightly to deserve it. The term is appropriate therefore to the sacred apothegms of Jesus as preserved in the Synoptic Gospels or independently. As against the simple λόγοι, it is probably a later form involving tacit comparison with the (sacred) precepts of the OT. It is less common than λόγοι, and certainly much less applicable to the discourses of the Fourth Gospel, where, even if traditional *logia* are embodied, dialogue, the favourite form for philosophic and religious exposition, predominates, and the traditionary interest is subordinated to that of expounding the Evangelist's Christology.

(*b*) The use of 'Logia' or 'the Logia' to designate a certain type of Gospel-composition is open to serious objection. The discovery by Grenfell and Hunt of papyri of the 2nd or 3rd century, in which Sayings attributed to Jesus are agglutinated with no more of narrative framework than the bare words, 'Jesus saith' (λέγει Ἰησοῦς), proves that such compilations actually circulated, fulfilling a function similar to the *Pirḳe Aboth*, or 'Sayings of the Fathers' in the contemporary and earlier Synagogue. But the later discovered superscription of the Oxyrhynchus collection itself (published 1904) condemns the editors' hasty application of the title Λόγια Ἰησοῦ to the fragment of 1897, by using the simple λόγοι (οἱ τοῖοι οἱ λόγοι, κ.τ.λ).* There is, in fact, absolutely no evidence that any book ever received the title λόγια, though there is a certain significance in the use of the word by Papias and Polycarp interchangeably with λόγοι to designate the precepts of Jesus, whether in literary embodiment or otherwise. For Papias these precepts are 'commandments delivered by the Lord to the faith' (ἐντολαὶ τῇ πίστει δεδομέναι), and hence comparable with 'the oracles of God committed to Israel' (ἐπιστεύθησαν τὰ λόγια τοῦ θεοῦ, Ro 3[2]) ; but he refers to just the same precepts as λόγοι, when in a connected clause he declares that Peter had no design of making a *syntagma* of the 'sayings' (οὐχ ὥσπερ σύνταξιν τῶν κυριακῶν ποιούμενος λόγων). Indeed, in all the earlier evidence we possess of the formation of such *syntagmata*, the expression used is always λόγοι, and never λόγια. Thus, besides the references already given to Acts, Clem. Rom. *ad Cor.*, and Polycarp *ad Phil.*, the Pastoral Epistles have two references to 'wholesome words' (ὑγιαίνοντες

---

* This of course is ungrammatical. The editors propose to delete the first οἱ. Professor Swete prefers to read οὗτοι for οἱ τοῖοι (see *ExpT* xv. [1904] p. 490).

λόγοι) which are more closely defined as 'sayings of the faith' (λόγοι τῆς πίστεως, cf. Papias, ἐντολαὶ τῇ πίστει δεδομέναι) 'of the excellent teaching,' and even explicitly as ' the sayings of our Lord Jesus Christ' (οἱ λόγοι τῆς πίστεως καὶ τῆς καλῆς διδασκαλίας, οἱ ὑγιαίνοντες λόγοι οἱ τοῦ κυρίου ἡμῶν Ἰησοῦ Χριστοῦ, καὶ ἡ κατ' εὐσέβειαν διδασκαλία, κ.τ.λ., 1 Ti 4⁶ 6³).

More important for its bearing on the question of the name to be applied to the Matthæan *syntagma* are the structural phenomena of the canonical Mt., to be discussed later. At present we note only that, apart from the Markan narrative outline, the main framework of this Gospel consists of five great agglutinated discourses, each marked off by the resumption of the narrative in a stereotyped formula, 'And it came to pass when Jesus had finished these words.' In this formula the expression λόγοι is varied only by the expressions 'parables' and 'directions to the Twelve,' where the context requires (11¹ 13⁵³), while the final group concludes : ' And it came to pass when Jesus had finished all these words ' (πάντας τοὺς λόγους τούτους, Mt 26¹), in spite of the fact that the narrative continues : 'he *said* to his disciples.'

In view of this earlier evidence it is manifestly unwarrantable to infer from the use by Papias of the term λόγια alongside of λόγοι, that 'he refers to three documents, (1) St. Mark's version of St. Peter's teaching, (2) an anonymous collection of *Sayings of the Lord*, (3) *the Logia* of St. Matthew' (K. Lake, *Hibbert Journ.* iii. 2 [Jan. 1905], p. 337). Papias is defining his authority for 'the commandments given by the Lord to the faith.' If he refers to these now, with 1 Ti 4⁶ 6³, as 'sayings,' of which Peter might have made a *syntagma* but did not, and now, with Polycarp *ad Phil.* vii., as 'oracles,' of which Matthew did make a *syntagma*, the difference is only that in the latter embodiment they seemed to him comparable with the 'oracles of God' given to Israel (Ac 7³⁸, Ro 3², He 5¹², 1 P 4¹¹).

The relatively late date of Papias (145–160 A.D.) makes it certain that for him, if not already for Polycarp, τὰ λόγια meant the precepts of Jesus *as embodied* in narrative Gospels, pre-eminently in canonical Matthew. In later authorities, who take over the tradition, the term is gradually extended to cover the embodying narrative as well, until with Irenæus and Tertullian the Divine utterance is coextensive with the canonical Gospel (' ait Spiritus Sanctus per Matthæum,' applied by Irenæus to utterances of the Evangelist). Whether at a stage anterior to its adoption by Papias the tradition regarding the λόγια had a narrower application, must be settled by a consideration of the expression in its context.

3. *Tradition on transmission of the Sayings.*— The fragments from the preface (προοίμιον) of Papias' work in five books, entitled *Exposition(s ?) of the Oracles of the Lord*, as given by Eusebius (*HE* III. xxxix. 2. 16), are closely related to one another, and to the passage already referred to in the Epistle of Polycarp, Papias' earlier contemporary and friend. As regards the 'commandments' which Papias sought to hear and to expound as 'oracles,' the fragment states as a tradition (probably from the same authority, 'John the Elder,' who gave that regarding Mark) that 'Matthew made a compend (συνετάξατο, *v.l.* συνεγράψατο) of the *logia* in the Hebrew (Aramaic ?) tongue, and every man translated them as he was able.' For Papias, and *a fortiori* for the later authorities who repeat the tradition in partly independent forms, it was a testimony to our canonical Matthew. This to them *represented* the *syntagma* of which the tradition spoke, though it was admitted not to be identical with it. That was in ' Hebrew,' this in Greek. Possibly a differ-

ence of contents as regards the narrative framework was also recognized, since Papias has no scruple in contradicting Mt 27⁵⁻¹⁰ (cf. Lightfoot-Harmer, *Apost. Fathers*, Frgt. xviii.), and Jerome recognizes the independence of what he regarded as the *ipsum Hebraicum*, and which was in his day 'called by most the authentic Gospel of Matthew,' by translating it anew into both Greek and Latin. Surviving fragments, however, prove this work, the so-called *Gospel according to the Hebrews*, to have been another and much later product. In Papias' time the Hebrew *syntagma* had disappeared from use (ἡρμήνευσεν), if ever known in his region ; his idea of its relation to canonical Mt. was probably as vague as his successors'. He valued the tradition because it gave him Apostolic authority for the Gospel on which he relies in all known instances for his *logia* of the Lord (Frgt. xi. *ibid.* is *not* related, as Lightfoot supposed, to Lk 10¹⁸, but to Mt 12²²⁻²⁹ ; see *Heads against Caius*, Frgt. v., and cf. Apollinaris, Frgt. ii. in *Chron. Pasch.*). It also gave him a convenient explanation for their variation of form in the Greek Gospels current in his own day (Mt., Lk.) ; both went back to a common Apostolic original, but were more or less perfectly translated.

4. *Criticism of the tradition.*—Modern critics attribute great value to the tradition reported by Papias, partly because of its inapplicability to canonical Mt., which shows it to be in his hands an heirloom, not a manufacture ; partly because it is independently attested ; partly because it seems to be connected internally with the tradition concerning Mark explicitly ascribed to 'the Elder' (John of Jerusalem [d. A.D. 117]), and *in that relation* becomes both intelligible and historically probable in view of known conditions in the Palestinian Church.

Its inapplicability to canonical Mt. appears in that our Mt. is not a translation, whether from Hebrew or Aramaic ; not (strictly) a *syntagma of the Oracles* ; and, as concerns derivation from immediate 'followers of the Lord,' *less* authentic in its 'order' than Mk., since practically its entire historical outline is borrowed from our Second Gospel with arbitrary alteration (in chs. 1–14) of the order (see the *Introductions to NT*). The tradition is also attested, however, by Pantænus (*ap.* Eus. *HE* v. x. 3), Irenæus, Origen, Cyril of Jerusalem, Eusebius, Chrysostom, Theophylact, Jerome, Augustine, and Euthymius Zigabenus. Not all of these can have derived all their data from Papias, so that the tradition cannot be his invention, although he clearly adapts it to his own use (cf. ὡς ἔφην in the Mk. fragment, referring probably to an inference of his own from 1 P 5¹³ [Eus. *HE* II. xv. 2, III. xxxix. 16]. Finally, the internal evidence of the tradition itself indicates a close relation to the testimony of 'the Elder' as to Mk., and agrees with known conditions in the Palestinian Church.

(*a*) Holsten has pointed out (*Drei urspr. Evang., ad init.*) that the original motive of the Mark fragment is apologetic and harmonistic. It accounts for the incompleteness and lack of system in Mk. by contrast with some other writing which could be regarded as a complete σύνταξις τῶν κυριακῶν λόγων. No such compendium did Mark make, but only a transcript of certain discourses of Peter, accurate and complete so far as secondary testimony could go, but suffering from the inevitable limitations of one who had been a follower, not of the Lord (like Matthew), but, 'as I (Papias) said, of Peter, afterward.' The result was a mingled account of narratives about Christ, now a saying, now something done (ἢ λεχθέντα, ἢ πραχθέντα), incomplete (ἔνια, ὅσα ἐμνημόνευσεν) and without system (οὐ μέντοι τάξει), because Peter's preaching,

Mark's only source of knowledge, had brought out the material in such irregular order as the occasion demanded (πρὸς τὴν χρείαν).

Our first concern must be with the motive of this conception of Mk., reserving the question of its historicity. Clearly, while unwilling to reject the narrative Gospel, it contends for the superiority of some other, whose characteristics may easily be inferred from what is denied to its rival. This authority of superior standing in the region whence Papias obtained his traditions (Palestine) emanated from one who had been a follower of the Lord Himself, not (like Mark) of an Apostle. It was more complete, and afforded a systematic, *not necessarily chronological*, arrangement of the Lord's words (σύνταξιν τῶν τοῦ κυρίου λόγων, συνέταξεν τὰ λόγια, οὐ μέντοι τάξει) serviceable to those in search of the 'commandments given by the Lord to the faith.' For, as soon as the general point of view is considered, the real significance of the complaint against Mk., so puzzling to modern critics, and perhaps not clear to Papias himself, becomes intelligible. The deficient τάξις of Mk. is explained by the contrasting statements regarding Peter and Matthew respectively, the former of whom did not aim at a σύνταξιν τῶν κυριακῶν λόγων [*v.l.* λογίων], whereas the latter actually made such a compend (συνετάξατο [*v.l.* συνεγράψατο] τὰ λόγια). The two fragments are parts of a single tradition, and the general point of view is that of a church to which the Gospel was primarily a new Torah, wherein the object of system (τάξις) is completeness in presenting 'the commandments given to the faith.' The historian-evangelist's idea of 'order' as chronological sequence in the biography (καθεξῆς Lk 1³) is not that in consideration. In short, the tradition of Papias reflects the attitude of the Palestinian Church towards the rival claims of its own autochthonous Matthæan tradition, and the Petrine or Roman. It aims to adjust the two with recognition of the merits of the latter, while holding to the superiority of the former, just as the appendix to the Fourth Gospel (Jn 21) adjusts the secondary Petrine to its own primary authority, the Johannine (Asiatic).

Looked at thus, from the point of view suggested by its own internal relations, the tradition of Papias becomes not only intelligible but probable. It defines (no doubt correctly) the primary authority for the λόγια κυριακά which Papias proposed to expound in the light of the traditional authorities. If the Gospel of Lk. does not come into Papias' consideration, and Mk. is treated as quite subordinate, it is because the object in view is the ἐντολαί delivered by the Lord, and tradition and Church usage were at one in pointing to Matthew as the fountain-head for such purposes.

Nor does the tradition stand alone in its distinction of *syntagmata* of the Logia of the Lord from Gospels of the Markan type. Ac 1¹ refers to its author's 'former treatise' as relating what 'Jesus began both to do and to teach' (ποιεῖν τε καὶ διδάσκειν), thereby properly classing Lk. with Mk. and similar Gospels made up of 'both works and teachings' (ἢ λεχθέντα ἢ πραχθέντα). Moreover, the implied distinction from *syntagmata* of the Sayings is precisely what we should expect in a church whose institutions and traditions were almost invariably based on the practice of the Synagogue. The teaching of the Synagogue was divided into (1) *Halacha*, *i.e.* 'the Way,' authoritative applications of the Mosaic law, precepts of life, and (2) *Haggada*, *i.e.* 'tales,' unauthoritative preaching, based mainly on OT narrative. Just so in the primitive Palestinian Church we soon find two types of Gospel composition—(1) the catechetic, for the converted, generally connected with the name of Matthew. Then (2) the evangelistic,

for the unconverted, similarly associated with the name of Peter. To the latter type would belong the 'testimony of the cross' (τὸ μαρτύριον τοῦ σταυροῦ) rejected by the opponents of Polycarp (*l.c.*); to the former not only the 'Sayings of the faith' or 'of the Lord Jesus' (1 Ti 4⁶ 6³) compiled by Matthew and others, but examples of Christian catechesis, such as the little manuals of ethics or 'teachings of baptisms' which survive to us under such titles as 'the Two Ways,' or the 'Teaching' (Διδαχή, Διδασκαλία) of the Apostles. These were primarily of Jewish origin, and were intended for the instruction of neophytes and catechumens. Such writings, on the other hand, as the *Preaching of Peter*, of the apologetic or evangelistic type, are clearly addressed to the unconverted, and if we go back to the examples furnished in Acts of this evangelistic preaching, still attributed to 'Peter,' we may identify the already stereotyped outline of Synoptic story in Ac 10³⁸⁻⁴¹, the so-called 'lesser Gospel of Mark.' Long ago the resemblance of this Synoptic outline to the *haggadic* type was observed by Jewish scholars such as Wünsche and Hirsch. Both types accordingly were current in the Palestinian Church. We might, in fact, presuppose it from the nature of the situation. But both would not there be equally esteemed. The indigenous product, adapted to the requirements of a church more given to the perpetuation than to the propagation of the gospel, a church where Jesus was pre-eminently the 'Prophet like unto Moses,' giver of 'the perfect law of liberty,' would be the authoritative *syntagma* of the Lord's Sayings, *halachic* in the fundamental sense of the term. The Greek version of the *Preaching of Peter*, imported probably from Rome, would be received; but it would stand upon the lower footing of *haggadic* narrative. The lateness of the combination is attested not only by the reluctance manifest in the tradition, but by the fact that when Mk. was added to the Matthæan *syntagma*, the editor had so little else to add.

The correspondence of Papias' tradition of the Matthæan *syntagma* with known Palestinian conditions is strongly confirmatory both of the tradition itself and of that interpretation of it which emphasizes the distinction between catechetic works and Gospels of the evangelistic type. It is characteristic of the Gospels which continued to circulate in Palestine independently of the canonical four so late as the time of Jerome and Epiphanius, that, while they conflate material drawn from the Greek Gospels with their own, they continue to represent their tradition in all cases as delivered by the Apostle Matthew (Preuschen, *Antilegomena*, Frgs. 2. 3. 12 of *Ev. Hebr.* and 6 of *Ev. Naz.*).

(*b*) The internal evidence of our Synoptic Gospels is the decisive factor in the question of the historicity and meaning of the tradition. Here we have only to subtract the material coincident with Mk. from Mt. and Lk. respectively, to see that what is left is in Lk. to a great extent, in Mt. almost exclusively, a mass of discourse-material, much of it reproduced in common by the two. So convincing is this general result of an application of the representations of early tradition to the actual structure of our Synoptic Gospels, that since the time of Schleiermacher the so-called 'two-document' theory of the Synoptic Gospels, which rests upon it, has won wider and wider assent, and is to-day in its general outline an almost universally accepted canon of criticism (see art. GOSPELS). Synoptic tradition consists in the main of the Markan story, filled out and expanded by masses of discourse-material which are otherwise almost devoid of historical setting.

But there is a great and significant difference in result when the subtraction is made from Mt. and when it is made from Luke. Subtract Mk. from Mt. and the *narrative* material which remains is exceedingly meagre in amount, somewhat apocryphal in character, and unconnected with any other source. It includes the Genealogy and Birth-stories (chs. 1. 2), Peter's walking on the sea (14^{28-31}), the stater in the fish's mouth (17^{24-27}), and a few traits in the story of the Passion and Resurrection—the suicide of Judas (27^{3-10}), Pilate's wife's dream, and his washing of his hands (vv.$^{19-24}$), the earthquake (vv.$^{51-53}$), watch at the tomb (vv.$^{62-66}$ 28^{11-15}), and appearance to the women and to the Eleven in Galilee ($28^{9-10.\ 16-20}$). A few other apparent Matthæan additions to the narrative of Mk. are illusive. The story of the centurion's son ($8^{5-10.\ 13}$) is the one great exception in character and attestation, being shared not only by Lk. (7^{2-10}), but even by Jn. (4^{46-54}). The real surplus of Mt. over Mk. consists pre-eminently in great aggregations of *discourse*-material, grouped in the five principal masses already referred to. These groups of agglutinated λόγοι consist of (1) the Sermon on the Mount (chs. 5–7), showing the new Way of Righteousness; (2) the Mission of the Disciples (ch. 10), showing the duty of Witness-bearing; (3) the Parables (ch. 13), treated as fulfilling the Scripture Is $6^{9\text{ff.}}$ against a generation which had rejected both the Baptist and Christ; (4) Rules of conduct towards brethren in 'the church' (ch. 18); (5) Warnings of the Judgment (ch. 25) attached to the eschatological chapter (24) parallel to Mk 13. Each of the five groups is marked off by the formula καὶ ἐγένετο ὅτε ἐτέλεσεν ὁ ᾿Ιησοῦς, κ.τ.λ., where the narrative is resumed; but groups (3) and (5) are enlarged by prefixing the two denunciatory sections (chs. 11–12 and 23), which are unaccompanied by the formula, and expand the total number of discourses to seven (cf. the seven parables of ch. 13, seven woes of ch. 23, seven petitions of the Lord's Prayer expanded from five of Lk.). Thus our First Gospel, minus the Markan biographic outline and the few late narrative accretions, really consists of a systematic compendium of the teachings of the Lord, once framed in the favourite pentad structure of Torah, Psalm-book; and the Christian Διδαχή, but later expanded to a sevenfold form.

The same process applied to Lk. yields a very different but equally enlightening result. The subtraction of Mk. leaves a much more considerable narrative element, including, besides the Centurion's Son, a whole series of incidents elsewhere unknown, of kindred animus. Such are the Penitent Harlot and Penitent Thief, Zacchæus, the Ministering Women, the Samaritan Leper, the Crooked Woman, the Widow of Nain. But more important than the new incidents is a series of parables and teachings in the same vein, of which the Prodigal Son, Good Samaritan, Rich Man and Lazarus, Pharisee and Publican, are examples. The so-called Infancy chapters of Luke show the same favour towards the lowly, and partake otherwise to so high a degree of the linguistic and stylistic peculiarities of this material, that we must either suppose Luke to have had at command a 'special source' equally abundant in narrative- and discourse-material, and characterized by the humanitarian interest so manifest here, or else ascribe to him an extremely one-sided selection from a much more copious stream of tradition than would seem probable from Matthew and Mark. Thus the great outstanding difference in structure between the non-Markan element in Mt. and in Lk. is that in the former it is almost exclusively the λόγοι, arranged in groups as such; whereas in Lk. the *logian* material does not stand apart from narrative, but is connected with and framed into a narrative independent of Mk. and

found in no other Gospel. Moreover, the combination of discourse with narrative in Lk. is not, as sometimes stated, a mere adaptation by the Evangelist of *logian* material to narrative settings of his own composition. There are examples (14^{1-7}) of such fictitious settings, but who would dream of so describing the incident of the Repentant Harlot (Lk 7^{36-50}), which forms the setting of the parable of the Two Debtors? No explanation will here suffice but an admission that narrative and discourse have come down together from the earliest and most authentic sources. The same conclusion must be reached when the relation of this 'pre-canonical Luke' to Mk. and to the added sections of Mt. (11 f. and 23) is studied (see art. WISDOM). Priority will be found to belong in both cases to the Lukan source.

Luke's distribution of his discourse-material under various heads of narrative description, and his disposition of the non-Markan material at various points of a shorter and longer journey (Lk 6^{12}–8^3 9^{51}–18^{14}), indicate in what sense we should take his proposal to write 'in order' (καθεξῆς, 1^3). He aims, like the historian that he is, at chronological sequence; but certainly not without some better authority than his own conjecture. For while his discourse-material is sometimes without true connexion, it has a basis of order which indicates that, in the region whence this Gospel is derived, narrative and teaching had been combined at a much earlier time and with better resources than in our Matthew.

Critics who have attempted to reconstruct the *Logia* from Mt. and Lk. have unfortunately neglected this fundamental distinction, reconstructing their ultimate source, without regard for the difference in type (with Mt 28^{20} cf. Lk 1^4, Ac 1^1), from the mere coincidence of Mt. and Lk. in a certain part of the discourse-material. This ultimate source, however, cannot be reached from the side of Lk. without first taking account of the so-called 'special source' from which some elements seem to have passed into Mt. (*e.g.* 3^{7-12} 4^{1-11} 6^{19-34} 8^{5-10} 11^{1-27}), and can even be shown with great probability to have affected canonical Mk. (With Mk $1^{2.\ 5f.}$, cf. Lk $7^{24-27.\ 33f.}$; with Mk 1^{13}, Lk 4^{2-12}; with Mk 2^{1-22}, Lk $7^{33f.}$; with Mk 3^{22-30}, Lk 11^{14-22}; with Mk 7^{1-23}, Lk 11^{37-54}. Comparison with Mt. will in all these cases prove dependence by Mk. upon the source more fully recoverable from Mt. and Lk.). But the elements most naturally to be sought in a purely *logian* common source, such as the Sermon on the Mount and the Parables, display a very different degree of resemblance in Mt. and Lk. respectively. Instead of the exact verbal identity of long sentences in the sections outside the Matthæan pentad, there is within it for the most part an extreme divergence from the Lukan parallels. In general it would be difficult, if not impossible, to prove from this material any *direct* acquaintance with the *Logia* on the part of our Third Evangelist.

5. *Conjectural reconstructions of the source.*— Lost works have nevertheless been so frequently reconstructed in modern times by process of extraction from later documents into which they had been independently incorporated, as to offer a standing challenge in this supreme instance of the Matthæan *Logia*. If Krawutzky (to cite a single example) could reconstruct the *Teaching of the Twelve* from the *Apostolic Constitutions* and *Apostolic Epitome*, in advance of its discovery by Bryennios, why should not our First and Third Gospels yield up out of their common discourse-material the substance of the lost *Logia*? There have been thus far but two notable attempts to meet this challenge. Wendt's *Lehre Jesu* (1886) presents in the first (untranslated) volume the author's attempted reconstruction from Mt. and Lk. of the (Greek) *Logia* of Matthew. Unfortunately no account is taken of the third factor, Luke's 'special source,' which certainly afforded much discourse-material not likely to have been connected with the Matthæan *Logia*, and may even have contained all that Luke shares with Matthew. Equally unfortunate was the failure to distinguish the difference in point of view between a '*syntagma* of the Lord's commandments' in which 'order' must be topical, and a διήγησις καθεξῆς such as Luke's, where the λόγοι are λόγοι τῆς χάριτος (Lk 4²²) illustrative of the message of the Divine wisdom. The problem must not be treated as if a mere question of arithmetic: Elements common to Mt. and Lk., *minus* Mk. = the *Logia*. As a pioneer in the field, Wendt deserves credit for his work, but a process so simple could not be expected to solve so complicated a problem. Wendt himself could find no place for a non-Markan διήγησις such as the Centurion's Son, Lk 7²⁻¹⁰ = Mt 8⁵⁻¹³ = Jn 4⁴⁶⁻⁵⁴, which could not naturally be connected with the Matthæan *Logia*, but falls into place at once when account is taken of its relation to the Lukan context. Wendt's results were not unjustly pronounced 'a heap of interesting ruins, without beginning, without conclusion, without connexion' (Resch).

A much more elaborate and detailed analysis is that of Alfred Resch, *Die Logia Jesu nach dem griechischen und hebräischen Text wiederhergestellt*, Leipzig, 1898 (Hebrew text separately סֵפֶר תּוֹלְדוֹת יֵשׁוּ: דִּבְרֵי יֵשׁוּעַ הַמָּשִׁיחַ, τὰ λόγια 'Ιησοῦ). Here the attempt is made to restore the original Apostolic source not only in the Greek form assumed to be utilized in common by Mt. and Lk., but to retranslate into the Hebrew (*sic*) assumed to have been employed by the Apostle as the classical religious language in preference to the colloquial Aramaic spoken by Jesus Himself. Resch brings to his task an immense amount of learning and patience, especially in the accumulation of all possible (and many impossible) traces of extra-canonical *logia*. Unfortunately the process is again vitiated, not only by an extremely indiscriminate use of unsifted material, but by highly uncritical assumptions. Of these one of the most fatal is that the order of Lk. must be nearest that of the *Logia* because, in Resch's judgment, nearest the historical; while another, wherein may be traced the influence of B. Weiss, attributes to the *Logia* the features of a narrative-Gospel. As will be apparent from our criticism of the tradition, and criticism of canonical Mt., all the evidence we possess should commend precisely the reverse principle. The Apostolic *syntagma* of Matthew was not a narrative, and cannot have had a historian's order, and the structure of Mt. and Lk. respectively shows that in the one case the *halachic*, in the other the *haggadic*, principle was predominant from the first. On the other hand, Resch's gathering of the material was indispensable. His renewed consideration of the careful and scrupulous work of B. Weiss (*Matthäusevangelium*, 1876; *Markusevangelium*, 1872) looking toward an Apostolic (?) source utilized in common by these Gospels, did better justice to another factor not to be neglected, namely, use of the *Logia* (?) in Mk.; and his tracing of the tradition of Matthæan authorship to a direct claim embodied in at least one of the early Palestinian Gospels (*Ev. Naz.* Frg. 6 [*Preusch.*] σὲ τὸν Ματθαῖον), are contributions of permanent service. The experience of both Wendt and Resch, however, should warn against indiscriminate combination of Mt. and Lk., without regard for the structural evidence of the Gospels as we have them, or even for the avowed purpose of the Third Evangelist himself.

Besides Wendt and Resch, mention should be made of the disposition of material in the Greek *Synopticon* of A. Wright, who devotes Division 2 of his presentation to material supposedly derived from the *Logia* of Matthew. The arbitrariness of the dealing with the Lukan material is amply demonstrated by the two supplementary divisions which follow. The work is unfortunately affected by inadmissible presuppositions regarding oral tradition.

6. *Conclusions.* — These may be briefly summarized in the following outline:—

(1) The term *logia* was applied to the Sayings of Jesus early in the 2nd century by those who held them as Divine utterances, but not as displacing the earlier λόγοι.

(2) The same individuals report a tradition of Palestinian derivation which contrasts the Markan type of Gospel with another, of Matthæan origin, consisting of *syntagmata* of the Sayings.

(3) Our present representative of the Matthæan tradition, disembarrassed of its Markan framework, displays this type-form, combining the teaching of Jesus in five agglutinations of Christian precepts corresponding to the five books of the Torah.

(4) Our Third Evangelist presents the discourse-material which he holds in common with Mt. from the historical point of view, and seems to have received it in a collection wherein narrative and discourse were intermingled from the first, the agglutination being effected with an eye to illustrate Jesus' mission of grace rather than to form a new Torah (see art. WISDOM).

(5) If the actual work of the Apostle Matthew (Matthias?) be not too remote for recovery, it should be sought primarily in, or rather under, the accumulated aggregations of *logian* material in the five discourse groups of our First Gospel, with secondary comparison of the added groups (chs. 3 f. 11 f. 23) which have special affinity by language and content with Lk., together with the rest of the Lukan material. It is not probable that the Matthæan *syntagma* can have been lost in any other way than through superimposition of new material. To extricate it from the mass of superimposed accretion is a task which still challenges the utmost skill of the critic.

LITERATURE.—Besides the works of Wendt, Resch, and B. Weiss, above referred to, the reader should consult the excellent discussions of Hawkins, *Horæ Synopticæ*, and in *Expos. Times* xii. (1900–1901) pp. 72 ff. and 471 ff., also *ib.* xiii. (1902) p. 20, on 'Some Internal Evidence for the use of the Logia in our First and Third Gospels,' and 'Use of Materials in Mt 8–9'; also four articles by C. A. Briggs, *ib.* vols. viii. ix. (1897–1898) on 'The Wisdom of Jesus the Messiah.' Many excellent observations are made by A. Wright in his *Synopsis*², 1903. A valuable discussion of the history of the *logia* embodied in the Sermon on the Mount will be found in the Extra Vol. of Hastings' *DB*, *s.v.* 'Sermon on the Mount' (C. W. Votaw). For an analysis of this and related principal discourses of Jesus, see the present writer's *The Sermon on the Mount—its Literary Structure and Didactic Purpose*, Macmillan, 1902. On the *logian* material of Lk. see art. WISDOM.   B. W. BACON.

LOGOS.—The conception of Christ as the Logos, or eternal Word, is peculiar to the Fourth Gospel. In the Epp. to Colossians and Hebrews (writings which are likewise touched with the Alexandrian influence) the Logos theory of Christ's Person is in some points implied (cf. Col 1¹⁵⁻¹⁸, He 1²⁻⁴). In Revelation (19¹³) the 'Word of God' is announced as the new and mysterious name which Christ bears when He comes forth to execute judgment. But only in the Fourth Gospel is the conception deliberately adopted and worked out in its full significance.

The idea of a Logos, an immanent Divine reason in the world, is one that meets us under various modifications in many ancient systems of thought,

Indian, Egyptian, Persian. In view of the religious syncretism which prevailed in the 1st and 2nd centuries, it is barely possible that these extraneous theologies may have indirectly influenced the Evangelist; but there can be no doubt in regard to the main source from which his Logos doctrine was derived. It had come to him through Philo after its final elaboration in Greek philosophy.

In the 6th cent. B.C. Heraclitus first broke away from the purely physical conceptions of early Greek speculation, by discovering a λόγος, a principle of reason, at work in the cosmic process. From the obscure fragments of this philosopher that have come down to us we gather that he was chiefly interested in accounting for the æsthetic order of the visible universe. In the arrangement of natural phenomena, in the adaptation of means to ends, he discerned the working of a power analogous to the reasoning power in man. His speculation was still entangled with the physical hypotheses of earlier times, and on this account dropped out of sight, and had little influence on the greater systems of Greek thought. Plato and Aristotle were engaged in the development of the theory of ideas, with its absolute separation of the material world from the world of higher reality. Their work was of profound significance for the after history of Logos speculation, but belongs itself to a different philosophical movement. It was in the reaction from Platonic dualism that the Logos idea again asserted itself, and was worked out through all its implications in Stoicism.

The Stoics, animated chiefly by a practical interest, sought to connect the world of true being, as conceived by Plato, with the actual world of man's existence. They abandoned the theory of supersensible archetypes and fell back on the simpler hypothesis of Heraclitus, that the universe is pervaded in all its parts by an eternal Reason. Man in his individual life may raise himself above all that limits him, and realize his identity with this Logos, which resides in his own soul, and is also the governing principle of the world. The Stoic philosophy not only furnished the general conception of the Logos to later thinkers, but also emphasized the distinction which became of prime importance in the later development. The faculty of reason as it exists in man reveals itself in speech, which is denoted by the same Greek word, λόγος. To the universal λόγος Stoicism ascribed the two attributes that mark the reasoning power in man. On the one hand it is λόγος ἐνδιάθετος,—reason in its inner movement and potentiality,—and on the other hand λόγος προφορικός,—reason projected and made concrete in the endless variety of the visible world.

1. Philo appropriates the main Stoic conception, but combines it with other elements borrowed eclectically from previous systems of thought. The Logos idea is loosened from its connexion with Stoic materialism and harmonized with a thoroughgoing Platonism, which regards the visible things as only the types and shadows of realities laid up in the higher world. It becomes identical in great measure with Plato's idea of the Good, except that it is further regarded as creatively active. Philo's grand innovation, however, is to press the Logos theory into the service of a theology derived from the OT. The same problem which Stoicism had tried to solve had in a different manner become urgent in Jewish thought. Here also all progress, alike in the moral and intellectual life, was like to be arrested by an overstrained dualism. The effort to conceive of God as absolutely transcendent had resulted in separating Him entirely from the world, of which He had yet to be regarded as the Creator and Governor. Already in the later books of the OT, much more in Rabbinical speculation, we can trace the idea of an intermediary between God and the world. 'Wisdom' is described in Job and Proverbs, with something more than a poetical personification, as God's agent and co-worker. Peculiar significance was attached by the later expositors to the various OT allusions to the 'word' of God. By His 'word' He had created heaven and earth and revealed Himself to the prophets. The actual hypostatizing of the Word in the doctrine of the Memra was subsequent to the time of Philo, but it was the outcome of a mode of thinking already prevalent in Jewish theology. God who was Himself the High and Holy One, of purer eyes than to behold iniquity, mediated His action through the Divine Word. It was natural for Philo, with his Hellenic and philosophical culture, to advance a

step further and identify the Word of the OT with the Stoic λόγος.

The Logos of Philo requires to be understood in the light of this double descent from Greek and OT thought. The Stoic conception, as we have seen, took account of the two meanings of λόγος as reason and uttered speech, but the distinction was of little practical importance. What the Greek thinkers sought to affirm was the rationality of the world. The Logos under all its aspects was simply the principle of reason, informing the endless variety of things, and so maintaining the world-order. To Philo, on the other hand, the idea of reason is combined with that of the outgoing of Divine power. While describing his Logos in terms directly borrowed from Plato and the Stoics, he regards it as in the last resort dynamic, like the creative word in Genesis. This difference between Philo and the Greek thinkers is connected with another and still more vital one. To the Stoics the eternal Reason was itself an ultimate principle, and the necessity was not felt of explaining it as the reason of God. The doctrine of the Logos may, indeed, be regarded as an attempt, more or less conscious, to escape from the belief in a Divine Creator. Philo could not content himself with this notion of an absolute Logos. He started from the Hebrew belief in a supreme, self-existing God, to whom the immanent reason of the world must be related and subordinated. To this clashing of the primary Greek conception with the demands of Hebrew monotheism, we may largely attribute one of the most perplexing peculiarities of the Philonic doctrine. The Logos appears, sometimes as only an aspect of the activity of God, at other times as a 'second God,' an independent and, it might seem, a personal being. There can be little doubt that Philo, who never ceased to be an orthodox Jew, had no intention of maintaining the existence of two Divine agents; and the passages in which he appears to detach and personify the Logos must be explained mainly in a figurative sense. The Word which is described as speaking, acting, creating of itself, is the word of God, vividly realized by an imaginative thinker. But this separate existence assigned to the Logos may also be set down in some measure to the composite origin of the idea. The Stoical doctrine of an independent Reason could not be wholly reconciled with the Jewish belief in one supreme God.

2. The Fourth Gospel sets out from a conception of the Logos which to all appearance is closely similar to that of Philo. In the Prologue the main features of the Philonic doctrine are reproduced one by one;—the eternal existence of the Word, its Divine character (ἦν θεός), its relation to God as towards Him, and yet distinct (πρὸς τὸν θεόν), its creative activity, its function in the illumination and deliverance of men. The Evangelist assumes that the idea of the Logos is already a familiar one in Christian theology. It is introduced abruptly, as requiring no explanation, and its different aspects are lightly indicated, by way of reminding the reader of truths sufficiently known to him. We can thus infer that the conception of Philo had already naturalized itself in Christian thought, but there is reason to believe that the author of the Gospel was acquainted more or less directly with the Philonic writings and consciously derived from them.[*]

To what extent does the Logos idea of Philo change its character as it assimilates itself to the theology of the Gospel? Before an answer can be offered to this question, it is necessary to consider a preliminary difficulty with which Johannine criticism has been largely occupied since the ap-

[*] Cf. the list of parallel passages collected by Grill (pp. 111-138).

pearance of Harnack's famous pamphlet.* Is the Prologue to be regarded as an integral portion of the Gospel, or is it, as Harnack contends, a mere preface written to conciliate the interest of a philosophical public? The idea of Christ as the Divine Logos is nowhere resumed in the body of the Gospel. Although the term Logos is constantly used, it always bears its ordinary sense of spoken discourse, while the categories of Light, Life, Love are substituted for the Logos of the Prologue. The work, as we have it, is no metaphysical treatise, such as we might expect from the opening verses, if they truly set forth its programme, but a historical document, the narrative of the earthly life of Christ. In spite, however, of Harnack's powerful argument, the almost unanimous voice of Johannine criticism has declared against him. The statement of his view has led to a closer examination of the Prologue in its connexion with the Gospel, resulting in multiplied proof that the ideas presented at the outset are woven in with the whole tissue of the work. The Prologue supplies the background, the atmosphere, which are necessary to a right contemplation of the history. Nevertheless, while Harnack's main argument cannot be accepted, it serves to remind us of one fact which cannot be emphasized too much. St. John is not concerned merely with the Word, but with the Word made flesh. After the first few verses, in which he treats of the pre-existent Logos, he passes to the historical Person of Jesus, who is more than the abstract Word. In Him it had become visible, and acted on men through a human Personality.

St. John therefore accepts the Philonic conception in order to assimilate it to his account of a historical Person, through whom the Word declared itself under the conditions of human life. It is evident that the conception could not be so adapted without submitting to profound modifications. (1) The Logos, which was to clothe itself in flesh and act on men with the force of a personality, must in its deepest ground be a personal Being. We have seen that Philo, partly in imaginative fashion, partly because of the composite origin of his thought, attributes a semi-independence to the Logos. This prepared the way for a complete personification; but Philo himself thinks only of a Divine principle, the creative reason of God. St. John, however, makes it an essential moment in his conception that the Logos has a ground of independent being within God ($\pi\rho\grave{o}\varsigma\ \tau\grave{o}\nu\ \theta\epsilon\acute{o}\nu$, standing over against Him as a distinct Being). His view even of the pre-existent Logos is coloured by his knowledge of the ultimate Incarnation. (2) The creative activity of the Logos, which in Philo is central and all-determining, falls into the background. Only in 1[3] ('All things were made by him') do we have any clear trace of this aspect of Logos doctrine, and the sequence of thought would still be complete if the brief allusion were omitted. It is thrown out, apparently, by way of acknowledgment of the recognized theory. Some reference to the cosmic significance of the Logos was necessary if any link with previous speculation was to be preserved. The Gospel, in point of fact, knows nothing of the absolute transcendence of God, which Philo's whole theory is designed to mitigate. It assumes that 'the world' is the direct object of God's love and providence (3[16]). It maintains that God acts immediately on the human soul and so makes possible the redeeming work of the Logos (6[44] 17[6]). (3) In the Gospel, much more emphatically than in Philo, the term $\lambda\acute{o}\gamma o\varsigma$ denotes Word as well as Reason. The Greek philosophical meaning is, indeed, discarded, or

retained only as a faintly colouring element. The Word is regarded throughout as the expression of God's will and power, the self-revelation of His inward nature. It does not represent the Divine reason but the Divine energy. Its sovereign attribute is Life, the life which it derives from God and transmits to men. Under the form of Alexandrian speculation St. John preserves the essential Hebrew conception of the living, quickening Word.

Thus, in accepting the Philonic idea, St. John does not commit himself to the precise interpretation that Philo placed on it; on the contrary, whether consciously or not, he departs from the characteristic lines of Philo's thinking. The differences, however, do not alter the main fact that he rested his account of the Christian revelation on a hypothesis which was metaphysical rather than religious. The Jesus who had appeared in history was identified with the Logos of philosophy, and this identification involved an entirely new reading of His Person and life. St. John does not, indeed, press to its full extent his theory that the Logos became manifest in Christ. Behind his speculation there is always the remembrance of the actual life, which had arrested him as it had done the first disciples, and been to him the true revelation of God. His worship is directed in the last resort not to the Logos whom he discovers in Jesus, but to Jesus Himself. Nevertheless the acceptance of the Logos idea imposes on him a mode of thought which is often alien to his deeper religious instinct. On the one hand, he conceives of Jesus as revealing God to men and lifting them to a higher life by His ethical personality. On the other hand, he is compelled to interpret the work of Jesus in terms of metaphysic. God was manifest in Him because He was Himself the Logos, and the life He imparted was the Divine life, different in essence from that of man. The Gospel wavers throughout between these two parallel interpretations of the life of Christ,—that suggested by the history and that required by the Logos hypothesis. Superficially the two conceptions are drawn together, but they are disparate by their very nature and will not admit of a true reconciliation.

St. John does not concern himself with the questions that arose in later theology regarding the nature of the union between the Logos and the human Jesus. He assumes the union as a fact incapable of further definition. 'The Word became flesh,' appeared in Jesus as a human personality. How and when this Incarnation was effected, to what extent the Divine nature in Christ could be distinguished from the human,— these are questions which he does not try to answer, and which he probably never asked himself. His silence is mainly to be explained by the practical intention with which he wrote his Gospel. It was not his purpose to discuss the Divinity of Christ as a theological idea, but to impress it on his readers as a fact, by the knowledge of which 'they might have life' (20[31]). At the same time, the problems which came to light in the course of later controversy are all legitimately suggested by the simple thesis 'the Word became flesh.' From St. John's silence in regard to them we are compelled to infer that he did not reason out his doctrine with any fulness or clearness. He had set himself to combine ideas which in themselves were radically incompatible, and succeeded in doing so only by a certain confusion of thought.

3. The Evangelist, then, sets out from the fact that the historical Jesus was also the Divine Logos. In the body of the Gospel this hypothesis is never directly alluded to, but it is assumed throughout and modifies profoundly the whole picture of the earthly life of Jesus. (1) Peculiar

* *Über das Verhältniss des Prologs des vierten Evgl. zum ganzen Werk* (1892).

stress is laid on His miracles as the 'signs' by which He 'manifested forth his glory.' The motive of compassion, to which the miracles are for the most part ascribed by the Synoptic writers, falls into the background. They are regarded as sheer exhibitions of power, intended by Jesus to inspire belief in His Divine claims. The marvellous element is uniformly heightened, in such a manner as to preclude all natural explanations. (2) Apart from direct works of miracle, certain attributes are assigned to Jesus which witness to His possession of the Logos nature. He partakes even on earth of the Divine omniscience (1^{48} 2^{25} 4^{17} 11^{14}). He appears where He will, with something of a Divine omnipresence (6^{19} 8^{59} 9^{35}). There is a majesty about His Person which quells and overawes (7^{46} 12^{21} 18^{6}). An impression is borne home on us in every episode of the history that, while He dwelt with men, He was a heavenly being, who could exercise at will the prerogatives of God. (3) The aloofness of Jesus, as of one who belonged to a different world, is everywhere brought into strong relief. In the Synoptic narratives, what separates Him from other men is His matchless wisdom and moral purity. St. John ascribes to Him a radical difference of nature. He does not participate in human weaknesses and distresses (even His sorrow over Lazarus is that of a Divine being who stands apart and contemplates the tragedy of our mortal lot). In His intercourse with the disciples He is conscious all the time that He has come from God and returns to God ($13^{3.\ 4}$). (4) A still more striking emphasis is laid on the absolute freedom, the self-determination of Jesus. While submitting for a time to earthly limitations, He vindicates His higher nature by acting in everything on His own sovereign will, without compulsion from without (2^{4} $6^{5.\ 6}$ 7^{6} 11^{33}). From the beginning He has fixed His 'hour,' and Himself ordains all the conditions that will lead up to it. His enemies are impotent until the hour willed by Himself has come (7^{30} 8^{20}), and meanwhile He goes about His work in perfect security (11^{9}). In this well-marked strain of Johannine thought we have little difficulty in discerning the influence of the Logos idea, penetrating the actual reminiscence of the life of Christ. (5) The Logos character of Jesus, which is thus illustrated on various sides by His actions, comes to clear expression in His spoken words. These are concerned almost wholly with the assertion, under many different types and forms, of the Divine significance of the Speaker Himself. Hence the peculiar value which is ascribed to them ($6^{63.\ 68}$ 15^{3}). They convey more clearly and emphatically than actions could do the inner secret of our Lord's personality. Being Himself the Logos, one in essence with God, He had power to impart the higher life (see WORD).

In all these directions, therefore, St. John gives effect to the idea of the Prologue that the nature of Christ was a Logos nature. His acceptance of this doctrine involves him in a new reading of the Gospel history—a reading which in some respects is artificial and inadequate. The life of Jesus becomes that of a heavenly being, and all traces of moral struggle (as in the Temptation and the Agony) disappear from it. The attributes of faith in God and infinite sympathy with men are replaced by metaphysical attributes, which are supposed to belong more essentially to the Divine nature. Jesus is the revelation of God because He is the eternal Logos, who manifests in an earthly life the absolute being and self-dependence of God. This, however, is to divest the revelation of its real worth and meaning. What we desire to know and what was actually revealed to us in the life of Jesus, is the moral character of God, and of this the Logos doctrine can render no account. In so far as the Fourth Evangelist has subordinated his conception of Christ to a philosophical speculation, we cannot but feel that he defeats his own purpose. He desires so to assert the majesty of Christ that men may be drawn to believe in Him as the Son of God, and enter into life-giving fellowship with Him. But in the endeavour to exalt the Lord's Person by means of the Logos hypothesis, he obscures those very elements in the Divine life which constitute its true glory.

4. It is necessary at the same time to recognize that much was gained for Christian theology by the adoption of this hypothesis. (1) A middle term was discovered between Christianity and the forms of Hellenic thought, and a wider development was thus rendered possible. The new religion could now interpret itself to the Græco-Roman world, and assimilate whatever was congenial to its spirit in the intellectual life of the time. With the help of the categories which it henceforth borrowed from Greek philosophy, it was enabled in many ways to convey its message more clearly and adequately. (2) The claim of Christianity to be the absolute religion was definitely formulated in the Logos doctrine. Jesus was identified not merely with the Jewish Messiah, but with the eternal Word who had been with God from the beginning. His revelation was not one out of many, but the supreme and final revelation. This idea is prominent throughout the Prologue, in which the 'true Light' is contrasted with the manifestations of God through John the Baptist and Moses. These, although burning and shining lights, were only 'for a season' (5^{35}). (3) By identifying Him with the Logos, St. John declared, in a manner that could not be mistaken, the uniqueness of Jesus, and assigned Him His central place as the object of Christian faith. The Logos category was in itself insufficient, and tended to confuse Christianity with metaphysical issues which were alien to its real import. But it provided a form within which the innermost truth of the religion could maintain itself for ages following. Jesus Christ in His own Person is the revelation of God, and believing on Him we have life through His name.

5. The vital and permanent message of the Fourth Gospel is little affected by any estimate we may form of the value of the Logos hypothesis. It is evident that, while the Evangelist ostensibly sets out from a philosophical theory, he derives in reality from a religious experience. From the impression created in him by the earthly life of Jesus, still more from the knowledge he had received of Him in inward fellowship, he has arrived at the conviction that this is the Christ, the Son of God. He avails himself of the doctrine of the Logos, the highest that the thought of his time afforded him, in order to express this conviction, and in some measure explain it. But the speculative idea belongs to the form, not to the essence of St. John's teaching. It represents the attempt to interpret, in terms of an inadequate philosophy, a truth which has been grasped by faith. See also art. DIVINITY OF CHRIST, vol. i. p. 478[b].

LITERATURE.—Aall, *Geschichte der Logosidee* (2 vols., 1896, 1899); Heinze, *Die Lehre vom Logos in der griech. Philosophie* (1872); Drummond, *Philo Judæus*; J. Réville, *Le Quatrième Évangile* (1901), and *La doctrine du Logos dans le 4ème Évang. et dans les œuvres de Philon* (1881); Grill, *Untersuchungen über die Entstehung des vierten Evang.* (1902); Bousset, *Die Relig. des Judenthums* (pp. 405–431); Simon, *Der Logos* (1902); Meyer, *Der Prolog des Johannesevang.* (1902); Baldensperger, *Der Prolog der vierten Evang.* (1898); Harnack, *Über das Verhältniss*, etc. (1892); Kaftan, *Das Verhältniss des evangelischen Glaubens zur Logoslehre* (1896); art 'Logos' in Hastings' *DB.*

　　　　　　　　　　　　　　　　　E. F. SCOTT.

LONELINESS.—To speak of the isolation of Christ would give a wrong impression as far as the everyday circumstances of His life are concerned. He was most often either in crowds, teaching and healing, or else seeking loneliness without success; He was lonely in the same sense as that in which Nazareth and Syria were lonely—placed close to the world's highways, yet living a life of their own (cf. G. A. Smith, *HGHL*, p. 432; Edersheim, *Life and Times of Messiah*, i. 147). We may notice four aspects of what may be called the loneliness of Christ.

1. *Solitude for the purposes of prayer, meditation, and rest.* The outstanding instances are—the Temptation in the Wilderness (Mt 4[1], Mk 1[12], Lk 4[2]), the retirement after the excitement consequent on the feeding of the five thousand (Mt 14[22], Mk 6[45]; cf. Jn 6[15]), and the retirement for prayer, soon interrupted (Mk 1[35]; cf. also Lk 6[12], and 9[18] where Mk 8[27] has 'in the way he asked his disciples'). It should be noted that at times of peculiar spiritual intensity Jesus withdrew from the other disciples, but kept by Him Peter and the sons of Zebedee, as at the Transfiguration (Mt 17[1], Mk 9[2], Lk 9[28]), at the raising of Jairus' daughter (Mk 5[37]), and at Gethsemane (Mt 26[37]—'watch with me,'—Mk 14[35], Lk 22[43]).

2. *Retirement from possible persecution, or from unwished for notoriety*: *e.g.* after the death of John the Baptist (Mt 14[13]; in Mk 6[31] this retirement immediately follows the return of the Twelve); from the opposition of the Pharisees (Mt 16[13], Mk 8[27], Lk 9[18]; also Mt 15[21], Mk 7[24]). Similarly, He was extremely anxious that His miracles should not become known (Lk 5[43], Mt 8[4], Mk 8[26] 9[9]; the chief exception, where there were special reasons, is in Mk 5[19]). The opposite reason for solitude and concealment is given in Jn 6[15] ('perceiving that they were about to come and take him by force, to make him king'). On the other hand, it must be remembered that (*a*) Jesus was constantly accompanied, at least in Galilee and at the end in Jerusalem, by twelve friends and disciples specially appointed (Mt 10[2], Mk 3[16], Lk 10[1] imply a larger circle from which to draw); to these we must add a number of women (Lk 8[3]; cf. Mt 27[55], Mk 15[40], Lk 23[49]). In connexion with the visits to Jerusalem recounted in the Fourth Gospel, the disciples are hardly mentioned; Jn 7[10], coupled with the absence of reference to the disciples in chs. 7 to 10, seems to make it certain that Jesus was alone; we find the disciples with Him again in Jn 11[16]. (*b*) In the earlier part of His ministry Jesus was constantly inconvenienced by the thronging of the vast crowds drawn to His side (cf. Mt 4[23] 8[18] 9[35], Mk 1[37], Lk 4[42] 12[1]; see Swete, *St. Mark*, p. lxxx); in the last visit to Jerusalem He sought retirement at night by leaving the city either for Bethany or the Mount of Olives (Mt 21[17], Mk 11[19], Lk 21[37]). (*c*) His conduct was social enough—as distinct from that of John and of the Essenes—to give rise to the slanders about 'a gluttonous man and a winebibber' (Mt 11[19], Lk 7[34]); He went to the marriage at Cana (Jn 2[1]); He was found at the feast in Simon's house (Mt 26[6], Mk 14[3], also Lk 7[36]); with Matthew (Mt 9[10], Lk 5[29]), and Zacchæus (Lk 19[6]); and contrasted Himself with John as one who 'comes eating and drinking' (Mt 11[19], Lk 7[34]).

3. *The inevitable result of His own attitude.* The question in Mt 12[48] seems to be that of one who wilfully cuts himself off from human ties; as He faced death more nearly, isolation could not but grow on Him (Mt 17[12], Mk 9[30], Lk 9[22. 44], cf. also Mk 10[32]); as early as the feeding of the five thousand, 'many of his disciples went back, and walked no more with him' (Jn 6[66]). The disciples remained with Him till the end, when the arrest proved too much for their loyalty, although we find John, with the women, at the foot of the cross (Jn 19[25. 26], Mt 27[55], Mk 15[40]).

4. *The uniqueness of Christ's Person.* This is emphasized chiefly in the Fourth Gospel; though that it was soon felt is shown in Lk 5[8] ('Depart from me; for I am a sinful man, O Lord'; compare the timidity of the disciples in Jn 21[12]); and easily gathered from the manner in which the disciples misunderstood Him and His purposes for themselves (Mt 20[21], Mk 10[37]; cf. Lk 9[54. 55], and Mk 9[32], Lk 9[46] 22[24]). When Christ speaks of His own nearness to the Father, distance from mankind must naturally follow; see Jn 5[18ff.] 8[16. 27. 29] 10[30] 20[17]. On the other hand, this special relation of Christ to the Father is one which is, through Christ, to be shared by His disciples (see Jn 10[4], ch. 17 *passim*, and 20[17]). The extreme of loneliness, as it is heard in the cry upon the cross (Mt 27[46], Mk 15[34], cf. Lk 23[46], Jn 19[30]), lasted, it would seem, but for a moment. See DERELICTION.

LITERATURE.—In addition to the Commentaries and Lives of Christ, see F. W. Robertson, *Sermons*, 1st Series, p. 220; J. Caird, *Aspects of Life*, p. 111; H. P. Liddon, *Passiontide Sermons*, p. 138; J. Martineau, *Endeavours after the Christian Life*, p. 159; E. B. Pusey, *Sermons from Advent to Whitsuntide*, p. 188.

　　　　　　　　　　　　　　　W. F. LOFTHOUSE.

LONG-SUFFERING (μακροθυμία), like another fruit of the Spirit, love (ἀγάπη), has almost entirely non-pagan connexions. The Gr. word occurs 14 times in the NT, while its cognate verb is found 10 times, and the adverb only once (Ac 26[3]). Only the verb occurs in the Gospels: Mt 18[26. 29] (EV 'have patience'), Lk 18[7] (AV 'bear long,' RV 'is long-suffering'). It is both a Divine attribute and a Christian virtue. The word 'long-tempered' as opposed to 'short-tempered' is not in ordinary English use, but it expresses with fair accuracy the central thought in μακροθυμία. The Latin equivalent is *longanimitas* (Vulg.), and Jeremy Taylor amongst others tried to transplant the word into English soil under the form of 'longanimity,' but without success.

OT use.—Long-suffering is one of God's noblest attributes, and is made the subject of a special revelation in Ex 34[6]. The Heb. phrase 'erek 'aph (אֶרֶךְ אַף) is found frequently in the books that follow, and Joel (2[13]), Jonah (4[2]), and Nahum (1[3]) specially dwell upon this element in God's character.

NT use.—It is significant that the word μακροθυμία is rare in pre-Christian Greek. In the NT it occurs several times in context with ὑπομονή (patience, endurance), from which it must be carefully distinguished (2 Co 6[6], Col 1[11], 2 Ti 3[10], Ja 5[10. 11]). Trench (*Synonyms*) says μακροθυμία is used of persons, and ὑπομονή of things. As regards NT usage alone, this is near the truth (but see Ja 5[7], and cf. in OT Is 57[15] [LXX] and in Apocr. 1 Mac 8[4]). Perhaps we may more truly say that patience keeps a man from breaking *down* in despair, while long-suffering keeps him from breaking *out* in word or action because of some unsatisfied desire. This latter distinction is probably the key to several passages where μακροθυμία has been said to approximate to the meaning of ὑπομονή. In He 6[12. 15], for instance, Abraham not only waited patiently for the promise; he did not in heart or word break out into murmurs against God's delay, and this right attitude won him his reward. So in Ja 5[7] the husbandman without patience would break down with despair, but if his long-suffering gave out he would probably break out into pulling up his tardy plants. Long-suffering, then, is a passive virtue, and waits God's time. It is the exact opposite of hasty action or hurried speech. Nevertheless it is not carelessness. If God is long-suffering, He waits to give further opportunity for repentance, and this may not be presumed upon without risk (Ro 2[4] 9[22], 1 P 3[20], 2 P 3[9]).

1. *Christ's long-suffering character.*—The word itself is not often used of, or by, Christ Himself, but the virtue which it expresses is frequently exemplified in the Gospels. It was His long toleration of manifest injustice that puzzled John the Baptist (Mt 11[3]), and there is long-suffering too in His quiet reception of John's complaint (v.[4]). In long-suffering He refused to call down fire from heaven on inhospitable Samaritans (Lk 9[54]). It was long-suffering too that made Him yield to arrest without resistance (Mt 26[52. 53], Ja 5[6. 7]), and refrain from returning scorn for scorn or threat for threat at His trial (Mt 27[12]). And after His ascension we see Him exhibiting the same long-suffering spirit towards those who persecuted the disciples as they had persecuted the Master (1 Ti 1[16], Ac 9[4]; cf. 2 P 3[15]).

In His teaching He bids His people be partakers of His own long-suffering character. The tares are not rooted up, but grow together with the wheat until the harvest (Mt 13[30]). In the parable of the Unmerciful Servant the prayer of that unworthy man was for long-suffering (Mt 18[26]), but a full pardon was given instead, until his subsequent conduct caused the withdrawal of the boon (v.[29]). In the parable of the Unjust Judge the word μακροθυμεῖ (Lk 18[7]) occurs in connexion with a difficult piece of interpretation, for the full discussion of which we have scarcely space here. Christ possibly had in mind a verse in Sir 35[18] [Gr. 32[22]]. If ἐπ᾽ αὐτοῖς refers to the elect, we may say that μακροθυμεῖ here means the vindication of the cause rather than the punishment of the foe. But if we may refer the words to the enemies of the elect, the phrase will be parallel in thought to Ro 2[4].

2. *Long-suffering a Christian duty.*—In Mt 18[26. 29] we noted the obligation resting on those who enjoy Christ's long-suffering to exhibit it to others. This habit we find enforced in the Epistles (1 Co 13[4], 2 Co 6[6], Gal 5[22], 1 Th 5[14], 2 Ti 3[10]). It is not a natural characteristic: it has to be acquired (Col 3[12]). In Eph 4[2] it is explained as forbearance, or cessation of hostilities (ἀνοχή). This implies that there may be wrong on *both* sides. But there is a power from without (Col 1[11], Gal 5[22]), the Spirit of God, who will enable Christ's people to reproduce His long-suffering in face, for instance, of opposition to the truth they teach (2 Ti 4[2]). In Ja 5[7-10] the word occurs four times. The Christian who is persecuted is to be as long-suffering towards his foe as the farmer who waits till the unproductive field bears a crop after fertilizing showers. There is, perhaps, in addition, a thought of man's attitude towards God in times of trial. Christ's long-suffering man refuses both to rail at his enemies and to question the dealings of his God.

LITERATURE.—Trench, *Synonyms*; Cremer, *Lex. s.v.*; art. 'Long-suffering' in Hastings' *DB*; Paget, *Studies in the Christian Character*, 177; Morrison, *Unlighted Lustre*, 188.

H. C. LEES.

LOOK (CHRIST'S).—The Gospels give no direct information as to the look of our Lord, if the word 'look' be regarded as a synonym for His outward appearance. The first natural request of a child—'You are going to tell me about Jesus, then tell me what He was like'—puts a question the Evangelists do not even begin to answer; and in a tale generally so frank and childlike this fact is not without significance. No description of Jesus' 'face' is ever given in the Gospels, except when, in the story of the Transfiguration, it is said that the fashion of His face was altered (ἐγένετο τὸ εἶδος τοῦ προσώπου αὐτοῦ ἕτερον, Lk 9[29]). Even then, it is stated to have become like the sun (Mt 17[2]); and, as it happens, the figure is of something which, though it lights the world, is not in itself directly to be gazed upon (cf. Rev 1[16]). While it may be possible, therefore, to deduce from the Epistles a message figuratively termed 'the Gospel of the Face' (see Bushnell, *Sermons on Living Subjects*, 73 ff.), the Evangelists afford no opportunity of making this study of Christ 'after the flesh.' See art. CHRIST IN ART.

It is further to be observed, in the same connexion, that even the more vivid words for looking, as a synonym for 'seeing,' 'beholding,' are never used of Christ so as to draw attention to the *manner* of His look. Such a word, *e.g.*, as ἀτενίζω, 'to gaze fixedly' (employed to describe a congregation gazing *at* Jesus, Lk 4[20]; the maid staring at St. Peter, 22[56]; St. Paul flashing an indignant look at Elymas the sorcerer, Ac 13[9]), is never associated with our Lord. Even διαβλέπω, a milder though

still pictorial word, is not connected with Him. It is as though every mental image of Christ's outward appearance were designedly excluded. We must be content, therefore, to study Christ's look in the more objective sense in which it expresses simply the act of vision. Here we may roughly divide the references into four classes.

1. The look of Christ is sometimes disclosed as an *upward* look, expressing dependence on the Father. This uplifted glance is recorded on four occasions—during the miracle of the feeding of the 5000, while giving thanks and blessing the loaves (Mt 14[19]); in the healing of a man deaf and dumb, when Christ looked up to heaven and sighed (Mk 7[34] [in both passages ἀναβλέψας εἰς τὸν οὐρανόν]); in the raising of Lazarus (Jn 11[41] ἦρεν τοὺς ὀφθαλμοὺς ἄνω); and during the great High-Priestly prayer (Jn 17[1] ἐπάρας τοὺς ὀφθαλμοὺς αὐτοῦ εἰς τὸν οὐρανόν). In all these instances the action and gesture must have imprinted themselves very deeply on the memory of the disciples. They were an outward sign of a lifelong inward attitude. They evidenced the direction of the appeal which Christ made in His human nature to God. Of Him the words are pre-eminently true, 'Mine eyes are ever toward the Lord' (Ps 25[15]).

2. The look of Christ is often disclosed as an *outward* look of calm clear-eyed discernment on the world around Him. 'He beheld (ἐθεώρει) how the people cast money into the treasury' (Mk 12[41])—appreciating not only the matter of their gift, but the manner of it. He 'entered into the temple, and looked round about upon all things' (Mk 11[11] περιβλεψάμενος πάντα); and it appeared on the following day how piercing and comprehensive His glance had been (v.[15ff.]). 'He looked up' (ἀναβλέψας) and saw Zacchæus in his post in the tree (Lk 19[5]). When the scribes brought Him a crafty question, 'He perceived (κατανοήσας) their craftiness' (Lk 20[23])—'saw at a glance,' the word might be rendered. If there were space to offer a complete list of those things which Jesus is said in the Gospels to have beheld or seen, the impression would at least be strong that those calm eyes *missed* nothing. Retaining God continually in the field of vision, Jesus' sight was not thereby dimmed, but only purged and purified for all other exercise. On one occasion His disciples were permitted to share a deeper gaze into the world behind the veil—'And He said unto them, I beheld (ἐθεώρουν) Satan as lightning fall from heaven' (Lk 10[18]).

3. A special look of Christ is recorded as directed to a man or an audience during the utterance of some *statement* or *address*. The simplest record of this is when it is said that He 'looked round' before speaking (Mk 3[34] 10[23] περιβλεψάμενος); or that 'he beheld (ἐμβλέψας) them and said' (Mt 19[26]); or when more fully St. Luke states in reporting the Sermon on the Mount, 'And he lifted up his eyes (ἐπάρας τοὺς ὀφθαλμούς) on his disciples, and said' (Lk 6[20]). This is the look of the sower scrutinizing the field. It is a look adding personality to the word spoken. It is a silent 'Verily, verily, I say unto you.' More individual instances of this look are when Jesus 'beheld' (ἐμβλέψας) Peter, and said, 'Thou art Simon . . . thou shalt be called Cephas' (Jn 1[42])—a look sealing the new name upon Peter's heart; or when He 'beheld' (ἐμβλέψας) the chief priests and scribes, and said, What is this then that is written?' (Lk 20[17])—a grave look of reproach, 'to add solemnity to His reference to their own Scriptures.' Christ and His words can never be separated. He is Himself the Word made flesh—the greatest utterance in the greatest Person; and the language of the Apostles is 'what we have *seen* and heard declare we unto you' (1 Jn 1[3]).

4. A few passages form a group by themselves, wherein strong *feeling* is expressed or implied as accompanying some look of Christ. The most notable instance of this is when 'the Lord turned and looked upon (ἐνέβλεψεν) Peter' (Lk 22⁶¹), 'No word, no gesture of reproach'; but

> 'Oh to render plain,
> By help of having loved a little and mourned,
> That look of sovran love and sovran pain'
> (Mrs. Browning, *Sonnets*).

Akin to this is the look directed by Jesus upon the young ruler, 'And Jesus beholding (ἐμβλέψας) him loved him' (Mk 10²¹); or the look of the King upon Jerusalem, on 'what should have been the City's bridal day,' 'He beheld (ἰδών) the city, and wept over it' (Lk 19⁴¹). As a last instance, though expressing a very different emotion, we may adduce Mk 3⁵ 'He looked round about on them (περιβλεψάμενος αὐτούς) with anger, being grieved for the hardness of their hearts.' Of Christ, too, might the words have been written, He

> 'loved well because he hated,
> Hated wickedness that hinders loving' (Browning).

R. STEVENSON.

LORD.—This title is used as the translation of three different words in the Gr. Gospels: (1) ὁ δεσπότης. This word occurs only once in the Gospels, in the prayer of Simeon, 'Lord, now lettest thou thy servant depart in peace, according to thy word' (Lk 2²⁹). It is the proper correlative of δοῦλος. In thus addressing God, Simeon thinks of himself as His slave. (2) οἱ μεγιστᾶνες. This word also occurs but once in the Gospels, in Mk 6²¹ 'Herod . . . made a supper to his lords.' It describes the chief men or nobles of a city or kingdom. (3) κύριος, ὁ κύριος. Except in the above instances, this is the word which stands for 'Lord' and 'lord' in the Gospels. It occurs with great frequency. With or without the article, it is found at least 244 times. The frequency of its use is concealed from readers of the English versions. It is sometimes translated 'master' ('Yet the dogs eat of the crumbs which fall from their master's table,' Mt 15²⁷), or 'sir' ('I go, sir, and went not,' Mt 21³⁰), or 'owner' ('the owners therefore said, Why loose ye the colt?' Lk 19³³). Fundamentally the title describes one who has power or authority (ὁ ἔχων κῦρος) over persons or things. Strictly speaking, it implies ownership, but it is also used as a title of reverence or courtesy. In the Gospels it is applied in a wide variety of relationship.

1. It is frequently used as *a name for God*.—(1) In most cases as a name for God, it is used without the article. It occurs in all 59 times (17 in Mt., 8 in Mk., 30 in Lk., and 4 in Jn.). It is found in quotations from the OT, as 'Thou shalt not tempt (the) Lord thy God' (Mt 4⁷); and in phrases of OT origin, as 'the angel of (the) Lord' (Mt 1²⁰ ‖ Lk 1¹¹); 'the law of (the) Lord' (Lk 2²³); 'the power of (the) Lord' (Lk 5¹⁷). It is noteworthy that the only instances in the Gospels where the title is used in direct address to God, are found in the prayers of Jesus: 'I thank thee, Father, Lord of heaven and earth' (Mt 11²⁵ ‖ Lk 10²¹). In both cases the title is found in exactly the same phrase. (2) The use of the name with the article is infrequent, occurring in all 11 times (twice in Mt., once in Mk., and 8 times in Lk.): *e.g.* 'Perform unto the Lord thine oaths' (Mt 5³³); 'Tell how great things the Lord hath done for thee' (Mk 5¹⁹); 'Pray ye therefore the Lord of the harvest' (Lk 10²). In the application of this name to God, with and without the article, the Gospels follow the usage of the LXX.

2. It is also used with great frequency as *a general title of courtesy*, or as *a name for a master or owner*. (1) Without the article, it is employed in direct address, as the salutation of a son to a father, 'I go, sir' (Mt 21³⁰); of servants to their master, 'Sir, didst not thou sow good seed in thy field?' (Mt 13²⁷); 'Lord, let it alone this year also' (Lk 13⁸); of the Greeks to Philip, 'Sir, we would see Jesus' (Jn 12²¹); of the Pharisees and priests to Pilate, 'Sir, we remember that this deceiver said' (Mt 27⁶³). This use of the title, as a general term of courtesy in direct address, is not found in Mk., but it occurs 9 times in Mt., 8 times in Lk., and twice in John. As the name for a master, without the article it is found only in Mt 6²⁴ 'No man can serve two masters,' and in Lk 16¹³, the parallel passage. (2) With the article, it is a frequent name for a master or owner, as 'the lord of the vineyard' (Mt 20⁸), 'the lord of that servant' (Lk 12⁴⁶), 'the servant knoweth not what his lord doeth' (Jn 15¹⁵). In Lk 16⁸ it is the 'lord' of the unjust steward who commended his dishonest method of providing for himself.

3. It is most frequently of all employed as *a title of courtesy in direct address to*, or as *a name for Jesus*. (1) Without the article, it is used (*a*) by His disciples, as 'Lord, if it be thou, bid me come unto thee on the water' (Mt 14²⁸). This title in direct address to Jesus by disciples is never found in Mark. It is most frequent in Jn., as is to be expected, since he records most of the private intercourse between Jesus and His disciples. (*b*) By others than disciples, as 'Lord, if thou wilt, thou canst make me clean' (Mt 8²). In Mk. it is employed only once in this relation, by the Syrophoenician woman, 'Yes, Lord' (Mk 7²⁸). In most cases, the title as used by others than disciples is found in narratives of miracle. (*c*) By Jesus Himself, as 'Not every one that saith unto me, Lord, Lord, shall enter into the kingdom of heaven' (Mt 7²¹). (*d*) It is also found in the words of the angel to the shepherds, 'Unto you is born this day . . . a Saviour, who is Christ (the) Lord' (Lk 2¹¹). This phrase (χριστὸς κύριος) is found in Ps-Sol 17³⁶. Briggs (*Messiah of the Gospels*, pp. 34, 35, notes) says it is probably to be interpreted on the basis of אדני Ps 110¹ ('The LORD said unto my *Lord*'), but adds that Schürer, Ewald, Wellhausen, and W. R. Smith regard the phrase in Ps-Sol as a mistranslation of משיח יהוה ('Anointed of (the) Lord,'—a phrase which is found in Lk 2²⁶ '(the) Lord's Christ'). Dalman, on the other hand (*Words of Jesus*, T. & T. Clark, p. 303 f.), thinks it incredible that a translator should have made such a mistake. We agree with him in regarding κύριος (Lord) as a word added by the Evangelist to interpret the Jewish title Messiah (χριστός) to his Gentile readers. (The same necessity of interpretation accounts for the phrase 'Christ, a king' (Lk 23²), in the accusation made before Pilate. The claim that Jesus was 'the Christ' had no political significance to the Gentile governor. It had to be interpreted to him as 'king' before he could receive the charge as an accusation). In Ac 2³⁶ the phrase 'God hath made that same Jesus . . . both Lord and Christ' (κύριον καὶ χριστόν), is to be explained in the same way. 'Lord' is an addition by the Evangelist, to interpret 'Christ' to Gentile Christians. We may add that the same necessity of interpreting 'Christ' to Gentiles accounts for the curious phrase in the address of Peter to Cornelius, which has been found so difficult—'Jesus Christ (he is Lord of all, πάντων κύριος),' Ac 10³⁶. The clause in brackets is added to interpret the confessional title 'Christ.' It may be due to Lk., but it is more likely that it was added at the time by Peter. He was speaking to a Gentile, who, though he was 'a devout man and one that feared God,' may not have understood the confessional significance of the term 'Christ.' Without the addition of the interpretation, Cornelius might have regarded it as part of the name of Jesus. The title 'Christ' did become a proper name, but that use of the term did not arise till a later date.

If the interpretation was given by Peter when speaking to Cornelius, it provides an interesting illustration of the way in which the first preachers of Christianity adapted themselves to the new conditions in which they found themselves, when they began to preach to Gentiles. The Saviour of the world must not have a local or national confessional title, (cf. the words of Paul and Silas to the Philippian jailer as they are given in אAB, and accepted by Westcott and Hort, Tischendorf, and other critical editors, 'Believe on the Lord Jesus (*i.e.* believe on Jesus as Lord), and thou shalt be saved,' Ac 16³¹. Also, 'No man can say that Jesus is Lord but by the Holy Ghost' (1 Co 12³), and 'every tongue should confess that Jesus Christ is Lord, to the glory of God the Father,' Ph 2¹¹). To the Jewish Christian, Jesus was the 'Messiah,' to the Hellenistic Christian Jew He was 'the Christ,' and to the Gentile Christian He was 'the Lord.' The Hellenistic and Gentile terms are combined in our familiar name 'the Lord Jesus Christ.' The interpretation of 'Christ' as 'Lord' enables us to understand that the essential idea of the first term is that of Sovereignty or Lordship. The Saviour is the Lord, the Possessor and Ruler of the Kingdom of God.

This title readily acquired its highest significance as one of Divine honour among the Gentile Christians, especially in the East. 'Oriental religions are fond of expressing the relationship between the divinity and the devotee, as that of the "Lord" or "Lady" to a slave' (Deissmann). The higher significance of the title was most likely assisted also by the fact that among Hellenistic Jewish Christians κύριος was in use as a Divine title applied to God.

(2) With the article, the title is applied to Jesus (*a*) by Himself, directly, as 'Ye call me Master and Lord' (more literally, 'the Teacher and the Lord') (Jn 13¹³), and indirectly, as '(The) LORD said unto my Lord (τῷ κυρίῳ μου), Sit thou on my right hand till I make thine enemies thy footstool' (Mt 22⁴⁴). (*b*) The historical application of the title, with the article, to Jesus is specially significant. Tischendorf and Westcott-Hort omit the title in this form, in the only place where it is found in Mt. (28⁶). It occurs twice in Mk. (16¹⁹·²⁰), *i.e.* in that part of the Gospel which is regarded by critical editors as not belonging to the original MSS. Therefore it is only in the Gospels of Lk. and Jn. that the title in this form is applied historically to Jesus. This is a strong argument for the earlier composition of Mt. and Mk., for the title became so common in the Apostolic Church that its absence from these Gospels can be explained only by their early date. The title occurs 18 times in Lk. and 12 times in John. Twelve of the instances in Lk. are found in passages which are peculiar to that Gospel, as 'the Lord appointed other seventy' (Lk 10¹). The other instances may be regarded as editorial additions (7¹³ 11³⁹ 12⁴² 17⁵·⁶ 24³). Three of the instances in Jn., which are found in the early part of the Gospel, are plainly editorial additions (4¹ 6²³ 11²). The remaining instances are found in the last two chapters of the Gospel, and in passages which are peculiar to it. They deal with the risen life of Jesus, and were written at a time when the higher conceptions of His personality gave a deeper significance to the title, and when its confessional meaning was universally known. The adoring cry of Thomas, 'My Lord and my God' (ὁ κύριός μου καὶ ὁ θεός μου) Jn 20²⁸, is an illustration of how among Jewish Christians the title of respect addressed to a teacher became one of Divine honour. Yet, as Dalman says, 'it must . . . be remembered that the Aramaic-speaking Jews did not, save exceptionally, designate God as "Lord," so that in the Hebraic section of the Jewish Christians the expression "our Lord"

was used in reference to Jesus only, and would be quite freh from ambiguity' (p. 329).

4. In comparing parallel passages in which the title occurs, it is to be noticed that other titles are sometimes employed as equivalent terms in addressing Jesus.—

i. Mt 8²⁵ (κύριε) 'Lord, save us : we perish.'
  Mk 4³⁸ (διδάσκαλι) 'Teacher, carest thou not that we perish?'
  Lk 8²⁴ (ἐπιστάτα) 'Master (teacher), we perish.'

ii. Mt 17⁴ (κύριε) 'Lord, it is good for us to be here.'
  Mk 9⁵ ('Ραββεί) 'Rabbi, it is good for us to be here.'
  Lk 9³³ (ἐπιστάτα) 'Master (teacher), it is good for us to be here.'

iii. Mt 26²² (κύριε) 'Is it I, Lord?'
  Mt 26²⁵ ('Ραββεί) 'Is it I, Rabbi?'
  Jn 13²⁵ (κύριε) 'Lord, who is it?'

The variety in the title used in addressing Jesus is not confined to the parallel passages. It is to be seen throughout each of the Gospels. Arranging the titles in the order of preference, Mt. uses κύριος, διδάσκαλος, and 'Ραββεί ; Mk. διδάσκαλος, 'Ραββεί, 'Ραββουνεί, and κύριος ; Lk. κύριος, διδάσκαλος, and ἐπιστάτης ; Jn. κύριος, 'Ραββεί, 'Ραββουνεί, and διδάσκαλος. Sometimes the variety of the title is seen even in the same passage. It cannot be without intention or meaning that in (iii.) Mt. represents the eleven disciples as asking, 'Is it I, Lord?' while Judas, the traitor, says, 'Is it I, Rabbi?' (Mt 26²²·²⁵). Possibly Judas indicated his position of detachment or opposition by using 'Rabbi' instead of the title employed by the rest of the disciples. It is only by Judas that Jesus is addressed as 'Rabbi' in Mt. (26²⁵·⁴⁹). There must also be some difference of feeling in the use of different titles in Lk 5⁵ 'Master (teacher, ἐπιστάτα), we have toiled all night'; and Lk 5⁸, where Peter, after the miraculous draught of fishes, falls at the feet of Jesus with the cry, 'Depart from me ; for I am a sinful man, O Lord' (κύριε). But it is possible that the variation of title in the parallel passages may have taken place in the process of oral transmission, or in translation from the Aramaic.

5. The variation of title in addressing Jesus suggests that in the original language of the Gospels at least two titles were employed. Of these 'Ραββεί was one, cf. 'ye call me Master (teacher) and Lord,' Jn 13¹³, and the frequent use of 'Rabbi' in the Gospels. Evidently 'teacher' (διδάσκαλος) is a translation of 'Rabbi' in some of its forms (רב, רבי, רבן). In 7 places Lk. uses ἐπιστάτης as a synonym for διδάσκαλος (5⁵ 8²⁴ *bis.* ⁴⁵ 9³³·⁴⁹ 17¹³), and, without doubt, some form of רב lies behind this also. As to the title κύριος (Lord), which is used so frequently in addressing Jesus, it is most probably a translation of מרי or מרנא. It was a common name for a master, and was used as a title of courtesy. It was used by a servant to a master, by a debtor to a creditor, and by a layman to a learned man. It is possible, however, since many of the people of Palestine were bilingual, that κύριος was used by itself when one who knew Greek spoke to Jesus.

6. We thus suggest a twofold origin of the title as applied to Jesus. First, as the translation of the Aramaic titles in use among the disciples ; and second, as the substitute for χριστός with confessional meaning among Gentiles. These distinctions of origin and meaning were soon lost in the gradual but rapid adoption of the title as one expressive of Divine honour. It is possible that this use of the title first became common among Eastern Christians.

7. In regard to the application of κύριος to God, it may be said that this was entirely due to the influence of Hellenistic Judaism. It is very unlikely that it was in use among Aramaic-speaking Jews at the time of our Lord. In reading the Scriptures in the synagogue in Hebrew, the name אדני (Lord) was read wherever the sacred name יהוה was found in the text. When it became necessary to translate the Scriptures into Aramaic in public reading, אדני still took the place of the sacred name.

In quoting from the Scriptures אדני was not employed for the name of God, but הַשֵּׁם ('the Name') in Hebrew, and שְׁמָא in Aramaic. In phrases of OT origin like 'the angel of (the) Lord,' the name of God was entirely omitted or merely hinted at.

LITERATURE.—Dalman, *The Words of Jesus*, 324 ; Bruce, *Apologetics*, 398 ; Naville, *The Christ*, 144 ; Somerville, *St. Paul's Conception of Christ*, 295 ; Spurgeon, *The Messiah*, 649 : *Expository Times*, vol. xii. [1901] p. 425 ff., vol. xiii. p. 236 ff., vol. xv. p. 296 ff. ; Deissmann, *ibid.* vol. xviii. p. 195 ff. ; *Lexicons* of Cremer and Grimm-Thayer, *s.v.* κύριος.   JOHN REID.

LORD'S DAY.—See CALENDAR (THE CHRISTIAN).

LORD'S PRAYER (I.)—1. Place in NT.—Mt 6[9-13], Lk 11[1-4].

The former passage has been more influential in the later history of the Lord's Prayer, but the latter seems to give it in a more historical setting. In the Sermon on the Mount, the Prayer is, to all appearance, a later insertion ; Lk. leads into the neighbourhood of Bethany (10[38-42]) or Gethsemane ; see J. A. Robinson, 'On the Locality in which the Lord's Prayer was given,' in F. H. Chase, 'The Lord's Prayer in Early Church' (*TS* iii. [1891] pp. 123–125). Not far from the traditional site of Gethsemane, on the slope of the Mount of Olives, stands to-day the Church of the Paternoster, showing in the quadrangle the Lord's Prayer engraved in thirty-two languages.

The Lord's Prayer has been frequently published in Polyglot editions ; the oldest at Rome, 1591, in 26 languages ; then by H. Megiser, Frankfort, 1593, in 40 [2nd ed.], 1603, in 50 ; 3rd ed., Linz, 1616, in 52] ; by Andr. Müller, 1660, in 100 ; Chamberlayne, 1715, in 150 languages. J. Adelung (*Mithridates*, 1804–1817) made the Lord's Prayer the basis of a scientific classification of languages. Further Polyglot editions by Bodoni (Parma), J. J. Marcel (Paris), Auer (Vienna), Dalton (St. Petersburg, 1870, in 108 languages of Russia), S. Apostolides (London, no date, in 100 languages, published for the benefit of the poor Cretan refugees now in Greece) ; *The Lord's Prayer in Three Hundred Languages* . . . with a Preface by Heinrich Rost, 1891 ; in 300 dialects of Africa, 1900. But most of these compilations lack scholarly supervision. A pleasant task would be for a united band of scholars to trace the historic development of those languages for which this is possible, on the basis of the Lord's Prayer, and to show the character of the rest on the same basis. The Lord's Prayer has also been frequently turned into *metre* and *rhyme*. Whether there exists a collection of this kind in English, is unknown to the present writer ; in German, cf. *Das Gebet des Herrn : Eine Sammlung metrischer Umschreibungen des Vaterunsers*, Reutlingen, 1821 ; E. W. Scripture, 'A Record of the Melody of the Lord's Prayer,' in *Die neueren Sprachen*, ed. by W. Vietor, x. 9.

For early English translations of the Lord's Prayer, see Albert S. Cook, 'Study of the Lord's Prayer in English' (*Amer. Journ. Philol.* vol. xii. pp. 59–66), and *Biblical Quotations of Old English Prose Writers* (London, 1898, pp. xxv, liii, lix, lxiv, 147 ff.). Cook refers to Wanley's *Catalogus*, where separate versions of the Lord's Prayer are either given or their existence noted, pp. 51, 160, 169, 197, 202, 221, 224, 239 (?), 240, 248. Cook gives the first from MS. Bodl. Jun. 121. Three poetical paraphrases of the Lord's Prayer of uncertain date are given by Greiss in his *Bibliothek der Angelsächsischen Poesie*, ii. 285–290 (new ed. ii. 227–238), the last two published by Wanley, *Catalogus*, pp. 48 and 147 f., and by Ettmüller, *Scopas and Boceras*, pp. 230–237 ; the first by Thorpe, *Codex Exoniensis*, p. 468 f. On p. 147, Cook gives the Lord's Prayer from Ælfric's *Homilies*, and an isolated quotation in Cnut's *Laws* (Schmid, *Gesetze der Angelsachsen*, p. 270). We may quote : 'urne daeghwamlican hláf,' 'ure gyltas,' 'on costnunge' ; 'fram yfele,' 'hláf userne oferwistlic,' 'instondenlice,' 'scylda' (Cook, pp. liii, lix). For the expression 'costnunge,' it is interesting to note that the corresponding German word 'Bekorung' was declared by Luther better than the received 'Versuchung.'

In the new and enlarged edition of *The Lord's Prayer in Five Hundred Languages, comprising the Leading Languages and their Principal Dialects throughout the World, with the Places where Spoken* ; with a Preface by Reinhold Rost (London, Gilbert & Rivington, 1905), the Lord's Prayer is given in English in sixteen forms, namely : Charles II. Prayer-Book, 1662 ; Edward VI. Prayer-Book, 1549 ; as sent from Rome by Pope Adrian, an Englishman, about 1160 ; from two MSS of the 13th cent. ; from Wyclif, about 1380 ; Tindale, 1534 ; Cranmer, 1575 ; Rheims Version, 1582 ; AV, 1611 ; RV, 1881 ; *The Twentieth Century NT* ; further, in Anglo-Saxon.

A disciple—it is not said whether one of the Twelve—asked Jesus, as He was praying in a certain place, when He ceased, 'Lord, teach us to pray, as John also taught his disciples.' That the disciples of John were wont to make prayers or supplications, besides their fasting, is told by St.

Luke only (5[33]). On a form of prayer ascribed to John, see 'Lord's Prayer' (by present writer) in *EBi* 2817, n. 6, and the Catalogue of the Syriac MSS preserved in the Library of the University of Cambridge (p. 529). There it begins : 'Bright Morning, Jesus Christ, Who was sent by God the Father.' Where fixed forms of prayer are in use, as was the case, it seems, with the Jews in the time of Christ, it is but natural that petitions on particular subjects should be added to them ; such additions are mentioned as made, for example, by R. Eliezer and by R. Johanan (see Lightfoot, *Hor. Heb.* on Mt 6, and art. 'Schemone Esre' in Hamburger, *RE* ii. [1883] 1098).

2. Sources.—The sources whence our Mt. and Lk. took the Lord's Prayer are quite unknown. The Gospel of Mk., which, according to the common view, was used by our Mt. and Lk., does not give it. On Mk 11[24f.], where Mk. speaks about prayer, see A. Wright, *Synopsis*[2], 1903, p. 115, and Wellhausen, who thinks that Mk. may have known the Lord's Prayer as a prayer of the Church, but did not dare to refer it in its wording to Jesus ; the expression (ὁ πατὴρ ὑμῶν) ὁ ἐν τοῖς οὐρανοῖς, occurring there, is not found elsewhere in Mk. If the first Gospel was originally written in (Hebrew or) Aramaic, its author may have had the Lord's Prayer before him, written or oral, in (Hebrew or) Aramaic, and given it in one of these dialects ; then the translator may have formed the Greek under the influence of Lk. (cf. the *hapaxlegomenon* ἐπιούσιος). This is the view especially of Th. Zahn. The opposite view, that ἐπιούσιος was first coined by Mt. or one of his fellow-workers, is maintained, for instance, by A. Wright, *The Gospel acc. to Luke*, 1900, p. 102.

3. Text of the Lord's Prayer.—As there are two traditions about the place of origin of the Lord's Prayer, so even its wording is given in two different forms. In the Received Text, it is true, they differ very little ; in the AV, for instance, the variations are but four :

Matthew.	Luke.
(1) in earth as it is in heaven.	as in heaven, so in earth.
(2) this day.	day by day.
(3) debts, as we forgive our debtors.	sins, for we also forgive every one that is indebted to us.
(4) For thine . . . Amen.	omits.

In the Greek TR they differ even less, the first of the above variations has nothing to correspond in Greek. (In Mt. the AV preserved the order of the Pr. Bk. version, which differs both from Mt. and Lk. in the fifth petition, 'trespasses' against 'debts' and 'sins').

There can be no doubt that in the TR the form of Lk. has been assimilated to that of Mt. The modern critical editions agree almost to the letter ; see the editions of Scrivener, Weymouth, Nestle. Weiss retained in Mt. the form ἐλθέτω instead of ἐλθάτω, and the article τῆς before γῆς. The critical apparatus of Tischendorf and WH [the 2nd ed. of 1896 is enriched by some additional notes] may be supplemented by the following notes :

(1) The *Didache* (8[2]) has the singular τῷ οὐρανῷ ; the *Apost. Const.* in both places, 3[18] and 7[24] (here reproducing the *Didache*), the plural.

(2) On the form 'veni ad regnum tuum' in the oldest Latin MS (Cod. Bobbiensis), see F. C. Burkitt (*Cambr. Univ. Reporter*, 5th March 1900).

(3) Syr[cur] and the Syr. *Acts of Thomas* have the plural for 'thy will' as the first hand of Cod. א in Mt 7[21] (τὰ θελήματα).

(4) On the article for 'on earth,' see *EBi* 2818 ; on the new punctuation of the third petition, see below.

(5) With τὴν ὀφειλήν of the *Didache* cf. Mt 18[32], and the difference of the singular and plural in German and Dutch : *Schuld* and *Schulden*. Two MSS of the *Apost. Const.* give παραπτώματα = 'trespasses,' καθὼς for ὡς, and omit the verb. Syriac forms combine 'debts' and 'sins' ; see, besides *EBi* 2818, Burkitt in his ed. of the *Evangelion da-Mepharreshe*, Mrs. Gibson's ed. of the *Didascalia*, and Mrs. Lewis' MS of the *Acts of Thomas*.

(6) In some Oriental translations 'deliver' is rendered by different roots in Mt. and Lk., and then both are combined in liturgical use of the Lord's Prayer.

(7) Of the Doxology the *Didache* omits 'the kingdom and'; in the *Apost. Const.* (7²⁴) one MS, on the contrary, omits 'and the power and the glory'; and the same two clauses are omitted by another MS at 3¹⁸, which with its ally ends 'of the Father, and the Son, and the Holy Ghost, for ever and ever.' In this connexion it is worth while to remark, that Funk, in his new edition of the *Didascalia* and *Apost. Const.*, puts at 3¹⁸ and 7²⁴ the final quotation marks after τονηροῦ, implying by this that he does not regard the Doxology as part of the quotation from the NT. Compare with this the above statement about the MSS of the *Constitutions*, and Brightman's *Liturgies Eastern and Western*, p. 353 f.

In Lk. the modern editions differ even less than in Mt.—only in a single letter, Weiss retaining here also the spelling ἐλθέτω. With this unity contrast the judgment of Dean Burgon (*The Revision Revised*, pp. 34–36; *The Traditional Text*, p. 84):

'"The five Old Uncials" (אABCD) falsify the Lord's Prayer as given by St. Luke in no less than forty-five words. But so little do they agree among themselves, that they throw themselves into six different combinations in their departures from the Traditional Text; and yet they are never able to agree among themselves as to one single various reading: while only once are more than two of them observed to stand together, and their grand point of union is no less than an omission of the article. Such is their eccentric tendency, that in respect of thirty-two out of the whole forty-five words they bear in turn solitary evidence.'

Any one who is unwilling to believe that the TR of Lk. is due to assimilation with Mt. may compare the critical apparatus of the *Latin Testament* of Wordsworth-White, or of the pre-Lutheran *German* Bible as edited by Kurrelmeyer. There he can watch the same process for the German and the Latin texts. Even the Vulgate of Sixtus V. (1590) has the addition in Lk., *Fiat voluntas tua sicut in cœlo et in terra*; but not the rest.

The chief question about the Lord's Prayer in Lk. is, What about the petition ἐλθέτω τὸ ἅγιον πνεῦμά σου ἐφ' ἡμᾶς καὶ καθαρισάτω ἡμᾶς, which is witnessed for Marcion and found since in one MS (604, or Scrivener's *b*, Gregory's 700, von Soden's ε 133, pub. by Hoskier, 1890). Perhaps a trace of it is found in D, which has ἁγιασθήτω ὄνομά σου ἐφ' ἡμᾶς, ἐλθέτω σου ἡ βασιλεία, etc. Another reading of Marcion is '*thy* bread' for '*our*'; whether he read the second clause of the fifth petition we do not know, the sixth (and last with him) had the form καὶ μὴ ἄφες ἡμᾶς εἰσενεχθῆναι εἰς πειρασμόν. The same or similar forms are found independently from Marcion down to the present day. Harnack (*Sitzungsber. Acad. Berl.* 21st Jan. 1904) was inclined to see in the petition, 'Thy holy spirit come (upon us) and cleanse us,' the original for Lk., comparing 11¹³ with Mt 7¹¹.

4. Arrangement of the Lord's Prayer.—Augustine tells us (*Enchir.* 116): 'Lucas in oratione dominica petitiones non septem sed quinque complexus est'; thus it became the custom in the West to count seven petitions; but Origen, Chrysostom, and the Reformed Churches count six, connecting 'but deliver us from evil' closely with what precedes. WH print in Mt. the Lord's Prayer in 2×3 *stichi*, in Lk. without strophical arrangement, seeing in 'as in heaven, so on earth' the common burden for the first triplet of single clauses; see § 421. This has been adopted now for the Pr. Bk. version by Parliamentary Papers, 1903, No. 53, removing the comma from behind 'on earth' to behind 'done.' For the AV, the editions of the *Parallel NT* give a comma after 'done' as well as after 'on earth'; but Scrivener's *Paragraph Bible* (1873), the *Two Version Edition* (1900), and the *Interlinear Bible* (1906) omit the first comma. Whether the RV agrees with WH is not quite clear from its comma (in this case we should have expected a colon). This arrangement was already put forward by the *Opus imperfectum in*

Mt. (Migne, lvi. 712): 'Communiter autem accipi debet quod ait, Sicut in cœlo et in terra,' *i.e.*—
'Sanctificetur nomen tuum, sicut in cœlo et in terra.
Adveniat regnum tuum, sicut in cœlo et in terra.
Fiat voluntas tua, sicut in cœlo et in terra.'

On the fact that in mediæval explanations the beginning was construed 'Pater noster qui es. In cœlis sanctificetur nomen tuum,' see below.

5. Contents. —(*a*) *The exordium.*—The short πάτερ in Lk., the fuller πάτερ ἡμῶν in Mt., would both correspond to an Aram. אַבָּא, which is connected with ὁ πατήρ in Ro 8¹⁵, Gal 4⁶, Mk 14³⁶. Cf. J. H. Moulton's *Prolegomena*, pp. 10, 233, and art. ABBA in vol. i. That πάτερ ἡμῶν may also correspond to אַבָּא and does not necessarily presuppose the form with suffix (אָבִינוּ) in Heb., אֲבוּנָן in Aram., אֲבוּנָא in Galilæan), is shown by Dalman, *Worte Jesu*, 157, though for the beginning of a prayer the more solemn form appears to him more probable. Among Jews it is customary to add שֶׁבַּשָּׁמַיִם in Hebrew (דְּבִשְׁמַיָּא in Aramaic) to אָב where it is used of God, but the isolated אַבָּא is not unusual. In the NT ὁ ἐν τοῖς οὐρανοῖς is almost exclusively used in Matthew. On the question whether from Ro 8¹⁵, Gal 4⁶ an acquaintance of St. Paul and his churches with the Lord's Prayer may be concluded, see Gerh. Bindemann, *Das Gebet um tägliche Vergebung der Sünden in der Heilsverkündigung Jesu und in den Briefen der Apostel*, Gütersloh, 1902.

(*b*) On the imperatives ἁγιασθήτω, γενηθήτω, see Origen, *de Orat.* 24. 5; Blass, *Grammar*, § 20. 1; Moulton, *Proleg.* p. 172, who quotes from Gildersleeve on Justin Martyr, p. 137: 'As in the Lord's Prayer, so in the ancient Greek Liturgies the aor. imper. is almost exclusively used. It is the true tense for "instant" prayer.' Moulton adds: 'To God we are bidden, by our Lord's precept and example, to present the claim of faith in the simplest, directest, most urgent form with which language supplies us.'

(*c*) With the first petition cf. *SE* * 3, and the beginning of the *Ḳaddish* יִתְגַּדַּל וְיִתְקַדַּשׁ שְׁמֵהּ רַבָּא; afterwards eight more such verbs are placed together about 'the name of holiness (Blessed be it).' A benediction without mentioning הַשֵּׁם (=יהוה) is no benediction at all (*Ber.* 40b).

(*d*) Likewise a benediction with no מַלְכוּת is no benediction at all (*ib.*; cf. *SE* 11, in opposition to 12, 14, 17, *Ḳaddish*).

(*e*) γενηθήτω is tr. יֵעָשֶׂה by Shemtob, Delitzsch, Salkinson-Ginsburg, Resch; יְהִי by Alexander (McCaul-Hoga), Margoliouth, by the old Syriac versions except the Syro-Palestinian; from *SE* cf. 13, עֲשֵׂי רְצוֹנֶךָ; in the *Ḳaddish*: 'May your prayers be accepted, and may *your* petition be done.' To רָצוֹן of Biblical Hebrew would correspond צִבְיוֹן in post-Biblical Hebrew and Aramaic.

(*f*) For ἐπιούσιος the remark of Origen, *de Orat.* 27, still holds good, that the word is found nowhere else in the whole range of Greek literature. Jerome compares it with the LXX περιούσιος; but this stands almost everywhere for סְגֻלָּה (*ap.* Aquila, Gn 14²¹ for רְכוּשׁ, Ps 16¹⁴ for יֶתֶר). On περιούσιος, see Jerome's remark (*Anecd. Mareds.* iii. 1, p. 92): 'Verbo περιούσιος, i.e. *substantialis*, exceptis sanctis scripturis nullus foris disertorum usus est.' The *Gospel according to the Hebrews* had for ἐπ., as Jerome states, *māḥār* (=מָחָר). His most explicit statement has been published by Morin, *Anecd. Mareds.* iii. 2, p. 262: 'In Hebraico evangelio secundum Matthæum ita habet: Panem nostrum *crastinum* da nobis hodie.' This lends a strong support to the view that ἐπιούσιος is formed from ἡ ἐπιοῦσα, 'the coming day,' even if this *māḥār*

---

* *SE*, used hereafter as abbreviation for *Shemone Esre*, the daily Prayer of the Synagogue; see the edition in Dalman, *Worte Jesu*, p. 299 ff.; and cf. on it, *e.g.*, Hirsch in *JE* x. 270–282.

were nothing but a retranslation of the Greek. But another view is that it is the original word used by Jesus and preserved by the Jewish-Christian communities. This is the view of Zahn, *Gesch. Kan.* ii. 193, 703, *Einl.* ii. 312; Ambrose: 'Latinus hunc panem *quotidianum* dixit, quem Græci dicunt *advenientem*, quia Græci dicunt τὴν ἐπιοῦσαν ἡμέραν *advenientem diem*'; Athanasius: τὸν ἐ. ἄρτ. τουτέστι τὸν μέλλοντα; Cyril Alex.: οἱ μὲν εἶναί φασι τὸν ἥξοντά τε καὶ δοθησόμενον κατὰ τὸν αἰῶνα τὸν μέλλοντα; the Sahidic Version, on which see Lagarde, *Mitt.* ii. 374.

But the Oriental versions took another view: Syr[cur] לחמן אמינא, *i.e.* 'our continual bread,' in Luke Syr[cur sin] and *Acts of Thomas* 'the continual bread' (לחמא אמינא); the same tradition seems to be followed by the *cotidianus* of the Latin, the *sinteinan* of the Gothic, especially by לחמו תמידי of Shemtob ben Shafrut, with which cf. Nu 4[7] לֶחֶם הַתָּמִיד 'the continual bread.' [The Armenian version of 2 Mac 1[8] used for the shewbread the same expression as in the Lord's Prayer, wherefore Holmes-Parsons remarked: '*tres codices Sergii* ἄρτους ἐπιουσίους,' which remark led Deissmann (*Neue Bibelstudien*, p. 41) and Hilgenfeld (in his *Ztschr.*, 1899, p. 157) to the belief that ἐπιούσιος was actually found in some Greek MSS. This was corrected by the present writer in *ZNTW* i. 250, *EBi* 2820, n. 1; but it is repeated by Wellhausen in his Com. on Mt. and not recalled in that on Lk.]. The Vulgate (Jerome?) has *supersubstantialis* in Mt. and *cotidianus* in Lk. How the Peshiṭta (Rabula?) came to translate 'the bread of our need,' לחמא דסונקנן, is not quite clear, while the translation 'our bread of richness' in the Syro-Palestinian version rests on confusion with περιούσιος.

The following is a conspectus of the different renderings that have been tried:

(1) Shemtob: לחמנו תמידי. (2) J. B. Jona, Rome, 1668: לחמנו על הקיום, a literal rendering of the *supersubstantialis* of the Vulgate, as *überstantlich* in three editions of the pre-Lutheran German Bible. (3) Delitzsch, Salkinson, Resch: לֶחֶם חֻקֵּנוּ, after Pr 30[9]. (4) Taylor: לֶחֶם תָּמִיד or לַחְמָא הַדִּירָא. (5) Schultze: *laḥma di çorkâna* (=Pesh.). (6) Rönsch: לֶחֶם סְגֻלָּתֵנוּ, like the Syro-Palestinian version. (7) Arn. Meyer: מַכֵּת (sufficient). (8) Chase: 'our (or the) bread of the day.' The *Variorum Bible* quotes the readings: 'our bread in sufficiency,' 'the bread proper for our sustenance,' 'the bread for the coming day,' 'needful bread,' or 'bread for the life to come.' Others tr. 'bread of second quality,' 'the bread that we shall need' (*Twentieth Cent. NT*); see on the word, *ExpT* ii. [1891] 184, 242, 254, iii. [1891-92] 24, 31, 77.

The meaning of the word is certainly not far from the ἐφήμερος τροφή of Ja 2[15]. The change of σήμερον into καθ᾽ ἡμέραν (and of δός into δίδου) has been explained by the daily use of the prayer; but the *Didache*, which already enjoins the use of it three times a day, does use δός and σήμερον.

(*g*) In the fifth petition ὀφειλήματα is rather = חובותינו (Shemtob, Delitzsch, Margoliouth), not אשמתינו (Salkinson, Resch). On the variant ὀφειλήν and the dogmatic changes of εἰσενέγκῃς, see above. In the Latin Church it became customary in the time of Jerome and Hilary to say 'in tentationem quam ferre (or, sufferre) non possumus.'

(*h*) The last ambiguity is πονηροῦ, *malo*, which also in Heb., Aram. and Syr. may be masculine or neuter. The tr. of Shemtob, מכל רע 'from all evil,' finds its parallel in Ethiopic (see Brightman's *Liturgies*, p. 234), 'Deliver us and rescue us from all evil,' while the Nestorian Liturgy equally combines the two verbs by which the Pesh. (not Sin[cur]) renders ῥῦσαι in Mt. and Lk., 'Save and deliver us,' but continues, 'from the Evil and his host.' The neuter is found (in a different connexion, 10[5]) already in the *Didache*: μνήσθητι, Κύριε, τῆς ἐκκλησίας σου, ῥύσασθαι αὐτὴν ἀπὸ παντὸς πονηροῦ. Nevertheless, it seems to the present writer, on the whole, more probable that it should be taken as masculine.

For the Greek NT see the exhaustive investigation of Chase, and cf. Ac 10[38] where διαβόλου (Cod. E σατανᾶ) is rendered (by Shemtob) באשא 'the Evil One.' The most decided view that the word is masculine is in the *Clem. Hom.*, where Peter uses the passage as one of his proofs for the fact that his Master frequently spoke to them of the existence of an Evil One (19[2] ἐν ᾗ παρέδωκεν ἡμῖν εὐχῇ ἔχομεν εἰρημένον· ῥῦσαι ἡμᾶς ἀπὸ τοῦ πονηροῦ, along with Mk 1[13], Mt 12[26], Lk 10[18], Mt 13[39] 5[37], as proof for the statement: πολλάκις οἶδα τὸν διδάσκαλόν μοι εἰπόντα εἶναι τὸν πονηρόν = τινὰ κακίας ἡγεμόνα). Zahn and Wellhausen take it as neuter, as in 5[37].

(*i*) That the Doxology formed no original part of the Lord's Prayer needs no longer to be proved, in spite of Dean Burgon. The very discovery of the oldest witness outside of the NT, the *Didache*, where it occurs, corroborates the view that it originated in liturgical use. Its peculiar form there does not agree with any of the forms known to occur in the authorities for the text of Matthew (see *The NT in the Apostolic Fathers*, by a Committee of the Oxford Society of Historical Theology, 1905, p. 28 f.). The statement of WH on the Doxology in the *Apost. Const.* must be supplemented as above from the new edition of Funk. See also art. DOXOLOGY in vol. i. p. 492.

6. The Lord's Prayer as a whole.—True prayer, says Wellhausen, is a creation of the Jews, and so the Lord's Prayer follows Jewish examples, though it is not a mere composition 'ex formulis Hebræorum.' On the latter exaggeration, put forward by Grotius, Wetstein, and others, and strongly maintained by modern Jewish writers, see *The Lord's Prayer no Adaptation of existing Jewish Petitions*, by the Rev. M. Margoliouth (London, Bagster, 1876). The *Ḳaddish*, which is justly quoted for comparison, does not begin with 'Abba,' but it, too, has as first petition, 'Hallowed be thy name,' with the addition, however, 'in the world to come.' The national, eschatological, or Messianic element which goes through the *Ḳaddish* and the *SE* from beginning to end is remarkably thrown into the background in the Lord's Prayer. A petition like 'Give us this day our daily bread' would be impossible in the *Ḳaddish*, though a similar petition is not wanting in *SE*.

It is, however, wrong to deny completely the eschatological character of the Lord's Prayer; see esp. the Com. of Th. Zahn, who insists on the force of the aorists ἁγιασθήτω, ἐλθάτω, γενηθήτω. Even the first petition looks forward to the time when the name of God, which in this world is so much blasphemed, especially among the heathen, through the sins of Israel (Ro 2[24]), shall be glorified, when He brings about the inward purification and outward restoration of His people, separating the godless out of their midst. Zahn declares it erroneous to believe that the Lord's Prayer had a specifically Christian character. A Jew knowing nothing of Christ, and having no wish to have anything to do with Him, was able and is still able to-day to pray it. The saying of Mt 5[17], that He 'came to fulfil,' is true also of the Lord's Prayer.

That the first three petitions touch God and the rest refer to man is too clear a point to be missed.[*] The second half may perhaps be arranged under the heads of *present* (daily bread), *past* (debts of the past), *future* (temptation and deliverance); but a reference to the last trial (Mt 24[22]), the hour of temptation (Rev 3[10]) and deliverance from it, does not seem to be implied in the words.

'Thy kingdom come' is again the second petition in the *Ḳaddish*.

Instead of the third petition, which Wellhausen calls hard to understand, we have in the *Ḳaddish*,

[*] It is, however, wrong to accentuate the word 'thy'; only codex D has in Lk. the emphatic order of words, σου ἡ βασιλεια.

'Your petition be done.' Whether it was under the influence of the fact that it is missing in the true text of Luke or not, at all events it is remarkable that Luther, in his *Catechism*, gave to the third petition no contents of its own, but treated it as a mere combination of the first and second ('Wenn Gott allen bösen Rat und Willen bricht und hindert, so uns den *Namen* Gottes nicht heiligen und sein *Reich* nicht kommen lassen wollen,' etc.).

Dogmatics and Ethics seem to be combined in every one of these three petitions : That we do not dishonour the name of the Heavenly Father (1) by mistrust, (2) by disobedience ; that His Kingdom may come (1) with its blessings, (2) with its tasks and duties ; that we (1) gladly accept all that is God's will concerning us, and (2) willingly do what He demands of us. To take the fourth petition as merely spiritual, like Marcion and afterwards Luther in his monkish days, is certainly wrong.

The sixth petition reminds us much more of the temptation of Jesus Himself at the beginning and end of His work, in the wilderness and in Gethsemane. The Jewish morning prayer contains the petition ליִדֵי נִסָּיוֹן . . . אֵל תְּבִיאֵנוּ 'Bring us not . . . into temptation'; but the age of this part is unknown. Jesus speaks, however, throughout in the second person, advising His disciples, not including Himself ; on the other hand, He could not have taught them such a prayer if He had not Himself lived in that atmosphere which the prayer breathes. When He bids them pray after this manner (οὕτως), He gives them an example from which they might learn with few words to say to God what the pious soul has to say to Him, and He did not prescribe the use which was made very early of this prayer, so that it became, to use Luther's expression, the greatest martyr.

7. Later history of the Lord's Prayer.—Only a few hints can be given here. It is very sad to observe how early a mechanical use of the Lord's Prayer set in. The same *Didache* which turned the warning of Mt 6[16] into the precept, 'Your fastings shall not be with the hypocrites, for they fast on Monday and Thursday, but you fast on Wednesday and Friday,' goes on to write : ' Nor do ye pray as the hypocrites, but as the Lord commanded in His Gospel, Our Father, etc. Thrice in the day do ye pray so.'

This was enforced by the *Apost. Const.* (iii. 18) : προκατασκευάζοντες ἑαυτοὺς ἀξίους τῆς υἱοθεσίας τοῦ πατρός, lest Mal 1[6] and Is 52[5] find application to the Christians. Tertullian styled the Lord's Prayer *breviarium totius evangelii*, and pronounced the judgment : ' Oratio hæc quantum substringitur verbis, tantum diffunditur sensibus.' Cyprian called it *cœlestis doctrinæ compendium* ; Origen wrote on it the treatise *de Oratione* (vol. ii. in the Berlin edition). On its use in the Liturgy, Brightman (p. 58) says : ' It occurs in all liturgies except *Apost. Const.* as the conclusion of the central action and summing up of the great prayer (533–534), and the transition to the communion, with a proem and a conclusion (*Embolismos*) ; it is also otherwise used.' For instance, in the liturgy of the Nestorians it is three times repeated.

Of mediæval explanations, the *Glossa ordinaria* draws a rather artificial parallel between the seven petitions of the Lord's Prayer and the seven gifts of the Holy Ghost (Is 11[12]) and the seven Beatitudes. The Com. of St. Thomas Aquinas has been translated from the Latin by Edw. Male (1893). Of special interest is the block-book of Henricus ex Pomerio (Henri van den Bœgaarde, 1382–1441), *Explanatio figuralis super Pater noster.*

See on it Alvin in *Bulletin de l'Académie R. de Belgique*, 2 Ser. vol. xvii. 674–94 ; *Monuments iconogr. et typogr. de la Bibliothèque R. de Belgique* ; and P. Weizsäcker in *Christliches*

Kunstblatt, 42 (1900), Nos. 4, 5. It is characterized by joining *in cœlis* with the first petition,* and a thoroughgoing tripartition ('in *cœlo tres* sanctorum affectiones ; in *purgatorio tres* animarum afflictiones ; in *sæculo tres* virorum defectiones ; *tres* panes in via necessarios (naturæ, gratiæ, gloriæ) ; *triplex* debitum (commissionis, omissionis, remissionis) ; *triplex* tentatio ; damnandorum *triplex* malum ; salvandorum *triplex* bonum. The illustrations remind one of the task which has yet to be executed, of writing a monograph on the artistic illustrations to the Lord's Prayer.

LITERATURE.—The literature on the Lord's Prayer is immense. Strangely enough, an art. 'Lord's Day' is found in Smith, but not one on 'Lord's Prayer.' Under 'Paternoster,' Murray mentions that the first example of this term in English is one from about 1000. Of Queen Mary the saying is quoted that she 'got the crown by Our Father and held it by Pater noster.' The Latin designation was so frequently used, esp. in connexion with the rosary, that it was taken over into the language of architects, engineers, and anglers (see Murray). In German both its components in the form 'Patter' and 'Nuster' became expressions for collar-chains. As a measure of time, cf. a 'Paternoster cricket.'

Out of the literature on the Lord's Prayer, Th. Zahn in his *Com. on Matth.* (1903) selects : Tertull. *de Orat.* cc. 1–10 ; Cypr. *de Oratione Dominica* (Vienna ed. i. 267) ; Origen, περὶ εὐχῆς (Berlin ed. ii. 346) ; Gregory of Nyssa, Or. 2–5, *de Oratione* (Opp. ed. Paris, 1638, i. 723–761) ; Kamphausen, *Das Gebet des Herrn*, 1866 ; Chase (see above) ; E. v. d. Goltz, *Das Gebet in der ältesten Christenheit*, 1905, pp. 35–53 ; *EBi* 2816 ff. We may add Plummer in Hastings' *DB* iii., and the following list of writers which is arranged chronologically as far as possible : 1626, Alex. Huish ; 1798, N. B. Cadogan ; 1814, Isaac Mann ; 1826, Samuel Saunders ; 1832, J. Knight ; 1835, W. Howells ; 1846, Henry Alford ; 1849, H. Caunter ; 1852, Dan. Moore ; 1854, Thomas Hugo ; 1855, Charles Parsons Reichel ; 1858, Hope Robertson ; 1861, Navison Lorain, Rob. Hemley, W. H. Karlslake, F. D. Maurice ; 1863, Geo. Wagner ; 1864, W. Denton ; 1865, Jos. T. Parker ; 1866, Octavius Winslow ; 1869, Claude Bosanquet ; 1870, Ad. Saphir ; 1872, J. W. Lance, Edw. J. Robinson ; 1876, C. J. Vaughan (Dean of Llandaff) ; 1883, Newman Hall ; 1884, Charles Stanford ; 1885, Marcus Dods, W. S. Carter ; 1886, A. M. W. Christopher, Wash. Gladden ; 1889, Gilb. Karney ; 1890, H. N. Grimley, A. Hastings Ross ; 1892, Rob. Eyton ; 1893, Alb. Stolz ; 1894, Arth. C. A. Hall, F. W. Farrar ; 1895, G. Milligan ; 1898, Dean E. M. Goulburn, Eliz. Wordsworth ; 1900, J. E. Roberts ; 1902, John Wakeford ; 1903, J. D. Jones.—Without date (alphabetically) : F. C. Blyth, J. J. Busfield, Rich. Glover, Thom. Griffith, Aug. W. Hare, J. Knight, B. Lambert, J. W. Lance, Rob. Leighton, Thom. Manton, Marcus Rainsford, Rigaut, Dean Stubbs, Caleb Webb, Will. R. Williams.

In *ExpT.*, besides the passages already quoted, may be compared : vi. [1894–95] 50, 140, 146, 190, xiii. [1902] 378, 431, xvi. [1905] 5, 10.

See also O. Dibelius, *Das Vaterunser : Umrisse zu einer Gesch. des Gebets in der alten und mittleren Kirche*, Giessen, 1903 (chiefly pp. 59–72—'Die Auffassung des Vaterunsers bei griechischen Schriftstellern' ; cf. Ed. v. d. Goltz in *Theol. Litztg.* 1904, No. 2) ; C. F. Georg Heinrici, *Beiträge zur Gesch. und Erklärung des NT*, iii. (Leipzig, 1905, pp. 65–68 [Heinrici is inclined to agree with Harnack as to the petition, 'Thy holy spirit come upon us,' collects parallels from the OT, questions direct relation to *SE*, and republishes (p. 109 ff.) the explanation of the Lord's Prayer ascribed to Petrus of Laodicea (published by Mai, *Bibl. Patrum*, vi. 543, Migne, *Patr. Gr.* 86[2], p. 3321)] ; together with Fed. Morelli, *Interpretis reg.*, *Notæ ad orationem dominicam*. Petrus explains : ἐπιούσιον ἢ τὸν συνιστῶντα τὸ σῶμα ἡμῶν, τουτέστι τὸν ἐφήμερον, εἴτε τὸν ἐπόντα, τὸν μέλλοντα. πονηροῦ Petrus understands of the διάβολος : κατ' ἐξοχὴν δὲ οὗτος καλεῖται διὰ τὴν ὑπερβολὴν τῆς κακίας.

On the Lord's Prayer on a papyrus of the 6th cent., as amulet, brought to Europe by Willken, but destroyed by fire in Hamburg, see *Egyp. Explor. Rep.* 1902, p. 42, 1903, p. 12 ; *Æg. Urkunden aus Berlin*, iii. No. 954 ; on the clay tablet, from Megara, containing the Lord's Prayer, see *ZNTW* ii. 228, 357.

EB. NESTLE.

LORD'S PRAYER (II.).—This name for the prayer which Jesus taught His disciples (Mt 6[9-13], Lk 11[2-4]), though used so generally by Christians, does not occur in the NT, and objection to it has sometimes been offered. It might suggest that the prayer was one which Jesus Himself employed, while not only is there no evidence of His having done so, but the petition for forgiveness is a sufficient assurance that He cannot have made it His own. 'When ye pray,' He said to His disciples, 'pray thus'; but His own manner of praying would be different—how different we may judge from the recollections preserved in the Fourth Gospel of one of His prayers (Jn 17). And so it has sometimes been suggested that we should speak not of 'The Lord's Prayer,' but of 'The

---

* O. Dibelius, *Das Vaterunser* (1903, p. 165 ff.), knows, for this construction, only Theodoricus of Paderborn, *Com. in Or. Dom.* M. 147, 333 f.

Disciples' Prayer,' or that we should content ourselves with designating it by its first two words, calling it the 'Our Father,' just as German Protestants call it the 'Vaterunser' and Roman Catholics the 'Paternoster.' But apart from the consecration of long and hallowed use, the name is appropriate as giving expression to the fact that the prayer comes to us from the very lips of our Lord. In this sense it is the Lord's Prayer. When we use it, we are approaching God with no words of our own, but in the very words which our Master has taught us.

1. Occasion.—Of the two accounts, in Mt. and Lk. respectively, of the occasion when Christ gave the prayer, it is generally agreed that if we must choose between them, Lk.'s is to be preferred as the more historical. It may be that the author of the First Gospel, after recording the Lord's injunctions with regard to the spirit and manner of prayer (Mt 6^{5-8}), thought this a suitable opportunity to set down the prayer-form which was really given at a different time. And yet there seems no positive reason why we should set aside Mt.'s statement as to the connexion at least in which the prayer was spoken. If Jesus gave a form of prayer at all, and meant it to be used as He gave it, it seems likely that He would repeat it, more especially when dealing with different sets of hearers. And if it was natural that He should impart it when one of His disciples, not necessarily one of the Twelve, asked to be taught to pray, it was also natural that, when He had just been warning His disciples against hypocrisy in prayer and the vain repetitions of the Gentiles, He should instruct them to pray after the brief, simple, and filial manner of this model of approach to God.

2. Structure.—This is exceedingly simple. Apart from the Doxology, which occurs only in Mt., and even there forms no part of the original, but is a later insertion due to liturgical usage, we have only an invocation and a series of six petitions. Since Augustine, the number of the petitions has commonly been reckoned at seven, the last clause in Mt.'s version being regarded as two separate requests. But the view that now commends itself to most scholars is that the two members of the sentence are to be taken as one and the same petition negatively and positively expressed. This view is confirmed by the fact that in the critical text of Lk. (see RV) the petition runs simply, 'Bring us not into temptation,' and it is further borne out by the RV rendering (almost certainly correct) of Mt.'s τοῦ πονηροῦ by 'the evil one' instead of 'evil.' The petition is that we may not be brought into temptation, but may be delivered from the Tempter; and these are two aspects of the selfsame request.

Looking now at the six petitions, we observe at once that the first three have a Godward, the second three a manward reference. Because of this the prayer has often been compared to the Decalogue with its summation of human duty first to God and then to man (cf. Mt 22^{40}, Mk 12^{31}). But beneath this resemblance there lies a great difference between the Ten Words and the Lord's Prayer, the familiar difference between law and grace, between the Old Testament and the New. For while in the one case our debt to God and to man is laid upon us from above as a commandment that must be obeyed, in the other we look up to God, crying like Augustine, 'Da quod jubes, et jube quod vis' (*Conf.* x. 60).

When we examine the prayer more closely, a beautiful continuity and symmetry of thought becomes apparent. In the invocation God is addressed by His new name of 'Father'; and it is with a petition for the hallowing of this name that the prayer proper begins. If we take the three petitions of the first group, God appears to be addressed: (1) as the Father whose name must be hallowed, (2) as the King whose Kingdom is to come, (3) as the Lord of heaven and earth whose will must be fulfilled. And when we pass to the three petitions of the second group, the same threefold view of God may be traced, coming, too, in the same order, so that the successive clauses of this group correspond respectively to those of the first. For the prayer for bread naturally suggests the request of the child to the Father, the prayer for forgiveness the petition of the subject to the King, and the prayer for deliverance from the Tempter the cry of one who feels in the presence of the world's evil his utter dependence upon the strong and holy will of his Master and Lord.

3. Contents.—Without entering here into the questions raised by the twofold text (see preceding art.), we shall for convenience follow Mt.'s version as the one which has passed into general use in the Christian Church.

(*a*) *The Invocation*: 'Our Father which art in heaven.' These words mark a new epoch not only in the history of prayer, but in the history of revelation. In the OT, God is occasionally spoken of as the Father of the Jewish people (Dt 32^6, Is 63^{16} etc.), but individuals do not venture to address Him by this name (Ps 103^{13} is only a comparison). And though in some of the extra-canonical writings there appears a dawning consciousness of a personal relation to God as a Father (Wis 2^{16}, Sir $23^{1. \ 4}$ etc.), it was Jesus Christ who first turned the dim hope of pious hearts into the assured certainty of faith. 'Father' is the distinctive Christian name of God, the name which Christ taught us, and which, apart from Him, we have no proper right to use (cf. Jn 1^{12}, Gal 4^6). The Fatherhood here appealed to is not the general Fatherhood of Creatorship, but the special Fatherhood of grace. It is for those who are the children of God by Christian faith that this prayer is meant, those who turn to Him with filial hearts, prepared to say: 'Hallowed be thy name. Thy kingdom come. Thy will be done.'

But God is called not 'Father' only, but 'Our Father,' and thus the invocation acknowledges the brotherhood of man as well as the Fatherhood of God. There is a human brotherhood which rests on the Divine Creatorship (cf. Mal 2^{10}). But just as there is a special sonship, the sonship of believers, so there is a distinctive brotherhood, the brotherhood of saints; and it is this brotherhood that finds immediate expression in the invocation of the Lord's Prayer.

Our Father is 'in heaven.' The phrase speaks to us of His greatness and holiness, of the reverence we owe Him, of His power to bless. But it also reminds us that if we are the children of the heavenly Father, His home is the true home of our souls, and that, as always, so especially when we bow before His throne with our requests, we must set our mind on the things that are above.

(*b*) *First Petition*: 'Hallowed be thy name.' In the OT the 'name' of God is a constant expression for His revealed character (cf. Ps $9^{10} \ 20^7$, Pr 18^{10}). Without doubt it is in this sense that the word is used by Jesus. But His immediate reference here must be to that character of Fatherhood under which He had just presented God to His disciples. It is our Father in heaven whose name is to be hallowed. To hallow that name is to set great store by it, to exalt it and revere it and glory in it. To pray that it may be hallowed is to pray that God as revealed to us by Christ may be accepted and honoured by ourselves and others —that we may turn to Him as our Father with loving, trustful hearts, and give Him the honour that is due.

(c) *Second Petition* : ' Thy kingdom come.' The Kingdom of God was the hope of Israel before Christ's advent, and when He came it formed the constant and central theme of His teaching. When we examine the Synoptic Gospels to learn what His teaching upon the subject was, we find Him speaking of the Kingdom of God in two ways. (1) It was a present reality set up on earth (Mt 12[28], Mk 1[15], Lk 17[21]), gathering round His own person (Mt 13[41] 16[28] 25[31. 34] etc.), the coming of which meant its entrance (which is really His own entrance, Mt 8[10ff.] 11[28-30] etc.) into the individual heart (Lk 17[20. 21], Mt 18[3] ||, Jn 3[3]), its steady growth (Mk 4[26-32]), and its gradual spread like leaven through society (Mt 13[33] = Lk 13[20f.]). (2) But again it was a hope of the future, a Kingdom not realized as yet, but one day to be revealed in power by the Parousia of the Son of Man Himself (Mt 13[41f. 49f.] 22[13] 25[30]). And so, when we pray for the coming of God's Kingdom, we are praying that Christ the King may enter into our hearts, that He may take full possession of them, that the gospel of the Kingdom may spread throughout the world, and that its principles may work in human society with subduing power. But we are praying also for the hour of the final consummation when the Lord Himself shall appear in His glory, when the kingdom of this world shall become the Kingdom of our Lord and of His Christ, when out of that Kingdom there shall be cast all things that offend, and God shall be all in all.

(d) *Third Petition* : ' Thy will be done.' This may be described as the dominant note of the Lord's Prayer. The petitions that precede lead up to this, and those that follow must be brought into harmony with it. We frequently use these words as if they were nothing more than a prayer of submission and resignation in the day of sorrow, an echo of the Saviour's cry in the Garden of Gethsemane (Mt 26[39] ||). And no doubt this is part of their meaning, and one of the uses to which they may be applied. They are a cry to God to enable us to bear what He sees fit to send, and to make us meek and patient under His chastening hand. But while this is implied in the petition, it is not its first intention. The added words, ' as in heaven, so on earth,' should keep us right here, since from heaven all sorrow and sighing have fled away. This is the prayer of active rather than of passive obedience, an obedience like that of God's angels who excel in strength and do His commandments. Before we think of Jesus in the garden of shadows, we should think of Him as He sat by the well of Sychar and said to His disciples, ' My meat is to do the will of him that sent me, and to accomplish his work' (Jn 4[34]). When we pray this prayer we are asking that we and all men, being delivered from the spirit of wilfulness, may attain to a joyful alacrity like that of angels in doing the will of God.

(e) *Fourth Petition.*—' Give us this day our daily (ἐπιούσιον) bread.' We pass now from the Godward to the manward aspects of the prayer. The first petition of this second group shows that it is right and proper to pray for material as well as for spiritual blessings. The prayer is not to be spiritualized, with most of the Fathers, into a request for the Bread of Life ; it is literal bread, bread for bodily sustenance, that Jesus means us to ask for.

The one expository difficulty of this petition lies in the word ἐπιούσιος, which has been called ' the most untranslatable word in the NT.' It appears here (in both Mt. and Lk.) for the first time in Gr. literature, and within the NT occurs nowhere else. Of the three principal renderings—' daily ' (EV text), ' for the coming day ' (RVm), and ' needful ' (Amer. RVm, alternat.)—there is least to be said for the first, familiar as it is. It reproduces the Old Lat. *quotidianum*, but finds no support in etymology, and may be regarded perhaps as nothing more than a guess suggested by what the sense of the passage appeared to require. For the coming day ' is more likely from the etymological point

of view (ἐπιούσιος fr. ἡ ἐπιοῦσα [sc. ἡμέρα] = ' the coming day,' fr. ἐπιών, pres. part. of ἐπειμι [εἰμι, ' to go or come ']), but seems out of keeping with Christ's teaching elsewhere in the Sermon on the Mount (Mt 6[34]). If this rendering is accepted, Chase's view (' Lord's Prayer in Early Church,' *Texts and Studies*, Cambridge [1891], *in loc.*) is plausible, that the word was a liturgical insertion intended to adapt the prayer for use at evening service. In the morning the petition would run, according to its original form, ' Give us this day our bread,' while in the evening there would be substituted, ' Give us our bread for the coming day.' Cf. Lk.'s ' day by day,' which obviates any inappropriateness in asking at night for the bread of the day.

Perhaps, however, there is most to be said for the view that ἐπιούσιος is a word specially coined, after the analogy of the LXX περιούσιος (Ex 19[5], Dt 7[6] 14[2] 26[18], for Heb. סְגֻלָּה, EV ' peculiar.' It is evidently derived from περιουσία = wealth, abundance [περί and οὐσία]). ἐπιούσιος in contrast to περιούσιος would thus denote what is needful or sufficient as distinguished from what is abundant or superfluous. If this is the proper rendering of the word, the petition would correspond almost exactly with the prayer of Agur, ' Feed me with the food that is needful for me ' (Pr 30[8] RV).*

(f) *Fifth Petition.* — ' Forgive us our debts (ὀφειλήματα), as we forgive our debtors.' Lk. has ' sins ' (ἁμαρτίας), while in the explanatory addition given by Mt. (vv.[14. 15]) ' trespasses ' (παραπτώματα) is used—the word which in the *Bk. of Com. Prayer* is substituted for ' debts ' in the Lord's Prayer itself. ' Debts ' is particularly suggestive. In the first place, it reminds us of the personal accountability to God into which we are brought by every act of sin. We may look at sin in many aspects— as the transgression of an ideal law, as a wrong done to our neighbour, as a harm inflicted upon ourselves. But most solemn of all is the thought that sin makes us debtors before God, debtors who have wasted our Lord's money and are called to render account. But further, ' debts ' reminds us of a class of sins we are most apt to forget—our sins of omission. It is when we ask ourselves, ' How much owest thou unto thy Lord?' that the full extent of our shortcoming begins to appear. Perhaps we have striven hard against wrongdoing, but what of the things we have left undone ? In Christ's great vision of the Judgment, ' Inasmuch as ye did it not ' is the preface to the sentence of condemnation (Mt 25[45]).

By teaching us to offer this petition our Lord teaches that God is ready to forgive all our debts. But a condition is laid down. Those who pray for forgiveness must be ready to forgive. On this Jesus placed great emphasis, so great that He does for the fifth petition what He does for no other, adding at the end of the prayer (vv.[14. 15]) a sentence of explanation and enforcement, in which He makes it perfectly clear that if we will not forgive those who have trespassed against us, neither will our Father in heaven forgive our trespasses.†

(g) *Sixth Petition.*—' Bring us not into temptation, but deliver us from the evil one.' This petition follows naturally after the fifth, for the recollection of past falls makes us conscious of weakness and fearful of future possibilities. But is it not an impracticable petition ? How can we hope to escape from being tempted ? The world and the flesh and the devil are ever with us, and still ' in the midst of the garden ' ; just where all life's daily cross-paths meet, the tree of temptation grows and the Tempter himself lies waiting. And is it not also a mistaken petition ? Is not temptation a means of grace, an opportunity of ' winning our souls ' ? Does not St. James write, ' My brethren, count it all joy when ye fall into divers temptations ' ? (Ja 1[2]). Yes, but there is another side to

* In support of this interpretation see A. N. Jannaris in *Contemp. Rev.*, Oct. 1894 ; *ExpT* vi. [1894] p. 51. Cf. also the preceding article.

† If the view is taken that vv.[14. 15] have been imported here by the Evangelist from another connexion such as 18[35] (so Meyer-Weiss and Bruce ; cf. Holtzmann in *Hand-Com.*), the words testify at all events to the fact that Jesus was accustomed to lay stress on the relation between human and Divine forgiveness ; see Mk 11[25. 26], Lk 6[37], and esp. the parable of the Unmerciful Servant, Mt 18[23-35].

the question. Temptation is a means of grace, but it may prove to be an occasion of stumbling and even of utter destruction. Blessed is the man that endureth it (Ja 1[12]) ; but what of him who is drawn away by his own lusts and enticed, and so falls into the snare of the devil? By putting this petition into our lips Jesus reminds us that the hour of temptation is always a dangerous hour. He hangs out a red lamp of warning on the dark and crooked road along which we have to pass, and summons us to ' watch and pray ' (cf. Mt 26[41]=Mk 14[38]).

And yet temptations must come, we cannot hope to escape meeting them, and this petition, like every other in the Lord's Prayer, is subject to the rule of the guiding petition of all, 'Thy will be done.' But 'Deliver us from the evil one' is a prayer that Satan may not gain the victory over our souls. That ' the evil one ' is the right rendering of τοῦ πονηροῦ is now commonly accepted by scholars on grounds of exegesis. It is in keeping, too, with our Lord's teaching about the presence and influence in the world of a hostile and malevolent will, an ' enemy ' of God's Kingdom and its King (cf. Mt 13[25.39]). From him we may well pray to be delivered. Jesus Himself prayed for Simon that in the hour of Satan's sifting his faith might not fail (Lk 22[31f.]). And we know that faith need never fail. God will not suffer us to be tempted above that we are able (1 Co 10[13]), and this petition is an appeal to Him for strength in the evil day to endure and to overcome.

4. Uses.—(1) This is a *breviary* of Christian prayer, in which all Christian petitions are summarily comprehended. As the commandments of the moral law are all gathered up in the two tables of duty to God and to man, so the petitions of the gospel are all represented in the two divisions of this little prayer. Apart from requests of a personal and particular kind, everything that the universal Christian heart need ask for is explicitly stated or implicitly enfolded here, whether things on earth or things in heaven, things human or Divine, things of the body or the spirit, things of the life that now is or of that which is to come.

(2) It is a *model* or *directory* of prayer. According to Mt.'s account, Jesus, when He gave it, had just been warning His disciples against the formalisms of hypocrites and the vain repetitions which the Gentiles use (vv.[5-8]), and it was in contrast with these that He said, ' *After this manner pray ye.*' Looking at the manner of the prayer we are struck by its direct sincerity, its brevity, its simplicity, its calmness and quietness of spirit, its entire submission to the will of God. It teaches us that we are not heard for our much speaking, that long and elaborate prayers are unnecessary, that a simple request like that of a child to a father is enough. It teaches also the right relation and proportion in prayer between what belongs to God and what concerns ourselves. The earthly has its claims, but the heavenly comes before it ; and all requests must be made in subordination to the Divine will.

(3) It is a *form* of prayer. The prayers which John the Baptist taught his disciples (Lk 11[1]) must have been forms ; and when a disciple of Jesus, reminding Him of John's custom, said, ' Lord teach us to pray,' it was doubtless a prayer-form for which he asked. And Jesus justified the request by replying, ' When ye pray, *say*, Our Father,' etc. Not that He wished His disciples to restrict themselves to this form or to repeat it incessantly. It is significant that, apart from these two passages in Mt. and Lk., we do not hear of the Lord's Prayer in the NT again. The recorded prayers of the Apostolic Church bear no resemblance to it. When God sent forth the Spirit of His Son into men's hearts, they prayed with freedom

as the Spirit gave them utterance. And yet from the first this must have been, and must ever continue to be, a specially consecrated form of prayer, which no one can sincerely use without being conscious that, in presenting his petitions in the very words that Christ has given, he is asking according to the will of God (cf. 1 Jn 5[14]).

(4) It is a prayer especially for *social* use. There are prayers which can be offered only in secret, and Jesus had already spoken of these. ' *Thou*, when thou prayest, enter into thy closet,' He said (v.[6]). But this was a prayer for the whole Christian society : ' After this manner pray *ye*,' ' When *ye* pray, say.' The invocation is addressed to ' *our* Father,' the requests are on behalf of others as well as ourselves : ' give *us*,' ' forgive *us*,' ' bring *us* not,' ' deliver *us*.' And so this prayer, which is an appeal to the Fatherhood of God, is also a constant reminder of our human and especially of our Christian brotherhood. It teaches us to join our desires with those of the universal Church as we pray for the coming of the Kingdom. It teaches us when we ask for bread, or forgiveness, or guidance and deliverance, to bear the needs of others along with our own on our hearts before God, and to remember that the unspeakable privilege of intercession is of the very essence of Christian prayer.

LITERATURE.—See preceding article.

J. C. LAMBERT.

LORD'S SUPPER.—(I.)

Introductory.—The Lord's Supper has been for centuries, and is to-day, a theological storm-centre; though the blasts have shifted, recent critical scholarship having occasioned a new incidence of forces. Former controversies raged round the meaning of the institution. At present the discussion is even more vital, for it is a matter not of interpretation only, but of the trustworthiness of the sources. The Gospels as they now stand are said to owe so much to the thought and practice of the growing Church, that it is necessary to read between the lines in order to detect the simple form of the Eucharist on the day of its first celebration, when ' it signified rather the abrogation of the old worship and the near approach of the Kingdom than the institution of a new worship.' It is denied that Jesus, with His views as to the speedy consummation of His Kingdom, could have instituted the Supper as a perpetual memorial of His death ; and the connexion between the Last Supper and the Passover in the Gospels is regarded as a later overlying deposit, which can be easily detached from the primitive stratum. To take an example, Jesus is supposed to have uttered the words of the Supper recorded in the Gospels on the impulse of the moment. Feeling Himself already victor over death and the world, He wishes to inspire His disciples with His own conviction, and by an act of vivid imagination conceives Himself as already dispensing the blessings of the completed Kingdom, their simple farewell meal having been transformed into the great Messianic banquet of the future, which commonly served as a figure for the joys of Messiah's sovereignty. Professor Gardner is even more drastic in his treatment of the Gospel tradition, eliminating all evidence except that of St. Paul, who, he thinks, was the real originator of the rite, having 'turned a pagan ceremony to Christian use' in a moment of ecstasy under the influence of what he had seen of the Greek mysteries in Corinth. But the great majority of impartial scholars who have discussed the question do not adopt such a highly critical attitude towards the narratives of the institution of the Supper, or reverse so completely the ordinarily accepted views as to its origin and purpose. No sufficient treatment of the Lord's Supper can pass in silence these problems which have been raised with great learning and acuteness, but they must be discussed in relation to the method of Jesus the Messiah, who brings Israel to its fulfilment.

1. The Sacramental in Hebrew worship.—The term 'sacrament' denotes an outward and visible sign of an invisible spiritual reality. By means of symbol, which is metaphor transformed into action or concreteness, truth is conveyed to the participants in a sacrament much more readily than by the bare word. Language conveys truth, but symbol does what language cannot compass. The worship of the OT was full of the symbolic, for it is almost certain that the cultus was in its essence no arbitrary prescription of meaningless forms. The sacrificial system was held to be a means of grace, of Divine appointment, whereby the worshipper could approach Jehovah. It must have been educative, so that the obedient and leal-hearted Israelite became in the actual observance more receptive of moral and spiritual truth. In that sense the sacrificial system of Israel was truly sacramental. But whether the average Hebrew recognized the sacramental character is doubtful, for the great prophets constantly warn the people that the mere ritual performance of sacrifice is inefficacious. Some, especially the earlier prophets, often seem to disparage offerings entirely, as though the only worship with which Jehovah is well pleased is the spiritual service of moral character and a contrite heart. And yet the prophets employ symbolic action again and again in the service of an ideal spirituality, so that in itself symbol has been a widespread and perfectly legitimate means of grace. The transcendental element in worship, however brightly or faintly the contemporary life of Israel may have been illumined by the spiritual truth of the prophets, had all but vanished from the official Judaism of our Lord's day. There was no open vision. No prophet or seer was abroad in the dull day of rationalism. Heroic faith had been displaced by a shrewd but commonplace conduct. The Law had come in alongside Temple service, and ritual was observed as an ordinance. The average Jew, having become a deist, could not feel sky, earth, and sea palpitate with the Divine Spirit, and so was impervious to sacramental conceptions (W. P. Paterson, art. 'Sacrifice' in Hastings' *DB* iv. 341 ; Bousset, *Rel. des Judenthums*, pp. 182–184). It was to the 'poor of the land' who cherished the prophetic ideal that the parabolic, the sacramental, the symbolical in the teaching of Jesus would appeal.

2. The Method and Teaching of Jesus.—The Gospel narratives represent the Supper as a solemn final act in the life of the Messiah. But the Messiah of their delineation is a Person of startling originality. He penetrates through the crust of unimaginative moralism to the living prophetic stream which in His day found its way to the surface only in tiny rivulets. On His own authority He claims, while purifying and enlarging the hopes of prophecy, to fulfil all that was truest in the religion of Israel, having accepted in His Temptation the Divine ideal of a Kingdom unalloyed by any earthly aspirations. He discovers and applies to Himself the title 'Son of Man,' and in virtue of His position inaugurates changes in religion which constitute a breach with the past, for His doctrine concerning worship, foreshadowed by the prophets, antiquates bloody sacrifices and opaque ritual. To say that Jesus could not have instituted the sacraments of Baptism and the Lord's Supper, because He looked for a speedy realization of the Kingdom, is to deny that He had the complete vision of the destiny of the Servant of the Lord whose function is assumed by the Son of Man, whereas it seems certain that He foretold a spiritual inheritance among the Gentiles in return for His faithful service even unto death (Is 42$^{1\text{ff.}}$ 52$^{13\text{ff.}}$ 62$^{1\text{ff.}}$, Mk 1^{11}, Lk 4$^{16-21}$, Mt 12^{18}, Mk 10^{45}). Another unique prophetic ideal was the consummation of the Kingdom in the Day of the Lord. In respect to this also we must assume that Jesus was a creator of spiritual truth, for the consistency of the Synoptic portraiture of Jesus, and the purity of His own views as to His mission, demand that our interpretation of His outlook into the future of the Kingdom should not be limited by the current ideas of Jewish apocalypses, or by the literal symbolism of OT prophecy.

We infer from the Gospels, (1) that before the close of His ministry in Galilee Jesus had looked forward to His death as the goal of His service (Mk 8^{31}) ; (2) that this death was to result in the redemption of the new Israel to which the prerogatives of the old would be transferred (Mk 10^{45} 12$^{1-12}$) ; (3) that He expected an earthly future for His Kingdom outlasting the earthly Jerusalem, and involving its establishment among the Gentiles (Mk 4$^{30-32}$ 12$^{1-12}$ 13$^{10.\ 14\text{ff.}}$, Lk 13$^{32-35}$ 21$^{20-24}$). No less evident, however, was the inability of the disciples to understand that the road of service even unto death was the road to the crowning glory of the Kingdom. For Him thus steadily to set His face towards Jerusalem, was, they thought, a sheer and fatal fascination (Mk 10$^{32-34}$, Lk 18$^{31\text{ff.}}$).

Nor is the institution of the sacrament of the Supper inconsistent with the method of Jesus. The day for symbolism was not past, provided the symbolism was adequate ; and this Supreme Teacher surpasses all others in the use of parable and symbol. Every meal with His disciples becomes sacramental through its prayer of thanksgiving, a symbol of the spiritual truth that in Him God was giving to the world the food that was real indeed (Jn 6$^{51-58}$). Nor would such a procedure be altogether strange to men who would remember that in the OT the common meal was the symbol of a completed covenant (Gen 26^{30} 31^{54}, Ex 24^{11}, 2 S 3^{20} ; see König, 'Symbols, Symbolical Actions' in Hastings' *DB*, Ext. Vol., 171^{b}). In order to understand the significance of this institution, it must be borne in mind that the disciples had committed all their fortunes to Jesus. Their faith had been for them a heroic venture, and the death of the Messiah meant little less than His desertion of them. That night, death like a dark shadow hovering over them was forcing their loved one within its portal. They could not see that a glorious light was shining on His back, that He was in reality an angel of blessing. They needed a pledge of love significant of the future and yet full of tender memories. This the Lord's Supper becomes to them. That it was a mark of supreme wisdom thus to perpetuate the significance of His death for the completion of

His Kingdom in concrete symbolism, is evident from their misinterpretation of their Lord's promise as to the future of His Kingdom on earth and His own return ; but we are led to expect only such words and symbolic action as would illuminate the spiritual idea of the Kingdom ; not precepts and ritual ordinance for its external organization.

3. Passover Eve.—Jesus came into Jerusalem on the morning of the first day of the week, and for several days escaped the plots of His enemies. But Judas entered into a conspiracy with the chief priests apparently two days before 'the Passover and the feast of unleavened bread' (Mk 14[1. 10. 11]). Ignorant of this accomplished treachery, the other disciples, observing that Jesus has as yet made no arrangement for the celebration of the feast, say unto Him 'on the first day of unleavened bread, when they sacrificed the Passover, Where wilt thou that we go and make ready that thou mayest eat the Passover?' (14[12]). Now we are embarked upon a sea of difficulties. The Gospels separate very distinctly — the Synoptics on the one side, the Fourth on the other. Did Jesus eat the regular Passover with His disciples, or did He not? At first sight the Synoptic Gospels seem to say that He did. But, according to John, Jesus died on the afternoon when the Passover lamb was slain (Jn 13[1. 29] 18[28]).

(a) *The Synoptic Gospels.*—(α) Evidence that the last meal was eaten at the conclusion of the regular Passover meal is offered by Mk 14[12. 14], Mt 26[17-19], Lk 22[7. 8. 11. 15. 16], the last verses laying especial stress upon the desire of Jesus to eat this Passover with His disciples. Many features of the meal also suggest the Passover,—the family group with Jesus presiding, the prayers of thanksgiving, the cups (Lk 22[17. 20]), the breaking of the bread, the solemn demeanour, the exposition, the conclusion with a hymn.

(β) But the Synoptics contain hints that the Supper was not a regular Passover meal. It is stated in Mk 14[1. 2], that two days before the feast the priests resolved to capture Jesus, and to execute Him before any sympathizers among the populace could interfere ; and, since nothing is said to the contrary, it is reasonable to conclude that the purpose was carried out. It would appear that, according to contemporary Jewish practice, Passover, the 14th Nisan, was spoken of as the beginning of the feast *Mazzoth*, though originally Unleavened Bread began on 15th Nisan (Wellhausen, *Evangelium Marci*, 115 ; Schürer, *ThLZ*, 1st April 1893, col. 182 ; as against Chwolson in *Das letzte Passamahl*). But only work necessary for preparing food was permitted from sunset on the 14th to sunset on the 21st, and it would have been illegal or contrary to custom to arrest Jesus that night with swords and staves, to hold a meeting of the Sanhedrin, to release a prisoner, to purchase grave-clothes, and to take the dead body down from the cross, if He ate the regular Passover meal on Thursday evening Nisan 14. Further, there is no mention in the Synoptic narrative of their eating the lamb (*Jewish Encyc.* x. art. 'Passover'). Jesus died on a Friday, so that we may probably assume from Mk 14[1. 2] that Passover (Nisan 14) fell on the Sabbath, which began on Friday at sunset. Nevertheless the preponderating impression of the Synoptic Gospels is certainly in favour of this meal having been related in some way to the Passover feast. It is distinctly so stated, and it is difficult to suppose that there were not good grounds in the primary sources for such united testimony.

(b) *The Fourth Gospel.*—From Jn 18[28] we must infer that Jesus died on the afternoon before Passover—'between the two evenings' (Dt 16[6]). This inference is so strongly reinforced by Jn 13[1. 29], that

Dr. Hort, with whom Dr. Sanday and Mr. C. H. Turner agree, believes that the Fourth Evangelist is silently correcting a false impression left by the Synoptists (*Expos.* iv. v. [1892] p. 182 ; Hastings' *DB* i. 411[a]. On the other side see Edersheim, *Life and Times of Jesus the Messiah*, Bk. v. ch. x.). St. John neither here nor elsewhere refers directly to the institution of the Supper, but in 6[53-59] his conception of the truth that underlies the Sacrament is set forth in the conversation of Jesus. He states that the miracle of the feeding of the 5000 took place at Passover time (6[4], so true reading), probably seeing in it a figure of the Christian Passover. Notwithstanding, therefore, his fixing of the day of our Lord's death before the regular Passover, there is good ground for holding that he implicitly relates the Last Supper to the Passover (Westcott, *St. John*, pp. 96, 113 ; Holtzmann, *NT Theol.* ii. 503 ; Wendt, *St. John's Gospel*, 137–139). See, further, artt. DATES, vol. i. p. 413 ff., LAST SUPPER, PASSOVER (II.).

(c) *The Apostle Paul.*—Though 1 Co 5[7. 8] is often interpreted so as to make St. Paul agree with the Fourth Evangelist, that Jesus died when the lambs for the feast were slain, it is very doubtful whether this idea was in his mind. He is comparing the Christian life with the old Passover upon which the Feast of Unleavened Bread followed (Ex 12[19] 13[7]). So now, since the Christian Passover has begun through the sacrifice of Christ, all impurity must be removed from their lives. Perhaps 1 Co 10[1. 2. 6. 15. 16] have the imagery of the Passover ; 'the cup of blessing' (v.[16]) was one of the most sacred elements of the Paschal meal (Edersheim, *op. cit.* ii. 510 f. ; but for opposite view, see Holtzmann, *op. cit.* ii. 184 f.).

The figure of 1 Co 5[7. 8] may refer to an actual celebration of the Christian Passover in the Corinthian Church, for we know that in the middle of the 2nd cent. Easter was the most important annual festival of the Catholic Church, and there is no evidence of its having been introduced after the Apostolic age. The great Quartodeciman controversy (c. 165 A.D.) was not concerned with doctrinal differences, but with the date on which the universal Christian feast was to be held—whether the Jewish date, Nisan 14, or the Sunday of Easter week. No inference can be drawn from it as to the connexion between the Eucharist and the Passover, inasmuch as the Christian Passover was not a memorial of the Passover only, but of redemption in which Christ's death and resurrection both were the essential factors. The Supper would be at most one element in the celebration, and possibly had little direct Paschal significance. The Church of the last half of the 2nd cent. assumed that there was agreement among the four Evangelists with regard to the time of Christ's death, and apparently accepted the Synoptic chronology, Origen and Eusebius making definite attempts to bring Jn. into conformity with the other Gospels. Zahn, however, holds that the Quartodecimans interpreted the latter in accordance with the former (*Gesch. NT Kan.* i. 1. 191). For a fuller discussion, with older literature, see Zahn, *op. cit.* i. 1. 180–192 ; J. Drummond, *Character and Authorship of Fourth Gospel*, 444–513 ; Stanton, *The Gospels as Historical Documents*, 173–197 ; Preuschen in *PRE*[3] xiv. 725–734 takes a different view.

The easiest explanation of this conflicting evidence is that Jesus did not eat the regular Passover feast with His disciples, but that He did eat a meal by anticipation on Nisan 13, the night before the regular Jewish celebration, which was in some sort a keeping of the Passover by this little group (but see Robinson, art. 'Eucharist' in *Encyc. Bibl.* i. § 3). The words of Jesus in Lk 22[15. 16] become intelligible when we remember what the Passover meant, and also His method in promulgating His Kingdom. Passover was the greatest national feast, gathering into itself whatever was most sacred in the religious life of Israel. It was the memorial of national redemption. Through its families—each a part of the larger whole—Israel entered annually into renewed covenant relationship with Jehovah, who had graciously preserved and ransomed the people. It was a sacrificial feast allied with the *shelamim* or peace-offerings. The sprinkled blood denoted atoning efficacy (v. Orelli, 'Passah,' in *PRE*[3] xiv. ; art. ' Passover' in Hastings' *DB* iii. and in *Jewish Encyc.*). Now Israel is on the point of being transformed. A new redemption is to be completed. Jerusalem and the Temple, with its bloody sacrifices and ritual worship, are soon to disappear. But while the Messiah is abrogating the letter of the old, He fulfills its spirit. He is supplying new wine-skins for the new wine. Just as He has provided the new Israel with a new conception of worship (Mt 6[1-18], Jn 4[21-24]), a new standard of righteousness (Mt 5[17-48]), and a reinter-

pretation of the Sabbath (Mk 2[23-36] 3[1-5]), so now He transfigures, while yet He preserves the identity of, the central institution of Israel's national life. By 'a masterpiece of practical skill as a teacher' Jesus enshrines, in this symbolic action, for the spiritual representatives of the new Israel, the memory of its ransom through the death of Messiah, whereby a new covenant relationship with Jehovah is possible.

4. The Institution.—Mk 14[22-26], Mt 26[26-30], Lk 22[15-20], 1 Co 11[23-26] :

Mk	And as they were eating	He	took bread and when He had blessed
Mt	And as they were eating	Jesus	took bread and blessed
Lk	And	He	took bread and when He had given thanks
1 Co	In the night in which He was betrayed	the Lord Jesus	took bread and when He had given thanks
Mk	He brake it and gave to them	and said, Take ye	this is my body
Mt	And brake it and He gave to the disciples	and said, Take eat	this is my body
Lk	He brake it and gave to them	saying	this is my body which is given for you
1 Co	He brake it	and said	this is my body which is for you
Lk	This do in remembrance of me.		
1 Co	This do in remembrance of me.		
Mk	And He took a cup and when He had given thanks He gave to them and they all drank of it. And He said unto them		
Mt	And He took a cup and gave thanks and gave to them saying drink ye all of it		
Lk	And the cup		in like manner after supper saying
1 Co	And the cup		in like manner after supper
Mk	This is (covenant) my blood of the covenant		
Mt	For this is (covenant) my blood of the covenant		
Lk	This cup is the new covenant in my blood		
1 Co	This cup is the new covenant in my blood		
Mk	which is shed for many		
Mt	which is shed for many unto remission of sins		
Lk	which is shed for you		
1 Co	This do as often as ye drink it in remembrance of me		
Mk	Verily I say unto you I will no more	drink of the fruit of the vine	
Mt	But I say unto you I will not henceforth	drink of this fruit of the vine	
Lk (v. 18)	For I say unto you I will not from henceforth	drink of the fruit of the vine	
Mk	Until that day when I drink it new in	the Kingdom of God	
Mt	Until that day when I drink it new with you in my Father's Kingdom		
Lk	Until the Kingdom of God shall come		

1 Co adds : For as often as ye eat this bread and drink this cup ye proclaim the Lord's death till He come.

We read in Matthew and Mark that, during a meal, Jesus took bread and brake it. Possibly it was one of the unleavened cakes used at the Feast, though the foregoing discussion renders unnecessary any attempt to fix this action into the order of the regular Passover. The procedure was peculiarly solemn, with an added gravity, because for the first time, a few moments before, Jesus had announced that one of the little group was a traitor (Lk 22[21-23], which puts this after the narrative of the Supper, is probably a displacement). Ruin without, treachery within, the disintegration of the brotherhood may well have seemed to have already begun, and collapse was staring them in the face. Nothing but the serene assurance of Jesus could brace them against such disaster. Like a father presiding at a family meal, He rallies them, in full view of His own death, by such a thanksgiving as they had often heard from Him before (Mt 14[19] 15[36], Jn 6[11]). There is no suggestion here of exaltation or ecstasy. His demeanour is that of confidence, subdued by sorrow for His betrayal and the hatred of His enemies. The presumption from the order of Mk 14[18-21] and Jn 13[21-30] is against the traitor having remained throughout the Supper.

(*a*) *The common underlying Tradition.*—The action of Jesus in solemnly breaking bread and handing it to His disciples must mean that His body is likewise to be broken, destroyed by men ; but, when assimilated by His disciples, He in His complete Person will become their spiritual food. It is parabolic, or rather, it may be illustrated by the allegories of the Fourth Gospel, as *e.g.* Jn 15[1], where Jesus claims to be 'most really and yet not materially the true vine' (Westcott). Quite apart from the question of its historical value, the discourse of Jesus in Jn 6[47-59] may be used to illuminate this procedure, because the same truth is expressed in Jn. in words as in the Lord's Supper by words and symbol.

The second part of the Supper is another solemnly acted allegory. Old is passing over into new. At Sinai sprinkled blood had ratified a covenant (Ex 24[4-8]). Jeremiah, all but submerged in the flood which was carrying on its surface the fragments of the old system, sees like a rainbow of hope the new covenant which, with its promise of forgiveness of sins, was to be established on a perfect knowledge of God ; and later came the profound truth that this new covenant between God and man could be inaugurated only by the death of the Servant of the Lord, whose sufferings would bring salvation to the whole world (Is 42[6] 49[8] 52[13. 14. 15] 53[11. 12] ; see Kautzsch, 'Religion of Israel,' in Hastings' *DB*, Extra Vol. 708).

The new covenant is about to be ratified by Messiah's blood. The many are to be ransomed (Mk 10[45]), these representatives of the true Israel being but the first to appropriate the benefits of the new covenant. Parabolic or symbolic this meal was, but both parts do not convey the same truth. The first action is a vehicle for the truth that Jesus Himself will continue to be for His disciples their heavenly food unto eternal life ; the second that, in virtue of Messiah's death, salvation from sin is possible through the covenant grace of God. To attribute the conception of the second half of the institution, as it is recorded in Mk., to the influence of Pauline thought, is to do injustice to the fact that its roots are deeply imbedded in OT prophecy, although, like many other ideas, its flower first appears in the teaching of Jesus.

His closing words have a future outlook. Death will end in victory, and when the Day of the Lord shall usher in the Kingdom, He will again hold fellowship with His disciples at the eternal Messianic banquet. That Day began to come with power as the Spirit-filled Church received the Gentiles for her inheritance, and the eagles gathered upon the carcase of official Judaism.

(*b*) *Differences in detail.*—The records, as preserved in the TR, divide into two types—Mark-Matthew and Luke-Paul. In the shorter recension of Luke, to be referred to later, there is an independent narrative. We begin with the Markan tradition, reproduced mainly in Matthew, as the earliest source.

(i.) *Mark-Matthew.*—The words 'take (eat)' may perhaps be intended to emphasize the representative action of the disciples. As those who are to sit on twelve thrones, they are not eating a common meal but accepting this blessing for Israel. Some justification of this view may be found in the fact that in Luke and Paul the addition ' which is (given or shed) on your behalf' is qualified by the words ' do this in remembrance of me,' whereas in Mk.-Mt., which omit this injunction altogether, the words run ' which is shed for many,' as though the meal had a wider reach than an ordinary supper. The omission from Mk.-Mt. of the command to repeat the meal as a memorial is the most remarkable difference between the two sources for the Supper. Mt. differs from Mk. in minor points, the most important being the addition of the words ' unto remission of sins,' which may have been a current or ritual interpretation, but in any case merely render explicit the idea of the new covenant (Jer 31³¹).

(ii.) *Luke* 22¹⁵⁻²⁰.—The difficulties of the text are such that so far no final decision has been reached with regard to them, some scholars indeed thinking that the textual problem is involved in the Synoptic problem. The evidence is as follows: (1) The TR is supported by אABCL. (2) Old Latin b e (k defective) have the order 16. 19ᵃ. (καὶ λαβὼν ἄρτον . . . τὸ σῶμά μου) 17. 18, and omit 19ᵇ. 20. Old Syriac (Syr ˢⁱⁿ and Syr ᶜᵘʳ) agree in the main with old Latt., though with interpolations. Their order is 16. 19. 17. 18. 21. ' And he took bread and gave thanks for it and brake it and gave and said : This is my body which is for you (Syr ˢⁱⁿ + ' is given') : do this in remembrance of me. And (Syr ˢⁱⁿ ' after they had supped') he took a cup and gave thanks over it and said: Take this and share it among yourselves (Syr ˢⁱⁿ + ' this is my blood of the new covenant'). I say to you that from this time on I shall not drink of this growth of the vine (Syr ˢⁱⁿ ' fruit') until the kingdom of God comes.' The Pesh. omits 17. 18 ; Egyp. omits 16–18 ; Marcion omits 16. 18. 19ᵇ, and after 19ᵃ comes the cup, but there is only one. (3) D a ff² i 1 omit 19ᵇ and 20. Hort, with whom Nestle agrees, is strongly of opinion that vv.¹⁹ᵇ⁻²⁰ were not part of the original text of Luke. Weiss, Schürer, Zahn, and others also believe in a shorter text, but Zahn looks to the oldest versions rather than to D a, etc., for the proper order. Their testimony is uniform for the order of Mk.-Mt.-Paul (for 1 Co 10¹⁶ even with the *Didache* can hardly, in the face of 1 Co 11²⁴, be cited for primitive practice) and for only one cup. However, Mark and Paul seem to have influenced the oldest Syriac directly, in its additions ' this is my blood,' etc., and the command for repetition. If the longer text be accepted, as it is by many scholars, the mention of the two cups may be due to the recapitulatory propensity of Luke (Thayer), or the first cup may signify the close of the Old Covenant in the last Passover (16–18), while the second cup belongs to the New Covenant (19ᵃ. 20). In favour of the latter view it may be observed that ' a cup' occurs in v.¹⁷, but in v.²⁰ ' the cup,' as though well known in the Church (Holtzmann). There is, however, other evidence in this chapter of unsuitable order if not disarrangement, as *e.g.* vv.¹⁸·²¹⁻²³, where a change of position would fit the narrative better : and if Jn 13¹⁻³⁰ may be taken as a guide, it would seem that Lk 22²⁴⁻²⁷ should come before the institution of the Supper. Hence Hort's excision of vv.¹⁹ᵇ·²⁰ is as

yet the simplest solution of the difficulty. In that case Luke did not intend to give the detailed account of the institution of the Supper, but rather its meaning. Whatever the original order may have been, there can be no doubt that he desires to lay stress on the Paschal character of the meal. The old dispensation is closing. For the last time Jesus hands His disciples the Passover cup : in the coming Kingdom He will provide for them a heavenly vintage (cf. Jn 15¹). (See Hort, 'Notes on Select Readings,' p. 63 f. ; Nestle, *Textual Crit. of Gr. Test.* p. 276 f. ; Zahn. *Einl. in d. NT*, ii. 357 ff. ; Sanday, Hastings' *DB* ii. 636 ; Plummer, *St. Luke*, 496.)

(iii.) *Paul.*—1 Co 11²³⁻²⁶ is evidently drawn upon by the author of the longer account of the Supper in Luke. The Apostle gives unimpeachable authority for his view of the Supper, claiming that he had a revelation from the Lord, though it is highly probable that he derived it indirectly through the Apostles (ἀπό seems to involve a remote source ; see Schmiedel, *Hand-Com.* ii. 162). Of the variations from Mk.-Mt. the most important are the repetition of ' Do this in remembrance of me,' and the change of ' This is my blood of the covenant' into ' This cup is the new covenant in my blood ' : while the common Synoptic prophecy of Jesus that He will drink the new fruit of the vine in the Kingdom with His disciples, gives way to a Pauline interpretation of the forward aspect of the Supper —' ye proclaim the Lord's death till he come.'

In 1 Cor. the subject is introduced incidentally. There is no formal description of the first Supper, with full historical detail. The narrative is intended to correct abuses among light-hearted Greeks, who seem to have degraded the Supper to the level of their former heathen club-banquets (συσσίτια, ἔρανοι). They had few such sacred associations as the Jews, whose annual Passover was a valuable discipline in reverence for Jehovah their Redeemer. These Corinthians had poor ideas of the awful cost of their redemption, when they failed to recognize the meaning of this memorial of Christ's redeeming death, and by their selfish party-spirit profaned the Lord's Supper, instituted as it was at such a time as the night on which preparations for His betrayal were being matured (παρεδίδετο). The rite as described here is essentially the same as in the Gospels ; but in the Gospels we have the historical account of its creation ; while 1 Cor. describes an ideal celebration for the Christian brotherhood.

According to 1 Co 11²³⁻²⁶, the ruling idea of the Supper is the symbolical display of redemption through the death of our Lord, and the same conception, under the figure of the Christian Passover, is involved in 1 Co. 5⁷. Another truth also underlying 11²³⁻²⁶, but especially taught in 10¹⁶⁻²², is that all those who partake of the spiritual food and drink in this Sacrament are brought into fellowship with Christ Himself, and are thus united into one body (vv.³· ⁴· ¹⁶· ¹⁷).

(iv.) *The Fourth Gospel.*—Though the institution of the Supper is not found in Jn., the final discourses of Jesus (13–17) are coloured with the thought of it and of the love-feast, like brilliant clouds irradiated by the sun which they hide. It is in a measure true to say that, while the Synoptists are concerned with the Supper, St. John lingers upon the memory of the love-feast, for the conversations have the one great theme fittingly introduced by the deed of humility on the part of Him who having loved His own, loved them unto the end. He had exhibited the new law of love of which His death would be the crowning expression, and He becomes at once their example and their Sanctifier (see esp. ch. 17). The Evangelist, as we have seen, seems to correct the Synoptists as to the day of Christ's death, but he relates the discourse of ch. 6 to the Passover, and in the theme he agrees substantially with them, for the words 'this is my body . . . this is my blood,' with their symbolic accompaniments, find an excellent interpretation in Jn 6[41-58], which can hardly be dissociated from the later institution of the Supper (see Westcott, *St. John*, 113 ; Holtzmann, *NT Theol.* ii. 501–503 ; Loisy, *Quatrième Évangile*, 702–722, 760, 811).

RESULTS.—(*a*) The Lord's Supper was instituted by Jesus as a perpetual memorial of His death. It is true that the words 'Do this in remembrance of me' do not occur in the oldest tradition, and may, perhaps, in their present form be traceable to St. Paul ; but it is incredible that he should have originated this sacrament, and that it should have been adopted from him by the Jewish Christians. The ordinance was in existence among the Jerusalem Churches before his conversion, and the symbolism and narrative which he received must have been invested with a peculiar sacredness, for, as preserved in the written Petrine source (Mark) at least twenty years later, while different and distinctly more original, they are essentially the same. It is difficult to see how the early Christians would have turned every meal into a commemoration of their Lord's death without His command, for even after the death they failed for a while to understand its full significance. After Pentecost they might have found their meals to be symbols of His perpetual presence to nourish them, but that they should have combined with this the necessity of His death, which remained a solemn mystery, would be inexplicable except under the example and instruction of their Lord.

(*b*) The Evangelical records relate the Supper to the Passover either directly or indirectly, but no such transformation of the original feast as we find in the Supper would have been made by the primitive Church, which remained thoroughly Jewish, except under the guidance of Jesus.

(*c*) Like all other teaching of Jesus, this does not prescribe new ritual dependent for its validity upon a set of fixed terms. Possibly freedom was allowed even with regard to the order of the action (see shorter text of Luke, 1 Co 10[16] and *Didache*) : certainly the spirit was not to be enslaved by an inerrant repetition of sacred words. Complete verbal accord is not to be found in the records, nor even in St. Paul is there a fixed liturgical formula such as might be repeated by a presiding officer ; but the import of the Supper was preserved and conveyed mainly by a generally uniform Christian practice.

(*d*) The Lord's Supper was a 'visible word' conveying the truth of the awful mystery of Redemption. Until He came, however long or short might be the interval, His followers, Jew and Gentile, would in this acted parable read their Master's mind in regard to His death, the culmination of His service of love on their behalf. 'The Passion of Christ was itself a sacrament or mystery of an eternal truth : it was the supreme sacrament of human history : the outward and visible sign of a great supra-temporal fact' (W. R. Inge, *Contentio Veritatis*, p. 298 ; see also art. FELLOWSHIP, § ii.).

5. The Apostolic Church. — (*a*) *The Jewish Christian Community.*—'To break (or 'the breaking of') bread' (κλᾶν—ἡ κλάσις τοῦ ἄρτου) is almost a formula in the NT (Mk 8[6] ||, Mt 26[26], Lk 24[35], Ac 2[42. 46] 20[7. 11], 1 Co 10[16.] 11[24]). The term does not seem to have been employed for the ordinary meals of the Jews or their sects in any formal way (see Jer 16[7. 8], La 4[4]). Undoubtedly sacrificial feasts shared in by fellow-worshippers were common not only in heathen circles but among the Jews ; they were consecrated by thanksgivings and other religious ritual (Schürer, *ThLZ*,

1891, 32), and it would have been quite natural for the Christians thus to associate themselves together ; but a widespread religious custom is not sufficient to account for the usage, and its nomenclature among the early disciples. Why was it distinguished from the 'fellowship' (κοινωνία) and singled out by a different terminology ? Partly because of the memory of their Lord's constant table-fellowship, to which His thanksgivings, with their intense reality, had given religious significance, but much more because of the Last Supper carrying His command. That Supper made every common meal more sacred. Enshrining the love of their Master in the symbolism of its closing scene, it gave new meaning to the communion of brethren at their common board. It became the source of a renewed joy, and the daily inspiration of a richer hope. So the term 'breaking of bread' covers more than the observance of the Eucharist. It designates the meals of which this ordinance formed an integral part, the action of breaking bread, which was the largest factor of their meal, being used to denote the whole feast. We may assume that the disciples followed their Lord's example, celebrating a love-feast, which would be enriched with memories of their Master and teaching from His nearest disciples, and closing with the more solemn thanksgiving for the broken body and the cup of blessing which Jesus had consecrated.

(*b*) *The Pauline Churches.*—There are signs in the letters of St. Paul that there was a widespread doctrine and practice to which his own churches would conform (Ro 6[17]), so that his influence over any churches but those of his foundation must not be exaggerated, especially in matters so vital as the sacred observances on which the personal disciples of Jesus would be regarded as primary authorities (cf. 1 Co 1[12]). Nevertheless the Church underwent a profound change when it passed from Jerusalem and the village churches of Judæa to the large cities of Syria, Asia Minor, and Greece. All ranks now contributed their share to the brotherhood. Thus of necessity the disciples could no longer meet daily, and their regular gatherings were held on the first day of the week (Ac 20[7], 1 Co 16[2], Rev 1[10]). Probably the conduct of the service at Troas (Ac 20[7-11]) was that of the average Gentile congregation, but little can be gathered from it except that there was a weekly meeting of the church on Sunday night, followed by a common meal, at which, in this case, St. Paul presided, and protracted the discourse till daybreak. The Lord's Supper may have been observed at some time during the common meal.

Thanksgiving was such an outstanding feature of the meal that already in 1 Co 10[16] there is mention of 'the cup of blessing which we bless' (some think it is so called in distinction from the cups at heathen banquets), and afterwards the meal is called 'the Eucharist' (Ignat. *Philad.* 4, *Smyr.* 6 ; Justin Martyr, *Apol.* i. 64–66, *Trypho*, 116, 117). This Supper, originated and presided over by the Lord (τὸ κυριακὸν δεῖπνον), did not owe its validity to any official president or to any Apostolic blessing. It was a celebration of the brotherhood as a whole ; indeed, the sacrilege of the Corinthians consisted partly in destroying the bond of love which united into one body the brethren who ate one bread (1 Co 10[16f.] 11[20ff]). Only brethren seem to have been admitted to the Supper, though unbelievers and strangers attended other gatherings of a hortatory or didactic nature (14[23]). It is noteworthy that the direct references to the Lord's Supper in the epistolary writings of the NT are confined to 1 Cor., so that we may possibly attach a larger importance to the function of the Lord's Supper in the Christian life than the Apostle Paul (see 1 Co

1^{14-17}), though he did undoubtedly regard it as a powerful means of grace (1 Co 10^{16-21}).

(c) *The Agape and the Lord's Supper.*—While the word 'Agape' occurs only once in the NT (Jude [12], for the reading of 2 P 2^{13} is almost certainly ἀπάταις), there can be no doubt that the common meals of the primitive Christians, and the table-fellowship which the Corinthians abused, answer to the later Agape. A new name was given to what was really a new thing, for there is nothing elsewhere like the spirit of love which called into existence and pervaded the common intercourse of the brotherhood. The occasion for the origin of the name may be found in Jn 13–16, though the technical term probably did not come into use till long after the brethren had been enjoying the reality.

What did 'the Lord's Supper' (τὸ κυριακὸν δεῖπνον, 1 Co 11^{20}) precisely mean? Was it the concluding part of the Agape, later called the Eucharist, or did it include both the Agape and the Eucharist? Or was the Lord's Supper a distinct Eucharistic meal separate from the Agape? The decision turns partly on the interpretation of 1 Co 11^{20}. Jülicher is of the opinion that 'the Lord's Supper' was quite unlike all other congregational gatherings, and holds that St. Paul found fault with the Corinthians because by their greed they turned a meal, which was meant to serve the brotherly unity of the Church, into a means of satisfying their appetites (see Stewart, *Expos.* July 1898, and also Drews, *PRE*[3] v. 562 f.). But there are two decisive objections to this view. (a) The Apostle says that the ordinance was instituted 'after supper' (μετὰ τὸ δειπνῆσαι, 11^{25}). (β) Bread and wine would not occasion the gluttony which he rebukes. It is much more difficult to decide between the other views. Those who hold that the Agape culminated in the Eucharist, and that the whole was called 'the Lord's Supper,' explain that the selfish conduct of the Corinthian cliques rendered impossible any table-fellowship like that of the first Lord's Supper, when the feast of love culminated in the Eucharist (Keating, *Agape and Eucharist*, Appendix B; Robertson in Hastings' *DB* i. 490[b]). Perhaps this agrees with the term 'breaking of bread,' and the practice as outlined in Acts, but the words of St. Paul seem to separate this part of the feast from the rest. It is a 'Lord's meal' because of the institution by the Lord which he proceeds to relate. 'It is impossible for you to eat a real Lord's Supper when you have acted so disgracefully in the Agape.' Further, the institution 'after supper,' and the subsequent history of the ordinance, seem to be most easily explained on this view (Weizsäcker, *Apost. Age*, Eng. tr. vol. ii. 283 ff.; Zahn, 'Agapen,' in *PRE*[3] i. 236 f.). The abuses which led eventually to a separation of the Agape from the Eucharist were abundant in Corinth, though the process of dissociation proved to be slow, and varied in different localities.

6. The sub-Apostolic Church.—(a) *Clement of Rome.*—To counteract the disturbances resulting from the Corinthian rivalries, Clement urges the necessity of order and reverence in the service, which will be effected by every one abiding in his own part (14). The bishops must offer 'the gifts blamelessly and holily' (44), *i.e.* 'the prayers and thanksgivings, the alms, the Eucharistic elements, the contributions to the Agape, and so forth' (Lightfoot). His stately prayers and insistence upon orderliness may point to a developing liturgical service, but the epistle sheds no real light upon the place or meaning of the Eucharist in the worship of the Church.

(b) *Pliny's Letter to Trajan (A.D. 112).*—This letter is of importance, but raises vexed questions. How far the practice described extended beyond the Church of Bithynia, and the trustworthiness and interpretation of evidence which he drew from apostate Christians, are doubtful. He says: 'Essent soliti stato die ante lucem convenire carmenque Christo quasi deo dicere secum invicem, seque sacramento non in scelus aliquod obstringere, sed ne furta, ne latrocinia, ne adulteria committerent, ne fidem fallerent, ne depositum appellati abnegarent : quibus peractis morem sibi discedendi fuisse, rursusque coeundi ad capiendum cibum, promiscuum tamen et innoxium' (*Ep.* 96. 7).

Just what is involved in the word *sacramentum* has divided scholars. Lightfoot (*Ign.* i. 50 ff.) and Ramsay (*Ch. in Rom. Empire*[3], 219 f.) believe that the Eucharist and the Agape were separated at this time, and that the social meal, which was held in the evening, had been repressed in accordance with the Roman Imperial policy against associations (Keating, 54 ff.). Weizsäcker is not very clear (*op. cit.* ii. 249, 285), but Zahn *PRE*[3] i. 236, art. 'Agapen'.) and J. A. Robinson (*Encyc. Bibl.*, 'Eucharist,' § 17) are unwilling to draw such a conclusion. Possibly the abolition of the Agape was local and temporary (Mayor, *Clem. of Alexandria Strom.* vii. 376 ff.). In any case, undue emphasis should not be placed upon the Imperial policy as a uniform influence, for there were other contributory local forces at work, introducing changes into worship ; and when Ignatius wrote, the Eucharist and the Agape were still united 'in some parts of Asia Minor, and probably at Antioch' (Lightfoot).

(c) *The Teaching of the Twelve Apostles.*—The uncertainty of the date and local origin of the *didache* renders its witness doubtful. Quite different in tone from Paul, and not influenced directly, it would appear, by John, it may be taken as a type of widespread Jewish Christian life within the limits of Palestine, and possibly Egypt, about the end of the 1st century. The Supper, called 'the Eucharist,' and associated with 'the breaking of bread,' is mentioned in chapters 9, 10, and 14. The Eucharist is not yet separated from the Agape, if, indeed, they are not identical, for the latter is not mentioned, though some take ch. 9 to contain the closing prayers of the Agape, and ch. 10 those of the Eucharist (Zahn, Weizsäcker, Weiss, Loofs). It is held on the Lord's Day, and is preceded by confession, for only pure hearts make praise and thanksgiving possible. The order, as in the shorter form of Luke, is cup and bread ; but nothing is said as to the method of celebration, except that, while a set form of prayers is given for ordinary use, prophets are allowed freedom. There is no sign of a priest, and the celebration is the common act of the whole Church. Only the baptized are to partake of the Eucharist, which is that holy thing that cannot be given to the dogs, though not because the Eucharistic elements are regarded as conveying some mysterious power, or are, in any sense, sacrificial ; for there is not much advance on Ro 12^1.[*]

The *Didache* is mystical, like the Fourth Gospel. Life and knowledge come through the appropriation of Jesus Christ as Messiah, but no reference is made to redemption through His blood. A unique figure—that of the grains of wheat being brought together to form one loaf—is applied to the sanctification of the Church in a unity. Thanks are given for knowledge of God, for faith and immortality brought through Jesus the Servant, and for daily food, but especially for the spiritual food through Jesus. After the stress of the present evil age, which may soon close with the advent of the Lord, will come the peace of perfect mystical union in the Church of the completed Kingdom (Bartlet, 'Didache,' Hastings' *DB*, Extra Vol. 439 ff.; Drews in *Neutest. Apokryphen*, 182–188).

(d) *Ignatius.*—The Lord's Supper assumes large

---

[*] εὐχαριστία in Christian usage has two concrete senses besides the abstract sense : (1) a thanksgiving in words, and (2) a thanksgiving in offerings ; and in early times it appears to denote always the offering or thing offered itself, not the ceremony or service, or the institution' (Hort, *JThSt*, vol. iii. 595).

importance. By a transference of the name for the prayer of thanksgiving to the whole meal it is called 'the Eucharist' (*Eph.* 13, *Phil.* 4, *Smyr.* 6, 8). It is still associated with the Agape (*Smyr.* 8. 1, 2), and the term 'breaking of bread' seems to include both (*Eph.* 20). His utterances often stand out untoned in the atmosphere of controversy with the Docetists, against whom he is never wearied of insisting upon the reality of the human nature of Jesus Christ which is essential to salvation. Only in the one Church is this full truth preserved, and the Eucharist is the symbol of unity, for there the gifts of salvation which are the full fellowship of life with Christ find fleshly expression. So, to be valid, it must be celebrated by the bishop, who, as opposed to all heretics, performs the sacrament as an act of the Church as a whole. For Ignatius the spiritual supersensible world is intensely real, but it becomes illusory without an earthly or material form, and only through the appropriation of the flesh and blood of Christ do believers enter into mystical union with God. This is most fully realized in the breaking of bread, an action efficacious as an antidote to spiritual death — 'a medicine for immortality' (φάρμακον ἀθανασίας, *Eph.* 20). Some hold that Ignatius regards the elements of the Supper as purely symbolic, for in *Phil.* 5. 1, the gospel is called 'the flesh of Jesus'; in *Trall.* 8. 1, faith is 'the flesh of the Lord,' and love is 'the blood of Jesus Christ'; and in *Rom.* 7, *Eph.* 5, 'the bread of God' is an image of the blessings of salvation without any reference to the Lord's Supper (v. d. Goltz, *Ignatius von Antiochien*, pp. 72, 73 ; Lightfoot, *Ign. ad Rom.* 7 ; Loofs, *PRE*[3] i. 40). Harnack's most recent view is that in Ignatius, sixty years after St. Paul, the whilom clear theology has become fouled by the Mysteries and their lore (*Expansion of Christianity*, i. 289). Apparently Ignatius does not think of magical powers as being inherent in material elements, but, influenced by Johannine mysticism, holds that the material forms must be interpreted by a spirit of faith, love, and thanksgiving in order to convey spiritual gifts. Yet he is ambiguous, and his realistic language, partly due to a mind more imaginative than penetrating, opens the door for the cruder conceptions which follow. Perhaps we may go further, and see in his use of the term 'medicine for immortality' the first evidence of the later view of Greek theology, which laid the chief stress of redemption rather on the annihilation of physical corruption by the infusion of the Divine Nature of the Son of God, than on spiritual regeneration through the eternal Divine Person (Lightfoot, *Ign.* ii. 45, 171, 258 ; Inge, *Christian Mysticism*, 257, and Appendix C ; Swete in *JThSt*, iii. 168 ; Sanday, *The Fourth Gospel*, 241–245).

(*e*) *Justin Martyr.*—The ecclesiastical term for the Supper is henceforth 'the Eucharist.' Justin makes no mention of the Agape. The Eucharist ceases to be a meal of the congregation and becomes a regular part of the Sunday service, and seems to require the presence of a bishop or some other official for its valid celebration (*Apol.* i. 65–67). Under the growing tendency towards ritual it began to gather to itself some of the Jewish, or perhaps heathen, sacrificial ideas centring in a special priesthood. Indeed Justin sees in the mysteries of Mithras a demonic imitation of Christian symbolism (*Apol.* i. 54, 62, 65–67 ; *Dial. c. Trypho*, 70, 78). The ideas of Ignatius are in Justin losing their purity. He continues to speak of the Supper as a spiritual life-giving food, but holds that a material change passes upon the elements of the sacrament, so that they nourish our bodies and make them incorruptible, the Logos becoming united by the Eucharistic prayer with the bread,

as He took flesh and blood when He became incarnate in Jesus (*Apol.* i. 66 ; Loofs, *PRE*[3] i. 40, 41, 45, 46 ; Swete, *JThSt*, iii. 169 f.). Harnack put forward a theory that bread and water were the usual elements in the Eucharist at the time of Justin, but it has received little approval, for the most that can be said is that the practice existed among some small sects in Africa (*TU* vii. 2, 117–144, outlined by Stewart, *Expos.* July 1898, 43 ff.).

A variety of causes led to the discontinuance of the celebration of the Agape along with the Lord's Supper. (*a*) The increase of abuses as they are found already in 1 Cor. and Jude. (*b*) The growth of the Church in large cities, where it became impossible for the Christians to meet together in house-celebrations. (*c*) The increasing power of the bishop and clergy, who found in house-gatherings a menace to the unity of the Church, together with the development of the dogma that the presence of a bishop was necessary to make a Supper valid. (*d*) Charges of child-murder and cannibalism (θυέστεια δεῖπνα, οἰδιποδείους μίξεις). (*e*) The enforcement of the Imperial law against associations (see Drews, *PRE*[3] v. ' Eucharistie '). The change, already widespread in the time of Justin Martyr, whereby the Supper is definitely called 'the Eucharist' and becomes the central part of public service, was of vast consequence, and gradually spread over the whole Church, transforming the conception of worship. In Tertullian's circle the Eucharist is celebrated in the early morning and the Agape is held in the evening (*Apol.* 39, *de Corona*, 3). But authorities differ as to the completeness of the separation at Alexandria in Clement's day, Bigg, *e.g.*, saying that 'the Eucharist was not distinguished in time, ritual, or motive from the primitive Supper of the Lord' (*Christian Platonists*, 102, 103), while Mayor is doubtful (*Clem. Alex. Strom.* vii. 382), and Zahn is strongly of the contrary opinion (*PRE*[3] 'Agapen,' 234).

7. The Lord's Supper and the pagan Mysteries. — Dr. Percy Gardner may be taken as a representative of a few scholars who trace the influence of the pagan Mysteries on St. Paul.

'The great difference between the teaching of the Synoptic Jesus on the one hand, and the teaching of Paul, of the Fourth Evangelist, and of the author of Hebrews on the other, is just that the latter is permeated, as the former is not, by the ideas of spiritual communion, of salvation, of justification, and mediation—ideas which had found an utterance, however imperfect, in the teaching of the *thiasi*. . . . Christians are, like the Pagan Mystæ, called upon to be ὅσιοι and ἅγιοι. The language of the Pauline and Johannine writings shows the translation of Christianity on to a new level by the reception and baptism into Christ of a set of ideas which at the time, coming from a Divine source, were making their way into the various religions of the human race ' (*Explor. Evangel.* p. 340 ff.). H. J. Holtzmann also holds that in separating the sacrament as a specifically religious act unrelated to the kernel of his gospel, Paul opened the gates to 'mystery' conceptions (*NT Theol.* ii. 186, 187).

But the sacrament of the Supper was in existence before St. Paul, and its import well established in the Jewish section of the Church before the gospel went to the Gentiles, who for many decades were not sufficiently influential to stamp the sacrament with 'mystery' conceptions even if they had so desired. All this type of thought was alien to the Jewish mind, the only section of the nation that was in sympathy with these ideas being the Essenes, who derived their sacramental meals—in some sort 'mystery' associations—from foreign sources, and they cannot be regarded as a factor in the shaping of the Christian rite (Bousset, *Rel. des Judenthums*, 431–443). It is quite gratuitous to say that the ideas of spiritual communion, salvation, justification, and mediation are especially Pauline or Johannine. They had, in fact, a long history in Hebrew thought, and while they are frequent in 'mystery' ritual, their import is different. The pagan Mysteries, even in their purest expression, were tainted with the religious conceptions of old nature-worships. Fellowship through sacraments with the Divine was thought to bring an infusion of the subtle material essence of the god, who thus held present communion with the initiated, and vouchsafed immortality to him. This was the result not so much of a moral act of faith as of an impression produced upon the character by the vision of the Divine drama. Contemplation and ecstasy crown the course of the initiated. A rigorous ethical discipline was also required by way of preparation for the vision of the Divine, but inasmuch as the purpose was to free the soul from its prison-house in the flesh, the purification was chiefly of a ceremonial character. The soul cleansed of earthly impurities would ascend after death into final union with the Supreme (see Dill, *Roman Society from Nero to Marcus Aurelius*, Bk. IV. chs. v. vi.). Of sin in the Christian sense there is little trace in pagan thought. Such sin as the worshipper was freed from in the heathen Mysteries was inherent in him by reason of human frailty, or was an outward taint of the body (Anrich, *Das antike Mysterienwesen*, 38). When in the 2nd cent. these subtle shades began to colour Christian thought, it was a sign that the full summer was passing.

St. Paul is ruled by the Hebrew idea of sin as it became heightened by the life and death of Jesus. God is for him the supremely moral Person, and sin is treason against His Sovereignty. On His Son, the Redeemer from sin, he lavishes all his loyalty and worship. Indeed, Christ becomes his intimate personal friend and Lord. For him it is Christ to live, which is only another way of saying that Christ is his spiritual food as it is symbolized in the Supper (1 Co 10⁴·¹⁷). He does not, it is true, lay inordinate emphasis on the celebration of Baptism or the Supper (1 Co 1¹⁴⁻¹⁷), but he finds in the common meal of love the most perfect earthly expression of the fellowship of the saints with the Head of the body. The living Christ draws the believers, who have abandoned their former pagan fellowship, into a new communion with Himself. He is the most real of all persons, dwelling in the hearts of a loving company as their thought is focussed upon Him by the symbols of His redemption, and pledged by this memorial of His death to return (see Dobschütz, *Probleme d. apost. Zeitalters*, 72, 73 ; Ramsay, *Expos.*, Dec. 1900, Jan. 1901). Even the use by St. Paul of such words as 'mystery' and 'to initiate' (τελειοῦν), 1 Co 2⁶·⁷, 2 Co 1²², Ph 3¹², hardly justifies the assumption of conscious influence (Heinrici, *Com.* [1887] *zu 2 Kor.* 121 ; Anrich, 112). Nor is there any more reason for discerning 'mystery-doctrine' in John, for the conception of God and of true worship which rules this Gospel is unsurpassed (4²ᴵ⁻²⁴), while in 6⁶³ words which might be thought to have a materialistic sense are expressly said to be spirit and life. In the final discourses of Jesus the conditions for receiving the Spirit of Christ are ethical. Those abide in Christ who show their love to Him by obeying His command to love one another. In the First Epistle the final vision of God is promised for the world to come, but only those can know God now who love, and who have had their sins taken away through the Lamb of God who is the propitiation for the sins of the whole world (1 Jn 2², cf. Jn 1²⁹). 'Faith' in Paul, 'love' and 'knowledge,' almost convertible terms in John, are the subjective conditions for communion with God, who dwells in the individual heart attuned to the loving fellowship of the brotherhood.

It may be partially true to say that without the sacraments Christianity would not have conquered Europe, and yet such a judgment should be qualified by the fact that non-sacramental Judaism was the most effective proselytizer of all the religions of the old world. Widespread as the 'mystery' cults were, the Jews became a church within the Roman Empire, exceeding other foreign worships in numbers, the attention it attracted, and the privileges it extorted from a hostile power. Philo, the only 'mystery' philosopher of the Jews, was an isolated phenomenon (Bousset, *op. cit.* 78, 79).

Unquestionably, the heathen Mysteries satisfied many deep religious longings. The contemplation of impressive ceremonial and a Divine drama concealed from all but the initiated, the litany, the rhythmic music, appealed to the feeling of the worshipper, and swept him into an attitude of mind in which he enjoyed Divine communion and received a pledge of his immortality. By means of a common meal he entered into mystical union with the god, and began the process of deification through the infusion of the imperishable Divine nature. Degraded though these Mysteries often were by magic and superstition, they were felt by their purest votaries to be the guarantee of salvation here in fellowship with God and of a blessed future life (Anrich, pp. 39, 46, 47 ; Dill, 609–614). And yet Judaism was the most powerful factor in that religious world, because it satisfied more perfectly than any 'mystery' cult the more insistent ethical and spiritual needs of human nature. But Christianity brought to the world a richer boon than either Judaism or the heathen Mysteries. It offered all that was best both in the Mysteries and in Judaism. By its sacraments it disclosed its 'open secret' to Jew and Gentile ; and in these sacraments the believer, as one of a brotherhood of saints, was brought into perfect communion with the eternal God who had redeemed him.

The most sacred symbol of this redemption, 'the core of religious worship,' was the Lord's Supper, and it remained truly symbolic until, after the first decade of the 2nd cent., the stream of Christian life, making its way through pagan soil that was saturated with ideas drained off from mystery-practice and thought, began to grow discoloured. How far in the succeeding years there was direct imitation between Christianity and the mystery religions, or how far resemblances were due to ideas that had by a long process of religious development become almost essential to the thought of the early centuries, is a problem that still awaits solution. But it was the Gnostic sects that were first invaded and overcome by distinctly heathen influences. The Christian Church, with its immense reserve of spiritual power, performed a masterly and slow retreat from the more exalted positions of the Apostolic age (Harnack, *Expansion of Christianity*, i. 285–299 ; Hatch, *Hibbert Lectures*, 283–309 ; Mayor, *Clement of Alexandria*, ch. iii. ; Inge, *Christian Mysticism*, Lect. ii. and Appendix B ; and esp. Dill and Anrich, *ut supra*).

LITERATURE.—Schultzen, *Das Abendmahl im NT*, 1895 ; J. H. Thayer, 'Recent Discussions respecting the Lord's Supper' in *JBL* xviii. [1899] 110–131 ; Cremer and Loofs, 'Abendmahl,' i. and ii., in *PRE³* i. ; Drews, 'Eucharistie,' *ib.* v. ; Zahn, 'Agapen,' *ib.* i. ; Plummer, 'The Lord's Supper,' in Hastings' *DB* iii. ; J. A. Robinson, 'Eucharist' in *Encyc. Bibl.* ii. The views of Harnack, Jülicher, and Spitta are clearly outlined by G. Wauchope Stewart in *Expos.* 5th ser. viii. [1898] 43–61, 86–102, and by Grafe in *Ztschr. f. Theol. u. Kirche*, 1895, pt. 2. See also Percy Gardner, *Origin of the Lord's Supper*, 1893 ; J. F. Keating, *The Agape and the Eucharist*, 1901 ; J. C. Lambert, *The Sacraments in the NT*, 1903 [excellent] ; G. H. Box, *Jewish Antecedents of the Eucharist*, and reply by J. C. Lambert in *JThSt*, vols. iii. iv. ; H. B. Swete, 'Eucharistic Belief in the Second and Third Centuries,' *ib.* vol. iii. ; W. B. Frankland, *The Early Eucharist*, 1902 [useful for textual material] ; Bishop A. J. Maclean, art. 'Agape' in Hastings' forthcoming *Encyc. of Religion and Ethics*.   R. A. FALCONER.

LORD'S SUPPER (II.).—The NT passages bearing on this subject may conveniently be divided into the following groups :—

1. Preparation for Institution.—(1) *Feeding of Five thousand* (Mk 6[41. 42] = Mt 14[19. 20], Lk 9[16. 17], Jn 6[11. 12]). In connexion with this miracle it is important to observe that (*a*) it is recorded in all four Gospels ; (*b*) the record contains the following significant phrases, which it is well to compare with the phraseology in the accounts of the institution : λαβών (Mk., Mt., Lk. ; ἔλαβεν, Jn.), εὐλόγησεν (Mk., Mt., Lk. ; εὐχαριστήσας, Jn. ; cf. Jn 6[23] εὐχαριστήσαντος τοῦ Κυρίου), κατέκλασεν (Mk., Lk. ; κλάσας, Mt. ; Jn. omits), ἐδίδου (Mk., Lk. ; ἔδωκεν, Mt. ; διέδωκεν, Jn.) ; (*c*) the event carried on and emphasized the idea of a sacred meal, which, as a means of communion with God, had been profoundly impressed on the minds of the Jews by the sacrificial system.

(2) *Feeding of Four thousand* (Mk 8[6-8] = Mt 15[36. 37]). In connexion with this must be observed : (*a*) the same type of phrases as in the Feeding of the Five thousand : λαβών (Mk. ; ἔλαβεν, Mt.), εὐχαριστήσας (Mk., Mt.), ἔκλασεν (Mk., Mt.), ἐδίδου (Mk., Mt.), εὐλογήσας (Mk. only) ; (*b*) the same idea of a sacred meal as in the Feeding of the Five thousand. With the Feeding of the Five thousand and the Four thousand should be compared the meals after the Resurrection in Lk 24[30. 31. 35] and Jn 21[13], where, though neither appears to have been the Eucharist, the idea of a sacred meal is maintained, and the phraseology should be noticed (λαβὼν τὸν ἄρτον εὐλόγησεν καὶ κλάσας ἐπεδίδου αὐτοῖς and ἐν τῇ κλάσει τοῦ ἄρτου in Lk 24[30. 35], and λαμβάνει τὸν ἄρτον καὶ δίδωσιν αὐτοῖς, καὶ τὸ ὀψάριον ὁμοίως in Jn 21[13]).

(3) *Discourse in the Fourth Gospel in connexion with Feeding of Five thousand*. This miracle, like others, is called σημεῖον in the Fourth Gospel (Jn 6[14. 26]), *i.e.* it has a place in the group of 'signs' which are so called because 'they make men feel the mysteries which underlie the visible order' (Westcott). The peculiar significance of this 'sign' in particular was drawn out by our Lord in the discourse at Capernaum which followed it. That it was an acted parable of Divine truth He asserted to the multitude which sought Him at Capernaum, in the words : 'Ye seek me, not because ye saw signs, but because ye ate of the loaves, and were filled. Work not for the meat which perisheth, but for the meat which abideth unto eternal life, which the Son of Man shall give unto you : for him the Father, even God, hath sealed' (Jn 6[26. 27]). Thus it supplied the starting-point for the conversation with the multitude, in which our Lord identified 'the bread out of heaven that is genuine,' which 'the Father giveth,' with Himself as 'the bread of God which cometh down out of heaven, and giveth life unto the world,' 'the bread of life,' 'the bread which cometh down out of heaven, that a man may eat thereof, and not die,' 'the living bread which came down out of heaven' ; and further declared, 'the bread which I will give is my flesh, for the life of the world' (vv.[32-51]). As the conversation proceeded, our Lord spoke, in still clearer terms, of the reception of His flesh and blood as the means whereby there was to be participation in Himself, and as requisite to the possession of life : 'Except ye eat the flesh of the Son of Man, and drink his blood, ye have not life in yourselves. He that eateth my flesh, and drinketh my blood, hath eternal life' ; 'My flesh is true food, and my blood is true drink. He that eateth my flesh and drinketh my blood, abideth in me, and I in him' ; 'He that eateth me, he also shall live because of me. This is the bread which came down out of heaven' ; 'He that eateth this bread shall live for ever' (vv.[52-58]). Recognizing the difficulty caused to His hearers by this teaching, our Lord laid stress on the deep spiritual significance of what He had said : 'The Spirit is the life-giver ; the flesh profiteth nothing :

the words that I have spoken unto you are spirit, and are life' (vv.[61-63]). By this conversation, the idea of a sacred meal is carried further than it had been in the miracle itself. An act of eating the flesh and drinking the blood of Christ is anticipated as the way in which His disciples will participate in the life which is in Him.

To dissociate this teaching from the Eucharist is to take away the key to its meaning which is supplied by the comparison of the phraseology used in it with that employed by our Lord at the Institution. This fact may be illustrated by the view of Arthur Wright (*Synopsis of the Gospels in Greek*[2], p. 140, *NT Problems*, pp. 134–146) that the Eucharist had been observed by our Lord from the first as 'a covenant of service' or 'union,' since the language of Jn 6 would not have been intelligible unless the Eucharist had been already in common use. Wright's view must be rejected as (*a*) lacking positive support ; (*b*) not really affording a parallel to the existence of a rite of baptism (3[22] 4[1. 2]) before the institution of Christian Baptism (Mt 28[19]) ; (*c*) being contrary to the tenor of Jn 6, which implies that, to the disciples as well as to the multitude, the teaching had the element of difficulty which shows that the Eucharist was not yet instituted ; and (*d*) as contrary to the parallels by which the discourse about Baptism in Jn 3 is prior to the institution in Mt 28[19], and the teaching about forgiveness in Mk 2[5-11] (= Mt 9[2-8], Lk 5[20-24]) is prior to Jn 20[21-23] ; but its plausibility at first sight is a significant indication of the truth that the discourse in Jn 6 was destined to find its explanation in the Institution of the Eucharist. Thus the teaching may be taken as anticipatory of the Eucharist. As such it suggests (*a*) a real spiritual participation on the part of the communicant in the human nature of Christ by the power of the Holy Ghost, and a consequent union with His Divine Person ; (*β*) connexion with His death, indicated in the words 'the bread which I will give is my flesh, for the life of the world,' and with His resurrection, indicated by the references to 'the bread of life' and 'the living bread.' Consequently the communicant feeds on the living risen body and blood of the Lord which have passed through death.

The interpretations of the discourse which need be mentioned are the following : (1) that there is no connexion with the Holy Communion, but the feeding on Christ referred to is simply acceptance of His teaching or faith in His work, a view which obviously fails to allow for the distinctive character of the phraseology ; (2) that the primary and special reference is to the Holy Communion, the interpretation which best satisfies all the conditions ; (3) that the teaching, while not excluding the Holy Communion, is rather to the general verity of spiritual communion with our Lord than specifically to the Holy Communion, a view which, though it may be expressed so as to come very near the interpretation here accepted, does not account for the peculiar phrases used in the discourse and their remarkable likeness to, and explanation by, the words used in the Institution of the Eucharist. The objection that, if the primary reference were to the Eucharist, Jn 6[54-58] would require that mere reception of Communion, even by one who should receive unworthily, would confer the gift of life, is not weighty, since any reasonable treatment of the passage regards it as referring to those who communicate with such dispositions as may preserve them from receiving unworthily.

2. Accounts of the Institution.—(1) 1 Co 11[23-25]. The earliest history of the Institution which we possess is that here given by St. Paul. It records our Lord's words with reference to the bread : 'This is my body, which is for you : this do as my memorial' ; and with reference to the cup : 'This cup is the new covenant in my blood : this do, as oft as ye drink it, as my memorial.' The interpretation of these words is concerned with two subjects :—

(*a*) The meaning of 'This is my body.' The word 'this' is the subject of the sentence. Viewed in connexion with the introductory words 'took bread,' 'He brake it and said,' it cannot reasonably be understood to denote bread in general or anything else except the actual pieces of bread which our Lord gave as He spoke. The word 'is' is the logical copula between the subject 'this' and the predicate 'my body.' In the Aramaic sentence which our Lord spoke, the predication was probably expressed simply by the juxtaposition of the subject and the predicate without any copula. Either the Greek copula, as used in the record which we possess, or the juxtaposition in the Aramaic sentence which it probably represents, denotes that the subject ('this,' *i.e.* the bread which our Lord gave to His disciples) and the predicate ('my body') are viewed as identical. The interpretation of the sentence then depends on the sense in which the word 'body' is to be understood. It must be remembered that (a) the idea of communion with God by means of a sacred meal was familiar, as in many religious rites outside Judaism, so also in the literature and the religion which were well known to the disciples, as shown in the Levitical peace-offerings with the threefold division into the portion for God, the portion for the priest, and the portion for the worshipper (Lv 3 7$^{29-34}$) ; the bread and wine brought forth by Melchizedek, the 'priest of God Most High' (Gn 14^{18}) ; the eating of the lamb in the Passover (Ex 12) ; the meal of Moses and Aaron, Nadab and Abihu, and seventy of the elders in the presence of God (Ex 24$^{1-11}$) ; the prophecy by Isaiah of the feast to be made by the Lord of hosts (Is 25^6) ; and the invitations to a meal evidently of profound spiritual significance given by the personified 'Wisdom' of the Sapiential books (Pr 9$^{1-5}$, Sir 24$^{19-21}$). (β) This idea had been emphasized in our Lord's ministry in the Feeding of the Five thousand and the subsequent discourse, and the disciples had been taught that in eating His flesh and drinking His blood they would have participation in Divine life (Jn 6$^{53-57}$). (γ) There is nothing to indicate that the word 'body' is used in any unreal or metaphorical sense, and the added words, 'which is for you,' alluding to the sacrificial efficacy of our Lord's body, appear to identify that which is spoken of with His actual body. (δ) The close connexion of the words 'The Spirit is the life-giver ; the flesh profiteth nothing' (6^{63}) with the teaching about eating the flesh of the Son of Man and drinking His blood, suggests that in the rite which our Lord was instituting there would be the operation of the Holy Ghost and a work of spiritual efficacy. (ε) However accomplished at the Institution, as in the parallel instances of anticipation in the walking of our Lord on the water and His Transfiguration during the days of His humiliation, the gift contemplated in the rite instituted must be viewed in the light of the spiritual nature and powers of the risen body of Christ. (ζ) The assertion of this spiritual aspect of the body denoted is confirmed when the language in which St. Paul describes Christians as 'the body of Christ' (1 Co 12^{27}) is compared ; but this comparison would be pushed beyond its proper force if it were held to imply that the meaning in the two passages is the same, since in St. Paul's teaching the gift in Baptism, which makes men 'the body of Christ' (12^{13}), is not identified with the gift in the Holy Communion. The exegesis of this part of our Lord's words at the Institution, then, as recorded by St. Paul, indicates that the gift in the Eucharist is the spiritual food of the risen and ascended body of our Lord. The same method of exegesis involves a similar interpretation of the words 'in my blood,' though, in view of the spiritual nature of the risen body, it is impossible to make a sharp severance between the body and the blood.

That this line of exegesis, which is that which is naturally deduced from the study of the Holy Scripture by itself, is right is strongly confirmed by the traditional interpretation in the Church from St. Ignatius onwards.

Other interpretations are (1) that the words 'this is my body' mean, 'This conveys the efficacy of my body but is not my body' ; (2) that they mean, 'This represents my body but is not my body.' Both of these interpretations are vitally distinguished from that which has here been adopted, namely, 'This not only represents my body and conveys its efficacy, but also is my body.' To adopt either of them involves putting aside the cumulative argument which has already been briefly detailed ; the main argument by which they have been supported is the supposed merely metaphorical character of certain phrases, alleged to be parallel, in which our Lord described Himself as 'the bread of life' (Jn 6$^{35.\ 41.\ 48}$), 'the living bread' (6^{51}), 'the light of the world' (8^{12} 9^5), 'the door of the sheep' (10$^{7.\ 8}$), 'the good shepherd' (10$^{11.\ 14}$), 'the way' (14^6), 'the true vine' (15$^{1.\ 5}$). In regard to these phrases it must be observed that (1) neither the phrases themselves nor the circumstances in which they were used were really parallel to the words and circumstances at the Institution ; and (2) the phrases in question are as a matter of fact very far from being simply metaphorical. In each of them an actual fact about Christ is set forth. Christ in spiritual reality feeds Christians, and gives them light, and admits them into the Church, and tends them, and affords them access to the Father, and unites them in Himself. Similarly, in spiritual reality the bread which He gives in the Holy Communion is His body.

(b) The meaning of 'This cup is the new covenant' ; 'this do, as oft as ye drink it, as my memorial.' The interpretation of these sentences turns on three words : (i.) 'covenant,' (ii.) 'do,' (iii.) 'memorial.'

(i.) The sentence 'This cup is the new covenant in my blood,' while recalling the phraseology and promise of Jer 31$^{31-34}$, inevitably suggests a comparison with Ex 24$^{1-11}$. The making of a covenant between the Lord and Israel is there described. A sacrifice was offered by the slaughter of oxen and the sprinkling of part of the blood of the victims on the altar. After the reading of the book of the covenant in the audience of the people by Moses, and their promise to be obedient to all that the Lord had thus spoken, the rest of the blood was sprinkled by Moses on the people with the words, 'Behold the blood of the covenant, which the Lord hath made with you concerning all these words.' The sacrifice was consummated, and the covenant completed, by the sacred meal wherein 'the nobles of the children of Israel' 'beheld God, and did eat and drink.' The analogy between this series of actions and the Eucharist which the words 'This is the new covenant in my blood' suggest, is worked out with some detail in He 9$^{11-28}$. The death of Christ and His entrance into heaven with His own blood are there represented as the highpriestly actions of which the slaughter of the beasts and the sprinkling of their blood in the Mosaic sacrifices, alike in the covenant of Ex 24$^{1-11}$ and in the ceremonies of the Day of Atonement in Ex 30^{10}, Lv 16, were an anticipation. The words 'This is the new covenant in my blood' thus bring the Eucharist into close connexion with the highpriestly work wherein Christ offered Himself a sacrifice in His death on the cross, and His entrance into heaven at the Ascension. They denote that the gift by Christ of His body and blood, and the reception of these by Christians, are the means of a covenant relation in the sacrificial action ; and that Christians by participating in this rite are in contact with the death of Christ and His high-priestly acts in heaven.

(ii.) The command 'this do' conveys the injunction for the perpetuation of the rite instituted by our Lord in the Church. It has been much discussed whether the word 'do' (ποιεῖτε) suggests sacrificial associations. The truth appears to be that in itself ποιέω is simply negative as to this point. Apart from other indications of sacrifice, it would not suggest any such thing, since in the very large number of instances in which it is used in LXX and NT it is in a merely general sense. In a sacrificial context, however, like the Heb. עָשָׂה, it acquires the idea of 'sacrifice' or 'offer,' as, e.g. in Ex 29³⁹, Lv 9⁷, Ps 66¹⁵, where עָשָׂה (LXX ποιέω) is rightly translated 'offer' in AV and RV. In NT cf. Lk 2²⁷. In this possibility of a special use, side by side with the ordinary use, ποιέω is not greatly dissimilar from the Shakspearian use of 'do,' by which 'do' constantly has its ordinary general sense, but in a sacrificial context in *Jul. Cæs.* II. ii. 5 acquires the sense 'offer' (' Bid the priests do present sacrifice,' *i.e.* 'offer sacrifice immediately'). Consequently, the word 'do,' as used by our Lord at the Institution, is in itself wholly negative, and does not suggest or deny the idea of sacrifice. In relation to the context, however, it will be held to be appropriate or inappropriate to the idea of sacrifice according as the suggestion of sacrifice is recognized or ignored in the general surroundings of the Last Supper and in the words 'covenant' and 'memorial.'

(iii.) The primary thought suggested in the word 'memorial' (ἀνάμνησις) is that of a memorial before God, though without excluding the idea of a memento to man. It occurs five times in the LXX, namely in Lv 24⁷, Nu 10¹⁰, Ps 37¹ (= Heb. 38¹) 69¹ (= Heb. 70¹), Wis 16⁶. In Wis 16⁶ it denotes a reminder to man ; in the other four passages it denotes a memorial before God. The only place in NT where it occurs besides 1 Co 11²⁴· ²⁵, and the same phrase in Lk 22¹⁹, is He 10³, where it refers to the remembrance of sins in the Jewish sacrifices. When all the circumstances are taken into account, the thought most naturally suggested is that of a memorial of Christ presented by Christians before the Father, which is at the same time a memento to themselves. If so, the idea differs little from that way of regarding the Eucharist in much Greek theology, whereby it is viewed as the act in which the Church remembers Christ and in remembering Him makes the memorial of Him before the Father. In the sentences 'This cup is the new covenant in my blood : this do, as oft as ye drink it, as my memorial,' then, our Lord associated with the command for the observance of the rite which He instituted, indications that by means of it Christians would have access to His high-priestly work on the cross and in heaven, and would possess a memorial before God and a memento to themselves.

(2) Mk 14²²⁻²⁵. As here recorded, our Lord's words at the Institution were : 'Take ye : this is my body' ; 'this is my blood of the covenant, which is poured out for many. Verily I say unto you, I will no more drink of the fruit of the vine, until that day when I drink it new in the kingdom of God.' The words in connexion with the species of bread are the same as those in 1 Co 11²⁴, already discussed, and do not need further comment, except to notice that Mark does not add 'which is for you : this do as my memorial.' In connexion with the cup Mark differs from 1 Cor. in that (1) he has 'this is my blood of the covenant' instead of 'this is the new covenant in my blood' ; (2) he omits 'this do, as oft as ye drink it, as my memorial' ; (3) he adds 'which is poured out for many' ; (4) he adds 'Verily I say unto you, I will no more drink

of the fruit of the vine, until that day when I drink it new in the kingdom of God.' As to these differences, it may be noticed : (α) The blood in Mark's phrase is described as being Christ's and as being 'of the covenant,' *i.e.* it is Christ's because it is the blood which He personally took in the Incarnation, and it is 'of the covenant' because by means of it the covenant between God and man which Christ makes is ratified and sealed. Consequently the meaning of the expression is not substantially different from that used by St. Paul in 1 Co 11²⁵ ; (β) the consideration of the omission of 'which is for you : this do as my memorial,' 'this do, as oft as ye drink it, as my memorial,' does not belong to this section of the article ; (γ) the words 'for many,' *i.e.* 'on behalf of many' (ὑπὲρ πολλῶν), indicate the sacrificial and expiatory power of Christ's blood. Similarly the words 'which is poured out' (τὸ ἐκχυννόμενον) are connected with the sacrifice of His blood. In the LXX ἐκχέω is often used both of the shedding of blood in slaughter and of the pouring out of the blood of slain victims at the altar. Instances of the latter use are Ex 29¹², Lv 4⁷·¹⁸·²⁵·³⁰·³⁴ 8¹⁵ 9⁹ ; cf. 1 K (= 1 S) 7⁶. The close connexion with the word 'covenant' in Mk 14²⁴, and the general sacrificial surroundings, give strong probability that the meaning here is 'poured out' rather than 'shed,' and that the sense is 'this is my blood,' 'which is sacrificially poured out,' as in the Jewish sacrifices the blood of the slain victim was poured out as the culmination of the sacrifice ; (δ) like much else in the Gospels, the words 'when I drink it new in the kingdom of God' appear to have a twofold reference. They refer in part to Christian Eucharists ; the 'kingdom of God' is the Christian Church ; the drinking 'new' is in the 'new covenant' of 1 Co 11²⁵ ; thus is denoted the fellowship between Christ and His people in the Eucharistic feast. In a further sense they refer to the 'marriage supper of the Lamb' (Rev 19⁹) ; the 'kingdom of God' is the consummated Kingdom of glory ; the drinking 'new' is in that state in which 'all things' are made 'new' (Rev 21⁵), newness being a characteristic feature of the future as well as of the present Christian life. See art. COVENANT.

(3) Mt 26²⁶· ²⁹. As here recorded, our Lord's words were : 'Take, eat, this is my body' ; 'Drink ye all of it ; for this is my blood of the covenant, which is poured out for many unto remission of sins. But I say unto you, I will not drink henceforth of this fruit of the vine, until that day when I drink it new with you in my Father's kingdom.' There is little here different from Mark's account which calls for comment : (α) 'unto remission of sins' is added to 'poured out,' specifying distinctly the object of the sacrificial offering of our Lord's blood ; (β) the words 'with you' are added in the description of the future 'new' drinking of 'this fruit of the vine' ; (γ) the phrase 'my Father's kingdom' is used instead of 'the kingdom of God,' both phrases alike being descriptive of both the Christian Church and the future perfected Kingdom.

(4) Lk 22¹⁴⁻²⁰. The account here given is as follows : 'When the hour was come, he sat down, and the apostles with him. And he said unto them, With desire I have desired to eat this passover with you before I suffer : for I say unto you, I will not eat it, until it be fulfilled in the kingdom of God. And he received a cup, and when he had given thanks, he said, Take this, and divide it among yourselves ; for I say unto you, I will not drink from henceforth of the fruit of the vine, until the kingdom of God shall come. And he took bread, and when he had given thanks, he brake it, and gave to them,

saying, This is my body which is given for you; this do for my memorial. And the cup in like manner after supper, saying, This cup is the new covenant in my blood, even that which is poured out for you.' From the point of view of exegesis, this account of the Institution does not need further comment than what has already been said in connexion with the accounts in 1 Cor., Mk., Mt. From other points of view it would be necessary to discuss (1) the cup which our Lord 'received' (δεξάμενος) before He 'took bread' (λαβὼν ἄρτον); and (2) the shorter reading of the text according to which some authorities omit from 'which is given for you' to 'which is poured out for you.'

3. Pauline teaching.—(1) 1 Co 10[16-21]. 'The cup of blessing which we bless, is it not a communion of the blood of Christ? The bread which we break, is it not a communion of the body of Christ? seeing that we, who are many, are one bread, one body: for we all partake of the one bread. Behold Israel after the flesh: have not they which eat the sacrifices communion with the altar? What say I then? that a thing sacrificed to idols is anything, or that an idol is anything? But I say, that the things which the Gentiles sacrifice, they sacrifice to demons, and not to God; and I would not that ye should have communion with demons. Ye cannot drink the cup of the Lord, and the cup of demons; ye cannot partake of the table of the Lord, and of the table of demons.' The following points here call for comment: (a) St. Paul describes the 'bread' and the 'cup' as being the means by which Christians participate in the 'body of Christ' and the 'blood of Christ'; (β) there is nothing to suggest that the phrases 'body of Christ' and 'blood of Christ' are used in any other sense than that in which they would ordinarily be understood; (γ) the phrases 'which we break,' 'of blessing which we bless,' seem to connect the efficacy of the elements as means of conveying the body and blood of Christ with the consecration of them, not simply with their reception; (δ) this participation by Christians in 'the one bread' is a means of their unity, so that they are 'one bread, one body'; (ε) this description of the 'bread' and the 'cup' as the 'body of Christ' and the 'blood of Christ' must be compared with St. Paul's description elsewhere of Christians being made by means of baptism the body of Christ (see 1 Co 12[12. 13. 27], Eph 5[30]); (ζ) the communion of Christians is analogous to the Jewish sacrifices and to the sacrifices of the Gentiles. As the object of the Jewish sacrifices was to hold communion with God, and as the object of the Gentile sacrifices was to hold communion with the false gods who are more properly regarded as demons, so also the Christian feast aims at communion with Christ.

(2) 1 Co 11[26-29]. 'As often as ye eat this bread, and drink this cup, ye proclaim the Lord's death till he come. Wherefore whosoever shall eat the bread or drink the cup of the Lord unworthily, shall be guilty of the body and the blood of the Lord. But let a man prove himself, and so let him eat of the bread, and drink of the cup. For he that eateth and drinketh, eateth and drinketh judgment unto himself, if he discern not the body.' (a) Christian communion is here declared to be a proclamation of the death of the Lord, a setting forth of it so that it may not be forgotten between the time of His visible departure from the earth and the time of His return. So far as the indications of a sacrificial aspect which have already been noticed are held to be of weight, this proclamation may be regarded in a double manner as a memory among Christians and as a memorial before God. (β) The reception of communion unworthily is said to be an offence of so great gravity as to make the offender 'guilty of the

body and the blood of the Lord,' so that his communion is an act of judgment upon himself in his failure to discern or appreciate or estimate the significance of the Lord's body.

(3) 1 Co 12[13]. 'We were all made to drink of one Spirit.' This probably refers to the gift of the Holy Ghost in Baptism, though the use of the word 'drink' has led some to refer it to such a gift in Communion.

4. He 13[8-16].—The starting-point in this passage is the assertion in v.[8] of the unchangeableness of Christ: 'Jesus Christ is the same yesterday, and to-day, yea and for ever.' From this is derived the thought of v.[9], that since Christ, the centre of Christian life, is unchangeable, Christian belief must have stability and consistency. Hence 'divers and strange teachings,' such as those in Judaistic forms of Christianity, and the externalities to which Judaizing teachers would have led Christians, are to be avoided; and the power that stablishes the heart is to be sought in Divine grace. This contrast leads on to v.[10], the point of which is to emphasize the sharp line which divides Christianity from Judaism; since Christians 'have an altar, whereof they have no right to eat which serve the tabernacle.' Vv.[11. 12] pass on to the likeness between the Jewish sacrifices and the sacrifice of Christ, in that in the former bodies were 'burned without the camp,' and in the latter Christ 'suffered without the gate.' V.[13] notes the conclusion from the sacrifice of Christ that it is right for Christians to abandon what is distinctively Jewish. V.[14] takes up the frequently-implied thought of this Epistle, that the old covenant is earthly, and that the new covenant, both now on earth and in its future perfection, is heavenly. The Christian gets beyond the old earthly covenant. He reaches the new heavenly covenant in the city of the living God, which on earth he does not realize as an abiding possession, though even now he has the life of Christ which makes his citizenship, and through which he is eventually to reach perfect holiness and fruition of God. Vv.[15. 16] point out that through Christ Christians can offer up to God a 'sacrifice of praise,' and that with this are to be associated the 'sacrifices' of doing good and communicating, with which 'God is well pleased.' These two verses, then, describe the worship and life of Christians as being a sacrificial offering to God. The Epistle as a whole regards the heavenly centre of this earthly worship and life as being the high-priestly work of our Lord in heaven. If the 'altar' mentioned in v.[10] is the altar of the Eucharist, this implies that the earthly centre of the sacrificial worship and life of Christians is in the Eucharist. This would be in harmony with the traditional Christian view of the Eucharist as the means whereby Christians enter into and partake of the heavenly offering of Christ. The interpretations of the word 'altar' which need be mentioned are that it denotes (1) Christ Himself, (2) the cross of Christ, (3) the altar of the Christian Church. Any one of these three interpretations would give a good meaning to the verse. It might be truly said that the Jews have no participation in Christ, or in His cross, or in the Christian altar. But the use of the word 'eat' makes it difficult to suppose that a reference to the Eucharist was not at any rate included by the writer. Thus there is the idea of the priesthood of Christ as an abiding priesthood, and the sacrifice of Christ as an abiding and continually pleaded sacrifice in heaven, and of the Eucharist as the means of entering into and pleading that heavenly sacrifice on earth, and as the earthly centre of the sacrificial worship and life of Christians.

5. Rev 5[6].—'A lamb standing as slain.' The offering of our Lord's living ('standing') created human nature ('lamb'), which had passed through death ('as slain'), is here represented as the centre of the heavenly worship. This passage, therefore, has an indirect relation to the Eucharist as the corresponding earthly centre (see above on He 13[8-16]).

6. Summary.—The results of the exegesis of the NT passages relating to the Eucharist may be summed up as follows: (1) In the reception of Holy Communion there is a gift of Christ's body and blood to sustain and increase His life in those who receive it. (2) The consecrated elements are the spiritual body and blood of the risen and ascended Christ. (3) Those who receive the communion grow thereby in that living union with Christ which their baptism conferred. (4) The feast of communion is also a sacrificial presentation of Christ. (5) It is important to observe that the tradition found in the teaching of the writers of the Church corroborates what is thus seen to be taught in the NT.

LITERATURE.—Frankland, *The Early Eucharist*; Gore, *The Body of Christ*; Strong, *The Doctrine of the Real Presence*; Stone, *The Holy Communion*; Thomas, *A Sacrament of our Redemption*; Adamson, *The Christian Doctrine of the Lord's Supper*; Lambert, *The Sacraments in the NT*; Franzelin, *Tract. de SS. Eucharistiæ Sacramento et Sacrificio*, pp. 12-74, 356-363; Lobstein, *La doctrine de la sainte cène*; Schultzen, *Das Abendmahl im NT*; Batiffol, *Études d'histoire et de théologie positive*, 7ième série; Abbott, *Essays chiefly on the Original Texts of the OT and NT*, pp. 110-128, also *A Reply to Mr. Supple's and Other Criticisms*; Alford on Mt 26[26], 1 Co 10[16. 17], and He 13[10]; Cornely on 1 Co 10[15-22] and 11[23-32]; Ellicott on 1 Co 10[16-18] and 11[23-32]; Evans on 1 Co 10[16-18] and 11[24-31]; Plummer on Lk 22[19. 20] (*ICC*), and in Hastings' *DB* iii. 148-150; Sanday, *ib.* ii. 636-638 (=*Outlines of the Life of Christ*, pp. 157-169); Swete on Mk 14[22-24]; Westcott on Jn 6 and He 13 [10]; Wordsworth on Mt 26[26-23] and Jn 6[51-56].

DARWELL STONE.

LOST.—The word 'lost' has come to be invested with a sinister theological significance. A moral sense hopelessly degraded, a sullen abandonment to evil, a persistent closing of the heart, and a future determined beyond the possibility of alteration—are some of the ideas which it compels in the mind. As it fell from Christ's lips, however, the word did not, as a rule, convey any such harsh suggestions. It was rather a word of infinite pathos and of Divine pity. Used in its Middle voice, the verb ἀπόλλυμι denotes irretrievable ruin, as in the great text, Jn 3[16] (cf. also 17[12] 'None of them is lost, but the son of perdition'; see JUDAS ISCARIOT); but as a participle used passively, the form in which we find it in Lk 19[10], and in the group of parables in Lk 15, which bear especially on this subject, it signifies simply a condition of peril, grave, yet with the glad prospect of recovery.

What moral condition of humanity is meant by the word 'lost' appears from the character of those to whom Jesus directed His message. Broadly speaking, the society of His day was split up into two classes. There were those who, with the advantage of wealth, or, if wealth were denied them, with praiseworthy self-denial, contrived to satisfy the demands of the Law; and, on a platform infinitely lower, stood those who had neither the will nor the means to bear so heavy and so doleful a burden. These latter comprised the sinners, the lapsed, and those recreant Jews who so far forgot themselves as to take service under the conquering Power. They had no share in Israel's hopes; they had ceased to cherish the ideals of the race. It was precisely to this class, called by the Pharisees in a bitter hour 'an accursed multitude which knoweth not the law' (Jn 7[49]), that Christ mainly appealed. He ate and drank with them: He made the conditions of entrance to His Kingdom such as were possible for them all. With a profound sense of what they had missed in life, He summed up their imperfections under this term, 'the lost.' Reviving a beautiful OT figure, He compared them with sheep that had gone astray. If the reality of the case

demanded sterner language, His supreme pity covered that fact from His eyes. They were simply 'lost'; and the word, sorrowful as it was, yet with a ring of hope in it, expressed, while at the same time it concealed, the heinousness of their sin. It was a moral condition full of danger, because they acquiesced in it, and were in some measure content to abide under the shadow of the contempt of their fellow-men. It was a condition full of hope, because it was due partly to circumstances that were invincibly against them, and partly to a merely thoughtless divergence from the true way of human life.

But the delicate shades of meaning which Christ imparted to the word may best be appreciated from its use in the trilogy of parables in Lk 15. From them we learn that, however sinister may be the suggestions which the word carries to our minds, it did not, as employed by Christ, indicate any supreme or singular degree of vice. To be lost was to wander, aimlessly and thoughtlessly, or in wantonness and self-will. It was to live in vain, as a coin that lies hidden among the dust; to turn aside from life's true way, and therefore miss life's true end. There is a suggestion in the term of the lost ideals that one used to hold, and of the forlornness of the mind from which those ideals have fled. There is a hint of the entanglement of the wandering soul in influences that hold it back from safety. There is the generous implication that sin is always in a greater or less degree the result of ignorance, of a thoughtless and wild pursuit after unknown pleasures into unknown paths, until the true path is lost to view, and the unhappy wanderer does not know where it lies. The term leaves also upon the mind the impression that to be lost one does not need to wander far. A man need step but a little way aside to find himself among circumstances that stand up about him and shut out the light, and then, equally with him whose 'feet stumble on the dark mountains,' he is lost. But the singular and appropriate beauty of the idea lies in the prospect of recovery which it implies. Whatever is lost may be found, if in its ignorance it cannot find itself. It may be found by him who has lost it, and whose heart, tortured by anxiety and thrilled with exquisite devotion, will carry him in his search over difficult and perilous roads.

LITERATURE.—Cremer, *Bib.-Theol. Lex. s.v. ἀπόλλυμι*; Bruce, *Parab. Teach. of Christ*, 261, 293, *Gal. Gospel*, ch. vii.; H. E. Manning, *Teaching of Christ*, 105; A. Maclaren, *Beatitudes*, 243; Stopford A. Brooke, *Unity of God and Man*, 34; C. H. Spurgeon, *Parables of our Lord*, Nos. 57, 58, 59; F. W. Robertson, *Sermons*, ii. 190; G. S. Barrett, *Intermediate State*, 187.

A. G. CAMPBELL.

LOT.—The suddenness of the Divine Parousia and the unpreparedness and want of expectation on the part of the world, find illustration from 'the days of Lot' (Lk 17[28]), when the people of Sodom continued their social and commercial activity until 'the day that Lot went out' (v.[29]).

Lot's wife.—to whom in Jewish tradition the name עֵרִית Edith is given—is recorded in Gn 19 to have been turned into a pillar of salt as a result of her looking back upon Sodom while escaping to the mountain. Her fate, as one failing to escape imminent and foretold destruction, is referred to in Lk 17[32], though without specific mention of the form in which destruction overtook her.

Our Lord's word 'Remember' neither confirms nor rejects the tradition. It is with the spiritual fact and its lesson, not with the memorial, that He is concerned. The folly of unreadiness, of the longing for things left behind, of the desire to retain a transient little in the face of impending judgment and at the cost of a greater and eternal loss, is the lesson He would teach in connexion with His Parousia, from the remembrance of Lot's wife.

Literature. — Hastings' *DB*, Smith's *DB*, *Encyc. Bibl.*, Kitto's *Encyc.*, *Jewish Encyc. s.v.*; G. A. Smith, *HGHL* p. 505; Jos. *Ant.* i. xi. 4; Jon. Edwards, *Works* [ed. 1840], ii. 64; Comm., esp. Driver on *Genesis*; and the following expository sermons, J. A. Alexander, *Gospel of Jesus Christ*, 88; H. E. Manning, *Teaching of Christ*, 38; F. Temple, *Rugby Sermons*, ii. 312; S. Cox, *Expositions*, iv. 280; B. Herford, *Courage and Cheer*, 79; G. Matheson, *Representative Men of the Bible*, ii. 22; A. Whyte, *Bible Characters*, i. 129.

J. T. L. MAGGS.

LOTS (Casting of) (λαγχάνω, κλῆρον βάλλειν).— Among the Jews the lot was in frequent use (see Hastings' *DB*, art. 'Lots'). It was the recognized method by which the order of service and most of the individual duties of the priesthood were determined. The order of the 24 'courses' or priestly families was arranged by lot. The 'course' to which Zacharias (Lk 1⁵⁻⁹) belonged was that of Abijah, which stood eighth on the list (1 Ch 24¹⁻¹⁹). Each family or 'course' was on duty for a week, from one Sabbath to another, twice a year (2 K 11⁹). The priests from whom the officiating ministers for the service of the day (ἐφημερία) were to be chosen, had to present themselves 'washed' (Ex 40¹²⁻¹⁵) before the officer who had special charge of the lots. The lots were cast in the 'Hall of Hewn Polished Stones' in the Temple. The distribution of duties for a day among the priests required that the lot should be cast four times. The priest who had to offer incense was chosen by the third lot. This duty was regarded as one of special honour, and the lot by which it was assigned was cast after prayer and confession. The decision was accepted as indicating the man whom God had chosen to offer the prayers of the people. The third of April or the first week of October is by some reckoned as the time when Zacharias was appointed to offer incense (Lk 1⁹). It may have been at the morning or the evening service.

At the Crucifixion the soldiers cast lots for the clothes of Jesus. As they were divided into 'four parts, to every soldier a part' (Jn 19²³), it was evidently a quaternion of soldiers that was on duty. The Synoptists simply record the parting of the garments by lot (Mt 27³⁵, Mk 15²⁴, Lk 23³⁴). In Jn. special reference is made to His 'coat.' It is impossible to say whether the 'coat' was added to one of the four parts, or if a separate lot was cast for it. The precision and detail of the narrative in Jn. have been regarded as proofs that the Fourth Evangelist was an eye-witness of the things which he records. In the casting of the lot for the 'coat' he saw the fulfilment of one of the predicted woes of the Messiah (Ps 22¹⁸). The quotation is in the exact words of the LXX. Critical editions of the NT omit the quotation in Matthew.

There is no indication as to the particular method by which the lot was cast in the two incidents in which it is employed in the Gospels.

It may be noted under this heading that the idea of the lot as giving expression to the Divine will runs through all the words which relate to inheritance (κληρονόμεω, -ομία, -ονόμος). With this fundamental significance all such words become part of the language of grace. The right of inheritance in the Kingdom of God, or to eternal life, does not spring from legal enactment or personal merit, but from the will of God.

Literature. — Edersheim, *Life and Times of Jesus the Messiah*, i. 133–187, ii. 592 f.; Jos. *Ant.* VII. xiv. 7; Godet on *Luke*, vol. i. 71; Muirhead, *Times of Christ*, p. 79; Godet on *John*, vol. iii. 266. See also art. Chance.

JOHN REID.

LOVE.—In the word 'love' is concentrated, we may say, the essence of the Christian religion. It is love that is the outstanding feature in the revelation Christ has given us of the nature of God, love that is the controlling power in the life of the Son who claimed that he that had seen Him had seen the Father (Jn 14⁹). On the two commandments to love God and to love our neighbour, Christ declares that all the Law and the Prophets hang (Mt 22⁴⁰). In the commandment to love one another as He has loved them, He sums up the new law which He lays upon His disciples, declaring that by their fulfilment of it the faithfulness of their discipleship shall be known (Jn 13³⁴ᶠ·). We propose to exhibit from different points of view the place which love holds in the doctrine of Christ.

1. The love of God for man.—It is certainly true, as has been pointed out, that Christ does not, in the Synoptic Gospels, speak directly of the love (ἀγάπη) of God. But if He does not thus expressly *predicate* love of God, it is because He has already endowed Him, as *subject*, with this love in the highest degree. The doctrine of the Fatherhood of God, which is the foundation of the whole gospel of Christ, contains within it the fullest recognition of the love of God. If the Apostolic writers of the NT expand with greater fulness the doctrine of the Divine love, they are only making explicit the truth involved in the assurance of the Fatherhood of God set forth on every page of the Synoptic Gospels. The God whose love is the constant theme of St. Paul's preaching is the Father-God of Jesus Christ (so H. Holtzmann interprets the Pauline formula ὁ θεὸς καὶ πατὴρ τοῦ κυρίου ἡμῶν Ἰησοῦ Χριστοῦ, *Neutest. Theol.* i. 171). In the one word 'Abba,' which Christian lips have learned to repeat after the Master, there lies to St. Paul the assurance of the Divine love which can banish the old feeling of bondage and inspire the spirit of adoption (Ro 8¹⁵). The Johannine doctrine that God is love (1 Jn 4⁸) is but the statement in abstract terms of the truth to which Christ has given concrete expression in the doctrine of the Fatherhood of God. For it is the love of God that Christ will express by this name which is so constantly on His lips. He speaks of God not only as His own Father ('My Father'), or as the Father of those who are members of the Kingdom of God ('your Father'), but as 'the Father' absolutely (Mt 11²⁷, Mk 13³², Lk 11¹³). The title suggests more than the relation in which God stands to mankind as their Creator. In Mt 5⁴⁴⁻⁴⁸ Christ urges His hearers to become God's sons by showing a love like to that of their Father in heaven, 'for he maketh his sun to rise on the evil and on the good, and sendeth rain on the just and on the unjust.' Did Fatherhood mean merely Creatorship, there could be no question of *becoming* the sons of God. All men are God's creatures. The fact that Christ speaks of our becoming God's sons, proves that He is using the terms 'Father' and 'sons' in an ethical sense. By Fatherhood He indicates the love which God cherishes for men, by sonship the love by which they may prove themselves like in character to this Father whose nature is love. This love suggested by the name 'Father' is the very essence of the Divine nature. It is not merely one among the various attributes of God. It is the supreme and dominating element in the Divine character. It is in it that the Divine perfection lies; and when Christ urges us to be perfect as our Father in heaven is perfect (Mt 5⁴⁸), it is evident from the context that it is of the love of God that He is thinking, a fact recognized by Lk., who substitutes 'merciful' for the 'perfect' of Mt.'s version (Lk 6³⁶).

This love of the Father in heaven is the foundation upon which the gospel of Christ rests. It is all-embracing. God is the Father not only of those who are members of the Kingdom of God, *i.e.* of those who by the love which animates them prove themselves to be His sons (Mt 5⁴⁵), but of all men. The evil as well as the good, the unjust as well as the just, are the objects of His love (*ib.*); and if the facts to which Christ refers, in this connexion, in proof of the universality of the Father's love, do not go beyond such natural blessings as the sunshine and the rain, that is explained on the ground that these blessings require for their appreciation no special receptivity on the part of those who enjoy them (Beyschlag, *Neutest. Theol.* i. 81). The Father cares for all. Each individual is precious in His sight. ' It is not the will of your Father which is in heaven, that one of these little ones should perish' (Mt 18¹⁴). The very hairs of our head are all numbered (10³⁰). There is joy in heaven over one sinner that repenteth (Lk 15⁷· ¹⁰). In the fact of God's Fatherhood there lies the assurance that He will certainly give good things to them that ask (Mt 7¹¹ 18¹⁹), and that He will welcome the penitent sinner who turns to Him (Lk 15¹¹⁻³²). It is the Father's good pleasure, Christ assures us, to give us the Kingdom (12³²), that greatest of all blessings, to obtain which a man might well be willing to sacrifice everything else (Mt 13⁴⁴⁻⁴⁶) ; and with it He gives us all such material blessings as He sees to be necessary for us (Lk 12³¹, Mt 6³³). When we thus gather together the various utterances of Christ with regard to the God whom He reveals to us as Father, when we think of the assurance that name breathes of bountiful providence, of watchful care, of forgiving love, when we remember, above all, how Christ points to the Father's unfailing goodness towards the undeserving as an instance of the Divine perfection, we must confess that though the Synoptic Gospels contain no direct mention of the love of God, the Being whose character the Saviour seeks to reveal to us by that name 'Father' is one whose very nature is love.

In the Fourth Gospel it is the same representation of the nature of God that meets us. Here, too, 'Father' is the favourite designation. It has been questioned, indeed, whether the title 'Father' has the same significance in the Fourth Gospel as in the Synoptics. H. Holtzmann (*Neutest. Theol.* ii. 433 f.) maintains that in the constantly recurring designation of God as 'the Father' there is always either an express or a tacit reference to the Son. [For a full discussion of the use of the word 'Father' in St. John, see Westcott, *The Epistles of St. John*, pp. 29–34]. But there are occasions on which we feel that the title is used in a manner which suggests a reflexion on the love of God quite in the manner of the Synoptics, as when Christ says to the disciples that whatever they shall ask the Father in His name He will give (15¹⁶ 16²³), or when He tells them that He does not say that He will pray the Father for them, for the Father Himself loveth them (16²⁶ᶠ·). And in any case the question of the significance attaching to the title 'Father' in the Fourth Gospel is of minor interest in our present inquiry, since that Gospel contains many express declarations of the love of God, the absence of which makes the question of the significance of that title in the Synoptics matter of importance. These express references to the love of God in the Fourth Gospel occur specially in connexion with that aspect of the Divine love which we proceed to consider under the following head.

2. The love of God for man as manifested in Christ.—The highest proof of the Father's love is given in the mission and Person of the Son. This aspect of the Divine love, which is emphasized in the Fourth Gospel, is not unknown in the Synoptics, though it is rather implied than expressed. If the love of the Father is manifested in the bestowal of the Messianic Kingdom (Lk 12³²), that Kingdom which has been prepared for His children from the foundation of the world (Mt 25³⁴), and which is now about to come with power (Mk 9¹), then the sending of the Son (Mt 10⁴⁰ 21³⁷) to inaugurate the Kingdom must in itself be an evidence of the love of God. All things are delivered unto the Son of the Father, and He alone can reveal the Father to man (Mt 11²⁷, Lk 10²²). And this revelation is not confined to His preaching. It embraces the whole of His Messianic work. That work was from beginning to end animated by the spirit of love. He pointed to His works of healing as proof that the Messianic era had arrived (Mt 11⁵ 12²⁸). He described His daily work on one occasion as 'casting out devils and doing cures' (Lk 13³²). He called to all who laboured and were heavy laden to come to Him and He would give them rest (Mt 11²⁸). As He had assured men of the forgiving love of God, so He declared that He came not to call the righteous but sinners (Mk 2¹⁷), and on occasion announced the forgiveness of their sins to those who approached Him (Mk 2⁵, Lk 7⁴⁷ᶠ·). His whole ministry was one continual mission of love, culminating in the willing sacrifice of His own life as a ransom for many (Mk 10⁴⁵). If we look for the revelation which the Son gives of the Father, not only to His preaching but to His Person and work, then we must admit that that revelation is one which confirms at every point the assurance of God's boundless love for man conveyed by the gracious title by which Christ designates Him.

But this aspect of the matter is not emphasized in the Synoptics as it is in the Fourth Gospel. Here the mission of the only-begotten Son for the salvation of man is expressly cited as a proof of the vastness of the love of God (3¹⁶ᶠ·) ; and whatever question there may be as to the metaphysical relation suggested by that word 'only-begotten,' there can be none as to the depth of the love involved in the sacrifice of the Son so designated. We may note not only the depth but the wideness of the love here proclaimed. God gives His Son for the salvation of the *world*. This wider outlook in connexion with the work of Christ is characteristic of the Fourth Gospel (O. Holtzmann, *Johannes-evangelium*, 49 f., 80 ff.). Christ is the Saviour of the world (4⁴²), the Lamb of God which taketh away the sin of the world (1²⁹). He speaks to the world (8²⁶), gives His flesh for the life of the world (6⁵¹), is the light of the world (9⁵ 12⁴⁶). Into this world burdened with sin (1²⁹) and animated by a spirit of hostility to Himself (12³¹ 17¹⁴), God in His infinite love has sent His Son for its deliverance (3¹⁷). Throughout the whole Gospel there is far more prominence given than in the Synoptics to the fact that Christ has been sent by the Father (5³⁷ 7¹⁶ 8¹⁶· ²⁸ etc.). He repeatedly refers to Himself as Him whom the Father hath sent (5³⁸ 6²⁹ 10³⁶ 17³). He is not come of Himself (7²⁸), but is come in the name of His Father (5⁴³) from whom He has come forth (8⁴² 16²⁷ 17⁸). Not only does the Son, as in the Synoptics, claim to reveal the Father as none other, He asserts that He is in the Father and the Father in Him (10³⁸ 14¹⁰· ²⁰ 17²¹· ²³). He and the Father are one (10³⁰ 17²²). The words that He speaks have been given Him by His Father (7¹⁶ᶠ· 12⁴⁹ᶠ· 14¹⁰· ²⁴ 17⁸). The works that He does are the works of His Father who dwelleth in Him (14¹⁰). He that hath seen Him hath seen the Father (14⁹). As it is love that has inspired the Father in the mission of His Son, so it is love that is the animating principle in the life of the Son who is one with the Father—love to the Father on the one hand (14³¹), and love to His own in the world on the other (13¹ 15¹³). As the Father has loved Him, so He has loved His disciples (15⁹). He sets His love before them as an example, and bids them love one another as He has loved them (13³⁴ 15¹²). The highest proof of His love is given in His death (10¹⁵ 15¹³). The Son lays down His life willingly in obedience to the commandment of the Father (10¹⁷ᶠ·). For this the Father has given the Son (3¹⁶ ἔδωκε, if not to be restricted to the giving to the death, may be taken, in view of 3^{14}, cf. 12^{32}, to include this reference); and the result will be the consummation of the gracious purpose which animated the Father in the giving of the Son. The cross will become the centre of attraction. Through it Christ will draw all men unto Him (12^{32} 8^{28} 11^{52}, cf. $10^{15f.}$), and gain the victory over the prince of this world (12^{31}). Thus will the love of the Son which impelled the Father to the sacrifice of the Son gain the end it seeks to attain, man's deliverance from the destruction which threatens him, and participation in the blessing of everlasting life ($3^{15f.}$ 6^{40}).

Such is the aspect under which the love of God is presented in the Fourth Gospel. It is in the Person of Christ that we have the full and complete revelation of that love. He is God's love incarnate. The Prologue gives the keynote to the whole Gospel. Christ is the Word become flesh, the perfect revelation in human personality of the Divine nature. He is the only-begotten Son (or only-begotten God, if we adopt the reading θεός instead of υἱός), who has declared the Father to us (1^{18}). With God in the beginning (v.²), He was made flesh, and dwelt among us (v.¹⁴). The glory that we behold in Him is a full revelation of the Divine glory, for His relation to the Father is that of an only son who receives the whole of his father's inheritance (ib.). And that glory is the glory of one who reflected in His own person the Divine love, who was full of *grace* and truth (ib.), and of whose fulness we have received, in ever increasing measure, participating in the grace which flowed from Him.

3. The mutual love of God and Christ.—The words 'Father' and 'Son' as applied by Christ to God and man in their relations to one another have, as we have seen, an ethical significance. It is by His love that God proves Himself the Father. It is by exhibiting a love like to that which God displays that man becomes the son of God (Mt 5^{45}). The terms do not lose their ethical content when used to describe the relation in which God and Christ stand to one another. The God whom Christ revealed to men as 'the Father' He had known first of all as His own Father. Such He had felt Him to be from His childhood (Lk 2^{49}). So He addressed Him in prayer (Mt $11^{25f.}$, Mk 14^{36}, Lk 23^{46}); so He spoke of Him to others (Mt $10^{32f.}$ 11^{27} $18^{19.\ 35}$, Lk 22^{29}). He knew Himself to be in a special sense the object of the Divine love. He had been anointed of the Spirit for the performance of the work for which He was sent (Mk 1^{10}, Lk 4^{18-21}), and endowed with a power whereby He might triumph over every hostile influence (Lk 10^{19} 11^{20}). In a remarkable utterance (Lk 10^{22}, Mt 11^{27}) Christ describes the intimate relationship in which the Father and He stand to one another, ' All things are delivered to me of my Father ; and no man knoweth who the Son is but the Father ; and who the Father is but the Son, and he to whom the Son will reveal him.' The mutual knowledge which Father and Son have of one another is based upon that mutual love indicated by the terms Father and Son. Christ claims to be able to reveal God in His character of Father (τίς ἐστιν ὁ πατήρ) as no one else, for none can have such knowledge of the Father's love as the Son, who knows Himself to be in the supreme degree the object of that love (Mk 1^{10}), and can say of Himself that all things are delivered unto Him of His Father, *i.e.* all things necessary for the fulfilment of the Father's gracious purpose. And the Father can reveal Himself thus to the Son because of the love with which that Son responds to His love, and the meekness and submission with which He surrenders Himself to the Father's will (Mt 11^{29}, Mk 14^{36}). It is evident that in this striking word

of Christ's regarding the mutual knowledge of the Father and the Son, the words ' Father' and ' Son' are not mere names to denote the persons concerned, but are used to suggest that mutual love upon which the knowledge is based. And indeed all through the Synoptic Gospels there is always a suggestion of this relationship of mutual love in the manner in which God and Christ are spoken of as Father and Son. Whether, when Christ is spoken of in the Synoptics as the Son of God, there is more than this ethical relationship implied, is a question upon which there is difference of opinion. But it is admitted, even by those who attach a deeper significance to the designation, that, in the first instance at any rate, it has an ethical content, and that, when Christ is called the Son of God, whatever more may be implied, so much in any case is suggested, that on the one hand He is the supreme object of the Father's love, and that on the other He exhibits in His Person in its perfection that loving obedience whereby man may become the son of God.

In the Fourth Gospel the references to the love of the Father and the Son to one another are more frequent and more express. Christ is the only-begotten Son (3^{16}), loved by the Father before the foundation of the world (17^{24}), and now returned to the bosom of the Father (1^{18}). He and the Father know one another intimately (10^{15}). The Father loves Him, and has given all things into His hand (3^{35}). As in the Synoptic account of the announcement at the Baptism, Christ is called the beloved Son in whom God is well pleased (Mk 1^{11}), so in Jn. the love of the Father is occasionally represented as being based upon the Son's obedience to the Father's commandment (15^{10}) and willing sacrifice of Himself (10^{17}). The Father never leaves Him alone (16^{32}), for He does always those things that please Him (8^{29}). Because He keeps His Father's commandments He abides in His love (15^{10}). No higher estimate can be given of the Saviour's love for His disciples than to say that He has loved them as His Father has loved Him (15^{9}), nor of the love of God for believers than to compare it to that of the Father for the Son (17^{23}). Sometimes the love of God for believers is represented as based upon that of the Father for the Son ($14^{21.\ 23}$ 16^{27}).

And as the Father loves the Son, so the Son loves the Father. He alone has seen and known the Father ($3^{11.\ 32}$ 6^{46} 7^{29} 8^{55} 10^{15}). He does nothing of Himself, but only what He seeth the Father do (5^{19}). He speaks only as His Father hath taught Him (8^{28} 12^{50}). His meat is to do the will of Him that sent Him (4^{34}). It is love to the Father (14^{31}) no less than love to His brethren (13^{1} 15^{13}) that is the motive that animates Him in the fulfilment of His vocation. In virtue of the love which unites them one to the other, each may be said to be in the other, the Son in the Father and the Father in the Son (10^{38} $14^{10.\ 20}$ $17^{21.\ 23}$). They have no separate interests. Whatever belongs to the one belongs to the other (17^{10}). The Father and the Son are one (10^{30} 17^{22}).

4. The love of man for God.—There is comparatively little under this heading to be found in the Gospels. It is true that Christ has Himself given as the first commandment of all, that which enjoins the love of God with the whole heart and soul and mind and strength (Mk $12^{28ff.}$), and in the same spirit in the Fourth Gospel He finds the final explanation of the unbelief of the Jews in their lack of this love of God (5^{42}). But so far as the former of these passages is concerned, it is evident that Christ's answer to the scribe is purposely couched in language borrowed from the Old Testament ; and it is a noteworthy fact that at other times, when He has no occasion to conform to OT modes of expression, Christ does not give prominence to the duty of love towards God.

Ritschl has drawn attention to the fact of how small a part the love of man towards God plays throughout the NT as a whole. 'Love is reserved as the characteristic of God and God's Son in the foundation and guidance of the congregation, while of its members faith or trust in God and His Son is demanded' (*Rechtf. u. Vers.* ii. 100 f.). B. Weiss thinks that Christ keeps the commandment of love to God in the background, because where the love of God does not awaken such love in return it would be of no avail to demand it (*Bib. Theol. of NT*, § 25b). Wendt, while recognizing that the idea of love corresponds well, on the whole, to the filial relationship, believes that it is too general, and does not give sufficient prominence to the relation of subordination and complete dependence in which man stands to God. To express the feeling of whole-hearted devotion to God suggested by the idea of love, while at the same time giving full recognition to His infinite love and power, Christ selected the term 'trust' (πίστις) as the one most suitable to describe the disposition man should display (*Lehre Jesu*, ii. 227).

Whatever the reason, we must recognize the fact that neither in the Synoptics nor in the Fourth Gospel, with the exception of the passages referred to, do we find Christ dwelling on the love which man should cherish towards God. But though He speaks of man's trust in God rather than of his love towards Him, we must not overlook the fact that this trust which Christ seeks to inspire is but love under a slightly different form. It is the response of the human heart to the infinite love of God,—love on the part of man awakened by the love of God, yet humbling itself in the presence of One who, though the Father, is yet Lord of heaven and earth. Without trust there can be no such trust as Christ seeks to inspire. The prayer in which this trust finds expression must be the outpouring of a heart full of love to God and of zeal for the establishment of His Kingdom. The righteousness which becomes the members of the Kingdom must be righteousness not of outward conduct alone, but of a heart which takes delight in the performance of the Divine will. The believer is to seek first the Kingdom and the righteousness of God (Mt 6[33]), to have his heart fixed on the heavenly treasure (6[21]), to be filled with whole-hearted devotion to the service of God (6[24]), and to renounce, no matter at what cost, whatever may hinder him in the attainment of the great end set before him (Mk 9[43-48], cf. Mt 13[44ff.]). Though there may be little explicit reference in the teaching of Christ to the love for God which man is required to cherish, we feel that in the case of the believer no less than in that of Christ Himself, it is the source from which springs all the strength for the performance of duty and the endurance of suffering, and that, just as Christ accounted for the unbelief of the Jews by the utter lack in them of this love of God (Jn 5[42]), so, if we trace back to its beginnings the faith which the gospel inspires, it will be found to issue from the love to the Father who has revealed Himself in Christ.

5. The love of man for Christ.—Of love for Christ there is almost no mention in the Synoptics. In one utterance, indeed, Christ requires His followers to love Him more than their closest earthly relatives (Mt 10[37]). But the purpose of that saying, as is proved by the parallel passage, Lk 14[26], is not so much to insist on a personal affection for Himself as the condition of discipleship, as to emphasize the supreme worth of the good represented by His own Person, compared with which the joys of family life are to be esteemed as nothing. The nearest approach to any reference to love of Himself as a motive for conduct is to be found in those passages in which He puts His own Person in the foreground, requiring of His disciples a readiness to sacrifice themselves for His sake (Mk 8[35] 10[29]), and attaching high importance to the most trivial acts done in His name (Mk 9[37. 41]). On these occasions He identifies Himself with

His cause. When He requires devotion to Himself, it is only another way of requiring devotion to the truth revealed in His Person. Thus He speaks of sufferings borne for His sake and the gospel's (8[35] 10[29], cf. Lk 18[29]), and of being ashamed of Him and of His words (Mk 8[38], Lk 9[26]). In this spirit He welcomed the love displayed by the woman who anointed His feet in the Pharisee's house, as a proof of the sincerity of the repentance which filled her heart, and of the vastness of the blessings she was conscious of having received (Lk 7[47]).

In the Fourth Gospel, where the personal relation to Christ is so strongly emphasized, there is more direct reference to love as the disposition the believer may be expected to display towards Christ. Jesus tells the Jews that if God were their Father they would love Him, for He proceeded forth and is come from God (8[42]). Of the disciples He says, on the other hand, that the Father loveth them because they have loved Him, and have believed that He came from God (16[27]). Something is, indeed, still lacking in their love. He tells them in His farewell address that if they loved Him they would rejoice because He said that He went unto the Father (14[28]). But though their love be not perfect, He can confidently reckon upon it. He would only remind them, as He does more than once in the course of that address, that a true love for Him will manifest itself in the keeping of His commandments (14[21. 23f.]). So it had been with His own love for the Father (14[31]). So let it be with the disciples. Let them prove the sincerity of their love to Him by the loyalty of their obedience. Such a relationship to Himself, love manifesting itself in faithful fulfilment of His commandments, is the condition upon which the giving of the Paraclete is promised (14[15ff.]). Where it exists, Christ promises the enjoyment of the closest communion with the Father and Himself (14[21. 23]). It is quite in keeping with the emphasis that has been laid upon love throughout the Gospel as the relation which must exist between the disciple and Christ, that in the final scene with Peter in the Epilogue He should thrice address to him the question, 'Lovest thou me?' (21[15-17]), as if to suggest that such love is the indispensable qualification on the part of one who would be a true shepherd of Christ's flock.

In view of these quotations, it is difficult to understand Ritschl's statement (*Rechtf. u. Vers.* iii. 560), that, apart from Jn 21[15. 16], there is no reference in the NT to love towards Christ. Certainly it is the case that, for the most part, faith is the usual formula to indicate the relation of the believer to Him. But it is quite in accordance with the general character of this Gospel, with its conception of a mystical union between the believer and Christ (15[1ff.]), to use warmer colours to paint the devotion of the believer, and to describe that complete self-surrender to Christ, which is the true relation to Him, as the work of love.

6. The love of man to man.—Alongside of the first great commandment to love the Lord our God, Christ places a second, 'Thou shalt love thy neighbour as thyself' (Mk 12[31]). The high importance He assigned to this duty is evident from the place He gives it alongside of the commandment to love God. 'There is none other commandment greater than these' (*ib.*). Both are ethical in their nature. The ceremonial observances in which Christ's contemporaries thought to find the fulfilment of this first commandment are never to be allowed to stand in the way of the performance of the offices of love towards our fellow-men. These latter, because they are ethical, are the weightier matters of the Law which are on no account to be omitted (Mt 23[23]). To refuse to support one's parents, on the plea that one desires to make an offering of the money that might be used for this purpose, is to make a travesty of religion (Mk 7[9-13]). The ethical stands above the ceremonial. God desires mercy, not sacrifice (Mt 12[7]). The first commandment may be to love the Lord our God, but when it is a question of showing love towards our brother man or performing some act of worship towards God, there can be no doubt which is to come first, 'Leave there thy gift before the altar, and first go thy way; be reconciled to thy brother, and then come and offer thy gift' (5[23f.]).

In the enunciation of this second great commandment, Christ specifies the love which men are required to show for one another as the love of one's *neighbour*. Doubtless the word was suggested by the precept from Leviticus which He quoted, just as the form of the first commandment is based, as we have seen, upon the language of Deuteronomy. When we inquire as to the wideness of the circle denoted by the term 'neighbour,' we seem to find an answer in the parable of the Good Samaritan, which was told, according to Lk., in response to the question that had been put, 'Who is my neighbour?' (Lk 10[29-37]). But in its present form that parable gives no satisfactory answer to the question. After telling the story of what befell the traveller, how he was maltreated by the thieves and passed by in his miserable plight by the priest and the Levite, and how at last the Samaritan took compassion on him, Christ asks, 'Which now of those three, thinkest thou, was neighbour unto him that fell among the thieves?' The answer is, the Samaritan; and the conclusion of the parable seems to be that it was the traveller's duty to love the Samaritan, *i.e.* that the term 'neighbour' is wider than the lawyer who had put the question seemed to imagine, and must be held to embrace any who by their conduct prove themselves worthy of the name, whether they be Jews or not (so Wendt, *Lehre Jesu*, ii. 268). This is certainly the logical conclusion from the parable as it at present stands, but it is questionable whether this can have been the lesson Christ desired to enforce by it. It starts with the object of proving who is one's neighbour in the sense of *diligendus* (v.[29]), and ends by proving who is the traveller's neighbour in the sense of *diligens*, v.[36] (Jülicher, *Die Gleichnisreden Jesu*, ii. 596). The nearest approach that it reaches to a definition of the term 'neighbour' in the sense required is contained in the 'Go and do thou likewise' with which it concludes. The usual method of interpreting the parable is to find the answer to the question in the practical lesson enforced by that exhortation, and to conclude that our neighbour is anyone who requires our help. But in view of the immediately preceding statement that the neighbour of the traveller was the Samaritan who had compassion on him, it seems utterly incongruous to conclude that the design of the parable is to teach that one's neighbour is not one's benefactor, but anyone that one can benefit, *i.e.* in this case that the traveller was the neighbour of the Samaritan. So we can only conclude that Lk. is responsible for the introduction of the parable in connexion with this question of the lawyer's, and that whatever the original purpose for which it was related, it was certainly not designed to give an answer to the question, 'Who is my neighbour?' in the sense of 'Who is the person I am required to love?'

But the precise scope of the term 'neighbour' in the mouth of Christ is of the less importance, as it is only on the occasion of His interview with the scribe (Mk 12[28-34], Mt 22[35-40]) that He thus defines the limits within which one is to show love towards one's fellow-men, and there, as we have seen, He is evidently formulating His answer in the language of the OT commandment. In opposition to the narrow sense in which the term 'neighbour' was interpreted by His contemporaries, who could add to the injunction to love their neighbour a corollary to the effect that they were to hate their enemy (Mt 5[43]), Christ enjoined a love which was to embrace both friend and enemy (v.[44f.]). The Golden Rule which Christ has given men to guide them in their offices of love takes us far beyond the circle of neighbours in the narrow Jewish sense. The command runs, 'All things whatsoever ye would that men (not your neighbours) should do unto you, do ye even so to them' (7[12]). We are to show love to all. 'Whosoever shall smite thee,' 'if any man will sue thee,' 'whosoever shall compel thee,' 'he that asketh thee,' 'he that would borrow of thee,'—these are the phrases with which Christ introduces those to whom He commands His disciples to show love (5[39-42]). Sometimes He describes them as 'brothers' (5[22. 24] 7[3-5] 18[15. 21f. 35]), not in the sense of those who are bound to us by natural ties, in which sense brotherly love is practised by the Gentiles as well (5[47]), nor in the sense of fellow-citizens of the Kingdom of God (so B. Weiss; Westcott, *The Epistles of St. John*, note on 1 Jn 2[9]), in which sense the word would reproduce in a new form the limitation that attached to the Jewish interpretation of the term 'neighbour,' but in the same wide sense as He applies the term 'Father' to God. He is the Father not only of the members of the Kingdom, but of all mankind (5[45]), and by using the term 'brother' to denote the objects of our love, Christ will suggest that it is to be a love as wide and all-embracing as that of the Father in heaven, who bestows His bounties on good and evil,—a love not only of those who are members of the Kingdom of God, but of all who have the right to look up and claim God as their Father in heaven (Wendt, *Lehre Jesu*, ii. 270 f.). The command to forgive our brother his trespasses (18[35]) is interpreted in the widest sense in 6[14f.], when, in place of forgiving our *brother*, Christ speaks of forgiving *men* their trespasses.

From various occasional utterances of Christ we can form a general idea of the nature of the love which He expects men to display in their relations to one another. Its unselfishness on the one side, and its interest in the welfare of others on the other, are features which continually appear in the exhortations in which He seeks to inculcate it. In illustration of the unselfish spirit which He commends, He urges His hearers to invite to their banquets not their friends and kinsmen who may invite them in return, but the poor, the maimed, the lame and the blind, who cannot recompense them (Lk 14[12ff.]). In the same spirit He bids men lend, hoping for nothing (6[35], according to the translation of μηδὲν ἀπελπίζοντες best suited to the context). Another aspect of the unselfishness which is characteristic of the spirit of love Christ would instil, is the suppression of those vindictive feelings which are prone to rise when we experience ill-treatment from others. We are required to forgive those who have wronged us, not seven times, but seventy times seven (Mt 18[21f.]); to be so far from resenting injury we receive from another that we turn the other cheek to the smiter, allow him who would take away our coat to have our cloak also, and go two miles with him who would compel us to go one (5[38-42]); to love our enemies, and to pray for them that persecute us (5[44]). Again, this unselfishness will exhibit itself in the absence of all self-assertion or desire to attain pre-eminence among our fellows. Such self-exaltation is characteristic of the scribes and Pharisees (Mk 12[38f.], Mt 23[5ff.]), and of the Gentiles (Mk 10[42], Lk 22[25]). But the follower of Christ, who came not to be ministered unto but to minister, and who was among His disciples as he that serveth, will be ready to stoop to the lowliest service (Mk 10[43-45], Lk 22[26f.]), and will seek for self-exaltation only through self-abasement (Lk 14[11]).

But while love is thus regardless of self, it will ever seek to advance the good of others. It will give readily to supply their demands (Mt 5[42], Lk 6[30]). Nay, it will be quick to anticipate them. It will teach us to put ourselves in their place and realize what they stand in need of. 'All things whatsoever ye would that men should do to you, do ye even so to them' (Mt 7[12], Lk 6[31]). We shall not hesitate to share with them our earthly goods. 'It is more blessed to give than to receive' is a saying of Christ's preserved by St. Paul (Ac 20[35]) which is not recorded in the Gospels. In the picture which Christ has painted of the Judgment, He claims as offices of love performed towards Himself acts of kindness done to our unfortunate fellow-creatures (Mt 25[34-40]). That is the wise use of our riches whereby we make to ourselves friends of those whom we benefit (Lk 16[9]). But we shall care not only for our brother's worldly interests, but also for his spiritual welfare. We are solemnly warned to give heed lest we cause him to stumble (Mk 9[42], Lk 17[1f.]). It is not the will of our Father which is in heaven that one of these little ones, *i.e.* the humblest member of the Kingdom of God, should perish (Mt 18[14]). And while we are careful to avoid the censorious spirit which takes delight in uncharitable judgment of the faults of others (7[1f.]), we shall still feel it our duty to rebuke our brother when he trespasses, and to endeavour to reclaim him from his sin (18[15f.]).

One other point worthy of notice in connexion with the duty of brotherly love which Christ inculcates, is the light in which this duty is presented in view of the love which we experience at the hands of God. At the root of all that Christ says regarding the love which we should display to one another lies the great truth of the Fatherhood of God. That word of St. John's, 'We love because he first loved us' (1 Jn 4[19]), expresses the position which Christ takes up. To forgive another his trespasses and to recompense an injury with kindness, to love one's enemies and to pray for them that persecute one, appears the height of magnanimity from the standpoint of the natural man. But Christ puts the matter in a new light. He reminds us of the love with which God treats man, undeserving as he is, and of the readiness with which He forgives us our offences. In the parable of the Unforgiving Servant (Mt 18[23-35]) He exhibits in its true light the conduct of the man who, freely forgiven at the hands of God, yet refuses to forgive his brother who has offended him. And as our indignation burns at the behaviour of the unforgiving servant in the parable, we realize that so far from the forgiveness of those who have offended us being the magnanimous conduct we had imagined, it is a simple duty, the non-fulfilment of which calls for severest condemnation.

In the Fourth Gospel the duty of love to our brother is laid down with the utmost distinctness, though the references are comparatively few. As in the Synoptics Christ had summed up the Law and the Prophets in the Golden Rule to do unto others whatsoever we would that they should do to us, so here He concentrates His ethical teaching to His disciples in the new commandment to love one another as He has loved them (13[34] 15[12]). It was a new commandment in the new emphasis with which it was enjoined, in the new place assigned to it as the one principle in which the Law and the Prophets find fulfilment (Mt 7[12] 5[17ff.], cf. Ro 13[9], Gal 5[14]), in the new sanction it received through the appeal to Christ's own example. He declares that the keeping of this commandment is

the sure test whereby His disciples may be recognized by others (13[35]). It is by their fulfilment of it alone that they may enjoy such close communion with Him as He enjoys with His Father (15[10. 12]). He has given them an example in His own Person of the love they are to practise. At the last meal with His disciples, at which this new commandment was given, He had Himself washed their feet, to enforce the injunction to lowly service which He laid upon them (13[14ff.]). But this act of condescension on the part of the Master was typical of the self-denying love which He had displayed throughout His whole intercourse with them, that love which reached its culminating point in the willing sacrifice of His life. It is to this that He points when He urges them to love one another as He has loved them. 'Greater love hath no man than this, that a man lay down his life for his friends' (15[13]).

It has been urged that the brotherly love which is thus commended in the Fourth Gospel falls short of that enjoined in the Synoptics, in respect that it is limited to the circle of the Christian brotherhood. While Christ in the Synoptics commands us to love our neighbour, and insists that the love which He enjoins must embrace not only our friends but our enemies, we read in the Fourth Gospel of a love *for one another* (13[34. 35] 15[12. 17]). The reciprocal pronoun points to a limitation of the love to the Christian brotherhood. The Christians are known not by their love for others, but by their mutual love amongst themselves (H. Holtzmann, *Handcom.* on Jn 13[13], *Neutest. Theol.* ii. 388 f. ; O. Holtzmann, *Johannesevang.* 76, 266). And as the love which the believer is exhorted to practise is limited to the Christian brotherhood, so also, it is maintained, is that of Christ Himself, which is held up as an example. The Fourth Gospel and St. Paul both cite the death of Christ as the highest proof that can be given of His love ; but St. Paul finds in it a proof of His love for His enemies (Ro 5[6ff.]), whereas the Evangelist adduces it as a proof of His love for His friends (15[13]). Such love of friends, it is maintained, is the highest love the Gospel recognizes. Of love for one's enemies it knows nothing (O. Holtzmann, *ib.* 87, 276 ; H. Holtzmann, *Handcom.* on Jn 15[13], *Neutest. Theol.* ii. 477).

We must admit that there is so much truth in the contention that, as a matter of fact, the love referred to in 13[34f.] 15[12. 17] is a love of Christian brethren for one another. It would be quite unwarrantable to find the novelty of the commandment 13[34] in the wideness of its scope, to which there is no reference at all in the context. But it is equally unwarrantable to explain that novelty as consisting in the narrowness of the circle within which Christ, in the context, insisted on its fulfilment, as if this commandment to practise brotherly love were an advance upon the old injunction to love one's neighbour. (So Grotius: 'Novum autem dicit, quia non agit de dilectione communi omnium, sed de speciali Christianorum inter se, qua tales sunt' ; cf. Kölbing, *SK*, 1845, pp. 685–694). It is a mistake to take the commandment in any exclusive sense, as if there were any contrast implied to the wider commandment of the Synoptics. Christ speaks of the love of Christian brethren for one another, either because He had had occasion immediately before to give His disciples a lesson on the manner in which they should be ready to render loving service to one another (13[4-17]), or because it was natural to look for the display of this spirit of love He would inculcate first of all within the smaller circle of those who stood in close relation to Him and to one another. It is not a question of confining their love to their Christian brethren, but of displaying it towards those with whom they come into closest contact.

In the same way as Christ urges them to show their love to those who stand nearest to them, He represents His own love as issuing in the sacrifice He made for them, His friends. He does not mean that it was because of the love they had shown Him as friends that He responded with this culminating proof of love in return. On the contrary, He calls them friends because they are the objects of His love (15[15f.]). His sacrifice has not been evoked by the friendship they have displayed. It is rather their friendship that is the response to the love He has cherished for them, of which that sacrifice was the culminating proof.

While we recognize, then, that in this farewell conversation with His disciples, the love which Christ urges them to display is in the first instance a love of one toward another, we cannot admit that there is any intention on the part either of the Evangelist or of Christ Himself to limit the practice of it to the Christian brotherhood. The circumstances in which the address was spoken sufficiently explain the form in which the commandment is given, and the manner in which Christ's example is appealed to. The Teacher who had inculcated a love which was to embrace friend and enemy alike might well feel constrained to give His own disciples the commandment to love one another. And He who had given His life as a ransom for many might well remind those who stood nearest to Him that they were among the many for whom the sacrifice was made, and appeal to them to love one another as He had loved them.

LITERATURE. — Sartorius, *The Doctrine of Divine Love*; Wendt, *Die Lehre Jesu*, ii. ; *NT Theol.* of B. Weiss, Beyschlag, H. Holtzmann, Stevens ; Ritschl, *Rechtfertigung und Versöhnung* ; Rothe, *Theol. Ethik* ; Secley, *Ecce Homo*, chs. xiii. xiv. ; F. W. Robertson, *Serm.* iv. 222 ; Law, *Serious Call*, ch. xx. ; Butler, *Serm.* xi.-xiv. ; C. A. Briggs, *Ethical Teaching of Jesus*, 97, 114.

                                      G. WAUCHOPE STEWART.

LOWLINESS. — The modest attitude of mind and demeanour which characterized our Lord as a man. It is in contrast with, though not in contradiction to, the greatness both of His station and of His claims. He describes Himself (Mt 11[29]) as 'lowly in heart,' and the word employed ($\tau\alpha\pi\epsilon\iota\nu\dot{o}s$) is accurately translated by the Eng. 'lowly' and the Lat. *humilis* as denoting that which is near the earth, low as opposed to lofty, bowed down as opposed to erect. Though sometimes used in a bad sense, as indicating meanness of spirit, this is not at all its necessary or common signification. In the moral sense it is opposed to proud, haughty, self-assertive. The adjective occurs elsewhere in the NT (Lk 1[52], 2 Co 10[1], Ja 1[9] 4[6], 1 P 5[5]) ; and the noun $\tau\alpha\pi\epsilon\iota\nu o\phi\rho o\sigma\dot{\nu}\nu\eta$ and the verb $\tau\alpha\pi\epsilon\iota\nu\dot{o}\omega$ are even of more frequent occurrence. Both noun and verb are used by St. Paul (Ph 2[3. 8]) in describing the $\kappa\dot{\epsilon}\nu\omega\sigma\iota s$ of Christ, where a twofold lowliness is declared of Him : (1) in *becoming* man, (2) *as* a man. In the prophecy of Zechariah (9[9]) the Messianic King is foretold as being 'lowly and riding upon an ass' ; but in the passages where the prophecy is quoted (Mt 21[5], Jn 12[15]), the action is given in both cases. The adjective is altogether omitted by St. John, and is rendered 'meek' ($\pi\rho\alpha\hat{\upsilon}s$) by St. Matthew. See also artt. MEEKNESS and HUMILITY.   E. C. DARGAN.

LUKE. — The only reliable sources for the life of Luke are his Acts of the Apostles, and, in a very slight degree, his Gospel, and the Epistles of St. Paul. The biography found in many MSS of the Gospel in Latin, and printed, for example, in Wordsworth and White's *Novum Testamentum Domini Nostri Iesu Christi Latine*, Pars i. (Oxonii, 1889–1898), pp. 269–272, can hardly be considered reliable, by whomsoever composed. Some of its statements will be quoted below.

1. *Name.*—The name Λουκᾶς appears to be unexampled elsewhere. The modern accentuation is no doubt correct, and this at once proclaims it as a contraction or shorter form of some other name. It belongs in fact to the class of pet names (*Lallnamen*, *Kosenamen* in German), as a glance at the long list of such in Jannaris' *Historical Gr. Gram.* (London, 1897), § 287, will show. The NT itself is not without examples of such names ; Σίλας (Σιλέας) for Σιλουανός, Ἀμπλιᾶς (Ro 16[8]) for Ἀμπλίατος, Ὀλυμπᾶς (Ro 16[15]) for Ὀλυμπιόδωρος, Δημᾶς (Col 4[14]) for Δημήτριος, Ἐπαφρᾶς (Col 4[12]) for Ἐπαφρόδιτος, Ἀπολλώς for Ἀπολλώνιος, Ζηνᾶς (Tit 3[13]) for Ζηνόδωρος, Ἀντιπᾶς (Rev 2[13]) for Ἀντίπατρος, Στεφανᾶς (1 Co 16[15]) for Στεφανηφόρος. The shorter names are less technical and more friendly than the others. There can be little doubt that Λουκᾶς is short for Λουκανός, and indeed this latter form is very frequent in the oldest forms of the Latin Bible, in the title of the Gospel. There appears to be no example of the nominative in MSS, but the accusative CATA LUCANUM is regular (see C. H. Turner in *JThSt*, vi. (1904–1905), pp. 256–258). Monsignor Mercati, of the Vatican Library, has found an instance even of the nominative, on the sarcophagus of Concordius at Arles, MATTEUS MARCUS LUCANVS IOANNES (*ib.* p. 435).* The name *Lucanus* suggests 'Lucanian,' a native of the district of Southern Italy ; it also suggests the Latin poet, a member of the *gens Annæa*, nephew of Seneca the philosopher. But neither of these suggestions seems to lead us further in the attempt to trace the ancestry or family of the Third Evangelist.

2. *Origin.*—The Latin biography above referred to calls Luke a Syrian of Antioch. This is almost certainly due to a mistaken interpretation of Ac 13[1], where a different person, with a different name, Lucius, is mentioned. If that be not the explanation, the selection of Antioch may be due to a guess, which sought to connect him with an important city. Some have thought that 'Antiochensis' is right, but that 'Syrus' is wrong, and would claim him for Pisidian Antioch, a place of much less importance. In the absence of other evidence, this second theory would be possible, as Pisidian Antioch is much nearer the historical scene on which he first appears and figures prominently in the missionary journeys of St. Paul. The Book of Acts itself, however, seems to yield up the secret. If we concentrate our attention on that part of the narrative which tells of St. Paul's visit to Philippi, we observe certain peculiarities about it which distinguish it from the other parts. In the first place, we observe that in 16[9] 'a certain man of Macedonia' ($\tau\iota s$ implies that the author could name him if he chose) is mentioned as appearing to St. Paul in a dream at Troas, and inviting him to cross over into Macedonia. In the following verse, the first 'We' passage begins :— 'we sought immediately.' The Macedonians did not differ from other Greeks in their appearance or dress, and why should the author conceal the name of the Macedonian, if not from modesty ? The present writer can feel no doubt that Luke and Paul met in Troas, and conversed together, expectant of a sign of the Spirit's will ; that, as the result of their impressive talk, St. Paul saw a vision of his companion of the previous day, who appeared to be addressing him in the words of v. 9 ; and, in accordance with the belief of the time, considered—who shall say wrongly ?—that the Spirit had spoken through this dream. V.[12] of ch. 16 is even more important in this connexion for the information it supplies :—'Philippi, which

* The present writer has recently seen it on the mould of this sarcophagus at the Museum of St. Germain near Paris.

is a city of Macedonia, the first of its district, a *Roman* colony.' The characterization of Philippi might almost be styled gratuitous. Since the battle of B.C. 42 this place was well known to all persons of any education. Further, one might judge from this passage that it was the only Roman colony mentioned in Acts. This is far from being the case. Corinth, Lystra, Ptolemais, and Pisidian Antioch, to mention no others, were also Roman colonies; yet the author affixes the title to Philippi only. Again, we know that Philippi was not regarded by all as the chief town of its district. The author is clearly taking a side as against those who regarded Thessalonica or Amphipolis as the chief town of that district. The rivalry between cities was a characteristically Greek quality, which finds a parallel in the more modern rivalry between Dôle and Basançon. An instance in Asia Minor was that between Smyrna, Ephesus, and Pergamum. We shall not be wrong in regarding the author as a native of Philippi. His fondness for the sea and all matters nautical, as well as his choice of a profession almost entirely confined to Greeks, already proclaim him a Greek. There are other indications that point to Philippi as his native place. V.[13] of ch. 16, 'where *we thought* there was a place of prayer,' is quite natural, if the author, being a Gentile, had only a rough idea where the Jewish place of prayer in his native town was. Again, when Paul and Silas go to Thessalonica (Ac. 17[1]), Luke is left behind in Philippi, and reappears in that neighbourhood afterwards (20[4,5]).

3. *Notes on his Life.*—Of Luke's early life little can be said, and that little is inference derived from his two books. If he were the son of a Greek freedman of a Roman master, this would account both for his name and his history. From the character of the language of his writings it is evident that he had a good education, both rhetorical and medical. It is impossible to say where he was educated, as higher education was widespread in the Greek world. About his disposition something can be said. From the frequent references to the poor in his Gospel and his loving attachment to Paul, as well as his self-effacement, it seems not too fanciful to picture him as a man of modest, tender, sympathetic, and constant nature. His circumstances appear to have been good; otherwise he could hardly have followed Paul as he did, ministering to his ailing body. The present writer has little doubt that the reason why Titus, though a valued coadjutor of St. Paul, is not mentioned in Acts, is that he was Luke's brother, especially as the only natural way to take the words τὸν ἀδελφόν in 2 Co 12[18] is as 'his brother,' *i.e.* the brother of the man previously mentioned, that is, of Titus. Luke as a teacher was not so prominent as Titus, and hence is not named there. The true meaning of the passage would have been understood long ago, had it not been for the obscuration produced by the ecclesiastical sense of the term 'brother.'

The only part of Luke's life of which we know much is the part he spent travelling in St. Paul's company. They met first at Troas, and journeyed together from there by Samothrace and Neapolis to Philippi (Ac 16[10-12]). In Philippi Luke remained after Paul had gone, and they appear to have been separated for a little over five years (according to Ramsay's chronology). After meeting again, almost certainly at Philippi (Ac 20[3-5]), they appear to have remained together till the death of St. Paul. Certainly they were together on St. Paul's last journey along the coast of Asia Minor and Syria, up to Jerusalem (Ac 21[15]), and on the eventful voyage to Puteoli and Rome (ch. 27). In Rome he appears with St. Paul (Col 4[14], Philem 24).

It is probable that he devoted himself mainly to medical and literary work, and not so much to evangelization. The Latin biography states that he never married, and that he died at the age of 74 in Bœotia (some MSS., Bithynia). Another tradition has it that he died at Constantinople, and his sarcophagus, said to have been brought from there, is now pointed out in the Church of Santa Giustina, at Padua.

LITERATURE.—The above art. is largely indebted to Sir W. M. Ramsay's *St. Paul the Traveller and the Roman Citizen*[8], the most sympathetic study of Luke in existence. See also his *Was Christ Born at Bethlehem? A study in the Credibility of St. Luke*[3]; cf. R. J. Knowling's Introduction to the Acts of the Apostles in *The Expositor's Gr. Test.*, vol. ii. (Lond. 1900); Hobart, *The Medical Language of St. Luke* (Lond. 1882); Harnack, *Lukas der Arzt* (Leipzig, 1906).

A. SOUTER.

LUKE, GOSPEL ACCORDING TO.—

i. The Synoptic Problem.
  1. Solutions offered in the past.
  2. Priority of St. Mark.
  3. The doctrine of a proto-Mark, of a deutero-Mark, and of a trito-Mark.
ii. Analysis of St. Luke's Gospel according to the sources used.
  1. First Source—St. Mark.
  2. Second Source—St. Matthew's *Logia*.
  3. Third Source—a Pauline Collection.
  4. Fourth Source—Anonymous Fragments.
  5. Fifth Source—a Private Collection (from the Holy Family?).
  6. Editorial Notes.
iii. Points of contact with St. John.
iv. St. Luke's characteristics.
v. Date of writing.

Literature.

i. THE SYNOPTIC PROBLEM.—To a student of the Synoptic Problem St. Luke's Gospel is the most interesting of the three. Indeed, we may confidently affirm that, but for St. Luke, the Synoptic Problem would never have existed. For the connexions between St. Matthew and St. Mark are comparatively simple and are easily explained. It is only when we read St. Luke that the perplexing questions which constitute the Problem arise. We have first to explain the fact of his omissions (*a*) of Markan matter, (*b*) of Matthæan; next, his additions (*a*) of narrative, (*b*) of discourse; thirdly, his variations from the other Gospels in arrangement (*a*) of Markan matter, (*b*) of Matthæan; then we must examine his editorial work, which consists (*a*) of prefaces to introduce a section, (*b*) of conclusions to wind it up, (*c*) of explanatory notes, (*d*) of corrections, alike in fact, in style, and in grammar; lastly, we must consider cases where he agrees with St. Matthew against St. Mark, and cases where he alone of the Synoptists has some contact with St. John. Anyone who attempts to solve the Problem by neglecting one or more of these factors, may fascinate the reader by the simplicity of his proposals, but he does so at the expense of success. He has not really grappled with the Problem, and therefore has not solved it. If, on the other hand, the reader thinks the proposals which are here offered too intricate; if he accuses the writer of vacillation, because two or more solutions are frequently offered of the same difficulty, let him reflect that in mathematics—the most exact of sciences—a similar fact may be observed. For every quadratic equation has two solutions, and when the Radcliffe Observer published his calculation of the distance of the sun from the earth, the answer came out as a double quadratic with four variations. Similar complications should be expected in an intricate literary problem like this. Let the beginner cultivate patience and suspense of judgment. He will have made good progress, if he learns to suspect the man who is too simple or too confident.

1. Solutions offered in the past.—Augustine, bishop of Hippo, at the close of the 4th cent., was the first writer who made a serious attempt to solve the Synoptic Problem. He was guided partly by tradition, but chiefly by a careful examination of the internal evidence which the Gospels offer. In that age it was perhaps inevitable that he should assume, what modern critics are almost united in denying, that the Apostle Matthew was the author of the First Gospel in its present form. From this fundamental error it inevitably followed that he assumed the priority of St. Matthew, and spoke of St. Mark as the 'abbreviator and humble follower of St. Matthew.' St. Luke he held to have copied from the other two. Augustine's influence in the Western Church was so transcendent, that his opinion on these intricate questions was accepted without examination until quite modern times. Strange to say, the founders of the famous Tübingen school in theology, though they reversed most of the traditional beliefs, adhered to this. They upheld the priority of St. Matthew, not for any literary reason, but for a dogmatic one. The miraculous element is somewhat less prominent in St. Matthew than it is in St. Mark; therefore, they argued, he must be the earlier writer.

2. Priority of St. Mark.—The notion of the priority of St. Matthew has, however, been so completely beaten off the field, that we need not spend time in refuting it. Suffice it to say that even so conservative a writer as Dr. Salmon, the late Provost of Trinity College, Dublin, admitted that St. Mark's is the archaic Gospel. And no wonder, for it is simple where the others are complex; it is meagre where they are rich; it is a chronicle while they are histories; it contains Latin and Aramaic words which they have translated or removed. For example, in Mk 15³⁹ we find the Latin word κεντυρίων, but in the parallel passages St. Matthew writes ἑκατόνταρχος and St. Luke ἑκατοντάρχης. Both Evangelists felt that they must not disfigure their pages with St. Mark's 'barbarism,' and the different forms which they used indicate independent action. Who, on the other hand, could suppose that St. Mark found ἑκατόνταρχος in St. Matthew, and deliberately altered it into κεντυρίων, or that St. Luke found ἑκατόνταρχος, and deliberately altered it into ἑκατοντάρχης? For these and other reasons it is maintained in all orthodox schools of criticism that St. Matthew and St. Luke made use of St. Mark. Indeed, St. Mark's Gospel furnishes the historical framework for the others. Equally certain is it that St. Matthew and St. Luke were unacquainted with each other's writings. Whatever agreement exists between them in non-Markan sections comes from their use of a common source. Augustine therefore is wrong in every particular.

3. The doctrine of a proto-Mark, of a deutero-Mark, and of a trito-Mark.—It has, however, long been debated whether St. Mark's Gospel in its complete form lay before St. Matthew and St. Luke. Many critics have held that St. Luke, at any rate, had only an *Urmarkus*—a term which has been used in Germany to signify a document shorter than our St. Mark, earlier in date, and free from those 'picturesque' additions which strike the reader of St. Mark's Gospel. Of late years there has been a growing tendency, both in Germany and in England, to repudiate the doctrine of an *Urmarkus*. Dr. Swete, without arguing the question at length, expresses the opinion that we can dispense with it. The Dean of Westminster is more positive in setting it aside. Nor is this surprising. Those who reject the oral hypothesis are beginning to feel that they cannot multiply documents at pleasure. *Litera scripta manet.* If St. Mark's Gospel circulated in the Apostolic age in three widely different editions, it is impossible to believe that the first and second editions perished without being noticed by such scholars

as Origen and Jerome. Nor is it conceivable, as some maintain, that St. Mark entrusted his first edition to St. Luke, who incorporated it into his Gospel, but allowed no one else to make use of it. No wonder that with men who have an historical sense such hypotheses are unpalatable. But the oral hypothesis readily admits of, nay requires, these gradual growths in St. Mark. Under it there is no difficulty whatever in believing that St. Luke's (oral) St. Mark was much shorter than St. Matthew's, and that St. Matthew's had not received the final touches. In fact, the oral hypothesis solves the Synoptic Problem. The documentary hypothesis fails to do so. Both are equally hypothetical. And those who declare the oral hypothesis to be incredible have never, as yet, fairly tackled the arguments on which it rests, or sufficiently taken into account the habits of the East and of that age. This, however, is not the place to plead for the oral hypothesis, nor has the present writer any wish to do more than demand for it a dispassionate consideration. In the examination which follows he will not assume its truth.

ii. ANALYSIS OF ST. LUKE'S GOSPEL ACCORDING TO THE SOURCES USED.—**1. First Source—St. Mark.**—St. Mark's Gospel (oral or written) was not merely used by St. Luke, it forms the backbone of his Gospel. It is hardly too much to say that without St. Mark there would have been neither a St. Luke nor a St. Matthew. But, as we have already intimated, there is strong reason for concluding that St. Luke used a much shorter work, not merely than our St. Mark, but than the St. Mark which lay before the redactor of St. Matthew. In short, he used an *Urmarkus* or an (oral) proto-Mark. By adopting this view we account at once (a) for his omissions, (b) for his variations from St. Mark's order. He omitted nothing which his St. Mark contained: he adhered to St. Mark's order in every section which he took directly from St. Mark. The marvellous simplification of the Synoptic Problem which this view offers can be appreciated only by those who have seriously endeavoured to explain to themselves and justify to others St. Luke's omissions and his order.

But St. Luke's omissions are so important that we must consider them at some length. In the *Synopsis* St. Mark's Gospel is divided into 223 sections, of which St. Luke omits 54. A group of sections is omitted between Mk 3²² and 4¹. A much larger group—amounting to more than two out of St. Mark's 16 chapters—is omitted between Mk 6¹⁷ and 8²⁶. The remaining omissions consist of single sections scattered over the rest of St. Mark's Gospel. Only from Mk 2 and 5 are no sections omitted. It is manifestly the duty of the critic to account for these omissions, and attempts have been made by harmonists to do so. Thus they have suggested (1) that St. Luke omitted what his readers would not value: being a Gentile himself, and writing for Gentiles, he naturally omitted sections which dealt with questions of Jewish interest; (2) that he objected to repetition, and left out what he regarded as dittographies; *e.g.* having given the feeding of 5000, he thought it unnecessary to narrate the feeding of 4000; having described the anointing of our Lord's feet, he deemed it superfluous to record the anointing of His head. These reasons, however, are quite inadequate. St. Luke is particularly fond of alluding to Jewish customs, and Gentile Christians have always taken a deep interest in them. Furthermore, the great majority of his omissions cannot be accounted for under either of the above heads. Thus he omits 25 out of St. Mark's 86 proper names. He does so in defiance of his instincts as an historian (Wright, *NT Problems* 56–90). Again, he omits the healing of the Syrophœnician's daughter (Mk 7²⁴⁻³⁰)—the only case in which our Lord is recorded to have healed a Gentile. He omits the only journey which our Lord is said to have taken through Gentile lands (7³¹⁻8¹⁰). He omits our Lord's teaching about the inferiority of he moral precepts of the Old Testament to those of the New (Mt 5²⁷·³¹·³³·³⁸·⁴³). All these topics were of overwhelming interest to Gentile readers, and we find it impossible to believe that St. Luke deliberately rejected them. The only satisfactory hypothesis is that he was not acquainted with them, as he would not be if he used a shorter recension of St. Mark and of the *Logia*.

(*a*) Now, if St. Luke used an earlier recension of St. Mark, whether oral or written, it is reasonable to suspect that in several places he has preserved for us the primitive Petrine wording. He will occasionally be nearer to St. Peter's teaching than is either St. Matthew or St. Mark. For, if the trito-Mark has made many additions to the primitive records, so also has he sometimes altered the tradition. In the index to the *Synopsis* nine passages are pointed out in which St. Luke's account is held to be the oldest, but there are probably many more. At any rate it is of the greatest advantage to the critic to feel that he is not always bound to vindicate the priority of St. Mark in details, however highly he may value it on the whole. And although subjective reasoning must always be received with caution, it ought not to be altogether discarded.

(*b*) Although St. Luke omits, as we have seen, 54 out of St. Mark's 223 sections, he does not always omit them entirely, but has preserved short fragments or 'scraps' of 24 out of the 54. These 'scraps' are always misplaced in his Gospel. In fact, the departure from St. Mark's order is our chief means of detecting them. (They may be seen in the *Synopsis*, Table I. a.) No one is likely now to maintain that these 'scraps' were copied directly from a written St. Mark. It is surely incredible that they should have been torn from their context and misplaced. But if these 'scraps' came to St. Luke orally, is it conceivable that he was so careless as never to have discovered that he had a full account of them in writing before him? To the present writer's mind the very existence in St. Luke's Gospel of these 'scraps' is conclusive proof that he used an abbreviated St. Mark. When, therefore, these 'scraps' reached him, he was not aware that they were Markan. For, if we mistake not, there were in the Apostolic age two kinds of oral tradition, both of which contributed much to the composition of St. Luke's Gospel. First there was a vast body of uncodified fact, *rudis indigestaque moles*. Striking sayings were remembered apart from their surroundings, striking deeds were recorded without mention of place or person. These passed from mouth to mouth informally. Secondly, there was the regular course of catechetical teaching preserved by those catechists to whose ill-requited toil St. Paul bears testimony in Gal 6⁶. From these men St. Luke derived the sections of the proto-Mark in their invariable order: from the former source he derived the 'scraps' of the deutero-Mark together with much other matter.

(*c*) St. Matthew's redactor frequently introduces non-Markan material into a Markan section, mixing the two together to the reader's confusion. St. Luke avoids doing this, as a rule, rightly feeling that his sources ought to be treated with respect. But, of course, all the 'scraps' are amalgamated with and lost in other matter.

(*d*) There are cases in which St. Luke corrects the proto-Mark or forsakes it in favour of other sources. Not only does he polish St. Mark's style in a multitude of instances, but in his third chapter he gives (with some additions) the account of the Baptist which he found in the second Source, preferring it to the much shorter account which is found in St. Mark. The same thing is done in Mk 3²²⁻²⁶. He differs from the proto-Mark in holding that only one of the malefactors who were hanged reviled our Lord, the other turned to Him for help (Lk 23³⁹). In the account of the Eucharist (according to the true text) he puts the administration of the Cup before that of the Bread (Lk 22¹⁷⁻¹⁹), following in all probability a local liturgical usage of which several traces remain. These changes must have been made deliberately. And in all cases in which St. Luke or St. John corrects St. Mark, it is reasonable to believe that they had good warrant for doing so.

(*e*) It used to be argued that the testimony of four men is true, and those passages which are found in more than one Gospel were held to be doubly or trebly attested. Criticism has considerably altered our view of this matter. No doubt the 'Triple tradition' deserves special respect. When three Gospels agree *verbatim* (as they seldom do for more than a few words at a time), they are reproducing a source which must be as old as, and may be considerably older than, any of them. Tradition assigns St. Mark's Gospel to St. Peter's teaching, and we are entitled to claim that at least the proto-Mark may in large measure be regarded as his work. In this there is scope for apologetics. But it is evident that, if three Evangelists are reproducing the same Source, they may be reproducing its defects as well as its excellences. Their agreement proves the antiquity, but not the infallibility, of the original. Now Papias expressly asserts that St. Mark's Gospel is defective in order. And when we examine it critically we find that it is arranged topographically. It takes us first to the Jordan valley for our Lord's Baptism, then to Galilee for His ministry; after that comes a journey to Jerusalem, followed by the Passion. Finally, the lost verses must have contained a journey into Galilee, for such a journey is expressly enjoined on the disciples. All three Synoptics adopt this arrangement, except that the final journey into Galilee is omitted by St. Luke, belonging, as it does, to the deutero-Mark. Can we accept St. Mark's arrangement, supported, as it is, by St. Matthew and St. Luke? Is the testimony of three men true? No one until quite modern times has ever thought so. The traditional account is that it is partly true. The Galilæan ministry was broken by visits to Jerusalem, which St. John alone records. In ignoring them the Synoptists were wrong. But the ministry in Jerusalem which the Synoptists give is assumed to have been unbroken by visits to Galilee, and must therefore merely be adjusted with Jn 12–20. This is improbable. St. Mark assigns 360 verses to the ministry in Galilee, which is commonly supposed to have lasted three years, 251 to the ministry in Jerusalem, which lasted about a week. Events in real history seldom move so rapidly. Our contention is that St. Mark is, as Papias says, and as his contemporaries probably well knew, defective in arrangement. Not only ought the ministry in the North to be broken by several visits to Jerusalem, but St. Mark's account of the ministry in Jerusalem ought to be broken by several visits to Galilee. Both ministries must be split up and dovetailed together, if we would attain to the true sequence of events. St. John corrects St. Mark by putting the Cleansing of the Temple into the first year's ministry (Jn 2¹³⁻²²) instead of the last. The traditional view that there were two cleansings is discredited in every other case, and is particularly incredible here. But if St. Mark has misplaced it, he has misplaced also some other sections which adhere to it. And although we cannot with any confidence decide at which particular visit to Jerusalem each of the recorded events happened, it is an enormous gain to the historian to be at liberty to distribute them.

2. Second Source—St. Matthew's Logia.—When Papias wrote that 'St. Matthew compiled the *Logia* (or Utterances of our Lord) in the Hebrew dialect, and each man interpreted them as he was able,' he cannot, as the traditionalists suppose, be alluding to our First Gospel, which was written (at Alexandria?) in Greek. Critical opinion is fast coming round to the view that St. Matthew compiled, not a formal Gospel, but a collection of our Lord's Utterances, which was incorporated into our First Gospel, and formed so distinctive a feature of it, that the whole book was with some justice called 'the Gospel according to St. Matthew.' And if this collection was originally oral, as many who deny an oral Mark are ready to admit, there is nothing strange in our contention that St. Luke used it, when it was much shorter: in fact, he used a proto-Matthew. In that way we explain his omissions, which are more glaring even than his omissions from St. Mark.

The question of order, which was complex in the case of the first Source, is simple here. For St. Luke's order is entirely different from St. Matthew's. Except on the rare occasions when St. Mark furnishes a clue, as he does in the account of the Baptist and of the Temptation, St. Luke arranges the *Logia* in one way, St. Matthew in another. Which, then, of these arrangements is to be preferred? Which Evangelist reproduced St. Matthew's order? Not the redactor of the Gospel according to St. Matthew, for he has massed most of the *Logia* into five huge Discourses, which are impressive for Church reading, but can hardly correspond to any actual Sermons. Many critics, however, incline to believe that St. Luke has preserved the original order, because he has so scrupulously followed the order of the proto-Mark. Even if he has done so, we must not assume that he is any nearer the truth, for we have no right to suppose that St. Matthew, any more than St. Mark, had regard to anything else in arrangement than convenience in Church teaching. It seems to us, however, that there is considerable evidence to show that originally the *Logia* were piled one upon another in confused disorder, as they are in the Oxyrhynchus fragment, with no other prefaces than 'Jesus said' or 'John said.' Their arrangement into speeches was the work of later hands (*Synopsis*, xxv). If so, this was done by the art of conflation, which consists in picking out all the Utterances which dealt with one subject and arranging them into an artificial speech on that subject. Such speeches, of which the Sermon on the Mount is a typical example, do not correspond to any Sermon that was ever preached, but are compiled for the simplification of teaching, and for the preservation of important Utterances which were in danger of being lost. St. Matthew prefers long conflations. One of these covers three chapters (Mt 5-7), another two (24. 25), and three more one each (10. 13. 23). St. Luke's conflations are shorter, never filling one chapter. They are therefore more numerous (we reckon nineteen of them) and more compact; for, whereas it is difficult to say what is the subject of the Sermon on the Mount or of the Charge to the Twelve, there is no such difficulty with St. Luke. In St. Matthew's Eschatological Discourses (24. 25) the prophecies respecting the destruction of Jerusalem and those respecting the Second Coming of the Son of Man are inextricably blended together, as though the redactor regarded the two events as synchronous, whereas St. Luke separates them (Lk 17^{20-37} 21^{5-38}), and it may well be that our Lord habitually did so.

The hypothesis of conflations may come as a shock to those who have been brought up in the belief that the Sermon on the Mount is a single discourse. We credit the Evangelists with some audacity. Their literary morality must not be judged by the standard of this century They were composing Gospels and not formal histories. They were providing for the need of an age which lived in daily expectation of the return of their Lord. The work was done wisely and well, for it has stood the test of time; but we must understand its limitations if we really care to attain to the truth.

That the art of conflation was a real thing, actually practised by the Evangelists, can be fully proved only by a detailed examination into all the conflations; and for that we have no space now; but it may help to remove prejudice if we compare St. Matthew's Sermon on the Mount (Mt. 5-7) with St. Luke's Sermon on the Plain (Lk 6^{20-49}). Both begin with Beatitudes, and both end with the same Warning. We conclude, therefore, that the source contained the nucleus of a sermon. But the proto-Matthæus had only three short and one long Beatitude, for St. Luke gives no more. In St. Matthew five others have been added by the deutero-Matthæus. St. Luke's Beatitudes, short and long, are all expressed in the second person, owing to an editorial change made by him for the purpose of securing literary uniformity. In St. Luke, Woes follow the Blessings. St. Matthew contains Woes, but not here. Either, therefore, St. Luke borrowed these Woes from another source unknown to us, or they are mere editorial work to enhance the Blessings. Their close uniformity to the Blessings favours the latter view. The wording of the Warning, with which the Sermons end, has been slightly altered in St. Luke to suit the comprehension of readers who did not live in Palestine, and would not know the action of winter torrents on a wady. Between the Beatitudes and the Warning the Source must have contained some Utterances setting forth the Law of Love. Besides these, St. Matthew has collected much material, St. Luke comparatively little; for St. Matthew's Sermon contains 107 verses, St. Luke's only 30. Yet we cannot regard St. Luke's Sermon as an abbreviation of St. Matthew's. True, he reproduces 26 out of St. Matthew's 107 verses; but he reproduces 32 more of them in other parts of his Gospel, spreading them over no fewer than seven chapters. Again, he gives in his Sermon four passages (Lk $6^{24-26. 27. 34. 37. 38}$) which are not found in St. Matthew at all, and therefore do not come from the *Logia*. He adds two ($6^{39. 40}$) which are given by St. Matthew in a different context. We are justified, therefore, in regarding the Sermons as in large part independent conflations. St. Luke's subject, as usual, is precise, being simply the statement of the Law of Love; but the most that we can say for St. Matthew is that he seems here to be setting forth the duty of Christian laymen, while in the charge to the Twelve he gives our Lord's teaching about the duty of the clergy.

It is a further proof of the fact of conflation that in some cases, where the subject-matter is so clearly marked that two Evangelists have collected the utterances respecting it, which may have been widely separated in the Source, into one conflation, they have nevertheless arranged the sections in different order. Thus in the Temptation, St. Matthew gives the second and third Temptations in one order, St. Luke in another. In the passage about the Ninevites, and Solomon and the Queen of the South (Mt 12^{38-45}, Lk 11^{24-32}), two such differences of arrangement occur. In the Woes on the Pharisees, St. Luke's order (Lk 11$^{37-54}$) differs repeatedly from St. Matthew's (Mt 23$^{13ff.}$), and the deutero-Matthæus supplies fresh Woes. It is, of course, possible that St. Luke was dissatisfied with St. Matthew's order, and thought to improve upon it; it is more probable that he was not acquainted with it.

In cases where the subject is less clearly marked, the Evangelists collect the utterances into independent conflations. But there is one very instructive example. Both Evangelists have gathered together our Lord's teaching on the subject of prayer. St. Matthew has put it into the Sermon on the Mount (Mt 6$^{5-13}$), St. Luke into an independent conflation (Lk 11$^{1-13}$). St. Luke, however, has very properly included in his conflation the utterance, 'Ask, and it shall be given to you,' etc. St. Matthew has put this also into the Sermon on the Mount, but in a different department (Mt 7$^{7-11}$). Why is this? The words 'pray' or 'prayer' do not occur in it, and the redactor of St. Matthew, acting, as we are all liable to do, mechanically, did not perceive that this *Logion* dealt with prayer. St. Luke was more observant.

That the original *Logia* had no prefaces beyond 'Jesus said,' etc., is shown by four remarkable cases in which St. Matthew (3^7 12$^{24. 38}$ 16^1) applies to the Scribes and Pharisees, *i.e.* to the ruling class, denunciations which in St. Luke (3^7 11$^{15-29. 16}$) are addressed to the lower orders. Plainly the Evangelists were left to gather from the contents of the *Logion* the persons to whom it was addressed. St. Luke's pronounced dislike of the rabble made him incline to them, while St. Matthew's indictment of the upper class led him into the opposite direction. It may well be that both Evangelists were mistaken. At any rate the limitations under which they worked must be acknowledged by all seekers after truth.

The contents of the second Source may be seen in the *Synopsis*, 187–239. St. Luke's parable of the Pounds is identified with St. Matthew's parable of the Talents, and St. Luke's parable of the Great Dinner with St. Matthew's of the Marriage Feast.

3. Third Source—a Pauline Collection.—If the first Source contained a good deal of triple tradition, and the second Source a good deal of double tradition, the remaining sources consist almost entirely of single tradition. Again, St. Mark contains a small quantity of single tradition, added (we believe) by the trito-Mark. St. Matthew gives a considerable amount; but St. Luke surpasses them both in respect of quantity and interest. And first we must recognize in his Gospel a collection of nineteen discourses, parables, and stories which stand by themselves, and may be called Pauline from their character (*Synopsis*, 241–250). We do not mean that St. Paul had much, if anything, to do with their wording; but some one in sympathy with Pauline teaching must have edited them. Our Lord spoke the words, but credit must be given to the collector who preserved them from oblivion. And if in St. John's Gospel it is more and more recognized that the mind of the Evangelist cast the utterances of our Lord into the peculiar form which they there hold, the same process of redaction may be observed in St. Luke, who comes nearest of the Synoptists to the methods of St. John. The story of the Prodigal Son is the crown of this division, but the stories of the Good Samaritan, of the Pharisee and the Publican, of the woman who washed our Lord's feet with her tears, are scarcely of inferior interest, while the parable of the Unjust Steward, when properly interpreted, is full of interest, and that of the Rich Man and Lazarus of difficulty. The more we consider this collection, the more entranced we are with it. It

is the very cream of the Gospel, and yet (strange to say) it is peculiar to St. Luke.

In all cases, but especially in those of the single tradition, the question arises, How near do our records come to the actual words of Christ? The traditionalists, although they are forced to admit that in the triple and the double tradition some doubt may exist through the divergences in three, or two, Gospels, quietly assume that in the single tradition we have a *verbatim* report. To this assumption the critic is unable to assent. If the triple tradition was first taught by St. Peter, and confirmed by the general consent of the Churches; if the double tradition was taught by St. Matthew and diffused extensively, the single tradition was later in formation, lays no claim to Apostolic origination, and must have been known to few, or else by its intrinsic interest it would often have found its way into more Gospels than one. It is possible that St. Philip the Evangelist was the worker to whom we are indebted for the third Source; but it is mere guesswork to say so; there are no solid grounds for argument. We do not therefore claim for the single tradition the same authority that we claim for the others. The work of an editor is often conspicuous in it, and always to be suspected. And yet it would be mere scepticism to throw much doubt on these utterances, many of which vindicate their claim to have been given by Him who spake as never man spake. When a witness recollected only one or two sayings of our Lord, his memory would be specially trustworthy. The apologist has no cause to fear, but he must recognize the human element which plays its part in all Scripture. In this division the human element, if we are not mistaken, may be most clearly seen in the narrative of the washing of our Lord's feet by the woman who had been a sinner (Lk 7$^{36-50}$). Our view of this most perplexing section is that its groundwork belongs to the deutero-Mark, being identical with the Markan account of the anointing of our Lord's head. It has been misplaced by St. Luke, but he misplaces all the deutero-Markan sections which he gives. St. Luke agrees with St. John in saying that the feet, not the head, were anointed. In this, according to our contention, St. Luke and St. John are simply following St. Mark's original narrative. In the Gospels according to St. Matthew and St. Mark the feet have been changed into the head, because the Psalmist wrote, 'Thou anointest my head with oil' (Ps 23^5). The early Christians were always searching for fulfilments of Scripture, and in some cases the primitive records have been changed to secure a more complete fulfilment. Such changes appeared legitimate to the literary morality of that age, and we have no right to object (*Synopsis*, 269).

4. Fourth Source—Anonymous Fragments.—To this Source we assign 80 fragments of St. Luke, of which nine are found also in St. Matthew, but, of course, in a different context. If the sections in the third Division lack Apostolic authority, still more probable is it that these do so. Nay, to some of us it may appear their chief glory, as it is of the Epistle to the Hebrews, that their authors are unknown. Hundreds of Christians in Palestine had seen our Lord in the days of His flesh, and every one of them would treasure up some personal reminiscence. The great majority of these have inevitably been lost, but a few were so widely known and so much valued that they forced their way into local Church tradition and so passed into one—seldom into two—Gospels. All this is quite certain to the historian. But, of course, difficulties about chronology arise. Probably most of these fragments are widely misplaced. Thus St. Luke (5$^{1-11}$) by a conflation blends the Draught of fishes with the deutero-Markan account of St. Peter's Call. St. John places it (in what we believe to be its true position) after the Resurrection (Jn 21¹⁻¹⁴). Now, as St. Luke leaves no room either in his Gospel or in the Acts for a visit to Galilee after the Resurrection, it is at last being confessed that he was not aware of such a visit, and therefore it was quite natural for him to infer that the Draught of fishes belonged to St. Peter's Call, and indeed explains his readiness to rise and follow Christ without question. But, if this had been the true connexion of events, it is incredible that St. Mark, if he gives St. Peter's account of the call, did not mention it (*Synopsis*, 13).

If in the deutero-Mark and in the *Logia* St. Luke was content to find a literary connexion for many of our Lord's Utterances, it is no wonder if he did so in the fourth Source. He certainly endeavoured to write, as he says, ' in (chronological) order,' but in many cases he had not the detailed information which was necessary for doing so. St. Luke's Gospel is probably the least chronological of the three (as we shall show hereafter more fully), but in all the Gospels criticism teaches us to value the picture more than the frame ; to treasure the Utterance, but esteem at a much lower value the setting which the Evangelist has given it.

5. Fifth Source—a Private Collection (from the Holy Family ?).—St. Luke's first two chapters, together with the Genealogy, the Sermon at Nazareth, and the Raising of the widow's son at Nain, form our fifth and last Division. Marcion rejected the first two chapters and many other sections from his canon. Wellhausen omits them from his edition of St. Luke. The Bishop of Ely infers from Ac 1¹·²² that they were no part of the first edition of the Gospel. The present writer has long taught that they are among the latest additions to the Gospel, and that they never were part of the oral teaching : beyond that we can hardly go. The idea that St. Luke issued two editions of his Gospel has gained few converts, and Dr. Blass, its chief advocate, assigns these chapters to both supposed editions. That they proceed from St. Luke is shown by the literary connexion which Sir John Hawkins has traced.

This Division bears testimony to the fact, which Irenæus records, that there was difference of opinion in the early Church on the question of the Virgin Birth. St. Paul is silent on that subject, showing, perhaps, that it had not been raised in his day. St. John alludes to it in his own peculiar way (1⁴⁵). Both Genealogies seem to have issued from Ebionite circles, in which our Lord's descent from Joseph was affirmed. They have been altered with some rather clumsy editorial changes, to make them square with orthodox belief. But the trito-Mark has altered the wording of a passage (6³) with a view to support the Virgin Birth (*Synopsis*, xli), while St. Matthew's first chapter and St. Luke's second strenuously assert it. There can be no doubt that, when once the question was raised, it was answered in widely different Churches in no hesitating way. East and West, at Rome and in the provinces, belief in the Virgin Birth became a test of orthodoxy.

In St. Matthew, Joseph is the hero, and all action is taken by him. Mary is kept in the background, in accordance with Eastern feeling. But in St. Luke, Elisabeth and Mary are brought forward. Honour is claimed for women, as it is throughout the Third Gospel.

It is obvious that the story told in these chapters, unless it be regarded as a free invention, must have been derived, directly or indirectly, from the Virgin Mary herself. The style is strangely Semitic, in striking contrast to the four verses of preface. Not only was the original narrative told in Ara-

maic, but the translator has closely imitated the language and manner of the LXX, feeling that he could thus best convey the meaning. Few parts of the Gospel have been more popular than this. The Sermon at Nazareth (4¹⁶⁻²⁹) is conflate, much of a (misplaced) deutero-Markan section having been worked into it. But it shows additional information; and long ago the observation was made, that St. Luke's knowledge of events at Nazareth is unique. If he had intercourse with some member of the Holy Family, the mystery is explained.

6. Editorial Notes.—The editorial element in all the Gospels is very great, for ancient authors took immense pains to reduce the crude chronicles which they used into literary form. In Herodotus, Thucydides, Livy, and Tacitus the charm of style is all their own, and it must have been gained by unsparing labour. Nor did inspired authors deem it unnecessary to take pains. Nay, the Divine treasure which they held in earthen vessels demanded and received all the skill which they possessed. Both St. Luke and the redactor of St. Matthew are artists of a high order.

Editorial changes, however, though they often improve upon the original, do so at some sacrifice. The substitution of a more elegant word alters the precise meaning of the original. The critic's endeavour must always be to recover the primitive wording. And in the triple tradition he can generally feel sure of his ground; in the double tradition there is more room for subjective preferences; while in the single tradition he has little else to guide him. Just where the records are most likely to be obscured, the means of verifying them disappear. We cannot attain to greater certainty than God has given.

St. Luke's editorial contributions are manifold and important. He had sources of information which are closed to us. Even his own opinion is of high value. But, nevertheless, he worked under limitations, and an exact scrutiny throws some doubt upon many of his assertions.

Let us first consider the general arrangement of his Gospel, which, as we have said, depends almost entirely on St. Mark. The first thing which strikes us is the extraordinary fact, that whereas St. Mark describes our Lord's last journey to Jerusalem in 52 verses, which St. Matthew expands to 64, St. Luke devotes to it no fewer than 408 : more than one third part of his whole Gospel. How are we to understand this amazing disproportion ? First, let us look at the 'Travel Narrative' in itself. It contains a very few and slight Markan 'scraps': so few, that we are entitled to call the whole of it non-Markan. There is a good deal of matter which has been taken from the second Source; this, of course, is arranged by St. Matthew in an entirely different way. But much of the material is peculiar to St. Luke. For example, sixteen out of the nineteen sections of the third Source are embedded here.

Harmonists say that St. Luke is giving us a Peræan ministry, in which our Lord repeated much of what He had taught in Galilee. But who were these Peræans, that the wealth of the third Source should have been reserved for them ? St. Luke gives us no help in answering that necessary question. Not a single town or village is named until we reach the Markan Jericho. If there was a door open to our Lord at all in Peræa, it would seem to have been among those Galilæan pilgrims who passed through Peræa on their way to keep the Feast. But there are other difficulties. We are distinctly taught that our Lord gradually withdrew from public teaching, first speaking only in parables, and finally confining Himself to the training of the Twelve. But here within a fortnight of His death (though harmonists try to lengthen the journey, and, indeed, change it into several journeys, with visits to Jerusalem and retirements into Galilee of which St. Luke says nothing) some of the simplest and plainest of His teaching is set forth. Again, why does St. Matthew put so many of these sayings into the Sermon on the Mount or the Charge to the Twelve? The theory of repetition is entirely unsatisfactory (*NT Problems*, 30–39).

We have little doubt that a different explanation must be found. If St. Luke's sole guide to chronology was St. Mark, what was he to do with non-Markan matter? The difficulty confronted him continually. New materials reached him, while he taught at Philippi, by every ship which arrived. Seldom did the new fragments contain any clue to their date or occasion. If they were not worked into his oral teaching they would soon be forgotten. Some niche must be found for them. And he began, it would seem, by placing them into this last journey. Slowly they accumulated until they reached their present proportions. The famous 'Travel Narrative' is therefore really a collection of undated material. The extraordinary vagueness which characterizes this Division favours that view. It is discourse matter, but quite indeterminate. Some of the most striking parables have no further preface than 'He said,' and there are no indications of locality except that He was still on the journey. St. Luke's idea was that our Lord brought forth the best of His treasures as the time of His departure drew nigh: it is a noble conception, but not in agreement with what we learn from the other Gospels. The matter (we believe) is scarcely arranged at all, and always wrongly.

If this be so, it is no wonder that we attach low historical value to those editorial prefaces with which St. Luke introduces so many sections in this 'Travel Narrative,' and, indeed, outside it also. Such prefaces appear usually to be inferences from the contents of the passage or transferences from other occasions. Thus the parable of the Marriage Feast according to St. Matthew (22¹⁻¹⁴) was spoken in the courts of the Temple. But the parable of the Great Dinner, which we identify with it, was, according to St. Luke (14¹⁵⁻²⁴), part of a long discourse at a Pharisee's dinner table: the machinery of the dinner table is made much of by St. Luke in binding the conflation together. St. Luke stands alone in telling us that our Lord on three occasions (7³⁶ 11³⁷ 14¹) accepted hospitality from Pharisees. There is reason to think that the last two of these occasions are due to transference or assimilation.

St. Luke, like the other Synoptists, seems to have thought that our Lord's ministry lasted one year only—'the acceptable year of the Lord' (*NT Problems*, 182–194). He appears to have placed our Lord's Birth after Herod's death, though St. Matthew distinctly places it before that event. For a discussion of this difficult question the present writer may be allowed to refer the reader to his edition of St. Luke's Gospel. Suffice it here to record the conviction that, though St. Luke has done much for us in connecting our Lord's life upon earth with secular history, his Gospel is very far from being arranged with the chronological accuracy at which he aimed. He was working in a place and amid surroundings which precluded historical research, and, when he visited Palestine, it was too late to recast the whole work of his life.

Philosophy was sedulously cultivated among the Gentiles for whom St. Luke wrote. All the more earnest thinkers, who were attracted by Christianity, had been brought up as neo-Platonists or Stoics. They would, of course, bring their philo-

sophy with them into their new religion. Christianity became to a considerable extent leavened by Hellenistic thought. This is what our Lord foretold in the parable of the Leaven, rightly interpreted. Now Plato taught the indestructibility of the soul. But in Mt 10²⁸ God is declared to be 'able to destroy both soul and body in hell,' which is the usual Biblical doctrine. St. Luke (12⁵) has altered this into 'him who has power to cast into hell.' It would seem that he, or his informant, did this to avoid giving offence to the Platonists. In the Markan account of the Agony in Gethsemane (Mk 14³²⁻⁴²) there is much to perplex a Stoic, who believed that a good man is never perturbed. All trace of agony is absent from St. Luke's account (cf. RVm at 22⁴³ᶠ.); perhaps because the proto-Mark did not contain it; more probably because St. Luke has deliberately struck it out.

St. Luke has long been accused of Ebionism, because the rich are severely handled in his pages, and because he expressly commands us to part with all our property (12³²⁻³⁴); whereas St. Matthew (according to the Greek) bids us only think more highly of the heavenly than of the earthly treasure (6¹⁹⁻²¹). St. Luke was certainly not an Ebionite, or he would not have defended the Virgin Birth or praised Joseph of Arimathæa. In speaking words of severity against the rich he is probably faithfully reproducing our Lord's words, which were wont to be incisive. The strongest of all these sayings against the wealthy is preserved in the proto-Mark (Mk 10²⁵), and it is followed by a declaration in which our Lord Himself cautions us against interpreting His utterances with prosaic literality. Nor have Christians generally supposed that He intended us to pluck out our right eye or cut off our right hand and foot.

The most striking example of editorial addition in St. Luke is that in which he attributes the three hours' darkness to a solar eclipse (23⁴⁵). In saying so he cannot be right for many reasons (*Comp. of the Gospels*, 119).

iii. POINTS OF CONTACT WITH ST. JOHN.—If St. John's teaching was esoteric, intended for advanced disciples only, we shall better understand the rarity of the occasions on which allusions to it are found in the sub-Apostolic age. But that it existed orally for many years before it was committed to writing, is indicated not only by its own characteristics, but by several cases in which it is simpler to assume that one of the Synoptists learned a fact from St. John than that St. John learned it from him. Many passages are pointed out in the index to the *Synopsis* in which the trito-Mark is held to have drawn from St. John's oral teaching. There is one case where St. Matthew does so. And we have now to consider cases where St. Luke appears to have followed their example. We have already seen that St. Luke agrees with St. John that our Lord's feet were anointed and not His head. But in that matter we held that St. Luke is reproducing the original deutero-Markan statement which has been corrupted in St. Matthew and in the trito-Mark. The trito-Mark tells us that the day of the Crucifixion was Friday (Mk 15⁴²). This statement St. Luke repeats (23⁵⁴), but in a different context and in different language. The simplest explanation of these peculiarities and of the absence of the words from St. Matthew is that both Evangelists, directly or indirectly, derived their information from St. John. Finally, St. Luke and St. John tell us that the sepulchre in which our Lord's body lay was a new one, 'where no one had yet lain' (Lk 23⁵³).

iv. ST. LUKE'S CHARACTERISTICS.—St. Luke the Gentile was cosmopolitan in his sentiments. St. Luke the beloved physician had sympathy for the sorrows of mankind. The words of pity which he records were drawn from the all-compassionate heart of the Saviour, but to St. Luke is due the credit of preserving them from oblivion. To his literary skill we are probably right in attributing some of the beauty of their form. St. Luke the disciple of St. Paul tells of the publican, who durst not so much as lift up his eyes to heaven, but kept smiting his breast and saying, 'God be merciful to me the sinner' (18[13]). He tells of the traveller by the wayside, stripped, wounded, and half-dead, and how the good Samaritan had pity upon him (10[30-37]). He tells of the Prodigal, wandering in thoughtless levity from home, spending his substance in riot and revelry, and then eating the husks which were thrown to the swine ; and how the father had compassion upon him and welcomed him home (15[11-32]). He tells of the poor woman who had been a sinner in the city, coming behind and washing the Saviour's feet with her tears (7[36-50]) ; of the robber's appeal on the cross, 'Lord, remember me when thou comest in thy kingdom' (23[39-43]). These and other passages which set forth the freeness and fulness of pardoning love have been preserved to us only in the writings of St. Luke, who had more pity for the weak and for the suffering, for widows and for the poor, than any other NT writer.

St. Luke was no idealist. He had a literal, matter-of-fact mind, which blurted out facts without glossing them. We have seen how he records without reservation the command to part with our possessions, as St. Barnabas and others in their first love did (Ac 4[36. 37]). Being a physician, he nevertheless had the strongest belief in the truth of demoniacal possession, understanding literally what was originally given as a burst of insanity (Mk 5[9] with parallels). He stands alone in affirming that our Lord, after His resurrection, ate a piece of broiled fish before His disciples (24[41-43]). To this he refers, probably in Ac 1[4], certainly in Ac 10[41]. Many persons in modern times have felt some difficulty in reconciling this with the general Scripture account of the nature of our Lord's resurrection body. It may be one side of the truth which is apt in these days to be ignored ; in a coarser age it was the only side that was accepted. Ignatius supports it in the saying which he preserves: 'I am not an incorporeal demon' (*Smyr.* iii. 1).

v. DATE OF WRITING.—St. Luke's Gospel is not, like St. Mark's, a bare record of our Lord's deeds and words, but, to a considerable extent, a theological exposition of their meaning. St. Luke, like his master St. Paul, has reflected on them, and is anxious to impress on the reader his own ideas about them. Such action demands time. In spite of 1 Ti 5[18], we cannot admit that St. Luke wrote before St. Paul's death.

Again, if we observe the treatment in his pages of the destruction of Jerusalem, contrasting his precise language (21[20]) with the vague predictions in St. Mark (13[14]), we can hardly doubt that he wrote after the event, and edited the wording accordingly. The end of the world was not with him, as it was with the redactor of St. Matthew, synchronous with the burning of the Temple. He carefully puts our Lord's teaching about the last days into a separate conflation, which he prefaces with a remarkable saying which warns us against a literal interpretation : 'The kingdom of God is within you' (17[21]).

But there are no 2nd cent. ideas in the Gospel, nor anything to throw doubt upon the unanimous and early tradition of St. Luke's authorship. Nor would so obscure a member of the Church have been selected as author if there had not been good ground for the belief. Probably his name stood on the original title-page.

We are, therefore, probably right in assigning the date to about 80 A.D.

LITERATURE.—Plummer's Commentary (T. & T. Clark) is good on the linguistic side. The Commentaries of Meyer (German) and of Godet (French) have been published in English by T. & T. Clark, but the later German editions of Meyer, edited by B. and J. Weiss, are preferable. In the *Expositor's Greek Testament* the Synoptic Gospels are treated from the side of the higher criticism by A. B. Bruce, but unfortunately the TR is used. Wellhausen has translated the Gospel into German with a few critical notes. For comparative study Wright's *St. Luke* and his *Synopsis* may be used. In *Horæ Synopticæ* Sir J. C. Hawkins has collected statistics of great value. Hobart's *Medical Language of St. Luke* needs some weeding out, but has never been refuted. A. Resch, in *Das Kindheits-Evangelium*, as in his other writings, collects an immense quantity of illustrative matter, but the critical standpoint which he adopts is not generally acceptable. Ramsay (*Was Christ born at Bethlehem ?*) successfully defends St. Luke as an historian of high rank, but insists too much on his accuracy in editorial details. Blass, in his edition of St. Luke's Gospel and of the Acts, follows Lightfoot in suggesting that St. Luke published two editions of his works—one for Theophilus and another for use by the Church. In this way he accounts for the Western readings, which, however, are found in other books of the NT.

A. WRIGHT.

LUNATIC.—
Introduction.
i. Difficulty of classifying NT cases.
   1. From the medical side.
   2. From the Biblical side.
ii. Leading cases reported in Gospels.
   1. Capernaum lunatic.
   2. Case at foot of Mt. of Transfiguration.
   3. Gerasene victim.
   4. Other cases.
iii. Question as to possession by evil spirits. Prevalent misconceptions. Truer conception.
iv. Our Lord's method of restoration. Kinship with modern medical treatment.
Literature.

The word 'lunatic' in the AV of NT is the tr. of σεληνιάζεσθαι (from σελήνη, 'the moon') which occurs in Mt 4[24] 17[15], and nowhere else in the NT or in classical or Biblical Greek. Literally its meaning is 'to be moonstruck.' The Vulgate translates it *lunaticus*, and in Mt 17[15] *lunaticus est*, where Tindale gives 'is frantick,' and other versions practically follow the Vulgate. Sir John Cheke (1550) has the expression 'is moond' as the equivalent of 'lunatic,' putting into plain English the ancient thought expressed by the word. The influence of the moon on persons was believed to be injurious, and to be able to cause them to become moonstruck (Ps 121[6]), an idea which has been widely prevalent and still persists. The fact that certain forms of insanity are periodical, no doubt gave rise in part to the idea. Dr. Menzies Alexander says: 'The popular idea that there is some connexion between the moon and epilepsy is partly due to the confusion of epilepsy with epileptic insanity. The bright moonlight of the Orient has a curious stimulating effect on such creatures as crows and dogs, making them restless and noisy. It has an exciting effect also on those afflicted with epileptic insanity. In both cases darkness acts as a sedative.'

The RV of the two passages in Mt. above cited prefers 'epileptic' and 'is epileptic' as tr. for σεληνιάζεσθαι, but without substantial warrant. The ground for the preference according to *Encyc. Bibl.* is that a Greek medical writer of the 7th cent. gives ἐπιληπτικός as the correct scientific term for the disorder referred to, and that δαιμονιζόμενος and σεληνιαζόμενος were the popular terms for the same disease.

But the word 'lunatic' covers more than the cases in which Mt. uses σεληνιάζεσθαι. The mentally deranged also are described by the Evangelists as δαιμονιζόμενοι, and no kind of doubt is possible that the latter term included many sufferers who are now called lunatic, as well as simple epileptics and epileptic idiots. The uncontrollable explosions of nervous energy which characterize these cases were not unnaturally attributed solely to demonic agency. The explanation is so simple and direct and apparently so adequate, that none other was sought for. But the term 'lunatic' must be restricted in its use to those who were mentally deranged, and ought not to be applied to those who were simply epileptic, or suffering from mental feebleness or imbecility.

The attempt to trace a differentiation between mental diseases on the part of the Evangelists cannot be pronounced successful, being based upon far too slender ground in a simple NT passage, Mt 4²⁴, where δαιμονιζόμενοι and σεληνιαζόμενοι are placed side by side. (1) We have no grounds for expecting such precision in writers like the Evangelists. (2) The same writer uses (Mt 17¹⁵) the word σεληνιάζεσθαι of a case which is not simple epilepsy (see below). (3) He does not use the word for the Gerasene demoniacs of Mt 8²⁸, where we have undoubted cases of lunacy. (4) Luke the physician knows nothing of the distinction so far as his own usage is concerned. (5) It is not to be thought that Mt. alone of the Evangelists traced a distinction between the epileptic and the possessed, or that he would not attribute an attack of simple epilepsy to the domination by evil spirits.

The Evangelists class all the cases together, and use both words to cover the same trouble of mental derangement, while the latter word δαιμονιζόμενοι is also employed with a wider signification. The fact that the description given in the Gospels enables us to classify the instances under the broad types of mental disease is evidence of the faithful unsophisticated narration of what the Evangelists had seen or heard, not of their having any scientific understanding of the phenomena in question.

i. DIFFICULTY OF CLASSIFYING NT CASES.— The Gospels record and describe three clear cases which may be included under the general head of lunacy. Others are probably indicated with no kind of description; or only the very vaguest is given. But the task of determining to which particular class of lunacy the cases described are to be assigned is not without difficulty, and perhaps cannot at present be accomplished without some degree of uncertainty. The difficulty is twofold.

1. The current classifications, in vogue amongst alienists, of the various insanities are very numerous, and by common consent far from being final. Certain of these systems, some adopted by International Congresses and others determined by representative associations, and generally in use among the leading mental physicians of Great Britain, are valuable chiefly as giving facilities, the one for international conference, the other for national comparison and correspondence. Clouston in his *Clinical Lectures* provides a good working classification. Following the example of many illustrious predecessors, he divides mental diseases : (1) according to the mental symptoms manifested, and (2) according to the causes of the disorder and to the relationships of the disease to the great physical periods of life and to the activities other than mental. But the researches of the present day, and especially in respect of the causes of mental derangement, with their suggestions of toxic and bacteriological origin, are profoundly modifying the generalizations which only a few years ago were accepted as satisfactory. Brilliant and enthusiastic investigators in Italy, France, Germany, America, and in our own country are 'settling much and unsettling more' (Clouston), and while this condition of science is full of promise for the ultimate goal of all such research in the alleviation and recovery of the malady and the removal of its causes, the prevalent uncertainty does not lessen the difficulty of classifying the NT cases. The difficulty arises largely from the facts that (a) the symptoms from one class are combined in ever-varying proportions with symptoms of other classes, rendering the task of deciding which is the predominant symptom according to which the malady must be classified well-nigh impossible; and (b) a similar combination is discovered among the causes producing the disorder. Accordingly some have scoffed at the attempt to classify mental diseases with all the divisions and technology of a botanical or zoological system. And perhaps it is more important to mark carefully all the symptoms in each case and study the predisposing and actual causes so far as they can be ascertained.

2. The difficulty from the Biblical side lies in the following facts. (a) The descriptions of the cases mentioned in the Gospels are non-scientific. They do not profess to give a complete methodized account of the ailments with which the power of Jesus dealt. The Evangelists give no sign that they themselves understood what they describe. (b) They deal only with symptoms. Causes of the disorder were not sought for, the prevalent theory of demonic possession being to them adequate to account for the trouble, and this possession the only possible cause. Our Lord Himself speaks and acts as though upon the whole He shared the conceptions of the time. Possibly because in this realm, as in others, He in His incarnate condition shared the limitations of the race, *or* because He could not take upon Himself the task of correcting and remoulding the deep-lying misconceptions of that generation with respect to these matters, without withdrawing His strength from far more vital concerns on which in the short time at His disposal He must concentrate all His attention. (c) The Evangelists' descriptions probably do not give all the symptoms which a modern alienist would have noted, but only those which for one reason or another were pressed particularly upon their observation.

ii. LEADING CASES OF LUNACY REPORTED IN NT.—1. *The case in the synagogue at Capernaum* (Mk 1²¹⁻²⁸, Lk 4³¹⁻³⁷). The symptoms indicated by the Evangelists are—

(1) The predominance of unclean habits and instincts. Mk. speaks of the man as being under the influence of an unclean spirit; Lk. of the spirit of an unclean demon. This might possibly mean no more than that the victims of this malady habitually haunted unclean places, as tombs, and desert regions believed to be the habitation of demons. But the greater probability is that it points to 'moral alienation,' which Esquirol (*Maladies Mentales*) declared was the proper characteristic of mental derangement. 'The subtle influence of epilepsy, or rather of that condition of the nervous system which gives rise alike to epileptic seizures and certain mental symptoms, is most strikingly manifested in the change which takes place in the moral character' (Bucknill and Tuke).

(2) Convulsive seizures. This feature is not made prominent in the case before us, but is indicated by the words of Mk 1²⁶, 'And the unclean spirit tearing (RVm 'convulsing,' σπαράξαν) him and crying with a loud voice.'

(3) Uncontrolled impulse, leading the victim in defiance of all that was fitting and customary to burst into the assembly at the hour of worship.

(4) The patient's belief in and identification of himself with an alleged evil spirit. He speaks of himself and the evil power as one—'What have we to do with thee?' This may be explained as an example of a well-known delusion classed as demonomania, but the question must not be foreclosed (see below). At least, however, an element of delusion may be traced in the feeling of entire and inevitable subjection to the monstrous control.

(5) The acknowledgment of Messiah. This has been claimed as the classical criterion of demonic possession, all cases where it is not found being regarded as not due to this cause even although the Scripture so attributes them (Menzies Alexander). But argument from silence is always perilous, and especially so in dealing with the Gospel narratives. And other cases might yet be genuinely demonic where the confession is apparently or really absent. And, on the other hand, the acknowledgment might reasonably be regarded as the last vestige of rationality in the otherwise deranged nature.

Attempting to classify the above, it may be ranged symptomatically under Clouston's head— 'States of Defective Inhibition, or Impulsive Insanity,' the chief characteristic of which is uncontrollable impulse, and which includes general impulsiveness, epileptiform impulse (indicated by the convulsions), animal, sexual and organic impulse (pointed to by the term 'unclean' applied to this and other instances). Clinically considered (according to the causes) it most nearly approaches epileptic insanity. This 'means insanity with epilepsy, whether the convulsive affection has preceded the insanity and has seemed to be the cause, or whether it has appeared during the course of the mental disease only as a symptom or complication' (Bucknill and Tuke). The presence of epileptic insanity is not always indicated by epileptic fits but by the character of the mental disturbance, the paroxysmal gust of passion, the blind fury. And therefore Defective Inhibition is difficult to distinguish from Mania. Out of 385 epileptic women observed by Esquirol (*Maladies Mentales*, vol. i.), only 60 were free from mental derangement, and nearly all were unstable, peculiar, easily enraged.

2. *The case at the foot of the Mt. of Transfiguration* (Mt 17[14-20], Mk 9[17-29], Lk 9[37-43]).—Two sides are plainly marked in this disorder : (1) The physical. Uncontrollable paroxysms accompanied by foaming at the mouth and gnashing of teeth, succeeded by utter prostration. The affliction had been from infancy, pointing to some congenital disease involving the other physical features— deafness and dumbness. (2) The mental. At least idiocy, but more probably lunacy, a feature of which was the suicidal mania manifested. The indication is that during the time while he was free from convulsions and their effects the patient was not mentally disturbed. The suicidal impulse was apparently spasmodic and periodical, but no very solid ground is given to theorize upon.

The epilepsy is more pronounced than in the previous case, and the suicidal tendency is added. But possibly, if the previous instance had been fully described, it might more nearly approximate to the one under consideration. The classification must be under the same general head—Defective Inhibition or Epileptic Insanity (rather than Epileptic Idiocy—as Alexander).

3. *The Gerasene victim* (Mt 8[28-34], Mk 5[1-20], Lk 8[26-39]).—The physical symptoms, the convulsions, that characterize 1 and 2, are here absent, and the features of mental derangement become all-prominent. The victim is possessed by an ungoverned violence, having the command of a morbid muscular energy. This uncontrollable power was one that increased, for the description implies that in the earlier stages they had been able to control him in some measure by binding, but that the binding had increased the violence of the power so that he could no longer be bound (Mk 5[3, 4]). 'The tenses used ($\delta\epsilon\delta\epsilon\sigma\theta\alpha\iota$, $\delta\iota\epsilon\sigma\pi\tilde{\alpha}\sigma\theta\alpha\iota$, $\sigma\upsilon\nu\tau\epsilon\tau\rho\iota\phi\theta\alpha\iota$) denote the relation of these past acts to the present inability' (Gould, *Internat. Crit. Com.* on 'St. Mark'). The malignant power controlling the life drove him into the tombs and mountains, causing him to utter frenzied cries and leading to impulses of self-mutilation, apparently also to homicidal tendencies (Mt 8[28]). Loss of personality is the dominant feature of the case, evidenced by the absence of the sense of all fitness, causing him to destroy his clothing and rush about in nakedness, and by his positive feeling of being possessed by a legion of devils which tore his life asunder. At times he thoroughly identifies himself with the power that controlled his life ('we are many'), and is terrified by the fear lest he and they should be driven from their hiding-place. A

conspicuous feature also was the homage paid by the evil power, or by the man in spite of the evil power, to the authority of Jesus (Mk 5[7], Lk 8[28]).

The case belongs to those described by Clouston as 'states of mental exaltation or mania,' which includes the varieties simple, acute, delusional, chronic, ephemeral, homicidal ; and the indications all point to acute mania with delusions. The fixed idea of plural possession would lead to the medical classification 'Demonomania,' a variety of 'religious mania.'

4. *Other cases.*—(1) The daughter of the Syrophœnician woman, Mt 15[21-28], Mk 7[24-30]. (2) The dumb demoniac, Mt 9[32-34], Lk 11[14, 15]. (3) The blind and dumb demoniac, Mt 12[22-24]. These cases are not described except in most obscure terms. In (2) and (3) the interest of the narrator was fixed upon other elements of the occasion. And they would all be doubtfully classified as cases of lunacy. (4) Mary of Magdala (Mk 16[9], Lk 8[2]), with whom are classed other women healed of evil spirits and infirmities. Mary Magdalene is said to have been delivered from seven demons. The expression may be due (a) to the Evangelist's sense of the violence of the derangement to which she had been subject, or (b) to the current idea of manifold possession among the disciples, to which Jesus gave no sanction, or (c) to mania and delusion of manifold possession. But nothing can be determined beyond the fact that Jesus had delivered her from grievous bodily or mental distress, or a combination of these.

The Evangelists give full prominence to the physical side of these distressing afflictions, not because they understand the symptoms they describe, but because they testify simply and artlessly to what they had themselves witnessed, or what had become part of the common tradition from the testimony of eye-witnesses. But the physical is not the only side. Even in bodily disorders it is being more fully recognized that there is the mental or psychical factor in the problem as it faces the physician (see art. CURES). And the NT plainly sets forth this psychical element in the cases now before us. They ascribe the trouble directly to an intangible spiritual influence which possesses the being of the sufferer, takes the use of the bodily organs, and controls the will. And thus emerges—

iii. THE QUESTION AS TO POSSESSION BY EVIL SPIRITS.—How far does the NT in attributing these disorders to demonic possession give a true account of the phenomenon ? The question is not to be determined by invoking authority, either that of the NT or of our Lord Jesus Christ. The authority of the Gospels is of a totally different order, and moves in a higher sphere than that of writers who were 'supernaturally' lifted above the current conceptions of their generation. We have no warrant for believing the Evangelists to have been granted knowledge of mental disease in advance of the scientific attainments of their own day. Nor can inquiry be silenced by the appeal to the fact that our Lord Himself habitually spoke and acted as if He recognized the presence of evil spirits in mental disease. The Christian apologist takes unnecessarily perilous ground when he declares that for our Lord to have been limited in knowledge invalidates His authority as Prophet and Saviour. In His condition as incarnate our Lord did share the limitations that belong to our human lot, and advanced in knowledge of human affairs and scientific problems by normal human processes.

But it is equally important that the matter should not be dogmatized off the roll of discussion by those who claim to speak in the name of science and declare that the NT explanation is 'impossible' on the ground that *spiritual agencies do not exist.* The question, if left open, must be open on both sides; and there are certain considerations which must be borne in mind while we examine the possibility of spiritual agencies being concerned, as concomitants of the physical disease or nervous instability, in cases of mental derangement, whether in NT times or in the present day.

(1) We must guard ourselves from the conception of these evil spiritual agencies as semi-sensuous beings, possessed of bodily form, appetites and passions. The conception has vitiated human thought from early Semitic times, in the NT age, through the Middle Ages down to the present, when it is even yet strangely persistent. The popular thought of Satan is grotesquely dominated by that idea, and much of the prevalent disbelief in the existence of a spiritual adversary can be traced to that gross misconception.

(2) Kindred to this is the thought of a multiplicity of demons being concerned in the possession of a human life. This idea has been responsible for much false conception in the case of the Gerasene sufferer. And it cannot be too strongly emphasized that nowhere does our Lord give the least sanction to any such notion. He never speaks of more than one evil or unclean spirit (see Alexander, *Demonic Possession*, ch. vii.).

(3) In place of misconceptions, a right conception needs to be grasped of the malignant powers that can make a prey of an otherwise disordered human life. So far from the idea of semi-sensuous beings representing the truth, it would be far truer to think of possession as akin to the condition seen in intense anger, or extreme fear. 'Anything is a possession that dispossesses the man of himself, from whatever world it comes' (Bushnell). We are yet far from being able to define the nature of mind or spirit. We believe in mind on the ground of its manifest action in the directing of our human activities, because of the things it creates and destroys. But what mind is, passes our power to conceive and define. And the same is true of spirit. But we can make no progress in understanding the Universe and our human life within it, except on the assumption of a Supreme and Holy Intelligence and Will behind all physical and mental phenomena. We believe in a living Personal God, and the faith illumines all life and being. Moreover, we are ourselves personalities constantly acting upon, and being acted upon by, other personalities. A moral world is inconceivable on any other terms. And is it unreasonable if we decline to admit the impossibility of other superhuman personalities, some of them centres of benignant and others of malignant moral energy, being present and active in and upon our life here? Who can reasonably deny that such evil agencies may conceivably take advantage of an unstable nervous system or a disordered physical constitution, and possess and control the whole being?

(4) It must also be made clear that the physical disease may be the effect of a potent psychical disorder. The whole mischief may come from the side of the mental or psychical. A long-continued yielding of the mind or spirit to evil agencies may result in physical deterioration, just as truly as physical deterioration may give the opportunity for an evil spiritual possession. 'Prolonged mental enfeeblement is followed by brain atrophy, and prolonged mental disturbances by structural brain changes' (Clouston). A consideration of our Lord's method in dealing with this disaster in humanity will increase our unwillingness to bar out the 'demonic' element in lunacy. See also artt. AC-COMMODATION, vol. i. 20 f., and DEMON, *ib.* 441 ff.

iv. OUR LORD'S RESTORATION OF THE 'LUNATIC.'—The Synoptic Gospels all ascribe to Jesus a unique command over these afflicted persons and over the alien power that possessed them. He was able to restore the lost self-control and also to deal with the disease which was commonly the physical basis of the mental derangement. The latter portion of the process is akin to our Lord's healing of bodily diseases (see CURES); but the action of Jesus is upon the body through the mind, and upon the mental or psychical directly. Mental physicians who treat lunacy from the physical side yet fully recognize the existence of the psychical, and the possibility and actuality of alleviation being brought by action upon that side of the ailment. 'The action of "mind on mind" in healthy brains is direct, intense, and most subtle. The same is the case when the brain is disordered, and hence in psychiatry mental therapeutics are a most important means of treatment' (Clouston). Such facts are truly illuminative of the action of Jesus, and we may not unreasonably attribute His restoring power to a master-influence which, while it transcends all that is known of the human, yet is not on a totally different plane. In Jesus the power of mind was at its fullest and finest by reason of : (1) His intense and penetrating sympathy with mankind ; (2) His vigorous will to bring help and deliverance to all human sufferers ; (3) His continual and perfect alliance and moral union with the Divine Power in which He lived and moved and had His being. The Divine Will can and does manifest itself in every human unselfishness and sympathy and generous helpful impulse, and through a human personality healing forces of God Himself are at work amidst all human distress and oppression. And in our Lord that Divine healing might find full scope and unhindered freedom of activity, so that the Name of Jesus was a healing, restoring, life-giving Name, even empowering feeble disciples to cast out devils (see art. MIRACLES, C.).

The method of Jesus clearly suggests the exercise of a Holy Divinely-informed Will and Personality upon other wills and personalities. The features which most impressed those who witnessed His action were the rebuke, the command, the authority which claimed and obtained unhesitating homage and obedience (Mk 1$^{21-27}$, Lk 9$^{37-43}$), inevitably reminding them of 'the majesty of God.' Especially does His dealing with the Gerasene lunatic indicate His secret. He goes direct to the lost self-control, seeks to recover the submerged personality, and to remove that self-identification with the evil power. He endeavours to awaken the man to the true sense of his own individuality and to set it free from an alien domination. 'What is thy name?' He asks. By the efficient co-operation of the man He would break up that terrible sympathy and alliance which caused the victim to say, 'We are many.' (The suggestion of Schmiedel that in asking this question Jesus was, like a modern alienist, seeking to discover the delusions of the patient, amounts to an anachronism). And the unique Personality of Jesus had the power to evoke, and give once again its commanding controlling place to, this essential energy of the man.

Modern treatment of the insane bears a most suggestive likeness to the method of Jesus. By cheerful surroundings, by healthful labour, by the encouragement of all existing faculty in the patient, by amusement and music and religious exercises, and not least by human sympathy, the endeavour is made to conserve every vestige of self-possession, to keep alive and to develop all available capacity. The constant effort is to penetrate through all physical and psychical disabilities to the real and effective personality. It may fairly be said that medical skill and investigation into causes and remedies of this distressing malady are yet in their preliminary stages, and the progress of the years may be followed with the utmost hopefulness because in all such investigation the Divine Spirit energizes.

LITERATURE. — Griesinger, *Mental Pathology and Therapeutics* (tr.), 1867 ; D. Hack Tuke, *Dictionary of Psychological Medicine*, 2 vols. 1892 ; Bucknill-Tuke, *Manual of Psychological Medicine*, 1874 ; Maudsley, *Physiology and Pathology of Mind*, 2 vols. 1879 ; Clouston, *Clinical Lectures on Mental Disease*[6], 1904 ; Macpherson, *Mental Affections*, 1899 ; *Traité de Pathologie Mentale*, by various writers, ed. Ballet, Paris, 1903 ; Kraepelin, *Clinical Psychiatry* (tr.), 1904. On Biblical aspects of the question, consult artt. on 'Medicine,' 'Satan,' 'Demonology,' 'Exorcism,' etc., in Hastings' *DB* ; also kindred artt. in *Encyc. Bibl.* ; R. Bennett, *Diseases of the Bible*, 1887 ; Menzies Alexander, *Demonic Possession*, 1902 [brings together most valuable data for the discussion of the whole question]. See also Literature at end of artt. MIRACLES and CURES, and chapter on 'Demoniacs' in *The Finger of God*, by the present writer.

T. H. WRIGHT.

LUST.—The noun 'lust' (ἐπιθυμία) occurs only twice in EV of Gospels (Mk 4[19], Jn 8[44]), and the verb 'to lust' (ἐπιθυμέω) only once (Mt 5[28]). Both noun and verb, however, are of common occurrence in the rest of the NT. In modern usage, 'lust' is confined to sexual desire ; but, when the AV was made, the word had a much greater elasticity of meaning, corresponding in this respect to ἐπιθυμία and ἐπιθυμέω. In NT, as in classical Gr., these words properly denote strong desire whether good or bad, then evil desire in particular, and finally sexual desire specifically. Even in the Gospels we find illustrations of these varying connotations of both the Gr. and the Eng. terms. When our Lord says of His desire to eat of His last Passover ἐπιθυμίᾳ ἐπεθύμησα (Lk 22[15]), He simply expresses a deep longing. When He speaks of the seed of the word being choked by the lusts (ἐπιθυμίαι) of other things (Mk 4[19]), these lusts are desires not necessarily evil, though the taint of evil is beginning to enter, because, while in themselves they may be harmless, these desires are allowed to hinder the operation of the word. When He says to the Jewish leaders, 'Ye are of your father the devil, and the lusts (ἐπιθυμίας) of your father it is your will to do,' both 'lust' and ἐπιθυμία have passed into a distinctly bad meaning. And in Mt 5[28] the Gr. and the Eng. word are alike equivalent to lascivious desire. See also art. DESIRE, vol. i. p. 453.

Very little is said explicitly about lust in the Gospels, because little is needed. Lust is not to be dallied with or compromised with ; it is to be totally and continually shunned and avoided. Inward lust is as heinous as outward adultery to the eye of God, which views alike the inside and the outside of man (Mt 5[28]).* The lustful eye will make the whole body full of darkness (Mt 6[23]). The single eye and mind are free from lustful fancies and thoughts (Lk 11[34]). The honest and good heart brings forth only good fruit (Lk 8[15]). Either the heart must be pure, and its fruit pure ; or else impure, and its fruit impure (Mt 12[33]). Adulteries, covetings, lasciviousness,—these defile a man (Mk 7[22]). And lust, in its very nature, is unholy. Hence Christ's Holy Spirit is opposite to, and inconsistent with, the lustful *demon* which makes its foul abode in the neglected heart of the careless or heedless or wanton. There is no limit to the iniquity and abandonment to which such evil possession or corruption may drag the blinded, besotted soul intent upon brutish delights never realized. Herod's course was impeded only a little by the rebuke of a John Baptist (Mk 6[18]). No man can serve two masters (Lk 16[13]) ; and he that committeth sin is the bondservant of sin (Jn 8[34]).

W. B. FRANKLAND and J. C. LAMBERT.

LYSANIAS.—This name is given by St. Luke (3[1]) among those who ruled in the various parts of Syria and Palestine at the time when John the

* See discussion of this passage in art. ADULTERY.

Baptist entered upon his public work. The name does not again occur in the NT. A Lysanias is mentioned by Dio Cassius (xlix. 32) as having been made king of Ituræa by Mark Antony and afterwards put to death by him. This same Lysanias is also spoken of by Josephus (*Ant.* XV. iv. 1), who adds that Antony was moved to the step of putting Lysanias to death by Cleopatra, on the ground that he had conspired against her with the Parthians. The same Lysanias and his connexion with the Parthians are alluded to also elsewhere by Josephus (*BJ* I. xiii. 1 ; *Ant.* XIV. xiii. 3). The data agree in making him the son of Ptolemy, and locating his reign between B.C. 40 and 36. A Lysanias is mentioned again by Josephus in *Ant.* XVIII. vi. 10 and XX. vii. 1. In both of these passages the territory over which he ruled is designated a tetrarchy (cf. *BJ* II. xi. 5, xii. 8 ; *Ant.* XIX. v. 1).

The question raised by these data is, Does Josephus know two men of the name or one ? If he knows two, the Lysanias of St. Luke is evidently the second, and no further difficulty exists. If, however, he has the same man in mind throughout, the question next emerging is as to whether St. Luke knew and alluded to another and younger Lysanias, or erroneously identified the only ruler of that name with the times of the public appearance of John the Baptist and Jesus. In favour of the latter view, it is alleged that Josephus never gives any intimation of a difference between the two men of the name, and in fact does not at first reading seem to know two. His readers were bound, it is argued, to suppose that the Lysanias who was executed in B.C. 36 is meant wherever the name is used. St. Luke was acquainted with the writings of Josephus, but did not use them with accuracy, and an error is quite probable. He makes an error in defining the limits of the realm of Philip, Ituræa. It is not held that an error can be demonstrated in his statement regarding Lysanias, but the probability is said to be for such an error, and the grounds for believing in a second Lysanias are regarded as unsatisfying. This view was propounded by Strauss, and has been supported by Keim, Krenkel, and Schmiedel.

Per contra, that there were two men of the name is argued from various considerations. (1) Though Josephus does not explicitly say that he is speaking of two distinct persons, his descriptions imply such a distinction. Lysanias the son of Ptolemy was not a tetrarch, but bore the title of king (so he is also called by Dio Cassius). (2) The limits of the territories over which the Lysaniases of Josephus ruled are different. The elder Lysanias inherited from his father a kingdom including Chalkis on the Lebanon. This was not, however, included in the realm of the tetrarch Lysanias. (3) Abila was associated with the name of the tetrarch, but not with that of the son of Ptolemy. (4) During the reign of Tiberius, or at least 50 years after the death of the first Lysanias, a certain Nymphæus built a road and erected a temple, and left an account of these acts in an extant inscription (*CIG* 4521). In this inscription he calls himself 'a freedman of Lysanias.' It is impossible that he should have been the freedman of the son of Ptolemy. He must be regarded as living under the tetrarch. (5) Another inscription at Heliopolis, whose *lacunæ* have been filled out by Renan, renders it exceedingly probable that there were more than one ruler bearing the name in question. (6) A coin discovered by Pococke at Nebhi-Abel (Abila) bears the superscription Λυσανίου τετράρχ. καὶ ἀρχιερέως. But as Dio calls the first Lysanias a king, it is at least doubtful that the lower title of tetrarch should appear on his own coin. In that case the coin must have been struck by the second Lysanias. (7) Finally, an inscription (*CIG* 4523) informs us that Lysanias the son of Ptolemy left children behind him. It is probable that the names Lysanias and Zenodorus were dynastic names, and that the second Lysanias was given the name of him who was put to death in 36. This is the view supported by S. Davidson, Wieseler, Renan, Schürer, Plummer, and others.

An earlier effort to establish the historical accuracy of St. Luke's statement regarding Lysanias was made by Paulus (*Com.* i. 1) through the suggestion that the word τετραρχοῦντος should be erased from St. Luke's text, or that it should be connected with Φιλίππου, making Philip the 'tetrarch of Ituræa, Trachonitis, and the Abilene of Lys

i.e. of that province of which Lysanias had been tetrarch in his day. But this has always been considered an arbitrary way of dealing with the text, resorted to solely for the purpose of saving the historical precision of the Evangelist, and has not found much favour in any quarter.

LITERATURE. — Strauss, *Leben Jesu*, 1835, pp. 310–313 ; S. Davidson, *Intr. to NT*, i. pp. 214–221 ; Wieseler, *Chron. Synop. d. vier Evang.* 1843, pp. 174–183, *Beitr. z. Würdigung der Evang.* 1869, pp. 194–204 ; Herzog - Plitt, *PRE*[2], 1877, art. 'Abilene' ; Renan, *Mém. de l'Acad. d'Inscr.* 26. 6, 1870, pp. 49–84 ; Keim, *Gesch. Jesu von Nazara*, i. 618, ii. 384 ; Krenkel, *Jos. u. Lucas*, 1894, pp. 95–98 ; Schürer, *GJV*[3], 1901, i. pp. 716–720 [*HJP* i. ii. 335] ; Plummer, *Com. on St. Luke*, 1900, p. 84 ; Schmiedel, *Ency. Bibl.* art. 'Lysanias.'

A. C. ZENOS.

M

MAATH.—An ancestor of Jesus (Lk 3[26]).

MACHÆRUS.— A fortress on the east of the Dead Sea, in which, according to Josephus (*Ant.* XVIII. v. 2), John the Baptist was imprisoned and put to death by Herod Antipas (Mt 14[3-12], Mk 6[17-29], Lk 3[19]). It had been originally fortified by Alexander Jannæus (Jos. *BJ* VII. vi. 2), and afterwards destroyed by Gabinius (*ib.* I. viii. 5 ; *Ant.* XIV. v. 4). It was restored by Herod the Great, who used it as a residence (*BJ* VII. vi. 1, 2.). On his death it passed into the hands of Antipas, as it lay in the Peræan portion of his tetrarchy. At the time of the Jewish revolt it was occupied by a Roman garrison, which was constrained to abandon it in A.D. 66 (*ib.* II. xviii. 6). After the fall of Jerusalem it was recaptured, and finally destroyed by the Roman general Lucilius Bassus (*ib.* VII. vi. 4). The ruins, called *Mkawr*, on a projecting height near the Dead Sea on its eastern side, are supposed to mark the site of the fortress.

LITERATURE.—Hastings' *DB*, art. 'Machærus,' and the Lit. there cited ; to wh. add *PRE*[3] ix. 326 f.

JAMES PATRICK.

MADNESS.—It is somewhat remarkable that the OT ideas about madness should differ so much from those of the Gospels. In the OT madness is due to the influence of a spirit from God (1 S 16[14] 18[10]), in the Gospels to a demon ; in the OT it is conceived of as being closely connected with the 'spirit of prophecy' (which likewise came from God) ; this is clear from such passages as 1 S 10[6. 10-13] 19[23. 24], Hos 9[7], 2 K 9[11], Jer 29[26] ; there is no sign of this in the Gospels.* It was, no doubt, owing to the belief that madness was a sign of the indwelling of a spirit from God that a madman was looked upon (in the OT) as, in some sense, sacred ;† in the Gospels the reverse of this seems to be the case, if one regards the demoniac described in Lk 8[26-39] as a madman [see DEMON].

There are very few references to madness in the Gospels ; in Lk 6[11] the word ἄνοια is used (the RVm renders it 'foolishness'), its meaning is certainly nearer to 'foolishness' than to the modern notion of madness ; perhaps its meaning is best expressed by the German *ausser sich*, lit. 'outside of oneself,' resulting in a temporary loss of mental balance ; in 2 Ti 3[9] the same word is translated 'folly,' which, taken with the words 'corrupted in mind' in the preceding verse, brings out the sense more fully. Another expression, used in Mt 4[24] 17[15], is σελη-

* See, however, Ac 16[16ff.].
† This is still the case in the East.

νιάζεσθαι 'to be lunatic,' or 'moonstruck,'* but from the context in the second passage there can be no doubt that this was epilepsy. Neither of these expressions answers to modern ideas of madness. There is, however, one other word (μαίνεσθαι, Jn 10[20]) which seems to correspond with what would be understood by madness nowadays, viz. to be bereft of reason ; in the passage in question it is certainly used in this sense ; at the same time it must be remembered that μαίνεσθαι is connected with μαντεύεσθαι, which implies possession by some supernatural being.† The same word, as well as μανία, is used in Ac 26[24. 25], where ἀλήθεια and σωφροσύνη are placed in opposition to it, which confirms the meaning implied in Jn 10[20].‡ [See, further, DEMON, LUNATIC].

On two occasions in the Gospels we find madness or insanity definitely attributed to our Lord Himself. Once by His own friends, among whom, apparently, His mother and brethren were included (Mk 3[21], cf. v.[31]). We read that 'they went out to lay hold on him : for they said, He is beside himself' (ἐξέστη). Commentators are for the most part agreed that in this passage ἐξέστη denotes insanity, or at least a mental excitement bordering upon it (cf. a similar use of the word by St. Paul, 2 Co 5[13]). The other occasion is that already referred to, when, according to St. John, certain of 'the Jews' said of Jesus, 'He hath a devil, and is mad' (δαιμόνιον ἔχει καὶ μαίνεται, Jn 10[20]). In this case the madness is evidently ascribed to Satanic possession, and is not regarded merely as a derangement due to overwork and excitement. It is worth noting, however, that μαίνομαι is applied to St. Paul in a less offensive way (μαίνῃ, Ac 26[24]) by Festus. AV renders, 'Thou art beside thyself,' which RV consistently changes into, 'Thou art mad,' to correspond with 'I am not mad (οὐ μαίνομαι), most excellent Festus,' in the next verse. The charge of madness brought against Jesus is characteristic and significant, and has many parallels in the history of Christ's followers in the early (cf. Ac 2[13] as well as 26[24. 25], 2 Co 5[13]) and in the later Church. It is an illustration of the inability of the natural man to receive the

* Macalister (in Hastings' *DB* iii. 328a) quotes Vicary, who says of the brain that 'it moueth and followeth the mouing of the Moone : for in the waxing of the Moone, the Brayne followeth upwards : and in the wane of the Moone the Brayne discendeth downwardes, and vanishes in substance of vertue . . .'; according to the Jewish conception, which connects epilepsy with demoniacal possession (Mt 17[18]), the light of the moon drove demons away. [See DEMON].
† See Trench, *Synonyms of the NT*[11], pp. 21, 22, cf. Ac 16[16-18].
‡ A somewhat similar meaning belongs to παραφρονῶν in 2 Co 11[23] and παραφρονία in 2 P 2[16].

things of the Spirit of God (2 Co 2^{14}; cf. Jn 15^{18} 17^{16}).

W. O. E. OESTERLEY and J. C. LAMBERT.

MAGDALA.—The word 'Magdala' occurs once only in the TR of the NT (Mt 15^{39}). In B and ℵ the reading is '**Magadan.**' This reading is followed by Tisch., Alford, WH, and is adopted in the RV. In the parallel narrative in St. Mark's Gospel (8^{10}) the place to which Christ came is designated as 'the parts of *Dalmanutha*' (wh. see). These names evidently refer to the same district, but not necessarily to the same place. They seem to have been in such proximity, however, that the adjacent district might be named from either. With respect to their location, various sites on the south and south-east border of the Lake of Galilee have been suggested, but none of them can be regarded as satisfactory. There is no site in this locality whose name bears any resemblance to Magadan; and the only place which suggests a resemblance to Dalmanutha is a village known as *ed-Delhemiyeh*, near the mouth of the Jarmuk river. Apart from the name there is nothing else in or about the place to justify its identification with the town to which St. Mark refers in the passage above cited. Caspari and Edersheim would place Magadan within the limits of the Decapolis, but do not assign it to any definite location. The suggestion of Ewald that its site is identical with Megiddo, on the southern border of the Esdraelon plain, does not harmonize with the facts of the narrative, and apparently rests upon a very slender foundation.

In the light of all the information attainable at the present time, the probabilities strongly favour the view, which has long been held by eminent writers and explorers, that the district in which these places were located was on the *western* shore of the Lake of Galilee, and that Magadan represents the village now known as *el-Mejdel*, the traditional site of the town of Mary Magdalene. While the words in their present form are not identical, they may be regarded as variations of the same name. Stanley's suggestion is worthy of note in this connexion : ' It may be observed that, as Herodotus (ii. 159) turns Megiddo into Magdalum, so some MSS in Mt 15^{39} turn Magdala into Magadan' (*SP* 451, note 1). It has been suggested also by another writer, as a possible explanation of the substitution of one name for the other, 'that owing to the familiar recurrence of the word Magdalene, the less known name was absorbed in the better, and Magdala usurped the name and possibly also the position of Magadan' (art. 'Magdala' in Smith's *DB* ii. p. 1734). On the supposition that Magadan was on or adjacent to the site of *el-Mejdel*, the probable location of Dalmanutha is at or near '*Ain el-Barideh*, where the ruins of an ancient village have been traced and described by Porter, Tristram, and other explorers. This site is about a mile south of *el-Mejdel*. An incidental testimony in support of this identification is given by Rabbi Schwarz, who asserts that the cave of Teliman or Talmanutha was in the cliffs which overlooked the sea behind the site of *el-Mejdel*. In the same connexion he identifies Migdal (*Mejdel*) with Magdala (p. 189). To this may be added the testimony of the Rabbins, that Magdala was adjacent to the city of Tiberias (Otho, *Lex Rabb.* 353). In the travels of Willibald (A.D. 722), 'Magdalum' is located between Tiberias and Capernaum; and in the time of Quaresmius (17th cent.), Mejdel is mentioned as identical with the Magdala of Scripture (ii. 866).

The generally accepted view that the descriptive surname of Mary — 'Magdalene' — used several times in the NT, and by all the Evangelists, was derived from her home or birthplace, is confirmed by the testimony of Edersheim, who asserts that several Rabbis are spoken of in the Talmud as 'Magdalene' or residents of Magdala. From the same source he gathers the statements that Magdala, which was a Sabbath-day's journey from Tiberias, was celebrated for its dye-works and its manufactories of fine woollen textures, of which eighty are mentioned. It was also noted for its wealth, its moral corruption, and for its traffic in turtle-doves and pigeons for purifications. The suggestion made by Lightfoot, that the name meant 'curler of hair,' is rejected by Edersheim, who regards it as founded upon a misapprehension (*Life and Times of Jesus the Messiah*, vol. i. p. 571).

Magdala is favourably situated at the S.E. corner of the plain of Gennesaret. It is three miles north of Tiberias, and almost the same distance south of *Khan Minyeh*. Before it lies the northward expanse of the Plain and the Lake; behind it rises a dark background of beetling cliffs, broken in one section by the deeply-cleft gorge of the *Wady Hamam* (Valley of Doves). Its precipitous sides are honeycombed with caves, which for centuries have been the refuge of robbers and outlaws. Mt. Hattin, the traditional mountain of the Beatitudes, is a conspicuous landmark on the plateau at the upper end of the wady. Through this natural passage-way the caravan route from the Mediterranean coast follows the line of the old Roman road to Khan Minyeh, and thence northward over the hills of Naphtali. A perennial stream, which waters the southern portion of the Plain, finds its way to the Lake a short distance north of the outskirts of the town.

Mejdel, which has little in itself to commend or distinguish it, is the only place of permanent habitation in the once densely populated 'land of Gennesaret.' It consists of twenty or more low, flat-roofed, grass-covered hovels, built of a conglomeration of dried mud, shells, and pebbles. Its degenerate inhabitants are the only resident farmers of the Plain, and go out from the town to cultivate a few patches of cleared ground in favourable locations. Near the centre of the village a palm-tree rises conspicuously above the objects around it, and a few thickly set thorn-trees on the outskirts afford a grateful shade to the loungers of the place in the heat of the day. A watch-tower on the north border of the town is a present suggestion of the derivation of the name *Mejdel* or its Greek form *Migdol*. It is possible also that Migdal-el (Jos 19^{38}) stands for the same place. The tower gives evidence of a date of construction comparatively modern, but it is doubtless the successor of an older outlook or watch-tower, which commanded the gateway to the southern section of the Gennesaret plain. The remains of substructions of a substantial character, hidden beneath the earth and its dense covering of undergrowth, afford satisfactory evidence of the antiquity of the site.

LITERATURE. — Edersheim, *Life and Times of Jesus the Messiah*, vol. i. pp. 571-572; Andrews, *Life of our Lord*, pp. 337-338; Tristram, *Holy Land*, p. 253; Thomson, *Land and Book*, 'Central Pal.' p. 394; Smith's *DB* vol. ii. p. 1734; Robinson, *BRP* ii. 397; Ewing, art. 'Magadan,' in Hastings' *DB*; also art. 'Dalmanutha'; Baedeker, *Pal. and Syria*, p. 255.

ROBERT L. STEWART.

MAGDALENE.—See preceding art., and MARY, No. 2.

MAGI (μάγοι, AV and RV '**wise men**').—The only reference to Magi in the Gospels occurs in Mt 2, where we have the well-known story of the visit of the Oriental Magi to the infant Jesus. The following article will deal with (1) certain difficulties in the narrative, (2) the historical value of the narrative, (3) the legendary additions to the narrative.

1. The *difficulties* are occasioned chiefly by the vague and indefinite character of the record. The first question that suggests itself is, What class of people had the Evangelist in his mind when he used the term μάγοι? Now, according to Herodotus (i. 101), the Magi were a Median tribe which in the time of Gaumata, the pseudo-Smerdis, made a determined attempt to substitute Median for Persian rule (*ib.* iii. 61 ff.; Ctesias, *Pers.* 41 (10) ff.; Justin, i. 9, 10; Agathias, ii. 26). Through the failure of this revolt the Magi lost all political importance, but they were influential as the priestly caste (Herod. i. 132; Amm. Marc. xxiii. 6; cf. the Levites among the Hebrews, *SBE* iv. pp. lxii, lxiii), and as religious instructors of the Persian kings (Cic. *de Divin.* i. 41; Philo, *de Special. Leg.* 18; Pliny, *HN* xxx. 1). The introduction of this Magian priesthood is ascribed to Cyrus (Xen. *Cyr.* viii. 1. 23); and classical writers conversant with Persian affairs use the word *magus* as synonymous with 'priest' (Apul. *Apol.* i. 25, 26; cf. Strabo, pp. 732, 733; Philo, *Quod omn. prob. lib.* 11; Dio Chrysost. *Or.* 36, p. 449, 49, p. 538; Diog. Laert. *proœm.* 6; Porphyr. *de Abstinent.* iv. 16; and the lexicons of Hesych. and Suidas). Darius Hystaspis made Mazdaism the religion of the Empire (Behistun inscr., and Sayce, *Ancient Empires of the East*), and from his time, at any rate,—for how long before, if at all, is disputed,— the Magi are identified with the Zoroastrian worship, and are represented as the disciples of Zoroaster (Plato, *Alcib.* i. 122; Plutarch, *de Is. et Os.* 46, 47; Pliny, *HN* xxx. 1; Apul. *Apol.* 26; Diog. Laert. *proœm.* 2; Amm. Marc. xxiii. 6; Agathias, ii. 24; Aug. *de Civ. Dei*, xxi. 14). In the Avesta, however, the priests are called, not *magi*, but *âthravans*; though even in the sacred texts the word 'magi' is found in a few instances. Finally, it may be noted that these Median magi are credited with skill in philosophy (Strabo, pp. 23, 24; Nicol. Damasc. *fr.* 66; Diog. Laert. *proœm.* 1), natural science (Philo, *Quod omn. prob. lib.* 11; Dio Chrysost. *Or.* 49, p. 538), and medicine (Pliny, *HN* xxx. 1, cf. xxiv. 17). They are also described as interpreters of dreams (Herod. i. 107, 120, vii. 19), astrologers (*ib.* vii. 37; Pliny, *HN* xxxvii. 9; Amm. Marc. xxiii. 6), soothsayers and diviners (Cic. *de Divin.* i. 41; Strabo, p. 762; Pliny, *HN* xxx. 2; Diog. Laert. *proœm.* 7; Aelian, *Var. Hist.* ii. 17; Amm. Marc. xxiii. 6).

In a technical sense, then, *magi* denoted the members of the sacerdotal class in the Persian Empire. But in the LXX Daniel the word is used to render the Heb. *'ashshâphim*, AV 'astrologers,' of Babylonia (Dn 1²⁰ 2². ¹⁰. ²⁷ 4⁷ 5⁷· ¹¹· ¹⁵. Some would explain the title Rab-mag in Jer 39³· ¹³ as= 'chief magian,' but without probability). Moreover, classical writers sometimes confuse the words *magi* and *Chaldæi* (Ctes. *Pers.* 46 (15); Justin, xii. 13). The latter term, however, is properly used in Daniel (1⁴ 2². ⁴· ⁵· ¹⁰ 4⁷ 5⁷· ¹¹) and by classical authorities (Herod. i. 181, 183; Diod. Sic. ii. 29–31) to represent a class, or the class, of Babylonian priests or learned men (Driver, *Daniel*, pp. 12–16), renowned for their skill in astronomy, astrology, and sorcery (Cic. *de Divin.* i. 41, *de Fato*, 8, 9; Diod. Sic. ii. 29–31; Strabo, p. 762; Curtius, v. 1; Apul. *Flor.* 15; Porph. *Vit. Pyth.* 6; Diog. Laert. *proœm.* 6; cf. Lenormant, *La magie chez les Chaldéens*; R. C. Thompson, *Reports of the Magicians and Astrologers of Nineveh and Babylon*; W. L. King, *Babylonian Magic and Sorcery*; Chantepie de la Saussaye, *Lehrbuch der Religionsgeschichte*; Jastrow, *Religion of Babylonia and Assyria*).

Lastly, the words *magi* and *Chaldæi* came to be applied not only to the members of a sacerdotal caste, but in a secondary sense to all those who cultivated magic arts (Soph. *Œd. Tyr.* 387; Tac. *Ann.* ii. 27, xii. 22, 59; Juv. *Sat.* x. 94, with Mayor's note; Dio Chrysost. *Or.* 36, p. 449). In Rabbinical writers this bad sense is predominant (Edersheim, *Life and Times*, i. p. 210), and the same may be said of the passages in the NT (other than Mt 2) in which magi are referred to (Ac 8⁹· ¹¹ Simon Magus, 13⁶· ⁸ Elymas). In the LXX the Egyptian conjuring is described as μαγικὴ τέχνη (Wis 17⁷). And Jerome says: 'Consuetudo et sermo communis magos pro maleficis accepit' (Hieron. *Com. in Dan.* 2, cf. Isid. *Ety.* viii. 9).

In what sense, then, did the author of Mt 2 understand the term? The majority of the Fathers affix the worst interpretation, and lay stress on the idea that magic was overthrown by the advent of Christ (Ign. *Ephes.* 19; Justin M. *Dial.* 78; Tertull. *de Idol.* 9; Origen, *c. Cels.* i. 60; Max. Taur. *Hom.* 21; Hilar. *de Trin.* iv. 38. *Com. in Matt.* 1; Aug. *Serm.* 200, § 3; Theophylact, *in loc.*); and this was the common opinion even in the Middle Ages (Abelard, *in Epiph. serm.* 4; Aquinas, *Summa*, III. xxxvi. 3). But the consensus of later commentators rejects this view. There is no hint or suggestion of reprobation in the Gospel narrative. On the other hand, there is no indication that the Evangelist is alluding to any particular class of magi. He appears, on the contrary, to use the term in the general sense of sages from the East, who busied themselves with astronomy (vv.²· ⁷· ⁹· ¹⁰) and perhaps with the interpretation of dreams (v.¹²). There is certainly no attempt in the narrative to contrast Christianity with Zoroastrian or Babylonian worship.

Closely connected with the above is the further question of the region whence the Magi are supposed to have come. Mt. calls them simply μάγοι ἀπὸ ἀνατολῶν, *i.e.* 'Oriental magi.' The expression is quite indefinite (cf. Mt 8¹¹ 24²⁷, Lk 13²⁹, Rev 21¹³). Various attempts have been made, however, to identify the particular part of the East whence the Magi may have come (Patritius, *de Evang.* iii. p. 315 ff.; Spanheim, *Dub. Evang.* ii. p. 291 ff.). The oldest opinion inclines to Arabia (Justin M. *Dial.* 77, 78; Tertull. *Jud.* 9; Epiphan. *Exp. Fid.* 8, and most Roman commentators, *e.g.* Corn. a Lapide, *in loc.*), partly on account of references such as Ps 72¹⁶, Is 60⁵, partly on account of the character of the gifts, partly by reason of the close intercourse that subsisted between Arabia and Palestine (Edersheim, i. p. 203). On the other hand, Arabia is to the south rather than the east of Judæa (cf. Mt 12⁴² βασίλισσα νότου), and in the NT it is usually specified by its geographical name. Other places suggested are Persia (Clem. Alex. *Strom.* i. 15; Chrysost. *in Mt. Hom.* 6. § 1, 2, 3, 4; 7. § 5; *Op. Imp. in Mt. 2 ap.* Chrysost. vi.; Diodorus Tars. *ap.* Phot. cod. 223; Theophylact, *in loc.*; Juvencus, *Evang. Hist.* i. 276), Chaldæa (Max. Taur. *Hom.* 21; Origen, *c. Cels.* i. 58), Parthia (Wetstein, *in loc.*; Hyde, *Rel. Vet. Pers.* c. 31), and Egypt (Möller, *Neue Ansichten*). But the language of the Evangelist is 'too indefinite, and perhaps intentionally too indefinite, to justify any decision' (Trench, *Star of the Wise Men*, p. 4), and it is unsafe to draw any inference from the nature of the presents (Weiss, *Life of Christ*, i. p. 266). One thing alone seems clear—the Magi were heathen and not Jews (see references in Meyer, *Com. in loc.*). The form of their question (Mt 2²) would be sufficient to establish this, apart from the ecclesiastical tradition which represents their homage as the first-fruits of the Gentile world (Aquinas, *Summa*, III. xxxvi. 8).

The cause of the coming of the Magi is roughly

indicated in the words, 'we have seen his star in the rising' ($\dot{\epsilon}\nu \tau\hat{\eta}$ $\dot{\alpha}\nu\alpha\tauo\lambda\hat{\eta}$). It seems clear that they were induced to make the journey by some sidereal appearance; but what exactly this appearance was is not conclusively determined (see art. STAR). From this phenomenon, however, whatever it may have been, the Magi inferred the birth of a Messiah-king of the Jews. We cannot say precisely by what means they arrived at this inference. It is unlikely, for chronological and other reasons, that their expectations had been excited by the Zoroastrian prediction of the coming of Soshyos (*SBE* iv. p. xxxvii); nor is it probable that an independent tradition of Balaam's prophecy (Nu 24[17]) had been preserved by their ancestors and handed down to them (Origen, *c. Cels.* i. 60, *Hom. in Num.* 13. 7; *Op. Imp. in Mt. 2 ap.* Chrysost. vi.); nor is there any historical evidence that there was at this time among the nations any widespread expectation of the advent of a Messiah in Palestine (Tac. *Hist.* v. 13 and Suet. *Vesp.* 4 are derived from Jos. *BJ* VI. v. 4, and refer to the Flavian dynasty). On the other hand, the Jews themselves were undoubtedly expecting the Messiah (Charles, *Eschatology*, p. 304; Toy, *Judaism and Christianity*, p. 330), and a Rabbinical tradition, which may be previous to Christ's birth, declared that a star in the East was to appear two years before the Messiah's advent (Edersheim, i. pp. 211, 212; Strauss, *Life of Jesus*, Eng. tr. p. 174 and references; cf. the name Bar-Cochba). Hence the source whence the Magi derived their inference that a king of the Jews was born may well have been the Jews of the Diaspora, whose tenets would doubtless be known to the wise men of the lands in which they sojourned.

The time of the visit of the Magi is quite uncertain. By ancient writers it was usually supposed that they arrived at Bethlehem on the 13th day inclusive after the birth of Christ, *i.e.* Jan. 6 (Aug. *Serm.* 203. 1). Most commentators, however, place their coming after Christ's presentation in the Temple; and some, as an inference from Mt 2[16], delay it till Jesus had reached or nearly reached His second year (see Patritius, iii. 326 ff.; Spanheim, ii. p. 299 ff.; Trench, p. 109 ff.; Ramsay, *Was Christ born at Bethlehem?* pp. 215–220). Here also the evidence is insufficient to warrant a definite conclusion.

2. The *historical value* of the narrative has been frequently impugned, the principal objections being as follows. The account of the Magi is found in the First Gospel only, and is not corroborated by either Lk. or Josephus or any pagan historian. (The references in Macrobius, *Sat.* ii. 4. 11, and Chalcidius, *Tim.* 7. 126, cannot be regarded as independent evidence). Moreover, it is not easy to see how Mt.'s narrative can be harmonized with that of Luke. Many of the details, again, are suspicious; the conduct of Herod, as here represented, seems inexplicable (Meyer, *in loc.*). Finally, the story in general is vague, and on *a priori* grounds may even be held to be improbable. These objections are not without force. Doubtless too much stress has been laid on the absence of confirmatory evidence, and the argument from the silence of Josephus can scarcely be sustained (Edersheim, i. pp. 214, 215; Trench, p. 102 ff.). The difficulties in connexion with Herod's attitude have also been overestimated (Weiss, i. p. 219). Yet the divergence between Mt. and Lk., though certainly not incapable of explanation (Ellicott, *Huls. Lect.* p. 70), is sufficiently serious; and the positive evidence for the truth of the narrative is slender. It may be urged, however, that there is no reason for denying the existence in the narrative of at least a substratum of historical fact, though possibly the facts have been treated with a cer-

tain amount of freedom. Such a view, at any rate, appears to account for the story better than any rationalistic explanation hitherto put forward.

Of these attempted explanations the most important may briefly be summarized. (*a*) The older school of critics sought for the basis of the history mainly in the prophecies of the OT. Thus Strauss laid great stress on Nu 24[17], while Keim emphasized Is 60. From these and other prophetical passages (*e.g.* Is 9[2] 42[6] 49[6. 7], Ps 68[29. 31] 72[10]), supplemented possibly by Jewish or pagan tradition, the Evangelist is supposed to have built up his story. But it is incredible that the history could have been constructed from such material, or that such a fulfilment could have been deliberately devised for prophecies which at the time were understood to have so different a significance (Edersheim, i. p. 209). Moreover, it should be noted that 'the Evangelist who at other times searches zealously for the fulfilment of OT predictions, nowhere refers in this narrative to one of these prophetical passages, from which it is said to have arisen' (Weiss, i. p. 267). (*b*) A different, and very fanciful explanation has been offered by W. Soltau, Usener, and others (Soltau, *Birth of Jesus Christ*; Usener in *Encyc. Bibl.* art. 'Nativity,' cf. his *Religionsgeschichtliche Untersuchungen*, i. 'Das Weihnachtsfest'). According to this, Mt.'s account is the outcome partly of the operation of heathen superstitious ideas, partly of the transformation of a story recorded by Dio Cassius and Pliny. Thus, for the incident of the star, Soltau appeals to the widespread belief that such portents were manifested in connexion with the birth and death of kings and heroes (for instances see Wetstein, *in loc.*; Winer, *Biblisches Realwörterbuch*, vol. ii. p. 613); and, for the Massacre of the Innocents, Usener refers to the story of Marathus concerning the birth of Augustus (Suet. *Aug.* 94). The visit of the Magi is represented as a Christian transformation of the story related by Dio and Pliny about the visit of Tiridates and his Magians to Nero (see the passages quoted by Soltau, *op. cit.* pp. 73, 74). In the year A.D. 66 the Parthian king Tiridates, the Magus, bringing other Magi with him, journeyed to Rome, worshipped Nero as the sun-god Mithra, and afterwards travelled home by another way through the cities of Asia. Now to the Christians of the East Nero was Antichrist: hence it is argued that just as, in the early legends, the miraculous events of Christ's life were transferred to Antichrist, so the story of being worshipped by Magi may have been transferred from the Antichrist Nero to the Christ. The whole narration of the Magi, then, Soltau dismisses as an insertion 'of Hellenistic origin' (*op. cit.* p. 49). But he does not explain how this insertion received so characteristic a Jewish form, or why such alien elements should have 'crystallized themselves in just the most markedly Jewish part of the New Testament, while they are passed over in silence elsewhere' (*Interpreter*, Jan. 1906, pp. 195–207). On the whole it is easier to suppose that the events recorded actually took place, than to believe the far-fetched explanations of them offered by Soltau and Usener. (*c*) Other critics, again, resort to a mythological solution, and regard the adoration of the Magi and the attendant events as 'not history, but pious transformations of current mythic stories.' Réville believes that it was suggested by the Mithraic legend, though he admits that the supposition is incapable of proof (*Études publiées en hommage à la faculté de théologie de Montauban*, 1901, p. 339 ff.). Pfleiderer and Cheyne maintain that the star, the worship of the wise men, and the persecution of the Holy Child have many prototypes in tales concerning heroes of old, and belong to a pre-Christian international myth of the Redeemer (Pfleiderer, *Early Christian Conception of Christ*; Cheyne, *Bible Problems*); on which it may be remarked that although striking parallels can undoubtedly be produced, yet resemblances do not necessarily presuppose an imitation. (*d*) Another suggestion is that the narrative exhibits the characteristic features of Jewish Midrash or Haggādā, and is governed by an apologetic purpose. The writer's object is to show that the prophecy of Dt 18[15] was fulfilled in Jesus, and he endeavours to do this by drawing a parallel between the early career of Moses and that of the Christian Messiah (see the *Midrash Rabbā* to Exodus in the section which deals with the birth of Moses, and cf. Jos. *Ant.* II. ix. 2). Jesus is throughout represented as the antitype of Moses. This is the underlying motive of the narrative, to which may be added another influential idea, viz. the desire to suggest the homage of the Gentile world (G. H. Box in *Interpreter*, *loc. cit.*). The simplicity of the Gospel story, however, seems to be at variance with this hypothesis.

Allusion may here be made to the theory that the history of the Magi was added to the Gospel as late as the year A.D. 119. The evidence for this is a Syriac document, ascribed to Eusebius of Cæsarea, which was published with an Eng. translation by W. Wright in the *Journal of Sacred Literature*, vols. ix., x., 1866, from a 6th cent. British Museum codex, Add. 17, 142. The title is, 'Concerning the star; showing how and through what the Magi recognized the star, and that Joseph did not take Mary as his wife.' This tractate relates that the prophecy of Balaam about the star was recorded in a letter written by Balak to the king of Assyria, and preserved in the Assyrian archives. At last, in the reign of king Pir Shabour, the star appeared, and the Magi were sent with great pomp to do homage to the Messiah. The colophon at the end states : ' And in the year 430 (= A.D. 119), in the reign of Hadrianus Cæsar . . . this concern arose in (the minds of) men acquainted with the Holy Books ; and through the pains of the great men in various places this history was sought for and found and written in the tongue of those who took this care.' As to the meaning of this statement, however, critics are not agreed (see F. C. Conybeare, *Guardian*, April 29, 1903 ; and, on the other side, *Church Quarterly Review*, July 1904, p. 389). The more probable explanation seems to be that ' the Holy Books' refers, not to the OT but to the narrative in Mt 2, already, therefore, incorporated in the Gospel in A.D. 119 ; and that the 'history' is not Mt 2, but the legend about the preservation of Balak's letter and the coming of the Magi in the reign of Pir Shabour.

To conclude this part of the subject, it may be pointed out that the story of the Magi must stand or fall with the other Matthæan narratives of the Infancy. All were probably drawn from some written source, Jewish-Christian in character, and perhaps originally Aramaic in language. The value of this source cannot here be determined (see artt. BIRTH OF CHRIST, MATTHEW). It is sufficient to point out that if a Palestinian or semi-Palestinian origin of the narratives can be sustained, the hypothesis of direct pagan influence in their formation must be rejected.

3. Of the *legendary accretions* to the story of the Magi, the following deserve notice. From the 6th cent., if not before (Tert. *Marc.* iii. 13, *Jud.* 9 are not decisive), the opinion prevailed that the Magi were kings. This belief is first unambiguously stated in a sermon ascribed to Cæsarius of Arles (Aug. *Opp.* v. Append. *Serm.* 139. 3) ; and it prevailed universally during the Middle Ages (cf. Paschasius, *Exp. in Mt.* ii. 2). Hence the festival of Epiphany received the name *Festum Trium Regum.* The idea would, of course, find support in such passages as Ps 68[29. 31] 72[10], Is 49[7. 23] 60[3. 10. 16] ; but there is no suggestion of it in the Evangelic narrative. (For discussions see Patritius, iii. p. 320 ff. ; Spanheim, ii. p. 273 ff. ; Barradius, *Com.* ix. c. 8).

The number of the Magi is not specified in the Gospel. Eastern tradition fixed it at twelve (*Op. Imp. in Mt. 2 ap.* Chrysost. vi. ; cf. the curious MS fragment quoted in *Classical studies in honour of Henry Drisler*, p. 31—' Twelve kings set out from Persia to go to Jerusalem,' etc.), or thirteen (Bar Bahlul in Hyde, *Rel. Vet. Pers.* c. 31). But in the West the number of the Magi was reckoned at three (Max. Taur. *Hom.* 17, 20 ; Leo M. *Serm.* 31. § 1, 2 ; 34. § 2), probably on account of their threefold gift (Abelard, *Serm.* 4 : ' Quot vero isti magi fuerint, ex numero trinæ oblationis tres eos fuisse multi suspicantur '), though allegorical reasons were also found (Patritius, iii. 318 ff.).

The familiar names of the Magi — Melchior, Gaspar, and Balthasar—first occur in Bede, where also is given a remarkable description of their persons, derived most probably from some early work of art. ' Primus fuisse dicitur Melchior, senex et canus, barba prolixa et capillis . . . aurum obtulit regi Domino. Secundus nomine Gaspar, iuvenis imberbis, rubicundus . . . thure, quasi Deo oblatione digna, Deum honorabat. Tertius fuscus, integre barbatus, Balthasar nomine . . . per myrrham filium hominis moriturum professus est' (*Collect.* v. 541. For the association of the gifts with the several Magi, contrast the familiar verse, ' Gaspar fert myrrham, thus Melchior, Balthasar aurum '). Other names are found, *e.g.* Appellius,

Amerius, Damascus : Magalath, Pangalath, Saracen : Ator, Sator, Peratoras, etc. (Patritius, iii. p. 326 ; Spanheim, ii. pp. 288, 289 ; Hebenstreit, *de Magorum nomine, patria et statu dissert.*, Jenæ, 1709). Hyde quotes thirteen names, among which the three familiar to Western tradition do not occur (*Rel. Vet. Pers.* c. 31).

Symbolical meanings were early attached to the gifts. Thus Irenæus says : ' Matthæus autem Magos ab Oriente venientes ait . . . per ea quæ obtulerunt munera ostendisse quis erat qui adorabatur : myrrham quidem quod ipse erat qui pro mortali humano genere moreretur et sepeliretur : aurum vero quoniam rex, cuius regni finis non est : thus vero, quoniam Deus, qui et notus in Judæa factus est, et manifestus eis qui non quærebant eum' (*Hær.* iii. 9. 2, cf. Max. Taur. *Hom.* 21 ; Leo, *Serm.* 34. 3 ; Origen, *c. Cels.* i. 60 ; Ambros. *in Lk.* ii. 44 ; [Aug.] *Serm.* 139. 2 ; Hilar. *Com. in Mt.* 1 ; and Christian poets, Juvencus, *Ev. Hist.* i. 285 ; Prudent. *Cath.* xii. 69 ff. ; Sedulius, *Carm. Pasch.* ii. 96 ; [Claudian] *Carm.* Append. 21). Mediæval tradition invented histories for these gifts. The gold consisted of thirty pennies, which had once been paid by Abraham for the cave of Machpelah, and which were afterwards given to Judas. Some of the myrrh is said to have been administered to Jesus on the cross (*Quarterly Review*, vol. lxxviii. p. 433 ff.).

Miraculous elements were increasingly introduced into the narrative, and the whole history was gradually amplified. Thus the star is alleged to have shone with surpassing brilliance (Ignat. *Ephes.* 19 ; Leo, *Serm.* 31. 1 ; *Protevang. Jacob.* 21 ; and pass. quoted in Barradius, *Com.* ix. 9), having the sun, moon, and other stars as ' chorus' to it (Ignat. *loc. cit.*). According to Eastern tradition, there was in the star an appearance of the Virgin and Child (Lightfoot, *Ap. Fath.* ii. 81), or of a young child bearing a cross (*Op. Imp. in Matt. 2 ap.* Chrysost. vi.). The star was alleged to be an angel (Suicer, *Thes. s.v.* ἀστήρ) ; and according to Greg. of Tours it was still, in his time, to be seen in a well at Bethlehem (*Mirac.* i. 1). Similarly a mass of details were invented about the Magi themselves, their journey, and their later life and death. Here it need only be noticed that they are reported to have been baptized by St. Thomas. (A full account of the Magi-legends will be found in Crombach's monumental monograph, *Primitiæ gentium sive historia et encomium SS. Trium Magorum.* See also the epitome in the *Quarterly Review*, vol. lxxviii. p. 433 ff., of the mediæval stories collected by John of Hildesheim ; and the *Boll. AA. SS.* Jan. d. i. vi. and xi.).

The bodies of the Magi are said to have been discovered in the East in the 4th cent. (according to one tradition, by St. Helena herself), and to have been brought to Constantinople and deposited in the Church of St. Sofia. When Eustorgius became bishop of Milan, they were transferred to that city, whence, in the year 1162, they were again removed by Frederic Barbarossa to Cologne (*Boll. AA. SS.* Jan. d. vi.). The festival of Epiphany (the celebration of which in the West is mentioned first by Amm. Marc. xxi. 2) commemorated originally Christ's manifestation to the Magi, together with His baptism, His miracle at Cana (Max. Taur. *Hom.* 29 ; Isid. *de Off. Eccl.* i. 27 ; Abelard, *Serm.* 4), and the miracle of feeding the 5000 ([Aug.] Append. *Serm.* 36. 1). But soon the manifestation to the Magi became in the West, if not exclusively, yet principally, dwelt upon (see, *e.g.*, Leo's *Epiphany Sermons*) ; and the common Western synonym for Epiphany was *Festum Trium Regum* (Bingham, *Ant.* xx. 4 ; *DCA* i. p. 617 ff. ; *Boll. AA. SS.* Jan. d. vi.). In the Middle Ages the Magi were considered the patron saints of travellers, and inns were called after them. Their names were also used as charms to cure epilepsy and snake-bite (Spanheim, ii. pp. 289, 290). See also art. STAR.

LITERATURE.—Besides the books referred to above, see Hastings' *DB*, art. 'Magi'; *PRE*³, vol. viii. art. 'Magier'; *Encyc. Bibl.* art. 'Nativity'; Kraus, *RE*, vol. ii. art. 'Magier'; Moroni's *Dizionario*, vol. xli. art. 'Magi'; Hamburger's *RE*, art. 'Zauberei'; Smith's *DB*, artt. 'Magi,' 'Star'; Suicer, *Thesaurus*, artt. λίβανος, μάγος; Winer, *Biblisches Realwörterbuch*, vol. ii. artt. 'Magier,' 'Stern der Weisen'; Hone, *Everyday Book*, Jan. 6; and the various Comm. on Matthew. An English monograph by F. W. Upham, *The Wise Men*, is of little value. The discussions of Spanheim and Patritius should be consulted, while Crombach's elaborate study is a treasury of curious information.   F. HOMES DUDDEN.

MAGISTRATE.—This English word occurs only twice in the Gospels (AV), viz. in Lk 12¹¹ and ⁵⁸, where the RV gives the same translation. By our use of the word we usually mean one entrusted with the duty and power of putting laws into force, but the Greek ἄρχων (of which 'magistrate' is the translation in the passages before us) has a wider meaning, and may denote *ruler*, *captain*, *chief*, *king*. In the Gospels, ἄρχων (as well as the similar word ἡγεμών) occurs frequently, and will be referred to in the articles RULE and RULER.

In the first of the instances to be noticed here our Lord prepares His disciples for the persecutions that await them. One form of persecution will be arrest and accusation before magistrates. In such an event, however, Christ's followers are not to concern themselves unduly about their defence, for the Holy Ghost shall teach them in the same hour what they ought to say. Their presence before the magistrates and their utterance in such a situation will constitute a twofold testimony—a testimony against the unbelief and injustice of their accusers, and perhaps also of the magistrates (Mk 13¹¹)—and a testimony to the truth of the gospel and to their own fidelity (Lk 21¹³). The Lord's prediction and promise were alike fulfilled. Persecutions did ensue, and nothing is more remarkable than the dignity and wisdom of the words spoken by disciples thus accused before magistrates, the Holy Ghost being a mouth and wisdom unto them (Lk 21¹⁵; cf. Ac 4¹³ *et al.*).

This policy of submissively trusting to the Holy Ghost for defence is not to be taken as justifying Tolstoi's theory of non-resistance. But our Lord's counsel indicates that He looked upon existent magistracies as a part of the providential order, not to be overturned in any revolutionary way by His first disciples. Similarly, Christ taught that, the political circumstances being what they were, tribute should be paid to Cæsar, the supreme magistrate (Mt 22²¹). The capital instance of submission to the magistrate is Christ's own demeanour before Pilate (styled ἡγεμών in Mt 27², Lk 3¹). The subject of the relation between Christ and the magistrate runs into questions of Church and State, the spiritual and the civil power, individual conscience and public law.

In the second instance (Lk 12⁵⁸) Christ seems to warn against a litigious spirit, and to commend that 'sweet reasonableness' which is one of the gifts of His own Spirit, and which may obviate the necessity of going before a magistrate. This does not condemn as un-Christian all reference to a magistrate, but Christ hints that to agree with an adversary quickly may prove to be the highest prudence as well as the most Christian-like conduct. The advice is sometimes spiritualized to mean that the sinner ought to settle accounts with God quickly.   R. M. ADAMSON.

MAGNIFICAT.—Our primary interest in the hymn *Magnificat* (Lk 1⁴⁶⁻⁵⁵) is centred in the question of (1) its authorship, upon which must largely depend the scope of (2) its interpretation. Then (3) the history of its liturgical use may be briefly summarized.

1. *Authorship.*—Opinions are divided as to the source from which St. Luke derived the materials of his first chapter. Völter suggests that it is based on an *Apocalypse of Zacharias*, a Jewish document which has been edited by a Christian, who found the *Magnificat* attributed to Elisabeth, and transferred it to Mary. Weizsäcker thinks that St. Luke simply inserted an early Christian hymn. A more satisfactory view is that of Sanday (Hastings' *DB* ii. 639, 644), who suggests that St. Luke was supplied with a special (written) source, through one of the women mentioned in Lk 8³ 24¹⁰, possibly Joanna, who, being the wife of Herod's steward, may also have supplied information about the court of Herod. We know from Jn 19²⁵ (cf. Ac 1¹⁴) that the Virgin Mary was brought into contact with this group. Ramsay (*Was Christ born at Bethlehem?* p. 88) calls attention to 'a womanly spirit in the whole narrative, which seems inconsistent with the transmission from man to man, and which, moreover, is an indication of Luke's character; he had a marked sympathy with women.' On the supposition that St. Luke used an Aramaic tradition or document, it is possible to account for all the characteristics of style by which Harnack (see below) seeks to prove that he was the author both of the *Magnificat* and of the *Benedictus*.

Having described the visit of the Virgin Mary to Elisabeth, and Elisabeth's salutation, the TR has καὶ εἶπεν [Μαριάμ] with the variant reading Ἐλισάβετ. Then follows the hymn, the text of which has been excellently preserved, the only other doubtful reading being μεγάλα, for which we should probably read μεγαλεῖα.

Μαριάμ is the reading of all Greek MSS, of the great majority of Latin MSS, and of innumerable Patristic testimonies, back to the 2nd cent., when Tertullian wrote (*de Anima*, 26): 'Exsultat Elisabet, Johannes intus impulerat, glorificat dominum Maria, Christus intus instinxerat.'

Ἐλισάβετ is the reading of three Old Latin MSS. *a* (Vercellensis, *sæc.* iv.), *b* (Veronensis, *sæc.* v.), *rhe* (Rhedigeranus-Vratislaviensis, *sæc. fere* vii.), in Burkitt's phrase 'a typical European group,' to which may be added the testimony of Niceta of Remesiana, *de Psalmodiæ Bono*, c. 9: 'Nec Elisabeth, diu sterilis, edito de repromissione filio, Deum de ipsa anima magnificare cessat; c. 11: Cum Elisabeth Dominum anima nostra magnificat.'

So also Origen, or his translator Jerome, in the 5th *Homily* on Lk. 5 (Lommatzsch, *t.* v. p. 108 f.): 'Inuenitur beata Maria, sicut in aliquantis exemplaribus reperimus, prophetare; non enim ignoramus, quod secundum alios codices et hæc uerba Elisabet uaticinetur Spiritu itaque sancto tunc repleta est Maria,' etc. Harnack thinks that Jerome, if he had been responsible for this reference, would have mentioned whether the reading was in Latin or Greek MSS. But as Jerome was writing in Latin, and the evidence of Niceta shows that the reading *Elisabeth* was more persistent and widespread in the very district from which Jerome came,—having been born in Pannonia, not a great distance from Remesiana,—it must be considered still possible that he interpolated the reference.

Lastly we come to Irenæus, iv. 7. 1 (*Cod. Clarom. et Voss.*): 'sed et Elisabet ait: Magnificat anima mea dominum,' etc. *Cod. Arund.* 'Maria.' In iii. 10. 1: 'Propter quod exultans Maria clamabat pro ecclesia prophetans: Magnificat anima mea dominum,' etc. Here the context proves that Irenæus intended to write 'Maria.'* Thus it

* In iii. 14. 3, Irenæus refers to Lk 1⁴²⁻⁴⁵ as *exclamatio Elisabet*.

seems probable that it was the translator of
Irenæus, or a copyist, who introduced the reading
Elisabet from his Old Latin Bible, and we may
safely carry it back to the 3rd century. *

How then are we to account for the reading?
Bardenhewer thinks that, Μαριάμ having dropped
out, Ἐλισάβετ was supplied by a copyist. But most
critics (Burkitt, Harnack, Wordsworth) agree that
the original text must have been καὶ εἶπεν without
either name. Burkitt puts it concisely : ' "Mary"
was read by Tertullian as well as by all Greek and
Syriac texts. This is fatal to "Elisabeth"; yet, if
"Mary" were genuine, the actual occurrence of
"Elisabeth" in the European branch of the Old
Latin would be inexplicable. But if the original
text of the Gospel had καὶ εἶπεν Μεγαλύνει, κ.τ.λ.,
without either name, all the evidence falls into
line.'

On the question, which is the right gloss, critics
are divided. Harnack and Burkitt argue for
'Elisabeth,' Wordsworth and Spitta for ' Mary.' (1)
Harnack does not think that the exclamation of
vv.[42-45] covers all that is implied in v.[41] καὶ ἐπλήσθη
πνεύματος ἁγίου ἡ Ἐλισάβετ. In v.[67] similar words
are used about Zacharias, and are followed by the
Benedictus. Nothing is said about Mary being
filled with the prophetic spirit. It does not seem
necessary, on the other hand, to resort to the
extreme remedy of Spitta, who refuses to consider
that the *Benedictus* supplies a parallel case, because he thinks that it has been interpolated at
this point. The 'glowing words' of Elisabeth's
address need some reply. ' Could St. Mary, who
answered so freely and so bravely, yet so humbly,
to the angel, have been silent at such a moment
when addressed by one whom she knew so well?'
(Wordsworth). Though undoubtedly she is kept,
or more probably keeps herself, in the background
of this history, and is not spoken of as 'filled with
the Holy Ghost,' there is no question of deepest
communing with God (*Gottinnigkeit*, Spitta), and
this suffices to explain the outpouring in devotion
and faith of a mind stored with OT phrases.

In the OT ' when any question is addressed to
a person or persons whom the reader knows to be
present, the formula of reply is frequently and
perhaps generally without proper name and without pronoun'; cf. Lk 2[49]. Later in his Gospel Lk.
generally uses ὁ δὲ εἶπεν ; but the first chapters have
' a special OT colouring' (Wordsworth), in view of
which Harnack's argument, that 'if in v.[46] the
subject was to be changed, Lk. would have written
εἶπεν δὲ Μαριάμ,' falls to the ground. Further, the
words μακαριοῦσί με πᾶσαι αἱ γενεαί of v.[48] seem to be
a reply to Elisabeth's μακαρία ἡ πιστεύσασα. On the
other hand, it is only fair to point out that Prof.
Burkitt seeks to prove that St. Luke was ' remarkably fond of inserting καὶ εἶπεν or εἶπεν δέ
between the speeches of his characters without
a change of speaker.' † (2) Another argument has
been based on the words ἔμεινεν δὲ Μαριὰμ σὺν αὐτῇ,
which are said to make it probable that Elisabeth
has been the speaker, otherwise Lk. would have
written ἔμεινεν δὲ Μ. σὺν τῇ Ἐ. or ἔμεινε δὲ σὺν τῇ Ἐ.
' The Peshitta as well as the Sinai Palimpsest
renders, "Now Mary remained *with Elisabeth*."
But the Greek has retained "the tell-tale αὐτῇ"'
(Burkitt).

In the OT the personality of the singer is, as a
rule, sunk in the song, and the name is mentioned
at the end as if to pick up the thread (cf. Balaam,
Nu 24[25]; Moses, Dt 32[44] 34[1] etc.). It is true that
Hannah's name is not mentioned in 1 S 2[11], but it
has been mentioned at the beginning. The name

---

* Prof. Burkitt still adheres to his view, that 'Irenæus
regarded *Elisabeth* as a type of the ancient Jewish Ecclesia
prophesying by a Divine Spirit about the Christ.'
† *JThSt* vii. p. 223.

---

marks 'the whole section vv.[39-56] as what we may
call a " Mary section,"' the Syriac reading being
an attempt to clear up ambiguity (Wordsworth).

On the whole, then, so far as external evidence
goes, the balance of probability is in favour of the
reading or gloss ' Mary.' But the more difficult
question of internal evidence remains for discussion. Does the *Magnificat* seem more suitable
on the lips of Elisabeth?

Harnack thinks that it was modelled on the lines
of Hannah's song, that it expresses the feeling
of a mother from whom has been removed what
Jewish women felt as 'the reproach of childlessness.' Burkitt suggests that 'the Λόγος ἀπὸ Σιγῆς
προελθών more corresponds to the fitness of things
than a burst of premature song.'

Apart from the question raised by Wellhausen
whether Hannah's song has been interpolated in
1 S 2, Spitta thinks that it is the song of a warrior
rather than a woman, and looks elsewhere for
parallels to the *Magnificat*. Any way, either
Mary or Elisabeth would regard it as the song of
Hannah, which is the main point before us. We
cannot do better than quote the text at this point,
with Harnack's parallels, to introduce his argument that St. Luke is thereby proved to be the
actual author of the hymn which he puts into the
mouth of Elisabeth.

vv.[46. 47] Μεγαλύνει ἡ ψυχή μου τὸν κύριον, καὶ ἠγαλλίασεν τὸ πνεῦμα μου ἐπὶ τῷ θεῷ τῷ σωτῆρί μου'	(1) 1 S 2[1] Ἐστερεώθη ἡ καρδία μου ἐν κυρίῳ, ὑψώθη κέρας μου ἐν θεῷ μου.
v.[48] ὅτι ἐπέβλεψεν ἐπὶ τὴν ταπεί-νωσιν τῆς δούλης αὐτοῦ· ἰδοὺ γὰρ ἀπὸ τοῦ νῦν μακαριοῦσίν με πᾶσαι αἱ γενεαί·	(2) 1 S 1[11] ἐὰν ἐπιβλέπων ἐπι-βλέψῃς ἐπὶ τὴν ταπείνωσιν τῆς δούλης σου ; Gn 30[13] μακαρία ἐγώ, ὅτι μακαριζοῦσίν με πᾶσαι αἱ γυναῖκες.
v.[49] ὅτι ἐποίησέν μοι μεγάλα ὁ δυνατός, καὶ ἅγιον τὸ ὄνομα αὐτοῦ,	(3) Dt 10[21] ὅστις ἐποίησεν ἐν σοὶ τὰ μεγάλα. Ps 111[9] ἅγιον καὶ φοβερὸν τὸ ὄνομα αὐτοῦ.
v.[50] καὶ τὸ ἔλεος αὐτοῦ εἰς γενεὰς καὶ γενεὰς τοῖς φοβουμένοις αὐτόν,	(4) Ps 103[17] τὸ δὲ ἔλεος τοῦ κυρίου ἀπὸ τοῦ αἰῶνος καὶ ἕως τοῦ αἰῶνος ἐπὶ τοὺς φοβουμένους αὐτόν.
v.[51] ἐποίησεν κράτος ἐν βραχίονι αὐτοῦ, διεσκόρπισεν ὑπερηφάνους διανοίᾳ καρδίας αὐτῶν·	(5) Ps 89[11] σὺ ἐταπείνωσας ὡς τραυματίαν ὑπερήφανον, καὶ ἐν τῷ βραχίονι τῆς δυνάμεώς σου διεσκόρπισας τοὺς ἐχθρούς σου.
v.[52] καθεῖλεν δυνάστας ἀπὸ θρόνων καὶ ὕψωσεν ταπεινούς,	(6) Job 12[19] δυνάστας δὲ γῆς κατέστρεψεν, 5[11] τὸν ποιοῦντα ταπεινοὺς εἰς ὕψος.
v.[53] πεινῶντας ἐνέπλησεν ἀγαθῶν καὶ πλουτοῦντας ἐξαπέστειλεν κενούς.	(7) 1 S 2[7] κύριος πτωχίζει καὶ πλουτίζει, ταπεινοῖ καὶ ἀνυψοῖ. Ps 107[9] ψυχὴν πεινῶσαν ἐνέ-πλησεν ἀγαθῶν. Job 12[19] ἐξ-αποστέλλων ἱερεῖς αἰχμαλώτους.
v.[54] ἀντελάβετο Ἰσραὴλ παιδὸς αὐτοῦ, μνησθῆναι ἐλέους	(8) Is 41[8] σὺ δέ, Ἰσραήλ, παῖς μου, οὗ ἀντελαβόμην. Ps 98[3] ἐμνήσθη τοῦ ἐλέους αὐτοῦ τῷ Ἰακώβ.
v.[55] —καθὼς ἐλάλησεν πρὸς τοὺς πατέρας ἡμῶν—τῷ Ἀβραὰμ καὶ τῷ σπέρματι αὐτοῦ εἰς τὸν αἰῶνα.	(9) Mic 7[20] δώσει . . . ἔλεον τῷ Ἀβραάμ, καθότι ὤμοσας τοῖς πατράσιν ἡμῶν ; 2 S 22[51] καὶ ποιῶν ἔλεος . . . τῷ Δαυεὶδ καὶ τῷ σπέρματι αὐτοῦ ἕως αἰῶνος.

In regard to these parallels Spitta argues with
some force that there are nearer parallels in the
Psalms ; *e.g.* Ps 33[3. 4] ἐν τῷ κυρίῳ ἐπαινεθήσεται ἡ ψυχή
μου . . . μεγαλύνατε τὸν κύριον σὺν ἐμοί ; 34[9] ἡ δὲ ψυχή
μου ἀγαλλιάσεται ἐπὶ τῷ κυρίῳ, τερφθήσεται ἐπὶ τῷ
σωτηρίῳ αὐτοῦ ; 34[27] = 39[17] = 69[5] ἀγαλλιάσαιντο καὶ εὐφ-
ρανθείησαν ἐπὶ σοὶ πάντες οἱ ζητοῦντές σε κύριε, καὶ
εἰπάτωσαν διὰ παντός, Μεγαλυνθήτω ὁ κύριος, οἱ ἀγα-
πῶντες τὸ σωτήριόν σου. * This is true ; but at the
same time we cannot doubt that a Jewish woman
would turn to Hannah's song as, so to speak, a
model, even though the phrases of the psalms
which she used often in devotion would come more
readily to her lips while working out her idea.

Harnack picks out certain words as having no
place in his parallels, and suggests that they are
not found in the LXX, and being characteristic of
Lk.'s style, prove that he was really the author
of the hymn. Spitta, however, proves that the
phrases in question are not only found in the LXX,

---

* He quotes Ps 9[14f.] 124-6 30[8] as parallels to v.[53].

but are not so characteristic of Lk.'s style ; *e.g.*
(1) ἰδοὺ γάρ is found not only in Lk 1[44] 2[10] 6[23] 17[21],
Ac 9[11], but also in 2 Co 7[11] ;* (2) ἀπὸ τοῦ νῦν, said to
be found in Lk 5[10] 12[52] 22[18. 69], Ac 18[6] only, is also
found 2 Co 5[16].† These instances alone will suffice
to prove how unsafe the foundations are upon
which Harnack's argument is based.

There is one other possible source for some of
the phrases which has not been mentioned, *i.e.* the
18 Benedictions of the Synagogue (quoted by
Warren, *Liturgy of Ante-Nicene Church*, p. 243).

v.[49]　　*Ben.* 2 : 'Thou art mighty, O Lord, world without end.'
v.[51]　　*Ben.* 12 : 'Let the proud speedily be uprooted, broken,
　　　　crushed, and humbled speedily in our days. Blessed
　　　　art Thou, O Lord, who breakest down the enemy and
　　　　humblest the proud.'
vv.[54. 55]　*Ben.* 1 : 'Blessed art Thou who rememberest the pious
　　　　deeds of our fathers, and sendest the Redeemer to
　　　　their children's children. Blessed art Thou, O Lord,
　　　　the shield of Abraham.'

On the whole, then, in spite of Harnack's arguments, there is still room to believe that St. Luke
translated, or perhaps to some extent worked up into
a Greek hymn, the materials supplied to him in an
Aramaic tradition or document. There was no
unnatural seeking after effect. In reply to Elisabeth's address no conventional answer would seem
in place. On the other hand, Prof. Burkitt regards
the whole of Elisabeth's words as the acknowledgment of Mary's salutation, and finds 'a striking
parallel in Lk 2[25-35], *i.e.* the conversation of Mary
and Simeon. In both cases Mary's interlocutor is
said to have a holy Spirit, in both cases the whole
of the words recorded is assigned to the interlocutor, and the words themselves consist partly of
pious meditation, partly of words addressed exclusively to Mary' (*JThSt* vii. p. 225). This is
a question perhaps of sentiment. But few devout
believers in the Incarnation would hesitate to
express their profound gratitude for the words of
simple faith and hope, grounded, as Spitta has
certainly shown, as much on the Psalms as on
Hannah's song, a spontaneous offering of praise
from a lowly spirit continually in communion with
the Divine, and therefore never lacking words of
praise. We may regard these words as spoken in
substance by the Virgin Mary, and yet maintain
the truth of the phrase of Ignatius about 'the
Word proceeding from silence.' The silence remains unbroken. No personal dread of the possible
reproach not of childlessness but of shame, no personal exultation in this transcendent blessedness
among women, find expression.

2. *Interpretation.*—The scope of interpretation
varies in accordance with the view held concerning
the authorship. Harnack's description is correct
so far as it goes : 'The artistic arrangement of
the pronouns, which governs the hymn, expresses
exactly the progress of thought, advancing from
the subjective to the objective in order to return
again to the subjective, though in a higher form.'
But he fails to express the situation so clearly
described by Liddon (p. 13) from the internal
evidence.

'Like the songs of Zacharias and Simeon, it is something
more than a psalm, and something less than a complete Christian hymn. A Christian poet, living after the Resurrection of
Christ, would surely have said more ; a Hebrew psalmist would
have said less than Mary. In this Hymn of hers we observe a
consciousness of nearness to the fulfilment of the great promises, to which there is no parallel even in the latest of the
psalms ; and yet even Mary does not speak of the Promised
One, as an Evangelist or an Apostle would have spoken of Him,
by His Human Name, and with distinct reference to the
mysteries of His Life and Death and Resurrection. Her Hymn
was a native product of one particular moment of transition in
sacred religious history, and of no other ; when the twilight of
the ancient dispensation was melting, but had not yet melted,
into the full daylight of the new.'

_____

* Ps 50[7. 8] 53[6], Is 32[7] 38[17] 44[22] 62[11] 66[15].
† Gn 46[30], 2 Ch 16[9], To 10[13] 11[9], Is 48[6], Dn 10[17].

In Strophe I. (vv.[46. 47]) she offers praise to God as
His due, with all powers of the soul, that is, of
imagination and impulse ; and of the spirit, with
the faculties of reason and memory and will.

In Strophe II. (vv.[48. 49]) she dwells on the distinction vouchsafed to her in becoming the Mother of
the Incarnate Son. She is to live in the memory
of mankind not because she deserves it, but because He whose Name is holy so wills.

In Strophe III. (vv.[51. 53]), turning away from self,
she rises, as in moments of spiritual enlightenment
any one may rise, to larger views of God's purposes
in the shaping of human history. His presence
and power are vindicated in the humbling of the
proudest dynasties and the triumph of the meek.
This thought is characteristic of a group of psalms
(9. 10. 22. 25. 35. 40. 69. 109 ; cf. 4 Ezr (2 Es) 11[42],
Ps-Sol 5[13f.]) which must often have been in the
minds of the little group—Joseph, Mary, Zacharias,
Elisabeth, Simeon, Anna—who were looking for
the redemption of Israel.

In Strophe IV. (vv.[54. 55]) she comes back to the
thought of the Messianic time now beginning : the
assurances given to the fathers should be fulfilled.
The source of the Incarnation is found in God's
attributes of loving-kindness and truth.

3. *Liturgical use.*—In the Eastern Church the
Magnificat is sung as a morning canticle. This
also was its use in the West at one time. In the
directions at the end of the Rule of Aurelian, bp.
of Arles, *c.* 540, it is mentioned as used in the
Office of Lauds 'with antiphon or with alleluia,
following OT psalms and canticles, and followed
by *Gloria in excelsis.*' *

In the treatise of Niceta, *de Psalmodiæ Bono*,
to which we have already alluded, the primary
reference is to Vigils, to the use, therefore, of the
Magnificat in the evening. The list of canticles
mentioned corresponds to that in use in the Church
of Constantinople at that time. When the later-
hour offices were developed in the West, it was, in
accordance with such usage, attached to Vespers,
with varying antiphon. Thus it passed into the
first Prayer-Book of Edward VI., and has since been
used in Evensong after the first Lesson.

In Julian's *Dict. of Hymnology* there are references to several metrical versions which found
favour from the 16th century. But these are of no
importance.

LITERATURE.—O. Bardenhewer, *Biblische Studien*, vi. (1901)
p. 187; F. C. Burkitt in A. E. Burn's *Niceta of Remesiana*,
1905, and *JThSt* vii. 220 ; A. Harnack, *Sitzungsberichte der k.
preuss. Akad. der Wissenschaften*, 1900, xxvii. p. 537 ; F. Jacobé,
Revue d'hist. et de litt. religieuses, ii. p. 424 ; H. P. Liddon, *The
Magnificat*, 1889 ; W. Sanday, art. ' Jesus Christ' in Hastings'
DB ; F. Spitta, 'Das Magnifikat ein Psalm der Maria und nicht
der Elisabeth,' *Theol. Abhandlungen*, 1902 ; Völter, *ThT* xxx.
(1896) p. 224 ; Bp. Wordsworth in A. E. Burn's *Niceta of
Remesiana* ; T. D. Bernard, *Songs of the Holy Nativity*, 1895, pp.
56, 65.　　　　　　　　　　　　　　　　A. E. BURN.

MAHALALEEL.—An ancestor of Jesus, Lk 3[37].

MAID.—The English words 'maid,' 'maiden'
represent three Greek words : κοράσιον (Mt 9[24f.]
AV 'maid,' RV 'damsel') ; ἡ παῖς (Lk 8[51] AV and
RV 'maiden' ; v.[54] AV 'maid,' RV 'maiden') ;
and παιδίσκη (Mt 26[69], Jn 18[17] AV 'damsel,' RV
'maid' ; Mk 14[66. 69], Lk 22[56] AV and RV 'maid' ;
Lk 12[45] AV 'maidens,' RV 'maidservants'). The
first two clearly signify 'young girl,' answering
to the Aramaic *ṭalitha* (cf. Mk 5[41] and Lk 8[54] : for
a discussion of the Aramaic form see art. TALITHA
CUMI). *Talitha* seems to have been frequently
employed in the sense of 'young woman.' In
the Targums it is used of Dinah, Miriam, and
Esther. It and its Greek equivalents have almost
that meaning as applied to the daughter of Jairus.
κοράσιον seems to have lost its diminutive force in

_____

* Migne, *Patr. Lat.* lxviii. 393.

later Greek and to have been no longer employed as a familiar term, but to have been virtually equivalent to κόρη. παιδίσκη, the feminine of παιδίσκος, originally a diminutive of παῖς, meant in the first instance 'girl' and then 'domestic female servant' or 'slave.' It has the latter meaning in the Gospels. In some passages in the LXX (Ex 20[10], Lv 25[44] etc.) it represents 'āmāh (cf. art. HANDMAID). It seems to have been used especially of a doorkeeper (Gospels, Ac 12[13], Lysias cited by Wetstein). That it often referred to a slave, not a hired servant, is evident from the passages quoted by Wetstein from the grammarians, and seems to be implied in the contrast between παιδίσκης and ἐλευθέρας in Gal 4[22].

LITERATURE. — Wetstein on Mt 26[69]; Levy, *Chaldäisches Wörterbuch*, i. 303b; Swete on Mk 14[66].

W. TAYLOR SMITH.

MAIMED. — This term signifies disabled by wounding or mutilation; deprived of the use of a necessary constitutive part of the body; mutilated; rendered unable to defend oneself or to discharge necessary functions. In Mt 15[30] and Mk 9[43] κυλλός is the word employed and is tr. 'maimed' in both AV and RV. It is kindred with κοῖλος, 'hollow,' and signifies originally 'crooked,' 'bent,' and so crippled and halt. κυλλὴ χείρ is the hand with its fingers bent so as to make a hollow palm. ἔμβαλε κυλλῇ (*sc.* χειρί)='put it into the hollow of the hand.' In Lk 14[13. 21] the word used is ἀνάπηρος, *i.e.* πηρός='deprived of some member of the body' (Lat. *mancus*), preceded by ἀνά intensive. The composite word indicates an extreme form of bodily mutilation, and Jesus is never said to have restored one so suffering. The word is not employed in connexion with our Lord's miracles, but only in His invitation to the blessings of the Kingdom, to which all outcast sufferers were with Divine compassion called.　　　　T. H. WRIGHT.

MAJESTY.—1. The term.—In the NT the word 'majesty' is associated with Christ in three different connexions. (1) In RV of Lk 9[43a] we read that the people 'were all astonished at the majesty (μεγαλειότης, AV 'mighty power') of God.' The immediate occasion of their astonishment was the healing of the lunatic boy, but v.[43b], and esp. the ἐποίει which critical editors substitute for ἐποίησεν of TR, seems to show that the miracles of Christ generally are to be thought of as producing this impression that the Divine μεγαλειότης was manifesting itself through Him.

(2) In 2 P 1[16] the writer, who claims to have been present with Jesus on the Mount of Transfiguration, says of that experience, 'We were eyewitnesses of his majesty' (AV and RV; Gr. μεγαλειότης). The word μεγαλειότης is found in only one other passage of the NT, viz. Ac 19[27], where it is used to describe the 'magnificence' (AV and RV) of the great goddess Diana. It is thus an interesting coincidence that the two instances of its use in connexion with Christ belong to the episode of the Transfiguration and the incident of the healing of the lunatic boy which followed immediately after. On the 'holy mount' the favoured three received a revelation of Christ's inherent μεγαλειότης (the word ἐπόπται, 'eyewitnesses,' is a technical term denoting those who had been admitted to the highest grade of initiation into the Eleusinian mysteries. And when He came down from the mountain, the μεγαλειότης of God shone forth through His works in the eyes of all the multitude.

A comparison of the uses of μεγαλειότης in Lk 9[43], Ac 19[27], and 2 P 1[16] raises a doubt whether 'majesty' is the most adequate rendering of the word in the first and third passages, and whether 'magnificence' (as in Ac 19[27] EV) or 'splendour' would not more correctly reproduce the original idea. This is suggested by the ordinary use of the adj. μεγαλεῖος in class.

Greek, and even by the two instances of its employment in the NT (Lk 1[49], Ac 2[11]). The evidence of the LXX also points in the same direction; for while μεγαλειότης is used in Jer 33[9] to tr. הָדָר (AV 'honour,' RV 'glory')—a word which is usually rendered by δόξα—the terms ordinarily taken to express the idea of greatness or majesty are μεγαλωσύνη and μεγαλοπρέπεια (*e.g.* 2 S 7[23], Ps 145 [LXX 144] 3. 5. 6. 12).

With this idea of Christ's miracles, or of His miraculous being, as an effulgence of the Divine splendour or magnificence, compare the statement of Jn 2[11] that by the miracle of Cana Jesus 'manifested his glory' (ἐφανέρωσε τὴν δόξαν αὐτοῦ). Cf. also the ἐπόπται τῆς ἐκείνου μεγαλειότητος of 2 P 1[16] with what is said in v.[17] of the 'glory' (δόξα) which Jesus received upon the mount from God the Father.

(3) In He 1[3] 8[1] we see Jesus seated 'on the right hand of the Majesty on high.' The word for 'Majesty' in these two cases is μεγαλωσύνη, a term that does not occur again in the NT except in the doxology at the end of Jude (v.[25]). The idea of Christ as seated at God's right hand, which is so frequent in the NT (Mt 26[64] ||, Ac 2[33] 7[55f.], Ro 8[34], Eph 1[20], Col 3[1] etc.), was no doubt taken in the first case from Ps 110[1] (cf. He 1[3] with v.[13]). It seems always to be used with reference not to His pre-existent dignity, but to the exaltation that followed His incarnation and suffering. Moreover, in the two passages in Hebrews there is no direct ascription of the Divine majesty to Jesus. The idea is that of His exercise of a supremely exalted office as the Great High Priest who is the Mediator between God and men.

2. The quality of majesty in Christ.—Apart from its infrequent use of the word, the NT affords abundant material for a consideration of the majesty of Christ, whether in His estate of humiliation or of exaltation.

(1) With regard to His *life on earth*, (*a*) it is evident that there was nothing of the majestic in His *outward circumstances*. From His birth in a stable to His death on a cross, it was a life of 'no reputation,' His form being that of a servant and not of a king (cf. Ph 2[8]). And on the one occasion when He assumed a kind of royal state, and suffered the multitudes in the streets and the children in the Temple to hail Him with Hosannas (Mt 21[9. 15f.]), His majesty, after all, as the Evangelists subsequently perceived, was but the majesty of meekness, for Zion's King came to her gates, as the prophet had said, 'lowly, and riding upon an ass, and upon a colt the foal of an ass' (Mt 21[1ff.], Jn 12[14ff.]; cf. Zec 9[9]).

(*b*) Was there no majesty, then, in His *personal appearance*? The Gospels are completely silent on this point, and in the lack of any trustworthy tradition the Fathers seem to have fallen back chiefly on the prophetic pictures of the Messiah, with the result that a wide diversity of view came to exist, according as one passage or another was taken as the norm. The earlier tendency, inspired without doubt by prevailing ascetic ideals, was to fasten upon the words of Deutero-Isaiah with reference to the Suffering Servant (53[2. 3]), and to represent Jesus as utterly devoid of all beauty and dignity of face or form. 'Base of aspect' (αἰσχρὸς τὴν ὄψιν) is the verdict of Clement of Alexandria (*Pæd.* iii. 1), who was preceded in his estimate by Justin Martyr, and followed by Tertullian. There came a reaction by and by, represented in the East by Origen and in the West by Jerome, when men bethought themselves of such a prophetic Psalm as the 45th, with its vision of One 'fairer than the children of men' (v.[2]) and girded with glory and majesty (v.[3]). Jerome in particular maintained this high view of the majesty of Christ's outward aspect. There was 'something starry' (*sidereum quiddam*), he affirmed, in the Saviour's face and eyes (*Ep. ad Principiam*); 'the brightness and majesty of His Divinity . . . shed their rays over His human countenance' (*in Matt.* i. 8). This was the view that ultimately prevailed in the Church, and finds expression in the so-called 'Letter of Lentulus' (see vol. i. p. 315). It gave rise to a type of presentment that has dominated Christian art ever since; but it is right to remember that this conventional conception of a Christ who was tall in stature, beautiful in countenance, dignified and even majestic in figure and bearing, rests upon no real basis of authentic tradition, as it is supported by no single word of the NT; and that Augustine has stated the simple truth when he says, 'Qua fuerit ille facie penitus ignoramus' (de Trin. viii. 5).

(c) But there is a *moral majesty*, a majesty of purity and truth and goodness, that is independent of all outward seeming; and the Gospels give abundant illustration of Christ's endowment with this majesty of soul. Milton tells us how, face to face with the cherub:

> 'abash'd the devil stood,
> And felt how awful goodness is' (*Par. Lost*, iv. 846).

And no one can read the Gospel narratives without perceiving how good men and bad alike were smitten at times with a sense of subduing awe as they stood in the presence of Jesus Christ. This was the experience of the Baptist when he exclaimed, 'I have need to be baptized of thee, and comest thou to me?' (Mt 3[14]). It was the feeling of Simon Peter when he cried, 'Depart from me; for I am a sinful man, O Lord' (Lk 5[8]). This majesty of Christ's character forces itself upon us at every point, rising higher and higher until it reaches a culmination in the awful scenes of the judgment-hall and the cross. Was it not this majesty of a pure soul that arrested and troubled Pilate himself in the midst of his keen concern for his own selfish interests and his lofty Roman contempt for a mere Jew? And was it not this same majesty of holiness that smote upon the heart of the very centurion who carried out the sentence of crucifixion, so that he exclaimed, 'Certainly this was a righteous man' (Lk 23[47])? Sometimes we see Christ's moral majesty flashing out so overwhelmingly that it works with a kind of physical effect, as when the profane traffickers in the Temple cringe and flee before Him; or when, in the Garden, as He steps out of the shadows, saying, 'I am he,' His enemies go backward, and fall to the ground (Jn 18[5f.]).

(d) But besides the unconscious majesty of goodness, we see in Jesus Christ throughout His public ministry a *conscious majesty* of the most positive kind. This man, so meek and lowly in heart, does not hesitate to make the most astounding claims. He claims a personal authority that sweeps aside in a moment all the traditional learning of the nation's religious teachers (Mt 7[28. 29]). Never, surely, in the world's history has there been another series of utterances so clothed in the majesty of spiritual power as the Sermon on the Mount. And this poor Carpenter of Nazareth further assumes without the least hesitation the name and dignity of the promised Messiah of Israel; He affirms, in a sense altogether unique, that He is the Son of God, unto whom all things have been delivered of the Father (Mt 11[27], Lk 10[22]; cf. Jn 14–17); He invites every burdened and weary soul to come unto Him for rest (Mt 11[28]). And what could be more majestic than the language in which Christ assumes the office of the universal Judge of men, and describes the events and issues of that solemn day when the Son of Man shall come in His glory, and all the nations shall be gathered before Him? (Mt 25[31ff.]).

(2) It is unnecessary to dwell in any detail upon the majesty of *the exalted Christ*. From St. Peter's first sermon on the Day of Pentecost (Ac 2[33ff.]) down to the last utterance of the Apostolic Church, the Christ of the NT is the Christ enthroned in glory, dignity, and power. His followers do not think of Him 'according to the flesh' (2 Co 5[16])—as the Prophet of Galilee or the Man of Sorrows. The Christ of whom they do habitually think is risen, ascended, glorified, and set down on the right hand of the Majesty on high (cf. Ro 8[34], 1 Co 15[14ff.], Gal 2[20], Ph 2[9ff.], 1 Th 4[13ff.], He 1[2ff.] and *passim*). Apart from the evidence of their own writings, no better proof of this can be found than the fact that for more than a century after the death of Jesus the Church appears never to have concerned itself in any way as to His earthly appearance, or to have had any desire for pictorial representations of His human face and form. And is it not highly significant that, on the one solitary occasion on which a NT writer has set himself to describe the Lord's personal appearance, the attempt is based upon no recollections or traditions regarding Jesus of Nazareth, but upon a splendid conception of the majesty of the exalted Christ—His eyes as a flame of fire, His voice as the sound of many waters, in His right hand seven stars, and His countenance as the sun shineth in his strength (Rev 1[13ff.])?

LITERATURE.—The Lexx. and Comm.; Farrar, *Christ in Art*, bk. ii.; P. Dearmer's art. 'Christ in Art' in vol. i.; Dora Greenwell, *Patience of Hope*, pt. i.; Seeley, *Ecce Homo*, ch. iv.; Denney, *Stud. in Theol.* 169.   J. C. LAMBERT.

MALCHUS (Μάλχος).—The name of the man whom Peter wounded in the right ear at the arrest of Jesus (Jn 18[10]).

Malchus was a common Semitic name, though not certainly met with among the Jews proper. By both Delitzsch and Salkinson it is vocalized מֵלְכּוֹם, which is no more than a transliteration. Josephus (see Niese's index) mentions five persons who bore it under the form of Μάλχος or Μάλιχος, whence an original מָלִיךְ has been inferred (Dalman, *Gram. Aram.* 104). But the true Greek form seems to have been Μαλίχας (*Periplus maris Erythræi*, cf. Müll. *Geogr. Gr. Min.* i. 272); and מלכו, pronounced מָלְכוּ, appears in three inscriptions (*CIS* ii. 158, 174, 218) that may be dated with some confidence between B.C. 40 and A.D. 40. In these inscriptions the name is Nabatæan; but the root מלך is common to all the Semitic languages, and appears to belong to the unhistorical period prior to the separation of the various peoples. In Assyrian it is a designation of a subordinate ruler (Schrader, *COT* i. 23), a prince rather than a king. While there are instances of its use in relation to a god (cf. Boehmer in *Expos. Times*, xvi. [1905] 473 ff.), there is no need to see in it anything more than an allusion, serious or playful, to superiority in rank or in pretence.

The bearer of the name in the Gospel narrative held a position of trust in the household of the high priest, probably Caiaphas (Jn 18[13]). It has been assumed that the other Evangelists suppressed the name (Mt 26[51], Mk 14[47], Lk 22[50]) with a view to protect Peter from revenge or an action at law on the part of the Jews. It is at least as likely that they were ignorant of the name, or of opinion that no purpose was to be served by its mention. There is no evidence that Malchus was exceptionally active in the arrest, or anything more than an onlooker. Peter's forward rush, when his indignation could be restrained no longer, towards the group of which Jesus was becoming the centre (Jn 18[4]), suggests rather that Malchus was on the skirt of the group, and not immediately engaged in binding Jesus. He happened to be in Peter's way in his attempt to rescue his Master, and may well have been personally unknown to the majority of the disciples. If John was the unnamed disciple who was 'known unto the high priest' (v.[15]), possibly because he supplied the family of Annas with fish (according to an old tradition; cf. David Smith, *Days of His Flesh*, 465), he would be acquainted with both Malchus and his kinsman (v.[26]); and the mention of the name in the Fourth Gospel may be taken as one of the undesigned indications of Johannine authorship. The healing of the ear of Malchus is recorded by Lk. alone, but is an essential part of the story (cf. *Expos. Times*, x. [1898–99] 139, 188), and exactly such an incident as would be likely to attract the notice of a physician, and so to calm the soldiers as to make the subsequent remonstrance preserved by each of the Synoptics possible. The natural order of events was first the healing of the wound, followed, while Malchus' friends were crowding around him, by the rebuke of Peter, and then, as soon as the people were ready to listen, by the taunting protest in regard to the manner of the arrest. Thereupon Jesus consented to be seized, and in perfect self-possession passed on to His trial and death.

R. W. Moss.

MALEFACTOR.—Two Gr. words, whose shades of meaning are indistinguishable, are thus translated in NT: (1) κακοποιός or κακὸν ποιῶν (lit. 'evildoer'), Jn 18³⁰, 1 P 2¹². ¹⁴ 4¹⁵; (2) κακοῦργος (lit. 'evil-worker'), Lk 23³². ³³. ³⁹, 2 Ti 2⁹. AV renders κακοποιός 'malefactor' in Jn 18³⁰, 'evil-doer' elsewhere; but RV gives 'evil-doer' throughout. Again AV renders κακοῦργος 'malefactor' in Lk 23³². ³³. ³⁹, 'evil-doer' in 2 Ti 2⁹, while RV makes it always 'malefactor.' This illustrates the NT Revisers' uniformity in the translation of words.

In Lk 23³² the best attested text is ἕτεροι κακοῦργοι δύο, not ἕτεροι δύο κακοῦργοι (TR). Hence it is maintained by Alford and others that we ought to read 'two other malefactors' (without a comma after 'other') instead of 'two others, malefactors' (AV and RV). There is really no difficulty about adopting this rendering, which does not imply that St. Luke assents to the judgment that Jesus was a malefactor, but merely states the fact that He was led to execution as such.

D. A. Mackinnon.

MAMMON, or more accurately 'Mamon,' is the transliteration of the Gr. equivalent for a late Aram. or Syro-Chald. term denoting 'wealth' or 'riches' or 'treasure,' whose etymology is still a matter of dispute (cf. the articles *s.v.* in Hastings' *DB* and *Encyc. Bib.*). In the Gospels it means worldliness in the form of wealth, and occurs twice —(*a*) in Mt 6²⁴ = Lk 16¹³ ('ye cannot serve God and mammon'); and (*b*) in Lk 16⁹. ¹¹, where it is defined, or rather described, as *unrighteous*, the latter epithet being applied to it not only in the Targums, but as early as En 63¹⁰ ('our souls are satisfied with the mammon of unrighteousness, yet for all that we descend into the flame of Sheol's pain').

The genuineness of the logion (*a*) there is no need to question, although its present position is probably due to editorial arrangement. Of the two settings, Matthew's seems preferable. Mammon here represents a sort of personified worldliness, a Plutus of the age, and Christ exposes the impossibility of combining devotion to this end with devotion to the true God. The spiritual life, He explains in 6¹⁹⁻²⁴, must have the two notes of inwardness and unity. Compromise here is out of the question. The object of a man's confidence determines ultimately his character; and singlemindedness is the supreme condition of health and effectiveness in religion. Jesus 'warns them that it is impossible to be at once high-minded and just and wise, and to comply with the accustomed forms of human society, seek power, wealth, or empire, either from the idolatry of habit, or as the direct instruments of sensual gratification' (Shelley). Objection is sometimes taken to this counsel as inapplicable to a group of good disciples. But Jesus had rich people among His adherents, and besides it is not the rich alone who are tempted to make a god of their money. Poor people are just as prone in some ways to attach an exaggerated importance to wealth, to overestimate its power, and thus to let it exercise a control over their desires. No

written comment on the verse, however, can equal the impression made by Mr. G. F. Watts' picture of 'Mammon,' with its coarse, gross limbs crushing human life; to which one pendant is the same painter's picture entitled, 'For he had great possessions.'

The Lukan setting is as apt in its own way, placing the same logion amid a cluster of characteristic (see THEOPHILUS) sayings and parables on the dangers and abuse of money (cf. v.¹⁴). Lk 16¹³ forms one of several rather heterogeneous fringes to the parable of the Unjust Steward (16¹⁻⁸ or 16¹⁻⁷), arranged with almost as little connexion as the logia in 16¹⁶ᶠ. So far as it stands, however, it has the same meaning as in Mt 6²⁴. The main difficulty is to correlate it with what immediately precedes, and this opens up the unpersonified use of mammon in the second class of passages (*b*). The point of 16¹⁻⁸, which is certainly a genuine parable of Jesus, is to inculcate the wisdom of making provision in the present life for the life which is to come. The temper commended by Jesus is that of a man who has wit enough to see that his future prospects depend on his present exertions, and who inferentially has no illusions whatever about himself. He is open-eyed to the present situation. He does not flatter himself into a rosy view of his case, or look to some happy chance to bear him through. A prudent regard to self-interest is the saving feature of his character and conduct. So much is clear. The trouble is to adjust vv.⁹⁻¹³ to this standpoint. If, with critics like J. Weiss, Wernle, and Jülicher, all five verses are regarded as editorial glosses, the solution becomes fairly simple, the original parable having nothing to do with the use of money at all, as Christ meant it. But v.⁹ may well be the original sequel to v.⁸ (so Wellhausen recently), in which case 'the mammon of unrighteousness' there and in v.¹¹ is explained by 'what belongs to another' in v.¹². Wealth, Jesus teaches, does not really belong to a Christian. It is something alien to him. Yet, as the steward used wealth that was not his own for his own ends, so the Christian can and must employ his wealth in order to promote his eternal interests. Money given in alms makes friends for him in heaven, just as it lays up a treasure for him there (11⁴¹ 12²³ etc.). Instead of serving God and mammon alike, he is to use mammon wisely in the interests of his relation to God and the heavenly Kingdom, the wisdom consisting in the practice of charity (cf. v.¹⁹ᶠ). If not, the prospect held out is ominous. 'God,' as Kingsley once said, 'will yet take account of the selfishness of wealth; and His quarrel has yet to be fought out.' This is true to the spirit of the Lukan sayings, except that they threaten an eschatological ruin rather than one wrought out on this side of the grave.

In any case vv.¹⁰⁻¹³ (v.¹⁰ coming from 19¹⁷) form a conglomerate appendix, added to prevent misconceptions, 'another instance of editorial solicitude on the part of an Evangelist ever careful to guard the character and teaching of Jesus against misunderstanding' (Bruce). V.¹¹, especially, indicates the right use of money (as in the parable of the Talents): Use it faithfully, *i.e.* for the good of the needy, instead of hoarding it up selfishly. Honesty in money matters (v.¹⁰) *is* vital to the Christian. And honesty, in this particular application, is viewed under the light of liberality (v.¹¹), in accordance with the tenor of Luke's social sympathies throughout his Gospel. Thus the use of mammon brings out two elements in the teaching of Jesus upon money—(*a*) the need of administering it wisely, and (*b*) the essentially inferior and even irrelevant position of money in the religious life. The latter is brought out by the epithet *unrighteous* (almost equal to 'secular' here); money is *less* by far than a Christian's other interests (v.[10]), *alien* (v.[12]), and *unreal* (v.[11]), even when it is not allowed to be a positive rival to God (v.[13]). By its nature it belongs to *the present* (*i.e.* this evil) *generation*, not to the real order of things which forms the sphere of *the children of light*, *i.e.* Christians. Yet even so it is a test; it furnishes opportunities for the exercise of certain virtues (cf. Morley's *Voltaire*, p. 107). Christians are trusted with money, as the steward was. But what in his case was fraud, in their case is both honest and shrewd. Forethought is the quality commended by our Lord, as opposed to a selfish and shortsighted policy. Faithfulness in dealing with money means giving it away. And the two, faithfulness and forethought, are different sides of the same habit— pretty much as in the proverb, 'What I gave, I have' (cf. Pr 11[24]). The steward dispensed his goods; no doubt, for selfish ends. Still he dispensed them, and so proved his wisdom at least.

On this interpretation 'the mammon of unrighteousness' does not mean money or worldly advantages wrongly gained, as though the point of the parable were that wealth, dishonestly come by, should be disbursed in charity (so Strauss, and O. Holtzmann in Stade's *Geschichte Israels*, ii. 584– 585). The steward is not commended because he atoned by beneficence for ill-gotten gains, as if he represented a sinner who insured forgiveness and welcome in heaven by means of charity to his fellows on earth, finding it impossible to restore, as Zacchæus did, his fraudulent profits (so even Bruce, *Parabolic Teaching of Jesus*, pp. 373–374). 'The mammon of unrighteousness' means money as essentially secular and unchristian (cf. Weinel's *Wirkungen des Geistes*, 1899, p. 15), pertaining to the order of the Evil One. Jesus does not deal here with any question of reparation. The object of the parable is to point out how one may best use this tainted possession in view of the future, and the teaching is on the lines of the later Jewish Rabbis, who attached high religious significance to alms (cf. Lk 12[15-21] 18[22] etc.), though it must be borne in mind that some allowance has to be made for St. Luke's 'ascetic' bias in estimating some of Christ's sayings on wealth in the Third Gospel, where logia, perhaps originally genuine, have been sharpened (*e.g.* in 6[24f.]) into exaggerated emphasis. In calling mammon 'unrighteous,' Jesus means that great wealth is seldom gained or employed without injustice. The stain of abuse is upon it. The mark of the evil world is stamped on it. At best, then, it is a means, not an end, for the Christian, and a means which demands care and conscience for its wise employment, lest life degenerate into the mercenary and narrowing spirit which devotes itself to what Bacon called 'a Sabbathless pursuit of fortune,' a culpable love of acquisition and material goods, and an insidious appetite for self-gratification which deadens the higher faculties of the soul and stunts the instinct of self-sacrifice.

LITERATURE.—See the commentators on *Matthew* and *Luke*, the various Lives of Jesus, and the current works upon the Parables, in all of which the mammon questions are handled; also Zahn's *Einleitung*, i. 11–12. On the parable of the Unjust Steward, cf. the critical discussions of Feine (*Eine vorkanon. Ueberlieferung d. Lukas*, p. 80 f.), J. Weiss (in Meyer's *Luke*[8], 528–535), Schmiedel (*Encyc. Bibl.* 1863–1864), and incidentally Rodenbusch (*ZNTW*, 1903, 243 f.). For Christ's attitude to wealth, consult H. Holtzmann, *Neutest. Theologie*, i. p. 448 f.; Titius, *Jesu Lehre vom Reiche Gottes*, 72–79; Pfleiderer, *Urchristenthum*[2], i. p. 649 f.; Keim, *Jesus of Nazara*, iv. p. 80 f. (extreme); and Peabody, *Jesus Christ and the Social Question*, p. 244 f. Further discussions on the significance of the parable may be found in *Expos.* 4th ser. vii. 21 f.; *Expos. Times*, 1903–1905, *passim*; Latham's *Pastor Pastorum*, p. 386 f.; *Expos.* 1903, 273–283 (Oesterley); and *Christliche Welt* (xvii. 218–227); besides F. W. Robertson's *Sermons*, iv. (No. 22); J. Martineau, *Endeavours after the Chr. Life*, p. 76; R. F. Horton, *Commandments of Jesus*, p. 249. On mammon-worship, see Carlyle, *French Revolution* (iii. bk. 3, ch. vii.) and *Past and Present* (bk. 4, ch. iv.); Ruskin, *Mornings in Florence*, § 50; also

Morley, *Gladstone*, iii. p. 548, for modern war as the most remarkable 'incentive to mammon-worship'; Coleridge in his *Friend* (Essay xvi. written during 1818) said that Lk 16[8] would form a suitable motto for a collection of Machiavelli's most weighty aphorisms, by some vigorous mind, in order to illustrate thereby the 'present triumph of lawless violence' as due to the imprudent neglect of such worldly-wise maxims.—In *Academy* (1888), pp. 416–417, C. Bezold criticises unfavourably Mr. Pinches' derivation of the term from an Assyr. *mimmu* or *memmu* = 'anything,' 'everything,' 'property,' etc.

               J. MOFFATT.

MAN.[*]—1. Christ's relation to men.

—(1) The first aspect of Jesus in His relation to men, is the relation of a *Master* to His disciples, and of a *Brother*, who is also Leader and Teacher, to His brethren. This relationship is unmistakable. 'Ye did not choose me, but I chose you' (Jn 15[16]). The disciple is not above his master, nor the servant above his lord' (Mt 10[24]). They were not to accept the title 'Rabbi'; they were brethren; they had but one teacher, even Christ (Mt 23[8-10]). The relationship was no external one. The disciples were not simply the servants of Jesus; they were His friends (Jn 15[14. 15]), and knew His thoughts and purposes. To them He was about to show the very height and greatness of His love by laying down His life. The best way for them to show that they were His friends was by keeping His commandments (Jn 15[14]). They were also under His Father's care; they were the Father's flock, and no one should snatch them out of His hand (Lk 12[28. 32], Jn 10[29]). They were called to a vocation in some respects similar to His own: they were to be 'fishers of men' (Mt 4[19]); they, too, would know persecution and trial and death; but these, in their essence, were but temporal things, and could not really injure or destroy (Mt 10[17. 18. 28], Lk 10[19]). As contrasted with others who were 'wise and prudent,' the disciples were but 'babes'; but it was to them that God had made the revelation of Himself in Jesus Christ (Mt 11[25. 26]). The disciples responded to this attachment. When they found the teaching of Jesus difficult and obscure, and were almost tempted, like many others, to go no more with Him, He asks them plainly, 'Will ye also go away?' and the answer rises within them with all the strength of passionate loyalty and conviction: 'Lord, to whom shall we go? Thou hast the words of eternal life' (Jn 6[66-68]). It is significant also that one of the strongest utterances of devotion is recorded of Thomas. Other references to this disciple show him as a practical man, who lives on the earth and not in the clouds, and who withholds his faith and support until plain proof be shown (Jn 20[24. 25]). But when Jesus expressed His determination to go up to Bethany and wake His friend Lazarus out of his sleep, it was Thomas who first saw his Master's danger, and that death was near at hand, and who exclaimed with vehemence, 'Let us go up also with him, that we may die with him' (Jn 11[16]). Peter is called blessed when, at Cæsarea Philippi, he answers Christ's question and confesses, 'Thou art the Christ of God' (Lk 9[20]); and John is the disciple whom Jesus loved (Jn 19[26]), the man who at the Last Supper sat next to His Master and leaned upon His breast (Jn 21[20]), and the one to whom Mary the mother of Jesus was entrusted by Jesus as He hung on the cross (Jn 19[26. 27]). When His disciples are weary, Jesus bids them go with Him to a desert place and rest a while (Mk 6[31]); and after their last meal together, He kneels down and washes their feet, thus teaching

[*] ἄνθρωπος and ἀνήρ are used by Jesus with the ordinary classic distinctions. Generally ἄνθρωπος = a human being, male or female (*e.g.* Mt 4[4] 5[16]); ἀνήρ, a man as distinguished from a woman (Mt 7[24. 26], Lk 14[24]). In keeping with this distinction, and by a Hebrew idiom (cf. the use of אִישׁ), He employs ἄνθρωπος in the sense of the Gr. τις, Lat. *quidam*, to denote 'someone,' 'a certain one' (Mt 21[28] 22[11] etc.). As the converse of this, it may be noted that not infrequently (esp. in Jn.) where τις occurs in the teaching of Jesus, EV renders it 'a man.'

them the duty of service (Jn 13³⁻⁵). The discourses recorded in Jn 14–16 are doubtless in some measure ideal; but they are true to the main lines of Christian tradition. The relationship between Jesus and His disciples was very intimate and sacred, and the disciples were filled with sorrow at the prospect of that relationship being snapped.

(2) But Jesus was also a *Jew* and a *citizen*. His mission was, first and foremost, to the lost sheep of the house of Israel (Mt 15²⁴); and it was only when they repeatedly rejected Him and His doctrine that He turned and went elsewhere. Jesus found that His own people were spiritually dead. They had now no prophets, and scarcely any teacher who might quicken their interest in things beyond the present hour and day. They had made the Temple (which was to Jesus His Father's house) a den of robbers (Mt 21¹³), and they had forgotten that mercy was better than sacrifice (Mt 9¹³); and Jesus, in the strength of His moral indignation, upset the tables of the money-changers, and drove those who sat there out of the Temple. His people honoured the prophets, but in their lifetime they stoned them; and now the greatest of the prophets had come, and they knew it not (Mt 23²⁹⁻³⁹, Lk 11²⁹·³²). He had come to His own, and they that were His own received Him not (Jn 1¹¹). There was woe to come upon Chorazin and Bethsaida. Had Tyre and Sidon seen the things which they had seen, they would have repented long ago in sackcloth and ashes (Mt 11²¹). Jesus looked upon Jerusalem and its people with a citizen's and a patriot's love, and was moved even to tears (Mt 23³⁷, Lk 19⁴¹). Let them weep for their city, themselves and their fate, and not for Him! (Lk 23²⁸⁻³¹). How often would He have gathered her children together as a hen gathereth her brood under her wings!

(3) It seems certain that the Jews, as a body, could never have accepted Jesus as their Messiah. It was the Pharisee who, with all his faults, had remained true in some measure to his national tradition; and it was in him that the teaching of Jesus found its strongest opponent. It was, above all, the *universalism* of Jesus that the Pharisee could not bear. He despised the Greek and Roman, and especially his kin and neighbour the Samaritan, as 'Gentile' folk—outsiders. If the God of the Jews should show Himself favourable unto such, it would have to be by some special act of grace. But Jesus followed out the prophetic ideal. He submitted to be baptized by John, and He expressed in no stinted way His feeling about the Baptist and his work. In His first public utterance Jesus reminded His hearers of the nature of Israel's God. He was the God of *men*, no matter what their race and no matter what their moral character. It was this God who despatched Elijah to Zarephath on an errand of mercy, when there were many widows in Israel. Elisha also was sent to heal Naaman the Syrian, although there were many lepers nearer home (Lk 4²⁵⁻²⁷). It was by utterances such as these that Jesus gained at the outset the opposition of the national party. Men felt—and felt rightly—that if Jesus triumphed Judaism was undone. The Pharisees were also deeply troubled by Jesus' manner of life. He received 'sinners,' and ate with them; He dined with tax-gatherers, and spoke kindly and compassionately to a woman of ill fame (Lk 5²⁷⁻³⁹ 19¹⁻¹⁰, Jn 8¹⁻¹¹). The official class—the Sadducees and priests—also felt that new wine like this would burst the old skins, and that a new society might arise, in which they themselves might be anywhere save at the top. And from the moment Jesus set foot in Jerusalem, the priests and Sadducees, as the ruling official party, set themselves to work, not to confute Him, but to compass His death (Mt 21²³ 26³·⁴, Lk 19⁴⁷·⁴⁸ 20·²²).

It follows from this that Jesus was a lover of man, irrespective of his race or condition. He began His ministry with teaching and healing. He was often moved to compassion by the multitudes which followed Him; they were as sheep without a shepherd; they heard Him gladly, and even tarried with Him a whole day, and that in a desert place (Mk 1⁴¹ 6³⁰⁻³⁶). On one occasion they would have made Him their king (Jn 6¹⁻¹⁵). And to Jesus, though He refuses their proffered sovereignty, they were as 'fields white unto the harvest' (Jn 4³⁵). Many of the most striking sayings of Jesus, however, occur in utterances addressed to individuals. It was while sitting and talking with a Samaritan —a Samaritan *woman*—that He said: 'God is Spirit' (Jn 4²⁴); it was in the house of Zacchæus that men first heard that 'the Son of man came to seek and to save that which was lost' (Lk 19¹⁰); while it was in answer to 'a certain lawyer' that Jesus related the parable of the Good Samaritan (Lk 10²⁵⁻³⁷). Men were amazed at and charmed by Jesus' power of speech; they 'wondered at the words of grace which proceeded out of his mouth' (Lk 4²²). Police officers on one occasion were disarmed by it. 'He taught,' says the Evangelist, 'as one having authority, and not as the scribes' (Jn 7⁴⁵⁻⁴⁷, Mt 7²⁸·²⁹).

What was it that led Jesus to teach and to associate Himself, not simply with Jews, but with men as men? What was it that carried Him willingly and of set purpose into all classes of society, and especially among the outcast and unfavoured folk? What led Him to seek, not the righteous, but sinners, and not the whole, but the sick? To answer this question we must pass to—

2. Christ's teaching on man.—With Jesus the doctrines of God and man are closely akin. They pass into each other, and are deeply interfused; so much so, that at times we seem but to have been looking at different sides of the same fundamental truth. Central, basal, a pole around which everything else centres and revolves, is His conception of God. To know Him is to share His life, and to seek His Kingdom and His righteousness is alike the highest duty and the highest joy of man (Jn 17³, Mt 6³³). He is Spirit (Jn 4²⁴). Without Him nature would cease to be; its beauty, its order, and the creatures which have within it their home, derive all their life and sustenance and joy from Him. The hairs of a man's head are all numbered; not even a sparrow falls to the ground without His notice. The common flowers and grass owe their life to Him (Mt 6²⁵⁻³⁴ 10²⁹·³⁰).

What, then, does Jesus, with this high doctrine of God, say about man? He tells us that man is distinct from the natural world and natural creatures; he is God's child; God is his Father; he is God's son (Mt 5⁴³⁻⁴⁸ 6²⁵⁻³⁴). Such words may not define man's present condition; they look at him in the light of the ideal; they describe his duty, his highest destiny and ambition. The loftiest hope and purpose that any man may cherish is to become a son of his Father who is in heaven, and to become perfect as his heavenly Father is perfect (Mt 5⁴⁵⁻⁴⁸). It is noteworthy that Jesus never mentions the fall of man, nor is there any very conclusive passage in which He speaks of man as a sinner. But He implies that man is such in that He makes 'Repent' the keynote of His opening ministry (Mt 4¹⁷). There is but one who is good, even God (Lk 18¹⁸·¹⁹); yet men, who are evil, can render good gifts to their children (Mt 7¹¹). It is possible for a man's eye to be evil, and for his whole body to be filled with darkness rather than with light (Mt 6²³). Men cannot serve two masters, mammon and God (Mt 6²⁴). A rich man can with difficulty enter into the Kingdom of God (Mt 19²⁴). Ultimately, too, men are sifted out and their destiny is determined by their attitude to Himself and His brethren; some will sit down with Abraham and Isaac and Jacob in the Kingdom of God; others will be cast into the outer darkness, where there shall be weeping and gnashing of teeth (Mt 25[31-46]).

But, generally, it is the ideal which is present with Jesus; He prefers to look at the possibilities; He does not see capacity for evil; He tries rather to discover the latent powers and potencies of good. An incident such as that recorded in Jn 8[1-11] is striking proof of this. Jesus there sees not simply the sinner, but the possibility of good in the sinner. His final word to her, therefore, is not one of condemnation: 'Neither do I condemn thee; go thy way; from henceforth sin no more.' Man, therefore, is crowned with high dignity and solemn grandeur because he is akin to the Divine. If Jesus had not believed in the capacity for good even in the most unlikely and unexpected people, what we read recorded of Him and His work would never have happened. Of set purpose He turned from folk who were reputable, respectable, and, in the conventional sense, righteous and holy. He came not to the whole, but to the sick; not to call the righteous, but sinners to repentance (Lk 5[31, 32]). He turned to those without repute, to the so-called 'sinners,' in the faith that goodness lived within their hearts; and history tells us that He was not disappointed. He sought for the common man, unsophisticated, unconventional; and we read that He was often surprised and astonished at what the common man revealed to Him (Mt 8[5-13]); Jesus may thus be said to have been the first to discover the true significance of common men and common things. They were significant because they led up to and implied more than themselves; at the base and heart of each there was God.

But to Jesus man was not one object or thing among other objects or things in the natural world. He was not simply a part of Nature. 'How much then is a man of more value than a sheep!' (Mt 12[12]). If the recovery of one sheep brought joy to the shepherd in charge of the flock, a man, by his choice and pursuit of the good, could bring joy to the heart of God (Lk 15[3-7]). He was *of value*, as a lost coin is of value, for which a woman sweeps the house and searches diligently until she finds it (Lk 15[8-10]); or as a son is of value, who, even if he has left home for a far country and there wasted his substance in riotous living, is still dear to his father's heart (Lk 15[11-32]).

To Jesus, man, as a spiritual being, made in the image of God, who is Spirit, took precedence of all material things. The death of the body was merely a temporal event; but to think and believe and act as if the material world was all, was the death of the soul (Lk 12[13-21]). It was to deny God by forgetting Him, and at bottom meant the surrender of one's life as a *person* and the endeavour to become a *thing*. Such was the act of a fool. To Jesus the spiritual side was all; or, in relation to other things it was the central, controlling principle, the *fons et origo* of all besides. The life is 'more than the meat, and the body than the raiment' (Mt 6[25]). 'A man's life consisteth not in the abundance of the things which he possesseth' (Lk 12[15]). 'What shall it profit a man if he gain the whole world, and forfeit his life?' (Mt 16[26]).

From a strictly moral standpoint the same truth held good of man; he alone of all natural creatures was capable of good and ill; *things* could not defile; they were unmoral, and knew neither good nor bad; defilement could come only from spirit, from man, and it proceeded from the thoughts and purposes of his heart (Mt 15[10. 11. 18-20]). If the inner life was watched, and its waters and streams kept pure, all was well; from without there was no danger, because things had no power. It was similar in regard to the nature of the true good. It was an inward possession; moth and rust consumed material things, but they could not touch spiritual treasure, which made up the wealth of the soul; this was treasure in heaven, and as such would abide (Mt 6[20]). It was the good incorporated, as it were, into the very life and spirit of man. Such also was the Kingdom of heaven. Men could not see it; it did not come by observation; it was within (Lk 17[20, 21]).

There is a revelation of God in Nature; there is a revelation of God in man; above all, in the moral consciousness of man. People often asked Jesus for a sign or miracle to show them that His teaching was true. But Jesus gave no sign. The teaching itself was its own sign and witness (Lk 11[29-32]); its presence was also an argument; it 'doth both shine and give us sight to see.' The rich man in the torments of hell-fire might ask that a messenger be sent to his brethren—that some one should rise from the dead to warn them from his fate;—surely at a miracle they would repent? But the appeal of Jesus ever addressed itself to the moral consciousness of man. 'They have Moses and the prophets; let them hear them. . . . If they hear not Moses and the prophets, neither will they be persuaded though one rise from the dead' (Lk 16[19-31]). In this aspect John also, in the Prologue to his Gospel, defines for us the nature of man. There was a light which lighted every man as he came into the world. The source of this light was God. Its supreme manifestation was in Jesus; in Him was life, and the life was the light of men (Jn 1[1-9]).

Man, then, as spiritual, takes precedence of everything else that is. He is not a means or a thing; he is an end in himself. In the time of Jesus, however, as has also happened in other periods of history, the customs and institutions which man had made had become his master, were obscuring his vision and keeping him from his true good. One of these institutions was that of the Sabbath. A man might not heal another man on the Sabbath; yet if a sheep had fallen into a well he might get it out, or if his ox or his ass were thirsty he might lead them to the pool. Jesus enforces the true order; the Sabbath was made for man; it was a means for his good; it was a custom, an institution, a thing, and, as compared with spirit, occupied a strictly subordinate place. It was similar with every custom and institution man had made (Mt 12[1-21], Mk 2[23-28]).

In saying this, Jesus stood emphatically for progress; He practically said also that there was something in the life of man which neither institutions nor the social order nor civic legislation could ever fully express; man bore the infinite within him; deep and ineradicable, within his life, there was the life of God. Man was therefore immortal. If we admit the premises, no other conclusion is possible. The fact, said Jesus in effect, that we can stand in relation to God, that we can speak with Him and commune with Him, is itself the promise and pledge of immortality. Because He lives, we live also (Jn 14[19]). God 'is not the God of the dead, but of the living, for all live unto him' (Lk 20[38]). And thus the chief end of man was to know God and Jesus Christ whom He had sent (Jn 17[3]); his true vocation was to seek the kingdom of God and His righteousness (Mt 6[33]). Because he was made in God's image, and was able, in some measure, to represent Him and reveal Him, man was endowed with a peculiar dignity. But here again Jesus spoke in the language of the ideal. Immortality was a possibility for man; it was in some sense an achievement ; it was also something that could be lost. But it was something of which every man was capable.

In conclusion, the strongest argument for the dignity and worth of man is to be found in Jesus Himself. He called Himself the Son of Man ; whatever touched man and his well-being was His concern. His teaching and His life were such that men find it impossible to regard Him from the ordinary human standpoint. They have conceived of Him as Divine ; they say that His entry into human life to share the common pain and toil and death was a purely voluntary act. Such is not only a view held by theologians, but one which is entertained to-day by men of science. Sir Oliver Lodge speaks of Jesus as being willing to share the life of a peasant, and as being the best race-asset that men possess (*Hibbert Journal*, Oct. 1904). From whatever standpoint, however, He is viewed, the presence of Jesus in humanity can only add incalculably to its worth and dignity. In set doctrine Jesus taught very little as to the nature of man. To really see what He thought about man and the value He set on him, we must look at Jesus' life. He came to do the will of His Father and to accomplish His work (Jn 6^{38} 9^4) ; He came to give life, and to give it abundantly (Jn 10^{10}) ; He came not to be ministered unto, but to minister, and to give His life a ransom for many (Mt 20^{28}). That He loved men is a commonplace. He, beyond all other teachers and leaders whom we know, 'stood stoutly for the human,' and made the cause of man—the true well-being of man—take precedence of every other thing and cause. It was not that men were better in His than in any other age ; it was that He ever saw men in the light of the ideal, and ever found at the root of man's life the life of God. To say this is to say also that among all the benefactors of humanity, Jesus of Nazareth is, *par excellence*, the Friend of Man. He thought that the common weal—man and man's true cause and good—was worth living for with absolute devotion ; should things so require, it was also worth dying for. And, as Jesus Himself has said, greater love hath no man than this (Jn 15^{13}).

Psychologically, man, in the thought of Jesus, is made up of two parts, soul and body, or spirit and flesh. But He speaks, as a moral teacher, of man in his broad general aspect, and is not concerned with minute psychological distinctions (cf. Mt 10$^{28.29}$ 16^{26} 26^{41}, Mk 8^{36}, Lk 16^{22}).

Literature.—Grimm-Thayer, *Lex. s.vv.* ἀνήρ, ἄνθρωπος ; Hastings' *DB*, art. 'Man' ; A. B. Bruce, *The Kingdom of God*, and other works ; John Caird, *Introduction to the Philosophy of Religion* ; A. M. Fairbairn, *Studies in the Life of Christ* ; Laidlaw, *Bibl. Doct. of Man* ; Wendt, *Teaching of Jesus* ; N. T. Theol. of Weiss, Beyschlag, etc. ; H. E. Manning, *Sermons* (1844), p. 47 ; H. Bushnell, *The New Life* (1860), p. 16 ; J. Martineau, *Hours of Thought* (1879), ii. p. 286 ; F. Paget, *Faculties and Difficulties*[2] (1889), p. 132 ; W. Gladden, *Burning Questions* (1890), p. 67 ; J. B. Lightfoot, *Cambridge Sermons* (1800), p. 229 ; R. W. Dale, *Christian Doctrine* (1894), p. 170 ; H. van Dyke, *Manhood, Faith and Courage* (1906), p. 1.

E. Wheeler.

MANAEN (Μαναήν, Ac 13^1 = Menahem, מְנַחֵם, 'comforter,' 2 K 15^{14} etc.).—Two facts only are recorded in Scripture concerning Manaen. In his old age he was a Christian minister ; in youth he was foster-brother of Herod the tetrarch, *i.e.* Antipas (Ac 13^1). But this must be read side by side with a statement of Josephus, who tells us (*Ant*. XV. x. 5) that, some few years before, another Manaen (or Manaem) had come into touch with another Herod,—the Great. The double parallel appears too striking to be mere coincidence. It seems more reasonable to assume a connexion between the two stories, and from them we may inferentially derive much light.

1. *The connexion between the Manaen of Josephus and Herod the Great.*—When Herod was yet a schoolboy, he was one day greeted in the street by this Manaen, who patted him on the back, and saluted him as future king of the Jews. As Antipater, Herod's father, was only a military governor, the prediction seemed absurd. But Manaen was an Essene, one of the stalwart Puritans of that day, who had a reputation not only for austerity but for predictive powers (*Jos. BJ* II. viii. 12) ; and the words induced the lad to make further inquiry. Manaen persisted, adding that the coming dignity would not be accompanied by righteous living, and that God's punishment would visit his later life. About fifteen years later (B.C. 37), when the first part of the prophecy was fulfilled, Herod sent for the old Essene, and ever after honoured him and his sect. If, as Lightfoot conjectures, he was the same Manaen who, being vice-president of the Sanhedrin under Hillel, led away eighty others to the service of Herod, and inaugurated a system of laxer living, then the connexion did not issue in the moral profit of the older man, and he may have been alluded to (as Plumptre thinks) by our Lord under the figure of the shaken reed (Mt 11^7), and as a soft-clad dweller in royal households. Perhaps, too, this defection was the origin of the sect of the Herodians (Mk 3^6, etc.).

2. *Connexion between the later Manaen and Herod Antipas.*—The facts related above seem to constitute an intelligible foundation for the circumstances of Manaen's life noted in Ac 13^1. Antipas was a son of Herod the Great, and if the old king had an elder Manaen living in his household, nothing would be more natural than that a young Herod and a young Manaen (perhaps a grandson, since Manaen the elder was a man of standing when Herod the Great was a boy) should be brought up together. What this implied it is difficult to determine, since 'foster-brother' (σύντροφος) has both a narrower and a wider meaning. It may only indicate that the children were much together. Manaen may well have shared both the home-life and the subsequent education, under a private tutor at Rome, which Antipas and Archelaus enjoyed (*Ant*. XVII. i. 3). On the other hand, Archelaus is not mentioned here, so perhaps the narrower sense of σύντροφος may be pressed, that Manaen's mother was also nurse to Antipas. In either case it is suggestive to contemplate the murderer of John the Baptist and paramour of Herodias, side by side with the man of ascetic Essene stock, subsequently a teacher in the Church of Christ.

3. *Manaen's religious development and influence.*—One wonders how the companion of Herod became the servant of Christ. His name ('consoler') may indicate that his parents were of that spiritually watchful circle who waited for the consolation of Israel (Lk 2^{25}). According to the Talmud (Jerus. *Ber.* ii. 4), *Menahem* was to be one of the titles of the Messiah, and indeed it became so (see 1 Jn 2^1 παράκλητος, used in Job 16^2 [Aq. Theod.] as tr. of מְנַחֵם). The name was sometimes given to children at this period, with Messianic thoughts and hopes. Manaen is like a ferry-chain whose ends are visible and whose centre is submerged. We know of his childhood and old age : his mature manhood we can only conjecture. But we know at least that he passed through the Gospel period of John the Baptist's preaching and Jesus Christ's ministry. He may have been amongst the number of those who listened on the Jordan's banks, and brought tidings to Antipas. At any rate, in Herod's household he must have heard the stirring words of the rugged prophet of the old Essene type, and if Herod 'heard gladly,' how much more Manaen ! The twin-texts, 'Repent ye' and 'Behold the

Lamb,' may well have become the head-lights of his course, and the forerunner's words have led to Christ one more fruitful servant. There is much to indicate that the lonely ministry in the castle of Machærus was not barren of results. Besides Manaen, we know of spiritual interests kindled in Joanna, wife of Herod's major-domo (Lk 8[3]), in the king's courtiers (βασιλικός, Jn 4[46]), perhaps in Herodion (Ro 16[11]), whose name indicates court connexions; we know, further, that there were servants to whom Herod talked on religious topics (Mt 14[1f.]). And among these Manaen may well have been one of those unseen influences for good which alone can account for some of the better impulses of Herod's inconsistent life. What passed between the foster-brothers after John's murder? Was Manaen a silent or a protesting spectator when Jesus was mocked? Did the death of Christ complete a work of grace already begun at the death of John? Did the Resurrection of Christ (no rumour this time, Mt 14[2], but a well attested fact) seal for ever the allegiance of a halting disciple? Did he remain in the train of his foster-brother till the latter left for Rome in A.D. 39? If so, he may have gone to Antioch at that date, and been one of the founders of the Church in that city, which comes into view about A.D. 41 (Ac 11[19]). He would then rank amongst that honoured company whose consistent practice of the faith they professed first won them the name 'Christian,' Christ's man,—honoured since with world-wide acceptance wherever the gospel message has spread. At Antioch, in any case, we find him four years later occupying a position of authority (Ac 13[1]). If he was a prophet, we have an interesting link with the old Essene foreteller of Herod the Great's reign. But perhaps the copulative particles, strictly pressed, rank him as teacher and not as prophet. He must by this time have become somewhat advanced in years. If St. Luke also came from Antioch (Euseb. HE 3. 4), it may have been from Manaen that he learned certain details concerning Herod and John which are peculiar to his Gospel. We last catch sight of Manaen in that hallowed gathering when he and his fellows in the ministry willingly surrendered their two ablest men, Barnabas and Saul, for the evangelization of the world. He who was called by his parents 'the comforter' cheerfully yielded to the higher voice of the heavenly 'Comforter' (Ac 13[2]), and tarried by the stuff, while others went forth to the fight.

LITERATURE.—Lightfoot, Pitman's ed. iii. 211; Jos. Ant. xv. x. 5, BJ II. viii.; Plumptre, Bib. Educ. ii. 29. 82; art. in Smith's, Hastings', and Fairbairn's DB (by Hackett, Cowan, and Dickson respectively), and in Encyc. Bibl. (by Cheyne).

H. C. LEES.

MANASSEH.—The well-known king of Judah, mentioned as a link in our Lord's genealogy, Mt 1[10].

MANGER.—The AV and RV tr. of φάτνη in Lk 2[7. 12. 16]. In Lk 13[15], the only other place where φάτνη occurs in NT, AV and RV both render it 'stall,' though RVm gives 'manger.' The precise meaning of φάτνη is somewhat uncertain, opinions differing as to whether it denotes a *stall* or a *manger* within a stall.

Tristram (*Land of Israel*, p. 73) supposes that Mary and Joseph, who could not find room in the κατάλυμα, were obliged to go to some poor house hard by, where there was 'an upper platform' for people and 'a lower platform' for cattle, and that 'in the lower portion allotted to the cattle the Infant when born was naturally laid at once in the long earthen trough which serves for a manger, and into which the fodder is pushed from the floor.' If the κατάλυμα was like a modern Eastern khan, and if the φάτνη belonged to it (see below), Mary and Joseph went to one of the stalls for cattle and beasts of burden within the outside wall, and there the babe was born. Meyer (on Lk 2[7]) favours the view that φάτνη means a feeding-trough placed in a stable. In any case, φάτνη, as its derivation implies, designates a feeding-place for animals.

Opinions further differ as to whether the φάτνη in question was a *cave* or grotto in the limestone rock of the neighbourhood used as a stable, or an *enclosure* fenced in.

The former view, which has the weight of persistent tradition, is due to Justin Martyr, who tells us that Christ was born 'in a certain cave near the village,' which cave, he says, had been pointed out by Isaiah as 'a sign.' For this latter circumstance he founds upon Is 33[16] LXX, 'He shall dwell in the lofty cave of the strong rock' (*Trypho*, 70 and 78). A similar statement is made by Origen, who affirms that in his day there was shown at Bethlehem 'the cave where Jesus was born, and the manger in the cave where He was wrapped in swaddling bands' (c. Cels. i. 51).

There is, of course, nothing improbable in this traditional view that the place where Mary sought shelter was a cave, for throughout Palestine such caves or grottoes were and are commonly used as stables. The other view, that the φάτνη was an enclosure, is favoured by many. According to Schleusner, it was the open courtyard attached to the inn and enclosed by a rough fence, into which the cattle would be shut at night, and where poorer travellers might lodge, when from want of room in the inn, or want of means to pay for room, they could find no other place. This view is supported by the Vulg. (*præsepium*) and the Peshiṭta. It is, moreover, significant that the earliest Christian artists represent the Nativity as in an open courtyard.

Stanley, who opposes the view that the φάτνη was a cave, does so partly on the ground of Mt 2[11] and partly on the ground of the superstitious tendency to associate sacred events with caves. He says (SP p. 440): 'As soon as the religion of Palestine fell into the hands of Europeans, it is hardly too much to say that it became "a religion of caves."' He further notes that when the Convent of the Nativity was dismantled during the invasion of Ibrahim Pasha, it was found that the traditional cave had been, in pre-Christian times, a place of sepulture, and was therefore not at all likely ever to have been used by Jews as a manger.

It has been commonly but too readily assumed that the precise meaning of φάτνη in St. Luke's account must be determined by our interpretation of κατάλυμα. This appears to be a groundless assumption. It is not said by St. Luke that the φάτνη was connected with the inn. In 2[7. 12] the definite article is not used; for, though it appears in the TR and a few MSS of minor importance, in which it was probably inserted to designate the well-known φάτνη, preponderating evidence is altogether against it. It occurs, as the best MSS show, in v.[16], but there it clearly refers to the φάτνη spoken of in vv.[7. 12]. It is at least possible that the φάτνη did not belong to the κατάλυμα at all, and it is worth noting as subordinate evidence for this that the *Protevangel of James* and the *Arabic Gospel of the Infancy* do not connect 'the cave' of which they both speak with the inn.

Our conclusion, then, seems clear that, whether the φάτνη was a cave or an enclosure, it was certainly a place where cattle were housed or fed. It cannot be maintained that there is anything improbable or unreasonable in the continuous Christian tradition which goes back to the first decade of the second century. Nor is the pious sentiment groundless which has pictured the birth of the world's Redeemer in circumstances so humble, and has lingered in loving and grateful meditation over His manger cradle. See also artt. BETHLEHEM and CAVE.

LITERATURE.—Schleusner, Lex. s.v. φάτνη; Meyer-Weiss on Lk 2[7]; Keim, Jesus of Nazara (Eng. tr. ii. 80); Edersheim, Life and Times of Jesus, i. 185; Stanley, SP, and Tristram, Land of Israel, as quoted; Hepworth Dixon, Holy Land, i. ch. 13.

J. CROMARTY SMITH.

MANIFESTATION.—1. *The historic manifestation.*—We shall not attempt in this article to say anything about such manifestations of Christ as those alluded to in Jn 1[9], where He is spoken of as the Light which lighteth every man coming into the world. Our first point must obviously be that manifestation in the flesh of which St. Paul speaks in his letter to Timothy (1 Ti 3¹⁶). We are so accustomed to its outward form that to some extent we have lost its significance. Not in the court as a king's son, not in the Temple as the member of a priestly family, not in the wilderness as the son of some aged solitary who had given up the world, but in the familiar commonplace surroundings of a peasant family, as the Son of Mary, the wife of a village carpenter. This was the presentation of God to the world. Any of the other forms would have been more in accord with human expectations. But we are learning more and more every day that God loves the natural, not the out-of-the-way, as a means for manifestation. And this manifestation, first in the manger at Bethlehem, then in the home at Nazareth, was the outward setting of the Divine Life, both simple and natural. There were no miracles, no strange exhibitions of unseen powers, no external signs that led the men of Nazareth to mark out that home as being specially remarkable. Mary and Joseph, who alone knew the secret, read the wonder of it in the spotless life which from infancy to manhood unfolded new beauties every day. Nothing like it had they ever seen or heard.

2. *Manifestation by signs.*—But this manifestation of God in human character, though the only one seen during thirty out of thirty-three years, was not the only one. His mother evidently expected something further. When He left His home to begin His ministry, she felt sure that this reserve and silence would be broken. It might come at any place, and at any time. And it was in accord with the humility and kindness of her character that she should believe it might come at a small village feast to meet a temporary social need. It is plain from our Lord's reply (Jn 2⁴) that she was looking for some manifestation, for He told her that the hour for such had not come. It is equally plain that she read in His words only a correction of her eagerness and supposition that she best knew the occasion. She had no doubt that He would help, and gave directions accordingly. And in that secret miracle, apparently unperceived at the time, and discovered only when there was an opportunity to ask the servants, He manifested forth His glory.

This is typical of the many manifestations that followed during the three years. They were not wonders wrought to force men's belief, but signs of Divine character. They were bits of teaching by illustration, object-lessons as we should call them. He never would work a miracle for the sake of astonishing men, though He was often asked to do so (Mt 12³⁸ᶠᶠ· 16¹ᶠᶠ·). They were all signs of God's sympathy with the needs of men, and the desire He had to relieve them. (See Wace, *Some Central Points of Our Lord's Ministry*, p. 133).

3. *Manifestation of the Transfiguration.* — For some eighteen months there had been wonderful manifestations of Divine character and power, but no personal manifestation. Like any one else, Christ was seen tired, hungry, asleep, and in pain through the infirmities and sicknesses of others that He carried. He did not strive nor cry, neither was His voice heard in the streets (Mt 12¹⁹). All was singularly quiet and unassuming, and men might well wonder what there was at the back of this astonishing teaching and these wonderful works. But once the disclosure was made (Mt 17¹ᶠ· ‖ Mk 9²ᶠ·, Lk 9²⁸ᶠ·). See art. TRANSFIGURATION.

4. *Manifestations after the Resurrection.*—It is very difficult to realize the character of these revelations of the Risen Lord. In one He is like a gardener (Jn 20¹⁵), in another, a traveller walking to a country village (Lk 24¹⁵), in another, a stranger standing on the beach of the Lake (Jn 21⁴). Mk. speaks of the appearance to the two disciples on the road to Emmaus as being in 'another form' (Mk 16¹²). They were manifestations marked by sudden appearances and disappearances. His home was elsewhere, but He came and went according to the disciples' needs. The body was real—could be touched as well as seen. Indeed, He was anxious that they should not suppose Him to be mere spirit, and actually ate a piece of broiled fish before them in order to show them the reality of His bodily existence (Lk 24⁴²). But these manifestations are characterized by two features: (1) they were made only to His friends; (2) they were not apparently surrounded with glory and majesty.

With regard to (1), we may believe that only His friends could have perceived them. They might have seen *something*, as St. Paul's companions did on the road to Damascus (Ac 9⁷), but not the face of Christ. Faith and love were necessary to interpret the manifestations. (2) They were not apparently surrounded with glory and majesty. They disturbed and frightened, not because they were expressions of His eternal majesty, as that of the Transfiguration was, but because they were unexpected and sudden. This, we think, is singular, and certainly one of the marks of the truthfulness of the narrative. We expect it to be so different, as is shown by the shining figures that represent the Risen Lord in picture and stained-glass window. But just as the graciousness of a king leads him to adopt the dress of his guest so as to make him more completely at home, so our King, when He comes to those poor labouring folk whom He had chosen for His Apostles, comes as one of them.

5. *Manifestations to disciples since the Ascension.*—There is a striking promise in the words our Lord spoke after the Last Supper, in which He declares that He will manifest Himself to the man that loves Him. That this does not refer to the manifestations of the Resurrection, which were so soon to follow, is clear from His reply to Jude's very natural question as to how He would manifest Himself to the disciples and yet not to the world (Jn 14²²). It is interesting to note that St. John does not use the ordinary Greek word (φανερόω) for manifestation, but takes another word (ἐμφανίζω), which is employed in this sense in only one other passage (Mt 27⁵³), where the dead bodies of the saints are said to have appeared to many in the holy city. That passage would seem to indicate a bodily appearance; but our Lord's explanation contradicts such an interpretation. When asked how He could appear to the men who loved Him and yet not to the world, He replies that in the first place the man who loves Him will keep His word, *i.e.* will give his mind to Him, and observe His teaching, and then in his fixed contemplation and obedience will realize not only His own presence, but the presence of the Father. Such manifestations as these, then, are secret, personal realizations of Christ's presence, according more nearly with the revelations of a friend's character that we have in his letters, or in his pictures if he is an artist, in his music if he is a musician. Not, however, that we are to think of them as entirely subjective. The words 'We will come unto him' teach an actual spiritual movement on our Lord's part towards those who love Him, which they will feel and enjoy.

To St. Paul, who did enjoy some actual appearances of Christ, the spiritual revelations were everything; and in one difficult passage he declares that though he had known Christ after the flesh, *i.e.* in bodily form, henceforth he knew Him no longer in that way (2 Co 5¹⁶), evidently finding more in the indwelling manifestation of Christ than he had known in the joy of Christ's visible form.

6. *Manifestation of the Second Advent.*—In 2 Th 2⁸, where AV gives 'with the brightness of his coming,' RV renders 'by the manifestation of his coming,' the Gr. word being ἐπιφάνεια. Similarly RV substitutes 'shall be manifested' for AV 'shall appear' in Col 3⁴, 1 P 5⁴, 1 Jn 2²⁸ 3², the Gr. word in each case being φανερόω. See artt. PAROUSIA, SECOND COMING.

G. H. S. WALPOLE.

MANLINESS.—To the Christian, Jesus is the perfect man, and therefore in His character is to be found the perfect type of manliness. At the same time, when we speak of the manliness of Jesus, there is an element of challenge in the phrase, and we make an assertion that is felt to require justification. This is due partly to the fact that the conventional idea of manliness seems too poor a standard to apply to Jesus, and partly to the fact that the courage of Jesus is not often emphasized. Gentleness, meekness, and forgiveness are the qualities by which His character was pre-eminently distinguished, and it is too often assumed that these preclude the possession of courage. A somewhat complex problem is thus raised by the discussion of manliness in relation to Jesus, which involves two questions: (1) What is the conventional or worldly conception of manliness? (2) How far do the character and teaching of Jesus agree with this, and how far do they modify it?

1. *The conventional or worldly conception of manliness* cannot be described in a word, for a number of qualities go to make up what the world accepts as a manly man. (1) There must be a basis of *adequate physical strength.* Men have always admired the athlete, and they reject the claim to manliness of those who are puny and feeble in body. The vigour and energy of a strong, well-disciplined body form the substratum of the world's idea of manliness. A proof of this is to be found in the many efforts made by Christian people to remove the prejudice that there is an opposition between Christian faith and bodily strength. The combination of Christian faith with athletic vigour has seemed and does seem to many extremely desirable (cf. 'muscular Christianity'). (2) There must be a sufficient degree of *intelligence.* As, however, the standard of intelligence demanded for manliness is not very high, this element is not greatly emphasized. (3) There must be the *moral qualities* of courage, temperance or self-control, perseverance, and love of personal honour. Of these courage is fundamental, and it may be defined as the assertion of self against opposing influences. It is recognized by the world in many forms, from the animal quality of bold disregard of physical danger up to steadfast adherence to conscientious conviction. At the same time, however courageous a man may be, the world holds him to come short of true manliness if he is not able to control his impulses, whether of mind or body, to persevere patiently in any course of action he has adopted, and to be scrupulous in guarding his personal honour with life itself if necessary.

There are three points which may be noticed in connexion with this analysis of the conventional idea of manliness. (a) All the virtues involved are compatible with pride, and indeed are conceived as ministering to and supporting pride. This is obvious in regard to courage and love of honour. Self-control, again, is desirable largely because its opposite brings ridicule; and perseverance, because to give in is intolerable to the proud man. (b) This idea of manliness corresponds very closely to the ideal of the perfect man of the Greek and Roman moralists. The starting-point of pagan ethics is the analysis of the term 'happiness' (εὐδαιμονία), regarded not as a subjective state of feeling, but as an objective form of being. Happiness is held to be found in the harmony of character and experience.

Hence the qualities which give a man rule over his circumstances are to be desired as good. By Plato and Aristotle an optimistic view of the world's capacity to satisfy the requirements of a good man is assumed. With the Stoics, pessimism about the world leads to strong emphasis being laid on the power of the individual to be sufficient to himself. With the Epicureans the optimistic assumption that the world will not fail to give the gratification necessary to happiness, leads to the emphasis being laid on the regulation rather than the suppression of desire. The ethics of Greek and Roman writers may be generically described as the science of the relation of man to his environment. The variations in theory are determined by the view taken of the responsiveness of the environment to man's needs. Thus, from the practical point of view, all the various theories aim at self-development. Self is the beginning, centre, and aim of pagan ethical thought. Harmonies with Christian teaching are largely accidental. The essence and root are different. The virtues of the pagan are 'inflated and arrogant' (Augustine), even where they inculcate the same conduct as the Christian virtues (cf. Luthardt, *Hist. of Christian Ethics,* i. 25). (c) This idea of manliness corresponds very closely to the ideal of manhood to be found in the Ethics of Evolution. Phrases such as the 'survival of the fittest' and the 'struggle for existence,' which suggest that men are engaged in a constant war from which only the conquerors emerge, indicate at once an ideal of manliness of which self-assertion is the fundamental quality.

2. *How far do the character and teaching of Jesus agree with the worldly conception of manliness, and how far do they modify it?*—Was Jesus a manly man according to the world's idea? To this the answer must be that His manliness can be vindicated in relation to all the qualities which go to make a manly man, but that allowance must be made for the very different ideal in relation to which these qualities were exercised. About physical strength and intellectual ability it is not necessary to say anything. There is a degree of human excellence which makes even the latter inconsiderable, and we have passed that degree when we discuss the character of Jesus. Courage, however, is on quite a different plane, and the courage of Jesus can be triumphantly vindicated. The cleansing of the Temple (Mt 21¹², ¹³, Mk 11¹⁵⁻¹⁸, Jn 2¹³⁻¹⁶), the attitude of Jesus towards the throng who would have made Him king (Jn 6¹⁵ᶠ·), His denunciations of the Pharisees (Mt 23), His woes against the cities of Galilee (Mt 11²⁰⁻²⁴), His acts of healing upon the Sabbath, His rebuke to the people of Nazareth (Lk 4¹⁶⁻³⁰), His statement about the Temple (Jn 2¹⁸⁻²²), His refusal of a sign to the scribes (Mt 12³⁸⁻⁴² 16¹⁻⁴, Mk 8¹¹, ¹², Lk 11¹⁶ᶠ·), His last journey and entrance into Jerusalem (Lk 9⁵¹), His demeanour before the high priest and before Pilate (Mt 26⁵⁷ᶠ·, Mk 14⁵³ᶠ·, Lk 22⁶⁶ᶠ·)—all show courage of the very first quality. He is undismayed before an unparalleled combination of adverse forces. And the overwhelming forces opposed to Him give an added lustre to His courage in dealing faithfully with those who took or were ready to take His part. His disciples are fearlessly rebuked when they are in the wrong (Lk 9⁵⁴⁻⁵⁶, Mt 16²³, Mk 8³³, Mt 18¹ᶠ·, Mk 9³³, Lk 9⁴⁶ 24²⁴ᶠ·, Mt 19¹⁴, Lk 10¹³⁻¹⁵, Lk 18¹⁵⁻¹⁹). He never modifies His demands in order thereby to secure influential supporters (Jn 3¹ᶠ·, Mt 19¹⁶ᶠ·, Mk 10¹⁷ᶠ·, Lk 18¹⁸ᶠ·, Mt 8¹⁹⁻²², Lk 9⁵⁷⁻⁶²). Moreover, the inevitable result of His faithfulness was clear to Him from an early point in His public career. So there was not lacking in His courage that element which arises from the vision of the cruel and shameful death awaiting Him. The self-control of Jesus, again, is very apparent in His life. We see it in the fact that He remained subject to His parents (Lk 2⁵¹), and was 30 years of age before He began His ministry. It is displayed in a different relation in the temptation in the wilderness (Mt 4¹⁻¹¹, Lk 4¹⁻¹³), when neither the pangs of hunger nor the splendid prospect of world-wide dominion could overcome His resolution. And once more, before the high priest, before Pilate, and in the brutal hands of the soldiers, He never spoke one bitter or unworthy word, even though Peter denied Him and the other disciples had forsaken Him. Of His perseverance it is only necessary to say that He was 'obedient even unto death, yea, the death of the cross' (Ph 2[8]).

It is in regard to love of personal honour that the transcendent difference between the world's idea of manliness and the manliness of Jesus becomes apparent, just as also very varying views are to be found even among worldly men as to what honour really is. However, an integral element in honour in the worldly sense is the good opinion of a man held by his fellows. To be an inconsiderable person was regarded by Aristotle as incompatible with happiness. High-mindedness is one of the virtues which go to make the perfect man, and 'by a high-minded man we seem to mean one who claims much and deserves much' (*Nic. Eth.* iv. 3, § 3 ; cf. Mt 23[12]). Even the proud indifference of the Cynic to the opinion of his neighbours by its vehemence betrayed its hollowness. It is the last refuge of pride to despise all who do not acknowledge the superiority on which it is based. In the life and teaching of Jesus the centre of morality is changed from self to God. Right conduct consists in obedience to the law of God. The essential nature of the Law is to love God and one's neighbour (Mt 22[37-40], Mk 12[30. 31], Lk 10[27]). The approval of God is thus the supreme practical consideration for the Christian, while his relations to others are to be governed by love and a desire for their good. There is no exception to this rule. It is to guide the conduct of Christians towards those who have injured them. Now the right and duty of avenging an affront or an injury have always seemed to men bound up with the love of honour, and the division of others into friends and enemies has seemed inevitable. But Jesus teaches that His followers are to forgive injuries, and to love their enemies (Mt 5[39f.] 18[21. 22], Lk 6[27f.] 17[3. 4]). Moreover, they are not to meet violence with violence. And of these precepts He has given a perfect illustration (Lk 4[24-30], Mt 26[52-56], Mk 14[65], Mt 27[30], Jn 8[59] 10[39] 19[17]).

It is in regard to this duty of forgiveness that the world has found the greatest difficulty in assimilating the views of Jesus, and has been inclined to treat them as counsels of perfection which cannot be put in practice. Three degrees of opinion on this question may be distinguished : (1) that of those who altogether ignore the teaching of Jesus as impracticable ; (2) that of those who find in His teaching the condemnation of all resistance to evil, whether private or public, and so condemn alike war between States and private quarrels, whether settled by physical force or by an appeal to courts of law, the decisions of which ultimately rest on force ; (3) that of those who find in the teaching of Jesus primarily the inculcation of a spirit of love the manifestation of which is determined in every case by the circumstances, and which accordingly condemns neither war nor an appeal to force, nor an appeal to courts of law, apart from the occasion which gives rise to them.

With the first of these opinions we are not concerned. The second has always been held by many Christians. It is based especially on Mt 5[18-48] 26[52], Lk 6[27] 17[3]. In the early Church it led to a strong feeling against the propriety of Christians serving as soldiers (cf. Tertullian, *de Idol.* ch. 19—'the Lord in disarming Peter unbelted every soldier'). In later times the Society of Friends have been the most prominent adherents of similar ideas. And Tolstoi, among modern writers of distinction, holds such views in their most extreme form. It has to be remembered, however, (*a*) that the illustrative sayings of Jesus cannot wisely be generalized into universal precepts. To do this is to ignore the clearly marked feature of His teaching, in which He aimed 'at the greatest clearness in the briefest

compass.' (*b*) If Jesus said, 'To him that smiteth thee on one cheek offer also the other' (cf. Mt 26[52], Jn 18[11]), He also told His disciples to sell their garments and 'buy a sword' (Lk 22[36], cf. Mt 10[34. 35]). (*c*) Jesus laid down a method of dealing with one who has trespassed against another which cannot be brought within the boundary of strict non-resistance, though, indeed, the motive of this dealing is undoubtedly to be a desire for the good of the offender (Mt 18[15-17]). The third opinion is that which has generally prevailed among Christians. According to it, the ruling principle of a Christian's conduct is love towards all. This involves at once and without question or limit the forgiveness of all injuries and the crucifying of the spirit of emulation and self-esteem which so often leads to strife. But the manifestation of heart-forgiveness is to be regulated by a wise conception of the injurer's welfare and the welfare of others. These principles, in their mutual interaction, condemn all personal vindictiveness and malice, such an appeal to violence as duelling, that litigious spirit which aims at getting the better of another in a law-court, and all wars of aggression, as well as those which spring from national or personal pride. They do not condemn, however, the establishment of just government by force of arms, nor an appeal to justice and a desire for its vindication by force, nor the use of arms in the protection of the weak.[*]

There is thus open to the Christian a sphere for the exercise of aggressive courage consecrated to the furtherance of noble ends. To right wrong and to protect the weak are the natural aims of Christian manliness. At the same time it remains true that the Christian is called upon to exercise the courage of endurance much more frequently than that of aggression. And the endurance of the martyr shows a quality of manliness which transcends all others, inasmuch as his courage is made sublime by self-sacrifice.

LITERATURE.—Sidgwick, *Hist. of Ethics* ; Paulsen, *A System of Ethics* ; Knight, *The Christian Ethic* ; Martensen, *Christian Ethics* ; Luthardt, *Hist. of Christian Ethics* ; Benjamin Kidd, *Social Evolution* ; *Ecce Homo*, chs. 20, 21, 22 ; Wendt, *Teaching of Jesus* ; Speer, *The Principles of Jesus* ; Tolstoi, *The Christianity of Christ* ; Hughes, *The Manliness of Christ* ; Phillips Brooks, *The Candle of the Lord*, p. 253.

ANDREW N. BOGLE.

MANNA.—The miracle of the loaves and fishes, by which Jesus fed five thousand men, stirred the multitudes to fanaticism (Jn 6[1-15]). Their first impulse was to make Jesus king by force. On the morrow they followed Him across the sea to Capernaum, hoping that He would feed them again in some supernatural way, and suggesting the giving of bread from heaven as a suitable sign in confirmation of His high claims. Would not the prophet of Nazareth imitate the great lawgiver, who gave their fathers bread from heaven? Jesus turns their thoughts away from Moses to God : 'It was not Moses that gave you the bread out of heaven, but my Father giveth you the true bread out of heaven.' As God gave the fathers literal bread from heaven, so now He is giving to their children spiritual food that nourishes the soul eternally. 'I am the bread of life ; he that cometh to me shall not hunger, and he that believeth on me shall never thirst.' 'Your fathers did eat the manna in the wilderness, and they died.' God has a far better gift than the manna that was gathered day by day in the wilderness. 'I am the living bread that cometh down out of heaven : if any man eat of this bread, he shall live for ever ; yea, and the bread which I will give is my flesh, for the life of the world' (v.[51]).

---

[*] Tolstoi, with remorseless logic, declares that a Christian should not interfere with force to prevent murder—a precept which ignores the moral nature of the murderer no less than the claim of the person attacked for protection.

In Rev 2[17] the spiritual blessing promised by the glorified Christ to the victor in life's battle is called 'hidden manna.'   JOHN R. SAMPEY.

MANSION (μονή, Jn 14[2. 23]).—**1.** 'Mansion,' like μονή, is properly an abstract noun, meaning 'a staying,' 'an abiding.' In English literature it is first found in Hampole's *Psalter*, 5. 8 (*c.* 1340 A.D.), 'þai entire in til Godis house of heuen and takis þaire joy and þaire mansyon in þaire perfeccioun.' So in the B text of *Piers Plowman*, Langland says of Pride (B xiv. 26): 'Arst in the maister than in the man some mansioun he hath' (he dwelleth in the master rather than in the man). The C text (*c.* 1393) keeps the word while it extends the limits of Pride's abode (xvii. 59): 'Other in the maister, other in the man, some mancion he shewith.' But Hampole and Lydgate (1420) also use 'mansion' of a dwelling-place. A charter of Henry VI. (1444) uses it of a hostel, and Fabyan (1512) of the chief residence of a lord, whence it gains its modern meaning of 'an imposing abode,' which is seen even in Shakspeare (2 *Henry IV.* III. ii. 351). Bacon, however, still uses the word in its abstract sense in the *Advancement of Learning* (1605), and both Shakspeare and Milton use it of 'an abiding-place' without the suggestion of a building (*Timon of Athens*, v. i. 218; *Paradise Lost*, i. 268, viii. 296). From the Vulgate *mansiones* it is used by Wyclif for 'halting-places' in Ex 17[1], but in translations from the Greek (as Whiston's *Josephus*, 1737) this meaning represents σταθμός, not μονή, and so has no bearing upon the sense of Jn 14[2]. The Vulgate also uses *mansiones* in Jn 14[2], and is responsible for Hampole's use of the English form of the word in the sense of 'dwelling-places.' That sense was confirmed in the language, partly by Chaucer (*Knight's Tale*, 1116), but mainly by the influence of Tindale's Version of the NT (1526), 'In my fathers housse are many mansions,' and (2 Co 5[1]) 'Our erthy mancioun wherein we now dwell,' copied by Milton in *Il Penseroso*, 92.

2. But while the English 'mansion' and the identical French word *maison* have retained from their common original only the developed meaning of 'dwelling-place,' the Greek μονή is nowhere in extant literature found with this meaning, save only in Jn 14[2]. Westcott (with Liddell and Scott) explains its use in this verse by the supposed occurrence of the word in Pausanias (x. 31[7]) in the sense of 'a halting-place for the night.' But the ordinary reading in that passage seems impossible Greek, and is certainly corrupt (see J. G. Frazer's note): τέτμηται δὲ διὰ τῶν μονῶν ἡ ὁδός is not an intelligible expression for the traditional meaning, 'there are halting-places at intervals upon the road.' One MS reads μηνῶν, from which W. M. Ramsay conjectures διὰ τῶν Μηρηνῶν, 'the road has been carried through the country of the M. (beside Minos' tomb).'

Apart, then, from Jn 14[2], μονή remains a purely abstract noun, meaning (1) *abiding*, (2) *continuance*, (3) *rest*. The ease with which it passes from the first to the last of these meanings can be seen from Plato, *Crat.* 437 B, where μνήμη is defined as a μονή, and not a φορά; Ar. *Phys.* v. 6. 8 (ὥστε κινήσει μονὴ ἐναντία); Polybius, iv. 41. 4, 5, where it is twice coupled with στάσις; and most of all in Plutarch, whose writings (A.D. 80–120) are contemporary with St. John's Gospel.

Like the classical authors, Plutarch still uses μονή in the literal sense of 'a stay' or 'a continuance': οὔτε μονὴν ἐν τῷ βίῳ τοῖς ἀγαθοῖς οὔτε ἐξαγωγὴν τοῖς κακοῖς (1042 D), ἀλλὰ καὶ τούτοις μονὴν οἴονται καθήκουσαν εἶναι κἀκείνοις ἐξαγωγήν, 1063 D. But in 1024 F, though μονή answers to τὸ μένον, Plutarch opposes it, like Aristotle, to κίνησις : ἔστι γὰρ ἡ μὲν νόησις τοῦ νοοῦντος κίνησις περὶ τὸ μένον, ἡ δὲ δόξα μονὴ τοῦ αἰσθανομένου περὶ τὸ κινούμενον. So in 927 A the material elements as conceived by Empedocles are reduced to order by the introduction of the principle of love (φιλότητος ἐγγενομένης), ἵνα . . . τὰ μὲν κινήσεως τὰ δὲ μονῆς ἀνάγκαις ἐνδοθέντα

. . . ἁρμονίαν καὶ κοινωνίαν ἀπεργάσηται τοῦ παντός, where μονή has the complete meaning of *rest* as opposed to motion. And in 747 C he uses the plural of 'rests' in dancing; ἐνταῦθα δὲ αἱ μοναὶ πέρατα τῶν κινήσεων εἰσίν.

In Jn 14[2], however, the immediate mention of 'a place' seems to demand a concrete meaning for μοναί, though it has no parallel elsewhere. If so, the senses of 'abode' in vv.[2] and [23], concrete and abstract respectively, will be derived from the idea of *rest* that has become attached to the word, as well as from the original idea of *remaining*. The difference is seen at once when the μονὴν ποιεῖσθαι of Jn 14[23] is compared with the same phrase in Thuc. i. 131: Pausanias the victor of Plataea, intriguing with the Persians in Asia Minor, was 'prolonging his stay to no good purpose' (οὐκ ἐπ' ἀγαθῷ τὴν μονὴν ποιούμενος), μονήν, as the Scholiast remarks, being practically equivalent to ἀργίαν, 'idleness.' In Jn 14[23] the phrase combines, like μοναί in v.[2], the meanings of 'abiding' and 'rest' with that of the 'home' in which the rest is found. All the same suggestions are found in 1 Mac 7[38], the only passage in the LXX where μονή occurs: μνήσθητι τῶν δυσφημιῶν αὐτῶν, καὶ μὴ δῷς αὐτοῖς μονήν ('and suffer them not to live any longer,' RV).

3. The μονή of the Christian in the spiritual world (v.[2]) and the μονή of God in the Christian (v.[23]) are evidently intended to be correlative: 'Abide in me, and I in you' (Jn 15[4]). Their consummation realizes the ideal of Jn 17[21. 23]; meanwhile they are the NT fulfilment of the two OT ideals of rest: 'Rest in the Lord and wait patiently for him' (Ps 37[7]), and 'Arise, O Lord, into thy resting-place; thou, and the ark of thy strength' (132[8]). Jn 14[2], that is, refers not only to the perpetual 'rest' or 'home' in the life hereafter, but, like v.[23], to the 'abiding' fellowship with the Divine in this life (Mt 28[20], Rev 21[3]). See artt. ABIDING, and FATHER'S HOUSE.

LITERATURE.—For the English word see *Oxford Eng. Dict.*, where its history is fully illustrated; Aldis Wright's *Bible Word-Book*, 387, 388; Hastings' *DB* iii. 238. The Greek word is very insufficiently treated both in Stephanus and in Liddell and Scott; for Plutarch's uses see Wyttenbach's Index, where, however, some references are misprinted. Reference may further be made to *Expos. Times*, viii. [1897] 496, x. [1899] 303; *Expositor*, II. ii. [1881] 281, iii. [1882] 397, IV. vi. [1892] 209; A. Maclaren, *The Holy of Holies* (1890), p. 12; R. W. Dale, *Christ and the Future Life* (1895), pp. 33–84; J. Parker, *City Temple Pulpit*, i. (1899), p. 259.   FRANK RICHARDS.

MANUSCRIPTS.—The aim of the present article is to give a select list of the more ancient or interesting MSS of the Gospels, with a description of the most important or interesting of these. The simplest course will be to divide them into the languages in which they are written, premising that the Gospels were originally written in Greek, and that the versions in other languages are translations, generally direct, from the Greek. The symbols employed to indicate these manuscripts, whether letters or numbers, were invented for the sake of brevity, when they are referred to in an apparatus of variant readings. The standard collection of variants contained in Gospel manuscripts is that of C. Tischendorf (*Novum Testamentum Graece*: Editio Octava Critica Maior, vol. i., Lipsiae, 1869), and the standard lists of MSS are those contained in the *Textkritik des Neuen Testamentes* (2 vols., Leipzig, 1900, 1902) of C. R. Gregory, an American scholar domiciled in Germany. The new numbers which von Soden (*Die Schriften des Neuen Testaments*, Band i., Berlin, 1902) has given to the Greek MSS are added for the sake of completeness, but it is very doubtful whether they will gain wide currency. Capital letters are used to indicate MSS with uncial writing, which is never later than the 10th cent.; numbers, for those in minuscule writing (9th to 15th centuries and later).

I. GREEK MSS:—(a) *Uncials* :—

ℵ (= δ 2, von Soden), Codex Sinaiticus (of the 4th or 5th cent.), now in the Imperial Library, St. Petersburg, with the exception of a small portion, which is in the University Library, Leipzig, contains OT (with considerable losses), NT (complete), followed by Ep. Barnab. and the *Shepherd*. The MS, found by Tischendorf in the Convent of St. Catharine, Mt. Sinai, in 1844, consists of 346½ (NT 147½) leaves of fine parchment, measuring 48 × 37·8 cm., with four columns to the page and 48 lines to the column. The ink is now brownish ; the letters are not very large, and are painfully regular, without breathings or accents, the use of which is only sporadic till the 9th century. The hands of seven revisers, dating from the 4th (5th) to the 12th centuries, can be observed in the MS. This MS shares with B the honour of being considered the purest MS of the Gospels. Tischendorf has been charged more than once with having stolen this MS, but the charges are successfully refuted by Gregory.

A (= δ 4, von S.), Codex Alexandrinus, in London, British Museum, Reg. I. D. v.–viii. (the NT is in showcases). This MS is of the 5th cent., and consists of 773 leaves (NT 143 leaves) of parchment, measuring 32 × 26·3 cm., with 2 columns to the page and 49–51 lines to the column. It contains, with some losses, the whole Greek Bible. It was probably written in Egypt, and came in 1098 into the possession of the patriarch of Alexandria, from which place it gets its name. Cyril Lucar, patriarch of Constantinople, and former patriarch of Alexandria, sent it as a gift to Charles I. of England in 1628. About a century afterwards it was presented to the nation. A few lines at the beginning of each book are written in red. The following portions of the Gospels are lost: Mt 1¹–25⁶, Jn 6⁵⁰–8⁵². It is quite clear that Jn 7⁵³–8¹¹ never formed a part of the manuscript. A complete facsimile was published in 1878–1880.

B (= δ 1, von S.), Codex Vaticanus, Vat. Lib. MS Gr. 1209 (in showcases). The MS is of the 4th cent., and consists of 759 (NT 142) leaves of parchment, measuring 27 cm. square, with 3 columns to the page and 42 lines to the column. The parchment is very soft and fine. The uncial letters are small, simple, and written without breaks between the individual words ; the first hand wrote no breathings or accents, and punctuation is very rare. The MS is of uncertain origin, and, when complete, contained the whole of the Greek Bible with perhaps the exception of the Books of Maccabees and the Prayer of Manasses. No gaps occur in the Gospels. It has been twice revised, once by a corrector contemporary with the original scribe (called B²), and again by another of the 10th or 11th cent., who worked over the letters and often added accents and breathings. WH consider it our very best MS, and regard the combination Bℵ as practically infallible. A splendid facsimile of the NT part was published by Hœpli of Milan in 1904 (see the notice of it by Nestle in the *Theol. Literaturblatt* for 6th Jan. 1905), superseding the inferior photograph issued by Cozza-Luzi at Rome in 1889.

C (= δ 3, von S.), Codex Ephræmi rescriptus, Paris Bibl. Nat., gr. 9, a palimpsest of the 5th century. Contains, in present form, 209 leaves, written in single columns. The NT portion consists of 145 leaves, and contains parts of every book except 2 John and 2 Thessalonians. Edited by Tisch. (Leipzig, 1843 and 1845).

Dᵉᵛᵛ· ᵃᶜᵗ· (= δ 5, von S.), Codex Bezæ, in Cambridge University Library, Nn. 2, 41 (in a showcase in Cockerell's Building). This MS is of the 6th cent. (according to Burkitt, of the 4th), and is bilingual (Greek and Latin). It is on parchment,

26 cm. in height and 21·5 in breadth, and contains now 415 (406 + 9 added later) leaves, with one column to the page. When the book is open, the left side is Greek, the right side Latin. Originally it contained probably Mt., Jn., Lk., Mk. (the regular Western order of the Gospels), Apoc., 1, 2, 3 Jn., Acts (Dom Chapman in *Expositor*, 1905, ii. p. 46 ff.). Now the Gospels and Acts are almost complete, the Apocalypse and 1st and 2nd Jn. have disappeared, and of 3 Jn. there remain only a few verses in Latin. Many hands have been engaged in correcting the MS. It was probably written in Italy, or South France, where it was when Beza acquired it and gave it to the University of Cambridge in 1581. The MS is the only representative of the Western text in Greek, a form of text which was widespread already in the 2nd century. It contains, therefore, many original elements, which have been worked over at a very early date. In spite of this revision, it often agrees with the neutral MSS, ℵB. Scrivener published an accurate and handy edition of the MS at Cambridge (1864), which retains its use side by side with the gorgeous facsimile published by the Cambridge University Press in 1899.

N (= ε 19, von S.), Codex Purpureus Petropolitanus, incomplete and mutilated, the parts being distributed between St. Petersburg, Rome, Patmos, London, and Vienna. It is an uncial, probably of the 6th cent., measuring 32 by 26·5 cm. ; has 2 columns to the page, 16 lines to the column, and 227 leaves. The leaves are stained with purple, and the writing is silver, the Divine names being in gold. The MS is very like Σ both in text and external character. The only complete edition is that of H. S. Cronin in *TS*, vol. v. No. 4 (Cambridge, 1899). He considers N and Σ to be copies of the same lost original. The text is of a mixed character, representing a sort of transition stage between the purity of the older uncials and the corruption of the majority of cursives. While it sometimes supports the former, it also at times provides the earliest known authority for readings which are subsequently almost universal. For particulars see Cronin's valuable introduction.

Σ (= ε 18, von S.), Codex Purpureus Rossanensis, in the charge of the Archbp. of Rossano, S. Italy. An uncial of the 6th cent., probably later than its brother MS N, it is, like it, purple with silver writing. It measures 30·7 by 26 cm., has 2 columns to the page, 20 lines to the column, and comprises 188 leaves. It contains Matthew and Mark (the latter without 16¹⁴⁻ᵉⁿᵈ). Edited by von Gebhardt (*Die Evangelien des Matthäus und des Marcus aus dem cod. purp. Rossan.*, Leipzig, 1883). See under **N.** The credit of the discovery of this MS belongs to von Gebhardt and Harnack (1879). It contains eight pictures of Gospel scenes, the oldest known.

Ψ (= δ 6, von S.), Athos, Laura 172 (β 52), an uncial of the 8th or 9th cent., measuring 20·8 by 15 cm., has 31 lines to the page, and comprises 262 leaves. It contains the greater part of the NT, but lacks Mt., and Mk. down to 9⁵. The ending of Mk. is like that in L and T¹. After 16⁸ ἐφοβοῦντο γάρ, it proceeds as follows : πάντα δὲ τὰ παρηγγελμένα τοῖς περὶ τὸν Πέτρον συντόμωσ· ἐξήγγειλαν : Μετὰ δὲ ταῦτα, καὶ αὐτὸσ ἰησοῦς ἐφάνη ἀπὸ ἀνατολῆσ καὶ μέχρι δύσεωσ ἐξαπέστειλεν δι' αὐτῶν τὸ ἱερὸν καὶ ἄφθαρτον κήρυγμα τῆσ αἰωνίου σωτηρίασ ἀμήν : ἔστιν καὶ ταῦτα φερόμενα μετὰ τὸ ἐφοβοῦντο γὰρ :— Ἀναστὰς δὲ, κ.τ.λ., up to v.²⁰, and at the end Εὐαγγέλιον κατὰ Μᾶρκον. It is only in this Gospel that the text is of interest. The character of its readings is set forth in Lake's edition (*Studia Biblica et Ecclesiastica*, vol. v. (Oxford, 1903) pp. 94–122) [pp. 89–186 can be obtained separately].

Tˣ (= ε 02, von S.), Oxyrhynchus Papyri, vol. ii. No. 208. We mention this papyrus uncial fragment of the 3rd cent. (Jn $1^{23-31.\ 33-41}$ $20^{11-17.\ 19-25}$), because it is probably the oldest fragment of Gospel MS in existence.

(b) Minuscules :—

1 ($= \delta\ 50$, von S.), Basel University Library, A.N. iv. 2 (formerly B vi. 27), of the 12th (others say 10th) century. This MS was used for Erasmus' Gr. Test., the first published edition. It gives a good text, which is often in agreement with 118 ($= \epsilon\ 346$, von S.), 131 ($= \delta\ 467$, von S.), and 209 ($= \delta\ 457$, von S.). Lake has edited the four, taking **1** as the basis, and showing the variants in the others ('Codex 1 of the Gospels and its Allies' in *TS*, vol. vii. No. 3, Cambridge, 1902). He has also discussed with thorough-ness the relations between them. The reader will find his Introduction a valuable lesson in textual criticism. It is sufficient here to quote his conclusion with regard to the text in Mark, which escaped a good deal of the assimilating process which affected the texts of Matthew and Luke : '(1) *fam*^{1} in St. Mark seems to form part of a larger family of which the most certain members are *fam*^{13} 22, 28, 565, 700 ; (2) this larger family seems to represent a local text or local texts which were current in a comparatively limited region in the East ; (3) the only definite localities which there is any reason to suggest are Jerusalem and Sinai, and even for these the evidence is insufficient to justify confident assertion' (p. liv). The most noticeable features in the other Gospels are an element akin to ℵB and a Western element (cf. p. lv).

13 ($= \epsilon\ 368$, von S.), Paris, Bibl. Nat., gr. 50, of the 13th century. This MS is one of the group 13–69–124–346–543–788–826–828–983–ϵ 1053 (von S.)–ϵ 1054 (von S.), conveniently named by Lake *fam*^{13}. The group is also called the Ferrar group, because the relation between 13, 69, 124, and 346 was discovered by Ferrar of Dublin (*A Collation of Four Important Manuscripts of the Gospels*, by W. H. Ferrar and T. K. Abbott, Dublin, 1877). The studies of Rendel Harris (*On the Origin of the Ferrar Group*, Cambridge, 1893 ; *Further Researches into the History of the Ferrar Group*, London, 1900), Lake (*JThSt*, vol. i. [1899–1900] pp. 117–120), and von Soden have shed further light upon this group. The archetype appears to have been in Calabria or Sicily in the Middle Ages. Its most remarkable characteristics are the transposition of Jn 7^{53}–8^{11} to Lk 21^{38}, and Lk $24^{43f.}$ to Mt 26^{39} (on the first transposition see von Soden, *Die Schriften des Neuen Testaments*, i. (Berlin, 1902) p. 486 ff.). The importance of the group lies in the great support which it gives to the Western text.

II. SYRIAC MSS :—

(a) of the Old Syriac translation (Evangelion da-Mepharreshe, 'Gospel of the Separated Ones') :—

1. London, British Museum, Additional MSS, No. 14,451 (No. 119 in Wright's catalogue), and Berlin, Royal Library, Orient. Quart. No. 528. This MS, Codex Nitriensis Curetonianus (Burkitt's *C*), consists of 82½ leaves in the British Museum and 3 leaves in Berlin ; and came from the great Library of the Convent of St. Mary Deipara in the Nitrian Valley, west of Cairo. The greater portion of the MS reached England in 1842. In its original state it contained Mt., Mk., Jn., Lk. (in this unusual order). The portions still extant are Mt 1^1–8^{22} 10^{32}–23^{25}, Mk 16^{17-20}, Jn 1^{1-42} 3^5–8^{19} $14^{10-12.\ 15-19.\ 21-24.\ 26-29}$, Lk 2^{48}–3^{16} 7^{33}–16^{12} 17^1–24^{44}. The early part of the 5th cent. is the latest possible date for it. Each page has two columns, each with lines varying from 22 to 26. Each leaf measures 30 by 24 cm. The first edition of this MS is that of Cureton (London, 1858) supplemented by Rödiger (Berlin, 1872), but the definitive edition is that of F. C. Burkitt, who has edited this MS and the following together, the

only representatives of the Old Syriac version, with an English translation, copious Introduction and Notes (*Evangelion da-Mepharreshe*, etc., 2 vols., Cambridge, 1904). From this work the details here are taken. A photograph of a page of *C* is in vol. ii. opposite p. 7, also p. 38 two pages ; also in Kenyon's *Our Bible and the Ancient MSS*, facing p. 155.

2. Sinai, Monastery of St. Catharine ; Syr. 30, Codex Palimpsestus Sinaiticus (Burkitt's *S*). The MS was discovered by Mrs. Lewis and Mrs. Gibson, of Cambridge, in 1892, and has been since studied repeatedly by Mrs. Lewis and other scholars. The MS consists of 182 leaves of vellum (one leaf was stolen in 1902, but afterwards restored ; see *Exp. Times*, xiii. 405 ; xvii. 396). The upper writing is of the 8th cent., and consists of Lives of Saints. In its original form the MS had 166 leaves, containing the four Gospels in the usual order. Its date is early 5th, perhaps 4th century. Each page contains 2 columns, with from 29 to 21 lines each, and measures 21·9 by 15·8 cm. The Gospels are nearly complete. Of the two MSS this must be regarded as the better representative of the original translation. Complete photographs of it are in Cambridge University Library ; Westminster College, Cambridge ; Rylands' Library, Manchester : photos of separate pages in Burkitt, vol. ii. pp. 28, 257, and elsewhere.

The *Evangelion da-Mepharreshe* was so called to distinguish it from Tatian's *Diatessaron* or Harmony, in which form the Gospels were regularly read in the Syrian Church at first. This Church had its centre at Edessa near the Euphrates, and its language must not be identified with the Aramaic our Lord spoke. The value of the Old Syriac Version consists in the fact that it reproduces the Greek text current in Antioch at the end of the 2nd cent., with a certain amount of contamination from the use of the *Diatessaron*, which is in origin Italian. It is of the first authority for the constitution of the text of the Greek Gospels. For all problems connected with it the reader is referred to Burkitt's second volume.

(b) of the Peshiṭta ('simple') translation :—

2. Earl of Crawford's MS 1, now Rylands' Library, Manchester, of the 6th cent. (Gwilliam, No. 11).

13. London, British Museum, Addit. MSS 14,470, of the 5th or 6th cent. (Gwilliam, No. 17).

15. London, British Museum, Addit. MSS 14,453, of the 5th or 6th cent. (Gwilliam, No. 14).

22. London, British Museum, Addit. MSS 12,140, of the 6th cent. (Gwilliam, 31).

There are many other codices, complete or incomplete, of equal antiquity, in other libraries. See Gwilliam's list of 42 MSS in the *Tetraeuangelium Sanctum* by Pusey and Gwilliam (Oxonii, 1901), which is the best edition of the Peshiṭta, and is provided with a literal Latin translation. As to the date of the Peshiṭta itself, Burkitt's view that it was prepared by Rabbula, bp. of Edessa from 411 to 435 A.D., has gained wide acceptance. He regards it as 'a revision of the *Evangelion da-Mepharreshe*, undertaken mainly with the object of conforming the translation more closely to the Greek text as read at Antioch early in the 5th century' (*Evangelion da-Mepharreshe*, vol. ii. p. 5).

(c) of the Palestinian or Jerusalem translation :—

1. Rome, Vaticanus Syr. 19 (formerly 11), of the year 1030 (Codex A, Lewis-Gibson).

6. Sinai, Monastery of St. Catharine, of the year 1104 (Codex B, Lewis-Gibson).

7. Sinai, Monastery of St. Catharine, of the year 1118 (Codex C, Lewis-Gibson).

Edited by Mrs. Lewis and Mrs. Gibson in the *Palestinian Syriac Lectionary of the Gospels* (London, 1899). This version is perhaps more closely related to the Old Syriac than to the Peshiṭta, and may be a revision of the former.

(d) of the Philoxenian-Harklean translation :—

1. Belonging to the Syrian Protestant College in Beirut, but lent to the Union Theological Seminary of New York. Of the 9th cent., and somewhat defective.

22. Florence, Laur. i. 40 (Assem. 3). Of date 757.

25. Rome, Vat. Syr. 266. Of the 7th century.

26. Rome, Vat. Syr. 267. Of the 8th century.

This, the youngest of the Syrian versions, is a revision by Thomas of Harkel (Heraclea) in the first half of the 7th cent. of an earlier version made at the instance of Philoxenus, Monophysite bp. of Hierapolis (Mabog) in the early 6th century. The earlier translation was perhaps made from the Peshiṭta by reference to the 'corrected' form of the Greek text, and Thomas found in Egypt older Greek MSS, which had escaped the enthusiasm of the destroyers, who favoured the 'corrected' text, and inserted some readings from them, adding others in the margin.

III. EGYPTIAN (COPTIC) MSS:—
(a) of the Bohairic translation :—

Complete manuscripts are all of late date, none being earlier apparently than the 12th century. On all questions connected with this translation and its MSS, see *The Coptic Version of the New Testament in the Northern Dialect* [ed. G. Horner], 4 vols. (Oxford, 1898–1905).

1. Oxford, Bodleian Library, Huntington, 17,* Horner's A, printed entire by him as the basis of his edition. This MS was written in 1174, and contains the Gospels complete, both in Bohairic and Arabic. It is on paper, contains 457 (+5) leaves, and 2 columns to the page, with 20 lines each. It measures 34·5 by 26 cm. The MS has a number of omissions : see the valuable tables of omissions in the chief Bohairic MSS in Horner's edition, vol. i. p. cxxvi ff.

21. Paris, Bibl. Nat., copt. 16, Horner's C. The MS was written in 1196, and contains the Gospels almost complete, both in Bohairic and Arabic. It is on paper, contains 369 (+2) leaves, and 2 columns to the page, with 26 lines each. It measures 28·5 by 21 cm. The text is perfect, with the exception of a small lacuna, Jn 16^{6-18}.

33. Paris, Institut Catholique, Horner's H. This MS was written in 1250, and contains the Gospels complete, both in Bohairic and Arabic. It is on paper, contains 235 (+2) leaves, and 2 columns to the page, with 33 lines each. It measures 25 by 17·5 cm., and contains some beautiful pictures.

(b) of the Sahidic translation :—
Of this there exists only a considerable quantity of short fragments (Gregory gives 91). Some are as old as the 5th century. One is still older (No. 48 Rome, Propag. 65).

(c) of the Fayyum translation :—
Gregory gives fragments of 5 Gospel MSS only, one (No. 2), in the possession of Flinders Petrie, of the 4th century. Of (*b*) and (*c*) there is as yet neither a comprehensive edition nor a complete study. Further fragments of both are certain to be discovered.

The Ethiopic, Armenian, Georgian, Persian, and Arabic translations may be here passed over.

IV. LATIN MSS :—
(a) of the pre-Vulgate (otherwise called 'Old Latin,' or 'Itala') translation(s) :—
a: Vercelli, Cathedral. This MS is of the 4th cent., measures 25·5 by 16 cm., has 2 columns to the page, and 24 lines to the column. The order of the Gospels is Mt., Jn., Lk., Mk., the regular Old Latin order. Much is wanting in Mt 20–27 ; Jn. is slightly defective ; in Lk. much of chs. 1. 11 and 12 has disappeared ; in Mk. chs. 1. 4. 5. 15. 16 have suffered greatly ; a second but ancient hand has supplied Mk 16^{7-20}. The text is good, and was, according to tradition, copied by the famous bishop Eusebius of Vercelli, martyred in 371. The book has suffered greatly from neglect and bad treatment. Editions by G. A. Irico (*Sacrosanctus Evangeliorum Codex S. Eusebii Magni*, Milan, 1748), J. Bianchini (*Evangeliarium Quadruplex*, Rome, 1749 ; very accurately reprinted in Migne's *Patrologia Latina*, vol. xii.), and J. Belsheim (*Codex Vercellensis*, Christiania, 1894).

b: Verona, Cathedral Library (Biblioteca Capitolare). The MS is of the early part of the 5th cent. (or of the end of the 4th), and is written in silver.

* Gregory wrongly 'Huntingdon 11.'

The following parts are wanting : Mt 1^{1-11} 15^{12-23} 23^{18-27}, Jn $7^{44-8^{12}}$, Lk $19^{26-21^{29}}$, Mk 13^{9-19} $13^{24-16^{20}}$. Edited by Bianchini (see under **a**) and by J. Belsheim (*Codex Veronensis Quattuor Euangelia*, Prag, 1904). It was probably a MS like this which was the chief basis of Jerome's revision known as the Vulgate. It is perhaps the best representative of the European Latin versions of the 4th century. There is a photograph of one page in *Monumenta Palæographica Sacra* (Turin, 1899).

c: Paris, Bibl. Nat. 254 (Colb. 4051), of the 12th century. Edited by P. Sabatier (*Bibliorum Sacrorum Latinæ Versiones Antiquæ*, vol. iii., Paris, 1751 ; there is also an edition with 'Reims' on the title-page), and by J. Belsheim (*Codex Colbertinus Parisiensis*, Christiania, 1888). The work of P. Sabatier is still unsuperseded as the most complete repertory of the readings of the Old Latin Bible.

d : This symbol indicates the Latin side of Codex Bezæ (D).

e: Palatinus ; all that is left is in Vienna (Kais. Lat. 1185) except one leaf, which is in the Library of Trinity College, Dublin (N. 4, 18). The MS is of the 5th cent., and is, with **k** (see below), representative of a form of text used in the Roman province of Africa (corresponding to modern Tunis). It is very defective, containing about half of Mt., nearly the whole of Jn. and Lk., and about half of Mark. A copy of the MS made before its present mutilation exists in the Vallicellian Library, Rome, as U. 66. The Vienna part was edited by Tischendorf (*Evangelium Palatinum*, Leipzig, 1847), the Dublin leaf by T. K. Abbott (*Par Palimpsestorum Dublinensium*, etc., London, 1880) ; reports on the copy in the Vallicellian Library were published by H. Linke (*Sitzungsberichte der Königl. bayer. Akad. der Wissenschaften* [Phil - Philolog. und Hist. Classe], Munich, 1893, Heft 2, pp. 281–287). See also Belsheim (*Evangelium Palatinum*, Christiania, 1896), and *Old-Latin Biblical Texts*, vol. ii. (Oxford, 1886), pp. lxvii–lxxxv, by W. Sanday.

f: Brixianus ; in the Capitular Library of Brescia. It is of the 6th cent., and is written in silver. It lacks the last quarter or so of Mark. It was edited by Bianchini (see under **a**), and is also printed under the Vulgate in Wordsworth and White's edition (Oxford, 1889–1898), as in the opinion of these editors and Hort the type of text which Jerome used as the basis of his revision. The other view with regard to it, namely, that of Burkitt, is that it is an Old Latin text deeply contaminated with the Vulgate (see *JThSt*, i. [1899] pp. 129–134). With Burkitt's view the present writer agrees. If it be correct (see under **q**), the result is the disappearance of Hort's 'Italian' class altogether.

ff¹: St. Petersburg, Imperial Library, formerly Corbeiensis 21 (10th cent.) : Matthew.

ff²: Paris, Bibl. Nat. 17225, formerly Corbeiensis 195. It is of the 5th cent. (C. H. Turner in *JThSt*, vol. vi. [1904–1905] p. 257), not the 7th (Tischendorf, Gregory, and the Paris authorities). The following parts of the four Gospels are wanting : Mt $1^{1-11^{16}}$, Lk $9^{48-10^{20.\ 21}}$ $11^{45-12^{6.\ 7}}$, Jn 17^{15-18^9} 20^{22-21^8}. Published reports of this MS are incomplete and inexact. An exact edition is expected from Rev. E. S. Buchanan, who has made a very careful study of the MS, and has already published a translation of its text of some Gospels (*e.g. The Latin Gospels in the Second Century*, Part I. 'S. John,' Sevenoaks [1904]), and prolegomena (*JThSt* vii. 99 ff.).

g¹: Paris, Bibl. Nat. 11553, formerly Sangermanensis 15, of the 8th cent., edited by the Bishop of Salisbury (Dr. John Wordsworth) in *Old-Latin Biblical Texts*, No. I. (Oxford, 1883).

k: Turin, Nat. G. vii. 15 (formerly of the Irish monastery of Bobbio). This, perhaps the most precious of all Old Latin MSS, is of the 4th

(Burkitt) or 5th cent., and represents the text habitually used by St. Cyprian in the early 3rd century. The MS measures 18·7 by 16·7 cm., and consists now of 96 leaves. It contains Mk 8⁸⁻¹¹· ¹⁴⁻¹⁶ 8¹⁹⁻¹⁶⁸, Mt 1¹⁻³¹⁰ 4²⁻¹⁴¹⁷ 15²⁰⁻³⁶. The only reliable edition is that of Wordsworth, Sanday, and White (*Old-Latin Biblical Texts*, No. II., Oxford, 1886), which is enriched by discussions of the greatest value for the study of all Biblical texts. Side by side with this edition should be consulted the article of Turner and Burkitt, 'A Re-Collation of Codex k of the Old-Latin Gospels' (*JThSt*, vol. v. [1903–1904] pp. 88–107).

m: Rome, Sessorianus lviii. This MS, of the 8th or 9th cent., contains the so-called *Speculum*, falsely attributed to St. Augustine, a series of extracts from nearly all the books of the NT. The compilation appears to be of Spanish origin, as the text closely resembles that used by the Spanish heretic Priscillian. Edited by F. Weihrich in the *Corpus Scriptorum Ecclesiasticorum Latinorum*, vol. xii. (Vienna, 1887).

q: Munich, Lat. 6224, formerly of Freising. It is of the 6th cent., and contains the Gospels, except Mt 3¹⁵⁻⁴²⁵ 5²⁵⁻⁶⁴ 6²⁸⁻⁷⁸, Jn 10¹¹⁻¹²³⁹, Lk 23²²⁻³⁶ 24¹¹⁻³⁹, Mk 1⁷⁻²² 15⁵⁻³⁶. This, like **f**, belongs to Hort's 'Italian' class, and stands or falls with **f** (see above). Edited by H. J. White as *Old-Latin Biblical Texts*, No. III. (Oxford, 1888).

(*b*) *of the Vulgate revision* (made by St. Jerome in 383), the two best MSS out of thousands which exist are :—

am: in the Laurentian Library, at Florence, formerly in the monastery of Monte Amiata, No. 1. This MS was written about the year 700 in the North of England, probably by an Italian scribe, and was taken by Ceolfrid, the abbot of Jarrow, to the Continent as a present to the Pope in the year 716. It measures 50 by 34 by 20 cm. (without the cover), and comprises 1029 leaves, with 2 columns to the leaf, and 43 or 44 lines to the column. It contains the whole Bible. The NT was published by Tischendorf (Leipzig, 1850, and again 1854), but not with perfect exactness. (See *Nouum Testamentum Domini Nostri Iesu Christi Latine*, rec. Wordsworth and White, Pars Prior, Oxonii, 1889–1898, p. xi; and *Studia Biblica et Ecclesiastica*, vol. ii., Oxford, 1890, pp. 273–324). Wordsworth and White's A.

fuld: in the library of Fulda, Prussia. The MS was written about the year 540 at the wish of Victor, bishop of Capua. The Gospels are written in the form of a harmony. Edited by E. Ranke (*Codex Fuldensis*, Marburg and Leipzig, 1868), with specimens of the handwriting. (See *Nov. Test. etc. Latine*, rec. Wordsworth and White, Pars Prior, p. xii). Wordsworth and White's F.

V. GOTHIC MSS :—

1. Upsala University, the 'Codex Argenteus.' The MS is of the 6th cent., and now consists of 187 leaves, which are stained with purple and bear silver writing. The contents are fragments of Mt., Jn., Lk., Mark. (The translation was made by Ulfilas (Wulfila) in the 4th cent., and all surviving fragments are collected in Gabelentz and Loebe's *Ulfilas* (Altenburg and Leipzig, 1836–1843).

LITERATURE.—Most of the important literature has already been indicated in the course of the article. Reference should also be made to *The NT in the Original Greek* : The Text revised by Westcott and Hort, vol. ii. Introduction and Appendix (London, 1881 and 1896); Kenyon, *Handbook to the Textual Criticism of the NT* (London, 1901); Nestle, *Introduction to the Textual Criticism of the Greek NT* (London, 1901); Hammond, *Outlines of Textual Criticism applied to the NT* (Oxford, 1902).

ALEX. SOUTER.

MARK.—1. Name and identity.—One, two, and even three Marks have been discovered in the NT. But the identity of the 'John Mark' of Acts with the 'Mark' of St. Paul's Epistles is clearly proved by Col 4¹⁰, where he is called the cousin of Barnabas, and his identity with the 'Mark' of 1 Peter is clearly proved by Ac 12¹². These two passages show that in all the nine places where the name occurs (Ac 12¹². ²⁵ 13⁵. ¹³ 15³⁶ff., Col 4¹⁰, 2 Ti 4¹¹, Philem ²⁴, 1 P 5¹³) the same person is referred to. The curious notion has widely prevailed that the 'young man' of Mk 14⁵¹· ⁵² was the Evangelist himself, but there is no evidence whatever in its support. Indeed, the words of Papias, 'he neither heard the Lord, nor accompanied Him,' would seem to exclude this and other similar suggestions. In accordance with a well-known custom (cf. 'Jesus Justus,' Col 4¹¹), Mark had both a Hebrew and a Latin name, and the Roman *prænomen* Marcus is of frequent occurrence. From Ac 12¹¹ff· we gather that Mark occupied a position of some prominence socially in the Church at Jerusalem. His mother's house was evidently a well-known rendezvous for believers. When St. Peter is released from prison, he turns naturally to this place, and on his arrival finds a company of Christians at worship. Several slight indications in the description suggest the house of a person of means (the porch, the slave-girl, the large upper room). The only other information we possess as to Mark's family history is his connexion with Barnabas, who seems to have been a man of standing in the Christian community.

2. Relations with Paul and Barnabas.—When Paul and Barnabas returned to Antioch from Jerusalem, whither they had gone with the offering for the poor, they took Mark with them as assistant, perhaps owing to his kinship with Barnabas (Ac 12²⁵). A little later, he again accompanies them on their first missionary journey as their 'attendant' (13⁵). This word (ὑπηρέτης) emphasizes his secondary position and function. Probably his work was of the nature of business management. He had to look after such matters as lodging, routes, conveyance, and the like. At Perga, Mark withdrew from the mission, for what reason is not stated. That Paul deeply resented his conduct is shown by the refusal to employ his services on a later occasion. It has been assumed that he shirked the dangers of the enterprise, or that he tired of the work. But Ramsay (*Ch. in Rom. Emp.* p. 61 f.) has taken a more favourable view of his conduct. He holds that there was a change of plan at this point, that the journey into the interior was not in the original arrangement, and that Mark might consider this a good ground for refusing to go on. He had not the same necessity laid upon him as those who had been solemnly designated by the Spirit for this service. He was an 'extra hand,' taken on for casual labour. Barnabas, at any rate, judged Mark's conduct more leniently than Paul, and later on Paul himself modified his attitude. At the outset of the second missionary journey, however, his objection to Mark's co-operation was so strong that it led to a separation between himself and Barnabas (Ac 15³⁶ff·). The latter took Mark with him on a mission to Cyprus, and we hear no more of him in the Book of Acts. When Mark next appears (Col. and Philem.), it is as the 'fellow-labourer' of Paul, who had by this time become completely reconciled to him, and had found him a comfort (παρηγορία, Col 4¹¹) in his imprisonment. Paul speaks in Col 4¹⁰ of a projected visit of Mark to the Colossian Church, and urges his friends there to receive him kindly, 'if he comes' to them. It is probable, therefore, that Mark's previous desertion had created an unfavourable impression over a wide area. Harnack thinks the visit was paid, and that, when St. Paul wrote to Timothy to bring Mark with him (2 Ti 4¹¹), Timothy was to pick him up at Colossæ on his way from Ephesus. Paul had evidently missed the attentions which Mark had been able to give.

3. Relations with Peter.—St. Peter refers to Mark in his First Epistle (1 P 5[13]) as 'my son.' This may imply only a peculiarly close intimacy, but more probably it means that Mark had been converted through Peter's influence. Peter was evidently a frequent visitor at Mark's home (Ac 12), and the friendship had begun there which afterwards became so deep and fruitful. St. Peter's reference in his letter shows also that at this date Mark was with him at 'Babylon,' which most writers now consider to mean Rome. From the familiar words of Papias (see MARK [GOSPEL ACC. TO], ii. 1) we learn that Mark had become the 'interpreter' of Peter, and that Mark 'accompanied' or 'attended' him. Swete thinks he acted as Peter's dragoman, and translated the Apostle's words for his audiences. Peter, it is supposed, would not be fluent in Greek. It is not easy to fit in this ministry to Peter in Rome with the ministry to Paul. Swete thinks it occurred after Paul's death; but it is at least doubtful whether Peter survived Paul. Harnack and Lightfoot may be quoted to the contrary. It is by no means impossible, of course, that Mark may have 'attended' Peter in Rome, and transferred his services to Paul. It would be much simpler, however, to suppose that the ministry was exercised much earlier, and in the real, not the spiritual, Babylon. In any case, Mark's association with Peter was a fruitful one, as it resulted in the composition of the Second Gospel. In this matter Mark seems to have been little more than an amanuensis. According to Papias, the Gospel is really Peter's, and Mark was simply his 'interpreter' on this as on other occasions.

4. Character and position in the Apostolic history.—Mark was thus associated with three notable men in turn, and always in the same subordinate capacity. Jülicher calls him 'Apostelschüler.' Swete thinks this humble position decidedly implied in the terms used of him in Acts and the Epistles. The συνπαραλαβόντες of Ac 12[25] suggests an assistant 'of inferior rank.' The ὑπηρέτης of 13[5] indicates personal and not spiritual service. Ramsay (*St. Paul the Traveller*, p. 71) holds that Mark's subordinate character is displayed by the 'haphazard reference' to him in Ac 13[5]. The same conclusion may be drawn from St. Paul's language in 2 Ti 4[11] ('he is useful to me εἰς διακονίαν'). His services to the Apostle in prison probably concerned his comfort and convenience. If, again, Mark was Peter's dragoman, he exercised very much the same 'ministry' for Paul also. We gather, then, from these references, that Mark was a person with a large capacity for being useful in practical matters, but without any special spiritual gifts, and probably without any very great force of character. This opinion may be regarded as receiving confirmation from his conduct at Perga, on the most charitable view of that incident. He does not appear to have been fitted for heroic enterprise, or for a separate responsibility, or for spiritual functions. It is only fair to say, however, that a more favourable opinion has been expressed by writers like Westcott (*Introd. to Study of Gospels*) and Jülicher (in *PRE*[3]). Jülicher points out that St. Paul ultimately came round to the lenient judgment of Barnabas, that Mark never lost his missionary zeal, and also that he remained unaffected by the prevalent party spirit, serving both St. Paul and St. Peter with equal loyalty.

5. Traditions.—Tradition has been busy with Mark's name. The most widely spread is that which assigns to him a mission in Egypt, and the evangelization of Alexandria. This mission is re-

garded as occupying the gap between the history in Acts and the later ministry to the Apostles. It was also widely believed that he died at Alexandria, receiving (according to some versions) the crown of martyrdom. These traditions cannot be traced back further than a hundred years after the supposed events. One curious fact is preserved in some of the Western traditions. Mark is said to have been κολοβοδάκτυλος, which means either mutilated or stunted in one or more of his fingers. Explanations of this deformity have been offered which possess no probability. But the reminiscence itself may quite possibly preserve a genuine fact; and it is not impossible that this defect may have had some influence in determining the possibilities of Mark's career.

LITERATURE.—The best accounts of Mark are given by Swete (*Gospel acc. to St. Mark*, 1898) and Lindsay ('St. Mark' in T. & T. Clark's *Handbook* series) in their introductions. The following may also be consulted : Harnack, art. 'Mark' in *EBr* (esp. for its good account of the traditions concerning the Evangelist); Jülicher, art. 'Marcus' in *PRE*[3]; Morison and Salmond in introd. to their Comm. on this Gospel.

FREDERICK J. RAE.

MARK, GOSPEL ACCORDING TO.—

i. THE PROBLEMS TO BE DISCUSSED.—No book of the NT has experienced such a change in public estimation as the Second Gospel. Formerly regarded as comparatively unimportant and receiving little attention from commentators, who in effect re-echoed Augustine's opinion that it was but an abbreviation of the First Gospel, it has of late years been more carefully studied, and has received a juster appreciation. It has now been recognized as a book of supreme importance, as giving us the narrative of the life of Christ in a most primitive form, and as being not improbably the foundation, if not directly at least indirectly, of all the Gospels. It will be necessary, then, in this article first to investigate the statements about its composition in the earlier Fathers and their use of it, and then to examine the Gospel itself, to see what picture it gives of our Lord's Person and work, and what relation it bears to the other Synoptic Gospels. We shall then be able to come to a conclusion about questions of date, authorship, and place of writing, of the original language, and of the integrity of the Gospel. Finally, we will consider the question of an 'Ur-Marcus,' that is, if the Gospel in our hands is the original work of St. Mark.

It will be convenient here to state the results arrived at in this article with regard to some points. The present writer thinks it most probable that the Second Gospel as we have it, or at any rate with the very slightest differences, was in the hands of all the other Evangelists when they wrote ; and that the latter freely used the material before them, altering it, or adding to it, or omitting parts of it, as they thought right when following other guides. The theory put forward by Alford (*Prolegomena to his Greek Testament*, i. 2) and other holders of the 'oral hypothesis,' that the later writers would not have so treated a book which they regarded as inspired or even as authoritative, does not greatly commend itself, as it appears to interpret the feeling of the Christians of the 1st cent. by those of a later age.—The very style of Mk., with its roughness and inelegances, is of great value, and still more is its description of the Saviour in words which were often in after times misunderstood, of the utmost importance as showing a very early record. For these and other reasons a date at least before the Fall of Jerusalem seems to be probable. Further, it is considered likely that the Gospel was written in Greek, and primarily for Roman readers, the last twelve verses being an appendix, not composed as an ending to the Gospel, but having once had an independent existence, and being added later to the Gospel to supply a lost leaf.

ii. THE SECOND GOSPEL IN THE EARLY CHURCH. —1. **Statements as to its composition.**—We will first consider those passages of early writers which may be thought to throw light on the composition of Mk., before discussing those which only quote or refer to it ; later (§ vii.) we will consider whether the Gospel known to these writers is the same as our Mark.

The first passage which *may* refer to Mk. is St. Luke's prologue. This shows that some who were not from the beginning eye-witnesses and ministers of the word had already written narratives of the Gospel history, and by implication avers (Lk 1³) that these narratives were incomplete in not beginning 'from the first' (ἄνωθεν) ; also we perhaps gather that they were not in St. Luke's judgment in good chronological order (καθεξῆς, cf. ἀκριβῶς just before). Internal evidence leads us to think that not improbably St. Luke knew Mk. (see below, § iii.), and, if so, we may have here the first criticism on the Second Gospel ; it has some striking resemblances to Papias' account, for which we are indebted to Eusebius (*HE* iii. 39). Eusebius says :

Ἀναγκαίως νῦν προσθήσομεν ταῖς προεκτεθείσαις αὐτοῦ [sc. τοῦ Παπίου] φωναῖς παράδοσιν, ἣν περὶ Μάρκου τοῦ τὸ εὐαγγέλιον γεγραφότος ἐκτίθειται διὰ τούτων. 'Καὶ τοῦτο ὁ πρεσβύτερος ἔλεγε' Μάρκος μὲν ἑρμηνευτὴς Πέτρου γενόμενος, ὅσα ἐμνημόνευσεν, ἀκριβῶς ἔγραψεν, οὐ μέντοι τάξει, τὰ ὑπὸ τοῦ Χριστοῦ ἢ λεχθέντα ἢ πραχθέντα. οὔτε γὰρ ἤκουσε τοῦ Κυρίου, οὔτε παρηκολούθησεν αὐτῷ, ὕστερον δὲ, ὡς ἔφην, Πέτρῳ, ὃς πρὸς τὰς χρείας ἐποιεῖτο τὰς διδασκαλίας, ἀλλ' οὐχ ὥσπερ σύνταξιν τῶν κυριακῶν ποιούμενος λογίων [v.l. λόγων], ὥστε οὐδὲν ἥμαρτε Μάρκος, οὕτως ἔνια γράψας ὡς ἀπεμνημόνευσεν. ἑνὸς γὰρ ἐποιήσατο πρόνοιαν, τοῦ μηδὲν ὧν ἤκουσε παραλιπεῖν ἢ ψεύσασθαί τι ἐν αὐτοῖς.' Ταῦτα μὲν οὖν ἱστόρηται τῷ Παπίᾳ περὶ τοῦ Μάρκου. Lightfoot's translation (*Apost. Fathers*, compend. ed. p. 529) is here appended, and some points where Schmiedel (*Encyc. Bibl. s.v.* 'Gospels') differs from him are noted : 'For our present purpose we will merely add to his [Papias'] words which have been quoted above, a tradition which has been set forth through these sources concerning Mark who wrote the Gospel : "And the Elder said this also : Mark, having become the interpreter of Peter, wrote down accurately everything that he remembered [Schmiedel : 'mentioned'], without, however, recording in order what was either said or done by Christ. For neither did he hear the Lord, nor did he follow Him ; but afterwards, as I said, (attended) Peter, who adapted his instructions to the needs (of his hearers), but had no design of giving a connected account of the Lord's oracles [*v.l.* 'words']. So then Mark made no mistake [Schm. 'committed no fault' ; but see Lightfoot's *Essays on Sup. Rel.* pp. 8, 163], while he thus wrote down some things as he remembered them [Schm. 'repeated them exactly from memory '], for he made it his one care not to omit anything that he heard, or to set down any false statement therein." Such, then, is the account given by Papias concerning Mark.'

Here Papias vindicates Mark from inaccuracy, and from errors of omission, as far as his knowledge went, but finds fault with his chronological

order, which was due to his being dependent only on Peter's oral teaching. If this is a correct interpretation of Papias, which account of the Gospel story did he prefer ? Lightfoot (*Essays on Supernatural Religion*, pp. 165, 205 f.) thinks John, Salmon (*Introd.* Lect. vii.) thinks Luke ; while Schmiedel, in a not very convincing argument, thinks that Papias did not recognize Jn. and Lk. as being of equal authority with Mt. and Mk. (*Encyc. Bibl.* ii. 1813 ; see, further, § vii. below). Schmiedel takes no account of Lightfoot's essay 'On the Silence of Eusebius' (*Sup. Rel.* ii.). However this may be, Papias describes the Second Gospel as being limited to Peter's reminiscences, the writer being the 'interpreter' of that Apostle. This phrase may mean (Zahn, *Einleit.* ii. 209, 218) that Mark, being Peter's scholar, made Peter's teaching widely known through his written Gospel, or (Swete, *St. Mark*, p. xxiv) that he was the secretary or dragoman who translated Peter's words into a foreign tongue during the Apostle's lifetime. Papias does not call the work of Mark a 'gospel,' and the word εὐαγγέλιον is not undoubtedly found in the sense of the record of good tidings before Justin (*Apol.* i. 66, see below), though some find this sense in Ignatius, *Philad.* 5, 8, and in the *Didache* 8, 11, 15. In these places, however, it is probably not the written word that is referred to. [For a complete discussion of the Papias fragment see Lightfoot, *Ess. on Sup. Rel.* v., vi., and Sanday, *Gosp. in Second Cent.* v. 2].

Justin Martyr (*Dial.* 106) says that Christ changed Simon's name to Peter, and that this is written 'in his memoirs' (ἐν τοῖς ἀπομνημονεύμασιν αὐτοῦ), and also that He changed the name of the sons of Zebedee to 'Boanerges, which is Sons of Thunder.' But these last words actually occur only in Mk 3¹⁷, where we read of both names, Peter and Boanerges, together, and in no other Gospel. We may probably dismiss the idea that αὐτοῦ refers to Christ, as if Justin meant 'Christ's memoirs,' and conclude that Justin is speaking of a Petrine Gospel. Harnack (*Bruchstücke d. Ev. . . . d. Petrus*, p. 37) proposes to find this in the apocryphal Akhmîm Fragment which goes by St. Peter's name, and Sanday (*Inspiration* ² [Bampton Lectures], p. 310) agrees that Justin used pseudo-Peter. But as there is no other reason to suppose that this apocryphal Gospel ever contained the passage in question,—the fragment lately discovered beginning in the middle of the story of the Passion, —and as Justin elsewhere probably refers to our Second Gospel (see below), it is more reasonable to suppose with Swete (*Gospel of St. Peter*, p. xxxiii), Salmond (Hastings, *DB* iii. 256), and Stanton (*JThSt* ii. 6, and *Gospels as Hist. Doc.* p. 93 ff.) that he refers to it here. If so, we have another authority for regarding St. Peter as a chief source of Mark. In considering the question whether Justin refers to Mk. or to the apocryphal Gospel, we must note that while some points of contact are found between pseudo-Peter and Justin, there are also some considerable differences (see esp. Stanton, *loc. cit.*), and that if one borrowed from the other, it is as likely that pseudo-Peter is the borrower as Justin.—The Evangelic narratives are in Justin commonly called 'memoirs'—*e.g. Apol.* i. 66, 'the memoirs composed by them [the Apostles] which are called Gospels.' From *Dial.* 103 it appears that he included in the term some not composed by the Apostles themselves but by their followers. He speaks of 'the memoirs drawn up by the Apostles and by those who followed them,' and in this context recalls the (Lukan ?) account of the Agony and the drops of blood.

Tatian, Justin's pupil, affords evidence that Mk. was received in his time (*c.* 170 A.D.) as one of the four Gospel narratives pre-eminently above, and on a different platform from, all others. His *Diatessaron* is now known to be a harmony of our four Gospels, and probably it was not the first of its kind.

Irenæus is the first explicitly to expound the doctrine of the necessity of a fourfold Gospel (ἔδωκεν ἡμῖν τετράμορφον τὸ εὐαγγέλιον, iii. 11. 8). As the world has four quarters, and as the Church is spread over the whole world, and as the pillar and ground of the Church is the Gospel and the Spirit of life, so it is right that there should be four Gospels. Irenæus finds other equally fanciful reasons for a fourfold Gospel, and identifies our Evangelists with the fourfold appearance of the cherubim, St. Mark being the eagle (see § iii. **1** below). This reasoning, however erroneous, shows that our four Gospels had a position entirely by themselves in Irenæus' estimation; and Dr. Taylor conjectures that he borrowed the idea from Hermas (*Witness of Hermas*, § 1). In an earlier passage (iii. 1. 1) Irenæus says that Mark was Peter's disciple and interpreter (ἑρμηνευτής, as Papias), and that he handed on to us in writing the things preached by Peter, after the departure of Peter and Paul. In iii. 10. 6 (where the Greek is wanting), Irenæus calls Mark 'interpres et sectator Petri.'

Tertullian (*adv. Marc.* iv. 5, Migne, *P. L.* ii. 396) gives similar witness ('. . . licet et Marcus quod edidit, Petri affirmetur, cujus interpres Marcus').

The Muratorian fragment (*c.* A.D. 170? or perhaps a little later) begins in the middle of a sentence thus: '. . . quibus tamen interfuit, et ita posuit. Tertium Evangelii librum secundum Lucan . . . Quarti evangeliorum Johannes ex discipulis. . . .' Thus the writer had been speaking of *two* Gospels, which were neither Luke nor John. It is generally recognized that the opening words of the fragment refer to Mk. rather than to Mt., and that the latter had come first, as in Irenæus; but there is some difference of opinion as to their meaning. Swete, Lightfoot, and Chase interpret them to mean that Mark was present at *some* discourses of Peter; he reported Peter's teaching as far as he had the opportunity. The first word 'quibus' may be the second half of 'aliquibus' *some*; Chase (Hastings' *DB* iii. 24) takes 'quibus tamen' as the equivalent of an original οἷς δέ—for the fragment is a Latin translation from Greek. Zahn (*Einleit.* ii. 200 f.) thinks that the author of the fragment had quoted Papias as saying that Mark was not a hearer of our Lord, and then qualified Papias' assertion by saying that Mark had been present at *some* of our Lord's discourses. Compare this with the idea of some later writers (*e.g.* Epiphanius, *Hær.* xx. 4, li. 6) that Mark was one of the Seventy (Seventy-two) Disciples; and with the modern opinion that the young man of Mk 14⁵¹ was the Evangelist. But, as Swete shows (*St. Mark*, p. xxxiii), this is against the words that follow about Luke: 'Neither did he [Luke] himself see the Lord in the flesh.'

Clement of Alexandria (*Hypotyp.*, *ap.* Euseb. *HE* vi. 14) says that while Peter was preaching the gospel at Rome, many of those present begged Mark to write down what was said. Peter neither forbade nor urged it. There is a story similar to this told in the Muratorian fragment about John. In *HE* ii. 15, Eusebius says, on the authority of Clement and Papias, that Peter confirmed the writing; but the passage afterwards quoted by Eusebius from Papias does not bear out this detail. Origen (quoted by Euseb. *HE* vi. 25) says that Mark composed the Gospel at Peter's instruction (ὡς Πέτρος ὑφηγήσατο), being acknowledged as his son (1 P 5¹³).

It is unnecessary to quote later writers, who could scarcely have other means of information

than we have; but we may notice that Eusebius (*HE* ii. 16) makes Mark go to Egypt and found the Church at Alexandria after he had written his Gospel, and says (*ib.* 24) that Annianus succeeded him as bishop there in the eighth year of Nero, a statement which Jerome improves upon by saying that St. Mark died then (*de Vir. Illustr.* §8). It is also desirable to quote Augustine, as his opinion has had such weight in the Church. He says (*de Consensu Evangelistarum*, i. 3, *aliter* i. 6) that of the four Evangelists, Matthew wrote first, then Mark, and that Mark was, as it were, Matthew's follower and abbreviator ('Marcus eum subsecutus tanquam pedissequus et breviator ejus videtur'). Seldom has one short sentence had such an unfortunate effect in distorting a judgment on a literary work; and largely in consequence of it Mk. has been generally neglected. The Second Gospel seems hardly to have engaged the attention of commentators; and the writer known as Victor of Antioch (quoted by Swete, *St. Mark*, p. xxxiv) in the 5th cent. (or later), says that he had not been able to find a single author who had expounded it.

2. Early quotations, references, and use.—The use of Mk. by the Apostolic Fathers is not certain, though in some cases quite probable. The quotation in Clement of Rome (*Cor.* 23) and pseudo-Clement (*Ancient Homily*, 11), which in the latter is introduced by λέγει γὰρ καὶ ὁ προφητικὸς λόγος, is more likely to be from some lost Christian writing than to be a fusion of Mk 4²⁶ᶠᶠ· and other NT passages; but Polycarp, *Phil.* 5, διάκονος πάντων, seems to come from Mk 9³⁵. In other cases it is probable that one of our Gospels is referred to, but we cannot be sure that it is Mk. in particular that is before the writer. As an example we may take Polycarp, *Phil.* 7, which quotes Mt 26⁴¹ and Mk 14³⁸ exactly, and both in Polycarp and in the Gospels the context is about not going into temptation. Pseudo-Clement (§ 2), after quoting Is 54¹ LXX, continues: 'Another Scripture saith, I came not to call the righteous, but sinners,' exactly as Mt 9¹³, Mk 2¹⁷, where 'to repentance' is not in the best manuscripts, but comes from ‖ Lk 5³². But Mt. and not Mk. might have been before Polycarp and pseudo-Clement, though in the latter case the omission of the γάρ of Mt. makes Mk. more likely. And so with Clement of Rome, Ignatius, and others. The *Didache* apparently refers to Mt. and Lk., and the name itself seems to be derived from Ac 2⁴²; but though a probable reference (x. 5) to 1 Jn 4¹⁸ makes the writer's knowledge of Jn. likely, there is no trace of his knowing Mark. For the possible references to the last twelve verses in Barnabas, etc., see below, § vi. The use of Mk. by Hermas is very probable. He apparently refers to Mk 3²⁹ 10²⁴ where they differ from Mt. and Lk., in *Mand.* ii. 2 (οὕτως οὖν ἔνοχος ἔσῃ ἁμαρτίας τοῦ καταλαλοῦντος), and *Sim.* ix. 20. 3 (τοῖς τοιούτοις δύσκολόν ἐστιν εἰς τὴν βασιλείαν τοῦ Θεοῦ εἰσελθεῖν). Indirectly the *Shepherd* of Hermas supplies a great argument for the antiquity of the Gospels, because it shows the uniqueness of our Lord's parables as there narrated. Hermas essays the same method of teaching, but his attempt is utterly feeble. If the Gospels were 2nd cent. productions, and the words of our Lord had been handed on only by oral tradition, the parables could never have been kept so pure. They would in the course of time, before the narratives reached us in their present form, have assimilated features such as we find in Hermas. [For further references in the *Shepherd* see Zahn, *Hirt d. Hermas*, p. 456 ff.; Stanton, *Gosp. as Hist. Doc.* p. 45].

To Justin's probable reference to the Boanerges passage (see above) must be added *Dial.* 88, where he speaks of Jesus as 'supposed to be the carpenter' (τέκτονος νομιζομένου ; but Otto's text has νομ. Ἰωσὴφ τοῦ τέκτ. υἱοῦ ὑπάρχειν). Only Mark (6^3) calls Jesus a carpenter (see § iii. 4 (j) below). Justin also probably quotes from the last twelve verses (below, § vi.).

The use of Mk. by heretics is presumed from references to it in Heracleon, the Valentinians, pseudo-Peter, and the *Clementine Homilies* (the first two as reported by Clement of Alexandria and Irenæus), for which reference may be made to Swete's *St. Mark*, p. xxxi ; and Sanday's *Gospels in the Second Century*, ch. vi. p. 177 ff.

The Gospel is found in all the old Versions—Curetonian and Sinaitic Syriac (of the former only 16^{17-20} is extant), Old Latin, Bohairic, Sahidic ; and in all catalogues and Greek manuscripts of the Gospels.

Putting together the statements, references, and quotations, and deferring the question of an editor later than the original writer of the Gospel (see § vii.), we may conclude, (a) that there is valid evidence that Mk. was *in circulation* before the middle of the 2nd cent. ; (b) that ecclesiastical tradition almost uniformly connects the Second Evangelist with St. Peter—the *Apostolic Constitutions* (ii. 57, Lagarde, p. 85, c. A.D. 375) being the only writing which undoubtedly connects him with St. Paul (οἱ συνεργοὶ Παύλου . . . Λουκᾶς καὶ Μάρκος, cf. Philem.[24], Col. 4^{11}) ; (c) that there was a difference of tradition as to whether he wrote while St. Peter was alive or after his death (see § iv. below). Further, (d) the Alexandrian Fathers Clement and Origen do not mention Mark's preaching at Alexandria—a strange silence ; and (e) there is no hint till Hippolytus that there was more than one Mark ; apparently the other writers identified the cousin of Barnabas and the disciple of Peter.

iii. The CHARACTER OF THE GOSPEL AS SHOWN BY ITSELF AND BY COMPARISON WITH THE OTHER GOSPELS.—If we had no information from ecclesiastical writers, we could have made no conjecture as to the authorship of the Second Gospel, as we can in the case of Lk. (by comparing it with Acts) and Jn. (by comparing it with the Synoptics). But from internal evidence we should gather that the author was either an eye-witness of the events described or at least that he had first-hand information. Further, a close examination of the Gospel makes it exceedingly probable that the writer's informant was St. Peter. So that, while we should never from the NT itself have arrived at the name Mark, yet the internal evidence fully corroborates the external, that the author was the 'interpreter of Peter.' The impression left from a study of Mk. is that we have here in effect, though not in form, and not without some additions due to the Evangelist himself, that Apostle's Gospel. It begins the narrative at the point when Peter could give his own recollections—at the preaching of the Baptist and the baptism of Jesus. This, not the Birth-narratives, as in the case of Mt. and Lk., nor yet the account of our Lord's pre-existence, as in the case of Jn., was to Mark 'the beginning of the gospel of Jesus Christ the Son of God' (1^1), whether these words are part of the record or are the title prefixed by an early scribe.

1. Presentation of Christ's Person and work.—Beginning with the preaching of John and our Lord's entering on His ministry, St. Mark describes at length the Galilæan ministry and the slow unfolding of Jesus' claims. Our Lord, for example, does not at once proclaim His Messiahship, nor does He allow evil spirits to proclaim it inopportunely (1^{25} 3^{12}, cf. 1^{44} etc.). Even after Peter's confession at Cæsarea Philippi, when the Galilæan ministry was nearly ended, the disciples were charged to tell no man (8^{30}). At first Jesus begins by calling Himself the Son of Man (2^{10}). Then

the crowds begin to see in Him a prophet ; His own people and the learned scribes from Jerusalem think Him mad. We might even think, at first sight, especially if we have the Matthæan account (16^{16}) of Peter's confession chiefly in mind and not the Markan, that the disciples then and then only found out that Jesus was Messiah. But this deduction would be precarious. The account in Jn., which makes the Baptist begin by calling Jesus the Lamb of God and the Son of God, and makes Andrew, Philip, and Nathanael at once recognize Him as Messiah (Jn $1^{29.\ 34.\ 41.\ 45.\ 49}$), bears all the marks of probability. A Judæan ministry, as to which the Synoptists are almost silent, must have been carried on simultaneously with the Galilæan preaching. We should expect Jesus, as a religious Jew, to visit Jerusalem frequently ; and indeed, if the last Passover were His first visit during the ministry, we could not explain the sudden enmity of the Jerusalem Jews, or the fact of there being Judæan disciples—Judas Iscariot (probably from Kerioth in Judæa), Joseph of Arimathæa, the owners of the colt at Bethphage and of the room where the Last Supper was celebrated (these evidently knew Jesus), the household at Bethany, and Simon 'the leper.' Also non-Markan portions of Mt. and Lk. imply visits to Jerusalem or a wider ministry than that in Galilee (Mt 23^{37}, Lk 4^{44} BCℵ, $13^{21.\ 33f.}$) ; and in Acts the Apostles at once make their headquarters at Jerusalem, which would have been unlikely if they had only just arrived there for the first time. On that occasion they were perfectly familiar with places and people. But if this be so, we should expect two methods of proclaiming the Person of Christ to have been adopted for these two quite distinct people, of such different characteristics, and separated by hostile Samaria. In Jerusalem, where religious controversy was rife, the question of Jesus' Personality and office could not be postponed ; this is shown by the way in which the Pharisees questioned the Baptist. But in Galilee this was not the case, and the revelation consequently was much more gradual. The Apostles, doubtless, had heard the questions asked in Judæa, and did know the claim of Jesus to be the Christ, though perhaps they did not fully realize all that it meant until the incident at Cæsarea Philippi. Thenceforward Jesus speaks to them of His future glory (8^{38}, cf. 9^7) and of His Passion (8^{31} $9^{12.\ 31}$ etc.). After the Galilæan ministry (which ends at 9^{50}) Mark gives some short account (ch. 10) of journeys in Judæa and Peræa, and it is only on the final approach to Jerusalem that all reserve passes away. In common with all the Evangelists, Mark gives a detailed account of the last days at Jerusalem.

In describing our Lord's Person, Mark emphatically brings out His *Divinity*. Jesus claims superhuman authority—e.g. 2^{28} (lord of the Sabbath), 8^{38} and 14^{62} (coming in glory, the latter in answer to Caiaphas' question, 'Art thou the Christ?'), $12^{6ff.}$ (the beloved Son and Heir) ; and especially authority to forgive sins, $2^{5.\ 10}$ (the paralytic). He is a supernatural Person : 1^{11} 9^7 ('my beloved Son'), 1^{24} ('the Holy One of God'), 3^{11} ('the Son of God'), 5^7 ('Son of the Most High God'), 15^{39} ('the Son of God' *or* 'a son of God'). He knows the thoughts of man, 2^8 8^{17} 12^{15}, and what is to happen in the future, 2^{20} (fasting), 8^{31} and 9^{31} etc. (the Passion), 8^{38} (the Second Advent), 10^{39} (the sufferings of the Apostles), 13^2 (destruction of the Temple), 13^{10} (the universal gospel), 14^{27} (scattering of the sheep). His death has an atoning efficacy, 10^{45} (λύτρον ἀντὶ πολλῶν), 14^{24} ('my blood of the covenant which is shed for many').

But still more striking is the emphasis laid on the true *humanity* of our Lord. The reality of His human body is referred to much as in the other

Evangelists—*e.g.* He is wearied and sleeps (4^{38}; sleep is perhaps implied also in 1^{35}); He eats (14^3) and drinks (15^{36}); His 'touch' is frequently spoken of (1^{41} etc.) (see GESTURES); the burial of His body is dwelt on in 15^{43ff}. But Mark pre-eminently describes the human soul and spirit of our Lord. Note especially His human compassion (1^{41}) and love (10^{21}), and the more painful emotions (1^{43} 3^5 6^6 10^{14} $14^{33f.}$ 15^{34}), for which see below, § iii. 3. Note also the reference to our Lord's human soul and spirit in 2^8 14^{34}, and to His human will in 14^{36}. Mark also refers to the sinless limitations of Jesus' human nature. Questions are asked apparently for information (5^{30} 8^5 9^{16})—for in these cases an 'economical' questioning seems scarcely worthy. The Evangelist also records the one perfectly certain instance of Jesus' ignorance *qua* man, 13^{32} (the Day of Judgment—so Mt.). It is because so much stress is laid in Mk. on our Lord's true human nature that St. Augustine assigns to the Second Evangelist the symbol of the man. Other Fathers vary much in assigning the four symbols, but it is remarkable that each one of the four is assigned to St. Mark in some one or other of the Fathers, Irenæus making him the eagle, Victorinus the lion, Augustine the man, pseudo-Athanasius the calf (see Swete, *St. Mark*, p. xxxviii).

2. Autoptic character.—In many passages Mk. shows, equally with Jn. and much more than Mt. and Lk., clear signs of first-hand knowledge. In these places Mk. often gives a lifelike touch, though Mt. and Lk. in their parallels have lost it. Such are the stooping down of the Baptist to loose the shoe-latchet (1^7), the heavens in the act of opening ($\sigma\chi\iota\zeta o\mu\acute{e}\nu o\upsilon\varsigma$ [present], 1^{10}), the 'incoherent and excited remarks of the crowd' at the healing of the Capernaum demoniac (1^{27} best text, see RV; they are softened down by later scribes of Mk. and by Lk.), the 'house of Simon and Andrew' (1^{29}, where || Mt. and Lk. omit Andrew; in the East it is common for several brothers, even when married, to live in one house, but it required first-hand knowledge to know that Andrew and Peter lived together), Simon starting in pursuit of Jesus (1^{36}), the breaking up of the mud roof to let the paralytic down through it, with other details (2^4, where Mt. tells none of the small points, and Lk., writing for a Roman nobleman, as has been conjectured, translates these, to him, unintelligible details into the language of Western Europe, and says that the man was let down through the *tiles*; see Ramsay, *Was Christ born at Bethlehem?* p. 63), the *single* pillow, $\tau\grave{o}$ $\pi\rho o\sigma\kappa\epsilon\phi\acute{a}\lambda\alpha\iota o\nu$, probably a wooden head-rest, in the boat in the storm (4^{38}, Mk. only), Jesus turning round in the crowd to see who touched Him (so Mt., not Lk.), and His glance at the woman ($5^{30ff.}$, Mk. only), His not allowing the crowd who were with Him to come near Jairus' house, a very probable and lifelike detail (5^{37}, Mk. only; Lk. makes Jesus dismiss the crowd on His entering). The scene at Jairus' house is especially vivid in Mk., and is instructive as showing who the Evangelist's authority was. It must have been one of the inner circle of Apostles, *i.e.* Peter, James, or John (Andrew was not here present. As James died early, and another Gospel was written by (or, at least, depends on) John, we are led to think of Peter as the source. Further instances of lifelike touches are: the five thousand arranged 'like garden beds' $\pi\rho\alpha\sigma\iota\alpha\grave{\iota}$ $\pi\rho\alpha\sigma\iota\alpha\acute{\iota}$ (Mk. only) on the green grass (6^{40}), the details in the account of the Transfiguration ($9^{2ff.}$, where Mt. and Lk. also are vivid), but especially of the healing which followed, where the story is told from the point of view of the three Apostles, not of those who remained behind (9^{14} $\grave{\epsilon}\lambda\theta\acute{o}\nu\tau\epsilon\varsigma$ . . . $\epsilon\grave{\iota}\delta o\nu$ $\acute{o}\chi\lambda o\nu$, Mk. only), and where Mk. only

has the delicate touch (9^{17}) that the man brought the cataleptic boy to *Jesus* and applied to the disciples only when he found that Jesus was absent, and other autoptic details; Mt. and Lk. greatly abbreviate this narrative. So Mark alone relates that in the dispute about precedence and in the blessing of the little ones Jesus took the children into His arms ($\grave{\epsilon}\nu\alpha\gamma\kappa\alpha\lambda\iota\sigma\acute{a}\mu\epsilon\nu o\varsigma$, 9^{36} 10^{16}), and in the latter case that He blessed them *fervently* ($\kappa\alpha\tau\eta\upsilon$-$\lambda\acute{o}\gamma\epsilon\iota$). Notice also how Mk. alone tells us of the searching glance of love cast by Jesus on the rich young man and the clouding over of the young man's brow ($10^{21f.}$), and of the colt tied at the door without in the open street (11^4; probably Peter was one of the two disciples sent), of Jesus refusing to permit vessels to be carried through the Temple (11^{16}), of the command to *bring* a denarius, the Roman coin, into the Temple (where only Jewish coins were current) at the question of paying tribute (12^{15}). For the Agony in the Garden, see below, **3**; but here again we note that the source must have been Peter, James, or John. The account of Peter's denials is indecisive, as he must have been the ultimate authority for all the narratives; but the $\grave{\epsilon}\pi\iota\beta\alpha\lambda\grave{\omega}\nu$ of Mk 14^{72} (see below, **4** (*h*)) argues the priority of our Evangelist. Exceptional knowledge is evidenced by the mention of the names of Levi's father (Alphæus, 2^{14}), of the father of the blind man at Jericho (Timæus, 10^{46}), and of the sons of Simon of Cyrene (Alexander and Rufus, 15^{21}). These and other instances lead us to see in the Second Gospel a graphic account of one who had first-hand knowledge at his command, and, to a large extent, confirm Papias' description of Mark as Peter's interpreter. Mk. consists almost entirely of things of which Peter had personal knowledge. As Eusebius noticed long ago (*Demonstr. Evangel.* iii. 5, Cologne ed. p. 120 f.), it is silent on matters which reflect credit on Peter. It alone records several Petrine touches. We have, in fact, here in all particulars the Petrine tradition in a far more exact form than in the other Synoptics.

3. Description of the inner feelings of our Lord and of the Apostles.—This is found in Mk. to an extent which argues an early narrative based on intimate personal knowledge of Jesus and of the Twelve. In Mt. and Lk. the painful emotions of our Lord are not mentioned, except in the case of the Agony, and even that disappears in the Westcott-Hort text of Lk. ($22^{43f.}$); a fact probably to be accounted for by a feeling of reverence due to a slightly later age. In Mk. we find a more childlike boldness in describing Jesus' feelings. See the following instances, which are found in Mk. only: 1^{43} $\grave{\epsilon}\mu\beta\rho\iota\mu\eta\sigma\acute{a}\mu\epsilon\nu o\varsigma$ (denoting sternness: not necessarily anger, but deep feeling); 3^5 righteous anger and grief; 6^6 wondering at the people's unbelief (here Mk. retains $\delta\iota\grave{a}$ $\tau\grave{\eta}\nu$ $\grave{a}\pi\iota\sigma\tau\acute{\iota}\alpha\nu$ $\alpha\grave{\upsilon}\tau\grave{\omega}\nu$, but omits $\grave{\epsilon}\theta\alpha\acute{\upsilon}\mu\alpha\sigma\epsilon\nu$; on the other hand, Mt 8^{10}, Lk 7^9 have the wonder of Jesus' human mind at the centurion's faith—an incident which was not part of the Petrine tradition and is not in Mk.); 10^{14}, indignation when the disciples kept back the little children; and especially $14^{33f.}$, the Agony in the Garden, where Mk. alone speaks of the surprise ($\grave{\epsilon}\kappa\theta\alpha\mu\beta\epsilon\hat{\iota}\sigma\theta\alpha\iota$) added to the distraction from grief ($\grave{a}\delta\eta\mu o\nu\epsilon\hat{\iota}\nu$) of Jesus' human soul. Mt. changes the former to $\lambda\upsilon\pi\epsilon\hat{\iota}\sigma\theta\alpha\iota$ while retaining the latter, and Lk. omits the whole passage. If, as seems probable, the passage Lk $22^{43f.}$ is not an original part of the Third Gospel, it is perhaps a fragment older than Lk. and reflects the same stage of thought as Mark. It is referred to in Justin, *Dial.* 103.—It is not unlikely that the difference between Mk 10^{18} (the rich young man) and Mt $19^{16f.}$ in the best text (BDℵ, Origen, etc.; see Westcott-Hort, *Notes*) is due to the same feeling. Possibly when the First Evangelist wrote, the Markan phrase, 'Why callest thou me good? none is good save one, even God,' may have been misunderstood to imply a merely human Christ. Or perhaps the Westcott-Hort text of Mt. is not original, but is due to an early scribe or editor who disliked the Markan form of the incident. Another example is the πτῶμα of Mk 15⁴⁵ (so אBDL ; Westcott-Hort with AC, etc., read σῶμα). This was a word used of the carcase of a dead animal or of a human being, with a touch of contempt. Mt. and Lk. have therefore altered πτῶμα to σῶμα, as also have some scribes in Mk., from feelings of reverence.

The same thing is true of another matter almost peculiar to Mk., the account of the inner feelings of the Apostles.' See 4³⁸, showing the Apostles' resentment against the Lord ('Carest thou not?'), and similarly 4⁴¹, showing their awe or holy fear at the revelation of Jesus' power and Divinity (cf., however, St. Peter at the miraculous draught of fishes in Lk 5⁸); so 10³², showing their amazement and fear, apparently arising from our Lord's manner as He went before them; and 14⁵ ἐνεβριμῶντο, here (unlike 1⁴³) of anger.

A similar result follows from the passages where Mk. tells us that Jesus 'could not' do a thing. The inability is, doubtless, relative and conditional. Jesus 'could not' do that which was inconsistent with His plan of salvation. Yet here the other Synoptists, feeling that the phrases might be misunderstood as taking from the Master's glory, have altered or omitted them. See 1⁴⁵ 7²⁴, and the specially significant 6⁵ᶠ⁺, where οὐκ ἐδύνατο ἐκεῖ ποιῆσαι οὐδεμίαν δύναμιν εἰ μὴ, κ.τ.λ., καὶ ἐθαύμασεν διὰ τὴν ἀπιστίαν αὐτῶν = Mt 13⁵⁸ οὐκ ἐποίησεν ἐκεῖ δυνάμεις πολλὰς διὰ τὴν ἀπιστίαν αὐτῶν, the two possible causes of offence being removed in Mt.

4. Comparison with the other Synoptics.—The indications given in the last two subsections will lead us to believe that the Second Gospel, either in the form in which we have it now, or at least in a form very like that which we have, is chronologically the first of the Synoptics, and that it lay before the writers of the First and Third Gospels. This impression is greatly strengthened by the considerations which follow. We still postpone the question whether the Markan Gospel known to Matthew and Luke is the same as our Mark.

(a) *Scope of Mark.*—Except about thirty verses, all the narrative that we find in Mk. we find also (and in the same order) in either Mt. or Lk., or in both. This might tell both ways. If Mark were only an abbreviator, borrowing from Mt. and Lk., without much independent information, it would stand to reason that he would have little to tell us that was not found in them. But, then, his Gospel would not be the fresh and vivid, first-hand and autoptic, composition that it is. Therefore we are led to the conclusion that Matthew and Luke borrowed from Mark, and that one or other of them took almost everything that was found in his Gospel.

That Luke borrowed from Mark is seen from another fact. In the Third Gospel there is a long section which is not in the Second (Lk 9⁵¹–18¹⁴). For this, Luke is dependent on some other source. But, having followed the Markan order somewhat closely up to the point where the section begins, he goes back, when the section ends, to within a few verses of the place in Mk. where he dropped it. Thus, Lk 9⁵⁰ = Mk 9³⁹ᶠ⁺; Lk 18¹⁵ = Mk 10¹³. This looks as if Mk. (or something very like it) was lying open before the Third Evangelist as he wrote.

(b) *Diffuseness and redundancy of Mk. as compared with parallel passages of Mt. and Luke.*— The idea that Mark is an abbreviator of Matthew

is at once shown to be wrong when we compare parallels. When we do so, we shall find, in almost every case, that Mk. is much fuller than either Mt. or Lk. taken singly. The greater bulk of the two latter is due to their relating many incidents and speeches which are not in Mark. The style of Mk. is somewhat diffuse, and it was necessary for the other Synoptists, if they were to make room for the new matter which they desired to introduce, to prune it considerably. This they did. Instances are: 1³² (Mt. omits 'when the sun did set,' Lk. omits 'at even'); 1³⁵ πρωὶ ἔννυχα λίαν (= Lk. γενομένης ἡμέρας); 2¹⁵ᶠ⁺ 4¹ᶠᶠ⁺, where the shorter form in Mt. and Lk. really omits nothing from the sense; 5²²ᶠ⁺ ³⁵ (Mt., abbreviating, puts together the arrival of Jairus who said that the child was dying, and of the messenger who said that she was dead); 5²⁵ (Mt. omits all the Markan details about the woman with the issue of blood, Lk. omits some of them); 6¹⁷ᶠᶠ⁺ (the parenthetical explanation about the Baptist's death interrupts the course of the narrative in Mt. and Mk., but is greatly abbreviated in the former; in Lk. the story is put in its proper place, but abbreviated to one or two sentences; note Mk.'s redundant εὐθὺς μετὰ σπουδῆς, 6²⁵); 8¹ (the feeding of the four thousand, shortened in Mt., left out in Lk.); 8¹⁴ (the omission to take bread, abbreviated in Mt., whence we should have gathered, if we had not had Mk., that they discovered the omission only after landing, instead of when in the boat, as Mk., which is much more likely); 9³⁸ᶠᶠ⁺ (the stranger exorcist, omitted in Mt., shortened in Lk.); 13¹⁹ ἀπ' ἀρχῆς κτίσεως ἣν ἔκτισεν ὁ θεός (= Mt. ἀπ' ἀρ. κόσμου, Lk. different). Many other examples might be given, e.g. 7¹³ 8¹⁵. ³⁷ (cf. Lk.) 12¹⁴. ⁴⁴ 14⁶⁸ 15¹ 16⁸. See also Hawkins, *Horæ Synopticæ*, pp. 100 ff., 110.

A similar instance of redundancy is the use of pleonastic forms in Mk., e.g. ἐκ παιδιόθεν 9²¹ (A omits ἐκ, D has ἐκ παιδός), ἀπὸ μακρόθεν 5⁶ 8³ 11¹³ 14⁵⁴ 15⁴⁰. These are very seldom found in Mt. and Luke.

(c) *Correction of Markan details in Mt. or Luke.*—In two or three instances we find a small slip of the pen corrected, as when Mark (1²ᶠ⁺) cites as from Isaiah a passage which is really partly from Mal 3¹ and partly from Is 40³, perhaps through using a book of quotations in which these passages followed each other, with 'Isaiah' at the top of the page; here the other Synoptists omit the Malachi passage (though they give it elsewhere, Mt 11¹⁰ = Lk 7²⁷), thus silently correcting Mark. So Mk 2²⁶ has ἐπὶ Ἀβιάθαρ ἀρχιερέως, which can only mean 'during the high priesthood of Abiathar' (AC, etc., insert τοῦ, which might give the meaning 'in the time of A., who was afterwards high priest'; D, syr ˢⁱⁿ, and some Old Latin MSS omit the whole phrase; these are scribes' corrections). The ‖ Mt. Lk. have the Markan sentence almost exactly, with the exception of these three words which they omit, no doubt because it is not correct to say that the events happened when Abiathar was actually high priest. In the account of the women at the tomb (Mk 16²) there is some confusion of time (λίαν πρωΐ . . . ἀνατείλαντος τοῦ ἡλίου), probably due to compression, different events being put together, unless, indeed, we accept Wright's suggestion (*Synopsis of the Gospels ²*, *in loc.*) that μήπω has dropped out before ἀνατείλαντος. In ‖ Mt 28¹ there is a similar obscurity :' 'late on the Sabbath day, as it began to dawn toward the first day of the week, came Mary Magdalene.' But this is corrected in ‖ Lk 24¹. The women came on the first day of the week ὄρθρου βαθέως (so Jn 20¹ πρωΐ, σκοτίας ἔτι οὔσης).

Cases of explanations, or corrections of matter, as opposed to corrections of phraseology, may be seen in Mk 12⁸, where the killing of the heir precedes the casting out of the vineyard, the order being inverted in Mt. and Lk. to make the parable fit the heavenly counterpart; in Mk 13¹⁴ ('abomination of desolation') where ‖ Mt 24¹⁵ adds 'spoken of by Daniel the prophet,' and ‖ Lk 21²⁰ explains by altering to 'Jerusalem compassed with armies'; and Mk 15³⁹ where the words 'Son of God' (so Mt.) are explained by Lk. as 'a righteous man.' In this last case the Markan phrase is probably original, though the centurion would have borrowed it from the Jews without understanding it; Luke gives what the centurion meant in his own mind.

In several cases additions in Mt. or Lk. imply the priority of Mk., the added words probably coming from a non-Markan source, as in the confession of St. Peter, where the account in Mk. (8²⁹) could hardly have been derived from Mt. by abbreviation; and in the warning (Mk 13¹⁸) to pray that the flight be not in the winter ($\chi\epsilon\iota\mu\hat{\omega}\nu os$), where Mt. (24²⁰) adds $\mu\eta\delta\grave{\epsilon}$ $\sigma\alpha\beta\beta\acute{\alpha}\tau\omega$, changing the case. Or, in some instances, the added words are a gloss; e.g. Mk 8³⁴ (taking up the cross—Lk. adds 'daily'), 10⁴⁰ (to sit on Jesus' right hand or left hand is for those for whom it has been prepared —Mt. adds 'by my Father'), 12¹ (the owner of the vineyard goes away—Lk. adds $\chi\rho\acute{o}\nu ovs$ $\acute{\iota}\kappa\alpha\nu o\acute{v}s$, showing special knowledge of viticulture, as it would be several years before the grapes were allowed to ripen).

In some cases, by a turn of phrase, Mk.'s accuracy in minute points is lost in Mt. and Luke. Thus in Mk 4³⁶ our Lord was already in the boat (4¹); the other Synoptists, by an oversight, make Him embark here. In the Charge to the Twelve Mk 6⁸ has 'take nothing . . . save a staff only'; ‖ Mt. and Lk. show an early exaggeration of the command (see Swete, *St. Mark, in loc.*). In Mk 10¹ Jesus comes 'into the borders of Judæa and beyond ($\kappa\alpha\grave{\iota}$ $\pi\acute{\epsilon}\rho\alpha\nu$) Jordan'; Mt. (19¹) omits $\kappa\alpha\acute{\iota}$, as do some lesser MSS. in Mk. (A, etc., have $\delta\iota\grave{\alpha}$ $\tauο\hat{v}$ $\pi\acute{\epsilon}\rho\alpha\nu$); but doubtless Mk. is right here, —Jesus went both into Judæa and into Peræa. The passage is not in Luke. On the general question of the alterations and omissions of Markan matter in Mt. and Lk. see Hawkins, *Hor. Synopt.* p. 96 ff. He suggests that several Markan passages might be misunderstood as derogatory to Jesus or to the Apostles, or might otherwise cause offence; and therefore were altered by Mt. or by Lk. or by both.

(*d*) *Correction of Markan phraseology in Mt. or Luke.*—The Second Gospel is distinguished by a rough and unpolished style, reflecting the Greek commonly spoken by the Jews in the 1st century. In the parallels of the other Synoptics there are numerous instances of toning down and pruning Mark's unliterary forms of speech.

As an example, take Mk.'s frequent use of *diminutives*, often altered in Mt., almost always in Luke. Such are $\theta\upsilon\gamma\acute{\alpha}\tau\rho\iota ο\nu$ 5²³ 7²⁵ (not elsewhere in NT)= $\theta\upsilon\gamma\acute{\alpha}\tau\eta\rho$ Mt. Lk. (no Lukan parallel to 7²⁵); $\pi\alpha\iota\delta\acute{\iota}ο\nu$, $\kappa o\rho\acute{\alpha}\sigma\iota ο\nu$ (the latter a late colloquial word condemned by the Atticists) 5³⁹ᶠᶠ·= $\kappa o\rho\acute{\alpha}\sigma\iota ο\nu$ Mt. *bis* = $\pi\alpha\hat{\iota}s$ Lk.; $\pi\alpha\iota\delta\acute{\iota}\alpha$ 10¹³ (so Mt.)= $\beta\rho\acute{\epsilon}\phi\eta$ Lk.; $\iota\chi\theta\acute{v}\delta\iota\alpha$ 8⁷—Mt. has it once, but soon corrects to $\iota\chi\theta\acute{v}\alpha s$ (not in Lk.); $\pi\lambda o\iota\acute{\alpha}\rho\iota ο\nu$ 3⁹ (so Jn.), not in Mt. and Lk. (all the best MSS in Mk 4³⁶ have $\pi\lambda o\hat{\iota}\alpha$ as in Mt. and Lk., not $\pi\lambda o\iota\acute{\alpha}\rho\iota\alpha$ as TR); $\dot{\omega}\tau\acute{\alpha}\rho\i002ον$ אBD 14⁴⁷ (also in Jn.)= $\dot{\omega}\tau\acute{\iota}ο\nu$ Mt.= o$\mathring{v}$s Lk.; $\pi\alpha\iota\delta\acute{\iota}\sigma\kappa\eta$ 14⁶⁶· ⁶⁹ (so Mt. Lk. once, but Mt. soon changes it to $\acute{\alpha}\lambda\lambda\eta$, Lk. to $\acute{\epsilon}\tau\epsilon\rho os$); $\kappa\upsilon\nu\acute{\alpha}\rho\iota\alpha$ 7²⁷ᶠ· (so Mt., no Lukan parallel); $\psi\iota\chi\acute{\iota}\alpha$ 7²⁸ (so Mt., no Lukan parallel in Lk 16²¹ is not in the best MSS).

(*e*) Other *colloquialisms* are frequent in Mark. These are often corrected in Mt., oftener still in Luke. [Those here marked with an asterisk are

expressly condemned by the Atticists]. Such are $\kappa\rho\acute{\alpha}\beta\beta\alpha\tau os$* or $\kappa\rho\acute{\alpha}\beta\alpha\tau\tau os$* 2⁴· ⁹· ¹¹ (Mt. and Lk. $\kappa\lambda\acute{\iota}\nu\eta$, Lk. also $\kappa\lambda\iota\nu\acute{\iota}\delta\iota ο\nu$) and 6⁵⁵ (Mt. omits, Lk. has no parallel, Jn. also has the word); $\sigma\upsilon\mu\beta o\acute{v}\lambda\iota ο\nu$ $\acute{\epsilon}\delta\acute{\iota}\deltaου\nu$ [*vv.ll.* $\acute{\epsilon}\pi o\acute{\iota}\eta\sigma\alpha\nu$, $\acute{\epsilon}\pi o\acute{\iota}ου\nu$] 3⁶, σ. $\pi o\iota\acute{\eta}\sigma\alpha\nu\tau\epsilon s$ 15¹, neither elsewhere in NT (Mt. has σ. $\lambda\alpha\mu\beta\acute{\alpha}\nu\epsilon\iota\nu$ five times, Lk. different); $\acute{o}\rho\kappa\acute{\iota}\zeta\omega$.* 5⁷, avoided by Mt. and Lk. (Mt 26⁶³ has $\acute{\epsilon}\xi o\rho\kappa\acute{\iota}\zeta\omega$); $\acute{\epsilon}\sigma\chi\acute{\alpha}\tau\omega s$ $\acute{\epsilon}\chi\epsilon\iota$* 5²³, corrected by Mt. and Lk. (Josephus has $\acute{\epsilon}\nu$ $\acute{\epsilon}\sigma\chi\acute{\alpha}\tauο\iota s$ $\epsilon\hat{\iota}\nu\alpha\iota$, *Ant.* IX. viii. 6); $\sigma\phi\upsilon\rho\acute{\iota}s$* [best reading] 8⁸· ²⁰ (so Mt.), colloquial for $\sigma\pi\upsilon\rho\acute{\iota}s$ (see Deissmann, *Bibl. Stud.* p. 158, Eng. tr.); $\beta\lambda\acute{\epsilon}\pi\epsilon\tau\epsilon$ $\acute{\alpha}\pi\acute{o}$ 8¹⁵ 12³⁸, probably colloquial or coined by Mark, corrected or avoided in Mt. and Lk.; $\mu ο\nu\acute{o}\phi\theta\alpha\lambda\mu os$* 9⁴⁷ (so Mt., Lk. has no parallel); $\tau\rho\upsilon\mu\alpha\lambda\iota\grave{\alpha}$ $\acute{\rho}\alpha\phi\acute{\iota}\delta os$ 10²⁵=Mt. $\tau\rho\hat{\eta}\mu\alpha$ $\acute{\rho}$. = Lk. $\tau\rho\hat{\eta}\mu\alpha$ $\beta\epsilon\lambda\acute{o}\nu\eta s$ best text ($\tau\rho\upsilon\mu$. is a late rare word, doubtless colloquial; $\acute{\rho}\alpha\phi\acute{\iota}s$* is colloquial); $\kappa ο\lambda\lambda\upsilon\beta\iota\sigma\tau\acute{\eta}s$* 11¹⁵ (so Mt. and Jn., Lk. omits; Jn 2¹⁴ᶠ· has $\kappa\epsilon\rho\mu\alpha\tau\iota\sigma\tau\acute{\eta}s$ in addition); $\acute{\epsilon}\kappa\epsilon\phi\alpha\lambda\acute{\iota}\omega\sigma\alpha\nu$ 12⁴, $\acute{\alpha}\pi$. $\lambda\epsilon\gamma$. in Greek, altered in Mt. and Lk. (see § iii. 5 and § vii. below); $\acute{\alpha}\gamma\rho\epsilon\acute{v}\sigma\omega\sigma\iota\nu$ 12¹³ (=Mt. $\pi\alpha\gamma\iota\delta\epsilon\acute{v}\sigma\omega\sigma\iota\nu$, both $\acute{\alpha}\pi$. $\lambda\epsilon\gamma$. in NT; Lk. has $\acute{\epsilon}\pi\iota\lambda\acute{\alpha}\beta\omega\nu\tau\alpha\iota$); $\kappa\alpha\tau\acute{\alpha}\lambda\upsilon\mu\alpha$ 14¹⁴ (so Lk., but Mt. omits), a colloquialism, though the verb $\kappa\alpha\tau\alpha\lambda\acute{v}\omega$ is classical in the sense of 'halting to rest'; $\epsilon\hat{\iota}s$ $\kappa\alpha\theta$' ($\kappa\alpha\tau\grave{\alpha}$) $\epsilon\hat{\iota}s$ 14¹⁹ (altered in Mt., no parallel in Lk., a colloquialism, $\epsilon\hat{\iota}s$ being made an indeclinable numeral, or else $\kappa\alpha\tau\acute{\alpha}$ an adverb, see Deissmann, *Bibl. Stud.* p. 138); $\sigma\acute{v}\sigma\sigma\eta\mu ο\nu$* 14⁴⁴ (=Mt. $\sigma\eta\mu\epsilon\hat{\iota}ο\nu$); $\acute{\rho}\acute{\alpha}\pi\iota\sigma\mu\alpha$* 14⁶⁵ (so Jn., but altered in Mt. and Lk.); $\epsilon\acute{v}\sigma\chi\acute{\eta}\mu\omega\nu$* 15⁴³ in the sense 'rich' or 'of honourable estate' (altered in Mt. and Lk.). It is noteworthy, however, that Luke is more particular when correcting Mark than when composing his later treatise, for we find $\kappa\rho\acute{\alpha}\beta\beta\alpha\tau os$ in Ac 5¹⁵ 9³³, $\acute{o}\rho\kappa\acute{\iota}\zeta\omega$ in Ac 19¹³ (cf. 1 Th 5²⁷ $\acute{\epsilon}\nu o\rho\kappa\acute{\iota}\zeta\omega$ best text), and $\epsilon\acute{v}\sigma\chi\acute{\eta}\mu\omega\nu$ in the above sense in Ac 13⁵⁰ 17¹².

(*f*) Mark's so-called *Latinisms* must probably be reckoned as being in reality colloquialisms; see § iv. below. Such are $\kappa\epsilon\nu\tau\upsilon\rho\acute{\iota}\omega\nu$ *centurio* 15³⁹· ⁴⁴ (= $\acute{\epsilon}\kappa\alpha\tau\acute{o}\nu\tau\alpha\rho\chi os$, $\acute{\epsilon}\kappa\alpha\tauο\nu\tau\acute{\alpha}\rho\chi\eta s$ Mt. Lk.); $\xi\acute{\epsilon}\sigma\tau\eta s$ *sextarius* 7⁴, not in the best text of 7⁸ (Mt. omits, abbreviating; no parallel in Lk.); $\sigma\pi\epsilon\kappa o\upsilon\lambda\acute{\alpha}\tau\omega\rho$ *speculator* 6²⁷ $\acute{\alpha}\pi$. $\lambda\epsilon\gamma$. in Greek (omitted in Mt., no parallel in Lk.); $\kappa o\delta\rho\acute{\alpha}\nu\tau\eta s$ *quadrans* 12⁴² (omitted in Lk., no parallel in Mt., but the word is found in Mt 5²⁶); $\lambda\epsilon\gamma\iota\acute{\omega}\nu$ or $\lambda\epsilon\gamma\epsilon\acute{\omega}\nu$ *legio* 5⁹· ¹⁵, *i.e.* 'a large number,' which seems to have been its meaning in colloquial Greek (the ‖ Lk 8³⁰ has it, but ‖ Mt 8²⁹· ³⁴ omits it; Mt 26⁵³ has the word in its literal, military sense); $\kappa\hat{\eta}\nu\sigma os$ *census* 12¹⁴ (so Mt., but Lk. $\phi\acute{o}\rho os$); $\tau\grave{o}$ $\acute{\iota}\kappa\alpha\nu\grave{o}\nu$ $\pi ο\iota\epsilon\hat{\iota}\nu$ *satisfacere* 15¹⁵ (omitted in Mt. and Lk., cf. Ac 17⁹ $\lambda\alpha\beta\acute{o}\nu\tau\epsilon s$ $\tau\grave{o}$ $\acute{\iota}\kappa\alpha\nu\grave{o}\nu$ *satis accipientes*). To these must be added $\delta\eta\nu\acute{\alpha}\rho\iο\nu$ *denarius* 6³⁷ 12¹⁵ 14⁵ and $\mu\acute{o}\delta\iο s$ *modius* 4²¹, which both the other Synoptics have retained.

(*g*) *The Aramaic transliterations* in Mk. are a source of some perplexity when we ask the cause of their presence (see below, § v.). But in this connexion they are significant, because almost all of them have been removed by the other Synoptists. Even in Mk. they are nearly always accompanied by an interpretation; the other Evangelists, writing later, probably thought it useless to retain them. They are marks of an early hand, desirous of retaining the *ipsissima verba* spoken.

(*h*) *Corrections of grammar, awkward and difficult phrases*, etc.—Under this head we note many instances of smoothing an unpolished style. Thus in 3¹⁵ᶠᶠ· Mark writes $\kappa\alpha\grave{\iota}$ $\acute{I}\acute{\alpha}\kappa\omega\beta ο\nu$, $\kappa.\tau.\lambda$., forgetting that he had added a clause about Peter after (אBC*, etc.) $\kappa\alpha\grave{\iota}$ $\acute{\epsilon}\pi o\acute{\iota}\eta\sigma\epsilon\nu$ $\tau o\grave{v}s$ $\delta\acute{\omega}\delta\epsilon\kappa\alpha$ (Westcott-Hort insert a bracket in endeavouring to make Mk. grammatical—surely a desperate expedient)—the difficulty disappears in Mt. and Lk.; in 4¹¹ $\acute{v}\mu\hat{\iota}\nu$ $\tau\grave{o}$ $\mu\upsilon\sigma\tau\acute{\eta}\rho\iο\nu$ $\delta\acute{\epsilon}\delta o\tau\alpha\iota$ is awkward—in Mt. and Lk. $\gamma\nu\hat{\omega}\nu\alpha\iota$ is inserted and makes the phrase easy—this probably is not a correction proper, but a case of taking a smoother phrase from the non-Markan source of Mt. and Lk. rather than the rough phrase in Mk. (see § vii. 2 below). Note also 4^{15} οὗτοι δέ εἰσιν οἱ παρὰ τὴν ὁδόν . . . καὶ ὅταν, κ.τ.λ., for οἳ ὅταν—simplified in Mt. and Lk.; 4^{21} where ἔρχεται is very awkward—Luke removes it, as also Matthew, who narrates the passage in a different connexion; 4^{24} βλέπετε τί ἀκούετε—Luke's gloss is πῶς (for τί), doubtless a true one (no parallel in Mt.); 4^{31}, anacolouthon, removed in Mt. and Lk., which both insert ὃν λαβὼν ἄνθρωπος, here probably following in preference their non-Markan source (as in 4^{11}); $7^{11f.}$ ἐὰν εἴπῃ ἄνθρωπος . . . Κορβάν . . . οὐκέτι ἀφίετε αὐτόν, κ.τ.λ., which is grammatical enough though the sense is rather strained—this is smoothed in Mt. (no parallel in Lk.); 9^{1} εἰσίν τινες ὧδε τῶν ἑστηκότων more awkward than the ‖ Mt. τῶν ὧ. ἑ. or the ‖ Lk. τῶν αὐτοῦ ἑ.; $9^{11. 28}$ ὅτι in the sense ‘why?’ (i.e. ‘how is it that . . .’)=Mt. τί or διὰ τί, not in Lk. (so ὅτι in 2^{16}=Mk. Lk. διὰ τί); 9^{12}, no δέ corresponding to μέν, καὶ πῶς being used instead—in Mt. the order is inverted and the λέγω δέ provides the requisite antithesis; 9^{41} ἐν ὀνόματι ὅτι, an awkward phrase for ‘because’=Mt. εἰς ὄνομα μαθητοῦ (the converse change would be impossible; Swete finds a classical parallel to Mk. in Thuc. iv. 60; there is no parallel in Lk.); 11^{3} the words in the best text: ‘And straightway he will send (ἀποστέλλει, historic present) him back (πάλιν) hither,’ are part of the message, but (perhaps as being ambiguous) have been omitted in Lk., and altered in Mt. to a prediction that the owner of the colt would comply with the request; 13^{14} βδέλυγμα is made ungrammatically masculine (ἑστηκότα), because it is taken to be a man (the participle corrected in Mt. to ἑστός—Lk. completely different); 13^{19}, the harsh phrase ‘those days shall be tribulation’ (softened in AV to ‘in those days,’ etc.) is altered and smoothed in Mt. and Lk. to ‘there shall be,’ etc.; 14^{65}, the difficult phrase ῥαπίσμασιν ἔλαβον is omitted in Mt. and Lk. (the reading of TR ἔβαλλον in Mk. arises partly from confusion of βαλ- and λαβ-, partly from harshness of the original); 14^{72}, the difficult ἐπιβαλὼν ἔκλαιεν altered both in Mt 26^{75} and Lk 22^{62} to καὶ ἐξελθὼν ἔξω ἔκλαυσεν πικρῶς, but Westcott-Hort bracket the clause in Lk. as doubtful (it is wanting in some Old Latin MSS)—if it is genuine in Lk. (and it has almost overwhelming attestation) we probably have here a case not of correction proper, but (as before) of both Matthew and Luke preferring their non-Markan source to the ambiguous Mk., which was perhaps misunderstood in early times as much as now; whether it means ‘when he thought thereon he wept,’ or ‘ covering his head he wept,’ or as D and the Latin, Syrian, Armenian, and other versions have it, ‘ he began to weep.’

The corrections under this head are most significant, and appear to be conclusive as to the early date of Mk. as compared with the other Synoptics. For no writer, having before him a smooth text, would gratuitously introduce harsh or difficult phraseology, whereas the converse change is natural and common.

(i) We may notice some changes made for *greater precision*, especially by Luke, who, as one would expect, uses more correct medical language. Cf. Mk $2^{3ff.}$, Mt $9^{2ff.}$ παραλυτικός = Lk $5^{18ff.}$ παραλελυμένος; Mk 2^{17}, Mt 9^{12} ἰσχύοντες = Lk 5^{31} ὑγιαίνοντες. [In Mk 5^{42} =Mt 9^{25}=Lk 8^{55}, Lk. Mk. (not Mt.) add the command to give the maiden something to eat,—cf. Lk 7^{15} where Jesus gives the widow's son back to his mother : ‘ in each case He intimates that nature is to resume its usual course’ (Plummer, *St. Luke*, on 8^{55})].

Similar corrections for precision are: Mk 6^{14} ὁ βασιλεὺς Ἡρῴδης (cf. $6^{22. 26f.}$)=Mt. Lk. Ἡ. ὁ τετραάρχης (though Mt. has retained ὁ βασ. in 14^{9}); perhaps also 6^{22} τῆς θυγατρὸς αὐτοῦ Ἡρῳδιάδος if the

reading of ℵBD (so Westcott-Hort) be right, in which case either the girl was not Salome but her half-sister, or perhaps more probably αὐτοῦ is used in a loose way to denote that she was Herod's step-daughter—Mt 14^{6} has ἡ θυγάτηρ τῆς Ἡρῳδιάδος, which is more likely to be the truth (the Markan reading is, however, very doubtful); 1^{16} etc., where Mark calls the Lake of Gennesaret ‘the *sea* (θάλασσα) of Galilee’ (so Mt.), but Luke always, with his superior nautical knowledge, changes the word to λίμνη; and 15^{32} which says that ‘they that were crucified (pl.) with him reproached him’ (so Mt.)—the plural is perhaps used only impersonally, or possibly both robbers began to revile and one repented; but Luke, who had independent knowledge of this incident (for he alone relates the penitence of the robber), emphatically corrects the phrase to εἷς δὲ τῶν κρεμασθέντων κακούργων (Lk 23^{39}).

(j) *Doubtful cases.*—We must finally consider some passages in which it is doubtful whether we must attribute to Mk. priority or posteriority. In Mk 6^{3} we find οὐχ οὗτός ἐστιν ὁ τέκτων; where Mt 13^{55} has ὁ τοῦ τέκτονος υἱός and Lk 4^{22} υἱὸς Ἰωσήφ. Here the correction might be on the part of the First and Third Evangelists, who disliked the name ‘the carpenter’ being given to Jesus, and the fact that they use different phrases points to the probability that they are not here borrowing from their common source or sources; while the correction might be on the part of Mark, who thought that the phrase ‘son of Joseph’ might be misunderstood by his readers, inasmuch as they had not the birth-narrative before them to explain it. Origen asserts that ‘in none of the Gospels current in the Churches is Jesus Himself ever described as being “the carpenter”’ (*adv. Cels.* vi. 36), and perhaps this reading was not in his copy of Mark—a few authorities now extant have a different phrase (but see Westcott-Hort, *Notes on Select Readings*, p. 24). If the correction is on the part of the Second Gospel, it is probable that our Markan reading is the work of an editor later than Mt. Lk. (but see § vii. below).—In $14^{30. 68. 72}$ the cock is said to crow twice, according to the usually received readings; in Mt. Lk. Jn. only one cock-crowing is recorded. Some MSS omit δίς in Mk 14^{30}, many (ℵBc syr^sin etc.) omit καὶ ἀλέκτωρ ἐφώνησεν in 14^{68}, some omit ἐκ δευτέρου in 14^{72}, others omit δίς in 14^{72}. If a second cock-crowing was in the Petrine tradition, it is difficult to understand why the other Evangelists should have so completely omitted all trace of it; but it is equally difficult to understand why, if it belongs to the original Mk., and if that Gospel was later than Mt. and Lk., the Second Evangelist should have introduced it; or again why, if it is an editorial addition to Mk., the editor should have introduced it. Perhaps Dr. Salmon's solution is the right one (*Textual Criticism*, ch. v.)—that originally Mk. had only one cock-crowing, that of 14^{72} (i.e. not in the same place as in Mt. and Lk.); that the omission of ℵB, etc., in 14^{68} is right; and that some early scribe having by error put in these words, without intending to introduce two cock-crowings, other scribes added δίς and ἐκ δευτέρου in the other places to produce consistency. On the other hand, it must be remembered that the omissions in some MSS of Mk. are easily explicable on the supposition that a harmonizing scribe, not finding two cock-crowings in the other Gospels, omitted these words in Mk.; if this be so, the enigma is inexplicable.—In Mk 14^{58} the words χειροποίητον, ἀχειροποίητον may be a comment of the Evangelist's, the simpler words of Mt 26^{61} being what the false witnesses really said (Lk. has no parallel). If so, the Markan form would probably be later than the Matthæan (see Schmiedel in

Encyc. Bibl. ii. 1851). But the introduction of comments such as these, however much in the style of Mt., is not in that of Mk., and there is no reason why Jesus should not actually have used the words, and, if so, why the false witnesses should not have quoted them; their false testimony lay in giving a wrong sense to our Lord's words, rather than in quoting Him wrongly.

A case of possible correction of Mk. may be briefly noticed here, though it does not concern Mt. or Luke. In 15^{25} we read that the Crucifixion took place at the third hour; Jn 19^{14} says that the trial was hardly over by the sixth hour (ὥρα ἦν ὡς ἕκτη), and this looks like a correction of Mk. as to time. But probably this is no correction, whether we take Westcott's solution that John's 'sixth hour' is our 6 a.m., or that of Ramsay (*Expositor*, 4th ser. vii. 216, 5th ser. iii. 457) and others that the word 'hour' is used in a loose and ill-defined way, or the more probable and ancient view (Euseb. *ad Marin.*) that there is an error of the digamma, F (=6) for Γ (=3) or *vice versa*, in the text of the Gospels. If so, our copies of Jn. are probably wrong, since Mk. has three separate notes of time which hang all together, $15^{1.\ 25.\ 33}$ (see Wright, *Synopsis*[2], *in loc.*, and *New Test. Prob.* p. 147).

(*k*) *Conclusion from the evidence.*—The detailed comparison of Mk. with Mt. and Lk. leads us to the conclusion that either Mk. as we have it now, or at least a Gospel which differs from our Mk. in unessential particulars only, lay before the First and Third Evangelists when they wrote. If the doubtful cases mentioned above, and the instances given below in § vii., be held to argue the priority of Mt. or Lk. over Mk., that would apply only to editorial additions, and the main conclusion would not be affected. Some of the deductions made above may be questioned, yet the cumulative force of the whole is very great. And a careful study of them will at once dissipate the idea that Mark is an abbreviator of Matthew, and will lead us to the conclusion that here we come much closer to the bed-rock of the Gospel story than in either Mt. or Luke. This is the great value of Mk., and it has been left for modern scholars to discover it.

5. Other characteristics of diction in Mark.—The style of the Second Gospel may be gathered to a large extent from what has preceded. For its Aramaic tinge see below, § v. A few favourite modes of speech remain to be noticed. The use of the historic present is especially common, and this contributes largely to the vividness of the narrative. Yet there is great freedom of tenses; we find changes in the same sentence from a past tense to a historic present, and *vice versa*. Of a few particles Mark is very fond—*e.g.* εὐθύς 41 times; πολλά as adverb, 1^{45} 3^{12} $5^{10.\ 23.\ 38.\ 43}$ 6^{20} אBL 9^{26} 15^3; πάλιν $2^{1.\ 13}$ $3^{1.\ 20}$ etc.; πᾶς is used in exaggeration, *e.g.* 1^5 2^{13}; accumulated negatives are common, *e.g.* 1^{44} 2^2 $3^{20.\ 27}$. In ch. 4 καὶ ἔλεγεν or καὶ λέγει is so frequent (8 times) that Swete has raised the question (on 4^{21}) whether Mark had before him a number of detached sayings of Jesus which he here introduces.

Our Gospel has about ten somewhat striking words which are, as far as we know, ἅπαξ λεγόμενα in all Greek literature. Such are: ἔννυχα 1^{35} (cf. πάννυχα—A, etc., have ἔννυχον); ἐπιράπτει 2^{21} (D has ἐπισυνράπτει); σπεκουλάτορα 6^{27} (see above, § iii. **4** (*b*)); πυγμῇ as adv. 7^3, *i.e.* 'with arm and elbow' (a late Greek meaning—in classical Greek 'with the fist'), so 'completely' or 'diligently' (D has πυκμῇ, א πυκνά 'frequently,' and so several VSS, obviously a correction); ὑπερπερισσῶς 7^{37} (D has ὑπερεκπ.) and ἐκπερισσῶς 14^{31} (A, etc., have ἐκ περισσοῦ); τηλαυγῶς 8^{25}, *i.e.* 'clearly, though at a distance' (א*CLΔ have δηλ-); ἐπισυντρέχει 9^{25}; ἐκεφαλίωσαν 12^4 (*v.l.* λαίωσαν), see below, § vii.; προμεριμνᾶτε 13^{11}. There

are also about 70 other words which occur nowhere else in NT, though many are found in the LXX. This, as compared with the other Gospels, is a small number; Lk. has some 250 words not found elsewhere in NT (see Swete, *l.c.* p. xliv, for careful lists of words peculiar to Mk., or used by him in common with one or more of the other NT writers).

6. Matter peculiar to Mark.—The Second Gospel relates very few incidents not given, or at least referred to, in Mt. or Luke. We have only one parable peculiar to Mk., that of the seed growing secretly ($4^{26ff.}$), and only two miracles, the healing of the deaf stammerer (μογιλάλος—the *v.l.* μογγιλάλος, from μόγγος 'thick-voiced,' is not well supported) ($7^{31ff.}$), and of the blind man at Bethsaida ($8^{22ff.}$). Other paragraphs peculiar to Mk. are: the questions about the dulness of the disciples when they forgot to take bread ($8^{17f.}$), and about the disciples disputing (9^{33}); and the incidents of the young man with the linen cloth ($14^{51f.}$), of the smiting of Jesus by the servants (ὑπηρέται) of the chief priests (14^{65}), and of Pilate's wonder, and his question put to the centurion (15^{44}). See also § vii. below.

iv. AUTHORSHIP, DATE, AND PLACE OF WRITING.—There is no reason to dispute the Patristic statements (§ ii. above) that Mark, the ὑπηρέτης of Paul and Barnabas (Ac 13^5) and the disciple of Peter, was the author of the Second Gospel. And there is much probability that the statement of Clement of Alexandria, that Mark wrote in Rome, is correct. We cannot, indeed, argue from the Latinisms (see § iii. **4** (*f*)) that he wrote for the Romans, for these words are probably mere colloquialisms in common use in the whole Empire, and, moreover, the Christian Romans undoubtedly spoke, at least in the ordinary way, Greek and not Latin (see § v. **2**). But that it was written for Gentiles appears from the general absence of OT quotations, except when our Lord's words are cited ($1^{2f.}$ is an exception; 15^{28} must almost certainly be expunged from the text, being omitted by אABC*D k syr[sin] etc.); also from the interpretation of Aramaic transliterations and the explanation of Jewish customs: *e.g.* $7^{2ff.}$ (washing of hands, etc.) 12^{42} (two mites making a farthing; the λεπτόν or half quadrans, being a Jewish coin, has to be explained), 15^{42} ('the Preparation, that is, the day before the sabbath'); from the absence of mention of the Jewish law; and from the geographical description of 13^3 ('the Mount of Olives * over against the temple'). Chrysostom's statement (*Prœm. in Matt.*), that Egypt was the place of writing, is negatived by the silence of the Alexandrian Fathers Clement and Origen, and is probably a mistaken inference from Eusebius, *HE* ii. 16, which says that Mark was sent to Egypt and preached there the gospel which he had composed. Some moderns have supposed a double publication, one in Rome and one in Alexandria.

The question of *date* is more difficult. From internal considerations we should certainly assign an early date to Mk., at any rate before the Fall of Jerusalem. The Discourse on the End (esp. $13^{13f.\ 24.\ 30.\ 33}$) is reported as if the fulfilment were only in prospect, and in a manner that would be hardly possible if the siege of Titus had already taken place. This conclusion becomes still more likely when we compare Mk. with Mt. and Luke. The discourse seems to join together two separate things, the destruction of Jerusalem and the end of the world. All the Synoptics begin with the destruction of the Temple. In Mk. and Lk.

---

* Mk. uses τὸ ὄρος τῶν Ἐλαιῶν here and in 14^{26}; but in 11^1 we must probably accentuate the last word as oxytone—πρὸς τὸ ὄρος τὸ Ἐλαιῶν (B k r)—*i.e.* the substantive is Ἐλαιών, 'an olive grove' (as in Ac 1^{12} ἀπὸ ὄρους τοῦ καλουμένου Ἐλαιῶνος). See Deissmann, *Bibl. Stud.* p. 208 f., and Swete, *St. Mark* on 11^1.

follows a discourse which apparently speaks of the destruction of Jerusalem, and then the passage Mk 13²⁴⁻²⁷ seems to refer to the end of the world. But Matthew in his accustomed manner weaves together Jesus' sayings which in the other Evangelists are distinct, and mingles together the two events spoken of. Thus the compiler of the Matthæan discourse (we need beg no question as to authorship) evidently thought that the two events would be synchronous, and therefore must have written his account of the prophecy (not necessarily the whole Gospel) before the Fall of Jerusalem. If so, the Markan discourse is earlier still.

So the reference to the shewbread (2²⁶ οὐκ ἔξεστι, present) seems to imply that the Temple was at the time of writing still standing, and that the presentation of the shewbread still went on. Also the considerations mentioned above in § iii. **3, 4,** as to the description of Jesus' inner feelings, the style and details of the Gospel, point strongly in the same direction. If, again, we were to hold the theory of an Aramaic original (but see § v.), we could hardly avoid supposing a still earlier date.

We have then to consider if the external evidence contradicts the internal. The date of two other NT books affects our judgment. (*a*) If we adopt the early date for Acts (*c.* A.D. 62), *i.e.* if we suppose that St. Luke tells us no more of St. Paul's history after the two years at Rome simply because nothing more at the time of writing had happened, we must assign a still earlier date to Lk., and *a fortiori* to Mark. There is much to be said for this early date of Acts, though many hold that Lk 21²⁰ ('Jerusalem compassed with armies'), when we compare it with Mk 13¹⁴, Mt 24¹⁵ ('abomination of desolation'), betokens a writing *after* the event described. (*b*) Papias by implication, and Irenæus (iii. 1. 1) explicitly, say that Mark wrote after Peter's death (see § ii. above)—Irenæus also asserts that Matthew wrote first—while Clement of Alexandria and Origen say that he wrote in Peter's lifetime. Now, if we take the former statement as true, the date of 1 Peter is a difficulty in the way of accepting the internal evidence for the date of Mark. For we can hardly assign a very early date to it (*e.g.* 1 P 4¹⁶ '[suffer] as a Christian'). There is no great reason for believing that St. Peter died *in the same year* as St. Paul, and it is quite possible that he survived him for some considerable time, during which St. Mark acted as his interpreter. The indications of a later date in 1 Peter do not then militate against the Petrine authorship of that Epistle. But if Mark wrote his Gospel after Peter's death, the early date to which the internal evidence leads us becomes difficult. While, therefore, we might have agreed with Swete (*St. Mark*, p. xl) that the witness of Irenæus and Papias is more probable than that of Clement and Origen, if we had nothing else to go by, yet, in view of the strong internal indications of an early date, we are perhaps led to prefer the Alexandrian view that Mark wrote in the lifetime of Peter. Nevertheless Swete's date, just before A.D. 70, is chronologically possible (the order would then be 1 Peter; death of St. Peter; Mk.), but it allows very little time for the Mt. Discourse on the End to be written. Possibly the theory of a double publication might reconcile the Patristic testimony; but, if so, the second edition probably differed hardly at all from the first (see §§ vi. vii. below).

§ v. THE ARAMAIC CHARACTERISTICS AND ORIGINAL LANGUAGE OF MARK.—The external evidence would not lead us to any other conclusion than that the Greek St. Mark as we have it is an original composition, and not a translation from any Aramaic document. We have, however, to consider a noteworthy phenomenon which the Gospel itself brings out—the strong Aramaic tinge which goes all through it. This tinge has led some to postulate an Aramaic original, and to suppose that the Gospel which we possess is a translation. We may first collect together and comment on instances of this characteristic, and then consider how they bear on the question of the original language.

1. Aramaisms.—A characteristic of Mk. is the retention of several Aramaic words transliterated into Greek. Such are :—βοανηργές 3¹⁷ (=בְּנֵי רְגֶו ?, the *o* or the *a* being probably an intrusion in the text, or βανηρογές being perhaps the original reading, see Dalman, *Words of Jesus*, p. 49, *Gramm. d. Jüd.-Pal. Aramäisch*, p. 112 ; the syr ^sin ^psh is ܒܢܝ ܪܓܫܝ, which the Nestorians pronounce *bné raγsh*, the Jacobites *bné* [or *bnai*?] *r'γesh*, both with mute *yudh*—for a possible origin of these forms see Burkitt, *Evang. da-Mephar.* ii. p. 280 ; the Armenian is 'Banereges') ; ταλειθὰ κούμ 5⁴¹ (=טְלִיתָא קוּמִי, syr ^psh ܛܠܝܬܐ ܩܘܡܝ with *yudh* quiescent, syr ^sin wanting : some Greek MSS read κούμι ; see also below) ; κορβάν 7¹¹ (=קָרְבָּן, syr ^sin ܩܘܪܒܢ, syr ^psh ܩܘܪܒܢܐ, ܩܘܪܒܢܝ being the usual Syriac name for the Eucharist) ; ἐφφαθά 7³⁴ (=אֶתְפְּתַח) ; ἀββά 14³⁶ (=אַבָּא, again in Ro 8¹⁵, Gal 4⁶, see ABBA). These occur in Mk. only of the Gospels, as does the redundant Βαρτίμαιος (ὁ υἱὸς Τιμαίου Βαρ.) 10⁴⁶ (Mt. Lk. give no name ; Bartimæus could not be the blind man's own real name, though he may have been known by it ; cf. Bar-jona, Barabbas). Two others are found also in Mt. and Jn., ῥαββεί Mk 9⁵ 11²¹ 14⁴⁵ (=רַבִּי, syr ^sin ^cu ^psh ܪܒܝ), ὡσαννά 11⁹ (=הוֹשַׁעְנָא, syr ^sin ^cu ^psh ܐܘܫܥܢܐ) ; a third in Jn., ῥαββουνεί Mk 10⁵¹ (=רַבּוּנִי, syr ^sin ܪܒܘܠܝ, syr ^cu wanting in Jn. also, syr ^psh ܪܒܝ, syr ^hkl ܪܒܘܠܝ, perhaps a diminutive) ; these three are not found in Luke. The Heb.-Aram. ἀμήν (אָמֵן, syr ܐܡܝܢ) is retained by all the Evangelists, but much less often by Luke than by the others ; note also that Mk 3²⁸ ἀμὴν λέγω becomes in Mt 12³¹ διὰ τοῦτο λέγω, and so sometimes elsewhere. The Aramaic Word from the Cross is remarkable, Ἐλωΐ, Ἐλωΐ, λαμὰ σαβαχθανεί Mk 15³⁴ (אֱלָהִי א' לְמָא שְׁבַקְתָּנִי, syr ^sin ^psh ܐܝܠ ܝܘܢ ܐ ܠܡܢܐ ܫܒܩܬܢܝ with both *yudhs* quiescent ; *vv.ll.* are ἠλεί D and some old latt., λεμά and ζαφθανεί D, zaphtani *d*, zaphani *k*). The Divine name here is a Hebraized form of the pure Aramaic אֱלָהִי (syr ܐܠܗܝ). Ἐλωΐ recurs in the אB text of Mt 27⁴⁶ (so Westcott-Hort), but the AV and RV text, following other MSS, have ἠλεί or ἠλί (so syr ^sin ܐܝܠ, syr ^psh ܐܠ ; syr ^cu wanting), and this would be a correction by Matthew, or (as Westcott-Hort, *Notes*, p. 21) by a Matthæan scribe or editor, to suit the Hebrew form אֵלִי, which was no doubt familiar from liturgical worship. This reading is probably confirmed by pseudo-Peter, for it apparently underlies his strange phrase ἡ δύναμίς μου, ἡ δ., κατέλειψάς με, being mistaken for חַיִל (syr ܚܝܠܐ) 'strength.' The object of the Matthæan correction would be to make it more obvious why the people thought that Elijah was being invoked, the form Ἐλωΐ being much farther from Ἠλείας than Ἠλεί is ; and this consideration would point to our Lord Himself having used the pure Hebrew form of the Divine name rather than the Aramaic.

Certain Aramaic (or Hebrew) proper names should also be noted : Κανανᾶος 3[18] (so Mt., =Lk.

Ac. Ζηλωτής ; = Aram. קַנְאָנָא, syr[sin psh] ܩܢܢܝܐ) ; Ἰσκαριώθ 3[19], also -ώτης (so also Mt. Lk. ; Heb. אִישׁ קְרִיוֹח, syr[sin psh] ܣܟܪܝܘܛܐ ; syr[cu] ܐܣܟ in Lk 22[3]) ; Βεελζεβούλ or, as B, Βεεζεβούλ 3[22] (so Lk., and so Mt. elsewhere), a word of uncertain meaning, perhaps 'lord of dung' or 'lord of habitation' (syr[cu sin psh] ܒܥܠܙܒܘܒ 'lord of flies') ; perhaps Δαλμανουθά 8[10] (εἰς τὰ μέρη Δ.= למנותא דלמנותא, the second word being inadvertently repeated and the real name being dropped (Harris, *Study of Codex Bezæ*, p. 178 ; but see Dalman, *Words of Jesus*, p. 66 ; D has Μελεγαδά, d Magidan, syr[sin] ܡܓܕܘ, syr[psh] ܕܠܡܢܘܬܐ ; in ‖ Mt 15[39] the best Greek text has Μαγαδάν, syr[sin] as above, syr[cu] ܡܓܕܘ, syr[psh] ܡܓܕܘ) ; Γολγοθάν 15[22] אB, etc. (ἐπὶ τὸν Γολγοθὰν τόπον)=Γολγοθά Mt. Jn. (Mt. Mk. translate it by Κρανίου τόπος, Jn. leaves it without translation, Lk. has Κρανίον only ; the Aram. is גֻלגֻלתּא, syr[sin] ܓܓܘܠܬܐ in Mk. but ܓܓܘܠܬܐ in Mt., and so syr[psh] throughout, syr[sin] is wanting in Jn. ; syr[cu] is wanting in all these places ; in Lk. syr[sin cu psh] have ܩܪܩܦܬܐ).

The frequent use of a participle and the substantive verb in Mk. may well be due to Aramaic influence, the Aramaic participle with הוא, for example, forming an imperfect (see W. C. Allen in *Expositor*, 6th series, vol. i. p. 436) ; *e.g.* 1[6] ἦν ὁ Ἰωάνης ἐνδεδυμένος, 1[22] ἦν διδάσκων (so Mt.), 1[33] ἐπισυνηγμένη ἦν, and so 2[6. 18] 5[5] 6[52] 9[4] 10[22. 32] 13[25] 14[4. 40. 54] 15[7. 26. 43. 46] ; and in some 'Western' texts of 1[39] (ἦν κηρύσσων for ἦλθεν κ.) 2[4] (ἦν κατακείμενος for κατέκειτο) ; similarly also perhaps a participle with ἐγένετο, as 9[3] ἐγένετο στίλβοντα, 9[7] ἐγ. ἐπισκιάζουσα, both altered in Mt. and Lk. ; and so whichever way we read 1[4] (ἐγένετο Ἰωάνης ὁ βαπτίζων . . . κηρύσσων, *v.l.* ἐγ. Ἰ. βαπτ. . . . καὶ κηρ., altered in Mt. and Lk.).

The use of some prepositions after verbs, etc., is thought to be due to the same cause (Allen, *loc. cit.*), as ἔρχεται ὀπίσω 1[7], ἐν σοὶ εὐδόκησα 1[11], πιστεύετε ἐν 1[15], λέγουσι περὶ 1[30], ἐσθίει μετά 2[16], ἴαται ἀπό 5[29], ὕπαγε εἰς εἰρήνην 5[34], ὑγιὴς ἀπό 5[34], διὰ τῶν χειρῶν αὐτοῦ 6[2] (but the Aramaic would have the singular), ἐλάλησε μετά 6[50], λάβῃ ἀπό 12[2]. Similarly also prepositions repeated after compound verbs, as ἐξελθε ἐξ 1[25], and so 1[26. 42. 45] 2[1] 5[2. 8. 13. 17] 6[54] 7[17. 26. 29. 31] 9[25. 28. 45. 47] 10[15] etc. ; the suggestion apparently being that these represent Aramaic forms like על ל פק מן.

Phrases like δύο δύο 6[7], συμπόσια συμπόσια 6[39], πρασιαὶ πρασιαί 6[40] are Aramaic or Hebrew idioms. Also several other Aramaic phrases have been noted, as 'sons of the bridechamber' 2[19] (so Mt. Lk.), 'sons of men' 3[28] (see § vii. 2 below), εἶπε δοθῆναι 5[43], μία τῶν σαββάτων 16[2] (positive for superlative), γίνεται καί 2[15] (so Mt., not Lk.), ἐγένετο ἦλθεν 1[9] (Mk. only) ; and the indefinite use of εἶς = חַד (for τις) 9[17] 10[17] 12[28] 13[1] 14[18. 66] (Allen, *loc. cit.*). Dalman also has made a collection of Hebraisms and Aramaisms in the Gospels (*Words of Jesus*, p. 20 ff.), though he considers that they do not constitute a proof of a Hebrew or Aramaic original. Of these the following are found in Mk. :—ἐλθοῦσα redundantly used with a finite verb 7[25] (ἐ. προσέ-

πεσε) ; ἀφείς with a term signifying departure where the idea of 'leaving' is not emphasized 4[36] 8[13] 12[12] ; καθήμενον and στήκετε where they are superfluous 2[14] 11[25] ; ἀναστάς used redundantly 2[14] 7[24] 10[1. 50] (AC) ; 'answer and say' 3[33] 7[28] 9[5] 10[51] 11[14] 12[35] 15[9], often when no question has been asked ; ἐλάλησεν . . . καὶ λέγει 6[50] (?) ; ἤρξατο (-αντο) with infinitive when nothing follows developing the action, 26 times ; εὐθέως or εὐθύς, a favourite form in Mk. (45 times)=Aram. מִיָּד ; the use of πρόσωπον, not only in a quotation like 1[2], but in the phrase βλέπεις εἰς πρ. ἀνθρώπων 12[14], and some others.

2. Original language of Mark.—The Aramaic tinge in our Gospel is thought by some, *e.g.* Blass (*Philology of the Gospels*, ch. xi.) and Allen (*loc. cit.*), to show that it was originally written in Aramaic. A large number of the real or alleged Aramaisms given above are found in Mt. and Lk. ; but it is argued that as they had *ex hypothesi* Mk. before them, they merely retained a certain number of the Aramaisms of their source. Moreover, the Aramaisms are found not only in the words of our Lord, in which case they might be explained as being due to the faithful reporting of His *ipsissima verba*, but also in the framework of the Gospel. On the theory of an Aramaic original, Allen explains the frequent use in Mk. of καί as a connecting link (cf. Aram. ו), and of five particles constantly used, εὐθύς (see above), πάλιν, δέ, γάρ, ἀλλά, other particles being rare. He also explains the favourite historic present in Mk. as coming from the use of an Aramaic present participle for this purpose. In Syriac it is so found only in the verb אמר 'to say' (Nöldeke, *Syr. Gramm.* § 274, p. 190), except in syr[hkl], where it is a literal translation. But in the other Aramaic dialects this usage is not so limited ; the idiom is found with other verbs, *e.g.* in Daniel and Tobit, and its presence in an original Aramaic Mk. would bring us to the frequent historic presents in the Greek Mk. The irregularity noticed above (§ iii. 5) of their being mixed up with past tenses occurs also in Aramaic. It is also thought that the difficult εἰς τριάκοντα καὶ εἰς (*v.l.* ἐν Westcott-Hort) ἑξήκοντα καὶ εἰς (*v.l.* ἐν WH) ἑκατόν in 4[8] (cf. 4[20]) is explained by the εἰς (*i.e.* εἷς) representing חַד, cf. Dn 3[19] (but equally well εἷς might represent an Aramaic בְּ 'at the rate of') ; and that the ἔρχεται of 4[21] and ἐν ὀνόματι ὅτι of 9[41] and ἐπιβαλών of 14[72] (see above, § iii. 4 (h)) come from a mistranslation of some (unknown) Aramaic original. In the *JThSt* ii. 298, Allen suggests that the word ἐκεφαλίωσαν (12[4]) is due to a confusion of אבאיש 'they injured' with אראיש, which would be a puzzle to the translator, who rendered it by this coined word, taking it from Aram. שׁא 'a head.' Similarly, Prof. Marshall (*Expositor*, 4th series, iv. 377) thinks that Mk 5[10] ἔξω τῆς χώρας and ‖ Lk 8[31] εἰς τὴν ἄβυσσον (Mt. different) are the result of translations of one Aramaic original, אֲרַע meaning both 'earth' or 'land' and 'below.'

Blass brings different arguments on the same side. They run in two lines. (*a*) He suggests that St. Luke in Ac 1–12 used an Aramaic source, while the rest of the book was his own independent work. In these twelve chapters Aramaisms abound, while in the rest of the book they are comparatively scarce ; and the style of the twelve chapters is rough as compared with St. Luke's own. Blass conjectures that Mark, who, as son of a prominent Christian lady in Jerusalem, was well fitted for the task, wrote the Aramaic source. [With this we may compare Weiss's idea that Mark ended his Gospel at 16[8] because he went on to write a second work, which began with the Resurrection appearances]. If so, the first work, *i.e.* the Gospel, would be in Aramaic. (*b*) Blass thinks that the various readings in the present MSS of Mk., and those shown by Patristic quotations, are relics of different translations of an original Aramaic.

In reviewing these considerations, we must remark that Dr. Blass's first argument rests on pure conjecture. Why should Mark be the writer of the supposed Aramaic source of Ac 1–12? And if so, why must he have written two books in the same language? He was confessedly bilingual, able to write in both Greek and Aramaic. This argument, then, is a halting one. And the second seems scarcely less precarious. The suggestions of Mr. Allen are more substantial. But these also appear to be inconclusive. They certainly show that the Aramaic tinge, strong in all the Synoptics, is strongest in Mark. But this need mean no more than that Aramaic was St. Mark's native language, that in which he thought, as most of the Palestinian Jews would do. The Greek spoken in Palestine was doubtless saturated with Aramaic forms and idioms, and Mark, whose style is comparatively unpolished, discarded them less than the other Synoptists. The theory of an Aramaic original has some formidable difficulties to overcome. Papias had evidently never heard of any but a Greek Mk., and no ecclesiastical writer suggests that the latter is a translation. The external evidence is all against the hypothesis which we have been examining. But so, also, when we look closely, is the internal evidence. It is true that there are many Aramaisms in Mark. Of these, however, we may dismiss, for our present purpose, the proper names, which would be used in Palestine equally whether an author wrote in Aramaic or in Greek. The influence of Aramaic grammar and diction may also probably be dismissed, seeing that the writer doubtless thought in Aramaic. There remain, then, the suggestions of mistranslation, which, however, are too ingenious for verisimilitude, and the transliterations like *Talitha Cumi*. But the fact that practically in each case of transliteration a Greek interpretation is added, is fatal to the idea that we have here traces of a conservative translator who incorporated bodily the words which he found in the book before him. As Swete remarks (*St. Mark*, p. xlii), a translator might have either translated the Aramaic or transliterated it; but transliteration followed by interpretation savours of an original writer. A still more fatal objection is the freshness of the style of our Gospel. Even the best translation loses the individuality of the author. But here we have a book in which the individuality is most strongly marked. It can hardly be a second-hand reproduction of any one's work.

If the Aramaic-original theory be true, we must put back the date considerably, as Mr. Allen (*loc. cit.*) sees, probably to a date before A.D. 60; and then the Gospel is not likely to have been written in Rome. In this last detail the ecclesiastical testimony is again contradicted by the theory.

There is a line of argument which, though interesting, does not really bear on this question. In 5⁴¹, for ταλειθά or ταλιθά, D has θαβιτά, supported by Old Latin *tabitha*, or *thabitha*, or *thabita*, as if the girl's name were Tabitha (cf. Ac 9²⁰). In a Syriac text the transition from ﺗﺒﻴﺜﺎ to ﻃﺒﻴﺜﺎ would be easy. The Old Latin MS *e* has the curious reading 'tabea acultha quod est interpretatum puella tibi dico exsurge.' But these variations show nothing as to the original language of Mk.; they show only that D and the Old Latin MSS were directly or indirectly influenced by the Syriac versions (see Chase, *Syro-Latin Text of the Gospels*, p. 109 f.).

Finally, we must consider the statement of some cursive Greek MSS, that the Gospel was written in Latin ('Ρωμαϊστί). They add that it was written in Rome, and this is no doubt the explanation of the other statement. It was supposed that if Rome was the place of writing, the Gospel must have been written in Latin. But this deduction is known to be without warrant. Those in Rome for whom the Gospel was written would speak Greek. St. Paul wrote to the Christian community in Rome in Greek, and St. Clement wrote from Rome in the same language. Further, even a cursory examination of Mk. shows that, whatever it is, it is not a translation into Greek from Latin. Thus this idea may be very briefly dismissed.

vi. THE LAST TWELVE VERSES.—The question of the end of the Gospel is one of great difficulty, whatever view we take of the paragraph which now brings it to a close. An endeavour will be made in this section to state and weigh all the principal arguments; it would seem that neither the supporters nor the impugners of the present ending have quite done justice to the strength of the arguments on the other side. The facts to be considered are as follows. There are three ways of ending the Gospel. The first, here called the 'Short Ending,' stops at 16⁸ ἐφοβοῦντο γάρ. The second, here cited as the 'Long Ending,' is that of our ordinary Bibles (16⁹⁻²⁰), the last twelve verses. But there is also a third, here called the 'Intermediate Ending,' which runs as follows: πάντα δὲ τὰ παρηγγελμένα τοῖς περὶ τὸν Πέτρον συντόμως ἐξήγγειλαν. μετὰ δὲ ταῦτα καὶ αὐτὸς ὁ Ἰησοῦς [ἐφάνη αὐτοῖς καὶ] ἀπὸ ἀνατολῆς καὶ ἄχρι δύσεως ἐξαπέστειλεν δι' αὐτῶν τὸ ἱερὸν καὶ ἄφθαρτον κήρυγμα τῆς αἰωνίου σωτηρίας. 'And they immediately (*or* briefly) made known all things that had been commanded (them) to those about Peter. And after this Jesus himself [appeared to them and] sent out by means of them from the East even to the West the holy and incorruptible preaching of the eternal salvation.' This ending is found in four minor uncials, L (Codex Regius, 8th cent.), ٦¹² (Fragmentum Sinaiticum, 7th cent.), ρ (Fragm. Parisiense, 8th cent.), and Ψ (Codex Athous Lauræ, 8th or 9th cent.), in all of them as an alternative to the Long Ending, though it would appear that the archetype of the first three, at any rate, ended at 16⁸. The Intermediate Ending is also found in the Old Latin *k*, standing alone, in several MSS of the Ethiopic prefixed to the Long Ending, and in the margin of syr ʰᵏˡ, of two Bohairic MSS, and of a cursive Greek MS. No one maintains its genuineness; it is clearly written as an end to the Gospel, and is not an independent fragment. It is probably due to an early scribe, who wrote it either because he had before him the Long Ending and objected to it, or because he had before him the Short Ending and thought it abrupt. Swete (*St. Mark*, p. cviii) conjectures that he was a Western, because of the emphasis laid on the West. Nestle makes him an Egyptian, without giving reasons (Hastings' *DB* iii. 13). Dobschütz (*TU* xi. 1, p. 73 f., quoted by Swete) thinks that the ending is part of the 'Preaching of Peter'; but the internal evidence is against this (see above). It is not found in any of the Fathers. Its presence, however, bears materially on the whole question. The only variation in the readings that need be mentioned is that ἐφάνη αὐτοῖς καί, which the sense clearly demands, is omitted by L٦, αὐτοῖς καί is omitted by Ψ, and καί by all the Greek codices,—it has to be supplied from the versions.

The Short Ending is found in אB, syr ˢⁱⁿ, and also in the oldest MSS of the Armenian and Ethiopic versions. Eusebius says (*ad Marin.* Quæst. 1, vol. 4) that the Long Ending was not in the 'accurate copies' of his day; later writers copy Eusebius, and do not add to our knowledge. Tertullian, Cyprian, Athanasius, and Cyril of

Jerusalem are silent about the Long Ending; and this would be very significant if it were not that Cyril of Alexandria and Theodoret are also silent, though they must have known verses which were in wide circulation in their time. Here we must note, further, that the fact that the Short Ending could scarcely have been the original close of the Gospel (see below), is no argument for the genuineness of the other two extant endings.

The Long Ending is found in practically all the authorities except those mentioned above—in almost all the uncials and cursives, the lectionaries, in the great majority of versions. It is explicitly quoted by Irenæus as a genuine part of Mk. (iii. 10. 6: 'in fine autem evangelii ait Marcus, Et quidem Dominus Jesus,' etc. = Mk 16[19]). It is also probably referred to by Justin (*Apol.* i. 45: ἐξελθόντες πανταχοῦ ἐκήρυξαν = Mk 16[20]); possibly by 'Barnabas' (xv. 9, φανερωθεὶς ἀνέβη εἰς οὐρανούς; cf. Mk 16[14] ἐφανερώθη) and Hermas (*Sim.* IX. xxv. 1, 2; cf. Mk 16[15]). But these last two cases are quite uncertain, and there is no evidence at all that any Father before Irenæus knew these verses *as part of the Gospel*; they may have known them from some other writer. Dr. Salmon argues with some force (*Introd.*, appendix to Lect. ix.) that though אB have not got these verses, yet in this part they are copied from one archetype which probably did contain them. The scribes seem to have purposely omitted something which was in the archetype, leaving a blank or distending the writing, and that something must have been of about the same length as the Long Ending. Salmon conjectures that the scribes of א and B were of the school of Eusebius, and that they left out these verses, though they had them in their original, because Eusebius disapproved of them. No writer before Eusebius is known to have rejected them, and their presence in all later MSS shows that the successors of Eusebius, in spite of his great authority, did not follow his judgment in the matter. If, however, Salmon's argument on this part of the subject is sound, and if אB when cross-examined give evidence, as he says, *for* the disputed ending and not against it, yet the absence of the ending in syr[sin] and in Eusebius' 'more accurate copies' remains a stumbling-block to accepting the further inference that the Long Ending is genuine. Mr. F. C. Conybeare has suggested (*Expositor*, 4th series, viii. 241) that these verses are the work of the Aristion mentioned by Papias as one of our Lord's disciples. In an Armenian MS. of the Gospels written A.D. 986 (only discovered in 1891), the Long Ending is said to be 'of the presbyter Ariston,' and it is not unreasonable to understand Aristion to be meant, the iota having fallen in transcription into Armenian. But the evidence is too late to be of much worth.

The internal evidence is important. It is freely admitted by the supporters of the Long Ending that its style and vocabulary are entirely different from those of the main part of the Gospel; and this consideration is decisive against the authorship being the same. But this does not at once bring us to a solution of all our difficulties. As far as style goes, it does not necessarily follow that the Long Ending is not by St. Mark. Salmon (*loc. cit.*) suggests that our Second Gospel is, in its present form, the latest of the Synoptics, St. Mark having, indeed, followed the written Petrine tradition more faithfully than the others, and having incorporated it in his Gospel almost in its own words, prefixing 1[1-15] and adding 16[9ff.], inserting also various editorial touches (for which see § vii. **2** below). Certainly both the first fifteen and the last twelve verses of our Gospel show the same system of summarizing events,—Salmon suggests that it was these two passages which led Augustine to call Mark an abbreviator of Matthew,—and so far they might be by the same author. Yet the style of the 'preface' and that of the 'appendix' are not similar. A greater objection to this view is that it supposes in reality a Peter-Gospel not written by St. Mark; but ecclesiastical writers never represent St. Peter as writing a Gospel, either by himself or by any scribe or 'interpreter' except St. Mark. For we notice that this theory will not bear the weight of the additional hypothesis (not Salmon's), that St. Mark wrote a first edition, perhaps at Rome, and afterwards a later one, *with added matter*, perhaps at Alexandria. The style-argument is decisively against this; moreover, some traces of the original ending would have survived, and the Church to which he gave his first edition would have preserved the words with which that edition closed.

There is one consideration which seems to the present writer decisive against Dr. Salmon's view. The Long Ending could not, like the Intermediate one, have been written—whether by Mark or by another—expressly to finish the Gospel left unfinished at 16[8]. For the beginning of v.[9] is not continuous with v.[8]. The subject of ἐφάνη had evidently been indicated in the sentence which had preceded; yet the necessary 'Jesus' cannot be understood from anything in v.[8]. Further, Mary Magdalene is introduced in v.[9] as a new person,—she is indicated as one παρ' ἧς ἐκβεβλήκει ἑπτὰ δαιμόνια,—though she had just been mentioned by name in 15[40, 47] 16[1], and though she was one of the women spoken of throughout the eight verses preceding the Long Ending. This paragraph, then, must be a fragment of a larger work, and could not have been composed on purpose to end the Gospel. It is, indeed, too much to say that it is a summary of events of the Forty Days, complete in itself, but at least it fits very badly on to the rest of the Gospel.

The presence of the Intermediate Ending also militates against the last twelve verses being the work of St. Mark. It shows that in very early times, how early we cannot say, these verses were not unanimously received. The evidence of Irenæus, however, shows that they were adopted as an ending to the Gospel not later than the middle of the 2nd century.

We must probably, then, dismiss the idea that either the Long or the Intermediate Ending was the work of the Second Evangelist. We have, however, still to consider the problem suggested by the Short Ending.

It is inconceivable that 16[8], with its abrupt and inauspicious ἐφοβοῦντο γάρ, could possibly be the end of a Gospel; indeed, it seems to stop in the middle of a sentence. Against this it is said that abrupt terminations are not unknown in Greek literature (see Salmond in Hastings' *DB* iii. 253). Yet in this case such an idea is hardly tenable. It is very unlikely that the Gospel should deliberately end without any incident of the risen life of our Lord and with a note of terror. We have therefore to suppose a *lost ending*; and the difficulty of accounting for its total disappearance is the strongest argument of the supporters of the last twelve verses. It is not sufficient to pass it by, as is often done by those who impugn them, as a matter of little importance.

It is suggested that the last leaf of the original was early lost, and that the other extant endings were supplied to take its place. The last leaf of a MS is undoubtedly the very one which is most likely, after much use, to disappear. Dr. Salmon points out (*loc. cit.*) that this idea is based on the supposition that the original *completely* disappeared. The hypothesis of a lost leaf would account for a partial circulation of shorter copies, but for the complete disappearance of the old ending only if it was Mark's own autograph that lost its leaf before any copy was made from it. But it is difficult to suppose that only one MS of the Gospel existed in Mark's lifetime, and that his autograph was not copied till he died ; and if the leaf fell in Mark's lifetime before the autograph was copied, why did not Mark write another ?

There is an equal difficulty in the kindred supposition that the Gospel was left accidentally unfinished at 16⁸. Salmon asks why, if Mark died before completing his work, the disciple who gave the work to the world did not add a suitable ending, as Tertius added something to Romans (16²²), and the presbyters (probably) to the Fourth Gospel (Jn 21²⁴)? If suitable endings were added afterwards, why not at the time when the Gospel was first published ? And this supposition is against the ecclesiastical testimony, which makes Mark finish his Gospel, and in some cases makes him take it to Egypt.

It cannot be said that these difficulties have been very satisfactorily met. Perhaps in our present state of knowledge the best solution of them is that of Dean Armitage Robinson, who suggests (*Study of the Gospels*, p. 5) that the Second Gospel was not highly esteemed in the 2nd cent., and that all copies perished but one, which lost its leaf. We know that the Gospel was neglected later on (see above, § ii.), chiefly on account of its shortness, and because it apparently adds little to our information. This may well have been the case early in the 2nd cent.; and if that be so, the circulation of it would not have been nearly so large as that of the other Gospels. It is not, however, necessary to put the loss of the leaf so late. The same state of things might well have existed immediately after St. Mark's death.

The difficulties on neither side can be neglected. But our verdict must be given after weighing probabilities, and to the present writer they seem overwhelmingly to preponderate against the Markan authorship of the last twelve verses, or even against their being a real ending of the Gospel at all. But they are, nevertheless, like the *Pericope Adulteræ*, an exceedingly ancient and authoritative record of the words and deeds narrated in them.

vii. Is our Second Gospel the original which lay before the First and Third Evangelists?—Those who in the present day answer this question in the negative usually take a different line from that taken by Baur and his school. They regard our present canonical Gospel as an edited and augmented form of the original, yet as retaining almost all the characteristic features of that original. This hypothesis is much more tenable than the Tübingen theory, which made all our Synoptic Gospels 2nd cent. productions, and held that the Mk. known to Papias was not our Mk., but something entirely different. These two hypotheses are, in reality, inconsistent, and must be considered separately. [For an attempt partially to combine them see Sanday's *Gosp. in Sec. Cent.* v. 2, written in 1876, and not since reprinted. It is not known if Dr. Sanday would still maintain the opinions which he then held].

1. Baur, Schleiermacher, Wendt, Davidson, Renan, and others substantially agree in holding the latter hypothesis. Papias says that St. Mark wrote Christ's words and deeds 'accurately' but 'not in order' (see above, § ii.). From this it is concluded that the Mk. of Papias ('Ur-Marcus') was not written 'in order,' but was a disjointed collection of speeches and anecdotes ; and, further, was not a Gospel in our later sense of the word, but something of the nature of the *Clementine Homilies*, a record of the sayings and teachings of *Peter*. Again, Papias says that Matthew com-

posed the 'oracles' (λόγια) in the Hebrew language, and each one interpreted them (ἡρμήνευσε, aorist— the interpreting did not go on in Papias' own day) as he could. We need not here discuss the question of the original language of Mt., but the argument which we are now considering is that, whereas our present Gospels resemble one another in general plan, and to a great extent in detail, the Mt. of Papias was very different from his Mk., the former being a collection of discourses, the latter a narrative of the words and deeds of Christ. Renan (*Vie de Jésus*, p. xxii) supposes that Matthew wrote the discourses and Mark the anecdotes about Christ, and that by assimilation our present Mt. and Mk. took their shape, the former assimilating the anecdotes and adding them to the discourses, the latter adopting the reverse process. A further argument on the same side has been drawn from the evidence of Justin Martyr (see above, § ii.), who constantly quotes the Evangelic narrative, but in words that in many cases differ from our canonical Synoptics, so that if he had the latter before him, we cannot always be sure which he is quoting ; we need not here consider whether he used the Fourth Gospel. The conclusion which at one time used to be drawn from Justin's quotations, and from his mentioning one or two things not found in the canonical texts, *e.g.* that Christ was born in a cave, and that the Magi came from Arabia, was that he used Gospels different from those which we now have. Perhaps also we should insert under this head the fact that a comparatively long section in Mk. (6⁴⁵-8²⁶) is omitted by Luke, from which it is argued by some that Luke's Mk. was not the same as our own. It is also argued that the records of the Two Feedings show that our Mk. is a compilation from two separate originals, one of which narrated the feeding of the 5000, the other of the 4000, and that it cannot be the work, directly or indirectly, of an eye-witness.

When we consider these arguments, we are struck by the fact that they assume several disputable points. It is not at all clear that Papias meant that his Mk. was an unconnected collection of anecdotes ; it is quite as probable that he meant that he did not approve of the chronological order of Mk.; and, as we have seen (§ ii.), St. Luke was perhaps of the same opinion. It is also assumed as obvious that Papias meant only 'discourses' by λόγια. Certainly that is the primary meaning of the word. But its use in the sense of 'oracles,' *i.e.* the inspired Scriptures, is quite common in early Christian times. In Ro 3² τὰ λόγια τοῦ Θεοῦ may, indeed, refer only to God's sayings (as Sanday-Headlam, *in loc.*; see also Sanday, *Gosp. in Second Cent.* p. 155), but it is more natural to refer it to the whole of OT. Sanday-Headlam remark that from the time of Philo onwards the word was used of any sacred writing, whether discourse or narrative. Thus, then, we cannot assume without argument that Papias meant only discourses by λόγια. Eusebius (*HE* iii. 39) tells us that Papias' own work was called Λογίων κυριακῶν ἐξηγήσεις (*v.l.* ἐξήγησις), and Papias clearly did not deal only with our Lord's sayings. It is at least quite possible that Papias uses the word λόγια as equivalent to our 'Gospel' (so Westcott, *Canon*, p. 80 n.; Lightfoot, *Ess. on Sup. Rel.* pp. 155 n., 171 f.). If so, the argument from the dissimilarity of Papias' Mt. and Mk. breaks down. But even supposing (as living scholars are more willing to grant than were Lightfoot and Westcott) that λόγια in Papias means 'discourses,' his words do not necessarily mean that Matthew wrote sayings *only*; and we shall be led to the contrary opinion by a great difficulty that meets the hypothesis in question at the outset. There was no time for the process imagined by Renan to take place. Such a process would take a very much longer time in its development than can by any possibility be allowed. And a fatal objection to the hypothesis is that the result would not be that which as a matter of fact has taken place. We should have had a great number of variant Gospels, and the earlier the copies the greater would have been the variations. We should have had no certainty as to which Gospel could rightly claim any given incident, and there would have been in an aggravated form the textual conditions that we find in the case of the *Pericope Adulteræ*, which appears sometimes in one Gospel and sometimes in another. In reality the four Gospels are perfectly distinct, and have been so as far back as we have any copies of them, the earliest MSS showing as distinct a division between them as the later ones (see Salmon, *Introd.* Lect. vii.; Lightfoot, *op. cit.* p. 172 ff.). Justin Martyr tells us that the 'memoirs of the Apostles' (*i.e.* the Gospels) were read at Christian worship in his time (*Apol.* i. 67). If the Gospels then read were our canonical Gospels, there is not sufficient time between Papias and Justin for such a revolution to have taken place as is supposed. If, on the other hand, Justin used the supposed 'original Matthew' and 'original Mark,' there is not time between him and Irenæus for the same thing to have happened. As a matter of fact, it is now generally held that Justin knew at least our Synoptic Gospels. This does not mean that he had no other sources of information, such as oral tradition, or even that he did not borrow from an 'apocryphal' Gospel; the 'cave' at Bethlehem, for example, may well have come from some one or other of such sources. But a careful analysis of his quotations from OT shows that he varies from the true text in these quite as much as in his Gospel quotations; and most of the variations probably arise from his trusting to memory. The difficulty of turning to a manuscript without divisions, even for words, is so great, that the memory would be trusted in a far greater degree than with us who have printed Bibles. And, as we should have conjectured, Justin is much more accurate in his longer quotations, where he would be obliged to refer to his manuscript, than in his shorter ones, where it would be less necessary to do so (see, further, Sanday, *Gospels in Second Cent.* ch. ii.; Salmon, *Introd.* Lect. vi.). Moreover, we may remark that an 'original Mark' could not have disappeared without leaving any trace; we should have found some quotations from it, or some reference to its being dispossessed by a more modern successor. And the autoptic argument (above, § iii. 2) comes in here with overwhelming force. Our Mk. could not have had its fresh, lifelike character, its evidence of first-hand knowledge, if Renan's idea were true.

The argument from the omission by Luke of a Markan section is inconclusive. He had a long section to introduce (§ iii. 4 (*a*) above), and it was natural for him to omit something, to make room for his new matter. The section of Mk. is found, in the same order, in Mt., and therefore, if this argument held good, it would be necessary to suppose that, while Luke used an 'original Mark,' the First Evangelist used our present one. Also, two incidents in this section are referred to shortly in Lk., the seeking of a sign and the leaven of the Pharisees (Lk 11¹⁶·²⁹ 12¹). The conclusion from .'doublets' is very insecure. There is no reason why there should not have been two Feedings.

2. The hypothesis that our present Mk. is an 'edited' form of the Gospel which was used by Matthew and Luke, is in reality quite different from that which has just been considered. For it supposes that our Second Gospel is very like the original, differing from it only by the insertion

of a few editorial touches, at the most by the addition of a few paragraphs; whereas the other hypothesis supposes our Mk. to be entirely different from the original Gospel. Dr. Salmon proposes one form of the hypothesis which we have now reached (*Introd.* Lect. ix. s.f.). He suggests that our Second Gospel is at once the oldest and the youngest of the three Synoptics; the oldest as giving most nearly the very words in which the Apostolic traditions were delivered, the youngest as respects the date when the independent traditions were set in their present framework. This opinion is largely influenced by his view that the Long Ending is really Markan (see above, § vi.). He supposes that Mark added, besides the first fifteen and the last twelve verses, some other slight portions; and that the remarks about unbelief 3⁵ 6⁶·⁵², which are not found in the other Synoptics, are by the writer of the Long Ending (cf. 16¹¹·¹³f·), *i.e.* by St. Mark, as the editor of the Petrine Tradition. From an opposite standpoint, Schmiedel (*Encyc. Bibl.* ii. 1844, 1848, 1850 f.) thinks that the canonical Mk. is a later edition, and that several things in it are 'secondary' to Mt. and Luke. One leading consideration urged by him (also by Sanday, *Gosp. in Second Cent.* v. § 2, p. 149) is that Mt. and Lk. often agree against Mk.; therefore, unless the First Evangelist knew the Third Gospel, or the Third Evangelist the First (both of which suppositions are confessedly improbable), they must have had a form of Mk. which is not ours. But this assumes too much; it supposes that the First and Third Evangelists had no other source (besides Mk.) than a collection of discourses, *i.e.* that the 'non-Markan document' could not have been a history parallel to Mark. As Schmiedel himself rightly says, this assumption is not necessarily true. But if so, his argument, given above, has little weight. There is no reason why Mt. and Lk. should not have got their agreements as against Mk. from the non-Markan source. There is no reason to believe that the latter carefully avoided everything contained in the Petrine tradition; and if it included some things which were in that tradition, there is no reason why Matthew and Luke should not sometimes have followed it in preference.

As this question of agreement of Mt. and Lk. against Mk. is of great importance in forming a judgment about the Second Gospel, it is necessary to consider some details. As examples, it will suffice to give instances from the first few chapters: Mk 1⁸ πνεύματι ἁγίῳ = Mt. Lk. πν. ἁγ. καὶ πυρί; 1³¹, Mt. inserts ἠγέρθη καὶ, Lk. ἀναστᾶσα; 1⁴⁰·and 2³, Mt. Lk. insert (but in different ways) ἰδού; 2³ φέροντες, Mt. Lk. insert (but in different ways) ἐπὶ κλίνης; 2¹² ἐξῆλθεν ἔμπροσθεν πάντων = Mt. Lk. ἀπῆλθεν εἰς τὸν οἶκον αὐτοῦ; *ib.* ἐξίστασθαι = Mt. ἐφοβήθησαν = Lk. ἐπλήσθησαν φόβου; 2²² ὁ οἶνος ἀπόλλυται, κ.τ.λ., Mt. inserts ἐκχεῖται, Lk. ἐκχυνθήσεται, and both transpose ἀπόλλ.; *ib.* ἀλλ' οἶνον νέον, κ.τ.λ., Mt. inserts βάλλουσι, Lk. βλητέον, but both come from the βάλλει (Mt. βάλλουσι) which had just preceded; 3¹⁸ᵃ, Mt. Lk. insert 'his brother' (Mt. nominative, Lk. accusative), and both transfer Andrew to a place just after Peter; 3²³, Mt. inserts εἰδὼς δὲ τὰς ἐνθυμήσεις αὐτῶν, Lk. αὐτὸς δὲ εἰδὼς αὐτῶν τὰ διανοήματα; 4¹¹, Mt. Lk. insert γνῶναι (see above, § iii. 4 (*h*)); 4³¹, Mt. Lk. insert ὃν λαβὼν ἄνθρωπος; 5²⁷ ἥψατο τοῦ ἱματίου αὐτοῦ, Mt. Lk. insert τοῦ κρασπέδου. The other chapters give similar results; *e.g.* Mk 14⁶⁵, Mt. Lk. insert τίς ἐστιν ὁ παίσας σε; 14⁷², Mt. and (?) Lk. insert καὶ ἐξελθὼν ἔξω ἔκλαυσεν πικρῶς (but see § iii. 4 (*h*) above). These changes, or most of them, could not, as Sanday (*loc. cit.*) points out, have been accidental. The same cannot be said of the great majority of the instances often quoted of supposed agreement of Mt.–Lk. against Mk.; most of them are so minute and unimportant that they do not argue any common bond between the First and Third Evangelists except common sense.

Now, the argument which we are considering suggests that these inserted phrases were originally in Mk., but were omitted or altered by a later editor. Is this in the least probable? There is no reason that we can conceive why they should have been omitted or altered. In some cases it is most improbable that anything of the kind should have happened, for it would mean the introduction by a later editor of harsh or difficult phrases not found in Mt. or Lk. (see § iii. 4 (*h*) above). On the other hand, the theory that the non-Markan source or sources used by Matthew and Luke contained narrative as well as discourses has all the marks of probability, to put the matter at the lowest. See, for example, the non-Markan paragraphs collected in the second division of Wright's *Synopsis*, which contains the narratives of the Temptation and of the Baptist's preaching; and there are many others. If this be the case, the result is exactly what we should expect. Matthew and Luke sometimes follow Mark rather than the non-Markan source; sometimes one follows the one and the other the other; and sometimes both follow the non-Markan source. Probably no one would have thought otherwise but for presuppositions founded on the λόγια sentence of Papias.

But Schmiedel (*loc. cit.*) finds in certain passages indications of our Mk. being 'secondary' to Mt. and Luke. Such are 3^{28} πάντα ἀφεθήσεται τοῖς υἱοῖς τῶν ἀνθρώπων, where ‖ Mt $12^{31f.}$ has ἀνθρώποις, but goes on to say: 'Whosoever shall speak a word against *the Son of Man*, it shall be forgiven him.' The supposition is that the editor of our Mk. did not like this latter phrase, which had been common to Mt. and the original Mk., and omitted it, but kept the words 'Son of Man' by altering the ἀνθρώποις of Mt. to τοῖς υἱοῖς τῶν ἀνθρώπων. It seems much more probable that Matthew got the additional sentence from the non-Markan source; and Mark's 'sons of men' as equivalent to 'men,' a common Semitic idiom, is on a par with his other Aramaisms (see § vi. above). In 7^{27} occurs a phrase, 'Let the children first be filled,' which is not in Mt., and is thought by Schmiedel to be an insertion in our Mk., showing 'some aversion to Jewish particularism,' as toning down our Lord's answer. Yet Mt 8^{11} shows much more 'aversion.' In 9^{1} the phrase 'the kingdom of God come (ἐληλυθυῖαν) in (with) power' is thought to be a correction of 'the Son of man coming (ἐρχόμενον) in his kingdom,' Mt 16^{28}, as postponing the Parousia, which the result showed to be not so near as was at first believed. Here Luke (9^{27}) has 'the kingdom of God' simply, which at least shows no priority to Mark. It is much more likely that 'the kingdom of God,' with or without the addition 'come in (with) power,' was our Lord's own phrase, and that Matthew, as is his wont, gives the explanation, no doubt prompted by the belief of the first age that Jesus would return in the lifetime of those 'standing here' (see Sanday in Hastings' *DB* ii. 635). The awkward turn of the wording in 9^{12}, used above (§ iii. 4 (*h*)) as an indication of Mk.'s priority, Matthew smoothing down an awkward phrase, is held by Schmiedel to show our Mk.'s 'secondary' character; he thinks that our Mk. has introduced a 'sense-destroying parenthesis'—surely a very strange thing for an *editor* to do, whatever an original author might have done. In 11^{25} we find ὁ πατὴρ ὑμῶν ὁ ἐν τοῖς οὐρανοῖς (where ‖ Mt. has ὁ π. ὑ. ὁ οὐράνιος), the only Markan instance (perhaps 11^{26} of TR is an interpolation) of an express characteristic of Mt., and it is thought to

be an editorial addition. This argument, however, would necessitate the supposition that the first clause of the Lord's Prayer, as given in Mt., was an invention of the First Evangelist, which is very unlikely. It is true that the shorter or Lukan form shows much of Luke's style, and some of the differences between it and the Matthæan form seem to be due to Luke himself (see Plummer on Lk 11^{1}), the Matthæan form being probably nearer the original; and Dr. Chase supposes that the first Christians adapted the prayer for liturgical use (*TS*, Camb., i. 3). But it is quite unnecessary to suppose that the phrase 'Our Father which art in heaven' was first found in Matthew. From Mark's account of the Wicked Husbandmen ($12^{2ff.}$), where one messenger is mentioned on each occasion, and then, 'in a quite unnecessary and even disturbing manner,' many others, Schmiedel argues the priority of Mt., where several servants are sent on each occasion. It is hard to see any force in this. Matthew is as likely to have corrected Mark (if it be a correction) as our Mk. to have introduced a gratuitous inconsistency (if it be an inconsistency) under the influence of Matthew. In the discourse on the Coming of the Son of Man, after the account of the afflictions, Mk 13^{24} has: 'In those days, after that tribulation, the sun shall be darkened,' while ‖ Mt. has 'immediately after,' etc. This is said to show the posteriority of a supposed Markan editor who desires to postpone the Parousia, as in the case of 9^{1} (above); but as there, so here, it is more probable that Matthew's εὐθέως is an explanation, and Mark's ἐν ἐκείναις ταῖς ἡμέραις is our Lord's own phrase, or nearly so.

Thus, although there is nothing in the nature of things why our Second Gospel should not be an edited form of the original document that lay before Matthew and Luke, the reasons alleged by Schmiedel will hardly convince us that this is the case. Salmon's argument really depends on the view taken of the last twelve verses (see above, § vi.). If on other grounds we believe them to be by the writer who put our Second Gospel into its present shape, then we may accept his theory; but if otherwise, the theory falls.

If, however, we were to accept the hypothesis of a later editor, it would be of interest to trace the portions due to him. We may put aside Dr. Salmon's suggestion (see above) of 1^{1-15} 3^{5} $6^{6.52}$ $16^{9ff.}$ unless we accept the appendix as a real ending to the Gospel. But we might hold that several paragraphs peculiar to Mk. are due to this supposed editor; such as $3^{19b. 20. 21}$ (accusation of madness by Jesus' friends: though here we might equally hold that the omission in Mt. and Lk. is due to the same feeling as in § iii. 3 above), 4^{26-29} (the seed growing secretly), $7^{3f.}$ (explanation about washings), 7^{32-37} (the healing of the deaf μογιλάλος), 8^{22-26} (the blind man of Bethsaida), $14^{51f.}$ (the young man who fled naked), 15^{21} (the names Alexander and Rufus). It might also be thought that the Aramaisms and Latinisms were due to such an editor (but see above, §§ iii. 4 (*f*), (*g*), v.). These are points which are peculiar to our Gospel.

But a consideration which militates against such a large amount of editing is that our Mk. retains at once the original roughness and the original freshness of style. If the canonical Mk. is later than and influenced by Mt. and Lk., why did not its editor correct the mistakes and prune the vulgarisms and roughnesses as did Matthew and Luke? While, however, this seems to forbid the idea of any large amount of editing, it is certainly possible that a later editor has introduced a few phrases. Sir J. Hawkins (*Hor. Synopt.* p. 110) suggests the following as additions: 1^{1} Ἰησοῦ Χριστοῦ [also υἱοῦ Θεοῦ?], 5^{13} ὡς δισχίλιοι, 6^{37} δηναρίων διακοσίων; 8^{35} καὶ τοῦ εὐαγγελίου, 9^{41} ὅτι Χριστοῦ ἐστέ (but see above, § iii. **4** (*h*)), 10^{29} καὶ ἕνεκεν τοῦ εὐαγγελίου, 10^{30} μετὰ διωγμῶν, 14^5 ἐπάνω δηναρίων τριακοσίων, 14^{56} καὶ ἴσαι αἱ μαρτυρίαι οὐκ ἦσαν, and so in 14^{59}. But even this hypothesis is not necessary ; and on the whole the more probable solution seems to be that our Second Gospel is that which was used by the First and Third Evangelists ; in fact, that Mark wrote first of all the Four, and that his work was known to the others.

LITERATURE.—*COMMENTARIES*: (1) On St. Mark specially : those by Swete, 1902 (the fullest Commentary in English, with text, apparatus criticus, introduction, and notes) ; A. Menzies, (*The Earliest Gospel*), 1901 ; A. B. Bruce, 1897 ; Gould, 1896 (in the *International Critical Commentary* series) ; J. Knabenbauer, 1894 ; P. Schanz, 1881 ; J. Morison, 1873 ; B. Weiss, 1872 ; A. Klostermann, 1867 ; J. A. Alexander, 1858 ; K. Fritzsche, 1830 ; and several smaller ones on a popular scale. (2) As part of general Commentaries on the NT, those by Alford (1st ed. 1849) ; Chr. Wordsworth, Davidson, Cook (in *Speaker's Commentary*), 1878 ; Lange (1st ed. 1858). (3) Old Commentaries, by ' Victor of Antioch' (in Cramer's *Catenæ*, 1840) ; Bede (Migne, *P. L.*), Theophylact (Migne, *P. G.*), Euthymius Zigabenus (Migne, *P. G.*), Bruno Astensis (Migne, *P. L.*), Rupertus Tuitiensis (Migne, *P. L.*), Thomas Aquinas (*Catena Aurea*, authorship not certain), Albertus Magnus, Dionysius Carthusianus, Faber Stapulensis, Erasmus, Maldonatus, Cornelius a Lapide. [For information about these, see Swete's *St. Mark*, p. cxiv ff.]
RELATION OF MK. TO THE SYNOPTIC PROBLEM: Wright's *Synopsis of the Gospels in Greek* (1st ed. 1896, 2nd, 1903 ; supports the Oral Theory ; the first edition for mere purposes of comparison is the more useful as being simpler) ; Huck's *Synopse* ; Rushbrooke's *Synopticon*, 1880 ; Wright's *Some NT Problems* ; Campbell's *First Three Gospels in Greek* [?], 1899 (supports priority of Mt. and Lk. over Mk.) ; F. H. Woods in *Studia Biblica*, vol. ii. ('Mk. the groundwork of Mt. and Lk.') ; Sir J. Hawkins' *Horæ Synopticæ*, 1899 (esp. part iii.) ; Salmond, art. ' Mark (Gospel of)' in Hastings' *DB* ; Schmiedel, art. 'Gospels' in *Encyc. Biblica* ; Salmon's *Historical Introduction to the NT* ; Westcott, *Canon of the NT* and *Introduction to the Study of the Four Gospels* ; J. A. Robinson's *Study of the Gospels*, 1903 ; A. B. Bruce's *The Synoptic Gospels* ; Vincent Rose, O. P., *Studies on the Gospels* (Eng. tr. 1903, by Dr. Rob. Fraser) ; Zahn, *Einleit. in das NT and Geschichte des NT Kanons* ; Burkitt, *The Gospel History and its Transmission*, 1906.
THE SECOND GOSPEL IN THE EARLY CHURCH: J. B. Lightfoot's *Essays on the Work entitled Supernatural Religion* (collected in one volume, 1889) ; Sanday's *The Gospels in the Second Century*, 1876 ; Stanton's *The Gospels as Historical Documents*, part i. 1903 (the rest not yet published) ; and most of the above works on 'Introduction.'
THE ENDINGS OF THE GOSPEL : The modern Commentaries, as above ; Burgon's *The Last Twelve Verses of the Gospel according to St. Mark* ; Salmon's *Introd.* Lect. ix. ; Zahn's *Einleit.* ii. 227, and *Geschichte*, ii. 910 ff. ; Harnack's *Bruchstücke des Evangeliums und der Apokalypse des Petrus* [2], p. 33 (*Text. u. Unt.* ix. 2) ; Westcott-Hort, *New Testament in Greek*, Notes on Select Passages ; Scrivener's *Introduction to the Criticism of the NT*.
ON SPECIAL POINTS: Blass's *Philology of the Gospels* (original language, and the text) ; Deissmann's *Bible Studies*, Eng. tr. 1901 (the language) ; Dalman's *Words of Jesus*, Eng. tr. 1902 (esp. on the Aramaisms) ; Westcott-Hort's *New Testament in Greek*, as above, and Salmon's *Textual Criticism* (the Greek text) ; Burkitt's *Evangelion da-Mepharreshe*, 2 vols. 1904 (the Sinaitic Syriac text) ; Pusey - Gwilliam's *Tetraeuangelium Sanctum*, 1901 (the Peshitta Syriac text) ; also many articles in the *Expositor* and the *JThSt*. Of the latter may be mentioned : i. 278, Burkitt on 15^{34} ; i. 290, Lake on the text of Codex Ψ ; ii. 1, Stanton on pseudo-Peter and its bearing on Justin and Mk. ; ii. 111, Burkitt on 8^{32} ; ii. 298, Allen on Aramaic Gospels ; v. 321, Sanday on our Lord's ' silence,' esp. in Mk. ; v. 330 and vi. 121, Burkitt and Bartlet on Mk. in the Early Church ; v. 451, Burkitt on 14^{61} ; v. 628, Burkitt on 'St. Mark and Divorce' (cf. v. 621, Lyttelton on ' Divorce') ; vi. 237, Jackson on 10^{40} ; vi. 563, Chapman on Irenæus and the date of Mt. and Mark.

A. J. MACLEAN.

MARKET, MARKET-PLACE (ἀγορά).—**1.** *Locality and appearance.*—The landscape of Palestine was characterized by the number of its villages and the absence of isolated dwelling-houses on the cultivated lands. This was due to the joint ownership and tillage of the village fields and to the importance of living together for common safety. The Oriental always lived in the midst of neighbours (Lk $15^{6.9}$), and sought his home in ' a city of habitation' (Ps 107^{36}). The Palestine village had a path of communication leading through it to other villages, and this thoroughfare, or the widest and most central part of it, became the market-place. A few small shops opened upon the roadway representing the simple village traffic in food and clothing, and the manual skill of the carpenter and the blacksmith. In the larger towns the single shop of a kind became a street, row, or enclosed square devoted to the manufacture and sale of particular articles, each being thus known as the fruit-market, the shoe-makers' street, or the *khan* of the silver-smiths (Jer 37^{21}, Jn 5^2).

2. *Uses and associations.*—Beside the fountain or large tree of the market-place to which the village often owed its name and choice of locality, muleteers and other travellers rested their baggage animals, and told of what had happened by the way. There the elders of the village could be met with (Ac $16^{19. 20}$), and the children naturally collected and played where there was most to be seen and heard (Lk 7^{32}). In the market-place, day-labourers gathered at dawn from different quarters and waited to be engaged (Mt 20^3). There men met and greetings were exchanged, a scale of distinction being carefully observed, from the recognition accorded to equals and neighbours up to the salutation offered to those whom it was prudent or becoming to hold in honour on account of seniority, family connexion, worldly prosperity, or religious position (Mt 23^7, Lk 11^{43}). On account of the coming and going of strangers and the importation of foreign wares, the Pharisee washed his hands on returning from the market, as he might have unavoidably or inadvertently touched something that was classified as defiling, or that had itself previously come into contact with what imparted such ceremonial defilement (Mk 7^4).

3. *In Gentile towns.*—Under the Græco-Roman influences the market-place of an Oriental city became a broad paved way, with a colonnade on each side marking off two side-walks for foot-passengers. Such was the agora of Ephesus (Ac 16^{19} 17^{17}), leading in a direct line, with branching side streets of the ordinary kind, from the canal quay to the amphitheatre at the other end. The street called 'Straight' (9^{11}) in Damascus was thus laid out. In Rome, the Forum was a similar localizing of trade and municipal business.

G. M. MACKIE.

MARKS OF JESUS.—See STIGMATA.

MARRIAGE (I.).—**1. Oriental estimate of marriage.**—Of the three great events in family life —birth, marriage, and death—that of marriage was rendered important by the amount of consideration devoted to the choice of son-in-law or daughter-in-law, to the settlement of the customary financial conditions, and to the arrangements connected with the wedding festivities. It was recognized as a step leading to grave consequences, for, in the case of a daughter, if the marriage should prove unsatisfactory, she would likely return to her former home discredited and unhappy, and there would be a feeling of irritation and injustice between the families concerned. An almost equal anxiety attended the arrival of the young wife to live with her husband's parents, and to perform her duties under the often exacting superintendence of her mother-in-law. In a decision thus affecting the whole circle of relatives, it was considered natural and inevitable that both the selection of the individual and the settlement of all financial matters should be decided by the parents and guardians of those about to be married. The impulsive self-will of Esau which showed itself in the contempt of his birthright, led him to set aside the above tradition by marrying two of the daughters of Heth (Gn $26^{34. 35}$ 27^{46}). Woman was not thought of as having a personal existence at her own disposal, but as a unit in the family, and under the protection and authority of her male relatives. In marriage she was practically the purchased possession of her husband, becoming *beʽûlah* to him as her *baʽal*, or owner and master.

2. Betrothal.—This was a binding transaction declaring the fact of prospective marriage, and specifying the terms agreed upon by the contracting parties, that is, by those acting on their behalf. Although in both families the intention of marriage might have been decided upon by the parents from the infancy of their children, yet the formality of betrothal was not proceeded with until marriage could be regarded as a possibility in the near future. On the one hand, it was undesirable to make gifts or pay an instalment in a compact that might never be implemented by marriage, and, on the other hand, it was equally undesirable to dedicate a daughter to one who might not live to undertake her support, and thus cause her to be regarded as a widow. During a prolonged interval the man might move to another part of the land or fail to carry out the betrothal stipulations, and then the intended bride would require to get a writing of divorce or separation before she could be betrothed or married to another. While the act of betrothal by the presence of witnesses and the assemblage of friends had the importance of a ceremonial function, yet the spirit of bargaining was generally so keenly aroused, and the process of compromise so protracted and complex, that the situation scarcely admitted of immediate marriage rejoicings. Besides, it frequently happened that an interval of time was needed in order that the bridegroom might render the stipulated service, or acquire the sum of money agreed upon as the present to be given to the father and brothers of the bride. Thus there was usually an interval of a year or two, or it might be of several years, between the betrothal and the celebration of marriage.

3. Ceremony of marriage.—As a welcome sequel following in due time upon the discussion and settlement of the marriage portion and similar matters, the wedding itself was always an occasion of joyful festivity and congratulation. (a) *Place.* —While in ancient times the marriage doubtless took place occasionally in the home of the bride, yet the fact that the bridegroom came to claim one who had become his by the fulfilment of assigned conditions, and further, the widespread tradition of forcible opposition to her removal from her people, point to the greater frequency of marriage in the house of the bridegroom's parents. Thither the bride was conducted by a company of friends, carrying also her personal outfit and household belongings. If her people were of the peasant class, and she was merely passing to a neighbouring village, she would be already in her bridal dress and seated upon a led horse or mule, while in front of the procession young men and maidens individually engaged in sword-play and dancing. In the larger villages, such as Bethlehem and Nazareth, the robing of the bride was more elaborate, and was carried out by the help of women after her arrival at the new home. On that day, the bridegroom, instead of following the primitive custom of going to claim his bride or to meet her procession on the way, remained absent from the house with his relatives or friends until all preparations had been fully made.

(b) *Time.*—The marriage generally took place in the evening, so that those coming from a distance might not fail to arrive, and those who were occupied during the day might have liberty to attend. During the evening, as he sat among his friends, the bridegroom, in the exercise of his prerogative as the chief person concerned, signified his desire to move homewards. Upon this the wedding procession was formed. Lanterns and torches were lit to guide him and his companions through the dark, silent streets. Those who were waiting to see the procession pass raised the peculiar Oriental cry of marriage festivity, and thus, as the cry was taken up, the fact of his approach was known along the path in front of him up to the house in which the bride and her attendants were waiting. Owing to the stillness of the air and the slow pace of the illuminated procession, the cry might be heard half an hour before the arrival of the bridegroom. Then those who had merely come to do honour by joining in the procession returned to their houses, and the relatives and invited guests passed in to the wedding ceremony and festivity. These rejoicings were maintained for several days or even a week, according to the worldly circumstances of the family.

Many of these marriage customs are alluded to by Christ in His teaching, as the subject was familiar to His hearers, and any parabolic lessons deduced from it would be easily understood. Thus the bridegroom could excuse himself for not attending the wedding of another, seeing that his own invited guests were returning to pay visits of congratulation and good-will, and would feel offended if they found him absent (Lk 14[20]). It was a privilege and honour to the guest to be invited to the wedding feast, and an affront to those who invited him if he failed to attend (Mt 22[3. 9]). It was late when the wedding guest returned to his own house (Lk 12[36]). It was for the bridegroom to tarry until he was pleased to appoint the hour of his coming (Mt 24[42] 25[6. 13]). The reference to marrying and giving in marriage, with the Flood at the door, exemplified that preoccupation of the mind with worldly interests and ambitions by which men forget the transitoriness of life and the precariousness of its possessions. One of the marks of the new Kingdom was to be its power of carrying disruption into the closest and strongest family relationships at the call of loyalty to its larger and higher citizenship (10[35-37] 12[46-49]). With such a background of tradition and custom Christ gave to marriage the support of His own presence, and spoke of its Divine origin and temporary nature (Jn 2[2], Mt 19[4-6] 22[30]). In the Epistles it is evident that the higher conception of marriage prevalent among the Jews was gravely endangered by the inherited views still familiar to the mind, though condemned by the conscience, in the Gentile membership of the Church (1 Co 7). The marriage relationship was used to typify the intimate vital affinity between Christ and the Church (Eph 5[22-33]). In Rev 21[2] the comparison of the New Jerusalem to an Oriental bride adorned for her husband, appropriately sets forth the protracted development and perfected beauty of the Kingdom of God.

The bridegroom's friend (Jn 3[29]) must be distinguished from 'the children of the bride-chamber' (Mt 9[15]), who were simply the invited guests. In Judæa there were two such 'friends,' one acting for the bridegroom, the other for the bride. They conducted all the preliminary inquiries, made the bargains as to dowry, etc., arranged the betrothal, and finally led the betrothed couple to the bride-chamber. They were responsible for the legality of the whole proceedings, and were guarantors of the bride's virgin chastity. The bridegroom's voice, in converse with the bride, assured them pleasantly that their work had been successful. The discharge of the 'friend's' functions was liable to gross abuses (see Mishnic tractate *Middoth*). There was no corresponding functionary in Galilee, and so there is no allusion to him in the account of the marriage at Cana. Similar offices are discharged by the friends of would-be bridegrooms in Palestine to-day. An ardent suitor once sent to the present writer a sum of £40, with the request that it be given to a friend, on condition that he should secure the goodwill of a certain maiden, and the consent of her parents to his suit.

The bride-chamber is probably = Heb. *ḥeder*, 'the nuptial chamber' (Jg 15[1]), in which stood the *ḥuppah*, the bridal 'bed with a canopy' (Jl 2[16]; Gesenius, *s.v.*). In all the lands of their dispersion the Jews still apply this name, *ḥuppah*, to the richly embroidered canopy under which the contracting parties stand during the marriage ceremony.

G. M. MACKIE and W. EWING.

MARRIAGE (II.).—Jesus does not treat of the family from the point of view of the sociologist, but from that of the teacher of religion and morals. The high estimate which He places upon it is to be seen, not alone in His regard for His mother, but more particularly from His use of the institution as His most characteristic analogy for the Kingdom of God. As far as the condition of its future members in the present evil age is concerned, He describes the Kingdom as a social order in which the relationship of men to God is analogous to that of sons to a father ; and their relation to each other, therefore, is like that existing between brothers. Jesus also frequently uses figures drawn from marriage customs to illustrate His teaching concerning the coming of the Kingdom. It would be a mistake to see in this use of the paternal and filial relations a survival of that primitive religious concept which made members of a clan the sons of its gods. The usage of Jesus contains no reflexion of such a primitive thought, but rather springs from His high appreciation of marriage as it existed in the conventionalized civilization of the Jews of His day.

1. As an institution Jesus regards marriage as *essentially physical, and intended only for the present age.* Those who were to share in the blessings of the eschatological Kingdom would neither marry nor be given in marriage, but would be possessed of the non-physical body in the resurrection (Mt 22[23-30], Mk 12[18-25], Lk 20[27-36]). His teaching at this point is not an endorsement of the view that immortality is to be without personal relations, but is rather a relegation of physical relations to physical conditions.

The Sadducees, in their query which gave rise to this teaching of Jesus, raised the question of the levirate marriage. Jesus' answer does not touch upon that peculiar institution, but deals rather with the nature of marriage itself. He was no social reformer. In all the records of His teaching there is nothing to indicate that He gave to marriage any new social content or custom. Like His Apostles after Him, Jesus accepted marriage as an existing institution which gave rise to practical moral questions. His use of the customs of the time (cf. Mt 22[2ff.], Jn 2[1ff.]) was for the purpose of illustration rather than in the way of either approval or disapproval. It follows that Jesus did not look upon marriage as psychical or spiritual. Such transcendental teaching is foreign to the practical temper of Christianity. In its place is the assumption that the family, like all other members of social life, comes within the region of the great commandment of love. Jesus assumes that the father loves the child, and that brothers love each other. Farther than this His discussions do not go, but the inference is imperative that the relations between husband and wife fall within the great teaching of Mt 5[44-48] quite as truly as other social relations of individuals. If quarrelsome brothers are to be reconciled, most assuredly should there be reconciliation between husband and wife.

2. Marriage as a social institution Jesus regards as *of Divine origin.* It is one of the primal facts of humanity, established by God before the giving of the Law (Mt 19[5. 6], Mk 10[6-8]). Jesus grants that because of the exigencies of social development Moses modified the institution to the extent of permitting and regulating divorce ; but such modification Jesus evidently regarded as out of harmony with the institution. According to the original Divine purpose, man and wife were no longer two persons but one flesh. That is, marriage was to be monogamous. Any form of polygamy is thus excluded from His ideal.

It is noteworthy that Jesus in His quotation of Gn 2[24] does not follow the Heb. reading, in which οἱ δύο of the LXX has no equivalent. Polygamy is not excluded by the Hebrew, but is obviously inconsistent with the LXX statement, and even more so with the inference drawn from the passage by Jesus. It is from this point of view that one must approach the subject of divorce. (See DIVORCE).

3. Jesus, however, *does not make marriage a supreme good.* Rather is it one of those great goods of an imperfect age which are to be subordinated to the supreme good of sharing in the Kingdom of God, *i.e.* eternal life. Yet at no point is the sanity of His teaching more in evidence than here. He Himself was unmarried, but He never counsels celibacy. He does not even take the mediating position of St. Paul (1 Co 7[7. 29. 32-40]). In this particular, as in so many others, He is in such opposition to the Essenes of His day as quite to overbalance any of those superficial resemblances which have been discovered between His teaching and the ascetic doctrines of that sect. At the same time, just because marriage, though a good, is one which must pass with the present age, He teaches that in some cases it must be avoided. Mt 19[12] speaks of those who have made themselves eunuchs for the sake of the Kingdom of heaven, *i.e.* who, because of exceptional circumstances, have become celibates. In certain other expressions He distinctly recognizes the necessity for some among His followers to leave their families in the interests of a devotion to His cause (Mt 18[25], Lk 14[26]). These sayings, however, are not to be interpreted as in any way a prohibition of marriage, or as an elevation of the unmarried state to a plane superior to that of marriage. To draw such an inference is to misinterpret the entire tendency of His teaching, and to elevate into a controlling position His recognition of exceptional and particularly difficult situations in which one is compelled to practise a supreme self-sacrifice in order to remain loyal to a supreme ideal. The sayings are to be interpreted in accordance with those others in which Jesus concedes the fact that the family circle is not proof against evil influences — sayings which aroused hostility against His followers (Mt 10[34ff.], Lk 12[49-53]).

The Early Church under the influence of extra-Christian ideals moved along the line suggested by St. Paul towards the approval of the highest state of celibacy. Rev 14[4] gives the highest honours to those men who have not been married. Clement of Alexandria (*Strom.* iii. 9. 63) refers to the unauthentic saying of Jesus preserved in the Gospel of the Egyptians, 'I came to destroy the works of the female.' Similarly Clement (*ib.* 16) reports Jesus as having said, 'Eat every herb, but that which hath bitterness (*i.e.* maternity) eat not.'

A consideration of this teaching of Jesus leads naturally, therefore, to the genuinely Christian conception of marriage as a relationship which, though in the very nature of the case limited to the physical mode of existence, is yet sacred. The ascetic ideal is thus utterly lacking here as in all the teaching of Jesus, and in its place is to be found all that is normal in the so-called Greek ideal of life, together with the ennobling Christian ideal of love. See, further, ADULTERY, CELIBACY, DIVORCE.

LITERATURE. — Westcott, *Social Aspects of Christianity* ; Mathews, *Social Teaching of Jesus*, ch. iv. ; Peabody, *Jesus Christ and the Social Question*, ch. iii. ; M. J. Savage, *Jesus and Mod. Life*, p. 162 ; W. Cunningham, *The Path towards Knowledge*, p. 1 ; cf. also the standard treatises on the teaching of Jesus.

SHAILER MATHEWS.

MARTHA (of Bethany, sister of Lazarus and Mary). — The name (כְּרְהָא 'mistress' or 'lady'), though unique in the Scriptures, is common in the

Talmud.* She appears in the Gospel-story on three occasions: (1) when she entertained Jesus on His way to Jerusalem at the season of the Feast of Tabernacles (Lk 10^{38-42}); (2) when Lazarus died and was revived by Jesus (Jn 11^{1-46}); and (3) when Jesus, on His way to the Passover from His retreat at Ephraim (Jn 11^{54}), was honoured with a public entertainment at Bethany in the house of a leading man named Simon the Leper (Jn 12^{1-11} = Mt 26^{6-13} = Mk 14^{3-9}). Being a notable housewife, Martha was entrusted with the management of the banquet. See ANOINTING, I. 2.

The idea that the scene of this entertainment was Martha's house has given rise to the unfortunate surmise that Martha was a widow, Simon the Leper being her deceased husband. On the supposition that Κυρία in 2 Jn $^{1.5}$ is a proper name, the Greek equivalent of *Martha*, 'lady' (Volmar), it has been surmised that St. John's 2nd Epistle is addressed to our Martha. This is ingenious but untenable, since (1) 'the elect Kyria' would be, not ἐκλεκτῇ Κυρίᾳ (v.¹), but Κυρίᾳ τῇ ἐκλεκτῇ (cf. 3 Jn¹); (2) the Epistle is probably addressed metaphorically to a church and not to an individual.

Martha and Mary exhibit a peculiarity frequently observable in families. They were, like the brothers Jacob and Esau, utterly diverse in disposition and temperament. While Mary was impassioned and imaginative, Martha was unemotional and practical.† When Jesus visited her house at the season of the Feast of Tabernacles, He found her busy preparing the festal cheer (see MARY, No. 3). His arrival redoubled her housewifely solicitude, and it angered her when she saw her sister seated at His feet and listening to His discourse, leaving to her unaided hands the offices of hospitality. And when Jesus came to Bethany in tardy response to the sisters' appeal, 'Lord, behold, he whom thou lovest is sick,' Mary was in the darkened home overwhelmed with grief, but Martha had repressed her emotion, and, when word was brought her that Jesus had been sighted making His toilsome approach by the Ascent of Blood, the steep and robber-haunted road up the eastern slope of Olivet, she went out and met Him ere He entered the village. She greeted Him calmly, not without upbraiding for His delay; and when He assured her that her brother would rise again, she took His words in her matter-of-fact way as a reference to the current doctrine of the resurrection of the righteous at the last day, seeing in them merely a commonplace of pious consolation. Very different was her sister's behaviour. When Martha returned home and told her that the Master had arrived and was calling for her, she sprang up and ran to Him, and, in a passion of love and sorrow, flung herself at His feet.

It were, however, unjust to disparage Martha. She was of a practical turn, but she was very far from stupid. She was mistress of the house, and she was as a mother to her unworldly sister. There was evidently a close sympathy between them. During the dark days which succeeded their brother's death, they had been each other's comforters and had unbosomed their grief one to the other. Their constant plaint had been, 'Had the Lord been here, our brother had not died'; and this was the cry of each in turn when they met Jesus (Jn $11^{21.32}$). Martha was calm and self-possessed, but a great tenderness was concealed beneath her unemotional exterior. She wept less than Mary, but she mourned as deeply. Nor was she lacking in love and reverence for Jesus. Her impatience of Mary's inactivity amid the bustle of preparing the meal was due less to resentment at being left alone to serve, than to anxiety that nothing should be wanting for the comfort of the dear Master. And she believed in His power to

help even when Lazarus had been dead four days (Jn 11^{22}). She lacked some qualities which Mary possessed, but she had others of her own, and Jesus appreciated the excellence of her character. He loved Martha no less than her sister and Lazarus (v.⁵).

It is no slight attestation of the historicity of the Lukan and Johannine narratives of the family of Bethany that they faithfully accord in their delineations of the two sisters. On the pages of St. John each sustains the character which she exhibits in the little scene so exquisitely depicted by St. Luke. Here are no imaginary pictures, but portraitures of real personages. St. John says that the village where Martha and her sister dwelt was Bethany; but St. Luke does not name it, and he has been charged with placing the incident of the meal in Martha's house in Galilee. This idea, however, arises from a misconception of his literary method. Like the other Synoptists, St. Luke was not an original author but an editor of the Evangelic Tradition, and his aim was not chronological accuracy but the exhibition of Jesus. He sifted the ample material at his disposal, and arranged his selections topically rather than historically. Thus at $9^{49.50}$, recounting what befell in Galilee, he records the Lord's rebuke of His disciples' mistaken zeal; then, finding another incident which teaches a like lesson (vv.$^{51-56}$), he inserts it in this connexion, though it belongs to the last journey to Jerusalem (cf. v.^{51}). Having begun this section of the Tradition, he continues it, giving various other incidents of the journey, down to the close of ch. 12. Then he returns to what befell in Galilee, resuming the narrative of the journey to Jerusalem at 17^{11}.   DAVID SMITH.

MARY.—1. Mary the mother of James the Little and Joses, one of the women who followed Jesus from Galilee, stood beside the cross, watched the burial, and visited the sepulchre on the Resurrection morning (Mt $27^{55.56}$ = Mk $15^{40.41}$, Mt 27^{61} = Mk 15^{47}, Mk 16^{1} = Mt 28^{1} = Lk 24^{10}). From Jn 19^{25} it appears that she was wife to Clopas. This name is distinct from Cleopas (Lk 24^{18}), and is perhaps identical with Alphæus, both representing חלפי. Cf. J. B. Lightfoot, *Gal.* p. 256. WH write Ἀλφαῖος (see *NT*, vol. ii. § 408). If this identification be allowed, then (1) James the Little was probably one of the Twelve (Mt 10^{3} = Mk 3^{18} = Lk 16^{15}); (2) he was perhaps brother to Levi (Matthew), the son of Alphæus. The latter inference is favoured by (a) the v.l. Ἰάκωβον for Λευείν in Mk 2^{14}; (b) the tradition that James, like Matthew, had been a tax-gatherer (Chrysost. *in Matth.* xxxiii.: δύο τελῶναι, Ματθαῖος καὶ Ἰάκωβος; Euth. Ζιγ.: Ματθαῖος δὲ καὶ Ἰάκωβος ὁ τοῦ Ἀλφαίου, τελῶναι). See artt. ALPHÆUS and CLOPAS.

Hegesippus (in Eus. *HE* iii. 11. 32, iv. 22) mentions a Clopas who was brother to Joseph, our Lord's foster-father; but there is no evidence that he was identical with this Clopas. Jerome, in support of his theory of 'the Brethren of Jesus,' construes Μαριὰμ ἡ τοῦ Κλωπᾶ in Jn 19^{25} as in opposition to ἡ ἀδελφὴ τῆς μητρὸς αὐτοῦ, thus reducing the number of the women by the Cross to three, and making 'Mary the [wife] of Clopas' the Virgin's sister. See J. B. Lightfoot, *Gal.* p. 255 ff. But (1) it is improbable that two sisters bore the same name, and (2) 'the sister of his mother' was apparently Salome, the mother of the sons of Zebedee (cf. Mk 15^{40} = Mt 27^{56}).

2. Mary Magdalene.—She is first mentioned (Lk 8^{2}) as one of a company of women who attended Jesus on His second mission through Galilee in the course of the second year of His ministry. She is distinguished by two significant epithets: (1) 'the Magdalene,' i.e. the woman of Magdala (*Mejdel*), a town on the Lake of Galilee, some 3 miles from Capernaum, at the southern end of the Plain of Gennesaret. The modern Mejdel is a miserable village, but the ancient Magdala was a wealthy place, one of three cities, according to the Talmud, whose tribute had to be conveyed in waggons to Jerusalem (cf. Lightfoot on Jn 12^{3}). It had, however, an evil reputation, and was destroyed, according to the same authority, for harlotry, so that 'Mary the Magdalene' might be equivalent to 'Mary the harlot' (cf. 'Corinthian Lais'). It is only fair, however, to add that many regard this as very precarious.

(2) 'From whom seven demons had gone forth.' In Jewish parlance, immorality was a form of

* See Lightfoot on Jn 11^{1}.
† Euth. Ζιγ. on Lk 10^{42} δύο μερίδες πολιτείας ἐπαινεται, ἡ μὲν πρακτικὴ ἡ δὲ θεωρητική.

demonic possession,* and, just as the grace of the Holy Spirit is called 'sevenfold,'† so sevenfold possession might signify complete abandonment to the dominion of unclean passion. Cf. Mt 12[45] = Lk 11[26]. It is possible that Mary had been a harlot, that Jesus had rescued her from her life of shame, and that she followed Him out of gratitude. She was one of the devoted women who stood by the cross (Jn 19[25], Mt 27[56] = Mk 15[40]), watched His burial (Mt 27[61] = Mk 15[47]), and came on the Resurrection morning to the sepulchre (Jn 20[1] = Mt 28[1] = Mk 16[1] = Lk 24[10]). Finding it empty, she waited beside it weeping, and was rewarded with the first vision of the risen Lord (Jn 20[11-18], cf. Mt 28[9. 10]).

3. Mary of Bethany.—She is first introduced by St. Luke (10[38-42]), who tells how Jesus, probably on His way to the Feast of Tabernacles (Jn 7[2. 10]) in the third year of His ministry, reached 'a certain village,' and was hospitably received by 'a certain woman by name Martha,' who had a sister called Mary. The Feast of Tabernacles was a season of feasting and friendship. 'They ate the fat and drank the sweet, and sent portions unto them for whom nothing was prepared, and made great mirth' (Ex 23[16], Lv 23[33-44], Nu 29[12-38], Neh 8[9-18]). Martha, a good housewife, was busy making ready the festal cheer; but Mary, oblivious of all save the Lord's presence, seated herself, in the posture of a disciple (cf. Ac 22[3]), at His feet and listened to His discourse. Martha, 'distracted about much service,' interposed: 'Lord, dost thou not care that my sister left me alone to serve? Tell her then to lend me a helping hand.' 'Martha, Martha,' He answered, gently protesting against the sumptuousness of His hostess's preparations, 'thou art anxious and troubled about many things, but a few are all we need: or rather,' He added, 'only one thing;‡ for it is the good "portion" that Mary chose, one which shall not be taken away from her.' At that season, when they were all feasting and sending 'portions,' Mary was thinking not of the meat that perisheth, but of that which endureth unto eternal life.

St. Luke does not name the village where Martha and Mary dwelt. St. John tells us that it was Bethany, and that they had a brother named Lazarus (Jn 11[1-46]). Some months later, when Jesus was at the other Bethany beyond Jordan, whither He had retired from Jerusalem to escape the fury of the rulers (Jn 10[40]; cf. 1[28] RV), Lazarus fell sick, and his sisters sent Jesus word. For two days after He heard the news He remained where He was, and only when Lazarus died did He set out. His approach was reported to Martha, apparently the elder sister and mistress of the house; and she went to meet Him and sorrowfully upbraided Him: 'Lord, hadst thou been here, my brother had not died.' Assured of His sympathy and help, she returned home and, finding her sister among the mourners, whispered to her that the Teacher had come. Mary arose, and, hurrying to Him, fell at His feet, crying in the very words which Martha had used, the words which had been on their lips all those sorrowful days: 'Lord, hadst thou been here, my brother had not died.' Cf. art. MARTHA.

Mary appears a third time six days before the Passover, when Jesus was entertained in the house of Simon the Leper at Bethany, and she came in during the feast and anointed His feet (Jn 12[1-11]; cf. Mt 26[6-13] = Mk 14[3-9]). See ANOINTING, I. 2.

* Lightfoot on Lk 8[2]. Cf. Jer. *Vit. Hil. Erem.*: a *virgo Dei* at Majumas possessed by *amoris dœmon.*
† Cf. Od. Clun. *Hymn. de S. Mar. Magdal.*:
　'Qui septem purgat vitia
　Per septiformem gratiam.'
‡ אBL, WH ὀλίγων δέ ἐστιν χρεία ἤ ἑνός.

LITERATURE.—Lightfoot, *Hor. Heb.* ii. pp. 23, 388, 652; Hengstenb. on Jn 11[1-46]; Andrews, *Life of our Lord*, pp. 281-286; artt. 'Mary' in Hastings' *DB* and in *Encyc. Bibl.*
DAVID SMITH.

MARY, THE VIRGIN.—Historical data for the life of the mother of our Lord are astonishingly meagre. Legendary matter there is in abundance, with regard to her life both before the Annunciation and after the Ascension, but this art. will not touch on this except incidentally.

1. The Virgin Mary was born, we may suppose, at Nazareth. Tradition names Jerusalem (Cuinet, *Syrie, Liban, et Palestine*, p. 523), but this is quite untrustworthy. Her parents, according to a not improbable tradition, were Joachim and Anna (*Protev. Jacob.*). There is no reason to doubt that the Virgin, as well as Joseph, belonged to the tribe of Judah and to the family of David (Lk 1[32. 69], Ro 1[3], 2 Ti 2[8], He 7[14]), although it is almost certain, on the other hand, that both Mt. and Lk. give, not her genealogy, but Joseph's.

The statement of the *Test. XII. Patr.* (Simeon vii.), which makes Mary a woman of the tribe of Levi, is clearly an erroneous inference from the relationship between her and Elisabeth (cf. Plummer on Lk 1[27. 36]). Syr sin reads, Lk 2[5], 'because they were both of the house of David.'

Only one member of her immediate family is alluded to in the NT, viz. her sister (Jn 19[25]). This sister of the Virgin was most probably Salome, wife of Zebedee, and mother of James and John. We know from the other Gospels (Mt 27[56], Mk 15[40]) that Salome was present at the Crucifixion, and it is quite in accordance with St. John's manner to allude thus to his own mother without mentioning her name. The other opinion, that this sister was Mary 'of Clopas,' would (cf. Westcott, *in loc.*, also Mayor, *St. James*, pp. xix-xx) 'involve the most unlikely supposition that two sisters bore the same name.' The family of the Virgin was connected in some way with Elisabeth (ἡ συγγενίς σου, Lk 1[36]), but what the degree of relationship was cannot be known. According to a theory brought forward in connexion with the harmonizing of the two genealogies of our Lord, Mary was a cousin of Joseph her husband (art. 'Genealogy of Jesus Christ' in Smith's *DB*), but such a theory has little to recommend it. That her family was but a humble one may be inferred from her betrothal to Joseph 'the carpenter,' especially if there be any truth in the tradition as to the disparity of their ages.

2. Some time after their betrothal, which came generally among the Jews a year before the marriage, the angel Gabriel was sent from God to Nazareth to tell her of One who was to be born of her, and who should 'be called holy, the Son of God' (Lk 1[35]). The simplicity of the narrative bears on it the stamp of truth. Mary was troubled (διεταράχθη), we are told, at the saying, yet she believed at once. Her words, 'How shall this be?' ought not to be taken as an expression of doubt, like the words of Zacharias, 'Whereby shall I know this?' They are rather to be regarded as an 'involuntary expression of amazement' (Grot. 'non dubitantis sed admirantis'). Equally impossible is it to suppose that she believed that the child promised would be the fruit of a future union with Joseph. The words of the angel forbid any such idea. Yet, on the other hand, we need not suppose that the full meaning of the angel's words was at once grasped. There are evident signs in the narrative that this was not so, but nothing that we read mars the exquisite simplicity of her words of humble submission, 'Behold the handmaid of the Lord; be it unto me according to thy word.' Soon after ('in these days,' Lk 1[39]) the departure of the angel, Mary set out to pay the visit to her kinswoman, which his words would naturally suggest to her. The supposition that her journey was due to the intention of Joseph to put her away is a baseless one. Rather, as it has been said, 'the first but the ever-deepening desire in the heart of Mary, when the angel left her, must have been to be away from Nazareth, and for the relief of opening her heart to a woman, in all things like-minded, who perhaps might speak blessed words to her' (Edersheim, *Life and Times*, i. p. 152). She arose with haste and set out to seek that relief in the house of her kinswoman in the far-off hills of Judah.

What the city of her destination was we cannot know for certain. Whatever it was, it was distant from Nazareth by almost the whole length of the land. According to a tradition which may be correct (cf. *ExpT* xv. [1905] 245 f.), it was *'Ain Karim*, a village an hour and a half west of Jerusalem.

The opinion held for so long that this city was Juttah is, according to Buhl (*GAP* p. 163), quite worthless, having originated with Reland in the beginning of the 18th century.

When Mary reached her kinswoman's house, a fresh surprise awaited her in the greeting of Elisabeth : 'Blessed art thou among women.' No longer is Mary to Elisabeth simply 'kinswoman,' she is 'the mother of my Lord.' Doubtless what she had heard from Zacharias of the promises made in regard to their son would fill Elisabeth with hopes of a speedy appearance of the Messiah, and now, by inspiration (Lk 1⁴¹), she knows that the mother of her Lord is before her. Her greeting is in reality a psalm, brief though it is and overshadowed by the still more wonderful hymn which it called forth in response. The 'Song of Mary' is 'modelled on the OT psalms, especially the Song of Hannah (1 S 2¹⁻¹⁰), but its superiority to the latter in moral and spiritual elevation is very manifest.' That Mary should 'fall back on the familiar expressions of Jewish Scripture in this moment of intense exultation' is very natural (cf. Plummer, *St. Luke*, p. 30).

Niceta, bp. of Remesiana, in his treatise *de Psalmodiæ Bono*, names Elisabeth as the author of the *Magnificat*. This is supported by the Old Latin MSS Vercellensis, Veronensis, Rhedigeranus, and by Irenæus. Origen also knew of the reading, though he did not accept it. The evidence adduced, however, does not seem sufficient to override the verdict of all the rest of antiquity, that the Hymn is Mary's and not Elisabeth's. See, further, art. MAGNIFICAT.

3. Mary remained with her kinswoman in Judah 'about three months,' probably waiting (cf. Lk 1⁵⁶ with v.³⁶) till after the birth of John the Baptist, and then returned to Nazareth. It is probably at this point that we ought to put the commencement of the narrative in Mt., which records Joseph's intention to put Mary away privily when her condition became known to him, and speaks of his subsequent marriage with her in obedience to the angelic messages. The marriage would afford 'not only outward but moral protection' both to the mother and to the unborn Babe. That the Virgin is still spoken of as ἐμνηστευμένη in Lk 2⁵ is not to be taken as necessarily indicating that the marriage had not yet taken place. Had she not been Joseph's wife, Jewish custom would have forbidden her making the journey along with him. When Joseph went up to Bethlehem to get himself enrolled, Mary went also, not because it was necessary, but because 'she would be anxious at all risks not to be separated from Joseph' (Plummer, *in loc.*). At Bethlehem, perhaps in the cave where now is the Church of the Nativity, she brought forth her first-born Son, and there, too, she received the visit of the shepherds, whose words as to the sign given them from heaven she 'kept, pondering them in her heart.'

4. There is no need to linger on the next events, —the Circumcision, the Presentation and Purification in the Temple, the visit of the Magi, the Flight into and Return from Egypt,—for these all belong rather to the life of Christ than to that of Mary. Before leaving this part of her history, it may be well to emphasize how much of what we know of the Birth, Infancy, and Childhood of our Lord we owe to accounts given by His mother. That St. Luke's source in the first two chapters of his Gospel was one connected with the Virgin is generally admitted. Whether he received his information directly from her, as Ramsay supposes (*Was Christ born at Bethlehem?* p. 85 ff.), or whether the information came to him indirectly through another (perhaps, as Sanday conjectures, Joanna), may not be determinable. At least we can say that St. Luke believed that he wrote what he wrote on her authority.

'He does not,' writes Ramsay (*ib.* p. 74), 'leave it doubtful whose authority he believed himself to have. "His mother kept all these sayings hid in her heart"; "Mary kept all these sayings, pondering them in her heart"; those two sentences would be sufficient.'

5. The Return from Egypt was followed by a life in retirement at Nazareth. Very little do we know of those years. Two verses in Lk. (2⁴⁰, ⁴¹), which tell us of the growth of the Child and the custom of His 'parents' to go every year to Jerusalem at the Feast of the Passover, are all we have in the way of direct statement. Here in Nazareth it was that those brothers and sisters of the Lord, of whom we read in the course of the Gospel narrative, were born to Mary and Joseph (for other views see art. BRETHREN OF THE LORD). Four brothers are named (Mt 13⁵⁵, Mk 6³), but the sisters are mentioned only once (Mk 6³), without any mention of their names.

The silence of the life at Nazareth is broken but once before the commencement of the Ministry. The scene in the Temple (Lk 2⁴²⁻⁵⁰) would claim a fuller consideration in the Life of Jesus Christ. As regards its relation to His mother, we have to notice only two points which emerge from St. Luke's narrative. Mary did not yet understand all the meaning of the angel's words to her regarding the Child that was to be born. The Child's own words would be a reminder to her of His true nature. He must be 'about his Father's business' (or 'in his Father's house'). Then again we see from the passage the lasting impression which the scene left on Mary's mind. 'His mother kept (συνετήρει) all these sayings in her heart.' The tense of the verb covers a long period, up to, and even during, the Ministry. Yet of the Virgin's life during the interval between our Lord's twelfth year and His Baptism we know nothing but what is contained in these words and those which immediately precede, as to her Son's subjection to her and Joseph. It is, however, an easily drawn inference from the absence of any mention of Joseph in the later Gospel narrative, that he died during this interval. Beyond this it is useless to conjecture. 'The Arabic *Historia Josephi* (cc. 14, 15) places his death in our Lord's eighteenth year, when Joseph had reached the age of 111' (Swete on Mk 6³).

6. The remaining allusions to the Virgin in the Gospels may be briefly recorded. She was present at the marriage feast at Cana (Jn 2¹), after which she went down to Capernaum (v.¹²) with Jesus and His brethren and His disciples. She would seem to have been among 'his friends' (οἱ παρ' αὐτοῦ) at Capernaum, who 'went out to lay hold on him' (Mk 3²¹), for the next paragraph tells us of the coming of His mother and His brethren (v.³¹). She is mentioned by the unknown woman out of the multitude (Lk 11²⁷), 'Blessed is the womb that bare thee, and the breasts that thou didst suck.' She was present at the Crucifixion, whence the loved disciple, into whose care she had been committed, took her to his own home (Jn 19²⁵ff.). It is not a little remarkable, in view of later developments, that no fewer than three of these allusions seem to guard against an undue feeling of veneration for the mother of our Lord. In the story of the feast at Cana, His words, though not wanting in respect, 'show that the actions of the Son of God, now that He has entered on His Divine work, are no longer dependent in any way on the suggestion of a woman, even though that woman be His mother. . . . The time of silent discipline and obedience is over' (Westcott, *in loc.*). In the scene at Capernaum the lesson is much the same, though the interference of Mary and our Lord's brethren on this occasion seems to have arisen from a different motive. They are seeking to oppose His work. Before they reach Him He understands their purpose, and declares that the true kinship to the Son of God consists in obedience to the will of God, and not in mere earthly ties. It is, of course, as Swete observes (*St. Mark*, p. 70), 'a relative attitude only, and is perfectly consistent with tender care for kinsmen, as the saying on the cross shows.' These two scenes at Cana and Capernaum belong to the beginning of the Ministry, and similarly, almost at its close, we have Christ's words, during the last journey from Galilee to Jerusalem, in answer to the saying of the woman above mentioned, 'Yea, rather ($\mu\epsilon\nu o\hat{\nu}\nu$), blessed are they that hear the word of God and keep it (Lk 11[28]).' This adds to and corrects the woman's words. There is no denial of the Virgin's blessedness, only a declaration of that wherein her blessedness consists, a blessedness which may be shared by all who, like her, hear the word of God and keep it.

Why it was that the Virgin was committed by our Lord on the cross to John can be only a matter of conjecture. It may be, as Mayor suggests (*St. James*, p. xxvii), that her sons, as married men (1 Co 9[5]), were already dispersed in their several homes, while John her nephew was unmarried, and so could more readily accept such a charge. All we know is that 'from that hour that disciple took her unto his own home (Jn 19[27]).

7. After this the only glimpse we get of Mary is in Ac 1[14], where she is mentioned as continuing steadfastly in prayer with the other women and the brethren and Apostles of the Lord, after the Ascension. Whether she lived the rest of her life in Palestine, or accompanied St. John to Ephesus, cannot be known. Traditions there are, but they vary. According to one, found in Nicephorus Callistus (*HE* ii. 3), she continued to live with St. John in Jerusalem, and died there in her fifty-ninth year. Another tradition, found in the Synodical Letter of the Council of Ephesus (A.D. 431), makes her accompany St. John to Ephesus, and speaks of her as having been buried in that city.   J. M. HARDEN.

MASTER (Lat. *magister* from root of *magnus* = 'great.' Hence 'master' corresponds to **rabbi**, which is from רב 'great'; and in AV $\rho\alpha\beta\beta\epsilon\iota$ is frequently tr. 'master,' *e.g.* Mt 26[25], Mk 9[5], Jn 4[31], though in all such cases RV retains 'rabbi'). — The word most generally rendered 'master' is $\delta\iota\delta\acute{\alpha}\sigma\kappa\alpha\lambda o\varsigma$, which strictly means **teacher**; and this meaning is given in every case as an alternative reading in RVm, *e.g.* Mt 8[19] 22[16], Mk 5[35] 10[17], Lk 3[12] 8[49], Jn 11[28] 13[13. 14]. In Lk 8[24] and 9[33] the Gr. word for 'master' is $\epsilon\pi\iota\sigma\tau\acute{\alpha}\tau\eta\varsigma$, a word generally used in the sense not of 'teacher' but of 'chief' or 'overseer.' In Mt 23[10] $\kappa\alpha\theta\eta\gamma\eta\tau\acute{\eta}\varsigma$, rendered 'master,' is more correctly tr. 'leader' or 'guide.' 'Master' was the ordinary title of courtesy and respect paid to a religious teacher. See art. RABBI.   DUGALD CLARK.

MATTATHA.—A grandson of David, named in our Lord's genealogy, Lk 3[31].

MATTATHIAS.—Occurs twice in our Lord's genealogy, Lk 3[25. 26].

MATTHAN.—Grandfather of Joseph the husband of Mary, Mt 1[15].

MATTHAT.—**1.** The form of the name (Mt. *Matthan*) of Joseph's grandfather given in Lk 3[24]. **2.** Another link in our Lord's genealogy, Lk 3[29].

MATTHEW ($M\alpha\theta\theta\alpha\hat{\iota}o\varsigma$, Lachm., Tisch., WH; $M\alpha\tau\theta\alpha\hat{\iota}o\varsigma$, TR) is to be identified with **Levi**, son of Alphæus, since the Synoptists agree in their description of the feast associated with the publican who is named Levi in Mk. (2[14]) and Lk. (5[29]), and Matthew in Mt. (9[9]).* *Levi*, according to the analogy of *Simon* and *Peter*, may have been the original name and *Matthew* the acquired; though, according to Edersheim (*Life and Times*, i. 514), it was common in Galilee for a man to have two names, one strictly Jewish and the other Galilæan. Matthew was chosen one of the Twelve, and is placed seventh in the lists in Mk. and Lk., and eighth in those in Mt. and Acts. When called to be a disciple, he was sitting at a toll-house, his place of business. Along the north end of the Sea of Galilee there was a road leading from Damascus to Acre on the Mediterranean, and on that road a customs-office marked the boundary between the territories of Philip the tetrarch and Herod Antipas. Matthew's occupation was the examination of goods which passed along the road, and the levying of the toll (cf. Hausrath, *NT Times*, ii. 179). The work of a publican excited the scorn so often shown beyond the limits of Israel to fiscal officers; and when he was a Jew, as was Matthew, he was condemned for impurity by the Pharisees. A Jew serving on a great highway was prevented from fulfilling requirements of the Law, and was compelled to violate the Sabbath law, which the Gentiles, who conveyed their goods, did not observe. Schürer makes the statement that the customs raised in Capernaum in the time of Christ went into the treasury of Herod Antipas, while in Judæa they were taken for the Imperial *fiscus* (*HJP* I. ii. 68). Matthew was thus not a collector under one of the companies that farmed the taxes in the Empire, but was in the service of Herod. Yet the fact that he belonged to the publican class, among whom were Jews who outraged patriotism by gathering tribute for Cæsar, subjected him to the scorn of the Pharisees and their party (cf. Edersheim, *Life and Times*, i. 515); and his occupation itself associated him with men who, everywhere in the Empire, were despised for extortion and fraud, and were execrated (cf. Cic. *de Offic.* i. 42; Lucian, *Menipp.* 11). Even Jesus Himself named the publicans with harlots (Mt 21[31]). See PUBLICAN, and SEA OF GALILEE, § vi.

Before the call of Matthew, Jesus had resided at Capernaum, had left it, and had gone back to it (Mk 1[21. 38] 2[1]); and it is safe to conclude that Matthew, a dweller in or near the city, had heard the fame of Jesus, and perhaps he may have been among those who sought Him (Mk 1[37]). Jesus, too, may have noticed the publican, and the fact may have led to the call. According to the narrative of that call, which is almost identical in the Synoptics, Jesus said to him, 'Follow me,' and he arose and followed Him (Mt 9[9]). After the call and the answer there was a feast, probably to celebrate the new departure in the life of the publican, at which Jesus met him and his friends.

Certain critics (cf. Keim, *Jesus of Nazara*, iii. 268 n.) take the words $\kappa\alpha\grave{\iota}\ \dot{\epsilon}\gamma\acute{\epsilon}\nu\epsilon\tau o\ \alpha\dot{\upsilon}\tau o\hat{\upsilon}\ \dot{\alpha}\nu\alpha\kappa\epsilon\iota\mu\acute{\epsilon}\nu o\upsilon\ \dot{\epsilon}\nu\ \tau\hat{\eta}\ o\dot{\iota}\kappa\acute{\iota}\alpha$ (Mt 9[10]) as indicating that the house was that of Jesus; but they can bear this interpretation only if taken in connexion with the preceding words, $\kappa\alpha\grave{\iota}\ \dot{\alpha}\nu\alpha\sigma\tau\grave{\alpha}\varsigma\ \dot{\eta}\kappa o\lambda o\acute{\upsilon}\theta\eta\sigma\epsilon\nu\ \alpha\dot{\upsilon}\tau\hat{\omega}$. It is, however, not necessary to establish this connexion, as the writer may simply have made a sudden transition to a paragraph beginning $\kappa\alpha\grave{\iota}\ \dot{\epsilon}\gamma\acute{\epsilon}\nu\epsilon\tau o$.

* Levi's father was not the father of James the Little (cf. Zahn, *Einleitung*, ii. 263).

If, on the other hand, the connexion must be made, then it is possible to take the narrative as recording that Matthew rose and followed Jesus to the house which belonged to Jesus. Mk. does not indicate the ownership of the house, while Lk. says distinctly that it was Levi's. If we accept the description of Mk. or Lk., we need not conclude that the feast followed immediately after the call, since it may have taken place just before the assembling of the Twelve (Mk 3¹⁴, Lk 6¹³), in the period between that event and the calling of the individual disciples.

At the feast were Jesus and His disciples, and at the table with them were many publicans and sinners. These disciples were also many in number (Mk 2¹⁵), and they must therefore have included others beyond the individuals who had been specially called. The sinners mentioned along with the publicans at the feast were those who violated the Law, or did not try to keep its innumerable commands as set forth by the scribes or interpreted by the Pharisees. Certain scribes and Pharisees had been spectators of the feast, and they asked the disciples concerning Jesus' eating and drinking with sinners; and Jesus Himself, answering them, declared that He had not come to call the righteous, but sinners to repentance. The call of Matthew and the feast with publicans and sinners were the comment of Jesus on Pharisaic separatism; but the action itself did not prevent the separatism which showed itself in the primitive Church, and which involved the rebuke of Peter by Paul.

Beyond the call and the inclusion of the name in the list of the Twelve, there is no mention of Matthew in the NT. On the question of the authorship of the First Gospel, see following article.

LITERATURE.—*Expos. Times*, viii. [1897] 529; *Expos.* i. i. [1875] 36, iii. ix. [1889] 445, v. viii. [1898] 37; Keble, *Chr. Year*, 'S. Matthew the Apostle'; W. B. Carpenter, *The Son of Man*, p. 141; J. D. Jones, *The Glorious Company of the Apostles*, p. 150.

JOHN HERKLESS.

MATTHEW, GOSPEL ACCORDING TO.—'*The power of God unto salvation—to the Jew first, and also to the Greek.*'—The Gospels of St. Matthew and St. Luke may be characterized respectively as the Gospel of the Jew and the Gospel of the Greek. St. Luke gives us the conception of the Christ as His Person presented itself to the Greek Churches of the West. To them Christ was the Saviour of the world, the Divine Redeemer, whose Good News was equally available for all the children of men, regardless of distinctions of race, or class, or sex. St. Matthew, on the other hand, presents to us the Christ as He was conceived by the Jewish Christians of Palestine. To them Christ was the King of Israel; and the glad tidings of His coming Kingdom were intended first for the Chosen People. It was true that He had foretold the coming of many from the east and the west to sit down in the Kingdom of God (8¹¹), and had bidden His Apostles baptize all nations (28¹⁹); but then it had always been a part of the Divine plan to suffer aliens to enter as proselytes into the fold of Israel, and to partake of the blessings promised to the Chosen People. So it was to be with the new Israel. In the period of preparation for the Kingdom, the gospel was to be preached to all nations for a testimony (24¹⁴), and those who entered by baptism into the Christian Church would become members of that new Israel, which in the days of the Kingdom should be judged and governed by the twelve Apostles as viceroys of the King Messiah (19²⁸).

Of course the distinction here drawn makes itself felt in two respects. First, in the selection of material by the two writers. Each Evangelist has a certain amount of matter peculiar to himself; and it will be found that whilst in the First Gospel this is very largely matter which lends itself to the Christianity of one who was glad to emphasize the prior claim of the Jew to the blessings of the Kingdom, that in St. Luke is predominantly material capable of a more universalistic interpretation. Secondly, in the treatment of the large amount of material which is common to the two Gospels. A good example is to be found in the discourse on the Last Things. Whilst St. Matthew emphasizes the close connexion between the fall of Jerusalem and the Coming of the Son of Man (24²⁹), thus limiting the period during which the gospel could be preached to the Gentiles, St. Luke expands this period to an indefinite length, during which Jerusalem was to be trodden under foot (Lk 21²⁴), thus making space for a long and protracted preaching to the Gentiles.

In the present article we propose to discuss the chief features in the picture of the Person of Christ drawn for us by the First Evangelist, and to consider the bearing of this upon the questions of the author, the sources, the date, and the historical value of the Gospel.

1. Theology of the Gospel.—(1) *The Messiah.*—Jesus the Messiah was legally descended from David, and through him from Abraham, the father of the Israelite people (1¹). He was the culminating point in the history of His family. In David it had risen to monarchical power (1⁶), but at the period of the Captivity it had lost this dignity. But now again in Jesus the anointed King it had regained it (1¹⁶). He was therefore born 'king of the Jews' (2²). As King He entered Jerusalem (21⁵). As King He suffered the death of crucifixion (27³⁸·⁴²), and as King He would sit to judge all nations at the Last Day (25³¹ᶠᶠ·). But He was no mere scion of the Davidic stock. Though legally descended from David through Joseph ben-Jacob, He was also in a unique sense Son of God. As such He was born of the Holy Spirit from a virgin (1¹⁸⁻²⁵). Hence He was 'God with us' (v.²³), and this Divine Sonship placed Him in a unique relationship to God. He could speak of God and of Himself as 'the Father' and 'the Son,' as though these terms could only be applied to this relationship (11²⁷); and David himself had recognized by the Divine inspiration this Divine Sonship of his promised descendant, when he applied to Him the Divine name 'Lord' (22⁴⁴). The history of the supernatural birth was, of course, an easy mark for Jewish calumny, but nevertheless it was a fact which had been Divinely foreordained (1²²); and in the history of the Davidic family there had been women of old time (Rahab, Bathsheba, Tamar, Ruth) whose lives should have taught the calumniators of the Virgin that God overrules and uses circumstances for His own Divine ends. Moreover, if in Jesus the prophecies of a Coming Davidic king, supernaturally born, had found at last their fulfilment, so also in Him were summed up all the many strands in the web of Jewish anticipation. He was 'the Beloved' (3¹⁷ 17⁵) whom God had eternally chosen (3¹⁶ 12¹⁸), and to whom God had eternally given all things (11²⁷) and all power (28¹⁸). He was the supernatural Son of Man, who was to come upon the clouds of heaven (16²⁸ 26⁶⁴ 24³⁰), and to sit upon the throne of His glory to judge all men (16²⁸ 19²⁸ 25³¹). And the events of His life down to the minutest details had been foretold in the OT. Thus Isaiah had foretold the circumstances (1²²), and Micah the place, of His birth (2⁵). Hosea had foreseen the flight into Egypt, Jeremiah the massacre of the infants at Bethlehem (v.¹⁷); and the settlement of His parents at the ill-famed village of Nazareth had been the subject of prophecy (v.²³). His herald John had been fore-announced by Isaiah (3³), and the same prophet had foreseen the Christ's ministry in Galilee, with Capernaum as His headquarters (4¹⁴). That He healed the sick was in accordance with a prophecy of Isaiah, and the contrast between His gracious and gentle work and the noisy clamour of His opponents, found anticipation in another passage of the same prophet (12^{17-21}). Zechariah had foreseen His entry as King into Jerusalem (21^5), His betrayal (26^{24}), and the desertion of His disciples (v.^{31}); and the whole course of His tragic end had been Divinely foreordained, and foretold in Scripture (16^{23} [τὰ τοῦ θεοῦ] $26^{54. 56}$).

Such was the Person of Jesus. He was the Divinely foreordained Messiah, the supernaturally-born King of Israel, the unique Son of God. What then had been His work? It is clear that the editor of the Gospel is much more concerned with Christ's doctrine than with His work, with what He had said than with what He had done. He is interested in the events of the life chiefly in so far as they proved Jesus to be the Messiah of the OT, and with His actions either as proofs of His supernatural power over all the known forces of life, or as illustrative of His attitude towards the orthodox Pharisaism of the day. He could, e.g., heal disease, even leprosy, without use of drugs or medical appliances, by the simple exercise of His will (8^8 'Speak the word only,' v.^{16} 'with a word'), the cure being immediate and complete (v.^{13} 9^{22} 15^{28} 17^{18}). He could control the forces of nature ($8^{26. 27}$), and could drive out demons from the unhappy beings of whom they had taken possession (vv.$^{28-34}$). He exercised upon earth the Divine prerogative of forgiving sin (9^{1-8}), and raised the dead to life (9^{25}). He could feed multitudes with a few loaves and fishes (14^{13-21} 15^{32-39}). On the other hand, He associated with people who were regarded by the leaders of religion as ill friends for a devout man (9^{11}), and seemed negligent of the rules which the Pharisees had framed as the guides of a pious life. His disciples did not fast (9^{14}), and broke Sabbath regulations (12^2). He Himself performed acts of healing on the Sabbath day (v.^{10}), and His disciples neglected the regulations about purification of the hands before meals (15^2). After a ministry marked by acts like these, He had been put to death by the Romans at the instigation of the Pharisees and Sadducees. He had expected this fate, and had foretold it to His disciples as being ordained of God and prophesied in Scripture (16^{21} δεῖ, v.^{23} τὰ τοῦ θεοῦ, $17^{12. 22. 23}$ $20^{18. 19}$). He had promised that on the third day He should be raised again, and this was fulfilled; and He had ascended into heaven.

Now it is clear that the details thus sketched furnish a very small part of the significance of the Gospel to the editor. The miracles proved Christ's power, or illustrated His attitude towards Pharisaism, or showed Him to be the Messiah of the OT. But to what end was He powerful, and, if the Messiah, where was His Kingdom? We might have expected to find a good deal more emphasis laid on the significance of Christ's death, but such emphasis is strikingly absent. The death is rather regarded as without significance in itself, but as a necessary stage in the revelation of the Messiah. He had come to found a Kingdom, but in accordance with the Divine plan had been put to death. Clearly then the Kingdom remained yet to come, and the death was a necessary prelude to glorification. The insistence on the fact that the death *had* to take place, because it had been foretold in the Scriptures, suggests the inference that to the editor it was a fact which required explanation, a difficult phase in the history of the Messiah rather than the central fact which itself explained everything else in His life. In two passages only is the death referred to as having any purpose or effect, rather than as being simply a thing which had happened as a necessary transition stage from the earthly life to the heavenly monarchy of the

Messiah. In one of these Christ is represented as saying that He came to give His life as a ransom for many (λύτρον ἀντὶ πολλῶν, 20^{28}); in the other He speaks of His blood as shed for many for the remission of sins (26^{28}). It is easy to see how sayings like these could be made the foundation of a theology which would explain the whole of Christ's life from the significance of His death. But it is equally clear that the editor of the First Gospel has recorded them because they formed part of the tradition which had come to him, without seeing in them an explanation of the entire earthly life of the Messiah. They are incidental rather than fundamental to his Gospel.

Thus the facts of Christ's life as here recorded would have been meaningless to the editor without the teaching which he records. It is in that that he finds the explanation of Christ's life. The facts alone were obscure and difficult. Jesus was the Davidic Messiah and also the Son of God. He had entered into human history through the Virgin's womb. He had evinced His supernatural power in all that He did. But then He had allowed Himself to be put to death, because, as He said, the Scriptures had foretold it; and rising from the dead, He had gone into heaven again. But how then was He the Messiah, and where was the Kingdom? The main object of the Gospel is to explain this, and the explanation is given in the great discourses which the editor has formed by massing sayings or groups of sayings.

(2) *The Kingdom.*—The central subject of Christ's doctrine had been the near approach of the 'kingdom of the heavens.' With this He began His ministry (4^{17}), and wherever He went He taught this as a good news (v.^{23}). The Kingdom, He taught, was coming, but not in His lifetime. After His ascension He would come as Son of Man upon the clouds of heaven ($16^{27. 28}$ 19^{28} 24^{30}), would send His angels to gather together the elect (24^{31} 13^{41}), and would sit on the throne of His glory (16^{28} 19^{28} 25^{31}). This would happen in the lifetime of the generation to whom He spoke (16^{28} 24^{34} 10^{23}), immediately after the great tribulation accompanying the destruction of Jerusalem (24^{29}); but God alone knew the exact day and hour (v.^{30}). Then the twelve Apostles should sit on twelve thrones judging the twelve tribes of Israel (19^{28}). In the meantime He Himself must suffer and die, and be raised from the dead. How else could He come upon the clouds of heaven? And His disciples were to preach the good news of the coming Kingdom (10^7 24^{14}) among all nations, making disciples by baptism (28^{19}). The body of disciples thus gained would naturally form a society bound by common aims (16^{18} 18^{17}). They would be distinct from the existing Jewish polity, because the Jews as a people, the 'sons of the kingdom,' *i.e.* those who should have inherited it (8^{12}), would definitely reject the good news ($21^{32. 42. 43}$ 22^7). Hence the disciples of the Kingdom would form a new spiritual Israel (21^{43} 'a nation') which would include many who came from east and west (8^{12}).

In view of the needs of this new Israel of Christ's disciples, *i.e.* of the true sons of the Kingdom (13^{38}), who were to await His coming on the clouds of heaven, it is natural that a large part of the teaching recorded in the Gospel should concern the qualifications required in those who hoped to enter the Kingdom when it came. They were still to live in allegiance to the revelation of God made in the OT, which was permanently valid. Not a letter was to pass away from it (5^{18}). Its permission of divorce still held good (v.^{32} 19^{3ff}). Christ had not abolished the Mosaic distinctions between clean and unclean meats (see notes on 15^{20}). His disciples were still to take two or three witnesses (18^{16}); and the Sabbath was still to be held sacred

(24^{20}). But they were to search beneath the letter of the OT for its spiritual meaning. Their 'righteousness' was to exceed that of the scribes and Pharisees, because they were to interpret the Law of Moses in a sense which would make it more far-reaching in its effect upon conduct than ever before (5^{21-48}). In particular, their 'righteousness' was to be less a matter of something done that men might see it, and more a right relation to God, taking effect in action known only to God Himself (6^{1-34}). In relation to their fellow-men they were to cultivate humility, and to suppress self-assertiveness (18^{1-14}); to exercise forgiveness (vv. $^{15.}$ $^{21-35}$); to be slow to judge their fellows (7^{1-5}); to do to others what they would have done to themselves (v. ^{12}). In relation to wealth, they were not to hoard up treasure upon earth, but to trust in God's care for them (6^{19-34} 19^{28}), seeking first His righteousness and Kingdom. In relation to sexual morality, they were to be chaste in thought (5^{28}); marriage was an indissoluble bond, broken only by adultery (19^{9}). But some were called to live single lives for the Kingdom of the heavens (v. ^{12}). In relation to God, they were to pray to Him for their daily needs, for His forgiveness, and for deliverance from the evil that is in the world (6^{9-13} 7^{7-11}).

In the above sketch of the picture drawn for us in the First Gospel of the Person and teaching of the Messiah, we have purposely omitted the parables. Most of the parables in this Gospel are parables of the Kingdom. With the exception of $18^{21.35}$, they do not, as in the case of many of St. Luke's parables, inculcate some Christian virtue or practice, such as love of one's neighbour, or earnestness in prayer, but convey some lesson about the nature of the Kingdom and the period of preparation for it. Their interpretation will often depend largely upon the conception of the Kingdom with which the reader approaches them. We are not now concerned with the meaning which they were intended to convey when they were originally spoken. But it should be sufficiently obvious that if we ask what meaning they had for the editor of the First Gospel, and why he selected them for insertion in his Gospel, the answer must be that he chose them because he believed that they taught lessons about the Kingdom of the heavens in the sense in which that phrase is used everywhere else in his Gospel, of the Kingdom which was to come when the Son of Man came upon the clouds of heaven. Thus the parable of the Sower illustrates the varying reception met with by the good news of the Kingdom as it is preached amongst men. That of the Tares also deals not with the Kingdom itself, but with the period of preparation for it. At the end of the age the Son of Man will come to inaugurate His Kingdom. A phrase here, 'shall gather out of his kingdom,' has been pressed to support the interpretation that the Kingdom is thought of as present now. But it need convey no such meaning. The 'good seed' is interpreted as equivalent to the 'sons of the kingdom,' i.e. according to Jewish usage, not they who already live in or possess the Kingdom, but those who are destined to inherit it when it comes. It is not inaugurated until the 'end of the age.' Then when the 'Son of Man' comes, the 'Kingdom' comes; and the method of its foundation is not a gathering of the elect out of the mass of mankind, but a gathering of the wicked from amongst the elect, a gathering of them out of the Kingdom that the righteous may inherit it and shine forth in it. There is nothing here or elsewhere in this Gospel to suggest that the scene of the Kingdom is other than the present world renewed, restored, and purified (cf. παλινγενεσία, 19^{28}). The parables of the Mustard Seed and of the Leaven describe the way in which the good news of the Kingdom spreads rapidly and penetrates deeply into human society. Those of the Hid Treasure and of the Goodly Pearl emphasize its value, and teach the lesson that a man must give up all else to enter into it. That of the Drag-Net has much the same application as the parable of the Tares. The doctrine of the Kingdom attracts good and bad alike. But at the end of the age, when the Kingdom is inaugurated, there will be a separation. In 20^{1-16} occurs the parable of the Labourers in the Vineyard. In its present context this seems to be intended to teach the lesson that in discipleship of the Kingdom priority, whether in date of entrance upon discipleship or of position now, will not carry with it special privilege within the Kingdom when it comes. All shall receive the same reward—eternal life. Of the other parables in the Gospel, $18^{21.35}$ does not bear directly upon the doctrine of the Kingdom, but emphasizes forgiveness as a qualification in all who wish to enter it. 21^{28-32} illustrates the perverse attitude of the Pharisees towards the Baptist's preaching. 21^{33-46} and 22^{1-10} are historical forecasts of the fate of the Jewish nation. 22^{11-14} emphasizes the necessity for all who hope to enter the Kingdom of possessing the necessary qualifications. 25^{1-13} and vv.$^{14-30}$ teach the suddenness of its appearance and the necessity of watching for its coming. Vv.$^{31-46}$ describes the test by which the King when He comes will admit the righteous into His Kingdom.

Of several of these parables it will rightly be felt that, as originally spoken, they had a wider meaning and scope than that here given, and one which is inconsistent with the narrow limits of the Kingdom to be inaugurated immediately after the fall of Jerusalem. That is quite true. But the question is not, What did these parables mean when they were originally spoken? but, What interpretation did the editor put upon them when he incorporated them into his Gospel? He everywhere seems to use the phrase 'kingdom of the heavens' in its eschatological sense. In four or five passages he has, instead, the 'kingdom of God.' In 6^{33} τοῦ θεοῦ is probably not genuine (omit אBg¹k). As regards 19^{24}, a passage borrowed from Mk., the fact that Mt. in 13 other places where 'kingdom of God' occurs in Mk., substitutes 'kingdom of the heavens,' or omits or paraphrases the passage, makes it very probable that 'kingdom of the heavens' should be read here also. In 12^{28} $21^{31.}$ ^{43} the editor has retained 'kingdom of God,' not because he regarded it as equivalent to 'kingdom of the heavens,' but because he felt that in these passages the idea conveyed was different from that which his phrase 'kingdom of the heavens' everywhere carries with it; and he therefore retained 'kingdom of God' to mark the difference.

Thus the conception of Christianity as expressed in this Gospel may be summarized as follows. Jesus was the King-Messiah of the OT. He was also the Son of Man of apocalyptic anticipation. But how could the functions ascribed to these two ideals be combined? Only if the King passed through death that He might come again on the clouds to inaugurate His Kingdom. And to those who could read the OT aright, all this had been foretold. Hence the Crucifixion. When Jerusalem fell, the end of the age would come, and the Son of Man would appear. In the meantime the good news was to be preached, and men were to be gathered into the society of disciples of the Messiah.

2. Date and place of composition. — If the dominant conception of the book has been rightly sketched, very important conclusions can be drawn as to its *provenance* and date. It must have been written by a Jewish-Christian, probably by a Jewish-Christian of Palestine, and it cannot date from long after the fall of Jerusalem. For it is inconceivable that any one should so arrange the words of Christ as to convey the impression that He had taught that He would return as Son of Man immediately after the fall of Jerusalem, if many years had elapsed since that event. And this conclusion as to the early date and Palestinian origin of the Gospel is supported by other features of the book. It is markedly anti-Pharisaic, and strongly Jewish-Christian in outlook.

(1) *Its anti-Pharisaism.* — This already underlies the stories of the first two chapters, which are most easily explained as a narrative of facts written to rebut Pharisaic calumnies. Christ was born of a virgin, but He was legally of Davidic descent, and the Virgin Mary's marvellous history already found prototypes by contrast in the history of women connected with the ancestors of the Christ. If He went into Egypt, it was in the days of His infancy, and He brought no magical arts thence. If His parents settled at Nazareth, it was that the tenor of prophecy might be fulfilled.

So far the anti-Pharisaic polemic of the writer has been defensive and implicit. In the third chapter it becomes manifest and open. The sayings of the Baptist are so arranged as to form a sermon of denunciation of the Pharisees and Sadducees. They are a 'brood of vipers,' who pride themselves on their descent from Abraham. But right action based on repentance is the only ground for hope of God's favour. The Messiah is at hand, and will sweep away all such false claims with the fire of judgment. In the Sermon on the Mount the same anti-Pharisaic polemic is found. Their 'righteousness' will not admit them into the Kingdom (5^{20}). They are 'hypocrites' whose religious observances are based on desire for personal credit (6^{1-17}). In 8^{12} they are 'the sons of the kingdom,' but nevertheless they will be cast into the outer darkness. It was the Pharisees who complained that

Christ ate with tax-gatherers and sinners (9^{11}), and it was they who ascribed His power to cast out demons to Beelzebul (v.^{34} 12^{24}). They accused His disciples (v.^{2}), and Christ Himself (v.^{10}), of doing illegal actions on the Sabbath. They plotted to destroy Him (v.^{14}), and asked a sign from Him (v.^{38}). They condemned His disciples for eating with unwashen hands (15^2), and were shocked at His teaching about things clean and unclean (v.^{12}), being themselves blind guides (v.^{14}). The disciples were to beware of their teaching (16^{12}). In the last days of the Messiah's life the Pharisees took a prominent part in the events that led to His death. They plotted with the chief priests to arrest Him (21^{45}). They planned to entrap Him in His speech (22^{15}). They tried to entangle Him in argument (vv.$^{34. 41}$). All this leads up to the tremendous indictment of the scribes and Pharisees in ch. 23. In the narrative dealing with the Crucifixion we read naturally rather of the chief priests and elders than of the Pharisees; but it is the latter, with the chief priests, who effect the sealing of the tomb ($27^{62ff.}$).

(2) *The Jewish-Christian element.*—Of course the whole conception of the Kingdom of the heavens as sketched above is Jewish-Christian in character. But there are other Jewish-Christian features in the Gospel. (*a*) One is the interest shown in St. Peter. He was one of the earliest of Christ's disciples (4^{18}), and Christ had healed his wife's mother (8^{14}). He was in some sense 'first' of the Twelve (10^2), and it was he who walked on the waters at Christ's command ($14^{28ff.}$). It was he who first confessed Christ's Messiahship (16^{16}), and received the promise of high rank in the Kingdom (v.^{19}). By inserting this passage the editor blunts the severity of the rebuke (v.^{23}), which St. Luke altogether omits. It was Peter who was prominent amongst the three who were privileged to be on the Mount of Transfiguration (17^4), and it was he to whom the tax-gatherers came as to one who was the representative of the other disciples. It was Peter who acted as the spokesman of the rest (15^{15} 18^{21} $26^{33. 35}$), or who was addressed as representing the others (v.^{40}). It was he who penetrated into the palace, and there denied that he knew Christ (vv.$^{58-75}$). If all the Apostles were to sit on thrones in the new age (19^{28}), Peter was to have administrative and legislative power in the Kingdom (16^{19}).

(*b*) Another Jewish-Christian feature in the Gospel is the presence in it of sayings which seem to limit Christ's mission and doctrine to the Jewish nation. In His own lifetime He had expressly asserted this of His own activity. 'I was not sent save to the lost sheep of the house of Israel' (15^{24}). On two occasions He had extended His mercy to pagans (8^{5-13} 15^{21-28}), but on the latter occasion He made it plain that the grace thus extended to a Gentile woman was only as it were a crumb which had dropped from the table of the Jews, to whom He was sent, and had been devoured by a Gentile dog. He bade His disciples 'go not to the way of the Gentiles, nor to the cities of the Samaritans, but to the lost sheep of the house of Israel' (10^6); and said they should not have exhausted the cities of Israel before His coming (v.^{23}). In the new age the Apostles were to rule over a new Israel (19^{28}). Of course, side by side with these sayings from his Palestinian sources, the editor has incorporated others from other sources, which prove that he himself was well aware that Christ had on other occasions foreseen and commanded the admission of Gentiles to the discipleship of the Kingdom. 'Many were to come from east and west' (8^{11}), and the three parables in 21^{28}–22^{14} seem to convey the same truth. Further, the good news was to be preached among all nations for a testimony (24^{14}), and the Apostles were to make disciples of all nations (28^{19}). But there is nothing in any of these

passages to suggest that the editor anticipated the admission of Gentiles to discipleship save on terms similar to those on which proselytes had been admitted to the old Israel;* and it is clear that he saw no difficulty in the preaching to all nations being accomplished within a generation, for the 'end' (24^{14}) which was to close this preaching was the period of great tribulation accompanying the siege of the city, followed immediately by the coming of the Son of Man (v.^{30}).

(*c*) A third Jewish-Christian feature is the insistence on the permanent obligations of the Mosaic Law; see above, p. 144^b.

Now all these characteristics of the Gospel point irresistibly to Palestine, and to Palestine in the period before or very soon after the fall of Jerusalem, as the place and date of the composition of the Gospel. The most obvious feature in this connexion is the belief that the coming of the Son of Man would immediately follow the period of tribulation accompanying the siege of the city. But the other features above mentioned point in the same direction. The prominence given to St. Peter is natural enough in traditions which had been collected and preserved in Palestine in the early days of the Church at Jerusalem. The limitation of Christianity to Jews or proselytes, and the insistence on the permanent validity of the Law, reflect the same primitive Christian atmosphere as we breathe in the first few chapters of the Acts, before the pressure of circumstances had compelled the Apostles to recognize that St. Paul must be right, and that under Christianity Jew and Gentile stood on the same plane in the sight of God.

Lastly, the anti-Pharisaic attitude of the editor would be natural in one who knew something of the difficulties of the Jewish-Christian Church in the early days when Pharisaic hatred pursued its members from city to city.

The date thus arrived at affects the whole Gospel and not only portions of it. It is a literary unity, and apart from a few possible later interpolations, *e.g.* 6^{14} (the doxology) 22^{43} 23^{35} ('son of Barachiah'), belongs to one editor, and to one period of final composition. The attempts made to argue for a late date for the composition of the whole book from isolated phrases, or to mark large sections as late additions, fail to account for the unity of idea and conception that runs through the whole work, and neglect the cumulative evidence of the conceptions that characterize it for an early date.

1^{18-25} has been claimed as late because the idea of virgin-birth is 'quite foreign to Judaism.' As a matter of fact this idea is thoroughly Eastern (as well as Western), and must have been familiar to every Palestinian Jew who had read the Septuagint. And in other respects the narrative is Jewish throughout. The occurrence of the word ἐκκλησία (16^{19} 18^{17}) and the Baptismal Formula (28^{19}) have been said to betray late date. But there is no possible reason why a Jewish Christian writing about the year A.D. 70 should not have used ἐκκλησία to represent whatever Aramaic word was originally uttered; and if the Triune name in v.^{19} is not a later gloss, it may well have been used by a Palestinian Christian who was contemporary with St. Paul (cf. 1 Co 12^3, 2 Co 13^{14}, and 1 P 1^2, 1 Jn $3^{23. 24}$).

3. The Sources. — If, then, we take the year A.D. 70 as an approximate date for the composition of the Gospel, there remain the questions of its sources, its author, and its historical value. The facts about the sources are these :—

(1) The editor has borrowed the greater part of the Second Gospel, and has made it the framework of his narrative. He has altered the order of Mk 1–7^{24} in order to group the material under subject-heads. He has greatly expanded the discourses. He makes omissions and alterations in phrases relating to the Person of Christ, omitting especially expressions which attribute to Him inability, or de-

* At least the Mosaic Law was to be binding upon them.

sire for information, and terms of human emotion; and makes a series of somewhat similar changes in clauses relating to the Apostles. For the details of his editorial revision of the Second Gospel, see art. MARK (Gospel), and the Com. on 'Matthew' in *ICC*, pp. xiii–xl.

(2) The Gospel contains, besides this Markan material, a good deal of matter, almost entirely sayings, which is found also in substance in the Third Gospel. It is generally supposed that this was borrowed by the two Evangelists from a common source, viz. a collection of Gospel material compiled by the Apostle Matthew, and referred to by Papias (Eus. *HE* III. xxxix.).

The present writer has elsewhere attempted to prove that, so far as St. Luke goes, this is not a very probable theory. Besides these sayings which he has in common with St. Luke, the editor of the First Gospel has also a number of sayings found only in his Gospel. The probability is that he borrowed these peculiar sayings, and most of those common to him and to St. Luke, from the Apostolic collection of sayings mentioned by Papias. If so, it is not very likely that St. Luke had also seen this collection. Rather material from it had passed into some of the many sources which he had used (Lk 1[1]), and were borrowed by him from them. See 'Matthew,' *l.c.* pp. xli–lxii. Thus Mt.'s second source was the Matthæan *Logia* or collection of discourses.

(3) What remains of the Gospel, when we have put aside the matter borrowed from Mk. and the sayings drawn from the *Logia*, consists of a number of narrative traditions. These deal with Christ's Birth and Infancy (chs. 1. 2), with a few incidents connected with St. Peter (14[28-31] 17[24-27]), and with some details connected with Christ's trial and Resurrection (27[3-10. 19. 24. 25. 51a-53. 62-66] 28[11-15]). They were all drawn, it may be supposed, from current Palestinian Christian tradition.

(4) Lastly, a number of quotations of a peculiar type, which are introduced by a special formula (1[22. 23] 2[5. 6, 15. 17. 18. 23] 4[14-16] 8[17] 12[17-21] 13[35] 21[4. 5] 27[9]), were drawn from a catena or list of OT Messianic passages, which had already been translated into Greek when the editor borrowed them.

4. The Author.—Now, who was the writer who thus welded together the Second Gospel, the Matthæan *Logia*, a number of Palestinian traditions, and a series of OT quotations, into our present Gospel? From the end of the 2nd cent. the work has been ascribed to St. Matthew. But there are the following difficulties in this ascription:

(1) The same writers who attribute our Gospel to St. Matthew state that he wrote it in Hebrew or Aramaic. Now it is clear that our Gospel was composed in Greek, and is based upon Greek sources. This is certain so far as the material drawn from the Second Gospel is concerned, and probable for the sayings drawn from the Matthæan *Logia*.

(2) It does not seem very probable that the Apostle Matthew should have written a Gospel from second-hand materials. The work lacks that freshness of presentation which we should expect from an eye-witness of many of the events.

How then explain the ascription of the Gospel to him? Because the book, in a sense in which the statement is not true of St. Luke's Gospel, is based directly upon the collection of sayings compiled by the Apostle. We must, therefore, suppose that the author was an otherwise unknown Jewish Christian of Palestine, who about the year A.D. 70 compiled his Gospel, using as his framework the Second Gospel, but borrowing largely from the Matthæan *Logia*, and inserting also some Palestinian traditions with which he was familiar. The Gospel, as it left his hand, represents the concep-

tion of Christ's Person and work which was dominant in the Palestinian Church in the middle of the 1st cent. A.D. To Christians there Jesus was the Jewish King-Messiah. His life on earth was only the prelude to His sovereignty. For He was to come again as Son of Man at the end of the age, and that was imminent, and would follow immediately upon the final downfall of the Jewish polity.

5. Historical value.—So far as the question of the historical value of the detail given in the Gospel is concerned, we may set aside for our present purpose all that is drawn from St. Mark's Gospel. The value of that is a consideration for a writer on the Second Gospel (see above, p. 133 ff., and cf. the Dean of Westminster's *Study of the Gospels*, and Burkitt's *The Gospel History and its Transmission*). The sayings drawn from the Matthæan *Logia* have behind them Apostolic authority, and, allowing for some change of emphasis and possible accretion in the process of transmission, may safely be taken as representing actual utterances of Christ.

The Palestinian traditions peculiar to the Gospel are probably not all of equal weight. The narrative of the supernatural birth is best attested, because the main fact of the story is supported by the tradition known to St. Luke. Of the rest it is difficult to say more than that they are early Palestinian traditions, and we must abstain from condemning them upon purely fanciful grounds as legendary.

But the question of historical value can be raised in a different form, and one of much greater importance. Allowing the substantial accuracy of the bulk of the detail in the Gospel, and without discussing the precise value and importance to be attached to each separate tradition, how far do the main conceptions of Christ and of His doctrine which run through the Gospel correspond to the historical Christ? Did He teach what is here ascribed to Him?

Something may be learned in this connexion if we consider the method of the Evangelist. He presents to us selections from Christ's sayings, arranged in what is clearly often an artificial and literary manner. A good example of this is the Charge to the Twelve. The nucleus of this consists of a few sayings, recorded by St. Mark, addressed to the Twelve when Christ sent them forth on a journey of preaching in Palestine. But the editor of the First Gospel is so little concerned with the actual historical facts that he omits altogether the statements descriptive of their going forth and of their return. The local and temporary mission in Palestine merges itself in his mind in the wider and universal mission to all nations. He draws from his sources many other sayings which had reference to this wider mission work, and adds them to St. Mark's short discourse, regardless of the fact that some of them were not spoken on that particular occasion. Now, selection and artificial grouping of this kind, useful as it is, inevitably involves over-emphasis. Teaching, which would have explained and counterbalanced that which is recorded, is left out, and impressions are given which would be qualified, if the selection given had been larger, or the grouping less artificial. And combined with this feature of arbitrary selection and artificial grouping may be linked the local character of the Gospel, and the early date of its material. For it is clear that the Jewish-Christian disciples in the early Church stood too near to the life of the Christ to be able to form any adequate conception of the true meaning of His person or His work. Jesus had, we may be sure, said many things that were obscure at the moment of utterance, had spoken sometimes in parable, sometimes in symbol, sometimes in paradox. And the first Christians of Jerusalem did, it is clear, what, after all, others since them have often done, *i.e.* they interpreted the life of Christ in the light of their own historical surroundings, and selected from His teaching those elements which enabled them to adapt their ideas of His meaning to their own lives, without making an absolute breach with all that life had hitherto meant for them. The development of history is, as we now see, the truest interpreter of much that Christ said, and not until Jerusalem fell could His teaching about the future of Christianity become clear.

We shall expect, then, to find in the Gospel an over-emphasis upon certain points arising from artificial grouping of sayings, and from omission of other aspects of Christ's teaching. We shall also not be surprised to find interpretations of His sayings which the later developments of history have proved to be mistaken. Let us apply this to the chief conceptions of the Gospel.

(1) *The permanence of the Law.* — If we may judge from the general tenor of the NT evidence, Christ laid down no hard and fast rules for dealing with the difficult problem of the obligations of the Mosaic Law. But on special occasions He seems to have given expression to the idea that particular precepts or sanctions belonged to a bygone age, and had lost their validity. St. Mark (who is here supported by St. Luke and St. Paul) represents Him as teaching that the tacit sanction of divorce by Dt 24^{1-4} should be set aside as a concession to weakness, and should, from a Christian point of view, be superseded by an ideal view of marriage as a tie which could not be broken. St. Mark again represents Him as implicitly annulling the Mosaic distinctions between clean and unclean meats, on the ground that defilement was moral and internal, not external and ceremonial. And the fact that He taught views of the Law which were not those of orthodox Judaism, is suggested by the statements that the Pharisees attempted to entrap Him into some statement about the Law, or upon subjects with which the Law dealt, which could be used as an accusation against Him (Mk 10^2 [$\pi\epsilon\iota\rho\acute{a}\zeta o\nu\tau\epsilon\varsigma$], Mt 22^{35} [$\pi\epsilon\iota\rho\acute{a}\zeta\omega\nu$]). But the history of the early Church proves that it was difficult for the first Jewish disciples to suppose that the Messiah had ever countenanced the view that any part of the OT Scriptures had lost its original hold upon the consciences of men. This is the standpoint of the editor of the First Gospel. Christ had taught that not a letter should pass from the Law until all had been fulfilled, and that anyone who relaxed the authority of the least commandment of the Law should be least in the Kingdom of heaven (5^{17-20}). And not only was there this general statement of the permanent validity of the Law in general, but special laws had been sanctioned and reaffirmed by Christ as still valid and obligatory. Divorce must be sanctioned when there had been fornication ($\pi o\rho\nu\epsilon\acute{\iota}a$) ($5^{32}$ 19^9). The saying about clean and unclean had reference not to the Mosaic Law, but to the Pharisaic traditions about eating with unwashen hands (15^{20}). The Christian disciple who had a case against his brother was to take two or three witnesses, that the Mosaic Law might be satisfied (18^{16}). And in the great tribulation Christians were to pray that their flight might not fall on the Sabbath, lest the Law should be broken (24^{20}). It is clear that the editor regarded the Mosaic Law as still binding in all its details on Christian men. Now it is probable that we must make allowance here for some over-emphasis due to local and national prejudice which interpreted Christ's sayings in the direction which the history of the Jewish people seemed to warrant, and which took

effect in the selection, and arrangement, and interpretation of such of His sayings as lent themselves to the impression which it was desired to produce.

The most obvious instance of this process may be found in Mt.'s treatment of Mk 10^{1-12}. That narrative is perfectly clear, coherent, and decisive. The Pharisees, who knew well that Christ taught a doctrine about the sanctity of marriage which seemed to set aside the sanction of divorce by the Law (Dt 24^{1-4}), came to test Him, *i.e.* to get from Him a direct statement which would enable them to say that He was attacking the Mosaic ordinance. He met their challenge with the expected answer. The permission of divorce by the Law was a concession to human weakness. From an ideal standpoint, the marriage tie was indissoluble. The man or woman * who put away their partner committed adultery. Nothing can be clearer than this, and it is in accordance with the tradition of Christ's teaching, preserved by St. Luke (16^{18}) and by St. Paul (1 Co $7^{10.\ 11}$). But the editor of the First Gospel has introduced hopeless confusion into the narrative. He represents the Pharisees as asking for an interpretation of Dt 24^{1-4}. The Jewish theologians were divided upon the point. Some—the school of Shammai—argued that by דבר ערות some act of unchastity was intended. Cf. *Giṭṭin*, 90*a* : 'No one shall divorce his wife unless there be found in her something unchaste' (ערוה דבר). They thus placed the emphasis upon the word ערוה. But others—the school of Hillel—allowed divorce for any idle pretext, emphasizing the word דבר. Accordingly, the Pharisees in Mt. ask, 'Is it lawful to put away a wife for every cause?' Christ answers, as in Mk., that from an ideal standpoint marriage is indissoluble. The Pharisees appeal to Dt 24. Now clearly Christ should be represented as reaffirming and supporting what He has said by declaring (as in Mk.) that the permission of Dt 24 was a concession to human weakness, and that a higher principle was to be found in the purpose of God as declared in Gn 1^{27}. But, instead, He is represented as saying that $\pi o\rho\nu\epsilon\acute{\iota}a$ constituted an exception to the ideal principle. Thus He is made to reaffirm the Law of Dt 24, interpreted in the sense of the school of Shammai, and to acknowledge the permanent obligation of a sanction which He had just criticised.

It seems clear that the editor of Mt. has confused Mk.'s consistent narrative by introducing into it a clause which entirely confuses the point at issue. Now, if we ask why he has done this, we remember that earlier in his Gospel (5^{32}) he has inserted a saying (probably from the Matthæan *Logia*) in which this same exception to the general rule occurs. The words are not identical. In 5^{32} they are $\pi a\rho\epsilon\kappa\tau\grave{o}\varsigma$ $\lambda\acute{o}\gamma o\upsilon$ $\pi o\rho\nu\epsilon\acute{\iota}a\varsigma$, but in 19^9 ($\epsilon\acute{\iota}$ $\mu\grave{\eta}$ $\epsilon\grave{\pi}\grave{\iota}$ $\pi o\rho\nu\epsilon\acute{\iota}a$ (but BDS^2 33 latt have $\pi a\rho\epsilon\kappa\tau\grave{o}\varsigma$ $\lambda\acute{o}\gamma o\upsilon$ $\pi o\rho\nu\epsilon\acute{\iota}a\varsigma$ here also). The two clauses look like alternative renderings of the phrase דבר ערוה, which the school of Shammai declared to be the ground of divorce. That is to say, in 19^9 the editor has blended with Mk.'s narrative another tradition of the Lord's words, which was furnished to him by his Palestinian source; and we have a clear case of a saying of Christ altered in process of transmission to bring it into accordance with the Mosaic Law. Of course the saying of 5^{32} may be as genuine and original as Mk $10^{11.\ 12}$. It is quite possible that Christ should have on one occasion taught as Mk. represents Him, and on another have sanctioned the necessity of divorce for $\pi o\rho\nu\epsilon\acute{\iota}a$. But there is a good deal of probability in the supposition that, as a matter of fact, He appealed to the ideal view of marriage as a principle which should guide men, leaving it to the common sense of His disciples to realize that when the sin of men makes a breach in the ideal law, such sin drags with it the necessity of divorce. In this case the clause which allows an exception will be an accretion to His words, added in the early Palestinian Church to His simple statement that no man must divorce his wife and no woman her husband, in order to harmonize it with the supposed teaching of the OT, and then transferred by Mt. into Mk.'s narrative.

Another somewhat similar case may be found in Mk $7^{14-23}=$ Mt 15^{10-20}. The reading and interpretation of Mk 7^{19} are obscure. According to one reading, $\kappa a\theta a\rho\acute{\iota}\zeta\omega\nu$ $\pi\acute{a}\nu\tau a$ $\tau\grave{a}$ $\beta\rho\acute{\omega}\mu a\tau a$ may be a comment of the Evangelist, to the effect that Christ's teaching on this occasion 'purged all meats,' *i.e.* cancelled the Mosaic distinctions between clean and unclean meats. But however this may be, the narrative leaves on the mind of the reader the impression that the inevitable effect of such teaching as is here recorded would be to make null these distinctions of the Mosaic Law. Now the editor of Mt. clearly wished to avoid this inference. He omits the clause $\kappa a\theta a\rho\acute{\iota}\zeta\omega\nu$ $\pi\acute{a}\nu\tau a$ $\tau\grave{a}$ $\beta\rho\acute{\omega}\mu a\tau a$, and at the end of the discourse turns the mind of the reader from the inevitable inference by adding the clause, 'But to eat with unwashen hands defileth not a man,' as though the whole discourse had been dealing with the Pharisaic regulations about ceremonial hand-washing. Thus he carries the reader back at once to the previous question, and, so far as possible, prevents him from drawing the natural and inevitable conclusion from the discourse as recorded by Mk.

A somewhat similar desire to avoid words which might seem out of harmony with OT regulations has probably caused the omission in Mt 12^8 of the clause, 'The Sabbath was made for man, and not man for the Sabbath,' found in Mk 2^{27}.

Lastly, an example of over-emphasis due to arrangement of

---

* For divorce by a woman amongst the Jews, cf. *Aramaic Papyri discovered at Assuan*, p. 12 (London, G. Moring, 1906).

sayings may be found in Mt 5¹⁷⁻²⁰. It is quite probable that vv.¹⁸·¹⁹ are genuine sayings of Christ spoken on some occasion when their meaning could not be mistaken, as a paradoxical expression of the permanent value of the moral elements in the OT. But as they now stand they hopelessly confuse the plain tenor of the Sermon. The illustrations given in vv.²¹⁻⁴³ make it clear that the 'fulfilling' of v.¹⁷ meant to make clear the true spiritual meaning of the Law. But vv.¹⁸·¹⁹ interpret πληρῶσαι in another sense ; namely, to reaffirm and carry out in detail, which is indeed in harmony with the teaching of Rabbinical Judaism, but is inconsistent with the plain meaning of the rest of the chapter. If vv.¹⁸·¹⁹ be omitted as extraneous to this context, and due to the practice of the editor of bringing together sayings which in any way bear upon the same subject, the meaning of vv.¹⁷·²⁰⁻⁴³ is quite clear. Christ did not, as His adversaries argued, subvert the Law. He reaffirmed its spiritual principles, and gave to it a deeper meaning than that arrived at by Rabbinical exegesis. The 'righteousness' of His disciples was to exceed that of the Pharisees, because it would be based upon a more spiritual understanding of the principles underlying the OT revelation.

(2) *The near approach of the Kingdom.*—A still more difficult problem is raised by the question, Did Jesus Christ promise that He would come again on the clouds of heaven within the lifetime of the generation to which He spoke ? The Palestinian Church, as represented by the First Gospel, certainly believed that this was the case. But did they misunderstand Him ? And the question may be raised in an earlier form. Nearly all the terms used in sayings of this nature were familiar technical theological terms in use in the apocalyptic writings, which expressed one side of contemporary Messianic expectation. *E.g.* 'the Son of Man,' 'the clouds of heaven,' the 'coming' of the Son of Man, 'the throne of glory,' 'the coming age,' 'the day of judgment,' the division between righteous and wicked, the condemnation to Gehenna, the inheritance of the Kingdom by the righteous, the feast in the Kingdom, and 'eternal life'—all these formed part of the ordinary mental equipment of every writer who tried to express the hopes of Israel under apocalyptic imagery. Did the Lord use them of Himself, or did the Palestinian Church try to express her faith and belief in Him as the Divine Messiah by transferring to Him the phrases and the imagery of current Messianic belief ? Attempts have been made to show that the second supposition is the more probable,* but, so far as the present writer can judge, they have failed in their aim. For it is impossible to disentangle all apocalyptic imagery from Christ's teaching, without entirely destroying the credit of the Gospels as historical records. This kind of imagery and metaphor is, of course, more accumulated in the First Gospel than in the others, and one or two phrases, as, *e.g.*, the 'end' or 'consummation of the age,' and 'the throne of glory,' occur only in it, but still all the Gospels contain a good deal. If Christ did not speak of Himself as the 'Son of Man' and of His 'coming' at the Last Day, and of other similar things, then we have no solid ground for believing that any saying recorded of Him is genuine.

But if we assume that Christ did use of Himself this apocalyptic language, what shall we say of the more important question, Are, then, the conceptions which His sayings, as they are arranged in the First Gospel, seem to convey, to be taken as a part of the real teaching ? And here we shall necessarily have to take into consideration the following facts amongst others.

(*a*) It seems clear that Christ must have given utterance to words which left upon the minds of the early disciples the impression that He had promised to come again shortly. For this conception not only pervades the Synoptic Gospels,

* *E.g.* it has been argued on linguistic grounds that Christ could not have spoken of Himself as the 'Son of Man,' and that much of the apocalyptic imagery in Mk 13, Mt 24, is due to the blending of a Jewish Apocalypse with genuine sayings of Christ. But the former theory is still unproven, and the second is an unsuccessful exegetical device to solve a difficulty.

but is found in almost every part of the NT literature.

(*b*) It was, however, inevitable that any expressions of time to which He gave utterance should have been interpreted by His Jewish adherents to imply a short time literally. For if we grant for a moment, for the sake of argument, that He had foreknowledge of the future development of history, it is clear to us now that it would have been inconsistent with His methods of teaching to have unveiled to His disciples the historical details of future ages. On the other hand, He may well have wished that His return should be, as it has been, the soul's pole-star of His lovers in every successive age, and have left the period of His Coming veiled in ambiguous language. In that case the early Jewish Church has been influenced by the contemporary Messianic belief which always placed the coming of the Messiah in the near future, and has selected from Christ's sayings those which were most easily interpreted to convey the impression of the nearness of the Kingdom.

This will partly explain the large part which sayings referring to the near approach of the Kingdom play in the First Gospel. Some of these occur only in this Gospel, as, *e.g.*, 10²³ 13²⁴⁻³⁰·³⁶⁻⁴³·⁴⁷⁻⁵⁰ 19²⁸ᵃ 25¹⁻¹³·³¹⁻⁴⁶. In other cases a saying, the original form of which was found in the Second Gospel, has been modified so as to make it express clearly this idea. For example, in Mk 9¹ occur the words 'until they see the kingdom of God come with power.' Although a reference to the immediately preceding verse would naturally suggest that this coming of the 'kingdom of God' was identical with the coming of the Son of Man with His angels, the words taken by themselves might be interpreted by the reader to refer to the Transfiguration which follows, or to some later event, such as the Day of Pentecost, or the Fall of Jerusalem. The editor of the First Gospel has been unwilling to leave them in this ambiguity, and by changing them into 'the Son of Man coming in His kingdom,' interprets them unmistakably of the coming in glory with the angels (16²⁷), which he then believed to be about to take place during the lifetime of some to whom the words were originally spoken. Again, in Mk 14⁶² occur the words 'you shall see the Son of Man sitting at the right hand of the power, and coming with the clouds of heaven.' The editor of the First Gospel (Mt 26⁶⁴) inserts before 'you shall see' the words ἀπ' ἄρτι. This phrase is difficult, because the words should mean 'from this present moment' (cf. 'Matthew,' *l.c.*). But since the period between the Crucifixion and the Resurrection must on any interpretation be excluded, it is probable that the words mean 'you shall soon, shortly, see,' etc. That is again an expression of the belief of the editor that the Second Coming was near at hand. A similar case is found in Mt 24²⁹, where the editor inserts into Mk.'s discourse the word 'immediately,' thus again linking the Second Coming closely with the Fall of Jerusalem.

These facts suggest irresistibly the conclusion that the editor or the tradition which he follows has, by accumulating sayings of one kind, and by modifying others to some slight extent in order to give them the required meaning, given the impression that the Lord taught a nearness of His coming to inaugurate the Kingdom, which goes beyond what He Himself originally intended. He spoke, no doubt, of the coming of the Son of Man in glory, using apocalyptic language, which He may or may not have intended to be taken literally. The early Jewish Church has interpreted it quite literally, and read into it that element of immediacy which is presupposed in all apocalyptic writings. He forecast, no doubt, the catastrophe to which the shortsighted policy of the Jewish authorities was hurrying that ill‑starred people. The early Church linked together these two classes of utterance, and believed that both would receive their fulfilment at the same period.

If, then, we must allow for some over-emphasis, some foreshortening in the presentation of this conception in the First Gospel, we shall naturally ask if there is not evidence that Christ's teaching anticipated, in fact, a longer development of history than that here presupposed. Even within the First Gospel itself many of His sayings suggest a different interpretation from that put upon them by the editor (*e.g.* the parables of the Mustard Seed, the Drag-net, and see below). And when we pass to the writers who have emancipated themselves from Jewish theological conceptions, we see that Christ's words were regarded as presupposing a longer development of historical events than that suggested by the First Gospel. This, of course, is true of the later Epistles of St. Paul, of the Fourth Gospel, and of St. Luke. And the verdict of the historian must be that the Jewish-Christian interpretation of Christ's words upon this point is not likely to be most accurate, because it is Jewish and because it is early. Rather these two factors would, in the nature of things, concur to impel the first Jewish Christians to an interpretation of His sayings which is one-sided, and in part over-emphasized, just because it is local and early. The best interpreter of much that Christ taught has been the later development of history.

(3) *The scope of the Gospel.*—It is known that the later Jewish theologians had no strictly formulated views of the relation of the Gentiles to the future Messianic salvation. In some few passages of their writings, especially in the Sibylline Oracles, it would seem as though they looked forward to the admittance of Gentiles into the Kingdom on equal terms with the Jews, simply on the ground of obedience to God (cf. Sib. Or. iii. 740). But the prevailing tendency was very different. When the Kingdom came, the Gentiles would be annihilated; or they would be condemned to everlasting punishment in Gehenna; or they would, if they were righteous, participate in the Messianic salvation, but only as proselytes, or as subjects of the Jewish people.

To the early Jewish Christians, who had been trained in such conceptions as these, it was inevitable that Christ's teaching, if it were universal in ultimate scope and intention, implicitly rather than explicitly should seem to point to a national rather than a universal Kingdom. That this was the belief of the first disciples at Jerusalem, the first half of the Acts bears witness. Only the pressure of circumstances could force the Apostles to go back to Christ's words, and to see that they bore within them the seeds of a belief in a universal, spiritual monarchy, which was quite unlimited in scope. It needed a vision to convince St. Peter of this, and Gal 3 shows how difficult the lesson was for him. In this respect the First Gospel has a twofold outlook. Underlying the surface there may clearly be seen, in the words of Christ which are recorded, expressions which would naturally convey the implication that Christianity was intended to influence all mankind. The gospel was to be preached to all nations (24[14]). The disciples were to make disciples of all nations (28[19]). Many were to come from east and west, and sit down within the Kingdom (8[11]). The Kingdom was to be given to another nation, and to be taken from the Jews (21[43]). But these sayings have all the appearance of words which were interpreted in a limited sense by the editor of the Gospel. If the Kingdom was to come immediately after the fall of Jerusalem, then the preaching to the Gentiles

could be but a superficial process. It was to be 'for a testimony.' Moreover, there is nothing in the Gospel to suggest an unconditioned equality of Jew and Gentile. The supposition is rather probable that the editor assumed that such Gentiles as became Christians would do so as proselytes of the Jewish‑Christian Church. They were to be 'made disciples,' that is to say, to be merged in the Jewish-Christian Church. If they had not the fitting wedding garment, they would be excluded from the Kingdom; and the garment probably symbolizes, in the editor's mind, the 'righteousness' which was to be greater than that of the Pharisees, only as being based upon a deeper insight into the spiritual intention of the Mosaic Law, which by no means permitted any relaxation of its obligations.

Here again we must, as it would seem, make some allowance for over-emphasis, due partly to artificial arrangement of Christ's sayings, partly to a limited insight into their true scope and meaning, which was due to past religious training. Some lapse of time, some clearing of spiritual vision by the actual facts of life when Christianity came into contact with pagan peoples, was needed before it could be realized that if Christianity was intended for the Jew first and also for the Greek, it nevertheless was to include them both in a position of absolute equality, and to appeal to men without respect to differences of race or creed. See also GOSPELS, LOGIA, LUKE (Gospel), MARK (Gospel), PAPIAS, SERMON ON THE MOUNT, etc.

LITERATURE.—Willoughby C. Allen, Com. on 'St. Matthew' in *ICC*, 1907 (see List of Authorities on p. lxxxix ff.); Th. Zahn, *Das Evangelium des Matthäus*, 1903, the same author's *Forschungen f. Gesch. d. NT Kanons*, 1881–1903, *Gesch. d. ,NT Kanons*, 1888–1890, and his *Einleit. in das NT*, 1897–1899; H. J. Holtzmann, *Handkom.* 'Die Synoptiker,' 1901; Wellhausen, *Das Evangelium Matthœi*, 1904, the same author's *Skizzen u. Vorarbeiten*, 1899, and his *Einleit. in die drei ersten Evangelien*, 1905; A. Merx, *Das Evangelium Matthäus*, 1902; Burkitt, *The Gospel History and its Transmission*, 1906; the Comm. of Broadus (1887), Morison (1875), Alford [7] (1874), Schanz (R. C., 1879), Meyer-Weiss (1898), Maclaren (1892), A. B. Bruce (in *EGT*, vol. i.). See also Scholten, *Das Aelteste Evangelium*, 1869; Renan, *Les Évangiles*, 1877; Roehrich, *La composition des Évangiles*, 1897; Bruce, *With Open Face*, 1896, pp. 1–24; Sir J. C. Hawkins, *Horœ Synopticœ*, 1899; Dalman, *Die Worte Jesu* [Eng. tr. 1902]; P. Wernle, *Die Synopt. Frage*, 1899; F. Blass, *Textkritische Bemerkungen zu Matthäus*, 1900; the Introductions of Hilgenfeld, S. Davidson, Bleek-Mangold, Westcott, Salmon, B. Weiss, H. J. Holtzmann, Jülicher, Godet; artt. 'Matthew' (by J. V. Bartlet) in Hastings' *DB* and 'Gospels' (by Schmiedel) in *EBi*. Special points are dealt with in such works as Resch's ´ Kindheitsevangelium' in *TU* x. 5; Hoelmann, *Bibelstudien* (on the Eschatological Discourse), 1860; Weifferbach, *Der Wiederkunftsgedanke Jesu*, 1873; Schwartzkopff, *Die Weissagungen Jesu Christi*, 1896 [Eng. tr. 1897].   WILLOUGHBY C. ALLEN.

MEALS.—The prevalent custom amongst the Jews in the time of Jesus was to have two formal meals in the day. Both these are referred to more than once in the Gospels by the terms ἄριστον and δεῖπνον (cf. Lk 14[12], where both words occur in the same context), and we know from these writings that it was to either of these meals that guests were invited to partake of the festive hospitality of their friends (cf. 14[12] 11[37] 14[16f.]). Besides these, it was customary to have an informal meal at an early hour of the day (ἀκράτισμα or ἄριστον πρωϊνόν), which was a very light repast, consisting of a piece of bread, or bread with some accompanying relish, such as oil or melted butter (Robinson, *BRP*[2] ii. 18). This meal is only once referred to in the NT (Jn 21[12. 15]), and there the word used is the same as that which occurs in the Lukan narrative of Jesus 'dining' (ἀριστᾶν) in the Pharisee's house (Lk 11[37f.]).

It is probably this meal which 'the virtuous woman' of Proverbs rises so early to provide (Pr 29[33] [LXX]=31[15] [Heb.]), and which at the present time constitutes the breakfast of the populace in Palestine. It is, moreover, probable that it is this meal which is called in the Talmud the 'early snack' (פַּת שַׁחֲרִית),

though Edersheim refers this descriptive title to the ἄριστον of the NT (see his *Life and Times of Jesus the Messiah*, ii. 205 n. [3]; cf. also Plummer, 'St. Luke,' in *Internat. Crit. Com.* on Lk 11[37]).

The mid-day meal, corresponding somewhat to the modern luncheon, was partaken of at hours varying, according to rank and occupation, from 10 a.m. till noon (*Shabbath*, 10*a*). It was partaken of immediately after the business of the forenoon was concluded, whether in the market-place (Mk 7[4]), in the synagogue (Edersheim, vol. ii. p. 205; cf. 1 K 13[7]), or during the heat of the middle of the day, when the labourers were compelled to desist from their field work (cf. Ru 2[14]). Josephus informs us that the Jews were required by their Law to make their breakfast (ἀριστοποιεῖσθαι) at noon on Sabbath days (*Vita*, 54, cf. also Gn 43[16. 25] and 2 S 24[15], where the LXX has ἕως ὥρας ἀρίστου, which is rendered by Pesh. 'till the sixth hour'). This, too, was generally a meal of a simple character, consisting of bread with parched corn, the former being moistened with a little vinegar (Ru 2[14]), or of bread broken down into a bowl of pottage, together with some weak or diluted wine (στάμνον οἴνου κεκερασμένον, Bel [33] [LXX, Swete's ed.]). Fish grilled by laying it upon the hot charcoal (ἀνθρακιά) was also a common article of food accompanying the bread (see Jn 21[9]).

The principal meal of the whole day was the δεῖπνον, which was eaten after the day's work was finished (see Lk 17[7]). This would naturally be about the time of the going down of the sun, which will explain the Lukan narrative of Jesus and the two disciples at Emmaus (πρὸς ἑσπέραν, Lk 24[29f.]). This was the time of the day when Jesus is recorded by the three Synoptists to have miraculously fed the multitudes (ὥρα πολλή, Mk 6[35]; ὀψίας δὲ γενομένης . . . καὶ ἡ ὥρα ἤδη παρῆλθεν, Mt 14[15]; ἡ δὲ ἡμέρα ἤρξατο κλίνειν, Lk 9[12]). The Passover was also eaten during the evening, and it was at the conclusion of that festal meal (μετὰ τὸ δειπνῆσαι) that Jesus instituted the Feast memorial of His death.

We find numerous references to the δεῖπνον in the writings of Josephus, from whom we learn incidentally that this was usually an elaborate meal and closely connected with sacrificial feasting; that sometimes it was prolonged to a late hour, which may explain the Preacher's reference to the dangerous habit of over-eating before retiring to sleep (Ec 5[11], cf. To 8[1]; Jos. *Vita*, 44, 63, *Ant.* vi. iv. 1, xiv. xv. 11, etc.; 3 Mac 5[14]).

The principal constituent of every meal was bread, which was regarded, indeed, as the meal itself. So much so was this the case, that the word 'bread' (לֶחֶם) was used by the ancient Hebrews either for bread in particular or for food in general (see *Encyc. Bibl.* art. 'Bread,' vol. i. col. 604). It was over the bread that the blessing was pronounced which was thus supposed to have been spoken over all the rest of the solid food eaten during the first part of the meal. So strongly was this held by all Jews, that for them bread assumed a *quasi*-sacred character, and elaborate rules were devised for its treatment at table (see Edersheim, *op. cit.* vol. ii. pp. 205–210).

The Hebraistic φαγεῖν ἄρτον occurs again and again as a synonym for an ordinary meal (Mt 15[2], Mk 7[2], Lk 14[1. 15], cf. Jn 21[13], Gn 43[16] [LXX], Ex 32[20] [LXX], etc., see art. BREAD above and in Hastings' *DB*, vol. i. p. 315[b]). Keeping this fact in mind, we are enabled to feel the force of Jesus' words in His great sacramental discourse (Jn 6[26-59]), and also to understand the true reason for the rejection by the Jews of His reiterated claims. It was not that their interpretation of His words was carnal (cf. vv.[52-58]). 'There was no gross misunderstanding on their part, but a clear perception of the claim involved in the Lord's words' (Westcott, *Gospel of St. John, ad loc.*). The phrases in which He couched these claims were such as would present no real difficulty to a thinking Jew, as they might easily be paralleled out of his sacred literature (ὁ ἄρτος τῆς ζωῆς, ὁ ἄρτος τοῦ θεοῦ, ὁ ἄρτος ὁ ζῶν, ὁ ἄρτος ὁ ἐξ οὐρανοῦ καταβάς). Bread, which is the representative and symbol of all earthly food, is the type of Him who is the Representative Man, imparting life to all who will partake of His Spirit.

On three different occasions we are told that Jesus was the invited guest of a Pharisee; and, so far as the circumstances in each instance testify, it was at one of their ordinary meals that He was present. It is remarkable that it is St. Luke who records all these occurrences, and at the same time it is noteworthy that he uses three different expressions in his wording of the formal invitations (ἵνα φάγῃ μετ᾽ αὐτοῦ, Lk 7[36]; ὅπως ἀριστήσῃ παρ᾽ αὐτῷ, 11[37]; σαββάτῳ φαγεῖν ἄρτον, 14[1]). Not only are the invitations couched in varying phrases, but St. Luke uses different words when referring to the attitude of the guests at the meals (κατεκλίθη, 7[36]; ἀνέπεσεν, 11[37]; συνανακειμένων, 14[15]). There is every probability that in each case it was the mid-day meal to which Jesus was invited. It became customary amongst the Jews to make three elaborate meals on the Sabbath day ('Observa diem Sabbati; non Judaicis deliciis,' quoted by Plummer, *op. cit.* p. 354). So much so, indeed, was this the case, that specially devised rules were made for carrying out the observance of the Sabbath feasts, and special spiritual benefits were supposed to be conferred on those who, overcoming the difficulties interposed by poverty, supplied themselves with the choicest procurable food for that day (see *Peah*, viii. 7, and the examples quoted from *Shabbath* by Lightfoot in his *Hor. Heb. et Talm.* on Lk 14[1]; cf. Edersheim, *op. cit.* ii. 52, 437; Farrar, *Life of Christ*, ii. 119 n.[2]). It was on the occasion of one of these Sabbath meals that a fellow-guest of Jesus, on hearing Him speak, answered with the exclamation, 'Blessed is he that shall eat bread (φάγεται ἄρτον) in the kingdom of God' (Lk 14[15]), referring, of course, to the popular Jewish idea that the Messianic Kingdom was to be ushered in by a banquet, and that feasting was to be the chief occupation of those who shared its glories (cf. Is 25[6]),—an idea which finds a place in the illustrative teaching of Jesus on the universal character of the future Kingdom of God (cf. ἀνακλιθήσονται ἐν τῇ βασιλείᾳ τοῦ θεοῦ, Lk 13[29]; see Wendt, *Lehre Jesu*, Eng. tr. vol. i. pp. 217, 221).

At first sight it may seem strange that Jesus should countenance the Jewish custom of Sabbath banqueting, which was carried to such excess that its character for luxury became proverbial. At the same time we must remember that the principle which lay at the root of this method of feasting was the honour of the Sabbath day (cf. three quotations from *Shabbath* illustrative of this in Lightfoot, *op. cit.* iii. 149). Nor was this practice out of harmony with Jesus' views and teaching on the Sabbath rest, so long as it was conducted in a spirit of humility, mutual toleration, and charity (cf. Lk 14[7-14]). It is of interest, and in this respect not without significance, to notice that, on the last Sabbath spent by Jesus before His Passion, He was the chief guest at a festive meal (ἐποίησαν οὖν αὐτῷ δεῖπνον ἐκεῖ, Jn 12[2]). This was probably on the evening of the Sabbath day as it was drawing to a close and passing away, when festivities were of the most liberal and elaborate character (*epulæ lautiores*); and it is evident from the three narratives (St. Luke's story of the anointing of Jesus by the 'woman who was a sinner' [7[37]] can scarcely be a record of the same event [see, however, Hengstenberg, *Com. on St. John*, Eng. tr. pp. 1–33, etc.]) that it made a deep impression on the minds of Jesus' followers (cf. Mk 14[3], Mt 26[6f.], Jn 12[2]). From the way in which St. John dispenses with the use of the nominative before the verb, it would seem that this meal was of a semi-public character, designed to do honour to Jesus, and that the house of 'Simon the leper' was made the meeting-place for all who wished to meet Him (cf. Westcott, *ad loc.*, and Edersheim, *op. cit.* ii. 357 f.). It is impossible not to be struck with the way in which Jesus makes use of the opportunity afforded by His presence at these meals on the Sabbath, to inculcate lessons of large-hearted charity even when His host is inclined to be the discourteous critic (Lk 7[39] 11[38. 45ff.] 14[1ff.], cf. Jn 12[7f.]). There is no appearance of disapproval in His attitude towards what was tending to, if it had not already become an abuse, because there were latent possibilities for good in the joyous and festive Sabbath. It was to these possibilities that He directed His attention.

Acting on these principles, we can understand His words and deeds on the evening when He instituted 'the Lord's Supper' (κυριακὸν δεῖπνον, 1 Co 11[20]). As we have seen, the Jewish custom was to constitute the bread the representative food at their meals. In the same way wine was considered the representative drink. Many and elaborate rules were formulated as to the manner in which blessings were to be said over these, and the discussions arising out of the etiquette to be observed degenerated into meaningless verbalism (see Berakhoth, 35a, 36a, 41b, referred to by Edersheim, ii. 206). In spite of this spiritual decadence and barren ritualism, Jesus did what was characteristic of His general teaching. He rescued the primitive act from its debased surroundings, and the wine blessed (τὸ ποτήριον τῆς εὐλογίας) became the means of a participating of 'the blood of Christ' (κοινωνία τοῦ αἵματος), and the loaf blessed and broken (τὸν ἄρτον ὃν κλῶμεν, ἄρτον εὐλογήσας) became the joyful (εὐχαριστήσας) communion of 'the body of Christ' (cf. 1 Co 10[16f.] 11[23-27], Lk 22[19f.], Mk 14[22f.], Mt 26[26f.]). In a spirit somewhat similar He dealt with the elaborate ceremonial washings which His Jewish contemporaries sought to elevate to the rank of a compulsory religious rite (Mt 15[2] = Mk 7[2ff.], Lk 11[38]; for a description of this Jewish practice during meals, see Edersheim, ii. 207). Not the least remarkable of the lessons, objective and spiritual, inculcated by Jesus was that in which He transformed what had become a tedious and worse than meaningless series of forms into a beautiful example of social service and personal humility (see Jn 13[4ff.], cf. Lk 22[27]). By this single act He gathered up into one the various customs of His day, including the hospitable one of the guests' feet being washed by their host's servants before they sat down to eat, and taught His disciples the dignity of labour in the service of humanity (cf. Mt 18[1-14], see Westcott on 13[4], and Plummer, 'St. John' in Camb. Gr. Test. ad loc.). Nor must we omit to note here that the Church's Eucharistic meal constitutes the most emphatic object-lesson of the essential oneness of all Christian people in a brotherhood as extensive as her own borders, as intensive and real as any of the claims of Jesus to rule within the sphere of human thought (cf. πάντες δὲ ὑμεῖς ἀδελφοί ἐστε Mt 23[8]; and Philem [16]).

Several different words are employed by the Evangelists to denote the bodily attitude of the Jews at their meals, all of which, however, imply that the custom was to recline with the body stretched out (cf. Edersheim, ii. 207). In this respect it is interesting to note the differences in usage, and the preferences for one or more of these words which characterize each of the writers. St. Luke, for example, uses a word no fewer than 5 times which occurs nowhere else in the NT (κατακλίθηναι, 7[36] 14[8] 24[30]; κατακλίνειν, 9[14. 15]). Hobart states that in his use of the active voice St. Luke is employing 'the medical term for laying patients, or causing them to lie in bed, placing them in certain positions during operations—making them recline in a bath, etc.' (The Medical Language of St. Luke, p. 69; cf., however, Luke 2[7] 12[37]). As might be expected, this Evangelist exhibits a richer and more flexible vocabulary than the others. On the only occasion of his using the verb κατακεῖσθαι (Lk 5[29] [D has here ἀνακειμένων]) for sitting at meals, he seems to employ it because he has already, in the immediately preceding context, made use of the same word to express a different idea (cf. 5[25]). The same might, of course, be said of St. Mark, who has this word in the same two senses in the parallel narrative. It is not probable, however, that St. Luke sacrificed his customary literary independence by a verbal copying of St. Mark, who, moreover, uses the same word for Jesus' reclining at Supper in Bethany (Mk 14[3]).

Of the 5 different words employed by the four Evangelists when speaking of sitting down to meals, St. Luke uses all (ἀνακλίνειν twice, ἀναπίπτειν 4 times, ἀνακεῖσθαι with its compound συν- 5 times, κατακεῖσθαι once, κατακλίνειν 5 times); St. Matthew uses three (ἀνακλίνειν twice, ἀναπίπτειν once, ἀνακεῖσθαι and its compound συν- 7 times); St. Mark uses four (ἀνακλίνειν once, ἀναπίπτειν twice, ἀνακεῖσθαι and its compound συν- 5 times, κατακεῖσθαι twice): St. John is characteristically limited in his use, and employs only two of these words (ἀναπίπτειν 5 times, ἀνακεῖσθαι 4 times without any employment of its compound).

In the narrative of the conversion and call of Levi (Matthew), which is common to the three Synoptists, St. Luke is the only one who expressly states that Jesus was the guest of the new disciple (Lk 5[29]), the latter having made a feast in honour of his recently discovered Master. St. Matthew uses the vague expression ἐν τῇ οἰκίᾳ (Mt 9[10]), which may mean 'inside' as contrasted with 'outside' (ἐπὶ τὸ τελώνιον, 9[9]), where lay the scene of Levi's call (cf. Plummer, ad loc.). St. Mark, on the other hand, seems to have understood that Jesus was the host and not the guest (cf. κατακεῖσθαι αὐτὸν ἐν τῇ οἰκίᾳ αὐτοῦ, Mk 2[15], where his use of the same pronoun in the same sentence would point to this interpretation; see also συνανέκειτο τῷ Ἰησοῦ, 2[15]; τῶν συνανακειμένων σοι, Lk 14[10]; τοῖς συνανακειμένοις [sc. τῷ Ἡρώδῃ], Mk 6[22]). On the other hand, it does not seem at all certain that either of these two writers connected the conversion of Levi with the entertainment (cf. καὶ ἐγένετο, Mt 9[10]; καὶ γίνεται, Mk 2[15], which marks the commencement of a fresh narrative). It is improbable that St. Luke acted merely the part of interpreter by introducing his categorical assertion as a gloss (καὶ ἐποίησεν δοχὴν μεγάλην Λευεὶς αὐτῷ κ.τ.λ., Lk 5[29]), thus doing away with a previous ambiguity. It is more likely that he had sufficient oral, if not documentary, authority to justify his statement (the word δοχή is peculiar to St. Luke, and is used by him only once afterwards as a general equivalent for ἄριστον ἢ δεῖπνον, 14[12f.]); and we have St. Mark's authority for connecting the conversion of Simon and Andrew with hospitality to their newly-found Master and His other disciples (Mk 1[16ff. 29ff.]). Whether, however, this partaking by Jesus of a Sabbath-meal in the house of Simon Peter was secondary to the purpose of healing the fever-stricken πενθερὰ τοῦ Σίμωνος, would be difficult to determine. Nor must we forget the possibility that St. Luke's authority for the statement that Jesus was the guest of His latest convert Levi may have been influenced by the parallel case we are here noticing—the conversion of the brothers Simon and Andrew and the subsequent entertainment in their own house of the newly discovered Messiah (cf. Jn 1[41]).

LITERATURE.—See for discussions of the last-mentioned questions, Wright, Synopsis of the Gospels in Greek, pp. 16 f., 23, etc.; Plummer, 'St. Luke' in Internat. Crit. Com. p. 159 f.; Gould, 'St. Mark,' ib. p. 41; O. Holtzmann, Leben Jesu, Eng. tr. p. 206; cf. art. 'Matthew' in Encyc. Bibl. col. 2986 f.; B. Weiss, The Life of Christ (T. &. T. Clark), vol. ii. p. 125 n.[2]; Bengel, Gnomon of the NT on Mt 9[10]; and, for the problem as to the identification of Matthew and Levi, which is germane to that we are discussing, see Zahn's Einleit. in das NT, ii. p. 264.

J. R. WILLIS.

MEASURES.—See WEIGHTS AND MEASURES.

MEDIATOR.—*Introductory.*—The title 'Mediator' is applied to our Lord in the NT only by St. Paul (1 Ti 2⁵) and the author of Hebrews (8⁶ 9¹⁵ 12²⁴). In Gal 3¹⁹· ²⁰ St. Paul's argument implies that there is an important sense in which Christ cannot be fitly called a mediator. Here Moses is described by this title, and the *mediator* (generic) is sharply distinguished from *God.* Moses was a person coming between two contracting parties, God and Israel, with the consequence that the law administered by Moses is apparently in opposition to the promises of God which depend upon God only. Obviously Christ is not such a mediator as Moses. He does not come between two contracting parties, for He Himself is the representative human receiver of God's promise, and the Divine Son through whom we receive that promise. He includes both parties in His own Person, instead of coming between them. He is not the instrument of a contract, but the embodiment of a Divine gift. This passage implies that Christ united God and man, two parties previously at variance, in a wholly unique manner. And the same truth is asserted in the verse which calls Him 'the one mediator between God and men' (1 Ti 2⁵). In what sense St. Paul calls Christ a mediator will be shown more fully in § 3.

1. The Synoptic Gospels.—Although these do not employ the title 'mediator,' they throughout imply that the teaching, life, and death of Jesus were mediatorial. The familiar old division of His mediatorial functions into those of Prophet, Priest, and King is roughly correct, though it may be better to designate them as those of Prophet, King, and Redeemer. By such a division we are able to find a more natural place for those passages in the Synoptic Gospels which speak of His atoning work, than if we use the word 'Priest.' We are also able to do more justice to the truth that He revealed Himself as already the Messiah during 'the days of his flesh,' and did not teach that His Messianic Kingdom was only an affair of the future.

(*a*) The 'wisdom' of our Lord impressed His hearers at Nazareth, and when they were offended at the difference which they noted between Him and His humble family, Jesus said, 'A prophet is not without honour, save in his own country, and in his own house' (Mt 13⁵⁴⁻⁵⁸). Here He seems in some way to claim the office of a *prophet.* And there are several passages which show that the ordinary people inclined to regard Him as a *Prophet.* See, fully, under art. PROPHET.

(*b*) He is also *King.* He claimed to fulfil the Jewish expectation of an ideal King, the Messiah. This cannot be reasonably disputed, in spite of the fact that this claim did not represent all that He was and all that He demanded. The confession of His Messiahship by St. Peter, the dispute between His disciples for places of honour, and especially the desire of the sons of Zebedee to sit on His right hand and His left, cannot be thrown aside as legendary inventions. Nor can we fail to see the Messianic meaning of His triumphal entry into Jerusalem, His trial and answer to the high priest (Mk 14⁶²), and the inscription 'The King of the Jews' upon the cross. Apart from His Messianic claim, His life and His death become unintelligible, although He used the actual title very seldom, and rather avoided it on account of the political associations which clung to it. See, further, artt. KING and KINGDOM OF GOD.

(*c*) Jesus, who is Mediator in revealing God, is also Mediator in *redeeming man.* He offered to the Father a sacrifice of perfect human obedience which effected a new relation between God and mankind. It was a reparation to God for the disobedience of man.

In dealing with the redemptive work of Christ, we have to consider as of primary importance the place occupied by His death in the theology as well as in the history of the Synoptics. It is frequently asserted or hinted that He did not foresee His death until an advanced period in His ministry, and that, when He found that it was inevitable, He did not attribute to it any power of obtaining the remission of sins. These two theories do not elucidate the Gospels, but simply contradict them. All the accounts of our Lord's baptism represent Him as hearing the words which declare that He is the Son in whom the Father is well pleased (Mt 3¹⁷, Mk 1¹¹, Lk 3²²). He was, therefore, from the first conscious that He fulfilled the Isaianic picture of the Servant of the Lord, who dies as a *guilt-offering* for the people. In submitting to baptism, He identified Himself with a race that has sinned ; in submitting to the subsequent temptation, He identified Himself with a race which suffers when Satan lures it to sin. He also predicted His death early in His ministry. He is the bridegroom who will be taken away in the midst of joy, and His disciples will fast at that day (Mk 2¹⁹· ²⁰). Later, He tells how He has to submit to the baptism of His Passion, and feels anguish until it is accomplished. He dreads it ; but He desires it, because it is the necessary preliminary of His kindling a sacred fire on earth (Lk 12⁴⁹). With these words we must compare the question addressed to the ambitious sons of Zebedee, whether they can drink of His cup and be baptized with His baptism (Mk 10³⁸). The baptism and the cup represent the will of the Father with all the suffering which the doing of that will entailed. What that suffering was the story of Gethsemane tells us. It was there that He, with a final effort of His human will, identified Himself wholly with the Servant 'wounded for our transgressions.' But this identification had been outlined long before in the words, 'Whosoever would be first among you shall be servant of all.' For verily the Son of Man came not to be ministered unto, but to minister, and to give his life a ransom for many' (Mk 10⁴⁵). This acceptance of death was not a mere example of perfect resignation. He had taught His disciples not to fear those who kill the body (Mt 10²⁸), He had assured them that 'he that findeth his life shall lose it ; and he that loseth his life for my sake shall find it' (10³⁹). But the disciple who loses his life for Christ's sake does not necessarily win any life except his own, whereas Christ's death avails 'for many.' With this prediction we must connect the words used at the institution of the Lord's Supper. Assuming that Christ did institute this sacrament, we may also assume that He who taught His own not to fear those who kill the body, did not mean that when His blood was shed 'for many' it was shed to save them from being killed by the Jews or Romans. Whether He did or did not add the words 'for the remission of sins,' He must have meant that a new covenant was being made between God and man. His death had some special value in itself, or else the Church would not have continued to show forth the Lord's death (1 Co 11²⁶). The special value which He attached to His own death is made plain by the account of the Lord's Supper contained in the Petrine Gospel of St. Mark no less than in the Pauline Gospel of St. Luke. The shedding of Christ's blood seals a covenant similar to the initial covenant made by Moses between God and the people (Ex 24³⁻⁸) ; it consecrates a new people to God. It also fulfils Jeremiah's prophecy of a new covenant, of which the very foundation was the forgiveness of sins (Jer 31³¹). And, like the blood of the Paschal lamb, the blood of Jesus saves His people from a destruction that comes from God. With this sacrifice of Jesus His disciples are to hold communion. They appropriate the atonement, and as they appropriate it, it becomes for them a propitiation.

2. Acts of the Apostles and Epp. of St. Peter, St. Jude, and St. James.—The simple teaching about our Lord conveyed in Acts, more especially in chs. 1–12, and in the First Epistle of St. Peter and that of St. Jude and of St. James, justifies us in placing these books in a class by themselves. They represent a theology which in character, if not in date, is primitive, and in close touch with Judaism.

(a) In *Acts* Jesus is set forth as Prophet, Messiah, Son of God, and Redeemer. From the first He is the *Lord Jesus* ($1^{6.\ 21}$). And at Pentecost St. Peter proclaims that 'God hath made him both Lord and Christ, this Jesus whom ye crucified' (2^{36}). He is the *Prophet* whom Moses had foretold, and those who will not hearken to Him will be utterly destroyed ($3^{22.\ 23}$). His *Messianic lordship* is repeatedly preached; He is the Holy and Righteous One, the Prince of life, the Saviour, the Stone or foundation of the true temple, the Stone now exalted to be the Head of the corner ($3^{14.\ 15}\ 5^{31}\ 4^{11}$). He is Lord of all ($10^{36}$), and there is salvation in none other (4^{12}). Miracles are regarded as His work, though He is no longer visibly present. He is preparing for the 'Day of the Lord,' when the Divine Kingdom will be vindicated, and He has Himself poured out the Holy Ghost to fit the disciples for that day (2^{33}). Moreover, His unique *Sonship* is implied in the expression 'the Father' as used in the beginning of the book ($1^{4.\ 7}\ 2^{33}$). Fitly does St. Stephen direct to Him his dying prayer, and Saul declare that He is the Son of God (9^{20}). The whole mission and work of Jesus is therefore mediatorial. His death has also an atoning mediatorial worth. Of great importance in Acts is the identification of our Lord with the suffering Servant of the Lord in Is 53. Our Lord had so identified Himself, as is shown not only by the quotation in Lk 22^{37} but by the whole tenor of His life from the time of His baptism. In Acts a keynote is struck by St. Peter's words, 'the God of our fathers hath glorified his Servant Jesus' (3^{13}). When Philip meets the Ethiopian eunuch he finds that he is reading Is 53, and resolves his doubts by explaining that the vicarious sufferer is Jesus. Acts shows plainly that the Christian Church of the most primitive period applied to Jesus this prophecy. 'Of a truth in this city against thy holy Servant Jesus, whom thou didst anoint, both Herod and Pontius Pilate, with the Gentiles and the peoples of Israel, were gathered together, to do whatsoever thy hand and thy counsel foreordained to come to pass' ($4^{27.\ 28}$).

These Apostolic words show precisely how the Church regarded the death of Christ. He died, not as any ordinary martyr, but as the Messiah and the atoning Servant. The death was a necessity, not because it was simply inevitable from the surroundings in which Jesus lived and against which He struggled, but because God Himself required it as an indispensable means for the realization of His will for man. It took place by His foreknowledge (2^{23}), it was foretold by His prophets (3^{18}). Further, it would have been impossible for the Apostles to attribute this meaning to the death of Christ, unless they had been able to point to the empty grave, to assert that the Messiah lives, and that a direct relation can be established between Him and His sinful people. The Servant in Isaiah, though he died, lived again to 'prolong his days.' And because they were able to assert positively that Christ had risen, the first Christians were able to make the death of Christ a fundamental thing in their gospel. Repentance, faith, baptism, the gift of the Holy Spirit, are the distinctive gifts which flow from the death and resurrection of Jesus Christ. St. Peter exerts himself to deepen a sense of sin in his hearers by pointing to the cross. They tried to destroy the Saviour, but God thwarted their effort by raising Him from the dead. Their act, so far from accomplishing what they desired, fulfilled God's counsel. Let them repent while there is time, before Christ returns to judgment ($2^{14-21}\ 3^{19.\ 20}\ 4^{10.\ 11}\ 5^{30.\ 31}\ 10^{36-43}$). God offers forgiveness to those who are baptized in the name of Jesus Christ, and He offers the bestowal of the Holy Spirit to make a new life possible (2^{38}).

If we compare this very early doctrine with that of St. Paul, we see that, simple though it is, it is radically the same. And against all modern attempts to represent St. Paul as the first man who inseparably joined together the thought of Christ's death, of sin, and of atonement, St. Paul's own words protest: 'I delivered unto you first of all that which also I received, how that Christ died for our sins according to the Scriptures' (1 Co 15^3). He affirms that he *received* it, and his testimony is true.

(b) In *First Peter* the mediatorial character of Christ's death is always present to the writer's mind. The doctrine of this Epistle may possibly have been influenced by that of St. Paul, but it is considerably less developed, and is such as we might well expect from St. Peter. The doctrine with regard to our Lord's Person is simple. It is taught that 'He existed before He was born on earth, for He was not only 'foreknown indeed before the foundation of the world' (1^{20}), which might not necessarily imply a personal pre-existence, but His Spirit was in the prophets before the Incarnation (1^{11}). To Him, as to a Divine Being, glory and dominion are ascribed (5^{11}). In consequence of His resurrection, baptism 'saves' us (3^{21}). It has an inward power to cleanse the soul in response to the interrogation of a good conscience, because Christ rose and lives.

But it is the Passion of Christ, the 'precious blood,' that fills this letter with its peculiar glow. By that blood, 'as of a lamb without blemish and without spot,' we were 'redeemed' ($1^{18.\ 19}$). It is a moral redemption, changing a former 'manner of life' into a better type of conduct. His action involved a patient endurance which it is the Christian's duty to imitate ($2^{21}\ 4^1\ 3^{17.\ 18}$). But it is, nevertheless, an objective external fact before it becomes subjective and inward. Christians are 'elect according to the foreknowledge of God the Father, in sanctification of the Spirit, unto obedience and sprinkling of the blood of Jesus Christ' (1^2). The life of obedience involves sprinkling with the blood. As the Israelites were received into a unique relation with God at Sinai by being sprinkled with sacrificial blood, so by the blood shed on Calvary, a new elect race is dedicated to God. It is this blood that has an abiding power to cancel sin. What Christ did in His Passion is clearly stated, 'His own self bore our sins in his own body upon the tree' (2^{24}). The word 'bear' means both 'endure,' and 'carry' a sacrifice to the altar. So Christ both endured the consequences of our sins, and carried them to the cross as if they were His own. He suffered for sins which were not His own, and He did it that we might be 'healed.' Again, St. Peter says that Christ 'suffered for sins once, the righteous for the unrighteous, that he might bring us to God' (3^{18}). He is urging his readers to be prepared to suffer for righteousness' sake; he hopes that their conduct may silence opposition, perhaps that it may bring others to God. But all the power to suffer rightly rests on an event now past. It is the solitary death of Christ 'for sins' that enables us to go to God and sets us right with God. Like St. Paul and like the author of Hebrews, St. Peter regards the death of Christ as the supreme event which established for mankind a free communion with the Father.

(c) The *Epistle of St. Jude* and the *Second of St. Peter* do not add to the doctrine of Christ's mediation. The lascivious sect against which the former is directed seems to have denied the reality of the Incarnation and of the Lordship of Christ (v.⁴), which the writer regards as essential. He mentions the Holy Spirit, God, and our Lord Jesus Christ together (v.²¹), and ascribes glory to 'God our Saviour' through Jesus Christ. 2 Peter also simply assumes the Divinity and mediatorial work of Christ. The writer describes himself as 'the bond-servant and apostle of Jesus Christ' (1¹), describes Jesus as 'Lord and Saviour' (2²⁰), speaks of growing 'in the grace and knowledge of our Lord and Saviour Jesus Christ' (3¹⁸), and of entrance into His 'eternal kingdom' (1¹¹).

(d) In the *Epistle of St. James* little is said, yet much is implied, respecting the Person of Christ. He is 'Lord' and 'the Lord of glory' (2¹). His is the 'honourable name' (2⁷) which was named over Christians in baptism. He is unquestionably regarded as the Mediator of salvation. For the 'word of truth,' 'the implanted word' (1¹⁸·²¹), which the Christians have received, has come to them through Christ, and He is called 'the judge' who 'standeth before the doors' (5⁸·⁹). Moreover, the opposition manifested by St. James towards a misuse of Christian freedom is of a kind which implies that he, like the people whom he desired to refute, believed that faith gains blessings from God through Christ. He illustrates the necessity of good works by instances in which 'works' can hardly be distinguished from faith, but are its necessary expression. He insists that God requires a good life; but, no less truly than St. Paul, he insists that a living faith is requisite for salvation. There is no developed Christology, but the writer who calls himself a 'bond-servant of God and of Jesus Christ,' and is so faithful both to the letter and to the spirit of Christ's moral teaching, must necessarily have believed that He is the Mediator between God and man.

3. The Pauline Epistles.—(a) St. Paul's doctrine of *the Person of Christ* is fundamentally the same in all his Epistles. And his whole teaching concerning the work of Christ is inseparable from the doctrine of His Person. Jesus is the Son of God, who, as such, possesses a superhuman and Divine nature. God is 'the Father of our Lord Jesus Christ' (2 Co 1³), and the Son shares in the spiritual immaterial nature of the Father. In his earliest Epistles, those to the Thessalonians, Jesus is called 'the Lord Jesus,' and each letter closes with the prayer that His 'grace' or unmerited kindness may be with His people. It is assumed that Jesus is exalted to heaven, is the Lord ruling the Church, and that He will return to judge the world. In the second group of Epistles—1 and 2 Cor., Gal., Rom.—there is much teaching about our Lord's Person. He is God's 'own Son' (Ro 8³), and to Him alone belongs the privilege of being 'the image of God' (2 Co 4⁴). St. Paul applies to Christ passages which in the OT refer to Jehovah (Ro 10¹³, 1 Co 2¹⁵ 10²²), and in Ro 9⁵ says that He is 'over all, God blessed for ever.' The Son of God is more ancient than all creation, and 'through him all things were made' (1 Co 8⁶). He existed in heaven before He was 'sent forth' on earth, and this coming to earth was for Him the humiliation of exchanging riches for poverty (2 Co 8⁹). The last two facts are fundamental in the next group of Epistles (Col 1¹⁵⁻¹⁷, Ph 2⁵⁻¹¹).

The third group of Epistles—Phil., Col., Eph.—illustrates these doctrines more fully. Ph 2⁵⁻¹¹ lays special stress upon the self-sacrifice involved in the Son of God taking 'the form of a servant.' In heaven He had 'the form of God,' but He 'emptied himself, taking the form of a servant, being made in the likeness of men.' This likeness is elsewhere called 'the likeness of sinful flesh' (Ro 8³). In Colossians, St. Paul attacks a superstitious theosophy which taught that worship ought to be paid to some intermediate beings who come between God and the world—a theory which implied that God could not come into direct contact with matter. Against this St. Paul insists upon the mediatorial work of the Son of God in both crea-

tion and redemption. He declares that the Son is the 'image' or adequate counterpart of the Father, and the 'firstborn of all creation,' *i.e.*, not the first being created, but, as the context shows, 'born before all creation' (Col 1¹⁵·¹⁶). All things were created *in Him*, since their existence was conditioned by His thought; *by Him*, since it was through His power that they came into being; *unto Him*, since all creation finds in Him the summit of its evolution. All things cohere in Him (Col 1¹⁷), and it was God's purpose that all things should be summed up in Him (Eph 1¹⁰). The sum total of God's attributes dwells in Him *bodily* (Col 2⁹). And the Church is an organism without which Christ deigns to regard Himself as incomplete, because without the Church His incarnate life would not continue to be manifested. It is an extension of the Incarnation. It is a body in which Christ Himself lives and works (Eph 1²³), the suffering of its members completes His own (Col 1²⁴) by making possible a further application to mankind of His saving power.

The Church therefore exists to promote a certain relation between God and man. That relation is one of union and communion. The new confession which is taught to us by the Spirit of God's Son is expressed in the words 'Abba, Father.' The very Aramaic word used by Jesus in His communion with the Father in Gethsemane (Mk 14³⁶) is used by St. Paul to describe the Christian's attitude towards God. The prominence given by St. Paul to the love of God for man, for all men, for sinners, is unceasing. His certainty of God's love rests on all that Jesus did and does, but the most fundamental proof of it was that Jesus died. By this God commends His love toward us (Ro 5⁸). This makes it obvious that God will give us all things (8³²). And this equally proves the love of Christ (2 Co 5¹⁴, Eph 5²·²⁵). The death of Christ is, therefore, the highest proof of the love of the Father and the love of Jesus for mankind. The mediatorial work of the Son of God is a process involved in the whole relation of His Divine Person to the world. But it was focussed in one great event—His death.

(b) St. Paul's teaching about *the death of Christ* is entirely consistent. He teaches that there are two great elements in the process of the individual man's reconciliation with God. The first is his faith in Christ, who died as a sacrifice on our behalf. The second is that inward, vital, and ethical union with Christ, the 'life-giving Spirit' (1 Co 15⁴⁵), involved in our baptism 'into Christ.'

To suppose that his language about dying as our 'ransom' or 'price' (1 Co 6²⁰ 7²³, 1 Ti 2⁶, Tit 2¹⁴) is inconsistent with our need of identification with Christ, or that the moral identification excludes the need of a sacramental identification, is to create an imaginary false antithesis. Sacrifice, rightly understood, implies communion with the object sacrificed. And sacraments convey the power which is taken and used by that moral choice which is called 'faith.' Baptism begins our new supernatural life (Ro 6⁴ᶠ), the Lord's Supper imparts to us sustenance for that life (1 Co 10³ᶠ). In both we enter into union with a Christ who died, and died 'for us' and 'for sins' (e.g. 2 Co 5¹⁴, Gal 1⁴, Ro 8³², Eph 5²⁵). That death had a special meaning for mankind as a whole, for God the Father, and for Christ Himself.

(i.) *The death of Christ effected a reconciliation.*— By it we were reconciled to God (Ro 5⁹·¹⁰, Eph 1⁷). This is because God was in Christ reconciling the world unto Himself (2 Co 5¹⁹), and those who were 'alienated and enemies' Christ has reconciled in the body of His flesh through death (Col 1²²). The action of Christ is identical with the action of God. In Christ living and Christ dying God was present, 'not reckoning trespasses.' He came to pardon when He might have punished. The cross, therefore, manifests the love and pity of God. And the reason why the love of Christ specially 'constraineth us' is 'because we thus judge that one died for all (therefore all died); and he died for all, that they which live should no longer live unto themselves, but unto him who for their sakes died, and rose again' (2 Co 5¹⁴ᶠ·). We feel the constraint of love when we see that Christ died a death which was a substitute for our death. If the Son had not died, we should have been left to experience the death of a sinner who is alienated from God. The work of reconciliation was done by the

Father through the Son,—done outside us before it was done in us.

(ii.) *The death of Christ removes the wrath of God.*—Sinners are exposed to God's wrath (Ro 1[18. 32] 2[3] 5[10] 11[28]). This wrath is not vindictiveness, but the attitude of a loving Father towards that which destroys the very life of His children. The wrath of God is removed when, 'through faith,' the sinner accepts Jesus as a 'means of propitiation' (Ro 3[25]). God justifies, acquits as righteous, those who avail themselves of that force which wipes away their sins. In providing this means of propitiation, God did something to counterbalance all His previous forbearance towards sin. He manifested His righteousness, His disposition to treat men according to a perfect moral law. When sin is passed over, righteousness is not manifested. But it was demonstrated when God showed that He could not forgive except at the tremendous cost of sending His Son to be a means of propitiation by His blood. The death of the Son was an oblation and a sacrifice to the Father (Eph 5[2]), wholly acceptable to the Father on account of the sinlessness and love of the Sufferer; and it is wholly adequate to the needs of the human soul, because it simultaneously removes the sinner's sin and his fear of the judgment of God.

(iii.) *Christ is not regarded by St. Paul as literally punished for the sins of all mankind.*—These sins are not transferred to Jesus, for men who do not accept Him as their Saviour have still to answer for their sins. They are still under the wrath of God (Ro 1[18]). Nor were the sins of those who God foresaw would repent literally transferred to Jesus. In the Hebrew conception of the sin-offering, the offering was 'most holy,' which would have been impossible if sin had been transferred to it in any literal manner. At the same time, Christ is said to have been made 'sin' (2 Co 5[21]) and to have been made 'curse' for us (Gal 3[13]).

The first passage may mean that Christ was made a sin-offering; the second may mean that Christ in some way fulfilled the type of the scape-goat (Lv 16[21]), which symbolized the disappearance of the iniquities of the children of Israel. Both these interpretations are somewhat uncertain. What is certain is that in 2 Co 5[21], Gal 3[13] St. Paul means that Christ was treated as a sinner in order that sinners might become righteous; that He chose to die by crucifixion, a death which in Jewish eyes was symbolical of God's curse; and that in dying He realized God's curse or condemnation on the sins of the race of which He had chosen to be a member. There is no question of a literal personal punishment of Christ. It was a voluntary entrance on His part into a state in which, by a profound sympathy, He felt our calamity as though it were His.

Our Lord Himself had shown the connexion between His death and the forgiveness of our sins. The primitive Church had believed and experienced the reality of this connexion. And St. Paul, in preaching what he calls 'the word of the cross' so fully and vividly, was 'faithful' to 'the much' which was committed to Him by the risen Christ. He preached, as no other man has done, the Name which means that Christ saves His people from their sins.

4. The Epistle to the Hebrews.—(*a*) The subject of the Epistle to the Hebrews is 'the world to come' (2[5]). This world to come already exists and has existed from the Creation. But it is regarded as still to come, because it has not yet been fully realized in time. It is a heavenly spiritual counterpart of this temporal material world in which we live. The material world, and the Jewish system of worship which belongs to this world, are not, in the strictest sense of the word, real. Christianity is the perfect religion, and is superior to Judaism, because its origin, worship, and priesthood belong to the heavenly world of which Judaism is only a shadow. The Revealer of Christianity belongs to the heavenly world. It is on His mediation that the existence both of the material and of the spiritual world depends. He is the 'effulgence' or 'radiance' of God's glory, *i.e.* of God's nature as shown to things created, and the impress of His essence; 'upholding all things by the word of his power' (1[3]). The Son, through whom the Father made the worlds, was appointed heir of all things prior to creation. By His almighty word (cf. 'God said' in Gn 1)—a word which is itself an act—He carries the world to its goal. This Son, as essentially Divine, is above the angels, and is the object of their worship (1[7]). He is above Moses, as the son of a house is superior to a servant, and as the founder of a house is superior to one who is only a part of the edifice itself (3[2. 3]).

(*b*) But Jesus is especially our sympathetic High Priest 'who hath passed through the heavens' (4[14]). Great stress is laid upon the fact that He endured all that we endure, sin apart. Having taken flesh and blood, and become in all things like His 'brethren,' He passed through temptations, shed tears, suffered death. His human prayer to God, offered during His agony, was heard on account of His 'godly fear.' He was strengthened to bear His burden, and was made perfect for His saving work by the discipline of His sufferings. He manifests the highest degree both of sympathy and of probation, and is therefore the Representative of man to God. He is able to enter with full sympathy into the lot of ignorant and erring man. He also possesses the other essential qualification of a High Priest, for He was Divinely appointed. He who proclaimed Him to be His Son, declared Him to be a priest for ever after the order of Melchizedek (5[5. 6]). In the reality of His human experience and sympathy, and in the fact of His Divine calling, He resembled the Levitical priests. But He differed from them profoundly. They were sinful: He was sinless. They must offer sacrifices for themselves: His offering was solely for others. They served a temporary sanctuary: He ministers perpetually in heaven. He further differs from them because He is a priest after the order of Melchizedek. The priesthood of Melchizedek had these two great characteristics: it was especially royal, and it was independent of any genealogy; whereas the priesthood of the Levitical priests was not more royal than that of all the Israelites, and their title to it rested on their descent from Levi. Christ is King as well as Priest; and as His Being had no beginning, the silence of Scripture about the ancestry of Melchizedek assimilates him to Christ. And since Abraham the father of Levi paid tithes to Melchizedek, he acknowledged his inferiority, and compromised the Levitical priests by so doing. Their priesthood is lower than that of Melchizedek, which was an archetype of that of the Son of God (7[1-10]).

(*c*) The sacrifice of Christ had these notes. (i.) It was the expression of *the perfect obedience of His will to the will of the Father.* No animal sacrifices can take away sins. They rather bring sins to remembrance than purge them away. Bulls and goats cannot give to God a conscious, voluntary, moral sacrifice. This the Son gave: He satisfied the will of God by so doing: 'When he cometh into the world he saith, Sacrifice and offering thou wouldest not, but a body didst thou prepare for me. . . . Lo, I am come to do thy will, O God' (10[5-7]). By the offering of Christ's body, which was prepared by God to make this great sacrifice possible, the will of God was satisfied, and by that will we are 'sanctified.'—(ii.) *It is one, and need not be repeated yearly.* Every day the Levitical priests offer sacrifices which cannot cancel sin. In contrast with the ineffectiveness of those sacrifices, offered by priests still standing day by day,

Christ offered one sacrifice on the cross, and then the adequacy of His offering was proved by His sitting down on the right hand of God (10^{12}). His offering is valid for both past and future, and delivers men from ' the transgressions that were under the first covenant ' (9^{15}), in addition to giving a new power to those who live after the Incarnation has taken place.—(iii.) *It is the basis of a* '*new covenant*' *between God and man.*

The best commentators differ somewhat with regard to the meaning of $9^{15. 16}$. But the natural explanation is that since the word διαθήκη meant both *covenant* or alliance and *testament* or will, the word is used in both senses, and the author was conscious of no logical difficulty in so using it. He means that God's people, their sins having been taken away by Christ, are able to enter upon that inheritance, that rest of God, bequeathed to them by Christ, who Himself removed the encumbrance of past sins which barred access to it. But the idea of covenant is more fundamental. The only sacrifice of the Old Covenant which the Jews never repeated was that which established the original relation between God and the Hebrew people (Ex 24^{3-8}). This was dedicated with blood. So was the New Covenant, the blood of the Son being ' the blood of the covenant' (10^{29}). And by it the whole region of man's approach to God, the system of 'the heavenly things' themselves, was cleansed from the taint of sin. In 10^{29} the writer has in mind the words spoken by our Lord in instituting His Supper.

(*d*) The effect of Christ's death on man is specially described by the ritual words 'purify' (καθαρίζειν), 'sanctify' (ἁγιάζειν), and 'make perfect' (τελειοῦν). These words do not exactly correspond with the terms of later theology. They are primarily ritual words, though they involve a truly ethical conception as used in this Epistle. They mean to remove the sense of guilt (9^{14}) or ' evil conscience,' to dedicate to God ($10^{10. 29}$ 13^{12}), to bring to that full enjoyment of spiritual privileges which the Levitical priesthood could not effect (7^{11}). The result of this work done by Christ is our sense of forgiveness and free access to God through Christ (4^{16}).

(*e*) The Ascension is the culminating point of the Atonement as offered by Christ to God. As a High Priest after the order of Melchizedek, *i.e.* with an eternal priesthood which belongs to the world to come, Christ offered Himself upon the cross (7^{27} 9^{24-28}). But as the Aaronic high priest carried the sacrificial blood on the day of Atonement into the Holy of Holies, so Christ entered heaven ' through his blood' having obtained ' eternal redemption' (9^{12}). He now exercises a priesthood which is after the order of Melchizedek, but at the same time fulfils the type of the Aaronic high priest's action within the veil. He still remains High Priest and acts as such (6^{20}). Because He abideth for ever He hath His priesthood unchangeable (7^{24}). He manifests Himself to God for us (9^{24}), continuously interceding on our behalf (7^{25}). Into all His intercession the value of His offering is put, so that He is ' the minister of the sanctuary' above. His work is still of a sacerdotal nature, 'it is necessary that this high priest also have somewhat to offer' (8^{1-3}). The ' somewhat' is His blood or life. His blood retains its sacrificial efficacy, pleads to God for pardon, and speaks peace to man.

'We have an altar' (13^{10}). Unlike the Jews, even the Jewish priests, who were unable to partake of the sin-offering offered on the Day of Atonement, Christians may partake of Christ.

The 'altar' of which they eat has been variously interpreted as the cross, the altar in heaven, and the Lord's table. The first seems to be excluded by the fact that according to the writer's argument the cross corresponds with the place outside the camp where the sin-offering was burnt, not with the altar in the tabernacle. Whether the altar here is the heavenly altar or the Lord's table (cf. Mal $1^{7. 12}$, Ezk 44^{16} 41^{22}), a reference to the Eucharist is included. And in that rite the pleading of Christ's death by the Church is joined with the present intercession which He makes in heaven.

The special value of the Epistle to the Hebrews is that it presents to us the mediatorial work of Christ as a work of Divine worship. Without worship, Christianity would be merely a philosophy. And the author satisfies one of the deepest needs of the human soul when he teaches us the relation between Christ and His people in the life of intercession, a life which is for the Christian one of faith and confidence by virtue of all that Jesus did and does. The author also teaches us something of the philosophy of religion. St. Paul's view of Judaism is wholly true, but it is not the whole truth. And this Epistle, with its peculiar dignity and calm, and a devotion to Christ not less real than that of the Apostle of the Gentiles, gives us a fresh insight into the Divine wisdom which made Judaism ' a sacred school of the knowledge of God for the world.'

5. The Johannine writings.—(*a*) *The Apocalypse.*—Whether the Apocalypse be the work of John the Presbyter, or, as the present writer believes, the work of John the Apostle, its doctrine of the mediatorial work of Christ is of high importance. The book is full of the exaltation of Jesus. He is the Messiah, the unique Son of God (1^6 3^5 14^1), the Divine Word (19^{13}). He is the lion of the tribe of Judah, the root and offspring of David (5^5 22^{16}). He is the Lord's Messiah (11^{15}). By His resurrection He has become Ruler of the kings of the earth, many royal diadems are on His head, and He is King of kings and Lord of lords (1^5 19^{12} 17^{14} 19^{16}). He has all authority, an authority given Him by God (3^{21}). His terrible might is suggested by the description of His feet, His voice, His eyes, and the sound from His mouth ($1^{14ff.}$). With God He shares the throne of heaven ($22^{1. 3}$), with Him He receives ascriptions of praise from the angels and the redeemed (5^{13} 7^{10}). He comes seated on a white cloud, like the figure in Daniel's vision (14^{14}). He is the Morning Star who brings in the day of grace (22^{16}). The coming of Christ is the coming of God, and when the coming is accomplished God is called He 'who is and who was,' and no longer ' the coming one' ($1^{4. 8}$ 4^8, cf. 11^{17} 16^5). He holds the keys of death and Hades (1^{18}), He is ' the first and the last, and the living One,' ' the Alpha and the Omega' ($1^{17. 18}$ 22^{13}).

From the beginning to the end the book contains deep appreciations of the mediatorial work effected by Christ's death. (i.) *It is a great demonstration of the love of Jesus* (1^5). (ii.) *It is a death which implies that a redeeming work was then accomplished, and that the Christian enjoys a liberty which was won by that death*; 'He loosed us from our sins by his blood ; and he made us to be a kingdom, to be priests unto his God and Father' ($1^{5. 6}$). And in 5^{6-14} the Lamb is praised in the words, 'Thou wast slain, and didst purchase unto God with thy blood men of every tribe and tongue.' The Lamb is ' standing, as though it had been slain'; it is not dead, but has the virtue of its death in it. (iii.) The abiding power of the death of Christ is shown in this, that it is *the source of moral purity and of moral victory under persecution.* Even the virgins who follow the Lamb reach heaven only because Christ 'purchased' them ($14^{3. 4}$), And the martyrs slain by persecuting pagan Rome overcame the dragon ' because of the blood of the Lamb, and because of the word of their testimony' (12^{11}). The blood of the Lamb therefore did something in the past, for it released mankind from sin by the ransom paid to God. And it does something now, for it enables us to live and witness as Christ lived and witnessed. The mediatorial power of the blood of Christ is therefore a power without which the Christian life can be neither begun nor continued.

(*b*) The *Prologue of St. John's Gospel* contains an assertion which is of essential importance for all subsequent Christian theology. The Divine

Λόγος, the Word who 'was God,' became flesh, and was incarnate as Jesus. This Word is both the expression of God and God expressed. The origin of the title is to be sought mainly in the OT and in Palestinian tradition. But St. John's use of it was probably partly determined by its common occurrence in Greek philosophy, and more especially in the writings of the Alexandrian Jewish philosopher Philo. His doctrine of the Λόγος is more moral and less metaphysical than that of Philo, more Jewish and less Greek. Philo's dominant idea is that of the Divine *Reason*, St. John's is that of the Divine *Word*, the manifestation of the Divine will. The Jewish Targums use the phrase *Memra* or Word for God as manifested in His action on the world, and in Wis 18¹⁵ the almighty Word of God is described as leaping down from heaven to smite the Egyptians. The term as used by St. John denotes inherence in God, as a thought or conception inheres in the mind—mediatorship between God and the universe of a kind which implies that God Himself comes into touch with the universe—and it requires as its complement the other title 'only-begotten Son.' In Philo the Λόγος remains a vague cosmic force, in St. John it is a definite Divine Person who becomes Man. See, further, art. LOGOS.

(c) Although in the *Fourth Gospel* the word Λόγος is applied to the Son of God in the Prologue only, the same doctrine pervades the whole book. 'We beheld his glory' (1¹⁴) is shown to be true by the record which follows. In the Synoptics, Jesus seems to speak most of His own ministry and of men; here He rather speaks of Himself and His relations to the Father. There He frequently distinguishes Himself from His disciples in His relations to the Father; here He takes the same attitude more decisively. He declares Himself the Son of God (5²⁵ 9³⁵⁻³⁷ etc.), the Son in a unique sense (3¹⁶· ³⁵ 5¹⁹⁻²² etc.). Distinct from all others there exist *the Father* and *the Son* (3³⁵· ³⁶ 5¹⁹⁻²²). The Father is the Source of the Son's being and action (5¹⁹· ²⁶). He does works in the Son; the Father and the Son know one another (10¹⁵ 8⁵⁵). They love one another (5²⁰ 14³¹ 15⁹); they abide in one another (8²⁹ 14¹⁰· ¹¹). They are one, ἕν (10³⁰ 17¹¹· ²¹· ²²). As the Father has life in Himself, He has given to the Son life in Himself (5²⁶). So to see or to reject the Son is to see or reject the Father (8¹⁹ 14⁹ 15²¹⁻²⁴). Men must render similar honour to the Father and to the Son (5²³). The Son existed before He came into the world: He was before Abraham (8⁵⁸), He was glorified with the Father before the world existed (17⁵): He came from heaven and returns to heaven (6⁶²). The Father sent Him into the world (3¹⁶) to fulfil a certain mission (5³⁶ 14³¹ etc.), to speak, judge, and act in His Name (8³⁶ 10³²· ³⁷).

But the chief object for which the Son came was to save the world (3¹⁷) and to give it eternal life (3¹⁶· ³⁶ 4¹⁴ etc.). And Jesus is Himself the life (14⁶), and came that men might have it more abundantly (10¹⁰). He is also the light of the world (3¹⁹ 8¹² 12⁴⁶), because He teaches men to know God and His Son, and this knowledge is eternal life (17²· ³). Jesus is therefore the Mediator of the life and the light of God for men. How are they to receive it?

We receive eternal life by attaching ourselves to the Person of Jesus Christ. We must believe on Him (3¹⁶). We must obey the Son if we are to escape from the wrath of the Father (3³⁶). We must believe His claim or die in our sins (8²⁴). We must abide in Him, as the branches in the vine, and abide in His love as He abides in His Father's love (15¹⁻¹⁰). Other conditions of salvation remind us of our Lord's teaching in the Synoptics. It is necessary to be born again of water and the Spirit

(3³⁻⁷), and to eat His flesh and drink His blood (6⁵²⁻⁵⁹).

The last injunction reminds us that the Divine life which is in Jesus becomes available for the Christian by virtue only of His death. It is sometimes held that Jesus is represented in this Gospel as saving men by revealing to them the truth about God, a revelation made in His own Person. But it cannot be said with justice that the mediatorial work of Jesus in this Gospel is only of this prophetic nature. St. John records a great deal about the death of Jesus which implies that the death has a propitiatory character in the Gospel as well as in the First Epistle. In 1²⁹ the Baptist describes our Lord as the Lamb that taketh away the sin of the world. This must have a sacrificial meaning, for only by sacrifice could a lamb be conceived as taking away sin. In three passages (3¹⁴ 8²⁸ 12³²) our Lord speaks of Himself being 'lifted up.' Men will look to Him for life as the Israelites looked to the brazen serpent which Moses uplifted in the wilderness. Again, after He has been lifted up by the Jews, they will know that He is the Messiah. Lastly, He says, 'I, if I be lifted up from the earth, will draw all men unto myself'; the Cross, followed by the Ascension, will be the means of attracting Gentile as well as Jew. So He is the Good Shepherd, whose very vocation it is to lay down His life for the sheep (10¹¹). His laying it down is wholly voluntary, but it is God's purpose and His own for His earthly life (10¹⁷ᶠ·). St. John regards Caiaphas as unconsciously prophesying that Christ would die for the well-being and the union of all God's children (11⁵²). In 12²⁷ He dreads the appointed 'hour' or crisis, which He nevertheless knows to be the hour when He will be glorified (12²³), this glory being the manifestation of His character in the great passage from His trial and death to His Ascension (cf. 17⁵). He ascends to heaven by the way of the cross; and this ascent shows, as nothing else can, what He is. He also compares Himself in 12²⁴ to a grain of wheat which bears fruit only if it dies, otherwise 'it abideth by itself alone.' Here our Lord makes His whole influence depend upon His death; because He is to perish, He will be the source of life to others. 'Greater love hath no man than this, that a man lay down his life for his friends' (15¹³) His death is therefore the fullest revelation of His love. And in 17¹⁹ He sanctified Himself, deliberately dedicated Himself to the Father in death, that so He might establish for men a dedicated relationship with God.

Ch. 6 throws further light on our Lord's teaching about His Atonement. The great discourse therein contains three sections, the first Christological (6²⁶⁻⁴⁰), the second more definitely Soteriological (6⁴¹⁻⁵¹), the third Eucharistic (6⁵²⁻⁵⁹). In the first, Jesus requires belief in Himself as the living Lord, and *bread* of God. In the second, He asserts that He is the *living bread*, and that He will give His *flesh* for the life of the world. In the third, He speaks of the necessity of eating His *flesh* and drinking His *blood*. The flesh and blood must mean not Himself merely, but Himself as affected by a violent death, and a death endured, as He has declared, for the life of the world. The act of communion is represented as an exalted act of faith by which man appropriates Christ's atoning self. All this implies that the death of Christ is propitiatory; the sacrifice is dedicated to God, and it cleanses man's sin when man appropriates it. If we consult 8²⁴ and 3³⁶, we see quite certainly that the result of this sacrifice is that God's wrath is removed. The sin of the world is exposed to His wrath, and this wrath on His part means death on man's part. It is such wrath as can be felt only by perfect love. And the saving effect of Christ's death is this, that it established between God and man that relationship which enables individual men to escape from sin, wrath, and death, and attain a vital union with God.

(d) In St. John's *First Epistle* the doctrine of Christ's mediation is clear. The Apostle insists upon the historical truth of the atoning work of Christ, and upon the existing witness of that work. In 5[6, 8] he opposes the Docetic theory concerning Jesus and His work, and declares that the crucifixion was as true an experience of Christ as His baptism. He who by baptism associated Himself with repentant sinners, by crucifixion endured what that baptism foreshadowed. The Holy Spirit makes these two saving events penetrate our hearts, and the water of Christian baptism and the blood of the Eucharistic cup bear testimony to His witness. In 2[1, 2] 4[9, 10] 1[7] it is shown that the death of Jesus has a direct relation to the sins of the world, for it is their propitiation; to His own righteousness, for only the perfectly Righteous could establish God's law of righteousness; to His present intercession for man, for He is the Advocate of man by virtue of what He has already done for us. The Apostle further implies in 1[7, 9] that the Christian needs a continuous purification. He is unforgiven and uncleansed unless he continues to 'walk.' His salvation is ethical. It is made possible by something which he did not do, and could not do, for himself. But it is not something which he can secure eternally by a momentary choice.

Conclusion. — The writers of the NT unite in various ways in teaching that Jesus is the Mediator between God and man in the whole work of reconciliation which the human conscience requires. In the whole of His teaching and His contest with evil He satisfied the Divine law of Righteousness. Further, by His perfect sympathy He entered into the situation and the misery of sinful man; a truth which is unintelligible when regarded as an external legal transference of guilt, but intelligible and moral when regarded as the voluntary act of love. In giving Himself for man, He gave Himself to God, offering in His own Person to God all that devotion which God, who is holiness and love, could desire from His children. In so surrendering Himself to death, He acquiesced in the justice of God's condemnation of the sins of the human race, of which He had chosen to become a member. All sin inevitably tends to death, not by any arbitrary appointment but by its very nature, and Christ accepted death as the symbol of God's judgment on man's sin. Lastly, Christ is our propitiation, because He gives us inwardly that power, that communication of His own life, which cleanses us from sin. He enables us to die to sin, and thus within us, as outside us, does not suspend but establishes the law of Righteousness. All this is possible if Jesus is truly God and perfectly man; having an actual original solidarity with our race previous to the choice of any individual member of it, and that new solidarity which He establishes between Himself and all who consciously come into a moral and sacramental union with Him.

See also artt. ATONEMENT, DEATH OF CHRIST, PROPITIATION, RANSOM, RECONCILIATION, REDEMPTION, and the Literature there referred to.

LEIGHTON PULLAN.

MEEKNESS. — **1. The quality defined.** — The Christian virtue of meekness has suffered the misfortune of being seriously misunderstood. In the popular mind it has been so conceived as to forfeit the right to be considered a virtue at all, being regarded as the equivalent of weak compliance— the temper of one devoid of manly vigour, who tamely allows himself to be slighted and injured without protest or resistance. That this concep-

tion is a caricature of meekness, is apparent in view of Christ's Beatitude (Mt 5[5]); for not only is it incredible that our Lord should have pronounced a blessing on those of feeble character, but the nature of the promise attached to the Beatitude implies that in some sense meekness is a strong and victorious quality. Whatever it be, we must presume it to be a virtue replete with energy, robust and manly, the very opposite of everything that is weak. Otherwise Christ's words are reduced to an absurdity.

In the NT use of the word, meekness (πραΰτης, πραότης) is commonly interpreted as meaning gentleness of disposition, peaceableness of temper in the face of provocation and wrong. It is the spirit of one who is not easily provoked, but keeps under control the natural instinct to assert oneself and to retaliate. It is the opposite of irascibility and the spirit of revenge. That is to say, it is conceived as a disposition restricted in its exercise to a man's relation with his fellow-men. But in reality meekness has a deeper and wider significance. It is, to begin with, a disposition towards God, the humble submission to the Divine will, the quiet acceptance of the discipline of life as coming from One who in infinite wisdom and love directs the destinies of men. This is made clear by the Biblical history of πραΰς. In the LXX, πραΰς is most frequently employed as the tr. of עָנָו —one who bows himself down in lowliness beneath the hand of God. The πραεῖς are the class of afflicted ones who accept their sorrows without murmuring, and yield themselves in trust and in hope to the will of God. When Jesus pronounced His blessing on 'the meek,' it was this class of humble, uncomplaining, God-fearing sufferers that He had in view. His appropriation of the words in Ps 37[11] is conclusive proof of that. That 'the meek' of the Beatitude have so often been exclusively conceived as those who are peaceable and unvindictive in their dealings with their fellow-men, is due to the fact that the Greek conception of πραΰτης [*] has governed the interpretation, instead of the conception represented by the underlying Hebrew word. At the same time, this common interpretation of πραΰτης is not to be rejected as alien to the NT meaning. The attitude of humble submission to the will of God carries with it of necessity a disposition of gentleness and forbearance towards men who are harsh and provocative in their dealings, not only because they are to be regarded as the instruments of the Divine discipline, but because only through the loving restraint of angry and vindictive feelings can the gracious will of God be done in human relationships. The primary significance of meekness is the calm and trustful acceptance of God's will, when it is adverse, as meaning our good; but this involves in regard to our fellow-men the quiet and patient endurance of scorn, annoyance, and opposition.

2. Meekness in relation to God. — Regarded as the submissive attitude of the soul towards God, meekness has its root in a humble, childlike faith. To use the words of Gregory of Nyssa, humility is 'the mother of meekness.' Humility and meekness are kindred virtues; hence they are often mentioned together (Eph 4[2], Col 3[12], cf. Mt 11[29]). Humility is the soul's attitude induced by a proper sense of one's creaturely weakness, ignorance, and unworthiness in presence of the Most High; meekness is the attendant disposition, born of humility, which constrains the soul to bow without complaining before the will of God in the hard and perplexing experiences of life. The soul that thus bows meekly beneath the Divine discipline is not open to the reproach of feebleness or insensibility;

[*] See, for the Greek conception of πραΰτης, Aristotle, *Nic Eth.* iv. 7.

it is meek, not because it is too callous to feel the pain of sorrow and misfortune or too spiritless to protest against it, but because it bends in lowly and childlike trust before the unsearchable wisdom and love of God. Where there is faith in the universal operation of the all-wise love of God, meekness shows itself in the unmurmuring surrender to the Divine will and in the patient endurance of that will. And from this attitude towards God there flows the blessing of peace. Meekness is the channel by which the gracious love of God is communicated to the soul as waters of refreshment and rest. This is the truth taught under a different figure in Mt 11[29]. Meekness is the easy yoke of Jesus which enables the weary and heavy-laden to bear the discipline laid upon them without chafing and complaining. Amid outward conditions which are hard and oppressive, they who like Jesus are 'meek and lowly of heart,' who bow before God with a profound sense of His infinitely wise and perfect will, find 'rest unto their souls'; they are freed from that inward restiveness and discontent which aggravate the outward burden and wear away the strength. Not only is meekness a strong and heroic quality which curbs the natural impulse to fume and rebel against God's will, but it is the means whereby the soul is reinforced by a Divine power to endure life's discipline with courage.

Meekness before God is, then, the natural ethical outcome of humble faith in the Divine Father who in unerring wisdom and holy love orders the life of men. It is seen in its crowning manifestation in Jesus Christ (cf. 2 Co 10[1]), for whom alike in the tasks which He undertook and in the sorrows which He bore the Father's will was supreme. When faithfulness to His mission brought upon Him unmerited suffering, He endured it in meekness, assured that it was God's holy will for Him. That His meekness was not merely a passive virtue, but one that was pervaded by a moral vigour and strength of purpose, is made clear by the conflict in Gethsemane. In the prayer of lowly submission, 'Not my will but thine be done,' we see the meekness of Jesus, in respect of God's dealings with Him, in its Divinest light. The agony and the bloody sweat, the prayer, 'If it be possible, let this cup pass away from me,' not only set in vivid relief the moral grandeur of Christ's willing acceptance of His Father's will, but they show with convincing power that true meekness is not the easy outcome of insensibility or tameness of spirit, but the victory of a strong nature over personal desires which conflict with the will of God.

3. Meekness in relation to men.—When we think of meekness in regard to the wrongs and opposition of men, we find that it is characterized by the same heroic qualities and is attended by similar blessed results. It is a virile and noble thing. The outward garb of meekness may, indeed, be worn by men in whom there are none of the robust and gracious qualities which make true meekness so worthy of admiration and honour. There are those who, by natural disposition, are timid and compliant, who have not manliness enough to resent injustice, who do not retaliate when they are wronged simply because they dare not. Similarly, there are those who, when slighted, show no sign of resentment, because they are too dull to feel an affront, or because they are controlled by feelings of scorn or by considerations of self-interest and policy. Of none of these can it be said that he is meek, nor does his conduct deserve our admiration. True meekness, which is worthy of all honour, is seen only in those who, with an acute sense of wrong, control the natural impulse to show anger and to retaliate, not from fear, or pride, or policy, or scorn of others, but because in obedience to the will of God they accept the provocation or wrong as discipline, and as an opportunity for showing the Divine spirit of patience and love. The meek man is not quick-tempered or vindictive, because, swayed by feelings of benevolence and love, he remains master of himself. Where there is no love, there is no meekness. 'Meekness is the power of *love* to quell the ebullition of anger, to restrain the violent and hasty temper' (Martensen). The irritation may be keenly felt; the temptation to retaliate may be very strong; but love keeps the upper hand and imposes calmness and self-restraint. It follows from all this that true meekness is not open to the contemptuous charge, so often brought against it, of softness and mean-spiritedness. It is a strong quality, for it means victory over the hot desire to retaliate; it is a gracious quality, for it means love triumphing over the selfish and self-assertive impulses of one's nature, in its anxiety to avoid the embittering of friendly relations and to subdue ill-feeling by gentleness and kindness.

Meekness, then, is an expression of the love which 'is not easily provoked' (1 Co 13[5]). It is the self-restraint imposed by love when one is irritated or suffers a personal wrong. But this gentle and peaceable disposition is not inconsistent with a burning indignation at the injustice and evil conduct of men, when wider interests are concerned. The meek man is not bound over to keep the peace at any price. Meekness does not mean incapacity for indignation. When the interests of the Divine Kingdom are at stake, in the face of flagrant and defiant wrongdoing, the duty of the meek is not silence and self-repression, but indignant and active opposition to evil. Indignation has a vastly greater moral value and influence when it proceeds from one who in personal matters endures provocation with calmness and self-restraint. It is the meekness of Jesus that makes His anger so terrible. When He was subjected in His own person to insult or wrong, He bore it with patience and with compassion on those who wronged Him (1 P 2[23]). When He was wounded to the heart by the treachery of Judas, and the betrayal was sealed by a hypocritical kiss, His answer to the traitor showed how superior He was to the natural resentment of men: 'Comrade, is it for this that thou art come?' (Mt 26[50]). When He hung upon the cross in agony, He was so far master of Himself and so deeply moved by compassion for His enemies, that He found some ground for extenuating their conduct and prayed for their forgiveness. But when the interests of the weak and helpless were involved (Mt 18[6]), when the sacred name of religion was profaned (Mt 21[12]), and the Kingdom of God was thwarted by those who were so blind as to imagine they were defending it (Mt 23[13ff.]), 'the wrath of the Lamb' flamed on the heads of the wrong-doers. So far from anger being inconsistent with meekness, it is only when meekness is associated with it that anger has a pure moral worth. The wrath of an irascible and violent man is deservedly discounted; that of a meek man scorches where it falls. Even when it is most vehement, the indignation that is associated with meekness is kept within bounds. It is not allowed to degenerate into uncontrollable and self-willed passion. Behind its severity there is the moderating power of love, which even in the act of showing indignation regrets its necessity (cf. Mk 3[5]).

In the matter of personal wrongs, meekness is shown in the refusal to retaliate in the spirit of the aggressor. It will not requite evil with evil. Much rather will it endure the wrong and yield no room in the heart to the spirit of revenge. The motive for this meek endurance of wrong is love, which does not suffer us to forget that the wrong-doer is a brother-man, whom we should strive to win to penitence and friendly relations by patience and forbearance (Gal 6[1], 2 Ti 2[25], Tit 3[2]).

Whether there should be any bounds to this acceptance of personal wrong is a question which has been brought into great prominence in our day by the teaching of Tolstoi. According to the Russian moralist, who has preached with great power the Quaker doctrine of non-resistance to evil, the old right of requital was abolished by Christ; not only should there be no private retaliation against wrong, but there should be no recourse to any legal tribunal when one has suffered injury or injustice. The law of non-resistance in Tolstoi's view is absolute; when we are wronged, we should suffer meekly in the hope that through our meekness evil will be overcome of good. Against this interpretation of the law of Christ in an absolute sense we have to set not only Christ's own example, when in the sacred name of justice He challenged the man who smote Him at the bar of judgment (Jn 18[23]), but also the whole tenor of the Christian law. When Jesus, in inculcating meekness and love to our enemies, said, 'Resist not evil' (Mt 5[39]), the context shows that He was not laying down a law which should be rigidly interpreted according to the letter, but that He was requiring a new spirit—the spirit of forbearance and love in dealing with those who wrong us. Christ's aim in requiring meekness of His followers was a moral aim—the furtherance of the Divine Kingdom, the lessening of the amount of evil in the world—a result which the meek endurance of wrong often brings with it in the disarming of enmity and in the quenching of the fires of ill-will, whereas retaliation adds to the evil and inflames the bitterness that already exists; but when it has become clear that forbearance and patience with a wrong-doer only confirm him in his evil courses, Christian love not only does not forbid but actually requires, in the interest both of public righteousness and of the wrongdoer himself, recourse to a civil tribunal that requital may be given. So long as there is any reasonable hope that meek endurance of wrong will turn the wrongdoer to a better frame of mind, we should be willing to suffer injustice; but when that hope has proved itself vain, there is nothing inconsistent with the spirit of meekness and Christian love in securing that justice shall be done and evil defeated by the procedure of civil law.

4. The dominion of meekness. — Meekness, though feeble to all outward seeming, is 'a world-conquering principle' (Tholuck). 'Blessed are the meek,' Christ said, 'for *they shall inherit the earth.*' 'To inherit the earth' (or, rather, 'the land') was originally the formula for the Israelitish possession of the Promised Land (Gn 15[7], Dt 4[38]). In OT times, however, it had already, as in Ps 37[9. 11], become 'a symbolic expression for the totality of Divine blessing and Messianic happiness' (Holtzmann). On the lips of Jesus the phrase has a spiritual significance; it expresses the highest good along with the collateral idea of world-wide influence. The inheritance of the earth by the meek does not come through outward possession, but by spiritual sovereignty. The meek, in accepting God's will in His disciplinary dealing with them, are not in bondage to earthly things, but are their true masters. They derive from life the highest good that it can bestow. They who rebel against the appointments of Providence miss the real gains of life. Only when the conditions of life are seen to be instinct with spiritual significance and intention as the expression of God's will, do they yield up the purest blessings that are hidden in them, and become the means of inward enrichment (cf. 1 Ti 6[6]). Further, they who are meek under provocation and wrong have a large spiritual dominion. They are the true rulers of men. Human hearts are won only by gentleness and love. God's Kingdom on earth grows not by requiting evil with evil, but by overcoming evil with good. That is the sovereignty of the Cross. And the future is with the meek. They are destined to have a world-wide dominion. Because God reigns and they accept and do the will of God, they are on the winning side. Meekness will one day claim the whole earth for its own, when men, conquered by the meek endurance of the Cross, bow humbly before God and live together in peace and brotherhood.

LITERATURE. — Trench, *NT Synonyms*, 142 ff.; Comm. on Mt 5[5]; works on the Sermon on the Mount (Tholuck, Dykes, Gore, Boyd-Carpenter, etc.); art. 'Sermon on the Mount' in Hastings' *DB*, Ext. Vol. 19 (Votaw); Sermons by MacLaren ('The Beatitudes'), Leckie ('Life and Religion' [excellent]), Channing ('Self-Denial'), etc.; Tholuck, *Hours of Christian*

Devotion, 378 ff.; Martensen, *Christliche Ethik*, Spec. Th. i. 307 ff.; Moulton, *Expos.* Aug. 1906; Tolstoi, *My Religion*, and *The Kingdom of God is within you*.   A. F. FINDLAY.

MELCHI.—Occurs twice in our Lord's genealogy, Lk 3[24. 28].

MELCHIZEDEK.—See PRIEST.

MELEA.—An ancestor of Jesus, Lk 3[31].

MENNA.—An ancestor of Jesus, Lk 3[31].

MENTAL CHARACTERISTICS. — There can be no full appreciation without some analysis: the friend who is understood is loved the better. That 'love is blind' is singularly false, save when the word is restricted to an unworthy meaning. True love gives insight always; and the power it gives of divining what to others is invisible is a species of analysis. There is no question, however, of analyzing Divinity. Divinity realized in humanity is what we know in Jesus Christ. In God Incarnate there can be nothing which is not human, though nothing which is human only. An attempt to analyze the mental characteristics of the Lord Jesus is therefore an attempt to appreciate the human manifestation which God has made of Himself. The first condition must be reverence, and the study is best undertaken with St. Paul's teaching (1 Co 2[6-16]) in mind, for success is to be reached only if 'we have the mind of Christ.'

1. Perhaps the first characteristic to notice is the way in which the mind of the Lord Jesus was always so thoroughly *alive to everything around Him*. In the single glimpse afforded of His boyhood this appears strikingly; for no one can read Lk 2[41-51] without feeling the eagerness with which He looked on Jerusalem for the first time consciously, and threw Himself into the best life of the festival. He was instantly at home in the Temple, and ready to listen and to inquire of the Rabbis there with a keen grasp which amazed them. Later on, the same ready observancy, which not merely noticed but entered into every phase of life, is again and again to be remarked. Now it was the flowers of the country side that won His attention (Lk 12[27]), now the games of the children in the market-place (7[32]), now the habits of the wild creatures (9[58]), or their unconsidered treatment in captivity (12[6]), now the details of the yeoman's employment (Mt 13[3-8] 12[11], Lk 13[11]), now the unnoticed self-denial of a poor woman in a crowd (Mk 12[43]). Just as readily He gave keen attention to the life of long ago told in the Scriptures of His race. For Him the characters appearing in the stories of the past were all real and vivid; *e.g.* Naaman (Lk 4[27]), David (Mt 12[3]), Zachariah (Mt 23[35]). With no less alacrity He noted the current events which made a popular impression (Lk 13[4]), and the far more momentous movements of national life which others too often overlooked (21[20], Mt 16[1-3]).

2. In close connexion with the foregoing characteristic stands *the fulness of vital force* in the Lord Jesus. Of most persons it is true that the emotional, or the intellectual, or the volitional faculties dominate and give the general colour to the temperament, but in Him *all* were supremely strong. The vehemence of His feelings was such as would have overbalanced the will or unsteadied the intellect of another; but He never lost balance or clarity. The lucid understanding which never failed in things great or small would have subordinated feeling, or even sapped its strength, in most; but the calm sweep of His discernment never made Him less warm-hearted towards 'one of the least of these my brethren,' and He condemned at once any use of reason which restrained responsiveness, as when His disciples were inclined to check the children brought to Him and He was 'moved with indignation' (Mk 10[14]), or when He promptly defended the woman's 'waste' of the costly ointment which her uncalculating love so gladly spent on Him (14[6]). Yet neither warmth of feeling nor reach of understanding ever warped His will to excuse or palliate in any wise, or made His resolution waver. Nothing could be sterner or more unsparing than the way in which He turned on almost the best-loved and aptest of His disciples, and this, too, directly after His whole heart had gone out to him in welcome and in grateful sympathy for the trust and insight he had just shown (Mt 16[17. 23]). The narrative of the Temptation in the wilderness, which must have been derived from the Lord Himself, can hardly be paralleled in its dauntless determination, except indeed by the narrative of how He followed out in His work the ideal here resolutely formed, and never faltered in following it still when it led Him through the valley of the shadow of death.

3. What has been said of the poise of these three mental factors, which are found in every living action of every living soul, though hardly ever balanced evenly, must be extended in Jesus' case to a wider range. There is nothing more remarkable than *the perfect proportion of His nature.* Those characteristics which are found singly in others, and which are commonly antithetic and even incompatible, are found alike, and at one in Him. He was passionate : ' He looked round with anger ' (Mk 3[5]) ; ' Jesus wept ' (Jn 11[35], cf. Lk 19[41]) ; ' Jesus looking on him loved him ' (Mk 10[21]) ; ' Ye serpents, ye offspring of vipers ! ' (Mt 23[33]). But who was ever so patient ? cf. Mk 4[40], Jn 16[12], and the whole scene of His trial and crucifixion. He was full of reverence for the past ; scrupulous in His respect for authority (Mt 23[2]), and very sensitive to the sacred associations of ancient institutions (Mk 11[15-17], Lk 19[41. 42]22[15]). But He held Himself entirely untrammelled by either precedent or outward enactment (Mt 5[17. 18ff.]), and appealed without hesitation to the conscience and instinct of every man, as to a sufficient and trustworthy test (Lk 13[15. 16]). His was an imaginative and contemplative mind ; He loved to withdraw to the desert country by Himself, or with a handful of intimate friends, and to spend long hours in personal devotions. Even when work pressed upon Him, and He 'had no leisure so much as to eat' (Mk 6[31]), feeling the harvest waiting to be reaped was far too great for His little band of fellow-labourers to cope with, He still spent what seems to have been an astonishingly large proportion of His time in seclusion. But never was a dreamer of dreams so intensely practical. Hard and prolonged work He undertook with zest, then slept at once and soundly, and woke ready for any effort or emergency at the instant (4[1. 2. 33-39]). And His practical ability is strikingly apparent in other ways ; *e.g.* He was so sure in the handling of men (Lk 9[57-62], Jn 3[1-15] 11[6-16]), so capable of picking out and dealing with the precise thing needing to be done at any given stage or moment (Mt 17[24-27], Jn 7[3-8] 11[6-16]). He was remarkably tolerant, and again and again gave offence to narrower minds by the width of His sympathies and the leniency of His judgments. Particularly is this illustrated by His relations with 'publicans and sinners,' which exposed Him to disgraceful calumny (Mt 11[19]), of which He recked nothing ; but His tolerance was also too great for His own followers to understand it (Mk 9[38-41]), and great enough sometimes to shame the bitterest opponents into silence (Jn 8[7-11]). Yet no one could be more rigid on occasion, as in His treatment of the Phœnician mother (Mt 15[23-28]), or more inexorable in condemnation (23[13-36], Mk 3[28. 29]). His humility was profound,

and has changed the estimation of this quality in the eyes of mankind. 'I am in the midst of you as he that serveth' (Lk 22[27]), He would say, or show them even more vividly in deed (Jn 13[15]). 'I am meek and lowly in heart' (Mt 11[29]) was what He felt as He welcomed the weary, and gave thanks that the highest wisdom was 'revealed unto babes.' Yet never were such tremendous assertions made by any one about himself, or such unfaltering emphasis laid upon the place he must hold in the eyes of others, and the claims he made upon them : 'He that loveth father or mother . . . son or daughter, more than me, is not worthy of me. And he that doth not take his cross and follow after me is not worthy of me' (10[37. 38]) ; 'The Spirit of the truth shall glorify me, for he shall take of mine and shall declare it unto you. All things whatsoever the Father hath are mine' (Jn 16[13-15]). Again, the stern independence which would not bend to make a 'hard saying' more easily acceptable, but would let all who would not receive it go their way, even if His closest intimates were to be included (6[66-68]), and which justly called forth F. W. Robertson's rejoinder, 'Don't care was crucified on Calvary,' was no less characteristic of Him than that craving for sympathy which went with His sensitive and affectionate nature, and led Him to beseech the companionship of those whom He could best trust in such hours of agonized prayer as are recorded on the Mount of Transfiguration and in the Garden of Gethsemane. On the one hand, He always saw things just as they are, undistorted by His own feelings, unconcealed by custom or convention, neither excused nor glorified, if faulty, by their associations, nor hackneyed or degraded by their common abuse. This holds equally of the smallest details of the natural world (Mt 11[7]) or of human life (Lk 14[7] 15[8. 9]), and of the greatest forces at work in the world (Mk 13[2]). All this marks Him out as a genuine realist. But, on the other hand, beyond all others He was an idealist. For Him the most real world was that Kingdom of heaven which He always felt to be 'at hand'—within direct and instant reach. It was His own most positive experience not to 'live by bread alone,' but to satisfy the needs of His nature with food and drink that were spiritual (Jn 4[13. 14. 34]). The story of the Temptation is perhaps the purest idealism ever written : but glimpses into His thoughts which are subsequently afforded show how the habitual working of His mind was on no lower level of idealism (Lk 10[17-24]). Again,. He was intensely individualistic in His point of view (Mt 6[3. 6. 17]), and, even in the widest sweep of forecast on the fate of the world, did not fail to regard each several individual in and for himself ; in fact, His influence has given the world a different and a deeper conception of the worth and meaning of individual lives, and has gone far towards the making of the best modern thoughts of personality. But none the less He was quite free from the segregative and disintegrating individualism which has been the bane of Puritanism and Benthamism and other phases of thought in which the individualist standpoint has been prominent. And the aims He set forward were always communal. *E.g.* His followers were described as 'a flock,' 'a church,' 'a vine,' in which the severance of a member involved its utter futility. The 'Kingdom of God' was the one great end for which all were to live and work (6[33]), careless of personal needs ; and no condition for association with Himself was more imperative than that every one should 'disown himself' completely (Mk 8[34-37]). But what is most remarkable of all is not that these and other antithetic characteristics, which are in other cases met with singly, were found in concurrence and in full development in the mind of the Lord Jesus, but that in Him they were in such perfect proportion and such intimate relation that they were not opposing tendencies at all. To say that it is impossible to indicate which way the balance of contrasted impulses inclined, so stable was the equipoise, is not enough. These things, which in other natures are conflicting, were in Him mutually supporting and at one. In nearly all minds one can detect more or less cleavage and internal strain, but that of the Lord Jesus was wholly annealed, showing only the finest temper without any tension.

The fulness, balance, and unity of the Master's nature make it impracticable to use in His case what is the commonest and readiest way of portraying a person. This is to throw into the foreground of the picture those features in which the character is exceptionally strong, or those deficiencies which mark it off from others, and to leave as an unelaborated background the common stuff of human nature. Thus by sketching the idiosyncrasies, and casting a few high-lights, the man is set forth sufficiently. But what traits are there in the Lord Jesus which stand out because more highly developed than other features? Where are His foibles or defects? Nothing truly human was wanting in Him, nothing was exaggerated. The fact which distinguished Him from all others was His completeness at all points, so that in the first and in every succeeding generation of His followers the greatest have declared, 'Of his fulness we all receive' (Jn 1¹⁶). And this surely is what we must expect to be its mode if we try to conceive of a Divine Incarnation. Even as Christ's power and presence give to such as trust Him 'perfect wholeness' (τὴν ὁλοκληρίαν ταύτην, Ac 3¹⁶), so the power and presence of the Infinite realized in humanity is disclosed in a 'perfect wholeness' which raises every human feature and faculty above itself, and compels the confession, 'In him dwelleth all the plenitude of the Godhead bodily-wise' (Col 2⁹). It is difficult to mention more than four features which can fairly be called personal traits of the Lord Jesus. These are : His keen appreciation of the beauty of the natural world ; His fondness for little children, whom again and again He held up for the reverence of His disciples, and whom He Himself looked upon with a feeling akin to awe (Mt 18¹⁰) ; His love of being on a height (many of the cardinal points in His career were on the hill-tops, just as the crises of temptation were on 'an exceeding high mountain,' and when He was 'set on the pinnacle of the temple,' cf. Mt 5¹ 14²³ 15²⁹ 17¹ 28¹⁶ ‖ Mk 3¹³) ; and His love of being often alone. On the other hand, if one seeks for personal characteristics due to the marked absence of anything that most men share, there is nothing that can be named, except that, unlike others, He was without 'the defects of His qualities.' Thus exaltation never passed into ecstasy ; zeal never into rashness or one-sidedness ; sympathy never into sentimentality ; determination never into obstinacy ; conscience never into scrupulosity ; the habit of moral discrimination never into casuistry ; standing indignation against the hypocrisies of the day never made Him censorious ; a wonderful tenderness of heart left Him stern and uncompromising ; and an energy which rejoiced in work, and shrank from nothing, never led Him to become exacting towards others or inconsiderate of their weakness.

In this connexion a word must be said on His relation to the stock of Israel. All His personal habits and customs, all His information, His religious premises, found their starting-points in the national life and customs of Israel, and in the Scriptures and other current ideas of its noblest minds belonging to previous days. And He never hesitated to adopt and use freely the practices and religious language which He found in the Israel of His age. But it is impossible, for all that, to regard Jesus as a typical, or as a perfect Jew. He had indeed all the best characteristics of the greatest sons of Israel, and notably of the prophets of the past ; their zeal for righteousness, their fear of God, their tenacity of purpose, their noble scorn of the littleness of the earth and all that is in it in comparison with 'the high and lofty One that inhabiteth Eternity, whose name is Holy' (Is 57¹⁵). But He was likest them just where they were least representative of the race from which they sprang, just where they towered above their fellow-countrymen and were least appreciated by the latter. He rose above them all ; and while nothing truly Jewish was discarded or denied, the Jew was left below. He was fully conscious of this Himself, and so the term by which He continually named Himself was at once the simplest and the greatest that a human being can bear—He was the 'Son of Man.' It is a title all can use, but He alone exhausts. And to this day it continually receives corroboration from many quarters, for His disciples, drawn from many

races, never find Him alien to their own needs. To the Oriental believer Jesus is an Oriental, to the Western He has all the Western nature. The ancient Greek philosopher, the modern Hindu, and the Negro slave, no less than the British subject, see indeed different aspects of Him salient, but none feels in Him a national character which makes Him a foreigner from their several points of view.

4. A few negative observations are required, as they serve to define more clearly some of the characteristics of the Lord Jesus. (a) He was *sinless*. Amidst men whose eyes were sharpened by envy to detect the least fault, and who tried many times to ensnare Him in His words because they despaired of tripping Him in wrong conduct, He threw down the challenge without misgiving : 'Which of you convicteth me of sin?' And none dared take it up, either then or later (Mk 14⁵⁵) : nor in the sixty generations that have passed since then have any such ethical advances been made that, looking back from our present vantage ground, we can point to anything as sin in Him. But His sinlessness did not consist merely in the fact that no act of fullgrown sin could be discovered. There was no *taint* anywhere in Jesus' mind. Everything bore the bloom of perfect spiritual health and maturity. Spiritual disease could find no foothold whence to spread its poison, not even in the hours of spiritual conflict and internal agony. 'One that hath been tempted in all points like as we are, apart from sin' (He 4¹⁵), is the only possible description of Him. (b) He made *no use of limiting qualifications in His sayings, or similar reservations in His action*. He did not use 'ifs' and 'buts,' but spoke with simple decisiveness on the most complex questions. At times He would carry this to the length of paradox, and bid a man struck on one cheek turn the other to invite a blow. At other times He would restate a problem to strip it of those adventitious difficulties with which it is enveloped in common minds ; as when He met the unuttered question whether He would break the Law by healing on the Sabbath, by putting the inquiry, 'Is it lawful on the Sabbath day to do good, or to do harm? to save a life, or to kill?' (Mk 3⁴). But more often He went straight to the centre of the matter in hand with a simple directness which made all qualifications needless : His dealing with the Sadducees' puzzle (12¹⁸⁻²⁷) is a striking instance. This can be done only by one whose 'eye is single.' (c) *Jesus was never critical*. More nearly than anywhere else one seems here to discover a deficiency in Him ; for the critical faculties are of great value, and in some minds are in admirable vigour. In Him they were in abeyance. And yet it is plain this resulted from no want of faculty. He could on occasion prove Himself matchless in dialectic ; and in more than one controversy with skilled opponents He used this dialectic power with crushing effect. What could be finer than His appeal to the image and superscription of the tribute-money when plied with the insidious question, 'Shall we give, or shall we not give?' (12¹⁴) ; or than His rejoinder to the challenge of His own authority, 'The baptism of John, was it from heaven, or from men? answer me' (11³⁰),—a rejoinder which not only silenced objectors, but went to the root of the question they raised as to the criterion of 'authority'? His dialectic skill sometimes passed into biting sarcasm, as when He pointed out how the scribes and Pharisees witnessed to themselves that they were the sons of them that slew the prophets, by the way they garnished their tombs (Mt 23²⁹⁻³¹). Here are all the faculties for critical efficiency, but the Lord Jesus was never critical. The fact seems to be that His mind was too creative. In minds of lesser stature, criticism may hold an honourable place,

and often serves a very useful purpose; but it is always a second-hand way of winning truth. The truly creative mind does not need it, and does not use it, but reaches truth by direct intuition, or makes it spontaneously. He did so.

5. The last observation leads on to the mention of three mental characteristics which can hardly be separated, and which are all inwoven in the very fabric of Jesus' mind. His thoughts were always *concrete*, not abstract; His intellectual processes were *intuitive*, not argumentative; His views were ever *positive*, not negative. It has been very truly pointed out that 'only the widest generalizations and concrete facts are definite' (Hort); whatever lies between these extremes is more or less indefinite. Most minds are occupied mainly with this intermediate region, adding some degree of generalization to each fact of experience, and qualifying the largest generalizations by some accommodation to groups of facts observed. And to this is due not a little of the indefiniteness of most men's thoughts. But it was otherwise with the Lord Jesus. If He dealt with generalizations at all, He generalized out and out, dropping all half-way descriptions and limitations. He did not, therefore, shrink from inculcating principles which have often since been questioned on the ground that they are not of universal application. *E.g.* 'Give to him that asketh of thee' (Mt 5^{42}),—though experience shows too surely how much moral mischief may be done by indiscriminate charity; 'Ask, and it shall be given you' (7^7),—though prayers by no means always win what has been prayed for; 'It is easier for a camel to go through a needle's eye than for a rich man to enter into the kingdom of God' (Mk 10^{25}),—though wealth used worthily is no such bar to entry, and must itself be regarded as a 'loan from the Lord.' There is a definiteness in these unrestricted duties which could not have been attained by any carefully qualified rules of conduct. But more often the Lord Jesus adhered to concrete facts, and did not generalize at all. So, when any case came before Him, He dealt with *that*, and did not treat it as a precedent to govern others generally similar. Thus He told the rich young ruler to 'sell all he had and give to the poor, and follow him' (10^{21}). He certainly meant this to be done literally and at once; but it would be ruinous to turn this counsel into a command binding upon all rich men. It was never so intended, but was the particular remedy for the 'one thing lacking' in that one young man. No rule is to be directly drawn from the Lord's treatment of the woman in the Temple, or of Zacchæus, or of Judas Iscariot, which would apply to all adulteresses, or renegades, or traitors: each was dealt with as the particular need required.

This was one leading reason why the use of parables was such a very characteristic feature in Jesus' teaching; they have been said, in fact, and not without reason, to be the most characteristic of the Lord's recorded sayings. They enabled Him to put the lesson He desired in the concrete instead of the abstract. So, when asked, 'Who is my neighbour?' He gave no general answer, but an actual instance occurring on the road (Lk $10^{30ff.}$). Probably the scribe to whom this was first spoken never found himself in circumstances that were similar; but if he gained the higher standpoint which this story gave him, and saw into the very heart of truth in that one case, he would be able, like thousands of others who have heard the story since, the better to answer his own question in his own circumstances.

It was a consequence of this love of the concrete, and avoidance of that vagueness which belongs to all that lies short of the widest generalization, that Jesus never gave definitions. Instead, He fixed the *type* in some particular fact or instance. In His teaching there was no theorizing, no abstract discussion, no systematic theology. Nor was there any care to lay down principles for the organization or policy of His Church in times to come. The nearest approach to this last is in such passages as Mt 18^{15-17}, or the directions given before the first mission (10^{5-23}); but in these nothing is more noticeable than the utter absence of all abstractions, and all provisions for distant contingencies, every idea being expressed in concrete form, and in immediate connexion with the conditions of the work in hand. And yet in all this there is no mere particularism. Each single fact on which He looked was seen by Him in its real relations to all else, and in the light of the highest and widest principles. There is true insight into human needs in the saying that 'little thoughts do not suit with little duties. It is in the fulfilment of simple routine that we need more than anywhere the quickening of the highest thoughts' (Westcott). With Jesus that was instinctive. Any fact in His sight was serious, was sacred; for it was not merely an illustration of a wider truth, rather it was an actual embodiment of eternal reality. He looked on the 'flower in the crannied wall'—no more—and saw it with such penetrating insight that to Him it was eloquent of 'what God and man is.' He showed just the same intuitive recognition of truth in His estimate of a man, or His grasp of a religious principle. Whether it were the purpose and use of the Temple, or the religious customs and conventions of the day, or practical problems involving conflicting considerations, like that set to Peter by the question, 'Doth not your Master pay the half-shekel?' (17^{24}), or inquiries on the outer confines of human thought, such as those concerning eschatology and the life beyond death, the Lord Jesus always looked into the very heart of the facts before Him, so that all accessories and accidents seemed to drop away and leave the truth in its naked simplicity under His eyes. He completely disregarded the things which for most minds overlie and confuse the essential issues, and fixed His gaze on those positive points round which all the rest was accretion. His mind therefore concerned itself but little with negatives in any case. One most important consequence of this was that He always saw whatever good there was in any man, and paid comparatively little heed to the evil which might be there also. He did not stay to combat or correct the latter, but freed and reinforced the former so that it grew till no place was left for the evil, and it was expelled. In His hands all the old negative commandments were transformed into positive ideals; and all were summed up in the one great ideal of loving God and one's neighbour (Mk 12^{29-31}), which was itself set forth in no lower form than the very highest, 'Ye shall be perfect, as your heavenly Father is perfect' (Mt 5^{48}). And in full accordance with this habit of mind, the judgments which from time to time He passed on men about Him were determined rather by what moral worth they had or lacked, than by what faults were in them. The most unsparing condemnation fell upon the Pharisees, whose lives were strict and reputable, and free from the gross and careless vices of the multitude. He denounced their whole moral and religious activity as an 'hypocrisy,' because it was one great negation. They were not 'sinners'; but with all the opportunities for good which more than others they possessed, their hearts and lives were empty. He portrayed them, and showed the futility of their whole religious method, by describing a man out of whom the unclean spirit has been driven, and whose house is then cleaned and left vacant. The cleaning out is not disputed, but all the more surely does the vacancy invite new tenants; and if no good spirit occupies the house forthwith, 'the last state of that man becometh worse than the first' (Lk 11^{26}). So in His pictures of God's final judgment the condemnation falls not usually on those against whom crimes may be alleged (though these find mention, *e.g.* Mk 12[9], Mt 22[7]), but on the thoughtless maids found without oil; on the servant who took good care of his talent but never used it; on the guest without a wedding garment; on those to whom it is said, 'I was an hungered, and ye gave me no food; I was thirsty, and ye gave me no drink; I was a stranger, and ye took me not in; naked, and ye clothed me not; sick, and in prison, and ye visited me not' (Mt 25[42f.]). The whole point of view of Jesus in this is in strong contrast with that of the Judaism of His age, which aimed at attaining holiness by an earnest and elaborate endeavour to eliminate unholiness and defend the shrine of the soul from trespass.

One aspect of these last-mentioned characteristics may be summed up in a word, by saying that the make of Jesus' mind was that which is found in the greatest poets. They all combine, as lesser men cannot, the realist and the idealist. Their ideas are concrete, not abstract. Their minds work by intuition, not by argument. Their interests and thoughts are positive; and they are all more or less insistent that—

'The evil is null, is nought, a silence implying sound.'

And much of the Lord's teaching shows that the sense of form and the feeling for language which belong to them were His in a remarkable degree. Perhaps it was not entirely the power of His own personality, nor yet the substance of what He said, but also in part the music of its expression, that enabled Him so often to throw a spell over His hearers: *e.g.* 'All bare him witness, and wondered at the words of grace which proceeded out of his mouth' (Lk 4[22]); 'The people all hung upon him, listening' (19[48]); 'The officers answered, Never man so spake' (Jn 7[46]). There is, of course, the truest poetry in many of His sayings and in His parables; and His teaching teems with flashes of imagery such as only the highest poetry presents. Even in form of language some of His sayings lack little of the rhythm and music of poetical expression. But we have to remember that He wrote nothing that remains, and that nothing has been reported in His original words. The best we can expect to find in the NT is a good and faithful translation; and who can translate poetry? But a doubt must remain whether any literary vehicle could carry the full poetic inspiration of the Lord Jesus. Poems, however truly living, are the reflexions of life. The Life itself was inherent in Him (Jn 5[26]), and He came to impart it, not to reflect it (10[10]). So His 'poems' (ποιήματα) are the souls which, generation after generation, He has created anew, the ideals which have transformed, and are transforming, the world: even as St. Paul said of his disciples, 'Ye are an epistle of Christ ministered by us, written not with ink, but with the Spirit of the living God' (2 Co 3[3]). See, further, art. POET.

6. There are some things more properly described, perhaps, as features of character than as mental characteristics, but the distinction is such a narrow one, being a difference in the point of view and not in the facts, that they must be mentioned, though as briefly as possible. The *profound reverence* of Jesus' mind is one. Not only does this appear in every relation to His Father in heaven, and in the way He taught His disciples to look up to Him, but also in His delicate respect for all those who sought His help, and the sensitive regard He showed for the spiritual responsibility of each person, on which He never trenched. Another is His *simplicity*. He loved a simple life in outward things, rebuking Martha for her too ample provision when so little was needful (Lk 10[41]), and teaching His followers to spend little care on the wealth and comfort which He held so lightly, and to pray only for 'daily bread.' But simplicity is still more strikingly characteristic of the nature and process of His mind. Though more than any other that has ever lived He was 'many-sided,' He never gave the impression of a complicated nature. With the directness of a child He always turned to the point in hand; and no one was ever more free from that hesitancy which is so often found in those who are the best able to see both sides of a question. With sympathy unfailing and unlimited, He still was simple, and could put the loftiest thoughts into simple terms. That is always a characteristic of a really great—though not of every great—mind: never was an instance of it comparable with this one. Closely akin to this is the fact that *Jesus was never disconcerted* or bewildered, nor did He

ever lose presence of mind in the most difficult or dangerous situations. Rather, in times of trial, there was a heightening of His serenity of mind; for trial and sorrow made stronger appeal to His faith, which was always responsive. μὴ μετεωρίζεσθε was a counsel most characteristic of Him (Lk 12[29]); and it was this habitual trust in the Father that enabled Him in the very hour of impending agony to make His followers the bequest of peace—His peace (Jn 14[27] 16[33]).

7. Two matters of importance remain to be mentioned, distinct but by no means unconnected—(*a*) *Jesus' characteristic outlook upon life*, and (*b*) *His method as the Saviour of the world.*

(*a*) One cannot escape the feeling that while others look only at the surface of life, the Master looked through its surface and saw its depth: we see life usually in two dimensions, He looked at it in three, and so saw *reality*. Of course, from His standpoint all its proportions were very different from those which appear to us. The most striking expression of what is meant is to be found in Browning's description of Lazarus as given in the *Epistle of Karshish*. But while Browning had learnt the nature of this larger view, converting all proportions, from Him who called back Lazarus to earth, he represents it as a double prospect in Lazarus, with none of that translucent unity which is its essential feature in the Lord Jesus. The Beatitudes are an instance. Their chief effect, and it cannot be doubted their chief purpose, is to set the hearer on a new standpoint, and so enable him to gain a new view of life. It is no paradox that the poor are blest, while all men congratulate the rich; and this is not said to give emphasis to the aspect which is too much overlooked. It is simply the truth of life, seen as the eyes of the Lord Jesus saw it when He looked round on His disciples gathered there, all destitute of earth's possessions, but with a light in their eager faces as they 'hung upon him listening' which told of the 'righteousness and peace and joy in holy inspiration' which showed that theirs *was* the Kingdom of God (Ro 14[17]). All whose reading of experience goes deep can see, or partly see, why He counted sorrow blest, and gentleness, mercy, purity, and love the treasures of man's real enrichment. Another instance is the prayer He gave to His disciples when they felt the need of being taught how to pray. There is an unearthliness in it, and a grasp on the real depths of life, such as no other prayers disclose. God's glory, and His Kingdom, and the joy of fulfilling His will, fill up all the foreground; and the remainder of the view includes brief mention of bare needs here, and then fuller appeal for the deeper needs of forgiveness, and of the shelter of Him who is our 'shield and our exceeding great reward.' Hardly less striking is the way in which He enforced the duty of simple truthfulness, His words calling up vividly the awful picture of the Evil One leaning over the soul that talks loosely, to ply it with 'suggestions' which then find unsuspecting utterance as readily as those which the hypnotist gives to his unconscious 'subject' (Mt 5[37], with which cf. Lk 22[31]). There were times when the Lord expressed strongly this contrast between the view which men took of life and that which He took (Lk 16[15]), but more often His reference is a mere allusion. The difference culminated in that most characteristic and central idea on which He so often dwelt, that a man must 'lose his life to find it' (Mk 8[34-37]‖, cf. Mt 10[39], Lk 17[33], Jn 12[25]). Death itself was accordingly transfigured in Jesus' eyes: it neither put a limit to life nor made a breach which destroyed its continuity. Death was for Him 'sleep'; a sleep from which He awaked more than one, and from which 'in the last day' He would awake and raise up 'every one that beholdeth the Son and believeth on him' (Jn 6⁴⁰). For Himself, He looked through death to His own resurrection, which He again and again told His disciples to expect as the day of His departure drew nearer ; and for the rest, He recognized death with all its miserable and misleading associations as little as might be, and refused even to speak of it if this could be avoided (11¹¹⁻¹⁴). With His strong sense of the continuity of life there went, however, a very remarkable reserve about the future. Concerning it He disclosed nothing of detail ; nothing that trust in the love of God and the assurance of life's continuity do not themselves imply. He plainly said He did not know the course of the future, and His disciples must not expect to do so (Mk 13³², Ac 1⁷). But He never showed Himself averse to adopting the current religious language which rested on the prophecy and apocalyptics of the past, to clothe those ideas which He wished to impress about the life to come ; though it may well be that the eschatological passages in the Gospels are considerably coloured and confused by the fact that they have come through the medium of disciples who were not equal to following their Master's higher thoughts.

It is in connexion with this far profounder view of life which we find in Him that we are best able to understand the 'powers that worked in' the Lord Jesus (ἐνεργοῦσιν αἱ δυνάμεις ἐν αὐτῷ, Mk 6¹⁴), and His consciousness in regard to them. The term 'miracles' can hardly fail to prove misleading, as it is so closely associated with the 18th cent. point of view, which considered them as exceptions to natural law, and as owing their evidential value to the fact that they were exceptions. That view is quite obsolete and impossible now to a really scientific mind : it was always singularly unappreciative of 'the mind of Christ.' There can be no doubt that Jesus Himself felt complete certainty that He did wield powers of an extraordinary and practically limitless kind (cf. Mt 26⁵¹⁻⁵³), and that His contemporaries never dreamt of disputing the fact. But to Him they were certainly neither 'unnatural' nor 'supernatural.' The distinction drawn by the latter term is quite alien to His mind, and inconsistent with His point of view ; for Him the continuous character and flow of life was a fundamental idea, and the one unbroken reality included equally what we describe as 'natural' and 'supernatural.' The 'powers' of which He was conscious had their proper place and scope in life as He saw it ; and if it is not possible for us to assign this, or to explain them, that is due probably to the single fact that, as already said, we try to see the reality of life from the standpoint of two dimensions, and can succeed so little in seeing it from that of three as He did (cf. Mt 16¹⁹ 18¹⁸, Jn 20²³).

(b) The method which the Lord Jesus followed in carrying out His purpose as the world's Saviour was no less unique than His outlook on life, and it was the direct result of the latter. In the ordinary sense of the term He was no reformer ; He did not try to make the institutions which He found serve their end better, nor did He seek to substitute one expedient for another, to attain more successfully the aims before Him. He felt that His Kingdom was 'not of this world,' and all He sought was to open its portal to believers. He did not pit His Kingdom against those of the world to overthrow the latter ; rather He refused to let His followers do this or to do it Himself (Mt 26⁵²⁻⁵⁴). Nor did He attempt to withdraw His followers from the world, as other religious leaders often have done, that they might serve God with less distraction. Even His prayers were not for change of the world itself, or the delivery of His disciples from it (Jn 17⁹⁻²¹). Though His whole life was sacrificed to save the world, He just left the world alone. As in His teaching there was little that was negative, so in His work He tried to undo nothing. It is very surprising how content He always seemed to be to accommodate Himself to the use of any means or circumstance that lay ready at hand, while so unbending in aim throughout. Thus He spoke the religious language of Judaism, practised the customs in Israel, and respected its institutions, however much they were degraded and abused. He paid His half-shekel to the Sanhedrin and His tribute-money

to the Cæsar without protest. Browning again brings out with striking effect this feature of the Master's in his portrait of Lazarus, whose 'especial marking . . . is prone submission to the heavenly will,' so that he tries to change nothing ; but here again this characteristic, being isolated, lapses into quietism as it never did in Lazarus' Master. For, however willing Jesus was to use and leave unreformed the things around Him, none of these ever bound Him. If there was fault or falsehood mingled with what He borrowed for the moment, He left that on one side and moved on towards His goal unaffected. He saw the truth too clearly to be diverted by aught else, and the truth made Him free. And He led His followers into the freedom that was His own. So, while He abstained from all political intervention, and declined to be mixed up with the ordinary business of life (Lk 12¹⁴), and left religious institutions and traditions where He found them, He nevertheless revolutionized all life. There is no department of human activity in the world to-day—except in some of its backwaters which have not yet felt His influence—which is not profoundly altered in consequence of His life and work and words. His confidence that it would be so never faltered ; He saw here the supreme scope of the law of 'life through loss.' So He declared beforehand the result which is yet in progress under our eyes—'I, if I be lifted up out of the earth, will draw all men unto myself' (Jn 12³²). Of what import are the foam flakes which float upon its surface to him who plunges into the mighty stream of life? Jesus' view of life, and His method of saving men, both so original, both so characteristic, are both vindicated in full by the results. They are alike summed up in the joyous conviction which many and many a soul has uttered when lifted to His higher plane, and which even the world itself has been forced to suspect, though not to share : 'If any man be in Christ, there is a new creation !' (2 Co 5¹⁷, Gal 6¹⁵).

LITERATURE.—Bernard, *Mental Characteristics of the Lord Jesus Christ* ; Adamson, *Studies of the Mind in Christ* ; Latham, *Pastor Pastorum* ; Du Bose, *Gospel in the Gospels* ; art. CHARACTER OF CHRIST, and the Literature there cited.

E. P. BOYS-SMITH.

MERCHANT.—See TRADE AND COMMERCE.

MERCY.—1. Mercy of God. — Mercy is 'that essential perfection in God whereby He pities and relieves the miseries of His creatures' (Cruden). In the OT the mercy of God (חָנַן, רַחֲמִים ; חֶסֶד, 'to show mercy') is sought and celebrated in view of distress caused by sin (Ps 51¹, La 3²²), or more frequently where no connexion with sin is expressed (Ps 89¹ 118¹). Sin and the distress which is the consequence of it are not always separated in thought (Ps 41⁴ 79⁸⁻⁹).

In the NT a clearer division can be made of places where the mercy spoken of is temporal or spiritual. Those who came to Christ for help asked for *mercy*, that is, for pity and relief (Mt 9²⁷ 15²² 17¹⁵ 20³⁰ ; cf. Mk 5¹⁹). The word used is ἐλεεῖν, while Christ's twofold response is expressed by σπλαγχνισθείς, 'moved with compassion,' and by His act of healing (Mt 20³⁴). Along with these may be placed Lk 1⁵⁸, Ph 2²⁷, 1 Co 7²⁵, where particular instances of mercy are mentioned. On the other hand, the words ἔλεος, ἐλεεῖν are used of the whole of God's saving work in Christ (Lk 1⁷²⁻⁷⁸, Ro 11³⁰, 2 Co 4¹, Eph 2⁴, 1 Ti 1¹³⁻¹⁶, Tit 3³⁻⁷, Jude 21). In the publican's prayer, 'God, be merciful to me the sinner' (Lk 18¹³), the more exact translation is 'be propitiated' (ἱλάσθητι), as also in He 8¹² (ἵλεως). In these places the obstacle of sin is recognized, and the mercy described is such as overcomes sin.

Generally in the NT sin is described not only as the source of human misery, but as itself the greatest evil from which men need to be delivered ; and accordingly the work of God's mercy is to save from sin (see Eph 2$^{1-10}$, Tit 3$^{3-7}$). In Ro 11$^{30-32}$ something is said of the Divine purpose in permitting sin, so that we may believe that the severities of God's judgments are not inconsistent with 'that essential perfection of mercy whereby He pities and relieves the miseries of His creatures.' But of this as creatures we have not the final right to judge (Ro 9$^{15.\ 23}$). A deepened sense of the hopelessness of separation from God brings it about that no other deliverance is to be for a moment compared with salvation from sin (Eph 2$^{1-4}$; cf. Gal 1^4, Jude ^{21}).

This is also seen to be the meaning of mercy when the *method* of God's mercy in the Gospel is considered, and the *aim* of it.

(1) *Its method.*—Christ's work teaches us that God's mercy seeks a higher good for men than the relief of temporal distress. We must think of Christ as abiding in the constant sense of the mercy of His Father, and communicating the same to men in word and deed. 'Be ye therefore merciful (οἰκτίρμονες), as your Father also is merciful' (Lk 6^{36}). 'Love one another, as I have loved you. Greater love hath no man than this' (Jn 15$^{12.\ 13}$). That is to say, the mercy of God beginning with compassion went on to action, in the Incarnation and Atonement. 'This is he that came by water and blood' (1 Jn 5^6). 'I lay down my life that I may take it again. . . . This commandment have I received of my Father' (Jn 10$^{17.\ 18}$, cf. 1 P 1^3).

Following upon the work of Christ, it is said of believers that they have obtained mercy (2 Co 4^1, 1 Ti 1$^{13.\ 16}$, 1 P 2^{10}); and that they look for the mercy of the Lord Jesus Christ unto eternal life (Jude ^{21}). And mercy is still continuously needed, asked for, and received by believers (He 4^{16}, Ph 2^{27}, 2 Ti 1$^{16.\ 18}$). Also the prayers in 1 Ti 1^2, 2 Ti 1^2, Gal 6^{16}, 2 Jn ^{3}, Jude ^{2}, indicate that it becomes us to go in prayer to seek the mercy which it remains always with God to bestow. It is noteworthy that mercy is added to the usual 'grace' and 'peace' of the salutations just in those places where some more intimate affection and tender sympathy is naturally to be expected (*e.g.* Gal 6^{16}, the Letters to Timothy, and Jude's Epistle). Whatever there is painful in the experience of believers constitutes for them a new need of the Divine mercy, and is to be explained as a part of God's purpose of greater good by saving them more and more completely from sin.

(2) *Its aim.*—The aim of God's mercy is expressed in Christ's words, 'That ye may be the children of your Father which is in heaven' (Mt 5^{45}). The parable of the Unmerciful Servant (Mt 18^{23}) sets forth the purpose of God negatively, and in 1 Jn 2^5 4$^{12.\ 17}$ the positive side is given. God's mercy or love to us comes to perfect realization when we have learned to be like Him. Because He loves us He will have us to be merciful, that we may be at our best. In this way also the progress of the Kingdom of God among men is assured, as we see in a concrete instance in 2 Co 4–7 (cf. Ac 20$^{18-35}$).

2. Mercy of man to man.—We have seen that it is the aim of the Divine mercy to reproduce itself in the spirits of men. As mercy has two parts, pity and active beneficence, we are commanded to love not in word, neither in tongue, but in deed and in truth (1 Jn 3^{18}). This is Christ's teaching in Mt 9^{13} 12^7 23^{23}, and in the parables of the Good Samaritan (Lk 10^{30}) and of the Sheep and the Goats (Mt 25^{31}), as well as in that of the Unmerciful Servant (Mt 18^{23}). From these we learn that if gratitude to God does not avail to make men merciful to one another, they will be dealt with by penalties (see also Ja 2^{13} 3^{17}, 1 Jn 2$^{9-11}$ 3^{15}). This right disposition of heart is a product not so much of enlightenment of the mind as of such experiences as touch the springs of affection. The passage in 2 Co 4–9, beginning 'as we have obtained mercy' (and, indeed, the whole Epistle), is a treasury of evangelical motives to philanthropic conduct. 'Our mouth is opened unto you, our heart is enlarged' (6^{11}). Similarly, in the case of St. Peter, 'Thou knowest that I love thee. . . . Feed my sheep' (Jn 21^{17}; cf. Ro 12^1 'I beseech you . . . by the mercies (οἰκτιρμοί) of God that ye present your bodies a living sacrifice').

Selflessness, and the constraint that Christ's love lays upon a believer, are the important features of his behaviour in this matter of mercifulness. 'Though I be nothing'; 'I will very gladly spend and be spent for you' (2 Co 12$^{12.\ 15}$). 'I am debtor . . . as much as in me is, I am ready' (Ro 1$^{14.\ 15}$). 'The love of Christ constraineth us' (2 Co 5^{14}). 'We ought to lay down our lives for the brethren' (1 Jn 3^{16}). When we look at Christ's own life for an example, we do not find in His case the indebtedness of one who has been forgiven, but we do find the readiness of unreserved surrender to His Father's will. 'I came not to do mine own will' (Jn 6^{38}). 'My doctrine is not mine, but his that sent me' (Jn 7^{16}). 'I have not spoken of myself' (Jn 12^{49}). Thus the mercy of God does not work *in vacuo*, but in the concrete example of Christ and of men possessed by His spirit, and made vehicles of His mercy (Ro 11^{31}, 1 Jn 4^{12}).

In the OT the word חֶסֶד 'mercy' is used of the duties of piety between kinsmen (Gn 20^{13}), or persons who are in covenant with each other (21^{23}). And it might seem in conflict with this that one of the most striking instances in which an appeal for mercy is disallowed in the NT is that of the rich man to his father Abraham (Lk 16^{24}). Similarly, Christ subordinated the ties of kindred (Lk 14^{26}) even with Himself (Mk 3^{33}, Lk 11^{28}) to the higher bonds of the Kingdom of God. Nevertheless the effect of Christian faith is to strengthen, and not to weaken, all the ties of human affection, raising them into the region of religion. The early motto of Christ's ministry was, 'I desire mercy and not sacrifice' (Mt 9^{13} 12^7); the same thought pervades the later chapters of the Gospel of John (13–17) and his First Epistle, *passim*, while both in Acts (20^{38} 21^{13}) and in his Epistles there is evidence of the overflowing, self-forgetting affection of St. Paul for the Christian Churches. The rule of pity and of active helpfulness is the teaching and the practice of Christ and His disciples. Mercy is the note of the Christian temper. See, further, artt. GRACE, KINDNESS.

LITERATURE.—Cremer, *Lexicon, s.v.* ἔλεος ; Hastings' *DB*, art. 'Mercy'; Seeley, *Ecce Homo*, chs. xix. xx. ; Dykes, *Manifesto of the King*, p. 101 ff. ; Paget, *Studies in the Christian Character*, p. 221 ff. ; Butler, *Serm.* v. vi. ix. xi. xii. ; Browning, *Ring and the Book*, x. ; C. Watson, *First Ep. of John* ; Dean Stanley *Corinthians*, vol. ii.   T. GREGORY.

MERIT.—The idea of merit in general is one which attaches to human conduct on the presupposition of the existence, in the first place, of a moral law ; in the second place, of free-will in man, enabling him to obey it ; and, in the third place, of some system of rewards and punishments, by which the worth of obedience to the Law is recognized, and equally the unworth of disobedience is demonstrated. That conduct is meritorious, or possesses merit, which corresponds with the moral law, and at the same time is voluntary ; and, as meritorious, it claims honour or reward. This is the general ethical conception of merit (cf. Martineau, *Types of Ethical Theory*^{3}, ii. 80 ff.). The theological use, however, of the conception, and still more of the term ('merit,' *meritum*), involves further specifications, which follow, on the one hand, from the connexion of the idea with other theological ideas, *e.g.* those of God, of His grace, and so on ; and, on the other hand, from the different analogies under which, from time to time, the relation of God to men has been conceived. Here we have two special cases of the use of the conception to consider : (1) its use in the Gospels ; (2) the use not only of the idea, but also of the theological term ' merit' in reference to the work of Christ.

1. The idea of merit in the Gospels.—We note, first, that the use of the conception is frequent in the Gospels in connexion with a general view of God as the Judge and Rewarder of good and evil deeds. This conception of God was in fact that dominant at the time of the ministry of our Lord, God's relation to men being commonly viewed under legal analogies. Compare the statement of Schultz (*op. cit. infr.*) :—

' When Christianity entered into the world and found its first expression in the dominant Jewish circles, as well as among the spokesmen of the idealistic Hellenic popular culture, the thought of a Divine repayment deciding according to legal standards, and therefore of a merit or demerit of men according to which their fate was to be settled, was a self-evident axiom. . . . With faith in God as the representative of the moral order of the world, there appeared to be self-evidently given the faith that He rewards and punishes according to the rule of human law.'

This statement of Schultz may be supplemented, with regard, in particular, to the doctrine of the Pharisees, which forms at once the background and the contrast of the teaching of Jesus, by the accounts of H. J. Holtzmann, *NT Theol.* i. p. 62 ff., and of Weber, *Jüd. Theol.*[2] p. 277 ff. In the Pharisaic theology the legal conception of God takes the sharpest possible form. The Law is thought of as the sum of so many precepts, the performance of each one of which establishes a separate and definite merit or claim to reward (Weber, p. 380 ff.).

' Just like a heavenly book-keeper, God reckons and calculates according to a standard quantitative as well as qualitative—here the sum of performances of the law and meritorious works, there the sum of transgressions and misdeeds' (Holtzmann, p. 63).

The idea of merit, however, does not end with the performance of the Law : it also attaches to ' good works,' *i.e.* voluntary acts beyond the strict requirement of the Law, but which are taken account of in the same way before God's judgment-seat, and avail to make up the shortcomings of a man's account. The principal of these good works are almsgiving and works of charity (Weber, p. 284). Finally, the idea of merit is brought specially into connexion with the question of ultimate salvation.

' The judgment on men before the heavenly court of justice takes place with reference to the question whether the man shall live or die—whether he shall be found worthy of the future Kingdom of God or not' (Weber, p. 278).

The teaching of Jesus now proceeds in agreement with the theology of the Pharisees, in so far as He not only continually speaks of the rewarding of our works by God, but also represents the Kingdom of God itself under the point of view of a reward, which is awarded to the performance of ' righteousness.' We have the general idea of work and reward in Mt $6^{1.\ 2.\ 3.\ 4.\ 6.\ 16.\ 18}$ $10^{41.\ 42}$ 20^{1-7} 24^{45-51} 25^{14-28}, Mk 9^{41}, Lk 6^{35} 10^7, Jn 4^{36}. For the Kingdom of God (life, or eternal life) as reward, cf. Mt 6^{20} 19^{17} 25^{31-46}, Mk $10^{29.\ 30}$.

The limitations set to the idea of merit in the teaching of Jesus, as compared with its use in the theology of the Pharisees, are, however, very striking. (*a*) First of all, we have to notice the change involved by the difference in the conception of God. While with the Pharisees the idea of God as Lawgiver and Judge is dominant, with Jesus this idea is subordinated to *the conception of God as Father*. The idea of reward itself, in fact, is

connected with that of God's Fatherhood (Mt $6^{1.\ 4.\ 6.\ 18}$). What this implied is thus stated by Schultz :—

' Since Jesus has taught His disciples to see the true understanding of their relation to God in the figure of child and father, then the thought of merit in the sense of the law is in general completely irreconcilable with the figure' (p. 15).

Only an *ethical*, not a legal, conception of merit is therefore possible along the lines of the teaching of Jesus.

(*b*) Jesus criticised the Pharisaic doctrine of reward according to strict legal merit, by teaching that the reward which God gives is *not according to debt, but according to grace*. We have here to remember that when Jesus illustrates, as He frequently does, the relation of God to men by that of a master and his household servants (cf. Mt 24^{45-51} 25^{14-30}, Lk 17^9), this excludes the idea of legal merit.

' A servant in the sense of antiquity cannot win merit. He is δοῦλος ἀχρεῖος, even when he has done all he should (Lk 17^9). The Lord can reward him, but that remains at bottom an act of good-pleasure' (Schultz, p. 15).   •

The point is made still clearer by the one parable where Jesus introduces a relation in which merit and reward are possible, speaking not of household servants, but of hired labourers (Mt 20^{1-16}). Here

' He emphasizes in intentional paradox that the lord in his goodness will not bind himself to this rule—that he indeed redeems his promise, but reserves to himself the right to transcend the measure of the law in free sovereignty' (*ib.*).

Cf., on the same point, Holtzmann (i. p. 196) :—

' This remarkable parable annuls the idea of reward in applying it, completely destroys the relation of merit and right, of performance and reward in general.'

We note, finally, to the same effect, the *gracious abundance* of the reward in Mk 10^{30}, Mt $24^{46.\ 47}$ 25^{21-23}, Lk 6^{38}.

(*c*) Another criticism which Jesus passes on the legal idea of merit is that it is *too external*. God, the Father, looks at the heart. The better righteousness, which admits to the Kingdom, is an inward righteousness (cf. Mt 5^{20}–6^{18}). But this affects the whole conception of merit and reward.

' The reward belongs to the personality which reveals itself in the work, not to the performance as such. . . . Thus, what appears as reward is at bottom the recognition of the worth of the personality. . . . It is the conduct of life, the πρᾶξις, which appears in the single acts, and is rewarded (Mt 16^{27}) . . . as it is the love shown to the brothers of Christ which is recognized in the judgment (Mt 25^{34ff}.)' (Schultz, p. 14).

To sum up, then, we do not in the teaching of Jesus get a completely unified doctrine of merit, but we get clear indications of the lines which such a doctrine must follow. It must be ethical rather than legal ; must connect itself with the conception of God's Fatherhood, and with the idea of His free grace, rather than with that of His strict retribution according to law ; and must have regard not to external actions only, but to the inward motive. The conditions are fulfilled if we recognize human merit as the worth to the Heavenly Father of the conduct of His sons when judged by the inward motive of filial obedience, and its reward as the recognition of this worth by His Fatherly love, which gives to His children who seek His Kingdom both this chief good and all things else that they need (Lk $6^{31.\ 32}$). As regards the individual actions of God's children, the idea of merit is not to be connected with them apart from the general context of filial conduct in which they stand ; nor is the idea of reward to be connected with particular Divine gifts apart from the gift of the Kingdom. Only on the background of the general conception of the reward of filial conduct by the gift of the Kingdom can particular gifts appear as the reward of particular actions.

2. The merit of Christ.—The definite theological doctrine, in which the term ' merit' is employed as a *terminus technicus* of the subject, lies beyond the NT. But it is anticipated in the latter, in so far as we there have a doctrine of Christ's work as man, in which ethical standards are applied to the subject. (*a*) In this doctrine it is above all upon His *death* that attention is concentrated, as the point in which the character of His saving work specially appears. We have first the idea of Christ's death as an act of *obedience* to God (Ro 5[19], Ph 2[8], He 10[5-10]). Further approximation to the idea of a merit of Christ is contained in the references to the *worth* of His death in procuring the salvation of men. It is a ransom (Mk 10[45]), a price (1 Co 6[20]). In the idea of *sacrifice* once more we have both the idea of the worth to God of Christ's death as self-surrender, and of its worth for men in procuring salvation (Eph 5[2], He 10[5-10]). [The important series of passages further defining the sacrifice of Christ as an expiatory sacrifice is not brought in here; since these passages, so far as they contain this additional idea, belong properly to the Scripture proof of the doctrine of Christ's work, not as *directly* meriting salvation, but as making satisfaction for sin, and so making salvation possible. In virtue of the general idea of sacrifice contained in them, apart from the specification of it as expiatory, they may, however, be added to the proof of the doctrine of merit]. We have, further, references in the NT to the *recognition* of Christ's death by God. On account of it the Father loves Him (Jn 10[17]); because of His obedience in it God exalts Him to universal lordship (Ph 2[9-11]). [Compare the Divine recognition of the worth of the work of the Suffering Servant in Is 53[10-12]]. (*b*) The conception of the work of Christ is not, however, confined to His death. His *life* is a ministry to men (Mk 10[45]). His work (Jn 17[4]) includes the manifestation of the Divine name to the disciples (v.[6]), the giving to them of the words received from the Father (v.[8]), the keeping of them from the evil in the world (v.[12]), as well as His final sacrifice (v.[19]). Moreover, it is not only the death of Christ, but His work throughout His life, that God recognizes in glorifying in turn the Son who has glorified Him (vv.[1-4]). And, finally, both Mk 10[45] and Jn 17 imply that the work of Christ in His life and death is all of a piece; since in both passages, but especially in Jn 17, there is no break in the way in which the culminating work of the death is added on to the work of the life.

Summing up our results, we have in the NT the basis of a doctrine of Christ's merit as the worth to God (and men) of His human work carried on throughout His life, and culminating in His death. This worth of Christ's work is estimated by God along the lines of Christ's obedience to His will (the work of Christ being that which the Father has given Him to do (Jn 4[24] 17[4])). It is recognized by God in the special love with which He regards Christ in the accomplishment of His work, and outwardly by His exaltation or glorification. It is to be noted, however, that while the position of lordship is viewed as the reward of the work of Christ, the salvation of men is not viewed in the NT as its direct *reward*, but rather as its *fruit* or *effect* (Jn 12[24]). Christ saves, according to NT conceptions, by His earthly work, but not by means of it as a *quantum* which can be detached from His Personality, and rewarded by the salvation of men [as in the conception of the ecclesiastical doctrine of Christ's merit, presently to be discussed]. Instead of this, we have the conception that through His work He becomes a saving Personality, or, as Rothe puts it, that through it He 'qualifies Himself to become a Redeemer' (*Theol. Ethik.*[2] iii. p. 104). Our salvation follows from His work; since the Christ, who lived to minister

to men, to make known to them the words which the Father had given Him, and to keep them from the evil, and persevered in His work to the death in perfect obedience to the will of His Father, thus offering up His life as a sacrifice to God, by this very work and the Personality achieved through it, exercises a saving authority and influence over men (Jn 12[32]; cf. the similar idea in Is 53[11], where the righteous Servant justifies many through his *knowledge*, and thus sees of the travail of his soul and is satisfied. But the open recognition of Christ's work by God in the exaltation of Christ, which begins with the Resurrection, also contributes to His saving power over men (cf. Ro 4[25] 'raised for our justification'); inasmuch as a human personality influences us not only by its inner worth, but also through the outward manifestation and revelation of that worth. Thus in the NT the Saviourhood of Christ is connected specially with His Lordship (Ac 5[31], 2 P 1[11]). The name which is above every name (Ph 2[11]) is the name of salvation (Ac 5[12]). Cf. also the use of the name *Christ*, which implies both Saviourhood and Lordship, in special reference to the state of exaltation (Ac 2[36]; St. Paul also always thinks of the *risen* Lord as the Saviour). It is at this point that the way in which human salvation can be regarded as the 'reward' of the work of Christ becomes clearest, inasmuch as the exaltation which is His direct reward puts Him in the position to reap the full fruit of His travail in the salvation of souls.

Two more points are necessary to complete our outline of the suggestions of the NT towards a doctrine of Christ's merit. In the first place, there is required (*c*) a closer definition of Christ's *saving power*. What is the work by which He saves? It is, above all, the revelation of the holy love of God in Christ's life and death, which moves men at once to faith in God as revealed in Him, and to repentance (μετάνοια, change of mind from love of sin to love of God), and thus brings them into that communion with the Father which is the essential ground of all the blessings of salvation. Christ's love towards men and His holiness, in the absolute unity of His Person, are a manifestation of the love and the holiness of God, as existing in a similar absolute personal unity; and the trust and repentance which Christ inspires are directed through Him to God. For proof of these statements, the following passages, amongst others, may be referred to. According to Jn 1[14-18] the grace and truth of Christ declare the invisible God. In Ro 5[15] the grace of Christ is equivalent to the grace of God. In Ro 8[35-39] the love of Christ reveals the love of God. Further, in Jn 17[11. 25] the Father whom Christ reveals is the holy, the righteous Father. Jesus awakes not only trust in the love of God (Ro 5[8] 8[35-39]), but also repentance towards God (Ac 5[31]; cf. the Pauline idea of baptism into Christ's death and resurrection as involving a death to sin and new life unto God, Ro 6[1-11]). Finally, to know God as revealed in Christ is eternal life, or the sum of all blessings (Jn 17[3]).

(*d*) In the second place, the above definition of the work of Christ as the revelation of the holy love of God, throws further light upon the 'reward' of Christ. We saw that while this meant primarily the recognition of Christ's work by God in His exaltation, it involved indirectly the fruit or effect of the work of Christ, as realized through this. But now it appears that the whole conception of the reward of Christ by God is subordinate to the idea of the *immanence* of God in His work. The work of Christ is not only the work which God has given Him to do (Jn 4[34] 17[4]), but God works through Him; so that the value to God of the work of Christ consists ultimately in His voluntary self-surrender to be the personal instrument in the world of the saving revelation of God, and the recognition of this work by God in the exaltation of Christ, which yields Him the fruit of His work in the salvation of men, is, at the same time, included in the execution of God's own purpose of salvation. Thus the *ethical* doctrine of the work of Christ culminates ultimately in the wholly *religious* view of it (2 Co 3[19]; cf. the subordination of the work of Christ to the grace of God in Ro 3[24-28]).

Such is the outline of a doctrine of Christ's merit, as sketched in the NT. The agreement of it with the ethical lines of Christ's own general teaching on merit, as previously stated, is apparent. There is the same stress on the inner motive of obedience, the same domination of the whole subject by the idea of God's Fatherhood; while the exaltation of Christ is the analogue of the gift to His people of the Kingdom, in which they share His Lordship (Lk 22[29], 2 Ti 2[12]).

Very different is the ecclesiastical doctrine of Christ's merit, which, beginning with Anselm's *Cur Deus Homo*, extends throughout both the Catholic and the Protestant scholasticism. Here an idea of merit is applied to the work of Christ, which is essentially the same as that of the Pharisaic theology, rejected by Jesus. This idea exists as a general conception illustrating the relation of man to God from the time of Tertullian onwards, who introduced from the vocabulary of Roman law the term *meritum*, and its cognates *mereri, promereri, demereri*, to define it (cf. Harnack, *Dogmengeschichte*[3], iii. p. 16, n. 1). As employed by Anselm to elucidate the work of Christ, it includes the following points. (1) The work of Christ is regarded as a voluntary work or performance, lying outside of the sphere of Christ's proper obligation to God. Anselm thinks of Christ as bound as man to obedience to God in His life, but as sinless man, free from obligation to die: hence His voluntary death is a work, which He can and does offer to God to procure the salvation of men. (2) The value of this work to God is estimated, not qualitatively by its motive, but quantitatively by the dignity of the Person who performs it. (3) The reward of Christ's work follows from God's justice, and the conception of this is equally external with that of the work itself, the reward being transferable from Christ to His people just like a sum of money 'Whom could He more justly make the heirs of His debt (*i.e.* the reward which God owes Him), which He does not Himself need, than His relatives and brethren?' (*Cur Deus Homo*, lib. ii. cap. 9).

The Catholic schoolmen after Anselm, and the Protestant schoolmen after them, continue the Anselmic doctrine of merit, not, however, without many changes. Of these the most important are as follows. Peter Lombard, following Ph 2[9-11], adds that Christ merited not only salvation for us, but exaltation and glory for Himself (*Sent.* lib. iii. dist. 18). Thomas Aquinas and Duns Scotus no longer deduce the reward of Christ's merit from God's justice, as does Anselm, but either from a relative justice or equity, such as that implied in Roman law by the relation of father and son, or lord and slave (Aquinas, *Summa Theologiæ*, II. i. 104. 1), or from God's mere good pleasure (Scotus in *Sent.* lib. iii. dist. 20, qu. 1). By the Protestant schoolmen the material content of Christ's merit is enlarged by the addition of the general obedience of Christ's life, as voluntary, to the special voluntary obedience of His death (which latter they view not as a gift to God, but as an endurance of the penalties of sin). None of these changes, however, *essentially* alters the Anselmic conception of merit. Two points in particular stand fast throughout, viz. the idea of Christ's work as something voluntary and unowed, and the entirely external conception of it as a *quantum*, whose value can be assessed and rewarded by another quantum of corresponding value. Only in the idea, first fully developed, after Bernard and Lombard, by Aquinas, and continued especially in the Reformed theology, that the 'transfer' of Christ's merit to His people is mediated through His mystic unity as Head with them as His members, is the hard, juristic outline of the Anselmic doctrine transcended (cf. *Summa Theol.* iii. 46. 1). By the end of the Protestant scholasticism, however, the disparateness of the traditional idea of merit from anything in the NT had become clear to the theologians within Protestantism of a critical tendency. The Arminian Limborch says of this idea, along with that of satisfaction : 'Since they do not stand in Scripture, but have been invented by men, no one is bound to the meaning of them any further than it can be construed from the phrases of Scripture, to elucidate the sense of which they have been applied' (*Theologia Christiana*, lib. iii. cap. 21. 1). In the period of theological reconstruction since Schleiermacher, the general tendency of theologians, so far as they have not simply repeated older ideas, or dissolved theology into philosophy, has been either to reject the term 'merit' altogether, as being too much associated with the scholastic conception of it, or, if it has been retained, to reinterpret it along more Scriptural lines. Ritschl, above all, has succeeded in transforming into firm dogmatic conceptions the outlines of the NT doctrine, as above stated. See his exhaustive treatment of the whole subject in *Justification and Reconciliation*, vol. iii. [Eng. tr. p. 434 ff.].

LITERATURE.—Schultz, 'Der sittliche Begriff des Verdienstes

und seine Anwendung auf das Verständniss des Werkes Christi' in *SK*, 1894, p. 9 ; Ritschl, *Rechtfertigung und Versöhnung*[3], 3 vols. 1889 [Eng. tr. (*Justification and Reconciliation*) of 1st vol. from 1st ed. 1872, of 3rd vol. from 3rd ed. 1902] ; H. J. Holtzmann, *NT Theol.* 1897 ; Wendt, *Lehre Jesu*[2], 1901 [Eng. tr. from 1st ed. 1893] ; Anselm's *Cur Deus Homo* in Migne's *Patr. Lat.* tom. 158, also in separate ed. (Nutt), 1894.

ROBERT S. FRANKS.

MESSENGER.—The word is formed from 'message' with intrusive nasal. It is used as the equivalent of ἄγγελος in its primary meaning of one sent on a message or to make an announcement. So it occurs frequently in the OT (representing מַלְאָךְ of Heb. and ἄγγελος of LXX), and in the Gospels in Lk 7[24] 9[52]. It is to be observed, however, that in 'messenger' the emphasis is on the sending or mission, while in ἄγγελος it is on the message or proclamation. Philologically a truer equivalent is ἀπόστολος; and accordingly in two instances (2 Co 8[23], Ph 2[25]), where missionary preachers are so described and where some special mission is in view, the latter is the Greek term used.

1. Towards the close of the OT the term seems to have acquired the meaning of a special or inspired teacher. Thus in Hag 1[13] the prophet styles himself 'messenger' as the bearer of Jehovah's message. A similar meaning is at least probable in Job 33[23]. And this usage is in some degree paralleled in the modern tendency to seek a definite 'message' in the literary works of distinguished poets and thinkers. The most important use of the term is in Malachi, a prophet whose name [if מַלְאָכִי be, indeed, his *name* ; cf. Mal 1[1] and the Comm. *ad loc.*] means 'my messenger.' He uses the term three times and in three applications. First, it is a designation of the true priest, whose work is to conserve spiritual knowledge and teach the law of God (2[7]). Secondly and thirdly, in 3[1] it is applied to a forerunner, and to the 'messenger of the covenant,' who seems to be identical with the Person styled 'the Lord whom you seek.' These two applications are in the NT interpreted of the Baptist and the Messiah respectively. The words of the prophet with reference to the forerunner are with a change of pronoun ('thee' for 'me') repeated in identical form in each of the Synoptics (Mk 1[2], Mt 11[10], Lk 7[27]). In these quotations, as in Lk 9[52], the messenger is one sent before to proclaim or to prepare. The direct application of the term to Jesus is not made in the NT, though a kindred idea is frequently expressed : in the saying which occurs in all the Gospels, 'He that receiveth me receiveth him that sent me' (Mt 10[40], Mk 9[37], Lk 9[48] 10[16], Jn 13[20] 12[44]) ; in the frequent Johannine phrase 'whom God hath sent,' and in the commission (Jn 20[21]) ; and even in the term 'gospel' (εὐαγγέλιον), which is expressive of what Jesus described Himself as anointed of God and sent to preach (Lk 4[18]). The conceptions of Christ as the Revealer of the Father and the incarnate Word are also kindred ; and it might be argued that the language of Malachi was in the mind of the writer of the Epistle to the Hebrews in 1[2] 3[1] 7[22] and throughout.

R. SCOTT.

2. In He 6[20] our Lord is spoken of as our **Forerunner** (πρόδρομος) 'within the veil.' This is the only place in the NT where the title is used. A πρόδρομος (in the literal sense) was a messenger sent in front of the main army to examine the ground, clear the front of obstacles, or notify the presence of an enemy to the main body advancing behind (*i.e.* a scout, light-armed soldier, or spy). Here it is connected with the priestly work of our Lord. He has entered within the veil 'for us,' as our 'high priest for ever after the order of Melchizedek, *i.e.* in our interest, namely, to obtain pardon for us (9[12]), to represent us in the presence of God

(v. [24]), and to open up for us an entrance into heaven itself (10[19])' (Lünemann in Meyer's *Com.*). Probably, however, the military connotation is not to be entirely ignored. Just as an army advances securely under cover of its scouts far in front, so the army of believers moves on through the valley of the shadow of death without fear, knowing that our great Forerunner is in front. He has encountered and conquered death for us, so that we have no need to fear anything. This thought is beautifully elaborated from another point of view in Jn 14[2. 3]. When Jesus came back for a moment from the silent land, it was not with an air of terror or defeat, but as a conqueror, crying 'All hail!' (Mt 28[9]). There is nothing to fear in the Beyond whither Jesus has gone before us 'to prepare a place for us.'   E. GRIFFITH-JONES.

MESSIAH is the English word based on the Greek representation of the original Hebrew or Aramaic. The Gr. reproduction assumes the varied forms Μεσίας, Μεσσίας, and Μεσείας, corresponding to the Hebrew מָשִׁיחַ and the Aramaic מְשִׁיחָא. The Heb. is the normal *katîl* form, meaning 'anointed,' which is tr. into Greek in the term which has become so familiar, χριστός, the *agnomen* of our Lord. The Heb. מָשִׁיחַ was a term applied pre-eminently to the king, who was designated to office by the ceremony of anointing (1 S 9[16] 10[1], 2 K 9[2. 3. 6]). Priests were consecrated to office in like manner (Lv 8[12], cf. 4[3. 16]).

i. *ANOINTING OF KINGS.*—The custom of anointing the king, from which his designation as 'messiah' arose, is connected with magical usages of hoary antiquity, based on the conception that the smearing or pouring of the unguent on the body endows the human subject with certain qualities. Thus the Arabs of Eastern Africa believe that an unguent of lion's fat inspires a man with boldness, and makes the wild beasts flee in terror from him. Other illustrations may be found in Frazer's *Golden Bough*[2], ii. 364 ff. The Tell el-Amarna inscriptions show that this custom of anointing the king with oil prevailed in Western Asia at least as far back as B.C. 1450. The passage to which we refer occurs in a letter from a certain Rammân-nirâri of Nuḫašši in Northern Syria addressed to the king of Egypt, in which it is stated that a former king of Egypt [Thothmes III.] had 'poured oil on the head' of Rammân-nirâri's grandfather and established him as king of Nuḫašši.[*] Frazer's great work has rendered us familiar with the supernatural endowments of a king who was regarded as a *quasi*-deity.[†] That ancient Israel also believed that the royal dignity involved supernatural Divine powers, and that the oil poured upon the king conveyed these powers (like the 'laying on of hands'), can hardly admit of doubt. The oil, like the sprinkled blood in a covenant-rite[‡] (Ex 24[6ff.]), possessed a magical virtue.[§]

Like the priest, the king was regarded as a Divine intermediary, and assumed the supreme ritual functions of a priest in his own person. Among the ancient Semites, especially the Babylonians and Assyrians, the earthly ruler or king was considered to be the supreme God's representative or viceroy. Sometimes he declares himself the 'son of the deity' (*e.g.* in the opening line of Ashurbanipal's cylinder-inscription he calls himself *binutu Ashûr u Bêlit*, 'offspring of Ashur and Beltis'; cf. the language of Ps 2[7]), or 'favourite of the deity' (cf. the name of the Bab. monarch *Naram-Sin*, 'beloved of Sin.' Sargon calls himself in the opening of his Nimrûd insc. 'the favourite of Anu and Bel'). Further parallels in the case of Nebuchadrezzar may be found in Schrader, *COT* ii. 105 ff. See also Tiele, *Bab.-Assyr. Gesch.* 491 ff. Tiglath-pileser I. (B.C. 1100) calls himself *issakku* (PA-TE-SI) of the God Ashur (Prism-Insc. col. vii. 62. 63), *i.e.* Ashur's plenipotentiary. That in this sacred function priestly office was involved may be readily inferred. Thus Ashurbanipal (like Sargon) calls himself not only the *saknu* or vicegerent of Bêl, but also the *sangu* or priest of Ashur. Similarly the Homeric kings offer sacrifice on behalf of the people. As Robertson Smith remarks ('Priest' in *EBr*[9]), the king in both Greece and Rome was the acting head of the State-religion. So also in ancient pre-exilian Israel, David and Solomon offered sacrifices (2 S 6[17ff.], 1 K 8[63]) in accordance with the tradition of the age.

ii. *UNIQUE POSITION OF DAVID IN HEBREW THOUGHT.*—Among the Hebrew anointed kings or messiahs, *David* came in course of time to have a special significance. His importance was enhanced by the history of the three centuries that followed his reign. No Israelite or Jew living in the year B.C. 730 could have failed to note the striking contrast between the unbroken continuity of monarchs of the seed of David sitting on the throne of Jerusalem and the succession of brief dynasties and usurping kings who followed one another on the throne of Samaria. The swiftly passing series of short reigns terminated by violence which filled the space of 15 years in Northern Israel from the close of the dynasty of Jehu (which lasted nearly a century) to the accession of Hoshea, Assyria's nominee, to the dismembered kingdom, deeply impressed the prophet of Ephraim, who exclaims :—

'They have appointed kings, but not from me (*i.e.* Jahweh); Have made princes, but I knew them not' (Hos 8[4]).

It is not surprising, amid the rapid changes of rulers and the disasters wrought by foreign invasion, that Hosea should have prophesied the discipline of exile for his faithless countrymen, and as its final issue that they should return and seek Jahweh their God and 'David their king.'[*] For amid all the vicissitudes of the last three centuries the seed of David had survived every peril. The 'sure mercies of David' to which the Jews still clung, though with feeble hope, in the dark days of exile (Is 55[3]), began in the age of Isaiah to take root in the national imagination. Though Judah was destined to suffer terrible chastisements, yet as a result of the disciplinary trial 'a remnant would return' (*i.e.* be converted) to Jahweh, and Jerusalem would be preserved from the onslaughts of the Assyrian foe. The Immanuel prophecy, which contained the assurance of God's presence among His people, delivered to the doubting Ahaz and his unbelieving court during the dark days of B.C. 735, became the germ of a great series of Messianic passages which are found in Is 9[1-6] [Eng. [2-7]], which was probably composed soon after B.C. 701, in 11[1-9], and, lastly, in 32[1-3]. In the first the Messiah is portrayed as a military conquering hero, 'breaking in pieces the oppressor's mace'; in the second, the sounds of discord cease, and He, sprung from Jesse's stock, is the ruler of justice and peace in God's 'holy mountain' of Zion, where even the

---

[*] Winckler, *Thontafeln von Tell el-Amarna* (vol. v. in Schrader's *KIB*), Letter 37 (p. 98).

[†] *Golden Bough*[2], i. 137–156; cf. also his *Lectures on the Early History of the Kingship* (1905).

[‡] According to Westermarck, the blood shed possesses a magical power of conveying a curse ('Magic and Social Relations' in *Sociological Papers*, vol. ii. p. 160). In the case of a covenant the curse falls if the covenant be not fulfilled.

[§] Thus shields were smeared with oil to render them or their owners immune (2 S 1[21], cf. Is 21[5]). Saul's shield was *un*anointed, and so its owner perished).

[*] There is not a shred of evidence to show that this clause is not genuine in Hos 3[5]. It is difficult to see why, if the idea 'had its roots in Isaiah's time' and not in that out of which Ezk 34[23] 37[24f.] 45[8. 9] and Jer 30[9] arose (Harper, *ad loc.*), we should follow Wellhausen in rejecting the clause. Nowack rejects the entire verse.

powers of violence and injustice are turned into submission to a Divine authority. In the last He is again the King who shall reign in righteousness, 'a hiding-place from the wind, a covert from the tempest.'

All these passages, as well as Is 2²⁻⁴, are regarded by Duhm as Isaianic. On the other hand, Cheyne, Hackmann, and Marti hold that they are post-exilic,* but on what the present writer considers to be insufficient grounds. The subject is discussed by Cheyne in his *Introd. to Isaiah*, pp. 44 ff., 57 ff., and 173–176 ; also by Hackmann, *Die Zukunftserwartung des Jesaia*, pp. 126–156, and by Marti in his Commentary on the above passages ; cf. also his *Gesch. der Isr. Religion*⁴, p. 191 footn., 255 ff. On the other side, see the Commentaries of Duhm and Dillmann-Kittel (1898) on these passages, and the *Century Bible*, Com. on 'Isaiah' by the present writer. Kautzsch, in his elaborate art. 'Religion of Israel' in Hastings' *DB* (Extra Vol. p. 696ª), admits the reasonableness of the view here advocated.

After the gleams of hope awakened by Hezekiah and the deliverance of Jerusalem, and after the glowing anticipations of an ideal Messianic King clothed with Divine powers, to which Isaiah in the early years of the 7th cent. gave expression, there followed a time of reaction when these high hopes suffered temporary eclipse. Men's hearts became sick of waiting. The long reign of Manasseh, followed by the brief reign of Amon, was a period of religious as well as political decline. On the other hand, the reign of Josiah reawakened the hopes of the faithful adherents of Jahweh, and it is significant that Messianic expectation revives in the oracles of Jeremiah. In 23⁵⁻⁸ (cf. 30⁹) he foretells the coming days when a righteous branch or shoot shall be raised unto David, who shall reign prudently and execute judgment and justice. In his days Judah shall be saved and Israel shall dwell secure, and the name by which he shall be called is 'Jahweh is our righteousness.' This fragment probably belongs to the earlier utterances of Jeremiah, and upon it Zechariah in the opening years of the post-exilic period bases his well-known prophecies (3⁸ 6¹²), in which Joshua and his comrades are addressed as tokens of the coming of Jahweh's servant 'the branch' (3⁸). In 6¹² it is made clear that Zerubbabel of the seed of David is meant, who is destined to complete the building of the Temple.† With the passage in Jer 23⁵⁻⁸ cf. also 30⁹ 33¹⁵ as well as Ezk 21³² 34²³⁻³¹ 37²⁴. In Jeremiah less stress is laid on the personal and material features, more emphasis placed on the ethical. Also it appears from several passages that Jeremiah thought rather of a succession of rulers of Davidic descent than of a single ruler. But in determining this question the utmost critical caution is required. Thus 33¹⁴⁻²⁴ is regarded by most critics as a later addition to the oracles of Jeremiah (see, *e.g.*, Giesebrecht's Com., and Cornill in *SBOT*). Certainly after the time of Jeremiah the personal features in Messianic prophecy became fainter. 'There shall not be cut off from David one that sits upon the throne of the house of Israel' (Jer 33¹⁷), points to a succession of rulers at a time when the hopes of Israel still clung to the 'sure mercies of David.' But this utterance, as we have already seen, belongs to a later time than that of Jeremiah. Zephaniah and Obadiah make no reference to the Messianic King. When we consider their historic environment, this is not surprising. For royalty in Judah was rapidly

* Recently Prof. R. H. Kennett has discussed Is 9¹⁻⁷ in *JThSt* (April 1906), and would assign it to the Maccabæan period. The epithets are referred to Simon the Maccabee.

† Duhm deals very arbitrarily with these passages. Jer 23⁵⁻⁸ was not the genuine utterance of Jeremiah, but a post-exilic addition. Zec 3⁸ 6¹² are badly corrupted, and later editors have sought to eliminate the name of Zerubbabel from the original oracle, because Zechariah's prophecies with respect to him were not fulfilled.

Probably Mic 5¹⁻⁸, like Jer 23⁵⁻⁸, may be assigned to the earlier years of the reign of Josiah, when the religious and political outlook of Judah appeared more hopeful, and the overthrow of Assyria seemed as probable as it did to Isaiah after B.C. 701 (Is 9³ ⁴ [Heb.]). We may assign Nah 2²⁻3¹⁹ to the same period.

declining in power and prestige. The last kings of Judah became mere puppets in the hands of foreign princes, who pulled the strings from the banks of the Nile or of the Euphrates. Under these circumstances the ideal of a Davidic ruler ceased to appeal as powerfully as it did a century earlier, and ultimately gave place to another. It is marvellous that it continued to survive after the rude shocks of a hundred years.

Its survival is probably due to *Ezekiel*, the priest-prophet, herald of restoration, of hope and of reconstructive effort. This prophet was an earnest student of Israel's past, and read its records and its oracles. The influence not only of his great elder contemporary Jeremiah, but also of the earlier prophets Hosea and Isaiah, is unmistakable. The influence of the first and the last is clear in Ezk 34²³⁻³¹ 'And I will set over them a shepherd, and he shall feed them, even my servant David ; . . . and I the Lord will be a God unto them, and my servant David a prince in their midst.' Here, as in the case of Jer 23⁵⁻⁸, David represents a succession of Davidic descendants sitting on his throne. When we turn to Ezekiel's ideal scheme of the restored Jewish theocracy (chs. 40–48), we find that the secular prince of Davidic lineage falls into the background, and his functions are subordinated to the ecclesiastical routine. The same fate in the early post-exilic period befalls the somewhat shadowy, if stately, figure of Zerubbabel in Zec 4 and 6 (cf. Hag 2²²), who was soon destined to subside into the background in the presence of Joshua the high priest, the natural and legitimate head of the newly constituted Church-nation. In truth, the Messianic King rapidly becomes a vanished ideal of prophecy. In the closing verses (¹⁴⁻²⁰) of Zephaniah (obviously an addition belonging to the late-exilic or early post-exilic period) it is Jahweh who is Israel's King in the midst of His people, their mighty Hero who wards off the nation's foes (vv. ¹⁵⁻¹⁹).

When we turn to the *Deutero-Isaiah* (40–55), we find that an entirely new ideal, to which reference has already been made, had displaced the earlier and older one created by Isaiah. In place of the national-Messianic King we have the national-prophetic ideal of the Suffering Servant of Jahweh, through whose humiliation and sorrow the sinning nation shall find peace. God's anointed king, who is not of Davidic descent at all, but the *Persian* Cyrus, is the chosen instrument for accomplishing the Divine purposes with respect to His servant Jacob (44²⁸ 45¹⁻⁴). We shall have to note how profoundly the Deutero-Isaianic portraiture of the Suffering Servant came in later times to modify the Hebrew ideal of the Messiah, and to constitute an entirely new conception which the Hebrew race only partially and very slowly assimilated, and whose leaven worked powerfully in the Messianic ideal of the 'Son of Man' in the consciousness of Christ and His immediate followers.

When we pass to the *Trito-Isaiah* (56–66), which probably arose in the years that immediately preceded the advent of Nehemiah, we find that the old ideal of the Davidic Messiah, which Ezekiel and Haggai attempted with poor success to revive, has altogether disappeared. Not even in the lyrical collection (60–62) is the faintest note to be heard of a Messianic Jewish King. The prophecies of Malachi are equally silent. We have to wait for centuries—perhaps as late as the declining days of the Hasmonæans—before the Davidic Messianic King definitely and clearly reappears.

Before we pass to the Greek period (B.C. 300 and later), it is necessary to refer briefly to a series of OT passages of a Messianic or reputed Messianic character. (1) Gn 3¹⁵ (belonging to the earlier Jahwistic document, J¹) can only by a strained interpretation be regarded as Messianic at all. The seed of the woman and the serpent (representing the power of evil) are to be engaged in prolonged conflict, in which both suffer injury. In this struggle it is not expressly stated which side will triumph (so Dillmann). (2) Gn 49¹⁰ is exceedingly obscure. The rendering, 'as long as one comes to Shiloh' (Hitzig, Tuch), is doubtful in point of Hebrew usage, and difficult to sustain historically ; 'until one comes to Shiloh' seems quite as difficult to sustain historically. The Greek versions attribute to the phrase an obscure Messianic reference, but interpret שלה as a late Hebrew compound form with a relative, which can be accepted only after making violent assumptions.* Giesebrecht ingeniously proposed to read in place of שלה the form מֹשְׁלָה 'his ruler.' He rightly argues that to read שִׁלֹּה as the LXX presupposes, immediately followed by וְלוֹ, constitutes a very awkward and intolerable combination.† If we accept this emendation, the passage may be regarded as Messianic. But it is most probably an insertion moulded on Ezk 21³², for it stands in no immediate relation to the verses that precede or follow.‡ (3) 2 S 7⁴⁻¹⁷. Here vv.¹⁵. ¹⁶ are the expression, placed in the mouth of the prophet Nathan, of the sentiment of reverence to the House of David, which took its rise in the latter part of the 8th century. Budde refers this speech of Nathan and the following prayer of David to a later period than the other more primitive sections of the historical narrative, and we may reasonably follow him in ascribing this passage to the 7th cent.—not improbably the same period as that in which Jer 23⁵⁻⁸ and 30⁹ arose.§ (4) Nu 24¹⁷ 'A star hath marched (? gleamed) out of Jacob, and a sceptre hath arisen out of Israel, and hath broken in pieces the sides (temples) of Moab, and hath destroyed all the sons of Seth' (?). The text is here difficult, and 'many points are uncertain. The entire series of Balaam's oracles are brought together by the redactor of the J and E documents, and the reference of the lyric passage just cited may be either to David (2 S 8²) or to Omri (cf. insc. of Mesha, lines 4–8, and art. 'Omri' in Hastings' DB).‖ Its Messianic interpretation by early Christian writers (Justin Martyr, Irenæus), as well as by Rabbi Aḳiba, who referred it to Bar Cochba in the days of Hadrian (cf. also the Targums of Onkelos and Jon.), need not detain us. (5) Dt 18¹⁵ 'A prophet shall Jahweh thy God raise up unto thee from thy midst from thy brethren, like unto me. To him shall ye hearken.' This passage is quoted in Ac 3²² 7³⁷ as having an individual Messianic reference. But the context (cf. the verses that immediately precede) clearly proves that the reference is general, and not individual. The Israelites are not to pay heed to the magician or soothsayer, but to God's true prophet, like Moses, whom He will raise up in Israel from time to time (see Driver's Com. in ICC). (6) Lastly, we have a series of Psalm passages. Pss 2 (esp. v.5ff.). 72. 89. 110 may be taken as the most conspicuous examples of the revived Messianic expectation. They all belong to the Greek period. Ps 2, like Ps 1 (both without superscription), was evidently placed by the redactors at the head of the Psalm collection, and belongs to a late period. Ps 2, like Ps 110, originates from the Maccabæan days, when the old conception of the national deliverer from foreign enemies, which was created by Isaiah after Judah's emergence from a desperate crisis, once more revived.

Before we come to deal with the later phases of Messianic expectation, we would here note the historic evolution of three distinct lines of anticipation respecting the human agency whereby Israel's salvation and the establishment of a Divine and righteous rule would be effected. (1) The *righteous Messianic warrior-king* of Davidic descent. (2) The *prophetic sufferer* portrayed in Is 40–55, and esp. in 52¹³–53¹² — a conception which may also underlie the obscure passage Zec 12¹⁰. ¹¹. (3) The *prophetic ideal*, based mainly on Dt 18¹⁵, which came to be identified with the heraldic prophet of 'the great and terrible day of the Lord,' the Elijah of Mal 4⁴ᶠ· [Heb. 3²²ᶠ·], or was identified with the Messiah Himself (Ac 3²²ᶠ·). Cf. Mk 6¹⁵ 8²⁸, Jn 1²¹ 6¹⁴ 7⁴⁰, and Wendt's *Teaching of Jesus*, i. p. 67 f.

iii. *TRANSFORMATION OF THE MESSIANIC IDEAL THROUGH APOCALYPTIC.*—The kingdom of righteousness and the fear of the Lord, or what is expressed in the Biblical phrase the *Kingdom of*

* LXX τὰ ἀποκείμενα αὐτῷ, 'that which is reserved for him.' The LXX in some variants has ἕως ἂν ἔλθῃ ᾧ ἀπόκειται, 'till there comes he to whom it (? the sceptre) belongs,' which is the rendering of the Targ. of Onḳelos and also of Jerusalem. This most clumsy and almost impossible construction is apparently due to the influence of Ezk 21³², where, however, we have a subject for the relative clause, viz הַמִּשְׁפָּט.

† *Beiträge zur Jesaiakritik*, p. 29, footnote. It is difficult to understand the acquiescence of Gunkel in the construction presupposed in the alternative rendering of the LXX variant (cited in the previous footnote).

‡ See Driver in *Expositor*, July 1885 ; *EBi*, art. 'Shiloh' ; and Bennett's 'Genesis' (*Century Bible*), ad loc.

§ Budde's Com. on the Books of Samuel (J. C. B. Mohr), p. 233 ; cf. also his *Richter u. Samuel*, pp. 244, 247.

‖ The Com. of Dr. Buchanan Gray (*ICC*) should be consulted.

God, was not to be attained without a struggle against opposing forces political and moral, or without the instrumentality of a personal leader, sometimes an anointed king of Davidic descent, through whom the victory was to be won for Israel. For throughout we find that Israel, or a purified remnant, stands at the centre of the whole movement towards righteousness, and becomes more or less identified with it. Accordingly, the closest connexion subsisted between the national Messiah and that future state of blessedness, a restored theocracy, which became the steadfast expectation of the Jewish race since the destruction of Solomon's temple in B.C. 587. At first it was believed that the desired consummation would not long be delayed. The existing generation and the earthly scene in which the prophet lived would behold the great day of the Lord and the advent of the salvation foretold. But ever since the days of Amos, and still more· after the discipline of the Exile, the horizons of time and space expanded.

1. After the Exile and the return of the *Gôlah* (exiled Jews), the advent of the fulfilled hopes of a Divine kingdom of righteousness was still delayed, and the Messianic age seemed as far off as ever, even after Nehemiah and Ezra had worked at their task of reform. As time went on, the disappointed expectations of post-exilic Judaism bred among the spiritual leaders a spirit of hopelessness as to the political outlook, and this is echoed in their religious hymns : 'Does Jahweh cast off in abhorrence for ever ; will he no more be gracious ? Is there an end to his kindness for evermore' (Ps 77⁸. ⁹ [Heb.]) ; cf. Pss 22. 37, etc. Trust in Jahweh still survived, and His faithful followers clung to the Tôrah (Ps 19⁸⁻¹² [Heb.] and 119 *passim*), but Messianic expectation languished. The outlook of the present time was hopeless. But amid the enlarged horizons of time as well as space to which we have referred, the thoughts of some of the most spiritual minds in Judaism were directed to the transcendental and ultimate. In *that* world God would finally vindicate Himself and His ways to the expectant faith of Israel. A distinction began to be established between the present and the future age or æon. The former is corrupt, and hopelessly delivered over to Satan and the powers of darkness. Victory will come in the latter. As we approach the time of Christ, the distinction between the present age (עוֹלָם הַזֶּה or αἰὼν οὗτος) and the age to come (עוֹלָם הַבָּא or αἰὼν μέλλων) becomes sharply contrasted, and the transcendental features and colouring which invest the latter, and the final conflict with the heathen or demonic powers (Gog and Magog in Ezk 38. 39, attributed by some recent critics to a later hand than Ezekiel) characterize the new and later phase of Messianic expectation. This final agony or conflict, called in later times the 'Messianic sufferings or pangs' (חֶבְלֵי מָשִׁיחַ), which was to usher in the new age, was no longer confined to earth. It was universal and cosmic. These apocalyptic features (which first meet us clearly in that latest addendum to the Isaianic oracles, Is 24–27) now impress themselves on Messianic expectation, though by no means always ; cf. Mk 13⁶⁻³⁷, Jn 16¹¹. ²⁰⁻²².

2. Another feature of equal importance, which begins to emerge in apocalyptic literature, left its impress on Messianic expectation, viz. the belief in the *resurrection of the dead*. The first clear intimations of this faith are to be found in Is 26¹⁹, Dn 12². In the older apocrypha (Sirach, Judith, Tobit, 1 Mac.) it is absent. In the later (2 Mac 7⁹. ¹⁴. ²³. ²⁹. ³⁶ 12⁴³. ⁴⁴) it is obviously present. In the Wisdom of Solomon it takes the form of a happy life after death for the just (3¹⁻⁹ 4⁷ 5¹⁶ 6²⁰).* It is

* Schürer, *GJV*³ ii. 508.

hardly necessary to emphasize how profoundly this belief in the resurrection of the righteous (the most primitive form of the doctrine limited the resurrection to them) moulded the Christology of St. Paul. For to St. Paul, Christ is the Second Adam, endowed with the πνεῦμα ζωοποιοῦν (1 Co 15⁴⁵), in whom all His faithful followers are made alive (v.²²); cf. Ro 6³⁻¹¹. See Volz, *Jüd. Eschatologie*, pp. 237–248.

3. The *pre-mundane existence of the Messiah* was another mode of the larger transcendental mould of thought which apocalyptic reveals. Belief in the ante-natal existence of the Messiah was only part of a general tendency of Jewish speculation. The new Jerusalem, the Temple, and Paradise existed before the creation of the world (Apoc. Bar 4³ 59⁴, Assumpt. Mosis 1¹⁴·¹⁷). The Midrash on Pr 8⁹ even goes beyond this, and expressly mentions the Messiah among the seven things created before the creation of the world, viz. the Throne of Glory, Messiah the King, the Tôrah, ideal Israel, Repentance, and Gehenna.* The pre-mundane existence of the Messiah is also certified in the Targ. on Is 9⁶ and Mic 5². In these metaphysical conceptions, stimulated, as we may with considerable probability believe, through the Platonic doctrine of archetypal ideas which passed in the great stream of Hellenic influence over the Jewish Diaspora, we clearly discern what Charles aptly calls a Semitic philosophy of religion.† By this doctrine of pre-mundane existence the things of God were lifted above the universal lot of change and decay, and brought into the realm of adamantine permanence. As Baldensperger acutely remarks, it became, in the minds of reflective and pious Jews, a guarantee against loss.‡ We need not labour to set forth how profoundly it affects NT thought, especially Pauline and Johannine (2 Co 8⁹, Ph 2⁷; cf. 2 Co 4⁴, Col 1⁵, He 1² 2¹⁰, Jn 1¹⁻³).

4. *Messianic titles.*—(*a*) Among the most significant for students of the NT is that of 'Restorer,' which is probably involved in the epithet *Ta'eb*, which occurs in the apocalypse of the Samaritan liturgy for the Day of Atonement. In the day of *Ta'eb* it was believed that the sacred vessels of the Temple would reappear which had been concealed on Mount Gerizim,§ and it has been conjectured that this same idea of Restorer underlies the epithet *Taxo* (Greek τάξων) in Assumpt. Mosis 9¹. In the literature of the time of Christ we frequently meet with this conception of the Messiah. Thus in the Testaments of the Twelve Patriarchs (Test. Levi, 18), which may have originated about a century before Christ's birth, the Messiah is regarded as the coming restorer of the Paradise lost by Adam's transgression. In Ac 3²¹ the καιροὶ ἀποκαταστάσεως clearly reflect this tradition. This function of 'restorer' was evidently ascribed to the Messiah and not to God's messenger Elias, referred to in Mal 3¹·²³ᶠ·. [Heb.].

(*b*) Other significant epithets, as 'Son of a woman,' prob. in allusion to Is 7¹⁴, appear, if the text be sound, in the Book of Enoch (*Similitudes*) 62⁵ 69²⁹.‖ This is of interest when we compare the Pauline 'son of a woman' (Gal 4⁴). On the other

hand, the designation 'horned,' or 'two-horned' (*Bᵉrēshîth Rabbâ*, 99), based apparently on Dt 33¹⁷, belongs to Jewish literature subsequent to the 1st cent. and need not detain us here. Far more significant is the title which plays so large a part in the Synoptic Gospels, viz. :

(*c*) '**Son of Man.**'—The employment of this phrase as a Messianic title dates from the Maccabæan period, and in this specific sense meets us for the first time in Dn 7¹³. Its earlier occurrence in the OT requires no exposition here. At the time when the Book of Daniel was written, Jewish apocalyptic was directed to the conception of a great final Divine judgment at the close of the present age, whereby the coming age was to be ushered in. We no longer see the figure of a Messianic King of Davidic descent. His place is taken by a mysterious symbolic portraiture which, as Volz correctly argues,* is not angelic. It stands contrasted with the four animal symbolical shapes previously described, and especially with the last beast with the ten horns, 'dreadful and exceedingly strong,' which had 'great iron teeth that devoured and brake in pieces.' In sharp distinction from these monstrous and bestial world-powers which are finally to be destroyed, we have a mysterious figure in human shape.† In v.²⁷ its significance is explained. It represents 'the people of the saints of the Most High.' As H. J. Holtzmann correctly observes, it is intended to express 'a world-empire which is human and not brutal, which is ethical and noble and not immoral, which is like man, stamped with the likeness of God' (Gn 1²⁶). That this human and humane world-empire was to be Jewish and not Gentile, is obvious to the reader of Daniel's apocalypse.

The 'Son of Man' has a yet more definite and distinguished rôle in the *Similitudes* of the Book of Enoch (chs. 37–71), written probably after B.C. 100. Here He is obviously a supernatural personality and not a symbolic figure, or indefinitely expressed as 'like a son of man.' The Son of Man is not mere man. This is clearly shown in ch. 39, where a cloud and whirlwind carry Enoch away and set him down at the end of the heavens. There he sees the mansions of the holy, and among these latter 'the Elect One of righteousness and faith,' which is another name for the 'Son of Man' (v.⁶). Moreover, He sits on God's throne (51³), which is also His own throne (69²⁷·²⁹), possesses universal dominion (62⁶), and all judgment is committed to Him (69²⁷). Various alternative titles are given to Him, viz. 'the Righteous One' (38²·³ 53⁶), and 'the Elect One' (39⁶ 40⁵ 45³ᶠ·). We note meanwhile that the Son of Man is also *Judge*.

Accordingly, we conclude that while the term in Daniel is symbolical of the human rule of God's people Israel, in Enoch it is the designation of a supernatural personality, who holds universal empire and wields the office of Judge.

When we pass from this apocalyptic use of the title 'Son of Man' to its employment in the Synoptic Gospels, we observe a great change. It was without question Christ's favourite designation of Himself. It is noteworthy that in the Synoptics the term relatively occurs twice as often as it does in the Fourth Gospel. It occurs 30 times in Matthew, 14 times in Mark, and 25 times in Luke. In John it is found only 12 times.

Christ's employment of the term is by no means uniform. Consequently we are in danger, as Bousset points out, of giving a one-sided interpretation to the expression, either by taking it predominantly in the eschatological sense of Daniel or the Book of Enoch, or as signifying ideal typical man (as

---

* Edersheim, *Life and Times of Jesus the Messiah*, i. p. 175.

† *Book of Enoch*, Introd. p. 23, in his description of Apocalyptic generally. It is quite possible that we have a trace of it in that profoundly speculative Psalm, 139 (note vv.¹⁵·¹⁶). With reference to the pre-existence of the Messiah (not His name only, as Volz seems to assume in *Jüd. Eschatologie*, p. 217), see Enoch 48²·⁶, and cf. Charles' notes (and 62⁷). 'Name' here connotes *existence* as in the Babyl. Creation tablet (lines 1, 2). On the other side, as against the *Jewish* belief in Messianic pre-existence, see Dalman, *Worte Jesu*, p. 245.

‡ *Selbstbewusstsein Jesu*², p. 89; Volz, *Jüd. Eschatologie*, p. 218.

§ Bousset, *Religion des Judentums*², pp. 258, 267, 274.

‖ Here, however, it should be noted, in both passages Charles adopts the reading 'Son of Man.'

* *Jüd. Eschatologie*, p. 10 f.

† On the element of mystery attaching to the use of the preposition כְּ (in כְּבַר אֱנָשׁ), see Volz, *ib.*

Schleiermacher assumes).* Probably Charles is on the right path when he interprets the Synoptic use of the phrase as involving a combination of two contrasted ideas — the transcendent conception of apocalyptic and the Deutero-Isaianic ideal of Jahweh's Suffering Servant.† It is certainly possible that the latter was the prevailing conception in Christ's personal consciousness rather than the former or eschatological use of the phrase ; while the former was the interpretation of the title which dominated the thought of the Synoptic writers, and came to be impressed on the utterances of Jesus. This view seems to be sustained by the fact that in Aramaic the term 'Son of Man' (ﻧﺎﺵ ﺑﺮ) means simply 'man.' On the other hand, it is difficult to believe that Jesus could have employed so colourless and vague a designation of Himself ; and Bousset is probably right in his contention, as against Wellhausen, that such a term, employed in Aramaic, could easily come to acquire a special eschatological significance.‡ In all probability, Jesus on certain momentous occasions so used it. How far it was weighted with the significance that the phrase conveys in the Book of Enoch, when the expression was actually employed by Jesus, it is difficult to say. It is hardly necessary to believe that in the personal consciousness of Jesus the superadded notion of pre-mundane existence was attached to the term, though Jn 8[58] ('Before Abraham was, I am') would fairly point in this direction. We certainly have no clear right to infer it from Mk 12[6]. Moreover, there is some weight in the suggestion which a few scholars, including Bousset, have put forth, that the term 'Son of Man' has been placed in the mouth of Jesus in many cases when He simply used the first personal pronoun.§ That He did, however, employ the phrase in an eschatological sense of Himself, and with a full consciousness of the sublime dignity which it conferred, cannot be denied. Thus, in answer to Pilate's question (Mk 14[62]; cf. Mt 26[64], Lk 22[69]), He quotes the well-known Daniel passage (7[13]), declaring that men would see Him, the Son of Man, sitting at the right hand of power (i.e. of God), and coming in the clouds of heaven. This utterance is certified by the three Synoptic Gospels ; and all three agree in giving it a decisive influence in the trial of Jesus before the Sanhedrin. This testimony, however, carries us one step further. It is hardly possible to dissociate in the consciousness of Jesus the assumption of this high eschatological dignity without including in it the judicial function. The Oriental king was also judge. As King or Messiah, Jesus had, with full consent from Himself, been already acclaimed (Mk 11[7-11]), and, with the title of 'King of the Jews' placed on the cross by the Roman governor, He was crucified (Mk 15[26]; cf. vv.[12. 18. 32]). Moreover, His preaching of the Kingdom of God was closely bound up with the conception of impending judgment. 'Just as He could not dispense with the ideas of the kingdom and the judgment, if He wished to make Himself intelligible to His countrymen, so He could not dispense with the Messianic idea if He wished to be intelligible to

Himself' (Bousset).* It is easy to draw the necessary corollary. In the designation 'Son of Man' applied by Jesus to Himself in an eschatological sense, there was involved the other conception which meets us in the *Similitudes* of the Book of Enoch, that of universal judge.†

But the eschatological side is not the only, nor is it the most important, aspect of the conception of 'Son of Man' in the mind of Jesus and the Synoptic writers. Far greater, viewed from the ethical standpoint, was the human aspect of the lowly Suffering Servant suggested by the Deutero-Isaiah. This certainly could never have been invented by the Synoptic writers. It is of the very essence of Christ's thought respecting Himself. It is nevertheless remarkable that the *locus classicus* of the NT writers who reflected on the mystery of the Messiah's crucifixion, viz. Is 53, was never, so far as we can gather from the Synoptic writers, quoted by Jesus Himself, with the doubtful exception of Lk 22[37]. That this prophecy, however, must have been in His mind, seems fairly clear from Mk 10[45] 12[6-10]; cf. Jn 13[12-17] and Lk 24[25. 26]. Accordingly, the title 'Son of Man' had a twofold significance. It is employed when Christ's claims to power and authority are asserted, both now and in His future Kingdom and glory. The 'Son of Man' has power to forgive sins (Mk 2[10]). He is Lord over the Sabbath (Mt 12[8]). He will appear clothed in power at the last day (Mk 14[62]). But the title is also used in immediate connexion with His human nature, lowliness, poverty, suffering, and death. 'The Son of Man came eating and drinking' (Mt 11[19], Lk 7[34]); 'the Son of Man hath not where to lay his head' (Mt 8[20], Lk 9[58]); 'is betrayed' (Mk 14[21]); 'came not to be ministered unto but to minister' (Mk 10[45]); suffers and is condemned (Mk 8[31]). The paradox of this twofold antithetic significance is solved by the positive truth which underlies it. The peculiar and special function of dignity and privilege which belongs to the 'Son of Man' rests on an ethical basis. He that has come to serve, suffer, and give His life a ransom for many, will pass through agony and death to His place of exaltation in the clouds of heaven (cf. Ac 3[18] 8[32] 17[3] 26[23]). Upon this basis St. Paul and his successors have built. We also are to suffer with Him, that we may share in His glory (Ro 8[17]). The Kenotic doctrine of Ph 2[6. 7] is reared on this foundation of the teachings of Jesus respecting Himself as 'Son of Man,' whereby we learn that He was 'made perfect through sufferings,' and became 'the leader of our salvation' (He 2[9. 10]).

(*d*) '**Son of God**' is a designation frequently applied to Jesus in the Gospels, and is applied by Jesus to Himself as the expression of His vivid consciousness of God's presence in His life, and the intimate bond that united Him to the Father (Mt 11[27]). In His native Aramaic, *Abbâ* was the mode of address in prayer that came most naturally to His lips, and became a tradition in the worship of the early Christian Church (Ro 8[15]). That the relation claimed by Jesus was a special one, is indicated by His use of the expression 'my Father' in Mt 11[27] 18[35] 20[23], whereas in Mt 6[32] 10[29] God is spoken of to the audience before Jesus as 'your Father.' More significant still is the designation of Himself as 'beloved Son' in the parable of the Vineyard let out to Husbandmen (Mk 12[6]), and also by the voice which spoke to Him from heaven at His baptism (Mt 3[16. 17], Mk 1[10. 11], Lk 3[21. 22]). Upon this unquestionable basis of language employed by Jesus respecting Himself, the frequent application of this designation 'Son of God' to

---

* *Jesu Predigt in ihrem Gegensatze zum Judenthum*, p. 112 f.
† Book of Enoch, Appendix B, p. 315 ff.; cf. also Bartlet, *Expositor*, Dec. 1892.
‡ *Religion des Judentums*[2], p. 305, footnote.
§ Bousset's *Jesus* (Eng. ed.), p. 188. Bousset thinks that it was not till the closing months of His ministry that this title was assumed ; 'in face of the threatening doom of final failure . . . only briefly and sparingly did He adopt the name' (p. 192 f.). Some colour is given to this view, that the Synoptic writers have frequently supplied the phrase in Christ's discourses, by comparing ἕνεκεν ἐμοῦ in Mt 5[10] with the parallel ἕνεκα τοῦ υἱοῦ τοῦ ἀνθρώπου in Lk 6[22]. But in the extremely severe limitation imposed by Bousset on Christ's employment of the term we are unable to concur.

* *Jesus*, p. 178. Bousset, however, refuses to include in Christ's conception of the title 'Son of Man' the idea of His own judgeship (p. 194).
† Cf. Mk 13[26. 27], Mt 25[31-32], 2 Co 5[10]. See also Friedländer, *Die religiösen Bewegungen innerhalb des Judentums im Zeitalter Jesu*, p. 325.

Christ in the Pauline Epistles, and of the same phrase with the epithet μονογενής in the Johannine writings, was obviously founded. In the memorable scene at Cæsarea Philippi, when Jesus questioned His disciples as to their belief respecting Himself, Peter, according to the Matthew tradition, replied, 'Thou art the *Messiah, the Son of the living God*' (Mt 16[16]). This would seem to imply that the expression 'Son of God' was a Messianic title. But in this connexion two things should be noted : (1) Mk 8[29] gives Peter's reply in the briefer form 'Thou art the Messiah.' (2) There is scarcely any evidence in later Jewish literature to indicate that the phrase 'Son of God' was used as a Messianic title.[*] This is the more remarkable when we remember Ps 2[7] 'Jahweh hath said unto me, Thou art my son, this day I have begotten thee,' and the old Semitic conceptions of divinity which attached to kingship, reflected in Assyrian inscriptions (see above, p. 171). Probably the stern monotheism of later post-exilic Judaism tended to suppress language which seemed to attribute Divinity to an earthly human personality.

(*e*) **'Son of David'** is the most characteristic, as it is the most traditional and historic, designation of the Jewish Messiah. It expresses the most representative type of Messianic expectation, if we understand by that term an anointed Jewish king who was to be the national deliverer. This conception, as we have already seen, had its roots in the days of Isaiah of Jerusalem, and revived in the age of Jeremiah and Ezekiel, and even survived in attenuated form to the early days of post-exilic Judaism. But in later Jewish literature belonging to the Greek period we notice a remarkable absence of any allusion to a Messianic king of Davidic descent who at the end of the ages will erect his throne. That the expectation still survived, and at times found expression, especially as we approach the period of the Maccabæan struggle, seems fairly clear from such Psalms as 2. 72. 110. On the other hand, we find no reference to a Messianic deliverer of the seed of David in Joel, Is 24–27, Sirach, Daniel, Enoch (chs. 1–36, the Vision of Weeks and the hortatory discourses), Book of Jubilees, Assumpt. Mosis, Sib. Or. 3[36-91]. The figure of the Messiah is absent also from Tobit, Judith, 1 and 2 Maccabees, Wisdom, Baruch. It is true that we do find mention of the Messiah, or allusion to Him, in the visions of animals in Enoch (chs. 85–90), in Sib. Or. 3, in Philo (*de Præm. et Pœn.* 16), and also in Apoc. Bar 29[3] 30[1] and 2 Es 7[28f.] ; but the figure holds a secondary position, and is far more shadow than substance.

Bousset, in reviewing this literature (both pre-Christian and extending to A.D. 100), endeavours to solve the problem of this absence of Messianic expectation.[†] The causes are twofold. *First* comes the patent fact to which reference has already been made in a previous page. The Jew had entered into a larger world, and his eschatology was therefore framed on these larger dimensions of time and space in which the final catastrophe was to be vast and world-wide. The world of the Jew was no longer Palestinian or even Western-Asiatic. It was the world ruled by the successors of Alexander, and the yet greater world ruled by the Cæsars. Moreover, Greek culture had begun to enter deeply into the mind of Judaism. To the cultured Jew the figure of a Davidic-Messianic king seemed incongruous and provincial amid these larger political and intellectual horizons. *Secondly*, the establishment of the line of Maccabæan rulers left large circles of pious Jews well content. In the latter part of the rule of Jonathan, and during the days of Simon and Hyrcanus,

the Jew might well have believed in the advent of a Messianic age. Now, the Maccabees were of priestly descent, and came, therefore, from the tribe of Levi. It is therefore not surprising that the seed of David of the tribe of Judah faded for awhile into comparative insignificance ; cf. Charles' note on Enoch 90[37].

But the old hopes bound up with the Messiahking of David's line were by no means extinct, though they appeared sometimes to be dormant. There were Palestinian Jews as well as Jews of the Diaspora, and there were uncultured Jews both in the countryside and in the towns, influenced by old traditions and the expectations still kept alive by the Law and the Prophets read in the synagogue, as well as the literary Jews who pored over the Book of Wisdom or consoled themselves with the Visions of the Book of Enoch amid their blighted political hopes. Moreover, the spell of the Hasmonæan line of princes did not last for ever. The 1st century B.C. witnessed a great change as compared with the second. Life was no longer under Aristobulus I. and Alexander Jannæus what it was in the great days of Judas, Simon, and John Hyrcanus. The Hasmonæan princes were regarded as usurpers, and the political aspirations of the race began to turn once more to the seed of David. The ordinary uncultured Jew did not trouble himself with apocalyptic dreams of new heavens and a new earth, and probably there were many cultivated Jews who had little taste for the Book of Enoch. These would read with far greater satisfaction the Psalter of Solomon, especially Ps 17[5ff.], with its references to the familiar words of Prophecy and Psalm :—

'Thou, Lord, didst choose David to be king over Israel, and didst swear unto him concerning his seed for ever, that his kingdom should not fail before thee [2 S 7[13-16], Ps 89[4. 5]]. Then, through our sins, sinners[*] arose against us, attacked us, and thrust us out. Those to whom thou didst make no promise took away with violence (our honour[†]). . . . They laid waste the throne of David with insolent shouting. But thou, O God, wilt cast them down and remove their seed from the earth, when one that is a foreigner [‡] to our race arises against them. According to their sins wilt thou recompense them, O God . . . (v.[23]). Behold, O Lord, and raise up for them their king, the son of David, at the time which thou, O God, knowest, that he may reign over Israel thy servant ; and gird him with strength that he may break in pieces unjust rulers. Purge Jerusalem with wisdom and righteousness from the heathen that trample her down with destruction. May he thrust out the sinners from the inheritance, utterly destroy the pride of the sinners, and as potters' vessels with an iron rod break in pieces all their substance' [Ps 2[9]].

The Psalter of Solomon, not inaptly called by Ryle and James 'the Psalms of the Pharisees,' clearly reveals by its contents that it belongs to the period B.C. 70–40. Its chief interest for us consists in the strong indications which it gives of the reviving Messianic hopes of Israel at this time under the Roman yoke. Palestine was ready to respond to any bold or able adventurer like Judas, Theudas, or Bar Cochba, the last of whom was supported even by the distinguished Rabbi Aḳiba. The Synoptic Gospels furnish clear evidence that the national expectations which were directed to a Davidic Messiah in the middle of the last cent. B.C. still prevailed in the days of Jesus. The very form of the Matthew and Luke traditions respecting our Lord's birth exhibits an endeavour to conform to the prevalent expectation that the Messiah would be of Davidic descent. (1) The divergent pedigrees in the two Gospels trace the genealogy of Joseph, the reputed father of Jesus, from David. (2) Both lay stress on Bethlehem as Christ's birthplace, in conformity with the oracle in Mic 5[2].

Quite apart from the form of the Gospel narra-

---

[*] The passages where the term 'Son' occurs in 2 Esdras (7[28] 13[32. 37. 52] 14[9]) as well as in Enoch (105[2]) are all extremely doubtful. The Aramaic original is lost ; and it is held by many scholars, including Drummond, Spitta (*Zur Gesch. und Lit. des Urchristentums*, ii. 9), as well as Charles, that Christian hands have worked over these texts and have inserted the expression 'Son.' See Volz, *Jüd. Eschatologie*, p. 213, who regards Drummond's conjecture as probable, that the phrase 'Son' of God may sometimes have arisen from the Gr. rendering παῖς for 'servant' (עֶבֶד). See also N. Schmidt's art. 'Son of God' in *EBi*, col. 4694.

[†] *Religion des Judentums*[2] *im neutest. Zeitalter*, p. 255 f.

---

[*] A reference to the Hasmonæan princes who usurped the high priesthood (so Ryle and James).

[†] The Greek ἀφείλοντο has no object, and these words may probably be supplied.

[‡] Pompey is undoubtedly meant. See the interesting and full discussion in Ryle and James' *Com. on the Psalms of Solomon*, Introd. p. xlii ff.

tives and the predisposition of the writers, the facts of the life of Jesus furnish conclusive evidence of this strong current of Messianic expectation.* We know that on repeated occasions, especially towards the close of His career, He was acclaimed as Son of David : Mt 9²⁷ (cf. Mk 10⁴⁷· ⁴⁸) 12²³ 15²², Mk 11¹⁰ (Mt 21⁹· ¹⁵). A survey of the facts, however, leads to the conclusion that Jerusalem in South Palestine was the centre of this national movement of Messianic anticipation, and that its pulses become weaker as we pass to the Jewish populations farther removed from this centre.

(f) We also find the title 'comforter' (מנחם *mĕnaḥēm*) bestowed on the Messiah of Davidic lineage. In Jn 14¹⁶· ²⁶ 15²⁶ 16⁷ παράκλητος is forensic in origin = 'advocate,' hence comes to mean 'helper' (see Weiss, *ad loc.*). It has therefore nothing to do with the above Messianic title. See Wünsche, *Leiden des Messias*, p. 112 ; Bousset, *Relig. des Jud.²* p. 261. We find a Menahem, son of Judas the Galilæan, appearing in Jerusalem as a messiah, and after a brief interval overthrown (Volz, *Eschat.* p. 210).

iv. *ATTITUDE OF JESUS TOWARDS THE MESSIAHSHIP.*—This subject involves some delicate problems which do not admit of easy or immediate solution. Several questions present themselves, and the answers to these enable us to define approximately the attitude of Jesus towards the Messiahship. (1) What was the popular impression created by the Personality and ministry of Jesus ? (2) In what form did Jesus regard Himself as Messiah, and how was this related to the popular impression or the current Messianic expectation ? (3) At what time did the Messianic consciousness possess Jesus, and when was it proclaimed ?

1. In reference to the first question, the following facts may be noted : (a) During the Galilæan period of His ministry Jesus was designated a *prophet* ; and of this He was plainly conscious (Mk 6⁴). Yet in popular estimation He was considered to be endowed with powers so remarkable that some supposed Him to be Elijah (6¹⁵), the precursor of the Messiah (Mal 3¹ 4⁵), or one of the great prophets returned to life (Mk 8²⁸ ; perhaps Jeremiah or Isaiah, cf. 2 Mac 2⁵ 15¹⁴ᶠ·, 2 Es 2¹⁸). This seems to have been the general opinion respecting Jesus down to the close of His life (Lk 24¹⁹ 'a prophet mighty in deed and word '). (b) On the other hand, when Jesus passes into Judæa, He is confronted by the powerful current of Messianic expectation which looked for a king of David's line (Mk 10⁴⁸ 11⁹· ¹⁰). Probably an attempt to draw Him into this path of Messianic claim and revolt against Roman imperial authority underlies the question as to tribute-money (Mk 12¹⁴).

2. As to the form of Christ's own Messianic consciousness and its relation to the popular impression and the South Palestinian expectation, we note : (a) That the narrative of the Temptation (Mt 4⁵ᶠᶠ·, Lk 4⁵ᶠᶠ·) points to the conclusion that early in His public ministry the path of a material or worldly Messiah-king was deliberately renounced (cf. Jn 6¹⁵ 18³⁶). (b) At an early period Jesus promulgated the fundamental principles of the Kingdom of God, and was fully conscious of His plenary authority to declare them even in opposition to the sacred Mosaic *Tôrah* which He announced Himself prepared to fulfil (' Ye have heard how it hath been said . . . but *I* say unto you '). Yet though the expression ' kingdom of God (or heaven)' is often on His lips, He does not name Himself as ' king.' (c) He was evidently conscious of a higher vocation and dignity than the designation ' prophet' involved. For (i.) He never called Himself ' prophet,' though popularly acclaimed as such ; (ii.) the prevailing designation

* Cf. Keim, *Jesu von Nazara*, i. 244, iii. 103.

of Himself which He adopted was, according to the Synoptics, ' Son of Man,' which, we have already shown, implied a high eschatological function and dignity ; (iii.) He also regarded Himself as ' Son of God ' (cf. Mk 1¹⁰· ¹¹), though He restrained the announcement of the title (Mk 3¹¹· ¹²). (d) He was wholly out of sympathy with the popular national and materialistic conceptions of Messiahship with which Southern Palestine at this time was rife. This we can clearly discern in His warning against false prophets and messiahs (Mk 13²², Mt 24¹¹⁻²⁴), who attempted by violent revolutionary means to force on the advent of the ' kingdom of God ' (Mt 11¹²). From these data the conclusion may be derived, that Jesus from very early times—even as early as the date of His baptism, according to the triple tradition of the Synoptics—was conscious of His unique relation to God as His Father, and of His Messianic dignity and mission, but that He filled it with an ethical as well as apocalyptic content. It was for this reason that He hesitated to declare Himself as Messiah at the opening of His public ministry, knowing the perils of the material and unspiritual conceptions with which the national expectations of the Jews invested the name. The true representation of His Person and of His mission was to be found in the apocalyptic title ' Son of Man.' He was thinking of the exalted cosmic spiritual dignity which attached to this title when, in answer to Pilate's question, He acquiesced * in the ambiguous honour ' King of the Jews' (Mk 15²). The name connoted to Him the same personal authority as He claimed in the previous reply to the high priest (Mk 14⁶²). So the Fourth Gospel interprets the enigmatic answer of Jesus to Pilate (Jn 18³⁶, cf. also 19²¹).

3. With reference to the time when the Messianic consciousness possessed Jesus, and when His Messiahship was proclaimed, few will dissent from Bousset's dictum, that it is highly probable that the tradition is right in dating Jesus' awakening to the Messianic consciousness from the moment of His baptism, that is, before the opening of His ministry.† As we have already indicated, there were, nevertheless, powerful motives which dictated the withholding of His claims from immediate public announcement. It is evident that the significant declaration which He drew from Simon near to Cæsarea Philippi, that He was the Messiah, and more than prophet, marks the decisive point after which His Messianic title was generally proclaimed. Though He still imposed upon His followers great reserve (Mk 8³⁰), we find that shortly after this He is hailed by the blind Bartimæus (Mk 10⁴⁸) and by His enthusiastic followers (Mk 11⁹· ¹⁰) as ' son of David,'—a title which He probably regarded with mixed feelings.

v. *VARIED FEATURES IN THE MESSIANIC EXPECTATION CURRENT IN THE TIME OF CHRIST.*—**1.** That the Messiah of Jewish traditional expectation *would be endowed with the virtues of justice and understanding through the Spirit of God*, was an obviously fundamental conception derived from the old Isaianic prophecy, Is 9⁷ [Heb.⁶] 11²ᶠ·, cf. Ps 72. These ethical qualities are reproduced in varied forms in, *e.g.*, Ps-Sol 17, Test. of the XII. Patr., Levi 18. In this last passage the Hasmonæan priest-princes seem to hover before the writer's imagination. In this portraiture the Messiah is king and priest of the whole earth ; the nations of the earth and the angels in heaven rejoice over him. All iniquity disappears under his sway. He again opens Para-

* The present writer, though with considerable hesitation, differs from Swete's comment upon the words σὺ λέγεις in Mk 15² (Mt 27¹¹). For Pilate appears to have understood these words as an affirmation of His own suggestion (Mk 15⁹) ; so also the Roman soldiers (Mk 15¹⁸, cf. v.²⁶). Cf. Lk 22⁷⁰ᶠ· with 23³.
† *Jesus* (Eng. ed.), p. 174.

dise, and the devil (Beliar) is bound by him. It is not easy to be quite sure whether Christian elements have been interpolated here as elsewhere in the Test. of the XII. Patriarchs. Moreover, in the Sibyll. Oracles (3[36-92]) the Messiah is called a 'holy king' of universal sway. In the Psalms of Solomon (17[36. 41. 42]) the sinlessness of the Messiah is emphasized, and expressly referred to his endowment with the Holy Spirit (cf. Mt 3[16. 17], Ro 1[4]).

2. *The element of mystery and marvel shrouds the appearance of the Messiah,* cf. Apoc. Bar 29[3] (text, however, somewhat doubtful ; see Charles) 32[1], 2 Es 7[28], Test. of the XII. Patr., Levi 18, Sib. Or. 3[652]. According to Targ. Jon. on Mic 4[8], the Messiah is already in the world, but is concealed owing to the sins of the people ; see Schürer, *GJV*[3] ii. 531 ff. With this tradition cf. Jn 7[27].

3. *The Messiah is to be preceded by a messenger of God who is to purify Israel* (Mal 3[1. 3]).—This angel of the Covenant is identified by Malachi (or perhaps by an interpolator) with the returning Elijah (4[5f.] [Heb. 3[23f.]]). This passage, we know, exerted a far-reaching influence over later times ; cf. Sir 48[10. 11] and Mt 17[10-13] (Mk 9[11f.]).

4. *The scattered tribes of Israel are to be gathered together to Jerusalem, and Jerusalem and its Temple rebuilt.*—Often we find that the *apocalyptic features of a heavenly Jerusalem* usurp the place of the terrestrial lineaments of the older forms of Messianic anticipation ; cf. Rev 7[4ff.] 21[10ff.]. Here, again, the sources of these traits are found in the OT, *i.e.* in exilic and post-exilic literature : Ezk 39[27ff.], Is 11[11. 16] (which tell of the gathering of the Diaspora from Assyria, Babylon, Egypt) ; cf. Is 27[12. 13] 35[8ff.], Mic 7[12], Is 60[4. 9] 66[20]. In many cases these expectations may be called by the general term 'Messianic,' but are without the presence of a Messiah. God brings about the blessed change, not by a gradual evolution of the earthly order, but by a mighty destruction of world-empires, in which Israel's foes (pre-eminently Edom) are overthrown without the instrumentality of any human or superhuman intermediary. Perhaps the most characteristic passage is Is 27[13] 'In that day the great trumpet shall be blown, and all who are being lost in Assyria, and are driven into Egypt, shall come and bow to Jahweh in the holy mount in Jerusalem.' Similarly in the earlier Enoch 90[33f.], Ps-Sol 11, and Bar 4[36]-5[9], and even in Philo (*de Exsecrationibus,* § 8-9, *de Præm. et Pœn.* ; see Schürer[3], ii. p. 515), where the ethical traits are not forgotten.

Moreover, the rebuilding of Jerusalem is the reflex of the Deutero-Isaianic utterances, and also of Ezk 40-44. 47, Sir 35[13ff.], To 13[15-18] 14[5], Enoch 90[28]. According to Ps-Sol 17[33], this restoration of Jerusalem is to be the work of the Messiah.

5. The *Messiah as a martial personality* is based on the portraiture of Is 9[3. 4] 11[4], Ps 2[7-9], and this trait frequently recurs in the literature of the 1st cent. B.C. and later ; cf. Sib. Or. 3[652], 2 Es 12[31. 33] (where the Messiah is the lion which is to destroy the Roman empire), also Apoc. Bar 70[9,*] and esp. Ps-Sol 17[22-25]. It is significant that this trait is absent from the NT except in Rev 19[11-21], in which the atmosphere is Judaic rather than Christian.

6. The conception of Messiah *ben-Joseph* or *ben-Ephraim* belongs to much later Jewish literature, and need not detain us. See Bousset, *Rel. des Judentums*[2], p. 264 f.

7. The *ethical* and *universal* traits of the Jewish Messiah and of Messianic expectation are, however, *meagre* and *even conspicuous by their absence.* The blight of materialism or national exclusiveness

* Bracketed, however, by Charles as an interpolation ; it comes in abruptly and forestalls the reference to the Messiah in ch. 72.

rests upon most of the later Jewish literature of Messianic hopes. We scarcely have a hint of the Messiah as the bearer of a new and higher revelation of God's nature or will to mankind, or of His function as a redeemer from sin. The horizons are the horizons of the Jew. With the exception of Philo and the writer of Sib. Or. 3, who were evidently Hellenic in sympathy and culture, we have but little to remind us that the Jew felt any interest in other nationalities and their future. Jewish apocalyptic presents a singularly contracted world, though it be an entire universe. For that universe, when it is not limited to Palestine, is to be governed by Israel only. The visions of the Book of Enoch suffer from these painful limitations. The *Similitudes* in the description of the last struggle with the heathen restrict the scene to the Holy Land (Enoch 56). Similarly in the Psalms of Solomon the eschatology is limited in its scope to Palestine. Seldom do we meet with any hint or suggestion of the conversion of the Gentiles. Is 49[6], with its glorious ideal of Israel's mission as a light to the Gentiles, is almost wholly forgotten. The might of the Gentiles is to be broken, and world-empires are to be destroyed. The heathen nations are to be tributary vassals to the new Israelite power which Jahweh will erect, and of which the restored Jerusalem will be the centre. The Gentiles may make pilgrimages to the Holy Land, but only Israel may dwell there. See Bousset, *op. cit.* pp. 268-270.

The features of the 'Suffering Servant' portrayed in Is 53 are almost totally absent in the version of the Targum of Jonathan, composed in the first two centuries of the Christian era, when the influence of the Maccabæan age still affected the Messianic conceptions of Judaism. The traits of Is 53 and 49[6] are quite foreign to the Messianic ideals of Judaism in the 1st cent. A.D. The cross of Jesus was to the Jews a stumbling-block (1 Co 1[23]) ; cf. Volz, *op. cit.* p. 237 ; Dalman, *Der leidende und sterbende Messias,* p. 6 f. ; Schürer[3], ii. 554 f.

vi. *JESUS THE TRUE SPIRITUAL FULFILMENT OF PROPHECY AND ISRAEL'S REAL MESSIAH.*— The volcanic uprising of the Jewish race under Judas Maccabæus and his brothers against the efforts of Antiochus Epiphanes to suppress the national worship, exercised a profound influence upon the Hebrew nation and its ideals. For the future spiritual progress of Israel the results were permanently injurious. Religious ideas became warped by particularism, and the thoughts of the race diverted from the noble universalist conceptions of prophecy, especially of the Deutero-Isaiah, to the study of the *Tôrah,* as Israel's national heritage, with its ever growing mass of legal requirements and ceremonial punctilios. Piety then became a rule of thumb, and an elaborated endeavour to secure merit took the place of the old prophetic ideals of righteousness. All this is summed up in the single word *Pharisaism.* Pharisaism was born of the strong national movement of which the heroic episodes of the Maccabæan struggle were the outward embodiment. Out of this movement emerged, on the one hand, a vehement reaction against Hellenic ideas and usages, and the exaltation of the *Tôrah* as Israel's *palladium* ; while, on the other, there emerged the Napoleonic legend of the Jewish race, which became the prolific source of messiahs whose abortive careers were quenched in blood, until the final heroic effort of Bar Cochba, hailed as the fulfilment of Balaam's prophecy by Rabbi Akiba, was extinguished in the reign of Hadrian. But the noble spiritual ideals of Hebrew prophecy—of Jeremiah and the Deutero-Isaiah—could not be entirely suppressed by Pharisaism. As Friedländer in his recent stimulating work has pointed out,[*] the liberal movements which prevailed in the Jewish Diaspora which was surrounded and penetrated by Hellenic influence, prepared the way, especially through the writings of Philo, for the advent of Christ; and the same writer enables us to discern more clearly how the highest ethical ideals of the Hebrew Messiah were realized in Jesus. The husk of nationalism, which clung to Jewish apocalyptic and left no place in its Messianic conceptions for the redemption of the Gentile world, was remorselessly cast aside by Jesus: 'I say unto you, that many shall come from the east and west, and shall sit down with Abraham, and Isaac, and Jacob in the kingdom of heaven, but the children of the kingdom shall be cast out into outer darkness' (Mt 8[11. 12]). What the Messiah-prophet of Nazareth declared in His oracles, St. Paul, His greatest disciple, fulfilled. For Judaism had been diverted by Pharisaism from its true prophetic mission marked out for it in the dark days of its exile, but was enabled at last, by its greatest latter-day Prophet, the Divine 'Son of Man,' and by His great Jewish disciple and Apostle to the Gentiles, to accomplish its real vocation in spite of itself; cf. Is 42[19], 2 Co 3[14].

LITERATURE.—This has been partially indicated in the course of this article. The article on 'Messiah' in Hastings' *DB* and in *EBi* and *PRE*[3] should be consulted. A selection only of the most important works need be given here: Drummond, *The Jewish Messiah*; Edersheim, *Life and Times of Jesus the Messiah*[2], i. 160–179, ii. 434 ff., 710–711; Stanton, *The Jewish and the Christian Messiah*, 1886; Wendt, *Teaching of Jesus*, i. pp. 60–84, 176–181, ii. pp. 123–339; Holtzmann, *NT Theol.* i. pp. 81–85, 234–304; Baldensperger, *Das Selbstbewusstsein Jesu*; Wellhausen, *IJG*[2] (1895), pp. 198–204; Charles, *Book of Enoch* (see esp. Introduction). The last named writer's editions of the *Apocalypse of Baruch* and his artt. in Hastings' *DB* and the *EBi* will also be found useful. Specially important is the section (§ 29) entitled 'Die Messianische Hoffnung' in Schürer's *GJV*[3] ii. 497–556; cf. also Bousset, *Religion des Judentums im neutest. Zeitalter*[2], pp. 245–308; and Paul Volz, *Jüd. Eschatologie von Daniel bis Akiba*, pp. 213–237, also pp. 55–68; Dalman, *Der leidende und sterbende Messias*; Castelli, *Il Messia secondo gli Ebrei*; Neubauer and Driver, *The Jewish Interpreters of Isaiah liii*. For a more complete list the reader is referred to Schürer, *op. cit.* p. 496 ff.

OWEN C. WHITEHOUSE.

METAPHORS.—A *metaphor* is a blossom of one tree on the branch of another; it is a figure of speech by which a word or phrase is lifted to a meaning to which it is not literally entitled. A simple *trope* is a metaphor condensed. *Similes* are metaphors explained. *Parables* and *allegories* are similes or metaphors elaborately extended, and do not come into the scope of this discussion (see PARABLE). In this article we shall not attempt to catalogue or classify the metaphors used in the Gospels, or to distinguish in any technical way between the metaphors and other closely-related figures of speech, but shall use the word in its broadest sense.

Macbeth (*Might and Mirth of Literature*) restricts the term 'metaphor' unduly (cf. Gardiner, Kittredge and Arnold, *Mother Tongue*, 1902). Wendt (*Lehre Jesu*), notwithstanding the classic character of his general treatment of the figurative language of the NT, does not give specific attention to the metaphors in the speech of Jesus and their relation to the more extended symbolic and parabolic teaching of the Gospels. Votaw, in his valuable art. 'Sermon on the Mount' in Hastings' *DB*, Ext. Vol., classifies NT figures of speech as metaphorical, symbolical, hyperbolic, and figurative. But evidently the last term includes all the classes previously mentioned, while many of the hyperbolic expressions, even in the instances cited by Votaw, contain veiled metaphors. Every one who listened to Jesus mentally supplied the resemblance between the 'gnat' and the ritual peccadilloes which these men, so scrupulous of their meat and drink, 'strained out,' and between the 'camel' and the gross sins against the moral law which they swallowed so complacently. So the 'eye' which was to be plucked out (Mt 5[29]) and the 'beam' which was not plucked out (7[3]) evidently were the man's pet sins.

A simple metaphor expresses the resemblance (or identity) between two dissimilar objects or ideas

by applying to one a term which can literally designate only the other, as 'This is my body' (Mt 26[26]). An abbreviated or veiled metaphor is one in which the assertion of resemblance is not expressed but implied. Sometimes a veiled metaphor sparkles in a phrase, as: 'water of life,' 'sons of thunder'; or even in a single word used in a non-literal, ideal, or peculiar sense, to be determined by the context or by current usage, as: 'cross,' 'yoke,' 'grace,' 'flesh,' 'the Day,' 'the Wrath,' 'darkness,' 'to wash,' 'to sleep' (cf. use in Synoptt., John, and Paul, of ποτήριον), 'to drink,' 'to walk' (περιπατέω), and scores of other words constantly used in the NT with an ethical meaning, the force of which is grasped only after the mind has made the connexion between their literal and non-literal meanings. All the Gospels refer to 'death' as a 'sleep.' This was not uncommon among the Jews of that era. But John's Gospel uses a different and more tender word (κοιμάομαι), and adds to the usual metaphorical conception the idea of sleep being an invigorator which brings health to the sick and makes the tired man ready for the work of a new day (Jn 11[12. 13]). Other expressions, such as 'Get thee behind me, Satan' (Mt 16[23]), 'Destroy this temple, and in three days I will raise it up' (Jn 2[19]), may be taken at random as examples of veiled metaphors, the connexion between the literal and spiritual meanings being mentally supplied. Many of the deepest teachings of the NT are embodied in words or phrases which cannot be fully understood until their metaphorical meaning is grasped.

All Oriental language is pictorial. This is especially true of the words of Jesus, not only as reported in the NT, but in other sayings reported by the early Fathers and in the recently-discovered Logia. To insist upon taking the Sermon on the Mount 'just as it reads,' would often mean to insist upon taking it as no one listening to Jesus would have understood it. This metaphorical method of speech was habitual with Jesus (Mt 13[34], Mk 4[11], where παραβολή does not mean 'parable' in the modern sense, but metaphorical comparison), and was used, so His disciples thought, to hide the meaning of His words from all except the inner circle of believers. It certainly, however, as Wendt has suggested, quickened the attention of His hearers, and enabled His teaching to be carried more easily in the memory.

Notwithstanding the marked difference in vocabulary, style, and thought found in the various Gospels, they all agree, when reporting the speeches of Jesus, in putting a metaphorical spiritual meaning into even the simplest words, such as 'sheepfold,' 'door,' 'key,' 'lamp,' 'bread,' 'water,' 'fish,' 'life,' 'birth,' 'travail,' 'death,' 'love,' 'hell' (γέεννα), 'paradise,' etc. This is true even in the case of reporters who themselves lacked poetic and spiritual insight, and who not infrequently misunderstood the inner meaning of Jesus' words.[*] Sometimes, as in the references to 'meat' and 'leaven' (Jn 4[32. 34] 6[27. 55], Mt 16[12], Mk 8[17], Lk 12[1]), the deeper meaning of our Lord's words was understood before the Gospels came into existence. In other cases it is plain that even the Gospel writer did not catch the meaning of the words which he reports.

In all parts of the NT, social, civil, and regal terms are applied, often with a new depth of meaning, to our Lord and His Kingdom. Not only such terms as 'king,' 'Lord,' 'Master,' etc., but υἱὸς θεοῦ and σωτήρ are titles given to the Roman

---

[*] *Die religiösen Bewegungen innerhalb des Judentums im Zeitalter Jesu*, pp. 237–264.

[*] Such misunderstanding does not seem so strange after one examines the contemporaneous literature. In the Talmud (Peṣachim) an entire section is given to the discussion whether a man may eat the leaven of a Gentile, and with what kind of water dough must be kneaded.

emperors of the 1st and 2nd cents., while ἀδελφός was the common term used for members of various heathen esoteric associations of that period, and 'birth' the technical term for the rite of initiation. So the papyri have shown that 'presbyter,' 'scribe,' 'prophet,' etc., were technical terms used for officials in the heathen temples. This means only that the members of the early Christian community were accustomed to use the ordinary language of their times. It is difficult to tell what new ecclesiastical colouring was originally given to the titles of the early Christian officials, or what new ideas were from the very beginning expressed by the old terms 'faith,' 'salvation,' etc. That the latter terms, though identical in form, expressed ideas radically different from what they did when used in the LXX, is acknowledged by all critics—how much more, then, did these ideas differ from those conveyed by the same terms when used in the heathen Mysteries? *

The command to baptize or believe on, in, or into the name of Jesus,—found in all parts of NT,—receives a new force from the papyri, where, in heathen temples, the property bought 'into the name of God' emphasizes the Divine ownership.†

The different NT writers are marked by certain striking peculiarities in their use of metaphors. St. Mark, in his peasant's Gospel, rustic but picturesque, uses many metaphors which all writers following him could but repeat. So his simple metaphors grow into extended metaphors or illustrations in the later Gospels. Yet certain strong expressions, evidently metaphorical, are, either because of their uncouthness or implications, ignored by the later and more reflective writers. That the disciples are to be 'salted with fire' (9⁴⁹), and that even in this life they are to be rewarded with a hundred 'mothers,' etc. (10³⁰) are peculiar to Mark.‡ But when the force of these metaphors is caught, each statement strengthens our Lord's argument.

So the statement that Jesus spat on the blind man's eyes and on the dumb man's tongue (8²³ 7³³), though omitted for obvious reasons from the other Gospels, becomes peculiarly impressive when we remember that spittle, according to all ancient thought, represented the essence of a man's inner spirit, the quintessence of himself, and therefore played, from the earliest ages, a leading part in magic and witchcraft. By this acted metaphor Jesus proclaimed symbolically that it was His very essence that healed. Cf. also Jn 9⁶, where the action of Jesus possibly receives a new meaning when we rememember that in the Talmud the dust of certain districts in Jerusalem was clean and of other districts unclean—not because of the district being insanitary, as is suggested in the Talmudic text. If, instead of spitting on the tongue, He 'spat out,' this would receive explanation from the custom of the Jews to spit in contempt when idols were mentioned; as also in the early Church, where converts coming to baptism spat out as a sign that they renounced the kingdom of Satan. Cf. JE, art. 'Alenu.'

In Mk., believers who have 'salt' within them (9⁵⁰) have brotherly love; in Mt., those who love their enemies are salt (5¹⁰⁻¹³).§ In Mk., the word is a lamp (λύχνος) which must not be hid (4²¹, cf. Lk 8¹⁶, ¹⁸); in Mt., it is the believer (5¹⁵), or his 'eye' (spiritual vision or intent), if clear and healthy (ἁπλοῦς, 6²²), which is the lamp shining forth from the inward centre of life (φῶς, 5¹⁴)—which Jn. sees to be the eternal Word, Christ Jesus (1⁴). In Mk., disciples are compared to sheep (6³⁴ 14²⁷); in Mt. they are sheep (10⁶ 15²⁴ 26³¹, cf. 18¹²), while in Jn. (10²⁻²⁷) a long, elaborate discourse is based upon this well understood metaphor.||

* See, e.g., Deissmann, Bible Studies, 1901, pp. 73, 233; Percy Gardner, Exploratio Evangelica (1899); cf. Ramsay, 'Greek of Early Church and Pagan Ritual' (Expos. Times [1898], p. 9).
† See Deissmann, pp. 142, 147, 197; Moulton, Gram. NT Greek, (1906), has shown that the prepositions are practically identical in meaning as used in the papyri.
‡ Mt 19²⁹ is doubtful, and at any rate νῦν is omitted.
§ Compare the proverb yet to be heard in Jerusalem, 'What salt is it that keeps money good?' Answer: 'Charity.'
|| Jülicher (Die Gleichnisreden Jesu, p. 120) looks upon the narrative as contradictory and suspicious, because at one time Jesus is represented as the Door and at another as the Shepherd

Both Mk. and Mt. teach that he who 'findeth his life shall lose it,' but Lk. enlarges the meaning of ψυχή until it includes the whole man (9²⁵). Mt. alone says, Have no anxiety for your life, 'for each to-morrow will be anxious for itself' (6²⁵⁻³⁴), though both Mt. and Lk. remark that even the birds, which have neither farming implements nor granaries, are cared for (6²⁶ 8²⁰, cf. Lk 12²²⁻²⁴). The metaphorical allusion to new wine in fresh wine-skins, Mk 2²², is explained in Mt 9¹⁷ and enlarged in Lk 5³⁷. The patch which in Mk. and Mt. tears out a larger hole from the old garment, is in Lk. condemned for two altogether different reasons (5³⁶)—the necessity of tearing a new piece of cloth in order to get the patch, and because it would be a different kind of cloth. Every one who heard this remark in either form would be caught by the unspoken metaphor: Judaism cannot be patched by this new doctrine of Jesus; it must be replaced by it. The gospel is no patch; it must replace the old and worn-out garment. In Mk. there is only a brief allusion to the coming of the Son of Man (13²⁴⁻²⁷), in Mt. an extended description.

'Let the dead bury their dead' (8²²); 'Cast not your pearls before swine' (7⁶); 'Do men gather grapes of thorns, or figs of thistles?' (7¹⁶), are some of the striking expressions found in Mt. alone, as also the declaration that no man should be called 'father' (23⁹); cf. the acted metaphor (17²⁶), nowhere else recorded, by which Jesus metaphorically claims that the God of the Temple is His Father, when He declares His legal exemption from the Temple tax. There are a number of peculiarly picturesque and humorous metaphors for which we are indebted to Matthew. The Pharisees are 'whitewashed tombs' full of putridity (23²⁷); 'blind guides of the blind' (15¹⁴ 23¹⁶, ²⁴); 'wolves in sheep's clothing' (7¹⁵). One who truly exhibits the law of righteousness (which is unselfishness and love) does not let his left hand know what his right hand doeth (6³); but these men blow a trumpet before them, not only when they give alms, but when they pray (cf. the remark in the Teaching of the Twelve Apostles [xii. 1], that a teacher of the true doctrine is known to one who 'has understanding of the right hand and the left'). They make long prayers and 'devour widows' houses' (23¹⁴ or ¹³?). These hair-splitting theologians, so particular in their eating, strain out the gnat but swallow the camel (23²⁴).* Christ's yoke does not gall (11³⁰), but these men lay upon the shoulders of others burdens which they will not move even with the finger (23⁴). For such is the 'weeping and the gnashing of teeth' (8¹² 13⁴². ⁵⁰ 22¹³ 24⁵¹ 25³⁰, elsewhere only Lk 13²⁸). These satiric pictures of the theologians of the day are peculiar to Matthew. Both Mt. and Lk. refer to the same individuals as hyper-critics, who are greatly disturbed by the mote in their brother's eye, although they have a beam in their own. Forgetting their own infirmity and need of immediate surgical assistance, they use the other eye, which must also have been sympathetically afflicted, in spying out and ridiculing the speck of dust in the eye of their neighbour (Mt 7³⁻⁵=Lk 6⁴¹ᶠ.). Nothing in Hogarth is better than that.

In Lk., several of the Beatitudes concerning the poor and hungry take on a distinctly different meaning from what they had in Mt. (5³. ⁶); the words 'poor' and 'hungry' (6²⁰. ²³) having perhaps obtained a settled ecclesiastical, non-literal meaning.

who enters it; but no Oriental would have criticised the use of these varying metaphors.
* All the Synoptics report the saying of Christ that it is easier for a camel to go through a needle's eye than, etc. (Mk 10²⁵, Mt 19²⁴, Lk 18²⁵). The Talmud has the same expression, excepting that an elephant takes the place of the camel (quoted by Arthur Wright, Some NT Problems, p. 127).

The storming of the Kingdom of heaven by those who upset the Law in their anxiety to hurry into the Kingdom of the gospel, while obscured in Mt. (11¹²), is explained in Lk. (16¹⁶· ¹⁷). The mixed figures used by Mk. (4¹⁴⁻¹⁶) and Mt. (13¹⁹),—sometimes similes and sometimes metaphors,—representing men in one breath as both soil and seed, disappear in Lk.'s beautiful symmetrical narrative (8⁵ff·). He, too, is responsible for the injunction 'Make for yourselves purses which wax not old' (12³³), and for the attractive Orientalism 'son of peace' (10⁶) added to Mt 10¹³, and for the less commendable addition that the descent of the Spirit at the baptism of Jesus, which Mk. and Mt. had said to be 'like a dove,'—and which Jn. explains to have been 'as a dove,' i.e. in a softly, floating manner (Moulton),—was 'in bodily form' (3²²). Instead of Mt.'s metaphorical reference to the Pharisees as painted sepulchres (23²⁷), beautiful to look at but foul within, Lk. makes Jesus speak of them as unsuspected graves (μνημεῖα) which defile every one who comes near them (11⁴⁴). The 'mountain' of Mt. (17²⁰), which can be cast into the sea by any disciple who has faith as fully alive as a mustard seed, becomes a 'tree' in Lk. (17⁶). The 'seventy-seven' acts of forgiveness required of Jesus' disciples, according to Mt. (18²²), are expressed with equal truth and vigour by Lk. when he reduces that number to 'seven' (17⁴). The satirical remark that wealth can build a man an 'eternal tent' (Lk 16⁹), and the hyperbole that one must 'hate' (μισέω) his father and mother in order to be a true disciple of Jesus (14²⁶), are original with Lk.; as also the statement that the disciples must 'win their souls' (21¹⁹), and that the Pharisees take away the 'key of knowledge' (11⁵², cf. Mt 16¹⁹).

Lk., which shows more attention to literary style than any other NT writing except the Hebrews (Moulton), uses far fewer original metaphors. This is because it was not a first-hand work, but a compilation (1³). Even the beautiful reference to Jesus as the Sun-rise (1⁷⁸) looks back to the OT; and the terms 'torment' and 'fixed gulf' in the Dives parable, which are peculiar to Lk., are found in the medical works of that period; while the word used for the life immediately after death—Paradise—is the word for the garden of delight in which our first parents dwelt (Gn 2⁸ LXX). In Lk., as truly as in Jn., the Baptist not only preaches the whole gospel, social, ethical, and sacrificial, but uses the favourite metaphors of Jesus; while Elisabeth and Mary, Zacharias and Simeon, all speak in blank verse, every line being filled with OT imagery. The nautical metaphors of Lk. are few and doubtful (cf. Expos. VI. viii. [1903] 130). It does not even use the striking phrase 'fishers of men' common to both Mk. and Mt.

In the Fourth Gospel we have not many new figures of speech, but all the old ones are filled with new contents. Even the old title 'Son of Man' becomes exalted (1⁵⁷ 5²⁷). In the Synoptt. Jesus points out the way; in Jn. He is 'the Way' (14⁶). In the Synoptt. He gives life; in Jn. He is 'Life,' and 'the Life' (1⁴), and large inferences are drawn from this. He is also called 'the Resurrection' (11²⁵). In the Synoptt. Jesus is like a shepherd, but in Jn. He has become both Shepherd and Gate of the fold (10⁷· ¹¹). In the Synoptt. Jesus speaks the word; in Jn. He is 'the Word,' and the term has taken into itself a new and mystic meaning: ὁ λόγος has come to mean the eternal thought of Jehovah given visible utterance, the sacred Tetra-grammaton manifested in flesh (1¹⁴), whose word (ὁ λόγος) or words (τὰ ῥήματα) are a part of His own Divine essence, to abide in which is to abide in Him (5³⁸ 8³¹). Either term expresses the creative, cleansing, protecting power of the Divine Name.

The unity of the spoken word with the speaker is metaphorically regarded as an identity equivalent to that between Christ and the Father (14¹⁰, cf. 10³⁰). But the unity of the word with the speaker, or of Christ with His Father, is no closer than that between the Christ and His true disciples. He abides in them and they abide in Him (6⁵⁶ 15⁴ 17²⁶; cf. 6⁷⁰, where Judas, because of his relationship with Satan, becomes diabolos). So all believers may become one 'as thou, Father, art in me and I in thee' (17²¹). The Christ, the 'only begotten' (1¹⁴· ¹⁸ 3¹⁶· ¹⁸), is the Vine (15¹), His body a sanctuary (2¹⁹); even while on the earth He is 'in heaven' (3¹³), and holds His disciples and all things in His hand (10²⁸ 3³⁵). Those in whom the Word abides (15⁷) and who abide in the Word (8³¹) — these metaphors being interchangeable — cannot 'taste death' (8⁵²), nor even 'look on death' (8⁵¹).*

In Jn., more than in any other Gospel, metaphors become an important factor in doctrinal development. These mystic figures of speech indicate the growth of the Church in theological development, and have also played no little part in shaping the later doctrines of Christendom. A freely translated expression in the Psalms concerning the manna which came from heaven is made the occasion, metaphorically interpreted, of deep and beautiful teachings concerning the heavenly origin of the Christ and His power to give life (6³³· ³⁵· ⁵¹). To eat Him is the only way to gain life (6⁵¹· ⁵³· ⁵⁸). So Jesus is the well of salvation out of which men may draw water with great joy (cf. Is 12³); not only satisfying their own thirst thereby, but becoming living fountains which send forth floods of life-giving water such as came from Jesus Himself (4¹⁰⁻¹⁴ 7³⁸). In the Acts (8³²) Jesus goes as a lamb to the slaughter; in Jn. He is the Lamb (1²⁹· ³⁶) 'exalted' upon the cross-altar (3¹⁴ 12³²· ³⁴ [ὑψόω is peculiar to Jn.]).

CAMDEN M. COBERN.

METHUSELAH.—Mentioned as a link in our Lord's genealogy, Lk 3³⁷.

MILE.—See WEIGHTS AND MEASURES.

MILL (μυλών), **MILL-STONE** (μύλος, λίθος μυλικός).—The hand-mill used in Palestine consists of two stone discs, from a foot to a foot and a half in diameter, the upper being about 2 in., the lower 3 in. thick. A porous stone of black basalt is preferred, as being sufficiently hard and not so liable as ordinary limestone to become glazed by the friction of the two surfaces against each other (Job 41²⁴). The stones are usually flat, but not infrequently the concave face of the upper stone rests upon the corresponding convex of the lower one, so as to facilitate the passing out of the flour in the act of rotation. The lower stone is always the heavier of the two, because it is thicker and because it is often a little wider, with a rebate or raised rim; and the upper stone fits into the recess thus formed. The flour then escapes from an opening several inches long where the rim of the lower stone has been cut away. The upper stone has an opening through the centre for the reception of the upright wooden pin projecting from the centre of the lower stone. Into this hole the wheat is poured in the process of grinding. The upper stone has near the circumference a wooden peg a little over two handbreadths in height, and when the stone is being turned by two women (Mt 24⁴¹), sitting on opposite sides of it, each grasps the peg continuously with one hand and alternately draws it to herself and pushes it away. Partly on account of their position in sitting, and

* For Oriental parallels to the Logos in other Oriental religions, see *JRAS*, April 1906.

partly to keep the edge of the skirt away from the cloth spread for the flour, they usually draw up the dress to the knee (Is 47[1. 2]). The sound of the hand-mill grinding the flour for the daily bread was suggestive of home life under conditions of peace and prosperity, and its cessation betokened turmoil and distress (Ec 12[3. 4], Jer 25[10. 11]). The μύλος ὀνικός, or donkey stone of Lk 17[2], may simply mean the revolving upper stone of the common hand-mill, as having the more active share in the work of grinding. If the reference be to the larger kind of stone driven by animal or water power, the allusion would be a case of emphatic hyperbole, like the passage of a camel through the slit of a needle (Mt 19[24]). In Rev 18[21] it is a strong angel that is described as casting such a stone. See, further, art. 'Mill,' with illustration, in Hastings' *DB*.   G. M. MACKIE

MINA.—See MONEY.

MIND.—See MENTAL CHARACTERISTICS.

MINISTER, MINISTRATION.—**1.** ὑπηρέτης : Lk 1[2] ὑπηρέται τοῦ λόγου, 4[20] ἀποδοὺς τῷ ὑπηρέτῃ.

ὑπηρέτης is originally 'a rower' (from ἐρέσσω,—the ὑπό pointing to his being under the direction of the κυβερνήτης or steersman, who was the navigating officer : *Encyc. Brit.*[9] xxi. 808). It is commonly used in class. Gr. in the sense of 'a doer of hard work,' 'an assistant' or 'apparitor' or 'inferior officer,' but still retains the meaning of 'one who is under the direction or control of another' (*e.g.* ὑπηρέται is the term employed by Xenophon for the adjutants or orderlies of a general).

In Bibl. Greek 'the word covers a wide range of offices,' but still retains this meaning : *e.g.* Mt 5[25] (the officer of a court of justice = πράκτωρ, Lk 12[58]), Mt 26[58], Mk 14[54. 65], Jn 7[32. 45. 46] 18[3. 12. 18. 22] 19[6], Ac 5[22. 26] (the Temple police, or apparitors of the Sanhedrin ; cf. Hastings' *DB* iv. 715[b] ; *Encyc. Bibl.* iv. 4650 ; Swete, *St. Mark*, xii. 329, 335). In Jn 18[36] our Lord says, 'If my kingdom were of this world, then would my ὑπηρέται ('officers,' RVm) fight' ; with which cf. (for a similar connexion of ὑπηρέται) LXX Pr 14[35] δεκτὸς βασιλεῖ ὑπηρέτης νοήμων, Wis 6[5] (kings) ὑπηρέται ὄντες τῆς αὐτοῦ (*i.e.* God's) βασιλείας. In Ac 26[16] ὑπηρέτην points to the service of complete subjection into which St. Paul was called to enter, when Jesus appeared to him as the Risen Lord. He and Apollos and Cephas are ὑπηρέται Χριστοῦ (1 Co 4[1]). Lk.'s ὑπηρέται τοῦ λόγου may be due to his having heard St. Paul use this and similar expressions, and describes the αὐτόπται τῶν πεπληροφορημένων πραγμάτων in their service of entire subjection to the gospel (here τοῦ λόγου= 'the gospel' as in other Lukan passages, Ac 6[2. 4] 8[4] 10[44] 11[19] 14[25] 16[6] 17[11]). 'ὑπηρέτης and διάκονος are often used interchangeably' (Hort, *Ecclesia*, 210 ; cf. Trench, *Synon.* ix. (near end) ; Hastings' *DB* iii. 378[a]).

In Lk 4[20] the ὑπηρέτης is the synagogue official called the *ḥazzān*, who during public worship 'hands the copy of the Scriptures to the reader, and receives it back from the hands of the man who has read the final lesson. . . . The *ḥazzān* rolls up the Torah roll after the reading, and, after holding it up to view, deposits it in the press' (Hastings' *DB* iv. 640[b] ; cf. Edersheim, *Life and Times of Jesus*, i. 438). Chase conjectures that John Mark was originally a *ḥazzān* or synagogue attendant (Ac 13[5] ; Hastings' *DB* iii. 245[b]).

2. λειτουργία : Lk 1[23] αἱ ἡμέραι τῆς λειτουργίας αὐτοῦ, 'the days of his ministration,' *i.e.* the week during which he was on priestly duty in the Temple.

λειτουργία is of common occurrence in LXX in the sense of ritual service (=עֲבֹדָה Nu 8[22] 16[9] 18[4], 2 Ch 31[2] ; cf. Diod. Sic. i. 21 (of the Egyptian priesthood), τὰς τῶν θεῶν θεραπείας τε καὶ λειτουργίας). At Athens the λειτουργίαι (from obsol. ἔργω= ἐργάζομαι, and λεῖτος, λήϊτος [fr. λαός]) were State burdens of a peculiar kind laid on the citizens, *e.g.* defraying the cost of

public choruses, or of the training of athletes, or of feasting one's fellow-tribesmen (Xen. *de Rep. Ath.* i. 13 ; Becker, *Charicles*, sc. iv. n. 23 ; *Dict. Antiq.* ii. 27). The use of λειτουργία in a ritual sense is not peculiar to LXX, the Papyri having shown that it was common in Egypt, and in particular that the services in the Serapeum were designated by this title (Deissmann, *Bible Studies*, 138 ; cf. Moulton, *Expositor*, VI. vii. [1903] 116).

Lk. speaks of the prophets and teachers at Antioch λειτουργούντων τῷ Κυρίῳ, by which prayers to Christ are probably meant (Ac 13[2]). λειτουργεῖν and the group of words connected with it are used, as in LXX, by the writer of Hebrews of the ministry of the tabernacle (9[21] 10[11]) ; metaphorically, of the more excellent ministry of Christ as High Priest in the heavenly sanctuary (8[2. 6]) ; they are also applied to the ministry of angels (1[7. 14]). St. Paul speaks of civil rulers as λειτουργοὶ θεοῦ, thus ascribing to them a sacred function (Ro 13[6]). Evidently the ritual sense of this group of words is always present to the mind of the Apostle when he has occasion to use them (Ro 15[16] 'Paul the ministering priest, the preaching of the gospel his priestly function, the believing Gentiles his offering' [Gifford], Ro 15[27], 2 Co 9[12], Ph 2[17] 'the Philippians the priests, their faith the sacrifice, the apostle's life-blood the accompanying libation' [Lightfoot], Ph 2[25. 30] ; cf. Westcott on He[1], p. 231). Those passages also show that Christ's ministers are sacrificing priests only in the same sense as the rest of the members of the Christian brotherhood, who render λειτουργίαι to God and to men by 'the work of faith, and the labour of love' (cf. Hastings' *DB* iii. 377[a] ; Lightfoot, *Philip.*[2] p. 182).—The application of λειτουργία to the prayers offered at the dispensation of the Lord's Supper is a comparatively late ecclesiastical usage (Cheetham, *Dict. Chris. Antiq.* ii. 1018 ; Lightfoot, *l.c.* 261 ; Trench, *Synon.* xxxv).

3. διάκονος, διακονεῖν, -εῖσθαι (διηκόνουν, διηκόνησα, later impf. and aor. for ἐδιακόνουν, ἐδιακόνησα).—

The derivation of διάκονος is uncertain. If Buttmann's conjecture is right (*Lexil.* i. 218), that the root of the word is an obsolete verb διάκω=διώκω, it may have originally meant 'a messenger.' Prellwitz (*Etymol. Wörterbuch*, 74) connects it with=ἐγκονέω, 'to be active,' the long α being explained as arising from διά+α=a weak form of the ἐν in ἐγκονέω. The original meaning would then be 'one who is quick and active in service.' The Greek usage of the word is fully dealt with by Hort (*Ecclesia*, 202 ff.), who quotes, amongst other passages which bring out its menial associations, Plato, *Gorg.* i. 518 A, where it is¹ said that, except gymnastics and medicine, 'all other arts which have to do with the body are servile and menial (διακονικάς) and illiberal.' Hort also shows that by later Greek writers it was sometimes used in a lofty figurative sense, *e.g.* by Epictetus, *Dissertationes*, iv. 7. 20, 'For I think that what God chooses is better than what I choose. I will attach myself as a minister and follower (διάκονος καὶ ἀκόλουθος) to Him ; I have the same movements as He has, I have the same desires ; in a word, I have the same will (συνθέλω).' *Long's translation*, 348.— 'The true proper Greek sense' is 'an attendant whose duty it is to wait on his master at table.'

In the Gospels, διάκονος and its derivatives are used in the sense of preparing or serving a meal, Mk 1[13] (|| Mt 4[11]), Mk 1[31] (|| Mt 8[15], Lk 4[39]), Lk 10[40] 12[37] 17[8], Mt 22[13], Jn 2[5. 9] 12[2] ; in the same sense, figuratively, Mk 9[35] (not exactly || Mt 23[11], Lk 22[26. 27]), Mk 10[43. 45] (|| Mt 20[26. 28]), Jn 12[26] ; of ministering service generally, Lk 8[3], Mk 15[41], Mt 27[55] 25[44]. διάκονος does not occur in St. Luke, who uses ὁ διακονῶν (22[26. 27]).

The passages in which 'minister,' 'to minister,' are the renderings adopted in AV and RV, are the following : (i.) Of the ministry of angels, Mk 1[13] (|| Mt 4[11]) οἱ ἄγγελοι διηκόνουν αὐτῷ, cf. Gn 28[12], 1 K 19[5], Dn 10[21], Jn 1[51], Lk 22[43], He 1[14], 1 P 1[12]. Christ's nativity, His temptation, His agony, His resurrection, His ascension, were all accompanied by their sympathetic ministrations.—(ii.) Of Peter's wife's mother, Mk 1[31] (|| Mt 8[15], Lk 4[39]) διηκόνει αὐτοῖς at the Sabbath meal immediately after the fever left her. 'Et nos ministremus Jesu' (Jerome, quoted by Swete, *in loc.*).—(iii.) Of the ministering women, Lk 8[3] (Mk 15[41], Mt 27[55]) αἵτινες διηκόνουν

αὐτῷ [αὐτοῖς] ἐκ τῶν ὑπαρχόντων αὐταῖς, and continued doing so till the close of Christ's life on earth. αἵτινες (=tales quœ) may imply that they had the heart as well as the means to minister to Him. Lk. has much to tell us about the women friends of Jesus (e.g. 10³⁸⁻⁴² 11²⁷ 23²⁷ 24²²).—(iv.) The great sayings about service being the path to true greatness, Mk 9³⁵ πάντων διάκονος, 'minister of all,' RV (not exactly ‖ Mt 23¹¹, Lk 22²⁶· ²⁷), Mk 10⁴³· ⁴⁵ (Mt 20²⁶· ²⁸, which is followed by an extensive interpolation of a similar tenor in DΦ, Hastings' DB, Ext. Vol. 345ᵃ) ἔσται ὑμῶν διάκονος . . . καὶ γὰρ ὁ υἱὸς τοῦ ἀνθρώπου οὐκ ἦλθε διακονηθῆναι ἀλλὰ διακονῆσαι.— Promotion to true greatness is not effected by such methods as are adopted by 'the princes of the Gentiles' to gain or to retain supreme power ; nor does it depend on an act of partiality, such as the sons of Zebedee imagined might be exercised in their favour if they applied for it in time. It is regulated by fixed spiritual laws, or by the general principle that honour comes in the Kingdom of God by disinterested love. As 'to get pleasure you must forget it' (Seth, Eth. Principles, 66 ; W. L. Davidson, Theism, 372), so to be great you must cease to think of greatness and humble yourself to serve others, which includes the being quick to discern and open-hearted to minister to their needs, even to the sacrificing of yourself for their good. They who shall have the highest place in God's household are they who take the duties of its humblest member, the δοῦλος, upon themselves ; and they who shall be qualified to sit down at the feast of salvation are they who fulfil the work of the διάκονος at table, who wait upon those whom God regards as His guests, and minister to their wants (cf. Menzies, Mark, 200). Jesus sets forth this principle in the most touching manner as that of His own life (cf. Ac 10³⁸). He is Himself the living embodiment of the truth which He teaches. In saying that He 'came not to be ministered unto, but to minister,' He does not mean that the ministrations He is receiving are not welcome, but He defines the main object of His sojourning in this world, and speaks of Himself not as the Guest whom the whole world will delight to honour, but as the humble attendant upon those who are in want ; not as the Benefactor who is to be raised by men to the highest earthly glory, but as One who is come to serve them (seeing that on account of the state they are in there is no other way in which He can effectually and completely serve them) by the surrender of life itself (cf. Mk 15³¹). This was Jesus' path to the most exalted greatness. It led to there being given Him by God 'the name which is above every name' (Ph 2⁹, cf. He 2⁹), and also to His receiving from man the undying homage of his heart, together with the confession of the tongue that his highest ideal of human goodness and service is now realized in Jesus. So, when we follow His example and are lifted out of ourselves by His Spirit of ministering love, everything that came to Him will come to us, according to the measure in which we, who are infinitely inferior to Him, will be found meet for it,—God's approval of our life, increasing influence for good, that true greatness which consists in our becoming better able to elevate and bless our fellow-men (cf. Caird, Univ. Serm. 260), and to minister to them in the highest way by leading them to righteousness (Dn 12³), and which may also comprehend the power to minister to them in a higher state of being (cf. Mt 25²¹, Lk 19¹⁷).*
—(v.) Mt 25⁴⁴ πότε . . . οὐ διηκονήσαμέν σοι ; those words supplement in a solemn way the sayings just commented upon. Ministering love is not only the path to true greatness, it is also the indispensable

* ' My idea of heaven is the perpetual ministry of one soul to another ' (Tennyson, Memoir by his Son, ii. 421).

condition of future exaltation with Christ. He who 'for our sakes became poor,' who turned the light of His infinite pity upon the world of hunger, poverty, and misery, still calls the hungry and poor and miserable ' His brethren,' and accounts their cause His own. Not to have ministered to their needs is not to have ministered to His (cf. Lowell, 'The Vision of Sir Launfal' ; and 'The Legend of St. Martin's Cloak,' Farrar, Lives of the Fathers, i. 630). At His coming in glory, Christ will declare His love to those who have loved, and will admit them as ' joint-heirs with Himself ' ; but He will reject as unmeet for companionship with Him those who have not taken the position among their fellow-men which He showed them how to take when He said, Ἐγὼ δέ εἰμι ἐν μέσῳ ὑμῶν ὡς ὁ διακονῶν (Lk 22²⁷, cf. Jn 13⁵).—These sayings of Jesus virtually create a new standard of social ethics. They give to the prophetic teaching of the OT on considerate and brotherly conduct (חֶסֶד, see W. R. Smith, Proph.¹ 160, 407 ; Driver, Sermons on OT, 221, 232) the breadth and completeness which it yet lacked. ' If we wish to feel the contrast of the Pagan and the Christian ideals of greatness, we have only to compare the Aristotelian picture of the μεγαλόψυχος, the proud aristocrat who lives to prove his independence and superiority, with that other picture of a Life that poured itself out in the service of others ' (Seth, Eth. Principles, 264).

Later Stoicism ' sometimes expressed with much warmth the recognition of the universal fellowship and natural mutual claims of human beings as such ' (Sidgwick, Hist. of Ethics, 120), but this was really inconsistent with the hard isolation of the individual that was the fundamental basis of Stoicism (Lightfoot on Ph², ' St. Paul and Seneca,' 296), and the practical results of such teaching were small (Lecky, Europ. Morals¹², ii. 78–79). Numerous coincidences are found between the teaching of Jesus and the humane sayings of Seneca, Epictetus, and Marcus Aurelius. But, as Lightfoot observes (l.c. 291), ' an expression or a maxim, which detached from its context offers a striking resemblance to the ethics of the Gospel, is found to have a wholly different bearing when considered in its proper relations.' Stoicism was wholly wanting in humility, which is the very foundation of ministering love as taught by Jesus (cf. Westcott in Smith's DB ii. 857ᵇ, iii. 1380). With Him, such love is not an occasional precept of benevolence, but, as Harnack says (What is Christianity? 98), it is ' the religious maxim.'

The following passages will show some of the results produced by our Lord's teaching in Christian thought and life. There are differences of διακονίαι (1 Co 12⁵), but the manifold faculties for ' the work of ministering ' are gifts from the Exalted Lord (Eph 4¹²), and each disciple has received a gift of some kind to be laid out in Christian service (1 P 4¹⁰· ¹¹). Some are called to the ministry of the word (Ac 6⁴, 2 Co 3⁶ 6⁴, Col 4¹⁷, 1 Th 3², 2 Ti 4⁵), to testify the gospel of the grace of God (Ac 20²⁴) and win men to faith (1 Co 3⁵) ; God has committed to such ' the ministry of reconciliation ' (2 Co 5¹⁸). Some as attendants and comrades can strengthen the hands of those engaged in this work : St. Paul was thus helped by Timothy and Erastus (Ac 19²²), by Tychicus (Eph 6²¹, Col 4⁷), by Onesiphorus (2 Ti 1¹⁸), by Mark (2 Ti 4¹¹), by Onesimus (Philem 13). Some can render invaluable help in the local churches, as Stephanas and his household at Corinth (1 Co 16¹⁵), and Phœbe at Cenchreæ (Ro 16¹). Ministering to the wants of the poor, the sick, the stranger, the prisoner, was constantly called for (Ac 6¹· ², Ro 12⁷, He 6¹⁰, cf. 10³⁴, Rev 2¹⁹). A collection (two are mentioned) is a διακονία (Ac 11²⁹ 12²⁵, Ro 15³¹, 2 Co 8⁴· ¹⁹· ²⁰ 9¹· ¹²· ¹³), and St. Paul speaks of his journey in charge of the latter as itself a part of the ministration (Ro 15²⁵ πορευόμαι . . . διακονῶν τοῖς ἁγίοις, see Gifford's note). The above passages show that 'a faithful minister of Christ' (Col 1⁷, cf. 1 Ti 4⁶) is one who combines with the stated ministry of the gospel the service of his fellow-men in things temporal and external.—Thus διάκονος, διακονεῖν, in showing men the path to greatness, have themselves attained to greatness. It is true of words as well as of persons, that God as revealed in Christ 'hath exalted them of low degree' (Lk 1⁵²).

LITERATURE.—Stephanus, Thesaurus (Hase and Dindorf's ed.); Hastings' and other Dictionaries of the Bible ; Dict. of Antiquities ; Dict. of Christian Antiquities ; Hort, The Christian Ecclesia ; Lightfoot, Philippians ; Deissmann, Bible Studies ; Swete, St. Mark ; Menzies, Mark ; Trench, Synon. ix, xxxv ; F. W. Robertson, Human Race, 143 ; R. W. Dale, Fellowship with Christ, 247 ; P. Brooks, Mystery of Iniquity, 327 ; R. W. Church, Human Life, 125 ; W. Sanday, Conception of Priesthood, 35.   JAMES DONALD.

MINISTRY.—The word 'ministry' as now used in English has two leading senses : (a) service rendered, and (b) an official class, especially ecclesiastical. The latter has no place in this discussion, which has regard to the public service rendered by our Lord during His life on earth. In this connexion it describes both the period of the service and its contents. The word comes from the Latin *minister*, properly an adjective, but in its substantive use signifying an 'attendant' or 'servant' who usually performed services of a personal and more or less menial nature. It was also sometimes used of public or religious functionaries. In Greek there are three words which more or less nearly correspond to the Latin *minister*, namely, διάκονος, λειτουργός, ὑπηρέτης. See preceding article.

i. **The Nature of our Lord's Ministry.**—In the mind of Jesus Himself there lay the ideas of both sacrifice and service as the essential principles of His mission among men.

1. The first element to be noticed is *service*. This presents a threefold aspect: (a) It was notably and characteristically a ministry of *teaching*. The frequent mention of His teaching, the reports of His discourses and sayings, and the fact that He was often called 'Teacher,' emphasize as all-important this function of His ministry. The varied character, the weighty contents, the marvellous power and the sweet charm of His teaching, are familiar thoughts to students of His life. But we must remember also the arduous nature of this work. The bodily toil, the mental strain, the spiritual intensity, all were great; and these were increased by the constant opposition of critics and foes, and by slowness of comprehension on the part of His friends. (b) But incidental to and accompanying this work of teaching was Christ's great ministry of *help and healing*. All the narratives show how large a place this occupied in His public life. Here, too, His labours were vast in sum, and made extraordinary demands—as many indications show—upon His sympathy and strength. (c) Closely related to His teaching, but not exactly identical with it, was our Lord's ministry of *founding His Church*. The selection and training of His Apostles and other disciples, involving many details of precept in regard to both the principles and the positive institutions of the Kingdom of God, were elements of the first importance in the earthly work of Jesus.

2. The other element is that of *sacrifice*. This was no less prominent in the ministry of Jesus than service. (a) In the Synoptics there is a progress of thought in regard to the fact and meaning of His sufferings. After Peter's confession near Cæsarea Philippi, Jesus began to impress on His disciples the certainty of His approaching death (Mt 16[16. 21]); at the Transfiguration, Moses and Elijah talked with Him of His 'decease (ἔξοδος) which he was to accomplish at Jerusalem' (Lk 9[31]); soon after (Mt 17[22f.]) He again spoke of His coming death. The self-giving character of His sufferings is indicated in the manner in whch they are spoken of in Lk 9[22-24], Mt 20[22], as compared with Lk 12[50]; and the severity of this experience as being something more than death alone, however painful, is indicated in the passages noted, and powerfully enforced by the Agony in Gethsemane and the events of the Crucifixion. Finally, the atoning value of Christ's sacrifice is pointed out in Mt 20[28]—the words 'and give his life a ransom for many,' and in the accounts of the Last Supper (Mt 26[27. 28], Mk 14[24], Lk 22[19. 20]). (b) In the Fourth Gospel the sacrificial note is even more distinct. It appears in the announcement of the Forerunner (Jn 1[29. 36]), in the great saying to Nicodemus (3[14-16]), in the discourse at Capernaum (6[32. 33. 48-51]), in the parable of the Good Shepherd (10[11. 15. 17. 18]), in the remarks on the visit of the

Greeks (12[20-33]), and in the words of comfort to the disciples (15[13]). (c) How strongly the Lord must have impressed this view of His ministry upon the minds of His disciples, is shown in utterances of Peter and of Paul in their addresses and in their Epistles, in the elaborate argument of the Epistle to the Hebrews, and in the representations of the Lamb in the Apocalypse.

ii. **The Extent of our Lord's Ministry.**—In regard to the extent of the public ministry of Jesus, three main questions present themselves: How long did it last? How much territory did it cover? How much labour did it include?

1. *Duration.*—On the point of duration the principal things to be considered are the limits, the dates, and the resultant theories of scholars. (1) The limits of the public ministry of Jesus are properly placed between His baptism and His burial, leaving out at the beginning the thirty years of retirement and preparation at Nazareth, and at the end the forty days of occasional appearances after His resurrection. The determination of the time between is a hard problem.

(2) The principal dates to be determined in our Lord's life are those of His birth, baptism, and crucifixion—the duration of the ministry depending upon the latter two, but involving the first. If it were possible to fix with certainty any two of these, the problem would practically be solved; or, if even one could be placed beyond doubt, it would be greatly simplified. But as a matter of fact scholars have never been able to decide positively on any one of the dates. A full discussion is not called for here (see art. DATES), but the salient points must be presented.

(a) For the Birth of Jesus, we know that it occurred in the reign of the emperor Augustus (Lk 2[1-6]), and not long before the death of Herod the Great (Mt 2[1. 19]). Herod died probably not later than B.C. 4, as is made out from statements of Josephus (see DATES), and thus it appears that by an early error (of Dionysius Exiguus, an abbot of the 6th cent.) the generally accepted era of Christ's birth has been irrevocably fixed a few years later than the actual time. The probable date of the Nativity is somewhere between B.C. 6 and 4.

(b) For the Baptism, we know that it took place at some time within the 'fifteenth year of Tiberius Cæsar' (Lk 3[1. 2]), for this was the time that John began to baptize, and Jesus was among those who received the rite at his hands (Mt 3[13], Mk 1[9], Lk 3[21]); but none of the accounts gives any definite note as to the exact point during the ministry of John when the baptism occurred. St. Luke states (3[23]) that 'Jesus when he *began* (presumably His ministry or teaching) was *about* thirty years old.' But neither His exact age nor the exact point of His 'beginning' is indicated. The probability is that He was either just thirty, or from one to three years past that—hardly under thirty. So that here we have no certain number of years to add to the already uncertain year of the Lord's birth. If we take B.C. 4 as the Birth date and add thirty years, it brings us to A.D. 26 as the probable year of the baptism; but if St. Luke's 'about thirty' be extended two years, it would be 28. Now, as to the 'fifteenth year of Tiberius,' that was probably the year 28, but may have been 26. Augustus died in A.D. 14 (Aug. 19), and, if the beginning of the reign of his successor Tiberius be reckoned from that date, the 'fifteenth year' would begin in Aug. 28, and the baptism of Jesus would be at some time in the twelve months following. But it is possible that St. Luke dates the beginning of Tiberius' reign from the time he was associated in the government with Augustus, *i.e.* in A.D. 12; and so the 'fifteenth year' could begin in Aug. 26.

On this, however, it is proper to remark that the more common mode of reckoning would be from the actual sole reign, and not from the previous association of an emperor in the government.

(c) For the Crucifixion, we know that it occurred during the governorship of Pontius Pilate in Judæa (all the Evangelists), and this administration covered about ten years, from A.D. 26 to 36. Other data (see DATES) help to fix upon near the central part of this period as the time of the Crucifixion, between 28 and 31, more likely 29 or 30.

(3) These uncertainties have given rise among scholars to a number of different theories of the duration of our Lord's ministry. It will be sufficient to mention three, among which choice, according to what seems to be the greatest probability, should be made.

(a) The *short period* theory. This assigns but a little over a year to the ministry. According to it, the Baptism probably occurred early in the year 29, that is, during the fifteenth year of Tiberius, reckoning that to have begun in Aug. 28, and the Baptism to have taken place early in the year following. The first Passover (Jn 2¹³) came soon after, and the last Passover just a year later. Between these two Passovers lay the whole ministry, hence this theory is called the *bipaschal* view. To obtain this result, the feast of Jn 5¹ is held not to be a Passover; the text of Jn 6⁴ is regarded as incorrect (on slight documentary evidence), and read as omitting 'of the passover,' and so leaving this also an unnamed feast. After disposing of these two feasts, the order of feasts mentioned in John is fixed as follows: Passover (2¹³), A.D. 29; Pentecost (5¹), nameless or omitted (6⁴), Tabernacles (7²), Dedication (10²²), and Passover (11⁵⁵), spring of A.D. 30. With this scheme derived from the Fourth Gospel, the data furnished by the Synoptics is made to harmonize by slighting the indications of a time of nearly ripe grain (Mt 12¹, Mk 2²³, Lk 6¹), which it is hard to locate if there were only two Passovers in the whole series of events. But this theory is defended (see von Soden in *Encyc. Bibl.*) on the following grounds: (i.) That the correct interpretation of the 'fifteenth year' of Tiberius is from the date of his sole reign, and therefore is A.D. 28–29. (ii.) The events of the Gospel narrative are too meagre to have extended over more than a year. (iii.) This view was held by many of the Fathers as early as the 2nd century. The only one of these grounds that has any real force is the first, and as to that it may be replied that we are not compelled to put the Crucifixion in 30, and thereby limit the time to one year. The second ground is entirely subjective—to many other scholars it seems far too short a time for all the events (with their implications of others and of intervals) to have taken place. As to the third ground, it may be said that the Fathers were not unanimous, and they had only the same data for forming opinions that modern and more accurate chronologers have. Besides its inadequacy to account for all the facts, this theory deals in an arbitrary way with the text of Jn 6⁴ and with the indication furnished by the incident of the grain fields (Mt 12¹ etc.).

(b) The *long period* theory. This holds that there were four Passovers in the ministry, and is hence called the *quadripaschal* theory. It dates from Eusebius in the 4th cent., and is held by many modern scholars. This takes the unnamed feast of Jn 5¹ to be a Passover, holds to the commonly received text of Jn 6⁴, puts the Baptism early in 27 and the Crucifixion in 30, thus making the ministry extend over three years. But there is

difference of arrangement of details even among those who hold this view, and it is not at all certain that the feast of Jn 5¹ can be fixed as a Passover.

(c) The *medium period* theory. This holds that the feast of Jn 5¹ is not a Passover, and that there were only three Passovers in the ministry—so the *tripaschal* theory. As to what feast it was, and as to the arrangement of all the details, there is much difference among the advocates of the medium period. But from a year and a half to two and a half is the time allowed by those who reject both the other theories. If the Baptism occurred in the autumn of 28 and early spring of 29, then to get in three Passovers it will be necessary to put the Crucifixion in 31—to which there are serious objections. But if the Baptism was in 26–27, then the Crucifixion could be assigned to 29, which is not improbable. It must be said in view of all these difficulties, that no positive convictions in regard to the duration of the ministry are, in the present state of knowledge, tenable, but the probabilities are upon the whole in favour of a ministry of more than one and less than three years' duration.

2. *Localities.*—In regard to the topographical extent of our Lord's ministry we have a much simpler question to deal with. His labours extended throughout Palestine, and on a few occasions to contiguous lands. (a) Judæa, in several different places, and more especially Jerusalem, witnessed some of His most important deeds and teachings. (b) Galilee, however, was the principal scene of His teaching and healing work. The Lake and its cities,—Capernaum with others,—Nazareth, Cana, and other towns and a number of villages, the plains and mountains of populous Galilee shared in the deeds of His busy life. Two certainly, and probably three, separate tours of the whole of Galilee are mentioned: (1) Mt 4²³, Mk 1³⁹, Lk 4⁴⁴; (2) Lk 8¹; (3) Mt 9³⁵, Mk 6⁶,—though it is possible that (2) and (3) are the same. (c) In passing through Samaria several times (Jn 4ff., Lk 9⁵²f. 17¹¹) He paused to perform some work of mercy. (d) Into Phœnicia, 'the region of Tyre and Sidon,' He went at least once (Mt 15²¹, Mk 7²⁴). (e) Several visits to districts contiguous to Galilee, to the east and north, are mentioned, namely, the visit to Gerasa or Gadara during His Galilæan ministry (Mt 8²⁸, Mk 5¹, Lk 8²⁶), to Decapolis (Mk 7³¹), to the unknown Magadan (Mt 15³⁹) or Dalmanutha (Mk 8¹⁰), and Cæsarea-Philippi (Mt 16¹³, Mk 8²⁷). (f) In regard to the region beyond the Jordan commonly known as Peræa, there are interesting notices, but some uncertainties. The first notice is in the account of John's baptism as taking place at Bethany beyond Jordan (Jn 1²⁸). Much later there was a ministry of uncertain duration in Peræa (Jn 10⁴⁰, Lk 13²². ³²), and still later a journey through the same region on His last visit to Jerusalem (Mt 19¹, Mk 10¹).

3. *Labours.*—The extent of our Lord's ministry is also to be regarded from the point of view of the labours He performed during its course. (a) The actual labours recorded by the Evangelists are considerable in sum. (b) That these were only samples and specimens of His work is distinctly and repeatedly implied. (c) Pointed allusions to the magnitude of His work are frequent (Mt 4²³⁻²⁵, Mk 1³². ³⁴, Lk 4¹⁴. ¹⁵, and many similar passages). (d) There are many indications of the insistent demands upon His attention (e.g. Mk 1³⁵⁻³⁷ 2¹. ² 3⁷⁻⁹. ²⁰ and similar ones), of His weariness and need of rest (Jn 4⁶, Mk 4³⁵ff. 6³⁰⁻³², and others), once of the anxiety of His relatives (Mk 3²¹. ³¹). (e) The enormous amount of His unrecorded labours is distinctly asserted (Jn 21²⁵).

The following conspectus may serve to present

in clearer view some of the points already discussed :

I.	The Thirty Years.	Birth to Baptism.	Bethlehem. Egypt. Nazareth.	B.C. 5 or 4 to A.D. 26 or 28.
II.	Opening Scenes.	Baptism to First Miracle.	Beyond Jordan. Wilderness. Judæa. Cana of Galilee.	26 or 28.
III.	Earlier Ministry.	First Miracle to Beginning of Work in Galilee.	Capernaum. Jerusalem. Samaria.	Between 27 and 29.
IV.	Central Ministry.	Preceding Events and FIRST TOUR in Galilee.	Nazareth. Capernaum. Other Cities of Galilee.	Probably 28, 29.
		Events connected with SECOND TOUR in Galilee.	Cities and Villages of Galilee. Gadara. Nazareth.	..
		THIRD TOUR, and Departure from Galilee.	Cities and Villages. The Lake. Capernaum. Tyre and Sidon. Decapolis. Cæsarea Philippi.	..
V.	Later Ministry.	Close of Galilæan Ministry to Triumphal Entry.	Galilee. Judæa. Peræa.	Probably 29 or 30.
VI.	Closing Scenes.	Triumphal Entry to Crucifixion and Burial.	Jerusalem and vicinity.	..
VII.	The Forty Days.	Resurrection to Ascension.	Jerusalem. Galilee. Olivet.	..

iii. **Results of our Lord's Ministry.** — When we attempt to sum up the results of our Lord's ministry, we have to distinguish between those which were gathered during His life and those which have been maturing through the centuries following.

1. *During His life.*—Briefly, we should here have in mind : (*a*) the multitudes who were reached by His personal influence both in His teaching and His healing ; (*b*) the number of particular adherents won, including the Twelve and all other disciples mentioned in the Gospels, together with those mentioned or alluded to in the early chapters of Acts ; (*c*) the training of the Twelve for their work after His departure ; and (*d*) the establishing of the institutions of the Kingdom of God— preaching, the ordinances, the Church.

2. *Since His ascension.*—The history of Christianity for nineteen centuries only partially describes the outcome of Christ's short ministry upon earth. It is indeed a commonplace, but withal a glorious truth, to say that no other term of service in any man's life, whether longer or shorter, was ever so potent an influence or so formative a force for all that is best in human affairs.

LITERATURE.—The Lives of Christ, esp. Andrews, *The Life of our Lord* ; Broadus, *Harmony of the Gospels*, with Notes on dates by A. T. Robertson ; art. 'Chronology' in Hastings' *DB*

(Turner) and in *Encyc. Bibl.* (von Soden), and the literature adduced ; art. in *The Biblical World* (Chicago) for Dec. 1905, by Professor Votaw.   E. C. DARGAN.

MINSTRELS.—See FLUTE-PLAYERS.

MINT (ἡδύοσμον, *mentha*) is mentioned only in Mt 23[23] and the parallel passage Lk 11[42], where it is represented as being subject to tithe. It is a familiar garden herb, belonging to the natural order Labiatæ. The species commonly grown in Palestine is horse-mint (*M. sylvestris*), and there can be little doubt that this is the mint of Scripture. It is extensively used for culinary purposes, and is also highly valued as a carminative. Mint was probably one of the 'bitter herbs' with which the Paschal lamb was eaten.

HUGH DUNCAN.

MIRACLES.—The process of thought and research, both theological and scientific, has led to a position where belief in the actuality, in the career of Jesus, of those remarkable activities and manifestations summed up under the comprehensive and popular term 'miracle,' is made possible if not inevitable. The prevailing negative attitude of science shows signs of being abandoned in view of enlarging understanding of the possibilities both in Matter and in Spirit, and theology is coming to see that the miraculous events recorded of Him who was the Son of God and the Regenerator of the Race must not be conceived of as in any sense or degree a violation of the order of Nature ; and that viewed in this way they become, instead of difficulties and stumbling-blocks in the way of faith, some of its most convincing reinforcements. It is scarcely too much to affirm that a belief in these occurrences as vital parts of the Christian revelation is rising, compared with which all previous belief is feeble and superficial. Without being unduly optimistic, we may anticipate that the 'ages of faith' in every department of Christian truth, and not least in that of miracle, are yet to come. This consummation is being prepared for in modern conceptions of the Order of Nature, of Human Personality, and of the Divine Being.

1. Modern conceptions of *the Order of Nature.* Christian advocates are becoming thoroughly disposed to accept unreservedly the scientific teaching of the Unity of Nature, carefully guarding the admission from being read as the Uniformity of Nature. They recognize and take account of the inalienable connexion between cause and effect by which the Universe consists. They do not regard the miracles of the Gospels as in the least degree arbitrary interruptions of the Order of Nature, but rather as a revelation of the infinite extent of that order. The ancient antagonism between the Natural and the Supernatural has broken down, and the two spheres are seen to be one, regarded from opposite poles. Grave objections lie against the term 'supernatural,' which is entirely un-Scriptural, and many modern thinkers prefer the term 'spiritual' to express the animating and sustaining Power which pervades all things. Without the spiritual the physical universe has no ground of being, and nothing exists, not the least fraction of the material, still less anything of human affection and sympathy and personal life-force, apart from the Universal Life. If the term 'supernatural' be retained, it must be on the distinct understanding that while all things may be conceived of as supernaturally sustained, it may with equal propriety be asserted that the whole Universe, including not only the physical but the mental, moral, and spiritual in human personality, is a part of the Order of Nature. The powers and sympathies that work in man cannot be separated from that order, and it is most natural, most agreeable to the whole constitution of human nature, that it shall be animated, sustained, and governed by the Divine Power and Life. Men of science, moreover, are increasingly willing to admit the necessity of the spiritual and rational as the ultimate ground of the physical; and recent investigations into the make of the so-called 'atom,' and the vast potentialities of Matter, will further develop the distrust of all dogmatic assertion that nothing in the nature of the events recorded in the Gospels and called 'miracles' is possible or credible. Sir Oliver Lodge (*Hibbert Journal*, October 1902) writes:

'The root question or outstanding controversy between science and faith rests upon two distinct conceptions of the universe: the one, that of a self-contained and self-sufficient universe, with no outlook into or links with anything beyond, uninfluenced by any life or mind except such as is connected with a visible and tangible material body; and the other conception, that of a universe lying open to all manner of spiritual influences, permeated through and through with a Divine spirit, guided and watched by living minds, acting through the medium of law indeed, but with intelligence and love behind the law; a universe by no means self-sufficient or self-contained, but with feelers at every pore groping into another supersensuous order of existence, where reign laws hitherto unimagined by science, but laws as real and as mighty as those by which the material universe is governed.'

2. *The nature of Human Personality.* — Researches, anthropological and psychological, into the nature and possibilities of man have greatly multiplied during the present generation, and something of the vast region of potentiality lying above and beneath and beyond all that is actually realized has been revealed. The conception of the ideal human personality has been immeasurably enlarged and exalted. Psychological investigation is only in its infancy, and yet enough has been arrived at to make it certain that the powers of humanity remain essentially unfathomed. Beneath or above the ordinary consciousness of man, and beyond the powers which at present his will controls and organizes, are other and larger powers at present uncontrolled and unorganized by the personal force, but manifest in exceptional phases of human life, such as dreams, hypnosis, clairvoyance, clairaudience, somnambulism, or unwonted excitement and spiritual exaltation. We may call man, as we are acquainted with him, a personality, a living centre of original will and action, made in the image of the Deity. But yet it is far truer to regard him as a personality which has not yet arrived, the mere rudiment of a personality whose powers, as he controls them, reach out beyond his control to regions of potentiality as yet unrecognized, and showing that the true personality is vastly greater and mightier than the present actual. 'Man partly is, and wholly hopes to be.' The powers at present possessed and controlled by man are the veriest suggestion of the powers that are his by right of nature, made as he was for intimate alliance with the Divine Being. But the perfect Personality was realized in the Son of Man who was also Son of God. The perfect Personality cannot be conceived of apart from the Divine Personality, for it is of the very essence of the Ideal Man that his nature shall be possessed and controlled by the Divine. By the Divine power the human nature consists. And the Lord Jesus plainly marked it as the essential condition of His power that He was morally and spiritually one with God.

3. *The Divine Nature.* — A wholesome feature of modern conceptions of the Being of God is their sense of mystery. Holding fast, on the one hand, to the essential knowableness of the Deity and to His self-revelation as the centre of all Divine action, theologians, on the other hand, admit the impossibility of giving dogmatic expression to the mode of the Divine Being. 'In mys-

tery the soul abides,' not only the Divine but even the human soul. But taking the teaching of the Lord Jesus, interpreted as it was by His life before God and man, and as it is by an increasing Christian experience, they conceive of God as the Infinite Will and Intelligence that animates while it transcends the whole creation, visible and invisible, a Divine Presence ever seeking self-realization and self-revelation in His creation, in some true measure expressing Himself in all the works of His hands, even in the non-human creation; but most really of all in human life with its manifold sympathies and powers, actual and potential, conscious and sub-conscious (or super-conscious). The conception is of a Living God present and active in all life, but supremely in the nobler impulses and humanities that glorify mankind. In the life of men as they are, in their poor actual, the Divine Mind finds a real though feeble and fragmentary expression, and as that nature is developed and its latent powers are evoked and made part of the conscious life, is destined to find a fuller channel for its living action. And the nature which was fitted to be a complete channel, and more than channel—an active co-operator with Himself—the Divine Being, revealing Himself as Father, finds in Him who was perfectly one with man and at the same time morally, spiritually, and essentially one with God.

In this fact, that the Divine Power dwelt in its fulness in the personality of Jesus, we find the unifying principle for all the miracles of the Gospels. The master-principle of them all is contained in our Lord's own declaration, 'If I by the finger of God cast out devils, then is the kingdom of God come upon you' (Lk 11[20]). This declaration is in complete harmony with His repeated affirmations that the ultimate power by which He wrought His beneficent and mighty works was the same as that by which He knew and taught the truth—the Divine power dwelling in Him (Jn 5[19. 30] 14[10]).

The great deeds of healing and of revelation were due to the direct action of the Infinite Life and active Power by which all things consist (1) on the nature of Jesus, and (2) through Him, so empowered, upon the life of man and upon the world. Our Lord makes it perfectly plain that the miraculous deeds were morally conditioned, were therefore a moral achievement, and depended upon His living faith in and union with God. Of Himself He could do nothing (Jn 5[19]). But He also has the feeling and knowledge that in His own nature there was a potentiality of superhuman working. And the chief point to emphasize is that the Personality of Jesus cannot be conceived of even momentarily as apart from the Divine Life. He perfectly lived in God. The purpose of all was to accomplish the Divine will by the establishment of His Kingdom among men. Here and elsewhere the miracles are represented, not as an arbitrary putting forth of a supernatural power altogether out of relation to any human capacity or possibility, but as arising spontaneously out of the unique relation He sustained to the Infinite Life; not as something given, while it could have been withheld, for the sake of commending the moral and spiritual and personal claims of Jesus, but as vital and essential parts of the Divine Revelation. The evidential value of the work was secondary, the need of man and the Divine impulse primary.

In order to get an intelligent faith in the Gospel miracles, it is of great consequence at what point we approach the problem. The important matter is to begin with the less obscure, with those works which are most closely and obviously related to what may be called the innate forces of human nature. This gives us as our starting-point the healing works of Jesus. Careful study must be given to the principles and methods employed in these cases of restoration from sickness, infirmity, and distress. A growing disposition is evident to receive these as genuinely historical, on the ground that they are not in themselves inconceivable, related as they are to the forces perceived to be at work in the complex nature of man. Psychical research has brought, and is more fully bringing, to light a vast wealth of resource in the depths and heights of human personality. And a close study of the method of Jesus convinces us that He worked upon this complex nature (see art. Cures). His miracles were not simply the output of an alien force, but the living exercise of a Divine force, deeply akin to all human powers, already working in the capacities, sympathies, and lifeties of humanity, utilizing the known in all their unknown ramifications, and also the unknown and unsuspected. These works are no less Divine because they are not emphasized as supernatural, the Divine energy being more truly conceived of as the normal and natural. If these deepest principles which our Lord followed are duly recognized in our faith and conception, then the remaining miracles, most of which are rejected by many who receive the healings, become not only not incredible, but inevitable as the completion of a revelation otherwise essentially incomplete. One who has gained a rational and imaginative faith in the healing of body and mind, by the incarnate pity and power of God in Christ Jesus, will be prepared to believe that it is extremely unlikely that Christ should so freely reveal the power of God in this sphere, and not go beyond to give visible expression to the power that resides in and animates and at the same time controls all Nature. And those miracles which are associated with the life and career of Jesus, being wrought not so much by the power of our Lord, as by the Divine Power acting upon Him, have a strong presumption in their favour, congruous as they are with the whole method of His mighty works and with the one revelation given in Him.

A. Miracles of Jesus.—1. *Our Lord's own description of them.*—A distinction must be made between what Jesus Himself said of the miracles and the description given by the people of the time, who were under the influence of low and vulgar ideas of a Divine revelation, and by the Evangelists, who were not altogether emancipated from current conceptions. (1) It must be borne in mind that the Synoptics give very few specific terms which our Lord applied to His own supernormal action. They are the record of His deeds, not of His speech concerning them. But the Evangelists' description may be taken without much deduction as a faithful reflexion of the Master's usage. Jesus does refer to His works, as in Mt 16⁹·¹⁰; He speaks of casting out demons by the Spirit of God (Mt 12²⁸) or by the finger of God (Lk 11²⁰), and declares that 'this kind' (τοῦτο δὲ τὸ γένος) goeth not out except by prayer (Mt 17²¹ TR). He refers to the deed itself and its blessed result, without characterizing it by any specific term. (2) His favourite term for them, according to the Fourth Gospel, was ἔργα, 'works' (Jn 5³⁶ 10²⁵·³²·³⁷·³⁸). He uses the same word also of the good and beautiful acts of others (καλὸν ἔργον, Mk 14⁶). He makes no great distinction between His ordinary works of mercy and the extraordinary, regarding them all alike as wrought simply and naturally in the way of His life and vocation. The miracles were not the highest works; they belong to a lower level of manifestation as compared with His moral and spiritual revelation of God (Jn 14¹¹). But He also qualifies ἔργα: 'the works that none other man did' (Jn 15²⁴), probably including under that category the healing and other mighty deeds. Utility was the

chief element in His view of all His deeds and actions. (3) He also calls them δυνάμεις ('powers' or 'mighty works'), emphasizing the striking manifestation of Divine Power overpassing all human capacity (Mt 11²¹). The Evangelists also commonly employ this term (Mt 13⁵⁸, Mk 6⁵). (4) He also speaks of His works as σημεῖα, 'signs' (Jn 6²⁶), carefully separating Himself from the popular estimate of what constituted a Divinely significant act (see art. Sign). The Fourth Gospel consistently applies this word to the works of Jesus. Probably we must see in the fact a feature due to prolonged reflexion on the events in the light of after-history. But the term is singularly fitting to describe the Divinely significant works of our Lord as signs of another and higher order of things, leading on the thought and imagination to higher spheres of being, fuller powers of soul, Diviner possibilities for humanity. (5) The word τέρατα ('prodigies') is never applied by Jesus to His own working. Only once He uses the word, and then to disavow the idea involved in it and to sever His action from it (Jn 4⁴⁸). In the Apocalyptic discourse these τέρατα are associated with false Christs and false prophets (Mt 24²⁴, Mk 13²²). (6) The popular use of σημεῖον was most akin to the τέρας. With this the English word 'miracle' has most affinity. It is not the equivalent of any word used by Jesus. The AV uses it to translate σημεῖον and δύναμις. The RV practically abandons it. The idea of the word 'supernatural' also is not found in the NT or in the whole Bible, and the term should be relegated to the region of the obsolete. The word 'spiritual' is an excellent substitute, conserving the idea expressed by it without committing the mind to any untenable and indefensible philosophy.

2. *Characteristics of our Lord's miracles.*—Briefly, the features of the miracles which commend them to our judgment and affection may be stated as— (1) Spontaneity. They arise out of the occasion —are never deliberated, unless the raising of Lazarus be an exception (Jn 11⁴), but spring from the present practical impulse of compassion and desire to help man, and the prompting of the Divine Spirit (Jn 2⁴ff·, Lk 18⁴⁰⁻⁴² etc.). (2) High moral purpose. The miracles of Jesus ever sought the highest and Divinest ends, and were never ends in themselves. In all His works there were no signs of any ostentatious exercise of power. Sternly He forbade any public advertisement of His healings, etc., which might rouse the popular excitement. (3) Strong restraint in use of supernormal power. The Temptation of the wilderness witnesses to what was characteristic of all His life, His constant refusal to use His power for personal ease, gratification, or convenience. Nothing was done by extraordinary which could be done by ordinary means. (4) Moral dignity and congruity with the whole spirit and life of Jesus. His miracles spring out of His innermost nature, and reveal the moral harmony and winsomeness of His Person. Herein lies a most fruitful comparison with other alleged miracles, ecclesiastical and mediæval and modern. The vast majority of these latter fail to commend themselves to us as worthy exercises of a Divine power. The criterion must not, however, be unduly pressed, for natures differ widely in what they regard as morally fitting and suitable for Divine action. But, employed broadly, it may help us to discriminate between alleged miraculous events as to how far they are worthy of credence. (5) Helpfulness to mankind was the abiding characteristic of our Lord's miracles. In most cases they were wrought for the immediate succour of suffering humanity, and for the revelation, in and through this, of the Divine love and pity. In His works on the non-human world also the need

of man was continually served, more especially his need for vision of the higher facts of existence. His action never issued in meaningless marvels or needless wonders and in those that seem farthest removed from the requirements of mankind a revelation was given of the kind of power which animated and sustained all nature, and ordered its course.

3. The whole texture of the Gospel narratives is *complicated with the supernormal.* They presuppose a unique relation to God in Jesus, and His possession of a miracle-working power. 'In most of the reports the action of Jesus is so interwoven with unmistakably authentic words, that the two elements cannot be separated' (A. B. Bruce, art. 'Jesus' in *Encyc. Bibl.*). If excision be made from the Evangelic records (1) of all that directly narrates His unique action as a healer and wonder-worker, (2) of all that presupposes the possibility and actuality of such unique action, (3) of all that testifies to His authority and power due to a unique relation to God—the Gospels are left bald and bare and mutilated beyond description. The very warp and woof of the fabric is destroyed.

As an example, apply the process to Mk 1-3. As a residue we have—
1. The account of the Baptist's preaching (without the reference to the prophetic witness).
2. The Baptism of John (robbed of the spiritual endowment of Jesus and its accompaniments).
3. The bare mention of a temptation in the wilderness (with angels excluded. The story cannot be filled up by reference to the other Evangelists, for their account presupposes a miracle-working power in Jesus).
4. John's imprisonment, and announcement of the Kingdom by Jesus.
5. Call of Peter, Andrew, James, and John.
6. Teaching of Jesus in the synagogue, and spread of His fame (the latter left like a pyramid on its apex without the restoration of the demoniac).
7. Entrance to house of Peter (healing of wife's mother excluded).
8. Account of solitary prayer (with no action of Jesus to account for such prolonged prayer).
9. Preaching in synagogue (mere repetition apart from healing of leper and casting out devil).
10. Account of sudden popularity (with no adequate reason given for it).
11. Another repetition of the statement that He taught the people (2³⁻¹² all being excised as entirely complicated with miracle).
12. Call of Matthew.
13. Conflict with scribes and Pharisees in regard to eating and drinking with publicans and sinners, and fasting, and His teaching consequent thereon.
14. Pharisees and Herodians take counsel to kill Him (but no reason given—the healing of withered hand being removed).
15. Withdrawal of Jesus (following by multitude being omitted because of motive given in v.⁸).
16. Call of disciples (commission reduced to preaching and teaching. Teaching in 3²⁰⁻³⁰ cut out as entirely dependent on His exorcism of demons).
17. Teaching of true relationship to Himself (strongly savouring of presumption, apart from reasons which have disappeared in process of excision).
The whole narrative is rendered colourless and dislocated, the only section which is left fairly unmutilated being 2¹³⁻²⁸. 'That the healing ministry was not only a fact, but a great outstanding fact, is attested by the popularity of Jesus and by the various theories which were invented to account for the remarkable phenomena' (A. B. Bruce, *l.c.*). The above analysis forcibly illustrates this assertion.

4. *Chronological list of miracles of Jesus.*

(a) PRELIMINARY PERIOD, FROM BAPTISM TO CALL OF LEADING APOSTLES.

	FOUND IN
1. Water made wine	Jn.
2. Cleansing of the Temple	Jn.
3. Son of nobleman restored	Jn.

(b) FIRST PERIOD OF GALILÆAN MINISTRY, TO DEATH OF JOHN THE BAPTIST.

	FOUND IN			
4. Escape from hostile crowd	..	..	Lk.	..
5. Draught of fishes	..	..	Lk.	..
6. Capernaum demoniac	..	Mk.	Lk.	..
7. Peter's wife's mother	Mt.	Mk.	Lk.	..
8. General healings and exorcisms	Mt.	Mk.	Lk.	..
9. Leper	Mt.	Mk.	Lk.	..
10. Palsied man	Mt.	Mk.	Lk.	..

	FOUND IN			
11. Impotent man of Bethesda	..	..	..	Jn.
12. Man with withered hand	Mt.	Mk.	Lk.	..
13. General healings and exorcisms	Mt.	Mk.	Lk.	..
14. Centurion's servant	Mt.	..	Lk.	..
15. Son of widow of Nain raised	..	..	Lk.	..
16. General healings and exorcisms	..	..	Lk.	..
17. Dumb demoniac healed	Mt.	..	..	..
18. Tempest stilled	Mt.	Mk.	Lk.	..
19. Gadarene demoniac or demoniacs	Mt.	Mk.	Lk.	..
20. Raising of Jairus' daughter	Mt.	Mk.	Lk.	..
21. Issue of blood	Mt.	Mk.	Lk.	..
22. Two blind men healed	Mt.	..	..	..

(c) SECOND PERIOD OF GALILÆAN MINISTRY, TO ITS CLOSE.

	FOUND IN			
23. Five thousand fed	Mt.	Mk.	Lk.	..
24. Jesus walks on sea	Mt.	Mk.	..	Jn.
25. Daughter of Syro-Phœnician woman	Mt.	Mk.	..	..
26. Deaf and dumb restored	..	Mk.	..	..
27. General healing of infirmities	Mt.	..	..	..
28. Four thousand fed	Mt.	Mk.	..	..
29. Blind man restored	..	Mk.	..	..
30. Deaf and dumb epileptic	Mt.	Mk.	Lk.	..
31. Stater in fish's mouth	Mt.	Mk.	..	..

(d) MINISTRY IN JUDÆA AND PERÆA.

	FOUND IN			
32. Man blind from birth restored	..	..	..	Jn
33. Impotent woman restored	..	..	Lk.	..
34. Man with dropsy healed	..	..	Lk.	..
35. Ten lepers cleansed	..	..	Lk.	..
36. Lazarus raised	..	..	..	Jn.
37. Two blind men near Jericho	Mt.	Mk.	Lk.	..

(e) CLOSING DAYS OF LIFE.

	FOUND IN			
38. Withering of fig-tree	Mt.	Mk.	..	..
39. Cleansing of Temple	Mt.	Mk.	Lk.	..
40. Healing of Malchus	Mt.	..	Lk.	Jn.
41. Falling to ground of soldiers	..	..	..	Jn.

Examining the above list, we may remark—
(1) The same event is probably referred to in 2 and 39. Possibly also, but on the whole not probably, 3 and 14 refer to same healing.
(2) Instances which seem to come so near to familiar human experience as to need no assumption of miracle are 2, 4, 41.
(3) In 31 no indication is given that the command of Jesus was meant to be obeyed. It may readily have been understood by the disciple as a parabolic expression of the surety of providential care.
(4) Cases where the reporting of the healing is so casual that nothing as to the method of Jesus can be securely built upon the narrative are 10, 12, 33, 34, 40. The chief interest of the Evangelist lies in the other part of the story. In the case of Malchus, St. John, who reports the injury, makes no mention of any healing, and the interest of St. Luke is evangelical rather than medical, emphasizing the generosity and compassion of Jesus.
(5) 'Nature miracles' are found (a) in each period; (b) in the Fourth Gospel; (c) in the Synoptic tradition, both in the Double and Triple Synopsis. They are therefore as well attested as the works of healing. The walking on the sea is found in the Double Synopsis; the stilling of the storm and the withering of the fig-tree in the Triple Synopsis; the feeding of the multitude in all four Gospels.
(6) The healings of nervous diseases, which many are more willing to accept on the ground of their likeness to well-known medical facts of to-day, are not better attested than those involving physical disorder and disease. The healings of fever, leprosy, issue of blood, and blindness are all recorded in the Triple Synopsis. The raising of the dead is found in all four Gospels; one case, the daughter of Jairus, is attested by the three Synoptics. The NT makes no distinction between these classes of miracles, but the evidence for all the classes is equally strong (see art. CURES, § 11).
5. *Classification of miracles of Jesus.* — As a

typical example of the customary classification of miracles, may be given that of Westcott (*Introd. to the Gospels*)—

I. Miracles on Nature. 1. Miracles of creative power: (α) water made wine, (β) bread multiplied, (γ) walking on the water. 2. Miracles of Providence: (α) miracles of blessing: (1) first draught of fishes, (2) storm stilled, (3) stater in fish's mouth, (4) second draught of fishes; (β) Miracle of judgment: withering of fig-tree.

II. Miracles on Man. (α) Miracles of personal faith: (1) organic defects (blind): (a) faith special (Mt 9²⁹⁻³¹), (b) faith absolute—Bartimæus restored; (2) chronic impurity: (a) open (leprosy)—faith special, the one leper—faith special and absolute contrasted, the ten lepers; (b) secret—woman with issue. (β) Miracles of intercession: (1) organic defects (simple intercession): (a) the blind (Mk 8²²⁻²⁶), (b) the deaf and dumb (Mk 7³¹⁻³⁷); (2) mortal sicknesses—intercession based on natural ties: (a) fever (Jn 4⁴⁶⁻⁵⁴), (b) paralysis—centurion's servant and man borne of four. (γ) Miracles of love: (1) organic defect—blindness (Jn 9); (2) disease—(a) fever, (b) dropsy, (c) withered hand, (d) impotent man, (e) woman with spirit of infirmity; (3) death—(a) death chamber, (b) the bier, (c) the tomb.

III. Miracles on Spirit World. (α) Miracles of intercession: (1) simple intercession—(a) dumb man with devil, (b) blind and dumb man; (2) intercession based on natural ties—(a) Syro-Phœnician's daughter, (b) lunatic boy. (β) Miracles of antagonism: (1) in synagogue—unclean spirit cast out, (2) in tombs—the lepers cast out.

The chief defect in the above is its endorsement of the term 'Nature miracles' as applied to the first class. If 'Nature' be rightly measured, the term may legitimately be used to cover the whole ground of our Lord's working, for the complex nature of man cannot be severed from the universal order. Moreover, the distinction is, apart from that consideration, an arbitrary one, for several of these so-called 'Nature miracles' are wrought in the sphere of our Lord's human nature, and are conceivably extensions of human, mental, and psychical faculty; and some of them are wrought in and upon the bodily form of Jesus Himself. The walking upon the water is an example of the latter. The draught of fishes is a miracle of vision, an extension of human perception, as well as an example of Divine control of the animal creation. A similar element must be traced in the instance of the coin in the fish's mouth, if we are to understand a miracle here.* Other defects are: 'Miracles of Providence,' 'Miracles of Blessing' and of 'Love,' are terms that may be applied to other than the classes given.

A truer classification may be suggested as follows:

I. Healings of bodily ailments—as blindness, leprosy, lameness, dropsy, deafness and dumbness, fevers, and manifold ailments and infirmities.
II. Healings of nervous diseases—as paralysis or palsy, simple epilepsy, possibly the woman with the spirit of infirmity (unless her ailment be physical).
III. Healings of nervous and psychical disorders—epilepsy associated with idiocy or insanity, and varieties of mania.
IV. Revelations of power in the nature of Jesus—walking on the sea.
V. Revelation of Jesus in nature and upon the organic world—as draughts of fishes, and stater in fish's mouth.
VI. Power upon the organic world—multiplied loaves and fishes, water made wine, fig-tree withered.
VII. Power upon the inorganic world—stilling of the tempest.
VIII. Raising of the dead—Jairus' daughter, son of widow of Nain, Lazarus.

B. 'MIRACULOUS' EVENTS ASSOCIATED WITH CAREER OF JESUS.—

	FOUND IN			
1. Annunciation by angels . . .	Mt.	..	Lk.	..
2. Virgin-birth	Mt.	..	Lk.	..
3. Angels' song	..	..	Lk.	..
4. Other appearances of angels in protection of the Child . . .	Mt.	..	..	..
5. Star of Magi	Mt.	..	..	..
6. Voice at Baptism of Jesus . .	Mt.	Mk.	Lk.	..
7. Descent of dove	Mt.	Mk.	Lk.	Jn.

* The power of the mind over the body may reasonably be conceived as at work in these instances, for it is impossible, with the growing knowledge of the inter-relations of mind and body, to set an arbitrary limit to that influence.

	FOUND IN			
8. Transfiguration	Mt.	Mk.	Lk.	..
9. Voices at Transfiguration . .	Mt.	Mk.	Lk.	..
10. Opening of graves after death of Jesus	Mt.	..	..	..
11. Rending of veil of Temple . .	Mt.	Mk.	Lk.	..
12. Darkness over land	..	Mk.	Lk.	..
13. Earthquakes	Mt.	..	..	..
14. The Resurrection	Mt.	Mk.	Lk.	Jn.
15. The Ascension	..	Mk.	Lk.	Jn.

In the above, noteworthy facts are—

(1) Only one Evangelist in each case records 3, 4, 5, 10, 13. Number 10 stands by itself, and is not found in other Gospels, although these speak of the rending of the veil of the Temple. The latter event (11) is also possibly an accompaniment of the remarkable physical phenomena 12 and 13, which were associated with the time of our Lord's death. 1, 2, 12 are recorded by two Evangelists only.

(2) While the historicity, as objective events, of 1, 3, 4, 6, 7 cannot be reasonably denied with any dogmatism, especially if the principles enunciated above be intelligently accepted, yet we are free to admit that they are such as were not unlikely to be added to the Gospel tradition by disciples and by the first Christian community, who were not entirely freed from Jewish prepossessions (see art. SIGN). It would be grossly disproportionate to give the same weight of authority to the details of the Birth, Baptism, and Death of Jesus as to the personal experience which He underwent, and to the significance of the Incarnation, Spiritual Endowment, and Atonement for human salvation.

(3) The Voice at the Baptism is well attested, but it is not clear if we are taught to regard it as more than subjective to Jesus Himself. Mt. and Mark seem to attribute the whole experience —the vision of the opening heaven, the seeing of the dove, the hearing of the voice—to Jesus; and the Baptist's vision of the Descent (Jn 1³²) may express his special insight into the whole event as it affected our Lord at that critical time and experience. It is noteworthy that Luke simply records the facts.

(4) The chief events that demand consideration are the Virgin-birth, the Transfiguration, the Resurrection, and the Ascension, for which we must refer to the separate articles on these subjects.

C. MIRACLES WROUGHT IN THE NAME OF JESUS BY HIS FOLLOWERS.—The Evangelists make it plain that the disciples and other followers of Jesus were commissioned by the Master to go forth in His name to combine healing and exorcism with the teaching and preaching of the gospel (Mt 10¹·⁷·⁸, Mk 3¹⁴⁻¹⁶ 6⁷, Lk 10⁹). They also declare that a signal success was achieved by the Seventy, for they return to Jesus rejoicing greatly in the power of His name, extending even to the control of the evil spirits (Lk 10¹⁷). Of this great success our Lord was aware, and it became to Him the occasion of a spiritual exultation, in which He saw, as already accomplished, the downfall of the Satanic power with all its accompanying ills and afflictions of mankind (Lk 10¹⁸).

The evidence favours the idea that Jewish exorcists had a certain measure of success in their arts, even although much charlatanry may be believed to have mingled with their practices. The names they invoked, including the Ineffable Name, together, no doubt, with the drastic physical remedies they applied, were possibly efficacious in some cases (Mt 12²⁷, Lk 9⁴⁹). And we may be confident that the Name of Jesus, which was of vast import and of awful and mysterious significance (especially after the Resurrection), would make for healing and for liberating disordered minds and evil-controlled natures. There is reason, also, to make a distinction between these healings and exorcisms and the other works of Jesus, for nothing is said of these latter supernormal powers being possessed by the disciples and first Christians. It must also be remembered that St. Paul's Epistles are clear witness to somewhat kindred phenomena having been experienced in the *Charismata* of Apostolic circles (1 Co 12, etc.). The closing section of Mark's Gospel, too, is a reflexion of 2nd century belief in the continuance of these miraculous endowments among the Apostles. Coming down to sub-Apostolic times, the evidence is too strong to be discredited that the same powers together with prophecy were familiar to those generations; and the question cannot be entirely avoided, as to whether we have any sufficient reason to draw the line at the close of this age, or, with other apologists, at the time of Constantine, and declare that, beyond it, all assertions of a manifest and direct Divine action through any servant of Christ are due to chicanery, or illusion, ignorance, or superstition.

If this question be left *sub judice*, and the story of the Christian Church of the following centuries be read without prepossession, an impression may well be produced that some of the alleged supernormal phenomena are far too well attested to be scornfully and summarily dismissed. In all generations of the Christian era, certain natures, specially God-sensitive, conspicuously consecrated to God and sympathetic with man and with all living things, appear to have wielded a real though imperfect control over the physical processes of life. Both through them and in them remarkable forces have been at work which we cannot but believe are God-sustained and God-energized, producing supernormal phenomena. In regard to all these, as well as to kindred manifestations of modern times, the right attitude is that of a watchful but unprejudiced and patient examination. Forces that make for healing undoubtedly lie in human nature, in certain gifted souls, and in others not conspicuously gifted spiritually, but 'sensitives'; and in times of great spiritual awakening, when the sense of the reality of the Unseen and Divine is quickened and God's presence is freshly and acutely realized, startling manifestations of these sub-conscious or super-conscious forces may occur, and need not surprise any who understand how closely the Divine power has access to all forces of human life. Such phenomena, and indeed all things that belong to the human race, must not be met with a *non possumus*, but with careful, scientific, and withal reverent, investigation. The miracles of Jesus are available as a criterion, and basing our judgment upon them we may demand: (1) an adequate and worthy moral purpose to be served [this must be clearly distinguished from personal or ecclesiastical convenience, advantage, or ambition, traces of which, together with offerings at the shrine of the saint, discredit so many mediæval miracles]; and (2) a proper moral dignity —in which many alleged workings of the thaumaturgist are conspicuously wanting. It is by no means easy to say how far healings and other powers kindred to those wrought by Jesus are meant to be expected in our human life on earth. It seems natural to make a distinction between the healings and other restorations from human infirmity on the one hand, and works of revelation in the non-human sphere. The latter may not be expected in this earthly scene, although they point to large powers of soul in the evolution of our psychical capacities in some further stages of being. But the healings and exorcisms we have good reason to expect among men on earth; for in all investigation and experiment and self-devoted labour, in all spiritual prayer and aspiration for the physical, mental, and eternal welfare of the race, His presence is ever active who said, 'Lo, I am with you always.'

LITERATURE.—For general, dealing with the various themes comprised in above art., see the many Lives of Christ, Commentaries on the Gospels, and artt. in Hastings' *DB*, *Encyc. Biblica*, and other Dictionaries. For the argument concerning the miracles in general and in particular—

(1) Adverse on whole: E. A. Abbott, *Kernel and the Husk*, *The Spirit on the Waters*, and *Philomythus* (a reply to Newman's *Essays on Ecclesiastical Miracles*); M. Arnold, *Literature and Dogma*; Percy Gardner, *Historic View of NT*, and *Exploratio Evangelica*; Harnack, *What is Christianity?* and *Christianity and History*.

(2) In favour of miraculous: Origen, *contra Celsum*; Pascal, *Pensées*; Row's, Mozley's, and Temple's *Bampton Lectures*; A. B. Bruce, *Miraculous Element in the Gospels*, and *Chief End of Revelation*; Trench, *Miracles*; Lyttelton's *Hulsean Lectures*; Fisher, *Ground of Theistic and Christian Belief*; *The Supernatural in Christianity*, by Drs. Rainy, Orr, and Dods (a reply to Pfleiderer's *Gifford Lectures*); Lias, *Are Miracles Credible?*; Thomson, *Miracles and Modern Science*; Illingworth, *Personality Human and Divine*, and *Divine Immanence*; to which may be added *The Finger of God*, by writer of the present article.

For larger and wider discussions bearing closely on the conception of the miraculous, consult the works of John Fiske, esp. *The Idea of God*; Dr. E. Caird's *Evolution of Religion*, 2 vols. (Gifford Lectures); and *Human Personality* by F. W. H. Myers.

T. H. WRIGHT.

MIRACULOUS CONCEPTION. — See VIRGIN-BIRTH.

MISSION.—The following article deals with the mission of the Lord Jesus Christ only as presented in the Gospel narratives. The Lord Jesus frequently manifested *consciousness of being commissioned by God*. Now the general ($\pi\acute{e}\mu\pi\omega$) and now the specific term ($\dot{a}\pi o\sigma\tau\acute{e}\lambda\lambda\omega$) for sending is used in reference to His work, the latter word signifying an intimate connexion between sender and sent (Cremer, p. 529). As God's trusted messenger He felt that there was a decree ($\delta\epsilon\hat{\imath}$) for Him to execute (Lk 2[49] 4[43] 9[22] etc.), that He had His Father's authority (Jn 5[43] 8[42]), and that as the Father had sanctified Him and sent Him into the world (Jn 10[36]), it was not for Him to do His own pleasure (6[38]). The Fourth Evangelist, deeply impressed with the idea of the commission received by his Lord, mentions the fact repeatedly, and in one place stops to brood over the mere name of a place because it suggests a mission (97). Instead of considering Himself as being merely one among a number of Divine messengers, Jesus knew Himself to be the Messenger-Son (Mk 12[6. 7]). The Lord's consciousness refers to (1) the *objects* of His mission, (2) the *means* to be adopted to gain His wondrous ends, (3) the *extent*, and (4) the *credentials* of His mission.

1. The objects of the mission.—These are exhibited in various forms. Prophecy has to be fulfilled (Mk 12[10. 11] 14[21. 27. 49], Lk 4[21] 10[24] 24[27], Jn 5[46] 13[18]). It is the function of Jesus to be the King (Ps 2), the Son of Man (Ps 8, Dn 7[13. 14]), the Servant of Jehovah (Is 42. 53), the founder of a New Covenant (Jer 31[31-34]); and thus to glorify God (Jn 12[28] 17[4]) and save men (Mt 1[21], Lk 2[11] 19[10], Jn 3[17] 10[10] 12[47] 17[2] 20[31]) by attracting men to Himself (Mt 11[28], Jn 5[40] 12[32]) and by giving Himself as a sacrifice (Mk 10[45], Jn 1[29] 6[51] 10[15] 12[24]).

2. Means to the ends of the mission.—The nature of these aims required that the Heavenly Apostle (He 3[1]) should manifest the Kingdom and the character of God, together with the greatness of man's calling. The sacrificial death at Calvary sums up all the revelations. The speech, the life, the death of the Lord Jesus are the means whereby He discharges His unique mission to mankind.

(*a*) To succeed, it was imperative that Jesus should ensure *the recognition of the sovereignty of God*. The Kingdom of God must be established upon the earth (Mt 4[17], Lk 19[11ff.]). Where there are minds that gladly defer to God's will, there the Kingdom is. Submission may be incomplete (Mt 13[24-30. 47. 48]) and transient (vv. [20-22]). In Jesus alone were the claims of God fully and constantly heeded : therefore the leadership of men is His prerogative (Mt 23[10]). He called men to Himself in order to make them loyal to the heavenly throne. God's subjects renounce evil habits (Mt 4[17]), enjoy pardon (Lk 24[47]), possess sincerity (Mt 7[21-27]), are plastic and trustful as children (Mt 18[2-4], Lk 18[16. 17], Jn 3[3]), are willing to render costly service in meekness (Mt 20[25-28]) ; they transcend national distinctions (Mt 8[11]) and set all interests below those of the Kingdom (Mt 6[33] 13[45. 46], Lk 9[57-62] 18[29-30]). The presence of the Kingdom is known by its conquering power (Lk 11[20]). Its growth cannot be accounted for unless the activities of God are adduced ; albeit man's co-operation is required (Mk 4[26-29]). A river (as the Nile) may not originate in the land that it waters, and yet may be indispensable thereto ; similarly Christ's Kingdom is the blessing the world needs most, and its coming must be uppermost in prayerful minds (Mt 6[9. 10]), yet it takes its rise in the unseen heaven (Jn 18[36]). Diseases, defects, excrescences of all kinds—physical, mental, spiritual—are foreign elements (Mt 13[27. 28], Lk 13[16]). It was the function of the Lord Jesus to reveal verbally and in His life the nature of God's reign. His loving and unswerving devotion to the Father's will is the central orb of the moral world, and all human wills should be planets ruled and lighted by His filial homage. Union with Him, harmony with Him, would bring about union and harmony among the races of mankind, and earth according to the great prayers (Mt 6[9. 10], Jn 17[20. 21]), would be a province of heaven. In all its particulars—its purity, might, obedience, joyful loyalty, friendliness, prayerfulness, catholicity—the Kingdom of God is the life of Christ expanded. It was His task to give mankind, on the scale of His earthly experience, a clear and distinct conception of subjection to the authority of God. The Kingdom is where He is ; it is He working through the wills, intellects, affections of His people. The laws of the Kingdom are those to which Christ conformed His purposes and deeds. The Beatitudes (Mt 5[1-12]) are songs that first were sung in His own heart. Hence a description of the Kingdom is a description of the character of Jesus from the point of view belonging to duty and common service. If the precepts of the gospel—which were indeed citations from His own book of life as child, friend, artizan, preacher, sacrifice—were heeded in home and Church and State, we should see the Kingdom of God an organism with Christ as its soul, devout, righteous, beneficent.

(b) He to whom the human will ought to be surrendered must be known to be supremely worthy of reverence, trust, and love. Inasmuch, then, as *knowledge of God* is essential to eternal life, it was one of the aims of Christ to impart this knowledge (Jn 17[3]). God had often been represented as the Father of the Chosen People, and here and there individuals had thought themselves to be sons of God ; but in the teachings of Jesus the Divine Fatherhood is asserted and illustrated so copiously, that some chapters of the Gospels consist almost solely of variations to the music of these good tidings (Mt 5. 6. 7). Jesus made men think of God trustfully as well as reverently, with love as well as with awe. The revelation could be made only by the Son of God (Mt 11[27], Lk 10[22]), and it was contained in Himself (Jn 1[18] 14[7-10]). The love and obedience of the Son have as their counterparts the Father's love and instructions ; and so the paternal and the filial dispositions are mutually illuminating. The purposes of the Father are exe-

cuted by the Son, and therefore to come to Jesus, to receive and honour Him, are acts that reach to God (Lk 9[48], Jn 5[22. 23] 13[20]). The message is the Messenger. Not merely does a veil fall from before the Divine character ; for Jesus, standing where the veil had stood, manifests the eternal righteousness and pitying love that cannot be content unless men are rescued from unrighteousness and wrath. Salvation is man's progressive advance (Jn 17[3] γινώσκω) to God, his growing communion with the Father, his increasing faith, love, and reverence. The Saviour invites men to come by penitence and trust to Himself, that they may become one with Him and, through Him, with the Father (Mt 11[28], Jn 17[21]), whose holiness He discloses.

(c) The fulfilment of Christ's mission required the *revelation of man*. What is the moral condition of men ? What is man in God's idea ? What can make man's sin to be seen and hated ? What can make God's thought and purpose concerning man attractive to sinners ? Inasmuch as penitence, faith, hope, love are essential elements of a true life, to create them was included in Christ's gracious task. To produce the consciousness of guilt was an indispensable preliminary. His speech made sin exceeding sinful, and in His conduct there were presented such contrasts to man's misdoings that the evils were exposed. A sense of sin actually was produced (Lk 5[8] 7[37ff.] 19[7. 8]), and men learned to trust God's Son and to desire to be taught His life (Lk 11[1]). He encouraged men to hope that His experience of pleasing the Father (Jn 8[29]) might become theirs, seeing that they could become as intimately related to Him as the branches are related to the vine (15[1-8]). The appearance of the Son of Man was a gospel, because, while it condemned sin, it affirmed moral evil to be an intrusion into man's nature, and it invited the sinful to receive forgiveness and enter into union with that victorious life which from the first had overcome the world (Mt 4[1-11], Jn 8[29] 16[33] 17[4]). Corrupted man rejected and killed the Holy One, thereby disclosing human guilt and need ; man, as God intended him to be, and as he may become by 'believing in him' (Jn 2[11] 3[16]), is revealed in Christ's meekness, devoutness, filial obedience and fraternal service. 'The Son of God' gives men authority to become God's sons (1[12. 13]), thereby causing men fully to unfold their manhood.

(d) *The mission of the Saviour involved His death.*—His death was a chief part of His work. The Evangelists record sayings which prove that the great sacrifice was present to our Lord's mind at an early stage of His ministry, so that there is no need to regard the explicit references to the death by violence made near Cæsarea Philippi (Mk 8[31ff.]) as indicating a new outlook to the Lord's own mind. The tragic note that is heard early in the Fourth Gospel (2[19-21] 3[14. 15] 6[51]) is not left to the last in the Synoptic accounts (Mt 9[15], Mk 2[19. 20], Lk 5[34. 35]). Moreover, the saving purpose of the sacrifice (Mt 26[28], Mk 10[45] 14[24], Jn 10[11] 12[23. 24. 32. 33]), its necessity (δεῖ Mk 8[31], Lk 24[26]), and its voluntary character (Mt 26[53], Jn 10[18]), are affirmed. 'Through death to life' is illustrated in His experience. The enjoyment by Him of a fuller life in countless redeemed ones is conditional upon His uttermost self-renunciation (Jn 12[24]). The life of the Saviour passes to men through His surrender, and it enters into them so far as they adopt its principle. The way of sacrifice is thus the way whereby the Saviour gives and the saved receive (Mt 16[24. 25]). The New Covenant (Jer 31[31-34]) is connected with the shedding of the Lord's blood (Lk 22[20]), and it is necessary that the saved should participate in this fundamental law of Christ's being (Jn 6[53-57]). It was the Son's gracious will to come to earth on an errand which meant exposure to temptation (and therefore exposure to the possibility that He might not return to heaven) in order to destroy sin and to allure mankind to the paths of rectitude and peace. It was not the purpose of the Lord to ascend to God unless He could do so as the head of a new race,—a race healed (Jn 3$^{14. 15}$), vivified and nourished by His sacrificial offering (6$^{51-58}$). This death, with its victory over death, and its sequel—the return to the Father—were intended to provide, through the gift of the Holy Spirit, those saving resources whereby the true life is initiated (16$^{7-11}$) and sustained (14$^{16. 26}$ 15^{26} 16$^{13-15}$).

3. The extent of Christ's mission.—While the regeneration of men was His first concern, His numerous miracles evince His care for man's physical needs. As all departments of life were to be purified and enriched by His example and teaching, so all men were to feel that they could be saved by His grace. It has been supposed that Jesus had no outlook beyond the Chosen People, and that the universalism of the Gospels is an interpolation; the catholicity which the Church subsequently manifested being read back into the teachings of the Lord. This conjecture is applied to the Fourth Gospel, to the world-wide commission (Mt 28$^{18-20}$, Mk 16^{15}), and to the universalism of St. Luke. True it is that at first the area of labour was restricted (Mt 15^{24}), but this was a necessity of the situation, and is no indication that the Gentiles were to be excluded from salvation. Sin is not local or racial, and Jesus hated *it*; and man, as man, was loved by Him. Any devout Jew would think that somehow the Gentiles were to reap advantage from the Messianic reign (Lk 2$^{80-32}$), and though it was deemed absurd to suppose that preference could be given by the Messiah to heathen men (Jn 7^{35}), even the Pharisees were zealous in making proselytes (Mt 23^{15}). Why should it be thought incredible that Jesus hoped ultimately to win men of all nations? Was not exclusiveness distressing to Him? Was He not ready with a reference to mercies granted to the woman of Zarephath and to Naaman the Syrian (Lk 4$^{25-27}$)? The outer court of the Temple was the only part of the sacred structure to which a Gentile had access, and all the Evangelists report that Jesus insisted that this enclosure should be kept clean and quiet 'for all the nations' (Mt 21$^{12. 13}$, Mk 11$^{15-17}$, Lk 19$^{45. 46}$, Jn 2$^{14-16}$). Jesus rejoiced in the centurion's faith—not found by Him in Israel (Lk 7^9), and the Syrophœnician woman cheered His heart by her trust and loving ingenuity (Mt 15^{28}). At first the disciples were forbidden to preach to Samaritans (Mt 10^5), though, when they were fully equipped, the restriction was withdrawn (Ac 1^8): He Himself laboured in Samaria (Lk 9$^{51-56}$, Jn 4), and called attention to the beneficence of one Samaritan (Lk 10$^{33-35}$), and to the faith and gratitude of another (17$^{15-19}$). It is quite in harmony with the Saviour's love for the outcast and despised, the publicans and sinners amongst the Jews (Mt 9$^{9-13}$, Lk 7$^{37-50}$ 15$^{1. 2ff.}$ 18$^{9-14}$ 19$^{1-10}$), that He should foresee the approach of all men to Himself (Jn 12^{32}), and anticipate a time when He should be the Shepherd of one flock consisting of sheep gathered from far and near (10^{16}). The interest manifested by the Magi (Mt 2) and by the Greeks (Jn 12$^{20. 21}$) is not alien to Christ's mission. Moreover it is clearly declared that strangers will become workers in the vineyard (Mt 21^{41}), and that before His throne all nations are to be assembled for judgment (Mt 25$^{31. 32}$). 'The Saviour of the world' (Jn 4^{42}) has grace and power wherewith to meet the needs which belong to every man in every age and country; for He is the Light (1^9 8^{12} 9^5 12^{46}), the Water (4^{10} 7^{37}), the Bread (6$^{35. 48-51}$), the Life (11^{25} 14^6).

4. Credentials of the mission.—Jesus entered

upon His task with the confidence that He was anointed with the Holy Spirit (Lk 4^{18}). John the Baptist declared that he saw the Spirit descending upon Jesus, and that he had been prepared for this sign (Jn 1$^{33. 34}$). The testimony thus borne by the last of the Old Covenant prophets is referred to by the Saviour together with other credentials,—as the witness of His works, that of the Father and that of the Scriptures (Jn 5$^{32-47}$). Messengers came from the Machærus prison, saying, 'John the Baptist hath sent us unto thee, saying, Art thou he that cometh, or look we for another?' In that hour Jesus wrought miracles which He adduced, together with His habit of announcing good tidings to the poor, as proofs of His Messiahship (Lk 7$^{18-22}$). The deeds were signs ($\sigma\eta\mu\epsilon\hat{\iota}\alpha$) that the Divine messenger could quicken body and soul (Mk 5$^{41. 42}$, Lk 7$^{14. 15}$, Jn 11$^{25. 43. 44}$); cure physical and spiritual diseases; render efficient withered powers (Mk 3$^{1-5}$, Jn 5$^{5-9}$); add faculties, contrary to what might be expected, as in the case of the man born blind (Jn 9); redress evils caused by circumstances—for instance the fever due to the Capernaum district—(Lk 4$^{38. 39}$); cleanse all the fountains of life, as in cures wrought for lepers (Mk 1$^{40-42}$, Lk 17$^{12-14}$); bestow abilities, receptive (Mk 8$^{22-25}$) and communicative (Mt 9$^{32. 33}$). While the miracles were wrought in pure kindness, they afforded evidences to the thoughtful of the validity of Christ's claims (Jn 3^2 7^{31} 10$^{37. 38}$ 14^{11} 15^{24}), and they were intended by the Lord to give assurance to men of His redeeming grace (Mk 2$^{10. 11}$). The very term employed for saving processes ($\sigma\acute{\omega}\zeta\omega$) will serve equally for temporal and spiritual blessings (Mt 1^{21}, Mk 10^{26}, Lk 7^{50}, Jn 3^{17}), even as the Worker shows Himself in reference both to the inner and the outer life to be the Great Physician (Mk 2^{17}). Some persons were allowed to have extraordinary aid to the belief that Jesus came from God, for they were with Him when He was transfigured, and heard a voice saying, 'This is my Son, my chosen: hear ye him' (Lk 9^{35}); nevertheless there was adequate support for the faith of all men in the remarkable interest Jesus took in the neglected (Lk 7$^{22. 23}$ 15$^{1ff.}$), in His readiness to pray (Jn 17^1) and to serve (Mk 6^{34}, cf. v.^{31}), and in the union of qualities of character which are rarely found together. The credentials of Christ's mission are in Himself. The grandeur and simplicity of His life, the meek and beneficent use of marvellous powers, the sinless One's friendship with sinners, the strength and gentleness, the zeal and patience, the ardour and purity of His character—prove that He came forth from the Father (Jn 6$^{68. 69}$ 16^{27}). Believers in Him discover with more and more clearness, as they trust Him more and more fully, that His gracious promises are fulfilled. He is to their consciences the Goodness,—to their intellects the Truth,—to their hearts the supreme Beauty, the Way, the Truth, the Life.

LITERATURE.—Cremer, *Lex. s.v.* $\dot{\alpha}\pi o\sigma\tau\acute{\epsilon}\lambda\lambda\omega$; Wendt, *Teaching of Jesus*, ii. 184 ff.   **W. J. HENDERSON.**

MISSIONS.—1. *The prophetic background.*—The missionary spirit and aims of Christianity have their beginnings in the history, literature, and character of the Jewish people. The OT, especially in the portions which express the ideals and spirit of prophecy, is full of principles and promises which find their fulfilment in the world-wide mission of Christianity (Horton, *The Bible as a Missionary Book*). The proselytizing energy of the Jews in the last cent. B.C. and in the time of our Lord ('Ye compass sea and land to make one proselyte,' Mt 23^{15}) is a partial outcome of ideas and instincts which were long inherent in the race. These wide and lofty prophetic aims had to struggle against particularist tendencies, which made the Jews one of the most narrow and exclusive of the races of mankind. It is one of the paradoxes of history, that the missionary propaganda which aimed at the conversion and blessing of the world, sprang from a people whose predominant characteristics were pride in racial privileges, expectation of national greatness, and contempt for all who were not of the seed of Abraham. But the missionary activities and aims of Christianity cannot be rightly understood apart from the gradual development of missionary ideas which took place in the course of Jewish history. The words applied to John the Baptist in relation to Christ might be applied to the Jewish race, 'Behold, I send my messenger before thy face, which shall prepare thy way before thee' (Mk 1²). These germinal missionary conceptions and movements found their end and fulfilment in the Person and work of Jesus Christ, and in the work which He originated. He absorbed and enlarged them, giving them such definiteness and fulness that they appear to be derived entirely from Him ; for the spirit, aims, and motives of missions are distinctively Christian, and Christianity is essentially a missionary religion.

2. *The missionary character of our Lord.*—He regarded Himself as a missionary. At the beginning of His work in Galilee He applied to Himself the words of Isaiah (61¹), 'The spirit of the Lord God is upon me, because he hath anointed me to preach the gospel to the poor, he hath sent me to heal the brokenhearted,' etc. (Lk 4¹⁸. ¹⁹). He frequently describes Himself as one 'who was sent,' as when He says, 'he that receiveth me, receiveth him that sent me' (τὸν ἀποστείλαντά με, Mt 10⁴⁰); 'as the living Father hath sent me' (ἀπέστειλέν με, Jn 6⁵⁷); 'the Father which hath sent me' (ὁ πέμψας με, Jn 6⁴⁴). The references to His being 'sent' are most frequent in John.

It may be remarked that the verb ἀποστέλλειν is applied to Jesus 17 times in Jn. and 10 times in the Synoptics, while πέμπειν is applied to Him 25 times in Jn., but only once in the Synoptics. The distinction between the two verbs is slight. In most cases in the Gospels πέμπειν applies to the sender and ἀποστέλλειν to the person sent (cf. 'Neither is he that is sent (ἀπόστολος) greater than he that sent (πέμψαντος) him,' Jn 13¹⁶); but the distinction is not always followed (cf. 'As thou hast sent (ἀπέστειλας) me into the world, even so have I also sent (ἀπέστειλα) them into the world' (Jn 17¹⁸). Wilke and Grimm distinguish πέμπειν as the general term, which may imply accompaniment (as when the sender is God), while ἀποστέλλειν includes a reference to equipment, and suggests official or authoritative sending. But the frequency with which both words are applied to Jesus in the Gospels (at least 53 times in all) is an emphatic indication of the missionary character of His work. (Under this heading it is not necessary to discuss the distinctive aims and character of His mission. See artt. KINGDOM OF GOD, ETERNAL LIFE, SALVATION).

3. *In the call and training of the disciples* the missionary idea is also strongly emphasized. They were to be 'fishers of men' (Mk 1¹⁷ ‖ Mt 4¹⁹). Jesus ordained them that 'they might be with him, and that he might send them forth to preach' (κηρύσσειν, Mk 3¹⁴). The training was not only educative but practical. After a period of private intercourse He sent the Twelve forth two by two, as heralds to proclaim (κηρύσσειν) that 'the kingdom of heaven (or of God) was at hand' (Mk 6⁷ ‖ Mt 10⁵⁻⁷ ‖ Lk 9³). There is recorded by Lk. (10¹⁻¹⁷) another mission of Seventy, also sent forth two and two, who were to go with the same message to every city and place to which He Himself was about to come. From the words 'also others' ([καὶ] ἑτέρους, Lk 10¹) it is probably to be understood that the Twelve were not included in this mission. In both missions of the disciples, the work they had to do was evangelistic in relation to the people, and educative in relation to themselves. There may have been other missions which have not been recorded, for Mk. uses the suggestive phrase, 'He began to send them forth two by two' (6⁷); but the influence of such work on the training of the disciples, especially in giving them a firm grasp of the gospel they had to

preach, is incalculable. Not a little of the teaching of Jesus which we have in the Gospels may have taken its present shape from the frequent repetition of their message.

4. *The limits within which the personal work of Jesus was confined were declared by Himself* : 'I am not sent but unto the lost sheep of the house of Israel' (Mt 15²⁴). During the time of His personal ministry the work of the disciples was similarly limited. In sending them forth, He said, 'Go not into the way of the Gentiles, and into any city of the Samaritans enter ye not : but go rather to the lost sheep of the house of Israel' (Mt 10⁵. ⁶). This restriction, given at such a time, is of great importance, for it is an indication that the idea of a mission outside the bounds of the Jewish people was in the minds of the disciples when they were sent out on their first missionary journey. The restriction would have been needless if the disciples had not thought of such a mission as a possibility. It is an entire misreading of the Gospel history to imagine that the glorious conception of a world-wide mission was an afterthought, which only occurred to the disciples, or was suggested to them, after the resurrection of our Lord. The limitations which were so carefully laid down were temporary, and were evidently regarded as temporary. Even in declaring that He was sent but to the lost sheep of the house of Israel, He had also said, 'Let the children first be filled' (Mk 7²⁷). The reasons for the limitation were adequate. The disciples had to be fully trained ; the Kingdom of God had to be preached to the people who had been disciplined by the providence of God to receive it ; the gospel had to be completed by the full disclosure of the redemption of grace, in the death and resurrection of the Saviour.

5. *Indications of a world mission in the teaching of Jesus.*—Apart from the essentially universal character of the gospel, which inevitably involved a universal mission, there are indications that the world-wide view was brought before the minds of the disciples prior to the time when the great commission was given. The disciples were to be 'the salt of the earth' and 'the light of the world' (Mt 5¹³. ¹⁴). When Jesus praised the faith of the centurion of Capernaum, He said, 'Many shall come from the east and from the west, and shall sit down with Abraham, Isaac, and Jacob in the kingdom of God' (Mt 8¹¹; cf. also the same passage in Lk. in another connexion, where He adds, as if in reference to the preference which the Jews had received, 'Behold there are last which shall be first, and there are first which shall be last,' Lk 13²⁹. ³⁰). So also, when defending the woman who had anointed Him with the box of ointment, He said, 'Verily I say unto you, Wheresoever this gospel shall be preached in the whole world, this . . . shall be told for a memorial of her' (Mt 26¹³). Then He warned the disciples, saying, 'Ye shall be brought before governors and kings for my sake, for a testimony against them and the Gentiles' (Mt 10¹⁸). Many of the parables have references to or suggestions of a future extension of work among the Gentiles. In the interpretation of the parable of the Tares (one of the earlier parables) it is said that 'the field is the world' (Mt 13³⁸). In the later series of parables, as in that of the Vineyard and the Husbandmen, it is said, 'The kingdom of God shall be taken away from you, and shall be given to a nation bringing forth the fruits thereof' (Mt 21⁴³); in the Marriage Feast the direction is found, 'Go ye . . . into the highways, and as many as ye shall find, bid to the marriage' (Mt 22⁹, Lk 14²³); in the Sheep and the Goats there is a picture of the judgment of 'all nations' (Mt 25³²). Direct intimations of a world mission are not awanting, as in the apocalyptic discourses in the Synoptics, which are prefaced with a declaration of the destruction of the Temple ('There shall not be left one stone upon another which shall not be thrown down,' Mt 24^2, Mk 13^2, Lk 21^6), and contain the announcement that 'this gospel of the kingdom shall be preached in all the world, for a witness to all the nations' (Mt 24^{14} || Mk 13^{10}). In the Fourth Gospel the evidence of a world view as part of the instruction given to the disciples is very plain. After saying that He lays down 'his life for the sheep' (Jn 10^{15}), Jesus adds, 'Other sheep I have, which are not of this fold : them also I must bring, and they shall hear my voice' (v.^{16}). In connexion with the visit of the Greeks, He uttered the pregnant and impressive prophecy, 'I, if I be lifted up from the earth, will draw all men unto me' (12^{32}); and a little further on in the same chapter we find the words, 'I came not to judge the world, but to save the world' (12^{47}). In the private converse of our Lord and His disciples, in the last days of the earthly ministry, the vision of the world is repeatedly brought before the minds of the disciples as the object of the Saviour's thought and the scope of the disciples' mission, as—'That the world may know that I love the Father . . . even so I do' (Jn 14^{31}); 'As thou hast sent me into the world, even so have I also sent them into the world' (17^{18}; also $12^{46\text{-}48}$ $16^{8\text{-}11}$ $17^{2,\,21}$). Judas (not Iscariot) is even represented as asking, 'How is it that thou wilt manifest thyself unto us and not unto the world?' (14^{22}), as if the limitation of His work was a source of perplexity to him. Unless we are to regard the Gospels as entirely unhistorical, and all such universal references as due to the mind of the Church (which would then be greater than its Lord) at a later time, it must be admitted that the disciples were aware of the world-wide character of the work they were to undertake. The frequency of the world references in the earthly ministry may to some extent account for the fact that the missionary commission is mentioned only once in each of the Gospels (Mt $28^{16\text{-}20}$ || Mk 16^{15} || Jn 20^{21} || Lk $24^{46\text{-}48}$), and in Ac 1^8. For it is recognized that it is only in the brief records of the risen life of Jesus that the universal mission of the disciples is explicitly expressed in the form of a command. But that is no reason for imagining that it was an afterthought of Jesus, or an addition put into His mouth by followers of a later time. The universal commission is given then, because that is the time to which it belongs. The work of redemption had been 'finished'; the gospel was completed; the limitations which had restricted its extension were no longer necessary. The intimations of a universal mission, which had been given before, were carried to their inevitable conclusion in the majestic commission : 'All authority is given unto me in heaven and in earth. Go ye into all the world, make disciples of all nations, baptizing them in the name of the Father, and of the Son, and of the Holy Ghost : teaching them to observe all things whatsoever I have commanded you : and, lo, I am with you all the days, unto the consummation of the age' ($\pi\acute{a}\sigma a\varsigma$ $\tau\grave{a}\varsigma$ $\dot{\eta}\mu\acute{\epsilon}\rho a\varsigma$ $\ddot{\epsilon}\omega\varsigma$ $\tau\hat{\eta}\varsigma$ $\sigma\upsilon\nu\tau\epsilon\lambda\epsilon\acute{\iota}a\varsigma$ $\tauο\hat{\upsilon}$ $a\dot{\iota}\hat{\omega}\nu o\varsigma$, Mt $28^{16\text{-}20}$). The universal note predominates the whole passage. There is (i.) the claim of universal authority; (ii.) the direction to a universal field; (iii.) the universality of what is to be taught ('all things whatsoever I have commanded you'); (iv.) the promise of a universal presence, 'Lo, I am with you all the days, unto the consummation of the age.'

6. *The genuineness of the missionary commission* has been gravely questioned. In Mk. it appears in the closing section ($16^{9\text{-}20}$), which is now generally regarded as an addition by a later hand, possibly by the presbyter Aristion, who, according to Papias, was 'a disciple of the Lord' (F. C. Cony-

beare, *Expositor*, IV. viii. [1893] 241 ff. ; but see ARISTION). All critics admit the antiquity of the passage, and it may be accepted as 'embodying a true Apostolic tradition' (Salmond in Hastings' *DB* iii. p. 253^b).

The passage in Mt. ($28^{16\text{-}20}$) is characterized as 'a later appendix' (Moffatt, *Historical NT*, p. 647) entirely on account of its contents. The indications (in a different order) of its lateness are said to be—(i.) its incipient Trinitarianism, (ii.) the Trinitarian formula of baptism, which is found nowhere else in the NT. To these is added, (iii.) that the first disciples could hardly have known of the universal mission, or else they lived in flagrant disobedience to their Master's solemn command, and only reluctantly recognized its fulfilment in the Pauline gospel. But it may be said, on the other hand, as to (i.), that the incipient Trinitarianism of the NT is such a daring conception, especially to men who had been trained in the strict monotheism of Judaism, that its existence can hardly be explained without some word of the Lord Jesus in relation to it, such as that which Mt. records. How are we to account for the 'incipient Trinitarianism' of the Pauline benediction—'The grace of the Lord Jesus Christ, the love of God, and the communion of the Holy Ghost' (2 Co 13^{14}) —if there were no words of the Lord Jesus to justify it? As to (ii.), the baptismal formula, as it has been called, may not have been a formula. It may have been the mistake of a later time to regard it as such. If it was not a formula, there was nothing to hinder the Apostles and others from baptizing in the name of the Lord Jesus ('The Baptismal Formula,' by J. H. Bernard in *Expositor*, VI. v. [1902] 43 ff.). (iii.) The apparent inaction of the disciples may not have been due to ignorance or disobedience. The command as given in Lk. and Acts indicates a gradually widening sphere of operations, in Jerusalem and Judæa, in Samaria, and unto the uttermost parts of the earth. The difficulties and persecution which the Apostles encountered at the beginning of their work may have been to them a proof that the time had not yet come when they could leave the nearer and narrower fields and go forth to the Gentiles. If any reliance is to be placed on Acts as an historical document, it is abundantly evident that the first disciples did know of the world mission, and that they were moving in the line of their instructions. For in his first recorded utterance St. Peter strikes the universal note repeatedly. He quotes the words of Joel in explanation of what had happened at Pentecost, saying, 'It shall come to pass in the last days, saith God, that I will pour out of my Spirit upon *all flesh*' (Ac 2^{17}), 'And it shall come to pass, that whosoever shall call on the name of the Lord shall be saved' (v.^{21}). He closes his appeal to the people with the assurance that 'the promise is unto you, and to your children, and to all that are afar off, even as many as the Lord our God shall call' (v.^{39}). Then in $3^{25\text{f.}}$ there is the recognition of the coming of Christ as a fulfilment of prophecy, as a carrying out of the covenant made with Abraham ('And in thy seed shall all the families of the earth be blessed'); further, in the words, 'Unto you first God, having raised up his Servant ($\pi a\hat{\iota}\varsigma$), sent him to bless you,' there is the recognition of a wider field to be entered in due time. The great declaration, 'Neither is there salvation in any other : for there is no other name under heaven given among men, whereby we must be saved' (4^{12}), is meaningless, if there was not behind it a consciousness of the universal character of Christianity, and, as a consequence, the consciousness of a universal mission.

The disciples are also seen to be moving in the line of their instructions. They certainly preached the gospel in Jerusalem and in all Judæa. It is also seen that they preached it among the Samaritans, towards whom Jews had as strong an antipathy as they had towards Gentiles (' Philip went down to the city of Samaria and preached Christ unto them. . . . (Peter and John) preached the gospel in many villages of the Samaritans,' Ac 8[5. 25]). In a few years after the Crucifixion (Harnack says 1, Ramsay 3, Lightfoot 4, Turner 6 or 7 [in fixing the date of St. Paul's conversion, see Hastings' *DB*, art. 'Chronology of the NT ']) the faith of Christ had spread to Damascus, and had gained such hold there, that Saul was sent thither by the Sanhedrin to bring 'any of the Way,' whom he might find, bound to Jerusalem (Ac 9[2]). Lastly, some of those who were scattered abroad upon the persecution which arose about Stephen went as far as to Antioch, and preached the word to the Greeks ("Ελληνας, the reading adopted by Tischendorf, Nestle, etc.); and when tidings of these things came to the Church at Jerusalem, they sent forth Barnabas to visit and help them (which he did by finding Saul of Tarsus, Ac 11[19-26]).

Taking Turner's estimate as above (though we prefer Ramsay's), the gospel was firmly established in Damascus (and in Antioch) 6 or 7 years after the Crucifixion. The trouble which arose about Stephen marked the close of the comparatively peaceful progress of the Church. The hidden cleavage between Judaism and Christianity then became apparent, and an entirely new situation resulted, which affected those within and without the Church. The sympathy of the Jews (Ac 2[47]) towards the Christians had become antipathy (12[2. 3]). The persecution created anxieties which naturally absorbed the attention of the leaders. Coming as it did when the Church had been extended throughout Palestine, the persecution may have arrested the forward movement which, in accordance with the line of progress sketched out in Ac 1[8], had then become due. A little consideration of the difficulties which affect the progress of modern missions in different countries might lead to a better understanding of the situation in the Apostolic age, and to a higher appreciation of the results which the first missionaries achieved.

The dispute in the early Church in relation to the Gentiles, regarding which so much has been made, was not about preaching the gospel to them, but about the conditions on which they were to receive salvation and be admitted into the Church. No instructions on these matters had been given by the Lord Jesus, and difference of opinion was inevitable until the truth was made plain. St. Peter's reluctance to go to Cornelius did not arise from any unwillingness to preach to him, but from the natural shrinking of a strict Jew from entering the house of a Gentile. The accusation which was brought against him at Jerusalem by those who were of the circumcision was, not that he had preached the gospel to a Gentile, but that he had gone in to 'men uncircumcised and had eaten with them' (Ac 11[3]). It was 'they of the circumcision,' and not the first disciples, who glorified God, saying, 'Then hath God also to the Gentiles granted repentance unto life' (Ac 11[18]). These considerations are sufficient to establish the knowledge of the missionary command by the first disciples, and to account for the apparent delay (if any) in carrying it out.

7. *The progress of mission work within the NT record.*—The order is admirably given by Turner in his art. 'Chronology of the NT' in Hastings' *DB*. He says that 'the picture in Acts is cut up, as it were, into six panels, each labelled with a general summary of progress'; and his arrangement is adopted here. First stage, the beginning at

Jerusalem (Ac 1[1]-6[7]); second stage, the extension of the Church throughout Palestine (Ac 6[8]-9[31]); third stage, the extension of the Church to Antioch (Ac 9[32]-12[24]); fourth stage, the extension of the Church to Asia Minor, as a result of St. Paul's first missionary journey (Ac 12[25]-16[5]); fifth stage, the extension of the Church to Europe, resulting from St. Paul's second missionary journey (Ac 16[6]-19[20]); sixth stage, the extension of the Church to Rome (Ac 19[21]-28[31]). While that is the view of progress which is presented in Acts, it is not to be taken as complete. It exhibits for the most part the movement as connected with the great missionaries, St. Peter and St. Paul. The labours of the majority of the company of the Apostles are not recorded, and their activity might to some extent modify the above order of progression. Missionary enthusiasm also was not confined to the Apostles. Unnamed disciples, as in the case of Antioch (Ac 11[20]), and certainly also in the case of Rome, may have carried the gospel into many places of which no mention is made. But for general purposes the sketch as given above represents the line of advance up to the year A.D. 70. Progress after that belongs to the general history of missions.

LITERATURE.—Horton, *Bible as a Missionary Book* ; Bruce, *Training of the Twelve* ; Latham, *Pastor Pastorum* ; Hort, *Judaistic Christianity* ; Selby, *Ministry of the Lord Jesus*, pp. 86–118 ; Moffatt, *Historical NT*, pp. 647–650 ; Lambert, *Sacraments in the NT*, pp. 38 ff., 234 ff. ; F. C. Conybeare, *Expositor*, IV. viii. [1893] 241–254 ; J. H. Bernard, *ib.* VI. v. [1902] 43 ff. ; H. B. Swete, *ib.* VI. vi. [1903] 241 ff. ; art. 'Baptism' in Hastings' *DB*.   JOHN REID.

MITE.—See MONEY.

MOCKERY. — The Evangelists relate in the Passion history a series of narratives describing the brutal mockery of Jesus by the authorities and by their soldiers and servants. The passages are the following : (*a*) Mk 14[65] = Mt 26[67. 68] = Lk 22[63. 64] ; (*b*) Lk 23[11] ; (*c*) Mk 15 [16-20] = Mt 27[27-31] = Jn 19[2. 3].

There is no necessity to regard these stories as duplicates. A person who was condemned for the claims that Jesus was supposed to put forward was likely to meet with derision and brutality at every turn. Of course, if the story that Jesus was sent to Herod, which is peculiar to Lk., is unhistorical, the second of the stories would have to be struck out. If, however, that narrative is historical, and there is no cogent reason for doubting it, it was perfectly natural that Herod and his guards should mock one who claimed to be king. It is possible, indeed, that the narratives may have exerted an influence upon each other; but nothing compels us to affirm that any of them is unhistorical.

The first narrative records the mockery and ill-treatment inflicted on Jesus immediately after His condemnation by the Sanhedrin. Two stages are mentioned in Mark. The first consisted of spitting, blindfolding, buffeting, and the request that He should prophesy. Then, following this, we have a statement as to the attendants, the meaning of which is not perfectly clear. The better reading in Mk 14[65] is ἔλαβον. Several MSS, however, read ἔβαλλον or ἔβαλον (see Field). It is not quite clear how we should translate or explain the better reading. Swete renders 'they caught Him with blows,' others 'they took Him in charge with blows.' ῥαπίσμασιν means blows with the open hand, not blows with the rod. Another question touches the authors of this outrage. According to Mt., it is the members of the Sanhedrin. This seems to be Mk.'s meaning also, except that he limits it to 'some.' He mentions the servants at the close. Lk. represents the attendants who had charge of Jesus as alone concerned. Difficulties are also raised by the command to prophesy. Mt. and Lk. both explain it as a challenge to Jesus to prophesy who it was that smote Him. This in itself is perfectly natural, but it implies that Jesus was blindfolded, though there is no reference to this in Mt., and it is omitted by D and Syr ^{sin} in Mark. Even if original in Mk., it may imply that Jesus was condemned to death (cf. 'they covered Haman's face,' Est 7⁸), rather than that He was blindfolded so that He might be asked to prophesy who struck Him. Accordingly, the meaning may be 'foretell the future,' either generally or with a specific reference to His own fate, or to the destruction of the Temple, which He had been accused of predicting.

The second mockery, that before Herod, is free from the element of physical ill-treatment. Jesus is simply arrayed in royal garments, and a mocking homage is paid to Him; then He is sent back to Pilate. Lk 23¹⁰⁻¹² is omitted, it is true, in Syr ^{sin}, and is regarded by Wellhausen as a later addition (see his note on the passage and on 23¹⁵).

The third mockery is that by the Roman soldiers after the condemnation by Pilate. This narrative is omitted by Lk. but recorded by John. The soldiers take Jesus into the Prætorium and summon the whole of their company. Then they clothe Him in purple and put a crown of thorns upon His head; then they do homage to Him, saluting Him as king of the Jews. They keep on striking Him on the head with a reed, spitting upon Him, and bending the knee to Him in mock homage. To this account (of Mk.) Mt. adds, first, that before clothing Him in the robes they divested Him of His garments, and that they put a reed in His right hand, and subsequently took it from Him and struck Him on the head with it. Here Mt.'s account deserves preference, for it is intrinsically probable that the reed should have been given Him as a sceptre before it was used to smite Him. Jn.'s account is brief; he does not mention the reed, but says that they gave Him blows with the hand. It is a mark of historicity in the Gospel narratives that the Sanhedrists are represented as mocking the claims of Jesus to be a prophet, whereas the Roman soldiers, quite uninterested in His prophetic character, mock His claims to be a king, which would not be so ready a subject of jesting with the Jews, though they mocked Him for His pretensions to be a king of Israel as He hung upon the cross.

In recent years quite new significance has been attached to the mockery. Wendland in his art. 'Jesus als Saturnalien-König' (*Hermes*, xxxiii. 175–179) put forward the view that the Roman soldiers ridiculed Christ's royal and Divine claims by attiring Him in the dress of king Saturn. J. G. Frazer urges as an objection to this that, while it is possible that the Saturnalia may have been celebrated in Jerusalem at what seems to have been its original date in March, it is much more likely that it was really held in December, which, of course, does not harmonize with the time of year at which the Crucifixion took place. Frazer himself thinks that it resembled much more closely the treatment of the mock king of the Sacæa. He translates Dio Chrysostom's description as follows : 'They take one of the prisoners condemned to death and seat him upon the king's throne, and give him the king's raiment, and let him lord it and drink and run riot and use the king's concubines during these days, and no man prevents him from doing just what he likes. But afterwards they strip and scourge and crucify him' (Frazer, *Golden Bough* ², iii. 187).

Frazer argues that the Jewish Feast of Purim was a continuation of the Sacæa, and he conjectures that the Jews regularly compelled a condemned criminal to play a tragic part in that festival, and that Jesus perished in the character of Haman. He admits the difficulty caused by the fact that Purim fell a month before Passover, but he puts forward various suggestions to mitigate this difficulty. He thinks that possibly the Christian tradition may have shifted the date of the Crucifixion to coincide with the Passover, though he admits that this is perhaps not possible. He points out that the Bab. festival seems to have

fallen near the time of the Passover, and that the date of Purim was altered to a month earlier so as not to clash with it. He conjectures that the Jews may have sometimes, for a special reason, celebrated the Feast of Purim, or at least the death of Haman, at or near Passover. A further suggestion is, however, that possibly the licence of thirty days allowed to the mock king of the Saturnalia was allowed to the human representative of Haman. Yet as the mockery in question was not by Jews but by Roman soldiers, the question arises whether they would have been likely to take part in a Jewish celebration. To this Frazer replies that they may have fallen in with the local customs, but, quite apart from this, it was natural that without sharing Jewish beliefs they would be quite ready to join in the sport. He points out, however, that according to Lk.'s account, it was Herod's soldiers who mocked Jesus, and they were presumably Jews. Thus the Crucifixion on this view was not a punishment specially designed for Christ, but merely the fate which annually befell the malefactor who played Haman. It is argued that certain difficulties in the narrative thus gain relief. Pilate was reluctant to give up Jesus and yet acquiesced, though he had the power to release Him. This is due to the fact that someone had to be given up to play the part of Haman. Again, would Pilate have ventured to put over the cross the inscription declaring that Jesus was king of the Jews with a tyrant so gloomy and suspicious as Tiberius, unless it had been a formula of long standing and regarded as quite innocuous? Since Jesus represented Haman, it is suggested that Barabbas represented Mordecai ; and if so, he was probably released in order to play the part of a buffoon king (cf. the story of the mockery of Carabas in Philo, *adv. Flaccum*, ii. 520–523, and the 'Ride of the Beardless One' in Persia, referred to by Lagarde in his *Purim*). The name Barabbas, Frazer suggests, was an official title mistakenly regarded as a personal name. Originally Haman and Mordecai were the same, but one personated the dead and the other the risen deity. The same person probably played both parts, he who was Mordecai one year was Haman the next.

This ingenious theory is open to the most serious objections. Some of these have been stated by Mr. Andrew Lang in the very elaborate investigation he gives in *Magic and Religion*. It is very difficult to make good the identification of Purim with the Sacæa even if Frazer's interpretation of the Sacæa could hold good, which is very doubtful. It is also very improbable that a victim was actually crucified in the character of Haman by the Jews. There is not a shred of evidence to make such a suggestion plausible. And when we come to apply it to the Gospel history, the theory becomes more improbable than ever. The licence allowed to 'the Beardless One' was such that he was permitted, if the shopkeepers did not give him what he wished during his ride through the city, to appropriate everything they had in their shops. It is not easy to see any real parallel between this and the overturning of the money-changers' tables and driving out of their sheep and oxen from the Temple by Jesus. There is all the difference between a raid on the shopkeepers for personal plunder and the cleansing of the Temple from an intolerable abuse. Jesus would not have been asked by the authorities by what right He did these things, if it had been a perfectly legitimate exercise of a power He possessed as the representative of Haman. Moreover, Frazer's theory involves our rejection of the Johannine date for the cleansing of the Temple, although that date has much that can be said in its favour. Apart from this, however, one insuperable difficulty remains. It is quite possible that Jesus should have suffered in any character chosen for Him by those who compassed His death. In that respect He was a passive victim. But it is quite incredible that He should have participated in these ceremonies of His own free will, or have given any colour whatever to superstitions of that kind. It is accordingly out of the question to interpret the cleansing of the Temple as Frazer does, since that would imply that Jesus lent Himself to this festival. Moreover, unless the Gospel narratives are altogether misleading, Jesus was not in the hands of His enemies till the night before His death, and therefore His triumphal entry and His attack on the desecration of the Temple could have been no part of the programme of a Purim festival. There would have been no need for secrecy through the fear of the people, or for the services of the traitor, if the mockery and death were but the last acts in a longer drama. Nor are the difficulties in the Gospel narratives really mitigated by this hypothesis. The ordinary explanation of Pilate's vacillation and surrender is perfectly adequate. The procurator was so unpopular that he dared not risk the charge of treason that might have been launched against him before Tiberius if he had let a claimant to Messianic dignity go free. However convinced Pilate may have been that Jesus was harmless to Rome, nothing would have been easier than to bring a very damaging charge against him before the emperor. Nor is the title over the cross to be interpreted along Frazer's lines. To have let Jesus go would have constituted a much more valid basis of accusation than to write the title 'This is the king of the Jews' over His cross, for that meant 'This is the king of the Jews, and thus I serve pretenders to the throne.' It mocked Jesus and exasperated the Jews. To imagine that by one course Pilate would have escaped the charge of treason which he would have incurred by the other, is indeed to strain out the gnat and swallow the camel. If, as Frazer says, Pilate was obliged to give up a prisoner, and all he could do was to choose him, he had others whom he might have chosen besides Jesus and Barabbas. It was a choice that was dictated by his position. He was in the grip of his past and of his dread of Tiberius. Another point that deserves mention is that the mockery of Christ's prophetic claims is precisely parallel to the mockery of His royal claims. In the one case they bid Him prophesy, in the other they dress Him up as a mock king and pay Him a ribald homage. The parallelism shows us how unnecessary it is for us to seek for far-fetched reasons to explain the conduct of the Roman soldiers. Nothing was more natural than that the supporters of an alien empire should mock royal claims put forward by one who belonged to the subject people, and no derision was more effective than the dressing up of their victim as king. The sceptre served to beat Him, and the jest of the coronation was all the more piquant that the crown was studded with thorns. As Mr. Lang reminds us, 'Wallace was crowned at his trial with laurel'; and Atholl, who was a pretender to the crown, 'was tortured to death with a red-hot iron crown' (*Magic and Religion*, p. 203).

Lastly, it should be observed that the passage from Dio Chrysostom will not bear too much weight. There is a resemblance in the clothing with royal robes, in the stripping, the scourging, and the death, but there is no resemblance to the royal privileges accorded to the condemned prisoner, and it is also not clear that the victim was crucified. The Greek word used (ἐκρέμασαν) may mean simply that he was hanged, though the other view is more probable. No stress can be laid on the scourging in the case of Jesus, for it was the usual preliminary to crucifixion, and crucifixion was unhappily among the Romans no exceptional form of execution.

LITERATURE.—In addition to the Commentaries and Lives of Christ, see Frazer, *Golden Bough* 2, iii. 186–198 ; A. Lang, *Magic and Religion*, 76–204, 298–305 ; Vollmer, *Jesus und das Sacœenopfer* ; Reich, *Der König mit der Dornenkrone*.

ARTHUR S. PEAKE.

MONEY.—We propose to treat first of money in general as referred to in the Gospels, and afterwards of the definite sums or coins which are there named.

I. *MONEY IN GENERAL.*—In the AV six Greek words are rendered 'money,' 'tribute money,' or 'piece of money.' In two cases this is a mistranslation, and is rectified by the RV. The words are as follows: **1.** ἀργύριον (Mt 25[18. 27] 28[12. 15], Mk 14[11], Lk 9[3] 19[15. 23] 22[5]). (In three of the above passages it occurs in the plural without the sense being

altered ; thus, cf. Mt 25[18] with 25[27]). This word originally means silver, hence silver money (also tr. 'pieces of silver,' Mt 27[3. 5. 6. 9] ; see below, under 'Stater') ; finally, as silver was the chief medium of exchange in the ancient world, money in general (cf. Fr. *argent*). **2.** χαλκός (Mk 6[8] 12[41]). This word originally means brass, hence coins of brass (or copper), and, as copper money circulated largely among the common people, money in general. **3.** κέρμα (Jn 2[15]) comes from a verb meaning *to cut*, and means originally change or small coins. It is appropriately used in this passage for the stock-in-trade of the money-changers, a part of whose business it was to supply change for larger sums. **4.** νόμισμα (Mt 22[19]) comes from a verb meaning *to acknowledge as customary or lawful*. It means, accordingly, money in the sense of lawful coin. The νόμισμα τοῦ κήνσου, or tribute money, was the currency in which the Roman tribute had to be paid, that is, the *denarius*. **5.** τὰ δίδραχμα (Mt 17[24] AV 'tribute money,' RV 'the half-shekel'). As is rightly indicated by the RV, this word is the name of a definite sum of money which was levied for the maintenance of the Temple (see below, under 'Didrachm'). **6.** στατήρ (Mt 17[27] AV 'piece of money,' RV 'shekel'). Here, too, the AV is at fault, the word meaning a definite coin (see below, under 'Stater').

To the above words used for money in general (though under slightly different aspects) may be added the comprehensive description of money in Mt 10[9] in terms of the three metals used as specie—gold, silver, and brass (or copper). This verse may be taken as evidence that gold as well as silver and copper coins circulated in Palestine in the time of our Lord, although no gold coin is mentioned in the Gospels. The current gold coin was doubtless the Roman *aureus*, frequently referred to in the Mishna as a golden *denarius*. In silver there was more variety. The Roman *denarius* was, of course, largely in evidence, and was probably the silver coin in most common use. But there were also coins of larger size, bearing Greek names. When Pompey made Syria a Roman province (B.C. 65), he found in circulation tetradrachms of two different kinds. There were those issued chiefly from Antioch by the Seleucid kings on the Attic standard, weighing 262 grains troy. There were also those issued by the semi-autonomous cities of Phœnicia on the Phœnician standard of 224 grains to the tetradrachm. Tetradrachms of both standards were recognized by Pompey as equivalent to four denarii (Mommsen, *Gesch. des Röm. Münzwesens*, 36, 715). Both would still be lawful coin in the time of our Lord, though, as Mommsen surmises (*ib.* 72), the heavier royal tetradrachms would tend to be driven out of circulation by the lighter Phœnician coins, which, besides, as corresponding exactly to the Hebrew shekel, were in special demand in Palestine for religious purposes (see below, under 'Didrachm'). The supply of silver from the mints at Tyre and Sidon, which continued to issue tetradrachms and didrachms under the Emperors,* was reinforced from the time of Augustus onwards by the tetradrachms coined in large numbers at Antioch for circulation in the province of Syria. These ranged in weight from 220 to 236 grains, and were no doubt reckoned for ordinary purposes as equal to four *denarii*, although, in accordance with the regular practice of the Romans of giving a preference to their own

* According to most numismatologists ; *e.g.*, Head (*Hist. Num.* 675) says : 'From B.C. 126 down to the reign of Vespasian, we possess a plentiful series of Tyrian tetradrachms and didrachms.' On the other hand, Mommsen (*op. cit.* 36) holds that from the time of Pompey the Phœnician cities lost the power of issuing silver money, and points out that the extant Phœnician tetradrachms never bear the names of Emperors or any other indication of Roman sway.

silver, they were tariffed for purposes of taxation as only equal to three *denarii*.

A vexed question, which cannot be held to be yet decided, is whether prior to the time of the first Jewish revolt any silver coins had been produced in Palestine itself. Until lately it has been usual for numismatologists to assign to Simon Maccabæus certain silver shekels and half-shekels struck on the Phœnician standard, and bearing the inscription in Hebrew, 'Jerusalem the Holy' (Madden, *Coins of the Jews*, 65–71; Head, *Hist. Num.* 681, 682). Strong historical reasons, however, have been brought by Schürer (*HJP* I. ii. 379–383) and others for dating these coins rather in the time of the revolt under Nero; and the opinion seems to be making headway that at the time of our Lord, and previously, the Jews were dependent for their silver money upon foreign sources. (For an able statement of the case, see Kennedy in Hastings' *DB*, vol. iii. *s.v.* 'Money,' § 5).

On the other hand, the supply of copper money must have been almost, if not quite, exclusively of native production. There were the copper coins of the Hasmonæan princes, those of the various Herods, and those which had been struck since A.D. 6 by successive procurators of Judæa. Unlike the foreign silver money, they have, in deference to Jewish feeling, no Imperial effigy or the likeness of any living thing; even those of the procurators have only the name of the reigning Emperor, and innocent ears of corn, palm-trees, lilies, and the like. As to their denomination we have no sure evidence. Schürer holds that the Romans imposed their monetary standard more rigorously in Palestine than elsewhere, and that even the Herodian coins followed the Roman system (*HJP* II. i. 38). Other writers consider it to be more probable that the copper coinage of Palestine followed the subdivisions of the drachm common in Greek-speaking countries. The extant coins contain no indication of value, nor can any safe inference be drawn from their weight, seeing that, where a silver standard prevails, the copper coinage must always be very much of the nature of token money. (See, further, under 'Assarion,' 'Kodrantes,' and 'Lepton,' below).

Before proceeding to speak in detail of the coins named in the Gospels, it will be well to give in tabular form the main elements of the two systems, the Greek and the Roman, which obtained concurrently in Palestine at the time of our Lord. For convenience of reference the average value in sterling money is put opposite the larger sums.

Greek system.

1 Talent (£240) = 60 Minas.
1 Mina (£4) = 100 Drachms.
1 Drachm (9½d.) = 6 Obols.
1 Obol = 8 Chalki.

(To this system belong also the stater of four, and the didrachm of two, drachms; and the lepton, whose relation to the chalkus is uncertain. See below, under 'Lepton').

Roman system.

1 Aureus (£1) = 25 Denarii.
1 Denarius (9½d) = 16 Asses.
1 As = 4 Quadrantes.

The point of connexion between the two systems is found in the identification of the Roman *denarius* with the Attic drachm. This identification was rendered easy by the fact that at the time when Rome began her career of conquest in the East the drachm of the Attic standard had fallen to a weight which only slightly exceeded that of the *denarius*; but there can be little doubt that it was made deliberately by the Romans as a matter of policy. Alexander the Great had made the Attic drachm the unit of his Imperial coinage, which he imposed upon all the lands he had conquered; and in adopting the Alexandrine drachm as equal to their own *denarius*, the Romans wished to indicate that they served themselves heirs to his kingdom in the East (Mommsen, *op. cit.* 691). In Imperial times the identification was so completely established that Hellenistic writers regularly refer to the *denarius* as 'the Attic drachm.' This identification enables us to assign values to those coins which follow the Greek system. The weight of the gold *aureus* is known, and its value admits of easy calculation (see Hastings' *DB* iii. 427), and the other values, as given above, follow at once. This method of ascertaining the value of the silver coins of the Gospels does justice to the fact that, in the Roman Empire then, as in Britain now, the value of silver coins was legally defined in terms of the gold standard.

II. *DEFINITE SUMS OF MONEY AND COINS MENTIONED IN THE GOSPELS.*—These may most conveniently be treated of under three heads: money of account, silver coins, and copper coins.

(i.) *Money of account.*—Two sums of money, to which no actual coin corresponded, receive a special name in the Gospels. These are the *talent* and the *mina*.

1. Talent (τάλαντον, Mt 18[24] 25[15. 16. 20. 22. 24. 25. 28]) is originally the name of the highest weight in the various systems of antiquity, hence the sum of money represented by that weight in gold or silver. The talent of the Gospels, which is, of course, a talent of silver, might conceivably be the Phœnician talent, but is far more probably to be identified with the talent on the reduced Attic scale which had been formally recognized by the Romans (see above). It contained 6000 Attic drachms or *denarii*, and was thus worth 240 *aurei* or £240.

The talent is mentioned twice by our Lord. In the parable of the Unmerciful Servant (Mt 18[23-35]) the one servant owes the king 10,000 talents, or nearly two-and-a-half millions of our money—an enormous sum, of which the 100 denarii (= £4) owed him by his fellow-servant represents but an insignificant fraction (ππ̂πη̂). (It may be remarked that the juxtaposition in this parable of the talent and the *denarius* is a confirmation of the view that it is the *Attic* talent that is meant). In the parable of the Talents (Mt 25[14-30]) the master intrusts his capital of eight talents or £1920 to his three servants in sums of £1200, £480, and £240 respectively. It will be seen that even he who received but one talent had yet quite a respectable capital to trade with, so that the excuse which is sometimes made by commentators on his behalf, viz. that he was discouraged by the smallness of the sum committed to him, is as little valid as that which he offered for himself. The real reason for his conduct was, of course, just his slothfulness.

2. Mina (μνᾶ, Lk 19[13. 16. 18. 20. 24. 25] AV and RV **pound**) is the sixtieth part of the talent. Like the latter, it is to be calculated on the Roman-Attic scale. It contains 100 *denarii*, and is thus equal to £4.

The only mention of this sum in the Gospels is in the parable of the Pounds (Lk 19[12-27]), where a nobleman, going to a far country to get a kingdom, gives one mina to each of his ten servants, bidding them trade with it till his return. The smallness of the sum in such a connexion is remarkable, especially when compared with the companion parable of the Talents. The explanation (as far as the story is concerned) seems to be that the master is not in this case a trader making provision for the suitable employment of his capital in his absence, but one who, having in prospect the acquisition of a kingdom, desires to test the capacity of his servants for high office in that kingdom. Ingenuity and diligence would be more thoroughly tested in multiplying a small sum than a large one.

(ii.) *Silver coins.*—Of these there are mentioned by name, the *denarius*, the *drachm*, the *didrachm*, and the *stater*. The 'piece of money' of the AV in Mt 17[27] is the stater, the 'pieces of silver' in Lk 15[8] are drachms, while the 'pieces of silver' in Mt 26[15] are probably staters, and are discussed under that heading.

1. Denarius (δηνάριον, AV and RV **penny**; American Revisers, more happily, **shilling**).— This is the most frequently mentioned coin in the Gospels (Mt 18[28] 20[2. 9. 10. 13] 22[19], Mk 6[37] 12[15] 14[5], Lk 7[41] 10[35] 20[24], Jn 6[7] 12[5]). It is the name of the most important Roman coin, which circulated throughout the Empire, and in terms of which all public accounts were made up. It received its name from being originally the equivalent of ten copper asses, but from B.C. 217 onwards it was equivalent to sixteen asses, and weighed $\frac{1}{84}$ of the Roman pound, or 60 grains troy. Under Nero (c. A.D. 60) it was reduced to $\frac{1}{96}$ of the pound, or 52½ grains. At the time of our Lord its value was fixed at $\frac{1}{25}$ of the *aureus*, which may be taken under the early emperors as equal on the average to our sovereign; thus the *denarius* was worth 9·6 pence, or roughly 9½d.

We find the *denarius* used in the Gospels for the reckoning of even fairly large sums. Thus in the parable of the Unmerciful Servant (Mt 18[23], see above under 'Talent') a sum of 100 *denarii* is mentioned, while in the parable of the Two Debtors (Lk 7[41]) the two debts are stated at 500 and 50 *denarii* respectively (£20 and £2). In Mk 6[37] = Jn 6[7] the disciples estimate that it would need bread to the value of at least 200 *denarii* (£8) to provide for the five thousand. (There is no probability in the suggestion that this figure was named as the amount of money then in 'the bag.' It is intended to indicate a sum far beyond the means of the little company). In Mk 14⁵=Jn 12⁵ the vase of ointment with which Mary anointed our Lord is valued at 300 *denarii* (£12). The 'exceeding costliness' of this loving tribute is realized when we remember that the sum named represents at least the annual income of a labourer of those days. This appears from the parable of the Labourers in the Vineyard (Mt 20¹⁻¹⁵), where a *denarius* is evidently looked upon as liberal pay for a day's work ; for we may be quite sure that the employer who dealt so generously with the labourers engaged late in the day had struck no niggardly bargain with those hired in the morning. (A passage which may be quoted in confirmation is To 5¹⁴, where the disguised angel is promised by Tobit a drachm a day—at that time a little less than a *denarius*—for acting as companion to his son. It is true that this was to be exclusive of his necessary expenses ; but, on the other hand, the position was one of trust, and would naturally be more highly remunerated than field labour). In the parable of the Good Samaritan (Lk 10³⁰⁻³⁷) two *denarii* are given to the innkeeper as a reasonable payment in advance for the keep of the wounded traveller for a day or two, to be supplemented if necessary on the return of the Samaritan. (This is the most natural way to explain the reference ; see Jülicher, *Gleichnisreden*, ii. 591. On the other hand, Ramsay in Hastings' *DB*, Ext. Vol. 394, holds that the two *denarii* were simply payment for the one night that the two had spent in the inn).

Of special interest is the reference to the *denarius* in Mt 22¹⁹=Mk 12¹⁵=Lk 20²⁴ in connexion with the Pharisees' question as to the lawfulness of paying tribute to Cæsar. The *denarius* was 'the money of the tribute' (Mt 22¹⁹), all Imperial taxes being payable in terms of it in accordance with a rescript of Germanicus (*c.* A.D. 18). It bore upon it the name and title of the reigning Emperor, along with the effigy either of himself or of some member of the Imperial family—the 'image and superscription' to which our Lord alluded. It was issued by the Imperial authority, even the Roman Senate having only the right to mint copper coins, and could thus most appropriately be spoken of as 'that which is Cæsar's.'

2. Drachm (δραχμή, Lk 15⁸·⁹ AV and RV **piece of silver**).—This is the name of the unit of the Greek system of silver coinage, and, as such, might be applied to a great variety of coins from different mints and of different standards. In the Gospels it occurs only in the parable of the Lost Coin, where, of course, it must be understood of some coin current in Palestine. Few coins of this denomination were issued from the Phœnician cities or from Antioch, and the city of Cæsarea in Cappadocia had only recently begun to coin drachms on the Phœnician standard (of 55 grains) for use in the provinces of Syria and Cappadocia (Mommsen, *op. cit.* 734, 897 ; Head, *op. cit.* 634). Thus, while it is not impossible that the coins in question may have been drachms of the Phœnician standard, they are with greater probability to be identified with the 'Attic drachms'* of the Hellenistic writers, that is, with Roman *denarii*. In any case, the value for ordinary purposes was the same—about 9½d. of our money. The 'ten pieces of silver' possessed by the woman thus amounted to eight shillings.

3. Didrachm (δίδραχμον, Mt 17²⁴ AV 'tribute money,' RV 'half-shekel').—As the name implies, this is a coin of the value of two drachms. τὰ δίδραχμα in the passage quoted refers to the tax of half a shekel (Ex 30¹³) levied each year in the month of Adar from all Jews above the age of twenty for the maintenance of the Temple. The only coins then current in Palestine which answered exactly to the 'shekel of the sanctuary'—leaving out of

* It may not be out of place to remind the reader that the word 'Attic' in this connexion implies only a remote association with the coinage of Athens. In his *Notes on the Parables*, Trench assumes that this drachm was Athenian, stamped with 'an owl, a tortoise, or a head of Minerva,' and reluctantly surrenders 'the resemblance to the human soul, originally stamped with the image and superscription of the great King,' which earlier expositors had delighted to trace. A sound method of parable exposition will indeed dispense with this fanciful suggestion, but not for Trench's reasons (see Bruce, *Parabolic Teaching*, 279).

account the shekels commonly but probably erroneously assigned to Simon Maccabæus (see above) —were those which had for long been coined in the Phœnician cities ; and the Temple tax, along with other sacred dues, was paid in this currency.

The well-established correspondence of the didrachm to the half-shekel has been obscured for some writers by the fact that the LXX regularly translate שֶׁקֶל by δίδραχμον. From the narrative in Mt. it is evident that the tax was a voluntary one, although the Mishna declares that the goods of those who had not paid it by the 25th Adar might be distrained (Edersheim, *Life and Times*, ii. 112). After the destruction of Jerusalem, Vespasian made compulsory a poll-tax of the same amount to defray the cost of rebuilding the temple of Jupiter Capitolinus.

4. Stater (στατήρ, Mt 17²⁷ AV **piece of money**, RV **shekel**).—The word στατήρ is derived from the verb ἵστημι in the sense of *to weigh*. It hence means, in the first place, a standard weight, and then derivatively a standard coin. In Athens it was at first applied to the didrachm, which was looked upon as the standard coin of the monetary system, but afterwards to the tetradrachm or piece of four drachms. It is evidently so used in the passage before us, for the stater to be found in the fish's mouth was to pay the Temple tax of a didrachm for two persons, our Lord and Peter. The tetradrachm of the Phœnician standard corresponded to the Hebrew shekel, and is no doubt the coin here indicated. Josephus refers in one passage (*BJ* II. xxi. 2) to 'the Tyrian coin which is of the value of four Attic drachms,' and in another (*Ant.* III. viii. 2) he gives the value of the Hebrew shekel as four Attic drachms. The stater would thus be worth 4s. 2d. of our money.

In Mt 26¹⁵ Cod. D reads τριάκοντα στατῆρας ; and though this reading is rejected by critical editors, it probably embodies a correct paraphrase of the ἀργύρια (AV and RV 'pieces of silver') of the TR. That is, the thirty pieces of silver paid to the traitor as the price of blood were staters of the Phœnician standard. This appears from a comparison of the passages in Mt. where they are spoken of with Zec 11¹². ¹³, in which shekels are plainly intended. It has been pointed out (O. Holtzmann, *NT Zeitgesch.* 110) that just as in Zec 11¹² the word שֶׁקֶל does not occur but is suggested by שָׁקַל, so also the word στατήρ is latent in the verb ἔστησαν in Mt 26¹⁵. Reckoning the stater at 4 *denarii*, the sum paid to Judas amounted to £4, 16s. Thirty shekels of silver was the price that had to be paid (Ex 21³²) as blood-money for a male or female slave ; and this coincidence has frequently been used as a striking illustration of the truth expressed in Ph 2⁷ that our Lord took upon Himself the form of a servant.

(iii.) *Copper coins.*—There are three copper coins mentioned in the Gospels : the *assarion*, the *kodrantes*, and the *lepton*. The last is tr. 'mite' in the EV, while the two others are called, without distinction, by the name 'farthing.'

1. Assarion (ἀσσάριον Mt 10²⁹, Lk 12⁶, AV and RV **farthing**, Amer. RV **penny**).—The name is derived from the Latin *assarius*, a variant of *as*. It may either be the name given in Greek-speaking countries to the Roman *as*, or else the name of some local copper coin which in some way corresponded to it. Both views have been taken, by different scholars, of the significance of the word in the above passages. On the one hand, Schürer (*HJP* II. i. 39) and others hold that it is the Roman *as* that is here mentioned, in value the sixteenth part of the *denarius*. In support of this view, it may be urged that copper coins were issued, by authority of the Senate, from the Imperial mint at Antioch for circulation in the province of Syria, that these coins bear Latin inscriptions, and that of the two sizes in which they are found one has been identified (*e.g.* by Mommsen, *op. cit.* 718, and Madden, *op. cit.* 301) with the *sestertius* or quarter-*denarius*, and the other with the *as*. Moreover, the Vulgate not only renders ἀσσάριον back into *as* in the passage in Mt., but in the corresponding passage in Lk. has *dipondio*, thus identifying the 'two farthings' which are named as the price of two sparrows with the Roman *dupondius* or piece of two *asses*. Schürer points out, besides, that the name אִסָּר (*'issar*, evidently the Heb. form of ἀσσάριον) occurs frequently in the Mishna, and is sometimes expressly called אסר אימלק or Italian *assarion*. If this view is correct, the *assarion* of the Gospels will represent ·6d.—roughly a halfpenny—in English money, or exactly 5 German pfennigs. On the other hand, this simple solution of the problem is challenged, and chiefly on account of those very references in the Mishna to which Schürer appeals. The qualification of certain *assaria* as 'Italian'— which is also found in Greek on certain Cretan coins of the time of Claudius (Head, 384) and in a quotation from the Rescript of Germanicus in the Palmyra tariff—seems to imply that there were other coins of the same name, but of different value. And, as a matter of fact, the Mishna speaks of the *dinar* or *denarius* as containing 24 *'issārîm*, which cannot therefore be Roman *asses* of 16 to the *denarius*. If this distinction existed already in the time of our Lord, it is to be presumed that He used the word in the more popular sense.* In this case the price of the two sparrows (Mt 10²⁹) would be ·4d., or rather less than a halfpenny — almost exactly 4 centimes.

2. Kodrantes (κοδράντης, Mt 5²⁶, Mk 12⁴², AV, RV, and Amer. RV **farthing**).—There can be no question as to the identity of the coin that is intended in these two passages. It is the *quadrans* or quarter - *as*, the smallest coin in the Roman system, equal in value to ⅔ of a farthing, or a little more than the pfennig. It may, however, reasonably be doubted whether any coin known by this name was in circulation in Palestine in the time of our Lord. The word does not occur in the Mishna, and it has not been found in any of the inscriptions in Greek-speaking provinces (see *ExpT* x. [1899] 232, 336, where Sir W. M. Ramsay takes Prof. Blass roundly to task for assuming that the name κοδράντης was familiar in the East, and that the provincial cities coined copper money with Roman designations). Nor are the allusions in the Gospels conclusive. Mk.'s explanatory note (λεπτὰ δύο, ὅ ἐστιν κοδράντης) is obviously intended for non-Palestinian (possibly Roman) readers. As for the use of the word in Mt., the fact that the parallel passage in Lk. has τὸ ἔσχατον λεπτόν instead of τὸν ἔσχατον κοδράντην, suggests that it may have been inserted by the First Evangelist as the name of the smallest coin in the Roman system in place of the *lepton*, the smallest coin in the Palestinian system. It is, however, open to us to suppose that there was a local coin which for some purposes was identified with the *quadrans*, though rarely so named. A coin of Agrippa II. has been found bearing the name χαλκοῦς (Madden, 146). In the ordinary Greek system the *chalkus* is equal to 1/48 of the drachm ; but if we suppose that for purposes of taxation local copper was only accepted subject to a discount of 25 per cent., the *chalkus* would be tariffed as equal to the *quadrans*, which is 1/64 of the *denarius*. (Cf. note to last paragraph, and see the already quoted art. by Prof. Kennedy, who works out in detail the relations of the 'tariff' and 'current' values of the various coins).

3. Lepton (λεπτόν, Mk 12⁴², Lk 12⁵⁹ 21², AV and RV **mite**).—This name is originally an adjective meaning 'thin' or 'small.' It hence denotes a very small coin, but is otherwise indeterminate.

* Prof. Kennedy in Hastings' *DB, s.v.* 'Money,' § 8, draws an interesting and instructive distinction between the 'tariff' and the 'current' value of the local copper money. Just as the tetradrachmon of Antioch was tariffed as only equal to three *denarii* for purposes of taxation, so he supposes that the local *assarion* (1/24 of the drachm) was rated as equivalent to half of the Italian *assarion* or *as*. But this does not affect the calculation made above, for of course the purchase of sparrows would be one of those 'ordinary purposes' for which the coin would retain its current value.

'In the Oriental provinces of the Roman Empire,' says Babelon (*Monnaies Grecques et Romaines*, I. i. 466), 'the word λεπτόν regularly denoted local copper money as distinguished from coppers of the Roman mint.' At different times and in various places it was used of coins of very different value. As used in the Gospels, however, there is no ambiguity. It is agreed on all hands that it denotes the smallest coin current among the Jews, known to the Mishna as the פְּרוּטָה (*pĕrûṭāh*), of which we are expressly told that it was an eighth of the Roman *as* (see reff. in Lightfoot, ii. 453, and Schürer, II. i. 40),—a statement which exactly agrees with that of Mk. about the value of the *lepton*. If, therefore, the *quadrans* is to be identified with the *chalkus*, the *lepton* is a coin of half the value.

Nevertheless, the statement of Mk. (λεπτὰ δύο, ὅ ἐστιν κοδράντης) has given much trouble to numismatologists, who, to quote the words of one of them, 'have serious difficulty in finding among the small coins of Judæa separate denominations for chalkous and lepton' (G. F. Hill in *EBi, s.v.* 'Penny'). Accordingly, many attempts have been made to identify the *lepton* with the *chalkus-quadrans*. Thus Madden, following Cavedoni, cuts the knot by supposing Mk. to have meant the ὅ ἐστι to apply to the λεπτόν and not to the λεπτὰ δύο (*Coins of the Jews*, 304), and appeals for corroboration to the correspondence of the *kodrantes* to the *lepton* in Mt 5²⁶ = Lk 12⁵⁹. Hill, on the other hand, following up the suggestion of Prof. Kennedy referred to in the preceding paragraphs, contends that the difference between the *lepton* and the *chalkus-quadrans* was only a matter of accounting. The difficulty, as stated by Mr. Hill, depends upon the assumption that the *chalkus-quadrans* was a current Palestinian coin. This, however, has not been proved. Agrippa's *chalkus* need not have been considered as equal to a *quadrans*.* As stated by Mr. Madden, 'it is impossible to get over the fact that at this period the quadrans of the Empire, which still retained the name of χαλκοῦς, had the same weight as the lepton of the time of the Seleucidæ' (*Coins of the Jews*, 304). The difficulty depends, further, upon an inference from weight, —an inference which, in the case of coins which were little more than tokens, is unusually precarious. In any case, the arguments advanced would need to be much stronger in order to upset the positive statement of St. Mark.

The value, then, as men reckon values, of the widow's gift was little more than a farthing. But the fact that it consisted of *two* tiny coins,—a fact which we constantly obscure by talking, in our careless way, of 'the widow's *mite*,'—is full of significance. She might have kept back one.† But of her penury she cast in all that she had ; and so of her, too, as of another woman who from her larger resources made an equally lavish gift, it is true that, wherever the gospel is preached throughout the whole world (Mt 26¹³), this that she did is told as a memorial of her.

LITERATURE.—Madden's *Coins of the Jews* (vol. ii. of *Numismata Orientalia*) contains an exhaustive account of all the extant Jewish coins, and an appendix (289–310) on the money of the NT. The subject is treated briefly, but clearly, in Schürer, *HJP* II. i. 38–40, and O. Holtzmann, *NT Zeitgesch.* 110–116. Mommsen's *Gesch. des Röm. Münzwesens* is a mine of information on all that concerns the money of the Empire. Articles on 'Money' in the various Bible Dictionaries can be read with advantage, esp. the admirably comprehensive and lucid art. by Prof. Kennedy in Hastings' *DB*.

NORMAN FRASER.

MONEY - CHANGERS. — See preced. art. and BANK, No. **1.**

MONOTHEISM.—At whatever period in their early history the people of Israel may be supposed to have passed through the obscure and uncertain stages of belief that precede a clear and reasoned theism, that period had been left behind long before the days of Christ and the NT writers. The bitter experiences of exile and suffering on the one hand, and on the other the lofty teachings of prophets and men of God, had eradicated all tendencies to polytheism, and had fixed immovably in the conscience and conviction of the entire nation the faith that Jehovah was the one God of

* Babelon (606) identifies the *quadrans* with the δίχαλκον and the χαλκοῦς with the *lepton* of the Gospels.
† 'Quorum unum vidua retinere potuerat' (Bengel).

the whole earth. If Israel's early beliefs, as some contend, were henotheistic, and conceded a place and right to other national gods, as Chemosh, Molech, or Rimmon, as equal and paramount lords of their own peoples, such recognition of external divinities had long since ceased to be permissible. There were not really gods many and lords many ; there is one God the Father, and one Lord Jesus Christ (1 Co 8[6]).

This monotheistic belief, however, is assumed rather than formulated or defined in the Gospels. The doctrine that God is one, universally supreme and without rival, does not need to be explained or defended, for it runs no risk of being assailed. Like the belief in the existence of God, it is an article of faith accepted on all sides, by Jesus and by His opponents, and is rather implicit in the thought than explicit in the teaching of Christ and of His disciples.

While, however, this is true, and all the more so because His controversy with the Jews turned largely upon the question of His claim to equality with God, and the blasphemy which this claim appeared to them to imply, epithets and phrases may readily be quoted from the Gospels which have no meaning except as presupposing an absolute and pure monotheism. Such phrases, as would naturally be anticipated, are more generally employed by St. John than by the Synoptists. Thus the Prologue of the Fourth Gospel, tracing all things back to God with whom the Word is one (Jn 1[1]), asserts nothing less than the uniqueness as well as the eternity and sovereignty of Him from whom they proceed ; and the true Light entering into the world enlighteneth not this or that nation only, but every man (v.[9]). To the same effect and with the same background of accepted and common belief are the repeated declarations of His oneness with the Father (Jn 10[30. 38] 14[10], cf. 17[21. 23]). The area and claims of the Divine Kingdom, the Kingdom of God, are explicitly enlarged beyond any mere national limits, and made to embrace the whole world (Lk 16[16], Jn 4[21ff.]), and so the disciples are taught to pray that it may come upon earth, as it is in heaven (Mt 6[10]). It is indeed not bodily or material (Lk 17[21]), but transcends the world (Jn 18[36]). In the Last Judgment, again, all nations are gathered before the throne, and all receive sentence. 'The field' in which the seed is sown is 'the world' (Mt 13[38]) ; and the final injunction to Christ's followers is that they are to go into all the world to make disciples of all the nations (Mt 28[19]).

The same teaching is conveyed with more or less directness in the assertion of the subordination and judgment of the prince of this world (Jn 16[11]) ; in the stress laid upon the unique obligation and importance of love to God as constituting the first and greatest commandment (Mt 22[37] ‖ Mk 12[30] Lk 10[27]) ; in the appeal made by Christ Himself to a similar unique obligation of worship and service to the one only God (Mt 4[10] ‖ Lk 4[8]) ; in the emphatic affirmation of a common Fatherhood and Godhead (Jn 20[17], cf. 8[41]) ; and in the solemn declaration of the permanence and inviolability of the words of the Son (Mt 24[35] ‖ Mk 13[31], Lk 21[33]), while elsewhere there is ascribed to Him that omniscience which is an attribute of God Himself (Jn 16[30]).

There are also passages in which the epithet 'one' or 'only' is directly applied to the Divine Ruler, thus claiming for Him with more or less emphasis the sole dominion and the exclusive right to homage. 'The Lord our God is one Lord' (Mk 12[29] from Dt 6[4], cf. v.[32]). The God who forgives sins is εἷς (Mk 2[7]), or μόνος (Lk 5[21]) ; He is unique in goodness (Mt 19[17] ‖ Mk 10[18], Lk 18[19]) ; the sole Father (Mt 23[9]) ; and the only God (Jn 5[44]).

Some of these expressions might, it is true, be satisfied by a wide conception, such as the ancient prophets had formed, of a God of Israel to whom the sons of Israel were a first interest and charge, or even of a Sovereign the limits of whose sway left room for other sovereigns beside Him. Not all of them, evidently, if read apart and by themselves, will bear the weight of a full monotheistic inference. Taken together, however, and in their context, their joint and several significance is unmistakable. They assume on the part of speaker and hearer alike a belief in the sole supremacy of one God. Nor is this inference as to their meaning seriously contested.

Moreover, in one passage (Jn 17[3]) there is found a perfectly distinct and unequivocal assertion of monotheistic doctrine ; eternal life is to gain a knowledge of the only true God (τὸν μόνον ἀληθινὸν θεόν). Other phrases, in themselves less definite or comprehensive, must clearly be received and interpreted in the light of this, if an adequate conception of Christ's teaching concerning the Father is to be reached. The principle is applicable to other elements of His instruction than that under consideration. The whole is to be construed and expounded by means of the loftiest and most comprehensive statements of doctrine, not to be attenuated to those which may be more particular or obscure.

The conclusion, therefore, is that a monotheistic belief is everywhere assumed in the Gospels ; and if it is rarely formulated, the reason is to be sought in the universal assent with which it was received. Christ did not need to teach with definiteness and reiteration, as though it were a new truth, that there is one only Lord of heaven and of earth ; for this belief was common to Himself and to His hearers, and formed the solid and accepted foundation of their religious faith.

LITERATURE.—Treatises on the Theology of the NT discuss the conception of God, and the general doctrine is treated in works on Theism ; cf. Ed. Caird, *Evolution of Religion*[2], 2 vols., Glasgow, 1894 ; Orr, *Christian View of God and the World*[1], pp. 91–96.

A. S. GEDEN.

MONTH.—See TIME.

MOON.—In the NT the moon (σελήνη) is part of the established natural order. So when Christ prophesies the end of the world, 'The moon shall not give her light' (Mt 24[29], Mk 13[24]). Twice in the Gospel of Matthew (4[24] 17[15]) σεληνιάζεσθαι (literally *to be moonstruck*) is used to describe mental derangement, as in our 'lunacy,' 'lunatic,' from Lat. *luna*, 'the moon.' See above, pp. 91[b], 96[b].

The Passover always took place at full moon, for it was held on the 14th of the month Nisan, and it was the lunar month that was used, as it is still used by the Jews (Jos. *Ant.* III. x. 5 ; cf. Col 2[16]). Thus there was moonlight in Gethsemane when Christ went there with His disciples, and when He was betrayed. Also, the darkness which lasted for three hours during the crucifixion could not be due to an ordinary eclipse of the sun by the moon. See also art. TIME.

T. GREGORY.

MORALITY, MORAL LAW.—See ETHICS, and LAW.

MORNING.—Mt 16[3] 20[1] 27[1], Mk 11[20] 13[35] 16[2] ; cf. Mt 28[1], Lk 24[1], Jn 20[1]. There was no exact division of the day into parts among the Jews until after the Exile. The broad divisions current were 'evening,' 'morning,' and 'mid-day,' which followed this order usually, after the Jewish method of reckoning the day prevailed 'with the triumph of the Law.' The Roman division of the night into four 'watches,' extending from six o'clock to six o'clock, is brought into striking view in Mk 13[35], where ὀψέ (in the evening), μεσονύκτιον (at midnight), and ἀλεκτοροφωνίας (at cock-crowing), are given in connexion and contrast with πρωΐ (in the morning). The passages in the Gospels in which πρωΐ (morning) plays the most interesting and puzzling part are those connected with the visit of the women to the sepulchre after the resurrection of Jesus (Mt 28[1], Mk 16[2], Lk 24[1], and Jn 20[1]). Here Mt. has 'late on the sabbath' (RV), while Mk. says 'very early on the first day of the week,' and Jn. 'while it was yet dark.' No explanation will prove satisfactory to all. But Mt.'s 'late on the sabbath' may be taken as reckoning the following night as a part of the Sabbath—a departure from Jewish usage (Meyer). In short, we may suppose that the Babylonian method of adding diurnally the night to the day, rather than the day to the night (Israelitish), had come at this time, more or less, into common use among the Jews, so that there were two ways of reckoning complete astronomical days : namely, first, by 'night-days,' and, secondly, by 'day-nights.' Then we need only to suppose Mt. to be thinking of the 'day-night,' and the difficulty vanishes ; for 'late' in that 'day-night' would mean about the end of the night which followed the end of the Sabbath. This would accord perfectly with Mk.'s note of time, 'very early on the first day of the week.' Another solution of the difficulty is suggested by J. H. Moulton (*Prolegomena*, p. 72), that, according to the usage represented in the papyri, Mt.'s words rendered in RV 'late on the sabbath,' should be rendered 'late from the sabbath,' which is equivalent to saying 'after the sabbath.' This, too, would bring the words into harmony with those of Mark and John.   GEO. B. EAGER.

MOSES (Heb. מֹשֶׁה in accordance with the derivation from משה 'to draw,' given in Ex 2[10] ; LXX and NT usually Μωϋσῆς [Vulg. *Moyses*], following the derivation adopted by Philo and Josephus from the Coptic *mo* 'water' and *ushe* 'saved,' occasionally, however, Μωσῆς in conformity to the Hebrew. On its declension see Blass, *Grammar of NT*, § 10). —For an estimate of the position occupied by Moses in the Gospels, and his relation to the Person and work of Christ, a good starting-point is afforded by the words of He 3[2-6], which may be paraphrased thus : Moses was intrusted by God with an influence which was to affect and permeate not only his own generation but the whole of the Old Dispensation ; and he proved himself worthy of the trust. Christ was similarly faithful, but in two ways He far transcended Moses.—(*a*) Moses, for all the influence which he exercised, was yet a member, a portion, of the 'house' throughout which that influence extended ; but Christ is God, the Builder and Maker of the 'house.' (*b*) Moses had a delegated authority in the house ; he acted under orders as a trusted servant in the early stages of man's spiritual evolution ; but his authority vanished when the Son came into possession. Moses may thus be considered under two aspects, which, however, are not entirely distinct, but blend into one another. (1) He is not so much a person as an instrument. He represented the Old Dispensation because he was the instrument through which the Law was given. (2) He is an historical personality. But, because he represented the Old Dispensation, many of his acts, and of the events of his career, and of the characteristics of his person, prove to be types—inferior and prophetic counterparts — of various factors in the Kingdom and the Person of Christ.

1. (*a*) It was the opinion universally held among Jews and Christians in Apostolic times, that Moses was the *author* of the Pentateuch. (On our Lord's acceptance of this opinion, see below).

Mk 12[26]. The passage in Exodus relating God's appearance in the bush is said to occur 'in the book of Moses.' And in | Lk 20[37] Moses 'pointed out' (ἐμήνυσεν) the truth of a resurrection of the dead in the passage about the bush, 'when he calleth the Lord the God of Abraham . . .' It was God Himself who used these words (Ex 3[6]), but Moses is spoken of as the author of the passage.

Mk 12[19] || Lk 20[28]. The Sadducees, in referring to the Levirate law, claim that 'Moses wrote unto us.' On || Mt 22[24] see below.

Jn 1[45]. Philip speaks of 'him of whom Moses in the law, and the prophets, wrote.'

Lk 16[29. 31] 24[27]. Moses being the author of the Pentateuch, his name stands as synonymous with that which he wrote.

To these must be added the passages which speak of 'the law of Moses' : Lk 2[22] (the offering after childbirth), 24[44] ('the law of Moses, and the prophets, and the psalms'), Jn 7[23] (circumcision ; cf. Ac 15[1. 5]). See also Ac 13[39] 26[22] 28[23], Ro 5[14] 10[5], 1 Co 9[9], 2 Co 3[15], He 10[28].

(*b*) Besides this somewhat impersonal use of the name of Moses, there are passages which invest him with a more conscious responsibility and authority in connexion with the Law.

Mt 8[4] || Mk 1[44], Lk 5[14]. The healed leper is told to offer the gift which 'Moses enjoined.'

Mt 19[7] || Mk 10[3f.]. The Pharisees, 'tempting' Jesus, argue on the assumption that 'Moses commanded' a man to give his wife a writ of divorcement. And our Lord answers them— 'Moses allowed you to put away your wives (Mt.), he wrote you this commandment (Mk.), with a view to (πρός) your hardness of heart.' Moses is here conceived of as looking out with a prophetic eye over the ages, and seeing that all future generations of Israel would alike harden their hearts against God ; and that it would therefore be advisable to permit divorce as a necessary evil under certain circumstances, in order to limit and check man's sinful disposition. The words 'recognize the validity of the husband's act, but do not create the situation' (Swete). In Mk. our Lord anticipates the appeal to Moses by saying, 'What did Moses command you?' Mt. misses this, putting the τί ἐνετείλατο into the mouth of the Pharisees (see Swete on the whole passage, Mk 10[1-6]).

Mt 22[24]. In citing the Levirate law, the Sadducees claim that 'Moses said'—for which the other Synoptists have the less personal 'Moses wrote.'

Mk 7[10]. Our Lord quotes the Fifth Commandment of the Decalogue, together with Ex 21[17], with the words 'Moses said.' || Mt 15[4] has 'God said.'

Mt 23[2]. Moses, as the great teacher of the Law, used to sit (cf. Ex 18[1f.]), and deliver *ex cathedra* decisions. And the recognized teachers of the nation, the scribes and Pharisees, took up the same authoritative position (ἐπὶ τῆς M. καθέδρας ἐκάθισαν) when they became the exponents of the traditional rules by which the old Law was 'hedged.' Jesus does not find fault with the position ; He says, in effect, 'as interpreters of the Law of God, show them all due reverence ; as keepers of the Law of God, beware of following their example' (see Hastings' *DB* iii. 74[a]).

In the Fourth Gospel this view of Moses' authority appears no less prominently.—

Jn 1[17]. 'The Law was given through Moses.' But this very tact places him and it on a lower plane than Christ and the Gospel. Moses was merely a channel, through whom the Law —which was something separate from himself—was given ; whereas 'grace and truth came into being (ἐγένετο) through Jesus Christ,' because He Himself was, and is, grace and truth ; so that we received the fulness of grace and truth 'because we all received of his fulness' (see Hort, *The Way, the Truth, and the Life*, p. 43 f.).

Jn 5[45]. The national adherence to the Law is the resting of the national hopes upon Moses ('Moses on whom ye have placed your hope'). But (v.[46f.]) this adherence on your part ought to mean a loyal acceptance of his words, even though their true meaning is at variance with national expectations. Moses' words accuse you ; for belief in his writings really involves belief in My words. 'He wrote of me.'

There are two senses in which it may be said that Moses wrote of Christ. Christ said (Mt 22[36-40], cf. Dt 6[5], Lv 19[18]) that on the two commandments—love to God, and love to man—'all the Law is hung, and the prophets.' So that the true underlying meaning and motive of the whole Law was reflected in the spirit of Christ (see 'Christ the Interpreter of Prophecy,' by Kennett, *Interpreter*, Jan. 1906). But the Pentateuch contains more than the laws. A further sense in which Moses wrote of Christ is indicated in the whole of § **2** of the present article. Moses was quite unconscious that he wrote of Christ when he 'hung' the Law upon love ; and he was similarly unconscious of it when he related events which were afterwards to receive a spiritual fulfilment in the religion of Christ.

Jn 7[19. 22]. Our Lord shows the Jews that a strict observance of the letter of the whole Law is, in practice, impossible ; and that He is therefore, from their own standpoint, entitled to heal on the Sabbath. 'Did not Moses give you the law? and yet not one of you carries it out in actual practice (ποιεῖ τὸν νόμον).' For instance—Moses has given you circumcision ; but in keeping that ordinance, you do not hesitate to break the letter of another, for you circumcise on the Sabbath. There is irony in the ἵνα μὴ λυθῇ ('that the law of Moses be not broken') of v.[23]. But a further thought seems to be implied in the διὰ τοῦτο ('for this cause') with which v.[22] opens. Not only did Moses give you a law which it is impossible to keep with rigid exactness, but he gave it to you on this very account, *i.e.* that you might discover by experience its weakness and unprofitableness. A parenthesis, however, is thrown in to modify the δίδωκεν. Moses 'has given' you circumcision in the sense that he has authoritatively endorsed it as a binding ordinance; but it did not originate from him; it was handed down 'from the fathers,' *i.e.* from the days when Abraham circumcised himself and his sons. (Our Lord uses a similar argument with regard to the Sabbath in Mt 12[5]).

Jn 9[28f.]. The Pharisees taunted the man who had been healed of his blindness with being a disciple of Jesus, while they were 'Moses' disciples.' In their eyes Moses held a position analogous to that of Mohammed or Buddha, or any great founder of a religion. They were Moses' disciples because they revered his writings and obeyed his commands. But Christ's true followers, while they are His disciples, are at the same time far more, because they are partakers in His Divine life.

See also Ro 10[19] (the expression 'Moses saith' introducing the words of God, Dt 32[21]), He 7[14].

The thought of this section finds concrete illustration in the narrative of Mt 17[1-8] || Mk 9[2-8], Lk 9[28-36]. Moses and Elijah, the two grandest figures of the OT, who both fasted forty days and nights, who were both privileged to behold a theophany on Mt. Horeb, and who were both taken from the earth in a supernatural manner, represented 'the Law and the Prophets.' And they appeared to Him who was the fulfilment to which both pointed, and conversed with Him (Lk.) concerning His impending departure (ἔξοδος). Among other factors in the vision which taught a lesson to the watching disciples was the vanishing of Moses and Elijah when 'Jesus alone' remained. 'It helped them to see that the OT being fulfilled by Christ is done away in Christ' (Plummer in Hastings' *DB* iv. 808[a]).

In all the above passages, both in (*a*) and (*b*), Moses does not appear strictly as a personality. He is not a man, possessed of individual character—of moral or spiritual attainments. He is the instrument through whom the Law was given to Israel (Ac 7[38])—the hand which wrote and the voice which spoke. And Jesus, together with the Jews of His day, thought of him as such. This fact is held by some to cut away the ground from the critical arguments which go to prove that Moses was not the author of the Pentateuch as it stands, and, indeed, that the greater part of the Pentateuchal law is in its present form later than the age of Moses. The question has been very fully discussed by many writers, so that only a brief notice is needed here. If, as Hebrew scholars contend, the evidence is overwhelming that the Pentateuch and the Laws contained in it are the result of a long growth, which was not completed until a period after the return of the Jews from exile, it is impossible for us to shut our eyes to this evidence on the assumption (for it is only an assumption) that our Lord's use of the name of Moses precludes further argument. An explanation sometimes given is that Jesus must have known the exact truth about the authorship of the Pentateuch, but that He made a *concession* to the ignorance of the Jews of His day. But a growing body of students rejects this as untenable, because it detracts from the complete humanity of our Lord. If, as man, He had a full knowledge of the results which modern study has reached with regard to the literary problems of the OT, He must also, as man, have known all future results which will be reached by the study of generations to come. In other words, as man He was omniscient. But this conflicts alike with our conception of complete manhood and with the explicit declaration that He 'advanced in wisdom' (Lk 2[52]). We know that He could feel hungry and thirsty and weary, that He could be overcome with sleep, that He could manifest surprise; and on one occasion at least He spoke of something which 'no

one knoweth, not the angels of heaven, *nor the Son*, but the Father only' (Mt 24[36], Mk 13[32]). He was subject, therefore, to the ordinary limitations of manhood, and, as man, He acquired His knowledge by the methods which other men follow. The problem is a part of a larger one—the problem of determining to what extent, or in what sense, His Divine powers and prerogatives were in abeyance during His earthly life. Although fully and completely man, He did not cease to be God, and He did not cease to be conscious of His Divinity. 'It is this continuous self-consciousness of the Son of God that gives the true measure of His transcendent humility' (Gifford, *The Incarnation*, p. 90). We can venture the statement with respect to His knowledge, that though, as God, He never ceased to be omniscient, yet *He refused to know*, as man, anything which could not be learnt by human means. But when we have said that, we have only enunciated and not solved the problem. This is not the place to enter into it further. But there can be no doubt that it is along this line of thought that we must move, to justify modern criticism in denying to Moses the authorship of the Pentateuch which our Lord and His Apostles ascribed to him. See also artt. HUMANITY OF CHRIST and KENOSIS.

2. But because Moses was the representative of the Old Dispensation, Jesus and the NT writers thought of him as something more. He was an historical personage of such unique prominence in Israel's history, that his whole career affords parallels to spiritual factors in the New Covenant. The history of the old Israel repeats itself in that of the new. To say this is not to affirm that the OT writers had the slightest idea that the events which they described were one day to receive a spiritual fulfilment. The mind of God alone knew it, when He guided the events and inspired the writings.

The series of Mosaic events which NT writers cite as affording points of comparison with things spiritual, form an extremely interesting study, since they cover so many of the distinctive features of the New Dispensation, and illustrate in a striking manner the essential unity of the 'Divine Library.'

(*a*) 2 Co 3[7-18]. The centre of Christianity is the Incarnation—the dwelling of God's glory among men in the Person of Jesus Christ (Jn 1[14]). And St. Paul argues that the 'glory' upon Moses' face,[*] which accompanied his reception of the Law, was so great that the Israelites could not bear to gaze upon it, although that law was merely a ministration of death, and of condemnation: much more will the ministration of the spirit, and of righteousness, be of surpassing glory. Again, Moses realized that the 'glory' on his face was transitory, and so he could not boldly leave his face uncovered. And the veil which he wore still lies, spiritually speaking, on the hearts of the Jewish nation, and will not be removed till they 'turn to the Lord,' as Moses used to remove it when he returned to the Divine presence. But we Christians can speak boldly, and with unveiled face gaze at the glory of the Lord. If we are told that our gospel is obscure and hidden by a veil, it is only so in the case of those who are spiritually perishing. It is they who have been blinded by the 'god of this age,' to prevent the 'glory of God,' which is, in fact, the Incarnate Christ, from dawning upon them.

(*b*) Jn 3[14]. The Incarnation had its issue in the Passion. The connexion of this verse with v.[13] by the opening 'and,' and the repetition of the title 'Son of Man,' express this thought (see Westcott, *in loc.*). The difficulties in arriving at the ideas attached to the brazen serpent in the original story (Nu 21[7-9]), and of our Lord's application of it, are great. Patristic writers deal with it in a variety of ways—some of them deeply suggestive (see Westcott, p. 63 ff.). Two points stand out clearly—the lifting up of the Son of Man upon the Cross, and the spiritual healing of those who look up with faith to Him. But two others suggest themselves, though we cannot estimate the exact part which they played in our Lord's thought. (1) The serpent on the pole symbolized the evil from which the people had suffered; and Christ identified Himself with sinful humanity so completely, that when He was crucified He took sin 'out of the way, nailing it to his cross' (Col 2[14], cf. Gal 3[13], 1 P 2[24], with RVm). (2) The word 'be lifted up' (ὑψωθῆναι,

---

[*] His use of the narrative is rendered easier by the LXX, which renders קרן ('shone') by δεδόξασται and δεδοξασμένη (Ex 34[29f.]).

exaltari) is applied elsewhere, not only to the Passion (Jn 8[28] 12[32-34]), but also to the Ascension (Ac 2[33] 5[31], cf. Ph 2[9] ὑπερύψωσεν). Christ 'reigned from the Tree' in the supreme moment of victory, but that was only the first stage in a triumphal progress upwards.

(c) Jn 19[36]. Christ's death and the shedding of His blood procured atonement. This, in the minds of all Christians, has its counterpart in the Passover (He 11[28]). St. John traces a fulfilment of a particular detail in the fact that no bone of our Lord's body was broken. And see 1 Co 5[7f.].

(d) Christ's sacrifice is more clearly connected with the covenant sacrifice at Horeb (Ex 24[4-8]). Our Lord explicitly refers to it in the words of the institution of the Eucharist (Mt 26[28], Mk 14[24], Lk 22[20], 1 Co 11[25]; see also He 9[18-20], 1 P 1[2], with Hort's note).

(e) He 12[18-24]. Though pleading in heaven, Christ is still present among men ; He is still incarnate ; hence the existence of the Church which is His Body. In these verses the position and condition of the Church under the New Covenant is contrasted with that of the Israelites at Sinai, the characteristics of the two covenants being summed up in the words 'terror' and 'grace' (cf. Keble's *Christian Year*, ' Whitsunday ').

(f) 1 Co 10[2]. Sacramental incorporation into Christ's Divine life had its counterpart in the old Jewish Church ; all the Israelites were ' baptized into Moses in the cloud and in the sea.' Jn 6[30-35 41-58]. By the other great sacrament, the Divine life is fed and nourished in the members of the Church. Our Lord teaches that ' it was not Moses, but God revealing Himself through Moses, who gave the manna ; and again the manna—the perishable bread—was not in the highest sense " bread from heaven," but rather the symbol of spiritual food.' [It is not here asserted that our Lord's discourse had reference exclusively to the Sacrament of the Holy Communion, which He was afterwards to institute. But it must have been impossible for St. John—and it is impossible for us—having heard the words spoken at the Last Supper, not to see in the present passage their fullest and deepest application].

1 Co 10[3. 4]. As Christ is the Bread of Life, so He is the Water of Life. The Israelites, in the mind of St. Paul, did not eat and drink mere physical food and water, but spiritual. The two accounts of the striking of the rock by Moses for the production of water (Ex 17[6], Nu 20[11]) gave rise to the Rabbinic explanation that the rock which was struck followed them through the desert, affording a continual supply. That rock, says St. Paul, is typical of Christ.

(g) Ac 3[22] 7[37]. Besides the spiritual nourishment, which fosters the Divine life in the soul, Christians need a Teacher, who will at all times reveal the will of God. Both St. Peter and St. Stephen see in Christ the fulfilment of the declaration in Dt 18[15-18] that God would raise up a prophet like unto Moses. And John the Baptist, in his truthfulness and self-effacement, declares that he himself is not ' the Prophet,' but only a voice heralding His coming (Jn 1[21ff.]). And see Jn 6[14] 7[40] [Lk 7[39]].

(h) While the Israelites are the counterpart of the Christian Church, their enemies who opposed Moses (cf. 2 Ti 3[8]) afford a parallel to those who obey not the gospel. In Rev 8[5. 7. 8] 9[2-4] 15[6ff.] 16[2-4. 10. 13. 18. 21] the symbolism of punishment is clearly based on the plagues of Egypt. On the other hand, those who have been redeemed from the slavery of sin can, like the Israelites rescued from Egypt, ' sing the song of Moses the servant of God ' (Rev 15[3]).

LITERATURE.—Besides the works mentioned in the article, reference should be made throughout to the principal commentaries on the NT. See also, for our Lord's relation to the Law, artt. ACCOMMODATION, AUTHORITY OF CHRIST, LAW, LAW OF GOD.

A. H. M'NEILE.

MOTE.—See BEAM AND MOTE.

MOTH (σής).—The Bible frequently makes reference to the destructive action of the moth as a fit symbol of the perishableness of man and his earthly possessions. In Oriental countries, where so large a part of ' treasure ' consisted of costly silken and woollen fabrics, the figure was peculiarly appropriate and impressive. Specially referred to is the ' clothes ' moth,' one or more (not readily identified as to its particular member of the family) of the genus *Tinea*, which may be said to have an almost cosmopolitan distribution. The larva of this moth feeds on wool, silk, hair, fur, feathers, etc. Out of the material on which it feeds it forms a portable case or house, supposed to be alluded to as an image of instability (though Cheyne [*EBi*, ' Moth '] denies this) in Job 27[18a]. The moth first finishes its case, which is often motley-coloured on account of the variety of material from which it draws supplies, and afterwards feeds voraciously on the substance from which the tent or house has been produced. For building purposes it selects the long straight fibres, but for food the shortest and thickest, and in order to get the latter it eats down below the surface pile to the fabric itself. The feeding pro-

cess is therefore the most destructive to the fabric. The yellowish-brown pupa is either formed in this structure which the larva constructs, or in a slight cocoon. Before the perfect insect appears the mischief is accomplished, for large patches are eaten in the clothes, carpets, or tapestry where the parent moth has laid its eggs. If the action of the insect is undiscovered, or by carelessness allowed to be completed, it makes the fabric into a mere flimsy shell which falls into nothingness on the least touch or breath. 'Crushed before the moth' (Job 4[19]) is a faithful description of this most effective destruction—an apt figure of the insidious, deadly work of evil in the human character.

Our Lord refers to this well-known phenomenon in the Sermon on the Mount (Mt 6[19-20], Lk 12[33]). Along with the corroding work of the rust—due to chemical action on metals left unused and exposed—He classes the ravages of the moth, as illustrations of the inevitable corruption and decay which overtake all earthly things apart from the heavenly and Divine. Men are not to set their affections on things that belong to the earth (things which contain no higher and heavenly element), are not to make these their treasures, for in that case their heart, the centre of their life, set upon these decaying, perishing things, is itself subject to similar destructive forces—'Where your treasure is, there will your heart be also.' All earthly things are to be valued, not in themselves as ends, but as means to the higher spiritual life. The affection is to be positively fixed on the enduring things of human virtue, knowledge, and character, formed and obtained by fellowship with the Divine—elements which all lower things are adapted to subserve, and which themselves 'neither moth nor rust can corrupt.'   T. H. WRIGHT.

MOTHER.—Concerning the relations of Jesus with His mother, and her influence upon His training, we can but infer that the mother of such a son must herself have been an exceptional personality. See art. MARY (VIRGIN). Professor W. M. Ramsay, in his *Education of Christ*, shows how thorough was the instruction given to the Jewish youth. With this the mother had much to do. Granted that religious genius is not to be accounted for by environment, there still remains the overwhelming probability that the feminine qualities in the character of Jesus—His graciousness, gentleness, and sympathy—found a congenial setting in the home at Nazareth. Had it been otherwise, some hint of the fact must have been given in the records of His public ministry. It has been contended that such a hint is given in Mk 3[31ff.], an incident which also finds a place in the other Evangelists. Another is Mt 10[35-37] ‖ Mk 10[29], Lk 12[53] 14[26]. But it should not be overlooked that these hyperbolical expressions by no means involve the repudiation of the filial tie. They are rather designed to mark the thoroughness with which the religious life should be embraced, the higher love absorbing and transforming the lower. The emphasis with which, in other connexions, Jesus denounces contemporary sins against the filial relationship is a proof that with Him the ideal life did not consist with holding it in contempt (Mk 7[10-13], Mt 15[4-9]). The filial relationship is to be superseded only by the greater sacredness of the conjugal (Mt 19[5], Mk 10[7]). In His response to the question of the rich young ruler Jesus emphasizes the command to honour father and mother (Mt 19[19] etc.), but (Mt 19[29] etc.) loyalty to the truth as expressed in Himself is made to take precedence of all other ties. The reason for this insistence is obvious, and has been abundantly illustrated in the history of the world's benefactors.

Concerning our Lord's dealings with other mothers than His own, few details are given in the Gospels. It is noteworthy that the mother of Zebedee's children (Mt 20[20]) goes unrebuked, as does the action of the mothers who brought their children to Him (Mk 10[13]). His sympathy with motherhood may be inferred from these incidents, as also from the healing of the daughter of the Canaanitish woman (Mt 15[22], Mk 7[26]). The same is implied in the pathetic phrase (Lk 23[28]) uttered on the way to Calvary. In nothing is the uniqueness of Jesus more clearly seen than in this kind of reverence for womanhood, so unexpected in a religious teacher of His time (Jn 4[27]). See WOMAN.

LITERATURE.—F. W. Robertson, *Serm.* 2nd ser. xviii. xix.; Rendel Harris, *Union with God*, ch. iv.; Stalker, *Imago Christi*, ch. ii.; A. Morris Stewart, *Infancy and Youth of Jesus*, p. 105.

R. J. CAMPBELL.

MOUNT, MOUNTAIN (ὄρος).—Mountains figure often in the narratives of Christ's life. This is natural, considering the highly mountainous character of the country in which He lived. At no point in His journeyings were the mountains out of sight; and if He was not actually on or among them, they were never a great way off.

The Mount of Olives (wh. see) alone is named in the Gospels—the mountain that rises beyond the Ḳidron Valley, east of Jerusalem, from the S.E. slope of which Bethany looks out over the wilderness. In two passages we see from the context which mountains are referred to. In Mt 21[21] 'to this mountain' points clearly to Olivet, on which Jesus and His disciples stood, viewing the cursed and withered fig-tree. In Jn 4[20] 'this mountain' can be no other than Gerizim, on whose rocky summit, amid the ruins of ancient splendour, the remnant of Samaritans still annually chant their weird service at the feast of the Passover. In other places, such as Mt 24[16], 'mountain' must be taken generally as meaning the wilder and more inaccessible parts, forming natural places of refuge, Judæa itself being almost entirely mountainous (cf. Rev 6[15]). So also with the haunts of the demoniac (Mk 5[5]). The 'mountain' on (Lk 8[32]) or near (Mk 5[11]) which the swine were feeding must have been the western edge of the great plateau which stretches from the desert to the lip of the *Ghôr*, and drops a distance of some 2000 feet to the eastern shore of the Sea of Galilee. The place intended is probably a little north of the old fortress of Gamala, where the foot of the swift slope runs almost to the water.

Perhaps only men familiar with the steep cliffs and beetling crags of Palestinian mountains would think of calling in their terror upon the mountains to fall and cover them (Lk 23[30]).

Regarding the position of three mountains there has been much discussion—the mountain of the Temptation (Mt 4[8], Lk 4[5]), the Mount of Beatitudes (Mt 5[1]), and the Mount of Transfiguration (Mt 17[1] etc.).

The evidence we possess is mainly negative, tending to show that traditional identifications are impossible. As to the first, if any actual height is intended, *Jebel Ḳuruntul*, with its cave-fretted brows frowning over Jericho, and the district to the south, are bleak and inhospitable enough, and there certainly the sojourner by night would be 'with the wild beasts' (Mk 1[13]). But there is no height at all suggesting the description 'an exceeding high mountain.'

The tradition identifying *Ḳarn Ḥaṭṭin* with the scene of the Sermon on the Mount dates only from Crusading times. To the traveller journeying towards Tiberias from Nazareth or Tabor, the double-peaked hill seems easy of approach. But from any part of the seashore the ascent is steep, and from Gennesaret, where our Lord was at work, the way, as the present writer knows from much experience, is both long and toilsome. With so many heights near the plain, quite suitable for the Master's purpose, the necessity for this difficult journey is not apparent. Further, certain traces of ancient buildings lend colour to the idea that, in our Lord's time, the hill may have been occupied.

The Roman and Greek Churches still maintain the traditional identification of Mount Tabor with the scene of the Transfiguration, and, in accordance with their separate calendars, that august event is annually commemorated there. It must be remembered, however, that they have much valuable property on the mountain—the great monasteries—which an admission of error would render worthless, while the contributions received from streams of pilgrims would be diverted. Most modern students of the question locate the Transfiguration on Mount Hermon; if not on the summit itself, on one of the lower spurs. This would satisfy the requirements of the narrative; whereas the journey south to Tabor, through Galilee, and back again to Capernaum, within the time specified, while possible, is highly improbable. The present writer spent some weeks in the summer of 1891 on the top of Tabor, and was led to emphatic agreement with the opinion that the presence of a town or fortress on the mountain in the days of Christ makes the traditional identification utterly impossible. See art. TRANSFIGURATION.

On a mountain in Galilee the risen Jesus gave His disciples their great commission (Mt 28[16]). The circumstances suggest some height familiar to all, not far from the scenes of the Galilæan ministry, commanding a wide prospect. Certain identification is, of course, impossible; but these conditions are well fulfilled by *Jebel Kan'ān*, a bold headland projecting southward from the great bulk of Naphtali. The spacious view ranges from Carmel and the Mediterranean to the eastern ridges of Bashan, and from snowy Hermon to the dim mountains guarding the Dead Sea. In the great hollow below sleep the blue waters of Galilee, the white-sailed fishing boats recalling imperishable memories.

In hours of devotion Jesus seemed to long for the solitude and stillness to be found only on lonely heights by night (Mt 14[23], Mk 6[46], Lk 6[12] 9[28], Jn 6[15]). From a mountain at last He passed into the invisible (Lk 24[50], Ac 1[9. 12]). See also art. HILL.

LITERATURE.—G. A. Smith, *HGHL*, p. 47 ff.; W. M. Ramsay, *Education of Christ*, cf. *ExpT* xiv. [1903] p. 194.

W. EWING.

MOUNT OF OLIVES (τὸ ὄρος τῶν ἐλαιῶν, Mt 21[1] 24[3] 26[30], Mk 13[3] 14[26], Lk 19[37] 22[39], Jn 8[1]; and τὸ ὄρος τὸ καλούμενον ἐλαιῶν, Lk 19[29] 21[37]).—One of the universally accepted holy sites around Jerusalem. It is to-day known as *Jebel eṭ-Ṭûr* (the mountain of the elevation or tower) by the Moslems, and as *Jebel ez-Zeitûn* (the mount of olives) by native Christians and, indeed, also by Moslems. By the Jews, besides the above mentioned, the name 'mountain of light' has also been given, from the fact that here used to be kindled the first beacon-fire to signalize through the land the appearance of each new moon.

The mount due east of Jerusalem forms the culminating height of a range which, separating itself from the central plateau near the village of *Sha'phat*, runs for two miles, first S. and then S.W., and terminates beyond the village of *Silwân* at the *Wady en-Nâr*. The beginning of the range has very generally been accepted as the Scopus (prospect) of Josephus, and the part running S.W. —*Batn el-Hawa*—considerably lower than the part east of the city and not higher than the Temple area itself, has by many been identified as the Mount of Offence. Although these have been described by some authorities as parts of the Mount of Olives, there seems no real reason for including them in the description, and to do so is confusing.

The natural boundaries of Olivet are to-day well defined by two ancient roads. To the N. a very ancient highway to Jericho, after traversing a deep bay * in the range, which from the city side seems to separate the range into two, crosses a low neck cutting off the northern part, now crowned by the house of Sir John Grey Hill, from the

* This open valley, in which to-day are many olives and also at least one ancient olive press, is an attractive site for Gethsemane (which see), though it must be admitted that tradition is all against it.

southern loftier mass—the true Mount of Olives. To the S. the road which runs to Bethany forms a convenient if somewhat arbitrary division, cutting off Olivet from the so-called 'Mount of Offence' and from other spurs to the south. To the W. the boundary is sufficiently plainly marked off by the deep valley of the Kidron, while to the E. there are indications (see Lk 19^{29} 24^{50}; cf. Ac 1^{12}) for including within the limits the projecting spur on which Bethany stands. Probably the limits were never defined geographically, but the whole area was distinguished, as it is to some extent to-day, by its thick plantations of olives, figs, and palms,—hence the names Bethphage (house of figs) and Bethany (house of dates). This fertility, though no doubt most constantly observed by the city dwellers, to whom the beautiful slopes, then as they do to-day, would appeal most refreshingly as viewed from the dirty, squalid streets, must also have held out to the tired and thirsty travellers, ascending the dry and dusty wilderness from the Jordan to the city, an enchanting prospect of coolness and refreshment. For this alone it would appear only reasonable to include the sites of the villages on the eastern side, with their abundant gardens, as an essential part of the Mount. There can be little doubt that in the days of Christ the hill was thickly spread with verdure over parts which to-day are given up to churches, hovels, and extensive cemeteries.

Viewing the mountain thus, two principal summits and two subsidiary spurs may be described. The N. summit is that known as *Karem es-Sayyâd* (the vineyard of the hunter), and also as the *Viri Galilæi*; it reaches a height of 2723 feet above the Mediterranean, and is separated from the S. mass by a narrow neck of land traversed to-day by the new carriage road. As far back as 530 this hill is spoken of as Galilee, and in the *Acts of Pilate* (about 350) a mountain near Jerusalem called 'Galilee' is mentioned. It is said to have first received its name Γαλιλαία because the Galilæans attending the feasts used to encamp there, or as Sæwulf (1102) says, it 'was called Galilee because the Apostles, who were called Galilæans, frequently visited there.'* The S. summit, of practically equal height, is the traditional Mount of the Ascension, and has for some years been distinguished by a lofty tower erected by the Russians. Here, too, Constantine erected his Church of the Ascension in 316 on the site where now stands its successor (erected 1834–5) of the same name. Here also is the Church of the Creed and the Paternoster Church, the latter a modern building on the site of one of that name destroyed long ago. Scattered over the summit is a modern Moslem village—*Kefr et-Tûr*—which combines with the noisy conduct of its rapacious inhabitants in spoiling the quiet beauty and holy associations of this sacred spot.

A small spur running S. is sometimes known as the Hill of the Prophets, on account of the interesting old 'Tomb of the Prophets'—a sepulchre generally believed, until recently,† to have been originally Jewish—which is situated there; and the other somewhat isolated spur to the S.E., on which stands the wretched, half-ruined village of *el-'Azarîyeh*, on the site of Bethany, should, for reasons given, be included in the Mount.

Along the W. slopes facing the city lies the reputed Garden of Gethsemane (part, too, of the

* Attempts have been made to harmonize the accounts of the appearances of Jesus after His resurrection by supposing that this was the place where He appointed His disciples to meet Him. A recent discussion of the subject by Lepsius will be found in *Das Reich Christi*, Nos. 7 and 8 (1902).

† According to Father Vincent and M. Clermont-Ganneau, it is not Jewish, but belongs to the 4th or 5th cent. A.D. (see *PEFSt*, 1901, pp. 309–317).

Mount, cf. Lk 22^{39}; see GETHSEMANE) of the Latins and its Greek rival; and a little higher up the hill to the S. the great Russian Church of St. Magdalene. The greater part of the slopes of the S.W. part of the hill is filled with a vast number of graves, those from the valley bottom till a little above the Bethany road being Jewish, while higher up are some Christian cemeteries. The Jews have a strong sentiment about being buried on this spot, the slopes of the 'Valley of Jehoshaphat' being traditionally, with them and with the Moslems, the scene of the resurrection and final judgment.

Traversing this side of the Mount are three steep paths, all probably ancient. The most evident and important is the N. one, which continues the line of the path from the St. Stephen's Gate and the Tomb of the Virgin. It runs along the depression between the two summits, and is the direct route for travellers crossing the Mount from or to Bethany. Too steep for riding, it is essentially the short cut for the pedestrian. The second path, still steeper, branches off from this just above the Garden of Gethsemane, and after passing the traditional scene of the lamentation of Jesus over the city, leads to-day to the Russian tower and buildings. It is the path of the modern pilgrim. The third, more gradual in ascent, starts from the Garden of Gethsemane and ascends the hill through Russian property in a S. direction, passing near the 'Tomb of the Prophets.' Whether the first or second of these lies most in the direction of our Lord's frequent passages from the city to the Mount of Olives and to Bethany, it is difficult to say, but it can hardly be supposed that He came by such a path on the morning of His triumphal entry into the city. The only likely course for the highroad of Roman times must have been in the general direction of the present Bethany and Jericho road; and, as Dean Stanley has suggested, the most natural site for the scene of the lamentation over the city is the point where this highroad crosses the S.W. shoulder of the Mount and the first full view of the city is obtained. A viaduct appears to have connected the Mount with the Temple hill, probably on the site of one of the two bridges which to-day span the dry torrent bed of the Kidron.

The Mount of Olives in the days of Christ must have presented rural fertility, verdure, and quiet very grateful to country visitors to the great metropolis; fresh mountain breeziness in contrast to the closeness and foulness of the city atmosphere, and a view of the beloved and sacred city in which all that was sordid was lost, and only the beauty and grandeur remained. This view is, when the historical associations are taken into consideration, probably the most fascinating in the Holy Land. It is seen at its best about the hour of sunset. In its essential details it is one on which the eyes of Christ must frequently have rested.

To the immediate W. is the Holy City, separated from the onlooker by the deep Valley of Jehoshaphat; just within the wall lies the 'Dome of the Rock' and the *al-Aksa* mosque, and in the open space of the great Temple area figures of people may be discerned moving about. Beyond this enclosure lie, pile above pile, the domed houses of the modern city, interspersed with the minarets, the synagogue domes, and the church towers of the followers of the three great Semitic religions: most prominent of all are the two domes and the massive tower which go to make up the Church of the Holy Sepulchre. Far to the W. lie the battlements of the so-called Tower of David, and behind that, on the horizon, the W. mountains of Judæa shut off the distant sea. The roar of the city is deadened, but the fresh breeze carries the chiming of many bells, the blast of a military bugle or the roar of a salute from the barracks, reminding the onlooker that it is no dead city of the far past he is looking at. Somewhat to the N. the eye passes from the close-packed streets of the Moslem and Christian quarters, past the long line of the N. wall, to the many buildings of the newer Jerusalem, chiefly mean Jewish houses, but among them many handsome buildings like the great French Hospice, the Russian Cathedral, or the Abyssinian Church. Here lies all that is progressive and of promise for the days to be. Beyond again, against the sky line to the N., rises the outline of *Nebi Samwîl* crowning the height of Mizpeh.

Turning S. the spectator sees the bare slopes south of the city walls, once thickly covered with the houses of the poor, terminating in the two deep valleys of Ḳidron and Hinnom, while on the opposite slope some of the houses of *Silwân* may be distinguished. Far to the S. in a gap in the hills lies the convent of *Mar Elias* on the road to Bethlehem; and to its left a crater-shaped hill —the Herodium—the burial-place of Herod the Great.

As the eye passes gradually E. over the wilderness of Judæa, it is caught by the still beauty of the Dead Sea lying nearly 4000 feet below, but in the clear atmosphere looking very near, while behind lies the long level line of the beautiful hills of Moab. More in the foreground a few houses of Bethany appear, and behind them the village of *Abu Dis*—inhabited by the hereditary robbers of the Jericho road. Northward of the great lake, beyond a vista of tumbled hills and parched valleys, lies the Jordan Valley, through the centre of which may be traced, by a serpentine line of green, the course of the famous river itself. Eastward of this the line of Moab is continued N. as the mountains of Gilead, with their one distinct summit—*Jebel Ôsha*—almost directly E. of the onlooker.

Gospel incidents connected with the Mount of Olives.—Although, with the single exception of Jn 8[1], all the incidents expressly connected with the Mount of Olives belong to the Passion week, there can be no doubt (Lk 21[37]) that this quiet spot was one beloved and frequented by the Master. Here He withdrew from the city for rest and meditation (Jn 8[1]) and for prayer (Mt 26[30] etc.). Once we read of His approach to the Mount from the Eastern side 'unto Bethphage and Bethany, at the Mount of Olives' (Mk 11[1] ‖ Mt 21[1] ‖ Lk 19[29]). Over a part of the Mount He must have made His triumphal progress to the city (Mt 21, Mk 11, Lk 19), and on this road He wept over Jerusalem (Lk 19[40-44]). During the whole of that week 'in the daytime he was teaching in the temple; and at night he went out and abode in the Mount that is called of Olives' (Lk 21[37])—the special locality on the Mount being Bethany (Mt 21[17], Mk 11[11]). Crossing over from Bethany, Jesus illustrated His teaching by the sign of the withering of the barren fig-tree (Mt 21[18. 19] ‖ Mk 11[12-14. 20-22]), and ·on the slopes of this hill, with the doomed city spread out before them, Christ delivered to His disciples His wonderful eschatological discourse (Mt 24[3f.] ‖ Mk 13[3f.]). Then here, in the Garden of Gethsemane, occurred the Agony, the Betrayal, and the Arrest (Mt 26[36-56], Mk 14[26-52], Lk 22[39-53], Jn 18[1-12]). Lastly, on the Mount, not on the summit where tradition places it, but near Bethany, occurred the Ascension (Lk 24[50-52], Ac 1[12]).

To these incidents where the Mount of Olives is expressly mentioned may be added the scene in the house of Martha and Mary (Lk 10[38-42]), the raising of Lazarus (Jn 11), and the feast at the house of Simon (Mt 26[6-13], Mk 14[3-9], Jn 12[1-19]); for, as has been shown, Bethany was certainly a part.of the Mount of Olives.

‒ LITERATURE.—*PEF* Mem., 'Jerusalem' volume; papers by Schick and others in the Quarterly Statements (*PEFSt*); Groves, art. 'Mount of Olives' in Smith's *DB*; R. Hofman, *Galilæa auf dem Oelberg*, Leipzig, 1896; Porter in Murray's *Handbook to Palestine*; Robinson, *BRP* vol. i. (1838); Stanley, *SP*; Socin and Benzinger in Baedeker's *Palestine and Syria*; J. Tobler, *Siloahquelle und Oelberg*, 1852; Vincent (Père), 'The Tombs of the Prophets' in *Revue Biblique*, 1901; C. Warren, art. 'Mount of Olives' in Hastings' *DB*.

E. W. G. MASTERMAN.

MOURNING.—An expression of grief for death or disaster. See also artt. LAMENTATION and RENDING OF GARMENTS. Mourning is associated in the Gospels (1) with 'the appearance of the sign of the Son of Man,' Mt 24[30]; (2) with the removal of the visible presence of the Saviour, Mt 9[15]; (3) with the death of friends. It is also one of the conditions mentioned in the Beatitudes as bearing a special blessing (Mt 5[4], but cf. Lk 6[21]). The laws of mourning were very minute. The general time of mourning was seven days, during which the mourner was forbidden to work, wash, anoint himself, or wear his shoes. This last provision might, however, be evaded by putting earth or ashes into his boots. For seven days the mourner might not read in the Law, the Prophets, or the Talmud, because it was a 'joy' to do so; but a teacher could teach others through an interpreter. The mourner was allowed during this period to read only the books of Job, Jeremiah, Lamentations, and the הלכות אבילות (Laws of Mourning). He had to sit away from his dead, with his head tied up, and on the first day he might not wear his phylacteries. He was forbidden to shave his head or his neck, or do anything which might be considered to be for his comfort. He could take no part in rejoicings, and the rent in his garments was to be seen for thirty days. Even a poor man, or one who lived on charity, was forbidden to work for three days; but after that time he might do work secretly, for his maintenance, or his wife might spin in his house. Travelling with goods was forbidden, and no business even at the risk of loss could be transacted by himself or his family or his servants. It was allowable, however, to have a business carried on, if he assigned it to another before the departure of the soul. The mourner was allowed to eat only in his own house; he might eat no flesh and drink no wine; nor could he ask blessing before or after food. Extra-Talmudical regulations enjoined that the mourner should sit on the floor and take his food from a chair instead of a table, and, as is still the custom, that he should eat eggs dipped in ashes with salt. He might not leave town for thirty days; and in the case of mourning for a parent he might not go out of town for the first year, till his friends told him to do so. After the death of a wife, a widower might not marry for a year (*i.e.* till after three feasts had passed); but if his wife had died childless, or if she had left young children, he might marry after seven days. A mourner being 'free' must attend the synagogue; when he appeared, the congregation faced him as he entered, and said: ברוך מנחם אבל 'Blessed is He that comforteth the mourner.' Immediately on a death, all water in the house and in three houses on either side was emptied out, because of the belief that the Angel of Death procured death by means of a knife which he washed in water close at hand. Between death and burial the mourner was free from all the Law, because he was supposed to be beside himself with grief. The following is the prescribed prayer before meat to be used in the house of the mourner after burial :—

'Blessed art thou, O God our Lord, King of the universe, God of our Fathers, our Creator, our Redeemer, our Sanctifier, the

Holy One of Jacob, the King of Life, who art good and doest good ; the God of truth, the righteous Judge who judgest in righteousness, who takest the soul in judgment, and rulest alone in the universe, who doest in it according to His will, and all His ways are in Judgment, and we are His people and His servants, and in everything we are bound to praise Him and to bless Him, who shields all the calamities of Israel and will shield us in this calamity, and from this mourning will bring us to life and peace. Comfort, O God our Lord, all the mourners of Jerusalem, and all the mourners that mourn in our sorrow. Comfort them in their mourning, and make them rejoice in their agony as a man is comforted by his mother. Blessed art Thou, O God, the Comforter of Zion, and that buildest again Jerusalem' (Jewish prayer-books from יורה רעה).

The practice of hiring mourners was common with such as could afford it, and, as in the story of Jairus' daughter, these hired mourners used flutes to increase the sounds of woe. The apostasy of a member of the family was the occasion of mourning as for the dead, and a blasphemy spoken in the presence of the high priest was also a reason for a demonstration of mourning. See also FLUTE-PLAYERS, RENDING OF GARMENTS.

LITERATURE.—See under RENDING OF GARMENTS.

W. H. RANKINE.

MOUTH (Mt 4⁴ 12³⁴ 15¹¹ 18¹⁶ 21¹⁶, and Lk 1⁷⁰).— In conformity with Oriental usage, 'mouth,' considered as the organ of speech, is used in the NT, as in the OT, in the sense of 'language,' 'utterance,' etc.—a notable instance of the primitive employment of the concrete for the abstract. Indeed, among the ancient Hebrews 'mouth' was even personified, e.g. in such expressions as 'The mouth of the Lord has spoken it,' etc.—a usage that helped not a little to prepare the Jewish mind at last to apprehend the meaning of *the Word made flesh*. Most passages of the Gospels where 'mouth' is found are quotations from the OT (LXX), e.g. 'Every word that proceedeth out of the mouth of God' (διὰ στόματος θεοῦ, Dt 8³) ; 'in the mouth of two or three witnesses' (ἐπὶ στόματος, Dt 17⁶ 19¹⁵) ; 'out of the mouth of babes and sucklings' (ἐκ στόμ., Ps 8² etc.) ; cf. Zacharias' words, Lk 1⁷⁰ 'as he spake by the mouth of his holy prophets' (διὰ στόματος) ; and Jesus' words to His disciples, 'I will give you a mouth (στόμα) and wisdom' (21¹⁵).

GEO. B. EAGER.

MULTITUDE.— This word is used in EV to translate ὄχλος and πλῆθος.

(1) ὄχλος is defined by Grimm-Thayer as 'a casual collection of people, a multitude of men who have flocked together in some place, a throng.' The plural οἱ ὄχλοι, which often occurs in Mt. and Lk., is found twice in Mk., viz. 6³³ [TR ; all the best MSS omit] and 10¹ without the article ; once only in Jn. (7¹² where אD Vulg. give sing.), meaning probably the various groups or companies (cf. Lk 2⁴⁴) which had come up to the feast. In AV it is rendered 'multitude' and frequently 'people,' also 'press' (Mk 2⁴ 5²⁷·³⁰, Lk 8¹⁹ 19³) and 'company' (Lk 5²⁹ 6¹⁷ 9³⁸ [but 'people' in v.37]12¹³, Jn 6⁵). RV usually gives 'multitude,' but in some passages prefers 'crowd,' from A.S. *crúdan*, 'to push,' 'throng,' apparently in cases where the ὄχλος would cause inconvenient pressure, cf. Mk 3⁹ (διὰ τὸν ὄχλον ἵνα μὴ θλίβωσιν αὐτόν), also Mt 9²³, Mk 2⁴ 5²⁷·³⁰, Lk 8¹⁹ 19³ ; yet in Mk 5³¹ where συνθλίβοντα is used of ὄχλον (tr. 'crowd' in the previous verse), and in Lk 5¹ where the ὄχλος is described as pressing upon Him (ἐπικεῖσθαι), RV rather inconsistently uses 'multitude.' The following phrases may be noted—(a) ὄχλος ἱκανός, which RV in Mk 10⁴⁶ translates 'great multitude' (AV a 'great number of people'), yet in Lk 7¹² renders, as AV, 'much people,' probably because in the preceding verse 'great multitude' is used for a different collection of persons ; (b) ὁ πολὺς ὄχλος or ὁ ὄχλος πολὺς forming almost a composite term 'the common people' (Mk 12³⁷, Jn 12⁹ and 12¹² RVm) ; (c) ὁ πλεῖστος ὄχλος, Mt 21⁸ RV 'the most part of the multitude,' AV 'a very great multitude,' Vulg. *plurima turba* ; in Mk 4¹ ὄχλος πλεῖστος is read by אB, al.; (d) τῶν μυριάδων τοῦ ὄχλου, Lk 12¹ 'the many thousands of the multitude' (RV), 'an innumerable multitude of people' (AV), *multis turbis* (Vulg.) ; this ὄχλος appears to be the largest mentioned in the Gospels, and the words 'in the mean time' (ἐν οἷς) at the beginning of the verse suggest that it was drawn together by the conflict between Christ and His adversaries which is narrated 'n the previous chapter.

(2) πλῆθος occurs 12 times in the Gospels, of which 8 are in Lk. (1¹⁰ 2¹³ 5⁶ 6¹⁷ 8³⁷ 19³⁷ 23¹·²⁷), 2 in Mk. (3⁷·⁸), and 2 in Jn. (5³ 21⁶) ; in only two cases is it used otherwise than of a collection of persons (Lk 5⁶, Jn 21⁶ a 'multitude of fishes'). AV renders the word by 'multitude' in all passages except Lk 23²⁷ where it gives 'company.' There is more variety in RV, which

employs 'multitude' in 9 places, but also 'company' (Lk 23¹), 'number of the people' (6¹⁷), and 'people' in 8³⁷, where Humphry (*Commentary on the Revised Version*) says it would not be in accordance with English idiom to say 'the whole multitude of the country' ; yet the latter is the tr. of AV, which does not usually err in this respect. 'People' is elsewhere almost invariably reserved by RV to tr. λαός. All three Gr. words occur in Lk 6¹⁷ ὄχλος πολὺς μαθητῶν αὐτοῦ καὶ πλῆθος πολὺ τοῦ λαοῦ (AV 'the company of his disciples and a great multitude of people,' RV 'a great multitude of his disciples and a great number of the people').

The multitude occupies a distinct position in the Gospels ; those of whom it was composed are marked off from the disciples (cf. Mk 8³⁴, Lk 9¹⁶·¹⁸, and Mt 23¹, where the disciples appear round Jesus in the foreground, the multitude farther off, and the Pharisees in the background). They are also distinguished from the ruling classes who despised them and held them in contempt, regarding them as accursed through their ignorance of the Law (Jn 7⁴⁹), and a prey to any designing teacher (7¹²·⁴⁷ᶠ·). Thus the 'multitude' answers to 'am hā'āreẓ, 'people of the land,' 'common persons,' which was the name given to those who were not ḥăbērîm, i.e. not strict observers of the Law (see Hastings' DB iii. 743ᵃ, 826). Hillel used to say, 'No brutish man is sin-fearing, nor is one of the people of the land pious,' and Rabbinical writers used such contemptuous expressions as 'the ignorant is impious ; only the learned shall have part in the resurrection' (Godet on Jn 7⁴⁹). Yet it was felt that the multitude would be formidable from its very numbers if it were only united under a leader in one common purpose. Accordingly we read that Herod was restrained from putting John the Baptist to death since he feared the multitude, because they counted him as a prophet (Mt 14⁵). For the same reason the chief priests and elders dared not say that John's baptism was of men (21²⁶). This same fear prevented the chief priests and the Pharisees from laying hold on Jesus (21⁴⁶) ; they decided not to arrest Him on the feast day (Mk 14²), 'lest haply there shall be a tumult of the people' (λαοῦ, note the future ἔσται, which shows their positive expectation of trouble) ; and they arranged with Judas for His betrayal 'in the absence of the multitude' (RVm 'without tumult,' ἄτερ ὄχλου, Lk 22⁶, cf. 19⁴⁷ᶠ·). The multitude, however, at ordinary times was greatly under the influence of their rulers, looking up to them as guides in religious matters, cf. Jn 7¹²·¹³ 'there was much murmuring among the multitudes concerning him : some said, He is a good man ; others said, Not so, but he leadeth the multitude astray. Howbeit no man spake openly of him for fear of the Jews.' This whole chapter is important as showing the relations between the ruling classes and the multitude, and also the discussions between different sections of the latter as to the claims of Jesus, and the gradual development into belief or disbelief (see especially vv. 25-27. 31. 40-44 and art. MURMURING. Here also perhaps may be noted Lk 12¹. The violent scene of ch. 11 'had found its echo outside ; a considerable crowd had flocked together. Excited by the animosity of their chiefs, the multitude showed a disposition hostile to Jesus and His disciples. Jesus feels the need of turning to His own, and giving them, in presence of all, those encouragements which their situation demands' (Godet). The power of the same influence is seen in the account of the Trial, cf. Mt 27²⁰ 'the chief priests and the elders persuaded the multitudes that they should ask for Barabbas and destroy Jesus '—words which suggest that if left to themselves they might have listened to Pilate's proposal, but their leaders turned the scale against Jesus. It must be remembered that this multitude which cried for His blood was mainly, if not entirely, composed of Jews of Jerusalem. It was therefore quite distinct from the multitude which had accompanied Jesus at His triumphal entry, and which largely consisted of pilgrims from Galilee coming to the feast. For the meeting of the two multitudes see Mt 21[10. 11], and note how the answer of v.[11] is already greatly modified from the Hosanna cries of v.[9]. Accordingly the favourite use of these incidents as illustrations of the proverbial fickleness of a crowd—shouting Hosanna and waving palm branches one day, and crying 'Crucify him' the next — though attractive, is without justification.

Jesus regarded with deep pity the multitudes who came to Him. We read that on one occasion He had compassion on them because they were ἐσκυλμένοι καὶ ἐρριμμένοι, as sheep not having a shepherd. (Mt 9[36]).

If these words primarily describe the physical aspect of those who came to Him on this occasion, then ἐσκυλμένοι, which properly means 'flayed,' 'mangled,' will signify here 'distressed and wearied by long travelling'; and ἐρριμμένοι, 'prostrated by fatigue, lying down like tired sheep' (cf. Vulg. *jacentes*). Thus they will express mute misery, and a half unconscious appeal to the Divine compassion, and they are so taken by Meyer, and Bruce in *Expos. Gr. Testament*. But if, as seems more likely, the expressions are mainly figurative, ἐσκυλμένοι will mean 'harried and distressed by spiritual foes,' harassed by the tyranny of the scribes and Pharisees with their 'heavy burdens' (cf. Mt 23[4]); and ἐρριμμένοι, 'scattered,' without true spiritual shepherds, John the Baptist being imprisoned and their regular teachers shamefully neglecting their duties. This agrees better with the Lord's remark in v.[37] that 'the labourers are few,' and with the commission of the Twelve immediately following in ch. 10, as the result of His compassion; so RV 'distressed and scattered'; AV 'they fainted,' following TR, which reads ἐκλελυμένοι for ἐσκυλμένοι, with very little MS support.

On other occasions His compassion for the multitude led Him to heal their sick (Mt 14[14]), and to feed the 4000 (Mt 15[32], Mk 8[2]).

The astonishment and wonder with which the multitude regarded Jesus is a very marked feature in the Gospels, especially in Mk. and Lk. (see art. ATTRIBUTES OF CHRIST, ii. 9). These feelings were excited by the manner and substance of His teaching (Mt 7[28] 22[33], Mk 1[22], Lk 4[32]), by His words of grace (Lk 4[22]), and also by His mighty works (Mt 9[8. 33] 15[31], Mk 2[12] 5[20] 7[37], Lk 4[36] 5[26] 7[16] 9[43] 11[14]). The people never became so familiar with His miracles as to take them as a matter of course. It is noted that they received His words and acts with gladness (cf. Mk 12[37] and Lk 13[17], where there is a contrast to the feeling of His adversaries who 'were ashamed'). They greatly enjoyed the discomfiture of His enemies when He easily replied to their subtle questions and escaped their cleverly-laid snares. Jesus was very popular with the ordinary people; it is frequently recorded that great multitudes followed Him (cf. Mt 4[25] 8[1] 12[15] 19[2]). At other times we read that, attracted by His teaching and His miracles, 'all the city was gathered together at the door' (Mk 1[33]); 'they came from every quarter' (1[45]); their attendance was so persistent that Jesus and the disciples 'could not so much as eat bread' (3[20]); it was necessary to address them from the boat (Mt 13[2]); they brought their sick and maimed to Him (Mt 15[31], Mk 1[32]); they pressed upon Him and heard the word of God (Lk 5[1]); and their rapt attention to His preaching, even during the last days at Jerusalem, is described by St. Luke (19[48]) in emphatic language, 'the people all hung upon him, listening' (ἐξεκρέματο αὐτοῦ ἀκούων). The feeding of the 5000 produced such an effect that they were 'about to come and take him by force to make him king' (Jn 6[15]), proclaiming Him the Son of David (cf. Mt 12[23] 21[9. 15]); and His enemies bore striking testimony to His popularity when they said, 'Lo, the world is gone after him' (Jn 12[19]). Even in the region of Cæsarea Philippi, whither He had gone for retirement, we are surprised to find mention of a multitude, which may indeed have consisted mainly of Gentiles (Mk 8[34]). Edersheim (*LT* ii. 45 f.) thinks there is a previous men-

tion of a non-Israelite multitude in Mt 15[31] 'the multitude wondered . . . and they glorified the God of Israel' (but see Alford's note). 'By the reiteration of this word we are constantly reminded that our Lord, wherever He went, drew about Him eager crowds of the common people, who sometimes thronged and pressed upon Him too closely, sometimes followed Him far from their own homes, and always heard Him gladly' (Humphry, *Commentary on the Revised Version*, on Mt 7[28]).

Christ, however, was not deceived as to the depth of these impressions; He did not court their applause or seek their favour. On the contrary, it is recorded that on several occasions He withdrew Himself from the multitude (cf. Mt 8[18], Jn 6[15]), and the expression ἀφεὶς τοὺς ὄχλους, used in Mt 13[36], Mk 4[36], means 'leaving the multitude' (RV), not 'sending them away' (AV). Knowing that such popularity would not further the Kingdom of God, and would lead afterwards to serious disappointment, He sought at times to repress it, and showed the danger and loss and self-sacrifice involved in being His disciples; cf. His teaching as to the necessity of being willing to forsake everything (Lk 14[25f.]). The parables of Mt 13 give a very sober estimate of the value of the professions of the multitude. Yet His popularity with the simple-hearted people of Galilee continued until the end, as was shown at His triumphal entry into Jerusalem.

Certain sections of Christ's teaching were specially addressed to the multitude, viz. the discourse about defilement (Mt 15[10f.], Mk 7[14f.], where, turning from the Pharisees and the scribes, 'he called to him the multitude, and said unto them, Hear and understand'; ἐκείνους μὲν ἐπιστομίσας καὶ καταισχύνας ἀφῆκεν ὡς ἀνιάτους· τρέπει δὲ τὸν λόγον πρὸς τὸν ὄχλον ὡς ἀξιολογώτερον, Euthym.); the first three parables of the Kingdom (Mt 13); the passage showing the need of renunciation and of counting the cost (Lk 14[25f.]||); the section dealing with the Bread of Life (Jn 6[24f.]); the questions concerning John the Baptist, and the statement as to his character and mission (Mt 11[7f.]); and the passage dealing with the scribes and Pharisees (Mt 23[1f.]), which was spoken to the multitudes and to His disciples; cf. also Mk 2[13]. See also CROWD.

LITERATURE.—In addition to the notes on the various passages in Commentaries, two suggestive sermons may be mentioned: Vaughan, *Earnest Words for Earnest Men*: 'The Christian aspect of a multitude'; A. K. H. B., *The Graver Thoughts of a Country Parson*: 'A great multitude a sad sight.'

W. H. DUNDAS.

MURDER.—The observance of the Sixth Commandment, as of the rest, is taken for granted in the Christian system (Mt 19[18], Mk 10[19], Lk 18[20]). It concerns those who are outside of the society founded by Jesus. Thus the guilt of murder is predicated of Barabbas (Mk 15[7], Lk 23[19. 25], Jn 18[40] 'robber'), and of the unwilling guests (Mt 22[7]), and Satan is designated the original ἀνθρωποκτόνος (Jn 8[44]). In the doctrine of Jesus, the crimes of the Mosaic codes are traced to their source in the heart (Mt 15[19], Mk 7[21]), and murder to the passion of anger. He who is angry with his brother, or who says to him 'Raca,' or 'Thou fool,' is accounted guilty of murder (Mt 5[22]). With this saying of Jesus may be compared one of Mohammed, 'Whosoever shall say to his brother, Thou unbeliever, one of the two shall suffer as an unbeliever.' It is also interesting to note that the Arabic verb *katala* means both to kill and to curse (Koran, lxxx. 16). In the Koran murder is atoned for by retaliation (cf. Mt 5[38]), a free man dying for a free, a slave for a slave; or the relatives of the slain may accept a money payment, which in practice does not exceed £500 (Koran, ii. 173; Lane's *Arabian Nights*, vi. 8). The Jewish Rabbis distinguished between manslaughter and murder (Ex 21¹³· ¹⁴) : only in the latter case did capital punishment follow (Edersheim, *History of the Jewish Nation*, p. 375 f. ; W. R. Smith, *RS*² p. 420). Self-murder is rare among Semitic peoples, though cases do occur (Mt 27⁵, Ac 1¹⁸ ; Jos. *BJ* III. viii. 5).   T. H. WEIR.

MURMUR, MURMURING (Lat. *murmur*, a reduplication of an imitative syllable *mur* ; cf. Gr. μορμύρω).—A low continuous sound, as of a stream or of bees, hence a whispering, something said in a low muttering voice. The verb represents :—

(1) γογγύζω, to murmur, say in a low tone ; according to Pollux and Phavorinus, it was used of the cooing of doves, like τονθρύζω and τονθορύζω of the more elegant Greek writers. It is found in the Gospels with the accusative of the thing said (Jn 7³²), with περί τινος (Jn 6⁴¹· ⁶¹ 7³²), κατά τινος (Mt 20¹¹), πρός τινα (Lk 5³⁰), and μετ’ ἀλλήλων (Jn 6⁴³). (2) διαγογγύζω only in Lk. (15² 19⁷), where διά seems to give the idea of a general pervasive murmuring through the whole assembly, or perhaps it means alternative murmuring ‘among one another,’ ‘certandi significationem addit’ (Hermann). (3) ἐμβριμᾶσθαι is used in one passage (Mk 14⁵) of the disciples murmuring against Mary ; it implies that they were moved with indignation. The noun γογγυσμός occurs only once in the Gospels (Jn 7¹²) ; it as well as γογγύζω and διαγογγύζω are frequently used in LXX of Israel in the wilderness.

The word ‘murmur’ appears in itself to have a neutral meaning, the context deciding whether it expresses favour, doubt, or hostility ; hence in several cases ‘muttering’ or ‘whispering’ might be a better rendering. For its use in a friendly sense see Jn 7³¹· ³², where the murmuring was that of persons who believed on Jesus, and who said, ‘When the Christ shall come, will he do more signs than those which this man hath done?’—a dangerous omen to the Pharisees. The noun γογγυσμός, as used in 7¹², includes both favour and hostility : ‘There was much murmuring among the multitudes concerning him ; some said, He is a good man ; others said, Not so, but he leadeth the multitude astray.’ It implies a discussion low and whispered, not free and open ; it was hardly safe to speak out plainly, for they feared the Jews (cf. 7⁴⁰· ⁴¹). The development of such differences of opinion is recorded in Jn 6⁵² ‘they strove (ἐμάχοντο) one with another’ ; 7⁴³ ‘there arose a division (σχίσμα) in the multitude because of him’ ; cf. also 9¹⁶ 10¹⁹ 11⁴⁵· ⁴⁶. The sense of doubt and dissatisfaction predominates in Jn 6⁴¹· ⁴³, as also in 6⁶¹ ‘his disciples murmured at this,’ namely, at the ‘hard saying.’ There is some uncertainty as to what precisely is here meant : whether the new teaching of life through death (Westcott) ; the paradoxical nature of the words just spoken by Jesus, the need of eating His flesh and drinking His blood (Godet) ; His claim to have come down from heaven (Lampe and others) ; the apparent pride with which He connected the salvation of the world with His own Person (Tholuck, Hengstenberg) ; or the bloody death of the Messiah (de Wette, Meyer). Dissatisfaction is seen highly intensified in Lk 5³⁰ 15², where the Pharisees and the scribes murmured because He ate with publicans and sinners. Compare also 19⁷, where all, apparently even the Twelve, shared in it with a sense of outrage done to propriety ; Edersheim calls it a murmur of disappointment and anger ; but perhaps Bengel is more correct, ‘ex hæsitatione potius quod ad majorem partem attinet quam cum indignatione.’ Hostile murmuring is found in the parable of the Labourers in the Vineyard (Mt 20¹¹), and in the story of the Anointing in the house of Simon the leper (Mk 14⁵).
           W. H. DUNDAS.

MUSIC.—The Jews cultivated music from the earliest times, perhaps the more because sculpture and painting were practically forbidden (Ex 20⁴). It gave expression to all their emotions, and found a place in all the chief events of public and private life (cf. OT, *passim*).

1. References in the Gospels are few and indirect. (*a*) *Song* : Mt 26³⁰ ‖, Lk 15²⁵ (?) seem to be the only instances. (*b*) *Instruments* : Mt 9⁻³ 11¹⁷ ‖ pipe (wh. see) or flute (see FLUTE-PLAYERS) ; 24³¹ trumpet (wh. see), probably the curved trumpet as in Ex 19¹⁶. In Dn 3⁵· ¹⁵ (LXX) συμφωνία is usually taken to mean a bagpipe ; but such a meaning in Lk 15²⁵ is unlikely. It is in the OT that the various national instruments appear, of which the following are the principal types :—(1) *Stringed* : lyre (EV ‘harp’), harp (EV variously ‘psaltery,’ ‘viol,’ ‘lute’) ; (2) *wind* : pipe, of wood ; curved trumpet, of horn or (in later times) of metal ; straight trumpet, of silver ; (3) *percussion* : handdrum (EV ‘tabret,’ ‘timbrel’) of skin ; cymbals (EV once [Zec 14²⁰] ‘bells’) of brass, used, especially the precentor as it appears from 1 Ch 16⁵, no doubt for rhythmical purposes. Several others are mentioned, but some are foreign, and the nature of the rest is unknown.

2. The general character of Jewish music in the time of Christ is wholly a matter of inference. There were no theoretical writers, as among the Greeks ; of their instruments sculpture portrays the silver trumpet alone ; and, notation not having been invented, specimens of their music contemporaneously committed to writing do not exist. Yet within definable limits inference amounts to certainty. (*a*) As to rhythmical structure, all ancient music was of the free form, in contrast to the measured form of modern music : ‘time,’ in our sense, was then unknown. (*b*) The variety and combination of instruments employed, together with the musical arrangements generally (*e.g.* 1 Ch 15¹⁶⁻²²), imply at least some definite system whereby the intervals of melodic progression were regulated. The existence of scales or modes, of some sort, cannot therefore be questioned. (*c*) They seem to have been in accord with those in use at Babylon (Ps 137¹⁻³). Moreover, habitual contact with Greek influences in Alexandria and elsewhere probably produced (or at least goes to prove) an affinity with the Greek modes. (*d*) The ‘traditional melodies’ now used in Jewish synagogues are, in some cases, similar in kind to the music that we may infer to have existed in the time of Christ. Tradition might preserve melodies down to the invention of notation, much as it preserved the vowel-system down to the invention of ‘points.’ But the Jews themselves seem to have discontinued the Temple melodies after its destruction ; so that the synagogue melodies, whatever their origin, would not be those of the Temple. It may be supposed that Jewish Christians imported some of their Temple melodies into the Christian Church. Perhaps it was they who introduced antiphonal singing : and even Greek liturgies are held to have been largely ‘affected by Mosaic rites’ (Swainson, *Gr. Liturgies*). It is therefore not impossible that a Jewish element still survives in some of the ancient ecclesiastical plainsong. But no one can say for certain that this is so, or identify any particular instance.

LITERATURE.—Chappell, *History of Music* ; Stainer, *The Music of the Bible* ; Edersheim, *The Temple*, etc. ; art. ‘Music’ in Hastings’ *DB* ; Helmore, *Plainsong*, etc. The traditional Jewish melodies can be seen in E. Pauer’s *Hebrew Melodies* (Augener), and in the collection of music for the synagogue edited by Cohen and Davis.   F. S. RANKEN.

MUSTARD.—In a simile the word (σίναπι) occurs in Mt 13³¹, Mk 4³¹, Lk 13¹⁹ ; as a bold metaphor, in Mt 17²⁰, Lk 17⁶. It used to be strongly contended that the mustard referred to is not any of the familiar wild species of the Holy Land (such as the *Sinapis nigra*), but an arboreal plant (*Salvadora persica*) found in the extreme south or sub-tropical part of Palestine, and said to be called among the Arabs by the same name (*Khardal*) as mustard.

This theory, however, may now be said to be exploded (cf. Hastings' *DB*, art. 'Mustard'). The passages concerned clearly suggest, not a perennial shrub, but an annual sown among and comparable with other garden herbs; and if the expression 'tree' be a difficulty ('great' in Lk 13[19] is of weak authority, cf. RV), it is to be remembered that, when Jesus spoke to the multitude, it was in popular language. He meant that the tiny seed became to all intents a tree. An accurate botanist (Dr. Hooker) found the black mustard on the banks of the Jordan 'ten feet high, drawn up amongst bushes, etc., and not thicker than whipcord.' And Dr. Thomson says that he has seen it 'on the rich plain of Akkâr as tall as the horse and his rider' (*LB*, p. 414).

Equally prosaic is the criticism that the mustard is not 'the least of all seeds' (Mt.), or 'less than all the seeds that be in the earth,' *i.e.* annuals (Mk.). Enough, as before, that the language is not absolute and scientific. The mustard was probably the smallest a gardener ordinarily sowed. But the fact is, the saying is proverbial (found as such in the Talmud and in the Koran), and in good proverbs there is often the suppressed note of poetic licence (cf. the Semitic form of poetry in the introductory verse of the passage Mk 4[30], Lk 13[18]). The broad effect of the image is plain, that out of a speck of seed there was to come in due course marvellously great growth—a plant towering among the pulse and pot-herbs like a Titan, and with branching sprays on which the birds of the air find shelter and rest.

The Arabs are given to special cultivation of mustard as a condiment (Hooker), and there is clearly emphasis on the statement that it was 'a grain' (not a handful) which was taken 'by a man' (Mt. and Lk.) and cast 'into his own garden' (Lk 13[19] RV)—the garden ('field' in Mt 13[31]) being a place where, as observation attests, wild plants attain more than the normal size. Elsewhere this is the thought of Jesus—that God's Kingdom is taken from the world and developed on lines of its own (cf. the fig-tree favoured by being put in the choice and carefully protected place usually devoted to vines, Lk 13[6]).

The essential point in the application is not any seeming rapidity of growth; rather it is the striking contrast between the initial insignificance and the amply beneficent result. Jesus, the spokesman of the coming Kingdom, was derided in His teaching, persecuted in His Person, doomed to violence and degradation; but He felt, and knew, and here affirms that the cause was supremely great, and that its greatness should be manifested to the world.

The remaining passages (Mt 17[20] and Lk 17[6]) describe the wonder-working power of faith, which, within its own sphere, produces miraculous results (cf. art. FAITH in vol. i. p. 569).

GEORGE MURRAY.

MYRRH (σμύρνα, Mt 2[11], Jn 19[39]).—A gum-resin, the exudation of a shrub (*Balsamodendron myrrha*) and some other allied species of shrubs growing in the dry regions of Arabia, in Somaliland, and in certain districts bordering on the Red Sea. The myrrh shrubs are of a low stature, unattractive, rigid, spiny, with scanty foliage and minute flowers and small oval berries. Myrrh exudes from the bark, or is obtained by incisions made in the bark, and appears in resinous, yellow drops, which gradually thicken and become harder. The smell is balsamic, and the taste bitter and slightly pungent. Myrrh has been known to mankind from the remotest times, and was among the most precious articles of ancient commerce. It is used in medicine as a tonic and stimulant, and was much employed by the ancient Egyptians in embalming. It is collected in great quantities to-day by the Somali tribes and sold to traders. There has been considerable controversy as to the real nature of the ancient myrrh, and particularly as to the regions from which it came; but the σμύρνα of NT appears, on the whole, to have been the substance described above.

Myrrh was one of the gifts brought by the Magi to the Infant Christ (Mt 2[11]), and it was used, along with aloes, by Nicodemus to anoint the body of Christ before burial (Jn 19[39]). All the ancient commentators affirm that each of the three gifts—gold, frankincense, and myrrh—offered by the Magi is replete with spiritual significance. Thus it was widely accepted in early times that the myrrh was emblematic of the death of Christ, inasmuch as myrrh was used for embalming. It was 'offered to' Christ as to one who is about to die for all' (Aug. *ad loc.*). Others regarded it as setting forth His true human nature, and therefore as teaching the mortification of the flesh by abstinence. The well-known ancient hymn, part of which refers to this, says:

> 'Gold, a monarch to declare;
> Frankincense, that God is there;
> Myrrh, to tell the heavier tale
> Of His tomb and funeral.'

Though we may admit that in the gifts presented there was an unconscious fulfilment of prophecy (Is 60[6]), no symbolism of the nature referred to can have been designed by the Magi. So far as their intention was concerned, they simply offered to the new-born King, whom they came to worship, the choicest and most precious products of their country, and thus expressed their homage.

In Mk 15[23] we are told that there was offered to Christ, probably just before He was nailed to the cross, ἐσμυρνισμένον οἶνον, 'wine mingled with myrrh.' It was offered, of course, as an anodyne; but as myrrh was often infused into wine to give it a more agreeable flavour and fragrance, it has been held by some that Mt.'s expression οἶνον μετὰ χολῆς, 'wine mingled with gall,' is the more correct, because the mingling of gall with wine to render it anæsthetic was a well-known practice. It is, however, possible that the *gall* of Mt. was the same as the *myrrh* of Mk., the corresponding Hebrew words being from the same root, and both signifying 'bitter.' The mingling of myrrh with the wine would certainly render it more potent as an anodyne, and we must therefore accept the word given by Mk. as conveying the purpose for which the draught was offered. Such a draught, called by the Romans *sopor*, was regularly offered to criminals just before their crucifixion. It was provided by an association of wealthy women in Jerusalem, who prepared it for the purpose. But, having tasted it and ascertained its object, He would not drink. This action is in contrast with what He did at a later period of the day; for when, in response to His cry 'I thirst,' one of the soldiers soaked a sponge in 'vinegar' and, holding it up to Him on a reed, gave Him to drink, He received it. This was not to soothe His agony, but only to moisten His parched tongue and lips, perhaps that He might be able to utter 'with a loud voice' His triumphant τετέλεσται, perhaps also to sanction and sanctify the friendly office which is often the only one that can be rendered to the dying, and possibly in fulfilment of the prophecy of thirst (Jn 19[28], cf. Ps 69[21]). However this may be, His purpose in refusing the draught offered as an anodyne is clear. He would 'look death in the face,' and meet the King of Terrors in full possession of all His faculties. He was dying of His own accord, fulfilling His words, 'No man taketh my life from me' (Jn 10[18]). His death was an act of voluntary self-surrender, and He would 'taste death for every man' (He 2[9]). He 'endured the cross, despising shame' (12[2]).

LITERATURE.—Birdwood in *Bible Educator*, ii. 151; an exhaustive article by Hanbury, 'The Botanical Origin and Country of Myrrh' in the *Pharmaceutical Journal*, 19th Apr. 1873.

J. CROMARTY SMITH.

MYSTERY ($\mu\nu\sigma\tau\dot\eta\rho\iota\sigma\nu$ from $\mu\dot\nu\sigma\tau\eta\varsigma$ 'one initiated'; stem $\mu\dot\nu\omega$ 'to close,' 'shut' (cf. Lat. *mutus*, Eng. 'mum').—**1.** In classical Greek $\mu\nu\sigma\tau\dot\eta\rho\iota\sigma\nu$ means *a hidden thing, a secret*; in Biblical writers primarily *a hidden or secret thing*; in the plural (usually) individual matters of revelation or superhuman knowledge (Mt 13[11], Lk 8[10], Ro 11[25], 1 Co 4[1] 15[51]). In the singular with the article $\tau\dot\sigma$ $\mu\nu\sigma\tau\dot\eta\rho\iota\sigma\nu$ is used, principally by St. Paul, of the hidden counsel of God, especially His redemptive plan culminating in the final judgment (Ro 16[25], 1 Co 2[7], Eph 3[3. 9], Col 1[26f.]). This counsel of God is further characterized as the 'mystery of his will' (Eph 1[9]) 'which he formed' (Col 2[2] [1 Co 2[1], text of WH]) 'respecting Christ' (Col 4[3]), and constitutes the contents of the gospel (Eph 6[19]). It is consummated in the *parousia* (Rev 10[7]). In antithesis to 'the mystery of the faith' or 'of godliness' (1 Ti 3[9. 16]) stands that of 'lawlessness' (2 Th 2[7]), the purposed impulse of an antagonistic power operative in the world.

Besides this primary sense, the word $\mu\nu\sigma\tau\dot\eta\rho\iota\sigma\nu$ is also used like רָז and סוֹד in Rabbinic writers to designate the hidden or mystic sense of a Scripture (Eph 5[32]), a name (Rev 17[5]), or the image or form seen in a vision (Rev 1[20] 17[5]).

It is important to observe that the connotation of *intrinsic* difficulty of comprehension, obscurity, which has become inseparable from the word in modern use, is misleading. In Biblical and in ancient use generally the 'mystery' is simply that which is made known only to the initiated, be its content easy or hard to understand, hence *revealed* as against *reasoned* knowledge.

2. In a looser sense the term 'mysteries' was transferred from the teaching symbolized to (*a*) the rites enacted in certain cults or rituals known to classic authors as $\tau\epsilon\lambda\epsilon\tau\alpha\dot\iota$ (Wis 14[23]), and (*b*), still more loosely, to the $\tau\epsilon\lambda\epsilon\tau\alpha\dot\iota$ themselves. From the former sense (*a*) the designation of the sacraments, or even the Church service generally, as 'the mysteries' becomes common from the 2nd cent. onward. From the latter is doubtless derived the designation of mediæval religious dramas or pantomimes as 'mysteries' (cf., from the same stem, 'mummery').

3. The $\tau\epsilon\lambda\epsilon\tau\alpha\dot\iota$, loosely called 'mysteries,' are of importance to our consideration as affecting the application of the term 'mystery' to the gospel as a whole in Mk 4[11]. They consisted of secret rites in honour of certain divinities especially representative of the drama of life, vegetable and animal, annually failing and renewed. These divinities are always chthonic, as against the Olympian (national) divinities of the upper air; and their worship, maintained by guilds, was commonly associated with the rites of ancestor- and hero-worship. Mystery-religion transcended all lines of mere nationality, substituting its own brotherhoods of initiates, and offered the idea of personal deliverance and immortality as the goal; as the means, it offered sacramental (instead of sacrificial) union with a Redeemer-god ($\theta\epsilon\dot\sigma\varsigma$ $\sigma\omega\tau\dot\eta\rho$), who, in contrast with the Olympian divinities, participated in the suffering and death of humanity, and won for men victory over their spiritual foes. Its strong monotheistic tendency, added to these other traits, gave it an obvious resemblance to the gospel as preached to the Gentile world, and made it a much more formidable rival than the various religionized forms of Greek and Oriental philosophy, in bidding for the adherence of popular faith in the Empire, after the dissolution of the national religions. Christianity itself, in the transition from a national to a universal religion, necessarily passed through some of the same phases as the mystery-cults; for these had already connected themselves in a syncretizing spirit with the mythology of every people. Their influence is most apparent, as we should expect, in the development of the Pauline Church, supremely in the ultra-Pauline or Gnostic. The resemblances were in fact so striking alike in dogma, terminology, and ritual, as to lead early apologists to account for them by the theory of diabolic travesty (Justin M. *Apol.* i. 66, *Dial.* lxx.). Some modern students of the history of religion find it impossible to deny a relation of dependence on the side of the Church, especially in the Pauline and post-Pauline period. [For an able presentation of the view that it is impossible to establish any direct relation during the Pauline or early post-Pauline period, see Anrich, *Das antike Mysterienwesen*]. This appears not only from terminology, but even from the Pauline doctrine and ritual, in particular as regards the theory of the sacraments. In the Gospels this influence is scarcely traceable outside the Fourth, wherein the type of the $\delta\rho\hat\alpha\mu\alpha$ $\mu\nu\sigma\tau\iota\kappa\dot\sigma\nu$ and the sacramental interest are very apparent (Harnack, *Mission und Ausbreitung*, pp. 169–173— John and Origen the profoundest mysteriosophists of the Church); but in the single passage Mk 4[11]= Mt 13[11]=Lk 8[10] even the Synoptic writers must be admitted to have been affected through St. Paul both as to phraseology and as to thought.

4. Mk 4[11] seems to be earlier in form than its parallels; for the context shows that the thing given or withheld is not certain *elements of the gospel*, conceived as $\mu\nu\sigma\tau\dot\eta\rho\iota\alpha$ and therefore uttered only in parables (understood as enigmas; cf. Mt 13[35], Jn 16[29])—the sense conveyed by the use of the plural in the parallels ($\tau\dot\alpha$ $\mu\nu\sigma\tau\dot\eta\rho\iota\alpha$, Mt 13[11]=Lk 8[10])—but is the gospel as a whole conceived as a 'mystery' in the Pauline sense, *i.e.* a Divine revelation (cf. Mt 13[16. 17]). The teaching in parables is regarded by Mk. (and still more by Mt.) as a fulfilment of Is 6[9] conceived as a sentence of judicial blindness. In answer to the question (Mt 13[10]), 'Why speakest thou to them (the motley Galilæan multitude) in parables?' (*i.e.* enigmas), Jesus answers that it is a fulfilment of the prophetic curse of Isaiah upon a disobedient and gainsaying people, of whom such fruitless hearing had been foretold. The inner circle (Mk 4[10], cf. 3[13. 34. 35]) are alone intended to receive more than the husk. The parallels, in altering to $\tau\dot\alpha$ $\mu\nu\sigma\tau\dot\eta\rho\iota\alpha$, give a dilution of this sense (cf. the secondary sense above under **1**).

5. Not the word alone, but the entire context of Mk 4 and parallels are Pauline in aim. Ro 9–11 attempts a theodicy of the rejection of Israel the covenant people in favour of the Gentiles, based upon the same idea of judicial hardening, and employing the same passage from Isaiah. In Ro 11[8] Paul writes after 30 years of disappointing experience in preaching to the Jews: '*It is written*, God gave them a spirit of stupor, *eyes that they should not see, and ears that they should not hear*, unto this very day.' To St. Paul, accordingly, must be attributed the first utilization of Is 6[9], which henceforth becomes the *locus classicus* to account for the rejection of the Messiah by His own people (with Mk 4[11] and parallels, cf. Jn 12[39-41], Ac 28[24-28]). Manifestly an interpretation of parabolic utterance which supposes it adopted in order to fulfil the prophetic sentence of judicial blindness on Israel cannot be attributed to Jesus, since the end sought in the parables themselves is the reverse of intentional obscurity. Mk 4[11], accordingly, which does not stand alone in this

Gospel as regards its Pauline phraseology (cf. Mk 1¹⁵ with Mt 4¹⁷), is equally Pauline in the employment of this theory of the intention of the parabolic teaching.

6. Linguistically the results are at least equally conclusive. The word μυστήριον occurs 21 times in the Pauline Epp., elsewhere in the NT only here, and 4 times in the Apocalypse. The conception of the gospel itself as a 'mystery' is found nowhere else save in the Pauline Epistles. With St. Paul it is fundamental (1 Co 2¹⁻¹⁶, Eph 1⁹ 3³⁻¹¹, Col 1²⁷, Ro 16²⁵⁻²⁷), usually involving the contrast of philosophy *versus* revelation, the 'wisdom of this world' *versus* the spirit of prophecy. It is noteworthy that the removal of vv.¹¹·¹² from the context of Mk 4¹⁰⁻²⁰ produces a simpler and more intelligible connexion (cf. v.¹⁰ 'asked of him the parables.').

7. The *agraphon* quoted by Clement of Alexandria (*Strom.* v. x. 69) from 'a certain Gospel': 'My mystery belongs to me and to the sons of my household' (μυστήριον ἐμὸν ἐμοὶ καὶ τοῖς υἱοῖς τοῦ οἴκου μου), and also found in *Clem. Hom.* XIX. xx. in the form, 'Keep the mysteries for me and the sons of my house,' is manifestly connected with Mk 4¹¹, but probably not dependent upon it, nor upon St. Paul. This, however, does not counteract the above conclusions. It is quite probable that Mk 4¹¹ rests upon a traditional *logion* of some such form as this, rather than directly or exclusively on Ro 11⁸. The utterance in this form is not indeed attributable to Jesus, to whose doctrine its suggestion of esoteric teaching is abhorrent (cf. Philo, *de Vict. Off.* i. f., on the superiority of the Mosaic to heathen 'mysteries' as concealed from none; also Wis 6²²); but proper appreciation of the Pauline use of the word μυστήριον will show a common basis in the real teaching of Jesus. Mt 11²⁵⁻²⁷ = Lk 10²¹⁻²² is the canonical equivalent of the *agraphon*, and affords the real point of connexion between the teaching of Jesus and the Pauline and post-Pauline application of the term μυστήριον to the gospel. In respect to the superhuman, Divinely revealed character of the one message, Jesus and St. Paul are both emphatic. The expressions of 1 Co 2¹⁻¹⁶ from this point of view are not only in agreement with Jesus' whole teaching as 'with authority and not as the scribes,' but form a striking parallel to Mt 11²⁵⁻³⁰. However open to suspicion the *logion* of Mk 4¹¹ may be in its present canonical or post-canonical form, the words are at bottom nothing more than the translation into Greek equivalents of a claim of Jesus that is unquestionably historical, namely the claim for His teaching to be by *revelation*, a wisdom of God accessible to His 'little ones' though 'hid from the wise and prudent.'

LITERATURE. — On the word μυστήριον see, besides Grimm-Thayer, Hatch, *Essays on NT Greek*, p. 58; Lightfoot, *Com.* on Col. 1²⁶; Stewart, *s.v.* 'Mystery' in Hastings' *DB*; Ramsay, *s.v.* in *Enc. Brit.*⁹; and A. Jülicher, *s.v.* in *Encyc. Biblica*. On the influence of the Greek mysteries on early Christianity, see Lobeck, *Aglaophamus*, 1829; Anrich, *Das antike Mysterienwesen in seinem Einfluss a.d. Christenthum*, 1894; and Wobbermin, *Religionsgeschichtliche Studien zur Beeinflussung des Urchristenthums durch d. Mysterien*, 1896; also Cheetham, *The Mysteries Pagan and Christian*, 1897; and Hatch, *The Influence of Greek Ideas and Usages upon the Christian Church*, ch. x. On NT use of terminology from the mysteries, see Carman in *Bibliotheca Sacra* L (1893). On the mysteries generally as a phenomenon in the history of religion, see Rhode, *Psyche*; Frazer, *Golden Bough*²; Harnack, *Mission und Ausbreitung des Chr.* 1902, Bk. II. ch. v.   B. W. BACON.

MYTH.—Neither the word μῦθος nor the conception of a myth occurs in any of the Gospels. Outside of the Gospels the word appears in the NT several times (in plur. μῦθοι) in the Pastoral Epistles (1 Ti 1⁴ 4⁷, 2 Ti 4⁴, Tit 1¹⁴), and once in 2 Pet. (1¹⁶). In all these cases a myth is a story unworthy of credence, a foolish tale without sufficient foundation in fact or significance in principle to make it worth while to give heed to it. This is not, however, the ordinary meaning of the word in the Classic period or in modern usage. A myth in the Classic writers is either (1) akin to parable or legend; *i.e.* a story constructed with a specific design or conveying a moral or philosophical truth —Æsop's *Fables*; Plato's *Phædo*, 61 B, *Prot.* 320 C, 324 D; or (2) a story in which, through a process of growth, has come to be embodied a truth of nature or of conscience. Of this class of myths, illustrations are such as those in Plato, *Legg.* 636 D, *Rep.* 330 D (cf. Grote, *Hist. Gr.* i. 480). Modern historical terminology would make myth a story whose basis is past verifying. An account is said to be mythical when external evidences for its being a true narration of facts are not forthcoming, and when its internal characteristics render it incredible.

In the Platonic sense of the word no myths can be said to exist in the Gospels unless, contrary to all usage, the parables of Jesus be called myths (against this cf. Trench, *Parables*). In the modern sense it has been alleged that the Gospels are a tissue of mythological material (Strauss, *Leben Jesu*). This was the mythical theory of Gospel history, which for a time disputed the ground with the Tübingen hypothesis of 'tendency' literature, on the one side, and the earlier traditional view that the Gospels should be taken as precise and accurate history, on the other.

With the rise of the critical method all these theories have been compelled to yield the field to the view that the Gospels are the *sources* of history rather than history strictly so called; and that they are to be used as sources precisely upon the same principles as all other first-hand documentary testimony. But this view does not exclude the possibility of some mythical elements in these sources. The question, then, is whether there actually exist mythical accounts in the Gospels, and, if so, whence and how they came there. Whereas, therefore, the mythical theory propounded by Strauss has been entirely set aside, a new one has arisen to take its place.

The grounds on which the Straussian theory had been set aside were that the age of Jesus was not a mythopœic age in the sense assumed by its propounder. No matter what the truth may be about a mythology in the OT, where a prehistoric period certainly comes into view, the age of Jesus falls within a clearly lighted historic period, and the conditions for mythological growth of the nature assumed do not exist.

Accordingly the new mythical theory does not posit that these Gospel myths are the creation of the period and country in which Jesus lived. It rather undertakes to affiliate the narratives with the mythology of the environing heathen world. They are not creations of, but importations into, the Christian tradition. The age of Jesus was not a myth-making age, but a large stock of myths was already in existence among the peoples to whom the gospel came. These myths were diffused in the atmosphere, and could not but be absorbed into the very texture of the history. The search for the origin of Gospel myths is therefore not to be made in the Gospel story itself, but in the field of Comparative Religion.

The special passages of the Gospel history where, according to the new mythical theory, these myths were drawn in and found ready lodgment, are the account of the birth of Jesus, the accounts of His miracles, and the accounts of His death and resurrection. The accounts of the birth (Mt 1¹⁸⁻²⁵, Lk 1³⁴ᶠ·) are to be regarded not as parts of the original story of Jesus, but as 2nd cent. additions to it. They owe their origin to Gentile-Christian imagination. Like all true myths, they embody an idea, that of the Divine sonship of the founder of a great religion. The conception and phrase of Divine sonship are not foreign to the more direct Hebrew and Jewish antecedents of the gospel (Ps 2[6ff.], Enoch 45–51, 2 Es 13). Yet it is among the heathen that the idea was more commonly ascribed to great personages, especially rulers and sages. In Egypt, even to the latest days, the Pharaohs were regarded as incarnations of the deity (Wiedemann, *Egyp. Rel.* p. 92 ff.). Alexander the Great deemed it wise, upon conquering Egypt, to permit himself to be called the son of the god Ammon-Ra. In Babylon, from the time of Sargon I. onwards, the kings were considered emanations of the godhead (Radau, *Early Hist. of Babylon*, p. 308 ff.). These incarnations are, moreover, often associated with a virgin birth. Pythagoras and Plato were both regarded as born of virgin mothers and the god Apollo (Olympiodorus, *Vit. Plat.* p. 1). The mother of Alexander the Great was believed to have been visited by Zeus in the form of a serpent before king Philip had consummated his marriage with her. In the narratives of the birth of Buddha (which are of pre-Christian origin) there are some marked similarities to the Gospel accounts of the birth of Jesus.

The myths alleged to have grown about the career of Jesus as a wonder-worker are prefaced by parallel accounts of a temptation and a conquest of the power of evil. The prince Siddhartha was tempted by the spirit of evil, who urged him to abandon his foolish and futile purpose of living a simple and abstemious life, and to return to the comfort, glory, and power of the royal palace; but he resisted. The prophet Zarathustra had been urged by the evil spirit Ahriman to 'renounce the good law of the worshippers of Mazda,' and thereby to win dominion over the nations of the earth. But he had declined to do so. All the subsequent miracles recorded of Jesus are said to be abundantly paralleled in the legendary lore of the Orientals. The miraculous element did, in fact, persist through the Patristic age and down into the mediæval period.

The last portion of the Gospel story is said to be specially overlaid with myths of this genus. All that is apparently distinctive and remarkable here is represented as the reflexion and counterpart of the myths current among pagans. The idea of the death of Christ as the propitiation for sin is paralleled by the numerous instances of vicarious human sacrifices. The burial and resurrection are the Christian equivalents of the Egyptian myth of Osiris, who was slain by his brother Set, 'the demon of the withering heat of summer,' and who lives again in the person of his son Horus. Likewise the fabled death, resurrection, and translation into heaven of Adonis, the rape of Persephone, and her rescue upon the compromise that she thereafter spend part of the year with her mother upon earth and part in Hades, are expressions of the same thought.

These cases are associated with mystic rites. In fact, it seems to be a peculiarity of mysteries that death and restoration to life again should be symbolically represented in them. In their best form these rites occur in the Dionyso-Orphic festivals. Here the death of the god was enacted in the sacrifice of a bull, whose flesh was then torn and devoured by the worshippers without being drained of its blood. Thus, it was supposed, the immortal life of the god passed into and conferred immortality upon the worshippers (Clem. Alex. *Protrept.* i. 12, 17; Frazer, *Golden Bough*[2], ii. 165).

If the death of Jesus is pictured as a voluntary descent into the realm of shades that He might there conquer death, the same thought is seen to run through the Babylonian myth of Ishtar (Schrader, *Höllenfahrt d. Istar*), the Mandæan myth of Hibil Ziwa (Brandt, *Mandäische Religion*, p. 213 ff.), and the myths of Orpheus and Herakles, both of whom accomplished descents into Hades, and, according to the Greek classical mythology, achieved conquests there.

The Gospel account of the ascension is paralleled first of all in the OT by the ascensions of Enoch and Elijah, then in the Græco-Roman legendary lore by the ascensions of Romulus and Herakles. Legends of ascensions were, in fact, common even in the later periods. Some of the Roman emperors were said to have been raised at their death into equality with the gods (Rhode, *Psyche*, p. 663). The case of Peregrinus Proteus, recited by Lucian, is quite noteworthy. Peregrinus took Herakles as his ensample. As Herakles had made his exit from the world by consigning himself to a funeral pyre, so Peregrinus built a pyre and cast himself into it; but at the moment of his doing so a trustworthy old man reports that he saw an eagle issuing from the flames and flying up into the heavens. Further, the same old man testifies that he beheld Peregrinus clothed in a white garment, and with a garland of victory on his head. Apollonius of Tyana is also reported to have disappeared quite mysteriously, either in the temple of Athene at Lindus or in that of Dictynna at Crete. Philostratus, his biographer, appeals to the fact that nowhere on earth could a grave of him be found, in proof of his ascension and deification.

To the question how these myths filtered into the Gospel story there is no clear answer given. It is simply assumed that they were in the air, and that a new religion must somehow adopt them, and embellish the life and personality of its founder with them. This is a serious difficulty with the new mythical theory. For it is precisely the manner of their infiltration into the Christian tradition that is the crucial point in it. The existence of the myths themselves among the pagans has always been known, and is no new discovery. It is not by simply re-telling these stories that the theory can gain support to itself, but by substantiating the claim that they actually passed from the world of heathen thought into the Christian tradition. This difficulty is enhanced and made practically insuperable when it is further borne in mind that the Hebrew antecedents of the Gospel had resolutely and effectively resisted the incorporation of such myths for a thousand years. Moreover, there is no room in the time interval between the life of Jesus and the writing down of the Gospel accounts of Him for such a process as is assumed, unless we except the birth-narratives of St. Matthew and St. Luke upon purely textual grounds. Criticism has been busy with the origin of the Gospel story as found in the extant narratives, and the more light it throws on the subject the more clearly it appears that the main data come from eye- and ear-witnesses. The old Strauss theory, assuming that the myths were constructed by the disciples of Jesus under the power of an excited and vivid imagination, was at this point stronger than the new one.

Furthermore, when these parallels are closely scrutinized, the first aspect of plausibility given to the mythical theory by them vanishes. The parallels are in most cases far-fetched. In some instances the resemblances are striking indeed. But a relation of derivation of one from the other or from a common source seems to be out of the question. In other instances where a genetic connexion might be possibly established, the parallelisms are forced.

In the case of the birth-narratives (Mt 1[18-25], Lk 1[34f.]), the question is one of evidence. The effort to reduce these to mythology is based upon the *a priori* conception that they are mythical. If it could be proved, apart from the theory itself, upon purely critical grounds, that these accounts are of later origin, a basis for the theory might be found; but, as a matter of fact, the assumption that they are mythical furnishes the strongest consideration for their critical rejection—a process which can scarcely be called scientific.

LITERATURE.—D. F. Strauss, *Das Leben Jesu*, 1835–1836 (4th ed. 1840), also *Das Leben Jesu, f. d. deutsche Volk bearbeitet*, 1864 (4th ed. 1877); Gfrörer, *Die Heilige Sage*, 1838; Ullmann,

Historisch oder Mythisch? 1838 (2nd ed. 1864); Schenkel, *Charakterbild Jesu*[4], 1873; Luthardt, *Die modernen Darstellungen des Lebens Jesu*[2], 1865 (for products of the Strauss controversy, see, further, Grimm, *Glaubwürdigkeit d. Evang. Gesch.* 1845, pp. 128–131); Pfleiderer, *Early Christian Conception of Christ*, 1905; J. May, *Miracles and Myths of NT*, 1901; Kalthoff, *Entsteh. Christenthums*, 1904. For the influence of the Babylonian Marduk myth and other myths on Jewish thought, and indirectly on the Gospel history, cf. Gunkel, *Schöpfung u. Chaos*, also Bousset, *Antichrist*, and A. Jeremias, *Babylonisches im NT*. For incarnation parallels, R. Seydel, *Das Evang. in sein. Verhältnissen z. d. Buddha-Sage u. Buddha-Lehre*, Leipzig, 1882, *Die Buddha-Legende u. d. Leben Jesu*, 1884; Verus, *Vergleichende Uebersicht d. vier Evang. in unverkürztem Wortlaut*, Leipzig, 1897.　　　A. C ZENOS.

N

NAAMAN (Lk 4[27] Νεεμάν, TR; Ναιμάν, Tisch., WH; Heb. נַעֲמָן = 'pleasantness').—The famous captain of Benhadad II., whose cure by the instrumentality of Elisha is related in 2 K 5, and who was referred to by our Lord as 'Naaman the Syrian' in His discourse in the synagogue at Nazareth.

Whether our Lord's visit to Nazareth took place early in His ministry as here related by St. Luke, or later on as some think (cf. Mt 13[54-58], Mk 6[1-6]), or whether there were two distinct visits, does not concern this article, since the purpose of our Lord's reference to Naaman is the same at whatever period of His ministry He may have made it. He suggested to His audience that they were ready to quote the proverb 'Physician, heal thyself,' and to say, 'Whatsoever we have heard done in Capernaum, do also here in thy country.' 'And (better 'But') he said, Verily I say unto you, No prophet is accepted in his own country.' His hearers apparently inferred from these words that He had determined to work no miracle among them, and were irritated accordingly, although perhaps our Lord intended to imply no more than that He had little hope of being able to do so (cf. Mt 13[58], Mk 6[5]). Then, to justify and to illustrate His action in working miracles outside the limits of His own city, He referred to the cases of the widow of Sarepta and of Naaman, which were instances of blessings bestowed through the instrumentality of two of Israel's greatest prophets on persons who were not of the house of Israel at all. This afforded a complete justification of His own action, and was, further, a very pointed rebuke to them if, as seems the case, they were annoyed that He had neglected them for Capernaum, which, situated in that region known as 'Galilee of the Gentiles,' might be considered as less a Jewish town than their own. And, further, our Lord in these words rebuked Jewish exclusiveness in general, and quite clearly indicated the great truth that the benefits of His gospel, whether bodily or spiritual, were not only for the Jew, but also for the Gentile. It is probable that it was this underlying suggestion, coupled with His application to Himself of the great passage from Is 61, which caused the final outbreak of His hearers' wrath (cf. Ac 22[22] 28[28. 29]).
　　　　　　　　　　　　　　ALBERT BONUS.

NAGGAI.—An ancestor of Jesus, Lk 3[25] (= OT *Nogah*, 1 Ch 3[7] 14[6]).

NAHOR.—Grandfather of Abraham, named in our Lord's genealogy, Lk 3[34].

NAHSHON.—An ancestor of Jesus, Mt 1[4], Lk 3[32].

NAHUM.—An ancestor of Jesus, Lk 3[25].

NAIL.—See CRUCIFIXION, and FEET.

NAIN (Ναΐν אBCD Ti WH, etc.; Ναείν EGΓΔ, etc., Ναείμ 1 and 209, al pauc) is named only once in Scripture. St. Luke mentions it (7[11]) as the 'city' to which the widow, whose dead son Jesus raised to life, belonged. The miracle was wrought near to the 'gate,' and in the presence of 'much people.' This Nain cannot be the same as the village on the E. side of the Jordan mentioned by Josephus (*BJ* IV. ix. 4). Robinson (*BRP*[2] ii. 361) identified Nain with the modern *Nein*, a collection of squalid huts on the N. slope of *Jebel ed-Duhy* (Little Hermon), 2 miles W. of Endor and about a day's journey from Capernaum (cf. Lk 7[1. 11 (margin)]). Robinson's view has been generally accepted. It agrees roughly with the statements of Eusebius and Jerome, both of whom place it S. of Tabor and not far from Endor. Eusebius reckons it 12 miles to the south (*Onom. s.v.* Ναείν), Jerome (*ib. s.v.* 'Naim') says 2 miles. The situation of the present village is bleak and uninviting, though it commands a wide and interesting view. A few hundred paces above the huts, to the S.E., are rock-tombs in the hillside. Ramsay (*Education of Jesus*, Preface, p. ix) says he has 'little doubt that the ancient city was on the top' of the hill, somewhere above the modern village. He expresses his belief that this site has more claim to be the 'city set on a hill' (Mt 5[14]) than Safed. It should be noted that Cheyne doubts the correctness of the reading Ναΐν here (*Encyc. Bibl.* iii. 3263), and claims Nestle (*Philol. Sacra*, 20) as also recognizing 'the doubtfulness of the locality assigned in Luke.'

LITERATURE.—Hastings' *DB* iii. 477; Stanley, *SP* 357; Thomson, *Land and Book*, 445; Tristram, *Land of Israel*, 127; Buhl, *GAP* 217; Guérin, *Galilée*, i. 115 f.; Neubauer, *Géog. du Talm.* 188; Sanday, *Sacred Sites of the Gospels*, 24, 101; Baedeker-Socin, *Pal.* 346; Murray, *Handbook for S. and P.* 349.
　　　　　　　　　　　　　　A. W. COOKE.

NAKEDNESS (γυμνότης).—Oriental dress is generally a draping of the figure in one or more continuous gowns or cloaks. The clothing may be drawn to the body by the waist-band or sash, but the tendency is to avoid as far as possible any exact shaping and rigid fastening of the costume, as such close adaptation to the figure is considered both immodest and undecorative, and in a warm climate would cause friction and perspiration (Ezk 44[18]). With Orientals, to a greater extent than in the West, out-door dress carries a meaning of investiture and embellishment, with a consciousness of self-appreciation and an expectation of comment. This is partly because in the daytime, in the retirement of the family, they undress more than is customary in the West. In the OT, the garments that were continually put on and off, as one went out and returned to the house, were called suits of apparel or exchange (Jg 17[10], Is 3[22]). The cotton or linen gown worn beneath these is the permanent under-garment, and any one wearing only this is conventionally said to be naked or unclothed. In this loose costume—a long robe reaching to the feet—members of the family, both male and female, attend to their active household duties, or enjoy the passive luxury of the unoccupied hour. It is, however, unbecoming to receive visitors in such undress, and hence the impropriety of entering without due announcement and permission received, or of looking down from the flat roof of the house into a neighbour's enclosure. The linen cloth mentioned in Mk 14[51. 52] was a substitute for the ordinary under-garment. The solitary fisherman when diving from the side of the Lake of Galilee after his cast-net usually divests himself of all clothing. The same is frequently done in summer weather when fishermen haul the drag-net into the boat (Jn 21[7]), or a loincloth is worn, as in the case of the tanner and potter at their work.

Nakedness thus means: (1) the state of undress permitted in Oriental family life, and preferred as an adaptation to the climate; (2) insufficiency, amounting sometimes to complete want, of clothing, involving discomfort and suffering in the case of the poor and destitute (Mt 25[36], Ro 8[35], 2 Co 11[27]); (3) the nudity connected with immodest behaviour (Ex 20[26]), or inflicted as a humiliation on prisoners of war (Is 20[4]); and (4) in a metaphorical sense, unnatural and shameless disloyalty to God (Ezk 23[29], Rev 3[18]).   G. M. MACKIE.

NAME ($\mathring{o}νομα$).—**1.** In the Gospels the word is frequently used in the ordinary sense of a distinctive appellation or title, and especially to denote personal proper names (e.g. Mt 10[2], Mk 5[22], Lk 1[5. 27], Jn 1[6]). See following article.

2. Rarely it is found in the sense of 'reputation,' 'fame,' 'glory'—the result of a person's name being on every tongue. So it is said of Jesus, 'His name was spread abroad' (Mk 6[14]; cf. 'a name which is above every name,' Ph 2[9]).

3. But especially $\mathring{o}νομα$ is used, like Heb. שֵׁם, not as a mere external designation, or distinguishing label attached to an individual, but with the suggestion of its significance as characteristic of personality. Hence the importance attached, just as in the OT, to the choosing of a name (Mt 1[21], Lk 1[13. 31. 63]); hence also (cf. Gn 17[5. 15] 32[28]) the alteration of a name, or the addition of another name, when some vital fact of experience has made the character different from what it was before (e.g. Mt 16[17. 18], Ac 13[9]). It is when we remember that 'name' stands for character that we see the force of such an expression as 'to receive a prophet in the name of a prophet' (Mt 10[41]). This does not mean to receive him in the name or for the sake of someone else, but to receive him in his character as a prophet—for his work's sake, and on the ground of what he himself is.

4. This use of $\mathring{o}νομα$ as significant of character is of very frequent occurrence with reference to God —corresponding here again to the employment of שֵׁם in the OT. When Mary sings in the *Magnificat*, 'Holy is his name' (Lk 1[49]), it is the revealed character of God that is meant. When Jesus teaches His disciples in the Lord's Prayer to say, 'Hallowed be thy name' (Mt 6[9]=Lk 11[2]), it is that Divine quality of Fatherhood which He has just set in the very forefront of the prayer that He desires them to hallow. When He did works in His Father's name (Jn 10[25]), He did them by appealing to His Father's self-revelation, and hence by His Father's authority. When He exclaims, 'Father, glorify

thy name' (Jn 12[28]), He is asking the Father to complete in the eyes not only of the Jewish people, but of the great Gentile world represented by those Greek seekers who now stood before Him, the manifestation of His holiness and love given in the Person and ministry of His Son. And when He says in the Intercessory Prayer, 'I have manifested thy name' (17[6], cf. v.[26]), He is speaking once more of that Fatherhood of God of which His own earthly life had been the revelation and the pledge.

5. Corresponding to the foregoing use of $\mathring{o}νομα$ as expressive of the revealed character of God, is the constant employment of the word, not only in the Gospels, but throughout the whole of the NT, to denote the character, dignity, authority, and even the very Personality of Jesus Christ. This is the use made of it by the First Evangelist (Mt 12[21]) when he applies to Jesus the words of Deutero-Isaiah according to the LXX reading, 'And in his name shall the Gentiles hope' (Is 42[4]). The meaning of the author of Acts is similar when he writes, 'The name of the Lord Jesus was magnified' (19[17]). When our Lord speaks of those who 'receive a little child in my name' (Mt 18[5] ||), or gives a gracious promise to the two or three who in His name are gathered together (v.[20]), or assures us that whatsoever we shall ask in His name the Father will bestow (Jn 16[23f.]), He is certainly not speaking of the use of His name as a species of magical formula —nothing could be further from the mind of Christ (cf. Mt 7[22])—but of a service and worship and prayer undertaken for His sake or inspired by faith in His Person. And when in the Johannine writings the very same blessings are assured to those who 'believe on his name' (Jn 1[12] 2[23] 3[18], 1 Jn 3[23] 5[13]) and to those who believe on Himself (Jn 3[16] 6[40], 1 Jn 5[10]; cf. esp., as occurring in close juxtaposition, Jn 3[16] with v.[18], and 1 Jn 5[10] with v.[13]), it seems plain that by 'the name of Jesus' is meant the Personality of Jesus as that has been summed up in 'the name'—the name, above all, of 'only-begotten Son of God' (Jn 3[18], cf. 1 Jn 5[13]).

6. There are certain phrases in which 'the name of Christ' occurs that call for more particular consideration. (1) *Persecution for the name.*— When our Lord said to His disciples that they should be hated and persecuted 'for his name's sake' (Mt 10[22] 24[9], Mk 13[13], Lk 6[22] 21[12. 17]); when 'for his name's sake' shame and suffering actually fell upon the Apostles and the early Church (Ac 5[41] 9[16] 15[26]); and when St. Paul expresses his readiness not to be bound only, but also to die 'for the name of the Lord Jesus' (21[13])—what are we to understand by these expressions? No doubt in several of these cases 'name' is practically synonymous with Person; and so to suffer for Christ's name is equivalent to suffering for His sake—an alternative phrase which is also employed (Jn 13[37. 38], 2 Co 12[10], Ph 1[29]). But sometimes it seems more natural to think of the primary meaning of 'name' as an external designation. The expression $\mathring{υ}πὲρ τοῦ$ $\mathring{ο}νόματος$ used in Ac 5[41] (RV 'for the Name') and 3 Jn [7] (RV 'for the sake of the Name') suggests that 'the Name,' like 'the Way' (Ac 9[2] 19[9]), was a technical term, and that to suffer for 'the Name' meant to 'suffer as a Christian' (1 P 4[16]), *i.e.* as one who bore the name of being a disciple of Christ. It is true that the name 'Christian' (wh. see) does not appear to have been originally used by Christ's followers themselves. But at all events it was employed by outsiders (Ac 11[26] 26[28]), and came to be employed especially by enemies (1 P 4[16]). And if the name Χριστιανοί was not current within the Church, there was a party in Corinth that claimed to be distinctively 'of Christ' (Χριστοῦ, 1 Co 1[12]), while St. Paul not only protests, with reference to this claim, 'Is Christ divided?'

(v.[13]), but says a little further on in the Ep., with regard to the whole Christian body, 'Ye are of Christ' (ὑμεῖς δὲ Χριστοῦ, 3[23]). When, again, St. Peter writes, 'If ye are reproached for the name of Christ, blessed are ye' (1 P 4[14]), it is evident that the reproach is brought not so much against the name of Christ itself as against those who bear it (cf. v.[16]). And this view is confirmed when we find St. James speaking of 'the honourable name which was called upon you' (Ja 2[7] RVm), the reference being apparently to Christ's name as a designation that came to be applied to His people — probably from the fact that His name had been invoked over them at the time of their baptism.

(2) *Working of miracles in the name.*—In the Gospels references to the working of miracles (esp. the casting out of evil spirits) with the use of the name are found in Mt 7[22], Mk 9[38f.] = Lk 9[49f.], Lk 10[17], and in the Appendix to Mk.'s Gospel, where, before His Ascension, Jesus is represented as assuring His disciples that those who believe shall have the power of casting out demons in His name (16[17]). In Ac 3[6ff.] (cf. v.[16] 4[10. 30]) St. Peter cures the lame beggar at the gate of the Temple by commanding him in the name of Jesus Christ of Nazareth to walk. In 16[18] St. Paul, with the invocation of the same name, casts the spirit of divination out of the slave-girl at Philippi. In 19[13ff.] certain vagabond Jews, exorcists, take upon themselves to call over those possessed by evil spirits the name of the Lord Jesus, and the sons of Sceva in particular do this to their own confusion; but the implication of the narrative evidently is that the 'special miracles' which had just been wrought by St. Paul himself were accomplished with a like invocation (cf. vv.[11. 12] with v.[13]). In Ja 5[14] the elders of the Church are told to pray over the sick man, 'anointing him with oil in the name of the Lord.'

The view has been taken that this use of the name of Christ for the working of miracles was nothing more than the employment of a theurgic formula, which finds its analogue in the invocations and incantations of ancient magic (so esp. Conybeare, *JQR* viii, ix). We may be sure that in so far as such a use of His name was commanded or approved by our Lord Himself, this view is quite impossible (cf. Mt 7[22]). And as for the Apostolic Church, while it is clear that the name of Jesus was invoked by both Peter and Paul before the performance of a miracle, Peter's prayer, after the miracle at the Temple gate, that God would accompany the use of the name by stretching forth His hand to heal (Ac 4[29. 30]), points to the conclusion that the name of Jesus was invoked by the Apostles in these cases simply because every appeal to God was made through the Person of the Mediator. The influence of Greek and Oriental superstition soon brought into the Church a magical and theurgic element, which gathered specially round the use of Christ's name in formulas of exorcism. But within the Apostolic sphere, at all events, it was not a formula, however sacred, that was believed to cast out demons or work cures. St. James, after enjoining the use of the Lord's name at a sick-bed, adds that 'the prayer of faith shall heal the sick' (Ja 5[15]). And in the case of the impotent man, St. Peter, when the people came crowding into Solomon's Porch, greatly wondering (Ac 3[11]), said, 'By faith in his name hath his name made this man strong . . . yea, the faith which is through him hath given him this perfect soundness in the presence of you all' (v.[16]).

(3) *Baptizing in* (or *into*) *the name.*—Christian baptism, as we meet with it in the Apostolic Church, is performed in (or into) the name of Christ (Ac 2[38] 8[16] 10[48] 19[5], Ro 6[3], Gal 3[27]). On the other hand, in our Lord's parting instructions to the Eleven, as given at the end of Mt., He directs them to baptize 'into (or in; but εἰς is the preposition used) the name of the Father, and of the Son, and of the Holy Ghost' (28[19])—a formula that is found nowhere else in the NT. This is not the place to discuss the genuineness of the logion (in support of it see Resch, *TU* x. 2, summarized by Marshall in *ExpT* vi. [1895] p. 395 ff.; Bruce, *Kingdom of God*, p. 258 ff.; against it, Holtzmann, *NT Theol.* i. 378 ff.; Harnack, *Hist. of Dog.* i. 79; Moffatt, *Hist. NT*, p. 647 ff. See, further, art. BAPTISM, § 5). But if we accept the triple formula as coming from the lips of Jesus, the fact that we have no direct evidence of its use in the Apostolic Church certainly creates a difficulty. The suggestion that the shorter form is simply a designation of the fact that baptism was administered on confession of Jesus as Christ and Lord, and that the Trinitarian formula would invariably be employed in the actual administration of the sacrament, does not meet the case, for we know that in the 3rd cent. a baptism in the name of Christ was still common, and that in the time of Cyprian the controversy about re-baptism gathered round this very point.

The solution of the problem may lie in the fact that at first the efficacy of baptism was not attached to any set form of words. The Trinitarian formula itself occurs in different versions. Justin gives it after a paraphrastic fashion (*Apol.* i. 61); Tertullian associates the name of the Church with the names of the Three Persons of the Trinity (*de Bapt.* vi.), and a like usage is found in the Syrian Church (see Scholten, *Taufformel*, p. 39). Corresponding to this lack of fixity in the longer form is the absence of anything like uniformity in the shorter one. The name used is 'Jesus Christ,' or 'the Lord Jesus,' or perhaps even simply 'Christ' (1 Co 1[13] suggests the last); while the relation to the name is variously expressed by εἰς, ἐν, ἐπί (ἐπὶ [or ἐν] τῷ ὀνόματι Ἰησοῦ Χριστοῦ, Ac 2[38]; εἰς τὸ ὄνομα τοῦ Κυρίου Ἰησοῦ, Ac 8[16] 19[5]; ἐν τῷ ὀνόματι τοῦ Κυρίου, Ac 10[48]; εἰς Χριστὸν Ἰησοῦν, Ro 6[3]; εἰς Χριστόν, Gal 3[27]). It is hardly legitimate to simplify this diversity by assuming, with Dean Armitage Robinson, that εἰς and ἐν are really synonymous in every case, and that 'in the name,' not 'into the name,' is always the proper English rendering (*EBi* i. 473). No doubt it is true, as he says, that 'the interchangeability of the two prepositions in late Greek may be plentifully illustrated from the NT' (cf. J. H. Moulton, *Gram. of NT Gr.* i. 62, 66, 234 f.). But this is far from deciding the question whether in the case of baptism they are used indifferently, and passages like Ro 6[3], 1 Co 12[13], Gal 3[27] strongly suggest that they are not.

All this diversity of usage seems to show that slight importance was attached at first to the question of a formula, provided that it was clearly understood what Christian baptism meant, and what it implied. Relation to Christ was the essential matter. And as Christian baptism in the NT is invariably conditional upon confession of Christ, so it was administered with an appeal to Christ's authority (ἐν τῷ ὀνόματι); it depended for its reality upon a faith that rested on His name (ἐπὶ τῷ ὀνόματι); and it was the outward symbol of an actual union with His Person (εἰς τὸ ὄνομα).

LITERATURE.—The Lexx. of Grimm-Thayer and Cremer, *s.v.* ὄνομα; Hastings' *DB*, art. 'Name'; *PRE*[3], art. 'Name'; Böhmer, *Das biblische* '*Im Namen*' (1898); Conybeare, 'Christian Demonology' in *JQR* viii, ix; Scholten, *Das Taufformel*; Deissmann, *Bibelstudien*, 181 ff.; *ExpT* vi. [1895] 247, 395, xi. [1899] 3, xv. [1904] 294; *Expositor*, Oct. 1902, p. 251 ff.; F. H. Chase and J. A. Robinson in *JThSt*, July 1905 (vi. 481), Jan. 1906 (vii. 186), Jan. 1907 (viii. 161). J. C. LAMBERT.

NAMES.—Jewish children usually received their names very soon after their birth; in the case of male children, at the time of their circumcision on the eighth day (Lk 1⁵⁹ 2²¹). The name was selected in honour of a parent or relative (1⁵⁹), or because of some circumstance connected with the birth of the child, as in the case of Thomas (Aram. תְּאוֹמָא, Gr. Θωμᾶς), meaning 'twin'; in the case of our Lord and of John the Baptist the name had been selected beforehand by special Divine communication (Mt 1²¹, Lk 1¹³). Indeed, Jewish names generally were significant, referring to some trait in the child, actual or prophetic; some feeling or hope of the parent, at the time of the birth, though this was perhaps not so generally true as in the early OT period. Such old-fashioned names still survived in names like *Nathanael* (Ναθαναήλ, Heb. נְתַנְאֵל 'God gave'); *Zachariah* (Ζαχαρίας, Heb. זְכַרְיָה 'Jehovah remembered').

Surnames were quite common in NT times. Frequently one person was distinguished from another of the same name by the adding of the father's name, joined by the Aramaic word *bar* (בַּר), 'son of,' as in *Simon bar-Jona* (Mt 16¹⁷), and also in such names as *Bartholomew*, 'son of Tolmai,' and *Barabbas*, 'son of a father.' The Greek idiom is frequently followed, however, as in Jn 21¹⁷ 'Simon of Jonas'; or, written more fully with υἱός, 'son,' 'Simon son of Jonas' (1⁴²).

The presence of two names for the same person in the Gospels is sometimes to be accounted for by the fact that many of the people of Palestine in Christ's day were bilingual. Hence persons would have an Aramaic and a Greek name, the second translating the first, or being quite similar in sound. The Greek for *Thomas* ('twin') was *Didymus* (Jn 11¹⁶); for *Cephas* (כֵּיפָא 'stone') it was *Peter* (Πέτρος, 1⁴²). Many of the Jews mentioned in the Gospels are known to us only by Greek names, so widespread had the influence of that language become; cf. Φίλιππος, *Philip* (1⁴⁵), and Ἀνδρέας, *Andrew* (Mt 4¹⁸).

A noteworthy feature of personal names in Christ's day—though the custom existed much earlier and was widespread (cf. Gn 32²⁸, Dn 1⁷)— was that of changing the name or adding a new name at some important crisis in the life, or because of some manifest characteristic of the person so named (Mt 16¹⁸, Mk 3¹⁶, ¹⁸).

Surnames were sometimes given from the place where one lived or from which one came, as in the case of Judas Iscariot (wh. see), Mk 3¹⁹; or from the party to which one belonged: Simon the Zealot (Ζηλωτής), Lk 6¹⁵.

On names applied to Christ see following article.

LITERATURE.—Hastings' *DB*, art. 'Names, Proper'; *EBi*, art. 'Names'; Schürer, *HJP* ii. i. 47; A. Wright, *Some N.T. Problems*, 56 (in St. Mark), 74 (in St. Luke).

E. B. POLLARD.

NAMES AND TITLES OF CHRIST. — That special significance is attached in the Gospels to the names which are applied to our Lord, is clearly suggested by the reason assigned by the angel of the Lord for the name which he directed Joseph and Mary to bestow upon the Babe whose birth he foretold. 'Thou shalt call his name Jesus: for he shall save his people from their sins' (Mt 1²¹). This explanation of the name Jesus suggests that the other titles that are used to distinguish our Saviour have each its own didactic purpose, and are intended to shed light on some special aspect of Christ's mission and nature.

1. Jesus.—The name Divinely bestowed upon our Lord, 'Jesus' (Ἰησοῦς, the Gr. equivalent of the Heb. *Joshua* or *Jeshua* יְהוֹשׁוּעַ, יֵשׁוּעַ), 'Jehovah is salvation,' was one of the commonest of male names among the Jews. Its bestowal upon Christ had, as is expressly stated in Mt 1²¹, peculiar and special significance. It meant that the bearer of the name should in this unique instance of its application be in the fullest sense all that the word meant, the Divinely sent Saviour of His people, and in particular that the salvation which He should work out should be a moral and spiritual, not a temporal deliverance. The name Jesus, as being that by which He was commonly known among His countrymen, is used by the Evangelists as a proper name, with or without the addition of other names or titles employed by way of distinction. See separate article and also SALVATION.

2. Immanuel.—In connexion with the miraculous birth of Jesus and with the assurance that in Him should be fulfilled the promise of the Messiah, St. Matthew applies the prophecy (Is 7¹⁴), 'Behold, a virgin shall be with child, and shall bring forth a son, and they shall call his name Immanuel, which is, being interpreted, God with us' (Mt 1²³). The thought present to the Evangelist, in his use of this prophecy of Isaiah, is that which was embodied in the OT types of the Tabernacle and the Temple, and may be compared with the use in the Fourth Gospel of the expression, 'The Word was made flesh and dwelt (ἐσκήνωσεν, lit. 'tabernacled') among us' (Jn 1¹⁴). The name Immanuel, as applied to Christ in respect of His Incarnation, thus denotes the union of the Divine and the human natures in the person of the God-man. See also separate article.

3. Christ.—This name (Χριστός, 'anointed,' the exact equivalent in Greek of the word 'Messiah' מָשִׁיחַ) holds a very important place among the titles of our Lord.

The word is variously applied in the OT. It is used of the high priest, who is called 'the anointed priest' (ὁ ἱερεὺς ὁ χριστός [הַכֹּהֵן הַמָּשִׁיחַ]), or more fully, ὁ ἱερεὺς ὁ χριστὸς ὁ τετελειωμένος, 'the anointed priest who has been consecrated,' the participle τετελειωμένος, 'consecrated,' being added to the translation apparently in order to call attention to the meaning of the anointing (Lv 4⁵, cf. 6²²). Its use as a designation of kings is familiar, as in the title 'the Lord's anointed' (ὁ χριστὸς τοῦ Κυρίου [מְשִׁיחַ יְהוָה]) applied to Saul (2 S 11⁴ etc.), to David (2 S 19²¹, Ps 89³⁸. ⁵¹ 132¹⁰. ¹⁷), to Cyrus, in connexion with his mission as the deliverer of God's people (Is 45¹). It is applied even to the people of Israel as a nation consecrated to God (Ps 105¹⁵ || 1 Ch 16²², Hab 3¹³). It occurs as a title of the expected Messiah in Ps 2² and Dn 9²⁵. In the latter book it occurs with special reference to royal authority, as a result of which it came to be regularly used as the recognized title of Israel's promised deliverer; cf. its use in the Book of Enoch (48¹⁰ 52⁴), an apocalyptic work which strongly influenced the theology of the Hebrews.

The word is used in the Gospels, but very rarely, as a proper name, in the first chapters of St. Matthew and St. Mark, where the subject of the narrative is mentioned in such expressions as 'Jesus Christ, son of David, son of Abraham' (Mt 1¹), 'Jesus Christ' (Mk 1¹, where υἱοῦ τοῦ θεοῦ is omitted by the best authorities), or where Jesus of Nazareth is distinguished from others who bore the same name, as in the phrase 'Jesus who is called Christ' (Mt 27¹⁷. ²², cf. Mt 1¹⁶). It appears as a proper name in the passage in which St. Matthew, commenting upon the genealogy of the family of Abraham, notes that 'from the carrying away to Babylon *unto the Christ* there were fourteen generations (Mt 1¹⁷); and probably also in the one passage in which the word occurs without the article (Mk 9⁴¹), where Jesus uses the words 'because ye belong to Christ.' With these exceptions the name has in the Gospels some special reference to our Lord's offices and claims, or to the Messianic expectations of the Jews. Thus it is said of Simeon (Lk 2²⁶) that it was revealed to him that he should not see death till he had seen 'the Lord's Christ' (τὸν χριστὸν Κυρίου—the familiar LXX translation of מְשִׁיחַ יְהוָה 'the Lord's anointed,' the title of all Hebrew kings), and the angel announced to the shepherds the birth of a Saviour 'who is Christ the Lord' (Lk 2¹¹). We learn from St. Matthew (2²) that the Magi inquired in Jerusalem, 'Where is he that is born King of the Jews?' Herod, who took this as referring to the current form of the Messianic hope, and regarded the Messiah concerning whom the inquiry was made as a possible rival to himself, called the chief priests and scribes, and put the question of the Magi in another form, demanding 'where *the Christ* should be born.' Herod and the Jewish rulers evidently considered the title 'Christ' as synonymous with that of 'King of the Jews,' in accordance with the general expectation current at the time. To them the Messiah was a king who should derive his royal authority from his Davidic descent and reign as a temporal prince. The Jews, in fact, influenced largely by their apocalyptic literature, had so narrowed their conceptions of the meaning of the title 'Messiah' as to make it signify little more than a king by Divine right, and, leaving out of account all other elements of the Messianic promise, to associate it with thoughts of a kingdom which was of this world. Our Lord, probably for this reason, refrained from claiming the title for Himself, and discouraged its use by others. He forbade the demons whom He cast out of those possessed to confess that He was Christ (Lk 4[41], cf. Mk 1[25. 34] etc.). When Peter, in reply to the direct question, 'Who say ye that I am?' confessed His Messiahship, Jesus strictly commanded the disciples to tell no man that He was the Christ (Mt 16[20]). On the other hand, He revealed Himself as the Christ to the woman of Samaria (Jn 4[25. 26]). He answered the doubting message of John, 'Art thou he that should come, or do we look for another?' by pointing in proof of His Messianic claims to His teaching and His works of beneficence (Mt 11[2-6] || Lk 7[19-23]). Even at the beginning of His ministry He accepted the confession of the first disciples when they acknowledged Him to be the Messiah (Jn 1[41ff.]), as He afterwards accepted the confession of Peter (Mt 16[16]); and when the high priest adjured Him to declare whether He was the Christ, He answered in the affirmative (Mt 26[63] || Mk 14[61] || Lk 22[67]); and before His final rejection, when the Jews challenged Him, 'How long dost thou make us to doubt? If thou be the Christ, tell us plainly,' He replied that He had already told them, and that His claim was confirmed by the works which He did in the Father's name (Jn 10[24. 25]). The murmuring of the people when He spoke of the lifting up of the Son of Man, showed that by that time the impression produced by His ministry was that He did claim to be the Christ. Jesus had just said, 'I, if I be lifted up from the earth, will draw all men unto me,' to which the people replied, 'We have heard out of the law that Christ abideth for ever: and how sayest thou, The Son of Man shall be lifted up?' (Jn 12[32ff.]); and again St. John tells us, in connexion with the incident of the cure of the man who had been born blind, that the Jews had agreed that if any man should confess that Jesus was the Christ, he should be put out of the synagogue (Jn 9[22]).

From these various instances the conclusion appears to be, that Jesus discouraged the application to Himself of the title 'Christ' in every case in which it was likely to be misunderstood or to lead the people, with their narrow views as to what the Messiah should be, to form inadequate conceptions of the nature and scope of His actual claims and His actual mission.

His aim throughout His ministry was to correct the current conceptions of the expected Messiah by calling attention to the spiritual significance of the national hope, and to the true meaning of that word which was so often upon their lips, thus gradually preparing them to accept Himself as the Deliverer who had been promised and whom

they required. This explains, on the one hand, His reticence on most occasions as to His personal claim to be the Christ; and, on the other hand, His frankness at other times, as when He revealed Himself as the Christ to the woman of Samaria, who had learned to look upon the promised Messiah as One who should reveal the Father and the Father's will.

Jesus sought to effect His purpose in various ways. To adduce one conspicuous example, He called the attention of the Pharisees to a well-known Messianic prophecy, evidently in order to correct that popular belief which they shared. He asked them, 'What think ye of Christ? Whose son is he?' (Mt 22[42f.], cf. Mk 12[35f.] || Lk 20[41]), clearly treating the matter as a question in Biblical theology or Scripture interpretation. They answered His question in terms of the belief then current, 'The son of David.' Then Jesus, by quoting from the Psalms a passage which they understood to be not only distinctly Messianic, but an utterance of David himself (Ps 110[1]), showed some of the practical difficulties involved in the belief that the Messiah of prophecy owed his authority to his Davidic descent. 'How is David's son David's Lord?' Thus our Lord suggested the need there was of carefully revising the whole question of Messianic prophecy, that the people should ask themselves whether they had taken into account not one element or aspect of the problem only, but all that the prophets had spoken concerning the Christ. Until they had done this and were in a position to judge the Person, mission, work, and claims of Jesus by the light shed upon the subject by such a careful study of the whole question, they must necessarily find not merely the teaching and work of Jesus, but the OT revelation itself, a dark problem full of insoluble enigmas.

Thus Jesus sought gradually to lead His countrymen to rise above their narrow views, and, instead of making an unintelligent use of words and names, mere signs of spiritual truths, to apprehend the thing signified by them. Thus He taught them that 'the Christ,' 'the Messiah,' 'the Lord's Anointed,' simply meant 'him whom the Father sanctified and sent into the world' (Jn 10[36]) that He might 'do the' Father's 'will and finish his work' (Jn 4[34], cf. 17[4]). The anointing which the name denoted, and of which under the old economy priests and kings, as types of the coming Deliverer, were the subjects, was only a symbol of the Holy Spirit by whose effectual working God's will was done. The Christ of God, the Anointed One by way of eminence, the Antitype to which those types more or less clearly pointed, was He upon whom the Spirit of God rested and abode according to the prophecy (Is 11[2. 3]), and who was thus equipped for the fulfilment of the Father's will. We may compare with this what we learn from the Fourth Gospel of the manner in which the Baptist knew that Jesus was the Christ. The appointed sign was the descent upon Him of the Spirit in the form of a dove. 'Upon whom thou shalt see the Spirit descending, and remaining on him, the same is he which baptizeth with the Holy Ghost' (Jn 1[33]). That was the anointing which constituted Him the Christ, and by which He was publicly set apart for the perfect accomplishment of the Father's purpose of redemption. This truth was not fully learned, and therefore the name in which the truth was enshrined could not be used, with a correct understanding of its meaning, even by the most intimate disciples of Jesus, until after the Resurrection, when they knew that the doing of the Father's will, for which He had been anointed with the Spirit, involved the sufferings, death, and resurrection of the Christ (Lk 24[46]), after which, and as a result of which, Christ should impart to His followers the gift of the Holy Ghost, and so communicate to them all the benefits of His redemptive work. See also art. MESSIAH.

4. Son of David ; King of Israel ; King of the Jews.—These titles, closely connected with that of 'Christ,' and, like it, associated in the minds of the people with inadequate conceptions of Messianic prophecy, were little favoured by our Lord. They had, however, their own significance for the Evangelists in respect of their bearing upon the fulfilment of prophecy. St. Matthew in the beginning of his Gospel calls Jesus 'son of David,' and prefaces his narrative with a genealogical table in which he notes Christ's place in history as a descendant of the royal house of David (Mt 1$^{1ff.}$), while in ch. 2 he calls attention to the general expectation prevalent among the nations that the Messiah should appear as a Prince of the house of Judah (Mt 2^2). St. Luke also traces the genealogy of Jesus, and calls attention to His descent from David, in connexion with which he explains how it happened that He was born in Bethlehem, though the home of Mary and Joseph was in Nazareth in Galilee (Lk 2$^{1ff.}$ 3$^{23-38}$). The Evangelist further emphasizes the point of our Lord's Davidic descent by recording the words of Gabriel at the Annunciation : 'The Lord God shall give unto him the throne of his father David' (Lk 1^{32}). The aim of these Evangelists in noting these points is to show that in Jesus of Nazareth, OT prophecy, and, in particular, the promise that the Christ should come of the house of David, find their fulfilment. The connexion between the Old Covenant and the New having been thus established, and Jesus proved to be the subject of OT prophecies of the coming Deliverer, the title ' Son of David ' ceases to be used or referred to until the Gospel narrative reaches the closing scenes of the life of Christ. Then we learn that Jesus was addressed as 'Son of David ' by the two blind men (Mt 9^{27}), by the Syrophœnician woman (Mt 15^{22}), by the blind men at Jericho (Mt 20^{30} ‖ Mk 10$^{47.48}$ ‖ Lk 18$^{38.39}$) ; and that He was saluted as such by the multitude at His triumphal entry into Jerusalem (Mt 21^9 ‖ Mk 11^{10}). That the popular belief made the Davidic descent of the Messiah an essential element, is illustrated by the exclamation of the multitude on the occasion on which He healed one 'possessed with a devil, blind and dumb,' 'Is not this the son of David ?' (Mt 12^{23}) ; by the objection raised at another time by those who maintained that Christ should come not from Galilee, but 'of the seed of David, and out of the town of Bethlehem, where David was' (Jn 7^{42}) ; and by the answer of the Pharisees to our Lord's question, 'What think ye of Christ ?' (Mt 22^{42}, cf. Mk 12^{35} ‖ Lk 20^{41}).

Closely connected with the title ' Son of David ' are those of 'King of Israel ' and 'King of the Jews.' Jesus is spoken of as a 'King of the Jews' by the Magi (Mt 2^2, cf. Lk 1$^{32.33}$), and the first recorded instance of His being addressed as 'King of Israel ' is the confession of Nathanael, 'Thou art the Son of God, thou art the King of Israel' (Jn 1^{49}). All other instances of the use of these titles belong to the narrative of the last week of Christ's ministry. He was hailed as 'King of Israel ' (Jn 12^{13}, cf. Lk 19^{38}) at His triumphal entry, when He seemed to be on the point of acceding to the popular desire, and when He so far countenanced it by literally and in the most public manner fulfilling the prophecy of Zechariah (9^9), riding into Jerusalem upon a young ass, the use of which He had claimed on the ground that ' the Lord hath need of him ' (Mt 21^3 ‖ Mk 11^3 ‖ Lk 19^{31}). The title appears after this in direct connexion with the sufferings and death of Jesus, whose claim to be ' Christ, a King,' was the pre-

text used by the chief priests for delivering Him over to Pilate (Lk 23^2). Pilate, hearing this charge brought against his prisoner, asked Jesus, ' Art thou the King of the Jews ?' (Mk 15^2 ‖ Lk 23^3). Jesus replied in the affirmative, but explained that the Kingdom which He claimed was spiritual, not temporal (Jn 18$^{33-37}$). After this the titles ' King of Israel ' and ' King of the Jews ' are ' applied to Jesus by Pilate, the Roman soldiers, and the Jews, with associations of mockery and abuse (Mt 27$^{29.42}$ ‖ Mk 15$^{18.32}$ ‖ Lk 23^{37} ‖ Jn 19$^{3.14.15}$) ; and with the same associations the title ' King of the Jews ' was affixed to the cross (Mt 27^{37} ‖ Mk 15^{26} ‖ Lk 23^{38} ‖ Jn 19^{19}). The explanation already suggested of our Lord's avoidance of the name Christ has special force here. Misunderstood as those titles were, Jesus systematically discouraged their use as being calculated to create a false impression of His actual claims. The trial before Pilate and Herod and the scene at the Crucifixion themselves illustrate the reason for Christ's refusal to accept the royal honours which the people would have pressed upon Him. In the opinion of Jew and Gentile the royalty of Jesus and His crucifixion as an impostor and malefactor involved a grotesque contradiction. The cry of derision, ' He is the King of Israel, let him come down from the cross ' (Mt 27^{42} ‖ Mk 15^{30}), was but another form of the popular belief that a suffering Saviour was a contradiction in terms, that the Christ could not be subject to death (Jn 12^{34}). See also art. KING.

5. Son of God.—This title, as it was known among the Jews, had in it a very considerable element of ambiguity. We can understand why this was so when we reflect upon the fact that in OT Scripture the expression is more than once used of others besides a Divine Being. It is used of 'angels (Gn 6$^{2.4}$, Job 1^6 2^1 38^7), of kings, and even of the nation of Israel (2 S 7^{14}, Ps 82^6, Ex 4^{22}). In the New Test., again, it is applied to Adam (Lk 3^{38}), where the reference is to the relationship in which by his creation he stands to God ; and Jesus Himself uses the expression ' sons of God ' with reference to believers, where He says that in heaven ' they are equal unto the angels ; and are the ' children (Gr. υἱοί, " sons") of God ' (Lk 20^{36}).

The use of the name as a title of the Messiah is traceable to OT prophecies like that of Ps 2^7 ' Thou art my Son ; this day have I begotten thee.' Thus ' Son of God ' came to be synonymous with ' Christ.' It is possible that it was so used even by Peter in his confession at Cæsarea Philippi (Mt 16^{16}, cf. Mk 8^{29} ' Thou art the Christ,' and Lk 9^{20} ' the Christ of God,' with Jn 6^{69} ' the Holy One of God,' ὁ ἅγιος τοῦ θεοῦ), and it was certainly understood in that sense, *i.e.* as strictly Messianic, by the Jews generally in the time of our Lord. To them the Messiah as such was Son of God. Thus in Nathanael's confession the latter name occurs in conjunction with the Messianic title ' King of Israel '; and John the Baptist, after relating the incident by which the Spirit of God showed him that Jesus was the Christ, concludes with the words, ' I saw and bare record that this is the Son of God ' (Jn 1^{49}, cf. v.^{34}). It is of rare occurrence in the Synoptic Gospels. We find it in the Annunciation : ' That holy thing which shall be born of thee shall be called the Son of God ' (Lk 1^{35}). In the Synoptic accounts of the Baptism and the Transfiguration we learn that on both occasions Jesus was hailed as God's Son by a voice from heaven (Mt 3^{17} ‖ Mk 1^{11} ‖ Lk 3^{22}, cf. Mt 17^5 ‖ Mk 9^7 ‖ Lk 9^{35}). Again, the Synoptists give various instances in which Jesus was called ' Son of God ' by others, as by Satan (Mt 4$^{3.6}$ ‖ Lk 4$^{3.9}$), by the demons whom He cast out of those who were possessed (Mk 3^{11}, Lk 4^{41}), and by the occupants of

Peter's boat after the second stilling of the storm on the lake (Mt 14³³). Again, as already noted, Peter confessed 'Thou art the Christ, the Son of the living God.' To these may be added the testimony at the cross by the centurion and others (Mt 27⁵⁴), 'Truly this was the (a) son of God.' Of its use by Jesus Himself the Synoptists record no direct instance, though they record allusions in His parabolic teaching which clearly point to Himself as the Son of the King (Mt 22²⁰·) or of the Lord of the vineyard (Mt 21³⁷⁻³⁹ || Mk 12⁶⁻⁸ || Lk 20¹³⁻¹⁵), and take note of His acceptance of the title as involved in His answer to the direct questions of the chief priests and scribes, 'Art thou the Christ, the Son of the Blessed?' (Mk 14⁶¹); 'Art thou then the Son of God?' (Mt 26⁶³, cf. Lk 22⁶⁷·⁷⁰). Further, in the baptismal formula Jesus instructs the disciples to baptize in the name of the Father, the Son, and the Holy Ghost (Mt 28¹⁹).

In addition to the instances already cited in which He was called 'Son of God' by others, there are those in which Jesus was challenged to prove Himself Son of God by coming down from the cross, though in the latter case the title is used in its purely Messianic sense as that was currently understood among the Jews (Mt 27⁴⁰).

In the Fourth Gospel, on the other hand, considerable prominence is given to our Lord's claim to be the Son of God. In the discourses of our Lord as recorded by St. John, Jesus clearly conveys the impression that the Divine Sonship there spoken of means very much more than was involved in the popular Messianic use of the name. But even in that Gospel the actual use of the title is confined to a very few passages. Jesus applies it to Himself in the narrative of the man who was born blind (9³⁵⁻³⁷); again (10³⁶) where He says, 'I said, I am the Son of God'; justifying His claim to the title in that passage in which He says 'The Father loveth the Son,' etc. (Jn 5²⁰); in His remarks on the illness of Lazarus: 'This sickness is . . . for the glory of God, that the Son of God may be glorified thereby' (11⁴); and in the Intercessory Prayer (17¹). Elsewhere He is acknowledged as the Son of God by Nathanael (1⁴⁹) and by Martha (11²⁷). Among the charges brought against Him by His enemies this is specially emphasized, that 'He made himself the Son of God' (19⁷).

The conclusion to which we are led by a careful consideration of such instances as we find in the Gospels of the use of the name 'Son of God' is, that, as it had come to be employed by the Jews, it was at best a vague and indefinite term. It did not necessarily involve the conception of essential Deity, eternal participation in the attributes of Godhead. The object of the Gospels was to show how Jesus appeared as the Revealer of the Father, and that salvation could come only through One who was Himself equal with God assuming the nature of humanity, dwelling among men, and suffering in their place. Such a revelation so far transcended the current expectations of the people as to the nature and work of the promised Messiah, that the full realization of the significance of Christ's mission could not be attained until His work was completely accomplished and Jesus was revealed as the Son of God with power. This view of the history of the title 'Son of God' is well illustrated by Wendt (*The Teaching of Jesus*, ii. p. 133): 'According to the Jewish idea, the Messianic King was also Son of God; according to Jesus' idea, the Son of God as such was the Messianic King.' Here as elsewhere Jesus sought to enlarge and elevate the current conception of the Messianic hope, and to show that the Redeemer of Israel and the world was none else than the Son of God, by nature and essence equal with God, and not

in that secondary sense in which that name had hitherto been understood. Such a revelation could be made only gradually, hence the sparing use by Christ of the title 'Son of God.'

The Fourth Gospel gives special prominence to the doctrine of the essential Divine Sonship of Jesus. That indications of it are found in the Synoptists themselves is evident not only from the cases already cited, the testimony of the voice from heaven at the Baptism and at the Transfiguration, and our Lord's argument from Ps 110¹ that Christ must be more than Son of David since David himself calls Him Lord, but from such an utterance as this of our Lord Himself recorded by St. Matthew and St. Luke: 'All things are delivered unto me of my Father: and no man knoweth the Son, but the Father; neither knoweth any man the Father, save the Son, and he to whomsoever the Son will reveal him' (Mt 11²⁷ || Lk 10²²). But our Lord's claim to be Son of God κατ' ἐξοχήν is one of the central features of the Johannine discourses no less than of the teaching of St. John himself. St. John identifies Christ with the Eternal Logos, and calls Him 'the only-begotten of the Father' (Jn 1¹⁴); and Jesus applies to Himself the same expression (3¹⁶·¹⁸) in terms which distinctly assert His essential Sonship and His pre-existence, and declares that the unbelieving are 'condemned already' because they have 'not believed in the name of the only-begotten Son of God' (3¹⁸). Jesus associates His work with that of the Father (5¹⁷), and that in such a way as at once to expose Himself to the charge of blasphemy. So the Evangelist tells us that the Jews sought the more to kill Him, because 'He said also that God was his Father, making himself equal with God' (5¹⁸), their interpretation of His words being justified by His language on other occasions, as when He said, 'Before Abraham was, I am' (8⁵⁸), an expression at once suggestive of the Tetragrammaton, the sacred name Jehovah itself. And notwithstanding the fact that the Jews put such a construction upon His words, Jesus enlarged upon the theme, and claimed for Himself power and authority to give life to the dead and to execute judgment (5¹⁹⁻³⁰). In the same connexion He declares it to be the Father's will 'that all men should honour the Son, even as they honour the Father' (5²³); and in other places asserts His essential oneness with the Father (10³⁰), and claims to have shared His glory 'before the world was' (17⁵). He claims, moreover, to have received from the Father 'power over all flesh,' to 'give eternal life to as many as' the Father has 'given him' (17²); while in more than one passage emphasis is laid upon the fact that He came from God and should return to Him (13³ 6³⁸·⁴⁶·⁶² 7²⁸·³³·³⁶ 8¹⁴·¹⁶·¹⁸·²⁶·⁴² 16²⁸·³⁰). Again, while He teaches His disciples to regard God as their Father (so 20¹⁷, where He says 'My Father and your Father'), and to pray to Him as such (as He does also in the Synoptic Gospels), 'He never places His filial relationship on a level with theirs' (Weiss). On the contrary, He speaks at times of the Fatherhood of God with exclusive reference to Himself, as, *e.g.*, where He says (6⁴⁶), 'Not that any man hath seen the Father, save he which is of God, he hath seen the Father,' a passage which, as Holtzmann points out, 'shows clearly that there the historical appearance of the Son is connected with the supra-historical being of the pre-existent Logos.'

From all this it is evident that while the title 'Son of God,' which had come to be associated with essentially theocratic ideas, as of the election of Israel by the adoption of grace as sons of God, and of the Messiah as King of Israel, and was therefore open to misunderstanding and misconstruction, was seldom used by Jesus or His disciples as a title of our Lord ; the testimony of all the Gospels, and especially of the Fourth, distinctly shows that Jesus claimed to be the Son of God in the strictest sense of the term, as essentially and eternally One with God the Father (cf. St. John's summary of the aim of his Gospel in 20³¹ 'These are written, that ye might believe that Jesus is the Christ, the Son of God ; and that believing ye might have life through his name'). See also sep. article.

6. The Word or The Logos. This name is peculiar to the Fourth Gospel, and there it occurs only in the Prologue (Jn 1¹· ¹⁴). Much controversy has arisen as to the probable sources from which the Apostle derived his conception of Christ as the Logos—a controversy the more natural that the term 'the Word' as used by St. John represents the meeting point of Hebrew theology, Hellenic philosophy, and the religion of Jesus Christ. To that controversy little reference need here be made. See art. LOGOS.

The Logos doctrine of St. John may be summarized thus. God's revelation of Himself in the history of mankind is a complete unity. Creation, Providence, and Redemption are parts of the same grand purpose, whose object is the highest well-being of God's creatures, and especially of man, the head and crown of the creation. In each we have God revealing Himself, and that through a Mediator. This Mediator, more or less darkly imagined by mankind from the beginning until these last times, and more or less clearly revealed to God's chosen people in the days of the fathers as the Angel of the Covenant or the Angel of the Presence, is the same in whom He has now manifested Himself, the Christ by whom God has now spoken to those to whom the promise was given, and who had long been expecting their Messiah, and to all the sons of men, as many as will receive Him. Thus is the Christ, the Redeemer of Israel, the very Word of God, the last, the perfect revelation of the Most High, and the Redeemer of the world.

The Prologue of the Gospel is St. John's appeal to the nations, and speaks thus : ' In Christ Jesus, whom we knew, who as a man among men companied with us, God has spoken, has manifested Himself to us who beheld His glory, and to all that have welcomed that Word of the Father. In Christ the Word was made flesh and dwelt among us. In Him was life, and the life was the light of men.' This conception of Christ as the Logos, the same that was in the beginning with God, necessarily involves the doctrine of the essential Deity and eternal pre-existence of Christ. But the point which St. John specially brings out by his use of the term is that in Christ God perfectly reveals Himself to man, and gives to all that receive Christ that adoption by which they may become ' children of God ' (τέκνα θεοῦ, not υἱοί, Jn 1¹²; cf. 1 Jn 3¹). Having in the Prologue established this point, St. John makes no further use of the term Logos in his Gospel, where ' Son ' or ' Son of God ' takes its place.

7. Son of Man.—This title seems to have been most favoured by our Lord, and occurs with great frequency, especially in the Synoptic Gospels. Two typical instances may be given of our Lord's preference for this name. One is found in the Gospel of St. John, where the title least frequently occurs — that of Christ's answer to Nathanael, who had just acknowledged Him as Son of God. Jesus, accepting Nathanael's confession, replied thus : ' Because I said unto thee, I saw thee under the fig-tree, believest thou ? thou shalt see greater things than these. And he saith unto him, Verily, verily, I say unto you, Hereafter ye shall see heaven open, and the angels of God ascending

and descending upon the Son of Man ' (Jn 1⁵⁰· ⁵¹). The other is His reply to the adjuration of the high priest, who asked Him whether He was the Christ the Son of God, in which again, immediately after acknowledging that such was His claim, He spoke of Himself as Son of Man, and that in connexion with a prophecy of His appearing on the right hand of power, and coming in the clouds of heaven (Mt 26⁶³· ⁶⁴ ‖ Mk 14⁶¹· ⁶² ‖ Lk 22⁶⁷⁻⁷⁰). For the origin and history of the title ' Son of Man,' see separate article.

With regard to the question as to the sense in which Jesus used the title ' Son of Man,' the answer is suggested by the connexion in which at various times He so described Himself. It may be briefly stated in this way : God manifesting Himself to man in a form which man as man can understand. Comparing the passages in which the title is used by Christ, the first thing that strikes us is that He uses it in connexion both with His humiliation and with His exaltation. We find it associated with thoughts of the privations and sufferings of Jesus,—as where He says : ' Foxes have holes, and the birds of the air have nests ; but the Son of Man hath not where to lay his head ' (Mt 8²⁰ ‖ Lk 9⁵⁸). It occurs repeatedly in connexion with His sufferings and death, as where He tells His disciples that as John was slain by Herod, so shall it be done to the Son of Man (Mt 17¹² ‖ Mk 9¹²). Again, that the Son of Man must ' be delivered into the hands of men ' (Lk 9⁴⁴ ‖ Mt 17²², cf. Mt 20¹⁸ ‖ Mk 10³³ ‖ Lk 18³¹⁻³³, Mt 26⁴⁵ ‖ Mk 14⁴¹), ' and suffer many things ' (Mk 8³¹ ‖ Lk 9²²). Thus also Jesus states this as the mission of the Son of Man, that He ' came not to be ministered unto, but to minister, and to give his life a ransom for many ' (Mt 20²⁸ ‖ Mk 10⁴⁵). Again, the title is used where the thought expressed is that of the sympathy of Jesus with human joys as with human sorrows, in the contrast drawn between the asceticism of John and the sociable disposition of our Lord (Mt 11¹⁸· ¹⁹ ‖ Lk 7³³· ³⁴); while the same thought appears in another form, where Jesus, justifying His acceptance of the hospitality of Zacchæus, says : ' The Son of Man is come to seek and to save that which was lost ' (Lk 19¹⁰). In other passages the use of the name suggests the coexistence of Messianic authority with the lowliness of Christ's human nature, as in the narrative of the healing of the paralytic, in connexion with which Jesus says that ' the Son of Man has power on earth to forgive sins ' (Mt 9⁶ ‖ Mk 2¹⁰ ‖ Lk 5²⁴); and St. Matthew notes the impression produced upon the multitude, as that ' they marvelled, and glorified God which had given such power unto *men.*' To this class of passages may be referred also our Lord's saying concerning blasphemy against the Son of Man and that against the Holy Ghost (Mt 12³²). The Son of Man, in His humiliation, veiling His Divine nature, appearing to men like one of themselves, may not be recognized for what He is. Blasphemy against Him, therefore, as resulting only from ignorance and unbelief, admits of forgiveness ; whereas blasphemy against the Spirit of God, a presumptuous offence against the Deity, cannot be forgiven. Again, the title is used of Jesus in respect of His representative character, where He asserts His right as Son of Man to interpret the Sabbath law (Mt 12⁸ ‖ Mk 2²⁷· ²⁸). ' Jesus regarded the institution from a philanthropic point of view, and He claimed lordship over it for the Son of Man on the ground of His sympathy with mankind, which He deemed a far more reliable interpreter of the Divine purpose and guide in observance, than the merciless rigour of the Rabbis ' (Bruce, *Kingdom of God*, p. 174). A connecting link between these uses of the title and those which specially refer to Christ's

Exaltation is found in those passages in which Jesus so calls Himself with reference to His mission as Founder of the Kingdom of God. So in the parable of the Tares. 'He that soweth the good seed is the Son of Man' (Mt 13³⁷). 'The Son of Man shall send forth his angels' (v.⁴¹). Here Jesus identifies the Founder of the Kingdom of God in the world with the Judge of the world, using the same title in both connexions. He who as Son of Man seeks with all patience and forbearance to establish His Kingdom by manifestation of the grace of God, is He who must judge mankind according as they have accepted or rejected His message of salvation.

But undoubtedly the most remarkable use of the name Son of Man is that which is directly and specially connected with the thought of Jesus in His Exaltation. We see this in all His predictions of His Second Coming. Thus, speaking of the suddenness and unexpectedness of His appearing, He says : 'At an hour when ye think not the Son of Man cometh' (Mt 24⁴⁴ ∥ Lk 12⁴⁰). The Son of Man is to appear with the suddenness of lightning (Mt 24²⁷ ∥ Lk 17²⁴), and the circumstances of His appearing are compared to those of the world in the days of Noah and of Lot (Mt 24³⁷ ∥ Lk 17²⁶⁻³²). He is to come after the great tribulation (Mt 24³⁰ ∥ Mk 13²⁶ ∥ Lk 21²⁷). His advent is to be announced by 'the sign of the Son of Man appearing in the heavens' (Mt 24³⁰). He is to sit as a King upon the throne of His glory (Mt 25³¹), when His Apostles shall be associated with Him, judging the tribes of Israel (Mt 19²⁸, cf. Lk 22²⁹⁻³⁰).

In the Fourth Gospel the name 'Son of Man' is used in connexion with the pre-existence of Christ : 'No man hath ascended up to heaven but he that came down from heaven, even the Son of Man which is in heaven' (3¹³, cf. 6⁶²). As Son of Man He is Mediator between Heaven and Earth (Jn 1⁵¹). Judgment is committed to the Son of Man as such (Jn 5²⁷). Special emphasis is laid upon associations of this title with the coming judgment (cf. besides the passages just noted, Mt 26⁶⁴ ∥ Mk 14⁶² ∥ Lk 22⁶⁹). Again, Jesus concludes one of His discourses on 'The Last Things' with an emphatic warning to His own disciples to watch and pray that they 'may be accounted worthy . . . to stand before the Son of Man' (Lk 21³⁶). The meaning of all this is plain. The Son of Man as such is the Judge of man. Man is, as it were, to be 'tried by his peers.' The Son of Man, as bearing the nature of man, capable of understanding and sympathizing with him, is to appear at last as the Judge of the human race.

It is clear that the meaning of the title cannot be limited to any of those conceptions which have been suggested of Christ as the ideal of humanity, still less to the thought of the humanity as distinguished from the Divinity of our Lord. It was rather used, as Wendt puts it, very much ' to raise problems and to incite,' among Christ's hearers, ' reflexion and the use of their own judgment.' ' It contained, *in nuce*, through reference to the testimony of OT Scripture,' 'a solution of the paradox of the coexistence' in Jesus 'of lowly humanity with lofty Messianic dignity' (Wendt, *Teaching of Jesus*, ii. p. 148).

8. To these characteristic titles of our Lord may be added those of **Lord, Master** (κύριος, ἐπιστάτης, διδάσκαλος), **Rabbi,** which are variously used. The title 'Lord' appears most frequently as the equivalent of 'Master' (ἐπιστάτης), 'Teacher' (διδάσκαλος) simply. So Martha addressed Jesus as 'Lord' (Κύριε) when complaining of Mary's conduct in the household of Bethany (Lk 10⁴⁰). The same word is used by the disciples in peril on the Sea of Galilee (Mt 8²⁵), in which case the parallels 'Teacher' in St. Mark's account (διδάσκαλε) and

'Master' (ἐπιστάτα) in St. Luke's, illustrate the sense in which it occurs (Mk 4³⁸, cf. Lk 8²⁴). So again, in the narrative of the Transfiguration, where Peter says, 'Lord, it is good for us to be here,' the word κύριε in St. Matthew corresponds to 'Master' (ἐπιστάτα) in St. Luke and 'Rabbi' ('Ραββεί) in St. Mark. Peter addressed Jesus as 'Lord' (Κύριε) when he remonstrated with Him at Cæsarea Philippi (Mt 16²²) ; and the same title is used by the disciples when they ask Jesus to teach them to pray 'as John also taught his disciples' (Lk 11¹) ; again, when they say of Lazarus, 'Lord, if he sleep, he shall do well' (Jn 11¹²), and by Martha and Mary in the same narrative (Jn 11³· ²¹· ²⁷) ; and Jesus Himself uses the title 'Lord' in connexion with that of 'Teacher' (Jn 13¹³) : 'Ye call me Master (teacher) and Lord.'

The title 'Lord' (κύριος) is also applied to Christ, especially by St. Luke, as an alternative for Jesus or Christ, apparently by anticipation, speaking of Jesus in the manner which became current after the Crucifixion. Thus we read that 'the Lord said' to the widow of Nain : 'Weep not' (Lk 7¹³) ; that 'the Lord said, Who then is that faithful and wise steward ?' etc. (12⁴²) ; 'the Lord said, Hear what the unjust judge saith' (18⁶) ; and again, that 'the Lord appointed' the seventy disciples (10¹). Again, in St. John we read, 'When therefore the Lord knew that the Pharisees had heard,' etc. (Jn 4¹) ; that 'the Lord gave thanks' (6²³) ; and that Mary of Bethany was she ' who anointed the Lord with ointment' (11²). Occasionally also the title 'Lord' (κύριος) is applied to Christ where text and context plainly demand that it should be interpreted in the highest sense of the word, as where Elisabeth calls Mary 'the mother of my Lord' (Lk 1⁴³) ; where the angel says, 'a Saviour which is Christ the Lord' (Lk 2¹¹) ; where Thomas addresses Christ, 'my Lord, and my God' (Jn 20²⁸) ; and by Jesus speaking of Himself in connexion with the Last Judgment (Mt 7²¹· ²², cf. 25¹¹ etc.). See also separate articles.

9. The various figurative or parabolic names of Christ do not call for any special remark, as their use by Christ in the passages where they occur sufficiently explains their meaning. Such is that of the **Good Shepherd** (Jn 10²· ¹¹ etc., cf. Lk 15³ff.), where He shows how, like the Shepherd of Messianic prophecy, He tends and protects the sheep entrusted to His care, and how He must lay down His life for them ; and again, that of **the Door of the Sheep,** an expression which means simply that acceptance of Christ by faith is the first condition of entrance into the Kingdom of God (Jn 10⁷· ⁹, cf. 14⁶). Again, impressing upon His hearers the dependence of His disciples upon Himself as the source of their spiritual life, He described Himself as **the Bread of Life** (Jn 6³⁵ff.). The same truth is taught in the parable in which He calls Himself **the True Vine,** with the added thought of fruit-bearing as the legitimate test of life in all that are joined to Him by faith (Jn 15). Again, in justification of His work among the outcasts of society, He compares Himself to **the Physician,** of whose aid only the sick stand in need (Mt 9¹² ∥ Mk 2¹⁷ ∥ Lk 5³¹). Speaking of the conflict of good and evil in the heart of man when first he looks to Christ for help, our Lord uses the similitude of a strong man armed, successfully defending his house against all assailants until there comes one stronger than he who overpowers and binds him, where the meaning of the passage is that Christ is that Stronger One, who breaks the power of the strong man—Satan (Lk 11²¹, Mt 12²⁹ ∥ Mk 3²⁷). Lastly, Christ's mission to save sinners by His vicarious sufferings and death is shadowed forth by the words of John the Baptist (Jn 1²⁹), 'Behold **the Lamb of God** [see SHEEP, § 4] which taketh away the sin of the world.'   See also artt. OFFICES OF CHRIST and PRINCE.

LITERATURE.—Cruden's *Concordance* (sixth ed. unabridged), Preface ; Cremer, *Bib.-Theol. Lex. s.vv.* Χριστός, Κύριος, Λογος, μονογενής, υἱός ; Thayer, *Lex. NT. s.vv.* ἅγιος, Ἐμμανουήλ, Ἰησοῦς, Χριστός, Κύριος, Λογος, μονογενής, υἱός ; Comm. of Meyer, Alford, etc.; Bengel's *Gnomon* ; Wendt, *The Teaching of Jesus*, ii. p. 122 ff. ; Beyschlag, *Christologie d. NT*, p. 10 ff., also *NT Theol.* i. pp. 57 ff., 240 ff., ii. pp. 412-424; Reuss, *Hist. of Chris. Theol. in the Apostolic Age*, i. pp. 72-201 ; H. J. Holtzmann, *Lehrbuch d. NT Theologie*, i. pp. 73-96, 241-268, ii. 397-434 ; Weiss, *Bibl. Theol. NT*, i. 73-92, ii. 325-347 ; Schmid, *Bib. Theol. NT*, pp. 63-90 ; Bruce, *Kingdom of God*, 166-186 ; E. H. Plumptre, *Christ and Christendom*, 131 ; A. Maclaren, *God of the Amen*, 19 ; J. Cairns, *Christ the Morning Star*, 39 ; D. G. Monrad, *World of Prayer*, 219; A. M. Fairbairn, *Christ in Mod. Theology*, 358.   **H. H. CURRIE.**

NAPHTALI (Νεφθαλείμ).—**1. Description.**—With the Captivities all practical use of the tribal divisions came to an end, and, but for such a reference as that given in Mt 4[15] to the OT prophecy of Is 9[1], the lands of Zebulun and Naphtali could scarcely appear as geographical names in the NT. The boundaries of these divisions we can know at best only approximately. Many of the towns named in Joshua's description of the tribal territories are unknown to us, and, besides, the tribes are not likely ever to have had the unbroken compactness the maps would lead us to believe. Villages among the mountains of Naphtali have to this day their arable lands near the shores of the Sea of Galilee, and similarly in Zebulun the inhabitants of Nazareth cultivate portions of the plain of Esdraelon. Thus the tribes might in many cases possess detached portions, and difficulties connected with their extent and boundaries may sometimes be explained from this fact. This uncertainty as regards the boundaries of these tribes is of no consequence to our present purpose, as the indefinite statement in Mt 4[15] cannot be used in any argument regarding the site of Capernaum ; nor can we fix the boundaries from any supposed relationship to that city, as Reland has sought to do (*Pal.* p. 161). The lands of Naphtali then, generally speaking, occupied the N.E. portion of Galilee, together with the west and south of the Lake. Josephus (*Ant.* v. i. 22) defines its northern boundary as Mount Lebanon and the Fountains of Jordan. The Rabbis tell us that ' Naphtali rejoiced in his portion, having seas and fish.' They assign the Sea of Galilee to the portion of Naphtali, and give him also ' a full measure' to the south of the Lake (Bab. *Baba Kama*, 81*b* ; *Sifri* on Dt 33[23]). In Naphtali were represented the three divisions of Galilee —of varying elevation (Mishn. *Shebiith* ix. 2) ; (1) Upper Galilee, from Kefr Hananyah (Kefr Anān) northwards, which is described as the portion ' where the sycamores do not grow' ; (2) Lower Galilee, extending downwards till we reach (3) the third division, which is designated טבריה תהום or העמק—' the depression of Tiberias' or ' the valley.' For description of the last of these districts, see artt. SEA OF GALILEE, and GENNESARET (LAND OF).

From the north end of the Plain of Gennesaret and the Sea of Galilee (-682·5 ft.) the land rises through a series of steep ascents and small plateaux to Safed (+2750 ft.) and Jebel Jermuk (4000 ft.), the highest peak in Western Palestine. To the north of these points, and until the valley of the Litani is reached, we have an undulating tableland, with vast stretches that are arable and everywhere tilled, with swelling hills in view all round, covered with prickly shrubs and trees and forests of small oak. This district is broken into by two deep valleys, somewhat like but narrower than Wady Ḥamam. From the N.W. of the Plain of Gennesaret the Wady Leimon, otherwise called Wady Amūd, and in ancient times מעלת מרון, the ' ascent of Meiron,' extends to the neighbourhood of the village of that name. It is a narrow gorge,

for the most part enclosed by steep rocky walls and natural pillars. It is now impassable, but in ancient times it was accessible to passengers in single file (*Erubhin*, 22*b* ; *Rosh-hash.*, 16*a*). About half-way up this ravine a smaller wady branches off eastward, to beyond the great rock of Akbara— a cliff as grand and impressive as anything met with in Wady Ḥamam. In later days there grew up under its shadow a famous Rabbinical school, and the district was renowned for its coverts of pheasants. Farther north, Upper Galilee is divided by another valley (Wady Fara), almost equally deep, but less rocky. It extends eastward from the neighbourhood of el-Jish, and opens out into the plain beside Lake Ḥuleh and the Jordan.

In the neighbourhood of el-Jish and Taitabeh (said to be the Tishbe of 1 K 17[1]) we meet with three *extinct craters* and quantities of black volcanic rock, and by it the slopes to the Ḥuleh valley and the Jordan as far as the Sea of Galilee are also fringed. Between Kerazeh and Tell Ḥum great quantities of basaltic boulders cumber the ground, and the stones of Tiberias again are black. Volcanic forces have been active in the past. They have created for us these wild gorges and gigantic cliffs, and their continued existence is proved by the hot springs, as also by the frequent earthquakes in ancient (*Ant.* xv. v. 2 ; *Joma* v. 2 ; *Soṭa* viii. 7) and in modern times. Of these latter the most terrible known is that which occurred on 1st Jan. 1837. Elsewhere the rocks of Naphtali are generally a species of limestone, known in Palestine by the name of *nāri*. On the hills above the Lake there are great stretches of these white rocks, hard as flint, bare, desolate, and painful to the eye, especially under the summer sun. But though the surface is hard and glossy, we have only to get below it to find that the rock is really soft. It may be cut with a saw with even greater facility than wood. All sorts of trees—olives, figs, and vines—can send their roots through it and draw nourishment thence, while the hard exposed surface is there to conserve the moisture below. With little trouble these rocky desolations may be turned into vineyards, olive groves, and orchards, and we have every reason to believe that they were such in the early Christian centuries (Bab. *Megilla*, 6*a*).

Naphtali will thus be seen to have, in virtue of its lands of varying altitude and deep depression, a greater variety of climate, scenery, and possible variety of production than any other tribe of Israel. To it more than to any other could be applied the words of promise uttered ere the Land was yet entered—' a land of brooks of water, of fountains and depths that spring out of valleys and hills ; a land of wheat and barley and vines and fig-trees and pomegranates, a land of oil olives and honey ' (Dt 8[7. 8]). Apart from the barren stretches mentioned, these words describe most naturally the state of Naphtali to-day. Different parts are renowned for their varied products—Rameh for the excellence of its olives and its oranges, el-Jish for its vineyards, the north and the Ḥuleh valley for their fine crops of wheat and barley. Elsewhere we meet with the lemon, fig, mulberry, apricot, and even tobacco and tomatoes, in great abundance. As the Targum (on Gn 49[21]) has it, ' Naphtali's lot was cast in a pleasant land.' From shortly after the commencement of the rainy season it is brilliant with flowers—anemones of many varied tints, cyclamens, and lilies, while all its water-courses may be traced by the red bloom of the oleander. The hills are greener than those of any other tribe, and the grass and the spring flowers continue among its uplands long after the rest of Palestine is burned black and bare. This arises from the fact that Naphtali enjoys first and most of all the much praised ' dews of Hermon that descend upon the mountains of Zion' (Ps 133³). When the N.E. wind has come gently blowing over the great mountain, we have seen the dew-clouds rolling down in great volumes over its fields, supplying all nature with fresh vigour and sensations of pleasantness. Modern products, such as oranges, tobacco, and tomatoes, were absent in our Lord's time, as was also another feature that attracts the eye in these days, viz., the great hedges of prickly pear or cactus, by which many of the villages are practically fortified. This plant is of modern importation, though, unfortunately, it has often found its way into pictures of Bible scenes. Compared with the present day, the hills of Naphtali were much more wooded in NT times. Just after such another period of unrest and unsettlement as Galilee had passed through before the Advent, Arculphus, a pilgrim (A.D. 670), found that the hills in his time were wooded down to the shores of the Lake. The woods of Naphtali are mentioned in the Palestinian Talmud (*Baba Bathra* v. 1).

Of the productiveness of the soil there is ample testimony. We are told that Gush Ḥalab (Gischala ; el-Jish) was famous for the quantity of its oil (*Erakhin* ix. 6 ; *Menakhoth*, 85b), and as this was considered to be a border town adjoining the tribe of Asher, the Rabbis saw here a fulfilment of Gn 49²⁰, Dt 33²⁴. Josephus, speaking of the same place, tells us that its people were generally husbandmen, and applied themselves to the cultivation of the fruits of the earth (*BJ* IV. ii. 1). The quality of the wheat of Chorazin and Capernaum is well spoken of (*Men.* 85a). It is elsewhere stated that Naphtali possessed vines and fruitful fields (Bab. *Meg.* 6a), and we meet with incidental reference to the honey of Ṣafed, the indigo of Magdala, and the raw silk of Gush Ḥalab. And, in so far as productiveness is concerned, it must be remembered that whatever may be said of the hills of Naphtali applies with tenfold more force to the Plain of Gennesaret and the southern shore of the Lake (Jos. *BJ* III. x. 8). If the evidence of Josephus and the Talmuds does not all refer to the time of our Lord's ministry, at least it shows us clearly what the district was becoming during that period.

2. The people.—Zebulun and Naphtali were in the year B.C. 135 practically Gentile (1 Mac 5²³), but from that time onward they became gradually reoccupied by a population of Jewish blood, and from the time of this resettlement its people were pre-eminently patriotic (*Ant.* XIV. ix. 2, xv. 10). It was a district of great memories and inspiring scenes, and the new settlers acted up to them. The kind of immigrants—those who sought a freedom unknown at the court of Herod—would guarantee their quality, and, besides, there is something in the free air of the mountains—especially mountains that have a past heroic history—that goes a long way to make heroes and warriors. In B.C. 4, Judas the son of Hezekiah had made an unsuccessful attempt to revolt, and again in A.D. 6, Judas of Galilee and his Zealots (cf. Lk 6¹⁵), declaring 'There is no king but God' (*Ant.* XVIII. i. 6). [With this saying we may compare that in the Jewish Morning Prayer, אֵין לָנוּ מֶלֶךְ אֶלָּא אַתָּה, and its repudiation in the cry of the Jews to Pilate (Jn 19¹⁵), as well as the Galilæan Arabic proverb met with in el-Jish to-day, '*Mā fish sulṭān ghêr alla*,' 'There is no king but God']. The milder government of Antipas, and his presence, as a 'half-Jew,' between them and their conquerors, kept the Zealots at peace during a long period in the 1st cent. (A.D. 6 – A.D. 66), and allowed the population to grow, so that probably all the villages of to-day represent cities of that time (*BJ* III. iii. 2). The population did not in peaceful days sink into sloth and indulgence. They were essentially sturdy sons of hardy toil ; and where commerce, agriculture,

and fishing did not afford employment, they engaged in trades, as in dyeing at Magdala, weaving at Arbela, and pottery manufacture at Kefr Hananyah. Though despised by the people of Jerusalem, Naphtali was itself becoming a centre of learning, and, even before the Christian era, had given birth to one in the direct line of succession as transmitters of the oral law or traditions of the elders (Mt 15²) —Nitai or Mattai of Arbela—who has left us this saying, which is almost characteristic of the people : 'Remove from a bad neighbour, have no partnership in evil, and despair not of reward' (*Pirḳē Aboth* i. 7).

3. Christ's sojourn. — Our Lord's settlement in the lands of Naphtali began probably about January of the year A.D. 27 (Mt 4¹³), a short visit of 'not many days' having been made before the previous Passover (Jn 2¹²). The time of sojourn would then extend till Sept. A.D. 28—a period of about 20 months ; but this was broken in upon by circuits in Galilee (Mk 1³⁴, Lk 8¹⁻³, Mt 9³⁵, Mk 6⁶), to Tyre and Sidon (Mt 15²¹), to Decapolis (Mk 7³¹), to Cæsarea Philippi (Mt 16¹³), and a visit to Jerusalem to the Passover (Jn 5¹). In virtue of Christ's being asked for and paying tribute in Capernaum (Mt 17²⁴), we may conclude that He was recognized as a citizen there ; and the light thrown on this transaction by the Talmud enables us to infer that He had been domiciled in Naphtali one year before the 15th Adar preceding the request for payment (cf. *M. Sheḳalim* i. 3 ; *Baba Bathra* i. 6 ; *Sanhedrin* 112a). As the circuits through Galilee took place for the most part during the hot season, when the inhabitants are in the mountains, we can see, when we consider the smaller Galilee of those days, that the greater part of one year at least would be spent among the people of Naphtali. It was from among them that the Lord chose most of His friends and disciples. It was in Naphtali, too, that He made the selection. It was there that He did most of His mighty works (Mt 11²⁰). Its towns were the best known in Gospel history—Capernaum, Bethsaida, Chorazin, Magdala, and Tiberias—and it was over three of these that He uttered the sentence of woe because they believed not (Mt 11²¹⁻²⁴). It was in Naphtali that most of His teaching, as recorded in the Synoptics, was given. Its flowers, its fruits, its crops, its birds and beasts, its mountain torrents, its manners and customs, were all used to illumine the Gospel message, and to bring light first to its people, and then, through them, along the world's highways to all that sit in darkness. In this, Matthew (4¹⁵), and with him the whole Christian world, sees the fulfilment of Isaiah's old prophecy, and, apart from individual opinions that it might be understood of the glory to which Rabbinism attained here in the 2nd and 3rd cents., the older Synagogue teaching is so far at one with them that all the *midrāshim* declare that the Messiah ben Joseph should appear in Galilee. So also writes Sa'adiah ha-Gaon in his work on *Faith and Knowledge*, § v. ; while the Book of Zohar on Ex 1⁸ clearly states that the 'Messiah shall arise and be revealed in the land of Galilee.'

LITERATURE.—See the authorities cited under artt. PALESTINE, GALILEE, CAPERNAUM, etc. For homil. use, C. H. Waller, *The Names on the Gates of Pearl* ³ (1903), p. 129.

W. M. CHRISTIE.

NAPKIN.—The Gr. σουδάριον, tr. 'napkin' in the Gospels (cf. Ac 19¹² 'handkerchief'), is Lat. *sudarium*, and became current in the East through the extension of the Roman Empire. The piece of cloth, a yard or so square, of which the σουδάριον consisted, was turned to various purposes. It usually served as a head-dress to protect the head of the living from the sun, and to give a finish to their costume, but it served other purposes as well. Two of these are mentioned in the Gospels. In Lk

19^{20} the unfaithful servant confesses that he had wrapped up his master's pound in a napkin. In Jn 11^{44} and 20^7 we are told that the head of the dead had been bound about with a napkin.

With regard to Lk 19^{20} the words put into the lips of the unfaithful servant are an example of Christ's irony, and help to show us the true character of the servant. The fact that he admits having put the pound in a *sweat-cloth* is significant. It stamps him not only as a man who was discontented with his pound, but also as a man of indolent character, unwilling to use the opportunities of service which were given him. The misuse of the napkin, revealing as it does the lazy habit of the man, is of importance for the right understanding of the parable.

The reference to the napkin in Jn 20^7 is worthy of special attention in connexion with the Resurrection of Christ. Unfortunately neither the AV nor the RV gives the exact translation of the Greek text. The literal rendering of the passage makes it clear that the napkin which had been placed about Christ's head before burial was discovered by the two disciples lying where His head had been, in the undisturbed form of a coiled or twisted head-wrapper. The verb ἐντετυλιγμένον should be rendered 'coiled' or 'twisted up,' and not 'wrapped together' as in AV, or 'rolled up' as in RV, and implies that the napkin was found coiled or twisted together in turban-like fashion, just as if His head had somehow slipped out of it, while the words χωρὶς . . . εἰς ἕνα τόπον, translated in both AV and RV 'in a place by itself,' would be better translated 'separately (not touching the linen clothes which had been swathing the body) into one place,' εἰς ἕνα τόπον being the equivalent of εἰς ταὐτό in classical Greek. This rendering of the passage is confirmed by the impression made upon the two disciples by what they witnessed on entering the tomb. It is said that they 'saw and believed'—saw something, that is, which persuaded them so completely that their Master was risen from the dead that their doubts were immediately resolved, and they proceeded at once to their own home (Jn 20^{10}) to await the development of events. For a full discussion of the passage and its bearing on the Resurrection, see H. Latham, *The Risen Master*, p. 40 ff.

LITERATURE.—Geikie, *Holy Land and the Bible* ; G. M. Mackie, *Bible Manners and Customs* ; Trench, *Notes on the Parables* (Parable of the Pounds). 　　　MORISON BRYCE.

NARD (Heb. נֵרְדְּ, from Skr. *naladurtha*, probably through Persian ; Gr. νάρδος, Arab. *sumbul-i-hindi* [=Indian spike]). — The chief ingredient in the costly unguents used in the East, and from thence imported to Rome. The word is found in the OT (Ca 1^{12} 4$^{13.14}$), and twice in the Gospels (Mk 14$^{3-5}$, Jn 12$^{3-5}$), occurring in both cases in the account of the anointing of our Lord, in a house at Bethany, by a woman whom St. John identifies as Mary the sister of Lazarus.* In classical literature there are frequent references to nard. Theophrastus speaks of it as a root (*de Odor.* 28), and says it came from India (*Hist. Plant.* ix. 7. 2). Dioscorides, a physician who flourished about A.D. 100, also tells us that it came from India, being found in the Ganges district, and that it had many shaggy (πολύκομος) spikes growing from one root (i. 6. 77). Athenæus (xv. 691 B), Horace (*Od.* II. xi. 16, IV. xii. 16), Ovid (*Ars. Am.* iii. 443), and Tibullus (ii. 2. 7) make references to it. But our chief authority is Pliny the Elder (*Nat. Hist.* xii. 26, 27, xiii. 2). He speaks of its great value,†

*Mk. connects this incident closely with the last Passover, but Jn. makes it clear that it happened on the night before the triumphal entry into Jerusalem.

† Mk. and Jn. mention 300 denarii (about £10) as the cost per

its adulteration, and the means by which genuine nard may be distinguished from spurious. Genuine (*sincerum*) nard is known by its lightness, its red colour, its sweet smell, and its peculiar taste (*gustu maxime siccante os, sapore iucundo*). He also speaks of the use of alabaster boxes to preserve it. (See ALABASTER).

It was formerly supposed by Linnæus and other botanists that nard was an Indian grass ; but Sir W. Jones and Dr. Royle, director of the Government Botanical Gardens at Saharunpore from 1823 to 1831, have conclusively proved that it is to be identified with *Nardostachys Jatamansi*, a plant of the order Valerianaceæ, found at great altitudes in North India. This plant bears small spikes of purple flowers, each with four stamens. The part used for making the perfume was the root and lower portion of the stems, which are shaggy 'like tufts of ermine,' and to which the skeletons of former leaves adhere, giving them a bristly appearance. It is probably these stems, rather than the flower heads, which Pliny calls *spicæ*. The epithet πιστική applied in Mk. and Jn. to νάρδος may possibly be an attempt to reproduce *spicata*, which, in vulgar Latin, may have become *spicita* (see Swete's *St. Mark, ad loc.*, and art. SPIKENARD in present work).

LITERATURE.—Besides the authorities quoted in the article, see *Asiatic Researches*, ii. 405–417 ; W. Dymock, *Pharmacographia Indica* (1891), ii. 233–238 ; Tristram, *Natural History of the Bible*, p. 485 ; articles 'Spikenard' in *Encyc. Brit.*9, Smith's *DB* (by Houston), Hastings' *DB* (by Post), *Encyc. Bibl.* (by Thistleton-Dyer and M'Lean). 　　H. W. FULFORD.

NATHAN.—A son of king David, named in our Lord's genealogy, Lk 3^{31}.

NATHANAEL (=Θεόδωρος, 'Gift of God' [Heb. נְתַנְאֵל Nu 1^8, 1 Ch 2^{14} etc.] ; cf. *Adeodatus, Deodatus, Deusdedit*).—We know nothing about him except what is told us in Jn 1$^{45-51}$ 21^2. On the question of his identity with Bartholomew, see art. BARTHOLOMEW, i. p. 173^a. The place at which Nathanael was found by Philip and brought to Jesus is not mentioned ; but it is not improbable that Nathanael was returning from listening to the preaching of the Baptist. He may have been baptized by him. The very detailed account of the calling of Nathanael leads one to suppose that it was an important event, such as the calling of one who was afterwards to be an Apostle. In any case, the local knowledge shown in v. 44f. is very real, and, so far as it goes, it tells in favour of Johannine authorship ; for St. John would possess this knowledge, and a later writer would not, and would not care to invent such details. Philip, like Nathanael, was a Galilæan, the one of Bethsaida, the other of Cana (21^2) : they were therefore neighbours, and evidently friends. Like Andrew and John, Philip no sooner finds, or is found by, Christ, than he seeks to make Him known to others. The plural, '*We* have found him,' etc., seems to imply that Philip, with Andrew and Peter and John and James, was now a disciple of Jesus. These five formed the beginning of the Christian Church. The order of the words in the Greek is noteworthy : 'Him of whom wrote Moses in the law' comes first, 'and the prophets' being added as an afterthought ; and the whole of this comes with emphasis before the verb, 'we have found.' It looks as if Nathanael and Philip had at times discussed the OT descriptions of the Messiah. At this time Philip would know nothing of the virgin birth at Bethlehem : he quite naturally describes Jesus as He was

pound of the unguent. Pliny (xii. 26) says that the 'spicæ' were worth 100 denarii a pound, and in xiii. 2 mentions the price of a similar unguent as rising to 300 denarii per pound.

commonly known. The Scriptures to which he specially refers would be Gn 17[7] 49[10], Dt 18[15].

Nathanael's question, 'Can any good thing?' etc., does not imply that Nazareth had a bad reputation, but that the insignificant village, so close to his own home, was not a likely birthplace for the Messiah. Was a petty place, so familiar to them both, thus honoured? What prophecy said anything of the kind? The prophecy alluded to in Mt 2[23] is not known to us, and was probably unknown to Nathanael. In any case, Nathanael's question confirms the statement that the miracle at Cana was the first of Christ's signs. If Jesus had worked miracles at Nazareth, Nathanael at Cana must have heard of them.

Philip's 'Come and see' is in harmony with the practical bent of his mind (12[21] 14[8]), and is the best answer to anything like prejudice. 'He that doeth the truth cometh to the light' (3[21], cf. 1[9]); and this is what Nathanael does, with good results. It is part of his guilelessness that he is willing to have any prejudice removed, and he at once accepts Philip's proposal; cf. 4[29. 30]. Christ praises him as truly an Israelite, i.e. as one who has something more than the blood of the patriarch, viz. a character which corresponds to the dignity of the name (Ps 73[1]). In him the guile of Jacob the supplanter has given place to the righteousness which wins a victory with God. He is one whose death a prophet may desire (Nu 23[10]).

Nathanael overhears the praise of himself, and the question with which he replies to it has been criticised as arguing a want of modesty on his part. But his reply does not mean, 'I know that I am all that: but how do you know it?' Rather, he exhibits surprise that a total stranger should express any opinion about him. He somewhat coldly intimates that he doubts the value of praise which can hardly be based upon experience. But, like Mary's 'How shall this be?' (Lk 1[34]), his question does not so much ask for proof as express astonishment. In both cases the proof which was not demanded was granted. Gabriel gave Mary a sign that he could read her future, for he showed that he knew all about Elisabeth's prospects of a son; and Jesus gives Nathanael a sign that He could read his character, for He shows that He knows all about his private conduct (cf. what we read of Elisha in 2 K 5[26] 6[12]). Nathanael at once recognizes the significance of this knowledge, and in his reply 'the true Israelite acknowledges his King.'

It is right to allow for the *possibility* that in Nathanael's confession (1[49]), and in that of the Baptist (v.[34]), the Evangelist may be putting into the mouths of others language which had become natural to himself, but was not actually used by them. St. John was so full of the doctrine that Jesus as the Messiah was the Son of God, that he may have made those who accepted Him as the Messiah express their belief in a form which was not used until somewhat later. We must admit that thus to antedate the terminology of a fuller appreciation of the truth would be possible. But Ps 2[6. 7] will suffice to explain the language which the Evangelist attributes to the Baptist and to Nathanael. This Psalm was generally recognized as Messianic, and seems to have been very familiar (Ac 4[25-28] 13[33], He 1[5] 5[5]). In the fulness of his conviction Nathanael quite naturally uses the fullest Scriptural designation of the Messiah with which he was acquainted. Experience of Christ's miraculous knowledge had convinced him, as it convinced the Samaritan woman (4[29]) and Thomas (20[27. 28]), that Jesus stood in the closest relation to God. Hence he uses this title of the Messiah (11[27], Mt 26[63], Mk 3[11] || 5[7] || 15[39] ||, Lk 4[41]) rather than the common 'Son of David' (Mt 9[27] 12[23] 15[22]

20[30. 31] 21[9-15] 22[42] etc.). Although 'Son of God' and 'King of Israel' both indicate the Messiah, the titles are not quite synonymous, as is shown by the repetition of 'Thou art.' 'Son of God' gives the relation to God—a relation which would be only vaguely understood by Nathanael; 'King of Israel' gives the relation to the Chosen People. Thus the two titles complete one another.

Nothing is gained by suggesting (Cheyne in *Enc. Bibl.* iii. col. 3338) that 'when thou wast under the fig-tree' ought to be 'when thou wast making supplication,' because the Hebrew for the one (וְאַתָּה מִתְחַנֵּן *wĕattā mithḥannēn*) would resemble the Hebrew for the other (וְאַתָּה תַּחַת הַתְּאֵנָה, *wĕattā taḥath hattĕʾēnā*). What the Evangelist gives us is intrinsically more probable, as being more definite, and therefore more likely to impress Nathanael. Nathanael seems to have believed that Jesus knew what he was thinking about under the fig-tree, just as the Samaritan woman believed that He knew all about her past life. Fresh from the teaching of the Baptist, Nathanael may have been meditating on the coming of the Messiah as near at hand. It was under a fig-tree that Augustine heard the '*Tolle, lege*' (*Conf.* VIII. xii. 1). See OT reff. to 'fig-tree.'

'Believest thou?' implies something of surprise at the rapidity of Nathanael's conviction (contrast Mk 6[6]); but 'thou believest' is perhaps right. Christ approves of his faith and of its basis; and He forthwith promises him an ampler basis, and therefore the prospect of a loftier faith. This wider basis of 'greater things' refers to the public signs which are to follow, and which seem to be alluded to in 'the angels of God ascending and descending upon the Son of man.' Angels are instruments of the Divine power in nature (Rev 14[18] 16[5]). Nathanael has believed because of a miracle of knowledge which could be appreciated by himself alone: he is hereafter to witness miracles of power which can be appreciated by all. And here it is to be noted that, while the 'Israelite indeed' enters upon a new life in recognizing his King by the sign granted to him, the Messiah Himself enters upon a new career in granting the sign. This private sign to Nathanael was a prelude to those public miracles in which Christ 'manifested His glory' to the Jewish nation and through it to all the world. The angels, who are to be instruments of the manifestation, are represented as being already on earth, the 'ascending' being placed first. They are ready to carry men's prayers to heaven, and to bring down the blessings which prayer wins. But there is a reference to Jacob's dream (Gn 28[12]), suggested possibly by the place; for Bethel, Mahanaim, and the ford Jabbok all lay close to the route which Christ would take in going from Judæa to Galilee; and in the narrative in Genesis the ascending angels are mentioned first. What Jacob had dreamed was fulfilled in Jesus. Heaven was opened and remained so (perfect participle) to mankind. Heaven came down to earth in the Person of the Son of God, and, by a regular intercourse between His place of sojourn and His home, man became capable of attaining to heaven. It narrows the meaning far too much when the promise to Nathanael is interpreted of the angels who appeared after the Temptation, at the Agony, and after the Resurrection and Ascension.

The change in the designation of the Messiah is significant. Nathanael had called Him 'the Son of God': He calls Himself 'the Son of Man,' and it is the earliest occasion on which He does so. In the Synoptic Gospels the title 'Son of Man' occurs 69 times, and Christ is represented as using it (always of Himself) on about 40 different occasions. In John the title is used 11 or 12 times, 9[35] being doubtful; and none of these passages is parallel to anything in the Synoptics. Here the point may be that He is come, not to revive the old theocracy, nor to ' restore the kingdom to Israel' (Ac 1[6]), but to redeem the whole human race. It may also be that at this beginning of His ministry Jesus will not definitely accept the title 'Son of God.' Without rejecting it, He substitutes for it a title which seems to have been adopted by Him to veil, rather than to reveal, the fact that He was the Messiah. But here again we must allow for the *possibility* that the Evangelist is wording Christ's reply according to language which he had often heard from His lips, but which was not used quite so early in the ministry as this.

In Nathanael we have an instance of a good man hampered by prejudice, but quite willing to be enlightened. He comes to the Light, and is searched, approved, and illuminated. In Christ's treatment of him we have an instance of His knowledge of what was in man (2[25]), not only in the case of mankind in general, but with regard to individual character; also of the working of the law that 'whosoever hath, to him shall be given.'

The narrative of the call of Nathanael, like the rest of Jn 1, strongly confirms the belief that the writer is a Jew of Palestine, well acquainted with the Messianic hopes, and with the traditions and phraseology current in Palestine at the time of Christ's ministry; able also to give a lifelike picture of Christ's first disciples.

Literature.—B. F. Westcott, *Gospel of St. John*, 26 f., 33 ff.; R. C. Trench, *Studies in the Gospels*, 66; H. P. Liddon, *University Sermons*, 2nd ser. 4; Phillips Brooks, *Mystery of Iniquity*, 129; A. Maclaren, *A Year's Ministry*, 2nd ser. 169; W. Boyd Carpenter, *Son of Man*, 163; J. G. Greenhough, *Apostles of our Lord*, 74; H. T. Purchas, *Johannine Problems*, 68; G. Matheson, *Representative Men of the N.T.* 71; *Expos.* 5th ser. viii. (1898) 336.   A. PLUMMER.

NATION.—This word has two meanings, according as it distinguishes Israel from other peoples, or as it concerns Israel within itself. In the former sense it signifies a State more or less organized, and its keynote is *independence*; in the latter, a race of common speech and religion, and its keynote is *unity*. There are two pairs of Greek words corresponding to this distinction. Ἰουδαῖοι is used under the former category, and most frequently by John, who wrote when the Jewish and Christian communities were decisively separated from one another; * whereas Ἰσραήλ is used always with a note of affection and pride by those who count themselves as its members, sharers in the Divine choice and covenant. There is a similar contrast between the words ἔθνος and λαός, the former and ἔθνη (in the phrase 'all nations') being used generally of political States. τὰ ἔθνη has the special meaning of 'the Gentiles,' the non-Jewish peoples (Heb. גוים), and gradually became ethically blackened, so that AV instinctively translates 'heathen' (Gal 1[16] 2[9], cf. Mt 6[7] ἐθνικοί). But the common noun which corresponds with Ἰσραήλ is λαός. It conveys the sense of God's possession and purpose, which are creative of the national unity maintained by the sacrifices and observances of the Law. Its analogue in Heb. is עם. As ἔθνη sank down into the meaning of heathen, so λαός is at length appropriated by the Christian consciousness. The few exceptions to the above rules should be noted. In Lk 7[5] 23[2], and throughout the Fourth Gospel, ἔθνος is used in the place of λαός; for, as was just stated, in the later Apostolic circles the old prerogatives of Israel were claimed for the 'Israel of God,' *i.e.* the Christians. In Lk 2[10] λαός

* St. Paul, too, puts Ἰουδαῖοι on the same secular footing as Ἕλληνες; cf. the phrase καὶ Ἰουδαίοις καὶ Ἕλλησιν καὶ τῇ ἐκκλησίᾳ τοῦ θεοῦ (1 Co 10[32]).

is translated in AV as if it were ἔθνη; but RV corrects it from 'all people' to 'all *the* people.'

1. Ἰουδαῖοι, ἔθνος, ἔθνη.—In so far as the Jews constituted a body politic, they had lost their *independence* since Pompey's occupation of Jerus. in B.C. 63, and the Roman hold was tightened by the rule of the Imperial protégé Herod the Great, B.C. 37–4. He obtained from Augustus the title of 'king' in B.C. 30, and large slices of territory, first Samaria, Jericho, and towns in the west, and afterwards the regions between the Lebanons and the Lake of Gennesaret, and eastwards. He greatly enhanced the material glories of the Holy Land, especially by wealth expended on the Temple (Mt 23[16] 24[1], Jn 2[20]), by which he hoped to secure the loyalty of the nationalists. But, though he gave lavishly with one hand, he took away cynically with the other. He filled the high priest's office with his own creatures; and by building theatres and pagan temples showed scant respect for the national ideal. 'He founded Καισάρεια (*i.e.* temples of Cæsar) in many towns' outside Judæa (Jos. *Ant.* xv. ix. 5). His strength lay in his bodyguard of 3000, who were drawn from the Samaritan population, and in the fortified palaces which he built at Jerusalem and Cæsarea. By intrigue and assassination he exterminated the rival Hasmonæan house, including his favourite wife and her popular sons. The frenzied act of massacre of the babes of Bethlehem, for which Mt 2[16] is the only authority, is quite in accord with his temper in the later years of his life.

On the death of this Idumæan tyrant an even sadder chapter from the standpoint of national independence began. For Herod's kingdom was divided among three sons: Philip having the newly added territories of Trachonitis, Ituræa (Lk 3[1]), etc.; Antipas succeeding to Galilee and Peræa; and Archelaus, after a long suit at Rome, obtaining the most important part with an allotted income of 600 talents. In A.D. 6, the last-named was finally summoned for his evil courses to Rome, and the unhappy people sank one stage lower in the scale of national independence, being placed under a procurator. This was an exchange for the worse, even from the tyranny of Herod the Great and the iniquities of his son. For although these were only half Judæans, and in subtle and sometimes pronounced antagonism to the nationalist party, they did not fail to give it some regard; whereas Pontius Pilate and his four predecessors mostly gave up even the attempt to understand so impracticable a people. No wonder 'the revolutionary current was continually increasing among the Jewish people in the time of Christ' (Schürer).

These procurators (ἡγεμών in NT, ἐπίτροπος more often in Josephus) were not of senatorial or prætorian, but only of equestrian rank, and not absolutely independent of the Syrian governor, though their dealings were mostly direct with Rome. Their power included (*a*) *military and police control.* The Jews were themselves free from conscription for military service. But there were plenty of Gentiles in the land to supply the small garrisons required. The centurion (Lk 7[2] 23[47]) and his cohort would be required only in a few of the larger towns. The Temple was dominated by the tower of Antonia. The procurator had also (*b*) *judicial authority.* His confirmation was required for capital sentences (Jn 18[31]), and his executive force carried them into effect (Mt 27[27]). Ordinary civil and criminal cases, however, affecting Jews were dealt with at the sessions of the Sanhedrin, and when they appeared to have the people behind their verdict, Pilate was loth to deny them (Mt 27[18. 24]). He also used his powers of release with a view to propitiating the populace (Mt 27[15]). But the name of procurator conveys a special reference to the duties respecting (c) *the Roman treasury.* Being an Imperial province, the taxes of Judæa were paid to the account not of the Senate, but of Cæsar (Mk 12¹⁴). The country was divided into some ten toparchies for fiscal purposes. Tacitus (*Annals,* ii. 42) speaks of Judæa in A.D. 17 as *fessa oneribus.* The taxes (land and poll) were collected by State officers; but the customs were farmed to *publicani* such as Zacchæus (ἀρχιτελώνης, Lk 19²) of Jericho.

The rights of the procurator were also enjoyed by the tetrarchs, as well as the right to issue copper coinage. Herod Antipas built Tiberias, S.W. of the Lake, for his capital. Like his father, he tried to propitiate or rather seduce national sentiment by his outlay on public works; and he was at any time ready to use it for his own ends (Mk 3⁶ 12¹³). Jesus warned His fellow-countrymen against the leaven of Herod (Mk 8¹⁵); and, in response to a crafty attempt to get rid of Him, described the tetrarch as a fox (Lk 13³²). John the Baptist, whose preaching was in his territory, was his victim (Mk 6¹⁷ff.). But though his partisans were hand and glove with the Pharisees in their hostility to Jesus (Mk 3⁶ 12¹³), and though we learn from Luke that he associated himself with the condemnation of Jesus, he was not ready to take that awful responsibility upon himself **(Lk** 23⁷⁻¹²). The advent of Jesus apparently raised no political excitement in the regions under Philip, because the bulk of the population was non-Jewish. But there was often danger in Galilee (Lk 4²⁹); and infinitely more in the furnace of fanaticism at Jerusalem (Mk 10³²f., Jn 11⁸).

When Herod the Great died, his policy of getting material benefit for the nation at the cost of its religious ideals was continued by the priests, who exercised the highest civil as well as religious functions. They constituted the majority of the Sanhedrin, which, as the supreme court of appeal, professedly represented the remnant of Jewish independence. But it represented no cause so truly as the vested interests of an order dependent first on the favour of Herod, and then on the pleasure of Rome. Thus in the name of a bastard independence, which meant that they had leave to grow rich and their country leisure to grow outwardly splendid, they opposed any national movement which might provoke the Romans to take away not only the nation, but also 'our place' (Jn 11⁴⁸). It was, *e.g.,* the high priest Joazar who checked the threatened revolt in A.D. 7 on the taking of the census by Quirinius. There were even some of the Pharisees who, whether because they were satisfied with the measure of religious liberty accorded under the Imperial administration, or because they shut their eyes to the facts (Jn 8³³), or because they saw in the foreign yoke the discipline of God, resented any movement towards national independence; and perhaps it was some of these who associated themselves with the Herodians in Mt 22¹⁶.

2. Ἰσραήλ, λαός.—But while the independence of the Jewish people was irretrievably mutilated, and the State as a geographical or governmental entity about to perish, the other note of national existence, viz. *unity* as focussed in the word λαός, was very completely realized. Indeed, as the outer husk decayed, the inner shell grew the harder and tougher. The succession of Pharisees and scribes proved a far surer defence than the dynasty of David. The soul of Judaism was not devoured even by the omnivorous influences of Greek culture. The first steps in this movement were taken by Ezra and Nehemiah, who put an end to mixed marriages among those who had returned from the Exile. The race was adulterated, however, even so late as B.C. 125, when the Idumæans, being de-

feated by Hyrcanus, submitted to circumcision. And in respect to language, the Jews of the Dispersion spoke Greek, and read the Scriptures therein; while 'the people of the land' understood Aramaic only (Ac 21⁴⁰). Religiously, however, the nation was undivided after the Exile, feeling itself to be the special property and instrument of God (Mt 2⁶ 3⁹, Lk 1⁶⁸, Jn 8⁴¹). This unity was expressed not only by the rite of circumcision (Jn 7²²), but also by the keeping of the Sabbath (Mk 3⁴), the abstinence from unclean foods, and the worship, without images, of one only God. And these distinctions were guarded by a multitude of observances, which called into requisition the school of scribes trained in the principles of the Pharisees.

But although the scribes claimed to sit in the seat of Moses (Mt 23²), their authority was not recognized in what may be called the outer circles of Judaism. The Samaritans declined to follow the national Church in its later developments. Hence they were referred to with contempt (Jn 8⁴⁸) as outsiders (Lk 17¹⁸), because of their particular objection to the religious monopoly of Jerusalem (Lk 9⁵³, cf. Jn 4³⁰). But for all that, they were counted Jews, though grudgingly, as heretics —'the foolish people who dwell in Sichem' (Sir 50²⁵f.), and were proud of the Israelite strain in their blood (Jn 4¹²). More than that, their doctrinal shortcomings received some countenance in high places; for 'the Sadducees say only what is written is to be esteemed as legal . . . the tradition of the fathers needs not to be observed' (Jos. *Ant.* XIII. x. 6).

Taken as a whole, however, in despite of the home-land being penetrated under Herodian and priestly influence with Hellenistic speech and culture, and although, what with Essenes on the one hand, and Samaritans on the other, they did not all keep step, the people preserved such unity that they became, if not politically independent, socially isolated. On the one hand, their exemption from military service, from Sabbath employment, and their refusal of market food, drew out the dislike of the populace and the contempt of the cultured classes, so that they were regarded as 'haters of mankind.' On the other hand, the word ἔθνη, meaning the nations outside the Law of the chosen λαός, gathered more and more of moral connotation, as it passed through the meanings of 'Gentile,' 'heathen,' and finally 'sinners' (Mt 26⁴⁵; cf. Gal 2¹⁵). The symbol of this rejuvenated Judaism was still the Temple, whither the tribes went up at the national festivals; but its rallying-point was the synagogue, where men were instructed in the Law and Hope of Israel, and where the Pharisees ruled supreme. Their rivals, the Sadducees, had no influence beyond the aristocratic circles at Jerusalem, in the Hellenized cities, and perhaps in Samaritan villages; and though they had a large place in the Sanhedrin, they had to comply with Pharisaic watchwords.

Thus the national life was knit from within, and ruling functions were exercised through officers of the synagogue, such as πρεσβύτεροι (Mt 21²³ 26⁴⁷), πρῶτοι (Lk 19⁴⁷), γραμματεῖς (Mk 9¹¹), or νομικοί (Lk 10²⁵). Although Palestine was not politically the mistress of her own territories, she was religiously the mother of a people throughout the Empire. The Jews of the Dispersion could but rarely visit the Temple, and they read the Scriptures in the Greek tongue; but in their separate communities they maintained the precepts as to Sabbath rest and clean food under the protection of Roman governors and the Emperor (cf. Ac 18¹²⁻¹⁵). The Jews could say with Josephus, 'Even if we were deprived of wealth, of towns and of other possessions, the Law remains to us for ever. And no

Jew will be so far from his native land, or so much fear a hostile ruler, as not to fear the Law more than him' (c. Apion. ii. 38).

If it was by the hands of the priests, in the name of national independence, that the Lord was betrayed to the 'nations,' so the chief antagonism which He met in His ministry, and which His spirit encountered afterwards in the Apostolic mission, came from this close-knit theory and practice of national unity. The Pharisees pursued Him from the first because they instinctively saw that the tendency of His teaching (see NATIONALITY) was to break the bonds their traditions had woven, and to act as a solvent on the rigidity of national isolation, which was the only thing left to their pride.

LITERATURE. —Cremer, Bib.-Theol. Lex. s.vv. ἔθνος, λαός; Schürer, HJP [indicates all possible sources of information, the fullest of these being the Antiquities and Wars of Josephus]; Ewald, Hist. of Israel, vol. vi.; Hausrath, Hist. of N.T. Times; Milman, Hist. of the Jews, vol. ii.; Keim, Hist. of Jesus of Nazara, vols. i. and ii.; Stanley, Lectures on Jewish Church; artt. 'Gentiles' and 'People' in Hastings' DB.

A. NORMAN ROWLAND.

NATIONALITY.—This term includes the characteristics created by national ideals and facts. The national environment of Jesus and His disciples has been set forth in the preceding article under the two ideals of independence and unity. Of these ideals the former rested on the Messianic Hope, the latter on the Mosaic Law, which were the key-notes of the most ancient Scriptures of the Jews—the Prophets and the Pentateuch respectively. They provide the clue to all that was distinctive in the nationality which appeared in, around, and against Jesus.

1. *The Messianic Hope, with its meaning for independence.*—The expectations aroused at the birth of Jesus were by no means of a cosmopolitan character (Mt 1^{21} 2^6, Lk 2^{10}—'all the people,' not 'all people'), even as they appear in the perspective of St. John's transcendental point of view (Jn 1^{29}; but cf. v.^{31}). It was with the hope of keen patriots that the disciples remained with Him to the end (Ac 1^6, Mk 10^{28}). St. Matthew especially represents Him throughout with a glow of nationalist pride, as son of Abraham and of David (Mt 1^1 9^{27} 21^{15}), and the heir of the prophets (Mt $2^{15.\ 23}$ 4^{14} 8^{17}).

As to Jesus Himself, it cannot be denied that He so far shared the patriotic hopes of His fellow-countrymen as to believe they were to be fulfilled in His own person (Lk 4^{21} 7^{23} 20^{13}). We may even venture to say that He counted it a temptation to make His ministry succeed on popular lines (Mt $4^{5f.}$). At any rate He withdrew from advertisement (Mk $1^{36f.}$), and from the popular desire to make Him king (Jn 6^{15}), refused to give a 'sign' (Mk 8^{12}), and seemed to repudiate any claim that rested on succession from David (Mt 22^{43-45}). But He took as the very keynote of His acceptable and authoritative preaching the phrase which the nationalists used in the name of independence, 'the kingdom of God' or of 'Heaven.' He spoke of His disciples sitting on twelve thrones judging the twelve tribes (Mt 19^{28}). And though He baffled their material hopes over and over again, and left them dumb, He quickened enthusiasm to the highest pitch by His entry into Jerusalem (Mt $21^{5ff.}$) on lines sketched out by prophecy. And these advances were no accommodation to the popular feeling; they were the expression of His own patriotic consciousness. He declared to the Samaritan woman that salvation is of the Jews (Jn 4^{22}). He forbade the disciples to address themselves to others than the lost sheep of the house of Israel (Mt $10^{5f.}$). He was loth to discount the value of nationality by admitting a Syrophœnician woman, an alien both in race and in religion, to an equal claim on His brief ministry with the elect people (Mt $15^{24.\ 26}$). Although He allowed the rights of Cæsar (Mt 22^{21}),

and authorized His disciples to pay the tribute-money that was due, He reserved the right to consider it an unrighteous infliction (Mt 17^{26}). With the love of a patriot He wept over Jerusalem because it knew not the day of its visitation, and was near its final ruin (Lk 19^{41-44}). Though rejected by those who had formulated their own material notions of the Messianic Hope (Mt $16^{20f.}$, Jn 7^{45-52} 9^{22}), it was after all on the ground of His patriotism that Jesus was betrayed into the hands of the Gentiles. When Caiaphas urged this policy, he was moved more by fear for 'our place' than 'our nation.' It was on the charge of having spoken against Cæsar (Lk 23^2) that Pilate was induced to condemn Jesus (Jn $19^{12.\ 16}$). It was in the name of the Messianic Hope that He was mocked by the soldiers, and over His cross were written as accusation the words, 'The King of the Jews' (Mk 15^{26}).

2. *The Mosaic Law in its bearing upon unity.*—National pride also centred in the unity which was epitomized in the Mosaic Law. Before the death of Herod the Great, two Pharisees were burnt alive for leading an assault upon the golden eagle he had fixed over the gate of the Temple court. And the passion for the Law was no less exaggerated throughout the period of direct Roman rule, as when there was a riot on the occasion of Pilate's bringing the Roman ensigns within the city walls. Jesus Himself was very conscious of the national unity through the Law. He kept the feasts, being found in Jerusalem at the Passover, the Feast of Tabernacles, and of Dedication (cf. Mt 26^{55}). He was a regular attendant at the synagogue at Nazareth (Lk 4^{16}); and His interest in these nurseries of nationality was so far recognized that the liberality of Jairus in providing one was assumed to be a claim on His favour (Lk $7^{4.\ 5}$). His works of healing were kept so far as possible on the lines of the Law (Mk 1^{44} $5^{12.\ 13}$). He thought of Israel as the Chosen People, and spoke of them as 'the children' (Mt 8^{12} 15^{26}). Indeed His reverence for the Scriptures (Lk $4^{4.\ 8.\ 12}$ 16^{31} 24^{25-27}), for the Law (Mt 5^{19}, Lk 10^{26-28}, Jn 5^{45}), and for the Temple (Mt $23^{17.\ 21}$, Jn $2^{16.\ 17}$), went far deeper than was appreciated by worldly-minded ecclesiastics (Jn 2^{18} 7^{46-49}).

But with all this tenderness for the obligations of Jewish religion as ties, He resented them as bonds. His perfect allegiance to the truth and grace of God (Jn 1^{17}) made every lesser loyalty stand in subordination. He withdrew Himself more and more from the passion of nationality as embodied in the religious pedantry and exclusiveness of the Pharisees, until at last it was almost wholly arrayed against Him and He against it (Mt 23^{15} etc.). The disparagement of Gentiles with which He began (Mt 6^{32}, cf. 20^{25}), turned to denunciation of the false children and unfaithful servants (Mt 21^{28-44}, cf. 8^{12} 11^{21}). And Luke especially records His kindly attitude towards Samaritans (Lk 9^{52} 10^{33} 17^{16}). In regard to the terms of the Mosaic Law, He did not hesitate to act as Lord of the Sabbath in the interests of humanity (Mk 3^4). And, further, He taught that a man could not be defiled by the eating of meats (Mk 7^{15}), or cleansed by the washing of pans (Mk 7^8). He distressed His disciples by sending away sorrowful a young devotee of the Law (Mk 10^{17-22}), and offended religious sentiment when He kept company with publicans and sinners (Mt 9^{11}, Lk 15^2 19^7).

Thus at length the devoted Student of the Scriptures and whole-hearted Champion of the Law was ejected from the national party as a deceiver (Jn 7^{12} 9^{22-28}, Mt 27^{63}), and delivered up to the priests and the Romans. While He was finally accused to the Romans as a pretender in the cause of independence, He was attacked from the beginning by the legalists as an enemy to the cause of unity. Though He embodied the Hope of Israel and fulfilled the Law of Moses, it was in the name both of the Hope which the priests mistook and of the Law which the scribes misinterpreted, that Jesus was brought to the cross.

But the essential attitude of Jesus in respect to nationality can be better read in the varied witness of His disciples even than in His own. Within the limits of His short career He conformed to the Law, for He was born under it (Gal 4[4]); and He spoke out of a Messianic consciousness (Lk 4[21]), because He came unto His own (Jn 1[11]). But when He was departed, His disciples 'saw greater things than these.' They perceived that the use of current speech and even contemporary ideals was compatible with a more perfect independence of their limitations than the most antagonistic and revolutionary attitude could express. The ideals of Christ moved with such ease in a plane of thought which is as universal as it is inward, that they could be embodied in the contemporary forms as well as in any other. Whereas the most ardent of reformers, ready to deny standing room to everything established, may be quite exclusively the product of his age, and governed by the most pedantic ideas. Thus the gospel of Jesus was released at once and instinctively from its nationalist setting, with this unique result that it lost nothing but gained everything by its liberation. It is true the company of original Apostles remained Christian Jews; but the leaders came to recognize that they enjoyed no distinctive privilege of the Kingdom which was withheld from the Gentiles. And St. Paul, son of Benjamin and pupil of Gamaliel as he was, drew out to the full logical issue the universal implication of the gospel.

The influence of Jesus upon nationality has been of a composite nature. On the one hand, He has loosened its bonds by enlarging the conception of God and emphasizing the fact of human brotherhood. Nationality was at first constituted under the ægis of the national deity, and provided the practice-ground and range for social ethics. Thus nationality and religion were virtually the same thing, where either meant anything, and where Rome had not obliterated them both by the triumph of material force and the deification of the reigning Emperor. It was to the sacred union of these two ideas of nationality and religion that Jesus was sacrificed. But the sacrifice enabled religion to pass into the higher stage of association with *humanity* (cf. Jn 12[24. 32]), for which, through the providential advance of Rome, the world was craving, and towards which in the region of philosophy the Stoics had already felt their way (Ac 17[26]). What nationality had hitherto done for religion, in providing the scope for its practice of social ethics, humanity was to do henceforth. The barriers had been broken down between Jew and Gentile, Greek and barbarian, bond and free; they being brought by the blood of the Cross near to God, and so to one another, in order that henceforth the bonds of brotherhood might be of a purely human character, and that the parables of the Good Samaritan and of the Shepherd-judgment might be the pattern and sanction for next-door philanthropies and world-wide missions.

LITERATURE.—Matheson, *Growth of the Spirit of Christianity*, as well as more formal works; Wilson Harper, *The Christian View of Human Life* (1901), chs. vii.-x.; Forrest, *The Authority of Christ*, (1906), ch. v.; J. Martineau, *National Duties* (1903), 1; B. F. Westcott, *Social Aspects of Christianity* (1887), 35; F. W. Robertson, *Sermons* (1874), iv. 287; D. J. Vaughan, *Questions of the Day* (1894), 12.

A. NORMAN ROWLAND.

NATURALNESS.—Few terms are more fruitful of fallacious thought than the group including 'nature,' 'natural,' 'naturalness.' In modern usage they are very frequent, and the range of varied meanings which they cover is wide. Thus we speak

of natural instinct, natural conduct, natural religion, natural science, and the natural creation, though the single epithet has a different sense in every case. Two phrases like 'the law of nature' and 'natural law' are verbally equivalent, yet they are very different in significance, the one drawing its connotation from Roman jurisprudence, the other from modern science; the one being concerned entirely with human thought and conduct, the other mainly with inanimate phenomena or those regions of Biology which include creatures of lower organization than man. It is always needful to be on one's guard against the fallacies which so easily arise through such changes in the meaning of a term; for they are apt to be unnoticed when the term itself is constant. But the danger becomes greater when these terms are carried back to a period in which they were in far less frequent use, and when they covered a smaller range of meaning. This was the case in the age of the NT. We have now generalized our ideas, and we speak of 'Nature' in the sense of the Cosmos. It is commonly with a reference more or less definite to the observed order of the Cosmos as a whole that we employ the words 'natural,' 'naturalness'; although there are many instances also in which they have a narrower reference. But in antiquity it was either a particular person or thing, or else a particular class of persons or things—a kind—which was in view; and the nature of this group of instances was the standard of naturalness. So 'life according to nature' meant, not what was in harmony with the universe, nor even what corresponded with environment, but what fulfilled the nature of the man himself. What was 'contrary to nature,' on the other hand, was not what put a man into antagonism with his surroundings, but what amounted to violence done to his better self. The later Stoics, indeed, made approach to the modern use in some directions, and in turn influenced legal principles, and later movements of thought which sought a 'return to nature,' such as that with which the name of Rousseau is connected; but they afford no more than an exception to the general truth that in ancient times the use of the terms under consideration was particularist, while to-day it is commonly generalized or even cosmical.

An examination of the passages in the NT in which naturalness is spoken of bears out this difference fully. In Ja 3[7], *e.g.*, the 'nature of beasts' (φύσις θηρίων) is contrasted with human nature (ἡ φύσις ἡ ἀνθρωπίνη); and St. Paul opposes the teaching of nature in the case of the Gentiles to the teaching of law in the case of Jews (Ro 2[14. 27]); while in 2 P 1[4] we read of 'a Divine nature' (θεία φύσις). But all such instances which develop the idea of naturalness lie outside the Gospels, and most of them occur in the writings of St. Paul. It is not necessary, therefore, to discuss them fully here; it may suffice to refer to an instructive note by Dr. Armitage Robinson in his Com. on the Epistle to the Ephesians (on 2[3]), pp. 49–51.

The words which are rendered by 'nature' or the like in the EV are φύσις, φυσικός, ὁμοιοπαθής, and ψυχικός, but the last is only translated 'natural' where it stands opposed to πνευματικός, and there the rendering is not satisfactory though none better is easily found. None of these words, however, occurs in the Gospels at all: and the entire absence from the Gospels of terms directly expressive of naturalness is in itself a warning against attempting to bring the facts of Jesus Christ's life under this category without care and caution.

There is, however, profound truth in Tertullian's saying, 'Anima naturaliter Christiana,' and it is no false extension of this if one speak of the naturalness of Jesus Christ as perfect, since in Him the best and highest nature of man is shown complete and unalloyed for once. Such a mode of expression would only serve to heighten the supplementary aspect of the truth which comes out in the contrast that St. Paul emphasizes between the first Adam as the 'natural man' (ψυχικός), and the last Adam as the 'life-giving spirit' (1 Co 15⁴⁵). It is along this line that the explanation must be sought of what some have felt as a serious difficulty, namely, that few principles in Christ's teaching can be instanced to which parallels of earlier date may not be adduced. Not only the writings of the OT Prophets and Psalmists, but also the religious teachers of other races, such as Gautama, Epictetus, or those collected in the Tao of China, afford numerous anticipations of the Lord's words. It could not be otherwise if the true nature of man be realized in Him ; if God purposed 'to sum up all things in Christ' (Eph 1¹⁰) ; if He was 'the true light which lighteth every man' (Jn 1⁹). A similar consideration enables one to understand the remarkable fact that Christ's appeal is to men of all races. 'One touch of nature makes the whole world kin': apart from this, the fact, to which ever-widening experience bears witness, that in all races 'his sheep hear his voice,' would be most wonderful, not to say inexplicable.

It is quite in keeping with this view of the facts, that the Lord Jesus never hesitated to appeal to the natural instinct of men on questions of conscience. *E.g.* 'Doth not each one of you on the Sabbath loose his ox or his ass . . .? And ought not this woman to have been loosed from this bond . . .? (Lk 13¹⁵ᶠ·, cf. 14⁵). He also employed expressions in reference to Himself which may be said implicitly to make naturalness the criterion of conduct. *E.g.* 'Thus it becometh us to fulfil all righteousness' (πρέπον ἐστὶν ἡμῖν, Mt 3¹⁵) ; 'Behoved it not the Christ to suffer?' (οὐχὶ ταῦτα ἔδει παθεῖν τὸν Χριστόν, Lk 24²⁶). This last usage is very characteristic of the Ep. to Heb. (cf. 2¹⁷ ὤφειλεν . . . ὁμοιωθῆναι ; v.¹⁰ ἔπρεπεν αὐτῷ ; and the similar expression in 7²⁶ ἡμῖν καὶ ἔπρεπεν ἀρχιερεύς, which bases on the nature God has given us the natural expectation which must be formed of Christ). See Newman Smyth, *Old Faiths in New Light*, 105.

E. P. BOYS-SMITH.

NATURE AND NATURAL PHENOMENA.—1.

The inquiry as to the attitude taken up by Jesus towards the natural, visible, tangible world which is the physical environment of the soul, is affected and limited by the fact that our Lord was not a philosopher or a scientist, but *a spiritual teacher*. His only mission was to preach the doctrine of the Kingdom of God, and to this He rigidly restricted Himself. Thus He nowhere enunciates a cosmology ; He gives us no explicit theory of the providential order ; He leaves the scientific conceptions of His day where they were, correcting no current mistakes as to the meaning of natural phenomena, and giving no intellectual synthesis of His own of the facts of the physical universe (see Wendt's *Teaching of Jesus*, i. pp. 151–153). This at once both hampers us and frees us in dealing with our special subject. It hampers us because we have to glean such hints as are possible for our purpose from scattered references to natural phenomena and to the order of nature as a whole, which occur incidentally in His teaching. But it also assists us by enabling us to understand that no sinister or misleading suggestions lurk behind the silence of Jesus on the innumerable problems that try the modern mind in its outlook on the natural order. The revelation of Jesus does not contain a complete conspectus of the facts of the world in all their aspects : it is a *spiritual* revelation, which aims at the enlightenment of the soul as to the vital truths of conduct, and as to the ideal relations between it and its Heavenly Father. Every element in the teaching is subordinate to this central consideration. In seeking for such light as is possible on the attitude of our Lord to the physical world, we must, therefore, bear this limitation constantly in mind.

2. We also find here the key to the kind of references which are made by our Lord to the facts of nature. These references are, fortunately for our purpose, very numerous in proportion to the bulk of His teaching as it has come down to us, and this for a reason we shall presently deal with. But they all belong (1) to the class of facts that were quite familiar to His hearers. His aim was always entirely practical, and His illustrations and references to nature are thus extremely simple and obvious. We seek in vain for any recondite, or technical, or unusual allusions ; they all lie consistently in the path of common observation ; so much so that hardly any of them need interpretation to the simplest modern minds. And (2) they are of that class which lend themselves obviously to the uses of illustration, being vivid, pictorial, and frequently recurrent in the lives of ordinary men and women, so that anyone familiar with His teaching could not fail afterwards to be reminded of the spiritual truths He had taught, because no one could go through a single day of average experience without coming across one or more of the natural facts used in His matchless collection of illustrations. By this means He turned nature into a whispering gallery of spiritual truths, and filled each common day with perpetual reminders of His central teaching, thus enlisting both the understanding and the memory of His followers in His permanent service as a revealer of religious truth. Any devout and careful student of the Gospels will readily find the justification of these remarks in the pages of the Evangelists.

3. Incidental, however, as are the references to nature and natural phenomena in the words of Jesus, they are full of suggestiveness as to His attitude to the material world. Through the rigid self-limitation which He imposed on Himself we catch the glow of His spirit ; through the narrow windows of His imagery rays of light pour out in many directions on the mysteries of life and providence. It is not, perhaps, possible to construct a complete Christian *Weltanschauung*, or 'View of the World,' out of the scattered references of Jesus to nature ; but in the light of His teaching it is certainly possible to suggest the lines along which such a theory must run. His doctrine of the Fatherhood necessitated an attitude towards nature as well as man, and this attitude is consistently maintained by Him in all His words and habits of thought as recorded in the Gospels.

4. *Christ's theory of Providence in the natural order.*—(1) The first characteristic in the attitude of Jesus towards the facts and arrangements of the organic world is a certain beautiful *calmness and serenity*. The facts which so deeply disturb us in our view of nature—suffering, the preying of one animal on another, death—were just as familiar to Him, who was an accurate and careful observer, as to ourselves ; moreover, He who was so sympathetic with men in their sorrows, must have been equally accessible to the sorrows of dumb creatures. Yet there is no trace of any disturbance of mind in Him as He met these familiar facts. His profound trust in God's goodness to His creatures enabled Him to view their sufferings with an equanimity in which there could have been no trace of hardness or indifference. It is the calmness of a mind so firmly centred in the idea of the Divine love and care that it suffers no shock at the most disturbing and harrowing of natural events. His references to the Providence that looks after the interests of flowers and birds, which are 'clothed' and 'fed' by God Himself, are full of a sense of the Divine benignity and good-will towards His meanest creatures, and He uses this fact as an argument to quell the needless anxiety of men, who belong to a far higher order of being (Mt 12¹²), as to the sources and sureness of the natural provision for their own life and well-being. If God so 'clothes the grass of the field,' and 'feeds the fowls of the air,' He will surely much more attend to the temporal wants of His children so that they may consider themselves free to attend to their proper spiritual interests (6²⁵⁻³⁴). That the optimism of Jesus is not the result of careless observation or lack of sympathy is seen also in His acknowledgment of the evanescence and perishableness of vegetable and animal life (v.³⁰). Jesus teaches us that 'God feeds the sparrow and also attends his obsequies' (Lk 12²⁴, cf. Mt 10²⁹). The sufferings peculiar to animal life and the incidence of natural death are clearly normal facts in our Lord's view of nature, and need contain no problem for faith.

(2) Another feature of our Lord's view of the providential order is His recognition of the *orderliness and faithfulness of natural law*. There is every indication that in realizing this He found a deep and constant pleasure. The world to Him was the home of order, and, as such, an indication of the will and character of the Creator and Sustainer of all things. He loved to notice and draw attention to this characteristic of the natural world (cf. Mt 5¹³ 7¹⁶⁻¹⁸. ²⁴⁻²⁷, Mk 4⁴⁻⁸. ²⁶⁻²⁸ 9⁵⁰, Lk 10¹⁸ 12²⁴ 13⁸ 19³⁴, Jn 3⁸ 10³⁻⁵ 15¹⁻⁴ etc.) Specially interesting to Him were all the phenomena of growth, which He so often uses as a symbol of the laws of the spirit (Mk 4⁴⁻⁸. ²⁶⁻²⁸. ³¹ᶠ. 13²⁸, Lk 13⁸. ²¹, Jn 15²⁻⁴), and of the habits of animals (Mt 6²⁶ 7¹⁵ 10¹⁶, Lk 13³⁴ 17³⁷, Jn 10³⁻⁵. ¹² etc.).

(3) This leads us to the most important of all the characteristics exhibited in our Lord's treatment of natural phenomena—His profound sense of the function they fulfil *as suggesting spiritual facts and laws*. His purpose in using natural imagery is not summed up in the fact of its picturesqueness and mnemonic aptness. However handy it may have been as a mould into which to throw His teaching, He evidently believed that there was in addition to this a real correspondence between the laws of organic and of spiritual life. He lived in two worlds, with an intensity of interest that has seldom been approached—the world of sense and the world of spirit. These two worlds to most men are divided by a deep chasm; but to Him there were innumerable bridges of connexion between them, and His thoughts traversed these in a perpetual play of happy insight, finding in both unending correspondences that were real and true, each shedding light into the heart of the other. Or, to vary the simile, we may say that to Him nature was the mirror of the spirit, in which He ever caught glimpses of the profoundest laws and operations of the higher life of the soul and of the character of God as the Lord of both. When He said, 'The kingdom of God is like . . ,' He was exercising no mere ingenuity of fancy, neither was He inventing fictitious similarities between disconnected spheres of existence; rather He was holding up the gold and silver sides of the same bright shield of Truth.

(4) In entire consistence with this view of our Lord's imagery, we notice the complete *absence, in His view of the world, of any such distinction as has been drawn by modern thinkers between the natural and the supernatural*. Living, as He did, in the perpetual sense of His Father's presence and power and love, such a distinction would be to Him utterly unreal. In His cosmology there was no third term, such as 'force,' or 'energy,' or 'law,' coming in immediately between the Divine will and its result. There was only God—the Creator and Sustainer—and nature was the material expression of His loving care and energy. What we would attribute to a secondary or efficient cause He always attributed to the direct activity of the Father. 'Your heavenly Father feedeth them. . . . Shall he not much more clothe you . . .?' 'Not one of them falleth to the ground without your Father . . .' 'My Father worketh hitherto.' In this sense of the immediacy of the Divine activity we find one of the most characteristic traits of the religious attitude of Jesus towards the natural world. The same consideration throws a suggestive light on the way in which He exercised His 'miraculous' gifts. To Him there was nothing 'supernatural' or inexplicable in the wonderful deeds He wrought. They were rather perfectly natural signs of the activity of God in and through Him: 'My Father that dwelleth in me, he doeth the works' (Jn 14¹⁰). Even in the case of an act of healing which was performed without any overt reference to the Divine power, as when He said, 'I will, be thou clean' (Lk 5¹³), the same attitude of dependence on the Father's favour and power must be presupposed (cf. Jn 5¹⁹). To Jesus, therefore, the wonderful works which He wrought were but the expression of the will of God through Him, and were as natural as the forces that eventuate in the 'blowing clover and the falling rain.' If this were borne in mind, perhaps the difficulty of the miraculous would not be what it is to many nowadays. The key would be seen to lie in the region of personality rather than of a 'supernatural' law over-riding a natural law. Jesus being who and what He was, it was as natural for Him to work 'miracles' and to exercise an exceptional control over the 'forces' of nature, as it was for Napoleon to do extraordinary things through his gift of control over men, or for a great scientist to initiate fresh changes in the forms and conditions of matter. The *differentia* of the soul of Jesus was an unbroken fellowship with God as His Father, which manifested itself in all He did, and, among other ways, in the power to use natural forces in a unique way in order to fulfil His filial mission.

5. There is another aspect of the attitude of Jesus to nature and natural phenomena which must not be overlooked, and which, however incidental it may be to His mission as such, is replete with suggestion and helpfulness. We have pointed out that His *scientific* and *philosophic* interest in nature was merged into the *religious* interest which always controlled His soul. What of the *artistic* interest which is so strong in the highest type of mind? Here again we must speak of the subordination of all to the spiritual outlook and temper. None the less is it clear that Jesus was profoundly sensitive to the *beauty* of the world. He loved Nature for her own sake, and because she ministered to His love of what was fair and good to look at. And if it is true that the 'function of art is (1) to teach us to *see*, (2) to teach us *what* to see, and (3) to teach us to see *more than we see*,' then the discourses of Jesus reveal the artistic temperament in all His references to the facts of the natural order. See art. POET.

(1) His faculty of *observation* was extraordinary. His eye took in the smallest detail of the outward world with loving appreciation. We have references to the march of the seasons (Mt 24³², Mk 13²⁸); to the orderly stages of growth (Mk 4²⁸); to the varying response of various kinds of soil (4⁴⁻⁸); to the mystery of development (vv.²⁷. ³¹); to the habits and dispositions of animals (Mt 10¹⁶, Lk 9⁵⁸ 13³⁴ 17³⁷, Jn 10³⁻⁵. ¹², cf. M t7¹⁵); to the customs of the household (Lk 13²¹, cf. the many references to the law of hospitality, and to human intercourse and social life). He was never at a loss, indeed, in drawing upon the resources of His observation for the purpose of illustrating His own teaching, but was like a householder, 'bringing forth from his treasure things new and old' (Mt 13⁵²).

(2) In the same way He teaches us *what* to see. A wise selection must be made in storing the mind with facts and impressions, so that the multiplicity of Nature may not overwhelm the mind, or cause us to lose our way in the confusion of her wealth. And while, as we have seen, there was nothing too great or too small to arrest His eye or interest His mind, there is one interest which evidently dominated His mind in His watchful observation of natural phenomena. That was the *ordinary human* interest. And this is always true of the highest art. The painter, the poet, the sculptor, are eminently and broadly *human* in their approach to Nature ; what has no reference to human experience and action and passion lies outside the scope of her appeal to them. A glance at our Lord's parables and illustrations at once reveals this dominant human interest. He refers only to those aspects of nature that in some more or less definite way intermingle with the daily or occasional experience of human beings. There was a practical as well as artistic purpose in this ; for He was thus able to interest His hearers more readily in the higher truths which He was anxious to impress upon their minds and to commend to their sympathies.

(3) He teaches us to see *more than we see*, for the natural became in His hands a translucent veil through which the spiritual poured its light and inspiration into the hearts of men. Here art once more became handmaid to religion ; and the beauty of nature became a vehicle for the higher beauty of holiness and truth. The same artistic gift is seen in the beautiful, vivid, and balanced *form* in which He clothed His imagery and parabolic teaching. His language is wonderfully clear and pictorial and apt : the mould into which He runs His illustrations is in keeping with the simplicity and beauty of its content. There is the happiest marriage of word and fact, type and antitype, in His teaching. This reveals the Master both of material and of expression. The earthly forms in which the Incarnate Word enshrined His message have caught something of His own Eternal quality and beauty, and will stand for ever as unique and unforgettable as the truth they embody. 'The words that I speak unto you, they are spirit, and they are life' (Jn 6^63).

LITERATURE.—Mozley, *Univ. Sermons*, 122 ; Shairp, *Stud. in Poetry and Philos.* 310 ; *Expositor*, III. ii. [1885] 224 ; F. W. Robertson, *Human Race*, 163 ; J. Caird, *Univ. Ser.* 300 ; S. J. Andrews, *Man and the Incarnation*, 105 ; W. G. Elmslie, *Memoir and Ser.* 240 ; D. W. Forrest, *Authority of Christ* (1906), 143.

                     E. GRIFFITH-JONES.

NATURES, TWO.—See DIVINITY OF CHRIST, and INCARNATION, vol. i. pp. 481, 812 f.

NAZARENE.—**1.** *Introductory.*—'Nazarene' is a descriptive term applied in the Gospels and Acts to Jesus and His followers. The epithet is also regularly applied in the Talmud to Jesus (יֵשׁוּעַ הַנּוֹצְרִי *Sanh.* 43*a*, 107*b* ; *Sota*, 47*a*) and His disciples (הַנּוֹצְרִים *Taan.* 27*b*). As usually understood, 'Nazarene' in the first place meant 'of [the town of] Nazareth,' and indeed this explicitly appears in some passages in the Gospels (*e.g.* Mk 1^9 ' Jesus came from Nazareth of Galilee,' Lk 2^4 etc.) ; but, according to Cheyne, the name Nazareth in its original significance was the designation not of a town but of a district, and 'Nazarene' is primarily equivalent to 'Galilæan' (see, further, below, and art. NAZARETH).

Sometimes a descriptive clause with ἀπό followed by the place-name appears : *e.g.* Mt 21^11 'This is Jesus the prophet from Nazareth of Galilee' (ὁ ἀπὸ Ναζαρὲθ τῆς Γαλιλαίας) ; cf. Ac 10^38 ('Ἰησοῦν τὸν ἀπὸ Ναζαρέθ).

2. *The two Gr. equivalents of* 'Nazarene.'—In the Greek Test. two words correspond to 'Nazarene,' viz. Ναζαρηνός and Ναζωραῖος. In WH's text

the former occurs in Mk 1^24 10^47 14^67 16^6, also in Lk 4^34 (where it may be dependent on the Markan source).* In Mt., Jn., Acts (and perhaps originally in Lk.), Ναζωραῖος is exclusively used. Probably Ναζαρηνός was employed in the earliest source, and this was given up later for Ναζωραῖος.

Ναζαρηνός is derived from Ναζαρά, like Μαγδαληνή from Μαγδαλά. The forms Ναζαρά, Ναζαρέτ, Ναζαρέθ imply Heb. forms נָצְרָה, נָצְרַת.† The Talmudic form נוֹצְרִי may be derived from נָצְרַת (or its masc.) with change of ā to ō (ô). See Dalman, *Gram. d. Jüd.-Pal. Aram.*[2] p. 152 n. The same scholar thinks Ναζωραῖος implies a Heb. form נָצוֹרִי (connected with a by-form of the place-name נָצוֹרַת), *op. cit.* p. 178, n. 2. Does Ναζωραῖος (= נָצוֹרִי) represent the dialectical form current in Judaea (cf. esp. Jn 19^19, Ac 24^5)? This is possible. For a different view, see below.

The exact relation borne by these two forms to one another, as well as the significance to be attached to this relationship, raise a difficult problem. The points involved come to a head in Mt 2^23, where it is stated that the child Jesus was brought to Nazareth that 'it might be fulfilled which was spoken by the prophets, that he should be called a Nazarene' (Ναζωραῖος). Of the various explanations of this passage that have been proposed the most important are : (1) those that connect it with the Hebrew word *nēzer* ('branch,' 'sprout') in the Messianic passage, Is 11^1. (2) The interesting view of Hitzig that Ναζωραῖος (Ac 24^5) was suggested by נצורי in the (unpointed) text of Is 49^6 regarded as = σωζόμενοι ('those who are being saved') in contradistinction to ἀπολλύμενοι (1 Co 1^18. 21 'them that are perishing'). Later the word נצורי was taken to be a singular to correspond with the parallel עבר ('servant'), and applied to Jesus (with a play upon the place-name Nazareth). This is very ingenious, but hardly convincing. It would be better to suppose that the (unpointed) נצורי of the passage was read נָצוֹרִי, the Heb. form implied, as Dalman thinks, by Ναζωραῖος, and applied by Jewish-Christian exegesis to Jesus.‡ (3) Cheyne § doubts whether Nazareth was 'originally the name of a town (or village) at all.' The earlier and more correct form of the word is *Nazara*, implying a Heb. form נַצְר (or נָצְרָה, also desiderated by the Talmudic נוֹצְרִי) : and this again is a by-form of the same word which enters into the second element of the name *Gennesar* (Gennesaret). This Nazara is really a name of Galilee, and Ναζωραῖος = Galilæan. The word of the 'prophets' referred to in Mt 2^23 becomes, on this view, Is 9^1f. ('the land of Zebulun, and the land of Naphtali . . . Galilee of the Gentiles') rather than Is 11^1.

It seems clear from the NT data that the term 'Nazarene' was an early designation applied to Jesus and His disciples generally. It thus was the Jewish (Oriental) equivalent of the specifically Gentile term 'Christian.' 'Nazarene' was not the title given by the Christians of Palestine to themselves, but by others outside the Christian fellowship. The names for, and used by, themselves were much more probably such as 'believers,' ‖

---

* It occurs again only in Lk 24^19, where, however, the reading is doubtful (AD read Ναζωραῖος).

† Cf. such forms as צָרְפַת (1 K 17^9) in Bibl. Hebrew.

‡ The verse so interpreted would run : 'It is too light a thing that thou shouldest be my servant to raise up the tribes of Jacob, and (shouldest be) the Nazarene (נצורי) to restore Israel ; I will also give thee for a light of the Gentiles,' etc. This is one of the Servant-passages which was undoubtedly applied to Jesus in early Jewish-Christian circles. Cf. Lk 2^32.

§ Developing a theory suggested by Neubauer and Grätz. See *EBi*, col. 3360, *s.v.* 'Nazareth.'

‖ See FAITH. It is always important to distinguish the names used by a body of itself from those given by outsiders. Another case is probably 'Pharisees,' Heb. = פְּרוּשִׁים = (?) 'separatists.' Their own name for themselves in the earlier period may have been *ḥăsîdîm*, 'pious' : later, such terms as חֲכָמִים 'wise,' תלמיד חכם, חבר 'colleague,' were used. Cf. also remark on Ebionites at end of article.

'brethren' (*e.g.* Ac 9[30]), 'saints' (v.[13] etc.), 'elect.' In time 'Nazarene' seems to have acquired a somewhat contemptuous or, at any rate, hostile *nuance* (cf. Jn 1[46]). The followers of 'the Nazarene' had evidently been made to feel the reproach of the alleged Galilæan origin of their Messiah.* Moved by these influences, the Jewish-Christians seem to have transformed the title Ναζαρηνός—which had now become in the mouths of their opponents an opprobrious one—into the honorific one Ναζωραῖος, and to have substituted the latter for the former. In this way, at any rate, Mt. seems to turn the edge of the reproach levelled at the Christian Messiah in the characteristically Jewish-Palestinian designation of Jesus as 'the Nazarene' (יֵשׁוּעַ הַנּוֹצְרִי). Assuming, then, that the term Ναζωραῖος is an honorific title educed in this way by the Jewish-Christians themselves, it remains to elucidate the process by which the form was arrived at, and its exact significance.

Ναζωραῖος may be a Greek form of *nāẓûrâ* (נָצוּרָא),[†] the Aram. equivalent of the Heb. Messianic term נֵצֶר 'Branch' or 'Shoot.' The selection of this particular Messianic term was dictated by the necessity of finding a counter-term to Ναζαρηνός. Ναζωραῖος is thus an honorific title given by the disciples themselves to Jesus, and expresses the conviction that He was the *nezer* of Is 11[1]—the 'Branch' of Messianic Prophecy. Its application to members of the Christian community naturally followed. See also following article.

3. '*Nazarene*' *as a community-designation.*—It is clear not only from Ac 24[5] but also from Mt 2[23] that the Christian communities of Palestine, and even outsiders, at first bore the name of 'Nazarenes.' The writer of Mt 2[23] evidently belonged to a community so designated. The name is, of course, specifically Jewish, and it remained the characteristic Oriental-Jewish term for Christians generally (*e.g.* in the Talmud), though primarily it was the Jewish Christians of Palestine who were thought of. An interesting piece of early evidence of this usage has in recent years come to light in the Palestinian recension [‡] of the *Shemoneh Esreh.* As is well known, the 12th of these 'Benedictions' contains the famous imprecation on 'slanderers' or 'heretics.' In the Palestinian version an explicit reference is made to 'Nazarenes and Sectaries' (*mînîm*).[§] Though the clause containing these words may not belong to the earliest form of the prayer (early 2nd cent. A.D.), it is, at any rate, not very much later. Jerome (*Ep.* 112) makes allusion to the use of this 'cursing' prayer in the Jewish synagogues throughout the East.

A Jewish-Christian sect of 'Nazarenes' is referred to both by Jerome and Epiphanius. They are apparently to be distinguished from the Ebionites, though very little exact information is extant concerning them.[‖]

* The Galilæan population seems to have been by no means strict in carrying out certain legal enactments regarded as important by the Rabbis. A feeling of distrust, if not of contempt, of the Galilæan population seems to have prevailed in Rabbinical circles. For a full and minute investigation of the relevant data, see the valuable monograph of A. Büchler (*Der galiläische 'Am-ha-areẓ des zweiten Jahrhunderts*, Vienna, 1906).

† Or rather the adjectival form of this, נְצוּרָא. The Aram. word נְצוּרָא is guaranteed by the Syr. ܢܣܘ݂ܪ = *surculus* (Heb. נֵצֶר); see Payne-Smith, *Thes.* col. 2443.

‡ Discovered by Prof. S. Schechter among the Cairo Genizâh MSS, and published by him in the *JQR*, vol. x. [1898] pp. 654-659.

§ See, further, an art. by the present writer in *Church and Synagogue*, vol. v. [1903] p. 167 ff. ('The Jewish Prayer against Heretics').

‖ Possibly 'Ebionites' (Heb. אֶבְיוֹנִים = 'poor men') was a more general term, and may have been given by Jewish-Christians to themselves. See art. EBIONISM.

LITERATURE.—The artt. 'Nazareth,' 'Nazarene' in Hastings' *DB*, the *EBi*, and *JE* ; 'Nazareth' (by Guthe) in *PRE* [3] and in Hamburger's *RE* ; the Comm. on Mt 2[23] (esp. Zahn, 1903); J. Halévy, *Études Évangéliques*, vol. i. p. 231 f. (on Ναζωραῖος : ὁ most valuable and suggestive essay. Halévy suggests the derivation of Ναζωραῖος from the Aram. word adopted above); Neubauer, *Géog. du Talmud*, 1868 ; Biesenthal on Mt 2[23] (*Sacred Lit.* 1859). The bizarre theory as to the existence of pre-Christian 'Nazarenes' set forth by W. B. Smith, *Der vorchristliche Jesus* (1906), does not call for discussion here.

G. H. BOX.

NAZARETH (Ναζαρά, Ναζαράτ, Ναζαρέθ, Ναζαρέτ).—The town of Nazareth, the modern *en-Nâṣira*, was situated in Lower Galilee, 5½ miles almost due west of Mount Tabor, and nearly as far in a south-westerly direction from Kefr Kennâ, the site that is usually identified with Cana of Galilee. The road that ascends from the latter place winds through the high valley in which Nazareth lies, and divides a short distance south of the town, the south-eastern branch finding its way to Jezreel, and thence down the valley to Beth-shean and the Jordan, the western crossing the low pass of the Samaritan hills, by ancient Megiddo, to join eventually the great trunk road north and south, on the plain by the sea. The town itself, however, lay retired from the great highways of commerce, though within easy reach, almost within sight of them ; and its secluded position explains the absence of any mention of Nazareth in the OT or Josephus. The modern village, with a population of seven or eight thousand, clings to the foot of the hill. But the ancient town seems to have spread considerably higher up the slope, and from 'the brow of the hill on which the city was built' (Lk 4[29]), 1600 ft. above the level of the sea, one of the finest views in Palestine is said to be obtained, embracing on the one side the valley of the Jordan and the mountains of Gilead, and on the other the blue waters of the Mediterranean.*

That in our Lord's time Nazareth was a place of considerable importance is indicated by the fact that it is always referred to in the NT as a city (πόλις, Mt 2[23], Lk 1[26] 2[4, 39]) not a village (κώμη). It was in touch with, but not harassed by the currents of popular, commercial, or political life. And there appears to be no real justification for the belief that Nazareth or its people were in any sense insignificant or despised.[†] The words of Nathanael (Jn 1[46]), which have given currency to this view, are perhaps misunderstood. He must himself have shared the universally accepted belief that the Christ could come only from Bethlehem (cf. Mt 2[5], Jn 7[42]) ; and if his language is intended to express disdain, it is no more than that of the polished town-dweller for the uncultivated rural population who know nothing of his artificial rules of propriety and manners. As to the Athenian every native of Bœotia was a dullard, so to the refined *habitué* of Jerusalem the rustic of Galilee may well have appeared uncouth and contemptible. These characteristics might not improbably have become accentuated in the case of Nazareth, owing to its withdrawn position in a self-contained upland valley. Under any circumstances Nathanael's words bear witness only to a personal opinion, and are no evidence of a widespread or general belief.

With the exception of the events of the early ministry recorded in Lk 4[16ff.], the direct references to Nazareth in the Gospels are all associated with the birth and boyhood of Jesus. It was to Nazareth that the angel Gabriel was sent, to Mary

* For a description of Nazareth and its site see G. A. Smith, *HGHL*, London, 1894, p. 432 ff. ; Baedeker's *Palestine* ; *PEF Memoirs*, i. pp. 262 f., 275-79, 328 f. ; A. P. Stanley, *SP*, London, 1860, p. 365 ff. ; cf. W. Sanday, *Sacred Sites of the Gospels*, Oxford, 1903, p. 49 f., with plates ; Ramsay, *Education of Christ*, p. 47.

† See especially Selah Merrill, *Galilee in the Time of Christ*, London, 1886, chs. xvii. xviii.

His mother (Lk 1[26]); and thither His parents came to find a home after the flight into Egypt (Mt 2[23]). From Nazareth they journeyed into Judæa for the purpose of the Roman enrolment (Lk 2[4]), returning to the same city when the requirements of the Jewish law for the purification of Mary had been satisfied (2[39]). Twelve years later a similar visit to Jerusalem, in accordance with His parents' annual practice (2[41f.]), and return to Nazareth (v.[51]), make it evident that the home during this period had been at the latter town. On the occasion of His baptism, it is from Nazareth that, according to St. Mark (1[9]), Christ came to the Jordan; the other Synoptists merely state that the journey was made from Galilee (Mt 3[13]), or name no place (Lk 3[21]). His early life, therefore, was spent at Nazareth, and only in consequence of the opposition aroused by His preaching in the synagogue and the murderous attempt upon His life (Lk 4[28f.]) did He abandon Nazareth and take up His abode at Capernaum (Mt 4[13]). Thenceforward He does not appear to have visited, or to have had any direct relations with, His former home. Its name, however, continued to cling to Him, and by that designation He is known to the 'multitudes' at Jerusalem at the Passover, the stranger-pilgrims from Galilee His native province (Mt 21[11]). Philip uses the name when he calls Nathanael to Jesus (Jn 1[45]); and later in the history it is employed by Peter at Cæsarea (Ac 10[38]) as a well-known title with which Gentiles also would be familiar.

The precise form of the word and its signification are alike uncertain. In two passages (Mt 4[13], Lk 4[16]) the oldest MSS read Ναζαρά, and are followed by all recent editors. Elsewhere in the Synoptic Gospels WH print Ναζαρέτ, with the exception of Mt 21[11] (Ναζαρέθ), Tischendorf reads Ναζαρέθ consistently in all passages of Matthew and Luke (except Ναζαρά, as above), adding with reference to the usage of the latter a note (on Lk 1[26]) that on a comparison of all the instances in which the name occurs in St. Luke, including Ac 10[38], the decision must be that the Evangelist wrote Ναζαρέθ not Ναζαρέτ, a variable usage between the two forms being inconceivable.* In Mark and John the form Ναζαρέτ and in Acts Ναζαρέθ is accepted by all with the more ancient MSS; and in Mk 1[9] the form Ναζαρέτ is found in AP. Dr. Hort also states that in eight out of the eleven passages in the Gospels the Codex Sangallensis has Ναζαράθ, but that the form 'has little other attestation.' It would seem probable that the variations in spelling, where they are not merely accidental, are due to local or dialectic peculiarities,† and are to be ascribed to the transmitters of the tradition or the copyists of the documents rather than to the original authors.‡

The adjective also appears in two different forms. The Second Gospel uses only Ναζαρηνός (Mk 1[24] 10[47] 14[67] 16[6]); Matthew and John have always Ναζωραῖος (Mt 2[23] 26[71], Jn 18[5.7] 19[19]). St. Luke has both in his Gospel (-ρηνός, 4[34] 24[19]; -ραῖος, 18[37]), but in the Acts only Ναζωραῖος (2[22] 3[6] 4[10] 6[14] 22[8] 24[5] 26[9]). In no instance is there any important difference of reading. Neither the noun nor the adjective is found in the Epistles or the Book of Revelation.

There is no agreement, again, with regard to the meaning or derivation of the name. St. Matthew sees in the return to Nazareth a fulfilment of the prophecy of Is 11[1] ('a branch (nēzer) out of his roots shall bear fruit'), thus connecting Nazareth with the Hebrew נצר 'shoot,' 'sprout'; and some have therefore supposed that the name was given to the town in reminiscence of Isaiah's language, and on account of the circumstances of our Lord's early life there. Such an origin of the term is perhaps not impossible, although it hardly commends itself as probable; and of course no such thought was in the mind of the writer, or is intended to be suggested by his words. Others have sought a connexion with the root נצר in the sense of keeping watch or guard; e.g. Dr. Swete would follow Delitzsch and Dalman in explaining Nazareth to mean 'watch-tower.' § This would imply either that the town itself

was on the top of the hill, or that it took its name from the hill on the slopes or at the foot of which it stood; the former would seem to be contrary to fact, and the latter improbable. It would be preferable to understand the word in a passive sense from נצר, to preserve, protect (Old Aram. נְצַר, Assyr. naṣâru),* so that Nazareth is the town secluded, protected, and the name describes its position in a valley surrounded by hills. The word might also be explained as a Niphal participle of צור, נצר, with the same meaning of 'confined,' 'shut in'; compare the adjectival form Ναζωραῖος. Heb. or Aram. צ, however, usually becomes σ in Greek, e.g. צִיּוֹן=Σειών, Σιών, צבאות=Σαβαώθ מצפה=Μασσύχ, Μασσηφά, etc.; or a dental, e.g. צור=Τύρος. But עץ is represented by Ζόγορα in Gn 13[10]. A derivation from נור, denom. of נויר, has also been suggested; Nazareth would then be 'the town of the Nazirites.' נויר becomes in the Greek of the Septuagint ναζίρ, ναζιραῖος. Compare the modern name of the town en-Nāṣira. The latter, however, is more likely to be a conscious or unconscious assimilation of the sound and perhaps the spelling to a well-known descriptive title. See also preceding article.

LITERATURE.—In addition to the references given above, the articles in the Bible Dictionaries may be consulted; add Edward Robinson, BRP, London, 1841, iii. pp. 183–200; A. Edersheim, Life and Times of Jesus the Messiah, London, 1883, i. pp. 145–148, 456 f.; Cunningham Geikie, Holy Land and the Bible, London, 1887, ch. xxxix.; G. le Hardy, Hist. de Nazareth et de ses sanctuaires, Paris, 1905.   A. S. GEDEN.

NAZIRITE (Heb. nāzîr), in AV spelled 'Nazarite,' means etymologically 'one separated,' a religious devotee. The historical references are in Judges (13[2ff.] the case of Samson) and Am 2[11.12]; the 'law of the Nazirite' is found in Nu 6. A comparison of these passages reveals the fact that there was considerable difference between the earlier and the later type of Nazirite. Samson had been 'a Nazirite unto God from his mother's womb' (Jg 16[17]); his Nazirate was lifelong, and due not to any vow, but to the appointment of God (13[1.4.5.7]). In his case the abstinence from wine, which is emphasized in the 'law of the Nazirite,' is not specified, and the avoidance of contact with the dead is apparently excluded. On the other hand, great stress is laid on the hair being left unshorn even from childhood (vv.[4.7.14]). This, which may be taken to be the most marked feature of a Nazirite in early times, rests upon the belief that the hair is part of a man's vital being, and a symbol of his vitality. Thus to let it grow unpolled or to offer it in sacrifice was an expression of the devotion of the entire manhood to God. From the reference in Amos it may be inferred that the Nazirites formed a numerous class in the 8th cent., and that abstinence from wine was then a marked feature in their outward life. According to W. R. Smith (Prophets of Isr. 84), this prohibition 'was undoubtedly a religious protest against Canaanite civilization in favour of the simple life of ancient times. This appears most clearly in the case of the Rechabites, who had received from their father Jonadab the double precept never to drink wine and never to give up their wandering pastoral life for a residence in cities (Jer 31).'

The 'law of the Nazirite' describes the obligations of the Nazirite, the ceremonies to be observed on the accidental interruption of his vow, and the sacrifices to be offered at its termination. It is clear that the vow is now contemplated as one which might be taken for a specified time only. A passage in Josephus (BJ II. xv. 1) suggests that in his time thirty days was regarded as the minimum duration of the vow. It included three points: abstinence from intoxicating drink of every kind, and from the fruit of the vine in any form, avoidance of all contact with the dead, and the letting the hair grow with a view to offering it on the sacred fire (Nu 6[18]). Accidental defilement was followed by seven days of uncleanness, after which the period recommenced, and the vow was

---

* 'ναζαρέτ, c.ℵBKLXII al permu e q. Conlatis omnibus hujus evangelii locis (quibus accedit Ac 10[38] -εθ ℵBCDE) Lucam ναζαρεθ scripsisse statuendum est non ναζαρετ, nisi quod 4 16 formam eum ναζαρα adhibuisse suadent testes. Inter -εθ enim et -ετ eundem scriptorem fluctuasse incredibile est.'

† Compare shibboleth and sibboleth (Jg 12[6]).

‡ Dr. Hort, however, writes:—'The evidence (for the spelling of the name Nazareth) when tabulated presents little ambiguity. Ναζαρά is used at the outset of the Ministry in Mt 1/3 (4[13]) and Lk 1/5 (4[16]); Ναζαρέθ in Mt 1/3 (21[11]), the only later place in the Gospels where the name occurs, and in Acts; and Ναζαρέτ certainly or probably in all other places' (New Testament in Greek, Notes on Orthography, p. 160).

§ See his note on Mk 1[9]; Aram. נצרה. Cf. also Merrill, loc. cit. p. 122.

* Cf. G. A. Cooke, North Semitic Inscriptions, pp. 185, 189; Oxf. Heb. Lex. s.v. נצר.

renewed with elaborate and costly rites. In like manner the termination of the vow is marked by offerings and libations, and specially by the shaving of the hair 'at the door of the tent of meeting,' followed by its being 'put on the fire which is under the sacrifice of peace-offerings' (vv.[13-20]). 'After that the Nazirite may drink wine.' 'It appears most probable that the combination of observances in the law is not ancient, that in the regulations for the Nazirite of later times we see a fusion of several originally distinct customs, which, like many others, had lost much, and, in some cases, all of their original meaning' (G. B. Gray, *ad loc.*). 'Through this change, however, it lost its value; in old times it was Jehovah who raised up the Nazirites as He did the prophets. These were men of God, ensamples of the genuine Israelite God-pleasing life, and therefore of great significance for the whole people. Under the Law the Nazirate had sunk to a private practice of asceticism, through which the individual obtains favour from God' (Benzinger).

Later allusions to the practice of the Nazirite vow are found in 1 Mac 3[49], and in Jos. *Ant.* XIX. vi. 1, *BJ* II. xv. 1 (case of Berenice). John the Baptist, in some respects at least, resembled the Nazirites (Lk 1[15]; cf. the account of James the Just in Eus. *HE* II. xxiii. 3). It has been supposed by some that the vow taken by St. Paul at Cenchreæ, and discharged by him at the Temple, was Nazirite in its character (Ac 18[18], cf. 21[23-26]); but the information given in the Acts is not sufficient to warrant the conclusion (see Knowling, *ad loc.*, in *Expos. Gr. Test.*).

Literature.—Spencer, *de Leg. Heb.* III. i. 6; G. B. Gray, 'Numbers' in *Internat. Crit. Com.*; W. R. Smith, *Prophets*, p. 84 f., *RS*[2] p. 332 f.; W. R. Harper, 'Amos and Hosea' in *Internat. Crit. Com.* p. li ff., 56 f.; Benzinger, *Heb. Arch.* pp. 429 ff.; art. 'Nazirite' in Hastings' *DB*.   C. A. Scott.

NECESSITY

NECESSITY.—We exclude from this article all problems not directly raised by the Four Gospels.

1. Necessity and the Divine nature. — Metaphysicians distinguish between (1) *contingent* existence, and (2) *necessary* existence. A thing exists *contingently*, of which the beginning or end or change can be conceived. A thing exists *necessarily*, of which neither the beginning, nor the end, nor the change can be conceived. The Universe exists *contingently*, for we can imagine its annihilation; the laws of Nature also exist contingently, for we can imagine them altered. On the other hand, the laws of Reason, of Mathematics, and of (fundamental) Morality exist *necessarily*, for we can imagine no beginning or end or change in them.

Thus there never was, or will be, or could be, a time when things which are equal to the same thing could be *unequal* to one another. Nor can we imagine a time, or a world, in which cruelty would be other than odious, and lying other than contemptible. If cruelty and deceit were seated on the throne of the universe, they would still be what they are, odious and contemptible; and benevolence and truth, their opposites, would still be what they are, admirable and praiseworthy. Time and the vicissitudes of things can make no difference to the laws of Reason and the Moral Law. These are eternally and immutably true,—true not only to the human mind, but to every rational mind that does or can exist; valid not only in this universe but in all possible universes.

There exists, therefore, a body of eternal and necessary truth. But this conception of necessary truth carries with it the further conception of *necessary Being*, or *necessary Substance*. A truth cannot exist as it were 'in the air,' or in an infinite void: it must be true to *some mind*. And since the truths in question are independent of all created minds, there must exist some *Eternal Uncreated Mind*, to which these truths are eternally true. Moreover, since the truths are partly *moral truths*, this Mind must be *moral*, or,

to use the language of religion, *holy*. Now it is obvious that to this Infinite Mind the predicate of necessary existence belongs in a higher degree than it belongs to what is called necessary truth. The laws or truths which are called necessary derive their necessary character from the fact that they are the laws of His Mind; but He, the Ultimate and Absolute Mind itself, exists with a degree of necessity transcending theirs. They inhere in Him, not He in them, and consequently He, the Infinite, Absolute, Ultimate Substance, is not only *necessarily* existent, but also *self-existent*.

The self-existence, or necessary existence, of the One True, Living, Personal God is a fundamental doctrine of Scripture. It was taught, according to the traditional exegesis of Ex 3[14], to Moses at the bush, and our Lord endorsed this view of the meaning of the Mosaic revelation (Jn 8[58]). According to the Johannine theology (with which the Pauline is in essential agreement), necessary existence belongs primarily and originally to the Father, who is emphatically ὁ θεός (with the article), and the Living One (ὁ ζῶν πατήρ, Jn 6[57]). To Jesus also, as consubstantial Son, belongs eternal and necessary existence (8[58]). He has 'life *in himself*' (5[26]), and is to creatures 'the resurrection and the life' (11[25]). Yet He has this 'life in himself' by derivation from the Father (5[26] 6[57]), and consequently is (in this aspect) an *Effect*, of which the Father is the *Cause*.[*]

2. Necessity and the Divine freedom. — The Divine freedom, though absolute in the sense that God is free to achieve all that is possible, is limited by the laws of necessary truth and necessary substance as defined in § **1.** Thus, since the laws of Reason are eternally valid, He cannot achieve the essentially irrational, or (what is really the same thing) the essentially impossible. For instance, He cannot annihilate the past, or make the angles of a plane triangle *unequal* to two right angles. Similarly, since He is a *necessary* Substance, He cannot will His own annihilation; and since He is the *supreme necessary Good* (Mk 10[18]), He cannot cease to be good, or will what is evil.

The necessary character of the Divine perfections is fully recognized in Scripture † (Ps 102[24-27], Mal 3[6], Nu 23[19], He 13[8], Ja 1[17]), as also is the doctrine that God's freedom is limited by His character. All that is worthy of Him, He can perform, but deceit, cruelty, and injustice are to Him impossible (Gn 18[25], Job 8[3] etc.).

3. Necessity and the laws of Nature.—It is an important corollary of the Divine freedom, that the laws of Nature do not possess immutable and necessary validity. So far from Nature being a self-contained system of blind, inexorable, materialistically determined forces, it is a realm of *Providence*, in which a Being friendly to man guides the course of events providentially, with the object of securing ultimately to each individual his proper good (Mt 10[29ff.]).

In both Testaments the laws and operations of Nature are regarded as expressions of Jehovah's *free will* (Gn 1, Ps 104, Job 26, Mt 5[45] 6[26ff.] etc.), and consequently as capable of being providentially or miraculously interfered with (Ex 3-15, etc.). The NT lays particular stress upon Christ's control over the forces of Nature (Jn 2[1ff.], Mt 14[22ff.] etc.; see esp. Lk 8[25] 'Who then is this that commandeth even the winds and water, and they obey him?').

4. Necessity and human affairs.—The recognition of God as the sole Absolute and Ultimate Being, excludes the heathen conception of an inscrutable Fate or Necessity (ἀνάγκη) to which gods and men are subject, but it does not of it-

---

[*] Quite Scriptural, therefore, is the Greek theology which regards the Father as αἴτιος, and the Son and Spirit as αἰτιατά.
† The perfections of the Son of God have the same necessary character as those of the Father (see He 13[8]).

self exclude the doctrine of *Theological Determinism* as taught by Calvin. The advocates of this view can appeal plausibly to a considerable number of NT passages.

Thus there are texts which teach that the general course of events is predetermined from eternity (Eph 1[4] 3[11], 2 Ti 1[9], Tit 1[2], 1 P 1[20] etc.), and others which seem to deny human freedom of choice. Most of these are in the Fourth Gospel; see, *e.g.*, Jn 6[37] 'All that the Father giveth me shall come unto me' (cf. 6[39]); 6[44] 'No man can come unto me, except the Father draw him' (ἑλκύσῃ αὐτόν); 10[28] 'they shall never perish, and no one shall snatch them out of my hand'; 12[39] 'for this cause they could not believe, for that Isaiah saith again, He hath blinded their eyes, and hardened their heart'; 17[9] 'I pray for them, I pray not for the world'; 17[12] 'not one of them perished, but the son of perdition, that the scripture might be fulfilled' (cf. 13[18] 17[12], Mt 26[24]). Even in the Synoptics we have Mt 13[11ff.] 'unto you it is given to know the mysteries of the kingdom of heaven, *but to them it is not given*,' etc.; 18[7] 'it *must needs be* that offences come' (ἀνάγκη γάρ ἐστιν ἐλθεῖν τὰ σκάνδαλα); see also 24[6] and 26[24].

But these passages of deterministic tendency are balanced by others of opposite import.

Thus Christ's invitation to be saved is addressed not to selected individuals, but to *all men* : 'Come unto me, *all* ye that labour and are heavy laden' (Mt 11[28]); 'it is not the will of your Father which is in heaven, that *one* of these little ones should perish' (18[14]); 'And I, if I be lifted up, will draw *all men* unto myself' (Jn 12[32]); cf. 1 Ti 2[4] 'God will have *all men* to be saved, and to come unto the knowledge of the truth.'

Since, however, some reject God's benevolent purpose, and refuse to be saved (Mt 25[41] 26[24], Jn 17[12]), it follows that the human will is *free*, and that the apparently deterministic passages of Scripture must be so interpreted as to leave room for human freedom. We are led, therefore, to some such view as this, *that only the main events of human history are absolutely determined beforehand. The persons by whom, and the times when, the Divine purposes are to be realized, are not predetermined absolutely, but only conditionally.* Thus God willed conditionally that the Chosen People should play the leading part in winning the world to the gospel of Christ (Is 60–62, etc.), but, when they proved unfaithful, the Gentiles were called (Mt 21[43] 8[11, 12] etc.). Similarly the time of the Last Judgment is not fixed absolutely, but only conditionally (Mk 13[32] compared with 2 P 3[12] RVm). Applying the same principle to the interpretation of the apparently deterministic passages quoted above, we conclude that Eph 1[4] 3[11] etc. refer mainly to *conditional* predetermination; that 'all that the Father giveth me' (Jn 6[37]) are simply those whom the Father foresaw would be genuine disciples; that the statement that 'no one (*i.e.* no hostile power) shall snatch them out of my hand' (10[28]) does not preclude the possibility that they may *snatch themselves* out of Christ's hand by unfaithfulness; that the 'drawing' of the Father (6[44]) is the attraction of Divine Love, not the Irresistible Call of Calvinism; that the 'I pray not for the world' of Jn 17[9] is to be read in the light of 17[23], that the 'blinding' and 'hardening' of 12[40] are a penalty for past sin; and that even the case of Judas was not one of individual predestination. The general principle bearing upon the case of Judas is laid down in Mt 18[7] 'Woe unto the world because of occasions of stumbling! for it must needs be that the occasions come; but woe to that man through whom the occasion cometh.' That is to say, in a wicked world great crimes are morally certain to be committed, but there is no need for any individual to commit them, therefore woe to that individual by whom they are committed. To apply this to the case of Judas—the world being what it was, alienated from God and full of treachery and malice, *some one* was morally certain to betray Jesus to death. *But that some one need not have been Judas.* He freely undertook the evil business, and therefore his condemnation is just (Mt 26[24]).

5. The predetermination of the events of Christ's life.

—Much stress is laid by the Fourth Evangelist on the predetermination of the events of Christ's life, even with regard to such details as their precise dates and incidental circumstances.

See, *e.g.*, Jn 2[4] 'Mine hour (for changing the water into wine) is not yet come' [it came a few minutes later]; 7[8] 'I go not [yet] up unto this feast, because my time is not yet fulfilled' [it was fulfilled a few days afterwards]; 7[30] 'no man laid his hand on him, because his hour was not yet come' (cf. 8[20]); 12[23] 'the hour is come that the Son of Man should be glorified' [by death]; 12[27] 'for this cause came I unto this hour' [of my death]; 13[1] 'knowing that his hour was come that he should depart out of this world unto the Father'; 17[1] 'Father, glorify thy Son [by death and resurrection], that thy Son may glorify thee.' Cf. Mt 26[39. 53], Lk 13[33], which imply that the length of Christ's ministry and the time of His death were predetermined; also the very strong expression in Lk 22[22] 'the Son of man indeed goeth *as it hath been determined*' (κατὰ τὸ ὡρισμένον). In all these passages the language is strongly predestinarian, but, for the reasons given in the preceding section, the present writer holds that *conditional* predestination is, for the most part, meant.

6. The necessary fulfilment of prophecy.

—According to the ordinary view, it is the nature of the future event that determines the nature of the prophecy. But often in the Gospels it is the nature of the prophecy that is regarded as determining the nature of the future event. This conception is specially characteristic of the First and Fourth Gospels, but it is not peculiar to them.

In St. Matthew, Christ is born of a virgin at Bethlehem, is named Jesus, sojourns in Egypt, resides at Nazareth, migrates to Capernaum, heals the sick, speaks in parables, enters Jerusalem riding an ass, is deserted by the disciples, is betrayed and put to death, 'that it might be fulfilled which was spoken by the Lord through the prophet' (ἵνα πληρωθῇ τὸ ῥηθὲν ὑπὸ τοῦ Κυρίου διὰ τοῦ προφήτου λέγοντος, κ.τ.λ.: so, with slight variations of phrase, 1[22] 2[15. 23] 8[17] 12[17] 13[35] 21[4] 26[53]; cf. 2[5] 13[14. 15] 26[31] 27[9]). Similarly, St. John regards the blindness of Israel as the result of a prophecy of Isaiah (12[39], referring to Is 6[9]); the betrayal of Jesus as happening 'that the scripture (*i.e.* Ps 41[9]) might be fulfilled' (ἵνα ἡ γραφὴ πληρωθῇ); the prevalent hatred of Jesus as coming 'to pass that the word may be fulfilled that is written in their law [viz. in Ps 35[19] 69[4]], They hated me without a cause.' See also Jn 17[12], where 'the son of perdition' perishes 'that the scripture might be fulfilled'; 19[24], where the casting of lots is necessitated by the prophecy, 'They parted my garments among them' (Ps 22[18]); 19[36], where the piercing of Christ's side takes place to fulfil Ps 34[20], and the refraining from breaking His legs to fulfil Ex 12[46]; cf. also 18[9] and 20[9]. For Synoptic parallels see Lk 24[26. 44].

Without entering deeply into the philosophy of the question, we may point out that the two views in question do not necessarily exclude one another. We may suppose that God has a plurality of motives for causing or allowing events to happen, and that when events have been predicted by a duly accredited prophet, *one* of His motives in causing or allowing them to happen, is to maintain the credit of the prophet. This, at any rate, seems to be the view of the Evangelists, who esteem prophecy so highly that they regard a prediction once uttered by a prophet as (in a sense) placing God under a moral obligation to fulfil it. Jesus Himself, on several occasions, acknowledged the obligation of fulfilling the ancient prophecies (see Mt 26[53] 16[21] 21[4], Jn 19[28], etc.).

7. The necessity of means to ends.

—The 'musts' of Christ, of which there are numerous examples in the Gospels, generally refer to the necessity He was under (in order to fulfil the purpose of His Incarnation) to do or to suffer certain things. His original purpose to become incarnate, and to redeem the world, was freely chosen (Ph 2[7], 2 Co 8[9] etc.); but the choice once made, a whole series of experiences (many of them painful and humiliating) became necessary.

As a child of twelve, He was already conscious, according to one interpretation of Lk 2[49] (see RVm), of the necessity of being about His Father's business, and the same idea frequently recurs during the ministry. Almost at the beginning of it He declares to Nicodemus that His purpose to give eternal life to believers can be achieved only by His death: 'As Moses lifted up the serpent in the wilderness, even so must (δεῖ) the Son of Man be lifted up' (Jn 3¹⁴).* He frequently declared the necessity He was under of working during the appointed time—'We must (δεῖ) work the works of him that sent me, while it is day : the night cometh, when no man can work' (Jn 9⁴) ; 'Howbeit I must (δεῖ) go on my way to-day, and to-morrow, and the day following, for it cannot be (οὐκ ἐνδέχεται) that a prophet perish out of Jerusalem' (Lk 13³³) ; 'My meat is to do the will of him that sent me, and to accomplish his work' (Jn 4³⁴, cf. 5¹⁷. ¹⁹ etc.). His visit to Zacchæus was determined by a redemptive purpose (Lk 19⁵ 'to-day I must (δεῖ) abide at thy house.' From the time of Peter's confession at Cæsarea Philippi, intimations of the necessity of the Passion and Resurrection become more frequent ; 'From that time began Jesus to show unto his disciples how that he must (δεῖ) go unto Jerusalem, and suffer many things of the elders and chief priests and scribes, and be killed, and the third day be raised up' (Mt 16²¹) ; 'but first must (δεῖ) he suffer many things, and be rejected of this generation' (Lk 17²⁵) ; 'Behoved it not (οὐκ ἔδει) the Christ to suffer these things, and to enter into his glory ?' (24²⁶).

Corresponding to Christ's obligation of doing and suffering all that is necessary for man's salvation, is man's obligation of appropriating (if he would be saved) the necessary means. Frequent stress is laid upon the latter obligation in the Gospels : see, e.g., Mt 4¹⁷ (the necessity of repentance), 18³ (of conversion), 22³⁷ (of love), Jn 3⁵ (of baptism), 6⁵³ (of the Holy Supper), 15⁴ (of abiding in Christ), etc.

LITERATURE.—See under FREE WILL, and add W. James, 'Necessary Truths' in Principles of Psychology, ii. 617 ff. ; Boutroux, La contingence des lois de la nature ; J. Edwards, Freedom of the Will ; Momerie, Personality ; Martineau, Study of Religion, bk. iii. ch. 2 ; Lotze, Microcosmus, i. 144 ff. ; Sturt, Personal Idealism (iii.) ; A. Moore, Essays (vii.) ; J. S. Mill, Hamilton's Philosophy Examined (xxvi.), and Logic, bk. vi. ch. 2.
C. HARRIS.

NECK.—(1) In the embrace of family salutation the smooth part of the neck below the ear is the part that is kissed, first on one side and then on the other (Lk 15²⁰). This is implied in Hebrew by the use of the dual form (Gn 46²⁹). (2) Prisoners and those condemned to punishment had the chain attached to a metal ring around the neck (Lk 17²). (3) It was on the neck of the oxen that the yoke was placed in ploughing. The freedom from all other bondage, which is conferred and naturalized by the grace of Christ, is conditioned by the yoke of service to Him (Mt 11²⁹. ³⁰). G. M. MACKIE.

NEEDLE.—Although the needle is of prehistoric origin, having been made out of fish bones before the discovery of bronze, it is mentioned only in one passage in the Bible : 'It is easier for a camel to go through the eye of a needle,' etc. (Mt 19²⁴ ‖ Mk 10²⁵, Lk 18²⁵). The eye of a needle is, in Hebrew and Greek, called simply 'the hole,' but in later Arabic it is also called 'the eye.' Thus one modern Arab poet (Mej. Ad. ii. 231) asks, 'What animal has its hoof in its head, and its eye in its tail ?' and another (ib. iii. 273) speaks of 'the eye which never tastes of sleep and is never filled with tears.' The needle is often used as a symbol of self-neglect, in that it clothes all the world and itself remains naked (Burckhardt, 563).

The phrase cited above from the Gospels was used in the schools, with the substitution of an elephant for a camel, to express something which does not happen. Thus in Baba Mezia, 38b, in the course of a discussion on dreams and their interpretation, R. Shesheth says to R. Amram, who had tried to convince him of something incredible : 'Perhaps you are from Pumbeditha [where there flourished a famous academy of the Babylonian Rabbis], where they can drive an elephant through the eye of a needle'—that is, can prove that black is white. Similarly, Berakhoth, 55b : 'No one ever saw a golden palm, nor an elephant entering the eye of a needle.' For other occurrences of the phrase, see Buxtorf's Lex. s.v. אלב.† T. H. WEIR.

* Some critics assign this saying to the Evangelist, not to Jesus.
† The proposals that have been made to identify the 'needle's eye' with the small door in a large city gate, or to substitute 'cable' (κάμιλος) for 'camel' (κάμηλος), have nothing in their favour. See Hastings' DB iii. 505ᵃ, and Expos. Times, ix. (1898) 388, 474 ; A. Wright, Some N.T. Problems, 125.

NEIGHBOUR.—To the people of Israel, God had given the commandment, 'Thou shalt love thy neighbour as thyself' (Lv 19¹⁸) ; but in their hardness of heart they had put a limit to it. They had deduced from the commandment, 'Thou shalt love thy neighbour'—its converse—'and hate thine enemy' (Mt 5⁴³) ; and they had made the latter as binding as the former. To a people who regarded themselves as the sole recipients of Jehovah's favour, the limitation was not unnatural ; but with the revelation of God as the universal Father, who showers His blessings equally upon all the world, just and unjust alike (Mt 5⁴⁵), the limitation must of necessity be swept away. To make men like to God was the essential aim of the life and teaching of Jesus Christ ; and as the love of God is limitless, the love of man to man must be no less. All His doctrine in reference to man's treatment of his neighbour He summed up in the words, 'Be ye therefore perfect, even as your Father which is in heaven is perfect' (Mt 5⁴⁸). 'Neighbour,' then, upon our Lord's lips becomes a term synonymous with 'humanity.' 'Who is my neighbour ?' asked a scribe ; and Christ made answer with the parable of the Good Samaritan (Lk 10²⁵⁻³⁷), seeking by a picture of pure compassion to shame him of his question. 'Dost thou ask,' He seems to say, 'who thy neighbour is ? Set about at once to relieve the misery of every one thou meetest. Make thyself the neighbour of all who need thy help.' It is to be noted that in the application of the parable He does not ask which of the three was, but which of the three became (γεγονέναι, v.³⁶) neighbour unto him that fell among thieves. In the Sermon on the Mount He makes the same thing clear by direct statement—that 'neighbour' includes all the world of men, even those who hate and persecute us (Mt 5⁴³. ⁴⁴).

To the old commandment, 'Thou shalt love thy neighbour as thyself,' Christ gives a new and striking form in the words, 'Whatsoever ye would that men should do to you, do ye even so to them' (Mt 7¹²) ; and that the all-importance of this rule may be made plain, He adds, 'for this is the law and the prophets.' He thus makes a man's own longing for love and kindness and compassion the measure of the treatment which he should extend to others. But this love and compassion must not be the outcome of any selfish motive. To do good to others that we may receive the same again, is to miss wholly love's reward (Mt 5⁴⁶. ⁴⁷ ‖ Lk 6³²⁻³⁴) ; for the joy of love is loving : it is more blessed to give than to receive (Ac 20³⁵). To ask to our feasts only those who can invite us in return is no manifestation of love—is but a bid for earthly recompense. To obtain God's blessing we must invite the poor, the maimed, the lame, the blind, who can give nought in return (Lk 14¹²⁻¹⁴). The presupposition of our Lord's teaching, then, is this, that love is its own reward, that to lose one's life for love's sake is to find it (Mt 10³⁹ ‖ 16²⁵, Mk 8³⁵, Lk 9²⁴). The true servant of the Kingdom, therefore, must be ever ready to give unstintingly and ungrudgingly of all that he has and is ; and even to those who would take from him by violence must offer no resistance (Mt 5³⁹⁻⁴²).

It follows naturally that the Christian must be as ready to forgive as to give. When a brother seeks forgiveness, it must be granted gladly, even unto seventy times seven (Mt 18²¹ ‖ Lk 17³. ⁴). There can be no refusal of pardon to the penitent, for so the Heavenly Father treats His erring children (cf. the parable of the Prodigal Son, Lk 15¹¹ff.). To refuse to remit the offences of others means to remain unpardoned by God ; for the Heavenly Father cannot forgive His children if they will not in turn forgive their brethren, who also are His children : for thus they cut themselves off from the family of God, exclude themselves from His love (Mt 6[12] 18[35]). The hatred of a brother becomes a sin which cannot be pardoned except it be repented of, except the hatred be wiped out and love restored. The universal Fatherhood of God is thus once more the basis of the argument (1 Jn 4[20. 21] 5[1]). And not only towards those who are fellow-subjects of the Kingdom is love inculcated : it must extend even to those who are our enemies and the enemies of God (Lk 6[37. 38]) ; for Christ came to seek and to save the lost, and the Christian must follow in his Master's steps. Yet, on the other hand, forgiveness must in no case flow from mere weak benevolence which foregoes revenge for injury, and leaves the matter there. An entrance must be won for pardon into the heart of the offender before the Christian's work is done ; for pardon must be accepted as well as granted. It is not for his own but for his brother's sake that a man must forgive ; and forgiveness is spiritually useless to the offender unless he repent of his offence. To win souls for God's Kingdom is the Christian's noblest work, and it is to that end that his whole treatment of his neighbour must be directed (Mt 18[15]). Reproof, therefore, must not be wanting. The offence must be pointed out, and the sinner urged to amendment. In Mt 18[15-21] (|| Lk 17[3ff.]) a course of treatment is prescribed for the impenitent. He is to be dealt with privately as a first step ; if that fails, in the presence of witnesses ; and as a last step the Church is to be called in to aid in effecting a reconciliation. Only when all has proved vain is he to be regarded as a heathen man and a publican. But even then love's offices may not cease. The publican and the heathen still remain the Christian's care, are still sharers in the love of God. Love must still strive with him, by returning good for evil, by heaping coals of fire upon his head, to win him back to God and love (Mt 5[44], Ro 12[20]). When all else has failed, there still remains the duty of prayer to God, who in His providence may find a way to penitence.

It follows from the humble self-forgetting attitude which this implies, that all loveless judgment of the weaknesses and sins of others is wholly forbidden. To judge is to usurp the prerogative of God, and to bring upon ourselves His condemnation of our lovelessness (Mt 7[1. 2]). Yet men are not to close their eyes to the characters of those about them. They must certainly seek to find the best that is in every man, and to draw it to the light even as Christ did ; but to treat the notoriously wicked man as if he were good and upright is to make him a cause of offence to others, and at the same time to tempt the man himself to greater wickedness. To act thus is to cast pearls before swine (Mt 7[6]). There is no more grievous sin against love than to disregard or to play upon the weaknesses of others. We must know others' weaknesses that we may avoid offending them and causing them to stumble. But that we may be able to do this—to help the weak brother and to save him from his defects—it is first needful that we should be conscious of our own. If our own eyes are blinded by the beam of self-righteousness and pride, we cannot see clearly to cast out the mote out of our brother's eye (Mt 7[3-5] || Lk 6[41] || Gal 6[1]). In the very strongest terms our Lord warns against the giving of offence to others, even to the least. It were better, He says, to suffer the most miserable death than so to endanger the salvation of another, and sin against God's love (Mt 18[6. 7. 10]). In 1 Co 8 St. Paul treats of the matter in reference to a particular instance, pointing out that even Christian liberty must be willingly laid aside if it in any way tends to hurt the conscience of a weaker brother. Love for souls is so absolutely the law of the Christian life that it makes right wrong

and wrong right. Charity is the greatest virtue of all, so that the want of it makes every other virtue worthless (1 Co 13).

To summarize the doctrine, the revelation of the new relationship between God and man, and the new law which rests thereon, make of love the highest principle in life, and make the love of God and the love of man one and the same ; and since love is the divinest element in human nature, it must be love's object to beget and to increase love in others. Hence towards all who are our brethren in the Lord we must be humble and meek and forgiving, 'in honour preferring one another' (Ro 12[10]), seeking greatness not in dominion but in service (Mt 20[26. 27] || Lk 22[26]) ; for it is ever the overestimate of self that takes offence and causes hate (Mk 7[22]) ; and to the sinner and the unbeliever who are ignorant of love, there is but the greater need to make love manifest by unwearying self-sacrifice and unceasing kindness ; for so the evil in the other's heart will be overcome, and the Divine germ of love within him will be fanned into a living flame, and he also will become a true son of God (Mt 5[38-48] || Lk 6[28-31] || Ro 12[19-21]). It is those whose whole lives make for peace—the peace that springs not from indifference but from love—who shall be called the children of God (Mt 5[9]).

LITERATURE.—Works on *NT Theol.* by Beyschlag and by Weiss ; the Comm. on the NT, and works on the Parables ; J. H. Thom, *Laws of Life after the Mind of Christ*, 330 ; M. Creighton, *The Mind of St. Peter*, 38.
                                             W. J. S. MILLER.

NERI.—An ancestor of Jesus, Lk 3[27].

NEST.—Orientals, while often indifferent to the study and explanation of natural processes, have always been attracted by the provisions of instinct for the preservation of animal life. They observed the home-like motive of rest and safety in the selection and construction of birds' nests (Job 29[18], Ps 84[3] 104[17], Jer 48[28] 49[16]). In the Gospels the word tr. 'nest' (κατασκήνωσις) means generally the place of night shelter for birds (Mt 8[20]), or where they alight in search of food during the day (13[31. 32]). By contrasting His own with the more fortunate condition of the birds, Christ intimates that whoever, like the scribe, would follow Him to the uttermost, may for His sake have to endure loneliness, misunderstanding, and rejection. The reference to the mustard seed, which in its wild state produces a shrub reaching to the seat of a horse's saddle, indicates that power of rapid expansion inherent in Christ's Kingdom which has often surprised both its friends and its foes.
                                             G. M. MACKIE.

NETS.—Nets were in ancient times used not only in fishing but in hunting beasts and in birdcatching. In the Gospels they are mentioned only in connexion with fishing, which was an important industry on the very prolific inland waters of Palestine. See FISH. Three terms occur. **1.** δίκτυον (perhaps from δικεῖν, 'to cast '), Vulg. *rete*, is the general term, including various kinds of nets. It is found in the parallel accounts of the call of the disciples (Mt 4[20. 21], Mk 1[18. 19], Lk 5[2-5]) always in the plural. In St. John's narrative of the great draught of fishes (21[6. 8. 11]) it is found in the sing., possibly referring to a net of larger size. See **3** below.

2. ἀμφίβληστρον (which may perhaps be an adjective, δίκτυον being understood), a casting-net (deriv. ἀμφιβάλλω, which verb stands, without a noun, for the action of the fisherman in using the net, Mk 1[16]), bell- or pear-shaped, thrown by hand from the shore or from a boat, which was skilfully wielded so as to fall upon the water with its circular mouth fully extended. The edges, being weighted, sank immediately to the bottom, and the fish within the area of the mouth were enclosed. This net is still much used in Palestine. The individual skill required in its employment is in point if it was with this kind of net in mind that our Lord invited the fishermen to become 'fishers of men.' In the Gospels the word is found only in Mt 4[18] and (in the TR) Mk 1[16].

3. σαγήνη (Lat. [so Vulg.] *sagena*; French and English, 'seine'), from σάττω, 'to load, fill': a drag-net (Mt 13[47] RVm) or sweep-net, often of immense size (Manilius, 'vasta sagena'). Such nets have been in use from early times down to the present day, and are extensively employed on our own coasts, as, for instance, in Cornwall. A common way of working the seine is to have one end of it attached to the shore, while the other is taken seawards by a boat in a wide circuit, and at length brought to land again. The upper side of the net is sustained by corks, while the lower, being weighted, sweeps along the sea-bottom. The ends are gradually drawn in till the whole net is brought up on the beach, carrying with it all the fish in the area through which it has passed. The seine may also be worked entirely from a boat or boats. In classical Latin this kind of net is called *everriculum* (*verro*, 'to sweep'); cf. Hom. *Il.* v. 487, λίνον πάναγρον, a take-all net. σαγήνη is found in the Gospels only in Mt 13[47] (tr. 'net,' the word 'draw-net' is not in the Eng. text, but only in the AV chapter-heading), where the choice of this term instead of δίκτυον or ἀμφίβληστρον greatly strengthens the meaning of the parable. See DRAW-NET. It occurs in LXX Is 19[8], Ezk 26[5]; and ἀμφίβληστρον and σαγήνη are mentioned together in Hab 1[15].

LITERATURE.—R. Flint, *Christ's Kingdom upon Earth*, 245; H. S. Holland, *God's City*, 206; W. C. E. Newbolt, *Counsels of Faith and Practice*, 169.   A. E. ROSS.

NEW BIRTH.—See REGENERATION.

NEW COMMANDMENT.—The definition of the Christian law of love as a 'new commandment' is peculiar to the Johannine writings (Jn 13[34] 15[12], 1 Jn 2[7. 8], 2 Jn [5]). In the Fourth Gospel the Supper is regarded as the prototype of the Agape rather than of the Eucharist, and the institution of the 'new covenant' gives place to that of the 'new commandment' of brotherly love. The commandment, like the covenant, is inaugurated by a symbolical act, the washing of the disciples' feet.

In the Synoptic Gospels our Lord repeatedly insists on love for one's neighbour as the paramount ethical duty (cf. Mt 5[43-48], Mk 12[31], Lk 10[30-37]); He contrasts this new conception of the Moral Law with the rule that held good 'in old time' (Mt 5[43-44]). The words in the Fourth Gospel thus sum up with an exquisite simplicity the authentic substance of the social teaching of Jesus. At the same time there are elements in the Johannine idea which differentiate it from the apparent parallels in the Synoptics.

(1) Jesus in His teaching, as given in the Synoptics, does not impose His ethic under the form of 'commandment.' Accepting the moral code of the Decalogue as Divinely given, He contents Himself with 'fulfilling' it by a deeper and more inward interpretation. The effect of His 'fulfilment' is indeed to replace the ancient Law by a new one, but in this Christian law the idea of commandment is altogether transcended. It is a 'law of liberty,' which the enlightened conscience originates for itself. The Fourth Gospel reverts to the idea of 'commandment'—of a moral law enforced from without. Jesus as the Son of God has power to impose a new law, equally binding with that of the Decalogue; and it is henceforth valid in virtue of His authority.

(2) The divergence from the Synoptics is still more marked in regard to the scope of the 'new commandment.' The love which it requires is the φιλαδελφία that found expression in the Agape; not love to one's neighbour in the universal sense, but love of Christians to one another. Here more signally than elsewhere the Fourth Evangelist betrays the influence of the later Church-idea which had narrowed the original intention of the teaching of Christ. A sharp distinction had grown up between the community of believers and the 'world,' and the duty of Christians was primarily, if not exclusively, to their brethren. The passage in the Fourth Gospel already contemplates a time when mutual love within the Church was the γνώρισμα τῶν Χριστιανῶν (Jn 13[35], cf. Tert. *Apol.* 39). There is no indication of a wider demand, in the spirit of the Sermon on the Mount and the parable of the Good Samaritan.

The commandment is expressly called a *new* one, although in its Synoptic form it appears as a direct quotation from the ancient Law (Mt 22[39] ‖ Mk 12[31] = Lv 19[18]). The newness has been explained in various ways. (*a*) According to the Greek commentators (Cyril, Theod. Mops. etc.) it consists in the higher degree of love implied in καθὼς ἠγάπησα ὑμᾶς—not 'as thyself' but 'more than thyself,' with the self-forgetting love of Christ. This, however, overstrains the meaning of καθώς, which says nothing of the quality of Christ's love, but states the simple fact of His example. (*b*) Several modern commentators (*e.g.* Meyer, Godet, Bugge) have still sought the explanation in the words 'as I have loved you.' The love of Christ experienced by the believer is to be the motive power to a new and higher kind of love. Our love to one another is henceforth to be Christian love—not grounded in a mere natural instinct, but in an inward fellowship with Christ. This idea is certainly present in the Gospel, and in the Epistle it comes to definite expression. 'Hereby we know love, because he laid down his life for us; and we ought to lay down our lives for the brethren' (1 Jn 3[16]). The love required in Christians is the greater love which was revealed for the first time in the Cross of Christ. This, however, does not seem to be the idea involved in the 'new commandment.' The newness is ascribed to the commandment itself, not to the motive or the quality of the love enjoined in it. (*c*) An attractive explanation is that suggested by Olshausen. The commandment of love is new in the sense that it is for ever fresh, always renewing itself. Such a meaning seems to be plainly implied in the beautiful antithesis in the Epistle (1 Jn 2[7. 8]), 'I write no new commandment unto you, but an old commandment. Again, a new commandment I write unto you.' This passage, however, is a kind of poetical expansion of the idea of a 'new commandment,' and cannot be construed as an exegesis. (*d*) The simplest and most natural explanation is that Christ has in effect established a new morality by His insistence on love as the fulfilment of the Law. In outward form the demand was an old one, and this is acknowledged in the Synoptic parallels by the quotation from Leviticus. But the place assigned to it by Jesus as the sum of the Law, the sovereign principle of the moral life, invests it with a new significance. The ancient morality is superseded by the Christian law of love. The words in the Fourth Gospel thus give expression to the truth which had emerged ever more clearly in the course of later reflexion,—that the teaching of Jesus, based as it was on the religion of the OT, was something radically new. The Law had been not only fulfilled but abrogated. In its place there was a new commandment, a new determining principle for the moral life.

As indicated above, the definition of the Christian ethic as a 'new commandment' is in one respect inadequate, and even involves a self-contradiction. The true originality of the moral demand of Jesus consisted in its breaking away from the idea of outward requirement. The Law imposed from without was replaced by the inward spirit of faith and love and obedience. In the Fourth Gospel we have probably the earliest phase of the reaction which ended in the formulation of Christianity as *nova lex*. The development of the Church as an institution was accompanied by a certain externalizing of moral and religious ideas, while at the same time the influence of the OT favoured the relapse into a modified legalism. Thus where St. Paul, in full accordance with the Synoptics, demanded a new spirit (cf. Ro 12[2], Gal 5[16]), the later Church was satisfied with obedience to a 'new law.' The Fourth Gospel appears to mark the transition between these two conceptions of Christian morality. The true character of the 'commandment' is still safeguarded by the profound religious spirit of the Gospel, but the idea of outward ordinance has begun to re-establish itself. In a subsequent age, which had drifted out of sympathy with the original teaching of Jesus, the 'new commandment' became literally the *nova lex*.

Literature.—The Comm. on Jn 13[34f.] 15[12], *e.g.* Holtzmann, *Hdcom.* (1893); Godet (Eng. tr. 1892); Oscar Holtzmann (1887); Bugge (Germ. tr. 1894); Loisy, *Le Quatrième Évangile* (1903); J. Réville, *Le Quatrième Évangile*, 245 f. (1901); cf. also H. J. Holtzmann, *NT Theol.* i. 494 f., ii. 344 f., 389 f. (1897); Stevens, *Johannine Theol.* 266 f. (1900); R. F. Horton, *The Commandments of Jesus*, 319 ; F. W. Robertson, *Ser.* i. 234 ; T. T. Carter, *Spirit of Watchfulness*, 206.   E. F. SCOTT.

NEW TESTAMENT. — The expression 'New Testament' (καινὴ διαθήκη) has a double meaning. (1) The New Covenant itself (Lk 22[20], 1 Co 11[25], 2 Co 3[6] etc.). See artt. COVENANT and TESTAMENT. No other meaning is possible in the Bible. (2) The books that contain the New Covenant. The latter is the subject of this article.

1. The genesis of a NT literature.—This is to be assigned, humanly speaking, to the slowly developing needs of the Christian society. The Apostles were commissioned not to write but to preach. The OT, interpreted in the light of its fulfilment in Christ, contained both for them and for their earliest converts the whole deposit of Divine truth (2 Ti 3[15] etc.). (*a*) Epistles, as a class, were needed first, in order to settle questions that soon arose on the conversion of Gentiles (Ac 15). Many of the Epistles plainly show their 'occasional' origin (1 Co 7[1], 2 Co 9[1], Gal 1[6], 2 Th 2[1f.] etc.). Formal communications were evidently no new thing in Jewish communities (Ac 9[2] 28[21]). (*b*) Narratives of Christ's words and works, such as the Gospels, were not at once so necessary. Men were looking for Christ's speedy return (2 Th 2[2]), and eye-witnesses of His ministry were at first plentiful (Ac 1[22], 1 Co 15[6]). The demand for written and authentic narratives was forcibly realized only when Apostles and eye-witnesses began to pass away (2 P 1[15ff.], 2 Ti 4[6ff.]), and irresponsible persons took in hand to supply the want (Lk 1[1f.]). Yet even in the next generation there lingered a preference for traditional reminiscences, cf. Papias (*c.* A.D. 140) *ap.* Eus. *HE* iii. 39. On the shortest reckoning no Gospel was committed to writing in its present shape within twenty-five years after Christ's Ascension.

2. The canonical reception of NT writings.—This may be said to have passed through three stages, not wholly separable in point of time.

(1) The first stage is that of *collective recognition* (extending roughly to A.D. 170). Christian writers of this period exhibit—(*a*) Coincidences of language with NT expressions : *e.g.* Clem. Rom. (*c.* A.D. 95) ; Ign. (*c.* A.D. 110) ; Polyc. (*c.* A.D. 116) ; Barn. (*c.* A.D. 70–130) ; *Didache* (*c.* A.D. 90–165) ; Herm. (*c.* A.D. 140–155) ; Heges. [*ap.* Eus.] (*c.* A.D. 155). —(*b*) Anonymous references—which seem to have been the set rule for all writers of 'Apologies,' whatever their custom in other works : *e.g.* Just. M. (*c.* A.D. 150) ; *ad Diogn.* (*c.* A.D. 170 ?) ; also 2 Ep Clem. (*c.* A.D. 140).—(*c*) Direct references : *e.g.* Clem., *ad Cor.* xlvii., alludes to 1 Co. ; Polyc., *ad Ph.* iii., to Philippians ; Papias (before A.D. 150), *ap.* Eus. *HE* iii. 39, mentions a record of Christ's words and deeds by Mark, and 'logia' (originally in Hebrew) by Matthew ; Just. M., *Dial.* ciii., speaks of 'Memoirs by Apostles and those that followed them,' and refers to the Apocalypse (*Dial.* lxxxi.) by name.—(*d*) Dogmatic recensions: Tatian, *Diatessaron* (*c.* A.D. 150), harmonized the four Gospels ; Marcion (*c.* A.D. 140) mutilated Luke and (acknowledging ten Pauline Epistles) rejected the three Pastoral Epistles.—(*e*) Catalogues : *e.g.* the Muratorian fragment (composed *c.* A.D. 160), which, according to Westcott, gives 'a summary of the opinion of the Western Church on the Canon shortly after the middle of the 2nd century.'

(2) The second stage is that of *unique authority*. —(*a*) A succession of contrasts is drawn by Christian writers. (α) Apostles and themselves : cf. all the Apostolic Fathers—Clem. Rom. vii. xlvii. ; Polyc. *ad Ph.* iii. ; Ign. *ad Rom.* iv. ('not as Peter and Paul') ; Barn. i, iv ('not as a teacher'). (β) Apostolic records and traditions : Justin M., *Ap.* i. 33, says the Memoirs of the Apostles relate 'all things concerning Jesus Christ.' 'These words (Westcott observes) mark the presence of a new age. . . . Tradition was definitely cast aside as a new source of information.' (γ) Canonical (ἐνδιάθηκοι) and uncanonical (ἀπόκρυφοι) books : *generally, e.g.* Dionysius of Corinth (*c.* A.D. 176), *ap.* Eus. *HE* iv. 23, says, 'the Scriptures of the Lord . . . and those that are not of the same character'; and *in detail, e.g.* Clem. Alex. (*c.* A.D. 165–200) *ib.* vi. 14 ; Origen (A.D. 286–353), *ib.* vi. 25 ; Dionys. Alex. (*c.* A.D. 248) *ib.* vii. 25—representing the opinion of Alexandria ; Tertullian (*c.* A.D. 160–240), *de Pudic.* 20, that of Latin Africa ; Caius (*c.* A.D. 213), *ap.* Eus. *HE* vi. 20, that of Rome ; Irenæus (*c.* A.D. 135–200), *ib.* v. 8, cf. Iren. *Hær.* iii. 7, that of Asia Minor and Gaul ; Serapion (*c.* A.D. 190), *ap.* Eus. *HE* vi. 12, that of Syria. These exhibit substantial agreement, together with variety in detail. From Tertullian's time the general estimate was much as it is to-day.

(*b*) Illustrations of this developing consciousness are seen in two matters arising from constant use of the books. (i.) *The descriptive titles.* Barnabas, *Ep.* iv., is the first to use the formula 'as it is written' in quoting words taken from the N.T. [= Mt 22[14]]. In Justin M., *Ap.* i. 66, the term 'Gospels' is first applied to books. Melito of Sardis (*c.* A.D. 170), *ap.* Eus. *HE* iv. 26, refers to 'the books of the Old Testament,' implying undoubtedly by contrast 'the books of the New.' The latter description is expressly used by Irenæus, *Hær.* ii. 58, and the two Testaments are from that time on a level. Chrysostom is said to have been the first to adopt the expression 'Bible' (τὰ βιβλία) for the two Testaments as one whole. (ii.) *Public reading.* For some considerable time (varying much in different places) *profitableness* seems to have been the only absolute test required. Dionys. of Corinth (*c.* A.D. 170–175), *ap.* Eus. *HE* iv. 23, refers to the public reading of a letter from Soter, as well as to the better known instance of the Ep. of Clem. of Rome. Eusebius (*ib.* iii. 3) relates that Hermas had formerly been read in public on account of its usefulness for 'elementary instruction.' *Apostolic nature* (*i.e.* practically inspiration') was subsequently the regular test : cf. Eus. *l.c.* and Cyril of Jerus. (*c.* A.D. 340), *Catech.* iv. 33–36. Hence δημοσιεύεσθαι under the former conditions refers merely to the fact of public reading ; under the latter it is a declaration of canonical authority.

(3) The third stage is that of *formal definition.*— Diocletian's persecution (A.D. 303–311), directed against the Christian Scriptures, proves that their unique position and influence was a matter known to the heathen throughout the Roman Empire. It also made the identification of those Scriptures, as distinct from other Christian books, a vital matter (cf. the history of the Donatist schism on the question of 'traditores'). Eusebius, writing A.D. 313–325, sums up the general consent of that time (*HE* iii. 3, 24, 25), in three classes of books—'acknowledged,' *i.e.* of undisputed authenticity and Apostolic power ; 'disputed,' *i.e.* defective in either of those qualities ; and 'heretical.' The Emperor Constantine (A.D. 331) caused to be prepared, under the direction of Eusebius, fifty copies of the Divine Scriptures for use in the churches of Constantinople (cf. Eus. *Vit. Const.* iv. 36). These must have become a standard in the Greek Church. It may be added that the evidence of ancient versions, old Latin, Syriac, and Egyptian, is of great importance ; but it is of too complicated a nature to be briefly discussed. Succeeding Councils dealt with the Canon, esp. that of Laodicea (*c.* A.D. 363) and the third of Carthage (A.D. 397). The catalogue of canonical books which bears the name of the former is held to be spurious : to the catalogue of Carthage Christendom adheres to-day.

LITERATURE.—The NT (as a whole or its separate portions) forms the subject of well-known 'Introductions,' Commentaries, etc. For special information see Sanday, *Inspiration* ; Wright, *Synopsis* (oral theory) ; Westcott, *Canon of NT* and *Bible in the Church* ; Moffatt, *The Historical NT.* A work on the 'Canon and Text of the NT' (Gregory) is to form part of the *International Theol. Library* series.   F. S. RANKEN.

NICODEMUS.—One of the persons mentioned only in the Fourth Gospel. He is described as a Pharisee and a ruler of the Jews. He had an interview with Jesus by night (Jn 3[1ff.]) ; and though he did not become an avowed disciple, he protested in the Sanhedrin against the hasty condemnation of Jesus (7[50f.]) ; and after the Crucifixion he brought spices to embalm the body of the Lord (19[39]).

The name *Nicodemus* is Greek (from νίκη and δῆμος—'conqueror of the people'). Josephus (*Ant.* XIV. iii. 2) gives Nicodemus as the name of an ambassador from Aristobulus to Pompey. In the Talmud we have the form נַקְדִּימוֹן as the name given to a certain Bunai ben Gorion, because, it is said, of a miraculous answer to his prayer. This ben Gorion was a rich man, and is reported to have spent a vast sum on the marriage of his daughter, who afterwards sank into abject poverty. He appears to have had charge of the supply of water to the pilgrims at Jerusalem ; and he was accused of being a Christian. Some have identified this man with the Nicodemus of the Gospel ; but the positive grounds of identification are insufficient ; and there is the negative consideration that ben Gorion is spoken of as living till the siege of Jerusalem, whereas Nicodemus, already in Jn 3 an elderly man (γέρων, v.[4]), could hardly have survived to so late a period. Some writers, who regard the Fourth Gospel as unhistorical, suggest that our Nicodemus is simply a typical character, constructed by the Evangelist from the traditions of ben Gorion, with the aid of the Synoptic references to Joseph of Arimathæa. Thus E. A. Abbott (*Ency. Bib.* art. 'Nicodemus') says : 'Nicodemon ben Gorion passes into the Gospel under the shadow of Joseph of Arimathæa'; and speaks of 'a conflate development of Joseph into two persons.' He says that N. ben Gorion was one of three or four who were sometimes called βουλευταί, 'rich men,' 'great men of the city,' and suggests that as an official provider of water he was an appropriate character for a dialogue on regeneration. He concludes that Nicodemus is 'a Johannine conception representing the liberal, moderate, and well-meaning Pharisee, whose fate it was to be crushed out of existence in the conflict between Judaism and its Roman and Christian adversaries.' This reconstruction can hardly be persuasive except to those who on other grounds have already judged the Fourth Gospel to be without historic value. The general discussion goes beyond the limit of this article. It is enough to say here that there is nothing in what is related of Nicodemus, or in the circumstances of his connexion with Jesus, which is in itself improbable, or out of harmony with what we

are told elsewhere. It is altogether probable that some men of the upper classes and of the Pharisees would be attracted by the personality and teaching of Jesus, and that they would seek with varying degrees of caution to know more of Him. To a certain extent the Synoptics confirm this (cf. Lk 7[36] 8[3] 19[5]). We may add that the personality of Nicodemus stands out clearly in spite of the brevity of the reference to him. The protest in the Sanhedrin shows the same blending of courage with caution as the interview by night. There was a sufficient sense of truth and justice, and of personal interest in Jesus, to enable him to risk the anger of the majority by a protest, but enough of caution or timidity to put the protest into an indirect and tentative form rather than into a bold defence of the Master. The personality of Nicodemus and the conduct ascribed to him do not weaken the case for the historic credibility of the Evangelist.

It has been urged with some measure of plausibility that the conversation in Jn 3 bears the marks of artificial construction. It is said that it is really a brief sermon by the Evangelist, and follows the regular plan of the Johannine discourses :—a pregnant saying by the Master ; a remark by an interlocutor who misunderstands the text by taking it literally and not spiritually ; then a further exposition by the speaker : the whole being 'a thoroughly artificial construction on a set plan' (Gardner, *A Historic View of the NT*, sec. vi.). There is a very general agreement that the discourses in the Fourth Gospel owe something of their form to the Evangelist. Differences of opinion on that point are almost entirely confined to the question of the extent to which the writer has gone in condensing or re-shaping the Master's utterances. Without surrendering the conviction that we have a faithful report of the substance of a real conversation, we may readily admit that the Evangelist has put his material into the form which seemed best fitted to make the truth clear to his readers. He is, we may suppose, chiefly interested in Nicodemus 'as instrumental in eliciting from Jesus' the sayings which he records. But this does not make Nicodemus a mere lay figure, and his questions mere 'rhetorical artifice.'

Dr. Gardner says of the question in v.[4] : 'Such crassness is scarcely in human nature.' Yet when we give due weight to the prejudices of a Pharisee and allow for the deadening effect of respectable religious legalism, it is not hard to understand the sheer bewilderment of Nicodemus at the idea that he—no Gentile, no publican—needed to be born anew. How common it is for men of such a type to be utterly unable to understand even an elementary spiritual truth, if it cuts across their conventions and challenges their privileges. Nicodemus did not at all suppose that a second physical birth was meant. He was simply unable to conceive what kind of new birth could be needed by one who was already a Jew and a keeper of the Law. His questions are simply his bewilderment beating the air.

The last reference to Nicodemus (Jn 19[39]) appears to show greater boldness and a more definite discipleship on his part. His gift of spices was certainly an expression of respect and reverence for the Master, and its amount is the lavish gift of a rich man. Whether it expressed faith in the Messiahship of the Crucified, 'the Saviour typified by the brazen serpent which Jesus had explained to him beforehand (3[14])' (Godet), is less certain. Nicodemus may have regarded Jesus simply as a martyred teacher, whose cause had perished, but who deserved to be held in loving memory. He could hardly at that moment have anticipated the Resurrection. He may even have been encouraged to bring his gift by the thought that Jesus dead was no longer feared by the authorities, and that it was no longer a serious risk to show respect to His name.

Christian tradition records many legends of Nicodemus, and his name is associated with one of the Apocryphal Gospels ; but nothing further is recorded that has any historical value.

LITERATURE.—Hastings' *DB*, art. 'Nicodemus'; Edersheim, *Life and Times*, i. 381 ; W. Boyd Carpenter, *Son of Man*, 185 ; W. M. Clow, *In the Day of the Cross*, 279 ; A. B. Davidson, *The Called of God*, 247 ; G. Matheson, *Representative Men of the N.T.* 115 ; *Expos. Times*, iv. (1893) 382, 478, 527, xii. (1901) 210, 307, xiv. (1903) 194 ; J. Reid, *Jesus and Nicodemus* (1906).
        E. H. TITCHMARSH.

NIGHT.—1. **Associations of the word 'night.'**—
(*a*) It was the season for all that demanded *secrecy*.
Travellers on a dangerous errand went by night, as
Joseph did, after he had received warning in a
dream (Mt 2[14]). Nicodemus for fear of his colleagues came to Jesus by night at the Passover
season ; the interview may have been on the roof
of some friendly house, or in one of the tents used
by the pilgrims (Jn 3[2] 19[39]) ; night was also the time
for theft, and drunkenness, and revelling (Lk 12[39],
cf. 1 Th 5[2. 7], Ro 13[12]), and was convenient for plots
and stratagems (Mk 14[11]). The chief priests bribed
the guard to say that the disciples had taken away
the body of Jesus *by night* (Mt 28[13]).

(*b*) Night had its peculiar *dangers and annoyances* (cf. Ps 91[5]). Travellers might be delayed
through stress of circumstances till after nightfall,
and even till midnight (Lk 11[5]), and such journeys
were not without danger ; 'if any man walk in the
night, he stumbleth' (Jn 11[10], cf. Job 5[14]). A modern
traveller has spoken of 'the villages by night, without a light, when you stumble on them in the darkness, and all the dogs begin barking' (G. A. Smith,
HGHL, p. 99). Such annoyances would be encountered by the host in the parable, who, coming
to beg bread, arrived at midnight after stumbling
through the narrow streets of the village (Lk 11[5]
etc.).

(*c*) It was the season when *Divine guidance* might
be looked for. Joseph and the Magi were warned
in dreams (Mt 2[12. 13. 19]). Pilate's wife suffered
many things in a dream because of Jesus (Mt 27[19]).
To the Israelites the thought of night would always
bring the memory of visions and revelations of God,
given to their seers, beginning from the nights
when Jacob saw the ladder, and wrestled with the
angel.

(*d*) It was the season of *rest* (Jn 11[9] 9[4]), but not for
all men ; shepherds guarded their flocks by night
(Lk 2[8]) ; though from November to March the
sheep were probably in the fold. The fishermen
toiled all night (Lk 5[5], Jn 21[3]), when the Lake was
often swept by sudden gales (Mk 4[37]) ; the men who
could not watch one hour in Gethsemane were
accustomed to sleepless nights. In Palestine, as in
all Eastern lands, the marriage ceremony was
celebrated after nightfall ; lamps and torches were
always the accompaniment of weddings (cf. Rev
18[23], where the light of the lamp and the voice of
the bridegroom are mentioned together). In the
parable of the Ten Virgins the guests assembled
at nightfall, but they had to tarry till midnight
before the bridegroom came, the hour being chosen
for the purpose of the parable, because then they
would most likely be off their guard (Mt 25[6]).

(*e*) Night was the season of *surprises*. The day
of the Lord was to come as a thief in the night
(1 Th 5[2]). In the night the soul of the rich fool
was required of him (Lk 12[20]). At the coming of
the Son of Man 'in that night,' it is said, 'there
shall be two in one bed ; the one shall be taken, the
other shall be left' (Lk 17[34]). The disciples must
guard against a surprise : 'for ye know not when
the Lord cometh, whether at even, or at midnight,
or at cock-crowing, or in the morning ; lest coming
suddenly he find you sleeping' (Mk 13[35]). Especial
stress is laid upon the mid-watches (Lk 12[38]) ; it
would be easy to keep the first watch, and almost
impossible to sleep during the watch before the
dawn.

(*f*) The phrases 'day and night,' 'days and
nights,' are used to give a *comprehensive* idea of
time (Mt 4[2]) ; or to give an impression of a continuous practice [as when we read that Anna served
God night and day (Lk 2[37])], or to indicate the
monotonous passage of time : the sower 'sleeps and
rises night and day,' and nothing happens day after
day (Mk 4[27]).

2. **Divisions of the night.**—It is important not to
seek the scientific accuracy of modern usage in the
NT. Time was divided by natural phenomena.
The night varied in length with the seasons of the
year ; and the length of the four watches into
which the night was divided must also have
varied (Mt 14[25], Mk 6[48], Lk 12[38]). In NT times
four watches were recognized, in the OT only three.
The division into hours could not be made for the
night-season.

'The division of the day into hours sprang from the use of
the sundial, and its peculiar character, the varying length of
the hour, was conditioned by its origin ; hours of the night
could be measured only by water-glass or some similar means,
which would give divisions of equal length during all seasons of
the year, and not varying hours like those of the day' (Ramsay,
Expos. IV. vii. [1893] p. 219).

The watches of the night are indicated in Mk
13[35] : evening (ὀψία)—midnight—cock-crowing—
full morning. It was at eventide, for example,
that Jesus sat down with His disciples ; before
'cock-crowing' Peter denied Him ; and in the
'morning' Jesus was carried away to Pilate.

3. **In the life of Jesus.**—Before Jesus called His
disciples, He went out into a mountain to pray,
and continued all night in prayer (διανυκτερεύων,
Lk 6[12]). After the 'feeding of the five thousand'
also He departed into a mountain to pray (Mk
6[46] ‖ Mt 14[23]), and not till the fourth watch did He
come to the disciples, spent with their 'bootless
toil.' From these and other references it is clear
that Jesus often made the night His season of
prayer. He whose mind was saturated with the
OT may have recalled how the prophets had withdrawn to the mountains.

'So, separate from the world, his breast
  Might duly take and strongly keep
    The print of Heaven.'—(Keble, *Chr. Year*, 13th Sund.
                after Trin.).

In the neighbourhood of the Lake, night was the
only time of solitude.

'Save in the recorded hours of our Lord's praying, the history
of Galilee has no intervals of silence and loneliness ; the noise
of a close and busy life is always audible ; and to every crisis in
the Gospels and in Josephus we see crowds immediately swarm'
(G. A. Smith, *HGHL* p. 421).

It may be urged that Jesus teaches by His example the value of prayer in the silence of night.
There are many references to such prayer in the
Psalms (cf. Ps 119[62]) ; and it is not without significance that the time is midnight in the parable in
which Jesus teaches the lesson of 'shameless'
prayer (ἀναιδία, Lk 11[8]). 'The thing could never
have taken place in the daytime. It is a story of
midnight importunity' (Whyte).

There is no reason to doubt the preference of
Jesus for an abode where He would be sure of
mountain solitude ; we have no record that He
entered Tiberias, which was a walled city (*HGHL*
p. 449). 'He entered Jericho only to pass through
it.' 'This freedom Jesus had from childhood' in
Nazareth, Capernaum, Bethany, and other resting-
places. When men did not need Him, He must be
free to leave them. It is substantially true that
'Jesus never slept in a walled city' (see *Expos.*
III. iii. [1886] p. 146). The scenes of rescue on
the Lake were in the night-time ; then it was He
walked upon the sea and stilled the waves (Mk
6[49], cf. 4[39]).

The closing incidents of the life of Jesus cannot
be pictured except against the background of
night. It was dark when they sang a hymn, and
went to the Mount of Olives (Mt 26[30]). The approach of the soldiers was marked by their lanterns
(Jn 18[3]). Peter warmed himself in the chilly air
before a fire of coals (Jn 18[18]). It was possible in
the dark to follow undetected afar off (Mt 26[58]).
The panic of the disciples owed something to the
night. It was at cock-crowing that Peter remem-

bered his Master's warning, and wept bitterly.
The air of night is over all these scenes. It was
'the night in which Jesus was betrayed' (1 Co 11²³).

After the Resurrection, night was falling when
Jesus revealed Himself to the two at Emmaus in
the breaking of the bread (Lk 24³¹). They, on
returning to Jerusalem, found the disciples gathered
together, and Jesus appeared amongst them. When,
for fear of the Jews, the disciples met at eventide,
Jesus came to them (Jn 20¹⁹); and it was when the
day was breaking that He welcomed His weary
disciples to the shore (21⁴).

It is impossible to discover with accuracy the
character of these Syrian nights, so wide is the
variation in the climate between place and place,
season and season; it is not clear whether, for
example, it is literally true to say, 'For thee I
trembled in the nightly frost.' Even when we know
the impression made upon the Western traveller,
we cannot tell how Jesus and His disciples, hardened
by the bracing uplands of Galilee, endured the cold
and the mists of night. It is clear that the nights
are often as cold as the days are hot (cf. Gn 31⁴⁰,
Jer 36³⁰; see Geikie, *The Holy Land and the Bible*,
i. 73). At certain seasons in late summer Jesus
would be exposed in His nightly vigils to the dense
chilly clouds of mist of which the Song of Songs
(5²) speaks: 'For my head is filled with dew,
and my locks with the drops of the night.' For
modern descriptions of nights spent in the sacred
scenes, reference may be made to Warburton's
Crescent and the Cross, and Kinglake's *Eothen*.
But in order to discover the colours, the lights and
the half-lights of the Syrian night, those modern
painters are the best guides who, like Holman
Hunt and William Hole, have studied the Holy
Land in the lights and shadows, which are the
same as when Jesus watched through the hours of
night.

4. Metaphorical applications of 'night.'—The
contrast between night and day, darkness and
light, belongs to the stock of ideas common to all
religions, to the most ancient vocabulary of
thought. It is freely used in the OT and NT.

(a) In the opening of the *Synoptic Gospels*, quotations are used to depict as darkness the state of
the world before the dawn of Christ (Mt 4¹⁶, Lk 1⁷⁹,
cf. 2 Co 4⁶). It is upon such darkness that the
gospel shines; and at the consummation of the
Kingdom it is the outer darkness that awaits the
evil-doers (Mt 8¹² 25³⁰). Between the two areas of
darkness there is the kingdom of light brought in
by Jesus, whose disciples were to be the light of
the world (Mt 5¹⁴). When Jesus was arrested, He
said that the darkness had prevailed (Lk 22⁵³), for
the high priests were the emissaries of darkness.
The night was therefore an emblem of all that was
set against the Kingdom of God, of the ignorance
and corruption of the world which crucified Christ.

(b) *The Fourth Gospel* has a certain framework
of contrasts, amongst which is the opposition between the light of Christ and the darkness (1⁵ 8¹²
11¹⁰ 12³⁵⁻³⁶, 1 Jn 2⁸⁻¹¹). While Christ is revealed as
the source of light, His enemies are unmasked as
the story proceeds. Though 'darkness' is used in
this connexion, it is impossible to escape from the
thought of this conflict when we read of 'night' in
this Gospel. It is used to denote the close of the
divinely appointed day of service (Jn 9⁴). The
healing of the man born blind was part of the
manifestation of God, for which there was a set
time. This day being past, neither Jesus nor His
disciples could work. 'In the application to Jesus
the night is His death, and His retreat into the
invisible world' (Loisy). When Jesus persisted, in
spite of the warnings of His disciples, in returning
to Judæa, He said that the hours of the day were
given for work; so long as it was the appointed

time, He would be safe. The one danger was lest
the day should be prolonged 'beyond God's appointment.' So prolonged, the day would be as night,
in which the traveller stumbles. With both these
passages Lk 22⁵³ should be compared. Night
stands also for the close of the day of grace in the
life of Judas (Jn 13³⁰). Judas went out, 'and it
was night.' The darkness is his place. Across
the darkness 'less deep than his own soul' he
moves from the light of Christ. Night stands for
the new environment which he has chosen, 'loving
darkness because his deeds were evil.'

(c) *In the Apostolic writings* the night stands for
the waning order, which will be ended by the
coming of Christ. The day was at hand; the
disciples must put off the garments of night, and
put on the armour of light (Ro 13¹² etc.). The
difference in the metaphorical use of the night may
be seen by a comparison of the word of Jesus,
'the night cometh,' with St. Paul's 'the night is
far spent.' For those who are of the fellowship of
Christ the darkness is already past (Eph 5⁸, 1 Th 5⁴,
1 P 2⁹): 'Some daylight it is, and is every moment
growing.' The darkness and the light are alternatives, and contemporary.

> 'But he that hides a dark soul, and foul thoughts,
> Benighted walks under the midday sun.'

Night has other associations for the modern
mind. It is still the emblem of peril and evil, but
it speaks also of quietness and peace; this value it
has had for poets from Milton to Whitman.

> 'Dear night! This world's defeat;
> The stop to busie fools; care's check and curb;
> The day of spirits; my soul's calm retreat,
>   Which none disturb!'—(Vaughan).

It is important that the reader should not carry
such associations into the study of the NT. There,
night has always a sinister suggestion. It speaks
of all that is hostile to God, who is light, and in
whom there is no darkness at all. The word has
changed its value in the commerce of ideas. It is
with the night as with the sea. In the OT and
NT both are emblems of fear and evil: in the City
there will be no night (Rev 21²⁵), and the sea is no
more (21¹). But in the modern mind they awaken
other thoughts of attraction and kindliness. The
writers and teachers of the NT use the coinage of
their age; and though we may conjecture that
Jesus had other memories of night than those of
fear, yet He did not depart from the customary
usage, in which the men of His time took night as
significant of terror and evil.

LITERATURE.—W. R. Nicoll, *Ten Minute Sermons*, 103; W. C.
E. Newbolt, *Counsels of Faith and Practice*, 62; J. Parker,
Studies in Texts, vi. 89; W. J. Dawson, *The Evangelistic Note*,
133; W. T. P. Wolston, *Night Scenes of Scripture*.

                            EDWARD SHILLITO.

NINEVEH, NINEVITES.—The great city of
Nineveh was on the eastern bank of the Tigris,
opposite the modern city of Mosul. (For account
of it see art. in Hastings' *DB* iii. 553 f.). In
Mt 12 and Lk 11 are grouped several *logia* of our
Lord, short pithy passages, each of which appears
to be a whole in itself. Two of these contain
references to Jonah and the Ninevites.

1. Mt 12³⁸⁻⁴⁰ ‖ Lk 11²⁹·³⁰. It would seem that on
two occasions, the second of which is narrated in
these passages, the Pharisees asked for a sign.
Christ's preaching and miracles were not enough
for them. They wanted Him to prove His Divine
mission by some overwhelming marvel that would
force them to believe in it, if it were truly Divine.
The first occasion is in Mk 8¹¹ᶠ· ‖ Mt 16¹⁻⁴, where
they asked for 'a sign from heaven.' This He met
with a definite refusal (Mk.). St. Matthew, however, adds to the answer words which really belonged to the second occasion—'except the sign of
Jonah.' The answer on the second occasion con-

tains this exception in both Gospels. (In St. Matthew the Pharisees are addressed, in St. Luke the multitudes 'when they were coming crowding up,' ἐπαθροιζομένων). But the meaning of the explanation which our Lord adds is somewhat obscure: 'for as Jonah became to the Ninevites a sign, so shall also the Son of Man be to this generation' (Lk.). It is important to notice that the 'sign' did not consist in the *preaching* of Jonah and of the Son of Man. Jesus had been preaching already, whereas the sign was still future ('shall be'). And the story of Jonah in the OT does not, of itself, throw any light on the difficulty. Jonah started from Joppa to sail westward (Tarshish), and the storm occurred near enough to the shore to make the sailors try to row back for safety. When Jonah, therefore, was vomited up by the fish on to the dry land, it was presumably near Joppa. Then he received the second command to go to Nineveh. According to the story, therefore, Jonah was in no sense a sign *to the Ninevites.* One of two conclusions is inevitable: either that there was a current Haggadic tradition about Jonah and Nineveh which was known to our Lord and His hearers but has been lost to us, or that the word 'Ninevites' has supplanted some other word in the original text of St. Luke, having been introduced by the influence of v.[32]. St. Matthew obviates the difficulty by omitting the name altogether; but he (or some later writer, cf. Sanday, *Bampton Lectures*, p. 433) represents our Lord as teaching that 'as "Jonah was three days and three nights in the belly of the whale" (=Jon 1[17]), so shall the Son of Man be in the heart of the earth three days and three nights.' The 'sign of Jonah' is thus the sign of the resurrection. That, and that only, will be the supreme vindication of Christ's Divine mission. [In St. Luke's passage, after v.[30] D and some Latin MSS add the harmonistic statement καὶ καθὼς Ἰωνᾶς ἐν τῇ κοιλίᾳ τοῦ κήτους ἐγένετο τρεῖς ἡμέρας καὶ τρεῖς νύκτας οὕτως καὶ ὁ υἱὸς τοῦ ἀνθρώπου ἐν τῇ γῇ, 'and as Jonah (was) in the belly of the whale three days and three nights, so also (is, or shall be) the Son of Man in the earth.' It is conceivable that this was the more original form of the words in St. Matthew]. The question whether this passage necessitates the belief that our Lord accepted the story of Jonah as historically true is dealt with in art. JONAH.

2. Mt 12[41] ‖ Lk 11[32]. The words in the two Gospels are identical. [D omits the whole passage in St. Luke]. St Matthew places side by side the two *logia* relating to Jonah, and then introduces the one that relates to Solomon and 'the queen of the south.' St. Luke transposes the latter two, 'either for chronology, or effect, or both' (Plummer). Our Lord again addresses the 'evil generation.' 'Ninevites (ἄνδρες Νινευεῖται, no article; EV 'the men of Nineveh') shall stand up (as witnesses) in the judgment with this generation and shall condemn it, because they repented in accordance with the message preached by Jonah (εἰς τὸ κήρυγμα Ἰωνᾶ),' whereas this generation has not repented though a far greater than Jonah is preaching to it; 'something greater (πλεῖον, cf.v.[31], Mt 12[6]) than Jonah is here.'   A. H. M'NEILE.

NOAH.—The hero of the Hebrew version of the Semitic tradition of the Flood; mentioned twice in the Gospels. In the genealogy of Jesus (Lk 3[36]) he appears in the ninth generation after Adam, as in the OT narrative. The second mention is in Lk 17[26. 27] ‖ Mt 24[37. 38], where Jesus uses the Flood in the days of Noah to illustrate the sudden and unexpected coming of the Son of Man; the indifference of the people in the time of Noah is paralleled by the indifference of men to this approaching event.

The use of the illustration shows the familiarity of the Jews with the story of Noah. In the OT there is but the slightest mention of him outside of the immediate Flood-story in Genesis. The writer of Is 54[9] describes the present distresses of Israel 'as the waters of Noah,' to be followed by peace, according to the unchangeable covenant of peace, as surely as the promise and the covenant followed the Flood. Ezekiel (14[14. 20]) knows of three men, Noah, Daniel, and Job, efficient mediators to deliver the people by their righteousness; but in the present case, even the three shall be able to deliver only themselves (see also He 11[7]).   O. H. GATES.

NOBLEMAN.—This word is derived from the Lat. *nobilis* (=gnō-bilis), 'well-known,' 'notable.' In usage the ennobling which makes a man notable may come (a) from rank inherited or conferred, (b) from office, or (c) from character. With the meaning (c) 'nobleman' does not occur in the NT, nor has it often this significance in English authors. 'A noble man' should be used, when it is desired to convey the thought expressed in Dryden's lines:

'A nobleman is he whose noble mind
Is filled with inborn worth.'

In the EV 'a certain nobleman' is the translation of two different Gr. phrases, viz. (1) ἄνθρωπός τις εὐγενής, Lk 19[12]; (2) τις βασιλικός, Jn 4[46. 49].

1. In the parable of the Pounds (Lk 19[11ff.]) the literal rendering of the Gr. phrase is 'a certain well-born man,' or, more idiomatically expressed, 'a man of noble family' (Weymouth). The nobility comes from inherited rank. Inadequate translations are those of Wyclif 'a worthi man,' and of most early English versions 'a noble man.' The 'nobleman' of this parable is probably Archelaus, who, on the death of his father, Herod the Great, went to Rome in order to urge his claims to the kingdom. An 'ambassage' of fifty Jews followed Archelaus from Jerusalem to the 'far country' in order to protest against his being made king; in other words, they went to Rome to say, 'We will not that this man reign over us' (Lk 19[14]).

2. The Gr. word used in Jn 4[46. 49] means 'belonging to a king' (cf. Ja 2[8] 'royal'). Wyclif 'a litil kyng,' like the Vulg. *regulus*, follows the false reading βασιλίσκος. More adequate renderings are AVm 'courtier,' or 'ruler'; RVm 'king's officer.' The nobility comes from office. Weymouth expresses the meaning well: 'a certain officer of the king's court.' Josephus (*BJ* VII. v. 2, *Ant.* XV. viii. 4) uses the word to distinguish the courtiers and other officers of the king from those of Rome. The 'king' in whose court this officer served was Herod Antipas, tetrarch of Galilee. The title 'king' was not his by right, but was given to him in courtesy (Mt 14[9]). It is not known who this king's officer was, nor whether his duties were civil or military. He has wrongly been identified with the 'centurion' (ἑκατόνταρχος) referred to in Mt 8[5] and Lk 7[2],—a Gentile officer in the army of Antipas. To identify the healing of the nobleman's son with the healing of the centurion's servant is not only to manufacture discrepancies, but also to lose the light which the earlier miracle casts upon the later one. This is well brought out by Chadwick (*Expositor*, 4th series, v. 443 ff.); the strong faith of the centurion (Mt 8[10]) 'becomes intelligible, without ceasing to be admirable, when we reflect that he was evidently aware of the miracle formerly wrought for another inhabitant of the same city, an eminent person, one of the court which his own sword protected.'   J. G. TASKER.

NON-RESISTANCE.—See RETALIATION.

NUMBERS.—In this article it is above all things necessary to distinguish carefully between passages in which numbers are used only in the ordinary way and those in which they are connected with some custom or belief, or have for any reason symbolic significance, whether secular or sacred.

Three facts must be borne in mind throughout the inquiry : (1) the Oriental preference of round numbers to indefinite statements ; (2) the close association in Western Asia from early times of numbers and religion. It seems to be proved that each of the chief Babylonian gods had his number : Anu, for example, 60, Bel 50, Ea 40, Sin 30, Marduk, as identified with Jupiter, 11, etc. ($KAT\,[ZW]$ 454). And it is equally certain that number often played an important part in ritual. (3) The gradual obliteration of the original reference from the popular consciousness. By the time of Christ the process by which certain numbers had acquired special significance would be wholly or partially forgotten by most of the Jews resident in Palestine. They had received their use from their fathers, and found it expressed in literature and ceremonial and daily life, but knew little, if anything, of the way in which it had originated, so that it is very unsafe to credit them with conscious application of ideas current elsewhere. The Jews who lived in Babylonia from about B.C. 600 to the completion of the Babylonian Talmud unquestionably adopted in course of time many Babylonian thoughts and expressions ; but this cannot be assumed, at any rate in the same degree, of the Jews of the Holy Land.

Seven.—Of the significant numbers met with in the Gospels the most prominent is that so freely used in the OT and the other literature of the Semitic area—the number seven, represented in the Gr. Test. by ἐπτά, ἐπτάκις, ἑπταπλασίων, ἕβδομος. In three contexts it must be understood literally, although perhaps in the first two with an underlying reference to another use : in the statement that Anna's married life lasted 7 years (Lk 2^{36}), in the accounts of the feeding of the 4000 (7 loaves, 7 baskets, Mt $15^{34.\ 36f.}$, Mk $8^{5.\ 6.\ 8}$; cf. also the references in Mt 16^{10} and Mk 8^{20}), and in a note of time, 'the seventh hour' (Jn 4^{52}). In all other passages : Mt 12^{45} $18^{21f.}$ $22^{25f.\ 28}$, Mk $12^{20.\ 22f.}$ $16^{[9]}$, Lk 8^2 11^{26} 17^4 18^{30} (a doubtful reading) $20^{29.\ 31.\ 33}$; in the number of the Beatitudes relating to character (Mt 5^{3-9}) ; in the 7 disciples at the Lake (Jn 21^2) ; and in the grouping together of 7 parables of the Kingdom in Mt 13—it has some kind of special significance. In the Apocalyptic passages which come within the scope of this study, the literal meaning combined with the symbolic may be recognized in the 7 churches (Rev $1^{11.\ 20}$), the 7 candlesticks ($1^{12.\ 20}$ 2^1), the 7 stars ($1^{16.\ 20}$ 2^1 3^1), and the 7 angels (1^{20}). Elsewhere, in the 7 seals ($5^{1.\ 5}$), the 7 horns, the 7 eyes, and the 7 spirits (4^5 5^6), the use is purely symbolic.

This symbolic or, to speak more generally, non-literal use is very frequent in the Jewish literature of the period extending from about B.C. 150 to about A.D. 100, the period which includes the time covered by the Gospels. The following are a few examples out of many. We read of 7 heavens (Slav. Enoch 3 ff. ; Test. of Levi, 2 f. ; cf. Charles in *ExpT* vii. [1895] 57 ff.), 7 angels (To 12^{15}, Eth. Enoch 81^5), and 7 high mountains, 7 large rivers, and 7 great islands (Eth. Enoch $77^{4.\ 5.\ 8}$). Man is said to have been made by the Divine Wisdom of 7 substances (Slav. Enoch 30^8), and to have received 7 natures (30^9). Seven great works were made on the first day of creation (Jub 2^3) ; Adam and Eve lived 7 years in Paradise (3^{15}) ; at the Deluge 7 sluices were opened in heaven, and 7 fountains of the great deep in earth (5^{24}) ; and Jacob is said to have kissed his dying grandfather 7 times (22^{26}).

In this non-literal use of the number, three shades of significance can perhaps be traced. (a) It was a favourite *round number*. Instead of 'many' or 'a considerable number,' an Oriental in many cases preferred to say 'seven.' This is probably the force of the number in Peter's question about forgiveness (Mt 18^{21}) ; in our Lord's command of sevenfold forgiveness for sevenfold injury (Lk 17^4) ; in the promise (Lk 18^{30}, according to some MSS) of sevenfold reward (ἑπταπλασίονα instead of the usual reading πολλαπλασίονα) ; in the

references to the 7 evil spirits (Mt 12^{45}, Mk $16^{[9]}$, Lk 8^2 11^{26}) ; in the question of the Sadducees about the 7 brothers (Mt 22^{25} etc.) ; and in the passages alluded to in the Book of Jubilees.—(b) Seven often expressed the idea of *completeness*. So in 7 churches, 7 parables of the Kingdom, the 7 Beatitudes above mentioned, perhaps in the 7 loaves and the 7 disciples, and some of the passages referred to in the Books of Enoch. This use of 7 in the ancient East is directly attested by some cuneiform texts which explain a sign consisting of 7 wedges as meaning 'totality,' 'whole' (Zimmern in *Busspsalmen*, p. 73).—(c) Seven was for the Jews and all their neighbours from early times a *sacred number*. In our Lord's day there were many features of Jewish religious life which kept the sacredness of 7 continually before the mind : the observance of the 7th day and the 7th year ; the 7 days of unleavened bread and of the Feast of Tabernacles ; the 7 sprinklings of the leper (Lv 14^7) ; the 7 sprinklings of the blood of the bullock in the Holy of Holies on the Day of Atonement (Lv 16^{14}) ; the 7 he-lambs prescribed as an offering for several important occasions (Nu $28^{11.\ 19.\ 27}$ 29^{36}) ; the 7 days of seclusion for uncleanness or suspected uncleanness (Lv $13^{4.\ 6.\ 26}$ 14^9 $15^{13.\ 19.\ 24.\ 28}$, Nu $12^{14.\ 15}$ etc.) ; the sevenfold march round the altar on the 7th day of the Feast of Tabernacles (Mishna, *Sukkah* iv. 4) ; and the seven-branched candlestick in the Temple (Jos. *Ant.* III. vi. 7, the Arch of Titus). For all classes of Jewish society in the period of our Lord's ministry the number 7 was inseparably associated with the most solemn seasons and the most important acts of worship. There is no direct illustration of this sacredness of 7 in the Gospels, but it can be confidently traced in Apocalyptic imagery : in the 7 candlesticks (Rev $1^{12.\ 20}$ 2^1) which evidently allude to the seven-branched candlestick in the Temple, and in the 7 horns of the Lamb, and the 7 eyes which are the 7 spirits of God sent out into all the earth (Rev 5^6, cf. 4^5). In non-canonical literature it is found in the 7 heavens and the 7 angels, and in the remarkable description in the so-called Fourth Book of Maccabees of the 7 brothers put to death by Antiochus Epiphanes as a most holy 7 (παναγία συμφώνων ἀδελφῶν ἑβδομάς), who circled round piety in choral dance like the 7 days of creation round the number 7 ($14^{7f.}$, according to the emended text followed by Deissmann in Kautzsch's *Pseudepigraphen*, p. 169). The rise and development of these shades of meaning, which to some extent melt into one another (for the use of 7 as the number of completeness was probably connected with its sacred use, and its employment as a round number may have been facilitated by the other uses), are questions which hardly come within the range of this article, as the process must have been completed millenniums before the Christian era. Seven is distinctly a sacred number in the inscriptions of Gudea the ruler of Lagash some centuries before the time of Abraham (*RP*, new series, ii. 83, 94 ff.). Whatever the primary impulse, whether the observation of the phases of the moon, or of the 7 planets, or of the 7 brightest stars of the Pleiades, or of the 7 stars of Arcturus, or of the 7 stars of the Great Bear, which all attracted the attention of early star-gazers, the Jews of our Lord's age (with a few exceptions) will have used the number simply as their fathers had used it for many generations, as they found it in ritual, in proverbial lore (Pr $6^{16.\ 31}$ 9^1 $26^{16.\ 25}$, Sir 7^3 20^{12} 35^{11} 37^{14} 40^8), in other literature, in history (Jos 6^4, Jg 6^1 $16^{7.\ 13}$, 2 S 24^{13}, 2 K 5^{10} etc.), and in common life (7 days of the marriage feast, To 11^{19} ; and 7 days of fasting and mourning, 1 S 31^{13}, Job 2^{13}, *Mo'ed Katon* 27^b). A few highly educated men associated the number with astral phenomena ; the pseudo-Enoch, for example (Slav. Enoch

30³), and Josephus, who affirms that the 7 lamps of the candlestick imitated the number of the 7 planets (τῶν πλανητῶν τὸν ἀριθμὸν μεμιμημένοι, *Ant.* III. vi. 7); but most will have had little or no acquaintance with such speculations.

One use of the number in the Gospels which has been already briefly referred to needs fuller treatment. In three or four passages, which are really but two, mention is made of 7 evil spirits. Our Lord cast 7 devils or demons out of Mary Magdalene (Lk 8², Mk 16[9]), and He spoke of an evil spirit which had been cast out as returning with 7 other spirits worse than himself (Mt 12⁴⁵, Lk 11²⁶). It has been suggested, cautiously by Zimmern (*KAT*[*ZW*] 462–463), positively by R. C. Thompson of the British Museum (*Devils and Evil Spirits of Babylonia*, I. xliii.), that these 7 are connected in some way with the evil 7 so often referred to in Babylonian incantations, and identified to some extent with winds and storms. That the Babylonian belief was widely diffused in the regions affected by Babylonian civilization is probable enough, and that it lingered in one district at any rate into Christian times is attested by a curious Syrian charm cited by Thompson; but there seems to be no clear allusion to it in the extant Jewish literature of the period inclusive of the time of Christ. The 7 spirits put by Beliar into man, according to the Test. of Reuben (2 f.), are mere abstractions. The whole passage seems to be a sort of allegory. And it must be remembered that the Test., as we have it, has been manipulated by a Christian, who would be familiar with the passages in the Gospels under consideration. The use of 7 in the latter can be fully accounted for without any reference to Babylonia.

In the Holy Land and amongst the Arabs there are still many echoes of the ancient use of 7 as shown in the preceding paragraphs. Dalman's *Diwan* contains several examples of it as a round number in popular poetry (pp. 260, 287, 305, 309). Mourning for relatives and marriage rejoicings extend amongst the Arabs over 7 days (Forder's *With the Arabs in Tent and Town*, 216, 218). If the person is stained with blood, the stain is washed 7 times (Robinson Lees, *Village Life in Palestine*, 2nd ed. 218). A festival at Nebi Musa lasts 7 days (Curtiss, *Primitive Semitic Religion To-day*, 163). These illustrations show that the modern Oriental not only employs 7 as a round number, but sometimes associates it in some measure with the ideas of completeness and sanctity.

Three and a half.—Of the symbolic use of the half of seven there is one instance in the Gospels, viz. the reference to the famine in the time of Elijah as lasting three years and six months (Lk 4²⁵, cf. Ja 5¹⁷). This number, the half of the number of completeness, seems to have been often used by the Jews of periods of trial and judgment. According to Josephus (*BJ* I. i. 1, v. ix. 4), the worship of the Temple was discontinued in the time of Antiochus Epiphanes for three years and six months; and, according to the Midrash on La 1⁵, the siege by Vespasian continued for the same period (cf. Dn 7²⁵ 9²⁷ 12⁷, Rev 11², and Wetstein's note on the last passage).

Fourteen.—The double of 7 in the genealogy at the beginning of Matthew can hardly be accidental. When the Evangelist carefully divides the generations from Abraham to Christ into three groups of 14 each (Mt 1¹⁷), he must intend the number to have some meaning. He does not forget that it is the double of a favourite round number which is at the same time suggestive of completeness. This multiple of 7 seems to have been common in old Canaan, for scores of the Tell el-Amarna Letters from Canaanites to the Pharaoh have some form of the salutation: 'Seven and seven times I fall at the feet of the king my lord.' A striking example of the use of a multiple of 7 in a scheme of history is supplied by a writing composed probably within a hundred years of our Lord's ministry, 'the Book of Jubilees' or 'Little Genesis.' The writer

arranges the whole period from Adam to the giving of the Law in about 7 times 7 jubilees, the interval between two jubilees being 7 times 7 years (50⁴).

Seventy.—Of another much used multiple of 7, $7 \times 10 = 70$, there is only one instance in the Gospel narrative, the sending out by Jesus of the 70 disciples (Lk 10¹· ¹⁷). It must be noted, however, that WH read (with BD, some OL, Vulg., Syr cur and Syr sin) 72, the multiple of 6 by 12. In either case the use of 70, of which there are so many examples in the OT and elsewhere (Gn 50³, Ex 1⁵ 15²⁷, Nu 11¹⁶, Jg 1⁷ 8³⁰, 2 K 10¹, 2 Ch 29³², Ps 90¹⁰, Jer 25¹¹, Ezk 8¹¹, Dn 9²⁴, Eth. Enoch 89⁵⁹ 'the 70 shepherds,' Test. of Levi, c. 8, 2 Es 14⁴⁶; Jos. *Vita*, 11, *BJ* II. xx. 5; Bk. of Jub 11²⁰ clouds of ravens returned 70 times; *Sanhedrin* i. 6 the high court of justice with 70 members and president) as a round number for 'very many,' with perhaps the added idea of comprehensiveness, may be safely recognized as influential.

The Rabbinic idea of 70 languages for the 70 peoples is found in the Mishna (*Ṣoṭa* vii. 5), and so may be as old as the time of Christ, but can hardly be alluded to in a mission intended only for Jews. Dr. A. Jeremias (*Babylonisches im NT*, 93) regards 70 as used in the Gospel as 'a round number with astral character;' but any reference to the stars is unnecessary and improbable. Babylonian astrologers might be credited with it, but not the Galilæan Jews of our Lord's time and the Evangelists.

Seventy times seven.—The 70 times 7 of Mt 18²², the multiple of 10 times 7 by 7, is a very strong way of saying 'very many times,' almost equivalent to 'without limit.' The alternative rendering of RVm 'seventy times and seven,' which yields a much less emphatic meaning, rests on the LXX tr. of Gn 4²⁴ where the same Greek ἑβδομηκοντάκις ἑπτά represents Hebrew words which clearly mean 77. In Mt. the familiar rendering is distinctly preferable. Wellhausen (*Das Evangelium Matthæi*, 94) notes that D reads ἑπτάκις for ἑπτά, which is strictly correct (but cf. Moulton, *Proleg. Gr. Gram.* 98).

Ten (δέκα, δέκατος, ἀποδεκατεύω ἀποδεκατόω).—The number ten is probably a round number in the parables of the 10 virgins (Mt 25¹), the 10 pieces of silver (Lk 15⁸), the talents (Mt 25²⁸), and the 10 servants who received 10 pounds (Lk 19¹³· ¹⁶f. ²⁴f.); and in the prediction to the Church of Smyrna of tribulation 10 days (Rev 2¹⁰). In other passages (Mt 20²⁴, Mk 10⁴¹, Lk 14³¹ 17¹²· ¹⁷, and the references to the payment of a tenth to God, Mt 23²³, Lk 11⁴² 18¹²) it is used literally. As a round number significant of completeness (although without the idea of sacredness associated with 7), its use was facilitated by the decimal system, which may have been suggested in the first instance by the number of fingers on the two hands. Be that as it may, the Jews of our Lord's day found 10 again and again in their sacred books and in history; for example, in the 10 patriarchs from Adam to Noah (Gn 5); the 10 righteous men whose presence would have saved Sodom (Gn 18³²); the 10 commandments (Ex 34¹²⁻²⁶ and 20²⁻¹⁷, Dt 5⁶⁻²¹); the 10 temptations with which Israel tempted God in the wilderness (Nu 14²²); the 10 curtains of the tabernacle (Ex 26¹); the 10 lavers (2 Ch 4⁶); the 10 candlesticks (v.⁷) and the 10 tables (v.⁸) in Solomon's temple; the 10 servants of Gideon (Jg 6²⁷), and the 10 elders of Boaz (Ru 4²).

The non-canonical literature of later times supplies many additional examples. The Book of Jubilees knows of 10 temptations of Abraham (19⁸), a thought found also in the Mishna ('*Abôth* v. 4), and the Test. of Joseph of 10 temptations of Joseph (ch. 2). The fondness of the Rabbis for the number receives striking illustration from the long series of significant tens in '*Abôth* v. 1–9. The number was also applied in daily life. Ten persons constituted the minimum required for a community or congregation (Mishna, *Sanhedrin* i. 6), and for a company at a Paschal supper (Jos. *BJ* VI. ix. 3). Later authorities fix 10 as the number of persons drawn up in a row to comfort mourners (*Sanh.* 19a) and as the number requisite for the utterance of the nuptial benediction (*Kethuboth*, 7b). The 10 virgins of the parable may possibly receive illustration from an Arab custom mentioned by some mediæval Jewish writers. They affirm that in the land of the Ishmaelites, when the bride was taken from her father's house to her new home on the evening preceding the completion of the marriage festivities, 10 torches or lamps were borne in front of her. The authority is, it is true, very late, but the custom described may have been of ancient origin (given in the gloss to *Kelim* ii. 8, 9*b*, and in Latin in Wetstein's note on Mt 25[1]). The payment of a tithe or tenth to the Deity, referred to twice by our Lord (Lk 18[12], Mt 23[23] ‖ Lk 11[42]), must have been connected in the first instance with the symbolic use of 10. The custom has been traced among Hebrews, Babylonians, Phœnicians, Greeks and Romans. The prominence of the subject in later Judaism is attested by the great space devoted to it in the Mishna, three treatises with 150 *hălăkhôth*.

Five.—Five, the half of ten, is met with in a considerable number of passages in the Gospels, in some of which it may have more than mere numerical significance. So perhaps in the 5 loaves (Mt 14[17. 19] 16[9], Mk 6[38. 41] 8[19], Lk 9[13. 16], Jn 6[9. 13]), a great multitude fed by an amount of food strongly suggestive of smallness and incompleteness; the 5 talents which bring in 5 more (Mt 25[15f. 20]); the fivefold profit of the second servant in the parable of the Pounds contrasted with the tenfold profit of the first (Lk 19[18f.]); perhaps the 5 sparrows worth two farthings (Lk 12[6]); and the 5 disciples of Jesus at the beginning of His ministry (Jn 1[35-51]; cf. the 5 disciples of R. Jochanan ben Zakai, *c.* 80 A.D. ['*Abôth* ii. 10], and the 5 disciples ascribed to Jesus in a *baraitha* removed from the censored editions of the Talmud [*Sanh.* 43*a*, see Laible's *Jesus Christus im Talmud*, Anhang 15]). In the other passages (Mt 25[2], Lk 1[24] 12[52] 14[19] 16[28], Jn 4[18] 5[2]) it is safest to find only the ordinary meaning. Five, as a small round number, is repeatedly met with in the OT (Gn 43[34] 45[22], Lv 26[8], Is 30[17] etc.) and in the Tell el-Amarna letters. In one of the latter (ix. 20 in Winckler's edition) it seems to be regarded as a number so small as to need an apology.

Forty.—An important multiple of ten is 40, found in the accounts of the Temptation (Mt 4[2], Mk 1[13], Lk 4[2]) and of the period intervening between the Passion and the Ascension (Ac 1[3]). That it is in both cases more than a mere number is evident. The 40 days of fasting in the wilderness clearly point back to the 40 days spent by Moses on Sinai (Ex 24[18] 34[28]) and the 40 days' journey of Elijah in the same region (1 K 19[8]). The 40 days of temptation remind us of the repeated use in the OT of the number 40 of periods of testing or punishment. The rain at the Flood fell 40 days and 40 nights (Gn 7[4. 17]). The spies were absent 40 days (Nu 13[25]). The punishment and proving of the people extended over 40 years (Nu 14[34]). Nineveh was granted 40 days of respite (Jon 3[4]). The Philistine oppression lasted 40 years (Jg 13[1]), and Ezekiel predicted that Egypt should be desolate 40 years (Ezk 29[11]). That this application of the number was not confined to Israel is probable from the statement on the Moabite Stone (lines 7 f.), that the occupation of Mehedeba by Israel lasted 40 years. Even if king Mesha intended the number to be understood literally, which is very doubtful, he may have recorded it with a view to its special significance. In another group of passages, also, 40 seems to be a normal or ideal number. Three periods of rest from foreign invasion, each of 40 years, are mentioned in the Book of Judges (3[11] 5[31] 8[28]). Eli was judge for 40 years (1 S 4[18]); and the reigns of David and Solomon are reckoned at 40 years each (2 S 5[4], 1 K 11[42]: add from tradition the reign of Saul, Ac 13[21], Jos. *Ant.* VI. xiv. 9).

How did 40 come to be used in this way? The most satisfactory answer is suggested by the following passages in the OT and other Oriental literature and history. Isaac and Esau married at 40 (Gn 25[20] 26[34]). Moses came forward as a friend of his people about 40 (tradition recorded in Ac 7[23]; cf. Ex 2[11] 'when Moses was grown up'), and began his work as their divinely appointed leader 40 years later (Ac 7[30] and Ex 7[7]).

Caleb was 40 years old when sent out as one of the spies (Jos 14[7]). Hillel is said to have entered on his Rabbinic career at 40 (*Sifre* referred to in *Jewish Encyc.* art. 'Forty'), and Jochanan ben Zakai to have exchanged commerce for study at 40 (*Rosh ha-shanah*, 31*b* : the same is affirmed of 'Aḳiba in the late writing, the '*Abôth* of Rabbi Nathan, c. 6). Mohammed, according to a tradition referred to by König (Hastings' *DB* iii. 563[b], *Stilistik*, 55 ; cf. Muir, *The Coran, its Composition and Teaching*, 11), appeared as a prophet at or about 40. These passages suggest that 40 was regarded in the ancient East as the age of intellectual maturity, and there are not wanting direct declarations of that belief. In the addendum to the fifth chapter of '*Abôth*, 40 is described as the age of reason or understanding (בן ארבעים לבינה), and a passage in the Ḳoran cited by König (*ll.cc.*) runs : 'until he reached his full strength and attained the age of 40 years.' Forty years, therefore, represented a generation, and thus the number 40 became a round number for a full period, a complete epoch, and more generally for 'many.'

It is still used in this way to some extent in the modern East. There is a Syrian proverb : 'If you live 40 days with people, you will then either leave them or become like them' (Mackie, *Bible Manners and Customs*, 111 ; Bauer, *Volksleben im Lande der Bibel*, 236, gives it rather differently, but with the same use of 40). As the ancient star-gazers noted the disappearance of the Pleiades for 40 days, some recent writers (Cheyne, perhaps, *Bible Problems and their Solution*, 114 f., and Winckler cited there ; Zimmern, too, in *KAT[ZW]*, 389, thinks the reference possible) connect the interval between the Passion and the Ascension, through a pre-Christian myth, with this astronomical period. This need not be seriously debated. The explanation given above is quite sufficient to account for the 40 days of the Temptation and 'the Great Forty Days.'

A Hundred (ἑκατόν, ἑκατονταπλασίων).—That the product of 10 by 10 should be frequently used in a general way to express a large number, could be expected only in a civilization which was acquainted with the decimal as well as the sexagesimal system. There are instances in the OT, etc. : Lv 26[8], 2 S 24[3], Pr 17[10], Ec 6[3] 8[12], Sir 18[9] (RV: 'The number of man's days at the most are 100 years'), and the Moabite Stone (lines 28 f. : 'I reigned over 100 chiefs'). In the Gospels the number is used mainly in this way : in the parable of the Sower (Mt 13[8. 23], Mk 4[8. 20], Lk 8[8]), in the parable of the Lost Sheep (Mt 18[12], Lk 15[4]), and in Mt 18[28] 19[29] (not WH), Mk 10[30], Lk 16[6f.]. In Mk 6[40], Jn 19[39] it is employed in the ordinary way.

The division of 100 into 99 and 1 (Mt 18[12f.], Lk 15[4. 7]), with the preference of the 1, is found in the Mishna, *Peah* iv. 1 f. The same division is also met with in a remarkable passage in the Jerus. Talmud (*Shabbath* xiv. 3), which, however, is not earlier than the 3rd cent. A.D. Perhaps the contrast of 99 and 1 was not unknown to the Rabbinic teaching of our Lord's day.

Ten Thousand.—In the two passages in the Gospels in which the multiple of 10 by 1000 occurs (μυρίος, Mt 18[24] ; μυριάς, Lk 12[1]), it is best regarded as hyperbolical. The intention in the one case is to name an amount quite inconceivable in ordinary life, a debt which could not possibly be discharged by a private person ; in the other, to impress on the reader the enormous magnitude of the crowds which gathered round Jesus at that period of His ministry. There are many examples of this use in the OT (Lv 26[8], Dt 32[30], 1 S 18[7f.], Ca 5[10], Ezk 16[7] RVm, Dn 11[12], Mic 6[7] etc.). In the Tell el-Amarna letters 100,000 is used in this way. Dushratta, king of Mitani, prayed that Ishtar might protect him and his royal brother the Pharaoh for a hundred thousand years (No. xx. in Winckler's edition).

Two.—There seems to be no special significance of the number 2 in the Gospels, unless, with König (*Stilistik*, 51 f.), we regard it as, in some passages, an equivalent for 'a few.' This idiom seems to be proved for the OT. 'Two days,' in Nu 9[22], may well mean 'a few days'; and 'the 2 sticks' of the widow of Zarephath (1 K 17[12]) can hardly be understood literally. It *may* be illustrated in the NT by the 2 fishes (Mt 14[17. 19], Mk 6[38. 41], Lk 9[13. 16], Jn 6[9]), and the 2 who agree in prayer concerning anything (Mt 18[19]) ; but the ordinary interpretation seems not inadmissible in both these cases. The custom of sending out representatives in pairs, of which there are several examples in the Gospel story (the 2 disciples sent by the Baptist to Jesus [Lk 7[19]], the 12 sent out by two and two [Mk 6[7]], the 70 sent out by two and two [Lk 10[1]], the 2 sent out near Jerusalem [Mt 21[1], Mk 11[1], Lk 19[29]], and the 2 sent out to make preparations for the Paschal supper [Mk 14[13], Lk 22[8] ; cf. the 2 going to Emmaus, Lk 24[13ff.] Mk 16[[12]]], the 2 angels at the sepulchre [Lk 24[4], Jn 20[12]], and the 2 on Olivet [Ac 1[10]]), was probably known to the Jewish society of our Lord's time.

A comparatively early tradition enjoined that the collectors of charity should travel in couples (*Baba Bathra*, 8*b*). When the son of Rabban Gamaliel (the grandson of St. Paul's Gamaliel) was ill, the distressed father sent two of his disciples to R. Chanina ben Dosa to request his prayers (*Berak.*, 34*b*). The 5 *zŭgôth* or couples of eminent teachers, the last of which consisted of Hillel and Shammai, referred to in the Mishna (*Peah* ii. 6, '*Abôth* i. 4–16), may also be mentioned. The expression ' pairs ' was probably used of them in Rabbinic circles in the time of Christ.

The two ways of Mt 7[13f.] probably represent a widely current mode of teaching. They are met with in Jer 21[8] (cf. Dt 30[15], Sir 15[17]), Slav. Enoch 30[15] ' I showed him the two ways, the light and the darkness ' (cf. the note of Charles), in the Jewish manual probably incorporated in the early chapters of the *Didache* (cf. Ep. of Barnabas, 18 ff.), and in a remarkable passage in the Talmud. When R. Jochanan ben Zakai (*c.* 80 A.D.) was on his deathbed, he said to his disciples, who wondered at his tears : ' There are two ways before me : one leading to the Garden of Eden and the other leading to Gehenna, and I do not know in which I am about to be led ' (*Berak.* 28*b*).

Three.—A number of peculiar interest to the student of the Gospels is three—τρεῖς, τρίς, τρίτον, τρίτος. It is purely numerical in the following passages : Mt 15[32], Mk 8[2] ; Peter's words about the three tabernacles on the Mount of Transfiguration (Mt 17[4], Mk 9[5], Lk 9[33]) ; Mt 18[16-20] 20[3] 22[26], Mk 12[21] 15[25], Lk 1[56] 2[46] 12[38. 52] 20[12. 31] 23[22], Jn 2[1. 6]. In a much greater number of passages it obviously or probably means more : in the allusion to Jonah (Mt 12[40]), in the parables of the 3 measures of meal (Mt 13[33], Lk 13[21]), the friend asking for 3 loaves (Lk 11[5]), the Good Samaritan (Lk 10[36]), and the barren fig-tree (Lk 13[7]), in the 3 temptations (Mt 4||), and the 3 prayers of Jesus (Mt 26[44], Mk 14[41]), in the references to Peter's threefold denial (Mt 26[34. 75], Mk 14[30. 72], Lk 22[34. 61], Jn 13[38]), in the allusions to the 3 days' interval between the Passion and the Resurrection (Mt 12[40] 16[21] 17[23] 20[19] 26[61] 27[40. 63f.], Mk 8[31] 9[31] 10[34] 14[58] 15[29], Lk 9[22] 13[32] 18[33] 24[7. 21. 46], Jn 2[19f.] : add Ac 10[40], 1 Co 15[4]), in the 3 manifestations of the risen Lord recorded in the Fourth Gospel (Jn 21[14]), and in the threefold question, ' Lovest thou me ? ' addressed to Peter (v.[15ff.]). In this latter and larger group can be traced a reference to the use of 3 as a significant number, of which there is a multitude of examples in the OT and other Jewish literature : the 3 feasts (Ex 23[14]), Job's 3 friends (Job 2[11]), the 3 times of prayer (Ps 55[17], Dn 6[10]), the threefold shooting of Joash (2 K 13[18]), the 3 sanctuaries—Eden, Mount Sinai, Mount Zion (Bk. of Jub 8[19]), the 3 branches of a vine and the 3 baskets representing 3 days (Gn 40[10. 12. 16. 18]), 3 days' journey (Ex 3[18], Nu 10[33], Jon 3[3]), the 3 days' search for the body of Elijah (2 K 2[17]), Esther's 3 days' fast (Est 4[16]), the 3 days of rejoicing for the honour done to Enoch (Slav. Enoch 68[7]), the perfuming and anointing of the body of Abraham for 3 days (Test. of Abr. text A, ch. 20), the 3 sayings of the men of the Great Synagogue ('*Abôth* i. 1), the 3 things on which the world standeth (Shim'on the Righteous in '*Abôth* i. 2, and Shim'on ben Gamaliel in '*Abôth* i. 19), and the 3 sayings ascribed to each of the 5 disciples of Rabban Jochanan ben Zakai ('*Abôth* ii. 14 ff.).

It is not difficult to see how the number came to be used in this manner. Several wholes which are often met with can be readily divided into 3 parts : the head, trunk, and legs of a body ; the source, stream, and mouth of a river ; the root, trunk, and corona of a tree (König, *DB* iii. 562[b]) ; the van, centre, and rear of an army ; morning, noon, and evening. Early Eastern speculation grouped all things under three heads ; heaven, earth, and the abyss (cf. the Babylonian triad of gods, Anu, Bel, Ea). It will have been noticed in very early times that 3 is the smallest number with beginning, middle, and end. So it naturally came to be used of a small, well-rounded total, especially, as shown above, in reference to time.

The 3 days' interval between the Passion and the Resurrection may perhaps receive additional illustration from the Jewish rule that evidence for the identification of a corpse could not be received after 3 days (*Yebamôth* xvi. 3). A reason for the rule is given in a tradition ascribed to Bar Kappara, who was associated with the compiler of the Mishna (*c.* A.D. 200). This Rabbi is reported to have said that for 3 days the soul hovers near the body, waiting for an opportunity of returning into it, but that at the end of that period, seeing that the features are altered, it goes away (Midrash on Genesis, c. 100 ; Midrash on Ecclesiastes 12[6] : cf. Bousset, *Die Religion des Judenthums*, 285 note). The resurrection of Jesus evidently took place before the close of the period of identification. Be that as it may, there can hardly be a doubt that the belief expressed by Bar Kappara, or something like it, underlay the words of Martha : ' Lord, by this time he stinketh : for he hath been dead four days ' (Jn 11[39]). The 3 days were ended, and decay, she thought, had advanced so far that the features would be unrecognizable. That the 3 days between the Passion and the Resurrection had even the remotest connexion with the 3 days' disappearance of the new moon in spring (Zimmern in *KAT[ZW]*, 389), is highly improbable.

Two other passages cannot be entirely passed over, although little or nothing can be said in illustration : the reference to the Father, the Son, and the Holy Ghost in the baptismal formula (Mt 28[19]), and the words ascribed to the risen Lord in the Apocalypse : ' I am the first, and the last, and the living one ' (Rev 1[7]). There is no parallel to the use of the number in the former in pre-Christian Jewish literature, and connexion with Babylonian and Egyptian triads is out of the question. The triple priestly blessing (Nu 6[24-26]) and the Thrice Holy in the song of the seraphim (Is 6[3]) are remarkable, but cannot be safely regarded as foreshadowings of the doctrine of the Trinity. The number 3 is in both cases strongly emphatic, but it is not advisable to find more than emphasis. ' Holy, holy, holy ' is a very strong superlative. The passage in the Apocalypse is, no doubt, like the preceding words ' him which is, and which was, and which is to come ' (Rev 1[4]), an expansion or interpretation of the name I AM THAT I AM (Ex 3[14]), and has a partial parallel in Plato, *de Legibus*, 716 : ὁ μὲν δὴ θεὸς (ὥσπερ καὶ ὁ παλαιὸς λόγος) ἀρχήν τε καὶ τελευτὴν καὶ μέσα τῶν ὄντων ἁπάντων ἔχων, but must not be connected with it.

Four.—The number 4 (τέσσαρες, τεταρταῖος, τέταρτος, τετράμηνος, τετραπλόος) is found in the Gospels in the following passages : in the 4 months before harvest (Jn 4[35]), the 4 bearers of the paralytic (Mk 2[3]), the 4th watch (Mt 14[25], Mk 6[48]), the fourfold restitution promised by Zacchæus (Lk 19[8]), the 4 days of Lazarus in the grave (Jn 11[17. 39]), the division of the garments of Jesus among the 4 soldiers (Jn 19[23]), the 4 winds (Mt 24[31], Mk 13[27]), and the 4 kinds of soil in the parable of the Sower, with the types of character which they represent (Mt 13[4ff.] and parallels). We may add the 4 Gospels, the number of which was early regarded as significant. The four last references constitute a group. The 4 winds, associated with the 4 points of the compass, are met with in the OT and elsewhere in Oriental literature and symbolism : 1 Ch 9[24] RVm, Jer 49[36], Ezk 37[0] 42[20] RVm, Dn 8[8] 11[4], Zec 2[6] 6[5], Babylonian Flood Story, col. iii. line 42, Book of the Dead, c. 161 (in Budge's smaller edition, p. 531 f.). This use of 4 suggested world-wide extent and then comprehensiveness. So we find in the OT : 4 heads of the river going out of Eden (Gn 2[10]), 4 cherubim each with 4 faces and 4 wings (Ezk 1[5f.], cf. Rev 4[6ff.]), 4 horns (Zec 1[18]), 4 smiths (1[20]), 4 chariots (6[1]), and 4 empires (Dn 2[40] 7[3ff. 17ff.]). An Assyrian royal title ran ' king of the 4 quarters,' that is, of the world. Some of the divine figures in Assyrian sculptures have 4 wings, for example No. 1 in the Nimroud Gallery of the British Museum. Adam's name is said to have been given from 4 substances, that is, the east, the west, the north, and the south (Sl. Enoch 30[13]). Abraham is said to have pitched his tent where 4 roads met (Test. of Ab. text A 1). The 4 kinds of soil in the parable, therefore, and the 4 types of character which they represent, cover the whole area of human life ; and the 4 Gospels give a complete outline-portrait of Christ. The use of 4 in the grouping of persons or things seems to have been a favourite method with Jewish teachers. There are several examples of it in Amos (1[3. 6. 9. 11. 13] 2[1. 4. 6]) and in Proverbs (30[15f. 18f. 21ff. 24ff. 29ff.]). Later instances are Sir 37[18] ' good and evil, life and death,' Test. of Judah, ch. 16, ' 4 spirits in wine,' and the remarkable series of paragraphs in 'Abôth v. 16–21, in which people generally, dispositions, scholars, almsgivers, college-goers, and those who sit under the wise, are in each case grouped in 4 classes. May we suppose that our Lord, in accordance with His habit of utilizing current methods, adopted in the parable a familiar mode of classification ?

Twelve.—Twelve, as the number of the tribes of Israel according to ancient tradition, became naturally a favourite number among the Jews, especially as it carried with it the suggestion of Divine choice and Divine faithfulness. So it figured in religious ritual, symbolism, and history. There were 12 jewels in the high priest's breast-plate (Ex 28[21]), and 12 cakes of shewbread (Lv 24[5]). Solomon's sea stood on 12 oxen (1 K 7[25]), Elijah's altar on Carmel consisted of 12 stones (1 K 18[31]), and the altar-hearth in Ezekiel's visionary temple was 12 cubits long by 12 cubits broad (Ezk 43[16]). It is, therefore, not surprising that the number 12 is prominent in the Gospels. The 12 disciples referred to in Mt 10[1f. 5] 11[1] 20[17] 26[14. 20. 47], Mk 3[14] 4[10] 6[7] 9[35] 10[32] 11[11] 14[10. 17. 20. 43], Lk 6[13] 8[1] 9[1. 12] 18[31] 22[3. 47], Jn 6[67. 70f.]. 20[24] (in 22 of these passages simply as οἱ δώδεκα, ' the Twelve' ; cf. also Ac 6[2], 1 Co 15[5], Rev 21[14]), the 12 baskets of broken pieces (Mt 14[20], Mk 6[43] 8[19], Lk 9[17], Jn 6[13]), the 12 legions of angels (Mt 26[53]), are all more or less reminiscent of the 12 tribes. In the promise in Mt 19[28] ‖ Lk 22[30] is a direct reference which puts beyond doubt the association of the number in our Lord's day with the tribes.

This use may have been aided by the constant recurrence of the 12 months of the year, but it is not safe to follow Dr. A. Jeremias (*Babylonisches im NT*, 88) in connecting the number of the Apostles even indirectly with the 12 signs of the zodiac. He does not, indeed, venture to affirm that this lay in the consciousness of Jesus, although he thinks the promise of the 12 thrones (Mt 19[28], Lk 22[30]) might point at that ; but he is confident that ' the mystical cosmological reference,' as he calls it, lies in the words of the writer of the Apocalypse about the 12 Apostles of the Lamb (Rev 21[14]). However it may be with the latter, it is unnecessary to find any allusion of the kind in the Gospels. Men familiar in some degree with Gentile culture and the astrological-astronomical speculations which were in

vogue about this time, such as Philo and Josephus, might connect the 12 gems of the high priest's breastplate with the signs of the zodiac, and might therefore regard 12 as a perfect number (Philo, *de Profugis*, § 33, cited by König, *DB* iii. 563*a*, τέλειος δ' ἀριθμὸς ὁ δώδεκα ; Josephus, *Ant.* iii. vii. 7) without the idea ever entering the minds of the majority.

In several passages a period of 12 years is referred to. The woman healed by touching the fringe of the Lord's garment had been ill for 12 years (Mt 9[20], Mk 5[25], Lk 8[43]). The daughter of Jairus was 12 years old (Mk 5[42], Lk 8[42]). Jesus was 12 years old when found in the Temple (Lk 2[42]). In all these cases the number must be understood literally, but the second and third admit of illustration from Oriental life. At 12 childhood ceased for the Jewish boy. In the addendum to the fifth chapter of 'Abôth two of the rules run : ' At 10 the Mishnah, at 13 the Commandments.' A boy of 12, therefore, was on the threshold of manhood. A tradition recorded by Josephus affirms that Samuel was 12 years old when he received the Divine call (*Ant.* v. x. 4). Another tradition, found in a Christian writing, but probably of Jewish origin, represented Solomon as 12 years old when he gave his famous judgment about the child (pseudo-Ignatius, *ad Magnesios*, iii.). At 12 a girl was marriageable. According to the Book of Jubilees (30[2]), Dinah was 12 years old at the time referred to in Gn 34[2].

One more passage remains : ' Are there not twelve hours in the day ?' (Jn 11[9]). Here, no doubt, Babylonian influence can be traced, although in the time of Christ most of the Jews living in Palestine will have been wholly unconscious of the fact. The full day was divided by the Babylonians, who in this matter as in so many points set the rule for all their neighbours, and through the Greeks for the whole Western world, into 12 parts. As this day consisted of two halves, the daylight portion and the night portion, the division into twelve was applied to each, without regard to the season of the year. An hour was one-twelfth of the day or the night (*KAT* [*ZW*] 328, 335 f.). The old way of speaking still survives in Syria. The day is regarded, as in the time of Christ, as consisting of 12 hours (Bauer, *Volksleben im Lande der Bibel*, pp. 274 f.).

Sixty.—The use of the number 60 in the parable of the Sower (Mt 13[8. 23], Mk 4[8. 20], not in Lk 24[13]) may possibly have indirect connexion with the sexagesimal system of Babylonia (for this, cf. Bezold, *Ninive und Babylon*, 90, 92), which must have been current throughout western Asia, especially through its use in the subdivision of the talent (talent = 60 manehs ; maneh = 60 shekels), and would naturally lead to the employment of the number with more or less significance. There are many passages in the OT and other Jewish literature in which 60 can hardly be accidental : Nu 7[88] (60 rams, 60 he-goats, 60 he-lambs of the first year), Dt 3[4] (60 cities, cf. Jos 13[30], 1 K 4[13], 1 Ch 2[23]), 1 K 6[2] (Solomon's temple 60 cubits long, cf. 2 Ch 3[3]), 1 K 4[22], 2 Ch 11[21], Jer 52[25] (60 men of the people of the land found in Jerusalem by the Babylonians, cf. 2 K 25[19]), Ca 3[7] 6[8], Test. of Judah, ch. 3 (stone weighing 60 lbs.), ch. 9 (60 men slain), Test. of Abraham, text A 10 (cherubic chariot attended by 60 angels). The many examples in the Babylonian Talmud (fire the 60th part of Gehenna, *Berak.* 57[b] etc.) will be largely due to the Babylonian atmosphere of the compilation.

Thirty.—Thirty, the half of sixty, may be used in the same context (Mt 13[8. 23], Mk 4[8. 20]) in somewhat the same way, through the same association. In Lk 3[23], where it is said that Jesus was about 30 years of age at the beginning of His ministry, there is probably an allusion to the belief that 30 years marked the attainment of manly vigour. Joseph entered on his career as a statesman at 30 (Gn 41[46]), and David was 30 when he ascended the throne (2 S 5[4]). In the appendix to the fifth chapter of *'Abôth*, 30 is defined as the age of strength (בֶּן שְׁלֹשִׁים לכּה). The 30 pieces of silver paid to Judas (Mt 26[15] 27[3, 9], cf. Zec 11[12f.]) would remind every Jew of the average value of a slave as fixed in the Law (Ex 21[32]), 30 shekels. The Babylonian average was lower, but the Assyrian coincided with the Hebrew (Johns in *Babylonian and Assyrian Laws, Contracts, and Letters*, p. 182 f.). In the remaining passage, Jn 6[19], the number is purely historical.

LITERATURE. — Art. 'Zahlen' in Winer, *RWB*[3]; Riehm, *HWB*[2], and Guthe, *Bibelwörterbuch*; artt. 'Forty' and 'Number' in the *Jewish Encyc.*; art. 'Number' in *Encyc. Bibl.* and in Hastings' *DB* iii. 560[b] ff.; König, *Stilistik*, 51–57.

W. TAYLOR SMITH.

NUNC DIMITTIS (Lk 2[29-32]), so called from the opening words in the Latin version, is the third and shortest of the hymns of the Incarnation preserved to us by St. Luke. Like the other two, it speaks of Christ; but whereas *Benedictus*, the Song of the priest Zacharias, is naturally of His Priesthood, and *Magnificat*, the Song of the royally-descended Virgin Mary, of His Kingdom, this, the Song of Simeon (wh. see), as beseems the utterance of a prophet, is of Messiah fulfilling the prophetic function assigned to Him in the OT (cf. Dt 18[15]), and especially by Isaiah.

The feature in Simeon's character which is to the Evangelist the climax of his virtues is that he was 'waiting for the consolation of Israel.' The words are a reminiscence of Jacob's, 'I have waited for thy salvation, O Lord' (Gn 49[18]); and they describe what was precisely the attitude of Abraham in regard to God's promise of the land (Ac 7[9] and He 11[13]), and of David in regard to the kingdom (1 S 26[9-11]), both of whom did not 'fret themselves in anywise to do evil' (Ps 37[8]), but waited till the Lord would give what He had spoken. So our Lord, speaking of those in danger of being led away by false Christs, bids His followers 'in patience possess their souls' (Lk 21[19]). This was part of the faith of Simeon: his waiting for '*the Lord's* Christ' (Lk 2) saved him from going after any turbulent pretender, or accepting, with the Herodians, a mere king of this world. The '*consolation of Israel*' was a phrase with the Rabbis for the times of Messiah: Lightfoot (*Hor. Heb.*) gives five illustrations of its use.

The repeated mention of the Holy Spirit guiding Simeon at each successive step evinces the fact that prophecy, silent since the days of Malachi, is again about to stir (de Wette, Oosterzee); yet the difference also is to be observed between the repeated comings of the Spirit upon Simeon, and His abiding on Jesus (Jn 1[33]) and remaining with the Church (14[16]). By what sign Simeon was taught of the Spirit to recognize the child of Mary as the Christ we are not told: perhaps the Virgin's poverty, evidenced by her offering of doves, was the token to him, as the manger-cradle had been to the shepherds (Lk 2[12]). Anyhow the Child was pointed out to him; he went up to Him, received Him in his arms, and, as he held Him, he 'blessed God,' and uttered his *Nunc dimittis*. There are no different readings in the text of it; but the Syriac renders the verb in the first clause, which in Greek, Latin, and English is in the *indicative* mood, by an *optative*, 'My Lord, now release thou thy servant in peace.' The mistake has been followed by several in this country who should have known better: *e.g.* by Logan, in the *Scottish Paraphrases* (Par. 38):

'Now, Lord, according to thy word,
Let me in peace depart.

. . . . . .

At length my arms embrace my Lord,
Now let their vigour cease,'

and even by John Keble, usually so accurate:

'Whose prayers are struggling with his tears,
Lord, let me now depart.'

As a matter of fact, Simeon does not pray for death. He thanks God for permitting him to see, what many prophets and kings had desired to see and were not permitted (Lk 10[24]), the salvation He had promised; and having seen it he says that he is ready to go when God wills.

The hymn is in three couplets:

(1) Thanksgiving for permission at last to leave his post, as the sentinel when the hour of his watch is over (Godet). Death will be to him as sleep to a labouring man (Bruce).

'Now *thou art letting* thy servant depart, O Lord,
According to thy word, in peace.'

The 'word,' of course, is the promise of v.[26] that he should not see death before he had seen the Lord's [own] Christ; and the fulfilment of the promise has brought him peace, because in Christ there is sure *salvation* for him and for all God's people.

There are two fine Patristic comments—Cyprian's (*On the Mortality*, 3), 'He bears witness that the servants of God have peace, are free, and tranquil when, withdrawn from the whirlwinds of this world, they reach the port of the eternal home, and pass through death to immortality'; and Ambrose's (*Exposition of St. Luke*, Bk. II. ii. 59), 'Let him who wishes to depart come into the Temple; let him come to Jerusalem; let him wait for the Lord's Christ; let him take in his arms the Word of God, embracing Him by the arms of faith.' Servant (δοῦλον), Lord (δέσποτα)—'slave,' 'master' are terms appropriate at all times to express the relation between God and men, yet savouring of the Law (Bruce).

(2) The reason of Simeon's peace in the prospect of death:

'For mine eyes have seen thy salvation,
Which thou preparedst before the face of all peoples.'

What we see with our eyes is sure (cf. Jn 1[14] 19[35] and 1 Jn 1[2]). And Jesus Christ is salvation (Is 49[6]), for salvation is in Him and in none other (Ac 4[12]). Moreover, He is the salvation which God Himself provided, not which man might have fancied. 'Preparedst' is a more correct rendering than AV 'hast prepared,' for the tense refers to a definite historical fact (cf. Lk 1[47]); and this God means *for all peoples* (2[10]) (plural)—both the sections of mankind of whom, in the next verse, Simeon is to speak, viz. the Gentiles and Israel. The Greek word used (λαός) usually means Israel only, the people [of the Lord]. But now the privilege is extended, and they who were not a people are to be the people of the living God (Hos 2[1], Ro 9[25, 26], 1 P 2[13]).

(3) The different prophetic functions Christ is to discharge towards the Gentiles and the Jews respectively:

'A light to lighten the Gentiles,
And the glory of thy people Israel.'

(*a*) To the Gentiles who sat in darkness (Is 9[2]) He is to be a Light (49[6]); but not only by giving them light. The thought is greater than merely that Christ is to reveal truth *to* the Gentiles. He is a Light 'for their revealing' (εἰς ἀποκάλυψιν ἐθνῶν) —to show what the Gentiles are, how dear to Almighty God (cf. Ro 3[29]), and how capable they are through His grace of producing saints. The prophecy of Simeon is thus akin to that of John the Baptist (Mt 3[7]), and has its OT roots in such passages as Is 25[7] and Hos 2[3]. How wonderfully has it been fulfilled—that out of Judaism He could bring a Peter, a John, a Paul; out of decadent Rome an Augustine and an Ambrose; out of the wild Irish a Columba; out of the Saxon 'knifemen' a Wilfrid and a Bede! We have yet to see what He will make of China and Japan, when they are Christianized. (*b*) Of Israel, who had produced so many saints, prophets, and teachers, the 'lights of the world in their several generations,' Christ is to be the supreme Glory, of more honour than

Moses (He 3³), with a better priesthood than Aaron (7²⁷), Himself the very Brightness of the Father's glory (1³), which was beheld in Him (Jn 1¹⁴). St. Paul saw, in the 1st cent., how true is this prophecy of Christ (Ro 9⁴⁻⁶), and all subsequent history is its confirmation.

A parallel is given by Carpenter (*The Synoptic Gospels*) from Buddhist legend of one who, discerning in a babe the signs of perfection, predicted, 'Thou wilt be a Buddha, and remove the veils of sin and ignorance from the world.' But the Indian seer could not rejoice with Simeon, he could only weep that he would not be alive to share the light; which reminds us that Simeon's peace is through the Christian hope of a better life to come, when we shall be with Christ.

Simeon's attitude towards the Gentiles, while in full accord with that of the OT (Gn 22¹⁸ 49¹⁰, Ps 98³ 100¹, Is 42⁶ 49⁶ 60³), is in striking contrast to that of the nearest contemporary Jewish writings, the Psalms of Solomon, in which, though there is the same longing for Messiah and His kingdom, the lot of the heathen is not light or salvation, but only judgment (Ps-Sol 16⁴).

The singular sweetness—the calm beauty, as of a perfect pearl—of the Song of Simeon has always been recognized; and for ages it has entered into the evening service of the Church. Both the Roman Catholic and the Anglican Churches have appointed it as a hymn at Vespers, teaching us (as it does) to live each day as if we knew it to be our last; and, embracing Christ by faith, to thank God for Him and be ready in peace to depart in Him. In the Church of Scotland, while Knox's Prayer-Book held its place, and again after the introduction of the Paraphrases (1781), it became customary to use it at the close of the Communion Service; while in a few churches, both Episcopal and Presbyterian, it is sung at funerals when the body is being carried out of the church.

LITERATURE.—T. A. Gurney, *Nunc Dimittis* (1906); A. M. Stewart, *Infancy and Youth of Jesus* (1905), 53; T. D. Bernard, *Songs of the Holy Nativity* (1895), 120, 131; S. Cox, *Expositions* (1888), iv. 1.   JAMES COOPER.

O

OATHS.—Christ's teaching on the subject of oaths is set forth in one of the sections of the Sermon on the Mount, in which He contrasts His doctrine with that of the earlier dispensation (Mt 5³³⁻³⁷). The position of the Law on the subject is summed up in the statement, 'Thou shalt not forswear thyself, but shalt perform unto the Lord thine oaths.' This is a combination of different passages in the Law (Lv 19¹², Nu 30³, Dt 23²²), of which the first deals specially with oaths, the others with vows. But in point of obligation oaths and vows were recognized in the Rabbinical schools as on the same footing (Wünsche, *Neue Beiträge zur Erläuterung der Evangelien aus Talmud und Midrasch*, p. 57), and the statement in which Christ here represents the position of the Law was, no doubt, the current formula in which, in these schools, the doctrine of the Law on the question was summed up. In opposition to this dictum of the Law, Christ lays down an absolute prohibition, 'Swear not at all' (v.³⁴), and proceeds to draw out the full meaning of the 'at all' (ὅλως) by showing that His prohibition covers every appeal to anything beside us in confirmation of our word, and not merely such as expressly introduce the name of Jehovah. The casuists among the scribes made a distinction between more and less binding oaths. The former class consisted of those which invoked the name of God; the latter used such forms as 'by heaven,' 'by earth,' 'by Jerusalem,' 'by the life of my head.' An oath by heaven and earth, for instance, was not considered to be binding, because one did not require to think of the Creator; whereas if one swore by one of the letters of the Divine name, or by one of the Divine attributes, that was regarded as binding, and he who treated such an oath lightly was punishable (Wünsche, *op. cit.* p. 59; Schürer, *HJP* II. ii. 122).

Our Lord Himself gives other examples of such casuistical distinctions in the matter of oaths in Mt 23¹⁶⁻²². He refers to them here because the full import of His prohibition of oaths might not be realized by those who were familiar with such distinctions. It might be thought that He was merely forbidding a direct appeal to the name of Jehovah. And so He proceeds to show how utterly different is His standpoint on the question of oaths from that of the Rabbinical authorities. They en-

deavoured to empty the oath of reference to God, so as to narrow the scope of the commandment against perjury. Christ sought to make explicit the reference to God virtually contained in every asseveration, so as to widen the scope of His prohibition of swearing. With this object He takes some of the common forms of oaths which were regarded as less binding, and shows how, though the name of God be not expressly mentioned, they are meaningless unless they involve an appeal to Him. Thus to call heaven or earth to witness our statement is an empty form, unless we be thinking not merely of heaven or earth, but of the Power they suggest, who will punish unfaithfulness (vv.³⁴·³⁵ᵃ), *i.e.* God, of whom heaven is the throne and earth the footstool (Is 66¹). To appeal to Jerusalem (v.³⁵ᵇ) is meaningless unless we be thinking of the great King, who has made Jerusalem His city (Ps 48³). And to swear by one's head (v.³⁶) involves an appeal to Him in whose hands our destiny lies, and who alone can bring upon our heads the punishment of perjury. For ourselves, we cannot make one hair black or white. Black hair is here used as the symbol of youth; white, of old age. The very colour of our hair, Christ would say, reminds us that we are in the hands of a higher Power. It is to that Power we appeal when we swear by the life of our head. Every form of asseveration, then, Christ concludes, every appeal to anything beside us in confirmation of our word, is an oath, for it virtually involves an appeal to God. All such forms come under Christ's prohibition. His command is: 'Swear not at all; but let your speech be, Yea, yea; Nay, nay' (vv.³⁴·³⁷).

These last words have received different interpretations. Beza renders them, 'Let your affirmation be yea, and your negation nay,'—an attempt to bring the present verse into harmony with Ja 5¹² at the sacrifice of grammar. Equally unjustifiable grammatically is Grotius' attempt to secure the same object by his translation, 'Let your yea and nay of speech correspond to a yea and nay of fact,' with the additional fault that it is questionable whether that is the meaning of the passage in James. The simplest way of taking the words is to regard the ναὶ ναί, οὒ οὔ, as a repetition, such as was common in actual speech (cf. 2 K 10¹⁵, 2 Co 1¹⁷), to confirm a statement. 'Let your speech,' says

Christ, 'be a clear and forcible yes or no. For whatsoever is more than these,' He continues, 'cometh ἐκ τοῦ πονηροῦ.' Again there is difference of opinion as to these last words. Many take them as equivalent to ἐκ τοῦ διαβόλου. But B. Weiss (*Matthäusevangelium, ad loc.*) contends that such a view is incompatible with the fact that the OT requires oaths (Ex 22[11]), and even puts them into the mouth of God (Gn 22[16] 26[3]). It is better to take the πονηροῦ as the gen. of the neuter; so that the statement will mean that the oath springs from evil, either in the sense that it is the presence of evil in the world that leads to the oath in confirmation of one's word, and that in the Kingdom of God, in which truth prevails, the oath must altogether disappear (so Weiss), or that the practice of confirming one's statement by an oath springs from the tacit assumption that when one does not so confirm it, one is not bound to speak the truth (so Wendt, *Lehre Jesu*, ii. 210).

Before proceeding to discuss the conclusion to be drawn from the passage, we must note an interpretation of vv.[34-36] which has gained considerable acceptance, but which puts quite a different meaning upon Christ's prohibition in v.[34] from what we have given above. It is suggested that the prohibition is not meant to embrace all oaths, but merely the thoughtless swearing of everyday life whereby the name of God is profaned (so Calvin, Ewald, Tholuck, and many others). The ὀμόσαι ὅλως of v.[34], it is contended, does not include swearing by God; for, as Ewald (*Die drei ersten Evangelien*, p. 267) says, that was done only in courts of law, and Christ is not referring to this at all. If He had meant to forbid oaths absolutely, He would certainly have mentioned the direct oath in which the name of God is expressly invoked. As He has not done so, we must conclude that His prohibition is not meant to apply to it, *i.e.* that He means to forbid only such thoughtless oaths of common life as He proceeds to exemplify.

This attempt to empty the ὅλως of its meaning does not commend itself. It is evidently inspired by fear of the consequences which seem to ensue from the absolute prohibition Christ lays down, and such a motive does not tend to sound exegesis. It fails to do justice to the original. The only permissible translation of μὴ ὀμόσαι ὅλως is that which regards it as an absolute prohibition. Only thus does Christ's position present a proper contrast to that of the Law. The Law forbids swearing falsely; Christ forbids swearing at all. Thus we have a sufficient contrast to, and advance beyond, the position of the Law. But on the present interpretation Christ sets over against the commandment against perjury in the name of God a prohibition merely of frivolous swearing, and that of a kind which does not mention the name of God at all, which is somewhat of an anti-climax. It is true, as the supporters of this interpretation point out, that Christ does not expressly mention the oath by the name of God in the instances He adduces. But it is much more reasonable to suppose that He omits it because it is evident that it is included under the swearing He prohibits, while there may be doubt as to these indirect oaths He specifies, than to argue that, when He prohibits swearing ὅλως, He includes under the prohibition only those forms of oath which were hardly regarded as oaths at all by His contemporaries, and omits the one oath that was universally so esteemed.

We conclude, then, that Christ's word in v.[34] is to be understood as an absolute prohibition of swearing, and that it cannot be restricted to the thoughtless, irrelevant oaths of common life. And it remains to consider in what spirit this absolute prohibition is laid down, and what are the con-

clusions that follow from it. Christ has Himself given the reason for His prohibition of swearing. Whatsoever goes beyond the distinct and forcible affirmation and negation, He says, cometh of evil (v.[37]). As we saw above, this saying may be interpreted in different ways. It may be taken to mean that it is the presence of evil among our fellow-men that necessitates oaths, to convince them of the good faith of the speaker. So Augustine (*Sermon on the Mount*): 'Tu autem non malum facis, qui bene uteris juratione, quæ, etsi non bona, tamen necessaria est, ut alteri persuadeas quod utiliter persuades, sed a malo est illius, cujus infirmitate jurare cogeris.' But, as Tholuck (*Sermon on the Mount*, Eng. tr. p. 252 f.) remarks, this is open to a twofold objection—first, that in such a case the evil in question rests with him who *requires* the oath, whereas all the stress of the prohibition is directed against *taking* oaths; and, second, that on this interpretation the fulfilment of our Lord's command would be deferred to the realization of that ideal state in which no evil exists, in which case the present command would stand on a different footing from the others of the Sermon on the Mount, which plainly apply to a world in which evil is prevalent. For this reason we accept the other interpretation of the words given above—that whatever goes beyond the plain affirmation and negation cometh of evil, in the sense that behind it is the tacit assumption that, when our word is not confirmed by an oath, we are not bound to adhere strictly to the truth. This brings the present passage into harmony with the general spirit of the Sermon on the Mount. The theme of that Sermon is righteousness of the heart. When Christ opposes His commands to those of the Law, it is to show that He requires more than the Law demanded, that He insists not only upon righteousness of outward conduct, but upon righteousness of the heart. The Law required strict truth whenever an oath was taken. The tendency of the Pharisaic formalism of Christ's day was to keep the letter of the Law by strict fulfilment of one's promise and scrupulous adherence to the truth whenever the Divine name was invoked, but to break its spirit by assuming that whenever such an oath was not taken, greater latitude was allowed. Christ insisted upon such a regard for truth that the absence of the oath should make no difference. To feel that one is more bound by an oath than by one's simple word is to have the spirit of falsehood in one's heart. In such a case whatsoever is more than the direct yea and nay cometh of evil.

Once we realize what is the spirit in which Christ's prohibition is given, we are in a position to decide some of the questions raised as to the practicability of the observance of the command in existing social conditions. If the prohibition is absolute, on what ground can the practice of taking oaths in courts of law be defended? The answer is that the spirit in which the oath is taken in such a case is very different from that which our Lord condemns in the present instance. In a court of law we take the oath to convince our fellow-men, who cannot see our heart and judge of our regard for truth, of our good faith. That is a very different thing from thinking that we are not required to speak the truth unless bound by an oath; and it is the latter view that Christ condemns in His dictum upon swearing. We may still keep the spirit of our Lord's command though we break the letter of it by taking an oath in court, just as we may keep the spirit of many other injunctions of the Sermon on the Mount, *e.g.* that with regard to praying in private (Mt 6[6]), though we break them in the letter. Christ Himself, according to the Gospel in which the present passage occurs, did not refuse to answer when the high priest adjured Him by the living God (26[63]). And though Mark omits the adjuration, so that we cannot with confidence appeal to the conduct of Christ Himself on this occasion, all the Gospels represent Him as frequently strengthening His declarations by the solemn ἀμήν, which in the Fourth Gospel becomes ἀμὴν ἀμήν. In a word, while the prohibition of swearing is absolute, and is on no account to be modified in the manner we have referred to above, we must remember that what Christ is aiming at is not the mere outward oath, but the spirit of evil which inspired it, and regard as an infraction of His command only such conduct as cometh of the evil He seeks to destroy. When we regard the commandment in that light, there is no need to defer the fulfilment of it to an ideal state. It does not describe the conditions which should prevail between the members of the Kingdom of God only in their relations to one another, but lays down a principle which should guide the member of the Kingdom in his relation to all with whom he comes in contact. And though, owing to the conditions of the society in which he lives, he may have to depart from the strict letter of the precept by taking a solemn oath on occasion, so long as he does not do so from the unworthy motive which inspires the oaths against which Christ contends, he may still claim to remain faithful to the command of Christ.

LITERATURE.—The various Commentaries; Hastings' *DB*, art. 'Oath' and Extra Vol. p. 28; *PRE*[3], art. 'Eid'; Tholuck, *Sermon on the Mount*; Wendt, *Lehre Jesu*, ii. 210–213; Gore, *Sermon on the Mount*; Rothe, *Theol. Ethik*, § 1067; Dykes, *Manifesto of the King*, p. 265; Martensen, *Christ. Ethics*, ii. 226. A full list of the relative literature will be found in Tholuck and Rothe.　　　　G. WAUCHOPE STEWART.

OBED. — Father of Jesse, mentioned in both genealogies of our Lord (Mt 1[5], Lk 3[32]).

OBEDIENCE.—i. The Obedience of Christ.— 1. Christ as a man (see HUMANITY OF CHRIST) *came under the obligations of men*, and principal among these was the obligation of obedience. This He Himself recognized explicitly. His parents had Him circumcised (Lk 2[21]), and brought Him to Jerusalem according to the custom, to observe the law of the Passover (possibly every year, Lk 2[41. 42]), which custom He subsequently continued personally (Jn 2[23] 5[1], cf. 7[2. 10], Mt 26[17ff.] etc.). He felt Himself called upon to join in the great religious movements of His day, though not commanded by the Law (Mt 3[15]), as well as to observe the political customs (Mt 17[27]). It was therefore more than a mere expression as to a definite example when He said : ' It becometh us [me] to fulfil all righteousness' (Mt 3[15]).

2. *The fact of His obedience.*—If we test this by the Ten Commandments as substantially embracing the whole moral law, we find His obedience complete. They are mostly prohibitions, and we do not find Him infringing them. It cannot be said that this silence of the Scriptures as to transgressions does not prove His entire conformity to them, and leaves room for the doubt whether His obedience was perfect; since He was surrounded by watchful enemies who magnified variations that were not disobedience, and would have mentioned any real disobedience with eagerness. The honour which He paid to God was as perfect as His perception of the spiritual nature of His worship was clear (Jn 4[24]). He observed the Sabbath, being found regularly in the synagogue on that day (Lk 4[16] 'as his custom was'). The fact that He did no work that was contrary to the Sabbath commandment, is shown clearly by the fact that He was repeatedly attacked for immaterial things and for exercising His healing power upon that day,

for which He successfully defended Himself (Mt 12[3. 7. 11. 12]). To those of another race and time He may seem to have been lacking on one occasion in respect for His mother, viz. at the marriage in Cana of Galilee (Jn 2[4]). But the appellation 'Woman' was not disrespectful, for it was used in the tenderest way at the cross (Jn 19[26]); nor was it disrespectful to reprove officious interference; nor was Mary left unsatisfied (v.[5]), but expected His compliance with her hinted request. So much for the negative side of the moral law. On its positive side, as comprehensively stated by Him in the words, 'Thou shalt love the Lord thy God with all thy heart, and thy neighbour as thyself' (Mt 22[39]), none was ever so zealous of God's honour, or of preserving His own communion with Him (Jn 10[30] 17[11. 21-23. 25]), as Jesus. And love of neighbour, as interpreted first fully by Himself (Lk 10[30ff.]), He exemplified in all His contact with suffering and needy humanity. Nor did He fail in that harder sort of obedience which consists in quick response to the personal will of God manifested in providence (Mt 4[4], Lk 2[49], Jn 12[7. 28]). His care for the ceremonial law, besides the cases already cited, may be seen by His recommending the lepers whom He cleansed, on two occasions, to observe the law of Moses provided in their case (Lk 5[14] 17[14]).

3. *His sinlessness.*—We thus see in the life of Jesus no offence against the law of right. There is no evidence of sinfulness. But this would not in itself establish His sinlessness. Many a man gives the impression of a perfect life, is, according to the Scripture phrase, 'blameless,' who is not 'sinless,' because he sees sin in himself, and charges himself with it. But Jesus claimed sinlessness for Himself. He challenged the Jews to convict Him of sin (Jn 8[46]); and He affirmed of Himself that the 'prince of this world' had nothing in Him (Jn 14[30]). True, this sinlessness was first *attained* through conflict (cf. Mt 4[11], Jn 12[27], Mk 15[34]), and 'learned' (He 5[8]), and Jesus Himself shrank from the application to Him of the word 'good' in the absolute sense (Mk 10[18]); but it was attained and learned, and this without the experience of failure. Its necessity to the work of redemption gives it its complete dogmatic establishment (cf. He 9[7. 14] 5[9] 4[15]); but the proof of its actuality depends, finally, upon the word of Jesus Himself. Were this the testimony of the Jews, who were self-righteous, and thus incapacitated for judging of their true spiritual condition, it would have no value; but it is the testimony of a specially sensitive conscience, one which saw deeper into the meaning of the Law than others, which enjoyed perfect communion with God (Jn 14[9] 12[45]). As such it stands, and is subject to no diminution from our ability to point out defect in Him. As a challenge, it was not met by His adversaries, evidently because they could not meet it. See, further, art. SINLESSNESS.

4. *His superiority to the Law.*—His obedience may be conceived, on the one side, as His perfect subjection to the Law. But, on the other side, He was superior to the Law. In respect to infringements of the law of the Sabbath with which He was charged, He did not simply defend Himself by saying that He alone rightly interpreted the law, but He proclaimed His superiority to it. 'The Son of Man is Lord even of the sabbath' (Mk 2[28]). He set aside certain of the provisions of the Law (Mt 5[38]); but He did a more significant thing in deepening the meaning of others (Mt 5[27ff.]). He revealed the true meaning of the Law when He brought it back to its foundation in the all-embracing law of love. The element of the Law which He modified was, therefore, the external, the scaffolding or clothing of the legal principle, not the fundamental meaning of the Law. He came also to 'fulfil' the Law (Mt 5[17]); and this meant to *fill out* (πληρόω), and

hence to set it aside as completed and its design accomplished. In the later form of the Apostolic doctrine Jesus was called the 'end of the law' (Ro 10[4]), in the sense that He provided a new way of salvation, which had formerly had to be attained through the observance of the Law. This was particularly through the sacrifice of Himself (He 10[8-14]) by which He brought the whole OT system to an end, and for ever cancelled the ceremonial law. When the same idea appears in St. John's Gospel (3[14. 16] 6[51] 10[17]), it may be thought to belong to the same stratum of later teaching; but it is reflected in the earliest form of the Gospel (Mk 10[45]), it appears in the institution of the Lord's Supper (Mt 26[28]), and is accordingly to be regarded as the primal and unvarying substance of the Gospel. The Law, then, is abrogated because its object has been attained, and its definite and peculiar prescriptions may give way to more general and spiritual forms of precept. The emphasis is hereafter to be laid not upon the letter, but upon the spirit (2 Co 3[6]). See LAW, LAW OF GOD.

5. *The capital article of His obedience—the Death upon the Cross.*—The later strata of the Gospel history lay emphasis upon the fact that the death of Christ was a subject of the Divine command. Thus Jesus says, according to St. John, 'This commandment [viz. to lay down my life] I received from the Father' (10[18]). In 12[27], shrinking from the foreseen suffering of the cross, He says, 'For this cause [viz. to suffer the death of the cross, cf. v.[32]] came I unto this hour.' The same idea, that His death upon the cross was the essential part of His work which He came into the world to do, and which was laid upon Him by the Father, appears in many other texts in this Gospel, implied where not explicitly stated (cf. 3[14] 6[38. 50. 51. 58] 8[21] 10[11] 14[30. 31] 17[13] 19[30]). The same conception is fully developed in the other portions of the NT which belong to the same period of development with this Gospel, particularly in Philippians (2[8]) and the Epistle to the Hebrews (5[7. 8] 10[10]). But it is also indicated in the earliest strata. In Mk 10[45] Jesus Himself says that He has come, 'not to be ministered unto, but to minister, and *to give his life* a ransom for many.' The whole Gospel story is displayed, as it were, upon the black background of the darkness and sufferings of Calvary. Prophecies by Jesus Himself of His own death begin to appear at an early period by intimation (Mt 10[38], cf. 16[24]), and at a period still long before the final Passion in more explicit and frequent utterance (Mt 16[21-28] ‖ ; 17[3ff.] according to ‖ Lk 9[31] ; 17[22. 23] ‖ ; 20[17-19] ‖). There is evidence in these passages, taken as a whole, and regarded as containing the concurrent and consistent Evangelical idea of the death of Christ, that to Christ the burden of death consisted partly in its physical pain, from which One shrank who possessed the instinct of life among other human qualities (see HUMANITY OF CHRIST), but still more as something unbecoming to the pure and holy Son of God, associated, as it was in human history, with the idea of sin and condemnation. Or, as St. Paul expresses it (Gal 3[13]), it was a curse which He did not lightly take upon Himself. Two things result from this method of considering the death of Christ : (1) that it measures the highest degree of devotion to the salvation of men ; and (2) that it was effective because it lay in the will of God, to which Christ was obedient, not assuming it Himself, as a desperate and uncertain remedy, but accepting it as the God-designed path of propitiation and redemption.

6. *The relation of Christ's obedience to the salvation of men.*—The relation of the sacrifice, which was the main article of His obedience, to the salvation of men is considered elsewhere (see ATONEMENT, PROPITIATION, SACRIFICE, etc.). No text

of the Gospels presents the obedience of Christ, strictly considered, as having a connexion with our salvation, except as His moral perfection was among the qualifications for the office of Saviour. The inference which has been made, that the obedience of Christ itself formed a part of His saving work, has been drawn from such texts as Ro 5[19] ('through the obedience of the one shall the many be made righteous'). But this idea receives no support from the Gospels, and none from the text cited itself, when carefully interpreted. The thought of the Apostle is unfolded here in a series of parallel expressions, in which, on the one side, Adam's 'trespass,' 'sin,' 'disobedience,' and, on the other side, Christ's 'grace,' 'gift by grace,' 'free gift,' 'righteousness,' 'act of righteousness,' 'obedience,' are mentioned as equal to one another, and as contrasted, the one side with the other. The obedience of Christ here considered is, therefore, His *act* of obedience, or His atoning death. The act of obedience saves, not *as* obedience, but as atonement.

7. *The significance of Christ's obedience for religion* arises from the exaltation which it affords of the Person of Christ. As the victorious contestant and the perfect character, He calls out the veneration and enthusiastic loyalty of His followers, incites them to greater efforts, and fills them with loftier courage than any imperfect prophet could do, however excellent otherwise, and thus becomes the true 'exemplar and leader' (ἀρχηγός, He 12[2]) of our faith.

LITERATURE.—Hastings' *DB*, art. 'Obedience'; Ullmann, *Sinlessness of Jesus*; Forrest, *Christ of Hist. and Exper.* 17 ff. ; R. Mackintosh, *Christ and the Jewish Law*; Dale, *Atonement*, Lect. IX.

ii. Our obedience.—Christ came not only as a Teacher and Redeemer, but also as an Example. It might be said of all His life, as He said when He washed the disciples' feet, 'I have given you an example, that ye also should do as I have done to you' (Jn 13[15]). As the object of all His work was to reveal the Father, and he that had 'seen him had seen the Father' (Jn 14[9]), so he who did as Jesus did obeyed the will of the Father, which was perfectly exemplified in Him (Jn 8[29]). Indeed, this was the necessary consequence of His teaching office, for He always said in fact if not by word, 'Take my yoke upon you, and learn of me' (Mt 11[29]). It was His purpose in the world to bear witness to the truth (Jn 18[37]), and to do this not merely by word, but by right deed. Hence the obedience of Christ is the standard of our obedience. We are to be 'perfect as our Father in heaven is perfect' (Mt 5[48]), and that perfection is the perfection which is manifested in the Son. At the same time, as performance falls far short of ideal in other human things, so here. There is no example given us in the Gospels of the attainment by a disciple of such perfection as was in the Master. Peter who denied Him, Thomas who could not believe His resurrection, John and James who were fired by an unholy ambition, were the chief among the Twelve, and doubtless as successful as the others. Even after Pentecost, Paul and Barnabas had a sharp contention. All had 'the treasure in earthen vessels.'

The obedience which Christ asks of us is an obedience of the spirit rather than of the letter. He says in one place, 'If ye keep my commandments, ye shall abide in my love' (Jn 15[10]) ; but when we ask what the commandments of Jesus are, we find few which, in the form in which they are given, have direct application to the conditions of modern life. He refers to the Ten Commandments when the young man asks what he shall do to inherit eternal life (Mt 19[16]) ; but when the young man is not satisfied, He gives him a test which was not in any of the Commandments nor of any general application to men, 'Go, sell, and give to the poor' (Mt 19²¹). His own observance of the Sabbath was not according to the customs of the Jews (Mt 12⁸). He went beneath the letter of the Law to its spirit, and this was His demand of men, that they should obey the spirit of the Law. Hence He reduces the Law to its essential and comprehensive element of love (Mt 22³⁷⁻³⁹), which, if a man observe, will constitute the fulfilling of the Law (cf. Ro 13⁸). And thus the attitude of one who is evangelically obedient is not that of an anxious inquirer as to every specific commandment and consequent duty, but that of one who freely wills to do the will of God, is animated by the spirit of love, and out of its abounding fulness, by the indwelling Spirit (Ro 8⁴, cf. Jn 16¹³ 17¹⁷), does what is well-pleasing to God. Such a person might conceivably err as to duty in some specific case, because of lack of enlightenment, but if he has the spirit of obedience, he has substantially obeyed. The spirit will bring him into eventual accord with the objective demands of reason and conscience.

At the same time, none of the specific commands of the Decalogue are set aside. Even the Sabbath was observed by Jesus Himself and by His disciples after Him. The ethical results of the Jewish development were, therefore, conserved by Jesus, who added to them the more spiritual interpretation of the facts of history and experience, and to this extent made them richer and more comprehensive. Not merely judicial false witness (Ex 20¹⁶ (עֵד שָׁקֶר), but every form of lying (ψεῦδος, as the absence of all ἀλήθεια, Jn 8⁴⁴), come under His disapproval (as already in Pr 26²⁸).

The great standard and guide of our obedience therefore becomes the will of God as manifested both in His written word and in His providence. It is not so much the general will of God that we are to seek to learn. This is generally easy to understand and recognize. It is His specific will, as manifested in the course of events, in the unfoldings of our personal history, that we are to learn how to understand and fulfil. Thus obedience rests upon the study of history both general and individual to ourselves (Mt 26³⁹, cf. Jn 4³⁴ 5³⁰), and consists fundamentally in submission to the Divine will.

Sin is therefore not to be conceived of as merely disobedience to specific precepts of the Law. It is this; but it has its secret in the failure to adjust oneself to the will of God as such. Obedience is not profession empty of definite good works (Mt 7²¹); it is not even always to be found with those who 'prophesy' and perform miracles (Mt 7²²). The emphasis in the Gospels is laid upon 'faith' in Jesus Christ as fully as it is in the Epistles. This granted, as the important and controlling element of the religious life, obedience follows from it as a matter of course. Such obedience, however defective in form, is genuine obedience, acceptable in God's sight. This is because God wants the man, not his acts; his heart, and not any material gift. With the heart will naturally be given to God every other desirable service.

Hence the penalty of disobedience, since this is essentially difference with God, is first of all separation from Him. It is 'darkness' because men refuse the 'light' (Jn 1¹¹ 3¹⁸⁻²¹). The sinner is in his 'own place' (Ac 1²⁵), the place fit for him because he is what he is. The penalty involves pain (Mt 13⁵⁰, cf. Rev 14¹¹), is judicial (Mt 25³¹ etc.), and involves the personal disapproval of God (Mt 25⁴¹); but it is, in a high sense, natural and inevitable. The wicked man, being what he is, cannot meet with any other lot than what he has. Obedience, on the other hand, leads to reward. This is not 'deserved,' and so given as a matter of justice.

Sinners will always 'deserve' punishment. But God freely rewards the forgiven sinner whose heart is right with Him, because of His own goodness, that He may express His favour. Thus the lot of the saved man is the reverse of the sinner's, and is a state of blessedness in the presence of God.

Literature.—Hastings' DB, art. 'Obedience'; Martensen, Christ. Ethics, i. 293; F. W. Robertson, Sermons, ii. 94; W. A. Butler, Sermons, ii. 164; Channing, The Perfect Life, xi; Dale, Evangel. Revival, 104 ff., 125 ff., Laws of Christ for Common Life, 273.   FRANK HUGH FOSTER.

OBSCURITY.—Those who are called from darkness to light do not perform the journey instantaneously, and so must be conscious of obscurity, in various ways and to different degrees, in their progressive apprehension of the gospel of Christ. Yet we are assured that nothing is hid, save that it should be manifested (Mk 4²²); and the Holy Spirit is promised us for guidance into all the truth (Jn 14²⁶ 16¹³). All four Gospels speak of a clouding of the eyes and dulling of the ears of the perverse (Mt 13¹³, Mk 4¹², Lk 8¹⁰, Jn 12⁴⁰). To the heedful and amenable the teaching will be made plainer and plainer (Lk 8¹⁸ 10²¹). To the haughty and cunning nothing clear can be vouchsafed (Lk 13³²). In teaching by parables there was necessarily an element of obscurity; but this stumbling-block Christ frequently removed (Mt 13¹¹), and promised the clearance of all hindrances to the perfect knowledge of God (Jn 16¹³. ²⁵). Obscurity was not infrequently felt by the Apostles in their efforts to discern the meaning of the Lord's other utterances. The teaching about the eternal food of His flesh and blood for the life of the world was felt to be 'a hard saying' (Jn 6⁶⁰). The foretelling of His cruel death and glorious resurrection was not at first understood (Lk 18³⁴). Indeed, the Apostles experienced a signal opening of mind after the Resurrection in respect of the prophecies implying His Passion (Lk 24⁴⁵). Thus in the Last Discourse they are found exclaiming, 'We know not what he saith' (Jn 16¹⁸); and a little later they gratefully confess, 'Lo, now speakest thou plainly, and speakest no proverb' (Jn 16²⁹). Obscurity there must often be when spiritual realities are expressed by the inadequate vehicle of human vocabulary. Such an instance may be: 'This is your hour, and the power of darkness' (Lk 22⁵³). The living spirit cannot be expressed by the dead letter except in similitudes and allegories (Jn 3⁸). When the Infinite strives to find portrayal in the finite, there must be what we call obscurity. Richness of significance and application attaches to heavenly truths which might at first seem obscure (Jn 3³¹). Obscurity must disappear more and more, for the darkness cannot confine the Light of the world within any bounds (Jn 1⁵ 8¹² 9⁵). The steadfast disciple will learn to understand His speech (Jn 8⁴³), and release from obscurity will convey increase of freedom (Jn 8³²). The gospel is not meant to remain obscure (Mt 5¹⁵).

Literature.—Butler, Analogy, p. 269 ff.; F. W. Robertson, Sermons, ii. p. 94 ff.; Expositor, 2nd ser. i. [1881] pp. 372–387; Ker, Sermons, 1st ser. p. 302 ff.; Wendt, Teaching of Jesus, i. 109 f.   W. B. FRANKLAND.

OBSERVATION.—This word occurs only once in the NT, viz. Lk 17²⁰ 'The kingdom of God cometh not with observation' (μετὰ παρατηρήσεως). The verbal form (παρατηρέω) is used: (a) for watching carefully, especially in a bad sense, as a spy or with the object of finding fault (e.g. Lk 20²⁰); (b) for keeping a religious ordinance (Gal 4¹⁰). This second sense is impossible in the place where the substantive occurs; nor can the malignant sense of (a) be here suggested. The meaning seems to be that the Kingdom will come in such a way that even the close watchers may not discover its approach. The reason given for this assertion is that 'the kingdom of God is within [(ἐντός) or "among" (so Syr sin)] you' (Lk 17²¹). Whichever meaning we give to the preposition, a spiritual and therefore invisible presence is indicated. This statement appears to be contradicted by v.²⁴, where 'the Son of Man in his day' is compared to 'lightning when it lighteneth out of the one part under the heaven' and 'shineth unto the other part under the heaven.'

Four explanations of the apparent contradiction have been proposed: (1) that the earlier verse refers to the Pharisees, who are blind to the signs of the new age, and the later to the disciples, who will have their eyes opened to see it (cf. 2 K 6¹⁷); (2) that the coming of the Kingdom is a different event from the Parousia of Christ, 'the Son of Man in his day'; (3) that there is no contradiction between the two passages; because while, on the one hand, there will be nothing for the watcher to discern as indicative of the drawing near of the great event, this being sudden as a flash of lightning, when it has come it will be universally apparent; (4) that the reference to the lightning manifestation is an apocalyptic element from a foreign source that has been inserted, with other similar elements, among the genuine teachings of Jesus. Against (1) is (a) the lack of any discrimination between two classes of hearers, and (b) the breadth of the lightning-like manifestation, which does not indicate a secret revelation for the few, but what all the world can see. Against (2) is the fact that elsewhere the coming of the Kingdom and the coming of Christ are regarded as the same event (e.g. cf. Mt 16²⁸ with Mk 9¹). Against (3) is the indication of signs, such as, 'Now learn a parable of the fig-tree,' etc. (Mt 24³², Mk 13²⁸, cf. Lk 21²⁹). Explanation (4) is to cut the knot, and against it is the fact that not this passage only but many other equally inconvenient passages would have to be removed by an arbitrary process. Thus all four proposed explanations are beset with difficulties.

H. Holtzmann points out that παρατήρησις should be understood in an active sense; it is not to be regarded as a conceivable attribute of the Kingdom, but as associated with the bringing about of the Kingdom. Accordingly, perhaps, we should reconcile the sayings thus: Sharp, critical watching will not bring it. They who busy themselves with this unsympathetic action will neither hasten its coming nor perceive the first signs of its appearance. In its beginning it is already present (ἐντὸς ὑμῶν ἐστίν). Yet those who practise παρατήρησις do not perceive this. Nevertheless, the complete revelation of the Christ in His Kingdom will be universally manifest.

Literature.—Wendt, *Teaching of Jesus*, i. 366; *ExpT* vi. [1895] 358; H. E. Manning, *Sermons* (1844), 172; J. H. Newman, *Plain Ser.* ii. 107; R. C. Trench, *Ser. New and Old*, 196.

W. F. ADENEY.

OCCUPATION.—This word is not found in the Gospels. It occurs elsewhere twice in the AV (Ac 18³ [τέχνη] and 19²⁵ [περὶ τὰ τοιαῦτα]). 'Occupy,' in the sense of 'do business,' 'traffic,' 'trade' (so RV), is found in AV of Lk 19¹³ as the rendering of πραγματεύομαι. Christ, as well as His reputed father, was Himself an artificer in wood, or a carpenter (τέκτων). Every Jewish boy, indeed, had to learn a trade (τέχνη), that it might stand between him and destitution if other resources failed. And however far removed our Lord might be in later life from *quondam* fellow-craftsmen, this technical education kept Him in touch with His industrial compatriots.

Our Lord's attitude towards the various occupations in which men are engaged is of more interest than details regarding the occupations themselves.

Judaism in Christ's day had lost hold of the masses, because its ministers urged a law viewed by themselves in false perspective. Christ denounced them for tithing mint, anise, and cummin, while omitting the weightier matters, judgment, mercy, and faith (Mt 23²³). Hence work and worship were largely divorced. People indulged in pagan-like worry over the question, What shall we eat, and what shall we drink, and wherewith shall we be clothed? instead of seeking first the Kingdom of God and His righteousness (Mt 6³¹ff.). But Christ's strenuous example proved the possibility of being diligent in business, fervent in spirit, serving the Lord. 'I must work the works of him that sent me, while it is day: the night cometh, when no man can work' (Jn 9⁴). He never allowed danger to interfere with duty—'Are there not twelve hours in the day? If any man walk in the day, he stumbleth not, because he seeth the light of this world. But if a man walk in the night, he stumbleth, because there is no light in him' (Jn 11⁹. ¹⁰). Christ poured contempt on that monastic spirit which creates artificial distinctions and exalts religious officials, devoid of religious motives, at the expense of those who, though engaged in less responsible callings, are more devout. He reprobated the Pharisee who thanked God for his superiority to other men; and justified the Publican who was a butt for his fellow-worshipper's sneers (Lk 18¹⁰ff.). He rebuked Simon, haughtily hospitable, and commended the kindly woman, whose love exceeded her pride (Lk 7⁴⁴ff.). He held up the priest and Levite to perennial scorn; and crowned with approbation that Samaritan who proved more humane, if he did not profess to be as holy as they (Lk 10³⁰ff.). St. Luke relates with professional delight how Jesus defended His own act of healing on the Sabbath day, against the false spirituality that saw in it a breach of the Fourth Commandment (13¹⁵f. 14³ff.).

A legitimate inference from all this is that our Lord—with His healthy outlook on life—would encourage all the honest occupations which ministered to man's varied needs. The Apostles' teaching surely reflected the mind of their Master on this subject. If eating and drinking could contribute to the glory of God (1 Co 10³¹), then all the occupations which provided food and drink could be pursued in the same spirit. St. Paul enjoins on bishops and other teachers of the gospel to inculcate upon Christians that they should maintain good works for necessary uses (Tit 3¹⁴). That means for the support of themselves and families, and relief of the needy. This is a duty as imperative in its own place as the duty of the ministry, and the Apostle lays great stress on it. 'This is a faithful saying, and these things I will that thou affirm constantly, that they which have believed in God might be careful to maintain good works. These things are good and profitable unto men' (Tit 3⁸), *i.e.* of general benefit and advantage to mankind. Thus a man's occupation, instead of being a hindrance to religion, is a part of it,—that sphere in which he can prove himself a doer of the word,— and faithfulness is required there as much as anywhere else (Lk 16¹⁰). See also artt. BUSINESS, CARPENTER, TRADES.

Literature.—Besides Lexicons, see articles on 'Craft,' 'Trade,' and 'Trades' in Hastings' *DB*; Tillotson, Sermon 101 vol. vi.; Delitzsch, *Jewish Artisan Life*.

D. A. MACKINNON.

OFFENCE.—This article deals with the ideas connected with the words σκάνδαλον and σκανδαλίζειν, and, in so far as they are applied in the same moral sphere, with those suggested by προσκόπτειν, πρόσκομμα, and ἀπρόσκοπος. The literal meaning of σκάνδαλον, which is probably the Alexandrian form of σκανδάληθρον, may be the part of a trap to which the bait is fastened, and which, when it is touched, springs up and catches the victim; but in Scripture the sense is not so definite. It may be questioned, indeed, whether it is ever used literally; and the figurative or ethical use of it, which is peculiar to Scripture, is what we are now to investigate. The one idea which is constant in every use of the word, literal or figurative, is that of hurt sustained; it may even be of ruin incurred, by the person who encounters the σκάνδαλον. It will be convenient to exhibit the Scriptural view of the subject by referring (1) to the experience of Jesus; (2) to the teaching of Jesus; and (3) to the application of this in the Apostolic Church.

1. Experience of Jesus.—When Jesus visited Nazareth, and taught in the synagogue so that all were astonished, astonishment soon passed into a kind of carping criticism. 'Whence hath this man these things, and what is the wisdom that has been given to him? And these mighty works that are being done by him? Is not this the carpenter?' And so on (Mk 6²ᶠ· ‖). The people had been used to Jesus in one aspect or character, and they could not adjust themselves to Him in another. There was something in His present appearance and claims which they could not get over: as the Evangelists put it, ἐσκανδαλίζοντο ἐν αὐτῷ. Jesus Himself was the σκάνδαλον with which, for the time at least, they collided: it was to their hurt even at the moment (He could do no mighty work there because of their unbelief, 6⁵), and it would be their ruin if it were their final attitude. Probably before Jesus can become a σκάνδαλον, men must have felt the attraction in Him: it is only when closer acquaintance reveals something in Him, or in the consequences of attachment to Him, which is repellent to the natural man, that He becomes a σκάνδαλον, and those who were once attracted fall away. They stumble at something which attachment to Him involves; they cannot get over it, and so they desert Him. This is the connexion in which σκανδαλίζεσθαι occurs in Mk 14²⁷· ²⁹ and ‖. Jesus on the last night of His life recalls to the Twelve the prophecy of Zechariah (13⁷): 'I will smite the shepherd, and the sheep of the flock shall be scattered,' and applies it by adding, 'All ye σκανδαλισθήσεσθε ἐν ἐμοὶ ἐν τῇ νυκτὶ ταύτῃ.' They had felt the charm of Jesus, and continued with Him in His temptations so far; but a Messiah who should be seized, tortured, and crucified by sinners would be too much for them. In spite of all they had seen and felt in Him, they would stumble at this, and leave Him in the lurch. It is the same idea, *mutatis mutandis*, which is found in Mk 4¹⁷ and ‖ Mt.; the rocky ground hearers, who have shown a warm appreciation of the word, are taken aback when they find that they have to endure persecution because of it, and 'immediately they are offended.' Lk 8¹³ gives the correct interpretation: 'in time of temptation they fall away.' The parable of the Sower, standing where it does, is not so much a prophecy, though it is prophetic, as a summary of the disenchanting experiences of Jesus. He had seen many enthusiasms chill, the moment fidelity to Him exacted any sacrifice. In one sense this is 'the offence of the cross,' though it is not what St. Paul means by this expression. We are in the same circle of ideas in Mt 24⁹ᶠ·, Jn 16¹ᶠ·. Jesus warns His disciples of coming persecutions; they as well as He have the cross to bear; and while many will stumble at it,—that is, find it too much for them, a thing which they cannot get over, and must simply decline, — He tells the Twelve beforehand, that being forewarned they may be forearmed against the peril of apostasy. One of the most striking instances of σκάνδαλον in the experience of Jesus is that which is connected with John the Baptist. John was evidently dis-

appointed somehow in Jesus. He had had reason to regard Him as the Messiah, but He was not the Messiah John had expected. Where were the axe and the fan and the consuming fire? Why, if the Messiah had really come, were not all wrongs irresistibly righted? Why was a true servant of God like himself left to suffer for fidelity to his Master? It is to this temper in John that Jesus says, 'Blessed is he whosoever shall not be offended in me' (Mt 11⁶, Lk 7²³). We must not impose our preconceptions on God, and dictate to Him the terms on which He may have recognition from us. This always implies the risk that we may stumble at what He actually does—refuse to recognize Him in Jesus because the manifestation does not square with our demands. The Baptist here is a perfect illustration of St. Paul's words, written in immediate connexion with his idea of Christ as σκάνδαλον: 'Jews claim signs.' They say, Let God signalize His presence; let Him make bare His holy arm, and break in pieces the oppressor, and we will see and believe Him; and when they see nothing of this in Jesus, they stumble at Him. He becomes a σκάνδαλον to them. And just as Jesus in His acts may become an offence to those who anticipated something quite different, so may He be by anything disconcerting or too challenging in His teaching. Thus the Pharisees in Mt 15¹² were offended by the word in which He seemed to abolish the distinction between clean and unclean meats: they could not get over the idea that a distinction on which so much of their sanctity depended should be so summarily swept away. It finally repelled them from Jesus. And in Jn 6⁶¹ we find disciples put out, as it were, by the hard sayings about eating the flesh of the Son of Man, and drinking His blood: it is almost more than they can stand, and Jesus asks τοῦτο ὑμᾶς σκανδαλίζει; 'Doth this cause you to stumble?' Almost anything in Jesus may become a ground of stumbling—the demands He makes, the sacrifices which fidelity to Him entails, His disappointment of our expectations, the paradoxical and apparently impossible elements of His teaching. And all these become grounds of stumbling to those who have made some acquaintance with Him, been to some degree attracted and held by Him. To be offended in Him is the sin of those who have had the opportunity of being disciples.

Even though the words σκάνδαλον, σκανδαλίζειν, are not used at every point, the whole of the central division of the Gospel according to Matthew (chs. 11–18) may be read as a series of illustrations of them. In ch. 11 we have the Baptist, the whole generation (v.¹⁶ff.), the favoured cities (²⁰ff.), and especially the wise and prudent (v.²⁵), offended in Jesus. In ch. 12 we have first the Pharisees, and then His mother and brothers. In ch. 13 the parable of the Sower gives the keynote: it is the experience of one who knows what it is to be an offence: cf. vv.²¹· ⁴¹. In ch. 14 there is the miraculous feeding with which the great 'offence' proved in Jn 6¹⁴ᶠ· ⁶⁶ is connected. Then cf. 15¹² 16²³ 17¹⁷· ²⁷ 18⁶ᶠ·.

There is another side to the experience of Jesus, that in which the σκάνδαλον is not found in Him, but presented to Him. In Mt 16²³ He says to Peter σκάνδαλον εἶ ἐμοῦ. He had been telling His disciples for the first time of the necessity of His death, and Peter had made a vivacious remonstrance. He had tried, in short, to put Jesus at fault about the path appointed for Him by the Father. He had the human temper which avoids suffering at all costs, not the Divine love which at any cost is faithful to its calling; and in yielding to his human temper he had made himself a stumbling-block in Jesus' way. It is a signal illustration of 'a man's foes shall be they of his own household.' But Jesus does not stumble: in ὕπαγε ὀπίσω μου, σατανᾶ, He sweeps the σκάνδαλον from His path.

2. Teaching of Jesus.—It is remarkable that almost the only thing approaching to a discourse of

Jesus in our earliest Gospel (if we omit the chapter of parables (ch. 4) and the eschatological discourse (ch. 13)) deals with the subject of offences, and this in both the aspects in which we have seen 'offence' appear in the experience of Jesus: Mk 9[42ff.].

(a) There is first *the giving of offence to others.* The others are conceived as disciples—'little ones who believe' (Mt 18[6] says 'who believe in me'). To 'offend' such means to be responsible for leading them into sin; and when we think what and whose they are, it means to be responsible for their separation by sin from Christ. Thus to mislead 'the little ones who believe' is for Jesus the sin of sins: all the Evangelists record the terrific words in which He denounced it (Mk 9[42], Mt 18[6], Lk 17[2]). It is singular that side by side with this both Mt. and Lk. preserve a saying in which the inevitableness of offences coming is admitted, while unabated woe is pronounced on him through whom they come. Nothing is said by Jesus about how they come, that is, about the ways in which the little ones who believe are led into sins which put them at fault about Him; but what has been said above about Jesus as a σκάνδαλον has its application here. What is meant is in principle to seduce them to ways of thinking or acting such as led men to stumble at Jesus while He lived. It is only in the Christian society that this sin can be committed, and there is something peculiarly solemn in the picture of the Last Judgment in Mt 13[41]: the Son of Man shall send His angels, and they shall gather *out of His kingdom πάντα τὰ σκάνδαλα.* There is in the life of Jesus one very interesting illustration of His own care in avoiding what might cause others to stumble (Mt 17[24-27]). Here we see—what will repeatedly come up later—that an inconsiderate use of our spiritual liberty as children of God may prove a stumbling-block to those who do not understand it; and we are taught by the example and word of Jesus that conduct is never to be decided merely by the abstract principle that this or that is in itself legitimate; part of the motive on which a Christian must always act is consideration for others, and the moral significance of his conduct for them. Of course, there is the complementary consideration of what the principle requires, and though it is not to be pressed to the hurt of 'little ones who believe,' it is not to be sacrificed to obscurantists or hypocrites (see for an illustration of this Mt 15[12-14]). All this will reappear in what is sometimes regarded as the characteristically Pauline part of NT teaching.

(b) Equally important with His sayings on causing others to stumble are those in which Jesus warns His disciples against *allowing anything to cause themselves to stumble.* There are three of these in Mk 9[43. 45. 47] (vv.[44. 46] are spurious), and they are found twice in Mt. (5[29f.] 18[8f.]). It is a fair inference from this that, though Lk. does not give them, they were found in the collection of discourses used by him and Mt. as well as in Mk. (Mt. inserting them in his Gospel from both sources), and therefore that they belong to the most surely authenticated words of Jesus. What Jesus contemplates is that one's hand or foot or eye may cause one to stumble—in other words, that something in his nature, something which is in itself legitimate, may mislead one in the spiritual region and alienate him from Christ; and He declares that to prevent such a catastrophe no severity to nature can be too great. The right eye is to be plucked out, the right hand or foot cut off and cast away: it is better to enter into life halt or maimed or with one eye, than to go with two eyes and feet and hands into the everlasting fire. It is easy to argue against this from the point of view of self-realization and the development of all sides of our nature, but the per-

emptory and vehement tone of Jesus does not suggest arguing. For men whose nature is what ours is, living in the world in which we live, and called to discipleship to Jesus, situations will emerge in which salvation depends simply on whether we have it in us to subject nature to summary and surgical treatment. If a man will do no violence to his nature, but claims liberty for it on every side,—if he will go wherever his feet can carry him, do whatever his hands itch to do, look at whatever his eyes long to see,—the end will not be a complete and rounded character, it will be the forfeiture of all character; it will not be an abundant entrance into life, it will be hell fire. This is the philosophy of Puritanism. It is relative no doubt to human nature as Jesus knew it and as we know it; but as that is the only human nature we have to do with, it is absolute enough. It is as much a matter of life and death in the teaching of Jesus that we should not allow natural impulses to put us at fault about Him, as that we should not become responsible for putting others at fault. The most passionate words that ever fell from His lips deal with σκανδαλίζειν and σκανδαλίζεσθαι in both these vital aspects.

3. The Apostolic Church.—When we pass from Jesus to the Apostolic writings, we find new illustrations and applications of His teaching, but no new ethical ideas. Thus the conception recurs (a) of Christ Himself as σκάνδαλον. In the gospel which presented a crucified man as the power and the wisdom of God, there was something which people could not get over; they stumbled at it and turned away. This was especially true of the Jews (1 Co 1[23]). They could not accommodate themselves to a Messiah who had been hanged, especially when they thought of Dt 21[23]. As the act of striking against an obstacle is often painful and irritating, it was this offence of the cross which explained the persecution of St. Paul by the Jews, and even by Christians who did not know what Christianity meant (Gal 5[11]): it was the reaction of their soreness against what caused it. The early Christians, who had naturally difficulty in understanding how Christ could be a stumbling-block, found relief for their minds in this as in similar perplexities by discovering that the disconcerting fact had been predicted in the OT. It lay not outside of, but within the Divine counsel and plan. In Ro 9[33], 1 P 2[8], Christ is spoken of as λίθος προσκόμματος (a loose stone on the road against which the traveller strikes his foot = אֶבֶן נֶגֶף) and πέτρα σκανδάλου (a rock projecting through the soil, over which he falls = צוּר מִכְשׁוֹל). [On the relation of these two passages to each other and to Is 8[14] 28[16], see Sanday and Headlam on *Romans,* and Hort on *1 Pet.*]. What it was in Christ over which men stumbled, Peter does not say; but in Paul it is clear that what the Jews could not get over was the demand involved in Christ's atoning death, that they should renounce the pursuit of a righteousness of their own, and humble themselves to receive in faith the gift of a Divine righteousness. It was the cross that was a stumbling-block, and it was a stumbling-block to pride.

(b) In the main, however, σκάνδαλον is discussed in the Apostolic writings in connexion with the possibility that Christians may cause others, especially weaker Christians, to stumble, and so to forfeit their connexion with Christ. The danger of doing this is the more serious that it is possible to do it (so to speak) with a good conscience. It comes up mainly in 1 Co 8-10 and Ro 14. In both these passages the central idea is that of Christian liberty, and the problem is what are the Christian conditions of its exercise. There are minds which are intoxicated by it, and will not hear anything of conditions. They know what the Christian principle is, and to determine their conduct they do not need to think of anything else. They know, for example, that an idol is nothing in the world, and that is enough to answer all questions about their relation to idolatry—about buying and eating meat which had been sacrificed in a pagan temple, about attending a pagan friend's feast in the temple, and so forth. They know that the earth is the Lord's, and all that it contains; and that is enough to answer all questions about eating and drinking. In this region all things are lawful for them. It is at this point that St. Paul interposes in the spirit of Mt 17[24-27] (see above, **2** *a*). The knowledge of the Christian principle, he insists, is not enough. He accepts the principle, with a half-ironical depreciation of it: 'We know that we all have knowledge'—as if he would say, but *that* does not carry us far (1 Co 8[1]). In dealing with conduct we must always consider its moral consequences, both to others and to ourselves; we must consider not only an abstract principle, which may in itself be sound enough, but the practical effect of acting upon it in given conditions. We must consider, in particular, whether it may not cause others or ourselves to stumble. These are distinct questions, yet involved in each other. If we cause another to stumble by what we do, our own ruin is inseparable from his. St. Paul accepts the principle of liberty, but qualifies it in both directions to avoid σκανδαλίζειν and σκανδαλίζεσθαι. Thus he writes, 'All things are lawful for me, but all things do not edify,' *sc.* the Church (1 Co 10[23]); and the edifying or building up of the Church is the rule of all Christian action (1 Co 14[26], Ro 14[19] 15[2]). To be Christian, in other words, conduct has to be guided not merely by knowledge, but by love. It has to include a reference to Christ's interest in others, especially in the weak; a Christian sins grievously when he asserts his liberty in disregard of that. The extraordinary vehemence of St. Paul's language in discussing this subject reminds us vividly of our Lord's words in the same connexion. 'For meat destroy not the work of God' (Ro 14[20]). 'Through thy knowledge he that is weak perisheth, the brother for whose sake Christ died' (1 Co 8[11]). 'If meat maketh my brother to stumble, I will eat no flesh for evermore' (1 Co 8[13]). 'Who is made to stumble, and I am not on fire with pain?' (2 Co 11[29]). These are flashes of the same fire which glows in Mt 18[6-9]. The use of Christian liberty in an environment of paganism no doubt presented many moral problems, all with possibilities of σκάνδαλον in them. A false solution, legitimating a free relation to pagan worship and its ordinary festive and sensual accompaniments, which no doubt caused many to stumble, is denounced in Rev 2[14]; possibly in the 'Apostolic decree' of Ac 15[28f.] we have a more considerate and Christian solution for a special set of circumstances. (For the interpretation of the decree, practically in this sense, see Lightfoot, *Galatians*, 306 ff.; Chase, *Credibility of the Acts*, 96 f.). In the whole region in which liberty can be asserted, it is to be exercised only in subordination to love; to violate this rule and so injure others in their conscience and in their relation to Christ is the most un-Christian sin of which a Christian can be guilty. But Paul is aware of the other side of σκανδαλίζειν also—that in which a man so acts as to lead to his own stumbling, and the perdition of his own soul. 'All things are lawful for me,' but not only do all things not build up the Church, but '*I* will not be tyrannized over by any' (1 Co 6[12]). A man may be befooled by his wisdom: if he is puffed up in the consciousness that he comprehends the

principles of Christianity, he is quite capable of yielding to his natural appetites under the delusion that he is exercising a Christian liberty. St. Paul dreaded this for himself. 1 Co 9[24-27]—especially after v.[1] 'Am I not free?'—is written in the very spirit of Mk 9[43-47], and in 1 Co 10 the Apostle warns his converts of the peril which awaits them, if secure in their Christianity they slip into easy relations with paganism. In the end of this chapter the idea of offence is generalized. 'Show yourselves ἀπρόσκοποι—persons in whom there is no occasion of stumbling—both to Jews and Gentiles and to the Church of God' (1 Co 10[32]). This is a final if not the supreme maxim of Christian ethics; there must be nothing in the Christian's conduct which could mislead, disconcert, or repel any person seeking or enjoying relations with Christ. Put positively, it is the rule of the Apostle's own action: 'I have become all things to all men if by all means I might save some' (1 Co 9[22]); which again is but one form of the Golden Rule. Hence the teaching of the NT on 'offences' can be summed up in Mt 7[12]. The only passage in which σκάνδαλον occurs in Jn. (1 Jn 2[10]) perhaps combines the two references which it has elsewhere. When a Christian loves his brother, there is no σκάνδαλον in him; he does not cause others to stumble, and he does not create difficulties in his own path. 'The triumph of love is that it creates no prejudice against the Truth' ('Wescott, *ad loc.*).

LITERATURE.—Cremer, *Bibl.-Theol. Lex. s.vv.*; Hastings' *DB* iii. 586; Sanday-Headlam, *Romans*, p. 390; Hort, *First Peter*, p. 121; Carr, *Hor. Bibl.* 58; F. W. Robertson, *Sermons*, 3rd ser. xvi.; Bushnell, *Serm. on Liv. Subjects*, xix.; Dale, *Week-day Serm*, p. 216; Martensen, *Chr. Ethics*, i. 418 ff.; *ExpT* v. [1894] 147; *Life of John Cairns*, 438; J. B. Lightfoot, *Cambridge Sermons* (1890), 248; W. G. Rutherford, *The Key of Knowledge* (1901), 134.

JAMES DENNEY.

OFFERINGS.—

In the technical sense, implying a formal ceremonial act, three Gr. words are represented by 'offer,' 'offering,' in the RV: (1) προσφέρω, *to bring to or near*, the general term for the act of worshipper or priest, Mt 5[23. 24] 8[4] (=Mk 1[44], Lk 5[14]), Jn 16[2]; (2) ἀνάθημα, *a votive offering set up in a temple* (Lk 21[5]); (3) δίδωμι, *to give* (Lk 2[24], cf. Lk 21[4]).

The attitude of Jesus to the ceremonial law is, in part, indicated in these references. Speaking to Jews He uses language appropriate to their condition, and illustrates the truth He would teach from their everyday life. He assumes that they will bring their gifts to the altar, and so far 'He respects the practice,' but He adds the all-important truth that the reconciliation of man to man must come before the altar-offering. Forgiveness of injuries (Mt 5[23f.]), filial piety (15[5f.]), and mercy (9[13] 12[7]) condition all acceptable service of man. In this Jesus takes His stand with the Hebrew prophets, and fulfils their moral law. The command to the leper, now cleansed, 'show thyself to the priest, and offer the gift that Moses commanded,' Mt 8[4] (=Mk 1[44], Lk 5[14]), ought not to be pressed beyond this. The leper was ostracized, and the priest alone could remove the ban, and grant a certificate of health (Lv 14). Freewill offerings, over and above the requirements of the Law, were provided for in the Temple treasury (Mk 12[41], Lk 21[1]). Of the 13 trumpet-shaped boxes of the treasury 4 were for voluntary gifts. (See Edersheim, *The Temple*, p. 26; and for the general subject, see GIVING; cf., further, artt. LAW and SACRIFICE).

W. H. DYSON.

OFFICER.—

The term 'officer' is used in the Gospels (and Acts) as a tr. of ὑπηρέτης in the ordinary secular applications of that term (Mt 5[25], Jn 7[32. 45] 18[3. 12. 18. 22] 19[6], Ac 5[22. 26]). In other two cases (Mk 14[54. 65] ‖ Mt 26[58], Jn 18[36]) the AV tr. 'servants'; the RV in the former adhering to 'officers' and in the latter putting it in the margin. In most of these cases the officers are servants of the Jewish

Council; in Mt 5[25] and Jn 18[36] they may be regarded more generally as servants of the State. In Lk 12[58] 'officer' is the tr. of a still humbler term, πράκτωρ, a prison official, described in RVm as 'exactor' from his duty of collecting fines. In Jn 4[46] RVm 'king's officer' appears as an alternative to 'nobleman' for a term meaning 'courtier.'

It is evident that in the 16th or 17th century 'officer' had a lower meaning than now.* These ὑπηρέται belong to the rank and file. They are subordinate officials, with duties purely instrumental, virtually on a level with our policemen. As emphasized in Jn., they are the creatures of the Jews, accompanying the chief priests for the doing of their will; or they may take orders from a captain of the Temple (Ac 5[26]), or they carry into execution the sentence of a judge (Mt 5[25]). St. Luke in his narrative of the Arrest and Trial and in 12[58] avoids the term, but he uses it in Ac 5[22, 26] as above (where, possibly, he is following a source), and four times of religious service—in Lk 4[20] of a minister of the synagogue, in 1[2] and Ac 26[16] (Paul) of Christian preachers, and in Ac 13[5] of John Mark, who was, in some sense, assistant to Barnabas and Paul. So also St. Paul uses it in 1 Co 4[1]. In all these cases the AV renders 'minister'; in two (Lk 4[20], Ac 13[5]) the RV, without much lucidity, substitutes 'attendant.'

ὑπηρέτης, originally 'rower,' was used in Greece of an assistant or inferior agent in any sort of work. In particular, it was used in a military sense of attendants on heavy-armed soldiers, and also of adjutants to officers of rank. A similar indefiniteness, but always involving subordination, belongs to the NT usage. The term 'officer,' owing to the secular and especially the military associations of the name, was manifestly unsuitable for the description of a Christian minister of any rank. Such terms of ancient administration as ἀπόστολος (commissioner) and ἐπίσκοπος (inspector) were received into modern languages, not by translation into an equivalent, but by a process of adoption and adaptation. But the ὑπηρέτης, whose title, like these, was extended from the secular to the sacred sphere, was too inferior in dignity and too indefinite in character for such distinction. We have indeed in ordinary usage a somewhat similar rank expressed by the term 'office-bearer,' and there is a special episcopal use of 'official'; while a still humbler dignity, parallel with the secular use in Scripture, is denoted by the designation 'church officer.' Of such terms, and of the term 'officer' as representing the servants of the Sanhedrin, the interest pertains merely to the study of language. No theological or ecclesiastical idea is involved; and for practical utility or correctness the only duty of new Revisers towards this term is to eliminate it entirely from the sacred page.   R. SCOTT.

OFFICES OF CHRIST.—As the specific offices of Christ are handled in this work under their several heads, the treatment in the present article will be general.

Etymologically the word 'office' is from officium, the shorter form of opificium, the root meaning of which is 'a doing of a work' (Gr. πρᾶξις). The meaning of officium being wide enough to include any service or kindness, a more precise connotation is supplied by munus, the technical term employed by writers like Calvin to describe the capital functions discharged by Christ. In the Bible the word is nowhere used of Christ's work, though it occurs in other connexions in OT (פְּקֻדָּה) and in NT (διακονία, Ro 11[13] [RV 'ministry']),

πρᾶξις, Ro 12[4]). The idea, however, abounds in connexion with the Jewish Messiah and the Christ of the Gospel. Under the OT dispensation the three principal offices were those of prophet, priest, and king; and 'the innermost pulse, so to speak, of the history of prophecy is to be found in the effort to interweave these three offices together, and to contemplate them in the Messianic image instead of in their distribution among several persons' (Dorner, System of Christ. Doct. iii. 388). Jesus, being the Messiah, fulfilled these three offices, as the supreme prophet, arch-priest, and Divine king. So repeatedly does He appear in these capacities in the NT, that it would be superfluous to enumerate loci.

Passing to theology, we may find beginnings of the official conception of Christ in the Testaments of the Twelve Patriarchs, Eusebius, Gregory of Nyssa, etc. Thomas Aquinas departs from the triple division of the offices, and makes them coincide with the two states of humiliation and exaltation; the high-priestly office, to which the prophetic is merely introductory, coinciding with the state of humiliation, while the kingly is to be reserved for the state of exaltation (Dorner, op. cit. iii. 391). Discussions as to the relations of Christ's two natures (Eutychians and Nestorians) involved different views as to the way in which He performed official functions. But it was the Reformation, magnifying the sufficiency of Christ in every capacity, that was most fruitful in the exposition of His offices.

'The theologians of the Lutheran Church,' writes Hagenbach, 'further developed the locus de persona Christi by distinguishing between three different genera of the communicatio idiomatum, which were brought into connexion with the two states of Christ's exaltation and humiliation (status exaltationis et exinanitionis). To this they added the theory of the three offices of Christ, viz. the prophetical, priestly, and kingly offices. These definitions owed their origin in part to temporary controversies within the Lutheran Church, such as the controversy between the theologians of Giessen and those of Tübingen, at the commencement of the 17th cent., concerning the κένωσις and κρύψις of the Divine attributes, and the controversy carried on by Æpinus in a previous century respecting the descensus Christi ad inferos' (Compend. of Hist. of Doctrines, Buch's tr. p. 317). Those of Tübingen said that Christ in His humiliation possessed omnipotence, omnipresence, etc., but that these attributes were concealed; whereas those of Giessen said that Christ laid these prerogatives aside. Æpinus said that Christ's soul suffered the punishments of hell while His body lay in the grave, whereas Calvin said that the only hell suffered by Christ was anguish of soul. The Lutherans, again, held that Christ's visit to hell was a part of His exaltation. Such controversies had a reflex influence upon ways of stating how Christ exercised His offices. Our subject is admirably treated by Calvin in the second book of his Institutes, Christ's priesthood being magnified as against Romish usurpations (ch. xv.). Arminius is especially full and interesting in the present connexion. 'Two things,' he writes, 'were necessary on Christ's part: that He should undertake some offices for the sake of men to obtain eternal salvation for them, and that God should bestow upon Him dominion or lordship over all things' (Private Disputations, Nichols's tr. ii. p. 380). Both these things were comprehended under the title of Saviour and Mediator. In respect of Christ's priesthood, the preparation consisted in imposition of office, sanctification by the Spirit, obedience, sufferings and death, and resurrection; and the discharge of the office consisted in His offering His body and blood. Re Christ's prophetic office, Arminius raised the question as to whether He received knowledge from the Logos as well as from the Holy Spirit. The functions of Christ's kingly office were legislation, giving of remission of sins and of grace, and judgment. The results of Christ's official work are the gathering of the Church, the obedience of His people, the actual remission of sins, resurrection from the dead, and life eternal. The means of Christ's rule are His Church, Word, and Holy Spirit. To all this the corollary is that no one is admitted even subordinately to participation in Christ's proper offices; therefore no pope can be tolerated.

The Westminster Confession of Faith contains a chapter (viii.) 'Of Christ the Mediator,' from which we give the third section. 'The Lord Jesus, in His human nature thus united to the Divine, was sanctified and anointed with the Holy Spirit above measure; having in Him all the treasures of wisdom and knowledge; in whom it pleased the Father that all fulness should dwell: to the end that being holy, harmless, undefiled, and full of grace and truth, He might be thoroughly furnished to execute the office of a Mediator and Surety. Which office He took not unto Himself, but was thereunto called by His

---

* The most frequent application of the term was not to commissioners in the army or navy, but to petty officers of justice, as in 'sheriff's officer,' 'peace officer.' It is this usage that is reflected in the NT.

Father ; who put all power and judgment into His hand, and gave Him commandment to execute the same.' Along with this may be taken the answers to questions 43–45 in the *Larger Catechism*. 'Christ executeth the office of a prophet in His revealing to the Church in all ages, by His Spirit and word, in divers ways of administration, the whole will of God, in all things concerning their edification and salvation.' 'Christ executeth the office of a priest in His once offering Himself a sacrifice without spot to God, to be a reconciliation for the sins of His people ; and in making continual intercession for them.' 'Christ executeth the office of a king in calling out of the world a people to Himself, and giving them officers, laws, and censures, by which He visibly governs them ; in bestowing saving grace upon His elect, rewarding their obedience, and correcting them for their sins, preserving and supporting them under all their temptations and sufferings, restraining and overcoming all their enemies, and powerfully ordering all things for His own glory and their good ; and also in taking vengeance on the rest, who know not God, and obey not the gospel.'

In our day it is less common than formerly to speak of the official character of Christ ; and this for several reasons. Definite doctrine as to the Person and work of our Lord is unacceptable in many quarters, and a reaction from the terminology of the schools is common. Questions as to the metaphysical nature of Christ are thought to be too abstract. That Jesus should embody a fulfilment of OT prophecy as to the Messiah is of remote interest to many. The richness of Christ's humanity has been so energetically unfolded, that there is an aversion to contemplate Him in any aspect which might be suspected of dehumanizing Him by representing Him more in the light of a formal functionary than of a loving Son of Man and Elder Brother. Ritschl, *e.g.*, attacks the word 'office' as unsuitable, because office is a special calling with a view to realizing a legal or moral community upon conditions of law (see Dorner, *op. cit.* p. 383).

As against such objections we would submit that the theological category in question possesses too much historic and intrinsic worth to be discarded. Historically it has its roots in Scripture, and controversially it has served to clarify doctrine and to safeguard certain aspects of Christ's Person and work. But, above all, Christ in His official character meets the entire needs of sinful man. On account of that moral evil which blinds the soul to the knowledge and perception of God, we need a Mediator to reveal God and to enlighten the conscience ; and here Christ, as the Light of the world, appears in His prophetic office. Next, the effect of light is to disclose the fact of sin and awaken the sense of guilt and the fear of judgment ; and here Christ, by putting away sin, by affording access to God, and by blessing us from God, discharges the priestly office. Lastly, by creating an eternal society in which we may live as His loving subjects, serving Him willingly according to His laws, He acts as a Divine king. Nor is there any subordinate office performed by Christ which may not be classified under one or other of these constitutive three.

LITERATURE.—Hodge, *Syst. Theol.* ii. 459 ff. ; Martensen, *Chr. Dogmat.* 295–329 ; Macpherson, *Chr. Dogmat.* 328 f. ; Litton, *Dogmatic Theology*, 222 ; Denney, *Stud. in Theol.* 137 ff., 163 ff. ; art. 'Jesu Christi dreifaches Amt' in *PRE*[3] and the Lit. there given.   ROBERT M. ADAMSON.

OIL (שֶׁמֶן, ἔλαιον), by which we are to understand olive oil, was from the very earliest times one of the main products of Palestine, for already in days prior to the Hebrew settlement, Canaan was 'a land of oil olives' (Dt 8[8]). The importance of this valuable commodity cannot easily be overestimated. It afforded light (Mt 25[3]) and nourishment (1 K 17[12]) to the household ; it was valued for its healing and medicinal virtues (Is 1[6] RV, Lk 10[34]) ; it had its place in the Hebrew ritual (Ex 29[40], Lv 2[1]) ; and it was an important article of commerce (2 K 4[7], Lk 16[6]).

The oil was obtained by subjecting the berries

of the olive-tree to pressure. The earliest method of expression seems to have been that of treading the olives with the feet, to which allusion is made in Mic 6[15], and perhaps also in Dt 33[24]. This process is unknown in modern times (Thomson, *LB* pp. 207, 339). Van-Lennep, however, states that the pulp from the olive-press is still 'trodden with the bare feet of women and girls' (*Bible Lands*, p. 130). At what period this primitive method was abandoned, and made way for more thorough processes, we do not know. The OT has no references that are clear enough to guide us : those that occur (*e.g.* Job 24[11] 29[6]) are vague and general, and in none of them is the oil-press specifically mentioned. But from the Mishna (*Menāḥōth* viii. 14) we learn that the processes commonly employed were bruising in a mortar, and crushing in the oil-press and the oil-mill, these processes being consecutive, not alternative.

The quality of the oil depended partly on the time at which the olives were gathered, and partly on the mode of crushing. The best quality was that yielded by berries gathered before they became black (as they do when fully ripe), and pounded in a mortar. Of this kind was 'beaten oil' (Ex 27[20] 29[40], Lv 24[2], Nu 28[5]). This first quality of oil was got by putting the pulp from the mortar into wicker baskets, through which the strained liquid ran into receptacles placed beneath. A second and a third quality were obtained by further crushing of the pulp in the oil-press, and then in the oil-mill.

In the NT allusions to oil are not very frequent ; those occurring in the Gospels have reference to its use :—(1) As an *illuminant* (Mt 25[3. 4. 8]). The lamps in common use were of earthenware, and small in size (see LAMP). When they had to be kept burning for any considerable period, it was necessary to replenish them with oil from time to time. (2) *Medicinally* (Lk 10[34], Mk 6[13], cf. Ja 5[14]). The healing virtues of oil were highly esteemed by the Jews, and it was much employed by them and by other ancient nations. It was applied, *e.g.*, to wounds (Is 1[6] RV) to soothe their pain and to hasten the process of healing. A similar usage is found in the parable of the Good Samaritan (Lk 10[34]). In this instance, wine as well as oil was employed, the added wine imparting to the mixture an antiseptic quality (cf. Pliny, *HN* xxxi. 47 ; Talm. *Shabbāth* xiv. 4). Oil-baths were sometimes used, as in the case of Herod the Great (Jos. *Ant.* XVII. vi. 5). The anointing of the sick with oil (Mk 6[13], Ja 5[14]) was doubtless based on the current belief in its remedial powers, but may also have been a symbolic act, as was the anointing of lepers (Lv 14[15ff.]). Plumptre suggests that 'it served as a help to the faith of the person healed ; perhaps also, in the case of the Apostles, to that of the healer' ('St. James' in *Camb. Bible for Schools*, p. 103). (3) For *anointing* (Mt 6[17], Lk 7[46]). The custom of anointing the head or the body with oil was a very common one in ancient times, and was practised by the Egyptians (Wilkinson, *Anc. Egyp.* ii. 213), the Greeks (Homer, *Il.* x. 577), and others (Pliny, *HN* xiii. 1 ff.). Among the Jews the anointing of the head with oil seems to have accompanied the daily ablutions (Mt 6[17], cf. Ru 3[3], 2 S 12[20]), except in time of mourning (2 S 14[2], Dn 10[3]). It was also a mark of honour paid to guests by their host (Lk 7[46], cf. Ps 23[5]). Anointing the feet (Lk 7[38. 46], Jn 11[2]) was very unusual. The dead were anointed as a tribute of respect (Mk 16[1], Lk 23[56] 24[1], cf. Jn 12[3. 7]), aromatic spices being added. (4) As an article of *merchandise* (Mt 25[9], Lk 16[6]). In common and daily use, and to the Eastern one of the necessaries of life, oil played a large part in the home trade of Palestine (2 K 4[7]), and was, further, a most valuable export. We find special mention made of trading in oil with the Tyrians (Ezk 27[17]), who probably re-exported it, and with Egypt (Hos 12[1]). It formed an important part of the supplies sent by Solomon to Hiram in return for the timber and other materials furnished for the building of the Temple (1 K 5[11]).

HUGH DUNCAN.

OINTMENT (μύρον).—Nard oil, from a plant found especially in Arabia (*nardus*), and highly prized at Rome. St. Luke mentions it in connexion with the anointing of Christ by the unnamed woman in the house of Simon the Pharisee (7[38. 46]), and again (23[56]) as one of the things prepared by the women for the intended completion of the burial of the Master. See art. ANOINTING.

In the account of the anointing of Jesus at Bethany, St. Matthew describes the unguent as μύρου βαρυτίμου, 'exceeding precious ointment' (26[7] RV); St. Mark as μύρου νάρδου πιστικῆς πολυτελοῦς, 'ointment of spikenard [marg. pistic nard] very costly' (14[3] RV); St. John as μύρου νάρδου πιστικῆς πολυτίμου, 'ointment of spikenard very precious' (12[3] RV, with ref. to Mk 14[3] [marg.]). As this word πιστική is found only in these two places, it is rather difficult to give its true equivalent. It is used by Plato (*Gorg.* 455) and by Aristotle (*Rhet.* 1. 2), where it is synonymous with πειστικός, 'persuasive'; but that meaning would be irrelevant in this connexion.* Scaliger would translate 'pounded nard,' from πτίσσω, 'to pound,' which is a possible rendering, but lacks analogy. The RV has translated it 'spikenard,' following, apparently, the Vulgate rendering of Mk 14[3], *spicati*. Some would translate 'liquid nard,' deriving πιστικός from πίνω, 'to drink'; others regard it as a local technical term (see Mk 14[3] RVm; cf. Westcott, *St. John*, 12[3]). The most natural rendering would appear to be 'pistic nard,' an ointment prepared from the oil of the pistachio nut, which is used to this day in Syria for similar purposes. See especially a long note by Morison, *Com. on Mark*, 14[3], and cf. artt. NARD and SPIKENARD.

HENRY E. DOSKER.

OLD TESTAMENT (I. Christ as fulfilment of).†—
1. The ideals of life found in the OT by Jesus.—Jesus' conception of the life of the OT is that of the life which is proper to the children of God (Mt 5–7). It is the normal relation of fellowship between God and His children, obedience to God and to His messengers (7[24]). The life for which the prophets laboured, that which they represented as the ideal, was adopted by Him as the ideal, and their labours were continued by Him. He claimed no less an authority to carry on the development of the ideal than the greatest of the prophets had exercised. As the prophet taught (Is 50[10]) that those loyal to Jehovah should obey His representative, so did Jesus when He combined such sayings as 'He that doeth the will of my Father' (Mt 7[21]), and 'He that heareth these sayings of mine, and doeth them' (v.[24], Lk 6[46-49]).

The OT ideal of religious life was the earlier stage of a religious development which He came to continue. It needed no essential change to become that which He wished to establish. It was characterized by an imperative demand for a righteousness which consisted in a thoroughgoing obedience to God, and this was just what Jesus demanded and exemplified. Moreover, while Jesus taught that the ideal of life was to be found in the OT, He was far from teaching that all that was in the OT contributed to this ideal. When He had occasion, He expressly taught that even the lawgiver, Moses, permitted practices which belonged

<hr>

* In later Greek, however, πιστικός = trustworthy, and the meaning may thus be 'genuine,' 'unadulterated,' 'pure.'
† On the OT of Jesus see following article.

to a lower plane of living than that of the principles contained in the OT. There was so much in the human heart that was hostile to these principles, that for a time a standard of life lower than these ideals was permitted (Mt 19[8]).

Jesus, like the prophets, was certain that the religious life for which He laboured was to become a universal religion. His claim of permanence for His utterances (Mt 24[35], Mk 13[31], Lk 21[33]) was also a claim that His teachings had the changeless quality of the word of God under the Old Covenant (Is 40[8] 55[10. 11], cf. 51[6]), and of God's law under the New (Mt 5[18], Lk 16[17]). Words uttered by Him when the Greeks sought to see Him (Jn 12[32]), were an assumption to Himself personally of the universal significance for human history which the prophets (Is 11[9], Hab 2[14]) had claimed for the religion of Jehovah. This claim to a unique place in human history and identification of Himself with those lofty utterances of the OT, show that in the mind of Jesus the religious life of the OT had a unique place among the religions of the world. This is equally seen in His declaration to the Samaritan woman (Jn 4[22]), 'Ye worship that which ye know not: we worship that which we know: for salvation is of the Jews.'

Jesus addressed His hearers constantly as having the true religion, as nominally recognizing the true and living God, and as needing to do no more than live up to their own religion. He saw in the OT a universal ideal of society, and the principles for a programme of its establishment. The ideal society was one in which the lost should have been saved; into which the called and chosen should have been gathered; in which the repentant should have found pardon, the distressed and scattered should have found comfort; the members of which should love God supremely, and each other as themselves, and should be humble, meek, and pure in heart. During the progress of the establishment of this society, those who belonged to it would be called upon to be merciful, to hunger and thirst after righteousness, to be peacemakers, to endure persecution for righteousness' sake patiently, to love enemies, to devote themselves to God without pretence and with singleness of mind; and yet to live lives of radiant goodness, to bring forth an abundant fruitage of beneficence for the sake of Jesus and in His name, to observe the duties which grow out of the natural relations of life, to lose their lives for His sake and the gospel's, to seek first this ideal society and God's righteousness, to go to Jesus and take His yoke upon themselves, and look upon a life of lowliest ministry as the life of highest honour.

In these conceptions Jesus was developing the OT ideal, as will be seen later. An important element in developing the ideal was a maturing of the conception of God. Since Jesus was an 'OT saint' (A. B. Davidson, *Theology of the Old Testament*, 520), the OT God was His God. Moses had been able to add new elements of meaning to Israel's conception of God in connexion with the name 'Jehovah.' Jesus made a further advance by using the OT word 'Father' as applied to God, making it the dominant name in His own thought, and reading into this dominant conception of Fatherhood all the OT elements of the thought of God. Jesus so enlarged the conception of God that He practically gave a new revelation as the basis of the new development of religious life which He was promoting. This enlargement came in part from replacing the name 'Jehovah' by the name 'Father,' partly by the assumption on His part of a unique Sonship into which none of His disciples might enter (Mt 11[27]), partly by the new place given to the Spirit which was no more than adumbrated in the OT.

In these views Jesus was at variance with many of the people among whom He lived. The Jews at large were incapable of understanding them. For Pharisees and Sadducees the OT was a finality. It was a full and complete law incapable of further development. It was to be accomplished, fulfilled, simply by obedience to its letter. Prophecy was formal and literal, and their interpretations were often puerile. The Apocryphal literature shows how far short they fell of the ideals of the ancient prophets in spite of their ethical zeal. There was attachment to noble ethical ideals, and desire to attain them, and yet blindness to the real nature of these ideals. There was a lack of insight into the nature of their own religion, and an incapacity to live anywhere except on the surface of things.

2. Jesus and the Law.—Jesus found in the OT not only the ideal of a life, but also commandments, moral and ritual, by which this ideal was to be realized. It is certain that He regarded the OT as supremely authoritative for the conduct of life. He so accepted it and used it. He emphasized it as giving an authoritative revelation of the mind and will of God. He met temptation (Mt 4[4. 7. 10], Lk 4[4. 12. 8]) with precepts for life (Dt 8[3] 6[16. 13]), which exactly fitted the emergency. He also referred to the Ten Commandments as specific directions for conduct (Mt 15[4], Mk 7[10a]; Mt 19[18. 19a], Mk 10[19], Lk 18[20]). He treated the OT as giving authoritative legislation when (Mt 22[37. 39], Mk 12[29-31], Lk 10[28]) He quoted or approved other commands found in the Law (Dt 6[4. 5], Lv 19[18. 34]) as chief rules for life. His practice is not the only indication of His mind. He made a definite declaration of principles, and gave abundant illustration of what He meant by it. The Sermon on the Mount is luminous on this point: Mt 5[17f.] 'Think not that I came to destroy the law or the prophets: I came not to destroy, but to fulfil'; cf. Lk 16[17].

His words to John the Baptist (Mt 3[15] 'Suffer it now: for thus it becometh us to fulfil all righteousness') show that His conception of fulfilment included His own personal performance of any and every duty which was incumbent upon Him according to the Law, so that nothing should be wanting to His full performance of every human duty. In other utterances, as Jn 4[34] 5[36] 17[4], His use of τελέω shows that His idea of fulfilment meant the completion of the tasks laid upon Him to accomplish. It should be borne in mind that He considered, and even claimed, that His conduct and will were in perfect harmony with the will of God (Mt 7[21] 12[50], Mk 3[35], Mt 26[39], Mk 14[36], Lk 22[42], Jn 5[30] 6[38] 8[46]). This is a real and important mode of His fulfilment of the Law. If He did no more, it would be small help to those who were to preach the gospel. He did it because He was able to do far more, He was able to complete the Law as a law, *i.e.* to bring it to its perfection as a law. See, further, artt. LAW and LAW OF GOD.

One wishes to find a clear utterance of the mind of Jesus respecting the imprecatory Psalms. Perhaps it is to be found in Mt 5[44]. If the basis of the current Jewish morality respecting revenge found support, as some think, in Ps 41[11. (10)] ('But thou, O Lord, have mercy upon me, and raise me up, that I may requite them') and the imprecatory Psalms, then we find the mind of Jesus in respect of those Psalms an expression of feelings which belong to the individual relations in life. Hate, divorce, and revenge are contrary to the principles of the society which Jesus came to establish, and they have no place in His ideal Kingdom.

The OT often had an ideal in solution, as it were, which in the mind of Jesus was precipitated into crystals of perfect and imperishable form. An illustration is the inchoate ideal of Job 31[29] 'If I rejoiced at the destruction of him that hated me, or lifted up myself when evil found him'; cf. Pr 24[17] 'Rejoice not when thine enemy falleth, and let not thy heart be glad when he is overthrown'; 24[29] 'Say not, I will do so to him as he has done to me, I will render to the man according to his work'; 20[22] 'Say not thou, I will recompense evil; wait on the Lord, and he will save thee'; 25[21] 'If thine enemy be hungry, give him bread to eat; and if he be thirsty, give him water to drink'; Ex 23[4. 5] 'If thou meet thine enemy's ox or his ass going astray,

thou shalt surely bring it back to him again. If thou see the ass of him that hateth thee lying under his burden, and wouldest forbear to help him, thou shalt surely help with him'; 1 S 24[4-8] the example of David in sparing the life of Saul when he had him in his power; also the similar instance of Elisha in sparing the Syrians (2 K 6[22]); Ps 7[5b (4b)] 'Yea, I have delivered him that without cause was mine adversary.' These were expressions of an ideal as yet unformed; passing through the mind of Jesus they appear in the form, 'Love your enemies, and pray for them that persecute you' (Mt 5[44]), or more completely in Lk 6[27b. 28] 'Love your enemies, do good to them that hate you, bless them that curse you, pray for them that despitefully use you.' And they are exemplified in His prayer on the cross, Lk 23[34] 'Father, forgive them: for they know not what they do' (on this verse see Westcott–Hort, *Gr. Test.* ii. pp. 67, 68).

The ideal of true life found in the OT was fellowship with God. The necessary condition of such a life was perfect obedience to the law of love. Jesus found these principles in the literature of the OT, and their authority came from the Spirit, who moulded the life of which the OT was a growth.

3. Jesus and prophecy.—The recorded utterances of Jesus seem to indicate that He laid as real stress on the fulfilment of the prophecies of the OT as He did upon the fulfilment of the Law. This was a necessary consequence of the conviction that the ideal was to be realized. In Law and Prophets alike Jesus found declarations of the Divine purposes in human history, and intimations of the programme of the accomplishment of this purpose. In respect to the latter He expressed a firm confidence that the will of God as declared in the Law should be accomplished. In the Law and the Prophets He found intimations of Himself, of His experiences, and of the relation of these experiences to the establishment of the Kingdom. 'Ye search the scriptures, because ye think that in them ye have eternal life' (Jn 5[39]). Were the intimations which Jesus found in the Prophets detailed and exact predictions which He was to fulfil? How did He look at the OT in relation to His own life? Did the Messianic conceptions of Jesus come chiefly from predictions which He found in the OT? Early in His ministry (Lk 4[21]), after reading from Is 61[1. 2] He said, 'To-day hath this scripture been fulfilled in your ears.' He continued, and the contents of His speech are described (v.[22a]), 'And all bare him witness, and wondered at the words of grace which proceeded out of his mouth.' What these words of grace may have been is left to our conjecture. They may have been like the answer sent to John the Baptist at another time, which seems to show that Jesus regarded the work He was doing in preaching good news to the poor, healing the sick, restoring sight to the blind, as the fulfilment of the utterance of the prophet in this passage. But also the fact that He Himself was doing this work was seen by Jesus as a fulfilment of that prophecy. It is only reasonable to interpret the words of Jesus as affirming that He regarded Himself personally as included within the scope of the passage. Again, 'For I say unto you, that this which is written must be fulfilled in me, And he was reckoned with transgressors: for that which concerneth me hath fulfilment' (Lk 22[37]). 'That which concerneth me' probably means that which in the Divine counsel concerned Him, whether written or unwritten. The words quoted by Him from Is 53[12] were a part of the Divine counsel, according to the thought of Jesus. He says in effect: This utterance includes me within its scope and finds its culmination and perfect realization in my experience. The same may be said of the following, 'But that the scripture may be fulfilled, He that eateth my bread lifted up his heel against me' (Jn 13[18]); 'But this cometh to pass that the word may be fulfilled that is written in their law, They hated me without a cause' (15[25]), *i.e.* 'the words of the OT find their completion in my experience.'

All the most important utterances of Jesus concerning fulfilment of OT prophecy found in His work or experience were attached to no specific Scripture passage, and furthermore we are unable to find a specific OT utterance as the basis. This is a very significant fact, and deserves more careful attention than was needed in the case of the passages just mentioned; cf. Mt 26⁵⁴ 'How then should the scriptures be fulfilled, that thus it must be?'; v.⁵⁶ 'But all this is come to pass, that the scriptures of the prophets might be fulfilled'; less fully in Mk 14⁴⁹ 'But *this is done* that the scriptures might be fulfilled'; Lk 18³¹ 'And he took unto him twelve, and said unto them, Behold, we go up to Jerusalem, and all the things that are written by the prophets shall be accomplished unto the Son of Man.' Most important of all are Lk 24²⁶. ²⁷. ⁴⁴⁻⁴⁷ 'Behoved it not the Christ to suffer these things, and to enter into his glory? And beginning from Moses and from all the prophets, he interpreted to them in all the scriptures the things concerning himself. . . . And he said unto them, These are my words which I spake unto you, while I was yet with you, how that all things must needs be fulfilled, which are written in the law of Moses, and the prophets, and the psalms, concerning me. Then opened he their mind, that they might understand the scriptures, and he said unto them, Thus it is written, that the Christ should suffer, and rise again from the dead the third day; and that repentance and remission of sins should be preached in his name unto all the nations, beginning from Jerusalem.' In these passages Jesus taught plainly that the OT testified that His death and resurrection were necessary antecedents to the preaching of repentance and the forgiveness of sins. In other words, according to Jesus, the OT clearly showed that His death and resurrection were a necessity in the Divine economy. The exact nature of this necessity has not been preserved in the record of the teachings of Jesus. We may say that in harmony with Scripture we should regard this necessity as not due to any arbitrariness on God's part, or to any necessity of a mechanical conformity to the utterances in the OT. Rather, in the nature of things, it was due to the hardness of the human heart, which necessitated such experiences on the part of a Saviour in order to overcome its hardness.

It is quite significant that no one passage is quoted or mentioned in the reports of the teaching of Jesus given by Him after His resurrection. Yet He taught His disciples explicitly that His sufferings, death, and resurrection were necessary in order to fulfil the OT. Further, the disciples, after they understood the Scriptures, also saw the necessity of the death and resurrection. For the most part, the early utterances of the Apostles, as recorded in the Book of Acts, show the same reticence respecting specific OT passages which Jesus had shown.

We must believe that in its general tenor the Apostles taught what they had learned of Jesus. Is it not possible that the speech of Stephen before the Sanhedrin gives us very nearly the character of the teaching of Jesus? This is an argument from broad historical analogies and principles rather than a use of particular passages. In support of this suggestion we may turn to the utterances of Jesus, before His crucifixion, respecting His sufferings. See art. ANNOUNCEMENTS OF DEATH.

The only passages of the OT which Jesus is recorded as having quoted in any relation to His sufferings are Ps 35¹⁹ 41⁹ (Heb. ¹⁰) 69⁴ (Heb. ⁵), Is 53¹², and Zec 13⁷. Did Jesus see specific predictions in these passages?

Before attempting to answer this question, it will be well to note what He said respecting the suffering of others than Himself which was due to their religious activities. He affirmed

that in the past the world had been bitterly hostile towards those who worked for the doing of God's will on earth. In Mt 5¹¹ᶠ., Lk 11⁴⁷⁻⁴⁹, and similar passages, Jesus called to mind the fact that God's messengers to His people had encountered bitter hostility throughout the past. In passages like Mt 10¹⁷⁻²². ³⁴⁻³⁶ 23²⁹⁻³¹. ³⁴. ³⁷, Mk 10³⁰, Lk 12⁴⁹⁻⁵³ 13³⁴, Jn 15¹⁸⁻²⁵ 17¹⁴. ¹⁵ He showed that such hostility is inevitable in the progress of His Kingdom. The spirit and methods of the world in the midst of which His Kingdom must develop are wholly alien to those of the Kingdom, therefore Jesus must meet hostility, and so must His disciples. The work of Jesus in the establishment of the Kingdom was conditioned by a long historical development which had already been centuries in progress when He came.

A long-continued historical movement, however complex, tending toward one goal has a substantial unity of character in all stages of its development. The various attitudes assumed by men towards the great features of such a movement are substantially the same from generation to generation, from age to age. Human beings persistently manifest their attitude in modes that are practically identical. Hence arise the oft-noted historical parallels. The fact that at one stage of a movement persons may act as persons do at another stage is the essential element of a historical parallel. In a long-continued development of a specific character nearly identical situations will often be repeated, and nearly identical experiences will often occur.

More noteworthy than mere historical parallels is the substantial identity of moral attitude and conduct seen in the persons whose experiences constitute the historical parallels. These facts can be verified from the political life of all peoples which has been recorded and transmitted to us. Nay, even movements separated widely in time and place, and not in the direct lines of historical development, give striking instances of historical parallels, and substantial identity of human character and conduct. This is notably exemplified in the entire history of the attempt to establish an ideal society, from Moses until the present day. Every attempt of men to establish the coming perfect society had some likeness to the labours which were to follow it. Every person, therefore, who shared in the earlier parts of the work in some respect foreshadowed those who should come later, including Him who should complete it. The earlier is the type of the later. So the persons in the earlier stages were typical of those in the later stages. So also were the institutions which were auxiliary to the labours of these persons, or instrumental in their hands, typical of elements involved in the final accomplishment of the work to which they contributed. The later experiences are more complex than the earlier ones. For this reason we may say that the earlier ones foreshadowed the later, but we do not say that the earlier ones show with anything like exactness what the later ones were to be. Nevertheless, there is so much of likeness that similar language may often be used respecting them both. The names or descriptions of the earlier may, in a measure, fit the later. It was thus that Jesus properly gave the name Elijah to John the Baptist (Mt 17¹⁰⁻¹³), and appropriated for him the utterance in Mal 4⁵ (Heb. 3²³), as He had done more explicitly (Mt 11¹⁰⁻¹⁴) in the use of Mal 3¹.

It is a most noteworthy fact that men who would gain power over others to secure their transformation of character, must gain that power by self-denial and suffering. This was the philosophy of history given by Deutero-Isaiah. It was recognized by Stephen in his address before the Sanhedrin. Is it likely that Jesus had any less insight into the meaning of the history of His race, and the nature of the work which He had to do, than the prophet of the Exile? The teachings of Jesus show that He saw that the ideal state of society could come only by means of a contest with human selfishness and victory over it. The conflict presents essentially the same aspects in all stages of its progress. A successful issue of any long struggle is the consummation of all the previous stages of that struggle. Any complete realization of an ideal sought in the past is the consummation of that ideal. Also any conflict or experience securing the consummation of the ideal is equally the consummation of those seemingly fruitless conflicts and sufferings in the previous stages of the striving after the ideal. The history of redemption is organic. All the earlier stages typify the later ones.

Among other things, two facts have come to clear recognition at some stage in this discussion. One is that Jesus knew that the society which He was labouring to establish, the Kingdom of God, was certain to be established, and that both the chief place in the establishment of it and the supreme place in it after its establishment belonged to Him. The other fact is that Jesus recognized the inevitable and deeply rooted antagonism which He and His society must encounter and overcome, and that the way of suffering was the only path by which He could reach the goal of success. The conviction of the certainty of the establishment of the Kingdom of God must accordingly carry with it the conviction that all the conflicts and sufferings necessary to the establishment of this Kingdom were equally certain. Without doubt, Jesus saw in the OT Scriptures those experiences narrated and depicted which were necessary as the conditions of accomplishing the work which belonged to the establishment of the Kingdom of God. He claimed that He was establishing the Kingdom, that the foremost place in it belonged to Him, and that the position of men in the Kingdom was determined by relation to Himself. Accordingly He, the pre-eminent agent in the establishment of the Kingdom, in order to accomplish the purpose for which He was labouring, must accept into His experience all the trial and conflict which could befall any person engaged in the same work. OT prophecy, therefore, as a programme of the establishment of the Kingdom, depicted the experiences and labours of God's servants, which were an unavoidable part of their work in achieving the results which they sought. The Synoptics record the sense of Jesus that sufferings prophesied in connexion with the establishment of the Kingdom were necessary ($\delta\epsilon\hat{\iota}$, Mt 16²¹ et al.). He saw that the goal was certain to be reached, and that the OT representation of the toils, sufferings, and experiences necessary for the accomplishment of the labour which He was to perform concerned Him more fully than they concerned any one else, because the chief place in the Kingdom was His. So all the partial successes and the unsuccessful attempts in past generations to establish the ideal society were prophetic of what must come before the goal should be reached.

We must believe that this typical nature of the OT records and prophecy was that which Jesus had in His mind when He applied the OT prophecies to Himself. This is a principle, and the use which Jesus made of the OT in ethical and spiritual matters was so prevalently that of principle, that it is most natural to regard the use of prophecy as that of principle. Like the Semitic mode of presenting principles by concrete examples, so was His use of the OT Scriptures by definite illustrations and allusions to individuals. The instances noted above of the use of Is 53¹², Zec 13⁷, Ps 41⁹ (Heb. ¹⁰) 35¹⁹ 69⁴ (Heb. ⁵), may all without violence be interpreted as concrete illustrations of principles, instead of being regarded as citations of specific predictions of His individual experience. Jesus saw in Himself the fulfilment of all that belonged to the life of conflict which must be met by any of the members of the Kingdom of blessing, and of all that belonged to the work of deliverance of the people from those habits of life which enslaved them, and which might render them liable to re-enslavement after having once experienced some release.

The view thus derived from the broad consideration of the teaching of Jesus is supported by the various words conveying the idea of fulfilment in respect to the OT utterances and their relation to the experiences of Jesus ($\pi\lambda\eta\rho\delta\omega$, Mt 26⁵⁴·⁵⁶, Mk 14⁴⁹, Lk 4²¹ 24⁴⁴, Jn 13¹⁸ 15²⁵ 17¹² ; $\dot{\alpha}\nu\alpha\pi\lambda\eta\rho\delta\omega$, Mt 13¹⁴ ; $\pi\dot{\iota}\mu\pi\lambda\eta\mu\iota$, Lk 21²² ; $\tau\dot{\epsilon}\lambda\omega\varsigma$, Lk 22³⁷ ; $\tau\epsilon\lambda\dot{\epsilon}\omega$, Lk 18³¹ 22³⁷, Jn 19³⁰). The study of these passages gives the idea of the completion of the incomplete, the culmination of a process, as was the case in the use of the first of the above words when applied to the Law. E.g. Mt 13¹⁴ : the generation of Jesus exemplified in their conduct, more fully than any previous generation could have done, that wilful blindness, that spiritual insusceptibility described in Is 6⁹·¹⁰. Thus in the experience of Jesus He thought that nothing was to be lacking of the element of suffering which was the indispensable condition of His entering into the fulness of power needed by the Messiah. Since He was the One who should perfect the work for which so many before Him had toiled and suffered, He must gain His power by the same method as they, for the very nature of things made this a necessity, and His experience must fulfil theirs by taking up into it every variety known by them, and fill out to complete realization every type of suffering by which one must enter into power. He needed greater power than others, hence He must suffer much more than they.

It is to be noted that the large and broad conception of prophecy which is evident in the words of Jesus is not equally evident in the writings of the Evangelists. Mark and Luke make little use of prophecy, and present no variation from the method of Jesus. Matthew and John had much more use for OT prophecy. As Orientals, they also naturally follow the example of Jesus in the use of the common method of teaching by illustration. Those passages which in the mouth of Jesus would be of illustrative value were often stated by the Evangelists so as to seem the fulfilments of strict predictions.

The following are passages of this sort: Mt 1²²·²³ 2¹⁵·¹⁷·¹⁸·²³ 8¹⁷ 12¹⁷·²¹ 21⁴·⁵ 27⁹·¹⁰, Jn 2¹⁷ 12¹⁴⁻¹⁶ 19²⁴·³⁶·³⁷. See, further, art. PROPHECY.

LITERATURE.—Beyschlag, NT Theol., Eng. tr. bk. I. chs. i.-v.; Stevens, NT Theol. 1904, pp. 17–28, Edinburgh ; B. Weiss, Bibl. Theol. of NT, Eng. tr. 1888–1889, vol. i. § 24 ; Nösgen, Gesch. der NT Offenbarung, erster Band, 'Gesch. Jesu Christi,' 1891 ; Wendt, Teaching of Jesus, vol. i. p. 173 to vol. ii. p. 48 ; Tholuck, Die Bergrede Christi⁵, 1872 [Eng. tr. from 4th German ed., Edinburgh, 1860, pp. 115–144] ; Votaw, art. 'Sermon on the Mount' in Hastings' DB, Ext. Vol. pp. 22–25 ; see also the Comm. on Mt 5¹⁷·¹⁸ ; Baur, NT Theol. 46–60 ; Kähler, Jesus und das AT, 1896 ; Lechler, SK, 1854, p. 787 ff., 'Das Alte Testament in den Reden Jesu' ; Macfarland, Jesus and the Prophets, 1905 ; R. Mackintosh, Christ and the Jewish Law, 1886 ; S. Mathews, The Messianic Hope in the NT, 1905, pp. 57–133 ; Meinhold, Jesus und das AT, 1896 ; Osiander, 'Die Stellung Jesu zum Gesetz' in SK, 1890, p. 103 ff. ; Peters, 'Christ's Treatment of the OT' in JBL, 1896, vol. xv. pp. 87–105 ; P. Ewald, 'Zu Mt 5¹⁷·¹⁹' in ZKWL, 1886, pp. 499–518 ; cf. also Orelli, ib. 1884, pp. 283–291.
　　　　　　　　　　　　　　　F. B. DENIO.

OLD TESTAMENT (II. Christ as student and interpreter of).

1. Importance of the subject.—In studying the Gospels, it is hardly possible to exaggerate the importance of the subject of Christ's knowledge of and use of the Scriptures of the OT. These constituted the main part of the literature of His fellow-countrymen, and by all of them were regarded with a reverence second to nothing else.

In our own day it has become possible to study this subject as no previous generation has ever had the opportunity of doing. Careful textual investigation of the NT has enabled us to be much more sure of the actual form of the text than ever before, and the patient comparative study of the Gospels has set forth their inter-relation and dependence upon one another in a clearer fashion for the ordinary reader than at any other time. Much more care has also been expended on the study of the OT, both in Hebrew and in Greek, and, consequently, the influence of the latter version upon the language of the NT has been rendered clearer. Much study has also been given to the language of the NT, so that we are better able to tell when the LXX influences it, and when the vocabulary is less that of the OT than it is of the common contemporary speech. The discoveries of recent years among the papyri of Egypt have given us much insight into the ordinary Greek of the period, so that many words formerly supposed to belong exclusively to the LXX are now known to belong to the everyday language of the market-place. Investigations of another order have made us better acquainted than before with the vast amount of literature current in the circles of Judaism, only a small portion of which is contained in the Apocrypha of our English Bible. The various Apocalypses in particular exerted an immense influence upon the generation to which our Lord belonged, and much of their language and ideas can be traced in the pages of the Gospels. Again, the mere improvement in the methods of printing has made the study of this subject easier for present-day students. Take such a copy of the Greek text as that of Westcott and Hort. A cursory examination of it shows that not only actual quotations, but even reminiscences, when these consist of not more than a word or two, are printed in uncial type, and so reveal at a glance the fact that there are traces of the OT in the passage. It is very striking to run through the Gospels in such a form, and to find how large a portion of them, comparatively speaking, is made up of OT phraseology. A similar expedient is carried out in the Twentieth Century NT, save that there quotations and reminiscences from the Apocryphal literature are also indicated. In Weymouth's translation, The NT in Modern Speech, the actual quotations from the OT are also indicated in special type, and more clearly still these various sources are indicated in Weizsäcker's German translation of the NT. All these are indications of how thoroughly modern scholars realize the importance of setting forth the presence of OT language in the text of the NT. This, however, is not mainly of antiquarian or historical interest, but derives its greatest significance from the bearing that it has upon the personal thought and action of our Lord. It is always of the greatest interest and significance to discover the intellectual forces that have moulded any great personality. 'Books that have influenced me' always constitute an illuminative section of the autobiography of any great thinker or writer ; and to discover that the recorded conversations and addresses of our Lord reveal to us as clearly as they do the literature upon which He has nurtured His own soul, is a great help both in the interpretation of His teaching and in the understanding of His message and mission.

2. Difficulties of the subject.—Fascinating as this study is, it is beset with many peculiar difficulties. (a) First among these is the question of language. It is now generally recognized that the language our Lord spoke was Aramaic, the then current colloquial speech of Palestine. This is, as is well known, revealed in certain expressions in that language quoted in the Gospels, as, for example, the words upon the Cross and those spoken at the raising of Jairus' daughter. The fact that our Lord commonly spoke Aramaic implies, of course, that all the reports of His speeches and conversations are translations, and this at the outset necessarily complicates the question we wish to investigate, for the references that are clearly obvious to the OT or other writings may be the work of the translator ; and, on the other hand, many traces of OT language present in the original address may now be lost sight of. It is a further question whether and how far the existing Gospels depend upon an Aramaic original or originals. The well-known tradition, derived from Papias, that Matthew's Gospel was originally composed in Aramaic, has been taken as a basis for various theories, that seek to account for existing divergences among the Synoptics by the supposition that these consist of different translations of the same original.

(b) The second difficulty that attaches to the preliminary investigation of the subject is as to *whether our Lord Himself quoted from the original Hebrew text of the OT, or from the Septuagint.* A knowledge of Hebrew was not usual among the common people, and in the synagogue services the reading of the Hebrew text was always accompanied by that of an Aramaic paraphrase ; * but, of course, it is impossible to tell whether in any one individual case a knowledge of the sacred language might not in some way have been acquired. But the evidence goes to show that the Greek version of the OT was that most commonly in use, and the majority of the quotations in the Gospels are made from it. Swete has pointed out that the large number of citations common to the three Synoptics, or to two of them, are directly taken from the LXX, while in the case of citations that are peculiar to one Gospel a larger proportion show independence of the LXX text. Some of these peculiar instances will be examined in detail later in this article ; but a curious discovery has been made, namely, that certain quotations contained in the Gospels reveal a closer agreement with Cod. A than with any other existing text of the Greek OT—a tendency that has also been discovered in the writings of Josephus and of Philo, while Swete also points out that there is an 'occasional tendency in NT quotations to support Theodotion against the LXX' (*Introd. to the OT in Greek*, p. 395). It would thus appear that the NT writers may have employed a form of text different from that of the LXX as now known to us in what we reckon its best textual form ; but whether, of course, this is only a peculiarity of the writer or was also the form of text familiar to and used by our Lord Himself, is impossible to decide.

An interesting illustration of our Lord's apparent intimate acquaintance with the LXX, where that differs from the Hebrew, is given by Dr. Horton in the case of the Book of Proverbs. In Pr 9¹² there is a long addition in the LXX text to that of the ordinary Hebrew, the latter part of which runs as follows : 'For he hath forsaken the ways of his vineyard, and gone astray in the paths of his field ; for he walketh through a desert without water (διαπορεύεται δι' ἀνύδρου ἐρήμου), and over a land that is set in thirsty places ; and with his hands he gathereth that which is without fruit.' The phrase used above for 'through a desert without water' is that employed in the description of the conduct of the unclean spirit in our Lord's parable in Mt 12⁴³. Again, in Pr 4²¹ the LXX, instead of 'Let them not depart from thine eyes,' reads 'in order that thy fountains may not fail thee,' using a metaphor which recurs frequently in the pages of the book (see 18⁴ 14²⁷ 16²²), and is frequently employed by our Lord Himself in His language with reference to the 'water of life' (cf. Jn 7³⁸, and what is said of that passage below).

(c) The third difficulty is that which attaches to

* It has been thought that a trace of this Aramaic paraphrase of Pr 15²⁷, which uses the expression 'mammon of unrighteousness,' may be found in our Lord's use of the phrase, Lk 16⁹ (see *Expos.* III. vii. [1888] p. 112).

the *method of the Evangelists in reporting our Lord's sayings.* For instance, in Lk 11²⁹· ³⁰ our Lord says that no sign shall be given to the men of His own generation save the sign of Jonah ; 'for even,' He adds, 'as Jonah became a sign unto the Ninevites, so shall also the Son of Man be to this generation . . . the men of Nineveh shall stand up in the judgment with this generation and shall condemn it : for they repented at the preaching of Jonah, and behold a greater than Jonah is here.' It is obvious that in Lk.'s understanding of the saying the parallel between Jonah and Christ is that of the preacher of righteousness, and the result that his preaching had upon his hearers ; but when we turn to the parallel in Mt 12⁴⁰, we find the sign distinctly given as the fact of Jonah's being three days and nights in the maw of the sea-monster, and as a parallel with the Son of Man's being three days and three nights in the heart of the earth. But the close of the passage is the same as that given by Lk., so that it seems pretty certain that this fantastic and allegorical interpretation was not due to our Lord Himself, but to the Evangelist, a fact that is made the more probable by the consideration that He seems never to have hinted at His resurrection except to the immediate circle of His disciples. Another instance is to be found in Mk 7¹¹· ¹² and its parallel in Mt 15⁵· ⁶, where Mk. in the explanation of the custom of Corban makes our Lord say, 'Ye no longer suffer him to do aught for his father or his mother,' while Mt. says, 'He shall not honour his father (or his mother).' A further study of these two parallel passages will also reveal the fact that a passage from Isaiah quoted in each of them has a different connexion in each Evangelist, and that either considerable freedom must have been used in reporting our Lord's words, or the Evangelists have themselves introduced the passage as appropriate to the occasion. The well-known method of Mt., in particular, of introducing OT passages as illustrative of incidents in our Lord's history or as explicative of His teaching, makes it the more difficult in the case of the First Gospel to feel certain when we have our Lord's own words and when the sayings are attributable to the writer.

3. How Jesus learned to know the OT.—Jewish boys were from their earliest years made familiar with the contents of the OT, particularly with the books of the Law (see BOYHOOD, and EDUCATION). They were not only taught to commit many passages to memory, but there seems to have been a pretty widespread knowledge of reading. While the primary steps in such education were no doubt carried out in the home, there is pretty clear testimony that everywhere schools for at least elementary education were established. Within the home circle also children were accustomed from a very early age to observe certain practices enjoined by the Law, *e.g.* the keeping of the Sabbath, fasting on the Day of Atonement, the simpler forms of prayer, and grace at meals. Boys at least, as soon as they could walk the requisite distance, were required to be present at the chief festivals in the Temple, and in particular were bound to observe the Feast of Tabernacles. At the earliest manifestation of manhood's estate being reached, the full observance of the Law was enjoined upon the youth, and, consequently, our Lord's appearance in the Temple at the age of twelve is quite in accordance with the regular practice of the time. On this occasion the boy Jesus gained His first insight into the Temple worship. Whether He returned at all, or frequently, during His youth and early manhood, to the Holy City, we have no means of ascertaining ; but in Nazareth He would seem to have been a constant attender at the synagogue services, for such is noted in the Gospels as being

His practice ; and when He returned to the town, after His public ministry had begun, it was not His presence in the synagogue that surprised His fellow-townsmen, but the learning of one whom they had previously regarded as an ordinary comrade.   In the services of the synagogue He would be familiar not only with the recognized reading of the Law in accordance with the prescribed practice and order, and may even have been frequently called upon in His youth to read, but in the chief Sabbath service He would also become familiar with passages read from the Prophets. These might be chosen at will by the appointed reader, a practice of which Jesus probably availed Himself (Lk 4[17]).   The Scriptures were not only read in these services, but were paraphrased into the popular language of the people.   It is uncertain whether the interpreter was a fixed official, or whether his function was left open to be undertaken by any competent member of the congregation.   It is at least permissible to think that Jesus may Himself have played this part many times in the quiet of the Nazareth synagogue, and by the exquisite appropriateness of His language have already shown Himself capable of making the word of God an attractive message to the common people.   This is at least a possible fancy, and if it is true, it would form an excellent training for His subsequent service as a deeper interpreter of the inner meaning of both Law and Prophets.

It is almost certain that our Lord would have another advantage in gaining a familiar knowledge of the OT, and in enabling Him to use that knowledge for the benefit of His countrymen, the advantage, namely, of being familiar with another language that was then the common speech of the civilized world, namely, Greek.   The LXX was, as we have already seen, the Bible most generally used by the Jewish community, and it is quite possible that Jesus Himself read it.   In any case, if He could speak Greek (see art. LANGUAGE OF CHRIST), He would have the immense advantage that belongs to any one who grows up able to speak and think in two languages almost indifferently.   It seems as if the condition of affairs then prevalent in Palestine was similar to that which exists in many parts of the Highlands of Scotland, or in Wales, at the present moment.   The people will always read a book like the Bible by preference in their own tongue, and its language will naturally be most familiar to them in that form, but they can at will translate it into English, though that English may not, and very likely will not, agree verbally with the version in use.   Some such process as this may account for many variants that are found in the Greek quotations from the OT in the pages of the NT.   But the alacrity thus attained in mental processes and in the rapid change, not only from the idiom of one speech to that of another, but also from the mental atmosphere of one to that of another, is a great education, and helps the man with a natural gift as a teacher to develop his inborn genius in directions very valuable for those he has to teach.

4. Jesus as interpreter of the OT.—Having now seen how Jesus acquired His knowledge of the OT Scriptures, the next matter of importance is to discover how He attained to His position as an interpreter of them.   There was a class of official interpreters, and neither by training nor by personal claim did He belong to this section.   Yet His methods of interpretation created far more surprise among His hearers than did the teaching of the orthodox and recognized men of learning. It was not only that His methods possessed the charm of novelty, but that they enabled the people to feel that for the first time their Scriptures had become a new and living book, which no longer

pressed upon their souls like a heavy burden, but itself enabled them to bear life's greatest loads. He became, therefore, a popular interpreter of the Book to the weary heart of humanity ; while He became, on the other hand, a hated teacher to the privileged class, who felt their profession endangered both by His methods and by the reception they met with at the hands of the crowd.   He regarded the OT with much more real reverence than did the scribes, and, indeed, He spoke of it in a way that might almost sound extravagant in its praise, but He also treated its message with a freedom that was surprising, and broke through the husk of the letter till He found for men the strength and the sweetness of the kernel they had not before tasted.

(a) The great *ideas that were regulative of the OT revelation* were also those which guided the conduct and practice of our Lord, ideas that were central to His thinking, and loyalty to which He demanded not only from all His followers, but from the people who themselves professed to reverence them.   The OT idea of righteousness of conduct as consisting in both outward obedience to the ceremonial observance of the Law and inward obedience to its spiritual precepts, were the two points round which His own teaching and practice appear to have centred.   It was this, we are told (Mt 3[15]), that led Him to undergo the ceremony of baptism at the hands of John, as it was this also that on more than one occasion made Him quote the great spiritual commandments of the Law as containing within themselves the secret of eternal life.

(b) It is not, of course, possible to judge fully from the scanty references preserved in the Gospels as to how far our Lord employed *the histories of the OT* to illustrate His teaching ; but inasmuch as we have no material other than these upon which to form a judgment, we must examine the records that we possess.   The difficulty is increased, moreover, by our uncertainty as to when the statements are clearly those of the Master Himself, and when they are due to the editing hand of the Evangelist.

In the passage, for example, in which He refers to Noah's flood (Mt 24[37ff.], Lk 17[26f.]), He has been dealing with the question of the future history of the world.   In Mt. the words occur in the middle of the great apocalyptic passage, which is more than likely to have been much influenced by later ideas, and more altered than many sections of the Gospel.   As Lk. reports the reference, it is contained in a short section of teaching to the disciples that follows upon a question asked by the Pharisees ; but it is a section which also bears upon it the impress of apocalypse, and may be a passage extracted by the Evangelist from what the present writer regards as most probably the first collection of the sayings of Jesus, *i.e.* His apocalyptic utterances about the future.   Apocalypse was so favourite a form of literature in our Lord's day, and exercised so strong an influence upon His contemporaries, that it seems more than likely that the first series of His words to be reduced to writing would be that which in form and substance most readily fell in with current conceptions.   Such a collection of sayings also best accounts for the variety of form in which this particular section appears in the first three Gospels, and may also lie behind St. Paul's well-known passages in the Epp. to the Thessalonians. If the theory here suggested is a sound one, that collection of our Lord's sayings would be in the hands not only of St. Paul, but probably also of his correspondents ; and consequently his language and imagery would not only be familiar and intelligible, but would have the authority of Christ behind it.   In the parallel passage in Lk., above referred to, there is added to the reference to Noah a reference to the history of Lot, and the fate of Sodom and the Cities of the Plain is again referred to by our Lord when He utters His judgment upon the generation that rejected Him, and declares that in the Final Judgment it shall be more tolerable for Sodom than for them (Mt 10[15] 11[24], Lk 10[12]).   In the same connexion He makes reference to the fate of Tyre and Sidon.   According to Mt 12[40], our Lord speaks of Jonah's being swallowed by the sea-monster, but from the parallel in Lk. we should judge that the reference was made only to Jonah's preaching and the subsequent repentance of the Ninevites (Lk 11[29. 32]).

All the Synoptics (Mt 12[3f.], Mk 2[25f.], Lk 6[3f.]) contain a reference to an incident in the life of David, viz. his eating the shewbread, and, according to Mk. and Lk., his sharing it with his companions.   The account of Mk. has a peculiar difficulty, inasmuch as 'Abiathar' is given as the name of the priest, where the OT narrative (1 S 21¹¹ff.) states that it was 'Ahimelech' (see ABIATHAR). To Elijah the prophet there is more than one reference. In answer to the question asked by the disciples as to what is meant by the statement of the religious authorities that Elijah must be the precursor of the Messiah (a doctrine founded on Mal 4⁵), our Lord replies that the advent of Elijah has already taken place—a statement which in one connexion (Mt 11¹⁴) is directly referred by Jesus in its fulfilment to John the Baptist, whereas in another place (Mt 17¹³) this interpretation is given by the Evangelist himself. Another reference to the history of the same prophet is that to his visit to the widow of Sidon in the time of the great famine (Lk 4²⁵f.), where also an illustration is taken from Elisha's cleansing of Naaman the Syrian. In the former passage there is again a divergence from the OT as to the length of the period of famine. The latter two passages occur in the address in the synagogue of Nazareth, for which, of course, we have only the authority of Lk. ; but inherent probability is in favour of our Lord's using such illustrations to show the wider reach of His mission, though it is not perhaps quite probable that He would have done so, as Lk. represents, at the very outset of His ministry. We may therefore, perhaps, regard the fact of the reference as a correct tradition, but the place and manner of it as due to the Evangelist himself.

The glory of the court of Solomon is twice referred to in the Gospels, and that in words of Christ. The first instance is the unfavourable comparison between the splendour of the great monarch and the beauty of the field flowers (Mt 6²⁹, Lk 12²⁷). The second occasion is the reference to the story of the visit of the 'queen of the South' to the court of Solomon, and the argument that inasmuch as 'a greater than Solomon is here,' she will bring into condemnation Christ's contemporaries. A general reference to the ill-treatment of the prophets at the hands of their countrymen is made in the pathetic lament over Jerusalem, attributed to our Lord in Mt 23³⁷, Lk 13³⁴, while a more specific reference is contained in the immediately preceding verses in Mt.—a passage, however, that is fraught with peculiar difficulties. The whole section is that which contains the woes uttered against the scribes and Pharisees, and bears considerable trace of later editing, even if it is to be attributed, in very much of its present form, to the writer of the Gospel. The passage referred to is contained in Mt 23²⁹⁻³⁶, where the religious teachers are spoken of as those who 'build the sepulchres of the prophets and garnish the tombs of the righteous, and who say, If we had been in the days of our fathers, we should not have been partakers with them in the blood of the prophets.' The passage then proceeds to a prophecy of what is to happen later to further witnesses that will be sent, and of their ill-treatment ; they are to be scourged and persecuted from city to city—an obvious reference to the treatment of the early Christian missionaries, and, in all likelihood, with the knowledge of their fate before the writer's mind. The conclusion of the passage speaks of the judgment that is to come upon the men of that generation for all the blood shed on the earth, from that of 'Abel the righteous unto the blood of Zachariah, son of Barachiah, whom ye slew between the sanctuary and the altar.' It is very difficult to decide what is this last reference, the supposed original passage (2 Ch 24²¹) having a different name for the father of Zachariah (see BARACHIAH). In John's Gospel there is a reference (3¹⁴) to the brazen serpent raised by Moses in the wilderness, and in His controversy with the Sadducees our Lord shows His acquaintance with the passage in the life of Moses that relates the revelation at the burning bush (Mk 12²⁶).

These historical references may seem very slight, but they are sufficient to show Jesus' intimate acquaintance with the history of His people, seeing that He was able to employ at will illustrations from what one might consider remote and unlikely incidents in the national story. We must remember also that He was not dealing with historical questions in His teaching, and that all references to these are purely casual. He seems to have accepted the history as it stood recorded, and not to have dealt with it in any critical spirit ; for what concerned Him most was its spiritual significance, and this He could best show by accepting the narratives as they stood in the recognized Scripture.

(c) It is of extreme interest to discover, if we can, *what books of the OT Jesus turned to with the greatest interest and affection.* So far as the available evidence is concerned, it would seem, as we might expect, that the writings which were most familiar to Him were those in which the spirit of the prophets reached its highest level, and on which His countrymen and fellow-religionists had most perfectly matured their own spiritual life— such books as Isaiah, the Psalms, and that most spiritual setting forth of the Law, the Book of Deuteronomy. There is another of the prophets —in *all* likelihood a native of Galilee, where our

Lord Himself was brought up—who seems to have influenced His thought and teaching not a little, viz. Hosea. Out of the 39 books which compose the OT, 14 are directly quoted by Jesus in the records we possess. These are Gen., Ex., Lev., Num., Deut., Sam.–Kings, Ps., Is., Jer., Dan., Hos., Zech., Malachi. His particular interest in Deut. is shown in the fact that in the narrative of the Temptation all the quotations with which He meets the assaults of Satan are taken from that book ; and when He declares the essence of the Law to inquirers who ask for it, He invariably states it in the Deuteronomic form. Passages from the Psalms were apparently not only frequently upon His lips, but He used their language on various occasions to describe the real significance of His mission, as when He refers (Mt 21⁴² ||) to the 'stone which the builders rejected' as being significant of Himself, and so consecrated the passage to the later usage of the Church. That He used the Psalms to strengthen His own spiritual life, is pretty clear from various instances in His recorded language of their phraseology underlying His own forms of expression ; but most clearly from His words upon the cross, where it seems that one of the Psalms, the 22nd, was the subject of His reflexion in that supreme hour. Of the prophet Isaiah He evidently made frequent use. According to the narrative in Lk. (4¹⁷f.), His ministry opened with an appropriation and interpretation of the great passage in Is 61, which is elsewhere (Mt 11⁵) employed as part of the proof that He Himself is carrying out the Messianic programme. If the reference to the 'keys of the kingdom of heaven' (Mt 16¹⁹) be authentic, the phrase probably comes from another passage in Isaiah (22²²), which reads, 'The key of the house of David will I lay upon his shoulder, and he shall open and none shall shut, and he shall shut and none shall open.' In the case of Hosea it is not only that the suggestive words from 6⁶ are twice quoted (Mt 9¹³ 12⁷), but that the words in which He is accustomed to speak of His resurrection are also found in Hos 6². Hosea is a prophet who is fond of parables, and some of his illustrations from nature are those also employed by Jesus ; *e.g.* husbandry (Hos 10¹²), grape culture (14⁷), the flowers of the field (10⁴), the chaff on the threshing-floor (13³ ; see, further, *ExpT* x. [1899] p. 281). It is very remarkable that the Wisdom literature of the OT should not be directly quoted by Jesus, and that, in particular, there should be no specific quotation from the Book of Proverbs, though it will be shown in a later section of this article that much of its language finds an echo in His teaching. We shall find, too, traces of the later Wisdom literature in the words of Jesus, who came Himself to be regarded as the incarnate Wisdom.

(d) *Jesus' attitude to current modes of interpretation.*—The teaching of Jesus was recognized by His contemporaries as being different in character from that of the scribes ; yet He employed, to some extent, the same methods. He based His teaching upon that of the OT, which He interpreted not in their manner, but on authoritative lines of His own. The objections that He urged against the current modes of interpretation were that they hid under an accumulation of worthless tradition the real truths which the Divine word was designed to teach ; while His own method, in the first place, made clear the meaning of the original utterance ; and, secondly, interpreted it in a clearer and fuller manner to those whom He addressed. His method of dealing with current interpretation can best be studied in the records of His controversies with His opponents. For example, they based their teachings on divorce on the permission given in the Law of Moses ; Jesus goes behind it to the narrative of the Creation, and shows how husband

and wife were destined to be one higher and distinct unity from the very beginning. This note of idealism and spirituality is manifest in all our Lord's teaching, and marks it out as distinct from the verbal trifling of His contemporaries. He was not afraid to tell some of those who prided themselves on the subtlety of their arguments that they were in error, and unable to understand those very Scriptures which they professed to interpret (Mt 22²⁹, Mk 12²⁴· ²⁷). In His judgment many of those who were the professional interpreters of Scripture were doing more harm than good by their methods. ' Ye have made void the word (or law) of God because of your tradition' (Mt 15⁶, Mk 7¹³), He said, meaning that what they considered to be an improvement upon the original commandment was so contrary to its spirit as absolutely to make of none effect its purpose. But in the case of His own teaching, however revolutionary it might at first sight appear, He claimed that it constituted a fulfilment of the Law ; and not only so, but He asserted that loyal obedience to the commandments, both in act and precept, would be the ground of advancement in the Kingdom of heaven (Mt 5¹⁷· ²⁰). There is even a stronger passage in the same Gospel, where our Lord is represented as enjoining upon His disciples observance of all the precepts taught by the scribes and Pharisees, since they are the legitimate successors of Moses (Mt 23²) ; but the whole passage in which the words occur shows considerable traces of the influence of later ideas, and can scarcely be pressed into the service of a definite statement of Christ's own personal teaching. There may be in it a trace of Jewish prejudice in favour of the letter of the Law ; but the immediate context, in which the Pharisees are most severely criticised, proves that the prejudice, if it existed at all in the mind of the writer, cannot have gone very deep, and we may be justified in seeing in the words at least an accurate reflexion of the teaching of Jesus in this matter. If we may so regard it, it is then clear that He had the very highest estimate of the spiritual and ethical teaching of the OT, and objected only to such interpretation of it as obscured its meaning or altered its emphasis.

(e) We now turn to the very important and somewhat difficult section of our subject which deals with *Christ's discussion or use of special passages in the OT.* The first passage in which we meet this is in the narrative of the Temptation. This is, of course, a pictorial representation of an inward struggle, which must have been related to His disciples in the parabolic form in which we now possess the story. But it is nevertheless extremely important to find Him reverting time and again to that one book in the OT (Deut.) which we have already discovered was one of His favourites. In its highest spiritual teaching He seems to have found the best antidote against the poison of the evil suggestions that reached Him from the current conception as to the Messianic Kingdom prevalent among His contemporaries, and which also affected even the inner circle of His disciples. In following the course of the First Gospel, we next come upon the long series of teachings contained in the so-called ' Sermon on the Mount,' and there (5²¹) the first passage to be considered is that which consists of a condemnation of quotations from Ex. and Deut. where the old Law had spoken of killing. Jesus interprets its meaning as signifying an attitude of the inward temper rather than an outward act, and, according to the form in which the saying has reached us, increases the severity of the judgment in proportion to the contempt shown in the expression of inward hatred used against a brother. Here again, however, the whole nature of the expressions employed

seems to point toward a colouring of this original saying under the influence of a later Christian tradition ; and it is probably a narrowed and intensified form of some simpler word of Jesus which the early Christian community edited in such a way as to contain a severe and solemn warning against careless speech—a fault which, as is evident both from the Gospels and the Epistle of James (3⁵⁻¹² 4¹¹· ¹²), was sadly prevalent. In the same passage of Mt. (5²²) we have the first reference to Gehenna, a word which occurs frequently in the records of our Lord's teaching. This name for the place of punishment of the dead had become familiar in the literature of later Judaism, meeting us frequently, for instance, in the Book of Enoch (see 27² 84² 90²⁶). A similar elevation and intensification of the law of purity is found in vv.²⁷⁻³². In Mt 5³³ we have quotations from Num. and Deut. with reference to false swearing. Here, in interpreting the passage, Jesus goes much further than the precept of the older Law, and inculcates such perfect truthfulness as not to necessitate any form of oath. Again we are reminded of the Epistle of James (5¹²), so that we feel ourselves in the atmosphere of the early Christian assemblies. But there is nothing to prevent the statement, substantially as we find it, being attributed to Jesus. Such teaching had already been given in Judaism, and a close parallel is found in Sir 23⁷⁻¹¹, in the course of which we read : 'Accustom not thy mouth to an oath, and be not accustomed to the naming of the Holy One. A man of many oaths shall be filled with iniquity, and the scourge shall not depart from his house.' In the book of the Slavonic Enoch also (48¹) the sons of Enoch are taught not to swear by heaven, by earth, or by any other creature. The next citation deals with the law of retaliation (v.³⁸), and here again the interpreter goes even further, and practically reverses the theory of the OT. In place of exacting an equivalent for any injury, He definitely inculcates the principle of rendering voluntary service where unreasonable exaction has already been practised. To the next quotation (v.⁴³) no direct parallel can be discovered, the nearest equivalent to the sentiment, 'Hate thine enemy,' being Dt 23⁶ 'Thou shalt not seek their peace nor their prosperity all thy days for ever' ; so that we are compelled to assume that the form of the word here quoted by Jesus either represents some traditional form of the Law which has not been otherwise preserved, or that it embodies in a succinct form an idea that had hardened itself into ordinary practice.

In the eulogy of John the Baptist, reported in Mt 11, Jesus is represented as quoting the passage in Mal 3¹ with reference to His great predecessor. Inasmuch as this verse is elsewhere used by the Evangelists as descriptive of John, and as we have other traces of the fact that they did not, till a later time, understand our Lord's reference to him as fulfilling the function of Elijah, and as we remember also Mt.'s fondness for introducing OT quotations on every possible occasion, we cannot feel certain about the attribution of these words to Jesus, but they seem quite probable. Later in the same chapter (v.²³) the form in which the judgment is pronounced on Capernaum is taken from the Greek of Is 14¹³⁻¹⁷, and serves to show not only how, on solemn occasions, Jesus would readily fall into the familiar language of OT prophecy, but how He was always prepared to apply its teaching to the needs and moral issues of His own time.

We pass next to the passage in Mt 15⁴, where again our Lord is discussing a definite commandment of the Law, which He cites in a double form contained in Ex 20¹² and 21¹⁷, combining the passages without strict verbal accuracy. Starting from this precept, He proceeds to discuss and to condemn the casuistical tradition that had been reared upon it, and reveals perhaps an acquaintance with Pr 28[24], where the writer is in sympathy with Jesus in condemning the man who regards the robbery of father and mother as being no transgression. In the same context our Lord is made to quote Is 29[13] in a form that diverges even from the LXX. The usual difficulty has here, of course, to be faced,— Did Jesus actually use the words, or are they inserted by the Evangelist in order to give a definite completion to his paragraph, and to carry out his theory of finding appropriate illustrative passages from the OT for as many as possible of his events? The rebuke which our Lord gave to the defilers of the Temple (Mt 21[13]) consists of a combination of Is 56[7] and Jer 7[11], but does not call for more than a simple note of the fact that here also we see that intimate knowledge which could seize at once on the phrases most appropriate for His purpose. In Mt 22 we find three special discussions of passages recorded. The first (v.[31f.]) is that of Ex 3[6], which Jesus uses as an argument for the reality of the life after death. We cannot tell whether this was His own original interpretation of the passage, or whether He was here giving His assent to some ideas about it that were then current; but in any case it is a striking instance of the high level to which He was able to raise the frequently trivial discussions of the literalists. In vv.[37-39] He shows Himself in sympathy with the most spiritual teachers of His own day, insisting on the primary importance of the inward precepts of the Law, and upon Love as its most perfect and adequate fulfilment. According to another version of the same incident (Mk 12[32]), His answer won from His interlocutor the response, 'Of a truth, Master, thou hast well said that he is one, and there is none other but he: and to love him with all the heart, and with all the understanding, and with all the strength, and to love his neighbour as himself, is much more than all whole burnt-offerings and sacrifices.' If this, as it appears to do, represents the actual circumstances of the case, it shows how Jesus won the sympathy of the finest spirits of His day, and by His interpretation of the Law was enabled to appeal to their better nature.

The final example in this chapter (v.[42ff.]) is the difficult one of Christ's question about Ps 110[1]. An altogether exaggerated importance has been attached to this passage, because of its supposed bearing on questions of criticism. It is, of course, obvious that Jesus speaks under the limitations of the literary knowledge of His time, and that He and His hearers regarded the Psalm as representing David's own personal sentiments. But a matter that is often overlooked is that the point of the argument lies in David's being regarded as under the influence of the Divine Spirit in what he said. He designates the expected Messiah as his Lord, and yet the Messiah is regarded as being, according to the flesh, David's son. This seems to involve a contradiction in terms. All that Jesus does is here to state the dilemma, and enjoy the discredit of His adversaries when they were unable to solve it. He Himself offers no solution. In this case it appears that, as on one or two occasions, He was suggesting to the thoughtful among His auditors that the ordinary literal interpretations of Scripture were perfectly inadequate to meet the needs of the religious soul, and that His main endeavour was to lead them to revise their methods, and to understand that only the spiritually minded could understand the Divine revelation. Cf., for the same purpose, His statement that John the Baptist was the Elijah spoken of by Malachi.

The difficulties that we have encountered in Mt. are even more pronounced when we pass to the dis-

cussion of several passages in John's Gospel. There the idealizing process has been carried so far that we cannot be definitely certain, especially when we are dealing with quotations, that we have the words of Jesus at all. In 6[45], where Jesus is speaking of the impossibility of any man's attaining a knowledge of Him without the previous influence of His Father, this statement is supported by a quotation from Is 54[13], wherein the prophet speaks of the people being directly enlightened by God. This is one of the references that would suggest themselves to a writer familiar with the OT, but it has no special bearing on the argument of the passage, and has all the appearance of a gloss. The next passage is a very difficult one, though its very difficulty makes it more probable that it is to be referred in its present form to Jesus Himself, since it is not at all likely that a later writer would have added to his own problems by quoting as Scripture something of which the origin is so obscure. The words referred to are those in 7[38] 'He that believeth in me, as the scripture has said, out of his belly shall flow rivers of living water.' Now the passages suggested as the origin of this saying—*e.g.* Is 12[3] 43[20] 44[3-5,1] 58[11], Ezk 47[1-12], Zec 13[1] 14[8], and Jn 4[14]—have, it must be confessed, very little resemblance to it. The passage last cited, with its phrase, 'a well of water . . . unto eternal life,' has the closest resemblance to the form of the words, but we can scarcely suppose it to be the actual source. One seems driven to conclude, with Hühn, that the reference must be to some passage in a writing not now known to us (see, for some interesting suggestions as to the possible origin of the phrase, H. J. Holtzmann, *Hdcom. ad loc.*).*

(*f*) It is not only, or perhaps mainly, in such definite quotations as we have already considered that our impression of Jesus as a student of the OT is most clear, but when we read through the body of His teaching, and see how it is everywhere *permeated by OT ideas and coloured by OT language.* When, for example, we read the Beatitudes in Mt 5, we can almost parallel them from passages in the OT. For example, Ps 37[11] 'The meek shall inherit the land'; Pr 2[21] 'The upright shall dwell in the land, and the perfect shall remain in it.' Again, as illustration of vv.[5-8], we have the words in Ps 24[3] 'Who shall ascend into the hill of the Lord? He that hath . . . a pure heart'; while the very form in which these great utterances are couched is reminiscent of OT language, where the Beatitude is a favourite form of stating great and precious truths. When, again, we regard the continual teaching of Jesus as to God's Fatherhood, which many have considered to be the central point of His revelation, we are reminded how widespread a basis He found for this in the OT, in such passages as Dt 32[6], Mal 2[10, 16], Is 63[16], and elsewhere. The idea of the catholicity of the Kingdom of God, which is so often upon His lips—*e.g.* in Mt 8[11] 'I say unto you, That many shall come from the east and the west,' etc.—finds its prototype in such passages as Is 43[5f.], and more closely still in Ps 107[3]. For the darker as well as for the lighter colours of His picture He seems also to be dependent on the words of His predecessors, since we find that the foreshadowing of trouble within the

* Albert J. Edmunds (*Buddhist and Christian Gospels*) contends that the words are quoted from a Buddhist writing, the *Patisambhida-maggo* ('Way to Supreme Knowledge'). See *ExpT* xviii. [1906] p. 100. Cf. also Clemen, *Der Gebrauch des AT in den NT Schriften*, pp. 36, 37, who regards the words as referring not to one passage, but to the general teaching of the OT on the gift of the Holy Spirit. A third passage in John's Gospel should also be noted where (10[34]) Jesus quotes Ps 82[6], where the words are applied *a fortiori* to Himself. In Jn 8[44] we have a reference to the story recorded in Gn 48. 9. Cf. Wellhausen, *Erweiterungen und Aenderungen im Vierten Evangelium* [1907], pp. 19–24. Cf. also Jn 15[25] and 13[18].

family circle, owing to obedience to His message as set forth in Mt 10[21], has the closest parallel in Mic 7[6]. One is sometimes tempted to think that the actions of Jesus, as well as His words, were prompted by reminiscences of the OT. For instance, the story of Elisha, recorded in 2 K 4[42-44], may have suggested the providing of a meal for the multitude in the desert place, the words of Ps 69[9] the cleansing of the Temple (see Jn 2[17]), and the memory of the prophecy in Zec 9[9] may have been the thought that prompted the triumphal entry into Jerusalem. Sometimes also the OT seems to have afforded a theme for a parable, as in the case of the Vineyard (cf. Is 5[1] with Mt 21[33]), or the Lost Sheep (Lk 15[3]); and the allegory of the Shepherd in Jn 10 may have as its literary origin Ezk 34[11]. Jesus' great utterance about the future of His Church, as well as about the perils that were about to come upon His fellow-countrymen, has many points of contact with the OT (cf. *e.g.* Mt 24[21] with Dn 12[1] 24[24], Dt 13[2-4]; 24[29] with Is 13[10], Am 8[9]; 24[31] with Is 27[13], Zec 12[10]). A careful examination of the passage will reveal many more. Very pathetic is the interest of the sayings recorded from the Cross, where Jesus is reported to have quoted, in the language of His childhood, the first verse of the 22nd Psalm. The appropriateness of the whole of this to the circumstances has been frequently pointed out; and, according to Lk 23[46], His last words were an adaptation of Ps 31[5].* These are to be taken only as instances of what a careful examination of the Gospels, by the help of such a guide as Hühn, will reveal to any student in frequently unsuspected places; and the great significance of the study does not, of course, arise from the interest or ingenuity of the parallel that can be drawn, but from the fact that such a study reveals how thoroughly imbued Jesus was with the thought and spirit of the OT.

(*g*) A subject of wider reach, though also of greater difficulty, is the endeavour to discover to what extent Jesus was familiar with, and employed, *the Jewish literature that lies outside the OT*. It is only in comparatively recent times that much attention has been given to this subject; but the more carefully it is investigated, the more clear does it become that if He does not actually quote from any of that literature, He was either Himself familiar with it at first hand, or its ideas and language had so influenced Himself and His contemporaries that many of His ideas, and even forms of speech, are practically identical with what we find in that literature.

In the extra-canonical Wisdom literature we are familiar with many personifications of Wisdom, and traces of this are found in two passages given in Mt 11[19] and Lk 7[35]. The ordinary text of the former passage reads, 'Wisdom is justified by her works'; but some MSS read 'children' in place of 'works,' thus conforming it to the passage in Lk. where the verse stands, 'Wisdom is justified of all her children,' and a comparison may be made with Wis 7[22-8][1] and Sir 1[1-20]. Again, the passage at the close of Mt 11 has several reminiscences of the same literature, *e.g.* Sir 24[19] reads, 'Come unto me, ye that are desirous of me, and be ye filled with my produce'; 51[23] 'Draw near unto me, ye unlearned, and lodge in the house of instruction'; cf. also 17[24]. The whole tenor of the passage suggests the manner in which Wisdom speaks in the books referred to. Again, the longer and more elaborate addresses in Jn. have a suggestion of the speeches of Wisdom, and may well be modelled upon them. In some such way the marked difference between the addresses in the Fourth Gospel and the Synoptics may be accounted for. Wisdom is always represented as addressing her disciples, and so these words delivered in the hearing of the innermost circle of His chosen friends may have been modelled by the Incarnate Wisdom on the lines of His great forerunners. In this connexion there is one very interesting reference also contained in

---

* Traces of the Book of Proverbs are to be discovered in several places in the teaching of Jesus, *e.g.* the metaphors of the way and the light (cf. Pr 6[23] 14[12] 4[18, 19] with Mt 7[13], Jn 11[10] 12[35]), those of hid treasure and merchandise (cf. Pr 2[4] 3[14, 15] with Mt 13[44-46]). The germs of certain parables are also to be found there: *e.g.* Pr 3[28] as that of the parable recorded in Lk 11[5-8]; Pr 9[1-6], cf. Lk 14[16], Mt 22[10]; and even more clearly Pr 25[6, 7], cf. Lk 14[10]; and Pr 24[27], cf. Lk 14[28].

Lk. (11[49]), 'Therefore also said the wisdom of God, I will send unto them prophets,' etc. No OT parallel can be discovered for these words, and we are driven to the conclusion either that they are quoted from some work now lost, or that our Lord here uses the term 'wisdom of God' in the most general sense as indicative of the Spirit which moved in all the prophets. In Jn 4[37] there is a saying quoted, 'One soweth and another reapeth,' which may, of course, be a popular proverb, though words of somewhat similar character are found in Job 31[8], and they may have occurred in the exact form quoted in Jn. in some writing now lost.

The well-known name whereby our Lord most commonly speaks of Himself, namely, 'Son of Man,' though derivable from Daniel (7[13]), is so common a title in the Apocalyptic literature that there can be little doubt that His use of it is influenced thereby. This is the more certain when we remember how in these writings the glorious manifestations of the Son of Man are paralleled by certain sayings in the Gospels, *e.g.* His coming in the clouds of heaven, and in the glory of the angels. Such ideas also as those of the imminence of the Redemption, the sitting on the twelve thrones, the authority given to the Son of Man, and the definite doctrine of Gehenna, are all familiar in the Book of Enoch, 'the influence of which on the NT,' according to Professor Charles, 'has been greater than that of all the other Apocryphal and Pseudepigraphal books taken together.' To the same book are attributable developments in the doctrine of Hades and of the resurrection,—ideas which appear in the parable of Dives and Lazarus, and in such sayings as 'sons of the resurrection,' and the answer to the Sadducees' question about marriage. In the same book also are found doctrines about demons, which throw light upon the conceptions of the NT; *e.g.* that they are disembodied spirits (cf. Mt 12[43-45]); that their punishment is to be deferred till the Final Judgment, hence the surprise expressed by the Gadarene demoniac (Mt 8[29]), who asks, 'Art thou come hither to torment us before the time?' The subjection of all the evil spirits to Satan or Beelzebub (cf. Mt 12[24-27]) is also a doctrine found in the Book of Enoch.

Another interesting group of writings is the 'Psalms of Solomon,' which at the latest were probably put into circulation about half a century before the birth of Jesus, and seem to have exerted a very powerful influence on His contemporaries. It may not be possible to point to any actual quotations from these writings in the NT, but they show the growth of certain important ideas which have sometimes been regarded as unique in our Lord's teaching; *e.g.* the use of the word 'Christ' as a title of the expected Deliverer; the definite statement that He is to be a son of David (cf. Ps-Sol 17[23] with Mt 22[42-45]). In the third of these Psalms we find a careful description of 'the righteousness of the scribes and Pharisees,' and the germ of the parable of the 'strong man' (Mt 12[29]) is found in Ps-Sol 5[4].

More important, however, than any reference to special passages is the effect upon the general intellectual atmosphere of the generation in which Christ lived and worked, created and moulded to a certain extent by the literature intermediate between the OT and the NT. We have to read that literature to understand many of the ideas that were then current, and to find the conceptions that underlay much of the phraseology which to us seems new and specifically Christian, but which had been gradually evolved in the preceding centuries. Jesus and His disciples were, of course, children of their time in this matter, and He was bound to speak in terms intelligible to His contemporaries. What is wonderful is the manner in which He cleared these ideas of many foolish interpretations, and delivered them from a merely fanciful exegesis.

5. Traditional sayings of Jesus that reveal dependence upon the OT.—When we turn to a consideration of the sayings that are attributed to Jesus in sources outside the NT, our difficulties are, of course, increased; for here we are on less certain ground of information, and there is a greater likelihood of the writers being influenced by the literature with which they were familiar. Still, it will not serve to allow any theory of imitation to account for all these recorded utterances, and some of the best authenticated of them must now be examined in the light of our present purpose.

There is, to begin with, the famous saying from the *Gospel according to the Hebrews*. In this work Jesus Himself is the speaker, and the saying referred to runs as follows: 'The Saviour himself says, Just now the Holy Spirit my mother took me by one of my hairs, and bore me away to the great mountain Tabor.' This seemingly extravagant figure is not so uniquely grotesque as might be supposed, for in Ezk 8[3] we read of the Lord taking the prophet by a lock of his head, and the spirit lifting him between heaven and earth ; and in the Apocryphal book of Bel and the Dragon the prophet Habakkuk is described as being lifted by the hair of his head, while the notion of transportation without specification of the method is by no means uncommon in prophetic narratives. There is the ascetic character of the passage quoted from the *Gospel according to the Egyptians*, where, in answer to the question of Salome, as to when the power of death shall end, the Lord says, ' So long as ye women bear children ; for I came to destroy the works of womankind.' These words do not seem at all in agreement with the general tenor of our Lord's teaching, though it must be confessed that the paradox is modified in the later part of the section ; but the words as they stand have a reference to such sayings as that found in Sir 25²⁴ and other passages where women are spoken of with great severity. In the saying contained in the first *Oxyrhynchus papyrus*, ' Except ye make the Sabbath a real Sabbath, ye shall not see the Father,' there may be a reference to Is 58¹³·¹⁴. There is a class of sayings found in one form or another in several of the early Christian writers, and attributed to our Lord ; *e.g.* ' He that is near me is near the fire ' (Or. *Hom. in Jer.* xx. 3), ' He that is near the Lord is full of stripes ' (Clem. Alex. *Strom.* ii. 7. 35). Both of these have a close parallel to a passage in Jth 8²⁷ ' For he hath not tried us in the fire as he did them to search out their hearts, neither hath he taken vengeance on us ; but the Lord doth scourge them that come near unto him to admonish them.' In the *Clem. Hom.* 19, 20, we find our Lord saying, ' Keep my mystery for me and the sons of my house ' ; and Westcott has pointed out that Theodotion's version of Is 24¹⁶ reads, ' My mystery for me, my mystery for me and mine.' The words now found in 1 P 4⁸ and there frequently taken as a quotation of Pr 10¹², viz. ' Love covers a multitude of sins,' is by Clem. Alex. (*Pæd.* iii. 12. 91) and others attributed to Jesus. It seems probable enough that He might have used the expression, and not less so even if it is a quotation from the OT. Another saying found in Justin (*Dial. Tryph.* xlvii.), and other authorities, is, ' In whatsoever I may find you, in this also will I judge you,' which is, of course, reminiscent of Jn 5³⁰ ; and both of these may go back upon Ezk 18³⁰ and 24¹⁴. A very remarkable passage is given in Iren. v. 33, on the authority of Papias, descriptive of the days of the final glory, and the extreme fruitfulness of the vines and grain, and also of the universal peace throughout the animal creation. The passage, which is extraordinary in character, has much resemblance to those found in Is 11⁶·⁹, Am 9¹³, and a very close one to Apoc. Bar 20⁹.

6. Christ's methods as suggestive of our attitude towards OT problems.

—From the foregoing discussion of our Lord's study and employment of the OT we may be able to discover several principles which seem to have guided Him in His use of that literature.—(*a*) *He subjected Himself to its spiritual authority*, but in no respect did He forego His intellectual right to judge for Himself about details of its teaching. The mere fact that words were written in the Scriptures did not suffice to render them authoritative for Him ; in fact, He selected teaching which seemed in consonance with the spirit of the Kingdom He had come to declare, and in His interpretation of sayings that He did accept He was not afraid to pass by altogether received opinion or current explanation, if He felt these to be at variance with the true spirit of the original declaration of the Divine will. Sometimes, as in the case of the words, ' I am the God of Abraham,' etc., Jesus seems to support fanciful interpretations of the words, and even to give His authority to the allegorists. But on more careful examination we find that His exegesis is really a spiritual one, and that if the actual words can scarcely be taken, in their original use, to bear the meaning He puts upon them, at all events His reading of them is not forced, but penetrates beneath the surface to the spiritual realities underlying them.—(*b*) As has been already pointed out, the *critical questions* connected with Jonah or the 110th Psalm *did not emerge in His time*, neither does His treatment of either passage depend upon the judgment formed as to the authorship of the original. Whatever the character of the Book of Jonah, and whoever wrote it, the hero of the book remains as significant as a sign to Christ's contemporaries ; and in the case of the Psalmist it is the significance of his words as the utterance of the Divine Spirit upon which Jesus lays stress ; and this is equally the case whenever the Psalm was written, and whoever was the author of it. The same things apply to our Lord's treatment of narratives in Genesis and other parts of the OT. His treatment of these

passages is of immense significance for us, therefore, as showing that it is the truths embodied in the writing which we have to discover and apply, and that the mere outward form of the revelation is of little significance.—(*c*) Again, it is helpful to find that *Jesus recognizes the process of evolution that took place in OT revelation.* It is not only that He sets aside certain precepts of the Law, but that He sees clearly that those who in the past were deprived of the privileges that a later age possessed would also be judged in accordance with their opportunities. Thus Tyre and Sidon and the queen of Sheba would find more lenient treatment in the Day of Judgment than the cities that had the opportunity of receiving Christ, but rejected Him. This great spiritual principle carries us very far in the treatment not only of OT problems, but in that of the relation of God to heathen peoples, and in the manner in which we regard the revelation contained in other religious systems. When He speaks of Abraham ' seeing his day,' it is also an indication of the same mental attitude, and recognizes the reality of the apprehension of great spiritual truths, even when these are veiled under forms of expression that render them difficult of apprehension.—(*d*) Of great significance also is *the manner in which Jesus used the OT as the source of His own spiritual life.* It is not only, as we have seen, that He was so imbued with its letter and spirit that He could employ it at all moments of temptation and trial, but also that He based upon it His greatest doctrines, developing and purifying the idea of the Divine Fatherhood, the Kingdom of righteousness, the Messiah, the Final Judgment, the Holy Spirit, and the mission of Israel (see Charles in *Expos.* VI. v. [1902] p. 258). He found also, it would appear, the very forms of His teaching in OT examples. The parable, which has been so often regarded as His most significant invention, is not infrequent in the pages of the prophets. The aphoristic forms in which so many of His utterances are cast seem based upon the language of the Book of Proverbs ; while, as we have seen, the longer addresses have a resemblance to sections of the Wisdom literature. He was Himself reckoned by His contemporaries to be a great prophet, so that they saw the resemblance between His words and those of His great predecessors. As a preacher, therefore, He found His models in the religious literature of His own people, and a careful study of the use He made of these, the modifications that He found requisite, and the development that His own religious genius effected, may all be of the greatest value to those who have in the present day to apply not only Christ's teaching, but that which He Himself received and accepted, and which is implied in all that He taught. (See for interesting and valuable discussions of this latter point, Bugge, *Die Haupt-Parabeln Jesu* ; and Fiebig, *Altjüd. Gleichnisse und die Gleichnisse Jesu*).

LITERATURE. —The two best books for a careful study of the subject treated in the above article are Hühn, *Die Alttest. Citate und Reminiscenzen im NT*, and Dittmar, *Vetus Test. in Novo*. Both of these works contain most careful references to the OT parallels, and also to the passages in the extra-canonical literature ; and, where questions of various readings or other difficulties occur, these also are noted and discussed. Probably the best work in English of a similar nature is C. H. Toy, *Quotations in the NT*. This has the advantage of printing in important passages the Hebrew, LXX, and NT texts side by side, and contains fuller discussions of many passages than the German volumes. But, on the other hand, its references are not so full. An older, but useful book, is Turpie's *The Old Test. and the New*, which has much information, not given, however, in very careful fashion ; and another work by the same author bears on the question, *The New Test. view of the Old*. A valuable chapter by S. Davidson on Quotations from the OT and the NT is contained in Horne's *Introduction*¹⁰, vol. ii. pt. 1, chs. 28 to 32. Of great value is the discussion of the subject by Clemen in his *Der Gebrauch des AT in den NT Schriften*, pp. 20–26. For a more popular treatment, see Rose

Rae, *How Jesus handled Holy Writ*; Peters, 'Christ's Treatment of the OT,' *Journal of Bib. Lit.* vol. xv. pp. 87–105; Leipoldt, *Entstehung des NT Canons* [1907], § 3. Reference may also be made to Grinfield, *Novum Testamentum Græcum*, Editio Hellenistica; Palfrey, *The Relation between Judaism and Christianity, illustrated in Notes on the Passages in the NT*; Swete, *Introd. to the OT in Greek*, pt. 3, ch. 2; Dalman, *The Words of Jesus*; A. Meyer, *Jesu Muttersprache*; Schürer, *HJP* II. ii.; Wendt, *The Teaching of Jesus*; Barth, *Die Hauptprobleme des Lebens Jesu*, pp. 7 to 18, 71 to 103; Meinhold, *Jesus und das AT*; H. J. Holtzmann, *Lehrbuch der NT Theol.*, vol. i. pp. 110–150; Ross, *The Teaching of Jesus*, ch. 12; Clarke, *The Use of the Scriptures in Theology*, c. ii. The Commentaries on the various Gospels should also be consulted, and the best editions of the Apocrypha and Apocalypses, as also Griffinhoofe, *The Unwritten Sayings of Christ*; and Preuschen, *Antilegomena* (a convenient edition of the original passages). See individual articles in the following: *ExpT* x. [1898–99] p. 281; *Expositor*, III. vii. [1888] p. 105 ff., VI. v. [1902] pp. 52 ff. and 135 ff., and xi. [1905] pp. 340 ff. and 440 ff.; cf. Westcott-Hort, *The NT in Greek*, vol. ii. pp. 174–178.

G. CURRIE MARTIN.

OLIVET.—See MOUNT OF OLIVES.

OMNIPOTENCE.—The infinite power that works in and through, or above, all things towards the realizing of Divine ends. It may be viewed either intensively, as the power which makes its way through all finite powers, finding in these no real obstacle to its purpose; or extensively, as the power which gathers within it all finite powers, and so achieves its ends throughout the universe.

1. As attribute of God.—Power is a fundamental attribute of Deity: it has even been called the Divine attribute *par excellence*, because it is found in all religious conceptions from the lowest to the highest, and forms the basal thought, so to speak, upon which all other conceptions are built. In primitive religion, however, the superhuman power is not yet conceived as infinite: it is not even centred in one being, but distributed among many. It is enough for the worshipper to be able to regard the deity he worships as higher than himself and able to give him what he needs. Even the polytheist, however, often sets logic at defiance by ascribing to the god he is worshipping at the moment an unrestrained power within his own domain, and even a universal sovereignty. A true omnipotence is logically attributable only under a monotheistic scheme, where the one Divine being is invested with all the powers formerly distributed among many deities. Here the conception naturally develops of a Being whose power is universal in space and time, and moulds all things and events irresistibly to its own purposes. So, in the great days of the prophetic period of Israel's history, all limiting conceptions are withdrawn from the notion of God, and Jehovah stands revealed as the One Being who has all creation in the hollow of His hand, maker and controller of all things in heaven and earth, the supreme power working irresistibly to the accomplishment of His great moral ends (Am 4¹³ 5⁸, Is 40¹²·²⁶, Ps 33⁹⁻¹¹ 115³). God is not merely conceived as transcendent, the wonder-working God, intervening when and where He will: the higher conception also prevails that the ordinary as well as the extraordinary events of history are ordered by the Divine hand, and made to effect His purposes. Not only the universal movement of human life, but nature in all its forms, pulsates with the energy derived from God, is a channel of His revelation, and conforms absolutely to His will (Ps 148). In the NT the teaching of the prophets is accepted in its entirety: the advance made concerns only the higher attributes of God, and His spiritual ends. God is the infinite power working above and within all things: with Him is *the* power (Mt 6¹³), to Him all things are possible (Mk 10²⁷ 14³⁶), He is the Lord God Almighty (Rev 4⁸ 11¹⁷), with no other limits than are set by His own nature ('He cannot deny himself,' 2 Ti 2¹³) or by the moral ends He has in view (Mk 14³⁵·³⁶).

2. As ascribable to Christ.—It is generally admitted that the ascription to Christ of the Divine power has passed through a certain development, which is partly traceable in the Gospels themselves.

(*a*) In the *Synoptic Gospels* we have to distinguish between the Divine power attributed to Him in His earthly life, and the fuller power belonging to Him as the risen Lord, and the future Judge of the world. In His *earthly life*, while He passes through a truly human development, and is subject to natural human weakness, He is clothed with unique power for the fulfilment of His mission. The powers of heaven are at His command (Mt 26⁵³); He has power to heal, exerted at will (Mt 8³), and apparently resident in Himself, though ultimately derived from God by faith and prayer (Mt 17²⁰, Mk 9²⁹). Sometimes this power is brought into play unwittingly on Christ's part (Mk 5²⁷⁻³⁰,

Lk 6¹⁹). His wonder-working power extends over nature: and even the winds and the seas obey Him. The only limits to His power seem to lie in the faith of those who receive blessing (Mt 13⁵⁸) and in the conditions set to His Messianic mission (Mt 15²⁴). It is a further extension of this power of doing miracles that He can bestow it also upon His disciples (Mk 3¹⁵, Lk 9¹, Mt 10¹), to be used within the same limits and under the same inward conditions of faith and prayer—the channels of the Divine omnipotence. *As the risen and exalted Christ*, He enters into a still wider range of Divine power. He is now clothed with a limitless authority in heaven and earth for the triumphant fulfilment of the Messianic work (Mt 28¹⁸), and shares in the omnipresent government of God the Father (28²⁰). When He comes again as Messianic King to judge the world, He will come clothed with the full power and glory of God (Mk 13²⁶ 14⁶², Mt 25³¹ff·).

(*b*) In the *Fourth Gospel* the sphere of Christ's Divine power is still further enlarged. He is the incarnation of the Logos, by whom the world was made; the source, under God the Father, of all light and life. While the marks of human weakness are still found, the Christ of this Gospel is invested more thoroughly with the basal attributes of Divinity—eternity (8⁵⁸), omniscience (1⁴⁸ 6⁶⁴ 11⁴), and omnipotence. Thus His miracles are manifestations of Divine glory, and are painted in the most striking colours, as the miracle at Cana and the story of Lazarus. He speaks as if He were already at the right hand of power; for all judgment is already committed to Him, and life, even life eternal, is in His hands (5²¹·²² 10²⁷f·). His death on the cross is no longer a matter of untoward circumstance, and human violence prevailing over right; Christ permits His seizure only after proving His power to resist (18⁶); and as He has freely laid down His life, so He freely takes it again (2¹⁹ 10¹⁸). It seems clear, then, that in the Fourth Gospel the conception of Jesus as a man subject to ordinary human limitations of weakness, ignorance, and moral growth is giving place to the thought of a Christ-Logos, who, even while on earth, is invested with all the metaphysical attributes of Divinity. At the same time it must be recognized that the earthly Christ exercises His Divine powers under certain limitations. His power (ἐξουσία is the word preferred) is a delegated power, given Him of the Father; and it is exercised within the definite limits of His saving mission.

(*c*) Without following in detail the progress of thought in the Apostolic teaching, and the development in later ages, we may notice one or two points in Christology where the question of Christ's omnipotence comes more prominently into view. The Logos theory developed into the Two-nature conception of Christ's Person, which last remained as the authoritative doctrine of the Church. The problem of Christ's Person was not thereby solved; and ever-recurring attempts were made to harmonize the facts of weakness, ignorance, and growth with a Divine φύσις possessed of all Divine powers. Either the human nature was conceived as exalted to the Divine, or the Divine was conceived as limiting itself, and so placing itself on a level with the finite human nature. The boldest attempt in the first direction was that made by the Lutheran theologians of the 16th and 17th cents., who taught that all Divine powers were personally communicated to the human nature of Christ, but that in His earthly state the use of these powers was ordinarily veiled, if not surrendered. The other direction of thought is seen, *e.g.*, in Thomas Aquinas, who strives to bring the Divine omnipotence of Christ into harmony with His human life, by affirming that He shared in the Divine omnipotence only so far as He needed it in His mission, and, further, that He ordinarily limited His own power voluntarily so as to be able to partake of human weakness. A more strenuous attempt in the same direction is to be found in the Kenotic doctrine of last century, which affirms that Christ in becoming man emptied Himself of the attributes of omnipotence, etc., and so became subject to the ordinary conditions of a real human life (see KENOSIS). All such attempts to unify inconsistent characters end in depleting the Person of Christ either of His Divinity or of some part of His humanity, and so serve only to show the inadequacy of the Two-nature theory from which they start. The problem is to be solved only by (1) a new conception of what constitutes Divinity, and (2) by pressing back to the historical Christ as presented in the Synoptic Gospels. So long as God is characterized mainly by His basal attributes, the doctrine of the God-man is a simple unintelligibility: it is here that the proposition *finitum non capax infiniti* verifies itself to our minds. But as religious faith presses on to a recognition of the inner being of God, it comes upon attributes that are at once more central and at the same time essentially communicable to humanity. Holiness, justice, faithfulness, love, are the innermost attributes of God, and they also represent the goal of human life; and in the measure man attains to these, does he attain to union with God. It is through the possession of these qualities that Christ is one with the Father, and approves Himself as the Son of God. This must be the starting-point for a revision of the thought of Christ's omnipotence. Christ's power is not coextensive with God's; it is the power of omnipotent goodness and faith, the omnipotence of One who makes Himself the channel of the Divine will. Even His miraculous power must be subsumed under the same category; it is a power granted to faith (Mk 11[23], Mt 17[20]). If it be said that this spiritual power and sovereignty are not yet omnipotence, we shall not quarrel about words. Christ does not possess absolute omnipotence, any more than He is God *simpliciter*. But He who lives in fullest fellowship with the Father, who is one with God in heart and purpose, and who consciously makes Himself the instrument of the Divine will in carrying out His work of grace among men, may surely claim to share in the Divine omnipotence.

LITERATURE.—Köstlin, art. 'Gott' in *PRE*[3]; Schultz, *Gottheit Christi* and *OT Theol.* [Clark's tr.]; Kaftan, *Dogmatik*, 41–47; A. B. Bruce, *Miraculous Element in the Gospels*, ch. vii.; Thomas Aquinas, *Summa*, iii. Qu. 13; B. B. Warfield, *The Power of God unto Salvation* (1903), 91.   J. DICK FLEMING.

OMNIPRESENCE.—The distinctive conception of omnipresence which meets us in the Gospels may briefly be expressed thus: God is able to exert His activity anywhere. God's children cannot be where He is not. He is spiritually present with all earnest, seeking souls everywhere.

1. If this be so, it is evident that Christ's distinctive teaching on this subject was *not metaphysical*. He does not speak of God in terms of philosophy. Such terms as 'the Absolute,' or 'the Infinite,' or 'the Unconditioned' are never found on Christ's lips, and, what is more, the ideas implied by these terms are absent from His horizon. We do not find in Christ's discourses any disquisition on the nature and attributes of God. With the exception of the solitary phrase 'God is Spirit' (Jn 4[24]), which is certainly rich in implications, but, when originally uttered, was meant merely to check material and local conceptions of the Deity, we have no instance in which Jesus expounded the nature or even the attributes of God as such. His method was rather to reveal the character of God by portraying His activities in relation to the lives of men, and especially of Christian men. Not only so, but *Christ's starting-point* was different from that of the metaphysician. To the latter, God is a postulate of the *Reason*. God is a necessary assumption to explain the origination and continuance of the world. Reason claims satisfaction; and therefore insists that God must essentially be that which will subsume mind and nature under the unity of an intelligible notion. The metaphysician seeks for *proofs* of the existence of God—for indications of the real behind the phenomenal, the great First Cause behind the congeries of events which seem to be effects. In the teaching of the Lord Jesus, God is the postulate of the *religious consciousness*. When religious experiences are reduced to terms of thought, and the religious consciousness of the individual and the community is expressed in terms which are intelligible to the intellect, it is at once recognized that the God who is so real to His people, wherever they may be,—who is the source of strength and joy and light to His people everywhere,—must have the attribute of omnipresence predicated concerning Him. Christ's conception of the presence of God is thoroughly religious. It is always a presence to the religious consciousness, trust, prayer, and fellowship.

2. The Lord Jesus *never associated omnipresence with infinitude*. Hebrew philosophy, in the person of its supposed founder, might exclaim: 'Behold, heaven and the heaven of heavens cannot contain thee' (1 K 8[27]); but no such thought ever came from the lips of Jesus. To Him the distinctive conception of omnipresence was: The child of God cannot go where his Father is not. He did not associate omnipresence with the infinitely great, but rather with the infinitely little. He was chiefly concerned to show that in the minute events of life God is present and observant; and that there is nothing so trivial as to elude the vigilance of our Father in heaven. The Lord Jesus left it for philosophers to lash their weary imaginations so as to trace the ubiquity of God in the infinite recesses of space, and to prove that everywhere there are indications of the same law and order as in the world around us, and that the indications of the presence of a supreme Mind are as apparent in the sidereal heavens as here. If we may so say, Christ's conception was microscopic rather than telescopic. To trace the tokens of the presence of God's workmanship in the colours of the lily, or in the provision God has made for feeding the ravens, yielded great joy to the Saviour's heart because it suggested so strikingly that God is 'round about us,' and enabled Him the better to impress on the hearts of His disciples, when their faith was so feeble, that God was very *near* to them, to sympathize, to succour, and to bless, as well as to further the interests of His Kingdom.

3. It is probable that Christ's teaching on this subject was intended to be a *corrective to much of the current Jewish theology* of that period. An outstanding peculiarity of the religious thought of Christ's time was the emphasis placed on the doctrine of God's aloofness. The Jews had imported, probably from Persia, the belief that matter is essentially evil. Hence it was considered to be beneath the dignity of the Divine nature that God should be supposed to have direct contact with inert matter, or immediate intercourse with sinful men; and under the influence of this belief God was gradually pushed further away from His world. This conception was operative in two ways: (*a*) To the Palestinian Jews God was conceived of as enjoying the otiose majesty of an Oriental monarch, who is kept informed of the deeds of men and the events of the world by the 'angels of the Presence,' who 'at His bidding

speed o'er land and sea,' and report what they have
seen and heard. (b) The Alexandrian Jews, of
whose beliefs Philo was the chief exponent, treated
the matter more philosophically, and they pushed
the doctrine of God's 'separateness' from all that
is material, earthly, and human, to such an extent
as to deny that God has any qualities at all.
Philo maintained, as some moderns have done,
that to assign any quality or attribute to God is to
limit Him : which is inadmissible, since God is the
absolutely unlimited, eternal, unchangeable, simple
substance. 'Of God,' said Philo, 'we can only
know *that* He is, not *what* He is' (Drummond,
Philo Judæus, ii. 23–30). Knowing as we do that
this was the trend of Jewish thought in Christ's
day, it is difficult to believe that Christ's teaching
as to the Divine omnipresence and fatherly care, in
the Sermon on the Mount and elsewhere, was not
meant to be a corrective of the current theology,
which in its endeavour to de-humanize God was in
danger of un-deifying Him.

And now we are prepared to consider in detail
the intimations of omnipresence which meet us in
the Gospels ; and we may conveniently arrange
them in three groups, according as they refer to
the Father, Son, or Holy Spirit.

4. Passages which teach or imply *the omnipresence
of God the Father*. We know what kind of intimations to expect. We shall not meet with
much that will satisfy our intellectual, philosophical nature, but with much that will appeal
deeply to our religious nature.

As Dr. Stevens says: 'He (Jesus) aims to rescue the idea of
God from the realm of cold and powerless abstraction, and to
make it a practical, living power in the heart. He sought to
inspire in men an intense and constant sense of God's presence
and care' (*Theol. of NT*, 66). Similarly, Dr. Orr teaches that
'Christ's doctrine of the Father is entirely unmetaphysical. . . .
He takes up into His teaching all the *natural* truth about God.
He also takes up all the truth about God's being, character,
perfections, and relation to the world and man, already given
in the OT.' But 'the attributes of God . . . are never made by
Christ the subject of formal discourse, are never treated of for
their own sake, or in their metaphysical relations. They come
into view solely in their religious relations' (*Christian View*,
77 f.).

The distinctive feature as to the omnipresence of
God in the Sermon on the Mount is to be found in
the words, 'Thy Father who *is* in secret' (Mt 6[18]).
Others may expatiate on the fact that God transcends the heaven of heavens, our Lord was concerned to bring home to the religious consciousness
of His disciples, that God is in the secret place of
their lowly dwelling, where no other eye can see
them. To use the words of Beyschlag—Christ
taught that—

'God is as present and operative in the world as He can be,
without denying His absolute goodness, and without interfering
with the freedom of the creature, which is the fundamental
condition of all development of good in the world. The world
is . . . His work and workshop. If the Judaism of the time
separated God and the world from each other almost deistically,
. . . Jesus, on the other hand, conceives the relation of His
Father to the world as one instinct with life. God has by no
means withdrawn Himself from the world He once created'
(*NT Theol.* i. 95 f.).

'Presence' and 'activity' are equivalent with
God, and therefore He 'who *is* in secret' must also
'*see* in secret' (Mt 6[18]). He is actively present
with those who 'give alms' in secret (6[4]), who
'pray' in secret (6[6]), and who 'fast' in secret (6[18]).
The omnipresent activity of God is evidenced also
in His unceasing care and fatherly solicitude over
His creatures. His children are encouraged to
rely on His care from the fact that the Heavenly
Father feeds the fowls of heaven (6[26]), and clothes
the grass of the field and the beautiful lilies (6[30]) ;
notices the fall of every sparrow, and numbers the
very hairs of our heads (10[29f.]). Wherever God's
children may be, He knows what things they have
need of (6[8. 32]), gives good things to them that

ask Him (7[11]), and reveals the truth to earnest
souls (16[17]). We learn from these passages that
wherever God's children are, there God is, without
any need of moving from place to place. All the
activities of God are available everywhere at the
same time. 'Whatever God can do, whether by
way of knowing, loving, creating, or controlling,
He can do anywhere, and everywhere at once'
(W. N. Clarke, *Outline of Chr. Theol.* 79).

5. We turn now to the profound and really inexhaustible words which Jesus let fall in His conversation with the woman of Samaria : 'God is
Spirit' (Jn 4[24]), not '*a* spirit,' which might mean
that God belongs to the class of spiritual beings.
Jesus wished simply to describe what the essential
nature of God is ; it is spiritual. This declaration
of Christ, which, as Westcott says, is 'unique in
its majestic simplicity,' has many implications.
It certainly implies omnipresence. This is the
very fact which the words were employed by our
Lord to teach—that God's presence is not confined
to any temple, Judæan or Samaritan ; and that
therefore in the new dispensation His presence is
everywhere operative, and equally real and near
to men wheresoever they may be.

Taking in our hand this clue that 'God is Spirit,' we shall
find it useful to guide us in regions which lie beyond the
immediate purview of our Lord in His conversation with the
woman of Samaria. For instance, it is a disputed point whether
we ought to say that 'God *fills* all space.' Martensen expresses
himself thus : 'All is *filled* with God. The omnipresent God is
the inmost fundamental being of everything that exists,—the
life of all that lives—the Spirit of all spirits' (*Chr. Dogmatics*,
93). Dr. Strong says : 'By omnipresence we mean that God in
the totality of His essence, without diffusion or expansion,
penetrates and *fills* the universe in all its parts. Like birds in
the air, like fish in the sea, we are surrounded still with God'
(*Man. Theol.* 132). Whereas, on the other hand, W. N. Clarke
teaches : 'By omnipresence we do not mean a presence of God
that fills all space in the manner in which we think of matter
as filling certain parts of space. It is not a universal diffusion
of the essence of God, like diffusion of the atmosphere' (*Outline*,
79). Following the analogy of 'spirit,' we learn that we must be
very careful lest we fall into any statements that are strictly
applicable to matter only. Spirit is in every respect the
antithesis of matter. Every quality which belongs to matter
is, *ipso facto*, to be excluded from spirit. Matter *fills* space,
and on that very account we may *not* say that 'spirit *fills*
space,' or that 'God *fills* all things.' To introduce the idea of
God's filling space is at once inevitably to suggest materialist
analogies, as air fills the atmosphere, or the luminiferous ether
fills all space ; and all such analogies are misleading. The
saving clause introduced by Dr. Strong and others, that God fills
the universe 'without diffusion or expansion,' does not help us ;
it merely makes the definition self-contradictory. It is well
that we should avoid all metaphors which suggest that which is
extended and materialistic, and adhere closely to dynamical
analogies. It is not a *substantial*, but an *operative* presence of
God in creation which is suggested to us by the word 'spirit.'
It is God's almighty *energy* that is present everywhere. If we
could penetrate into the realm of ontology, doubtless God *is*
somewhat which infinitely transcends our thought, but *what*
that is we lack the capacity even to imagine.

While thus maintaining the Divine omnipresence,
we must try to find room for those numerous
passages which speak of God as *dwelling in heaven*.
In the First Gospel we have the frequently recurring phrase 'Your Father which is in heaven'
(5[16. 45] 6[1. 9] 7[11. 21] 10[32] 12[50] 18[14. 19]). In the prohibition
of oaths in the Sermon on the Mount, Christ
speaks of heaven as 'God's throne' and the earth
as His 'footstool' (Mt 5[34]). In the Fourth Gospel
Jesus says that He 'came down from heaven' (Jn
3[13] 6[33]), and also that He 'came forth from God'
(16[27. 32]). And in looking forward to His death, He
says : 'I came forth from the Father, and am in
the world : again I *leave the world* and go unto
the Father' (16[28]). So also in 16[10] 'I go to the
Father, and ye behold me no more' ; and in 20[17]
'I ascend unto my Father and your Father.' How
in the light of the present article are we to conceive of God's being thus connected with heaven so
much more than with earth ? and of other passages
which assure us that '*in heaven* the angels do
always behold the face of our Father who is in
heaven' ? How are we to reconcile the statement

that God's throne, or God's face, is in heaven, with the doctrine of Divine omnipresence? The following seems to be the line along which we must seek for light:—While it is true that God's presence is everywhere, it does not follow that His presence is *manifested* everywhere alike. He is most fully manifested to those who are most like Him; and if we may believe in a home where there are assembled the spirits of just men made perfect, and also the varying gradations of angels—the holiest intelligences whom God has created, vastly superior to man in purity and capacity for knowledge—that will be the home where God is most fully manifested, because those who can best understand Him are there. There are 'the pure in heart' who 'see God.' But it will be said: 'Is heaven, then, a *place*?' Perhaps not; but so long as we are here, and endowed with our present faculties, we are compelled to *think* of it as a *place*; and it must ever seem to us probable that *created* spirits are possessed of some enswathement which enables us, more or less accurately, to assign locality to them. This is our justification for believing that heaven is a region in which, in a manner more glorious than we can conceive, God manifests His natural and moral attributes, and reveals tokens of His loving favour to pure and holy intelligences. 'In thy presence is fulness of joy; at thy right hand there are pleasures for evermore' (Ps 16[11]).

Considerable controversy has been waged around the passage we have quoted from Mt 5[34], which affirms that heaven is 'God's throne' and the earth is 'his footstool.' The early Socinians interpreted it to mean that God's essential or substantial presence is in heaven, and that elsewhere He is present by His efficacy only. To this it has been objected that 'it includes God in the heavenly space and excludes Him from the earthly space, and thus tends to Deism' (Macpherson, *Chr. Dogmatics*, 131); and that 'such limitation in the Divine essence manifestly abrogates the Divine absoluteness' (Dorner, *System*, i. 241). The Socinian interpretation is a fair illustration of the way in which we become entangled when we introduce terms of *space* into our descriptions of God's attributes. God's spiritual nature refuses to be compared with terms of space, and hence it is incongruous to say that God is existent in one part of space and not in another. He does not, being purely spiritual, *occupy* space at all; but for fuller knowledge of Him we must be content to wait till we have emerged from this state of existence, where all our perceptions are conditioned by space and time, and have entered into that state where we shall see our Lord '*as he is*,' and 'shall know' in the same manner as now 'we are known' (1 Co 13[12]).

6. We have now to speak of *those passages in which the Lord Jesus speaks of Himself as ubiquitous.*—In Jn 3[13] our Lord says: 'No man hath ascended into heaven but he that descended out of heaven, even the Son of Man *who is in heaven.*' It must be noted that the words ὁ ὢν ἐν τῷ οὐρανῷ are omitted in A B L T[b], 33, Cyril, Origen, and several Fathers. WH consider them 'a Western gloss, suggested perhaps by 1[18]'; but our Revisers retain the words in the text, remarking in the margin that 'many ancient authorities omit them.' If genuine, as is very probable, they are important, but not unique. They do but cause Jesus to say of Himself what the Evangelist says of Him in 1[18] 'The only-begotten Son, who *is* in the bosom of the Father, he hath declared him.' They teach us that Jesus was conscious of a state of glory which from eternity He had with the Father—was conscious of it not as a past memory, but as a continued reality. His earthly life had not severed the intimacy of His fellowship with His Father; and ontologically His presence as Son of Man on earth did not remove the presence of the Son of Man from heaven.

Beyschlag interprets the passage differently: 'Jesus thinks of Himself as pre-existent, not because He knows Himself to be a second God, and remembered a former life in heaven, but because He recognized Himself in Daniel's image as the bearer of the kingdom of heaven, and because this Son of Man, as well as the kingdom which He brings to earth, must spring from heaven. That the *ideal man* existed from eternity in God is the truth which He grasped, and to which He gave concrete intellectual form' (*NT Theol.* i. 253).

Another important passage is Mt 18[20] 'Where two or three are gathered together in my name, there am I in the midst of them.' The genuineness of this passage has been denied, not because it is lacking in any Greek MSS, but for *a priori* reasons. Starting from a humanitarian conception of Christ, some hold it to be improbable, if not impossible, that He should, as is here affirmed, foresee the development of His Church, legislate for its management, and promise His spiritual presence, wherever the members of the Church were assembled, however few in number they might be. Our purpose is not critical, but exegetical. If we assume the genuineness of the words above cited, they seem to show that Christ's Messianic consciousness included the ability to fulfil such OT predictions as Jl 2[27] 'Ye shall know that I am in the midst of Israel'; Zeph 3[17] 'The Lord thy God in the midst of thee is mighty.' As He was conscious of His identity as Son of Man before His advent, so He is confident that such powers as He has heretofore possessed will be continued to Him in the days which He foresees shall intervene, before the Son of Man shall come in His glory. Whatever the community of disciples shall bind or loose, make binding or leave optional, shall receive Divine ratification, because the presence of the Christ will be with them guiding and controlling them.

If we have followed this interpretation—and surely, unless St. John and St. Paul have misunderstood and misinterpreted Jesus Christ, there is nothing improbable in the interpretation—we are quite prepared to expect that the Lord Jesus after His resurrection should say to His disciples, 'Lo, I am with you alway, even unto the end of the world' (Mt 28[20]). This passage is also regarded by Wendt and others as a product of the developing Catholicism and Christology of the Church; but it is surely a blunder to ascribe so much to *developing* Christology, unless there were some germinal utterances of Jesus which the Church proceeded to develop. The eagerness of the primitive Christians to disseminate the gospel most probably rests on a command of the Master, and the readiness with which they assume the presence of Christ with them wherever they are, implies as its background some such promise and declaration as that before us. Christ's Messianic consciousness could hardly fail to include the conceptions involved in Is 42[1] 49[6] as well as Jl 2[27]. If Jesus could appropriate to Himself the statements of Is 61[1, 2] (cf. Lk 4[18f.]), it follows most naturally—and this is precisely what the Gospels presuppose—that He applied to Himself all the OT predictions of the Messiah, and was conscious that He possessed the properties and attributes which the OT assigns to Him who was to come—King, Servant, Prophet, and Messiah in one. It is perfectly in accordance with this conception that Jesus, in contemplating the spread of His Kingdom in 'all nations,' 'to the ends of the earth,' should say, 'Lo, I am with you alway.'

In the Reformation period there was bitter controversy as to the ubiquity of Christ's *body*. It arose chiefly from Luther's interpretation of the words of Jesus at the Supper, 'This is my body' (Mt 26[26]). Luther was persuaded that the word '*is*' denotes real and essential existence. In vain did Zwingli point out to him that Jesus also said, 'I *am* the door'; 'I *am* the true vine.' Luther was immovable in his belief that the consecrated bread *is* in some sense the body of Christ. He had repudiated the Romanist dogma that the particles of the bread are transmuted into substantial particles of the veritable flesh and blood of Christ, and therefore it remained to him to contend that the body and blood of Christ are 'in, with, and under' the bread and the wine. In order to show that this is compatible with Christ's ascension, Luther fell back on the Scholastic distinction as to the three ways in which a body can be *in* a place, *localiter*, *definitivé*, and *repletivé*. Locally, when the contents exactly fill the vessel. Definitively, when that which fills has the power of occupying a larger or a smaller space. Repletively (or, to use Luther's word, illocally), when a thing is everywhere, and yet measured or contained by no place.

Luther maintained the ubiquity of the body of Christ illocally. Then, in order to explain how we may without self-contradiction ascribe omnipresence to *body*, he adopted the theory known to theologians as *communicatio idiomatum*. In other words, he maintained that the Deity of Christ imparted all its essential attributes to Christ's humanity. And in this way Christ's *body* received the attributes of omnipresence, omnipotence, and omniscience. The body of Christ is present everywhere, especially in the consecrated bread, and thus can be literally manducated by those who partake of the Lord's Supper. (For further extreme and unreasonable positions of Luther's followers, one should consult Bruce, *Humiliation of Christ*, Lecture III.).

7. We have now merely to adduce the few expressions in the Gospels which imply *the ubiquity of the Holy Spirit*. We do not find any explicit statement in the Gospels of the absolute omnipresence of the Spirit. His attributes are disclosed in connexion with His activities in the spread of the Kingdom. Wherever believers are found, there 'the Comforter, who is the Holy Ghost,' is present with His benign power over human hearts. He will 'teach' the disciples 'all things, and call all things to their remembrance' (Jn 14[26]) ; and will guide them into all truth, and show them things to come (16[13]). But the activity of the Spirit is not limited to those who have believed and have become disciples : it is exerted also on those who are still in 'the world.' Our Lord declares, 'He shall convict the *world* in respect of sin, of righteousness, and of judgment' (16[8]). To those who believe and are thus 'chosen out of the world' the Spirit 'testifies of' Christ (15[26]) ; He 'dwells with' them and is 'in them' (14[17]) ; and they know Him, 'though the world seeth him not, neither knoweth him' (14[17]).

Ritschl maintains that our Lord limited the doctrine of God to its relation to the Kingdom of God. This is not quite true with regard to the Divine omnipresence any more than to the other natural attributes of God ; for did not Jesus say that God 'causeth his sun to rise,' and 'sendeth rain' (Mt 5[45]), and 'clothes the grass of the field and the lilies' (6[30])? Still it is only a slight exaggeration of an important truth. The distinctive teaching of Jesus on the subject before us is that God is with His people everywhere. They cannot go where He is not present, to succour and to bless.

LITERATURE.—In addition to the references given in the course of the article, various points of view are presented in Charnock, *Existence and Attributes of God* ; Fairbairn, *Philos. of the Chr. Religion*, 58 ff. ; Martineau, *Seat of Authority*, 30 f. ; D'Arcy, *Idealism and Theology*, 157 f., 269 ff. ; and all treatises on NT Theology and Dogmatics.   J. T. MARSHALL.

OMNISCIENCE (OF CHRIST).—There are such great differences in the mental grasp of different persons, that no one can prove that all knowledge may not have been open to the human mind of Christ. On the other hand, no one can assert that because of His Divine nature in union with His human nature He must have possessed and exercised such powers. It seems to be left quite open to us, unbiassed in the one direction or in the other, to deal with each department of His knowledge,—as of history before His coming, of nature, and of the future,—and to come to the conclusion that His knowledge included any matter or did not include it, without introducing the dogmatic fallacy that He must, because of His omniscience, have known this or that. Apart from assurance of what God has done, we cannot say what He must do. And this applies to the conditions of the earthly life which it seemed good to the Father that Christ should live.

When we come to the testimony of Scripture, we find Christ growing in knowledge (Lk 2[52]), and afterwards limiting Himself to be a teacher not even in matters of civil justice (Lk 12[14]), but only in the highest region of religion. In a sense, every prophet who says what God will do, claims a knowledge which dominates all the details of God's providence in every department (1 Jn 2[20] 'Ye know all things'). And in this sense, and in higher measure, Christ was omniscient. In the words of Luther, 'He was full of grace and wisdom, and able to judge upon and teach all that came before Him' (Dorner, *Person of Christ*, ii. 92). Thus His disciples said of Him, 'Thou knowest all things' (Jn 16[30] 21[17]). 'He knew what was in man' (Jn 2[25]).

It is usual to refer to Mk 13[32], where Christ disclaims knowledge of the day of His coming, as evidence that there were limitations to our Lord's knowledge. On the other hand, in His discourse with Nathanael and with the woman of Samaria, He showed supernatural knowledge. See, further, artt. ACCOMMODATION, KENOSIS.

LITERATURE.—Liddon, *Bamp. Lect.*[8] 456 ff. ; Gore, *Bamp. Lect.*[5] 147 ff. ; Wendt, *Teaching of Jesus*, ii. 341 ff. ; Beyschlag, *Leben Jesu*, i. 171 ff., *NT Theol.* i. 73 ff. ; Orr, *Christian View of God and the World*, p. 287 ff. ; Powell, *Principle of the Incarnation*, 125 ff.   T. GREGORY,

ONENESS. — The term 'oneness' (ἑνότης, tr. 'unity') occurs only in the Epistle to the Ephesians, where it is twice used (4[3. 13]) in what may be called a moral sense, *i.e.* to express not a physical but a mental or spiritual idea. In that Epistle, where the writer has in view the Gentile world, fundamental ideas of unity are set forth more distinctly and emphatically than anywhere else in the Bible. There is one God, one Lord, one Spirit (4[4-6]). Christ's work is to 'gather together in one' (1[10]), or, as it may be rendered, unite under one head, all created beings in earth or heaven. God had made 'of one' (Ac 17[26]) all nations of men, but in the course of history divisions had prevailed and walls of partition (Eph 2[14]) had been built. These separations were to cease. In the Kingdom of God, Jew and Gentile were reconciled, these two types being made 'both one' (2[14]) in a union based on the deeper reconciliation of both to God (2[16]). Hence the formation of one Body in which the individuals resemble the Head, and the whole is animated by unity of faith and character and life (4[13. 16]). These conceptions, so eloquently unfolded, are presuppositions of Christianity, and are implied, if not explicitly taught, in the Gospels. In Luke, in particular, emphasis is laid on the work of the Redeemer in the saving of the outcast, the sinful, and the lost. This is the subject of the three parables in ch. 15 and of the parable of the Banquet in ch. 14. To these may be added the parable of the Good Samaritan (ch. 10), the story of Zacchæus (ch. 19), and the description of the Kingdom of God as containing men from all parts of the world (13[29], cf. Mt 8[11]). These correspond with the saying of St. Paul (Gal 3[28]), that 'all are one in Christ Jesus.' In Mt., again, we have the doctrine of the Church (16[18]), of the mystic presence of Christ with His people (18[20] 28[20]), and of the power of union in commanding answer to prayer (18[19]). And in the closing verses (28[18]) the universal Headship of Christ is fully announced.

It is in St. John's Gospel, however, that conceptions of oneness are most pointedly set forth. We note the following :

1. *The oneness of Christ and God* (10[30] 14[9] 17[11. 22]). The declarations, 'I and the Father are one,' 'he that hath seen me hath seen the Father,' may or may not be designed to teach identity of essence ; they at least express a practical identity as far as human relations are concerned. They imply the moral perfection of Jesus so that His life and example become the manifestation of the Divine ; and not moral perfection only, for His character and teaching constitute the revelation of the Father. Other passages indicate the mutual knowledge and love of the Father and the Son, and their mutual indwelling (17²¹⁻²⁵); but the main lesson is that Christ is for us the revealer and representative of God.

2. *The oneness of Christ and His people.*—This thought is embodied in the allegory of the Vine (15¹⁻⁸). The branches are a part of the vine, and when separated are dead. The unity is therefore that of a common life, and it is indicated in the phrases that express mutual indwelling. The idea is substantially the same as in the figure of the Body which is the fulness of Him that filleth all in all (Eph 1²³), and even in the figure of the Temple or spiritual house of which Christ is the foundation and His people are as living stones (1 P 2⁵, Eph 2²¹). This oneness is not of equality; for the vine is greater than the branches; the head is the source of the life, and occupies a position of authority. Jesus possessed the Spirit without measure, and His life marks the ideal towards which His followers are to strive (Eph 4¹³). But it is a oneness of life, though in the conditions of normal human existence the Divine is often obscured, and at best is only partially exhibited. This oneness of Christ and His people is represented as parallel to the oneness of the Father and the Son; in respect of mutual knowledge (10¹⁴· ¹⁵), community of life (17²¹), and the love which issues from the Father and the Son (15⁹). Hence the loving obedience of the disciple to his Lord should correspond to the consecration of the Son to the Father (15¹⁰).

3. *The oneness of Christ's people* as constituting a Body or Church, is expressed in the metaphor of the one flock (10¹⁶ RV), divided amongst Jewish and Gentile folds. And to the same effect is the assertion that Christ is to 'gather together into one' the children scattered abroad (11⁵²). The first of these texts contradicts the claim of a particular organization to be the sole Church of Christ. Both of them belong to a far loftier sphere of thought, which conceives the Church as a great spiritual organism, embracing those of every land and age who are redeemed and sanctified, and who by the power of God live for His Kingdom and glory.

4. But the conception of *a catholic Church one and holy* carries us away from any visible condition of things; and the moral oneness of faith and love which every company of Christians should exhibit presents itself as an unrealized ideal. The first years of Christianity were indeed a period of singular oneness (Ac 4³²). But harmony gave place to discord as new questions of thought and practice had to be faced. Consequently we find St. Paul pouring out his heart in pleas and prayers for oneness of mind and heart and soul (Ph 2²). In anticipation of such troublous times, Christ makes oneness a main burden of His last prayer with His disciples (Jn 17¹¹· ²¹⁻²⁶), as He makes mutual love the sum of His closing commandments (15⁹⁻¹³). Such oneness, resting on the basis of Divine fellowship and the possession of Christlike excellence, becomes a means of the attainment of perfection (17²³). For, without social relationship and the mutual support of interdependent men, human nature cannot truly realize itself or completely fulfil the end of its creation.

Literature.—A. Maclaren, *Holy of Holies*, 168 ff., 199 ff.; Rendel Harris, *Union with God*, 41 ff., 127 ff.

R. Scott.

ONLY BEGOTTEN.—1. Meaning.—There is no doubt that the term 'only begotten' indicates a *nuance* of the Greek μονογενής which is very seldom emphasized. As H. Schmidt proves, the word γίγνεσθαι has in general usage entirely lost the early sexual sense of the root γεν. It means simply 'to arise,' 'to become.' It signifies 'that that which previously was not there and had no

existence comes into being'; μονογενής is 'what alone acquires or has existence,' it is merely a fuller form for μόνος (as πρωτογενής = πρῶτος, ὁμογενής = ὅμοιος, ἀειγενής = αἰώνιος). When we have to do with living beings—men or animals—the meaning 'born,' 'begotten' is, of course, congruous, but there is no emphasis whatever attached to this side. When Christ is designated μονογενής υἱός, the emphasis is laid not on the fact that He as Son was 'born' or 'begotten' (in contrast to being 'created' or 'made'), but that He is the 'only' Son, that as Son of God He has no equal. The Latin translators were quite right when originally they rendered the expression υἱὸς μονογενής simply by *filius unicus*, not by *filius unigenitus*. It was the dogmatic disputes as to the inner essential relations between Christ and God, especially those raised by Arius, which first gave occasion for emphasizing the point that Christ as the Son of God was a 'begotten' Son, *i.e.* that He did not form part of the creation. After that it became a general custom to render μονογενής by *unigenitus*, 'only begotten.' In the original form of the so-called 'Apostolic Symbol'—the 'Old Roman Symbol'—we read: καὶ εἰς Χριστὸν Ἰησοῦν τὸν υἱὸν αὐτοῦ τὸν μονογενῆ τὸν κύριον ἡμῶν; and in the Latin text, which in all probability belongs to the same date (*i.e.* in any case some time in the 2nd cent.): 'et in Christum Jesum filium eius unicum dominum nostrum.' In the Latin, there is nothing to distinguish whether '*unicum*' is to be connected with '*filium eius*' or '*dominum nostrum*.' The present writer, in an exhaustive inquiry into the historical meaning of the original form of the Apostolic Symbol (see Literature cited at end), has defended the hypothesis that the latter combination is the correct one. Then, of course, the τόν before μονογενῆ in the traditional Greek form must be an interpolation. Such an interpolation could easily arise in later times, because the title υἱὸς μονογενής was well known from the Johannine writings as an honorific designation of Jesus, whereas in the NT the title κύριος μονογενής does not occur (only εἷς κύριος occurs, 1 Co 8⁶). As far as the language is concerned, there is absolutely no reason why Christ should not be designated μονογενής κύριος; and the thought, which then finds a place in the Symbol, is a particularly pregnant one. The combination of μονογενής with κύριος, not with υἱός, is favoured by two considerations: first, that in the Symbol there is nothing that recalls Johannine ideas (much, on the other hand, suggesting Pauline thought); and, secondly, that there are a number of Latin texts where, undoubtedly, 'unicum' is connected with 'dominum nostrum.'

2. NT usage.—In the NT the expression υἱὸς μονογενής is used only of Christ by John (3¹⁶· ¹⁸, 1 Jn 4⁹). The passage Jn 1¹⁴ is a contested reading, and in any case comes only indirectly into comparison. Elsewhere in the New Test. the expression occurs in Lk 7¹² (the young man of Nain), 8⁴² (the daughter of Jairus), 9³⁸ (the demoniac boy), He 11¹⁷ (Isaac). In the LXX μονογενής is frequently the tr. of יָחִיד, especially wherever the idea of uniqueness or aloneness seems to be emphasized: Jg 11³⁴, Ps 22²⁰ 25¹⁶ 35¹⁷ (cf. also To 3¹⁵ 6¹⁰· ¹⁴ 8¹⁷). The expression μονογενής acquires a qualitative secondary meaning from the fact that what is 'unique' is naturally of special value. An 'only son' is a specially beloved son. This secondary meaning belongs in all likelihood to the expression υἱὸς μονογενής in Jn. also. Cremer compares with it the term used by St. Paul in Ro 8³²—υἱὸς ἴδιος. In the LXX, where this secondary meaning is emphasized, the rendering ἀγαπητός is chosen for יָחִיד: Gn 22²· ¹²· ¹⁶, Jer 6²⁶, Am 8¹⁰, Zec 12¹⁰. In the Synoptics (in the narratives of the Baptism and the Transfiguration), where Christ is called υἱός ἀγαπητός, μονογενής could hardly be substituted. The expression here corresponds to the בְּחִיר of Is 42[1] [LXX ἐκλεκτός] (for ἀγαπητός in Lk 9[35] Cod. אB and other MSS give ἐκλελεγμένος). In all the passages in Jn., with the exception of 1[14], it seems we might substitute the expression ἀγαπητός for μονογενής.

Jn 1[14].—This passage is of interest because the question arises whether instead of υἱὸς μονογενής we ought not to read θεὸς μονογενής. Hort strongly supports this view with a brilliant display of learning, and has proved that the latter reading was very widespread in the Ancient Church. It is to be found in a number of good MSS of the Gospel: אBCL 33 and in the Pesh. and Coptic versions. He also argues, in support of it, that 'the whole Prologue leads up to it, and, to say the least, suffers in unity if it is taken away.' Supposing that we have to accept this reading, it appears to the present writer probable that St. John, in applying this predicate to Christ, was influenced by regard to a non-Christian religious employment of the notions of μονογενής and θεὸς μονογενής, and that the expression υἱὸς μονογενής has thus in his writings a special secondary meaning in addition. For the term Μονογενής occurs in the Valentinian (Ptolemaic) system as the name of one of the æons (Irenæus, i. 1 ff., ed. Harvey). Wobbermin, however, has shown that the term was of special significance in the Orphic mysteries, seeing that it occurs there as the personal name of a powerful incomparable divinity. Just as St. John took over from the Hellenistic philosophy the title 'Logos' for Christ, in order to remove from the minds of Christians the fear that there was beyond Christ a higher mediator between God and man, so he might have taken over from the highly important Orphic cult the title 'Monogenes,' in order to show Christians that they knew Him who is in reality the θεὸς μονογενής. We should then have to suppose that St. John has invested the expression with a meaning which was foreign to general and popular usage, but which probably corresponded with the use of the word in Orphic circles. That is to say, it is possible to interpret the term μονογενής as designating Christ as ἐκ μόνου γενόμενος (cf. αὐτογενής—a name of an æon in the Barbelognosis [Iren. I. xxix. 1], γηγενής—a description of mankind in Clem. Rom. [First Ep. to Cor. xxxix. 2] etc.). Christ would then be the 'God' who proceeded from the 'only,' i.e. from the 'true God,' the Son who sprang from the 'unique One.' In that case the idea of ἀγαπητός, noted above as the secondary meaning which per se everywhere best suits the context, would recede into the background. But the present writer does not regard it as likely that St. John knew anything of Orphism. In the whole Gospel there is nothing else to suggest this. It might, indeed, be said that the conception of the Logos in the Prologue is the only trace of Hellenism in the Fourth Gospel. But in the first place this is not quite correct, and again in itself it is much more likely that John [the author of the Gospel is unmistakably a Jew] knew the philosophy of Philo than that he was acquainted with the Orphic system. Thus the present writer believes that it was persons like Clement of Alexandria who were first reminded of the Orphic titles of the æons by the predicate μονογενής applied to Christ as Son of God. He further holds that the Church so far thought she was acting wisely in making out of the υἱὸς μονογενής of Jn 1[14] a θεὸς μονογενής, in order to be able with more assurance to meet both Orphism and Gnosticism.

Literature.—F. J. A. Hort, Two Dissertations, I. 'On μονογενὴς θεός'; B. F. Westcott, The use of the term μονογενής in the Epistles of St. John, p. 169 ff.; H. Cremer, Wörterbuch der neutest. Graecität; J. H. Heinrich Schmidt, Synonymik der griech. Sprache, ii. p. 530 ff.; F. Kattenbusch, Das apostolische Symbol, ii. p. 581 ff.; G. Wobbermin, Religionsgesch. Studien zur Frage der Beeinflussung des Urchristentums durch das antike Mysterienwesen, p. 114 ff.; Beyschlag, NT Theology (Eng. tr.), ii. 414 ff. Ferdinand Kattenbusch.

OPPOSITION.—The reason for the opposition offered to Christ in proclaiming His Kingdom on earth was the hostility of the scribes, Pharisees, and others, who represented the religious element in the Jewish nation. The profession of religion was at that time fashionable among the Jews. To make a parade of religious observance was a sure passport to popularity, as the ostentatious display of wealth is in modern times. Christ decried this parade of religion as hypocritical. He inveighed against the Pharisees and scribes in no measured terms (see esp. Mt 23). He told them that their profession was a sham and their religion worthless. He assured them that their lineal descent from Abraham, on which they prided themselves so much, gave them no special plea for acceptance with God. It was the spiritual descendants of the patriarch, who imitated his faith and listened to the teaching of God, who were the true Israelites, the inheritors of the promise. He insisted upon a religion of the heart, and not the outward and formal rites and observances, on which they laid such stress because they brought them into favour with men.

The Sadducees, with the leading priestly families at their head, had a special grudge against Jesus, on account of His cleansing of the Temple and condemnation of the traffic carried on in its courts, —a traffic in which they had a direct interest.

The opposition to Christ was so bitter as to be satisfied with nothing short of His death. It culminated in the illegal trial before the high priest and the Sanhedrin, and the arraignment before Pontius Pilate. Its strength is shown in the preference for the release of Barabbas to that of Jesus. Though the Roman governor fully realized that this opposition was dictated by envy, and that Christ was innocent of any thought of treason against the Roman government, yet he was afraid, from motives of personal interest, to give a decision in accordance with his convictions.

As far as the people, as distinguished from the ruling classes, were concerned, their final opposition, or at least indifference, to Jesus arose chiefly from the way in which He had disappointed their carnal Messianic expectations. See artt. Popularity, Popularity of Jesus.

Christ in the Gospels warned His disciples constantly of the opposition with which they would inevitably meet (see esp. Mt 24[9], Mk 10[30], Lk 21[12-16], Jn 15[20]). C. H. Prichard.

OPPRESSION.—The word does not occur in the Gospels or in connexion with the activity of Jesus except in the verbal form in Ac 10[38] ('Jesus of Nazareth . . . went about doing good, and healing all that were oppressed [καταδυναστευομένους] of the devil'). In 'breaking the rod of the oppressor,' Jesus delivered men not only from sin, but from sorrow and sickness (Lk 4[18], Mt 11[4f.]), from the yoke of legalism (Lk 11[46]), the tyranny of worldly circumstance (Lk 12[4-7]), the fear of death (Ac 2[15]), etc. Oppression of guilt weighing upon the sinner's soul was a condition which never failed specially to elicit Christ's sympathy and pity (Mt 11[28-30], according to the interpretation that commends itself to the present writer). The sense of this oppression could not exist without an earnest desire to be rid of the burden, and it was this desire that was a sign of a tendency towards a higher life.

It was the oppression of sin that Christ came to take away, and not the yoke of the Roman government which proved so galling to the Jewish nation after their glorious past. It was partly the mistake about the object of His mission that stirred up against Christ the opposition which is so marked a feature in the Gospels. See OPPOSITION. C. H. PRICHARD.

ORCHARD.—See GARDEN.

ORDINANCES.—In the English versions of the Gospels this word occurs only once, Lk 1[6], where the parents of John the Baptist are described as 'walking in all the commandments (ἐντολαῖς) and ordinances (δικαιώμασι) of the Lord blameless.' From its etymology the word δικαίωμα means (1) a righteous enactment of rightful authority, and (2) a righteous act or deed. Here, of course, the first signification is the one intended, but the strict etymological force is not to be pressed, as the word is simply one of the oft-recurring practical synonyms for the injunctions of the Divine Law, both moral and ceremonial. E. C. DARGAN.

ORGANIZATION.—In the NT organization is visible, but in a rudimentary and experimental state. It lacks the rigidity of a fully systematized religion, but it is thereby the better evidence of the glorious vigour of primitive Christianity and its impatience of all that might restrain and hinder its mission. Christ imbued His disciples with an ideal; they accepted His declaration of a Kingdom of God unfettered in plan and method and time; they knew it was to come imperceptibly ('the wind bloweth where it listeth,' Jn 3[8]), and to one the Kingdom will appear with the surprise of a treasure found in a field (Mt 13[44]), while to another it will be the pearl gained at the willing cost of all else (v.[45]). In its earthly realization it was to be all-inclusive, a net that should gather of every kind (v.[47]), a field for tares as well as wheat (v.[30]), and this wide vision gave the Apostles zeal to seek sinners as well as saints, Romans as well as Jews, calling none unworthy or unclean (Peter's dream, Ac 10[28]). Yet Jesus knew that organization was the inevitable accompaniment, if not the necessity, of this heavenly Kingdom's appearance on earth. The sea might be full of fish, but fishers were needful (Lk 5[10]); the fields were ripe unto harvest, but labourers must be found for the reaping (Mt 9[37], Lk 10[2]); the broadest community will need the power of exercising discipline, even to the extent of excommunicating if that will make the wrong-doer feel the distance between his present and his best self (Mt 18[17]); the tree must have visible form if it is to shelter men in its branches (Mt 13[32], Lk 13[19]), though its vital force may be a hidden mystery, permeating, as it does, the whole body, as the leaven does the bread (Mt 13[33], Lk 13[21]). Jesus accepted the organization of the past, and made use of it. He referred to the rights of the Sanhedrin (Mt 5[22]), He honoured the Temple-sanctuary and the altar (23[16-22]), He sent the lepers to the priests to fulfil the Law (8[4]), He attended the synagogue on the Sabbath 'as his custom was' (Lk 4[16]). His race had learned in the Captivity and the Dispersion the value of some outward conformity, especially of holy seasons, holy books, and meetings for worship and edification, all aiming at that unity expressed in Ac 4[32] 'they had one heart and soul.'

His first step was to form a circle of disciples, learners (μαθηταί), those who would differ from the crowd of listeners by their whole-hearted obedience, becoming imitators (μιμηταί), actually doing the things taught after the Teacher's example ('if ye abide in my word, then are ye truly my disciples,' Jn 8[31]). Much of His teaching is given directly to them: they are distinguished as 'the' disciples, or

'my' disciples (Mt 5[1] 10[1] 12[1], Mk 8[27], Lk 8[9], Jn 3[22] etc.); and, though they may ultimately almost form a school of tradition, inheriting certain teachings (Ac 2[42]), still they remain learners in the school of Christ, rejecting the title of 'Rabbi' ('teacher,' 'master'), and keep their name of 'disciples' well into the next generation (Ac 6[2] 9[36] 11[26] 21[4. 16]). Jesus may call them 'servants' (Mt 10[24]), 'labourers' (Mt 9[37], Lk 9[62]), 'the salt of the earth,' 'the light of the world' (Mt 5[13. 14]), but the two most distinctive titles He bestows are 'disciple' and 'apostle.' They are first to learn of Him (Mt 11[29]) the secret of calm inward strength of peace, and then they shall become heralds, messengers, apostles of that peace to the world. The Apostolate has no status except for its missionary purpose, and though the Apostles may have the power to forgive sins (Jn 20[23]), or to exorcize evil spirits (Mk 6[7]), or to heal the sick (Mt 10[8]), these are secondary to the work of preaching (Mk 6[12. 13]).

In founding this first great order in His Church, a whole night of prayer significantly precedes the all-important choice. Next day the Twelve are chosen, and after them Seventy for special and local service, and sent to preach repentance and the Kingdom of God, and to heal (Mk 3[14. 15], Mt 10[1], Lk 9[1], Mt 11[1] ['teach and preach,' as though to indicate the true fervour which will give wings to the doctrine]). They are to lead men to repentance (Mk 6[12]), over which the joy of the angels is increased (Lk 15[7. 10], ending in the parable of the Prodigal Son). They are to sow the seed of the word of life broadcast, on all soils (Lk 8[4-18]); and the thought which will sustain them, even when the seed seems utterly fruitless, is that they are His representatives, and speak with His authority behind them ('He that heareth you heareth me,' Mt 10[40], Lk 10[16. 19], Jn 13[20]), for are they not His 'servants,' and 'of his household'? (Mt 10[25]). He points to one, possibly as indicating all, and says that upon him, upon the living rock of human faith and enthusiasm, and not upon the dead heights of Sinai or rock of Zion, will He build His Church (Mt 16[18]). That Church was to be distinguished by its component members. It should reveal to the world a type of character new in the combination of its qualities and representative of the Society's ideal. This perfect membership was of the future, and not immediate. Even in the inner circle of His associates Christ had to admit the lapses of the Boanerges or of Peter; they had to learn slowly what it meant to be members of the Church as Christ conceived it. The disciple must bear himself with an unswerving attitude towards the world, being filled with one overmastering idea and service (Mt 6[24], Lk 16[13]), from which he must never look back (Lk 9[62]). So complete is to be his obedience and devotion, that the nearest human ties must be broken if they conflict with this vocation (Lk 15[26], Mt 10[37]), and entire renunciation of 'all that he hath' become his rule (Lk 14[33]), though not with the impulse of a blind fanaticism, but with the calm and measured reasoning of the king going to war, or the builder of a tower (Lk 14[28-33]); for calmness, trust in God, absence of fretful anxiety, is the note of the single-minded disciple (Mt 6[22-34]). Hence he will need to make no elaborate apologies for his faith, for God will inspire him when the time for utterance arrives, prophecy being one of the marks of primitive discipleship (Mt 10[19], Mk 13[11], Lk 12[11]). As a soldier, he must look for hardship as his lot, expect no ready welcome everywhere, not bid the fire of heaven fall on those who heed him not (Lk 9[53f.]), but anticipate the burden of the cross (Lk 14[27]), submit to be 'hated of all men for my sake (Mt 10[22]), fearlessly enduring persecution even unto death (v.[28]). As being on active service, each member must guard against encumbrances, possessions that, accumulating, hinder. If the rich young man would be a 'perfect' disciple, he must part with that which now shares his care and attention (Mt 19[21], Lk 18[22]): the disciple must go forth wasting no thought upon purse, wallet, or clothes, losing no time in mere gossip, 'salutations by the way' (Lk 10[4], Mk 6[8], Mt 10[10]). He renounces for the sake of his high mission, not for the boastful and purposeless contempt of an Essene. His aloofness from possessions is consecrated by the lowly simplicity of his spirit, which, already dwelling in the Kingdom of heaven, proclaims it with the artlessness of a little child (Mt 18[1], Mk 9[34], Lk 9[48]), and with the same generous desire to share all his possessions, spiritual as well as temporal, with others (Ac 2[44 4[32] and the Pauline comment Gal 2[9]). He may find himself a lamb among wolves (Lk 10[3]), but he will still show his discipleship by that love of men which first commissioned him (Jn 13[35]). He will learn to see brothers in all workers for good, whatever name they bear, for 'he that is not against us is for us' (Mk 9[38], Lk 9[50]), and the 'false prophets' he will easily discern by their spiritual unfruitfulness, though they call on the Name and work miracles (Mt 7[22]). These signs of the perfect member of the body of Christ will be the gradual outcome of the hidden inward life: no school can make it; it will spring from the inner sincerity of devotion and character, the 'prayer, alms, fasting' 'in secret' of Mt 6[1-18].

In founding the Church, whose main purpose should be the reconciliation of man to God, Christ's chief act of organization was connected with the material that should form the Church,—the primary Apostles, and the larger group of disciples who should foreshadow the ultimate attainment. To perfect them was the chief necessity : to make them the shining, guiding lights of the world, who in the after-days should do even greater things on earth than He Himself (Jn 14[12]). Hence, perhaps, the little He says about the elements of external religion. He certainly accepted from the past the act of baptism as employed by John (Mt 21[25] ‖ Mk 11[30], Lk 20[4]), and commanded its practice (Mt 28[19]), though not Himself actually baptizing (Jn 4[2]), and clearly impressing one Apostle with the minor importance of baptism (1 Co 1[17]) as compared with preaching—the baptism of the Spirit (Mt 3[11] ‖ Mk 1[8], Lk 3[16], Jn 1[26]). He accepted the Sabbath of His people, but only subject to the good and needs of man (Mt 12[8], Mk 2[27], Lk 6[5]), so that His followers afterwards felt free to change the day. While He organized prayer to the extent that it should be always in His name (Mt 18[20], Jn 14[13] 15[16] 16[26]), and showed the spirit of that command in the prayer taught to His disciples, He would have it liberated from the formalism and 'vain repetitions' of the past and of the heathen (Mt 6[7]). He adopted no systematized body of teaching, or of technical Rabbinic discipline, and no casuistic expounding of Scripture. The one new institution He delivered into the keeping of His followers was in the consecration of that Last Supper destined to be the first of an ageless series, and to be the perpetual symbol of the vital union of the Church and its Lord in things visible and invisible (Mt 26[26. 27], Mk 14[22], Lk 22[19]).

If, then, we ask what organization appears to exist on the night of the Crucifixion, we seem to find little that could satisfy the representative ecclesiastical mind. There is throughout Galilee and in Jerusalem a vaguely connected number of believers in Jesus. These know, in more or less detail, the kind of witness that is expected of them before the world, a manifestation that, once realized, would mark them out from the world more plainly than Jew from Roman. They are bound together by this unity of character, which, once attained, will be the presence of the Kingdom of God to each one. Their leaders are eleven of their Lord's intimates, chosen by Him as teachers and preachers of His word. For outward helps they have the institutions of Judaism, with the baptism of John ; the continual remembrance of Christ through praying in His name, and in the prayer He had given ; and in the communion of the Lord's Supper.

But in the Acts and the Epistles we meet with a development of organization arising chiefly out of local necessities. Whilst remaining Jews and attending worship at the Temple (Ac 3[1]), the disciples gradually became more conscious of the necessity of something in the nature of a separate community. Meetings of sympathizers, which were also open to any who would come (1 Co 14[23]), were planned, and since they could not be held in the synagogues (Ac 6[9]), private houses were used (Ac 2[46] 5[42] 18[7], Ro 16[5], 1 Co 16[15], Col 4[15]). Here were held gatherings for common prayer, for the breaking of bread, for Apostolic teaching and fellowship (Ac 2[42]), and for the moral edification of those present. As the first community at Jerusalem increased in numbers, it was found to be necessary to organize a group of helpers for the distribution of charity and the general ministrations (διακονίαι, Ro 12[7], 1 Co 12[5]) of almonry (Ac 6[1-6]), though for the full 'work of the ministry' other gifts and opportunities would enter in (Eph 4[12]). The Apostles continued to spend themselves in preaching and in prayer ; and as they needed assistance in these, they would naturally turn to their 'helps' (1 Co 12[28]), those 'men of good

report, full of the Spirit and of wisdom' (Ac 6[3]), who would thus, by giving occasional instruction and spiritual guidance, become practising ministers of the word, though their almonry would remain the distinctive duty of these 'deacons,' and the key to their expected morality (1 Ti 3[8ff.]), especially during the brief period of Apostolic communion (Ac 2[44. 45]).

The Church still consisted of those called disciples, but slowly it assumed a more visible membership. Baptism became the recognized entrance ; baptism 'into the name of Christ' (Ac 2[38] 8[16] 10[48] 19[5], Ro 6[3], Gal 3[27]) — in St. Paul's thought a spiritual cleansing (1 Co 6[11]), a mystical burial before the rising of the new life (Col 2[12]). Each member was to offer sacrifices of praise and thanks (He 13[15]), might teach (Ja 3[1]), and pray with immediate access to God (Eph 3[12]), and would receive direct illumination (Jn 1[9], 1 Jn 2[27]). Each was a temple of the Holy Spirit (1 Co 6[19]), and was to be given up entirely (mentally, physically, and spiritually) to God (Ro 12[1. 2]), unto a renewed life of righteousness and holiness (Eph 4[24]). Their common name steadily underwent changes that marked a more organized body. From 'disciples,' the followers and learners of Jesus, they became more conscious of mutual bonds of faith and consecration, so that ἀδελφοί ('brothers') better described them (Ac 28[14]), since in the fellowship of Christ they had abolished the demarcations of nation, wealth, position, and sex (Gal 3[28], Col 3[11]), and had attained to that kinship which is as close as that of mother and brethren (Lk 8[21]). Afterwards the religious sense of the brotherhood led them to a new name for the members, οἱ ἅγιοι ('the saints'), those who are striving after holiness (1 Co 1[2], Ro 1[7]). They are already looked upon as a school, a sect, a party (αἵρεσις) by outsiders (Ac 24[5. 14] 28[22]), so that these first communities of 'the holy ones' were being welded together openly. Their government was not sacerdotal, the name 'priest' occurring in the NT only when used of the whole society (1 P 2[5. 9], Rev 1[6] 5[10]). At their head were still the Apostles, strong by their commission from Christ (Mt 10[2], Lk 6[13], Mk 3[14 marg.] 6[7. 30]), and increased in numbers through the guidance of the Holy Spirit, Paul, Barnabas, Matthias, and others being added (1 Co 9[6], Gal 1[19], Ro 16[7], 1 Th 2[6]). Their faith and zeal had been renewed by the vision of the risen Lord (Ac 1[21. 22], 1 Co 9[1] 15[7]), and in that faith they had wrought wondrous signs of their Apostolate (2 Co 12[12]). But with the growth of the membership of the Church, and the formation of many isolated congregations, superintendents or presidents (πρεσβύτεροι) were needed and appointed, whose duties soon included that of teaching as well as governing the general affairs (1 Ti 3[2] 5[17], Tit 1[9]). Their equivalent title in Greek cities would seem to have been 'overseers,' 'bishops' (ἐπίσκοποι, Ph 1[1], Tit 1[7]), and their duties the same, namely, attending to the poor and the sick, helping travelling brethren, exercising discipline towards wrong-doers, and the general administration of the community's business. So that, although St. Paul mentions many offices in the Church (1 Co 12[28], Eph 4[11]), two orders only stand out clearly in the NT after the Apostles, that of the presbyters or elders, and that of the deacons. The prophetic office is too nearly allied to the Apostolic to be easily distinguished, though Jesus speaks of it as of something known universally (Mt 7[22] 10[41] 23[34]) ; St. John speaks of the Church as 'the saints, apostles, and prophets' (Rev 18[20. 24]) ; and Acts names some (Ac 11[27] 21[10] 15[32]).

In the organization of the Church, doctrine began to be more settled. While Jesus lived, and in His own life could show the blessedness of the Kingdom of God within, men could not go far astray. But afterwards it was necessary to tell of Him, His sayings and doings, His warnings, His ideals, and the purpose of His life. The Apostles would question whether the future would guard these truly, or add to, alter, or take away. So a body of things needful to be taught was collected, and, for the Gentile world, the OT added as an introduction to the comprehension of Christ. To some such collection St. Paul alludes in Ro 6[17], 2 Th 2[15]; but for the knowledge of this the whole NT is our only source to-day. Thence we gather, besides many conflicting modern readings of great doctrines, a general agreement as to the practices of the early Church. We find them still meeting for a while on the Sabbath, the Lord's day commemorating the Resurrection and only later becoming the rest-day. At their meetings would be celebrated the Love-Feast, sometimes hardly distinguishable from the Lord's Supper. Here would be the gathering for common prayer, of the form of which we know nothing, the Epistles quoting no regular prayer, referring to no liturgical order, and not even alluding to the Lord's Prayer. Afterwards the fund for the poorer brethren would be collected (Ac 4[35], Gal 2[10], Ro 15[26]).

So that which comes to be known by the Greek pagan title ἐκκλησία, 'the Church,' is gradually organized. She begins in the mind of Christ, free, unlimited, the universal Kingdom of God, with no sacred seasons, sanctuaries, or priesthood. But her Founder knows that her work is among men, and that she must be humanly as well as Divinely developed. So the limitations of organized life are lightly imposed upon her, not to hinder but to increase effectiveness. Still will she cherish the liberty to which the past has brought her (Gal 3[24]), and receive both good and evil into her net (Lk 5[6], 2 Ti 2[20]), for she strives to save all. The outward organization develops, but, while we keep to the pages of the NT, the spirit of the Church is still master of her organization, still looks to the Invisible Church, yet to be, of those made perfect, where the unrighteous have no place (1 Co 6[9] 15[50], Gal 5[21], Eph 5[5]), the assembly of those made perfect through love (Ja 2[5]), the everlasting Kingdom of our Lord (2 P 1[11]), into which the few have already entered here upon earth—'Theirs is the kingdom of heaven' (Mt 5[3. 10], Lk 6[20]). See also CHURCH.

LITERATURE.—For detailed treatment of the Church offices and officers, the following may be consulted out of the abundant literature on these subjects: Hatch, *Organiz. of the Early Christian Churches*, Lightfoot, *Philipp.*, Dissert. i. (repub. as *The Christian Ministry*), and *Galatians*, Excursus on 'Apostle'; Ramsay, *Church in the Roman Empire*; Hort, *Ecclesia*; Weizsäcker, *Apost. Age*, Eng. tr. vol. ii. bk. 5; McGiffert, *Christianity in the Apost. Age*, 645 ff.; Hausrath, *NT Times*, vol. ii.; Lindsay, *Church and Ministry*; artt. 'Apostle,' 'Bishop,' 'Baptism' (esp. pp. 240–242), 'Church,' 'Church Government,' 'Deacon,' 'Lord's Supper,' and 'Lord's Day' in Hastings' *DB*.

EDGAR DAPLYN.

ORIGINALITY. — It is not surprising that attempts should have been made to dispute Christ's claim to originality. Under whichever aspect we regard His Person, whether we consider Him in His historical relations, or contemplate the eternal truth revealed in Him, on either side opportunity presents itself for disputing the originality of His doctrine. Under the former aspect this is manifestly the case. However fully we may be convinced of the novelty of the doctrine of the Saviour, nobody fancies that that doctrine was without historical connexion with what had gone before. As in the Saviour's Person the Divine revealed itself in human form, so in His doctrine the Divine truth which He had to communicate clothed itself in the language and thought of the time in which He lived. Though He was the Son of God, He was also the child of His own age and people. Though the truth that He revealed was eternal, it was addressed, in the first instance, to the people of the country and time in which He lived, and linked itself at countless points to the religious ideas and hopes of those who listened to His preaching. And under this aspect of the Saviour's doctrine the question presents itself, whether it may not be sufficiently accounted for on the lines of a natural development of the religious tendencies of the age in which He lived, and whether He has indeed contributed anything new and original to the religious history of the world.

But, on the other hand, the tendency to emphasize the eternal truth revealed in the Person of Christ, while it seems to rebut such attempts to reduce His doctrine to the product of the religious developments of the age in which He lived, may lead indirectly to the challenging of His originality from another side. The religion which Christ has founded is recognized as a universal religion—a religion destined not for any particular people, but for all mankind. As such it must appeal to the deepest cravings of the human heart, and satisfy those yearnings which had found expression in the thoughts and aspirations of the teachers who had gone before Him. Christ came in the fulness of time. The course of the world's history before Him had been one long preparation for the revelation given in His Person. The Spirit of God had been at work in the hearts of mankind from the beginning, guiding them gradually to the truth. The very fact that the truth which Christ proclaimed is eternal, may be regarded as a proof that He can lay no claim to originality in the declaration of it. There had been countless anticipations of it in the teachers who had gone before. He did but formulate the truth upon which the mind of man had been brooding from the beginning. 'Nam res ipsa,' says Augustine (*Retract.* i. c. 12), 'quæ nunc Christiana religio nuncupatur, erat et apud antiquos, nec defuit ab initio generis humani quousque Christus veniret in carne, unde vera religio, quæ jam erat, cœpit appellari Christiana.' It is easy to understand how, from this point of view, arguments might be urged against the originality of Christ, in a spirit very different from that which animates Augustine in his remark. Attempts have been made to prove that the truth revealed in Christ had been anticipated by the sages and religious teachers who had gone before Him. The literature of the ancient world has been ransacked to discover parallels to the doctrine of Christ. And on the strength of the occasional points of resemblance, which have been thus collected, between the teaching of the Saviour and that of those who have gone before Him, the originality of Christ has been disputed, and His claim to be the founder of a new religion denied.

We propose to consider some of the attempts which have thus been made from different sides to prove the indebtedness of Christ to those who preceded Him, and to discuss the worth of the charge of want of originality based upon the evidence thus adduced. In some of the cases we have to consider, it is the question of the originality not so much of Christ as of Christianity that is involved, as the Person of Christ is either left out of account as a pure piece of fiction, or reduced to such mean proportions as rob it of all historical significance. But inasmuch as in such cases the attempt is made to disprove the originality of that religious movement which we, at any rate, associate with the Person of Christ, we may fitly consider them here, so far, at least, as the criticism in question involves the doctrine of the Master as distinguished from the Apostles.

i. Christianity and Græco-Roman thought. — Occasional attempts have been made to trace the indebtedness of Christianity to Greek and Græco-Roman thought. We do not refer here to the endeavours of such men as Hatch and Harnack to prove the influence of Greek philosophy on the development of Christian doctrine, but to the much more revolutionary tendency of such writers as Bruno Bauer and Ernest Havet, who have sought to account not only for the development of Christian doctrine, but for the origin of Christianity itself, upon such lines.

In his work, *Christus und die Cæsaren: Der Ursprung des Christenthums aus dem römischen Griechenthum* (1377, 2nd ed. 1879), Bauer seriously undertakes to prove that Christianity is not Jewish in its origin, but is really the product of Græco-Roman thought. Its birthplace was not Palestine, but the two cities in which the blending of East and West took place,—Alexandria and Rome. Judaism in its monotheism did but give the skeleton; it was the West that gave the soul. Philo and Seneca were its real founders. At Alexandria, Judaism was enriched by a combination of the Platonic world of ideas with the Heraclitic Logos. Philo made of this Logos a priestly mediator who brings the extremes of the Divine and the human into relation to one another. Seneca gave to this mediator reality, brought him down to earth into touch with men, and made him approve himself by suffering. In the picture he has painted of the ideal man who would one day arise and fulfil the destiny of mankind, he is the real creator of the Christian Messiah. He introduced to the masses the wisdom of Greece, with its call to self-denial and renunciation of the world, whereby man may attain to God-likeness and eternal peace. It was Seneca who laid the foundation for Christian Rome. In the contrast which he presents between the old law with its formal requirements and the new with its higher, more spiritualistic demands, he has supplied the theme for the Sermon on the Mount. Many of his sayings have been reproduced in the NT, sometimes in a manner which conclusively proves the secondariness of the Scripture version. It is true that he is never mentioned by name in the NT. This Bauer would explain by the fact that the NT literature is so late in date that its compilers were ignorant of the fact that Seneca was the author of the maxims which were current among the society for whom they wrote. Still, in some cases the correspondence between the NT parallels and the original utterances of Seneca is so close, that Bauer is of opinion that the NT authors must have had the writings of the Roman sage before them.

Another factor to which Bauer attaches importance in accounting for the origin of Christianity, is the influence of the political conditions of the time. Despair over the downfall of the Republic, which seemed to portend the end of the world, awakened the yearning for a new spiritual world. The levelling of classes, which followed on the establishment of the Empire, begot a faith in human rights and inspired a feeling of mutual dependence such as the Republic had never awakened. Further, the emperors themselves contributed to the ideal which was gradually taking shape in the mind of the age. The Christian Saviour and the Roman emperors are both products of the same tendency, which sought to sum up the aspirations and immaterial goods of antiquity in one personal, all-powerful form. Augustus was the prince of peace who healed the wounds of the Civil War; Tiberius, the servant of the community; Caligula, the god-man and world-judge; Nero, the philanthropist who dedicated himself to the service of humanity; Vespasian caused the Jewish oracle, which had called him to be ruler of the world, to be carried before his legions; Nerva and his successors gave to the Roman world an example of mildness and tranquillity. The central figure of the new religion is a composite character constructed out of the aspirations and ideals of Greek philosophy and various traits borrowed from the occupants of the imperial throne, in whom the Roman world recognized the mediators between heaven and earth.

Such are the lines on which Bauer seeks to ascribe the origin of Christianity to Græco-Roman influence. It is evident that his theory involves not only the complete overturn of all but the most extreme theories as to the date of the NT literature, but also a very different reading of the course of profane history from that which has hitherto obtained. Bauer has no hesitation in setting aside the testimony of Tacitus, Suetonius, and the other Roman historians. A theory which represents Nero in the character of philanthropist, and finds in his reign an anticipation of the Messianic blessedness, makes the strongest demands on our credulity. Bauer's views as to the date of the NT writings are wild in the extreme. The Epistles to the Corinthians are a late composition of the 2nd cent.; the *Urevangelium* is ascribed to the first half of Hadrian's reign; the Apocalypse and Fourth Gospel to the time of Marcus Aurelius, the latter being an attempt to carry out systematically the Gnostic opposition to Judaism. The Jewish element in the NT is persistently denied. The author of the *Urevangelium* is 'an Italian by birth, who

was at home in Rome and Alexandria'; the author of Matthew, no Jewish Christian, but 'a Roman nourished by Seneca's spirit.' Such theories justify H. Holtzmann's characterization of Bauer as 'a critical Herostratus' (*Einl. in d. NT*, p. 183). If their very wildness calls for no serious refutation, it at any rate serves to demonstrate the impracticability of the attempt to assign a Hellenic origin to Christianity.

Havet's work, *Le Christianisme et ses Origines*, is on somewhat similar lines, but much more moderate in tone.

There are, Havet thinks, three elements to be taken into account in considering the origin of Christianity, the Hellenic, the Jewish, represented by the Prophets and the Psalms, and a third which he calls the Galilæan, by which he means the sentiments and ideas which developed at first among the turbulent population of Galilee under the misery of the Roman dominion, and then raised up Jesus, and determined His action and destiny, and which gradually spread throughout the great cities of the Roman Empire. He admits that Christianity is not to be found '*tout entier*' in Hellenism, but insists, on the other hand, that however large may be the share of Galilæan Judaism in the Christian revolution, far more considerable is that of Hellenism in Christianity once it was established. We must distinguish, he contends, between the essence and the accident, between the Christian spirit and the Christian revolution. The Christian revolution came from Judæa and Galilee. But the Christian spirit is essentially that of Græco-Roman philosophy and religion. On the appearance of Christianity it was not the faith and wisdom of Hellenism that were absorbed into Judaism, but Judaism that was absorbed into the common beliefs of the human race. In order to establish this contention, Havet gives an exhaustive examination of Hellenic literature from the earliest times, making an anthology of all the passages which seem to breathe anything of the Christian spirit. In summarizing his conclusions, he paints a picture of the heathen world designed to show how nearly it approached to Christianity in its beliefs and hopes. The heathen believed in the immortality of the soul, in the resurrection of the dead, in a future life with punishments and rewards, in the existence of gods who were offended by the faults of men, in the approaching end of this world and the coming of a new one. They had their temples, their altars, their prayers, their sacred songs; while there were not wanting among them loftier spirits who held that the divinity desired no other temple than the heart of man, nor other worship than the practice of virtue. Their moral code breathed the same spirit of self-denial as Christianity inculcated; taught men to despise riches, honours, pleasures, yea, happiness itself; inspired an abhorrence of sin, a consciousness of our moral infirmity, and a passionate longing for salvation; inculcated chastity, alms, charity, a horror of war, submission to authority. How is it possible, asks Havet, with such a picture before us, to speak of Christianity as renewing the face of the earth, or to hail its advent as something entirely new and unexpected? He believes that the heathen world, if left to itself, would not have remained heathen, that its mythology and superstition would gradually have vanished, and that the feeling of human fraternity and the need of equality and justice would have developed more and more and passed into its manners and laws. This natural development it was not permitted to pursue. The Judaizers precipitated the crisis; the reform was carried through with too great haste, with the result that the world, in becoming Christian, remained more pagan than if Hellenism had retained its mastery.

While Havet recognizes that Judaism thus played a considerable part in the origin of Christianity, he assigns but little importance to the Person of Christ Himself in the movement which bore His name. He believes that John the Baptist was the principal personage in the religious revolution of which Jesus has the honour. Of the life of Jesus Himself we know almost nothing. Havet denies that He claimed to be the Christ, and that He was tried before the Sanhedrin and condemned for blasphemy or any religious crime. He did not break with Judaism, nor was He the opponent of the Pharisees in the way He is represented in the Gospels. He was a Jew, ardent to fanaticism, a Galilæan zealot who had inflamed the people of His country, and, in the end, so agitated Jerusalem itself that the Jewish authorities, whom He had compromised, handed Him over to the Roman police, by whom He was put to death as a disturber of the peace. At the moment of His death, that which we call Christianity had no existence. He was Himself a Christian only in His manner of feeling; otherwise He was a pure Jew, and there is neither word nor act in His life that is not thoroughly Jewish. He introduced no new dogma or practice. He had no conception of the Trinity, or the Incarnation, or other mysteries,—no idea of Church or Sacraments. It was not till after His death that some began to ask, 'Was He not the Christ?', and the thought once started gained currency. In order to give the suggestion any plausibility, it was necessary to combine with it the belief that this Jesus who had perished miserably had been raised up from the dead to enter on a life of glory. If Jesus was the Christ, then all was not finished. He must reappear. He must come again as the Christ on the clouds of heaven to destroy this wicked world and restore Israel. The hope thus cherished was converted into actual fact. The step was taken from the thought, 'He must rise again,' to the belief, 'He has risen.' The news spread among the Jewish communities scattered throughout the Roman Empire, and from them to the Roman world in the midst of which they lived, that the Christ, who was to come to inaugurate the kingdom of the God of the Jews in place of that of the Romans, had actually appeared, that He had been crucified, and had risen from the dead, and was to reappear to destroy the sinners, and to raise up from the dead all the righteous, and reunite them in an eternal life with those who were still alive. With faith in Christ and His resurrection, the Gentile converts to the new faith accepted also the worship of the one God alone, and the denial of idolatry; while in their turn they set aside, in the name of Christ, the more repugnant elements of Judaism, particularly circumcision. This purified Judaism purified itself more and more as it spread among the Gentiles, and became permeated by the spirit of Greek philosophy. The two spirits came in time to be confounded.

Such is Havet's account of the origin of Christianity. Although his theories are not so extreme as those of Bauer, his attempt to assign Hellenic culture as the main source from which Christianity has sprung serves, equally with Bauer's, to illustrate to what desperate expedients such a theory is reduced in order to give itself even some measure of plausibility. Both essays result in the attempt to explain Christianity without the Person of Christ; for though Havet does not, like Bauer, deny the existence of Christ altogether, there are few Christians who will recognize, in the Jewish fanatic whom he presents to us, the Saviour whom they worship. We must allow to both authors—to Havet especially—a certain merit, in so far as they demonstrate how well Greek thought had prepared the soil for the seeds of Christian truth. As contributions to the study of the early history of the Christian Church and the development of Christian doctrine, their works may prove of value; but as accounts of the origin of Christianity itself, we cannot assign to them any worth (Harnack, *Hist. of Dogma*, Eng. tr. i. 52 f.). They virtually recognize the impracticability of any attempt to trace the indebtedness of the historical Jesus to Hellenic culture. Whatever parallels they may bring forward to any of the recorded utterances of Jesus, they make no attempt to show in what way He could have been brought into contact with the literature from which He is supposed to have derived inspiration. Only by critical theories regarding the Gospels which would deprive them of all historical worth, can they find room to introduce that Hellenic influence which they seek to trace.

ii. **Christianity and Buddhism.**—From the side of Buddhism, also, attacks have been made on the originality of Christianity. It is an undoubted fact, that long before the Christian era Buddhist doctrine had penetrated to distant regions, and the possibility of the indebtedness of the Christian Gospels to the Buddha legend is not so remote as to be dismissed without careful consideration. Various attempts have been made to prove that much of the material in the Gospel narratives may be traced to Buddhist sources—notably by Bunsen, Seydel, Lillie, and more recently by Stix, Pfleiderer, and van den Bergh van Eysinga (for titles of works see below in list of Literature). Among the earlier group of writers, Seydel is generally recognized to be the most scholarly; and we may devote our attention chiefly to him. In his book, *Das Evangelium Jesu in seinen Verhältnissen zu Buddhasage und Buddha-lehre*, he endeavours to construct a 'Buddhist-Christian Gospel Harmony' by drawing up a list of the parallels that may be traced between the two religions.

In all, Seydel collects 51 such parallels, which he proceeds to arrange in 3 groups. In the first he places those resemblances which may be accidental; in the second, those cases in which we are forced to conclude that there has been borrowing on one side or the other. The third group contains parallels in which it is clear not only that there has been borrowing, but on which side the borrowing has taken place. This last group contains only five parallels, and in each case Seydel concludes that the verdict must be given in favour of Buddhism. They are as follows:—(1) the presentation of the infant Jesus in the Temple, compared with that of Buddha; (2) the fast of Jesus and of Buddha; (3) the pre-existence of Jesus and of Buddha; (4) the fig-tree as the place of Buddha's first conversion, compared with Jesus' interview with Nathanael (Jn 1⁴⁶ff.); (5) the question of the disciples regarding the man who was born blind (Jn 9²), which seems to imply a former state of existence whose sinfulness might account for present affliction. The verdict in favour of Buddhism in this third group of parallels strengthens the probability that in the second group also it is Christianity that is the debtor. In this group the number of parallels runs to 23, 12 of which Seydel regards as of greater cogency than the rest. Among the Gospel facts which he introduces in this first division of his second group may be mentioned the annunciation to Mary, the gifts to the newborn child, the temptation, and the Beatitudes. Lastly, even in the first group of 23 parallels, which Seydel admits may be wholly accidental, he believes that in view of the conclusions reached by an examination of the two other groups, there is a possibility that in at least 15 cases the Gospels may have been subject to Buddhist influence.

To account for the presence of so much material in the Gospels borrowed from Buddhist sources, Seydel formulates the hypothesis that, in addition to the two sources generally recognized as underlying the Synoptic Gospels—the collection of Sayings, and the original Mark—there must also have existed a third source, a poetic-apocalyptic Gospel, in which the Christian material must have been worked up after the pattern of the Buddhist Gospels, with the incorporation of much that was derived from Buddhist sources. This poetic source was used by all the Synoptists and the Fourth Evangelist as well. That it has been lost is to be explained by the fact that the available material which it afforded had been incorporated in the Gospels, whose more historical form and genuine Christian doctrine caused the early poetical work to be quite forgotten.

Seydel claims a certain apologetic value for his investigations. If he has shaken our faith in much in the Gospel narratives which he has shown to be derived from Buddhism, we may comfort ourselves, he thinks, with the reflexion that those features in the life of Jesus to which he has found no analogy in Buddhist tradition,—such, *e.g.*, as the Passion and certain fundamental doctrines and personal characteristics of Jesus,—are thus indirectly confirmed. In what remains after we have taken away what may be traced to Buddhism, we have a kernel of historical fact which is unassailable.

When we turn to examine the various parallels upon which Seydel bases his contention, we find that the resemblance between the Christian and the Buddhist material is frequently exaggerated; that but little attention is paid to the underlying difference between the two sides, which in many cases is much more striking than the apparent resemblance; and that, even where the resemblance is strongest, Seydel has not made out his case, viz., that the fact which he instances from the Gospels is so unintelligible on Christian premises, that borrowing from an external source is the only feasible explanation. We shall endeavour to justify this contention in the case of the five parallels upon which Seydel lays the greatest stress.

(1) The Presentation in the Temple. Here Seydel's point is that such presentation of the infant Jesus was not required, and that Luke's appeal to the Law (2²³) is a mere device to introduce an incident borrowed from a foreign source. We admit that it was not necessary that the infant should be presented in person on the occasion of its being ransomed; but we have only to read the account of the presentation of the infant Buddha, which Seydel thinks may have suggested this incident, with its description of how 100,000 gods drew the waggon which bore him, of how the earth trembled as he entered the temple, of how the images of the gods left their places to throw themselves at his feet, to convince ourselves that among the various motives which might be assigned for the departure from the strict letter of the Law in the case of Jesus, a more unlikely one could hardly be conceived than a desire to institute a parallel with this fantastic story, to which the simple Gospel narrative offers the most striking contrast.

(2) Seydel finds the 40 days' fast of Jesus in the wilderness inexplicable in view of the contrast He Himself drew between His own conduct and the asceticism practised by John the Baptist, and suggests that this incident is borrowed from the example of Buddha. But if any parallel at all is required, we do not need to go so far afield. The 40 days' fast of Moses (Ex 34²⁸, Dt 9⁹) and that of Elijah (1 K 19⁸) at once suggest themselves as parallels which do not take us beyond the limits of Jewish history.

(3) Seydel finds a parallel to Christ's words to the Jews, 'Before Abraham was, I am' (Jn 8⁵⁸), in Buddha's assertion of his pre-existence. But the resemblance at once disappears when we realize what is the kind of pre-existence Buddha claims for himself,—not like that of the Johannine Logos who

has been with God from the beginning (Jn 1$^{1f.}$), but that of a being who has undergone countless different forms of incarnation.

(4) It was while sitting under the Bodhi-tree, which was a kind of fig-tree, that Gautama attained Budda-hood, and immediately thereafter converted two brothers, who became his first disciples. Seydel finds a parallel to this in the words of Jesus to Nathanael, 'When thou wast under the fig-tree, I saw thee' (Jn 1^{48}). But beyond the facts that a fig-tree and a disciple are mentioned in both cases, there is no resemblance between them. It was not Jesus, but Nathanael, who was sitting under the fig-tree; there is no suggestion of the 'enlightenment' of Jesus; and the disciple in connexion with whom the fig-tree is mentioned was not, as in Buddha's case, the first who was called.

(5) The question of the disciples with regard to the man who was born blind, 'Master, who did sin, this man or his parents, that he was born blind?' (Jn 9^2) is brought forward by Seydel as implying belief in the Buddhist doctrine of re-birth, according to which we are punished here for sins committed in a former state of existence. But the doctrine of the pre-existence of the soul was not unknown to the Jews (cf. Wis 8^{20}), and it is questionable, further, whether even this doctrine is necessary to explain the question of the disciples. They may have been thinking of some sin committed in the womb (cf. Gen 25^{22}), or may have regarded the blindness of the man as punishment in anticipation of the sins he would commit (cf. B. Weiss in Meyer's *Kommentar, ad loc.*).

These are the parallels upon which, as has been said, Seydel lays the chief stress. He admits himself that the force of the other analogies depends, in great measure, upon the verdict we pass upon the evidence afforded by these five parallels, which constitute his third group. And if, as we have endeavoured to show, he has not made good his case in these instances, much of the force of his argument is gone. As to his hypothesis of the existence of a poetic-apocalyptic Gospel imbued with Buddhist doctrine, there is absolutely no proof for the existence of such a document. Seydel can bring forward no particle of evidence to support his hypothesis. He merely invents this fictitious Gospel to supply the lack of historical connexion between Buddhism and Christianity, the want of which is one of the strongest objections to his theory.

As remarked above, attempts have been made more recently by Pfleiderer and van den Bergh van Eysinga to trace Buddhist influence on the Gospel narratives. Among the parallels which the latter finds specially important, may be mentioned Simeon in the Temple, the twelve-year-old Jesus, the baptism of Jesus, the temptation, the blessing of the mother of Jesus (Lk 11^{27}), the widow's mite, the walking on the sea, the Samaritan woman at the well, and the world conflagration. Pfleiderer does not descend so much into detail, but groups his parallels together under general heads, such as Christ as Son of God, as miraculous Saviour, as victor over Satan, as King of kings, etc. With regard to these more recent works, the same criticism applies as in the case of Seydel. Many of the suggested parallels, when closely examined, prove much less striking than appeared at first sight; and even where the resemblance is closest, a much more natural explanation can usually be given of the feature in question on the Christian side than the adaptation of Buddhist material. And due consideration should here be given to the fact to which Oldenberg has called attention (*ThLZ*, 1905, No. 3), that the Buddhist literature which is drawn upon to supply these parallels to Christianity is so extensive, so infinitely rich in legendary lore, that the wonder would rather be if we did not find occasional points of resemblance between the Buddhist narratives and those parts of the NT which deal with a similar sphere of life. Finally, while we must admit in the abstract the possibility of Buddhist influence upon Western culture, the fact remains that we have no historical evidence of the spread of Buddhist ideas to the regions in which Christianity had its origin till a much later time. Clement of Alexandria is the first who mentions Buddha by name. In this connexion we may quote the words of Max Müller (*India, what it can teach us?* p. 279):

'That there are startling coincidences between Buddhism and Christianity cannot be denied, and it must likewise be admitted that Buddhism existed at least 400 years before Christianity. I go even further, and should feel extremely grateful if anybody would point out to me the historical channels through which Buddhism had influenced early Christianity. I have been looking for such channels all my life, but hitherto I have found none. What I have found is that for some of the most startling coincidences there are historical antecedents on both sides, and if we once know those antecedents, the coincidences become far less startling. If I do find, in certain Buddhist works, doctrines identically the same as in Christianity, so far from being frightened, I feel delighted, for surely truth is not the less true because it is believed by the majority of the human race.'

iii. **Christianity and Judaism.**—When we come to consider the relation of Christianity to Judaism, we feel that the case is very different from what it was in the above instances. There the possibility of contact between Christianity and those influences to which its indebtedness was alleged was remote. Here we are in the line of direct historical connexion. The roots of Christianity go deep down into Jewish soil. Christ was a Jew by birth and education. His whole thought and teaching were cast in Jewish moulds. The very title He bears—the Christ—is meaningless apart from the background of Jewish history in which it had its origin. If we claim originality for Him, we recognize that originality does not mean an entirely new start, the severance of all the links which bind the new Teacher to the religious development of the nation to which He belongs. Such originality is an idle figment of the imagination. It never has existed; it never can exist. If the original teacher is to be a teacher at all, if he is to exercise any influence upon the men he addresses, then he must live in close contact with them and link on his doctrine to the beliefs and hopes which they cherish. So it was with Christ. He may be the world's Teacher, but He spoke first of all to His fellow-countrymen in Galilee and Judæa, and He used the modes of thought and speech familiar to them. He preached in their synagogues and taught in their streets like the Rabbis of His own day. That there was a certain novelty in His manner of preaching is proved by the astonishment with which the people listened to it (Mk 1^{22} 6^2). But was the content essentially different from that of the preachers of His own day, or that of the prophets of old? Had He any new doctrine to communicate? Or was He, as has been alleged by modern Jewish scholars, merely a teacher who gave expression to the best Jewish thought of His time?

We proceed to consider more closely some of the different elements in the Jewish religion to which Christ's indebtedness is alleged to be so great as to detract from His originality.

(1) *The Old Testament.*—There can be no question as to Christ's obligations to the OT. How much He was influenced by it in His personal life is shown by the frequency of His quotations from it. He seems to live in it. Parallels from it suggest themselves at every turn. In critical moments of His life His thoughts find natural expression in OT quotation. So it was at the temptation (Mt 4$^{4. 7. 10}$), at the cleansing of the Temple (Mk 11^{17}), even when He hung upon the cross (15^{34}). He recognized its authority in religious matters. He appealed to it in defence of His own conduct (2$^{25f.}$). He quoted it in condemnation of the Pharisees (7$^{6. 13}$), and in refutation of the Sadducees (12$^{24f.}$). He claimed that He came not to destroy, but to fulfil the Law and the Prophets (Mt 5^{17}). And when He was asked by the rich young man what He must do to inherit eternal life, instead of imparting to him any new doctrine, He simply referred him to the commandments (Mk 10^{19}).

In view of the attitude Christ thus takes up to the OT, and of His avowed intention of fulfilling the Law and the Prophets, we should expect to find great affinity between His doctrine and that of the OT. Is this affinity so great as to detract from our Lord's originality? It is alleged by some that it is. Nay, it has been questioned, indeed, not only whether Jesus has made any new contribution to the religious and moral teaching of the OT, but whether He even desired to do so (so B. Weiss, *Leben Jesu*, i. 274). There is hardly a feature in the teaching of Christ, it is maintained, to which there is not a parallel in the OT. The constant theme of His preaching, the Kingdom of God, is so manifestly not novel, that He assumes familiarity with it on the part of His hearers, and never even explains what He means by it. His work as a Prophet, sent to announce the coming of this Kingdom and to call men to repentance, was evidently nothing novel. The very words by which the preaching of Christ is introduced by Mk. (1^{15}) are practically the same as Mt. uses to describe the appearance of John the Baptist (Mt 3^2). The God whom Christ reveals is no new God, but the God of Abraham, of Isaac, and of Jacob (Mk 12^{26}), the God of Israel (Mt 15^{31}, Mk 12^{29}). The Fatherhood of God, upon which so much emphasis is laid as the most fundamental and distinctively characteristic doctrine of Christianity, is taught in the OT. The trust in this Father which Christ seeks to inspire already finds most beautiful expression in the Psalms. The new commandment of love which Christ inculcates is so far from being new, that He Himself formulates it on occasion in language borrowed from the OT (Mk 12^{31}). Not even the widening of the circle of those whom we are required to love, so as to make it embrace our enemy as well as our neighbour, goes beyond the teaching of the OT (Ex 23$^{4f.}$, Pr 20^{22} 24^{29} 25$^{21f.}$). How, it is asked, can originality be claimed for the teaching of Christ, when He Himself takes His stand upon the OT and recognizes its authority; when He claims to reveal no other God than the God of the OT, and to continue the work of the Law and the Prophets; when we find that even those which are regarded as the most characteristic doctrines of Christianity have been forestalled in the OT?

To this it may be replied, that while it is true that Christ generally recognizes the authority of the OT, and appeals to it at times quite in the manner of the scribes, still His attitude towards it is one of freedom and independence. He discriminates between the various parts of it, and leaves aside much that does not appeal to Him. In spite of what He says in the Sermon on the Mount about fulfilling the Law and the Prophets, He does not hesitate in that same sermon to set up His own authority in opposition to the teaching of the Law. He freely criticises the Mosaic law of divorce (Mk 10$^{2ff.}$), and on the question of Sabbath observance not only exercises a freedom which scandalized His contemporaries, but claims to be invested with authority on the question (Mk 2^{28}). By His doctrine that that only could defile a man which affected his heart, He brushes aside the whole Levitical legislation as to cleanness, and raises the question from the region of the physical to that of the ethical.

It is true, indeed, that most of the elements of Christian doctrine may be found scattered throughout the OT. But they are found side by side with much else which Christ has rejected, and which, in juxtaposition with them, prevents them from having the significance they acquire in Christianity. That God is represented at times in the OT as a Father, *e.g.*, is perfectly true. But the distinguishing feature in Christ's designation of Him as such, as compared with that of the OT, is that with Christ Father is *the* characteristic title for God, and He is never represented under any aspect that is inconsistent with His Fatherhood; whereas in the OT Father is only one, and not

even the prevailing one, among various other titles for God, and God is represented at times under very different aspects. It is the same with the various other elements of Christian doctrine that have been found in the OT. They receive a new meaning from the place Christ gives them, the importance He assigns to them, and the consistency with which He insists on them. That God looks not upon the outward conduct but upon the heart, was a truth known to the OT writers no less than to Christ; but it is Christ who first consistently follows it out to its logical conclusions. That we should love our enemies is a doctrine that had been taught even in the OT; yet how much there is in the OT that breathes an entirely different spirit! When we put, not isolated utterances of Christ and of the OT, but the doctrine of Christ as a whole and the OT as a whole, side by side, then, in spite of the fact that we can trace the roots of Christianity down into Jewish soil and can find OT forecasts of much that appears in the teaching of Christ, the conviction is forced upon us that this doctrine of Christ as a whole, by the consistently lofty spirituality of its tone, by the inner coherence and harmony of its various parts in spite of the unsystematic form in which it was delivered, by its indifference to much which held a high place in the Jewish religion, is a new creation as compared with the OT upon which it is based. We feel too that only a mind of the highest originality could have evolved out of a religion in which there was much that was imperfect and unspiritual, a system so pure and lofty as that which we have in the Christian religion.

(2) *Later Judaism.*—But it is not to the OT alone that Christ's indebtedness is alleged. There are later developments of Judaism which are said to have exercised marked influence upon Him. It has been the custom to regard Christ's position as one of pure antagonism to the prevailing religious tendencies of His time, and to represent Him as standing in such irreconcilable opposition to the teaching of the Rabbinical schools that there can be no question of His being influenced by them, save in the way of being repelled. But in spite of the attitude of opposition that Christ took up to the religious authorities of His day, there was, it is alleged, much affinity between them. Like the Rabbis, He preached in the synagogues and taught in the market-places. Like them, He gathered a group of disciples round Him who called Him Master, and whom He sought specially to instruct. His manner of teaching is modelled on theirs. He delights in aphorism. He makes frequent use of illustration and example. It is from them that He has derived the parabolic method of instruction which is so characteristic a feature of His teaching. But not merely the form of His teaching, the matter also is in many cases similar to that of the Rabbis.

Many striking parallels to Christ's sayings have been found in Rabbinical literature. Hillel summed up the whole Law in the words, 'What thou wouldst not have done to thee, do not that to others.' He bade men not judge their neighbour till they came into his place. 'Raise not thyself above others.' 'If thou art where no men are, show thyself a man.' 'Be among the pupils of Aaron, who loved peace and pursued peace, who loved all creatures and guided them to the Law.' 'Be not as servants who minister to their masters upon condition of receiving a reward.' 'Do God's will as if it were thy will, that He may do thy will as if it were His will.' 'Let your neighbour's honour be as dear to you as your own.' Such are some of the more striking sayings of the Jewish Rabbis, which seem to breathe as pure a religious spirit as the teaching of Christ. Even the prayer which Christ taught His disciples, we are told, is but a shortened form of some of the older prayers of the Jewish Liturgy. It is true that in a great many cases the Rabbinical literature in which we find these parallels to the sayings of Christ dates from the 2nd cent. A.D.; and Christian apologists have endeavoured to make the most of the fact, suggesting that if there is any borrowing, the indebtedness cannot rest on the side of Christ. But that argument would be valid only if it were shown that there was any possibility of the literature in question having been influenced by Christian thought. But there is no such possibility. The Christian and the Jewish literature, as Renan (*Life of Jesus*, ch. v.) says, had scarcely any influence on one another before the 13th century. Though these parallels are from a literature which was compiled at a date later than the appearance of Christ, they are themselves older than Christ, and represent a purely Jewish development of thought.

One may dismiss this evidence against the originality of Christ in the words of Wellhausen (*IJG*[2]), 'Jewish scholars think that all that Jesus said is found in the Talmud. Yes, all, and a good deal more. Πλέον ἥμισυ παντός. The originality of Jesus consists in this, that He had the feeling for what was true and eternal amid a chaotic mass of rubbish, and that He enunciated it with the greatest emphasis.' No doubt there are occasional parallels to the words of Christ to be found in the Talmud, but there is a vast amount in the Talmud to which no parallel can be found in the preaching of Christ, for it falls lamentably short of the lofty spiritual tone which characterizes every utterance of the Saviour. Even if it be the case that we can find something corresponding to every clause of the Lord's Prayer in the Jewish Liturgy, it might still be maintained that there was originality in selecting precisely these petitions and bringing them together in such a brief and simple prayer. But indeed we are not much concerned to defend the originality of the Lord's Prayer. Christ's object was not to teach His disciples some new form of prayer, but to give expression to the deepest longings of the human heart; and it would be strange if these cravings had not already found utterance in some measure in the prayers of His fellow-countrymen. When we turn to the parallels which have been traced between sayings of Christ and quotations from the Jewish Rabbis, it will be found, on examination, that in many cases they are not so striking as they appear at first sight. For instance, the saying of Hillel which has been often quoted as an anticipation of the Golden Rule of Christ really falls far short of it. Hillel merely warns us against doing to others what we would not that they should do to us. One might conform to that maxim on grounds of selfishness. At best it requires only that we do no evil. But Christ's maxim is positive. It insists not merely that we do no evil, but that we do good, and can be carried out only by one who has his heart full of love for his brother. And, further, with regard to the parallels that are drawn between the sayings of Christ and the words of the Rabbis, we must ask what place the quotations occupy in the respective writings from which they are taken. Quotations from the Talmud which have a striking resemblance to some words of Christ may prove, when we consider the context in which they occur, to bear a different meaning from what they assume when put into juxtaposition with similar words of Christ, or may lose a great deal of the impressiveness which attaches to them when regarded as isolated utterances. Upon the whole, we conclude that little weight is to be placed upon the occasional parallels which have been found in the words of the Jewish Rabbis to sayings of Christ. The general spirit of the Rabbinical teaching is very different from Christ's. When sayings are found which seem to approach to the teaching of Christ, they are rather to be regarded as isolated utterances which rise for the moment above the general level of Rabbinical theology.

There is another branch of late Jewish literature which, it is alleged, has had a marked influence upon Christ, and from which He is said to have derived many of His leading ideas, viz. the series of Messianic-Apocalyptic writings in which the hopes and aspirations of later Judaism found expression.

There are numerous points of contact between the teaching of Christ and the literature in question. His eschatology, *e.g.*, is said to be almost entirely drawn from this source. Certainly the expectation of His second coming was a novel idea, as it presupposed a want of success on His first appearance which had not been anticipated by any of the later Apocalyptic writers. But otherwise, for the most part, He simply accepts the general eschatological programme which they had outlined. The sharp contrast in which the present age (ὁ αἰὼν οὗτος, Lk 16[8] 20[34], Mt 12[32]; ὁ καιρὸς οὗτος, Lk 18[30]) and the future (ὁ αἰὼν ὁ μέλλων, Mt 12[32]; ὁ αἰὼν ὁ ἐρχόμενος, Lk 18[30]) are set to one another, the inauguration of the new era by the miraculous intervention of God, who is to bring in the Kingdom of God with power, the belief that the Kingdom thus to be set up is to come down from heaven, whence also is to come the agent to whom is entrusted its establishment, the series of dire calamities which are to herald the approach of the new era, the great judgment scene and resurrection of the dead with which it is to be ushered in,—all these familiar features of Christ's eschatology are to be found in the writings referred to. In painting the blessedness of heaven and the torments of hell, Christ uses the colours which the Apocalyptic writers have prepared, — Abraham's bosom, the great banquet, eating bread and drinking wine in the Kingdom of God, the furnace of fire and the outer darkness. Again, the Messianic hope which Christ cherished was largely influenced by the expectation which had found expression in the Apocalyptic literature. There was much, indeed, that was sensuous in the expectation of those writers which could not appeal to Christ, and which He put aside. But under their hands the Messianic hope of the OT writers had undergone a transformation which prepared the way for the more spiritual conception of Christianity. They had widened its scope so as to make it embrace not only the nation but the world; they had detached it from earthly political ideas, and raised it to the realm of the supermundane; they had deepened and developed that tendency to individualism which had begun to show itself in the later writings of the OT. In these respects they had prepared the way for Christ, and in much of His teaching He was in sympathy with the aims, and did but develop the doctrines, of the Apocalyptic writers of later Judaism.

One might admit the truth of most of what is thus said, without in any way detracting from the originality of Christ. It is no disparagement to that originality, as we have seen, to recognize that Christ stands in close and vital connexion with those who have preceded Him, and uses the modes of thought and speech which they have made familiar. Whether, indeed, the connexion between the Messianic views of Christ and those of later Judaism is as close as has been suggested, is a question upon which there is a difference of opinion. Baldensperger answers in the affirmative, maintaining that we must no longer regard Judaism as the dark background against which Christianity stands out as something quite different, but rather as a preparatory stage on the way to Christianity. He lays special stress upon the transcendent character of its Messianism as an advance towards the spiritualism of Christianity (*Die messian. - apocalyp. Hoffnungen des Judenthums*, 1903, p. 232). This view of the relation of Christianity to later Judaism has not been accepted by other authorities. Wellhausen finds in Christianity rather a protest against the prevailing tendency of Judaism (*Skizzen und Vorarbeiten*, p. 98). So also Bousset (*Jesu Predigt in ihrem Gegensatz zum Judenthum*, 1892), who has enumerated a number of points in which the teaching of Christ is in direct conflict with the spirit of later Judaism. In view of this difference of opinion, it is evident that no very strong case has been made out to prove Christ's indebtedness to the later Jewish Apocalyptic writings. That He used the eschatological data and many of the modes of thought which are to be found in this literature, may be readily admitted. But beyond that, His general line of thought must have been little in sympathy with its spirit. There is a wide gulf between the transcendence of later Jewish Messianism, which is sometimes coarse and sensuous, and the spirituality of the Messianic hopes of Christ. Many of the most marked characteristics of later Judaism, as Bousset points out, its withdrawal of God from the world, its asceticism, its world-weariness and lack of interest in the present and yearning for the future, are directly opposed to the spirit of the Saviour's teaching. In view of these and other points of difference between the doctrine of Christ and the tendencies of later Judaism, it seems rash to attempt to trace the origin of Christianity to a system of doctrine to which, in spite of certain superficial points of resemblance, it stands in deep and radical opposition.

(3) *Essenism.* — Attempts have frequently been made to connect Christ with the Essenes, and to account for many of the characteristic features of His doctrine by deriving them from the practices of this sect. But no evidence has been brought forward to prove that Christ had any connexion with them. It is true He never refers to them, while He frequently denounces the Pharisees and Sadducees. But that fact may be easily explained by the smallness and retiring character of the sect. Ginsburg (*Essenes*, p. 24) argues that every Jew had to belong to one of the three parties, Pharisees, Sadducees, and Essenes, into which the Jews were divided at the time of Christ, and that Christ would naturally associate Himself with the Essenes as most congenial to His nature; but as his premises are quite unsupported, his conclusion has no weight whatever. The only valid ground upon which any plausible case may be made out in favour of the view that Christ had some connexion with the Essenes is, that there are several points in which His doctrine bears a considerable resemblance to theirs. Among these points of resemblance the following may be noted: prohibition of oaths, exaltation of poverty, simplicity of life, celibacy (Mt 19^{12}), feeling of brotherhood issuing in mutual service. But most of these features merely represent the high moral tone which obtains on both of the sides thus compared, and no direct connexion is required to account for the resemblance. On the other hand, there are very marked features of difference which preclude any direct connexion of Christ with the Essenes. One of the most distinctive features of the sect was its withdrawal from the world and adoption of a monastic life. Contact with strangers was supposed to communicate defilement. The conduct of Christ presented a striking contrast. He mixed freely in the life of the people. He told His disciples not to hide their light under a bushel. And, so far from thinking that mere contact with strangers caused defilement, He did not shrink even from the touch of the woman who was a sinner, or hesitate to lay His hand upon a leper. In their asceticism the Essenes went to an extreme. 'The Son of Man came eating and drinking.' In their Sabbath observance they outdid the Pharisees. There was no point on which Christ gave such offence to the rigorists. The Essenes stood aloof from the Temple, and offered no sacrifice there. Christ repaired to Jerusalem to some of the great festivals, and taught daily in the Temple. The Essenes were scrupulous to a degree on the question of purity. They had washings innumerable. Christ paid no attention to such ceremonial observances, but esteemed only purity of heart. The differences which thus separate Christ from the Essenes are broad and deep. We cannot find any connexion between Him and a sect which, by its monastic tendency, its exaltation of ceremonial observances, its formal and precise rules, could have made little appeal to Him.

iv. **The original element in Christianity.** — When we turn from these attempts to disparage the originality of Christ, and proceed to consider wherein that originality consists, we find a great variety of opinions upon the subject. Some would place all the emphasis upon the Person of Christ; others lay weight upon His methods as a teacher; others think to find the original element in His doctrine, selecting now its universalism, now its individualism, now its practical moral tendency, now its

lofty spirituality, as the characteristic feature of it; while others, again, contend that the specifically novel feature in the teaching of Christ is His announcement that the Kingdom of God is at hand, that God is about to intervene and bring in the Kingdom of God with power. We shall not confine ourselves to any one of these points of view, but proceed to indicate what appear to us some of the more important characteristics which go to make up the originality of Christ.

1. Without doubt the fullest emphasis must be laid upon *Christ's personality.* This is the most strikingly original feature in Christianity. We cannot separate the doctrine from the Person of Christ. He taught by His life no less than by His words, and it is His Person as much as His doctrine that has converted the world. There could be no more unsatisfactory method of attempting to estimate the originality of Christ than to single out various statements scattered throughout the Gospels which we believe to be unparalleled in any teaching that had gone before. 'It is not difficult to set over against every article from the preaching of Jesus an observation which deprives it of its originality. It is the Person, it is the fact of his life that is new and creates the new' (Harnack, *Hist. of Dogma*, Eng. tr. i. 73). When we approach the portrait of Christ presented in the Gospels, we at once feel that we are in the presence of One who is in the truest sense original. The moral grandeur of His character alone bears witness to the fact. It dwarfs the attainment of the greatest of human heroes, and leaves the ideals even of our noblest thinkers far behind. The very fact of its sinlessness stamps it with an originality that cannot be gainsaid. The perfect harmony that pervades the whole life, the holy peace which no trial or danger can disturb, the sublime faith, the noble optimism, the unquenchable love, the tender sympathy, the meek humility, the genial, kindly spirit which drew men to Him — these are a few of the features which go to make up that portrait which has produced such an impression on the heart of the world. We feel we are standing in the presence of One who has given in His own Person the perfect revelation of the Divine. One trait we may specially note as characteristic of that originality we are considering, viz. the tone of authority with which He ever acts and speaks. Meek and humble as He is, there is a certain majesty about Him that shines forth all the more forcibly because of the lowliness of the service to which He stoops. He sets up His own authority over against that of the Law: 'Ye have heard that it was said to them of old time . . . but I say unto you' (Mt 5$^{21f.}$ etc.). He speaks of Himself as a greater than Jonah, a greater than Solomon (12$^{41f.}$). He claims to be able to reveal the Father as no other can (11^{27}), for He stands in a relation of such intimacy to the Father that He can speak of the hidden mysteries of the Divine will as things into which He has Himself looked. Hence the ring of absolute certainty about the revelation He gives of God. Hence the tone of authority in which He announces the Divine will. Either He was the victim of the grossest self-delusion, or He stood in such a close relationship to God, and knew Himself, as the appointed Messiah, to be endowed with such authority as justified Him in speaking in a tone which in any other would be nothing short of blasphemy. There is nothing incompatible with this tone of authority, which marks the teaching of Christ, in the fact that much of His teaching, as we have seen, is closely related to the OT. In a sense His teaching may be said to be based upon the OT, in so far, viz., as in the OT He found the food which nourished His spiritual life. But it is out of the fulness of the spiritual life thus nourished that He draws His doctrine, and not directly from the OT. He speaks that He knows, and testifies that He has seen (Jn 3[11]); and what of OT teaching is reproduced in His doctrine is so transmuted and ennobled, bears so unmistakably the impress of His own personality, that it may be fitly called original. We may apply to His relation to the OT the words of the poet, and say that He

'made nobly his what he did mould;
What was another's lead, became his gold.'

Closely akin to this tone of authority which Christ assumes in His preaching is another feature which contributes to the originality of His personality, viz. the feeling that with Him a new era has arrived in the history of the world. 'The time is fulfilled, and the kingdom of God is at hand' (Mk 1[15])—that is the new message of which Christ is the bearer. The hope which animated the prophets has become a reality to Him. He told His disciples that they were blessed in that their eyes had seen the things which many prophets and kings had desired to see (Lk 10[23f.]). His whole preaching rings with glad tidings that the long expected time has come. The period of waiting is past, the new era has begun. Already the Kingdom of God is in the midst of men (Lk 17[21]). Even the tragic catastrophe to which His life is tending cannot shake His conviction that with Him the Messianic age has come. He longs for the baptism of suffering which He has to undergo, as calculated to give a mighty impetus to the movement He has begun (12[49f.]). And when the hour came for Him to lay down His life, so far from seeing in His death any frustration of the gracious work to which He had dedicated His life, He taught His disciples to look upon His blood as the seal of the New Covenant which it had been His life's work to establish.

2. The originality which we have noted as characteristic of the Person of Christ, we should expect to find reflected in *His doctrine*. It was in His doctrine that He made His authority felt (Mt 7[29]). The impression made upon those who stood in the closest relation to His Person was that He had a wonderful and life-giving doctrine to communicate (Jn 6[68]). In place of His anointment to Messianic kingship, He substituted His anointment to the prophetic office (Lk 4[18-21]), and addressed Himself to the work of preaching in fulfilment of His vocation as Messiah. Was there anything original, we ask, in His preaching, anything to justify His feeling that with His entrance on His work as a preacher the new era might be said to have begun ?

The impression made upon the people who first listened to His doctrine was that it was something new. 'A new doctrine with authority,' they exclaimed (Mk 1[27]) as they listened to His preaching for the first time. Certainly there was much that was old in His doctrine, much that did but echo the teaching of the OT. The description He gives in one of His parables of the scribe instructed in the Kingdom of heaven, applies in the first instance to Himself. He was like a householder who bringeth forth from his storeroom things new and old (Mt 13[52]). But if there was much that was old, there was much also that was new and original. As compared with the teaching of the OT, to which it stands in such close connexion, Christ's doctrine was original, as we saw above, in the freedom with which He selected only what appealed to Him, leaving aside much which from the standpoint of His contemporaries was equally, if not more important ; in the new emphasis with which it restates certain OT doctrines, and the new value it assigns to them. It was original in the simplicity of its requirements, as against the multitudinous demands which Judaism made upon the individual ; in the consistency with which it pursued its few

leading ideas—such, *e.g.*, as the righteousness of the heart as that which alone avails in God's sight —to their logical issues, not hesitating to enforce the conclusions which follow, even when they conflict with the recognized standards, as in the above case with reference to the Levitical law of cleanness (Mk 7[14-23]). It was original in the feeling of confidence that it inspired in man in relation to God, banishing that spirit of bondage which the Pharisaic attitude to the Law had produced, and putting in its place the spirit of adoption whereby we cry, 'Abba, Father' (Ro 8[15]), assuring man of the love of the Father in heaven, of the preciousness of each individual in His sight, of His willingness to bestow blessings in rich abundance upon him, to forgive his sins and give him the Kingdom. But, indeed, to do justice to the originality of Christ's doctrine, we should have to mention every feature of it. The purity of the ethical tone, the loftiness of the ideal it sets before us, the comfort it breathes to the sinful and the sinning, the depth of the love it inculcates, the zeal for righteousness it seeks to inspire, its indifference to the ceremonial in religion and interest only for the spiritual, — these are among the features which contribute to its originality. If it is true that there is scarcely a single doctrine of Christ of which we cannot find some anticipation in the OT, it is also true that there is no OT doctrine which Christ reiterates but receives a new significance from the setting it obtains in His teaching. This is the strikingly original feature about His doctrine,—how He makes the old new by the new light in which He places it, and the new value He assigns to it. Much that He taught had been taught before. But never had it been proclaimed with such assurance, never had it been brought home to the heart of man with such conviction, as when it was taught by Him who embodied in His own Person the truth He taught, who, when He spoke of the love of God, could point to His own presence among men as the confirmation of the message that He bore, and who sealed with His blood the truth that He had proclaimed in His life.

LITERATURE.—Bruno Bauer, *Christus und die Cäsaren*[2], 1879, *Das Urevangelium und die Gegner der Schrift 'Christus und die Cäsaren*,' 1880 ; E. Havet, *Le Christianisme et ses origines* ; Bunsen, *The Angel Messiah of Buddhists, Essenes, and Christians*, 1880 ; Seydel, *Das Evangelium von Jesu in seinen Verhältnissen zu Buddha-sage und Buddha-lehre*, 1882, *Die Buddha-legende und das Leben Jesu nach den Evangelien*, 1884 ; Oldenberg in *ThLZ*, 1882, No. 18, 1884, No. 8, 1905, No. 3 ; Lillie, *Buddha and Early Buddhism*, 1881, *The Popular Life of Buddha*, 1883, *Buddhism in Christendom, or Jesus the Essene*, 1885, and *The Influence of Buddhism on Primitive Christianity*, 1893 ; Aiken, *The Dhamma of Gotama the Buddha and the Gospel of Jesus Christ*, 1900 ; Stix, *Christus oder Buddha*, 1900 ; Pfleiderer, *Das Christusbild des urchristlichen Glaubens in religionsgeschichtlicher Beleuchtung*, 1903 ; van den Bergh van Eysinga, *Indische Einflüsse auf evangelische Erzählungen*, 1904 ; v. Hase, *Neutest. Parallelen zu buddhist. Quellen*, 1905 ; Kuenen, *Hibbert Lectures*, 1882, Lects. iv. and v., notes xi. and xiii. ; Bousset, *Jesu Predigt in ihrem Gegensatz zum Judenthum*, 1892, *Jesus*, Eng. tr. 1906 ; Votaw, *The Modern Jewish View of Jesus* (reprinted from the *Biblical World*, vol. xxvi. No. 2, Aug. 1905) ; Montefiore, 'The Synoptic Gospels and the Jewish Consciousness,' *Hibbert Journal*, July 1905 ; Harnack, *Hist. of Dogma*, ch. ii. § 2, *Das Wesen des Christentums*, p. 30 ff. ; Drummond, *The Relation of the Apostolic Teaching to the Teaching of Christ*, p. 85 ff. ; O. Holtzmann, *Life of Jesus*, ch. xiv. ; Bachmann, *Die neue Botschaft in der Lehre Jesu*, 1905 ; Eschelbacher, *Das Judentum und das Wesen des Christentums*, 1905 ; Wellhausen, 'Gesch. Israels u. Judas,' c. 11 (*Skizzen u. Vorarbeiten*, 1884), also *IJG*, c. 24 (1904) ; Baldensperger, *Die messian.-apocalyp. Hoffnungen des Judenthums*[3], 1903, also *Das spätere Judenthum als Vorstufe des Christenthums*, 1900 ; Schürer, *HJP*, also *Die Predigt Jesu Christi in ihrem Verhältniss zum AT u. zum Judenthum*, 1882 ; Jülicher, 'Jesus' in *Die christliche Religion*, 1906 ; H. J. Holtzmann, *NT Theol.* 1897 (first two chapters) ; J. Weiss, *Die Predigt Jesu vom Reiche Gottes*[2], 1900 ; Haupt, *Zum Verständnis der eschatol. Aussagen Jesu*, 1894 ; Wünsche, *Neue Beiträge zur Erläuterung der Evangelien aus Talmud und Midrasch*, 1878 ; Lightfoot, *Colossians and Philemon*, pp. 395–417 ; Ginsburg, *Essenes* ; Conybeare, art. 'Essenes' in Hastings' *DB* ; Nesbit, *Christ, Christians, and Christianity*, bk. i. 'Jesus an Essene,' 1895 (2nd ed. 1899) ; A. Schweitzer, *Von Reimarus zu Wrede*, 1906.

G. WAUCHOPE STEWART.

OVEN (κλίβανος).—In the reference to fuel for the village oven (Mt 6[30], Lk 12[28]) the term 'grass' is used generally for any wild produce of the fields, including thorns and thistles.

The Bible references to the baking of bread correspond to the three principal methods now employed in Palestine. (1) The simplest is that in use among the Bedouin or migratory Arabs of the desert. It is to make a slight hollow in the ground at the tent door, and burn upon it dry grass or twigs until sufficient hot ash is made for the baking of the bread cakes (Gn 18[6], 1 K 17[12] 19[6]). An improvement upon this is seen in the small villages, where the conditions of life are more stationary. The hollow is deepened a little more, and covered with large pebbles in order to retain the heat, and the bread is either laid upon these after the ashes have been brushed aside, or, without removal of the ashes, the bread is laid upon a convex metal disc or griddle slightly raised above the fire-place. (2) The next stage of advance is seen in the large, pot-like hole dug in the ground, and lined with a smooth coating of plaster. The same kind of fuel is laid as before on the pebbles at the bottom, and the thin cakes are fired by being placed for a minute on the hot concave surface of the oven. The work of baking is done by a woman who sits beside the oven, and from time to time adds a few handfuls of fuel. She has on one side the tray of dough from which she tears out a small piece, and after rolling it out into a thin cake she distends it still further by slapping it over one arm and then over the other. She then lays it upon a circular cushion-like pad kept for the purpose, and thus applies it to the plaster surface of the pot oven. As each loaf, about a foot and a half in diameter and of wafer-like thinness, is rapidly fired, it is placed upon the pile of bread on her other side. This is the ordinary oven for home-made bread in the villages, the *tannûr* of the OT and the simpler form of the *klibănos* of the NT. In the warning of Lv 26[26], the predicted scarcity of fuel and flour would be such that ten women in one cluster or section of the village houses, instead of using in turn the same oven for their separate households, would have to unite their little stock of flour to make a baking to be done by one of them, and then receive by weight the share of bread belonging to each.

(3) The final form is that of the baker's oven. The ordinary village usually has one of these, in which baking is done on three or more days of the week, and the towns are furnished with a larger number in daily use on account of the increased demand. The oven recess, instead of being a hollow in the ground, is now a vault about twelve feet long, four feet high, and eight feet broad, built in the bake-house. The pebbles of the primitive form are represented by a pavement of squared stone along the length and breadth of the semi-cylindrical vault. Upon it is laid fuel of the same kind as before, with an addition of thicker twigs and pieces of cleft wood, and the fire is kept up until sufficient heat has been produced. The hot ashes are then brushed off and banked up on each side, and the bread is laid on this cleared space of the hot stone pavement (Is 44[19], Jer 37[21]). The heat is considerably greater than what is needed for the more gradual firing of our larger European loaf, and the Oriental oven thus became the emblem of vehement desire (Ho 7[6, 7]) and the indignant anger of God (Ps 21[9]).   G. M. MACKIE.

OWNER (κύριος).—The word is found only once in the AV (Lk 19[33] 'The owners said (to the disciples), Why loose ye the colt?'). Luke alone indicates that there was any question asked when the disciples prepared to take the colt away. Probably the answer which the disciples were instructed to give ('The Lord hath need of him,' Lk 19[31, 34]) was a prearranged sign between the owners and Jesus. Elsewhere in the Gospels the frequency of the occurrence of the word 'owner' is concealed from readers of the English versions by its translation as 'lord' (see art. LORD). 'Lord' (κύριος) has the sense of 'owner' in the phrases 'the lord of the vineyard' (Mt 20[8] 21[40] ‖ Mk 12[9] ‖ Lk 20[15]). In the phrases, 'the servant is not above his lord' (Mt 10[24]), 'the servant showed his lord these things' (Lk 14[21]), 'the lord of that servant' (Lk 12[46f.]), the relationship is that of master (owner) and slave (δοῦλος). By translating δοῦλος as 'servant,' the fact is concealed from English readers that slavery was an institution in the social life of the Jews. It was not so common among them as among the Greeks and Romans, and the condition of the slave in the Jewish social economy was much happier than in the Gentile world. The terrible punishment mentioned in Lk 12[46] ('the lord of that servant . . . will cut him in sunder [διχοτομεῖν], and appoint him his portion with the unbelievers') is probably taken from the punishments which were practised in the Gentile world. It is, however, mentioned as a punishment in He 11[37]. On the different interpretations of Lk 12[46] see Godet, *ad loc.*, and Meyer on Mt 24[51]. See also art. SERVICE.

     JOHN REID.

OX.—See ANIMALS, vol. i. p. 63[b].

P

PALACE.—In the Gospels the word is used in the text of Mt 27[27] and Jn 18[28, 33] 19[9], and in the margin of Mk 15[16]. In all cases it is the representative of πραιτώριον (see PRÆTORIUM), which was a term wide enough to include what would now be called a guard-room or the barrack-square adjoining (Mt 27[27], Mk 15[16]), as well as the actual place (referred to in the Johannine passages) in which a case was tried and the sentence pronounced.   R. W. MOSS.

PALESTINE.—The tendency, represented by historians like Buckle and his school, to write history in terms of environment, is one of those remarkable exaggerations of a valuable truth in which the 19th cent. was prolific. Every age which produces elemental theories and sweeping changes in the most widely accepted and venerable views, is liable to this kind of exaggeration. New ideas first stagger and then captivate men's minds, and the new names which these theories introduce assume magic powers for a time. The next generation smiles at the omnipotence of the catchwords of the first years of evolutionary doctrine, and remembers that other words—'sympathy' and 'perpetual motion' among the rest—had a similar vogue in their day. Most of all has the power of environment received undue emphasis and been credited with an influence far in excess of the facts, in the case of Jesus Christ. There is nothing which has doomed the work of His purely naturalistic biographers to premature obsoleteness so much as this. Nowhere was Carlyle's protest in favour of the effect of great personalities so applicable as here. If anything in history is certain, it is that here we have a case in which a unique personality is seen mastering circumstances, rather than one in which circumstances are seen creating a conspicuous personality.

Yet the influence of Palestine on Jesus is equally unquestionable.

'We must not isolate the story,' says Dr. Dale, 'from the preceding history of the Jewish race . . . Many people seem to suppose that they may approach the subject as if the Lord Jesus Christ had appeared in Spain or in China, instead of in Judæa and Galilee' (*Living Christ and the Four Gospels*, 89). 'If, negatively,' says Hausrath, 'it be self-evident that Jesus' mission would have assumed another character had He grown up under the oaks of Germany instead of under the palms of Nazareth, that the subject of Arminius or Maroboduus would have been different from that of Antipas, that the opponent of the Druids would have differed from the opponent of the Rabbis, so, positively, it is indisputable that for Jesus Himself the facts of His consciousness were given Him under those forms of viewing things in which Jewish thought in general was cast. Only by a freak of the imagination can it be supposed that an historical personality becomes conscious of the facts of its own inner life by conceptions other than those in which the thought of the age in general finds expression' (*Hist. of NT Times*, ii. 225).

Thus we may take it that there is no sentence in the Gospels which can be fairly understood if it be regarded *merely* as the remark or question of a member of the human race who might have belonged to any nationality. Every word derives something of its significance from the place and time at which it was spoken. Jesus is the Son of Man, but He is also a Syrian teacher. It is Syrian landscape, Syrian history, and Syrian human nature with which the Incarnation works; and we of the West are confronted at every turn by the need to Orientalize our conceptions as we study these records.

In this article we shall consider the influence on Jesus (1) of Syria as a whole; (2) of the Gentile elements in the land; (3) of the open field and of Nature as seen in Syria; (4) of the town and village life with which He was familiar; (5) of the city of Jerusalem.

1. Syria as a whole.—Syria is an *Eastern* land, and the relations and differences between East and West are the first aspects of this subject which demand attention. No phenomenon of the kind is so remarkable as the combination of Eastern and Western characteristics in the thought and work of Jesus. Such books as Townsend's *Asia and Europe* and Fielding Hall's *The Soul of a People* (to mention two out of many popular accounts of East and West), though their generalizations are not always convincing, are full of suggestive illustrations of this. 'Though Asiatic in origin,' says the former writer, 'Christianity is the least Oriental of the creeds.' To find lives most typically Christian, we have to look chiefly to Western nations, France and Germany, Britain and America. Indeed, the astonishing fact is evident that in certain respects we have in Jesus an Oriental too Western for Asiatics, so that to a certain extent they have to Occidentalize their conceptions in order to become Christian. This strange fact has commonly been brought as a charge against the methods of Christian missionaries in the East. But there can be no doubt that in some measure it is due to the mind of Jesus Himself. His doctrine of personal immortality, *e.g.*, and still more the triumphant and glad spirit in which He proclaimed it, have a far more congenial appeal to the West than to the East. 'Eternal consciousness!' exclaims Townsend: 'that to the majority of Asiatics is not a promise but a threat.' Similarly, the prominence given in Christianity to the command to love our neighbour as ourself, in the West will always find at least a theoretical assent, for it will be backed by the sentiment or at least the conscience of sympathy between man and man as such. The East, whose religion is fundamentally a matter of saving one's own soul, or at widest a matter of tribal loyalties, will find that a hard saying, and indeed has always so found it. Again, everyone must have noticed that in the battles of Jesus against the unintelligent and conventional doctrines of the Pharisees, His constant appeal was to commonsense and the facts of the case obvious to every unprejudiced observer. But that in itself was an instance of the Western type of intellect pitted against the Oriental.

Yet, at the depths, Christianity rests upon distinctively Oriental foundations. The very publicity of Eastern life has had its effect upon the Gospels. The whole ministry of Jesus was performed among crowds, in public places of assembly and on thronged highways. His thoughts were flung at once into the arena of public discussion, and even His protests and His disregard of ritual in such matters as hand-washing, fasts, etc., were made under the scrutiny of innumerable eyes. The whole Gospel shows traces of this lack of privacy, and the emphasis of its teachings is often fixed by the angle at which its detail was seen by the onlookers. Again, the great Christian doctrine of renunciation is essentially an Oriental doctrine, typical of Hebraism as contrasted with Hellenism; so much so, that it is to the surprise with which that doctrine broke upon the West that its conquest was in part due. The Oriental has been kept from perceiving how Divine self-sacrifice is, by his familiarity with it as a commonplace of human life. 'The qualities which seemed to the warriors of Clovis so magnificently Divine, the self-sacrifice, the self-denial, the resignation, the sweet humility, are precisely the qualities the germs of which exist in the Hindu' (*Asia and Europe*, 69). Consequently, 'the character of Christ is not . . . as acceptable to Indians as to Northern races,' the former seeking in the Divine a contrast rather than a complement to their human thoughts. Again, that free play of imagination touching even the most everyday subjects, that direct statement of truth, unguarded by qualifications and unbuttressed by proofs, are Eastern rather than Western characteristics. These are but random instances, a few out of very many, and varying in importance from the most casual to the most fundamental, yet they are enough to prove that the thought of Jesus was cast in an essentially Oriental mould.

The geographical features of Palestine are strongly marked; and they include, in a very small field, mountains, rivers, plains, lakes and sea-coast. The story of Jesus brings Him in contact with each of these; but the only ones which can be said to have left very distinct traces are the mountains. The Bible is full of mountain scenery, and it owes much to that. The religious thought of the great plains of the world is one thing, that of sea-girt islands is another, and that of mountain-land is a third. The long ranges of Lebanon throw off their southern spurs in Galilee, and the range ends suddenly in the line of steep mountain-side which runs along the northern edge of the Plain of Esdraelon. Not far from this edge, nestling in hollows or crowning heights, lay the towns and villages among which Jesus spent His early years. Hermon is the one great mountain which Anti-Lebanon rises to, standing off to the south, and detached from the continuous range by the deep-cut gorge of the Abana, but sending on the ridge again unbroken, though rugged in outline, past the Sea of Merom on the eastern side, to the shores of the Sea of Galilee. Samaria lies to the south of Esdraelon, a region of finely sweeping valleys and hills of soft and rounded outline. But these hills grow less distinct as the road strikes southward through Judæa. The general level rises to a bare and lofty table-land, from which, near Bethel, rounded heights rise like huge breasts of grey stone from the upheaved bosom of the land. South of that, sheer gorges (geological faults, or the work of flooded winter-torrents) slash across the land from east to west, and open grim and sombre through precipices upon the sunken valley of the Jordan, where Jericho lies steaming in the heat, 6 miles west of the Jordan's channel-groove, chiselled deep below the level of the valley. Soon Jerusalem is seen, like a round nest among low mountains—a city thrust up from the summit of the land, and moated by deep valleys on two sides.

South of that, through the pasture-lands about Bethlehem and the wilderness of Judæa to the east of them, the land slopes down the rolling 'South Country' to the Arabian desert.

The traveller to-day is often disappointed in the emotions he had expected at sacred sites. The belief in miracle is nowhere so difficult as on the spot, where every detail of the scene seems so uncompromisingly earthly. If, however, he will follow the example of the Psalmist, and 'lift up his eyes unto the hills,' he will find the realization of Christ an easier matter. The great sky-lines are for the most part unchanged, and the same edges and vistas are to be seen which filled the eyes of Jesus. This is not merely the result of the fact that local tradition and foolish ways of honouring sacred places have disfigured and stultified so many spots of Palestine. It recalls the fact that Jesus came from the highlands of Galilee, and that He chose to associate many of the most outstanding events of His life with mountains. From the hill above Nazareth He looked abroad on an endless field of mountain tops. Hermon dominated the landscape on the north-east, and Tabor thrust its irrelevant cone, conspicuous and unique, over the undulating sky-line of the mountains between Nazareth and the Lake—a gigantic intruder which had reared its huge head to look down into Nazareth from over the wall of mountains. It was there, with countless mountain summits of familiar name about Him, that the Youth first encountered those tremendous thoughts which finally led Him to the Jordan. Driven thence by the Spirit into the wilderness, He fought His long fight with rival schemes of greatness, in the tract which Judæa thrusts high into the air from the depth of the Jordan Valley, and holds balanced upon the edge of cliffs. Jericho looks up at that mountain of Quarantania, and sees its angular and tilted platform of a summit as a black space cut out of the brilliance of a living, starry sky. From the edge He looked down on Jericho (Mt 4¹ etc.), and knew the power of worldliness as He saw the palace-life of Herod there, and the glimmer of festive lamps among the palm-groves that had been Cleopatra's. Mountains were the congenial places for His great utterances in which the Old Law changed to the New, and the freshness as well as the exaltation of these words remind us from beginning to end of them that they are a Sermon on the Mount (Mt 5¹). Similarly, by a sure instinct, it was to the heights that He went to find by night the fullest sense of converse with His Father (Mt 14²³ etc.). Probably it was on some of the slopes of Hermon that such a season of communion brightened to the wonder of the Transfiguration (Mt 17¹ etc.). Hermon's summit is always white, and many a 'bright cloud overshadows' it, until it shines upon the plain for miles around, in a white glory of frosted silver. It is not without significance that Matthew gives as the trysting-place between Jesus and His disciples 'a mountain of Galilee' (Mt 28¹⁶). There is a perceptible air of relief in the words, as if after all those stifling days in Judæa—days of judgment-halls and shut doors in upper rooms, of clouded cross and sealed sepulchre—an irresistible longing had seized Him for the sunlight and the wind-swept heights of His happier early days. Nothing fostered the patriotism of Israel so much as her mountains. From time immemorial they had been her defences in war, and the platforms of her worship. In the story of Jesus they are seen in both these uses, and the feel of the heights is upon much that He has said.

Palestine is a little and compressed country, where not only geographical features, but the facts and associations of *national history* are gathered, so close as to force themselves upon the attention at every step. While travelling there, it is a constant source of wonder that so much could have happened in so small a place. These continual reminders of the past history of the nation, which thrust themselves upon Israelites everywhere, and kept patriotism vehemently alive, had their effect also upon Jesus. The heroes of the past were much in His thought, and His journeys from place to place reminded Him of them continually. Elijah and Elisha, Solomon, David, and Isaiah, were figures not merely remembered from reading in the sacred books. They were the unseen inhabitants of the places where once they dwelt in the flesh, peopling for Him tracts over which He led His disciples. His patriotism is evident continually (Lk 19⁹ 13¹⁶). It was a great thing in His eyes to be a son or a daughter of Abraham. Jerusalem, for Him as for the Psalmist, is the 'city of the great King' (Mt 5³⁵). The waysides are hallowed by the footsteps of the dead. The tombs of the prophets are conspicuous monuments to His imagination (Mt 23²⁹). He lived among the dead, and they lived unto God and unto Him in the land where their bones had long crumbled to decay. He receives and is taunted with the title 'King of Israel' (Jn 1⁴⁹, Mt 27⁴² etc.). The accusation on the Cross is 'Jesus, the King of the Jews' (Mt 27³⁷ etc.).

Two aspects of the land, taken as a whole, must be remembered, especially if we would understand what it meant to Jesus—*Palestine as an oasis, and Palestine as a focus.*

Palestine as an oasis.—It is shut off from the rest of the world by a complete ring of natural barriers. Mountains on the north; a vast desert on the east, with the deep and long trench of the Jordan Valley set as a second and inner barrier like a moat; desert again on the south; and the west wholly bounded by the alien sea which so few understood—these are the boundaries of Israel. And there was also a double ring of national barricades. At a distance had stood the great empires of the East, the Parthians having taken in His time the place of ancient Nineveh and Babylon. To the south-west lay Egypt. An inner ring of wild Arabian tribes wandered over the eastern desert, and now and then raided the land. Formerly an unbroken belt of neighbouring heathen enemies encircled Israel, and even cut her off from the sea by the Philistine wedge driven along her western coast, stretching from the Pillar of Egypt to the Phœnician seaports. All this was modified, and much of it broken up, in the time of Jesus; but the religious meaning of it all was thus being only the better understood.

The whole meaning of the land in OT times had been the isolation of Israel for religious ends. For her, 'to act like men' (*i.e.* to imitate the nations round about her) was denounced by her prophets as a betrayal (Hos 6⁷). As a matter of fact, every experiment which she made in such imitation of 'men' was a failure. Under Solomon she had adopted the 'Policy of Orientalism' of the great world-empires. Under Jeroboam she had sought to conform to the secular ideas of ritual then fashionable, and had even attempted something in the way of a democratic system of government. Under many kings she had sought greatness in aggressive wars. Under Omri she had, by her alliance with Phœnicia, tried for the position of a great commercial power. In every one of these attempts she had found herself defeated, and driven back on the one thing she could do as no other nation could. That one thing was religion, and the meaning of Israel's isolation was that worship of Jehovah which grew up with her institutions, and of whose revelations she was the destined recipient and repository.

For Jesus also Palestine was an oasis. It is indeed true that the Palestine of His time was no longer the 'garden enclosed' which the prophets had striven to keep it. All its hedges were by this time broken down and driven through by the resistless march of Rome. In the heart of the invaded country Jerusalem remained bitterly exclusive and hostile to all the world, so far as the Pharisees could keep it so. Galilee was much more open to the wider thought of the time than Judæa, and Jesus was in sympathy rather with the Galilæan than with the Judæan spirit. Yet, so far as His own work went, He retained and utilized the oasis view of His land. His three temptations were an epitome of the nation's temptations—'to act like men' for bread, or for fame, or for power. In resisting them He was thrusting from His Kingdom the ideals of commercial prosperity, military conquest, and political empire, just as the prophets of Israel had fought against these as national ideals. He remained, and set His speech and His works, among those relationships where God had placed Him. He confined His own ministry and the earlier ministry of His disciples to the land of Israel (Mt 10⁵); and that land was still sufficiently isolated from the thought and life of the world to provide a true cradle and fostering-place for those thoughts which formed the nucleus of the Kingdom of heaven. Thus, in the earliest years, they were sufficiently aloof to gain intensity.

Palestine as a focus.—If Palestine was no longer an oasis in the full sense in which it had been so in OT times, it was more a focus than it had ever been before. In the Church of the Holy Sepulchre, a little hollow place with a flattened ball in it is still exhibited to the incredulous visitor as the centre of the world. The cosmography of the

Middle Ages took this as serious science, Jerusalem being the antipodes of the island of Purgatory at the other pole. No doubt some such conception was in the minds of many who looked in early Christian times for new heavens and a new earth *and a new Jerusalem*. Such thoughts were true in a wider sense than the thinkers knew. At the time of Jesus, Palestine was the meeting-point of East and West.

For many centuries Israel had been a buffer State between the conflicting powers of Egypt and Mesopotamia. Now instead of Egypt there was Rome, at the height of its military power, and armed also with the spiritual weapons of Greece, whose national power it had destroyed and by the deed had set free its spirit. The eastern empires of Nineveh and Babylon were gone, and instead of them were those changing hosts of Persian and Parthian warriors who were soon to dispute the world with Rome. And behind them, more clearly visible since the campaigns of Alexander the Great, though still dim in the mists of vast distances, lay India and the Far East.

The Roman conquest of Syria had brought into immediate and hostile contact two nationalities whose whole history and thought placed them irreconcilably apart. Rome's ideal of secular empire confronted the Jewish hope of the universal reign of Messiah. Down to the minutest detail of life the two ideals were opposed. To Rome tribute was the obvious consequence of conquest; the theatre was at once a politic and a generous enrichment of the life of the conquered State. To Israel tribute was a sacrilege, and the theatre which rose in Jerusalem a blasphemy. So hateful was the Roman to the Jew, that Jews were a worthless commodity in the Roman slave-market. So unintelligible was the Jew to the Roman, that Tacitus speaks of the nation as 'given over to superstition, disinclined to religion' (Hausrath, i. 173–86). These facts are but illustrations of the wider principle, that when a nation with intense national sentiments encounters a nation with strong imperial sentiment, trouble of the most violent kind always ensues. For confirmation of this, one has only to remember the history of Switzerland, of Ireland, or of the Transvaal. In Israel the struggle was only the more acute and inevitable, because the Romanizing policy of the Herods had lent to it the additional aspect of a civil war. Nothing could be imagined more explosive than this state of affairs—a fact which was very clear to the enemies of Jesus (Jn 11⁴⁸).

That Jesus also saw this clearly there can be no question; and this, among other things, must have been in His mind when He spoke of Himself as sending a sword (Mt 10³⁴), and scattering fire on the earth (Lk 12⁴⁹). Towards the Roman power He, in contrast with such revolutionaries as Judas of Galilee, maintained a strictly neutral attitude. It is probable that no words ever uttered showed such consummate diplomatic skill as those in which He answered the question about the tribute money (Mt 22¹⁷ etc.). His prophecies (24² etc.) show how patent to Him was the coming explosion of the forces then at play. His policy was to set the word of the Kingdom so fully at the explosive centre, that when the crash came it would send Christianity across the whole world.

For that diffusion everything was ready. Great roads had long been open by land and sea for trade and commerce. Even then the Romans were laying down those indestructible causeways by which they united land with land. The Sadducees, who in some respects read skilfully the signs of their times, did all they could to encourage trade in Syria, and to break down the Pharisaic restrictions which hampered it; and in this Jesus was their powerful ally. From the heights of Nazareth He had seen the march of the legions on the Roman road across Esdraelon from Acre to the Jordan, and watched the long lines of laden camels moving slowly from the coast to Damascus and back, along the road that lies like a flung ripple along the hillsides to the north. When in after years St. Paul utilized the Roman roads for the spread of the gospel, he was but carrying out the work which Jesus initiated when He placed that gospel within the charged mine of Palestine.

In the light of one further consideration we see the extraordinary Providence which watched over the situation then. It is a commonplace of history, that civilization and all higher developments of human life spring forward at a bound at the

meeting-point of national currents. 'The great civilizations have always arisen in the meeting-places of ideas' (Martin Conway, *The Dawn of Art*, 76). The Norman Conquest offers one of the most conspicuous illustrations, but it is only one of many. The supremely influential meeting of national forces has always been that between the East and the West. 'The contact between East and West has always been the prolific source of the advancement of humanity' (*op. cit.* 59, 60). It was from this contact, induced by the Pilgrimages and the Crusades, that the Renaissance arose. But Christianity itself had arisen at that earlier point of contact, when the Eastern factor was the Hebrew religion, and the Western was Greece and Rome. At the focus of the world Jesus set the light of the world.

2. The relations of Jesus with Gentiles.—Not only was Palestine in close proximity with Gentile neighbours in the time of Jesus; the land itself was overrun with Gentiles, and no account of the meaning of Palestine for Jesus can ignore that fact.

His home in Galilee must have given from the first a very different outlook on the Gentile world from any that would have been possible in Judæa. Far from the centre of Jewish exclusiveness, crossed by great high roads from the sea to the east, and actually inhabited by multitudes of Gentiles from various lands, Galilee was the most open-minded and tolerant part of the land. Commercial and other interests made the Galilæans acquainted with foreigners, and established much friendly human intercourse. Thus at the outset it must be borne in mind that Jesus was from His childhood accustomed to a more or less cosmopolitan world, and to the ideas current in such a society. The temptation of 'the kingdoms of the world, and the glory of them' (Mt 4⁸), indicates no new discovery of worldly grandeur, but a knowledge which had been gathering during the experience of thirty years.

One fact of great significance in the life of Palestine was that it had to be lived in constant view of the desert tribes to the east of it. Kinglake has described the Jordan as the boundary-line between roofs and tents; and besides the tents of nomad tribes there were also those cities of Edom and the Hauran, where, in a rude kind of civilization, Arab kings ruled their kingdoms. The terror of the desert Bedawîn and the barbaric splendours of these kingdoms both contributed a romantic element, which was enforced by the eternal mystery of the desert, in which all things are seen in a strong light which magnifies their significance and fascinates the imagination. Most of Jesus' parables of kings and their wars (Mt 18²³ etc.), and certainly His picture of a strong man armed guarding his house against a stronger (Lk 14³¹ 11²¹·²² etc.), tell of just such a condition of unsettled government and expectation of surprise as existed on the borderline between Arabian and Israelite territory.

In this border region stood the cities of the Decapolis, in which a wealthy and strongly defended Greek life held its own, by force of Roman garrisons, against the desert and the south. The marvellous ruins of Jerash, the two theatres and ornate tombs of Gadara, and the débris of carved stones above the dam which retained water for the *naumachiai* at Abila, tell an almost incredible tale of luxurious and ostentatious grandeur. The blend of civilization and savagery which such places produce is a phenomenon of the most startling kind. The fact that Jesus visited the Decapolis (Mk 7³¹; cf. Mt 4²⁵ and Mk 5²⁰), bearing His high and pure spirituality into that region of the Syrian world, suggests some of the strongest and most dramatic situations which it would be possible to conceive. In this light we see the extraordinary realism of the story of the Gadarenes and their swine and their devils (Mt 8²⁸ etc.). It was inevitable that they should have besought Him to depart out of their coasts. And the reaction on His own thought was equally inevitable. He saw the ideals for which He lived and was to die, not as spiritual visions remote from the actual world, or as an advance on its honest endeavours after holiness, but against the background of a life whose gilded swinishness threw it up in all the high relief of the holiness of heaven against earth at its most sordid. And yet it was to this region that He often retired for refuge from the Galilæans of the western shore, and through this region that He chose to travel on His last journey to the Cross. The relief He sought in it was not wholly that of solitude. Even these degenerate races called for His sympathy; and being unprejudiced by religion, they at least let Him be alone.

The sea-coast comes little into the story of the Gospels. Afterwards, in the lives of Peter and Paul, Joppa and Cæsarea were to assume an important place. But, so far as we know, Jesus visited it only once, when He retreated to the coasts of Tyre and Sidon from the Pharisees who had followed Him from Jerusalem. The few references which He made to the sea appear to be all subsequent to that visit. They are in every case characteristic of the inland Israelite's thought of the sea as a place of horror rather than of beauty (Mt 18[6]; cf. art. Poet below, p. 375[b]). It was natural that the part of the sea-coast to which He went for concealment should have been that of Tyre and Sidon. We are not, indeed, told that He visited those towns, and the word 'coasts' may even refer to the landward district near them. Yet, obviously, no place could offer Him better hiding than a manufacturing seaport town, where He would be easily lost in the crowds of workmen which came and went about the dye-works and the glass-works and the shipbuilding yards, or in the many-coloured throngs of native and foreign sailors on the quays. It is characteristic of Jesus that the record of that visit ignores the whole splendour of the wealthy life of Phœnicia; its temples with their sun-pillars, its markets, and its ships might have been non-existent for all the notice given to them. The one fact that has been found worthy of commemoration is that story where, in inimitable sprightliness and vivacity, we see for a moment the foreign mother, and hear her tale of human sorrow assuaged.

Samaria (wh. see) divided Galilee from Judæa by the alien race that is supposed to have originated in a cross between Mesopotamians and Israelites after the first captivity. During the centuries that had intervened there had been time for this nation to settle into a fixed and distinct type of its own, but the race still bore all the marks of its bastard origin. Luxurious and soft morally, with the fertility of the land encouraging the effeminacy, they seem to have relaxed their standards of purity in all directions, and the life of the woman of Sychar (Jn 4[18]) was probably typical of current views of sexual relations. The palace life of Herod at the central city of Samaria, and his intercourse with Rome at Cæsarea, upon which he had spent fabulous sums, must have intensified the Bohemian and foreign elements in the national character. The tragedies of the palace, the wild story of the murder of Mariamne and what happened after it, and the subsequent strangling of her two sons in that same palace, were matters within the memory of living men. These, and the whole effect of Herod upon the place, must have been all on the side of those primitive and half-savage elements which entered largely into the Samaritan character. In religion the Samaritans had adopted a kind of blend of heathen and Israelitish worship, in which the centre of enthusiasm was a rival group of holy places set over against those of Jerusalem, and a passion for relic-hunting which, in Christ's time, took the form of a search for hidden treasure in Gerizim. This, too, reveals the primitive, in its frank blending of the greed of gold with worship, and it took so deep a hold as to draw the vengeance of Pilate upon a Samaritan religious assembly (Keim, ii. 334). The claims of Samaritan religion, and its compromise with relaxed morality, are reflected in the conversation of the woman at the well (Jn 4[16ff.]).

The Jews of the time were always ready for vigorous hatreds, and in their relations with the Samaritans they showed that extreme rancour which religious bigots keep, not for opposition, but for compromise. The attitude of Jesus to Samaritans is one of the most illuminative of all the side-lights thrown upon His mind and character by the Gospels. On more than one occasion He took the unpopular direct route through Samaria while journeying between Jerusalem and Galilee (Jn 4[4]). In religion, when it comes to be a question of localities, He holds by Jerusalem, and refuses to admit that any other shrine can rival its claims (4[22]). Yet the error calls for no anger in Him, inasmuch as His thought of worship transcends all place-limitations, and is as wide as the human spirit and truth (4[23]). He allows for the unthinking brutality of inhospitable villages, and sharply rebukes disciples who would meet it in a like spirit (Lk 9[54]). There is a most pleasant sense of tolerant and kindly interest in the alien Samaritans and their ways of thinking, which, while it asserts the higher morality (Jn 4[17]) and the higher worship, is yet ever friendly and gentle. He even goes out of His way to show how much nobler as a man a Samaritan may be than those Jews who professed superior nobility of faith. The parable of the Good Samaritan (Lk 10[33]), and Jesus' words about the grateful leper (17[17f.]), are direct protests in the name of fairness against the common judgment and attitude of His countrymen.

A few words on the attitude which Jesus assumed to Rome and the Romans are necessary to complete the view of Palestine as He knew it. Rome thrust itself then upon the inhabitants of Palestine in two forms. In such governors as Pilate it was seen directly, as the hostile imperial power governing the province of Syria. From Antioch its roads and armies had subdued the land, yet had never broken the spirit of its people, or quenched their fierce hopes of reprisals and of deliverance. At every centre its tax-gatherers had their stations. Its Prætorium in Jerusalem was occupied by the palace of the hated Pilate, whose cruelties were held in check only by his fear of the still more cruel emperor, and whose desire to quell revolutions was hindered by the fear of complaints on the score of his financial crimes. On the other hand, there were the Herods, Idumæan princes whose policy was that of Romanizing. With them, to a great extent, were the Sadducees, and under them the outward face of the country had rapidly assumed the appearance of a Western land. Architecture, commerce, amusements, and worship all showed the work of Rome through the Herodian house. There was a Roman theatre in Jerusalem, with lavishly appointed games; and a Roman eagle was set up on the Temple gates. Fortresses had risen along all the frontiers and in every part of the land, and it was Herod the Great who had cleared out the robbers from the Valley of Doves in Galilee, and so had opened Gennesaret and created Capernaum, thus unconsciously building the platform for a great part of the ministry of Jesus. At Jericho the palace-life was unrestrained in its luxury and licentiousness; in Jerusalem, Herod's palace overlooked the city from the Jaffa gate. Tiberias rose by the shore of the Galilæan sea; but as it was built on an old graveyard it was avoided by religious Israelites, and Jesus never visited it, so far as our records tell. But all round the lake, villas had been built, and the shores of Galilee seem to have been a fashionable watering-place for Romans, a development which every Herod must have found to his own heart. The disciples, who were Galilæan fishermen, must have found a market for their fish in many a Roman household.

The attitude of Jesus towards Rome is very clearly depicted in the Gospels. From first to last every point at which His life touches any of the Herods shows hostility of relations (Mk 8¹⁵, Lk 13³¹· ³² 23⁹, etc.). He appears studiously to have avoided Tiberias, Cæsarea, and the city of Samaria. Herodism and its effects He accepted without further protest as the actual state of the world in which He had to live; but for that Herod with whom He had most to do He showed open contempt. To the popular mind, Herod was the murderer of John, who would also kill Jesus unless He sought escape (Lk 13³¹). To Jesus he was but 'that fox,' by no means of sufficient importance to make Him change His plans (13³²). He manifested no admiration for the great stones and buildings of Herod the Great in the Temple which he had erected (Mk 13¹· ²). This scorn of Jesus reached its climax in His silence under Herod's examination at Jerusalem, and the contemptible revenge of the purple robe and crown of thorns (Lk 23⁹).

Towards the actual Roman Empire Jesus assumed another attitude. Galilee in Jesus' time was full of revolution. Along with its tolerant cosmopolitanism there always were elements of the most violent fanaticism there, — a combination by no means unusual in the history of nations. Judas of Galilee was the popular patriot and hero, and the sons of Judas, who grew up as boys near Jesus, were to perish on crosses after Him, for vain attempts against the Roman sway. Thoughts of such revolution may have been involved in the third temptation; but if so, they were immediately rejected. Pilate's eager question, 'Art thou a king?' (Jn 18³⁷), met with no response which could be used against Jesus as a serious charge. His payment of tribute, and the words He spoke about it on various occasions, show no sense of resented injury (Mt 22²¹). His absence of bitterness towards the tax-gatherers, and His calling of one of them to be a disciple, were among the bitterest sources of the hatred borne to Him by the Pharisees (Mt 9⁹⁻¹¹). He saw the publicans as human beings, and not as renegades and traitors. The absence of prejudice which enabled Him to adopt this attitude has been explained on the ground that He took 'no interest whatever in the burning questions of the times' (Hausrath, ii. 210). It would be more accurate to say that, so far as the political conditions were concerned, He accepted the facts and their inevitable consequences. He saw the coming destruction of Jerusalem with deep emotion (Mt 23³⁷), and He spoke of it as about to be trodden down by the Gentiles (Lk 21²⁴), but He put forth no effort politically to change the course of events. The words in which He spoke of Pilate's slaughter of the Galilæans, who were no doubt a band of revolutionary patriots, are certainly very remarkable. Not only did He refrain from any comment on the tragedy, or any tribute to their daring or their sacrifice; all He had to say of them was that they were not sinners above other Galilæans (Lk 13⁴).

By gathering these and other considerations together, we may gain a fairly accurate idea of the feeling of Jesus towards the Gentiles, who played so important a part in the Syrian world of His time. Around Him there was the Herodian attitude of Romanizing, and the Pharisaic and patriotic attitude which delighted in branding Gentiles with such names as 'dogs' and 'swine'; while between these two a considerable mass of the general opinion of the time regarded them neither with emulation nor with hatred, but simply accepted them as facts — 'uncomfortable, unaccountable works of God,' as the Hindus are said to regard the English (*Asia and Europe*). To none of them all had it ever occurred to say, 'Suppose I were a Gentile?' and to try to look upon the world earnestly from the Gentile point of view—a quite

different matter from imitating Gentile ways in the Herodian manner.

Was this the attitude adopted by Jesus? Whatever answer we give to that question, it is quite clear that His attitude was a different one from any of the three above indicated. Unlike the Herodians, He showed no interest in Gentile architecture or commerce, literature or art. He accepted their institutions in so far as these formed part of the ordinary life of the land, but He passed no judgment either of approval or of disapproval on them. He almost exclusively, and evidently with deliberation, confined His ministry, and that of His disciples during His lifetime, to Israel. While not going out of His way to avoid Gentiles, He did not cultivate them. On almost every occasion they came to Him, not He to them. On the other hand, He expressly forbade His disciples to go into 'the way of the Gentiles,' *i.e.* to utilize for the spread of the gospel, as St. Paul afterwards did, those great roads in which the ends of the earth met. He even forbade them to enter any village of the Samaritans (Mt 10⁵). In His initial words to the Syrophœnician woman He contrasts the children of the Promise with the Gentile dogs (Mt 15²⁶), though probably there was that in His manner which encouraged her to her clever repartee. To the woman of Samaria He pointedly asserted that 'salvation is of the Jews' (Jn 4²²). He saw the failings of the Gentiles, and spoke of them as a warning to Christians. His disciples were to avoid their vain repetitions in prayer (Mt 6⁷), their greedy search and labour for food and clothes (Mt 6³²), their servility with princes, and their desire of honour (Mt 20²⁵). There is little doubt that His words (regarding John) about those who are clothed in soft raiment and who live in kings' houses, were meant to be understood in scorn of Herod (Mt 11⁸).

On the other hand, it is equally clear that He refused to countenance the virulent spirit of antagonism, either religious or patriotic. Nothing met with more frequent or more unsparing condemnation than the sanctimonious exclusiveness of the Pharisees, who made a religion of avoiding their fellow-men. Nor did He intermeddle with the revolutionary politics or methods of His day. On the contrary, He paid tribute; and when the servants of the high priest came to seize Him, He strongly condemned the use of weapons even in defence, and with a quiet request permitted Himself to be bound. The general impression which the narratives give is certainly one of kindly feeling for Gentiles. His interest and appreciation were always frank and open. He shielded His Roman judge from 'the greater sin' in His condemnation (Jn 19¹¹), and pleaded the ignorance of His actual murderers in His dying prayer (Lk 23³⁴). He evidently liked to point out cases of Gentile superiority to Jews. At the outset of His ministry He offended the Nazarenes by His words about Naaman and the widow of Sarepta (Lk 4²⁶· ²⁷); and on a later occasion He made the men of Nineveh and the queen of Sheba a foil to the unbelief of His generation (Mt 12⁴¹· ⁴²). The phrase which He used on several occasions of Gentile believers has become proverbial, 'I have not found so great faith, no, not in Israel' (8¹⁰ etc.). The impression which such conduct must have produced was certainly one of strong Gentile sympathies, and Matthew aptly quotes regarding Him the words of Isaiah, 'in his name shall the Gentiles trust' (12²¹).

From this it is already evident that Jesus cannot be placed in the third class, with those who merely accepted the Gentiles as facts in the situation. Politically, that was His attitude towards them, but as individuals He often delighted in them. He appreciated their broader outlook and want of Pharisaic narrowness. He was frankly relieved by their unconventionality and naturalness, which gave Him air to breathe after the stifling atmosphere of Rabbinism. To Him, in general, they stood for human nature, plain and unsophisticated.

When we inquire into the reasons for that Jewish exclusiveness against which Jesus thus protested, we come upon a fact of far-reaching significance. The Pharisees had much to justify their narrow views and practices in the fear of heathenism. The dearly won victory of the prophets over idolatry seemed to be in danger of being undone by the Græco-Roman invasion of a new heathenism. The old struggle renewed itself, and in Jesus' time the religious men of Israel were keeping back the encroaching worship of idols with both hands. In Samson's country the new Philistines (for so the followers of Epiphanes seemed to the faithful) had built an altar to Zeus (Hausrath, i. 29). Herod was known to have taken part in the completion of Jupiter's temple at Athens (*ib.* ii. 4). Much of the modern style, with its pictured art, must have savoured of idolatry to men who still took the Second Commandment literally, and the religious men of Israel were filled with the gravest apprehensions as they watched the advancing tide. In the whole speech of Jesus there is no attack upon heathenism to be found, nor any sense of serious danger from it. At Cæsarea Philippi He had seen the temple raised by Herod to Augustus, and the rock-cut niches dedicated to Pan and the nymphs where Jordan issued from its cave, yet no word of His is recorded in protest. True, He might upon occasion use such a current expression as ' Let him be unto thee as a heathen man and a publican ' (Mt 18^{17}), but His own attitude to publicans would be sufficient commentary upon that for His enemies. Evidently He was not in the slightest degree afraid of heathenism as a real danger, and He set Himself systematically against those maxims and practices as to clean and unclean things in which the Pharisaic spirit saw one of its best safeguards.

The explanation must be found in His further doctrine of the Kingdom of God, and the methods of its coming. There are two ways of opposing heathenism. The Pharisaic way was the negative one of denouncing it and withstanding its encroachment. Jesus chose the positive method of supplanting it by the Kingdom of heaven. That strong leaven He cast into the lump of humanity, well knowing that it must work eventually far beyond the Jewish regions. This is the ultimate point in His relations with the Gentile world. When He spoke to Pilate of His Kingdom, the Roman was relieved to hear that it was ' not of this world,' and at once set Him down as a dreamer. But Jesus was no dreamer. He was deliberately setting an actual Kingdom over against the existing empire, and history was soon to show that this was in the region of the practical and effective forces of the world. The consequences of this leaven of the Kingdom could not possibly be confined to the sphere of religion. They must eventually take political shape, and indeed affect every department of human life and interest, and spread throughout every nation of the world.

All this was in the mind of Jesus. The Book of Jonah was a favourite with Him, and it is the OT manifesto of the imperial and world-wide power of faith. His parable of the judgment of the nations (Mt 25^{32}), and His prophecies of the coming of the East and West and North and South to the Kingdom of God (8^{11}), showed plainly His ultimate designs upon the Gentile world. He spoke of other sheep beyond those of the Israelite fold (Jn 10^{16}), and finally commanded His messengers to go out into all the world and teach all nations (Mt 28^{19}). When He spoke of Himself as the Light of the world (Jn 8^{12}), and of His life as given for the world (6^{51}), it *was* the world that He was speaking of, and His hearers understood that it was so (cf. also Mt 16^{21} 13^{38} 5$^{5. 13. 14}$).

At times there may have crossed His mind a thought of making the wider appeal in person before His death. The most striking instance is that of the coming of the Greeks shortly before the end (Jn 12^{20}). It may be, as has been held by high authorities, that He saw in that event the invitation to address to the Greek world the message which the Hebrew world was rejecting. He refused it, proclaiming, in the wonderful saying about the corn of wheat (12^{24}), His knowledge that it was through death that life must come. Yet He rejoiced in it with a sudden glory (12^{23}), and recognized in it the fulfilment of His life's far-reaching purpose. He rejected it only that He might attain it. His own light, like that of His disciples, must be set upon a candlestick if it was to give light to all that were in the house; and He reached the Gentiles most effectually by concentrating His ministry upon Israel.

3. The open field. — In order to estimate the influence of Nature upon the mind of Jesus, it is necessary, first, to distinguish between the various ways in which Nature has been conceived in relation to humanity. At the two extremes stand materialistic realism and the purely spiritual and idealistic views. The former sees in nature mere masses of living or dead matter, arranged in various shapes, quantities, and combinations, and moved by forces variously conceived. The latter sees in it the visual and sensuous revelation of the Divine life. It is ' the garment of God,' whose fine drapery at once hides and reveals the Spirit of the universe.

Between these extremes there are three main points of view. Art, searching for beauty, has discovered landscape, in which the detailed objects are grouped into larger unities invested with a larger and more composite character of their own. The experience of individuals and the history of nations have added to the facts of landscape or of single objects certain associations which give them their human interest. Thought, emotion, and imagination have discovered (some would say invented) a mysterious spirituality in Nature, variously described or confessed to be indescribable, but perceived or felt as in some way a haunting presence, a ' something more ' than meets the eye or ear.

Often we find more than one of these ways of regarding Nature combined in the mind of a single thinker. St. Paul, *e.g.*, seems to have had singularly little feeling for Nature in the modern sense. There is no landscape and hardly any reference to detail in his writings, though his travels had showed him much of the finest scenery of the Mediterranean and of Asia Minor. For him the open field apparently represented nothing but a set of distances to be traversed before reaching cities. Yet at times the mystery comes upon him, and he invests Nature with a dim life of her own, groaning and travailing in pain towards some grand event (Ro 8^{22}). Dante, amid much of the grandest scenery of Europe, sees only obstacles to the foot of the traveller. But for him every place has historical associations, in whose light it lives in his mind. Gray is the poet who discovered English landscape. Wordsworth reaches the highest point in spiritualizing nature :

> ' Great God ! I'd rather be
> A Pagan, suckled in a creed outworn,
> So might I, standing on this pleasant lea,
> Have glimpses that would make me less forlorn ;
> Have sight of Proteus rising from the sea ;
> Or hear old Triton blow his wreathèd horn.'
> WORDSWORTH, *Miscellaneous Sonnets.*

The age of Jesus was divided between the Greek and the Hebrew view of Nature, and both of these must have been familiar in Syria. The Greek view was devoid of landscape properly so called. It saw brilliant and well-defined masses of detail— the temple white on its hill, reeds in the river-bed, the numberless laughter of waves. Greece not only saw but felt these, as charged with a spiritual significance which could be apprehended only in fragmentary hints and glimpses, with more wistfulness than understanding. She sought to capture and retain that spiritual significance in the exquisite imagery of her mythological creations of nymph and faun, the dryad of the forest and the goddess of the fountain. Yet these delicate incarnations did not suffice for her expression of Nature. Behind them lay those unaccountable moods of delight and misgiving which Nature awoke in her soul. The unsolved mystery of ' the beauty and the terror of the world ' emphasized in the main the misgiving, and produced ' the melancholy of the Greeks.' Death and change oppressed her spirit, and seemed to be ever the last word that Nature strove to say. The voice heard by the steersman had been heard by Greece before— ' Great Pan is dead.'

How much of this may have directly presented itself to Jesus, we cannot tell. His answer, however, to the Greeks who came to Him in Passion Week, seems to be an answer to the spirit of their nation (Jn 12²⁴). It is to Nature that He leads them in His reference to the corn of wheat, and to the element of death in Nature. But He reveals in Nature what they had not strength to find, the promise of resurrection, and the assurance of life enriched and fructified by death.

The Hebrew view of Nature differs from the Greek somewhat as Browning's differs from Wordsworth's. To the Greek, Nature has a spirituality which is no doubt reflected, in part, from the soul of her observer, yet is conceived as residing in herself in one or other of many fashions of personification. To the Hebrew, Nature in herself is dead, and has no soul of her own. She is the tool of Jehovah or His weapon, according as He is working or warring against His enemies ; or she is visible as a background over against human life, or at least as accessory to man and his needs or works in some way. In either case the point is that Nature for the Hebrew has no independent life or spirituality of her own. She shines ever in the borrowed light of human or Divine interest.

The Hebrew view of Nature, in its three main aspects, has been admirably described in the three expressions—(1) A stage for God, the 'place of His feet' ; (2) a home for man ; (3) the assessor at the controversy between God and man (Is 1², Mic 6²), a view in which the solemnity and austerity of Nature found a fitting metaphor to express them. Of each of these three aspects many instances might be quoted ; but at present it concerns us only to remark that in none of them is Nature seen in herself, but always dependent on an inhabitant, Divine or human, who gives her soul. The third view, indeed, seems to conceive of Nature as independent, her mountains judging between God and man. But the personification does not go deep, nor is the consciousness of its figurativeness lost. The mountains, the heavens and the earth, are witnesses in much the same sense as a pillar set up by one who has made a vow. They are called upon to listen, to rejoice, to break forth into singing, not because they are conceived as living an independent life, but because the human or Divine event is conceived as of such vast import that even dumb Nature must feel its thrill, and for once awake from her inertness to do homage to the higher forms of being.

There is, properly speaking, no landscape in the Bible. Objects are seen in detail, or groups of objects, in connexion with the events or circumstances narrated. Through a cleft fissure in a mountain range a glimpse is caught of a 'land that is very far off' ; but it is as a destination rather than as a picture that it is seen. The language spends its strength on those sharp and clear-cut names for natural phenomena which express so much—*Jordan*, the down-rusher ; *Ghôr*, the scooped-out ; *Gilgal*, the circular, and so on. The Song of Solomon is full of exquisite detail, with the aromatic scents of the East lingering about its voluptuous gardens and glades. But that is pre-Raphaelite art, of the same sort as those descriptions which are so common in the OT of a single tree or plant, a vine, an olive, or a gourd. It is characteristic of the Hebrew view of Nature that the Feast of Tabernacles, with its booths and illuminations, seemed to the Hebrew mind satisfactory as a piece of genuine rural life.

The life of Jesus was much spent in the open air, and His thought was full of the breezy freshness of the hills and fields ; but they were Syrian and not European hills and fields, and their effect is that of Eastern nature, not Western. Samaria and Lebanon strike the traveller from England as most familiar. But there is no word of Lebanon in the Gospels, and Samaria was seen but casually in passing through. It was in one of Samaria's richest and broadest valleys that He told His disciples to lift up their eyes and look upon the fields white already to the harvest (Jn 4³⁵). The regions with which He was most familiar were the hills and Sea of Galilee, and the rocky heights of Judæa. These are the very regions where the scenery is most typically Oriental. The main difference between a Syrian and an English landscape is that in Syria there is none of that 'atmosphere' which softens outlines and tones down a wide stretch of country into a unity of vision. The colouring is faint, in delicate shades of grey and brown and lilac, broken by the most violently brilliant splashes of high colour, where a water-spring flings a patch of lush green vegetation upon the pale mountain side, or where in springtime a long thin flame of oleander blazes along the winding depth of a washed-out river-bed. The general impression of wide views either in Judæa or Galilee is that of a land sculptured out of tinted stones. In Judæa the hills are bare grey limestone, whose stoniness is intensi-

fied rather than softened by sparse and dingy olives. Along the sides of many valleys the strata run in many-coloured parallel bands, giving the effect of a gigantic but faded mural decoration ; while the plateau on the heights round Jerusalem and on to the north lies bare in whitish grey. Galilee has more woodland, and some thin remains of what may once have been forests, but it also owes its general effect to rock rather than to vegetation. Allowing for the denudation caused by so many centuries of war and neglect, it is likely that even at its best the prevalent note of the land was that of sharp outline in faint colour, and its general impression that of huge-scale sculpture-work. Arriving from the West upon the edge of the hillside above Tiberias, the traveller catches his first sight of the Sea of Galilee. The writer may be permitted to quote a former description of his impression :

'This is not scenery ; it is tinted sculpture, it is jewel-work on a gigantic scale. The rosy flush of sunset was on it when we caught the first glimpse. At our feet lay a great flesh-coloured cup full of blue liquor ; or rather the whole seemed some lapidary's quaint fancy in pink marble and blue-stone. There was no translucency, but an aggressive opaqueness, in sea and shore alike. The dry atmosphere showed everything in sharpest outline, clear-cut and broken-edged. There was no shading or variety of colour, but a strong and unsoftened contrast. To be quite accurate, there was one break—a splash of white, with the green suggestion of trees and grass, lying on the water's edge directly beneath us—Tiberias.'

Of course, the colour changes with the seasons, and we know that Jesus sat upon green grass upon the slopes at the north end of the Lake. Wild flowers of all shades cover the land with richest colours in their season. By the shore, close to Capernaum, lies the wonderful garden of Gennesaret, a reserve of shelter and of fountains filling a level fold of the hills, some three miles by one and a half in area, with exuberant fertility.

Such were the fields where the feet of Jesus trod. His speech of Nature has no landscape in it, but much clear vision of detail. There is singularly little mention of colour. He speaks of white sepulchres and a red sky (Mt 16²). He refers to the purple in which the rich man is clad (Lk 16¹⁹) ; and those lilies of the field of which He said that Solomon in all his glory was not arrayed like one of them (Mt 6²⁸ etc.), were purple irises. In the East every shadow turns to this colour, and it may perhaps have been a favourite of His. If so, the robe with which Herod's soldiers mocked Him gains a new and pathetic irony. His references to flowers (cf. art. POET) are pre-Raphaelite in their detail and delicacy. No Greek nymph was ever conceived more daintily than Christ's lily. He often refers to single trees, such as the fig-tree, but especially to the vine, from which He draws symbolic lessons in great detail (Jn 15¹). Thus He is true to that characteristic of Palestine which has given to it the true and happy epithet of ' the land of the single tree.'

But it was as a stage for human activities that Jesus chiefly viewed the earth. His delights and His interests were with the sons of men. Sometimes the exigencies of His own life force thoughts of Nature upon Him, as when the stones of the wilderness suggest loaves of bread (Mt 4³), or the holes of foxes and the nests of birds are contrasted with His own homelessness (8²⁰). He speaks much of those trees which grow fruit for the use of man, and acquiesces in their doom when they are barren. Yet there is a note of compassion in the parable of the Barren Fig-tree (Lk 13⁸) which reminds us of Jonah's ' pity ' for his withered gourd (Jon 4¹⁰), and there is a sudden and striking description of a tree bursting into the full glory of its leafage. These, however, are exceptions. Man is almost always doing something to Nature as Jesus sees it,—ploughing, sowing, reaping ; fishing, tending sheep, protecting them against wolves. Hot journeying and refreshing cups of cold water, wayside incidents of all kinds, abound in His parables. He sees the operations of the husbandman and fisher in minute detail, touches of nature everywhere telling of the keen eyes that let nothing escape their observation. Gennesaret (Mk 6⁵³, Mt 14³⁴) itself may have furnished Him with many of those vivid pictures of agricultural life and its occupations in which His parables abound.* He notes the robbers lurking by the highways (Lk 10³⁰), and the places where He stands are sometimes crowded with sick folk laid there of an evening for His healing (Mk 1³²). His world is always 'a field full of folk.'

The open-air character of His ministry lends a sense of freedom and of roominess to much of His thought. There is a feel of wandering in it, and a clean scent of cornfields and flowery meadows. There are references to the weather (Mt 16²), and He overhears His disciples remarking that in four months it will be harvest time (Jn 4³⁵). In such phrases as 'the birds of the air' (Mt 8²⁰) and 'the lilies of the field' (6²⁸), there is the delight in sky-space and field-breadth. Nothing could better express the leisurely and detached mood of the wanderer, in sympathy with wide open spaces, than such words as 'sufficient unto the day is the evil thereof' (6³⁴). While His days were spent in crowded thoroughfares of men, He felt the need of retreat and the refreshment of solitary places (14¹³). When no wider space was available, He frequented the Garden of Gethsemane. But that was at a time when the world had closed in upon His life, shutting Him in with men and human tragedy. There, in full view of the lights of Jerusalem, and with its murmur in His ear, He still found among olive trees a certain solitude. Earlier, there must have been many quiet days of retreat among the mountains or across the lake, when He felt the soothing and healing effect of Nature in all its power.

Yet the message of the open field was not for Himself alone. In contrast with modern views of Nature, the freedom and the beauty of the world filled Him with the most childlike and delightful thoughts. There was no shadow of separation between the Creator and His works, no sense of cruelty or savagery, no philosophizing consciousness of the tormenting questions of scientific doubt. In all simplicity, with the eyes of a child, He saw in Nature the handiwork of the Father. The heaven is God's throne, and the earth His footstool (5³⁴ etc.). Across the whole field of the world the Father's care is lavished, on birds (10²⁹) and beasts and the children of men. As to the mysteries of Providence, Jesus refused to admit the popular view of God's interference in such accidents as the fall of a tower in Siloam (Lk 13⁴). On the contrary, though without pursuing the subject to further consequences, He reminds us that the Father makes His sun to rise upon the evil and the good, and sends rain upon the just and the unjust (Mt 5⁴⁵).

There is a mysterious fact of sympathetic response between Nature and Humanity which has been variously explained, and yet never satisfactorily understood. It would seem as if Nature and Humanity had some mysterious understanding with one another, some subtle and occult system of signalling to one another across the gulf which separates the living world from the dead. In all the ancient religions of Asia this was a familiar idea. Baal-worship, in all its varieties, spread it across the Semitic world. The OT is full of references to spiritual presence associated especially with certain places or natural objects, or spiritual agency pass-

ing over from the deeds of man to the locality associated with them. The ground is cursed for man's sake in the story of Eden (Gn 3¹⁷) ; the place on which Moses stands is holy ground (Ex 3⁵). A 'hill of Jehovah' may often have been so called in rhetorical religious speech when all that was intended was emphasis on height or greatness ; yet there can be no doubt that the words originally were meant of literal and peculiar possession. The whole ritual concerning clean and unclean animals is an instance of the same habit.

It would be enough, to prove that Jesus felt and utilized this strange and intimate connexion between Nature and the supernatural, to point to the miracles which He openly performed and professed. The Jews have a name for Him which is very significant in this connexion. By many of them He has been called 'The Good Magician.' This interesting fact throws light on the taunt of His enemies that He was a Samaritan, and had a devil (Jn 8⁴⁸). Samaria was famous for its magicians, who were for the most part addicted to sorcery and necromancy. Such mistaken interfusion of the material and spiritual world was regarded by His enemies as of the same kind as that which they saw and heard in Him. His prophecies of future judgment (Mt 25³¹ etc.) mingle the material facts of the world with spiritual forces and thoughts in very much the same fashion as they are blended in those flame-pictures which so interested Him in the Book of Daniel. His miracles involved the blending of the two spheres in every instance. On the other hand, He cut through the doctrines of 'clean and unclean' with a ruthlessness which stirred up the animosity of His enemies (Mt 15¹¹ etc.). Regarding the food provisions of the Jewish law, He said nothing, though it is unmistakably His spirit that we recognize in the vision of Peter a few years after His death (Ac 10⁹⁻¹⁶). But as for the curse of uncleanness which the Pharisees saw everywhere falling like a shadow over the whole life of man, He would have none of it, and (proclaiming eloquently His belief in the fresh wholesomeness of Nature) declared all things clean (Lk 11⁴¹).

Galilee was very superstitious, though in a more naïve and less repulsive form than the necromancy of Samaria. On two occasions we hear of the disciples mistaking Jesus for a spirit (Mt 14²⁶, Lk 24³⁷), —in the former, apparently for the angry spirit of the Lake. On both these occasions Jesus reassures them, but says nothing to dispel or ridicule their views. On the other hand, there can be no doubt that He accepted the universal belief in demons, who haunted not men only, but places as well (Mt 12⁴³ ['dry places'], cf. Mt 8²⁸, Mk 5⁵).

Thus for Jesus Nature was indeed 'haunted.' The worlds of spirit and matter were, in His thought, full of interchange. Yet it is very remarkable how entirely He differs from the spirit of contemporary magic, as we know its development in the Rabbinical doctrines of the time, and in the later Asiatic and Egyptian schools. There is at once a reserve and a freshness about the narratives of the miracles of Jesus. They are not the dark ultimate result of fearsome dealing with the occult. They are the inevitable effect of the Divine love set free on the earth and in full play upon the facts of Nature—that same love which in less startling fashion He has already recognized in sunrise and rainfall (Mt 5⁴⁵). Consequently in Him the unwholesomeness of magic and spiritualism is entirely absent. He calls the dead as simply, and they obey as naturally, as we call the living and they come. He heals the sick just as a mother might caress her child.

One more note must suffice for this brief account of His connexion with Nature as Palestine showed

* For a very full set of examples of this, see Hausrath, i. 9, 10 ; ii. 134, 135, 136, 138, 139, 140, 191, 223, etc.

it to Him. We have already referred in passing to some of His parables. It is very noteworthy that in so many of them He saw and used the symbolism of Nature. It would seem as if for Him every process of the field, the life of trees, the springs of 'living water,' the softness of sand and the stability of rocks, the saltness of salt, the shining and the quenching of lights, were constantly suggesting symbols of that spiritual life of which He was at once the creator and the exponent. The earth was interesting to Him in its own right, but it was doubly interesting on account of its analogy with the Kingdom of heaven. Seeds of the earth, birds of the air, wind and flowing water and burning fire, were all unceasingly rehearsing under His eyes the operations of the Kingdom.

Nor did the analysis stop there. When the busy and thoughtful work of man had touched the natural world, new symbols sprang forth for His use on every hand. We shall understand better such a saying as 'I am the way,' when we remember how through His childhood He had watched the life of the great world passing along a Roman road and a caravan route in the north. We are reminded of more than one of His sayings (Jn 15[1] etc.) when we find that in vine-growing parts of Syria to-day the vine-plants are dug round and exposed to the depth of more than a foot, and all rootlets are cut off from the main root to that depth. If this were not done, the sun would scorch the roots near the surface, or the passing plough would bleed them. It is the deep roots only that are safe. At Hebron, a few years ago, a traveller noticing the fact that the sheepfolds were circles of stone wall broken by a gap in which there was never any door, asked a shepherd for the reason, and was answered, 'I am the door.' The shepherd lies down in the open space, and no wolf can enter nor can any sheep stray except across his body. That was a symbol worthy of the use of Jesus!

4. Towns and Villages.—For the understanding of anything connected with the life and history of a Semitic nation, nothing is of such importance as to study the growth and character of towns, and the changes which they produce upon those who exchange a nomad for a settled existence. To realize the times of Jesus, and still more those of the OT, we have to disabuse our minds of all that the modern world means by a *city* when we meet the word in the ancient writings. It is not without a feeling of amused surprise that one comes to identify those grotesque hamlets with the 'cities' of the Bible, and to recall the fact that their 'kings' must have often occupied a humbler station in the body politic of their times than the chairman of a parish council may occupy in ours. Of course, there have been incalculably great changes in a land which has been under the ploughshares of war for so many centuries, yet the sites remain, and it is often possible to rebuild the past. The very forces that have consigned so many of them to ruins have kept the rest alive through everything. The want of good roads, the uncertainties of government, the ancient feuds and avoidances, have preserved village communities apart and with little alteration.

Of cities in the Western sense, there were none in Syria. Yet Damascus, Beyrout, and Jerusalem stand out from the towns of Syria as places worthy of the name. Jerusalem we shall consider at a later stage. There is no record of any visit of Jesus to Berytus or Damascus, but Tyre and Sidon must have rivalled if not surpassed them in His time. G. A. Smith has suggested that in the story of the Prodigal Son we may have a reference to the fast city life where boys from country homes might be seen then, as in Beyrout they may be seen now, 'wasting their substance with riotous living' (Lk 15[13]). It was in Beyrout, only a year

or two ago, that an American, trying to persuade a lad to come to America, received the answer, 'Suffer me first to bury my father'—the father standing by and acquiescing in the filial sentiment.

With several of the towns Jesus was familiar. They have changed more than the villages, and yet there is much in them still which enables us to reconstruct the life He saw. There are about a dozen of them, and they shine from far, white splashes on the hill-tops, like Jaffa, perched with a conscious pose above the rocks of its seashore; or Jenin, gleaming like a white bird from its nest of palmtrees. The streets are usually aggressively irregular, at once ancient and unfinished in their appearance. The wider spaces, where tents are pitched and camels and horses tethered, are full of noise and colour, a patchwork of brilliant and crowded human life. There are narrower streets, which often become tunnels, in which laden asses brush the wares of shopkeepers with their burdens, and the shrill talk of men and women intensifies the disagreeableness of the smells. Closely huddled together from the first, and kept from lateral expansion by their walls and gates, and the dangers of the open country outside, the houses are forced upwards for expansion, and the sky of townsfolk is a narrow strip seen between lofty precipices of stone.

The villages are charming at a distance, but full of disillusion as one approaches. The difference between the distant view and the interior reminds one of the words of Jesus about the outward and inward appearances of whited sepulchres (Mt 23[27]). They are usually well set, on picturesque heights or hillsides, and the angular outline of flat roofs and walls lends them a suggestion of military fortification. Cultivated oliveyards or gardens give the promise of quiet prosperity, and groups of trees seem to have arranged themselves for a picture. But, on nearer approach, the trees appear to detach themselves and stand apart, and the houses to decay before the eyes of the spectator into ruinous heaps of débris. This is due partly to poverty, and partly to the pretence of poverty as a device for avoiding the rapacity of the tax-gatherer or of the robber. Even in the time of Jesus ostentation was dangerous. Those towns of which He speaks were walled and guarded. Towns and villages were eagerly watched by the tax-gatherers and sometimes ruined and burned by banditti, especially in outlying or frontier regions. When He spoke of an angry lord coming to avenge the murder of his son and destroy the city of the murderers (Mt 21[41]), the words would awaken no surprise.

Jesus was a dweller in towns. His longest homes on earth were Nazareth and Capernaum, both of them among the larger towns of Galilee. The significance of this fact is noteworthy. Most of the Syrian towns are to-day the mingling-places of the land, the crucibles wherein a composite race is molten out of many elements. One or two towns, indeed, like Nablus and Hebron, are fanatically Mohammedan, and the unwelcome alien elements of the population are kept apart, while the life of the whole community stagnates, immune to the infection of their uncleanness, but unprogressive as cities of the dead. But the other towns are open to the world. It is said that the sanitary conditions are such that if it were not for the freedom of intercourse the population would die off. The inhabitants often emigrate, and there is much intermarriage with people of other towns, so that the life is varied and has other than purely local interests.

From the earliest times the population of these towns was recruited by Canaanites, Arabs, and Israelites from other districts. In the days of

Jesus, Græco-Roman life was pouring into them, and there was always the presence of the imperial military contingent. The great roads and the Eastern campaigns of Rome had opened up and greatly developed foreign commerce, which found markets in all the larger centres. Jesus was a child and a man of the town. It was not, as in the case of John the Baptist, in desert places that He chose to teach, but in the crowded synagogues, clad in ordinary townsman's tasselled dress.

Urban communities arose from three main causes, viz. commerce (especially commerce in connexion with agriculture), war, and worship. In its various phases, town life bears marks of its threefold origin through all time. Christ touched this life on all its sides, and came into relation with each of these three aspects of it.

Commerce Jesus knew from the first in Nazareth. The town lies in the oval hollow of a high mountain valley. The carpenter's shop there led Him doubtless to a knowledge of house building, and He knew the reasons why some houses stood the underwash of rainstorms and some did not (Mt 7²⁴). Tradition mentions 'yokes and ploughs' as among the chief objects which He manufactured as a carpenter; and there can be little doubt that this is correct. For Nazareth was just the place in which commerce was most sure to be closely connected with agriculture; and He who said, 'Take my yoke upon you' (11²⁹), and spoke of the light burden and the easy yoke, had doubtless in His mind much experience of the choice of timber and of accurate fitting of yokes to the necks of oxen. He knew the markets, and may not only have seen children playing in them, but have played there Himself as a child. Capernaum was a place of importance for the collection of revenue, being situated at an important point on a great Roman road. Jericho, famous for its rich trade in balsam, was a still more important tax-collecting centre, where a leading publican could gather many of his friends to a feast (Lk 5²⁹). Matthew and Zacchæus are links connecting Jesus with the receipt of custom. Capernaum also had its fishing fleet, and its extensive fish-market, and Peter's family resided there (Mt 8¹⁴). The traveller coming in from the eastern desert towards the Lebanon is astonished by the aspect of the town of Homs (Emesa), whose high square blocks of masonry and many chimney-stalks give it a striking resemblance to a Midland English manufacturing town. No doubt that is a product of modern industry. Yet, as He looked southward from His disciples' boat, Jesus must have often seen the cloud of smoke rising from Taricheæ, at the southern end of the Lake, where in His time a large trade in fish-curing was carried on.

War, also, had left its traces. As one advances farther and farther to the north-east from Damascus, one is struck to find the walls of oasis-towns grow thicker and higher, and to note the pierced loopholes in them, testifying to the nearness of the raiding Bedawin, and the precarious terms on which town life is possible there. Many such fortress towns Jesus must have visited on His journeys. Ever visible from Nazareth itself, the crest of Tabor, to which some have seen an allusion in the 'city set on an hill' (5¹⁴), was crowned by a fort and occupied by a Roman garrison. The centurions whom Jesus met, and who impressed Him so favourably, were in command of detachments of Roman soldiers, who formed an important feature in all the town life of Syria, mingling at times in friendly intercourse with their neighbours (Lk 7⁴·⁵), and lending to the life of the place that unmistakable air of distinction which is ever to be found about the army of a great empire.

Worship, too, was an ancient and ineradicable feature of town life. Many towns owed their first origin to some holy place, whose associations were lost in the most remote antiquity, and many were glorified by historical associations of the religious past. Such holy places were scattered up and down the land, but the history of Jesus brings us into contact chiefly with two of them— Jacob's Well, near Shechem, and Bethlehem, the city of David. The concentration of the religious life of the nation in Jerusalem tended to discourage the attention paid to local shrines, and it is striking that to visit the former of the two above mentioned, Jesus had to journey into the heart of Samaria; while, as regards Bethlehem, we never hear of it after the stories of His birth. It was the synagogue which gave its religious aspect to the town life which Jesus knew. The first beginning of His ministry was in the synagogue of Nazareth. It is in connexion with the ruins of a costly synagogue that the controversy about the site of Capernaum still centres (cf. Sanday). While the Temple still gathered round it the national religious sentiment, the actual religious life of the people owed more to the synagogues than to the Temple. In them religion was surrounded by individual memories and family associations. In them the Scriptures grew familiar, and the Law was expounded and applied to the details of actual life. While the Temple revealed to every true Israelite Jehovah as the God of his nation, the synagogue kept about him the thought and presence of Jehovah as God of his home. Thus the idea of the city was more and more a religious idea in Israel, and her God was a city dweller. There is an Eastern proverb which speaks of homeless strangers as 'going to God's gate,' and the idea of the City of God, fostered indeed by Jerusalem, yet hallowed every city of Israel. Not of the capital only, but of all her towns she sang that 'unless the Lord keep the city, the watchman waketh but in vain' (Ps 127¹).

There can be no question that the city conception entered largely into Jesus' view of His Kingdom. Josephus describes (perhaps in exaggerated terms) the Essene conception of the Kingdom of God as a spot beyond the ocean 'which is oppressed neither with storms of rain nor snow, nor with intense heat, but soft, cooling, zephyr west winds always blow' (cf. Hausrath, i. 164). That was Utopia seen from the wilderness—the Kingdom of God seen from the desert. But for Jesus the desert was but an occasional resort. It was the crowded streets of towns that set His point of view; and the life—not the retreat from life—of men and women, was the ideal of His Kingdom. In every parable and prophecy of His which describe it, we hear the hum of man's activity, and see him busy with human business.

The town life, however, which Jesus knew in Syria was very far from the ideal. Of course, in estimating such matters, a large allowance must always be made for the different tastes of Easterns and Westerns, so that many things which impress us as disadvantages may have been either unnoticed or actually enjoyed by Orientals. Nothing, for instance, strikes the traveller more than the constant *publicity* of life in the East, to which reference has already been made. There seems, at first sight, to be no private life at all. Every one knows everything about everybody. The intimacy of family life appears to be everywhere, but without its affection, and the unceasing sound of speech keeps up an unbroken and unseemly exposure of private affairs. That Jesus felt this oppressive at times is proved by those periodic retreats to desert places and to mountains which are so familiar to readers of the Gospels. The note of intimacy, the personal quality of intercourse even in crowded thoroughfares, appear in countless touches of the narrative. He Himself refers to it when He gives it as a thing to be counted on, that that which is told in the chamber will be proclaimed on the housetop (Mt 10²⁷, Lk 12³), (from which at least ten families would hear it). There is, behind the main speech of the Gospels, the sound of an eternal chatter among the 'rustling crowds.' Remarks of disciples and bystanders are often overheard either by Jesus or by the reporter (Mt 13⁵⁵·⁵⁶, Jn 4³⁵ etc.). Sins of speech are more frequently referred to and rebuked than other sins.

This publicity, however, is but one part of the general sense of *comfortlessness* which depresses the Western visitor in the East. At one time, when Jesus was homeless, He evidently felt this, contrasting His own wandering life with that of foxes and of birds (Mt 8²⁰). But the homes themselves are often such as to seem very comfortless to the traveller. Of course, comfort is a matter which very largely depends upon custom, and the apparent want of it is often illusory. The streets are filthy, and often untidy in detail; but the inhabitants seem to have a singular lack of sensitiveness to smells, and the sordid litter of odds and ends appears not to distract their eye from appreciation of the fine building that rises out of it. In many houses the floor is on two levels, the upper portion being for the human inhabitants, and the lower for cattle, whose mangers are hollowed out of the raised floor along its edge. Even in better houses the rooms are bare; and jars for olives, oil, or water, along with corn-baskets and agricultural implements, give to the reception-rooms the appearance of outhouses. The main desiderata seem to be heat in winter and coolness in summer, so that the interiors are generally dark—a state of matters which is not conducive to cleanliness. There is no glass, and the strong sunlight penetrates the rooms in shafts which end in brilliant jewel-like flames of colour where they strike upon a garment or a piece of coloured pottery, and throws the rafters and walls into shadows of the richest brown and indigo, while all recesses and much of the floor are in darkness unrelieved. That this was the state of matters with which Jesus was familiar, is strikingly borne out by His parable of the Lost Coin, where the woman lights a candle and searches the house (Lk 15[8]). That He is thinking of daylight is proved by the fact that the candle has to be lighted. It is narrated by Conder of a visitor to the cave of the Holy House at Nazareth, the reputed home of Jesus in His boyhood, that he remarked to the monk who showed him it, that it was dark for a dwelling-house. The monk answered that 'The Lord had no need of much light.' Yet it is evident from many sayings that Jesus was peculiarly sensitive to the contrasts of light and darkness. The 'outer dark' (Mt 22[13]) of unlit streets affected Him with a sort of horror; and He gloried in the claim, which He often repeated, that He was the 'light of the world,' or the light of men. In the still more striking phrase, 'the light of life,' we see something of what light meant to Him. It may have been suggested by the contrast of the dark interior of a tomb with the sunshine that struck upon its whitewashed outer walls. But these words could have been used only by One to whom light meant quickened and exhilarated vitality.

However much custom and race may have mitigated the trials which these matters would impose on Westerns, we know that there were other characteristics of town life which were wholly distasteful to Him, and which He denounced. From His speech we can gather that He was often in conflict with that sophisticated provincialism which was the besetting sin of country towns. Mingling-places of the national varieties, the towns were yet sufficiently complete in themselves, and apart from one another, to foster jealousy and local conceit. In places like Cæsarea Philippi, for instance, where to this day any passer-by may pick up large fragments of Roman mosaic floors or panels, the wealthy and luxurious life had given rise to a system of servility. Jesus had noted this, and warned His disciples against the Gentile practice of encouraging sycophants to address them as 'sweet lords' (Lk 22[25]). Nor are the objectionable ways and manners of the town confined to the Gentiles. There are the local hypocrites among the natives, who love to pray standing at the corners of streets (Mt 6[2]). There is that feature of country-town life which appears to be ineradicable,—that excessive love for litigation (Mt 5[24]),—the combined result of leisure and petty interests. Nothing is more striking in the narratives of the Evangelists than the frequency with which litigation is referred to, both by Jesus and His hearers. Again, the littleness and personal character of the habitual outlook on the world are illustrated by the fluency with which the Nazarenes enumerate the relatives of Jesus (Mt 13[55, 56])—the speech this of tongues practised in the eloquence of local gossip. And it throws light on the meaning of Jesus when He spoke of Capernaum as 'exalted to heaven' (Mt 11[23]). Capernaum physically was on the level of the Lake shore, and 682 feet below sea-level. It was the self-importance of the small provincial town of which He spoke. Jerusalem had its own sins, and the villages had theirs; but it probably was especially to the towns that He referred when He warned the forthgoing Apostles of supercilious rejection, and instructed them to meet it by a symbol of still more emphatic rejection, shaking the dust of them off their feet (Mt 10[14] etc.).

Still worse, and still more obvious and common in these narratives, are the tokens of the violent contrasts of avarice and misery in the town life. The selfishness of the town is there, in all its heartlessness, portrayed in such parables as those of Lazarus and Dives (Lk 16[20]), the rich man and his barns (12[18]), and many others. Prosperity and adversity are in shameless and pitiless sight of one another. Cruelty and oppression have become the recognized convention of the powerful classes. Disease is rampant, and a class of rapacious quack doctors has sprung up to prey upon its victims (Mk 5[26]). The moral tone of the town is such as to permit a prostitute to enter the feast of a wealthy Pharisee, and it is only when it appears that she is penitent that any one is shocked by the incident (Lk 7[37]). The preference of Jesus for the town is part of His principle that the true physician goes where the sick are thickest, and the true saviour where sin is most unblushing.

The villages of Syria are a class of communities of a quite different order. The sheikh dwells in his ruined tower, overlooking the huddle of brown walls and roofs, and keeping his audience-hall open for the elders to assemble in and discuss the news of the countryside. They are inhabited now, as they have been largely all along, by fellahin, said to be to a considerable extent the descendants of the ancient Canaanites, practically unmixed in blood, owing to the almost unbroken custom of intermarriages. With these Jesus must have talked that Aramaic tongue which some five or six villages in the Kalamun mountain valleys still use as their vernacular, and which is heard to-day among the bakers of Damascus who come down to the city from the Syriac village of Ma'alula. So conservative is village life in Syria, that it is to village communities alone that we look to-day, in the assured confidence that we are seeing the very kind of life which Jesus saw. One result of this conservatism is, that extraordinary combination of ignorance and pride, superstitious fears and contemptuous effrontery, which is often the first impression produced on strangers. They preserve self-government of a kind, a hereditary rule within an imperial; but they appear to be very helpless against both nature and man. Usury and oppression cow the inhabitants, the insecurity of property renders them suspicious. The writer has accidentally roused a man sleeping through the night upon his haystack in an open field, and seen others sitting upon the top of the grain piled upon a truck on the railway. They are almost exclusively agricultural in their way of life, and their methods are primitive and leisurely. They leave their hardest work to be done by their women, and spend many hours of each day in absolute idleness. Over them hangs the acrid-smelling smoke of fires whose fuel is camel-dung, that has been dried by being plastered over the outside of ovens, which break the monotony of flat roofs by their rounded shape, and appear like blisters in the fierce heat of summer. The dirtiness of the streets and of some houses is incredible. The simple food and habits of life produce healthy bodies, but disease comes upon its victims unprotected by any skill of medicine, and the sick and the whole dwell together and mingle everywhere. The first impression is one of universal gloom, and the faces of the people are sullen and contemptuous. But that is in many cases but the first instinct of self-preservation in those who are accustomed to ill-treatment. A very little tact and kindliness soon changes the aspect of things, and threatening looks give place to a smiling childishness.

Such were the villages with which Jesus was familiar, although their life was then more prosperous, and at least some of their homes more habitable. To their inhabitants He spoke His parables of simple life, such as that of the Friend at Midnight (Lk 11[5]). In one of them He blessed the children whom village mothers brought to Him

(Mk 10[13]). In another He brightened the wedding feast with good wine (Jn 2[1]). In the gathering dusk, the two villagers at Emmaus recognized Him in the act of breaking bread at their table (Lk 24[28ff.]). From a village gate was heard the sound of swift footsteps, when a rich young ruler, within sight of the squalor which had enriched him, asked the question about eternal life, and was answered that he must sell all that he had and give to the poor (Mk 10[17]). Beside another village gate He stopped the funeral procession of an only son of his mother, and gave her back her dead restored to life (Lk 7[11]). That was at Nain, one of the villages of that hill of 'Little Hermon,' on whose sides Endor and Shunem also cling—a hill of villages of resurrection. Bethany hardly counts among the villages, being almost a suburb of Jerusalem, and differing from the rest in consequence. But of all the villages of Palestine none brings Jesus so near as the little hamlet of Ephraim, perched far off on its hill in the lonely uplands to the east of Bethel. It was perhaps the remotest of the inland villages of Israel, and its rustic inhabitants dwelt alone. It was to it that He retired for His last retreat before the Passover of Death (Jn 11[54]). To Him the sickness and helplessness of the villages of His native land appealed, and drew forth compassion and healing. The sullenness that sometimes rejected Him and would have none of His love awakened no resentment, but only a great and pitying distress (Mt 11[20ff.] etc., Lk 9[52ff.]). The childlikeness of the villagers refreshed Him after the sophisticated life of towns, and found response in His constant speeches in praise of children and the childlike spirit (Mt 18[3]).

5. Jerusalem.—For good or evil, no city in the world has exercised so strong and constant an influence on the world as Jerusalem. Some of her visitors have been filled with an unbounded enthusiasm, others have been depressed with a shattering disappointment; but in one way or other the city has influenced all comers. It has been the usual fate of sacred cities to gather to themselves much of the worst along with much of the best of earthly life. Jerusalem is no exception to the rule. It is the most sacred and the most sinister spot on earth.

From the day when David took it, the last stronghold of the Jebusites, and the battle-beaten old fortress-walls of rough stone opened their gates to the God of Israel, it had been the focus of the nation's life (2 S 6, Ps 24). Solomon glorified it as the secular and religious centre, drafting into it the wealth and nobility of Israel until the land became hydrocephalous—its metropolis magnificent and the rest shrivelled and impoverished. In a far more real sense Josiah made Jerusalem great; and now at length, after countless changes of fortune, Jesus found it a city of such unique importance and significance that it stood over against all the rest of the land, dividing the nation into 'dwellers in Jerusalem' and 'others'—a more effective division than any other of the time.

In the visits paid by Jesus to Jerusalem, from those of His infancy and the memorable first remembered visit—that paid when He was twelve years old—to the triumphal entry and the night journey as a captive from Gethsemane, there is an increasing intensity of interest. His arguments here are more of the nature of pitched battles than in the country (Jn 6, etc.); His acts of authority more decisive and dangerous (Mt 21[12]); even His healing of the sick more of the nature of a challenge (Jn 5[10]). Thus the history of Jesus fully confirms our sense of the importance of Jerusalem. The thrill of patriotic enthusiasm in such a word as His reference to 'the city of the Great King' (Mt 5[35]) has already been alluded to. But more

and more irrevocably that loyal sentiment changed its aspect as the facts thrust themselves upon Him. It was the impossible spirit of the city more than any other thing that changed Jesus' speech from the Sermon on the Mount to the terrible denunciations and warnings of the closing days. The sacred city, which at the first had been for Him, as for every religious man of Israel, the goal of pilgrimage and the embodiment and incarnation of spiritual thought and dream, came to be the arena of His life's supreme conflict, where spirituality would fight out its great battle with 'the world, the flesh, and the devil.' Here love would try the final issue with hate, and life with death. It is by a happy inspiration that Langland, in his *Piers the Plowman*, tells of Jesus 'going to a jousts in Jerusalem.' Nothing could more exactly describe His own view of the case during His later journeys (Mt 16[21], Jn 11[16]). His spirit as He journeyed was that of one who, having fought the battle of the Spirit across the whole field, is now going on to the storming of the citadel.

Such was the change in His own feeling as He approached the capital. Not less striking is the expression of His thought of its meaning and its fate. For the pious Jew, Jerusalem was Utopia; and the mediæval view, expressed in such enraptured poems as 'Pearl' (cf. Gollancz's tr.) and the Crusading dreams of *Gerusalemme Liberata*, were the natural continuation of the ideas of which Ezekiel's visions and the Apocalypse are the expression. Jesus accepted this estimate of its importance when He deliberately chose it as the one place on earth where the Messianic claim must be publicly made (Jn 5[19] etc.), but He did this in the full consciousness that when it had served this purpose it would pass away. To Him it was a doomed Utopia, doomed beyond all hope of recovery. Had it known (Lk 19[42]), had it understood the day of its visitation, it might have endured; as things were, it was for Him but a city of might-have-been. Yet, in the very hour when it was rushing to its doom, He seized upon it and forced it to fulfil the purpose towards which it had blindly struggled through all its eventful history. It linked on His work and Person with the past, and in crucifying Him sent on to the future the completed drama of redemption.

Subsequent history, with ruthless and terrific irony, has confirmed His view. The efforts of the Crusades to revive Jerusalem have only the more hopelessly marked it as the doomed Utopia. Every traveller is impressed with the same sense of its infinite loneliness and stony desolation. It looks like a gigantic fortress that has stood dismantled for ages, but retains for ever a weird air of petrified gallantry. It is a fossil city, fossilized when far gone in decay. The savage liveliness of the bugles which now shriek across its streets and houses, only adds to the sense of ancient death. Built for eternity, setting the pattern for men's dreams of the New Jerusalem, it stands for the sarcasm of promises unfulfilled, a city with a great future *behind it*. 'What,' we cannot but ask, 'has this relic to do with a blessed future for mankind?' History and religion seem to mourn here together, reiterating the lament of Jesus. One sees in every remembrance of it those two weeping figures, the most significant of all for its secular and religious life,—Titus, who gazed upon Jerusalem from Scopus the day before its destruction, and wept for the sake of the beautiful city so near its doom; and Jesus Christ, who, when things were ripening for Titus, foresaw the coming of the legions as He looked upon Jerusalem from Olivet,—'And when he was come near he beheld the city, and wept over it' (Lk 19[41]).

The appearance of the city, as seen from such a

lofty vantage ground as that which the approach from Bethany gives from the shoulder of the Mount of Olives, must always have been to a considerable extent the same as it is to-day. It is true that there are now two Jerusalems side by side, the ancient city packed together firmly, and the more loosely scattered masonry of the new Levantine city that has risen to the south and west of the Jaffa Gate. Yet to the north there is still the mound of ashes said to have been carried thither from the Temple sacrifices of old; and ancient tombs fill the valleys and stretch along the northern plain. It is easy for the imagination to detach the modern buildings, and to regain the ancient impression. It has been pointed out (Hausrath, i. 38, 39) that Athens stands on an unfruitful cliff; Rome between a marsh and a wilderness; Jerusalem on a barren tongue of stone, where 'the mountain land gathers itself as to a natural centre.' The 'mountains stand round about Jerusalem,' but they lift her up to their height, and she stands as a mural crown upon the mountain land. The surrounding peaks are but little elevated above her level, and she is the climax as well as the centre of the land, set up to be 'the mountain throne and the mountain sanctuary of God.' And that tongue of land is so stony that even the denudation of sieges and of centuries cannot very greatly have changed the general aspect of the scene. There is no river in her landscape to redeem the hardness of the outlines. She is 'a city of stone in a land of iron, with a sky of brass' (Disraeli's *Tancred*). She has nothing in common with the villages of Judæa, the variety of her buildings differentiating her from the rectangular sameness of theirs. As if to accentuate the contrast, the village of Siloam still lies on the eastern slope of the Kidron valley, a drift of square hovels seen across a field of artichokes. Jerusalem 'sitteth solitary,' as she has always sat; unique in the land as she is lonely in history. The colours of her walls and buildings change in the changing lights from grey with a touch of orange to grey with a touch of blue. For there is no one colour of Jerusalem. In the changing lights of sunrise, noon, afternoon, and evening, its colour changes. At one time it hangs, airy and dream-like, over the steep bank of the Valley of Jehoshaphat; at another time it seems to sit solid on its rock, every roof and battlement picked out in photographic clearness; again, in the twilight of evening all is sombre, with rich purple shadows.

We have noted in the towns of Syria those moral defects of petty quarrelsomeness and provincial self-importance which appear constantly in the records of Jesus' ministry. The metropolitan pettiness which confronted Him at Jerusalem—the tenfold provincialism of the capital city, whose modern counterpart is so familiar in many lands to-day—was a much more serious matter. All the dreams of Utopia, religious and secular, had run into personal pride and vanity; all those Divine promises and guarantees on which the glorification of Jerusalem rested were interpreted by the citizens as a species of flattering Divine favouritism shown to themselves.

In spite of much disappointment, there were still many things which must have seemed in some sort the fulfilment of the ancient hopes for Jerusalem. 'The dromedaries of Midian and Ephah' had come to her, indeed, and they from Sheba bringing gold and incense. The flocks of Kedar and the glory of Lebanon were swelling her trade. Ships were flying as a cloud and as doves to their windows, making for her seaport with wealth for her (Is 60⁶). And with that wealth came men also from east and west, from north and south. The Dispersion of the Jews had already made her Passover feasts

almost as cosmopolitan as Mecca afterwards became. The Roman road, while it brought humiliation, brought also much else to Jerusalem. Feeling its way inland from the sea across the mountains of Judæa, it ended in the Jaffa Gate. It was but one of many roads from all points of the compass which, as they approached the city, grew broader and more thronged with passengers. From the account of Pentecost given in the Acts (2⁹⁻¹¹), we can see that at certain times the polyglot crowds must have been like those which are now seen in the Meidan of Damascus to welcome the return of the Haj.

The wealthy and luxurious inhabitants were obviously spoiled by all this grandeur, and in all the shamelessness of Eastern cities paraded it in the face of the poverty they should have sought to help. Those who favoured the Roman domination, and sought to make capital out of it, like the Herodians, prided themselves openly in Jerusalem as a Roman city, and did all they could to make it so. Those who simply acquiesced, like the Sadducees, in what their superior intelligence convinced them was inevitable, found enough in their wealth and in their pride in their old city and family connexions to keep alive their aristocratic spirit. Those who, like the Pharisees, stood for the ancient religious and national claims, fostered a still more bitter fashion of bigotry and exclusiveness. From Jerusalem they too, in their surreptitious way, tried to manage the world. They spent their strength in making proselytes (Mt 23¹⁵), and they sent out deputations to interfere in local questions as far off as Capernaum (Mk 7¹, Jn 1¹⁹). The crowd, who watched and copied the great ones from below, readily caught their tone, and, in an ignorant sense of superiority, were ready at any moment to raise a tumult at their instigation, and to shout for the crucifixion of a selected victim (Mk 15¹³ etc.). Altogether, so mighty was the self-importance of this little metropolis, that for its inhabitants the rest of the world was practically non-existent; and, as happens in all poorly equipped moral natures, their consciousness of their own better privileges and good fortune ran neither to interest nor to compassion, but only to scorn.

Of the more vulgar aspects of this metropolitan superciliousness the narratives present abundant examples. The contempt of Jerusalem for Galilee is everywhere apparent. It was not only on the ground of Messianic tradition, asking whether it were likely that Christ should come out of Galilee (Jn 7⁵²). The proverb was ready on their lips about no good thing coming out of Nazareth (1⁴⁶ 7⁴¹). The facility for inventing opprobrious names, and the unsparing use of them, had developed with them into a fine art (8⁴⁸). A man was an ignoramus, a blasphemer, a lunatic, if he brought any new thing among them from the provinces. The maid in the palace of the high priest did not show any originality in laughing at the accent of country people (Mt 26⁷³). If a provincial gathered crowds of a morning to hear his preaching, and men felt in him the advent of the Spirit of God, Jerusalem coarsely explained it all by the supposition that he was intoxicated (Ac 2¹³). Any traveller might have retorted that while they were managing the world from a distance, they were neglecting it at their own doors. The fishermen of Galilee were probably far less rude, either in speech or manner, than the semi-barbarous shepherds of the Judæan mountains. But that was no concern of theirs. Their world was within their walls, and the curious and shameful result of their extravagant exclusiveness was that every Israelite was a foreigner in the capital city of his own country. Not Jesus of Nazareth alone, but every countryman was in Jerusalem 'despised and rejected of men'; and every son of man felt homeless when he entered the Holy City's gates.

The first impression made upon a stranger visiting the city in those days must have been that of an extraordinarily Roman city. Herod, the greatest of Romanizers, had utterly disregarded the lessons of past history, and repeated the mistaken policy of Solomon, which neglected the land to glorify the city. His architecture must have been as extravagant in costliness as it was poor in art. One of the grandest of all his palaces crowned the hill of Zion; his temple blazed forth its splendours from the grand platform on which it stood along the hillside of Moriah. The famous Tyropœon way spanned the ravine between the two, entirely Roman in its construction and design. Here stood a theatre whose Roman audiences listened to plays on such themes as Susanna and the Elders; there an amphitheatre at whose games rich prizes were offered. There was much barbaric splendour of a kind in the aspect of the city, but it was Roman splendour; and everything that caught the eye as impressive, led it back to the barracks and the courthouse near the tower of Antonia.

It was this aspect of Jerusalem which one might have expected Jesus to be most greatly influenced by. One of the most famous of the many would-be Messiahs, some years after this, went with a multitude of followers to blow his trumpets as the priests had blown their horns at Jericho. Jesus acted on principles directly the opposite of these. He saw the Roman buildings without either admiration or protest. His certainty of the end of all was no less positive than that of Theudas and such rash men, but it only made Him the more calm in His acquiescence until the providential moment should arrive. That was so sure—that day when the Rome which had glorified the city would destroy it—that the thought of hastening the doom, or of preventing it, never occurred to Him. Yet that very fact embittered and terrified His enemies. They did not, indeed, approve of the rebellious patriots; but that was because they regarded them as Galilæan bunglers who undertook work whose gravity they did not understand. Had any of them succeeded, Jerusalem would have welcomed him with shouts. But here was a far more serious offence. Macaulay's New Zealander on London Bridge represents to British readers a familiar and a quite legitimate kind of speculation. To Pharisees of Jerusalem such an idea was sheer treason even to think of, far more to discuss in public.

Not less directly did the attitude of Jesus to the Temple draw the nets of death around Him. Like all religious Israelites, He directed His steps to the Temple as to the natural seat and centre of His religious life. From the first it was in His Father's house that the Son of God found His appropriate home (Lk 2⁴⁶). But the pleasantness of that boyish visit yielded in later years to slow and deepening bitterness, as the accepted meaning of the Temple became more and more unmistakable. The Jews have a legend that in the sacred rock now covered by the Mosque of Omar there was inscribed the mystic name of Jehovah, and that Jesus alone of men had been able to discover and to read it. The heart of every Christian understands the unsuspected truth of that legend. Jesus ever went to that Temple as one going to His Father's house.

All the more tragic is the contrast, as it must have come upon Him, between the real and the ideal Temple of the Lord. The priestly families were Sadducees, men in whom the national hope had largely died out, and in whom His acquiescent attitude to Rome would awaken neither anger nor surprise. Indeed, it is probable that they mistook His views, and carelessly classed Him among the other revolutionaries of the time. At least the high priest frankly avowed that it was necessary that He should perish, to avert the Roman anger and revenge. But if it was only by mistake or by pretence that they found this ground of accusation against Jesus, there were other grounds on which they and He stood in plain and deadly opposition. The Sadducæan priestly families were the chief representatives of a spirit of scepticism regarding spiritual things (in reaction from the Pharisaic spirit) which had lapsed into a kind of hard secularism, a lax morality, and an unconcealed worldliness which were indifferent alike to the glory of worship and to the shame of its degradation. The shadow of Herod had fallen across the Temple and its services. Herod, who at one time had thought of himself posing as Messiah, had built the Temple; and while the Roman idolater Agrippa had offered sacrifice there, Herod had sacrificed to Roman gods at Rome. With such a patron at its head, secular life flowed into the Temple unchecked. The courts were made into a market where fraudulent bargains were driven with country-folk in connexion with the very rites of their religion, and we see how Jesus resented this in the strange outburst of holy anger with which He drove these merchants forth (Mt 21¹²). A large number of synagogues had arisen within the precincts, but there is no record of His visiting them. By preference He chose the streets for preaching in, or He spoke in the open Temple court. In the East, religion tends ever to degenerate into ritual pure and simple, devoid alike of meaning for the intellect and of emotion for the heart (W. R. Smith, Rel. Sem. p. 16). Never had this taken place more completely than in the Sadducæan priesthood at Jerusalem then. From the abode of holiness and the centre of truth, He found His Father's house become a den of thieves, and a patent sham of ritual whose performers never dreamed of treating it even as a symbol of realities. It is this that explains that most strange and ominous of records, where Jesus is described as sitting silently in the Temple during long periods of the latest days of His life (Hausrath, ii. 250). What thoughts were passing in His mind then we cannot know, and we hardly dare try to imagine. But one thing is clear. Just as He changed the conception of the Messianic Kingdom from the outward to the inner region, so He did that of the Temple. When the priests poured out the water from great jars at the feast, He cried aloud that out of those who believed on Him would come rivers of living water (Jn 7³⁸). And the words of which He was afterwards to be accused, as to the destruction and rebuilding of 'this temple,' were spoken 'of the temple of his body' (2²¹).

From all these points of view, Jerusalem had become a place of sinister prospects for Jesus. From the populace He had to expect the usual reception given to all provincials, and if more powerful enemies should require their aid, they might be counted on for darker deeds. By the orthodox religionists He would be treated as a heretic, disloyal alike to the traditions of the past and the pressing needs of the hour. By the latitudinarian priests He must be regarded with the double antagonism of worldly men to spiritual aspiration, and of ritual to spiritual reality. So Jerusalem came to be seen by Jesus under a death-cloud. Rome was free in her use of crucifixion for the better ordering of Eastern affairs, and Jesus must have seen many of His countrymen hanging on crosses beside village gates. So the certainty of the end would force itself upon Him, and the shadow of the cross fall ever more deeply. Tombs of prophets were everywhere to be seen, and many of them were martyrs' tombs (Mt 23²⁹). But it was round the walls of Jerusalem that such tombs were thickest, and for Him also Jerusalem was seen as the place for perishing in. From the far North He saw it so, saying at Cæsarea Philippi that He must go to Jerusalem to be killed (16²¹). The final journey, eager and yet deliberate, had death for its goal in the Holy City. The disciples felt a horror in the thought of Jerusalem, as if the City of the Great King had changed to a shambles (Jn 11⁸). Thomas, more ready than the others to face the worst, boldly urged them to go on and die with Him (11¹⁶). When He came near, and seeing the city realized its hopelessness, and felt the flood of old associations sweep over Him, He wept over it (Lk 19⁴¹). But He went on, nevertheless, when for Him Jerusalem meant Calvary.

It is true that, in the memory of the early Church, Jerusalem was the place of rising again as well as the place of death, and of the New Evangel that had the city for its starting-point. Yet as far as the earthly life of Jesus is concerned, the associations of Jerusalem are of almost unrelieved antagonism, sorrow, and shame. The modern aspect of the city seems to the imagination of lovers of Jesus profoundly symbolic. What the first eye-shot gives, as one sees it from Olivet, is this : a sharp angle formed by the two valleys of Jehoshaphat and Hinnom ; steep banks rising from their bottoms to the walls, which they overlap in an irregular and wavy line ; within the walls, glancing back from the angle which they form above the junction of the valleys, the eye runs up a gradually rising expanse of close-packed building, which is continued more sparsely in the long rolling slope beyond, to the ridge of Scopus in the north, and to the distant sweep of long level mountain-line to the west. It is as if the whole city had slid down and been caught by that great angle of wall just before it precipitated itself into the gorges.

These gorges themselves are part and parcel of the city, and they stand for the overflow of her sad and desolate spirit. Their sides are banks of rubbish —the wreckage and débris of a score of sieges, the accumulation of three thousand years. One looks from the lower pool of Siloam in the valley of Hinnom up a long dreary slope of dark grey rubbish, down which a horrible black stream of liquid filth trickles, tainting the air with its stench. Far above stands the wall, which in old days enclosed the pool. Here the city seems to have shrunk northwards, as if in some horror of conscience. The Field of Blood and the Hill of Evil Counsel are just across the gorge to the south. The valleys are full of tombs.

The impression of this is overwhelming, and there is one point in the view which appears more than all else to embody and explain it. Right in front, as one looks from Olivet, is the line of the Temple wall, and it is broken by a double gate, built up with closely mortared masonry. That is the ancient 'Beautiful Gate' of the Temple, by which the scapegoat, bearing the nation's sins, was led forth to the wilderness. It was built up because of a Jewish tradition that Messiah would return and enter the city by it. So Jerusalem has indeed built up the exit for her sins and the entrance for her Saviour. The land seems, as one travels over its desolate mountains and valleys, still inhabited by Jesus ; but He has forsaken Jerusalem.

Cf. also separate articles, such as GALILEE, JUDÆA, SAMARIA, JERUSALEM, NAZARETH, CAPERNAUM, JORDAN, etc.

LITERATURE.—Schürer, *HJP, passim* ; Hausrath, *Hist. of NT Times—Times of Jesus* ; G. A. Smith, *HGHL* ; Sanday, *Sacred Sites of the Gospels* ; Doughty, *Arabia Deserta* ; Conder, *Tent-Work in Palestine* ; Ramsay, *The Education of Jesus* ; cf. also the present writer's book, *The Holy Land* (illustrated by Mr. Fulleylove).

JOHN KELMAN.

PALM.—Palm trees, though frequently referred to in the OT, are mentioned in connexion with the life of Christ only once : viz. in the account of the triumphal entry into Jerusalem (Jn 12¹³). The English name (Lat. *palma*) is due to the similarity of the leaves of some kinds to the open hand. The term in Greek (applied only to a genus) is φοῖνιξ, which gave its name to a town in Crete (Ac 27¹²). The word also means 'a Phœnician,' 'a purple colour,' and the fabulous *phœnix*. In Rev 7⁹ it is used of the leaf (or so-called branch), which is usually called βαΐον.

The palm tree is amongst the foremost both in beauty and in utility. It grows with uniform trunk straight like the mast of a ship. The trunk is in some kinds smooth, in others clearly annulated, in others rough with the roots of former fronds. At the top the leaves (or fronds) spring out in a spreading circle or crown, while beneath them the flowers and clusters of fruit are formed. The tree is endogenous, without bark and without branch. The leaves vary in length from three to thirty feet. And along the stalk on either side long leaflets grow close, presenting in many kinds (pinnated) the shape of an enlarged feather, in others, including most of the fan-shaped palms, a rounder, broader form of palmate or webbed configuration, while in the bi-pinnate caryota and the mauritia they have a triangular (or fish-tailed or wedge-shaped) appearance. The fruit is often valuable, and by incision the juice is obtained that makes palm wine. Palm trees are tropical and semi-tropical. Some grow near wells, as the palms of Elim (Ex 15²⁷), but this may be attributed to culture ; others flourish in sandy deserts ; some are found in mountainous regions, and many rear themselves erect on wind-swept ridges. Besides yielding food, drink, and oil, they afford house-building material, and many are highly serviceable for the various uses to, which fibres are applicable.

Palms have been divided into five tribes, over a hundred genera, over a thousand species ; but there is a limited number of main kinds. The palm of Palestine is the date-palm. This tree (*phœnix dactylifera*, date being a contraction of *dactylus*, 'finger') rises gracefully to a height of from fifty to ninety feet. It grows in various climates and latitudes, but its fruit fails both in Europe and in India. The female tree (for the phœnix, unlike most others, is not hermaphrodite) bears a cluster which may contain 200 dates, and it may continue to bear for two hundred years. These fruits, which are half sugar, are a chief article of food in Arabia and North Africa. From an incision near the top the fermenting sap flows so as to yield in one month twenty gallons of wine or toddy. The pinnated leaves, which are of a deep green colour and from 9 to 12 feet in length, are used to make mats and baskets, and the fibres of their stalks make cordage. The leaves also make thatch, and the trunk is useful timber. This tree abounded in the valley of the Jordan, but Jericho was specially the city of palm trees (Dt 34³). A group of palms, with their magnificent crowns, might afford ample shade. Accordingly, we find that early in the history of Israel Deborah dwelt under her palm tree (Jg 4⁵), while in the time of our Lord many of the Essenes were said to live in palm groves. Fructification is artificial or accidental ; and forests may be cultivated that in years of famine will support the population of a country.

The palm, being upright, green, fruitful, and imposing, was an emblem of the righteous in their prosperity (Ps 92¹²). In appreciation of the beauty of its form it was carved on the walls and doors of the Temple (1 K 6²⁹·³², cf. Ezk 40¹⁶ 41¹⁸). Its leaves were borne as symbols of rejoicing at the Feast of

Tabernacles (Lev 23⁴⁰) and also at the Maccabæan Feast of Dedication, of which the special feature was the illumination. This tall, firm, unbending tree, with its magnificent crown of fronds, with fruit and leaves that served for sustenance and ornament, was readily reckoned emblematic of moral qualities—rectitude, constancy, gracefulness, usefulness—such as are the constituents of success. The palm came to be regarded specially as the symbol of victory and triumph. It is in that sense that the name has acquired its metaphorical meaning. The winner (we say) carries off the palm. A period of exceptional prosperity is remembered as 'palmy days.' 'Another race hath been, and other palms are won' (Wordsworth).

The carrying of palm leaves (τὰ βαΐα τῶν φοινίκων) by the people in honour of the Messiah (Jn 12¹³) was in accordance with the custom observed at feasts and on great public occasions. Jesus was saluted as a king proceeding to His coronation. The palms symbolized His triumph and the people's joy. He allowed the homage of the multitude as the spontaneous expression of pure-minded loyalty. On the other hand, the Pharisees and officials regarded it as a challenge of their authority. The incident has been commemorated since the 5th cent. by the Greek and Latin Churches in the Palm Sunday (*dominica palmarum*, or feast of palm-leaves), immediately preceding Easter, at which palms are consecrated and a procession takes place.

The supreme expression of the palm as the symbol of triumphant homage is in the Apocalyptic vision, where the innumerable multitude who have come through the great tribulation, and who serve God day and night, stand before the throne and before the Lamb, clothed in white robes and with palms in their hands (Rev 7⁹· ¹⁴).

LITERATURE.—Artt. in *Encyc. Brit.*⁹, *Chambers's Encyc.*, the *EBi*, and Hastings' *DB*; *Historiæ Palmarum* by Martius; Griffiths' *Palms of British East India* is a volume of illustrations.   R. SCOTT.

PALM.—The word occurs (Mk 14⁶⁵, Jn 18²², cf. 19³) in the tr. of ῥάπισμα, a blow with the open hand. It refers to the stroke on the cheek (Mt 5³⁹, Lk 6²⁹), one of the affronts and indignities that may have to be borne cheerfully in representing and serving the Kingdom of heaven. In Mt 26⁶⁷, Mk 14⁶⁵, a distinction is implied between the rough jest of hitting with the fist (κολαφίζω) by the soldiers standing in front of Christ and the smiting with the palm by the servants of the high priests as they stood behind and challenged Him to tell from whom the blow had come. For all Christ prayed that the sin committed in ignorance might be forgiven (Lk 23³⁴). It is only by a Christian that affront can really be put upon Christ (Ph 3¹⁸).   G. M. MACKIE.

PALSY.—See PARALYSIS.

PAPIAS.— 1. Papias as witness to Gospels.— There is no early evidence as to our Gospels comparable to that of Papias, bishop of Hierapolis, even in the fragmentary and obscure form in which it has reached us through the pages of Eusebius (*HE* iii. 39). Eusebius' own slighting estimate of Papias' judgment was due largely to distaste for the highly realistic form in which he set forth the common primitive expectation of an imminent reign of Christ on a renewed earth, which Papias held, with the Apocalypse of John (20⁴ff·), would last a thousand years. But, whatever his mental calibre, Papias' importance lies rather in his endeavour to keep in touch with historical witness, as far as possible first-hand witness, to the true or original meaning of the Lord's own teaching.

For realizing such an aim Papias had exceptional advantages. There is little doubt that after the destruction of Jerusalem and its Temple in A.D. 70, if not before, the Roman province of Asia was the chief centre of Christian tradition outside Palestine. The foundation for this had been laid by St. Paul, with Ephesus as base of influence ; and hither were attracted not a few of the leading personal disciples of Jesus, including, perhaps, several of the original Apostles. Chief of all, we must reckon John, the son of Zebedee, whose presence at Ephesus for a period of years cannot be explained away by any confusion with another John. The latter's title, 'the Elder.' itself implies the need for distinguishing him from a greater namesake residing in the same neighbourhood.

The statement in certain late writers that John, as well as his brother James, had been 'done to death by Jews,' even if correct, would not negative this. But it is very possibly a mistake, since Eusebius, who was on the look out for all facts bearing on the lives of Apostles, says nothing of the kind. It probably arose from the misunderstanding of a passage in which Papias explained the 'cup' of Christ in Mk 10³⁸f·, Mt 20²²f· as 'martyrdom'—which in James' case was unto death, but in John's stopped short of that.

Hierapolis, Papias' home in South Phrygia, was well within the province of Asia and near the main road to Ephesus from the East, while it actually lay on another road running N.W. through Asia to Smyrna and Pergamum. A man so situated, and with a passion for first-hand information as to Christ's teaching, had special chances of intercourse with such disciples of the first generation ('elders' he calls them) as visited or worked in Asia, so far as his youth or early manhood overlapped their later years. But how far was this the case? For an answer to this question we have to rely on the chapter of Eusebius already referred to, and particularly on certain of Papias' own words there cited.

2. Papias' book and the situation it presupposes.—Papias wrote a work in five books, entitled 'Exposition of the Lord's Oracles (*Logia*).' Quoting from this, Irenæus wrote, about A.D. 180: 'These things Papias, too, who was a hearer of John and a companion of Polycarp, a man of the old time (ἀρχαῖος ἀνήρ), further witnesses in writing.' This statement Eusebius, anxious to dissociate John from Papias' millenarian views, challenges, saying that he does not claim to have heard Apostles, but only associates of theirs. In support of this, he quotes a passage from Papias' preface which enables us to judge how far his own reading of it is warranted. In studying it, our chief care must be to read it in the light of what we can learn as to the scope of its author's preface as a whole.

(*a*) *The Lord's 'Oracles' and their record.*—We gather that Papias felt constrained to write by the needs of the times in the western part of Asia Minor, where much diversity of view existed as to the standard of Christian faith and practice, owing largely to uncertainty both as to the exact wording of Christ's sayings and as to their real meaning. Some, it is true, took no pains even to ground their practice in all things on Christ's own words as spoken to His personal disciples, but deferred to 'alien precepts' coming through doubtful media of Divine revelation, rather than direct from this supreme source of truth. But, to Papias, the only sure way of reaching the mind of Christ, the Truth itself, is to start from the Apostolic written collection of 'the Oracles,' as he conceived the Gospel according to Matthew to·be, the one directly Apostolic document of this character (the Johannine Gospel is in any case of another type). To this method some—probably typical Greek or 'Gnostic' Christians, to whom its markedly Jewish and eschatological colour may have been an offence —might object that the accuracy of this Gospel itself was not above question, pointing to the differences between it and the Petrine Gospel by Mark. To meet some such difficulty,* which was perhaps meant to lower the authority of both Gospels (since Mark also had Jewish features of the kind in question), Papias cites a tradition derived from a man of the first Christian generation, 'the Elder' (? John, see below), as he styles him—

'And this the Elder used to say: Mark, indeed (μέν), having been Peter's interpreter, wrote down with accuracy, yet not in order, everything he bore in mind—the things, namely, either said or done by the Christ (or Lord). For neither did he listen to the Lord nor did he follow Him, but later on, as I said, Peter, who adapted his instructions to the requirements, yet without intending to make a connected account of the Lord's sayings (σύνταξιν τῶν κυριακῶν ποιούμενος λόγων or λογίων). Accordingly Mark was in no way in fault in so writing certain things as he recalled them: for of one thing he took precaution, not to omit anything that he had heard or therein to state anything falsely.'

Here we have a defence of the trustworthiness of Mark's narrative, so far as it goes, save on the score of the arrangement of its material, which, having originally been delivered by Peter in an order determined by the exigencies of Christian instruction (διδασκαλίαι, as distinct from public preaching, κήρυγμα), was reproduced by Mark with simple fidelity. A Gospel so composed made no claim to comparison, as regards the order of the Lord's sayings (so far as it recorded them), with a Gospel written by one of Peter's fellow-disciples on a different principle, that of collecting the weighty utterances of the Lord (τὰ λόγια), disposed in orderly grouping. Such, however, was the Gospel composed by the Apostle Matthew, as we may infer that Papias went on to quote 'the Elder' as saying in effect.

Probably the sentence beginning 'But Matthew,' which the 'Mark, indeed (μέν), . . .' of the extract in Eusebius seems to imply, included a statement that Matthew wrote 'among the Hebrews,' i.e. in Palestine. At least this is an element common to Irenæus (III. i. 1), and the tradition preserved in Euseb. iii. 24, possibly from Clement of Alexandria, whose account of the Gospels as contained in 'a tradition of the elders of earlier times' (τῶν ἀνέκαθεν πρεσβυτέρων) he elsewhere cites (vi. 14). Now in ii. 15 Clement is cited by Euseb. for an expanded form of the Papian tradition as to Mark's Gospel, with the additional remark that Clement's account is confirmed by Papias of Hierapolis. Papias, in fact, was the nucleus of that tradition; and so his Matthaean tradition, as given already in iii. 24, is here omitted.

Thus the whole passage was a defence at once of Mark's Gospel and of Matthew's, with which Papias from the nature of the case is mainly concerned. Then in the extract which Eusebius immediately subjoins, Papias sums up (οὖν) the net result of his discussion touching the accuracy of 'the Oracles' as originally compiled by that Apostle.

'Matthew, then, for his part, in Hebrew compiled the Oracles; but their interpretation was determined by each man's ability.† In this rendering, which keeps as closely as possible to the order of the original,† emphasis no doubt falls on the fact that Matthew's authoritative collection of the Lord's Oracles was in Hebrew, or rather Aramaic, and not in Greek. Yet Papias does not seem to have said anything about the manner in which the Greek Matthew, as current in the region where he was writing, came into being, else Eusebius would have gone on to cite information so much to his purpose. Hence we may infer that the point of the citation lies in the words actually given, and that Papias is explaining why various versions of the Oracles (in whole or part) were then current side by side with the recognized Greek Matthew. They went back, that is, to the time when Matthew's collection of the Oracles existed only in

* Other views as to the exact reason for the comparison of the Gospels of Matthew and Mark are possible; but the above seems best to fit in with the passage in Papias' preface touching his aim and method dealt with below.

† Ματθαῖος μὲν οὖν Ἑβραΐδι διαλέκτῳ τὰ λόγια συνετάξατο (preferable to συνεγράψατο, cf. σύνταξιν above), ἡρμήνευσε δ' αὐτὰ ὡς ἦν δυνατὸς ἕκαστος. The Logia, then, is Papias' description of the main contents of Matthew's Gospel in terms of his special interest in it, not the actual title of any writing ever current under that name.

a non-Greek form, various imperfect renderings of which passed into currency before the final Greek version was made. In this way he is able to set aside rival forms of certain sayings to those on which, as standing in the Greek Matthew, he bases his own exposition of the Lord's teaching.

While it is likely that Papias based on the Elder's testimony his own assertion that Matthew himself wrote his collection of the Lord's Oracles, it seems precarious to lean much weight on the statement. Against this there are various objections. Thus the Preface to Luke's Gospel seems to exclude any such Apostolic record, and its disappearance would be hard to explain.

(b) *Papias' relation to 'the Elders,' the prime witnesses to the meaning of the Oracles.*—So much for the true text of such Oracles of the Lord as he chooses for comment. But what guarantee can he offer that his own exegesis of their meaning is preferable to that of other Christian teachers about him, abler perhaps than himself? This is the question to which the chief citation made by Eusebius is a reply. Its substance is as follows. He is far from piquing himself on his own insight or ingenuity in evolving, at no slight length, plausible views as to the meaning of such Oracles as may seem obscure even to a careful reader. His one object being to reach the true meaning of Him who was the Truth incarnate, he has no false shame in supporting his own 'interpretation' by such authoritative traditions as he had collected in years gone by—traditions derived from the men of the first Christian generation, particularly personal disciples of the Master Himself. His zeal in collecting such authentic oral comments, even at second-hand, was due, he explains, to the feeling that the *vivâ voce* method of continuous transmission was more helpful, for reaching the true sense of the Lord's Oracles, than any books bearing on their elucidation. But before proceeding to draw further inferences from Papias' preface, so far as cited by Eusebius, we will quote the passage (*HE* iii. 39) to which we owe our knowledge of it—

'But I will not scruple to set down for thee everything, too, that once on a time I learned right well from the Elders and right well bore in mind—in juxtaposition with the (=my own) interpretations, so confirming their truth. For I used not to delight, like the many, in those wont to have so much to say (by way of comment), but in those wont to teach things that are true; nor yet in those accustomed to bear in mind the precepts of other masters (τὰς ἀλλοτρίας ἐντολάς), but in those (wont to bear in mind) such as have been given once for all from the Lord to faith and reach (us) from the Truth itself as source (ἀπ' αὐτῆς παραγινομένας [al. οἷς] τῆς ἀληθείας). But if haply one also who had been a companion of the Elders came (my way), I used to make careful inquiry into the discourses of the Elders—what had been said by Andrew, or what by Peter, or what by Philip, or what by Thomas or by James, or what by John or Matthew, or by any other of the Lord's disciples, and what things Aristion and the Elder John, disciples of the Lord, have to say (λέγουσιν). For I did not conceive that the contents of (the) books [of comment] assisted me as much as *vivâ voce* communications preserved continuously (τὰ παρὰ ζώσης φωνῆς καὶ μενούσης).'

The exact exegesis of this famous passage is still an open question. Much depends on the relation of the clause, 'But if haply one also who had been a companion of the Elders (=the worthies of the first generation, e.g. "disciples of the Lord," as also above) came my way,' to what immediately precedes. If it expresses a less direct contact with the Elders, then Papias virtually claims himself to have heard some Apostles or personal disciples of Christ. But if, as seems preferable, it expresses a more direct relation, Eusebius' reading of the passage will hold, and Papias implicitly resigns all claim to have heard any Apostle, and so John in particular. In favour of the former alternative may be urged Eusebius' obvious desire to dissociate Papias from the Apostles, as also the positive statement of not a few later readers of Papias, who must have known of Eusebius' challenge, and so been the more careful in their own reading of Papias' meaning (with the full context before them). In particular, one might cite the witness of Apollinaris, bishop of Papias' own Hierapolis,* within half a century of the date of his predecessor's writing, when he calls him 'Papias, the disciple of John.' Besides, was Eusebius entitled to assume that Irenæus, in calling Papias 'a hearer of John and a comrade of Polycarp,'—whom Irenæus elsewhere explicitly makes a disciple of Apostles and of John in particular,—was drawing on this passage at all, seeing that it does not itself suggest the second of the two descriptions here given? Nevertheless Eusebius' exegesis of the passage, viz. that Papias had heard 'from the Elders' only indirectly, though in certain cases at only one remove, best suits the extract as a whole. Nor does Papias' date depend very much on acceptance of the one view rather than the other. In either case he may well have been rather older than Polycarp (whose birth was as early as A.D. 69), though, unlike him, he was won to Christ's Gospel only after the death of His last Apostle. Yet even at that date two of His personal disciples, Aristion and the Elder John, were still living, most likely in Ephesus or its neighbourhood, somewhere about A.D. 100.

(c) *Date of Papias' writing.*—Against the above result nothing can be said on the score of the date of Papias' book. Not only does Irenæus regard it as the work of 'a primitive worthy' (ἀρχαῖος ἀνήρ), but Eusebius himself classes Papias with Polycarp, Ignatius, Clement (in this order), and others of the next generation after the Apostles (iii. 36 *init.*, 37 *init.*, and *ad fin.*), all of whom he regarded as flourishing under Trajan (A.D. 98–117). Accordingly he deals with Papias before going on to describe events at the end of Trajan's reign (iv. 2), and the accession of Hadrian in 117, in connexion with whom he refers to the *Apology* of Quadratus. There is no external evidence, therefore, apart from a confusion long ago cleared up by Lightfoot, to lead us to assign to Papias' *Exposition* a date later than about A.D. 115. Many scholars, indeed, point to the sentence, 'Touching those raised from the dead by the Christ, that they lived until Hadrian,' following immediately on some Papian matter in an epitome (Cod. Barocc. 142), as though it also were based on Papias, so that his work must be at least as late as Hadrian's reign. But the epitome is really based on Eusebius (with a few touches added directly from Papias in this connexion), and here passes on from Papias in Euseb. iii. 39 to Quadratus as cited in iv. 2, as the very 'form of the sentence, 'Touching . . . that they lived . . .,' suggests.

With this agrees also the internal evidence, as it seems to emerge from a comparison of the erroneous tendencies implied by his work, on the one hand, and, on the other, the Epistles of Ignatius and Polycarp, which fall about A.D. 115. The affinities with Polycarp, whom Irenæus makes Papias' comrade at one time, are specially striking—

'Let us therefore so serve Him [Christ] with fear and all due reverence, even as He Himself gave injunctions, and the Apostles who brought us the Gospel, and the prophets who proclaimed beforehand the coming of our Lord. . . . For every one who shall not confess that Jesus Christ is come in the flesh is antichrist [cf. 1 Jn 4²ᶠ·]; and whosoever shall not confess the testimony of the Cross, is of the devil; and whosoever shall perversely interpret the Oracles of the Lord (μεθοδεύῃ τὰ λόγια τοῦ κυρίου) to his own lusts, and say that there is neither resurrection nor judgment, that man is the firstborn of Satan. Wherefore let us leave behind the vanity of the many ["vain and empty talk and the error of the many," ch. 2] and false teachings, and turn unto the message which was delivered unto us from the beginning. . . .' (chs. 6–7). Here we get the idea of safety in close adherence to the injunctions (ἐντολαί) of Christ

* Thus he, unlike most others, does not need to describe Papias as 'bishop of Hierapolis.'

and His Apostles, or 'the message which was delivered' by them 'from the beginning,' in contrast to 'false teachings' by which 'the many' were apt, in love of empty talk, to be led into error, especially through perverse interpretations of 'the Oracles of the Lord.' The motive of such misinterpretation was Docetic denial of the reality of Christ's human body and of the significance of bodily self-control in the Christian, since 'there is neither resurrection nor judgment.' This comes out more clearly in Ignatius, for instance in the warning, 'Keep your flesh as a temple of God,' in his letter to Philadelphia, which lay less than 50 miles from Hierapolis, on the main road to the coast. This letter affords marked parallels to the situation implied in Papias' preface. Its central idea is that Christ Himself is the Christian's standard, his law of thought and conduct (κατὰ χριστομαθίαν, ch. viii.; cf. 'having Christ as law,' χριστόνομος, *ad Rom.* inscr.), and that all exegesis, even of the Scriptures, is to be tested by this criterion. Only Ignatius and Papias apply the supreme test differently. The former appeals straight to the notorious central facts of Christ's life and of Christian experience: 'His Cross and Death and Resurrection, and the faith that is through Him' (ch. 8). Papias essays the detailed task of supplying a standard exegesis of the Lord's own Great Sayings, in virtue of his special contact with authentic Apostolic tradition in Asia. The difference turns not only on the fact that the two men represent different types of Christian attitude, but also on their respective local traditions and opportunities; and it does not point to any real difference in date between their writings.

The milder tone used by Papias towards the errors in question (which are largely similar, as we see from Polycarp, who is a link between Ignatius and Papias), as compared with both Ignatius and Polycarp, is against the notion of a considerably later date for his *Exposition.* Indeed, it is hard, in the absence of any reference by Eusebius to Papias as engaged, like Ignatius, in refuting any deadly heresy, to believe that Papias was writing after Ignatius' polemic had sharpened, as it must have done, the Asian Churches' sense of the gravity of Docetism in Christianity. Its prevalence may, indeed, have led Papias to lay special emphasis on the realistic aspect of the millennium—a feature in which he was followed by Irenæus and others, to Eusebius' keen regret. But his attitude to *gnosis* seems less severe than we should expect after A.D. 115.*

3. Gospels known to Papias.—We have seen that Papias knew our Matthew and Mark. Eusebius tells us that he also used proof texts from 1 John, probably, *e.g.*, the anti-Docetic 1 Jn 4²ᶠ· cited by Polycarp as above; and this certainly suggests knowledge of the Fourth Gospel, of which there seem also to be traces in the fragments of Papias' *Exposition* as known to us (cf. also Westcott, *Canon* (1889), p. 71, n. 2). Even the order in which he refers to Apostles by name in his preface is that of Jn 1³⁷ᶠᶠ·, while his reference to Christ as the Truth, and, as such, the Fountainhead of Divine precepts (ἐντολαί), points the same way. Probably, however, he used the Johannine Gospel only as a secondary source of exegesis for the standard Matthæan collection of 'the Oracles'—as, in fact, a 'book,' and so less 'helpful' than direct oral tradition. In the *Argumentum* to John's Gospel in a 9th cent. MS., we read : 'The Gospel of John was revealed and given to the Churches. . . , even as Papias of Hierapolis, a dear disciple of John, has related in his five books.' His knowledge of Luke's Gospel is probable both in itself (cf. Lightfoot, *Essays on Supernatural Religion*, p. 186) and in relation to a seeming knowledge of Acts, shown by his traditional amplification of the end of Judas as given in Ac 1¹⁸ᶠ·, which he apparently tried to harmonize with Matthew's account. But no doubt he preferred to cite Mt. where he could, as being to him a work of direct Apostolic authorship, while Luke's Gospel was not even, like Mark's, only one remove from an Apostle's witness.

Some not only see in the phraseology of Papias' apology for Mark's Gospel traces of the influence of Lk 1¹⁻⁴, but also infer

* Papias' very archaic use of οἱ πρεσβύτεροι, for the men of the first generation, particularly Christ's personal disciples, is another indication of early date. In Irenæus this phrase always describes those of the second generation at least.

that Papias is there meeting the criticism of a party in Asia who held to Luke's Gospel, if not exclusively (like Marcion later), yet in so preferential a way as to make it, and not our Matthew, the standard by which to criticise Mark's work (so Dom Chapman in *Revue Bénédictine*, July 1905). This is more than dubious.

In a word, if our reading of the situation which Papias had in view in writing be correct, his attitude to our Gospels is just what we should expect from other sources that it would be, if he were writing in Asia about A.D. 115–120. At that time, not the form but the substance of Christ's teaching, whether oral or written, was still the prime matter. The Canon, or 'rule' of faith, consisted of the Lord's *words*, however obtained, if only it were in purity (cf. Polyc. *ad Phil.* 2, 'remembering what things the Lord said when teaching'). These constituted 'the Gospel' that lay behind the Gospels, and secured their general use, particularly in public worship—out of which canonical authority itself gradually grew (see B. Weiss, *Manual of Introd. to the NT* [1887], i. 32 ff.). This must be borne in mind in estimating the use of all New Testament books in early Christian writers, and makes the task of identifying Evangelic quotations so delicate an art (cf. Sanday, *The Gospels in the Second Century*, and *The NT in the Apostolic Fathers*, Oxford, 1905). But once it is allowed for, Papias becomes a valuable positive witness to our Canonical Gospels, as distinct from other Gospel writings which, no doubt, existed at that time in considerable numbers. Whether he used any apocryphal Gospel is quite doubtful. Eusebius' statement that 'he has set forth another story also about a woman informed against to the Lord on the scope of many sins, which the Gospel according to the Hebrews includes,' by no means proves that Papias got his version of the story from the Gospel in question (cf. Bacon in *Expositor*, 1905, pp. 161–177).

4. General reflexions.—Although we are unable to conceive in detail the exact character of Papias' *Exposition of Oracles of the Lord*, even our meagre knowledge of it, especially when taken in connexion with other Christian writings of the period, helps us not a little to realize the way in which our Gospels, and Gospels generally, were viewed and handled early in the 2nd century. Both it and the Oxyrhynchus Gospel—fragments of which have been found by Grenfell and Hunt—teach us not only that Christ's sayings were the most prized part of the Gospel tradition, but also how strong were the tendencies at work making for change in their meaning and even wording. They were heard or read in environments of thought far other than those for which they were first spoken; and just because they were taken so seriously and practically as Divine 'oracles,' as religious laws of life, their historical or original meaning was apt to be lost as soon as they passed beyond Palestine, and the fresh meanings or glosses put upon them tended insensibly to replace the Master's *ipsissima verba*. Here the instances afforded by the Oxyrhynchus Gospel of how in all good faith such a process of transformation took place, are most suggestive. They show how needful something like a standard exegesis, based on knowledge of the original historical sense, was becoming to the genuine transmission of Christ's own teaching, if it was not to be sublimated away in terms of Greek idealism and Oriental mysticism. Such a consummation was averted only by strenuous insistence on the part of the local Church leaders, that every care was to be taken to keep in touch with the historic meaning of the Lord's earthly teaching, as certified by Gospels historically known to be of Apostolic or *quasi*-Apostolic authorship, and expounded in the first instance by the aid of continuous local tradition going back to similar sources. Thus was the mass of Gospels

LITERATURE.—The Fragments of Papias, and Patristic references to his book collected in Lightfoot's *Apostolic Fathers*, in one vol. (Macmillan, 1891), and (with a commentary) in Funk, *Patres Apostolici* (Tübingen, 1901), i. 346 ff. ; Discussions by Weiffenbach, *Das Papiasfragment, u.s.w.* ; Lightfoot, *Essays on Supernatural Religion*, pp. 142–216 ; Sanday, *Gospels in the Second Century* ; Westcott, *Canon of the NT* ; Salmon in *Dict. of Christian Biography* ; Zahn, *Gesch. d. NT Kanons*, i. 849 ff., *Forschungen*, vi. 109 ff. ; Harnack, *Chronologie*, i. 658 ff. ; Leimbach in *PRE*[3] xiv 642 ff.; Abbott, *EBi* ii. 1809 ff., also *The Oracles ascribed to Matthew by Papias of Hierapolis* (1894), and A. Wright's review in *Some N. T. Problems* (1898), p. 265 ; R. W. Dale, *Living Christ and the Four Gospels*[14], ii. 277–306.

VERNON BARTLET.

**PARABLE.—1. Definition and Classification.—The word 'parable' is an oft-recurring one in the Synoptic Gospels, appearing altogether 48 times. Otherwise it is found in the NT only in He 9[9] 11[19] (RV), where it has the meaning of 'type' or 'symbol' (AV 'figure'). The Evangelists' use of it suggests that for them it was a technical term designating a certain form of discourse or method of teaching, and they report Jesus as employing it in like manner. It is always introduced as something well known, and nowhere defined. The readers are assumed to be as familiar with it as are the writers. This occasions no surprise, for we know that the term had long been current in the circle to which the Evangelists belonged, appearing, as it does, often in the LXX. The connexion between the NT usage and that of the LXX is expressly pointed out by St. Matthew (13[35]), who sees in Jesus' use of parables the fulfilment of Ps. 78[2].

In the LXX παραβολή serves frequently, though not uniformly, to tr. the Heb. *māshāl* (לָשָׁמ). The practice is sufficiently constant to warrant the assumption that it had much the same range of meaning. But, accepting this as true, we have made little progress in determining the exact significance of παραβολή, for as yet agreement has not been attained with reference to the definition of the Semitic original (לשמ, Aram. אלתמ). By some scholars the root is thought to mean primarily *to represent* or *stand for something* (so Fleischer ; cf. Franz Delitzsch, *Com. zu Prov.*, Leipzig, 1873, p. 43 f. ; Gesenius-Buhl, *HWB* ; Bugge, *Die Haupt-Parabeln*, i. 20 f.) ; while others, following a different line of derivation, make the conception of *likeness* or *resemblance* to be fundamental (König in Hastings' *DB* iii. p. 661 ; cf. Jülicher, *Die Gleichnisreden Jesu*, i. p. 36 f.). An examination of the OT makes it evident that Hebrew writers employed the term in the broadest and most inclusive way. Allegory, similitude, parable, proverb, paradox, type, and even riddle could be so designated. Jülicher concludes (*op. cit.* i. p. 37) that the most that can be done in the way of definition is to say that in the OT *māshāl* is a discourse expressing or implying comparison. The limitations thus suggested are, that it be a complete statement and not merely a word or phrase, and that it employ or rest on comparison.

The modern understanding of the word 'parable' has not as yet become well defined. One naturally expects this to follow the Greek conception, but in many definitions one finds a considerable infusion of the Semitic point of view. παραβολή (from παρά 'beside,' and βάλλειν 'to throw or cast') signifies literally *a placing beside*, and in ancient rhetoric designates an illustration or comparison. The fundamental idea is thus in agreement with that which is found by some in the Heb. *māshāl* Aristotle classes parable and fable together as means of indirect proof, more convenient and easier to use than historical example for one who is able to detect resemblances, but less effective.

That the Synoptists should entertain this narrower and more definite view of Greek and Roman writers is not to be anticipated. One expects to find in them rather the wider and more indefinite application of Semitic authors, and in this one is not disappointed. Proverb (Lk 4²³), paradox (Mk 7¹⁷), similitude (4³⁰), allegory (4¹³), and example or illustrative instance (Lk 12¹⁶) are so named. The word appears with sufficient frequency to make evident its wide application. This does not prove, of course, that in the NT it has a meaning identical with that which it bears in the OT. It is Jülicher's view that a new element entered in during the period of the Jewish-Hellenistic literature. Besides being a complete thought and expressing or implying comparison, the parable is now understood to veil a hidden meaning. The real teaching is not in what the words seem to say, but in their deeper import. We shall have occasion to return to this topic after reviewing the range of the parabolic material.

It is not to be assumed that the Synoptists have prefixed a title to all the sections that they regarded as παραβολαί. On the contrary, they have done so only incidentally as occasion required, since they had no particular interest in rhetorical categories. In Mk. the word παραβολή is found 13 times, with reference to 6 different sections; 17 times in Mt., with reference to 12 sections; and 18 times in Lk., with reference to 13 sections. It is not used in Jn., but παροιμία occurs with much the same meaning. Deducting parallels, there are 20 passages in the Synoptic Gospels that are spoken of as parables. How far short this comes of full enumeration is made evident by noting the number of parables recognized by modern expositors : e.g. van Koetsveld, 79 (including Jn.); Bugge, 71 ; Weinel, 59 ; Jülicher, 53 ; Heinrici, 39 ; Lisco, 37 ; Bruce, 33, and 8 parable germs.

This divergence of opinion makes it evident that it is not easy to determine the precise extent of the parabolic material. Nor is it easy to discover a satisfactory principle for classifying it. This has been attempted from various points of view. Some have sought to make the truth taught a standard for grouping. So Bruce distinguishes (1) Theoretic parables, or those embodying a general teaching regarding the Kingdom of God ; (2) the parables of Grace ; (3) the parables of Judgment. Others have made the realm from which the illustration was taken the criterion of division. More satisfactory results are obtained by paying heed to the form of the parable, that is, to the character of the illustration and the manner of its introduction. From this point of view a large portion of the material falls within one general division. To this belong all the sections in which a spiritual or moral truth is established or enforced by the use of an express or implicit comparison. An appeal is made to common experience, to what is recognized and accepted by all, in support of less evident truths pertaining to a higher realm. The tacit assumption is that the same laws are valid for moral and religious as for daily practical life. If assent is yielded without hesitation in the one case, it cannot be withheld in the other.

At times the comparison is expressly made by some formula, or by some word or particle (e.g. ὅμοιον, ὥσπερ, or ὡς). Attention is in this way directed to the resemblance between two distinct relationships. The writer makes his readers aware that a concrete experience is being used to teach some moral or spiritual lesson. Parables of this kind have been happily called **Similitudes.** The passage regarding the Fig-tree, found in all the

Gospels (Mk 13²⁸ᶠ·, Mt 24³²ᶠ·, Lk 21²⁹ᶠ·), and designated in them all as a parable, is a good example. 'Now from the fig-tree learn her parable : when her branch is now become tender and putteth forth its leaves, ye know that the summer is nigh ; even so ye also, when ye see these things coming to pass, know that it is nigh, even at the doors.' All the dwellers in Palestine knew that the bursting buds and tender shoots of the fig-tree gave unmistakable indication that summer was at hand. The application is that the nearness of the Parousia can with equal certainty be inferred from the signs that immediately precede its coming. There is here no thought of the resemblance of details, as, for example, between summer and the Parousia ; but in both instances it is pointed out that with equal certainty, from the signs of the coming, the nearness of the coming itself can be inferred. The likeness is one of relationships and not of details. In the pair of parables of the Hidden Treasure and the Pearl of Great Price we have two illustrations of like character to enforce the one truth, that to gain a possession of greatest value no sacrifice is too great. The Synoptic records afford evidence that not infrequently Jesus thus employed a double illustration. The attempt to discover resemblances between the Kingdom of heaven and the treasure or the pearl may be homiletically admissible, but it is exegetically beside the mark. Equally irrelevant are the ethical discussions regarding the conduct of the man who found the treasure. Jesus no more approves the quality of his act than He does that of the younger brother, or that of the unjust steward.

The following inferences regarding the character of a *Similitude* are possible in view of what has been said : (1) Fundamentally it is a comparison. Often this is expressly indicated, as above. (2) It is a comparison of relationships and not of details. There may chance to be some suggestive resemblance in details, but this is immaterial to the real purpose of the illustration. (3) In each Similitude there is one main comparison and one application, one truth that is unfolded. (4) Since there are two parts, the statement needing proof and the illustration supplying this, it is wrong, as is often done, to speak of the illustration alone as the Similitude. (5) The purpose of the Similitude is manifestly to elucidate or to prove, to win assent for what is unfamiliar by an appeal to what is well known.

A group of passages of lesser extent than the one just considered makes a like use of sayings which were apparently proverbial. Lk 4²³ is an instance of this: 'And he said unto them, Doubtless ye will say unto me this parable, Physician, heal thyself: whatsoever we have heard done at Capernaum, do also here in thine own country.' Jesus' conduct is likened to that of the physician in question. The proverb by itself does not constitute the parable, but the proverb used as an illustration. Since such proverbs are the concise and pointed formulations of the truths of common experience, we need not differentiate these parables from those last discussed — no further, at least, than to make them a subdivision of the Similitudes. Besides the passage quoted, others, such as Mt 5¹⁴ᵇ· 6²⁴ (Lk 16¹³) 15¹⁴ (Lk 6³⁹) 24²⁸ (Lk 17³⁷), Mk 2¹⁷ (Mt 9¹²ᶠ·, Lk 5³¹ᶠ·), would be included.

Often the illustration from experience is not stated as a general inference, recognized always and by all, but is embodied in the form of a specific incident, in what was done by some person or persons, or in what happened to them. Thus Lk 15¹¹⁻³² begins, 'A certain man had two sons,' and Mk 4³⁻⁹ 'Behold, the sower went forth to sow.' In purpose and in the way the illustration is employed there is close resemblance between this group and the Similitudes. The difference is mainly in the definiteness of the experience. Here it is presented as a single occurrence. It may still be, and no doubt usually is, wholly imaginary. All that is required is a degree of naturalness and probability sufficient to command unhesitating assent. Such a story, formed by the imagination from the material of actual experience, might be classed as a **Fable**, had not this name gained in the course of time a restricted meaning. By many writers it is looked upon as applicable only to the small group of animal fables in which the main actors are animals or inanimate objects. Since such stories often serve merely to entertain or to teach worldly prudence and discretion, the difference between parable and fable is made by some to consist in the kind of truth enforced. The latter is restricted to the lower realm of worldly knowledge, while the former is assigned to the service of the higher truths of morality and religion. We need not further discuss the distinction, because fable has become exclusively associated in most minds with the type of teaching attributed to Æsop. To connect it with any of the discourses of Jesus would occasion misunderstanding. Jülicher's proposal is to retain for this group the name *Parable* in its narrower meaning. Until a better designation is found, it will be well to accept this.

The Gospel of Lk. contains at least four sections differing in character from any previously considered. They have the narrative form, but the illustration is taken, not from a different realm, but from that to which the truth under discussion belongs. A specific instance wherein this is exemplified is recited to win the approval or call forth the disapprobation of the hearer. The application is made, not through analogy, not by some word expressing likeness or resemblance, but by simple affirmation : ' So is it ' or ' so should it not be.' The Good Samaritan (Lk 10³⁰⁻³⁷), the Foolish Rich Man (12¹⁶⁻²⁰), the Rich Man and Lazarus (16¹⁹⁻³¹), and the Pharisee and the Publican (18⁹⁻¹⁴) belong to this group. Possibly, as Heinrici suggests (*PRE*³, vi. 692), we ought also to add the accounts of the Importunate Friend (11⁵ᶠᶠ·), and the Unjust Judge (18¹ᶠᶠ·), since the lesson is gained in these instances by reasoning *a minori ad majus*. It is often difficult, as here, to determine to which division a given section may be most properly assigned. Comparison enters into this class only through the demand made upon the listener to test his life and conduct by that depicted in the story. The abstract truth is commended to him in concrete form. We might call such illustrations, which stand apart from the groups previously enumerated, *Narrative Examples*, or perhaps it will be better to term them, with Jülicher, *Illustrative Instances*.

On the basis of the reference in Mk 7¹⁷ (Mt 15¹⁵) it has been proposed (cf. Bugge, *op. cit.* i. pp. 59, 15, and 16) to regard the **Paradox** as a class of parable. That the name might be so applied may, in the light of Semitic usage, be assumed as probable, though there is wide difference of view regarding this particular passage in Mk. and Mt. Expositors have not, however, generally made paradoxes a distinct group in their treatment of the parables.

It now remains to ask whether there is another class of passages that should be brought together under the head of **Allegory**. This question has recently been much discussed, and opinion is still widely divided. It is variously affirmed that, even according to the Synoptists, Jesus never spoke in allegories (Weinel, *Die Gleichnisse Jesu*, p. 30) ; or that He is mistakenly reported by them as so doing (Jülicher, *op. cit.* i. 61 ff. etc.) ; or that He did make use of allegories, and is correctly reported in this respect (Bugge, *op. cit.* i. 40 ff. etc.). *Allegory* (ἀλληγορία, ἀλληγορεῖν) comes from ἄλλο, ' other,' ' something else,' and ἀγορεύειν, ' to speak.' The word occurs as a substantive nowhere in the NT or in Biblical Greek, nor does the verb appear except in Gal 4²⁴, where St. Paul makes use of the participle ἀλληγορούμενος. It is a mode of speech whereby one thing is ostensibly described or narrated, while the primary reference is to something very different. It is thus closely akin to the metaphor (wh. see), differing from it in consisting not of a single word or concept, but of a series of concepts belonging to the same realm, and so related as to form together a continuous and intelligible narrative. Since the several details are introduced, not because they are the component parts of a vivid and artistic picture, but because of their suitability to portray the desired meaning, the best of allegories are marked by some degree of artificiality and incongruity. The attentive listener is made aware that the story is being told to convey some deeper meaning and not for its own sake. Often it will be impossible for him to determine what this is until the allegory has been wholly or in part interpreted. In other instances the setting in which it occurs may afford the needed clue. To understand it fully, he must be able to translate the terms one by one and read their hidden meaning. Naturally no one but the framer of the allegory can be his infallible guide in this. In the similitude and parable we do not feel the need of seeking for any meaning beyond that which the words usually bear, whereas in the allegory the deeper, hidden significance is of first importance. Are there sections in the Gospels of which this is true ? It seems to be, to some degree, in at least five. Three are in the Synoptic Gospels, namely, the accounts of the Sower (Mk 4³⁻⁹· ¹⁴⁻²⁰, Mt 13³⁻⁹· ¹⁸⁻²³, Lk 8⁵⁻⁸· ¹¹⁻¹⁵), of the Wicked Husbandmen (Mk 12¹⁻¹², Mt 21³³⁻⁴⁶, Lk 20⁹⁻¹⁹), and of the Tares (Mt 13²⁴⁻³⁰· ³⁶⁻⁴³) ; and two are from the Fourth Gospel, the Door of the Sheepfold (Jn 10¹⁻¹⁶), and the Vine and the Branches (15¹⁻⁸). In each of these, except the Wicked Husbandmen, an allegorical interpretation is expressly added, while in this latter the setting, the comments, as well as the character of the narration, suggest an allegory. According to the definition given above, none of the five passages can be regarded as a perfect and fully developed allegory, because each has unimportant details that are not, and clearly were not intended to be, interpreted. They are introduced as natural parts of the picture, without reference to a hidden meaning. For instance, in the Sower no deeper meaning attaches to the way, the thirty, sixty, and hundredfold, as would be the case in a carefully developed allegory. The Wicked Husbandmen and the Tares are better examples of allegory ; but even in these there are several features without allegorical significance. The passages in the Fourth Gospel differ quite markedly from those in the Synoptics. The literal and the figurative are blended in such an unusual way that it has not been possible for commentators to agree in their classification. In ch. 10, following the first interpretation (vv.⁷⁻¹⁰) comes a second (vv.¹¹⁻¹⁶), which seems to presuppose a closely related but really different allegory. Or we can regard these last verses as a new allegory with continuous interpretation. The discourse of ch. 15 is of exactly the same type ; parallel to ' I am the good shepherd ' we there have ' I am the true vine.' Besides lacking the unity that usually marks the allegory, these Johannine sections contain many terms that have no significance beyond that belonging to them in ordinary speech. It seems, nevertheless, more correct to class them as allegories than to call them parables with an allegorical interpretation, or collections of related metaphors.

In addition to these passages there are numerous others where little doubt can exist that the Evangelists understood some details allegorically, for they suggest, even if they do not give, such an interpretation. By way of illustration the reference to the whole and the sick (Mk 2¹⁷) may be cited, so also the taking away of the bridegroom 2²⁰), and the blind who lead the blind (Mt 15¹⁴, Lk 6³⁹). Jülicher maintains that they looked on all parables as allegories. They have given, it is true, few allegorical interpretations, and have not often indicated that they felt such treatment necessary, but this is only because their practice is not in accord with their theory. Whenever they reflect (as they do in Mk 4¹⁰⁻¹². ³³⁻³⁴ || Mt 13¹⁰⁻¹⁵. ³⁴ff., Lk 8⁹⁻¹⁰), they think of parables as always veiling a hidden meaning, one hard to be understood and intelligible to the disciples themselves only after interpretation. This conception, as was stated above, is not held to be their own creation, but is thought to be one that came to them from the age of the Jewish-Hellenistic literature. It was the product of scribal activity. Such an explanation is open to serious question. It may be doubted whether existing evidence proves that the notion of mystery belonged so exclusively to this later period. It is true that with the decadence of prophecy men looked for the message of God in what had been said rather than in what was being said, and that the allegorical method of exegesis was assiduously cultivated. It may also be true that the Gospels indicate that, at the time when the Evangelists wrote, the words of Jesus received to some extent like treatment; but that it went to the length that this theory supposes is not attested. Such a claim could be more reasonably made for the Church Fathers and the interpreters of later generations. From post-Apostolic days even down to the present the prevailing method of exegesis has been allegorical. (On its prevalence in Alexandrian and Palestinian circles before and after Christ, see Hastings' *DB*, art. 'Allegory,' i. p. 64.) Representatives (*e.g.* Chrysostom, Calvin, Maldonatus) of sounder interpretation have not been altogether wanting, but they have been little heeded. There is no parable or detail of a parable that has not received many and conflicting interpretations. The judge of Lk 18², for example, according to some stands for God, and according to others for the devil. Elsewhere results are no less incongruous (*e.g.* Mt 24²⁸, Lk 17³⁷ : Mt 24⁴³f., Lk 12³⁹f. ; Lk 11⁵⁻⁸). So great was the contradiction, that in the 17th cent. the thesis was proposed that parables should not be used as a source of doctrine, but only to illustrate and confirm what was otherwise established (' theologia parabolica non est argumentativa,' cf. Jülicher, *op. cit.* i. p. 277). The form of the disciples' question (Mk 4¹⁰f., cf. ³³. ³⁴) might at first incline us to agree that the Church Fathers were but following the Synoptists, were it not that so many parables are recorded without even suggestion that they need interpretation. Jülicher finds it *a priori* improbable that a popular teacher, who expressed himself without any considerable deliberation or preparation, should employ such a highly artificial, rhetorical form as the allegory. This tends to veil rather than to reveal, and belongs to the writer rather than to the speaker. He concedes that Jesus may on occasion have made metaphorical or allegorical application of certain suggestive details of some parable, but finds little or no evidence of His having done so. Everything indicates, rather, that all the passages to which we have alluded derive their allegorical features and interpretations from the writers. Originally, as spoken by Jesus, the Synoptic accounts were parables in the narrower meaning of the term.

This extreme position of Professor Jülicher has been opposed by many, and unqualifiedly approved by few. Admitting the proclivity of Jesus' hearers, by reason of their traditions, to give an allegorical interpretation to many details, admitting that this might be increasingly done as men recalled these discourses and reflected on their import and sought to apply them to existing conditions, still to deny to Jesus all allegorical application of details and restrict Him to simple comparison, is unwarranted. If along with comparison (*e.g.* Mt 23³⁷ [Lk 13³⁴] 16¹⁶ [Lk 10³], Lk 10¹⁸) He made frequent use of metaphor, as the Gospels indicate (*e.g.* Mk 5³⁴ 10²¹ [Mt 19²¹, Lk 18²²] 12⁴⁰ [Lk 20⁴⁷]), and if He expanded comparison into parable, is it unwarrantable to assume that occasionally metaphor might be so extended as to become virtually an allegory? As long as such an interpretation of suggestive particulars contributes in a natural way to the enforcement of the main lesson, it cannot be considered irrelevant or artificial. Weinel has pointed out (*Die Bildersprache Jesu in ihrer Bedeutung für die Erforschung seines inneren Lebens²*, 1906) that in its psychological origin the parable is closely akin to the allegory. It springs often from some suggestive analogy of detail which might well be made evident in the progress of the discourse. Such an assumption does not, to be sure, account for all the allegorical features that a sound exegesis will discover in the Gospels, but it enables us to understand how Jesus may, in the case of some parables, have added an application distinctly allegorical, as, for example, in the account of the Sower. And if He wished to address to His enemies such thoughts as are contained in the Wicked Husbandmen, could they have been more suitably presented? The great service of Jülicher and of B. Weiss before him in effectually discrediting false methods of interpretation and establishing true, can hardly receive too great recognition. But past extravagances and present danger of their perpetuation do not furnish adequate reason for denying to Jesus the use of allegory, or of parables so developed as to be hardly distinguishable therefrom. We accordingly admit allegory as a division of our classification.

2. Purpose.—Why did Jesus make use of parables? It would occur to hardly any reader of the Gospels to-day to be in doubt as to their purpose, were it not for the statements of the Synoptists. Parables have been used by teachers of all ages to unfold and enforce their instruction. Was it otherwise with Jesus? Is it otherwise, for example, in His use of the story of the Prodigal Son? The passage which occasions the perplexity is as follows : ' And when he was alone, they that were about him with the twelve asked of him the parables. And he said unto them, Unto you is given the mystery of the kingdom of God : but unto them that are without, all things are done in parables : that [ἵνα] seeing they may see, and not perceive, and hearing they may hear, and not understand ; lest haply they should turn again, and it should be forgiven them. And he saith unto them, Know ye not this parable? and how shall ye know all the parables? . . . And with many such parables spake he the word unto them, as they were able to hear it. And without a parable spake he not unto them : but privately to his own disciples he expounded all things ' (Mk 4¹⁰⁻¹². ³³. ³⁴, cf. Mt 13¹⁰ff. ³⁴ff., Lk 8⁹ff.). These words are beset with difficulty from any point of view. Taken by themselves they affirm that parables lead to the hardening of men's hearts, and were intended so to do. Notwithstanding differences in statement, all three accounts are in substantial agreement as to this. It is instinctively felt, however, that Jesus could not possibly have entertained a purpose so at variance with the spirit of His whole ministry. He went forth to seek and to save that which was lost. To win, not to harden ; to enlighten, not to mystify, was ever His endeavour. Otherwise, why should He express surprise at the failure of His hearers to comprehend His parables? Why should He exhort them to hear? Can we think that He would mock at their helplessness? Why should He speak to His own disciples as well as to the multitude in parables which they could not understand without interpretation? Does not the parable of the Sower, to which these words are joined, imply an understanding on the part of all classes, even though all do not alike heed and profit by what is heard? It is evident that the statements cannot be attributed to Jesus in their most obvious meaning. While this is generally conceded, there is disagreement as to how they are to be qualified and the extent to which this should be done. A few have resorted to text emendation for the removal of the difficulties, but most have preferred to keep the form and seek for a new interpretation. Some expositors suppose that the truths needful for salvation were not presented after this manner, but in a way intelligible to all. What is here said refers only to parables dealing with the mysteries of the nature of the Kingdom of heaven, or the one mystery of its gradual development. Or this reference is limited to the parables of this chapter, or to the parables of Judgment. Such teaching, being suited only to those who are already disciples, is so conveyed that they alone receive it, while outsiders hear without understanding. The improbability and unnaturalness of such a supposition are too apparent to need refutation. The harshness of the view is softened by assuming that the unreceptive and unworthy multitude already stood self-condemned because of their rejection of the message of salvation. Teaching in parables is part of their just punishment, and serves also to keep the door open for those who may become receptive. Another way of removing the harshness is to say that the parable, while executing God's judgment, was at the same time a merciful provision, preventing an increase of guilt. Had the unreceptive understood what was taught in these parables regarding Jesus and themselves, or had it been spoken openly, they would have added to existing sins those of hate and blasphemy, and fallen into a passion, making all hearing impossible for themselves and others.

A different explanation is proposed by those who see here the enunciation of a pedagogical purpose. No class of hearers, not even the disciples, can understand the truth so presented, but the receptive will reveal themselves by their questions as to the meaning of the parable, while the unreceptive remain indifferent, and thereby make clear the hopelessness of their condition. Plain speech would have been equally unintelligible to such hearers, whereas the parable was calculated to quicken in them a spirit of inquiry, if anything could. This, again, is a very improvable supposition. Another interpretation sees in these words a reference not to intellectual comprehension, but to the inner spiritual appropriation of the truth set forth. Jesus seeks for this on the part of all, but finds it wanting in those who were dulled and hardened in their short-sighted self-righteousness and superficial self-satisfaction. Their hearing is as though they heard not. The parables are thus a summons to the conscience of the hearer, and bring about a separation between the receptive and the unreceptive.

Professor Jülicher, together with other recent writers, accepts the verses in their most obvious meaning, but assigns them to the Evangelists. When Jesus' words were collected after His death, the large proportion of parabolic material attracted attention. An explanation was sought, and it was found in the character of those to whom the parables were addressed, and in their attitude toward Jesus. The multitude had not accepted Him as the Messiah. What had happened must have been in accord with the Divine plan. This plan had been fulfilled through the use of parables. Paul's teaching in Ro 9–11 is here applied by the Evangelists to the history of Jesus. J. Weiss, indeed, holds that Mk. was acquainted with Romans, and followed St. Paul (*Die Schriften des NT*, i. p. 101). Whatever may be thought as to the dependence, the likeness of conception is obvious.

This explanation has in its favour a full and frank recognition of the difficulty as well as the avoidance of forced and unnatural interpretation. Many who think that the passage goes back to Jesus admit that the Evangelists in their report have been in some measure influenced by the hostility and opposition of unbelieving Israel, so pronounced at the time when they wrote. The explanation gains added support from the fact that the existing difficulty is not confined to the words of Jesus, but is occasioned in part by the appended comments of the Evangelists. Still, it cannot yet lay just claim to the validity of a demonstration. That the Evangelists should feel the need of accounting for the large proportion of parabolic material in Jesus' teaching is not obvious. The proportion in Mk., with whom we have primarily to do, is not striking. We should need to postulate, what many deny, his acquaintance with the Logia. Again, if the Evangelists evolved this whole conception, it is certainly strange that they should make so little use of it. Writers are not wont thus to forget or neglect their own pet hypotheses, as Mk. apparently did, even in the course of ch. 4. Could he fail to notice, too, how his theory was contradicted by the readiness with which Jesus' hearers understood the account of the Wicked Husbandmen? With all their freedom in transmitting Jesus' words, is it probable that the writers would venture upon an entirely new creation of this kind at so late a date?

There is greater likelihood that we have to do in this passage with a saying of Jesus that, in the course of time, has been modified, or received a false emphasis. At what stage of the development of the Gospels the change took place we cannot be certain. The lack of responsiveness on the part of His hearers and the growing opposition of which we learn in the Gospels, may have caused Jesus to apply to His ministry the words of the prophet Isaiah (6[9f.]). The outcome of His mission might appear, on first thought, to be a repetition of this experience; but a deeper insight revealed as true what the parables of this chapter (Mk 4) teach. The despair of the prophet's words receives its answer. That it was the Evangelists who first brought this OT quotation into such connexion can be doubted, though we can no longer be certain of its exact application, and though the text does not seem here to be in order. If Jesus used the words ironically, they might be cherished by the Christians of the later days of conflict as a statement of the Divine purpose. There is, in any case, too much contradictory evidence to admit of our receiving them as the deliberate statement of Jesus' intention.

3. Interpretation.—In what sense is it permissible to speak of the interpretation of a parable? If we mean thereby an allegory, the need of translating its terms into their equivalents is evident. This will be required by the hearer in more or less fulness, according to circumstances. The statements of the Synoptists (Mk 4[10–13. 33–34] ||) are then comprehensible so far as they may refer to allegories, but can the same be claimed if the remaining parabolic material is likewise included? By some it is said that it can be for the narrative parables, or parables in the restricted meaning of the term. Similitude and Illustrative Instance are excepted, as necessarily clear from the way in which they are introduced, but narrative parables, being complete and independent accounts, require interpretation. The hearer is as little aware of their real significance as was David when listening to Nathan's story of the poor man and his lamb (2 S 12[1ff.]). This view evidently represents Jesus as wont to relate incidents that had no apparent connexion with what was being said or done, and then to add an application, as the moral is appended to the fable. One, for instance, who heard about the Treasure in the field (Mt 13[44]), or the Two Debtors (Lk 7[36–50]), would have no reason to think of the Kingdom of heaven, or the duties of the sons of the Kingdom, until it was demanded by the application. The Gospels are not responsible for this theory, for they do not give the impression that Jesus kept His hearers in suspense. Either an explicit statement, as in the first example, or the occasion, as in the second, left commonly no doubt as to the topic under discussion. Furthermore, there seems to be no good reason for making such a distinction between this group of parables and the Similitudes and Illustrative Examples. Two parts are here essential to constitute a parable, the illustration and the truth illustrated. That the illustration appears in a slightly modified form does not involve a change in the parable's essential character. And can we suppose that Jesus ever told the people one story, or a series of stories, and withheld all indication of His purpose? What could be expected to result therefrom beyond a little entertainment? And even this would be of short duration, unless the stories were longer than most of our parables. How can we harmonize the fact that the parables, as they now stand, set forth in unparalleled clearness and beauty the deepest truths of the gospel, with the assumption that they were used by Jesus as a means of punishing the unrepentant by hiding the truth?

It is not improbable that oftentimes the illustrative half of a parable alone was preserved by tradition. In such cases we can speak of interpretation if we mean thereby the discovery of the original setting and application, whether this service is performed by the Evangelists or undertaken by their interpreters. Such an understanding of the term is, however, misleading, as it obviously does not represent the thought of Mk 4 and parallels. The demand of these passages is satisfied only when we assume that interpretation means an unfolding of details such as is provided for the story of the Sower. This would not be required for all parabolic material, but only for those parables that were considered to be allegories. We have found above that it is not easy to decide how many were included by the Synoptists in such a point of view. A priori considerations or ingenious conjecture cannot decide the question, but only the internal evidence discovered by detailed exegetical study.

4. Transmission and Value.—Have the Evangelists rightly understood and faithfully reported Jesus' parables ? Had the tradition, upon which they were dependent, preserved an exact recollection of His words and their application ? The parables were quite certainly spoken originally in Aramaic, and many of them, after being preserved for a time by oral tradition, may have first been written down in this same language. But even if the bulk of them were first written in Greek, we should, of course, still possess them only in translation. The possibility of modification accordingly exists, even if an earnest endeavour at historical accuracy, as we conceive of it, could be postulated. A comparison of the records of even the shortest parable appearing in all the Gospels, or in two of them, reveals many variations. While the major part are trifling, others may affect materially the meaning and structure of the parable. In the description of patching the old garment, for instance (Mk 2²¹, Mt 9¹⁶, Lk 5³⁶), the casual reader of the English notes the striking variation in Luke. The defenders of the validity of the several accounts in all their details have been wont to explain the divergences by advancing the hypothesis of the use of the same parable on different occasions. In some parables common to Mt. and Lk. such a view may be advocated with a show of reason, but when these two Gospels are following Mk. it has little support. There are parables, furthermore, like the one just noted and the Sower and the Wicked Husbandmen, that are spoken under conditions and with applications so much alike and at the same time so peculiar as to exclude any thought of repetition. The differences in the accounts of the Evangelists are unquestionable, and they leave the interpreter no choice. He must seek to ascertain the original form of the parable. If we say that these differences existed in the sources, we simply carry the problem back to an earlier stage and contribute nothing to its solution ; and even then the personal equation of the Evangelist enters in, through the choice and arrangement of the details of his narrative. When we observe Mt.'s tendency to group material, revealed in so many connexions, we can but think that this purpose, rather than special knowledge of the occasion, has often determined the setting of his parables. A comparative study shows that each of the Synoptists has peculiarities which reveal themselves in his report. Lk.'s interest in the individual and his love of the beautiful are as noticeable as Mt.'s regard for the OT and discovery of allegorical meanings.

If the existing evidence proves that Jesus' words were not at first treated as unalterably holy, it does not, on the other hand, show that there was such freedom as to cast doubt on all His reported sayings, or justify giving them a value secondary to that of the narrative portions of the Gospels. Notwithstanding differences, the Synoptists show such essential agreement that we feel little doubt regarding most parables. The wonder is that there should be so little divergence, even though so short a period separated our records and their Aramaic sources from the original utterances. It can be urged in explanation that Jesus' teaching was too well remembered to admit of the incorporation of new creations. What He had said became early a precious heritage for all believers, and, besides, the parables are of a character to make them especially well remembered. Their freshness, beauty, and earnestness attest their originality and faithful transmission, as does also, in a special degree, their suitability to explain and enforce the teaching in whose service they are employed. That they can be so varied and at the same time so simple, excites wonder. One turns from Rabbinical literature to the parables of Jesus with an increased appreciation of their literary excellence, to say nothing of the marked contrast in dignity and grandeur of theme. Nor is there any writer of early Christian literature worthy of a place in this field beside the Master. An observation of the details and relationships of common life and an appreciation of their significance is revealed that is unparalleled. We gain an insight into the inner life of Jesus Himself, as well as into His teaching, that is afforded by hardly any other portions of the Gospels. The parables are rightly regarded as a most valuable part of the Evangelical tradition, and they will so continue when their right to be heard in their simplicity is generally recognized.

Literature.—The most important work of recent date on the Parables and their exposition is A. Jülicher's *Die Gleichnisreden Jesu*, Freiburg, 1899. See also C. A. Bugge, *Die Haupt-Parabeln Jesu*, Giessen, 1903 ; Heinrich Weinel, *Die Bildersprache Jesu in ihrer Bedeutung für die Erforschung seines inneren Lebens*², Giessen, 1906 ; ' Die Gleichnisse Jesu, zugleich eine Anleitung zu einem quellenmässigen Verständnis der Evangelien,' Leipzig, 1904 [a volume of the series *Aus Natur und Geisteswelt*]; Paul Fiebig, *Alt-jüdische Gleichnisse und die Gleichnisse Jesu*, Tübingen u. Leipzig, 1904 ; S. Goebel, *Die Parabeln Jesu methodisch ausgelegt*, Gotha, 1879–80 [Eng. tr. (Edin. 1883) *The Parables of Jesus*] ; A. B. Bruce, *The Parabolic Teaching of Christ*, London, 1882 ; F. L. Steinmeyer, *Die Parabeln des Herrn*, Berlin, 1884 ; R. Winterbotham, *The Kingdom of Heaven* (1898) ; A. L. Lilley, *Adventus Regni* (1907) ; artt. in Hastings' *DB*, the *EBi*, and the *PRE*³, vol. vi. pp 688–703 (Heinrici) ; *Commentaries* on the Gospels, and *Lives of Christ*. For further literature, see Jülicher, *op. cit.* i. pp. 203–322.

W. J. MOULTON.

PARACLETE (παράκλητος).—The term is used only in RVm; and is applied to Christ in 1 Jn 2¹, and to the Holy Spirit in Jn 14¹⁶. ²⁶ 15²⁶ 16⁷. For an examination of the Greek word and its cognates, see ' Paraclete ' in Hastings' *DB* iii. 665 ff., also art. ADVOCATE in present work. A passive meaning, ' called to one's help,' is required by both the form and the classical usage, in which generally the word is technical, and denotes the adviser of a defendant, or his representative and counsel in a court of law. Gradually the two ideas of previous engagement by a client and of action only in the court or presence of a judge fall away, and the word comes to denote one who, in something of a representative character, carries on the cause and promotes the interest of another.

In Philo the process of the widening of the meaning of the word, used by him sometimes in a technical and sometimes in a more general sense, may almost be traced (cf. Hatch, *Essays in Bibl. Greek*, 1889, 82 f.), without the assumption of any Johannine dependence upon Philo. In the Talm. and Targ. the word is transliterated פְּרַקְלִיט or פְּרַקְלִיּמָא. In the Targ. at Job 33²³ מֵלִיץ is rendered ' paraclete,' the idea being apparently that a special agency from God is needed ' to show unto man what is right,' and so produce repentance. *Pirke Aboth*, iv. 15, represents obedience to a single precept of the Law as a man's paraclete, averting punishment from him. In *Shabb*. 32a, the technical use of the word occurs, and the passage proceeds to assert that repentance and good works act in a similar way as paracletes for a man, ensuring his salvation. Similarly *Baba bathra*, 10a, makes all acts of charity and benevolence paracletes between Israel and the Father in heaven. The two daily offerings and the sin-offering (*Zebaḥim*, 7*b*) are paracletes, interceding for man and securing the favour of the King. In Talmudic times, consequently, the process of change had been carried so far that the word was capable of an impersonal use, and even the plants of Succoth might be spoken of as paracletes, praying in man's behalf for rain (*Ta'anith*, i. 63*c*). An earlier stage is occupied by the Johannine writings, where the word is still personal, though the strictly passive sense had already gone, and the judicial suggestiveness was disappearing.

A Babylonian origin has been claimed for the doctrine of the Paraclete on such grounds as that Nusku is persuaded by Ea and Marduk to join in the intervention against the revolted evil genii. But Nusku was only a messenger of Bel (Jensen, *ZA* xi. 29; Jastrow, *Rel. of Bab.* 220 f.); and though he continued for some time to be known to the northern Semites (cf. the Nêrab inscr. in Cooke, *North-Semitic Inscr.* 186 ff.), his assumed functions differed generally from those of a paraclete, and entirely from those referred to in the Fourth Gospel. The term is certainly not Babylonian in its origin; and preparations for its NT use may be found not only in Philo and the Targums, but even in Ps 34[7] and Job 33[23], though neither Jesus nor the author of the Johannine literature needed such preparations. Both had sufficient literary faculty to be able to pass without guidance from the literal to a metonymous sense of a word, and to place it appropriately amid new connexions.

The term is applied both to Christ Himself and to the Holy Spirit in meanings that may be classified. Christ is referred to as a Paraclete in two passages. **1.** During His historic manifestation (cf. 'another' in Jn 14[16]) He acted in two ways concurrently upon men, promoting the interests of God. Immanently He was in them 'the light which lighteth every man' (Jn 1[9]); and objectively He brought to bear upon them from without the influence of His example and teaching. It is in the latter sphere that His provisional work as Paraclete, agent for God amongst men, is to be found. Evidently He regarded it as less permanently valuable for man than the indwelling life, which the coming of the Spirit would enrich, securing thus the control and the development of the regenerate heart from within; and hence He could say, 'It is expedient for you that I go away' (Jn 16[7]). 2 Since Pentecost, Christ acts as Paraclete for man with God (1 Jn 2[1]). In His immanence He represents all, as His propitiation avails for all; but specifically His immanental union with believers is made more effective by their attitude of consent and devotion, and He carries on their cause with the Father, covering their sins and acting personally in their behalf (cf. He 7[25], Ro 8[34], Lk 22[32] 23[34], Jn 17[24]).

On the other hand, the Spirit is the Paraclete of God with and in man, sent to carry on His cause and to make perfect the surrender to Him and the service of His people. The term 'sent' is used officially of the Spirit, as of the Incarnate in regard to His historical manifestation. The distinction must not be unduly pressed; but the Paraclete's work in the hearts of the disciples themselves is the prominent assurance of Jn 14[16. 26], His work through them on the world that of Jn 16[7ff.], whilst Jn 15[26f.] is intermediate, and combines the qualifying grace with the incitement to witness.

The Paraclete is not mentioned by that name elsewhere in the Gospels; but His functions as such are referred to not only in the intimate conversation on the evening of the betrayal, but in such preparatory words as Jn 1[33] 7[38f.]. And though the word is Johannine, the teaching has its parallels in the Synoptics (Mt 10[20], Mk 13[11], Lk 11[13] 12[12] 24[49]); and the general idea which our Lord, according to the testimony of all the Evangelists, sought to communicate and to expand, seems to have been that since He could no longer remain in the flesh to promote the cause of God in His disciples, He would act in heaven as their representative with the Father, and the Holy Spirit would come to dwell in them and to further whatever tended to their perfection and to God's glory.

LITERATURE.—To the works cited in Hastings' *DB* iii. 668, add Welldon, *Revelation of the Holy Spirit*, 107 ff.; G. G. Findlay in *Exp. Times*, xii. (1901) 445; and Jastrow, *Dict. of Targ.* etc., *s.v.* פרקליט.　　　　　　R. W. MOSS.

PARADISE.—The word is a Persian one, and was adopted by the Hebrews from the mildest and most benevolent of their conquerors. Like most words with sufficient impetus to find their way into another language, it brings with it something of the character of the race from which it comes. It means something that the NT receives 'Legion' and 'Prætorium' from Rome, and 'Paradise' from Persia. It seems in its first home to have denoted a park-like garden, —an enclosure fenced in from evil influences outside, and yet not so artificial as to be solely the work of man and devoid of natural landscape beauties. Herds of deer and other wild animals found a happy home in the old Persian paradises (Xen. *Cyr.* i. 3. 14, *Anab.* i. 2. 7). But a word entering the speech of a strong nation does not remain unaltered. The strength of Israel was religious, and the word 'Paradise' became on her lips restricted to the great garden where God at the first had talked with man. Paradise became to her the lost Eden, the garden of the four rivers and the two mystic trees. It was impossible, however, to the Hebrew that anything religious should remain a mere memory. In process of time it became a heavenly and an inspiring hope. A cool and fragrant Paradise awaits the faithful Hebrew after death. The Golden Age creates the future home of the people of God.

It was to little purpose that the Alexandrian Jewish school combated this conception as too materialistic and earthy. The popular mind saw nothing attractive in the allegorizing which taught that Paradise meant 'virtue,' and the trees of the garden the thoughts of spiritual men. The strangely mingled life man lives, half in, half out of the spiritual world, will not suffer a system which ignores so large a portion of his consciousness.

This was its meaning to the mass of men in Gospel times. It appears thrice in the NT,—in Lk 23[43], in 2 Co 12[4], and in Rev 2[7],—and its history on the sacred page seems that of a spiral curve upwards. St. Paul's reference is so mystic as to remain somewhat indefinite, yet it is *up* to Paradise he is caught. But in Revelation the spiritual meaning shines through the thin veil of the pictorial promise to the Ephesian 'angel.'

It is not without interest to observe that in later times and outside Scripture the word seems in two directions to take a downward slant: first, among Mohammedans as applied to their carnal heaven, and afterwards in the Mediæval Church as indicating a place (the *Limbus Patrum*) reserved for departed souls who are only in partial and imperfect communion with the faithful.

Our Lord's solitary use of the word constitutes by far its greatest interest to Christians. He who spoke of 'the kingdom of God' or 'the kingdom of heaven' to the Apostles, used the word 'Paradise' to the dying brigand on the cross. The connotation of a term rises and falls with the mood of the speaker. But with the Speaker on this occasion, His mood is always regulated by the receptivity of the hearer. This man never knew much of any world beyond his own world of violence and rapine. He was dying now. What he needed was a form of comfort—real and true, no doubt, but such as he could reach and relish. He was writhing in thirst and agony, and the simple, common, current idea of Paradise, with its rest and relief, was to him, for the time being, the chiefest good. The hope of such a change was a simple hope; but a plain thought may be as true, as far as it goes, as a complex one; just as an outline may be as correct as a finished portrait. Anything more advanced would have meant nothing to the repentant robber. He who 'knew what was in man' gave the promise. See, further, art. 'Paradise' in Hastings' *DB*, and the Literature cited there.

LITERATURE.—As bearing upon Christ's use of the word, special ref. may be made to Salmond, *Christian Doct. of Immortality*, 346 ff. ; Edersheim, *LT* ii. 600 f. ; W. H. Brookfield, *Sermons*, 13 ff. ; Cairns, *Christ the Morning Star*, 270 ff. ; Maclaren, *Sermons Preached in Manchester*, i. 160 ff. ; C. H. H. Wright, *The Intermediate State*, 152 ff. ; R. E. Hutton, *The Soul in the Unseen World*, 155 ff.   M. P. JOHNSTONE.

PARADOX.—The paradoxes of the Gospels may be divided into three kinds. (1) Truth may be expressed in a way to shock opinion from its dogmatic slumber. Brief and vivid statements are made without qualification or explanation; metaphors are used to arrest the attention and stimulate the imagination, rather than to give a definite picture of the truth; a contrast which will force the hearer to think for himself is preferred to an argument which he need only follow. 'Paradoxes,' it has been said, 'are the burrs of literature—they stick.' (2) Truth often appears paradoxical at the time of its discovery, because it runs contrary to current conventions. Our view of men and things contains little knowledge, but much opinion. Custom alone makes us forget that we are living upon a volcano, until the revelation of some new truth revolutionizes all. So the fact that the world moves appeared paradoxical enough in the 16th century. Its strangeness was due to the environment into which it was thrust. (3) But sometimes the most adequate expression of a truth that we can reach still retains its paradoxical character in spite of time and familiarity, owing to the conflict of the conceptions united in its expression. We believe that the opposition is harmonized in reality, but we have as yet no clear and distinct idea of the reconciliation.

Each of these three kinds of paradox may be abundantly illustrated from the Gospels; and some of the most remarkable of the sayings of Jesus exemplify all three (Mt 5[39], Jn 12[24. 25]).

1. Much of the teaching of Jesus naturally took the form of condensed and vivid aphorisms. Systematic discourse, such as a moral philosopher might attempt, would not have been appropriate. It could hardly have been recorded; it would not have been understood. Moreover, Jesus was setting forth fundamental principles which could not be demonstrated, but appealed directly to the moral intuition for acceptance (Mt 5[3ff. 39ff.]). Further, He often suggested spiritual truths through analogies or metaphors, which, however suggestive, cannot be pressed in detail (Mt 11[12] 17[20], Lk 18[25], Jn 13[3-17]). Again we find contrasts that were clearly intended to enforce reflexion (Mt 7[1-6] 10[34-39], Lk 14[26], Jn 15[12. 17]). In short, Jesus would naturally avoid expressions which could be taken quite literally (Mt 5[38-41] 18[21. 22] 6[34] 25[1-13]). For He came to give a new spirit to the world, not to lay down a detailed scheme of life and order of society, which in time must have become antiquated, if not lifeless.

2. The moral and religious teaching of Jesus, though foreshadowed by the Law and the Prophets, came into sharp conflict with the formalism that petrified Jewish life in His day (Mt 15[10-20], Mk 2[18-28] 3[1-6]). More paradoxical still must have appeared His condemnation of the Pharisees (Mt 23[1-36]), His friendship with publicans and sinners (Mt 9[9-13], Mk 2[15. 16], Lk 19[1-10]), His conception of the Messiah (Mk 10[45] 8[27-38]).

3. Finally, there is the important class in which opposite and apparently conflicting aspects of truth, life, and duty are expressed in a form which does not completely harmonize them. In the teaching of Jesus we have unworldly simplicity united with worldly shrewdness (Mt 7[15] 10[16. 17] 16[6] 18[2. 3], Lk 16[1-12]), the universal beneficence and compassion of God bound up with severe and inexorable justice (Mt 5[45] 11[20-30] 18[15-35] 20[1-16] 25[14-30]) ; we have the great and deep conceptions of life through death, joy through suffering, love through severance, peace through conflict, victory through surrender, self-realization through self-renunciation, the conquest of the world through the cross of shame (Lk 14[25-33], Jn 12[24-26] 16[20. 33] 12[32]). Here are the profoundest truths, and yet the most paradoxical, for they are expressed through ideas that are partially contradictory to one another. We believe that if we could apprehend the whole truth, if we could understand through and through the whole meaning and purpose of creation, we could express these truths in a manner that would not shock our reason. But in the twilight of our knowledge we must be content to hold fast to half-truths, none of which is quite free from error or, at any rate, indefiniteness. Some who prefer consistency to comprehensiveness would sacrifice one part of the antithesis and elaborate the other. But though these may play a useful part in the dialectical movement of progress, they appear to be further removed from the whole truth than those who embrace the seeming contradiction, unable to fathom its depths, yet assured that in it is realized a perfect reconciliation. See also art. PARABLE, p. 314[a].   A. J. JENKINSON.

PARALYSIS.—In the NT the terms παραλυτικός (Mt 9[1-8], Mk 2[1-12]) and παραλελυμένος (Lk 5[17-26]) are employed to designate the nervous affection variously known as paralysis or palsy. **Palsy** commonly denotes loss of motor power in a muscle or set of muscles, and is equivalent to motor paralysis. When the power of transmitting sensory impressions to the brain centres is lost, we have sensory *paralysis*. The affliction is due to disease of the cerebral centres or of the nerves, owing to injury or morbid changes. In some cases the paralysis depends on removable causes; most commonly, however, upon alteration of structure involving permanent loss of function. There are two forms of paralysis : *hemiplegia*, where one side of the body is affected ; and *paraplegia*, where the lower limbs are rendered useless. In the instance above given in the Synoptics the term used by Lk. (παραλελυμένος) indicates that it was not a case of hysterical paralysis where a shock would be available to remove the trouble (Bennett), but that it was rather paralysis arising from serious nervous disease. All three Evangelists make prominent the impression of Divine power and majesty caused by this significant healing work of Jesus. And St. Luke prefaces his account with the additional reference to the power of God. 'The power of the Lord was with him to heal' (εἰς τὸ ἰᾶσθαι). All the accounts likewise record a mighty expectation of healing on the part of the friends, leading them to overcome all obstacles in the path to the great Healer—an expectation which we may believe energized also in the one to be healed. The combination of a vitalizing faith on the part of the people, and the activity of Divine power and healing purpose in Jesus, was precisely such as was most favourable to efficient curative action. St. Luke's account may be placed side by side with his record of our Lord's words ascribing His healing to the direct action of the Divine power (Lk 11[20]), and the whole compared with the statement repeatedly ascribed to Jesus in the Fourth Gospel, that the source of all healing power (as of true wisdom) was in the Divine indwelling (see art. MIRACLES). For the question arising here as to the connexion between the infirmity and human sin, see art. IMPOTENCE.

The case of the Centurion's servant (Mt 8[5-13], Lk 7[2-10]) is marked by one feature which is significant. The patient was 'grievously tormented' (δεινῶς βασανιζόμενος), where, however, the description is not given by Luke, but by Matthew. The indication may therefore not be medically so suggestive. Bennett (*Diseases of Bible*) inclines to regard it as a case probably of 'progressive paralysis attended by muscular spasms and involving respiratory movements,' while Macalister (art. 'Medicine' in Hastings' *DB*), on the ground of Matthew's description of the pain involved, prefers to regard it as one 'possibly of spinal meningitis.' The narratives are, however, not medical, and their central interest lies in the centurion's 'great faith' so warmly eulogized by Jesus, and in his simple straightforward conception of the nature of the power and authority possessed by our Lord. He compares it to the authority conferred upon and exercised by himself—on the one hand being a power derived from the supreme source of all authority, and on the other being absolute in enforcing and obtaining promptest obedience. It is significant that our Lord accepts this conception, and commends in the fullest fashion the faith of which it was a part (see art. CURES).

T. H. WRIGHT.

PARENTS.—**1.** *Jewish parents.*—A few introductory remarks on the conjugal relation are necessary. The husband was supreme in the household; his authority recognized by the wife—and here it may be noted that, while polygamy was permitted by the Jewish law, the principle of 'one man one wife' had won general acceptance. As for the legal status of the wife, the provisions in respect to some things (see DIVORCE) were one-sided; but her position, if subordinate, was by no means one of absolute dependence, nor was she relegated to the seclusion common in other Oriental nations. The husband ruled; the wife's influence in all domestic concerns was great. Fidelity was expected on both sides. The match might have been arranged by other parties (see MARRIAGE), but the relations of the wedded pair would be characterized by a growing love. The honourable position of the faithful wife (Pr 31[10-31]) would be evidenced in countless Jewish homes. To the strong attachment of husband to wife, of wife to husband, there is frequent and touching allusion in later Jewish literature. It would make itself felt in the whole family life.

This brief notice of the conjugal relation should help to a correct appreciation of the relations now to be considered, viz. the parental, and, by consequence, the filial. At once it may be set down that the requirements of the Fifth Commandment had taken deep hold in Jewish life. As Bousset (*Rel. d. Jud.* 402) remarks, it was not forgotten that in the Decalogue the duties of children to parents follow immediately upon those which turn on matters religious and ritual. The requirements, it should be noted particularly, place both parents on the same level. In practice the supremacy of the father as ruler of the household was, indeed, recognized; his power over his children was almost absolute: at the same time, the utmost respect and obedience to both father and mother were demanded and yielded. Domestic discipline was exceedingly strict; the behaviour of child to parent would be marked by that courtliness of etiquette which was once a feature of English family life; there was, perhaps, little demonstrativeness of affection in the case of the father. Restraint is, in short, observable; but it formed no barrier to a love deep and strong which knit child to parent and parent to child: the full pathos of the love which linked a Jewish father to his son cannot be set down in words. The joyousness of child-life was in no wise cramped; allusion is met with to the readiness of parents to provide for, and to enter into, the amusement of the children. Not

until the 2nd cent. was the maintenance of children the subject of legal enactment; fulfilment of the duty had probably been taken as a matter of course. It was certainly expected that children should minister to the necessities of aged parents. See, further, BOYHOOD.

2. *The home at Nazareth.*—Joseph was in any case the legal father of Jesus (Dalman, *The Words of Jesus*); hence the parental and filial relation as illustrated in the Holy Family may be discussed apart from questions treated of elsewhere (see VIRGIN-BIRTH). The glimpses afforded are but few: there are the stories in the opening chapters of Matthew and Luke, and some incidents in our Lord's ministry. Fragmentary notices; and yet a great deal may be read into them when studied in connexion with the preceding paragraphs.

What, then, is discernible in the parents of Jesus? Conjugal attachment; so also a genuine and simple-hearted piety. They are punctilious in the observance of religious duties (Lk 2[21. 22]); if attendance at the Passover was only demanded of men, Mary is quick to avail herself of a privilege which had been extended to women also (Lk 2[41]). That the child Jesus 'increased in wisdom' (Lk 2[40. 52]) is a statement not to be interpreted without thought of the parental care which watched over His ripening intelligence. If His 'understanding and answers' were cause of astonishment (Lk 2[47]), the explanation points, in part at any rate to early training given by His mother; to the careful discharge, by Joseph, of the paternal duties, so preparing Him for the eventful day when, arrived at the age of twelve years, He would become a 'son of the Law.' There was the further discharge of paternal duty as the lad was taught a trade (Mk 6[3]). The strict discipline above spoken of is implied in Lk 2[51] (καὶ ἦν ὑποτασσόμενος αὐτοῖς: the respect and obedience which Joseph and Mary claim as their due are promptly rendered by the boy, the growing youth.

There the narrative of the early life of Jesus breaks off; of Gospel record of the next eighteen years there is none. With the resumption of the narrative Jesus has arrived at manhood; Joseph disappears from the scene, and attention accordingly centres on the relations of Jesus with the widowed mother. No longer is He a member of the family circle; Mary is cared for by sons and daughters; but the respect, the affection, the loving solicitude of 'her firstborn son' is still enjoyed by her. He asserts His independence, but with perfect courtesy (Jn 2[4]; 'the address is that of courteous respect, even of tenderness,' Westcott). He is not to be understood in Mk 3[32-34] as disowning parental ties; rather as speaking of a family of God that is greater than the human family. The touching incident recorded in Jn 19[26. 27] is significant of maternal and filial devotion to the very end.

3. *Sayings of our Lord.*—Attention must now be directed to notes struck by Jesus where recorded sayings of His have reference to the parental and filial relations. Few in number, they are significant. For Him parents are the natural guardians (Lk 8[56]). He has scathing condemnation for the legal fiction which affords means of escape for children unwilling to contribute to their parents' support (Mt 15[3-6], Mk 7[9-13]); the Fifth Commandment, for Him, is paramount above other religious duties (see CORBAN). He takes obedience to the Fifth Commandment for granted (Mt 19[19], Mk 10[19], Lk 18[20]); its observance is a condition of 'eternal life.' If in days near at hand parent will betray child and child parent, the unnatural circumstance will be but evidence of tribulation predicted by Him (Mt 10[21], Mk 13[12], Lk 21[16]). What He says in Mt 10[37] (Lk 14[26]) is tantamount to a recognition of the strength of family ties. Very beautifully has it been said that His favourite illustration was drawn from the home. Thus in the Lord's Prayer it is the idea of the home that governs the Prayer. The relations between the Heavenly Father and His children are set forth in terms richly suggestive of the human relationships. 'Reverence and submission—that the parent has a right to obtain from the children; support, forbearance, and protection—that the children on their part have a right to ask from the parent' (A. W. Robinson, *Church Catechism Explained*).

Two sayings may present difficulty. One of them occurs in Lk 18[29]; it must be compared with Mt 19[29. 30], Mk 10[29. 30], where descriptions of the blessings of the Messianic Kingdom are set forth in terms familiar to the Jews of our Lord's day. Mention is indeed made of circumstances under which the renunciation of earthly ties may be demanded; they are, however, exceptional circumstances, where the ties in question are incompatible with a higher allegiance. The other saying occurs in Mt 8[21] (cf. Lk 9[59]). Request and rejoinder have been explained of proverbial allusion (Adeney); it has been held that the permission really sought was to remain and support an aged father until he died (Theophylact); and this is possible. It is certainly hard to believe that, with burial following so quickly upon death as is the case in the East, a request so thoroughly in accord with Jewish feeling (cf. To 4[2-4]) was abruptly refused by Jesus. His reply is, perhaps, capable of metaphorical interpretation: 'Think not only of the dead, remember the needs of the living.' There may be, however, a reminder in it of the exceptional circumstances above alluded to. Besides, the teaching of Jesus had its sterner aspect.

LITERATURE.—Schürer, *HJP*, II. ii. 27; Abrahams, *Jewish Life in the Middle Ages*, which goes back to earlier days; Joseph, *Judaism as Creed and Life*; Maurice, *Social Morality*; J. R. Seeley, 'The Church as a Teacher of Morality' in *Lectures and Essays*. For the subject in regard to modern life see Mason, *Home Education*; Turnbull, *Hints on Child Training*; Mrs. Craik, *Sermons out of Church*. H. L. JACKSON.

PARONOMASIA (Gr. παρονομασία, Lat. *annominatio*).*—A play on words of similar sound. This linguistic use, which in the present day is usually confined to humorous writing, is found in ancient, and especially Oriental, works in the most serious passages. In Hebrew it is frequent, largely with proper names. There are many examples in the OT, *e.g.* Gn 9[27] 25[26] 48[22], Ex 2[10], Ru 1[20], Is 63[1], Mic 1[10-15].† In the New Testament the writings of St. Paul, whose early training had been Jewish, furnish some instances of *paronomasia* (*e.g.* Philem[11], 'Ονήσιμον—ἄχρηστον—εὔχρηστον), but in the Gospels it is rare, being found chiefly, if not wholly, in the Hebraistic Gospel according to St. Matthew. The best known and most certain example is Mt 16[18] σὺ εἶ Πέτρος (a rock), καὶ ἐπὶ ταύτῃ τῇ πέτρα (? fragment of rock) οἰκοδομήσω μου τὴν ἐκκλησίαν. If, as seems probable, our Lord spoke in Aramaic, the word used would be *Kepha* (אֵפָא, cf. Heb. כֵּפִים Jer 4[29], Job 30[6] = 'rocks'). The *paronomasia* makes the reference to St. Peter certain, although there may still be room for doubt whether Christ meant that St. Peter, as the leader of the Apostolic band, should be the human founder of the new Church, or that it should be built on the foundation of the confession, Σὺ εἶ ὁ Χριστὸς ὁ υἱὸς τοῦ θεοῦ τοῦ ζῶντος. The former of these views is the more reasonable, and would probably have been almost universally ac-

* Winer in his *NT Grammar* (tr. Moulton, 1882, pp. 793–796) distinguishes between *paronomasia* and *annominatio*, defining the former as 'a combination of like-sounding words' (*e.g.* Lk 21[11], Mt 21[41]), and the latter as 'having respect to the meaning of the words as well as to their similarity in sound' (*e.g.* Mt 16[18]). See also Blass, *NT Grammar*, tr. Thackeray, 1898, p. 298.

† Cf. also Ec 7[1a] שֵׁם, שָׁמֶן.

cepted had it not been for the extravagance of some Roman Catholic commentators.

There are also possible examples of *paronomasia* in Mt 2[23] 3[9]. In the former of these passages the words Ναζωραῖος (= an inhabitant of Nazareth) κληθήσεται are not found in any prophet, but it seems not unlikely that they contain an allusion to the language of Is 11[1] where Messiah is called נֵצֶר (= a branch), and possibly also to the word נָצַר (to preserve); cf. Is 49[6]. In Mt 3[9] (cf. Lk 3[8]) the Baptist says δύναται ὁ θεὸς ἐκ τῶν λίθων τούτων ἐγεῖραι τέκνα τῷ Ἀβραάμ. The Hebrew words for λίθοι and τέκνα are similar in sound. There may therefore be a *paronomasia* here: 'God can from these stones (אֲבָנִים *ʾăbānîm*) raise up children (בָּנִים *bānîm*) to Abraham.' These passages have been used to support the view, which is as old as Papias, that parts at least of Mt. had a Hebrew or Aramaic original.*

LITERATURE.—C. B. Michaelis, *de paronomasia sacra* (Hal. 1737); J. F. Boettcher, *de paronomasia finitimisque ei figuris Paulo Apostolo frequentatis* (Lips. 1823); Hastings' *DB*, Extra Vol., p. 165 (by König). H. W. FULFORD.

PAROUSIA.—In connexion with the intimations of His approaching death, Jesus frequently spoke of His coming again to earth in a way that would give proof of His indestructible life and power. It is evident, however, that in those predictions of the future it was not always in exactly the same sense that He meant His coming to be understood. His sayings on the subject from time to time obviously pointed to several comings, each of which was to have its peculiar character and aim (see COMING AGAIN). But there was one coming which He foretold in language of exceptional emphasis and impressiveness,—His appearance in celestial majesty at the end of the world, to perfect the work interrupted by His death, but still to be renewed and carried on through the ages by His spiritual energy. This was to be the supreme manifestation of His glory; and to it the term Parousia (παρουσία) is distinctively applied (Mt 24[3. 27. 37]). It will signalize the final triumph of His cause, and the complete establishment and consummation of the Kingdom of God. It is the great crisis which has been designated in common usage the Second Coming.

It was at Cæsarea Philippi, after His first announcement of the tragic end awaiting Him at the hands of men, that Jesus made also the first announcement of His future glorious return (Mt 16[27], Mk 8[38], Lk 9[26]). He repeated it subsequently under varied circumstances and to varied groups of listeners, and towards the close of His ministry the Parousia, or Second Coming, assumed a marked prominence in His teaching.

In His utterances regarding it, as recorded in the Gospels, there are three points which call specially for consideration,—its time, its manner, and its decisive significance.

1. Time.—As to the time of the Parousia, we find two classes of statements that are somewhat perplexing to reconcile. In one set of passages Jesus looks forward to its early, and even speedy, approach. The existing generation was to witness it (Mt 24[34]). On one occasion He told those standing by that some of them should not taste of death till they saw the Son of Man coming in His Kingdom (Mt 16[28]; cf. Mk 9[1], Lk 9[27]), and the same idea of nearness is expressed in Mt 10[23] and Mk 14[62]. Yet we are confronted by another set of passages that suggest a lengthened period of waiting, and

* It is, of course, possible that in our Lord's discourses, spoken originally in Aramaic, there were examples of *paronomasia* which have been lost in the Greek version. Eichhorn (*Einl. in d. NT*, i. 504) and others have made conjectural attempts to restore some of these, but they are not convincing. Mt 10[25] may contain a *paronomasia* if Βεελζεβούλ is to be connected with זְבוּל and made = 'lord of the dwelling' (οἰκοδεσπότης).

the probability of the Parousia being deferred. Such are the parables of the Ten Virgins (Mt 25$^{1-12}$) and the Tyrannical Upper Servant (Lk 12$^{42-46}$ and Mk 13^{35}). Jesus did not Himself profess to define the time; indeed, in one memorable saying He disclaimed with the utmost distinctness all positive knowledge of the day and hour of the supreme consummation (Mt 24^{36} ‖ Mk 13^{32}). In the great Eschatological Discourse recorded in Mt 24 and Mk 13 (cf. Lk 21), the subject is complicated by the manifest reference in certain sections to the disastrous collapse which threatened the Jewish State.

Some, taking the discourse as a homogeneous unity, have been led to maintain that the predictions of Jesus respecting His coming were all fulfilled in the destruction of Jerusalem (Stuart Russell, *Parousia*). Many critics, however, find themselves unable to regard the discourse, in the form reported, as one continuous and connected deliverance of Jesus. Wendt and Charles, following Colani, contend that some parts of it are interpolations from an apocalyptic document of Judæo-Christian authorship, belonging to the year A.D. 67-68. It seems more reasonable to adopt the view, advocated by Professor Bruce and others, that in this discourse the Evangelists have gathered together in one place words spoken on different occasions, and have connected future events more closely than the utterances of Jesus justified. It is at least clear that certain passages in the discourse point to the judgment on Israel as a nation and the impending fall of Jerusalem and its Temple-worship, whilst it is equally clear that other passages refer to a crisis, certainly to be looked for, but still lying in the distance (Mt 24$^{43-50}$, Mk 13$^{34-37}$).

With the purport of these latter passages, indicating a possible delay in the coming, there are several other sayings of Jesus that distinctly agree, as, *e.g.*, the two parables already mentioned (Mt 25$^{1-12}$ and Lk 12$^{42-46}$), and also the parable of the Unjust Judge (Lk 18$^{1-7}$). We find, besides, that in a particular group of parables—the Mustard Seed, the Leaven (Mt 13$^{31-33}$), and the Growing Grain of Corn (Mk 4$^{26-29}$)—the Kingdom He came to establish is represented as subject to the law of growth. Evidently Jesus was not unmindful of the preparatory process it might be necessary for the world to pass through ere He could usher in the Kingdom in its full glory. His words can be interpreted as indicating a recognition of the natural course of human development as an essential factor in determining the time when the world would be ripe for the final manifestation of His power. Moreover, He spoke also of the evangelization of the Gentile races as a work to be undertaken ere the end should come (Mt 24^{14} 26^{13}, Mk 13^{10}). The gospel was first to be published among all nations, that they also might have an opportunity of accepting the offer of grace; 'the times of the Gentiles must be fulfilled' (Lk 21^{24}). Here again there is foreshadowed a lengthened process, requiring, not a generation only, but an era, for its accomplishment. Manifestly Jesus took into account the gradual evolution of human affairs in contemplating the triumph of His Kingdom, while at the same time His faith in that triumph was so real and assured, and His vision of it so intensely clear, that it seemed to Him imminent, on the eve of fulfilment; and when He spoke under this feeling His disciples gathered the impression that it was close at hand, and they naturally understood the supreme event to be synchronous with the fall of Jerusalem, though in this, as it proved, they were mistaken.

2. Manner.—As to the manner of the Parousia, a considerable number of passages represent it as altogether startling and unexpected. It is to break in upon the world as a sudden surprise, while men are busied with their earthly affairs, like the Flood in the time of Noah, or the destruction of Sodom in the time of Lot (Lk 17$^{26-30.\ 34}$). Its approach shall be as that of a thief, stealing into the house without warning (12$^{39f.}$), or as the arrival of an absent master at an hour when his servants are not looking for him (vv.$^{42-46}$), or as the return of the bride-

groom in the night-time, leading his bride and the marriage party to the wedding-feast (Mt 25$^{1-13}$). On the other hand, there are passages in the Eschatological Discourse in Mt 24 and Mk 13 which seem to represent the final coming as preceded by certain manifest signs which shall give evidence of its nearness—the appearance of false Christs (Mt 24^5, Mk 13$^{6.\ 22}$), wars, earthquakes, and famines (Mt 24^7, Mk 13$^{7-10}$), persecutions and tribulations (Mt 24^9, Mk 13$^{11-13}$), the darkened sun and falling stars (Mt 24^{29}, Mk 13$^{24.\ 25}$). If, however, the view of the composite character of that discourse, as we now have it, is accepted, the passages describing such arresting phenomena may be interpreted as vivid pictorial forecasts of the calamitous state of things by which the threatened Jewish crisis would be ushered in. But whether that view is accepted or not, special weight must be attached to the warning given by Jesus that even the most striking and palpable signs might be misread. The heralds of the great climax, He declares, must not be taken as the climax itself; 'All these things must come to pass, but the end is not yet' (Mt 24^6). After all, apparently, whatever may be the catastrophic social or other upheavals by which it is preluded, the signal event is to come suddenly and unexpectedly, at such an hour as men think not (Mt 24^{44}, Lk 12$^{40.\ 46}$). Yet, when it does come, there shall be no dubiety; the splendour shall be dazzlingly patent, like the lightning-flash illumining all the heavens (Mt 24^{27}).

3. Significance.—The decisive significance of the Parousia was expressed by Jesus in words of profound solemnity. What it will involve, according to His teaching, may be briefly summed up as follows:

(1) The Divine dignity of His Person shall then be disclosed. He will appear in heavenly majesty, attended by His holy angels, and His glory and power shall be fully revealed (Mt 24^{30} 25^{31} 26^{64}, Mk 8^{38}).

(2) His authority as Judge shall be put in force. Entrusted by the Father with supreme judicial functions (Jn 5$^{22.\ 23}$), He will gather all nations before Him to receive a reward according to their works (Mt 16^{27} 25^{32}); the secrets of all hearts shall be unveiled (Lk 12^2); there shall be a sifting and separation of the good from the bad, the spurious from the true (Mt 7$^{22.\ 23}$ 13$^{41.\ 49}$ 25^{32}); and the sentence of approval or of condemnation passed shall depend on the attitude and spirit towards Himself by which the life has been swayed (25$^{34-46}$).

(3) The future destinies of men shall be determined. The day shall at last have arrived—'that day' (Mt 7^{22}, Lk 10^{12}) so momentous to every soul—when there can be no more self-deception, and the results of the law of recompense shall have to be faced, the righteous and pure-hearted being raised to eternal life and blessedness in the presence of the Father, and the unworthy and insincere cast into the outer darkness (Mt 13$^{41-43}$ 22^{13} 25$^{34-46}$, Mk 8^{38}).

Thus (4) the Kingdom shall be exalted to its triumph and perfection. It shall be cleansed of all things that offend, and them that do iniquity (Mt 13^{41}); the supremacy of righteousness shall be vindicated by the elevation of the godly to salvation, the ingathering of all elect souls (24^{13}), and the exclusion of the wicked from the eternal inheritance.

Then (5) the existing world-order shall come to an end. In the teaching of Jesus Himself there is no trace of the thought that the Parousia would inaugurate an outward visible sovereignty on earth, when He should assume the reins of government, and rule as King in the realm of temporal affairs. That thought arose among His followers only at a subsequent period. The idea implied in His utterances is rather that His final glorious advent shall mark the definite close of the long drama of human life on the earth, by the removal of all His true disciples to the heavenly state, and the consignment of the unfaithful to the doom prepared for them. That shall be the Last Day, when the human race shall have had its full trial under the dispensations of the Divine truth and grace,—the winding-up of the world's history.

LITERATURE.—Charles, *Eschatology, Hebrew, Jewish, and Christian* (1899); Wendt, *Teaching of Jesus*, ii. 274–351; Weiss, *Bib. Theol. of NT*, ii. 145-158, and *Life of Christ*, iii. 80–97; Beyschlag, *NT Theol.* i. 190–204; Bruce, *Kingdom of God* (1889), 272–294; Stuart Russell, *Parousia* (1887); Warren, *Parousia* (1885); Muirhead, *Eschatology of Jesus* (1904); Adams Brown, art. 'Parousia' in Hastings' *DB*; Dorner, *Syst. of Chr. Doct.* iv. 373–428; Salmond, *Chr. Doct. of Immortality*, 300 ff., 425 ff.; J. A. Beet, *Last Things* (1905), 19; G. Jackson, *Teaching of Jesus* (1905), 207; G. B. Stevens, *Theology of NT* (1899), 150; Sanday-Headlam, *Romans*, 379 ff.   G. M'HARDY.

PASSION WEEK.—What origin can we assign to the sacred institution known variously as Holy Week, Passion Week, or the Silent Week? What documentary evidence have we for the belief that the Triumphal Entry took place on a Sunday, so that exactly a week elapsed between that event and the discovery of the empty tomb?

1. Investigators of the Life of Jesus find a fulcrum in Jn 12[1]. Even Keim, who puts no faith in the narratives of the Fourth Gospel, least of all in its chronology, accepts its testimony in this particular passage (see *Jesus of Nazara*, v. 274). It is there stated that Jesus 'six days before the Passover (πρὸ ἓξ ἡμερῶν τοῦ πάσχα) came to Bethany'; and (12[12f.]) that He went to Jerusalem next day. But it is a little difficult to understand what the narrator means by the 'six days' in question. The idiom of πρὸ ἓξ ἡμερῶν τοῦ πάσχα (cf. LXX, Am 1[1] πρὸ δύο ἐτῶν τοῦ σεισμοῦ), which bears a resemblance to the Latin formula *ante diem tertium kalendas* (cf. *Inscr. Insularum Mar. Æg.* iii. 325, πρὸ ἷε καλανδῶν Αὐγούστων), is genuine primitive Greek (Moulton, *Gram. of NT Greek*, i. 100 f.). The question is, then, whether the Passover day, the 14th Nisan, on which the Passover was eaten, is or is not included in the number 'six.' If it is included, Jesus must have arrived in Bethany on the 9th Nisan; if not, then on the 8th. The latter alternative is the more natural, since the six days are spoken of as coming *before* the Passover; and on this assumption Jesus must have entered Jerusalem on the 9th Nisan. Now, since according to Jn 19[31] the 15th Nisan was a Sabbath, the 8th must likewise have been a Sabbath, and the day of the Triumphal Entry a Sunday. It is to these Johannine data that we trace our Passion Week.

2. Now the Johannine reckoning appears to be corroborated by at least one of the Synoptics, viz. Mk. For one thing, Mk. assigns the death of Jesus to the παρασκευή (15[42], cf. Mt 27[62], Lk 23[54]), His repose in the sepulchre to the Sabbath, and the finding of the empty tomb to the Sunday (16[2], cf. Lk 24[1], Mt 28[1]), and consequently the Last Supper to the Thursday evening. Further, it is obviously the design of our Mk. to number the days in proper order, as may be seen in its striking succession of morning and evening, thus:

11[11] Evening of *1st* day (the Triumphal Entry): καὶ περιβλεψάμενος πάντα, ὀψὲ ἤδη οὔσης τῆς ὥρας, ἐξῆλθεν εἰς Βηθανίαν.

11[12] Morning of *2nd* day: καὶ τῇ ἐπαύριον ἐξελθόντων αὐτῶν ἀπὸ Βηθανίας ...

11[19] Evening of 2nd day: καὶ ὅταν ὀψὲ ἐγένετο, ἐξεπορεύετο ἔξω τῆς πόλεως.

11[20] Morning of *3rd* day: καὶ παραπορευόμενοι πρωΐ ...

13[1] Evening of 3rd day (?): καὶ ἐκπορευομένου αὐτοῦ ἐκ τοῦ ἱεροῦ ...

To this point the enumeration is quite clear. We may ask, indeed, whether the various colloquies of 11[27]–12[44] all took place on a single day.

But in view of the care with which Mk. distinguishes the previous days, we can only infer that the absence of time references in the disputations is likewise a matter of design.

We must now inquire, however, how 14[1] is connected with what precedes. Are the words ἦν δὲ τὸ πάσχα καὶ τὰ ἄζυμα μετὰ δύο ἡμέρας meant to imply that the foregoing discourse of Jesus on the Mt. of Olives was spoken two days before the Passover, *i.e.* on the very day the religious authorities held their conference? And must we suppose the Anointing at Bethany (14[3] καὶ ὄντος αὐτοῦ ἐν Βηθανίᾳ) to have taken place that day also, *i.e.* on the evening of the third day, and after the Parousia discourse? Again, on what day does Mk. place the betrayal by Judas (14[10f.] καὶ . . . ἀπῆλθεν . . . καὶ ἐζήτει . . .)? On the day following, *i.e.* the fourth? In truth, the Evangelist's chronology in these passages is as vague as in 11[11. 12. 19. 20] it was unmistakable.

Nor is Mk.'s enumeration of the days between the decision of the Sanhedrin and the Last Supper quite explicit. If we regard 14[12] καὶ τῇ πρώτῃ ἡμέρᾳ τῶν ἀζύμων, ὅτε τὸ πάσχα ἔθυον as referring to the 14th Nisan, then in all probability 14[1] synchronizes with the 12th Nisan, and 14[10f.] with, say, the 13th. But this is not said in so many words. Nevertheless, the writer possibly had in his mind some such synopsis as follows:

1st day, 11[1-11]: Sunday, 10th Nisan.
2nd day, 11[12-19]: Monday, 11th ,,
3rd day, 11[20–14]9: Tuesday, 12th ,,
4th day, 14[10f.]: Wednesday, 13th ,,
5th day, 14[12-72]: Thursday, 14th ,,
6th day, 15[1-47]: Friday, 15th ,,
7th day, 16[1a] διαγινομένου τοῦ σαββάτου, Saturday, 16th Nisan.
8th day, 16[1b]: Sunday, 17th Nisan.

It is also possible, however, that there is an interval between ch. 13 and 14[1], so that the Anointing would fall on the day after the Parousia speech. This would so far dislocate the above scheme by making the first day coincide with Saturday, 9th Nisan (as probably in Jn.), the second day with Sunday, the third with Monday, and the anointing with Tuesday. If this be so, we must allow for a period of *nine* days between the Entry and the Resurrection. In point of fact, we cannot solve the difficulty from Mk.'s data; its mode of reckoning still leaves a residuum of doubt. In particular, we are at a loss regarding what Jesus does and where He is during the day previous to the Anointing. But, notwithstanding these obscurities, it is an unmistakable fact that Mk. makes an attempt —though by no means an entirely effective one—to distinguish and enumerate the days between the Triumphal Entry and the Resurrection. Especially does the *sequence* of chronological references seem to postulate a definite calendar of the interval in question.

3. We turn now to Mt. and Lk. Mt. indicates a clear break only at the close of the Triumphal Entry day (21[17] καὶ καταλιπὼν αὐτοὺς ἐξῆλθεν ἔξω τῆς πόλεως εἰς Βηθανίαν καὶ ηὐλίσθη ἐκεῖ). The second day runs without interruption from 21[18] to the end of 25. In passing to the narrative of the Passion proper, Mt. exhibits the same ambiguity as we found in Mk. We cannot decide whether the words of Jesus in 26[1f.] were spoken on the second day, or whether we must assume an interval between chs. 25 and 26.

Possibly, however, we err in looking for chronology at all in this section of Mt. We can understand the narrative quite as well on the hypothesis that the writer was not in the least concerned to tabulate the days, but simply joined incident to incident without regard to time. We find a similar uncertainty in Lk.: the writer's own words in 20[1] ἐν μιᾷ τῶν ἡμερῶν clearly imply that he had no distinct idea of the number of days between the

Triumphal Entry and the Passover (cf. also 21³⁷ ἦν δὲ τὰς ἡμέρας ἐν τῷ ἱερῷ διδάσκων). This lack of precision admittedly extends also to the story of the actual Passion. Instead of the 'two days' (Mk 14¹, Mt 26²), Lk. says only ἤγγιζεν δὲ ἡ ἑορτὴ τῶν ἀζύμων (22¹), and in place of the precise reference of Mk 14¹² τῇ πρώτῃ ἡμέρᾳ τῶν ἀζύμων, ὅτε τὸ πάσχα ἔθυον, Lk. simply has it that the day of unleavened bread 'came' (22⁷). This loose way of indicating time in Mt. and Lk. strikes us as strange in view of the generally accepted theory of their common dependence upon Mk., which designedly and explicitly gives an all but complete diary of the time. How are we to explain the fact that the two Evangelists who make use of the oldest Gospel are here less precise in details than their common source?

4. The recognized explanation, viz., that the later writers did not trouble about such matters of detail, is most unsatisfactory, as all investigation of the growth and progress of the Evangelical record goes to show a constantly increasing interest in such minutiæ as time and hour, place and number, name and personality; witness, e.g., the NT Apocrypha. In fact, had we not other grounds for deeming Mk. the oldest of the Gospels, its ostensible precision in such things would lead us to regard it as the latest.—The present writer is of opinion that we can best explain Mt.'s and Lk.'s omission of the time references of Passion Week, by the hypothesis that the recension of Mk. used by them did not itself contain these references (*Ur-Markus Hypothesis*). Or, in other words, our Mk.'s enumeration of the days is the work of a later hand, a redactor, the Deutero-Mark. This view is so far confirmed by the presence of a certain artificiality in the arrangement. It would seem as if a definite scheme had been forcibly stamped upon the material. The *first* trace of this appears in 11¹¹. While Mt. and Lk. quite simply and naturally make the Cleansing of the Temple succeed the Triumphal Entry, upon the same day, Mk. has it that Jesus, having come to the city, spent the rest of the day in seeing the sights (as if He had not been often enough in Jerusalem during His thirty years), and that then, as it was late in the day (too late, *i.e.*, to begin His great work), He went out to Bethany with His disciples. This apparently so exact piece of information really strikes us as utterly trivial and pedantic. What interest could Mark suppose his readers to have in such a petty detail? or what concern had he himself, so indifferent, in general, to all chronology, in such exactitude at that particular point? There is, as it seems to us, but one explanation of the anomaly, viz., that the writer of 11¹¹ was anxious to intercalate one day more than the facts naturally allowed; that is to say, he figured to himself a definite number of days, and must distribute them somehow in the material before him. A *second* trace is found in the circumstance that Mk. divides the incident of the Barren Fig-tree between two days (11¹³ᶠ· ²⁰ᶠ·). Here, too, Mt. gives the more natural account. For, granting the miracle of judgment upon the ill-starred tree, it is much more in harmony with popular views that the blight should instantly follow the curse (Mt 21¹⁸ᶠ·). In Mark's report, according to which the word of Jesus takes a day to work its effect, we seem to discern a rationalizing tendency. The Evangelist, with all his belief in the miraculous, can more easily grasp the phenomenon by allowing for some sort of natural process.* Further, the partition of the Fig-tree incident enables the

redactor of Mk. to give a sharper distinction to the two days (11¹²⁻¹⁹ and 11²⁰⁻¹³¹) by means of two morning walks from Bethany to Jerusalem (11¹²· ²⁰). A *third* indication of the artificiality of Mk.'s arrangement is seen in 14⁴⁹, where Jesus speaks in such a manner as to imply that He had taught in the Temple for several days. But according to the said scheme, again, the whole of the teaching at this time occupies but a single day (11²⁰–12⁴⁴), or, at most, two days if we include also the day of the Cleansing. Hence we are justified in inferring that the diary is not only not organic to the events, but actually at variance with them. In fact, the sayings and discourses at Jerusalem, as set down in Mk., give no hint whatever of a chronological order. They are as exempt from time references as are the five controversies of Mk 2¹–3⁶. The true design of either series is to illustrate the antagonism between Jesus and the hierarchy, and they may have been uttered either on one day or on several successive days.

We would therefore hazard the suggestion that our Mk.'s tabulation of the interval under consideration, and notably the passage 11¹¹· ¹², is due to the redactor, and that the latter was imbued with the Johannine tradition. For our own part, indeed, we have been able to collate a mass of evidence in support of the theory that the text of Mk. has been very thoroughly revised from the Johannine standpoint, that a host of Johannine characteristics were inserted into it at some period subsequent to its use by Matthew and Luke. It is, of course, impossible here to submit the detailed proof of such a theory, and we can but invite the reader to test it for himself. The design of the present article does not carry us beyond the advocacy and proof of the thesis: As originally the Synoptic tradition neither contained a complete diary of our Lord's last visit to Jerusalem, nor implied that His stay covered exactly one week, it is in the last resort to Jn. that we must trace the order of our Passion Week. See also art. DATES.

LITERATURE.—J. Weiss, *Das älteste Evangelium*, 1903; C. A. Briggs, *New Light on the Life of Jesus* (1904), 101 ff.; A. G. Mortimer, *Meditations on the Passion* (1903); R. Winterbotham, *Sermons in Holy Trinity Church* (1900), 140–184.

J. WEISS.

PASSOVER (I.) (Heb. פֶּסַח *pesaḥ*, Aram. פַּסְחָא *pasḥa*, in Greek πάσχα, φασέκ, and φάσκα [Jos.], NT πάσχα).—The most distinctive festival of the Jewish religion. Its origin, significance, and method of celebration are given in Ex 12¹⁻⁴⁹ 23¹⁸ 34²⁵, Lv 23⁵⁻⁸, Nu 9¹⁻¹⁴ 28¹⁶⁻²⁵, Dt 16¹⁻⁸.*

Modern criticism has discovered certain variations in the ritual and significance, has distinguished layers and stages in the ideas the festival was to suggest, and has sought to connect it with earlier and ethnic rites. Without accepting all such contentions, it may be granted that there is, at least, the union of an agricultural feast with a commemoration of the Exodus out of Egypt, in which commemoration certain of the circumstances which marked the historic deliverance are more or less literally repeated. Jewish expositors distinguish between 'the Egyptian Passover' and those which were subsequently observed,—'the perpetual Passover' or 'Passover for the generations,'—and narrate the points in which they differ from each other; in the former the impure partook, the blood was sprinkled on the lintels, the fat was not burned, and no hymn was sung; with other details.

The references in the OT to the observance of this festival are comparatively rare. There was the observance at the time of the Exodus, in the second year after coming out of Egypt (Nu 9⁵), at the entry into Canaan (Jos 5¹⁰· ¹¹). The feast was apparently observed during the reign of Solomon (2 Ch 8¹³). Under Hezekiah there was a great act of observance, but in the second month, when the feast was prolonged by one week, and even the

---

* A similar tendency emerges in the two miracles of healing reported by Mk. alone, in which the spittle of Jesus comes to the aid of His omnipotence (7³³ 8²³); in the healing of the blind, the narrator pictures to himself a gradual advance towards perfect vision (8²⁴· ²⁵).

* The derivation of the word is uncertain. It may be derived from a root meaning to *leap* or *pass over*, used of the sun at the spring-time; or to *pass over*, in the sense of *sparing*, the traditional meaning.

Levitically unclean were permitted to participate (30¹⁵⁻²³). At the period of the revival of religion during the reign of Josiah, there was another celebration that stood out conspicuously among the memories of the festival (2 K 23²², 2 Ch 35¹⁻¹⁷). One Passover is also recorded as kept by the returning exiles (Ezr 6¹⁹). With the period of the NT writers, of Josephus, and the Mishna, the feast has become one of regular observance, drawing multitudes to Jerusalem from many lands, and forming a strong bond of unity to the scattered nation.

From the references outside of the Pentateuch little can be learnt as to the details of the celebration of this feast. Nor is much to be gathered from the NT apart from the history of the Last Supper, regarding which there is doubt as to whether it was a true Paschal celebration, and whether the ordinary ritual was observed, or whether it was purposely modified and departed from (see following art. and LAST SUPPER). We are driven for information as to the order and details of celebration to the Mishna (c. A.D. 200), the Gemara, an ancient supplement of the same, the commentaries of later Jewish Rabbis, as Maimonides and Bartenora. There is consequently a certain doubt as to how far the practices enjoined in the Mishna were observed in the time of our Lord ; but, since the traditions are for the most part very ancient, the regulations laid down give a fairly accurate representation of the feast as observed at the time of the Evangelists.

One month before the feast, preparations for the same were put in hand. Roads and bridges were repaired for the companies of pilgrims, and burying-places which were lying in the way, and likely to be unnoticed, were whitened, that the travellers might avoid defilement. Flocks and herds were tithed, and persons ceremonially unclean went up to Jerusalem out of the country to purify themselves (Jn 11⁵⁵). As the time drew nearer, the significance and laws of the feast were explained in the academies and synagogues, the last two Sabbaths before the Passover being specially occupied with this exposition.

The number of those who took part in this festival was enormous. Every male Jew residing within fifteen miles of Jerusalem, and not ceremonially unclean, was required to do so, and in addition, numerous visitors from other parts of the Holy Land, and from other countries near and far, travelling with their gifts, and with song, swelled the number of residents. Women as well as men were eligible for participation, and though the observance was not compulsory, the privilege was often embraced (1 S 1³⁻⁷, Lk 2⁴¹·⁴², Jos. BJ VI. ix. 3, Mish. Pesachim ix. 4). The nearest approach to a census is that given by Josephus, and, though certainly exaggerated, it shows the vast concourse which the feast brought together. He states that at the Passover of A.D. 65 there were 3,000,000 persons present (BJ II. xiv. 3), while in another place (VI. ix. 3) he relates that, at the request of Cestius, the priests counted the number of lambs slain as 256,500. Remarking that the minimum number permitted for a lamb was ten persons, Josephus calculates the number at 2,700,000. An ancient Jewish tradition gives the number of Passover lambs on one occasion as 1,200,000. It was customary to extend hospitality to the numerous visitors. This was done without charge, but as a return the host received the skin of the lamb and the vessels used by his guests. Many must have tented outside the city. In this vast crowd, with the sense of nationality strong, and its religious feelings at the highest tension, it is easy to understand the dread of possible disturbance which from time to time appears in the Gospel narratives (Mt 26⁵, Lk 23²⁴, Jn 18³⁹).

The feast proper began with the evening of the 14th Nisan ; it must be borne in mind that, according to Jewish reckoning, this was the first half of the day. It was succeeded by the days of Unleavened Bread, which sometimes gave a name to the whole festival (Lk 22¹). On the evening of the 14th it was the duty of the master of each house to take a lighted wax candle, in silence thoroughly to search all the house for leaven and to remove it to a safe place. This investigation was preceded and followed by prayer. A portion of leavened food sufficient for the family requirements had been put aside, and it was lawful to eat this until 11 o'clock on the morning of the 14th, though a stricter school drew the limit at 10 o'clock. At midday all leaven was to be completely and solemnly destroyed, by burning or otherwise. The times of this obligation were notified in the following way : ' Two cakes of thanksgiving offering which had been desecrated were exposed on a bench or gallery of the Temple. While they lay there all the people yet ate leaven ; when one was removed, they abstained from eating it but did not burn it ; when both were removed, all the people commenced burning the leaven ' (Pes. ʼ.. 5). Secular work was gradually ceasing. In Galilee the whole day was one of rest. In Judæa work continued till noon ; but only what had been begun could be finished ; no new work could be commenced. Only tailors, barbers, and sandal-strap makers were allowed to follow their avocations. At 1.30 o'clock the daily evening sacrifice was killed, and at 2.30 it was offered up. In each case this was one hour before the usual time of killing and offering ; if the 14th Nisan fell on a Friday (i.e. Thursday evening and Friday morning according to our reckoning), these times were made each yet an hour earlier to avoid possible desecration of the Sabbath. By the time this daily sacrifice was offered, the lambs had been brought to the Temple by those who had been selected to represent each Passover group at the slaughter of the victim. Each lamb was required to be not less than eight days or more than one year old. The great company was divided into three sections, the ritual observed being the same in each case. The first section entered the Court of the Priests, the gates being thereupon closed, and the trumpets blown three times. Although the priestly course on duty for the week attended to the daily sacrifice, to meet the necessity of the Passover the whole priestly body was in attendance. It stood in two lines which ended at the altar, one row holding silver, the other golden bowls. Each man representing a Passover group killed his own sacrifice, the nearest priest caught the blood in his bowl, passed it to a fellow-priest and he again to another, while each as he received the full bowl handed back an empty one. The bowls were made without bases, and could not stand if placed on the ground, coagulation being in this way avoided. When the bowl was received by the priest nearest to the altar, he cast it with one jet at the base. Meanwhile the ' Hallel ' (Psalms 113 to 118) was recited, the Levites leading the song, the people repeating the first line of each Psalm and also three others of the closing Psalm, but otherwise responding ' Hallelujah ' to each line. If the sacrifices were not completed, the Hallel was sung a second or even a third time.

The preparation of the sacrifice now took place. The lambs were hung on iron hooks fastened to the walls and pillars of the court, and when these were all in use, upon staves which rested on the shoulders of two men ; if the day were a Sabbath, the use of staves was not permitted, and two offerers laid one the left hand the other the right on his neighbour's shoulder and so suspended the lambs. The sacrifices were then skinned, the portions appointed for sacrificial use (Lv 3¹⁻⁵) were removed and cleansed, the fat separated and placed on a dish and then offered with incense on the altar. The company was then dismissed to their dwellings to partake of the feast, the incense was burnt, the lamps trimmed, and the Temple court washed. If the sacrifice fell on a Sabbath, the first and second divisions stayed in appointed parts of the Temple until the whole of the victims had been sacrificed, that they might not profane the Sabbath by bearing a burden.

It was required that careful attention should be given to the cooking of the lamb. It was to be roasted, in an earthenware oven; a spit of pomegranate wood was to be put in at the mouth and to pass through at the vent; Justin Martyr (*Tryph*. 40) states that a transverse spit was passed through the victim, thus forming a cross. If any part of the lamb touched the oven, it was to be pared off, as was also the case with any part on which fat from the oven had fallen. No bone of it was to be broken, no part was to be taken out of the house where the feast was held, and none of it was to be left over.

The meal was partaken of, not as at the first Egyptian Passover, in travelling dress, 'with loins girded, with shoes on the feet, and staff in the hands,' but in festive garments, and reclining on the left side 'as free men do, in token of their freedom.' The table was probably arranged as a triclinium, and this explains the position of St. John, the question addressed across the table by St. Peter, and the unheard conversation of our Lord with Judas Iscariot (Jn 13²³· ²⁴, Mt 26²⁵). See art. UPPER ROOM.

A cup of red wine, mixed with water, was poured out for each guest, not by the host but by a servant, for all things were on this night to be done with distinction; and over it the following blessing was spoken:

'Blessed art Thou, Jehovah our God, who hast created the fruit of the vine. Blessed art Thou, Jehovah our God, King of the Universe, who hast chosen us from among all people, and exalted us from among all languages, sanctified us with Thy commandments. And Thou hast given us, O Jehovah our God, in love the solemn days for joy, and the festival and appointed seasons for gladness; and this feast of unleavened bread, the season of our freedom, a holy convocation, the memorial of our departure from Egypt. For Thou hast chosen us, and hast sanctified us from among all nations, and Thy holy festivals with joy and gladness hast Thou caused us to inherit. Blessed art Thou, O Jehovah, who sanctifiest Israel and the appointed seasons. Blessed art Thou, Jehovah, King of the Universe, who hast preserved us alive, and sustained and brought us to this season.'

The use of wine at this festival was compulsory, even upon the poorest; it might be the gift of charity, or procured by selling or pawning raiment or hiring out one's labour; but used it must be, even by persons commonly abstaining and young persons. After this, each participant washed his hands, our Lord apparently varying the custom and teaching a new and deeper lesson by Himself washing the feet of His guests (Jn 13³ff·).

The Paschal table, with its appropriate viands, was then placed in position. These comprised the lamb, the bitter herbs (lettuce, endive, garden endive (or succory), urtica, and bitter coriander (or horehound)), and the *harōseth*, a paste of dates, raisins, etc., with vinegar, which was held to represent the mortar of Egypt, and salt water. The president of the company took some of the bitter herbs, dipped them in salt water, ate a portion the size of an olive, and gave a similar portion to his companions. A second cup of wine was now poured out, and this was followed by the *Haggādāh* or 'showing forth' (cf. 1 Co 11²⁶ 'ye proclaim'). The son of the family or the youngest member of the company inquired the significance of the feast in which they were participating: 'Why is this night distinguished from all other nights?' 'Then the

father instructs his child according to the capacity of his knowledge, beginning with our disgrace and ending with our glory, and expounding to him from ''A Syrian ready to perish was my father'' (Dt 26⁵), until he has explained all through, to the end of the whole section' (*Pes*. x.). This involved a recital of the national history from the Patriarchal times to the deliverance out of Egypt, and the constitution of the emancipated people by means of the covenant at Sinai. After this, the president explained the significance of the Passover-lamb, of the bitter herbs, and of the unleavened bread. In acknowledgment of the great redemption, the first part of the Hallel (Pss 113. 114) was sung, and a benediction added: 'Blessed art Thou, Jehovah our God, King of the Universe, who hast redeemed us and redeemed our fathers from Egypt.' The second cup of wine, which had been previously filled, was now drunk.

After a second washing of hands, one of the two unleavened cakes was broken, and pieces containing between them bitter herbs were, after dipping in the *harōseth*, handed to each one in the company. This was probably the sop which Judas Iscariot received (Jn 13²⁶). After this the Paschal lamb was eaten, the hands were again washed, a third cup of wine filled, a blessing said, and the cup drunk. This was known as 'the cup of blessing,' and was probably that in which our Lord instituted the cup of the Eucharist, which is called by St. Paul 'the cup of blessing' (1 Co 10¹⁶). There remained another cup to be drunk, for the number four was insisted upon, and became the subject of various interpretations; the second part of the Hallel (Pss 115–118) was sung — probably the 'hymn' after which 'they went out unto the mount of Olives' (Mk 14²⁶)—and the feast ended with a benediction, 'the blessing of the song.'

On the next day, the 15th Nisan, sacrifices additional to those offered ordinarily were brought (Nu 28¹⁹), and peace-offerings, the *ḥagigah*—which on this day was compulsory, but on the 14th needed not to be offered except where the lamb would not suffice for the feast—were presented. On the 16th day the barley for the omer (Lv 23¹¹) that was to be presented was cut; this was threshed in the Court of the Priests, parched, and then ground fine. When sufficiently fine, one omer by measure was taken and mixed with oil; frankincense was placed upon it, and it was 'waved'—moved to and fro—before the Lord. The 17th to the 20th days were the *Mō'ēd Ḳāṭon*, or 'lesser festival,' when no new work might be commenced. With the 21st Nisan the feast ended, the day being kept as a Sabbath.

In the case of persons Levitically unclean or living at a distance, it was permitted to celebrate the Passover on the corresponding day of the following month (Iyyar), according to the legislation of Nu 9⁹⁻¹², 2 Ch 30²; but in this case there was no search for and removal of leaven, no Hallel was sung at the supper, and no *ḥagigah* offered and eaten.

LITERATURE. — Comm. on Pentateuch, esp. Driver's *Deut*.; Bibl. Archæol. of Keil, Nowack, and Benzinger; Buxtorf, *Syn. Jud*.; Reland, *Ant*.; the Mishnic tractate *Pesachim*, with comm.; Maimonides, *Yad Hachazakah*; artt. in Hastings' *DB*, Smith's *DB*, Kitto's *Cyclopædia*, the *EBi*, Hamburger's *RE*, the *JE*; Edersheim, *The Temple*, etc.; Chwolson, *Das letzte Passamahl Christi*; J. P. Lilley, *The Lord's Supper* (1891), 35 ff.　　　　　　　　　　　　　　　J. T. L. MAGGS.

PASSOVER (II.: in relation to Lord's Supper).— **1. The historical relation.**—The chronological difficulty raised by this topic having been adequately discussed in previous articles (see DATES, vol. i. p. 413 ff., LAST SUPPER, and LORD'S SUPPER (I.)), it is unnecessary to reopen it here. It may be assumed as certain that the Last Supper of Jesus took place not on the night of the general Jewish

Passover, but on the evening preceding. It does not follow, however, that the Last Supper was not a Paschal meal. To the present writer it seems impossible to set aside the distinct evidence of the first three Gospels on this point, reinforced as that is by the language of St. Paul (Mt 26[17ff.], Mk 14[12ff.], Lk 22[7ff. 15]; cf. 1 Co 5[7. 8] and 11[23-26]).

(1) It has been objected by Spitta (see the essay, 'Die urchristl. Traditionen über Ursprung u. Sinn des Abendmahls' in his *Zur Gesch. u. Litt. des Urchristentums*; cf. G. H. Box, *JThSt*, Apr. 1902), the most prominent representative of the view that the Last Supper bore no resemblance to the Passover, that the descriptions of it given in Mt. and Mk. do not suggest a Paschal meal, and in particular that the lamb is never mentioned. This has been called a 'significant omission'; a remark which assumes that, if Jesus had been observing the Passover, the Evangelists would naturally have given some account of the proceedings at the Jewish meal. But, since they had already stated with the utmost plainness that the meal to which He sat down with His disciples was an eating of the Passover, it was quite unnecessary for them to describe it in detail, since all Passover suppers were exactly similar. What they were concerned with were those novel and significant acts and words of their Master by which, while sitting at the table of the OT feast, He instituted the sacrament of the New Covenant.

(2) A similar objection is that at the Passover supper each participant had his own cup to drink from, while in the celebration of the sacrament there was only one cup. But this is to confound two things that are perfectly distinct. The fact that at the Jewish meal there was a cup for each person present is surely no reason why Jesus, in appointing the new rite of the Christian brotherhood, should not have taken one cup and passed it round to His disciples, saying, 'Drink ye all of it.'

(3) A further ground of objection is found in the fact that Jesus draws no parallels between the Paschal meal and the Christian sacrament, and in particular that, when He is choosing a symbol to represent His body, He takes a loaf of bread for the purpose, and not a portion of the roasted lamb. To speak in this way suggests a poor conception of our Lord's insight into the nature and destiny of His own religion. For, unless Jesus was altogether lacking in this respect, He must have foreseen, as clearly as we can see to-day, that the broken loaf of bread was infinitely better suited than a piece of the Jewish Paschal lamb to serve to the Church of the future as the symbol of His sacrifice of love.

Criticisms like these seem trivial at the best. And it must be remembered, on the other hand, that those who deny that there is any outward connexion between the Passover and the Lord's Supper have to meet difficulties of the most pressing kind, and above all the difficulty of accounting for the unanimous testimony of the Synoptics on this very point. What are we to make of this testimony, and especially of the testimony of Mk., presumably the most original of all? It is suggestive that Spitta solves the difficulty by pronouncing the whole paragraph in which Mk. affirms the Paschal character of the Supper (14[12-16]), to be an interpolation that stands in no organic connexion with the rest of the narrative (*op. cit.* p. 228). But even if there were any grounds of textual criticism for regarding the statements of the first three Gospels as later interpolations, we should still have to explain how it came to pass that at a very early date in the history of the Apostolic Church a false tradition not only sprang up but became dominant, according to which the Last Supper of Jesus with His disciples

took the form of a Passover meal. Spitta admits that in St. Paul's view of the Sacrament the connexion with the Passover meal is evident (*op. cit.* p. 265; cf. Box, *op. cit.* p. 365). How, then, are we to explain this entire transformation of what, according to this theory, was the original tradition —a transformation so early that it must have been completed before Paul became a Christian and received from the first Apostles the story of what took place in the Upper Room on that night in which the Lord Jesus was betrayed? It is hard to see how, within a few years of Christ's death, and at the headquarters of the primitive Church, there could have grown up a tradition as to a simple matter of fact that was an entire falsification of what the Eleven knew to be the truth.

We regard it, then, as practically certain that the Last Supper took the form of a Passover meal. And since it was held on the evening before the general Jewish observance, it must have been an anticipated Passover (cf. Sanday, Hastings' *DB* ii. p. 634; Zöckler, *PRE*[3] ix. pp. 32, 42). It is sometimes affirmed that this view will not bear the slightest examination (Box, *op. cit.* p. 360; cf. Gwilliam, art. LAST SUPPER, p. 8[a]). It is assumed, *e.g.*, that it would have been impossible for our Lord and His disciples to procure the sacrifice of a lamb before the following day. But Chwolson, an expert in Jewish antiquities, anticipates these and similar objections, and shows how precarious the grounds are on which they rest (*Das letzte Passamahl Christi*, p. 37 ff.). And he further makes the interesting suggestion that a very slight textual error at this point in a supposed Aramaic source would account for the apparent identification by the three Synoptics (Mt 26[17], Mk 14[12], Lk 22[7]) of the occasion of the Last Supper with the regular night of the Jewish Passover (*ib.* p. 11).

2. The spiritual connexions.—In order to establish these, two things are necessary. First, we must understand what the Passover meal meant to Jesus and His disciples; next, we must trace the links between the Paschal supper in the Upper Room and the Christian sacrament that sprang out of it.

(1) *What did the Passover mean to Jesus and the Twelve?* For evidently it is with the Passover of our Lord's time that we have primarily to do. It is not uncommon to meet with doctrinal constructions of the Lord's Supper (*e.g.* Gore, *Body of Christ*, p. 12 ff.; Illingworth, *Divine Immanence*, p. 126 ff.) in which a leading rôle is assigned to ideas drawn from the modern study of Comparative Religion as to the significance of the ancient rite of the blood-covenant (see Trumbull, *The Threshold Covenant*, p. 203 ff.), or as to a sacrificial 'eating of the god' on the occasion of a harvest festival (see W. R. Smith, *RS* p. 461; Frazer, *Golden Bough*[2], ii. ch. 2). But it seems safe to conclude that archæological considerations such as these were not uppermost in the mind of Jesus when He said to His disciples, 'With desire I have desired to eat this passover with you before I suffer' (Lk 22[15]), and that what He and they alike were thinking of was the Passover of Jewish history and tradition. Nothing could be further from the minds of a pious Jewish company at the dawn of the Christian era than the notion that God would partake of human food, or that they could enter into communion with the Highest by drinking the blood of a slain animal, or even by drinking wine considered as a substitute for blood (cf. Ac 15[20. 29]). What, then, did the eating of the Passover primarily mean for Jesus and His disciples?

(*a*) In the first place, it was *the memorial of a great historical deliverance*—that redemption of Israel from her bondage in Egypt which was also her birth-hour as a nation (Ex 12[3ff. 26f.]).—(*b*) But further, the Passover was *a covenant-meal based on the fact of the covenant made by sacrifice at Sinai* (Ex 24[3-8]). It is certainly impossible to find within the circle of ideas suggested by the narrative of the first Passover in Egypt a full explanation of the words of Jesus at the institution of the Lord's Supper. One of the special merits of recent critical investigations into the nature of the sacrament is that they have brought fully into view the connexion between our Lord's words about the New Covenant (Mt 26[28] ||) and the story of the covenant at Sinai, taken along with the great prophetic anticipations (Jer 32[40], Ezk 34[25] 37[26], Is 55[3]) of what the author of Hebrews calls 'a better covenant established upon better promises' (He 8[6]). It does not follow, however, as some have thought, that the covenant idea excludes that of the Passover, much less that the combination of them was altogether impossible (so Schultzen, *Das Abendmahl im NT*, p. 40). On the contrary, the narrative of the first Passover in Egypt appears to anticipate that of the covenant made at Sinai, while apart from the former the latter would have no historical explanation. In any case, in the time of our Lord, the Jewish Passover was an annual covenanting feast at which the nation's covenant fellowship with Jehovah was solemnly renewed. The narrative of Ex 24[3-8] makes it clear that the original covenant rested on the fact of a covenant-sacrifice, and there seems little reason to question that in its essence this sacrifice was of a piacular nature (cf. A. B. Davidson in Hastings' *DB* i. p. 512). The annual renewal of the covenant at the Feast of Passover evidently rested in like manner on the sacrifice of the Paschal lamb, and that this sacrifice also was conceived of as having a propitiatory effect it is hardly possible to doubt. —(*c*) Once more, the Passover was a joyful social meal, *the meal of Jewish brotherhood*, in which the participants, as members of the Divine covenant, gave expression to their covenant fellowship with one another as well as with Israel's God.

(2) If the Lord's Supper in its external relations sprang out of an immediately preceding Passover meal, and if that meal had for those who partook of it some such meaning as has just been described, the spiritual connexions between the two are evident. *The thought of the Jewish Passover underlies the Supper*, helping us to determine its true nature and purpose and religious significance.

(*a*) This outward relation between the Passover and the Lord's Supper goes far to decide the question whether or not the Supper *refers to our Lord's death.* Spitta's elaborate efforts to dissociate the Last Supper altogether from the Jewish Passover find their chief motive in his theory that the Supper had no bearing whatsoever on the death of Jesus, but was meant to have a purely eschatological reference, as an anticipation of the glorious Messianic meal in the heavenly Kingdom (*op. cit.* pp. 266 ff., 282 ff.). But if, on the other hand, it was at the close of a Passover meal that Jesus broke the bread and gave it to His disciples, saying, 'This is my body for you,' the analogy between the slain lamb and the broken bread can hardly be mistaken.—(*b*) It bears, again, on the question whether or not the Supper *was meant by Jesus to be repeated.* From the fact that in the Mk.-Mt. text of the institution of the Supper we do not find that command for a repetition of the observance which is given in Paul-Lk. (1 Co 11[24. 25], Lk 22[19]), a number of critical scholars have concluded that Jesus never spoke the words, 'This do in remembrance of me'; that He had no thought of instituting a rite for perpetual celebration by the Church; and that His purpose in breaking the bread and passing the wine was merely to bid His disciples a solemn farewell, to set before them a

striking parable in action, or at most to point them forward to the hope of a glad reunion in the heavenly Kingdom (Jülicher, *Theol. Abhandl.* pp. 235 ff., 245 ff. ; Spitta, *op. cit.* p. 301 ff. ; cf. P. Gardner, *Origin of the Lord's Supper*). But to a Jew the Passover was essentially a memorial feast to be kept by Israel throughout all her generations (Ex 12[14]). And if the Supper was deliberately set by Jesus in the closest relation to the Passover,—so deliberately that He even anticipated by a day an observance which otherwise His death would have rendered impossible,—this goes to confirm the view, supported not only by the text of Paul and Luke, but by the unhesitating praxis of the earliest community from the first (Ac 2[42. 46] ; cf. 20[7], 1 Co 10[16]), and the Apostolic tradition as that was handed on to St. Paul at the time of his conversion (1 Co 11[23]), that Jesus both intended and commanded that the Supper should continue to be observed in remembrance of Himself.—(*c*) If the Lord's Supper sprang historically out of a Passover meal, it naturally *falls heir to the chief meanings and associations of the more ancient rite.* It is not only a memorial of Jesus, but a memorial of His sacrifice. 'Our passover also hath been sacrificed,' says St. Paul, 'even Christ' (1 Co 5[7]) ; and he tells us that as often as we eat the bread and drink the cup, we 'proclaim the Lord's death till he come' (11[26]). The Passover was a renewal on the part of the OT Church of the covenant with God that had been made at Sinai ; and every Supper is a renewal by the Christian people of the covenant made for them upon the Cross. The Passover was not only a renewal of the covenant fellowship with God, but a festive social meal at which the links of Jewish brotherhood were forged afresh. And the Lord's Supper is the occasion of a glad spiritual communion of those who belong to the household of faith, both with Christ Himself — the Elder Brother and the Head — and with their fellow-members in the one family of God.

LITERATURE.—Hastings' *DB*, artt. 'Covenant' (A. B. Davidson), 'Passover' (W. J. Moulton), 'Jesus Christ' (Sanday, vol. ii. p. 634) ; *PRE*[3], art. 'Passah, isr.-jüd.' (von Orelli) ; Bickell, *Passover and Lord's Supper* ; Spitta, *Urchristentum* ; Jülicher, *Theol. Abhandlungen* ; P. Gardner, *Origin of the Lord's Supper* ; Schultzen, *Das Abendmahl im NT* ; Chwolson, *Das letzte Passamahl Christi* ; Schaefer, *Das Herrenmahl* ; Lambert, *Sacraments in NT* ; G. M. Mackie, 'Jewish Passover in the Chr. Church,' *ExpT* xiii. (1902), 391 ; *JThSt*, Apr. 1902, p. 357 ff., Jan. 1903, p. 184 ff.   J. C. LAMBERT.

PAST.—'Let the dead past bury its dead,' is the unequivocal counsel we derive from the Lord's reply to a lukewarm disciple (Mt 8[22]). In Christ no past is irretrievable ; Divine forgiveness may blot out what men consider it impossible to forgive (Lk 18[27]). Habit and custom may be burst asunder in a moment, like the rocky tomb that could not imprison the risen Lord. The motto of the Cliffords (*Désormais*) may recall a Christian truth of priceless value : 'Henceforward' sin no more (Jn 8[11]). God gives a fresh start for Christ's sake to each one who prays for forgiveness in the spirit of forgiveness (Mt 6[14]). The tyranny of the past led the Galilæans to ask, 'Is not this the carpenter?' (Mk 6[3]) ; but, as signally in the call of Levi, the disciple of Christ must be ready to throw aside the past altogether for His sake (Mt 9[9]).—There is a dead past to be forgotten and forgiven, for God is God of the living (Mk 12[27]). And there is a living past to be remembered and commemorated. Thus all generations call her *blessed* who was the mother of the Lord (Lk 1[48]). The loving gift of a forgiven woman who had been a sinner is still told for a memorial of her (Mk 14[9]). Yet the Christian hope looks ever forward to the brightness of the coming day, when the shadows shall flee away.

                   W. B. FRANKLAND.

PATIENCE ($\dot{\upsilon}\pi o\mu o\nu\dot{\eta}$, Lk 8^{15} 21^{19}, and throughout NT ; $\mu\alpha\kappa\rho o\theta\upsilon\mu\iota\alpha$, 'long-suffering,' only in Epp. ; verbal form appears Mt $18^{26.\ 29}$, with significance 'Give me time'). — The moral attribute which enables men to endure afflictions and to employ strength wisely. It is essentially a Christian grace. The classical conception of virtue was mainly active. 'The old pagan world meant by a virtuous man, a brave, strong, just, energetic human being, who might be, but who probably would not be, also humble, submissive, self-subduing' (Liddon, *Christian World Pulpit*, vol. xxiv. 138). The Oriental idea touches the opposite extreme, in which virtue consists not in such qualities as patience, but in the passivity from which feeling is expelled (cf. Newman Smyth, *Christian Ethics*, pt. i. ch. 2, iii.). As a Christian grace, patience is inculcated in the NT (1 Ti 6^{11}, Tit 2^2, He 10^{36}, Ja 1^4, 2 P 1^6), and exemplified in the life of Christ. His patience is referred to directly only once in the NT, and then incidentally (2 Th 3^5 AVm and RV) ; but examples of it are mentioned in the Epp. as incentives to believers (He 12^2, 1 P 2^{23}).

1. The patience of Christ may be regarded (1) *in itself*. It constitutes one of the most remarkable features of His manhood. It is not visible upon the surface of the Evangelical narratives, but it becomes impressive the moment that reflexion begins to deal with His Personality in the light of the events of His life on earth. Whatever His consciousness of Himself, He was evidently aware that extraordinary forces were at His command (Mt 4^3 26^{53}). 'Just in proportion to the eminence of a man's sphere and the genius of a man's endowments, the quality of patience is necessary.' To none, therefore, was it more necessary and more difficult than to our Lord, and by none was it more perfectly possessed. He set before Himself an aim which marks Him as the supreme Dreamer of history ; yet, with the vision always before Him, and the longing for its fulfilment pressing on His heart (Lk 12^{50}), He moved unhasting, if unpausing, towards the goal. The second temptation (Lk $4^{5f.}$) was a trial of patience. In it He met the temptation to accomplish His purpose prematurely and superficially by means of an appeal to forces which lay ready to hand in the temper and expectations of the Jews. He preferred the patience that works perfectly, and therefore slowly, to the passion that strikes swiftly and works partially and imperfectly. At the same time, His temperament could not be described as phlegmatic. His patience was not the placidity of a pool secluded by surrounding woods from storm, it was rather the calm of an ocean which refuses to allow any gale to rouse it to anger. Not incapability of passion, but perfect self-control, lay at the heart of the patience of Christ.

(2) *In its manifestations*. (*a*) *As a man*, He had to endure the irritations from which none is exempt, *e.g.* interruptions (Mk $5^{21f.}$ $6^{30f.}$, Jn $4^{6.\ 7}$), the suspicions (Lk $14^{1f.}$) and the provocations (Lk 10^{25} 11^{53}) of His foes ; the spiritual dulness (Mk 9^{19}, Lk $10^{40f.}$ 24^{25}) and carnal expectations (Mk $9^{33f.}$ $10^{35f.}$) of His friends. 'He was subjected to trials of temper . . . ; He was harassed by temptations caused by nervous irritability, or want of strength, or physical weakness, or bodily weariness ; unfair opposition was constantly urging Him to give way to undue anger and unrestrained passion ; or rejection and desertion would, had it been possible, have betrayed Him into moodiness or cynical despair. The machinations of His foes, the fickleness of the mob, even the foolishness of His disciples, were scarcely ever wanting to try His spirit, and would often goad Him beyond endurance' (Bernard, *Mental Characteristics of the Lord Jesus*, cited in Stalker's *Imago Christi*, p. 192 f.). It is not enough to say

that our Lord endured these temptations without showing any impatience ; there was a positive radiance about His patience that makes it the supreme example of the grace as manifest in human life. (*b*) *As a teacher*, the patience of Christ was manifested (i.) in dealing with individuals, *e.g.* Philip (Jn 1^{45} $6^{5f.}$ 14^8), Thomas ($20^{27f.}$), Peter (1^{42}, Mt $14^{28f.}$, Lk $22^{31f.\ 61}$ 24^{34}, Jn $21^{15f.}$) ; (ii.) in training the disciples, *e.g.* explaining their parables to them (Mk $4^{10.\ 13}$) ; teaching them only as they were able to receive the truth (Mt 16^{21}, Jn 16^{12}) ; repeating lessons only partially understood (Mk 9^{31} $10^{32b\ f.}$). It was through His patience as a teacher that our Lord was able out of very raw material to educate the men who were the founders and Apostles of His Church. (*c*) *As a sufferer*, His patience is conspicuous in the scenes connected with His passion (see esp. Mt $26^{52f.}$, Mk $14^{60f.\ 65}$, Jn $18^{22f.}$, Lk 23^{34}, Mk $15^{29f.}$). No one ever suffered so terribly and so patiently as He. There was the extreme of physical pain, of mental torture, and of spiritual agony. The suffering was unjustly inflicted, and was accompanied by almost every possible indignity, but the patience of the Sufferer rose above it with a quiet dignity that makes those scenes the most wonderful in history.

(3) *In its limitations*. The patience of Christ had its limits, as every noble patience has. Those limits were not where, at first, we might expect to find them ; He was patient with His disciples' dulness, though it grieved Him (Lk $24^{25f.}$). He never lost patience under the opposition of His enemies (11^{53} $20^{20f.}$). But when it was suggested that He should avoid the cross (Mt $16^{22f.}$), and when He was confronted with the spiritual assumptions of the Pharisees, His patience reached its limits. Self-indulgence and self-deception were sins with which Christ had no patience (see Stopford A. Brooke, *Sermons*, 2nd series, 'Patience and Impatience')

(4) *In its implications*. The patience of Christ is set before believers, directly (2 Th 3^5) and indirectly (1 P $2^{21f.}$), as an example and an inspiration. There is in Christ 'a type and fountain of patience' in which the possibilities of endurance are exhibited, and from which the grace for endurance to the uttermost may be gathered. The patience of Christ represents the passive side of Christian goodness, 'its deliberate, steady, hopeful endurance, in the spirit of Him who was made perfect through suffering' (Denney, *Expos. Bible*, 'Epp. to Thess.' p. 372).

2. Human patience is mentioned : (*a*) in Lk 8^{15}, with reference to the perseverance with which the fruit of God is brought forth in the believer's life. Spiritual fruitfulness is not easily attained. A consistent Christian character is wrought only by long patience. Christ sets the staying power of vital faith in contrast with the passing fervour of those who lightly receive and as lightly abandon the word of truth (cf. Lk 8^{13}). (*b*) In Lk 21^{19}, in the course of Christ's prediction of the sorrows that should befall during the struggle with Rome. RV is much the preferable rendering. Its meaning may be summed up thus, 'Heroic perseverance wins the crown' (Lindsay, *Gospel of St. Luke, in loc.*).

LITERATURE.—H. Bushnell, *The New Life* (1860) ; A. Ritschl, *The Chr. Doct. of Justification and Reconciliation* (Eng. tr. 1900), 625 ; J. T. Jacob, *Christ the Indweller* (1902), 149 ; C. L. Slattery, *The Master of the World* (1906), 121 ; M. Creighton, *The Mind of St. Peter* (1904), 22 ; M. R. Vincent, *The Covenant of Peace* (1887), 234.   JAMES MURSELL.

PAUL.—See APPENDIX.

PAVEMENT.—The word occurs only in Jn 19^{13} as one of the names by which was known the locality otherwise called **Gabbatha** (wh. see). In classical usage λιθόστρωτον denotes a stone pavement, and later a mosaic or tessellated pavement, in which sense the word passed into Latin. Of recent years beautiful pavements have been found in many places in Palestine; but so far there is no evidence outside the NT that any locality in Jerusalem was generally known as either Gabbatha or the Pavement, and no attempted identification of the spot is quite satisfactory. The easiest course is to regard the passage as unhistorical, and the allusions as derived only from the writer's imagination and introduced to give verisimilitude to the narrative; but such an explanation is itself as subjective as the pleas it adopts. That the reference is to the paved forecourt of the Temple, or to the usual meeting-place of the Sanhedrin, is rendered unlikely by the absence of the designation from Jewish literature, as well as by the improbability that Pilate would choose any partially consecrated spot for the inquiry. On the other hand, there are Latin usages which seem to connect the locality with the governor's official or temporary residence. Julius Cæsar is described by Suetonius (*Vit. Div. Jul.* 46) as carrying about with him on his military expeditions a tessellated pavement, which was laid down in his encampments as marking the spot from which judicial decisions and addresses to the soldiers were given. Jos. (*Ant.* XVIII. iv. 6) reports that Philip the tetrarch similarly carried his tribunal with him (τοῦ θρόνου εἰς ὃν ἔκρινε καθεζόμενος ἐν ταῖς ὁδοῖς ἑπομένου), but there is no reference to a portable mosaic. In the case of Pilate, it is possible that he would be disposed to imitate the procedure of the Emperor, or even that of a petty sovereign, but in this matter no record to such an effect has been found; and whilst the course would not be without danger, it is not easy to think that a locality would derive its name from being one of many places on which a movable pavement was once or occasionally laid. That, moreover, there were, as a rule, in the larger centres of population, fixed places for the administration of justice is not unlikely. The provincial basilicas were often law-courts as well as exchanges, the tribunal being set in the semicircular apse, of which the raised floor was certainly paved, and exactly the kind of spot to attract a designer. There may not have been any such basilica at Jerusalem, or at least the remains of one have not so far been clearly identified. Jos. (*BJ* II. ix. 3: καθίσας ἐπὶ βήματος ἐν τῷ μεγάλῳ σταδίῳ) has been cited in support of a view that Pilate used 'the open market-place' (so Whiston, followed by many) at Jerusalem for the administration of justice; but the passage refers to Cæsarea, and the rendering of στάδιον as a synonym of ἀγορά is not well established. Each stationary camp, again, had its tribunal, sometimes formed of turf but more frequently of stone, and from it the general addressed the soldiers and the tribunes administered justice. In Jerusalem the garrison occupied the castle of Antonia, within which would be the tribunal used in cases of military discipline, but probably not for the hearing of Jewish complaints and causes. Pilate himself would reside in Herod's palace (cf. Philo, *ad Gaium*, 31, and the practice of Gessius Florus in Jos. *BJ* II. xv. 5), as did also the procurator at Cæsarea (Ac 23[35]). It was a magnificent building, lined outside with spacious porticoes. Here it was natural that the Jews should present themselves when seeking the execution of Jesus (Jn 18[28] 19[4]), who was apparently confined in the palace (19[9. 13a]). And one of these paved porticoes may well have been known within the palace as the Pavement, upon which stood the judgment-seat, under an open cupola or within a rounded porch.

LITERATURE.—Hastings' *DB*, art. 'Gabbatha'; *EBi*, art. 'Pavement.'

R. W. MOSS.

PEACE.—**1.** The word frequently occurs in the Gospels in the idiomatic phrase 'to hold one's peace,' *i.e.* to keep silence, representing (both in RV and AV) no fewer than four different verbs in the original —ἡσυχάζω, σιγάω, σιωπάω, and φιμόω. ἡσυχάζω (Lk 14[4]) is the most general term (fr. ἥσυχος, 'at rest'), denoting a state of restfulness in which silence is included (cf. Lk 23[56] τὸ μὲν σάββατον ἡσύχασαν, 'and on the sabbath they rested'). σιγάω (Lk 20[26]) has been distinguished from σιωπάω (Mt 20[31] 26[63], Mk 3[4] 9[34] 10[48] 14[61], Lk 18[39] 19[40])—the former as referring to a silence induced by mental conditions (fear, grief, awe, etc.), the latter as a more physical term denoting simply an abstinence from vocal utterance (so Schmidt in his *Synon. d. gr. Sprache*, quoted by Grimm-Thayer, *Lex.* p. 281). But in classical Gr. such a distinction between σιγάω and σιωπάω can hardly be said to be ordinarily observed (cf. Liddell and Scott, *Lex. s.vv.*), and in the NT ἡσυχάζω, σιγάω, and σιωπάω, when used in the sense of holding one's peace, appear to be employed without any real discrimination.

On the other hand, φιμόω is a stronger and rougher word, which properly means 'to muzzle' (fr. φιμός, 'a muzzle'). It is noticeable that our Lord addresses it only to an unclean spirit (Mk 1[25] = Lk 4[35]) or to the raging sea (Mk 4[39], where EV gives 'Be still!'). Once Mt. uses it to describe how Jesus put the Sadducees to silence (22[34]); and in the parable of the Wedding Garment it is used (v.[12]) to express the speechless condition to which the intruder was reduced when challenged by the king (cf. *Twent. Cent. NT*[1], 'the man was dumbfounded').

2. In the ordinary sense of *rest* or *tranquillity*, in antithesis to strife and war, 'peace' (εἰρήνη) is found, *e.g.*, in Mt 10[34] = Lk 12[51] (note the contrast with μάχαιρα), Lk 14[32]. Generally, however, εἰρήνη in the NT means more than this, and clearly inherits the larger suggestions of the Heb. שׁלום, which primarily denoted a state of wellbeing, safety, and blessedness, of which, however, peace in the common acceptation of the term would be one of the most important conditions. It is in this way that we are to understand expressions like 'Now lettest thou thy servant depart in peace' (Lk 2[29]), 'his goods are in peace' (11[21]), 'the things which belong unto thy peace' (19[42]). This also is the connotation of 'Peace!' when used as a form of salutation (Mt 10[12. 13] = Lk 10[5. 6] 24[36], Jn 20[19. 21. 26]); though, as employed by our Lord, and by His disciples according to His instructions, the salutation is weighted with the larger Messianic meaning (see below).

3. But in its predominating and characteristic use in the NT, εἰρήνη is distinctively *a Christian word*, being employed especially to describe the mission, the character, and the gospel of Jesus Christ.

(1) *Peace was a distinctive feature of Christ's mission.*—In prophetic anticipation the coming of the Messiah was to inaugurate a reign of peace (Is 9[7], Ps 72[3. 7]), and He Himself was to be 'the Prince of Peace' (Is 9[6]). In the Gospel story of His birth, the promise of peace heralds His advent (Lk 1[79]), and 'on earth peace' is sung by the angels on the night in which He is born (2[14]). His earthly ministry was a ministry and message of peace. 'Have peace one with another' was one of His injunctions (Mk 9[50]), while of those who not merely live in peace, but are peace-*makers* (εἰρηνοποιοί), He said that they shall be called sons of God (Mt 5[9]). 'Peace' was the salutation which both the Twelve and the Seventy were bidden to use when sent forth on their respective missions (Mt 10[12f.], Lk 10[5f.]); it was the word spoken by Jesus Himself in dismissing those whom He had healed of their physical or moral plagues (Mk 5[34], Lk 7[50]

8^{48}); and again the greeting with which He met His disciples after He was risen from the dead (Lk 24^{36}, Jn $20^{19.\ 21.\ 26}$). And in all these cases it seems evident that 'Peace be unto you !' and 'Go in peace !' are not merely conventional forms of salutation or farewell, but refer to the blessings guaranteed by Jesus as the Christ of God.

And yet there is a sense in which Jesus came 'not to send peace, but a sword' (Mt 10^{34}, cf. Lk 12^{51}). For there is a false peace (Jer 6^{14} 8^{11}); and with that He could have nothing to do. Jesus would never compromise, or permit His followers to compromise, with falsehood or error or sin ; and so, in a world where these things abound, His coming inevitably meant division and struggle and suffering (cf. Lk $2^{34.\ 35}$). Yet, for all that, peace was the purpose of His mission, even though it had to be attained by sending forth a sword—sharp and two-edged, as the seer saw it (Rev 1^{16})—a sword which will ultimately secure the victory of the good in the conflict with evil, and bring in the peace that rests on righteousness (cf. Ps 72^7 85^{10}).

(2) *Peace was a quality of Christ's character.*—The words 'Peace I leave with you ; my peace I give unto you' (Jn 14^{27}) strike one of the fundamental notes of His personal being as that is revealed to us in the Gospels. Men have been known to make bequests when they had nothing to leave ; but peace was a blessing which Jesus had power to bestow, because it was His own peculiar possession. At the very centre of His earthly life, amidst all its vicissitudes, there always lies a profound peace, which is quite different from impassivity, for it is something vital and flowing like a strong calm river (cf. Is 48^{18}). It was, without doubt, the magnetism of this peace-possessing and peace-diffusing strength of Jesus that drew troubled hearts around Him ; and it was the consciousness of having it and being able to bestow it that inspired that most characteristic invitation, 'Come unto me, all ye that labour and are heavy laden, and I will give you rest' (Mt 11^{28}).

This personal peace of Jesus must be distinguished, of course, from the peace of outward circumstances. When He said, 'My peace I give unto you,' He was just about to go forth to Gethsemane and the judgment-hall and the cross. But the peace He was conscious of lay deeper than all trials and sufferings, for it came from the assurance of a perfect union in thought and heart and will with His Father in heaven (Jn $14^{11.\ 20.\ 31}$). Christ's peace was like that of a white water-lily—tossed to and fro by the surface waves of the lake, but unshaken from its place because its roots are buried deep in the soil beneath (cf. Wordsworth, *Excursion*, v. 555). All through His earthly life He realized, as no other human being ever could, the full meaning of the prophet's word, 'Thou wilt keep him in perfect peace whose mind is stayed on thee' (Is 26^3).

(3) *Peace is a characteristic blessing of the gospel of Christ.*—Thus we find it constantly described when we pass from the Gospels to the Apostolic teaching. So characteristic of Christ's gospel is it that this gospel is itself described by St. Paul as 'the gospel of peace' (Eph 6^{15}), and St. Peter in the Acts speaks of those who publish the message of salvation as 'preaching good tidings of peace by Jesus Christ' (Ac 10^{36}). 'Peace,' indeed, becomes, like grace, a virtual summary for gospel blessings, and so in the benedictory salutations of nearly every Apostolic writer it is combined with 'grace' as the distinctive gift of 'God our Father and the Lord Jesus Christ' (Ro 1^7, 1 Co 1^3, 2 Co 1^2, Gal 1^3, Eph 1^2, Ph 1^2, Col 1^2, 1 Th 1^1, 2 Th 1^2, 1 Ti 1^2, Tit 1^4, Philem ^{3}, 1 P 1^2, 2 P 1^2, 2 Jn ^{3}, Jude ^{2}).

It is St. Paul, however, who works out most fully the place of peace in the Christian gospel and its immediate relation to Christ Himself. With him 'peace' has two distinct meanings, corresponding to two different facts of Christian experience. (*a*) First, there is an objective peace—the peace of *reconciliation with God* through our Lord Jesus Christ—which follows as the result of being justified by faith (Ro 5^1 [vv. $^{1-11}$ show that the εἰρήνη of v.^{1} is the same as the καταλλαγή of v.^{11}], Eph 2^{14-17} ; cf. 2 Co 5^{18-21}). (*b*) Next, there is a subjective peace —the peace of *conscious fellowship with God* — which results from a living union with Christ the Saviour. This subjective peace finds its ground in the objective peace of reconciliation, but it is clearly distinguished from it. The other is 'peace *with* God' (Ro 5^1) ; this is 'the peace *of* God which passeth all understanding' (Ph 4^7). This inward peace is one of the fruits of the Spirit (Gal 5^{22}), it forms part of our joy in believing (Ro 15^{13}), it is a power that guards our hearts and thoughts in Christ Jesus (Ph 4^7). And it is of this peace, as a glad sense of sonship and trust wrought in the soul by Jesus Christ, that the Apostle is thinking when he writes : 'The Lord of peace himself give you peace at all times, in all ways' (2 Th 3^{16}).

LITERATURE.—The *Lexx.* of Grimm-Thayer and Cremer ; Hastings' *DB*, art. 'Peace' ; Weiss, *Bib. Theol. of NT*, i. 449 ff. ; Sanday-Headlam, 'Romans' in *ICC*, on 5^1 ; Beet, *Romans*, *ib.* ; J. T. Jacob, *Christ the Indweller* (1902), 209 ; J. Martineau, *Endeavours after the Chr. Life*, 54 ; F. W. Robertson, *Sermons*, 3rd ser. 130, *The Human Race*, 305 ; E. B. Pusey, *Par. and Cath. Ser.* 1, 431 ; J. H. Thom, *Laws of Life*, 9, 159, 172 ; Phillips Brooks, *The Law of Growth*, 219 ; J. B. Lightfoot, *Serm. in St. Paul's Cath.* 136 ; W. C. E. Newbolt, *Penitence and Peace* (1892).　　　　　　　J. C. LAMBERT.

PEARL.—This jewel, specially esteemed and familiar in the East, is twice used by our Lord as an image of the preciousness of the Christian religion : once in the saying, 'Cast not your pearls before swine' (Mt 7^6), and again in the parable of the Pearl of Great Price (Mt 13^{46}). A distinction should be observed in the choice of this jewel as a metaphorical expression. In the case of coined money such as talents or pounds, the side of religion emphasized is the active life of good works, and the lesson conveyed is that of duty. The value of the pearl is not primarily a commercial value ; it is something which appeals to its possessor as a unique and priceless possession, precious for its own inherent qualities of beauty and rarity, something for which all that a man has may be sold, itself to be jealously treasured, not to be cast at the feet of those to whom it has no meaning. The pearl is not, from the purchaser's point of view, merely a counter of commerce, it has a beauty which is its own, and which can be appreciated only by him who knows. It stands not for any utilitarian aspect of religion, but for the secret shared between the soul and God, which loses its beauty and its value if it is paraded before those who do not understand its sanctity. The main points of the two passages would seem to be the transcendent beauty and preciousness of personal religion, and the need of reticent reverence to guard it.　　　　　　　M. R. NEWBOLT.

PELEG.—Mentioned as a link in our Lord's genealogy (Lk 3^{35}, AV *Phalec*).

PENITENCE.—See REPENTANCE.

PENNY.—See MONEY.

PENTECOST (ἡ πεντηκοστή) was one of the three great national festivals of Israel at which all the males of the people were required to present themselves every year before the Lord their God, with an offering according to their means (Ex 23^{17} 34^{23}, Dt $16^{16.\ 17}$, 2 Ch 8^{13}). There is evidence that in the time of Christ multitudes assembled for the Feast of the Passover, the Feast of Pentecost, and the Feast of Tabernacles, not only from all parts of the Holy Land, but also from the Jewish communities scattered throughout the Roman Empire. The attendance at the Passover would probably be the largest, while the numbers at Pentecost would embrace more Jews from foreign countries, the season being more favourable for travel. All three feasts have (1) a basis in the agricultural life of Canaan, (2) a reference to the history of the nation, and (3) a spiritual and typical significance. Of the three, the Feast of the Passover came first in the natural year, signalizing the commencement of the barley harvest and the dedication of the first ripe sheaf by waving it before the Lord ; commemorating the deliverance of the people from Egyptian bondage ; and pointing forward, by the lamb without blemish sacrificed on the occasion, to the Lamb of God which taketh away the sin of the world. Of the series, the Feast of Tabernacles was the last, celebrating with great rejoicings the completion of harvest and vintage ; commemorating, by the erection of booths in which the people dwelt for the week, the wanderings of their fathers in the wilderness on the way to settled life in Canaan ; and having its antitype in the rest that remaineth for the people of God, or, better perhaps, in that great Harvest Home yet to come, when there shall be gathered before the throne a multitude which no man can number, out of all nations, and kindreds, and peoples, and tongues, clothed in white robes and with palms in their hands.

Between these two national festivals came Pentecost. As Passover signalized the commencement of the grain harvest, Pentecost marked its conclusion ; and as Tabernacles was a great national thanksgiving for the completed vintage and fruit harvest of the year, Pentecost was a thanksgiving for the completed grain harvest.

1. Names.—The actual word ' Pentecost ' does not occur in the canonical books of the OT, but it is found in To 2¹ and 2 Mac 12³². Neither does it occur in the Gospels, where the Feast itself is not mentioned. It occurs in NT three times outside the Gospels (Ac 2¹ 20¹⁶, and 1 Co 16⁸), and in these passages it is employed not as a numeral adjective, but as a substantive. The Feast is called Pentecost because it fell on the fiftieth day counted from Nisan 16, the day after the Passover Sabbath (or festival day), and fulfilled the ancient command : ' Ye shall count unto you from the morrow after the sabbath, from the day that ye brought the sheaf of the wave - offering : seven sabbaths (or weeks) shall be complete : even unto the morrow after the seventh sabbath shall ye number fifty days, and ye shall offer a new meal-offering unto the Lord ' (Lv 23¹⁵·¹⁶, cf. Dt 16⁹). The names by which the Feast is known in the OT proper exhibit its basis in the agricultural life of the people. It is the ' Feast of Weeks,' called from the seven weeks reckoned from the morrow after the Passover when they began ' to put the sickle to the corn ' (Ex 34²², Dt 16⁹·¹⁰, 2 Ch 8¹³) ; the ' Feast of Harvest,' ' the firstfruits of thy labours which thou hast sowed in the field ' (Ex 23¹⁶) ; the ' Day of First Fruits,' a day of rest and holy convocation (Nu 28²⁶, cf. Ex 23¹⁶ 34²²), although, like the other Feasts, it was actually of a week's duration. By later Judaism it was styled *Azereth* (' conclusion '), which appears in Josephus as Ἀσαρθά ; and ' Day of the Giving of the Law ' in commemoration of the revelation of the Divine Will to the people at Sinai (Hamburger, *RE*, ' Wochenfest '; Edersheim, *The Temple*, p. 227).

2. Agricultural basis.— The distinctive features of the ritual observed at Pentecost are those of a harvest thanksgiving. When barley harvest was begun at Passover time, the omer or sheaf was brought to the priest to be waved by him before the Lord ; and this was followed by a burnt-offering of a ' he-lamb without blemish of the first year,' with appropriate meat- and drink-offerings (Lv 23¹⁰⁻¹⁴). When the grain harvest which had been proceeding through the following seven weeks reached its completion at Pentecost and the thanksgiving celebration for it took place, a larger offering was prescribed. Instead of the omer of barley—whether presented in the sheaf or, as would appear from later practice, threshed and parched and made into flour—there were now two wave-loaves of the finest wheaten flour to be brought by the people out of their habitations and offered as a new meal-offering unto the Lord. In contrast to the Passover bread, which was unleavened, these two loaves, forming the peculiar offering of the Day of Pentecost, were ' baken with leaven,' which, as the Mishna informs us, was the case in all thank-offerings. These loaves are declared to be ' the firstfruits unto the Lord ' (Lv 23¹⁶·¹⁷), and formed with the peace-offering of two lambs the public thank-offering of the nation to God for His goodness. Instead of the single lamb of the Passover, there were now to be presented as a burnt-offering ' seven lambs without blemish of the first year, and one young bullock, and two rams,' with appropriate meat- and drink-offerings ; whilst a kid of the goats was to be sacrificed as a sin-offering (Lv 23¹⁸·¹⁹). It was in keeping with an occasion of national thanksgiving that freewill offerings were to be brought by the people, each as the Lord had prospered him : ' And thou shalt rejoice before the Lord, thou, and thy son, and thy daughter, and thy manservant, and thy maidservant, and the Levite that is within thy gates, and the stranger, and the fatherless, and the widow, that are among you. And thou shalt remember that thou wast a bondman in Egypt : and thou shalt observe and do these statutes ' (Dt 16¹¹·¹²). Although the festival proper, as we have seen, was confined to one day, it continued in a minor degree for a whole week, and was celebrated with gladness and rejoicing. All this made it peculiarly popular ; and the season of the year being favourable, as we have seen, for travel, it seems from notices in Josephus, and from references in the Acts of the Apostles, to have been frequented by a large concourse of pilgrims from all the lands of the Jewish Dispersion. It is now the custom among the Jews to decorate the synagogue at Pentecost with trees and plants and flowers,—a modern substitute for the harvest festival of former times (see *Jewish Encyc.*, art. ' Pentecost '; Rosenau, *Jewish Ceremonial Institutions*, p. 86).

3. Historical reference.—Whilst the notices in the OT, mainly in the Pentateuch, regard Pentecost simply as a harvest festival, it came to be regarded among the later Jews as commemorating the giving of the Law at Sinai. The Book of Jubilees, in the 1st cent. A.D. (Schürer, *GJV*³ iii. 277), makes the Feast of Weeks as old as Noah, and associates it further with the later Patriarchs. Josephus and Philo do not mention the giving of the Law among the associations of the Feast, yet many authorities, like Edersheim (*loc. cit.*) and Ginsburg (Kitto's *Cyclopædia*, ' Pentecost '), hold it to be certain that the Jews as early as the time of Christ commemorated the giving of the Law ·at Pentecost. With this was incorporated the legend of the Law being delivered in seventy languages, the number of the nations of the earth, and therefore meant for all the families of mankind. (See Spitta, *Apostelgeschichte*, pp. 27, 28.)

4. Antitypical significance—Giving of the Holy Spirit.—As the Passover has its antitype in the Lamb of God which taketh away the sin of the world, Pentecost has its antitype in the shedding down of the Holy Spirit, by whom the Law is written upon fleshy tables of the heart, and the bonds of intercourse between God and man are re-knit in a spiritual and enduring communion. St. Paul describes the Pentecostal gift as 'the first-fruits of the Spirit' (Ro 8[23]), in accordance with the purpose of the day. Of this momentous event we have the record in Ac 2. If in Jewish tradition the first Pentecost after the great deliverance from Egypt was, through the giving of the Law, the birthday of Judaism, in Christian history the first Pentecost after the true Passover Lamb had been slain was, through the outpouring of the Spirit, the birthday of the Church. The presence and working of the Spirit within the Church form the distinctive characteristic of Christianity. Gracious and beneficent as was the presence of the Master with His disciples, it was better, so He Himself declared, that He should go away (Jn 16[7]), and that in His stead the Paraclete, with His threefold conviction for the world, should come (vv.[8-11]). 'Behold, I send the promise of my Father upon you,' said Jesus to the Eleven and them that were gathered with them as He was about to ascend up into heaven; 'but tarry ye in the city till ye be endued with power from on high' (Lk 24[49]). Then, as the Evangelist records, He led them out until they were over against Bethany; and while His hands were lifted up in blessing, He parted from them, and was carried up into heaven. 'And they worshipped Him, and returned to Jerusalem with great joy: and were continually in the temple, blessing God' (Lk 24[52. 53]).

The Temple was the chief resort of the disciples during the period of tarrying which their Master had enjoined; but they continued also to frequent the Upper Room, now hallowed to them by its memories of the Lord (Ac 1[13f.]), continuing 'steadfastly in prayer, with the women, and Mary the mother of Jesus, and with his brethren.' And so they waited and prayed; and, lest anything should be lacking to their readiness for the promised blessing, they filled up, by the questionable arbitrament of the lot, the place in the number of the Twelve rendered vacant by the fall of Judas. It was now the eve of the second return of the Resurrection-day since the Lord had ascended, and the city was crowded and astir with the pilgrim bands which had come up to Jerusalem for the great annual harvest thanksgiving. No doubt they had counted the days; and they may well have divined that on Pentecost, the fiftieth day since their Lord had suffered as the Passover Lamb, their expectations would be fulfilled (Baumgarten, *Apostolic History*, i. p. 41).

'The day of Pentecost was now come,' and at an early hour the disciples, filled with anticipations awakened by the day, were all together in one place. That this place was the Temple seems natural, considering the occasion. It is a fair inference from the passage in St. Luke already quoted (24[52. 53]), and it harmonizes with the statement that 'the multitude came together' (Ac 2[6]) when the descent of the Spirit became known abroad. It is said that the sound heard from heaven filled 'all the house' (ὅλον τὸν οἶκον) where they were sitting,—an exaggerated form of expression if only a private dwelling is meant, whereas 'house' is the regular designation of the Temple in the LXX and in Josephus. Hallowed as the Upper Room had become by the institution of the Last Supper and the fellowship the disciples had there enjoyed with the Risen Lord, there was a significance beyond even that in the Temple, which had been so long the earthly dwelling-place of Jehovah, now being the place of the inauguration of the dispensation in which the believing soul

is to be the temple and dwelling-place of the Spirit.

To those praying disciples, and to the Church of which they were the representatives, came on that eventful day the fulfilment of 'the promise of the Father.' Suddenly a sound from heaven as of a mighty rushing wind fell upon the ears of the expectant band, and filled all the house where they were sitting. It does not appear that there was an actual wind, but only the sound of it pervading all parts of the house. Then, as they looked around, they beheld tongues like as of fire distributing themselves through the building, and alighting each upon a disciple's head. 'And they were all filled with the Holy Spirit, and began to speak with other tongues as the Spirit gave them utterance.' 'They were all filled with the Holy Spirit' is the supreme and enduring blessing of Pentecost. It is the central fact of this remarkable narrative. Side by side with the Incarnation, and the Atonement, and the Resurrection, and the Ascension of the Lord, stands the Mission of the Comforter in the gospel scheme. As the Mosaic dispensation was inaugurated with miracles and supernatural signs, it was meet that the dispensation which replaced it should likewise be ushered in with miraculous manifestations.

These manifestations must be briefly noticed. Wind and fire are elemental emblems of the Spirit occurring from time to time in the OT. 'He shall baptize you with the Holy Ghost and with fire' (Mt 3[11]) was the Baptist's prediction concerning the Messiah, now clearly fulfilled. 'The wind bloweth where it listeth . . . so is every one that is born of the Spirit' (Jn 3[8]), was the Lord's own shadowing forth of the Spirit's power to Nicodemus.

To the miraculous associations of Pentecost belong the 'tongues' with which the Apostles spake. Not unknown tongues, however, nor such ecstatic utterances as became familiar afterwards at Corinth and in the early Church, but tongues in which the strangers from distant countries, who had come to Jerusalem for the Feast, at once recognized their own speech, and heard the mighty works of God proclaimed. That the gift of tongues was a permanent endowment of the Apostles for their great work of proclaiming redemption to all the kindred of mankind, cannot be maintained. There is no proof that any of the Apostles of whose labours we have a record in the Acts was thus saved the trouble of acquiring foreign tongues, and supplied with the linguistic qualifications necessary for ministering to people of other races than their own. In fact, within the Roman world of that day such tongues were by no means indispensable. The Roman world, whithersoever the Apostles went on their missionary journeys, was to all intents and purposes of one speech, and they could make themselves understood in Greek in almost every ordinary case. It was only when they travelled to the far East, or to the bounds of the West, or away up the Nile, that their message required another tongue. The Jews who had come to the Feast at Jerusalem, or perhaps, as was the case with some, were sojourners in the Holy City, from out of every nation under heaven, recognized at once the vernacular of the several peoples among whom they were scattered—the tongue of Parthia, of Mesopotamia, of Phrygia, of Egypt, of Arabia—on the lips of one or other of the Apostles; but Greek was yet the *lingua franca* by which they could almost everywhere make themselves understood. 'The tongues' served the immediate purpose on this historic occasion of conveying to the assembled multitudes the great facts of the completed redemption, in familiar speech, yet with unwonted impressiveness and solemnity. But they were, over and above this, a supernatural sign, not only affording a striking proof at the moment of the presence and power of the Holy Spirit with the Apostles, but also furnishing a symbol of the universality of the new faith, and pointing forward to the proclamation of the glad tidings of great joy to all the families of mankind. Thus the legend of the giving of the Law in seventy languages on Mt. Sinai was matched by the fact of 'the tongues' at Pentecost; and the preaching of the gospel, first in all the lands of the Jewish Dispersion and then in all the earth, was emphatically shown forth.

5. Abiding significance.—The gift of tongues which marked the effusion of the Holy Spirit at Pentecost was only one of several extraordinary gifts bestowed at first upon the Church by the Ascended Lord. These gifts continued through the Apostolic Age, and were not only varied in their character, but wholly distinct from the ordinary quickening, sanctifying, and ministerial gifts which abide in the Church through all her history. They have passed away, and though in an Edward Irving and other saintly and gifted souls some of them may seem for a little while to re-appear, it is His gifts of quickening, sanctifying, and enabling that are the abiding blessing of the Holy Spirit to the Church, and that perpetuate the grace of Pentecost. The permanent blessing is not for a few, but for all believers. The Spirit had at the Creation brooded over the face of the deep; He had moved holy men to utter the oracles of God; He had rested upon anointed kings, like Saul and David; and He had dwelt without measure in the Incarnate Son of God. Now the blessing was to be for all. 'They were all filled with the Holy Ghost,' is the fulfilment of the prophecy of Joel ($2^{28.\ 29}$). It is the realization also of our Lord's promise (Jn 7^{37-39}). And St. Peter in his discourse to the multitudes on the day of Pentecost confirms the universality of the gift (Ac $2^{38.\ 39}$).

Whilst the experience of the disciples on the day of Pentecost shows the universality of the gift, it also attests the working of a new power of spiritual quickening and transformation. The Apostles themselves were transformed into new men. By the baptism of fire they were made courageous and brave; their eyes were opened to see the spirituality of Christ's Kingdom; and they were filled with a great enthusiasm for the salvation of men through the preaching of the crucified Christ. And such was the power of the Spirit accompanying St. Peter's words, that the multitude who had assembled to see and to hear were pricked to the heart, and cried, 'Men and brethren, what shall we do?' And with three thousand souls added to the little band of Apostles and believers, a Church was born in a day. 'With great power gave the apostles witness,' and that power was the gift of the Holy Ghost. Under the working of the Pentecostal gift a new spirit of love takes possession of them that believe, a new fellowship is established, a new service and varied ministry instituted. Throughout the course of the Church's history it has been the mission of the Comforter to convince the world of sin, and of righteousness, and of judgment; to glorify Christ to His believing people; to lead the Church into all truth, and to show her things to come; to sanctify them that believe; and to bestow grace upon all who serve in any ministry according to the requirement of the office which they fill. It is His mission still; and the great hope of the Church and of the world lies in the renewal of Pentecost, with its breath of refreshing and its tongue of fire, in each successive age.

LITERATURE.—Besides the works mentioned above, see the Comm. on Ac 2, the articles 'Pentecost,' 'Feasts,' 'Pfingstfest,' 'Wochenfest' in the Encyclopædias and Bible Dictionaries; Benzinger's *Heb. Arch.*; Mackie's *Bible Manners and Customs*; Farrar, *St. Paul*, i. 83–104; *Expositor*, I. i. [1875], 393–408; William Arthur, *The Tongue of Fire*.

T. NICOL.

PEOPLE.—This collective term, which occurs about 120 times in the Gospels, is used to denote sometimes in a lesser or more general way the people (λαός) among whom Christ lived and fulfilled His mission, but oftener the smaller or larger *crowds* of people (ὄχλος) who, from time to time, and in the various scenes of His labour, waited upon His ministry (see art. CROWD). But 'people' (λαός) is several times employed in the religious sense that attaches to such phrases as 'the people of God,' or 'Christ's people' (Mt $1^{21}\ 2^6$, Lk $1^{17.\ 77}\ 2^{32}\ 7^{16}$). It is only in this latter sense that the word calls for special notice, and as so viewed it possesses considerable importance.

The most noteworthy thing in regard to the religious use of the word in the Gospels is, that it is never in any of them employed by Christ Himself. All the instances in which it is found are in narratives connected with His birth and infancy, except the one in Lk 7^{16}; and in this case it was the people who beheld the restoration of the widow's son to life who said, 'that a great prophet is risen among us; and that God hath visited his people.' The fact that Christ discarded the use of the word 'people' in its religious sense cannot be regarded as a matter of little or no consequence. In doing so He must have acted with deliberate purpose, and for reasons considered by Himself to be valid. This view is evident from a variety of considerations: (1) The religious sense of the phrase 'the people of God' had occupied a place of high importance in the historical relation between God and the Hebrew race. (2) It had been organically associated by the OT revelation with the prospective advent of the Messiah and His Kingdom. (3) According to Messianic prophecy, the one people of God would eventually consist of all the peoples of the earth united in a common relation to Him. (4) Christ was aware of these facts. He knew that He was Himself the Jewish Messiah and the Saviour of the world. And He was inspired and controlled by the idea that the object of His mission was to bring the true and full sense of the phrase 'the people of God' to perfect realization in the Kingdom of heaven. (5) If He had chosen to do so, it would have been easy for Him to express all the essential truths of His message to mankind in terms of 'the people of God.' Moreover, this phrase could not be without attractions for Him. Why, then, did He never let it fall from His lips when addressing His audiences in public and in private?

One of His reasons must have been the significance of the phrase as it presented itself to His own mind. The ideas with which He would charge it may be inferred from the essential nature of the truths embodied in the message He left behind Him. In thinking of God and His people, He would think of Him as a moral Being and of them as moral beings. He would think of the relations between Him and them as moral, and therefore as founded in this direct inward relation to them as *individuals*. He would think also of His relation to them as absolutely impartial, and of their relations to Him as absolutely equal. And for all these reasons He would think of the relation between God and His people, *as His people*, as in no sense legal, and as not permitting Him to show towards any people in particular either national favour or political privileges. Finally, all this implies that Christ would think of God and His people in terms of purely moral universality. But if such is the meaning that He would attach to the phrase alluded to, does not that seem to favour His use of it, and to make His rejection of it still more difficult to understand? Quite the reverse, as another reason shows.

As a teacher, Christ had to consider not only the meaning that He attached to the phrase Himself, but also the meaning attached to it by the Jews among whom He taught, and who believed that they themselves were the people of God, and they alone of all the peoples of mankind. The people of Israel were *the* people of God. This was one of the most essential and distinctive dogmas of the fully developed, orthodox, and official Judaism with which our Lord everywhere and always had to reckon as a teacher; and this dogma, adhered to and upheld by the fanatical zeal of the rigid and conservative devotees of Judaism, was the most embarrassing that He had to reckon with as a teacher sent from God. For what did the dogma in question mean and imply? It rested upon a denial of the essential oneness of the relation of God to all the peoples of the world, and of the essential oneness of the relation of all the peoples of the world to Him. It was founded in the notion that the relation between God and His people was national, and that the nature of the national bond was not moral but legal. For Divine righteousness and the obedience of faith, the only real and permanent, because moral, conditions on which the relations between God and His people repose, it substituted ancestral descent from Abraham, and the observance of the national rite of circumcision. And the only way, it contended, for Gentiles to obtain admission within the circle of the people of God, was to become Jews by observing this national rite. It is manifest, then, that the ideas of Judaism and the ideas of Christ on the subject of 'the people of God' were in direct and complete antagonism to one another. This fact Christ had to consider, and it was necessary for Him as a teacher to weigh the question as to what the inevitable consequences would be for Himself and His cause, if He attempted in the course of His teaching to present and explain His ideas on the subject of 'the people of God' in their real and inherent antagonism to the ideas on the same subject which had become fixed and hardened in the perverted Judaism of His time. Evidently He came to the conclusion that the handling of this subject would involve Himself and the interests of His mission in great risks and dangers. It is certain that such would have been the case. For if He had taught and insisted on the acceptance of the truths of moral unity and universality that belong to the relations between God and His people as He understood them, the bigoted adherents of Judaism would have forthwith resented His teaching and made Himself the object of their fanatical and malignant hostility. He therefore persistently ignored the phrase 'the people of God.' It was highly expedient for Him to do so.

But the adoption of this course did not entail any compromise of those truths of moral unity and universality that are of the essence of the relations in which God stands to His people and they to Him. He showed His sense of the greatness and validity of these as well as of other moral truths, and secured the interests attaching to them, by two other vastly important things that He did as a teacher. In the first place, He embedded all the truths of moral unity and universality referred to in His parables, which He spoke as illustrative of the rich and diversified order of ideas presented by Him under the designation of 'the kingdom of God.' His reason for couching these ideas in parabolic forms He Himself explained (Mt 13[10-16]). His explanation implies that He would have preferred to employ a more explicit way of communicating the ideas in question if circumstances had permitted; that the hearts of the adherents of the existing perverted Judaism had been blinded and hardened by the influence of their system; that it was impossible for them to see the truth and validity of these ideas; and that they were not in a mood to extend to them or to Himself toleration. Such was His reason for speaking of the Kingdom of heaven in parables. The true meaning of the latter was veiled from the enemies of the truth by the blindness of their eyes. But, on the other hand, the parables, He knew, would preserve the essence of the truth as He had taught it, and to all who were of the truth the latter would in due time become revealed.

But, secondly, Christ guarded and effectively secured the interests of the truths of moral unity and universality, which are of the essence of His gospel, in another way. In the Kingdom of God and in the relations between God and His people, moral unity and moral universality are founded on their human side on moral *individuality*. In any case, therefore, it would have been necessary for Christ to give to moral individuality a place of supreme importance in His teaching. And this is precisely what He did. He knew and never lost sight of the truth that moral unity and universality can never come to actual realization in the Kingdom of heaven, or, in other words, in the relations between God and His people, unless in so far as men are saved, and become morally perfect as individuals. And therefore He not only gave His just and constant consideration to the individual, but held up before His disciples the moral perfection of God, their Father in heaven, as the ideal which they should strive individually to realize in their own character and life (Mt 5[43-48]). This is the basis on which moral unity and universality are realized in the relations of men to God as His people.   W. D. THOMSON.

PERÆA.—1. Name and extent.—The name (ἡ Περαία), while constantly used by Josephus, is not found in LXX or NT, in both of which it is represented by the equivalent πέραν τοῦ Ἰορδάνου = עֵבֶר־חַיַּרְדֵּן (cf. Is 9[1] [Heb. 8[23]], Mt 4[25], Mk 10[1]). Judæa, Galilee, and Peræa were reckoned by the Jews themselves as the three Jewish provinces. The division is repeatedly assumed in the Mishna (Schürer, *HJP*, II. i. 2; cf. Jos. *BJ*, III. iii. 3). The population of Peræa was, however, never so thoroughly Jewish as that of Judæa, or even of Galilee. In both Galilee and Peræa political vicissitudes had occasioned a large intermingling of Jewish and Gentile elements. Notwithstanding the close neighbourhood of the three provinces, the differences of their experience had produced differences of customs and manners, which gave to each of them an independent life of its own, and caused them to be regarded as in certain respects different countries (Schürer, *l.c.*).

The name 'Peræa,' like the names of many of the districts east of the Jordan, was somewhat loosely used, having a wider and a narrower signification. Josephus (*l.c.*) states the length of Peræa as from Machærus to Pella, *i.e.* from the Arnon to the Jabbok, and its breadth as from Philadelphia and Gerasa to the Jordan, limits corresponding with those of the modern Belḳâ. But in *BJ*, IV. vii. 3, he calls Gadara 'the metropolis of Peræa.' In what sense he uses this term there is no means of ascertaining, but he must intend to include under the name 'Peræa' the region extending north from the Jabbok to the Yarmuk (Hieromax), close to which river Gadara stood, that is to say, all that the Hebrews meant by 'beyond the Jordan.' His usage may depend on whether he happened at the moment to be referring to the district which was more completely Jewish, or to the whole region, which was governed as one, and which included the Hellenistic towns of the Decapolis (*Ant.* XIII. ii. 3, iv. 9). Peræa in its more limited sense corresponded with the kingdom of Sihon, or Reuben and a part of Gad. In its larger signification it was from 80 to 90 miles from north to south, and about 25 from east to west.

2. Characteristics. — As regards its physical features, Peræa consists for the most part of an elevated tableland, rising rapidly from the Jordan valley, but broken by frequent gorges and mountain torrents. It was, according to Mukaddasi, proverbially cold. Josephus (*BJ*, III. iii. 3) says that, while larger than Galilee, it is mostly desert and rough, and much less adapted than that province for the cultivation of fruit. Still he admits that it is in parts very fertile, and produces all kinds of fruits, and its plains are planted with various trees, chiefly the olive, the vine, and the palm. It is sufficiently watered by streams from the mountains and by springs which do not fail even in summer.

Mukaddasi (*c.* 985 A.D.) says that the Belḳâ district is rich in grain and flocks, and has many streams which work the mills. He divides Syria into four belts, from the Mediterranean eastwards. Of the third and fourth he writes : 'The Third Belt is that of the valleys of the Ghaur (the Jordan valley), wherein are found many villages and streams, also palm trees, well-cultivated fields, and indigo plantations. . . . The Fourth Belt is that bordering on the desert. The mountains here are high and bleak, and the climate resembles that of the waste ; but it has many villages, with springs of water, and forest trees.' He also mentions the hot springs of the district, naming those of *Al-Hammah*. Guy le Strange, whose translation has just been quoted, thinks that the hot springs of Gadara or Amatha in the Yarmuk valley are those referred to, and he adds in regard to them, that 'round the large basin may still be seen the remains of vaulted bath-houses. The sanitary properties of these sulphurous waters are highly extolled by many ancient writers, and to this day they have maintained their reputation among the Bedawin and *fellaḥin* of Palestine, so much so that the bathing-place is regarded by all parties as a neutral ground' (*Description of Syria*, by Mukaddasi, tr. by Guy le Strange [Pal. Pilgr. Text Soc.]). Of the Jordan valley Merrill (*East of the Jordan*, p. 438) says : 'From the Zerka (Jabbok) to the Sea of Galilee (*ib.*) it is exceedingly fertile ; and in any period when the country was settled and a good government in power, it must have been one of the most wealthy and important sections of Palestine for the raising of wheat and other products, while the foot-hills would afford excellent pasturage.'

3. History, population, etc. — Under the will of Herod the Great, Galilee and Peræa were united for purposes of government under Antipas, and this arrangement was confirmed by Augustus. As these two provinces had but a very short common boundary where Galilee touched the Jordan north of Samaria, it might have seemed more natural to combine Peræa with the regions north of the Yarmuk, or with Samaria. But affinities of race and religion (cf. Jos. *Ant.* XX. i. 1 ; G. A. Smith, *HGHL*, p. 539) plainly suggested the wisdom of governing them together. For the same reasons Jews journeying between Galilee and Judæa often preferred to go by way of Peræa, where they were among their own countrymen, rather than pass through Samaria (the more direct route), where they incurred the risk at least of insult (Lk 9⁵³, Jn 4⁴·⁹ ; cf. Edersheim, *LT*, i. 394 ; Jos. *Ant.* XX. vi. 1). They used the fords opposite Beisan, north of Samaria, and Jericho, south of it. The northern parts of Peræa mingled with the region of the Decapolis, where in the towns there was a vigorous Hellenistic civilization, and apparently north of the Yarmuk the Jewish element of the population was inconsiderable. The strongly Jewish character of Peræa is indicated in the Gospels. John the Baptist worked there during part of his ministry (Jn 3²⁶ 10⁴⁰). In Peræa multitudes gathered round Christ, among whom were Pharisees who entered into controversy with Him and displayed all the animus of their sect (Mt 19³ff·). Mothers, evidently Jewish, brought their children to be blessed (Mk 10¹³), and the ruler who had kept the whole Law

sought an answer to his question (Mt 19¹⁶). The mission of the Seventy was to Peræa, and although the restriction laid upon the Twelve (whose number corresponded with that of the tribes of Israel), 'Go not into any way of the Gentiles' (Mt 10⁵·⁶), is significantly absent in the case of the Seventy (whose number is typical of the nations of the earth), yet the scope of our Lord's ministry makes it evident that they were to encounter, at least for the most part, Jews.

The immigration of Greek settlers into the country east of Jordan probably began with the presence there of Alexander the Great, and the towns of Pella (no doubt named from the Macedonian city which was Alexander's birthplace) and Dion may have been founded by him, as Steph. Byz. states in a somewhat corrupt passage, or by some of his followers. Besides these towns, many other powerful Hellenistic communities sprang into existence, and flourished in the midst of a population from which they were separated by their distinctive culture, and, in so far as it was Jewish, by the practice of heathen worship. The Maccabees (B.C. 166–135) endeavoured to withdraw the Jews (who presumably were at that time the smaller section of the inhabitants) to Judæa (1 Mac 5⁴⁵⁻⁵⁴). John Hyrcanus (B.C. 135–105) possibly first adopted the opposite policy, which was vigorously carried out by Alexander Jannæus (B.C. 104-78), who brought the country from Lake Merom to the Dead Sea completely under his control (Jos. *Ant.* XIII. xv. 4 ; Schürer, *HJP*, I. i. 192, 297, 306). He took Hippos, Gadara, Pella, Dion, and other important towns, and extinguished the Greek culture which had flourished in them. He forced them to assimilate Jewish manners and ideas, and those places which would not submit he destroyed. In B.C. 64 the Roman province of Syria was formed, and under Pompey and Gabinius the procurator the ruined cities were rebuilt, and the Hellenistic communities regained their independence. Indeed, the sympathy of Pompey was long remembered by them, as is attested by the numerous coins which have been found impressed with his era. It was probably he who organized the Decapolis (the term ἡ Δεκάπολις is found first in the Roman period). See DECAPOLIS.

In B.C. 20, Herod the Great obtained permission to appoint his brother Pheroras tetrarch of Peræa (*Ant.* XV. x. 3 ; *BJ*, I. xxiv. 5). Pheroras afterwards incurred the enmity of Herod, and retired or was driven to Peræa, where he died, not improbably by poison (*BJ*, I. xxix. 4). At his death (B.C. 4) Herod left Galilee and Peræa to his son Antipas (*Ant.* XVII. viii. 1). The tribute paid by these provinces was 200 talents (*Ant.* XVII. xi. 4). Antipas ruled with the title of tetrarch till his banishment in A.D. 39 by Caius Cæsar, who added his tetrarchy to the dominions of Agrippa (*Ant.* XVIII. vii. 2). Antipas was therefore in authority in Galilee and Peræa during the whole lifetime of John the Baptist and of Christ.

Among the towns of Peræa, Pella has a special interest as having been twice the refuge of the Christians fleeing from Jerusalem, in A.D. 68, and again in A.D. 135, when under Hadrian Jerusalem was taken for the second time and its name changed to Ælia. The fact that Pella was a heathen city may have been an inducement to the Christians of Jerusalem to seek refuge in it, as it would not attract the hostility of the Romans. Merrill (*East of the Jordan*, p. 462 f.) thinks that Christ probably several times passed through the Jordan valley and may well have visited Pella itself. His preaching may have been successful there, and His connexion with the town such as to suggest it as a refuge to the Christians.

LITERATURE.—Besides authorities cited above, see Hastings' *DB*, artt. 'Peræa,' 'Gadara,' 'Decapolis,' 'Machærus'; Thomson, *Land and Book.* For later history, Guy le Strange, *Palestine under the Moslems.*   A. E. ROSS.

PERDITION.—See DESTRUCTION.

PERDITION, SON OF.—See JUDAS ISCARIOT

PEREZ.—Mentioned as a link in our Lord's genealogy (Mt 1³, Lk 3³³, AV *Phares*).

PERFECTION (OF JESUS).—Christian writers generally take for granted the perfection of their Lord. They point to the records, and declare that such is the impression which they make on the honest reader. And that is not the mere begging of the question which it seems. Men judge of goodness by the eye. The vision of faith comes first; thought comes later with its justifications.

1. One note of perfection, though merely a negative one, is **sinlessness.** He 4¹⁵ says that though He was tried in all things as we are, Christ remained without sin. Can that be proved or made clear? Certain difficulties suggest themselves. (1) Only the merest fragment of that life is known. Before His story begins, Jesus had lived for thirty years in this world, which is full to overflowing of all manner of sin. How can we be sure that no stain ever touched the purity of His soul during all those buried years, silent for ever now in quiet Nazareth? (2) There is also the whole story of a man's inward life; the dreams of the secret heart, the fancies cherished in the recesses of fond imagination, the converse which the soul holds with itself. What record can lay bare that hidden and withdrawn, but most real and vital, region of the spirit's life, with all its startling depths and unexpected glories?

One witness can testify of that—the spirit's own consciousness in the presence of God, who has been the unseen companion of all that life. And we gather from the Gospels that Jesus was weighed down by no sense of sin. It is the saints who have the keenest sense of sin. Their inward thought has always placed them in a line with the publican in the Temple who would not so much as lift his eyes to heaven, but smote on his breast and cried, 'God, be merciful to me a sinner' (Lk 18¹⁹). Jesus, among the saints, is unique in this matter: no word of self-reproach, no hint of any thought or inward struggle which He deplored, ever falls from His lips. See, further, art. SINLESSNESS.

2. Another note of perfection is that *Jesus stands above the various types and classes of men.* Humanity is parcelled out among men. They have their peculiar excellences and differences; but these are usually only a part of our human nature. The most royally endowed among men are but fragments. Our life is composed of three elements—thought, and will, and feeling; and according as one or other of these may preponderate, we have men of action, men of thought, men of passion. Jesus eludes any such classification: He has affinities with each of them; their excellences inhere in Him with none of their defects.

(*a*) Jesus has affinities with the *artist* and the *poet.* His eye rested on the beauty of the earth with the poet's joy and understanding. The common sights mirror themselves in His teaching: the lilies in their glory, the birds among the branches, the ravens seeking their food from God, seed-time and harvest, sowing and reaping. The face of this goodly universe spake joy within His heart. And He looked with loving, discerning eyes on all the pageant of human life. When we read His words, the life of His day flows past us. And His glance was deep as well as wide. With what irony He sketches the indecision of the Pharisees,

in the story of the children who will play neither at funerals nor at weddings! What deeper criticism of a prudential morality is there than in the words 'he that saveth his life shall lose it'? what clearer perception of the hopelessness of a man's attempt at self-deliverance than the parable of the house swept and garnished but empty? There is His indictment of the Pharisees (Mt 23). It is the most passionate invective in literature. But the marvel of it, the inner justification of it, is that there with utter clearness and precision He lays bare the essential evil of Pharisaism. Passion easily contents itself with strong denunciation. The words of Jesus are a stream of lava seven times heated from a burning heart; but they are full of light; they track the hidden ways of pride and self-seeking in the religious heart. We see in them the thinker, the seer before whose glance secret things lie open and bare, as well as the prophet with his passion for simplicity and truth.

Jesus was an artist also in His teaching. He was not content to bring before men truths about God and the way of life. He clothed His teaching in beauty. He uttered the deep things of the Kingdom in parables. And these are simple, pellucid, beautiful as with the loveliness of waters stilled at even. See art. POET.

(*b*) There are the men of *action*, men in whom the will is predominant. Jesus shows them their ideal. He was no dreamer, but a man of deeds. Will was as mighty in Him as thought. He impressed all with a sense of power and mastery. The people recognized that note in His teaching: He spake with authority, and not as the scribes. It was felt at Nazareth when they took up stones to stone Him and He passed through their midst (Lk 4³⁰), and at Gethsemane when the soldiers fell back before the majesty of His bearing (Jn 18⁶). He dominated friend and foe by the calm strength of a sovereign will. And His days were filled with active service, teaching and healing, so that St. Peter summed up His life as that of One 'who went about doing good' (Ac 10³⁸). Men of action have their limitations. Their energy outstrips the illumination of their minds; they work for the day and its needs; their outlook is narrow and dim. But Jesus ever fed the springs of action with thought. He was no less than thirty years of age when He was baptized in Jordan. He had been content to live with His thoughts and simple duties, perfecting there, in patient obedience, mind and heart and will for the great work. And even after the baptism, when the call had come, He went first to the wilderness, there in prayer and meditation to understand His work and His own heart. And often He stole away from the crowd, from the blinding pressure of constant activity, to gather light and balance in prayer (Mk 1³⁵ 6⁴⁶, Lk 6¹², Jn 8¹). Hence the crown which rests on His activities. He never turned aside from His path. One purpose shapes every word and act from the beginning. Will sits untroubled on its throne, whatever dissonances of earth be round Him, though world and friend and foe conspire to turn Him aside. And peace rests upon all He does. There was no hurry in His hands, no hurry in His feet. His life was full, crowded with incident; but it flowed on quiet, unchanging, harmonious as a poet's dream. The mountain with its peace and quietness, its hours of prayer and still thought, was His place of transfiguration. There He looked into the Father's purpose, till the glory that lay beyond and the love that shone through it kindled their reflexion on His face, till He saw His way so clearly that He could never miss it, never be in any hesitation about it,—the way, amid the conflicting passions of men, to His throne on Calvary.

(*c*) There remains another great class, the men of

passion. Among them have been some of the greatest and sweetest of the children of men—gentle souls with the grace of sympathy and self-forgetfulness; generous and magnanimous souls like David, whose inspirations have been to men an abiding memorial of the beauty of chivalry; heroes of faith like Paul and Luther, who change the current of human life. Jesus is the Lord of all such. Men of thought or action grow great oftentimes at the expense of their heart; but in Jesus the heart has equal sway with the mind or the will. He was full of sympathy. The sick and the sorrowful never appealed to Him in vain; His hand was laid gently and lovingly on the loathsome body of the leper; the sinful and outcast knew there was understanding and gentle judgment with Him. And His miracles of healing were never demonstrations, seals of His Messiahship; personal sympathy was their source and regulator. But Jesus does not throw the reins to sympathy. ' His sanity of judgment is as extraordinary as His depth of sympathy' (Peabody, *Jesus Christ and the Social Question*, p. 85). He could not look on the adulterous woman brought to Him for judgment—He felt for her so; but though He would not condemn, neither did He excuse; He said, ' Go, and sin no more' (Jn 8²⁻¹¹). His gospel was that there is infinite patience and forgiveness with God; and yet there are no sterner words in the NT than His. He who told the parable of the Prodigal Son told also the parables of the Ten Virgins, the Man without the Wedding Garment, and the Talents. And the woman who bathed His feet in Simon's house, and Zacchæus who lodged Him for the night, and Peter who listened to Him in the boat, all bear witness how, in His gracious presence, the sincere soul felt the evil of sin and the inflexible order of righteousness as it had never felt them before.

3. *The law of His life, its ultimate value.*—It is objected that an essential imperfection cleaves to the individual, however balanced the elements of humanity in him may be. He belongs to one age and people; and the ideal of his day, which is only in a state of becoming, and is surely passing away into some higher, fuller ideal, as the thought and experience of the race widen, inevitably bounds his spirit. Growth is the mark of all things human. The ideal of the good man grows; it draws to itself elements from different nations and different times; it passes through subtle changes and permutations. God speaks to men at sundry times and in divers manners; and not only great men, but nations, are His prophets to the spirit of the wide world which is travailing with the perfect ideal of man. So the individual can never have permanent or universal value. As the Abbé Galieni says, ' One century may judge another century, but only his own century may judge the individual.' That may be true of the ordinary man, or even of national heroes and saints, whose character ever seems strange and partially distasteful or even unintelligible to men of other races and times; it is conspicuously untrue of Jesus. He stands not at the bar of His century. He judges it and all times: He judges His own people and all peoples. He took their highest ideas of God and of moral duty and purified these, making them the light of to-day. Jehovah, the Holy One of Israel, became the Father in heaven whose name is Love; and the chosen people of God, all the immortal spirits God has made in His own image. And that idea wrought itself out perfectly in His teaching and conduct. It is in particulars that the prophet's insight is tested. Jesus identified the will of God with the good of men; and He found that good in the universal elements of human life. He emptied religion of all national and accidental elements. He passed by all customs and observ-

ances that were of His day and race; He removed all barriers and limits which men put to human brotherhood. And so, though born among the most exclusive of nations, a son of Abraham after the flesh, He is no Jew: He is the first Citizen of the world; in Paul's revealing phrase, ' the last Adam.'

Nor is the ideal of Jesus subject to time. There is progress in all things, but not in the same way. Knowledge moves from point to point. In mathematics and in all the mechanical sciences we pass with sure foot from one thing gained to another. But as we enter the region of personality, all that is changed. The art of to-day, whether in literature, painting, sculpture, architecture, is not necessarily better than the art of even a distant yesterday. There are creative times in the world's history when a great idea is expressed, and it becomes the task of centuries to understand and assimilate it. Jesus is the Creator of a new spiritual era. His work was to found a Kingdom, spiritual in nature, world-wide in extent. That Kingdom is based on what is ultimate in our nature—the Fatherhood of God, whose name is Love, and the brotherhood of men. Such a Kingdom is the finer breath and inspiration, the inner meaning and end, of all the imperfect, transient societies of earth. And such alone will satisfy the individual; for the end of personality is love. The ideal of Jesus may gather content in and through all the experiences and relations and offices of those who live in this Kingdom. His spirit will bear fruit within the Kingdom beyond what it could bear during the days He lived on earth, revealing its infinite riches. But never will the mind of the world pass beyond the bounds of that ideal, or draw light from any further source.

Jesus is the Lord of the new society, not only because He enunciated with perfect clearness its ultimate law, but because He Himself followed this law unerringly in His own life ' without being let or hindered, as we are, by the motions of private passion and by self-will' (M. Arnold, *St. Paul*, p. 45). The absoluteness of this obedience is attested by the trials to which it was put. The perfectly good man must not merely show flawless, joyful obedience; he must be sifted as wheat; he must meet trial and temptation in their extremest rigour and subtlest form. Only so can the supremacy of goodness in him be affirmed. Jesus was thus tried. And the trial served only to make clear the perfect identification of His mind with the heart and will of the Father. (For the possibility of the temptation of a sinless Being, see art. TEMPTATION).

(1) *Filial relation to God.*—In the wilderness Jesus met the trials of the future. He had there to come to an understanding with Himself, to know precisely what His mission was and what were the means of its accomplishment. One suggestion was to turn stones into bread. The loving soul will be tempted from the side of pity. To the heart of Jesus His countrymen's need of bread and of help to a better social state would always be present. But He turned aside to His task, which was to feed them with the words that proceed out of the mouth of God.

Renunciations are the lowly gateways on the narrow road of obedience. They are a measure of a man's moral sagacity, his clearness of vision both of his duty and of the means of realizing it, his simplicity of spirit and freedom from vanity or self-will. Men are readily drawn aside, the lower sort by suggestions of vanity and self-importance, the higher by the vision of some good more quickly realized. The world of political and industrial and social problems is a lower world than that in which Jesus wrought. It is a realm of expediency; its conditions change from age to age. The leaders there are men of affairs, men of practical wisdom, taught to discern what is immediately possible. The world will never lack such guides, for riches and honour and power gather quickly to them. Jesus kept aloof from such questions. He walked a more self-denying road, though one more fruitful of good to the world. He was not sent save as the physician of sick souls and the shepherd of lost ones. It was His to found a Kingdom not of this world, the Kingdom of God: and to provide, by His teaching and by the manifestation of His own loving heart in suffering and in death, what would quicken faith, and hope, and love in men throughout all lands and all times.

The Messianic idea was another great temptation. Evil is here entwined in all things; temptation lurks within a man's purest and highest aspirations. Men must always work with the instruments at their hand. Jesus came with the consciousness of being 'God's final messenger, after whom none higher can come' (Wernle, *Beginnings of Christianity*, Eng. tr. i. 45). He had to appeal to the popular expectation, their hopes of the Messiah soiled by ignoble thought. The popular thought is ever on a lower plane than the Divine, and becomes a difficulty and a temptation to the servants of God. When Jesus saw Himself as the long-looked-for Messiah, all the worldly hopes that clung to the office in the thoughts of Rabbi or people flowed in upon Him. There were the expectation of political glory, and the worship of force, in the popular mind. There was the Rabbinic expectation of a kingdom of right obedience set up miraculously by God through the sudden appearance of the Messiah—a more refined, seemingly pious expectation, full of trust in God only and of zeal for His glory. These were the thoughts and hopes which rose up at the claim of Messiah. In the wilderness Jesus had to face them: He had to come to a clear understanding of the nature of the Messianic Kingdom and of the means He had to use to establish it. There everything material and external fell from His idea of it. The earthly kingdom became spiritual; the glory of Israel became universal; the way of its establishment was to be through an appeal to the honest heart's faith in God as the highest good and the convincing vision of goodness; and for Himself not any success and glory, but suffering, and shame, and death. These elements of His purification of the Messianic idea only emerged gradually in His teaching, but they were present to His consciousness at the beginning, when He determined to worship God only, and to serve Him in simple obedience to His highest thought, making no compromise with the Prince of this world (Mt 4[10]).

Jesus had to meet again in the world all those temptations which He had vanquished in His thought. The people desired to make Him king (Jn 6[15]). He made it the occasion of showing clearly the spiritual nature of His mission, and reaped for His faithfulness their disbelief. The temptation came closer. Peter, in love, took Him aside and rebuked Him when He sought to prepare the disciples' hearts for the shame and death before Him. Peter was the mouth-piece of the Prince of this world, pointing out the lower way (Mt 16[21-23]). From the lips of mother and brethren the same temptation came. His mother whispered, 'They have no wine' (Jn 2[3]); His brethren said, 'Go into Judæa (where the great and powerful are), that thy disciples also may see the works that thou doest' (Jn 7[3, 4]). Temptation thus entrenched itself against Him among the sanctities of the heart. Jesus, as in the wilderness, triumphed by simple obedience. He put the temptation aside with the words, 'Mine hour is not yet come' (Jn 2[24]). He had no ear for any of the suggestions of policy or worldly prudence, whose hour is alway ready; He was a man under authority, waiting for the call of the Father; and clear and sweet above the discordant voices of the world that call ever came, and He followed it to Calvary. There His obedience was perfected (Jn 14[31]).

(2) *Brotherly relation to men.*—There were no limits to Jesus' sympathy and love for men. (*a*) The religious prejudices of His day did not impair His brotherhood with the sinful and the outcast. He discerned clearly their worth. That is a witness to His brotherhood. For interest and affection are the lights which illumine the personality of others; only by them can we read their hidden worth, especially when obscured by the dominant thought and prejudices of the day. Jesus discerned the spiritual soundness which might underlie sins of passion, the capacity of generosity with its healing power, the quick and deep response to a gospel of forgiveness in the humility of self-accusing hearts, the sacred soil where love grows (Lk 7[47] 18[13], Mt 21[28-32]). And He drew nigh unto men in brotherly love as the physician of sick souls, the faithful shepherd seeking the lost sheep of God, though thereby He outraged the sentiments of the Pharisees (Mt 9[11] 11[19], Lk 15[2] 19[7]), though His friendship with them was helping to raise the cross on which He was slain. The simplicity of Jesus' feeling of brotherhood for them is witnessed by the fact that they drew near to Him gladly (Lk 15[1], Mt 9[10]).

(*b*) 'No single social type monopolized the sympathy or acceptance of Jesus' (Peabody, *op. cit.* p. 204). The zealot and the publican met in the inner circle of His disciples: Mary of Magdala, out of whom went seven devils, and Joanna, the wife of Herod's steward, united to minister to Him of their substance. He was equally at home in Simon the Pharisee's house and at the table of Levi or Zacchæus, with their different *clientèle*; in private talk with Nicodemus, a master in Israel, and at the wayside well with the woman of Samaria. His help in sickness was for rich and poor, in all circumstances and conditions—the solitary leper, and the mourning widow in the streets of Nain; the paralytic of thirty-eight years, friendless and helpless, and the bond-servant of the household of the Roman centurion, whose name was held in honour throughout all Capernaum; the daughter of Jairus, a ruler of the synagogue, and the daughter of a nameless Gentile woman of Syro-Phœnicia. And His brotherhood went beyond the bounds of nations. He made the Samaritan the hero of His story of neighbourliness; He praised the faith of the Roman centurion; He pointed to God's care of Naaman the Syrian captain, and the widow of Zarephath. Jesus might not formulate in express terms the doctrine of the brotherhood of man. That was not His way. He dealt not in notions or abstractions. He rather inspired a spirit which sooner or later would burst all the swaddling-bands that confined humanity, and which expressed itself in the words of him who understood best the spirit of the Master, 'Where there is neither Greek nor Jew, circumcision nor uncircumcision, barbarian, Scythian, bond nor free' (Col 3[11]). Illumination rises from the heart.

(*c*) In Him love won also its ultimate triumph, viz. over wrong and hate. 'I say unto you, Love your enemies,' etc. (Mt 5[44]). That is an ideal which thought may win; but it has been fully realized only in Him who suffered the contradiction of sinners with unfailing patience and serenity of heart, and who prayed on the cross for those who placed Him there, and who reviled Him in His agony, 'Father, forgive them: for they know not what they do' (Lk 23[34]).

Jesus' filial relation of love and obedience to the

Father and His brotherhood to man reach their absolute expression on Calvary. That death was no accident, provoked by the invectives against the Pharisees ; it was seen afar off as the end of His mission. It looks through the sad irony of His answer to the Pharisees when they complained of the religious light-heartedness of His followers and He said, 'The days will come when the bridegroom shall be taken away from them, and then shall they fast in those days' (Mk 2²⁰). And as soon as the disciples had come to clear faith in Him as the Messiah, He began to prepare them for disappointment and tribulation and His death. This was the inevitable end of the method He had chosen in the wilderness, when He renounced all powers of persuasion but that of an appeal to the heart. The Kingdom of loving and obedient souls could be established only on the perfect sacrifice of love and obedience, and Jesus gave Himself absolutely in response to that vision of faith. In this sacrifice the law of His life, ultimate law for man, declares its victory.

4. As a result of His perfect love and obedience the character of Jesus shows certain notes of perfection, qualities in which He is unique and unapproachable among men. (1) There was in Him the union of the loftiest self-consciousness and the utmost sobriety of mind and lowliness of heart. 'I am the light of the world' (Jn 8¹²) ; 'No man knoweth the Father but the Son, and he to whom the Son willeth to reveal him' (Mt 11²⁷). A self-consciousness more than human is in these words. And this self-consciousness dominates all His work. He brushes aside the teachings of the scribes and the traditions of their schools ; He speaks to the people as one having authority, who is greater than Jonah or Solomon (Mt 12⁴¹·⁴²), who stands above all the Law and the Prophets (Mt 5¹⁷·¹⁸ 21³⁴⁻³⁷). He made also the most tremendous claims on men. He bade the rich man sell all and follow Him ; His disciples were to hate wife and family for His sake. The experience of failure and the approach of the Cross availed nothing to abate these claims. At the visit of the Greeks He said that, were He lifted up, He would draw all men to Him (Jn 12³²) ; He told the high priest that He was the Son of God, and that he would see the Son of Man sitting on the right hand of power and coming in the clouds of heaven (Mk 14⁶²). And yet Jesus ever showed the utmost sobriety and lowly-mindedness. He always prayed humbly and submissively to God the Father. The Son did nothing but what He learned from the Father (Jn 5¹⁹). And in the wilderness He recognized that He was to tread life's common way. Savonarola and St. Francis might offer to pass through the fire, but Jesus expected no guarding or attesting miracle. He must not cast Himself from the Temple. He must accept all the ordinary conditions of life in His work. And He accepted them. Meekly He went down the darkening ways, accepting failure and disappointment and hatred and shame as the portion appointed by the Father ; and there is no sign of any inward rebellion or amazement. He walked humbly before God.

He was with men also in lowliness and meekness. When the Samaritan villagers would not receive Him, He restrained His disciples' indignation and went to another village (Lk 9⁵²⁻⁵⁶) ; He took a place in the lower seats in the Pharisee's house (Lk 14⁷⁻¹¹) ; He was infinitely approachable by all the outcast and needy. Though He proclaimed, when need was, His greatness as the Son of God, yet He turned aside from personal questions as to whether He was the Messiah. His aim was to create in men's hearts faith in God as their Father, and He was content to let that faith come to its own appreciation of Him and His claims. The man who would not follow Him, but yet wrought cures in His name, was not to be rebuked (Mk 9³⁸⁻⁴²) ; and any blasphemy against Him personally would be forgiven (Mt 12³¹·³²). His greatness among men was the greatness of service. This union of lowly-mindedness and loftiest self-consciousness is reflected, as in a mirror, in His parable of the Last Judgment. He sees Himself attended by all the holy angels, and seated on the throne of glory to judge men. But there His royal robe is the self-forgetting humility of love. For there no wrongs done to Himself are thought of, no disbelief in His claims, no offence against His majesty : it is the helpless and the suffering forgotten by their brethren who fill His mind. His glory vanishes within the light of love.

(2) Jesus faced the sorrow and sin of the world, and yielded nothing of His faith and joy. It has been said that He was a man of melancholy, one who never laughed, one marked and scored by the world's evil, grown old before His time. That is an *a priori* interpretation of His character. In the Gospels it is the note of joy that strikes us. Jesus Himself says to the complaining Pharisees, 'Can the children of the bridechamber fast while the bridegroom is with them ?' The joy of the bridegroom was in His heart. His life then was empty of all the things in whose abundance the world thinks that man's life consists. But the sources of happiness are all within. And Jesus' joy reveals His victory over the tyranny of things. He was rich inwardly. That arose from His cheerful faith 'that all which we behold is full of blessings.' This world, to His vision, was God's world. It is He who clothes the lily with beauty, and feeds the ravens, and knows when a sparrow falls to the ground, and numbers the hairs of His children's heads. And He had faith in man. He saw in the Temple's outcast children marks of good. They could love much : the authentic Divine seal was still on their hearts. Such an outlook brings riches of interest and joy to the whole nature.

But how did that faith and that joy fare in their encounter with the world's sin and sorrow ? It was tried to the uttermost. Jesus met with all the sorrows of life in others' experience, which His sympathy made real to Him, if not in His own. He met the world's sin ; He had to endure the disbelief of His brethren and the forsaking of His followers ; He was led to see the very throne of Satan in the hypocrisy of religious men, and in the cruelty and inhuman pride of earth's saints. But that did not touch the inward joy and peace of His faith. As He went up to Jerusalem, where alone the blood of the prophets was shed, there was a glory in His face which held His followers awed and silent (Mk 10³²⁻³⁴). It was the inward rapture of a heart that saw, beyond the darkness, light ; beyond the hatreds and crimes of men, the love of the Father turning sin to blessed account. It is true that Jesus' latest words are words of judgment. That could not but be ; for the days of Judah's visitation were hurrying by, and the truth which the hour revealed must be spoken. The shadow of Israel's rejection is over them. But peace, 'subsisting at the heart of endless agitation,' was His. It is present everywhere in His last discourse in the Upper Room (Jn 13³¹–17²⁶). A sober colouring as of even is there ; but it speaks quiet assurance of victory. 'Be of good cheer : I have overcome the world.' That is its note. Peace breathes through it, peace 'whose other names are rapture, power, clear sight, and love.' Only twice during that night was this peace greatly disturbed : in Gethsemane when He prayed, 'Father, if it be possible, let this cup pass from me' (Mt 26³⁹) ; and on the cross when the cry burst from Him, 'My God, my God, why hast thou forsaken me ?' (27⁴⁶). These are mysteries where we pass beyond mere moral questions into the theology of the sin-bearing. Could such an unique spirit pass through such an experience without striking notes too profound and strange for our conceiving? But only for a brief space rested His soul within the shadow. There was peace in His heart after Gethsemane, when Judas came, and when He stood before Caiaphas and Pilate, which made Him the Lord of all that evil night. And there was peace on the cross, that throne of love and obedience; peace before the darkness, when sympathy for others filled His heart, and He prayed for those who slew Him knowing not what they did, and comforted the repentant thief, and gave His mother into His loved disciple's care; peace after the darkness, when He surveyed His work, and seeing it finished thus in sacrificial death, commended His soul to the Father, whose will He was obeying. There is the perfection of Jesus' victory over the world. He yielded no hostages of joy or faith. He confronted the world's sin, the very darkness of evil where God seemed not to be, and He remained with inward glory crowned, His soul full of the joy and peace of the vision that He and all His lay in the bosom of the Father.

LITERATURE.—The Lives of Christ; Young, *The Christ of History*; Ullmann, *The Sinlessness of Jesus*; Channing's *Works*, vol. ii.; Bushnell, *On the Character of Jesus*; Lacordaire, *Jesus Christ*; F. W. Newman, *Phases of Faith*, with Martineau's reviews thereof, in *Essays*, vol. iii.; Martineau, *Seat of Authority in Religion*, bk. v.; Wernle, *Beginnings of Christianity*, vol. i.; J. Scott Lidgett, *The Spiritual Principle of the Atonement*, ch. vi.; Peabody, *Jesus Christ and the Christian Character*; Forrest, *The Authority of Christ*; Weinel, *Jesus im neunzehnten Jahrhundert*.   RICHARD GLAISTER.

PERFECTION (HUMAN).—Perfection is one of those 'terms which, however they may have been perverted to the purposes of fanaticism, are not only scriptural, but of too frequent occurrence in Scripture to be overlooked or passed by in silence' (Coleridge, *Aids to Reflection*, xli. c.). In the Sermon on the Mount the second grand division of the thought culminates in the command, 'Ye therefore shall be perfect, as your heavenly Father is perfect' (Mt 5⁴⁸). The verb in this sentence is a future indicative, but practically all scholars agree that it has the force of an imperative (Meyer, Holtzmann, Dods, Weiss, Votaw, etc.). As a command of our Lord, this saying clearly sets before His disciples the possibility and the necessity of their perfection in conduct and character; and it becomes of supreme importance to know what the adjective τέλειος, 'perfect,' here means. It cannot stand for absolute perfection, which is defined as 'entire freedom from defect, blemish, weakness, or liability to err or fail' (*Century Dictionary*). Such perfection is clearly incompatible with finite being. Every man must confess that he falls far short of this glory; it belongs to God alone. The NT has little to say about this absolute perfection of God. It is everywhere assumed, but the word 'perfection' does not occur in any direct statement of it anywhere. When we are told here that the Father is perfect, we know that His absolute perfection is not in view, since the Master says that men may and must attain unto a like perfection. The context must determine the meaning of the word in this command.

The first portion of the Sermon on the Mount sets forth the character of the citizens in the new Kingdom which Jesus preached (vv.³⁻¹⁶). The Beatitudes are pronounced upon those who meet the conditions for seeing God and becoming the sons of God. Since those who see God become like Him (1 Jn 3²), and the sons of God are to be like the Father who is in heaven (Mt 5⁴⁵), the character pictured in the Beatitudes is one of God-likeness (vv.³⁻¹²). The influence of such character is next

presented under the figures of the salt which preserves and the lamp which illuminates. The preserving and enlightening work of the Heavenly Father is to be manifest in the lives of His sons. Their works are to parallel His. They are to reproduce and represent Him. He is glorified in the good works of His children, because their works are like His own (vv.¹³⁻¹⁶). Like Him in character and conduct, what will be the law of their life? That question is answered in the second great division of the Sermon. It will not be any code of external regulations. The Father is governed by nothing of that sort. He is a law unto Himself. His conduct is the spontaneous outcome of His own being. Even so the life of His children will not be measured by the standard of any written code, but by the unwritten law of a heart in perfect sympathy with the will of God (vv.¹⁷⁻⁴⁸). This law of the highest and purest possible motive will preclude not only the external act of murder, but the cherishing of anger against a brother (vv.²¹⁻²⁶). It will render impossible not only adulterous acts but impure meditations (vv.²⁷⁻³²). It will render oaths unnecessary (vv.³³⁻³⁷). It will counsel the surrender of rights in the maintenance of peace (vv.³⁸⁻⁴²). It will demand the constant exercise of love towards enemies as well as friends, towards Gentiles as well as Jews, towards the just and the unjust alike (vv.⁴³⁻⁴⁸). This law of the inner life in harmony with the Father's will is in no danger of coming into conflict with any righteous system of legal regulations, and least of all with the Law of God as revealed in the OT. It will not destroy this Law, but fulfil it in a righteousness far exceeding that which any mere legalists can maintain (vv.¹⁷⁻²⁰). It will lift the life above the plane of morality into the realm of genuine religion, in which the thoughts and the affections will be as pure as the outward conduct is righteous. As all the Father's acts are the proof that His thoughts towards us are of good and of good alone, so all His children's deeds will evidence their desire for the universal good; and they will be blessed as the Father is blessed, and active for the good of all as the Father is active for the good of all, and their motives will be as single and pure as the motives of the Father Himself. In such case, said the Master, 'ye shall be perfect as your heavenly Father is perfect.' The statement is a culminating summary of all that the Master has said up to this point. The citizens of the Kingdom are to be the sons of God. The sons of God are to be like God. The children are to be like their Father in their character and their conduct and the law of their life. In love to all and in doing good to all they give the clearest and the most indubitable proof of their likeness to Him. In this their perfection consists. In this the end of their being is reached.

The root idea in the adjective τέλειος, 'perfect,' is that of τέλος, the 'end.' The perfect man is the man who has reached the end designed in his creation, the man who represents the ideal set before his own being. The Father may be said to be perfect, as completely and constantly realizing the end of His own being. God is love (1 Jn 4⁸). His providence is the continuously perfect manifestation of His love (Mt 5⁴⁵). Jesus commands His disciples to be perfect in the continuous maintenance and manifestation of the spirit of love. They must love the Lord their God with all their heart, and with all their soul, and with all their mind; and they must love their neighbour as themselves. On these two commandments hung the whole Law and the Prophets (Mt 22³⁷⁻⁴⁰). He who kept these two commandments was perfectly obedient. He met the whole requirement of loyal service. He realized the end for which he was created.

To many persons 'counsels of perfection' are synonymous with 'demands of the impossible.' A large part of the difficulty in such minds is relieved, however, when the Master's limitation to perfection in love and loving service is made. This is seen at once to be compatible with imperfections of other sorts. The child may love his father perfectly, though he be weak in body and immature in mind. Absolute perfection belongs to God, and is demanded of no one of His creatures. Perfection in love God shares with man. He asks man to love Him with undivided loyalty and affection, and to prove his love to God in the service of his fellow-man.

LITERATURE.—Channing, *The Perfect Life*; Ritschl, *Chr. Doct. of Justification*, 646; D. Steele, *Love Enthroned*; J. Mudge, *Growth in Holiness toward Perfection*; P. T. Forsyth, *Chr. Perfection*; H. C. G. Moule, *Thoughts on Chr. Sanctity*; Alvah Hovey, *The Higher Chr. Life*; O. A. Curtis, *The Chr. Faith* (1905), 371; F. W. Robertson, *Serm.* 3rd ser. 143; J. R. Illingworth, *Univ. and Cath. Serm.* 1; N. Smyth, *Chr. Ethics*, 108; G. Matheson, *Landmarks of NT Morality*, 250; J. Iverach, *The Other Side of Greatness*, 186; *Expos.* 4th ser. ix. (1894) 319, 5th ser. v. (1897) 30, 134, 211, 6th ser. iii. (1901) 73.

D. A. HAYES.

PERPLEXITY.—The word 'perplexity' (ἀπορία) occurs but once in the NT (Lk 21²⁵), in that reminiscence of Daniel which foretells the day of terrors that shall usher in the presence of the Son of Man. But the idea has remarkable associations with Christ in the Gospels. Not only is perplexity discernible in His own experience, but He was then (as now) a frequent cause of it in others. His powers, and the amazing insight of His wisdom, were a continual occasion of astonishment to the mere onlookers (Mt 13⁵⁴⁻⁵⁶, cf. Lk 4²²). To explain His exorcisms, the Pharisees were driven to the confusing theory of demoniac possession (Mt 9³⁴ ‖ 12²⁴, Mk 3²², Lk 11¹⁵). His disciples would listen to His unconventional judgments with blank perplexity. Had He not, for example, taught them the blessedness of charity, and the law of love for one's neighbour? What, then, could they make of His defence of 'this waste' of a box of precious ointment (Mt 26⁸ ‖ Jn 12⁴)? It was hard for a disciple to understand why He should resist an opportunity of helping the poor: men are slow to learn the value of a rightful surrender of our most beautiful and treasured possessions for the purpose of reverence only. Not a little of the disciples' perplexity arose from their own materialistic preconceptions. When Jesus used the language of parable or metaphor, they made no attempt to reach the deeper and more spiritual meaning—as when He spoke of the Sower (Mk 4¹³ ‖ Lk 8⁹), or of the 'leaven of the Pharisees and Sadducees' (Mt 16⁵⁻¹² ‖ Lk 12¹). Once the awful terror which is sometimes the accompaniment of perplexity seized them—when Jesus spoke with such dread certainty of the presence of one among them who was ready to give Him up, and they 'looked one on another, doubting of whom he spake' (Jn 13²²). Yet, while Christ perplexed others, especially those who knew Him least, they seemed powerless to perplex Him. Perfect obedience to the will of God in all things left no room for that flickering of faith which blurs the answer or the gospel of so many teachers. When questioners deliberately attempted to puzzle Him, He unravelled their tangles with instinctive ease (Mt 9⁵ ‖ Mk 2⁹, Lk 5²³; Mt 12⁴ ‖ Mk 2²⁶, Lk 6⁴). Sometimes in a phrase He re-tied the knot into a problem which they were unable to resolve, as when they asked by what authority He did these things (Mt 21²⁷ ‖ Mk 11²⁸, Lk 20²), or in the question of the tribute money being paid to Cæsar (Mt 22²¹ ‖ Mk 12¹⁷, Lk 20²⁵), or the casuistry of the woman with the seven husbands (Mt 22³⁰ ‖ Mk 12²⁵, Lk 20³⁵). The pain of perplexity seems to have come to Jesus only towards the end of His life on earth, and then it was more from within than from without. In those closing days the burden of His mission, and all that it would entail in the far future of the world, seemed to weigh heavily upon Him. Near at hand He felt the weakness of His disciples' loyalty, and was especially 'troubled in the spirit' about Judas (Jn 13²¹). As He looked forward into the days to come, there fell upon Him the knowledge of divisions, feuds, persecutions that would arise in His name 'to incarnadine the world.' He was face to face with the baptism of all leadership: it would be His to kindle the flaming passions of men, Prince of Peace as He is (Lk 12⁵¹). Is it any wonder that on the threshold of such a task He should be distressed, perplexed (συνέχομαι, RVm 'pained')? He is moved to hesitate: at least the temptation arises when He feels spiritual perplexity (Jn 12²⁷). And in Gethsemane the overstrained humanity utters the cry of longing for escape—'Father, if it be possible, let this cup pass away from me: nevertheless, not as I will, but as thou wilt' (Mt 26³⁹). In that last sentence He reveals to us the key of deliverance from all cankering perplexity, all that uncertainty which confuses and enervates the will. He shows the world the supremacy of a will resigned to God. It is the truism of the choice—'No man can serve two masters: . . . Ye cannot serve God and mammon' (Mt 6²⁴ ‖ Lk 16¹³). Try to serve both, and you have strife and confusion within and around: life becomes a war of irreconcilable ideals. But bend all thoughts, desires, will, towards God; learn the worth of Christ's word, 'Be not anxious' as to food, life, raiment, and the rest, 'for your heavenly Father knoweth that ye have need of these things' (Mt 6²⁵⁻³³ ‖ Lk 12²²⁻³⁶). There are no more troubled hearts and perplexed wills for those who rest in God and live in Christ (Jn 14¹), for to them the prayer, 'Thy will be done' (Mt 6¹⁰), finds its invariable answer in a sublime and heavenly peace. See also artt. AMAZEMENT, DOUBT.

EDGAR DAPLYN.

PERSECUTION.—(1) Christ foresaw that persecution would be His inevitable lot and that of His true followers. Repeatedly He foretold the main incidents of His Passion (Mt 16²¹ 17²². ²³ 20¹⁸. ¹⁹ 26², Mk 8³¹ 9³¹ 10³²⁻³⁴). (2) Christ also forewarned His disciples that they too must suffer persecution (Mt 24⁹, Mk 4¹⁷ 10³⁰, Lk 11⁴⁹ 21¹². ¹⁶, Jn 16²⁻⁴. ³³). (3) Persecution was the test of true discipleship. It was mentioned in the parable of the Sower as the cause of defection among superficial believers (Mk 4¹⁷, Mt 13²¹). (4) It was the sure means of gaining a blessing, and as such is particularly referred to in the Beatitudes (Mt 5¹⁰⁻¹²).

The methods of persecution adopted against Christ and His immediate followers were such as contempt and disparagement (Jn 8⁴⁸); ascription of Christ's miracles to the power of the Evil One (Mt 12²⁴); expulsion of those believing on Him from the synagogue (Jn 9²². ³⁴); attempts to entrap Him in His words (Mt 22¹⁵, Jn 8⁶); questioning His authority (Mk 11²⁸, Mt 21²³); (after the failure of the former) illegal arrest and the heaping of every kind of insult upon the Prisoner, who was entitled to protection from the authorities until the authorized penalty was laid upon Him (Mt 26⁶⁷ff. and parallels). See also art. NAME, p. 217ᵇ.

It was the fear of persecution that drove the disciples to forsake their Master at the hour of His arrest (Mt 26⁵⁶ and parallels).

C. H. PRICHARD.

PERSON OF CHRIST.—See DIVINITY, HUMANITY, INCARNATION, SON OF GOD, SON OF MAN, etc.

PERSONAL APPEARANCE.—See CHRIST IN ART, vol. i. p. 314 f.

PERSONALITY.—1. **Definition and analysis.**—Personality is the substance and summary of a man's qualities, or rather it is the man himself, discovered in the last analysis and in the highest category of being short of God. Indeed, 'complete personality can be in God only, while to man can belong but a weak and faint copy thereof' (Lotze, *Outlines*, p. 72). The truth is that through the limitations of bodily existence there are mental and moral workings which do not at once cross the threshold of consciousness, but may at any time surprise the soul, as in the flash of genius or the turn of conversion. But personality implies a grip of these things as our own. We know that we exist when self is revealed to us over against the world. There the self-conscious life begins. But it is not until God is revealed over against both self and the world that personality is fully exercised. The recognition of a moral authority is the touchstone of the self-determined life. Thus, for popular purposes, personality may be expressed in terms of character. 'It is made up,' says F. W. Robertson, 'of three attributes—consciousness, character, and will.' In other words, it is the power of self-assertion on lines of character. But, philosophically speaking, the two chief factors in personality, in so far as it can be analyzed, are self-consciousness and self-determination, the contents of which it will be necessary to examine. Put briefly, self-consciousness is the soul's utterance 'I am'; self-determination is the soul's assertion 'I will.'

(1) *Self-consciousness* is the soul's utterance 'I am.' (*a*) I am myself and nobody else (cf. Jn 9[9] ἐγώ εἰμι). Almost the first sense of personality is that it speaks from behind closed doors. It can look out on others, but they cannot enter uninvited to share its life. This point is brought out in Holman Hunt's famous picture 'The Light of the World,' in which the door has no handle outside. 'Each self is a unique existence, which is perfectly impervious to other selves—impervious in a fashion of which the impenetrability of matter is a faint analogue' (Seth, *Hegelianism and Personality*, p. 216). (*b*) I am myself amid the varied functions of my being. Spinoza based personality on the intellect, Schleiermacher on the feeling, Schopenhauer on the will. But personality subtly underlies thinking, feeling, and willing. They are only modes of the soul's self-expression. They are unified in the intuition 'I am.' In Jn 6[20] there is an illustrative use of ἐγώ εἰμι, when Jesus assured the disciples of His personal identity behind an unfamiliar appearance. (*c*) I am myself in a continuity of experience. In all movement of time and change of circumstances the soul still knows itself as the same. We cannot get rid of our own past; it is with us still. And no sceptical philosophy can dissolve this elemental fact. There is a corresponding sense of ἐγώ εἰμι in Jn 8[58], where Jesus says, 'Before Abraham was, I am,' and reveals the wonderful secret of His self-consciousness.—These modes of the soul's utterance 'I am' enter into the basis of our understanding, on which is erected that faculty of the soul called reason, by which we cognize and construe the world. But the soul must be considered not only in this static, but also in its dynamic aspect, in its—

(2) *Self-determination*, which is the soul's assertion 'I will.' The soul selects and pursues its own ends at the bidding of its own desires. It has music of its own to beat out, by appreciating and appropriating objects in its own environment. The whole range of enjoyment in the pursuit of happiness on the one hand, and of endurance in the path of duty on the other, rests on the use of this power of self-determination. But that which moralizes the human will is that it responds to two voices—(*a*) 'I can.' The sense of liberty therein expressed is an essential element of per-

sonality, and through the intuition of the soul it has held its own as an assertion of free will in spite of the affirmations of reason respecting the will of God (in theology) or the laws of nature (in science). Our moral sense is strictly bound up with this assertion of the soul, without which there can be neither merit, nor blame, nor any accountability. It is this which binds up our being with that of God.

> 'So near is glory to our dust,
>   So nigh is God to man,
> When Duty whispers low, "Thou must,"
>   The youth replies, "I can."' (Emerson).

(*b*) 'I must.' Not, however, until 'I will' is consummated in 'I must' is the height of personality reached, for its liberty of will is given for the sake of its voluntary obedience. When the personality has found its master, its resources are all enlisted on the side of self-determination, especially when for love's sake we lose ourselves. In other words, the highest outgoing and incoming of personality in self-determination is in the exercise of love.

> 'Love took up the harp of Life, and smote on all the chords
>   with might,
>   Smote the chord of Self, that, trembling, passed in music
>   out of sight.'

2. Christ's influence on the conception of personality.

—The full extension of the possibilities of personality is due to Jesus Christ. He opened up new vistas for the soul's self-consciousness by revealing the inherent but hitherto hidden natures of God, the world, and the soul, whereby the value of the personality has been infinitely enhanced; and higher ways for the soul's self-determination by bringing the gift of the Holy Spirit, in the strength of which the soul overcomes the world, submits to God, and thus realizes itself. This is what the world was waiting for. Prof. Bigg (*The Church and Roman Empire*) shows that the Eastern religions of Isis and Mithras were being welcomed because by their virtual monotheism and their proffer of peace and happiness they seemed to meet the needs of the newly discovered personality. Christ did this completely. He supplied the key of knowledge to self-consciousness and the nerve of power to self-determination. Henceforth the soul is a possibility to be realized through knowledge in obedience. These are the two factors of faith, for 'faith is at once a vision and an allegiance' (Hort). Prior to Christ, and still apart from Him, the conception of the world has largely absorbed both the notion of God (in Polytheism, Pantheism, and Fatalism), and that of the soul (in Naturalism and Materialism). But through Christ, God and man draw out apart from the world, apart from each other too (sin being the 'sunderer'); and yet more truly close to each other, under the common conception of personality in which both share as distinguished from the world. Illingworth has put the whole point finely at the end of his 5th Bampton Lecture: 'As reason qualifies and conditions our whole animal nature by its presence, so that we are never merely animals, spirituality also permeates and modifies all that we call our natural faculties; and our personality itself is, in this sense, as truly supernatural as the Divine Person in whom alone it finds its home.'

> 'God . . . soul . . . the only facts for me.
> Prove them facts? That they o'erpass my power of proving
> Proves them such.' (R. Browning, *La Saisiaz*).

Through Christ man has learned to read God and himself as being gathered under the same categories, perfect and infinite in the one, derivative and fettered in the other. But that is only the intellectual aspect of what we owe Him. And, as Martensen has said (*Dogmatics*, p. 154), 'No intellectual creation can ever be perfected by dint of a mere psychological possibility; it must first be fructified and awakened by a higher inspiration.' Christ has shown us the way to the consummation of our personality in the voluntary and glad surrender to God and in fellowship with Him through the Holy Spirit (1 Jn 1³), so that we learn to say—

> 'Our wills are ours, we know not how :
> Our wills are ours to make them Thine.'

There is such an utter absence of the language of the schools in the speech of Christ, that one might be tempted to think that He made no contribution to the subject of personality. And it is true He was no philosopher in the accepted sense of the term. But He gave philosophy a new world to discover. He roused and satisfied experiences of the soul which at length called into being a new terminology. The fact that the analysis of personality first went to the depths in Paul's Epistles, argues that the first perfect exposition of personality was in Paul's Master. For a thing must be before it is thought upon. Where even Plato and Aristotle had groped blindly because they had no true conception of personality, Christ moved with perfect assurance. What was hidden from them, 'the wise and prudent,' was all in all to Him. It might truly be said that personality is the pivot of the gospel. 'The gospel was in the highest and most perfect sense a personal religion' (Bousset, *Jesus*, p. 164). It does not move in the regions of mere intellect or will or feeling, nor even in the field of their joint exercise. It moves throughout in the region of the man himself, in his self-consciousness and self-determination, and finds its highest expression in the Divine passion for the soul and the human hunger for God. Christ did not coin terms, and yet there is what may be called with Rothe, a 'language of the Holy Ghost.' His psychological expressions do not travel beyond the accepted antitheses of soul and body, flesh and spirit, using the first to express simply the two elements in man's nature (Mt 10²⁸), and the second to emphasize their distinction in origin (Jn 3⁶) and divergence in character (Mk 14³⁸). Indeed, Jesus did not make use of the psychology available in His own day, *e.g.* μακάριος οὗ οὐ κατέγνω ἡ ψυχὴ αὐτοῦ (Sir 14²), which is a plain reference to conscience.

Although the word 'spirit' (πνεῦμα) is reserved in the Gospels chiefly for super- or sub-human agencies, it is also used indifferently as a synonym for ψυχή or 'soul,' to express the region of the inner life where the feelings especially have full play. In fourteen instances of such a kind, πνεῦμα occurs seven times (five times in reference to Jesus), and ψυχή also seven times (in reference to Jesus only twice). (With Paul, however, these two words fall apart in psychological connotation). The favourite word of the Evangelists, and presumably of Jesus Himself, is καρδία, which is not only the region of the feelings, but the seat of the will (θέλημα) and of the thoughts (διαλογισμοί). In fact, throughout the Bible it means the organ of the personality (cf. Hastings' *DB*, art. 'Psychology'). It is, by the way, suggestive of the moral emphasis of Christ's teaching that He never uses νοῦς, διάνοια, σύνεσις or their correlatives. But, while Jesus employed terms simply in their popular connotation, He sometimes transfused them with His own transcendental conceptions, and then they stand in excess of light. Thus, 'If thine *eye* be single, thy whole *body* shall be full of light' (Mt 6²²); 'Whosoever will save his *life* (ψυχή) shall lose it' (16²⁵); 'Blessed are your *eyes*, for they see' (13¹⁶); 'The things that proceed out of a *man* defile him' (Mk 7²⁰); 'He that believeth on me, out of his *belly* (κοιλία) shall flow rivers of living water' (Jn 7³⁸).

But Christ's exposition of personality was not vocal, but vital. It was essentially the realm in which He lived, moved, and had His being : it was the true life to which He invited the careworn and heavy laden, and those who were entangled in their material and worldly environment. Secure in the possession of His own personality, His self-consciousness being at one with God, His self-determination being merged in the will of God, He could affirm, 'The prince of this world cometh, and hath nothing in me' (Jn 14³⁰); 'I am in the Father and the Father in me' (14¹⁰); 'I do always the things that please him' (8²⁹). That personality

is the pivot of the gospel which Jesus lived and taught may be illustrated in detail.

(1) The personal *temptation* of Jesus is given as the record of a unique struggle within the chambers of personality. It was associated with that enhancing of His self-consciousness which was represented by the descent of the Spirit as that of a dove, and the hearing of a voice, 'Thou art my beloved Son' (Mk 1¹⁰). The *first* temptation was overcome by His affirmation that the soul is infinitely more precious than the natural life, and that there is eternal provision for it in communion with the Father (Mt 4⁴). As Christ said afterwards to His disciples, 'I have food to eat that ye know not of' (Jn 4³²). The *second* temptation was resisted on the ground that man has the responsibility of cherishing his life and using it wisely, as the vehicle of a God-given personality. To depend on the aid of angels would be an act of presumption (Mt 4⁶ᶠ·). God has chosen that they should minister only when personality has achieved its proper work (Mk 1¹³), or before personality is permitted to begin it (Mt 18¹⁰). A true man scorns the aid of impersonal forces when affairs of the soul are at stake (26⁵³). The *third* temptation was met in the confidence that personality is of itself worth more than all the world. It may subject itself only to God (4¹⁰), by whose gentleness it is made great ; for it is meant to be king of all, but not through the acknowledgment of Satan (cf. 1 Co 3²³). So Jesus taught elsewhere, 'What shall it profit a man if he shall gain the whole world and lose his own soul?'; but 'The meek shall inherit the earth' (Mk 8³⁶, Mt 5⁵).

(2) The public *teaching* of Christ never moved far from the personal character of true religion. (*a*) The *Kingdom of heaven* is essentially the realm of personality. It thus calls for no less an analogy than a new birth, and the breath of the Spirit (Jn 3⁷·⁸). Its boundaries are specifically in character, for it is inherited by such as are poor in spirit, pure in heart, and peaceable in will (Mt 5³·⁸·⁹), and those who revert to the attitude of children (18³). Deeds of themselves, however zealously performed, are outside this realm (7²²ᶠ·), for a house may be swept and garnished, yet vacant for evil spirits (12⁴⁴). But even our words will witness against us, for out of the abundance of the heart the mouth speaketh (12³⁵). The approach of this Kingdom, therefore, is a call to repentance (Mk 1¹⁵) : its entry involves the 'binding of the strong man' (Mt 12²⁹); and its extension needs such a personal influence as the word or the gospel incorporated in the lives of the disciples (5¹³ᶠ·). (*b*) The *inner righteousness* is only another way of stating that in true religion the personality must come to its own, as the character of fruit is fixed by the tree on which it grows (7¹⁷). Nothing done by rote or for show is worthy of the soul's approach to its God (6¹⁻⁸). The only genuine worship is in spirit and in truth (Jn 4²³), in the consciousness that the best things may be asked for from a Father (Mt 7¹¹), who in turn expects the inward attitude of a believing (6³¹), lowly (Lk 18¹⁴), and forgiving heart (Mt 6¹⁵). The only defiling thing in life is the effluence of a man's personality (Mk 7²⁰). The only unforgivable sin is the sin against the Holy Ghost, which is essentially a sin against one's own personality (Mt 12³¹). And behind Christ's teaching were His miracles of mercy, which were sacramental of this rescue of personality from its fetters (Mk 2⁵ᶠᶠ·, Lk 13¹⁶). In short, with Christ, religion is positive because it is spiritual. Saintliness is not by contraction, but by expansion. Keeping the Law is acting the Good Samaritan. In a word, religion is raised to personality-power.

(3) The private *training* of Christ was always and

wholly exerted on the personality of His disciples. He left behind Him no documents, nor any organization, only men who knew whom they believed (2 Ti 1¹²). He was satisfied, therefore, that they should be with Him (Mk 3¹⁴), sure that afterwards they would become 'fishers of men' (Mt 4¹⁹), 'lambs in the midst of wolves' (Lk 10³), all because of His influence on their character. They had nothing else to carry with them but the secret of this wonderful change (Mt 10⁷ᶠᶠ·). This change was due to something deeper than even the personal magnetism of Jesus. It was due to a revelation at the core of a man's nature (16¹⁷ᶠ·), by an organ of personality undiscovered by the wise (11²⁵), and unappreciated by the rich (19²³). The Church rests on the confession of a convinced personality (16¹⁸), in whom it has pleased God to reveal His Son (16¹⁷, cf. Gal 1¹⁵ᶠ·). And this revelation provides the clue to spiritual truth and the criterion of religious authority (Mt 10³⁴ᶠ· 23⁹, Jn 8³¹ᶠ·, cf. 1 Co 3²¹⁻²³, 1 Jn 2²⁷) [cf. art. AUTHORITY IN RELIGION (iii.)]. It is worth while for a disciple to 'lose his life' in order to gain the hidden life of his true personality (Mt 16²⁵); and if he finds stumbling-blocks to this in his nature, he must act with surgical severity (18⁸·⁹).

On the other hand, there is an infinite range to the possibilities of personality clear to the mind of Jesus, but hardly fathomable to ourselves, as where He says that to receive a disciple is to receive One who is greater than he (10⁴⁰), and the service even of the helpless and forlorn is done to Himself (25⁴⁰, cf. 26¹¹). (Is it on this account that 'the least in the kingdom of heaven' is greater than John the great individualist?) Another great saying which suggests that we are more than ourselves through Christ, is, 'Where two or three are gathered together in my name, there am I in the midst of them' (18²⁰); and yet one more, 'Lo, I am with you all the days' (28²⁰). In such utterances, which give ample support to Pauline and Johannine mysticism, Christ at least suggests that personality, when once released, is not bounded by the limits of the individual, but is only fulfilled when lost in union with Himself, as the Spirit of all Love. In the words of Dr. Moberly (Atonement and Personality, p. 254), 'Personality is the possibility of mirroring God, the faculty of being a living reflexion of the very attributes and character of the Most High.' But for the final expression of this profound truth we turn to the words of our Saviour in His intercessory prayer: 'I in them, and thou in me, that they may be perfected into one (εἰς ἕν) . . . that the love wherewith thou lovedst me may be in them, and I in them' (Jn 17²³·²⁶).

3. New factors introduced by Christ.—The way in which He directly met the needs of personality was twofold—by a revelation and a reinforcement. (1) To man's *self-consciousness* He revealed God as our Father, with the full illumination of man's worth, hope, and destiny which this truth brings. (2) To man's *self-determination* He brought the gift of the Holy Spirit, as a power in aid (παράκλητος) of the fettered personality. The essential conjunction, in the view of the early Church, of these two elements of redemption, which are ours through Christ, is well illustrated in the variant of St. Luke's recension of the Lord's Prayer. After the acknowledgment of the Fatherhood stands the petition, 'Thy Holy Spirit come upon us and cleanse us.'

(1) Jesus made the soul aware of its high origin and destiny, for the acceptance of *the Fatherhood of God* clears a path through Time and through Eternity. The issues of life become of supreme account to those who believe in One who lives and loves, watches and listens, provides and controls,

and will at length either welcome or reject. There is a place for the least, the last and the lost. The angels of the little ones, who have achieved nothing and possess nothing, are before the face of the Father (Mt 18¹⁰). Though uncounted in a nation (Lk 19⁹), though unvalued by society (7⁴⁷), though classed with publicans and sinners (15¹), a man is counted among the Father's children, and valued in the Father's heart (Mt 12⁹ᶠ·, Lk 15²⁰ᶠ·). 'It is not the will of your Father in heaven that one of these little ones should perish.' But the greatest hindrance to the full emergence of personality is not so much the lack of outward respect as the loss of self-respect through sin. Self-consciousness becomes thereby a conscience of slavery, of impotence (Ro 7, esp. vv.⁷⁻¹¹). When St. Paul speaks of having been once 'alive apart from the law' (v.⁹), he means a non-moral existence, before true self-consciousness was born. In the words of Schleiermacher, 'The sinner prior to conversion is overlooked, and is not in this respect a person at all in the eyes of God. He is a particle of the mass, out of which the continued operation of the same creative act of God which gave us the Redeemer does, through Him, call him into personality' (A. Vaughan, *Works*, vol. i. p. 87; cf. Aug. *de Pecc. Or.* 36). The process in the experience of many is a painful one. And although for others it is gradual and apparently natural, there does not seem to be much footing in the NT for those whom F. W. Newman designated as the 'once-born' (cf. James, *Varieties of Religious Experience*, p. 80 and Lect. 3 and 4).

'Thus conscience does make cowards of us all;
And thus the native hue of resolution
Is sicklied o'er with the pale cast of thought.'

The tying to a dead past cramps the soul's activities. 'Now was I sorry' (says Bunyan in *Grace Abounding*, 87, 88) 'that God had made me a man, for I feared I was a reprobate. . . . Yea, I thought it impossible that ever I should attain to such goodness of heart, as to thank God that He had made me a man.' Yet, as St. Paul implies in the above reference, this humiliation is the way to the heights of self-consciousness, for 'guilt is the awful guardian of our personal identity' (Illingworth). Simon Peter only half knew himself when he cried to Christ, 'Depart from me: for I am a sinful man, O Lord' (Lk 5⁸). The lost son did not 'come to himself' fully until he was at home with his father, reconciled. Here we come upon the great doctrine of Justification (wh. see), which is St. Paul's interpretation of the Father's forgiveness in forensic terms. In the experience of the justified man, the 'conscience of sins' is transmuted into a consciousness of 'peace with God through our Lord Jesus Christ' (Ro 5¹). 'Actually and in fact Justification is only accomplished by an act of human freedom, an act of the deepest self-consciousness in man, appropriating the redeeming love of the Son of God by the power of awakening and life-giving grace' (Martensen, *Dogmatics*, p. 391).

Starting from this point, the revelation of God as Father is the means of the enlargement of our personality in three ways, through (a) His forgiveness of us, (b) our imitation of Him, (c) the communion between Him and us.

(a) *God's forgiveness*, gratefully received, is the first stage of man's moral freedom. It must always be a factor in our filial consciousness, but at first it may be said to be the only, or at least the chief one. Thus it was the message in which Christ first expressed the meaning of the Fatherhood (Mk 2⁵), and which He ever delighted to bring to the children who felt themselves farthest from home (Lk 15⁴·³²). Their repentance made joy in heaven (15⁷), while the Divine forgiveness woke love in their hearts (7⁴⁷). For it is the spiritual release that goes to the root of our being, and sets free the wholesome springs of goodness, long sealed and ignored (18¹⁴ 19⁸). But forgiveness was more than a 'word of grace': it was a gain for the world at the cost of Calvary (Mt 26²⁸). And that cost was ultimately met out of the treasuries of the Father's heart, 'who so loved the world that he gave his only-begotten Son' (Jn 3¹⁶, cf. Ro 8³²). Forgiveness in the name of Christ is thus the measure of the estimate in which our personality is held in the sight of God.

(b) *Our imitation of God.*—Sonship, being ours potentially through forgiveness, becomes ours actually through imitation. If one may venture to say so, without seeming to undervalue the continuity of grace, in forgiveness God pays our debts, in order that in imitation we may pay our way. We are 'made nigh' (Eph 2[13]), that we may grow like our Father who is in heaven. Having 'received the adoption of sons' (Ro 8[15], Gal 4[5]), we are to become 'imitators of God as dear children' (Eph 5[1]). 'Even as God (or the Lord) forgave you, so also do ye' (Col 3[13]). For the standard of our new nature is nothing less than κατὰ θεόν (Eph 4[24]). This connexion of thought is as clear in John as in Paul. 'Herein is love . . . that God loved us, and sent his Son. . . . Beloved, if God so loved us, we ought to love one another . . . because as he is, even so are we in this world' (1 Jn 4[10. 11. 17]). These words point to their original in the teaching of Christ, who bade us give 'mind, heart, will, and strength' to this holy task (Mt 22[37]). To 'be perfect, as our Father in heaven is perfect' (5[48]), to forgive as He forgives (6[12] 18[35]), to make peace and love our enemies that we may prove ourselves His sons (5[9. 45]), is the Christian standard of conduct, and the final challenge to our personality.

(c) *Communion between God and man.*—If personality finds its release in the forgiveness, its scope in the imitation, of God, it finds its fulfilment in communion with Him. 'Religion is nothing if it is not the vital act by which the whole spirit seeks to save itself by attaching itself to its principle. This act is prayer' (Sabatier, *Philosophy of Religion*, p. 28). But prayer, to be real and effectual, must rest on faith in the Father revealed by Jesus Christ. 'He who makes prayer simply a way to reach God "invents a god for himself, and one that does not hear." . . . There can be no true worship unless we come through Christ into the relation of children towards God' (Luther, quoted by Herrmann, *Communion with God*, p. 244). This is the prayer that is surely answered by God (Lk 11[9-13], Jn 15[7]), the worship that is in spirit and in truth, which He Himself both inspires and seeks after (Jn 4[23. 24], Ro 8[26. 27]). This is praying after the manner of the Lord's Prayer, when 'the storm of desire dies away into stillness before God.' Yet 'whatever really so burdens the soul as to threaten its peace is to be brought before God in prayer, with the confidence that the Father's love understands even our anxious clinging to earthly things' (Herrmann, p. 247). There is no higher employment of the powers of personality than real (Mt 6[5. 6]), believing (Mk 11[24]), consecrated (Jn 14[13]), persistent (Lk 18[1]) prayer, from a forgiving heart (Mk 11[25]), when it throws itself without reserve upon the loving will of the Father (Mt 26[39. 42]). Such prayer is far more than an act : it invests all the outgoings and incomings of life with the sacred sense that the Father is 'over all, through all, and in all' (Eph 4[6]). Thus prayer has 'a natural effect in spiritualizing and elevating the soul. A man is no longer what he was before. Gradually—imperceptibly to himself—he has imbibed a new set of ideas, and become imbued with fresh principles. He is as one coming from kings' courts, with a grace, a delicacy, a dignity, a propriety, a justness of thought and taste, a clearness and firmness of principle, all his own' (J. H. Newman). Resting on life eternal as a principle, a man cannot sink into being the mere plaything of events, a puppet in his environment. Christ has invited him to ascend a higher storey of his being, whence he can see the hosts of God beyond the encircling enemy. 'Heaven lies about us in our infancy.' And the fulfilment of that truth is when the saint, with the heart of a little child, endures as seeing Him who is invisible.

On these three steps of heightened self-conscious-ness — forgiveness, imitation, and communion — stands the temple of immortality for the soul.

(2) Jesus made the soul capable of attaining its high destiny (in correspondence with its Divine origin) by *the gift of the Holy Spirit.* This was the one great object of His saving ministry besides revealing the Father. It is not that there was no Holy Spirit except for the ministry of Jesus Christ. The Holy Spirit, we must believe, was as truly at the centre and circumference of the universe as the Father Himself. But none the less, for the purposes of human personality, the Fatherhood and Spirit of God were alike the creation of Jesus Christ. On these twin pillars His Kingdom of the redeemed is founded ; Justification being the result of the Father's relation to personality, and Sanctification being the effect of the Spirit's influence on personality : both being secured through faith in the Lord Jesus Christ. It were of little use to heighten the soul's self - consciousness without increasing its powers of self-determination. The knowledge that God is our Father, with all it implies, must be completed by our receiving the 'spirit of adoption' whereby we cry 'Abba, Father' (Ro 8[15]), and the 'power to become sons of God' (Jn 1[12]). The connexion between this Spirit of God and our spirits is too subtle for our analysis. 'In the ephemeral and empirical Me, there is a mysterious Guest, greater than the Me, and to which the Me instinctively addresses its prayer and its trust' (Sabatier, *Religions of Authority*, p. 318). But there can be no doubt (and this is the meaning of Ro 8) that the result is an enhancing of the soul's power to realize itself in respect of character which is the real realm of personality. In other words, the Holy Spirit is pre-eminently the mainspring of the life inspired by Christ (*vis vicaria*, Tertullian), not, however, as substitute for the will, but as its partner and prompter (cf. Gal 2[20] with 5[25], and Eph 3[16] with v. [17]). 'The Spirit and faith,' says Dr. Denney (art. HOLY SPIRIT in vol. i. p. 738[b]), 'are correlative terms, and each of them covers from a different point of view all that is meant by Christianity. Regarded from the side of God and His grace and power in initiating and maintaining it, Christianity is the Spirit ; regarded from the side of man and his action and responsibility in relation to God, it is faith.' The bearing of the Spirit on man's self-determination (*i.e.* as a moral motive) may be viewed in two aspects.

(a) There is the *entrance* of the Spirit, which is sometimes called simply a gift (Lk 11[13]), but also 'a new birth' (Jn 3[3ff.]), because its origin is behind the will of man (1[13]), and a 'baptism' (Mk 1[8]), because its outcome is in the will of man, in his personal dedication (cf. Ph 2[12]).

'My heart was full ; I made no vows, but vows
 Were then made for me ; bond unknown to me
 Was given, that I should be, else sinning greatly,
 A dedicated Spirit' (Wordsworth, *The Prelude*, iv. 334 ff.).

And cf. Paracelsus :—

'As He spoke, I was endued
 With comprehension and a steadfast will ;
 And when He ceased, my brow was sealed His own.'

In any case, it brings the power of the Highest (δύναμις ὑψίστου, Lk 1[35]) to those who have high work to do. Christ began His public ministry (4[14]) in the power of the Spirit, who first brooded over Him and then drove Him forth (Mk 1[10. 12]). The Spirit also endowed the behaviour and bearing of Jesus with its unique characteristics (Mt 12[17ff.]). But this belongs more properly to the section below. The most critical act of the soul's self-determination is known as conversion, which is the final acceptance of the will and love of God as

revealed in Jesus Christ, so that the motives stored
in the gospel become henceforth dominant partners
in the life of the soul. 'In conversion' (says Starbuck, quoted in James, *Religious Experience*,
p. 210) 'a person must relax, *i.e.* must fall back on
the larger power that makes for righteousness,
which has been welling up in his own being, and
let it finish in its own way the work it has begun.'
This is the true leverage of all moral possibilities ;
and it is due to the entering of the Spirit, which has
its own heavenly ways (cf. Lk 9^{55} AV), and releases
the soul from the encumbrance of habit and the
tyranny of desire. The entrance of the Spirit
thus brings the release of the personality. 'The
unseen region is not merely the ideal, for it produces effects in this world. When we commune
with it, work is actually done upon our finite personality, for we are turned into a new man, and
consequences in the way of conduct follow in the
natural world upon our regenerative change'
(Professor James, *op. cit.* p. 516).

(*b*) The *indwelling* of the Spirit is the consummation of the Christian faith, its distinctive feature
and peculiar power (Lk 11^{13} 24^{49}, Jn 7^{38} 14^{16} 20^{22}, cf.
Ac 11$^{15-18}$ 19$^{1-6}$, Ro 8^{2}, 2 Co 3, Gal 5$^{16ff.}$). The human
problem is stated in a famous chapter (Ro 7) by
Paul, in a memorable sentence by Christ (Mk 14^{38}).
Without the higher inspiration the mind becomes
carnal instead of the body being consecrated.
Christ Himself suffered from no division in His
nature (cf. Harnack, *What is Christianity?* p. 32 f.),
because He was filled with the Spirit (Lk 4^{1}) : the
Prince of this world had nothing in *Him* (Jn 14^{30}).
And this is the *summum bonum* to which He invites His disciples : 'Peace I leave with you, my
peace I give unto you' (v.^{27}). It resolves the
antinomies of flesh and spirit, body and soul,
whereby the self-determination of man is tested,
enabling us to believe, and live by the truth, that
our bodies are 'temples of the Holy Ghost' which
is in us, which we have from God (1 Co 6^{19}) ; or,
using the original analogy of Christ, that we are
branches of the true Vine, into which, and through
which, the sap of His ever-living word is to flow,
producing fruit to the glory of God (Jn 15$^{1-8}$). The
fruitfulness of life in character, which is the crown
of personality, depends in short on the partnership of our personality with the Paraclete, whose
dominion brings us liberty from the Law, as the
obverse of our obedience to Love (Ro 8^{15} cf. v.^{9},
Gal 5$^{22. 23}$ cf. v.$^{16. 18}$, 2 P 1^{8} cf. v.^{4}). All this is the
process of sanctification. 'If it has come to pass
that the saints of the New Covenant have a higher
idea of holiness, have walked by a more perfect
rule, have shown forth a more excellent and lovely
character, these are the fruits of the blessed Spirit'
(Dean Church, *Village Sermons*, p. 121).

The manifestation of this spiritual fact was at
Pentecost (Ac 2), and it presupposed two prior
events—the advent of Jesus, and His ascension.
And the meaning of these three events for man's
self-determination lies here.

(i.) The Spirit as revealed in the earthly life of
Jesus was the unique illustration of a Personality
moving only in the direction of truth, holiness, and
love, and yet on the lines of human nature. And this
was manifestly due to the unhindered operation of
the personal Spirit of God. Henceforth the association between Christ and the Spirit is so close for
us, that we may say that the Spirit *is* Christ interpreted in terms of our experience ; even as the
Father is Christ read into the Eternal. To use
the fine analogy of Martineau (*Essays*, iii. 1, p. 50),
'If it has pleased God, the Creator, to fit up one
system with one sun, to make the daylight of
several worlds, so may it fitly have pleased God,
the Revealer, to kindle amid the elliptic of history
One Divine Soul to glorify whatever lies within

the great year of His moral Providence, and represent the Father of Lights.' Only we must go on
to say that, in the name of God the Redeemer,
Jesus represents the sunshine as well ; for it is
through Him the Holy Spirit is mediated to us.
'The truth is' (as against Beyschlag, vol. i. p. 279),
'not that the Spirit is identical with Christ, but
that it was from the first so entirely the principle
of His personality, and He was throughout so
completely one with it in His Divine humanity,
that He became its perfect organ and expression,
not merely in a temporal and impersonal sense, but
in a personal and abiding sense. . . . The Holy
Spirit as it comes to us in Christianity, therefore,
includes the personal presence of Christ' (Walker,
Spirit and Incarnation, p. 85).

(ii.) But it is equally true that the earthly life
of Jesus had to be superseded if it was to have its
full effect on man's personality. On the one hand,
He Himself said, 'I, if I be lifted up from the
earth, will draw all men unto me' (Jn 12^{32}) ; and,
on the other hand, the response came from the
experience of an Apostle : 'Even though we have
known Christ after the flesh, yet now we know
him so no more' (2 Co 5^{16}). 'If any one have not
the Spirit of Christ, he is none of his' (Ro 8^{9}).
Faith is more than an outlook ; it is also an up-
look and an inlook. The Christ of history must
become the Christ of experience. Just as the
painter passes from the stage of imitation to
origination before he becomes an artist, so a
Christian is one who, looking away to Christ,
loses himself in Him, and so finds himself again
as a new creation (2 Co 5^{17} ; cf. Mk 8^{35}). Thus 'the
Lord is the Spirit.' Christ in whose face was the
glory of God becomes 'Christ in us the hope of
glory' (2 Co 4^{6}, Col 1^{27}). 'He that descended is
the same also that ascended up far above all
heavens, that he might fill all things' (Eph 4^{10}).

(iii.) The significance of Pentecost is, in brief,
that Christ is now to be made known to the world
through 'living epistles, known and read of all
men, written by the Holy Spirit on the fleshy
tables of the heart,' *i.e.* in the promptings of
conscience and compassion, which prove the working of the Spirit of Christ (2 Co 3$^{2. 3}$). In other
words, the honour of Christ's name and the success of His cause are thrown upon the personality
He has evoked,—that personality which in partnership with the Spirit of God, and in union with
fellow-Christians, is to do even greater things than
Christ in His earthly life could accomplish. And
who is sufficient for these things? But we have
the mind of Christ and the ministry of the Spirit
(1 Co 2^{16}, 2 Co 2^{16} 3^{6}).

4. The redeemed personality.—For the redeemed personality, Justification is its liberty ;
Sanctification its law. These great words were
invented to express personality at its highest, and
in its fulfilment, from the point of view of self-
consciousness and self-determination respectively.
It may fairly be said that this redeemed personality has been the keynote of Christendom, the
secret of its history, the source of its progress—
often misleading and misled, but having the power
of an endless life. This sketch of the subject may
be completed by a few suggestions as to the
significance of the redeemed personality for the
history of Christendom. It has caused man (1)
to stand for his rights and liberties, (2) to recognize his debts and duties.

(1) *The rights and liberties of the soul.*—Modern
history is the steady unfolding of the powers of
the personality in answer to the challenge of
the civilization by which it is surrounded. The
world is so much with us through facilities of
knowledge, communication, and enjoyment, that
the inner life of the soul would have little chance

indeed were it not continually replenished in spirit and in truth. But because personality is conscious of its eternal environment, it can 'endure as seeing him who is invisible,' and must assert itself in the name of its Creator and Redeemer. Steadily it has been rising to the height of its possibilities against the weight of an accumulating tradition and venerable institutions, in the belief that the word of God comes most directly to this world through its dedicated personalities. That 'word' has always breathed Justice as the social, and Liberty as the personal ideal. And reformers have always found their inspiration for the former in the OT, for the latter in the NT. Constitutional history could not be explained but for the continual inflow of these principles upon the consciences of the people from their springs in the Christian faith. We cannot fail to observe that the action of the Christian conscience through the leaders of the Church had much to do with the Magna Charta. The uprising from the condition of villenage in the 14th cent. was vitally connected with the Lollard movement and the distribution of the Bible in the English tongue. The Peasants' Wars in Germany which followed, and the national movements in all the northern countries of Europe, found the secret of their power in the recovered gospel. It is the testimony of all who know, that the rights of the Christian man were the first objective of our own Puritan Revolution. Said Pym, its typical exponent : 'The greatest liberty of our country is religion.' The American Commonwealth was founded, as to its true nucleus, in the passion for 'freedom to worship God.' And although the French Revolution triumphed in an 'age of reason,' in defiance of Church and creed, its passionate hope was derived from the Christian conception of the rights of man which had certainly drifted into the mind of Voltaire.

Finally, in religion itself personality has played its true part only under the ægis of Jesus Christ. In Mohammedanism the political and social bonds are drawn very closely, and its military associations have tended to promote the type of the devoted soldier (Moslems)—'Theirs not to reason why, theirs but to do and die.' Under such a form of religion personality has little chance. The Hindu philosophy which underlies Buddhism regards personality as the chief seat of evil in the universe, and works towards its obliteration. Socially, this philosophy results in the caste system, which is well calculated to this end. The religion, if so it may be called, of Confucius, throws the weight of every moral sanction on the dead past, and, by the worship of ancestors, depreciates to the utmost extent the homage due to the living soul. Christianity has no doubt many points of contact with these and other religions ; but in this respect it is utterly antagonistic, in that its unit is the individual, whatever his race, colour, or class, on the sublime ground that God seeks him and needs him. Hence its life has always been fed by personalities, whose love to God has been with the heart, mind, soul, and strength. As Christ founded His Church on Peter, so on the man who adopts the motto of the Northern university — 'Men say : Quhat say they : lat them say'—in the spirit of Peter (Ac 4[19]), has the Church as a matter of history always been refounded. By the touch of Christ on the individual all bands and bars have snapped, and in the inspired personality the word of God has found free course and been glorified. It might almost be said that no other religion is anything but a framework. Only in the religion of Jesus Christ do we see the face of a renewed personality changed into the same image from glory to glory.

(2) But the new-found personality has not only rejoiced in rights and liberties, political and social, mental and spiritual ; it has also made an ever fuller discovery of *its debts and duties*. The Fatherhood of God means the promise at least of personality in every human being, and that means the essential brotherhood of men. The Incarnation has drawn them into one by declaring them one ; so that each must bear the others' burdens, and so fulfil the law of Jesus Christ. The Atonement on Calvary has focussed the conception of vicarious suffering, and summoned Christians to fulfil that which is lacking of the sufferings of Christ (Col 1[24]). In the train of Christian salvation mutual service becomes the truest expression of the bond of union (Jn 13[15-17]). So we are bidden to respect one another's personality, to 'honour all men,' to 'receive one another as Christ also received us to the glory of God' (Ro 15[7]). Being hopelessly in debt to God, we are to pay off all we can on the altar of humanity's need. Our indebtedness to God involves our forgiveness of others (Mt 18[32. 33]), our help of any one in every time of need (Mt 10[8], Lk 10[37]), and especially our hope and labour for their spiritual welfare (Mt 28[19], Lk 10[2]).

This consciousness of duty to humanity for Christ's sake soon showed itself in the breaking of yokes, although the yokes crumbled rather than snapped under His humane influence. It worked upon pagan notions of slavery and conquest, and after abolishing the gladiatorial shows, first eased and finally freed the human chattel. The rights of woman, too, as partner rather than subordinate, and the honour paid even to children, as against the Roman practice of infanticide, have gradually come into being through the changed standpoint from which personality is regarded through Christ. Continuing the story thus begun, the recognition of our debt and duty towards others on account of their personality has (a) secretly undermined the resistance of racial barriers. More than this can hardly be said in view of events East and West. But at any rate the Christian Church, now a fellowship of many peoples, kindreds, and tongues, has to a large extent anticipated the fulfilment of the ideal which leaped to the imagination of St. Paul, when there shall be 'neither Jew nor Greek, bond nor free, male nor female ; for all are one in Christ Jesus' (Gal 3[28]). (b) It has slowly produced an attitude of tolerance, i.e. a recognition of the rights of others in thought. That is a position far in advance of the claim to personal independence. Liberty of thought for others, with a resulting equality of opportunity, is an ideal hard of attainment. But because humanity is logical, though men are not, it will at length be established as the corollary to the rights of personality. (c) It has steadily permeated law with the larger justice of mercy. This is another comparatively recent development of the Christian consciousness. The criminal code and the service discipline were both administered on brutal lines, and the industrial system was beset by conditions hardly less degrading. But the claim of personality is steadily laying hold of the popular imagination and conscience, and asserting itself in the acts of our statute-book. (d) It has turned older methods of education upside down. The claim of the personality is now respected even when in the bud. The teacher now learns to sit first at the feet of the child, who is no longer trained to be a kind of imitation adult, but is desired to develop on the lines of its own personality. (e) It has inspired all crusades of compassion. Christianity has led the way, to the marvel of the world, in the provision of hospitals, asylums, orphanages, etc. And this consideration for the blind, the insane, the leper, and such afflicted ones, is the monument to Christ's care of the body as the home of the personality. (*f*) It has been the fulcrum of foreign missions ; for there are souls to be saved wherever humanity is to be found. This is the most beautiful and characteristic task of the Church of Christ.

These are some of the modern developments of personality as to its rights and duties. By means of their proper balance and mutual influence, Christendom makes its advance. And this balance is maintained so far as man is in Christ. For from Him alone comes the ultimate sense of human dignity both for oneself and for all. At His feet we learn that personality is given its full enfranchisement in order that it may co-operate with the Father in the employments of perfect love.

LITERATURE.—Besides the works alluded to above, see Illingworth, *Personality, Human and Divine*; Moberly, *Atonement and Personality*, esp. ch. ix. ; Martensen, *Ethics*; Dorner, *Ethics*; Seth, *Hegelianism and Personality*; W. Richmond, *Personality*; Newman Smyth, *Christian Ethics*; James, *Problems of Personality*; Lotze, *Microcosmus*, i. 248 ff. ; Green, *Proleg. to Ethics*; Augustine, *Confessions*, etc. See also A. Chandler in *A Lent in London* (1895), p. 193 ; C. C. Hall, *The Gospel of the Divine Sacrifice* (1897), p. 267 ; H. Rashdall, *Doctrine and Development* (1898), p. 268 ; T. G. Selby, *The God of the Frail* (1902), p. 22 ; J. Newton, *The Problem of Personality* (1905) ; W. N. Clarke, *Outline of Theology*, pt. 2 ; Lotze, *Outlines of Philosophy of Religion*, §§ 30–35 ; Oman, *Vision and Authority*, pp. 19–24 ; Myers, *Human Personality*, i. 10 ff.

A. NORMAN ROWLAND.

PERVERTING (διαστρέφω, Lk 23[2] ; ἀποστρέφω, v.[14]). —The word occurs principally in the trial of Jesus before Pilate, where the first charge brought against Him was that of 'perverting the nation.' Such a charge, though somewhat vague, implied that He was a conspirator against the State, spreading a spirit of disaffection and rebellion among the people, and thus turning them against the Imperial Government. The charge was utterly false, but it revealed the bitter malice of the Jews and their determination to bring about the death of Jesus. The power of life and death was not possessed by the Sanhedrin : no merely religious offence could be visited with capital punishment (Jn 18[31]), and therefore the object which they clamoured for could be accomplished only through the instrumentality of the civil power. Accordingly, the leaders of the Sanhedrin lay aside the charge of blasphemy, which really weighed with themselves, but of which they knew Pilate could take no cognizance, and they bring Jesus before the Roman governor as a political offender, guilty of setting Himself and others in opposition to the ruling power of Rome. A charge of this character Pilate was in duty bound to consider and examine. DUGALD CLARK.

PESTILENCE (λοιμός).—The word is found twice in the Gospels, in both cases in the prophecy of Christ regarding the last days (Mt 24[7] [AV ; RV, following WH and others, omits], Lk 21[11]). In the OT the word is used in a generic sense, and usually indicates a direct Divine visitation (Lv 26[25], Nu 14[12], 1 Ch 21[14], Ps 78[50] etc.). The disease, whatever its nature, is not rarely associated with war and its consequences (Jer 24[10] 29[17] 34[17], Ezk 6[11] etc.). Thus it seems to be used by Christ in the texts quoted.

The specific meaning of the word λοιμός is not easily determined. It seems to indicate a swiftly-developing and mortal illness, contagious or infectious in its nature, as we may infer from Ac 24[5]. It may point to the glandular or bubonic plague, well known and universally dreaded by the ancients, and the great scourge of the world in the Middle Ages. (See Hastings' *DB*, iii. pp. 324, 755).

HENRY E. DOSKER.

PETER.—The use of the names *Simon* and *Simon Peter* in the Gospels is instructive. Mt., when he first mentions the Apostle, calls him 'Simon who is called Peter' (4[18]) ; he uses the same language in his list of the Apostles (10[2]). Again, with most obvious appropriateness he calls him 'Simon Peter' at the time of his celebrated confession (16[16]), while on the two occasions on which our Lord addresses the disciple directly, he is 'Simon bar-Jona' (16[17]) and 'Simon' (17[25]). In Mk. the name 'Simon' is employed up to the selection of the Twelve, and thereafter 'Peter' is used ; but when our Lord accosts him in Gethsemane, He names him 'Simon' (14[7]). In Lk. also he is designated 'Simon' with a single exception (5[8]) till the choice of the Apostles, after which he becomes 'Peter' ; but when our Lord speaks to him he is 'Simon, Simon,' which is softened to 'Peter' (22[31, 34]). His fellow-believers give him the same name when they relate that our Lord appeared to him after His resurrection (24[34]). The practice of Jn. is equally notable. Before Peter appears on the scene at all, his brother Andrew is described as 'the brother of Simon Peter' (1[41]). This double name is that which the Evangelist chiefly employs ; in fact, he prefers it except when its repetition would seem pedantic. At the same time, he indicates clearly that the Apostle's original name was 'Simon' (1[42]), and he places this name on the lips of Jesus just as the other Evangelists do (1[43]).

The life of Peter has a triple interest. (*a*) His personality is attractive because of its naturalness, buoyancy, and vigour. Belonging to the class of men who are readily understood, his impetuosity, candour, freedom of speech, transparency of motive, his large and genial humanity, appeal strongly to our hearts. Peter is the Luther among the Apostles. (*b*) Again, he is the most representative of the Apostles. Were it not for him, our knowledge of their views, tastes, hopes, prejudices, and difficulties would be scanty ; but, owing to his words and acts, these stand out in bold relief. It is in Peter that we see the kind of men whom our Lord deliberately chose to be His closest friends and the agents for the fulfilment of His purposes. The methods, too, by which the disciples became qualified for their great functions are most fully revealed in the treatment of Peter by Jesus—the patient wisdom, the boundless charity, the humour, the severity, the perfect frankness, the unreserved intimacy. (*c*) Again, the career of Peter after the Ascension is the most striking evidence at once of his natural capacity and of the transformation effected in him by his friendship with Jesus. The disciple is now worthy of the designation 'Rock.' He shows himself to be the natural leader of the new community : its most powerful and energetic member both in counsel and in act.

The career of Peter falls into two great sections, divided by the Ascension : his life as a disciple and Apostle under our Lord, and his life as the first leader of the Christian Church.

1. Prior to our Lord's Ascension.—Simon Peter was the son of a man called Jonas (Mt 16[17]) or John (Jn 1[42]), or possibly Jonas John, a fisherman on the Sea of Galilee. His mother's name is not recorded. The place of his birth was probably Bethsaida (Jn 1[44]). No mention is made of the date of his birth ; but, as he was a married man when our Lord's ministry opened, it is likely that he was born about the same time as Jesus. How long his parents lived is not known : they may have died before he became intimate with Jesus. It may be assumed from his later life that he was brought up by them in habits of temperance, frugality, diligence, and piety. He could read and write, and had considerable acquaintance with the Greek tongue as spoken in Galilee. He followed his father's occupation, obtaining by it an income adequate to all the wants of his household. By the time he is first spoken of in the Gospels he is married, and living in Capernaum, where he has a house of his own, which at a subsequent date appears to have been the centre of the labours of our Lord in Capernaum (Mk 1²¹· ²⁹ 9³³).

Attracted by the Baptist, Peter and his brother Andrew became his disciples. Andrew was one of the two disciples of the Baptist who heard him declare that Jesus was the Lamb of God (Jn 1³⁵), and who, after their interview with Jesus, were convinced that He was the Messiah. He communicated to his brother the great discovery he had made, and brought him to Jesus, who, reading his very soul, and perceiving what he was and what he was capable of becoming, announced that he should bear the name *Peter* or 'Rock' (Jn 1⁴²). The acquaintanceship thus formed passed after an interval of a few months, during part of which Peter was with Jesus, into discipleship and permanent fellowship. When our Lord began His ministry in Galilee, the two brothers Peter and Andrew were summoned by Him to become, in His own striking language, 'fishers of men': and this call was immediately followed by that of two other brothers, their partners in business, James and John (Mk 1¹⁶· ²⁰). The final stage of Peter's relationship to Jesus was that of Apostle. Our Lord had determined to select a very few persons from the larger number of His adherents to be constantly in His society, and to act as His messengers. Peter was the first to be chosen (Mk 3¹³). This place was not given him by accident. He was the first of the Apostles, not in authority or rank or precedence, for ideas of this description were utterly foreign to the mind of our Lord; but his courage, resourcefulness, energy, and devotion constituted him the natural leader of the new body. He was their spokesman, the interpreter of their wishes, hopes, desires, and purposes. Many words specially uttered by him or spoken by our Lord to him are preserved in the Gospels, and in several of the miracles of our Lord he has a unique place. The perception of our Lord's character, and familiarity with His views of God, of man, of righteousness and of salvation, as well as with His hatred of unreality and formalism, and with the depth and range of His sympathies for the common people and even for social outcasts—set up an intellectual ferment in the mind of Peter which ultimately engendered a fixed and definite view of our Lord's Person. On two occasions that conviction was expressed in memorable terms. At Capernaum, Peter, undismayed and unmoved by the rapid fall in our Lord's popularity due to His refusal to become a political instead of a religious leader, affirmed Him to be the only possessor of the words of eternal life, the Holy One of God (Jn 6⁶⁶ᶠᶠ·). Then, not long after, when the common people had ceased to regard our Lord as the Messiah, and assigned Him only the subordinate place of a forerunner, Peter, without a moment's hesitation, clothed in fit words the conviction which had now attained maturity and consistency in his mind—the ripe fruit of his intercourse with our Lord; he affirmed that He was the Messiah (Mt 16¹³ᶠᶠ·). This confession was rewarded with the famous promise, the sense of which is still in dispute—'Thou art Peter, and on this rock I will build my church.' The common view among the Fathers that the rock is Jesus Himself has scarcely any support among the interpreters of to-day. A number of Protestant scholars agree with the Roman Catholic Church in understanding the rock of Peter himself; but this explanation fails to answer two questions. Why, if Peter is the rock, did not Jesus simply say 'on thee'? Whence, too, the distinction in the present text between the two words for 'rock' (πέτρος and πέτρα), a distinction which must surely have been found in some form in the original Aramaic? But be the rock Peter himself or his confession, it is clear that our Lord was deeply gratified with the declaration, and that He recognized in it a spiritual insight and capacity which qualified the speaker for high office and service in the Kingdom of God. But, though Peter had grasped the truth that Jesus was the Messiah, he was still in bondage to the traditional conception of the Messiah as a conqueror. For hardly had our Lord, relying on his confession, proceeded for the first time to announce plainly His impending death, when Peter, shocked at His apparent despondency, remonstrated with Him, and thus drew from His lips the rebuke, 'Get thee behind me, Satan' (Mt 16²³).

The prediction of His death was made by Jesus at least thrice, in language which admits of but one meaning; but neither Peter nor any of the Apostles appears to have believed that the words were intended to be taken literally. Not one among them seems to have accepted the truth that Jesus would be crucified. But that event drew near, and Peter, as was to be expected, figures largely in the closing scenes. He refuses to allow his Master to degrade Himself by washing his feet; but when told that this refusal involves forfeiture of all interest in Him, under the impulse of the reaction generated by this reproof, he wishes that his hands and head as well as his feet should be washed (Jn 13⁶ᶠᶠ·). Conscious of his devotion to his Lord, he declares that though all men should stumble at Him, he never will, but would die for His sake; and draws from our Lord's lips the sorrowful announcement that he is about to deny Him thrice (Mk 14²⁹). When our Lord is arrested in Gethsemane, he has the courage, perhaps rather the rashness, to draw a sword and seek to cut down the very person who, it may be, was making the arrest (Jn 18¹⁰); he follows our Lord into the palace of the high priest, and there, outworn, perplexed, thrown off his guard, unmanned, he three times declares that he knows nothing of Jesus. Then, having met the eye of his Master as He was led from one room to another, the sense of his guilt becomes intolerable, and he bursts forth into tears of deepest penitence and self-abasement (Lk 22⁵⁴ᶠᶠ·). What the Apostle did after he quitted the palace of the high priest, has not been told us. Whether he was too overpowered by emotion to draw near the cross we cannot tell, but it is certain that his hopes were buried in the grave of Jesus. He and the rest of the disciples must have poured out their hearts to one another, suggesting, doubting, fearing, unable to resolve as to the future.

Not two days after the Crucifixion, Mary of Magdala informed Peter and John that the grave of Jesus was open and no body there. The two disciples started off in hot haste to verify the statement. John, the younger and fleeter, reached the tomb first, but awe prevented him from entering. Peter, unaffected by this motive, went into the grave as soon as he arrived, and then both disciples saw the grave-cloths lying in orderly array, with the napkin which had bound the head rolled up in a place by itself: facts which excluded the view that the corpse had been removed by enemies. The meaning of the words which they had heard again and again from Jesus as to His rising again from the dead began to dawn on their understanding: He was risen from the dead (Jn 20¹ᶠᶠ·). Soon the testimony of the women confirmed the inference they had drawn, and if any doubts continued to haunt the Apostle's mind, they were finally dispelled by a personal appearance made by Jesus to himself. The interview stands with no record save the bare circumstance, but is possibly on that account only the more impressive (Lk 24³⁴). It formed perhaps the most important event of Peter's life, and certainly produced on him the most extraordinary effects. What was soft and fluid in his ideas and convictions now hardened into rock : his courage acquired a new temper : his passionate loyalty to our Lord became measureless trust and devotion, chastened by a new reverence and awe. All that he had ever ventured to hope regarding Jesus was now confirmed, and rested on a basis of adamant.

Another scene is related in the appendix to the Fourth Gospel (ch. 21), which forms the fitting close to the earthly relations of the Master and His disciple. Here again Peter and John are the two chief actors, and each exhibits his distinctive characteristics. John is the first to identify the solitary figure on the shore of the Sea of Galilee with the Lord; while Peter is the first to try to reach Him, casting himself into the lake in his eagerness to welcome Him. There followed the triple question to Peter touching his love for Jesus, with answers from the Apostle which show that he had now been purged of presumption, boasting, and rash self-confidence. Then he in his turn is entrusted with the weightiest and most honourable of all charges : he is commissioned and commanded to feed and tend the flock of Christ. Finally, and as if it were the natural sequel of the high trust just allotted him, he is told that he will end his days by martyrdom. Accepting this declaration without a shadow of doubt, he ventures to inquire as to the fate of his fellow-disciple John, but is forbidden to meddle with such questions, his task being to concentrate his energies on the fulfilment of the duties imposed on himself.

2. Subsequent to the Ascension.—If Peter was the foremost of the disciples before the Ascension, he was still more so, if possible, after that event. He is represented throughout the Acts as the leader of the Church; and this view is confirmed by the references that St. Paul (Gal $2^{7.\,9}$) makes to his position, which prove that his was the commanding personality in the Church. The suggestion that a successor to Judas should be appointed was made by him, and at once adopted by the body of believers (Ac $1^{15ff.}$). The explanation of the descent of the tongues of flame at Pentecost is given by him ($2^{14ff.}$). He performs the first Christian miracle ($3^{6f.}$). The defence of the new community when its leaders are arrested by the Sanhedrin falls on him ($4^{8ff.}$). The doom of Ananias and Sapphira is pronounced by his lips ($5^{4.\,9}$). When the gospel is preached in Samaria, John and he are appointed commissioners to investigate the new situation (8^{14}). He is the first to throw open the Church to the Gentiles on the condition of faith only (ch. 10). Herod Agrippa sentences him to death as the chief leader of the sect of the Nazarenes (ch. 12). He takes a foremost place in the deliberations of the Congress at Jerusalem which determined the relations that should thereafter exist between the Gentiles and the Jews, pronouncing that the Gentiles should be exempt from all Jewish ordinances (ch. 15). At this point the account in the Acts terminates, and the remainder of his career is obscure. That he travelled about preaching the gospel, accompanied by his wife (1 Co 9^5), is certain, but the one place he is known to have visited is Antioch (Gal 2^{11}) in Syria, the second capital of Christianity. He may have gone to Greece (Euseb. $H\!E$ II. xxv. 8); he may have preached in the provinces to which his first letter is addressed (1 P 1^1); it is possible that he spent some time in Babylon (1 P 5^{13}). From the far East he turned to Rome, where he died as a martyr according to our Lord's prediction, but when and under what conditions cannot be ascertained (Clem. Rom. *Ep. ad Cor.* v. 7).

Literature.—*Lives* of Christ; the Comm.; F. Godet, *Studies on the NT* (Eng. tr. 1879), 246; G. B. Stevens, *The Messages of the Apostles* (1900), 42; G. Matheson, *Representative Men of the NT* (1905), 93; H. T. Purchas, *Johannine Problems* (1901), 68; J. G. Greenhough, *Apostles of our Lord* (1904), 52, 221; W. M. Taylor, *Peter the Apostle* (1891); W. H. G. Thomas, *The Apostle Peter* (1904); H. A. Birks, *Life and Character of St. Peter* (1887); S. Cox, *Genesis of Evil* (1880), 280, 351; W. B. Carpenter, *Son of Man* (1893), 91; *Expos.* 3rd ser. iv. (1886) 183, ix. (1889) 187; *JBL* xvii. (pt. 2, 1898) 31.

W. PATRICK.

PHARISEES.—I. *ORIGIN AND DEVELOPMENT.* —**1. Outline of history.**—The Pharisees present the most characteristic manifestation of Palestinian Judaism in the time of Christ, and His work cannot be understood without a knowledge of them; for 'later Judaism is through and through Pharisaism and nothing but Pharisaism' (Bousset, *Jesu Predigt*, 1892, p. 32). The Pharisees were an outgrowth of the long conflict between the Jews and surrounding heathenism, from the Babylonian Captivity onward. That captivity impressed the following things upon Judaism : intense monotheism, the Synagogue service, the OT Scriptures and Scribal interpretations of them, the Sabbath strictly observed as a sign of God's covenant, and a Puritan hatred of heathenism, which put the stamp of *separation* for ever upon Pharisaic piety. The Reformers under Ezra and Nehemiah were forerunners of the Pharisees, as the priestly court party under Zerubbabel foreshadowed the Sadducees. In these international relations—Jews in Palestine and in the Dispersion—Judaism grew gradually into a Church, and as such had an inner circle of the pious in contrast with mere adherents —'children of the world.' This transition cannot be fully traced, but appears well marked under the Maccabees (B.C. 167–63). The Macedonian policy of Alexander made the East Greek; the Romans made the West Latin; Persia and Carthage were overthrown; then Rome absorbed the Hellenistic East; and a world-system for the first time appeared when Jesus was born under the first Emperor. The denationalizing process prepared by Greece and introduced by Rome affected even the Jews, and helped to produce the Synagogue church system. But Pharisaic Judaism reacted strongly against it at first, and under the Maccabees battled for religious independence. When, however, the Maccabæan princes fought further for civil liberty, the Pharisaic party withdrew and formed a theocratic group, democratic in a measure, which soon gained the leadership of the majority of the nation. These *Ḥăsîdîm*, or Puritans of the century before Christ, became the Pharisees of NT times. They received the name 'Pharisees,' or *separated*, when they withdrew from the Sadducee court party of the Maccabæan rulers under John Hyrcanus (B.C. 135–105). They were the men of ἀμιξία (2 Mac 14^{38}) from everything heathen and impure. Their aim was in daily life to be as ceremonially pure as the priests were in the Temple.

2. Differences between Pharisees and Sadducees. —The chief differences were the following : (1) the Pharisees 'delivered to the people a great many observances by tradition which are not written in the law of Moses' (Jos. *Ant.* XIII. x. 6). These the Sadducees for the most part rejected. (2) The Pharisees had an elaborate doctrine of immortality, resurrection, angels, demons, heaven, hell, intermediate state, and Messianic Kingdom, about all of which the Sadducees were agnostic. (3) The Pharisees taught both predestination and free-will, —much as St. Paul did,—while the Sadducees held the Greek doctrine of absolute free-will. (4) The Pharisees had a high theory of the theocracy, which led them to oppose foreign interference from the time of the Syrian kings to the Roman emperors, and reject also the Maccabæan rule as inconsistent with the high priesthood. The Psalms of Solomon are full of sharp utterances against the Sadducee rulers (*e.g.* 4^1 3^8 9^4). It was this theo cratic spirit which developed national Judaism into a Church, with a world-consciousness equal to that of Rome and a spiritual unity not inferior to that of Greece. (5) The Pharisees were also missionary, and made many converts (*Ant.* XX. ii.–iv.; *BJ* II. xix. 2; Mt 23^{15}). Hillel said : ' Love men and lead them to the Law ' (*Aboth* i. 2) ; and the international Synagogue, inspired from Jerusalem, compassed sea and land in making proselytes. The Sadducees had no such interest. This Pharisaic propaganda, however, when it met the successful missions of the Christians, ceased making converts, condemned the translation of the LXX, and buried itself in the Talmud. (6) The Pharisees differed from the Sadducees by the wide distance between the Synagogue, the centre of the one party, and the Temple, the stronghold of the other. The Temple was waning in influence. Jesus refers little to it, and when it disappeared the religion of the Jews went on without a break. The Pharisees even prescribed rules for the priestly Sadducees in the Temple (*Ant.* XIII. x. 5), and had their prayers introduced alongside the sacrifices. In fact, the Temple services were regarded as meritorious because done in obedience to the legal teachings of the Pharisees (cf. Kohler, art. ' Pharisees ' in *JE*). Some Pharisees seem in theory to have even abandoned the Temple worship (cf. Enoch 89$^{58.\ 73}$ 90^{28}, Ps-Sol 10^{8} 17^{18}). (7) The Pharisees formed a fraternity with peculiar vows, which separated them from the heathen, the common people, and the Sadducees. The great majority of Jews were Pharisees in belief, but only about 6000 or 7000 were members of the brotherhood. Edersheim compares them with the Jesuits in the Roman Church (*Sketches of Jew. Soc. Life*, ch. xiv.). They married, however, and their fellowship included the families of members. On entering the order, they took two vows in the presence of three witnesses, one to tithe everything eaten, bought, or sold ; the other not to be guest of the *'am-hā'ārez*, and to observe all ceremonial purification. They were the true Israel, ' the saints ' ; their opponents were ' the ungodly,' ' the profane ' (cf. Lk 18^{9}, Ps-Sol 14^{1} 17^{16}). (8) The Pharisees were the religious power in Palestine in the time of Christ. They represented the authority of the Scriptures in home, school, synagogue, courts of law, and daily life. John almost identifies them with ' the Jews ' (1^{19} 2^{18}). Though an outgrowth of the school of the Scribes, they eclipsed their teachers. They were in business, and their goods were legal tender everywhere. They were united, zealous, dogmatic, patriotic, stood for the people against rulers and hierarchs, preached the keeping of the Law and the coming world of blessedness as reward of obedience, and were everywhere active in moulding Jewish life according to their principles. In opposition to Sadducees and common men, the Pharisees developed a new conception of piety ; it was something that could be learned, and they were its teachers. The wise men were the good, and took the place of both prophet and priest. Hillel said : ' The uneducated fears no sin ' ; but ' he who acquires knowledge has attained eternal life ' (*Aboth* ii. 6, 8). All this made the Pharisees more and more proud, formal, and uncharitable. They despised the common people (Jn 7^{49}) ; they had reached the climax of their power in the time of Jesus ; and, half-feared, half-hated, they were declining in spiritual influence.

3. Pharisaic environment of Jesus.—Pharisaic Judaism in the time of Christ included the best, as well as the worst, of the people. The Jewish saints in the NT, the parents of the Baptist and of our Lord, Simeon, Anna, and others, Hillel too, and Gamaliel and Jochanan ben Sakkai, were noble types of Pharisaic Jews. Galilee especially was the home of the more earnest Pharisaic piety, with

its severe living and strong Messianic hope. Here the Zealots appeared, and the outbreaks against Rome had their seat ; and here Jesus grew up and began His ministry in an atmosphere of Pharisaic devotion. He did not denounce all Pharisees, or the Pharisaic Judaism amid which He grew up ; since it stood for the whole transmitted religion of Israel,—for that salvation which was of the Jews. He stood nearer the Synagogue than the Temple, and in some respects presented His teaching in the line of the Pharisees. The Rabbis taught their disciples to honour the Scriptures, to seek first after heaven and its righteousness (*Ant.* XVI. ii. 4, v. 4, vi. 8), to look past the present legal life to a future world of grace and glory, to make proselytes, to have baptisms and holy suppers in their brotherhood, to pray, to fast and give alms— these three were ' the chief pillars of the Jewish religion ' (Bousset, *Relig. Judenthums*, p. 159). All these things Jesus favoured also, and they passed, with many others, from the Synagogue into the Church. But Jesus was not a Pharisee. He rebuked them for their anti-scriptural traditions, as He did the Sadducees for ignorance of the word of God (Mk 7^{9}). Neither was He a heretic ; the Pharisees did not put Him out of the synagogue, though He was called a Samaritan and possessed of a devil. He preached from the common ground of the Scriptures ; and, just because the Pharisees held in theory so much that was true, He castigated the more their formalism and insincerity. But, while opposing Pharisaic superstition, He did not favour the agnosticism and rationalism of the Sadducees. From the heart of Divine revelation, illuminated by the Holy Spirit and in the full consciousness of Himself as Son of God, in and through and above all the Scriptures, He proclaimed the everlasting truth of the gospel, setting aside everything in Pharisaic teaching and life that was inconsistent with it.

II. *THEOLOGY OF THE PHARISEES AND THE TEACHING OF JESUS.*—Two views formerly held respecting the relation of Jesus and His teachings to the Pharisaic Judaism of His time may now be regarded as obsolete. One was that both He and the Jews drew so directly from the OT that their ideas of the Messiah and His work were essentially the same, the chief question at issue being whether or not Jesus was the looked-for Messiah (cf. Schöttgen, *Hor. Heb.* 1742 ; Bertholdt, *Christ. Jud.* 1811 ; Gfrörer, *Jahr. d. Heils*, 1838). The other was the theory that the gospel preached by Jesus was only a reformed Judaism (Grätz, *Gesch. d. Juden*, 1867, iii. 217 ; Kohler, *l.c.*). But ' such a reconstruction of history belongs wholly to the past ' (Lucius, *Der Essenismus*, 1881, p. 8) ;[*] and we can set forth the relation of Jesus to Pharisaic Judaism better by way of contrast than of comparison (cf. Bousset, *Jesu Predigt*, p. 7 ; Chamberlain, *Grundlagen d. 19 Jahr.* 1900, i. 221). ' Jesus' appearance was really not a fulfilment, but a contradiction of the Jewish religion.' If there was anything the Pharisees lacked, it was religious originality. Chamberlain says, ' The fable that the Jews had especial qualifications for religion has been finally destroyed ' (i. 29). Jesus did stand upon the soil of OT piety, and was in vital relation to current Judaism ; but His unique Divine consciousness as Son of God led Him to speak with absolute authority respecting both. Whatever might have been said to men of old time must yield to His ' I say unto you ' : and no word of prophet or scribe or Pharisee had any authority for Him (Jn 7^{17}). When He spoke, God spoke, and all must hearken and obey (7^{16}).

The theology of the Pharisees was crude and un-

[*] Cf., however, J. Weiss, Wernle, Wrede, Weinel, etc., of the *Religionsgeschichtliche* school, who incline again towards the position of Renan, Grätz, Geiger.

scientific,—'a terrible mass of conflicting statements and debasing superstitions' (Edersheim, *Life and Times*, i. 106), everywhere limited by national conditions. It was less reasonable than certain views of the Sadducees, and lacked the mystic freedom from sacerdotalism of the Essenes. It had no appreciation of that natural theology so dear to the Greeks, or of the immanence of God as Father which Jesus saw in every flower of the field. Art, philosophy, science, history, culture were avoided as secular and profane. The Pharisees 'killed nature by legal prescriptions' (Wellhausen, *Phar. u. Sadd.* p. 19). In their confused teachings drawn from the OT by traditional exegesis, three great groups of thought may be distinguished; they refer to God, His revelation in the Law, and the hope of a promised Messiah. The thirteen articles of the Jewish Confession of faith still show the same division (cf. Landau, *Die alten Gebete d. H.* 1843, p. 120) as appeared in Rabbinical preaching in the time of Christ. Honour God, keep His Law as far as possible, and through all failures hope for the mercy of God in the Messianic age—that is the prevalent course of thought in Pharisaic Judaism. NT writers follow it also. St. Paul teaches a just God, His holy Law, and peace through faith in the Messiah. St. Peter, when the Law convicted men of murder, preached to them repentance toward God and faith in the slain Messiah, Jesus (Ac 2[37. 38] 3[19f.]). St. John sums up the contrast between Jew and Christian in the Law of God given by Moses, and grace and truth coming in the Messiah (1[17]). And when the Jews attacked early Christianity, their opposition lay along these lines (6[11]). Stephen was stoned for blaspheming God, Moses, and the customs of the Pharisees, and doing so in the name of Jesus Christ. In like manner Jesus was accused of blasphemy against God, violating His Law, and claiming to fulfil the Messianic hope.

1. Doctrine of God.—(1) *Pharisaic view of Divine transcendence.*—The Pharisees had an abstract, transcendental view of God, which gave rise to the legalism that marks their teachings, and added colour to their Messianic hope (cf. Baldensperger, *Selbstbewusstsein Jesu*, p. 45). Opposition to heathenism, coupled with Rabbinical study of the OT, produced this conception. God was Creator in the beginning, and will be final Judge at the end; but meantime He is a far-off ruler of the Universe. His name, the mysterious τετραγράμματον, was no longer spoken; and all anthropomorphic and human-like features in God were set aside. The God who tabernacled in Israel was succeeded by 'the God of heaven' (1 Mac 3[60], Enoch 13[4] 106[11], 2 Es 8[20], Ps-Sol 2[34], To 7[18]). 'God' and 'heaven' became interchangeable terms; and in place of words about the personal care of Jehovah, we meet cosmological and meteorological discussions of the stars and rain and snow, with suggestions of sun-worship (Enoch 72[35], Ps-Sol 2[13-14] 4[21]). It was a deistic view of God that became prominent. Two important views grew out of this theology: one was the doctrine of middle beings between God and man—good and evil spirits, angels, especially the *Memra* or mediating Word of God, and the Holy Spirit; the other was a personal conception of God, which appeared in belief in individual immortality and personal resurrection as involved in responsibility to God and hope of entrance into the Messianic Kingdom. A further outgrowth of this theology was the teaching that keeping carefully the Law of God would hasten the coming of the Messianic Kingdom. Thus Divine transcendence, mediation, individual piety, legalism, and the Messianic hope were closely related elements in the Pharisaic teachings.

(2) *Jesus' doctrine of God as Father.*—The theology of Jesus set out from the Fatherhood of God. It had been foreshadowed in the OT (Dt 32[6], Ps

68[5]) and later Jewish literature (Wis 2[16]), but was first taught in its unique importance and fulness by Jesus. It was peculiar to Him because He was related as none other to the Father. None but God could know Him, as He alone knew the Father (Mt 11[27]). To Him alone could God appear as Father without wrath against sin in Him. This doctrine of God as Father is what was fundamentally new in the message of Jesus (cf. Bousset, *Jesu Predigt*, p. 4; Hausrath, *NT Times*, i. 146). Through it God appeared everywhere in His love, caring for flowers and sparrows, just and unjust; beholding sin and Satan in the world, but still declaring it the happy home of God's children. He here 'broke through, at the most decisive point, the transcendental ascetic spirit of Judaism' (Bousset, *Relig. Jud.* p. 65; Baldensperger, 225; Wendt, *Teaching of Jesus*, i. ch. 2). This new doctrine of God led to a new doctrine of man's relation to Him. If God is Father, then men who come to Him enter into all the liberty of children, but at the same time are lovingly bound to be holy and perfect like God. The confused view of the Pharisees, that the Jew was partly in national relations to God and partly member of a holy congregation, disappears. His blurred hope of partly keeping the Law, partly being resigned to Divine chastisement, and partly redeemed in a world to come—all resting on merit—is supplanted by a joyful gospel of present peace. Instead of the otherworldliness of Pharisaic piety,—an attempt to imitate the transcendent God,—Jesus taught a present joy in a present Father for all men, 'am-hā'ārez as well as scribe and Pharisee. Here love to God and love to man first met in reality. As the Father in heaven forgives, so men are to forgive; the latter is the proof of the former. Religion and ethics were in perfect harmony. Jesus did teach a certain separation from the world, a selling all to follow Him, a bearing the cross; but it was not separation on ceremonial or external grounds; it was a question of values, a putting the Kingdom of God first that all other things might be added thereto. So sunny and natural was His relation to the world and common life, that He was at once denounced as a gluttonous man and a wine-bibber, a friend of publicans and sinners. Next to the fundamental doctrine that God is our Father, came this second dominating teaching of man's social relation to the world about him. Here is the great point of departure from Judaism and the Ghetto, already erected by the Pharisees in Jerusalem, towards Christianity and the gospel of humanity.

2. The Law.—(1) *Written and oral.*—This was central for Judaism in the days of Jesus. It was regarded in both written and oral form as coming from God through Moses (*Aboth* i. 1). It took the place of the God of heaven. Every word was inspired, and he who 'gains the Law gains the life of the world to come' (Hillel). Obedience to God's Law under the awful Categorical Imperative of Sinai, as applied by scribes and Pharisees, was the dominant principle, the yoke upon the neck of the Jews, when Christ appeared (Ac 15[10], Gal 5[1]). The Oral Law of tradition arose because prophecy ceased; cases arose not provided for in the OT, and Rabbinical exegesis of the Scriptures sought the cover of ancient names.

(2) *Law as civil code.*—Here especially the OT exegesis and tradition were necessary in using the Bible as the source of civil law, when Israel changed from a small pastoral people to become a world-wide commercial race. The chequered history of centuries under heathen rule broke up many customs, as those of tithes, offerings, Sabbath, Temple service, contact with Gentiles, etc. Hence from Hillel onwards the Pharisees elaborated a

civil code by means of tradition and exegesis from the Scriptures. The great loss to religion in such a process was in making it largely negative. The Rabbis counted 248 classes of things to be done, and 365 of things forbidden.

(3) *Ceremonial law.*—This the Pharisees made to touch every detail of human life. They regarded nature and spirit as so related that impurity could pass from one to the other. A bad man's body was impure, and to touch it would bring uncleanness to another man's soul. Adam's sin extended evil to unclean beasts, and foods, and the dishes holding them. There was no end to this defilement and the consequent necessary purification by various kinds of water or by breaking ceremonially the unclean vessels. Twelve treatises of the Mishna deal with this subject. It is said : 'He who lightly esteems hand-washing will perish from the earth' (*Sota*, 4). Jesus felt the utter superficiality of all this washing of the body while the inner life was unclean. Delitzsch says (*Jesus und Hillel*, 1879, p. 23) there is no historical point of departure in the time and land of Jesus for His method of contrasting the moral with the ceremonial. He here 'turned His back upon the highway of Rabbinical traditions, and opened a path which until then had never occurred to any human heart.'

(4) *Rule of faith and practice.*—The Pharisees bound spiritual and moral living also under law. But law cannot produce affection, or win the heart, or find place for the Holy Spirit, or be a vessel of grace. The idea of religion as a supreme impulse from the depths of man's nature, as Jesus taught it, independent of both superstition and ethics, was peculiarly foreign to the Pharisaic Jew (cf. Chamberlain, ii. 29). He said : 'To do right and wrong is in the work of our hands, and in Thy righteousness Thou chastisest the children of men. He who works righteousness obtains life from the Lord' (Ps-Sol 9⁷⁻⁹). Do the best you can, and submit to God's punishment for your defects, was the substance of such legalism. One sad result of this national legal religion was that it had one standard for the Jew and another for the Gentile. Adultery with a Gentile was trivial compared with such offence against a Jew. Pharisaic ethics taught to hate Gentiles as enemies ; their morality had no unifying principle of application to man as man —while Jesus taught love even to enemies and Gentiles.

(5) *Jesus and the Law.*—Even the best legal maxims of the Pharisees fall far short of the teachings of Jesus. Hillel's golden rule was negative, while that of Jesus was positive, showing all the difference between justice and love. The greater principle of love to God and one's neighbour, which the scribe (Mk 12³²), and Jesus, and St. Paul, and Aḳiba all regard as fundamental (Gal 5¹⁴ ; Bacher, *Die Agada d. Tannaiten*, 1884, i. 7, 285), became a new thing in the application of Jesus. He made love to man a test of love to God ; He united organically the two OT texts, Dt 6⁵ and Lv 19¹³ ; He put love to man on the same level with love to God ; He widened the conception of neighbour from *ḥaber* to '*am-hā'ārez*, from '*am-hā'ārez* to Samaritan (Lk 10³⁶), and to all men— thus moving in direct opposition to that separation which underlay all Pharisaic holiness. Jesus dropped the whole Law as a way of salvation,— a way the Pharisees themselves could not keep (Ro 7⁸), as appeared in their numerous evasions of it, such as 'blending of courts,' and their ostentatious putting of appearance in place of reality. He threw aside the endless civil, ceremonial, and ethical rules of the Pharisees, and went back to the spiritual religion of the OT as fulfilled in Him and transformed in the gospel. The Law was, at its best, but a παιδαγωγός to the gospel. Salvation

by way of the Pharisees was impossible, hence Jesus declared they were either blind or hypocrites in claiming to please God in that way. The best Jews admitted this (Ps-Sol 9⁹⁻¹⁵ 13⁹ 14¹⁻⁶). Jesus led men to God as Father through a new birth by the Holy Ghost, into a family of loving children, by way of repentance, faith, and union with Himself (Mk 1¹⁴. ¹⁵, Jn 3⁵ᶠ.). This gospel of the loving father and the prodigal son, of the penitent publican and the proud Pharisee, was as a honeymoon compared with the funereal legalism of the Pharisees (Mk 2¹⁹). Gamaliel said : 'Get thyself a teacher that thou mayest be free from doubt' (*Aboth* i. 16) ; but Jesus showed Nicodemus that all Pharisaic learning could not give the new life of the Spirit of God and the Son of God. He brought a new cup of blessing full of the wine of the Kingdom, a sweet blending of religion and ethics as inseparable in thought as the inside and outside of the holy cup itself. Here was 'the appearance of a new kind of humanity,' springing from contact with Jesus, 'for through Him for the first time humanity received a moral culture' (Chamberlain, i. 204, 207). It was because the gospel was utterly incompatible with Pharisaic Judaism that Jesus gathered disciples, taught them, gave them His Spirit (Jn 20²²), and sent them out to evangelize the world (Mt 28¹⁹. ²⁰).

3. Religious hopes of the Pharisees.—(1) *Their views of the Messiah and His Kingdom.*—The void between God and man was partly filled from Daniel onwards by Apocalypses of the Messianic Kingdom. This hope roused the godly in Israel to greater obedience, that the coming of the Son of David might be hastened. Law and Messiah were two centres of Jewish thought when Christ appeared. The burden of the one led to greater expectation of the appearance of the other. In this expectation, the nature of the Messiah also took a more universal, and at the same time more personal character, corresponding somewhat to the growing sense of personal responsibility in religion among the Jews. The Messiah, as Son of Man, appeared sharing the majesty, glory, and heavenly nature of Jehovah (Enoch 47³ and often). 'The identification of Divine hypostases with the Messiah had already taken place in pre-Christian Judaism.' It was not related at all to Philo and his λόγος doctrine (cf. Baldensperger, p. 88). But there was also the human Messiah, the Son of David ; and two confused accounts arose among the Pharisaic theologians respecting these two views of the Messiah and His Kingdom (cf. Stanton, *The Jewish and Christian Messiah*, 1886, p. 135 f.). The one was more earthly, national, material ; the other more spiritual and universal. The material was usually regarded as leading up to the spiritual, and the millennium appeared as a transition from one to the other. A full account of the ordinary expectation is given in Ps-Sol 17²³⁻⁵⁰. The Pharisees had no idea that the Messiah would be a Saviour of all men. Even the Baptist thought He would come only to separate by judgment the evil and the good in Israel, and establish the latter in the Kingdom of God. That He would bring a new revelation, and by temptation and suffering attain victory, as Jesus did, was utterly foreign to them. Especially foreign was the conception of a suffering and dying Messiah, as Dalman has shown (*Der leid. u. sterb. Mess.* 1888, pp. iii, 22 f.). Even the Apostles did not know it (Mk 8³¹ 9¹²⁻³¹ 10³³). The usual explanation of two Messiahs did not arise till two centuries after Christ (Dalman, *l.c.*).

(2) *Messianic teachings of Jesus.*—The teachings of Jesus differed from those of the Pharisees on salvation, first, by showing it was not by law ; and, second, by presenting the Messiah as a sin-bearer. By repentance and faith in Him men would be

saved. From the time of His baptism He looked
toward the cross ; for He was to give men rest by
becoming a ransom for their sin (Mt 11²⁸ 20²⁸). He
did not infer He must die from the fate of the
prophets — a prophet need not be crucified, — or
borrow the idea from the scribes—they never had
it, and they thought that to kill Him would end
His Messianic claims,—nor did His disciples invent
it ; they fought against it, and nearly forsook Him
when He taught it. Out of His Messianic consciousness Jesus went forth to die as the great
Shepherd for His sheep (Mk 8³¹⁻³⁸ 9⁹ᶠ· 10³²). Messiah
and sufferer were inseparable thoughts ; and as
soon as He was confessed as Messiah and Son of
God, He declared He must suffer, be rejected, be
killed, and rise again (Mk 8²⁹ᶠ·, Mt 16¹⁶). His
preaching of the Kingdom, also, was very different
from that of the Pharisees. He proclaimed it as
present, not in the future ; a certainty, a reality,
not a hope ; both within men, and yet to be fully
realized in the future. Much that the Jews
expected He grouped under a new doctrine, that
of the second advent of the Messiah. He appropriated to Himself the lofty Messianic conception
of the Pharisees ; He was 'Son of God' (Enoch
105²ᶠ·, Jn 19⁷) ; 'Son of Man' (Dn 7¹³ᶠ·, Mt 17¹²) ;
'son of woman' (Enoch 62) ; and Κύριος (Ps-
Sol 17²³). He adopted their view that He was
pre-existent with God (cf. Baldensperger, p. 87) ;
and on the ground of such consciousness forgave
sins, wrought miracles, and answered prayers. It
is little wonder that such words on the lips of
Jesus amazed the Pharisees ; in fact, nearly all
He said contradicted their teachings. He had no
dread of God, His law, sin, or death ; and invited all
men to share His rest and peace. He set aside
the Law, and turned Jewish eschatology into soteriology. He and the Kingdom were one ; to have
Him was to share everlasting life. Jewish teachers,
leading away from Him, He called thieves and
robbers, and the Pharisaic conception of the Messianic Kingdom was earthly and devilish (Mt 4⁸,
Lk 4⁵ᶠ·). The new heavens bent already above
Him ; the new earth was beneath His feet ; and
here He gathered citizens of the Kingdom, men of
the Beatitudes. In all this lies the greatest possible
contrast to Pharisaic teachings ; and the gospel of
Jesus can by no possibility be understood in the
framework of later Judaism (cf. Bousset, *Jesu
Predigt*, p. 65).

III. *OPPOSITION OF THE PHARISEES TO CHRIST,
AND HIS CRITICISM OF THEM.*—**1. Pharisaic opposition to Jesus.**—The Pharisees quickly saw the
dangerous tendency of Jesus' teachings, and took
steps to crush His work. Messianic ideas were
abroad, zealots were appearing, and a false Messiah could work ruin. Jesus arose as a prophetic
man in Galilee, independent of them. From boyhood He had learned nothing from the scribes (Mk
1²² 6², Jn 7¹⁵), and everybody felt the authority
of His words. They questioned the Baptist (Jn
1¹⁹· ²⁶), who added to their anxiety by declaring the
Messiah was at hand with a baptism of the Holy
Ghost and of fire. As soon, therefore, as Jesus
began to preach, a delegation of the Pharisees and
scribes went to Galilee to oppose Him (Mk 2⁶ 7¹).
They roused the Nazarenes to cast Him out (Lk
4¹⁶ᶠ·) ; they called forth a reaction against Him in
Bethsaida and Capernaum (Mt 11²¹) ; induced His
own family to think Him insane (Mk 3²¹· ³¹) and in
danger ; and formed an alliance with the Pharisees
of Galilee to oppose Him. His first public appearances, cleansing the Temple and preaching in Nazareth, called for decisive action. He attacked money-
changers for disturbing the worship of Gentiles in
the outer court, and pointed out that the prophets
helped a Gentile widow and healed Naaman the
Syrian, while the people of Israel were passed by.

He talked with a woman of Samaria, and healed
the child of a Roman. He helped all in need,—
publicans, sinners, harlots, lepers, demoniacs,—and
told the multitudes that a sincere heathen was better
than a formal Pharisee. No wonder the Pharisees
opposed Him. They attacked especially (1) His
violation of the Law, and (2) His relation to God.

(1) He was assailed because He paid no attention
to the *separation* principle of the Pharisees, and came
in contact with the *'am-hā'ārez*, Gentiles, and the
diseased in a way that horrified them (Mt 9²⁵, Mk
3¹⁰). It is very likely these 'lost sheep,' this ripe
harvest field, these 'poor' that Jesus refers to as
'babes and sucklings' (Mt 11²⁵ 21¹⁶), perhaps also
as 'little ones' (Mt 10⁴² 18⁶). The Pharisees were
'the wise and prudent.' Jesus also violated the
Sabbath law, this second bulwark of the Pharisees,
and did so with such miraculous power as led the
people to hail Him as Son of David, and the Evangelist to recall the prophecy that He would save
both Jews and Gentiles. He spoke disparagingly
also of tithing rules (Lk 11⁴²). A crisis had come,
for the people felt Jesus could not be a sinner and
do such mighty works. This led to the inquiry by
what power He did these things.

(2) *Relation of Jesus to Jehovah.*—Jesus taught
that He wrought Sabbath miracles and all miracles
by the Holy Spirit and as Son of God (Jn 19⁷).
The Pharisees replied that He did wonders by
Beelzebub. It was the devil incarnate that went
about doing good in Jesus. His forerunner, the
Baptist, was also possessed by Satan (Mt 11¹⁸).
No wonder Jesus 'looked round upon them with
anger, being grieved for the hardness of their
hearts' (Mk 3⁵). It was worse ; Jesus called it
blasphemy against the Holy Ghost (v.²⁸ᶠᶠ·). They
expected the Holy Spirit to come with the Messiah ;
but when both came, neither was accepted (Ac 7⁵¹· ⁵²).
It was an age 'in the highest degree religiously
excited, but it did not possess the Spirit' (Gunkel,
Die Wirkungen d. H. G. 1888, p. 57). Jesus
claimed authority over all human affairs—to regulate the Sabbath, forgive sins, and adjudge future
rewards and punishments. The claim to pardon
sins especially provoked Pharisee attacks (Mk 2⁷),
for it made Jesus equal with God (Jn 5¹⁸). He had
called them blasphemers of the Spirit ; they now
called Him a blasphemer of God. The contrast
was complete. Jesus' teachings and miracles prevented the Pharisees from attacking Him openly ;
so they tried now to catch Him by questions on
purification, worship, the commandments, and
tribute to Cæsar. He told them they were so
wicked they could not see a sign from heaven,
silenced them, and declared them hypocrites.
Then came His last visit to Jerusalem, and the
secret plotting of the Pharisees against Him. He
appeared now openly as the Messiah (Mk 11¹⁰).
When Caiaphas asked Him, 'Art thou the Christ,
Son of the Blessed?' He answered, 'I am' (Mk
14⁶¹· ⁶²). The Pharisees asked Him to rebuke the
crowd for calling Him Son of David ; they sent spies
to profess to be disciples and betray Him to the
Romans (Lk 20²⁰) ; they cast the blind man healed
out of the synagogue ; and led Jesus to ask, 'Why
go ye about to kill me?' (Jn 7¹⁹). They said He
had a devil, mocked Him, and took up stones to
kill Him as a blasphemer in the Temple (Jn 8²²· ⁵⁹).
The Pharisees supported the Sadducee leaders in
the last assault upon Jesus. 'Chief priests and
Pharisees' (Mt 27⁶², Jn 18³) plotted to kill Him
(Mk 14²· ⁴³), sent men to seize Him and went with
them, judged Him in the high priest's palace,
sought false witnesses against Him, heard Him
say He was the Son of God and declared it blasphemy, spat in His face, smote Him, put Him on
a mimic throne and said, 'In this way let us honour
the Son of God' (so Justin M., 1 *Apol.* 35, and

Evang. Petri), mocked His prophecies, and led the multitude to cry 'Crucify Him.' They charged Him with being a false prophet, deceiver of the people, a false Messiah claiming to be the Son of God (Lk 22[67], Jn 19[7]), the enemy of Cæsar, forbidding to pay tribute to him, and claiming to be King of the Jews, able to save others but unable to save Himself, and a destroyer of the holy nation. 'Chief priests and Pharisees' made His sepulchre sure, sealing the stone and setting a watch over 'that deceiver' (Mt 27[63-66]).

2. Jesus' criticism of the Pharisees. — Jesus' criticism followed the line of Pharisaic attack, and showed (1) *the legalistic perversion of religion in Judaism.* He showed (*a*) that they were utterly wrong in limiting the grace of God to the Jew under the yoke of the Law. The man who was offended at Him for helping the poor and outcast was not among the blessed. The righteousness of the Pharisees centring in themselves would never admit to heaven. The Roman centurion had more faith than the best Pharisees (Mt 8[10]), and Gentiles would enter heaven while they went into outer darkness (vv.[11. 12]). (*b*) Jesus told them their ceremonial usages were worse than useless, for they led to transgression of God's commandments (15[3]). They not only killed obedience by legalism, but made it impossible by putting small and great commandments on the same level. He told them they were doomed unless they abandoned their theology and mode of life. (*c*) He especially upbraided them respecting the Sabbath. In healing on that day He imitated David, the priests, the prophets, the Giver of the Sabbath and the Lord of the Sabbath, all of whom they ignorantly opposed when they taught that a man could not do good on that day. Their Sabbath theory sprang from hardness of heart, which had no mercy for the withered hand, the hungry disciples, the sick folk, the demoniac. They were blind, and with their followers perishing for lack of the knowledge He offered them. He then exhausted language in describing their wickedness. He anticipated St. Paul's description of heathenism and applied it to the Pharisees (Mt 23, etc., Ro 1[28-32] 2[1f.]).

(2) Jesus upbraided them further for *rejection of God and His Christ.* He told Nicodemus he must be born again of the Spirit and Son of God. The Pharisees who opposed Him followed the old Serpent who deceived Adam, and did his deeds. They were liars and murderers, and could not believe Jesus, who was of the truth (Jn 8[44. 45]). They could not see the holy proofs that He came from God, because they were wicked and adulterers. The darkness could not comprehend the light. They were bewitched, under demoniacal influence, and their persecution of Jesus was a matter of course. Having no word of God, or love or life of God in them, they could not follow Jesus (Jn 5[38f.]). Their rejection of Him was proof that they had already forsaken God. Jesus had shown He did not break the Sabbath law. He then went on to tell the Pharisees they had no authority to criticise Him, for His works were the works of God (5[17]). But they did not know the works of God when they saw them; they did not even understand Moses (5[46]), or David, or the prophets, for they were utterly out of touch with Divine revelation; and the Law they thought they were defending would condemn them at the last day (6[45f.]). They stumbled especially at Jesus' forgiving sin as Son of God, and His calling men to Him as the way to God; but He told them that, unless they accepted Him as Saviour, they would die in their sins (8[24]). He mixed appeals and warnings in His last dealings with them; but all in vain. Many of the common people accepted Him, but none of the Pharisees (7[48]). His last words to them were a series of 'Woes,' which He closed with the terrible sentence, 'Ye serpents, ye generation of vipers, how shall ye escape the judgment of hell?' (Mt 23[33]).

LITERATURE.—Besides the works quoted in the text, of which Wellhausen's, Bousset's, and Baldensperger's are especially important, cf. Montet, *Essai sur les origines d. partis Sad. et Phar.* 1883; Schürer, *HJP* § 26, and *Predigt Jesu in ihrem Verh. z. AT u. z. Jud.*; Weber, *System d. altsyn. Paläst. Theologie,* 1880; Sack, *Die altjüd. Religion,* 1889; Sieffert, 'Pharis. und. Sadd.' in Herzog, *PRE*[3] xv. 264 ff.; Dalman, *Die Worte Jesu,* 1898 (*Words of Jesus,* 1902); Wernle, *Beginnings of Christianity,* 1903, i. chs. ii.-vii., ii. chs. iv.-vi.; Jost, *Gesch. des Judenthums,* i. pp. 197-226; Ehrhardt, *Der Grundcharakter der Ethik Jesu im Verhält. z. d. mess. Hoffnungen s. Volkes,* 1895; Haupt, *Die eschatol. Aussagen Jesu,* 1895; J. Weiss, *Die Predigt Jesu vom Reiche Gottes,* 1892; Toy, *Judaism and Christianity,* 1891, pp. 220-290, 331-362; *Pro Christo et Ecclesia* (1901), 16, 33; and art. 'Pharisees' in Hastings' *DB.* See also H. P. Liddon, *Sermons on Some Words of Christ* (1892), 221; J. B. Mozley, *Univ. Serm.*[2] (1876), 25; F. W. Robertson, *Serm.,* 1st ser. (1875), 115; and the controversy on the Gospel representation of the Pharisees by I. Abrahams in *JQR* xi. (1899), 626, and C. G. Montefiore in *Hibbert Journ.* i. (1902), 335, and reply by A. Menzies, *do.* 789.

HUGH M. SCOTT.

PHILANTHROPY.—Philanthropy (φιλανθρωπία) is the love of man as man. It is love unconditioned by self, or by partly selfish relations of family and nation. It is love unto the uttermost. The Greek word occurs twice in the NT. St. Paul uses it of the universal compassion of God for mankind (Tit 3[4]), and St. Luke uses it to describe the kindness of the 'barbarians' of Melita towards the aliens shipwrecked on their coasts (Ac 28[2]). In both cases the word is correctly used to describe the compassion which recognizes no limitation. It is the element of universality that transforms humanitarian feeling into philanthropy. We shall not therefore consider here the kindness that belongs in some measure to all human intercourse, nor even that special manifestation of it which is seen in the charity of the early Christian Church. We shall confine our attention to showing how Christ infused into the common human sentiment that which completely transformed it, giving to it a finer motive, a larger range of activity, an absolute sanction, until St. John could venture to use his striking paradox, and say that the old law which they had had from the beginning was now 'a new commandment' (1 Jn 2[7. 8]).

Human pitifulness for human suffering belongs to the nature of man. It has always made the tender grace in human intercourse, and not infrequently it has risen to such heights as to command the instinctive admiration of the world for all that is heroic. But at best it has been spasmodic in its manifestation, it has been uncertain in its degree of intensity, and it has been strictly limited in its range. Christ took the rudimentary instinct and made it into a universal law. It is limited now neither in the sphere of its operation, nor in the time of its application: it is valid over all the earth, and applies to all generations. It dominates all mankind, and lifts man up to those levels of life in which sacrifice is consummate and eternal. It is the germ out of which has sprung all the highest good in social intercourse; out of it have come not only the occasional amenities of life, but even the moral usages of men. It is the secret of civilization, and its hold upon the imagination and conscience has become so great that it is now woven into the moral consciousness of men. It is a commandment as definite and as binding as any in the Decalogue; it comprehends them all, and where it is not honoured its neglect is visited with the contempt and censure of the world, while he who fails to obey it realizes in himself the degeneration which is the natural outworking of all Divine law abused by men. The Gospel story reveals the process by which this transformation has been made good. The evolution by which *compassion* has been changed into *philanthropy* is so subtly described that it may easily escape the notice of the superficial reader, but to those who possess the necessary spiritual insight and enlightenment the story has all the charm of a natural development. It establishes the origin of the law: reveals Christ as its Author. Philanthropy is the immediate product of the Incarnation.

1. Jesus could scarcely have been born into a less promising sphere for the promulgation of such a law. He could scarcely have found a less likely milieu than Judaism afforded for the cultivation of such a principle of life; nor could He have made His attempt at a time when common human pitifulness seemed at a lower ebb, than in the days that marked the decadence of the Empire of Rome. The contempt of the Roman for the conquered, and of the Greek for the barbarian, has always been recognized. Plato speaks with commendation of 'the pure and innate hatred of the foreign nature,' and Aristotle condones the slavery of his age, and complacently regards the slave as 'a kind of animate machine.' It is not until we come to the Stoicism of the Christian era that we meet with any teaching that approaches philanthropy, though even here we have Seneca laying down, as motive for the high type of benevolence he inculcated, the 'consciousness of having a noble nature' (*de Benef.* iv. 12). Blood relationships have always and universally laid down marked boundaries in the empire of love, and these have found a complete and historic embodiment in caste as it may be studied in India to-day. But it may well be considered whether even this system is not left far behind by the Jew, who held that the Gentiles without the Law were accursed, thus excluding all foreigners not only from the regard of man but even from that of God. Yet the fact remains that Christ, born into such a system, created the philanthropy that ignores all frontiers, and does not hesitate to lay down life itself for those whose one claim is that they share in the common humanity.

There are not wanting in the Gospel narrative incidents which seem to show that Christ inherited this feeling of His countrymen and of His age, at least to some extent. He limits the ministry of His disciples to the villages of Judæa, bidding them avoid the villages of the Samaritans (Mt 10[5]); and in His interview with the Syrophœnician woman (Mk 7[26]) He not only repeats the limitation given to His disciples as binding also upon Himself, declaring that He was not sent save to the lost sheep of the house of Israel, but speaks of the woman as a dog, and claims for the Jews that they are the children of the household. Contempt could no further go, and the words fall strangely from the Saviour's lips. But without for the moment setting against these passages others in which the sympathy of Jesus is seen to be as catholic as it was tender, it may very well be argued that these two incidents do not establish exclusiveness in Christ, and in any case the exclusiveness broke down and gave way to the very opposite feeling in Him. But, apart from that, it may be shown that the limitation in the injunction given to the disciples was due not to any narrowness in the Saviour's sympathy, but rather to His recognition of the limitations of His emissaries. The Apostles, with their prejudices strong within them, had scarcely the tact and the culture necessary for those who would open the door of faith to the Gentiles, and subsequent events show how after many a lesson the leader of the band, St. Peter himself, was unable fully to recognize the truth so clearly seen and strongly enforced by St. Paul. At any rate it is most significant that when the lessons of Christ's life were drawing to a close the prohibition was taken away, and the Apostles were instructed to

'go into all the world, and make disciples of all the nations' (Mt 28[19]). A far greater difficulty is seen in the story of the Syrophœnician woman. Here the Saviour's words are so entirely at variance not only with His own act on that occasion, but with the tenderness and courtesy with which at all other times He dealt with women, that attempts have been made from the earliest times to reconcile the contrast between the Spirit of Jesus and His harsh and contemptuous words on the occasion. The words can scarcely be justified even on the supposition that it was a harsh discipline intended to bring out the triumphant faith of the woman. We hold that Christ used the words in irony, and that, feeling the utter falseness of the leaders and teachers of the Jews, driven in utter weariness from them into Gentile territory, He assumes for the time being the narrow spirit which belonged to them, that His disciples might see how Pharisaic doctrine looked when reduced to act in dealing with the sorrow and need of the world. He throws into contrast with that doctrine the quick intuition of the woman, as well as the humility of her trust as she declares that even the Gentiles have a place in the family of God. There could be no finer method of revealing to the disciples the contrast between that exclusiveness of spirit which He had come to destroy, and the larger trust in the all-comprehending love of God which He came to fulfil.

Christ gave, then, to the human feeling of pitiful concern for another the universality which it lacked. And He did this first by His full and generous recognition of good in the alien, whether He found him in the actual commerce of life or in the imaginary scenes which He made to live in parabolic teaching. He had not found in Israel such faith as He found in the centurion (Mt 8[10, 11]), and He closed His tribute to that faith by saying that many should come from the east and the west and sit down with Abraham in the Kingdom of God, while the favoured people themselves should be cast out. When He was asked for a definition of a neighbour, He pointed to a Samaritan, and described him as possessing qualities lacking in priest and Levite (Lk 10[27ff.]). He had spoken of His own people with a great tenderness as 'the lost sheep of the house of Israel' (Mt 10[6] 15[24]), but He extends that tenderness to the Gentile world when He speaks of 'other sheep not of this fold.' He says that they too are His, and them also He must bring (Jn 10[16]). Whether He spoke the words to Nicodemus or not, it is clear that John learnt from Him that the love of God was not the exclusive privilege of the Jew, but that God loved 'the world,' and that His salvation was within the reach of whosoever should believe (Jn 3[16]). In 'the Gospel to the Greeks' He speaks of 'all men' as coming within the attractive power of Himself crucified and ascended (Jn 12[32]). And when He gave to His followers His final commission, there was no limit to the sphere of their evangelic labours: they were to 'go into all the world,' 'to make disciples of all the nations' (Mk 16[15], Mt 28[19]). Christ not only widened the domain of this law of love, pushing back the boundaries marked out by social custom or selfish expediency or fear, but He also enriched the law by giving it a deeper note, an intenser spirit. The poor man for neglect of whom Dives found himself at last in torment, was 'full of sores,' he was licked by the dog, the common scavenger of offal. Such was the claimant upon the rich man's kindliness (Lk 16[20ff.]). Lowly service touched its lowliest when the Master stooped to the feet of the disciple (Jn 13[5]). Throughout the East the touch of the foot brings defilement and degradation. And when the service had been rendered to His followers, He spoke to them of 'a new commandment' which He had therein given them (Jn 13[15, 34]). He called upon those who would follow Him to be ready to sell all and follow Him (Mt 19[21]). The gift that won the approval of Heaven was not that which came out of the superfluity of the rich, but the widow's mite, for that was 'all that she had' (Mk 12[43]). Last of all, He declared that He Himself would give unto the uttermost, for as Good Shepherd He was ready to lay down His life for His sheep (Jn 10[11]). There was thus added to the length and breadth of universal love the height and depth of sacrifice, and these two elements wrought powerfully in the instinctive love of man until the neediness of each became the common burden of all, and philanthropy became a part of the spiritual equipment of men.

2. The expression of that spiritual equipment will develop from age to age. The forms of its expression in the early days of the Christian era are well known. Christ instructed His disciples to heal the sick, and generally to minister to the physically distressed. The relief of the poor seems to have been another marked form of Christian philanthropy from the first, and they were in addition to minister in spiritual things, and to seek to admit men into the Kingdom of God. It may at first sight appear as if this was a strictly limited form of philanthropy, but it is obvious that the form of expression was accommodated to the capacities of the agents chosen and to the simplicity of the life which they were accustomed to live. Such forms of sympathetic relief, we may be assured, existed long before Christ sent forth His disciples; that which He added was the twofold vitalizing principle which made the charity of the age a living reality. It became real (ἀληθές, 1 Jn 2[8]) in them, as it was already in Him. The universality and the intensity which were His contribution to the common love, the old commandment of mankind, were also notes of life. Love without limit in range or in intensity,—such was the new commandment illustrated in the washing of the disciples' feet. It was now ἀγάπη εἰς τέλος, it was love unto the uttermost (Jn 13[1]). And having dropped into the human instinct the vitalizing germ of a new principle, Christ was content to leave the new law to find wider and fuller expression as the years moved on. With the developing powers of man, that vitalized law would be certain to find a far more extended application than lay within the compass of His earliest followers. In that age the manumission of the slave, the education of the poor, the enforcement of laws of sanitation—such things as are the commonplaces of philanthropic measures in our time—were not within the power of the disciples of Christ. But we can see that that which gives them the sanction of law, that which comes into every social reform that has any promise of permanence or of helpfulness, is just that with which Christ filled the hearts of His followers as He sent them forth on their simpler mission:—all endowment is but a trust; 'freely ye have received, freely give' (Mt 10[8]); there is no limit in love; the neediness of each is the common burden of all. All social reform, happily increasingly recognized, advocated, accepted, in our age, is but the working out in the larger life of to-day of the vital principle contributed by Christ when He made love's range conterminous with the universe of God, and at the same moment made it instinct with His own passion and sacrifice.

But philanthropy as Christ has taught it in the Gospel story goes further than this. It not only is the spring of all true social reform, but it possesses the power to enforce observance. It gives the sanction of duty to all such observance. It be-

comes not merely an added quality in human intercourse, but a positive compelling force. It is a new commandment. Neglect to feed the hungry, clothe the naked, visit the prisoner and the sick, or to translate these special terms into the general terms for which they stand,—to meet all human need as it arises,—such neglect is not in the eyes of Christ a venial offence, a trifle of indifference; it is clear He took a far more serious view of it: He taught His disciples that it meant rejection in the judgment of God; it excludes him who so neglects from the Kingdom. Philanthropy was thus invested with the august powers of a moral law. If we consider philanthropy to be the common human instinct endowed with the range given to it by Christ, the εἰς τέλος of His own showing, we can see how this binding quality, this sanction, is imparted. For such a quality in love strikes at the root of that which is destructive of all morality, and that is briefly the calculating spirit. The immoral compromises which we so often make with ourselves become impossible when love unto the uttermost is the rule of our regard for our fellow-men. It opposes every tendency to evade law where possible. It adds strength and loyalty to obedience, and imparts to scrupulous observance the gladness of enthusiasm. This operation so refines and enlarges duty, that by the side of it all other duty seems the merest travesty of duty, and to fail to reach this height of moral observance becomes a positive failure, a moral offence, a breach of law. Christ accomplished this by striking clear and strong that personal note which is the key to all His influence. He attached men to Himself, and then exhibited in Himself the very law which He promulgated, until in after days the appeal might be made to the Christian Church that its members should bear one another's burdens, since only thus could they fulfil that LAW which Christ was (οὕτως ἀναπληρώσατε τὸν νόμον τοῦ Χριστοῦ, Gal 6[2]). This love unto the uttermost was lived; and lived by Him who by His own loveliness has drawn all men to Himself. It is for this reason that words which might easily have become the rules of another futile Utopia, or the striking maxims of an original teacher, have become instinct with the spiritual; and with the new law of love the power to realize it was given. When to His setting forth of the new philanthropy Christ added the words, 'Ye have done it unto me' (Mt 25[40]), He endowed His words with spirit and life.

This spirit the Christian Church has sought to realize in what are called Missions. No distinction need ever be made between 'Home' and 'Foreign' Missions. Least of all should any be made when we consider, as we do here, the spirit which belongs to both. The resource and ingenuity of love will appear in all such enterprise. There is no power of modern life but will be pressed into service by the love which recognizes no limit to its operation, no limitation to its spirit. Legislative powers will be used for what they are worth. Social organization, all that art or science can teach,—in a word, all the fulness of life,—will be permeated and freely used by this great law of love. That law will find its fullest application in the service of the alien and the foreigner. Here, if anywhere, the universality of love will be seen; when the missionary breaks every tie that makes the sweetness of his life, to carry the burdens of

'Sullen peoples, half devil and half child,'

he reveals the intensest manifestation of that love whose Divine note is sacrifice. It is no wonder that the story of the triumphs of the gospel, or of the devotion of the missionary in strange and remote regions or in circumstances of peculiar physical peril and distress, has so often come back to the Christian Church with a breath as of the ocean, a breath that infuses new life into the stale observance and gives new stimulus to the jaded servant, a breath that whispers of broad spaces, of elemental forces, of the fulness of the Infinite, the

'Deep where all our thoughts are drowned.'

Missionary service must always be the perfection of philanthropy. And philanthropy is love without limit, and love is of God, for God is LOVE.

LITERATURE.—Uhlhorn, *Christian Charity in the Ancient Church* ; Wernle, *Beginnings of Christianity* ; v. Dobschütz, *Christian Life in the Primitive Church* ; Seeley, *Ecce Homo* ; Harnack, *Expansion of Christianity* ; Storrs, *Divine Origin of Christianity* ; Brace, *Gesta Christi* ; Church, *Gifts of Civilization* ; and the following Sermons :—on Jn 13³⁴ by F. W. Robertson (i. 234), Mt 19¹⁹ by C. H. Spurgeon, Mk 12²⁹⁻³¹ by A. Alexander. The question is also treated on the basis of the Sermon on the Mount by Gore, Trench, and Tholuck.

W. W. HOLDSWORTH.

PHILIP (Φίλιππος, 'lover of horses').—**1. Philip the Apostle.**—For the little that we know regarding him, beyond the mere mention of his name in the lists of the Twelve (Mt 10³, Mk 3¹⁸, Lk 6¹⁴), we are wholly dependent upon a few scattered notices in the Fourth Gospel.

(1) The first of these tells the story of his call, which took place on the day after the call of Andrew and John with their respective brothers (Jn 1⁴³ff.). And the fact that it is expressly mentioned that Philip, like these men, belonged to Bethsaida, would seem to point to a certain amount of friendship as having already existed between them, while his Greek name (a peculiarity which among the Apostles he shared with Andrew) makes it at least possible that he himself was originally of Greek descent. This accords entirely with what we know of the mixed Gentile population of Bethsaida. Whether, however, this was so or not, Philip would seem to have belonged to the growing class of devout souls throughout the land who were 'waiting for the consolation of Israel,' even if he had not, along with the previously named disciples, been an open follower of John the Baptist. For when Jesus 'finds' him—evidently not by accident but as the result of a deliberate search— and addresses to him the first direct call which, so far as we know, He addressed to any man, 'Follow me,' Philip immediately responds, and once and for all throws in his lot with his new Master. So complete indeed is his surrender, that though as yet his knowledge of Jesus is very imperfect (cf. v.⁴⁵ 'the son of Joseph'), he shows himself endued with the genuine missionary spirit in proceeding in his turn to 'find' Nathanael, that together they may rejoice in the discovery of the promised Messiah. The very precision and minuteness of the terms, moreover, in which Philip announces that discovery, bring before us another aspect of his character, for they show him to have been a man of an anxious and careful turn of mind, asking for no conviction on the part of others until he has been first convinced himself, and ever ready to submit all doubts and prejudices to the test of actual experience (v.⁴⁶ 'Come and see').

(2) Of this latter trait of the Apostle's character we have further confirmation, from a somewhat different point of view, in the next incident in which he is specially mentioned. For at the feeding of the Five Thousand in the wilderness it was to Philip that Jesus addressed the question, 'Whence are we to buy bread, that these may eat?' (Jn 6⁵). Some have thought that the reason of this was that Philip had charge of the commissariat of the Apostolic band, just as Judas acted as their treasurer; but of this there is no proof, and St. John expressly adds that Jesus said this to 'prove' him. The Master knew His disciple's cautious

and deliberate disposition, and how little he had yet shown himself able to make any of the bolder efforts of faith. And He evidently hoped that on this occasion Philip would rise from the manifest inadequacy of the existing material resources to the thought of the unseen powers which He (the Christ) had at His command. But the hope was to be disappointed. Philip was so occupied with his own careful calculations as to what the actual feeding of the multitude meant, that he could think of nothing else. And even the matter-of-fact Andrew showed more imagination when, after the mention of the lad's little store, he at least hazarded the suggestion, 'But what are they amongst so many?'

(3) The case is similar when we turn to another occasion when we find the two Apostles together. It is in entire accord not only with Philip's (possible) Greek origin, but with his sympathetic, inquiring disposition, that the Greek visitors to the Temple should select him as their ambassador to Jesus (Jn 12²⁰ff.). But it is equally characteristic that, as he realized the greatness and significance of the request, coming as it did from pure Gentiles, he should hesitate to act upon it on his own responsibility. He would do nothing until he had consulted Andrew. And even when Andrew had approved, it was only in conjunction with him, and leaving him to occupy the foremost place ('Andrew and Philip'), that Philip went to tell Jesus.

(4) This 'faith without confidence' is even more marked in the last glimpse which St. John gives us of his brother Apostle. When, in His farewell discourse to the Twelve, Jesus announced that He was going to the 'Father,' and that no one could come to the 'Father' except by Him, it was left to Philip to say, 'Lord, show us the Father, and it sufficeth us' (Jn 14⁸). With him 'seeing' was 'believing.' He could not believe that any real knowledge of the Father was possible except such as resulted from an actual theophany; and so proved how blinded he had been to that higher manifestation of which he had for so long been witness in the words and the acts of the Son.

(5) With the pathetic personal appeal to him which this dulness of spiritual vision called forth (Jn 14⁹), Philip disappears from the Gospel story. And we hear nothing more of him in the NT except for the mention of his name amongst the Apostles who assembled in the upper room at Jerusalem after their Lord's Ascension (Ac 1¹³). Various traditions have, however, gathered round his memory.

The most interesting of these is the account preserved by Clement of Alexandria (*Strom.* iii. 4, § 25), which identifies him with the unknown disciple who, when the Lord's call came to him, asked that he might first go and bury his father—an identification at least in keeping with what we have seen of Philip's character. The apocryphal *Journeyings of Philip the Apostle* (3rd cent.) represent him as travelling through Lydia and Asia, and finally settling in Hierapolis. And it was there, according to Polycrates (bishop of Ephesus c. 190 A.D.), that he was 'buried' 'along with his two aged virgin daughters' (Eus. *HE* iii. 31; cf. Lightfoot, *Colossians* ², p. 45ff.). The same authority adds that another daughter who 'lived in fellowship with the Holy Spirit' was buried at Ephesus—a circumstance that may perhaps point to Philip's own residence there for a time, and consequently to a renewed intercourse with his old friend the Apostle John. If so, we have an additional reason why St. John should have introduced Philip's name so freely in the 'memoirs' on which at the time he was engaged. Of the later connexion with Hierapolis already alluded to we have now interesting confirmation in the discovery of an inscription showing that the church there was dedicated to the memory ' of the holy and glorious Apostle and theologian Philip' (τοῦ ἁγίου κὲ ἰνδόξου ἀποστόλου κὲ θεολογου Φιλίππου : see Ramsay, *Cities and Bishoprics of Phrygia*, i. p. 552 f.).

In the West, St. Philip's Day is observed along with that of St. James the Less on May 1st. In the East, St. Philip's Day is Nov. 14th, St. James', Oct. 23rd.

LITERATURE.—In addition to what has been noted above, see Westcott, *The Gospel of St. John*, p. lxxiii f. ; A. B. Bruce, *The Training of the Twelve* (see 'Philip' in the Index); H. P. Liddon, *University Sermons*, 2nd ser., i. 'Prejudice and Experience.' (Jn 14[46]); J. B. Lightfoot, *Cambridge Sermons*, p. 129 ff. 'Show us the Father' (Jn 14[8. 9]); R. C. Trench, *Studies in the Gospels*, p. 68; A. Maclaren, *A Year's Ministry*, ii. 155; J. D. Jones, *The Glorious Company of the Apostles*, p. 109; R. H. Lovell, *First Types of the Chr. Life*, p. 514; and the present writer's *The Twelve Apostles* (Dent), p. 49 ff.

2. Herod Philip.—See vol. i. p. 722[b].

GEORGE MILLIGAN.

PHYLACTERIES (OT 'frontlets').—The observance of phylacteries is based on Ex 13[9. 10] and Dt 6[8] 11[18]. For the Heb. and Greek terms see Hastings' *DB*, *s.v.* It is disputed whether the passages in the Pentateuch are to be understood literally (so most of the Rabbinic writers, and Ginsburg in Kitto's *Cyclop.*) or metaphorically (so Ibn Ezra, Rashbam, the Karaites, Jerome, Lyra, Calvin, Hengstenberg, Knobel, Keil, and Kennedy in Hastings' *DB*); some assign a metaphorical meaning to the passages in Ex. and a literal to those in Deuteronomy. Under the more legal and formal interpretation and observance of the OT which flourished after the Return, the literal interpretation became dominant. The exact date of the introduction of the literal observance of the precept cannot be given. No indisputable reference is found in the OT; passages like Pr 1[9] being indecisive. From the relatively large number of regulations referring to phylacteries—some of them connected with the Tannaim—it follows that they were used as early as the time of the Sopherim, the 4th or at least the 3rd cent. B.C. (see *JE* x. 26). The first explicit reference, and that to the hand phylactery, is in the letter of the pseudo-Aristeas, the date of which is variously assigned between 200 and 100 B.C., where they are regarded as an established custom. They are also mentioned in connexion with Simeon ben Sheṭach, brother-in-law of Alexander Jannæus (B.C. 105–78). Josephus (*Ant.* IV. viii. 13) speaks of them as an established and recognized custom. We may, therefore, regard them as having preceded by about two centuries the birth of Jesus Christ. For our knowledge of the customs associated with them we are indebted chiefly to the references in the Mishna (for which see Schürer, *HJP* II. ii. 113). Though the collection of these traditions took place in the 2nd Christian cent., they may be regarded, for the most part, as representing an earlier state of things.

In the later Jewish writers, phylacteries play a great part; their manufacture and use are elaborately described, and their significance and importance dwelt upon at length. 'There are more laws—ascribed to delivery by God to Moses—clustering about phylacteries than about any other institution of Judaism. Maimonides (*Yad Tef.*) mentions 10; Rodkinssohn (*Tef. le Mosheh*) mentions 18' (*JE*). According to the Kabbala, they were significant of the wisdom, reason, and greatness of God. Phylacteries were more holy than the gold plate worn by the high priest, since that contained the Divine Name once, the phylacteries twenty-three times. The Mishna taught that 'he who has Tephillin on his head and his arm, Tsitsith on his garment, and Mezuzah on his door, has every possible guarantee that he will not sin.' The wearing of them distinguished the cultured and pious from the common mass, the *'am-hā'ārez*, the 'people who knew not the law' (Jn 7[49]). Though worn probably at first all day, they became limited to the time of morning prayer. Careful directions are given as to the person (women, the unclean), the times (Sabbaths and festivals), and the places (cemeteries, etc.) where their use was prohibited.

Phylacteries are of two kinds, those for the hand and those for the head. In the case of the former, a box or house (בַּיִת) was made of the skin of a clean animal, which had been softened in water and shaped and stiffened on a mould. In this was inserted a parchment on which the Scripture passages, Ex 13[1-10] and [11-16], Dt 6[4-9] and 11[13-21], had been written in four columns; the parchment was rolled and tied with white, washed hairs from a cow or calf, usually from the tail. This box was then sewn on to a leather base, furnished with a loop through which a leather strap passed. In the case of the head phylactery a similar box was prepared, but with four divisions, in which were placed in order, beginning from the left side, the four above named passages of the Pentateuch. On the right hand side of the box of this phylactery was impressed a three-pronged *Shin* (ש), and on the left hand one with four prongs (ש). This, too, was sewn on a base and provided with a leather strap (see Illustration in Hastings' *DB* iii. 870).

In 'laying'—to use the technical term—the phylacteries, that for the hand was adjusted first. The box part was placed above the elbow on the inside of the left arm where it would press against the heart, a fact to which significance was given (Dt 6[6]). A knot in the shape of the letter *Yōdh* (י) was made, the strap was wound about the arm four times and three times, and three times round the middle finger of the hand. The box of the other was placed on the forehead, where the hair ceases to grow, the band taken round the head and fastened with a knot like the letter *Dāleth* (ד), while the two ends were made to hang down in front over the shoulders. The *Shin* on the box, the *Dāleth* knot on the head phylactery, and the *Yōdh* knot on the hand phylactery, made the letters of one of the Divine Names—שַׁדַּי *Shaddāi*, 'Almighty.'

The following benedictions are said. At the laying of the hand phylactery—'Blessed art Thou, O Lord our God, King of the Universe, who hast sanctified us by Thy commandments, and has commanded us to lay the Tephillin.' An almost identical one is uttered during the placing of that for the head, and when it is finished—'Blessed be His name, whose glorious kingdom is for ever and ever.' At the adjusting of the strap round the middle finger, which is left till the last, 'And I will betroth thee unto me for ever; yea, I will betroth thee unto me in righteousness, and in judgment, and in loving-kindness, and in mercy. I will even betroth thee unto me in faithfulness: and thou shalt know the Lord' (Hos 2[19]). In removing, the fastening of the hand is first undone, the head phylactery removed, then that on the arm; they are kissed and placed in a bag, as to the place and use of which careful directions are given.

It cannot be doubted that the Pharisees and scribes in the time of our Lord used phylacteries; but how far the custom was followed by the people generally is uncertain. In order to emphasize their profession of religion, these people 'made broad' (πλατύνουσι, Mt 23[5]) these mementoes of their Judaism, whether by enlarging the whole, the boxes and the straps, or, as the Sinaitic and Curetonian Syriac suggest, the straps only. It was the vain extension of the outward sign of an unreal religion that our Lord rebuked; it marked the externality and hollowness of contemporary Pharisaism. While this is the only NT reference to phylacteries, their use by a certain class should continually be borne in mind by the reader, as it may add to the vividness of the picture suggested by many incidents. Thus in Mt 22[34] || it may be considered as certain that the group of Pharisees with whom our Lord held His controversy wore their broadened phylacteries, and that the passage He quoted, the *Shema'*, the foundation of Hebrew religion, would be found in the phylacteries they carried on their heads and arms.

LITERATURE.—Comm. on Ex. and Deut., including long note in Kalisch's *Exodus*; Maimonides, *Yad Hachazakah*, *Hilcoth Tephillin*; Wagenseil, *Sota*; artt. in Hastings' *DB*, the *EBi* ('Frontlets'), Smith's *DB* ('Frontlets'), Kitto's *Cyclop.*, the *JE*, Hamburger's *RE*, Riehm's *HWB*; Schürer, *HJP* II. ii. 113; Buxtorf, *Lex. Chald.* and *Syn. Jud.* (which contains much curious information); Edersheim, *Sketches of Jewish Social Life*; Margoliouth, *Fundamental Principles of Judaism* (much information as to modern use). J. T. L. MAGGS.

PHYSICAL (φυσικός, 'natural,' 'inborn').—To this word a distinctive and conspicuous place has been given in the terminology of modern science, and that very appropriately ; for the object of science in every one of its branches is to acquire such a knowledge of the Universe as shall correspond exactly to the constituted and established nature of things. Neither the word 'physical' nor the word 'nature' ($\phi\acute{v}\sigma\iota s$) occurs in any of the four Gospels. But nevertheless many things which fall under the description of both terms, as scientifically used, occupy a large place in all the Gospels ; and there high importance is necessarily and designedly attached to them. It is true that one has only to run one's eye reflectively over the pages of the Gospels to discover that in them the *moral* order of things is the matter of supreme and controlling interest. But while that is so, it becomes also apparent that this moral interest is not only involved in the physical order of things, but is inevitably and to a vast extent dependent upon it. Thus, *e.g.*, it is everywhere manifest in these narratives of our Lord's earthly life and work that He appeared among men as an *individual* Being. This implies that the physical order of existence was epitomized in Him in the same way and to the same extent as it is in every individual human being. It implies that His body was the organ of the moral order of the world as the latter existed in the spiritual constitution of His being, and as it came to manifestation in the moral or spiritual activities of His life within the sphere of His moral relations to God and to men. It implies, also, that His bodily constitution and life placed Him in direct relations with, and in constant dependence upon, the whole order of the physical environment in which He lived and moved and had His being as 'God manifest *in the flesh*' (1 Ti 3[16]). And so it becomes obvious that if He had not entered into these incarnate relations with the physical order of things, He never could have become the Son of Man, and if He had never become the Son of Man He never could have revealed Himself to humanity as the Son of God (Jn 1, 2 Co 4[6]). For these reasons, then, and others that sprang out of them or were otherwise related to them, our Lord was necessitated to make the physical order of the world a subject of reflexion, and to embody in His teaching such ideas of it as He considered to be fit for communication as a part of His general message to mankind. That He did make it a subject of extensive and profound, careful and sympathetic study, is as evident as any other fact in the Gospels. It is equally evident, too, that as the result of this study He formed some very definite and highly important conceptions regarding the order of things in question, more than one of which were entirely original. It may be affirmed, moreover, that none of the ideas of this order, to which as a Teacher of humanity He attached momentous importance and value, can ever be superseded by the teaching of either Science or Philosophy. What, then, were the leading constructions that He as a religious Teacher put upon the physical order of the world ?

1. For one thing, this order of things presented itself to His mind as *a medium of Divine revelation* (*e.g.* Mt 5[44-48] 6[25-30]). The question as to the order of things physical, and its significance, must have shaped itself in His mind at an early stage in His life of observation and reflexion. What the result of His inquiry was appears in His teaching. The most general and important item in that result was the discovery of *the presence and activity of God in the established order of organic and inorganic existence*. To His mind God was immanent and operative in nature ; and it is in the same view of the relation of God to the physical order of the Universe that modern Theism and Philosophy have begun to rest. That such was

indeed His view appears from His own utterances on the relation of God to the order of things physical ; which show that nothing was further from His mind than the reckless idea in which God is conceived as existing only in a relation of externality to this order and as acting upon it from without. When, for instance, He saw the sun rise and rain fall, and pondered on the extensive and complicated orderly system of physical means and ends to which sunrise and rainfall belong, He perceived in these occurrences manifestations of the immediate activity of God (Mt 5[45]), and He was too unerring a thinker not to know that God's will and therefore God Himself must be immanent in the established system of things in which He conceived the Divine activity as displayed. Nor is there any real collision here between Christ and modern science in regard to the system of activity to which sunrise and rainfall are due. When He said, 'Your Father which is in heaven maketh his sun to rise . . . and sendeth rain,' He used words which are absolutely consistent with the strictest scientific ideas of the natural forces and laws by which the same events in the physical order of things are now explained. For if the scientist is able to explain, and right, from his own point of view, in explaining these events by the action of physical forces and the laws of their operation, this explanation does not account for the existence of these forces themselves, for their persistence, for the perfectly and constantly regulated mode in which their respective forms of activity are manifested, or for the originating cause of the complicated and exquisite adjustment of these forces and their activities to the ends they serve. For these things there is only one satisfactory explanation, and that is the immanent and immediate activity of God. And Science and Philosophy have been rapidly becoming aware that no better explanation is likely ever to be found.

But, further, for Christ the revelation of God and His activity in the physical order of the world possessed a *moral significance*. God as a Moral Being—and because as such He is perfect—can never act unless morally, even in the system of things physical. This truth regulated the whole of our Lord's conception of God's relation to this order, and of His ways of administering its provisions. And therefore it is that He saw in such physical events as sunrise and rainfall manifestations of God's beneficence and magnanimity. He 'maketh His sun to rise on the evil and on the good, and sendeth rain on the just and on the unjust'! These words are a striking revelation of the perfectly fresh, intelligent, discerning eyes with which Christ looked upon the physical order of things, and contemplated God and His activity as therein manifested. This appears when three things are noted. —(1) There is only *one* established physical order of things. (2) This order is constituted throughout on one and the same homogeneous plan, and it is necessarily regulated accordingly. (3) Therefore it is impossible for this order to be so administered as to make distinctions of any kind in the distribution of its provisions among men. Here distinctions cannot be made even between the evil and the good, between the just and the unjust. Therefore as the Author and the Administrator of this system of things God makes no such distinctions. Within this sphere of the relations between God and men, the good and the evil, the just and the unjust, are the same to Him. His impartiality to both sorts of men is as absolute and universal as the rising of the sun and the falling of rain. And God Himself has so ordered the physical universe that it should be so, and that it cannot be otherwise. And, so far as any one can say, Christ was the first to notice and fully to appreciate the true meaning of these obvious but vastly important facts. In sunrise and rainfall He saw nothing but instances of the manifestation of the loving-kindness of God to all men, good and evil alike, and of His magnanimity towards evil and unjust men. For it was one of Christ's governing ideas as a Teacher that God did not need to punish evil and unjust men for their sin by withholding from them any of the beneficent provisions of the physical order of things. He knew and taught in effect that it is with the *moral order* of things and God's unerring and all-sufficient administration of *it*, as the *moral* Governor of the world, that evil and unjust men have to reckon ; and therefore, in the exercise of the magnanimity alike of His love and of His justice, God dispenses to them, in common with good and just men, a full and free share of His sunshine and rain. So Christ understood this matter (cf. Mt 5^{21-30} $11^{25.\ 26}$, Jn 9^{39-41} with Mt 5^{45}).

2. But, further, these views that Christ held as to the physical order of the world suggest the inference that He must have looked upon this system as *an order of law*. That He did so regard it is evident from His teaching, when the latter is carefully and fairly examined from this point of view. The term 'law,' as defined by science, is of modern origin, and therefore it is never employed in this sense in the Gospels. But the Gospels are rich in recognitions of a large variety of those facts for which the term 'law,' as scientifically understood, stands ; and recognition of these facts was made by Christ Himself. The modern conception of the order of things physical, which the term 'law' is employed to denote, is, that it is an order in which perfect constancy and regularity reign universally and persistently, and that even in the case of its minutest phenomena and its subtlest processes. Did Christ, then, perceive and acknowledge the great features of the physical order on which this conception is founded ? He did. In all its essential forces and laws the physical order was the same in His time as it is to-day. Science has not created any of the forces or laws in question ; it has only discovered and formulated them. Moreover, it is evident that Christ's observations and His reflexions on nature were prompted and controlled rather by religious than by scientific motives or reasons. It is to be admitted, again, that He never made the physical order of things a direct subject of teaching, but always made it subservient to the religious or moral ends He had in view. Still He was deeply convinced of the constancy and regularity of the physical system of existence in the midst of which He lived and taught, and on which He depended (*e.g.* Mt 7^{16-20}, Mk 4^{3-32}). That it was so is evinced by the following facts :—(1) A large proportion of His teaching was based on the principle of comparison. (2) The most of His comparisons were indications of resemblances between the things of the physical order of the world and the things of the Kingdom of God, which are in reality the things of the moral order of the world, considered as an order in which the will and purpose of God are coming to realization in the moral relations of God to men and of men to Him and to one another in Christ. (3) In His comparisons it was His custom to lay conspicuous emphasis on those phenomena of the physical order of things in which the constancy and regularity of this order are prominent. (4) His manifest reasons for doing so were such as these—His whole conception of the Kingdom of God implies that He regarded it as an order of perfect moral constancy and regularity, *i.e.* as an order of moral law. But few, if indeed

any, of His hearers had any idea of the Kingdom of God as being such an order. On the other hand, however, they were familiar with many of the phenomena of constancy and regularity in the physical order of things. Therefore His object in calling the attention of His hearers to these phenomena was to lead their minds up from the things of sense to the things of faith, and thereby to convey to them the conception, and to awaken in them the conviction, that the things of the moral order of the world, like the order of things revealed to their sense-perception, were things that had real existence, things that were indeed founded in moral principles of absolute constancy and regularity, and things therefore to be relied upon with the utmost confidence. (5) These considerations, then, all imply that the physical order of things from which our Lord drew His comparisons must have been regarded by Him as a system of *order*, a system in which constancy, regularity, law reigns. The whole principle of comparison as thus explained is applied, *e.g.*, in Mt 7^{15-20}.

3. But the physical order of the world was regarded by our Lord as also *a sphere of Providential administration* (*e.g.* Mt 5^{44-48} 6^{25-34}, Lk 12^{4-7}). It is important to note the fact that all His allusions to this branch of the subject here considered, imply that He conceived of the Divine providence as exercised within the boundaries of the physical system of things. This system is, so to speak, the machinery employed by God in all the various manifestations of His providential care. But if this system is an order of physical constancy or law, all the exercises of the Divine providence must be regulated by this fact. So Christ's teaching represents it as being. He never spoke of providence as in effect a system of Divine activities in which God, interposing in the interests of the objects of His care, either ignored the established order of physical existence or made breaches in its established arrangements. All the ways in which He saw the providential activities of God manifested in care for His creatures were ways in which the established orderliness of the physical world came into effect, as in the case of the rising of the sun and the falling of rain. That is to say, in Christ's view the physical order of the world is constituted on a providential plan, in which a perfectly arranged and regulated system of means is adjusted to serve the beneficent ends contemplated by God.

What Christ's ideas were of the leading features of the administration of this system is suggested by those passages of His teaching to which attention has been called. He believed the providential activities of God to be at once universal and particular, and this belief is in accordance with the nature of things. He believed also that God's providential activities are not only immanent and immediate, but persistent. They are as unslumbering and restless as the physical energies or forces in the activities and effects of which they are manifested. He believed, moreover, that God's providential interest and care extended even to birds and flowers as well as to human beings ; and this belief, also, is justified by the necessities and arrangements of the physical order of things to which they as *living* beings in common with men belong. For they, as living beings, have each physical needs according to their own respective natures and places and destinies in nature ; and therefore it was not unworthy of Christ to form and take delight in the conviction that their Creator was providentially faithful to them.

But withal, it remains to be added here, that Christ believed that human beings have a higher value for God as the God of providence than the birds of the air. And this is why. The birds of the air have no place, or task, or destiny in the moral order of the Universe. But it is otherwise with men. They are endowed with a moral nature ; their life is a moral vocation ; they have a moral destiny to shape in co-operation with God. And this explains and manifests the perfect wisdom of Christ as a teacher, in including all men within, and in excluding all other living creatures on the earth from, the *moral government* of God and its system of administration. He constantly paid truthful and perfectly wise respect to these two great facts in His teaching :—(1) The fact that God is ever and always providentially and actively related to men as physical beings, having physical necessities and requirements in their life ; and (2) the fact that He is ever and always governmentally and actively related to them as moral beings, having moral necessities and requirements in their life (*e.g.* Mt 11²⁵). This distinction between the providential and the governmental activities of God, in His relation to men and in His ways with them, has a determinative place in the truth taught in the Gospels.

4. Finally, all Christ's allusions to the physical order of the world present a deep *religious complexion*. He saw in this order, and in the relations between God and men as therein revealed, conditions and opportunities provided for the manifestation of pure and high forms of religious life. Men are dependent on the beneficent ministrations of the Divine providence. As moral beings it is their duty to recognize this fact, to pay due respect to it, and to cherish and manifest gratitude to God for all the various forms of His providential lovingkindness and faithfulness. Within the domain of Providence, moreover, reasons constantly exist and occasions are ever arising for men to exercise trust in God. Here also as well as in their own hearts men may find the presence of God in their life. And here they are summoned to imitate the ways of God's providential beneficence. In all these various ways Christ related His religion to the physical order of the world and its providential administration. His Sermon on the Mount shows that He wished and intended them all to have an essential place in the life of every one of His disciples. And in His own life they were all fully observed and manifested. See, further, NATURE, PROVIDENCE.

LITERATURE.—Wendt, *Teaching of Jesus*, i. 151 ff. ; Bushnell, *Nature and the Supernatural* ; Drummond, *Nat. Law in the Spiritual World* ; Mozley, *University Sermons*, pp. 122–144 ; *Expositor* II. vii. [1884] 103, III. ii. [1885] 224.

W. D. THOMSON.

PHYSICIAN.—**1.** *Luke, the physician.*—It is a fact of special importance, in reference to Christ's miracles of healing, that one of the four Evangelists was himself a physician (Col 4¹⁴). Traces of this fact appear in his Gospel (Lk 8⁴³ ‖ Mk 5²⁶), and still more in Acts (cf. Hobart, *Medical Lang. of St. Luke*). His training would probably be Gentile (Col 4¹¹· ¹⁴, cf. Eus. *HE* iii. 4), and his medicines, like Gentile food, would be unclean in Jewish eyes. See, further, art. LUKE.

2. *Jewish physicians.*—Priests were inspectors of leprosy (Mt 8⁴, Lk 17¹⁴), but they were not the regular physicians. (*a*) The physicians whom a sufferer had consulted before she was healed by Christ are alluded to in one case (Mk 5²⁶ ‖ Lk 8⁴³). Elsewhere physicians are mentioned in proverbial sayings only (Mt 9¹² ‖ Mk 2¹⁷, Lk 5³¹ 4²³) : there is no censure of them in Christ's words, on the contrary He implies that the sick should resort to the physician ; but Mk 5²⁶ probably gives a fair impression of their general value. (*b*) References to remedies are few : *e.g.* a lotion (Lk 10³⁴), an anodyne (Mk 15²³), both, we may assume, customary amongst Jews, but in neither of these

cases administered by them ; operations (circumcision, Lk 1⁵⁹ etc.; castration, Mt 19¹²). The language of Mt 18⁸ᶠ· ‖ speaks of mutilation rather than of surgical amputation. Superstitious cures were much sought ; cf. the addition to Jn 5³, which Westcott (*ad loc.*) describes as 'a very early note added while the Jewish tradition was still fresh.' (*c*) A special defect of Jewish medical science was the want of anatomy, necessarily involved in the ceremonial uncleanness of contact with the dead (cf. Mt 23²⁷), *i.e.* (as explained in *Jewish Encyc.* art. 'Medicine') contact with a complete corpse, or an 'anatomical unit' (a bone covered with its soft parts), or a collection of bones equal in bulk or number to more than half a skeleton. An illustration of this want may be seen in the fact that a young criminal's corpse was dissipated by long boiling, in order that the bones of the skeleton might be counted (*ib.*). The inspection of the bodies of animals slaughtered for sacrifice or food could be no real compensation for this want.

3. *Christ, the great Physician.*—Such a title is not found in the Gospels, but is at least suggested by Lk 4²³ 5³¹ ‖ 13³². [The word ἰάομαι is used (literally) 20 times in NT, and always, except in Ac 28⁸, directly of Christ]. Indeed, the word 'Saviour' implies it (Mt 9²¹ᶠ·). The following points are observable in Christ's healings :—(*a*) *Variety* : blindness (Mt 9²⁷ᶠᶠ· 20²⁹ᶠᶠ· ‖, Mk 8²²ᶠᶠ·, Jn 9), deafness (Mk 7³¹ᶠᶠ·), palsy (Mt 9¹ᶠ· ‖), withered hand (12⁹ᶠᶠ· ‖), issue (9²⁰ ‖), dropsy (Lk 14¹ᶠ·), fever (Mt 8¹⁴ᶠᶠ· ‖), leprosy (8¹ᶠᶠ· ‖ Lk 17¹¹ᶠᶠ·), wound (22⁴⁹ᶠᶠ·), possession (Mt 8²⁸ᶠᶠ·‖, Mk 1²³ᶠᶠ· ‖ etc.) ; (*b*) *purpose* : not merely works of mercy (Mk 3⁴, Jn 10³²), but also 'signs' (Jn 4⁵⁴ etc.), parables of a spiritual healing (Lk 5²⁴· ³¹ᶠ·, Jn 9²⁵· ³⁹) ; (*c*) *universality* : without price (Mt 10⁸, ct. Mk 5²⁶), without exception (Mt 11⁵, Mk 1²⁷ 7³⁷, Jn 9³²), without fail (ct. Mk 5⁴· ²⁶ 9¹⁸) ; (*d*) *conditions* : (i.) on Christ's part,—the (Divine) will (Mt 8³) ; in some cases is added the (human) prayer (Mk 9²⁹, Jn 11⁴¹) ; (ii.) on the sick one's or the petitioner's part,—faith (Mt 8¹³ 9²· ²²· ²⁸ 15²⁸ etc.) and (though seldom requiring mention) desire or will (Jn 5⁶ ; Lk 22⁵⁰ᶠ· is altogether exceptional) ; (*e*) *preliminaries* : (i.) ordinarily an application, either personal (Lk 5¹² 17¹³ 18³⁸) or intercessory—with (Mk 2³ 7³² 9¹⁷) or without (Mt 8⁶, Mk 7²⁹ᶠ·, Jn 4⁴⁷ᶠᶠ·) the presence of the sufferer ; (ii.) often no application preceded (Mk 5²⁸, Lk 13¹² 22⁵¹—and so always in Jn., *e.g.* 5⁶ 9²ᶠᶠ· [11¹¹]) ; (*f*) *performance* : usually immediate (Mt 8³ᶠ·, Mk 5²⁹), sometimes delayed (7²⁷ᶠᶠ· 9²¹ᶠᶠ·), rarely a gradual process (8²³ᶠᶠ·) ; (*g*) *accompaniments* : a word (Mt 8⁸· ¹³ 12¹³), never otherwise in the case of possession (8¹⁶· ³¹), a touch (8³ 9¹⁸· ²⁵· ²⁹, Mk 5²⁸ 6⁵⁶), a symbolic action (Mk 7³³, Jn 9⁶ᶠ·) ; (*h*) *sequel* : an assurance (Mk 5³⁴, Lk 17¹⁹ 18⁴²), a command (Mt 8⁴ 9⁶, Mk 5¹⁹· ⁴³), a warning (Jn 5¹⁴). See also artt. CURES, DISEASE.

LITERATURE.—In addition to the ordinary books of reference and those already mentioned, the following touch the subject : Ebstein, *Die Medizin im NT und im Talm.*, Stuttgart, 1903 ; Bennett, *Diseases of the Bible* ; Trench, *Miracles*. See also C. H. Spurgeon, *The Messiah*, 483.

F. S. RANKEN.

PIECE OF SILVER.—See MONEY, p. 200ᵃ.

PIGEON.—See ANIMALS, vol. i. p. 65ᵇ, and DOVE.

PILATE.—Pilate's first name, that by which he would be known in his own household, has not been recorded ; we know only his second name 'Pontius,' and his third 'Pilatus.' *Pontius* may be derived from *pons* ('bridge'), or be cognate with πέντε ('five') ; and *Pilatus* meant, no doubt, originally, 'armed with the pike' (of the Roman legionary) ; but we are no nearer his origin. We know nothing of his parents, his birthplace, or the date of his birth. He was a Roman citizen, and was born probably in Italy. From the position which he afterwards occupied, it is certain that he belonged in manhood to the middle or equestrian class in the community ; but whether by favour of the Emperor or by birth is unknown. Admission to this class could be obtained only by those who possessed 400,000 sesterces (equivalent to about £3000 of our money, but with much greater purchasing power). The question whether he inherited this property qualification or not cannot be answered.

In order to reach the position of procurator of the Roman province of Judæa, he must have passed through a course of earlier appointments open to his order. He must have had considerable military experience, and have held one or more of the following appointments : prefecture (or tribunate) of an auxiliary cohort, or a legionary tribunate of the second class (those of the first being open only to the senatorial order), or the prefecture of a wing (*ala*) of cavalry (Cagnat, *Cours d'Épig. Lat.*[3] p. 109 ff.). The earliest age at which one could become a procurator was between twenty-seven and thirty years. These procuratorships differed in standing (see PROCURATOR), and that of a province like Judæa was not the highest. Further promotion was open to one who did well in that position. The date of the birth of Pilate cannot have been later than about B.C. 4–1. In Mt 27[19] he appears as married, but whether he left any descendants or not is uncertain.

In A.D. 26, Pilate was appointed by the Emperor Tiberius procurator of the province of Judæa. This province comprised the former kingdom of Archelaus, — roughly Samaria and the territory south of it to Gaza and the Dead Sea,—and the procurator's duties were both administrative and military. He was in a position of subordination to the governor of the province of Syria, but the exact nature of the subordination is not known. For all practical purposes his rule over all in the province, except Roman citizens, was absolute. At the same time, it must be remembered that in this, as in other provinces, certain communities were permitted a large measure of self-government —one of the secrets of Rome's success as a world-power. Thus in Jerusalem the Sanhedrin retained many judicial functions ; death sentences, however, had to be confirmed by the governor, and were carried out under his supervision (Jn 18[31] ; Jos. *Ant.* XX. ix. 1, *BJ* II. viii. 1). The religious and political zeal of the various sections of the population made the task of governing the province one of extreme difficulty, requiring statesmanlike gifts of no ordinary quality.

We derive most of our knowledge of Pilate's rule from Josephus, from whom the following incident is repeated, to illustrate the statement above made. The Jewish prejudice against images of gods was incomprehensible to the other ancient peoples ; but their attitude was officially respected by the Romans, whose practice it was to refrain from introducing such into the Jews' country. They carried their conciliatory policy so far as to remove the figures of the god-emperor from those military standards which bore them. In contravention of this custom, Pilate caused the standards with their usual decoration to be carried by night into Jerusalem. The people pleaded with him to remove the objectionable images, but he remained obdurate, and eventually ordered his soldiers to surround the crowd and put them to death if they persisted. This threat had no terror for men whose religious frenzy was worked up to the highest pitch, and Pilate had to yield, for it was impossible to massacre so many. His action in this matter showed want of tact, hot temper, and weakness ;

and as the occurrence took place early in his period of government, it was an evil augury for his rule (*Ant.* XVIII. iii. 1). On another occasion he used money from the Temple-treasury for the building of an aqueduct, and broke up the riot which threatened by introducing disguised soldiers into the crowd (*Ant.* XVIII. iii. 2). Lk 13[1] is the only authority for the mention of the Galilæans whose blood Pilate 'mixed with their sacrifices.' The cause of his action was doubtless some riot. Pilate is represented in the worst possible light by a passage in Philo, which is put into the mouth of Agrippa (*Legatio ad Gaium*, 38).—

[The Jews' threat to communicate with Tiberius] 'exasperated Pilate to the greatest possible degree, as he feared lest they might go on an embassy to the Emperor, and might impeach him with respect to other particulars of his government—his corruptions, his acts of insolence, his rapine, and his habit of insulting people, his cruelty, and his continual murders of people untried and uncondemned, and his never-ending, gratuitous, and most grievous inhumanity.'

We do not need to go beyond the Gospel narratives, and the fact that he was retained in his position for ten years by Tiberius, to realize that this picture is grossly overdrawn.

For our knowledge of the part Pilate played in the trial of Jesus we are dependent on all four canonical Gospels. As it may be assumed that Mark's narrative is the oldest, we shall take it first, then proceed to Matthew's and Luke's, which are probably almost contemporaneous with one another, and, lastly, we shall draw on the Fourth Gospel.

(1) According to *Mark* (14[53]), the chief priests and scribes and elders, after Jesus had been brought from Gethsemane, led Him away to the high priest, in whose residence they all assembled. This was an extraordinary meeting of the Sanhedrin. The Court sought evidence which would lead to the death of Jesus, but failed to find any that was reliable. Such evidence as they had was false and conflicting. Jesus' statement about the Temple was repeated and misconstrued. Then the high priest elicited from Him a declaration that He was the Messiah. This statement was decided to be blasphemy, and as a result He was judged worthy of death (Lv 24[16]). After the verdict He was subjected to every insult. The death sentence had by law to be confirmed by Pilate before it could be carried out. In their eagerness they lost no time in bringing Him before Pilate's tribunal (15[1]). The question was put by Pilate, 'Art thou the king of the Jews?'; to which Jesus answered, 'Thou sayest' (v.[2]). The chief priests, being permitted by Pilate to make their charges, brought many against Him ; the accused, on being asked by Pilate if He had anything to say, was silent, and caused His judge to wonder. It happened that the feast of the Passover was at hand, and on such an occasion it was the custom to release a prisoner. The crowd which stood around called for the release of a certain Barabbas, a robber and murderer. Pilate proposed instead to release Jesus, knowing that hatred had been the motive of the high priests in handing Him over. The chief priests instigated the crowd to beg for Barabbas. Pilate then asked what they wished to be done with 'the king of the Jews,' and they said, 'Crucify him.' On being asked by Pilate what evil He had done, their only answer was to repeat the cry. Pilate, being anxious to please the crowd, gratified both their requests. Such is Mark's narrative of the trial, baldly stated. It is so very brief that it is not surprising that the other Evangelists have been able to add to it. Mark has nothing further to say about Pilate except to tell that Joseph of Arimathæa begged and obtained from him the body of Jesus (15[43]).

(2) *Matthew* makes only two additions of any importance to this narrative. One is the warning

message sent to Pilate, when seated on the tribunal, by his wife (27¹⁹). The character of the incident stamps it as a reliable tradition. The second is Pilate's washing of his hands after he had acquiesced in the decision of the Jews and the wishes of the mob, and his proclamation of his innocence, followed by the Jews' invocation of the curse upon themselves and their children. At a later stage in the narrative, Matthew alone (27⁶²ff.) gives the incident of the deputation to Pilate with the request for permission to seal the tomb, and the granting of that permission.

(3) *Luke*, at the beginning of the accusation before Pilate, mentions the charge (23²): 'We found this man perverting our nation, and forbidding to give tribute to Cæsar, and saying that he himself was an anointed king.' The first part of this charge is directly contrary to the truth (Mk 12¹⁷ = Mt 22²¹ = Lk 20²⁵). It is Lk. also who mentions (23⁴⁻¹²) that when Pilate learned that Jesus was a Galilæan he sent Him to Herod, tetrarch of Galilee, to whose jurisdiction He belonged. Herod could elicit no answer from Jesus, and sent Him back to Pilate. This exchange of courtesy led to a renewal of the friendship between Pilate and Herod, which had been interrupted for some reason or other. On the return of Jesus, Pilate is represented as proclaiming His innocence and confirming it by the decision of Herod.

(4) *The Fourth Gospel* makes the following contributions to the story. The informal questioning by Annas (18¹⁹⁻²⁴) is special to Jn., which gives also (18³³⁻³⁸) a much longer conversation between Jesus and Pilate than the others, in which Jesus explains the nature of His Kingdom. It is quite certain that Pilate realized that Jesus' Kingdom was not an ordinary kingdom, else his conduct of the case would have been entirely different. The section 19⁴⁻¹⁵ contains a further examination of Jesus, and the terrorizing of Pilate by the Jews. The Johannine account, as it is the fullest, is also the best. It explains what is obscure in the others, and brings the whole situation before us with startling vividness. John makes Pilate the author of the inscription on the cross, and mentions his repudiation of the Jewish criticism of its wording.

The situation was for Pilate an extremely difficult one. The Jews in authority were determined that Jesus should die. Assassination was impossible, because of the people. They were therefore compelled to resort to the governor's power. In order to get him to sign the warrant, they had to show that Jesus had committed a crime worthy of death. They had to select a charge which in their opinion would leave Pilate no option. They seized upon that of treason, a charge which brought death upon some of the most influential Roman citizens during that period, as the early books of Tacitus' *Annals* show. Pilate examined Jesus on this charge, and soon found that this was no case of treason. A strong man might have defied the provincials, and set Jesus at liberty. In doing so, he would have risked all his future prospects, perhaps his own life. The procurator was in reality only an upper servant of the Emperor, and as such could be dismissed and ruined without appeal. The Jews, when they saw that Roman justice might win and Jesus be released, held over Pilate the threat of a report to the Emperor on his conduct. Pilate, as we have seen, was not a strong man. He yielded, though he knew the accused was innocent. It must be remembered that Jesus was not a Roman citizen, was, in fact, in the eyes of a Roman officer, merely a subject, a slave, a chattel. The life of a Roman citizen was precious, that of a mere subject worthless. That Pilate had a tender enough conscience or a sound enough idea of justice to try to save this

'slave,' should be remembered to his credit. He was not of the stuff of which heroes are made, though doubtless in many respects a competent governor.

Little is known of Pilate's later history. He used armed force to suppress a fanatical movement in Samaria, which does not appear to have endangered the Roman supremacy in the slightest (Jos. *Ant.* XVIII. iv. 1). So many were put to death that the Samaritans appealed to Vitellius, the then governor of the province of Syria. The governor ordered Pilate to Rome, to appear before the Emperor's council. Before he reached Rome, Tiberius had died. The result of this no doubt was that he escaped trial. Of his further career nothing is certainly known, but legend has naturally not neglected one of the most interesting figures of NT history. In the *Gospel of Peter*, which belongs probably to the middle of the 2nd cent., he is represented in a very favourable light; the author shows also anti-Jewish tendencies. As the fragment of this Gospel is put together almost entirely from the canonical Gospels, it yields in interest to another apocryphal work—the *Acts of Pilate*. In the 2nd cent. the Church began to busy itself with its own history, and to build up a defence of its faith and practice on a historical foundation. The person of Pilate was a subject of special interest, and was pressed into the service of the Church as a valuable witness to the truth of Christianity. In the *Acts of Pilate* he is acquitted of all blame, and represented as in the end confessing Jesus to be the Son of God (ch. 46). It was widely believed in ancient times that an official account of the trial of Jesus was sent by Pilate to the Emperor Tiberius and preserved in the archives at Rome. It is not impossible that such a report was sent; but this at least we can say with certainty, there is no real evidence of its existence or its use to be found in any apocryphal writing. Justin in his (first) *Apology* (chs. 35. 48) refers more than once to the *Acts under Pontius Pilate*. The *Acts of Pilate* (*Gospel of Nicodemus*) which we possess, however, with kindred pieces, is not of earlier date than the 4th or 5th century. Tertullian in his *Apology* (ch. 21) speaks of the report of Pilate to Tiberius as containing an account of the miracles, condemnation, crucifixion, and resurrection of Jesus, with the story of the guard at the grave. There still exists in various ancient works (e.g. *Acts of Peter and Paul*) a so-called *Letter of Pilate to Claudius* (*or Tiberius*), which, though possibly interpolated at a later date, gives an impression of real antiquity, and is no doubt the document referred to by Tertullian. As to the date of it nothing can be said, except that it is older than 197 A.D., the date of the *Apology* of Tertullian: it was probably written in Greek originally, though it is extant also in Latin. Tertullian says (*Apol.* 5) that Tiberius, as the result of a communication from Palestine, proposed to the Roman Senate that Jesus should be recognized as a god, but that the Senate rejected the motion. He further states that the Emperor held by his intention, and punished those who accused the Christians. All this must be regarded as pure legend.

Tradition has it that Pilate fell on evil days after the death of Tiberius, and ultimately committed suicide (Euseb. *HE* ii. 7, and also in his *Chronicle*). Another account has it that he was beheaded by Tiberius' order, but that he repented before his death. His wife is commonly reported to have become a Christian, on the strength, no doubt, of the warning which St. Matthew records that she gave to her husband. It is told that Pilate appeared before the Emperor to stand his trial, wearing the tunic of Jesus, and that this tunic acted as a charm to protect him from the anger of his Imperial master. His body is said to have been first thrown into the Tiber, but the evil spirits so haunted the spot as to terrorize the populous neighbourhood, and it was conveyed to Vienne in the South of France and sunk in the Rhone. Here also the evil spirits proved troublesome, and the body was removed to the territory of Lausanne in Switzerland, where it was sunk and walled up in a deep pit surrounded by mountains. The best known legend connects itself with that country, and the mountain still known as Pilatus. The corpse is said to rest in a lake on the mountain side, whence it comes forth periodically and goes through the act of washing its hands. The Coptic Church reveres Pilate as a saint and martyr (June 25th).

LITERATURE.—The art. 'Pilate' in Hastings' *DB* contains a very full bibliography. A few works only are mentioned here : G. A. Müller, *Pontius Pilatus der funfte Prokurator von Judäa* (Stuttgart, 1888) ; A. Taylor Innes, *Trial of Jesus Christ : a Legal Monograph* (Edinburgh, 1899) ; G. Rosadi, *The Trial of Jesus* (London, 1905) ; F. W. Robertson, *Serm.* 1st ser. 292 ff. ; *Expositor*, II. viii. [1884] 107, VI. ii. [1900] 59 ; J. B. Lightfoot, *Serm. in St. Paul's Cathedral*, 91 ; W. B. Carpenter, *The Son of Man*, 33 ; W. H. Simcox, *The Cessation of Prophecy*, 287 ; J. H. Moulton, *Visions of Sin*, 185 ; for the early apocryphal literature, see R. A. Lipsius, *Die Pilatus-Akten kritisch untersucht* (1871) ; F. C. Conybeare, 'Acta Pilati' in *Stud. Bibl. et Eccles.* vol. iv. pp. 59–132 (Oxford, 1896) ; E. Hennecke, *Neutest. Apokryphen*, pp. 74–76 (Tübingen and Leipzig, 1904), and *Handbuch z. neutest. Apokr.* p. 143 ff. (Tübingen and Leipzig, 1904).

ALEX. SOUTER.

PILGRIM.—1. Although the word is not found in the Gospels, they constantly indicate the place of the annual pilgrimages in the life and thought of the people. There is always an air of movement over the scenes, and a frequent change of setting in the lives of the men and women ; they are constantly moving to and fro as the festivals come round. The parents of Jesus kept this custom, and at the age of twelve Jesus made with them His first (?) pilgrimage (Lk 2⁴¹⁻⁴⁹). In the Fourth Gospel there are many references to other visits to the feasts (Jn 2¹³ 5¹ 7¹⁴ 10²² 11⁵⁵· ⁵⁶). No mention is made of them in the Synoptic Gospels ; but it may safely be assumed that Jesus had often made the journey to Jerusalem with the caravans of pilgrims (cf. Mt 23³⁷). The custom explains the rapidity with which news spread ; the name of Jesus had become a familiar word in such places as Jericho on the main route (Lk 18³⁷· ³⁸). The last journey to Jerusalem was made among pilgrims. There is an implied contrast where it is said that Jesus went in silence before His disciples ; pilgrims marched with song and rejoicing (Ps 42⁴), but silence and fear marked the disciples (Mk 10³²). The multitudes who hailed Jesus as He entered Jerusalem included many Galilæan pilgrims, not without a certain local pride (Mt 21⁹, Jn 12¹²). The rejection of Jesus by the Samaritan village (Lk 17¹¹· ¹²) was due to their knowledge that Jesus and His band, though taking the less familiar route, were pilgrims to the hated Jerusalem (Edersheim, *Jesus the Messiah* [abridged ed. of *LT*], p. 297). In estimating the rapid progress of the Christian faith, especially amongst the Dispersion, it must be remembered that many strangers, such as Simon of Cyrene (Lk 23²⁶), would be at the feast, and would carry away some knowledge to prepare their minds for the Apostolic message.

2. These pilgrim experiences illustrate some of the words of Jesus. The disciple must travel through the world with heart detached and his treasure laid up in heaven (Lk 12³³, Mt 6¹⁹). His must be the straitened way, not the broad path (Mt 7¹³) ; to follow in the way he must give up all (Mk 10²⁹, Mt 19²⁹). In their missionary journeys the disciples have the equipment and the mobility of pilgrims (Mt 10⁹ etc.). The would-be disciple must expect to be homeless (8²⁰). The disciples are to be sojourners who guard against the dangers of an alien world from which they must be detached

(cf. He 11¹³, 1 P 2¹¹, where the word 'pilgrim' [παρεπίδημος] is used). In the Fourth Gospel Jesus denies (Jn 4²¹) that the annual pilgrimage will be an abiding necessity. Everywhere He speaks of Himself as sojourning in the world for a Divine purpose (8¹⁴ 16²⁸ 13³⁷) ; the disciples must so look upon their life (12³⁵ 17¹⁶). They are in the world, but not of it (17¹⁵⁻¹⁸ 15¹⁹) ; their true home would be in God. But even in their earthly life they would be in one of the mansions (μοναί) of the Father's house (14²). At intervals along the road stood the caravanserais where travellers lodged. The disciples were like travellers, and His companionship had hitherto cheered them. Now He must leave them that He might go forward ; but when they arrived He would be waiting for them. (See D. Smith, *The Days of His Flesh*, p. 449). To complete the thought of life as a pilgrimage, it is to be remembered that the journey is through the outlying parts of the Father's Kingdom to the centre. See, further, art. FEASTS.

LITERATURE.—Jos. *BJ* VI. ix. 3 ; Schürer, *HJP* II. ii. 51, 220 ; Farrar, *Life of Christ*, ch. vi. ; A. S. Laidlaw, 'The Priest and the Pilgrim,' in *ExpT* xi. (1900) 345.   E. SHILLITO.

PILLOW.—Mk 4³⁸ ἐπὶ τὸ προσκεφάλαιον καθεύδων, RV 'the **cushion**.' The Gr. word occurs in LXX, Ezk 13¹⁸· ²⁰ (probably 'fillets' used as amulets, A. B. Davidson, *Ezekiel*, 89), 1 Es 3⁸ (pillow of Darius). Originally it meant a pillow *for the head*, but it came to be used for any cushion (cf. the English use of 'kerchief,' originally a covering *for the head*, as found in 'neckerchief,' 'handkerchief'). Pollux (*Onomast.* x. 40) says that the poet Cratinus, in his *Horæ*, used it of the sailor's cushion (τὸ ναυτικὸν ὑπηρέσιον) ; and Hesychius, *s.v.* ποτίκρανον, further defines it as 'the leathern cushion (τὸ δερματικον ὑπηρέσιον) on which the rowers sit.'

'To mitigate the roughness of the beams or other seats, every rower was provided with a cushion, which he carried about with him from ship to ship' (Cecil Torr, *Ancient Ships*, 47). The following passage in the *Stratiotai* (v.) of the poet Hermippus illustrates this : ''Tis time now to come along with me, taking the rowlocks and a cushion, that leaping on board thou mayest ply the dashing oar.'

Little is known about fishing-boats in the time of our Lord (Hastings' *DB*, Ext. Vol. 367ᵇ ; *Encyc. Bibl.* iv. 4481 ; Smith's *DB* iii. 1285). The fishermen's belongings mentioned in the Gospels are the boat itself (Lk 5³, Jn 21³), with the accompanying small boat (Jn 21⁸), the two kinds of nets (Mt 4¹⁸ 13⁴⁷), the hook (17³⁷), the baskets (13⁴⁸), the fisher's coat (Jn 21⁷), and the cushion. It is clear that the condition of the fishermen of the Lake of Gennesaret was considerably removed from one of absolute poverty ; we have other evidences of this in Mk 1²⁰ ('the hired servants'), Lk 8³, Mk 15⁴⁰ᶠ· (Salome, one of those who 'ministered of their substance'), Jn 19²⁷ (cf. *Speaker's Com.* i. 203, ii. 276) ; Jos. *Vita*, 33, *BJ* III. x. 1.

The τό before προσκεφάλαιον seems to imply that the cushion was one of the ordinary articles of the boat's furniture, while its position 'in the stern' suggests that the disciples were in the habit of resting on it by turns during the night fishing (Lk 5⁵, Jn 21³). It is, therefore, not probable that it had been placed there specially for our Lord's accommodation. On starting to cross the lake, He seated Himself on 'the cushion in the stern' ; and there, being wearied with prolonged teaching, He soon fell into a sleep so profound that not even the tumult of the elements was sufficient to disturb it. 'Sleep is attributed to our Lord in this context only ; but it is probably implied in Mk 1³⁵, and in passages which describe His vigils as if they were exceptional' (Swete, *St. Mark*, 85). Bushnell compares in a striking way the sleep of Adam in Paradise with that of Jesus in the storm (*Christ and His Salvation*, 127). See also art. CUSHION.

LITERATURE.—Stephanus, *Thesaurus Græcæ Linguæ* (ed. Hase and Dindorf) ; Cecil Torr, *Ancient Ships*, 1895 ; Hastings' and other *Bible Dictionaries*.   JAMES DONALD.

PINNACLE occurs only in Mt 4[5] ‖ Lk 4[9]. The word (πτερύγιον) so rendered means 'a little wing,' and refers to some lofty point about the Temple, from which Jesus is said to have been invited by the tempter to cast Himself down. The word used for 'temple' in both passages (ἱερόν) denotes the whole enclosure, and not merely the Temple building proper (ναός). The 'pinnacle' may therefore be sought for anywhere within the Temple precincts. It is evident, from the use of the phrase '*the* pinnacle of the temple,' that there was a definite point well known by this name when the Evangelists wrote ; but now we are in some uncertainty as to where it was situated. Some understand the apex of the roof of the Temple building to be meant. Others suggest the roof of Solomon's Porch, on the east side of the Temple area. But if 'the pinnacle' was not the summit of the Temple proper, the most likely position for it is the battlement of the Royal Portico, which ran from east to west across the south end of the enclosure, on the precipitous edge of a deep valley. Josephus (*Ant.* xv. xi. 5) says of this portico : 'While the valley was very deep, and its bottom could not be seen if you looked from above into the depth, this further vastly high elevation of the cloister stood upon that height, insomuch that if any one looked down from the top of the battlements, or down both these altitudes, he would be giddy, while his sight could not reach to such an immense depth.' By 'both these altitudes,' it need hardly be said, Josephus means the height of the precipice *plus* the height of the portico which crowned it. As the top of the portico, according to Josephus, was 100 feet above the pavement, the drop from this elevation to the bottom of the Kidron Valley would be about 300 feet ; and if 'the pinnacle,' as some suppose, was a turret or spire at the eastern end, marking the south-east corner of the enclosure, then its height would have to be added to this vertical distance.

The Church historian Hegesippus (A.D. 160), as quoted by Eusebius (*HE* ii. 23), gives an account of the death of James the Lord's brother, who, he says, was cast down by the Jews from the pinnacle of the Temple (ναός—the Temple proper). If this statement were reliable, it would be decisive in favour of the first supposition mentioned above ; but the accuracy of the whole story is doubtful, and it may be questioned whether Hegesippus, writing nearly a century after the destruction of the Temple, knew any better than we do where 'the pinnacle' really was. There is still, therefore, a choice of views. On the one hand, the apex of the Temple proper would undoubtedly be the loftiest point of the whole group of buildings. On the other hand, the battlement of the Royal Portico would afford the deepest and sheerest fall, and, on the whole, it is most probable that 'the pinnacle' was situated here.   JAMES PATRICK.

PIPE (αὐλέω).—The verb is found only in the Gospels (Mt 11[17] ‖ Lk 7[32]), where the children say : 'We have piped unto you and ye have not danced.' The noun αὐλός is found in 1 Co 14[7]. The pipe was a wind instrument. It was perforated with two, three, or four holes, and was either single or double. The single form was played vertically or horizontally ; in the latter case the word 'flute' would be a better rendering. The single instrument was played with two hands, the double with one hand for each pipe. Its range was naturally limited, its music monotonous. The word '*ûgâb*, also tr. by RV 'pipe,' in the Targums was an instrument of similar structure, and has been translated

by the Vulg. *organum* and AV 'organ' (Gn 4[21], Job 21[12] 30[31], Ps 150[4]).   HENRY E. DOSKER.

PIT (βόθυνος, φρέαρ).—In the Gospels βόθυνος is used only of a place into which animals or men might stumble by accident (Mt 12[11]), or in consequence of blindness (Mt 15[14], Lk 6[39], AV 'ditch,' but RV 'pit'). This might mean any opening or hollow dug in the ground. In Lk 14[5] ‖ Mt 12[11], however, φρέαρ is used, so that here we should, perhaps, understand 'pit' as an empty cistern, or artificial well. These are seldom covered in the East or guarded in any way. In the neighbourhood of towns and villages, especially those that have fallen on decay, they are often the cause of serious accidents to unwary pedestrians. In the Apocalypse φρέαρ appears as the bottomless abode of 'the beast' and his unholy hosts (Rev 9[1] 17[8] etc.).   W. EWING.

PITCHER (κεράμιον).—An earthenware jar with one or two handles, used chiefly by women for carrying water (Gn 24[15], Jg 7[16], כַּד ; RV and AV 'pitcher'). The only occurrence of the word in the Gospels is in Mk 14[13] ‖ Lk 22[10], in the directions given by our Lord for securing a room for the Paschal meal. It has been alleged (*Speak. Com.* Lk 22[10] note) that the sign of the pitcher was not so accidental as it appears. 'According to Jewish usage, on the evening of the 13th [of the month Nisan], before the stars appeared in heaven, every father of a family was to go to the well to draw pure water, with which the unleavened bread was kneaded. It was a real rite which they performed. . . .' But apart altogether from the chronological inaccuracy,—the disciples must have entered Jerusalem early in the day (Mk 14[17], Mt 26[20]),—this statement is not confirmed by Mk 14[14] and Lk 22[11], from which it may be inferred that the head of the house, who has been identified in turn with John Mark, Joseph of Arimathæa, and Nicodemus, is not the bearer of the pitcher.

There is, however, presumptive evidence that the pitcher was being used in the preparation of the unleavened bread, the making of which, together with the putting away of leaven from the houses, was part of the work in which many hundreds in Jerusalem (Jos. *BJ* VI. ix. 3) must have been employed on that day ; but the demand for water for ordinary purposes alone will suggest the inference that in a city whose population was so enormously increased, the pitcher borne by this slave could not be distinctive.

Whatever the probability of recognizing or of not recognizing the sign, the most important feature of the whole incident remains unaffected. For all time the pitcher will be a sign not of the need for secrecy and sealed orders, nor even of the prescience of Christ, though that is abundantly proved, but rather of the faith of the two disciples. Here also is presented a beautiful illustration of the co-operation of the human will with the Divine, the overruling of common events for Divine ends, a demonstration of the power that is laid under service to faith. Blessing in the ordinary affairs of life, as in the greatest crises of the soul, is attainable only by implicit and unquestioning confidence in the Master mind.

LITERATURE.—Art. 'Pitcher' in Hastings' *DB* ; S. Cox, *Expositions*, iv. 321 ; the Commentaries on the Gospels, *ad locc.* ; the various *Lives of Christ*.   ALEX. A. DUNCAN.

PITY. — This word occurs once in the Gospels (Mt 18[33] AV) as tr. of ἐλεέω ; apparently in accordance with the practice of the translators 'that we have not tied ourselves to an uniformity of phrasing or to an identity of words,' since the same word ἐλεέω is rendered by 'have **compassion**' in the verse immediately before, as elsewhere.

1. *In the Synoptic Gospels* four different words occur which carry with them the notion of 'pity' or 'compassion': σπλαγχνίζομαι (σπλάγχνά), ἐλεέω (ἔλεος and ἐλεήμων), συλλυπέομαι, and οἰκτίρμων.

Of these, the first three are used with reference to Jesus: (1) σπλαγχνίζομαι, 'moved with compassion,' found in Mt 9³⁶ 14¹⁴ 15³² 18²⁷, Mk 1⁴¹ 6³⁴ 8², Lk 7¹³ ; (2) ἐλεέω, used in Mk 5¹⁹ by our Lord Himself to describe His own work in the cure of the demoniac, 'and hath had compassion on thee,' καὶ ἠλίησέν σε ; (3) συλλυπέομαι, Mk 3⁵, tr. '*being grieved* (for the hardness of their hearts).' The word occurs nowhere else in NT, but is used by Herodotus and elsewhere with the significance of having pity or compassion (see Liddell and Scott).

By their usage in these passages the Synoptics plainly declare that in His manifestation of human nature our Saviour was drawn towards suffering humanity by that Divine gift of pity which has ever been regarded as one of the higher feelings: sickness, sorrow, being like tired sheep, even bodily hunger, filled Him with compassion for the suffering ones,—while in the solitary use of συλλυπέομαι alluded to above to describe His feeling at the unwillingness of men to receive truth, we can hardly hesitate to give to the word its classical meaning of 'pity,' when we remember the outburst of weeping which accompanied His wail over Jerusalem (Lk 19⁴¹). And while Himself manifesting forth pity towards men and inculcating the same feeling on His disciples, He also most clearly taught them to think of His Father in heaven as One moved with compassion for His earthly family. The 'tender mercy of our God' in the *Benedictus* (Lk 1⁷⁸) is the thought illustrated in the parable of the Good Samaritan, who was 'moved with compassion' (ἐσπλαγχνίσθη) at the sight of the wounded man (Lk 10³³) ; as in that of the king who forgave the debtor, being 'moved with compassion' (σπλαγχνισθείς, Mt 18²⁷) ; and even more strikingly so in the description of the father of the Prodigal, who, when he saw his son returning, ἐσπλαγχνίσθη καὶ δραμὼν ἐπέπεσεν ἐπὶ τὸν τράχηλον αὐτοῦ (Lk 15²⁰). So also the solitary use of οἰκτίρμων in the Gospels (used again only in Ja 5¹¹) is found in our Saviour's exhortation, 'Be ye therefore merciful, as your Father also is merciful' ; γίνεσθε οἰκτίρμονες καθὼς ὁ πατὴρ ὑμῶν οἰκτίρμων ἐστί (Lk 6³⁶).

It is true that in speaking of God as the 'Merciful One' our Saviour was repeating what is a familiar thought in the OT. רַחוּם, 'compassionate,' is there used exclusively as an epithet of God (Dt 4³¹), while in Sir 50¹⁹ we already find the simple רַחוּם as a name of God (see Dalman, *Words of Jesus*, p. 204) ; but in our Saviour's teaching we recognize a new fulness and meaning in the thought that would have been impossible for men to grasp before He came who could say, 'He that hath seen me hath seen the Father' (Jn 14⁹).

2. *The teaching of St. John's Gospel.*—It is striking that in St. John's Gospel we never find any word used which conveys the meaning of 'pity' or 'compassion' ; Christ is never described as 'merciful' or as 'showing mercy,' nor does He so speak of the Father ; while even the exhortation to mercy as a duty of man to man is not found there.

Can we give a reason for this ? or is the omission purely accidental ? We believe the reason is found in the fact that in St. John's mind the thought of 'pity' is absorbed in that of 'love.'

To St. John was given the task of presenting the life of Christ upon earth in all its eternal meaning. The human idea of pity, as a feeling called forth by man's needs, is but one manifestation of love. St. John does not stop to show that Jesus Christ both pitied and also loved men, but in passing at once to the thought of love as the bond of union between God and man manifested forth in the Saviour's life upon earth, he naturally ascribes to it those actions that the Saviour's contemporaries had felt as acts of mercy. As an illustration of this, we may take the story of the raising of Lazarus. Here is a miracle performed for those who knew more of Christ than merely that 'He pitied them.' The familiar cry for help, found so often in the first three Gospels (ἐλέησον ἡμᾶς), is not the message sent by the sisters, but instead, it is a direct appeal to love—'He whom thou lovest is sick' (Jn 11³). The delay in giving the prompt relief which pity would ask for is explained by 'Now Jesus loved Martha and her sister and Lazarus' (11⁵). At the sight of the sorrow of those about Him we are told 'Jesus wept' ; but the Evangelist apparently hastened to add the remark of the Jews, 'Behold how he loved him,' that the thought of His love should even here swallow up that of mere pity. And this fuller presentation of Christ's feelings for men, he shows, had also been accompanied by a teaching of Christ, both as regards man's duty to his fellow and also God's attitude towards the world, which went far beyond what had been already recorded in the Synoptic Gospels. St. Luke had preserved the saying, 'Be ye therefore merciful,' but St. John was the first to record how his Master had taught, 'A new commandment give I unto you, That ye love one another as I have loved you' (13³⁴).

Christians had already in their hands the teaching of Christ which spoke of God as the 'Merciful One,' but now St. John records words which tell them not of a merciful God, but of a loving Father (Jn 3¹⁶ 14²³ etc.). It is true that even this conception of God is found in the OT, but a perusal of the passages in which 'the love of God,' or God as 'loving,' are spoken of, will show that such are always equivalent to the 'pity' of God, or God as 'pitiful,'—that is, in direct relationship to man as a needy creature. In the Fourth Gospel, however, the thought is altogether different: the Father loves men with the same love with which He loves the Son (17²⁶) ; that same feeling of real affection with which Christ had let them feel He regarded them, He taught them was also the feeling of His Father towards them (14²¹·²³ 16²⁶ᶠ·). The common bond of fellowship between Christ and the Father and between man and God through the Son was the power of the Divine love (17²⁶). But whatever doubt may exist as to the meaning of the omission of the thought of pity in this Gospel, its very omission leads us to see how St. John supplies what might be felt as a want, in the first three Gospels, in another particular.

How are men to think of that pitiful, gracious Saviour who in His own life was so sorely tried and afflicted ? *Now nowhere in the Gospels*—nor indeed in any passage of the NT—*is Christ presented to men as an object of pity*. The thought that seems to underlie the words of some well-known hymns, and even Is 53, is not found in the NT. Pity is the demand for help, and as an object of our help Christ never appealed to men. On the contrary, He said to the women, 'Daughters of Jerusalem, weep not for me' (Lk 23²⁸) ; and to the disciple Peter, 'Thinkest thou that I cannot now pray to my Father, and he shall presently give me more than twelve legions of angels ?' (Mt 26⁵³). To the Father alone He cries, 'If it be possible, let this cup pass from me' (Mt 26³⁹). But if we are not allowed to pity the suffering Saviour, are we to view His passion with indifference ? St. John clearly and abundantly answers this question. While the mystery of pain is not revealed, the message of the Saviour's agony is declared to be the proof to mankind of His and His Father's love. 'Greater love hath no man than this, that a man lay down his life for his friends' (15¹³). That love manifested in dying is the same love spoken of in 3¹⁶ 16²⁷ 17²⁶.

It may well be doubted if any presentation of the Passion which moves our pity is in accordance with the Gospel (see, for a strong indictment against such, Ruskin's *Lectures on Art*, ii. §§ 56, 57) ; but even if we hesitate to accept this, we must confess that unless we are led through pity to understand love, the message of pity has failed. 'We must look through the suffering to the triumph. . . . The crucifix with the dead Christ obscures our faith. Our thoughts rest not upon a dead, but upon a living Christ. The closed eye and the bowed head are not the true marks of Him who reigns from the Cross, who teaches us to see through every sign of weakness the fulfilment of His own words, *I, if I be lifted up from the earth, will draw all men unto myself'* (Westcott, *The Victory of the Cross*, vi., which see throughout).

LITERATURE.—Trench, *NT Synon.*[8], 160 ff., 361; Westcott on He 10[28]; Lightfoot on Ph 1[8] and 2[1]; Liddell and Scott, *s.vv.*; also Maclear on Mk 3[5] (*Cambr. Bible for Schools*); Butler, *Serm.* v. vi.; T. G. Selby, *The God of the Frail* (1902), p. 1.

J. B. BRISTOW.

PLACE OF TOLL.—See RECEIPT OF CUSTOM.

PLAGUE.—The word 'plague' is used in the Gospels to render the Greek word μάστιξ, which means a whip or scourge (cf. Ac 22[24], He 11[36]). In the Apocalypse the word πληγή, from which the English word is formed, is exclusively used. In the Gospels the word occurs only four times (Mk 3[10] 5[29, 34] and Lk 7[21]). In each of these passages it is used of distressing bodily disease, and carries the implication that such afflictions are Divine chastisements. The word is therefore used in a figurative sense, and there is no reference to the bubonic disease which is the scourge of India to-day. See art. DISEASE.   W. W. HOLDSWORTH.

PLAN.—**1.** *Did Jesus enter on His ministry with a deliberate plan?*—If so, what was its nature, and how far was it subsequently modified by the pressure of events? These questions, of the first importance for a right understanding of the Gospel story, are doubly complicated by the insufficiency of our records and by the mystery in which our Lord's self-consciousness is shrouded.

The Fourth Evangelist, looking back on the Saviour's life when it had now receded into the distance, sees in it, from first to last, the unfolding of a vast design. He represents Jesus as bending outward circumstances to His will, and moving forward, without haste and without rest, towards the set 'hour' in which His purpose would fulfil itself. He assumes, in like manner, that the future development of the Church was foreseen and directed by Jesus Himself. All had happened in accordance with a Divine plan, already determined on before the Word became flesh. This Johannine view is largely the result of theological reflexion, but it also arises in part from a feeling which still impresses itself on every reader of the Gospel narrative. There is a harmony and completeness in this Life by which it is distinguished from all others. The events appear to follow each other in inevitable sequence, as if they had all been ordered beforehand in a conscious plan.

It cannot be assumed, however, that this inward necessity which we now discern in the life of Jesus was clearly present to His own mind. Such an assumption seems to be precluded by the prayer in Gethsemane, which appears to imply that our Lord was uncertain, almost to the very end, of the Father's will concerning Him. The absolute faith in God which finds its highest expression in that prayer was at all times the chief motive in the life of Jesus. In the face of a great darkness He surrendered Himself utterly to the will of God, assured that it would lead Him wisely. Whatever may have been the programme which He had set before Him, He was prepared at any moment to change or abandon it, if God should so direct Him. This must always be borne in mind in any

attempt to discover His inward purposes. The dogmatic conception that Jesus knew the end from the beginning, and gave mechanical fulfilment to a prearranged plan, is not only untrue to facts, but destroys the whole moral worth and significance of the Divine life.

At the same time it is at least equally unwarrantable to construe the life as nothing but the unforeseen result of fortuitous circumstances. It has been argued from the notices which describe the beginning of the ministry (and more particularly from Mt 4[17]), that Jesus at the outset had no distinctive plan. As a disciple of John, He took up the Baptist's work after he had been cast into prison, and awoke gradually to a new conception of the Kingdom of God and to a sense of His own special calling. According to this view, His Messianic work was in a manner thrust upon Him, and was never followed out deliberately except perhaps for a brief season at the very close. Granting, however, that the appearance of John may have given the immediate impulse to the ministry of Jesus, we have no ground for supposing that it, in any sense, produced it. The connexion between John and Jesus appears to have been at most a casual one. There is no indication that the two teachers ever met before the Baptism, and John's imprisonment must have followed almost immediately afterwards. From the beginning, moreover, the contrast between the work of Jesus and that of John was the subject of common remark. It was recognized that the new Teacher was not merely continuing the movement of His predecessor, but had begun another movement, different in its aim and character. The facts of the narrative all bear out the only conjecture which is psychologically probable, that Jesus in His years of retirement had already planned out an independent mission. What He owed to the Baptist was merely the occasion of declaring Himself and carrying His purpose into action.

2. We assume, then, that Jesus took up His ministry deliberately, with a programme, more or less definite, already formed in His mind. *Was the Messianic claim an original part of this programme?* We have here the crucial issue on which the whole question of the plan of Jesus may be said to hinge.

That Jesus declared Himself the Messiah is established beyond all doubt by the fact of His trial and crucifixion. The process against Him can admit of no other explanation than that He had laid open claim to the Messianic office. It has been maintained, however, by several modern writers (*e.g.* A. Réville) that this claim was an after-thought. The first intention of Jesus was, they say, simply to proclaim the Kingdom of God; and the assumption of Messiahship was forced upon Him by the failure of His original message. In order to retrieve His declining cause, He consented, though against His will, to bring it into line with the national hope, and appeared in Jerusalem as the declared Messiah.

It may indeed be accepted as one of the most certain results of the modern study of the Gospels, that in the earlier part of His ministry Jesus was silent regarding His Messianic claim. But the evidence is almost conclusive that He only held it in reserve, and intended from the first to make it. (1) The Messianic hope was inseparably bound up with the idea of the Kingdom of God. From the moment that He knew Himself called by God to inaugurate the Kingdom, Jesus must have recognized His title to the office of Messiah. No other form was possible, under Jewish modes of thought, by which He might express to Himself His own relation to the Kingdom. (2) The accounts of His earliest teaching all lay stress on the *authority* with which He spoke, reflecting in His manner of utterance the consciousness of a unique personal dignity (Mt 7²⁹, Mk 1²⁷). This sense of authority is especially marked in the Sermon on the Mount, with its repeated 'I say unto you.' It seems evident that even while confining Himself to the rôle of teacher, Jesus was fully aware that He was much more. As yet He made no open claim to the place of Messiah, but the knowledge that it belonged to Him coloured His whole action and thought. (3) At Cæsarea Philippi, when He at last broke the silence, He elicited a spontaneous confession from His disciples. If the incident has been rightly reported (and few passages in the Gospels bear stronger marks of authenticity), we are compelled to infer that, while concealing His claim, He had only been waiting till the disciples should recognize it of themselves. In His previous intercourse with them He had been leading them, step by step, to this final recognition. His choice of the title 'Son of Man' may have been determined by a like motive. The title was ambiguous, and did not necessarily involve the more explicit title ; but it served to awaken reflexion, and to prepare the way for the definite claim to Messiahship.

We are justified, therefore, in concluding that Jesus intended from the first to declare Himself, and that His silence was part of His deliberate plan. The two chief motives that weighed with Him can be gathered, almost with certainty, from the whole tenor of the Gospel narrative. (1) He had resolved on a method of working which would have been impossible if the people had immediately known Him as the Messiah. The Kingdom, as He conceived it, was a spiritual magnitude, and He could fulfil it only by effecting an inward change in the hearts and minds of men. As Messiah, He would have been committed at once to action of a conspicuous nature, and could never have pursued His work of teaching, healing, comforting. The story of the Temptation, which probably rests on some authentic communication of Jesus to His disciples, represents Him as choosing between the two methods of activity which were open to Him at the outset. He decided to trust Himself to the purely spiritual forces, and His silence was the necessary consequence of this decision. (2) He desired to rid the Messianic idea of the national and political character with which the popular imagination had invested it. By assuming the title prematurely He would have awakened false hopes and exposed His mission to a fatal misapprehension. It was necessary, first of all, to create a new ideal in the mind of the people by the revelation of His own character and life. When they had learned to replace their worldly conception of the Messiah by a truer and more spiritual one, He would be able to declare Himself. It was this that happened at last in the case of His immediate followers. Through their intercourse with Jesus they had attained to a higher knowledge of the Divine purposes, and recognized in Him the true Messiah. But 'he charged them that they should tell no man of him' (Mk 8³⁰). The nation as a whole was engrossed with its hope of a political deliverer, and was still incapable of receiving His secret.

Thus far we can regard our Lord as acting consistently on a plan, formed, most probably, before He commenced His public ministry. He knew Himself to be the Messiah, but had determined to conceal His claim until His teaching and His personal influence should produce a change in the minds of His countrymen. It is difficult, however, to avoid the conclusion that from Cæsarea Philippi onward His original plan was set aside. Instead of continuing His chosen work until the whole people should spontaneously confess Him as His

own disciples had done, He resolved to go up to Jerusalem and proclaim Himself openly at the Passover feast. That this was the express purpose of His journey to Jerusalem is indicated in the two symbolic acts by which He marked His arrival—the solemn entrance in fulfilment of an unmistakable prophecy (Zec 9⁹), and the cleansing of the Temple by right of His Messianic prerogative. The abrupt transition from a consistent reserve to a studied publicity can be accounted for only on the ground that He had entirely changed His plan. It had become evident to Him that the expectation with which He started had missed its fulfilment. The people, so far from responding to His message, had settled into a mood of apathy or even of declared hostility. There was no longer any purpose in maintaining silence, and He determined to assert Himself at the great gathering of the nation, and bring His Messianic work to a final issue.

3. A question rises here of the profoundest interest and importance. *When our Lord decided on this second plan, did He fully realize that it would involve His sacrificial death ?* To this question we can offer no definite answer. That He contemplated the possibility of His death at Jerusalem appears certain. Apart from the actual statement that He foretold the end to His disciples (Mk 8³¹ 9³¹ 10³²ff.),—a statement which may be influenced by later reflexion,—we cannot doubt that He knew the temper of the national authorities, and consciously hazarded His life. His teaching also in that closing period assumes a new character. He no longer speaks of the Kingdom as immediately at hand, but prepares His disciples for an indefinite delay. He dwells much on the thought that whatever may befall Himself, the triumph of His work is certain. But while He surmised, with an ever clearer conviction, that the assertion of His Messiahship would involve His death, it does not appear that He chose death deliberately as necessary to His plan. We may rather infer, from the prayer in Gethsemane, that up to the very end He entertained the possibility of a different fulfilment. This only can be affirmed with entire certainty : that He was resolved to pursue His vocation to the very uttermost, leaving the manner of its final accomplishment in the hands of God.

4. We have dealt hitherto with our Lord's plan as it concerned His personal life and calling ; but there is a further problem which cannot well be separated from this one. *How did He intend that His work should be completed?* How far did He contemplate the world-wide extension of the Christian community after His death? The answer must largely depend on the interpretation of His idea of the Kingdom of God, which is still in many points obscure. If He believed (as is maintained by Bousset, J. Weiss, and other recent writers) that the Kingdom would come almost immediately by a sudden act of God, there could be no anticipation in His mind of the gradual development of a Christian Church. If (as appears more probable) He allowed room for an interval, more or less protracted, before the dawning of the Kingdom, we have still to question whether He planned a development on the lines which were actually followed. The direct allusions to the Church (Mt 16¹⁸ 18¹⁷) bear evident traces of later modification, and it would be hazardous to employ them as the basis of any theory. More consideration is due to the sayings (Mt 8¹¹·¹² 21⁴³) which foretell the rejection of Israel and the opening of the Kingdom to those of every nation who were worthy of it. Such thoughts may well have been present to the mind of Jesus, especially in the later days, when the hostility of His own countrymen became more and more decided. It seems clear, however, from numerous indications in the Gospels, that His original plan was confined to a mission to Israel. He chose twelve disciples, with obvious reference to the number of the tribes (cf. Mt 19²⁸ = Lk 22³⁰). He hesitated to exercise His healing power in the Gentile province, lest He might exceed the limits of His mission (Mk 7²⁷). He charged His disciples to avoid the Gentile and Samaritan cities and confine themselves to the 'lost sheep of the house of Israel' (Mt 10⁵. ⁶). These indications are all sufficiently explicit; and they are confirmed by the actual history of the primitive Church. Peter and his fellow-Apostles, on the day of Pentecost and long afterwards, were still unaware that their Master desired them to proclaim His message to the wider Gentile world. The mission of Paul was a grave departure from the accepted programme, and was sanctioned only after long and anxious deliberation, and under strict conditions. It could hardly have been so regarded if the disciples had known that such a mission had been contemplated from the first, in the plan of Jesus Himself.

We can only conclude that our Lord made no definite provision for the establishment of an outward Church and its world-wide extension. He delivered His message to His own people, and formed no clear design of a work that should embrace all men. None the less He had entirely broken with Jewish particularism. Even the Messianic title, as claimed by Him, assumed a new meaning in which the traditional patriotic idea was wholly lost. His message was in its spirit universal, and made appeal to that which is permanent and central in our common nature. Whether He consciously planned the future expansion of His Church is not, therefore, a matter of the first importance. He gave the impulse which could not but result after His departure in the work of St. Paul, and in a missionary enterprise which can never know pause or limit. The inward purpose of Jesus, if not His express commandment, is rightly summed up in the closing words of St. Matthew's Gospel : 'Go ye therefore, and make disciples of all the nations.'

LITERATURE. Besides the many *Lives of Jesus* (e.g. Keim, A. Réville, O. Holtzmann), the following are among the most useful recent books : Baldensperger, *Das Selbstbewusstsein Jesu* (1891) ; J. Weiss, *Die Predigt Jesu vom Reiche Gottes* (1900) ; Bousset, *Jesus* (1904, Eng. tr. 1905) ; O. Schmiedel, *Die Hauptprobleme der Leben-Jesu-Forschung* ; T. Adamson, *Studies of the Mind in Christ*, 233 ; H. Bushnell, *The New Life*, p. 1 ; see also the earlier chapters of books relating to the Apostolic Age (*e.g.* Weizsäcker, McGiffert, etc.).   E. F. SCOTT.

PLATTER (παροψίς, Mt 23²⁵, πίναξ, Lk 11³⁹).— **1.** *The dish.*—The words thus translated in the above parallel passages referred probably to the same kind of tray or flat dish. The latter word (*pinax*) is also translated 'charger' in Mt 14⁸. ¹¹, Mk 6²⁵. ²⁸. Originally a circular mat about three feet in diameter made of closely woven wheat straw in the natural colour or of variegated pattern, it became a flat, low-rimmed tray of brass or copper, which was laid on the stool or low table around which the family gathered at meals. Similar to this, only with the rim somewhat deepened, are the smaller flat dishes, resembling saucepans, made of glazed earthenware and tin-coated copper, now used in Palestine for the serving of cooked food. The reference in the texts above quoted was probably to a dish of this sort. It is placed on the large tray, and into it each one at the table dips with a small scoop of thin bread torn from one of the loaves at his side, and thus lifts out the required mouthful of food. **2.** *Ceremonial reference.*—Christ rebuked the artificial scrupulosity that paid more attention to

contingencies of ceremonial pollution than to actual and necessary cleanliness. A dish might be soiled with dust and stains, and yet be technically free of impurity, unless it were laid on a table on which, for example, a few drops of milk had previously fallen. The table itself also (Mk 7⁴) had to be washed, not out of regard for simple and wholesome cleanliness, but to avoid the danger of such law-breaking contamination. At the present day, in a house or institution conducted on strictly Rabbinical lines, the utensils for the cooking of meat, and those used in the preparation of milk dishes, must be kept in different parts of the kitchen. This is done not in deference to delicate sensibilities with regard to taste and smell, but because the juxtaposition of such vessels might create a situation in which it would be possible to commit a conjectural infringement of the prohibition against seething a kid in its mother's milk (Dt 14²¹).

Rabbinical legislation with regard to food and dishes, and the relationship of Christ's disciples to such ceremonial pollution, formed one of the first difficulties encountered by the gospel. The concession on the Jewish side was a great testimony to the power of the new life in Christ, for such regulations were taught to Jewish children from infancy, and were commended by the venerated names of teachers who had ingeniously elaborated them. So great was the influence of such teaching, that St. Paul on one occasion remonstrated with his fellow-Apostle Peter for complying with it to the detriment of the gospel, and added, in language of personal compliment while condemning the dissimulation, that *even* Barnabas was carried away with it (Gal 2¹³ RV). See also art. DISH.

G. M. MACKIE.

PLAY.—See BOYHOOD, vol. i. p. 222, and GAMES.

PLEASURE.—Not passing pleasure but true happiness is to be sought by the disciple of Christ. Pleasure as such is transitory, but Christian joy and peace are continual and eternal. This life is a preparation for the fruition of eternal happiness, and not merely a series of opportunities for gratification to self and others (Lk 12³⁷). In itself pleasure is not evil, for all things were made by God through His Son (Jn 1³). He sanctioned and sanctified social festivity in due season (Jn 2¹⁻¹¹), and said of Himself, in contrast with the ascetic John the Baptist, 'The Son of Man came eating and drinking' (Mt 11¹⁹). But pleasures are not always expedient, and may work eternal mischief (Lk 8¹⁴). The days of Noah and Lot were days of pleasure and self-indulgence, when God's visitation fell suddenly on the devotees of eating and drinking and marrying (Lk 17²⁷. ²⁸). Such sensual pleasure absorbs too much of man's limited effort to be truly profitable (Jn 6²⁷). The *sons of this world* lead effortless lives (Lk 20³⁴), but Christ's Kingdom is *not of this world* (Jn 18³⁶). The citizens of Christ the King must beware of careless indulgence in pleasure, being ready for His sudden presence (Lk 21³⁴ 12³⁶). Yet, far more than all this, the pursuit of pleasures is disloyalty, because it is the following after will-o'-the-wisps (as it were) instead of the steadfast regard to the Light of the world (Jn 8¹² 9⁵). It is really a folly to accumulate the means of pleasure (Lk 12¹⁵. ¹⁹) ; but for the Christian it is treason to pursue pleasure instead of *leaving all and following Him* (Lk 5¹¹). In return, the Lord has unfailing promises of blessedness here and hereafter (Lk 18²⁹. ³⁰, Mk 10²⁹. ³⁰) ; but the true disciple must renounce everything this world offers, to be counted worthy of the eternal joy (Mt 16²⁴, Mk 8³⁴, Lk 9²³). The sensuous or sensual life of the soul (ψυχή) must not be striven after (Mt 16²⁵ 10³⁹, Mk 8³⁵, Lk 9²⁴

17³³, Jn 12²⁵). All the pleasure the world can afford will never compensate for what is lost in such a pursuit (Mt 16²⁶, Mk 8³⁶, Lk 9²⁵). In this comprehensive statement even intellectual and æsthetic forms of pleasure are included. The habit of daily self-denial is to be adopted (Lk 9²³). No delight in business, however laudable in itself, must rival the call of Christ (Lk 14¹⁸). A dreadful reversal awaits the Dives who clings to the pleasures of this age (Lk 16²⁵). Thus the rich are terribly handicapped in their heavenly course (Mt 19²⁴). The pleasures of this world may secure the horrors of hell (Lk 6²⁵). No, the disciple must be as his Master (Mt 10²⁵). The Master's prayer was always, 'Not what I will, but what thou wilt' (Mk 14³⁶). The pleasures of popularity (Jn 12⁴³) and of ostentation (Mt 6¹⁻¹⁸, Lk 20⁴⁶) are to be avoided. Hand or eye may well be sacrificed for the sake of faithfulness to Christ in the hope of eternal salvation (Mt 5²⁹·³⁰, Mk 9⁴³·⁴⁷). The blessed are those who 'hunger and thirst after righteousness,' not after pleasure (Mt 5⁶). The faithful disciple shall find tribulation rather than pleasure (Jn 16³³), inward peace but an outward sword (Mt 10³⁴), joy rather than enjoyment (Jn 15¹¹ 16²⁰⁻²² 17¹³). W. B. FRANKLAND.

PLOUGH (ἄροτρον).—The plough is mentioned but once in NT (Lk 9⁶²), and the act of ploughing twice (Lk 17⁷, 1 Co 9¹⁰). The Eastern plough appears to have changed but little since ancient times, the oldest representations closely resembling the implement now in use. It is almost entirely of wood, and is of slight construction, the furrow drawn being only 4 or 5 inches deep in light soil. It consists of a pole about 8 ft. long, in two pieces, with a joint in the middle. Through the butt-end is passed downward and made fast a piece of wood about 5 ft. long, the upper end sloping backward to form the handle. The under end is sharpened, and armed with a piece of iron. This serves as both coulter and share. The handle is grasped with the left hand, the right holding the goad to drive and guide the oxen. To the thin end of the pole is attached a crossbar with yokes which drop upon the necks of the oxen, and are fastened by the yoke-bands. See also art. AGRICULTURE in vol. i., and in Hastings' *DB*, i. 49ᵇ (where the plough is figured). W. EWING.

POET.—It may seem unnecessary to protest at the outset against the idea of any essential incompatibility of poetry with truth, as if, because a saying is poetry, it lay under the suspicion of being untrue, or even less true than prose. Yet that delusion has done so much harm even in regard to secular writings, that it is necessary to refer to it in the association of poetry with the most sacred writings in the world. The fact is, of course, that poetry is often the only medium of expression for a more direct and larger truth. Many truths are too subtle and too far-reaching to be expressed otherwise; and it was inevitable that God should have chosen to make use of poetry in His supreme revelation. Greek poets were prophets, and Hebrew prophets were poets. In every age and nation the connexion between religion and poetry has been so close that it excites no wonder when Lecky (*Hist. of Rationalism*, ii. 232, 253, 260) tells us that, in the past, religious dogma has been transformed into poetry, or Matthew Arnold (*Essays in Criticism*), that in the future this transformation will be complete. It excites no wonder, for these writers were so impressed with the interest and significance of the connexion, that they did less than justice to the equally clear phenomenon of the element of indisputable facts that are permanently claimed by history and by science in the Christian religion.

No definition of poetry is here offered. Matthew Arnold's definition of it as 'a criticism of life' is true, but inadequately true. It is one kind of criticism of life—one which utilizes emotion and imagination in a peculiar way, and often affects the style of utterance in the direction of music, through rhymed or rhythmical utterance more or less deliberate and formal. The result is that subtle and yet unmistakable quality which differentiates poetry from prose, the use of which is an art akin to the graphic arts, yet often unconscious, and generally instinctive rather than deliberate.

That Jesus was in this sense an artist is abundantly manifest. We shall see how in Him the poetic and the graphic qualities blended, and nothing about Him is more evident than the delicate and indeed exquisite sensitiveness, both of body and of mind, which accompanies these qualities. Even in His unusually speedy death (Mk 15⁴⁴) we see the result of an extremely sensitive frame. It was this that led to the constant perversion of His words by coarse-grained and vulgar persons (Jn 2¹⁹), and often led Him to keep silence (Mt 27¹²) when the uncomprehending demanded speech; He knew that whatever He might say, He could not have made them understand Him.

At the beginning of the Gospels we find the story of His life set deep in poetry. The stories of John the Baptist's preaching are full of the poetry of the desert, with its intense visual images of the vipers, the axe, the stones, the fires, and the fan of the wilderness (Mt 3⁹ etc.). The infancy of Jesus is cradled among songs of women and of men, in which the narrative breaks forth into the music of the earliest Christian hymns.

His biographers are poets. The Gospel which gives us by far the most intimate glimpses into His inner life is written by a man who was a poet to the very heart of him. Matthew, himself less poetical, interpolates his narrative with long swinging quotations from the poets of his native land, such as those recorded in 4¹²⁻¹⁶, or that tender and appropriate fragment from Isaiah concerning the bruised reed, introduced with so great a pathos in 12²⁰. Even Mark, the most prosaic and almost curtly practical of them, is turned into a poet when he is writing the life of Jesus. The simple pathos of such a word as 'When he thought thereon he wept' (14⁷²), or the sudden reminder that Jesus in the wilderness of His temptation had for His companions the wild beasts and the angels (1¹³), are inimitable.

It has been wisely said that all children are poets, and indeed there is no poetry so pure as that of the naïveté of the little child. Of the childhood of Jesus we know practically nothing but what He retained of its spirit through later years. In a very true sense the childhood of Jesus lasted to the end, and He retained a child's heart through all His years. Children knew this when He was near them, and seem to have come to Him without hesitation (Mt 18²) as to one of themselves. No doubt one bond between them and Him was that directness of vision and of thought and speech which characterized both. But the poetry of their minds and hearts must also be remembered.

Thus it came to pass that the Kingdom of God which He established was proclaimed as the Kingdom of the child (Mt 19¹⁴); He quoted a prophetic verse in confirmation of His saying that the praise of God was made perfect by passing through infant lips (Ps 8², Mt 21¹⁶); He thanked His Father specially for revealing to the instinctive minds of babes, truths which were unattainable by the wise and prudent (Lk 10²¹); and, in the finest reference of all, He told how the angels of the children dwell in heaven, always beholding the face of the Father (Mt 18¹⁰). When to these utterances we add the fact that He was interested in the very human children who played and quarrelled in the market-place at their games of marriages and funerals (Mt 11[16]), we have said enough to show very plainly His sympathy with the poetry of childhood.

Arrived at manhood, and having thoughts within Him that had long been struggling for utterance, and had now come to their hour, Jesus deliberately chose poetic forms of language as the medium of His speech. The characteristic mould in which Hebrew poetry was cast, was not rhythm as in the Greek and Roman poems, nor rhyme in the later Western fashion. It was a kind of measured anti-thesis, in which, in each saying, there was a fall balancing the rise. This antithetic balancing is seen in most of Jesus' sayings. Each of the Beati-tudes in Mt 5 illustrates this mode, while v.[12] of the same chapter adopts the more complex form of the balanced triplet instead of couplet. *

It is true that poetry, and art in general, are very far indeed from being wholly matters of expression. There is to-day a renewal of the thoroughly unreasonable fashion of exaggerating the importance of manner in art, until the matter has come to be considered a negligible quantity. While both elements must be recognized, it will eventually be found that Johnson was far nearer the truth when he said that it was impossible for a man to be 'the good poet without first being the good man,' than those for whom style is everything and matter wholly unimportant. You do not make poetry out of prose by dividing it into anti-thetic or other kinds of couplets. There is, besides the form, the subtle spirit, and much more, that really determines the classification. Yet, when all this is admitted, it remains true that form has much effect on matter, and there is an inevitable and strong reaction of the style upon the thought expressed. Thus when Jesus chose the poetic forms of His day and nation for the utterance of His speech, He drew it more and more com-pletely within the line of poetry.

If it be true that it is not the form alone that distinguishes poetic literature from prosaic, it is equally true that it is not the matter alone. Apart from what is said, and from the liter-ary medium through which it is expressed, there is what we have called a 'subtle spirit' which emanates from the tempera-ment of a writer and gives the poetic quality of the writing. It is an elusive spirit to those who would define it in scientific terms, and it can only be appreciated in concrete example by those who are themselves in sympathy with it. All poets write for poets and for poets only ; they count upon the poetic intel-ligence of their readers, and shrink back into silence when in the society of those in whom that sense is deficient. Yet there are two elements which certainly are never absent from the spirit in question, and which may be taken as essential to the building up of poetic work. These are a certain kind of emotion and of imagination, not (as we have said) definable, but un-mistakable by all who are in sympathy with the poetic mood of mind.

The mention of emotion in this connexion recalls inevitably the famous definition of religion as 'morality touched with emotion' (M. Arnold, Lit. and Dogma, ch. ii.). It is indeed a meagre and inadequate conception of religion. Yet there is a large element of truth in it, and the emotional element in all true religion allies it with poetry.

That the temperament of Jesus was in the highest way emotional, is so familiar a fact that it needs little dwelling on. Christ as man of feeling is almost too well known. Perhaps we should rather say misknown, for anything of that sentimentality which vulgar minds are accustomed to associate with Him is entirely absent from Him. His emotion is always reticent and controlled, and when it finds expression, it is always utterly real and virile, without a touch of either the fantastic or the effeminate. A splendid example of the sensitive response to emotion which produces literary effect of the most delicate though uncon-scious poetic quality, is to be found in the story of the Prodigal Son (Lk 15). From the beginning to verse 24 no one can fail to feel the rising exhil-aration, an effect manifestly produced by the corresponding crescendo in the narrator's feeling. Suddenly, on the entrance of the elder brother, all is damped down, and the story drags itself to the close like a stricken thing.

* This subject is discussed and illustrated in Griffenhoofe's Unwritten Sayings of Jesus ; and in Briggs' articles in the Ex-pository Times, viii. [1897] 393, 452, 492, ix. 69, which, however, carry the matter further than all readers will be prepared to follow the author.

There are many signs of the ebb and flow of feel-ing in connexion with the events of Jesus' own experience. At the critical moments of His life this is naturally most noticeable. There is the outburst on the occasion of His first appearance in the synagogue of Nazareth, with the memories of thirty years behind the exhilaration. One can feel yet the thrill of the opening quotation, 'The Spirit of the Lord is upon me,' etc. (Lk 4[18] quoted from Is 61[1]). Correspondingly deep is the depression manifest in His first intimation to His disciples of the inevitable cross whose shadow had begun to lie upon His path. In the words, 'Likewise shall also the Son of Man suffer of them' (Mt 17[12]), there is an almost intolerable pathos. But the cross, as it came nearer, changed its aspect for Him, and as He entered on its terrific pathway at the end, one hears a shout of exultation, almost of laughter, in the words recorded in Jn 12[23-31], when we are told that He 'rejoiced in spirit.' Yet unmistakable though these instances are, there is even a more poignant emotion in such little casual touches as the contrast between the homelessness He felt and the homes of foxes and of birds (Mt 8[20]) ; or in such a wayside incident as that in which He defended the woman who 'hath wrought a fine work upon me' (26[10]), and whose gracious deed affected Him as with the breath of burial spices.

Countless instances, and those of many kinds, might be gathered from His speech to others. The gardener's pity for the fig-tree (Lk 13[8]) is a real touch of nature. When He addresses the dead damsel in the homely Aramaic tongue (Mk 5[41]), we have the same tone in which a northern peasant of our own land might say 'Lassie !' Nor can we omit those words which must have seemed to the disciple to whom they were spoken to gather up together all the tenderness of boyish memories with that of grown man's patient suffering, 'When thou wast young, thou girdedst thyself, and walkedst whither thou wouldest ; but when thou shalt be old, thou shalt stretch forth thy hands, and another shall gird thee, and carry thee whither thou wouldest not' (Jn 21[18]).

Perhaps the point at which the emotion of Jesus reaches its deepest fulness and tenderness of sug-gestion is in regard to the men and women of His nation. The metaphor of the hen and her brood (Lk 13[34]) was spoken with sobs. But the figure round which His emotion unquestionably gathered most of all was the favourite Israelite figure of the shepherd and the sheep. The OT image repeated by later prophets from 1 K 22[17] ('I saw all Israel scattered upon the hills as sheep that have no shepherd') had evidently touched His heart most deeply. Carlyle points out in his Essay on Burns how the shepherd instinct of the poet puts him in the place of the suffering sheep ; and it was the same instinct which drew from Ps 23, and from the passage above quoted, so rich and wonderful a shepherd poetry as the sayings of Jesus afford. He knows the ways and the folding of the flock (Jn 10[14. 16]). He is touched with compassion for those lost ones of the House of Israel who are as sheep without a shepherd (Mt 9[36] 15[24]). His Good Shepherd is seen in such detail as only the pitiful heart could have suggested, 'leaving the ninety and nine in the wilderness' (Lk 15[4], Mt 18[12]), and 'going into the mountains' in search of the wanderer. When the Shepherd is smitten, the sheep will be scattered abroad (Mt 26[31]), neverthe-less He will 'go before them into Galilee' (Mk 16[7]), bringing the scattered flock home.

These proofs of Christ's emotion are very familiar, but His imagination has received less attention, and to it we shall devote a somewhat more minute study. That it was strongly in evidence is suffi-ciently proved by the fact that some of the Jews on one occasion took Him to be a devil-possessed Samaritan (Jn 8[48]). Nothing could be a surer tribute to imagination than this judgment of the un-imaginative. His actual experiences, His memories of past events, and His thoughts about even abstract truth, alike presented themselves in images to His mind. Generally the images were visual, and sometimes they were extremely vivid in outline. He thought in pictures, which rose either from what He had actually seen, or spontaneously in His imagination.

Scenes from the life—plant and animal—of nature occur in all His parables, and in very many sayings, which show the exactness and sympathy of His observations. The whitening harvest fields of the fertile valley of Samaria (4[35]), sparsely dotted with the few labourers whose brilliant garments shone like flowers among the corn, is one of the very few instances of landscape in His descriptions of nature. The mountain-lands of both the north and south attracted Him, and it is striking to find Him making straight for the highlands of Galilee when His task of life was over (Mt 28[10-16]). But more frequently it is a clear-cut piece of detail that He sees, sharp-edged and complete in itself. A spring of living water (Jn 4[10]), the trackless mystery of the night wind (3[8]), salt shining white upon the offal heap where it had been thrown out as savourless (Lk 14[34. 35]), two sparrows sold for a farthing (Mt 10[29]), are wayside pictures which He has engraved on the imagination of the world. His favourite image was characteristic of that land where there were few forests, but where the single tree was so precious, either for shadow or for fruit (cf. W. R. Smith, *Religion of the Semites*). His images of single trees,—the vine, the fig, and the olive,—with their roots, branches, leaves, all seen as it were in detail, will occur to every reader (Mt 12[33] etc., Jn 15[1] etc., Mk 13[28], Lk 13[6]). One of the finest and tenderest of all His imaginative descriptions is that mere touch of artistry which gives us in a flash the life of the reeds bending before desert winds (Mt 11[7]).

The picturesqueness of His metaphors is very great. From the peaceful joy of the children of the bridechamber (9[15]) to the storming of the Kingdom by the violent (11[12]), we pass through a wonderful gallery of vivid scenes. Who can tell what great tableaux were before His mind's eyes as He said such words as these—'the Son of Man is come to give his life a ransom for many' (20[28]); 'for crisis have I come into the world' (Jn 9[39]); 'I have overcome the world'? (16[33]). One figure has become so familiar through His use of it that we have almost forgotten that it is a metaphor—the figure of the cup (Mt 20[22], Lk 22[20. 42], Jn 18[11]). Three times He saw His appointed destiny in life under the image of a cup held to His hands or lips by the Father's hand; and Christendom, and indeed the world, has taken over the beautiful and great symbol.

No finer instances of His visual intensity of imagination could be quoted than those which refer to the play of light and darkness. Such references recur like a sort of chorus from beginning to end of His work; and it is not without significance that the stories of the healing of the blind are told in such detail. This imagination blazes out in full splendour in the magnificent sentence, 'I am the light of the world' (Jn 8[12]), and the figure is sustained and strengthened by the assurance that those who believe in the light become 'children of light' (12[36]) — i.e. themselves radiant, their upturned faces having caught and reflected the light to which they were turned. This is rendered all the more brilliant by the intense consciousness of darkness to which it is in opposition. John, in his description of the departure of Judas from the upper room (13[30]), significantly adds, 'and it was night.' In the same way Jesus utilizes the sudden contrast between the flashing lamps of the banquet-room, reflected from the vessels and from the white garments of the guests, with the 'outer darkness' of the unlit street (Mt 25[30]). To realize the full brilliance of this contrast we must remember that the rooms had windows only into the courtyard, and the street walls were of blank unpierced masonry. The thought of darkness always moved Christ to a kind of horror. No condition was described by

Him with such frequency or with such depth of feeling as that of those who 'had no light in them' (Jn 11[10]), or who deliberately loved and chose darkness in preference to light (Jn 3[19]). 'How great is that darkness!' (Mt 6[23]) He exclaims with a shuddering pause. He hastened men's work by the reminder of the night coming 'when no man can work' (Jn 9[4]), and as we read we feel the helplessness of hands folded in the dark. When His captors and their traitor guide had come upon Him, looking through the torchlight upon their faces, He said that this was 'the power of darkness' (Lk 22[53]).

His words abound in bright little sketch-pictures of the life and labours of men—etched, one might almost say, upon the margins of the Gospels. 'Fishers of men' (Mk 1[17]), one with his hand upon the plough-handles but his head turned back (Lk 9[62]), some with loins girt and lamps burning, waiting for the sound of their master's returning footsteps (12[35. 36]), another 'strong and fully armed' (11[21])—these are among the countless images which will recur to every reader. The hair upon men's heads is not vaguely referred to—it is seen as black or white (Mt 5[36]); the water in the cups they carry is cold water (10[42]). The pictures He draws, as in a flash, of the unconscious busy life of men and women before the most terrific catastrophes, show an extraordinary vivacity (Lk 17[27. 28]); and there is a wonderful perfectness about the description of the farmer's life, 'as if a man should cast seed into the ground; and should sleep and rise night and day, and the seed should spring and grow up, he knoweth not how' (Mk 4[27]). There is little colour in His pictures, and the rich man 'in purple and fine linen' (Lk 16[19]) is exceptional; but nothing could surpass the brightness of the scene where the King pauses as he comes to see the feast, his looks arrested by the dulness of the everyday garment in the midst of the shining raiment of his wedding guests (Mt 22[11]). Not less remarkable, though of a very different kind, are such realistic pictures as that of the blind leading the blind into the ditch (Lk 6[39]).

These are simple pictures, but sometimes His poetry is more elaborate. In the old Welsh songs there was a curious device by which, for mnemonic purposes perhaps, the lines of story or sentiment were interlined with references to nature, concerning the reeds in the water or the wind in the trees. Was it perhaps with the same instinct that Jesus interwove the three denials of St. Peter with the two crowings of the cock (Mk 14[30])? But some of the images are themselves complex. How subtle, for example, is the imaginative insight that first described 'the branch *abiding in* the vine' (Jn 15[4])! Again, who but the rarest of poets would have imagined the birds sowing, reaping, and gathering into barns (Mt 6[26]), or have separated in thought the idea of the lily and its robes, the flower 'clothing itself according to its nature,' or rather 'God clothing the grass of the field (6[30])'? In reference to this nature-work, Dr. Sanday contrasts Tennyson's 'Flower in the crannied wall' with the passage about the lily just quoted. 'The one,' he says, 'gives utterance to a far-off, unattainable dream or wish—the other is the expression of perfect insight and knowledge; it is not an aspiration after a glimpse of God's working in nature, but a clear unbounded vision of that working.' Thus is the Divinity of Jesus seen most plainly in His exquisite naïveté, the simpleness rather than the grandeur of His poetic vision; and we learn of Him 'not by a planet's rush but a rose's birth.'

Occasionally the images are elaborated into a pageantry, but this is generally held in check. The triumphal entry into Jerusalem was the one actual pageant which He sanctioned; and that was only after the days of His life were numbered, that the memory of the spectacle might impress men, and when it could lead to no revolutionary consequences among enthusiastic crowds (Mt 21[1] etc.). His disciples wanted the spectacular, and perhaps even missed it in His fellowship. The request of two of them for places on His right hand and on His left (Mk 10[37]) hints at gorgeous dreams on their part. Its appeal to Himself is portrayed in the temptation of the pinnacle of the Temple (Mt 4[5]), whose meaning undoubtedly was a magical display before the eyes of wondering crowds. Occasionally, as we said, He permitted His images this elaboration into pageantry. Now and then the canvas is crowded with angels. 'Twelve legions of angels' wait upon His prayer to the Father (26[53]); and by those who look with opened eyes, angels may be seen daily 'ascending and descending upon the Son of Man' (Jn 1[51]). The twelve

Apostles are seen seated on twelve thrones, judging the twelve tribes of Israel (Mt 19²⁸), and for them and for all believers there are 'many mansions' in the Father's house (Jn 14²). As to the connexion between the earthly and the heavenly life, whatsoever they bind or loose on earth shall be bound or loosed in heaven (Mt 16¹⁹). The accounts (Mt 24) of His Second Coming are among the most difficult parts of the New Testament. But, however their details may be interpreted, they are brilliantly poetic flame-pictures which gather up into themselves much of the wild beauty and wonder of the apocalyptic imagination then so universal. A favourite scene is that of the Son of Man sitting on the clouds of heaven (26⁶⁴); but a sublimer picture is that which the same Son of Man draws of Himself standing ashamed among His angels because of the pusillanimous spirit of some of His followers (Mk 8³⁸). Nor could anything surpass the brilliance of the scene where 'the righteous shine forth as the sun' (Mt 13⁴³), and we seem to see great shafts of light as the cloud rack of Judgment Day passes, and past its flaming edge are seen the seats of the glorified spirits in heaven.

It need not surprise us when we find the imagination of Jesus reaching its climax of realistic vividness in the field of the weird and the ghastly. It is a tragic world, and he who, with his imagination in free play, dares to confront its facts impartially, will certainly see and tell gruesome things. There is, accordingly, frequent reference to loathsome things, whose loathsomeness had evidently affected Him. A serpent or a scorpion among food (Mt 7¹⁰, Lk 11¹²), a foul cup or platter whose exterior gave promise of cleanliness (Mt 23²⁵), the corruption of moth and rust among treasures of garments or metal (6¹⁹), are among His casual notes of observation. More deliberate and (as it were) classical are such sayings as that about the carcase and the vultures (24²⁸), and the vipers crawling towards the flames (23³³). The bitterness of the spiritual life is driven in almost upon our senses as we read that every sacrifice must be 'salted with fire' (Mk 9⁴⁹), that He is come to bring not peace, but a sword (Mt 10³⁴), and that only those who eat His flesh and drink His blood can claim to have life in them (Jn 6⁵³). The same rises to its height in the wild picture presented in the words, 'I am come to cast fire on the earth; and what will I, if it be already kindled?' (Lk 12⁴⁹); while the whole of His reference to Mammon (Mt 16⁹ etc.) is so realistic that it used to be imagined that this was the name of some Syrian god, such as G. F. Watts has painted, with bloody feet and hands pashing out the life of humanity.

Among the most conspicuous of His images of the ghastly are two that are drawn from human life. The first is that of the cross-bearers (Mt 10³⁸). It is but too easy to ascertain whence this suggestion must have come, for men bearing crosses to the public places of execution were common enough in Palestine under the Romans. So we have from Jesus the weirdest of all allegorical pictures of the noble life. It is a procession of men bearing crosses, and Himself at its head. The procession is not staggering in weakness along the Via Dolorosa to Calvary. It is winding its way through the sunshine, by the waters of Galilee, in and out of villages where men are working, and women standing by wells, and children playing in the streets. The other figure is that of a spectral funeral procession, in which the dead are burying the dead (8²²). The phrase has become proverbial, but the imaginary scene in which it originated is surely one of the ghastliest. The corpse of a dead man is being carried to its tomb, but in place of the many-coloured robes of an Eastern funeral there are but shrouds like his own in the cortege; and the march of limbs bloodless and stark, and the sunlight falling upon closed eyes, are images which we may well believe never ceased to haunt the minds of those who first shuddered at them. We are not here concerned with the lessons which these images conveyed. They are among the most important of all His teachings, and the point to note is that He drove them deep into the imagination

of His hearers by the most daring and unrelieved use of the ghastly.

Nature, too, lent her sinister suggestion. The sea was always an object of fear and hatred to the Jews. It was strange to them, as to all inland nations, and for many centuries they were never permitted to become familiar with it on account of the Philistine and Phœnician Gentiles, who held its harbours and its coast. In later days it was significant to them chiefly as the path of the invaders, whose maritime base for Syria was conspicuous from many mountains of Israel at Cæsarea. Only on a very few occasions does Jesus refer to it, and always in ominous suggestion. He speaks of some who compass sea and land to obtain proselytes, only that they may make them children of hell (Mt 23¹⁵). Again, He speaks of a sycamine-tree or a mountain being removed by faith and cast into the sea, as a thing stupendous and silencing (Lk 17⁶). The most appalling doom that can be set against the sin of injuring His little ones, and which were still better for the injurer than what actually awaits him, is to be cast into the sea with a millstone about his neck to hold him among the wreckage and slime of decaying things in its bottom ooze (Mt 18⁶). Amid the terrors of the latter Day of Judgment we hear the booming of the breakers as a terrifying undertone—'the sea and the waves roaring' (Lk 21²⁵).

Nothing in nature strikes so cold a fear into the imagination as that strange and sinister combination which has been called 'the beauty and the terror of the world.' In the sweetest sunshine and under the purest light of stars, lurk ever the savage cruelties and the obscene putrefactions of earth. This also Jesus noted when He spoke of 'the whited sepulchres' (Mt 23²⁷)—the brightest spots on many a sunny landscape of the East, yet suggesting a condition of physical horror within, which it needs experience to realize. But the utmost extreme of poetic power of this sort is felt in the sudden introduction of the picture of a fig-tree, blossoming peacefully in the full beauty of its leafage, into the midst of the magnificent horrors of the picture of the Day of Judgment (24³²).

The person of the devil is very frequently present to the mind of Jesus, and generally he is addressed or spoken of without imagery. At other times, however, he is portrayed as a princely figure — 'prince of this world'—who vainly comes to find his own in Him (Jn 14³⁰), and who is, by the Cross, cast out from his dominion (12³¹). There is one picture, from which Bunyan probably drew some of the imagery of his Holy War, of an attack by the Lords of Hell upon the fortress of the Church (Mt 16¹⁸). And once, in an hour of triumph, Jesus 'saw Satan fall as lightning from heaven' (Lk 10¹⁸).

Yet no victory of Good over Evil is ever complete on earth, and a deep horror remains, haunting the mind as it thinks of those who persistently refuse the Good and choose the Evil. Nowhere has this horror been more manifest than in the speech of Christ, who tells men to 'fear him that hath power to destroy both soul and body in hell, yea, fear him!' (12⁵). He uses several figures to express this horror, all of them borrowed from the OT and its conceptions. Now it is 'the outer darkness' (Mt 8¹²) of the unlit street which serves for an image of it; again, it is the offal-heaps of the valley of Jehoshaphat, and the fires which were always consuming them (Mk 9⁴⁴ etc.). But, for the most part, His imagination pictures the abyss of Sheol, with the 'great gulf fixed' (Lk 16²⁶) between it and the home of Abraham. It is an image closely connected with that of the 'nether deep,' into whose dreary vastness the demons pray that they may not be sent (8³¹). It is suggestive of the homeless, empty spaces beyond the ramparts of the world, where in the thick darkness there is the sound of 'weeping and gnashing of teeth' (Mt 8[12] etc.). The words are repeated again and again until we seem to hear the low sound of that wailing which Dante heard within the gates of the Inferno. It is the undertone of horror which, even among merely human poets, is ever heard beneath the laughter and the voices of the world. But none has heard it and told the sound with the mingled pity and horror of the words of Jesus.

Hitherto we have noticed only the clear-cut character of the imaginative work of Jesus. But there is another side to this—a vagueness and a sense of transcending all limits and definitions—which is, as it were, the poetic obverse of the clear edge. This also enters into the true conception of the mind of Christ.

Both in regard to space and time His delight in room, and the spaciousness of His thought are evident. The most familiar example in regard to time is the much disputed word αἰώνιος (Mt 19[29] 25[46] etc.). The whole point of that phrase is taken from it when it becomes a pawn in the game of theological disputation. It neither fixes the furthest limit at eternity, nor denies that the stretch is eternal. In it the mind simply flings itself out into the future, and is aware of the flowing river of the ages. It is the poetic and didactic, but not the dogmatic, purpose that is aimed at and that is accomplished. The sense of enormous duration is given with almost aching realization. The hope or the denial of a *terminus ad quem* is not given.

His allusions to vague and immense spaces are so numerous as to reveal a strongly marked and favourite habit of imagination. He seems to delight in the width of the world for the mere feeling of its roominess. The sound of a trumpet (Mt 24[31]) is heard, and a flash of lightning seen (Lk 17[24]) from one end of heaven to the other. Even in His reference to the birds and the lilies, already quoted (Mt 6[28]), He is not satisfied till He has added 'of the air' and 'of the field' (8[20]). In these mere touches the whole expanse of sky and earth opens and broadens to the horizon as we read. They are the subtle touches which only a poet's mind would give. Again, one feature of the Kingdom to which He frequently alludes is the journeying of ancient people and of those of later days across huge distances of the world (8[11]). 'They shall come from the east and from the west,' to sit down at the table of Abraham, and the elect shall be gathered from the four winds of heaven (24[31]). His memories of the OT recall remote nooks and crannies of the world—the far-off home of the Queen of the South (12[42]), Sodom and Gomorrah, Tyre and Sidon (Lk 10[12. 13]), and Nineveh (Mt 12[41]). Many of the people of His parables are travellers who go long distances and return (Mk 13[34] etc.), and He speaks of Himself, in one of the most wistful of all His utterances, as 'a man going a journey into a far country' (Mt 25[14]). These allusions are not of so much significance in themselves as in their revelation of the stretch and travel instinct in the mind of Jesus. They become splendidly significant when we remember them in connexion with such other sayings as that about the Father who 'maketh his sun to rise on the evil and on the good, and sendeth rain on the just and on the unjust' (5[45]); and that also about the other sheep which the Good Shepherd has which 'are not of this fold,' which also He must bring, that there may be one flock and one shepherd (Jn 10[16]). In that promise there is the whole breadth of His heart, who looks across the world and counts it all His pasture ground. This whole habit of His mind throws out into strong relief the spirituality of Jesus, to which it offers a sort of parallel in the region of the physical as against the literalism and preciseness of the Pharisees. While He was out among 'the ages,' they were wrangling as to the number of stars visible which marked the hour of evening; while they were settling the inches permissible for a Sabbath-day's journey, His heart was gathering disciples from the ends of the earth.

Spirituality and poetry are connected in the most intimate way, and the remembrance that Jesus was a poet may lead us past many futile controversies and into many illuminative interpretations. Two results may be selected as of very special value to the understanding of the mind of Christ.

1. *His use of hyperbole.*—Both His laws and His gospel have suffered many things at the hands of prosaic literalists. There are few things, for instance, which have been more confusing and harmful of late years than the perversions of Christianity which literalists have extracted from the Sermon on the Mount. Even to those who are willing to accept the doctrine thus presented in its naked literalness, it becomes but a counsel of perfection, and life in every act of Christian service leads down a blind alley, until the discouragement of constant and inevitable failure becomes altogether intolerable. But on those who are repelled by the doctrine, the

effect is even more serious. To them Christ appears a doctrinaire teacher, whose precepts have created an impossible situation; and they turn, not from the doctrines only, but from Him.

The fact is that the poet's exaggeration is the only way in which many truths can be expressed at all. Life is far too complex for any words that men have found in which to describe it. Spiritual things have no adequate language which corresponds to them; and the only way in which such truths can be communicated is by stating one side of them with such startling strength and vividness that *that* phase of truth at least shall never be forgotten. Of this fact Christ took the most fearless and unquestioning advantage, trusting wholly to the sympathetic intelligence of His hearers. Even in trifles He acted thus. The seed of the mustard plant is not the smallest of all seeds (Mt 13[32]), and there is no necessity for the zeal of commentators who would search for some unheard-of variety of mustard whose seeds are smaller than the spore of ferns. No one would have been more amazed at such defence of His veracity than He who spoke the words. In the same way is to be understood the saying, 'This is my body' (Lk 22[19] etc.); and if Luther had allowed himself to perceive this most obvious of truths, what a world of unnecessary controversy would have been spared to the Church! Such licence is demanded, not for poetry only, but for the very continuance of human intercourse, which otherwise would at once become a mere interchange of pedantries. In the same way are to be interpreted such passages as that about the hatred of father and mother (14[26]), and many of those commands about property, non-resistance (Mt 5[38] etc.), etc., which have been so grievous and so unwarrantable a stumbling-block to faith in modern times.

2. These considerations reach their highest value when we remember that in the teaching of Jesus there is *the spiritual idealism of the poet*. The incident of His praise of Mary rather than of Martha (Lk 10[42]) has not unjustly claimed His sympathies for the dreamers and the mystics whose world is that of the ideal truth. At times this spiritual exaltation showed itself in physical effects which were recognized by onlookers. As He walked, they were amazed and afraid (Mk 10[32]). It explains many of His wonderful sayings. Without it, that strange journey of the disciples would be wholly unintelligible, when they were to provide neither scrip, nor money, nor even shoes, nor any possessions but their peace (Mt 10[9ff.]). Similarly must be regarded the command to take no thought for the morrow, neither for food nor for clothes (6[34]). These are ideal descriptions, not meant for the ears of literalists, but describing that world of spiritual conceptions in which His spirit dwelt. With these may be compared the exacting spirituality of His doctrine of marriage (19[4ff.]), which He Himself supplemented by the further statement that in the next world the life of the angels supersedes marriage altogether (Lk 20[36]), and which leads on to St. Paul's association of the marriage bond with the union of Christ and His Church (Eph 5[22] etc.). Such doctrine, He Himself declares, is for them that can receive it (Mt 19[11. 12]). And indeed the whole of Christianity introduces men into an ideal world which does not at all correspond to the actual world of public life, and towards which the individual Christian is but now feeling his way in isolated points of character. It is a life to lead with one's soul commanding and guiding the body. That is, if one has a soul; for Christ (in His poetic fashion) refuses to take it for granted that a man necessarily has a soul because he is a man, and reminds us that each man's soul has to be won (Lk 21[19]). But for those who have souls, and are willing to live lives corresponding to them rather than to the flesh, Christ constructs an ideal world in which all things have suffered a 'change into something rich and strange.' The heaven is God's throne, and the earth His footstool (Mt 5[34, 35]). The body is a temple where the spirit dwells (Jn 2[19]). The life is sustained by spiritual food which even the closest friends know not of (4[32, 34]). To live that life is to be citizens of the Kingdom which is within (Lk 17[21]) and of the other world (Jn 18[36]), and which cometh not with observation (Lk 17[20])—the Kingdom of the truth (Jn 18[37]). The worship of such souls is in spirit and in truth (4[24]), and their work is to believe (6[29]).

That ideal world—so far ahead of the most spiritual of us all, yet so persistently claiming us as its children and beckoning us to the courageous renewal of our broken attempts to reach it — is a world which could have been constructed for man only by God incarnate in One who was a poet.

LITERATURE. — Various modern *Lives of Jesus*; cf. Schürer, *HJP*; Hausrath, *Hist. of NT Times—Time of Jesus*; Peyton, *Memorabilia of Jesus*. In Oscar Wilde's *De Profundis* there is a passage in reference to Jesus as Artist, which, though marked by the paradoxical excess and wayward imagination of the book which contains it, is yet brilliant and suggestive.

JOHN KELMAN.

POLICE.—The traditional and unsettled character of governmental relations in Palestine in the time of Christ, and the scarcity of definite information as to the organization of civil procedure in the provincial courts, make it difficult to ascertain exactly what were the ordinary provisions for the administration of justice. We cannot positively say, for instance, how far the earlier methods which obtained under Jewish custom were overshadowed, and at times overridden, by the interference of Roman and military law. One fact, however, seems to emerge, viz., that as a rule, and as a matter of policy on the part of the Romans, the Jewish courts were left free to administer justice in their own way, and were permitted to retain a sufficient force of subordinate officers to execute the ordinary penalties of the law. It would only be in times of considerable disturbance, or in cases of the extreme penalty, that the Imperial power would come into evidence, and that soldiers would supplant the usual civil officers. 'The ordinary administration of the law, both in criminal and civil matters, was left in the hands of the native and local courts' (Schürer, *HJP* I. ii. 57). Generally, it may be safely affirmed, the Mosaic law still formed for the Jew the basis on which all such administration was conducted; justice was a department of religion, and the officers employed in its execution were Temple officials or servants of the local Sanhedrin.

There were two considerable exceptions to this rule—one arising from the arbitrary way in which the Herods exercised their power, and the other due to the invasion of Hellenistic ideas. In a city like Tiberias, *e.g.*, where the Greek element was very large, administration was on the Greek model. The city had a council (βουλή) of 600 members (Jos. *BJ* II. xxi. 9), with such officers as *archon, hyparchoi, agoranomos*, etc. (see Schürer, *HJP* II. i. 145). The Greek cities of the Decapolis, while their local authorities were always liable to be superseded by the Imperial power (G. A. Smith, *HGHL*, p. 605), had 'communal freedom, their own councils, . . . the right of property and administration in the surrounding districts' (*ib.* p. 594). Even in purely Jewish towns, Greek influence was modifying the old usage. The large number of Greek and Latin words found in the Mishna (Schürer, *HJP* II. i. 31-32) shows that after the 1st cent. A.D. the example of Hellenic institutions was producing a change in the methods of conducting civil government; and already in the Gospels we find traces of this, *e.g.*, in the passage in which Jesus makes His most explicit reference to the processes of law (Mt 5[25, 26]=Lk 12[58]): whereas Mt. uses terms which indicate Jewish usage (κριτής, ὑπηρέτης), Lk. employs as equivalents words which suggest the Roman procedure (ἄρχων, πράκτωρ); see below, and cf. Holtzmann, *Hand-Com. in loco*. In Mt 5[22] ('Every one who is angry with his brother shall be in danger of the judgment; and whosoever shall say to his brother, Raca, shall be in danger of the council') Jesus is referring to the ordinary Jewish courts, the 'judgment' (κρίσις) being the 'provincial court of seven' (see *EGT, in loc.*, and below), the 'council' the Sanhedriп.

In Jerusalem there appear to have been two stipendiary magistrates, who were precluded from engaging in other occupations, and whose special province it was to superintend the observance of the police regulations of the city (see Edersheim, *LT* ii. p. 287). The 'Unjust Judge' of Lk 18[1-8] is probably an instance of a provincial police magistrate; but, while his unprincipled character is only too typical of Oriental judges, past and present (cf. Bruce, *Parabolic Teaching of Christ*, p. 158), it is not to be inferred from this parable that Jesus intended to reflect on the administration of justice as a whole. The usual number of judges for each city was, in accordance with ancient custom, seven (Jos. *Ant.* IV. viii. 14). Josephus, when in Galilee, 'appointed seven judges in every city to hear the lesser quarrels; for, as to the greater causes and those wherein life and death were concerned, he enjoined they should be brought to him and the seventy elders' (*BJ* II. xx. 5).

The Mishna assumes the existence throughout the country of local Sanhedrins which possess very considerable powers. It is to these local Sanhedrins that Jesus makes reference when He tells His disciples: 'Beware of men, for they will deliver you up to councils' (Mt 10[17] = Mk 13[9]). The supreme court was the Great Sanhedrin of Jerusalem, before which Jesus was tried, and in this body the religious and hierarchical character of the Jewish courts of justice was naturally more clearly preserved than elsewhere. They had under their control a body of Temple police, who were Levites, and were under the command of στρατηγοί, at whose head was an officer called στρατηγὸς τοῦ ἱεροῦ (Jos. *Ant.* XX. vi. 2; *BJ* VI. v. 3; Ac 4[1] 5[24]; the plural is used in Lk 22[4, 52]). The latter office was one which would be no sinecure, the numbers of people who thronged the Temple courts, even at ordinary times, being so great as to necessitate special provisions for keeping order. These Temple police were not armed or regularly trained; 'the greater part of them were unarmed and unskilled in the affairs of war' (Jos. *BJ* IV. iv. 6; cf. Edersheim, *LT* ii. p. 540). During the great feasts the Temple was guarded by a Roman cohort, which was stationed in the Tower of Antonia (*BJ* V. v. 8). The force which arrested Jesus in Gethsemane clearly consisted of two parts: (1) a detachment of the Roman garrison; (2) a body of Temple police (Jn 18[3]; Westcott, *in loc.*). As to the guard which watched the tomb (Mt 27[65, 66] 28[11-15]), there is room for doubt whether this was a small body of soldiers detached by Pilate at the request of the Sanhedrin, or a band of the Temple *gendarmerie*. Pilate's words, ἔχετε κουστωδίαν (27[65]), are capable equally of the interpretation, 'Take a guard' or 'Ye have a guard.' The fact that they report to the chief priests (Mt 28[11]) suggests that they were the satellites of the Sanhedrin, and that Pilate scornfully permitted them to use their own measures; but v.[14] 'If this come to the governor's ears,' is in favour of the other interpretation.

The usual name for the officers charged with the execution of the law and the maintenance of order is ὑπηρέτης (Mt 5²⁵, Jn 7³². ⁴⁵. ⁴⁶ 18³. ¹²). It may be variously translated 'apparitor,' 'serjeant,' or 'warder.' They had the duty, among others, of inflicting the punishment of scourging (Mt 10¹⁷ = Mk 13⁹, Mt 23³⁴). Josephus says that each judge had two ὑπηρέται assigned to him (Ant. IV. viii. 14) ; but in this passage the word probably means 'clerks' rather than police constables. That the powers of the latter were extensive is evident from the drastic measures taken by Saul as the commissioner of the Sanhedrin in his persecution of the followers of Christ (Ac 8³ 26¹⁰. ¹¹ ; cf. 5¹⁸⁻²³). Another term, used apparently more particularly in reference to cases of fines and debts, but also having a general signification, is πράκτωρ (Lk 12⁵⁸) = 'bailiff.' The term σπεκουλάτωρ (Mk 6²⁷), used of the executioner of John the Baptist, denotes an officer belonging to the police attached to the military rulers. The weight of opinion inclines to the view that the *speculatores* were soldiers (Schürer, *HJP* I. ii. 62) ; but it is probable that Herod had armed satellites about his court who did not rank as regular soldiers, but would be called upon to play many parts, from apparitor to executioner. The plain-clothes detective was employed by the Herods (Jos. *Ant.* XV. x. 4), and the despotic use which they made of their power, backed up as it was by the command of soldiery, took little cognizance of the established civil authorities. The centurion in Mt 8⁵⁻¹³ = Lk 7²⁻¹⁰ was probably the captain of the troop quartered at Capernaum and in the service of Herod Antipas (Holtzmann, *Hand-Com. in loc.*). These troops served the purpose of clearing the country of gangs of robbers (Jos. *Ant.* XV. x. 1).

J. ROSS MURRAY.

POLITICAL CONDITIONS.—1. Reign of Herod the Great.—Christ was born nearly at the close of the reign of Herod (Mt 2¹), who died in the spring of B.C. 4. Herod's relation to Rome was that of an allied king (*rex socius*), whose title and authority alike were dependent upon the goodwill of the Emperor. He was expected to preserve order within his kingdom, and to bring it into a fit state for inclusion in the normal system of provincial government, and at the same time to protect the frontier of the Empire. With foreign policy he had nothing to do ; and the right of coining was probably limited, the only known Herodian coins being of copper. A certain tribute was exacted, which Herod raised on the other parts of his kingdom than Judæa ; and instructions from Rome had to be strictly and quickly followed, the Imperial consent being necessary also to any arrangement as to the succession to the royal property or domains. Within these limits his power was restrained only by the necessity of not provoking the people either to rebel or to appeal to Rome.

2. Tetrarchy of Philip.—Special permission had been given by Augustus to Herod to bequeath his kingdom as he liked (Jos. *Ant.* XVI. iv. 5), the will being subject, of course, to Imperial confirmation. Under the pressure of various palace intrigues, and with a view to separate elements between which at the time there was no possible cohesion, Herod left Judæa to Archelaus, Galilee and Peræa to Antipas, and the north-eastern districts beyond Jordan to Philip. This partition was eventually accepted at Rome, with a few slight modifications. To Philip, with the title of tetrarch, which originally implied the government of a fourth part of a tribe or kingdom, but gradually came to be used of any petty dependent prince, were assigned the comparatively poor districts lying to the east of the Sea of Galilee, and extending northwards as far as Mt. Hermon (Lk 3¹). Over these he reigned for thirty-seven years (B.C. 4–A.D. 34), when upon his death the territory was incorporated in the province of Syria, though without losing the privi-

lege of the separate administration of its finances (Jos. *Ant.* XVIII. iv. 6). Three years later it was given to Agrippa I., with the title of king. The population was predominantly Syrian and Greek, with Jewish settlements in the south-west ; and though Philip's sympathies were entirely Roman, he respected the sentiments of the different classes of the people, and his long reign was disturbed by no outbreak of popular feeling, and no peremptory interference from Rome. Like most of the Herods, he had a passion for building ; and to the quiet and well-governed city of Cæsarea Philippi, near the alleged source of the Jordan, Jesus withdrew (Mt 16¹³, Mk 8²⁷) when the multitudes were crowding upon Him and His enemies tempting Him (Mt 16¹) ; just as Bethsaida, another of Philip's cities, was His refuge when news reached Him of the Baptist's death (Lk 9¹⁰, cf. Mk 8²²).

3. Tetrarchy of Antipas.—The title of tetrarch was granted also to Antipas, whose dominions included the two districts of Galilee and Peræa, separated by the confederation of free Greek cities known as the Decapolis. Peræa, east of the Jordan and south-east of Galilee, bore a high reputation for the purity of its Judaism, but politically was of small importance. Its population was prevailingly Jewish ; though Antipas found an opportunity for the indulgence of his passion for building in the erection of Julias on the site of the ancient Beth-haram (Jos 13²⁷), opposite Jericho. But the main part of the tetrarchy, as far as numbers and industry are concerned, lay to the north of Samaria, where the Jews formed the majority of a population estimated perhaps too highly (see art. POPULATION) at three millions, and comprising almost every possible admixture of Canaanitish and Greek elements. The administration of Antipas must have been successful on the whole, for it continued for more than forty years, though his father's diplomacy became in him craft and meanness (Lk 13³² ; Jos. *Ant.* XVIII. iv. 5). His private friendship with Tiberius may be part of the explanation of the length of his reign ; in A.D. 39 he was banished by Caligula to Lyons, and his territories were added to the kingdom of Herod Agrippa I. (Ac 12¹ ; Jos. *Ant.* XVIII. vii. 2).

4. Ethnarchy of Archelaus.—On the death of his father, Archelaus succeeded to the lordship of Judæa, with Samaria and Idumæa. His accession was opposed by some of his own family, and by the popular party at Jerusalem, who aimed at the restoration of the theocracy, but pleaded meanwhile for the investment of the high priest with supreme civil power, in subordination to the Emperor alone. Archelaus went in person to Rome (cf. Christ's allusion in Lk 19¹²), whither also journeyed an embassy from the people. Augustus substantially confirmed Herod's appointment ; and Archelaus returned as ethnarch of the three districts. He was disappointed with the inferior title (which denotes literally the ruler of a nation living, with separate customs, in the midst of another race, and was possibly chosen, in contempt, to identify Archelaus with his unwilling subjects), and proceeded to make his administration (B.C. 3–A.D. 6) one of revenge. Twice, if not thrice, a change was made in the high priesthood by a ruler who was considered as of mixed blood—unclean in his birth and unclean in his practice. The tyrannical disregard of powerful sentiments was carried to such an extent that at length the Jews forgot their hatred of the Samaritans, and the Samaritans their kinship with the ethnarch, and a joint deputation proceeded to lay their complaints before Augustus. Archelaus was fined and exiled to Vienne, and his domains were made directly subject to Rome.

5. The Roman procurators.—The situation fo Judæa, on the confines of Egypt and Arabia, was of such military importance that Rome could not wisely concede the repeated request of the people for the investiture of their high priest with all the functions of civil government. Instead, the country was made a kind of annex to the province of Syria, with a governor (*procurator*) of its own, of equestrian rank, who was charged particularly with the control of the army and the finances, and with the task of turning the district into a bulwark of the Empire. The legate of Syria was invested with only a general supervision; he was expected to interfere at his discretion in cases of need, but generally to remain in the background, as an unseen support of the Roman rule. The first procurator was Coponius (A.D. 6–9), a knight whose name is otherwise unknown. Accompanied by the legate Quirinius, he appeared at Jerusalem, took possession of the property of Archelaus, and turned his palace into the official abode of the procurator during the festivals, Cæsarea becoming the seat of government. Their next administrative act was to arrange for the taking of a census, with a view to control the incidence of taxation, and to establish Roman methods of government. The process was to compile schedules, enumerating the local communities, according either to houses or to families, for the purposes of a poll-tax, and providing information for the levying of taxes upon capital (originally, in Syria, one per cent., but afterwards probably increased) and upon trade. At the same time the produce of the field was valued, and made chargeable to the extent of one-tenth in the case of corn and two-tenths in that of fruit and vine. This was the enrolment referred to by Gamaliel (Ac 5³⁷); and on religious as well as patriotic grounds, as seeming to involve even a competition with Jehovah for the tithes, the result was dismay on the part of the leaders of the people, and an actual revolt, headed by Judas of Gamala, who thereby founded the fanatical party of the Zealots or Cananæans (Mt 10⁴). On the present occasion the revolt was suppressed after some furious fighting; but the agitation smouldered, and eventually broke out in the insurrection in the course of which Jerusalem was burnt. The census schedules, when completed, would be sent to Rome for approval; but in levying the taxes there would be no delay. Such as were destined for the Imperial treasury were collected under the supervision of the procurator, who made use of the Sanhedrin and various local courts. The customs were leased to collectors, individuals or syndicates, who paid a fixed annual sum, retaining any excess in the actual yield and making good any deficiency. The contracts were then divided, and sublet to subordinate officials in the different localities, and thus an entire class of publicans of various grades (Lk 19²) was constituted, whose average morality was probably low, but is not to be taken at the valuation of the popular hatred. Nothing more is known of the procuratorship of Coponius beyond a breach in the temporary alliance between the Jews and the Samaritans. The quarrel was brought to an issue by a successful attempt of the latter to defile the cloisters of the Temple on the eve of the Passover. Through Coponius no redress could be obtained, and the Jews had to content themselves with more stringent regulations for the exclusion of the Samaritans, and with a large extension of the police system of the Temple, the night-watchmen being increased in number to twenty-four, and an official made responsible for a periodic visitation of their rounds.

The successors of Coponius were Marcus Ambivius (? A.D. 9–12), Annius Rufus (? 12–15), Valerius Gratus (15–26), and Pontius Pilate (26–36). Of the first two the dates cannot at present be fixed with precision, and no known change of administration

was introduced by them. Soon after his accession in A.D. 14 to the throne of the Empire, Tiberius adopted the policy of lengthening the term of service in these provincial appointments, in the hope of protecting the people from rapacity, by affording the governors a longer period over which to spread their exactions. The theory was not a compliment to this class of officials, and did not work well in Judæa. Of the administration of Valerius Gratus the least that can be said is that it was meddling. In eleven years he changed the high priest four times, and the changes would have been more frequent but for the temporizing character of the man (Joseph Caiaphas) upon whom his final choice lighted. The example of oppression in Rome, whence the Jews were expelled by Imperial edict, was imitated so closely in Judæa, that several deputations were sent to Tiberius to protest against the masterfulness and avarice of his representative, with little other result than that of additions to the army of occupation.

A similar policy of oppression was adopted by Pilate, who exceeded his predecessor in resentment, but whose violence was apt to collapse in the presence of a stubbornness greater than his own. His first act was characteristic alike of his contempt for precedents and of his docility when opposed. The new troops destined for the garrison of Jerusalem were ordered not, as before, to leave at Cæsarea the medallions of the Emperor that were attached to the military standards, but to proceed in full equipment to their quarters in the Castle of Antonia. To the Jews the sacrilege appeared of the worst kind, as involving them in the crime of idolatry (Ex 20⁴). From all parts of the country people flocked to Cæsarea, and, disdaining the threat of massacre, extorted from the procurator, by their superior resolution, an order for the removal of the medallions. This bad beginning was followed by an equally bitter quarrel over the restoration of an aqueduct that brought water to Jerusalem (cf. Lk 13⁴). The scheme was of the utmost value to the city, as the supply of water conveyed through an older aqueduct at a higher level was proving insufficient; but the offence was that Pilate proposed to throw the cost upon the Temple treasury, and actually seized some of the sacred funds. A riot was anticipated; but the soldiers, dressed as citizens, were distributed among the crowd, and at a given signal turned their weapons against the people. The scheme was proceeded with, and the popular hatred grew savage. So much did Pilate disregard Jewish sentiment, that certain Galilæans were put to death in the Temple, and their blood mingled with that of the sacrifices (Lk 13¹). By taking a prominent part in an insurrection, Barabbas endeared himself to the people (Mk 15⁷, Lk 23¹⁹). On the death of Sejanus, in A.D. 31, Tiberius assumed a more friendly attitude towards the Jews; and, soon after Vitellius added the legateship of Syria to his other high commands (A.D. 35), he found it necessary to interfere. Pilate was ordered to proceed to Rome to answer for the wanton cruelty of his administration, and Marcellus was entrusted provisionally with the duties of the procuratorship.

6. Administration, military and civil.—In Syria, as in Egypt, were regularly stationed three or four legions, to which recourse could be had in any emergency; but the ordinary garrison of Palestine consisted of auxiliaries, raised partially amongst the non-Jewish inhabitants of the country. The Jews were generally exempted at the time from military service, on account of their temperament and religious usages. The garrison was distributed over the country in such a way as to make itself everywhere felt. At Cæsarea, the headquarters, was a force of three thousand men, of whom five-sixths were infantry. A cohort of five or six hundred infantry, with a detachment of cavalry and a body of spearmen or slingers (Ac 23²³), was quartered in the fortress of Antonia. Smaller garrisons occupied Jericho, Machærus, Samaria, and any other centre whence an important district could be commanded. There is no evidence of the existence of a police corps apart from the soldiery, though a secret-service system upon a large scale was maintained by Herod, and probably also by the procurators. The military were employed in keeping order, in the arrest of persons under suspicion (Jn 18¹²), in guarding prisoners (Mt 27²⁷), and in superintending the execution of a sentence (Jn 19²³). Use was sometimes made of the officers of the local courts and of the armed retinue of the native dignitaries (Mt 26⁴⁷). The Temple police were under the command of a captain of high rank, who probably controlled also the officers of the Sanhedrin; and these functionaries were recognized and supported within limits by the military authorities. There are traces also of the existence of a body of paid spies or secret police under Jewish control (Lk 20²⁰, Mt 22¹⁶, Mk 12¹³). In the provincial towns and rural districts order was kept as in Jerusalem; the administration acted through the local courts and organizations, with soldiers at hand when needed. See also art. POLICE.

Taxation was of two kinds—Imperial and provincial. A poll-tax and a tax on landed property were collected by the procurator, and the produce remitted to Rome (Mt 22¹⁷). Custom duties and market tolls were collected by lessees, who paid for the privilege a fixed yearly sum, destined in the case of Judæa for the Imperial treasury, but in that of Galilee for the tetrarch. Besides these regular imposts, an arbitrary procurator might enrich himself by a variety of exactions, as the penalties of imagined offences or the condition of official support; but in Judæa the expenses of administration were met by authorized deduction from the revenue of the taxes and tolls. Economically the province was poor, though a few courtiers and ecclesiastical dignitaries were of great wealth. So heavy was the incidence of taxation, that in A.D. 17 a deputation was sent to Rome to plead for relief. Sixteen years later, the entire Empire was visited by a financial crisis so severe that bankruptcies multiplied beyond enumeration, and even some of the public treasuries suspended payments in cash. In this general distress Syria and Palestine shared, though the busy industrial centres in Galilee did not suffer so much as the crowded and unemployed population around Jerusalem.

7. Political parties (see the various articles under separate titles).—The *Samaritans*, though kindred in race with the Jews, were regarded by them as sectaries, and the bitterness on both sides was fatal to joint political action of any permanent kind. The *Sadducees* were a priestly nobility, tenacious of the prestige of their own order, but tolerant of any system of government that did not threaten their prosperity. Opposed to them were the *Pharisees*, whose national ideal was that of a theocracy, and whose endurance of an alien rule was reluctant or sullen. They were supported sometimes by the *Herodians*, who favoured the dynasty of Herod, but were not disposed to quarrel seriously with any established institution. An extreme party was gradually formed of irreconcilables, under the name of *Zealots* or *Cananæans* (Mt 10⁴, Mk 3¹⁸, Lk 6¹⁵), who were prepared to use the sword without delay for the restoration of a theocracy. In political theory the *Essenes* exaggerated the views of the Pharisees; but their comparatively small number in the early part of the 1st cent. and their segregation from ordinary life made them

a force of little consequence except in times of excitement.

LITERATURE.—Josephus; references to other sources in Schürer, *GJV*³ (or *HJP*), which is indispensable; Hausrath, *Hist. of NT Times*; Derenbourg, *Hist. de la Pal.*; Mommsen, *Rom. Provinces*; Madden, *Coins of Jews*; the *Archæol.* of Keil, Riehm, Benzinger, Nowack; Hastings' *DB*, the *EBi*, *PRE*, and the *JE*; O. Holtzmann, *NT Zeitgeschichte*; Moss, *Scene of our Lord's Life* [a useful elementary handbook].

R. W. MOSS.

POOR.—See POVERTY and POVERTY OF SPIRIT.

POPULARITY.—The word does not occur in the NT, but the thing itself is not infrequently treated of. There is a true and there is a false popularity. The latter belongs to him who makes the praise of men his object, and seeks it by ostentatious piety and hypocritical charity (Mt 6². ⁵. ¹⁶); the former is the accompaniment of that behaviour whose ruling aim is to do the will of God regardless of all worldly ends (Mt 6³. ⁴. ⁷. ⁸. ¹⁷. ¹⁸. ²⁰. ²¹). True popularity is that love and admiration which unselfish devotion to the welfare of others, springing from the whole-hearted love of God, cannot fail to arouse in the breasts of all who have eyes to see and hearts to understand the good and pure. 'They shall see your good works and glorify your Father which is in heaven' (Mt 5¹⁶; cf. Jn 15⁸). The hypocrites who sound a trumpet before them when they do their alms, who pray at the corners of the streets for all to see, who disfigure their faces that they may appear to men to fast, are examples of those who seek and obtain the reward of false popularity. Fasting and prayer that flow from a desire to hold communion with God, charity that is the outcome of gratitude to the Heavenly Father for His wondrous mercy, are ever done in secret, so that there can be no suspicion of any unworthy motive; but the effect of these things is revealed in the man's whole life and character; it must win for him the praise and love of all good men, and for God the glory.

All this is in perfect harmony with the inwardness of Christ's life and teaching. His aim was to change the world from within outward—not to attach good fruit to a worthless tree, but to make the tree good, and to await the fruit which in due time it was bound to bear. In the same sense true popularity is inward; false, outward. The latter springs immediately from outside acts which may not be—probably are not—the revelation of the true man: the former is the effect produced upon the world by the outspeaking of the whole man as he is in himself in his relation to God. At the very opening of His career Jesus rejected the outward, the false, popularity as a means of propagating the truth He came to teach. He perceived it to be the suggestion of the Evil One that He should obtain the dominion of the kingdoms of the world by the external method, by the force of His authority, by the admiration which He could so easily have produced. Even to employ His miraculous power to gain the ear of His own countrymen He put from Him as a temptation (Mt 4¹⁻¹⁰ ‖ Lk 4¹⁻¹³); and when, aroused to enthusiasm by their miraculous feeding, the multitude would fain have taken Him by force to make Him their king, He fled from them (Jn 6¹⁵). He would have nought to do with any enthusiasm, however sincere, that was based upon a false conception of the nature of His Messiahship, that sprang from admiration of His power and the hope of sharing its blessings, and not from the clear perception of His holiness and the longing to share it (Jn 2²³⁻²⁵). The kind of impression which He wished to make was that which expressed itself in such phrases as—'Never *man* so spake' (Jn 7⁴⁶); 'He taught them as one having authority, and not as the scribes' (Mt 7²⁹); 'The common people heard him gladly' (Mk 12³⁷). It was neither *to* nor *by* flesh and blood that He desired to reveal Himself and to win a place in the hearts of men, but *to* the Divine germ within each soul, and *by* the revelation of the Heavenly Father (Mt 16[17]). See following article.

And as with the Master so must it be with the servants. As the world had hated Him, so would it hate them. He had come to send not peace on the earth, but a sword and fire (Mt 10[34] || Lk 12[51]), the sword which would part brother from brother and father from son—the fire which should try and reveal the essential nature of each heart. This hatred and persecution are therefore to be to the disciples a cause of rejoicing (Mt 5[11, 12]), for these will be the signs that they are in truth the followers of Christ. 'If the world hate you, ye know that it hated me before it hated you. If ye were of the world, the world would love its own: but because ye are not of the world, but I have chosen you out of the world, therefore the world hateth you' (Jn 15[18, 19]). But the more the world persecutes them, the more must they bear testimony to the cause of Christ by their loving fellowship one with another. 'By this,' He says, 'shall all men know that ye are my disciples, if ye have love one to another' (Jn 13[35]); and again—'(I pray) that they also may be one in us: that the world may believe that thou hast sent me' (Jn 17[21]). Among the disciples there must be no selfish striving for place or power. The truest popularity, the truest greatness, is to belong to the humble heart that ever preferreth other to itself, that rejoiceth to minister and to serve, to give itself freely to all even as Christ did (Mt 20[28] || Mk 10[45]).

LITERATURE.—Comm. on the Gospels; works on *NT Theol.* by Beyschlag and by Weiss; Stalker, *Life of Jesus Christ*, ch. iv.; Pressensé, *Jesus Christ*[7], pp. 263–286.

W. J. S. MILLER.

POPULARITY (of Jesus).—The general subject of popularity, as treated in the foregoing article, is strikingly illustrated by the course of our Lord's public ministry; and in the present article we shall consider (1) the popularity of Jesus, (2) the grounds on which it rested, (3) the value He attached to it, and (4) the reasons of its decline.

1. The fact of His popularity.—Although the earthly life of Jesus began in a stable and ended on a cross, there was a period in His ministry when He was at once the most conspicuous and the most popular personage in Palestine. From Jn. we learn that His first definite appeal to the nation was made in Jerusalem (2[12ff.]). There, however, the dominant influences were hostile to His acceptance (vv.[18ff.] 3[2, 12]). He soon felt that the nation was not yet ripe for a direct Messianic ministry, and so for a time He fell back in Judæa on a work of preparation similar to that which the Baptist was still carrying on (3[22] 4[1, 2]). But when John was cast into prison, He knew that the time was come to make His own distinctive appeal to Israel, and having met with little favour in Jerusalem, He now chose Galilee as the scene of His labours (Mk 1[14ff.] ||). The Synoptic Gospels show that an extraordinary popularity was the almost immediate result (Mk 1[28]). Crowds flocked to Him from every quarter (1[45] 2[13] 4[1] 5[21] and *passim*), and followed Him about wherever He went (3[7] 6[33]). The people were astonished at His teaching (1[22, 27]), but also delighted with it (Lk 5[1, 15], cf. Mk 12[37]); they saw His miracles with joy and amazement, and glorified God in Him (Mk 2[12] ||). The enthusiasm and excitement soon spread far beyond the borders of Galilee; and from Jerusalem and Idumæa, from beyond Jordan, and even from the region of Tyre and Sidon, multitudes came to see and hear the great Prophet of Nazareth (3[8]). All along, it is true, the scribes and Pharisees persistently opposed Him (2[6ff. 16f. 24ff.] 3[2ff.]), coming from Jerusalem for

this express purpose (3[22] 7[1]). But with the great mass of His countrymen, during the earlier period of His Galilæan ministry, Jesus had a popularity of the most unqualified kind.

2. To what was this popularity due?—(1) Much must be ascribed to *His personal qualities*, and among these (*a*) to *His perfect accessibility and entire naturalness.* In His attitude to the people there was nothing either of the supercilious contempt of the scribes and Pharisees (Jn 7[48, 49]) or of the ascetic austerity of John the Baptist (Mt 3[4] 11[18]). Any one might approach Him at any time, with the certainty of being readily and kindly received. It mattered not who came to Jesus,—rough fishers of the Galilæan lake (Jn 1[37ff.], Mk 1[16] ||), anxious parents seeking a blessing for their children (Mk 5[22ff.] 7[25ff.] 10[13ff.]), publicans whom everyone else despised (Mt 9[10] 10[3] 11[19], Lk 19[2ff.]), sinful women from the city streets (Lk 7[37ff.], Mt 21[31]),—to all He presented Himself as a man and a brother. (*b*) No personal gift conduces more to popularity than the subtle, indefinable quality of *charm*, and Jesus appears to have possessed this in an exceptional measure. It may be that the χάρις or 'grace,' of which St. Luke tells us in his account of the sermon in the synagogue at Nazareth (4[22]), refers wholly to Christ's message, and not at all to the manner of His speech. But the way in which men and women and little children were drawn to the Saviour, as if by a kind of magnetism, testifies to a winsomeness of nature that must have gone far to secure the favour of every unprejudiced heart. (*c*) Still more the *intense sympathy* of Jesus must have appealed to the people. A man may make himself accessible for reasons of policy, and even the quality of charm sometimes proves to be a superficial gift of pleasing that is no guarantee for any expenditure of heart. But the Saviour's profound sympathy for the sick, the sinful, the sorrowful, could not fail to make an impression on the popular mind. We can hardly realize, perhaps, what it meant for Him to be besieged day after day by a pressing crowd of men and women with loathsome diseases and festering sores—all demanding the touch of His hand as well as the pity of His heart (Lk 4[40] ||). The nervous tension must have been tremendous, the physical and spiritual expenditure a constant drain upon His strength (Mk 5[30], Lk 6[19]). But the crowd, which not only read in His face that compassion which was one of His most characteristic qualities (Mt 9[36] 14[14] 15[32], Mk 1[41], Lk 7[13]), but saw Him in the thick of His daily deeds of grace, must have dimly perceived something of that vicarious sacrifice which lay at the root of the Redeemer's sympathy, as it lies at the root of all true sympathy, and which led an Evangelist to bethink himself of the prophet's words, 'Himself took our infirmities, and bare our diseases' (Mt 8[17], cf. Is 53[4]).

(2) But the popularity of Jesus was due not only to His personal qualities, but to *His methods as a Teacher and the gospel that He brought.* (*a*) Much lay in His methods—in the simplicity and directness, the homeliness and picturesqueness of His language, and its entire freedom from all the professional pedantries of the Rabbis (Mk 1[22], cf. 12[37]). The undying power of His parables, simply as literature, enables us to form some idea of what it must have been to hear those wonderful stories as they first fell from His own lips. (*b*) But these things were only the outer swathings of His message—the husk, not the kernel. The form of His teaching might appeal to the imagination, but it was the substance—the joyful Galilæan gospel of the Kingdom of God—that warmed and thrilled the listening multitudes. Christ's words were 'words of grace'—words about the Heavenly Father's love and the blessings that lay within the

reach of every one who was willing to be God's child ; words of forgiveness for the sinful, and liberty for the captive, of comfort for the mourner, and rest for the weary and heavy-laden soul. 'The gospel of the kingdom'—in that Christ's message was all summed up (Mk 1¹⁴). And if the fore-runner shook the nation to its centre when he cried, 'The kingdom of heaven is at hand !' (Mt 3²), what must have been the effect of Christ's pro-clamation that the Kingdom of God was already come (Mt 5³⁻¹¹ 12²⁸)—that *this* was the acceptable year of the Lord (Lk 4¹⁹· ²¹).

(3) But it is in *the miracles of Jesus* above all that we find the explanation of His popularity. His miracles of healing were evidently wrought upon a very wide scale — much wider than the enumeration of individual cases gives any idea of (cf. Mk 1³⁴ 3¹⁰ 6⁵⁵· ⁵⁶). And though there were un-grateful recipients of His mercy (Lk 17¹⁷· ¹⁸), we know that at other times both those whom He had cured and their friends and relatives were filled with a passion of gratitude and devotion to His Person (vv.¹⁵· ¹⁶, Mk 5²⁰ 10⁵², Jn 11² 12³). But these gracious miracles stretched in their effects far beyond the wide circle of the actual benefici-aries. They created great expectations in the popular mind—expectations that were immensely heightened by yet more astonishing miracles, in which Christ's 'compassion for the multitude' led Him to make them in their thousands the direct partakers of His bounty (Mk 6³⁴ff· ||, 8¹ff· ||, Jn 6⁵ff·). These great miracles were taken to be 'signs'—signs of wonderful events that might be about to happen in Israel. Jesus, it began to be surmised, was not merely a great prophet as His teaching showed, but much more than a prophet ; not merely a marvellous healer of the sick, but the expected Deliverer of Israel. Unfortunately, however, in spite of all His teaching as to the nature of the Kingdom of God, the popular ideas on the subject were still utterly astray. And so His popularity, just when it seemed to be soaring to its highest, was made to rest upon the least worthy foundations. This brings us to the sharp dividing line (see preceding art.) between a popu-larity that is true and a popularity that is false, a popularity that Jesus could desire and welcome and one that He inevitably loathed and repelled. Jn.'s narrative shows that it was Christ's fame as a miracle-worker, and most of all His feeding of the Five Thousand in the wilderness, that raised His popularity to its point of culmination (Jn 6¹⁴· ¹⁵). But it was just then that Jesus rejected most emphatically a kind of popularity He did not want. And it was also from that day that the tide of popular favour which had swelled so high began to ebb.

3. What value did Jesus attach to His popu-larity ?—'He did not care,' it has been said, 'for the thing called popularity, but He loved human beings' (Bruce, *Galilean Gospel*, p. 10). And it is quite true that there was a kind of popularity that Jesus not only did not care for, but always despised and shunned. And yet, just because He loved human beings so much, He desired a popularity of the right sort. Was it not in search of it that He came into Galilee preaching the gospel of the Kingdom, after He had been coldly received by the ecclesiastical authorities in the capital ? To be popular is just to be beloved of the people, and the highest kind of popularity is when a man is beloved of the people on grounds which God and his own conscience can approve. It is impossible for one who loves, not to wish to have his love returned ; and Jesus, loving men and women as no other human being ever did, undoubtedly desired them to love Him, and trust Him, and follow Him. This is the meaning of His invitations to them to

come to Him, and of His words of sorrow and reproach when they refused. His soul, accordingly, must have filled with gladness and thankfulness when He saw the multitude pressing upon Him to hear His word, and listening to it with evident joy, or when He received the assurance of heart-felt gratitude from those whom He had healed or enlightened or lifted from the depths of self-despair. But, on the other hand, when men came after Him in search of signs and wonders (Mt 12³⁸ 16¹ ||, Jn 4⁴⁸)—something to confirm them in their false ideals of the Kingdom of God, if not merely to gratify their gaping curiosity ; worse still, when the multitude began to follow Him in the hope of being furnished gratis with the bread that they might have honestly earned (Jn 6²⁶), and to look to Him to set up by the use of His miraculous powers a kingdom of meat and drink and political privi-lege, He knew that now, under the guise of a dazzling popularity, the same temptation was re-turning which He had faced and conquered in the wilderness at the very outset of His ministry (Mt 4¹⁻¹¹)—the temptation to love the praise of men more than the praise of God, and to attempt to set up the Kingdom of heaven upon earth by methods that were not Divine, but worldly and Satanic.

4. The decline of His popularity.—The miracle of the Feeding of the Five Thousand was a great turning-point in the life of Jesus. It marked, we have said, the culmination of His popularity, but also the beginning of its decline. And the reason for this decline was just that the popularity it brought was of a kind that Jesus could not accept. The people wished to take Him by force and make Him king (Jn 6¹⁵), while He wished to win in their hearts a spiritual Kingdom for His Father. They would have set Him on a worldly throne, and He knew that His Kingdom was not of this world (Jn 18³⁶). The two ideals were utterly incompatible. Henceforth, He who had sought the people and welcomed their coming began to avoid them (Jn 6¹⁵, Mk 7²⁴ 8¹⁰· ¹³· ²⁶· ²⁷ 9³⁰), and, when they still came after Him, spoke not only of the gladness of the Kingdom, but of the mysterious pathway of the Cross (Jn 6²⁶⁻⁶⁵, Mk 8³⁴ff· 10²¹ff·). The result was soon apparent. Nothing more quickly cools the enthusiasm of the multitude than the refusal of its object to be popular on the popular terms. After this many even of Christ's disciples went back and walked no more with Him (Jn 6⁶⁶). And though Peter answered nobly for the Twelve to that pathetic question, 'Will ye also go away ?' (vv.⁶⁷⁻⁶⁹), the Lord knew that one of the very Apostles whom He had chosen had admitted into his heart a devil of dissatisfaction with his Master (vv.⁷⁰· ⁷¹). Soon, with the vision of the Cross before Him, He 'sted-fastly set his face to go to Jerusalem' (Lk 9⁵¹). The disciples, as they followed, were afraid (Mk 10³²), and so He prepared them for what was coming, by those great 'Lessons on the Cross' which mark the stages of His progress towards the great act of sacrifice (Mt 16²¹⁻²⁸ ||, 20¹⁷⁻²⁸ ||, 26⁶⁻¹³· ²⁶⁻²⁹ || ; cf. Bruce, *Training of the Twelve*). Day by day the shadows lengthened across the Saviour's path. And though at His last Passover the raising of Lazarus (Jn 12⁹⁻¹¹) led to a transitory outburst of fresh en-thusiasm among the Galilæans who had come up to the Feast (cf. Mt 21¹¹ with v.¹⁰), the time of His national popularity was really over from the day of the Capernaum discourse (Jn 6²⁴ff·), and what lay before Him thereafter was a growing opposi-tion that could end only in national rejection and the death on Calvary.

LITERATURE.—Sanday's art. 'Jesus Christ' in Hastings' *DB* ; Andrews, *Life of Our Lord* ; Stalker, *Life of Jesus Christ* ; Bruce, *Training of the Twelve, Galilean Gospel ; Expositor*, v. ii. [1895] 69.   J. C. LAMBERT.

POPULATION. — Ancient statistics are proverbially unreliable, and in no department are they less trustworthy than in the reckoning of population. Except for military or fiscal purposes, the inhabitants of a Roman province were not liable to be counted, while, even in such cases, the estimate, when preserved, is at best approximate. The sole information, of any precise and fairly contemporary character, as to the population of Galilee in the days of Jesus, is to be found in Jos. *BJ*, III. iii. The historian there observes that the Galilæans have always been numerous. The fertility of the soil induced the inhabitants to cultivate it, and trading was carried on assiduously. 'Moreover, the cities lie very thick, and the numerous villages are everywhere so populous, owing to the richness of the soil, that the smallest of them contains over 15,000 inhabitants.' This is probably an exaggeration, due to the historian's desire of glorifying the country ; but even when one discounts his statements fairly, a residuum of fact remains, corroborated by the occasional allusions of the Gospels to the thickly populated districts in which Jesus lived and preached. If Josephus could muster 100,000 warriors from the province, some thirty years after the ministry of Jesus, and if the larger towns, like Scythopolis, included over 30,000 inhabitants, it is probable that the population of Galilee, during the first quarter of the first century, must have exceeded one million, if not two millions, since it included over 200 towns and villages within an area of about 100 square miles. Certainly, the Galilee into which Jesus brougbt His gospel (Mk 1[14]), with its cities like Capernaum (Mk 1[21]), its country-towns (v.[38]), and country-districts, was no thinly - peopled tract. Crowds repeatedly gather round Him (1[45] 2[13] 3[7f.] 4[1] etc.). His presence is the signal for multitudes to assemble, and although these were naturally drawn from the cities (cf. Mk 6[33f.]), the same holds true of the rural districts (cf. 6[53f.]). A motto for the Galilæan ministry might well be found in the words, 'In those days again there was a great crowd' (Mk 8[1]), whether Jesus was in the populous cities by the Lake or touring through the inland synagogues. 'Save in the recorded hours of our Lord's praying, the history of Galilee has no intervals of silence and loneliness ; the noise of a close and busy life is always audible ; and to every crisis in the Gospels and in Josephus we see crowds immediately swarm' (*HGHL*, p. 421).

Eastward, it was otherwise. Gaulanitis, on the opposite side of the Lake, was more bare and wild, and to this quarter Jesus resorted at least once (Mk 4[35f.]) for some privacy, when pressed by the crowds of Capernaum and the neighbourhood. The population here was thinner. Villages were more widely scattered, and, apart from the southern federation of cities known as the Decapolis, there was a comparative lack of important towns. On the later spread of Christianity in Peræa, see Harnack's *Mission und Ausbreitung des Christentums*, pp. 414 f. [Eng. tr. ii. 252 f.]. How far the Christian churches in that district were recruited from a mission of Jesus it is difficult to say, since it is uncertain how much St Luke has grouped from other sources under his account of the Peræan journey (9[51] etc., cf. Mk 10[1]), and since the outbreak of the Jewish War drove many Christians from the west to the east of the Jordan. In any case, Peræa was less thickly populated than Galilee, though larger in extent. Josephus (*loc. cit.*) describes it as 'for the most part desert and rough, and much less adapted than Galilee for the growth of cultivated fruits.' Samaria, on the opposite side of the Jordan, numbered a larger population proportionately. But if Jesus worked here, it was only *en route* from Galilee to Judæa.

The crowds which Jesus found at Jerusalem were naturally drawn from the country-districts, so that they afford no reliable clue to the exact population of the capital, although, if we may trust the calculations of Josephus (*BJ* VI. ix.), it must have been capable of including, at the Passover season, more than three millions of people. Over two and a half million orthodox worshippers were reckoned at one census under Nero.

LITERATURE.—Schürer, *HJP*, II. i. 2 f. ; Selah Merrill, *Galilee in the Time of Christ*; Besant, *The City and the Land*, p. 113 f. ; Keim, *Jesus of Nazara*, Eng. tr. vol. ii. p. 6 f.

J. MOFFATT.

PORTER (θυρωρός, Mk 13[34], Jn 10[3] 18[16f.] [in last passage, 'she that kept the door ']).—The English word 'porter' is ambiguous, meaning 'burden-bearer' as well as 'door - keeper.' 'Janitor' or 'gate-keeper' would be a better rendering. 'Porters' were employed to guard city gates, and to keep watch at the entrance of public buildings and of private houses. It would appear from Jn 18[16f.], where a 'damsel' acts as door-keeper of the high priest's palace, that in some instances women were thus employed (cf. Ac 12[13f.]) ; see, further, Hastings' *DB*, artt. 'Gate,' 'Porter,' 'Priests and Levites' (iv. 93[a]).

The identity of the porter of the sheepfold (Jn 10[3]) has been much discussed. Obviously, he is the guardian of the fold, whose office is to open the door to any shepherd (Jn 10[2] [Greek and RVm]) whose sheep are in the fold. See art. SHEEP. Thus the porter may be (1) *God* : so Calvin (*Com. on John, in loc.*), Bengel (*Gnomon, in loc.*), and Hengstenberg (*Com. on John, in loc.*) ; (2) *Christ* : so Cyril and Augustine (quoted by Hengstenberg), who remark that Christ is His own porter ; (3) *the Holy Spirit* : so Stier, Lange, Alford, and others. Others apply the figure to John the Baptist (so Godet) or to Moses. The most natural interpretation is that given by Westcott (*Gospel of John, in loc.*) : 'The interpretation will vary according to the special sense attached to the "sheep" and the "shepherd." The figure is not to be explained exclusively of the Holy Spirit, or of the Father, or of Moses, or of John the Baptist, but of the Spirit acting through His appointed ministers in each case.' For parallels to the symbolism of the passage, cf. Ac 14[27] 16[14], 2 Co 2[12], Col 4[3], Rev 3[7].

JAMES MURSELL.

PORTION (μέρος).—The different shades of meaning which in the Gospels are assigned to the word μέρος have their counterpart in OT usage ; it will, therefore, be well to glance briefly at those words which express 'portion,' in its varying meanings, in the Hebrew.

גּוֹרָל is the ordinary and frequently used word for 'lots,' *i.e.* little stones, or the like, cast into a vessel, or the folds of a garment, for answering questions, deciding issues, etc. ; it is used once in a different sense, that of 'retribution,' in Is 17[14]. חֵלֶק means, as a rule, 'portion' in the sense of a constituent part of a whole ; חֶלְקָה is used in the same way, but with special reference to land. מָנָה and מְנָת are generally used of portions of sacrifice. These meanings are, however, not invariably adhered to, cf. *e.g.* Ps 16[5] יְהוָה מְנָת חֶלְקִי וְכוֹסִי אַתָּה תּוֹמִיךְ גּוֹרָלִי 'The Lord is the portion of my lot and my cup : thou maintainest my lot.'

In the Gospels μέρος * is used : (1) just like חֵלֶק, for a constituent part of a whole, *e.g.* 'Give me the portion of thy substance that falleth to me' (Lk 15[12]) ; it is used in the same sense in Lk 24[42], Jn 19[23]. In this use of the word, μέρος can refer to things material, as in the last two references, as well as to something abstract, *e.g.* Lk 11[36] 'If therefore thy whole body be full of light, having no part (μέρος) dark . . .' (2) It is used much in the same sense, but with a somewhat extended application, of districts of land ; when

* The RV translates, according to the context, by 'portion,' 'piece,' 'part,' 'side.'

this is the case, the plural form is invariably employed, viz. the 'parts' or districts (τὰ μέρη) belonging to Galilee (Mt 2²²), of Tyre and Sidon (Mt 15²¹), of Cæsarea (Mt 16¹³), of Dalmanutha (Mk 8¹⁰). In this sense the word would correspond to the Hebrew חֶלְקָה. Once more, the word occurs in a technical sense of the right-hand side of a ship (τὰ δεξιὰ μέρη τοῦ πλοίου, Jn 21⁶). (3) μέρος is used in the sense of *fate*, *destiny*, or *lot*; as such it occurs only twice in the Gospels: Mt 24⁵¹ 'He shall appoint his portion with the hypocrites,' and Lk 12⁴⁶ 'He shall appoint his portion with the unfaithful.' * The nearest approach to this in OT usage would be in Is 17¹⁴, where גּוֹרָל has a special and restricted meaning. There is a slight variation in the force of the word as used in Jn 13⁸ 'If I wash thee not, thou hast no part (μέρος) with me'; for, while in the two former passages the reference is to a final doom, in this the meaning is rather, 'If I wash thee not, thou canst have nothing to do with me.'

In one single instance 'portion' or 'part' occurs in the unique sense of one of the ways in which God is served; but here the word is μερίς, not μέρος (Lk 10⁴² 'Mary hath chosen the good part'; the context seems to demand the sense of 'the best part').

W. O. E. OESTERLEY.

PORTRAITS (of Christ).—See CHRIST IN ART, vol. i. p. 314 f.

POSSESSION.—See DEMON, DEMONIACS.

POT.—There are two words rendered 'pot' in the Gospels, ξέστης and ὑδρία. The first is a corruption of the Lat. *sextarius*, and stands for a wooden vessel holding about a pint and a half, used at table for holding water and wine. This it is that is mentioned by Mk. (7⁴· ⁸) when he is relating how 'the Pharisees and all the Jews' kept 'the tradition of the elders.' 'When they come from the market,' he says, 'except they dip themselves' (βαπτίσωνται, v.l. ῥαντίσωνται) 'they do not eat'; and, among the 'many other things which they have received to hold,' he specifies 'the dippings (βαπτισμούς) of cups and *pots*' (ξεστῶν), etc. This he mentions to explain why the Pharisees and scribes came to ask Jesus, 'Why walk thy disciples not according to the tradition of the elders, but eat bread with unwashen hands?' thus giving Jesus occasion to apply to them the prophecy of Isaiah, 'This people honoureth me with their lips, but their heart is far from me,' and otherwise exposing and rebuking their 'hypocrisy.'

When Jn. (4²⁸) tells us of the Samaritan woman, in the excitement of her new-found joy, 'leaving her water-pot,' he uses the words τὴν ὑδρίαν, pointing doubtless to just such a portable earthen water-pot as women in Palestine are everywhere to-day seen carrying on their heads. But in 2⁶, where he gives an account of the miracle at the marriage feast in Cana of Galilee, he tells of 'six water-pots of stone' (λίθιναι ὑδρίαι), which were clearly 'pots' of a very different kind—too large to use at table, or to be portable in the ordinary way. Their size may be gathered from the next clause, 'containing two or three firkins a piece'—about nine English gallons. They were probably just such huge stone pitchers as are shown to tourists to-day at *Kefr Kennā*, and as may be found elsewhere in Palestine. Scarcity of drinking water in Palestine made it necessary to keep a supply on hand in large vessels that would serve as coolers, especially in hot weather. Then a copious supply would be needed according to Jewish custom ('after the manner of the purifying

* It is interesting in this connexion to recall the fact that μέρος is connected radically with Μοῖρα, the goddess of Fate.

of the Jews'), for use in the washing of hands and vessels before and after meals (Mt 15², Mk 7³).

GEO. B. EAGER.

POTTER.—'The Potter's Field' was the name of the property in the purchase of which the chief priests spent the thirty pieces of silver returned by Judas, and which they proposed to use as a burial-place for strangers (Mt 27⁷). Mt 27⁸ states that this spot came in consequence to be known as 'the field of blood'—that is, the field bought with the price of blood; but a different reason for that name is given in Ac 1¹⁸· ¹⁹, where Judas himself purchases the field, and commits suicide in it. The 'field of blood,' or AKELDAMA (חֲקֵל דְּמָא), is generally identified with a spot in which there are numerous tombs, and where also clay is found, lying to the south of Jerusalem, in the valley of Hinnom, not far from the point where it joins the valley of the Kidron (Baedeker, p. 103). St. Matthew believes that this incident of the purchase of the field happened in fulfilment of Zec 11¹²· ¹³, which he reads as a prediction, and ascribes to Jeremiah. This may be a mere slip due to the mention in the Book of Jeremiah of the potter's house (18²) and the Potsherd Gate (19²), just as in Jer 27¹ Jehoiakim is a slip for *Zedekiah*. Or, as Mede (d. 1638) supposed, Jeremiah may actually have been the author of these chapters. It is agreed that they are not by Zechariah. Although, however, there is no doubt that St. Matthew has this passage in his mind, his citation of it is quite free, and diverges largely from the Hebrew, and even more from the Greek, in which v.¹³ becomes an injunction to throw the silver into the smelting-pit (χωνευτήριον), thus reading some derivative of יָצַק or of צָרַף) in order to prove whether it were genuine. Neither does the Targum come any nearer to the text of Matthew. The Syr. of Zech. instead of 'potter' (יוֹצֵר) reads 'treasury' (אוֹצָר), which is generally accepted as correct.

LITERATURE. — Hastings' *DB*, artt. 'Potter,' 'Akeldama'; Edersheim, *LT* ii. 575 f. The difficulties of Mt 27⁷⁻¹⁰ are discussed with especial fulness in the *Comm.* of Meyer and Morison.

T. H. WEIR.

POUND (μνᾶ).—The value of the *denarius* (AV 'penny') being about 9½d., the *mina* (AV 'pound'), which was 100 of these, was = £4 in our money. It was the 60th part of a talent. The only Gospel reference in this sense is in the parable of the Pounds (Lk 19¹¹⁻²⁷). 'Pound' as a weight (λίτρα = 12 oz. avoird.) is alluded to in Jn 12³ and 19³⁹ (see artt. MONEY and WEIGHTS AND MEASURES).

Modern commentators of repute (including Calvin) treat the story of the Pounds (Lk 19¹¹⁻²⁷) as a variant of the parable of the Talents (Mt 25¹⁴⁻³⁰); and prevailing theories on the origin of the Gospels as we have them tend to the confirmation of this view. In Mt. the parable appears as part of the prophetic discourse delivered at Jerusalem, when days of disaster were impending, and our Lord's absence from this mortal scene became naturally an impressive theme (see art. TALENTS). Here in Lk., while activity during that absence is enjoined as a duty, colour is added to the story from local reminiscence. Jericho (v.¹) owed its magnificent palace to the son of Herod the Great, Archelaus, facts from whose history seem clearly drawn upon in the narrative. The Herodian princes, on coming to office (v.¹²), went to Rome to receive imperial investiture (Jos. *Ant.* XIV. xiv. and XVII. xi. 4), and this same Archelaus was in such bad odour that an embassy of protest followed him (XV. xi. 1, etc.). Compare with this the action of the citizens, 'We will not have this man to reign over us' (v.¹⁴). As if to accentuate the variation between Mt. and Lk., we have a further modification of the figures in the *Gospel according to the Hebrews* (c. 200 A.D.), where one servant wastes the goods of his lord among harlots and flute-players, another multiplies the pound, while a third conceals it ; in the end, one is acknowledged, another reproved, and the third committed to prison. That Jesus uttered the parable is not to be doubted, but there seems some uncertainty in the details. The harshness of v.[27], however, as coming from His lips, can be escaped, on the theory that these words were used with reference to Archelaus, who had proved himself amply capable of cruelty.

The entire sovereignty of the Christ being not yet manifested, the broad lesson stands forth, and is unexhausted in our age, that the true note of faithfulness is active zeal in His cause (v.[13]). Means diligently improved yield rich results (v.[17] and v.[19]) ; and although these may vary among individual men, rewards are in all cases manifold (v.[17] and v.[19]). The highly informing contrast comes when we turn to the Pharisaic class,— specially abhorrent to Jesus,—who not only do no sacrificing deeds, but even glory complacently in negative propriety (v.[20]). The ultimate reason of their remissness is the wrong idea of God (v.[21]), whom they figure as a taskmaster who exacts, instead of a kindly father who bestows. Hence the note of the 'austere,' which passes by reflexion into their own sorry travesty of the eternal life. Daily deeds of love are the familiar exchange (v.[23]),—a mart which such religionists thoroughly neglect, since none are harder with their fellows. But innate law must prevail (v.[26]), and indifference never ends in itself—the callous soon betray diminished receptivity. Steel rusts when never out of the sheath, and the saddest cases in religion are seen in those who start fair, but achieve nothing. The figure of reaping where one has not sown (v.[21]), charged falsely against the master, tells truly on the critics themselves. The seed of truth lay to their hand, but it could not grow and reproduce till it was planted in the soil. Cherished mechanically, in their fashion, it was bound to shrivel into a withered husk, from which the germ of life had expired. Hence the verdict of the Master, that in spite of all appearances to the contrary, only the semblance of spiritual power remained—'even that he hath shall be taken away from him' (v.[26]). Conversely, the more actively men employ the graces of the Christian life, the more susceptible their souls become to higher things. It is in order to emphasize this fact—and for no other purpose—that the gainers of the ten pounds and the five pounds respectively are specified and put side by side in the story. The forfeited 100 drachms are awarded to the former, not to the latter, for 'unto every one that hath shall be given' (v.[26]). Life for us all means stewardship, and psychology more and more reveals a delicate and automatic system of rewards and punishments, under sanction of the One Supreme Being, who is revealed in teaching such as this, and who offers all men the saving presence of His Spirit.

LITERATURE.—Trench and Bruce in their works on the Parables, in loc. ; Lynch, Serm. for my Curates, 103 ff.

GEORGE MURRAY.

POVERTY.—That the life of Christ was one of poverty is an impression very generally derived from the familiar words of Is 53, and also from Ph 2[7] ('took upon himself the form of a slave') and 2 Co 8[9] ('he became poor, that ye through his poverty might become rich'). But the general picture of the surroundings of Christ which we find in the Gospels is one of healthy active life. Throughout NT times, until the final agony, the resources of Palestine were well used, and the population was able to bear considerable taxation with comparative ease ; and though Judæa was

liable to scarcity (cf. St. Paul's care for the Jewish Christians, 1 Co 16[1], Ac 24[17]), Galilee was a hive of industry (see Swete, Gospel of St Mark, p. lxxxii ; and Buhl, art. 'New Testament Times' in Hastings' DB, Extra Vol. p. 45, with authorities cited at end). In accordance with this distinction, the contact of Jesus with the poor as described in the Gospels is almost confined to Judæa and Jerusalem (Mt 19[16], Mk 10[21] the rich young ruler ; Mk 12[42], Lk 21[1] the poor widow ; Mt 26[6], Mk 14[5] 'this ointment might have been sold for much and given to the poor' ; Mt 20[30], Mk 10[46], Lk 18[35] the blind beggars outside Jericho ; cf. Mt 25[35]).

1. The place of poverty in Christ's own life.— (a) *The home in Nazareth.*—That Christ's parents were not wealthy we gather from St. Luke's narrative of the Infancy (2[24]), where the offering of the poor is brought at the Presentation ; that 'there was no room for them in the inn' (2[7]) does not in itself show that they were badly off. Nor does the fact that Nazareth was an inconsiderable town [the question in Jn 1[46], if implying a bad reputation, is not quite borne out by the facts ; see Westcott, St. John, ad loc.] condemn all its inhabitants to poverty (see Edersheim, Life and Times of the Messiah, i. 183). Since we are entirely without direct information on either side, we can only conjecture that the form of the townspeople's question as given in St. Mark ('Is not this the carpenter?' 6[9] ; cf. Mt 13[55]), and the movements of His family (Jn 2[12], where His mother and His brethren are staying at Capernaum ; 2[2], where His mother and His disciples are guests at Cana) imply a certain position of independence (cf. Jn 1[38] 'Where dwellest thou?').

The story in Eusebius (HE iii. 19, 20) of the grandsons of Judas 'the Lord's brother' being summoned before Domitian, and removing his suspicion of them by the appearance of their horny labourers' hands, can hardly throw light on the circumstances of Christ's own home.

(b) *The active Ministry.*—Christ and His disciples certainly did not subsist on charity ; true, the Son of Man had not where to lay his head (Mt 8[20], Lk 10[58]) ; but this shows only that Christ was content not to have a home of His own, not that He could not have had one. The little party had a common 'bag' or purse (Jn 12[6]), from which they purchased necessaries (Jn 4[8] ; cf. Mt 16[5], Mk 8[14]) and gave to the poor (Jn 13[29] ; cf. Mt 26[9]). The disciples' question before the feeding of the five thousand, as given in St. Mark (6[37] 'Shall we buy two hundred pennyworth of bread?' cf. Lk 9[13]), though doubtless ironical, does not suggest actual penury. It would seem that Jesus was in the habit of paying the Temple tax (Mt 17[24]). As the firstborn, He would under ordinary circumstances have the larger share of whatever property His father might leave. That He was not without well-to-do friends, and used their hospitality, is certain. Zebedee would seem to have been in a good position (Mk 1[20] 'with the hired servants' ; one of his sons is personally known to the high priest, Jn 18[15]). Perhaps it was through his help that Jesus was able to have a small boat constantly in attendance on Him when preaching at the Lake of Galilee (ἵνα πλοιάριον προσκαρτερῇ αὐτῷ, Mk 3[9]). The same thing may be gathered of the household at Bethany (Lk 10[38] ; and still more Jn 11[3. 45] and 12[3]) ; certain women, including the wife of Herod's steward, 'minister' to Him (Mk 15[40], Lk 8[3]). He is able to secure an ass on which to enter into Jerusalem (Mt 21[3], Mk 11[3], Lk 19[31]), a lodging at night through the last week (Mt 21[7], Mk 11[19], Lk 21[37]), and the use of an upper room for the Passover (Mt 26[18], Mk 14[15]) ; nor is there anything to suggest that Christ's hunger when He was passing the barren fig-tree was the result of inability to procure food (Mt 21[18], Mk 11[12]).

2. Teaching about poverty.—The blessedness of the poor is the subject of the first Beatitude (see the following article). In the same discourse occur the prohibitions against taking anxious thought (Mt 6[25]) and laying up treasures (6[19]). Prayer for temporal wants is to be for 'daily bread' ('bread of the coming day' or 'bread of sufficiency,' ἄρτος ἐπιούσιος; see LORD'S PRAYER) alone (Mt 6[11], Lk 11[3]). Christ bids the disciples of John observe that the poor have the gospel preached unto them (Mt 11[5], cf. Is 61[1. 2], Lk 4[18]), and specially contrasts the widow with the rich donors to the Temple treasury (Mk 12[42], Lk 21[3]). The danger of wealth is constantly pointed out (Mt 19[23], Mk 10[23], Lk 18[24] 'How hardly shall they that have riches enter into the kingdom of heaven'; Mt 18[8] 'If thy hand or thy foot cause thee to stumble, cut it off'; Lk 16[19] the parable of Lazarus and Dives; Lk 12[16] the parable of the Rich Fool, following on Christ's peremptory refusal to divide the inheritance between the two brothers). Cf. the command to the rich young ruler, 'Sell all that thou hast,' Mt 19[21], Mk 10[21], Lk 18[22], in which there was evidently some personal appropriateness; the demand was not universally made. According to our accounts, the Temple was cleansed of buyers and sellers both at the beginning and the end of the ministry (Jn 2[14], and Mt 21[12], Mk 11[15]). That Christ had the true Israelite contempt for money and commercial prosperity is at least hinted in the story of the Temptation (Mt 4[10], Lk 4[8]), and shown quite plainly in the parable of the Labourers in the Vineyard: 'It is my will to give unto this last even as unto thee,' Mt 20[15],—a principle which, as Ruskin saw (*Unto this Last*), is a defiance of political economy as ordinarily understood. Compare the anti-commercial statutes in Dt 15[1f.], Ex 23[10f.], Lv 25[1-15] as to the remission of debts and the reversion of holdings in the Sabbatical year and year of Jubilee. If faithful to the Law, it was impossible for Israel to be anything but a comparatively poor nation (note, however, Dt 15[4]), as would necessarily be the case with the Christian community which obeyed the rules, 'Give to him that asketh thee,' and 'Lend, never giving up hope,' μηδὲν ἀπελπίζοντες (Lk 6[35]; cf. Mt 6[12], Lk 11[4]). Peabody (*Jesus Christ and the Social Question*) points out the further opposition to current Socialism implied in the parable of the Talents (Mt 25[29], Lk 12[48]; cf. Mt 13[12]).

An interesting echo of this teaching on poverty, or on the openhandedness that must prevent the dangerous accumulation of wealth, is found in the *Gospel of the Hebrews* (fragm. 11), where the rich man who came to Christ in the attitude of the young ruler is told that he could not have kept the Law, since people are dying of hunger at his gates. What we do not find, however, in the Gospels, is any eulogy of poverty for its own sake; it is enjoined simply as an almost indispensable aid to serving God aright. And the fact that Christ constantly mixes with what we should call the middle classes and the well-to-do, without rebuking them or bidding them give up all, shows that poverty must be understood in a relative sense, and not as the equivalent of penury. His life was one long protest against the attitude of 'virtus laudatur et alget.' To take Mt 26[11], 'Ye have the poor always with you,' to mean that the existence of poverty must be acquiesced in, is to forget all that was said about mercifulness and liberality by Him who, when He saw the multitudes, 'had compassion on them' (Mt 9[36] 14[14]). Christ demanded the surrender not of money in itself, but of everything that could interfere with

the interests of the Kingdom of heaven; in this sense the verb ἀφίημι, 'to give up, leave' (Mt 19[29], Mk 10[28], Mt 4[20], Mk 1[18]; cf. Lk 9[60]), is characteristic of the Gospels,—as characteristic as it is in its other meaning of 'to forgive.' The ideal is not poverty but service (Mt 20[27], 'Whosoever would become first among you shall be your servant').

LITERATURE.—Edersheim, *Life and Times of the Messiah*; Schürer, *HJP passim*; Delitzsch, *Artisan Life in the Time of Christ*; Vogelstein, *Landwirtschaft in Palästina*, 1894; Merrill, *Galilee in the Time of Christ*; for good remarks on the place of poverty in Christ's teaching, see Harnack, *Das Wesen des Christentums* ('Das Evangelium und die Armut'); *Expos.* 6th ser. xi. (1905), 321.   W. F. LOFTHOUSE.

POVERTY OF SPIRIT. — According to the Matthæan version of the Sermon on the Mount, our Lord pronounced the first Beatitude on the 'poor in spirit' (πτωχοὶ τῷ πνεύματι). In the corresponding passage of Lk. (6[20]) the words τῷ πνεύματι are omitted; and there can be little doubt that this simpler form of the Beatitude is the more original. It may be gathered, indeed, from quotations in the early Fathers (cf. Polycarp, ii. 3; *Clem. Hom.* xv. 10; Polycr. 2) that the primitive reading in Mt. also was 'Blessed are the poor,' and that the qualifying words were introduced later, in order to define the sense more exactly. Though formally an addition to the actual saying of Jesus, they were felt to be necessary for the right translation of an Aramaic term which had come to bear a peculiar shade of meaning.

1. Already in the later OT writings we find poverty associated with a certain religious temper. The 'poor' are also the contrite of heart (Is 66[2]); they are the 'meek ones' who lend a willing ear to the Divine message (Ps 37[11], Is 61[1]). This estimate of poverty is probably to be explained by historical circumstances. The foreign influences which began to operate in the period succeeding the Exile had chiefly affected the richer classes, while the poor still clung to the ancient traditions. Poverty thus acquired a moral significance, which was reinforced by the conditions prevailing in our Lord's own time. As a result of the externalizing process which had long been at work in religion, the rich were in a specially favoured position from the point of view of legal righteousness. They alone were at leisure to study the Law and to order their lives according to its requirements. They were not exposed, like tradesmen and artizans, to a constant risk of Levitical defilement. They could afford to give alms, and offer the stated sacrifices, and cast much into the Temple treasury. The distinction of wealth and poverty had, therefore, come to be a religious as well as a social distinction; and the Pharisaic spirit of pride and self-sufficiency was chiefly prevalent among the rich. In their consciousness of strict obedience to the Law, they could lay claim to peculiar privileges, and look down with contempt on the ignorant 'people of the land' (Jn 7[49]). It must always be remembered that, when Jesus speaks of wealth or poverty, He is thinking not so much of a social status as of the religious conditions involved in it. Much in His teaching that has been supposed to bear on present-day economic questions, belongs properly to quite a different sphere.

2. It is thus apparent that the words τῷ πνεύματι, although not literally uttered by Jesus, are necessary to the right understanding of His thought. He pronounces His blessing on the poor, in so far as their spiritual temper corresponds with their outward condition. Their poverty was commonly assumed to entail certain drawbacks which placed them at a hopeless disadvantage in their relations to God. Jesus declares that, on the contrary, it was their privilege. It served to foster in them the disposition which could most readily understand the message of the Kingdom and respond to it. 'Blessed are the poor who have allowed their poverty to fulfil its work in them,—who are poor in spirit as well as in worldly circumstances.' The truth of the saying may be best illustrated by the historical fact that our Lord's earliest disciples were drawn, almost wholly, from the poorer class. In this class alone He found those who were capable of entering into sympathy with Him and co-operating with Him in His work.

3. What, then, is the religious temper, the 'poverty of spirit,' which was associated in our Lord's mind with actual poverty? When we examine the saying in the light of the general context of the teaching of Jesus, we can discover three main ideas which are implied in it. (1) In the first place, poverty of spirit is the *receptivity* for the Divine message. It corresponds, in this sense, with the teachable, childlike spirit to which the Kingdom is elsewhere promised (Mt 18²ᶠᶠ). The wealthier classes, in their scrupulous obedience to the Law, had become enslaved to custom and tradition. Before the new teaching could make any appeal to them, they had everything to unlearn, freeing their minds entirely of the prejudices and conventional ideas which had encrusted them. In the poor, the instinct for truth had never been perverted by mistaken habit and education. They could listen to Jesus with an open mind, and allow His message to make its own impression. From those who would enter into His Kingdom our Lord demands this receptivity, which in His own time He found, almost exclusively, among the poor,—the common people who heard Him gladly (Mk 12³⁷).—(2) The idea of *humility* is likewise implied. Arrogance and self-complacency are at all times the peculiar vices of men of wealth; and in our Lord's day these vices bore a religious as well as a social complexion. The rich man could boast, like the Pharisee in the parable, that he was not as other men, since he had fulfilled to the letter every demand of the Law. His pride as a rich man became, in the religious sphere, self-righteousness. Our Lord perceived that to such a temper of mind no true desire for God or right relation towards Him was possible. God could not bestow His gift on those who had never, in a deep sense of personal unworthiness, realized their need of it. The Kingdom of heaven was for the 'poor in spirit,'—the poor who are conscious of their poverty, and so make their approach to God.—(3) A third idea, characteristic of the whole teaching of Jesus, seems also to be involved in the words. Discipleship is impossible without a *renunciation* of earthly possessions. The natural result of wealth is to hamper a man in his pursuit of the higher life, since he cannot help reflecting, like the young ruler, how much it is likely to cost him. The poor have little to lose, and need have no hesitancy. They can answer the call of Christ at any moment, with an instant, unquestioning obedience. It is not, however, an outward poverty that our Lord demands, but a 'poverty of spirit,' an inward renunciation. There may be no demand for a literal abandonment of worldly possessions, but the true disciple will hold them indifferent. He will not be retarded in any Christian service by the fear of losing them. Whatever be his outward condition, he will have laid aside every weight, detached himself from all earthly considerations, and will act in the poor man's spirit of instant readiness at the Divine call.

The effect, therefore, of the added words in Mt. is to attach a deeper, moral significance to the original idea of poverty. Among the poor of His own land and time our Lord discovered the truest examples of the receptive, humble, unworldly temper which He demanded in His followers. The idea of social status was subordinate in His mind to that of an inward spirit, which is not necessarily confined to any particular class. By whatever process the qualifying words were introduced into the saying, they correctly interpret the real thought of Jesus, and are necessary to guard it from misconstruction.

4. The Beatitude as a whole is clearly reminiscent of OT passages which comfort the 'poor in the land' with the promise of Messianic blessedness (cf. esp. Ps 37). As in the other Beatitudes, our Lord arrests attention by stating His idea in a bold paradoxical form. The poor, whom men despised and pitied, were the truly rich; a wonderful inheritance was reserved for them, and was already 'theirs,' in the midst of their seeming poverty. We may trace, likewise, an implied answer to current Jewish theories of worldly misfortune as evidence of God's displeasure. The poor, so far from suffering a deserved punishment, were to be regarded as 'blessed.'—Their hardships were the promise and guarantee of their entrance into the Kingdom.

5. This Beatitude is placed first in the versions of both Mt. and Lk., and evidently with a deliberate intention. Poverty of spirit is the fundamental requirement in the Christian life. It represents a condition of mind and heart without which a man is wholly irresponsive to the Divine influences. As Jesus began His ministry with a call to repentance, so He pronounced His first Beatitude on the 'poor in spirit.' He thus repeated, under a different image, the great declaration, 'Except ye turn and become as little children, ye shall not enter into the kingdom of heaven' (Mt 18³).

LITERATURE.—Titius, *Die NT Lehre von der Seligkeit*, 1895, Part i. (esp. p. 72 ff.); H. J. Holtzmann, *NT Theologie*, vol. i. 181 f. (1897); Loisy, *Le discours sur la montagne* (1903); also works of a popular or homiletical character, *e.g.* : Dykes, *Beatitudes of the Kingdom* (1876); Gore, *Sermon on the Mount* (1904); Griffith-Jones, *Sermon on the Mount* (1903); Iverach, *The Other Side of Greatness* (1906; cf. *ExpT* xviii. [1907], p. 146 f.).   E. F. SCOTT.

POWER.—The term indicates the efficient force by which personal commands and the claims of law receive obedient attention and fulfilment.

In AV of Gospels 'power' is used with about equal frequency to represent two words in the original, δύναμις and ἐξουσία. These words are thus distinguished by Grimm-Thayer :—' δύν. *power*, natural ability, general and inherent; ἐξουσ. primarily liberty of action, then *authority*—either as delegated power or as unrestrained, arbitrary power.' Cf. also Cremer, *s.vv.* In RV, except in the three cases named below, 'authority' is given as the rendering of ἐξουσία, usually in the text, sometimes in the margin. Lk 22⁵³ retains 'power' without any marginal alternative ; Jn 1¹² gives 'right' ; Jn 10¹⁸ retains 'power,' but has 'right' in margin.

1. *Power in the personal life of Christ.*—During His earthly ministry, in the impression made both upon His disciples and upon the hostile Pharisees, as well as upon the mass of the people, there is abundant testimony to the transcendent personality of Christ. With this accords also the estimate concerning Him in the Acts and the Epistles. A vague attempt at assimilation likened Him to one of the prophets (Mt 16¹⁴), and Herod saw in Him the risen John the Baptist (Mk 6¹⁶), but otherwise His life and character were ever recognized as unique and beyond comparison (see AWE). In His works of healing, wrought on mind and body, the evidence was open to all (Mk 5¹⁵, Lk 9⁴³). It was the same with His teaching (Mt 7²⁹). In dealing with the most venerated religious precepts and traditions, He acts with the ease and freedom of original authority, noting limitations and supplying enlarged meanings and higher applications (Mt 5³³⁻⁴⁸). He rejects the offer of world empire (Lk 4⁶·⁸), and warns those whom He sent forward to tell of His approach not to rejoice even in the exercise of His delegated power (Lk 10²⁰). The same qualities of range and originality are recognized in His sympathy with the outcast and suffering (Lk 7³⁴ 13¹¹, Jn 11³⁵), in His knowledge of the heart and its temptations (Lk 5²⁰ 7⁴⁷, Jn 4¹⁸), and in His controversies with the Jewish leaders (Mt 22¹⁵⁻⁴⁶). A still deeper insight into the uniqueness of His character is afforded by what was involved in following and serving Him (Lk 14²⁵⁻³⁵, Jn 14¹² 15⁸). His works were stated by Himself to have been wrought in God (Jn 14¹⁰), who also had sent Him (9⁴ 16²⁸) ; and His day had been foreseen by Abraham (8⁵⁶) and Isaiah (61¹, ²), and by the prophets generally (Lk 24²⁷). His Kingdom was to be coextensive with the world and its nationalities (Mt 8¹¹ 26¹³ 28¹⁹, Jn 10¹⁶ 17²⁰). The gift of His life, offered freely and apart from external constraint, was to be the bond of union among His disciples (Mt 26²⁶⁻²⁸, Jn 15¹², ¹³), and was to be the power that would draw the world unto Him (Jn 3¹⁴ 12³²). The impression thus made upon His disciples became in turn the testimony which they gave to the world—' The Word was made flesh and dwelt among us (and we beheld his glory, the glory as of the only-begotten of the Father) full of grace and truth ' (Jn 1¹⁴). See AUTHORITY OF CHRIST.

2. *Power in the Kingdom of Christ.*—Christ declared of His Kingdom that it was not of this world (Jn 18³⁶). Those worldly kingdoms were of the sword, established by and for physical dominion. As every created thing must, by the inward necessity of that condition, come to an end, so those kingdoms would perish by the sword (Mt 26⁵²). His Kingdom, on the other hand, did not rise from beneath, but descended from above, having its origin in the eternal thought of God, the Kingdom of heaven. With the first grasp of this meaning, its administration was spoken of as different from the law of a carnal commandment, being ' the power of an endless life ' (He 7¹⁶).

In the prophetic intimation of its advent through the mediation of the sorrows of Zion, the essential character and tendency of this Kingdom, the requirements of its citizenship, the extent of its dominion, the motive of its statesmanship, its estimate of heroism, and its rewards of service, were all so new and conflicting, that there seemed to be two Messiahs, one who should reign and deliver, and one who should serve and suffer (Is 53. 59¹⁶⁻¹⁹ 61¹⁻³). Only the accomplished fact was able to reveal, and in new areas of its expansion is still revealing, that for such a Kingdom the anointed Head must needs have suffered in order to enter into His glory (Lk 24²⁶). The new and wonderful element that made its citizenship not of blood, nor of the will of the flesh, nor of the will of man (Jn 1¹³), consisted in this, that whereas in the kingdoms of the world there had been an ever-ascending scale of power, man living unto himself, and governments existing for the sake of the governing classes, so there was in this Kingdom a correspondingly descending scale of service in which all those features were precisely reversed. Whereas previously in religion men were the suppliants, and sacrificed unto their deities, and propitiated them by gifts and promises of devotion, in this Kingdom God Himself was the chief sacrificer, offering His only-begotten Son ; and the Almighty sought to reconcile the weak unto Himself (Jn 3¹⁶, ³⁸ 12²⁷ 18³⁷). With this leading fact of the Kingdom all the others followed in complete agreement. He who would be accounted greatest must qualify for that distinction by becoming the servant of all (Mt 20²⁶, ²⁸). Women are declared to excel in faith (Mt 15²⁸), discernment (26¹³), and courageous sacrifice (Mk 12⁴¹⁻⁴⁴). Little children are regarded with reverence, and the loving trust of a child's heart gives direction to the wise, and ap-

points the duties of the great (Mt 18³, ⁴ 19¹⁴). The constitution and aspirations of the Kingdom, as embodied in the Sermon on the Mount, not only surpass all similar requirements of government, but seem to invert all that the world had hitherto counted great and noble. The innermost instinct of empire, the white ensign of this unique Kingdom, is the joy of harmonious relationship to the will of God. Government is by beatitudes. The crucifixion of self for the sake of others is the recognition mark of its people. This pervades all gradations of its society, for He who is on the throne emptied Himself, and what is done unto the least is regarded as done unto Him (Mt 25⁴⁰). Instead of pride and ambition, the lust of power and possession that had created and controlled other dynasties, its regalia and administration are entrusted to the poor in spirit who claim no homage. The dispensing of the beatitudes is given to those who have become acquainted with grief and discouragement, whose necks have felt the pressure of the harsh forces and sharp limitations of life. Here also for exalted office there is the partaking of the Divine nature, but it is reserved for the pure in heart. So rich is the provision for its subjects, that even the cry of hunger becomes a feast, and to bear a burden and cross with Christ is an immediate Paradise. By its connexion with the One Name of which the OT spoke it fulfilled the vision of the prophets which Judaism had obscured, and, on the other hand, included in due place and proportion those gifts for physical need and circumstance that had been the crown and consummation of Gentile desire (Mt 6³³). These are both represented in the familiar and venerated form of prayer which in its first part lifts the language of our possession above all gifts to God Himself, but makes it treason for His Church to covet the Name, the Kingdom, and the Will. In its second part it encourages the claim of our continual frailty, ignorance, and dependence.

Again, the same principle of looking and stooping downwards and of uplifting what is beneath is the main subject-matter of the parables of Christ. The power that is seen exemplified in them is the counterpart of what is set forth in the Sermon on the Mount. Under various aspects, in whole or in part, they unfold the meaning of discipleship, the power of the Kingdom, and the dangers that attend its service. Here also, to be in the Kingdom is beatitude ; and when this privilege of entrance has been prevented by any cause whatever, the regret over the one wasted life and its great opportunity is described as weeping and gnashing of teeth (Lk 13²⁸).

Thus in His life and death, in His teaching and labours, Christ conformed to the beatitudes of the Kingdom, and afterwards entrusted its advancement to His disciples. ' Come unto me—take my yoke — learn of me,' — salvation, self - devotion, sainthood,—these were the steps into the Kingdom, and the power of its service.

In His last message to the disciples our Lord gave two special commands about the Kingdom they were to establish and extend in His name. This communication was accompanied by a touching and solemn act of covenant, and endeared by the mention of all that He had been and would be to them. The first concerned the loyalty to Himself that was to carry with it the invincible power of the Kingdom. It was, ' Abide in me and I in you ' (Jn 15⁴). In His cherished presence they would know His purpose, and that would be their way of power. This presence, however, could be granted only where they loved one another as He had loved them (v. ¹²). It was in vain to go out to the conquest of the world unless this base of operations was safeguarded. They were to tarry in Jerusalem until it became in each heart a conscious experience beyond the reach of doubt or discouragement. This enabling supernatural power of the Kingdom came to be called the grace of God. In 1 Co 13 its essential meaning is breathed forth as from a vase containing the fragrance of what is no longer visible. Its power within the heart is exhibited in Ro 8, and its energy of diffusion in Ro 13.

The second charge affected the world that was to be His possession, the nations that were to bring each its special riches and glory into His Kingdom (Mt 28[19. 20], cf. Mk 16[15]). It was His greatest commandment, and is therefore the greatest test of love to Him. He recognized the right and claim of the world to wait until it received sufficient evidence that He had been sent to be its Ruler. He warned His disciples that the only evidence that could carry such conviction would be the sight of a Church so filled with the spirit of His Kingdom and so devoted to the fulfilment of His command, that all things would give way in order to the presentation of that proof. The world that will say the Church is one will say that Christ is Lord (Jn 10[16] 17[21-23]).

See also art. FORCE.

LITERATURE.—W. Arthur, *Tongue of Fire*, ch. ix.; A. Maclaren, *Holy of Holies*, chs. vi. viii.; Mason, *Conditions of our Lord's Life on Earth* (1896), 84; W. N. Clarke, *What shall we think of Christianity?* (1899), 106; Forrest, *Authority of Christ*.

        G. M. MACKIE.

PRÆTORIUM.—The word occurs in the text of Mk 15[16] only, but in the margin of Mt 27[27], Jn 18[28. 33] 19[9], with Ac 23[35] and Ph 1[13]. In the Gr. it is a transliteration of the Lat. *prætorium*, which originally meant the tent of the commander of an army, and then the official residence of a provincial governor; other senses, such as that of the Imperial bodyguard or even of a spacious country house, were gradually acquired. In most of the passages in the Gospels is used in reference to a part or the whole of Pilate's official residence in Jerusalem, which was probably the palace of Herod the Great (see PAVEMENT).

Two other identifications are supported by comparatively early tradition, but are not on the whole to be approved. That Pilate's house was in the lower city, a little to the north of the Temple, is altogether unlikely. The theory has failed to be confirmed by any discovery of the site; and it is not easy to see why Pilate should prefer such a locality, when the palace built by Herod was available as the official residence of the procurator. More can be said in favour of Pilate's occupation of the castle of Antonia, which stood to the north west of the Temple area. It was a fortress and prison, and served as the headquarters of the garrison at Jerusalem. Josephus (*Ant.* xv. xi. 4; *BJ* i. v. 4) describes it as a citadel, with abundant accommodation, and connected with the precincts of the Temple by a private way. But, again, Pilate was not likely, especially when accompanied by his wife and household (Mt 27[19]), to stay there, when the sumptuous palace of Herod, with its gardens and banqueting halls, was at his disposal. It is true that the proximity of Antonia to the Temple would be a convenience to the priests and Sanhedrists, and save them from the toil of attendance at the more remote palace; but Pilate was not the man to study the wishes or comfort of the Jewish leaders at the cost of any discomfort to himself. The arguments in favour of his adoption of the castle as his residence have been accepted, amongst recent commentators, by Westcott (on Jn 18) and Swete (on Mk 15[16]); but, on the other hand, Herod's palace has been preferred by Schürer, Edersheim, Sir C. Wilson, and commentators such as Alford and Meyer. The practice at Jerusalem would thus correspond with that at Cæsarea (Ac 23[33-35]).

Such a hypothesis leaves the passages in which the prætorium is referred to without any serious difficulty; and it becomes possible to follow the probable order of events. According to St. John, the trial of Jesus took place in one of the porticoes of Herod's palace. When sentence was pronounced, Jesus was led away by the soldiers to Antonia, where they were themselves quartered, and where prisoners were ordinarily detained. He was taken into a court, to which also the name of *prætorium* is given (Mt 27[27], Mk 15[16]), and mocked by such of the soldiers as were off duty. In this connexion *prætorium* denotes probably the place of meeting of the council of chief officers for the transaction of the business of the cohort and for the trial of offences in the absence of the procurator. Such a usage of the term is anticipated, if not illustrated, in Livy (*Hist.* xxx. 5, xxxvii. 5); and the existence of such a court would be necessary for the maintaining of order in Jerusalem and the vicinity. When the soldiers were weary of the mocking, they led Jesus away again to be crucified.

        R. W. MOSS.

PRAISE.—**1. Introductory.**—Both in the OT and the NT the predominant idea of 'praise' is that of a tribute of homage in utterance, publicly expressed and rendered to God by His creatures. It forms the essence of worship, whether as offered by angels (cf. Lk 2[13. 14. 20], Rev 14[6f.]) or men (cf. Lk 19[37f.]). The subject of this 'praise' is either the excellencies of God's attributes and revealed nature (cf. esp. Rev 19) or the beneficent action of His providence, as shown more particularly in creation, revelation, and redemption (thanksgiving); cf. Ac 2[47], Rev 15[3f.]. In the Gospels Jesus is sometimes the object of praise and homage (Mt 21[16]; cf. Lk 4[15]), and Himself often dispenses praise for certain qualities of human nature or character (cf. Mt 8[10] 11[11] etc.). The praise of man by man is usually applied in the Gospels to unreal and hypocritical commendation, and is condemned by Jesus (Mt 6[1], Lk 6[26]; cf. Jn 5[41-44] 12[43]).

2. Jewish usage.—In Jewish worship the element of praise occupies a dominant place, and has received rich and manifold expression. The title of the Bk. of Psalms in the MT, *Sepher Tĕhillim* * (and its variants) = 'Book of *Praises* or Praise-Songs,' is an indication of the emphasis which was laid on the note of praise in later Jewish worship. This note is already prominent in the Psalter itself (cf. *e.g.* 'O thou that inhabitest the *praises* of Israel,' Ps 22[3]). The close connexion existing between the ideas of praise and thanksgiving (cf. *e.g.* Ps 100[4] 'Enter his gates with *thanksgiving*, his courts with *praise*') has already been pointed out in this work (see art. BLESSING, § **1**). Indeed, thanksgiving (Heb. *hōdāh*)—esp. for God's beneficence in creation, revelation, and providence—is an essential part of praise. If a distinction can be drawn, *praise* pure and simple is rather to be associated with extolling God's perfections and holiness, while *blessing* (thanksgiving) is connected rather with thankful recognition of His goodness, beneficence, and mercy. But this is true only in a general sense; the two conceptions are so intimately related that one passes over into the other almost imperceptibly.

For the Hebrew terms employed with the meaning 'praise' and its cognates, reference may be made to the art. 'Praise (in OT)' in Hastings' *DB* iv. 33 f. The most frequent are—הִלֵּל 'praise' (esp. in the liturgical formula הַלְלוּ־יָהּ = Hallelujah), הוֹדָה 'give thanks' (RV), בֵּרַךְ 'bless,' זִמֵּר 'make melody'; rare synonyms are—שִׁבַּח 'laud' (but very frequent in Jewish liturgy), הִגְדִּיל, גִּדֵּל 'magnify.' Cf. also such phrases as 'Sing unto J" a new song.'

In the Synagogue Liturgy the element of praise has received splendid expression. The most classical examples of this are perhaps the great 'Benediction of Song' (ברכת השיר) † and the *Kaddish*.‡ The former of these, in its shortest form, runs thus :

'Be Thy name lauded for ever, O our King, the great and holy God and King, in heaven and on earth; for unto Thee, O Lord our God and God of our fathers, song and laud are becoming,

---

* The title of one of the late (synagogal) Psalms is תְּהִלָּה לְדָוִד, Ps 146[1] ('Praise-Song of David').
† Cf. Singer's Heb.-Eng. *Daily Prayer Book*, pp. 36, 125–127. See also an art. by the present writer, 'S. Peter in the Jewish Liturgy,' in the *ExpT* [1903], xv. 93 f.
‡ Singer, p. 37.

praise and psalm, strength and dominion, victory, greatness and might, renown and glory, holiness and sovereignty, blessings and thanksgivings, from henceforth, even for ever. Blessed art Thou, O Lord, God and King, great in praises, God of thanksgivings, Lord of wonders, who makest choice of melodious song, O King and God, the Life of all worlds.'

In the *Ḳaddish* the following characteristic paragraph occurs :

'Blessed, lauded, and glorified, exalted, extolled and honoured, magnified and praised be the name of the Holy One, Blessed be He ; though He be high above all the blessings and songs, hymns of praise and consolation, which are uttered in the world.'

These are simply specimens of what pervades the entire Jewish Liturgy. In the Gospels the Angels' Song of Praise (Lk 2[14]) is an example of pure praise in worship, parallels to which are to be found in the Apocalypse (4[11] 7[12] 11[17] 14[7] 19[1f.]). In Rabbinical theology, it is to be noticed, prayer and praise form the spiritual counterpart and fulfilment of the old daily sacrifice in the Temple. The words of Hosea (14[2]), 'We shall render as bullocks the offering of our lips,' were interpreted in this sense. Spiritual worship thus becomes a 'sacrifice of praise and thanksgiving.' Cf. He 13[15] ('Through him'—*i.e.* Christ—'let us offer up a sacrifice of praise') with Westcott's note ; cf. also our Lord's application of the words of Hos 6[6] ('I desire mercy, and not sacrifice') in Mt 9[13] 12[7].

For the close connexion of prayer and praise — which are sometimes intermingled in the Jewish Liturgy, *e.g.* in the 'Eighteen Blessings'—cf. Cheyne's note on Ps 42[9] (*Book of Psalms* [1888], p. 118 f.).

3. Usage in the Gospels.—The note of praise so characteristic of Jewish worship also pervades the Gospels. It is esp. prominent in the Third Gospel, where it appears not only in the Jewish-Christian Nativity-narrative (chs. 1. 2) [see HYMN], but also elsewhere (cf. 19[37]). It is noticeable how often the people (spectators, the assembled multitude) are represented as 'praising' or 'glorifying' God for some great exhibition of power wrought by Jesus (see below).

The Greek terms for 'praise' and its cognates used in the Gospels are—αἰνεῖν, 'praise' * (cf. διδόναι αἶνον τῷ θεῷ, Lk 18[43]), used in LXX for הֹלֵל, הוֹדָה ל ; δόξα 'glory,' δοξάζειν 'glorify' [in LXX δόξα most freq. = כָּבוֹד ; several times for הוֹד, הָדָר, etc.; δοξάζω usually = כָּבֵד in LXX]; διδόναι δόξαν τῷ θεῷ, Lk 17[18]; εὐλογεῖν 'bless' [LXX usually for ברך]; ἐξομολογεῖν 'to celebrate,' 'give praise or thanks to,' Mt 11[25] and ‖. See, further, art. BLESSING, §§ 2 and 4.

The following formulas of praise are to be noted :
(*a*) The Angels' Hymn (Lk 2[14])—
   'Glory to God *in the highest*,
   And *on earth* peace among men of his goodwill.'
For the arrangement in two, not three, lines, cf. Plummer, Com. on 'St. Luke' in *ICC, ad loc.* Here ἐν[τοῖς] ὑψίστοις = בַּמְּרוֹמִים 'in the heavenly places,' and refers to the adoration of the angels in heaven (cf. Ps 148[1] LXX : αἰνεῖτε αὐτὸν (τὸν κύριον) ἐν τοῖς ὑψίστοις) ; cf. Lk 19[38]. With this should be compared the doxological form (ᾧ ἡ δόξα . . εἰς τοὺς αἰῶνας). See below, § 4.
(*b*) 'Hosanna in the highest' ; see art. HOSANNA.
(*c*) 'Blessed is . . .'; especially in the phrase, 'Blessed is he that cometh in the name of the Lord' (εὐλογημένος ὁ ἐρχόμενος ἐν ὀνόματι Κυρίου), Mt 21[9] 23[39], Mk 11[9], Lk 13[35] 19[38], Jn 12[13]. The use of 'blessed' (μακάριος) in the Beatitudes is also notable ; cf. also its use in personal address, Mt 16[17] (Lk 11[27. 28]). To these may here be added—
(*d*) The use of the phrase 'give God (the) praise' (or 'glory'): διδόναι δόξαν τῷ θεῷ = (נתן) שִׂים כָּבוֹד ליהוה, and has various shades of meaning, according to the context—*e.g.* of thanksgiving for benefits received, Lk 17[18]; by confession (of sin), Jn 9[24]; cf. Jos 7[19]. The phrase is frequent in Rev. of celebrating God's *praises* (Rev 4[9] 11[13] 19[7]).

The frequent mention in the Gospels of the multitudes as 'praising' or 'glorifying' God, esp. for the wonderful works wrought by Christ, is worth noting. It shows how deeply this element of public worship had impressed itself upon the

popular mind and heart in Israel. A typical example is Mt 9[8] ('But when the multitudes saw it [the healing of the sick of the palsy], they were afraid, and *glorified* God, which had given such power unto men'). Cf. Mk 2[12], Lk 5[25. 26] ; Lk 2[20] (shepherds) 7[16] 18[43] 23[47] (the centurion at the cross) ; cf. also Lk 13[13] (healing of woman with spirit of infirmity : 'and . . . she was made straight, and *glorified* God') ; Lk 17[15f.] (healing of the ten lepers) is esp. notable, because the grateful one who returned to give thanks to Christ, combined his thanksgiving with 'glorifying God.' Our Lord's words in this connexion are striking : 'Were there none found that returned to give glory to God, save this stranger ?' (v.[18])—words which imply that the duty of grateful praise to God was not always fully recognized in individual practice.

Our Lord's emphatic word about giving 'glory' to God (Lk 17[18]) has already been referred to. As the spontaneous expression of a pure religious instinct, this would naturally be encouraged by Him whenever He met with it. According to Jn 5[41-44], He reproaches the Pharisees with seeking honour from one another rather than from God. But He does not hesitate to accept praise and homage offered to His own person when such is sincere and spontaneous (cf. Mt 21[16]). He dispenses praise in a manner implying a unique claim to appraise and publicly express moral judgments on human character : in this way He expresses His approbation of John the Baptist (Mt 11[11]), all acts of faith (8[10] 9[22] 15[28] 16[8], Lk 7[9]), good and loyal service (Mt 25[11. 23], Lk 19[17]), all generosity of gift (Mk 12[43] 14[6]), self-devotion (Lk 10[41]), prudence (Lk 16[8]).*

Outside the Gospels (viz. in the Epp.) the subject of Christian praise is, as is natural, mainly the great facts of redemption (cf. 1 P 2[10], Ro 15[9-11], Eph 1[3-14], etc.). Creation and redemption are combined in the Christian Liturgies.

4. Ascriptions of praise to Christ outside the Gospels.—It is noticeable that, in at least three (and possibly more) of the Apostolic doxologies, the address is directly to Christ, viz. 2 Ti 4[18] ('The Lord . . . to whom be the glory,' etc.) ; 2 P 3[18] ('the grace of our Lord and Saviour Jesus Christ. To him be the glory,' etc.) ; Rev 1[6] ('him that loveth us, and loosed us from our sins, . . . to him be the glory,' etc.). He 13[21] and 1 P 4[11] are possible cases also. In two cases the ascription of glory to God is made through Christ, viz. Ro 16[27] ('to the only wise God, through Jesus Christ') and Jude [25] ('to the only God our Saviour, through Jesus Christ our Lord, be glory, majesty, dominion, power'), etc. See, further, Westcott, Add. Note on He 13[21] (*Com.* p. 464 f.).

The doxology of the Lord's Prayer is probably a later liturgical addition, inserted in the text of the Gospels, perhaps, under the influence of liturgical usage. See Chase, 'The Lord's Prayer in the Early Church' (*Texts and Studies*), pp. 168-174, and art. LORD'S PRAYER, p. 59[b].

See, further, BLESSING, HALLEL, HOSANNA, HYMN.

LITERATURE.—In addition to the references in the text, see the *Gr. Test. Lexicons* of Grimm-Thayer and Cremer (*s.v.* δόξα).

G. H. BOX.

PRAYER.—For the Christian what is said in the Gospels is absolute as to the duty of prayer for himself and for others ; but he need not fear that in fulfilling this duty he is doing what reason cannot approve. It does not fall within the scope of this article to attempt to find a scientific basis for prayer ; nor need more be said about the reasonableness of prayer than to point out two considerations : (1) The practice of countless races of mankind throughout countless generations is not likely

---

* ἐπαινέω occurs once in Gospels (Lk 16[8] of the unrighteous steward whose lord 'commended' him for his worldly wisdom) ; ἔπαινος, never in Gospels.

* Cf. Lock in Hastings' *DB* iv. 38 ('Praise [in NT]'), whose summary is here adopted.

to be based upon a complete delusion. Untold millions of human beings, including a majority of the most gifted and enlightened, have prayed and continue to pray, because they believe that experience has taught them that prayer is efficacious. (2) We have been placed in a world that is full of good things which are suitable to our needs. Yet it is certain that the world is so ordered that very few of these good things can be enjoyed by us, unless we take the trouble to appropriate them. There is, therefore, nothing unreasonable in believing that the world has been so ordered that some of the blessings which are within our reach cannot be enjoyed unless we pray for them. In the laws which govern the Universe, provision has certainly been made for the operation of men's wills and activities. Consequently there is nothing illogical or unscientific in believing that in those laws provision has been made for the operation of men's prayers. The cases are not completely parallel, because demonstration is possible in the one case but not in the other ; for the connexion between work and its results can be proved, while the connexion between prayer and its results cannot, for the obvious reason that faith is an essential condition of prayer, and proof would destroy faith. Nevertheless, the analogy between the two cases is sufficiently complete to show that there is no necessary antagonism between knowledge of the reign of law and belief in the efficacy of prayer.

In discussing the subject of prayer in reference to Christ and the Gospels, we may consider these topics : (1) the words used to express the idea of prayer ; (2) places and times of prayer ; (3) attitude in prayer ; (4) Christ's example ; (5) Christ's doctrine.

1. There are a few **words for ' prayer '** in the NT which are not found in the Gospels : εὔχομαι, εὐχή, ἐντυγχάνω, ἔντευξις, ὑπερεντυγχάνω, ἱκετηρία. But the majority of such words occur in the Gospels, and their distribution is of interest.

(1) προσεύχομαι, very frequent in the Synoptics, not in John ; προσευχή, 8 times in the Synoptics, not in John ; (2) δέομαι, Mt 9³⁸, 8 times in Luke, not in John ; δέησις, Lk 1¹³ 2³⁷ 5³³ ; (3) ἐρωτάω, rare in this sense in the Synoptics, frequent in John ; (4) αἰτέω and αἰτέομαι, in all four ; αἴτημα, Lk 23²⁴. Of these four sets of words, the first alone is specially appropriated to the *worship of God* : it implies that the person addressed in prayer is Divine. The second implies *personal need* and a special petition to God and man for the supply of a want. The third (which frequently means to ask a question), when used of making requests, generally asks a person to *do* something (Mk 72³, Lk 8³⁷, Jn 4⁴⁰⋅ ⁴⁷ 14¹⁶ 17¹⁵⋅ ²⁰). The fourth indicates a simple request to *give* something (Mt 77⁻¹¹, Lk 119⁻¹³, Jn 14¹³⋅ ¹⁴), the middle voice sometimes adding intensity to the request. All except the first may be used of petitions to men, and have no necessary connexion with the worship of God.

2. Places and times of prayer.—The chief place was the *Temple* : 'My house shall be called a house of prayer' (Mt 21¹³, Mk 11¹⁷, Lk 19⁴⁶). Christ called it 'My Father's house' (Lk 2⁴⁹, Jn 2¹⁶), and, as such, it is the type of heaven (Jn 14²). St. Luke tells of others worshipping in the Temple : Zacharias (1⁹), Simeon (2²⁷), Anna (2³⁷), the disciples (24⁵³), and (in a parable) the Pharisee and the Publican (18¹⁰). The worship in the *synagogues* was frequently attended by Christ, especially in the earlier part of His ministry (Mt 12⁹ 13⁵⁴, Mk 1²¹ 3¹ 6², Lk 4¹⁶ 6⁶, Jn 6⁵⁹ 18²⁰) ; and no doubt His disciples frequently did the same. There is also the *inner chamber* (ταμεῖον, Mt 6⁶), and the *guest-chamber* (κατάλυμα, Mk 14¹⁴, Lk 22¹¹) or *upper room* (ἀνάγαιον, Mk 14¹⁵, Lk 22¹²), in which the prayer of the great High Priest seems to have been offered (Jn 17, although some would place the prayer of this in the Temple, cf. 14³¹), and in which Jesus and the Eleven 'sang a hymn' (Mt 26³⁰, Mk 14²⁶) before going to the Mount of Olives. Nathanael's fig-tree (Jn 1⁴⁸) and Gethsemane (Mt 26³⁶, Mk 14³²) lead us to think of *gardens* as places of retirement

for prayer. And there is also the *mountain-top* near Bethsaida (Mk 6⁴⁶), and that other which was the scene of the Transfiguration (Mt 17¹, Mk 9², Lk 9²⁸), and which St. Luke tells us was ascended for the purpose of prayer.

Not much is said in the Gospels about **times of prayer;** but we read of Christ rising up *before daylight* and going to a desert spot to pray (Mk 1³⁵), and of His continuing *all night* in prayer before the choosing of the twelve Apostles (Lk 6¹²). The *evening* before His arrest is another recorded instance.

3. The common **attitude in prayer** among the Jews was *standing* ; and this our Lord assumes in His teaching (Mt 6⁵, Mk 11²⁵, Lk 18¹¹⋅ ¹³). But He Himself *knelt* in the garden (Lk 22⁴¹) : and it was perhaps in consequence of His example on that occasion that in the NT the first Christians are always represented as kneeling. Outside the Gospels no other posture for prayer is mentioned.

4. Christ's example. — Much more important than terminology, or the mention of places, times, and postures for prayer, is the fact that Jesus Christ, by His own example, has taught us the duty of prayer. Not that we need suppose that He prayed merely in order to set us an example : prayer was one of those things which became Him, in order that He might 'fulfil all righteousness' (Mt 3¹⁵). But example, as set by Him, is of the very strongest. If in such a life as His there was not only room but need for prayer, much more must there be room and need in such lives as ours. Nor were His prayers always prayers for others. In most cases we are not told why or for what He prayed : this we have to gather from the context. On one great occasion, in the garden, just before His Passion, we know that He prayed for Himself (Mt 26³⁹, Mk 14³⁵, Lk 22⁴¹). An hour or two before this, just after the Supper, we know that He prayed for His disciples (Jn 17⁶⁻¹⁹) and for the whole Church (Jn 17²⁰⁻²⁶) ; and a few hours later He prayed for those who nailed Him to the Cross (Lk 23³⁴, a verse which is historically true, whether St. Luke wrote it or not). Moreover, He has left us an example of intercession, not merely for groups of persons, large and small, but also for an individual. He assured St. Peter, 'I made supplication for thee, that thy faith fail not' (Lk 22³²).

It should be noticed that the instances of Christ's praying which are recorded in the Gospels are found just before or just after leading events in the Lord's life ; also that the majority of them are given us by St. Luke, whose Gospel is sometimes called 'the Gospel of Prayer.' There are, indeed, three recorded instances of His praying which are omitted by St. Luke. St. Mark (1³⁵) mentions His retirement for prayer after healing multitudes at Capernaum, where St. Luke (4⁴²) mentions only the retirement. Both St. Mark (6⁴⁶) and St. Matthew (14²³) record His retirement for prayer after the feeding of the 5000, where St. Luke (9¹⁷) omits both retirement and prayer. And St. John (12²⁷⋅ ²⁸) tells of His prayer when certain Greeks were brought to Him, where St. Luke omits the whole incident. As we might expect, the prayer for Himself in the garden of Gethsemane is recorded by all three Synoptists (Mt 26³⁹, Mk 14³⁵, Lk 22⁴¹). Nothing in the Gospels is stronger evidence of the reality of our Lord's humanity than that prayer, and it evidently established itself firmly in the earliest traditions respecting Him. But there are seven instances in which St. Luke is alone in relating that Jesus prayed : at His baptism (3²¹) ; before His first collision with the Jewish hierarchy (5¹⁶) ; before choosing the Twelve (6¹²) ; before the first prediction of His Passion (9¹⁸) ; at His Transfiguration

(9^{29}); before teaching the Lord's Prayer (11^1); and on the Cross $(23^{34.\ 46})$.

There are three other cases where prayer on the part of Christ seems to be implied, although it is not expressly stated. *He looked up to heaven* before breaking the bread at the feeding of the 5000 (Mt 14^{19}, Mk 6^{41}, Lk 9^{16}). So also, before healing the deaf man who had an impediment in his speech, Jesus *looked up to heaven and sighed* (Mk 7^{34}). Still more clearly, before raising Lazarus, Jesus *lifted up His eyes*, and said, *Father, I thank thee that thou heardest me* (Jn 11^{41}). We venture to count all three of these as occasions on which Jesus prayed.

This gives us, in all, fourteen instances : two in all three Gospels, one in Matthew and Mark, two in Mark alone, two in John alone, and seven in Luke alone. They cover the whole of Christ's public life from His baptism to the moment of His death, and show His dependence upon His Father for help and strength and refreshment. To say with Victor of Antioch (Swete on Mk 1^{35}), that Christ prayed οὐκ αὐτὸς ταύτης δεόμενος . . . ἀλλ' οἰκονομικῶς τοῦτο ποιῶν, is not adequate, even if in some sense true. He $5^{7.\ 8}$ places us nearer to the truth. We ought to beware of suggesting that our Lord's prayers were in any way unreal. It was out of the fulness of His own experience in a life of absolutely unique difficulty, toil, and suffering that He said, ' Ask, and it shall be given you.'

5. Christ's doctrine.—In addition to His weighty example as to the duty and blessedness of prayer, we have Christ's frequent sayings on the subject. That men 'ought always to pray and not to faint' was evidently a marked feature in His teaching, and it appears in three different forms : (1) On two occasions, apparently, once spontaneously (Mt 6^{5-15}), and once at the request of a disciple (Lk 11^{14}), Christ gave His followers a *definite form of prayer*. If, however, as some think, there was only one occasion on which this was done, then St. Luke rather than St. Matthew gives the historic setting. (2) He devoted certain *parables* to the subject. (3) He uttered a variety of *sayings*, enforcing and completing the teaching of the parables.

(1) The LORD'S PRAYER is the subject of separate articles, to which the reader is referred.

(2). There are five *parables*, three of which bear directly and two indirectly on the subject of prayer. Two, both of them in St. Luke only, teach that prayer must be *importunate and perse-vering*. These are the Friend at Midnight (11^{5-8}), which follows the giving of the Lord's Prayer, and the Unjust Judge (18^{1-8}). So far as the two parables differ, the former teaches that prayer is never out of season, the latter that it is sure to bring a blessing and not a curse. But we must beware of supposing that either parable teaches that by constant prayer we at last overcome God's unwillingness. The argument in both parables is *a fortiori*, and is strongest in the second. ' If an unrighteous judge would yield to the importunity of an unknown widow, who came and spoke to him at intervals, much more will a righteous God be ready to reward the perseverance of His own elect, who cry to Him day and night.' God's desire to help is always present ; by perseverance in prayer we appropriate it. In the helpful illustration of the anchored ship, pointed out by Clement of Alexandria (*Strom.* iv. 23), the sailors who pull the rope seem to draw the anchor to the ship ; in reality they draw the ship to the anchor.

The parable of the Pharisee and the Publican, which also is preserved by St. Luke alone, and is placed by him immediately after that of the Unjust Judge, teaches the frame of mind in which God must be approached in prayer, viz. a *deep sense*, not only of need (as in the other two parables), but *of unworthiness*. Before Him we have no claim to merit, no ground for self-congratulation. The parable indicates that downcast eyes and beating of the breast are natural accompaniments of a penitent's prayer. Less directly, and apart from its main purpose, the parable of the Prodigal Son teaches a similar lesson. The lost son's prayer, as planned before his return and as actually uttered, is touching in its humility.

In both these cases, the Publican and the Prodigal, the chief thing prayed for is forgiveness, as must constantly be the case with sinful man. And there is yet another parable which teaches what is requisite, if this most necessary of all prayers is to be rightly offered : the sinner himself must have *a forgiving spirit*. The Unmerciful Servant (Mt 18^{21-35}) by asking for forgiveness for himself thereby bound himself to be forgiving to his fellows. His refusal to recognize this obligation became fatal to his own forgiveness. The great truth, that one who asks to be forgiven must be ready to forgive, had been clearly seen by the more spiritual among the Jews. There is a striking anticipation of Christ's teaching in Sir 28^{2-5}.

(3) Besides the parables, there are frequent *sayings* of Christ on the subject of prayer, and these are found in all four Gospels. The necessity of a forgiving spirit is repeated in Mt $6^{14.\ 15}$ and Mk 11^{25}, with obvious reference to the Lord's Prayer. Two other things are stated as necessary accompaniments of prayer : *watchfulness* (Mk 13^{33} 14^{38}, Mt 26^{41}) and *faith* (Mk 11^{24}, Mt 21^{22}). This last is specially emphasized, as being the test of reality and the condition of success. It is the result of the human will being brought into complete union with the will of God, producing absolute trust in the fulfilment of His promises. And we may be all the more sure of success in our prayers *if others join with us* in making them (Mt 18^{19}). Prayers which are approved by many are more likely to be right. Desires in which we cannot ask others to join are likely to be selfish.

And there are two things specially to be avoided : *parade* (Mt $6^{5.\ 6}$ 23^{14}, Mk 12^{40}, Lk 20^{47}) and *prating* (Mt 6^7). In the latter passage the 'vain repetitions' of AV and RV is apt to mislead. The 'bable' of Tindale and the Genevan is perhaps better. Repetition of prayers, even in the same form of words, is encouraged by our Lord, both by precept (Lk 18^{1-8}) and by example (Mt 26^{44}). It is the mechanical repetition of a formula (1 K 18^{26}), as if it were a magical charm, to compel the compliance of the Deity, that seems to be forbidden. Our petitions must have a worthy meaning, and we must think of the meaning.

Instruction is also given as to the *right objects of prayer*. We are to pray for spiritual progress (Lk 11^{13}) in ourselves, in others, and in the world at large. We are to pray that we ourselves may be delivered from temptation (Mt 6^{13} 26^{41}, Mk 14^{38}, Lk 11^4 $22^{40.\ 46}$), and that evil may be cast out from others (Mt 17^{21}, Mk 9^{29}), and that missionaries for the conversion of the world may be multiplied (Mt 9^{38}, Lk 10^2). In our intercessions our enemies are to be specially included (Mt 5^{44}, Lk 6^{28}). About temporal blessings we are not to be over anxious ; yet prayer for them is not merely allowed but enjoined (Mt 6^{11}, Lk 11^3) ; as also is prayer against temporal calamities (Mk 13^{18}, Mt 24^{20}). The prayer of the disciples for help in the storm was heard (Mt 8^{26}, Mk 4^{39}, Lk 8^{24}).

Parallels to some of the items of this teaching could be found in the OT. But there is one point with regard to the *method of prayer* which is absolutely new. Men had been taught to worship God and even to pray to Him as a Father ; now they are told to pray to the Father *in the name of the Son* (Jn 16²³·²⁴·²⁶). Anything that can be rightly asked in Christ's name will be granted (Jn 14¹³·¹⁴); and there is no other limit. Any request which is consistent with His character and office, as represented by His name, may be made to His Father, with confidence that the prayer will be heard (Jn 15⁷·¹⁶). The prayer of the sons of Zebedee for the right and left hand places in the Kingdom (Mt 20²¹, Mk 10³⁷) was not of this character, and was not commended. Nor, for the same reason, were they allowed to pray for a special judgment on the inhospitable Samaritans (Lk 9⁵⁴·⁵⁵). Both requests were made in spiritual ignorance. It confirms our trust in the historical fidelity of the Fourth Gospel, that this remarkable development in the teaching of Christ respecting prayer in His name occurs in the farewell discourses.

There is yet another particular which is absolutely new, viz. *worship offered to Christ Himself as to a Divine person* : and once more the clearest instances of this are in the Fourth Gospel. St. Matthew often, and St. Mark once, mention the fact that people 'worshipped' (προσεκύνησαν) Jesus. But even where this worship is accompanied by a request that He would cleanse a leper (Mt 8²) or raise the dead (Mt 9¹⁸), this act of prostration does not necessarily imply more than that He was regarded as a great prophet (1 K 18⁷, Dn 2⁴⁶). The worship of Him by the disciples after the Resurrection (Mt 28⁹·¹⁷, Lk 24⁵²) carries us further : yet it might be argued that this also is the worship of mere reverence. But about the meaning of the worship of the man born blind (Jn 9³⁸) there can be little doubt ; all the less so, because St. John always uses προσκυνέω of the worship of God (4²⁰⁻²⁴ 12²⁰), never of mere respect to great men ; and the use of the word in the Apocalypse is similar. Still less can there be any doubt as to the meaning of the adoring exclamation of the sceptical Apostle (Jn 20²⁸)—'the loftiest view of the Lord given in the Gospels' (Westcott), and the climax to which the scheme of St. John's Gospel steadily leads up. In none of these cases did Jesus reject the worship, or rebuke those who offered it to Him.

LITERATURE.—Works on the reasonableness and the efficacy of prayer abound, but they are outside the sphere of this article. Handbooks of Biblical Theology give little help. In Bible Dictionaries the art. on 'Prayer' in Hastings, iv. p. 42 ff., should be consulted ; also in Schaff-Herzog, iii. p. 1879, and in Herzog-Plitt, art. on 'Gebet,' some information will be found.

A. PLUMMER.

PREACHING.—In the Gospels three Gr. words are used for preaching, viz. κηρύσσω, 'proclaim as a herald,' with the corresponding substantive κήρυγμα ; καταγγέλλω, 'announce,' 'declare' ; εὐαγγελίζω, 'tell good tidings,' with the corresponding substantive εὐαγγέλιον, 'good tidings.' A fourth word, λαλέω, 'talk,' 'discourse,' is also rendered 'preach' in Mk 2² AV (as also in Ac 8²⁵ 11¹⁹ 13⁴² 14²⁵ 16⁶) ; but in RV this is rendered 'speak' ('he *spake* the word unto them'). In a general way it may be said that preaching, as the proclamation of a message, was distinguished from teaching (διδαχή), the explanation and vindication of truth. In some cases this distinction is marked. Thus John the Baptist was emphatically a preacher, he came to announce the coming of the Kingdom of God ; Jesus began where John left off by also preaching this message ; and the Twelve were sent out to preach (κηρύσσειν, Mk 3¹⁴, cf. Mt 10⁷, Lk 9²). The function of the Seventy was similar (Lk 10⁹). But in all but His earlier ministry our Lord was more occupied in what is expressly called 'teaching.' While John, and Jesus Himself at first, as well as His disciples throughout the Gospel period, only preached, announcing the message from heaven, it was reserved to our Lord to explain the great

truths of the gospel by teaching. The forerunner and the Apostles announced that the Kingdom was to come, without discussing its nature ; Jesus Christ went further, and laboured to show what this Divine Kingdom really was. So, while John was content to prepare for the Kingdom, with the assurance that it was 'at hand,' Jesus asked, 'Whereunto shall I liken the kingdom of God?' and proceeded to illustrate its characteristics. This was regarded as teaching. Further, while the preaching was for all who would hear, a public utterance designed to arrest attention, the teaching was more especially designed for disciples ; and while some of it was public, much of it was given in private. In the second year of our Lord's ministry, after the breach with the authorities and the defection of the multitude, there was less preaching and more teaching in the training of the Twelve.

This distinction cannot, however, be maintained throughout. Sometimes our Lord's most public utterances are described as 'teaching,' and are of the character of instruction (*e.g.* Mk 2¹³ 4¹·²). Moreover, teaching is blended with preaching. The difference is more carefully maintained in Mk. than in Mt. Thus Mk. states that Jesus came into Galilee *preaching* the Kingdom of God (Mk 1¹⁴)— the public open-air proclamation ; but that He went into a synagogue to *teach* (Mk 1²¹), where after the scripture had been read He would expound it (cf. Lk 4²⁰ff.). But in Mt. we have teaching and preaching both assigned to our Lord's work in the synagogues (Mt 4²³). We may infer from the earlier Gospel that Jesus did recognize the distinction between the two kinds of utterance, though probably one would often pass over into the other.

When we turn from verbal distinctions to the real differences, we may observe three methods followed by our Lord, according to circumstance and requirement : (1) The primitive proclamation, in making which He went on the lines laid down by John the Baptist ; (2) the public teaching of the laws and principles of the Kingdom of God, offered to all who would attend to it, whether in the open air or in the synagogues ; (3) the private training of His own disciples and discourse with inquirers. Both (1) and (2) come into our modern conception of Preaching, and we must understand the actual preaching of Jesus to comprehend them. See also the following article and art. TEACHING.

W. F. ADENEY.

PREACHING CHRIST.—The purpose of this article is to explain what is meant by 'preaching Christ.' It is assumed that to preach Christ is the preacher's function, and the intention is to show what such preaching involved in the beginning, and what it must include still if it is to be true to its original. Changing conditions may demand for it different forms, but presumably under all forms there will be a vital continuity or rather identity in the substance which is preached.

1. The NT as a whole presents Jesus in the character of *the Christ*. When the first preachers preached Him, it was in this character. 'God,' says Peter, 'hath made this same Jesus both Lord and Christ' (Ac 2³⁶). 'Saul confounded the Jews that dwelt in Damascus, proving that this is the Christ' (9²²). All the Evangelists agree with this : see Mt 1¹·¹⁸, Mk 1¹, Lk 2¹¹, Jn 20³¹. Now 'the Christ,' or 'the Messiah,' was not a meaningless expression for Jews : it had a distinct meaning, and a great range of ideas and hopes attached to it. There was a Messianic dogmatic, as it has been called, among the Jews, quite apart from the question who was to be the Messiah ; or, to put it otherwise, Jewish disciples had a Christology before they became believers in Jesus as the Christ. It is easy to see the dangers connected with this situation. If we take the sentence, 'Jesus is the Christ,' we may put the emphasis either on the subject or the predicate. We can conceive how a Jew, whose imagination was on flame with the apocalyptic hopes associated with the Messiah, might allow these hopes, when he accepted the Christian faith, to overpower the person of Jesus; Jesus, so to speak, would become nothing to him but the person through whom expectations were to be realized which in their origin had nothing to do with Jesus. There may be occasions in the NT where we have to ask whether something of this kind has not taken place, but they are not conspicuous. In the NT, when it is said that Jesus is the Christ, the emphasis is always as much on the subject as on the predicate. The proof of the proposition is always found in something which has been done by or to *Jesus*. In point of fact, it is found in the first instance in His resurrection and exaltation to God's right hand. It is this participation in the sovereignty of God that makes Him Lord and Christ; and the content of this, in all essentials, is not derived from the Messianic dogmatic of the Jewish schools, but from the experience of the Apostles themselves. This experience has two aspects, the one in the stricter sense historical, the other in the stricter sense spiritual. The one, put briefly, is, 'We have seen the Lord'; the other, 'He hath poured forth this—the new life at Pentecost—which ye see and hear' (Ac 2^{33}). The one is represented by the series of witnesses to the resurrection cited by St. Paul in 1 Co 15$^{5-9}$, the other by the series of new spiritual experiences and convictions to which he can appeal in 1 Co 15$^{12-19}$. It is the testimony of the Apostles to the resurrection of Jesus, and experience of the new life in His spirit, not any pre-Christian Christology, or Jewish Messianic dogmatic, that define for the first Christians the content of the title 'the Christ.' And it may safely be said, to begin with, that there is no such thing as preaching Christ unless it is the preaching of *One who lives and reigns*. If Jesus is at the right hand of God,—if He is behind every revival of spiritual life in the Church,—then He is the Christ, and can be preached as such; but if not, not.

2. At first, naturally, great stress was laid upon this. The Apostles sincerely believed that they had seen the Lord, and they could not conceive of their calling as having anything in it to take precedence of this—that they were witnesses of the resurrection, and therefore of the Messiahship of Jesus. No doubt this gave its whole character to primitive Christianity; but if we accept the testimony of the Apostles to the resurrection, we shall be slow to say that it transformed its character, and made it a new and essentially an inferior thing as compared with the religion of Jesus. Jesus was not forgotten when the Apostles, appealing to the resurrection and to Pentecost, argued that He was the Christ, God's King, through whom all the hopes which God had inspired were to be fulfilled. Harnack, indeed, has argued that in its eagerness to prove that Jesus is the Christ—that is, to discharge a task in apologetic theology—the Church spent too much of the force which ought to have been given to teaching men to observe all things whatsoever He had commanded (*Dogmengesch.*[1] i. 57 f.). But there is no necessary antagonism between the two things, and except for their faith in His exaltation as the Christ the Apostles would never have taught anything at all. Weinel (*Paulus*, 108 f.) represents the same tendency in a much less guarded form. 'After the death of Jesus,' he says, 'the ethical religion of redemption, which had entered the world with

Jesus, underwent its most decisive transformation of a formal kind; it ceased to be the religion of sonship to God, and became faith in the Christ-nature of the man Jesus. . . . The disciples demanded faith in Him as the Messiah exalted to God, and in the conception of His death as an atonement appointed by God for sins. With the experience of the resurrection and with this dogma of the death of the Messiah, the Christ-religion, Christianity in the narrower sense, begins.' One almost wonders if Weinel thinks it a pity that Jesus rose from the dead, or that His disciples believed that He did, and were overpoweringly influenced by a faith so tremendous; but this apart, the assumption in all criticism of this sort is that when the Apostles preached Jesus as the Christ they concentrated all their attention on the predicate of the proposition, which owed no part of its import to Jesus, and treated the subject as if it had no meaning. Even on *a priori* grounds we should say this was improbable, and there is a very significant piece of evidence that it is not true. This is found in the qualifications of the man appointed to take the place of Judas. His function was to be a witness to the resurrection—that is, to the Messiahship of Jesus; he was, in other words, to be a preacher of the Christ. But he was chosen from 'the men that have companied with us all the time that the Lord Jesus went in and went out among us, beginning from the baptism of John unto the day that he was received up from us' (Ac 1$^{21f.}$). To preach Christ, even in the days when belief in the resurrection was so overpowering, one required to have a full knowledge of Jesus. It is idle to say that Jesus is the Christ if we do not know who or what Jesus is. It has no meaning to say that an unknown person is at God's right hand, exalted and sovereign; the more ardently men believed that God had given them a Prince and a Saviour in this exaltation, the more eager would they be to know all that could possibly be learned about Him. If there were men alive who had lived in His company, they would wait assiduously on their teaching (2^{42}). They would be more than curious to know what spirit He was of, and whether they could detect in His appearance and career on earth 'the works of the Christ' (Mt 11^2). They would expect to find some kind of moral congruity between His life on the one hand, and His transcendent dignity and calling on the other; there would be a demand, from the very beginning, for facts about Him. From this point of view, then, we may say that preaching Christ is not taking leave of Jesus in any sense or to any extent; it is preaching Jesus exalted and sovereign.

The passage just quoted (Ac 1$^{21f.}$) is practically coterminous with the oldest form of Gospel which we possess. 'Beginning from the baptism of John unto the day that he was taken up': these are the limits within which lies the Gospel according to Mark. Hence we might say that to preach this gospel is to preach Christ, on condition, of course, that it is preached in its connexion with Jesus exalted. Merely to narrate the history of Jesus, even if we had the materials for it, would not be to preach Christ. We need, of course, to know the historical Jesus, as the qualifications for Apostleship show; but to preach Christ means to preach that Person as present in the sovereignty of His resurrection. It is not preaching Christ if we tell the story of the life and death merely as events in a past continually growing more remote. It is not preaching Christ though we tell this story in the most vivid and moving fashion, and gather round it, by the exercise of historical imagination or dramatic skill, the liveliest emotions; it is not preaching Christ to present the life and death of

Jesus as a high and solemn tragedy, with power in it to purify the soul by pity and terror. There is no preaching of Christ, possessed of religious significance, that does not rest on the basis on which the Apostolic preaching rested : His exaltation in power, and therefore His perpetual presence. The historical Jesus is indispensable ; but if we are to have a Christian religion, the historical must become present and eternal. This it does through the resurrection as apprehended by faith.

3. For the purposes of this article it is assumed that the Synoptic Gospels give such a knowledge of the historical Jesus as is sufficient for the preacher's ends. No doubt He is depicted for us there by writers who believed in Him as the Christ, and for whom the light of His exaltation was reflected on the lowliness of His earthly career ; but this light is not necessarily a distorting one. We have no reason to say that there is anything in these Gospels which is untrue to the historical personality of Jesus, anything which represents Him in mind, in will, in temper, in character, in His consciousness as a whole of His relations to God and man, as other than He really was. Extravagant things have been said by many writers of *Lives of Jesus*, from Strauss downwards, on the imperfection of our knowledge, and on the way in which the real Jesus has been disguised from the very beginning by the idealization of His figure in the faith and love of those who preached Him—and especially in the Gospels. If we concentrate our attention on the character of Jesus, on the spirit of His words and deeds and death, on His consciousness of His relations to God and men—in a word, on what He was and achieved in the spiritual world—it is the present writer's conviction that we shall feel the very reverse of this to be the truth. We may be dubious about this or that word, this or that incident in the Gospels, but we have no dubiety at all about the Person. The great life that stands out before us in the Gospels is more real than anything in the world ; and Jesus is so far from being hidden from us that it is no exaggeration to say that we know Him better than anybody who has ever lived on earth.

It does not follow from this that we accept the Evangelists' proofs that Jesus was the Christ, or that in preaching Christ we employ the same arguments as they to show that Jesus has the unique significance for religion which was represented for them by the Messianic title. Broadly speaking, these arguments were two—one from prophecy and one from miracles. Both may be accepted in principle without being accepted in form. The argument from prophecy is an assertion of the continuity of revelation, of the one purpose of God running through it all, and culminating in Jesus. Jesus is the fulfilment of all the hopes contained in the ancient revelation, and we look for no other : 'How many soever are the promises of God, in him is the yea' (2 Co 1²⁰) ; we recognize this, and the absolute significance which it secures for Jesus in religion. But we no longer prove it to ourselves by emphasizing, in the manner of the First Gospel, particular correspondences between incidents in the life of Jesus and passages in the OT. There is no religious and no intellectual value for us in such fulfilments of prophecy as Mt 2¹⁵. ¹⁸. ²³. We should apply the Pauline principle (2 Co 1²⁰) quite differently, recognizing that correspondence is one thing, fulfilment another. Jesus did not really come to fulfil prophecy in the sense of carrying out a programme the details of which were fixed beforehand ; He came to fulfil Himself, or to fulfil the will of the Father, as the Father made it plain to Him from step to step ; and though, on one occasion (Mk 11¹⁻¹⁰), He Himself arranged an incident in which a literal correspondence with a prophecy

was secured, it is not such a phenomenon which makes Him the Christ to us. Its value now lies in showing that He regarded Himself as the Christ, the promised King. And so with the argument from miracles, which, though not formally put, is perhaps as characteristic of the Second Gospel as the argument from prophecy is of the First. The works of Jesus, in the largest sense,—all that He did and the power which it implied,—go to give Him the importance He has in our minds. But we do not limit His works to the class commonly called miraculous ; the impression left on the minds of men by His whole being and action gathers up into itself much more than this. The arguments from prophecy and from miracles are formal ways of expressing truths which really contain much more than these forms can carry ; and our impression of the truths is too direct, immediate, and complex to have justice done it by such arguments.

4. While, however, the inadequacy of such arguments to their purpose must be admitted, the purpose of the arguments is not to be overlooked. What those who first called Jesus the Christ, or preached Him as such, intended to do, was to put Him in a place which no other could share. Whatever else the name meant, it meant the King ; and there was only one King. In the Christian religion Jesus was never one of a series, a person who could be classified, and be shown to His proper place in the line of great personalities who have contributed to the spiritual uplifting of the race. The study of Comparative Religion has fostered a tendency to regard Him in this light ; but it cannot be said too strongly that to admit the legitimacy of such a tendency is to abandon from the very root all that has ever been known to history as Christianity. The NT is quite unequivocal about this. From the beginning Christians call Jesus 'Lord' (1 Co 12³), and recognize that God has given Him the name which is above every name (Ph 2⁹). All other men in the NT meet as equals on the same level, and all bow before Him as King. In His exaltation He confronts men as one Divine causality with the Father, working for their salvation. Historical Christianity, said Emerson (*Works*, Bell's ed. ii. 195), has dwelt and dwells with noxious exaggeration about the *person* of Jesus. As a criticism of some kinds of interest in dogmatic Christology, this may be true ; but if it is meant to reflect on the devotion of Christians to Jesus as a Person, it is completely beside the mark. To Christians this Person has been from the beginning, and will be for ever, what no other can be. To talk of Him as the same in kind with other prophets or founders of religions,—with Moses and Isaiah, with Confucius or Buddha, or, what is even harder to understand, with Mohammed,—is to surrender anything that a NT Christian could have recognized as Christianity. To preach Christ at all we must preach Him as κύριος and μονογενής. The first name secures His unshared place in relation to men, as the latter does in relation to God ; and unless He fills such a place, Christianity has no *raison d'être*. That it has is the assumption of this article, as it is the fact presented in the NT. It is, in fact, the *differentia* of Christianity as a religion that the distinction which can sometimes be drawn between a person and the cause for which he stands is in it no longer valid. To preach what Jesus preached is not preaching Christianity unless the thing preached is preached in its essential relation to Him. The truth which He announces is not independent of Himself ; it is in the world only as it is incarnate in *Him*. Thus, to take as an example what many regard as the supreme category in the teaching of Jesus—the Kingdom of God : what is meant by preaching Christ here ? It is very likely impossible for us to understand precisely what the expression 'Kingdom of God' conveyed in the mental atmosphere of Judaism or of the 1st cent. generally. It may be impossible for us even to understand with certainty and precision what Jesus Himself on any given occasion meant it to convey. All shades of meaning run through it,—political, eschatological, spiritual; national, universal; here, coming: how can anyone tell whether in preaching the Kingdom of God he is preaching Christ? The answer is clear if we remember that the Kingdom of God in His sense could come only in and through Him, and that its character is ultimately determined by that fact. He Himself, in the sense at least of being God's representative, is King in it (Mt 13^{41} 20^{21} 25^{34}, Lk 23^{42}), and it is from what we know of Him, including ultimately His resurrection and exaltation, that all our conceptions of the Kingdom must be derived. To preach the cause and ignore the Person, or to preach the cause as of universal import and to assign to the Person an importance in relation to it which He only shares with an indefinite number of others, is to be untrue to the facts as the Gospels present them. Even preaching the Kingdom of God is not preaching Christ unless the Kingdom is preached as one which owes its character to the fact that Jesus is its King, and the certainty of its consummation to the fact that Jesus shares the throne of God. Christianity is not abstract optimism; it is optimism based on the exaltation of Jesus, and on the knowledge of God as revealed in Him.

5. If we bring these ideas to a point, we shall say that to preach Christ means to preach Jesus in the absolute significance for God and man which He had to His own consciousness and to the faith of the first witnesses; and to preach Him as exalted, and as having this absolute significance now and for ever. The question then arises, In what forms did Jesus Himself present this absolute significance to His own mind? How did He conceive it, and body it forth to others, so as to make an adequate impression on them? And are the forms of thought and of imagination which He employed for this purpose in a given historical environment as indispensable to us, and as binding in our totally different environment, as they were for those with whom Jesus stood face to face? To preach Christ it is necessary to be able to answer these questions not at haphazard, but on principle; and the answer may sometimes seem difficult.

To proceed by illustration: (*a*) One of the ways in which Jesus represented His absolute significance for the true religion was this: He regarded Himself as the Messiah. The Messianic rôle was one which could be filled only by one Person, and He Himself was the Person in question; He and no other was the Christ. But is 'the Christ' a conception of which we, in another age and with other antecedents, can make use for the same purpose? Only, it must be answered, if we employ the term with much latitude. What it suggests to us, as already pointed out, is the continuity of revelation, and the fulfilment through Jesus of all the hopes which, through history and prophecy, God had kindled in human hearts; it is the possibility of using it to express this that justifies us in retaining the name. But it is certain that for those who first came to believe in Jesus as the Christ the name was much more definite than it is for us; it had a shape and colour that it has no longer; it had expectations connected with it which for us have lost the vitality they once possessed. In particular, the eschatological associations of the term have not, in their NT form, the importance for us which they had for the first believers. In the teaching of Jesus these associations cluster round the title 'the Son of Man,' which, at least after the

confession of Peter at Cæsarea Philippi, is used as synonymous with 'the Christ'; the Son of Man is identified with Jesus, and comes again, after His suffering and death, to establish the Kingdom, in the glory of His Father with the holy angels (Mk $8^{31.\ 38}$, Mt 10^{33} 16^{27}). This coming again, or, as the original disciples conceived it, this coming (παρουσία) in the character of the Christ, was expected, by those who first preached and received the gospel, to take place in their own generation; and it is difficult to argue that this expectation could have any other basis than the teaching of Jesus Himself. Nothing was more characteristic of primitive Christianity; it was the very essence of what the early Church meant by *hope*; it was for it part of the very meaning of 'the Christ.' Account has been taken, in art. AUTHORITY OF CHRIST (vol. i. p. 149), of any considerations which go to qualify the certainty with which we ascribe to Jesus Himself this eschatological conception of the consummation of God's Kingdom, and especially this conviction as to its imminence; but if we do connect it with Him, and regard it as part of what is meant when He represents Himself as the Christ, clearly history requires us to recognize the inadequacy of that conception to be the vehicle of the truth. The Kingdom of God has been coming ever since Jesus left the world; but Jesus Himself, after nearly two thousand years, has not yet come in like manner as the disciples saw Him going into heaven (Ac 1^{11}). We still believe that the Kingdom of God is coming; we believe this because we believe in Jesus; we believe that it is coming only through Him and as He comes; that is what the Christian of to-day means when he says we believe in Him as the Christ. But even the belief in His exaltation to God's right hand does not make possible for us that particular kind of expectation of His coming which burnt with so intense a flame in the breast of the Apostolic Church; quite apart from any preference or effort, our outlook on the future is different from theirs; and, while we do not abate in the least our recognition of the sole sovereignty of Jesus, and our assurance that God's Kingdom can come and God's promises be fulfilled through Him alone, we are compelled, apparently, to recognize that in infusing into the disciples His own assurance of the final triumph of God's cause in His own person, our Lord had to make use of representations which have turned out unequal to the truth. He had to put His sense of the absolute significance of His Person for God and man into a form which was relative to the mind of the time. The eschatological Christ, coming on the clouds of heaven, and coming in the lifetime of some who heard His voice, was one expression for Jesus of this absolute significance; and it is as such an expression—that is, as an assurance of the speedy triumph of God's cause in and through Him, and not in its spectacular detail—that we believe in it. It is not rejecting the absolute significance of Jesus to say that this spectacular detail is relative to the age and its mental outlook; but it would be a rejection of it, and a repudiation of Jesus as the Christ, if we denied that the Kingdom of God—however experience enables us to picture its coming and consummation—comes and is consummated through Him alone. This truth must be preached if we really preach Christ.

(*b*) Jesus, however, has other ways of conveying His absolute significance. One of the simplest is that in which He represents Himself as judge of men, arbiter of their eternal destinies. It may be argued, no doubt, that the form in which this is expressed in Mt $7^{21ff.}$ $25^{31ff.}$ is, in part at least, due to the Evangelist; 'prophesying in the name of Jesus' was a phenomenon which came into the world only after His death, and such an allusion to it as Mt 7²², where it is treated as an obvious thing, would hardly have been intelligible in His lifetime. But there is no reason whatever to doubt that both this passage and the other convey the mind of Jesus about His own significance for men. Whatever be the rule of the judgment—doing the will of *His Father* (Mt 7²¹), or humanity exhibited in practice in relation to those whom He calls *His brethren* (Mt 25⁴⁰)—it is a rule which has been finally embodied in Him. It is in Him that we see what doing the will of the Father means; it is in Him also that we see the law of humanity fulfilled. It is what we are when measured by His standard, judged by His judgment, that discloses the very truth about us. It has been urged that this prerogative of judgment is merely an element in the Jewish conception of the Messiah, and as such has been formally transferred to Jesus in the Gospels; but nothing is less formal in the NT than the conception of Jesus as judge. It does not rest on any borrowings from a pre-Christian Messianic dogmatic, but on the most real experiences of men in the presence of Jesus: 'Depart from me, for I am a sinful man, O Lord' (Lk 5⁸); 'Come, see a man who told me all things that ever I did' (Jn 4²⁹). The experiences by which words like these were inspired give reality and solemnity to all the representations of Jesus as judge. Here again we may say that the spectacular representations of the judgment are a form which we may recognize to have only a relative value, while yet we do not dispute in the least the absolute truth that the standard of reality and of worth in the spiritual world is Jesus, and that no life can be finally estimated except by its relation to Him. The Gospel according to John is distinguished from the others by emphasizing the function of Christ as judge, and the continuous exercise of it in what might almost be called an automatic fashion. The Father has committed all judgment to the Son (Jn 5²³); and the process of judging goes on in the Gospel under our eyes. The very presence of Jesus sifts men; they gather round Him or are repelled from Him according to what they are. Something of absolute and final significance, it may be said, is transacted before our faces, as men show that they will or will not have anything to do with Jesus. It is eternal judgment revealed in the field of time, and Jesus is the judge. No one else could fill His place in this character, and we do not preach Christ as He was and is except by making this plain. Probably, however, in this case more than in any other it is rash to discount too cheaply what we think, rightly enough in principle, are but forms of conveying this truth, and forms unequal to the reality. The picture of the Last Judgment in Mt 25³¹⁻⁴⁶ may not be true as a picture, the moral reality of the judgment may not be dependent at all on the scenic details here presented, but whether or not it is true as a picture, it is true in the moral impression it leaves on the mind, and this is the truth that is important. There is such a thing, if there is any truth in Christ at all, as final judgment; there is a right hand of the judge and a left, an inside of the door and an outside, a character that abides for ever and a character that collapses in irreparable ruin; and to realize of what kind character is, or where it must stand at last, we have only to confront it with Him. The man who cannot withstand the attraction of Jesus does not come into judgment, he has passed from death into life (Jn 5²⁴); the man who will not yield to the attraction of Jesus is judged already (3¹⁸), and the judgment will be revealed at last. To recognize and proclaim the absolute significance of Jesus here is an essential part of preaching Christ.

(*c*) The supreme illustration of this incomparable significance of Jesus remains. It is given in what we may call *His consciousness of His relation to God*. To Jesus, God was the Father, and He Himself was the Son. It does not matter that God is a universal Father, and that all men are or are called to be His sons; Jesus recognizes this, and insists upon it, but He claims Sonship in a peculiar sense for Himself. He never speaks of Himself as *a* child of God, but as *the* Son, *simpliciter*. In speaking of God and Himself He uses ὁ πατήρ and ὁ υἱός in a way which implies that there could no more be a plural on the one side than on the other: see esp. Mt 11²⁷ᶠ·, Mk 13³². It is natural to suppose that in the account of Jesus' baptism (Mt 3¹⁷ ||) the heavenly voice which pronounces Him Son of God, in words borrowed from Ps 2, means the term there to be taken in the Messianic 'official' sense; it is the Messianic consciousness of Jesus, as the accompanying narrative of the Temptation proves, which is expressed in ὁ υἱός μου. What the relation may have been in His mind between this (which defines His calling by relation to OT hopes) and the Divine Sonship exhibited in Mt 11²⁷, we may not be able to tell. It has been argued by some that the official Messianic Sonship, the calling to be God's King in Israel, widened and deepened in the mind of Jesus Himself into the consciousness of a unique relation to God, which found its most adequate expression in the language of Mt 11²⁷; by others, that only such a consciousness as is disclosed in Mt 11²⁷ enables us to understand how Jesus could ever have regarded Himself as the Messiah. The Messianic categories have been considered above; what we have here to do is to look at the less specifically Jewish way in which Jesus here reveals His absolute significance for religion. 'All things have been delivered to me by my Father: and no one knoweth the Son, save the Father; neither knoweth any one the Father, save the Son, and he to whomsoever the Son willeth to reveal him' (see AUTHORITY OF CHRIST, vol. i. p. 149). Here Jesus claims in the most explicit terms to have had the whole task of revealing God to men—the whole task of saving men, so far as that depends upon their coming to know God—committed to Him.* It is a task to which He is equal, and for which no other has any competence at all. Everything connected with it has been entrusted to Him, and to Him alone; there is not a man upon the earth who can know the Father except by becoming a debtor to Jesus. There is no such thing as preaching Christ unless we preach this: He is the mediator for all men of the knowledge of God as Father; that is, of that knowledge of God on which eternal life depends. This is the loftiest, the most universal, and the most gracious form in which the absolute significance of Jesus can be expressed: the loftiest, because it declares Him unequivocally to be the μονογενής, having His being in a relation to God constituted by perfect mutual understanding, and belonging to Him alone; the most universal, because the relation of Father and Son, while it can only be symbolic of the reality, uses a symbolism based on nature, not on history, and is therefore intelligible to all men, and not only (like Messiah) to one race; and the most gracious, for it suggests directly not only mutual understanding but mutual love, the love which unites the Father and the Son in the work of enlightening and redeeming men (cf. Mt 11²⁸ᶠ·). It is not necessary, however, to dwell on this: the point is that in this central passage Jesus emphasizes His absolute significance in the two main directions in which it can be understood: He is to God what no other is, and He can therefore do for

* It is fanciful, on account of παρεδόθη, to suppose that Jesus is here contrasting His παράδοσις, which has its starting-point in the Father, with the 'traditions' of the elders.

man what no other can do. He is the only-begotten Son, and the only Mediator between God and man. In preaching Christ in this sense, we have much more to go upon than this single utterance. The truth which it conveys, indeed, is not so much a truth revealed by Christ, as the truth which is embodied in Him; in order to appreciate it, it is necessary to have the experience of coming through Him to the Father, and of recognizing the Father in the Son. The interest of the Fourth Gospel consists to a large extent in this—that it is an expansion and illustration of these words. Jesus is presented there as the Word made flesh—the principle of revelation embodied in a human life; it is His work, so to speak, to enlighten every man, and apart from His work men remain in darkness. 'No man hath seen God at any time: the only-begotten Son, who is in the bosom of the Father, he hath declared—or interpreted (ἐξηγήσατο)—him' (Jn 1[18]); 'He that hath seen me hath seen the Father' (14[9]); 'I am the way and the truth and the life: no one cometh to the Father but through me' (14[6]). This is the key to the peculiar passages in the Gospel in which Jesus says ἐγώ εἰμι without any expressed predicate (4[26]? 8[24. 28] 13[19]): we are meant to think of Him as the great decisive Personality, who stands in a place which is His alone, and by relation to whom all men finally stand or fall. It may be that the expression given to this in the Fourth Gospel owes something to the writer as well as to Jesus; but what the writer expresses is at least the impression made on him by Jesus, and, as Mt 11[27] and Mk 13[32] show, the impression is one which answers exactly to Jesus' consciousness of Himself. The words quoted above from Jn. only do justice to Jesus' sense of what He was in relation to God and man, and it is not possible to preach Christ in any adequate sense if we ignore or deny the truth they convey. To do so would be to reject both what Jesus said and what He was in the experience of those who first believed on Him.

6. With the rest of the NT in mind, the question is naturally raised at this point, whether Jesus gave any further definition to the idea of mediation than that which we find in this passage. All men owe to Him the knowledge of God as Father, but how does He impart it? All men must become His debtors if they are to have the benefit of this supreme revelation: is there anything which more than another enables us to estimate the dimensions of this debt? If there is, then in preaching Christ that thing would require to have a corresponding prominence. It is obvious that Jesus mediates the knowledge of God to men, not by His words only, but, as is shown elsewhere (AUTHORITY OF CHRIST, vol. i. p. 149), by His being and life as well. It is the Son in whom the Father is revealed, and everything in the Son contributes to the revelation: His teaching, His works, His intercourse with others, His sufferings and death. The revelation is made in and through all these, and none of them can be omitted in preaching Christ. To borrow words of Wellhausen which are not without a misleading element (*Einleitung in die drei ersten Evangelien*, p. 114): 'His religion is found not only in what He taught publicly, but in His nature and bearing under all circumstances, at home and on the street, in what He said and did not say, in what He did consciously or without being conscious of it, in the way in which He ate and drank and rejoiced and suffered. His Person, with which they had the privilege of intercourse in daily life, made an even deeper impression on His disciples than His teaching.' All this is true, but not the whole truth. The NT in all its parts lays a quite peculiar emphasis on the death of Christ, and in doing so it is not false

to His own conception of the way in which He mediated the knowledge of the Father to men. His death, it may be said, does not require to be interpreted otherwise than His life; it is His life carried to a consistent consummation under the circumstances of the time; it is part of His life, not something distinct from it. This also is true, but, according to the representation in the Gospels, it is less than the whole truth. His death is a part of His life which has an essential relation to His work as the revealer of the Father, and the King in the Kingdom of God; it was recognized by Jesus Himself as Divinely necessary, it was the subject of frequent instruction to His disciples, and it is commemorated by His will in the most solemn rite of Christian worship (see Mk 8[31] 9[31] 10[33] 10[45] 14[24] and ‖). It is a fair inference from this, combined with the place taken by the Passion in the Evangelic narratives, and the place given to the interpretation of Christ's death in the Epistles, that to preach Christ it is necessary to represent His death as a main part, or rather as *the* main part, of the cost at which His work of mediation is done. In what particular way it is to be construed is an ulterior question. Our general conception of the moral order of the world, our sense of individuality and of the solidarity of the race, our apprehension of sin as generic, or constitutional, or voluntary, the mental equipment with which we approach the whole subject, may determine us to interpret it in ways which are intellectually distinguishable; no given explanation of the death of Jesus can claim finality any more than any given interpretation of His Person. But just as we may say that Christ is not preached unless the Person of Christ is presented in its absolute significance for religion, as the one Person through whom the knowledge of the Father is mediated to men, so we may say further that Christ is not preached in the sense which answers to His own consciousness of what He was doing, unless it is made clear and central that His mediation necessitated and therefore cost His death. In the simplest words, it is necessary to say, in preaching Christ, not only that He is μονογενής and Mediator, but that He died for men. It was not for Him to insist on this as a doctrine; it was for the Church to apprehend it as a fact, and to put it into doxologies (Rev 1[5] 5[9]); but in doing so, it could go back to unmistakable words of Jesus Himself, and to the sacrament which speaks for Him more impressively than any words.

7. Jesus' consciousness of Himself, which, however hard it may be for us to apprehend it, has certainly the character just described—in other words, is a consciousness of His absolute and incomparable significance for all the relations of God and man—must lie at the heart of all preaching of which He is the object. He had this significance while He moved among men on the earth, and it was declared and made unmistakable to His disciples when He rose from the dead. It is on Jesus' consciousness of Himself, therefore, including His consciousness of His vocation, and on His exaltation to God's right hand, that the preaching of Christ rests. As has already been remarked (see **§ 3**), the writer of this article assumes that in the Synoptic Gospels we have a representation given of the consciousness of Jesus, on the truth of which we can quite securely proceed. No doubt this has been questioned, most recently and radically by Wellhausen. The Gospels (to put it concisely) were written by Christians, and Jesus was not a Christian. They contain the gospel, that is, the Christian religion; but He knew nothing about the gospel, although it is put into His lips. He was a Jew. He preached no new faith. He taught men to do the will of God, which like all Jews He found in the Law and the other sacred books. The only difference was that He knew a better way of doing the will of God than that which the scribes of His day enforced on the people, and that He called men to leave their traditions and learn of Him. Wellhausen not only removes from the mind of Christ in this way everything that in Christian preaching has ever been known as gospel, everything that could by any possibility be regarded as contributing to Christology and Soteriology, but the great mass of what up till now has been regarded by criticism as the best attested part of the Evangelic record, the words of Jesus common to Matthew and Luke. Most of the parables, too, are sacrificed. Even the few in Mark are not all genuine, and Wellhausen feels free to pass severe strictures alike on those of Matthew and of Luke. All that need be said of this is, that if Jesus had been no more than Wellhausen represents Him to be, then it is inconceivable that either the Gospels or the gospel could ever have been generated from any impulse He could impart to human minds. As Jülicher puts it (*Theol. Literaturztg.* 1905, No. 23), the primitive Church is thus made to appear richer, greater, and freer than its Head : in Jerusalem it surpasses Him by producing the marvellous Evangelic history, in St. Paul it surpasses Him by producing a new imposing theory of redemption. The historian looks in vain for anything analogous to this elsewhere. We do not understand how it could be done. We do not understand how the Church so suddenly lost the power of doing it. We do not understand how a man like St. Paul, we may say how men like those who wrote all the NT books except the Gospels, should have been so incapable of writing a page which reminds us of them. Although it is true to say that truth guarantees only itself, not its author, the truths exhibited by the Evangelists have a way of coalescing into a sum of truth which is identical with Jesus. As Deissmann has expressed it,* they are not separate pearls threaded on a string, but flashes of the same diamond. Separately they guarantee themselves, but collectively they are a spiritual evidence to the historical reality of the great Person to whom the gospel owes its being, and to whom all preaching is a testimony. There is a kind of criticism which tacitly assumes that it is a mistake to believe in Christ as those who first preached Him believed ; He was a Person who appeared in history, and therefore cannot have the absolute significance which must attach to the object of religious faith, and which does attach to Jesus throughout the NT. Such criticism makes it its business to reduce this figure to a true scale —which means to make His personality exactly like our own, and His consciousness exactly what our own may be. Wellhausen illustrates the direct application of this criticism to the Gospels ; we see how it is brought to bear on the Epistles in such a remark as Wernle's, that a faith in Christ like that of St. Paul (which as good as deified its object) implies a certain want of faith in the living God. The consciousness of God must have decayed or lost its vital intensity in the Apostle before he could write the Epistle to the Colossians. Such a writing, we are almost invited to think, is on the way to justify the Jewish sneer : the creed of Christians is that there is no God, but that Jesus is His Son. In the face of criticism of this type, we hold with confidence the trustworthiness of the Evangelic representation, and venture to say that no NT writer, not even St. Paul or St. John, has anything to say of the absolute significance of Jesus, in all the relations of God and man, which goes beyond Jesus' consciousness of Himself as

* 'Evangelium u. Urchristentum' in *Beiträge zur Weiterentwickelung der christlichen Religion*, p. 85.

the Gospels preserve it. And, further, we venture to say that no NT writing, however casual or informal, falls short of the testimony which Jesus, according to the Evangelists, bears to Himself. Everywhere Jesus has the place which He claims for Himself, and Christians are conscious of an absolute dependence on Him for their standing towards God. To give Him this place is the only way to preach Christ.

8. The earliest specimens of Apostolic preaching are the sermons of St. Peter in Acts. Their value is universally acknowledged. According to Schmiedel (*Encyc. Bibl.* i. 48), 'almost the only element that is historically important (in the early chapters of Acts) is the Christology of the speeches of Peter. This, however, is important in the highest degree. . . . It is hardly possible not to believe that this Christology of the speeches of Peter must have come from a primitive source.' It starts with the historical person as such : 'Jesus of Nazareth, a man approved of God to you by miracles and portents and signs which God wrought through him, as you yourselves know' (Ac 2^{22}). This approbation of Jesus by His wonderful works might seem confuted by His death, but to this the Apostle has a twofold answer. On the one hand, the death itself was Divinely necessary ; He was delivered up by the determinate counsel and foreknowledge of God, evidence of which was found in the Scriptures (Ac 2^{23}, cf. 1 Co 15^4). On the other hand, it was annulled by the resurrection of Jesus and His exaltation to God's right hand. It was this that made Him both Lord and Christ, and in this character He determined for the Apostles and for all men their whole relation to God. To Him they owed already the gift of the Holy Ghost ; and, as St. Peter explicitly states elsewhere (Ac $11^{15.\ 17}$ 15^8), to receive the Holy Ghost is to be religiously complete. To His coming they looked for times of refreshing, indeed for the 'times of the restoration of all things, whereof God spake by the mouth of his holy prophets that have been from of old' (3^{21}). All prophecy, to put it otherwise, is conceived as Messianic ; all the hopes which God has inspired are hopes to be fulfilled through Christ. He is Prince of life (3^{15}), Lord of all (10^{36}), ordained of God as Judge of living and dead (10^{42}). Those who repent, believe, and are baptized in His name receive remission of sins and the gift of the Holy Ghost (2^{38} 10^{43}). All these expressions imply that from the very beginning Jesus had for His disciples that absolute significance which we have seen belonged to His own consciousness of Himself ; but in addition to this, it is put with singular force in a passage which expresses nothing else : 'There is not salvation in any other : for there is no other name under heaven given among men, whereby we must be saved' (4^{12}). It may be possible to strip from the gospel of St. Peter, without detriment to its essence, some of that vesture of eschatological Messianism which it necessarily wore at the time ; but it is not possible that religion should be to us what it was to him,—it is not possible, in the original sense of the words, to preach Christ— unless we give to Christ that same significance in all the relations of God and man which He has in St. Peter's preaching. It is not too much to say that side by side with his frank recognition of Jesus as a man (2^{22}), whose career in history he could himself look back upon, St. Peter regarded Jesus in His exaltation as forming with God His Father one Divine causality at work for the salvation of men. It was only in virtue of so regarding Him that he could preach Him as he did, and essentially similar convictions are still necessary if preaching is to be called preaching *Christ*. It is not necessary to argue that the Christology of the

First Epistle of Peter is on a level with this. In many respects it is more explicit. There has been more reflexion on the absolute significance of Jesus in religion, on His relation to the OT, on the power of His resurrection, on the virtue of His Passion as connected with redemption from sin, and on the example set in His life and death. But two passages may be briefly referred to as going to the root of the matter. The first is 1²¹, where Christians are described as 'you who through him [Jesus] are believers in God.' It is to Him that Christian faith owes its peculiar qualities and virtues : men may be theists apart from Him, but to have specifically Christian faith in God we must be His debtors. The other is the longer passage, so much discussed, 3¹⁸⁻⁴⁶. Whatever else this passage reveals, it reveals the writer's conviction that for the dead as well as the living there is no hope of salvation but Christ. Not only in this world, but in all worlds, whatever is called redemption owes its being to Him. All spiritual beings, angels, principalities, and powers, are subject to Him. The Christian is a person who is in Him (5¹⁴), and accordingly by Him everything in the Christian life is determined. To give Christ this place in our spiritual world, though a different mode of conceiving the world of the spirit may modify the intellectual form in which we do so, is indispensable to preaching Christ. Apart from His holding such a place it is possible only to preach *about* Him, not to make *Him* the sum of our preaching.

9. To pass from St. Peter to St. Paul is to pass from one who had the most vivid personal recollections of the Man Christ Jesus to one who had no such recollections at all ; and it is all the more striking to find that both of them preach Christ in the same sense ; or, perhaps, we should say, mean the same thing by preaching Christ. St. Paul's acquaintance with Christ began when the Lord appeared to him on the way to Damascus, and for him Jesus is predominantly the Lord of Glory (1 Co 2⁸). When he preaches Him it is as Lord (2 Co 4⁵) ; that is, as exalted at God's right hand. To call Him 'Lord,' to acknowledge His exaltation, is to make the fundamental Christian confession (1 Co 12³, Ro 10⁹). It is often asserted that whatever differences may have existed between St. Paul and the Jerusalem Church, there can have been no difference of a Christological character ; but it is not vital to Christianity that this should be so. It is just as plausible to argue from 2 Co 1¹⁹ that the Corinthians had heard preachers who did not preach Christ precisely as Paul and Silvanus and Timothy did ; and the argument might be supported by reference to 2 Co 5¹⁶ 11⁴. Further, the fact that St. Paul has something which he calls 'my gospel,' a conception of Christianity and a mode of presenting it which had peculiarities due to the peculiarity of his religious experience, might be adduced on the same side. And the presumption thus raised could not be overturned simply by an appeal to 1 Co 15⁴· ¹¹, which would prove only that his gospel rested, exactly as did that of the Twelve, on the great facts of the death and resurrection of Jesus interpreted in the light of Scripture. What it is important to see is that, be the variations in mode of thought or conception what they may, the Apostle ascribes to Jesus that absolute significance for religion which we have already seen attach to Him both in His own mind and in the preaching of St. Peter. This is the basis and the content of preaching Christ.

It might seem enough to refer to the salutations of the Epistles, in which St. Paul wishes the Churches grace and peace from God our Father and the Lord Jesus Christ (Ro 1⁷), or addresses them as having their being in God the Father and the Lord Jesus Christ (1 Th 1¹). Here we have the Father and Christ confronting men, so to speak, on the same plane, co-operating as one Divine power for their salvation. When St. Paul preaches Christ it is as a Person who has this power and importance, and stands in this relation to God and men. Or we might refer to what perhaps comes closest in form to Jesus' own mode of expression, the passage in 1 Co 15²⁸, in which 'the Son' is used absolutely, as in Mk 13³². There is a subordination of the Son to the Father here, and yet no more here than in Mk 13³² or in Mt 11²⁷ could we conceive of either word in the plural. Or again, we might refer to such passages as those in which St. Paul contrasts all other persons with Christ. 'What is Apollos? what is Paul? Was Paul crucified for you? or were you baptized in the name of Paul?' (1 Co 3⁵ 1¹³). This is entirely in the line of the contrast between the many servants and the one beloved Son in Mk 12¹⁻¹², or of the sayings of Jesus in Mt 23⁸⁻¹⁰. Of course both these Evangelic passages have been disputed, but the present writer sees no reason to doubt that in substance both are rightly assigned to Jesus. What St. Paul means in the words cited is that any other person has only a relative importance in Christianity, while Christ's importance is absolute. The Church would have missed Paul and Apollos, but it would have been there ; whereas but for Christ it could not have been there at all. It existed only *in* Him. This is assumed in all preaching of which He is the object. His significance for the Church is not in the same line with that of Paul and Apollos ; it is on the same line with that of the Father. No matter what the mode in which St. Paul conceives of Christ, he always conceives of Him as having this incomparable significance, and it is worth while to note the ways in which it appears.

(*a*) Sometimes they are, so to speak, unstudied : the truth is put, and possibly with emphasis, but there is no particular reflexion upon it. Thus, in 1 Co 3¹¹ 'other foundation can no man lay than that is laid, which is Christ Jesus.' This comes very close to Ac 4¹¹ᶠ· (see above). Again, when we read in 2 Co 1²⁰ 'how many soever are the promises of God, in him is the yea,' we are confronted with the same truth. There is not a single promise God has made, not a single hope with which He has inspired human hearts, which is to have any fulfilment except in Him. The mental attitude is the same in Gal 1⁸ᶠ·. The form of St. Paul's arguments is sometimes more disconcerting to us in Galatians than in any other of his Epistles, yet nowhere does he keep closer to the heart of his gospel. What these two seemingly intolerant verses mean is that Christ is the whole of the Christian religion, and that to introduce other things side by side with Him, as if they could supplement Him, or share in His absolute significance for salvation, is treason to Christ Himself. Christ crucified—the whole revelation of God's redeeming love to sinners is there ; the sinful soul abandoning itself in unreserved faith to this revelation—the whole of the Christian religion is there. Whoever brings into religion anything else than Christ and faith, as though anything else could conceivably stand on the same plane, is, wittingly or unwittingly, the deadly enemy of the gospel. Such expressions as these exhibit the absolute significance which Christ had for the Apostle in the most unquestionable way, but they imply no speculative Christology. We may hold them, and to preach Christ we must hold them, but we may do so without raising any of the theological questions which have been raised in connexion with them. There is hardly a page of St. Paul's writings which could not be quoted in illustration.

Confining ourselves to the Epp. to the Thess., as his earliest letters, and omitting the salutations referred to above, we find everywhere the absolute dependence of the Christian on Christ,—a kind of relation which would be not only inconceivable but immoral if any other than Christ were the subject of it. Just as men in general are said to live and move and have their being in God, Christians live and move and have their being 'in Christ.' What space is to bodies, Christ is to believing souls: they live in Him, and all the functions of their life are determined by Him. St. Paul has confidence *in the Lord* toward the Thessalonians (II 3[4]); he charges and entreats them *in the Lord Jesus Christ* (II 3[12]); they stand *in the Lord* (I 3[8]); he gives them commandments *through the Lord Jesus* (I 4[2]); church rulers are those who are over them *in the Lord* (I 5[12]); the Christian rule of life is the will of God *in Christ Jesus* concerning them (I 5[18]); the Christian departed are the dead *in Christ* (I 4[16]); all benediction is summed up in the grace of our Lord Jesus Christ (I 5[28], II 1[12] 3[18]); Jesus and the Father are co-ordinated as the object of prayer (I 3[11]), and prayer is directly addressed to the Lord, *i.e.* to Christ (I 3[12]). Our Lord Jesus Christ, through whom we are to obtain salvation at the great day, is He who died for us, that whether we wake or sleep we should live together with Him (I 5[10]). It is as though all that God does for us were done in and through Him; so that He confronts us as Saviour in Divine glory and omnipotence. We may trust Him as God is trusted, live in Him as we live in God, appeal to Him to save us as only God can save; and it is only as we do so that we have in Him a Person whom we can preach. Such a Person we can have, as the passages cited show, without raising any of the questions with which St. Paul himself subsequently wrestled. But the right way to express all this—which does not first appear in Colossians, but is of the essence of Christianity from the beginning—is not to say with Wernle that the consciousness of God has been weakened, but that the idea of God has been Christianized: the Father is known in the Son, and is known as working through Him to the end of our salvation. And this, it need hardly be repeated, is identical in religious import with what we have found in the mind of Christ Himself.

(b) Sometimes, however, the Apostle presents us with more speculative conceptions of Christ. He is not simply a Person who has appeared in history, and has been exalted in Divine power and glory. He is what may be called a universal Person, a typical or representative Person, who has for the new humanity the same kind of significance as Adam had for the old. Adam was the head of the one, Christ is the head of the other. As in Adam all die, so in Christ shall all be made alive. The acts of Christ have a representative or universal character: the death that He died for all has somehow the significance which the death of all would itself have; in His resurrection we see the first-fruits of a new race which shall wear the image of the heavenly. Broadly speaking, this way of conceiving Christ, in which the individual historical Person is elevated or expanded into a universal or representative Person, pervades the Epp. to the Romans, Corinthians, and Galatians (see esp. Ro 5[12ff.], 1 Co 15[21-49]). As these Epp. are central in St. Paul's writings, there is a certain justification for laying this conception of Christ—the second Adam—at the basis of a Pauline Christology (as was done by Somerville in his *St. Paul's Conception of Christ*). It is the conception which lends itself most readily to 'mystical' interpretations of Christ's work and of Christian experience. To bear the Christian name we must 'identify

ourselves' with all the experiences of the Second Adam. But though it is eminently characteristic of St. Paul, it is neither his first nor his last way of representing the absolute significance of Christ. It belongs to the controversial period in which everything Christian was defined by contrast. What St. Paul wanted to annihilate was legalism, the influence of the statutory in religion; and he argues that the really important categories in the religious history of humanity, those of universal and abiding significance, are not law, but sin and grace. The great figures in the history are not Moses, but Adam and Christ. He works out the parallel or rather the contrast between them with enthusiasm; but when we realize what he is doing, we feel that this is only one way of giving Christ His peculiar place. It is, however, a way which will maintain itself as long as the antithesis of sin and grace determines the religious life; and as this is a limit beyond which we cannot see, it seems involved in any adequate preaching of Christ that He should be preached in this universal character as the head of a new humanity.

(c) In his later Epp., St. Paul preaches Christ in what seems a more wonderful light. Christ is presented to us not merely as a historical, or as a universal, but also as an eternal or Divine Person. That which is manifested to the world in Him does not originate with its manifestation. The explanation of it is not to be sought merely in the history of Israel (as though Jesus were no more than a national Messiah), nor even in the history of humanity (as though He were no more than the restorer of the ruin which began with Adam): it is to be sought in the eternal being of God. When St. Paul came in contact with Jesus, he came in contact with what he felt instinctively was the ultimate reality in the universe. Here, he could not but be conscious, is the Alpha and the Omega, the beginning and the end, all that is meant—all that has ever been meant—by 'God.' Here is 'all the fulness of the Godhead bodily' (Col 1[19] 2[9]); here is the revelation of what God essentially and eternally is, and here therefore is that by which all our thinking must be ruled. Christ belongs to, or is involved in, because He is the manifestation of, the eternal being and nature of God. How far does this carry us when we try to think it out? Possibly not further, in some respects, than we have come already. Christ, it may be said, is represented as an eternal Person when He is spoken of as *final Judge of all* (Ac 10[42], 2 Co 5[10]); that is eternity as apprehended in *conscience*. Again, He is represented as an eternal Person when we speak of Him as *final Heir* or *Lord of all things* (He 1[2], Mt 28[18]); that is eternity as apprehended in *imagination*. But in Col. it is not through the conscience or the imagination, but through a more *speculative faculty*, that St. Paul interprets his conception of the eternal being of Christ. If Christ really has the absolute significance which all Christian experience implies,—for in all such experience we meet with *God* in Him,—then *all things* must be defined by relation to Christ; the universe must be reconstituted with Him as its principle, its centre of unity, its goal. Nature must be conceived as an order of things brought into being with a view to His Kingdom, and this implies that He was present in the constitution of nature. To say that He was ideally but not actually present,—present only in the mind of God as the intended consummation of the process, —would have been to St. Paul to introduce a distinction which we have no means of applying where God is concerned. The true doctrine of Christ— this is what St. Paul teaches in Colossians—involves a doctrine of the universe. The doctrine of the universe is put only negatively, or so as to exclude error, when we say that God created all things out of nothing; such a formula teaches only the absolute dependence of nature on God. But it is put positively, or so as to convey the truth in which the world is interested, when we say that all things were created in Christ. St. Paul's conviction of this truth is based (he believes) on experience : in his consciousness as a Christian man he is assured that in Christ he has touched the last reality in the universe, the *ens realissimum*, the truth through which all other truths are to be defined and understood. In other words, a true apprehension of the absolute significance of Christ involves a specifically Christian conception of the universe. The Christian religion is not true to Christ (as St. Paul understood His significance) unless it has the courage to conceive a Christian metaphysic, or, in simpler words, *to Christianize all its thoughts of God and the world*. Put in this form, we can see that in the last resort it is still necessary to share the Apostle's convictions at this point if we mean to preach Christ. For if there is any region of reality which does not depend for its meaning and value on its relation to Him,—if the truth with which we come in contact in Him is not the ultimate truth of God, the master light of all our seeing,—then His importance is only relative, and He has no abiding place in religion which requires that He should be preached at all. But in reality He is a Person so great that all nature and history and religion have to be interpreted through Him. All we call being, and all we call redemption, need Him to explain them. The love revealed in Him is the key to all mysteries. The categories we use to make His redemption intelligible are the only categories by which we can completely understand anything. Once Christ's absolute significance has become clear to us,—and, as already said, it is involved in every Christian experience,—we discover that our task, if we would understand the system of things in which we live, is not to find natural law in the spiritual world, but rather to find spiritual law—indeed, specifically Christian law—in the natural world. So far as we do so we are providing scientific attestation for the conception of Christ as a Divine and eternal Person.

10. The Epistle to the Hebrews and the Fourth Gospel, it need hardly be added, share in this conception of Christ. In neither is it allowed to infringe on the truth of His human nature while He lived on earth : indeed, of all the NT writings, these two in various ways make most use of Christ's humanity for religious and moral ends. But as the subject of this article is not Christology, it is not necessary to go into details. The prologue to the Fourth Gospel has precisely the same Christian experience behind it as the first chapter of Col., and the same experience, when taken seriously, will always inspire the mind to think along the same lines. The conception of the Logos, as has often been remarked, is not carried by the writer beyond the prologue : it may in reality affect the Evangelist's way of representing certain things, but it is not formally embodied in the Gospel. It was a conception widely current in the writer's time, whatever its sources, and he used it to introduce Jesus in circles which naturally thought in such terms. It does not follow that to introduce or to explain Christ among men who think in other categories, the preacher is still bound to make use of this one. 'There is only one thing,' says Dr. Sanday (*Criticism of the Fourth Gospel*, 198) 'that he [the Evangelist] seeks. He wants a formula to express the cosmical significance of the person of Christ.' That in which we must agree with him if we in turn would preach Christ, is his conviction of this significance, not the formula in which it suited him at the close of

the first century to express it. That like Paul he *had* such a conviction, based on experience, there is no doubt. The Son of God was not to St. John a lay figure to be draped in the borrowed robes either of Messianic dogmatic or of Alexandrian philosophy. He was a Being so great, and had left on the soul of His witness an impression so deep, that the latter felt it could be satisfied by nothing but a reconstitution of his universe in which this wonderful Person was put at the heart of everything—creation, providence, revelation, and redemption being all referred to Him. In St. John as in St. Paul the absolute significance of Christ in the relations of God and man, which is the immediate certainty of Christian experience, stamps Him as a Divine and eternal Person, by relation to whom the world and all that is in it must be described anew. We may say if we will that he uses the Logos as a formula to describe the cosmical significance of Christ, but that is perhaps less than the truth. He uses it rather to suggest that truth, as truth is in Jesus, is the deepest truth of all, and the most comprehensive, and that under its inspiration and guidance we must Christianize all our conceptions of God, nature, and history. He who is not in sympathy with this conviction will not find it easy to preach Christ in any sense in which the NT will support him.

11. If, however, we are in sympathy with this conviction, it may fairly be argued that we can preach Christ without raising any further questions. We must find the absolute significance of Jesus in the area within which Jesus presented Himself to men, 'beginning from the baptism of John until the day when he was taken up' (Ac 1[22]). This was the basis on which the gospel was launched into history, faith evoked, and the Church founded. This was the gospel of the original Apostolic testimony, and it is within its limits that the power of Christ must be felt. Once we do recognize this power, and its incomparable and unique significance, we are prepared to let our minds go further, and to appreciate at its true value what the Apostles and Evangelists tell us of such things as the pre-existence of Christ and the condescension of His entrance into the world. But these can never be the first things in preaching Christ. To put them first is really to put stumbling-blocks in the way of faith. Faith is evoked by seeing Jesus and hearing Him, and we see and hear Him only within the range indicated above. It is only faith, too, that preaches; preaching is faith's testimony to Christ. Hence, although faith must amount to a conviction of Christ's absolute significance, it must find the basis of this conviction in the historical Saviour, and it is only by appeal to the historical Saviour that it can reproduce itself in others. Accordingly it may exist and may render effective testimony to Christ without raising questions that carry us beyond this area. How we are to think of the superhistorical relation to God of the Person whose absolute significance we recognize in history, how we are to think of what is usually called His pre-existence, and of the marvel of His entrance into the world of nature and of history : these are questions which faith's conviction as to Christ's significance will dispose us to face in a certain spirit rather than another, but they are not questions on which the existence of the gospel, or the possibility of faith, or of preaching Christ, is dependent. With such faculties as we have, and especially such an inability to make clear to ourselves what we mean by the relation of the temporal to the eternal,—a relation which is involved in all such questions,—it may even be that we recognize our inability to grasp truth about them in forms for which we can challenge the assent of others. We can be certain from

Christ's life that His very presence in the world is the assurance of an extraordinary condescension and grace in God, even if we are baffled in trying to think out all that is involved either in His coming forth from the Father or in His entrance into humanity. But if on the basis of an experience evoked by the Apostolic testimony we can call Him Lord and Saviour, recognizing in Him the only-begotten Son through whom alone we are brought to the Father, then we can preach Him, be our ignorance otherwise as deep as it may be.

12. It might have seemed natural, in the discussion of such a question, to refer more directly to the various *criteria* of Christianity which the NT itself suggests, *e.g.* Ro 10⁹, 1 Jn 4²ᶠ·. But the last of these two passages only emphasizes the historical character of Christianity, the truth of our Lord's manhood, and the first the exaltation of Jesus: and to both of these justice has been done. The combination of the two is indeed required in preaching Christ, and it is all that is required. The reality of Jesus' life on earth as He Himself was conscious of it, the life of One uniquely related to God, and present in our world to make us all His debtors for revelation and redemption ; and the exaltation of such a One to the right hand of God : it is on this that preaching Christ depends. Into this we can put all the convictions by which the NT writers were inspired, and all that we know of the words and deeds of Jesus; and while we share at the heart the faith of Apostles and Evangelists, we do not feel bound by all the forms in which they cast their thoughts. The faith which stimulated intelligence so wonderfully in them will have the same effect on all Christians, and they will not disown any who call Jesus Lord, and give Him the name which is above every name.

LITERATURE.—Harnack, *Wesen des Christentums* ; Seeberg, *Grundwahrh. der christl. Rel.*; Cremer, *Wesen des Christentums*; Adams Brown, *Essence of Christianity* ; Wernle, *Anfänge unserer Rel.*; Orr, *Christian View of God and the World*, Lectt. vi. and vii. JAMES DENNEY.

PREDICTION.—See PROPHET.

PRE-EMINENCE (OF CHRIST).—The expression is St. Paul's. We shall take the passage in which it occurs as our starting-point, and work from that.
I. St. Paul's conception.—1. *The statement of it.*—The *locus classicus* is Col 1¹³⁻²⁰. In that and its context St. Paul represents Christ as Head of both creations, the natural and the spiritual, the Cosmos and the Church. Of the former He is Creator, Upholder, and End. Its ground of existence is in Him (ἐν αὐτῷ) ; He is before it and over it, even its highest intelligences (πρὸ πάντων), and shapes it to His purpose (εἰς αὐτόν). Of the second He is ἀρχή, at once Source and First ; Redeemer, Reconciler, Saviour (v.²⁰ᶠ·) ; Fountain of Life (3⁴) ; Treasury of Wisdom (2³) ; Hope of Glory (1²⁷) ; All in All (3¹¹). He is sole Mediator in both (1¹⁶⁻²⁰), through whom all streams of creative, providential, redeeming light and power go forth, and in whom all lines of creaturely approach to God converge. Of both, therefore, He is rightful Lord, as is implied in πρωτότοκος (1¹⁵· ¹⁸ ; see Lightfoot, *in loc.*), βασιλείαν τοῦ υἱοῦ (1¹³), and ἐν δεξιᾷ τοῦ θεοῦ καθήμενος (3¹),—a phrase that everywhere carries with it (*a*) subordination to the Father, (*b*) rule over all else. In both He is pre-eminent (1¹⁸). And this, not for any arbitrary reason, but because of what He is, which explains both the place He occupies and the work He has done. For He is God's Son in a unique sense (1³· ¹³—the phrase 'the Father of our Lord Jesus Christ' in the former being common in St. Paul and other NT writers) ; He is the image—the visible Revealer—of the invisible God (1¹⁵) ; and in Him dwells permanently in a bodily manifestation

the fulness of the Deity (1¹⁹ 2⁹), *i.e.* 'the totality of the Divine attributes and powers' (Lightfoot). His eternal Divinity shines out in ἔστιν (1¹⁷), while γένηται (v.¹⁸) reflects the humanity which He has assumed and glorified.

Similar teaching is found in the other Epistles of the same group. In *Ephesians* the ἐν αὐτῷ of Colossians becomes the dominant note. Christ is Head, Husband, and Saviour of the Church (4¹⁵ 5²⁵). All blessing is in Him (1³) ; all things are summed up in Him (1¹⁰). In Him all, both Jew and Gentile, are built up a holy temple, Himself the Chief Corner-stone (2²⁰⁻²²). He is the Supreme Revealer of God's grace (2⁷) and wisdom (3¹⁰), the one Lord (4⁶ 6⁷⁻¹⁰) seated at God's right hand and exalted above every other present or future power (1²⁰⁻²²). Here, again, it is because of what He is—the Son of God (1³ 4¹³) —that He brings us to perfection, and that all these facts can be true of Him. In *Philippians* He is all-subduing Saviour (3²⁰· ²¹) ; through Him come righteousness (1¹¹), peace (4⁷), joy (4⁴), strength (4¹³). In Him we glory (3³) ; compared with Him all else is as refuse (3⁸) ; He is our life's mainspring (1²¹) and highest goal (3¹⁴). Essentially God, He laid aside the manifested glory of Deity, and assumed humanity with its sinless manifestations and deepest sufferings. Therefore God exalted Him, so that at the name of Jesus every knee shall bow and every tongue confess Him Lord (2⁶⁻¹¹). It is probable that the title 'Lord,' when used of Jesus by St. Paul, carries with it always (as, indeed, it does in the rest of the NT) the fulness of meaning which it has here. The letter to *Philemon* is saturated with the conception expressed by the phrase 'in Christ,' which indeed forms the basis and strength of St. Paul's appeal.

According to this group of letters, Christ is pre-eminent primarily because of His Divine dignity, and secondarily because of His work in nature and in grace—as Creator, Mediator, Saviour, Lord. In St. Paul's mind these ideas are bound up inseparably with Him, and the probability is that he meant to express them in the full title—the Lord Jesus Christ—which he so frequently employs.

2. *Genesis of this conception.*—(1) It must be prior to all St. Paul's Epistles, for it is clearly present in all of them. To take the second group first. In *1 Corinthians* Christ is God's power and wisdom (1²⁴· ³⁰), the only Foundation (3¹¹), the true Passover (5⁷), our perfect Example (11¹), and the Second Adam, who gives life to all in Him (15⁴⁵). The Church is His body (12²⁷), of which, though not expressly stated, Christ must be the Head (cf. 11³). Especially worthy of note are 8⁶ (where He holds the same place in both creations as in Col.) and 15²⁷ (which tallies with Eph 1²⁰⁻²² and Ph 2¹¹). In *2 Cor.* (5¹⁸⁻²¹) we have language substantially the same as Col 1¹⁹⁻²² ; 4⁴⁻⁶ answers to Col 1¹⁵ ; 8⁹ implies pre-existence (cf. 1 Co 10⁴) ; 4⁵ and 10⁵ claim for Him unreserved obedience. In both these letters He is God's Son (I 1⁹ 15²⁸, II 1¹⁹). There is no need to quote specific passages in *Gal.* and *Rom.* representing Him as the only Saviour, for they are full of that thought. His universal Lordship is declared in Ro 9⁵ and 14⁹ ; His Sonship in Gal 1¹⁶ 2²⁰ 4⁴⁻⁶ and Ro 1⁴ 5¹⁰ 8³· ³² ; His Deity implicitly in Gal 1¹· ¹⁰⁻¹² (in the contrast between Him and man), and expressly in Ro 9⁵. Even in *Thessalonians* we have the following : Deliverer (I 1¹⁰, II 3²) and Saviour (I 5⁹· ¹⁰) ; Victor over evil in its mightiest manifestations, and Judge (I 5²ᶠ·, II 1⁷⁻¹⁰ 2⁸⁻¹²) ; God's Son (I 1¹⁰), and associated with God in salutation and prayer (I 1¹, II 1¹ᶠ· and I 3¹¹). This linking of Christ and the Father in salutation, and the ascribing to Him what is ascribed to God, are regular features of St. Paul's writings. It should further be noted that in practically all these letters the comprehensive title—Lord Jesus Christ—is applied to Him, and that frequently the strongest statements are made incidentally in such a way as to indicate that they belong to the common Christian conviction.

(2) St. Luke's account of St. Paul's preaching harmonizes with this. Ac 16–28 is, roughly speaking, contemporaneous with the first three groups of St. Paul's letters. In these chapters Jesus is represented as Saviour and Lord, and, as such, worthy of our utmost devotion (16³¹ 20²¹⁻²⁴· ³⁵ 26¹⁸) ; as the Christ, the burden and goal of prophecy and the Hope of Israel (17³ 18⁵ 24¹⁴ 26⁶· ⁷· ²² 28²⁰· ²³) ; as Judge of the world (17³¹), and even as God (20²⁸ text of אB). The book closes by summarizing the subject-matter

of St. Paul's preaching as the Kingdom of God and the things concerning the Lord Jesus Christ, where the full title is significantly given, as it is by St. Peter in his summary of the creed-content of the faith of Cornelius and his friends (11[17]). Working backward, we have in ch. 13 an extended report of St. Paul's address at Pisidian Antioch, which stands as representative of his teaching, at least during the First Missionary Journey. Certainly it must represent the view of Barnabas also; and its striking resemblance to St. Peter's Pentecost address is also noteworthy. In it Jesus is the Son of David, predicted by the prophets, and surely, therefore, Messiah (v.[22f.]); God's holy and incorruptible One (v.[35]); God's Son (v.[33]); the Saviour (v.[23]), through whom alone is remission of sins and justification (v.[38f.]), who is the channel of grace (v.[43]), the source of eternal life (v.[46]), the light of the world (v.[47], cf. Eph 5[8-14], Ph 2[15f.]). In 14[23] He is called Lord in a way which implies that the thought of His lordship was inseparable from faith.

The conception of Christ's Sonship here may seem to be quite different from that commonly found in the Epistles. But a comparison with Ro 1[4] may show that the two at root agree. Both here and in Romans the Resurrection is due to His holiness (Ac 13[35]). In Rom., further, the holiness is due to His sonship, of which the Resurrection is God's formal declaration, or (as Meyer) into which the Resurrection instates Him. May this not be the idea here also? Linguistic usage permits; for the priest was said 'to cleanse' the leper when he officially pronounced him 'clean'; so may it not be that the thought in v.[33] is that in the Resurrection God formally *declared* Jesus to be His begotten Son? On the other hand, the occurrence of the term 'justified' (v.[39]) shows how precarious a procedure it is to assert development of doctrine according to the occurrence or non-occurrence of a particular expression in brief letters addressed to different local conditions. The word here shows that St. Paul's doctrine of justification was not born just at the time of writing to the Galatians, even though it is not formally stated in the Thessalonian or Corinthian letters. The three accounts of St. Paul's conversion in Acts (9[22. 26]) show how the details of an event may be varyingly presented according to the character of those addressed and the purpose of the speaker.

(3) To find the genesis of St. Paul's view of Christ, we must go back to his conversion. There his conviction, at least as to the Person and pre-eminence of Christ, seems to have been settled. For (*a*) the light that shone about him, brighter than the Syrian noon-day sun (cf. Rev 1[16]), was a light out of heaven. To him, as a well-instructed Jew, that was the Glory of God's revealed presence. Would it not be natural for Saul, with his great conscientiousness, zeal for God, and hope of attaining to the promise made to the fathers (Ac 26[7]), to conclude immediately that the Lord had again visited His people, and that the august Person who appeared to him was none other than Jehovah Himself (cf. Is 6 and 1 Co 9[1])? If so, we can understand the pre-eminent place that Person for ever after held in his thought. The words of rebuke and heaven-laden pity naturally stun and bewilder him, and lead to the strange mingling of surprise and faith that breaks out in his question, 'Who art thou, Lord?' The definite answer, 'I am Jesus whom thou persecutest,' however it may have wrenched his soul, compelled his conversion. He surrendered unreservedly, and henceforth Jesus is his unchallenged and peerless Lord. Would such an unqualified surrender be justifiable had he not identified Jesus with the Jehovah of his people's history? Does any other view as fully explain all the facts?* (*b*) Unquestionably Saul was at once committed to the acceptance of Jesus as He was preached by those whom he was per-

* A sample fact would be the use of the word Κύριος, which in LXX is used to translate Jehovah, in the Gospels 'usually designates God, and in the Epistles, especially St. Paul's, most frequently Christ' (Winer; cf. Cremer, and Somerville, *St. Paul's Conception of Christ*, p. 295; and esp. Knowling, *Witness of the Epistles*, 261 ff.). The view here taken obviates Cremer's difficulty. For it would then be natural to use θεός of the invisible God (as in Jn 1[18]), and Κύριος of God manifesting Himself as Jehovah in OT or as Christ in NT.

secuting. For he must have been quite familiar with the claims made on behalf of Jesus by the Apostles and their associates. That Jesus was the Messiah, for example, he must have heard again and again. And what they declared Him to be, Jesus here plainly endorses. These two facts touching Christ's Person as Divine and His office as Messiah, Saul probably apprehended in the order here given. The record of his early preaching seems to follow the same order. For there he is represented as first preaching that Jesus is the Son of God, and later proving that Jesus is the Messiah (Ac 9[20-22]).

Doubtless he experienced some intellectual bewilderment. It was one thing to feel that the Mighty One who had appeared to him was Jehovah, and another to understand how the Man Jesus of Nazareth could be verily God. It might seem to strike at Jewish monotheism, and yet the two facts are before him. His mind must find some solution. Possibly it flashed upon him that God was essentially invisible (hinted at in Ex 33[17-23]; cf. Col 1[14], 1 Ti 1[17] 6[16]), and that therefore Jehovah, the august Person who was wont to appear to men and had now appeared to him, did not exhaust the mystery of God. Possibly he remembered that in the OT the closest relation to God was expressed by 'sonship' (2 S 7[14], Hos 11[1]). Perhaps he had heard from Christians utterances which suggested distinctions of Persons in the Godhead. For certainly the language both of St. John and of the Synoptists implies them, and in the baptismal formula mention would be made regularly of Father, Son, and Holy Spirit. It is quite possible that in the light of his new experience some or all of these may have led him to the assertion that Jesus is the Son of God as the first declaration of his faith. But Gal 1[15] may mean that some special access of revealing light was given him. In either case, the probability is that when he proclaimed Jesus to be the Son of God he did so in a sense transcending the ethical, equalling in significance its use on the lips of Jesus, and in full harmony with the Trinitarian conception. Jesus is God, Jesus is also Son. Certainly, if the meaning of the expression was specially revealed to him, the term chosen by St. Luke (ἐκήρυσσεν, 9[20]) becomes peculiarly appropriate, as representing not so much something which he had laboriously reasoned out, as something which he received by so direct a revelation that he can come forward proclaiming it with all the certainty of a commissioned herald.

II. Conceptions of the Twelve and their associates in the Acts.—Our discussion has brought us to the early preaching of the Twelve. Let us see more particularly the way they had come. Their approach was the opposite of St. Paul's. They began with the Man Jesus of Nazareth, and advanced slowly to the higher thought of Him; he, as a believer, began with the Divine Lord, and swiftly adjusted all else to that. They marched from earth to heaven; he came down from heaven to earth. The two forms of expression—'Jesus Christ' and 'Christ Jesus'—may represent the two lines of experience as well as the two regular standpoints of thought to which Lightfoot has called attention.

1. *Statements by Peter, Stephen and Philip, and James.*—St. Peter may be considered as representing the Twelve, including St. John, and his teaching may be summed up thus: Jesus of Nazareth is Lord and Messiah, exalted at God's right hand (2[36] 10[36]); into His name, *i.e.* into allegiance to Him, believers are baptized (2[38] 10[48], cf. 1 Co 1[13]); He is the Holy and Righteous One, the Suffering Servant of God, the only Saviour for men anywhere under heaven, and so Prince (ἀρχηγός—Author as well as Ruler) of Life (3[14f.] 4[27-30] 4[12]); the

Corner-stone (4^{11}); the last and greatest of the prophets, who becomes the touchstone of desti..y ($3^{22f.}$); the Judge of living and dead (10^{42}). In St. Stephen's address several of these notes recur. Jesus is Lord ($7^{59f.}$); the Righteous One of whom the prophets spoke (7^{52}); the Son of Man who in Divine glory stands at the right hand of God (7^{56}), the designation being especially appropriate as indicating that He did not lay aside His humanity when He ascended (cf. Ph 2^{10} the name Jesus); while the whole trend of the argument is that as Joseph and Moses were God-appointed deliverers, so Jesus is the Supreme Deliverer and Saviour (vv. 9-14. 22. 35. 37). St. Philip preaches Him as the Messiah and as the Suffering Servant of Is 53, which carries with it the ideas of Saviourship and Supremacy ($8^{5.}$ $^{12.}$ $^{32\text{-}35}$). Of the passages quoted, three (2^{39} 4^{12} 10^{36}) indicate the universality of Christ's pre-eminence, at least so far as men are concerned. This involved His being Saviour and Lord to Gentiles as well as Jews. That great fact of Christ's personal relationship to all men St. Peter seems to have seen clearly: what it involved for Judaism he had not yet apprehended,—an illustration of the fact that a great central truth may be grasped long before it is fully understood in its implications.

Whether St. Peter's conception of Christ's pre-eminence went beyond the world of men to that of higher intelligences, and the universe generally, is not so clear. And yet is it not implied in the frequent phrase 'at the right hand of God'? And might it not be understood from the prefatory words to the great Commission (Mt 28^{18}), which would be still ringing in his ears? Further, does not the language employed compel us to see in his thought of Christ more than mere manhood? Is this not suggested by the use of the word Κύριος in the Pentecost discourse? (See, *e.g.*, vv. $25.$ $34.$ $36.$ 39, where it is certainly applied both to Jehovah and to Jesus). It is a phenomenon that persists in the NT. We have noticed it already in connexion with St. Paul's experience. Another phenomenon equally persistent is found in vv. ^{17} and ^{33}, where the outpouring of the Spirit is ascribed first to God and then to the exalted Christ. This, of course, if it stood alone, might be explained on the principle that what one does through another he does himself. But it does not stand alone. His sinlessness, here repeatedly asserted, demands some adequate explanation. To be Judge of the world demands knowledge more than human. Similar phenomena occur in St. Stephen's address ($7^{30\text{-}32}$), where God, the Lord, and the Angel appear to be the same One, between whom and the people Moses mediated (v. ^{38}).

We notice next the view of St. James, as gathered from Ac 15 and his Epistle, which is here accepted as of early date. On the understanding that the letter of Ac $15^{23\text{-}29}$ was drafted by him, we have two points worthy of note in that chapter. The full title 'our Lord Jesus Christ' is given (v. ^{26}), as well as the 'our' as well as the quotation (vv. $^{16\text{-}18}$) show that St. James saw clearly that the sovereignty of Jesus would be accepted by the Gentiles, as well as by the Jewish world. In his Epistle there is added to the full title the phrase 'of glory,' which 'certainly attributes to Jesus a superhuman character' (Stevens, *Theol. of NT*, p. 287), and probably a Divine one (cf. Ac 7^2). In $5^{7\text{-}11}$ Κύριος is used first of God and then of Christ. In 4^{12} the Judge seems to be God; in 5^9 Christ is Judge. Is there any simpler explanation of this than that they were regarded as the same Person, and identified with the gracious Jehovah of the OT? He is probably also the Righteous One of 5^6, and undoubtedly the Saviour in whom saving faith rests. Such expressions from a brother in the flesh who had lived with Jesus from childhood are surely commandingly striking. The Lord of Glory stands forth in the thought of St. James as at least the Supreme Lord and only Saviour of men.

2. *Genesis of their conception.* — This takes us back to the Gospel history, and that to the prophecies of the OT. (1) Andrew and John were led to follow Him through *the testimony of John the Baptist*. Others were doubtless directly or indirectly affected by John's ministry. And John links us inevitably to the OT and the prophecies that went before concerning the Messiah. With these John and most of his hearers, these first disciples among them, were familiar. It is not necessary to go into the details here (they may be found in Drummond, Stanton, Edersheim, Westcott, Kirkpatrick, and a recent book by Willis J. Beecher, *The Prophets and the Promise*). But the heart of prophecy is God's close personal relation to man, His loving interest in man and gracious purpose for him. Thus there was in it a fact and a promise—the fact of God's kindness and grace, the promise of a Divinely - wrought deliverance. The former was the vital religious force in Israel's history, the latter its hope. Through unequalled suffering and by the might of His power the promised Deliverer was to crush the adversary, save His people, and set up an everlasting Kingdom that should fill the whole earth. Language is almost exhausted in depicting the greatness of that Deliverer and the glory of His reign (*e.g.* 2 S $23^{1\text{-}8}$, Ps 72. 89, Ezk $37^{21\text{-}28}$, Is 26. 52. 53, Dn $7^{9.}$ ^{27}). Some passages identify the Deliverer with Jehovah Himself appearing among men as their Saviour and King (*e.g.* Is $9^{6f.}$ and, in its light and that of Mt 1^{23}, Is 7^{14} and $8^{8\text{-}15}$; Is $40^{3\text{-}5}$ comp. with Mt 3^3 ‖; Is $45^{21\text{-}25}$ comp. with Ac 4^{12} and Ph $2^{10f.}$; Jer. $23^{5\text{-}8}$, where Jehovah our Righteousness is the Branch and King; Zec $12^{1\text{-}10}$, where the pierced one is identified with Jehovah; and Mal 3^1).

Whatever may be dark or disputable in these Scriptures, the pre-eminence of the Coming One is clear. John the Baptist was the last of the prophets. In his utterances the earlier are summarized. Jesus is the 'Lamb of God' who bears the world's sin, and 'the Son of God' as possessing permanently and without measure the Spirit of God (Jn $1^{29\text{-}34}$, cf. the Evangelist's elaboration in $3^{34f.}$). He is executor of God's wrath as well as of His grace, baptizing in fire as well as in the Holy Spirit (Mt $3^{10\text{-}12}$); He is the Bridegroom, even as Jehovah was Husband to His people (Jn 3^{29}). In His presence John feels his own inferiority and confesses it. He is not fit to loose His sandal-strap. At best he is His herald and friend (Mt $3^{11.}$ ^{14}, Jn 1^{23} 3^{29}). John can tell them to repent, and can baptize them in water as a symbolic declaration of repentance; but only this greater One can deal with them in the realm of reality and baptize in the Spirit (Mt 3^{11} ‖ Jn $1^{26.}$ ^{33}). In the light of Christ's tribute to John's greatness (Mt $11^{7\text{-}11}$), what a testimony John's utterances form to the pre-eminent greatness of Christ. It was the beginning of the disciples' faith.

(2) John's testimony was confirmed to them and strengthened by *Christ's own personality, words, and deeds*. His personality captivated and mastered them. The hallowed influence of the first day's fellowship (Jn 1^{39}), issuing in strengthened faith and open confession, is a sample of what was continuously at work thereafter. The calm and confidence, serenity and majesty of His demeanour; His absolute rectitude and sinlessness; His artless yet reverent familiarity with God and absolute devotion to His will; His exquisite tenderness, quick sympathy, abounding compassion, and unwearying beneficence, filled them with wonder, awe, admiration, and affection, and steadily ripened their faith. His words were clothed with unparalleled authority, and were full of wisdom and grace. In this setting His deeds of might and mercy accredited Him as from God, and attested His Lordship over nature as well as His Saviourship to men (see Mk 1^{27} 4^{41}, Lk 4^{22} *et al.*).

To all this experience, and interpreting it, were added His own imperial claims, most fully presented in the Fourth Gospel (see art. CLAIMS OF CHRIST).

(3) To the testimony of John and that of His own character and claims was added *the testimony of His enemies*, both men and demons (Jn 7⁴⁶, 19⁶, Mk 1²⁴ 3¹¹), *of angels* (Mt 28⁶), and *of the Father Himself* (Mt 3¹⁷ and Lk 9³⁵). The last passage is especially strong, because intended to rebuke the thought of putting Moses and Elijah on the same level with Him.

The effect of this growing body of testimony is seen in the confessions made from time to time. The early ones in Jn. needed deepening. The disciples had misconceptions, the removal of which might stagger their faith. They had as yet but poor knowledge of their own sinfulness; while of the path of suffering Jesus must take to His glory they knew nothing. The new consciousness of sin which came to St. Peter as he beheld the miraculous draught of fishes (Lk 5⁸), and the deeper sense of it that came with his denial (Mt 26⁷⁵), are waymarks of progress on the one side; the testing times in the Capernaum synagogue, when not only most of the multitude but even professed disciples forsook Him (Jn 6⁶⁰⁻⁷¹), and at Cæsarea Philippi, whither He had gone from the growing hostility in Judæa and Galilee, mark their progress on the other. It is for this reason that that confession of His Messiahship is treated as so important (Mt 16¹³⁻²⁰); their faith in Him holds when others desert. Immediately the way of the cross and the stern terms of discipleship are announced. We can see how it shook them. The Transfiguration, with its double message of death and glory (Lk 9³¹ᶠ·), served to steady them during the dark months that were coming; and the voice of the Father declared Jesus' Sonship and superiority to the greatest of the olden day. That scene was perhaps a means of answering the Master's prayer that their faith should not fail. Nor did it fail utterly. Peter's tears are the proof. But though their faith in Him personally held, it was intellectually eclipsed. It was the Resurrection, His subsequent teachings, and the coming of the Spirit that finally established it in clearness and power. That great conviction is expressed emphatically by Thomas when he hails Him as his Lord and God (Jn 20²⁸)—a declaration which Jesus endorsed. In keeping therewith is the closing scene in Mt 28¹⁶⁻²⁰, where, on the one hand, Jesus claims all authority in heaven and on earth, and, on the other, they worshipped (προσεκύνησαν) Him,—a term which should perhaps be understood here and in Lk 24⁵² in the full religious sense. Thus in the closing scenes of the Gospels these men are consciously face to face with One whom they joyfully hail as their 'Lord and God,' and the closing words fold back and into the opening quotation from the prophet that the Coming One should be 'Immanuel—God with us' (Mt 1²²ᶠ·). When men so thoroughly steeped in monotheism as these Jews, and with the lofty thought of God all Jews had, so believe and receive Him, how for them could there be any doubt about His absolute pre-eminence? Many adjustments of their views on other things will yet be necessary; but this conviction will abide and become the centre, the touchstone of truth for them, the central fact into which all others must be fitted. As St. Paul expresses it, they will hold the Head and so increase with the increase of God (Col 2¹⁹).

III. Conception of the later NT books.—1. *Hebrews.*—The very purpose of this letter is to forestall apostasy by showing Christ's superiority to all others, including Moses and Aaron, the prophets, and all the angels. The first chapter is equal in strength and fulness to the great passages in Col. and Philippians. He is God's Son, the express image of His Person, the effulgence of His glory; Maker of the world; God's last and perfect Spokesman. The angels worship Him. The Father

Himself addresses Him as God, who made all things, and outlives all things; whose throne stands for ever, whose sceptre is righteousness, and to whom all enemies shall become subject. In subsequent chapters He is represented as Captain (ἀρχηγός, Author and Leader, 2¹⁰) of our salvation; eternal High Priest made higher than the heavens, a Son perfected for evermore (7²¹⁻²⁵), who by the sacrifice of Himself obtains for us eternal redemption (9¹²), and secures us in an eternal covenant (8⁷·¹³ 9¹⁵ 13²⁰); the Author and Perfecter of our faith (12²); and the great Shepherd of His sheep (13²⁰). He is the One who speaks from heaven, rejection of whom is doom (12²⁵). He is our supreme goal. Others change and pass away; He abides the same yesterday, to-day, and for ever (13⁸); and to Him belongs the glory for ever and ever (13²¹).

2. *First Peter.*—Many of the terms with which we have become so familiar are here. He is the Lord Jesus Christ (1³). We must sanctify Him as Lord in our hearts (3¹⁵). He is seated at God's right hand, angels and principalities being made subject to Him (3²²). As Saviour He bears our sin (2²⁴), redeems us with His blood (1¹⁹), is the Chief Shepherd, the Bishop of Souls (5⁴ 2²⁵), and mediates all God's gifts to man (2⁵ 4¹¹). He is the Chief Corner-stone (2⁶); Sonship unique is implied in 1³, His place in a Trinity in 1², pre-existence in 1¹¹ (cf. 'manifested' in 1²⁰); His identity with Jehovah in 2³ (where an OT declaration about Jehovah is referred to Him). In keeping with this is the contrast between His 'blood' and 'corruptible things' in 1¹⁹ᶠ· (cf. Ac 20²⁸).

3. *Second Peter* is equally emphatic about His lordship (1²·¹⁴·¹⁶), and more explicit about His Sonship (1¹⁷) and Deity (1¹, cf. v.¹¹ 2²⁰ 3²·¹⁸; for the order of words is the same, and the presumption is that in each case but one person is referred to— Jesus Christ is God and Saviour as well as Lord and Saviour). The day of the Lord, ushered in by His coming, marks the time of His full triumph and glory (ch. 3), and His Kingdom is eternal (1¹¹).

4. *Jude* has in common with 2 Peter the use of the full title and of the term δεσπότης (v.⁴, 2 P 2¹, cf. 2 Ti 2²¹)—a term expressive of special absoluteness of authority, and made the stronger here by the μόνον. This Epistle has in common with 1 Peter what looks like a knowledge of His place in a Trinity (v.²⁰ᶠ·).

5. *St. John's Writings.*—In Acts, St. John was linked with St. Peter, and it is instructive to note how emphatically he harks back in his Epistles to that which they had from the beginning (e.g. I 1¹ᶠ·, II 5ᶠ·). He seems anxious to guard against any change from that early conception of Christ which is summed up in his Gospel in the confession of Thomas and in his own declaration (20²⁸·³¹).

The Prologue of St. John's *Gospel* restates it in the light of all the currents of thought that he has been meeting with in the intervening years. It stands, in its lofty conception of Christ, beside Col 1, Ph 2, and He 1, and forms the great thesis which the historic testimony marshalled in the Gospel was meant to establish. That testimony has been already referred to. All its strands are bound together here,—Creator, Light, Life, Revealer of God, Saviour of Men,—and all are grounded in His Godhead. What 'the Son' on the lips of Jesus involves and what the Evangelist expresses by 'the only-begotten Son' (3¹⁶), is here (v.¹⁸) expressed by 'only-begotten God,' which after all is the only adequate explanation of the phenomena, however incomprehensible to us it may be in itself. For He was in the beginning; He was face to face with God; He was God. The last statement guards against any form of Unitarianism (θεῖος would admit that), while in the use of θεός it provides for the Trinitarian conception which ὁ θεός might be understood to exclude, and fits in with the previous πρὸς τὸν θεόν, which implies two Persons in face to face fellowship. Being God, He creates the Universe and becomes incarnate, and so reveals God. Of this fact John the Baptist had some glimpse (1[15]). It is here assigned as the reason for his sense of inferiority.

St. John's *Epistles* assume all this, as the opening verses show, and are intended to point out that a life of righteousness, truth, and love is necessarily involved in that fellowship with God which faith in Christ effects. The liar is the one who denies that Jesus is the Christ (1 Jn 2[22]); he who believes that is born of God (5[1]). He who denies the Son hath not the Father, and will deny both Father and Son. Such is antichrist (2[22f.]). Jesus Christ is the true God (5[20]). This is final truth, beyond which none can go and have God (2 Jn [9]).

In the *Apocalypse* the Apostle is given a vision of Christ in His ineffable glory, and a panoramic view of His march to acknowledged pre-eminence. All the main features already sketched reappear here in most striking fashion. He is the Lamb slain, the Redeemer who in His blood loosed from their sins (1[5]) and purchased unto God men out of every nation (5[8f.]); the Living One who holds the keys of death and Hades (1[18]) and gives life (22[17]); the Ruler of the kings of the earth (1[5]), the King of kings and Lord of lords (17[14]); the Son of God (2[18] 1[6]) worshipped as God is (5[8-14] cf. with 4[8-11]) and as no other should be (22[8f.]). Between Him and God other parallels are drawn that find explanation and warrant only in His Deity, *e.g.* each is the Temple and Light of the New Jerusalem (21[22f.]); they have a common throne (22[3]), and the title Κύριος is applied to both.

It is clear that all the NT writers regard Jesus Christ as pre-eminent by virtue of His Person, His work, and the place which the universe of created intelligences shall yet accord Him. For, though some of them have written briefly, all that they do say fits in with this general conception. And it must be remembered that these early leaders formed a compact body, consciously bound together by the holiest ties, breathing the same atmosphere, receiving the same body of historic facts, professing the same vital religious experience, and drawn the closer together by the very opposition they encountered; and that, however they may have differed in minor matters, there is no symptom of difference or dispute among them as to the unapproachable greatness of their Lord and Saviour Jesus Christ, or as to the fact that He is the coming Universal King. See also artt. DIVINITY OF CHRIST, INCARNATION.

LITERATURE.—This is very extensive. Material may be found in the leading Commentaries, Lives of Christ, and works on Biblical and Systematic Theology, esp. those that deal wholly with the Person and work of Christ. Valuable lists may be found in Cave's *Introd. to Theol. and its Literature*. Two very valuable books there named might easily be overlooked, namely, Alexander Maclaren's 'Colossians' (*Expos. Bible*), and R. W. Dale's *Ephesians*. With them may be named Guthrie's exposition of the Colossian passage, entitled *Christ and the Inheritance of the Saints*. The following may also be consulted with advantage: M'Whorter, *Jahveh Christ*; Stalker, *Christology of Jesus*; Somerville, *St. Paul's Conception of Christ*; Forrest, *The Christ of History and of Experience*; R. J. Drummond, *Apostolic Teaching and Christ's Teaching*; Broadus, *Jesus of Nazareth*; A. T. Robertson, *Keywords in the Teaching of Jesus*; A. H. Strong, *The Greatness and the Claims of Christ* (in First Baptist World Congress); D. Fairweather, *Bound in the Spirit*, p. 265; G. A. J. Ross, *The Universality of Jesus*.

J. H. FARMER.

PRE-EXISTENCE.—

The OT conception of the Messiah was, for the most part, limited by the horizon of this present world. The prominent thought is that of a king of the line of David, born of the human stock (Jer 30[21]), though supernaturally endowed and blessed. There are, however, traces of another and higher conception, in which the Messianic king tends to be identified or closely associated with the personal self-revelation of Jehovah. The most remarkable of these are the titles 'Mighty God' and 'Father of Eternity' in Is 9[6]; the statement of Mic 5[2], that the Ruler who is to come forth from Bethlehem will be one 'whose goings forth are from of old, from ancient days.' To these may perhaps be added Bar 3[37]. Such passages as these, whether they are understood as implying definitely the personal pre-existence of the Messiah, or only his existence in the eternal counsels of God, tended undoubtedly to raise the Messianic conception to a higher level, and to prepare for the claims of Christ Himself, and the developed teaching of the pre-existence of Christ which is found in NT and the Christian writers generally.

In the more 'popular' teaching of Jesus Christ which is recorded in the Synoptic Gospels, though His continued existence, even to the end of time, is clearly stated, there are but few hints of His pre-existence before His human birth. His question to the Pharisees concerning Ps 110 (Mt 22[41-45], Mk 12[35-37], Lk 20[41-44]) would seem to imply, in the background of the Speaker's mind, His pre-existence before His birth of the line of David. A similar conclusion might be drawn from the language of the parable of the Wicked Husbandmen (see esp. Mk 12[6]). And possibly the lament over Jerusalem (Mt 23[37], Lk 13[34], taken in connexion with Dt 32[11]) implies that the attempt to 'gather together' the children of Jerusalem had extended over a much longer past than the three years' ministry.

There can be no question that St. John was profoundly convinced of the eternal pre-existence of Jesus Christ as the personal Logos. This is most clearly stated in the Prologue to the Gospel (Jn 1[1-18]). Similarly John the Baptist is quoted as bearing witness of Jesus in this respect (v.[30]). And in the discourses of Jesus Christ which are contained in this Gospel, addressed apparently to a different type of audience from that of the Synoptics, and conveying a fuller self-revelation, there are most startling claims to pre-existence. To Nicodemus (3[13]), Christ claims to know the heavenly things as having Himself descended from heaven. The same claim was made in the synagogue at Capernaum (6[33-42]), and produced strife and astonishment. A little later the Jews of Jerusalem attempt to stone Christ for blasphemy. He claimed not only priority to Abraham, but apparently an eternal pre-existence (8[58]). And in the climax of self-revealing at the Last Supper, Jesus in His communing with the Father twice refers to His own personal relations with the Father before the world began (17[5. 24]).

The sermons in the Acts confine themselves to the historical manifestation of Jesus Christ, the prophetical preparation for it, and the Second Advent. But in the writings of St. Paul an increasing consciousness of Christ's pre-existence and definiteness in speaking of it can be traced. In 1 Co 15[47] Christ is 'from heaven,' in 2 Co 8[9] His earthly poverty is contrasted with an antecedent richness. It is, however, in the Epistles of the First Imprisonment that pre-existence is not only hinted at, but expressed and defined. The remarkable passage Ph 2[5-11] predicates deliberate will and choice of Christ Jesus, before His Incarnation. He willed to surrender (from a human point of view) His natural equality with God, and chose the glory which came through humiliation and sacrifice of self. And, still more definitely, in Col 1[15-17] not only priority, but an eternal priority to all creation is ascribed to Him: 'he *is* before all things.' With this passage should be compared the opening of the Epistle to the Hebrews, where not only similar descriptions are given of the nature of Christ, but the words of Ps 102, contrasting the eternity of the Creator with the transitoriness of creation, are boldly and without any explanation applied directly to Christ (cf. also Ro 10[9-15]). The language of the Apocalypse is strictly parallel (Rev 1[17] 3[14] 21[6] 22[13]).

See artt. DIVINITY OF CHRIST, INCARNATION.

LITERATURE.—Sanday, art. 'Jesus Christ' in Hastings' *DB*; Liddon, *Divinity of our Lord* (Bampton Lectures for 1866); Westcott, *Gospel of St. John*, 1882; Dorner, *Chr. Doct.* (Eng. tr.) iii. (1882) 283; Lobstein, *Notion de la préexistence du Fils de Dieu* (1883); Godet, 'Person of Christ' in *Monthly Interpreter*, iii. (1886) 1; Beyschlag, *NT Theol.* (Eng. tr.) ii. (1895) 249; Wendt, *Teaching of Jesus* (Eng. tr.), ii. (1892) 168; Denney, *Studies in Theology* (1895), 51; Orr, *Chr. View of God and the World* (1893), 508; Barton, 'Jewish-Chr. Doct. of Pre-existence of Messiah' in *JBL* xxi. (1902) 78; Du Bose, *The Gospel in the Gospels* (1906), 221; Barrett, *The Earliest Chr. Hymn* (1897), 23.   A. R. WHITHAM.

PREMEDITATION.—1. There is frequent evidence of this quality in the teachings of Christ, and in the experiences of His life. Regarding Him simply on the common level of humanity, as for this faculty we necessarily must, there is little ground for the assertion so often made that He was an enthusiast, dependent on the inspiration of the moment. The occasional intuitions of the Divine are no explanation of the great body of His teaching. There is an inborn forethought, a native endowment of premeditation, that, humanly speaking, goes to the building up of His greatest thoughts, uttered or wrought. No accident or impulse gave birth to the Sermon on the Mount. Its varied teachings, the keywords of a spiritual and moral revolution yet to be effected in the world, strike one as the result of most careful observation, comparison, and imagination—all the product of patient premeditation. From His entrance into the active Gospel story, in that prelude of the Boy in the Temple, to the calm strength with which He faced the last days, it is a gift of deep insight into human probabilities that we look upon. The Saviour of men foresees His task—its glories, and its awful cost.

As a boy He is surprised that His parents have not seen this, and known that His thoughts were so fixed on Divine things that in the looked-for Jerusalem He is sure to be found about the Temple and the teachers. 'How is it that ye sought me? Wist ye not that I must be in my Father's house?' (Lk 2^{49}). He 'cometh unto John to be baptized of him' with the decision already thought out that 'thus it becometh us to fulfil all righteousness' (Mt 3$^{13-17}$ ‖ Mk 1$^{9-11}$ Lk 3$^{21.\ 22}$). The choice of the passage from Isaiah as the text of His first sermon at Nazareth (Lk 4^{18}) is too distinctive to have been the chance of an opening of the roll. The more often we read and weigh it, sentence by sentence, word by word, the more wonderfully true do we find it as a summary of our Lord's mission. What care, what hesitation, must have preceded the selection of the twelve Apostles, and the delivering of that high commission that rings down through the ages with a strange attraction to all set apart for ministry. Only the deepest premeditation could have given them such a full charge—to preach the Kingdom, raise the dead, and reveal the secret of life in the cross on the one hand, and on the other to recognize the disciple's duty in the common needs of men, as in the giving of a cup of cold water (Mt 9^{37} 10 ‖ Mk 3$^{13-15}$ 6$^{7-12}$ Lk 9$^{1-6}$). He had found the incompleteness of the Law, and with deliberate purpose declared His mission to be one that was not to destroy but to fulfil: 'Except your righteousness shall exceed that of the scribes and Pharisees, ye shall in nowise enter into the kingdom' (Mt 5$^{17.\ 20}$). He sees the divisions that will come because of the gospel (Lk 12^{49}), but, as One who has thought out every step of the way, it can be written of Him, 'He set his face stedfastly to go to Jerusalem' (Lk 9^{51}). There He speaks of the inevitable destruction of the Temple and the officialism it had so long stood for (Mt 24^1 ‖ Mk 13^1 Lk 21^5); there He weeps over the lost possibilities of Jerusalem, that ancient home of faith (Lk 19^{42}); and there, from the midst of His own agony and

sorrow, He can bid the women of the city weep for the downfall that is to come, 'for yourselves and for your children' (Lk 23^{28}). Dwelling upon prophetic visions, He portrays the signs that shall herald the coming of the Son of Man (Mt 24^{29} ‖ Lk 21^{25}).

But most notable of all His personal premeditations is that which gives expression to His passion and death. As One who walked beneath the shadow of the cross, His thoughts bear frequent witness to that silent companionship. He comes to the last Passover, and Peter and John are sent ahead with instructions that suggest a prepared understanding with the householder (Mt 26^{18} ‖ Mk 14^{13} Lk 22^7), thus giving us the beautiful and precious thought that the first of the long line of celebrations of the Lord's Supper should have taken place in a room chosen beforehand by Christ Himself. The sufferings inherent in Messiahship are foreshadowed in His many utterances concerning the cross (Mt 20$^{17-19}$ ‖ Mk 10^{32} Lk 18^{31}, Lk 9^{22}, Mt 17$^{22.\ 23}$ ‖ Mk 9^{31} Lk 9^{44} Jn 12^{23},.16^{16}); the necessity for His imitators (disciples) to bear their cross (Mt 16^{24} ‖ Mk 8^{34} Lk 9^{23}, 14^{27}); the certainty that He would be delivered up to His enemies (Mt 26^{21} ‖ Mk 14^{18} Lk 22^{21} Jn 13^{21}); the desertion by His followers, who would leave Him alone, 'and yet I am not alone, for the Father is with me' (Jn 16^{32}, Mt 26^{31} ‖ Mk 14^{27} Lk 22^{31} Jn 13^{36}). But He looked beyond the cross and saw the power of the risen life, and gave the promise of the Comforter, 'the Spirit of Truth who would lead them into all truth' (Jn 15^{26} 16^{13}). See also art. PLAN.

There are occasions on which His teaching or His action seems entirely unpremeditated. The immediacy of an intuition is seen in His use of the opportunity given Him by the woman at the well (Jn 4^7), or in the call of Nathanael (1^{38}), or in the treatment of the woman taken in sin (8$^{1-7}$), or in the scene at Simon the Pharisee's (Mt 26$^{6-13}$ ‖ Mk 14$^{3-9}$ Lk 7$^{36-50}$ Jn 12$^{1-8}$), or the freeing of the Sabbath from Rabbinic tyranny (Mt 12^3 ‖ Mk 2^{25} Lk 6^3).

2. But Christ constantly advocates forethought, that yoke which brings ordered rest (Mt 11^{28}). The builder who chooses his site carelessly may build on sand instead of solid foundations, and all the finely dreamed temple of his faith be brought to the ground (Mt 7^{24} ‖ Lk 6^{46}); or he may commence a tower too great for him to finish, as a king may carelessly engage in a ruinous war (Lk 14$^{28ff.}$). The parables of the Hidden Treasure and the Pearl of Great Price are the records of those who thoughtfully weigh all lesser things against the great adventure (Mt 13$^{44.\ 45}$). The parable of the Wise and Foolish Virgins is obviously the story of premeditation and its worth. The Prodigal Son leaves nothing to chance when he thinks of returning: the very words with which he will meet his father are rehearsed (Lk 15^{11}). The first impulse of the Unjust Steward is to ask 'What shall I do?', and to form his plan which, though immoral in itself, shows a careful foresight that in its higher thought and morality is too often lacking in the Christian disciple; 'The children of this world are wiser in their generation than the children of light' (Lk 16$^{1-8}$). The disciple who offers himself too readily is bidden to count the cost, and is reminded of the hardships: 'The foxes have holes, the birds of the air have nests, but the Son of Man hath not where to lay his head' (Mt 8^{20}); and an unwearying watchfulness is demanded, that the servant may be ready whenever his Lord knocks (Lk 12^{36}). Strongly does Christ reprove those who watch the heavens for signs of weather and can read the skies, but cannot read the spirit of their day (Mt 16^2 ‖ Mk 8^{12}, Mt 12^{39} ‖ Lk 11^{29}).

3. And yet how plainly Jesus sees that premeditation has its dangers, and may sap away the energies and effective values of a man's life. It is easy to be over-cautious, to grow too anxious about the lesser things (Mt 6[25. 31] || Lk 12[22]), giving all our thought to the care of these rather than of the life that is life indeed (cf. the parable of the Rich Fool, Lk 12[15-21]). It was surely with this thought in mind that Jesus gave that command to His Apostles, 'Get you no gold, nor silver' (Mt 10[9]); and 'when they deliver you up, be not anxious what ye shall speak' (10[19]). Too calculating a spirit, too careful a measurement of possible dangers, too great a forethought as to an assured future different from that of other men, would paralyze the missionary spirit. The disciple must not be over-prudent: he must give himself ungrudgingly, and sow the seed broadcast, not being too careful about the purity and goodness of the ground in which he sows, even throwing some on the trodden pathways of the world, and on what seems the shallowest of soil (Mt 13[1-9] || Mk 4[1-9] Lk 8[4-8]).

EDGAR DAPLYN.

PREPARATION (παρασκευή, Mt 27[62], Mk 15[42], Lk 23[54], Jn 19[14. 31. 42]).—**1.** Since the Sabbath was a day of holy rest, the food for it was cooked and all else needful got ready on the previous day, the προσάββατον (Mk 15[42]); * and thus that day was designated by the Jews 'the Preparation.'† The Christians took over the term,‡ and it remains to this day the regular name for Friday in the Greek Calendar.

2. The term was also used of the day of preparation, whatever day of the week it might be, for any of the sacred festivals, especially the Passover. The Paschal Supper was eaten on the evening which, since the Jewish day began at 6 p.m., ushered in the fifteenth day of the month Nisan; and the fourteenth day, when all was got ready for the celebration, was called the Preparation.

The term occurs thrice in the Synoptics (Mt 27[62], Mk 15[42], Lk 23[54]), and in each instance it means Friday. In the Fourth Gospel also it occurs thrice (19[14. 31. 42]), and there would be no doubt that here also it means Friday§ were it not for two other passages. (1) At 13[1] St. John seems to put the Last Supper 'before the feast of the passover.' (2) At 18[28] he says that, when on the morning after the Last Supper the rulers brought Jesus before Pilate, 'they did not themselves enter into the Prætorium, that they might not be defiled, but might eat the passover'; whence it would seem that the Paschal Supper had not been celebrated the previous evening, but was to be celebrated that evening. It thus appears as though there were a glaring discrepancy between the Synoptics and the Fourth Gospel. They all agree that Jesus was crucified on Friday; but whereas according to the Synoptists that Friday was the 15th Nisan, and on the previous evening which ushered it in Jesus had eaten the regular Paschal Supper with His disciples (cf. Lk 22[7]), according to St. John it was the 14th Nisan, and the Supper in the upper room on the previous evening was either not the Passover at all,|| or was

eaten a day too soon.* In the Synoptics παρασκευή means simply Friday; in the Fourth Gospel it means the Preparation Day, being also, as it chanced, Friday.

The problem has been discussed from the earliest times, and nowhere has harmonistic ingenuity been more lavishly expended. In our day the harmonistic method is out of fashion, and the tendency of some critics is to pronounce the Johannine representation unhistorical, and to explain how it originated. Appeal is made to the idea, suggested, it is alleged, by St. Paul (1 Co 5[7]), and definitely enunciated by Clement of Alexandria,† that Jesus, being the true Paschal Lamb, must have been slain on the Preparation Day, 14th Nisan. It is pointed out that, by way of proving Him the true Paschal Lamb, St. John (1) throws back the anointing at Bethany to 10th Nisan (12[1]), the day on which the Paschal lamb was chosen (Ex 12[3]); (2) represents Jesus as still before Pilate at the sixth hour, i.e. noon, in order, it is alleged, to make the Crucifixion synchronize with the sacrifice of the Paschal lambs, which were slain between 3 and 5 p.m.;‡ (3) shows how the Law's prescription that the lamb's bones should not be broken (Ex 12[46], Nu 9[12]), was fulfilled in the case of Jesus (19[36]).§

This is ingenious rather than convincing. (1) The anointing at Bethany actually took place, as St. John represents, six days before the Passover; and St. Matthew and St. Mark, with that disregard of chronological sequence which is characteristic of the Synoptic editors of the Apostolic tradition, have brought it into connexion with the Betrayal (Mt 26[6-16] = Mk 14[3-11]); their idea being, apparently, that the traitor was angered by the Lord's rebuke (Mt 26[10] = Mk 14[6] = Jn 12[7]). His foul deed was a stroke of revenge.|| (2) If, as is possible, St. John computed the hours of the day, not, like the Synoptists, from 6 to 6, but, according to the method which probably obtained in Asia Minor, from 12 to 12,¶ then by 'the sixth hour' he means, not noon, but 6 a.m., thus agreeing with the Synoptists (cf. Mt 27[1. 2] = Mk 15[1]). (3) Jesus was none the less the true Paschal Lamb, though He was not crucified between 3 and 5 p.m. on the 14th of Nisan, but at 9 a.m. on the 15th. St. Paul spoke of Him as 'our passover,' (1 Co 5[7]); yet he regarded the Last Supper as the regular Passover, calling the communion cup 'the cup of blessing' (10[16]),** which was the name given in the Paschal rubric to the third cup at the Passover feast.

In the opinion of the present writer the difficulty is due to a misunderstanding of Jn 13[1] and 18[28]. When these two passages are rightly considered, the position seems to be established that παρασκευή means Friday alike in the Fourth Gospel and in the Synoptics. Jn 13[1] should be read as a separate paragraph. As the end approached, says the Evangelist, there was a marked access of tenderness in the Lord's deportment towards His disciples. He demonstrated His affection as He had never done before. It was the pathetic tenderness of imminent farewell. 'Before the feast of the passover, Jesus, knowing that his hour had

---

* Ex 16[5]. See Lightfoot on Mk 15[42]. Curiously enough the Sabbath was the day for feasting, and the viands were specially sumptuous; but they had to be cooked the previous day and eaten cold. See Aug. de Cons. Ev. ii. § 151; Lightfoot and Wetstein on Lk 14[1].

† Cf. Jos. Ant. xvi. vi. 2: ἐν σάββασιν ἢ τῇ πρὸ ταύτης παρασκευῇ; Wetstein on Mt 27[62].

‡ Didache, viii. 1.: ὑμεῖς δὲ νηστεύσατε τετράδα καὶ παρασκευήν; Clem. Alex. Strom. vii. § 75: τῶν ἡμερῶν τούτων, τῆς τετράδος καὶ παρασκευῆς λέγω. ἐπιφημίζονται γὰρ ἡ μὲν Ἑρμοῦ ἡ δὲ Ἀφροδίτης.

§ 19[14] παρασκευὴ τοῦ πάσχα, 'Friday of the Passover-season,' not 'the Preparation for the Passover,' which would require ἡ παρασκευή.

|| So Clem. Alex. (fragm. in Chron. Pasch. See Dindorf's Clem. Alex. Op. iii. p. 498): In previous years Jesus had kept the Passover and eaten the lamb, but on the day before He suffered as the true Paschal Lamb, He taught His disciples the mystery of the type.

---

* Jesus anticipated the Passover, knowing that at the proper time He would be lying in His grave. St. Chrysostom (in Joan. lxxxii.) gives this as an alternative explanation of Jn 18[28]; Calvin: Since the Passover-day, falling that year on Friday, was reckoned a Sabbath (Lv 23[6. 7. 11. 15]), the Jews, to avoid the inconvenience of two successive Sabbaths, postponed the Passover by a day: Jesus adhered to the regular day.

† Also, according to Chron. Pasch., by Apollinaris, Hippolytus, and Peter of Alexandria.

‡ Jos. BJ vi. ix. 3.

§ Strauss, Keim, Schmiedel (Encycl. Bibl., art. 'John, son of Zebedee').

|| Cf. Aug. de Cons. Ev. ii. § 153.

¶ Cf. Plin. HN ii. 79. Polycarp was martyred in the stadium at Smyrna 'at the 8th hour' (Mart. Polyc. xxi.), i.e., since public spectacles began early (cf. Becker, Charicles, p. 409), at 8 a.m.

** τὸ ποτήριον τῆς εὐλογίας (כּוֹס הַבְּרָכָה).

come to pass out of this world unto the Father, naving loved his own that were in the world, he loved them to the uttermost,' *i.e.* demonstrated His affection as He had never done before.[*] Then begins a new paragraph, which recounts the story of the Supper (v.[2ff.]), assuming an acquaintance on the reader's part with the Synoptic details of time and arrangement. It was St. John's wont to correct his predecessors wherever they had erred ; and had they put the Last Supper a day too late, he would have stated expressly when it took place, and would not have said vaguely 'before the feast.'

And what of Jn 18[28]? It does not imply that they were looking forward to the Paschal Supper in the evening, and that therefore that day, when Jesus was tried and crucified, was the Preparation-day, 14th Nisan. They would indeed have been defiled by entering a heathen house, but the defilement would have remained only until the evening (cf. Lv 11[24. 25. 27. 28. 31. 39. 40] 14[46] 15[5. 6. 7] 17[15] 22[6], Nu 19[7. 8. 10. 21. 22], Dt 23[11]), and they could then, after due ablution, have eaten the Paschal Supper.[†] The truth is that it was not the Paschal Supper that they would have been precluded from, but the *Chagigah* or thank-offering, which was presented in the Temple on 15th Nisan, and had to be presented by each worshipper *in propriâ personâ.*[‡] The phrase 'eat the Passover' comprehended more than participation in the Paschal Supper. Alike in the Scripture and in the Talmud it denotes the celebration of the entire feast, including the *Chagigah.*[§] In the Fourth Gospel 'the passover' invariably signifies not the Supper but the whole feast, τὴν ἑορτὴν πᾶσαν,[||] and it is unreasonable to suppose that in this solitary instance St. John has departed from his *usus loquendi.*

There remains a final consideration. After the Crucifixion, Joseph of Arimathæa visited Pilate, and petitioned for the body of Jesus (Jn 19[38] = Mt 27[57. 58] = Mk 15[42. 43] = Lk 23[50-52]). He was a Sanhedrist, and had no less reason than his colleagues to shun pollution ; yet he went without scruple to the governor's house. The explanation is that, when they refused to enter the Prætorium, it was the morning, and they must offer the *Chagigah* in the afternoon ; when he waited upon Pilate, it was the evening (ὀψίας γενομένης), and he had already offered it.

On the above theory there is no discrepancy between St. John and the Synoptists. Both he and they represent Jesus as celebrating the Paschal Supper with His disciples on the evening which ushered in 15th Nisan ; and both he and they use παρασκευή in the sense not of the Preparation-day, but of Friday. St. John says that 'that Sabbath-day was a great one' (19[31]), not because, being at once the weekly Sabbath and Passover-day, it was Sabbath in a double sense, but because, as Lightfoot puts it, (1) it was a Sabbath, (2) it was the day on which the people appeared before the Lord in the Temple (Ex 23[17]), and (3) it was the day on which the sheaf of the firstfruits was reaped (Lv 23[11]). See also, for different views, artt. DATES, LAST SUPPER, PASSOVER (II.).

[*] εἰς τέλος, not 'to the end,' but 'to the uttermost.' Chrysost. *in Joan.* lxix. : οὐδὲν ἐνέλιπεν ὧν τὸν σφόδρα ἀγαπῶντα εἰκὸς ἦν ποιῆσαι. Cf. Euth. Zig. : ἀγαπᾶν of 'tokens of affection ; Mk 10[21] ἠγάπησεν αὐτόν, kissed his forehead. See Lightfoot on Mk 10[21], Jn 13[23].

[†] Strauss argues that they 'would still have disqualified themselves from participating in the preparatory proceedings, which fell on the afternoon of 14th Nisan ; as, *e.g.*, the slaying of the lamb in the outer court of the Temple.' But they might legally have deputed the business of preparation to their servants, as Jesus deputed it to Peter and John. Cf. Lightfoot on Mk 10[26].

[‡] See Lightfoot on Jn 18[28], Mk 15[25].

[§] Dt 16[2], 2 Ch 30[1. 23. 24] 35[1. 8-19], Ezk 45[21-24]. Lightfoot on Jn 18[28].

[||] Cf. 2[13. 23] 6[4] 11[55] 12[1] 13[1]. Contrast Mt 26[17] = Mk 14[12] = Lk 22[7. 8].

LITERATURE.—Lightfoot, *Hor. Heb.* (see references in footnotes) ; Strauss, *Leb. Jes.* III. ii. § 121, and *New Life of Jesus,* ii. § 85 ; Keim, *Jesus of Nazara,* vi. pp. 195–219 ; Caspari, *Chron. and Geog. Introd.* §§ 151–164 ; Farrar, *Life of Christ,* Exc. x. ; Andrews, *Life of our Lord,* pp. 457–481 ; Westcott, *Study of the Gospels,* p. 43 ; Du Bose, *The Gospel in the Gospels,* p. 28. For the contrary view that παρασκευή does not mean Friday in both the Synoptics and the Fourth Gospel, see Sanday in Hastings' *DB,* ii. 634 ; Godet in his *Comm.* on Lk. and Jn. ; Lobstein, *La doctrine de la sainte cène,* p. 51 f. ; Zöckler in *PRE*[3], ix. pp. 32, 42 ; Chwolson, *Das letzte Passamahl Christi.*

DAVID SMITH.

PRESENCE.—The ordinary word in the Gospels for 'before' (= in the presence of) is ἔμπροσθεν. Lk. also uses ἐνώπιον, which, with the exception of Jn 20[30], is not in the vocabulary of the other three Evangelists. He nearly always uses it of the presence of God. Other prepositions employed are ἐπί, (ἀπ)έναντι, and ἐναντίον).—**1.** The value of a religion is the pledge it can give of the presence of God. In the heathen lands round Israel the Divine Being was localized in sacred places with the aid of idols. But the religion of Jehovah was rid of such a tendency through the work of the prophets, with the result that, when all other religions in the Roman Empire were vulgarized and eviscerated of power, Judaism remained like a Samson with locks unshorn, with a God who could keep His own secret, and with a faith still pregnant with possibility. True, the Divine presence had been manifested, according to the OT, in cloudy pillar and burning bush, had, indeed, been localized in the ark of the covenant. But steadily the conception of God had been clarified from material associations, and the way in which this was done may be gathered from Jer 7. So thoroughly did the moral view of God prevail, that 'the Law became God's real presence in Israel' (Schultz, *OT Theol.* i. p. 354). The 'angel of Jehovah,' so frequently mentioned in the OT, was simply 'the messenger' (מַלְאָךְ), so did all intermediaries dwindle in the blaze of the only God. But with this transcendence came aloofness. On the one hand, the Law became a very barrier between God and His people. Even those who followed hard after it, like Saul of Tarsus and the rich young ruler, thirsted only the more for the living God (Mk 10[17], cf. Ro 7[9-13], Gal 3[21-23]). On the other hand, Greek modes of thought, already affected by Oriental dualism, represented fully in Philo, but also anticipated in Palestinian theology (cf. Schürer, II. iii. § 33), bridged the seeming gulf by theosophical and Gnostic speculations. At the very moment when Judaism had its opportunity, it failed to give that abiding pledge of the presence of God which should satisfy heart, mind, and conscience. Even the religions of Mithras and Isis, impure though the latter was, had a vogue in the Empire because they did something to meet the need which arose between the barren speculations and brutal superstitions of the age.

2. At this psychological moment came Jesus with His gospel as a challenge to the world of the presence of God. St. John himself expresses this thought no more decidedly, though much more fully, than St. Mark, even though in Mk 1[1] υἱὸς θεοῦ is a secondary reading. The common testimony of the Apostolic circle may be summed up in He 1[2] 'God . . . hath in these last days spoken unto us in his Son.' But nowhere is the thought that Jesus Christ was the presence of God set forth with such sublime effect as in the Prologue to John's Gospel : 'We beheld his glory, the glory as of the only-begotten of the Father, full of grace and truth' (v.[14]). No need was there now of an impersonal Word or impersonated Wisdom, as between God and us (Ph 2[9], Col 2[8-19]) ; or of sacrifices and ceremonies, as between us and God (He 9[14], Gal 2[21]) ; for the entire gulf between God the holy and us the sinful has been bridged in Jesus

Christ our Lord (2 Co 5¹⁹, Eph 2⁴⁻⁷). Thus through Christ our access to the Father is immediate (Ro 5²) by one Spirit (Eph 2¹⁸). 'There were to be no more finite mediators between God and man ; no temple of Jerusalem, where alone men must worship ; no necessity for interposing angels to interpret between the Divine and the human. Man was himself to be brought into immediate contact with God, and was to experience the deep conviction that heaven and earth had met together' (Matheson, *Growth of Spirit of Christianity*, i. 78). This faith that through Christ a man is always in the presence of God as a child in his father's house was based on (1) the testimony, and (2) the teaching of Jesus.

(1) By the *testimony of Jesus* is meant the unconscious impress of His Personality. It is evident, to use with all respect a familiar phrase, that Jesus *had* a presence. The people marvelled because He spoke with authority, although an unlettered man (Mt 7²⁸·²⁹, Mk 6²). His eyes were as a flame of fire (Mk 3⁵, Lk 22⁶¹). In the awe of His presence the Temple - courts were cleared, and the tempest calmed (Mk 11¹⁵ 6⁵¹) ; so that His disciples cried, 'What manner of man is this, that even the wind and the sea obey him ?' (Mk 4⁴¹). He drew the children to Him, and cast out demons, and said, 'If I by the finger of God cast out devils, then is the kingdom of God come upon you' (Lk 11²⁰). These impressions upon His contemporaries simply correspond with His own self-consciousness. He gave up the workshop at Nazareth for the theatre of the world, because He knew Himself as God's beloved Son (Lk 3²² 4¹·¹⁴). His first address in the synagogue is not recorded, because it was all in one word, 'I am here' (4²¹). It was enough for the disciples that they should be with Him (Mk 3¹⁴). It was the last folly of the Galilæan cities (Mt 11²⁰ᶠᶠ·) that they did not believe Him for the works' sake ; and of Jerusalem, that it knew not the day of its visitation (Mt 23³⁷, Lk 19⁴¹ᶠᶠ·). There was only one legacy He had to leave, and that alone worth leaving, His spiritual presence (Mt 28²⁰, Lk 24⁴⁹), which was the true Shekinah (Mt 18²⁰, cf. 'Ubi sedent duo qui legem tractant, Shekina cum illis est,' *Pirke Aboth*, 3 (Schultz, ii. 67)). The difference in this respect between St. John and the Synoptists is that whereas with them the testimony of Jesus to Himself is mostly unconscious, with him it is altogether self-conscious. St. John never fails to lay stress on the autonomy of Jesus (Moffatt in *Expos.* VI. iii. [1901] 469), so that, even psychologically speaking, He is not of the world, though in it.

(2) Thus in Jn. the testimony of Christ is merged in *His teaching*. He speaks of His own presence as living water, heavenly bread, light and life to a needy world (Jn 4¹⁴ 6⁴⁸ 8¹² 11²⁵). To keep His word is to keep in the presence of God as He Himself does (14²³ 15¹⁰). And that presence is an inward abiding which nothing outward can disturb (16²²·³³). All His words in the Synoptics similarly illustrate that—

> 'To turn aside from Him is hell,
> To walk with Him is heaven.'

Only with them His Person is, as it were, so transparent that they present God *through* Jesus rather than *in* Him, and we are left to draw the Christian inference that He Himself is the *focus* of the Father's presence. It is the essential nearness of God that gives all significance to the Beatitudes (Mt 5⁸·⁹), to the teaching on prayer (6⁶·⁸), to the interpretation of worship (Mk 7⁸, cf. Jn 4²³), to the illustrations from nature (Mt 10²⁹), to the exhortations against anxiety (Lk 12³⁰⁻³²), towards watchfulness (vv.³⁵·³⁶), against covetousness (vv.²⁰·²¹), towards compassion (Mt 10⁴⁰⁻⁴²). The sphere in which all the teaching moves, which makes it simple and intimate to the heart, and transcendent

in its appeal and its authority, is the presence of God the Father, the truth that—

> 'Spirit with spirit can meet,
> Closer is He than breathing; and nearer than hands and feet.'

But the immanence of God reaches a further stage in the gospel of Christ. Not only does Jesus bring God close into His world, as if οὐρανός meant the atmosphere one breathes rather than the firmament above (cf. τὰ πετεινὰ τοῦ οὐρανοῦ, Mt 6²⁶ etc.), but, according to Jesus, God is immanent in the human nature that makes room for Him. This is expressed in terms of (*a*) relationship (Mk 3³⁵, Mt 5¹⁶·⁴⁴, Jn 1¹²), (*b*) identification (Mt 10⁴⁰ 25⁴⁰), (*c*) indwelling (Jn 14¹⁶·¹⁷). This last is called the doctrine of the Holy Ghost. In order to give His own outlook to all disciples, Jesus promised His other self, the Paraclete or Comforter, in whose company and through whose intercession we live on the plane of sons, not only being in the Father's presence, but He being present in us. Although this doctrine is fully allowed for by the Synoptists (Mt 10²⁰, Lk 24⁴⁹), it is the special contribution of St. John. 'Jesus answered, If a man love me, he will keep my word : and my Father will love him, and we will come unto him, and make our abode with him' (Jn 14²³). From different points of view it may be said that Jesus *enjoyed* the presence of God, that He *was* that presence, and that He *gave* it. This threefold presence is really the basis of the doctrine of the Trinity.

3. What then are we to gather from all this but that, according to Christianity, Christ as God incarnate is the pledge that God is present, not only Creator-like in the universe, but Father-like in the believing heart and the consecrated life ? That is really the meaning of His exhibition of God in human life, and the impartation of His own Spirit. And our safeguard against the errors of Pantheism and of all such systems as tend to merge the Divine in the human instead of moulding the human by the Divine, is to be found in one small but significant phrase, 'ἐν Χριστῷ.' The Christian consciousness must always testify with a modern thinker (W. S. Palmer, *An Agnostic's Progress*) : 'When I lifted up my eyes to God, I found God not only looking through my eyes but looking *into* them.' It is among a people redeemed from their sins and consecrated to service that God will tabernacle (σκηνώσει) as an abiding presence (*Shekinah*, fr. שָׁכֵן 'abide'). And when the brotherhood is perfected, there will be no need of a Temple (Rev 21³·²²⁻²⁷). The revelation of God immanent in a redeemed humanity is the ideal towards which Christianity points (Eph 1–3, Col 1⁹⁻²⁰, cf. 2 P 3¹³, Jn 17²⁰⁻²³), and to which it is slowly moving, but only by outgrowing many misconceptions and leaving them behind. See, further, Schultz, *OT Theol.* i. 353 f., ii. 7–11 ; artt. 'Ark of the Covenant,' 'Shekinah' in Hastings' *DB*; Beyschlag, *NT Theol.* i. 95 ff. ; Wendt, *Teaching of Jesus*, § 3, ch. 2 ; Westcott on Jn 14–17).

4. Christian history has been a long series of endeavours to realize the full meaning of the Divine presence. First it was caught into Jewish preconceptions, and projected into the doctrine of the Parousia. This had its effect on the inmost circle of Christian writers with the exception of St. John, and on most of the early Fathers except for the school of Alexandria. With all its inspiration of hope, it must have tended to obscure the truth that God is present through the working of His Spirit in the individual and in society, in the unfolding of truth and the employments of love.

Under the influence of Greek thought in the Gentile world, the Divine presence has been treated as a metaphysical substance, and at last identified with the elements of the Lord's Supper (see Art. ii.), after consecration. This sacerdotal view was virtually accepted by the time of Cyprian, who wrote (*Ep.* lxiii. 17) : 'The passion of the Lord is the sacrifice we offer.' The doctrine of Transubstantiation became the keystone of the ecclesiastical edifice, and was maintained as a theory, by means of the prevalent philosophy of Realism, whose greatest exponent was Thomas Aquinas. As far as English thought is concerned, it crumbled under the dialectic of John Wyclif

(Lechler, *Life of Wycliffe*, p. 351), and by the discovery made by simple men, during the next two centuries, of the spiritual presence mediated through the NT in their own experience.

The Docetic views of Christ's Person, however, which throughout the Middle Ages invested Him with apocalyptic splendours at the cost of all human sympathies, called for still other means of allaying the hunger of the religious imagination. 'The remedy was found in the reverence of the image, in the substitution of the symbol for reality. Gradually that Church, which had tried to centre its affections on an absent Lord, found that its affections must be rekindled by the mediation of some earthly form. It had dismissed from its thoughts the idea of a spiritual presence; it must regain that presence through the intervention of material agencies. It must find it in the water of Baptism, in the bread and wine of Communion, in the act of ordination, in the relics of saints, in the tombs of the martyrs, in the heart of monasteries, and in the walls of consecrated cathedrals. It must see it in the figure of a visible cross, in the monuments raised to a celestial hierarchy, in the observance of festivals in memory of the sainted dead,' above all in apotheosis of the Virgin Mother (Matheson, *op. cit.* i. 322). In the meantime, as applied to the working of the Holy Spirit, the doctrine of the presence stamped infallibility upon the Councils, and finally upon the Pope. While with J. H. Newman it signified the validity of ecclesiastical development throughout the centuries, 'being the germination, growth, and perfection of some living or apparent truth in the minds of men during a sufficient period' (*Development of Doctrine*, p. 37).

But while the popular religion found the presence in the images and relics, and ecclesiastical speculations discovered it in the Conciliar assemblies and the Sacrament of the Supper, there was a parallel movement known as Mysticism, which found the real presence in the soul. To the French mystics, greatest of whom was St. Bernard of the 12th century, the presence of God was the obverse side of their own absence from the world. The Germans Eckhart and Tauler, the Dutch Thomas à Kempis, and others took up the theme, and wove it into a kind of new Stoicism, by way of purification, illumination, and union. 'They taught (following ⸢Thomas Aquinas) that the soul can even here upon earth so receive God within itself as to enjoy in the fullest sense the vision of His being, and dwell in heaven itself' (Harnack, *Outlines of the Hist. of Dogma*, p. 440). This 'practice of the presence of God' (Brother Lawrence) was the religious side of the preparation for Luther and his gospel for the people. He taught that Christianity was not a matter of consent to doctrine, as with the scholastics; or a method of losing oneself in the eternal, as with the mystics; but realizing the Divine presence as found through faith in Christ in 'the freedom of a Christian man.' Luther, commenting in his pointed way on Gal 2[16], says: 'Faith is, if I may use the expression, creative of Divinity, not, of course, in the substance of God, but in ourselves.' And again: 'When we truly say that He is Christ, we mean that He was given for us, without any works of ours, has won for us the Spirit of God, and has made us children of God . . . so that we might become lords of all things in heaven and earth—that is faith' (Erl. ed. 13, 251; Herrmann, *Communion with God*, p. 125). The primary authority of the inward witness thus established by Luther has been most fully apprehended for practical purposes by George Fox and his followers. A bright example was John Woolman (b. 1720), who, in taking his stand against prevailing customs sanctioned by the Church, records in his diary (ch. 4): 'The fear of the Lord so covered me at times that my way was made easier than I expected.' And this independent standpoint, for the sake of humanity, has found poetical expression in Lowell, Whittier, and, in a fashion, Whitman. John Wesley, too, coming from his earlier devotion to Mysticism to his doctrine of assurance, repeated the experience of Luther, and, by means of an evangelical theology, helped men to see that humanity is the proper organ of the Divine presence. This has been the inspiration of modern reformers and philanthropists, but the full bearings of this truth have not yet been realized by the churches. A new vindication of the soul's authority in matters of faith has been undertaken by A. Ritschl and his disciples—Harnack, Herrmann, and the rest. With them the Divine Man Jesus, separated from every ceremony, doctrine, or dream, vouches for the inward presence of God to the soul that believes. By their theory of value-judgments they throw the whole proof of the presence of God upon the faculties of the soul.

LITERATURE.—Harnack, *Hist. of Dogma*, or *Outlines*; Matheson, *Growth of the Spirit of Christianity*; Fairbairn, *Christ in Mod. Theol.*, bk. i.; Herrmann, *Communion with God*; *Imitation of Christ*; *John Woolman's Journal*; J. Campbell Whittier, *Poems*; Stopford Brooke, *Christ in Mod. Life*; Watson, *Inspiration of our Faith*, 274; Moore, *From Advent to Advent*, 63, 98; D. Young, *Crimson Book*, 237; Phillips Brooks, *Mystery of Iniquity*, 277.　　　　A. NORMAN ROWLAND.

PRESENTATION (in the Temple) (Lk 2[22-40]).— When St. Paul had mentioned (Gal 4[4]) the sending forth of the Son of God into our world, he spoke of it in two stages, 'born of a woman,' 'born under the law' (RV); and in both those acts or stages the Pauline Evangelist St. Luke is able and careful in his history of Jesus to exhibit Him. To the narrative of His nativity accordingly he sub-

joins (Lk 2[21]) a notice of His circumcision on the eighth day, in obedience to Gn 17[12]; and now on the fortieth day He is brought to Jerusalem to be offered or presented (RV, παραστῆσαι) to the Lord, in accordance with the legal requirements of Ex 13[2] (freely quoted in v.[23]) and Nu 3. 12. 18. Along with the rite of the *Presentation of the Child* there was fulfilled on the same occasion another for the *Purification of the Mother*; but we shall consider that afterwards.

1. The law as to *the Child* is described in OT as having its origin in Egypt. From patriarchal times, indeed, the firstborn had been the priest in the family; but a new obligation was laid on the firstborn in Israel by the circumstances of the Exodus. When God sent Moses to Pharaoh, the Divine message to the king ran, 'Israel is my son, even my firstborn: if thou refuse to let him go I will slay thy son, even thy firstborn' (Ex 4[22. 23]). Pharaoh refused. Nine successive plagues were sent on him in vain. The time had come for the execution of God's threatening. The Lord was to pass through the land of Egypt to execute the judgment. Israel was not *so* guilty as her oppressors; but neither could she stand before God if once He were angry; and God provided for her in the Paschal lamb a victim under which each Israelite household that would believe His word and keep His commandment might find shelter. 'By faith they kept the passover and the sprinkling of blood' (He 11[28]); but in token that their firstborn had been due to death and rescued by God's mercy, all the firstborn ('every male that openeth the womb') were to be sanctified to Him (Nu 8[17]). God might have slain each, or kept him for His own especial service. He would not slay him: He permitted him (and required him) to be redeemed (Ex 13[13-15]). Instead of the firstborn, however, God took for the service of His sanctuary the tribe of Levi (Nu 3[12] 8[14-18]), requiring, at the time of this substitution, that as many firstborn as there were in Israel *in excess of* the number of the Levites must be redeemed by the payment of five shekels for each one (Nu 3[44-51]). Afterwards (Nu 18[15. 16]), *every firstborn son* must be presented and redeemed by the payment of this amount. Our Lord might have claimed exemption, as the Son of God; just as afterwards when they asked Him to pay the Temple rate He declared, 'Therefore the sons are free' (Mt 17[26] RV). But He came not to claim exemptions but to share our burdens, carry our sorrows, take away our sins, and, more particularly, to redeem them that are under the Law (Gal 4[5]). He 'came not to be ministered unto, but to minister, and to give his life a ransom for many' (Mt 20[28]); and 'thus it became him to fulfil all righteousness' (3[15]). Moreover, by being thus redeemed from the personal obligation of serving in the Temple, His love to it, which at His next visit to it He was to manifest (Lk 2[49] RV), and His zeal for it which devoured Him (Jn 2[17]), were brought into clearer light. They were not of constraint, but willing. Still, the leading thought in the history of His Presentation in the Temple is that of His having come 'that the scripture might be fulfilled' (Lk 2[22-24] 24[44]), 'and that the whole life of the God-man on earth might present a realization of that ideal depicted in the prophetic writings of the OT' (Oosterzee).

The act of presenting Him would be performed by Joseph (Ex 13[15]) as the putative father, at once the shield of Mary and the protector of her child (Lk 3[23]); not by the Virgin, as Cornelius à Lapide assumes, although there is some beauty in his interpretation of the five shekels, which constituted the redemption money, as 'symbolizing the Five Wounds at the price whereof Christ redeemed the race of man' (*Com. in loc.*). The Law does not seem to have prescribed any particular time for the redemption of the firstborn, but many fathers would doubtless act as Joseph did, and perform the rite on the day appointed by the Law for the sacrifice of his wife's purification. There is hardly time for the visit of the Wise Men, the Flight into Egypt, and the Return thence, between the Birth of Christ and His Presentation in the Temple ; moreover, a public service at Jerusalem would have been fraught with danger after the inquiries of the Magi had aroused the jealous fears of Herod. But neither is there any need for supposing that the Wise Men's visit came so soon after the Nativity. 'From two years old and under' (Mt 2^{16}) was the age which Herod supposed the newborn 'King of the Jews' might be. Mary's availing herself of the permission, as a poor woman, to offer the two doves instead of the costlier lamb is not consistent with the idea that the gold offered by the Wise Men was at her disposal : while St. Luke's mention of the Holy Family returning into Galilee and Nazareth (Lk 2^{39}) is of the nature of a foreshortening, and does not imply that no event intervened between the Presentation and the journey to the North.

2. The *Purification of Mary*, besides synchronizing with the Presentation of her Son, was an event belonging to the same moral and religious category. It also was an act of a humble-minded and becoming obedience to the Law of Moses, under which she lived. St. Jerome alone among the Fathers was of opinion that in her case too it was strictly obligatory, not, of course, on account of any *sin* on her part, her conception of the Child being spotless and holy (Lk 1^{26-35}) and an act of obedience to Almighty God ; but *ceremonially* because, the Birth being a real one, she had touched things which involved ceremonial uncleanness. Whether St. Jerome is right, or the other Fathers (for the discussion see Cornelius à Lapide), and whether or not she might have claimed exemption, she is to be praised for not doing so, but quietly and humbly accepting the law binding on ordinary mothers, and being willing, as her Son will also be, to be reckoned with transgressors (Mk 15^{28}, Lk 22^{37}). It was enough for her, as it would be enough for Him, that God knew.

The reading adopted in the RV (Lk 2^{22}), 'the days of *their* (not '*her*,' AV) purification,' has the highest MS authority, and is that expressly of Origen and Cyril : it is explained when we remember that while the ceremonial uncleanness was directly that of the mother only, Joseph and the Child could hardly help —especially while living in such circumstances as were theirs at Bethlehem—contracting a like defilement, in the legal sense, by contact with her. Our Lord, all holy from the first, was often to be so defiled (Lk 15^1 19^7). He regarded it as His glory, not His shame.

The legal ordinance (Lv 12) appointed that a woman who had borne a man child should be (ceremonially) unclean for seven days ; for three and thirty days more she might touch no hallowed thing, nor come into the sanctuary. Then, on the fortieth day, she must bring 'a lamb of the first year for a burnt-offering (expressive of devotion), and a young pigeon or a turtle-dove for a sin-offering (a testimony, St. Jerome says, to the doctrine of original sin), unto the door of the tent of meeting, unto the priest, and he shall offer it before the Lord, and make atonement for her ; and she shall be cleansed from the fountain of her blood. . . . And if her means suffice not for a lamb, then she shall take two turtle-doves or two young pigeons ; the one for a burnt-offering, the other for a sin-offering.' The Virgin's humility appears in her availing herself of this merciful provision ; she disdained not to admit her poverty ; we may be sure she did not (as some, thinking to exalt her, have imagined) assume a false appearance of it : even if Joseph and she had not been extremely poor before, the expenses of the

journey to Bethlehem, and of living there six weeks, and the five shekels for the Child, could not have failed to make deep inroads on their purse. The order of the combined rites would be as follows :— (1) The Holy Family would come into the hall of the unclean, and stand there. (2) Then would be offered the dove for her sin-offering, and perhaps they would be sprinkled with the lustral water and the ashes of the heifer (Nu 19^{17}). (3) Then the Child would be presented. And lastly, (4) the other dove would be offered in sign of Mary's thanksgiving and self-devotion to God. The Virgin would not go further—even when she had been cleansed—than the Court of the Women.

The Evangelist's use of the words '*parents*' (v.^{27}) and 'father and mother' (v.^{33}) have been urged as evidence that 'the idea of the supernatural conception of Jesus has not penetrated to this part of the legendary materials here collected together' (Schmidt and Holzendorff, *Short Protestant Commentary*) ; to which we may answer that he would have been a poor redactor who, having transcribed ch. i., did not observe an inconsistency of this kind, and that in point of fact the Third Gospel is marked by its homogeneity (see Ramsay, *Was Christ born at Bethlehem ?*). The explanation of the apparent inconsistency lies deep in the principle which led our Lord, sinless Himself (2 Co 5^{21}), to accept the lot of sinners, and lay this lot also on His blessed Mother ; and further, that His glory was not to be manifested till the time appointed of the Father. Till then, whatever brief epiphanies there might be were only for the favoured few. Even the Transfiguration was to be told to no man till the Son of Man was risen from the dead. The facts were secure in the hearts of sufficient witnesses (Lk $2^{19.51}$) ; they would come forth in due time. More especially, His birth of a Virgin Mother— told as it was to be by two Evangelists (Mt 1^{18-25}, Lk 1^{26-38}), and always an article of faith in the Church—was not a thing to be communicated to unbelieving ears and scoffing tongues ; even when His claim to have come down out of heaven was contrasted with what were supposed to be the known facts of His origin as Man (Jn 6^{42}, Mt 13^{55}). The feeling of the Early Church upon the subject is expressed in a famous passage of St. Ignatius of Antioch (*c*. 110) : 'Hidden from the prince of this world were the virginity of Mary, and her child-bearing, and likewise also the death of the Lord—three mysteries to be cried aloud—the which were wrought in the silence of God' (*ad Ephes.* 19).

Both the Purification of Mary and the Presentation of our Lord in the Temple are commemorated on the 2nd of February (Candlemas). Baronius says that the Church at Rome was led to the institution of this Feast in order to supersede the *Lupercalia*, the observances connected wherewith were of an extremely immoral as well as idolatrous character. See, further, artt. ANNA and SIMEON.

JAMES COOPER.

PRESS.—See CROWD and MULTITUDE.

PRICE OF BLOOD ($\tau\iota\mu\grave{\eta}$ $\alpha\ddot{\iota}\mu\alpha\tau\sigma\varsigma$, Mt 27^6).—An expression used by the priests of the Temple in reference to the money Judas Iscariot had received for the betrayal of his Master. The thirty pieces of silver were the price of a traitor's service, and so ultimately the price of a man's head ; and though the priests were willing to take advantage of the dastardly deed by putting the betrayed Man to death, they still regarded with feelings of disgust and abhorrence the money paid for His betrayal. It had been soiled by the hands of a traitor, and associated with blood - guiltiness of a kind that they had no desire to share. They would neither accept it for themselves, when Judas offered to restore it, nor, when flung down in the sanctuary, did they regard it as fit for the holy uses of the Temple. An appropriate use was found for it in the purchase of ground outside the walls for the burial of strangers to Jerusalem. (For the story of Judas' end, and the divergent account in Ac $1^{18.19}$, see AKELDAMA, JUDAS ISCARIOT).

The reasoning of the Temple priests here has been usually condemned as a piece of pious hypocrisy, implying a display of honourable diffidence that stands in suspicious contrast with their previous dealings with the traitor. If the money was soiled, who was responsible, if not those who had taken it (perhaps directly from the Temple-treasury) and sent it on its dastardly mission ?

Why should they, who had paid the price of blood, scruple about taking it back? 'If it was sinful to put back the price of blood in the sacred treasury, how was it any more permissible to take it out?' (Calvin, *NT Com.*). This is rather a one-sided judgment. It is true, their manifestation of scrupulous feeling was somewhat belated : it would have become them better to have no dealings whatever with Judas. But we may still give them the credit for the wish to be as little as possible involved in the crime of treachery. In point of fact, people will make use of a traitor who have no love for traitors. In this case the compact made with Judas was very much more dishonourable on his side than on theirs; for they were sworn enemies of Christ, he a professed friend. The °priests might believe the money was well spent on their part, though ill gotten on his. The curse of treachery was now associated with it, and would help to intensify their loathing when they spoke of it as the price of blood. It was unhallowed gain; and they could use it only for some purpose less sacred than those connected with the Temple, and in which they themselves had no profit. We may compare with this scruple of the priests the similar feeling manifested by David in a contrasted case (2 S 23$^{14-17}$). When the three mighty men at the risk of their lives brought the king a draught of water from the well of Bethlehem, he scrupled to drink it, because it was so closely associated with the blood of the men who had risked their lives to procure it. It had been procured at the price of blood, and he could not use it in the common way. It was hallowed by the sacrifice associated with it, just as the blood-money in Judas' hands was tainted and defiled by a betrayal equivalent to murder.

LITERATURE.—See under JUDAS ISCARIOT, but esp. Ker, *Serm.* i. 293.   J. DICK FLEMING.

PRIDE.—The condemnation of pride has always been very pronounced in Christian thought. It is one of the faults most distinctly incompatible with the ethics of the NT. Certain other systems of religion have not so strenuously combated this feeling. In fact, some may not unreasonably be regarded as having contributed to its indulgence. An elementary attribute in the Christian conception of character is humility.

1. It is remarkable that the word for 'pride' (ὑπερηφανία) occurs only once in the recorded conversations of our Lord, and the adj. 'proud' (ὑπερήφανος) only once in the Gospels (Lk 1^{51}). In Mk 7^{22} pride is classed as one of the things which defile a man. It is in the positive precepts and general example and teaching of the Master that we find the principles which have made pride so repugnant to the Christian consciousness. Chief of all these forces is the example of our Lord's own life. The Incarnation was itself the most transcendent exhibition of humility. In it men saw their Lord counting it not a prize to be on an equality with God, emptying Himself, and taking the form of a servant. In the essential abasement of this earthly life He humbled Himself to the particular extremes of endurance of personal ill-treatment and obedience even unto death. Henceforth lowliness of station and self-forgetting passivity were consecrated by the Divine example. In the same degree the possessors of power and place were taught the limitations and responsibilities of their position, and shown the insensate evil of scornfully regarding men of inferior circumstances.

2. Before the Birth of Christ this characteristic of His mission was heralded in Mary's song. She who described herself as a handmaiden of low estate could rejoice that in the coming Kingdom the proud would be scattered in, or by (Lk 1^{51} RVm), the disposition of their hearts. Princes would be brought down, and rich men sent empty away. On the other hand, those of low degree would be exalted, and the hungry abundantly satisfied. The Magnificat proclaimed the truths that whilst poverty and obscurity are not bars to acceptance with God, there are evils peculiarly belonging to high rank which utterly disqualify.

3. The Temptation (Mt 4$^{1-11}$ ‖ Lk 4$^{1-13}$) was largely an attempt to work on feelings of pride in the mind of Jesus. He was urged to prove His superiority to the conditions of ordinary humanity by a self-glorifying triumph over the laws of nature. The Tempter strove to make Him do so either (1) by providing for His special physical needs, or (2) by a public display of His might. In the offer (3) of universal sovereignty, the lures of authority and glory were especially emphasized.

4. In His definite teaching our Lord laid especial stress on the virtues of humility and lowliness of mind as fundamental requisites in His loyal followers. The Beatitude of the meek struck the dominant keynote in this respect. Men were invited to learn of Him, for He was meek and lowly in heart (Mt 11^{29}). His disciples could apply to Him the prophetic description that He was meek (Mt 21^5). More than once He seems to have uttered the apothegm, 'Whosoever shall exalt himself shall be humbled, and whosoever shall humble himself shall be exalted' (Mt 23^{12}, Lk 14^{11} 18^{14}). Various specific forms of pride were rebuked and cautioned against.

(1) Several times our Lord severely censured exhibitions of *spiritual pride*. This vice called forth peculiar indignation and detestation in Him. The religious ostentation of the Pharisees was unsparingly reprobated. The types are eternally stigmatized who can thank God they are not as others are, who from the heights of their own complacency can look down on the supposed inferior spirituality of their fellows (Lk 18$^{9ff.}$); who parade in public places their devotions (Mt 6^5); who do all their works to be seen of men, and obtrude their religious symbols (Mt 23^5); who for a pretence make long prayers (Lk 20^{47}). This species of religious self-satisfaction, of spurious spirituality, elicited the scathing invective of Christ in an altogether unparalleled degree. He declared that the publicans and harlots went into the Kingdom of God before such proud professors (Mt 21^{31}).

(2) The strictures our Lord passed on the *racial pride* of the Jews drew against Him their fiercest anger. He showed how vain were their boasted privileges when He proclaimed that many should be admitted to the Kingdom from all quarters of the earth, but the children of the Kingdom rejected (Mt 8^{12}). He tried to make them realize from their own Scriptures the futility of their reliance on descent, by referring to the favour shown Naaman the Syrian and the widow of Zarephath (Lk 4$^{25ff.}$). The parables of the Labourers in the Vineyard (Mt 20$^{1ff.}$) and of the Householder's rebellious servants (21$^{33ff.}$) were plainly intended to make His hearers see how little worth was in their lofty pretensions as the children of Abraham—the chosen people.

(3) *Intellectual haughtiness* was also decidedly condemned by Christ. The inclination that springs from the consciousness of ability or learning to scornfully depreciate those of more meagre mental equipment, is one of the most insidious forms of pride. To it certain natures fall victims who would consider family pretensions or religious assumptions of superiority vulgar and discreditable. Many who would loathe the commonly recognized vaingloriousness of the Pharisees are dangerously near sharing in the mental arrogance which prompted the latter to sneer, 'This multi-

tude which knoweth not the law are accursed'
(Jn 7[49]).

The tendency to indulge in lofty contempt from the 'intellectual throne' is strikingly portrayed in Tennyson's *Palace of
Art*—

'O God-like isolation which art mine,
    I can but count thee perfect gain,
What time I watch the darkening droves of swine
    That range on yonder plain.'

All such disdainfulness for the simple and unlearned was impressively forbidden by Christ's
warning, 'See that ye despise not one of these
little ones' (Mt 18[10]; cf. a striking sermon by Bp.
Boyd Carpenter on 'The Dangers of Contempt').
Again, our Lord bore witness to the supreme importance of simplicity and innocence, as opposed to
superciliousness and pride, when He said of the
little children, 'Of such is the kingdom of heaven'
(Lk 18[16]), and added that the only attitude which
qualified for admission was that of a little child.
It is noteworthy that the same dispositions of
receptivity and absence of hard preconceptions are
insisted on by scientists as prime requisites for the
student of the kingdom of nature.

(4) The pride that comes from the enjoyment of
high official or social rank was discountenanced in
one of the most surprising actions of our Lord's
earthly life—the episode of the Feet - washing
(Jn 13). It was a vivid, unforgetable lesson in the
duty of self-abasing service. No one who then was
present was likely to fall into the sin of presuming
on privileges of position, or treating subordinates
with selfish, slighting inconsiderateness. The imagination of succeeding generations has been intensely impressed by the spectacle of the Son of
God washing the travel-stained feet of His poor
followers. The pride that jealously exacts subservience could not be more effectually proscribed.
The homily against those whose self-importance
made them claim the place of honour at entertain-
ments (Lk 14[7ff.]) is directed against the same
grandiose assumptions. This social arrogance of
the Pharisees was one of the points in our Lord's
indictment of them. They loved the chief place
at feasts, and the chief seats in the synagogues,
and to be called Rabbi (Mt 23[5ff.]). Any tendency
among His disciples to assume lordship was
strictly, tenderly suppressed. Once He called them
together when such claims were mooted, and
pointed out to them how among the outside
Gentiles there were those who lorded it and exercised authority. In contrast to that should be
their practice. Whoever of them was ambitious
of greatness and supremacy could attain it only
along the lines of submissive service (Mt 20[25f.]).
They had Him as an example, who came not to
receive service, but to minister to the needs of
others, even to the point of giving up His life for
them (v.[28]). They were not to arrogate to themselves titles implying mastership (23[8, 10]). The
question of leadership among them was met by
Christ taking a little child and placing it 'beside
himself' (παρ' ἑαυτῷ), and saying that the reception
of a little child meant the reception of Himself and
of His Father who sent Him (Lk 9[46ff.]). In the
light of how so stupendous a glory was to be won,
their own shortsighted strivings after precedence
stood exposed. All such grasping at power and
place was a contradiction of the true conception of
honour. It was he who humbled himself as a little
child that was greatest (Mt 18[4]).

5. The essential vice of pride was glanced at in
one of these conversations when the Master said,
'All ye are brethren' (Mt 23[8]). Pride is an injury
to the bond of brotherhood; it is disloyalty in the
Christian household; it is a breach of fellowship.
The selfish despising of our fellow-creatures is a
contradiction of the law of love. It cannot coexist
with a true-hearted affection for all men. Pride is

self-centred, and plumes itself on the gap between
ourselves and those beneath us. It revels in the
feeling of superiority. Nothing could be more
opposed than this to the self-sacrificing love which
is bent on raising and helping. Pride also betrays
a lack of perception as to our own true position
before God. It reveals an undue magnifying of
relative differences.

6. The word 'pride' is often used in another and
a harmless sense which may imply no more than a
fit appreciation of benefits, a lofty sense of honour,
a dignified aloofness that will not stoop to what is
mean or defiling. In this better sense Milton can
speak of 'modest pride,' and Moore deplore the
loss of the 'pride of former days.' The distinction
is clear between this pardonable and highly useful
feeling—a feeling which may be accompanied with
real humility—and a haughtiness of spirit, a contemptuous looking down on others, a selfish glorying
in one's own superiority. See also HUMILITY,
MEEKNESS.

LITERATURE.—Aristotle, *Nic. Eth.* iv. 3; Kant, *Met. of Eth.*
(Clark's ed.), 241; Liddon, *Univ. Serm.* ii. 203, *BL*[8], 491; Medd,
The One Mediator, 416; Alford, *Quebec Chapel Serm.* ii. 15;
Stalker, *Seven Deadly Sins*, 1; Wickham in *Oxford Univ. Serm.*
(ed. Bebb), 332; Bunyan, *Pilg. Prog.*, Pt. ii. 'The Valley of
Humiliation'; Longfellow's 'King Robert of Sicily'; Bp. Magee,
The Gospel and the Age ('Knowledge without Love').

W. S. KERR.

PRIEST.—1. The Jewish priests.—The few passages in the Gospels where the word 'priest' (ἱερεύς)
occurs apply solely to the Jewish priesthood, but
of its position and functions very little is recorded either in the Gospels or generally in the
NT. The Gr. ἱερεύς is the equivalent of the Heb.
כֹּהֵן. The Jewish priesthood is brought before us in
the Gospels in the following connexions :—(1) The
work of Zacharias (Lk 1[5-9]), where we read of the
priestly courses with the duties assigned to them
by lot. The priesthood was divided into twenty-
four courses (ἐφημερίαι), and each course was on duty
twice during the year (Plummer, *in loc.*). (2) The
priests and Levites who interviewed John the
Baptist (Jn 1[19]). (3) The lepers cleansed by our
Lord were to show themselves to the priest (Mt 8[4],
Mk 1[44], Lk 5[14] 17[14]) in proof of their healing and of
the obedience of Jesus to the Law (Plummer, *in loc.*).
(4) The reference to the shewbread as eaten by
the priests only (Mk 2[26]). (5) The priest who passed
by the wounded traveller (Lk 10[31]). The Gospels
are much more concerned with 'chief (or high)
priests' (ἀρχιερεῖς) than with priests, the former
word being frequently found in all four Gospels.
See artt. CHIEF PRIESTS and HIGH PRIEST.

2. Priesthood of Christ.—(1) *The general position
of Christ's priesthood in the NT.*—The English
word 'priest' represents two different Heb. and Gr.
words. It is used to translate ἱερεύς and כֹּהֵן (Lat.
sacerdos). It is also the contraction of *presbyter*
('prester,' 'prest,' 'priest'), which is the transliteration of πρεσβύτερος and LXX rendering of זָקֵן
(elder). But the NT idea of the priesthood of Christ
is associated solely with the former of these words.
Christ is called a priest, or high priest, in the
sense of a sacrificing priest (ἱερεύς, ἀρχιερεύς). This
application of the term to our Lord is found only
in Hebrews, though the priestly functions connected with sacrifice and intercession are, of course,
found frequently in the NT (Mt 20[28], Jn 1[29] 14[6],
Ro 8[34], Eph 2[18], 1 P 1[19-21] 3[18], Rev 1[5, 13]). It should,
however, be carefully observed that it is only in
Hebrews that these functions are connected with
our Lord as priest. Elsewhere they simply form
part of His general work as Redeemer.

(2) *The specific purpose of Christ's priesthood in
Hebrews.*—It is important to inquire why, and
under what circumstances, the priesthood of Christ
is brought forward in Hebrews. The situation
there described is one in which the Hebrew Chris-

tians were in danger of spiritual degeneration (5¹²), backsliding and apostasy (6⁹ 10³⁵). The Epistle was written to prevent this, and the means of accomplishing it was personal experience of the priesthood of Christ. In some way, therefore, Christ's priesthood is associated with spiritual steadfastness, progress, assurance. In the full understanding and acceptance of this truth will be found the secret of growth and maturity of experience. It is evident that these Hebrews knew Jesus as Saviour, and had an elementary knowledge of the truths of redemption (6¹), but they did not realize what it meant to have Him as priest. The distinction between the two may be seen by a consideration of the time and circumstances under which priesthood appeared in connexion with Israel. Apart from foreign priesthoods like those of Egypt and Midian (Gn 47, Ex 3), the first mention of priesthood in Israel is at Sinai. There was no priesthood in Egypt, only redemption. There was none at the Red Sea, where deliverance was the one thing needful. At Sinai they were to realize for the first time their true relation to God and God's relation to them as dwelling among them (Ex 19⁴⁻⁶ 25¹⁻⁸). The priesthood was appointed to provide the means of access to God and prevent fear in approaching Him. The essence of priesthood, therefore, is access to God based on an already existing redemption. The Hebrew Christians knew Christ as Redeemer; they were now to be taught the possibility, power, and joy of constant free access to God in Him, and in this, the removal of all fear and dissatisfaction. Any sense of unworthiness would be met by His worthiness, all fear removed by His nearness to them and to God as at once Son of Man and Divine High Priest. There is thus a whole world of difference between knowing Christ as Saviour and as Priest. The former may involve only spiritual childhood, the latter must necessarily include spiritual maturity (He 5¹⁰⁻¹⁴). This is one of the great distinctions between the teaching of Romans and of Hebrews. The former is concerned with redemption which makes access possible (Ro 5²), the latter with access which is made possible by redemption. This practical purpose of Hebrews in close connexion with spiritual growth and maturity should ever be kept in mind. Herein lies the present and permanent value of the Epistle in Christian life and service, with its constant emphasis on 'Draw near' (10²²), 'Draw not back' (10³⁹), 'Let us go on' (6¹).

(3) *The essential meaning of priesthood.*—In order to obtain a true idea of the priesthood of Christ, it is necessary to inquire what were the essential characteristics of priesthood. What were the functions which the priest performed as priest, those of which he had the monopoly, and which no one else could perform under any circumstances? The best definition is in He 5¹, where we are told that the priest was 'appointed for men in things pertaining to God,' that is, he represented man to God. What was included in this representation we shall see later, but meanwhile it should be clearly observed that priesthood meant the representation of man to God, and was the exact opposite and counterpart of the work of the prophet, which was to represent God to man. The priest went from man to God, the prophet went from God to man. The two ideas are seen in He 3¹, where Christ is called 'Apostle and High Priest'—'Apostle' because sent from God to man, 'High Priest' because going from man to God. In this twofold capacity lies His perfect mediation. If the priest did other duties, such as teaching, receiving tithes, and blessing the people, these were superadded functions and not inherent in the priesthood. The Levites could teach and the kings could bless, but by no possibility could either do the essential

duties of the priesthood in representing man to God. This specific idea is clearly taught as the essence of priesthood both in OT and NT, where the Godward aspect of priesthood is always stated and emphasized (Ex 28¹, Nu 16⁴⁰, 2 Ch 26¹⁸, Ezk 44¹⁵, He 6²⁰ 7²⁵ 9²⁴). This essential idea of priesthood as representative of man to God carries with it the right of access to and of abiding in the presence of God. In primitive days, families were represented by the patriarch or head of a clan; but as the sense of sin grew and deepened, and as the Divine purpose of redemption was gradually unfolded, it became necessary to have men entirely separated for this office. Priesthood was thus the admission at once of the sinfulness of the race, of the holiness of God, and of the need of conditions of approach to God. It is of the utmost importance that we should define and keep clear these essential characteristics of the priesthood. They can be summed up in the general ideas of (*a*) drawing near to God by means of an offering, (*b*) dwelling near to God for the purpose of intercession (Ezk 44¹⁶, Lv 16¹⁷, Ex 28³⁰ 30⁷⁻⁸, Lk 1⁹⁻¹⁰).

(4) *The special order of Christ's priesthood.*—The unique feature of the discussion in Hebrews is the association of Christ's priesthood with that of **Melchizedek.** Three times in Scripture Melchizedek is mentioned, and each time the reference is important. (*a*) In Gn 14 he appears in history in connexion with Abraham. He is termed 'priest of God Most High.' (*b*) Then in Ps 110 he is mentioned again in a Psalm usually regarded as Messianic, and as such applied to Himself by our Lord (Mt 22⁴⁴, Mk 12³⁶, Lk 20⁴²). The underlying thought in the Psalm is of a priesthood other than that of Aaron, and suggests a consciousness, however dim, on the part of spiritually-minded Jews, of something beyond and superior to the Aaronic priesthood. The bare mention of another priesthood at all is significant and striking. (*c*) He appears in Hebrews as a type of Christ. The record of Gn 14 is taken as it stands and used to symbolize and typify some of the elements of the priesthood of Christ. (α) The position of Melchizedek as king indicates the *royalty* of Christ's priesthood. (β) The meaning of the name 'Melchizedek' is used to suggest the thought of *righteousness*. (γ) The meaning of the title 'king of Salem' suggests the idea of *peace*. The order and connexion of righteousness and peace are noted in Hebrews. First comes righteousness as the basis of relation to God, and then peace as the outcome of righteousness. Righteousness without peace vindicates the Law and punishes sin; peace without righteousness ignores the Law and condones sin. Righteousness and peace when combined honour the Law while pardoning sin. (δ) The absence in the record of Gn 14 of any earthly connexions of ancestry and posterity is used in Hebrews to symbolize the perpetuity of Christ's priesthood. What was true of the record about Melchizedek is present in actual fact in Christ. One point of great importance not to be overlooked is that in Gn 14 no priestly functions are attributed to Melchizedek. The gift of bread and wine to Abraham had, of course, nothing essentially priestly in it. In the record he is just called 'priest of God Most High,' without any characteristic priestly acts being stated. This exactly corresponds to the use made of the Melchizedek priesthood in Hebrews, which does not treat of any priestly acts or functions, but of the *order* of the priesthood. The fundamental thought of the Melchizedek priesthood in Hebrews refers to the person of the priest, not to his acts. The functions, or acts, are considered in connexion and contrast with the functions of the Aaronic priesthood. It is the priestly person rather than the priestly work that is emphasized in the

Melchizedek priesthood. He was a *royal* person (which Aaron was not) ; an *abiding* person (which Aaron was not) ; a *unique* person (which Aaron was not). It is the personal superiority in these respects over the priesthood of Aaron that is dwelt upon in connexion with Melchizedek. There is, of course, no comparison drawn between Melchizedek and Christ, but use is made of Melchizedek to symboliz. the personal superiority of Christ's priesthood over all others—a priest'.ood that is older, wider, more lasting than that of Aaron.

(5) *The particular functions of Christ's priesthood.* —It is in connexion with the Aaronic priesthood that the *work* of Christ's priesthood is considered. A contrast is made, as is shown by the recurring key word 'better' (7^{22} 8^6 *et al.*). Our Lord never was a priest of the Aaronic line ($7^{13.14}$ 8^4), but it was necessary to use the illustration of the Aaronic priesthood to denote Christ's priestly functions, because no characteristic priestly functions are recorded of Melchizedek. A series of comparisons between Aaron's and Christ's priesthood needs careful attention : (*a*) first generally in $2^{17.18}$ with reference to personal qualification ; (*b*) then after bare mention in 3^1, more fully in 4^{14-16}. (*c*) But it is in 5^{1-10} that we have the first definite comparison. In vv.$^{1-5}$ the requirements of the Aaronic priesthood are stated in regard to (*a*) office (v.^{1}), (β) character (vv.$^{2.3}$), (γ) Divine appointment (vv.$^{4.5}$). In vv.$^{6-10}$ we have the fulfilment of these requirements in Christ stated in the reverse order : (*a*) Divine appointment (vv.$^{5.6}$), (β) character (vv.$^{7.8}$), (γ) office (vv.$^{9.10}$). (*d*) Then in ch. 7 we have the comparison and contrast between Melchizedek and Aaron, with the superiority of the former, on three grounds : (*a*) Aaron was not royal, (β) Aaron did not abide, by reason of death, (γ) Aaron had many successors. The superiority of the person gives superiority to the functions. (*e*) Then in chs. 8–10 the superiority of the work of Christ is compared with that of Aaron under three aspects : (*a*) a better covenant (ch. 8), because spiritual, not temporal ; (β) a better sanctuary (ch. 9), because heavenly, not earthly ; (γ) a better sacrifice (ch. 10), because real, not symbolical. In the course of this entire discussion several elements of superiority emerge. A superior order (7^{1-17}), a superior tribe (v.^{14}), a superior calling (v.^{21}), a superior tenure (vv.$^{23.24}$), a superior character (v.^{26}), a superior sanctuary and a superior covenant (ch. 9), a superior sacrifice (ch. 10). After ch. 10 there is nothing priestly in the terms used, though ch. 13 refers to functions connected with the priesthood. The functions of priesthood may thus be summed up as (*a*) access to God for man, (*b*) offering to God for man, (*c*) intercession with God for man ; and the superiority of our Lord's priesthood is shown in the following particulars : (1) It is royal in character, (2) heavenly in sphere, (3) spiritual in nature, (4) continuous in efficacy, (5) perpetual in duration, (6) universal in scope, (7) effectual in results.

At this point there are three questions that call for attention. (*a*) There is no real distinction between 'Priest' and 'High Priest.' Christ is both ($5^{6.10}$ 6^{20} $7^{1.3.15.17.21}$). The difference is one of rank only, the High Priesthood being, as it were, a specialized form. The term 'high priest' occurs only nine times in the OT, of which but two are in the Pentateuch, and it is curious that the term is never once applied to Aaron. This clearly shows that there is no real distinction between the two offices, for if there had been an essential difference from the first, Aaron would have been called 'high priest.' Christ is never termed 'High Priest' in connexion with Melchizedek, but only when Aaron is under consideration. As, however, the distinction was current in NT times, it was necessary to show that Christ fulfilled both offices.

(*b*) Hebrews dwells very carefully on Christ's offering as connected with His death on the cross, and also on His entrance into heaven as connected with His Ascension. The absence of reference to the Resurrection (except in 13^{20}) is explained by the fact that there was no place for this event in the type. Attention is therefore called to the two parts of the one priestly function of offering which was connected with the Day of Atonement, the sacrifice of the animal without the camp ($13^{11.12}$), and the entrance into the Holiest with the blood of the animal sacrificed. Stress is laid on the Ascension because that is regarded as the moment of our High Priest's entrance into heaven on our behalf ($9^{12.24}$). It is the close association of these two parts that explains 8^3 'It is of necessity that this man have somewhat also to offer.' The view that this verse teaches that Christ is now continually offering Himself to God in heaven is clearly inconsistent with the rest of the Epistle, which lays such stress on the association of the offering with Christ's death, and which also dwells on the uniqueness and completeness of the offering ($\dot{\epsilon}\phi\dot{\alpha}\pi\alpha\xi$, 7^{27} $9^{12.28}$), and on the session at God's right hand (the attitude of a victor, not an offerer). Further, the great and essential characteristic of the New Covenant is remission of sins (8^8 $10^{11.12}$), and this was possible only after the offering was completed (4^{16} 9^{14-22}). The aorist tense in 8^3 seems decisive in associating the offering with the death. It may be 'timeless' (G. Milligan, *Theol. of the Ep. to the Hebrews*), but at least it is not continuous (Westcott, *in loc.*). If with A. B. Davidson we interpret this 'somewhat to offer' of the heavenly sanctuary, as seems only natural, the conditions are exactly fulfilled by the fact and at the moment of ascension, when Christ first appeared before God for us, and then sat down at the right hand of God, having fulfilled all the requirements of the work of offering and presentation of Himself on our behalf. The offering in Hebrews is invariably associated with sin, not with consecration ; with Christ's death, not with His life ; and offering is thereby shown to be the characteristic work of a priest. To regard our Lord as now offering, or representing, or re-presenting Himself in heaven, is to think of Him in the attitude of a worshipper instead of on the throne. His work of offering and presentation was finished before He sat down, and it is significant that what the author calls the 'pith,' or 'crowning-point' ($\kappa\epsilon\phi\dot{\alpha}\lambda\alpha\iota o\nu$) of the Epistle ($8^1$) is a 'high priest who is set down.' This exactly answers to the type on the Day of Atonement. When the high priest had presented the blood, his work was complete ; and if we could imagine him able to remain there in the presence of God, he would stay on the basis of that complete offering and not as continuing to offer or present anything. Besides, there was no altar in the Holy of Holies, and there could therefore be no real sacrificial offering. Christ is not now at an altar or a mercy-seat, but on the throne. If it be said that intercession is an insufficient idea of His priestly life above, it may be answered that offering and intercession do not exhaust His heavenly life. His presence there on our behalf as our Representative includes everything. He Himself is (not merely His death was) the propitiation (1 Jn 2^2). Does it not betoken a lack of spiritual perception to demand that Christ should always be doing something ? Why may we not be content with the thought that He is there, and that in His presence above is the secret of peace, the assurance of access, and the guarantee of permanent relation with God ? It is just at this point that one essential difference between type and antitype is noticed. The high priest went into the Holy of Holies '*with* blood'; but when Christ's entrance into heaven is mentioned, He is said to have gone '*through* his own blood,' *i.e.* His access is based on the offering on Calvary (9^{12}). It seems impossible, therefore, to extend the idea of Christ's offering to mean 'a present and eternal offering to God of His life in heaven' (W. Milligan, *Ascension*, p. 116). Such a view finds no warrant in the Epistle, and everything against it in the emphasis laid on the association of Christ's offering with His death (7^{27} 9$^{13. 14. 24-28}$ 10$^{10-14}$), and the uniqueness and completeness of that as culminating in the entrance into heaven. The death of Christ meant propitiation, the Ascension emphasizes access based upon this propitiation (Westcott, *Hebrews*, p. 230).

(*c*) The use of the two priesthoods, Melchizedek's and Aaron's, is not to be interpreted of two aspects of priesthood,—one on earth and the other in heaven successively realized by Christ,—for this would be quite opposed to 7^{18} 8^4. It means that there is one priesthood, of which Melchizedek is used for the person, and Aaron for the work. If Christ's death is associated with the Aaronic priesthood (against 8^4), then the entrance into heaven must also be associated with Aaron (against 6^{20} *et al.*), which would leave no room at all for the Melchizedek priesthood. It is impossible for the death to be associated with one priesthood, and the ascension with the other. The order or nature of the priesthood according to Melchizedek gives validity and perpetuity to the acts which are symbolized in the Aaronic priesthood.

(6) *The personal qualifications of Christ as Priest*. —The practical and spiritual use made of priesthood in Hebrews gives special point to the emphasis laid on the personal qualifications of our Lord as High Priest. These are dealt with mainly from the human side up to 5^9, and thenceforward from the Divine side. Both the human and the Divine are shown to be necessary. In regard to the human qualifications, we have : (*a*) His manhood, involving oneness with us for sympathy and help (ch. 2); (*b*) His perfect sympathy (4$^{14-16}$); (*c*) His perfect training by obedience through suffering (5$^{1-10}$). The Divine qualifications are: (*a*) His Divine appointment (5^{10}); (*b*) His indissoluble life (7^{16}), involving an uninterrupted tenure of office as contrasted with the constant deaths in the Aaronic priesthood; (*c*) His inviolable or intransmissible priesthood (7^{24}), involving the impossibility of succession or delegation (ἀπαράβατον); (*d*) His perpetual life of intercession (7^{25}); (*e*) His fitness through character (7^{26}); (*f*) the Divine guarantee in the Divine oath of appointment (7^{28}); (*g*) His position on the throne (8^1); (*h*) His perfect offering (9$^{12. 24}$ 10^{12}). These Divine and human qualifications of priesthood are based upon His Divine Sonship (ch. 1). His priesthood inheres in His Person as Son of God. It is this uniqueness as Son that gives Christ His qualifications for priesthood.

(7) *The spiritual work of Christ as Priest.*—The various aspects of His priestly work are shown in Hebrews as follows : (*a*) His propitiation (2^{17}); (*b*) His ability to suffer (2^{18}); (*c*) His ability to sympathize (4^{15}); (*d*) His ability to save (7^{25}); (*e*) His present appearance in heaven for us (9^{24}); (*f*) His kingly position on the throne (8^1); (*g*) His coming again (9^{28}). These are the elements connected with His priestly work, though there are others which are associated with His more general and inclusive work as Redeemer. The work is at once perpetual and permanent. He offered Himself through an eternal spirit (9^{14}); He has made an eternal covenant (9$^{13. 14}$); He is the cause of eternal salvation (5^9); He obtained eternal redemption (9^{12}), which culminates in eternal inheritance (9^{15}).

(8) *The practical uses of Christ's priesthood.*—The definitely practical purpose of the truth of priesthood is what must ever be kept in view. It is by means of the experience of Christ's priesthood that Christians come out of spiritual infancy into spiritual maturity (6^1 10^1). Nowhere is the practical character more clearly seen than in the various statements and exhortations which have to do with the daily life of the believer. In particular, there are the associated phrases, 'we have,' and 'therefore let us.' (*a*) 4^{14} Having the High Priest, let us hold fast. (*b*) 4$^{15. 16}$ Having a sympathetic High Priest, let us come boldly. (*c*) 10^{19} Having boldness of access, let us draw near with *faith* ; having a High Priest, let us hold fast our *hope*, let us consider one another in *love*. Then these three exhortations to faith, hope, and love are amplified respectively in ch. 11 (faith), ch. 12 (hope), ch. 13 (love). (*d*) 12^{28} Receiving a kingdom, let us have grace. (*e*) 13$^{12. 13}$ Jesus suffered ; let us go forth. (*f*) 13^{14} We seek a city to come, therefore let us offer the sacrifice of praise. The Epistle thus emphasizes one truth above all others. Christianity is 'the religion of free access' to God (Bruce, *Hebrews*, p. 171). It might be summed up in the exhortations, 'Draw nigh,' 'Hold fast,' 'Draw not back.' It is characteristic that the word for believers is οἱ προσερχόμενοι, 'those who come right up' to God, and its corresponding exhortation is προσερχώμεθα, 'Let us come right up' to God. Christianity is the better hope by which we 'draw nigh' to God (ἐγγίζειν τῷ θεῷ), and Christ is the surety (ἔγγυος) of a better covenant, that is, One who ensures our permanent access to God (Bruce, *Hebrews*, p. 275). In proportion as we realize this privilege of nearness, and respond to these exhortations to draw near and keep near, we shall find that element of παρρησία which is one of the essential features of a strong Christian life. It is this above all that the priesthood of Christ is intended to produce and perpetuate, to guarantee and guard. This truth of priesthood, as taught in Hebrews, is absolutely essential to a vigorous life, a mature experience, a joyous testimony, and an abounding work.

Literature.—Hastings' *DB*, artt. 'Priest (in NT),' 'Hebrews'; W. Milligan, *Ascension and Heavenly Priesthood of our Lord* ; Davidson, *Hebrews*, Special Note on 'Priesthood of Christ'; Dimock, *Our One Priest on High*, and *The Christian Doctrine of Sacerdotium*; Perowne, *Our High Priest in Heaven*; Rotherham, *Studies in Hebrews*; Soames, *The Priesthood of the New Covenant*; Hubert Brooke, *The Great High Priest*; H. W. Williams, *The Priesthood of Christ* (Fernley Lect. 1876); J. S. Candlish, *The Chr. Salvation* (1899), p. 6 ; G. Milligan, *Theol. of Ep. to Heb.* (1899) p. 111 ; R. C. Moberly, *Ministerial Priesthood* (1897); A. S. Peake, 'Hebrews' in *Cent. Bible* ; Beyschlag, *NT Theol.* ii. 315.

W. H. GRIFFITH THOMAS.

PRINCE.—There are four Gr. words occurring in the Gospels or applied to Christ in the NT which either in AV or RV are rendered 'prince.'

1. ἡγεμών, Mt 2^6. Both AV and RV here give 'princes'—the only occasion of ἡγεμών being so rendered in NT. Otherwise it is almost invariably translated 'governor,' and, in particular, is used to denote the Roman governor or *procurator*. So of Pilate (Mt 27 *passim*, Lk 20^{20}), as of Felix and Festus (Ac 23$^{24. 26. 33. 34}$ 26^{30}). The description of Bethlehem as 'in no wise least among the princes of Judah' is perplexing in view of Mic 5$^{2\,[1]}$ from which the quotation is taken. The Heb. expression is בְּאַלְפֵי 'among the thousands of' (LXX ἐν χιλιάσιν). Differently pointed, however, the word becomes בְּאַלֻּפֵי 'among the heads of thousands of,' *i.e.* the chieftains ; and this apparently is the sense assigned to it in the quotation. It is worth noting that in the Gr. there is a close correspondence between the 'princes' (ἡγεμόνες) of v.^{6a} and the 'governor' (ἡγούμενος) of v.^{6b}. The whole verse, however, is a very free rendering of the Heb. (see the Comm. ; and cf. Hastings' *DB* iv. 185^a).

2. δυνάστης, Lk 1[52]. Here AV has 'the mighty,' but RV 'princes.' Elsewhere in NT the word is used only in Ac 8[27] of the Ethiopian eunuch (EV 'of great authority') and in 1 Ti 6[15] of God (EV 'Potentate').

3. ἄρχων. In Mt 20[25] AV gives 'the princes of the Gentiles,' where RV has 'rulers.' Similarly in Rev 1[5], as applied to Jesus, we have 'prince [RV 'ruler'] of the kings of the earth'—an expression that was probably suggested by the LXX rendering of Ps 89[27] [88-8]. More important is the use of ἄρχων in two of the Gospels as applied to Satan in the phrases ἄρχων τῶν δαιμονίων (Mt 9[34] 12[24], EV 'prince of the devils'), and ἄρχων τοῦ κόσμου τούτου (Jn 12[31] 14[30] 16[11], EV 'prince of this world'). The Matthæan phrase calls for no remark, especially as in 12[24] 'the prince of the devils' is said to be Beelzebub (wh. see). 'The prince of this world,' on the other hand, is a title that belongs to the special Johannine conception of the world as an order of things that is alienated from God and hostile to Him, and of Satan as a power dominating this sinful world and operating in it and through it (cf. Eph 2[2] 'the prince of the power of the air, the spirit that now worketh in the children of disobedience'). But, according to the Johannine view (1 Jn 4[4]), 'Greater is he that is in you than he that is in the world (ὁ ἐν τῷ κόσμῳ).' The secret of the Saviour's superiority lay ultimately in His absolute sinlessness. The prince of this world came and had nothing in Him (Jn 14[30]; cf. the Temptation narratives (Mt 4[1ff.], Lk 4[1ff.]), and especially the offer of 'all the kingdoms of the world'). The world was Satan's, but Christ overcame the world (16[33]). So far from finding in Jesus anything that he could claim as his own, the prince of this world was himself judged by Jesus (16[11]), and by Him cast out (12[31]; cf. Lk 10[18]).

4. ἀρχηγός is twice applied to Christ in Acts in the expressions 'Prince [EVm 'Author'] of life' (3[15]) and 'a Prince and a Saviour' (5[31]). Elsewhere the Gr. word is used in NT only in He 2[10] 12[2], both times of Christ. In 2[10] AV renders 'captain,' RV 'author,' RVm 'captain'; in 12[2] AV and RV have 'author,' AVm 'beginner,' RVm 'captain.' For the precise force of the word in the two passages in Heb. reference may be made to art. CAPTAIN. The 'Prince' (Vulg. princeps) of Ac 5[31] is thoroughly justified in this connexion by both classical and LXX usage, and is particularly appropriate if, as Chase suggests (Credibility of Acts, p. 130), we may see in the expression 'a Prince and a Saviour' an echo of 'the current phraseology—liturgical and literary—of the Messianic hope.' In 3[15], on the other hand, 'Author of life' (Vulg. auctor vitæ) is more suitable than 'Prince of life.' The use of ἀρχηγός with a causative force (often making it practically synonymous with αἴτιος, with which it is sometimes joined) is common in Gr. writers from Plato downwards, more especially when it is followed by the genitive of the thing. Moreover, there is no suggestion here of that idea of 'leadership' which is in keeping with both of the passages in Hebrews, and seems best to bring out their full meaning.

LITERATURE.—The Lexx. s.vv.; Alford's Gr. Test.; Westcott's St. John; Bruce and Dods in EGT; Holtzmann in Hand-Com.; Hastings' DB, art. 'Prince'; Chase, Credibility of the Acts, p. 129 ff.; Spurgeon, The Messiah, 163, 175.

J. C. LAMBERT.

PRINT (τύπος, the mark of a stroke or blow; cf. Athen. τοὺς τύπους τῶν πληγῶν ἰδοῦσα). — In the Gospels 'print' is found only in Jn 20[25], where in most MSS it occurs twice: 'Except I shall see in his hands the print of the nails, and put my finger into the print of the nails, and put my hand into his side, I will not believe' (for other uses of τύπος in NT see Grimm-Thayer and Cremer, s.v.).

At the second occurrence of the word a v.l. τότον is found in אl, which Lach., Tisch., and Treg. [marg.] read (א has εἰς τὸν χείραν (sic) αὐτοῦ). There is considerable variety in the Lat. VSS; Cod. Brixianus (OL) gives 'nisi videro in manibus ejus locum clavorum et mittam digitum meum in foramina clavorum'; others read 'figuram' (so D lat. in both places), which occurs in Vulg. for τύπος in Ac 7[43], 1 Co 10[i. 11]; and 'fissuram' is also found. Vulg. gives 'nisi videro in manibus fixuram clavorum, et mittam digitum meum in locum clavorum.' 'Fixuram' seems to be a correction made by Jerome, since it is not found in the older codices; but it may mean the place where the nail was fixed. Augustine preferred the word 'cicatrix,' in one place (on 1 Jn 1[5]) quoting Thomas' words as 'non credam nisi digitos meos misero in locum clavorum, et cicatrices ejus tetigero'; in another (on Ps 21 (22)[17]), 'nisi misero digitos meos in cicatrices vulnerum, non credam.' See full note in Wordsworth-White's NT Lat. (Oxford). The reading τότος would bring out more strongly what is implied in the story, that Thomas required the evidence of his senses, both of seeing and feeling; he wished to see the τύπος, and put his finger into the τύπος; cf. Grotius, 'τύπος videtur, τότος impletur.' Westcott, however, holds that this reading is nothing more than an early and natural mistake; and Godet says that it takes away from the denial of the disciple precisely its marked character of obstinacy, which is shown in the deliberate repetition of his phrases.

When Jesus appeared on the evening of the Resurrection to His disciples during the absence of Thomas, it is related that He showed them His hands and His feet, evidently bearing the marks of the wounds, in order to convince them of the reality and identity of His risen body (Lk 24[39], cf. Jn 20[20]). He also offered them the testimony of their sense of feeling, 'Handle me, and see; for a spirit hath not flesh and bones, as ye behold me having.' Thomas refused to accept their account of what had taken place, and required that he himself should have proof similar to or even stronger than what they had received. The wounds inflicted upon Calvary were deeply engraven on his memory, and to all their repeated assurances (ἔλεγον, Jn 20[25]) he had but one answer (εἶπεν). 'Si Pharisæus ita dixisset nil impetrasset, sed discipulo pridem probato nil non datur' (Bengel). A week later Christ appeared again to the disciples, Thomas being present, and offered him just the test he had demanded, giving him back his own words, but making no mention of the prints of the nails, for 'He does not recall the malice of His enemies' (Alford). It is a moot question whether Thomas availed himself of this offer. Tertullian, Ambrose, Cyril, and others suppose that he did, but it is psychologically more probable that Thomas rose above such a material test; the presence of his Master, and the proof of His omniscience, shown in His knowledge of what Thomas had said on the former occasion, were sufficient; with a bound he rose to the vision of highest faith (so Meyer, Alford, Westcott, Edersheim, Dods, et al.). With this, too, agree the words of the Lord, 'Because thou hast seen me, thou hast believed,' not 'because thou hast touched me.'

If it be asked, how the prints of the wounds could be seen, and even remain open, in His risen and glorified body, it is but one of many difficulties arising from our ignorance as to the nature of that body. On the same occasion Christ entered the room with this same body in which the prints were visible, the doors being shut. Since, therefore, the account deals with matters of which we have no experience, we must accept the fact on sufficient evidence, even though we may not be able to account for it. Meanwhile there is deep significance in the fact that the marks of these wounds remain. They prove the reality of the Resurrection body, and its continuity with that body which was crucified; though Christ glorified was in many respects changed, yet He was essentially the same who suffered, seeing that the prints could become visibly present to Thomas and the others. They show also the abiding nature of His atoning work, and teach us to connect the issue of His Agony with His Work in triumph (cf. the use of the perfect tense, Ἰησοῦν τὸν ἐσταυρωμένον, in Mt

28^5, cf. 1 Co 1^{23}). 'The prints of the nails are not only signs of recognition, but also signs of victory. . . . He points to His wounded hands and feet as proving that He bears even within the veil the tokens of redeeming love. The conception is one on which Art has always loved to dwell. We must all have seen, again and again, figures of the Lord in glory raising His wounded hands to bless, or pleading even on the throne of judgment with those who have rejected Him by the marks of His death, so showing that by these He is still known ; that by these He still proclaims the unchanging Gospel, "Redemption through sacrifice"' (Westcott, *The Revelation of the Risen Lord*, p. 69 f.). ' He gave them confidence in His unfailing sympathy, by shewing that He bore even to the throne of heaven the marks of His dying love' (*ib.* p. 79).

The marks (στίγματα) which St. Paul bore in his body (Gal 6^{17}) have by some been connected with these prints of our Lord's passion, as if they were reproduced in the Apostle's body, comparing 2 Co 4^{10}, Ro $6^{5.6}$ etc., and referring to the well-known *stigmata* of Francis of Assisi. But an entirely different explanation of the passage is now generally accepted, according to which the allusion is to marks of ownership branded on the bodies of temple slaves and others (see RV, Lightfoot's note *in loco*, and art. ' Mark' in Hastings' *DB* iii. 245). See STIGMATA.

See also artt. CRUCIFIXION, BODY.

W. H. DUNDAS.

PRISON.—The fact that no fewer than eight different Heb. roots are used to express ' prison' (see Hastings' *DB* i. 525) in the OT, testifies to the number of prisoners in ancient times, and the variety of treatment which they experienced. Not only ordinary prison-houses, but also fortresses, barracks, palaces, and temples had commonly accommodation—more or less extensive—for prisoners, just as our rural police stations have cells attached to them for temporary confinement.

The Latin and Greek terms translated ' prison' are expressive and significant. *Carcer* (cf. Gr. ἕρκος) emphasizes restraint. *Ergastulum* (lit. workhouse) corresponds to our ' penitentiary.' Malefactors and slaves laboured therein, as in the building where Samson had languished. The *Tullianum* at Rome was a condemned cell. Perhaps the mildest form of imprisonment recorded in the NT was that of St. Paul (Ac 28^{30}), when he dwelt for two whole years in his own hired house (μίσθωμα,—see illustration in *Rome and its Story* by Tina Duff Gordon and St. Clair Baddeley, p. 114), guarded by, and probably chained to, a soldier. οἴκημα, in polite Attic usage used for a prison, is found once (Ac 12^7). τήρησις, ' the place of keeping' (Ac 4^3 5^{18}), tr. ' hold' (RV ' ward') and ' prison' (probably that attached to the Temple or the high priest's palace, Hastings' *DB* iv. 103), also suggests the mildest form of restraint. The φυλακή or place of guarding, in which John the Baptist was confined (Mt 14^3), is believed to have been in the royal palace of Machærus (Jos. *Ant.* XVIII. v. 2). Custody in a φυλακή might mean anything, from the comparative comfort of a guard-room to the misery of a dungeon. Another word translated ' prison' is δεσμωτήριον, the ' place of bonds.' It is used interchangeably with φυλακή in speaking of John the Baptist's prison (Mt 11^2), and became painfully familiar to the first preachers of the Cross in the course of their missionary journeyings. See also following article.

If those mutilations and other horrid cruelties, familiar to the older pagan world, were less common, still vindictiveness rather than reformation was a note of imprisonment at the dawn of the Christian era. The LXX translates the place of Zedekiah's imprisonment at Babylon οἰκία μύλωνος, ' the millhouse' (Jer 52^{11}). Grinding corn in a millhouse is a somewhat more humane punishment than hard labour on the treadmill, and some of the tasks allotted to inmates of an *ergastulum* may have been no more disagreeable than picking oakum. But much more severe treatment was often the unhappy prisoner's lot. In our Lord's parable of the Unforgiving Servant, that ungrateful wretch fell into the hands of *torturers* (τοῖς βασανισταῖς, Mt 18^{34})—a staff of officials whose very name is sinister. One means of torture was an instrument (ξύλον, Lat. *nervus*) in which the bodies of victims were confined. It is described as ' a wooden block or frame in which the feet and sometimes the hands and neck of prisoners were confined' (Robinson, *Gr. Lex. of NT*). In such durance

were Paul and Silas placed at Philippi (Ac 16^{24}). The condemned cell of a Roman prison resembled that dungeon in the court of the prison into which Jeremiah was let down with cords, and where he sank in the mire (Jer 38^6). 'They were pestilential cells, damp and cold, from which the light was excluded, and where the chains rusted on the limbs of the prisoners' (Conybeare-Howson, *Life and Epistles of St. Paul*, i. 358). The *Carcer Mamertinus* on the slope of the Capitoline of Rome, and the traditional scene of St. Paul's last imprisonment, is typical of Roman prisons all over the world during Rome's supremacy. It consists of two chambers, one above the other—the upper one an ' irregular quadrilateral.' The lower, ' originally accessible only through a hole in the ceiling, is 19 ft. long, 10 ft. wide, and $6\frac{1}{2}$ ft. high. The vaulting is formed by the gradual projection of the side walls until they meet.' This prison is supposed to have been built over a well named *Tullianum*, and hence traditionally attributed to Servius Tullius (see Varro, v. 151). An inscription records that it was restored in B.C. 22 (Baedeker, *Italy*, ii. p. 226). See also art. HELL (DESCENT INTO).

LITERATURE.—Besides the authorities referred to above, see the Commentaries, *ad loc.* ; Hastings' *DB*, artt. ' Crimes' and ' Prison'; Conybeare-Howson, *Life of St. Paul*, i. 357 f.; Farrar, *Life of St. Paul*, i. 497, ii. 390 ff., 547.

D. A. MACKINNON.

PRISONER.—The word ' prisoner' (δέσμιος) is found in the Gospels only in Mt $27^{15.16}$, Mk 15^6 (see also, however, Lk 23^{17} RVm), where it is used of the prisoner whom the Roman governor was wont to release to the Jews at the Feast of Passover, and in particular of Barabbas, a ' notable prisoner' of the time. But, apart from the word, we read of other prisoners in the Gospels, and both there and elsewhere in the NT we learn something of the attitude of Christ to the prisoner, and the prisoner's relations and obligations to Christ.

1. Of actual prisoners there are two in the Gospels much more ' notable' than Barabbas. The first is John the Baptist, who for righteousness' sake was ' cast into prison' (Mt 14^3, Mk 6^{17}, Lk 3^{20}, Jn 3^{24}), and whose imprisonment so affected his strong, free spirit that for a time his faith in Christ appears to have faltered (Mt $11^{2\mathrm{ff.}}$). The other is Jesus Himself, who was arrested (Mt 26^{50}) in the Garden, and taken in bonds (Jn 18^{24} δεδεμένος [which is practically equivalent to δέσμιος ; cf. Mk 15^6 with v.^{7}]) first before the high priest and then before Pilate (Mt 27^2, Mk 15^1, Jn $18^{12.24}$).

2. The fact that the prisoners of the Gospels include a robber (Jn 18^{40}) and murderer (Mk 15^7, Lk 23^{25}) like Barabbas on the one hand, and John the Baptist and Jesus on the other, shows the necessity of discriminating between prisoners, and especially of distinguishing those who deserve their punishment (cf. the admission of the penitent robber, Lk 23^{41}) from those who ' suffer wrongfully.' To the former class Barabbas certainly belonged. His imprisonment was the reward of his crimes (Lk 23^{25}) ; and so long as crimes like his are committed against society, imprisonment will still be necessary. With all His pity for the prisoner, Jesus recognizes that there are cases in which a just judge will cast the offender into prison (Mt 5^{25}). But there are wrongful imprisonments as well as merited ones ; and our Lord warned His disciples that a time would come when they themselves should be cast into prison for His name's sake (Lk 21^{12})—a warning that was soon abundantly fulfilled in the experience of the Apostles and the early Church (Ac 4^3 5^{18} 8^3 12^4 16^{24} etc.).

3. In the Gospels Jesus comes before us as the prisoner's Friend. He proves His friendship (1) *by the deliverance He brings*. In the synagogue at Nazareth, at the very outset of His ministry (Lk

4[17ff.]), He applied to Himself the glowing words of the great Messianic prophet (Is 61[1f.]), and so assumed the office of one who came 'to proclaim liberty to the captives, and the opening of the prison to them that are bound.' There is, of course, a spiritual sense in which Christ fulfils this promise —by pulling down the dungeon walls of ignorance and error, by giving liberty to the human spirit, by striking off the fetters of sin. But in a more literal fashion Christ brought deliverance to the captives by destroying the very foundations of earthly tyrannies, and making it impossible that in any society which had learned to breathe the air of His gospel men should be cast into prison to gratify the pleasure of a despot or the rage of the persecutor. 'Christ died on the tree,' Carlyle said to Emerson: 'that built Dunscore kirk yonder' (Emerson, *Works*, ii. p. 8). And in a like sense we may say that it was Christ's hand on Calvary that tore down the walls of the Bastille, and abolished the iniquities of the Spanish Inquisition.

(2) Again, Jesus proves His friendship for the prisoner *by the sympathy He gives.* We see an illustration of this sympathy in the message of consolation and blessing that He sent to John the Baptist (Mt 11[4-6]) when the forerunner's heart was like to faint in the gloomy vaults of Machærus. But above all we see it in those haunting words of self-identification with the prisoner: 'I was in prison, and ye came unto me' (Mt 25[36]); 'I was in prison, and ye visited me not' (v.[43]). It is not merely with the righteous man who suffers wrongfully that our Lord here identifies Himself, but with the prisoner as such—the criminal, it may be, the pest of society, the man who deserves to die. It was Christ's love and pity for the prisoner that inspired the philanthropic labours of John Howard and Elizabeth Fry, and led to that great transformation in the prisoner's immemorial lot which is as much one of the 'Gesta Christi' as the modern missionary movement.

4. In the letters of St. Paul's captivity we find the Apostle describing himself as 'the prisoner of Jesus Christ,' or 'the prisoner of the Lord' (Eph 3[1] 4[1], Philem[9]; cf. 2 Ti 1[8]). It is a striking expression, which is by no means exhausted when understood to mean that Paul suffered imprisonment for the sake of Christ. It means that, without doubt; but it means much more (cf. Eph 3[1] 'the prisoner of Christ Jesus in behalf of you Gentiles,' where 'the δέσμιος of Christ' represents himself as suffering *for the Gentiles' sake*). The man who so describes himself believes that Christ has laid His arresting hand upon him, and put him where he is, and shut to the door of his prison; and that it is no other than the Lord Jesus who carries the key of that door at His girdle. St. Paul, in short, thought of Christ as the Keeper of the prison, and the thought filled him with profound content (cf. Ph 4[11]). Like St. Peter, he had learned in his own experience that the Lord could unlock prison doors at His pleasure and set his servants free (Ac 16[26], cf. 12[6ff.]). And if some day the door should be opened only that the prisoner of Christ might be led forth to die, Paul knew that this would really mean his escape through Christ's grace to a larger liberty than he could find on earth (2 Co 5[1-8]). And so, as the midnight hymns that he and Silas sang to God in the prison at Philippi compelled all the prisoners to listen (Ac 16[25]), the world has had to hearken ever since to those notes of wonder, love, and praise that turn St. Paul's prison-Epistles into prison-songs.

J. C. LAMBERT.

PROCURATOR.—A 'procurator' (the exact Gr. equivalent is ἐπίτροπος) was properly a slave or freedman who looked after (*procurabat*) a man's property (cf. Mt 20[8], Lk 8[3]). The nearest Eng. equivalent is 'steward' (wh. see). This upper servant acted for his master, in the absence of the latter, in all matters connected with money, and it may safely be said that only a small estate amongst the Romans would be without one. The position was one of responsibility, but it is obvious that the importance of the person in the world was directly in proportion to the importance of his master. An agent of the Emperor, who always possessed vast landed and house property, as well as the whole or part of the taxes of every province of the Roman Empire, held a higher position in society than the procurator of any other person. The Emperor's financial interests were so varied, that he required a large number of such servants to look after them, and his high position enabled him to draw them from a higher class than that of freedmen and slaves. The majority of them were of equestrian rank, and some of these procuratorships were deemed of higher importance than others. The diverse character of their duties will be seen from the fact that Cagnat (*Cours d'Épigraphie Latine*[3], p. 121 ff.) enumerates thirty-nine different kinds of procurators, whose titles have reference to every possible aspect of the Emperor's revenue and expenditure.

Certain of the smaller Imperial provinces (see under GOVERNOR) were put under procurators as governors, to whom the Emperor delegated administrative and military functions. Such a procuratorship was, of course, one of the highest of the Imperial procuratorships, and carried with it a large salary; but it must be clearly understood that a procurator, however high, remained a servant of the Emperor, and owed his life and fortune solely to the favour of the prince, who advanced those quickest who served his interests best. The word 'procurator' is not used in the NT, but the participle of the verb (ἐπιτροπεύοντος) occurs as a variant in Lk 3[1] to ἡγεμονεύοντος, a more general term applicable to all governors of provinces, and even to the Emperor himself. Pontius Pilate was *procurator prouinciæ Iudaeae*. See also art. GOVERNOR.

LITERATURE.—Greenidge, *Roman Public Life*, pp. 414 ff., 435; Schürer, *GJV*[3], i. 454 ff. [*HJP* I. ii. 106 ff.]; art. 'Procurator' in Hastings' *DB* and the *Encyc. Bibl.*; Hirschfeld, *Untersuchungen aus dem Gebiete der röm. Verwaltungsgesch.*[2] (Berlin, 1905); Marquardt, *Römische Staatsverwaltung*, i. 554 ff.

ALEX. SOUTER.

PRODIGAL SON.—The details of this parable (Lk 15) seem to have been carefully thought out, as the structure of the story is fairly complete and its movement quite natural. The younger of a certain man's sons, dissatisfied with the quiet life he is leading, resolves to leave his father's house; and, having received the share of property that fell to him, goes to a distant country and gives himself up with the fullest abandonment to every indulgence that appetite craved. But his career of gaiety and dissipation soon comes to an end. He passes from one stage to another in his downward course till he reaches the lowest. Without a friend and in the direst straits, he is forced to take service as a swine-herd—a grade of employment esteemed by Jewish society as the lowest. The misery to which he had brought himself, however, and the neglect from which he suffers, show him how great has been his folly and how wrong his conduct. He therefore resolves to return home, confess his fault, and solicit the place of a servant in his father's household. He carries out his intention, but his father receives him with the greatest eagerness and affection, and orders a feast to be prepared in celebration of his safe return.

The elder brother, however, is very indignant, and refuses to take any part in the general rejoicing. His father entreats him to enter into the spirit of the occasion ; but he is obstinate and petulant, and complains that this display in honour of his brother is in marked contrast with the treatment accorded him. He who had lived at home in dutiful submission had not received the slightest token in recognition of his merits or services, whereas his brother who had squandered his means in a career of vice is being honoured in the most enthusiastic and lavish manner.

Here, then, we have a father and his son differing as to how a younger son who had grievously misbehaved himself ought to be treated. The fact of the young man's wrongdoing and the sincerity of his repentance are accepted by both ; but while the elder brother challenges the justice and propriety of rejoicing over the return of one who had been so headstrong and foolish, the father firmly defends the course he had followed, and, in terminating the discussion, speaks with a finality that is not to be questioned : 'It was *meet* that we should make merry and be glad : for this thy brother was dead, and is alive again ; and was lost, and is found.'

The prodigal is a minor character in the parable. The contrast is drawn between the father and the elder brother in reference to their treatment of the wrongdoer, and not between the brothers either in regard to character or conduct. The substance of the parable is this : a father who welcomes back an erring and repentant son has his action emphatically approved, and an elder brother who maintains an attitude of surly aloofness is shown to merit severe disapprobation.

The parable is thus practical in its aim—teaching men not only how they ought to treat their repentant brethren, but chiefly what is necessary to enable them to do so. For what was it that led the father to act as he did ? Was it not just the love he bore his son, foolish and erring though he had been ? The elder son reasoned on the lines of cold and rigid law, whereas the heart of the father spoke, and the voice of love was obeyed. And was it not just the want of this affectionate heart that allowed the elder brother to act so ungenerously ? Had he loved his brother, he would have vied with his father in the warmth of his welcome ; had he even loved his father, he would have acquiesced in his father's wish for his father's sake. It was poverty of affection that led him to display a selfishness that was offensive, and a temper that was childish and rude. What could the father do ? —a son he loved and had lost was home again safe and sound—a son who had gone forth to a rude world had returned disillusioned and chastened by his bitter experience.

In the first instance, no doubt, the parable was meant to point out the defect in the Jewish way of dealing with those who had sinned. What was clearly lacking there was a brotherly spirit. Those who had erred were treated with unrelenting severity ; the sinner looked in vain for mercy and hoped in vain for restoration, no matter how painful and prolonged his period of repentance had been. But what was true for the Jews is true for all. Love alone is capable of rendering the conscience sensitive to the finest shades of justice. Law rigidly applied does not scrutinize the motive, does not measure the force of temptation, does not take into account the fact of repentance, and is therefore often unjust when in appearance it is most just. The father showed mercy because he loved his son, and in showing mercy dispensed the truer justice ; for mercy is but justice perfectly applied. The elder brother failed in his duty to brother and father alike, because he lacked the affection that would have swept away his shallow notions of justice, and pointed out a better way.

The parable thus emphasizes one aspect of the great commandment of our Lord, that men should love one another ; and in this respect shows a close resemblance to several of His other parables. In that of the Good Samaritan, the Priest and the Levite saw no duty they owed to the wounded Jew, whereas the heart of the Samaritan—a member of a despised race—responded at once to the demands of the situation. And in that of the Labourers in the Vineyard, is it not the mean and grudging spirit of the whole-day labourers that is condemned, since their rights were not infringed nor their interests invaded by the generous treatment accorded to the late-comers ?

What men require in their dealings with one another is the loving heart, and in dealing with our erring and repentant brethren nothing else will give the insight and tenderness needed to fulfil the ends of real justice. In the sympathy of Christ lay the secret of His power. No one who had paid the penalty of his transgression in bitter repentance was refused His countenance or His help ; and the moral sense of mankind, quickened by a genuine brotherly love, will ever admit that His way is the right way—will ever say to the harsh and unforgiving, It is 'meet that we should make merry and be glad : for this thy brother was dead, and is alive again ; and was lost, and is found.'

LITERATURE.—Goebel, *Parables of Jesus* ; A. B. Bruce, *Parabolic Teaching of Christ* ; M. Dods, *Parables of Our Lord* ; Trench, *Notes on the Parables* ; Arnot, *Parables of Our Lord* ; W. M. Taylor, *Parables of Our Saviour* ; also F. W. Robertson's *Sermons*, iii. 253 ; Dale, *Ep. of James and Other Discourses*, 160 ; Ballard, *The Penitent Prodigal* ; Hancock, *The Return to the Father* ; Willcox, *The Prodigal Son* ; *Expositor*, i. ix. [1879] 137, iii. viii. [1888] 268, 388, x. [1889] 122 ; *ExpT* vii. [1896] 325 ; Parker, *People's Bible*. D. G. YOUNG.

PROFANING, PROFANITY.—1. The terms.—

The word 'profane' occurs only once in EV of the Gospels, and then in the verbal form (Gr. βεβηλόω), viz. in Mt 12⁵, where Jesus says, in defending His disciples and Himself from the charge of Sabbath-breaking, 'Have ye not read in the law, how that on the sabbath day the priests in the temple profane the sabbath, and are guiltless?' Elsewhere in NT the vb. (Gr. and Eng.) is found only in Ac 24⁶, where the Jews accuse St Paul of profaning the Temple. The meaning of βεβηλόω must be considered in connexion with the adj. βέβηλος from which it comes, and which is found 5 times in NT (1 Ti 1⁹ 4⁷ 6²⁰, 2 Ti 2¹⁶, He 12¹⁶), 'profane' being in each case the rendering of EV. βέβηλος is the almost exact equivalent of Lat. *profanus*, whence Eng. 'profane.' *Profanus* (fr. *pro* = 'before,' and *fanum* = 'temple') means 'without the temple,' and so 'unconsecrated,' as opposed to *sacer*. βέβηλος (fr. βαίνω = 'to go,' whence βηλός = 'threshold') denotes that which is 'trodden,' 'open to access,' and so again 'unconsecrated,' in contrast to ἱερός. Originally βέβηλος (like its opposites, ἱερός, ἅγιος, etc.) had a purely ritual meaning, but out of this there gradually arose ethical and spiritual connotations. The LXX affords plentiful illustration of these various uses of the word. In Lv 10¹⁰, *e.g.*, βέβηλος means no more than ἀκάθαρτος, as the context shows, *i.e.* ritually unclean. In 19²⁹ RV 'Profane [AV 'Prostitute'] not thy daughter,' the ethical meaning is apparent. In Ezk 22²⁶, with its clear distinction between βέβηλος and ἅγιος, together with its conception of a profaning of God Himself, we pass from the moral into the still higher realm of spiritual religion. Similarly, in the Gospels we find a lower and a higher conception of what is meant by profanation. There is a profaneness of the law and the letter, eagerly pounced upon by scribes and Pharisees. There is a profaneness of the soul and the spirit, which stands revealed to the eyes of Jesus.

2. The sin.—The sin of profaning consists in treating sacred things with irreverence or contempt, and in the Bible the charge of profanation is found especially in connexion with the desecration or violation of *the Sabbath*, of *the Temple*, or of *the name of God* Himself. In a study of Christ's life and teaching the sin of profaning comes up for consideration under each of these heads. (1) *Profaning the Sabbath.*—It is significant that the only occasion of the use of the word ' profane ' ($\beta\epsilon\beta\eta\lambda\delta\omega$) in the Gospels is in relation to a charge of Sabbath-breaking brought against Jesus (Mt 12⁵). For, though it is Our Lord Himself who employs the word, and employs it of the action of the priests under the Mosaic Law, He evidently does so with reference to an accusation of which He was the object.* And this, we must remember, was no solitary case. There was nothing that more frequently brought Jesus into hot collision with the ecclesiastical authorities than the question of Sabbath observance (with Mt 12¹ff· cf. v.¹⁰ff·, Mk 1²¹ff· 2²³ff· 3²ff·, Lk 6¹ff· 6ff· 13¹⁴ff· 14³ff·, Jn 5⁹ff· ¹⁶· ¹⁸ 7²²f· 9¹⁴ff· ; note esp. the Johannine passages). In their eyes He was repeatedly guilty of a profanation of the holy day. And, though on this occasion He defends Himself by appealing to Jewish law and history, thus meeting His accusers on their own ground, He immediately passes from this *argumentum ad hominem* to state the great principles on which He really stood in His free, though reverent (cf. Lk 4¹⁶), use of the day—that God desires mercy rather than sacrifice (v.⁷), and that ' the Son of Man is Lord of the sabbath ' (v.⁸). In other words, He shows that the charge of Sabbath profanation, as brought against Him, rested on a wrong conception of Sabbath sanctity; and the charge of breaking a Divine law, on an entirely false idea of God's meaning and purpose in giving the Law (cf. Mk 2²⁷ ' The sabbath was made for man, and not man for the sabbath '). There is a profanation according to the letter that is not a profanation according to the spirit ; and there is a seeming transgression of the commandment that is in reality a revelation of the benignity of the Law itself and the ' philanthropy ' of Him who gave it. See, further, SABBATH.

(2) *Profaning the Temple.*—Jealous as the Jewish authorities were, after their slavish fashion, in the guardianship of the Sabbath, they were not less jealous in defending the sanctity of the Temple against the least taint of what they regarded as profanation. The Temple police were ever on the alert. For any foot of Gentile or Samaritan to pass beyond the Court of the Gentiles meant death to the transgressor. And Josephus tells us how at one period the Samaritans were altogether excluded from the Temple enclosure because of an act of profanation committed by some of their people (*Ant.* XVIII. ii. 2). The indignation shown by the chief priests and scribes at the hosannas of the children in the Temple was apparently due not merely to the hailing of Jesus as the Son of David, but to the raising of those joyful shouts within the consecrated building (Mt 21¹⁶). But, as Jesus in meeting the charge of Sabbath-breaking showed how misplaced the Rabbinic and Pharisaic ideas of sanctity were, so in connexion with the Cleansing of the Temple (Mt 21¹²f· = Mk 11¹⁵ff· = Lk 19⁴⁵f·, Jn 2¹³ff·), He showed how low and poor were their views on the subject of profanation.

The presence of the stall-keepers and cattle-drovers and money-changers was strictly within the letter of the Law, since it was in the Court of the Gentiles that this market was held, *i.e.* outside of the sacred area proper. For the Temple authorities this was quite enough ; they had no compunctions about a traffic that was technically legal—least of all as the rents paid by the traders for the privilege of using the Temple court as a bazaar passed into their own pockets. To Jesus this was an illustration of the readiness of the Jewish leaders ' to blend religious rigorism and utter worldliness,' or, in His own words on another occasion, to ' strain out the gnat and swallow the camel ' (Mt 23²⁴). Thus they had made His Father's house ' an house of merchandise ' (Jn 2¹⁶) ; nay, a very ' den of robbers ' (Mt 21¹³ ‖)—an allusion either to the greed and extortion of the high-priestly family as landlords of the enclosure, or to the shameful and notorious cheating practised by the privileged traders on the ignorant country people who came up to the Feasts. Moreover, this was ' the house of prayer ' (Mt 21¹³ ‖)—the place to which pious folk came up for purposes of detachment and recollection and communion with God. And by reason of these abuses, such worshippers had first to make their way through the distracting scenes of this profane bazaar ; and even as they knelt at prayer on the other side of the boundary, to have their ears filled with the noisy cries of the merchants, the bleating of innumerable sheep, and the lowing of excited cattle.

In the eyes of Jesus all this, however it might be defended by ecclesiastical lawyers, was a desecration of His Father's house, inasmuch as it was a hindrance to true spiritual worship. And the principles He lays down here on the subject of worship and its profanation are far-reaching and penetrating. The Temple at Jerusalem has long since vanished from the world, but the acts and words of Jesus in driving out the profane traffickers still find abundant application. Our Lord condemns everything that brings the spirit of the world into the atmosphere of the sanctuary, and turns the house of prayer into a house of merchandise. Much more does He condemn anything that associates His Church with methods and practices that are not even those of honest merchandise, but have the savour of dishonest gain. See, further, TEMPLE, § ' Cleansing of.'

(3) *Profaning God's name.*—For this form of the sin of profanation the word ' profanity ' is usually reserved, a word that is to be distinguished from blasphemy (wh. see)—though the distinction is not always observed, nor, indeed, possible. Blasphemy ($\beta\lambda\alpha\sigma\phi\eta\mu\iota\alpha=$' evil-speaking ') is an insult offered to God's majesty, and, in particular, a deliberate reviling of God and of Divine things. Profanity, on the other hand, is a taking of God's name in vain (Ex 20⁷)—understanding ' name ' in the scriptural sense of ' anything whereby God maketh Himself known ' (*Shorter Catech.*, Qu. 55). Profanity may, and often does, run into blasphemy, but the word finds its proper application in an irreverent treatment of holy things without the motive of the scoffer. When Peter began ' to curse and to swear ($\kappa\alpha\tau\alpha\theta\epsilon\mu\alpha\tau\iota\zeta\epsilon\iota\nu$ $\kappa\alpha\iota$ $\delta\mu\nu\nu\epsilon\iota\nu$), I know not the man ' (Mt 26⁷⁴, cf. Mk 14⁷¹), he was not guilty of intentional blasphemy ; he was in reality employing the most solemn forms of Jewish asseveration (cf. Nu 5²¹ ' an oath of cursing,' and see *EBi*, art. ' Oath '). But he was guilty of profanity, for he was invoking the Divine name in support of a lie.

There was no kind of profanation against which the Jewish Rabbis were more anxious to guard than the sin of profane language. The hedge they made around the Law was particularly high at this point. Through a mistaken interpretation of Lv 24¹⁶ they forbade the very utterance of the name *Jahweh*, and so, in the reading of the OT,

---

* It is an interesting coincidence that in the LXX account of the incident at Nob (1 S 21⁴), to which Jesus alludes in the preceding verse, $\beta\iota\beta\eta\lambda o\iota$ $\alpha\rho\tau o\iota$ is Ahimelech's expression for ' common bread,' as distinguished from $\alpha\gamma\iota o\iota$ $\alpha\rho\tau o\iota$ or ' shew-bread.'

Adonai or *Elohim* was invariably substituted. Partly, no doubt, for similar reasons, there had grown up in the time of Christ a custom of swearing not by the Divine name, but by heaven or earth or Jerusalem or the Temple (Mt 5³³⁻³⁷ 23¹⁶⁻²²)—though there emerges here, alongside of the desire to avoid the use of God's name, the consideration that such oaths were less binding than those in which God was directly invoked (contrast the high priest's adjuration 'by the living God' at the trial of Jesus, Mt 26⁶³). And here again, as in His cleansing of the Temple, our Lord showed how poor and mean the thoughts of the Rabbis were on the subject of profanation. That system of diluted oaths was a miserable piece of casuistry at the best. For an oath has no meaning if it is not an invocation of the Divine Being Himself as a witness; and, besides, heaven is God's throne and the earth His footstool, Jerusalem is the city of the Great King, and the Temple the place of His indwelling (5³⁴ᶠ· 23¹⁶ᶠᶠ·). Moreover, those legal refinements lent themselves to all sorts of falsehood and deceit in the intercourse of men, and thus became a prostitution of the holiest realities to wicked ends. And so Jesus lays down the general principle, 'Swear not at all' (5³⁴). Make no distinctions among your statements by the use of a graduated scale of oaths, as if, while you are bound to be truthful in regard to some of the things you say, you are otherwise free to shade off your language into the veriest falsehood by diminishing grades of protestation. 'But let your communication be, Yea, yea; Nay, nay' (Mt 5³⁷, cf. Ja 5¹²). See, further, OATHS.

LITERATURE.—The Lexx. *s.vv.* βεβηλόω, βέβηλοι, βλασφημία; Hastings' *DB*, artt. 'Oath', 'Temple'; *EBi*, art. 'Oath'; *PRE³*, art. 'Eid bei den Hebräern'; Edersheim, *LT*; Schürer, *HJP* II. ii. 90–125; R. W. Dale, *Ten Commandments*, p. 61 ff.; J. O. Dykes, *Manifesto of the King*, p. 265 ff.; F. J. Coffin, 'The Third Commandment' in *JBL* xix. (1900) 166.

J. C. LAMBERT.

PROFESSION.—In Biblical usage, to 'profess' is to make a public declaration (Mt 7²³, Dt 26³); then to take a certain stand or attitude (1 Ti 2¹⁰ 'which becometh women professing godliness'); and, lastly, to make an unjustifiable pretension or claim (Ro 1²², 1 Ti 6²¹, Tit 1¹⁶). In general, profession and confession are so closely related that one Greek word (ὁμολογέω) is employed indifferently for both; and the AV has not clearly distinguished between them. Yet they are by no means identical; for while both words imply the utterance or declaration of faith or of fact, confession invariably implies that there is harmony between what is declared and the inward thought or feeling of the speaker, while profession carries no such implication.

Thus the word 'confess' answers in the OT to ידה, which always implies the utterance of genuine faith or feeling (Hiph. =*humbly and thankfully to acknowledge God's name and goodness*, 1 K 8³³·³⁵ [LXX ἐξομολογέομαι]; Hithp.=*contritely to confess sin*, Lv 5⁵ 16²¹ [LXX ἐξαγορεύω]); while 'profess' answers to הִגִּיד='tell out', 'declare,' 'make manifest' (it may be in the way of thankful acknowledgment, Dt 26³, or of not concealing one's sin, Ps 38¹⁸, or even of showing forth one's sin openly and impudently, Is 3⁹ 'They declare their sin as Sodom'). The difference reappears in the NT, where 'confess' is used as tr. of ἐξομολογέομαι, which is exactly parallel to ידה in both its senses, and also as tr. of ὁμολογέω in the specific sense of publicly owning one's relationship of faith and devotion to Christ, Mt 10³², Lk 12⁸; whereas 'profess' answers to ἐπαγγέλλομαι = *to make a profession*, whether sincerely or not; φάσκω=*to assert or pretend*; and to ὁμολογέω in the sense of making a formal declaration, or in the bad sense of making an outward pretence. Thus, while the one word has received a deep religious impress, the other is restricted to the sense of making a public declaration, a declaration which may or may not be sincere and justified by facts. The RV, in substituting 'confession' for 'profession' in the tr. of ὁμολογία, for the owning of the Christian faith (He 3¹) or the faith which the Christian owns (4¹⁴), has logically followed the rendering of ὁμολογέω in its specific Christian significance, and has helped to put the distinction between the two terms in clearer light.

The 'profession' of Christ or of Christianity is at once more and less than the confession of Christ. It is more than confession; for while the latter is the witness to actual faith or feeling, profession also covers all ill-grounded utterances to which there is little or nothing in the heart to correspond. And profession is also less than confession : it is limited to the verbal expression of faith, while confession gives evidence of itself in the tone and conduct of life as well. Confession shows itself in the exercise of faith as well as in the assertion of it. The distinction between profession and confession is valuable when we consider the varying emphasis laid by the Gospels on verbal testimony as an element in the confession of Christ. The duty of verbal profession is at times strongly insisted on (see CONFESSION [of Christ], ii. and iii.), mainly because it was the sign of loyalty and steadfastness of faith. Yet the value of such professions depended on the occasions that called them forth, as well as on their genuineness and their seasonableness. Christ regarded them as peculiarly valuable in times of stress and growing opposition. So He prized the bold testimony of Peter at Cæsarea Philippi as being a sign of the rock-fast loyalty of His disciple (Mt 16¹⁷⁻¹⁹); so also He mourned over the later weakness of the disciples and the verbal denial of Peter, as betokening a certain diminution of their allegiance (Mk 14²⁷·³⁰, Lk 22⁶¹). At the same time, Christ repudiated many kinds of profession, and taught to His disciples a certain duty of reserve in the utterance of their faith. It goes without saying that He repudiated all insincere professions; and He knew that these were to be found not only among the Pharisees, but also among His own followers (Mt 7²² 21³⁰). He also feared the egoism of professions of goodness (Lk 18⁹⁻¹⁴), and the boldness of professions of constancy that might not be realized. Hence the coldness of His attitude to professions like that of the new disciple who said, 'Lord, I will follow thee whithersoever thou goest' (Lk 9⁵⁷·⁵⁸), or to Peter's hasty word, 'If I should die with thee, yet will I not deny thee' (Mk 14³¹). But, further, Christ repeatedly cautioned His followers against all ill-timed testimony. As He Himself practised a certain reserve in His own teaching (Jn 16¹²), He also frequently laid upon His followers injunctions of silence. So in cases of healing He charges those who have seen or experienced His power to tell no man what He has done (Mk 3¹² 5⁴³ 7³⁶), and after the scenes at Cæsarea Philippi and on the Mount of Transfiguration the same injunction follows (8³⁰ 9⁹). No doubt there were temporary reasons for such reserve on Christ's part, and for such injunctions of reserve; and He looked forward to the time when the things He had taught and done in private should be proclaimed upon the housetops (Mt 10²⁷), and when the disciples should be so fully established in the faith that no further reserve should be necessary. But in any case Christ desired no hasty testimonies in His favour. It was as if He said : The profession of My name is not always needful : its value depends on its seasonableness, and the maturity of the faith lying behind it. Wait till the times are ripe and faith is ripe; till the private confession wells forth irresistibly from the lips; or till the crisis comes when everyone is called to proclaim his faith. There will come occasions when to refrain from declaring one's faith may be equivalent to disowning and denial, or at least to cowardice. Then those who have been confessing Christ in heart and life will also profess their faith boldly with their lips, and face all the consequences of their profession. It is then, when the day and hour are calling for a clear and living testimony, that profession becomes one with confession, and the word has fullest force : 'Whosoever shall confess me before men, him will I also confess before my Father which is in heaven' (Mt 10³²ᶠ·).

J. DICK FLEMING.

PROFIT.—

Two Gr. words are so rendered : (1) ὠφελίω, *to further, help, profit* : RV 'profit,' Mt 15⁵ (=Mk 7¹¹) 16²⁶ (=Mk 8³⁶, Lk 9²⁵ AV 'advantage'), Jn 6⁶³ ; 'prevail,' Mt 27²⁴, Jn 12¹⁹ ; 'be bettered,' Mk 5²⁶ ; (2) συμφέρω, *to bear or bring together* ; 'be profitable,' Mt 5²⁹·³⁰ 18⁶ ; 'be expedient,' Mt 19¹⁰ (AV 'good'), Jn 11⁵⁰ 18¹⁴ 16⁷.

The address of Jesus is, for the most part, to the highest in human nature ; but sometimes a less heroic note is struck, and there is direct appeal to the instinctive impulses of self-regard and self-preservation, and to the instincts of gain and the anxieties of the balance-sheet. The analogy of profitable trading gives force to the parables of the Talents and the Pounds (Mt 25¹⁴ᶠᶠ·, Lk 19¹²ᶠᶠ·), but in one great saying the appeal to what may be termed the business instincts is direct : 'What shall a man be profited, if he shall gain the whole world, and forfeit his life ? or what shall a man give in exchange for his life?' Mt 16²⁶ (=Mk 8³⁶, Lk 9²⁵). Here the terms of commerce are used, and the 'balance-sheet of the soul' (Morison) is struck. With this we may compare Plato's words : 'What will anyone be profited if under the influence of honour or money or power, aye, or under the excitement of poetry, he neglect justice and virtue?' (see Jowett's *Plato*, iii. 505). This weighing of advantages and gain finds its full force in Christ's doctrine of the supreme good of the Kingdom of God, the one secure treasure of unspeakable value, for the possession of which all other treasures may well be given in exchange (Mt 13⁴⁴⁻⁴⁶).

W. H. DYSON.

PROGRESS.

PROGRESS.—Christ and the essential truth of His teaching as preserved in the Gospels are entirely identified with the fact of human progress. Man's progress is a fact, a fact and not an idea, a fact, however, in which ideas are embedded and come to manifestation. This, moreover, is the greatest and most complex fact in the history of the individual and social life of humanity. It is of the highest importance, therefore, that Christ and His teaching should be set in the light of this fact ; that not only His teaching, but Christ Himself should be examined and tested in this light. He and His teaching have nothing to lose, but everything to gain thereby.

1. In order to understand Christ and His teaching from the standpoint of progress, there are several historical facts as to the latter which require to be noted and kept in mind. (1) Man's history has been upon the whole a history of progress ever since he entered upon the course of his civilization. (2) But this fact does not imply that the idea of his progress in the path leading towards his destiny has been familiar to man ever since he began his career of advancement. The truth is that even at so late a date in history as the time of Christ's advent in it, the mind of pagan antiquity had nowhere been awakened to the clear consciousness that man had been pursuing, and that he had still for unknown ages to continue pursuing, a progressive destiny. The only historical instance slightly, not entirely, at variance with this general statement is the Zoroastrian theory as to the existence of good and evil, their hostile relations to each other, and the eventual subjugation and extinction of evil by the triumph of good. (3) Further, it is only within recent times that the general mind of the more advanced civilized races of mankind has become possessed by the idea and moved by the sentiment of the progressive destiny to which man is called in this world, and those men constitute a small minority who have begun

in any true sense to realize the momentous importance of the meaning with which the fact of human progress is charged. (4) Again, it is of consequence to state expressly what is implied in the general truth just indicated, that neither the fact nor the importance of the fact of human progress, in any true sense of the word, was admitted for many centuries to a place of recognition in the ecclesiastical and theological developments of traditional Christianity ; and this remark is true even of Augustine's *Civitas Dei.*

These facts, then, seem to encourage the conclusion, which is too often, but most unfairly, adopted, that Christ concerned Himself very little, if at all, with the fact of human progress on the earth, and that His teaching sheds little or no light upon this subject, which in reality is—as the modern mind has begun to see—a subject of urgent importance for every man and for the whole human race. But this conclusion is groundless. For in the Gospels there is abundance of evidence not only to show that the fact of man's progressive destiny had due recognition paid to it by Christ Himself and in His teaching, but also to make it manifest that in Himself and in His teaching there is a revelation of all the essential principles of human progress, and also an adequate provision of the moral conditions necessary to bring these principles to realization in the individual and social life and destiny of humanity.

2. But at this point notice requires to be taken of two other historical facts with which the position of Christ and His teaching came inevitably into immediate and important relations. *First,* the Jewish people occupied a unique and pre-eminent place among all the peoples of antiquity as regards the fact of human progress. Among them there had been developed, many centuries prior to Christ's time, ideas and sentiments, aspirations and hopes relative to the progressive destiny of mankind, which were entirely phenomenal, and which possessed immense value, partly because in many points they were highly enlightened, partly because of their profound *moral* significance, and partly because of the service they rendered in the preparation of the way for the new, progressive era to be ushered into the life of humanity by Christ's advent (*e.g.* Gn 22¹⁵⁻¹⁸, Is 2²⁻⁵ 10¹⁻⁹ 42¹⁻¹¹ 62. 65¹⁷⁻²⁵, Jer 31²⁷⁻³⁴, Ezk 36²²⁻²⁸, Mic 4¹⁻⁴, Ps 67. 72. 102¹³⁻²² 145¹⁻¹³). The people of Israel, as the passages referred to show, conceived of their own 'golden age' and that of the Gentile peoples as lying not behind but ahead of them in the less or more distant future, and they were the first people in whose mind this idea shaped and rooted itself. In this outlook of theirs on the future all those elements which formed their general idea of the fact of progress came into play. What those elements were need not be stated here. But one other word may be added, viz., that if conditions had favoured the free and full development of all the ideas of progress and of all the progressive sentiments and strivings to which the worthiest leaders and teachers of the nation had attained in the noontide of the prophetic age, and if this development had continued until the fulness of the times had arrived for Christ's appearance, two things would have happened : the task of His Mission, on the one hand, would have been immensely lightened ; and, on the other, the task of Christianity in evolving the moral progress of mankind would have been less difficult, and its success greatly accelerated.

But, *secondly,* the progressive developments in the earlier stages of the nation's history had an arrest put upon them in various directions, and that while they were still immature. When Christ appeared, He found that the religion of

Israel, transformed into Judaism, had departed from the path of progress and committed itself to the position of finality. The religion of the Prophets, which in its ideas, sentiments, and strivings had begun to cross the boundaries of exclusive nationality, had been changed, as a system of law, as a method of Divine worship and service, as a way of salvation, and as a political ideal, into a narrow, rigid, national institution; and this institution, it was claimed, had a right to exist throughout all ages, although it was, in effect, a wall of separation not only between Jews and Gentiles, but also between the latter and God.

It was in these circumstances, then, that Christ appeared to reveal the principles of progress and to become a moral power making for their perfect realization in the life and destiny of man. And towards the two facts thus indicated He had necessarily to relate Himself, His teaching, and, indeed, His entire work and influence. Towards the first fact and the progressive elements and tendencies, He took up an attitude of appreciation and sympathy, and made it His aim and endeavour to promote their development to higher and wider forms of realization. Towards Judaism, on the other hand, so far as its anti-progressive vices were concerned, He took up what He knew would prove to be eventually an attitude of effective reaction. It is evident, however, that the finality which Judaism claimed for itself must have rendered it necessary for Him to put some restrictions on Himself as to His method of communicating and developing His ideas on the subject of progress. For any outspoken and persistent attack on Judaism on the point in question would have been sure to arouse against Him overwhelming opposition, as is manifest from what happened to Stephen the proto-martyr. This may have been one of His reasons for His persistent non-interference as a teacher either with the nature or the administration of any of the civil or political institutions that He found existing in Palestine, or knew to exist in the Roman Empire generally.

But He had another, a deeper, a much farther-reaching reason for silently letting civil and political institutions alone. It was not that He was indifferent to them, or that He considered them as not belonging to the nature and objects of His mission as the Saviour of the world. The civil and political state of society as He knew it was a matter of profound and sorrowful interest to Him (Mt 9^{36} 20^{25}). He must have been quite aware of the fact that the renewal of the civil and political life of mankind was needed everywhere in the existing civilized as well as uncivilized world. He was fully conscious of the fact that His own perfect self-devotion to the service of God and man endangered His life, and would bring Him to His cross to a large extent because of the vices of the civil and political condition of things under which He conducted His ministry (Mt 20$^{17-19}$, Jn 18^{28}-19^{16}). He also anticipated the fact that the continuance of this evil order of things, after He was gone, would involve His servants and His cause in suffering (Mt 24$^{1-13}$).

Lastly, He never uttered a word to indicate directly and explicitly that He entertained any hope of the regeneration of the civil, or political, or economical conditions and organizations of human society. Why was this? Why did He keep Himself so entirely and persistently aloof from these and all other great interests of a kindred nature pertaining to the external relationships and well-being of human life, declining to interfere with them even when requested to do so? (Lk 12$^{13, 14}$, Mt 22$^{17-22}$). He assumed and maintained this attitude because of the perfect understanding He had of the necessary conditions and requirements of human progress in every one of its departments. He had to consider what it was possible and what it was impossible for Him to accomplish during the short period of His lifetime on earth. In doing this He had to keep in view the existing state of society in all the various developments of its life at the time. And He must have known, as any one knowing and correctly interpreting the facts can see was actually the case, that if He had attempted to initiate or to achieve a reformation within any of the domains of human life in question, the result would inevitably have proved worse than useless for Himself and His cause, and for humanity. Knowing this, moreover, He, in the exercise of marvellous faith and patience, left, meanwhile, the renewal of man's social life in all its diversified forms of manifestation, in the hands, and to the times and ways, of God as the moral Governor of the world. For the time being He devoted Himself wholly and exclusively to the moral task which His Father had given Him to do; and in doing this, and doing it successfully, He rendered to the cause of human progress a service which will never cease increasing the glory of His name.

3. All that has been said makes it easy to show now how Christ Himself, His teaching, and, indeed, the whole of His work on earth and in heaven, can be explained in terms of progress. This explanation was adopted in effect and often used by Himself. So true is this that a great deal of His teaching—the most of it, indeed, when properly understood—can be construed into a theory of what is meant by the progress of humanity, —a theory never stated by Himself in abstract terms, but embodied in the general order of ideas that found such diversified forms of expression in His teaching. Briefly, the theory in question was this—(1) His teaching was all related to the cardinal facts of the moral nature of God and the moral nature of man. (2) A great deal of His teaching was concerned with the moral relations between God and men and between man and man. (3) In His teaching He dwelt much upon the inward and direct moral relations of men to God, which in every instance are relations of men to Him as *individuals*. For it is only in the individual that the moral conditions exist which make inward and direct relations of God to men possible. And this must have been one of Christ's reasons for the immense importance and value that He attached to men as individuals. (4) He also dwelt much on the subject of the rectifying and the perfecting of the moral relations of men to God and to one another. (5) He announced, and often alluded to and explained in various ways and connexions, the fact that it was His predestined task as man's Saviour to occupy the position and to exercise the function of Mediator within the sphere of the moral relations of God to men, and of men to Him and to one another. Though He never used the word 'Mediator' in this connexion, He often spoke of His relation to God and men in expressions meaning the same thing. And He taught also that His work of mediation would be continued after His work on earth had been finished (*e.g.* Mt 11^{27} 28$^{18-20}$, Jn 14–17). (6) It was within the domain of the order of these great facts and ideas, which are all of an essentially moral nature, that Christ conceived the fundamental need of human progress as lying. Here also He saw the essential nature of the progress needed, and found the grounds on which to His mind man's progress was guaranteed. (7) But it was not Christ's idea that the progressive realization of these moral facts and ideas would come to manifestation *only* within the invisible moral sphere of the individual and social life of mankind. He cherished the certain conviction and hope that they would come gradually, in the course of their realization, to manifestation in the regeneration of all the various external relations of men to one another in the conditions, organizations, and activities of their social life. (8) He was fully persuaded that the course of human progress, such as He conceived its nature to be and the conditions on which it would proceed in the individual and social life of humanity, would strictly and persistently follow the laws of evolution. It may be added, finally, that it is within the region of these facts that the greatness of the extent of Christ's originality as a teacher is to be seen, and also the momentousness of the position and task He claimed for Himself as Mediator between God and men.

4. But did Christ's teaching as to human progress actually follow the lines just indicated? It did. In Mt 5[17] He identified His position in history and His work with the essentially moral nature, and with the cause and the evolution of the progress of the individual and social life of humanity. That in the Law and the Prophets which had supreme interest and value for Him, was the nature and the extent of the revelation they contained of the will and purpose of God with reference to the moral relations between God and men and between one man and another, and with reference to the historical development of human destiny. He saw that this revelation was very incomplete and imperfect. And in strict accordance with the Law of Continuity, which is one of the greatest laws of evolution and of human progress, He sympathetically put Himself and His work in direct organic relations with it, in order to complete and perfect the revelation of the Divine will and purpose to mankind, and in order so to mediate, by means of His moral power, the moral relations of men to God and to one another, that the Divine will and purpose would eventually attain to full and universal realization in their life and destiny. And so, when He said He had come not to destroy the Law and the Prophets, but to fulfil, He must have had the thought in His mind that the fulfilling in question, and His task in achieving it, would be continued after the work of His earthly ministry was done. In Mt 6[9. 10] His mind is to be seen moving within the order of the same ideas and facts: 'Our Father which art in heaven, Hallowed be thy name. Thy kingdom come. Thy will be done on earth, as it is in heaven.' These words of prayer, as Christ understood them, are rooted in the truth of the moral nature of God and of man, and of the moral relations of God to men, and of men to Him and to each other. They imply that the sphere of the direct and inward moral relations of men to God and to one another in Him is the essential domain of God's Kingdom on the earth. They imply that the Kingdom of God on earth is predestined to arrive at universal realization in the individual and social life of mankind, and that *pervasively*, so that the Divine will and purpose will be manifested in all the external forms of man's existence and activities. They imply that this consummation will be reached by a progressive process of historical development; for the Kingdom of God is an order of things that is *coming*. And they imply that the Fatherhood of God and the brotherhood of man will be the supreme governmental principles in the perfected conditions of human existence, which Christ hoped would be ushered in in answer to His prayer.

But these were not the only forms in which Christ expressed His great and rich order of ideas as to human progress. Man's progress is evolved in the course of his history, and nothing is more wonderful or beautiful than the parabolic forms in which Christ embodied His ideas as to the various phases that human progress assumes in the history of its evolution. (1) The gradual realization of God's will and purpose in the lives of men as individuals is everywhere and always the basis of moral progress in the social life and history of humanity; and therefore our Lord—no doubt designedly—illustrated the evolution of the Kingdom of God in its relation to the individual's heart and life in His first parable, that of the Sower (Mt 13[1-8. 18-23]).—(2) The progressive realization of the will and purpose of God in the moral relations of men to Him and to one another in the various social forms and manifestations of life may be conceived as a fact, which indeed it is, without taking into consideration the entanglements and dangers in which the process is involved from the existence in the world of moral evil. As so conceived, the evolution of man's moral progress is destined gradually and surely to attain to complete and manifest realization in the Kingdom of God. It was from this point of view that our Lord illustrated His ideas of human progress in His parable of the Seed Growing Secretly (Mk 4[26-29]).—(3) But the progressive fulfilment of God's will and purpose in the history of man's social life and destiny may also be conceived as a process of historical evolution, and as actually entangled and endangered, which is the case, by the presence and developments of moral evil in the individual and social life of men. As thus conceived, then, the history of man's social progress towards the perfect and universal realization of God's will and purpose has the character of a conflict between moral good and moral evil. But this conflict, at every stage and in every section of its history, is presided over by the moral government of God, and is certain under His judgment to issue in a final crisis in which evil will be entirely and for ever separated from good, and in which righteousness will reign universally in the relations of men to God and to one another in His Kingdom. From these points of view also our Lord contemplated the evolution of human progress; and He so couched His ideas on the subject in His parable of the Wheat and the Tares (Mt 13[24-30. 37-43]).—(4) Again, the history of man's moral progress starts from a very small and simple beginning, and eventually develops into a result of vast dimensions and great complexity. This fact as to man's progress our Lord likewise fully realized, and He expressed His sense of its truth and value in His parable of the Mustard-seed (Mt 13[31. 32]).—(5) Finally, the end of moral progress in the life and history of humanity will be a destiny in which every department of its individual and social life, external as well as internal, will be interpenetrated and regulated by the will and purpose of God as perfectly realized and manifested in a universal and established order of righteousness and love. Could it be anything else than this that our Lord meant by His parable of the Leaven and the three measures of meal? (Mt 13[33]).

Thus it becomes manifest that our Lord's teaching embodied a philosophy of human history and progress. In this point of view His teaching was absolutely original. Nor can it ever be superseded. His ideas of human progress and His faith in it are a large part of essential Christianity. This part of His gospel is urgently needed by the present age. And multitudes are waiting to welcome it as a message from *Him* as the world's Saviour.

Literature.—Buckle, *Hist. of Civilization*; *Lux Mundi*, ch xi.; Loring Brace, *Gesta Christi*; Janet, *Theory of Morals*, 416; P. Granger, *The Soul of a Christian*, 246; Westcott, *Chr. Social Union Addresses*, 66; W. D. Mackenzie, *Christianity and the Progress of Man*, 217; A. R. Wallace, *Studies, Scientific and Social*, ii. 493; W. L. Davidson, *Chr. Ethics*, 56; Liddon, *Serm. on Some Words of St. Paul*, 246, *Serm. before Univ. of Oxford*, 1st ser. p. 25.   W. D. Thomson.

PROMISE.—The NT is full of the idea that in Christ had arrived the fulfilment of a promise made over and over again in preceding ages. The gospel is regarded by all the writers not as an event unexpected and unprepared for, but as the due and natural sequel and climax of God's dealings from of old. The εὐαγγέλιον is the fulfilment of the ἐπαγγελία. It was, indeed, the strength with which this idea was rooted in the mind of the Jew ('whose is the adoption and the glory and . . . the promises,' Ro 9⁴) that made it so hard for him to understand how the Gentile could come within the full scope of the gospel. How could the 'dogs' share equally with the 'children' (Mt 15²⁶ =Mk 7²⁷)? How could the uncovenanted and uncircumcised be 'heirs according to the promise' (Gal 3²⁹)? Whole passages, therefore, in some of the Epistles (esp. Rom., Gal., Heb.) have to be devoted to showing that the implication of the promise was vaster than any of the forms in which it had been conveyed. There is no literature which is so saturated with the spirit of anticipation as the Hebrew, no nation which has cherished so ardent and irrepressible a belief in its destiny,—' a people who were looking forwards from a great Past of Wonders to a Future of Good and Glory' (Mason, *Heb. Gram.*² p. 98). It is in the NT, however, that this note of anticipation becomes dominant. Anticipation, indeed, here gives place to realization. While the NT contains several passages which show kinship with current Apocalyptic literature and its eschatology, and indicate a lingering belief in the mind of the writer that the fulfilment of the promises lies still in the future, the unmistakably prevalent thought of the writers is that in the work of Christ they have already seen the promises fulfilled. The Evangelic records exhibit, each in its own way, the consciousness that Israel's hopes had found their fulfilment in Christ ; and, sober and restrained as is the narrative, one can hardly miss in it the note of jubilant realization. Mt. loses no opportunity of showing that what happened to Jesus was in accordance with ancient prophecy ; Mk., while seldom citing Scripture, describes Jesus as beginning His ministry with the declaration 'The time is fulfilled' (1¹⁵) ; Lk. commences and concludes his Gospel with episodes (1⁴⁵⁻⁵⁵. ⁶⁷⁻⁶⁹ 2²⁵⁻³⁸ 24²⁵⁻²⁸. ⁴⁴⁻⁴⁷) intended to show how men saw, or failed to see, in Jesus the Christ foreshadowed in the Scriptures, and Jn. (5³⁹) quotes Jesus as stating that the Scriptures bear witness to Him, and notes (12¹⁶. ⁴¹ etc.) how the reception of Jesus answered to the sayings of the prophets.

It was this aspect of Christ's appearance—as the fulfilment of an eagerly awaited promise—that occupied most room in the earliest preaching of the gospel. See Stephen's speech (Ac 7), Peter's (2¹⁴⁻³⁶ and 10³⁴⁻⁴³), Paul's (13³² ' We bring you good tidings of the promise made unto the fathers,' and 26⁶). The main line of address taken by the early preachers was always to prove that Jesus was the Christ (9²² 17². ³ 18⁵. ²⁸).

It is to be noticed, however, that Jesus Himself in His public preaching seldom, if ever, adopted this line of appeal. Not even in His more private teaching does He appear to have attached importance to it. When, *e.g.*, John the Baptist definitely inquired 'Art thou he that cometh?' (Mt 11²⁻¹⁹, Lk 7¹⁹⁻²³), Jesus deliberately appealed not to the correspondence between Himself and the expectations formed of the promised Messiah, but to the effect being at the moment produced by His ministry. When the same question was being discussed between Himself and His disciples (Mt 16¹³⁻¹⁶=Mk 8²⁷⁻²⁹=Lk 9¹⁸⁻²⁰), Jesus was not concerned so much about their identifying Him with the One who was to come, by means of signs and tokens which were expected to accompany His coming, as that the conviction should come in an inward and secret way ('Flesh and blood hath not revealed it to thee, but my Father which is in heaven,' Mt 16¹⁷). He objected to being proclaimed as the Christ, not simply because He knew that the people, when persuaded of this, would seek to make Him a king and expect Him to use temporal resources, but because the very tenacity with which His countrymen clung to their stereotyped notions of the promised Messiah would prevent them from gaining a true understanding of the scope and purpose of His mission. He had a sublime contempt for the petty and pedantic way in which the scribes took upon themselves to say how the anticipations of Scripture were, or were not, to be verified, and held their pretensions up to scorn (Mt 22⁴¹⁻⁴⁶=Mk 12³⁵⁻³⁷ =Lk 20⁴¹⁻⁴⁴). It was, in short, because His mind was so filled with the larger purpose of God that He assigned little weight to the recognition of that local and national theory which had so much more of patriotic bias and ambitious desire in it than of pure love of humanity. And it was precisely because the priests and scribes, in their blind attachment to their own interpretation of the promise, saw, in His comparative carelessness about the traditional view and His frequent insistence upon a purely spiritual interpretation, a danger to their own designs, that they resolved upon His death.

It is true, of course, that Jesus commonly used one term at least which in the current phraseology of the time was closely associated with the temporal and literally-understood fulfilment of the ' promise.' He constantly proclaimed the advent of the Kingdom of heaven or the Kingdom of God. But whatever critical view be held of the records, and leaving undecided the question whether Mt 24 and other similar passages which contain a considerable eschatological element are to be taken as representing a part of the actual teaching of Jesus, or rather His teaching as coloured by passing through minds steeped in the ideas of Jewish eschatology, it is sufficiently evident that Jesus habitually used the expression 'Kingdom of heaven' in a different sense from the ordinary and popular one, and preferred to divest it of the usual patriotic and eschatological associations. The *locus classicus* is the Sermon on the Mount beginning with the Beatitude, 'Blessed are the poor in spirit, for theirs is the kingdom of heaven.' The 'promise,' as Jesus gives it here in sevenfold form, is a promise to the spiritually-minded of a spiritual grace, having no reference whatever to Messianic considerations, and this holds good even if the alternative form in which the Beatitudes are given in Lk. is held to be the earlier. Jesus, in the most royal and absolute fashion, gave assurances to His disciples, but these, in the Synoptics hardly less than in the Fourth Gospel, are assurances not of any kind of material benefit, but of spiritual grace,' *e.g.* 'Thy Father which seeth in secret shall recompense thee' (Mt 6⁴ also vv.⁶. ¹⁸) ; 'He that loseth his life for my sake shall find it' (Mt 10³⁹ 16²⁵) ; 'I will give you rest,' and 'Ye shall find rest to your souls' (Mt 11²⁸. ²⁹) ; 'I will make you fishers of men' (Mk 1¹⁷, cf. Lk 5¹⁰) ; 'Your reward shall be great, and ye shall be sons of the Most High' (Lk 6³⁵) ; 'Ye shall know the truth, and the truth shall make you free' (Jn 8³²).

It is true, of course, that there are some passages in which the assurance of blessing includes material benefit : *e.g.* 'All these things (*i.e.* food, clothing, etc.) shall be added unto you' (Mt 6³³) ; the reply to Peter that those who for Christ's sake have forsaken earthly advantage 'shall receive a hundredfold now in this time, houses,' etc. (Mk

$10^{30} = $ Lk $18^{29} = $ Mt 19^{29}) ; but the very connexion in which such passages occur shows in each case that Jesus attaches importance only to the spiritual blessing ; better forego all earthly profit whatever than miss this (Mt 10^{39} $16^{25. 26}$, Lk $12^{20. 21}$). Anything like requests for a promise of personal advantage He sternly discourages (Mt $20^{20-23} = $ Mk 10^{35-45}).

Generally the promises of Jesus to His disciples may be classified as follows : (*a*) *particular assurances to individuals* : to the thief on the cross (Lk 23^{43}), to the woman in the house of Simon the Leper (Mt $26^{13} = $ Mk 14^9), to Nathanael (Jn 1^{51}), to Peter (Mt $16^{18} = $ Mk $9^1 = $ Lk 9^{27}, cf. Mt 18^{18}), to Peter again (Jn 13^7 and v.^{36}), also Mk $9^1 = $ Lk 9^{27} ; (*b*) *assurances about the prevailing nature of prayer and the power of faith* (Mt 7^7 18^{19}, Jn $14^{13. 14}$, Mt 17^{26} $21^{21. 22}$, Mk $11^{23. 24}$, Mt 18^{18}) ; (*c*) *assurances of His continued presence and of their support and ultimate triumph* (Mt $10^{19} = $ Lk 12^{12}, Mt 28^{20} [Mk $16^{17. 18}$], Mt $10^{32. 39. 42}$ 13^{43} 16^{25} 19^{28}, Lk 6^{38}, Jn $6^{40. 44. 54}$ 8^{51} 11^{25} 14^{22} 16^{20}). It is to promises of this kind that James refers in 1^{12} ' the crown of life which the Lord promised to them that love him,' and in 2^5 ' heirs of the kingdom which he promised to them that love him' (cf. 1 Jn 2^{25}) ; (*d*) the outstanding promise, however, is that of *the Holy Spirit*, and this is the one promise which is most explicitly recorded as made to the disciples (Jn $14^{16. 26}$ 15^{26} 16^{13} etc.), and is directly recalled at the foundation of the Christian Church : ' He charged them . . . to wait for the promise of the Father, which, said he, ye heard from me' (Ac 1^4, cf. 2^{23}). And this promise may be said practically to include and interpret almost all the foregoing.

LITERATURE.—Denney in Hastings' *DB* iv. 104 ; Sidgwick, *Methods of Ethics*[7] (1907), 295 ; Somerville, *Precious Seed* (1890), 233 ; Spurgeon, *Twelve Sermons on Precious Promises.*

J. ROSS MURRAY.

PROPERTY.—Under this title two questions arise : (1) Is the possession of private property right according to the principles of the teaching and example of Jesus ? (2) In what ways is a follower of Jesus to acquire and to use his property ? These questions touch one another when it is suggested that a Christian should give away all his property and not seek to gain any more. They may, however, be kept distinct, and the second discussed on the assumption that the possession of private property is justifiable.

1. A very large section of a man's interest is connected with his possessions. Therefore, inevitably, the teaching and example of Jesus have an important bearing upon the question of property. And further, inasmuch as He gave to men a very different ideal of character and conduct from that of the world, it is to be expected that in regard to property His teaching will show marked divergence from the prevailing worldly view. But it is not therefore to be assumed that the authority of Jesus can be claimed for the socialistic view of property, which may be called the direct negative of the ordinary view which men hold. The question to be settled is—May we infer from the teaching and example of Jesus that the private ownership of property is unjustifiable ? The relation of the teaching and example of Jesus to modern Socialism opens up a wide field for discussion, and this is seriously complicated by the difficulty of defining Socialism and disentangling it, as a clear economic theory, from the general revolt against the hardships of poverty and the tyranny of riches, from which it springs, and which is reflected in the generous literature and thought of all ages and countries.

The first point to make clear is that this revolt was certainly present among the Jews, and has left distinct traces in the OT (Is 5^8) and also in the extra-canonical Jewish literature. ' There came to exist among them what has been called a " genius for hatred " of the rich ' (Peabody, *Jesus Christ and the Social Question,* p. 206). The popular view among the Jews was that godliness invariably resulted in prosperity ; and one of their problems was the prosperity of the ungodly and the adversity of the pious. This problem was exceptionally acute in our Lord's day, through the dominance of the Romans, and the wealth of the publicans acquired by their faithlessness to the national cause. Thus precisely the condition from which modern Socialism springs was present. And not only so, but a well-defined socialistic experiment was being made by the Essenes, among whom ' the strongest tie by which the members were united was absolute community of goods ' (Schürer, *HJP*, II. ii. 195). It has been maintained that the teaching of Jesus was greatly influenced by that of the Essenes. But as Essenism was ' in the first place merely Pharisaism in the superlative degree ' (Schürer, *l.c.* p. 210), whatever other elements entered into it, this view must be given up (Lightfoot, *Col.* 397 ff.). However, from the popular feeling about the rich, and the existence of the Essenes as a socialistic community, we may gather that the way was quite open for Jesus to adopt the doctrines of Communism ; and the argument that in His teaching we find the seed of Socialism, which only required conditions of thought and life such as are found in modern times to become fully matured, is not justified.

This is the view of the matter which representative Socialists take. As a general rule, Socialists are opposed to the Christian faith, and recognize in it a basis for the present organization of society and a hindrance to the change they desire to see brought about (for citations, see Peabody, *op. cit.* p. 15). They quote with approval the sayings of Jesus about the blessedness of 'the poor and the woes of the rich, but they realize distinctly that the basis of His thought is fundamentally different from theirs. The special ground of objection on the part of Socialists to the Christian religion is its teaching as to the future, which they regard as having diverted the moral enthusiasm of religious people from the present to the ' other ' world. Some, no doubt, hold that this emphasis on the future is due to the corruption of the pure teaching of Jesus, and so are ready to claim His authority for their views. But even if the contrast between present and future in the teaching of Jesus could be adjusted to the satisfaction of the Socialists, it leaves the contrast between outward circumstance and inward character, in regard to which there is a vital and all-embracing distinction between the principles of Jesus and Socialism. The phenomenon, however, of what is known as Christian Socialism has to be noted. The fierce competition of modern industrial and commercial life, with the cruelties it produces, cannot be accepted as desirable by any man of sensitive Christian convictions. And, moreover, the great hold which Socialism has taken of multitudes, and the fact that it becomes to them the only religion they feel any need of, have led Christians to desire that its influence should be exerted on the side of the Church. The Christian Socialists in England (Maurice and Kingsley) were influenced mainly by the first consideration, and were enthusiastic supporters of the Co-operative movement. The second consideration, as might be expected, appealed more especially to Roman Catholics, who are represented by Abbé Lamennais ; Baron von Ketteler, Archb. of Mayence ; and Count de Nurn. In Germany, among Protestants, Christian Socialism has been represented by Victor Huber and Pastor Stöcker. The views of those who may be

regarded as entitled to the name Christian Socialists cannot be thought of as an isolated fact. They
have been partly the result and partly the cause
of a general shifting of the centre of interest from
the sphere of doctrinal theology to that of practical
teaching. The theological literature of the last
50 years has been largely occupied with the application of the teaching of Jesus to the practical
problems of life, and many have held that there
is nothing in the Christian faith which is antagonistic to Socialism as an economic theory. But
with some exceptions it is agreed that Jesus did
not lay down any economic theory of the State,
and indeed deliberately refused to take advantage
of openings in this direction which He received
(Mt 22[15-22] 17[24-27], Lk 12[13-21]). 'To speak of the
economics of the New Testament is in my opinion
as impossible as to speak of its dietetics (Ac 15[20-29]),
its hermeneutics (1 Co 9[4-10]), its astronomy (Mt
2[9, 24, 29]), or its meteorology (Mt 16[23], Lk 12[24, 25])'—
(H. Holtzmann, *Die ersten Christen und die soziale
Frage*).

Before the actual teaching and example of Jesus
on the subject are analyzed, it is desirable to consider how far the glimpses we receive in the
Acts of the Apostles of the social life of the first
Christians at Jerusalem form an authoritative
commentary upon them. We read that 'all that
believed were together, and had all things common' (Ac 2[44]). And again, 'neither said any of
them that aught of the things which he possessed
was his own; but they had all things common'
(4[32], cf. also 2[45] 4[34, 37]). It is worthy of remark that
these statements are from the pen of the author
of the Third Gospel, in which the sayings of Jesus
about the rich and the poor are given in their most
uncompromising form (cf. Lk 6[20], Mt 5[3]). We may
therefore suppose that the communistic aspect of
the life of the church at Jerusalem has received
full attention in the Book of Acts, and that no
inference which goes in the least beyond the statements of that book is justified.*

A careful scrutiny of the relevant passages of
the Book of Acts shows that: (1) the condition
which prevailed in Jerusalem did not continue;
(2) the churches organized by St. Paul (whose
companion St. Luke was) show no trace of the
community of goods, nor is any condemnation expressed because of this; (3) those who had houses
and lands *sold* them; (4) Peter in what he said to
Ananias (Ac 5[4]) clearly indicated that the right to
private property was not questioned ('Whiles it
remained, was it not thine own? and after it was
sold, was it not in thine own power?'). No theory,
therefore, can be established on the basis of what
we find prevailing among the first Christians in
Jerusalem. We must rather suppose that in the
special circumstances of that church an exceptional
condition in relation to property was produced.

An analysis of the teaching and example of Jesus
brings out quite clearly that the denial of a right
to the possession of private property cannot be
extracted from them. It is true that many strong
statements are found in the Gospels as to the
disadvantages of riches, and that the poor are
represented as having a special interest in the
Kingdom of God (Mt 6[19], Lk 18[22], Mk 10[23], Lk 6[20-24]
12[15], Mt 6[24] 19[24] 11[5]). Far-reaching deductions have
been drawn from these in condemnation of the
prevailing industrial order. And their spirit is
manifestly very different from that which the
modern industrial and commercial struggle tends
to produce. But their full force can be realized
in connexion with the common effect of riches upon

* For discussions on the relation of St. Luke to Ebionism,
see Keim, iii. 284; H. Holtzmann, *op. cit.*; Colin Campbell,
Critical Studies in Luke's Gospel; B. Weiss, *Life of Christ*, vol. i.
bks. iv., v.; cf. Peabody, *op. cit.* p. 192.

character, and they do not involve any condemnation of the possession of private property. It is
to be remembered, too, in connexion with this, that
no single statement of our Lord can be wisely
taken by itself and pressed to the extreme conclusion logically possible. This is to forget His
method of teaching, which aimed 'at the greatest
clearness in the briefest compass' (Wendt, *Teaching of Jesus*, i. p. 130). 'One who proposes to
follow literally the specific commands of Jesus
finds himself immediately plunged into contradictions and absurdities. He accepts the teaching
of Jesus concerning non-resistance, "to him that
smiteth thee on one cheek offer also the other,"
but soon he hears this same counsellor of peace
bid His friends sell their garments "and buy a
sword"' (Peabody, ch. i.).

We must therefore set over against the words of
Jesus in which He seems to condemn the possession
of riches, facts and sayings which forbid any communistic conclusion being drawn from them. Thus
Jesus and His disciples had a fund for their common necessities (Jn 13[14]). Moreover, the disciples
owned boats and nets, to which they returned after
the crucifixion (Jn 21[3ff.]). Peter's house appears to
have been the headquarters of Jesus at Capernaum
(Mk 1[29] 2[1]). There is no condemnation of the
settled life which Martha, Mary, and Lazarus lived
at Bethany (Lk 10[38ff.], Jn 12[1ff.]). Zacchæus, who was
a rich man, was not asked to give away all that he
had, but rather commended for giving a portion (Lk
19[1-9]). Mary's action in 'wasting' the costly cruse
of ointment (Mt 26[12]) was justified and praised.
The centurion who had built a synagogue for the
Jews in Capernaum (Lk 7[1, 10]) received the highest
praise, but nothing was said about his wealth,
evidently considerable. Nicodemus must have been
a man of substance, but no question of his relation
to his property was raised (Jn 3[1-21]). Again, some
force must be allowed to the fact that in several
of the parables (Lk 19[12], Mt 21[33]) Jesus used the
rights which men have over their property to
illustrate the duty which all owe to God. This
argument cannot be pressed too far, but still such
illustrations would be practically impossible to
one who held that the possession of private property, with the power it gives over others, is
wrong.

2. On the assumption, then, that Jesus does not
condemn the possession of private property, it remains to discuss the place which property is to hold
in the life of a Christian, and the use which he is
to make of what he owns. The ruling consideration in this discussion is that Jesus in His teaching
looks not so much to the circumstances of men's
lives as to the kind of men they are and may
become. His teaching, therefore, about property
must be considered in relation to the effects of its
acquisition and use upon character. In regard to
the acquisition of property, the teaching of Jesus
is directed against that greedy temper of mind in
which worldly advantage is regarded as of supreme
importance, and a man's wealth as the sole criterion
of his worth. He also condemns dishonesty and
oppression in the acquisition of wealth, which
spring from this temper (Mt 23[14], Mk 12[40], Lk 20[47]).
He warns men against covetousness on the ground
that 'a man's life consisteth not in the abundance
of the things which he possesseth' (Lk 12[15]). He calls
the man a fool who had much goods laid up for many
years, and was not rich towards God (Lk 12[16-21]).
He condemns over-care about making provision for
the necessities of this life (Lk 12[22-34], Mt 6[19-34]).
And He declares that 'whosoever will save his life
shall lose it; but whosoever shall lose his life for
my sake and the gospel's, the same shall save it'
(Mk 8[35], Mt 10[39] 16[25], Lk 9[24]). Thus it is clear
that Jesus expects His followers to cultivate a

spirit of aloofness and independence in relation to the world and its wealth.

The duty of work and of making provision for • worldly needs by work may be clearly inferred from the teaching and example of Jesus, though it is not specifically inculcated. He laboured as a carpenter in Nazareth (Mk 6^3,• cf. Mt 13^{55}). In the miracle of the miraculous draught of fishes (Lk $5^{1.\ 6}$, Jn 21^6) He set His seal of approval upon the industry of the disciples. In some of the parables the duty of faithfulness in secular pursuits is plainly taught (e.g. Lk 16^{1-11}). This may also be inferred from the words of Mt 6^{50-54}. If the fowls of the air are provided for and the lilies of the field are arrayed in glory in the way of their nature through the providence of God, so also will men be provided for *in the way of their nature*, which is declared in the words, ' In the sweat of thy face shalt thou eat bread ' (Gn 3^{19}). Again, the necessity of providing for those dependent upon us is no remote inference from Lk 11^{13}, Mt 15^5 and Mk 7^{11}. For the willingness of a father to give bread to his son is taken as an illustration of the willingness of God to hear and answer the prayers of His people. And the method adopted by the Pharisees to escape the practical force of the Fifth Commandment is sternly rebuked (Mt 15^{3-6} ∥ Mk 7^{6-13}).

About the use of property the teaching of Jesus is very full. In the first place, men are to realize that they are stewards of what they possess rather than its owners (Mt 24^{45-57} 25^{14-20}, Lk 19^{11-27}). They are to use their property, therefore, for the glory of God and the good of men, themselves and others. In relation to the true good of the owners, the danger of riches is very clearly and constantly insisted upon (Mk 10^{23-27}, Mt $6^{19.\ 24}$ 13^{22}, Lk 18^{24} 6^{20-24} 16^{19-31} 12^{15} 18^{14-25} 12^{21} 16^{11}). From these passages it is clear that the tendency of riches is to hinder spiritual wellbeing. To avoid this, the renunciation of wealth is required (Lk 14^{33}, Mt 19^{29}, Lk 5^{11}, Mt 18^{19-22}, Lk 6^{58-62}). This renunciation of wealth is a general command holding for all who would be followers of Jesus, but it receives special emphasis in regard to the rich from the way in which the young ruler who had great possessions was dealt with. That the alienation of wealth is involved of necessity in its renunciation cannot be maintained in view of considerations formerly advanced, but, on the other hand, these considerations by no means preclude it in special circumstances (Lk 9^{58-62}). The way in which renunciation is to be given effect to depends upon the circumstances of each case, and is a matter for the conscience of each individual.

Apart from the general use which a follower of Jesus is to make of all his property, which is to be determined in relation to his own spiritual welfare and that of others, he is called upon also to give (alienate) a portion of his possessions to the poor and to the support of religion. These two directions for giving were fully recognized among the Jews. And so we find that although specific injunctions as to the duty of giving are not wanting in the teaching of Jesus, it is more with the spirit in which this duty is discharged that His sayings are concerned. He definitely commands the duty of giving to the poor (Mt 5^{42}, Lk 6^{38}, Mt 19^{21}, Lk 18^{22}). We see that He and His disciples were accustomed to give alms (Jn 13^{29}). The parable of the Good Samaritan, again, is the charter of the Church for all the benevolent work of hospitals, infirmaries, etc. (Lk 10^{30-36}). Such giving, however, is never to be formal and impersonal, an easy way of satisfying a fugitive emotion of pity. It is the service done rather than the gift made, which is emphasized in the parable of the Good Samaritan. Again, almsgiving is not to be ostentatious (Mt

6^{1-4}), nor are gifts to be made in the expectation of a return (Lk 14^{12-14}). The measure of giving is to be generous (Mt 10^8), and response to a claim is to be ready and ungrudging (Lk 11^{5-8}), and is to be regulated by no consideration but that of need (Lk 10^{30-36}, Mt 5^{43-48}).

In regard to giving to the support of religion, the teaching of Jesus must be considered in relation to the ordinance of the law which required a tithe. He does not commend any definite portion of a man's possessions as that which he should devote to religious objects. His teaching in this matter, as in all others, deals with the spirit in which gifts are made rather than the law which regulates their amount. He condemns the ostentation of the Pharisees in their gifts (Mk 12^{42}, Lk 21^2), and also their idea that a gift to the Temple is acceptable to God from those who are neglecting the weightier matters of the Law (Mt 23^{23-26} $6^{23.\ 24}$, Lk 18^{9-14}). But He is very far from condemning the giving of a tithe (Mt 23^{23}), and suggests rather that this is not sufficient (Lk 21^2). He distinctly commands giving to God (Mt 22^{21}), and by the way in which Mary's devotion (Mt 26^{12}) was received we are warned against any narrow utilitarian view of the objects covered by this phrase. See also artt. SOCIALISM and WEALTH.

LITERATURE.—Wendt, *Teaching of Jesus*, vol. i. ; *EBr*[9] xxii. 205 ff., xxxii. 664 ff. ; Schürer, *HJP, passim* ; Robert E. Speer, *The Principles of Jesus* ; Rae, *Contemporary Socialism* ; Peabody, *Jesus Christ and the Social Question*, and also *The Message of Christ to Society* ; Kaufmann, *Christian Socialism* ; Kirkup, *An Inquiry into Socialism* ; F. Naumann, *Das soziale Programm der evangel. Kirche* ; Flint, *Socialism*, ch. ix. ; Martensen, *Chr. Ethics*, iii. 126 ff. ; H. Holtzmann, *Die ersten Christen und die soziale Frage* ; Nitti, *Catholic Socialism* ; Newman Smyth, *Chr. Ethics*, 448 ff. ; Schaefle, *Quintessence of Socialism* ; Dale, *Laws of Christ*, ch. ii. ; J. F. Maurice, *Life of Frederick Denison Maurice* ; A. Stöcker, *Christlich-soziale Reden und Aufsätze* ; Herron, *The Larger Christianity*, and *Between Cæsar and Jesus* ; Gore, *The Sermon on the Mount* ; Westcott, *Social Aspects of Christianity* ; Lyman Abbott, *Christianity and Social Problems* ; S. Mathews, *Social Teaching of Jesus* ; Keim, *Jesus of Nazara*, vols. iii. and iv. ; Lightfoot, *Colossians*, p. 397 ff. ; Renan, *Life of Jesus, passim* ; Colin Campbell, *Crit. Studies in Luke's Gospel* ; Dykes, *Manifesto of the King*, 449 ff. ; Gladden, *Tools and the Man*, 55, 86.

ANDREW N. BOGLE.

PROPHET.—I. **The Messiah a prophet.**—1. Our Lord's redemptive work is usually divided into the threefold—prophetic, priestly, and kingly functions; and for this there is *ancient precedent*. Eusebius (*HE* i. 3) speaks of Him as ' the only *High Priest* of all men, the only *King* of all creation, and the Father's only supreme *Prophet* of prophets ' (see also Ambrose on Ps 118^{79}, and Cassiodorus on Ps 132^2). The Church has rightly felt that the unction bestowed on Jesus as the Messiah separated and endowed Him to these offices. She recognized that the old dispensation was established and preserved by those who were anointed to be prophets, priests, and kings, and she believed that each of these offices found its perfection in the Person and work of Jesus Christ. When, therefore, we dwell separately on any one of these three vocations of the Messiah (as we do in this article), we must remember that we are necessarily taking a partial view of His Person ; for to hold that He is *only* a prophet, is to fall into a heresy that has ever faced the Church.

Early in the Church's history the Gnostic Ebionites rejected the Catholic doctrine of Christ's Person, but felt no difficulty in believing Him to be an inspired prophet of the highest order. They regarded Him as one of the προφῆται ἀληθείας, and as superior to προφῆται συνέσεως οὐκ ἀληθείας ; and, as such, placed Him in line with Adam, Enoch, Noah, etc. etc., upon all of whom had rested the pre-existent Christ ; and in their Gospel we find the following words ascribed to Him: ' I am he concerning whom Moses prophesied, saying, A prophet shall the Lord God raise unto you, like unto me' (*Clem. Hom.* iii. 53 ; cf. Dorner, *Hist. of Person of Christ*, I. i. 208 ff.) ; but they refused to accept the Church's teaching as to His Deity. Similarly, the Mohammedan Koran says : ' The Messiah, the son of Mary, is only a prophet' (v. 79, also iv. 160 and xix. 30) ; and the Racovian Catechism (A.D. 1605) of the Socinians (§ 5) accepts and accentuates the prophetic aspect of His work.

2. But while the Church thus early classified the redemptive activities of our Lord under this three-fold division, it must not be assumed that *the Jews of His own time* had reached this full conception. It is clear from our Gospels that His contemporaries did not regard the 'coming prophet' as one with the coming Messiah ; for when the multitude were astonished at Jesus' discourse at the Feast of Tabernacles, and were divided in opinion regarding Him, some saying, 'This is of a truth the Prophet,' and others, 'This is the Christ' (Jn 7[40]), none declared Him to be the Christ, and *therefore* the Prophet.

A similar distinction is found in their view of the Baptist (Jn 1[21]). The only exception in the Gospels is the words of the woman of Samaria : 'Sir, I perceive that thou art a prophet. . . . When Christ is come, he will *declare* unto us all things' (Jn 4[19. 25]). But probably the Samaritans generally had small reason to expect the coming of a *kingly* Messiah (see Westcott, *Study of the Gospels*, note 2, ch. 2 ; Stanton, *Jewish and Christian Messiah*, pp. 126, 293).

3. Nor does this separation of the offices of 'the Prophet' and 'the Messiah' seem to be due to any special obtuseness on the part of our Lord's contemporaries ; *the OT prophets* themselves appear also to have been unable to rise above it. Isaiah, prophesying during the monarchy, pictures the Messiah as a Davidic king, and foretells the out-pouring of a fuller revelation during His reign, predicting that *then* the God of Jacob would teach Israel His way (Is 2[3]), and *then* Israel's teacher(s) would not be hidden any more, but the people would see their teacher(s), and hear a word behind them saying, 'This is the way' (30[20]) ; but he does not unite these kingly and prophetic endowments in the one person of the Christ. Fuller light of truth is to be a mark of the Messianic reign, but Isaiah does not recognize the Messiah as the organ of the revelation.

The fullest references to a coming prophet are found in Deutero-Isaiah ; and here He is clearly identified with 'the **Servant of the Lord.**' There enters largely into the prophet's conception of this great Personality the idea of His being an anointed revealer of truth. Jehovah makes 'his mouth like a sharp sword' (49[2]), and 'puts his spirit upon him, so that he shall bring forth judgment to the Gentiles' (42[1], also 59[21] 61[1]). But, clear as is *our* identification of 'the Servant' with Jesus, we yet know that this union of 'the Suffering One' with the Messianic King has ever been the great stumbling-block to Israel. The truth appears to be : the prophets of Israel, influenced by the national circumstances and needs of their own day, predicted under the Spirit's influence, now a coming king, now a prophet, now a priestly sufferer with prophetic functions ; and these parallel lines of yearning thought found together their satisfaction in the Person of Jesus.

The Book of Malachi closes with a prediction of the return of Elijah (4[5]), and Israel's prophetic expectations centred thenceforth chiefly in him.

4. With the silence of prophecy, there came to Israel a deep yearning for the living voice of Jehovah. This was a characteristic of the Maccabæan age, when the anticipation of a coming prophet overshadows that of the Messiah (1 Mac 4[46] 14[41] 9[27], also Sir 48[10]).

The same longing is found in Ps 74[9] 'We see not our signs, there is no more any prophet, neither is there among us any that knoweth how long.' This Psalm is therefore thought to belong to the Maccabæan period ; on the other hand, similar complaints are found in the writings of the Exile (La 2[9], Ezk 7[26]).

The *Apocalyptic literature* is mostly silent on the point. But in the Book of Enoch (*Simil.* 45[3.6]) the Son of Man is portrayed as revealing 'all the treasures of that which is hidden, and there are seen an inexhaustible fountain of righteousness, and round about many fountains of wisdom.' These promises of fuller revelation presumably imply a personal agent for its dissemination. The prophetic gift is advanced in the Test. of the XII. Patriarchs (Levi viii. 15) as an implicit claim of John Hyrcanus to the Messiahship ; and he alone was said by the Jews to have held the threefold office (Jos. *BJ* I. ii. 8).

5. If the abeyance of prophecy added to the gloom of Israel during the interval between the time that the last OT prophet delivered his message and the beginning of the Christian era, *the coming of Christ was heralded by an outburst of the prophetic gift.* It is recorded as first appearing in the priestly house of Zacharias (Lk 1[41. 67]) ; it was granted to the Virgin, to Simeon, and to Anna (Lk 2[25. 36]), and reached its most notable height in the person of John the Baptist. The nation, galled by a foreign yoke, and meditating on the predictions found in their sacred books, and, above all, picturing the return of Elijah as a herald of emancipation, 'mused in their heart' whether the Baptist were himself the Messiah, or Elijah, or the Prophet, or one of the old prophets returned (Lk 3[15], Jn 1[20ff.]). But John, realizing himself to be only a forerunner, and wishing to turn the thoughts of the people from himself to Jesus, refused to be anything save an impersonal voice crying in the wilderness. Fittingly thus was the world's supreme Prophet ushered upon His prophetic career by a volume of reawakened prophecy.

6. Whatever difficulty His contemporaries felt in acknowledging His Messiahship, they had *none in recognizing Him as a prophet.* Both at the commencement and at the close of His career, this was the popular view of His ministry. As soon as He became known, the general judgment was pronounced that 'a great prophet had arisen, and that God had visited his people' (Lk 7[16]) ; and when at the close of His ministry He allowed the populace openly to express their feelings regarding Him, they, in answer to the question 'Who is this?' replied, 'This is Jesus, the prophet of Nazareth' (Mt 21[11] ; also Mk 6[15], Mt 21[46], Lk 24[19], Jn 4[19] 6[14] 7[40] 9[17]). Indeed, only those who were biassed by ecclesiastical bigotry could have concluded otherwise, for His miracles of mercy were external credentials recalling the powers of Moses and Elijah ; and the authoritative tone of His teaching showed that He claimed for Himself at least the position of a God-sent teacher.

7. But not only was the title generally given to Him ; He also *claimed it for Himself.* Thus He opened His ministry in His native village by reading in the synagogue the words of Isaiah (61[1]), 'The Spirit of the Lord is upon me, because he hath anointed me to preach good tidings to the poor,' and commenced His discourse upon them by saying, 'To-day hath this scripture been fulfilled in your ears.' (Lk 4[18. 21]). Later in His ministry, when His death was imminent, He openly placed Himself in line with the ancient prophets of Israel, foretelling that, similarly to them, He could not perish out of Jerusalem (Mt 23[29ff.], Lk 13[33]) ; and when He used, in the parable of the Vineyard, the familiar OT figure of the Kingdom of God, He deliberately made Himself the last of the long line of God's martyr messengers to His people ; and told the Jews that, notwithstanding the fact that they had 'shamefully handled' His predecessors the prophets ; yet He had been sent to them by God with a final call to repentance.

II. Jesus had the essential marks of a prophet.— When we turn to the records of the life of Jesus, we find predicated of Him every characteristic that marked the Hebrew prophets. **1.** If Isaiah, Jeremiah, and Ezekiel were all introduced to their prophetic career by a *vision* granted and a *voice* heard (Is 6[1-8], Jer 1[4-10], Ezk 3[10-14]), so Jesus commenced His ministry by receiving at His baptism a vision from heaven and by hearing His Father's voice.

The Gospel according to the Hebrews gives the words then spoken to Him in a form different from that given by the Evangelists, and interesting in the present connexion. We read : 'It came to pass when our Lord had ascended out of the water, the whole fountain of the Holy Spirit came down and rested upon him and said unto him, "My Son, in all the prophets I was looking for thee, that thou mightest come and that i might rest in thee. For thou art my rest, thou art my first-born Son who reignest to eternity."' This form shows how strong was the belief in the earliest days of the Church that Jesus at His baptism was anointed specially to the office of Prophet.

2. The OT prophets were *men of God*. This title, doubtless, was frequently used, as conveying little more than a customary appellation of those holding the office ; yet the fact of its having been chosen as a title shows the underlying conviction, on the part of the nation, that sanctity of character was a necessary condition of receiving communications from Jehovah ; and it thus suggests not only the Divine purport of their message, but also the personal religiousness of the prophets. Isaiah felt that, in order to hold intercourse with God, personal holiness was requisite (6[5]) ; and indeed so fully was this felt that the prophetic state was looked upon as closely related to *communion with God in prayer* ; and the expression which was generally used in the OT for the answering of prayer was frequently applied to prophetic revelation (ענה Mic 3[7], Hab 2[1ff.], Jer 23[35]. See Oehler, *OT Theol.* ii. 336).

That Jesus bore this characteristic of the prophetic office needs no showing. He, the one sinless Man, whose whole life was lived in conscious communication, full and continuous, with His Father, must necessarily, as regards the fitness of holiness, be the very Prophet of prophets. His perfect sinlessness rendered possible uninterrupted fellowship with God, and guaranteed the perfection of the message He delivered. The pre-eminence of that message rests on the fact that whereas 'God of old times spake unto the fathers in the prophets, he hath in these last times spoken unto us in his Son' (He 1[1]).

3. Further, as men of God, the message of the prophets was one of *moral import*. They, as Micah (3[8]), could say, 'I am full of power to declare unto Jacob his transgressions and to Israel his sins.' The greater prophets had developed far beyond the earlier prophets and still earlier seers, who used their gifts to reveal matters of mere personal interest : their message to the individual or to the nation was filled, as occasion required, with moral teachings ; rebuking sin, calling to repentance, and threatening Divine judgment.

It is evident that Jesus fulfilled this characteristic continuously and perfectly. For not only did He, like the prophets before Him, utter words pregnant with moral enlightenment but also by His every word and act He constantly manifested the perfection of moral being. Being Himself the revelation of God, His whole incarnate life was a continuous teaching of infinite moral import.

4. The prophets were conscious of being recipients of *direct communications from Jehovah*. In Amos (3[7]) it is said, 'The Lord God doeth nothing without revealing his counsel to his servants the prophets' ; and in Jeremiah (23[22]) we are told that the prophet stands in 'the counsel of Jehovah.' God spoke to them, and they received His words into their hearts and heard them with their ears (Ezk 3[10]). It might seem that here is a characteristic of the prophetic office that is not applicable to Christ. It might be thought that as He is very and eternal God, He required no revelation, having in Himself all the fulness of Divine knowledge, and that therefore when He taught, He taught not what He had *received*, but what was intrinsically His own. A careful study, however, of the Gospel of St. John, where naturally we seek for light on the mystery of His Person, as it is the Gospel of His self-manifestation, leads us to conclude otherwise. In a remarkable number of passages Jesus speaks of *receiving from the Father* the truths He disclosed. He says, 'I speak to the world those things which I have heard' ; 'as my Father hath

taught me, I speak.' 'I have given unto them the words which Thou gavest me' ; 'I spake not from myself, but the Father which sent me, He hath given me a commandment what I should say' (Jn 8[26. 28. 38. 40] 12[49] 15[15] 17[8. 14]).

In such words Jesus seems clearly to teach that His supernatural knowledge was a gift given to Him from the Father, 'administered to Him in His human nature on some economic principle,' so that He might be fitted perfectly to perform the functions of Teacher and Prophet to the Church. In emptying Himself of His glory in the Incarnation, He appears so to have self-limited His Divine Powers as to have been dependent upon His Father for supernatural illumination : while the reception by Him of that revelation must have been perfect through the complete sympathy that essentially existed between Him and His Father. Like the prophets of old, He received communications from God : but in virtue of His Divine Personality He perfectly heard and faithfully expressed every thought revealed to Him. (See, especially, a valuable charge by O'Brien, Bp. of Ossory, 1865 (Macmillan) ; and A. B. Davidson, *Biblical Essays*, p. 179).

5. A further characteristic of prophecy was its power of **prediction**. The apologetic use of prophecy in the past no doubt led to a too exclusive consideration of this aspect of the prophetic books ; and the Church has gained much by regarding the prophets as men inspired by Jehovah with special moral messages to the age in which they lived. But it is not less one-sided so to over-emphasize this aspect of their work as to exclude their undoubted predictive powers. The writings of the Hebrew prophets are saturated with prediction. They foresee and announce as much of the secret purposes of Jehovah as was needful for His people to know. And the power of Jehovah to reveal to them the future raises Him, in the eyes of Israel, at once above the heathen gods, and proves to them that He is the true God (Is 41[21-28] 42[9] 43[9-13] 44[25ff.] 48[3-7]). No doubt their predictions usually announced the *general* results rather than detailed accounts of Jehovah's future dealings ; nevertheless their predictions were clear unveilings of coming events. So that it may be said that a teacher without the power of foretelling would be no *prophet* (Dt 18[21-22]), for the prophet has 'his face to the future,' and can see more or less clearly, by the inspiration granted to him, the results that God's love and righteousness are about to accomplish.

Now, full of prediction as are the writings of the prophets, the sayings of Jesus are even more so. With clear vision He was able to follow throughout future time the workings of the principles He taught, and was able to state as a matter of certain knowledge that their adoption would be universal. With an unparalleled insight He disclosed to the world the mysteries of eternity. He drew back the curtain not only from coming events of time, but with equal certainty from the hidden secrets of the invisible world. Hades, heaven, hell are all open to Him. And with a calm boldness, found only with absolute certainty, He tells us of Dives and Lazarus (Lk 16[19]), of the many stripes and the few (Lk 12[47]), and of the principles upon which the Final Judgment will be carried out (Mt 25[40]).

If the Hebrew prophets received at times illumination which revealed to them glimpses of coming events, Jesus was at all times able to reveal hidden things of the future with as much certainty as He could speak of the things clearly seen in the present.

In addition to the predictions of *general* events, there is also found, but less frequently, among the Hebrew prophets, the power of foretelling *particular* events to individuals. Thus Micaiah foretells the death of Ahab (1 K 22), and Jeremiah the death of Hananiah (Jer 28[16]). Here also Jesus surpasses them. With a certainty and clearness far beyond theirs, He was able to announce particular coming events to His disciples. Following the Gospel narrative, we find that the treachery of Judas was open to Him for long (Jn 6[70f.]). The fall of Peter and his final martyrdom, and the prolonged life of John, were all equally clear (Lk 22[31], Jn 21[18. 22]).

Allied to His knowledge of the future of individuals was His unerring insight into character. This gift was partially granted to the prophets, and may in a measure account for their predictions. It may have been insight into character that enabled Micaiah to predict the coming cowardice of Zedekiah (1 K 22²⁵), and it certainly seems to have been this that gave Elisha power to read the future of Hazael (2 K 8¹²). Similarly, only in an infinitely greater degree, Jesus read the inner depths of those around Him. At once He saw the guilelessness of Nathanael (Jn 1⁴⁷) and the strength of Peter (v.⁴²), and was able to read the thoughts of Simon the Pharisee while Simon was misreading His (Lk 7³⁹·⁴⁰). The records of His life show repeated instances that exemplify the statement of John, 'He knew all men . . . he knew what was in man' (Jn 2²⁴·²⁵).

6. As a final mark of His fulfilment of the prophetic office, His *fate* must be mentioned. In His own Person He gathered together every insult and cruelty that had been shown in the past to the messengers of God. And if it seems strange that Israel, which more than all other nations had spiritual instincts, should have habitually rejected those sent to them with the very message they above all should have received, and if it be stranger still that they should have crucified the Messiah whom they so passionately desired, it must be remembered that mankind at all times has been unable to receive, with patience, rebukes that shattered its self-conceit and truth that attacked its vested interests. New light ever discloses ignorance, reveals the inadequacy of much that is thought perfect, and shows the sinfulness of much that is looked upon as innocent. And thus it follows that the fuller the new light, the greater the hatred and opposition its bearer will have to endure at the hands of those who fail to recognize its truth. If, then, the preaching of Isaiah raised the gibes of the drunkards of Ephraim, and if the unwelcome predictions of Jeremiah led to bitterest persecution, is it any wonder that the clear light of the revelation of Jesus infuriated 'the blind Pharisee,' and ended in His cruel mockings and death?

III. **Jesus is above all other prophets.** —But while Jesus fulfils every prophetic characteristic perfectly, and is thus the world's Supreme Prophet, it is also evident, from this very perfection, that He is essentially distinct from all others who bore the title. For not only is there found in Him a man called of God to receive communications from heaven and to give them forth, when received, to his fellow-men, but in Him we have God revealing Himself directly to His creatures. As the personal, uttered ' *Word of God* ' (λόγος προφορικός), He manifests Himself (that is, He manifests GOD) to mankind. And if the essence of the prophetic office consists in revealing the Almighty to His children, then, clearly, He alone is the one perfect Prophet, who from His very nature must have (1) constantly, (2) completely, (3) infallibly, and (4) finally revealed all that mankind may know of their Creator.

1. His revelation was *constant.* OT prophets, receiving their revelation only at such times as Jehovah desired to reveal His will, could exercise their functions only intermittently; whereas Jesus, living in uninterrupted communion with His Father, was in receipt of a constant revelation of the purposes and will of God. Indeed, even in His hours of silence, He must be thought of as fulfilling His prophetic office. His every *act* was a message, and His miracles, not less than His parables, were revelations to teach men of His Father. His spontaneous lovingkindness, as exhibited to the sinful and the suffering, revealed even more powerfully than His words the fact that ' God is Love ' ; the beauty of His sinless life, not less than the depth of His matchless utterances, ever taught men this, the central truth of His message. Jesus, *simply by being what He was,* constantly delivered His prophetic message to the world.

2. His revelation was *complete.* The OT prophets could be recipients of only a partial revelation. As their writings are studied, it is seen how gradually God revealed His truth through them. Their knowledge of God is seen to develop, through progressive stages, from little to fuller light ; prophet after prophet being sent to add his quota of truth, each being granted that amount of illumination necessary to enable him to advance the hopes and knowledge of Israel beyond the stage already reached. With Jesus it was far otherwise. He came to raise the spiritual wisdom and knowledge of men, once and for all, to the highest point attainable by them on earth. And if we find Him, at any time during His ministry, withholding truth which He might have revealed, we know that the cause of such reserve is to be found, not in His inability to declare, but in His hearers' inability to receive (Jn 16¹²).

3. His revelation was *infallible.* Great as was the usefulness of the prophets to God's chosen people, yet it is clear that in them they had no infallible guides. They had to distinguish between ' the false prophets ' and those who truly represented Jehovah. For succeeding generations it may have been comparatively easy to separate them, for time would demonstrate, by events, the correctness or incorrectness of prophetic utterances ; but not so for contemporaries. The false prophets were not as a class mere impostors trading on the religious feelings of the people, but rather they were men who, prophets by profession, lacked the spiritual discernment to interpret the mind of Jehovah. Their messages therefore rose no higher than current spiritual ideas. The people of Israel thus had constant need of spiritual discernment on their part to select the true and to reject the untrue in messages proffered to them, which claimed to come from Jehovah. But when experience had marked out to them a prophet as a true revealer of Jehovah's will, they were not even then certain of receiving infallible guidance. The true prophet might at times confuse his own natural judgment with the voice of God. Thus Samuel at first mistook Eliab for the Lord's anointed (1 S 16⁶) ; and Nathan too hastily sanctioned the project of David to build a temple (2 S 7ᶠᶠ·).

But the revelation of Jesus comes to us with infallible certainty. He does not, indeed, reveal *everything* ; for on earth He was not omniscient. He distinctly told His disciples that there was at all events one thing He did not know (Mk 13³²). Thus He willingly limited His knowledge while on earth ; and it is well for us to remember that He Himself was aware of the limitation, for He knew that He did not know. But this self-limitation in no way weakened His claim to infallibility in all He taught. *Ignorance* is one thing, *error* quite another. And being the Son of God, and so the perfect recipient of all that the Father willed to teach Him during His state of humiliation, He *knew perfectly all He knew.* Similarly, if He did not foresee everything, yet what He did foresee, *that* He foresaw perfectly. Very remarkable is the calm certainty of conviction with which He claims infallibility. The tone of authority in His utterances, the repeated ' I say unto you ' astounded the multitude (Mt 7²⁹) ; while the claim itself could not have been more strongly put forth than in His words, ' Heaven and earth shall pass away ; but my words shall not pass away ' (Mk 13³¹).

It is here especially that He stands pre-eminent. Throughout the whole course of His utterances there can be found no hesitation due to a possible conflict between His own judgment and His Father's will, but rather a claim in unmistakable language to absolute infallibility as a Teacher. In truth, His consciousness told Him that He could not be wrong, for He knew *where* He had received that which He taught. The words which He spake were not His own, but the Father's who sent Him. He spake that which He had seen with the Father, —*that* Father who was ever with Him (Jn 14[24. 10] 8[38]). He knew, as none else could know, the truth regarding 'the heavenly things,' for He was 'the Son of Man, who had come down from heaven' (Jn 3[12. 13]). He is the one infallible Teacher of our race.

Jesus, in His interview with Nicodemus, draws a distinction between 'earthly things' (τὰ ἐπίγεια) and 'heavenly things' (τὰ ἐπουράνια). The former are spiritual truths within the range of human spiritual knowledge ; the latter, spiritual truths which man can learn only by a revelation granted from God. Of these latter, Jesus is the one infallible revealer (see Adamson, *Mind in Christ*, p. 77 ff.).

4. His revelation is *final*. If the message of Jesus is thus complete and infallible, it is necessarily final. No doubt, the prophetic office of Christ is still an activity in the love of God for us ; and the Church has ever the presence of the Holy Spirit leading her into fuller truth ; nevertheless, the message that Jesus brought was complete in itself, and therefore final. For the office of the Holy Spirit is not to teach men something new, something outside that message, but rather to disclose truths which, though hitherto unrecognized, were implicit in His teaching. The Apostolic Church was furnished with prophets, and in a true sense prophets have appeared at intervals throughout the Christian era, and doubtless will yet appear ; but, no matter how new their message may seem to the men of their own day, they are, unless they are false prophets, in reality only 'taking of the things of Christ, and declaring them' to His people (Jn 14[26] 16[14. 15]).

IV. Christ's prophetic utterances. — When considering the prophetic utterances of Jesus, we must not confine ourselves to His predictions alone. If, as we have seen, foretelling is an essential element of prophecy, it is evident that forthtelling is no less so. The OT prophets not only foretold coming events, but also were the religious teachers of their own age ; each in turn adding to the moral and religious knowledge of the nation. So Jesus, speaking as the world's Prophet, not only revealed the future, but once and for ever delivered potentially all truth to the world. The prophetic utterances of Jesus, therefore, include not only His predictions but all His teachings, and, as such, come within the scope of this article. As, however, His teaching is dealt with in a separate article, it is sufficient to refer the reader to the latter, and only to add some general remarks on the subject.

A. *DIDACTIC UTTERANCES.* — **1.** The moral teaching of Christ concerned itself with general *principles* rather than with *precepts.* The Sermon on the Mount, which contains the chief elements of His ethical teaching, is not a code of injunctions, but a declaration of the fundamental principles that underlie His Kingdom ; and the particular instances of right conduct mentioned in that discourse are not commandments, but illustrations of these principles. When He teaches His disciples regarding righteousness and sin, He avoids laying down laws regarding special acts, but goes at once to the very heart of moral distinctions, revealing the general principles which rule all special cases. Thus He solved all questions of meat by a single sentence, which 'made all meats clean' (Mk 7[19] RV) ; and He answered all questions of casuistry regarding Sabbath observance by pointing out the beneficent principle which led to its institution. In a word, He reduced all right action, whether towards God or towards man, to a fulfilling, and all wrong action to an outraging, of the one all-embracing commandment of Love. And thus His teaching finds its application in every act in every age.

There is but one exception recorded in our Gospels,—that in reference to divorce (Mk 10[11. 12], cf. Mt 5[32] 19[9]). In this case He gives a concise and direct precept ; but a precept, obedience to which purifies the human race at its source.

2. But Jesus not only revealed the true principles underlying all sin and righteousness, He also taught that *in Himself*, and particularly in Himself *dying*, was to be found the true atonement for sin. As soon as He was able to teach His disciples, even if it were in dark words, regarding His coming death, He connected that death with the world's salvation. Comparatively early in His ministry He announced that He would give His body 'for the life of the world' (Jn 6[51]) ; later, He told them that, as the Good Shepherd, He would 'lay down his life for the sheep' (Jn 10[15]) ; and as the fatal result of His ministry drew nearer, He declared, with still greater clearness, that He would give 'his life a ransom for many' (Mk 10[45]). It is clear, then, that Jesus explicitly taught that His death was in the highest sense *sacrificial* ; that there was a necessary connexion between that death and man's salvation.

It is true that Jesus does not explain *how* His death wrought the Atonement, and that we must turn to the Epistles for this knowledge ; but we may with confidence assume that the early Church derived its light on the matter from Jesus Himself ; for St. Luke (24[47]) tells us that among the truths taught the disciples by Jesus during the forty days were those regarding His 'death' and 'repentance and remission of sins.' Therefore the developed doctrine of the Atonement, as found in the writings of the early Church, are not mere subjective theorizings, but are based on the teaching of the risen Lord.

3. Jesus in His teaching taught the absolute *value of the individual.* The prophets of Israel felt the majesty of their nation as the chosen people of God, and dwelt upon Jehovah's Fatherly care of the Jewish race ; but not until the preaching of Jeremiah was the Fatherhood of God over the individual brought into prominence. It was Jesus who first fully revealed the infinite value of the single soul. He insisted frequently on the madness of risking its loss, even if thereby the gain should be 'the whole world' ; and He warned men that it were better that they should miserably perish than that they should cause to stumble even one of God's 'little ones' (Mk 8[36] 9[42]).

4. But His teaching was also *social*. The individual who was so precious in his Father's sight was not to be left unsupported in isolation. Wide and manifold as are the meanings of 'Kingdom of God' as established by Jesus, it is certain that underlying all else is the thought of its members united in love by a common life. This is essential to the very idea of a *kingdom*. And in it is ideally presented the thought of a spiritual nation composed of spiritual individuals.

The Kingdom of heaven from its spiritual nature, and as a Kingdom of ideas and principles, rather than of codified laws, is necessarily invisible, save as to its results. But man ever wants the outward or concrete ; and Jesus therefore not only founded the *Kingdom of God*, but established a *Church* (Mt 16[18] 18[17]); the latter being an embodiment of the idea of the former, *visibly* presenting to the world its truths. *The Kingdom* is thus, in the teaching of Jesus, much wider and more fundamental than *the Church*.

5. When we pass from the ethical to the spiritual side of the didactic prophecies of Jesus, we enter upon an unparalleled field of revelation. As we have seen, He alone among men—and that because He was more than man — could disclose 'the heavenly things' (Jn 3[12]) to the world. When, therefore, He speaks of the nature and acts of God, our attitude is that of reverent humble reception ; and our activities are to be exercised rather in the devout investigation of the meaning of His words than in the questioning of their truth.

When we turn to the teaching itself, we find little regarding the essential *nature* of God. It was His method rather to describe how God *acts* than to define what God *is*. Indeed, the only statement approaching to an abstract definition of His Being is found in His words to the woman of Samaria, 'God is Spirit' (Jn 4²⁴).

The titles chiefly used by Jesus to describe the character of God are 'King' (Mt 5³⁵ 18²³ 22²) and 'Father.' God is *Father* : in a unique sense in relation to Himself (Mt 10³² 11²⁷, Jn 5¹⁷ 10³⁰ etc.) ; in a special sense of His disciples (Mt 5¹⁶, Lk 12³² etc.) ; and in a general sense of mankind (Mt 5⁴⁵, Lk 15¹¹ff·).

Further, His teaching concerning God reveals the doctrine of the Trinity. His own Deity, and the Deity and Personality of the Holy Spirit are plainly taught by Him ; and the three Persons of the Godhead are with equal emphasis combined in the formula for baptism (Mt 28¹⁹).

There seems no reason sufficiently weighty to cause us to regard this latter verse as an amplification of the actual words of Jesus, after the Church had grasped fully the theological doctrine of the Trinity. Rather it appears necessary to assume that some such statement must have been made by Him in order that this belief, which is found so distinctly stated in the earliest Epistles of St. Paul, may be accounted for (see Sanday in Hastings' *DB*, vol. ii. p. 624).

6. Christ as Prophet chiefly *revealed God by revealing Himself.* It is customary to emphasize as His prime revelation of God, His teaching regarding the Fatherhood of the Almighty ; but rather would we emphasize His revelation of Himself as His chief prophetic work. He stood before men, and said not, 'I will teach you about God,' but, 'I will teach you about Myself, and then you will know God.' Throughout the Gospel of St. John this self-manifestation of Jesus is the one central subject. His ministry, in that Gospel, commences with His convincing self-revelation to Peter and John, Andrew and Philip, and Nathanael (ch. 1) ; His first miracle 'manifested forth his glory' (2¹¹) ; He closes His interview with Nicodemus by declaring His mission as a bearer from heaven of spiritual truths (3¹²· ¹³) ; the highest point in ch. 4 is the declaration to the woman of Samaria, 'I that speak unto thee am he' (v.²⁶) ; in ch. 5 He declares His oneness in power with the Father by saying, 'What things soever the Father doeth, these also doeth the Son likewise' (v.¹⁹) ; the teaching of ch. 6 centres round the self-revelation of 'I am the bread of life' (v.⁴⁸) ; at the Feast of Tabernacles He cried concerning Himself, 'If any man thirst, let him come unto me and drink' (7³⁷) ; in ch. 8 He asserts His own pre-existence, saying, 'Before Abraham was, I am' (v.⁵⁸) ; while the lengthy account of the cure of the blind man reaches its climax in the declaration, 'Thou hast both seen him, and it is he that talketh with thee' (9³⁷). Every section of the Gospel up to this point culminates and finds its reason in a self-revelation of Jesus made to an individual or to a few chosen ones (2²) who were capable, by reason of their sincerity, of receiving it ; while the succeeding chapters record a similar revelation granted to groups of listeners and disciples. He is 'the Good Shepherd' ; 'the Door' ; 'one with the Father'; 'the Resurrection' . . . (10⁷· ¹¹· ³⁰ 11²⁵ . . .). Clearer and clearer grows the revelation of Himself, until at last the real fulness and power, humility and truth of His self-disclosure are seen in the words, 'He that hath seen me, hath seen the Father' (14⁹ 12⁴⁵) ; that is to say, 'I have revealed God while I revealed Myself.' It is this that makes Him in Himself, as also in His deeds and words, the Supreme Prophet, as forthteller of the truth of God.

B. *CHRIST'S PREDICTIONS.* — The predictive element enters very largely into the utterances of Christ. Not only do the Gospels contain prophecies spoken with the express intention of revealing the future to the disciples, such as those relating to His own death and the destruction of Jerusalem, but also numerous prophecies which occur incidentally. An example of the latter is found in His rebuke to those that 'troubled' Mary because of her costly offering ; a rebuke that foretells the universality of His Kingdom and the perpetual memorial of her deed (Mk 14⁹).

If the Gospels be studied with a view to noting those sayings of Jesus which are predictive, surprise will be felt at their number. It will be seen that the parables grouped in Mt 13 are predictions of the history of the Kingdom ; that His promises not only exhibit His love and power, but also are foretellings of His future action (*e.g.* Mt 18²⁰ 28²⁰). It will be found that His miracles are often prefaced by announcements beforehand of the cure to be wrought (*e.g.* Lk 8⁵⁰, Jn 11¹¹) ; that His discourse in Jn 6 is based on a prediction of His own sacrificial death, and that in Jn 14–16 on His foreknowledge of the Holy Spirit's descent. And, further, even in His High-Priestly prayer He shows knowledge of the future by pleading for those whom He foresees as His disciples in the coming age (Jn 17²⁰) ; and, if His first recorded word during His ministry is a prophecy of the immediate advent of the Kingdom (Mk 1¹⁵), His last is a prophecy of its spread to the uttermost part of the world (Ac 1⁸). His words are saturated with prediction.

The predictions of Jesus may be classified as follows : Those referring (1) to individuals, (2) to His Kingdom, (3) to the material world, (4) to His own career, (5) to the destruction of Jerusalem, (6) to the Parousia and the consummation of the age.

1. As His *predictions regarding individuals* present no special difficulties, it will be sufficient simply to mention them. In giving Simon the name of Peter (Jn 1⁴²), Jesus not only revealed his character, but foretold his pre-eminence ; a prediction justified at Cæsarea Philippi (Mt 16¹⁸). On this latter occasion He foretold that the Apostle would become the porter of the Church, and the Acts of the Apostles records the fulfilment. Jesus also predicted his fall and restoration (Lk 22³¹, Mk 14³⁰), and finally announced in hidden language the death by which he should ultimately glorify God (Jn 21¹⁸). At this time He also used words which obscurely foretold to the Apostle John a prolonged life (v.²²). From an early period in His ministry Jesus read the heart of Judas (Jn 6⁶⁴ 13¹⁸), shortly after the Transfiguration He announced His coming betrayal (Mk 9³¹), in the Upper Room He declared that the betrayer was one of the Twelve (Mk 14¹⁸), and finally by the sign of the given sop He marked Judas as the traitor (Jn 13²⁶). To Nathanael He foretold that he would see 'heaven opened' (Jn 1⁵¹) ; to Caiaphas, that he would see the Son of Man coming in the clouds of heaven (Mk 14⁶²) ; to James and John, that they would be baptized with His baptism (Mk 10³⁹) ; and to all the Apostles, that they would be persecuted like Himself, excommunicated, and in peril of death (Jn 15²⁰ 16²), that they would forsake Him in the hour of His greatest need (Mk 14²⁷), but that after His death they would do even greater works than He Himself had done (Jn 14¹²), and ultimately would sit upon twelve thrones judging the twelve tribes of Israel (Mt 19²⁸, Lk 22³⁰).

2. *Predictions regarding the Kingdom.* — The position of Jesus in reference to the idea of the Kingdom of God is partly that of a fulfiller and partly that of a foreteller. He established during His ministry the Kingdom in its simplest stage, and so far fulfilled what the OT prophets had foretold ; but having established it, He made it the subject of His own predictions, projected it into the future, with the OT limitations removed, revealed its struggles throughout time, and announced its ultimate victory.

That Jesus did establish the Kingdom of God during His lifetime can hardly be doubted. To make it entirely future, as some do, seems impossible in the face of such passages as 'The kingdom of God is among you' (or '*within* you,' ἐντὸς ὑμῶν, Lk 17²¹ ; see art. IDEAS (LEADING), vol. i. p. 770b) ; 'The kingdom of God is come upon you' (ἐφ' ὑμᾶς, Mt 12²⁸) ; 'From the days of John the Baptist the kingdom of heaven suffereth violence' (Mt 11¹², see Wendt's *Teaching of Jesus*, vol. i. p. 364 ff.).

In the parable of the Sower (Mt 13, see also Lk 14[18ff.]) He foretold the different classes of people that would become its subjects, and the varied reception they would give to its claims; and in the parables of the Tares and the Draw-net (Mt 13), the presence within it of unworthy members. He marked out for it a long career of struggle with evil, within,— false prophets deceiving (Mt 7[15, 22]), without,— malignant foes opposing (Mt 10[16, 33], Lk 21[12], Jn 15[20] 16[2]); but He promised the support of His abiding presence (Mt 28[20]), and guaranteed its invincibility (Mt 16[18]).

Though its beginning is unobserved (Lk 17[20]), yet He predicted, in the parable of the Seed Growing Secretly (Mk 4[26]), its reaching through steady growth its consummation; in the parable of the Mustard Seed (Mt 13[31]), its universal extension as a visible society; and in that of the Leaven, its gradually acquired power over the hearts of men (Mt 13[33]). No longer will its bounds be confined to the Chosen Race, for adherents from every quarter of the globe will enter it (8[11]), humanity becoming one flock under one Shepherd (Jn 10[16]); and towards this great end it will itself work, for it will evangelize the world before His return (Mt 28[19] 24[14]). And when He comes in the clouds, its struggles will cease, and He will gather its members to that heavenly feast which will celebrate His marriage with His bride, and then, purged from evil, it will enter upon its career of eternal glory (24[31] 22[1ff.] 25[1ff.] 13[41] 25[34]).

3. *Predictions regarding the material world.*—A renewal of the face of nature enters largely into the prophecies of the OT (Is 11[6-9] 30[23ff.] 35. 65[17], Hos 2[21f.], Ezk 34[25, 28]), and reappears in wider form in the Epistle to the Romans (8[21]), where St. Paul predicts the delivery of creation from the bondage of corruption; and in the Apocalypse (21[1]), where a new heaven and a new earth are foretold (see also 2 P 3[13]). Nor can the Church look forward to any less comprehensive issue, believing as she does in the Incarnation which for ever glorifies *matter* by its union with the Godhead. The comparative silence of Jesus upon this subject is remarkable. He can not be said to have alluded to it except in two passages, neither of which is of certain interpretation. The one is in the Sermon on the Mount, where we read, 'The meek shall inherit the earth' (Mt 5[5]). These words may mean no more than that meekness here on earth wins more than self-assertion; but, seeing that the meek do not, as yet at all events, receive their due, the words more probably may be eschatological in reference, and predict their ultimate recognition on a renewed earth. In the other passage Jesus promises His Apostles that 'in the regeneration' they shall sit upon twelve thrones (19[28]). But here again there is uncertainty of interpretation; for, while He calls the culmination of the Kingdom of Grace in the Kingdom of Glory 'the regeneration,' He leaves it uncertain whether that regeneration concerns merely the whole body of the redeemed (cf. Briggs, *Mess. of Gospel*, pp. 228, 315), or whether it includes, as seems more probable, the physical transformation of nature (cf. Schwartzkopff, *Proph. of Christ*, pp. 219, 232).*

4. *Predictions regarding Himself.*—We find in the Gospels frequent predictions by Jesus of His death, and almost invariably in connexion with them allusions to His resurrection. There may be difficulty in deciding as to when He Himself first became conscious of the fatal end to His ministry, but there can be no doubt that as soon as He realized His death as imminent, He must have realized His resurrection as certain. To suppose Him to have recognized Himself as the true

---

* Jesus tells us that not only the brute creation (Mt 10[29] 6[26]), but even the vegetable kingdom is under the Father's care (6[30]).

Messiah and then to have regarded His death as the end of all, is to suppose the impossible. Living as He lived in uninterrupted communion with the Father, He must have been conscious of the indestructibility of the Divine life that was His, and of the eternal value of His Person and work (cf. Schwartzkopff, *Proph. of Christ*, pp. 64, 147). And if a dead Messiah was a contradiction in terms to any one holding Messianic hopes, how much more was it so to the Messiah Himself?

It was not until after the confession of Peter at Cæsarea Philippi (see Mt 16[21] 'From that time forth . . .') that Jesus plainly foretold His death; but having done so, He repeated the warning three times at short intervals, each time adding more definiteness to the prediction. (1) He outlined the Passion, foretelling the Sanhedrin's rejection of Him, His death, and resurrection (Mk 8[31]); (2) after the Transfiguration, where the highest point of His ministry was reached, He repeated the prediction, adding the fact of the betrayal (9[31]); (3) on the journey to Jerusalem He foretold in very full detail the sufferings that awaited Him (10[33]), enumerating in their actual order the stages of contumely through which He was to pass. The betrayal, the judicial condemnation, the delivery to the Roman power, the mocking and spitting, the killing (Mt 20[19] 'crucifying'), and, finally, the resurrection, all in turn are mentioned (cf. Swete's *St. Mark, l.c.*). See, further, art. ANNOUNCEMENTS OF DEATH.

It is assumed by some that Jesus commenced His ministry with views as to His work very different from those with which He closed it, the rigour of events leading Him to modify the ideas with which He started (*e.g.* Weiss, *Life of Christ*, iii. 60). If this be true, then the delay in our Lord's plain announcement of His death until Peter had made his confession may well be due to the fact that He Himself had not before realized it as inevitable. But we should require the strongest proof to cause us to believe in such vacillation or change of purpose on His part. The argument from silence is always precarious, but never more so than in the case of One who distinctly tells us that He restrained His utterances because of His hearers' inability fully to bear the truth (Jn 16[12]). We have, therefore, more ground for assuming that His reticence was due to His loving consideration for His disciples, who had already many doubts and difficulties to conquer, rather than to His ignorance of what was before Him. Indeed, in His last discourse He stated that now at length He felt able to speak openly, and would from that moment (ἀπ' ἄρτι) tell them plainly what was to come to pass, in order that they might the more readily believe that He was the Christ (Jn 13[19]). His reticence and His openness alike are due to His consideration for their weaknesses.

5. *Predictions regarding the destruction of Jerusalem.*—The chief difficulties found in the predictions of Jesus regarding the destruction of Jerusalem are in the great eschatological discourse recorded in Mk 13, and in 'the lesser Apocalypse' in Lk 17. As both these passages will come up before us under the prophecies of the Parousia, it is not necessary to consider them here. We now refer only to those other passages which foretell it.

(*a*) In the parable of the King's Son, Jesus declared that those who spitefully entreated and slew the messengers would be punished by the king's armies destroying the murderers and burning up their city (Mt 22[7]). These words contain, doubtless, a prediction of the punishment that through the ages ever follows apostasy, but not the less do they foretell vividly the judgment that fell upon Jerusalem.

(*b*) In the next chapter (Mt 23) we find the denunciation of the scribes by Jesus, which concludes with His lamentation over the city He loved. And He closes with the words, 'Your house is left unto you desolate. For I say unto you, Ye shall not see me henceforth till ye shall say, Blessed is he that cometh in the name of the Lord.' Here, in foretelling the desolation of the Temple, He predicted its destruction; for while, no doubt, its desolation was a spiritual fact from the moment He finally quitted its precincts, yet the visible evidence of its being God-forsaken was given in its destruction.

Lk. (13³⁵) gives these words in a different connexion. In Mt. they are spoken at the close of His ministry, just as Jesus was leaving the Temple for the last time as a public teacher. In Lk. they arise naturally from His sad words telling that no prophet can perish out of the city. It is difficult to decide between these two occasions, and it is possible, though not probable, that the words were spoken twice by Him.

The interpretation of the last part of the prediction is also difficult. The desolation is to cease when they shall say, 'Blessed is he that cometh. . . .' What future event does this indicate? If the words were spoken in the connexion given by Mt., they cannot refer, as some think, to the cries of the multitude on Palm Sunday, as they would have been spoken *after* that occasion. If Lk. is right, then this is a possible, but very inadequate, interpretation. Thus they may be taken as referring either to the Parousia or to the ultimate conversion of the Jews (cf. Plummer, *St. Luke, l.c.*). If the latter interpretation be accepted, then they are a prophecy of the final restoration of the Chosen Race, and supplement the prediction of their rejection (Mt 21⁴³; see also Lk 21²⁴).

(*c*) The most minute prediction of the destruction of Jerusalem is found in Lk 19⁴¹⁻⁴⁴. On the occasion of His triumphal entry, when He saw the city before Him, He announced with cries of sorrow that He foresaw its inhabitants shut in, the city itself captured, the people slain, and the walls demolished. To some this minuteness of detail suggests that the Evangelist, writing after the event, coloured his description from facts which had already occurred. But if Jesus was able to foretell the fact of the city's destruction, He could with equal ease have described the circumstances here mentioned, which are really common to all sieges.

(*d*) Jesus gave His last predictive warning of the coming judgment on the city to the women who wept as He journeyed to Calvary. He told them the days would come (*i.e.* the days of their city's destruction) when they would call upon the mountains to fall on them (Lk 23³⁰). His grief for the sorrow that the catastrophe would bring on poor womanhood is also shown in His longer eschatological discourse (Mk 13¹⁷), where He says : 'Woe to them that are with child and to them that give suck in those days.'

6. *Predictions regarding the Parousia.*—The predictions of Jesus regarding the Parousia are among the most difficult of His utterances, and many weighty questions of criticism and interpretation arise which are beyond the limits of this article. We can only state the conclusions at which we have arrived, referring readers elsewhere for fuller information (see PAROUSIA, SECOND COMING). There are five chief passages in which Jesus speaks of His return, and in each of these He uses language difficult of interpretation. This fact must not be forgotten. It is not that He spoke of His return sometimes in clear and sometimes in cryptic language, but that whenever He referred to it He invariably spoke enigmatically. There must have been some reason for this persistent ambiguity ; and it is to be found in the dulness of spiritual insight of the Apostles, and their unpreparedness for clearer teaching. In this connexion, as in connexion with the predictions of His death, He was unable to speak openly.

His aim seems to have been to *prepare* them for the following facts :—(*a*) that He was about to leave them ; (*b*) that His death would be due to His rejection by the hierarchy and the antagonism of the populace ; (*c*) that the sin of that generation which culminated in His death would speedily receive its punishment in the utter destruction of their city and Temple ; (*d*) that He Himself would, by His spiritual might, be the just avenger on Jerusalem of His own death ; (*e*) that ages of gospel preaching would then follow, during which the curse on the Holy City would last until the times of the Gentiles were fulfilled ; (*f*) that not until the whole world was evangelized would He visibly appear ; (*g*) but that He Himself, though visibly withdrawn, would be spiritually present with them and succeeding generations. These facts, so plain to us, could not possibly have been grasped by those who, having found the Messiah, necessarily expected immediate victory at His hands. We know that even after the forty days' instruction they still were unable to shake

off their preconceptions, and still hankered after a material Messianic kingdom (Ac 1⁶) ; and we may therefore be certain that during the days spent with Him before His death and resurrection, they would have been absolutely unable to understand Him had He spoken openly of His continuous spiritual presence, of His spiritual coming during their lifetime to judge Jerusalem, of the long ages of the Gospel Dispensation, and of His final visible return at the end of the world. What He could do, He did. In words that hiddenly contained these truths, He revealed them enigmatically ; and the logic of events would, and did, interpret them to His hearers and to the Church after them.

This characteristic of the sayings of Jesus regarding His Coming accounts in a measure for the ease with which the early Church changed her view as to the time of His return. At first she lived in expectation of an immediate return of her Lord, but when events proved that this hope was in a literal sense illusory, she, without any great rupture of faith, accepted the view that a long period would intervene before she welcomed Him in His glory. And this revolution of thought can best be accounted for by the fact that when He did not come at the expected time, she turned back to the mysterious words with which He had announced His return, and learnt, what circumstances now made plain, the deeper meaning of His pregnant sayings.

We will now consider the five chief passages which foretell His Coming, taking them not in the order in which they were spoken, but in that which best helps our investigation.

(1) Jesus, in reply to the question of Caiaphas whether He were the Christ, replied : 'I am ; and ye shall see the Son of Man sitting at the right hand of power, and coming in the clouds of heaven' (Mk 14⁶²). Mt. has, 'Henceforth (ἀπ' ἄρτι) ye shall see . . .' (26⁶⁴) ; Lk. 'From henceforth (ἀπὸ τοῦ νῦν) . . .' (22⁶⁹). It may be that Mk. gives the exact words spoken, and that Mt. and Lk. make the addition to show what they conceived to be the meaning ; but more probably Mk. omitted the 'henceforth,' as not comprehending it. It is evident that Jesus here spoke not of His final Parousia, but rather of an immediate spiritual visitation which from that present moment Caiaphas would experience — a prediction that had not long to wait for its fulfilment ; for must not the quaking rocks, the rent veil, and the opened tomb, followed as they were by Pentecost and the victories of the Church, have been felt by Caiaphas as true comings in power of Him whom he once thought he had mastered ? This passage, then, is full of importance ; for here, without doubt, Jesus spoke of a 'Coming' other than the final. And it compels us, when considering His other references to the same subject, to inquire whether He refers to 'historic Comings' or to His ultimate reappearance at the end of the world. It is thought by some that to make His sayings refer to such 'historic Comings,' is to use a modern key, made merely for the purpose of getting out of difficulty (Schwartzkopff, *Proph. of Christ*, p. 246) ; but in this passage it can have no other meaning, unless indeed we hold that Jesus erroneously thought that His final return would be during the lifetime of Caiaphas—a view to most impossible, for it predicates of Him not ignorance but error. On the other hand, we shall find that by the use of His enigmatic words He suggested frequently that His Coming was 'not one but manifold,' and that by His frequent 'historic returns' in the great crises of the life of Humanity, He would prepare the way for and rehearse His grand final Parousia.

It is remarkable that while Lk. follows Mt. in adding 'henceforth' to the words of Mk., he separates from both by omitting the reference to the 'Coming'; substituting 'shall the Son of Man be seated at the right hand of power' for 'ye shall see the Son of Man sitting at the right hand of power, and coming in the clouds of heaven.' Did he feel that 'the clouds of heaven,' as an apocalyptic phrase, was difficult to be understood by his Gentile readers ; or did he miss the point of view that recognized many historic Comings ? The omission by him of the words 'ye shall see' points in the latter direction. He understood the Session of the Son of Man at the right hand, but failed to grasp a 'Coming' that would be visible and immediate to Caiaphas. A somewhat similar change is made by him in the great eschatological discourse, where he substitutes 'know ye that *the kingdom of God* is nigh' (21³¹) for '*he* is nigh' (Mk 13²⁹, Mt 24³³). It is not that, according to him, there is no final coming ; for previously he had recorded (Lk 21²⁵ᶠᶠ·) the prediction of the signs in the heavens which, following the 'times of the Gentiles,' precede the coming of the Son of Man in the clouds with power ; but rather that where the coming does not appear to him as the *final* coming, he substitutes the Coming of the Kingdom for the Coming of Christ. He makes a similar change in the passage which will next occupy our consideration, namely, Mk 9¹, Mt 16²⁸, Lk 9²⁷. Mk. has 'some . . . shall in no wise taste of death till they see the kingdom of God come with power.' Mt. enlarges it 'till they see the Son of Man coming in his kingdom,' while Lk. has 'till they see the kingdom of God'—a change which makes interpretation easy, but which removes from the words all the allusion to such historic Comings as are implied by Mt. and not excluded by Mk.

(2) 'The Son of Man shall come in the glory of his Father with his angels, and then shall he render unto every man according to his deeds. Verily I say unto you, There be some of them that stand here, which shall in no wise taste of death, till they see the Son of Man coming in his kingdom' (Mt 16²⁷· ²⁸). Jesus predicts here two 'Comings '— one at the end of the world, when He returns in the glory of His Father to judge the world, the other within the lifetime of some of those present. Opinions may differ as to when this latter was fulfilled, whether at the Transfiguration, or at the Resurrection, or at Pentecost, or at the destruction of Jerusalem, or at each of these in turn ; but un-less we are to convict Jesus of error of judgment, we cannot hold that He identified any of these with His final coming to judgment. So that here, as in the words to Caiaphas, we find necessarily a prediction in mysterious language of His 'historic Comings '—a prediction that time would explain to His disciples by fulfilling.

(3) 'Ye shall not have gone through the cities of Israel, till the Son of Man be come' (Mt 10²³). These words are a fragment peculiar to Mt., and occur in the charge of Jesus to the Apostles when sending them out. Much of this charge as given by Mt. is found in different connexions in the other Synoptics ; it is therefore impossible to say whether this particular prediction was spoken at the time given by Mt., but this doubt does not enable us to conclude that it never was spoken at all. On the contrary, the great difficulty on the face of the saying renders it the more certain that it was spoken by Him on some occasion. Further, it should be noticed that it occurs in that Gospel which, as we have seen, records most fully those sayings of our Lord which refer to His 'Comings' (16²⁷ 26⁶⁴). We therefore are right in seeing in the words a prediction of His 'Coming' at the Resur-rection, or at Pentecost, or at the destruction of Jerusalem.

(4) 'The lesser Apocalypse of Jesus' is a title sometimes given to His discourse found in Lk 17²² 18⁸. Having told the Pharisees that the Kingdom of God was 'among them,' He turned to His dis-ciples and told them that in the future they would desire to see 'one of the days of the Son of Man' but would not see it ; but that when 'his day' did come, there would be no mistaking it, as it would shine as lightning and come as suddenly. He, however, would have first to suffer many things and be rejected. He then told them that as 'in the days' of Noah and of Lot (vv.²⁶· ²⁸), worldliness predominated until 'the day' that Noah entered the ark and Lot left Sodom (vv.²⁷· ²⁹), so would it be in 'the days of the Son of Man' until 'the day' when He would be revealed (vv.²⁶· ³⁰). 'The days' of Noah and Lot were days of opportunity for repentance before 'the day' of retribution. So 'the days of the Son of Man' must be the period of grace that ever precedes 'the day' of His reve-lation in judgment, whether that judgment be the final judgment or such a penal visitation as the destruction of Jerusalem. That the immediate reference in the passage is to the latter, follows from the warning contained in the next verses, bidding those on the housetop not come down and

those in the field not return home (v.³¹). These words could not possibly apply to the final return of Jesus, but must have been spoken in reference to the flight from the city before its destruction. And as that impending doom drew near, as the atmosphere became weighted with forebodings of coming calamity, and as their hearts failed them for fear (21²⁶), then they would desire 'one of the days of the Son of Man '—one of those days of God's patient waiting ; but they would not see it, for all was ripened to judgment. 'His day' of vengeance was at hand. He concluded this section with 'where the body is, thither will the vultures also be gathered together' (17³⁷)—enigmatic words whereby He told His disciples that when the cir-cumstances became ripe, the event would happen. Then followed the parable of the Unrighteous Judge (18¹), bidding God's 'elect' pray importu-nately for relief during the days of trial ; and, lastly, came the sorrowful question of Jesus, whether, notwithstanding the certainty of His de-liverance of His people, He, when He comes, shall 'find faith on the earth' (v.⁸). The worldliness of the days of Noah and Lot supply the answer.

(5) The discourse found in its simplest form in Mk 13 (cf. Mt 24, Lk 21) is the most elaborate recorded prophecy of Jesus, and presents to inter-preters many and serious difficulties ; but what has been said on the four preceding passages lessens the difficulties and points to the solution. Some scholars get rid of all that puzzles by assum-ing that the Evangelists inserted portions of a cur-rent Jewish-Christian Apocalypse throughout the discourse of Jesus. (For a good statement of this position, and for the various authorities, see Moffatt, *Historical New Test.* p. 637 ; and for a good exposition on conservative lines, see Briggs, *Messiah of the Gospels*, pp. 132-165).

It might be enough to object to such a radical solution by pointing out the entire absence of any external evidence ; but, further, it should be said that it seems incredible that the Evangelists should, by this sort of literary patchwork, have concocted a discourse so difficult for themselves and their readers to understand. The undeniable difficulties of the passage lead us to think that Jesus spoke the words ; they also show the con-scientious regard for truth that actuated those who recorded them. It must also be remembered that the difficulties found in this discourse are precisely the same in nature as those found in the four pass-ages we have just considered, so that to suppose that extraneous Apocalyptic literature is inserted here would lead us to give a like explanation of all these other passages. But that is impossible, for no such supposition would for a moment hold, in the case, for example, of the reply of Jesus to Caiaphas. Neither on external nor on internal grounds is such a solution to be accepted.

The discourse itself must now claim our atten-tion. The disciples, having pointed out to Jesus the splendour of the Temple buildings, receive the reply that not one stone shall be left upon another : a prediction He had previously made regarding the *city* of Jerusalem (Lk 19⁴³). The words evidently sank deeply into their hearts, for when they sat with Him on the Mount of Olives they asked Him privately, 'When shall these things be, and what shall be the sign when these things are all about to be accomplished ?' (21⁷). They thus asked two questions : first, *when* it would be ; secondly, what *sign* would herald it. Mt. enlarges the latter ques-tion into 'What shall be the sign of thy coming and of the end of the age ?' ; showing that the disciples connected the destruction of the Temple with Christ's return, and that they sought instruc-tion as to whether it was not also the End or consummation of the age (συντέλεια τοῦ αἰῶνος, Mt

$13^{39.\ 40.\ 49}\ 28^{20}$, cf. He 9^{26}). Our Lord's reply is full, both as to the *time* and the *sign* of the Temple's destruction, and is also directed to the question of His return and the end of the world. The fact that He includes these latter subjects in His reply as given in all three Gospels, goes to show that they were implicit in the shorter questions of Mk. and Lk. He first tells them that it will *not* be when false Christs arise and when nation rises against nation, for these things are but 'the beginnings of travail'—the birth-throes preliminary to final pains issuing in a new age—(Mk 13^{5-8}); but it *will* be after the gospel has been preached unto all nations, they themselves in the meantime suffering persecution; and *then* the end will come (Mk 13^{10}, Mt 24^{14}).

He then spoke of the *sign*, which would be that predicted by Daniel, namely, 'the abomination of desolation,' which would warn of the imminent destruction of the Temple. He further told them that that would occur at a period of unprecedented affliction, and He bade them, when they saw the sign, escape at once to the mountains (Mk 13^{14-20}, Mt 24^{15-22}, Lk 21^{20-24}).

Having thus spoken of the *time* and the *sign* of the destruction, He passed on to speak of His 'Coming,' which He announced as following 'immediately' upon the tribulation which He had just described. In Mk. we read, 'In those days, after that tribulation (Mt 24^{29} 'immediately ($\epsilon\dot{v}\theta\dot{\epsilon}\omega s$) after . . .'), the sun shall be darkened . . . and *then* shall they see the Son of Man coming in the clouds, . . . and he shall send forth his angels and gather together his elect from the four winds . . .' Thus both Evangelists make the coming of the Son of Man follow 'immediately' upon the foretold tribulation which was to preface the destruction of the Temple.

Briggs (*Messiah of Gospels*, p. 155) ascribes to the $\epsilon\dot{v}\theta\dot{\epsilon}\omega s$ of Mt. a prophetic sense similar to קרוב of the OT. The events were near to the vision of the prophet, but not necessarily near in actual history. But this does not get over the 'in those days' of Mk., which is almost as definite as the 'immediately' of Mt.

The question at once arises, whether those words can be taken as describing the judgment of the city and Temple. As far as the signs in heaven are concerned, we may say Yes; for these theophanic signs may justly be taken as imagery of the spiritual. Thus Peter interprets the heavenly portents foretold by Joel as fulfilled in the outpouring of the Spirit (Ac $2^{16.\ 19}$). But as regards the gathering together of the elect from the uttermost parts of the earth, we must say No. In no sense can this be said to have taken place when Jerusalem fell. What, then, we are to conclude is as follows: Jesus here foretold His 'Comings'; He wished His disciples to look forward to an early judgment on the guilty city and church, and He wished them also to look forward to a time of ingathering to take place at the consummation of all things. As He had done before (Mk 8^{38} 9^1), so now He spoke of these two events, one nigh at hand, the other far in the distant future, both as 'Comings' of Himself; but the two Evangelists, untaught as yet by events, were unable to separate in their records that which to His own mind was distinct. This view is much strengthened by our finding that that Evangelist who wrote after the destruction of Jerusalem was able then to distinguish what to them was confused. It is very remarkable that Lk., instead of placing the final return of Christ immediately after the tribulation, inserts a clause which makes the entire Christian dispensation intervene. He writes, 'Jerusalem shall be trodden down of the Gentiles, until the times of the Gentiles be fulfilled' (Lk 21^{24}); and thus makes room for the ages of evangelization that intervene between the destruction of Jerusalem and the Parousia.

The discourse closed with two remarkable statements: first, that that generation would not pass away until all those things were accomplished (Mk 13^{30}, Mt 24^{34}, Lk 21^{32}); second, that none save the Father, not even the Son, knew 'that day and hour' (Mk 13^{32}, Mt 24^{36}). That the Evangelists should have placed side by side two such apparently conflicting utterances, can be explained only by assuming their certain knowledge that Jesus had spoken them, and by their extreme fidelity to truth. To apply both sayings to the same event makes Jesus say, 'I do not know the exact day or hour, but I know that it will occur within the lifetime of some of those present.' But the words are far too strong for such a meaning. He never would have asseverated so strongly in such a connexion the ignorance of the angels in heaven and of Himself as Son. What He evidently meant was, that He Himself would visit the Temple and city in judgment, and level them even with the ground within that generation; but that the day and hour of His final return in glory were unknown even to Himself. 'That day' is used frequently as synonymous with 'last day,' indeed appears to be always used in that sense where the antecedent is not plainly indicated, and so must be taken in that sense here (Mt 7^{22} 26^{29}, Lk 10^{12} 21^{34}, 2 Th 1^{10}, 2 Ti $1^{12.\ 18}$ 4^8).

Mt. appends a series of parables which illustrate and spiritually apply the great lessons of the discourse. Jesus told His hearers to watch; for if the master of the house had kept awake, the thief would not have entered. They are to be diligent and faithful as trusted servants, so that they may receive the blessing from their Master when He returns (Mt $24^{43.\ 51}$). By the parable of the Ten Virgins He cautioned them against indolence creeping upon them because of His delay in coming. By the parable of the Talents He taught them that definite duties are entrusted to them during 'the long time' of His absence, but that on His return He will proportionately reward faithful service and punish neglect. And, finally, by the parable of the Sheep and the Goats He pictured in majestic language the great culmination of His ministerial office, when, seated on the throne of glory, He will dispense to assembled humanity the justice which their deeds of love or selfishness have merited.

The historic Comings, which are, as we have seen, so largely predicted by the Synoptists, are as plainly taught by John; in fact, it is even more impossible in the Fourth Gospel than in the first three to narrow down the sayings of Jesus that refer to His 'Comings' to any one event. When He says, 'I will come again, and receive you unto myself' (14^3), His meaning cannot be exhausted by referring the words to Pentecost, or to death, or to the Parousia; rather does it include all these. Similarly, 'I will not leave you desolate: I come to you' (14^{18}), is not sufficiently interpreted by referring the words to the Resurrection, or to Pentecost, or to personal spiritual revelations; but must include all these.

In both these verses the Greek is not in the future tense but present ($\dot{\epsilon}\rho\chi o\mu\alpha\iota$), meaning not 'I will come,' but 'I come, at all times I am coming' (see Westcott, *l.c.*; see also $16^{16.\ 22}$ 21^{22}). This view of repeated 'Comings' does not prevent John from teaching the great Final Advent, for he records the words of Jesus which foretell the hour when the dead in their graves shall hear His voice (5^{28}); and in his Epistles uses the word $\pi\alpha\rho o\upsilon\sigma\iota\alpha$ in exactly the same sense as it is used by Matthew, James, and Paul (1 Jn 2^{28}; cf. Mt 24^3, Ja 5^7, 1 Co 15^{23}).

The predictions of Jesus carry us even beyond His Parousia. They tell us that His Coming will be the signal for the resurrection of the dead, both bad and good alike (Jn $5^{28.\ 29}$), and that that resurrection will be followed by the judgment of mankind. It is revealed that He Himself will be the Judge, and that before the throne of His glory will be gathered the entire human race in order that they may receive the just recompense for their deeds (Mt $25^{31ff.}$), each individual receiving his merited sentence (Mt 25^{32} 22^{11} 16^{27}). The judgment will thus be *universal* and *individual*. It is further revealed that the decisions of that judgment will be 'age-long' in their consequences. On the one hand, the guilty will suffer from 'the unquenchable fire' and 'the undying worm' (Mk 9[44. 46. 48]); they will be shut out from the marriage feast of the King's Son, and condemned to 'outer darkness' (Mt 22[13] 8[12] 25[30]). On the other hand, the righteous will pass in with the Bridegroom to the marriage (25[10]), will enter into the joy of their Lord (25[21]), will be received unto Himself (Jn 14[3]), and will behold His glory (17[24]).

As regards the predicted bliss of the pardoned, there can be no doubt that Jesus taught that it was of eternal duration, for that bliss is naught but the gift of life, and that life is the life of God Himself, and so necessarily is everlasting as He is everlasting (Jn 1[4] 5[26-29], cf. 1 Jn 5[11. 12]). His teaching regarding the duration of the punishment of the wicked, however, is less plain. Much of His language is highly figurative, and may have been used by Him only to express the terrible punishment that awaits unrepented sin in the next world, without precluding the hope that God will finally win all to Himself by love ; a hope that not a few passages in the later books of the NT suggest.

V. The prophetic office of the Ascended Christ.— We must not conceive of the prophetic office of Jesus as ceasing with His ascension ; for it, no less than the priestly and kingly, belongs to His essential activities as the Redeemer of men. Error as well as sin blights human life, and truth as well as righteousness is needed to restore the fallen, and therefore from the right hand of God He still teaches the world He loves.

1. His prophetic work is carried on by Him through the instrumentality of *His Church*, which is inspired by His Spirit. It is not that He has transferred His teaching office from Himself to the Church, but that He Himself still teaches the world through her. When the earliest preachers of the gospel proclaimed their message, He, though enthroned, worked with them and confirmed the word with signs following (Mk 16[20]) ; and it was His Spirit—'the Spirit of Jesus'—that prevented Paul the missionary from entering Bithynia (Ac 16[7]), and that thus directed his steps as a teacher to Europe. In a word, the Church in her teaching office is taught, confirmed, and guided by Jesus Christ, her ever-living Prophet.

2. Shortly after the Church started on her career, the inherent prophetic power, which she possessed by her union with Christ, exhibited itself in a recognized *order of prophets*,—men and women who preached under the influence of direct inspiration, and who at times were able to foretell the future. These prophets were placed by St. Paul second in his list of Church ministrants (1 Co 12[28], Eph 4[11]). Their natural tendency towards independence by and by brought them into collision with the Church's authoritative organizations ; and their ministry of enthusiasm, under the pressure of the more regular and constant ministrations, gradually fell into disuse.

3. But the many movements claiming inspiration throughout her history tell us that the prophetic Spirit is ever present, though perhaps slumbering, within the Christian body. It is difficult to see how such a gift as prophecy, which by its spontaneity refuses to be bound by fixed rules, can coexist, without confusion, as a power along with the stated ministry ; but not the least need of the present life of the Church is the discovery of means whereby she may develop her organized existence as a community, and at the same time permit the free utterance of those direct spiritual communications which she may receive from Christ her Prophet.

LITERATURE. — (1) On the Messiah as Prophet : Stanton, *Jewish and Christian Messiah*, pp. 126, 293 f. (2) On Christ's Prophetic Office : Martensen, *Chr. Dogmatics*, p. 295 ff. ; and esp. Dorner, *Syst. of Chr. Doctrine*, vols. iii. and iv. *passim.* (3) On distinctive marks of prophet : Oehler, *OT Theol.* ; A. B. Davidson, *OT Theol.*, also his art. 'Prophecy' in Hastings' *DB* ; Ottley, *Aspects of OT*, p. 275 ff. (4) On Christ's didactic prophecies : Edersheim, *LT* ; Weiss, *Life of Christ* [Neander's *Life*, though not modern, is very useful] ; Bishop D'Arcy's *Ruling Ideas of our Lord* (Hodder) is succinct but full and valuable, see also his art. IDEAS (LEADING). (5) On Christ's predictive prophecies : for those regarding His death see Schwartzkopff, *Prophecies of Jesus Christ* [Eng. tr. T. & T. Clark] ; but for conservative standpoint, Denney, *Death of Christ* ; for those regarding His Return see Stevens, *NT Theol.* pt. I. ch. xii. ; Briggs, *Messiah of Gospels*, ch. iv. and *passim* ; S. Davidson, *Doctrine of Last Things* ; Schwartzkopff, as above ; Muirhead, *Eschatology of Jesus* ; art. 'Parousia' in Hastings' *DB.*
                                              CHARLES T. P. GRIERSON.

PROPHETESS.—Among OT prophetesses may be named Miriam (Ex 15[20]), and esp. Deborah (Jg 4f.) and Huldah (2 K 22[14], 2 Ch 34[22]). The prophetess Noadiah opposed Nehemiah (Neh 6[14]). While it was the exception for women to be called to the prophetic office, they were by no means excluded from it, and it is manifest that Deborah and Huldah made a deep impress upon their contemporaries. The only mention of a prophetess in the Gospels is that of Anna, who recognized the infant Messiah when His parents presented Him in the Temple (Lk 2[36]). She was of the tribe of Asher, and had lived to a great age, being probably a good deal over a hundred years old. She spoke to the pious worshippers in the Temple concerning the work of Jesus. See ANNA.   JOHN R. SAMPEY.

PROPITIATION.—The idea of propitiation is directly expressed in the NT by the words ἱλάσκομαι, ἱλασμός, and ἱλαστήριον, which occur but six times. The verb is found in Lk 18[13], He 2[17], the substantive in 1 Jn 2[2] 4[10] ; ἱλαστήριον, be it adjective or substantive, in Ro 3[25], He 9[5]. As the ground of reconciliation and atonement, it is the innermost truth in reference to Christ's redemptive work.

The word ἱλάσκομαι came down from classic usage through the LXX into the writings of the NT. As used in the latter, it refers to the relation of Christ's work to sin. We are interested chiefly in this article, therefore, in tracing the meaning it had in the LXX in reference to the sin- and guilt-offerings. It was used to render the Heb. *kipper*, 'to cover.' That which constituted the emblematic cover which hid sin from God so that He could act as though it did not exist, was the shed blood (or life) of the sacrificial victim. In the narrow limits of this article it is only possible to refer to the conclusions reached by eminent scholars with whom the writer ventures in general to agree. He would mention especially Prof. W. P. Paterson's art. 'Sacrifice' in Hastings' *DB*, where the conclusion is reached that 'the expiation of guilt is the leading purpose of Levitical sacrifices,' and that the expiation is accomplished through the sacrifice taking the place of the offender, and its death being accepted in place of his. While this seems the manifest import of the Levitical sin- and guilt-offerings with which we are in this discussion concerned, it is pretty certain that this was the view of the Jews in our Lord's time. As Holtzmann says (*Neutest. Theol.* p. 68), 'Everything pressed towards the assumption that the offering of a life substituted for sinners according to God's appointment, cancelled the death penalty which had been incurred, and that consequently the offered blood of the sacrificial victim expiated sin as the surrogate for the life of the guilty.'

1. In the teaching of our Lord.—The single instance in which our Lord is reported to have used the word ἱλάσκομαι, in Lk 18[13], has little bearing on the question whether He thought His work a propitiation. This question must be considered on the broader ground of His thought of the relation in which His work stood to the Levitical sacrifices out of which the idea of propitiation grew. Now, the Evangelists believed much relating to His birth, lifework, and death to be the fulfilment of OT prophecy (Mt 1[23] 2[6. 18] 3[3] 4[15. 16] 12[18-21] 13[35] 21[5] etc.). They evidently got this impression from our Lord Himself, who saw the OT fulfilled in Himself (Mt 11[10] 13[14. 15] 21[42], but esp. Mt 5[17] and Lk 24[13-31]). He did not view His work and teaching as a break in the continuity of religious historical development, but as woven into its evolving progress. He came to fill the Law and the Prophets full of a new meaning by stripping them of Rabbinic accretions and revealing their deepest spiritual import. He saw His life and death related to Moses (the Law) and all the Prophets.

In view of this general conception, we must interpret our Lord's references to His death. The place His death had in His thought, apart from the more direct teaching as to its purpose and import, makes it plain that it was deemed of paramount importance in His mission work. Interpreting His words at His baptism (Mt 3¹⁵ 'Thus it becometh us to fulfil all righteousness') in the light of Mt 20²². ²³, but especially of His words in Lk 12⁵⁰ ('I have a baptism to be baptized with, and how am I straitened till it be accomplished'), it would seem that His death was before Him from the first as an essential part of His mission. Of the same meaning is Mk 2²⁰ (cf. Mt 9¹⁵, Lk 5³⁵) of the taking away of the bridegroom. He foretold that His resurrection would follow His death (Mt 12⁴⁰ ∥ Lk 11²⁹). He dwelt upon the details of His betrayal and death (Mt 16²¹, ·cf. Mk 8³¹ 10³²⁻³⁴, Lk 9²²). In connexion with these prophetic statements He gives the warning : 'He that doth not take his cross and follow after me, is not worthy of me,' and 'he that loseth his life for my sake shall find it' (Mt 10³⁸. ³⁹ 16²⁴. ²⁵, cf. Mk 8³⁴. ³⁵ and Lk 9²³. ²⁴, see also Jn 8²⁸), referring, doubtless, to the manner of His death.

On coming down from the Transfiguration, He forbade the three to mention what they had witnessed till He was risen from the dead (Mt 17⁹, cf. Mk 8³⁰), and Lk 9³¹ declares that Moses and Elijah talked with Jesus of His death as of supreme moment. As the end drew near, He dwelt more upon His death and resurrection (Mt 17²². ²³ 20¹⁸. ¹⁹ 21³³⁻⁴⁰, cf. Mk 12⁶⁻⁸, Jn 10¹¹). The great space given to the circumstances connected with our Lord's death seems to show that the Evangelists saw in it the culmination of His redemptive work.

But our Lord connects Himself more explicitly with the sacrificial system. In Lk 22³⁷ He identifies Himself with the Servant of Jehovah of Is 53, as ' he was reckoned with the transgressors.' In Mt 20²⁸ (cf. Mk 10⁴⁵) He says that He is to ' give his life a ransom for (ἀντί ' in the place of') many.' At the solemn institution of the Supper (Mt 26²⁸, cf. Mk 14²⁴, Lk 22²⁰), the wine is said to represent ' my blood of the new covenant, which is shed for many unto the remission of sins.' He was also to give His ' flesh for the life of the world ' (Jn 6⁵¹⁻⁵⁶). St. John also identifies Him with the Suffering Servant of Jehovah of Is 53, in Jn 12³⁸. The words of the Baptist : ' Behold the Lamb of God, which taketh away the sin of the world ' (Jn 1²⁹), probably also are in terms of Is 53⁵, as the Servant of Jehovah, ' bruised for our iniquities,' like the sacrificial lamb, endured death silently.

From all these lines of evidence it is impossible to escape the conclusion that our Lord and the Evangelists considered His death to be of paramount importance in His mission, and gave it this value because it stood to the sins of the world in a similar relation to that which the Levitical sacrifices held to the sins of the Jews.

If the conclusion be accepted that these sacrifices were expiatory and vicarious, we have a clear idea of the purpose our Lord supposed His death served. Neither need we wonder that He taught so little about the purport of His death. The false notions of His Kingdom entertained by His disciples made them invincibly opposed to His establishing it through the Cross instead of a crown. They were ' foolish and slow of heart ' (Lk 24²⁵). Consequently He had ' many things to say' to them which they could not bear before His death shattered their false ideas (Jn 16¹⁻¹³). It was only then that this

fuller instruction could be given and was promised. Immediately after His resurrection He began to instruct His disciples as to the meaning of His mission and death as they stood related to the Law and the Prophets (Lk 24²⁰. ²⁷). They were not the men to invent an interpretation of His death, or to go back to Levitical explanations without His sanction. They reverenced Him too much to break consciously with His thought. The confidence with which they taught, beginning with Pentecost, can be explained only by their receiving from our Lord Himself and from the promised Spirit a certain knowledge of the nature of His work. Any view which makes our Lord's mission a break with the religious development either before or after, but much more with both, has against it the strongest conceivable presumption. St. Paul, St. Peter, and St. John all believed themselves to be giving our Lord's own view of the purport of His work. They were in a better position to know His own thought of Himself and His mission than any at this late time of day. From them we can get the clearest light on our Lord's own conception of the purpose served by His life and death.

2. In the teaching of the Apostles.—While we may have the key to the innermost meaning of our Lord's mission work in the forms of the word ἱλάσκομαι, they must be interpreted in the perspective of the general teaching of the Epistles. While the word ' propitiation ' is used so seldom, the idea that our Lord's work was a propitiation is woven into the warp and woof of them all. The whole aim of Hebrews is to show that Christ, as a priest representing the people, and as a sacrifice, expiated their sin, and was the antitype of the old priesthood and sacrifices. He was, as the Passover lamb, sacrificed for men without the breaking of a bone (Jn 19³⁶, 1 Co 5⁷. ⁸, cf. Ex 12⁴⁶) ; He was a sin-offering (Ro 8³, He 13¹¹). As in the Levitical sacrifices for sin, the shed blood, representing the life given up, was the propitiation, so emphasis is laid upon the blood of Christ in His redemptive work (Ro 5⁹, Eph 1⁷ 2¹³, Col 1¹⁴⁻²⁰, Heb. passim, 1 P 1¹⁹, 1 Jn 1⁷, Rev 1⁵ 5⁹ etc.). The blood of Christ is said to be the blood of sprinkling, because the blood of the sacrifices was sprinkled (1 P 1², He 12²⁴). We must, then, interpret the definite words ἱλάσκεσθαι, ἱλασμός, and ἱλαστήριον in the light of the environing conception of Christ as the antitype of the old sin- and guilt-offerings, which was held by those who used them.

(a) St. Paul.—The earliest, as well as the most important, instance is in Ro 3²⁵. ²⁶ ' whom God set forth to be a propitiation (ἱλαστήριον), through faith, by his blood, to show his righteousness because of the passing over of the sins done aforetime, in the forbearance of God ; for the showing of his righteousness at this present season : that he might himself be just, and the justifier of him that hath faith in Jesus.' According to St. Paul's conception, Christ is a propitiation in (ἐν) His blood or death, and because He manifests or demonstrates the righteousness of God. The righteousness of God demanded this demonstration to vindicate it against the suspicion of its violation which might arise because of the passing over of sins done aforetime, and of the justification of the believer at the present season. The nature of this righteousness is also evident. It is that in God which demands that sins be punished and not passed over in forbearance, and that sinners be condemned and not justified. It is that in God which is cast under suspicion when the reverse of this is done, and therefore needs demonstration and vindication. It is subjective righteousness in God. It is true that God provided the propitiation which His righteousness demands, and He does this in love (Ro 5⁸), but all the same, the propitiation to demonstrate His righteousness had to be provided by love in order to vindicate righteousness in 'passing over' sins in forbearance and in 'justifying' on the condition of faith. To confound righteousness and love in their manifestations, would be to remove the very ground of the problem involved in being just and justifying. Neither is the faith which might be aroused by the setting forth of Christ in His blood that which has propitiatory value. The righteousness of God had to be vindicated by this very propitiation in the case of those who had faith in Jesus. Christ in His blood constitutes the propitiation. It becomes effective as a propitiation, through faith.

In what sense, then, does St. Paul regard our Lord as a propitiation? How could He in His blood or death demonstrate God's righteousness, which demanded that sins be punished and not passed over, and that the ungodly be condemned and not justified when the reverse of this took place? Could it be in any other way than that, in the death of Christ, the righteousness of God which made these demands received a satisfaction for the sins of men of the same kind as would have been paid if God had let His punitive wrath (Ro 1[18]) fall upon the transgressor? In His death Christ endured the just desert of sin (Ro 6[23]), as 'him who knew no sin he (God) made to be sin on our behalf' (2 Co 5[21]). He could in consequence pass over sins in forbearance, and justify the believer though ungodly (Ro 4[5]), and His righteousness would not be tarnished but demonstrated, because Christ stood for sinners, and all died in His death (2 Co 5[14]). This is the natural interpretation of the passage itself. It also brings it into accord with St. Paul's general circle of ideas. It is in harmony with the central idea of the Levitical sacrifices for sin from which the pivotal word ἱλαστήριον is derived. In it the thought of our Lord in Mt 20[28] ‖ Mk 10[45] ('give his life a ransom [λύτρον] in the stead of [ἀντί] all'), and Mt 26[28] etc., is reflected and expanded. The historical continuity of thought between the OT and our Lord, and our Lord and St. Paul, is also preserved.

(b) *St. John.*—As St. Paul, in viewing Christ as a propitiation, lays emphasis upon His demonstration of the Divine righteousness, St. John sees in His propitiation a demonstration of the Divine love. Taking the two instances where He is said to be a propitiation (ἱλασμός, 1 Jn 2[2] 4[10]), we find that He is a propitiation for sins. The sending of Christ as a propitiation was prompted by God's love, not as a return for man's love. The propitiation was for the whole world, and not for those alone who should be saved. It is Jesus Christ the *Righteous* who is the propitiation, apparently showing that His propitiatory work had a peculiar relation to righteousness. As St. John had just referred to our Lord's blood as cleansing from all sin (1 Jn 1[7]), it is plain that he thought of Christ in His blood or death as the propitiation. Neither is He the propitiation for sins because of any cleansing or other work wrought in men as a consequence of His work and death; for He is the propitiation for the whole world, many of whom will never be purified or subjectively changed by or through it. The propitiation is due to a work for us, and not in us, except as a consequence. It must then, in itself, have reference to God, and not to a work in men's hearts. This brings these passages into harmony with the Johannine conception in Revelation. There it is ever as the Lamb that was slain —the antitype of the sacrificial victim—that He is spoken of, and that His blood is said to purify and redeem (Rev 5[6. 8. 12] 6[1] etc., cf. 1[5] 5[9] 7[14] etc.). St. John's whole view of Christ as the antitype of the sacrificial victims, in connexion with his statement (1 Jn 2[2]) that He is the propitiation for the whole

world, can be explained only on the ground that he thought of Christ's propitiatory work as having primarily an efficacy Godward, and manward only as a consequence.

(c) *The Epistle to the Hebrews.*—According to He 2[17], propitiation is made for sin. It is made by Christ as the antitype of the high-priesthood of the OT. From the whole scope of the Epistle up to 10[30] it is made as He offers His own blood as the perfect antitype of the imperfect sacrificial system of the old economy, which was thereby fulfilled and then abolished. Through His sacrifice a 'purification of sins' (1[3]), a cleansing of the 'conscience from dead works' (9[14]), is wrought, and access to God assured (10[9-22]). The eternal takes the place of the temporal, the perfect of the imperfect, the inward of the outward and fleshly, the real of the symbolical and typical. To the question whether Christ's work effected something objectively for us as well as provided for a subjective work in us, the answer is clear. By His sacrificial death He 'made purification of sins' (1[3]), 'obtained eternal redemption' (9[12]), 'put away sin' (9[26]), 'perfected for ever them who are sanctified' (10[14]). All this is regarded as already accomplished for us in Christ's sacrificial death, and not as still to be wrought in us through its influence. This work *for* us, as prior to that *in* us, is its necessary condition and ground, as apart from the shedding of blood there is no remission (9[22]). The author of Hebrews uses 'sanctify,' 'purify,' and 'perfect' in these passages in the Pauline sense of 'justify.'

The sacrifices of which that of Christ was the antitype did not give access to God's favour by removing a hindrance within the soul of the offerer, but by removing one that was objective. The interpretation which would make the author of Hebrews restrict the efficacy of Christ's work to its influence upon men, dislocates it from its whole setting, destroys its plainest antitypical significance, and would make his meaning unintelligible to the Hebrew readers for whom it was doubtless prepared. Neither are there wanting hints as to how Christ's work had this objective efficacy. The emphasis put upon the fitness of Christ's sharing man's nature and condition in order to do His work for them as high priest and sacrifice (ch. 2) is significant, and the statement that He tasted death for every man (2[9]) and bore the sins of many (9[28]), taken in connexion with His antitypical relation to the sacrificial system, can scarcely mean less than that He represented men in some way, so that He could bear their sins for them and die on their behalf.

What, then, does 'to make propitiation for the sins of the people' (εἰς τὸ ἱλάσκεσθαι τὰς ἁμαρτίας) mean as embedded in the author's general thought? The verb is in the middle voice with an active sense. Doubtless Winer is right in regarding it as elliptical, and meaning 'to propitiate God for the sins of the people.' The condition of making the propitiation is Christ's identification with humanity in nature and condition. The propitiatory value is in His blood, as He tastes death for every man so as to bear the sins of all, in a way analogous to that in which the sacrificial victim bore those of the offerer. The propitiation thus effected was objective for us, and not subjective in us. Through it forgiveness and access to God are possible. The propitiation puts away sin once for all—puts it out of the way as an obstacle to the Divine favour and forgiveness. How the sin is removed by His death is not explicitly stated, but the whole sweep of thought is favourable to the view that it was as a satisfaction to that in God which sin offends—call it holiness or righteousness as one will—and is in substantial agreement with St. Paul's conception. The view that the author of Hebrews thought of propitiation as effected by a 'mysterious inherent quality' he attributed to Christ's blood giving it direct 'inherent power to cleanse the life' (Stevens, *The Christian Doctrine of Salvation*, p. 88 f.), is too vapid to be credited to him.

If the writer of this article has succeeded in correctly interpreting Scripture thought on this central doctrine, then our Lord neither broke with the thought of the OT, nor did the writers of the Epistles break with His conception. They were interpreting His death in the fuller light of His own teachings after His resurrection and with the Spirit's help. We are justified in interpreting His own allusions to what was done by His death in view of both. Beneath the superficial variations due to the aspects of truth treated and the special aim of each of the NT writers, there is an underlying unity of thought as to what was effected by the death of Christ, and how it had efficacy to this end. See also artt. ATONEMENT, DEATH OF CHRIST, RANSOM, RECONCILIATION, REDEMPTION, SACRIFICE, VICARIOUS SACRIFICE [the last two written from a different standpoint].

LITERATURE.—In addition to the works referred to above :— Bruce, *St. Paul's Conception of Christianity*, 164 ff. ; Driver, art. 'Propitiation' in Hastings' *DB* ; A. Schwoller, 'Das Wesen der Sühne der altest. Opfertora' in *SK*, 1891 ; H. Schultz, *AJTh*, 1900, p. 286 ; Denney, *The Death of Christ* ; Gess, 'Zur Lehre von Versöhnung' in *Jahrbücher für Deutsche Theol.*, vols. iii. iv. ; Lomas, 'Fernley Lect.' 1872 ; Du Bose, *Soteriology of NT* (1892), 107 ; Vincent Tymms, *Chr. Idea of Atonement* (1904), 191 ; W. M. Ramsay in *ExpT* x. (1899) 157 ; and also Literature under articles on ATONEMENT, RECONCILIATION, SACRIFICE, etc.

C. GOODSPEED.

PROSELYTE.—1. Derivation of the name.— προσήλυτος (from προσέρχομαι) means lit. 'one who has arrived at a place,' hence 'a stranger,' 'a sojourner.' In the LXX it is frequently used as the equivalent of the Heb. גֵּר (see *Expos.* IV. x. [1894] p. 264). By NT times it had acquired the technical meaning of 'one who was a convert to Judaism from heathendom,' without any indication of place of residence being involved. This special meaning had also been gradually acquired by גֵּר (see W. R. Smith, *OTJC*[2] p. 342 n. ; also *Oxford Heb. Lex. s.v.* גֵּר), and also by the Aramaic גִּיּוֹרָא (LXX γειώρας).

2. Classes of proselytes.— In the time of Christ many foreigners had fully embraced Judaism, and were called 'proselytes'; there were also others, far more numerous, who had partially adopted Jewish doctrines and customs. The latter are indicated in the NT by σεβόμενοι (Ac 13[43] 16[14] 17[4. 17] 18[7]) and φοβούμενοι [τὸν. θεόν] (10[2] 13[16. 26]). These words indicate that they reverenced Israel's God and in part obeyed the Law, but had not fully entered into the fellowship of Israel. These divisions correspond to those of the Mishna, where גֵּר is a fully admitted proselyte, and the term גֵּר תּוֹשָׁב (lit. a resident alien) is applied to those who were more loosely attached to the Jewish worship. Later Rabbis expressed the same distinction by the phrases 'proselyte of Righteousness' (גֵּר הַצֶּדֶק), as contrasted with 'proselyte of the Gate' (גֵּר הַשַּׁעַר).

(*a*) *Proselytes properly so called* (NT προσήλυτος ; Mishna גֵּר ; Rabbinic name גֵּר הַצֶּדֶק). These were heathen by birth, who had been admitted to full fellowship in Jewish worship. Three observances were required for their admission : (1) Circumcision. (2) Baptism, which was analogous to the ceremonial purifications so frequently required of the Jews (Schürer, *HJP* II. ii. 321 ; also Edersheim, *LT* ii. 745). Some have maintained that the baptism of proselytes did not originate so early as the time of Christ, but the Mishna incidentally refers to it as if it had been long in use. (3) The offering of a sacrifice, by which atonement was made for the sins of the proselyte. Those thus admitted undertook to observe the whole Law (cf. Gal 5[3]), and they were granted privileges almost equal to those of an Israelite. Such are referred to in Mt 23[15], Jn 12[20], Ac 2[10] 6[5] 13[43].

(*b*) *Those denominated in the NT* σεβόμενοι or φοβούμενοι (Mishna גֵּר תּוֹשָׁב ; by the Rabbis גֵּר הַשַּׁעַר). The Talmud represents these as keeping what were denominated 'the seven precepts of Noah'—comprising the duties which were considered incumbent upon all men, even outside Israel (*Aboda Zara*, 64*b*). These precepts were : (1) obedience to those in authority ; (2) reverence to the name of God ; (3) abstinence from idolatry, (4) from fornication, (5) from stealing, (6) from murder, (7) from flesh with the blood in it (*Sanh.* 56*b*). [The decision respecting the obligations incumbent upon Gentile converts (Ac 15[29]) shows some agreement with these precepts].

Since גֵּר תּוֹשָׁב means one permanently dwelling in the country of Israel, the Talmud involves that all who were allowed to dwell in Palestine were required to keep the precepts of Noah ; but this was never actually enforced—it was theoretical only.

Persons who, without becoming full 'proselytes of Righteousness,' inclined to a greater or less extent towards Jewish doctrines and practices are referred to in the NT, Mt 8[5-13], Lk 7[1-10], Ac 10[2] 13[16. 26. 43. 50] 16[14] 17[4. 17] 18[7].

3. Proselytizing in the time of Christ.— The religious restlessness of heathenism, which favoured the introduction of Oriental creeds into the West, afforded an opportunity for Jewish proselytizing. The moral earnestness and monotheism of Judaism commended it to those who, having lost faith in heathen deities, were seeking a more rational and ethical creed. The Greek-speaking Jews, who were to be found in all the great cities of the Roman Empire, carried the knowledge of the Mosaic Law into the midst of heathendom, and presented their faith in a form calculated to win the approval of their neighbours. This accommodation to their surroundings in the way of representing their creed was partly unconscious, through their contact with Gentile thought, and partly an intentional emphasizing of the moral side of Judaism, while merely national and ceremonial features which might repel inquirers were minimized (Schürer, II. ii. 297). Hence, in spite of the scorn which Roman writers heaped upon the Jews (Tac. *Hist.* v. 2–8 ; Juv. *Sat.* vi. and xiv.; Cic. *pro Flacco*, 28), numerous adherents were gained, who either fully or partially accepted Judaism (Jos. *c. Apion.* ii. 40, *Ant.* xx. ii. 3). Many of these converts were women (Jos. *BJ* II. xx. 2 ; also Ac 13[50] 16[14] 17[4]).

From these proselytes a very considerable revenue was received by the Temple authorities (Jos. *Ant.* XIV. vii. 2). This pecuniary advantage from the spread of Judaism stimulated activity in proselytizing, such as that noticed by Christ in Mt 23[15]. Some Jews fraudulently enriched themselves from the gifts of proselytes (Jos. *Ant.* XVIII. iii. 5). Such unworthy motives for proselytizing were condemned by Jesus (Mt 23[15]).

Illustrations of the fanatical zeal of the Jews in making proselytes are found in Jos. *Life*, 23, *Ant.* XIII. ix. 1, xi. 3, xv. 4, xx. ii. 1, *BJ* II. xvi. 10, XVII. x.

The account of the Acts shows that proselytes often became converts to Christianity, and this was an important factor in the establishment of the Gentile Christian Church. The struggle between St. Paul and the Judaizers (Ac 15 and Ep. to Galatians) was an attempt on the part of Christian Pharisees to compel Gentile Christians to become 'proselytes of Righteousness.'

4. Moral quality of Jewish proselytes.— Proselytes who had accepted Judaism from pure motives must have been men of high character ; nevertheless proselytes are spoken of slightingly by the

Talmud. Thus we read (Bab. *Middah*, fol. 13. 2) : 'Proselytes and sodomites hinder the coming of the Messiah.' This is explained to mean that proselytes often erred through ignorance of the Law. We can readily imagine that insistence upon the minutiæ of Pharisaic tradition (cf. Mt 23⁴) would tend to produce a debased character such as is charged against some in Mt 23¹⁵. Edersheim, however, suggests (*LT* ii. 412) that the word 'proselyte' in this passage may signify the winning of a convert to Pharisaism, rather than a convert from heathendom to Judaism.

5. Christ's relations with proselytes.—Although the number of proselytes in Palestine must have been very great, references to them in the Gospels are few. We find : (1) *The centurion* (Mt 8⁵⁻¹³, Lk 7¹⁻¹⁰), who was an officer in the army of Herod Antipas. There is no reason to think of him as a 'proselyte of Righteousness,' for in that case (*a*) he need have had no hesitation in asking Jesus to go to his house, and (*b*) the words of Jesus (Mt 8¹¹) would not be so suitable. But from the fact that he had built a synagogue (Lk 7⁵), he was clearly one of the wider class of adherents to Judaism, called in later days 'proselytes of the Gate' (see Edersheim, *LT* i. 546).—(2) *The Greeks* (Jn 12²⁰). From the fact that these came to attend the Feast, they would appear to have been 'proselytes of Righteousness.' (Geikie, however, *Life of Christ*, ii. 434, considers that they were 'proselytes of the Gate').—(3) On Mt 23¹⁵ see preceding paragraphs on 'Proselytizing' and 'Moral quality.'—(4) *Pilate's wife* (Mt 27¹⁹). Tradition (earliest recorded in the Gospel of Nicodemus, ch. 2) asserts that Pilate's wife was a 'proselyte of the Gate.' Origen says that she became a Christian.

LITERATURE.—Selden, *de Jure Nat. et Gent.*, Lib. ii. ; Buxtorf, *Lex. Talmud. et Rabbin. s.v.* גר ; Schürer, *HJP* II. ii. 291–327 ; Harnack, *Expansion of Christianity*, ii. 1–24 ; Hausrath, *NT Times: Time of Apostles*, i. 123 ; Allen in *Expos.* 4th ser. x. (1894) 264 ; art. 'Proselyte' in Hastings' *DB* and in *EBi.*

F. E. ROBINSON.

PROTEVANGELIUM.—See art. FALL in vol. i. p. 571ᵇ f.

PROVERB is the rendering of παραβολή in Lk 4²³ (RV 'parable') and of παροιμία in Jn 16²⁵·²⁹ (RVm 'parable'). In Jn 10⁶ παροιμία is rendered 'parable' (RVm 'proverb'). Ordinarily παραβολή means 'parable,' παροιμία 'proverb'; but the words are sometimes interchanged in Hellenistic Greek. Both represent the Heb. *māshāl*, the primary meaning of which is 'comparison.' Such comparison lies at the base of many proverbs as well as parables; in fact many proverbs are only condensed parables; and a proverb usually sets up a single case as the type of a whole class. In the LXX *māshāl* is nearly always rendered παραβολή, even when a proverb is clearly meant (1 S 10¹² 24¹³ ⁽¹⁴⁾, 1 K 4³² ⁽²⁸⁾, Ezk 12²²·²³ 18²·³; in some of these places Aq. or Symm. substitutes παροιμία. παροιμία is found in the canonical OT only in Pr 1¹ 25¹ (Aℵ²; Bℵ¹ have παιδεῖαι); it occurs 5 times in Sirach, παραβολή 10 times ; at 39³ and 47¹⁷ they stand together. Thus Lk., like the LXX, uses παραβολή for 'proverb' as well as 'parable'; while Jn., on the contrary, uses παροιμία in the sense of 'figurative language, allegory' (10⁶), or 'dark saying' (16²⁶·²⁹) rather than 'proverb'; perhaps 'figure' best represents his use of the word. On our Lord's use of proverbs see following article.

LITERATURE. — Cremer, *Lexicon, s.v.* παραβολή ; Trench, *Parables*, ch. 1 ; art. 'Proverb' in Hastings' *DB* (by König) and *Encyc. Bibl.* (by Paterson) ; Königsmann in Hase and Iken, *Thes. Nov.* ii. 501 ; Driver, *LOT*⁶ p. 349.

HAROLD SMITH.

PROVERBS (JESUS' USE OF).—It is a saying of the Rabbis that 'the Law spoke in the tongue of the children of men.' And so did our Blessed Lord. He did not use the jargon of the schools, but expressed His heavenly teaching, albeit profounder than either Jewish theology or Greek philosophy, in language which the simplest could understand. The Oriental mind delights in proverbs, and Jesus, in His gracious desire to reach the hearts of His hearers, did not disdain to weave into His discourse the homely and often humorous sayings which were current in His day.

1. '*It is yet four months, and the harvest cometh*' (Jn 4³⁵). It is usual to find here a note of chronology (cf. Meyer). The harvest began in April, early enough sometimes for the unleavened bread of the Passover to be baked with new flour (Orig. *in Joan.* xiii. § 39) ; and since, it is argued, the harvest was four months distant, it was in December that Jesus visited Sychar in the course of His journey from Jerusalem to Galilee. There are, however, insuperable objections to this view.

(1) December is the rainy season, and with every wayside brook running full, Jesus would not have needed to crave a drink from the woman's pitcher to slake His thirst (cf. Ps 110⁷). (2) It is incredible that, when after the Passover He retired with His disciples from Jerusalem 'into the land of Judæa' (Jn 3²²), in order doubtless to collect His thoughts and brace Himself for the commencement of His ministry, He should have protracted that season of repose for eight months. (3) Moreover, as Origen remarks, the Evangelist's explanation of the enthusiasm wherewith the Galilæans received Him on His arrival (Jn 4⁴⁵), implies that His miracles in the capital during the Passover season were fresh in their memories.

In truth there is here no chronological datum. The *logion* is a husbandman's proverb, like the other which follows immediately (v.³⁷). The seed was sown towards the end of December, and four months elapsed ere it was ripe (see Wetstein) ; and the proverb conveyed the practical lesson that results mature slowly (cf. Ja 5⁷). Jesus was prepared to sow the good seed of the Kingdom and have long patience until it should ripen, and it filled His heart with surprise and gladness when He beheld His seed ripening in an hour. He spied the woman returning in haste from the town accompanied by an eager throng (Jn 4²⁸⁻³⁰), and He broke out, 'Ye have a saying (λέγετε, cf. λόγος in v.³⁷), It is yet four months, and the harvest cometh. Lo, I say unto you, Lift up your eyes, and behold the fields, that they are white for harvest !'

2. '*A prophet hath no honour in his own country, and among his own kinsfolk, and in his own house.*' Jesus is reported to have quoted this proverb on two occasions (Jn 4⁴⁴, Mt 13⁵⁷=Mk 6⁴=Lk 4²⁴), and it was constantly exemplified in His experience. He was rejected by His townsfolk of Nazareth ; He was pronounced mad by His kinsfolk ; His brethren did not believe in Him.

Origen (*in Joan.* xiii. § 54) thinks that the proverb originated in the dishonour which the prophets of Israel had always suffered at the hands of their contemporaries (cf. He 11³⁶⁻³⁸) ; but in truth it was not peculiarly Jewish. 'Few of the most sagacious and wise,' says Plutarch (*de Exil.* § 13), 'would you find cherished in their own countries.' 'Quidquid enim domi est,' says Seneca (*de Benef.* iii. 3), 'vile est.' 'Sordebat [Protogenes] suis,' says Pliny (*HN* xxxv. § 36), 'ut plerumque domestica.' Pericles would never dine abroad, lest he should be cheapened in the estimation of the company by the familiarity of social intercourse (Plut. *Pericl.* § 7 ; cf. *de Imit. Chr.* i. 10, § 1 : 'Vellem me pluries tacuisse et inter homines non fuisse'). Cf. the ancient proverb still in vogue : 'Familiarity breeds contempt' (Chrys. *in Joan.* xxxiv. : ἡ γὰρ συνήθεια εὐκαταφρονήτους ποιεῖν εἴωθεν ; Bernard. *Flores* : 'Vulgare proverbium est, quod nimia familiaritas parit contemptum') ; and the saying of the witty Frenchman that 'no man is a hero to his *valet de chambre.*'

3. In the course of His dispute with the people of Nazareth, Jesus quoted another proverb, '*Physician, heal thyself*' (Lk 4²³). The Talmud has : 'Medice, sana claudicationem tuam' (cf. Eurip. fragm. : ἄλλων ἰατρὸς αὐτὸς ἕλκεσι βρύων (ed. Witzschel, iv. p. 302) ; Cic. *Ep.* iv. 5 : 'Malos medicos qui in alienis morbis profitentur se tenere medicinæ scientiam, ipsi se curare non possunt' (see Wetstein).

4. There is no saying of Jesus more astonishing

than His answer to the disciple who sought permission to go and bury his father ere casting in his lot with Him : '*Leave the dead to bury their own dead*' (Mt 8[21. 22] – Lk 9[59. 60]). It seems as though He were speaking here after the manner of the Rabbis, who forbade that even the burial of the dead should be allowed to interrupt the study of the Law (Wetstein on Mt 8[21]), and required that a disciple should put his teacher's claims before those of his father ; ' for his father indeed brought him into this world ; but his teacher, who has taught him wisdom, has introduced him into the world to come' (Taylor, *Say. of Fath.* iv. 17, n. 21 ; Schürer, *HJP* II. i. p. 317). Is it credible that Jesus should have rivalled the Rabbis in heartless arrogance ? The difficulty disappears when it is understood that the disciple's request was merely a pretext for delay. He was quoting a flippant phrase which is current in the East to this day.

A missionary in Syria once counselled a youth to complete his education by travelling in Europe. 'I must first bury my father,' was the answer. The old gentleman was neither dead nor dying ; he was in good health, and the youth meant merely that his home had the first claim upon him (Wendt, *Teach. of Jesus*, ii. 70, n. 1).

5. Jesus was quoting another proverb when, in answer to the man who volunteered to follow Him but craved leave first to bid his household farewell, He said : '*No one, having put his hand to the plough and looking back, is fit for the kingdom of God*' (Lk 9[62]). The OT story of Elisha's call from the plough (1 K 19[19-21]) seems to have leapt into His mind and suggested His reply, which is an adaptation of a common saying : 'A ploughman must bend to his work, or he will draw a crooked furrow' (Plin. *HN* xviii. § 49 : 'Arator nisi incurvus prævaricatur'; cf. Verg. *Ecl.* iii. 42 : 'curvus arator'). 'Conveniet,' says Erasmus, 'in negocium quod absque magnis sudoribus peragi non potest.'

6. The Sermon on the Mount abounds in proverbial phrases. '*A single iota or a single tip*' (Mt 5[18]) is like our phrase, 'The dot of an *i* or the stroke of a *t*.' It is frequent in the Talmud (cf. Lightfoot and Wetstein). 'Sound not a trumpet before thee' (6[2]) is a proverbial metaphor, though Calvin takes it literally, supposing that the Pharisees, those 'play-actors' (ὑποκριταί) in religion, actually blew a trumpet to summon the beggars (cf. the Greek proverb αὑτὸς ἑαυτὸν αὐλεῖ, 'play one's own pipe,' like our 'blow one's own trumpet'; Achill. Tat. viii. 10 : αὕτη δὲ οὐχ ὑπὸ σάλπιγγι μόνον ἀλλὰ καὶ κήρυκι μοιχεύεται).

'I have observed,' says old Thomas Fuller, 'some at the church door cast in sixpence with such ostentation that it rebounded from the bottom and rang against both sides of the bason (so that the same piece of silver was the alms and the giver's trumpet), whilst others have dropped down silent five shillings without any noise.'

'*With what measure ye measure, it shall be measured to you again*' (7[2]) is very common in the Talmud (see Wetstein ; Dalman, *Words of Jesus*, p. 225).—'*Why seest thou the chip that is in thy brother's eye, but the log that is in thine own considerest not ? Or how wilt thou say to thy brother, Let me cast out the chip out of thine eye, and, behold, the log is in thine own eye ?*' (7[3. 4]). This proverb is characteristically Oriental in its grotesque exaggeration, and there is no need to explain it away by supposing that 'eye' represents עַיִן 'a well': a chip in your neighbour's well, a log in your own (see Bruce in *EGT*). It is a carpenter's proverb, and has a special fitness on the lips of the Carpenter of Nazareth.

It is found in the Talmud (see Lightfoot). Cf. *Baba Bathra*, 15. 2 : 'Cum diceret quis alicui : "Ejice festucam ex oculo tuo," respondit ille : "Ejice et tu trabem ex oculo tuo."' The proverb is Jewish, but the fault which it satirizes is universal. 'Many,' says St. Chrysostom, 'now do this. If they see a monk wearing a superfluous garment, they cast up to him the Lord's law, though themselves practising boundless extortion and

covetousness every day. If they see him enjoying a somewhat plenteous meal, they fall to bitter accusing, though themselves indulging daily in drunkenness and excess.'

'*Give not what is holy to the dogs, neither cast your pearls before the swine*' (7[6]). Cf. 2 P 2[22] (Pr 26[11]), Pr 11[22], and see Wetstein. '*What man is there of you who, if his son shall ask of him a loaf, will give him a serpent ; or if he shall ask an egg, will give him a scorpion ?*' (7[10]). There was a Greek proverb, 'For a perch a scorpion' (ἀντὶ πέρκης σκορπίον) ; '*ubi quis optima captans pessima capit*' (Erasm. *Adag.*). 'For a fish,' Wetstein explains, 'a fisherman sometimes catches a water-snake.— '*Build on the sand*' (εἰς ψάμμον οἰκοδομεῖς ; cf. εἰς ψάμμον σπείρεις ; see Erasm. *Adag.* under 'Inanis Opera') was a proverb signifying vain and unenduring labour, and it seems as though Jesus had it in His mind in His similitude of the Two Builders (Mt 7[24-27]=Lk 6[47-49]).

7. '*If a kingdom be divided against itself, that kingdom is unable to stand ; and if a house be divided against itself, that house shall be unable to stand*' (Mk 3[24. 25]=Mt 12[25]). A maxim of statecraft. Cf. Soph. *Ant.* 672–674 :

ἀναρχίας δὲ μεῖζον οὐκ ἔστιν κακόν.
αὕτη πόλεις ὄλλυσιν, ἥδ' ἀναστάτους
οἴκους τίθησιν.

Xen. *Mem.* iv. 4. § 16 : ἄνευ δὲ ὁμονοίας οὔτ' ἂν πόλις εὖ πολιτευθείη οὔτε οἶκος καλῶς οἰκηθείη.

8. '*Prudent as the serpents and simple as the doves*' (Mt 10[16]). The serpent was a symbol of sharp-sightedness, and the dove, like the sheep, of simplicity and gentleness. Erasmus (*Adagia*) quotes the proverbs ὄφεως ὄμμα and πραότερος περιστερᾶς (cf. Rabbinical comment on Ca 2[14] 'Deus dixit Israelitis : "Erga me sunt integri sicut columbæ, sed erga gentes astuti sunt sicut serpentes"'; see Wetstein).

9. '*He that hath found his life shall lose it, and he that hath lost his life for my sake shall find it*' (Mt 10[39]). 'Proverbium est militare' (Wetstein). Jesus here addresses the Twelve like a general exhorting his troops on the eve of battle.

Cf. Xenophon to the Ten Thousand : 'I have observed that as many as yearn to live by every means in warfare, these, for the most part, die evilly and shamefully ; but as many as have recognized that death is common to all and necessary for men, and strive to die nobly, these I see rather arriving at old age, and, while they live, passing their days more blessedly' (*Anab.* III. i. 43). Epict. iv. 1. § 165 (of Socrates) : τοῦτον οὐκ ἔστι σῶσαι αἰσχρῶς, ἀλλὰ ἀποθνήσκων σώζεται, οὐ φεύγων· Juv. viii. 83. 84 :

'Summum crede nefas animam præferre pudori
Et propter vitam vivendi perdere causas.'

10. '*If a blind man guide a blind, both shall fall into a ditch*' (Mt 15[14]; cf. 23[24]). Cf. Hor. *Epp.* i. 17. 3–4 : 'Ut si cæcus iter monstrare velit.' Wetstein quotes Sext. Empir. *Hyp. Pyrrh.* iii. 29 : οὐδὲ τυφλὸν ὁδηγεῖν δύναται τυφλός.

11. One misses the spirit of the conversation between Jesus and the Syrophœnician woman (Mt 15[21-28]=Mk 7[24-30]) unless one observes that it is a bandying of proverbs. The scene was evidently the lodging of Jesus and the Twelve. The woman had followed them indoors [in Mk 7[25] Tischendorf, after אLD, reads εἰσελθοῦσα], and she pressed her suit as they reclined at table. Perhaps a dog was in the apartment begging scraps. '*It is not right*,' says Jesus, quoting an apt proverb, '*to take the children's bread and cast it to the whelps.*' Cf. the Greek adage : 'You feed dogs, and do not feed yourself' (αὐτὸν οὐ τρέφων κύνας τρέφεις), which Erasmus (*Adag.* under 'Absurda') thus explains :

'It was said of one who, while too poor to procure the necessaries of life, endeavoured to maintain an establishment of horses or servants. It will be appropriately employed against those who, by reason of the narrowness of their means, have scarce enough to maintain life, yet ambitiously endeavour to emulate the powerful and wealthy in fineness of dress and general ostentation. In short, it will be suitable to all who regard the things which belong to pleasure or magnificence, neglecting the things which are more necessary.'

There was another proverb: 'Never be kind to a neighbour's dog' (μήποτ' εὖ ἔρδειν γείτονος κύνα), otherwise put: 'One who feeds a strange dog gets nothing but the rope to keep' (ὃς κύνα τρέφει ξένον, τούτῳ μόνον λίνος μένει).

'The proverb warns you against uselessly wasting kindness in a quarter whence no profit will accrue to you in return. A neighbour's dog, after being well fed, goes back to his former master' (ib. under 'Ingratitudo').

It was some such proverb that shaped our Lord's speech to the woman. He was not speaking after the heartless and insolent manner of the Rabbis, who branded the Gentiles as 'dogs' (cf. Megill. Ex. 12. 6: '"An holy convocation to you": to you, not to dogs; to you, not to strangers.' Pirk. Eliez. 29: 'He who eats with an idolater is like one that eats with a dog: for, as a dog is uncircumcised, so also is an idolater'). And the woman replied in like terms: 'Yea, Lord, for even the whelps eat of the crumbs that fall from the table of their masters.' Here also, it would appear, there is a proverb. Damis of Nineveh, the Boswell of Apollonius of Tyana, was once sneered at for the diligence wherewith he recorded his master's sayings and doings, taking note of every trifle. 'If,' he replied, 'there be feasts of gods and gods eat, certainly they have also attendants who see to it that even the scraps of ambrosia are not lost' (Philostr. Apoll. i. 19). It may be added that there is an Arabic proverb: 'It is better to feed a dog than a man,' the reason alleged being that the dog will not forget the kindness, but the man may (PEFQSt, July 1904, p. 271).

12. 'The gates of Hades' (Mt 16[18]). Cf. Is 38[10], Job 38[17], Ps 9[13] 107[18]; Hom. Il. ix. 312–313:

ἐχθρὸς γάρ μοι κεῖνος ὁμῶς Ἀΐδαο πύλῃσιν,
ὃς χ' ἕτερον μὲν κεύθῃ ἐνὶ φρεσὶν ἄλλο δὲ εἴπῃ.

13. 'It is better if a heavy millstone were hanged about his neck, and he were flung into the sea' (Mt 18[6] = Mk 9[42] = Lk 17[2]). Cf. Kidd. 29. 2: 'Dicit Samuel, Traditio est ut ducat quis uxorem et postea applicet se ad discendam Legem. At R. Jochanan dicit: Non molâ collo ejus appensâ addicet se ad studium Legis.' The proverb was derived from the punishment of drowning. At Athens criminals were flung, with stones about their necks, into the Barathrum, a dark, well-like chasm (Aristoph. Equit. 1359–60; Schol. on Plut. 431). In B.C. 38 the Galilæans rose against Herod, and drowned his adherents in the Lake (Jos. Ant. XIV. xv. 10).

14. The narrow gate and the two ways (Mt 7[13. 14] = Lk 13[24]). There is here an allusion to a favourite image of the ancient moralists which had passed into a proverb. 'Vice,' says Hesiod (B.C. 850–800), 'even in troops may be chosen easily; smooth is the way, and it lieth very nigh. But in front of Virtue the immortal gods have put sweat. Long and steep is the way to her, and rough at first; but when one cometh to the summit, then it is easy, hard as it was' (Works and Days, 287–292). Pythagoras of Samos (B.C. 570–504) adopted the image and elaborated it. He employed as a symbol of the two ways the letter Υ, the archaic form of Υ, hence called 'the Samian letter' (Pers. iii. 56–57, v. 34–35). The upright stem represented the innocent period of childhood, and the divergent branches the after-course of youth and manhood, pursuing the straight path of virtue or the crooked track of vice. The image is found also in the Tablet of Kebes, an allegory in the style of a Platonic dialogue, a sort of Greek Pilgrim's Progress, purporting to be a description of a tablet which hung in the temple of Kronos, and emblematically depicted the course of human life.

'"What is the way that leads to the true Instruction?" said I. "You see above," said he, "yonder place where no one dwells, but it seems to be desert?" "I do." "And a little door, and a way before the door, which is not much thronged, but very few go there; so impassable does the way seem, so rough and rocky?" "Yes, indeed," said I. "And there seems to be a lofty mound and a very steep ascent with deep precipices on this side and on that?" "I see it." "This, then, is the way," said he, "that leads to the true Instruction"' (Tab. § 15).

15. 'A grain of mustard-seed' (Mt 17[20], Lk 17[6])—a proverbial instance of extreme littleness (cf. Mt 13[31. 32] = Mk 4[31. 32] = Lk 13[19]). Uprooting trees (cf. Mt 21[21] = Mk 11[23]) or mountains,—an expression used of wonderful feats (cf. 1 Co 13[2]). Some of the greater Rabbis were called 'uprooters of mountains' (see Lightfoot and Wetstein).

16. 'Easier for a camel to pass through the needle's eye' (Mt 19[24] = Mk 10[25] = Lk 18[25])—a proverb denoting an impossibility. The Talmud has 'an elephant passing through the needle's eye' (see Lightfoot). The absurd exaggeration is characteristically Oriental, and should not be toned down either by substituting κάμιλος, 'cable,' for κάμηλος, 'camel,' or by supposing 'needle's eye' to mean postern-gate; cf. Shak. K. Rich. II. v. v. :

'It is as hard to come as for a camel
To thread the postern of a needle's eye.'

The proverb is found in Koran, ch. vii. : 'Verily they who shall charge our signs with falsehood and shall proudly reject them, the gates of Heaven shall not be opened unto them, neither shall they enter into Paradise, until a camel pass through the eye of a needle.' Did Mohammed quote from the Gospels, or was the proverb current throughout the East in his day?

17. 'Straining out the gnat and gulping down the camel' (Mt 23[24]). Cf. Jerus. Shabb. 107. 3 : 'One who kills a flea on the Sabbath is as guilty as one who should kill a camel on the Sabbath.' Erasmus (Adag. under 'Absurda') quotes a Latin adage : 'Transmisso camelo, culex in cribro deprehensus hæsit,' and refers to the bantering remark of Anacharsis the Scythian when he found Solon busy drawing up his laws. 'They are exactly like spiders' webs : they will hold back the weak and insignificant and be broken through by the powerful and rich' (Plut. Sol. 5. 2). The proverb satirizes those who atone for laxity in important matters by scrupulosity in matters of no moment.

18. 'To every one that hath shall be given, and he shall have more abundantly; and from him that hath not, even what he hath shall be taken away from him' (Mt 25[29]). Cf. R. Hillel : 'He who increases not, decreases,' which means that one who does not improve his knowledge, loses it (Taylor, Sayings of the Fathers, i. 14). Jesus employs the saying in this sense in Mt 13[12], Mk 4[25] = Lk 8[18].

It raises an interesting question that several of these proverbs not only have heathen parallels but are heathen proverbs. How comes it that Greek and Latin sayings were current among the Jews? The Jewish attitude toward pagan culture was one of bitter hostility. It is true that the liberal school of R. Hillel had a more tolerant spirit. Its most distinguished adherent was R. Gamaliel, who advocated the study of the hokhmath Javanith. The prevailing sentiment, however, was that of the school of Shammai, which pronounced a common malediction on one who reared swine and one who taught his son Greek (Otho, Hist. Doct. Mishn. pp. 68–70).

The general sentiment is well illustrated by Origen's sneer at Celsus' imaginary Jew who quoted Euripides, that Jews were not wont to be so well versed in Greek literature (c. Cels. ii. 34). A Jew with Greek quotations at his finger ends was an absurd fiction. And it is certain that Jesus had no acquaintance with Greek literature. Celsus charged Him with borrowing from Plato His saying about the difficulty of a rich man entering into the kingdom of heaven, and spoiling it in the process (ib. vi. 16. The Platonic passage is Legg. v. 743 : ἀγαθὸν δὲ ὄντα διαφερόντως καὶ πλούσιον εἶναι διαφερόντως ἀδύνατον); and Origen's reply is most just : 'Who that is even moderately able to handle the subject would not laugh at Celsus, whether a believer in Jesus or one of the rest of mankind, hearing that Jesus, who had been born and bred among Jews, and was supposed to be the son of Joseph the carpenter, and had studied no literature, neither Greek nor even Hebrew, according to the testimony of the veracious scriptures that tell his story, read Plato?'

Nevertheless, despite their exclusiveness, it was impossible for the Jews to escape the leaven of external influences. (1) They carried on a very considerable commerce. They had several industries of world-wide fame. The Lake of Galilee abounded in fish, which were pickled and exported far and wide. Galilee was celebrated for its linen manufacture, and the flocks which pastured on the wilderness of Judæa furnished material for a thriving trade in woollen goods. Jerusalem had a sheep-market and a wool-market. There was also an extensive import traffic. Trade involves an interchange of ideas. The merchants imported words as well as wares, and one meets many an alien vocable, uncouthly transliterated, on the pages of the Talmud. What wonder if the Jews caught up also some of the foreign merchantmen's proverbs?

(2) The traders were not the only strangers who visited the Holy Land. There were Roman soldiers and Herod's mercenaries, the latter including Thracians, Germans, and Galatians (Jos. *Ant.* XVII. viii. 3). King Herod the Great had built a magnificent theatre at Jerusalem and an equally magnificent amphitheatre, and had instituted athletic contests every four years after the pattern of the Greek games. From every land (ἀπὸ πάσης γῆς) came competitors and spectators (*ib.* XV. viii. 1). Still more numerous, however, was the concourse of worshippers who frequented the Holy City at the festal seasons. They came from all quarters (Ac 2[8-11]). They were, indeed, devout and patriotic Jews, but they had settled in foreign countries, and had acquired the languages and manners of the strangers among whom they dwelt and traded. Is it not reasonable to suppose that they would introduce into the Holy Land many a pithy saying which they had learned in the countries of their adoption? DAVID SMITH.

PROVIDENCE. — The word 'providence' (Gr. πρόνοια) is found only once in EV of the NT, viz. in Ac 24[2], where it is applied to Felix by Tertullus. 'Providence' (Lat. *providentia*, fr. *pro* and *videre*) literally means 'foresight,' but in its recognized use a much nearer equivalent is 'forethought' (πρόνοια). But providence is more even than forethought. It implies not only thought about the future, but practical arrangements for the purpose of securing premeditated ends (cf. Ro 13[14] 'Make not provision [πρόνοιαν—the only other occasion of the use of the word in the Gr. NT] for the flesh, to fulfil the lusts thereof'). And in the specific and most familiar sense of the word, as applied to the providence of God, it carries with it, as follows of necessity in the case of the Divine Being, the actual realization of the ends which God has determined. Though the word nowhere occurs in the Gospels, the subject is one that meets us constantly. And while it is the providence of God that is especially brought before us, there are not wanting suggestive references to providence on the part of man.

1. The Divine providence. (1) In the *OT* the fact of God's providence—in nature, in history, and in the individual life—is everywhere prominent; and the problems presented by the doctrine of providence appear and reappear in the Prophets, and receive a special treatment in the book of Job and in certain of the Psalms (*e.g.* 37. 73). In the *Book of Wisdom* the very word 'providence' (πρόνοια) twice occurs. In 14[3] it is applied to God

as governing the waves of the sea ; and in 17[2] the heathen oppressors of Israel are described as 'fugitives from the eternal providence.' From Josephus we learn that *Rabbinical Judaism* was much occupied with the mysteries of Divine providence in its relation to human freedom ; and that, as against the Sadducees who held an exaggerated view of liberty, and the Essenes who maintained a doctrine of absolute fate, the Pharisees kept to the middle path represented by the OT teaching, affirming the freedom and responsibility of man on the one hand, and the Divine providence and omnipotence on the other (*Ant.* XIII. v. 9, XVIII. i. 3, *BJ* II. viii. 14).

(2) In the *Gospels*, as in the NT generally, there is everywhere assumed the faith in the Divine providence which characterizes the OT writings, and is continued in orthodox post-canonical Judaism. The confidence of the Evangelists in the fulfilment of Messianic prophecy in the Person of Jesus is a testimony to their belief in the far-sighted operation of the Divine counsels (Mt 1[22] 2[5. 15. 23] 3[3], and *passim*). Their statements as to the incarnation of the Son of God furnish a supreme proof of a Providence that overrules the laws of nature by an indwelling governance, and moves down the long paths of history to the accomplishment of its own ends (Mt 1[18ff.], Lk 1[34ff.], Jn 1[1-14]; cf. Gal 4[4]).

(3) A doctrine of providence underlies *the whole life and teaching of Jesus Christ.* As against a Deistic view which makes God sit aloof from the world He has created, and a Pantheistic view which identifies Him with Nature and its laws, Jesus always takes for granted the fact of God's free and personal providence. It is in this confidence that He turns to His Father for power to work His miracles—miracles which in turn become signs that His trust in God's providence was not misplaced. It is in the same confidence that He goes to God in prayer (Mt 11[25] 26[39ff.], Mk 1[35] 6[46], Lk 3[21] 11[1] 22[32], Jn 11[41f.] 14[16] 17), and teaches His disciples to do likewise (Mt 6[6. 9ff. 77ff.] 9[38] etc.). Such petitions as 'Give us this day our daily bread' (6[11]), and 'Lead us not into temptation' (v.[13]), would be mere hypocrisies apart from an assured trust in the loving providence of our Father in heaven.

(4) Not only is a doctrine of providence a constant implication of our Lord's life and ministry, it forms *an express part of His teaching.* Jesus told His disciples that God rules in nature, making the sun to shine and the rain to fall (5[45]), feeding the birds of the air (6[26]), and clothing the lilies of the field (v.[28ff.]). He taught them that God also rules in human lives, bestowing His blessings on the evil and the good (5[45]), supplying the bodily wants of those upon whom He has conferred the gift of rational life (6[25]), devoting a peculiar care to such as seek His Kingdom and His righteousness (v.[33]). As against the pagan notion of chance (wh. see), and the analogous idea that at most the Almighty cares only for great things and does not concern Himself with the small (cf. 'Magna dii curant, parva negligunt,' Cic. *de Nat. Deor.* ii. 66), He affirmed that there is 'a special providence in the fall of a sparrow' (10[29], cf. *Hamlet*, Ac. v. Sc. ii.), and that even the very hairs of our head are all numbered (v.[30]). As against a doctrine of providence which would turn it into a blind fate, and make the strivings of the human will as meaningless as the motions of a puppet, we have to set His constant emphasis on the momentousness of choice and effort and decision (7[13. 21] 13[45ff.] 16[24ff.] 18[3], etc.). As against a narrow philosophy of providence, according to which good men are openly rewarded in this life and wicked men openly punished, He taught that God governs the world by general laws (5[45]), that persecution is often the earthly portion of the righteous (vv.[10ff.]), that dis-

asters falling on the individual are not to be taken as Divine retributions upon special guiltiness (Lk 13¹⁻⁵), and that our views of Divine providence must be extended so as to include a coming day of judgment for nations as well as individuals (Mt 25³¹ff.). Thus in His teaching He anticipated most of those questions which have been so much discussed by theologians in connexion with this whole subject — questions as to the relation of God's government to secondary causes, of providence to free will, and as to distinctions between a providence that is special and one that is merely general.

(5) But besides the underlying implications of His teaching and its broad lines of treatment, our Lord brings forward in one well-known passage *some special views and arguments bearing on faith in the providence of God as a means of deliverance from anxious care* (Mt 6²⁵⁻³⁴ = Lk 12²²⁻³⁴). (*a*) The first thing that strikes us here is the emphasis He lays on the Divine Fatherhood (Mt 6²⁶·³²). The revelation of God as our Father in heaven is the central fact of Christ's teaching, and it illuminates His doctrine of providence just as it illuminates His whole message. This is the point at which His doctrine of providence rises above the highest and best teaching of the OT upon the subject. God's providence is a more individual and a more loving care than the saints of old had ever dreamed of, and this it is precisely because He is our Father. Once we have realized the fundamental truth about our relation to Him, we find it not merely possible to believe in His loving guardianship of our lives, but impossible to conceive of anything else (cf. 7¹¹ = Lk 11¹³). (*b*) Taking for granted that His hearers believe in God as their Creator, Jesus argues from creation to providence as from the greater to the less. The life is more than meat, and the body than raiment. He, therefore, who breathed into the body the breath of life will assuredly sustain the life He has inspired, and clothe the body He has framed (Mt 6²⁵). (*c*) Next He argues, we might say, from the less to the greater. If God feeds the birds of the air, shall He not much more feed His spiritual offspring? If He clothes the flowers of the field in their radiant beauty, how can He fail to clothe His own sons and daughters? (vv.²⁶·²⁸⁻³⁰). (*d*) Again, He argues generally that the fact of our Father's knowledge of our needs carries with it the certainty that all our needs shall be supplied—an argument based directly on the thought of Fatherhood, and the love that Fatherhood implies (vv.³¹·³²).

2. Human providence.—Christ's special teaching on the providence of God in the passage just considered has sometimes been misinterpreted into a pronouncement against any providence on the part of man. The language of the AV no doubt lends itself to this; for in modern English 'Take no thought' is a very misleading rendering of μὴ μεριμνᾶτε (vv.²⁵·³¹·³⁴, cf. ²⁷·²⁸). It was not forethought, however, but anxiety (see RV) that Jesus warned His disciples against, when He turned their minds to the great truth of the heavenly Father's providence (see art. CARE). That He believed in the value and the need of prevision and forethought we may learn from His own example. The long years of silence at Nazareth were evidently spent in a deliberate preparation of Himself for the high tasks that lay before Him. And when His public ministry began, so far from being careless of the morrow, He shaped all His days according to a pre-conceived plan (cf. Mt 3¹⁸ff., Mk 1¹⁴f., Lk 12⁵⁰, Jn 9⁴ 17⁴). In His teaching He lays frequent stress on the value of prudent forethought (see art. PRUDENCE), both in worldly matters and in the affairs of the Kingdom of heaven—witness the parables of the Unjust Steward (Lk 16¹ff.), of the Pounds (19¹³ff.), and the Talents (Mt 25¹⁴ff.), of the

Wise and the Foolish Virgins (v.¹ff.). His appeal, therefore, to the birds of the air and the lilies of the field was not meant to encourage a belief that God would work for the idle and provide for the improvident. The argument rather is, If God provides for His unconscious creatures who cannot exercise forethought, much more will He provide for His conscious children who can and do. If He feeds the birds that neither sow nor reap, much more will He prosper you in your sowing and reaping; if He clothes the lilies that toil not neither do they spin, be sure He will see to it that men and women, on whom He has laid toiling and spinning as a necessity, do not lack the raiment they require. Work you must; it is the law of your lives as God's rational creatures; but learn from the birds and the lilies not to be anxious in the midst of your toil. Sow your seed, trusting in God to send the harvest. Fulfil your appointed tasks, but leave the results with confidence in your Father's hands. Jesus, then, does not commend improvidence. On the other hand, He does condemn a providence that confines itself altogether to the provision of earthly things, or even gives these the chief place in the heart. He condemns the providence of the Rich Fool (Lk 12¹⁶⁻²¹), and urges His disciples to lay up their treasure in the heavens (vv.²¹⁻³³). 'Seek ye *first* the kingdom of God and His righteousness' (Mt 6³³) is the counsel with which He concludes His special teaching on the relation of His disciples to the providence of the heavenly Father.

Christ's doctrines of Divine and human providence are thus complementary to each other. The thought of God's foreseeing care does not do away with human freedom and responsibility. On the contrary, it accentuates these by assuring us that we are not the creatures of fate, but the free children of God, and that we live our lives and fulfil our tasks under His watchful and loving eyes. The realization of the need of forethought and preparation on our part for the duties and events of life does not render us independent of the Almighty care. On the contrary, man's providence rests altogether upon the providence of God, and apart from it is utterly vain. And so to win Christ's approval human providence must be the providence of religious faith, and must be directed above all to the securing of higher than earthly blessings. It is only when we seek *first* the Kingdom of God and His righteousness that we have the promise that 'all these things' — food and raiment and whatsoever else we require for the bodily life— shall be added unto us.

LITERATURE.—Schürer, *HJP* II. ii. 14 ff.; Wendt, *Teaching of Jesus*, i. 205, 289; Martensen, *Dogmat.* p. 214; C. G. Montefiore, 'Heb. and Greek Ideas of Providence and Retribution' in *JQR* v. (1893) 517; Ritschl, *Chr. Doct. of Justif. and Recon.* (Eng. tr. 1900) 614; F. H. Woods, *For Faith and Science* (1906), 93; E. A. Abbott, *Silanus the Christian* (1906), 109; W. N. Clarke, *Outline of Chr. Theol.* p. 147; Dykes, *Manifesto of the King*, p. 483; Dale, *Laws of Christ*, p. 157.   J. C. LAMBERT.

PRUDENCE. — This term has a wider and a narrower reference. It may denote practical sagacity, the right choice of means to ends, clear-sighted forecasting of consequences and the shaping of conduct in accordance therewith. This would bring under review the whole of Jesus' conduct, and His methods of teaching, with their adaptation to the ends of His mission. In its more common use, prudence refers to the more self-regarding acts. It is the narrower reference that we consider.

1. Jesus' *conduct.* — In the earlier part of His ministry Jesus withdrew from the approach of danger. When He came from the temptation in the wilderness to take up His mission, hearing that Herod had put John in prison, He departed from Jordan to Galilee (Mt 4¹²). Galilee was within the dominion of Herod Antipas, but it was remote, away from the palace where John was imprisoned, away also from the place where John had baptized, and whither the crowds had come. In Galilee He would be more withdrawn from Herod's observation. Later on, when opposition was growing, and the Pharisees and Herodians were taking counsel together against Him, He withdrew for a time to the sea (Mt 12[14], Mk 3[6]). And when He heard of the execution of John, He retired with His disciples to the desert (Mt 14[13], Mk 6[31]). The Fourth Gospel also gives instances of His shunning Judæa when passions were stirred there against Him (Jn 7[1. 10] 10[39. 40] 11[8. 54]). What relation had these acts of prudence to Jesus' sense of duty and of trust in the care of the Father? He shunned danger then for His work's sake. His hour was not yet come (7[6]). Then life, and not death, was the necessity of His mission. Again, Jesus taught the most absolute trust in the guarding care of the Father. Not a sparrow falls to the ground without Him (Mt 10[29]). Should He not then have committed Himself to the Father: could Herod defeat the mission of the Messiah, the Son who alone could reveal the Father? In the wilderness Jesus recognized that thought to be a temptation of Satan (4[5-7]). God has given us minds to look before and after; and to run into avoidable peril needlessly is to tempt God. Carefulness, even amid duty, is lowliness' way of escape from presumption. Jesus recognized that He had to accept the ordinary conditions of human life, and guard Himself, for His work's sake, from the confinement that would hinder it, or premature death that might destroy it. But there is both in the Synoptics and in the Fourth Gospel a beautiful reconciliation of Jesus' prudence with duty and faith. When He withdrew to the desert on hearing of John's death, the crowds followed Him; and Jesus, seeing them as sheep without a shepherd, had compassion on them, and began to teach them (Mk 6[34]). The death of Lazarus makes Him return to Judæa, whence He had prudently withdrawn Himself (Jn 11[4-8]). The emergence of a duty, an appeal from circumstances to His compassion, is a call from the Father, and then Jesus enters upon danger secure in the Father's guarding providence. When a man is doing the duty clearly laid down for him at the moment, he is walking in the day, and there is no stumbling for him (11[9]).

Did Jesus sin against that earlier spirit of prudence in His last visit to Jerusalem? He knew that He was going into danger. And He went thither not quietly, but making a public demonstration. He rode up to the city on an ass's colt as the Messiah, with an enthusiastic crowd strewing palm branches and singing hosannas to the Son of David. That would rouse the Pharisees, who regarded His claim as blasphemous, and the Sadducees, who might tremble for the peace and order of the city. He went to the Temple, and drove out with a scourge of small cords them that bought and sold in the holy place. And when at last Pharisees and Sadducees were united against Him, He uttered in the public hearing His invectives against the hypocrisy of scribes and Pharisees. Jesus has been blamed for thereby running upon death. But (1) it was necessary that He should openly make His claim to be the Messiah. He had not done so at first, for He did not desire any mere political following. It was to spiritual believers, won by His preaching of the Father, who felt that He, the meek and lowly One, had the words of eternal life, that He made known the fact that He was God's Messiah. But it was necessary that the claim should ultimately be proclaimed, after all His gospel had been declared, that Israel's rejection of Him should be their rejection of Him as Messiah. (2) It was necessary also that the Lord of man's life should lay bare in judgment the evil of Pharisaism, the master sin which dwells in the Temple, serving the very altar (see PERFECTION OF JESUS, p. 337). But the invectives came only after His enemies were banded together and had decreed His death. The hour was striking when He uttered the words that maddened His foes. He chose His time with forethought and sagacity. (3) The hour of sacrifice had come. This death was no way of escape from intolerable difficulties (Renan, F. Newman). It was the end foreseen from the beginning. It lies at the back of the victory over temptation in the wilderness when He put aside the suggestion to use methods of popularity. Its shadow is over the words which He spake to the Pharisees, when early in His

ministry they questioned Him about His disciples and fasting 'The days will come when the bridegroom shall be taken away from them, and then shall they fast in those days' (Lk 5[35]). And as soon as Peter had made his confession of belief in Him as Messiah, Jesus began to prepare His disciples for sufferings and death (Mk 8[30. 31]). That is clear evidence that though His disciples had never dreamed of the tragic ending, yet it had long been in their Master's thought. The joyousness and serenity of the early Galilæan ministry is no proof that Jesus dreamed then of success; it only proves how absolute was His conquest over all self assertion and all natural shrinkings of the flesh. Death was His goal, seen from the beginning. Love's kingdom could be set up only by love's absolute devotion and self-sacrifice. The Father had laid upon Him the task of laying down His life for the sheep. And when Jesus went up to Jerusalem, He recognized that this His hour was come. He read the signs of the times (Mt 16[3]).

2. Jesus' *teaching.* — His teaching follows the lines of His conduct. As in His conduct, there is a prudential side. He counsels men to lay up treasure in heaven, for that treasure abides (Mt 6[19. 20], Lk 12[33]). He bids them count the cost of discipleship (Lk 14[25-33]). In the parables of the Unjust Steward and the Ten Virgins, He expresses His surprise at the lack of forethought and consideration on the part of the children of light. (See FOOLISHNESS). And He bids them pluck out their right eye, cut off their hand or foot, whichever it be that gives offence, and enter maimed into the Kingdom of God rather than perish (Mk 9[43-49], Mt 5[29. 30]). This has been called 'the distinctive principle of Christian asceticism' (Gore); and this may be granted, with the proviso that such asceticism has nothing to do with self-appointed penances or mortifications, but only with the self-denial which wise self-knowledge brings amid the inflow of life upon one. But it is rather Christian prudence, as St. Augustine has defined it, 'love making wise distinction between what hinders and what helps itself': it is a vivid commentary on the prayer, 'Lead us not into temptation.'

In Jesus' teaching, as in His life, these prudential maxims are always subservient to the ultimate principle of conduct, love's paradox, 'Whosoever will save his life shall lose it, and whosover will lose his life for my sake shall find it' (Mt 16[25], Lk 17[33], Jn 12[25]). Self-forgetfulness through loving service of God enriches the spirit with life's treasures of wisdom and joy. That is the secret hid from the wise and prudent and revealed unto babes (Lk 10[20. 21]).

LITERATURE.—W. M. Sinclair, *The Servant of Christ* (1892), 102; H. P. Liddon, *Sermons on Some Words of Christ* (1892), 191; S. A. Brooke, *The Ship of the Soul* (1898), 4; D. T. Young, *The Crimson Book* (1903), 157; W. C. E. Newbolt, *The Cardinal Virtues* (1903), 25.   RICHARD GLAISTER.

PSALMS.—In discussing the relation of Christ to the Psalms, two questions must be kept apart: (1) His use of the Psalter, (2) His presence in the Psalter. Even if we did not know, by direct quotation and indirect allusion, that the Psalter was a favourite book of Christ's, we could have safely inferred as much from His general attitude to the OT. The Psalter, as, on the whole, the simplest and purest expression of the devotional life of Israel, must have commended itself peculiarly to Christ.

1. The influence of the Psalter upon the mind of Jesus was probably larger and more profound than His recorded allusions to it, numerous and subtle as they are, would lead us to suppose. There were indeed elements in it which He could not have appropriated—cries for vengeance upon foes (Ps 41[11 (10)], cf. 68[24 (23)]), or of an almost cruel delight at their defeat (18[43 (42)]), or sorrowful laments at the prospect of a death in which fellowship with God was believed to be interrupted (6[6 (5)] 39[14 (13)] 88[11-13 (10-12)]). But there were other elements which were well fitted to express, as they may have helped to nourish, His piety. Especially must He have been attracted by those psalms which breathe the spirit of quiet confidence in God : ' Thou art my God ; my times are in thy hand' (31[15f. (14f.)]) ; ' In thy presence is fulness of joy ' (16[11]) ; ' As for me, I am continually with thee : thou hast holden my right hand. Thou wilt guide me with thy counsel, and afterward receive me to glory' (73[23f.]). The joy which comes from fellowship with God and from the contemplation of His acts in history (95-100), the humble and childlike spirit which lifts meek eyes to the God who looks down in pity from the heavens (123. 130)—these and other such tempers and aspirations cannot have been without their influence upon the spirit of Jesus. Most welcome of all would be those fine interpretations of the character of God scattered throughout the Psalter—as of one who is not only Lord of all space and time ('90. 139), but who is also 'good and ready to forgive and rich in love to all that call upon him' (86[5] 103[8]), who opens His hand and satisfies the desire of every living thing (145[16]), who is father of the fatherless and judge of the widow (68[6 (5)]), who rises up at the oppression of the poor and the sighing of the needy (12[6 (5)]).

2. But in estimating the influence of the Psalter upon Jesus, we are not left to conjecture. On many occasions—notably at the beginning and the end of His public career—He uses it directly, and expresses, sometimes the truths of His gospel, sometimes the aspirations of His soul, sometimes His premonitions of the fate of Jerusalem, almost in its very words. The Sermon on the Mount has at least half a dozen references, direct or indirect, to the Psalter ; not only words of a more general kind, such as ' Depart from me, ye workers of iniquity' (Mt 7[23] || Lk 13[27], cf. Ps 6[9 (8)]), or the allusion to Jerusalem as the 'city of the great king' (Mt 5[35], cf. Ps 48[3 (2)]), but even such an assurance as that the heavenly Father feeds the birds (Mt 6[26], cf. Ps 147[9]) ; and some of the Beatitudes themselves are but echoes of the Psalter, e.g. 'the meek shall inherit the earth' (Mt 5[5], cf. Ps 37[11] (the land)), 'the merciful shall obtain mercy' (Mt 5[7], cf. Ps 18[26 (25)]). Occasionally a psalm is explicitly cited by Him, e.g. Ps 82[6] in Jn 10[34], and even prefaced by the words, ' Have ye never read ?' (cf. Mt 21[16. 42]), which assume a familiar knowledge of the book, or at least of these particular psalms (8. 118), on the part of His audience. But even where there is no such citation, the language is often saturated with reminiscences of the Psalter. There can be little doubt, e.g., that 'my soul is exceeding sorrowful' (Mt 26[38] || Mk 14[34]) is an echo of Ps 42[6. 12. (5. 11)]), or that ' he that eateth with me shall betray me' (Mk 14[18]) is an echo of Ps 41[10. (9)] (cf. Jn 13[18], where the treachery is expressly said to be in fulfilment of the utterance in the psalm), or that ' they shall dash to the ground thy children within thee' (Lk 19[44]) is a reminiscence of Ps 137[9]. In the words of a psalm (31[6. (5)]) Jesus commended His spirit into His Father's hands (Lk 23[46]).

3. These references are not quite exhaustive, but they are characteristic ; and they are very significant of Christ's general attitude to the Psalter. He makes its words of faith His own in the moment of His sorrow, He repeats its promises to those who are prepared to be His disciples (Lk 10[19], cf. Ps 91[13] ; Mt 5[5], cf. Ps 37[11]) ; but, with the single exception—if it be an exception—of Ps 110, to be afterwards discussed, He does not seem directly to countenance, by His own example, that Messianic interpretation of the Psalter upon which the Church has, from her earliest days, uniformly insisted. True, it is recorded that He said that ' all things must needs be fulfilled which are written in the law of Moses, and the prophets, and the psalms, concerning me' (Lk 24[44]). But within the teaching of Christ Himself there is no certain illustration of specific passages which He applied Messianically to Himself. And this omission would be very singular, if He had generally countenanced Messianic interpretation in the narrower sense in which that word has been commonly understood. He believed in His Messiahship, but He did not rest it upon the basis of individual passages. He claimed to fulfil the Law and the Prophets ; but, judging by His general practice, this appears to imply the large fulfilment of their spirit and tendency, rather than any minute and literal fulfilment of particular words. His method of dealing with the Psalms, when controversy is involved, is well illustrated by His citation of Ps 82[6] in Jn 10[34]. The Jews are incensed at what they regard as His blasphemy in calling Himself the Son of God. He appeals to the psalm, to show that men exalted to high office had been in the OT called ' gods' ; and argues that, if the title was appropriate for them, how much more for Him who had a unique commission and equipment from the Father.

4. It is instructive to turn from Christ's use of the Psalter to that of the writers and speakers in the NT ; and, in this connexion, it is important to remember that most of their citations from the Psalter are made from the LXX. Occasionally this seriously affects the argument. The author of the Ep. to the Hebrews, e.g. (1[10-12]), finds, in the great words of Ps 102[26-28 (25-27)]—' Thou, Lord, in the beginning, didst lay the foundation of the earth, and the heavens are the works of thy hands'—an allusion to Christ. In the LXX it is ' the Lord ' who is said to be everlasting, and to the author of the Epistle the Lord is Christ. But in the Hebrew psalm the address is to Jehovah, a title which no Hebrew could possibly have applied to the Messiah. Here is a case—and there are others—where the argument holds only on the basis of the Greek translation ; it would be irrelevant and inapplicable on the basis of the original Hebrew (cf. Eph 4[8], Ps 68[19. (18)]).

Again, with regard to the psalms customarily called Messianic, it has to be remembered that the songs of the Psalter have, generally speaking, a historical background. They spring, not perhaps always, but undoubtedly often, out of a definite historical situation ; that situation, or some aspect of it, is their theme. In many psalms this is obvious (cf. 44. 83. 137) ; and the question may fairly be raised whether this is not also the case in the Messianic psalms. Doubtless time might prove that the meaning of a psalm was larger than the original intention of its composer : this is true more or less of all great literature. But to understand truly its deeper meaning, we must start from its original intention, and from the situation in view of which it was composed. While to some of the psalms whose subject is a king a Messianic interpretation has been assigned (cf. 2), in others the actual contents and implications of the psalm render that interpretation impossible. The ' anointed,' e.g. (Heb. ' his Messiah,' LXX ' Christ '), in 20[7 (6)] is almost necessarily some historical king, and the psalm appears to have been composed on the eve of a battle. If, then, in some of the psalms which deal with a ' Messiah' or ' Christ,' the reference is to a historic king of Israel or Judah, the presumption at least is raised that all the Messianic psalms may be similarly interpreted.

The tendency to find in the Psalter predictive references to Jesus must have set in very early. In Mt 13[35], e.g., the parabolic method of teaching adopted by Jesus is said to be in fulfilment of the prophecy (attributed in one MS to Isaiah), ' I will open my mouth in parables, I will utter things hidden from the foundation of the world.' In point of fact these words simply form the introduction to one of the longer historical psalms (78[2]), and in them the Psalmist simply declares his intention to draw instruction from the ancient history of Israel. There is here no conceivable allusion to the parabolic teaching of Jesus. This interpretation would hardly even have been possible but for the LXX, which happens to render the Hebrew בְּמָשָׁל by ἐν παραβολαῖς—another good illustration of the control that the LXX exercised over Messianic interpretation. This tendency to ' messianize,' wherever possible, naturally is operative also outside of the NT. There is no warrant in its pages, e.g., for referring the latter part of Ps 24 to Christ ; but the Fathers applied it to His ascension, and the Te Deum addresses Christ as the King of Glory. Sometimes psalms which are commonly regarded as Messianic contain sentiments which are un-Christian, and which therefore render the Messianic interpretation, in any sense worth defending, untenable. Some exegetes have even held that Ps 18 is Messianic, in spite of such a verse as 43 [(42)]. Ps 2, whose claims are much more generally allowed, contains sentiments (cf. v.[9]) which could not legitimately be reconciled with the spirit of Him who was the Prince of peace.

5. We shall now examine the psalms which are most commonly regarded as 'Messianic—for convenience' sake in the order in which they occur in the Psalter.

Ps 2. A study of the NT allusions to this psalm is peculiarly instructive, as, though there is a general agreement that it is Messianic, there is a considerable variety in its interpretation. One passage, indeed, does not seem even to regard the psalm as Messianic, at least in the narrower sense: in Rev 2²⁷ the promise of Ps 2⁹ that the king would 'break' (LXX and NT read ποιμανεῖ(ς), 'shepherd,' 'rule,' pointing תִּרְעֵם instead of תְּרֹעֵם) the nations with a rod of iron, as the vessels of the potter are broken, is applied, in the message addressed to Thyatira, to the Christian who overcomes and keeps the works of Christ to the end.

This application of the passage shows that, even in very early times, the Messianic interpretation of such psalms was felt to be not the only possible one. It is just possible, however, that the words of the psalm were chosen simply because they were an apposite description of triumph. This becomes the more probable when we remember that elsewhere in this same book—Rev 12⁵ 19¹⁵—the passage is applied Messianically.

The first two verses of the psalm—'Why do the heathen rage?' etc.—are applied in Ac 4²⁵ᶠ· to the combination of Herod, Pilate, the Romans, and the Jews, against 'thy holy servant Jesus,' who is clearly therefore regarded as the king celebrated in the psalm. The verse which the NT most frequently lays under contribution is v.⁷ 'Thou art my son, this day have I begotten thee.' This verse, or the first part of it, underlies Nathanael's confession (Jn 1⁴⁹), Peter's confession (Mt 16¹⁶), the high priest's question (Mt 26⁶³), and the voice which is said to have been heard on the occasion of the Baptism (Mt 3¹⁷ = Mk 1¹¹ = Lk 3²²) and the Transfiguration (Mt 17⁵ = Mk 9⁷ = Lk 9³⁵). According to the Codex Bezæ in Mt 3¹⁷, the words heard on the occasion of the baptism were, 'Thou art my son, this day have I begotten thee.' This attests the belief in some quarters that the Divine sonship of Jesus, which the psalm is supposed to foreshadow, dated from the day of His baptism. But in Ac 13³³ St. Paul regards the Psalmist's utterance as fulfilled not in the baptism, but in the resurrection of Jesus; and this view appears to underlie the Apostle's statement in Ro 1⁴ that it was by the resurrection that Jesus was declared to be the Son of God with power. The verse is further applied in He 1⁵ (cf. 5⁵) as a proof of the superiority of Jesus to the angels. In the Hebrew OT, however, the term literally translated 'sons of God' is applied to supernatural beings whether they be regarded as gods or angels; cf. Job 1⁶ 2¹, where the LXX renders by οἱ ἄγγελοι τοῦ θεοῦ. As, however, there are passages in which even the LXX speaks of these beings as 'sons of God' (Ps 29¹ 89⁶), we must assume, if the writer has not forgotten them, that he is laying particular stress on the latter half of the verse, 'this day have I begotten thee.' According to the Epistle, however, Jesus took part in the Creation, and was pre-existent before all eternity (1²·¹⁰); consequently we must suppose that the 'begetting to-day' refers to His eternal generation. See art. BEGETTING.

Here, then, are three different interpretations of the verse within the NT: the Divine sonship of the Messiah is variously connected with His baptism, His resurrection, or His eternal generation. These interesting fluctuations of opinion are possible only because the historical interpretation of the psalm is ignored. The phrase 'son of God' did not necessarily imply Divinity in the technical sense, for we find it applied even to the people (Ex 4²²), and we have already seen how Jesus argues (Jn 10³⁴) from the acknowledged application of the term to human beings. In truth, the psalm seems to be addressed to some actual king of Judah, and to express the assurance of his victory and dominion, possibly on the occasion of his coronation. The day on which he was begotten as a son of God is the day on which he was installed in his regal dignity as the representative of Jehovah, the King and Father of His people. It is, we must admit, by no means impossible, especially when we consider the soaring language of the psalm, that its subject is not any reigning king, but some king yet to be; this would be the case if the psalm belongs, as it may, to the post-exilic period, when the monarchy was no more. But in neither case can it be strictly regarded as referring to Jesus, partly because the establishment of the king upon the holy hill of Zion would have no relevance in His case; partly because the conception of His function as dashing His enemies in pieces is un-Christian. Besides, as we have seen, the NT itself is not agreed as to the precise incident which the psalm is supposed to prefigure. But its solemn and emphatic predication of the Divine sonship of the king, possibly also its outlook upon a world-wide dominion, made it natural, and almost inevitable, under the conditions of early Christian interpretation, that it should be regarded as, in some sense, a prediction of Jesus.

Ps 8. It is interesting to compare the use made of this psalm by Jesus with that made elsewhere in the NT. V.3⁽²⁾ 'Out of the mouth of babes and sucklings,' etc., is quoted by Him against the chief priests (Mt 21¹⁶), who murmur when they hear the children cry 'Hosanna.' The NT follows the LXX, which reads 'praise' instead of the Hebrew 'strength,' 'bulwark'; but the *essential* meaning of the psalm is finely brought out by the citation—the power, on the one hand, or the insight, on the other, of the children (cf. for a very similar thought, Mt 11²⁵). In He 2⁶⁻⁸, however (cf. 1 Co 15²⁷ᶠ·), 'Thou madest him a little (or 'for a little while') lower than the angels,'—vv.⁵·⁶ of the psalm are interpreted as referring to Jesus, because the supremacy which, in the psalm, is asserted of the 'son of man' is not, as a matter of fact, true of the human race, but it is true of Jesus. This is a noble application of the passage, full of poetic and spiritual insight; but it does not justify us in supposing that the psalm was, in its original intention, Messianic. The Psalmist is undoubtedly thinking of the human race, he marvels at the love of the great God towards His apparently insignificant creature in making him lord of all. 'Thou hast put *all* things under his feet.' To the Psalmist this supremacy is a fact: he is content with man as he finds him, and he is not thinking of One in whom this lordship would be more perfectly realized.

Ps 16. In Ac 2²⁵⁻²⁸ (cf. 13³⁵⁻³⁷) St. Peter quotes four verses of the psalm (⁸⁻¹¹) in confirmation of the resurrection of Christ. The crucial verse is ²⁷ 'Thou wilt not leave my soul unto Hades, neither wilt thou give thy holy one to see corruption.' It is not quite certain whether the psalm is individual or collective. If it be collective, this verse implies no more than an assured faith in the future of Israel; if, however, it be individual, the speaker is probably expressing his own faith in immortality, though a more meagre meaning has been put upon the words, as if he were simply expressing his confidence in his recovery from a severe illness, or perhaps in his immunity from the sudden death which overtakes the wicked. In any case 'thy holy one'—an unfortunate translation—is undoubtedly the speaker himself. He is Jehovah's ḥāsîd, that is, a bond of love subsists between him and his God; and, in virtue of this bond, he is sure that Sheol cannot be his ultimate fate,—he will overleap it, and be received into glory (Ps 73²⁴). The last word of 16¹⁰ שַׁחַת, which means 'pit,' was, however, unfortunately rendered by LXX διαφθορά, 'corruption'; and part of St. Peter's argument, as of St. Paul's in Ac 13³⁵⁻³⁷, depends upon the mistranslation. The argument is that, as the Psalmist himself 'saw corruption' (Ac 13³⁶), he was really speaking, not of himself, but, prophetically, of Jesus, who saw no corruption. The psalm is therefore regarded as a prophecy of the resurrection of Christ, though it is, in reality, only a devout believer's confession of faith in his own immortality. But it is only fair to notice that, while the form of the argument in Acts is Jewish, and rests, in part, upon a mistranslation, in substance the argument is sound. What the psalm essentially asserts is, that where a bond of love subsists between God and a man, death has no power to destroy the man —*a fortiori* in the case of *the* Man. 'It was not possible that *He* should be conquered by *him*' (Ac 2²⁴)—such a one as Jesus by such an antagonist as death.

Ps 22. Nothing is more natural than that the early Christians should have interpreted this psalm Messianically, or that that interpretation should have persisted throughout the whol history of the Christian Church. It is not only that echoes of it are heard in the Passion story of the Gospels,—in the parting of His garments and the casting of the lot for His raiment (Mt 27³⁵=Mk 15²⁴=Lk 23³⁴, Ps 22¹⁹ (¹⁸)), the shaking of the heads of the passers-by (Mt 27³⁹=Mk 15²⁹=Lk 23³⁵, Ps 22⁸ (⁷)), the mocking cry, 'He trusted in God, let him deliver him' (Mt 27⁴³, Ps 22⁹ (⁸)),—but Jesus Himself upon the cross used at least the opening words of the psalm (Mt 27⁴⁶=Mk 15³⁴), and the parting of His garments is expressly said in Jn 19²⁴ to have taken place that the scripture might be fulfilled. It must be admitted that there is often a very startling similarity between the details of the psalm and the narrative of the Gospels. Still, many of those details are not strictly applicable to the crucifixion. Alike in the sufferings, in the triumphant issue from them, and in the contemplated conversion of the world which is to be produced by that triumph (v. 28 (27)), this psalm very powerfully recalls the Suffering Servant of Deutero-Isaiah ; and the theme of both is doubtless the same, that is, the people, or at least the pious kernel of Israel. More important, however, than the similarity of detail just alluded to, striking as that is, is the large and profound insight of the psalm. It is all aglow with the consciousness that suffering means, in the end, not defeat, but victory, and that the Suffering Servant, so far from being crushed, will one day win the whole world to Himself. These truths, of course, find their highest and truest exemplification in Jesus

Ps 34²¹ (²⁰). According to Jn 19³⁶ the legs of Jesus were not broken, in order that the scripture might be fulfilled, 'A bone of him shall not be broken.' In the psalm the verse is intended to express the general care which Jehovah exercises over the righteous, and therefore it could hardly be regarded as an apt citation in connexion with the crucifixion of Jesus ; but more probably it is intended to be, primarily, a reminiscence of Ex 12⁴⁶, Nu 9¹², which prescribe that the bones of the Paschal lamb shall not be broken. In that case the quotation would convey to a Jewish ear the subtle reminder that Jesus was the true Paschal lamb.

Ps 40. In He 10⁵⁻⁷ part of this psalm (vv. 7-9 (6-8)) is quoted, and interpreted as a prayer of Christ on coming into the world ; and here, again, a large part of the argument turns upon the faulty text of the LXX. The author is arguing that the continual sacrifices of the OT dispensation have been for ever abolished by the one sacrifice of Christ. In *the body* which God prepared for Him, He perfectly fulfilled the Divine will by the sacrifice of Himself. But the words 'a body didst thou prepare for me,' which the author adopts from the LXX, do not represent the Heb. of 40⁷ (⁶), which reads, '*ears* hast thou digged for me.' Fortunately the origin of the mistake is not far to seek. The word for 'ears' is ΩΤΙΑ, and for 'body' ΣΩΜΑ. The Σ

at the end of ΗΘΕΛΗΣΑΣ was apparently duplicated, and then the following ΩΤΙΑ was easily transformed into ΩΜΑ ; so that out of an originally correct translation, 'ears,' a new word arose, which unhappily lent itself to a dogmatic interpretation almost the opposite of that intended by the Psalmist. His point is that God demands not sacrifice but obedience—the ready ear to hear ; the point in the Epistle is, not the ever-recurring sacrifice, but the one sacrifice of Christ's body. As, however, the ethical worth, in one of its aspects, of Christ's sacrifice was the perfect obedience which it illustrated, we may say that here, as in the case of Ps 16, the conclusion is essentially sound, though the argument is fallacious, at least in so far as it rests upon a mistranslation. Historically considered, the psalm appears to be a prayer expressing the mingled feelings of the people after their return from exile. It is one of the three great psalms (cf. 50. 51) which emphatically assert the superiority of obedience and contrition over sacrifice.

Ps 41¹⁰ (⁹). In the Gospel of John, as in the Epistle to the Hebrews, there is a strong tendency towards the Messianic interpretation of passages in which, to say the least, that interpretation is not necessary. According to Jn 13¹⁸ the treachery of Judas is said to have taken place in accordance with the scripture, which must be fulfilled, 'He that eateth my bread lifted up his heel against me.' In other words, Ps 41¹⁰ (⁹) is supposed to have Christ for its theme. That this is impossible, however, is clearly shown by the very verse of the psalm which follows the quotation, 'Thou, Jehovah, have mercy upon me, and raise me up, that I may requite them.' It is much more probable that Jesus simply used the words which St. Mark records of Him,— words, no doubt, suggested by the psalm, 'One of you shall betray me, even he that eateth with me.' He may have cited the words of the psalm as apposite rather than prophetic.

Ps 45. For long Ps 45 has enjoyed among Christian expositors the reputation of celebrating the love of Christ for His Church. But a glance at the psalm is enough to show that it, like others, has its roots in history ; the pointed and definite reference to 'the daughter of Tyre' renders any other interpretation extremely improbable. It is apparently a song in celebration of the marriage of some king of Israel or Judah with a foreign princess. Vv. 7f. (6f.)—'Thy throne, O God, is for ever and ever,' etc.—are cited in He 1⁸f. and interpreted as referring to the Son. Considering that shortly before, v.², and immediately after, v.¹⁰, the author of the Epistle touches upon the pre-existence of Christ, the direct naming of the royal subject of the psalm as 'God' would be peculiarly welcome. With what admirable cogency could the psalm thus be interpreted of Christ, and how little could it be fairly referred to any one else ! For the passages which some have adduced to prove that אלהים could stand for 'judges' (cf. Ex 22⁷f.)—though they do not really prove as much—would in any case be insufficient to show that an ordinary human king could be addressed in the word *Elohim* ; the king of the psalm must therefore be Divine. It has been conjectured, however, with great acuteness and probability, that instead of אלהים 'God,' the original reading was יהיה 'shall be' (יהיה). This may have been carelessly read as יהוה, and then altered by the Elohistic redactors of Pss 42-83 to אלהים. In that case the important dogmatic text, 'Thy throne, *O God*, is for ever and ever,' becomes the innocent assertion that 'thy throne *shall be* for ever and ever,' and with the change in the text, the Messianic interpretation vanishes, especially as the next verse speaks of his companions. Of a human king this is intelligible, but who would the companions of the Messiah be?

Ps 69. It might seem surprising that a psalm marked by so vindictive a spirit as Ps 69 should ever have been interpreted Messianically, but several of its verses are even in the NT brought into relation with Christ. In his usual manner St. John (19[28-30]) sees in the offering of vinegar to Jesus on the cross a fulfilment of scripture, that is, of Ps 69[22 (21)] (cf. Mk 15[36], Lk 23[36]), while St. Matthew (27[34. 48]), who parallels the language of the psalm still more closely by speaking of the gall, does not explicitly connect the incident with the psalm, though doubtless it was in his mind. The zeal with which Jesus drove the money-changers out of the Temple, is said in Jn 2[17] to have reminded the disciples of v.[10 (9)] of the psalm ; and Ro 15[3], where the second half of this verse is quoted, shows that St. Paul interpreted the psalm Messianically (but cf. Ro 11[9f.] with Ps 69[23f. (22f.)]). In Ac 1[20], Ps 69[26 (25)] and 109[8] are regarded as inspired predictions of the fate of Judas (Ac 1[16]). Two difficulties, however, stand in the way of interpreting this psalm Messianically : (1) It plainly reflects a contemporary historical situation ; it is the product of a time when Judah is in misery and her cities are in ruins (69[36 (35)]); and (2) its fierce vindictive tone (cf. v.[24]) is altogether unlike the spirit of Him who said, 'Father, forgive them.' The similarity of incidents in the life of Jesus to certain features of the psalm may have led to its Messianic application ; but it has nothing like the claims to such a distinction which Ps 22 has.

Ps 72. The NT lends hardly any support to the Messianic interpretation of this psalm, though this interpretation has found much favour with Christian expositors. The description of the gifts of gold that were brought to the infant Jesus (Mt 2[11]) perhaps recalls, in part, the language of the psalm, cf. vv.[10f. 15] ; but in spite of the extravagant language of vv.[8-11] (which are possibly, as some hold, a later insertion, added after the psalm began to be interpreted Messianically), it was, in all probability, originally only a prayer for some historic king. V.[15], in which prayer is to be continually offered for the royal subject of the psalm, shows that the Messianic interpretation is hardly admissible.

Ps 110. No psalm is so frequently laid under contribution in the NT as Ps 110. V.[1], *e.g.*, is referred to, directly or allusively, in Mt 22[44] 26[64], Mk 12[36] 14[62] 16[19], Lk 20[42f.] 22[69], Ac 2[34f.] 5[31] 7[55f.], Ro 8[34], 1 Co 15[25], Eph 1[20], Col 3[1], 1 P 3[22], He 1[3. 13] 8[1] 10[12f.] 12[2] ; and v.[4] in He 5[6] 6[20] 7[11. 17. 21] etc. The first verse is interpreted of Jesus, who, as the Messiah, is bidden by the Lord (*Jehovah* in the Hebrew) to sit at His right hand till He has vanquished all His enemies ; while, according to the Ep. to the Heb., He is also the priest for ever after the order of Melchizedek. Other priesthoods were transitory, His is eternal and inalienable (7[16. 24]). The use of the psalm made by Christ, together with the very deliberate, if not solemn words in which He introduces the citation, certainly raise a strong presumption that He regarded the psalm as Messianic. But in this connexion two things have to be remembered : (1) that this allusion springs from an atmosphere of controversy, and (2) that the *essential* meaning of Christ is independent of the Messianic view of the psalm. (1) As against the Pharisees, the citation had a peculiar relevance and propriety. Christ desires them to feel that they have not carefully considered the consequences of their views regarding the Messiah. (2) The real intention of Christ is to suggest the indefeasible superiority of the spiritual to the material. Starting from the conception of sonship, the Pharisees ended in thoughts of a material and political kingdom like David's, whereas, had they considered the sense in which the Messiah was David's Lord, they would have found themselves in a spiritual sphere.

It is certainly very difficult to resist the impression that the psalm is Maccabæan. Without laying too much stress upon the singular fact that the initial letters of each verse from [1b] to [4], שמעי, spell the word Simon, the historical implications of the psalm point very powerfully to the Maccabæan period. It implies that the king celebrated also bore the title of priest, and not till that period could this have been appropriately said of any ruler. The language of the opening verse, which, in the Hebrew, runs 'Oracle of Jehovah to my lord,' most naturally suggests that the psalm is composed by a poet in honour of his king, whom he calls 'my lord,' and for whom he foretells victory. But the vigorous language of v.[6] hardly seems compatible with the idea that its theme is Christ.

The use made of the psalm by St. Peter in Ac 2[34f.] is thoroughly analogous to his use of Ps 16. Immediately after arguing that Ps 16, with its seeming prophecy of the resurrection, could not refer to David because he ' both died and was buried,' the Apostle goes on to argue that Ps 110 must also be referred to some other than David, because ' he did not ascend into the heavens.' But in truth the sitting at the right hand of God is simply a pictorial way of suggesting an idea similar to that of Ps 2[7], where a historical king is called the son of God. The grandeur of the phrase ' sitting at the right hand of God,' the contemplated completeness of the king's victory, the union in his person of the offices of priest and king, and the mysteriousness that gathered round the person and the priesthood of Melchizedek, all combined to make the Messianic interpretation easy and all but inevitable.

Ps 118. With this psalm as with Ps 8, Jesus assumed a certain familiarity on the part of His audience (Mt 21[42] ' Did ye never read ? '). His use of it strongly suggests, though perhaps in truth compels, the belief that He regarded it as Messianic. With the words, ' Blessed is he that cometh in the name of the Lord ' (Ps 118[26]), He was acclaimed by the multitudes as He entered Jerusalem (Mt 21[9. 15] = Mk 11[9f.] = Lk 19[38] = Jn 12[13]), and in the same words He ends His lament over Jerusalem (Mt 23[39]). The saying that ' the stone which the builders rejected is become the head of the corner ' (Ps 118[22]), is also understood to find its fulfilment in Him (Mt 21[42] = Mk 12[10f.] = Lk 20[17] ; cf. Ac 4[11], 1 P 2[4. 7]). In the psalm, the reference appears to be to Israel, despised yet victorious ; but as the career of Jesus is the most perfect illustration of the principle pictorially expressed in the saying, the citation is thoroughly in keeping with the spirit of the psalm, though it cannot be regarded as a prediction. Similarly, ' Blessed is he that cometh in the name of the Lord,' is more strikingly appropriate to Jesus than even to the original subject of the psalm.

6. In conclusion, it may be said that the exegetical methods and the Messianic outlook of the early Church rendered it very natural that they should find in the Psalter, as in other parts of the OT, predictions of incidents in the life of Christ, or that psalms descriptive, on the one hand, of malignant persecution and agonized suffering, or embodying, on the other hand, a large outlook upon a universal dominion, should be claimed for Him. Usually there is an appropriateness, sometimes very striking, in the application to Him of passages in the Psalter which, for various reasons, can seldom, if ever, be with any plausibility regarded as predictions of Him. Often, as we have seen, a psalm can be regarded as Messianic only by ignoring its historical background (Ps 69), or by selecting and emphasizing certain verses while ignoring others that suggest an inadequate or unworthy view of the Messiah (Ps 2). There are undoubtedly in the Psalter many true foreshadowings of Christ ; but, speaking broadly, it is in its general spirit rather than in its isolated expressions that we may find Him. Of course, it has been commonly urged that a psalm may be typically Messianic though it is not prophetic ; but it may be questioned whether it is worth while to interpret literature in this fashion. Christ's own use of the Psalter is strikingly different from the occasional use of it, *e.g.*, in the Book of the Acts. He did not commend His Messiahship after the fashion in which His Apostles sometimes do. Profound as is the insight with which they often cite and apply the Psalter, very much more than the Master do the disciples emphasize the letter, sometimes even the letter of an inadequate translation. From His use of it we learn to find in the Psalter a support of the devotional life rather than a mainstay of Messianic argument.

LITERATURE.—Binnie, *The Psalms, their History, Teaching, and Use*, pp. 155–217 ; Alexander, *Witness of the Psalms to Christ and Christianity* (*BL*, 1876) ; Jennings and Lowe, *The Psalms, with Introductions and Critical Notes*, vol. i. ch. iv. ; Kirkpatrick, *The Psalms* (Cambridge Bible), Introduction, ch. viii. ; Cheyne, *The Christian Use of the Psalms* ; A. B. Davidson, *Biblical and Literary Essays*, pp. 139–193 ; Briggs, 'The Psalms,' 2 vols. (*ICC*) 1906–7, esp. Introd. p. ci ff. Allusions to the Psalter in NT are collected in Alexander's *Witness of the Psalms*, pp. 257–264 ; but they can be most profitably studied in Toy, *Quotations in the NT* ; Hühn, *Die messianischen Weissagungen*, 2 Theil, 'Die Alttestamentlichen Citate und Reminiscenzen im NT ; Dittmar, *Vetus Testamentum in Novo.*

JOHN E. M'FADYEN.

PUBLICAN (Gr. τελώνης).—The Roman practice of selling to the highest bidder the task of collecting the taxes and dues of a province or district for a definite period is well known. The persons thus engaged were called *publicani*, and usually belonged to the wealthy equestrian order. They, in their turn, employed local agents to get in the revenues, who were also called *publicani*. This lower class are probably the men referred to in the Gospels, wherever they belong to Judæa (or Samaria), except possibly in the case of Zacchæus, who was ἀρχιτελώνης of Jericho (Lk 19[2]), and may have farmed the revenues of that important commercial centre on his own account (but see Ramsay as cited below).

In Galilee the publicans had to collect, not for the Imperial treasury (as in Judæa), but for Herod Antipas the tetrarch. Such an official was St. Matthew (Levi), who was called to be an Apostle from the place of toll (τελώνιον) on the shores of the Lake of Galilee at Capernaum (Mt 9[9], Mk 2[14], Lk 5[27]). And in his house afterwards our Lord met many other publicans of the tetrarchy at a great entertainment.

Whether in the service of the hated Roman Emperor or of Herod Antipas, who was in complete subservience to him, the tax-gatherer was most unpopular with the Jews ; for, apart from the obvious liability of the method to abuse, the mere fact of the money being thus raised for an alien power was detestable in their eyes. And no doubt the publicans were often drawn from the lowest ranks in consequence. Hence common talk associated them not only with the Gentiles (Mt 18[17]), but with harlots (Mt 21[31. 22]) and sinners in general (Mt 9[10. 11] 11[19], Mk 2[15. 16], Lk 5[30] 7[34] 15[1]).

John the Baptist's preaching attracted many publicans to him, and when they inquired in what they must mend their ways after being baptized by him, his answer indicated that extortion was their besetting danger, as we should expect (Lk 3[12. 13]).

The remarkable effect that our Lord's ministry also had upon these men, as in the case of St. Matthew and Zacchæus (cf. Lk 15[1]), is not to be held as implying that He laid Himself out more for them than for other sinners who realized their need of Him ; nor are we to infer that, in contrasting them with the Pharisees and scribes, as in the well-known parable (Lk 18[10ff.]), He intended to clear their character altogether from current prejudices and aspersions. Extortion and oppression were as abhorrent to Him in the one class as formalism and hypocrisy were in the other. Both stood equally in need of His salvation (Lk 19[10]), but without a consciousness of the need on their part His salvation could not take effect.

LITERATURE. — Schürer, *GJV*[3] i. 474 ff. ; Edersheim, *LT* i. 514 ff. ; Ramsay, 'The *telonai* in the Gospels' in Hastings' *DB*, Ext. Vol. p. 394[b] ff. ; art. 'Publican' in *DB* and in the *JE*.
C. L. FELTOE.

PUBLISHING (κηρύσσω, fr. κήρυξ, 'a herald').— It is a principle in the Divine economy for God to withdraw Himself from the perception of man, except in so far as the latter is able to receive a Divine revelation to his profit (Is 45[15] 53[1], Mt 7[6]). It is not that God is unwilling to manifest Himself, but that the condemnation for rejecting the light is so great, that He is constantly withdrawing and veiling Himself from men's gaze (Jn 15[22]). Thus it is that He is so frequently represented as shrouded in cloud (Ex 16[10], Lv 16[2], Nu 11[25]). Thus Christ's Divine glory at the Transfiguration was veiled in a bright cloud (Mt 17[5], Mk 9[7], Lk 9[34]) ; thus, too, He will come at the Last Day in a cloud (Lk 21[27]). It is one of the paradoxes with which we are familiar in the Gospels, that manifestation should be accompanied by concealment, and revelation connected with mystery. Just as our eyes cannot see where all is dark, nor yet again in a blaze of brightest light, but as a blending of the two is necessary for physical vision, so is the law in the spiritual life. Complete darkness would leave us hopeless ; a blaze of Divine glory would blind our spiritual faculties.

Christ's childhood was wrapped in concealment. Only one incident is recorded about that period in the Gospels, and that one shows that His mother did not then understand Him (Lk 2[48ff.]). Christ was always veiling Himself throughout His ministry. He did not publish abroad the truths of His Kingdom indiscriminately. His use of parables was to avoid the casting of pearls before swine. His sayings were to a great extent allegorical. Such expressions as 'leaven' for 'doctrine' (Mt 16[6. 11f.] ||), 'sleep' for 'death' (Mt 9[24] || Jn 11[11]), cutting off the right hand (Mt 5[30] 18[8] ||), the dead burying their dead (Mt 8[22] ||), the buying of swords (Lk 22[36]), the undying worm (Mk 9[44. 46. 48]), were not, of course, intended to be understood literally. All this seems to be due to His wish to spare the greater condemnation which would follow upon the greater revelation. Persons and cities who received the latter without profiting by it are specially denounced (Mt 11[23], Lk 10[15]). In the explanation of the parable of the Sower a special condition of fertility was the right understanding. 'He that hath ears to hear, let him hear' (Mt 13[9]). It was a spiritual and not an intellectual perception that was required, one that depended on the state of the heart and not on the shrewdness of the mind (Mt 11[25], Lk 10[21]). Christ taught people as they were able to hear (Mk 4[33], cf. Jn 16[12]). He did not force new wine into old bottles. He explained the meaning of His parables to His disciples in private (Mk 4[34]). Towards the end of His ministry He dispensed with parables in speaking to them (Jn 16[25. 29]). The time for concealment was past.

The same principle is observable with regard to Christ's miracles. They were worked only on those who had faith (Mk 9[23]). In Capernaum He did not do many mighty works, because of their unbelief. The crowd of mourners are excluded at Jairus' house because they laughed Him to scorn (Mk 5[40] ||). The post-Resurrection appearances were not given indiscriminately, but to witnesses chosen before, who had shared the intimacy of temptation and suffering. Thus it was that after the performance of so many of our Lord's miracles the recipients of healing grace were told not to publish the news abroad. It would only provoke calumny or misrepresentation. The Pharisees were not influenced favourably by the miracles which they saw (Mt 12¹⁴, Mk 3⁵ᶠ·, Jn 5¹⁸ 10³⁹ 11⁴⁷, Lk 6¹¹) or heard of. It was only increasing their condemnation to publish the accounts abroad.

But it was especially in the healing of demoniacs that the principle received illustration (Mt 9³⁴ 12²⁴). The evil spirits are anxious to publish Christ's Divinity. They are not allowed to do so. There was evidently something repulsive to Christ in the knowledge possessed by the demons unaccompanied by love and reverence (Ja 2¹⁹). Human beings, having this knowledge without corresponding affection, would become like the demons, with hardened hearts. It was the sin against the Holy Ghost which is so severely denounced (Mt 12³¹). This was the reason for Christ's manifestation of Himself to His disciples and not to the world (Jn 14²²). They had shown the requisite spirit of submission to the Cross. They had ears to hear.

We see, then, that it was not Christ's object to reveal Himself to every one indiscriminately, but to those only who had a desire for that knowledge, together with love and reverence. The training of such recipients was gentle and gradual. Manifestation to the hardened brought with it only condemnation. Concealment implied mercy. As man had deliberately put forth his hand and tasted of the forbidden tree, so must he show by his deliberate action that he wished to taste of the tree of life, the true knowledge of God and of His Son revealed in the Incarnation (Jn 17³).

But while we observe in our Lord's ministry this principle of reserve with regard both to the mysteries of the Kingdom and the truth about His own Person, He never concealed, or wished His disciples to conceal, the saving message of the gospel. The gospel was to be ' published among all nations' (Mk 13¹⁰, RV 'preached'). The vb. κηρύσσω, which is used to denote a publication such as Jesus forbade of His miraculous cures (Mk 1⁴⁵ 7³⁶), is the same word as is constantly employed with reference to His own proclamation of the gospel (Mt 4²³ etc.) and His instruction to His disciples to proclaim it (Mt 10⁷, Mk 3¹⁴, Lk 9² etc.). When κηρύσσω is used, however, in this specific sense, it is almost invariably rendered 'preach' in EV. In Mk 13¹⁰, as noted above, RV has substituted 'preach' for 'publish' of AV. See, further, PREACHING, REVELATION.

LITERATURE.—Isaac Williams, *The Study of the Gospels*; cf. also, on the confession of Christ's claims by demoniacs, J. Weiss, *Das älteste Evangelium*; and artt. by W. Wrede ('Zur Messiaserkenntnis der Dämonen'), and B. W. Bacon ('The Markan Theory of Demonic Recognition of the Christ') in *ZNTW*, 1904, p. 169 ff., and 1905, p. 153 ff.

C. H. PRICHARD and J. C. LAMBERT.

PUNISHMENT.—1. God's punishment of sin.— For the sufferings of Christ for sin, see ATONEMENT: the present article is concerned only with the punishment of men. The Gospel teaching on this important subject can be briefly summarized in a few paragraphs :

(*a*) *The fact of punishment.*—This fact is involved in certain explicit statements of our Lord Himself (Mt 13⁴¹· ⁴² 25⁴⁶, Jn 15²· ⁶), and clearly suggested in more than one of His parables (Mk 12⁹, Mt 13³⁰ 22¹³· ¹⁴, Lk 13⁹· ²²ᶠᶠ·). It is further implied both in the recognition of God's wrath upon men (Jn 3³⁶) and of a consequent difference in their destinies (Mt 13⁴¹· ⁴³ 25⁴⁶, Jn 5²⁹), and in frequent references to Gehenna (Mt 5²⁹ 10²⁸, Mk 9⁴³⁻⁴⁸, Lk 12⁵) or to the place of outer darkness (Mt 8¹² 22¹³ 25³⁰). So serious may this punishment be, that death would be a preferable alternative (Mk 9⁴²); and, unrestricted to individual transgressors, it may fall also both upon cities (Mt 10¹⁵ 11²¹ 23³⁸) and

upon nations (Mt 21⁴³· ⁴⁴ 23³⁵· ³⁸). The principle of punishment was illustrated in our Lord's action (Mk 11¹²ᶠᶠ· ¹⁵ᶠᶠ· ||) as well as inculcated in His words.

(*b*) *The expression of punishment.*—God's punishment of men for sin, the fact of which is thus recognized by the Gospels, finds expression in different ways. (*a*) Our Lord seems to hint that even in the conditions of a man's present life the penalty of sin may sometimes be perceived. At least it would appear that in certain cases He allows that a connexion exists between sin and physical sickness (Mk 2¹⁰· ¹¹ || Jn 5¹⁴). Nowhere, however, does He approve the view, which emerges in the OT, that a similar explanation accounts for the presence in the world of human sorrow. (On the contrary, sorrow even becomes, in His esteem, a ground for rejoicing [Mt 5⁴· ¹⁰⁻¹²]). Apart from these vague suggestions of a physical penalty, the Gospels recognize both a present and a future punishment of sin. (*β*) There is a sense in which a man's judgment, and hence his punishment, is immediate. And not only is this true in that his sin involves remorse (Mt 26⁷⁵ 27⁴· ⁵, Mk 6¹⁶), but also because his very attitude to Christ automatically enriches his personality or issues in its impoverishment (Jn 3¹⁸· ¹⁹ 9¹· ¹¹· ¹², Mt 25²⁸· ²⁹, cf. Lk 2³⁴). (*γ*) There is a second sense in which a man's judgment lies in the future (Mt 13⁴¹⁻⁴³ 25³¹ᶠᶠ· and frequently). A discussion of the punishment resulting from that judgment does not fall within the scope of the present article, and the reader is therefore referred to the separate study on ETERNAL PUNISHMENT. Here it will suffice to observe that, whatever be its accidents, the essence of punishment will consist in banishment from the presence of Christ (Mt 7²³ 25⁴¹); and that it will be marked by varying degrees of severity (Mk 12⁴⁰, Mt 10¹⁵ 11²²· ²⁴, Lk 12⁴⁸), each of us by his own use of opportunity providing his own criterion (Mt 5⁷ 7¹· ² 10³³, Mk 4²⁴).

(*c*) *The aim of punishment.*—Punishment may be conceived as either disciplinary or retributive in its purpose. Our Lord Himself, in all probability with deliberate intent, made no unmistakable pronouncement on the meaning of the doom of the rejected. All that we can do, therefore, is to deduce from His words certain general considerations bearing more or less closely on the end that punishment has in view. (*a*) On the one hand, the teaching of the Gospels confirms the verdict of our own moral sense, that so long as there is any hope of a sinner's recovery, the reformatory element must at least be prominent in the transaction. Inasmuch as judgment is self-acting (Jn 3¹⁹ 12³¹), it inevitably accompanies God's gift of His Son (Jn 3¹⁸; see Westcott, *in loc.*); yet we are specifically taught that not judgment but salvation is God's deepest thought for mankind (Jn 3¹⁷; so Mt 18¹⁴, Jn 6³⁹ 8¹¹, Lk 15, cf. also Jn 5²⁴). It is in keeping with this that of the two words denoting 'punishment,' κόλασις and τιμωρία, distinguished in classical Greek as respectively remedial and penal in their purpose (so Plato; see Trench, *Syn.* § vii.), it is the former that is preserved in the report of Christ's teaching (Mt 25⁴⁶). That the classical shade of meaning is retained in the NT is signified by the suggestive use of κολάζεσθαι in 2 P 2⁹, where the punishment precedes judgment, and therefore could scarcely yet be retributive. (*β*) On the other hand, the terms in which Christ refers to punishment (*e.g.* Mt 18³⁵, Lk 20⁴⁷ etc.) would seem to forbid us to reduce it to the mere equivalent of discipline; and He Himself, in speaking of sin that has no forgiveness (Mk 3²⁸ ||, cf. Mk 14²¹ and 1 Jn 5¹⁶), distinctly implies a punishment that is retributive in character. The proportion in which these two elements in the Divine punishment of men are combined, is beyond our knowledge. Human analogies can merely give us vague hints, every analogy being to some degree imperfect, and therefore to the same degree misleading. Instead of seeking to dogmatize on what does not at present fall within the sphere of our understanding, it would seem wise to confine our conclusions to two broad principles:

(i.) The punishment of the sinner is such as Love can inflict. If God *is* Love (1 Jn 4[8. 16]), there can be no act of His which is not an expression of His nature. Sometimes Love reveals itself as tenderness. Sometimes it reveals itself as wrath (cf. the striking sequence of verses in Mt 10[28. 29] and 21[13. 14]); for if sin is more than a fiction, the measure of God's love for the sinner will determine the severity of His anger against his sin. Indeed, the surest proof of the punishment of sin is to be found in the *love* of God. It is only something less than love that would palliate evil in the life of the loved one. If, therefore, punishment is an expression of Love, it will contain the elements of discipline and retribution in such proportion as Love demands. What that proportion is we cannot say : we must be content to leave ourselves in the hands of Perfect Love.

(ii.) Hence, too, it follows that the duration of punishment will be such as Love requires. It seems reasonable to expect that as soon as a sinner becomes forgivable, the retributive aspect of punishment is at an end, and discipline alone remains ; and that when discipline has utterly failed to reclaim a man, it in its turn must give place to simple retribution. Of the precise point at which either crisis is reached we have no knowledge. In one place our Lord appears to hint that it may be beyond the grave (Mt 12[32]), but, as we have already seen, He gave no clear guidance in the matter. Again, we must be content to leave ourselves in the hands of Perfect Love. (On the nature and purpose of punishment, see Moberly's valuable chapter in *Atonement and Personality*, ch. i.)

2. Forms of human punishment.—(*a*) Among punishments mentioned as of general imposition are several which demand no detailed treatment. Such are *decapitation* (Mk 6[27], Mt 14[10]), *drowning* (Mk 9[42], Mt 18[6]), *incarceration* (Mk 6[17], Mt 5[25] 18[30], Lk 23[19]), and *hanging* (Mt 27[5]), inflicted, according to Jewish custom, only for idolatry or blasphemy, and then only after the victim had already been put to death in some other way (Edersheim, *LT* ii. 584). With these, too, may be classed the less familiar penalties of *precipitation* (attempted in the case of our Lord, Lk 4[29]) and of *mutilation* (διχοτομεῖν, Mt 24[51], Lk 12[46]). *Stoning* (Lk 20[6], Jn 8[5], cf. Mt 21[44] || and Mt 23[35] ||) was imposed for many offences, including the unchastity of a betrothed maiden, idolatry, and blasphemy. On one occasion the Jews sought to inflict it on our Lord Himself (Jn 10[31]). See art. STONING. For *excommunication*, see art. *s.v.*

(*b*) The two prominent forms of human punishment inflicted upon Jesus were those of scourging and crucifixion. *Scourging*, used among the Jews as a penalty for debt (Mt 18[34]) or for offences of a religious character (Mt 10[17] 23[34]), was also the customary precursor to Roman crucifixion. The Roman scourge was of leather thongs, weighted with bone or some form of metal. The victim's suffering was so intense that it frequently led to death before the capital sentence proper could be carried into effect. According to His own prophecy (Mk 10[34], Mt 20[19], Lk 18[33]), our Lord was subjected to this cruel instrument of torture (Mk 15[15], Mt 27[26], Jn 19[1]). It was inflicted by Pilate in the hope that it would satisfy the passion of the Jews and render the crucifixion unnecessary (Lk 23[22] ; see Westcott on Jn 19[1]). For the details of our Lord's

crucifixion (Mk 15[22] ||, cf. Gal 3[10-23]) and their significance the reader is referred to the special article under that heading. Christ foretold this form of death for other witnesses to truth (Mt 23[34], and probably Jn 21[18]) as well as for Himself (Mt 20[18] 26[2], Lk 24[7], Jn 12[32. 33]).   H. BISSEKER.

PURIFICATION (1. καθαρισμός : of washings before and after meals, Jn 2[6] ; of baptism, a symbol of moral cleansing, 3[25] ; of the Levitical purification of women after childbirth, Lk 2[22] ; of cleansing of lepers, Mk 1[44], Lk 5[14]. **2.** βαπτισμός : of cleansing of vessels, Mk 7[8]).—From the time of the Exile onwards, the interest of the Jew had largely centred around ritual observance, conditioned, to begin with, by the necessity of maintaining the separateness of the Remnant that remained. These observances, so far as they concerned purification, had two main sources of origin. Some must have dated from a prehistoric period when religion had but little to do with ethics, and concerned itself rather with maintaining the favour of a deity, thought of as arbitrary, by avoiding practices that might trench upon his holiness. Other observances, of later date, may have had their origin in sanitary requirements. The result, however, as is well known, was that Jewish life became completely fettered by these ordinances, written and oral. When Christ came proclaiming liberty to the captives, He could not avoid running counter in many respects to the regulations dealing with purification. See art. PURITY. The various ceremonies of purification referred to in the Gospels are these :

1. In case of leprosy (Mk 1[44], Lk 5[14], Mt 8[2], Lk 17[11-19]).—The uncleanness of the leper seems to have been due not to the fear of contagion, for contagious diseases were not, generally speaking, regarded as unclean, but to the repulsive appearance of this particular disease. Leprosy (wh. see) was counted to be a special scourge ; and the leper was, like the madman, supposed to be smitten of God. This distinctiveness of leprosy in the view of the priest is shown by the word used of its removal. Almost invariably its cleansing is denoted by the word καθαρίζειν. The exception to this is in the account of the healing of the Ten Lepers (Lk 17[15]), where the word ἰᾶσθαι is used ; but this exception may be accounted for on the ground that the narrative is dealing with Samaritans, who were regarded as being an alien people. The regulations for the purification of leprosy had two parts (Lv 14[1-32]). In the first ceremony, on the conclusion of which the leper was admitted to the camp, though not to his tent, two living birds were taken. One was killed over an earthenware vessel filled with 'living' (spring) water, in such manner that the blood dropped into the vessel. The other bird, along with cedar wood, scarlet, and hyssop, was then dipped into the blood-stained water, and the leper was sprinkled with it seven times. The bird was then released 'into the open field,' and was supposed to fly away with the leprosy, the blood-brotherhood between the leper and the bird being established by the immersion of the bird in the water.

The ceremony is akin to that of the laying of the sins of the people upon the head of the scapegoat, which was then sent away into the wilderness (Lv 16[21]). By a similar ceremony, an Arab widow who is about to remarry makes a bird fly away with the uncleanness of her widowhood (W. R. Smith, *RS*[2] 422, 447).

The second part of the ceremony took place eight days after the first part. Probably the object of the interval was to ensure an additional period of quarantine in which it might be seen whether the cure had been effective. If the leper were in good circumstances, he offered two he-lambs and was anointed by the priest with blood and oil. If the sufferer were poor, he could offer, in place of two lambs, one lamb and two turtle-doves, or two small pigeons. Our Lord did not interfere in any way with the offerings for purifica-tion of leprosy (Mk 1[44], Lk 5[14], Mt 8[4]).

2. In connexion with food (Mk 7[1-23], Mt 15[1-20], Jn 2[6] 3[25]).—The particular ritual connected with the ceremonial washing of hands affected Jewish life many times a day. Of the six books of the Mishna, the longest (*Tohārôth*) is devoted to the question of purification, and thirty chapters of this book deal with the cleansing of vessels. Even if the hands were already ceremonially clean, they had to be washed before a meal. A washing of the hands between the courses, as also a washing at the conclusion of the feast, was practised fre-quently; but this custom may have had its origin in obvious convenience, and not in any striving after ritual cleanliness (2 K 3[11]). In the ceremony itself, the hands were held over a basin while water was poured over them. The water was allowed to run down to the wrist (? Mk 7[3], see Swete's note). Such was the ritual in the case of an ordinary meal. But if holy or sacrificial food was to be partaken of, the hands had to be com-pletely immersed in the water. If the hands were ceremonially unclean, there had to be two wash-ings. In the first, the fingers were elevated and the water was allowed to run down to the wrist. In the second, the finger tips were depressed, so that the water might run from the wrist down-ward, and might thus carry off the water that had, on the first washing, contracted the defilement of the hands. The water to be used in ceremonial washing was kept from possible defilement by being kept in large jars (ὑδρίαι, Jn 2[6]). The vessel by which the water was drawn from these jars had to contain at least a quarter of a log, *i.e.* a measure equal to one and a half 'eggshells' (Edersheim, *LT* ii. 9 ff.).

3. Before the Passover (Jn 11[55] 18[28]).—If the Jews were so particular to ensure ceremonial purity before an ordinary meal, they insisted on absolute ritual purity before the celebration of the Passover (Lv 7[20. 21]). The reason that kept Christ's accusers from following Him into the judgment-hall (Jn 18[28]) may have been simply the fear of the defilement they would incur by entering a heathen house. But it is still more likely that they re-mained outside for fear that the judgment-hall might contain somewhere within its walls a por-tion of leaven. The exclusion of leaven from all sacrifices offered to Jehovah was a very early custom (Ex 23[18] 34[25]), and must have been due to the desire to avoid the association of any form of corruption with the Feast. This seems all the more clear, when it is noticed that the exclusion of leaven is associated with the command that no fat or flesh shall remain over till the morning. The efficacy of the sacrifice lay in the living flesh and blood of the victim; thus everything of the nature of putre-faction had to be avoided. For this reason, milk, the commonest of foods in the East, had no place in Hebrew sacrifice (W. R. Smith, *RS*[2] 220).

4. After childbirth (Lk 2[22]).—That childbirth renders a woman unclean is an almost universal belief among primitive peoples. Among some Arab tribes it was customary to build a hut out-side the camp, where the woman had to stay for a time (Hastings' *DB* iv. 828[b]; Wellhausen, *Reste*[2], 170). The Priestly Code recognized two degrees of uncleanness (Lv 12). After the birth of a boy, the mother was to be counted unclean, as in men-struation, for a week, and was to continue 'in the blood of her purifying' for 33 days longer, during which she could touch no hallowed thing nor come into the sanctuary. She was thus unclean, in greater or less degree, for 40 days. But if the child were a girl, both periods of uncleanness were doubled. At the expiry of the 40, or of the 80, days, the mother offered a lamb of the first year for a burnt-offering, and a young pigeon or a turtle-dove for a sin-offering. But if she were poor (as was Mary, Lk 2[24]), she could substitute for the lamb a young pigeon or a turtle-dove.

5. Graves as causes of defilement are referred to in Mt 23[27], Lk 11[44] (cf. TOMB).

R. BRUCE TAYLOR.

PURIM.—A feast of the Jews occurring on the 14th and 15th of the month Adar, one month before the Passover. It had only the slightest religious character, and was devoted to feasting and holiday.

The Book of Esther purports to give the origin of Purim in the feast kept by the Jews when the afflictions that threatened them through Haman were turned into joy and blessing. This explanation is now generally regarded as fanciful, in part because of the antecedent improbability of the narrative in Esther and the lack of historical evidence for its truthfulness, and in part because of the impossibility of verifying in Persian the meaning of the word *purim* (= 'lot'), upon which the con-nexion rests.

Several different theories have been held of its origin. (1) The outgrowth of the Nicanor festival kept on the 13th of Adar, to celebrate the victory over that general in B.C. 161. (2) Derived from a New Year's festival of Parthian origin. (3) A Persian spring festival. (4) Connected with the Persian *Fardigân*, festival of the dead. (5) The Greek *Pithoigia*, corresponding to the Roman *Vinalia*. (6) Others most recently (Zimmern, Jensen, Meissner, Wildeboer) derive it from a Babylonian New Year's festival, and make Mordecai the same as Marduk, and Esther = the goddess Ishtar.

The feast is not mentioned by name in the NT, but is by some supposed to be the 'feast of the Jews' of Jn 5[1]. If so, this Gospel mentions three Passovers during the ministry of Jesus (2[13] 6[4] 12[1]), and His ministry thus extends, according to Jn., over two and a half years. On the other hand, if the alter-native view is held, that 5[1] is a Passover feast, there are four mentioned, and the ministry, accord-ing to Jn., extends over three and a half years. Before either figure can be assumed as giving the correct chronology of the life of Christ, the accounts in the Fourth Gospel must be subjected to criticism in connexion with those of the Synoptics. See artt. DATES, FEASTS, MINISTRY.   O. H. GATES.

PURITY.—To form a clear conception of purity in its Christian sense is a matter of some difficulty, for two reasons. Historically, the idea has under-gone great changes, and the terms by which it has been expressed have been applied to very different qualities, which to-day we should classify as physical, ceremonial, and moral purity,—qualities which have nothing necessarily in common. On the other hand, if the idea in its highest signifi-cance be considered, it is singularly elusive, and therefore exact treatment is hardly practicable. It will be necessary to meet these two difficulties separately, and therefore to subdivide the subject.

1. In the Jewish world, wherein Christianity arose, purity occupied a commanding position. Since the return from the Exile, and especially since the reconstruction under Ezra and Nehemiah, there had been a strenuous and sustained endea-vour to secure the purity of both the national and the individual life by means of the jealous exclu-sion of all that could cause impurity. The Law laid down in detail the requirements of 'clean' and 'unclean,' alike in matters of worship, of food, and conduct, and of relations with the heathen world. Purity of descent in Israel also involved great insistence on genealogical records. And all these questions had received further elaboration at the hands of the later scribes. In this way the idea of purity had become increasingly artificial and external; till at last it became an obsession which went far to destroy the spontaneity of life, and to obscure the positive aspects of virtue and religion (cf. Ac 15[10], Col 2[20-23]). It follows that in most of the passages in the Gospels in which purity is mentioned, it is this current conception of it which is referred to ; a conception which was almost entirely negative, and was mainly ceremonial, though not without confused intermixture of elements which were strictly physical, and others which were really spiritual.

There are two groups of words by which purity is expressed, alike in the Greek and in the English NT, though these do not answer strictly each to each. In the Greek the first group consists of καθαρός, καθαρίζω, καθαρισμός (frequently) ; καθαίρω, διακαθαρίζω (twice each) ; καθαρότης, κάθαρμα, περικάθαρμα (once each) ; and ἀκάθαρτος, ἀκαθαρσία. In the English (RV) these are most often rendered by 'clean,' 'cleanse,' etc. ; but often by 'pure,' 'purify,' etc. The other group consists of ἁγνός, ἁγνίζω, ἁγνισμός, ἁγνότης, ἁγνία, which are found less frequently, and which in the EV are always rendered by 'pure,' 'purify,' etc., never by 'clean,' 'cleanse,' or the like. The failure of the EV to distinguish these terms is, however, of no great importance, inasmuch as the Greek words themselves appear to be used as completely equivalent. This appears well in He 9¹³ ἁγιάζει πρὸς . . . καθαρότητα ; in the parallel use of αἱ ἡμέραι τοῦ καθαρισμοῦ (Lk 2²²) and αἱ ἡμέραι τοῦ ἁγνισμοῦ (Ac 21²⁶) ; and in the use of καθαρισμός twice (2⁶ 3²⁵) and of ἁγνίζω once (11⁵⁵) in St. John's Gospel to stand indifferently for the customary purifying of the Jews. It is, however, worth while to notice that, with the exception of the last mentioned instance, the second group of words is never met with in the Gospels. (For use of κοινόω in the sense of making impure, see below).

The important point is to observe how Christ altered the significance of καθαρός and its cognates, correcting and deepening the idea of purity which they served to express. Often He used these terms in the senses which they currently bore. He employed them in connexion with physical disease : 'The lepers are cleansed' (Mt 11⁵, cf. Lk 17¹⁷, Mk 1⁴¹) ; and of the vine in a figure where more is symbolized by the want of physical vigour (Jn 15²). He spoke also of 'unclean spirits' when treating those 'possessed' (Mt 12⁴³, Mk 5⁸). But His characteristic habit was to look below the outward and visible evidences of purity and impurity, whether these were physical or ceremonial, to the purity or impurity of the heart. The leading instance is Mk 7¹⁴⁻²³ 'Nothing from without the man going into him can defile (δύναται κοινῶσαι) him. . . . These evil things proceed from within and defile the man.' Here the Evangelist expressly notes that the saying 'makes all foods clean.' And other passages show the same teaching if less fully expressed : e.g. the Pharisees are denounced for their hypocrisy in cleansing the outside of the cup and platter while inwardly full of extortion and excess, whereas practical love shown in alms would have made all clean to them (Mt 23²⁵· ²⁶, cf. Lk 11⁴¹) ; and they are also condemned for being 'like whited sepulchres, full of dead men's bones and all uncleanness,' which is defined as 'hypocrisy and iniquity' (Mt 23²⁷· ²⁸). So He gave His blessing to the 'pure in heart' (5⁸), setting the ideal of purity which He would have His followers share with Him. And that this is to be understood in no negative sense is made very plain by Christ's teaching elsewhere. In Jn 13¹⁻¹¹ the practice of the Lord's own humility is taught as the means of purity in His followers : in 15³ He says, 'Ye are clean because of the word that I have spoken unto you,' with which should be compared St. Peter's words, 'cleansing their hearts by faith' (Ac 15⁹) ; while in Lk 11²⁴⁻²⁶ ∥ it is expressly taught that a merely negative purity of heart, due to the extrusion or exclusion of evil, is hopeless, and 'the last state of that man becometh worse than the first.'

It is in the fullest accordance with Christ's habitual standpoint and with His teaching elsewhere that He adopted baptism, which had long been a symbolic and ceremonial rite of purification in Judaism, as a fundamental ordinance for His followers ; but it is equally in character with His mind and teaching that in the place of its old negative significance He gave it a new and positive meaning, by making it baptism into the Divine Name He had revealed, and into the practical observance of His commands, and the enduring possession of His Spirit (Mt 28¹⁹· ²⁰). The reference of Christian baptism is thus far less to the past—which it was in Jewish usage—than to the future ; to the life, i.e., to be found and shared in the 'true Israel of God.'

2. But when the lesson has been learnt that purity can never consist in externals or negations, but must be a positive characteristic of the heart or inner man, there still remains the harder question, Wherein does such purity consist? This has often been discussed by moralists, and it is curious how little they have to give in answer. No definition based on acts can be framed, for the same act under different conditions may be pure or impure. Nor is it easy to find one by the analysis of motives, as the treatment of the matter by the casuists clearly shows ; for they have almost always ended in defining impurity only—a thing best left alone. A clue to the answer may, however, be found in Christ's teaching, though not one admitting of any formal analysis or definition. He laid it down emphatically that evil things proceeding from within can defile (δύναται κοινῶσαι). The word employed is most instructive ; and the more so when one recollects that it occurs again in this sense in the decisive lesson taught St. Peter as to the nature of purity (ἃ ὁ θεὸς ἐκαθάρισεν σὺ μὴ κοίνου, Ac 10¹⁵ 11⁹, cf. 21²⁸). To make common, i.e. to vulgarize, is the way to make impure : profanity is the ruin of purity. A well-spring of living water, fenced about by reverence—that is purity. When reverence is broken through, or when careless frequency leaves the bulwark open, every beast may enter and foul the spring after slaking its thirst ; then purity is gone. Not that purity is the flow of living water, but its characteristic so long as it is guarded. The water-spring may be a fount of truth, or love, or life ; it may be an aspiration, a resolve, an idea ; it may consist in an opportunity met with, or an experience felt ; it may be a holy memory, or an act of worship ; sometimes it will be the new perception of some beauty natural or moral, and sometimes an inborn faculty of service for others. Round any or all of these God sets reverence in our hearts for a fence, and bids us bare our heads as we draw near to what for us is holy ground. If we give no heed, but vulgarize by common use that opening which was afforded us to be a 'window in heaven,' we may do this, but at the cost of purity. God endows all with faculties of body, of intellect, of soul, which He means to be exercised and kept pure ; but used without reverence, and viewed without wonder, they miss their purpose. It was the sense of what true purity consists in that led an old writer to say, 'Keep thy heart above all that thou guardest, for out of it are the issues of life' (Pr 4²³),—a saying which half-anticipates the Beatitude promising the vision of God to the pure in heart. Reverence is the root from which purity grows ; and never was the essential nature of purity set in more vivid contrast with that blind and brutal profanity which is its opposite, than in Christ's striking utterance, 'Give not that which is holy to the dogs, nor cast your pearls before the swine, that they may never trample them between their feet, and, turning, rend you' (Mt 7⁶).

LITERATURE.—W. M. Ramsay, 'Greek of Early Ch. and Pagan Ritual' in ExpT x. (1899) 107 ; J. Smith, Chr. Character as a Social Power (1899), 143 ; H. Bushnell, The New Life, 176 ; W. J. Dawson, Threshold of Manhood (1889), 102 ; F. W. Robertson, Serm., 3rd ser. (1876) 122 ; A. Maclaren, Serm. in Manchester, 2nd ser. 112 ; R. W. Church, Village Serm., 2nd ser. 180 ; J. R. Illingworth, Univ. and Cath. Serm. 99 ; H. C. G. Moule, Need and Fulness (1895), 57 ; C. G. Montefiore, Truth in Religion (1906), 73.   E. P. BOYS-SMITH.

PURPLE.—The adj. πορφύρεος had originally no

connexion with a particular colour either by derivation or by use (see Liddell and Scott's *Lex. s.v.* πορφύρω). Similarly in the Latin poets *purpureus* regularly stands for nothing more than 'bright.' In Greek, after the discovery of the purple dye, the notion of colour became inherent. The gradations of colour were φοῖνιξ (darker shades—purple to crimson); πορφύρεος (brighter red, rosy), κόκκινος (scarlet). In Mt 27²⁸ || Mk 15¹⁷·²⁰, Jn 19²·⁵, the last two words are used indiscriminately for the same colour (see art. SCARLET). Manufactured purples were of various kinds, all extracted from the juice of sea molluscs. The following is a summary of their varieties, though the terms employed to describe them were not always confined to their proper use.

(1) Purple proper ; of a bright red hue ; obtained from the purple-snail (πορφύρα, *purpura*). This was used sometimes pure (called *blatta*), sometimes diluted (*conchylium*). Of the pure there were two sorts—(*a*) Tyrian, the most celebrated, which was 'twice-dyed' ; (*b*) amethystine, of a paler tint. One pound of wool dyed with Tyrian purple cost 1000 denarii, with amethystine 100 (Plin. *HN* ix. 38, 63). The use of such purples (especially the former) is mentioned frequently in satirists and historians as a feature of ancient luxury (cf. Juv. *Sat.* vii. 134 ff. ; Mart. viii. 10, etc.) ; hence Christ's expression in Lk 16¹⁹.

(2) Common purple ; of a violet hue (*i.e.* φοῖνιξ rather than πορφύρεος) ; obtained from the trumpet-snail (κῆρυξ, *buccinum*, *murex*). This was much less esteemed. Its colour apparently could even be compared to the dark blue of an Eastern sky (Jos. *Ant.* III. vii. 7) : but probably there were different tints.

The fiery-red purple (proper) of antiquity had practically no resemblance, as a colour, to the modern purple : the latter could never be described, even approximately, as 'scarlet' (Mt 27²⁸). Yet, independently of the hue, the name carries with it in both cases the distinction of being the royal colour. Under the Roman Empire restrictions were imposed from time to time as to its general use ; and the purple toga was the garb of the Emperor alone. It was as the badge of kingship that the purple formed part of the soldiers' mockery (Mk 15¹⁷·²⁰ ||).

LITERATURE.—Becker, *Gallus*, Excursus ii. p. 446 ff. ; Schmidt, *Forschungen auf dem Gebiet des Alterthums*, pp. 96–212. An older work upon the subject is Amati, *de Restitutione Purpurarum*.
F. S. RANKEN.

PURSE.—**1.** βαλλάντιον, peculiar to St. Luke, which occurs in LXX as the tr. of צְרוֹר (Job 14¹⁷)

and כִּיס (Pr 1¹⁴). 'The purse of the modern Syrian peasant is a little bag, sometimes of woven silk thread, but usually of yellow cotton. The open mouth is not drawn close by a string, but is gathered up by one hand, and then by the other the neck of the bag is carefully whipped round' (Hastings' *DB*, art. 'Bag') ; it, no doubt, corresponds to βαλλάντιον. The 'Seventy' were directed not to carry a purse (Lk 10⁴) ; in 22³⁵f· Christ asked the Apostles, 'When I sent you forth without purse, lacked ye anything?' and gave the new direction, 'He that hath a purse, let him take it.' In v.³⁶ RV gives 'and he that hath none,' *i.e.* no purse (so Cov., Rhem., Gen., Meyer, etc. ; on the other hand, Tind., Cran., Beza, Ewald, Godet prefer to supply μάχαιρα as AV ('he that hath no sword'). The passage, says Wendt, is to be explained from foresight of an impending period of persecution for the disciples : Jesus sets the necessity of buying a sword in contrast to the freedom from all want hitherto enjoyed by His disciples in their work as His messengers, and bases His exhortation on a reference to the doom about to fall on Himself ; a period would begin when the disciples would no longer be unharmed, but would be in the midst of conflicts and persecutions (see Wendt, *Teaching of Jesus*, ii. p. 358). In Lk 12³³ βαλλάντια is used in a figurative sense, 'make for yourselves purses (AV after Tind. 'bags') which wax not old, a treasure in the heavens that faileth not' ('continens pro contento,' de Wette).

2. ζώνη (Mt 10⁹ = Mk 6⁸ in the directions to the Twelve), properly the girdle, which is still in Syria made 'double for a foot and a half from the buckle, thus making a safe and well-guarded purse' (Hastings' *DB*, art. 'Bag'). RVm tr. 'girdle.'

'There was no extraordinary self-denial in the matter or mode of their mission. We may expound the instructions given to these primitive evangelists somewhat after the following manner—"Provide neither gold nor silver nor brass in your purses. You are going to your brethren in the neighbouring villages, and the best way to get to their hearts and their confidence is to throw yourselves upon their hospitality. . . ." At this day the farmer sets out on excursions quite as extensive without a para in his purse' (Thomson, *LB* p. 345 f.).

See also BAG.

LITERATURE.—The Lexicons of Liddell and Scott, and Grimm-Thayer, *s.v.* βαλλάντιον ; *ExpT* iv. [1893] 153 ff. ; *Expositor*, I. vi. [1877] 312 ff.
W. H. DUNDAS.

Q

QUARANTANIA.—See WILDERNESS.

QUATERNION (τετράδιον).—The word occurs only once in NT, and then not in the Gospels (Ac 12⁴) ; but we know that four soldiers at a time were ordinarily told off for work in the Roman army (Vegetius, *de Re Milit.* iii. 8), and that there were that number in charge of our Lord's Crucifixion (Jn 19²³·²⁴ ; cf. *Evang. Petr.* 9 ; see art. COAT).
C. L. FELTOE.

QUEEN (βασίλισσα).—A title occurring only once in the Gospels (Mt 12⁴², Lk 11³¹), in our Lord's reference to the queen of Sheba as 'the queen of the south.' The visit of the queen of Sheba to king Solomon is related in 1 K 10¹⁻¹³ and in 2 Ch 9¹⁻⁹, and the chief object of her journey was to satisfy herself as to his great wisdom, the report of which had reached her, although she was also attracted by the accounts which had been brought to her of his riches and magnificence. It is to the former of these two purposes of her visit that our

Lord refers. The Pharisees had demanded of Him a special sign, and He replied that no such sign should be given them, but that they should have a sign in Himself and in His burial and resurrection, as the Ninevites had had in Jonah. But the Ninevites, He added, would in the judgment condemn the men of that generation ; for they had repented at the preaching of Jonah, who was a sign to them, while the men of that generation, He implied, would not repent at the preaching of one greater than Jonah. Then, referring to the celebrated queen, He added : 'The queen of the south shall rise up in the judgment with this generation, and shall condemn it ; for she came from the uttermost parts of the earth to hear the wisdom of Solomon, and, behold, a greater than Solomon is here.'

The connexion between the case of the Ninevites and that of the queen of Sheba does not lie on the surface. Some have supposed that our Lord refers to a *woman* as the correlative to the *men* of

Nineveh previously spoken of. Others think that, having spoken of the Ninevites to whom without any seeking of theirs a preaching of repentance was brought, He refers, to complete the warning, to one who was herself a spontaneous seeker of wisdom. Without setting aside these suggestions, it is more to the point to observe that our Lord brings into juxtaposition the two characteristics— so strongly emphasized in the case of Jew and Gentile—of the desire for a sign, and the seeking after wisdom ; and it has been suggested that St. Paul may well have had this whole incident in mind when he wrote 1 Co 1[18-27] (see esp. v.[22]). We may also notice how our Lord in effect boldly claims to be what St. Paul says that He is, 'the wisdom of God.' Solomon was 'wiser than all men' (1 K 4[31]), and later Jewish literature delighted to magnify his wisdom (cf. Wis 7[17-21]). For our Lord, then, to claim before a Jewish audience to be 'something more' than Solomon, was to claim to be Wisdom itself. We may also remark how here again, as in the discourse at Nazareth, our Lord chooses His examples from among Gentiles (cf. also Mt 8[11. 12] 10[15] 11[22-24]).

Abyssinian legend has many strange tales of the queen of Sheba, declaring that she came from Ethiopia, that her name was Maqueda, and that she had a son by Solomon. (For many curious details, see Ludolf, *Hist. Aethiop.* ii. 3 ; *Vitæ sanctorum indigenarum*, ed. K. Conti Rossini ; *Legend of the Queen of Sheba*, ed. E. Littmann ; also Jos. *Ant.* VIII. vi. 5). All this, however, probably rests on a confusion between Seba (אבָס) and Sheba (אבְשׁ), cf. Ps 72[10]. Our Lord's phrase, 'the queen of the south,' falls in with the most widely accepted opinion, *i.e.* that Sheba was in South Arabia ; her land was accordingly more than a thousand miles from Jerusalem, a fact which justifies our Lord's words, ἐκ τῶν περάτων τῆς γῆς (cf. Jer 6[20]).

ALBERT BONUS.

QUESTIONS AND ANSWERS.—A full examination of the questions asked and the answers given by Jesus would involve a general consideration of the methods He employed in His teaching, and in meeting the difficulties of His hearers. Every good teacher must adopt the plan, associated for classical students with the name of Socrates, of using questions to make his hearers define their own position and ideas, and to help them to see clearly the admitted fundamental principles which underlie the discussion ; and he will further find in the questions they ask, since they give him an insight into the way in which their minds are working, opportunities for emphasizing, explaining, or developing his teaching according to their requirements. If any one will take the trouble to read through the Gospels, and note and mark in the margin all the questions and answers of Jesus, he can hardly fail to learn from the method employed by the world's greatest Teacher much that will be of use to one who has himself to teach others. It is personal work at the records themselves that has a real value, and the main object of this article is to suggest lines of study, since an exhaustive investigation is obviously impossible within the space available.

i. **Questions put by Jesus.** — 1. The prominence of interrogative sentences in the Gospels is due in part to the characteristic avoidance of indirect constructions ; but no doubt both in this particular and in the number of questions introduced they reflect the vividness of the Saviour's methods of teaching. The interrogative form was also particularly adapted to make people think for themselves, and we can trace all through our Lord's utterances the desire to promote thought. In a few cases the questions are simply requests for information. One instance is of special interest. According to Mk 6[38], Jesus asked the disciples, before the feeding of the 5000, 'How many loaves have ye?' This question is omitted in Mt. (14[16f.]) and Lk. (9[13]). Jn. (6[5f.]) relates that Christ asked a similar question of Philip on the same occasion,

'Whence are we to buy loaves, that these may eat?' But the Evangelist is careful to show that he does not understand this to be simply a request for information, by adding, 'And this he said to prove him : for he himself knew what he would do.' The following is a list of simple requests for information ; it will be noted that they occur mostly in Mk., and fall in with the simpler conception of the Person of Christ presented in that Gospel :

Mk 5[9], Lk 8[30] 'What is thy name?' [wanting in Mt.].
 ,, 6[38]. See above.
 ,, 8[5], Mt 15[34] 'How many loaves have ye?' [wanting in Lk.].
 ,, 8[23] 9[16. 21] [peculiar to Mk.].
 ,, 9[33] 'What were ye reasoning in the way?' [Mt. avoids the question ; it is wanting in Lk.].
 Jn 11[34] 'Where have ye laid him?'
 ,, 1[38] 18[4. 7. 34] probably do not come under this category ; in each of these instances the question seems to be intended to suggest some thought to the hearers. Jn 20[15], like Lk 24[17. 19], seems to be due to the character of a stranger assumed for the moment by Christ.

2. Instances of purely rhetorical questions occur with normal frequency (*e.g.* Mt 15[3], where the parallel Mk 7[9] has an assertion ; Mk 4[13], Lk 18[7], Jn 6[70]). Christ habitually used such questions as a form of mild rebuke, often implying a notion of surprise or of sorrow (*e.g.* Mk 4[40]=Mt 8[26]=Lk 8[25], Jn 3[10]).

3. The use of a rhetorical question to introduce parables or parabolic utterances is characteristic of Luke, but is found also in Matthew and Mark. In the latter Gospel the parable of the Mustardseed (4[30]) is introduced by the striking double question, 'How shall we liken the kingdom of God? or in what parable shall we set it forth?' which Swete (*ad loc.*) thus paraphrases : 'How are we to depict the kingdom of God? in what new light can we place it?' He adds, 'The Lord, as a wise teacher, seems to take His audience into His counsels, and to seek their help.' Lk 13[18] retains the double question in an obviously less original and really tautological form, in which the hearers are not taken into the Master's counsels ('Unto what is the kingdom of God like? and whereunto shall I liken it?'), but Mt 13[31] drops it. Cf. also Mk 2[19]=Mt 9[15]=Lk 5[34], Mk 8[36f.]=Mt 16[26]=Lk 9[25], Mk 9[50]=Mt 5[13]=Lk 14[34] ; examples peculiar to Mk. are found in 3[23] and 4[21]. This use occurs also in Mt. in passages where the matter is common to himself and Lk. (Mt 6[27]=Lk 12[25], Mt 11[16]=Lk 7[31], Mt 18[12]=Lk 15[4], Mt 24[45]=Lk 12[42]), but there do not appear to be any instances of it in matter peculiar to Matthew. Further examples in Lk. are 6[39] 11[5] (where the interrogative form in which the parable of the Friend at Midnight begins is not carried to a grammatical conclusion), 13[20] (=Mt 13[33] where the question is dropped) 14[28. 31] 15[8] 17[7f.]. A somewhat similar use is found in Jn 4[35] and 11[9], where a parabolic meaning is apparently given to popular proverbs.

This investigation throws an interesting side-light on the Synoptic problem : one of the four parables recorded by Mk. is introduced by a very striking interrogative formula, and many parables in the non-Markan document used by Mt. and Lk. seem to have been similarly introduced ; Mt., however, did not care for this use, and was inclined to avoid it.

4. Christ often asked a question also in order to make men draw their own conclusions from His parables : cf. Mk 12[9]=Mt 21[40]=Lk 20[15] (where He apparently answered the question Himself, though Mt. ascribes the answer to the audience), Mt 21[31], Lk 7[42] 10[36] 16[11].

5. Very frequently Christ, by means of a question, led His hearers to admit the truth of matters of common knowledge, or of generally accepted principles, on which He was going to base His teaching : some characteristic examples are here classified :

(*a*) Matters of common knowledge : Mt 10[29]=Lk 12[6] (price of sparrows), Mt 17[25] (tribute collected of strangers).

(b) Appeals to common sense : Mt 5⁴⁶ᶠ· = Lk 6³²ᶠ·, Mt 7³ᶠ· = Lk 6⁴¹ᶠ· (the mote and the beam—almost parabolic), Mt 7⁹ᶠ· = Lk 11¹¹ᶠ·, Mt 7¹⁶ (question-form dropped in Lk 6⁴⁴), Mk 7¹⁸ᶠ· = Mt 15¹⁷, Mk 12¹⁶ = Mt 22²⁰ = Lk 20²⁴ ('Whose is this image and superscription ?'), Lk 11⁴⁰ 22⁹⁷.

(c) Appeals to the conscience of the hearers : Mt 23¹⁷ᶠᶠ·, Mk 3⁴ = Mt 12¹¹ = Lk 6⁹, Lk 13¹⁵ 14³· ⁵ (cf. Mt 12¹⁰ᶠ·).

(d) Appeals to OT Scriptures : Mk 2²⁵ᶠ· = Mt 12³ᶠ· = Lk 6³ᶠ·, Mk 11¹⁷ (question-form dropped in Mt 21¹³ and Lk 19⁴⁶), Mk 12¹⁰ᶠ· = Mt 21⁴² = Lk 20¹⁷, Mk 12²⁶ = Mt 22³¹ᶠ· (question-form dropped in Lk 20³⁷ᶠ·), Mt 21¹⁶, Jn 10³⁴.

(e) To establish principles closely connected with the teaching of Christ in the immediate context : Jn 3¹² 5⁴⁴· ⁴⁷ 8⁴³· ⁴⁶.

6. Again, Jesus often asked questions to lead men to an exact understanding of the circumstances connected with a question addressed to Himself, or with a request asked of Him : Mk 10³ (contrast Mt 19⁷) leads to a clear statement of the position of the Mosaic Law in regard to divorce, and enables Christ to contrast with it the higher law of God ; Mk 10³⁸ = Mt 20²² corrects the false notions of the sons of Zebedee in regard to the Messianic Kingdom ; cf. also Mk 10¹⁸ = Mt 19¹⁷ = Lk 18¹⁹ ('Why callest thou me good ?'), Mt 11⁷ᶠᶠ· = Lk 7²⁴ᶠᶠ·, Lk 13²· ⁴. The instances of this sort of question in the Fourth Gospel are of interest ; sometimes the question seems intended to make people think what they are doing (1³⁸ 10³² 18⁵· ⁷· ²³· ³⁴ 20¹⁵) ; at other times, to make them consider how they really stand in regard to Christ (1⁵⁰ 3¹² 6⁶¹ᶠ· ⁶⁷· ⁷⁰ 7¹⁹· ²³). Similarly a direct question often made men state exactly what they wanted (e.g. Mk 10⁵¹ = Mt 20³² = Lk 18⁴¹, Jn 5⁶).

7. Questions were also employed by Christ to draw from men a confession of faith ; the chief example is Mk 8²⁹ = 16¹⁵ = Lk 9²⁰, where, after the disciples had stated the opinions of the crowds concerning Himself, a further question led to St. Peter's great confession (cf. also Mt 9²⁸, Jn 6⁶⁷ 9³⁵ 11²⁶).

8. Quite alone stands the awful question of human despair addressed from the Cross to the Almighty (Mk 15³⁴ = Mt 27⁴⁶). To attempt to examine the import of that question would be to enter on a discussion of the relation in which Jesus stood to His heavenly Father. See art. DERELICTION.

9. In two instances Christ asked questions of the learned men among the Jews which they were unable to answer : in each case He evidently intended to show that the fundamental principles on which their boasted knowledge rested were wrong. When they demanded by what authority He acted, He asked them whether the baptism of John was from heaven or of men (Mk 11³⁰ = Mt 21²⁵ = Lk 20⁴). Their inability to answer showed that they did not possess the spiritual powers necessary for forming a judgment on claims which rested on eternal principles of right and wrong. The question (Mk 12³⁵ = Mt 22⁴²ᶠᶠ· = Lk 20⁴¹) concerning the Davidic descent of the Messiah showed that their interpretation of the Scriptures was not consistent, even when judged according to their own principles.

ii. **Answers of Jesus to questions put to Him.** —**1.** We turn now to the answers which Jesus gave. Very striking are those instances where the silence of Christ was more eloquent than words could have been. It was useless to attempt any answer to the charges of witnesses, brought against Him before judges who had procured their false evidence (Mk 14⁶¹ = Mt 26⁶³), or to similar charges before Pilate (Mk 15⁵ = Mt 27¹⁴) and Herod (Lk 23⁹) ; it was useless to discuss with such a man as Pilate the nature of truth (Jn 18³⁸), or His heavenly mission (Jn 19⁹). Only when such questions are asked in a right spirit is it worth answering them. When Pilate asked Him (Mk 15² = Mt 27¹¹ = Lk 23³, cf. Jn 18⁵⁷) whether He was 'the King of the Jews,' He gave an ambiguous answer—'Thou sayest' : it

was a title He had not Himself claimed, and which belonged to Him only in a sense that Pilate could not understand. But Christ did not hesitate, in spite of the obvious danger, to give direct answers to questions concerning His own claims (Mk 14⁶² = Mt 26⁶⁴, cf. Lk 22⁷⁰). See art. SILENCE.

A very interesting problem arises, however, in regard to this last answer. The high priest asked (Mk 14⁶²), 'Art thou the Christ, the Son of the Blessed ?' (According to Mt 26⁶³ he said, 'I adjure thee by the living God, that thou tell us whether thou be the Christ, the Son of God ' : Lk 22⁷⁰ has, 'And they all said, Art thou then the Son of God ?'). Jesus answered, according to Mk. 'I am' (ἐγώ εἰμι), according to Mt. 'Thou hast said' (σὺ εἶπας), and according to Lk. 'Ye say that I am' (ὑμεῖς λέγετε ὅτι ἐγώ εἰμι). It is usual to interpret the answer in each Gospel as a strong affirmation, and, in view of the fact that the order of Lk. (who continues at once, 'And they said, What further need have we of witness ?') supports this interpretation, it may probably be accepted as the right one. But it is possible that the answer to the high priest was really ambiguous, as the answer to Pilate seems to have been (so Westcott on Jn 18³⁷), and that Mk. and Mt. each dropped a half of the answer which is more accurately preserved in Lk.

2. Often He answered a question somewhat indirectly, correcting the mental attitude, or some misconception, of the questioner. Thus in answer to, 'Who is the greatest in the kingdom of heaven ?' (Mt 18¹), He shows the character of true greatness in the judgment of God. When a man asked (Lk 13²³), 'Lord, are there few that be saved ?' Jesus puts the word 'strive' (ἀγωνίζεσθε) at the head of His answer, and thus corrects the spirit of the questioner : this was no matter, He evidently thought, for academic discussion such as the Jewish Rabbis delighted in, nor was it a question of privilege—it was a practical matter, in which personal effort was of vital importance.

The following passages will repay careful study, and show how ready the Master was to avail Himself of any opportunities of giving teaching, even if they were due to the hostile questions of His foes, and also how He always drew the questioner away from details and misconceptions to principles of vital importance :—Mk 2⁷⁻¹² and parallels (the parallel between physical and mental healing— both are proper functions of the representative Son of Man), Mk 2¹⁸⁻²² and parallels (formal fasting has no value), Mk 7⁵ᶠᶠ· = Mt 15²ᶠᶠ· (observance of the traditions of the elders), Mk 10¹⁷ᶠᶠ· and parallels ('What does the word *good* really imply ?'—then the young questioner is made to feel that his knowledge, that of the letter of the Law, is not enough to lead to goodness, and a counsel of perfection is given), Mk 12¹⁸ᶠᶠ· and parallels (distinction between carnal and spiritual things), Mk 13³ᶠᶠ· and parallels (men are not concerned with foreknowing the dates of future events, but with recognizing their import as they come), Mt 11²ᶠᶠ· = Lk 7¹⁹ᶠᶠ· (What are the true signs of the Messiah ?), Mt 15¹² (it matters not if the carnally-minded are offended, whatever their worldly position), Lk 9⁵⁴ᶠ· (where the TR evidently contains a correct exegesis), Lk 10⁴⁰ᶠᶠ· (there is something better than anxious outward service), Lk 12⁴¹ᶠᶠ· (those who have to teach others must learn all they can). It is evident that in most cases the answer was given in such a way as to cause thought, without which its reference to the question is by no means obvious ; this is notably the case in Lk 17³⁷ ; the epigrammatic answer to the question of the perplexed disciples —'Where, Lord ?'—finds a solution only when we remember that the Master's thoughts were fixed on eternal principles, not on the examples of them that take place in time.

3. Very characteristic of the Fourth Gospel is the way in which Christ is represented as making questions of quite ordinary import, or those caused by utter bewilderment, the occasion of spiritual teaching. When Nicodemus asks (3⁴) how a man can be born a second time, Christ does not attempt to explain the difficulty, but goes on to speak of being born from water and spirit. Each question of the puzzled crowd in the Capernaum synagogue (ch. 6) leads on to deeper teaching, so that those disciples who could neither follow it nor accept it on trust left Him. When the Jews ask where Christ got His education (7[15]), His answer points them to the Divine Author of His teaching. The disciples ask (9[2]) whether blindness from birth is the punishment of pre-natal or of parental sin.; the answer sets aside such a question as trivial, and embodies the only explanation of human suffering that can be given—it is necessary to the working out of God's plan. Judas (not Iscariot) asks in surprise (14[22]), 'Lord, what has happened that thou art about to manifest thyself to us and not to the world?'—the answer shows the condition of communion with the Father. The careful student will multiply instances for himself.

4. Christ made people answer their own questions by Himself putting leading questions. The image and superscription of Cæsar on the tribute money (Mk 12[16] and parallels) gave a practical answer to the question of the Pharisees and Herodians, and to the lesson thus taught He Himself added a spiritual one. Many instances in which the questioners were forced to think out the answers for themselves will be found referred to under i. §§ **5** and **6** above, for it was characteristic of Christ's methods to answer a question by a question.

5. The answers given by Christ to questions which were asked for the express purpose of placing Him in a difficult position, or of showing the falsity of His principles, may at first sight seem to require separate treatment; but further consideration will show that He avoided the pitfalls prepared for Him by using the same dialectical methods as in replying to the inquiries of disciples: either He made the hostile questioners practically answer their own question, as in the case of the paying of tribute to Rome (Mk 12[17] ||); or else He took occasion to state a great general principle, which included and forced into its right place the particular detail referred to in the question (Mk 2[18-22] ||, and other passages referred to under § **2** above).

LITERATURE.—Gore, *BL* 198 ff.; Denney, *Gospel Questions and Answers*; Knight, *The Master's Questions to His Disciples.*

P. M. BARNARD.

QUIRINIUS.—Lk 2[2] AV, 'And this taxing was first made when Cyrenius was governor of Syria' is better rendered in RV, 'This was the first enrolment made when Quirinius was governor of Syria.' From art. CENSUS it will be seen that this statement probably means that this was the first occasion of an enrolment of this nature, an enrolment of population by households as distinct from a rating-enrolment in reference to property, and that it took place during the governorship of Quirinius in Syria. Here, however, there seems to emerge a great discrepancy between St. Luke's account and what is known from secular history. It is certain that Publius Sulpicius Quirinius was the administrator of Syria from A.D. 6 to 9, and that in that period he took the rating-census mentioned in Ac 5[37] (Jos. *Ant.* XVII. xiii. 5, XVIII. i. 1). But the birth of Jesus took place before the death of Herod the Great (Mt 2), and that was in B.C. 4. The narratives of the two Evangelists seem to be at hopeless variance on a most important point. How are they to be reconciled?

One way of cutting the knot readily occurs. We might suppose that the clause Lk 2[2] was not in the original narrative, but was a marginal date inserted by an early copyist, who made a mistake as to the census intended; but the MSS afford no warrant for this suggestion. Now, assuming the text to be as St. Luke wrote it, we can have no doubt that he did so quite deliberately, for he was most care-

ful to give an accurate account (see Lk 1[1-4]), and he himself has chronicled the census of A.D. 6 to 9 in Ac 5[37]. This would lead us *a priori* to reckon that as in his view at least there was no discrepancy, there must be some explanation that does not lie on the surface. Dr. Lardner's method of solving the difficulty is to interpret the verse thus: 'This was the first census of Cyrenius, who (afterwards) was governor of Syria,' St. Luke taking pains to distinguish, according to this view, between the two enrolments, and giving the information that Quirinius was the man who at a later time became governor of Syria. Thus Herodian says that 'to Marcus the emperor were born several daughters and two sons'; yet we know that some of them at least were born before he became emperor. Dr. Lardner's interpretation, however, does violence to the construction of the text, and is at best a forced expedient to avoid a difficulty. Fortunately, later scholarship is able to dispense with it. Zumpt (*Commentatio de Syria Romanorum provincia ab Cesare Augusto ad Titum Vespasianum*) has shown that Quirinius seems to have been governor of Syria on two occasions; and this clue has been followed up by independent studies of Ramsay (*Was Christ born at Bethlehem?*). A fragment of an inscribed stone found at Tivoli in 1764 tells of the doings of a Roman official in the time of Augustus. The name has perished, but from the facts recorded antiquarians of note agree in believing that he was Quirinius. Now this stone distinctly mentions that he was twice *legatus* of Syria. [The actual word *legatus* is wanting in the fragment preserved, but some such word is required by the context]. Still the problem is not solved by this discovery, though secular as well as sacred history must share the difficulty: for it happens that we know who were governors of that province for the whole period prior to Herod's death in B.C. 4. In B.C. 9 Sentius Saturninus succeeded Marcus Titius, and Josephus (*Ant.* XVII. v. 2) says: 'Now Quintilius Varus was at this time at Jerusalem, being sent to succeed Saturninus as president of Syria'; and this statement is verified by coins of Antioch-in-Syria bearing his name with date. As we know that Augustus had a rule that no governor of a province should hold that office for less than three or more than five years, the whole period from B.C. 12 to 4 is covered, and there is no room to place the governorship of Quirinius at the time required. He cannot have been governor before B.C. 12, for he was then consul at Rome; and even if it were of any service, we cannot place him later, for he became tutor of Caius Cæsar and governor of Asia; so that there is a difficulty in fixing his earlier period of holding office in Syria, if, indeed, he was twice governor. Farrar has suggested that, the above-mentioned rule of Augustus notwithstanding, Varus was displaced 'because his close friendship with Archelaus, who resembled him in character, might have done mischief'; but of this there is no evidence, and the conjecture is but a make-shift. A better solution of the problem is to reckon that the governorship of which St. Luke speaks may have been of a different character from that held by Saturninus and Varus. Quirinius was a man who had shown himself very capable in military affairs. Now at this period there were troubles with various tribes in Syria and its frontiers. Tacitus (*Ann.* iii. 48) tells us that Quirinius waged successful war against the Homonadenses in Cilicia (which belonged to Syria) at a time prior at least to A.D. 2, when he became rector to Caius Cæsar. There is therefore, to say the least, no unlikelihood that while Varus, who had no military renown, was left as the ordinary governor to administer the internal affairs of the province, Quirinius was appointed an extraordinary governor in charge of the military operations in the same region, with the title of *legatus*, or more specifically of *dux*. Inasmuch as the Greek equivalent in the case of either civil or military governor is ἡγεμών, St. Luke would be justified in saying, as he does, that the first enrolment was made 'when Quirinius was acting as governor' (ἡγεμονεύοντος Κυρηνίου).* Those nearer the Evangelist's own day, for whom he was specially writing, and who were better acquainted with the secular history of the time than readers nowadays, would find the date he thus gives even more exact than if he had mentioned either Saturninus or Varus; for, as has been shown in art. CENSUS, the enrolment was determined during the rule of the former, but, so far as Palestine was concerned, probably carried out during the rule of the latter. The likelihood of there being two simultaneous governors, one for military the other for civil affairs, in the same province, is supported by parallel instances adduced by Ramsay (*op. cit.* 238 ff.).

Another theory in explanation of the passage about Quirinius is that he was neither civil nor military governor, but merely one of the commissioners appointed to take the enrolment throughout the whole Roman world, the district for which he was responsible being Syria. Palestine, though not at this period actually a Roman province, was under the Roman suzerainty, and from its proximity it would be included under Syria. St. Luke, having no better word for the enrolment commissioner, might use ἡγεμονεύων [ἡγ. τῆς σκέψεως 'taking lead in the inquiry,' Plat. *Prot.* 351 E]. Tertullian (*adv. Marc.* iv. 19) states that the census at the time of Christ's birth was taken by Saturninus, not Quirinius, and thus seems to correct the narrative; but that must be merely because he knew that the enrolment had been decided upon during the civil governorship of Saturninus: he cannot have meant that it was actually accomplished then; for that would be utterly inconsistent with the date he elsewhere (*adv. Jud.* 8) gives for the nativity, B.C. 3.

LITERATURE.—Lives of Christ; Commentaries on St. Luke; Bib. Dictt. of Smith, Kitto, and Hastings, and works by Zumpt and Ramsay mentioned in article. Schürer's latest expression of opinion (*GJV*³ i. 508 ff.) is strongly adverse to the accuracy of St. Luke as well as to Professor Ramsay's theory.

ARTHUR POLLOK SYM.

QUOTATIONS.—1. Use of the OT in the Gospels.—In general it is agreed that a quotation is the intentional reproduction of some thought or fact already expressed in language by the use of the very words previously employed. This is an exact quotation. A free quotation is one which fails to reproduce the self-same words, because, either through defect of memory or lack of care, the person making it employed language varying more or less widely from that of his source, or he may have intended merely to give the substance of the original. Ordinarily an unintentional use of the same thought or of identical words is not to be regarded as a quotation. The *intention* is essential, to constitute a quotation either exact or free. The quotations in the Gospels may be classed as follows:

(a) *Quotations which conform to both the Hebrew and the Greek of the OT:* (α) by Jesus, Mt 15^{4a} (Mk 7^{10a}) 15^{4b} (Mk 7^{10b}) 19^{5} (Mk $10^{7.8}$) $19^{18.\ 19a.\ 19b}$ 21^{13a} (Mk 11^{17a}, Lk 19^{46a}) 22^{39} (Mk 12^{31}), Mk 12^{36} (Lk $20^{42.\ 43}$), Jn 10^{34}; (β) by others, Mt $5^{21.\ 27.\ 38.\ 43}$ 21^{9} (Mk 11^{9}, Lk 19^{38}, Jn 12^{13}), Lk 10^{27}; (γ) by the Evangelist, Jn 19^{24}.

(b) *Quotations conforming to the Hebrew alone:* by Jesus, Mt 9^{13} 12^{7} 27^{46} (Mk 15^{34}), Lk 22^{37} 23^{46}.

* Plut. *Camill.* 23 uses ἡγεμονία for the division of an army under an officer.

(c) *Quotations conforming to the Greek alone:* (α) by Jesus, Mt 4^{7} (Lk 4^{12}) $13^{14.\ 15}$ 19^{4} (Mk 10^{6}) $21^{16.\ 42}$ (Mk $12^{10.\ 11}$, Lk 20^{17}); (β) by the Evangelist, Jn 12^{38}.

(d) *Free quotations varying from both Hebrew and Greek:* (α) by Jesus, Mt 4^{4} (Lk 4^{4}) 4^{10} (Lk 4^{8}) $4^{15.\ 16}$ 11^{10} (Lk 7^{27}) 18^{16} 22^{32} (Mk 12^{26}, Lk 20^{37}) 22^{37} (Mk $12^{29.\ 30}$) 22^{44} 26^{31} (Mk 14^{27}), Mk 4^{12} 10^{19} (Lk 18^{20}), Jn 6^{35} 13^{18} 15^{25}; (β) by others, Mt 2^{6} 4^{6} (Lk $4^{10.\ 11}$), Mk $12^{32.\ 33}$, Lk 10^{27}, Jn 2^{17}; (γ) by the Evangelist, Mt 2^{18} 21^{5} (Jn 12^{15}) $27^{9.\ 10}$, Mk 1^{2}, Lk $2^{23.\ 24}$, Jn 12^{40} $19^{36.\ 37}$.

(e) *Free quotations varying less from the Hebrew than from the Greek:* by the Evangelist, Mt 8^{17} 12^{18-21}.

(f) *Free quotations varying less from the Greek than from the Hebrew:* by Jesus, Mt $15^{8.\ 9}$ (Mk $7^{6.\ 7}$) 24^{15} (Mk 13^{14}), Lk $4^{18.\ 19}$ 8^{10}.

The variations in exactness of quotation and in the standard to which they conform are interesting. The importance of the variations is open to question. Few of them are noticeable. Yet more, if the teaching of Jesus had been confined to a few days or weeks, if He had spoken about the topics recorded in the Gospels but once or twice, and if there were evidence that He was particular about the exact phrasing of His teachings, the question might be of more importance. We remember, however, that Jesus lived three years with disciples, teaching them and speaking on a great variety of occasions; and these facts were inconsistent with a stereotyped mode of utterance. Moreover, the record of His deeds and teachings is brief at best. The Gospels give from one-fifth to one-third of their scanty space to a period of one week, and but slight, though vivid, glimpses of occasional scenes during the remaining three years. He must have spoken many times on the same subjects, and have uttered the same thoughts in many modes of expression. One who insisted, as He did, upon the supremacy of the spirit over the form would scarcely have permitted Himself to be bound by a strict conformity to the letter, while appealing to the OT for the authority of the truths which He taught. This fact makes it seem strange that the collection of His teachings is not much larger and the variety of His expressions much greater. Under the influence of such a Teacher it is not likely that the disciples were over anxious to conform with exactness to the text of the OT.

The passages cited give evidence of intentional use of the OT. Usually they are introduced by some formula of citation such as 'it is written,' 'the Scripture saith,' and the like. There are about fifty different variants in the mode of introducing explicit quotations found in the Gospels.

Some of the passages given above have no formula of introduction, but the context of the passage shows conscious and intentional use of OT material. It is also to be noticed that the Gospels vary in their representation of the same passage or fact. *E.g.* the Evangelist in Jn $19^{24.\ 28}$ connects the events with a passage in the OT; the parallel narratives in the Synoptics mention these facts without connecting them in any way with the OT, so that at the utmost, so far as these Gospels are concerned, the passage is, so to say, an accidental parallel having no proper classification with quotations. It cannot be regarded as in the slightest degree an instance of use of the OT by these Evangelists. This is equally true of all events narrated in the Gospels which are not explicitly connected with OT passages, no matter how striking the coincidence; *e.g.* Is 50^{6} might well have been referred to in the narratives in Mt 26^{67} 27^{26}, Mk 14^{65}, Lk $22^{63.\ 64}$, Jn 18^{22}, and so also might Ps $22^{8.\ 16}$, but neither of these notable OT passages was so used. Again, while Mt 13[14. 15] is unquestionably a quotation, the same thought expressed in the parallel passage, Mk 4[12], has no formula of quotation, and has such transpositions and omissions that if we did not know of the passages in Isaiah and Mt., we might well doubt if it were a real quotation. As it is, we think it was intentionally derived from Isaiah. Further, Lk 8[10] is parallel with the passages just cited from Mt. and Mk.; it has a sentence from Is 6[9], nothing from v.[10], and is much more brief than Mark. If the parallel passages in Mt. and Mk. were unknown, even though we were fully acquainted with Is 6[9. 10], we should think that the use of the OT thought and phraseology was due to familiarity with the language rather than to an intention to quote from it. As it is, we have little doubt that the writers had in mind to report the same utterances of Jesus, and that the report is more incomplete in one case than in the other. Yet it is quite possible that different discourses of Jesus are reported. These instances, the words recorded in Jn 9[39] as uttered by Jesus, and those of the Evangelist in Jn 12[40], lead us to think the passage in Is 6[9. 10] pointed many an utterance of Jesus.

How many more passages like this in Lk 8[10] do the Gospels contain? That is a matter of conjecture. It is desirable to add to the lists already given several other lists of passages which go to show the nature of the connexion between the OT and the NT.

(g) *Intentional and free use of OT laws, facts, or statements independently of the original form of expression*: (a) by Jesus, Mt 5[12b] (Lk 13[34a]) 8[4] (Mk 1[44], Lk 5[14]) 11[14] 17[10. 11] (Mk 9[12. 13]) 12[3. 4] (Mk 2[25. 26], Lk 6[3. 4]) 12[5. 40. 41] (Mt 16[4b], Lk 11[29. 30. 32]) 12[42] (Lk 11[31]) 23[35] (Lk 11[50. 51]) 24[37. 39] (Lk 17[26. 27]), Lk 4[25-27] 17[28. 29], Jn 5[39c. 46] 8[17]; (β) by others, Mt 22[24] (Mk 12[19], Lk 20[28]) 23[30. 31] (Lk 11[47. 48]), Lk 1[72b], Jn 5[10] 6[31. 49. 58] 8[5] 19[31]; (γ) by the Evangelist, Lk 2[22], Jn 4[5] (?).

(h) Another interesting group of passages consists of those which have *a formula of reference to the OT* as their source or authority, but *whose content cannot be referred to any specific OT passage*. These are all from the words of Jesus: Mt 26[24a] (Mk 14[21]) 26[34. 56a] (Mk 14[49]), Mk 9[12b. 13], Lk 11[49] 18[31] 21[22b] 24[44. 46], Jn 1[45] 17[12].

(i) Still another class of passages consists of *intentional allusions to something in the OT*, but they make *no formal use of OT material*, and are not quotations in any strict sense of the term. The allusion to the destruction of Sodom and Gomorrah is an illustration. (a) By Jesus, Mt 8[11] (Lk 13[29]) 10[15. 21] (Mk 13[12]) 10[35. 36] (Lk 12[52. 53]) 11[25] (Lk 10[21]) 21[13b] (Mk 11[17b], Lk 19[46b]) 24[30b] (Lk 23[37]) 24[30a. c] (Mk 13[26], Lk 21[27]) 26[64] (Mk 14[62], Mt 16[27] 25[31]), Lk 17[32], Jn 1[51] 3[14a. 15] 8[7. 35. 56] 9[39]; (β) by others, Mt 8[21], Lk 9[54], Jn 1[21. 25] 6[14] 7[40] 16[32].

The instances thus far classified come almost entirely under the head of the use of the OT as an authoritative Scripture. Another influence is quite as evident. It is the literary influence. This is the influence of any work of literature over the modes of thought and habits of expression of those who make much use of that work of literature. Men may be unconscious of this influence, or they may consciously use the forms of utterance which they have learned to love. It is doubtless more a matter of habit working within the region of the unconscious, while it is the appeal to authority which is operative within the region of the conscious use of the OT. These two causes produce phenomena which are not altogether easy to classify together.

(j) Such a passage as Lk 8[10] cited above compels the recognition of passages which *may have intentionally used the OT thought or language, yet do not give conclusive evidence that they were so used.* Its use may have been due to literary and unconscious influence. In any case there is such coincidence in thought and phraseology that an intimate connexion is shown between the thought of the Gospels and that of the OT. For example, when we read in He 12[29] καὶ γὰρ ὁ θεὸς ἡμῶν πῦρ καταναλίσκον, and learn that the last two words are found together in the LXX only in Dt 4[24] and 9[3], we think it likely that the writer either intentionally used the phrase, with a thought of the passages in Dt., or that he was so familiar with Dt. that unintentionally and unconsciously he used its words and phrases. Thus also may we connect οἱ πενθοῦντες of Mt 5[4] with אבלים or τοὺς πενθοῦντας of Is 61[2]. When we remember the fact that the mind of Jesus was saturated with the Book of Isaiah, we can easily be convinced that there is a literary connexion between the utterance of Jesus and the OT passage.

The following passages show a similar connexion : Mt 5[5. 8. 34. 35] 7[7. 8] (Lk 11[9. 10]) 7[23] (Lk 13[27]) 10[28b] 11[5] (Lk 7[22]) 11[23] (Lk 10[15]) 12[37] 13[16] 15[14] 16[27b] 19[17] (Lk 10[28]) 19[26] (Mk 10[27], Lk 18[27], Mk 14[36]) 20[28] (Mk 10[45]) 21[11. 12] (Mk 11[15], Lk 19[45], Jn 2[16]) 23[12] (Lk 14[11] 18[14]) 23[37] (Lk 13[34]) 23[38] (Lk 13[35a]) 24[2] (Mk 13[2], Lk 19[44]) 24[21] (Mk 13[19]) 24[29] (Mk 13[24. 25], Lk 21[25. 26a]) 24[30b] 25[32] 26[11] (Mk 14[7], Jn 12[8]) 27[46] (Mk 15[34]) 28[3], Lk 1[32. 33. 69] 6[21] 14[8-10] 16[15b] 23[30], Jn 1[14. 34] 3[21] 7[24] 9[39] 12[8a] 14[15. 21. 24].

(k) Prolonged examination brings to recognition a class of passages in which, *without marked literary relation, or intentional use of the OT, there is yet a genetic relation between the OT and the NT.* Jesus had the Spirit without measure, and was an authoritative interpreter of the OT. He had so absorbed the OT that its ideals were His commonplaces of thought, and the scattered suggestions of truth in the OT were apprehended by Him in their full and explicit meaning. Imperfect or fragmentary suggestions became positive principles. In dealing with divorce He went to the fundamental conception of marriage (Mt 13[5] = Mk 10[7. 8]). In dealing with the Sabbath, He said that the Sabbath was made for man, and not man for the Sabbath (Mk 2[27]). This is a universal statement which is suggested in Ex 23[12] and Dt 5[14]. Again Jn 4[37] 'For herein is the saying true, One soweth and another reapeth' may be a current proverb, or it may be derived in thought from Job 31[8], Mic 6[15]. Whatever be true about that passage, there can be little doubt that the words of Jesus given in Mt 5[44] 'Love your enemies, and pray for them that persecute you,' is the explicit statement of an ideal of conduct that finds suggestion in Job 31[29] and several other OT passages.

The following is a list of similar passages : Mt 5[3. 6] (Lk 6[21a]) 5[7. 9. 11] (Lk 6[22]) 5[14. 18a] (Lk 16[17]) 5[28. 30] 18[8] (Mk 9[43]) 5[42a] (Lk 6[30a]) 5[43. 44a] (Lk 6[27]) 5[44b. 48] 6[6. 9. 11. 14. 15. 19. 24. 25. 26] (Lk 12[24]) 7[6. 21b] (Jn 13[17]) 10[6] 15[24] (Lk 15[6] 19[10], Mt 18[12]) 10[10b. 19. 37. 28] (Jn 6[27] 7[37b]) 19[29b] (Mk 10[30], Lk 18[30]) 10[41] 12[29] (Mk 3[27], Lk 11[21. 22]) 12[32b] 13[39. 40. 41. 43. 44. 45. 46] 15[13] 16[26] (Mk 8[37], Lk 9[25]) 18[15] (Lk 17[3]) 21[33] (Mk 12[1], Lk 20[9]) 21[44] (Lk 20[18]) 24[16-18] (Mk 13[14-16], Lk 21[21. 22]) 24[35] (Mk 13[31], Lk 21[33] 16[17]) 25[35. 36. 40. 45. 42. 46] 26[28] (Mk 14[24], Lk 22[20]) 26[52c] 27[6] 28[18. 20], Mk 22. 27 9[48], Lk 6[28. 34. 35. 36] 12[47. 48] 13[6. 7] 14[13] 15[18. 19. 21] 16[15c] 19[8. 42] 21[24. 25. 26] 22[19] 31 23[34a], Jn 16. 11. 18 5[37b] 6[46] 2[16 35] (Ezk 36[25-27] 11[19] ?) 4[22b. 37] 5[17. 21. 22. 27. 29. 39b. 44] 7[37b. 38. 39a. 42] 8[11] 9[2. 31. 41] 10[3. 10-16] 13[34] 15[12. 17] 14[23] 15[1. 14. 15] 19[7] 20[31].

These lists of passages under (j) and (k) are by no means exhaustive. Dittmar (*Vetus Test. in Novo*) gives many more passages than have been enumerated, and Hühn (*Die alttest. Citate und Reminiscenzen im NT*) gives a far greater number. It is not always easy to discriminate to one's own satisfaction between classes (j) and (k). We must follow the more pronounced character of the passage as it appears to us at the moment of investigation. The border-line between a real literary reminiscence and an accidental coincidence is also difficult to determine. Not only would it be possible to increase the lists (j) and (k), but at least two other classes could be made out. One such class (l) would consist of expressions which belong to the life of the land, or the common utterances of the people of the land, such as Mt 9³⁶ 'as sheep not having a shepherd.' These have no real significance, literary or otherwise. Again, there is another class of expressions (m) in which imagery similar to that of the OT is found. 'Wise as serpents' (Mt 10¹⁶) is possibly a comparison suggested by Gn 3¹, or it may have been current rhetoric. Or, again, the image of sifting (Lk 22³¹) may have been a current phrase, or it may possibly have had a suggestion from Am 9⁹.

2. Use of other writings in the Gospels.—Are other writings than the OT used in the Gospels? This question recognizes the possibility (a) of explicit citations from writings outside of the OT as authoritative documents, or (b) of a general use of material as a source of historical example or explicit allusion, or (c) of literary relationship, or (d) of other writings with a genetic relation to the teachings of the Gospels.

(a) The passages which have been brought into debate are Mt 27⁹, Lk 7³²ᵇ 11⁴⁹, Jn 4³⁷ and 7³⁸.

Mt 27⁹. Is this a citation from some lost writing outside the OT and attributed to Jeremiah? Apparently the dictate of common sense is that the passage is really from Zec 11¹². ¹³, and that there was some slip in the memory of the writer of the Gospel, or that there was an error on the part of the earliest transcribers.

Lk 7³²ᵇ. Doubtless here Jesus was using as an illustration facts with which all persons who observed children at play were familiar. It seems an attempt to manufacture a difficulty. This passage should be dismissed from consideration.

Lk 11⁴⁹. This is a passage which is not so easily explained. (1) Is 'The Wisdom of God' the name of a book? No such book is known. (2) Is 'The Wisdom of God' a speaker in a book, after the manner of 'Wisdom' in Pr 8? Every trace of such a book now seems lost. (3) Is Jesus quoting Himself? See Mt 23³⁴, where Jesus says, 'Behold I send unto you prophets, and wise men, and scribes,' just as in this passage Wisdom says, 'I will send unto them prophets and apostles.' The words in Mt. are dated in the second day of Passion Week, while the passage in Lk. belongs to a time several weeks or months earlier. If Jesus in Lk. is quoting Himself, it is from an utterance of an earlier date, not elsewhere transmitted to us. Resch (*Agrapha*², p. 184) would show that 'The Wisdom of God' was one of the self-designations of Jesus like 'The Son of Man.' To these statements it must be said that while they are possible, Jesus is nowhere else designated in this manner, nor is He elsewhere represented as quoting Himself in this manner. (4) It is claimed that the passage is founded upon Pr 1²⁰⁻³¹, and this is supported by the fact that in the early Christian Church the Book of Proverbs was called a *Sophia*. The passage hardly seems adequate for the words of Jesus. (5) This passage is claimed as an amplification of 2 Ch 24²⁰⁻²². This is in reality the same as (7) below. (6) Used of Divine Providence, as manifested in history (cf. Pr 8²²⁻³¹), sending prophets and apostles, equivalent to saying 'God in His wisdom said.' This is supported by the passage Lk 7³⁵ 'and wisdom is justified of all her children.' This is quite tenable. (7) The personal wisdom of God in Christ. In support of this are the facts that Jesus says the same thing in Mt 23³⁷ in His own Person, that He is elsewhere said to send prophets and apostles (Lk 10³, Eph 4¹¹), and that this is a Logos conception of Jesus. Even so, a reason for the expression is not obvious, nor is it at all evident why Jesus should have used this unusual phrase. There are difficulties in regard to any explanation of this passage. The greatest of all is in the theory of an extra-OT source. The passage is perfectly intelligible with-

out such a theory, whatever be said as to the reason of the expression.

Jn 4³⁷. 'For herein is the saying true, One soweth, and another reapeth.' Is this an explicit quotation from some writing? The word 'saying' does not point back to a writing. It might readily be something of a proverbial character, which had its origin in the mode of thought and utterance which is found in Lv 26¹⁶, Dt 28³⁸⁻⁴⁰ 6¹¹, Job 31⁸, Mic 6¹⁵, thus having a literary connexion of some sort with the OT.

Jn 7³⁸. If this is a quotation from a writing outside the OT, a wholly unknown writing has to be assumed. Nowhere else in the NT is a writing outside the OT called γραφή, 'Scripture.' It is a tenable and adequate explanation to treat it as 'a free quotation harmonizing in thought with parts of various passages, especially Is 44³ 55¹ 58¹¹' (Meyer). See, on an attempt to trace the saying to a Buddhist source, *ExpT* xviii. [1906] p. 100.

The examination of these passages fails to show the slightest probability that Jesus, a speaker in the Gospels, or any writer of the Gospels, explicitly cited any writing outside the OT as authoritative Scripture.

(b) Examination of the facts gives no greater probability that historical illustrations from writings other than the OT occur in the Gospels, or intentional allusions to such writings, in any such manner as the illustrations taken from the OT, or as the allusions to the OT found in the Gospels.

(c) It is difficult not to believe that literary connexion is quite marked. Note, especially, the following passages : Mt 5³⁴. ³⁵ (Sir 23⁹) 5⁴²ᵃ (Sir 4⁴. ⁵) 5⁴²ᵇ (Sir 29²ᵃ) 5⁴⁴ (Wis 12¹⁹ᵃ) 6¹². ¹⁴ (Sir 28²) 7¹² (To 4¹⁵) 11²⁸ᶠ. (Sir 51²³ᶠᶠ.) 19²¹ (Sir 29¹¹) 23³⁸ (To 14⁴), Lk 6³⁸ (Sir 14¹⁶ᵃ) 10²⁵ 18¹⁸ (Enoch 40⁹, Sibyl. *proœm.* 85 = frag. ii. 47) 16⁸ (Enoch 108¹¹) 18⁷ (Enoch 47¹. ²) 18¹⁻⁸ (Sir 32¹⁷. ¹⁸) 20¹⁰. ¹¹ (Enoch 89⁵¹), Jn 6²⁷ᵃ (Sir 15³ 24¹⁹) 8⁴⁴ (Wis 2²⁴, Enoch 69⁶).

(d) Is the relation between these writings more important than a merely literary relation? If it is, how important is it? What does it signify? In the references above, the extra-OT books are all prior to the birth of Jesus. They reveal something of the thought of the Jews before His time, and doubtless of His own generation. The very tone of the words of Jesus to Martha (Jn 11²³. ²⁵. ²⁶) shows that He assumed the truth of beliefs which had no prominence in the thought and life revealed in the OT. The non-canonical literature gives abundant evidence that the belief in the resurrection had become an important factor in the beliefs of the Jews. Such a passage as Mt 25³¹⁻⁴⁶ can hardly be said to be suggested by the OT writings. Compare it with Enoch 90¹⁸⁻³⁸, and striking similarities are found. Mt 25⁴¹ᵇ 'Depart from me, ye cursed, into the eternal fire which is prepared for the devil and his angels,' and similar passages, as also 13⁴². ⁵⁰, may be compared with Enoch 103⁷. ⁸ and 108⁵. ⁶. In Lk 16²⁶ the picture of separation between the righteous and sinners in Sheol may suggest Enoch 22⁹⁻¹³, where the righteous and sinners, in separate divisions, await the Great Judgment.

Although there is often a striking likeness in outstanding features, there is also a lack of harmony in details with the spirit of Jesus, which shows why He could not use these writings as an authority. For the possible connexion between the Book of Enoch and Christian thought, see *The Book of Enoch*, tr. and ed. by R. H. Charles, pp. 48–53, where he enumerates 'doctrines in Enoch which had an undoubted share in moulding the corresponding NT doctrines, or at all events are necessary to the comprehension of the latter.' Without doubt the points of contact between the

Book of Enoch and Christian beliefs of the earlier Christian generations were more numerous and intimate than between the Book of Enoch and the Gospels. Also such literature as the extra-canonical Jewish writings had great influence in the early development of Christian doctrine. Their importance, so far as the Gospels are concerned, is chiefly that of explaining the surroundings of Jesus and the spiritual and mental conditions amidst which He worked. Instances such as have been given could be multiplied, but it is doubtful if they could change the conclusions already given. The centuries between the prophets of ancient Israel and Jesus had witnessed a development of thought, especially on eschatological subjects. 'Jesus was a true OT saint' (Davidson, *Theology of the OT*, p. 520), and joined the work which He did as closely as possible to that of the OT prophets, using their authority for His teachings. Jesus was also a Prophet greater than any that had gone before Him, and He appropriated such current beliefs as were in harmony with His mission, without thereby authenticating other associated beliefs, but rather discrediting them by the general spirit of His teachings.

See also artt. on OLD TESTAMENT.

LITERATURE.—Allen, 'OT Quotations in Matthew and Mark,' *ExpT* xii. [1900–1901] pp. 187 ff., 281 ff. [a careful examination of the relation of the quotations in these books to the OT passages]; E. Boehl, *Die Alttest. Citate im NT* [the treatise and discussion superseded by that of Toy]; August Clemen, *Der Gebrauch des AT in den NT Schriften*, Gütersloh, 1895 [a discussion of the meaning of the citations in the NT context and in their original context]; Wilhelm Dittmar, *Vetus Test. in Novo*, Göttingen, 1903 [gives not only five times as many parallels in thought or words in addition to the quotations. Almost invariably the Hebrew and Greek of the OT are given, and the Greek of the NT and of the Apocryphal books where they are cited. It is a valuable work]; Eugen Hühn, *Die AT Citate und Reminiscenzen im NT*, Tübingen, 1900 [a list of passages much more full than that of Dittmar, almost twice as numerous. Few citations are given. The passages are classified as Messianic and non-Messianic. Both classes are divided into citations with formulæ of citation, citations without formulæ, and reminiscences. The material is valuable, but needs sifting and further classification]; Johnson, *Quotations of the NT from the Old*, Philadelphia, 1896 [discusses the literary principles exemplified in the NT quotations and defends them]; Tholuck, *AT im NT*[6], Gotha, 1868 [tr. in *Bibliotheca Sacra*, vol. xi. p. 568 ff.]; Crawford H. Toy, *Quotations in the New Testament*, New York, 1884 [holds that the quotations were made from the Greek or from an oral Aramaic version, the existence of which is assumed. It contains an admirable b'bliography]; D. M. Turpie, *The Old Test. in the New*, London, 1868 [quotations classified according to their agreement with the Hebrew or Greek of the OT, and discussed accordingly], and *The NT View of the OT*, London, 1872 [quotations classified and discussed according to their introductory formulæ]; Woods, art. 'Quotations' in Hastings' *DB* iv. 184 ff.

F. B. DENIO.

R

RABBI (from Heb. רב, which means as adj. 'great' or 'much,' as subst. 'chief' or 'master.' The final syllable is the pronominal suffix, signifying 'my,' the force of which, however, is not expressed in the use of the word).—A title of honour and respect addressed to religious teachers; and in this sense frequently applied in the Gospels to Jesus, and also once (Jn 3[26]) to John the Baptist. It appears to have come into use in the time of Hillel, who was born *c.* B.C. 112. That St. John regarded it as a comparatively modern word, and not universally known in his time, seems evident from the fact that he deemed it necessary to explain its meaning (see Jn 1[38], where it is expressly stated to be equivalent to διδάσκαλος, rendered 'master' in AV, and 'teacher' in RVm). ῥαββί (ῥαββεί, WH) is frequently tr. 'master' in AV, but RV transliterates 'rabbi' throughout. See MASTER.   DUGALD CLARK.

RABBONI (from Heb. רַבִּן or רִבּוֹן) is another form of 'Rabbi,' but was considered a higher and more honourable title. Hence possibly its preference by the blind man (Mk 10[51]) in his natural anxiety to address Jesus with the title of greatest courtesy and respect that he knew. The word occurs only twice in the Gospels, viz. Mk 10[51] (RV following the reading of most authorities), and Jn 20[16] (ῥαββουνί, TR; ῥαββουνεί, WH). In the latter passage it is explained as a synonym for διδάσκαλος.

DUGALD CLARK.

RACA.—The word occurs only in Mt 5[22], and offers one of the little riddles of the Gospels which have not found as yet a sufficient explanation. It had been spelt 'Racha' in the AV of 1611; so in Tindale and other earlier versions. It was replaced by 'Raca' in 1638, and explained 'that is, *Vain fellow*, 2 S 6[20],' by one of the marginal notes added to the AV at various times, chiefly in 1762 (see the Introduction to Scrivener's *Paragraph Bible*, p. xxx). The RV confines itself to the marginal note, 'an expression of contempt.' The spelling of the Greek MSS is ῥαχα in א*D, adopted by

Tischendorf; ῥακα in א[c]BE, etc., with -â in B, -á in other MSS, as 13. 124. 556 (see Scrivener, *Adversaria*); ῥακκα, ῥακκαν, ῥακαν in *Apost. Const.* ii. 32; *racha* in most MSS of the Latin Versions; *raccha* in *d*; only *f k Z*[c] and the official Vulgate have *raca*; רקא in all Syriac Versions, vocalized רָקָא, רַקָא, רְקָא, רְקָא (see the edition of the *Tetraeuangelium* by Pusey-Gwilliam, and the *Thesaurus Syriacus*; it is explained as = שׁיט, *i.e.* 'despised,' by Barhebræus).

The puzzle in the word is the *a* of the first syllable, which is not found in the corresponding Hebrew word. It is true, J. Lightfoot (*Hor. Heb.*, new ed. by Rob. Gandell, Oxford, 1859, ii. 108) writes:

'*Raca*: A word used by one that despiseth another in the highest scorn: *very usual in the Hebrew writers*, and very common in the mouth of the nation.' Then he gives examples from *Tanchum*, fol. 5, col. 2; fol. 18, col. 4; fol. 38, col. 4; *Midrash Tillin* upon Ps 138; Bab. *Berak.* fol. 32. 2, of which the following are worth quoting: 'A heathen said to an Israelite, "Very suitable food is made ready for you at my house." "What is it?" saith the other. To whom he replied, "Swine's flesh." "*Raca*," saith the Jew, "I must not eat of clean beasts with you."' 'A king's daughter was married to a certain dirty fellow. He commanded her to stand by him as a mean servant, and to be his butler. To whom she said, "*Raca*, I am a king's daughter."' 'One of the scholars of R. Jochanan made sport with the teaching of his master; but returning at last to a sober mind: "Teach thou, O master," saith he, "for thou art worthy to teach, for I have found and seen that which thou hast taught." To whom he replied, "ריקה *Raca*, thou hadst not believed unless thou hadst seen."' 'A certain captain saluted a religious man praying in the way, but he saluted him not again: he waited till he had done his prayer, and saith to him, "ריקה *Raca*, it is written in your law,"' etc.

But in all these cases the Semitic word is spelt ריקה (with *yod*), which must be vocalized רֵיקָא, *i.e.* *Reca*; see Dalman, *Aram.-Neuheb. Wörterbuch*, p. 384; Jastrow, *Dictionary*, ii. 1476. In the first edition of his *Gram. d. Jüd.-Pal. Aram.* (1896) Dalman assumed that in the form of the NT *ai* had been contracted to *a*, and that the spelling with χ in the MSS אD was due to an aspirated pronunciation of the Hebrew *qoph*, by which it approached to the aspirated *kaph*. In the second

(1905, p. 174) he suggested at last a more probable solution, that the word in Greek assumed its form through assimilation to Greek ῥάκος, 'lump'='rag (a tattered piece of cloth, and then used of a shabby, beggarly fellow). This is possible. But there is another strange and not yet corroborated statement about the use of the word, found in Chrysostom, who was acquainted with Syriac as spoken in the neighbourhood of Antioch. He says (p. 214) that it was not a word 'of the highest scorn,' as Lightfoot styled it:

Τὸ δὲ ῥακὰ τοῦτο οὐ μεγάλης ἐστὶν ὕβρεως ῥῆμα, ἀλλὰ μᾶλλον καταφρονήσεως καὶ ὀλιγωρίας τινὸς τοῦ λέγοντος. καθάπερ γὰρ ἡμεῖς ἢ οἰκέταις, ἤ τισι τῶν καταδεεστέρων ἐπιτάττοντες λέγομεν· ἄπελθε σύ, εἰπὲ τῷ δεῖνι σύ· οὕτω καὶ οἱ τῇ Σύρων κεχρημένοι γλώττῃ ῥακὰ λέγουσιν, ἀντὶ τοῦ σύ, τοῦτο τιθέντες. ἀλλ' ὁ φιλάνθρωπος θεὸς καὶ τὰ μικρότατα ἀναστᾷ, καθηκόντως ἡμῖν κεχρῆσθαι ἀλλήλοις κελεύων, καὶ μετὰ τῆς προσηκούσης τιμῆς, καὶ ἵνα διὰ τούτων καὶ τὰ μείζονα ἀναιρῆται.

In contradistinction to ῥακά, Chrysostom considers μωρέ as χαλεπώτερον, as ῥῆμα τῆς ὕβρεως πληκτικώτερον, for which διπλῆ γίνεται ἡ πυρά. The same statement by a later hand is also found on the margin of codex B, τὸ ῥακὰ ἀντὶ τοῦ σύ being one of the few marginal notes of this MS; and a similar statement is made in the so-called Opus imperfectum, p. 62; but, at the same time, the common explanation is there given: 'Racha quidem dicitur Hebraice vacuus.' Euthymius Zigabenus is dependent on Chrysostom: Τὸ ῥακὰ δὲ ἑβραϊκή ἐστι φωνή, δηλοῦσα τὸ Σύ. Ἐπεὶ γὰρ ὀργιζόμενός τις κατά τινος οὐκ ἀξιοῖ καλέσαι τοῦτον ἐξ ὀνόματος, ὡς ἀνάξιον ὀνόματος· ἀντὶ ὀνόματος δὲ τὸ Σὺ τίθησιν. Augustine speaks of having heard from a Jew, that Raca is vocem non significantem aliquid, sed indignantis animi motum exprimentem. No example, however, has been found as yet of this use in Syriac. It is interesting to note that Maclean's Dictionary of the Dialects of Vernacular Syriac gives the vocalization ܪܹܩܵܐ

rēca (or rica) for the present dialect of the Azerbaijani Jews. This want of examples may, however, be due to the fact that a word was avoided, the use of which was denounced in the Gospel. The expression ἄνθρωπε κενέ in Ja 2²⁰ may be considered its Greek equivalent, as St. Paul's ἄφρων (1 Co 15³⁶) is the parallel to μωρέ. It may be added that the εἰκῇ in the first part of the verse has been believed by some to be the Greek explanation of this Raca, and to have crept into the text at the wrong place. But this is not likely. The Onomastica sacra (ed. Lagarde) are unanimous in the explanation 'κενέ, κενός, vacuus,' and spell ῥακά, ῥακκά, Racha, Raca (cod. F). See also art. FOOL.   EB. NESTLE.

RACHEL, the wife of Jacob and the mother of Joseph and Benjamin, is mentioned in Mt 2¹⁸, in a quotation from Jer 31¹⁵. The words of Jeremiah are understood in this passage as a prediction of the slaughter of the Innocents, but in their original connexion they refer to a historical incident in the prophet's own life. He accompanied the exiles on their way to Babylon as far as Ramah, 5 miles north of Jerusalem (Jer 40¹), and the impression produced by his last sight of them took the form of a poetic picture of Rachel, the ancestral mother of the Israelites (who according to one tradition— 1 S 10²—was buried in the neighbourhood), bewailing the fate of her descendants (Jer 31¹⁵). The application of this passage to the massacre at Bethlehem seems to have been suggested by the fact that another tradition placed Rachel's tomb in the vicinity of that town (Gn 35¹⁹· ²⁰ 48⁷). The supposed site of this sepulchre has been shown, at least since the 4th cent. A.D., about 4 miles south of Jerusalem, and one mile north of Bethlehem. See RAMAH.   JAMES PATRICK.

RAHAB.—The mother of Boaz, and thus an ancestress of our Lord (Mt 1⁵).

'These names [those of Tamar, Rahab, Ruth, Bathsheba] are probably introduced as those of women in whose case circumstances were overruled by the Divine providence which, as it might have seemed, should have excluded them from a place in the ancestral line of the Messiah. They were in a sense forerunners of the Virgin Mary' (W. C. Allen, Com. ad loc.).

The 'faith' of Rahab is extolled in He 11³¹, and her 'works' in Ja 2²⁵.

RAILING.—See REVILING and MOCKERY.

RAIMENT.—See DRESS.

RAIN.—See AGRICULTURE in vol. i. p. 40ᵃ.

RAM.—A link in our Lord's genealogy, Mt 1³ᶠ. (AV Aram).

RAMAH (Mt 2¹⁸) was a city of Benjamin (Jos 18²⁵), the site of which has been identified with er-Râm, a small village situated about 5 miles north of Jerusalem, at an elevation of about 2600 feet above the sea. Ramah was the point at which Jeremiah parted from the exiles who were being carried away to Babylon (Jer 40¹), and he associated it with Rachel in the passage (31¹⁵) which is quoted by the First Evangelist. This seems to imply that he considered Rachel's tomb to be in the neighbourhood; and the existence of such a tradition is supported by the account in 1 S 10², which states that Rachel was buried 'in the border of Benjamin.' The mention of Ramah in the NT quotation is a detail which has no significance in relation to the massacre of the Innocents, since Bethlehem was 10 miles away, on the other side of Jerusalem. See RACHEL.
                                        JAMES PATRICK.

RANSOM.—The word 'ransom' occurs twice in the NT, in both cases with reference to Christ's giving of Himself for the redemption of man : (1) in Mt 20²⁸=Mk 10⁴⁵, where it represents the Gr. λύτρον : 'the Son of Man came not to be ministered unto, but to minister, and to give his life a ransom for many'; and (2) in 1 Ti 2⁶, where it stands for ἀντίλυτρον : 'For there is one God, one mediator also between God and men, himself man, Christ Jesus (v.⁵), who gave himself a ransom for all.' The idea, however, is implicit in the verb (λυτρόομαι) and nouns (λυτρωτής, λύτρωσις, ἀπολύτρωσις) used to express the thought and fact of redemption (see REDEMPTION). It is probable from its structure that the second of the above passages (1 Ti 2⁶) looks back upon Christ's saying in the first (Mt 20²⁸); it has been thought also that the ἐλυτρώθητε in 1 P 1¹⁸ is an echo of the same saying (Denney, Death of Christ, p. 92). The word λύτρον itself is most probably the equivalent of the Heb. word כֹּפֶר (Wendt and others question this, but most admit the connexion), and the attempt to give a closer definition of its meaning in relation to Christ's redemption goes back on the usage of this OT word (cf. the elaborate discussion in Ritschl's Recht. u. Vers. ii. pp. 70–80).

כֹּפֶר, then, the word generally translated 'ransom' in the OT (Ex 21³⁰ 30¹², Nu 35³¹· ³² AV 'satisfaction'; 1 S 12³ AV 'bribe,' Job 33²³· ²⁴ 36¹⁸, Ps 49⁷, Pr 6³⁵ 13⁸ 21¹⁸, Is 43³, Am 5¹²), is derived, like the verb כִּפֶּר 'to propitiate,' 'to atone,' from a root meaning 'to cover.' It may thus be used, as in 1 S 12³ above, of a bribe given to blind the eyes from seeing what, in justice, they ought to see (cf. Ex 23⁸, Job 9²⁴). This connects itself with the old idea of a gift as 'covering the face' (cf. Gn 32²⁰) of an offended person, i.e. propitiating, appeasing him, or inclining him to favour. As, however, in the case of an offence, there is little difference between covering the eyes of the offended party from beholding the offence, and covering the offence from his sight, it can easily be seen how כֹּפֶר came to take this second sense of covering the sinful person or his iniquity. This leads to the idea, which is the common one in the OT, of כֹּפֶר as a 'ransom,' in the sense of something given in exchange for another as the price of that other's redemption, or for one's own redemption, or, what is at bottom the same idea, as satisfaction for a life. Thus in Is 43³·⁴ Jehovah is metaphorically said to have given Egypt, Ethiopia, and Seba as a ransom for ('instead of') Israel. Hofmann, in his *Schriftbeweis* (ii. p. 234, 2nd ed.), has a different interpretation. He takes the notion of 'covering' in this word to apply to 'covering in value' (one thing covering the worth of another), and so imports into כֹּפֶר the idea of strict equivalence. It is true that 'ransom' in the OT usually includes the idea of rendering what may be termed an equivalent; but it is more than doubtful whether this can be read into the etymological signification. The term has, on the other hand, in nearly every case the direct meaning of a redemption-price for another, or for one's own life. (1) In illustration of the latter sense, we have it declared in Nu 35³¹·³² that in no circumstances is a 'ransom' to be taken for the life of a murderer. Again, in Ex 21³⁰ it is provided that if, through its owner's carelessness, an ox gore a man or a woman, the ox shall be stoned, and the owner shall pay 'for the ransom of his life' what is laid on him (in the case of a slave, 30 shekels, v.³²). So at the taking of a census (Ex 30¹²), each Israelite above twenty years had to pay half a shekel—'atonement-money' (v.¹⁵ᶠ·)—as 'a ransom for his soul (or life).' (2) In illustration of the former sense—redemption-price for another (cf. Is 43³ above)—two instances stand out conspicuously. One is Ps 49⁷ 'None of them [the rich in this life] can by any means redeem his brother, nor give to God a ransom for him' (cf. v.8ᶠ·); the other is Job 33²⁴ 'Then he is gracious unto him, and saith, Deliver him from going down to the pit, I have found a ransom.' כֹּפֶר, in both of these passages, has clearly the sense of something given in exchange for a life, which redeems it from death.

In the above cases in the Law, the ransom is a sum of money; in the case of the firstborn, though the word כֹּפֶר is not used, it is a sacrifice—a life for a life (cf. Nu 18¹ᵇ·¹⁶). Here the fact is to be noticed—of interest in the NT connexion—that in all this range of meanings the word 'ransom' is never in the OT directly connected with the propitiatory sacrifices. It is connected with propitiatory payments (cf. Ex 30¹² above), and in 2 S 21³·⁷ the idea, if not the word, is connected with the propitiatory delivering up of Saul's seven sons to the Gibeonites (after refusal of a money-satisfaction, v.⁴). But the victim, even in sin- and trespass-offerings, is never spoken of as 'ransoming' the offerer. Its blood propitiates, atones for his sin, but the term 'ransom' is not employed. Yet it must be held that the connexion between the two ideas of sacrifice offered for the removal of sin (to make propitiation, כִּפֶּר) and of 'ransom' (כֹּפֶר) is very close; and that, whether the word is used or not, the expiatory sacrifice was also, in its own way, a כֹּפֶר for the life of the offerer (the LXX in Ps 49⁸ as in 1 S 12³ renders the word by ἐξίλασμα). Ritschl's generalization of the meaning of the term (applied also to the sacrifice) into 'a means of protection' (*Schutzmittel*), ignores the essential point of redemption (not simply protection) by the payment of a price, or offering of an expiation.

The way is now clearer for the understanding of the NT passages. There can be little difficulty, when his words are taken in the general connexion of his thought, in apprehending what St. Paul meant when he spoke in 1 Ti 2⁶ of Christ's having given Himself as an ἀντίλυτρον for all. 'Ransom' has here its true and proper sense of 'a price paid in exchange,' and the ideas of 'ransom' and expiatory sacrifice flow together in the unity of the thought of redemption through Christ's reconciling death (see REDEMPTION). In St. Paul's view, Christ has given Himself up as a sin-offering for the world upon the Cross (Ro 8³ 2 Co 5¹⁴·²¹, Gal 3¹³ etc.). He has redeemed the world by Himself dying for it (Ro 5⁶·⁹·¹⁰). His death, reconciling us to God (Ro 3²⁴·²⁵, Eph 2¹⁶, Col 1²⁰ etc.), brings life and salvation to mankind. St. Paul's mind is not troubled by the monetary analogy: it is not of a money price he is thinking, but of a great ethical reparation rendered to God's broken law of righteousness. It is to God the 'ransom' is paid, not to another. The Son of God, in humanity, renders it for the world.

If, therefore, St. Paul knew of the saying of Jesus recorded in Matthew and Mark, there can be little doubt how he would have interpreted it. Alike in his thought and that of St. Peter (cf. 1 P 1¹⁸·¹⁹), the idea of a λύτρον is involved in the conception of ἀπολύτρωσις. Redemption has the two aspects, which can never be separated—redemption by 'ransom,' *i.e.* from sin's guilt and condemnation; and redemption by power, from sin's bondage and other evil effects. The Apostolic gospel comprehended both. But what of Christ's own thought? The genuineness of the saying in

Mt 20²⁸=Mk 10⁴⁵ has been assailed (by Baur, etc.), but surely without the slightest grounds (cf. Ritschl, ii. p. 42 ff.; Denney, p. 36 f.). Its meaning also must be interpreted by the fact that Christ's own mind at the time of uttering it was full of the thought of His death. It is His 'life' He gives, and He startles by saying that He yields it up as a λύτρον ἀντὶ πολλῶν. He declares, further, that it was for this very end He came. His death was neither unforeseen, nor simply submitted to. He came to redeem the world by offering Himself as a 'ransom' for it. No doubt it is possible to empty the saying of most of its significance by generalizing it to mean that in some undefined way Christ's death would be of great saving benefit to mankind, and therefore might be spoken of metaphorically as a ransom for the good of many (cf. Wendt, *Lehre Jesu*, ii. p. 509 ff.). This interpretation fails, if account be taken of the redeeming efficacy which Jesus in other places (as in the words at the Last Supper) undeniably attributes to His death (see REDEMPTION). Ritschl, though he unduly weakens the force of the word λύτρον, does not fall into any such superficializing. He sees a solemn and weighty import in the words of Jesus, and interprets them to mean that Jesus, by His voluntary and guiltless death, directed to this end, redeems the members of His community from the doom of final annihilation impending over them in the judgment of God, gives death a new character to them, and delivers them from its fear (ii. p. 87). The interpretation cannot be accepted; neither is it explained how the death of Jesus should effect such a result. Yet Jesus assuredly did view the world as lying under condemnation of God, sunk in estrangement and evil, and needing both forgiveness and renewal to righteousness, and redemption from this state He connected with His own Person, and in a peculiar way with His death, which He here speaks of as a λύτρον, or redemption-price, to that end. Further investigation must be left to other articles (see ATONEMENT, RECONCILIATION, REDEMPTION).

The idea of Christ's death as 'a ransom for all' has ever been a favourite one in the preaching, theology, and hymnology of the Church. In certain circles it early became connected with the fanciful notion that the ransom was paid, not to God, but to the Evil One, who was supposed to have acquired rights over man through sin, which God, in righteousness, could not ignore. Christ's soul, therefore, it was taught, was given up to Satan as the price of the surrender of these assumed rights over mankind. But Satan was deceived in the bargain, for, having obtained possession of the sinless soul of Jesus, he could not hold it. That sinless soul was a torture to him. This theory, connected in the early Church with Origen and Gregory of Nyssa (though Origen, at least, frequently expresses himself in a quite contrary sense), prevailed extensively in the Middle Ages, but never really stood alone, or gained ascendency over the abler minds. Distinguished Fathers repudiated it, and Anselm reasons against it in his *Cur Deus Homo.*

LITERATURE.—Ritschl, *Recht. und Vers.* ii. pp. 51 ff., 192 ff.; Wendt, *Lehre Jesu*, ii. p. 511 ff.; artt. 'Propitiation,' 'Ransom,' in Hastings' *DB*; Denney, *Death of Christ*, p. 42 ff.; Stevens, *Theol. of the NT*, p. 126 ff. JAMES ORR.

RAVEN.—See ANIMALS in vol. i. p. 66ᵃ.

READER. — The Gospels frequently refer to private reading of Scripture, and Jesus Christ assumes that His hearers have the sacred books and read them for themselves, *e.g.* Mk 2²⁵ 12¹⁰·²⁶, Mt 12³, Lk 6³. At Nazareth, Jesus took the place of the public reader in the synagogue (Lk 4¹⁶),

The expression, 'Let him that readeth understand,' in Mt 24[15], cannot refer to the reading of Dn 9[27], because, although Daniel is mentioned earlier in this passage of Mt. (i.e. at v.[15]), in Mk.'s parallel passage there is no reference to Daniel (see Mk 13[14]). Therefore the words cannot be part of our Lord's utterance, and must be taken as a note interjected by the Evangelist, the writer of his source, or a reviser. Taken thus, they appear to point to the function of the reader in the primitive Church. That this function was known in very early times is indicated also by Rev 1[3], where public reading is unmistakably indicated, because it is associated with hearing by others : 'Blessed is he that readeth, and they that hear,' etc. In this respect, as in many other matters, the order of the Christian assembly was moulded on that of the synagogue. Among the Jews any member of the congregation—even a minor—might be the reader both of the Law and of the Prophets, although if a priest or a Levite were present he should have precedence (Giṭṭin, v. 8). Therefore it was quite in order that Jesus, although neither a scribe nor a synagogue official, should have the Prophet roll handed to Him to read. For this reason we may conclude that the reader in the primitive Church was not a man in any sense 'in orders.' For convenience, the same person might read on every occasion ; but there is nothing to show that this was the case. We do not meet with the reader among the Church functionaries referred to by St. Paul. Tertullian is the earliest Patristic writer to mention this official (de Praescr. c. 41). In the 3rd cent. he was included among the minor orders (Cyprian, Epp. 29, 38, etc.). See Schürer, GJV[3] II. ii. 27 ; Smith's DCA, vol. i. pp. 79, 80 ; Harnack, Sources of the Apostolic Canons, pp. 54–92.   W. F. ADENEY.

READINESS. — The expression γίνεσθε ἕτοιμοι, 'Be ye ready,' is employed by Christ to denote the necessity for constant readiness to receive Him at His Second Coming (Mt 24[44], Lk 12[40]). Closely akin to it in meaning is the more frequently used γρηγορεῖτε, 'Watch ye,' the word with which Christ demands constant watchfulness for the day of His Parousia (Mt 24[42] 25[13], Mk 13[34f. 37], Lk 21[36]). The two terms are used almost interchangeably in Mt 24[42. 44], as is evident from the fact that the illustration of the necessity for watchfulness by the case of the negligent householder who suffers his house to be broken through (Mt 24[43]), is followed by the exhortation to readiness in the next verse ; further evidence being found in the parable of the Ten Virgins, where the proper performance of the duty enjoined in Mt 25[13] ('Watch, therefore') is exhibited in the careful preparation made by the wise virgins, who are described as αἱ ἕτοιμοι, for the coming of the bridegroom.

The duty of being constantly prepared for the return of Christ is rendered urgent by the fact that the time of its occurrence is known only to the Father, and, being concealed even from the Son, cannot be communicated to the disciples (Mk 13[32]). It is the ignorance of the disciples as to the day and the hour of the final Advent which lends point and emphasis to Christ's exhortations in prospect of it (Mt 24[42. 44] 25[13], Mk 13[33. 35], Lk 12[40]).

If, as some (Weiss, Charles) maintain, He foretold that the fall of Jerusalem would be the immediate prelude to the end of the world, thus furnishing the disciples with a certain clue to the date of the latter event (Mt 24[32f.]), the need for such exhortations is far from obvious, and indeed inexplicable, based as they are on the utter uncertainty that prevailed as to the time of the end. In the case of the earlier event, exhortations to watchfulness are wanting, the signs of its approach being quite unmistakable ; in the case of the later event, they are frequent, the date of its arrival being quite unknown. Weiss admits that 'any determination of the day of His return, even if it had been possible, would only have rocked the disciples in false security'

(Life of Christ, iii. 93). The truth is, the question is one on which our Lord declined to dogmatize ; and while His confession of nescience regarding the end (Mk 13[32]) did not preclude the possibility of its speedy occurrence, neither did it preclude the possibility that it might be long deferred. He undoubtedly favoured the idea that the latter alternative was much the more likely one. 'There are distinct hints in some passages (Mt 24[48] 25[19], Mk 13[35]) that the end may be delayed beyond all human anticipation, and that "an indefinitely long night of history" may intervene before the return of the Lord' (Forrest, The Authority of Christ, p. 322).

The parables and parabolic sayings in the Synoptics (Mt 24[42]–25[30], Mk 13[32-37], Lk 12[35-48] 19[11-27]), intended to enforce the lesson of constant readiness for the Second Coming, may be described as parting counsels and admonitions to the disciples for the guidance of their conduct during the period, indefinitely prolonged, which must elapse between Christ's departure from the world, then impending, and His return at the close of the present dispensation. They all proceed upon the assumption that membership of the Kingdom during its earthly development does not, ipso facto, guarantee fitness for a place in the perfected Kingdom to be inaugurated at Christ's return. The period of His absence is a period of probation for His disciples, who are to be tested individually, and are expected to prove their individual fitness for the glorious Kingdom of the future. 'Every man' has his own proper sphere and work assigned him (Mt 25[14f.], Mk 13[34], Lk 19[13]), and the lack of personal preparedness cannot be made up for by connexion with the believing community, animated by the common hope of the Lord's appearing (Mt 25[1. 2. 9]).

Preparedness for the last Advent naturally depends on maintenance of the moral and spiritual qualities, and continued performance of the duties, pertaining to members of the Kingdom of God— qualities and duties fully described in the teaching of Christ throughout His ministry. The fact of His departure involves no alteration in His great requirements, which are ever the same ; it involves merely a deepened responsibility, an increased sense of gravity on the part of the disciples, whose conduct is to be constantly regulated and controlled henceforward by the thought of its bearing upon future destiny. Wendt remarks that 'since Christ's ideas of the future are comparatively general and indefinite, His admonitions regarding the future always retain a comparatively general character.' Directions in greater detail were not needed. The character and conduct required on the part of the disciples, as outlined in Christ's previous teaching, are calculated to satisfy the most stringent tests. The only difference is that they must now be formed under the altered conditions presented by the withdrawal of Christ's visible presence. The proper attitude of the disciple has to be preserved in face of the difficulties, perils, and temptations incident to (1) Christ's unexpectedly prolonged absence, and (2) His sudden and unexpected return.

(1) It is everywhere implied that Christ's withdrawal from the world affords His disciples the needful opportunity for the free and independent exercise of the gifts and powers entrusted to them. Their spiritual resources are to be developed to the utmost without the consciousness of being constantly overshadowed by His visible authority and supervision, but always in view of the day of reckoning (Mt 24[45-51] 25[14-30], Mk 13[34-36], Lk 12[42-48] 19[12-26]). The proof of readiness for His return is thoroughgoing devotion to the interests of the absent Lord, which are identical with the interests of His Kingdom, displayed in steadfast fidelity and unflagging diligence in the use of the gifts held in trust, under the severe test of indefinitely prolonged absence (Mt 24[45] 25[20f.], Lk 19[16f.]). But the same situation which creates the opportunity for freely utilizing the entrusted gifts, may lead to the misuse or to the absolute neglect of them. The

perils attending a delayed Parousia, which must be guarded against with ceaseless vigilance, arise from a weakened sense of obligation issuing in slackness and lethargy, the sin of 'the untrimmed lamp and the ungirt loin' (Mk 13^{36}, Lk 12$^{35f.}$), yielding to unbridled self-indulgence and the tyrannical abuse of authority (Mt 24$^{48f.}$), faithless and inexcusable failure to improve one's trust (Mt 25$^{26f.}$).

(2) The main strength of the appeal for constant readiness is drawn from the consideration that Christ's return will be sudden and unexpected. The frequent admonition to watch sounds a note of alarm, pointing to the danger of being taken unawares and found in a state of unpreparedness, due to the abrupt and startling manner in which the Parousia breaks in upon and breaks up the established order of things (Mt 24^{50} 25^6, Mk 13^{36}, Lk 12^{36} 21^{34}). Being of a catastrophic character, it leaves no time for the making or completing of preparations previously neglected (Mt 24$^{38f.\ 43}$ 25^{10}). The period of probation, and with it the possibility of repairing past negligences and failures, are ended, and future destiny determined by character and achievements, now to come under searching scrutiny.

As the Parousia immediately heralds the Last Judgment (Mt 25$^{19.\ 31}$), the manner in which the disciples have acquitted themselves during the period of Christ's absence is then passed under review, and appropriate destiny assigned them. Those who have proved their capacity in humbler spheres of service by fidelity to Christ's Person and interests are promoted to loftier spheres of service (Mt 24^{47} 25$^{20-23}$), raised to equality with Himself (Lk 12^{37}), and participate in the eternal blessedness of the consummated Kingdom (Mt 25$^{10.\ 21.\ 23}$). Those who have failed to reach the required standard are excluded, so far as appears, irrevocably, from such high fellowship (Mt 25$^{11f.\ 30}$), and incur penalties varying in degree in proportion to their unfaithfulness (Mt 24^{51}, Lk 12$^{47f.}$). See also artt. Parousia and Second Coming.

W. S. MONTGOMERY.

READING.—See artt. Boyhood in vol. i. p. 222^b, Education, Reader.

REALITY.—That a spirit of clear sincerity and genuine reverence for truth pervades the narratives of the Gospel writers and inspires the central Figure they depict, is an impression irresistibly forced on unprejudiced minds. Everywhere there is evident, in the writers themselves and in the Master about whom they write, a straightforward honesty and singleness of aim, and we find ourselves unmistakably in an atmosphere of reality.

I. **In the Gospel writers.**—Reality, as manifested by the Gospel writers, may be recognized by several notable features, such as :

1. *The absence in them of any straining after effect.*—They relate facts as they know them, and always with a certain artless simplicity ; and if occasionally they put an interpretation of their own upon the facts, it is still patent that it is an honestly framed interpretation. Invariably, in describing startling events, instead of dwelling on their startling character, they content themselves with such bare statements as that 'fear came upon all' (Lk 1^{65}), that 'all men did marvel' (Mt 8^{27}, Mk 5^{20}), that men were 'amazed' (Lk 4^{36} 5^{26}), that 'they glorified God' (Mt 9$^{8.\ 33}$, Mk 2^{12}, Lk 5^{26}), or that 'they were astonished with a great astonishment' (Mk 5^{42}). There is often a graphic force in the description, yet the events themselves are related without any rhetorical elaboration, and no attempt is made to heighten the colours. The narrative is plain, direct, and unadorned.

2. *Their frankness in recording incidents which reflect on the leaders of their cause.*—Notwithstanding every inducement to save the credit of the disciples first chosen by the Master, far from concealing the faults and perversities of those men, they tell the story of them with simple candour, this being in their view essential to an accurate understanding of the circumstances connected with the early beginnings of the faith. The jealous rivalries of the Twelve, and their disputes as to who should be accounted greatest (Mt 18^1, Mk 9^{34}, Lk 22^{24}), the failure of some of them to meet the duty of the hour (Mt 17^{16} 26$^{40-43}$, Mk 14$^{40.\ 50}$), the intolerant zeal (Lk 9^{54}) and ambitious scheming (Mt 20$^{20-23}$) of the two sons of Zebedee, the rash presumption (14$^{28-30}$ 16$^{22.\ 23}$) and weak denial (Mt 26$^{69-74}$, Mk 14$^{66-71}$) of Peter, the treachery of Judas (Mt 26$^{10-16.\ 47}$, Mk 14^{43}, Lk 22^{48})—are all told with an unvarnished plainness which betokens an inward pressure to be strictly faithful to the truth.

3. *Their genuine absorption in their subject.*— There is evident in these Evangelists a feeling that they are dealing with a theme too sacred to be trifled with. Their attitude towards the Lord whose life and actions they seek to portray is one of profound reverential affection, constraining them to a complete sinking of their own personality, with no other aim than that of presenting a picture worthy of Him who has won their hearts. They write as men who are impelled by a pure devotion to declare what they have learned and know about things which they believe to be precious and true.

II. **In Jesus.**—Reality, as seen in Jesus Himself, is superlatively arresting. In an age of affectations, formalisms, and general bondage to tradition, He stood out as uncompromisingly sincere, intent on getting close to fact and truth, and keeping resolutely in view the essential and permanent interests of life. He dared to think for Himself, and rose high above all artificiality and make-believe. This spirit of reality in Jesus is convincingly attested by the following points :

1. *His thorough naturalness as a religious teacher.* —With no demure, sanctimonious airs, and no pretentious tones such as the Rabbis were wont to assume, He spoke straight to the heart and conscience ; and common people felt that His utterances came home with an authority they were compelled to own (Mt 7^{29}). There was nothing of the professional about Him. His demeanour was that of unstudied simplicity ; and when occasion suited, He could unbend and let joy and cheerfulness have their genial flow,— looking with amused interest on the children at their games (Mt 11$^{16.\ 17}$), sharing the gladness of the social gathering (Jn 2$^{1-10}$), or lighting up His discourse with flashes of playfulness (Lk 11$^{5-8}$). While keenly alive to the seriousness of His vocation, He affected none of the Pharisaic rigour which would repress the healthy instincts of humanity—a witness for the highest truth, yet winningly human, and with a manner so gracious and open as to make Him easily accessible to all classes of men.

2. *His fearless directness in facing the actual facts of existence.*—No one ever looked with more straight and steady gaze than Jesus did on the solemn realities of human life and destiny. The distress and suffering that are in the world (Mt 4^{23} 12^{15}), the mysteries of Providence (Lk 13$^{1-4}$, Jn 9^3), the value and needs of the soul (Mt 16$^{26.\ 27}$, Lk 12$^{20.\ 21}$), the curse of sin (Mt 18$^{8.\ 9}$, Lk 13^3, Jn 8^{24}), the certainty of retribution (Mt 18^6 23^{32}, Mk 9$^{43-48}$), the necessity of spiritual renewal (Mt 9^{17}, Jn 3$^{3-7}$), the burden of responsibility (Mt 11$^{20-24}$ 23^{14}, Lk 10$^{13-16}$), the imperative obligations of duty (Jn 9^4), the supreme authority of God (Mt 19^{17}, Jn 4^{34} 10^{29}),—on all these Jesus kept His eye fixed with an intensity of vision and purpose that was never relaxed from the beginning to the end **of**

His career. Clearing His mind of all vague sentiment and easy superficiality, He confronted the grave problems and experiences, the mighty facts and forces, which affect man's well-being now and for ever, and dealt with them in a spirit of unwavering fortitude and sincerity..

3. *His steadfast determination to reach, and hold by, the fundamental elements of religion.*—Radical in the truest sense, Jesus displayed an incessant anxiety to get at the roots of things, to pierce beneath superficial respectabilities, and find the great eternal principles on which life should be based. This is seen (1) *in His teaching.* The outward observances of religion, He maintained, are nothing unless prompted by genuine gratitude and reverence (Mt 23²³, Lk 11⁴²). No matter how decorous the worship offered to Jehovah, if the spirit of devoutness does not fill the mind (Mt 15⁸, Jn 4²⁴). The show of goodness may look fair, but it has no value if it be the outcome only of calculating prudence or self-flattering pride (Mt 6²⁻⁵, Lk 16¹⁵). Purity, mercy, clear integrity of motive in the central springs of the life, He insisted on as the essentials of goodness. Everything had to be sterling, from the heart, real [see art. HEART].—(2) *In His private life.* The demand thus made was severely searching, yet it was fully met by Jesus in His own person. If the faithful application of high spiritual principles to the common, trivial concerns of existence be a sure proof of reality, that proof was given by Him in a superb degree. It is significant that the men who knew Him best and saw most of Him in daily intimacy were also the men who adored and believed in Him most fervently; and even the one who played the traitor was yet constrained to bear testimony to the goodness he had wronged (Mt 27⁴).—(3) *In His bearing towards the bigoted exclusiveness of His day.* Though threatened with the wreck of His own reputation by any association with the 'publicans and sinners,' Jesus had such profound sympathy with them in their despair of all good, begotten by the harsh ostracism to which they were doomed, that He seized every opportunity of coming into touch with them (Mt 9¹⁰⁻¹³, Mk 2¹⁵· ¹⁶, Lk 5²⁹· ³⁰ 15¹· ²). Bent on stirring the hearts of those outcasts of society by some ray of hope, He moved straight on to His gracious object, grappling with the moral necessities of the situation, indifferent to the censures of offended propriety. He even went so far as to choose a publican as one of His immediate disciples. The same superiority to the exclusive temper of His time is evinced also in His relations with the despised Samaritans (Jn 4⁴⁻⁴², Lk 17¹¹⁻¹⁹, cf. 10³²⁻³⁷)—His dominant concern always being to penetrate beneath surface appearances, and to reach and make manifest the capacity for righteousness in the innermost core of every human soul.

4. *His unworldly standard of personal worth.*—While drawing a sharp distinction between the two kinds of worth,—the material and the spiritual (Mt 6¹⁹· ²⁰· ²⁵),—Jesus did not denounce material success, though for Himself He never sought it. What He did denounce was the disposition to take material success as the measure of a man's value (Lk 12¹⁵⁻²¹). It is a false measure, and He refused to be judged by it Himself, or to apply it in judging any man. Content to be estimated by His soul-qualities, He estimated others by the same test, not by their temporal status or means (Lk 16¹⁹⁻²⁶, Mk 12⁴¹⁻⁴⁴).

5. *His perfect candour in the bestowal of appreciation or reproof.* — Though disdaining to flatter, Jesus was ever ready to recognize good, even when found in unexpected quarters, as we see in His praise of the faith of the centurion at Capernaum (Mt 8¹⁰), and of the offering of the poor widow at the Temple (Mk 12⁴²⁻⁴⁴). Prompt and warm, too, was His approval of the genuine feeling which He found struggling to assert itself in any soul, even when others condemned, as when He threw the shield of His graciousness over Zacchæus of Jericho (Lk 19⁹), the erring woman amid her penitence (7⁴⁴⁻⁴⁸), and Mary of Bethany in the scene of the anointing (Jn 12⁵⁻⁷). On the other hand, while benignly charitable towards natural human frailty, He could not suffer the flagrant follies 'and misdoings that met His eye to pass without remonstrance. The fault - finders who challenged the piety of His disciples because they did not fast (Mt 9¹⁴⁻¹⁷, Lk 5³⁵⁻³⁹), the illiberal formalists who sought to convert the Sabbath into a dreary bondage (Mk 2²³⁻²⁸, Lk 13¹⁵· ¹⁶), the hardened censors who had no mercy on a woman caught in transgression (Jn 8⁷), the scribes and Pharisees who turned religion into a pretentious show (Mt 23¹³⁻³⁵),—were made to feel the baseness of the spirit by which they were animated. There was a clear-purposed directness in the intercourse of Jesus with men; and even the chosen Twelve were not spared when they gave way to presumption, intolerance, or jealousy (Mt 16²²· ²³, Mk 9³⁴⁻³⁶, Lk 9⁵⁴⁻⁵⁶). At the risk of alienating those men, He shrank not from speaking the straight word when their errors or failings called for rebuke.

6. *His downrightness in dealing with popular expectations.*—Not even to gain a following would Jesus trifle in the slightest with truth and sincerity. When the multitudes, excited by the fame of His deeds, pressed round, expecting Him to take some step which would lift Israel to new heights of glory, instead of playing on their credulity, as for a while He might have done, He struck directly at their sensuous and extravagant hopes, insisting on their deeper needs and the more vital work which had first to be effected in their hearts (Jn 6²⁷ff.). With His eye on the moral and spiritual regeneration of men, He made it abundantly plain that He had no reliance on any such political and social revolution as they were looking for, unless it were brought about through a change of character. And when the inevitable reaction came, He let the once eager throng go their way, rather than accept their allegiance on a false understanding of what He was and sought to accomplish (6⁶⁰⁻⁶⁶).

7. *His reverent sobriety amid popular enthusiasm.*—Dazzling as the outbursts of such enthusiasm were, Jesus would never permit Himself to indulge in the luxury of self-gratulation, but, anxious to preserve the purity of His high spiritual aims, He deliberately seized the earliest opportunity of escaping to the mountains or the wilderness for solitary communion with the Father (Mt 14²³, Mk 3¹³ 6³¹). Even during the triumphal entry into Jerusalem He detached His mind from the ringing hosannas, and thought of the sins of the nation and the threatening doom (Lk 19⁴¹); and when the ovation was over He withdrew to the quiet of Bethany (Mt 21¹⁷), maintaining His spirit clear and true.

8. *His scrupulous honesty with regard to the risks of discipleship.*—That none might be misled by too sanguine expectations, Jesus took pains to give warning of the hardship and sacrifice which the adoption of His cause would involve. He told those willing to rally round Him to count the cost (Lk 14²⁸⁻³³), to be prepared for the endurance of privation and the rupture of old ties (Mt 10³⁷, Lk 9⁵⁷⁻⁶²), the severities of the world's disfavour (Mt 5¹¹), the cross of self-denial (Mt 16²⁴, Mk 8³⁴). Standing on the clear ground of truth, He spoke without evasion or concealment, and shrank from any homage that was not founded on a heartfelt sense of His spiritual worth.

9. *His consistent devotion to an unselfish purpose.* —The freedom of Jesus from strictly personal aims is 'writ large' on every page of the Gospel narratives. Even when constrained to assert His high claim as the bearer of a special Divine commission, there is not the slightest trace of His having any end to serve but the will of God and the good of men ; and from that end the world had no bribes by which He could be tempted aside (Jn 14³⁰).

10. *His calm resoluteness in facing the consequences of His teaching and work.*—Though fully alive to the deadly hostility which His teaching and general line of conduct would inevitably arouse, Jesus refused to make His path smoother by any prudential concessions to conventional taste. The policy of concession was urged upon Him at various stages, from the Temptation in the wilderness to the Agony in Gethsemane, but was always energetically repelled. When Peter at Cæsarea Philippi ventured to dissuade Him from carrying His principles to the point of personal danger, He treated the suggestion as a voice from the realm of darkness (Mt 16²²ᶠ·). Conscious of a testimony to bear for God to which He could not be untrue, and intent on disseminating ideas which He felt to be essential to the spiritual well-being of humanity, He confronted the malice of priests, Pharisees, and scribes, and amid gathering troubles 'steadfastly set his face to go to Jerusalem' (Lk 9⁵¹), where that malice at its fiercest had to be encountered. Knowing that a baptism of suffering awaited Him as the result of the work He had undertaken, He was 'straitened till it should be accomplished' (Lk 12⁵⁰), and with serene inflexibility of purpose He moved on towards the tragic climax, and braved the death which had cast its shadow over Him for many a day. See also art. SINCERITY.

LITERATURE.—In addition to the Lives of Christ, the following works may be consulted :—Ullmann, *Sinlessness of Jesus* ; Lacordaire, *Conferences on Jesus Christ* ; Seeley, *Ecce Homo* ; Bruce, *Training of the Twelve*, and *With Open Face* ; T. G. Selby, *Ministry of the Lord Jesus* ; Farrar, *Witness of History to Christ*, pp. 75–88 ; J. Watson, *Mind of the Master* ; Stopford Brooke, *Christ in Modern Life*, pp. 89–131 ; Smyth, *Truth and Reality.* Fruitful suggestions may also be found in the sermons of Channing, F. W. Robertson, and Martineau.

GEO. M'HARDY.

REAPING.—See AGRICULTURE in vol. i. p. 40ᵃ, and SICKLE.

REBUKE.—**1.** In restoring the man with the unclean spirit in the synagogue at Capernaum (Mk 1²⁵, Lk 4³⁵), and the demoniac boy at the foot of the Mount of Transfiguration (Mt 17¹⁸, Mk 9²⁵, Lk 9⁴²), Jesus is said to have rebuked (ἐπετίμησεν) *the unclean spirit.* The rebuke would help to calm the nerves and strengthen the will of the sufferer. But that was only incidental. It is clear to the present writer that Jesus recognized, in such cases, the presence of a personal evil spirit (cf. Mt 12²⁵⁻²⁸, Lk 11¹⁷⁻²⁰). He rebuked the spirit (1) because, being personal, he was susceptible of rebuke ; and (2) because of His malevolence in torturing the human patient (Mt 17¹⁵), or because of his testimony to Him as Messiah, which testimony, seeing it tended towards a faith founded upon marvels and not upon a simple love of goodness and joy in His revelation of the Father, really opposed His work (Mk 1²⁴· ²⁵· ³⁴, Lk 4⁴¹). St. Luke also says that Jesus, when healing Peter's wife's mother, rebuked *the fever* (4³⁹). This may be more figurative. Sickness was, undoubtedly, regarded as due in most cases to evil agencies (Lk 13¹⁶) ; but even popular opinion then did not class fevers with cases of demoniacal possession. Neither St. Matthew nor St. Mark speaks of any rebuke here ; it is therefore most probable that this is only the Evangelist's vivid description of Jesus' authoritative tone and manner of healing. On the sea of Galilee, Jesus is said to have rebuked *the wind* (Mt 8²⁶, Mk 4³⁹, Lk 8²⁴). It is a needless literalism to infer that He believed that the wind was demonic. It is a poetic account of His attitude (cf. Ps 106⁹, Nah 1⁴). His faith that God would guard Him till His work was done, was absolute ; and on His rising up in the dignity and calm of such a faith and bidding sea and wind be still, the disciples beheld the threatening wind die down as if rebuked.

2. Jesus had frequent need to reprove *His disciples* ; but only on two occasions were His reproofs so severe that it is written that He rebuked them. These were in the case of Peter (Mk 8³³), and James and John (Lk 9⁵⁵). The severity of His rebuke of Peter, 'Get thee behind me, Satan,' was not because Peter was, though unconsciously, acting the part of a tempter to Him. That would be contrary to the spirit of Jesus, who always forgot His own things in the presence of others' needs. It was His disciple's danger that moved Him. The test of a leader's sympathy and insight is his rebukes, whether they are addressed to mere casual faults or to those tendencies which spring from the roots of character. In these two cases, Jesus rebuked the most fatal tendencies of the two types of saintliness. 'St. John is the saint of purity, and St. Peter is the saint of love' (Newman's Sermon on 'Purity and Love' in *Discourses to Mixed Congregations*). The most dangerous temptation to loving souls is to smooth the path for those they love and reverence even at the cost of duty or of loyalty to their highest vision. Jesus here rebuked in Peter, this, love's subtlest disloyalty to righteousness. In the case of James and John, types of intensest purity, Jesus condemned that severity of judgment which is the temptation of men of integrity, and by which they may make shipwreck of their spirits, becoming narrow-minded and unbrotherly.

3. Various instances of rebukes by other persons are reported, whose value lies in their revealing by contrast the mind of Jesus. (1) The disciples' rebuke of those who brought little children to Jesus, serves to contrast their thought of the parents as inconsiderate and selfish, and of the children as beneath His notice because of their incapacity to understand His words, with His sympathy with the parents' desire to give their children a prophet's blessing, His warm love for the children simply as children (Mk 9³⁶), and His delight in the child-spirit as manifesting the true heavenly temper (10¹⁴). (2) The crowd's rebuke of Bartimæus brings into stronger relief the simplicity and brotherliness of Jesus' helpfulness (Mt 20³¹). (3) The repentant thief rightly rebuking his comrade for railing on Jesus (Lk 23⁴⁰), brings out strongly Jesus' silent endurance of contumely. It sets in a clearer light His prayer, 'Father, forgive them : for they know not what they do.' (4) The Pharisees' request that Jesus would rebuke His followers for hailing Him as Messiah, only served to make more clear and definite His acceptance of that homage with all it meant (19³⁹).

4. Jesus bids His disciples rebuke *a brother who sins* (17³). The following verse shows that the sin to be rebuked is a personal wrong. This resentment of wrong seems opposed to His blessing on the meek (Mt 5⁵) and His exhortation to turn the other cheek to the smiter (vv. ³⁹⁻⁴⁴). The context, however, shows that this rebuke is regarded only as the first step to forgiveness and reconciliation (Lk 17⁴). Repentance is necessary before forgiveness and reconciliation can be perfected ; and the rebuke is to be the act of brotherly love, showing the wrongdoer his fault to win him to that repentance.

RICHARD GLAISTER.

RECEIPT OF CUSTOM (AV ; 'place of toll,' RV ; 'tolbothe,' Wyclif) occurs in the parallel accounts of the call of the publican Matthew or Levi to discipleship (Mt 9⁹, Mk 2¹⁴, Lk 5²⁷), which took place as Jesus passed forth from His own city, *i.e.* Capernaum. The custom or toll referred to consisted of export dues on merchandise, and at Capernaum would pass into the treasury of Herod Antipas, the ruler of Galilee in the time of our Lord. Capernaum was close to the junction of the great north road to Damascus with the road that led eastwards round the northern end of the Lake of Galilee, and the important revenue station situated at this point is what we are to understand by the 'place of toll' in the Gospel story. See also PUBLICAN.   JAMES PATRICK.

**RECONCILIATION.—The gospel, in the Pauline acceptation, is peculiarly a message of reconciliation (καταλλαγή). The ministry of the gospel is a 'ministry of reconciliation.' Its preaching is a 'word of reconciliation.' Its design is that those who receive the message should 'be reconciled to God' (2 Co 5¹⁸⁻²¹). The word 'reconcile' is not found in this connexion in either the Gospels or the other writings of the NT. It is a distinctively Pauline term. The fact is one worth remembering by those who insist so much on the absence of certain other aspects of St. Paul's doctrine from the Gospels, yet see in 'reconciliation,' at least as relates to man, the truest expression for the end of Christ's mission. If, however, the *word* is absent from the Gospels, assuredly the reality is there. It is implied, on its Godward side, in Christ's doctrine of forgiveness of sins as a primary blessing of His Kingdom (Mt 6¹². ¹⁴. ¹⁵). It is the presupposition of Christ's whole ministry as directed to the salvation of the lost (Mt 18¹⁰⁻¹⁴, Lk 19¹⁰); is exhibited in His own gracious and merciful attitude to the sinful and burdened (Mt 11²⁸⁻³⁰, Lk 4¹⁷⁻²¹); in His mercy, especially to those whom society regarded as outcasts (Lk 7³⁶⁻⁵⁰ 'friend of publicans and sinners'; Mt 11¹⁹, Lk 15¹. ²); is involved in His whole revelation of the Father. On the manward side, as necessity, duty, and privilege, it is not less clearly implied in the invitation to come to Him (Mt 11²⁸); in the demand for 'repentance'—a changed mind and life (Mt 4¹⁷, Mk 1¹⁵ etc.); in the call to sonship in His Kingdom (Mt 5⁹. ⁴⁸, Lk 6³⁵. ³⁶ etc.), and to complete surrender of self, and trust in the Father (Mt 6²⁴ff.); in the requirement of a habitual doing of the will of the Father (Mt 5⁴⁸ 7²¹ff. etc.). The parable of the Prodigal Son is a typical parable of reconciliation (Lk 15¹¹ff.). If, in St. Paul's gospel, reconciliation is made dependent on Christ's Person and redeeming death, it is certain that in the Gospels also Jesus views the whole Messianic salvation as depending on Himself, and on repeated occasions connects it with His death (Jn 3¹⁴. ¹⁵, Mt 20²⁸ 26²⁸, Lk 24⁴⁶. ⁴⁷; see REDEMPTION). This circle of conceptions involved in 'reconciliation' is now to be more closely investigated.

In the OT the word 'reconcile' occurs several times in the AV in Leviticus and Ezekiel as the tr. of the verb כִּפֶּר, usually rendered 'to make atonement' (Lv 6³⁰ 8¹⁵ 16²⁰, Ezk 45¹⁵. ¹⁷. ²⁰ [RV tr., as elsewhere, 'to make atonement,' 'atoning']). The idea here conveyed is that of forgiveness and restoration to Divine fellowship on the ground of a propitiation. Similarly, in the NT, AV reads in He 2¹⁷ 'to make reconciliation for the sins of the people,' where the word is ἱλάσκεσθαι, and RV renders, 'to make propitiation.' In Dn 9²⁴, while the same Heb. word (כָּפַר) occurs (with direct object), RV retains the rendering 'to make reconciliation,' and puts in the margin, 'purge away.' In 2 Ch 29²⁴, again, where AV has 'made reconciliation,' RV

renders more accurately 'made a sin-offering.' These OT examples have only an indirect bearing on the NT word, the idea of which is not propitiation but change from variance into a state of friendship. Propitiation, in the OT, no doubt, effected a reconciliation, and, in the NT, reconciliation is made by atonement; but the ideas expressed by the words are nevertheless distinct. The NT term for 'reconciliation,' as already indicated, is καταλλαγή (Ro 5¹¹ [not 'atonement,' as AV] 11¹⁵, 2 Co 5¹⁸. ¹⁹). With this are connected the verbs καταλλάσσω (Ro 5¹⁰, 1 Co 5²⁰; cf. of a wife, 1 Co 7¹¹), and ἀποκαταλλάσσω (Eph 2¹⁶, Col 1²⁰. ²¹). A related form, διαλλάσσω, is used in Mt 5²⁴ (pass.) of reconciliation with a brother. But besides these terms, there is in St. Paul, as in other NT writers, a considerable range of words and phrases which express the same idea, *e.g.* 'made peace' (Col 1²⁰; cf. 'preached peace,' Ac 10³⁶, Eph 2¹⁷; 'have peace,' Ro 5¹); 'made nigh' (Eph 2¹³); 'turned unto God' (1 Th 1⁹. ¹⁰), etc. The general meaning of the Pauline expressions is well brought out in such a passage as Ro 5¹⁰ 'If, when we were enemies (ἐχθροί), we were reconciled to God through the death of his Son,' etc.; or in such a declaration (addressed to Gentiles) as that in Col 1²¹ 'You, being in time past alienated, and enemies in your mind in your evil works, yet now hath he reconciled in the body of his flesh through death.'

There is no dispute, then, that, in St. Paul's use, and generally, the word καταλλαγή denotes a change from enmity to friendship. The differences in regard to reconciliation in the gospel relate to two other points. (1) On whose side does the change from variance to friendship take place—on God's side as well as man's, or on man's only? Is God as well as man the subject of the reconciliation, or is man only reconciled? (2) By what means is the reconciliation effected? On the first point, the view is very widely held that the reconciliation is on the part of man only (Ritschl, Kaftan, *Cambridge Theol. Essays*, pp. 206, 217, etc.); God needs no reconciliation. God is eternally propitious to the sinner: it needs only that the sinner change his thoughts and his dispositions towards God. Yet it is very doubtful if, on exegetical grounds, even in regard to the use of the word, this can be sustained. God, indeed, is represented by St. Paul as already reconciled in Christ, *i.e.* everything is done on His side which is necessary for the restoration of the ungodly to favour, All that is needed now is the reciprocal reconciliation of men to God (Ro 5⁶. ⁸, 2 Co 5¹⁸⁻²¹). But it is still implied that a reconciliation was needed on God's side as well as on man's, and it is declared that this has been accomplished once for all in Christ's Cross (Col 1²¹.²²). It is on the basis of God's reconciliation to the world in Christ, that the world is now entreated to be reconciled to God (2 Co 5²⁰). This, which is the view taken of the meaning of St. Paul's expressions by the majority of exegetes, is the only one which fully satisfies the connexion of the Apostle's thought. Sinners, it is implied throughout, are, on account of their sins, the objects of God's judicial wrath. They are ἐχθροί, a word which, both in Ro 5¹⁰ and 11²⁸, is used in the passive sense of *objects* of wrath (cf., in latter passage, the contrast with ἀγαπητοί, 'beloved'). As Prof. Stevens, who disagrees with St. Paul, explains it: 'between God and sinful man there is a mutual hostility. Sinners are the objects of God's enmity (Ro 5¹⁰ 11²⁸), and they, in turn, are hostile to God (Ro 8⁷, Col 1²¹). Hence any reconciliation (καταλλαγή) which is accomplished between them must be two-sided' (*Christ. Doc. of Salv.* p. 59, cf. his *Theol. of the NT*, p. 414). Quite similar is the view taken by Weiss, in his *Bib. Theol. of the NT*, i. p. 428 ff. (Eng. tr.);

by Denney, in his *Romans*, on 5⁹ff., and *Death of Christ*, p. 143 ff. ; in art. 'Reconciliation' in Hastings' *DB*, etc. St. Paul's own explanation of his words, 'God was in Christ reconciling the world unto himself,' by the clause, 'not reckoning unto them their trespasses' (2 Co 5¹⁹), makes it clear that the reconciliation intended is on God's side. If this is granted, the second question is already answered—By what means is the reconciliation effected ? For the Apostle's consistent doctrine is that it was by Christ's death that God was reconciled to the world (see REDEMPTION).

The objection, however, will not unfairly be urged—Does it not conflict with a worthy view of God's character, and detract from the grace of salvation, to think of God as at 'enmity' with any of His creatures, and needing to be propitiated or reconciled ? Can such a thought have any real place in a Gospel of Christ ? It may be observed, first, that St. Paul did not regard his doctrine as casting any shadow on the love of God ; rather, it is to this love he traces the inception and carrying through of the whole work of man's salvation. The crowning proof of God's love is just this fact that Christ died for us (Ro 5⁹). If this seems a paradox, it is to be remembered, next, that displeasure against sin, and even the assertion of holiness against it in the form of wrath, are not incompatible with love to the sinner, and with the most earnest desire to save him. In human relations also there are cases in which a very genuine displeasure requires to be removed before relations of friendship can be restored (cf. Mt 5²³·²⁴). If God cherishes displeasure at sin at all—and would He be God if He did not ?—then there must be a measure of reconciliation on His side, as well as on man's, even if it be conceived that repentance on man's part is sufficient to bring it about. But this is the whole point—Does repentance suffice to repair the broken relations of the sinner with a Holy God ? And does repentance of the kind required spring up spontaneously in man, or is it not called forth by God first meeting man with a display of His own reconciling love ? That this is the truer and more Scriptural view cannot be doubted, and it throws us back on what it may be necessary for God to do in approaching a world yet ungodly with the message of His grace. That God has come to the world in the way of a reconciling work by His Son is certainly no abatement from the love on which depends the possibility of a salvation for the world at all.

The other, or manward, side of reconciliation is one on which a few words will suffice. Its necessity and importance are admitted by all. Estranged from God by his sense of guilt, and alienated in the spirit of his mind, the sinner needs, as the first condition of his salvation, to have this enmity of his heart broken down, and new dispositions of penitence and trust awakened. He needs to be moved to say, 'I will arise, and go to my Father' (Lk 15¹⁸). The great dynamic in producing such a change is again the spectacle of God's reconciling love in Christ. 'I, if I be lifted up from the earth,' said Jesus, 'will draw all men unto me'. (Jn 12³²). Along both lines, therefore, the Godward and the manward, we come to the Cross of Christ as the centre of the reconciling power of the gospel. By it we are redeemed from the curse (Gal 2²⁰ 3¹³) ; by it the world is crucified to us, and we unto the world (6¹⁴). The man who truly realizes his redemption lives no more unto himself, but unto Him who died for him, and rose again (2 Co 5¹⁵).

On the different views which have been held in the Church on Christ's reconciling work, see art. REDEMPTION.

LITERATURE.—Ritschl, *Recht. und Vers.* iii. (Eng. tr. *Justification and Reconciliation*) ; D. W. Simon, *Reconciliation by*

Incarnation ; *Cambridge Theol. Essays* (v.) ; art. 'Reconciliation' in Hastings' *DB*; works by Stevens and Denney cited above. See also F. W. Robertson, *Serm.* iv. 208 ; J. Caird, *Univ. Serm.* 92 ; T. Binney, *Serm.* ii. 51 ; Phillips Brooks, *Serm. for the Principal Festivals*, 97 ; W. P. Du Bose, *The Soteriology of the NT* (1892), 47. JAMES ORR.

REDEMPTION.

—An Apostle writes of Christ— 'in whom we have our redemption through his blood, the forgiveness of our trespasses' (Eph 1⁷). It is proposed in this article to inquire what redemption in Christ means, how Christ's redemption is effected, and what blessings are included in it.

i. THE BIBLICAL DOCTRINE.—

1. The vocabulary.—In the OT the idea of redemption is distinctively expressed by the two verbs גָּאַל and פָּדָה, with their derivatives. The former term is used technically, in the Mosaic law, of the redemption by price of an inheritance (by a kinsman or the man himself, Lv 25²⁵ff., Ru 44·7 Jer 32⁷·⁸), or of things vowed (Lv 27¹⁴ff.), or of tithes (v. 31ff.) : the latter of redeeming the firstborn of animals or of children (Ex 13¹³· ¹⁵ 34²⁰, Nu 18¹⁵ff.). Outside the Law, and in relation to Jehovah, both terms are used of simple salvation or deliverance, especially when attended by impressive displays of power, or the assertion or vindication of righteousness, or vengeance upon enemies. גָּאַל appears in this sense in Gn 48¹⁶, Ex 6⁶ 15¹³ ; repeatedly in the Psalms (69¹⁸ 72¹⁴ 74² 103⁴ 106¹⁰ 107²) and in Deutero-Isaiah (43¹ 44²². ²³ 48²⁰ etc.), and occasionally in other prophets. פָּדָה, on the other hand, is the favourite term in Deut. (7⁸ 9²⁶ etc.), is frequent in the *earlier* Psalms (25²² 31⁵ etc.), but occurs only rarely in Isaiah (1²⁷ 29²² 51¹). The person who has the right to redeem, or who undertakes the duty, is a גֹּאֵל, or 'redeemer' (Nu 5⁸, Ru 2²⁰ etc. EV 'kinsman') ; the term is used also to denote the 'avenger of blood' (Nu 35¹², Dt 19⁶ etc.) ; and elsewhere, as in the famous passage Job 19²⁵, in Ps 19¹⁴ 78³⁵, and Pr 23¹¹, but specially in Deutero-Isaiah (41¹⁴ 43¹⁴ etc.), is applied to Jehovah as the all-powerful, holy, and merciful vindicator, deliverer, and avenger of His people. A term related in idea to 'redemption' is כֹּפֶר 'ransom.' (See RANSOM.)

In the NT the terms by which the idea is directly expressed are ἀγοράζω, 'to buy' or 'purchase' (1 Co 6²⁰ 7²³, 2 P 2¹, Rev 5⁹ 14³·⁴—the last tr. in AV, 'redeem'), and its compound ἐξαγοράζω, used by St. Paul in Gal 3¹³ 4⁵ ; but specially λυτρούμαι (from λύτρον, 'a ransom'), and its derivatives (Lk 24²¹, Ti 2¹⁴, 1 P 1¹⁸). The special Pauline word for 'redemption' is ἀπολύτρωσις (Ro 3²⁴ 8²³, 1 Co 1³⁰, Eph 1⁷ etc.,—found also in Lk 21²⁸, He 9¹⁵). The simple form λύτρωσις occurs in Lk 2³⁸, He 9¹². The meaning of these expressions is more precisely considered below.

2. The OT preparation.—The foundations of the NT doctrine of redemption are laid in the OT conceptions of the holiness, righteousness, and grace of Jehovah, and of sin as something abhorrent to Jehovah's holiness, which He must needs condemn and punish, but from which He desires to save. He is the Holy One, who abhors iniquity. Sinners shall not stand in His sight. He visits with severest penalties those who disregard His counsels and persist in their wickedness. Yet He is the Lord God, merciful and gracious, full of compassion and ready to forgive (Ex 34⁶·⁷, Ps 103⁸ff.) ; He desires not the death of any sinner, but that he should turn from his wickedness and live (Ezk 18³² 3³¹²). More specially, He is the covenant-keeping God, who does not allow His promises to fail, but, even when the nation in the mass is rejected, fulfils His word in due season to the faithful remnant, or to the whole people when brought to repentance (Ps 103⁸· ⁹, Is 8¹⁶· ¹⁷, Jer 32³⁷ff., Hos 1¹⁰· ¹¹ 2¹⁴ etc.). In this it is already implied that Jehovah will manifest His power, righteousness, and love in helping and saving His people, in vindicating their cause when oppressed, in visiting their adversaries with judgments, and in working out great and astonishing deliverances for them when the hour comes for the fulfilment of His promises. It follows that His relation to them, and His concern for their good, will be seen in the course of their history in a succession of acts of *redemption*.

It has been seen, accordingly, that while, in their legal usage, the OT terms for 'redeem' and 'redemption' imply payment of a price, or, in the case of firstborn sons, substitution of a life, or a monetary ransom, these terms are often used in the more general sense of simple deliverance or salvation. The great historic instance of Jehovah's redemption of His people was their deliverance from the bondage of Egypt (Ex 6⁶ 15¹³, Dt 7⁸ etc.). That held in it already the pledge of every other deliverance which the nation or godly individuals in it might need. Prayers, therefore, are frequent that Jehovah would redeem from oppression, from violence, from sickness, from death, from captivity, etc. (e.g. Ps 25²² 49¹⁵ 72¹⁴ 103⁴), and thanksgivings for deliverance refer usually to the same things (e.g. Pss 116. 124. 126, Zec 10⁸ᶠᶠ·). Redemption in such passages is commonly from temporal calamities or ills, endured or feared. Only in one place is direct mention made of redemption from iniquities (Ps 130⁸). This last fact, however, must not mislead us. As, in the OT, outward calamities are usually connected with Jehovah's anger, or with the hiding of His face, so, it is everywhere implied, the first condition of the removal of these evils is return to God and the forsaking of iniquity; if the individual is righteous, this is the ground on which he looks to God for vindication against the ungodly oppressor (Pss 3. 4. 5 etc.). We must beware here, and throughout this whole discussion, of building too much on the mere occurrence of a term. The *fact* of redemption is often present, where the *word* is not directly used. Behind all interpositions for deliverance and help, whatever the words employed, stand Jehovah's unchanging character, His pledged word, His inflexible will to uphold the right, His compassion for the afflicted and oppressed. Righteousness, in His deliverances, always counts for more than the deliverance itself, which is conditioned by His unerring knowledge of the moral state. Where sin has been the cause of judgments on the individual or nation, redemption includes, in the removal of these evils, forgiveness and restoration to the Divine favour and to righteousness (cf. Ps 85, Is 1¹⁶ᶠᶠ·, Hos 14, etc.).

The Deliverer of His people in the OT is Jehovah Himself. Hence the affection with which Deutero-Isaiah dwells on the idea of Jehovah as the גאל, or 'Redeemer' of Israel. It is noteworthy, however, that in two passages redemption is attributed to the 'angel' of Jehovah—that mysterious personality, one with Jehovah, yet again distinct from Him, who figures so prominently, particularly in the earlier stages of revelation. 'The angel which hath redeemed me from all evil,' says Jacob, in the earliest instance of the use of the word גאל, in Gn 48¹⁶; and again in Is 63⁹ we have, with the use of the same word, the like idea: 'In all their affliction he was afflicted, and the angel of his presence saved them; in his love and in his pity he redeemed them,' etc. That is, Jehovah's interposition in redemption is by means of His angel (cf. Ps 34⁷). There is a foregleam here of what comes more clearly to light in the NT.

It may appear a point of contrast between the OT and the NT conceptions of redemption that in the OT the word is never brought directly into association with sacrifice, or the ritual of atonement. The use of 'redeem' in connexion with the firstborn (the substitution, e.g., of a lamb for the firstling of an ass) does not affect this statement, for these substitutions have not the character of atonement for sin. Here again, however, it is important to keep in memory the distinction between words and things. Apart from the use of terms, it is the case that the sacrificial ritual—so far as expiatory—was, in its own way, a means of deliverance from guilt, and, in that sense, of redemption. A direct connexion between the sacrifices of the Law and the forgiveness of sin is expressly affirmed (e.g. Lv 4²⁰. ²⁶. ³⁵; cf. Is 6⁷); a

fact irrespective of any theory of efficacy. Even in regard to words, there is the important point of connexion in the word כפר 'ransom.' (See RANSOM.)

But there is a yet closer link. There can be no question that a peculiar line of preparation for the NT doctrine lay in the development by Psalmists and Prophets of the idea of the Righteous Sufferer. The culmination of that development is reached in the matchless representation of Is 53, where the Servant of Jehovah is pictured as making expiation by His sufferings and death for the sins of the people. Here at length Prophetic and sacrificial teaching touch, for the language and whole idea of the sacrificial ritual are taken over upon the Suffering Servant. The iniquity of His fellows is laid upon One who is without sin; His soul is made a guilt-offering; He bears the iniquities of the people; He pours out His soul unto death; He bears the sin of many, and makes intercession for the transgressors (Is 53⁶. ¹⁰. ¹¹. ¹²). The later Prophetic teaching is not without refrains of the same ideas (Zec 13, Dn 9²⁴ᶠᶠ·). Malachi brings to a close the long preparation of the OT with his prediction of the Angel of the Covenant soon to come to His temple, whose work would be at once judging and saving (3⁴).

3. Redemption in the Gospels.—With respect to the sources, it is acknowledged that a distinction is to be made between the Synoptics and the Fourth Gospel. The last, however, is accepted in the present article as a genuine work of the Apostle John, embodying, if with a certain colouring from his own personality and interpretative comment, that Apostle's reminiscences of the sayings and doings of Jesus, especially those of the Judæan ministry. Comparison will show that, fundamentally, the teachings of the four Gospels on our immediate subject coincide.

St. Luke's Gospel begins by introducing us to the circle of those who 'were looking for the redemption (λύτρωσις) of Jerusalem' (2³⁸), or, as an earlier verse has it, were 'looking for the consolation of Israel' (v.²⁵). Of these there were not a few. Zacharias and Elizabeth, Simeon and the prophetess Anna, were among the number. From the hymn of Zacharias in 1⁶⁸ᶠᶠ· we see how far the idea of 'redemption' was from being confined to temporal deliverance from enemies. Such deliverance was only a means towards serving the God who had redeemed His people in holiness and righteousness (1⁷⁵). Redemption included the knowledge of (spiritual) salvation by the remission of sins (v.⁷⁷). This salvation was to be brought in by one from the house of David, in fulfilment of the promises made to the fathers (vv.⁶⁹⁻⁷³). John the Baptist was to prepare the way for the Redeemer's coming (v.⁷⁶, cf. 3³ᶠᶠ·). We are here, in short, on the threshold of the introduction of the Messianic salvation. In three of the Gospels, accordingly, we have preparatory notes struck, which show in what sense we are to understand this wonderful redemption of the Christ. The shepherds in Lk. are apprised of the birth in the city of David of 'a Saviour, which is Christ the Lord' (2¹¹). In Mt. the child is called Jesus, 'for it is he that shall save his people from their sins' (1²¹). In St. John's Gospel the Baptist points out Jesus to his disciples as 'the Lamb of God, which taketh away the sin of the world' (1²⁹. ³⁶). All the Gospels give prominence to the Baptism of Jesus, with its consecration of Himself 'to fulfil all righteousness' (in Mt.), its acknowledgment of Him as 'the Son of God,' and the descent upon Him of the Holy Spirit (Mt 3¹³⁻¹⁷, Mk 1⁹⁻¹¹, Lk 3²¹. ²², Jn 1³¹⁻³⁴); and the Synoptics relate His Temptation, in which false ideals of Messiahship were rejected, and His true vocation was definitely grasped and chosen (Mt 4¹⁻¹¹ ∥).

The important question now arises, How did

Jesus Himself conceive of the work of redemption which belonged to Him as Messiah ? The word itself is only once attributed to Him, and that in an eschatological connexion (Lk 21²⁸) ; it affords us, therefore, little help. His conception must be sought in a less direct way, by consideration of the aspects in which His saving activity is presented in the Gospels, and of the sayings and doings in which He connects the salvation of men with Himself. An error to be sedulously guarded against here is that of fastening on one or two isolated sayings of Jesus, for instance, on the passages about His death, and giving these an interpretation as if they were without any context in Jesus' own thought, or in His general Messianic claim, or in earlier Prophetic revelation, or in the events which succeeded them, and threw light on them. A broader method must be followed if Christ's idea of redemption is to be satisfactorily grasped.

It must impress us, then, that, in the idea of redemption, or what corresponds to it, in the Gospels, the spiritual elements are prominent as they were not in the OT. This was to be expected from the spiritual nature of the teaching of Jesus, and from the larger place given to the hope of the future life. The political aspect of redemption disappears altogether. The Kingdom Jesus came to found was not of this world (cf. Mt 18¹⁻⁵ 19²⁷⁻³⁰ 20²⁵⁻²⁸ 26⁵¹⁻⁵³, Lk 17²¹, Jn 6¹⁵ 18³⁶ etc.). Salvation from bodily evils, indeed, appears as an important part of Christ's ministry, as in the healing of disease, the casting out of demons, the raising of the dead, the feeding of the multitudes (Mt 4²³· ²⁴ 11⁴· ⁵ etc.). In these works of mercy Jesus revealed Himself as the Saviour of the body as well as of the soul. But the physical benefit was never an end in itself ; it pointed up to, and prepared the way for the reception of, the spiritual blessing (Mt 9²⁻⁸. Jn 6²⁶ᶠᶠ.). It was conditioned by faith (Mt 8¹⁰ 9²· ²²· ²⁸ etc.). The real evils from which Jesus came to redeem were spiritual evils ; the priceless good He came to bestow was a spiritual good. Spiritual evil had its root and origin in sin ; salvation takes its spring in the grace and mercy of God, and begins with forgiveness.

(1) We have first, then, to look at *sin and its consequences* as the evil to be redeemed from. The teaching of Jesus on the love and mercy of the Father should not blind us to the depth of His realization of the awful evil of sin, of the wrath of God against it, and of the peril of eternal death which overhung the sinner. Rather, in His view, is the Father's mercy to be measured by the depth of the sinner's lostness, the heinousness of his state in the light of the Divine holiness, and his inability to deliver himself from that state or its consequences. The sternness of Christ's teaching in this relation is sometimes very terrible. As the Baptist warned his hearers to flee from 'the wrath to come,' so Jesus has ever in the background of His most gracious teaching the thought of an awful Divine judgment, which surely one day will descend on the impenitent. He does not hesitate to speak of the fire of Gehenna (Mt 5²²· ²⁹· ³⁰), and of God, who is able to destroy both soul and body in Gehenna (10²⁸); of the worm that dieth not, and the fire that is not quenched (Mk 9⁴⁴· ⁴⁶· ⁴⁸); of the judgment, less tolerable than that upon Tyre and Sidon, or even Sodom, which awaits cities like Capernaum (Mt 11²⁰⁻²⁴); of a blasphemy against the Holy Spirit which shall not be forgiven, either in this world, or in that to come (12³¹· ³² ‖). His denunciations of the Pharisees are merciless in their severity (23¹⁴· ¹⁵· ³²· ³³) ; the language of judgment in many of the parables is hardly less strong (13⁴²· ⁵⁰ 18³⁴ 21⁴⁴ 22⁷· ¹³ etc.). Those who speak of supposed judgments on others are warned : 'Nay, but, except ye repent, ye shall all likewise perish'

(Lk 13³· ⁵) ; of a Judas it is declared, 'Good were it for that man if he had not been born' (Mt 26²⁴, Mk 14²¹) ; the parable of the Final Judgment has such a sentence as, 'Depart from me, ye cursed,' etc. (Mt 25⁴¹· ⁴⁶). The Synoptic teaching on this point is identical with that of St. John, who declares that the wrath of God 'abideth' on him who believes (or obeys) not the Son of God (Jn 3³⁶), and habitually speaks of the world as perishing in its sin (3¹⁶· ¹⁷ 5²⁹ 6⁵³ 8²⁴ etc.).

Exposure to the wrath of God, therefore, is one result of sin, from which, undeniably, redemption is needed ; but this, in Christ's view, is not the worst evil, but rather flows from the infinitely heinous and hateful nature of sin itself. Sin, considered in itself, is the real evil from which men need to be delivered. It is a fountain of pollution in the heart, defiling the whole nature (Mt 15¹⁸⁻²⁰ ‖ ; cf. 23²⁷) ; evolves itself in corrupt words and deeds (7¹⁶⁻²⁰ 12³²⁻³⁷) ; brings under subjection to Satan (6¹³ 12²⁹· ⁴³⁻⁴⁵) ; is the loss of the soul's true life (16²⁴⁻²⁶) ; entails misery and ruin (Lk 15¹¹⁻¹⁶, Mt 23³⁷· ³⁸) ; ripens into hateful vices (impurity, covetousness, pride, hypocrisy, mercilessness, etc.), and culminates in blasphemy against the Holy Spirit (Mt 12³¹· ³² etc.). Souls in this condition are 'lost' ; need to be, in their helplessness and misery, sought after and saved (Lk 15³ᶠᶠ· 19¹⁰). The teaching of Jesus in Jn. is here again in accord with that in the Synoptics ; only that in some respects St. John's Gospel goes deeper, in explicitly affirming the need of regeneration (3³· ⁵), in laying more stress on the element of bondage in sin (8³³· ³⁴), and in giving greater prominence to the idea of Satan as 'the prince of this world,' whose power over men has to be broken (8⁴⁴ 12³¹ 14³⁰ 16¹¹ ; cf. Lk 10¹⁷· ¹⁸).

One thing still requires to be said to exhibit in its full extent man's need of redemption. The deepest and most condemnable aspect of sin is that it is alienation from God Himself. The first requirement of the Law is love to God (Mt 22³⁷· ³⁸) ; the proper attitude of the soul to God is that of humble dependence and trust (4⁴· ⁷· ¹⁰ 7²⁵ᶠᶠ·, Mk 11²²· ²⁴· ²⁵ etc.). But sin is the negation of this right religious relation. 'I know you,' said Jesus to the Jews, 'that ye have not the love of God in you' (Jn 5⁴²). Other and contrary principles— pride, self-sufficiency, self-will, the love of the honour that comes from men (Jn 5⁴⁴ ; cf. Mt 6²ᶠᶠ·)— had taken the place of love to God ; hence estrangement from God, antagonism to His will and spirit, enmity to Him and to His messengers (Mt 23²⁹ᶠᶠ·). Redemption means here the effecting of a change of disposition towards God, and the restoration of a spirit of love and trust—of the filial spirit (*e.g.* Lk 15¹⁷ᶠᶠ·). It is synonymous with *reconciliation* (see RECONCILIATION).

(2) This description of the evil to be redeemed from already determines *the positive character of the redemption*. The preaching of Jesus is described as the preaching of a 'gospel' (Lk 4¹⁸· ¹⁹)— 'the gospel of God' (Mk 1¹⁴)—and the 'salvation' (Lk 19⁹· ¹⁰) proclaimed in this gospel included deliverance from the whole range of evil covered by the word 'sin,' with introduction into the whole sphere of privilege and blessedness embraced in the term 'Kingdom of God.' Jesus in His teaching has much to say on the condition of mind necessary for the reception of this blessing. There is naturally the initial demand for repentance (Mt 9¹³ 11²⁰· ²¹, Mk 1¹⁵ 6¹², Lk 13 ³· ⁵ etc.), which has the full weight of meaning involved in the etymology of the word μετάνοια, 'change of mind.' There is implied in this change of disposition a parting with all pride, sufficiency, and sense of merit (Lk 17¹⁰) ; a coming to be humble, simple, trustful as a little child (Mt 18¹⁻⁴) ; in a pregnant phrase,

becoming 'poor in spirit' (Mt 5^3, Lk 4^{18}). To those in this humble, trustful, self-renouncing state of mind every satisfaction and spiritual blessing are promised (*e.g.* Mt $5^{3ff.}$; see Iverach, *The Other Side of Greatness*, p. 1 ff.). This blessing is always represented as mediated through Jesus Himself. It is only through the Son that men can receive the knowledge of the Father (11^{27}); it is through coming to Him, learning of Him, taking His yoke upon them, that they obtain rest to their souls (vv. $^{28-30}$); men are called to follow Him, to become His disciples, to acknowledge Him as their Lord and Master (7^{21-23} 8^{19-22} 23^8 etc.). He requires from His disciples the most absolute surrender to Himself (10^{37-39} $16^{24.\,25}$); it is by relation to Him that men are judged at last ($25^{40.\,45}$). As King, He dispenses the awards of service (16^{27} 19^{28} $25^{34ff.}$). Of the dependence of salvation on His sufferings and death, more is said below. Those who stand in the above relation to Christ are 'the children of the kingdom' (13^{38}), sons of God, and heirs of eternal life. Received into the Kingdom, they have the blessedness of knowing that their sins are forgiven them (6^{12} 9^2 etc.), though, reciprocally, there is laid on those who are thus forgiven the duty of forgiving others ($6^{14.\,15}$ 18^{35}, Mk 11^{25} etc.). They have the privilege of calling God their Father, of trusting Him for all their need (Mt $6^{25ff.}$), of free access to Him in prayer (7^{7-11} etc.). They are acknowledged by Christ as His brethren ($12^{49.\,50}$ 25^{40}). From the Father they receive mercy, and the satisfaction of their hunger and thirst for righteousness ($5^{6.\,7}$); they are sustained in persecution and sacrifice by the promise of a thousand-fold reward (5^{12} 19^{29}, Mk $10^{29.\,30}$); it is theirs to share in the resurrection of the just (Lk 14^{14}); and as sons and heirs of God, they have the sure hope of 'eternal life,' in which is included blessedness and glory (Mt 13^{43}) and the perfect vision of God (5^8). These unspeakably lofty privileges and hopes imply corresponding responsibilities. It is constantly assumed that there cannot be true repentance, or genuine membership in the Kingdom, which does not manifest itself in 'good works' (5^{16}), or in the doing of the will of the Father (6^{10}). Only the doers of the Father's will can be received into the Kingdom of heaven (7^{21} 18^4 $25^{34ff.}$). The disciple is to have for his aim to be perfect as his Father in heaven is perfect (5^{48}).

Not a great deal, comparatively, is said in the Synoptic Gospels of the work of the Spirit in imparting these spiritual blessings. But the Spirit's presence and agency are nevertheless constantly assumed. Jesus was 'full of the Holy Spirit' after His baptism (Lk 4^1), and it was the Spirit of the Lord upon Him who fitted Him for His saving work (v. ^{18}). 'The spirit of the Father' speaks in the disciples (Mt 10^{20}). He is, in Lk., the supreme gift of the Father (11^{13}). Blasphemy against the Holy Spirit is the last and highest crime (Mt. 12^{32} ‖). The Baptist announced Jesus as the One who should baptize with the Spirit (3^{11} ‖), and the promise of the Spirit is Christ's final word to His disciples (Lk 24^{49}). In the Synoptics, as in Jn., it is assumed that the Spirit was not yet given in His fulness, because Jesus was not yet glorified (Jn 7^{39}).

The Johannine teaching on salvation is once more, in all essential features, identical with that of the Synoptics. The change of mind insisted on by the latter is, in St. John's Gospel, directly traced to a regenerating work of the Spirit ($3^{3.\,5}$), and the doctrine of the Spirit altogether is more developed (14^{26} 15^{26} $16^{7ff.}$); the condition of salvation is expressed generally by the term 'believing' (which includes in it the idea of 'obeying,' cf. $3^{18.\,36}$); sonship, as the fruit of regeneration, is viewed as a special supernatural gift, the preroga-

tive of believers (1^{12}); salvation is connected with Christ's being lifted up (3^{14-17} $12^{32.\,33}$); 'eternal life' is regarded as already begun in the experience of the believer (3^{36} 4^{14} 6^{47} 17^3 etc.). But the necessity of union with Christ (cf. 15^{1-8}), the salvation from wrath through Him ($3^{16-18.\,36}$ 5^{24}), the dispositions to be laid aside in entering the Kingdom of heaven (5^{44}), and the essentials of character to be acquired by its members (humility, love, self-sacrifice, etc., 13^{4-17} 15^{12} 12^{25} etc.), the hope of the resurrection ($5^{28.\,29}$ 6^{40} 11^{24-26}), and the prospect of ultimately sharing Christ's glory in the Father's house ($14^{2.\,3}$ 17^{24}), are outstanding features in St. John's teaching as they are in that of the earlier Gospels.

(3) The question now recurs as to *the connexion of Christ's own Person, and especially His sufferings and death, with this redemption*, the message of which constitutes His gospel. Certain obvious aspects of that connexion have already been indicated. Christ's ministry of teaching and healing was itself a means of redemption—of bringing men to the knowledge of it, of awakening in them the desire for it, of drawing them to the acceptance of it, of putting them in possession of part of its blessing. But in its substance also, as we have seen, Christ and His gospel could not be separated. He alone could reveal the Father, and give the world assurance of His grace; He already, as the Son of Man, exhibited in its perfect form what Divine sonship in the Kingdom of God meant; it was by coming to Him, and learning of Him, that men were initiated into His mind and spirit, which itself was salvation. His purity, conjoined with His sympathy and grace, acted as mighty moral motives in breaking down the enmity of the heart to God and in winning sinners to repentance. These also are the aspects of Christ's connexion with redemption,—these, not declarations about atonement,—which meet us on the surface of the Gospels. Christ is the Good Shepherd, seeking and finding the lost sheep (Mt 10^6 15^{24} 18^{12-14}, Lk 15^{3-7}). All-compassionating, forgiving love is the power He relies on to draw out love (Lk 8^{47-50}). The very majesty of His claims and the manifest authority with which He spoke gave an added power to His gentleness and grace (Mt 11^{27-30}).

We have still to ask, however, Is this the whole? Is this the only way in which redemption depends on Christ? If it is, what remains as the foundation of the Apostolic gospel, which undeniably connects redemption in a peculiar way, not with Christ's life and teaching, but with His sacrificial sufferings and death? The question is further pressed upon us by particular utterances of Jesus, which likewise appear to point to such connexion. Is this aspect of redemption, as some think, to be excluded from Christ's gospel? To find an answer we are driven back upon the wider question of how Jesus Himself viewed His sufferings and death. On this topic, it was remarked above that it is a very misleading method to confine ourselves to the exposition of isolated texts, without taking into account the whole context of Christ's thought, and the ideas of OT revelation in which His thought was grounded. It will be necessary to begin in order at this point to reach a satisfactory conclusion.

A sure *datum* to start with here is the indubitable consciousness of Jesus—attested by the two names 'Son of God' and 'Son of Man'—of His Messianic vocation, and consequently of the connexion of the Messianic salvation with His Person. It was He, as the whole Jewish hope implied, who was to bring in that 'redemption' for which Israel waited (Lk 2^{38}). That Jesus knew Himself to be the Christ, at least from the time of the Baptism, is implied in all the Gospels, though it was only to favoured individuals that the disclosure was directly made (in Jn. to Nathanael, 1$^{47-51}$; to Nicodemus, 3$^{13ff.}$; to the Samaritan woman, 4^{26} etc.).

It is to misinterpret Peter's great confession in Mt 16^{16} to take it to mean that up to that time the disciples had no knowledge that Jesus was the Christ. Apart from what is narrated by St. John (14$^{1ff.}$), the whole ministry of Jesus, as recorded by the Synoptics—the claims He made, the authority He exercised—was by implication an assertion of that dignity; while to the direct testimony borne by the forerunner (Mt 3$^{11.~12}$ ||) was added afterwards the answer given to the Baptist's doubts (11$^{2ff.}$). What was new in Peter's confession was the inburst of new illumination, and unshakable strength of conviction, with which the confession was made (16$^{17.~18}$).

On the other hand, if Jesus knew Himself to be the Messiah of OT prophecy and hope, it is not less certain that He apprehended this great vocation, and the salvation with which it was connected, in a quite different way from most of His contemporaries. Messiahship for Him, as the account of the Temptation shows, meant the definite renunciation of all self-seeking motives, the rejection of all political and worldly ideals, the repudiation of all swerving from the sole end of seeking His Father's glory. Holding such a conception of His mission, and rooted in His consciousness, as His habitual use of Scripture and manner of deducing deep principles from its simplest words show Him to be, in OT and specially Prophetic teaching, it is impossible that, from the first, He should not have clearly perceived the collision that must ensue between Himself and the ruling classes, and the persecution, and ultimately death, which their enmity must bring upon Him. With so clear a vision of the persecutions, scornings, and death that awaited His disciples (Mt 10$^{16ff.}$||), He could not be ignorant of His own future. If, however, He saw thus far, it must be that He saw further. The path of self-renunciation and suffering that lay before Him must have presented itself, as we know it did, as part of His Father's ordainment in the accomplishment of His vocation; not as a fate merely, or even as a martyrdom, but as a necessary step to the founding of His Kingdom, and procurement of the great end of His Coming—the end of salvation. If this, in turn, presented itself as a problem to His thought,—we speak, perhaps, too humanly of the way in which Jesus arrived at His convictions,—the light was near at hand for its solution in the Prophetic Scriptures, especially in the picture of the Suffering Servant of Is 53. His sufferings were *expiatory*. No one who reads the Gospels with care can doubt the familiarity of the mind of Jesus with this portion of Prophetic testimony. It is probably this prophecy that was in view in the Baptist's announcement to his disciples (Jn 1$^{29.36}$); it is contained in the section of Isaiah on the Servant of Jehovah which Jesus cited in the opening of His public ministry as fulfilled in Himself (Lk 4$^{17ff.}$); one interesting passage shows that it was directly before His mind in His last sufferings—'For I say unto you, that this which is written must be fulfilled in me, And he was numbered with transgressors: for that which concerneth me hath fulfilment' (22^{37}). It cannot have been absent from the numerous prophecies which Jesus declared were fulfilled in His death (Mk 9^{12} 14$^{21.~27}$, Lk 18^{31} 24$^{26.~27.~46}$). But, indeed, the same strain of thought, sacrificial and Prophetic, which inspired the representation of Jehovah's Servant as One who must and would take upon Himself the burden of the people's sins, and, in substitutionary love, offer Himself in atonement for them, must have wrought as powerfully in the mind of Jesus, conscious as He was of His peculiar relation to both God and man, and fully aware of what sin was, and of what the forgiveness of sin meant to a holy God. If atonement for the world's sin was possible, and Jesus in His representative capacity, and Himself sinless, could offer such atonement,

it cannot be doubted that He would desire to do so.

This point of the connexion of the sufferings and death of Jesus with redemption will receive elucidation afterwards; but already, perhaps, it is possible to see how, during His ministry, a relation of His sufferings to His saving mission might be present to His own mind, though He said little of it publicly, and only toward the end of His life spoke freely to His disciples of His approaching death. His reticence on His death would then be paralleled by His reticence on His Messiahship, which yet was present to His consciousness throughout. On such a view it may be found that the phenomena of the Gospels, as we have them, fall naturally into place,—His general silence on His death in His public teaching, the occasional disclosures in Jn. and the Synoptics, the connexion of the later announcements of His death with His resurrection, and, after His resurrection, of both with the preaching of remission of sins, and the promise of · the Spirit; the coherence of this teaching with the Apostolic gospel.

For now it is to be observed that this silence of Jesus on the connexion of His sufferings and death with His saving work is far from absolute; on the contrary, the intimations of such connexion, when brought together, and read with the help of such a key as Is 53 affords, are neither few nor ambiguous. It is not, indeed, till late in the ministry, after Peter's confession, that Jesus begins to speak plainly of His approaching death, and then of that death as Divinely ordained and foretold, and to be followed by resurrection (Mt 16^{21} 17$^{9.~22.~23}$ 20$^{18.~19}$ ||, see above). Thenceforth His death had an absorbing place in His thoughts. It was a 'cup' He had to drink, a 'baptism' He had to be baptized with. He was 'straitened' till it was accomplished (Mt 20^{22}, Mk 10$^{32.~38}$, Lk 12^{50}; cf. Lk 9^{51}). At the Transfiguration it was, according to St. Luke, the 'decease (ἔξοδος) which he was about to accomplish at Jerusalem' which was the subject of His converse with Moses and Elijah (9^{31}). But the very decision and circumstantiality of these first announcements to His disciples imply that the subject had long been before His own thoughts; and that, in conformity with what has already been said, this was really the case, we gather from such a passage as Mt 9^{15} ('When the bridegroom shall be taken away from them'), but much more clearly from the sayings preserved to us by St. John from the Judæan and Capernaum ministries. Here, in the line of the Baptist's opening announcement (1^{29}), the connexion between Christ's death and the salvation of the world is unmistakably declared. Thus, in the conversation with Nicodemus, 'As Moses lifted up the serpent in the wilderness, so must the Son of Man be lifted up,' etc. (3$^{14-16}$; cf. on the lifting up, 12^{33}), and in the remarkable discourse at Capernaum, in which Jesus dilates on His flesh as given for the life of the world, and on His blood as shed (we must presume) for the same end (6$^{51-56}$). In the light of these sayings we must, in consistency, interpret others more general in character (*e.g.* 10$^{11.~15.~17.~18}$ 12$^{24.~23}$).

When we return to the Synoptics, we have again, in the closing period, more than one significant utterance. There is first the well-known passage preserved in both Mt. and Mk.: 'The Son of Man came not to be ministered unto, but to minister, and to give his life a ransom (λύτρον) for many (ἀντὶ πολλῶν)' (Mt 20^{28}, Mk 10^{45}).

It does not rob this passage of its force that it occurs in impressing on the disciples the lesson that the true greatness lies in service. No one will suppose that Jesus could have used language such as He here employs about the disciples, or about any other than Himself. The incidental occurrence of the saying may rather suggest that there must have been other teaching on the subject, and that Jesus here assumes the saving purpose of His death as known to the disciples.

The significance of the word λύτρον is investigated in art. RANSOM; it is enough now to say that the word is most naturally taken as the equivalent of the Hebrew כֹּפֶר (allied to כִּפֶּר 'to atone'), used of that which is given in exchange for a life, whether money or another life. The thought in Jesus' mind may well have been that of Is 53. The meaning would then be that His death is the redemption-price by which the many are delivered from the ruin entailed by sin (including both the guilt and the power of sin). There is, again, the passage already cited, Lk 22[37], directly glancing at Is 53, and declaring it to be fulfilled in Christ's death. There are, finally, the words at the Supper, which, amidst the variations in the four accounts we have of them (Mt 26[26-28], Mk 14[22-25], Lk 22[19. 20], 1 Co 11[23-25]), present certain very distinguishable ideas. The bread is Christ's body, the cup is Christ's blood. The body is given or broken and the blood is shed for the disciples (in Mt. and Mk. 'for many'). The very variations support the general meaning put upon the act. If Mt. and Mk. have not the words 'given' or 'broken' spoken of the body (Luke, Paul?), both have 'shed for many' of the blood. Lk. has both 'given for you' and 'poured out for you,' St. Paul, on the other hand, has 'My body, which is [broken?] for you,' but not the corresponding 'shed for you.' All agree in the leading feature, that Jesus said: 'This is my blood of the covenant' (Mt., Mk.), or 'This cup is the new covenant in my blood' (Luke, Paul). Mt. adds: 'which is shed for many unto the remission of sins.' Even if it were conceded, what there is no necessity for conceding, that this *logion* is less original than the others [there is probably a reminiscence of Jer 31[34]], it has at least the value that it shows the sense in which Christ's words were understood in the Apostolic age. That Jesus, therefore, in the words at the Supper, represents His death as a sacrifice for the salvation of many, and definitely connects the shedding of His blood with the remission of sins and the making of a New Covenant, is nearly as certain as anything in exegesis can be. The question that remains is—With what special sacrifice does Jesus regard His death as connected (Passover, ratificatory sacrifices at Sinai)? Probably it is not necessary to decide between different views. Jesus may well have regarded His death as fulfilling the truth of all propitiatory sacrifice.

There is yet one other fact to which attention needs to be directed in this connexion. The death of Jesus is evidently dwelt upon by the Evangelists with a special sense of solemnity and mystery, and there are features in the story of His Passion which deepen this feeling of mystery, and compel us to seek some special explanation. Such features are the mental perturbation which the thought of His death awoke in Jesus ('Now is my soul troubled,' etc., Jn 12[27]); the sore amazement and sorrow even unto death in the Garden (Mk 14[33. 34]); the sweat as of drops of blood, and words about the Cup (Lk 22[42-44], Mt 26[39]); the awful words upon the Cross, speaking to a loss of the sense and comfort of God's presence (Mt 27[46], Mk 15[14]). We recall M'Leod Campbell's words : 'When I think of our Lord as tasting death, it seems to me as if He alone ever truly tasted death' (*Atonement*, ch. vii.). Is there nothing which connects itself with Christ's position as sin-bearer here? It is not thus martyrs are wont to die; not thus did Stephen, or Paul, or Ignatius die. Why, then, so strange a contrast in the Lord and Master of them all? On any hypothesis, must we not say that we have here something which takes *this* death out of the rank of simple martyrdom? Let us now take with this Christ's last cry upon the Cross, 'It is finished' (τετέλεσται, Jn 19[30]), and mark how this most unusual death is followed by a resurrection, and, after the resurrection, by an apparently changed relation of Christ to both God and man; by commissions and promises which imply that this death has been a turning-point in the history of salvation, the opening of a new dispensation of the Spirit, and of the preaching to mankind of the remission of sins in Christ's name (Mt 28[16-20], Lk 24[45-49], Jn 20[21-23], Ac 1[4-8]), and it may be found difficult to deny that, even within the limits of the Gospels, a saving significance is attributed to Christ's death, in perfect consonance with that ascribed to it in the Apostolic gospel.

4. The Apostolic doctrine (*Acts, the Epistles, the Book of Revelation*).—(a) It is told by St. Luke that Jesus opened the minds of His disciples to understand from the Scriptures that the Christ should suffer, and rise again from the dead the third day, and that repentance and remission of sins should be preached in His name unto all the nations (24[46. 47]). From the first, therefore, we find the Apostles giving prominence to the death and resurrection of Christ as Divinely ordained events, with which salvation was connected (Ac 2[23-33. 36. 38] 3[13-18] 4[10-12]). It would be unreasonable to look for theology in addresses which had for their primary object to bring home to the consciences of the hearers their *crime* in crucifying 'the Holy and Righteous One' (Ac 3[14]). We need not wonder, therefore, that we do not find it in these early discourses in the Acts. Yet the conviction was plainly there that, in some sense, Christ, as St. Paul says, had 'died for our sins' (1 Co 15[3]), and had been exalted to bestow salvation, and that through faith in Him, and *only* through faith in His name (Ac 3[12]), was the wrath of God averted (2[21]), remission of sins obtained (2[38] 3[19] 10[43] 13[38. 39], etc.), the gift of the Holy Ghost received (2[38] 11[16. 17] etc.), and the way prepared for 'seasons of refreshing' and 'the times of restoration of all things' (3[19-21]). Very early, however, through deeper reflexion and the growing illumination of the Spirit, there necessarily came to be given a more definite interpretation of this connexion of Christ's death with human salvation. Sacrificial and expiatory ideas were freely taken over upon it (cf. Ac 20[28]); a new vocabulary sprang up; there was speech, as in the common doctrine of the Epistles (cf. 1 Co 15[3] 'that which also I received'), of Christ 'bearing our sins' (1 P 2[24], He 9[28], cf. 2 Co 5[21]), 'suffering for sins, the righteous for the unrighteous' (1 P 3[18], cf. Ro 5[6. 8]), 'redeeming us by his blood' (Eph 1[7], 1 P 1[18. 19], Rev 5[9]); 'offering' Himself as 'a sacrifice for sins' (He 10[12]), 'giving himself a ransom for us' (1 Ti 2[6]), becoming a 'propitiation' (1 Jn 2[2] 4[10]), etc. This more definite mode of conceiving of everything in salvation as depending on the redeeming death of Christ led, in turn, to a change in the form of presenting the gospel. Instead of attention being directed primarily, as in the Gospels, to the nature of salvation, as flowing from the mercy of God, the mind is now turned, above all, to the Person by whom redemption is effected, to His sacrifice as the means of redemption, and to the necessity of faith in Him as the condition of salvation. In this new perspective, the whole state of salvation, and every blessing included in it, is viewed as the fruit of Christ's redeeming death. An immediate effect is forgiveness (Ac 2[38] 13[38], Ro 4[6-8], Eph 1[7], Col 1[14], 1 Jn 1[9] 2[12], Rev 1[5] etc.). But Christ redeems also 'out of this present evil world' ('delivers,' Gal 1[4]), 'from all iniquity' (Tit 2[14]), 'from your vain manner of life handed down from your fathers,' etc. (1 P 1[18]). St. Paul's special conceptions are referred to below. The efficacy of this redemption is placed by all NT writers, after the sacrificial analogy, in the 'blood' (Ac 20²⁸, Ro 3²⁵, Eph 1⁷, He 9¹² and *passim*, 1 P 1².¹⁹, 1 Jn 1⁷, Rev 1⁵ 5⁹ etc.), which here is the symbol of a sacrifice that culminates in death. This strain of teaching is so inwrought into the texture of Apostolic teaching that it is impossible by any ingenuity of exegesis to get rid of it, or make it mean essentially anything else than what the words naturally convey, viz. that the death of Jesus had a direct and indispensable redeeming efficacy, arising from its character as an expiation for sin.

(*b*) The NT writer who has given this redeeming character of Christ's death its most complete theological elucidation, it will be universally conceded, is St. Paul. A full exposition of the concatenation of his ideas hardly falls within the scope of this article, but the general import of the Apostle's teaching on redemption is not difficult to grasp. Starting with the fact of sin as bringing the world, both Gentile and Jewish, under the condemnation (κατάκριμα) of God (Ro 1–3. 5¹⁶. ¹⁸ 8¹ etc.), he proceeds to the exhibition of God's method of salvation, in bringing to mankind a new righteousness ('the righteousness of God'), to be received by faith (Ro 1¹⁷ 3 ²¹. ²². ²⁶. 5¹⁷⁻²¹, 2 Co 5²¹, Ph 3⁹ etc.). This righteousness comes through the propitiatory death of Christ (Ro 3²⁵); is initially realized in Christ's sacrificial death, which is at the same time the culmination of His obedience (Ro 5¹⁹, Ph 2⁸); proceeds from His Cross, and is applied in God's justifying act to the salvation of the individual believer (Ro 3²⁴. ²⁶ 5¹ 8¹. ³³), who thereby is constituted 'the righteousness of God in him' (2 Co 5²¹, Phil 3⁹), or is 'justified' (Ro 3²⁴ 5¹), *i.e.* pronounced righteous. The salvation thus provided in Christ is a 'redemption' (Ro 3²⁴, Eph 1⁷, Col 1¹⁴). The connexion of it with Christ's death is, that Christ honours the righteousness of God in Himself consenting to be 'made sin' for us (2 Co 5²¹), or endure sin's condemnation in His own Person, that sinners may be saved. He redeems from the curse of the law by being made a curse for us (Gal 3¹³ 4⁴. ⁵). *How* such vicarious endurance of another's κατάκριμα was possible, St. Paul does not explain; but we may gather from the context of his thought that he would find the explanation in the peculiarity of the representative relation which Christ sustained to our race (Ro 5¹²⁻²¹, 2 Co 5¹⁴. ¹⁵); in the perfection of His identification with the world in sympathy and love (Gal 1⁴ 2²⁰ 5² etc.); and in the fact that a vital union is constituted between the believer and Christ by faith, so that the acts of the Head are participated in by the members (Ro 6³ff.). St. Paul attaches great importance to the corporate idea (Ro 14⁷⁻⁹, 1 Co 12¹²ff.), and to the representative principle involved in it (Ro 5¹²ff.). Christ, in His complete identification with the race He came to save, took part in its responsibilities as under a broken law, and magnified the righteousness of God (Ro 3²⁵. ³¹) in His endurance of death, which is the wages of sin (6²³). Sinless Himself, the sin of the world met on Him, and was atoned for in His perfect response to the mind of God in His Judgment on that sin.

The attempt has been made to explain St. Paul's doctrine of the atoning character of Christ's death as a survival of his older Rabbinical notions, as well as to make out an inconsistency between this side of his teaching and his other doctrine of mystical union with Christ. But to the Apostle's own mind there was no inconsistency. St. Paul's conceptions of law, of righteousness, of sin and its desert, had their roots in something far deeper than Rabbinism—even in the OT; and there was to His thought no contradiction in setting forth Christ's death as the objective ground of man's acceptance with God, and at the same time in teaching that the end of salvation was holiness—a holiness which could only be realized through dying to sin with Christ, and rising again with Him to life in the spirit; in other words, through personal, vital union with the Risen Lord.

(*c*) In the remaining writings of the NT, while the ideas are less developed theologically, and the distinctive nomenclature of St. Paul is not used, emphasis is not less strongly laid on Christ's death as a propitiatory and redeeming sacrifice (1 P 1¹⁸. ¹⁹, 2 P 2¹, He 9¹². ¹⁵, cf. Ro 3²⁵), cleansing from the guilt and power of sin (1 Jn 5⁷. ⁹, He 2¹⁷ 9¹⁴ etc.), saving from wrath (He 2². ³ 9²⁶ff., 1 P 4¹⁷. ¹⁸, Rev 5⁹; cf. 7¹⁴ 14⁴ff. etc.), rescuing from the power of the world and the devil (He 2¹⁴. ¹⁵, 1 P 1¹⁸ 5⁸ etc.), giving access to God (1 P 3¹⁸, 1 Jn 4¹⁴⁻¹⁶ 10¹⁹⁻²² etc.), introducing into a new state of unspeakable privilege and felicity (1 P 1⁹. ¹⁰ 2⁹. ¹⁰, 2 P 1¹¹, 1 Jn 3¹⁻³ etc.). Occasionally there seem links of connexion between the Epistles and the teaching of the Gospels. It is difficult, *e.g.*, not to see in St. John's 'He was manifested to take away sins (ἵνα τὰς ἁμαρτίας ἄρῃ); and in him is no sin' (1 Jn 3⁵), a reminiscence of the Baptist's similar saying in Jn 1²⁹ (ὁ ἀμνὸς τοῦ θεοῦ, ὁ αἴρων τὴν ἁμαρτίαν τοῦ κόσμου); or in St. Paul's, 'Who gave himself a ransom for all' (ὁ δοὺς ἑαυτὸν ἀντίλυτρον ὑπὲρ πάντων 1 Ti 2⁶), an echo of the words of Jesus in Mk 10⁴⁵ (καὶ δοῦναι τὴν ψυχὴν αὐτοῦ λύτρον ἀντὶ πολλῶν). In 1 Peter there is a blending of both sacrificial and Prophetic language. Jesus redeems with His 'precious blood' (τιμίῳ αἵματι)—the blood of the Sinless One (1¹⁹ 2²²); but in other places we have a clear falling back upon the ideas and language of Is 53 (*e.g.* 2²³⁻²⁵). Christ's death did for believers all that the suffering of the Servant of the Lord in Is 53 was to do for the people, and all that redeeming sacrifices did under the OT, only now in a grander and more effectual way. And St. Peter says that his readers *knew* this (1¹⁸)—it was the familiar doctrine of the Church. In 1 John we have prominence given to the idea of 'propitiation' (ἱλασμός, 2² 4¹⁰). The term points to the effect of Christ's sacrifice, not on men, but on God, in averting His wrath or displeasure against sin (cf. Is 12¹). The Book of Revelation, again, moves in the distinctively sacrificial circle of ideas. The centre of worship is the Lamb that was 'slain' (5⁶. ⁹. ¹²), who, loving us, 'loosed (λύσαντι) us from our sins by his blood' (1⁵), and 'purchased (ἠγόρασας) unto God' with His blood men of every nation (5⁹. ¹⁰)—those described after (7¹⁴), in strong paradox, as 'having washed their robes, and made them white in the blood of the Lamb.' If the design was to ascribe an expiatory and redeeming efficacy to the death of Christ, it is difficult to see in what stronger way it could be done.

It is in the Epistle to the Hebrews, however, that the relation between Christ's redemption and the sacrificial ritual of the OT is most fully wrought out. The writer of the Epistle evidently proceeds upon the view which regards the Levitical sacrifices as having a propitiatory value through the vicarious shedding of the blood (9²² and *passim*) —the victim 'bearing the sins' of the transgressor, and atoning for them by its death. Yet he is as clearly conscious of the typical and shadowy character of the sacrificial system (10¹), and of its inability to effect a real redemption. He lays it down as a self-evident principle that 'it is impossible that the blood of bulls and goats should take away sins' (10⁴). The inadequacy of the OT sacrifices is seen in their number and their continual repetition (10¹⁻³); while the imperfection in the reconciliation wrought by them was signified by the barriers still interposed to complete approach to God (9⁶⁻¹⁰). But now, once for all (ἅπαξ), Christ has offered the perfect sacrifice which the Law could not provide, and has obtained 'eternal redemption' for us (9¹¹. ²⁶). He is at once high priest and victim, for the sacrifice He offers is the sacrifice of Himself (9²⁶). It is a true sacrifice for sins He offers. He is a high priest to make propitia tion for the sins of the people (εἰς τὸ ἱλάσκεσθαι τὰς ἁμαρτίας τοῦ λαοῦ, Heb. idiom, 2¹⁷). He was ' once offered to bear the sins of many' (9²⁸) ; He has 'offered one sacrifice for sins for ever' (10¹²). It was appointed unto men once to die (9²⁷); and Christ has died once for men. His sacrifice avails for 'the redemption of the transgressions that were under the first covenant,' sins which the sacrifices of the law could not remove (9¹⁵). To the question, Wherein lay the superior virtue of this sacrifice of Christ as contrasted with the typical sacrifices? the writer of the Epistle would answer, in the Divine dignity of the Offerer (the 'Son,' 1¹⁻³ etc.), in the true humanity He has assumed (2¹⁴⁻¹⁶), in the perfect sympathy and love with which He identifies Himself with His brethren (Himself being tempted and having suffered, 2¹⁰. ¹⁷. ¹⁸ 4¹⁴⁻¹⁶ 7²⁶⁻²⁸), above all in the obedient will in the offering itself. His sacrifice had in it this ethical element of surrender to God. The principal passage here is 10⁵⁻⁹. It is not meant in this passage that the simple doing of the will of God is itself the sacrifice, or takes the place of it; but it is the ethical quality of the sacrifice ; it is the fact that it is an act of holy, intelligent obedience which gives the sacrifice its value : ' by the which will we are sanctified through the offering of the body of Jesus Christ once for all' (10¹⁰). The sacrifice of Jesus, the Epistle teaches, at once redeems and consecrates.

5. Reasonableness of the Biblical doctrine.—The reasonableness of the Biblical doctrine of redemption, peculiarly, of the NT connexion of redemption with the suffering and death of Jesus as a sacrifice for sins, can be rightly appreciated only in the light of the Bible's own presuppositions on the character of God, on the infinite demerit of sin, on the necessity of a vindication of the righteousness of God in the forgiveness of sin, on the peculiar relation of Christ to God and man, qualifying Him to make atonement for sin, and effect a perfect reconciliation between God and humanity. More definitely, among the presuppositions of the doctrine are to be noted the following :—(1) The Biblical doctrine of *the righteousness of God.* By righteousness is meant that in God which grounds the moral order of the world, and pledges Him to uphold that order. While, in its connexion with mercy, righteousness is frequently represented as a saving, redeeming attribute, it cannot be merged wholly, as some (*e.g.* Ritschl) would have it, in either love or Fatherhood. There is an essential 'right' for God as well as for men, and righteousness is that attribute of His character which leads Him to establish, uphold, and vindicate that right in all His dealings and relations with moral beings.—(2) The Biblical recognition of *the organic constitution of mankind.* Humanity has a unity as a 'race' (cf. Ac 17²⁶), a corporate life and responsibilities, a 'solidarity,' in virtue of which 'none of us liveth to himself, and none dieth to himself' (Ro 14⁷). There is personal responsibility, but there is also a measure of responsibility which every one is called to assume for others. Good acts do not end with the doer, but their benefits overflow to others. Similarly the penalties of transgression are never confined to the transgressor, but overflow on all connected with him, and on society. One illustration of this principle is seen in heredity. As, however, through this principle it is possible for one to injure others, and for the penalties of evil-doing to be entailed on the innocent, so it is possible for one to act and suffer for the benefit and redemption of others. Scripture doctrine knows nothing of pure individualism. One is blessed in another ; one is helped by the intercession of another ; one would willingly, if he could, atone—sometimes, in a relative way,

does seek to atone—for the sin of another. (On the application to redemption, cf. Ro 5¹²ff.).—(3) The Biblical view of *the infinite evil and hatefulness of sin.* Sin is direct contrariety to the holiness of God. Eternally, therefore, holiness must react against it in condemnation and punishment (cf. Ro 1¹⁸). It follows that, even in forgiving sin, God cannot tamper with the condemning testimony of His law against it, but must provide for the vindication of His righteousness in the passing of it by (cf. Ro 3²⁶, He 9¹⁵).—(4) The Biblical truth of *Christ's essential and peculiar relation to our race.* This lies at the foundation of everything that is declared of Christ's redeeming activity. He is the 'Son of God, standing in a quite peculiar relation to both God and humanity. That relation to our race is grounded (*a*) in His general relation to creation (Jn 1²⁻⁴, 1 Co 8⁶, Col 1¹⁵ ¹⁷ etc.), and (*b*) in His condescending grace in becoming man—in His incarnation (Ph 2⁵ff., He 2¹⁴ etc.).—(5) In this relation also account is to be taken of *Christ's perfect sinlessness* (2 Co 5²¹, 1 P 2²², 1 Jn 3⁵ etc.), and of His complete identification of Himself with our race in sympathy and love. Here already the substitutionary forces of love come into fullest play.—(6) The Biblical assertion that, in this identification, *Christ made Himself one with us in our whole position of responsibility and ruin under the broken and dishonoured law of God* (Ro 8³, Gal 4⁴ etc.). In this position it is impossible but that Christ should take cognizance of the relation in which sin has placed the world, not only to the commanding, but also to the condemning and punishing will of God, and should desire, as man's Redeemer, to do the highest honour to that, as to all else in God's relation to sin.—(7) Historically, it is certain that Jesus *did enter,* in the fullest way possible to a sinless being, into what may be called the penal evil of our state; into the experience of the deepest meaning of that evil ; above all, into death, the culminating form of that evil. When even a Bushnell can speak of Jesus as 'incarnated into the curse' of our condition (cf. *Forgiveness and Law,* pp. 150, 155, 158) ; can describe Him as 'doing all that He does and suffers, in a way to honour the precept, enforce the penalty, and sanctify the justice of law ; the precept as right, the penalty as righteous, the justice as the fit vindication of the righteousness of God' ; and declares that 'no moral account of His gospel, separated from this, can be anything but a feeble abortion' (*Vic. Sac.* pt. iii. ch. vi.), it may be felt that there is no supreme difficulty in believing that Christ, in our name and nature, may, in His acceptance of suffering and death, have rendered that acknowledgment of the righteousness of God in His condemnation of sin, which holiness demands, in order that sin may be righteously forgiven.

ii. ECCLESIASTICAL DEVELOPMENT.—In a brief sketch of the ideas and theories which have prevailed in the Church on the subject of redemption, only leading points can be indicated. It was only to be expected that, in the multitude of aspects under which redemption is represented in Scripture, much diversity would appear in the manner in which the doctrine was apprehended by different minds in the Church. And this is what we find.

1. In the immediately post-Apostolic age, little was done to elucidate the connexion of Christ's suffering and death with redemption. The Fathers of that age, while profuse in their allusions to redemption through the blood of Christ, content themselves, mostly, with the repetition of the Apostolic phrases, and offer no theological interpretation. The age of the Apologists which succeeded was, if possible, even more barren in this direction. Still, even in this earliest period, it would not be difficult to show that the essential fact of redemption by Christ was never lost sight of. Clement of Rome (Ep. 49), as later Irenæus (v. xvii. 3), lays stress on Christ's giving His flesh for our flesh, and His soul for our souls; and sometimes, as in Polycarp and the *Epistle to Diognetus*, a remarkably clear and evangelical note is struck. Reflexion on the mode of redemption may be said properly to begin with the old Catholic Fathers—Irenæus, Tertullian, Origen, etc. A leading idea in Irenæus is that of the *recapitulatio* of the whole of humanity in Jesus Christ. Jesus, *i.e.*, sums up all history, all stages and experiences of human life, in Himself, and so can represent humanity as its Redeemer. He enters as a new Head into our race; retracts the disobedience of the Fall by His own obedience; gains a complete victory over Satan; and honours the justice of God by His submission to death for our sins (II. xxii. 4, III. xviii. 6, xxi. 10, v. ii. 1, etc.). This Father is sometimes credited with the idea of a ransom paid to Satan, but any allusion of this kind in him hardly gets beyond a rhetorical figure (v. i. 1). He teaches explicitly that Christ by His death has reconciled us to God, and procured for us forgiveness (III. xvi. 9, v. xvi. 3, etc.). Origen, as Harnack (*Hist. Dogm.* ii. 367) observes, regarded Christ's redemption from many points of view (victory over Satan, expiation offered to God, ransom paid to Satan). The grotesque theory of a ransom paid to Satan—the devil, however, being deceived in the transaction, as he found he could not hold the soul of Jesus—is, in Origen also, hardly more than rhetoric (on Mt 16[8]); but the idea took hold, and, sometimes alone, sometimes along with other conceptions, was propounded by subsequent theologians, and in the Middle Ages, as far down as Bernard and the Schoolmen, as a serious theory of redemption. Other prominent teachers, however, as Gregory of Nazianzus, Athanasius, Anselm, would have nothing to do with it (see RANSOM). Athanasius takes a further step, and in his treatise on *The Incarnation of the Word* makes a brief, reasoned attempt at the *rationale* of salvation. God had ordained death as the penalty of sin, and, as it was impossible for God to lie, it was necessary that this penalty should be inflicted (*incar.* 6, 8, 9, etc.). But it was not fitting that God should allow His creation to perish; the Logos, therefore, Creator of the world, having assumed our nature, endured this penalty in our stead, and brought into our race anew a principle of incorruption (*ib.* 8, 9). The Latin Church naturally (Hilary, Ambrose, Augustine) gave more prominence than the Greek Church to the idea of satisfaction to law or justice, but in Greek writers also (Cyril, Chrysostom, etc.) this idea is not wanting. It is important to observe that Augustine, and the Fathers generally, never lose sight of the fact that it is God's love which is the cause of Christ's reconciliation; not Christ's death, as an appeasement of justice, which is the cause of the love (Aug. on Jn 17[21-29]; Calvin endorses this view, *Instit.* II. xvi. 3, 4).

2. A new period in the history of this doctrine begins with Anselm in his *Cur Deus Homo.* Anselm's theory turns on the necessity of a 'satisfaction' to God's violated honour; but it is noteworthy that he does not find this satisfaction in the penal endurance of our curse. His theory moves rather in the circle of the Catholic ideas of supererogatory merit. Christ, as man, was bound to obey God's law, but, as sinless man, He was not bound to die. His voluntary submission to a shameful death, therefore, for the glory of His Father, was an act of such transcendent merit as infinitely to outweigh all the dishonour done to

God by humanity. Anselm is strong in basing the necessity for satisfaction in God's nature; but his theory is faulty in the idea of merit on which it turns, in its ignoring of the penal aspect, and in its too external character. Abelard represented the opposite pole of doctrine—the purely *moral* view of the effect of Christ's death. Bernard opposed Abelard, and gave prominence to the important thought of the vicarious suffering of the Head for the members (*vers. Abel.* vi. 15). Aquinas sought, but without real logical cohesion, to combine all these points of view in a comprehensive scheme. Meanwhile, in accordance with the scholastic tendency to exalt the will of God at the expense of His other attributes, atonement was removed from the ground of necessity in the Divine nature on which Anselm had placed it, and was rested on the mere *fiat* of the Divine sovereignty (Duns Scotus). To this tendency the whole body of the Reformers, in the great religious upheaval of the 16th cent., strenuously opposed themselves, and, with their clearer views of what was needed as the basis of the sinner's justification, definitely placed the Atonement on the ground of a satisfaction to eternal law. Sin they regarded as 'a violation of the order of public law that is upheld by God's authority, a violation of the law that is correlate with the eternal being of God Himself'; they 'estimated the atoning work of Christ by reference to that justice of God which finds its expression in the eternal law' (Ritschl). It is this view which it embodied in the Protestant creeds. Socinianism denied the necessity of all satisfaction for sin, and explained Christ's work, as man, in terms of His prophetic office. The later Governmental theory of Grotius likewise denied the need of satisfaction to essential justice, and sought a basis for the atonement in 'rectoral' considerations. Christ's death was a 'penal example' for the upholding of public law, and the deterring from future sin. The 'covenant' theology viewed redemption as flowing from a compact between the Divine Persons, in which Christ became surety for the elect, and purchased their salvation by His death in their room.

3. The increasingly mechanical and narrowly legal character which thus tended to be stamped on redemption led, as it was bound to do, to a reaction. Modern theology has been marked, accordingly, by a considerable revolt against every form of satisfaction theory, and by a return, in one form or another, to views more purely ethical.

(1) In certain of these theories Christ's redeeming work is brought mainly under the head of 'revelation.' Its essence lies in His revelation of the character and will of grace of the Father. His death is the culminating point in this revelation, and the supreme test of His fidelity to God in His vocation (thus, *e.g.*, Ritschl).—(2) Bushnell's theory attaches itself specially to the idea of 'sympathy' in Christ, and finds in this the key to His vicarious sufferings. The redeeming quality of Christ's sufferings lies wholly in their moral efficacy. Christ 'simply engages, at the expense of great suffering and even of death itself, to bring us out of our sins themselves, and so out of their penalties' (*Vic. Sac.* pt. i. ch. 1). Later, Bushnell felt the need of doing more justice to the idea of 'propitiation'; but, while allowing that Christ came under the 'penal sanctions' of sin, he still held that these sanctions were 'never punitive, but only coercive and corrective' (*Forg. and Law*, p. 132). But what does 'penal' mean, if not 'punitive'?—(3) A third class of theories lays main emphasis on the surrender to the Father of the 'holy will' of Christ. In this lies the essence of His redeeming sacrifice for humanity (Maurice, F. W. Robertson, Erskine of Linlathen, etc.).—(4) A profounder view,

in some respects, is that of M'Leod Campbell, whose ideas have considerably influenced later theology both at home (Moberly) and on the Continent (*e.g.* Häring). Campbell finds the essence of Christ's atonement in what he calls a ' vicarious repentance ' for sin. The language is unfortunate, for, in strictness, no one can ' repent ' for another, though he may ' confess ' the sin of another, and ' intercede ' for that other. The real value of Campbell's theory lies in its attempt to give an ethical and inward character to Christ's dealing with the wrath of God against sin. He recognizes that sin's guilt, and the reality of the Divine condemnation of sin, cannot be ignored. There is but one way, he holds, in which that condemnation can be met, namely, by entering fully into God's mind regarding sin, and rendering to His judgment upon it a perfect *response*. In his own words, there goes up an '' " Amen " from the depths of the humanity of Christ to the Divine condemnation of sin ' (*Atonement*, pp. 117–118). This ' Amen,' in Christ's case, is viewed by him as rendered, not ' in naked existence ' (*i.e.* in purely mental realization), but under actual experience of the power of evil, and of death, viewed as including ' the sentence of the law against sin ' (*ib.* pp. 259–262). A note is touched here which perhaps takes us very near the heart of the matter.—(5) Moberly's view in his *Atonement and Personality* has affinity with Campbell's, but differs from it in viewing punishment in this life as only disciplinary—chastisement inflicted for the good of the transgressor—and never retributive. [Punishment, however, must be felt to be one's *due*, or it has no good effect.] Punishment in itself does not atone ; atonement arises only when the punishment is met by a spirit of perfect contrition. The essence of atonement is ' penitential holiness.' This, it is held with Campbell, is perfectly realised in Christ alone. In Christ is offered a perfect contrition for the sins of the world. But it is offered in Christ only that it may be reproduced in the believer. Great difficulty, in this theory, must be felt to attach to the idea of ' penitence ' as an element in Christ's consciousness ; it is besides, after all, not Christ's perfect penitence which is held to be the ground of forgiveness, but the spirit of contrition awakened in the believer himself. Christ's work has its value as producing *that*. Forgiveness, it is further taught, is not complete at once, but is proportioned to the degree of penitence ; surely not a Scriptural notion.

The result of the total survey will probably be to impress upon us : (*a*) how defective the best of human theories are to express the whole truth on this great subject ; (*b*) the fact that elements of truth are embraced in nearly all the theories, which a more complete view must endeavour to conserve ; and (*c*) the need of continually reverting from human theories to the original statements in Scripture itself, which, in their breadth, variety, and fulness, refresh and satisfy as nothing else can.

Literature.—Ritschl, *Recht. und Versöhnung*, Bd. ii. ; A. B. Davidson, *The Theology of the OT* (viii.-x.) ; Dillmann, *Alttest. Theol.* ; other *Biblical Theologies of OT* (Schultz, Oehler, etc.) ; Curtiss, *Primitive Semitic Religion To-day* (1902), p. 194 ff. ; artt. ' Righteousness,' ' Redemption,' in Hastings' *DB* ; Stevens, *The Theology of the NT*, and *The Christian Doctrine of Salvation* (ethical aspects ; rejects penal view).—On NT teaching : Denney, *The Death of Christ* ; Walker, *The Cross and Kingdom* (' Sayings of Jesus,' pts. ii. iii.) ; Scott-Lidgett, *The Spiritual Principle of the Atonement* (ch. iii.) ; Crawford, *The Atonement* (pt. i.) ; Dale, *The Atonement* (ii.-vi.) ; *Bib. Theologies of NT* (Weiss, etc.).—On Christ's work in Redemption : F. D. Maurice, *Theological Essays* (vii. ' The Doctrine of Sacrifice ') ; Bushnell, *The Vicarious Sacrifice*, and *Forgiveness and Law* ; M'Leod Campbell, *The Nature of the Atonement* ; D. W. Simon, *The Redemption of Man*, and *Reconciliation by Incarnation* ; Ritschl, *Justification and Reconciliation*, vol. iii. ; Moberly, *Atonement and Personality* ; Kähler, *Die Lehre von der Versöhnung* ; Seeberg, *Der Tod Christi* ; Dale, Scott-Lidgett, Walker, Stevens, etc., as above.—On criticism of theories :

Ritschl, as above, vol. i. ; Crawford, Dale, Scott-Lidgett, Stevens, etc.—On history of doctrine : Harnack, *Dogmengeschichte* [Eng. tr. in 7 vols.] ; Orr, *Progress of Dogma* (vii.).
JAMES ORR.

**REDNESS OF THE SKY.—When the Pharisees and Sadducees (Mt 16[1f.]) demanded of Christ a sign from heaven (ἐκ τοῦ οὐρανοῦ), He replied by reminding them how, when the sky (οὐρανός, RV ' heaven ') was red at morning or evening, they were able to foretell foul or fair weather, and so showed that they themselves could discern the face of the sky (or the heaven). There is here an insistence on the various meanings of οὐρανός that is lost in the AV by the introduction of a second word to construe it (see SKY). The ' redness ' of the sky is denoted by the verb πυρράζω, *to glow*, literally, *to become fire*. The colour of fire (πυρρός) is used for ' red ' in Rev 6[4] 12[3]. In the LXX it stands for the Hebrew אדם. The consequences of a fiery hue in the sky at morning or evening, due to the condition of the atmospheric medium, is one of the commonest of weather maxims. It is familiarized in various old couplets.
W. S. KERR.

**REED. (κάλαμος).—This represents the Heb. *kaneh*, probably *Arundo donax*, a plant which grows in great abundance in the marshes of the Jordan Valley and along the river sides. The stem is tall and straight, and the head bends gracefully with a great feathery brush, sensitive to the slightest breath of air (Mt 11[7], Lk 7[24]). The wood is put to many uses. It forms the frames of the rush mats with which the Arabs of *el-Hûleh* make their slender houses. It serves as a walking-stick. When bruised, it is not only useless but dangerous ; because, giving way when one leans upon it, the splinters are apt to pierce the hand (Mt 12[20]). As a mock-sceptre, a reed was put into Christ's hand (Mt 27[29]), and with this He was smitten (27[30]). On a reed the sponge with vinegar was raised to His lips on the cross (27[48]). Pens are made from the smaller stems, the Gr. κάλαμος (3 Jn [13]) again corresponding to the Arab. *kalam* and the Lat. *calamus*. The ancients made the shafts of their arrows from the κάλαμος, and the divining-arrow of the Arab is also *kalam*. The flute and pipes played on all occasions of festivity are made from the reed (Mt 11[17], Lk 7[32]). Measuring-rods were so uniformly of reed that they came to be known generally by this term (Ezk 40[3], Rev 21[15] etc.).
W. EWING.

**REFLECTIVENESS.—This is the habit of *bending back* the attention of the mind from action and experience to scrutinize and contemplate the nature and meaning of self and the world. Deep, steady reflectiveness is rare amid the extraordinary preoccupation in business of the modern world, which like briers chokes the word. The parable of the Sower should help to restore the reflective habit to its high place among the duties and privileges of life (Mt 13[19. 22]). The refrain, ' Who hath ears to hear, let him hear,' is a direct appeal to the reflective man. The good scribe has thoughts new and old to reflect upon and dilate upon (Mt 13[52]). It is the reflective mind which appreciates the absolute truth and varied applicability of the reciprocal principle involved in Mt 7[12] or even Mt 7[4]. Nature and experience are full of suggestive facts to reflect upon (Mt 6[26-30] 12[12]), God's care for men being greater than for flowers, and His loving-kindness to men exceeding any shepherd's anxiety for his sheep. John the Baptist is told to reflect upon the beneficence of his successor's ministry (Mt 11[4. 5]). Martha was ' anxious and troubled about many things ' which her more reflective sister Mary was privileged to be free from (Lk 10[41]). The Virgin Mary herself is a beautiful and pathetic example of fruitful reflectiveness (Lk 2¹⁹·⁵¹). Without reflectiveness the Holy Spirit's work of illumination and guidance could scarcely have its full and due fruit (Jn 14²⁵ 16¹³). Reflectiveness is necessary to grasp the lessons of truth as well as to sift error therefrom.

W. B. FRANKLAND.

REFORM.—There is no mention of this word in the Gospels ; the only use of it in the NT is He 9¹⁰ ' until the time of reformation ' (Gr. διόρθωσις). It may be well to note in what sense Jesus may be said to have approved of ' reform.' There was much about the State that needed reform. Did He step forward to help it on ? The answer must be in the negative. He made no attempt to reform the political abuses of His time, yet by the general strain and spirit of His teaching He assuredly did much to help on society towards such reformation. In His own conduct, we find Jesus submitting to the civil authorities under whom He lived. He refused to be made a King, or a Governor, or a Judge, or to be involved in any way, however remotely, in political revolution. He was ready rather to die than to be engaged in any such work. When asked about the lawfulness of tribute, He said, ' Render unto Cæsar the things that are Cæsar's, and unto God the things that are God's ' (Mt 22²¹). Although the words may not be pressed to support a doctrine of passive obedience, nor, on the other hand, taken as an incentive to revolution, He probably meant to remind His countrymen that, in return for the benefits of Roman government under which they lived, they might well be expected to share the expense by paying taxes. Again, in Mt 17²⁷, we find Him providing for the payment of the Temple-tax for Himself and His disciples. He thus submitted to the ordinary ecclesiastical authority, with only a mild protest. Before Pilate, He said, ' Thou wouldest have no authority against me, except it were given thee from above ' (Jn 19¹¹). This surely means that all human authority is subject to the higher power of God, who regulates all by His Providence ; though it has sometimes been supposed that Jesus thus acknowledged the legitimacy of Pilate's power.

Jesus cannot be claimed with any justice as a victim on the altar of political reform. Yet it may well be affirmed that His teachings, if carried out by men, would certainly produce a reformed society. His disciples, being good men, would also be good citizens. He gave to the world principles, which have been the fruitful seed of true reform.

As to Christ's relation to the law of Moses, it may be asked, Did He become a Reformer ? While declaring that ' he came not to destroy but to fulfil ' (Mt 5¹⁷), we must believe that, at least, He desired some reform of abuses, which had grown up through the interpretations and applications of the Law, made by scribes and lawyers of the past. Even in regard to the law of divorce, He calls attention to the right spirit of the Mosaic legislation, rather than to the exact letter of the Law (Mt 5³¹·³² 19³ff, Mk 10²ff). And He treats with indignant scorn those evasions of filial duty, as in the case of the Corban, which had so long been sanctioned by the practice of Jewish society (Mt 15³ff, Mk 7⁹ff). In regard to such traditional abuses, as well as in regard to the State and general social arrangements, we may say that Jesus rather gave an impulse to reform than engaged actively in any attempt to bring the Law, as understood and practised in His day, into accordance with the eternal law of God.

When asked to consider a question about a disputed inheritance, He refused to be drawn into such quarrels, and bade men beware of a covetous spirit, remembering that man's life does not con-

sist in the abundance of the things he possesses (Lk 12¹³ff). He believed that by interfering with the Law, even to have justice done, His disciples might do their spiritual life more harm than such action would do good in a temporal aspect. Jesus' disciple ought to be able to renounce the pursuit of his rights, and ought to co-operate in forming a nation of brothers, in which justice is done, no longer by the aid of force, but by free obedience to the good, and which is united, not by legal regulations, but by the ministry of love ' (Harnack, *What is Christianity ?* p. 112). See art. LAW.

LITERATURE.—Denney, art. ' Law ' in Hastings' *DB* ; R. Mackintosh, *Christ and the Jewish Law* ; *Lux Mundi*, ch. xi. ' Christianity and Politics ' ; Bruce, *Galilean Gospel*, ch. xi., *Parabolic Teaching*, p. 300 ff. ; Dale, *Laws of Christ for Common Life*, ch. xii. ; *Expositor*, I. v. [1877] pp. 214 ff., 436 ff.

D. M. W. LAIRD.

REGENERATION.—Of all theological ideas, regeneration is probably that which has had the most unfortunate history. The figure is an apt and obvious one to express the completeness of the change which takes place when the non-Christian becomes a Christian ; but it is tempting to press it, and it has been pressed in the most inconsiderate fashion. As the beginning of Christian life (it is argued), it must be antecedent to every Christian experience ; faith, justification, conversion are. strictly speaking, its fruits. As a new birth, man can no more contribute to it than to his first birth, and hence must be regarded in it as purely passive, not acting or co-operating with God. As there is no middle state between being dead and being alive, it must be conceived as instantaneous ; and so on. We can see the motives in such a mode of thought, but it is full of delusions. Perhaps they have influenced Reformed theology more than Lutheran ; yet, while the Lutherans were more conscious of the figure in regeneration, the Reformed were guided by the justifiable desire to give faith a real basis in the believer,—to lay an act of God, as the only sure foundation, at the basis of the whole experience of salvation.

The word ' regeneration ' occurs in AV only in Mt 19²⁸, Tit 3⁵ (παλινγενεσία), and the figure of a new or second birth is most distinctly expressed in our Lord's conversation with Nicodemus, Jn 3 (γεννηθῆναι ἄνωθεν). But as the first of these passages is eschatological, and refers to the new world which is introduced with the παρουσία of the Son of Man, while the two others belong to the latest in the NT, it is not convenient to start with them. To see the real basis for the figure of the new birth, it is necessary to go back to the teaching of Jesus in the Synoptics, and to look at it in its substance and not merely in its formal expression. What the figure conveys, vividly and truly, is the idea that somehow a man has become another man : he has entered into a new order of being ; things once real to him have lost reality ; things once unknown are now alone real. If we find this idea in the teaching of Jesus, we find what is meant by regeneration, even though that figure should not expressly appear.

1. Our Lord's teaching.—It cannot be questioned that the idea of the newness or originality of His work, and of all that depended upon it, was familiar to Jesus. Without accepting the doctrine that the Kingdom of God, as He conceived it, was purely transcendent,—a new world not spiritually evolved from the present, but supernaturally descending upon it,—we must believe that however it came, and however it was related to the present, the Kingdom introduced an order of things which was entirely new. It was itself, in a comprehensive sense, a παλινγενεσία (Mt 19²⁸). (On this word see the excellent article on ' Regeneration ' in Hastings' *DB*. by Dr. Vernon Bartlet.) But everything connected with it, involved in it, or leading up to it, awoke in the mind the same sense of newness. In spite, for example, of our Lord's feeling of the continuity of His work with the OT ('I came not to destroy, but to fulfil,' Mt 5[17]), He has the equally strong feeling that with the time of fulfilment a new era has dawned ('The law and the prophets were until John : from that time the kingdom of God is preached, and every one presses into it,' Lk 16[16]). The newness is so complete, the distinction is so great, that the least in the Kingdom of God is greater than the greatest in the old dispensation (Mt 11[11]). The same truth underlies all the passages in which Jesus claims for Himself absolute significance in determining the relations of God and man. Of these the most explicit is Mt 11[27]. Jesus alone reveals the Father, and the man who knows the Father is no longer the same man. No words could be too strong to tell how completely he is another. This absolute significance of Jesus is the sum and substance of His self-revelation (cf. Mt 16[13ff.]), and the truth of 'regeneration' is an immediate inference from it. Further, though it is not put expressly in this form in the Synoptics, the 'newness,' which is the point to be emphasized, does break through in various ways. We see it in the parables of the New Patch on the Old Garment and the New Wine in the Old Bottles (Mk 2[21f.] ||). We see it in the new spiritual liberty which Jesus in Mt 17[24-27] claims for Himself and those who through Him become children of the Kingdom. We see it especially in the words at the Supper ; for there is no doubt that Mt. and Lk. give at least the thought that was in His mind when they speak of the new covenant based on His blood (Mt 26[28] D, Lk 22[2]). It deserves special mention, too, that in all the Synoptics (Mk 14[25], Mt 26[29], Lk 22[16-18]) the thought of the new covenant carries the mind forward to the new world in which it is to be consummated ; the new religious relation to God, determined by Christ and His death, cannot be fully realized apart from immortality. The inward regeneration of the soul (so to speak) is part of the ἀποκατάστασις πάντων, or of the παλινγενεσία in the sense of Mt 19[28]. But to use the term 'regeneration' here is to anticipate. We have not found any suggestion of it in the words of Jesus, and, in point of fact, the only such suggestion to be found in the Synoptics is Mt 18[3] 'Verily I say unto you, Except ye turn (ἐὰν μὴ στραφῆτε), and become as little children, ye shall in no wise enter into the kingdom of heaven' (cf. Mk 10[15]). To become as a little child is really to be born again ; it is what this figure of a new birth properly means, and it is the only key to it which the words of Jesus yield. In the words of Jesus, evidently, it describes a moral requirement ; it is something He demands from those who would be His disciples and enter the Kingdom, and it is achieved through 'turning.' The context defines what 'turning' means. It means giving up ambition, pride, self-seeking, by-ends in religion, and other unchildlike tempers ; it is, in short, identical with what is elsewhere in the Synoptics called μετάνοια, or repentance. It is through this moral change, the responsibility for which is laid upon man, that he becomes as a little child, that is, is born again.

It should be remarked, in passing, that John never uses μετάνοια or στρέφεσθαι in the moral sense (except in the quotation from LXX at 12[40]), and that the Synoptists never use 'regeneration' of the individual, or speak of a new birth (except by the allusion in Mt 18[3]) ; but it is one and the same experience which they respectively describe by these terms. When that experience is regarded from the side of God, as something due to His grace or Spirit, it is called *regeneration*, a being born again, from above, of God ; when it is regarded from the side of man, as an experience the responsibility for which lies with him, it is called *repentance*. But we have no meaning or substance to put into either of these terms which does not equally belong to the other.

Perhaps another approach to the figure of regeneration (though that of resurrection is equally obvious) may be recognized in the passages in which Jesus speaks of the sinful life as death, and of recovery from it as a return to or entrance into life. There are two of these in the Synoptics (Mt 8[32] || Lk 15[24. 32]) : obviously the emphasis in both is moral, not metaphysical. A change of character is in view, which, however deep and far-reaching, raises none but moral problems. More important, however, than these are the passages in which our Lord teaches that the new or higher life—the regenerate life, to call it so—can only be won through the sacrifice of a lower life. In other words, to have the life which is life indeed, we must surrender the other ; we must die to nature in order to live to God. We must renounce self (ἀπαρνήσασθαι ἑαυτόν: a new and radical idea, without formal analogy in the OT) if we are to share in the life of the Kingdom. The man who refuses to do so, who cannot find it in him to do violence to nature, is incapable of discipleship and of the life which is life indeed. This is the burden of our Lord's teaching in such passages as Mt 16[24ff.] || 10[39] 18[8f.] ||, Lk 14[25ff.]. It contains all that is meant by regeneration, but it does not use that figure to express it. And again it is all within ethical limits.

2. Pauline Epistles. — The Book of Acts is a picture of the regenerate life in its workings in the Church, but it is not specially so conceived. At Pentecost what we see is rather *a* new birth than *the* new birth of the Apostles. The Spirit is not so much the author of regeneration as the source of the peculiar gifts and powers of believers. But the newness of Christianity is nowhere more strongly felt and expressed than in this book. It brings us directly to St. Paul. The Apostle of the Gentiles became a Christian in a way which must have impressed him profoundly with the difference between the Christian life and that of the pre-Christian state. No one could say with greater truth than he, 'I am now another man.' But in him the change took place in a way which was in the highest degree startling and abnormal ; it could not possibly suggest to him anything so natural as being born ; and it agrees with this that, though no one has a more adequate sense than St. Paul of the absolute newness of the Christian life, he never uses the figure of regeneration to convey this. He speaks of the New Covenant of which he is a minister (2 Co 3[6]), of the new creature (καινὴ κτίσις, 2 Co 5[17], Gal 6[11]) which he has become, of the new world in which he lives (2 Co 5[17]), of the new man who has been created according to God in righteousness and holiness of truth (Eph 4[24]), and who is being renewed unto knowledge after the image of Him that created him (Col 3[10]) ; he speaks also of being transformed by renewal of the mind (Ro 12[2]), and (if Tit 3[5] be his) of a renewal wrought by the Holy Spirit at baptism ; of walking in newness of life (Ro 6[4]), and serving God in newness of spirit (Ro 7[6]) ; but he never speaks formally of being born again. Even when he contrasts the past and the present as death and life, the life is not conceived as coming by birth, but either by a creative act of God analogous to that by which at first He commanded light into being out of darkness (2 Co 4[6]), or by an exercise of the same almighty power with which God wrought in Christ when He raised Him from the dead, and set Him at His own right hand in the heavenly places (Eph 1[20ff.] 2[1. 5]) : when we were dead in trespasses He quickened us together with Him. It is essentially the same change which Paul represents elsewhere as translation from the tyranny of darkness to the Kingdom of God's dear Son (Col 1[13]), or from the state of condemnation to that of justification, or from life after the flesh to life after the Spirit (Ro. Gal. *passion*), or, in more mystical or metaphysical fashion, from being in Adam to being in Christ : *vid.* esp. Ro 5¹²⁻²¹, 1 Co 15⁴⁵ff. It is not necessary here to discuss what is called Paul's psychology, as though he had such a thing in the sense of modern mental philosophy ; he has really no psychology ; he knows what he was, and he knows what he is, in the way of moral experiences, and he generalizes his past and his present into the conceptions of the natural and the spiritual man, the ψυχικός and the πνευματικός. Every man in himself is ψυχικός, a descendant and representative of Adam ; every man has through the gospel the opportunity of becoming πνευματικός, a child of God and representative of Christ. But, as has been already pointed out, Paul never uses the figure of a birth to elucidate or make intelligible the process of this change. He approaches the figure indeed in two different ways. On the one hand, he speaks of himself as the father of those who receive the new life of the gospel through his ministry : ' in Christ Jesus have I begotten you through the gospel' (1 Co 4¹⁵ ; cf. Gal. 4¹⁹, 1 Ti 1² ' my true child in the faith '). On the other, he speaks of the spirit in virtue of which men are πνευματικοί, and walk in newness of life, as specifically the spirit of sonship (υἱοθεσία), by which men are made to be, and are identified as, children of God. It is usually the dignity and privileges of this relation to God on which Paul lays stress, and these are suggested by υἱός ; but he has also the sense of the kinship to God which it involves, and this is expressed by τέκνον. The latter, though relatively infrequent, occurs in passages so characteristic that we can say that Paul was no stranger to that intimate sense of kinship to God which is so notable in the Johannine type of Christianity (Ro 8¹⁶⁻²¹, Eph 5¹).

There are two points of contact between the Pauline presentation of truth on this subject, and that which we have found in our Lord's teaching, which require to be emphasized. (1) There is in both the same outlook to immortality ; the spirit in Paul which makes men children of God is also the earnest of a life which vanquishes death (Ro 8¹¹, 2 Co 5⁴ᶠ·, Eph 1¹³ᶠ·). Indeed the new life is often identified with the resurrection life of Jesus in such a way that the present spiritual experience of it seems rather a deduction from that transcendent possession than something having an independent existence of its own. This applies, *e.g.*, to Ro 6¹⁻¹¹, Eph 2¹⁻⁵. In the Gospel, and in the experience of the Christian, there is the revelation at once of ζωή and ἀφθαρσία (2 Ti 1¹⁰). (2) There is in both our Lord and St. Paul the same idea that the new life is entered on through a death. ' Our old man was crucified with Christ' (Ro 6⁴), and it it is through that crucifixion that the new man comes into being (compare what is said above, § 1 *ad fin.*). It is one process, one experience, in man, in which the Adam dies and the Christ comes to be. In Paul the process is normally connected with baptism, and in view of Ro 6²ff·, Col 2¹¹⁻¹³, it is not easy to maintain that Paul could not have written ' the laver of regeneration, and of renewing wrought by the Holy Spirit' (Tit 3⁵). No doubt it is against the Pauline origin of the last phrase that it introduces the figure of regeneration which is so conspicuously wanting in the undoubted Epistles. When St. Paul spoke of baptism, however, as involving men in the death and resurrection of Jesus, —making them mysteriously participant in all that was meant by both, a death to sin and a life to God, with the assurance of immortality at the heart of it,—he was not thinking of baptism as a sacrament which produced these effects as an *opus operatum*. He could only think of it as he knew it, that is, as an ordinance administered to people

confessing their sins and accepting the love of God in Christ,—an ordinance that gathered into it the whole meaning of Christianity, and in a high and solemn hour raised to its height the Christian's sense of what it is *to be* a Christian. He says expressly in Col 2¹³ that in this ordinance we are raised with Christ ' *through faith in the working of God who raised him from the dead.*' The same holds of Ro C²ff·. Baptism there is a picture of what is meant by the faith which looks to a dead, buried, and risen Saviour as its one object ; in faith we identify ourselves with Christ in all these aspects, and so are taken out of the region to which sin belongs : this is what baptism shows even to the malignant or unintelligent persons who carped at Paul's gospel of salvation by faith alone. The sacrament, as St. Paul was accustomed to it, shut the mouth of anybody who denied that the Christian life rested on a death to sin ; and in guarding this fundamental truth it guarded (as we have seen) one of the primary teachings of Jesus. It is an immediate inference from all this that when we ask whether any particular passage in Paul—say Ro 7¹⁴⁻²⁵—applies to the regenerate or the unregenerate man, we are asking a question which the Apostle himself does not formally enable us to answer. He does not think of his experience in terms of regenerate and unregenerate. He can speak of the old man and the new, of the natural and the spiritual, of being under law and under grace, in Adam and in Christ, dead to sin and alive to God, and so on ; but the distinction between the states is moral rather than metaphysical, and it is in doctrine rather than experience that it is absolute. One personality subsists through all experiences, all changes of state ; nature, or the old man, is not extinct even in those who are in Christ and have the earnest of the Spirit ; and though St. Paul, like all religious teachers, often speaks absolutely, not telling his converts to be what they should be, but to be what as Christians they are, he does not allow the religious interest to engulf the moral. It is to men *dead* in Christ, whose old man has been crucified with Him, that he says, ' *Put to death* your members that are on the earth ' (Col 3⁵), ' *Reckon yourselves to be dead* unto sin' (Ro 6¹¹). Experience is not a quantum but a process, and in the life of a spiritual being it cannot be dated ; the things that in a sense happened twenty years ago are also present experiences, and it may be only now that we are discovering their real meaning. This holds especially of such generalized experiences as are embodied in the passage referred to. Only the new man, who by becoming such has learned what the life of the old man meant, could have written it, but it is unreal to say that it is the experience of either, to the exclusion of the other. The new man understands it better than anybody, but the fact that everybody understands it in some degree is the evidence that all men are capable of the experience it describes.

3. Catholic Epistles.—We find the idea of regeneration both in James and 1 Peter. In Ja. (1¹⁸) God is the author of it, Christians its subjects, and ' the word of truth' the instrument. We are reminded here of the parables in which the word of God—that is, the gospel—is spoken of as a seed, and of 1 Co 4¹⁹, though in James it is the will of God and not the ministry of an Apostle to which the new birth is referred. When James contemplates Christians thus begotten as a kind of first-fruits of God's creatures, he has apparently in view the universal παλιγγενεσία of Mt 19²⁸. The regeneration of individual men has the promise in it of new heavens and a new earth. There is a similar connexion of ideas in Ro 8²¹ff·. Peter, who uses twice (1³·²³) the word which is exactly rendered by regenerate (ἀναγεννᾶν), connects the experience which he so describes first with the resurrection of Christ, and then with the incorruptible seed which he identifies with the word of God—the gospel message which has been delivered to his hearers. The first brings him closely into line with Paul: the new life is distinctively life in the power of Christ's resurrection, a living hope which has an incorruptible inheritance in view (cf. 1 P 1³ and Ro 6⁴ᶠ.). This resurrection life is, of course, ethical, because it is Divine, but its ethical character is more explicitly secured by reference to the incorruptible seed from which it springs. 'Love one another from the heart fervently, having been born again,' etc. (1 P 1²²ᶠ.). The figure is continued in 2¹ᶠ., where the readers are exhorted (precisely as in Eph 4²²) to 'put off' all that was characteristic of their former life, and as 'newborn babes' to desire the spiritual milk which is without guile. Another parallel to Paul (and to our Lord) in making the new life rest on death to the old is found in 4¹ᶠ.; but though the reality is the same, the figure differs.

4. Johannine writings.—It is in the Fourth Gospel and 1 Jn. that the figure of a new birth is most frequent and explicit. John does not indeed use ἀναγεννάω, but he says γεννηθῆναι ἄνωθεν (Jn 3³·⁷); he speaks nine times in the 1st Ep. of being born of God (ἐκ τοῦ θεοῦ), and twice in the Gospel and four times in the 1st Ep. of children of God (τέκνα θεοῦ). The fundamental passage here is that in Jn 3, in which Jesus explains the new birth to Nicodemus. No experience is described or demanded in it which has not already come before us independently; the new birth is only a new figure which gives vivid and suggestive expression to a truth which Jesus Himself in the Synoptic record, and the Apostles in their writings, have already expressed in other forms. It may fairly be argued, when we look to the general relation of the discourses in the Fourth Gospel to the indisputable words of Jesus, that the real text of this discourse is Mt 18³. The Evangelist is guided by the Spirit of truth into all the truth of this apparently simple saying (Jn 16¹³); he universalizes it, and sets it in the various relations which bring out its meaning; he shows the necessity of the new birth, the method of it (so far as experience enabled him to do so), and the seat of the power which produced it. But he gives no description of its contents—no analysis of it as an experience—which enables us to put more into it than we put into 'turning and becoming as little children,' or into 'dying to sin and living to God,' or into 'putting off the old man and putting on the new.' He does indeed put in the most general form the necessity for the new birth when he says, 'that which is born of the flesh is flesh.' This does not mean that human nature is essentially or totally depraved; it means that that which is natural is not *ipso facto* spiritual; it is not what we get from our fathers and mothers which enables us to appreciate Christ, or to enter God's Kingdom; it is something which we can only get from God. This is the same truth which St. Paul teaches in 1 Co 15⁴⁵ᶠᶠ. 'That is not first which is spiritual, but that which is natural, and afterward that which is spiritual.' The birth by which man enters into relations with the natural world has an analogue in the experience by which he enters into relations with the spiritual world. It, too, is a birth—which is variously described as a second birth, or a birth from above, a being born of God, or of the Spirit, or of water and spirit. It cannot be denied that in generalizing the necessity for the second birth, the Evangelist passes from the safe and intelligible moral ground of Mt 18³ into a more metaphysical region (as St. Paul also does in 1 Co 15⁴⁵ᶠᶠ.); but in the circumstances this is not of much consequence. What St. Paul means by τὸ

ψυχικόν and St. John by τὸ γεγεννημένον ἐκ τῆς σαρκός is not any metaphysical abstraction, but human beings as they are encountered in the world; and it needs no argument that they must become other than they are, through and through, if they are to dwell with God. It needs no argument, either, that they cannot make themselves other than they are. To be born again they must be born of a power which comes from above, and that power—as the whole experience of his life taught St. John, and had taught St. Paul before him—was the power of the Spirit. To be born again is to be born of God. When the truth is put in this way—in what we may call without offence the onesidedly religious way—its mysteriousness is apparent. The action of God through which the new life emerges in men cannot be prescribed or calculated; it is as unquestionable in its effects as His action in nature, but there is something in it which eludes control. The sense of this underlies all the predestinarian passages both in St. John and St. Paul, but, of course, these are not to be read alone. We should completely misrepresent both Apostles if we supposed that their sense of dependence upon God for being the new men they were impaired their sense of responsibility in this relation. The mind is apt, and perhaps the feeble or insincere mind is glad, to escape from the moral to the metaphysical, from Mt 18³ to Jn 3⁶; there is more to talk about and less to do; but there is no ground for bringing this charge against the Apostles. St. John's interest in this passage is not in the earthly truth (v.¹²) of the necessity of regeneration—it needs no revelation from above to make that plain; bitter experience teaches it to all men; his interest is in the possibility and the method of regeneration, the heavenly truths which only Jesus can reveal. The new birth is a birth of water and spirit (v.⁵): in other words, it is a birth which is realized through Christian baptism. That the Spirit is the important matter appears from the fact that the water is only mentioned once, and then the Spirit alone (vv.⁶·⁸). Here, as in the case of St. Paul (see above), baptism must be taken in the whole circumstances and conditions in which it was familiar to the Evangelist. It was not the baptism of unconscious infants, but that of penitent and confessing believers. The importance of it in this passage is seen when we look on to v.¹⁴ᶠ. The heavenly truth (v.¹²) of the passage is that the power through which men are born again is lodged in the Son of Man lifted up as Moses lifted up the serpent in the wilderness. The baptism through which the new birth comes is baptism in His name —baptism, as in Ro 6, into His death and resurrection—baptism which means the believing abandonment of the soul to the love of God revealed in that strange 'uplifting' which includes both the Cross and the throne, a believing abandonment for which man's responsibility is complete, and the refusal of which is the only fatal sin (3³⁶). When we realize that this is the connexion of ideas in the conversation with Nicodemus, we see that it falls into line with the teaching of St. Paul, entirely so far as its substance is concerned, and more nearly than is at first apparent even in form; while the teaching of both Apostles is securely based at once on their experience as Christians and on thoroughly attested words of Jesus.

It is as easy with regard to St. John as with regard to St. Paul to ask questions connected with his doctrine of regeneration to which he himself does not afford any answer. Thus the new birth is made dependent somehow on baptism; but it has been argued that in 1¹²ᶠ. 'children of God' are spoken of, who were 'born of God,' before the Incarnation, and that in 11⁵² 'children of God' are spoken of as 'scattered throughout the world' who are to be gathered into one by the death of Jesus. As to the first of these passages, the interpretation which refers it to the ages before the incarnation seems to the writer more than doubtful, but in any case the Logos doctrine is a way of expressing the truth that the meaning and power of the Incarnation and Passion are independent of time. In the second passage 'children of God' is probably prophetic; there are men everywhere who will gather yet round the Cross of Jesus, and by the power which descends from it into their souls be born again as τέκνα θεοῦ. Another kind of question with regard to those who are born of God is raised by some passages in the 1st Epistle. In ch. 1[8] it is said of Christians, 'If we say that we have not sin, we deceive ourselves,' and in v.[10] 'If we say that we have not sinned, we make him a liar.' But in ch. 3[9] we read, 'Every one that is born of God doth not sin, for his seed remaineth in him; and he cannot sin, because he has been born of God.' This is in another form the same difficulty which we encounter in St. Paul when he says in one breath, 'You are dead,' and in the next, 'Put to death, therefore'; or when we try to tell whether any given spiritual experience is that of the regenerate or the unregenerate man. The regenerate and the unregenerate man, for better or worse, cannot be separated in this summary way. The practical interest of the Apostles compels us to interpret them everywhere through experiences that we can understand; hence it is vain to seek in them any suggestion of what regeneration can mean in the case of baptized infants. There is no indication in the NT that they ever contemplated any such case. Regeneration is a moral experience regarded as the work of God, and repentance is the same moral experience regarded from the side of man; but neither in the one aspect nor the other can we speak of it in the case of beings who have as yet no moral experience at all.

Regeneration is not an exclusively NT idea, and those who regard NT Christianity as a kind of religious syncretism have sought the key to some of its ideas, its terminology, and its rites, especially where this doctrine and its sacramental connexions are concerned, in the Greek and Oriental mysteries which were so popular in the Roman Empire during the first two or three centuries of our era. That powerful influences from these sources—especially, perhaps, from the religion of Mithras—did at a certain period tell upon popular Christianity, cannot be questioned; but the period was not the creative one for Christianity, and the channel of these influences was not Jewish Apostles who held every kind of pagan religion in horror. The writer is convinced that there is nothing in the NT, either about the new birth or about baptism, which cannot be explained from experiences specifically and exclusively Christian; and that to drag in the *Taurobolium*, and the *renatus in æternum* of Mithraic monumental inscriptions, to explain NT ideas, while ignoring the historical connexions which these ideas assert for themselves, is mere wantonness.

LITERATURE.—The works on NT Theology (Holtzmann, Weiss, Stevens), books mentioned under the article HOLY SPIRIT; Gennrich, *Die Lehre von der Wiedergeburt*; Kaftan, *Dogmatik*, §§ 54, 55; Kähler, *Die Wissenschaft der christlichen Lehre*, 493 ff.; Orr, *God's Image in Man*, 278 f.; Ritschl, *Rechtfertigung u. Versöhnung*, iii. § 61; W. N. Clarke, Outline of *Chr. Theol.* 395; Laidlaw, *Bible Doct. of Man*, chs. xiii. xiv.; Denney in *Expositor*, Oct. and Dec. 1901. For kindred ideas in other religions, see Anrich, *Das antike Mysterienwesen in seinem Einfluss auf das Christentum*; Dieterich, *Eine Mithrasliturgie*; Reitzenstein, *Poimandres* (*s.v.* παλιγγενεσία in Index).
                                                    JAMES DENNEY.

REHOBOAM.—Son of Solomon, mentioned as a link in our Lord's genealogy (Mt 1[7]).

REJECTION.—The word 'rejection' does not occur in the Gospels, but the idea of 'casting-off, despising, rejecting' is familiar to the writers of the NT. Mt 21[42], under the figure of the cornerstone, refers to the rejection of Jesus by the Jews; and in Mk 12[10] and Lk 20[17] the same reference occurs. Jesus knew that He would be rejected, and anticipated the result to Himself (Mk 8[31], Lk 9[22] 17[25]), to the Jewish nation (Lk 19[43]), and to the world (Jn 12[48]). Regarding Himself as a prophet, He expected a prophet's treatment (Lk 13[33. 34], Mt 23[37]). Jesus regarded Himself as the test applied to nations and individuals, and, according to their acceptance or rejection of Him, would be their progress or decay. When the Jews rejected Jesus, they wrote their own sentence of doom, while the Gentiles who have accepted Jesus have secured the leadership of the world. As the national rejection of Jesus was attended by national disaster, so the individual rejection is marked by loss of character. See also art. DESPISE.
                                          COLL. A. MACDONALD.

RELIGION.—The Lat. word *religio* did not come into Christian usage until in the 4th cent. Lactantius (*Instit.* iv. 28) wrote, 'Religion is the link which unites man to God.' The reason was that the implications of the word were altogether external, and, in accordance with the Roman genius, almost administrative. But the Greeks were equally unable to supply a word which would correspond with the Christian faith and its fruits. θρησκεία, tr. 'religion' in Ac 26[5] and Ja 1[26f.], was also spiritually threadbare, and suggested nothing more than the ceremonial side of public worship. With this history behind it, religion has come to be a very complex conception; but for the present purpose it may perhaps be defined as the soul's response to the spiritual revelation by which it is illumined, kindled, and moved. With some the revelation does not pass beyond the mind, with others it calls for little more than an indulgence of feeling, with others, again, it brings out only a discipline of obedience. But in true religion all three elements are present. 'It includes the whole energy of man as reasonable spirit' (Fairbairn, *Phil. of Religion*, p. 201). The key-words of religion then are: (1) revelation, (2) response.

1. Religion as revelation.—The quality of the response depends on the character of the *revelation*. Religion must always mean something different from what it was before the revelation of grace and truth which came by Jesus Christ. Of what that consisted will appear later. Meantime it might be noted that the factor of revelation has been minimized in the workings of thought during the last two centuries, in reaction, no doubt, from the emphasis on external authority, not only in the Catholic Church, but in older theology generally. On the one hand, in the 18th cent. there was, if one may say so, an artificial construction of 'natural' religion, in which Christ was put out of court. On the other hand, in the 19th cent. the rise of psychological and humanitarian interests has created a tendency to lose the revelation in the response. Thus Schleiermacher in his *Reden über die Religion* has nothing to say on religious authority, and in a chapter on the nature of religion practically identifies revelation with intuition and original feeling (p. 89). Ritschl, again, in his theory of value-judgments, throws the weight of authority on the soul's response; while Sabatier, in his beautiful study of the genesis of religion, speaks of the spirit attaching itself to its principle, and seems also liable to the dangers of subjectivity (*Outlines of Phil. of Rel.* p. 28). The alteration of standpoint is thus expressed by F. D. Maurice (*Life*, i. p. 340):

The difficulty in our day is to believe in a revelation as our fathers did. . . . Our minds bear a stronger witness than the minds of our forefathers did to the idea of a revelation : so strong a witness, that we think it must have originated in them. We cannot think it possible that God has actually manifested Himself to us, *because* the sense of a manifestation is so near to us that we think it is only our sense, and has no reality corresponding to it.'

But no good end is served by minimizing that side of religion that is 'not ourselves.' For although, as Oman so well shows (*Vision and Authority*, p. 81), 'the supreme religious fact is the individual whose capacity of vision is the channel of authority,' yet if truth is ultimately one, it must proceed by way of revelation from some objective source. 'Faith,' says Dorner (*Syst. of Chr. Doctrine*, i. p. 133), 'does not wish to become a mere relation to itself, or to its representation and thought. That would be simply a monologue : faith desires a dialogue.' See, further, art. FACT AND THEORY.

Now, revelation finds its way to the soul both mediately and immediately. And it is essential to give due consideration to both these channels of religious authority. Jesus Christ, who is the norm of religion as well as the focus of revelation, made use of both. It must not be overlooked that He took over without hesitation the general conception of God's nature, kingdom, and law which He inherited from the teaching of home (Lk 2⁵¹), synagogue (Lk 4¹⁶), and Scriptures. The OT provided Him not only with illustrations of His own original thought (Mt 12³⁹⁻⁴², Lk 4²⁵⁻²⁷), but with canons of judgment and standards of authority (Mt 5¹⁸), and even with personal assurance in the time of moral temptation (Mt 4⁴ ⁷ ¹⁰) and of mortal weakness (27⁴⁶, Lk 23⁴⁶). But this attitude of our Lord must not be misunderstood. In leaning on the Word of God in the Scriptures of His people, He was not compromising the Church on critical questions. Moreover, it cannot be affirmed that He gave any guarantee of an infallible book. On the contrary, He handled it with perfect freedom, treating it as a guide but not as a goal (Mt 5²¹ᶠᶠ·). Its validity for Him, as for us, lay in its being the chosen testimony of those who gave the best response that was in them to the revelation they received, and so became witnesses of the truth.*

So far our Lord behaved Himself as the 'root and offspring of David.' But He was also 'the bright and morning star.' And religion was His by a revelation that was immediate, as well as by that which was mediated. Into the secrets of His sublime self-consciousness as the beloved Son of God and one with the Father we cannot penetrate. But His words are before us, with all their august claim : 'It was said by them of old, . . . but *I* say unto you' (Mt 5²¹ᶠ· etc.) ; 'Ye search the Scriptures, . . . but ye will not come to *me*,' etc. (Jn 5³⁹ᶠ·). The immediacy of revelation to Him is fully declared in Mt 11²⁷ 'All things are delivered unto me of my Father, and no one knoweth the Son save the Father ; neither doth any know the Father, save the Son, and he to whomsoever the Son willeth to reveal him.' None has ever challenged this solitary claim. Yet it is notable that our Lord did not shut up His followers to a revelation that is mediated even through His own blessed words.

'Christ found men everywhere ready to receive Him as a Rabbi. On the authorit yof other people they would accept anything. But He insisted on basing what He taught on the authority of their own hearts and consciences. To this end He spoke in parables that they might not understand on any other conditions' (Oman, *Vision and Authority*, p. 104).

And it is for us to remember that Christ has not left us His revelation, as it were, on deposit. The partial records of His life, first in the flesh and then in the spirit, which are ours through the NT, are certainly means whereby the Divine grace and

* The communication of religion, says Schleiermacher (*op. cit.* p. 150), is not to be sought in books. In this medium, too, much of the pure impression of the original production is lost.

truth are mediated to us, providing, indeed, our canon of spiritual judgment. But we are to trust also to the immediacy of Divine access to our minds, knowing that there is a Spirit to lead us into all the truth, enabling us to judge all things and approve those that are excellent (Jn 16¹³, 1 Co 2¹⁵, Ph 1¹⁰).* Thus Christianity is like an ever new commandment, being true in Him and in us (1 Jn 2⁸). See, further, art. REVELATION.

2. Religion as response.—The primary *response* to the revelation of God may be said to run on three lines, the sense of (*a*) dependence, (*b*) estrangement, (*c*) obligation.

(*a*) The soul's response in a sense of *dependence*. The soul, when it comes to itself, finds itself solitary and orphaned. The issues of life run up into eternity, and the soul first proves it is awakened by crying out for the living God. The fact that man is a spiritual being soon asserts itself in the life that is not wholly preoccupied with things temporal. In the words of St. Augustine (*Confess.*), 'Thou hast made us for Thyself, and our heart is restless until it find its rest in Thee.' Thus begins a 'commerce, a conscious and willed relation, into which the soul in distress enters with the mysterious power on which it feels that it and its destiny depend' (Sabatier, *Outlines*, p. 27). This need of security and rest is perfectly met by Christ. He satisfies the soul's sense of dependence by drawing it to Himself. In His Divine Personality men find their long-sought God. To the soul once awakened there is no resting-place except in the eternal Christ, 'the same yesterday and to-day and for ever.'

> 'Holding His hand, my steadied feet
> May walk the air, the seas ;
> On life and death His smile falls sweet,
> Lights up all mysteries.
> Stranger nor exile can I be
> In new worlds where He leadeth me.'

(*b*) A second primary response of the soul in religion is a sense of sin, or *separation*. Religion has found expression in sacrifices on account of the well-nigh universal instinct that something must be offered in order to avert the wrath or unkindness of the Deity, or at least to restore happy relations between the worshipper and the world that is beyond his control. Whether they were originally offered in fear of malevolent deities, or in commemoration of the ghosts of the departed, or to renew the covenant of a tribe with its proper deity, does not greatly matter. Suffice it that the sacrifice is intended to restore communion with God in such a way that in the place of guilt and fear there may come a sense of favour through prosperity and peace.

This strong sense of a separateness that may be bridged is more or less efficient in all human response to the Unseen, and is the basis on which the higher religions rest. The danger is that the interest may run out towards the material sacrifice and its attendant rites in such a way that the end is forgotten in the means. But here Christ meets the supreme need of reconciliation in the only worthy way conceivable. On the cross the soul's reliance can be securely planted. It so suffices that all other sacrifices can only be put aside as mistaken, superfluous, and vain (He 13¹⁵), unless they are the sacrifices of empty hands and a full heart.

(*c*) There is a third primary strand of religion in the sense of *obligation*, by which the soul is brought under a supreme law and purpose. There is a con-

* 'Not every person has religion who believes in a sacred writing, but only the man who has a lively and immediate understanding of it, and who therefore, so far as he himself is concerned, could most easily do without it ' (Schleiermacher, *op. cit.* p. 91).

straining influence in all religion, in addition to the feeling of dependence and the sense of estrangement. Religion really begins for us, says Lotze, 'with a feeling of duty' (*Phil. of Religion*, p. 150). It involves a committal of the life, the framing of its career on lines that often lie athwart the obvious advantages of life. The Indian fakir or Buddhist monk is moved strongly by this sense of obligation, and observes conditions of consecration even to the crippling of his life. But here, again, the faith of Jesus Christ fulfils this need of the soul in a way that liberates and enlarges it. He made that absolute claim on the soul's affection and the life's service to which so many have thankfully responded. He knew human nature too well to ask for a partial surrender, and an obedience in outward things which is hard and toilsome. But His yoke is easy, because it brings the whole life, love, and strength under contribution to a reasonable service; so that 'I ought' is transmuted into 'I must,' and the struggling life of division becomes the soaring life of dedication. And as *prayer* is the expression of the sense of dependence, and *sacrifice* of the consciousness of estrangement, so the *sacrament* is the symbol of the sense of obligation.

3. True religion embodied in Jesus Christ.—It is evident from this brief analysis of religion on its responsive side, that Christ has the key to all its intimacies, because the meanings of religion are consummated in Himself. The religion which we believe to be universal and everlasting in its character is just the fuller knowledge and obedience of Christ. He is His own religion, and therefore He not only harmonizes the various *feelings* of religion, as we have just seen, by satisfying the desire for security, for reconciliation, and for authority, but He also brings into unity its various *forms*. There are three chief forms which religion has taken, corresponding to the emotional, intellectual, and volitional elements in human nature: (*a*) the *ritual* side of religion, presided over by the priests, (*b*) the *speculative* side, represented by the theologians and philosophers, and (*c*) the *legal* or customary side, typified by the office of the scribes. All these departments are resolved in the NT into the headship and hegemony of Christ. He did not incorporate His religion in a hierarchic order (as with the Buddhists), or in philosophical books (as with the Brahmans), or in codes and customs (as with the Confucians and Muhammadans). He is Himself the Way, the Truth, and the Life (Jn 14[6]) for all humanity.

(*a*) Christ is the perfect expression of the Temple symbolism (He 9[11f.]). His name is the shrine (Mt 18[20], cf. 2 Co 5[17]); His will is the altar (Mt 25[40], cf. 2 Co 8[5]). In His self-surrender He is the sacrifice (Mt 26[36ff.], cf. He 10[10]); in His self-manifestation He is the priest (Mt 11[27], Jn 14[6]). 'Having then a great high priest, who hath passed through the heavens, Jesus the Son of God, let us hold fast our confession . . . let us draw near with boldness unto the throne of grace' (He 4[14. 16]). (*b*) Christ is also the final secret of revelation. The Spirit's work was to be focussed on Himself (Jn 16[14f.]), for to know Him is to know the Father (Jn 14[9]), and that is life eternal (Jn 17[3]). This is a wisdom that the rulers of this world never knew (1 Co 2[6ff.]), though prophets and kings have desired to look into it (Lk 10[24]). For the mystery of God is Christ, in whom are hidden all the treasures of wisdom and knowledge (Col 2[3]). (*c*) Christ is, moreover, 'the end of the law unto righteousness to everyone that believeth' (Ro 10[4]). His spirit of love is a law of liberty to His disciples (Jn 13[17] 15[14], cf. Ja 1[23]). Keeping the commandments is consummated in following Him (Mk 10[21]), *i.e.* walking in love (Eph 5[1f.]); for love is the fulfilling

of law (Ro 13[10]) and solves the complicated problems of social life (Ro 14[18]).

The three provinces of religious manifestation correspond with the three primary sensibilities of the religious life. The religious philosopher seeks to rationalize the consciousness of dependence on some theistic basis. The priest comes into being through the urgent need of reconciliation. The scribe meets the desire for some authority amid the tangled questions of practical life. Thus Christianity, which is essentially a life hid with Christ in God, is always in danger of being drawn down to the level of those who would reduce religion to a ritual of worship, a system of thought, or a fashion of life. But the fact that Jesus Christ is His own religion is the one guarantee of religion arriving at perfection. For it may truly be said that religion is in its essence the consciousness of personal being under the eye of the eternal Personality. It is surely too vague to define it, with Max Müller, as a 'perception of the infinite,' or, with Schleiermacher, as the 'immediate consciousness of the eternal in the temporal.' Lotze gives the following propositions as the characteristic convictions of the religious mind : (1) Moral laws embody the will of God ; (2) individual finite spirits are not products of nature, but are children of God ; (3) reality is more and other than the mere course of nature, it is a Kingdom of God. In each of these propositions the note of *personality* is sounded, both subjectively and objectively. And Ritschl states one side of this truth strongly when he explains religion out of 'the necessity which man feels of maintaining his personality and spiritual independence against the limitations of Nature.' But surely the religious man is at equal pains to assure himself of an all-embracing Personality at the heart of things, to which his own soul can return and be at rest (Ps 116[7]). That being so, we can see that only through Christ, the God-man, can this twofold consciousness be securely maintained, and the balance kept true between the objective and subjective elements in religion.

In Christ is perfected both the revelation and the response. He is the focus of revelation and the norm of religion. In fact, 'He reveals most because He awakens most' (Matheson, *Growth of Spirit of Christianity*, p. 8). He enables us to see in God our Father, because He quickens in us a filial consciousness and behaviour. As for His revelation of Godhead, men have seen in Him that interwoven authority of love and law, of truth and grace, which gives fulness of meaning to the conceptions of a Father in heaven, free will and human immortality. As for the response which He has awakened in men, they have been won to His ideal through His fulfilment of filial and fraternal obligations in His sacrificial life. The authority and the obedience were alike pre-eminent in the Cross. Thence came the kindling spark which made the Person of Christ a vital religious fact for humanity. Man had thought of himself as being in some sense on a cross because of the presence of suffering, sin, and death ; and, so far as he was religious, tried by ritual to propitiate the Almighty, by philosophy to vindicate His ways, by methods of conduct to reduce the mischief of evil. But in Christ crucified man has found God Himself on the cross ; and with Him there, there can be no injustice in suffering, no victory for sin, no sting in death.

4. Characteristics of Christ's religion.—Having set this corner-stone, it only remains to mention seven characteristics of the religion which is derived from Jesus Christ and lives upon Him still.

(1) Christ has made religion *personal in its authority*. He is the only and absolute Lord. His spirit has broken and broken again the bands of ecclesiastical systems which multiply the scruples of conscience. The authority which is *not* as that of the scribes has been in more or less effectual operation through all the history of Christendom. Unlearned men, the weak and foolish of this world, have more than held their own in the name of Jesus of Nazareth (Ac 4, cf. 1 Co 1[26ff.]). His people have gone forth, indifferent to praise or blame, favour or persecution, and even suspending their judgment of one another on the ground that to their own Master they stand or fall, before whose judgment-seat all must appear (Ro 14[4. 10f.]). Heroic exploits have been undertaken and meanest duties performed by those whose one desire is to be well-pleasing unto Him (He 13[21]) whom not having seen

they love (1 Pl⁸). Christianity loses its secret when it forgets the glorious egotism of the Master, who not only made Himself a law to the disciples who accompanied His ministry (Mt 23¹⁰), but gave Himself back to them as more than ever theirs after death (Mt 28²⁰, Jn 20. 21). Christian mysticism is not only in place, it is imperative for the believer. Though he may not rise to the full height of St. Paul's 'Not I, but Christ' (Gal 2²⁰), he must be in conscious touch with his Lord.

(2) Christ made religion *human in its sympathy*. It was stamped upon the remembrance of His disciples that He went about doing good. Jesus presented to a world much given to religiosity the problem of One who reserved His devotions for the solitude of night, and filled His days, including the Sabbaths, with helping the needy and the outcast. True, He went up to the national Feasts (Jn 2¹³ etc.), but He was most Himself when He provided a miraculous meal of His own (Mk 6³⁵ff·||). True, He revered the Temple; but the occasions of His triumphs, and the moment of His transfiguration, were in secular places (Mt 17¹ff·||). True, He was subject unto the Law; but He made its requirements a secondary consideration when the cause of humanity was at stake (Mk 2²³ff· 3¹ff·). These incidents are typical of the attitude of Jesus towards religious duty. He denounced the advocates of 'Corban,' and those who 'devoured widows' houses and for a pretence made long prayers'; demanded 'mercy instead of sacrifice, and reconciliation rather than ritual' (Mt 9¹³ 5²³f·); and declared that the service of the 'little ones,' the least of His brethren, was the true way of honouring the Father in heaven (Mt 10⁴⁰ 25⁴⁰, Jn 13¹⁴). Slowly the disciples were weaned from their contempt for the multitude, their disparagement of women and children (Mk 10¹³ff·), their vexation with men like Bartimæus and Zacchæus who interfered with their religious plans (v.⁴⁸, Lk 19⁷). At last they deserved the name of 'League of Pity.' Their first social experiment was to have all things in common (Ac 4³⁴). Their first economic problem was how to distribute alms most wisely to the widows (Ac 6¹). They invented a new virtue called 'brotherly love,' in which all shared who were of the faith, whatever their status or nationality. The revolution which Christ effected in humanizing the conception of religion may be clearly seen in a study of words. There were three Greek words for service: διακονία, which was used for service from man to man, chiefly reserved for slaves; λειτουργία, which was used for the service of a man to the commonwealth; and λατρεία, for the service rendered to the gods.

The Christian consciousness rejected the last word; but adopted and hallowed the other two, which stood for human, not Divine service. They appear in 'deacon' and 'liturgy' respectively: the third word is left embedded in idolatry.—See, further, below, § 5.

(3) Christ has made religion *moral in its character*, because He is pre-eminently the Saviour from sin. Religion under other auspices may mean almost anything but a moral conflict and victory. It may even, as in various Asiatic beliefs, spread its sanction over immorality. And even where there is a high ethical standard, as in Confucianism, goodness is rather a codified substitute for religion than the vital substance of it. Nowhere but in Christianity is love for God identified with a passion for real righteousness and inmost cleansing. Not that there is no teaching to this end in the OT. On the contrary, it is the main burden of the prophets. And John the Baptist stood in the true succession when he turned religion into the terms of a repentant and reconstructed life. But it too easily became a means to an end, so that personal

righteousness became subsidiary to national rights. And goodness became so degenerate in the chair of the scribes that their ideal was not so much rectitude as correctitude.

But the religion of the Sermon on the Mount breathes out a holiness which consumes every lesser thing, and carries the moral imperative into the inmost recesses of the soul. It is a remarkable thing that Jesus brought so few charges of sin against the irreligious people. If one might venture on a reason, it is that sin itself, *i.e.* the enthronement of self against God, meant so much to Him that He let other things pass in order to strike at the Prince of this world (Jn 12³¹ 16¹¹). His life and spiritual presence have made men conscious of sin without the aid of any catalogue of transgressions. On the other hand, Christ's conception of morality was always warm and positive, on the ground that 'no virtue is safe that is not enthusiastic' (Seeley, *Ecce Homo*, ch. i.). Every token of self-abandonment in humility, faith, and love drew forth His admiration, whether it was the quiet confidence of the centurion (Mt 8⁵ff·, Lk 17²ff·), the moral enthusiasm of the young ruler (Mk 10¹⁷ff·||), the sacrificial giving of the poor widow (12⁴²ff·||), or the overflowing repentance of the woman who wept at His feet (Lk 7³⁶ff·). Every human trait that escaped the imprisonment of self was in the eyes of Jesus the material of true religion. And it was a radiant goodness, unconscious and unlaboured, in the early Christians that chiefly arrested the attention of the world.

(4) Christ has made religion *individual in its responsibility*, because He is the Lord of all. Religion always tends to congeal into a system. There is, of course, a solidarity of mankind, of which religion must take note, of which indeed it is an expression. Sin is a common inheritance, and redemption, too, is a universal fact. It is on this truth that the gospel of Jesus rests. But starting from this truth the gospel lays a test and an obligation on individuals as such. There is no safeguard in being a son of Abraham or a disciple of Moses without giving personal credence, allegiance, and service. μόνον πίστευε is the keyword by which the individual escapes from 'an evil and adulterous generation,' and all that threatens the full exercise of personality. From the beginning Jesus kept the multitude at the distance of a strait gate and a narrow way, which can be traversed only by one at a time, by the giving of the will, and the crucifying of the self. And what is true of entrance to the Kingdom holds good of its final appointments. Punishment will be proportioned to knowledge and reward to fidelity. With all that He Himself brought, Jesus did not allow men to take anything for granted, but bade them 'watch, as if on that alone hung the issue of the day.'

(5) Christ has made religion *spiritual in its essence*, because 'the Lord is the Spirit' (2 Co 3¹⁷) as God is Spirit (Jn 4²⁴). Religion is apt to become a mere sediment of observance, a shell from which the life has departed. It certainly was so in the days of our Lord; it threatens to be so still. The words in vogue among the Greeks were λατρεία and θρησκεία, the latter word being translated 'religion' in Ac 26⁵ and Ja 1²⁶f·, the former 'service' in Jn 16², Ro 9⁴ 12¹, He 9¹· ⁶. But they only connoted rites of worship and sacrifice: they were old bottles which could not be entrusted with the new spirit of Christianity. St. James uses θρησκεία almost ironically when he says that 'pure religion and undefiled is visiting widows in their affliction and keeping one's self unspotted from the world.' St. Paul (Ro 12¹) takes up λατρεία and θυσία with equal scorn, qualifying the former word with λογική and the latter with ζῶσα, before allowing them to be applicable to Christianity.

It was in this way that Christ Himself had dealt with the prayers and almsgiving of pious Jews (Mt 6^{1-8}); and the whole tendency of professional separatism among the Pharisees (cf. *Pro Christo et Ecclesia*). His Father 'sees in secret,' and 'seeks those to be his worshippers who worship in spirit and in truth' (Mt 6^4, Jn 4^{24}). By resting religion on spirituality, and giving free access by the Spirit to the Father (Ro 5^5, Eph 2^{18}), the whole basis of the sacrificial system was undermined and sacerdotalism became an anachronism.

'The society as founded by Christ has in its collective being a priestly character, but is without an official priesthood. It has no temple save the living man ; no sacrifices save those of the spirit and the life' (Fairbairn, *Christ in Modern Theology*, p. 49).

(6) Christ made religion *independent in its action*, because, as He once said, 'My kingdom is not of this world' (Jn 18^{36}). Being the expression of His eternal Spirit, Christianity has never been stamped or cramped by the language of a given period or the fashion of a particular people. His gospel, being a secret of personal experience, has received a most varied witness even within the NT. It has continually broken through language and escaped. And while the Christian religion in its purity has always been able to shake itself free from the encumbrance of a theological system, it has been no less an independent spirit in regard to other departments of human activity. It has been free to enter and often able to renew them without being itself captured in the process. Political movements, new departures in art, and even advances in science, have as often as not received guidance and support from the Christian spirit. But to none of them has it remained captive, because it moves by right in a higher realm. Thus 'age cannot stale its infinite variety.' It exercises the royal prerogative of lending to all, but borrowing nothing in return, and so is free for every emergency which history unfolds in the whole compass of humanity.

(7) Christ has made religion *missionary in its outlook*, because He is the Saviour of the world. Christianity is not equipped like, *e.g.*, Muhammadanism, for capturing whole tribes at once, for it is not, properly speaking, nationalist in its range. But it stands alone among all other religions in its power to emancipate individuals, and ultimately to regenerate society in every race under the sun. It takes secure root in the universal soil of human needs and possibilities, and with such a grip it is in command of the future. All it waits for is that its professors should realize that it increases in proportion as it is given away, and is truly known only by those who try to make it known.

Christ always believed in small beginnings, but His hope was ever set on great and triumphant conclusions. That He was alone, with nowhere to lay His head, did not trouble Him, for He knew that when He was lifted up from the earth He would draw all men unto Him (Jn 12^{32}). That His disciples were not wise and learned satisfied Him perfectly, because He saw them (metaphorically speaking) seated on thrones judging the twelve tribes of Israel. That none of the rulers believed on Him did not perturb Him greatly ; for He foresaw the time when they would come from the east and the west, the north and the south, to sit down in the Kingdom of God (Lk 13^{29}). His parables suggested His confidence in the irresistible contagion of the lives of men who had once been won for the Kingdom. He likened His word to a fire (Lk 12^{49}), to leaven (Mt 13^{33}), to a seed (v.^{19}), so potent is its influence on life and on society. And because the needs of the world are so great and deep, and the fields white unto harvest, He gave

Himself up wholly to the ingathering work of the Father, and, more than that, He laid it as a last charge and responsibility upon His disciples that they should go out into all the world and preach the gospel to every creature (Mt 28^{19}).

LITERATURE.—Bruce, *Chief End of Rev.* ; Herrmann, *Com. with God*, and his art. 'Religion' in *PRE*[3]; Illingworth, *Div. Immanence*, and *Personality Hum. and Div.* ; Gore, *BL* ; Newman Smyth, *The Rel. Feeling* ; Coleridge, *Aids to Reflection* (esp. Introd. Aphor. xxiii); Menzies, *Hist. of Rel.* ; Schleiermacher, *Reden über die Rel.* [Eng. tr. by Oman]; Orr, *Chr. View of God and the World* ; Caird, *Fundamental Ideas of Christianity* ; Harnack, *What is Christianity?* ; Martineau, *Studies in Christianity* ; Seeley, *Ecce Homo* ; Oman, *Vision and Authority* ; Forrest, *Authority of Christ.*

A. N. ROWLAND.

RELIGIOUS EXPERIENCE. — **1. Evidential value of religious experience.** — Experience is the ultimate test of truth. All knowledge comes from within. World-knowledge, self-knowledge, God-knowledge, all equally depend upon the trustworthiness of this inner organ of information. A universal experience, or an intuitive consciousness, gives us knowledge lifted to the highest power. That which is most universal and most enduring is vouched for by the nature of things. The religious consciousness is as clear and universal as the world-consciousness. It is as natural to man as volition or mathematics. Every baby is born blind and dumb and without the power to will, and there may be some tribes with poor eyes and slow tongues and no theology ; but in normal humanity there is a latent capacity for sight and speech and volition, and at least a hope that the soul has relations with the supernatural. Religion is not something miraculous. It is as natural to man as eyesight and star-gazing. It is as normal as any physiologic function. Modern psychology has indisputably proved that religious experience is as closely related to the nerves and blood as puberty ; the vital organs and psychic mechanism are built with reference to it. Its importance and value to the race are doubly starred, for 'its best fruits are the best things history has to show' (James, *Varieties of Religious Experience*, p. 259). To doubt its veracity would be an insolence to the Providence of the universe. Modern psychology has only emphasized Augustine's decision : 'Lord, if we are deceived, we are deceived by Thee.'* It is because the NT grew out of, and is the record of, genuine first-hand religious experience that it has the gift of tongues, and can speak to every man in the language wherein he was born.

2. Pre-requisites of religious experience.—The great fundamental pre-requisites of religious experience the Gospels take for granted. There is no more of an attempt to prove God's existence than man's existence, or God's power of speech than man's. God loves to speak to man, and man can understand. God is the imperative preliminary to all religious life ; He is the chief factor in its continuance and perfecting. Each soul possesses as its birthright a knowledge of moral distinctions, a sense of moral obligation, a conscious power of obedience or disobedience to such law as the soul knows. All this, where not affirmed, is assumed by all the Gospel writers.

3. Pre-Christian religious experience.—Much of the religious experience described in the Gospels is pre-Christian. Primitive Christianity never imagined that a rich religious experience was not possible outside the Christian community. The Divine Shepherd has 'other sheep' besides the Israelites (Jn 10^6). Jesus Himself expressly affirms

* Professor James, from a study perhaps too largely devoted to abnormal developments of the religious emotions, reaches nevertheless the significant conclusion that, 'if intercourse between man and God is not a fact, then religion does not simply contain elements of delusion, but is rooted in delusion altogether' (*op. cit.* p. 465, cf. p. 547).

this, and refers to Naaman the Syrian, the widow of Zidon, the Roman centurion, and the Syro-phœnician woman as possessing better religious experience than their Jewish neighbours, and definitely announces that 'many' shall come from the heathen nations and enter the future Kingdom in peace (Jn 12²⁰· ²³, Lk 4²⁵⁻²⁸, Mk 7²⁴, Mt 8¹⁰ 15²⁸). So, the Samaritans were at various times praised by Jesus, and one of them was selected as the ideal type of brotherhood (Lk 7¹¹· ¹⁹ 10²⁵⁻³⁷). Yet, while Jesus proclaimed faith and gratitude and compassion to be religious virtues wherever found, and evidently preferred honest heresy to thoughtless orthodoxy, He nevertheless regarded Gentiles and Samaritans as heretics, and the Jews as the natural 'children of the kingdom' (Mt 8¹²; cf. 18¹⁷, Jn 4²²). The Apostles were all Jews, and the holy men and women whose prayers and hymns filled the earth with prophetic hope at the birth of John and Jesus were representative OT saints. They had been 'prepared for the Lord' (Mk 1¹⁷), and were 'prayer-ful,' 'devout,' and 'righteous' people who 'rejoiced in God,' being 'filled with the Holy Ghost,' and could depart this world 'in peace' (Lk 1⁶· ⁴⁷· ⁶⁷ 2²⁵⁻²⁹, cf. Jn 1⁴⁷). Such religious fruit does not grow on a tree with a rotten root.

4. Christian experience contrasted with all other religious experience.—Nevertheless, as compared even with the best religious experiences of the Old Covenant, those of the New seemed like 'new wine' (Mk 2²²), like newly discovered treasure (Mt 13³⁴), like a wedding day (Mt 9¹⁵), like the 'one pearl of great price' (Mt 13⁴⁶), like a king's banquet (Mt 22²), like the rising of the sun (Lk 1⁷⁹, cf. Jn 1¹⁷). The religious knowledge and outlook even of that holy prophet and herald of whom Jesus Himself said that there had been 'none greater born of women,' were to be so eclipsed that he who was 'little' in the New Kingdom should be greater than he (Mt 11¹¹). New standards, new ideals, new spiritual magnitudes, above all, a new spiritual dynamic had appeared, and with these a totally new spiritual experience. The new things introduced by the gospel have often been catalogued, but Jesus was the supremely new thing in the new religion. Much of the teaching, even its central Golden Rule, was old, but He was new. He, not His teaching, was the centre of the new gospel. He was the gospel; Himself the glad tidings of great joy. His coming brought a new morning to the world (Lk 1⁷⁸), and originated a new vision of righteousness and a new sunrise type of religious experience in the souls of men.

5. Religious experience of Jesus.—But although Jesus created a new religion characterized by strangely new religious dispositions, it is a difficult task to discover from the records the facts concerning His own soul life. That He prayed and had the inner certainty of reply; that He was tempted; accepted the Father's will even when unexplained to Him; that He had great confidence in God, and felt a peculiar harmony between Himself and the Infinite Goodness,—all this, and much more, is known. But did the self-identity with the moral law which He claimed (Jn 14⁶, cf. Mk 8³⁴ 10²¹ 13³¹, Mt 5¹⁷) involve the consciousness of self-identity with Jehovah? So St. John's Gospel certainly teaches. According to all the Gospels, He claimed a jurisdiction here and hereafter which no other sane man has ever ventured to claim. He showed no hesitancy in calling Himself 'meek and lowly,' while in almost the same breath He demanded absolute submission of intellect and will from all who expected to remain His 'friends,' or hoped to be at peace with God hereafter (e.g. Mt 7²¹ᶠᶠ· 11²⁸ᶠᶠ·, Lk 6⁴⁶, Jn 15¹⁴). Even in Mk. He is represented as claiming, without misgiving, to be the expected Messiah and Judge of the world (8²⁹),

who has power to forgive sins (2¹⁰), and to whom all men owe absolute spiritual allegiance (8³⁴· ³⁸). The other Synoptics, as well as Jn., specifically represent Him as claiming to be superior to the wisest lawgivers and prophets of the past (Mt 12⁴² 19⁸, Lk 11³¹, Jn 1¹⁷)—One whose mission in the world was to give His life a ransom for the race (Jn 3¹⁶, cf. Mk 10⁴⁵), Himself the centre and object of the devotion of all men loyal to the inner light (Lk 19¹⁴ 20¹⁸, Jn 5⁴⁰ 7¹⁷), the only Being who knew God (Mt 11²⁷), a Saviour and Judge whose 'Depart from me' was the severest penalty which could be pronounced on guilty man (Mt 1²¹ 7²³). Yet, notwithstanding all this, He is represented in every Gospel as being peculiarly calm, sincere, humble, and self-forgetful, possessing a heart of singular purity, having not the slightest doubt of His own right relationship to God, trusting the inner witness perfectly, and constantly possessing a peace 'deep as the unfathomed sea,' which peace He believed He could impart to others. The self-consciousness of Jesus was the spring underneath the Temple-altar, out of which flowed the healing waters of Christianity.

6. Christ's relation to Christian experience.—Whatever we think, who never ate at the same table with Him, there is not the slightest doubt as to what the earliest Christians thought of Jesus. They never attempted to analyze His states of consciousness,—He was to them the object rather than the subject of religion,—but of one thing they were absolutely sure, it was He who had worked the mighty change in them. Whereas they had been blind, they could now see; whereas they had been helpless, they now had conscious victory over sin; and new powers in many directions were theirs. These new experiences came through Him. In coming to Him they had found God, and a new type of thought and life had appeared within themselves. Jesus Christ was the source of this change of personality. All the NT writers agree as to this.

A writer in the *JE* (art. 'Jesus'), though believing that Jesus never claimed to be the Messiah, at the same time acknowledges that 'his most striking characteristic was his claim that spiritual peace and salvation were to be found in the mere acceptance of his leadership.' Nathaniel Schmidt (*Prophet of Nazareth*, 1905) also makes a suggestive admission when he says that, while Jesus never claimed to be the Messiah, yet all the hopes of OT prophets embodied in King, Redeemer, and Divine Manifestation were more than fulfilled in Him; and although He never, probably, claimed to forgive sins, yet He could forgive them, and historically He has actually been the Saviour of the world, and is saving men yet (pp. 8, 203, 317).

That Jesus Christ was the Saviour every man needed, One who could save up to and beyond the limit of the man's best hope, was the common thought of those who most thoughtfully observed His influence and reported His words. It is constantly assumed as a fact of consciousness, and often declared in unequivocal language, that every man has so flagrantly sinned against light and become such a slave to sin that he needs the very power of the Almighty to enable him to fulfil his moral duty and reach his spiritual ideal. He needs more than one act of omnipotence. He needs a God who will come and stay close to him, ruling the life, not from without but from within (Mk 7¹⁵, Mt 15⁸, Lk 17²¹, Jn 4²¹ 15¹⁻⁶). The earliest Christians are unanimous in the declaration that in coming to Jesus Christ they had found the Father, and that He was not afar off but within; and after Pentecost they speak of the inward Presence either as 'God,' 'Spirit of God,' 'Holy Spirit,' or 'Spirit of Christ.'

7. Origin of Christian experience.—Herein lies the explanation of the earliest typical Christian experience. The new religion was rooted in a new conception of the Holy Ghost. A perfected Christian experience was not possible until after Pentecost. There is no emphasis in the Gospels upon personal experience. They have to do with 'Jesus only.' His statements as to truth and His promise of future blessedness were sufficient grounds of certainty without any 'experiences' to corroborate them. Salvation, according to the earliest Christian Gospel, is proved not by personal experience but by practical morality, a compassionate spirit, and obedience to the inner law—this inner law being objectified in Jesus Christ when He is known (Mt 25^{14-45}). The proper use of talents, helpfulness, mercifulness, prayerfulness, and love for brother man—these are the marks of a Christian. To be humble and self-forgetful, to care for the poor, and the sick, and the sinful—this is to 'inherit the kingdom' (Mt 6^{14}). A man may be a member of Christ's Kingdom even though he has not consciously been serving Him (Mt 25^{37-39}). He who forgives shall be forgiven (Mt 6^{14}). To be a Christian is not to 'accept the word with joy,' but to live, bearing fruit (Mt 13^{20-23}, Lk 8^{13}). In Mk. it is not even remembered that Jesus ever promised 'joy,' or 'peace,' or 'rest.' These words do not meet us in this earliest Gospel. Jesus was the sole object of thought. How a disciple felt was of too little importance to be noticed. In Mt. the transforming principle is the word spoken by Jesus, and the result is 'rest' (e.g. 7^{28} 11^{29} 13^{23}). In Jn. the transforming principle is Jesus, who is 'the Word' and 'the Life,' and the result is 'peace' (3^4 6^{33} 14^{27} 17^3). With St. Paul the transforming principle is the Holy Ghost applying the redemption purchased by the blood of the cross, and the result is 'joy' and 'glory.' In the Synoptics the command is 'Come,' and if you endure to the end you 'shall be saved.' In Jn. the command is 'Believe,' and he that believeth 'hath everlasting life.' With St. Paul the central interrogation is, 'Have ye received the Holy Ghost?'—if so, you 'have been saved' (cf. Eph 2^8). In the Synoptics it is following Jesus that is emphasized; in Jn. it is being one with Jesus; in St. Paul's letters it is being united with Him in His death. In the Synoptics salvation is educational; in Jn. it is biological; in St. Paul's letters it is sacrificial. The first type of thought emphasized the fact of salvation, the second its psychology, the third its philosophy. In their deepest meaning these three are one; but they represent three types of Christian thought, from which resulted three types of Christian doctrine and Christian experience. Each type finds its root in the Gospel teaching; but the appeal to the 'inner witness,' the making prominent of Christian experience, and the rise of what may be called the emotional type of Christianity, are all post-Pentecostal developments. So long as Jesus remained with them, the disciples did not think it worth while to talk of themselves, or notice their own inward emotions or mental experiences. But Jesus left them, and in utter loneliness and sorrow they stood gazing into the heavens which had received Him. But at Pentecost they began to awaken to the fact that He was still alive, still near them, still able to talk with them, and make their hearts burn as He talked. Then their eyes were turned within, and Christian experience began to be of vital theological importance. It was the new Christian thought of the Holy Ghost which gave birth both to the Johannine and to the Pauline theologies and experiences. The Holy Spirit represented Christ in the believer's heart. It spake with the authority of God Himself, and in the very accents of the One now gone. Christ was with them again. He had promised to come, and to abide with them always (Jn 6^{56} 14^{18}). He had kept His promise. The Word was again incarnate, and was in each one of them. The believer's flesh was His flesh (cf. Eph 5^{30}, and especially the startling words of 2 Co 3^{17} ὁ δὲ κύριος

τὸ πνεῦμά ἐστιν). This discovery, that it was the Lord Jesus Himself who was speaking within them in the Person of the Holy Ghost, brought the experiences of the soul into new importance. It was this consciousness of the indwelling Christ which filled the hearts of the early Christians with joy, and made them a wonder to the heathen world.

Typical Christian experience did not begin until Pentecost (Jn 7^{39}, Ac 2^{17} 19^2); yet the Synoptic Gospels contain all the roots of the beautiful rod which budded in those later ecstatic experiences. Although, when a sinner repented and was forgiven, it was only the joy of God and the angels which the Synoptics thought important enough to mention (Lk $15^{7.\ 10}$), incidentally we learn that the return to God brings a kiss to the soul and a song to the lips (Lk $15^{20.\ 24}$). It was a home-coming. There can be no doubt that 'praising God,' and 'gladness of heart,' and an exhilaration which was like the exhilaration of wine, were characteristic of the earliest Christian experiences (Ac $2^{15.\ 46.\ 47}$). Every later Apostolic experience, however jubilant, appears prophetically in Jn. (e.g. 4^{36} 15^{11} $16^{20.\ 22.\ 24}$ 17^{13}).

8. Range and content of Christian experience. —No part of human nature is excluded from the influence of saving grace. Schleiermacher centred religion in the feelings, Hegel in the intellect, Kant in the will; but Jesus Christ centred it in the man. The Torah of Jesus brought into loftiest prominence the fact that all man's faculties of sensibility, intellect, and volition must be brought to focus in the act and state of loving self-surrender to God (Mk 12^{30}). Christian experience, as depicted in the NT, includes a new intellectual vision, a radical shifting of the emotional centre, and a rectification and strengthening of the will.

The first step in a typical Christian experience is the recognition of a new horror in sin. Sin is a more hateful and deadly thing to the Christian than to the Hebrew or the Babylonian. It is not only an epidemic universal and fatal (Jn 1^{29}), a blood-poisoning (9^{41} $15^{22.\ 24}$), worse than a lifelong paralysis (5^{14}), which may be eternal (Mk 3^{29}), a slavery (Jn 8^{34}), and an insanity (Lk 15^{17}); it is ungrateful (16^6), traitorous (Mk 22^6), unfilial (Lk 15^{11}); the assassination of one's higher self (9^{25}), and a fratricidal blow at Jesus Christ (Mt 21^{38}, Lk 9^{22}). The cross shows God's thought of sin, and those who have seen the cross get a totally new view of the guilt of sin. Jesus can never be seen as a Saviour, in the Gospel sense, until a man sees himself to be a lost sinner having no hope of help except from God (Lk 7^{42} 15^{4-32} 19^{10}). It is no sign of 'healthy-mindedness' to feel no terror of sin. The 'neurotic state' is not one of keen sorrow for sin, but a state of hardness and callousness (e.g. Lk 15^{17}, cf. Eph 2^1). Repentance is not a 'pathological condition of melancholia,' which is to be avoided; it is the sinner's only hope. It is the goodness of God which leadeth him to repentance. To be 'pricked to the heart' when one faces the cross is characteristic of a genuine Christian experience. When one reaches a state where he cannot feel these sharp goads of pain, then even God Himself cannot help him (Mt $12^{31.\ 41}$, cf. He 6^6). Sackcloth and ashes are the appropriate clothing for the penitent (Mt 11^{21}). Yet it is not the emotional drapery, but the decisive action of the soul away from the wrong and towards the right (i.e. Christ) which is made emphatic (Jn 14^6). The first call is to repentance (Mk 1^{15}). This is the first thing commanded, for it is the first possible active effort of the man co-operating with the constant effort of God—without whom he could neither will nor act aright—in his own salvation. It is the first active human preliminary to a conscious

Christian experience. It is a radical change of mind (μετανοέω), involving a radical change of front (ἐπιστρέφω). The response of the will to revealed duty is the 'Yea' or 'Nay' to God's call. With the 'Yea' his eyes open, and he gets new vision. Sin can shut out even the sight of God and blind the soul to the difference between good and evil (Mt 12^{24}). Purity of intent and purpose cleanses the lens of the intellectual telescope so that one can see God; and when one sees God, many other things previously obscured become visible (Jn 4^{29} 5^{40}).

Saving faith, according to the Gospels, centres in Christ. It is not faith in one's self or in one's own salvation, present, past, or future; it is a loyal surrender to Him who represents the soul's highest ideal of right, as Lord. Having accepted Him as Lord, the soul then finds Him to be Saviour (Jn 5$^{23. 24}$). In the Synoptics the words πίστις, πιστεύω do not mean as much as with St. John and St. Paul, because the words 'Christ' and 'Saviour' did not mean as much; but in every case the surrender is to Jesus up to the level of all the light received. Whosoever 'wills to do his will' shall know at least this, that Jesus can be trusted (7^{17}, cf. 9^{36}). The testimonies to conscious personal trust in Jesus Christ as the supreme standard of right and the never-failing and ever-present Helper of all sin-sick souls, fill every page of the NT. The result of the exercise of faith is not infrequently a change of opinion and judgment; it is always a change of affection and volitional relation to God. The man's whole nature changes. Jn. states this by the strongest possible figure—that of a second birth (3^{10}); but the Synoptics hint prophetically at the same thing. The man must make a new beginning, as radical as if he had become a child again (Mt 5^{45} 18^{3}, cf. Mk 10^{15}). A new seed of personality must be planted within him (Lk 8$^{4-15}$ 17^{21}). There must be a change of the life passion (Mt 6^{25} 10^{39}). New-born thoughts and feelings and powers must develop until the vital functions are practically reversed (Mk 8^{35} 12$^{30. 35}$, Mt 5$^{3-10}$ 16^{25}, Lk 17^{35}).

St. Paul constantly dwells upon this. The new life which one consciously obtains through faith in Jesus Christ is likened to that which would be needed in quickening a corpse or bringing about a resurrection from the dead (1 Co 15^{22}, Col 2^{13}, Eph 2^{5}). The man obtains a new self, as if he had been re-created (2 Co 5^{17}). Christ has started a new race, as truly as did Adam (1 Co 15$^{22. 45}$), and the result is a new manhood, a new humanity (τὸν καινὸν [τὸν νέον] ἄνθρωπον, Eph 4^{24}, Col 3^{10}), governed by a new law of life.

All the Gospel writers mention, though incidentally or prophetically, the liberty and the new strength and courage to will and to do the right which come with trust in Jesus, as well as the new and glad sense of love for both man and God (e.g. Mk 12$^{30. 31}$, Mt 11^{30} 25^{40}, Lk 6^{32} 11$^{21. 22}$, Jn 8^{36}). One is not merely conscious of his own sincerity; he can testify that a Father's welcome has been given him, and that Christ has 'manifested' Himself to him (Lk 15^{20}, Jn 14^{21}). Perhaps the Gospel doctrine most fully developed in the later writings of the NT is that of spiritual unity with Christ, through self-surrender to become one with Him. This doctrine is found in germ in every Gospel, but comes to complete flower in the profound teachings of St. John. Unity with Christ does not, however, mean identity. The disciple may be perfectly like his Lord, but magnitudes differ. The best experience has in it a good hope of a better experience. Unity with the Divine does not make man a god, but splendidly and fully human. The Ego not only finds peace when it turns to God, but finds itself (Mt 10^{39} 15$^{16. 25}$, Lk 15$^{16. 17}$). Progress is now possible. The man can now 'win' his own soul (Lk 21^{19}). Jesus lifts life out of the 'tragedy of the commonplace' by offering to it a perfect ideal and the highest possible impulse to reach it. This guarantees never-ending development. He who takes the Perfect for his ideal, and strives for an experience to match his vision, must have grace and more grace, life and more life (Jn 1^{16} 10^{10}).

LITERATURE. — See *Biblical Theologies* for main discussion. Among best recent books on validity of knowledge given by experience: Bowne, *Theory of Knowledge, Metaphysics.* On content of Christian consciousness: Starbuck, *Psychology of Religion*; Coe, *Spiritual Life*; Hall, *Adolescence* (vol. ii.); James, *Varieties of Religious Experience.* On content of consciousness of a pious non-Christian: art. by present writer in *Meth. Rev.*, Sixth Series, vol. xxiv. Best popular works on religious experience: Black, *Chr. Consciousness*; Newbolt, *Gospel of Experience*; Granger, *Soul of a Christian*; Forrest, *Christ of History and Experience*; Everett, *Psychologic Elements of Religious Faith*; Dale, *Living Christ*; Clifford, *Chr. Certainties*; Hall, *Universal Elements of Christian Religion*, and *Chr. Belief interpreted by Chr. Experience*; Stearns, *Evidence of Chr. Experience.*   CAMDEN M. COBERN.

RENDING OF GARMENTS.—The practice of signifying grief by tearing the clothes. There were four occasions on which rending of garments was enjoined by the Jewish Law: (1) death; (2) the apostasy of a member of the family; (3) the destruction, during persecution, of a copy of the Law; (4) blasphemy. In the case of a member of the family becoming apostate the clothes were rent as for his death, and the mourners sat for one hour on the ground and ate bread and ashes. The הלכות קריעה (Laws of Rending) are very minute, and embrace no fewer than thirty-nine rules. For the dead the rending was to be performed just before the body was finally hid from view, and it was to be done standing. Both sexes were ordered to rend the clothes 'to the heart,' *i.e.* to the skin, but in supposed obedience to Jl 2^{13} it was to be 'no farther than the navel.' For father or mother all the garments were rent till the breast was exposed, but a woman was enjoined to rend her under garment in private, and to wear it reversed. This was for the sake of decorum, and the outer garment was then rent in public without her skin being exposed. For other relations (brothers and sisters) the outer garment only was rent. For father and mother the rent was over the heart, but in the case of others on the right side. The rent garment was worn for thirty days. The rent was ordered to be of the size of a fist (מפח). It was not to be repaired in the case of mourning for parents till the time of mourning was past, but for others it might be loosely drawn together, leaving a ragged tear, after seven days, and properly repaired after thirty days. A woman, however, might in all cases repair after seven days. The rending of clothes was not to take place on the Sabbath, but if it were done on that day in excess of grief, it was excusable on account of the piety it betokened. No rending of garments was obligatory unless news of the death were received within thirty days, except in the case of the death of parents.

The action of Caiaphas (Mt 26^{65}, Mk 14^{63}) is an instance of the rending of garments for blasphemy. In this case the high priest was enjoined to rend 'both his outer and his inner garments with a rent that could never be repaired.'

LITERATURE.—Edersheim, *LT*; Mackie, *Manners and Customs of Bible Lands*; Thomson, *LB*; art. 'Mourning' in Hastings' *DB*.   W. H. RANKINE.

RENUNCIATION.—Ideas of renunciation in the teaching of Jesus may be classed under three heads: (1) renunciation of what is sinful, (2) surrender of worldly possessions, (3) special self-abnegation. It may not be possible to draw clear lines of demarcation, but these divisions are nevertheless distinct. The cares of this world and the deceitfulness of riches and the lusts of other things (Mk 4^{19}), that check the life of the soul as weeds choke the growth of the grain, may be said to indicate them in the reverse order.

1. *Sin*, of course, is to be renounced without qualification or compromise; and whatsoever leads to sin. The 'thou shalt not' of the Decalogue is carried into the inner sphere with an extent and thoroughness of application not known to the law-givers of the world. 'We have renounced,' says St. Paul, 'the hidden things of dishonesty' (2 Co 4²). But Christ's commands go farther. 'If thy right eye offend thee, pluck it out' (Mt 5²⁹· ³⁰ 18⁸· ⁹). These laws require not only the renunciation of whatever desire, impulse, aim, or intention is contrary to the will of God, but also of things innocent that might tend to 'lead into temptation'; the renunciation of that trebly manifested evil (1 Jn 2¹⁶) by which the world is placed in antagonism to the Father.

2. Renunciation in its bearing on *temporal possessions* is expounded in the address that followed the rebuke of covetousness (Lk 12¹³⁻³⁴, Mt 6¹⁹⁻³⁴). Here Jesus emphasizes the distinction of the inward and the outward, the primary and the subordinate, the essential and the accidental. The life is a far greater thing than the material means of sustenance, the body by which we live is much more important than its protecting garment. 'A man's life consisteth not in the abundance of the things which he possesseth.' If what is primary and essential is made secure, what is secondary will follow as a matter of course. The error of the Gentiles is that they devote themselves to the secondary and neglect the fundamental. Men feed the outward life and starve the soul, or they adorn the body and disregard its real dignity. They store up wealth, but are not 'rich toward God.' But 'treasure in heaven' is the true riches. The spiritual is supreme. Our prayer should be for 'daily bread' or the satisfaction of necessary requirements. We should seek the Kingdom of God, in the assurance that temporal matters will find adjustment according to providential law.

3. *Special self-abnegation* has its clearest statement in Mt 19¹². Whether that passage is literal or figurative is immaterial. The value is in the principle. The duty of abandoning good may be laid on men of hesitating disposition who need to be untrammelled, or on special ministers such as the disciples, who forsook all and followed their Master that they might give undivided effort to the preaching of the gospel. The things surrendered may be possessions, kindred, or even life (Lk 18²⁹). An important lesson on the subject is found in the interview of the rich ruler with Jesus (Lk 18¹⁸ etc.). This man was outwardly perfect, yet conscious of imperfection. He had rank, position, wealth, manners, and he had kept the Law. Jesus called on him to surrender his property and become a disciple. The first reflexion here is that formal is not real excellence; that not the outward life only, but the heart, and soul, and spirit are to be judged. Hence it is that not the right-eousness of the Law, but the righteousness by faith is the hope of the Christian. With this youth may be contrasted his contemporary St. Paul, who attained to the mind of Christ, and for the sake of the higher life counted all things but loss. The second reflexion (which is virtually the same) is the ethical principle that benevolence precedes prudence, that the cause of the community is prior to that of the individual. The command to 'sell . . . and give to the poor' was the form adapted to the individual case in which the principle of renunciation was expressed in the shape of social duty. In a religion which begins with the requirement of repentance and renovation of life, and which in all aspects exalts the spiritual, subordinating the temporal and earthly, nothing is more fitting than the childlike spirit; the graces of humility, meekness, and gentleness belong to the

new conception of the beautiful; while the strain of public duty requires the propelling motive of philanthropy and the ready acceptance of self-sacrifice. But renunciation is not without reward. The individual is one in a large family of brethren, and his own good is promoted by the health of the community. He who subordinates the self-regarding virtues to the altruistic, who abandons rights and possessions while he cherishes the love of God and of man, will find even in this life 'manifold more.' Sharing the life of others, he will receive from them more than he gives. By the frustration of false developments the basis of his personal life is strengthened; and by fellow-ship and service his life becomes richer, nobler, more blessed. Thus is realized the paradox (Mk 8³⁵) that the Christian loses his life to save it. The dethronement of self is the beginning of moral victory and power. The path of renouncement leads to spiritual wealth.

These principles derive strength from a study of Christ's own life. The Son of Man had no possessions, no fixed abode. He toiled for the relief of the suffering. The project of kingship He recognized as the temptation of Satan. He saved others—He could not save Himself. The model life was at all points a life of renunciation; a life, too, of uncomplaining endurance of wrong. But from the date when the cross came distinctly into view, renunciation was inculcated as a necessary condition of membership in His community. 'If any man will come after me, let him deny himself, and take up his cross' (Mt 16²⁴ etc.). Victory through cross-bearing, life through death, became the final maxims of duty. And the disciples were required at once to behold the career of their Master, and to be prepared to undergo a similar experience. The principle of renunciation took the form of a courageous facing of difficulties, a steadfast endurance of ills, a heroic encountering of persecution, and a submission even unto death. Perhaps the typical Christian is St. Paul. To him crucifixion is the image of his relation to established society. 'The world is crucified to me and I to the world' (Gal 6¹⁴). For Christians in general his language is more restricted but not substantially different: 'they that are Christ's have crucified the flesh' (Gal 5²⁴). But, nevertheless, his tones are triumphant: 'all things are yours' (1 Co 3²²). The cross is the centre of history, and cross-bearing is the soul of virtue; and the afflicted are 'more than conquerors' (Ro 8³⁷).

The law of Renunciation has been repeatedly restated in modern literature. 'Die and re-exist' was a maxim of Goethe. Self-renouncement was expounded by Matthew Arnold (*Lit. and Dogma*) as the *secret* of Jesus. 'Die to live' is a principle of Hegelianism. This latter axiom has been expounded by Dr. E. Caird (*Hegel, ad fin.; Evolution of Religion*, ii. 6–8) as the fundamental principle of a universal ethic. According to this authority, it is a law of the spiritual world, as contra-distinguished from the natural, that self-realization is to be attained by self-sacrifice. The theorem 'die to live' involves on the one hand absolute surrender of self and of every good to the Father of spirits, and on the other hand restoration in another form through the possession of an enlarged life filled with deeper and wider interests. The sacrifice of selfishness proves the birth of the true self, the individual deriving from the universal the good for which it exists. The death of Christ was no accidental phenomenon, but the highest revelation of the Divine in conflict with the world's evil. The surrender of a life as a sacrifice to a cause tends to give a universal value to the life so sacrificed. This, of course, does not differentiate the death of Christ from ordinary martyrdom; but we may agree with Caird that paramount moral doctrine must accord both with the lessons of history and with the highest reason of a universal spiritual philosophy. By such tests we distinguish the true from the false renunciation, and arrive at a clearer comprehension of the Divine intuition of Jesus.

On the other side, the reverse doctrine, that self-assertion is the essence of sin, has been rightly accepted as a fundamental truth of the moral sphere. The term so used includes the exaltation of the lower nature over the higher, and the placing of the individual or particular before the social or universal. This principle denies equality of right, repudiates the primary law of love, and treats with scorn the consciences of men. Its essential manifestation is in the lust of power and pride of life, though every other selfish gratification may be included. In mediæval ideas pride held the dark pre-eminence, and conceptions of Satan were formed therefrom. But in modern times, and especially since Milton, the historic view is modified. In the career of the master-fiend whose history is the history of evil (as that career is in *Paradise Lost* portrayed for all time) it is 'pride and, worse, ambition' that rule. True it is that down the Christian ages, and even within the Church, self-assertion has been as prominent (though not so abundant) as self-denial. But it is equally true that where such egotism has flourished spiritual life has died. See, further, art. SELFISHNESS.

LITERATURE.—Hastings' *DB*, art. 'Self-Surrender'; Newman Smyth, *Christian Ethics*, p. 372 ff.; Müller, *Christian Doct. of Sin*, ii. 362 ff.; Channing, *Complete Works* [ed. 1884], p. 259 ff.; W. Archer Butler, *Serm.* i. 27; A. Kempis, *Imit. of Christ*; George Eliot, *Mill on the Floss*, ch. iv. bk. 3; G. Macdonald, *The Religious Sense in its Scientific Aspect* (1903), 79; J. Strachan, *Heb. Ideals* (1902), 48. R. SCOTT.

**REPENTANCE.—In Christ's own life repentance has no place. The four Gospels contain no expression, direct or incidental, of any feeling of penitence or of regret for anything He ever did or left undone, for anything He ever said or left unsaid. He never prays for forgiveness. He never knows of a time when He was not in peace and harmony with God; He never speaks of coming into peace and harmony with God. Though He teaches insistently that all others must repent and become sons, and even then must pray for the forgiveness of their sins, yet He Himself knows nothing but that He is the Son of His Heavenly Father, and He never loses by any act the consciousness of the Father's approval. See, further, art. SINLESSNESS.

1. Christ's teaching on repentance.—In the teaching of Jesus the fundamental category was the Kingdom of God (βασιλεία τοῦ θεοῦ), *i.e.* the spiritual rule of God in the heart of a man or in the hearts of men. This βασιλεία simply means God's authority established, God exercising His will and having His way, whether it be in a single human soul, or in a Church, or in a Christian community (as in the primitive Church of Pentecost), or in the Church universal, or in the world. God's Kingdom has come, that is, His rule is established, when and where His will is done as it is supposed to be done 'in heaven,' that is, ideally, whether that be in a single heart or 'on (the whole) earth.'

This enables us to understand why Jesus has so much to say about righteousness. Righteousness was another name for the fulfilling of the will of God; it was doing what God wanted done; it was the realizing of *the rule of God*. Hence men were called on to repent and become righteous. Repentance, as conceived and taught by Jesus, meant a change of the whole life, so as to subject it and to conform it to God, a radical and complete revolution of one's view of God and attitude toward God. This meant a change of the whole of life in its inlook as well as in its outlook; a change, in short, of one's self, motives, aims, pursuits.

Jesus' primary thought was of a change *to*. For His starting-point was God. Hence the burden of His message was God and righteousness. But this implies that there was something to change from. Men were to free their mind from one thing and to fix it on another. They were to exchange one habitual, fixed state of mind for another—for its opposite, namely, for one that recognized, preferred, hungered after and sought for righteousness as the fulfilment of the will of God, as the realization of *the rule* (Kingdom) *of God*.

What was it then that they were to change *from*? Naturally it was from that which was the opposite of righteousness, that which refuses the rule of God and excludes Him from life. In other words, it was from sin. In turning to God it was necessary, in the nature of the case, to turn from that which is opposed to God, from that state of mind which loves, enjoys, chooses sin; which is permeated and dominated by sin, and which brings about the inevitable consequence of living in the practice of sin. So that, while Jesus had much to say about righteousness, He had much to say, and inevitably, about sin. We are now better prepared to understand what He meant when He called on people to repent. Popularly, repentance is understood to be a sense of regret and self-abasement looking to the forgiveness of the wrong-doings of the past. This is one part of repentance, but it is the least part. Sin lies deeper than the act. It is in the unrenewed, perverse nature behind the act. So repentance goes deeper than the act. Sin has its root in the inherent condition of man's nature; repentance contemplates a change in this condition. And until this change is effected, sin will inevitably continue to rule. Repentance then, while it is a sense of regret and sorrow for the wrong-doings of the past, is far more. It is an agonizing desire, leading to an agonizing and persistent effort, to realize such a radical change in the state of the mind as will secure and ensure against wrong-doing in the future. Born of a realization, more or less clear and pungent, of our natural sinward tendency and of our hopeless inability to correct it or control it, it impels us to desire above all things and to seek before all things that change of mind and moral condition which will not only lead us to choose righteousness, but also enable us triumphantly to realize righteousness. Repentance goes to the root of the matter. The very word goes to the root of it. For what is μετάνοια but a 'change of mind'? That this was the meaning of the word in the thought and intent of Jesus, the whole drift of His teaching implies. But it is specifically shown in those sayings of His which reveal His view of the inherent sinfulness of human nature: 'If ye being evil' (πονηροὶ ὄντες, Mt 7¹¹); 'a corrupt tree cannot (οὐ δύναται, v.¹⁸) bring forth good fruit'; and that terse statement of the whole situation which in one epigrammatic sentence sums up all that St. Paul says in the seventh and eighth chapters of Romans: 'That which is born of the flesh is flesh, and that which is born of the Spirit is spirit' (Jn 3⁶). It is what St. Paul calls 'the mind of the flesh,' and as good as calls *the mind of sin* (see Ro 7¹⁷·²⁰).

Repentance, as used in the Synoptic Gospels, covers, as a rule, the whole process of turning from sin to God (as in Lk 24⁴⁷). So that in the broad, comprehensive sense of the Synoptics, it includes faith, which is a part of the process, the last step of it. It is so used also in the discourses of the early chapters of the Book of Acts. There the comprehensive condition of admission to the brotherhood of believers and of participation in the life of the Spirit is repentance (Ac 2[38] 3[19] 5[31]). Faith is not mentioned, though, in the nature of the case, it is included.

In the Fourth Gospel the reverse is the case. There faith is the condition of salvation (Jn 3[15. 16. 36]). But while repentance is not specifically mentioned, it is included in the notion of faith. Faith is the trustful commitment of one's self to God for forgiveness of sin and deliverance from sin; but it is psychologically impossible to commit one's self thus to God without renouncing and turning away from all that is contrary to God. And this impossibility is expressed or implied in the discourses of the Fourth Gospel. For they clearly set forth the moral conditionality of faith. A man *cannot* exercise faith whose heart is not right, whose moral condition and attitude of will are opposed to the right (5[44]). And this moral conditionality of faith is exactly what is meant by repentance, in its narrower sense. Faith is the condition of entrance into the experience of salvation, the enjoyment of eternal life; but repentance is the psychological and moral condition of faith. As eternal life is unattainable without faith, faith is unattainable without repentance.

But Jesus was a preacher, not a theologian. Consequently His call to repentance is, as a rule, in the form of those exquisite parables that speak to the heart. Such is the parable of the Pharisee and the Publican (Lk 18[9-14]), and that of the Prodigal Son (15[11-24]). The latter of these is the truest, the humanest, and the tenderest picture of repentance to be found in the Bible. The essential elements, in the repentance of the Prodigal are (1) a realization of his desperate condition: 'He came to himself'; (2) a definite mental determination to reverse his course and retrace his steps at any risk: 'I will arise and go to my father'; (3) the decisive act of breaking away from his surroundings and going straight into the presence of his much wronged father: 'He arose and came to his father'; (4) his absolute, abject, self-effacing humility: 'I am no more worthy to be called a son of thine; make me as a servant'; (5) his open, outspoken, unreserved, unqualified confession: 'I have sinned to the very heaven, and my sin is against thee, O thou best of fathers.'

2. How Christ leads men to repentance.— If repentance means what we have seen, namely, the change from the self-centred life to the God-centred life, then Jesus is the author and inspiration of repentance. No other was ever able to reach down deep enough into human nature to effect this change. And He does it (1) by means of the revelation which He gives of the beauty and blessedness of righteousness in contrast with the ugliness and wretchedness of sin. This revelation makes one 'hunger and thirst after righteousness.' (2) By means of the revelation which He has given of God and the Fatherly compassion of God toward alienated and sinning men. (3) By means of the surpassing and compelling exhibition of His own love in renouncing self and enduring such suffering as He did for the reconciliation and redemption of men. (4) By working in man through His Spirit that sorrow for sin and hatred of sin which lead men to renounce it and to turn away from it, seeking forgiveness and deliverance. (5) By holding out to men and giving to men the power to forsake sin and to overcome the tendency to sin. (6) Through the convincing effect of examples of that moral transformation which He is continually working in men and women of all sorts and conditions. In short, the history of Christianity in the past and the Christendom of the present both form a solid commentary of fact on the pregnant and potent

words of St. Peter: 'Him hath God exalted as Prince and Saviour, to give repentance and forgiveness of sins' (Ac 5[31]).

LITERATURE.—Bruce. *Kingdom of God*; Wendt, *Teaching of Jesus*; Stevens, *Theology of NT*; Beyschlag, *NT Theology*; Alexander, *Son of Man*; Weiss, *Life of Christ*; Stapfer, *Jesus Christ before His Ministry*; Hastings' *DB*, art. 'Repentance'; Briggs, *Ethical Teaching of Jesus*; de Witt Hyde, *Jesus' Way* (1903), 55; Gilbert, *Revelation of Jesus* (1899), 62; C. A. Briggs, *Ethical Teaching of Jesus* (1904), 68; J. Watson, *Doctrines of Grace* (1900), 25; J. Denney, 'Three Motives to Repentance' in *Exp.* 4th Ser. vii. (1893) 232; C. G. Montefiore, 'Rabbinic Conceptions of Repentance' in *JQR* xvi. (1903) 209; P. J. Maclagan, *The Gospel View* (1906), 71; H. Black, *Edinburgh Sermons* (1906), 89. GROSS ALEXANDER.

REPETITIONS.—The word 'repetitions' is found in the Gospels only in the phrase 'vain repetitions' in Mt 6[7] 'When ye pray (RV 'in praying'), use not vain repetitions, as the heathen (RV 'the Gentiles') do: for they think that they shall be heard for their much speaking.' The original word (βατταλογέω, written by modern scholars with a in the second syllable, after אB) seems to be unknown to classical Greek, occurring only in the comment of Simplicius on Epictetus (*c.* 530 A.D.), and in Christian literature influenced by the Gospels.

Its origin has been explained in three ways: (1) as a word related to βατταρίζω, and derived from Battus (Βάττος), the name of a Libyan stammerer said to be associated with the early history of Cyrene, or a wordy poet; (2) as an onomatopoetic word imitating the utterance of a stammerer (Grimm, H. Holtzmann, Meyer); (3) as a hybrid composed of a Semitic element—Neo-Hebrew *batal*, Aram. *betal*, 'to be idle,' 'vain,' 'worthless,' represented in modern Arabic by *battal*, a term of contempt, *ExpT* xii. 60, and λογέω. The last derivation, which may have been in the minds of some of the Syriac translators (Syrsin and Pal. Lect.), has the powerful support of Blass (*ExpT* xii. 60), and apparently of Zahn. It is not wholly new, for some earlier scholars regarded the word as a hybrid, but found a different Semitic element. Zahn suggests that it was coined by Greek-speaking Semites, who, in writing the word with ττ, thought of βατταρίζω, and wished to connect their new formation with it. This ingenious explanation is not absolutely certain, but may be safely pronounced more probable than the first, and is, on the whole, preferable to the second.

The meaning of the word, or at least part of the meaning, is suggested by πολυλογία in the latter part of the verse. What our Lord condemns is clearly verbosity, the unthinking use of many words, and perhaps also the formal, careless use of expressions which are in themselves appropriate. The reference to Gentile errors in this respect is well illustrated by the cry of the priests of Baal on Carmel (1 K 18[26]), and the shout of the Ephesian mob, kept up for more than an hour (Ac 19[34]). Additional illustrations are supplied by Hindu practice (Ward, cited by Rosenmüller, *Das alte und neue Morgenland*, v. 38 f.) and Tibetan Buddhism (Rhys David, *Buddhism*, 209 f.). For an Egyptian condemnation of the practice see *ExpT* iv. 537. That the later Jews were liable to wordiness in prayer might be inferred from the Lord's warnings, and is put beyond doubt by a number of passages in the Talmud. It is noted with approval (*Berakh.* 32b) that the righteous of an earlier age used to devote three hours a day to prayer and six hours to waiting, an hour before and an hour after each hour of prayer. R. Meir (of 2nd cent. A.D.) is reported to have said that a man ought to utter a hundred benedictions in a day (*Menahoth*, 43b). R. Shimeon ben Nathanael, one of the disciples of R. Jochanan ben Zakai, warned his hearers against formalism: 'When thou prayest, make not thy prayer an ordinance, but an entreaty before God' (*Abôth*, ii. 17, ed. Taylor). The threefold repetition of the 'Eighteen Blessings,' a custom the germ of which may have begun to develop in our Lord's day, was of itself calculated to encourage formal repetition. Some of the Rabbis recognized the peril and tried to check the tendency. An instance of verbosity which elicited a rebuke from a Rabbi is given in *Berakh.* 33b, 'O God, great, mighty, awful, glorious, strong, terrible,' etc. Vain repetitions are still in favour in the East, in Islam and its sects (Robinson Lees, *Village Life in Palestine*[2], pp. 48, 51 f.; John P. Brown, *Dervishes*, p. 57).

LITERATURE.—Besides the authorities cited above, see Wetstein and Zahn on Mt 6[7]; Bischoff, *Jesus und die Rabbinen*, 1905, p. 71. W. TAYLOR SMITH.

REPOSE. — 1. It seems superfluous to labour (*e.g.* as Liddon, *Bampton Lecture*, p. 20; Edersheim, *LT* i. 599 f.) the point that Jesus needed repose, bodily rest, relaxation, as witnessing to His real human nature. This feature of His experience, along with others, appears as a quite simple and natural thing in the picture of the Prophet of Nazareth as presented by the primitive Evangelical tradition. The Synoptics repeatedly speak of the crowds that gathered about Jesus in the course of His work. The brief story is full of movement, press, and popular excitement. Withdrawal from time to time for rest and prayer was simply imperative. Mark conspicuously calls attention (as in 6[31] δεῦτε . . . κ. ἀναπαύσασθε ὀλίγον) to the various occasions when Jesus sought escape and relief from the crush. The Fourth Gospel, too, for all its peculiar portrayal of Jesus, accords with the Synoptics in this description of His ministry: see especially the mention of popular excitement in Jerusalem and elsewhere in chs. 6. 7 and 10. Nor must we overlook in another connexion the homely picture of Jesus resting, tired out with His journey, given in Jn 4[6]. This in a way matches the memorable picture found in the threefold Synoptic narrative, in which the Master beats a speedy retreat after one busy and exhausting day, and sleeps like a child through the storm (Mk 4[35-38] ‖). At the same time it is to be noted that undoubtedly Jesus sought by such withdrawals from public life not only repose and relief, but also opportunities for the special instruction of the Twelve. As particular instances of this, Mk 3[13] and 7[24-37] may be cited (see Bruce, art. 'Jesus,' § 11, in *EBi*, vol. ii.).

2. Repose of spirit as a trait in the character of Jesus abundantly appears in the Gospels. If in doing the works of Him that sent Him (Jn 9[4]) He often seems 'ohne Rast,' He is always in manner and spirit 'ohne Hast.' Suppliants for His help in healing the sick are often frantic in their appeals; He in responding ever displays composure and deliberation. Contrast, *e.g.*, the entreaties of Jairus (Mk 5[22f.]) and the calmness of the whole attitude of Jesus (v.[36]); the quiet response, 'I will come and heal him' (Mt 8[7]), and the hurried, eager request of the Roman captain on behalf of his servant. These are typical instances. John presents the same feature in the description of our Lord's behaviour on hearing of the sickness of Lazarus (ch. 11). The paroxysm of grief which shakes Him when He comes to His friend's grave (vv.[33-38]) only throws into relief the normal composure which recovers itself in v.[41f.]. Such, too, is the relation of Gethsemane's agony to the calm dignity which shows itself through all the rest of the *Via Dolorosa*. It is also a characteristic of the teaching of Jesus that there is an entire absence of the impatience, fuss, and strain which so often characterize the schemes of social and religious work launched by His well-meaning followers. With all the zeal and diligence that His sayings lay stress on, He always speaks with the accent of one who can afford to wait. It is not a mere matter of chance that serenity sits on the face of the Lord, as He is represented in the unbroken tradition of Christian art.

3. In the well-known passage Mt 11[28-30] Jesus offers the gift of repose (ἀνάπαυσις, EV **rest**) to those who will learn of Him. It is true, ἀνάπαυσις

strictly speaking denotes relief from labour, a break to afford rest to tired toilers (see Trench, *NT Synonyms*, § 41); and it seems also to imply the resumption of labour. The words of Jesus, however, teach that to take His yoke and bear His burden, to live and serve as He teaches and as He lived and served Himself, will itself be ἀνάπαυσις as compared with other modes of living and serving, the yoke of which is never to be resumed. 'A Christi *corde* manat quies in *animas nostras*' (Bengel, *in loc.*). Tranquillity of soul, then, is a promised accompaniment of true Christian discipleship. A temper eagerly cultivated by Stoics (*Æquanimitas* was the last watchword given by Antoninus Pius to his bodyguard) is also a precious Christian grace.

'Drop Thy still dews of quietness,
Till all our strivings cease:
Take from our souls the strain and stress,
And let our ordered lives confess
The beauty of Thy peace.' (Whittier).
J. S. CLEMENS.

REPROACH.—The word is found in EV as a rendering of four Gr. terms that either occur in the Gospels or are used in the NT with reference to Christ Himself—the nouns ὄνειδος, ὀνειδισμός, and the vbs. ὀνειδίζω, ὑβρίζω. ὄνειδος = 'shame,' as the ground of reproach (whereas ὀνειδισμός is the actual reproaching), is found only in Lk 1[25] (of Elisabeth's barrenness). ὑβρίζω is once rendered 'reproach' (11[45]), but properly means to 'insult.' ὀνειδισμός and ὀνειδίζω are the terms with which we are specially concerned. The subject comes before us in three forms: (1) *reproach as uttered by Christ*; (2) *reproach as borne by Him*; (3) *reproach as falling upon His people*.

1. As uttered by Christ.—The language of rebuke (ἐπιτιμάω) is several times ascribed to Jesus (see art. REBUKE), but seldom the language of reproach. When we distinguish between the two, the difference seems to be that rebuke denotes the simple censure of a fault, while reproach carries with it some emphasis upon the personal shame (ὄνειδος) attaching to it. And so it seems to be part of the method of Jesus, as understood by the Evangelists, to point out faults rather than to fasten the stigma of disgrace upon the culprit; He was more anxious to effect improvement than to inflict punishment— His eyes being ever towards the future rather than towards the past (cf. 'Neither do I condemn thee: go thy way; from henceforth sin no more,' in the *Pericope Adulteræ*, Jn 8[11]). Once in EV (Lk 11[45]) the word 'reproach' is used with reference to our Lord's utterances, but there by a misrendering; for the Gr. vb. is ὑβρίζω, which means to 'insult,' not to reproach. But the Evangelist, it is to be noted, does not say that Jesus insulted any one; it is 'one of the lawyers' who accuses Him of insulting the legal class. It was not our Lord's way, however, to insult people, even though they were His enemies; and, on examination, the charge of this lawyer serves only to illustrate the tendency of offended pride to regard a declaration of the honest truth as a ground of personal offence.

Only on two occasions is the vb. ὀνειδίζω employed to describe the language of Jesus, and both times AV renders 'upbraid,' which RV rather inconsistently retains. In Mt 11[20] Jesus reproaches the cities in which most of His mighty works were done, because they repented not; and in the Appendix to Mk. (16[14]) He reproaches the Eleven for their slowness to receive the testimony of His resurrection. These cases suggest that Jesus did not hesitate to add reproach to rebuke when He thought it deserved. Capernaum was 'his own city' (Mt 9[1], cf. 4[13]); Chorazin and Bethsaida had shared with it in the fullest manifestations of His power and grace. The men whom He is said to have reproached for their unbelief and hardness of heart were those whom He had specially chosen to be the depositaries and messengers of His gospel, and whom He had trained through long months for this very purpose, lavishing upon them all the wealth of His Divine treasures of knowledge and love. No wonder that in these cases the censure of Jesus became reproachful. And indeed His reproach was more frequent than we might gather from the occurrence of the word in the Gospel narratives, and was most frequent when He was dealing with those of whom, loving them the best, He expected the most. Was He not speaking reproachfully when He said, 'How is it that ye do not understand?' (Mt 16¹¹); 'How long shall I be with you? how long shall I bear with you?(17¹⁷); 'Have I been so long time with you, and dost thou not know me, Philip?' (Jn 14⁹). Was there not a more piercing reproach in His voice when He said to the traitor, 'Judas, with a kiss dost thou betray the Son of Man?' (Lk 22⁴⁸); and in His eyes when, as the cock crew, He turned and looked upon Peter (vv.⁶⁰· ⁶¹)?

2. Reproach as borne by Christ.—So far as the term is concerned, it is only by the two robbers who were crucified along with Him that our Lord is said to have been reproached (ὀνειδίζω, Mt 27⁴⁴, Mk 15³²; see RV). This reproach by the robbers belongs to the general subject of the reviling of Jesus Christ in connexion with His trial and crucifixion, for which see art. MOCKERY.

In the Epistles the word 'reproach' receives a much wider meaning, as denoting generally the shame and contempt, the hardships and suffering which Christ endured in the days of His flesh. In Ro 15³ St. Paul exhorts Christians to a life of unselfish consideration for others by pointing to the example of the Master, and quotes in this connexion the exact words of the LXX tr. of Ps 69⁹ (68¹⁰) 'The reproaches of them that reproached (οἱ ὀνειδισμοὶ τῶν ὀνειδιζόντων) thee fell upon me.' The Psalm describes the sufferings of the righteous man at the hands of the ungodly, and the verse quoted represents him as telling how he has to bear the reproaches directed against God Himself. The Apostle, however, transfers the words to Christ, and makes them describe how He bore the burden of reproach for others, and so serve to give point to an exhortation against self-pleasing.

In two passages the author of Hebrews uses the expression 'the reproach (ὀνειδισμός) of Christ,' or 'his reproach,' to denote the earthly shame and sorrow of Jesus. In the first case (11²⁶), Moses is described as 'esteeming the reproach of Christ greater riches than the treasures in Egypt.' The writer's idea appears to be, not only that by identifying himself with his despised people Moses took upon himself a burden of contempt and suffering resembling that which was afterwards borne by Christ on our behalf, but that he had Christ prophetically in view—saw Him afar off, even as Father Abraham did (Jn 8⁵⁶), and was strengthened by the vision to run his own race with patience (cf. He 12²· ³). In the second passage (13¹³), the Jewish-Christian readers are exhorted to a fellowship with the sufferings of Christ, in the words, 'Let us go forth therefore unto him without the camp, bearing his reproach.' The allusion apparently is to the sin-offering on the Day of Atonement without the camp of Israel, and to the suffering of Jesus without the city gate; and the meaning is that those Jewish-Christians must forsake the sphere of the OT religion, break off the old ties of national fellowship, and face all the pain and contumely that this would involve, so that they might share in the better blessings of the great Sin-offering.

3. Reproach as falling upon Christ's people.—

Both in Mt. (5¹¹) and Lk. (6²²) reproach forms a part of the last Beatitude—the Beatitude of Persecution. There are, we have seen, two kinds of reproach—a reproach that is just, and one that is unjust; such reproach as Christ uttered, and such reproach as He endured. In deserved reproach there lies great sorrow and shame. The Lord's backward look through the open door of the hall sent Peter out into the night to weep bitterly (Lk 22⁶¹ᶠ·); the remembrance of the last words addressed to him by his Master must have been as a barb to the arrow of remorse that sank so deep into the soul of Judas (Mt 26⁵⁰, Lk 22⁴⁸). On the other hand, both honour and blessing belong to undeserved reproach falling upon Christ's people for their Master's sake. Jesus frequently forewarned His disciples that persecution would come upon them through following Him (Mt 5¹⁰ᶠᶠ· ⁴⁴ 10²³·· ³⁸ 13²¹ 16²⁴, Mk 10³⁰· ³⁸, Lk 6²² 21¹², Jn 15²⁰). And in this Beatitude He specially forewarns them of the persecution of false and bitter tongues —more trying to some natures than the stones of the mob or the tyrant's scourge and sword.

The Apostles and the early Church had their full share of the reproach of evil tongues (cf. Ac 2¹³ 6¹¹ 17³² 21²⁸ 22²² 24⁵· ⁶, Ro 3⁸, Ja 2⁷, 1 P 4⁴). But the glory that lies in being reproached for Christ's sake, and the Lord's great promise regarding this experience, were never forgotten. It was this that taught St. Paul to bless when he was reviled (1 Co 4¹²). It was evidently with the very words of Jesus echoing in his ears that St. Peter wrote, 'If ye be reproached (ὀνειδίζεσθε) for the name of Christ, blessed are ye' (1 P 4¹⁴). And when the author of Hebrews speaks of the 'reproach of Christ'—telling of the manner in which it was esteemed by Moses, and urging his fellow-believers of the Jewish race to go forth without the camp with that reproach upon them—it may be that he also is recalling how Jesus taught His disciples to rejoice in reproach because their reward in heaven was great (Mt 5¹², Lk 6²²). For in the one case he represents Moses as forming his estimate of the reproach of Christ from his respect unto the recompense of the reward (He 11²⁶), and in the other he exhorts Christians to the bearing of the same reproach, on the ground that they look for the abiding city which is to come (13¹⁴).

J. C. LAMBERT.

RESERVE.—In Mt 7⁶ Jesus counsels reserve in the communication of religious truth. That maxim, which has had great and sinister developments in the Church, stands alone, both in its place in the Sermon on the Mount and in His teaching. Its meaning, then, can be gathered only from His practice.

1. It was never Jesus' custom to meet *religious curiosity or speculation.* As He was teaching, one said unto Him, 'Lord, are there few that be saved?' (Lk 13²²⁻²⁵). He did not answer; He said, 'Strive to enter in at the strait gate . . .' He turned His hearers' attention from that speculation, which has no saving power in it, to the clear duty and wisdom of the moment. When Peter asked if the parable of the Servants waiting for their Lord was addressed to the disciples specially, or to all, Jesus did not answer (12⁴¹). He painted, instead, another picture for the inward eye of the heart. In both cases it was the practical and most imperative needs of the soul's relation to God that He considered. That directing purpose shown in these cases, explains the silences of His teaching, the reserves of His revelation. When He spoke of those on whom the tower fell, and of the Galilæans whose blood Pilate had mingled with their sacrifices (13¹⁻⁵), the old problem of the suffering of the innocent was suggested; but He shed no light upon it. He made practical use of it, instead, as a call to repentance. The immortality of the soul is the presupposition of all His teaching about the love of the Heavenly Father for men, His children. 'The life after death, Lightfoot and I agreed, is the cardinal point of Christianity' (*In Memoriam*, Author's Notes, p. 227 n.). But Jesus, of His own impulse, only enunciates this truth at the end of His mission. And a practical need then impelled Him. His disciples needed consolation for the days after His death, and He left them the hope which would strengthen their faith and loyalty (Jn 14). With Jesus, the declaration of any truth depended wholly upon the needs of faith in the heart.

2. Jesus practised reserve as to *His personal claims.* The Jews came and asked Him, 'How long dost thou make us doubt: if thou be the Christ, tell us plainly' (Jn 10^{24}). They were surprised at His silence about what seemed to them so important. And His blessing of Peter (Mt 16$^{13-17}$) shows that He had been silent also in private, even among the inner circle of His disciples. His reserve is explained, not by the slow growth of His own conception of His Messiahship, but by the method of establishing the Kingdom of God which He had set before Him from the beginning. The weapons of His warfare were to be purely spiritual. His aim was to set up the Kingdom within men's hearts, to win their heart's love and trust in the Father. And for that end the appeal of all His activities, miracles of help and healing and words of teaching, was single. He aimed at the heart, the seat and source of faith, where the vision and the love of goodness, with their dynamic impulse, are. And Peter's confession was a joy to Him, because it came from his heart's assurance that Jesus had the words of eternal life (Jn 6^{68}, Mt 16^{17}). It was faith in goodness asserting itself against the appearance of things. To this faith Jesus confessed His greatness and Divine mission. He did so, because then He was merely certifying the Divine supremacy of that goodness which had, in its lowliness and simplicity, won the love and trust of their hearts. Through their faith they reached His authority. Jesus recognized no other path to faith in Him as Messiah, the revealer of the Father, and the founder of the Kingdom of God upon the earth. He sent the inquiring Jews back to this road (Jn 10$^{25-27}$); He withdrew from the people who, from material ideas and expectations, would have made Him king (6^{15}); and He declined to answer the chief priests and elders, who came inquiring for His authority, because they were not simple-hearted or honest inquirers (Mt 21$^{23-27}$). This single regard for the interests of faith in the heart explains also His reserve with the messengers of John (11$^{2-6}$). John belonged to the old economy (11^{11}); his prophecy of the Messiah's coming had been a prophecy of judgment (3^{12}). The simple acknowledgment by Jesus that He was the Messiah could never have brought to him enlightenment and faith as to that Kingdom of heaven whose least disciple was greater than he. Its inevitable consequence would have been to confirm him in his old expectations of judgment; it would have appeared to him a call to wait in patience the good time of the Messiah, when He would play the stern part John had foretold. Therefore Jesus gave no direct answer to John's question. He pointed rather to all the gracious activities which were partly the causes of John's doubting impatience. These were the signs of that Kingdom of love which Jesus was establishing; and if John were ever to gain the higher and richer conceptions of God and of man manifested there, he must see the Messiah through these quiet and lowly activities of loving helpfulness, and believe in Him as Him that should come, because of them and not despite them.

3. *The sufferings of the Messiah.*—It was immediately upon Peter's confession that Jesus began to teach the necessity of suffering and death for Himself (Mt 16^{21}, Mk 8^{31}). There are a precision and a fulness of detail in the account of this teaching, which are probably reflected back upon it from later experience. But the tragic note enters then and dominates the later teaching both in public and private. Its emergence at that time does not prove that Jesus entered then upon a new conception of His mission, taught by the progress of events. It is more probable that this tragic note was in His conception of the task of establishing the Kingdom from the beginning. His wilderness temptation argues that (Mt 4$^{8, 9}$); it is implicit in His Beatitudes upon the meek and the persecuted, and in His teaching of the earthly rewards of hypocrisy (6$^{2, 5, 16}$); and the deeper spirit of the OT, with its history of religious growth through the sufferings of the saints and the long-suffering patience of Jehovah's love, could not be veiled from the insight of His meditation thereon in the years of His preparation. The joy of the early days does not contradict this. It was the natural answer of the heart to those new thoughts of the love of the Father which Jesus preached. And in Jesus' own thought this tragic element was not in contradiction with that instinctive, buoyant joy in His gospel, though then He had many things to say to them which they could not bear (Jn 16^{12}). Peter's confession brought the opportunity of revealing further the depths of the riches of the wisdom and love of God.

Reserve, as practised by Jesus, was never a politic means of leading men's minds gradually to doctrines which might startle or offend them at first sight; it consisted only in seeking, with a single aim, the practical needs of faith in the heart—belief in that Divine Love whose outgoings are redemptive, and in whose fellowship and service stands eternal life.

LITERATURE.—Ker, *Sermons*, 1st ser. xx.; *ExpT* iv. [1893] 446; Paget, *Studies in the Chr. Character*, xxii.; J. Smith, *The Magnetism of Christ* (1904), 269; B. Whitefoord in *ExpT* vi. (1895) 22.   RICHARD GLAISTER.

RESISTANCE.—See RETALIATION.

REST. — **1.** There is in the Gospels frequent allusion to the value of rest as the purchase of preceding effort, the compensation that is provided for sore afflictions. The Sermon on the Mount, as the proclamation of the new Kingdom, guarantees such rest and peace to those who serve and suffer for the sake of that Kingdom (Mt 5$^{1-12}$). Prosperity in the world can make no such promises (Lk 12^{20} 16^{25}).

2. As rest, physical, social, and religious, is an organic necessity of life, and is protected by conditions of time and place, it should not be set aside for effort that is uncalled for, or that confuses the lower and higher forms of rest. Such was the lesson given in the home at Bethany (Lk 10^{42}). Similarly, the lilies of the field, while developing to the full their own character in their own place, are content to remain lilies (Mt 6$^{28, 29}$).

3. There is an ignoble state of rest that may slothfully or blindly oppose the call to a higher and truer contentment (Mt 11$^{17, 22}$, Lk 19^{40}). Christ's gift is life abundant (Jn 10^{10}), but the bestowal involves asking, and faith's exertion of knocking is expected at the entrance into life (Mt 7^7).

4. In the parable of the Sower, the recompense is in the abundant harvest. This increase is the way of nature where hindering things cease to operate. The list of obstacles typifies the things that impoverish or prevent altogether the fruitfulness of discipleship. In the Kingdom of heaven the instinct of citizenship is to be rich toward God.

Its gratification is not toil but rest (Mt 11²⁸ ; see art. REPOSE).

LITERATURE.—The subject is treated homiletically in many vols. of Sermons, as H. Allon, *Indwelling Christ* (1892), 41 ; Stopford Brooke, *Gospel of Joy* (1898), 123 ; R. Flint, *Christ's Kingdom* (1865), 22 ; E. W. Moore, *The Promised Rest* (1904) ; R. Rainy, *Sojourning with God* (1902), 37 ; J. H. Jowett, *Apostolic Optimism* (1901), 87. See also *ExpT* ii. (1891) 110, viii. (1897) 239, x. (1899) 48, 104, xii. (1901) 466.

G. M. MACKIE.

RESTORATION.—Round this word gather some of the most fascinating problems of our thought in regard to the possibilities of human destiny. Every lover of his kind, and everyone who has caught something of the spirit of the Lord Christ, is compelled, for his own mental and spiritual satisfaction, to ask, What is to be the issue of all this complex life of man, the beginnings of which we see on the earth, the final issue when the Divine purpose concerning the race is accomplished ? And naturally the Scriptures of the NT are eagerly scanned to discover what declarations are there made, or hints given, respecting the issue. Above all, has the Master of Truth left us any definite teaching on which a fair and inspiring hope may be built ? At first sight it must be confessed that to those who look for express statements of our Lord and His Apostles in regard to future destiny, the results of a restrained exegesis are disappointing. Isolated expressions and passages may be, and often have been, pressed into the service of preconceived hopes ; but, on the whole, the statements of Scripture afford too slender a basis on which to raise a structure of dogmatic assertion, and do not throw light very far into the great mystery of the future. The disappointment, however, is modified by two considerations : (1) Many of the references to the future life are quite incidental, and occur in writings which are themselves obviously of the most occasional character, in which, therefore, the immediate doctrinal or ethical concern is paramount, and no intention of dealing with the problems of Eschatology was before the writer's mind. (2) The mysteriousness which everywhere surrounds our human existence is an essential part of life's discipline. If all the mystery concerning the future were dispelled, the race would be without one of its most refining and sanctifying influences, much of life's interest would vanish and its finest essence evaporate. The Evangelists, the Apostles, and even our Lord Himself in His earthly life, were required to vindicate to themselves the Divine purpose in this mortal career without having all the future destiny of mankind revealed to them. Limitation of knowledge here seems to be essential to the very being of human nature.

In considering the Scripture intimations regarding the hope of a universal Restoration of humanity, it must be clearly seen that whatever hopes may, more or less distinctly, emerge in the expressed thought of the Apostles, are all clearly based upon, and inspired by, an enlarging thought concerning the Person of Jesus Christ, and the revelation given in Him and recorded in the Gospels.

The word 'restoration' (ἀποκατάστασις, AV 'restitution') is found only once in the Gospels, and in its verbal form, in Mt 17¹¹, in connexion with a hope current in our Lord's time of a moral renovation of the nation under the leadership of Elijah (cf. Mal 3¹ 4⁵· ⁶), and declared by our Lord to be fulfilled in the great spiritual movement initiated by John the Baptist (Mt 17¹⁰⁻¹²). The noun is employed in Ac 3²¹, where it would be extremely interesting if we could believe that St. Peter, in his anticipation of the χρόνος ἀποκαταστάσεως πάντων, had in his mind any thought of the universal restoration of mankind, and its final up-

raising to the life of fellowship with God. His need of mental enlargement, given later by means of the vision (Ac 10⁹⁻³³), to enable him to believe in the possibility of Gentile salvation, is decisive against such an interpretation. We may well inquire, however, how far the expression, calculated to express so much, was due to the writer of the Acts, St. Luke, to whom such a pregnant phrase and such a large hope for humanity would naturally commend itself.

But the question remains, Does the larger idea of the restoration of humanity as a whole to obedience, and to the condition of blessedness for which it was created, receive a warrant from the words and thoughts of Scripture ?

1. In examining, first, *our Lord's own teaching*, which we take as fundamental in the consideration of the question, it must be clearly understood what we are to ask concerning it. We desire to know if we have any evidence from the words of Jesus reported in the Gospels, that He Himself held the faith of the final restoration of all men. Was it for Him included in the possibilities of the future ? or have we any express declaration that in this life only is there a possibility of right moral decision being made, with the consequent attainment to a right and saving relation to God ? The last question stands on the threshold of the inquiry ; for if it be unmistakably answered in the affirmative, it must determine the whole problem for those who accept His authority as final ; while, if no such declaration is found, the way is left open for a redeeming process beyond the bounds of this brief mortal life.

Our Lord is reported to have spoken of everlasting or eternal punishment (κόλασιν αἰώνιον), apparently as the opposite of life everlasting or eternal (ζωὴν αἰώνιον, Mt 25⁴⁶). The use of the same term αἰώνιος of both life and punishment has inclined many to regard the passage as decisive on this momentous question ; but the majority of modern scholars consider that the æonian (literally 'age-long') life or suffering is to be understood as at least possibly terminable, and that the expression applied is qualitative rather than quantitative, referring to the relation of both life and death to God rather than to duration of time. 'Eternal' and not 'everlasting' is its true equivalent. It may also be said that even if the expressions are meant to refer to the endlessness of the punishment or of the blessedness, they may properly be understood as a very strong assertion of the undoubted fact that the suffering that comes of sin is eternally, endlessly bound up with the sin, even as the blessedness of the righteous is necessarily involved in their obedience. The hopelessness of the blasphemy against the Holy Ghost is summed up in the words 'he is guilty of eternal sin' (Mk 3²⁹). The latter possibility, however, is nowhere asserted of all who 'die in their sins' (Jn 8²⁴), and leave this world unrepentant. See ETERNAL SIN.

Similarly, the same fact of the eternal and necessary association of suffering with sin is expressed in Mk 9⁴³⁻⁴⁸ 'the worm that dieth not,' and 'the fire that never shall be quenched.' But in neither case is it declared that those who are sent away into that searching experience are doomed to abide there endlessly. The fire of the Divine wrath against sin is essential to the Divine Being, and while God is God it cannot but burn. Both passages convey a most solemn warning to men against being caught into that holy wrath, the fiery trial of suffering and remorse that inevitably waits upon all disobedience, against that dissolution of the life which elsewhere our Lord describes as the cutting of man asunder, and as that terrible portion of the unbeliever or hypocrite which is weeping and gnashing of teeth (Mt 24⁵¹, cf. Lk 12⁴⁶).

Unspeakable horror of the world to come for the impenitent and disobedient reveals itself in all that He teaches us regarding it ; in His sense of sin, and the mischief, corruption, and agony which it works ; in His urging that it were 'profitable,' good for a man, to make the utmost sacrifice of all that makes life good to live, even to the plucking out of the eye or the cutting off of the hand, rather than to be cast into that loathly Gehenna which our Lord glances at, rather than depicts (Mt 5$^{29, 30}$) ; but of the duration of that state of woe He gives no hint. Although it may with much force be maintained that the images He employs—the worm, the fire, the salting with fire—are all most naturally interpreted as purifying and cleansing agencies, yet it is wiser to see that He leaves the Divine purpose in all that mysterious process of retribution to be inferred from the whole revelation of God which He had given in His earthly life. See, further, ETERNAL FIRE, ETERNAL PUNISHMENT.

Due weight must be assigned to the remarkable reticence maintained by Jesus regarding the world to come, both concerning the nature of the blessedness of heaven, and the future destiny of the unrepentant. In His incarnate condition, under the limitations necessarily involved in the taking of a veritable human nature, much of that future was hidden from His view as from ours. The discipline of mystery concerning the future world, which is so salutary for our nature, was not without its value in the perfecting of the Redeemer. And therefore, while He possessed absolute knowledge of the moral conditions of that life, kindred as they were with the moral conditions of life here, He was not privileged to see all that future unfolded. And it is surely most significant that of the course of events in that ' sequestered state,' in that world to which the sinful pass at death, He speaks no word. And He nowhere precludes the possibility of moral growth and betterment in that vast Unseen ; the parable of Dives and Lazarus (Lk 16$^{19-31}$) speaks of ' a great gulf fixed' prohibiting a passage from either of the two contrasted states of being to the other, but it was not a gulf across which there could come no communication or redeeming influence, for Dives and Abraham can hold converse ; and the parable hints not obscurely at some betterment of the selfish rich man who begins to have a genuine concern for his brethren (unless it must be interpreted as a subtle form of self-excuse).

The Gospels contain no word of this life as being absolutely and finally decisive of all human destiny, and remembering the complexity of life not for the heathen only, and for nations chosen to play another part than a religious one, in the great purpose of God, but for men living in full gospel light, yet doomed from their birth and before it to an almost hopeless incapacity for truth and virtue, our moral nature shrinks irresistibly from such a thought. On the contrary, we have certain indications, not beyond question and yet full of hopeful suggestion, that the mind of Jesus reached out beyond all the complexity and travail to a glorious issue and consummation worthy of being called ' the glory of the Father.' He speaks in Mt 19^{28} of a coming Regeneration ($\pi\alpha\lambda\iota\nu\gamma\epsilon\nu\epsilon\sigma\iota\alpha$) in which those who have faithfully followed Him shall share His rule ; but we have no clue as to whether His words are intended to reach beyond the definite establishment of His Kingdom as an actual fact among men. But in that Kingdom once established He placed His hope, and He taught us to pray for its coming as the equivalent of the Divine will being done on earth as it is in heaven.

In Jn 12^{32} (cf. Jn 3^{14}) He declares that His ' lifting up' shall be the means of ' drawing all men' to Himself, and His words are naturally interpreted as expressing His hope and expectation of a complete redemption of mankind, and can scarcely be satisfied by saying that though this is the natural effect, it may never be the actual effect of His supreme sacrifice.

On the whole, while it must be confessed that we have no certain statement from our Lord as to the final issue of things, we have yet much to encourage a hopeful attitude, in harmony as that attitude is with the intuitions of the human heart, and with the whole disclosure of God's love ' in the face of Jesus Christ.' The Son of Man and Son of God has ' thrown light' not only upon the intimations of immortality which existed in the heart of man, but also upon the problem as to future restoration, not so much by what He says as by His whole Personality, His revelation of and abiding relation to the unseen Father.

2. Upon that revelation in the actual Jesus of Nazareth, and upon their increasing sense of the infinite importance of the Christ who ever liveth, *the Apostles* found their thought and speculation, so far as these find place in their writings, regarding the larger and ultimate issues of redemption. Whatever hopes they permit themselves to express, all centre in His Personality and power. The vagueness which characterizes most of the references to the question is due to the fact that the writings are all casual. In no case are the authors specifically or systematically dealing with the problem, being not theologians so much as practical Apostles, dealing with the ethical questions of the Churches and with individual salvation.

(*a*) In the Johannine writings are found many principles of truth on which far-reaching inferences may legitimately enough be founded, such as the assertion that ' God is light, and in him is no darkness at all' (1 Jn 1^5) ; but there is no evidence that the writer had apprehended these logical inferences.

(*b*) In the First Epistle of Peter two important passages are 1 P 3$^{18-20}$ and 4^6, which, in spite of a considerable weight of adverse exegesis which forbids any dogmatic assertion based upon the words, may fairly be taken as suggesting that the scope of redemption is not limited to the present scene. The Apostle has the conception of an underworld from which a moral process is not excluded.

(*c*) In the Pauline writings the most conservative exegesis reads a clear declaration of the Divine purpose that all men shall be saved, but denies that any certain hope as to the final issue can be built upon the fact. Here many will naturally diverge in judgment, and feel that they can raise their hope so securely nowhere else as upon the expressed purpose and will of God (Ro 11^{32}, 1 Ti 2$^{3, 4}$, cf. 2 P 3^9). When once the holy *will* of the Father, in its might and energy and Divine persistence, is realized, the Christian man may at least ' rest in hope' of an issue beyond our farthest vision. Martensen (*Christian Dogmatics*, Eng. tr. 474–484) is a type of those who regard Scripture as presenting two sides of the truth respecting future destiny which are at present unreconcilable ; but the antinomy which no doubt exists will largely disappear if the process of development in Apostolic and especially in Pauline thought be allowed for. In his earlier Epistles (1 and 2 Thess.), St. Paul is largely influenced by the apocalyptic ideas of traditional Judaism (1 Th 4$^{15-17}$, 2 Th 2$^{3-10}$). But in the later stages of his writing a larger conception of the Divine purpose begins to find expression. In Ro 8^{19} he anticipates a glorious ' revelation of the sons of God'—and in 11^{32} he expresses the widest design in the Divine mind, determining all the mysterious process of redemption, as ' that he might have mercy upon all.' And, as his thought matures, his hope expands under an enlarged sense of the central position of the ever-living

Christ in this world and in all worlds, and under his feeling of the larger spaces in the Divine purpose and working—the 'ages upon ages' (Eph 2⁷ 3²¹). In Col 1¹⁶·¹⁷ the Son is declared to be the creator of all things visible and invisible. All things (τὰ πάντα) find their cohesive principle in Him (συνέστηκεν), and their final consummation (εἰς αὐτόν). In Eph 1¹⁰ He is the Head of all, in which the whole creative and redeeming process is to be summed up (ἀνακεφαλαιώσασθαι τὰ πάντα ἐν τῷ Χριστῷ), and in Ph 2¹⁰ His is the Name at which the whole created universe is to bow with undivided acclamation. In Col 1²⁰ the blessings of redemption are extended to the whole system of things (cf. Eph 1²¹·²²), on which Toy (*Judaism and Christianity*, pp. 407–408) says: 'If we are to see here the conception of a final reconciliation between God and His creatures, a blotting out of evil in the sense that it shall be transformed into good, a complete harmonizing of the universe so that neither angel nor man shall be found to set himself against the Divine ethical order, then we must hold this view to spring out of a philosophical thought which does not find support elsewhere in the NT, and which did not afterward meet with wide approval in the Church.' And though this may be conceded, and though we must not be blind to the fact that the issues thus gloriously expressed were not fully thought out by the Apostle or applied to the question of Restoration, yet, based as they are upon the Person of Christ and supplemented by the principles of His teaching and revelation, they may be taken to express a sober and restrained hopefulness for the ultimate issue, which shall never for a moment be suffered to lessen the evangelic urgency that 'Now is the accepted time; now is the day of salvation' (2 Co 6²).

The hope of a final completion of the Divine purpose in the restoration from sin's dominion of all mankind must derive much of its force from a contemplation of the alternatives; from the difficulty of supposing a Divine purpose and will eternally active yet never attaining to its desire, or of conceiving of any human soul as eternally incapable of responding to the all-pervasive Love of God, or of thinking of any eternal felicity of the blessed which can be undisturbed by the knowledge of living souls abiding in a hopeless doom. Alleviations of the idea of eternal punishment such as that of 'Conditional Immortality' offend almost equally against the fundamental instincts of the human heart, which cannot think that the All-wise and All-loving has created any soul in His own image to prove but a waste and an abortion.

'Which else He made in vain—which must not be!'

Such thoughts are in the human intuition, and they are based upon the nature of God as made known to us in Christ Jesus, and upon the eternal Personality of Him 'who was dead, and is alive for evermore; and hath the keys of death and the unseen world' (Rev 1¹⁸). They are reinforced by the human love for its own kind, which at its highest finds voice in Browning (*Saul*):

'Would I fain in my impotent yearning do all for this man,
And dare doubt He alone shall not help him, who yet alone
can?'

And on these rests the conviction that 'faith in the exceeding grandeur of reality shall never be confounded' (Sir O. Lodge, *Life and Matter*).

LITERATURE.—The subject is treated, *in loc.*, by the following: various works on NT Theology; Salmond, *Christ. Doct. of Immortality*; Petavel, *The Problem of Immortality* (1892); Toy, *Judaism and Christianity*, ch. vii. (1892); Row, *Future Retribution*; Maurice, *Theological Essays*; R. H. Charles, *Eschatology*, chs. ix. x.; J. Fyfe, *The Hereafter* (1890); Wendt, *Teaching of Jesus*, Eng. tr. i. pp. 364–408, ii. pp. 340–374. W. R. Alger, *Critical History of the Doctrine of a Future Life*¹⁰ (1880), is critical from the point of view of a past generation, but contains, amid much strained and perverse exegesis, and consider-

able rhetoric, many illuminating suggestions in favour of a final Restoration. On the same or kindred lines, but with truer exegesis, are Farrar, *Eternal Hope* (1878), *Mercy and Judgment* (1881); Cox, *Salvator Mundi: Is Christ the Saviour of all Men?* (1877); Jukes, *The Second Death and the Restitution of all Things* (1888); Plumptre, *Spirits in Prison* (see pp. 193–204 for citation of divines, ancient and modern, in favour of Restoration); *Letters* of Erskine of Linlathen—one on 'Final Salvation of all.'   T. H. WRIGHT.

RESURRECTION OF CHRIST. — **1. St. Paul's summary of the Resurrection appearances** (1 Co 15) is, says Godet (*Com.* ii. 435), the most ancient and most official of the records we possess. If Harnack's chronology be made our basis (*Gesch. der Altchristl. Lit.* vol. ii. (i.) 236 ff.), our Lord's death was in A.D. 29 or 30; St. Paul's conversion in 30; his correspondence with Corinth, 53. His visit to St. Peter at Jerusalem would be in 33. Thus he had known this tradition for nearly 20 years, and recorded it within 23 years of the Resurrection. On St. Paul's list of the witnesses we note: —(1) That it is a list and not a narrative. It is the barest summary, expressed with the utmost conciseness (cf. *Cambr. Theol. Essays*, p. 331). (2) It is derived and not original (1 Co 15³ 'I received' [παρέλαβον], 'I delivered unto you' [παρέδωκα]). If we here possess a primitive tradition orally communicated to St. Paul by the older Apostles, then it would be uncritical to infer that St. Paul 'knows nothing' of any appearance which he does not record. (3) The order of the list is chronological. This is shown by the use of εἶτα, ἔπειτα: 'then to the Twelve; then . . . to above 500; then . . . to James; then to all the apostles.' (4) The purpose is not primarily apologetic (cf. *Cambridge Theol. Essays*, 395, 329, 330). The Resurrection of Christ was not disputed at Corinth. The introduction of the list here is due to that instinct for systematic completeness, that determination to go down to first principles, which is eminently characteristic of St. Paul, rather than to any apologist's desire to convince men who do not believe that Christ is risen. (5) The selection is evidently *official* (cf. Knowling, *Testimony of St. Paul*, p. 301)—St. Peter as the first of the Apostles, St. James head of the Church at Jerusalem. 'Peter and James were at the time of writing the two most prominent persons in the Christian Society, St. Paul himself not being excepted' (*Ch. Quart. Rev.*, Jan. 1906, p. 330). The same applies to the Apostles in a body. The other appearance is recorded for its numerical importance. Thus the omission of the Women from this official list is not surprising. It is noticeable that the Fourth Gospel, although recording the appearance to Mary Magdalene, yet omits it from the official enumeration (Jn 21¹⁴). Thus the Fourth Gospel supports St. Paul's procedure, and demonstrates that omission is not necessarily due to ignorance.

On St. Paul's list of the witnesses, see, further, *Ch. Quart. Rev.*, Jan. 1906, 327–331; Knowling, *Testimony of St. Paul*; Gess, *Das Dogma von Christi Person und Werk*, xvii.

2. The personal testimony of St. Paul to Christ's Resurrection.—A comparison of the three accounts of St. Paul's conversion in Ac 9. 22. 26, which may be respectively denoted A, B, and C, shows certain variations.

(1) The intervention of Ananias, contained in A and B, is omitted in C; the instruction given by him being in substance transferred in C to Christ. It may be, as Blass considers (*Act. Apost.* ix.), that the historic order is maintained in A and B rather than in C, since such instruction as to the Apostle's duty would come more naturally under calmer circumstances and at a later time. It should also be noted that of these three accounts the first is the historian's narrative in the course of the events, where Ananias would necessarily be mentioned. The second was spoken to the Jewish throng on the ascent to the Prætorium, where the mention of Ananias and his orthodoxy would be reassuring to the hearers (cf. Knowling, *op. cit.*). The third, spoken before the magistrates, omits him, because the reference would not in any degree strengthen the Apostle's case, nor be desirable on Ananias' account. Again, it is note-

worthy that the incident of Ananias is, as Blass says, separable from the main event. Its omission by St. Paul in 1 Cor. shows this. It does, however, entail the important loss of reference to St. Paul's baptism given in A and B. It may be psychologically difficult to separate Ananias' instructions from St. Paul's own reflexions. But this again is distinct from the momentous issue.

(2) The effect upon the attendants is recorded with variations. In A they are described as ἀκούοντες μὲν τῆς φωνῆς μηδένα δὲ θεωροῦντες. In B, τὴν δὲ φωνὴν οὐκ ἤκουσαν τοῦ λαλοῦντός μοι. In C the attendants are not mentioned. It is usually said that the distinction of case after ἀκούειν implies that the attendants heard the sound (genitive) but could not distinguish the substance (accusative) of the message (cf. Grimm-Thayer, Lex.).

But, taking the extreme case that these details cannot be reconciled, do they vitally alter the central affirmation? Is not some confusion between the effect on St. Paul and that upon the attendants very readily accounted for on the religious principle that receptiveness varies with spirituality? Zeller (followed by Pfleiderer, Ur-christentum, i. 61) has, indeed, made the most of these differences (Acts, vol. i. p. 287), on the ground that for the objective character of the appearance great importance must attach to the testimony of St. Paul's companions. But the essential points are perfectly clear; that the attendants were bewildered and confused by an external incident whose nature they evidently took for supernatural but could not further explain.

On the three narratives in Acts, see, further, Knowling, Testimony of St. Paul; Sabatier, L'apôtre Paul; Goguel, L'apôtre Paul et Jésus Christ; Chase, Credibility of Acts; Rackham, Acts.

So far as to St. Paul's personal testimony recorded in Acts. To this must be added the references in his Epistles. It is certainly remarkable that amid his courageous self-revelation no account of his own conversion is given in the Epistles. And yet any such account would obviously be necessary for his opponents rather than for his converts, who must have heard the story orally; and this is precisely what the allusions and inferences in the Epistles suggest. There are here three points to be remembered: (1) The external or objective character of the appearance outside Damascus; (2) the fact that this external appearance is not incompatible with intellectual preparation for the change; nor (3) with an inner revelation in the department of the intellect as to the significance and far-reaching character of the external revelation bestowed (cf. Maurice Goguel, L'apôtre Paul et Jésus Christ).

(a) Theologians were formerly disposed to confine the intellectual change in St. Paul to the period of reflexion subsequent to conversion. Modern writers place it chiefly in the period before. It may well have been in both. Consciousness of the impossibility of unaided compliance with the requirement of the moral ideal (Ro 7) may well have prepared the way for the acceptance of Christianity, although by no means necessarily even suggesting, still less involving, its truth. On this point the greatest caution is essential. We have no information. The elaborated hypotheses whereby St. Paul is supposed to have made the transition to Christianity in purely subjective ways are wonderful feats of critical ingenuity, but they have no necessary relation to history. What is certain is that he believed the transition to have been suddenly effected by the manifestation of the Risen Christ.

(b) Similarly with the question of the inner revelation of Christ within the mind of St. Paul (Gal 1[15, 16] 'to reveal his Son in me'). Because St. Paul received a mental enlightenment, it cannot possibly follow that he did not see an outward vision or hear a voice. Rather that which he heard and saw formed the external data of his inward thoughts and convictions. The careful distinction drawn by St. Paul between inner visions of the Lord (2 Co 12), as to which he cannot tell whether

they were in the body or out of the body, and the event appealed to in 1 Co 9[1] as the certificate of his Apostleship, show how vividly conscious he was of the external objective nature of that vision of the Risen Christ (see Goguel, p. 82). But that there was an inner revelation also as the result of the external vision is, of course, essential to the value of the vision. Indeed, it would not be easy to exaggerate the vastness of this inner revelation to St. Paul, provided always that space is left for the external circumstance which created it.

As to the external, objective character of St. Paul's vision of the Risen Christ, this and nothing less is required by the Apostle's language. 'The metaphor of an untimely birth, which he employs in regard to himself (1 Co 15[8]), implies a sudden, violent, abnormal change which brought him weak and immature into a new spiritual world' (Chase, Credibility, p. 72). Moreover, St. Paul places the appearance to himself in the same category with those to the Apostles in general (1 Co 15; cf. Gal 1[13, 14] and Lightfoot's paraphrase).

3. Evidence of the Evangelists.—The Synoptic problem must, of course, be studied elsewhere. Nor do our limits allow an analysis of the various documents. (1) The original of Mk., so far as we possess it, ends with the vacant grave, but no appearance of the Risen Master. [On the question of the last twelve verses of the present Mk. see above, p. 131 ff.]. (2. 3) But what the original Mk. no longer gives us is supplied by Mt. and Lk., who almost certainly wrote with Mk. before them; and whose agreements may partially supply the missing conclusion of the earliest narrative. To do full justice to the documents would require a careful analysis and comparison of the appearances given by Mt., Lk., and Jn., together with the existing conclusion to Mark.

From what source the distinctive features of the Resurrection narratives in Mt. and Lk. were derived is not known. Attention has often been drawn to their diversities. They are certainly difficult to harmonize. But the substantial identity as to the central fact is not less impressive because of the diversities. The peculiar difficulties as to locality will be considered presently.

(4) The existing conclusion of Mark.—'We may say with confidence,' writes Dr. Sanday (Criticism of the Fourth Gospel, p. 241), 'that its date is earlier than the year 140—whether we argue from the chronology of Aristion, its presumable author, or from its presence in the archetype of almost all extant MSS, or from the traces of it in writers so early as Justin and Irenæus.' 'It belongs at the latest,' says Dr. Swete, 'to the earlier sub-Apostolic age' (Apostles' Creed, p. 66). (See, further, Chase, Syriac Element in Codex Bezæ, 1893, pp. 153–157).

(5) The Fourth Gospel.—The value set on this evidence will vary with critical estimates of the Fourth Gospel, into which it is impossible to enter here. Suffice it to say that a very marked tendency exists in more recent writers to return to older views. So advanced a critic as Jülicher, for instance, dates the Gospel between A.D 100 and 110 (Introd. N.T. p. 401). In no case is reception or rejection more influenced by philosophic and theological presuppositions than here.

We note then that the documentary evidence, while certainly less than we might desire, is adequate for its purpose. Partial discrepancies are not only compatible with, they may be confirmatory of, substantial veracity (cf. Gwatkin, Gifford Lect. ii. 48).

4. Canonical as contrasted with Apocryphal Gospels.—The Canonical narratives form but a small portion of the early accounts of Jesus Christ. And it is important to consider why we lay exclusive stress upon the Four. The Canonical Gospels, as their name implies, cannot be regarded merely as documents; they are the property, and indeed the product, of a community, the Christian Church. The documentary evidence for the Resurrection requires to be supplemented by the evidence of the existence of the institution and its principles. The Church gave its recognition to certain Gospels, and refused it to others.

'It was not the prestige of an Apostolic name that made it canonical, for the "Gospel of Peter" was rejected. Great antiquity and respectful quotation by learned Church writers did not avail to include the "Gospel acc. to the Hebrews," nor did philosophical thought avail the document commonly called the "Oxyrhynchus Logia"' (Burkitt, *Gospel History and its Transmission*, p. 230).

What was the principle which led to their exclusion? What was it that the Four Gospels had which these had not? The answer manifestly is, that the contents of the Gospels called Canonical were in harmony with the principles of the Christian community which received them. The Church recognized the Four as possessing characteristics in which the others were more or less defective. 'And,' says Prof. Burkitt, 'it should not be forgotten that those of the non-canonical Gospels which we know enough of to pass judgment upon, show a sensible inferiority' (p. 259). 'Marcion's Gospel is in every way inferior to Luke, and the Gospel of Peter to either of the Synoptic accounts of the Passion' (*ib.*). Their extravagant wonder-workings and obviously fictitious character impress readers of any school of thought (cf. Pfleiderer, *Urchristentum*, ii. 121).

5. The empty grave.—This is witnessed to by (1) *the Evangelists*; cf. the original narrative of Mk. (16¹⁻⁸). 'There is no reason to doubt,' says O. Holtzmann, 'that the women could not carry out their purpose [of embalming the body], simply because they found the grave empty' (*Life of Jesus*, p. 497). According to the tradition accepted by St. Paul, the first manifestation was on the third day, and therefore in Jerusalem. This agrees with the Apostles' visit to the grave, which should be contrasted with their visit with our Lord to the grave of Lazarus. That the grave was empty, would also seem to be required by Jewish contemporary ideas on resurrection (cf. Dn 12²).

Considerable thought has of recent years been bestowed on St. John's description of the manner in which the grave-clothes were lying. As far back as Chrysostom's time, attention was called to the fact that myrrh was a drug which adheres so closely to the body that the grave-clothes would not easily be removed (in *Joan. Hom.* lxxxv). Cyril of Alexandria suggested that, from the manner in which the grave-clothes lay folded, the Apostles were led to the idea of resurrection: 'Ex involutis linteaminibus resurrectionem colligunt,' as the Latin version renders it (Migne, vii. 683). Latham's theory is that the word ἐντετυλιγμένον implies that the napkin which had been wrapped around the sacred head still partially retained the annular form thus given it (*The Risen Master*, p. 43). The grave-clothes still marked the spot where the body had rested, and still retained the general outline of the human form (cf. p. 50). If this interpretation be correct, that St. John saw the napkin which had been about the head of Jesus, not lying with the linen clothes, but apart, twisted round, away by itself, then the suggestion would be not only the emptiness of the grave, but that 'that which died had passed away into that which lived' (Richmond, *Gospel of the Rejection*, p. 109).

On the evidence, so far, to the empty grave, we are constrained to say that the weight of the Evangelists' united testimony is so strong that it cannot with any justice be rejected. (For critical acknowledgment of this see *Our Lord's Resurrection* in Oxf. Libr. Pract. Theol. p. 87 f.).

(2) But it has been asserted that, whatever the Evangelists might think, at any rate *St. Paul's* theory of the Resurrection was independent of all interest in the empty grave (O. Holtzmann, *Life of Jesus*). His theory of the spiritual body, so it is said, does not require the resurrection of the material elements of the buried corpse. And it is further remarked that St. Paul, in his evidences of the Resurrection, not only makes no appeal to the emptiness of the grave, but actually makes no reference to the subject at all in his teaching. This supposed indifference of St. Paul to the question of the empty sepulchre is based partly on the character of his theology, and partly on his omission of any reference to the fact. But here we must remember St. Paul's antecedents. He was educated in the principles of the Pharisees, and doubtless held the prevalent theory of physical resurrection. As Schmiedel truly says, 'His theology came into being only after his conversion to Christianity. When he first came to know of Jesus as risen, he was still a Jew, and therefore conceived of resurrection at all in no other way than as reanimation of the body' (*EBi* iv. 4059); cf. 1 Co 15³·⁴. The suggestion in the term 'rose' (ἐγείρειν) as applied to the dead is that death is compared with sleep, and the resurrection out of the former to the awakening out of the latter. Moreover, the fact of the burial implies that the Resurrection was not merely of one who died, but also of one who was buried. Thus resurrection refers to an experience affecting the body, and not to an isolated experience of the soul; cf. Ro 8¹¹, where resurrection is described as quickening our mortal bodies. Thus the grave of Jesus cannot be considered by St. Paul otherwise than as empty (see Schmöller in *SK*, 1894, p. 669). St. Paul believed in 'a highly objective resurrection, including a bodily somewhat, though of a non-fleshly order' (V. Bartlet, *Apost. Age*, p. 4; Riggenbach, p. 7).

(3) There is the further evidence of the application to Jesus Christ of the passage in *the sixteenth Psalm* (16¹⁰): 'Neither wilt thou suffer thy Holy One to see corruption' (Ac 2²⁷). St. Peter sees an exact parallel between this language of the Psalm and the physical experience of the dead Christ. It is a reference to the Resurrection. 'He [David] seeing this before, spake of the resurrection of Christ, that his soul was not left in hell, neither did his flesh see corruption' (v.³¹). No contrast could be greater than between this and the ordinary experience as exemplified in David. David manifestly saw corruption. 'He is both dead and buried, and his sepulchre is with us unto this day' (v.²⁹). Corruption its sad work had done. The foul engendered worm had fed on the flesh of 'the anointed one.' But St. Peter's contention is that, in the case of Christ, the physical frame saw no corruption. The fact of the empty grave is here involved, and is, moreover, thrown out as a challenge in the very city where our Lord was buried; and that within six weeks of the burial! It has well been asked: Was not St. Peter disturbed by the misgiving that the hearers might interrupt him with the crushing remark—We know where he was buried, and that corruption has begun its task (Ihmels, *Die Auferstehung Jesu Christi*, 1906, p. 26). The whole argument of St. Peter would be absolutely worthless, if any could refute the major premiss of the empty grave.

(4) The emptiness of the grave is acknowledged by *opponents* as well as affirmed by disciples. The narrative of the guards attempts to account for the fact as a fraudulent transaction (Mt 28¹¹⁻¹⁵). 'But this Jewish accusation against the Apostles takes for granted that the grave was empty. What was certain was that the grave was empty. What was needed was an explanation.' So far as the present writer is aware, this acknowledgment by the Jews that the grave was vacated extends to all subsequent Jewish comments on the point.

Here, for instance, is a 12th cent. version of the empty grave circulated by the Jewish anti-Christian propaganda. The story is that when the queen heard that the elders had slain Jesus and had buried Him, and that He was risen again, she ordered them within three days to produce the body or forfeit their lives. 'Then spake Judas, "Come and I will show you the man whom ye seek: for it was I who took the fatherless from his grave. For I feared lest his disciples should steal him away, and I have hidden him in my garden and led a waterbrook over the place."' And the story explains how the body was produced (*Toledoth Jesu*; see Baring Gould, *Lost and Hostile Gospels*, p. 88). It is needless to remark that this daring assertion of the actual production of the body is a mediæval fabrication, but it is an assertion very necessary to account for facts, when the emptiness of the grave was admitted and yet the Resurrection denied.

Substantially, then, St. Matthew's narrative is corroborated by the admissions made by opponents of Christ. That the disciples removed the body was a saying commonly reported among the Jews 'until this day' (Mt 28^{15}). And this admission by opponents is enough to show that the evidence for the empty grave was 'too notorious to be denied' (*Cambr. Theol. Essays*, p. 336).

(5) The grave, then, was assuredly empty. But *the emptiness of the grave does not demonstrate resurrection.* The alternatives are that this was a human work or a Divine. Either somebody removed the corpse, or the Almighty raised the dead. The momentousness of the alternative it is scarcely possible to exaggerate. The ultimate decision must be largely influenced by the entire range of a man's presuppositions. Two antagonistic conceptions of God and the world and mankind meet at the grave of Christ. It will always be possible to construct naturalistic hypotheses to account for the vacant grave, but it is impossible to conceal the rationalistic assumptions upon which such constructions are based. We may here quote a recent and extremely independent critic.

'It is admitted that with the Resurrection the body of Jesus also had vanished from the grave, and it will be impossible to account for this on natural grounds' (Wellhausen, *Das Ev. Matt.* p. 150).

(6) If we keep to the evidence, it is certain that *the empty grave was not the cause of the disciples' faith.* According to the Evangelists, the fact of the empty grave created no belief in the Resurrection in the case either of Mary Magdalene, or of the women, or of St. Peter. The only exception, and that under conditions of peculiar reticence and reserve, was St. John.

'Thus the oft repeated expression that the faith of the Christian Church is founded on an empty grave is one which requires explanation. The Easter faith did not really spring from the empty grave, but from the self-manifestation of the risen Lord' (S. Simpson, *Our Lord's Resurrection*, p. 103).

6. The locality of the appearances.—The narratives present us with a double series of manifestations of the Risen Lord, distinguished by locality: the Judæan series and the Galilæan series.

(1) Any true criticism should start from the data of the *original Mark.* According to this (16^{7}), not only did the women visit the grave on Easter Day and therefore were still present in Jerusalem, but the message sent to the disciples, 'He goeth *before* you into Galilee,' implies the presence of the disciples also in Jerusalem on that day. Accordingly the theory that 'they all forsook him and fled' (14^{50}) means fled direct home to Galilee, is refuted by the implications of the same Evangelist (cf. Rördam, *Hibbert Journ.*, July 1905, p. 781). On the other hand, the direction 'he goeth before you into *Galilee*' would seem to indicate that the lost conclusion of this Gospel must have contained a description of an appearance in Galilee. This may be true. But what we cannot determine is whether any Judæan appearance was also recorded.

(2) *Mt.* (28^{9}) relates that the first appearance took place to the women near Jerusalem, and then adds a manifestation to the Eleven in Galilee.

(3) *Lk.* contains an exclusively Judæan series of manifestations. He 'knows nothing' of appearances in Galilee. The significance of this must depend on St. Luke's worth as a historian. Harnack has recently exhibited a profound mistrust of the Lukan account (*Luke the Physician*). St.

Mark, who is assumed to have recorded nothing but a Galilæan series, is endorsed as correct. On the other hand, the high value of St. Luke as a historian is vigorously asserted by so critical a scholar as Ramsay, who came to the study greatly prejudiced against him. He places the author of the Acts 'among historians of the first rank' (*Paul the Traveller*, pp. 4 ff., 8, 14). Then, further, St. Luke cannot possibly, as St. Paul's companion, have been ignorant of the Jerusalem tradition. How could he conceivably have written a version of the Resurrection manifestation which the Jerusalem Church could not receive? It is quite possible that he derived his information as to the 40 days at Jerusalem itself. St. Paul gives no locality, but the natural view is that he considered the first manifestation to have occurred in Jerusalem. Is it possible that St. Luke's exclusive interest in the Judæan series is due to the purpose for which his Gospel was written? Writing for Greek believers, it would be natural that he should concentrate attention upon the Holy City. Is it not possible conversely that St. Matthew, as Palestinian and Jerusalemite, gives for that very reason the more distant and less known manifestations in Galilee?

Harnack seems reduced to the singular position that the only evidence for the Galilæan series is St. Mark's conclusion, and that does not exist. For he lays all stress, for St. Mark's value, on St. Matthew as his copyist. He depreciates the independence of St. Luke and rejects the authority of St. John. Thus, after all, the testimony to a Galilæan series is reduced to a solitary witness whose testimony is lost.

The first impression derived from Lk.—that the Ascension took place on the same day as the Resurrection—is partly corrected on further consideration of the Gospel itself. For there does not seem sufficient time to crowd all these events into a single day. Emmaus is reached towards evening when the day was far spent (24^{29}). The meal in the town must have taken some little time. And Emmaus is threescore furlongs (v.^{13})=7 miles from Jerusalem. The whole journey would take the greater part of two hours. Then follows the conversation with the two and the Eleven. Afterwards, Christ Himself appears and gives them an instruction in the Scriptures—the Law and Prophets and the Psalms (v.^{44}). This must have taken a considerable time. Finally is placed the journey to Bethany and the Ascension. This could scarcely be before midnight. Yet certainly (as Rördam says) the account gives the impression that the event was conceived as happening in the daytime (*Hibbert Journ.*, July 1905, p. 774). If the incident has suffered condensation, the difficulty is at once explained.

In this connexion it is worth noting that Ramsay describes St. Luke as deficient in the sense of time. 'It would be quite impossible from Acts alone to acquire any idea of the lapse of time' (*Paul the Trav.* p. 18). And the fault is not individual. It is the fault of his age. St. Luke 'had studied the sequence of events carefully, and observes it in his arrangement minutely,' but 'he gives no measure of the lapse of time implied in a sentence, a clause, or even a word. He dismisses ten years in a breath, and devotes a chapter to a single incident.' Thus 'Luke's style is compressed to the highest degree; and he expects a great deal from the reader. He does not attempt to sketch the surroundings and set the whole scene like a picture before the reader; he states the bare facts that seem to him important, and leaves the reader to imagine the situation' (p. 17). These are said to be characteristics of the writer of the Acts. And they will explain some of the difficulties in his narrative of the Resurrection.

But it is asked, Since our Lord's prediction was that He would meet the disciples in Galilee and the angel's direction was in accordance with the same, is it not contrary to the logic of the situation, as well as to the original command, that appearances should occur in Jerusalem?—To this difficulty Rördam's reply is:

'This apparently insoluble difficulty is very easily explained. We learn (24$^{11.24}$) that nobody believed the women's tale, and even those who had listened most to their words returned disappointed after having seen the empty grave. This fully explains why appearances followed in Jerusalem. For that such sceptics would not go to Galilee to meet Christ is obvious. Therefore, just as the original story was that Christ appeared to the women, because they doubted the *angel's* words, so the narrative goes on to relate how Christ had to appear to the apostles and the disciples together with them, as they did not believe the *women's* words ' (p. 778).

7. The nature of Christ's resurrection body.—

(1) *The statements of the Evangelists are commonly classified as of two kinds* : (*a*) Those which exhibit a purely materialistic view, the most impressive instance being Lk 24³⁹ ' Handle me and see : for a spirit hath not flesh and bones, as ye see me have.' (*b*) An immaterial series, illustrated in His vanishing and reappearing, in the difficulty of recognition and the alterations of form.

One school of criticism here endeavours to impose a dilemma, bidding us select between the two views, on the ground that it is impossible to accept both. Keim, for instance, says, ' There is a capricious alternating between a subtle and a gross corporeity . . . which is self-contradictory' (*Jesus of Nazara*, vi. 340). We may, however, decline the dilemma, and declare ourselves prepared to accept both series of statements, as forming parts of a perfectly conceivable and intelligible conception. This ' alternating between a subtle and gross corporeity,' to adopt Keim's expression, is, to begin with, profoundly original. The contemporary Pharisaic idea of resurrection had no subtlety about it. It was grossly and even repulsively animal. The martyred Maccabees expect to repossess the same physical organs and limbs in the same condition as on earth. This is expressed with a coarseness which cannot be mistaken in 2 Mac 7¹¹ and 14⁴⁶ (see also Gröbler in *SK*, 1879, p. 682 ff.). It is resuscitation of the same body to the same estate as before. The Book of Enoch, it is true, speaks of the resurrection state as resembling that of the angels, but it describes the latter in such physical and animal terms as to deprive the resemblance of much value (cf. Enoch 51⁴ with 15¹). The description of ' revealing every thing that is hidden in the depths of the earth, and those who have been destroyed by the desert, and those who have been devoured by the fish of the sea and by the beasts, that they may return and stay themselves on the day of the Elect One ' (61⁵, ed. Charles, p. 160), is equally suggestive of a grossly material view. The exact antithesis to the Pharisaic conception, which was prevalent in the Apostolic age, was the Greek conception of emancipation from the body and continued existence as pure spirit. See preceding article.

The view given by the Evangelists is independent of both of the above conceptions. It certainly possesses a strongly materialistic side. Yet with equal certainty it is no mere resuscitation of the animal frame. It is anything rather than a return to life under the same conditions. The broadest distinction is drawn by the Evangelists between the revivification of Lazarus and the Resurrection of Christ. Lazarus is obviously represented as granted a re-entrance into earthly life under the same conditions as before, to become again the possessor of a corruptible organism, subject to the same fleshly necessities, and destined again to expire in a second experience of physical death (cf. Kruger, *Auferstehung*, p. 21 f.).

(2) *The Pauline conception of the risen body.*—St. Paul's doctrine is condensed into the two crucial phrases, a ' psychical ' body and a ' pneumatical ' body. The psychical body is the organ and instrument of the animal force ; the pneumatical body is the organ and instrument whose vitalizing principle is the spiritual personality. The psychical body is that which discharges the functions of animal self-maintenance and reproduction. It is the organ adapted to life under terrestrial conditions. The pneumatical is the organ adapted to life under non-terrestrial conditions. It is the best self-expression of spirit (*Our Lord's Resurrection*, p. 164 f.). Now, St. Paul's doctrine firmly maintains two points, of which the first is *identity* between the body which died and the body which rose. This is implied in all that we have seen of St. Paul's interest in the empty grave ; in his illustration of the relation between the two states of the body as akin to that between the seed and the perfected plant. It is further taught by his

description of his vision of Christ under the idea of Christ's Resurrection.

But if, on the one hand, St. Paul affirms identity, he no less emphatically affirms a *distinction* between the characteristics and qualities of the body on earth and beyond it. ' Flesh and blood cannot inherit the kingdom of God' (1 Co 15⁵⁰). ' Thou sowest not that body that shall be ' (v.³⁷). The vastness of the distinction is so strongly asserted in the term the ' spiritual body,' that the identity might almost seem to be, what it never is, really obliterated. But the risen body of Christ was spiritual, ' not because it was less than before material, but because in it matter was wholly and finally subjugated to spirit, and not to the exigencies of physical life. Matter no longer restricted Him or hindered. It had become the pure and transparent vehicle of spiritual purpose' (Gore, *Body of Christ*, p. 127).

(3) A comparison of the Pauline doctrine with the Evangelists' statements does not lead, then, to the conclusion that their principles diverge. There is an extreme improbability that St. Luke, for instance, considering his relation to St. Paul, should be in hopeless contradiction with the Apostle's principles. But there is no manner of contradiction. The Evangelists are concerned with the historic manifestations of the Risen Christ, St. Paul with the intrinsic nature of the resurrection body. The former describe the body of Christ during the temporary periods in which its presence was ascertainable by the senses ; the latter considers the body as it is in itself. The former say, This is what we touched and saw, and our hands have handled ; the latter is concerned with the profound inquiry as to what constitutes the nature of the risen body. Thus the aspects are complementary, not antagonistic.

(4) If we attempt, then, to formulate the Christian conception of the nature of Christ's risen body, we shall affirm that, according to Christian doctrine, man consists of the personality or self together with a vehicle of self-manifestation. This vehicle is material. Under terrestrial conditions this vehicle must possess characteristics, properties, organs, adapted to such conditions. Otherwise it would be no self-expression at all. Such was the psychical body of Christ. But at death the self passed out of terrestrial conditions, leaving the fleshly condition of the body behind, but by no means continuing bodiless. The self is re-endowed with a vehicle of self-expression which is still material, only under the complete dominion of spirit. The self now exists under heavenly conditions. The fleshly organism would be impossible there, because hopelessly unadaptable to such conditions. Its whole system, construction, solidity, its parts and organs, its methods of self-maintenance, would be worse than meaningless under non-terrestrial conditions. We should suppose that the pneumatical or risen body of Christ was, in its normal state, as an ideally perfect utterance of spirit, imperceptible to the human senses as we now possess them. But the capacities of this ideally perfect self-expression are so great that it can manifest itself to persons living under terrestrial conditions. And we believe that this pneumatical body of Christ did temporarily assume such conditions of tangibility and visibility as to bring His ' subtle corporeity,' for evidential and instructive purposes, within range of our ' grosser corporeity.'

This leads to the difficult subject of the relation between the psychical and the pneumatical body of Christ. That they are related, in the Apostolic conception, is clear. But the question is, To what extent? Does the existence of the pneumatical body require the disappearance of the psychical ? or can they coexist? Can the one remain intact within the grave while the other is declared to have risen? Is the emptiness of the grave in Joseph's garden essential to belief in Christ's transition into the pneumatical estate? Since it is impossible for us to determine the precise relation between these two conditions of the bodily life, we must be prepared for the possibility of the co-existence of the psychical and the pneumatical body. Would it therefore follow that the emptiness of the grave in Joseph's garden is indifferent to Christian thought? No, not in the very least. We must surely here distinguish between the Resurrection of Christ and the resurrection of mankind. It was clearly necessary for evidential purposes that the risen Lord should reappear within a terrestrial environment, and that for the same reason His grave should be vacated. Belief in the reality of His Resurrection in presence of the corpse was to that age absolutely impossible.

Max Müller expressed years ago a regret that the Jews buried and did not burn their dead. For in that case, he thought, the Christian idea of the Resurrection would have remained far more spiritual. And the question has been quite recently asked, What kind of Resurrection would your gospel have exhibited if the body of Jesus had been cremated? Max Müller's regret is more than justified by the deeply materialistic conceptions which have heavily burdened the Christian mind. But it has no weight whatever in view of the teaching of St. Paul. The suggested cremation of the body of Jesus would not in the slightest degree have affected the Pauline conception of the pneumatical body. Nor would it have removed the necessity for visible and tangible manifestations under terrestrial conditions. Christ must in any case have reappeared with features and form as of old, whether His body had been buried or burned. The scars must have reappeared upon it. The facts of dissolution of ordinary human bodies have not altered the ordinary belief in their physical reappearance in the Resurrection. The disintegration of the body and its return to dust, the cremation of the martyrs, did not prevent mediæval discussions whether one who died in childhood would appear full-grown in the future life. The Maccabees, at any rate, knew nothing of the Resurrection of Christ, but that did not prevent their holding the grossest ideas of a resurrection state. 'As for cremation, Christian reverence shrinks from discussing the cremation of our Lord's sacred body,' says Dr. Liddon ; 'but cremation, had it taken place, could have made no difference except in the sphere of imagination' (Liddon, Easter Sermons, i. 111).

If the account given by Sir Oliver Lodge, in the Hibbert Journal (Jan. 1906), of Christianity and science may be viewed as representative of modern thought, it would seem clear that contemporary thought ought not to have much difficulty in accepting the Pauline doctrine of the resurrection body. The question is, What is the relation between the spiritual personality and the material side of human existence? 'It is plain,' he says, 'that for our present mode of apprehending the universe a material vehicle is essential' (p. 318). The only evidence of the existence of spiritual activity is the manifestation of that activity through matter. We are manifested to each other through the medium of the senses. 'Now,' argues the writer, 'this dependence of the spiritual on a vehicle for manifestation is not likely to be a purely temporary condition : it is probably a sign or sample of something which has an eternal significance, a representation of some permanent truth' (p. 319). 'To suppose that our experience of the necessary and fundamental connexion between the two things—the something which we know as mind and the something which is now represented by matter—has no counterpart or enlargement in the actual scheme of the universe, as it really exists, is needlessly to postulate confusion and instrumental deception' (p. 319). Consequently the conclusion is that, 'though it by no means follows that mind is dependent on matter as we know it, it will probably be still by means of something akin to matter—something which can act as a vehicle and represent it in the same sort of way that matter represents it now—that it will hereafter be manifested' (p. 320). Now, certainly this statement of the relation of mind to matter, of personality to the vehicle of self-manifestation, is one which St. Paul would find no reason to dispute. As the writer himself recognizes, 'This probability or possibility may be regarded as one form of statement of an orthodox Christian doctrine' (p. 320). Such advances of modern thought towards the Pauline conception are as hopeful as they are significant. 'What is wanted,' he adds, 'to make definite our thoughts of the persistent existence of what we call our immortal part, is simply the persistent power of manifesting itself to friends, i.e. to persons with whom we are in sympathy, by means as plain and substantial in that order of existence as the body was here' (p. 322). 'We may surmise that any immortal part must have the power of constructing for itself a suitable vehicle of manifestation, which is the essential meaning of the term "body"' (p. 323).

For the nature of the resurrection body see Goulburn, Bampton Lectures ; Skrine, Contemp. Rev., Dec. 1904, 870.

8. The sayings of the Risen Master are most significant. Their *manner* is perfectly distinct from that of the ministry. What Keim (*Jesus of Nazara*, vi. 354) describes as the 'simple, solemn, almost lifeless, cold, unfamiliar character of the manifestations,' calls attention to the striking aloofness and uncarthliness of the Easter tone. Familiarity is altered into distance and awful dignity. Yet with this difference, which is inevitaoie, if the circumstances are historic, the Personality is just the same. And as with their manner, so with their *substance*. They occupy, very marvellously, an intermediate position between the teaching of the ministry which they presuppose, and the teaching of the Apostles which they account for and explain.

9. Christ's Resurrection and modern thought.— *Non-Christian explanations of Christ's Resurrection.*—There are only two ultimate explanations possible : either the event was the action of God, which is the Christian explanation ; or else it must be accounted for within purely earthly and human limits. Rejection of the Christian or supernatural account leaves the necessity of providing a naturalistic explanation ; otherwise there would always be a danger that the supernatural, although cast out on principle, would nevertheless return again. Non-Christian theories of Christ's Resurrection form a series. No one has summarized them better than Keim (vi. 327 ff.).

(1) There was the theory, now quite obsolete, which denied Christ's death. He fainted away on the cross, and recovered in the grave. The valuable point in this theory is its recognition that the Apostles did really see their Lord alive again as a solid objective fact confronting them. Its monstrously irrational character lies in its impossible assumption that a half-dead form, with difficulty brought back to life, leading an exhausted existence, and finally dying over again, could ever have inspired in His adherents triumphant faith in Him as a risen conqueror and Son of God. The well-known sentences of Strauss have effectually disposed of this miserable fabrication, with all the wretched immoralities which it included. It is, says Réville, 'un tissu d'invraisemblances matérielles et morales' (ii. 455).

(2) Another theory was that the body was secretly removed from the grave—either by opponents or by friends. Imagination hovers between Pilate, or the Sanhedrists, or Joseph of Arimathæa, or the gardener, or Mary Magdalene. Of the attempt to account for the empty grave as an imposture, Keim justly remarks : 'All these assumptions are repellent and disgraceful ; they show that the holy conviction of the apostles and the first Christians . . . has not in the slightest degree influenced the hardened minds of such critics' (p. 325). This theory also has passed away. Critics, says Keim, have left off seeking an explanation from external facts.

(3) But there is still a world of mental facts. The naturalistic explanations of to-day are sought through psychology. There is the Vision hypothesis—a self-generated appearance, the product of reflexion on the uniqueness of the Personality. Jesus' followers, studying the Scriptures, came to the conclusion that it belonged to the vocation of the Messiah to pass through suffering to glory. From the principle, 'He must live,' they passed involuntarily to the assertion, 'He does live,' and to the further assertion, 'We have seen Him' ! Thus they took a leap from a conclusion of the intellect to a fact of history. Keim's criticism is that reflexion requires time. Its advocates postulate a year—ten years. But the Apostolic evidence concurs in asserting that the interval between the death and the belief in the Resurrection was exceedingly brief. Strauss himself gave up the theory, and adopted another. 'Not so much by way of

reflexion, it is now said, as by the quicker road of the heart, of the force of imagination, and of strong nervous excitement, the disciples attained to belief in the living Messiah' (p. 334). The invincible Jesus hovered before their minds (p. 343). When Mohammed died, his adherents swore to decapitate any one who dared to say that the Prophet had expired (p. 344). In reality Jesus was not dead to the disciples, since they had witnessed neither His Passion nor death nor burial. Back in Galilee the old associations revived, far from the disasters and the graves of Jerusalem—unbounded excitement, intensified by abstinence from food and by the feverish moods of the evening, caused the limits of the outer and inner world to disappear. They thought they saw and heard externally, while they only saw and heard within. Martineau adopted something of this subjective theory of emotion and reflexion combined. It is the most popular non-Christian explanation of the day. But Keim deliberately rejects it.

Keim admits that the Apostolic age was full of more or less self-generated human visions. But if these visions had been the same in kind as the appearances of the Risen Christ, St. Paul would certainly not have closed his list with the fifth or sixth manifestation. Why does the Apostle consider the manifestation to himself as last of a series (ἔσχατον, 1 Co 15^8), obviously last of its kind, carefully differentiating it from the visions which may have come either to himself or to others? 'Having made such a sharp and clean division, it is to be taken as proved that there lay between the first 5 or 6 appearances and the later often-repeated visions such a great and broad gulf of time, and indeed of character, as rendered it impossible to reckon the latter appearances with the former' (p. 353).

A vision of departed persons does not necessarily imply their resurrection. If Moses and Elijah were seen at the Transfiguration of Christ, did the disciples infer their resurrection? Contemporary belief in the Apostolic age had assumed that patriarch and prophet and saint of OT times lived on in Paradise, but this did not involve belief in their resurrection. Visions were perfectly compatible with the continuance of the dead body in the grave, and no belief in their resurrection would ensue. Why then did the Apostle, having seen Christ after His death, affirm His Resurrection (cf. Schmöller in SK, 1894, p. 689)? Was it not because this 'seeing' Him was consciously different from the seeing in a dream, or from any kind of seeing except one involving physical identity? The idea of resurrection introduces an after-death experience as it concerns the body. It affirms that that which rose is also, however altered, that which died.

Separating, then, the ordinary visions of the Apostolic age from those decisive earlier appearances of Jesus, the question is, says Keim, Were those visions of the Risen Jesus merely self-generated natural products explicable by psychology? This, he replies, is 'contradicted first by the evidently simple, solemn, almost lifeless, cold, unfamiliar character of the manifestations.' 'There are reserve and reticence in the face of the strange phenomenon. There is no trace of a happy, sweet, prolonged repose in the bosom of him who is again endowed with life and love.' And secondly, a merely subjective explanation becomes 'still more glaringly inadequate' when we consider the abrupt cessation of the appearances. Advocates of the Vision theory have consistently postulated an extended duration of time, years during which the appearances were reiterated. 'This is as true with regard to the hypothesis as it is false and frivolous with regard to the Apostolic account' (p. 356). 'There was no host of appearances, no exuberance, no indescribable irregularity, no violent transition.' 'Just when fervid minds are beginning to grow fanatical, the fanaticism absolutely and entirely ceases.' And thirdly, the immediate result of the visions is vigorous practical activity. Mere psychological phenomena do not move this way. 'The spirits that men call up are not so quickly laid' (p. 357). 'If, therefore, there was actually an early or immediate transition from the visions to a calm self-possession, and to a self-possessed energy, then the visions did not proceed from self-generated visionary over-excitement and fanatical agitation among the multitude' (p. 358).

Keim's judgment, then, upon the Vision theory, as a whole, is as follows : 'All these considerations compel us to admit that the theory which has recently become the favourite one is only an hypothesis which, while it explains something, leaves the main fact unexplained, and, indeed, subordinates what is historically attested to weak and untenable views' (p. 358).

(4) Keim then comes to his own explanation. 'If the visions are not something humanly generated or self-generated, if they are not blossom and fruit of an illusion-producing over-excitement, if they are not something strange and mysterious, if they are directly accompanied by astonishingly clear perceptions and resolves, then there still remains one originating source, hitherto unmentioned, namely, God and the glorified Christ' (p. 361). Keim accord-

ingly propounds a theory of *objective* Vision created by Christ Himself. 'If the power that produces the vision comes, as according to our view it does, entirely from without, and the subjective seeing is merely the reflex form of what is objective, the immediate cessation of the seeing and of the will to see, as soon as the operating power ceases to operate, becomes perfectly intelligible.' 'Even the corporeal appearance may be granted to those who are afraid of losing everything unless they have this plastic representation for their thought and their faith' (p. 362). Thus, according to this view, the Resurrection manifestations are a God-created message of victory. To quote Keim's oft-quoted expression, they are 'a telegram from heaven,' an evidence given by Christ Himself and by the power of God.

This objective Vision theory, although far beneath the Christian conviction, is nevertheless a very remarkable approximation towards it. It is a most significant recognition of the inadequate character of all purely subjective explanations of the Apostles' belief. It acknowledges a God-created reality in the Easter faith. The theories of fraud and fiction and self-delusion are hereby deliberately set aside. The Almighty produced the Apostles' faith.

On the objective Vision theory see, further, Steude, *Auferstehung*, p. 99 ; Lotze, *Microcosmos*, ii. 480 (Eng. tr.).

The ultimate reasons for rejecting the Resurrection evidence are not historical. As Sabatier truly says, 'Even if the differences were perfectly reconciled, or even did not exist at all, men who will not admit the miraculous would none the less decisively reject the witness. As Zeller frankly acknowledges, their rejection is based on a philosophic theory, and not on historic considerations' (*L'Apôtre Paul*, p. 42). Strauss long ago fully admitted that 'the origin of that faith in the disciples is fully accounted for if we look upon the Resurrection of Jesus, as the Evangelists describe it, as an external miraculous occurrence' (*New Life*, i. 399). Nothing can be more genuine than Strauss' acknowledgment that he was controlled by *a priori* considerations, to which the fact of a resurrection was inadmissible ; cf. p. 397 :—

'Here, then, we stand on that decisive point where, in the presence of the accounts of the miraculous Resurrection of Jesus, we either acknowledge the inadmissibility of the natural and historical view of the life of Jesus, and must consequently retract all that precedes and give up our whole undertaking, or pledge ourselves to make out the possibility of the results of these accounts, i.e. the origin of the belief in the Resurrection of Jesus without any correspondingly miraculous fact.'

This is his conscious, deliberate undertaking—to give an explanation of the evidence on the presupposition of a certain view of the universe. It invariably amounts to this. At the grave in Joseph's garden two antagonistic world-theories confront each other (cf. Ihmels, *Auferstehung*, p. 27 ; Luthardt, *Glaubenslehre*). Spinoza, it has been said, could not believe in the actual Resurrection of Jesus, because such belief would have compelled him to abandon his theory of the universe. Obviously the pantheist must account for the manifestation on naturalistic principles.

Those who are anxious to dissociate religion from facts will naturally resent the position which Christianity ascribes to Christ's Resurrection. The relation between eternal truth and historic incidents cannot, of course, be treated in the limits at our disposal. But it must be remembered that a religion of Incarnation cannot possibly be dissociated from the facts of history. The objection, therefore, to the connexion between doctrine and history is fundamentally an objection to the whole principle of an external and specialized revelation, or to a progressive revelation which culminates in Divine personal entrance into history and self-manifestation within its limits (see Gwatkin's *Gifford Lectures*).

Similarly, the attitude of individuals towards the evidence is affected by their conception of the relation of body and soul. . There are, says Grützmacher (*l.c. inf.* p. 120), ultimately three conceptions. Either body and soul are both integral portions of a complete humanity; or man is only body, of which the soul is nothing but a transient function; or man is only soul, and the body is its entanglement and its prison. Of these three theories, says the same writer, the last is the least congenial to modern thought. Psychology is strenuous in its insistence on the intimate and necessary relationship of soul and body (p. 121). The second theory is materialism pure and simple; but its unsatisfying character is to modern thought sufficiently obvious. There remains, in the long run, only the first conception, which places upon the body a very high value indeed. Immortality without embodiment is not a theory which harmonizes with the deepest reflexions of the day.

10. The Apostolic teaching on the meaning of Christ's Resurrection. — (1) *Evidential as to His Messiahship.* — According to the prevalent interpretation of Dt 21²³, adopted by the LXX, 'cursed of God is every one that is hanged upon a tree' (cf. Jos. *Ant.* IV. viii. 6), the crucifixion of Jesus had, in Jewish contemporary thought, finally condemned Him in the sight of God and man. 'To a Jew the cross was infinitely more than an earthly punishment of unutterable suffering and shame; it was a revelation that on the crucified there rested the extreme malediction of the wrath of God. The idea was no theological refinement. It could not but be present to the mind of every Jew who knew the Law. Within a few years (1 Co 12³) it was formulated in a creed of unbelief—ἀνάθεμα Ἰησοῦς. It found expression in the name by which in later days the Lord was known among the Jews—הַתָּלוּי, "the hanged one"' (Chase, *Credibility of Acts*, p. 149). '"Whom ye slew, hanging him on a tree" (Ac 5³⁰). Here was a public, an impressive, a final attestation of what Jesus of Nazareth was in the sight of God. Here was an end' (p. 150). There could be but one conclusion. Now here are appreciated the force and the meaning of the Resurrection. If 'the God of our fathers raised up Jesus' (Ac 5³⁰), then it was clear that the estimate inevitable from the hanging upon a tree had been mistaken, and must be reversed; that earth's rejected was God's accepted; then it was possible to believe of this Crucified One, 'Him hath God exalted to be a Prince and a Saviour' (Ac 5³¹).

Thus, on the basis of the Resurrection, St. Peter describes Jesus of Nazareth as Lord and Christ (Ac 2³⁶), Prince of Life (3¹⁵), only source of salvation (4¹²), ordained of God to be the Judge of quick and dead (10⁴²; cf. 17³¹).

'It is the expression,' says B. Weiss (*Bibl. Theol. NT*, i. 239), 'of the most immediate living experience, when Peter says that they were begotten again unto a living hope by the Resurrection of Jesus Christ (1 P 1³). Not till it took place was the dead Jesus manifested with absolute certainty as the Messiah.'

(2) *Evidential as certifying the redemptive character of His death.* — It required a new interpretation to be placed upon His death. The Resurrection showed the death to possess a Godward validity, affecting the Divine relations with mankind. It was the Divine response to the death, and the explanation to mankind of its meaning (see Gloatz in *SK*, 1895, p. 798; cf. Ro 6⁴· ¹⁰). The Resurrection, says Horn in a striking phrase, is the 'Amen' of the Father to the 'It is finished' of the Son (*NK Ztschr.* 1902, p. 548).

(3) Christ's Resurrection is *evidential of His Divinity.* — St. Paul begins the letter to the Romans with this thought: 1³· ⁴ '. . . the gospel of God . . .

concerning his Son, who was born of the seed of David according to the flesh, who was declared to be the Son of God with power, according to the spirit of holiness, by the resurrection of the dead.' Here the essence of the gospel, that is, of Christianity, is said to be concerning God's Son. And the expression 'God's Son' is, says Meyer, not by any means to be taken merely as a designation of Messiah; it is in St. Paul a Son who has pre-existed, and proceeded out of the essence of the Father, like Him in substance (cf. Liddon, *Analysis*, p. 4). The gospel of God concerning His Son is concerned with Sonship in the highest of all senses. It designates neither adoption nor official place, but personal equality.

God's Son, then, is viewed by the Apostle in two aspects, which both represent constituent elements of His nature,—according to the flesh, and according to the spirit of holiness. The former describes His humanity, the latter His higher Self. Regarded in the former aspect, He was born of the dynasty of David; regarded in the latter, He was declared to be the Son of God. The term translated 'declared to be' (ὁρισθέντος) might refer either to an actual appointment or to the declaration of a fact. If our exposition of the title 'Son of God' be correct, it is the second that is intended here. Jesus is, then, here declared to be the Son of God with power by the Resurrection. A powerful demonstration of His higher Self has been made in the sphere of resurrection (cf. Liddon, *Easter Sermons*, vi. 94, iv. 58; Gifford on *Romans*; contrast Du Bose, *Gospel acc. to St. Paul*, p. 31).

(4) *Instrumental in effecting Christ's Exaltation.* The Resurrection is in Apostolic theology by no means merely evidential. It is no mere certificate of acceptance. It is not merely an indirect means through which men have become believers, a matter which can be dispensed with so soon as faith is gained, or is unnecessary if faith is obtained some other way. It is also instrumental, and produces its own necessary and indispensable effects. It has primarily its own effect on Christ Himself. Obviously it does not only certify Him to be the Christ. It is instrumental in effecting His Exaltation. It is through the Resurrection that Christ 'enters into his glory' (Lk 24²⁶; cf. Ac 2³³, Ro 6⁹). St. Paul (Ac 13³³) applies to the Resurrection the Psalm, 'Thou art my Son, this day (*i.e.* Easter Day) have I begotten thee.' The primary reference (? to the coronation of Solomon) is here, accordingly, mystically transferred to the Exaltation of Jesus. Not that the Resurrection constituted Him God's Son (which He was throughout), but that it effected the transition into a glorified state. Jesus, as having expired on the cross, would be conceived by the Jews as transferred to the gloom of Hades. Jesus, as risen, was thereby exalted to a condition hitherto unprecedented among the occupants of the other world (cf. Rev 1¹⁸). As the result of the Resurrection, Jesus 'is at the right hand of God,' 'making intercession for us' (Ro 8³⁴).

(5) The Resurrection is also *instrumental in effecting justification.* The great passage is Ro 4²⁵ 'Who was delivered for our offences, and was raised again for our justification.' The two clauses are by no means identical—an antithesis of phrases without antithesis of meaning—as an attempt to transpose them ought to show. St. Paul could not conceivably have said, 'Who died for our justification, and rose again for our sins.' There is an intimate connexion between the categories of death and sin, and those of resurrection and justification. Moreover, both Death and Resurrection have their functions to discharge in completing the work of redemption. In the first place, Christ was delivered over to death as a Sacrifice on account of

our offences. Thereby objectively reparation was made in behalf of humanity by its representative, and reconciliation secured. But this, while complete on the Divine side, leaves the earthward yet to be effected. The reconciliation must be subjectively appropriated by each individual. Accordingly Christ was raised again on account of our justification. Our individual acceptance is said to be due to the Resurrection. This is for two reasons : (a) because we can appropriate justification only by belief in the saving significance of Christ's death. And we can attain to this belief only through the fact of the Resurrection (cf. B. Weiss, *Bibl. Theol.* i. 437). But it should be most clearly understood that this is only a partial statement of the truth. Our individual acceptance is also due to the Resurrection ; (b) because it was only by His Risen Life that Christ became the new life-principle for mankind. Justice will never be done to this great passage so long as the effect of Christ's Resurrection on our justification is restricted to its being a mere certificate of His acceptance with God (contrast Pfleiderer, *Paulinism*, i. 119, and Stevens, *Pauline Theol.* 254 f.).

The Resurrection becomes the medium through which the glorified life of Jesus is infused into the personality of the believer. Apostolic Christianity, we are profoundly persuaded, does not limit itself to the former of these two conceptions, but embraces the latter. It is not Christ outside us, but Christ within us that completes the Apostolic view. It is not the recorded Christ appealing to us across the centuries, but the Living Christ imparting His glorified strength, that is the ultimate Christian principle. This is the meaning of St. John's teaching on eating Christ (Jn 6). This assimilation of Christ becomes possible only through His Resurrection. And St. Paul can mean no less when he writes, 'raised again for our justification.' Thus, as B. Weiss says, the relation between the Death of Christ and His Resurrection is, that ' the former was the means of procuring salvation, the latter the means of appropriating it' (*Bibl. Theol.* i. 437).

On this most important passage see, further, Meyer on Ro 4²⁵ ; Liddon's *Analysis* ; Newman's *Sermon*, ' Christ's Resurrection the Source of Justification.'

(6) The Resurrection of Christ is also, according to Apostolic teaching, *instrumental in effecting the physical resurrection of all believers.* As early as 1 Th 4¹⁴ St. Paul appeals to Christ's Resurrection as the ground of consolation to the mourner. Similarly St. Peter is represented (Ac 4²) as ' preaching through Jesus the resurrection from the dead ' (cf. Ro 6⁵ 8¹¹, and above all 1 Co 15).

Specially noteworthy is St. Paul's argument in Ro 8¹⁰ᶠ·. On the supposition that Christ *is* in us—if Christ has really entered into the individual believer—if His power has taken possession—then the result is (a) that although the body—the human body—is dead because of sin—*i.e.* belongs to the category of dead things owing to the influence of moral evil—not merely mortal but dead—yet the spirit—the human spirit—is life because of (Christ's) righteousness. That is to say, a resurrection has taken place already *on the spiritual side.* We are already risen with Christ—in the region of personal renewal—because the righteousness of Christ is in us—imparted to us. (b) But if so (v.¹¹)—if the resurrection has already taken place in the spiritual,—the new vitality shall in process of time extend itself into the physical : ' He that raised up Christ from the dead shall also quicken your mortal bodies.'

The Christian doctrine proclaims both a moral and a physical resurrection. Attempts were made in the Apostolic age, under the influence of non-Christian presuppositions, to lay exclusive emphasis on the former and reject the latter. Men declared that the resurrection was past already (2 Ti 2¹⁸). Death was

to be understood in a moral sense, and resurrection was its moral antithesis, it was a restoration out of the death of ignorance, a giving of life to the morally dead. Attempts are also made in modern thought to maintain exclusively a moral resurrection. But nothing can be more paradoxical than endeavours to shelter this exclusiveness under the authority of St. Paul. To say that ' in St. Paul's ideas the expression [resurrection from the dead] has no essential connexion with physical death ' (Matt. Arnold), is to say what is preposterous to any one who has the great words of 1 Co 15 ringing in his mind. It is, as has been accurately said, ' claiming the authority of St. Paul's spiritual teaching in order to discredit the historical faith without which he declared his preaching vain ' (Waggett, *The Holy Eucharist*, p. 200). All attempts to limit St. Paul's idea of resurrection to the moral sphere are worse than useless. The fact is that St. Paul did not gratuitously attach a relic of incongruous materialism to a spiritual theory complete and consistent with itself. ' He believed, indeed, in our Lord's bodily Resurrection, but not in spite of his spiritualism ; rather because of the triumphant character of his spiritualism ' (Waggett, p. 201). The severance of human life into two distinct departments, the one the spiritual and moral over which resurrection prevails, the other the physical over which resurrection has no power, is not a true spirituality, but a false and timid spirituality. ' It is false precisely through timidity, and by failing to invade in the name of Spirit the regions of sensible experience' (Waggett, p. 200). The intimate connexion of the two spheres, the moral and the physical, is fundamental throughout the Christian revelation. Death in Christianity is physical, and death is also moral. And the two interpenetrate. Redemption involves an intimate association between the two. The Death of Christ is moral surrender and physical experience. Death physical is awfully real, as real in its province as is death in the moral sphere. It is therefore impossible, consistently with Christian principles of redemption, to separate sin and dissolution into two worlds having no connexion. The Christian religion is of a life-giving force which pervades the moral sphere already, and is to pervade the material hereafter. It has done both these already in the case of Christ. And the Spirit of Christ already pervades the Christian here in the present world. He is already morally risen with Christ. The force of the Resurrection of Christ is already at work in the sphere of mind and affection and will. But there is a redemption of the body yet to come. (On the relation of moral to physical resurrection, see also Du Bose, *Gospel in the Gospels* ; and Denney, *Atonement and the Modern Mind*).

(7) Consequently it is seen that the Resurrection of Christ is *the foundation of Apostolic Christianity*, and this for dogmatic just as truly as for evidential reasons. (a) Their consciousness of its basal character is shown in the position it occupies in their witness. An Apostle is ordained to be a witness of the Resurrection (Ac 1²²). The content of St. Paul's Christianity is thought at Athens to be ' Jesus and the resurrection ' (17¹⁸). The early sections in the Acts reiterate the statement, ' This Jesus hath God raised up, whereof we all are witnesses' (2³²). (b) Moreover, negatively, the consequences to Christianity of a denial of the Resurrection of Christ were drawn out with all the dialectic force of St. Paul. And it is surely significant every way that this acute and searching analysis of the doctrine was made by one of the first teachers of Christianity. The fearlessness with which he propounds his great dilemmas is in itself extremely valuable and reassuring. He saw, with a clearness never surpassed, what the Resurrection of Christ involved ; and seeing that, was calmly prepared to risk everything upon it. It would seem indisputable that St. Paul's entire exposition proceeds on the assumption that the Resurrection of Christ was not in controversy in the Church of Corinth. The section of Corinthian churchmen whom St. Paul has in mind accepted the Resurrection of Christ, but rejected the future resurrection of the dead. Their philosophic antecedents rendered such rejection entirely natural (see Heinrici, *in loc.*; Kennedy, *St. Paul's Conception of the Last Things*, 225), while their Christianity constrained them to make a concession to faith in the altogether exceptional case of Jesus Christ. They were practically combining incompatible elements from the Old and the New, and had not the clearness of thought to realize the incompatibility. There is certainly nothing abnormal to human religious experience in this. But to St. Paul's logical intellect it was intolerable. If there be no

such thing as a resurrection of dead persons, then is not Christ risen (1 Co 15[13]). The denial of the general principle will not permit the affirmation of particular instances.

St. Paul then proceeds to show the effect of this denial of Christ's Resurrection : first, on the proclamation of Christianity, whose sum and substance become words lacking in contents and in truth, if Christ be not risen ; secondly, on the believer's faith, which in that case becomes equally empty, being created by a baseless message ; and thirdly, on the Apostolic proclaimers, who have delivered as fact what in reality is fiction, and have misrepresented God by affirming as His deed what He has not done. Thus in all three departments the denial of Christ's Resurrection evaporates everything. The substance of Christianity has gone, the believer's faith has gone, the Apostolic veracity has gone. To dwell on the second of these : The faith of a Christian depends on Christ's Resurrection, because forgiveness depends on the redemptive power of Christ's Death, and this is certified by the Resurrection. If the Resurrection is not historic fact, then the power of death remains unbroken, and with it the effect of sin ; and the significance of Christ's Death remains uncertified, and accordingly believers are yet in their sins, precisely where they were before they heard of Jesus' name.

That St. Paul's estimate of the place of Christ's Resurrection in Christianity is profoundly true seems proved, conversely, by the invariable results which follow upon its denial. Without belief in the Resurrection there may easily exist a reverence for the moral sublimity of Christ's character, and a glad recognition of the religious value of His prophetic instruction. But these are widely different from faith in Him as understood by St. Paul. All distinctively Christian belief in Jesus has been founded on a knowledge of His Resurrection. It is this which has characterized and determined the nature of the faith which men have placed in Him. To their minds there has been a revelation which the Risen Christ has made, and which He could not have made otherwise than as having risen.

As a historic fact, it has been His Resurrection which has enabled men to believe in His official exaltation over humanity. It is not a mere question of the moral influence of His character, example, and teaching. It is that their present surrender to Him as their Redeemer has been promoted by this belief, and could not be justified without it. Indeed, those who deny His Resurrection consistently deny as a rule His Divinity and His redemptive work in any sense that St. Paul would have acknowledged. Pauline conceptions of Atonement are intimately bound up with Pauline conceptions of Easter Day. The former do not logically survive the rejection of the latter. Thus it comes naturally to pass that denial of the Resurrection issues ultimately in another religion, which, whatever may be said about it, is not Apostolic Christianity. The whole doctrine of reconciliation through the Word's assumption of the flesh, redemption by incarnation, moral death and rising again of the individual believer in and with Christ, are inseparable from Christ's own Resurrection.

LITERATURE.—On the doctrinal significance of Christ's Resurrection see Ph 3[10], Col 1[18] ; and cf., further, Grützmacher, *Moderne positive Vorträge*, 1906, p. 113 ; Goguel, *L'apôtre Paul et Jésus Christ*, p. 256 ; *Lux Mundi*, p. 235 ; Borg-Schüttmann in *NK Ztschr.* 1901, 667-693.

W. J. SPARROW SIMPSON.

RESURRECTION OF THE DEAD.—1. Jewish beliefs current in the time of our Lord.—The doctrine of the resurrection of the dead, symbolically applied to the nation (Hos 6[2] 13[14], Ezk 37[1-14]),

implicit as regards the individual in prophecy and psalm (Job 14[13-15] 19[23-27], Is 65. 66, Pss 49. 73), has its first explicit expression in Is 26[14-19] as the hope of the righteous, based on conviction of God's power and faithfulness and on their persistent relation to Him. It appears in the Canon as formal prediction and definitely in Dn 12[2], and became part of that 'consolation' which the devouter part of Judaism, in the absence of official prophecy, but upon the basis of past prophetic utterance and on the lines of prophetic indication, developed. 'The Pharisaic movement offered salvation to the Jewish race . . . partly by opening wider hopes to those who obeyed' (Swete, *Apoc. of St. John*, p. xxiii)—proximately the Messianic hope, and eschatologically the hope of the resurrection. The literature of the period preceding and following our Lord's appearance shows three views as to the future of the dead, viz. (1) the traditional doctrine of Sheol ; (2) a doctrine, variously held, of resurrection ; (3) a Platonic doctrine of immortality.

(1) Of these Sirach (17[27-30]) knows only the first unmodified, repeating the thought of Ps 6[5] and of Hezekiah's psalm (Is 38[8. 9])—the days of man are to the eternity of God as a drop to the sea,— wherefore the Divine pity (Sir 18[8-11]) ; the dead have lost the light and are at rest (22[11]) ; even of the righteous only the name and deed survive (44[9-15]) ; Samuel's death is 'his long sleep.' In Tobit death is dissolution ($\ddot{o}\pi\omega\varsigma$ $\dot{a}\pi o\lambda v\theta\hat{\omega}$) and permanent ($\tau\dot{o}\nu$ $a\dot{\iota}\dot{\omega}\nu\iota o\nu$ $\tau\dot{o}\pi o\nu$, 3[6]). As to the doctrine of 1 Mac. the evidence is negative ; no future life is referred to. 'We fight for our lives and our laws' (3[21]). In Judith the enemies of God in the Day of Judgment shall meet His vengeance in putting fire and worms $\epsilon\dot{\iota}\varsigma$ $\sigma\dot{a}\rho\kappa a\varsigma$ $a\dot{v}\tau\hat{\omega}\nu$ (Jg 16[17]), and shall feel the pain of it for ever ; but in the absence of more, this scarcely implies a doctrine of physical immortality. This traditional eschatology had still its adherents in the Judæa of our Lord's lifetime (Mt 22[23], Mk 12[18], Lk 20[27], Ac 23[8]).

(2) In 2 Mac. there is a clear statement of a developed doctrine of *bodily resurrection for the righteous*. God shall raise up those who have died for His laws ; the very members which have been stricken from the martyr being restored to him, and 'breath and life as at the first' 'unto an everlasting life' (7[8. 11. 23] 14[46]). The faith of such a restoration is felt as an ethical necessity. It is not so much a theory of human destinies as a conviction of the Divine justice and truth. The problem of martyrdom has compelled it—the problem whether supreme fidelity can issue in loss. That it should seem even for the present so to issue is realized as a difficulty, and is explained as a chastising, a temporal penalty ($\beta\rho a\chi\dot{v}\nu$ . . . $\pi\dot{o}\nu o\nu$) for personal and national sins ; the martyr's rôle being one of self-offering and expiation for these (7[18. 37. 38]). Resurrection is God's reconciliation with His servants, and is implied in their persistent relation to Him—they are 'dead under God's covenant of everlasting life' (7[33. 36]). But for the enemies of God there is no resurrection (vv.[14. 36]).

As to the *extent* of the resurrection, the case in 2 Mac. is that of the martyrs only ; but the confidence expressed with regard to them is probably based on a wider hope, including Israel, or at least the faithful in Israel ($\sigma\dot{v}\nu$ $\tau o\hat{\iota}\varsigma$ $\dot{a}\delta\epsilon\lambda\phi o\hat{\iota}\varsigma$ $\sigma o\upsilon$, 7[29], hardly implies this, the $\dot{a}\delta\epsilon\lambda\phi o\dot{\iota}$ are literal ; but the tone of the whole passage [see v.[14]] implies a faith for others than the actual speakers). In the apocalyptic literature, which did much to extend the doctrine of resurrection in Judaism, it is generally presented as limited to Israel. For the question with which the Apocalypses deal is one of fulfilment of promises to Israel, and the deeper question whether 'the righteous shall be as the wicked'—at what point and in what form the faithful in Israel are to be vindicated and the apostates meet Divine justice. The earlier section of Eth. Enoch seems to expect a resurrection universal to Israel, with the exception only of the absolutely evil : 'complete in their crimes' (22^{13}). The second section excludes none — all Israel is raised, but the righteous and holy are chosen from the rest for reward (51. $61^{4.5}$). In the third section 'the judgment appears to be followed by the resurrection of righteous Israelites only' (Charles, *Bk. of Enoch*, p. 27). The conception of a resurrection general to mankind does not occur in this literature until the close of the period under discussion, when the Apoc. of Baruch (1st cent. A.D.) expressly proposes the question of the number of those who shall rise (28^7 41^1, cf. Lk 13^{23}), and teaches a first resurrection at the Advent of the Messiah, of 'all who have fallen asleep in hope of Him'; but also apparently a resurrection of good and evil, Gentiles and Israelites, for the purpose of judgment ($50^{3.4}$ 51^{1-6}). 2 Esdras teaches one general resurrection of the same character (7^{32-35}).

With regard to this development, there seems no adequate reason for regarding it as introducing a mechanical and unspiritual conception of resurrection (Charles, *Eschatology*) as distinguished from a 'high and spiritual' conception of resurrection limited to the just. This also rises from an ethical root. It is based in apprehension of the necessity of Divine justice, conceived as requiring not only the vindication of righteousness, but the condemnation on equal terms of unrighteousness ; a justice from which death itself affords no hiding. The doctrine of a general resurrection of good and evil alike follows from the apprehension of God as Judge of the whole earth, dealing with man and not with Israel only, and marks a widening of eschatological outlook from being an interest in the fulfilment of promise to Israel to become an interest in the assertion of God as fulfilling righteousness for the world.

As to the *nature* of the resurrection body, in 2 Mac. only the facts of restoration and identity are insisted on. In Enoch, while the resurrection body is one in which the righteous shall 'eat and lie down and rise up,' it is changed to be imperishable and glorious—'garments of glory . . . garments of life' (61^{14-16}); they are 'clad in shining light,' and share the nature and rank of the angels (51^4 104^6). In Apoc. of Baruch the dead are raised as they have died, in order that the living may know the verity of their resurrection (49^{2-4}); but thereafter a judicial change passes upon both them and those who have been alive at the time (51^1), the wicked 'becoming worse' than those who presently occupy Gehenna ($52^{2.15.16}$), while the righteous are transfigured and are fitted for immortality and the eternal world ($57^{3.4.9-14}$). We have here much more than a doctrine of physical resuscitation ; resurrection is apprehended as advance to a new and higher plane of life.

(3) The doctrine of *immortality without resurrection* appears in two forms — Palestinian and Alexandrian. (*a*) In the Palestinian form the consummation of the soul's destiny is postponed to the end. There is an intermediate state, in which the righteous and wicked are already separated ; and there is Final Judgment, after which the righteous pass to the heavenly world of glory and felicity, and the wicked to eternal woe. Thus the Book of Jubilees speaks of the 'Day of the Great Judgment,' and goes on to say of the righteous : 'Their bones will rest in the earth and their spirits will have much joy' ($23^{11.13}$) ; and this is probably the view of the Assumption of Moses as well (10^{3-10}), and perhaps of the Slavonic Enoch. In the latter the translated Enoch does indeed receive a raiment of Divine glory instead of his 'earthly robe' (equivalent to the changed body, 'garments of glory,' of the *Simil.* of Enoch) ; but his case is exceptional, and he is destined for 'the highest heaven' (67^2). Nothing is said of any reclothing for those who have died. There is a place prepared for every soul of them (49^2), 'Many

mansions . . . good for the good, evil for the evil' (61^2), 'their eternal habitation' (65^{10}). With regard, however, to these two last-named writers, there is silence as to the resurrection rather than denial of it ; and it is difficult to say, especially of the Assump. of Moses, that they were conscious of divergence from current beliefs.

(*b*) Alexandrian Judaism, adopting a Hellenic philosophy, taught a doctrine of personal immortality of the individual soul, which it endeavoured more or less successfully to disentangle from the questions of the corporate destiny of the nation and of cosmic judgment. Accepting from Platonism the ideas of the eternity and evil of matter, it necessarily ignored that of resurrection ; and accepting from the same source the ideas of the soul's pre-existence and of salvation by wisdom, it was compelled to regard each soul as working out its own fate in this life, and as reaching that fate at the point of severance from the flesh ; immortality in its final form beginning from the moment of death. Thus in Wisdom the body is essentially 'subject to sin' (1^4) ; the soul is pre-existent and essentially good (8^{20}), but is entangled in matter which weighs it down (9^{15}) ; man is destined for immortality (2^{23}), which the wise attain ($8^{13.17}$), and find it in all blessedness as they depart from our sphere of knowledge (3^{1-5} 4^{7-14} 5^{15}). The despisers of wisdom, on the other hand, have neither hope nor comfort in death ; it is for them an immediate passage to judgment and retribution (3^{16-19} 4^{18-20} 5^{14}). The Hebrew idea of death as unnatural and punitive is nevertheless, however inconsistently, also present to the mind of the writer. God made not death, but the impious called it in (1^{13-16}) ; death entered by envy of the devil, and is the portion of his servants (2^{24}). The idea of a future Judgment, a 'day of decision,' also keeps its place in the writer's thought (3^{18} 4^{20}). Nor is his conception that of an immortality wholly immaterial ; the righteous shall receive a palace and royal crown ; they shall judge the nation and have dominion over the people, sharing their Lord's kingdom (3^8). He has not successfully assimilated his Hellenism, but requires the Hebraic eschatology to supplement it. The teaching of Wisdom on this subject is substantially that of Philo as well : 'Apparently he did not look forward to a general and final judgment. All enter after death into their final abode' (Charles, *Eschatol.* p. 260). The philosophy of 4 Mac. is Stoical, not Platonic ; but it agrees with Wisdom and Philo in ignoring the ideas of an intermediate state and of resurrection, and in teaching an immortality of the spirit only, commencing when this life ends.

2. The teaching of Jesus.—Our Lord found Himself in an atmosphere of thought in which ideas representative of these various forms of doctrine were more or less current. The Rabbinic teaching on the whole held the field as a popular orthodoxy, identified in the common mind with devoutness and earnest religion : and it asserted the resurrection of the dead. This was generally conceived of as twofold—a resurrection of the just, and a general resurrection preparatory to universal judgment (Muirhead, *Eschatol. of Jesus*, p. 91) ; the anticipation of resurrection was a commonplace of piety (Jn 11^{24}). At the same time, the Sadducaic party adhered to an unmodified Sheol doctrine and contended aggressively for it. No allusion to the Alexandrian doctrine of an immortality without resurrection appears in the NT ; but the Palestinian schools cannot have been unaware of its existence. Throughout His teaching Christ puts aside the second and third of these doctrines, and sets His seal to the first. He teaches a resurrection of the dead.

The teaching of Christ as to resurrection is widely scattered through the Gospels. The capital passages are Mt 22^{23-33}

(Mk 12¹⁸⁻²⁷, Lk 20²⁷⁻³⁸) and Jn 5¹⁹⁻³¹ 6³²⁻⁵⁶. The term used is commonly ἀνάστασις ; once (Mt 27⁵³) it is ἔγερσις. Verbal forms of ἀνιστάναι and ἐγείρειν seem used interchangeably, occurring consecutively in the same passages (as in Mk 12²⁵·²⁶, Lk 11³¹·³²), or in parallel passages (cf. Mt 16²¹ 17²³ with 17⁹), without apparent distinction of sense. ἀναστάσεως τῶν νεκρῶν occurs in Mt 22³¹, but in the parallel Mk 12²⁵ ἀν. ἐκ νεκρῶν, and in Lk 20³⁵ τῆς ἀν. τῆς ἐκ νεκρῶν (cf. Ac 2³¹). ἐκ νεκρῶν is the phrase used of Christ's resurrection predicted (Mt 17⁹, Mk 9⁷·¹⁰) ; of the supposed resurrection of the Baptist (Mt 14²), and of the case of one rising from the dead (Lk 16³¹). In the Epp. ἐκ is used of Christ's resurrection, ἀν. τῶν νεκρῶν of resurrection generally. A distinction of usage seems to exist, ἐκ implying an individual or a non-universal resurrection. ζωοποιεῖν occurs in Jn 5²¹ 6⁶³ (cf. Ro 4¹⁷ 8¹¹, 1 Co 15²²·³⁶·⁴⁵), but is more than a synonym for ἀνιστάναι or ἐγείρειν.

'To Jesus the OT Scriptures as a whole conveyed the pledge of the will and power of God to raise the dead who had lived unto Him' (Muirhead). In His reply to the Sadducees He does not instance the more precise predictions of the prophets, but argues from the broad relation of God to His servants, not as a covenant but as a vital relation. Their resurrection is so involved in the nature of the case that it requires no other demonstration than that God lives and that God is their God. He appeals to the common usage which called God 'the God of their fathers,' 'of Abraham, Isaac, and Jacob' (men who were dead), and to its authority in the oracle of the Bush ; and needs no more than the admission that such language conveyed a truth. As touching the dead that they rise, has not God confessed that He is theirs? recognized that in this life they had already entered into possession of Him ? Such possession, once established, cannot be lost. God is theirs— how can their life (for surely they live to Him) remain permanently mutilated ? Surely it shall again be for them life in fulness of their nature. They have fallen ; death is death : Christ does not minimize the penal and privative character of what was to Himself a great horror ; but they shall rise again—for God is theirs : they have a hold and right in God, who has life in Himself and is essentially the Giver of Life.

The argument appears excessive in simplicity, but involves more than it expresses. If man is capable of possessing God, then man is potentially akin to God ; if man has known and loved God (as man must, if God has in any sense become his), then God must have laid hold on him and must have given Himself to man. God is their God : they have then even in this life attained an interior contact with the Divine, and have so far entered the sphere of the imperishable ; they have gained an inheritance which is essentially eternal. In possessing God they have secured a place in God's future, and in whatever God will reveal or accomplish. Our Lord thus moves the question to a higher ground than that of promise or covenant or even of ethical necessity, and grounds upon a concrete relation which is recognized as vital and dynamic. The argument involves whatever is involved in the nature of human personality ; its reflexion of the Divine unity, its indestructibility and capacity to resist and survive the shock of physical dissolution, and its necessity of full self-realization in God. It is impossible to limit the destiny of that which possesses God. It is impossible to deny to it completeness of development along the lines of initial character. Death interrupts but cannot ultimately bar that development. As touching the dead, that they rise again—that life shall be for them reconstituted and perfected—have we not read that God calls Himself their God ?

The discussion in this case was with those who 'deny that there is any resurrection of the dead' (Lk 20²⁷), and it was enough for its purpose to consider the case of those who in life have possessed God. On the face of it the argument might seem to apply to these only. On the other hand, it seems to identify (at least for man) immortality with resurrection. What it proves is that the dead are living (οὐκ ἔστι θεὸς νεκρῶν ἀλλὰ ζώντων) ; what it assumes is that, if they live, they will rise again. Christ does not contemplate that they may be immortal apart from that destiny, or discuss the alternative conception (which cannot have been unfamiliar to his interlocutors) that the patriarchs might live in God for a merely ghostly eternity. The alternatives which He seems to oppose are that either they no longer live

(in any effective sense) or that they shall live completely—there shall be an ἀνάστασις, a reconstitution of that duplex life of spirit and organism which is characteristically human. The question whether the finitely spiritual can be conceived of as self-conscious, apprehensive or active apart from organism, or whether the fact of its limitations local and temporal and of relations to other finite existence does not imply organism, is involved, but is not the whole question. The question is of man, who is distinctively the meeting-point of two worlds, the spiritual and the material, at which the Creator has 'breathed into the dust,' and at which the creation becomes conscious of God. The differentia of humanity is this incarnation, making possible the ultimate Incarnation in which the Word became flesh. In virtue of this duplex nature man is essentially the priest of the material creation, interpreting its testimony to God, and capable of furnishing the medium in which Creator and creature reach an absolute unity in Him who is Head over all things and in whom all things consist. By death this dual constitution is broken—resurrection is its recovery ; reconstitution in the totality of the elements of our nature which condition fulfilment of man's distinctive vocation in the cosmos. The redemption which is to redeem man must reach his being in its completeness—the organism of the spirit as well as the spirit itself. It must reach even the body which has been 'the entrenchment of sin' (Gore). Not as resuscitation, but as 'change' ; so that on a new plane of life, unexplored by us and therefore meantime indescribable to us, it may be the adequate organism of a spirit perfectly correspondent with the Divine Spirit, and death be swallowed up 'not in life, but in victory.' The norm of Christ's personal resurrection may seem to imply this : His work in redemption is not completed by a sacrificial death, but must go on in a triumphant rescue of the body from death. It is not left as an 'outworn tool,' but is brought again, quickened and transformed, to be the instrument of a universal mediation ; its reassumption is for Him entrance upon an eternal priesthood. Incarnation is not a passing phase of Deity ; it is the realization of the Divine purpose in humanity. Death is privative ; disembodiment is incompleteness. Our salvation implies our reconstitution, not only in the spiritual which places us in correspondence with God, but in the organic which places us in correspondence with God's creation. God will not leave us 'hopelessly stunted and imperfect' (Milligan, Res. of the Dead, p. 161), but will 'give a body.' With regard to the scope of the resurrection, the question is not touched in the discussion with the Sadducees, unless in so far as the argument used may seem to identify immortality with resurrection. (St. Paul in 1 Co 15 has the same alternatives : 'if the dead are not raised . . . then they also which sleep in Christ have perished.' He recognizes no third possibility, of a merely spiritual immortality). Elsewhere, however, Christ teaches a general resurrection (Jn 5²⁸⁻²⁹) of 'all that are in the graves' ; not only an elect of them, but they who have 'done evil' as well as they who have 'wrought good'—and distinguishes 'the resurrection of life' from 'the resurrection of condemnation.' The rejection of these verses as an interpolation, on the ground that their teaching is not found elsewhere in the Synoptics or in Jn. itself, is not justified. A general resurrection of just and unjust forms at least the background of the thought in Mt 5²⁹·³⁰ (μὴ ὅλον τὸ σῶμά σου βληθῇ εἰς γέενναν) 10²⁸ (καὶ ψυχὴν καὶ σῶμα ἀπολέσαι ἐν γεέννῃ) 12⁴¹·⁴², Lk 11³² (ἄνδρες Νινευῖται ἀναστήσονται κ.τ.λ.), and in Mt 25³¹⁻⁴⁶. It is implied in the sequence to the statement that

God is not the God of the dead but of the living, reported by Lk. (20³⁸), 'for all live unto him'—the thought of which would seem to be that not such only as the patriarchs were have a link to God, but that men as men 'live to Him,' and that this must have its inference for all. The absence of bias on St. Luke's part towards a doctrine of general resurrection, peculiar to himself among the Evangelists, is evident from the extended form in his account (v.³⁵) of the saying more briefly reported in Mt 22³⁰, Mk 12²⁵. As reported by St. Luke ('they which shall be accounted worthy,' etc.), the saying would seem to contemplate a particular resurrection only. Nor can bias on St. Luke's part be argued from the fact that (Ac 24¹⁵) he reports St. Paul as preaching to Felix a resurrection of the just and of the unjust, while St. Paul himself in his Epp. deals only with the believer's hope in Christ; the one concerned Felix, the other did not. A doctrine of general resurrection does appear in the reports of the Synoptists. And in Jn 6³⁹. ⁴⁰. ⁴⁴. ⁵⁴ the emphasis laid upon a resurrection which is *by Christ Himself* (ἐγὼ ἀναστήσω αὐτὸν) seems to imply that there is also resurrection of another character, and to be consecutive with the teaching of 5²⁸·²⁹.

The salvation constituted and offered in Christ is a positive salvation, to be realized and possessed in Himself. With that salvation the gospel is occupied. Our concern is with that—with the hope which is declared to us and with the Kingdom which He has opened to believers. We know the end, for we know the way. There is an alternative —a way that is not to life and an end that is not with Christ. It is named only, for our fear. It is the background of outer darkness against which the glory in Christ is thrown up into splendour. But it is in no sense the subject-matter of revelation. That which is revealed is life and incorruption (2 Ti 1¹⁰). This is the general principle of Christian teaching. Two aspects of resurrection are accordingly discoverable in that teaching, and first in the teaching of our Lord. Of these the one belongs to the essence of positive gospel; the resurrection of Christ Himself is already its beginning and pattern, and the root for us of its power; it is matter of assurance and exposition; our present life in Christ is full of experiences referable to it, and is explicable only in its terms; it is dynamically identified with whatever we are in Christ now or hope to be in Him hereafter. The other, resurrection of condemnation, is only indicated as in some sense an element of final adjustment of the issues of life. It remains in the sphere of apocalyptic, out of which the resurrection of life has been brought into the historic present by the resurrection of Christ which already demonstrates and illustrates it. This resurrection, in which He is our forerunner, of which His victory over death is the operative force, which shall result in us as the effect of our vital union with Him, and is the extension to us of the life from death to which He has attained, is the subject of our faith and the topic of Christian doctrine. See preceding art. § **10** (6) (7).

LITERATURE. — Charles, *Eschatology, Hebrew, Jewish, and Christian*; Apoc. of Baruch, ed. Charles; Book of Secrets of Enoch, do.; Book of Enoch, do.; Muirhead, *Eschatology of Jesus*; Milligan, *Resurrection of the Dead*; Swete, *Apocalypse of St. John*; Westcott, *Gosp. of St. John*; Gore, *Ep. to Romans*; Schwartzkopff, *Prophecies of Jesus Christ*; J. M. Whiton, *Beyond the Shadow*; Church, *Cath. and Univ. Sermons*, p. 131; R. C. Moberly, *Christ our Life*, p. 98.

H. J. WOTHERSPOON.

RETALIATION (Mt 5³⁸⁻⁴⁸, Lk 6²⁷⁻⁴⁵). — **1.** The *lex talionis* must have been part of the most primitive Semitic law, as it was current in almost identical words in Babylon and Canaan. The Code of Ḥammurabi prescribes (§§ 196, 200): 'If a man has caused the loss of a gentleman's eye, his eye shall one cause to be lost'; 'if a man has made the tooth of a man that is his equal to fall out, one shall make his tooth fall out.' The verse Ex 21²⁴, which Christ quotes (Mt 5³⁸), belongs to the Book of the Covenant, the oldest stratum of Hebrew law.

2. In various ways the later Hebrew legislation mitigated the severity of the *lex talionis*. That law could be, at best, but a very rough-and-ready method of dispensing justice. The man who had only one eye, and who destroyed the eye of another, would suffer, by the loss of his remaining eye, a penalty infinitely greater than the damage he had inflicted. And, apart from actual difficulties in the working of this law as a hard-and-fast rule,— difficulties which were, in point of fact, settled by the judge as they arose (Ex 21²²ᶠᶠ·, Lv 24¹⁹⁻²²),—there was a growing feeling that the exaction of the full letter of the Law was out of harmony with what was known of the will of God (Lv 19¹⁸): 'Thou shalt not avenge nor bear any grudge against the children of thy people' (cf. Pr 20²² 24²⁹, Sir 28¹⁻⁷). It was in harmony with this sentiment that the Hebrews, in the later days of the kingship, mitigated the severity of the old desert law, by refusing to allow the children to suffer for the sins of the parents, and *vice versa* (Dt 24¹⁶); but this alleviation of the penalty was an innovation (1 K 21²¹, 2 K 9²⁶).

3. When Christ came to deal with the Pharisees, He found that this broader interpretation of the Law was lacking. The interest of the scribes lay not in the effort to do the will of God as between man and man, but in the academic discussion of the compensation to be awarded, in soulless casuistry instead of in the effort to make straight the way in the practical business of life (Mk 7¹¹). In nothing was His teaching more utterly at variance with the received traditions of His day than here. The law of the Kingdom was love. Men were to be moved not by the spirit which was always seeking its own, but by the spirit which desired the welfare of the other. Christ put forward a principle instead of insisting upon the observance of a multitude of details. The whole question of the treatment of the adversary was lifted into another sphere. And what Christ counselled in the Sermon on the Mount He practised in His own life and death. The disciples who wished to call down fire from heaven upon the inhospitable village were rebuked (Lk 9⁵⁴); the disciple who began to meet armed force by arms was told to put up his sword into its sheath (Jn 18¹¹); the false accusers were met by silence (Mk 14⁶¹).

The lesson that Christ taught was well learned by the Apostles. St. Paul, in his earliest letter, warns his readers to 'see that none render evil for evil unto any man' (1 Th 5¹⁵, cf. 1 P 3⁹). Again, he points out that men should not seek their own vindication, but should leave that to God (Ro 12¹⁷⁻¹⁹). Lawsuits of Christians between themselves are frowned upon by this same broad reading of Christ's teaching. When Christians are more concerned with gaining a personal victory than with seeking the honour of God, Christ's cause suffers (1 Co 6¹⁻⁷).

4. *Is Christ's teaching a new law?* — Literal obedience to Christ's teaching on this subject would destroy the structure of society. If no man were, in the strictest sense, to count as his own that which he had, there could be no such thing as private property; the home would disappear; the State would lapse into a condition of anarchy. And while a believer might, in his desire to obey his Lord, give to any one who took away his coat his cloak also, he might be doing the robber and society a very ill turn. The beggar is best helped not by indiscriminate charity, which does not attempt to get at the root of the trouble, but by being put in the way of earning a living for himself. The robber has information laid against him and is punished, not to satisfy a personal grudge, but to force him to amend his ways and to protect the fabric of civil life. It is clear that what Christ lays down in these particular verses, and in the Sermon on the Mount generally, is not a new code of law, but a broad principle of action. As much of the discourse is aimed at the Pharisees, who had made an idol of the minutiæ of the Law, it is wholly improbable that Christ meant to lay down a new set of rules, which could be worthily observed only by adhering to their letter. It was necessary, in order that men should remember His teaching, that He should put the truth He had to propound in vivid and concrete form. St. Matthew, the most Judaistic of all the Evangelists, does apparently read the new principles as being legal directions; but the version of the Sermon given by St. Luke shows that this was not how the Apostles, whose outlook was towards the Gentiles, understood them. The injunction to turn the other cheek is thus not an injunction to be fulfilled to the letter, but an illustration of the principle that is to guide a man in disputes. He is not in passion to smite the wrong-doer, and to requite one wrong by another; he is to try to win the offender by love. He is to consider the other.

'So far as our personal feeling goes, we ought to be ready to offer the other cheek, and to give, without desire of recovery, whatever is demanded or taken from us. Love knows no limits but those which love itself imposes. When love resists or refuses, it is because compliance would be a violation of love, not because it would involve loss or suffering' (Gore, *Sermon on the Mount*, p. 103).

5. Modern theories of non-resistance. — George Fox took the Sermon on the Mount as another law; and as he fulfilled the injunction to take no thought for clothing, by wearing a leather suit, so he practised to the letter the injunction with regard to non-resistance. 'Did we ever resist them? Did we not give them our backs to beat, and our cheeks to pull off the hair, and our faces to spit on?' is a familiar phrase in his *Journal*. But his followers have got below the letter into the spirit. With all their charity, they have not given indiscriminately. They have made their place in philanthropic work by their insistence on searching into the causes of social evils, and, while helping others, have themselves accumulated wealth.

The great modern representative of the non-resistance view is Tolstoi, who carries his adherence to the letter of Scripture to a point which involves a return to anarchy. He takes the case (*Letter on Non-Resistance*) of a robber found killing or outraging a child. The child can be saved only by killing the robber. Should the robber be killed? Tolstoi answers in the negative. Even the non-Christian should not kill the man, Tolstoi argues, because he cannot say whether the child's life is more needed or is better than the robber's life. He, therefore, has no sufficient rational ground for action. But the Christian, who sees the meaning of life in fulfilling God's will, has no ground at all for killing the robber. 'He may plead with the robber, may interpose his own body between the robber and the victim; but there is one thing he cannot do—he cannot deliberately abandon the law he has received from God, the fulfilment of which alone gives meaning to his life.' The answer, of course, is that the fulfilment of God's law may not mean the observance to the letter of one phrase. We are to manifest love towards others. In this case, should it not be shown to the child who is innocent and helpless rather than to the man who is proving himself by his deed to be dangerous to his human kind?

LITERATURE.—Butler, *Serm.* viii. ix.; Seeley, *Ecce Homo*, chs. xxii. xxiii.; Dykes, *Manifesto of the King*, 287; *ExpT* iv. [1893] 256, vi. [1895] 338, vii. [1896] 145; J. B. Mozley, *Leading Ideas*

in *Early Ages* (1877), 180, 201; C. F. Kent, *Israel's Lawgivers* (1902), 59; W. H. Hunt, *Sermons on Social Subjects* (1904), 196.

R. BRUCE TAYLOR.

RETICENCE.—See RESERVE.

RETRIBUTION.—We shall understand by this word the operation of the Divine justice, rewarding and punishing, in this world and the next. (For human justice see art. VENGEANCE).

1. The doctrine in our Lord's time.—As is well known, the primitive religious consciousness of the Jews expected earthly happiness to correspond strictly to merit and demerit. Facts made it impossible to hold such a theory, and we have the problem of the Divine justice as it is raised in the Psalms, Job, etc. The remarkable thing is that the next life is *not*, at least with any consistency of belief, called in to redress the balance of this (see, *e.g.*, Kirkpatrick, *Psalms*, p. xciv.). Later Jewish thought, developing the doctrine of immortality, found in it the natural answer to the problem, as in the opening chapters of the Book of Wisdom. But the conception of recompense moved mainly on external lines; the rewards and punishments which did not come in this life were expected in the next, or in a Golden Age on earth. And so in our Lord's day—

'The religious relation between God and His people was a legal one, upheld by God as righteous Judge, in the way of service and counterservice, reward and punishment.' Pious Jews here and there might remember that forgiveness and free grace were part of the character of Jahweh, 'but with most Jews this mode of view was overshadowed by the legalistic conception, whereby every act of obedience was regarded as having an exact recompense, and every blessing to be obtained as requiring previous service.' 'Desiring to earn a Divine reward, and as great reward as possible, they sought to practise a strict legal righteousness, and, wherever possible, to exceed what the law demanded. But yet again, anxious to attain that reward on the easiest possible terms, they wished to do no more than was absolutely necessary for attaining their purpose' (Wendt, *Teaching of Jesus*, i. p. 39 ff.).

The charge that religion is only an enlightened selfishness, is valid against this position and the popular conception of Christianity. The object of this article will be to show that it is not valid as against the teaching of Christ.

2. The teaching of Christ.—(1) *He showed once for all that there is no invariable connexion between individual suffering and sin in this world.* The Heavenly Father bestows His gifts on evil and good alike (Mt 5[45], Lk 6[35]). Lk 13[1ff.] is decisive on this point. ('Ye shall all in like manner perish' refers to the special doom of the Jewish nation, and falls under the exception mentioned below). It is true there may be a connexion between suffering and sin, but it is undefined (Mt 9[2], Jn 5[14]), and it must not be assumed in any given case (Jn 9[3]). There are in the Gospels no 'poetic justice' parables, no limelight scenes of sensational punishments of evil-doers or dramatic vindication of virtue. There is no hint of any special doom on the Herods, Pilate, or the priests as individuals (cf. *per contra* Ac 12[20]). Judas is an exception, though Christ Himself never speaks of his punishment in this world. The treatment of *nations and cities* is also an exception (Jerusalem [Mt 21[43] 23[35], Lk 19[41-44]], Chorazin, etc. [Mt 10[15] 11[20]]). The life of the nation or city is long enough to show the inevitable results of moral decay. Further, all desire for personal vengeance now is forbidden (Sermon on the Mount, Lk 9[51ff.]). There is nothing of the spirit of the imprecatory Psalms or the Apocalyptic literature.*

The clearest and most decisive proof of the truth we are considering is Christ's own death and the

---

* An exception is Lk 18[7], which is closely akin to Rev 6[10] and to the frequent prayers for vengeance which meet us in Enoch. But the vengeance in this passage is that of the Last Day, and is part of the final consummation, which is the real object to which the prayers of the elect are directed.

sufferings and persecutions promised to His followers. Suffering may be a mark of God's love no less than of His anger (cf. He 12) ; the grain of wheat must die to bring forth fruit (Jn 12²⁴), therefore death and all that leads to it cannot be regarded as retributive. The cup of suffering which the disciple drinks is the cup of Christ, not the wine of the wrath of God.

(2) *Christ teaches equally decisively the fact of retribution in the next world*, and uses freely the language of reward and punishment. The doctrine of personal responsibility is indeed fundamental to Christianity, and it is necessary to refer to only a few typical passages : *Parables* (Mt 13²⁴ 18²³ 22² 25, Lk 12¹⁶ 16), *Rewards* (Mt 19²⁸, Lk 14¹⁴), *Punishments* (Mt 5²⁶ 10²⁸ 12³⁶, Mk 9⁴² 14²¹, Jn 5²⁹).

(3) *Retribution is to the character rather than to the act, and is automatic.* 'Every act rewards itself, or, in other words, integrates itself, in a twofold manner ; first, in the thing, or in real nature ; and secondly, in the circumstance, or in apparent nature. Men call the circumstance the retribution. The causal retribution is in the thing, and is seen by the soul' (Emerson, Essay on 'Compensation'). The truth is seen most clearly in the Fourth Gospel. Life is the result of faith in Christ and of the knowledge of God (3¹⁸ 5²⁴ 17³). Judgment is immediate, the self-inflicted result of wilful blindness, and of the rejection of the message of life (3¹⁹ 8²⁴ 12⁴⁸). At the same time this is no purely abstract law ; behind it is the personal God, and the Son to whom judgment is committed (5²²) ; see Westcott, *St. John*, p. xlviii. So in the parable of the Rich Man and Lazarus, 'the gulf' is the character * which has been formed on earth and is unalterable. The spiritual condition of the two cannot be altered by a mere change of place. In the parables of the Talents and the Pounds, neglect of opportunity brings unfitness for trust ; use of opportunity automatically opens the door to the reward of greater opportunity. The cutting down of the fig-tree is the inevitable doom of its barrenness (Lk 13⁶ ; cf. Mk 11¹³ and the teaching of the Baptist, Mt 3¹⁰). The same principle is seen in the blindness men bring on themselves (Mt 6²² 13¹²), and if the blind lead the blind, they must fall into the ditch (15¹⁴). The measure we receive is in the nature of things the counterpart of that which we give to others (7²), the judgment the counterpart of our judgment, God's forgiveness of our forgiveness (6¹⁴). The house must stand or fall according to the foundation on which it is built (7²⁴⁻²⁷).

Accordingly, acts have their results rather than their rewards, and the idea of 'the punisher' tends to disappear.

'It is well to remember that infliction from without, by another, so far from being an essential element in all thought of punishment, tends more and more completely to disappear, as having no longer even an accidental place, in those deeper realities of punishment which human punishments do but outwardly symbolize. The more we discern their process and character, the more profoundly do we recognize that the punishments of God are what we should call self-acting. There is nothing in them that is arbitrary, imposed, or in any strict propriety of the word, inflicted. As death is the natural consummation of mortal disease, not as an arbitrary consequence inflicted by one who resented the mortal disease, but as its own inherent and inevitable climax ; so what is called the judgment of God upon sin is but the gradual necessary development, in the consistent sinner, of what sin inherently is' (Moberly, *Atonement and Personality*, p. 15).

It is from this point of view alone that we can harmonize the fact of *forgiveness* with that of judgment or retribution. So long as we look on the latter as the inevitable result of *acts* considered each on its merits, there can be no room for forgiveness, or at least it appears as an arbitrary

interference with law. As soon as we realize that both have to do with *character*, the difficulty largely disappears. Our retribution depends on character. Forgiveness affects the character, being bound up with μετάνοια, the change of character. The dying thief may have lived a life of sin ; under the attraction of the grace of Christ, his whole self experiences a change, and so his future can be changed too. The woman who loves much finds the sins of her past forgiven because she has become a new creature. The unmerciful servant finds his old debt back upon him, because the conditional forgiveness of his master has not touched his character. *

(4) *Christ spiritualized the conception of reward and punishment.*—Reward consists not in having certain things, but in seeing God. It is the result of character and the fruition of character. Punishment is the leaving of the self to be identified with sin, and so to depart from Christ into the outer darkness which is separation from God. Again we refer to the Johannine conception of life (17³). In the Synoptics, happiness is connected with the Kingdom, as particularly in the Beatitudes ; it consists of treasure in heaven (Mt 6²⁰, Mk 10²¹). Specially significant is Lk 10²⁰ ; the main cause of rejoicing to the disciples is not the possession of exceptional powers, but the knowledge that their names are written in heaven. All centres round the personal relation of the believer to Christ (Mt 25, Lk 12⁸). And this happiness is enjoyed even now ; the believer has life (Jn 3³⁶ etc.). He enjoys the good things of this life, not as specific rewards for good actions, but as gifts of the love of God which he has fitted himself to use (Mt 6³³). There can indeed be no thought of a claim against God (Lk 17⁷ 6³⁵). We cannot appear as litigants before His judgment-seat.

Accordingly we may say that Christ destroyed the distinction which existed in the Jewish thought of His time, and which still exists in popular ethics, between rewards in this world and the next. If men know where to find their happiness, how to seek for their reward, they have it now, just as the retribution of the evil conscience is immediate. Only this happiness will be a personal possession of the soul ; it may be accompanied by trouble and persecution in the world (Mk 10³⁰, Jn 16². ³³). The believer must not look for the twelve legions of angels to vindicate him ; none the less he will know the peace of Christ, and his joy will be fulfilled even here and now. The Beatitudes and the section on the rewards of discipleship (Mk 10²⁹) are particularly instructive on this point.†

To sum up, Christ did not so much change the place and time of happiness as alter its conception. He transformed the idea of retribution, connecting it not with the isolated act, but with the permanent character which lies behind the act. To find His deepest teaching we must go to the Fourth Gospel and to kindred sayings in the Synoptics. Few will dispute this method, whatever be our ultimate view of the nature of the Fourth Gospel. It is, of course, perfectly true that Christ uses more popular language without scruple, as all teachers must. He appeals to the fear of punishment, and speaks of many and few stripes (Lk 12⁴⁷). He figures the blessedness of the Kingdom under the current image

* The name 'Lazarus' ('God has helped')—the only name given in a parable—must be intended to be significant of character, no less than the names in the *Pilgrim's Progress*.

* The significance of the truth may best be emphasized by a contrast. Buddhism, strictly interpreted, leaves no loophole for forgiveness. Its doctrine of *Karma* is that every act has its strict and inevitable resultant in another existence, either by transmigration, or in heaven or hell. This effect depends on the act *per se*, and has nothing to do with the character. The embryo-Buddha in one of his existences destroyed a widow's hut in a fit of temper. Though he repented and built her a better house, and had performed innumerable other good deeds, yet for this he suffered in hell for eighty thousand years.

† It is obvious to compare Plato, *Republic*, x., on the rewards of the δίκαιος.

of a feast (Mt 22², Lk 14¹⁵), and He uses freely the motive of reward (Mt 6. 10⁴¹ 19²⁸, Lk 6²³ 14¹²) ; He even speaks as though it were the conscious motive of humility (Lk 14⁷⁻¹¹). We must interpret such language in the light of His profounder teaching. Even so, some have found it a fault that the thought of reward does not entirely disappear. Religion should be so completely unselfish that all thought of self should be eliminated. The connexion of virtue with the desire for happiness is one of the ultimate problems of Ethics, and cannot be fully treated here. But this we may say. The claim of extreme altruism must fail because it ignores personality (Gore, *Sermon on the Mount*, ch. vi.). We cannot think ourselves away. We can cease to look for our own happiness in our own short-sighted manner, at the expense of others, apart from God. We can come to identify our own ends with God's purpose for the world, but we cannot dismiss the hope that in the realization of that purpose we shall find our own happiness, that when the Kingdom comes we shall see it and have our place in it. In one sense we learn to do good, hoping for nothing again ; or else in seeking to save our life we shall lose it. And yet in the background there is always the consciousness that in losing our life for Christ's sake, we do in the fuller sense find it. In this paradox is summed up the teaching of Christ and the NT. See also REWARD.

LITERATURE.—Hastings' *DB*, art. 'Eschatology'; Wendt, *Teaching of Jesus* (esp. i. pp. 39 ff. and 210 ff.) ; B. Weiss, *Bibl. Theol. of NT*; Moberly, *Atonement and Personality* (chs. i. to iii.) ; Du Bose, *Gospel in the Gospels* ; Froude, Essay on 'Job' ; Emerson, Essay on 'Compensation' ; J. Drummond, *Via, Veritas, Vita* (1894), 269 ; A. T. Ormond, *Concepts of Philosophy* (1906), 533 ; C. A. Row, *Future Retribution* (1887) ; J. A. Beet, *The Last Things* (1905), 1 ; J. M. Schulhof, *The Law of Forgiveness* (1901), 94.   C. W. EMMET.

REU.—A link in our Lord's genealogy (Lk 3³⁵, AV *Ragau*).

**REVELATION.—1. The question stated. — Few theological or philosophical problems have received keener and more industrious examination than the problem which is suggested to us by the word 'revelation.' Does the word stand for any real disclosure of His secrets by the Eternal ? Does God stoop to unveil His face to men ? And if He does, what is the mode of such manifestations ? What are the conditions under which we may believe that a revelation has been given ? Is there any room in a rational scheme of the Universe for a revelation ? It is pointed out, on the one hand, that every great religion has been promulgated in the faith of its adherents that its message was a veritable message from heaven, not merely a well-reasoned theory about life ; while, on the other hand, it is a part of the claim of Christianity that the revelation of God in Christ is unique and final. 'Comparative Religion' has reached the dignity of a science, and it will not allow us to pass by the non-Christian religions of the world with a mere phrase of patronizing criticism or approval ; while the teaching of the Christian creeds will not allow us to regard our own religion as only one among the many in which men have sought and have found their God. And, within the last half-century, a yet more searching question has been suggested by the scientific view of man's gradual development in mental and moral, as in physical, stature, which dominates at this moment all scientific investigation. Is not revelation rather a gradual disclosure than a sudden unveiling ? And may it not be that what men have taken for an act of God should rather be described as an acquisition on man's part which came to him, as all natural knowledge has come,

by the gradual quickening of his spiritual faculty, in response to the discipline of life ? *

These are among the largest and most momentous questions on which the human mind can be engaged. It would require encyclopædic knowledge to answer them fully, and only the briefest treatment is possible here. But it may help to prepare the way for an answer if we examine the aspects under which the idea of revelation is set forth in the NT, and the presuppositions which it is necessary to make before the questions that have been rehearsed can be clearly apprehended. We cannot entertain the idea of a Divine revelation without making certain large assumptions as to God and man of which it is well to remind ourselves at the outset. They are all assumed in the NT.

2. Presuppositions.—(*a*) First, then, we take for granted the central fact of life—the fact that God is a living Being, Merciful and Just : that ' God *is*, and that he is a rewarder of them that diligently seek him ' (He 11⁶). One must begin somewhere, and we begin here. That is, we assume that, supposing God's creatures to be capable of understanding His purpose in Creation, He is capable, on His part, of making it known to them. He is the Giver of all good things, the Author of all knowledge ; and we recognize that the highest of His gifts may be the knowledge of His will and the stimulus of His grace. (*b*) To say this implies, secondly, that there is a certain capacity in the recipients of such Divine communications. No one will maintain that the Eternal Spirit could thus reveal Himself to the brutes ; for, to be sure, a revelation is limited by the capacity of those to whom it is addressed. Revelation, as Maurice said, is always the unveiling of a person ; and a revelation can be made to personal beings only in terms of personality.

Thus far, no assumption has been made which is peculiar to Christianity. The thesis is simply this : that whatever difficulties are found in believing that men could appreciate a revelation, there is no difficulty in believing that God could give them one, if He be indeed alive. Whether man could securely recognize it as *revelation*, and not as a mere *discovery* of new truth, is another question, to which we shall return later. All that is here asserted is that God *may* communicate with man. If He be a Personal Being, communication with Him is possible. This is the first principle of all religion worthy of the name.

(*c*) We assume, in the third place, that as revelation is thus *possible*, it may also be described as *probable*. Creation involves responsibility for the creature, and thus there is a probability that He who made the world will continue to guide it. Mankind is not perfect, and it is not doubtful that the progress of the race towards holiness and truth would be made easier by the grace of heaven bringing light and life.† To assert that revelation is *probable* is then only to assert that God has pity for human weakness, and that it is not His will that it should be left unaided to perish.

3. Aspects of idea of revelation.—We have now to consider the aspects under which the idea of revelation ‡ is presented in the NT. There are, as it seems, two lines of thought in St. Paul about this great matter which we must try to distinguish. Sometimes he speaks of Divine revelation in terms which would be acceptable to every believer in a spiritual religion ; at other times he uses language which can be interpreted only if we remember that

---

* This is, seemingly, the view taken in Canon Wilson's essay on 'Revelation and Modern Knowledge' (*Cambridge Theological Essays*, p. 229 ff.).
† This is the thesis expounded by Butler (in opposition to Tindal and the Deists of his day) at the beginning of Part II. of the *Analogy* : 'To say Revelation is a thing superfluous, what there was no need of, and what can be of no service, is, I think, to talk quite wildly and at random.'
‡ The word ἀποκάλυψις occurs in the Gr. OT (*e.g.* 1 S 20³⁰, Sir 11²⁷ 22²² 42¹), but never in the sense of a Divine communication.

to him Jesus Christ was a supreme, a unique, a final revelation of the character of the Eternal God. We may take these separately, although they are quite consistent.

4. Revelation in general.—There is a sense in which all religion must presuppose a revelation—that is, the unveiling of His purposes by the Supreme, and the response with which He meets the aspirations and the yearnings of human souls. No religion, *e.g.*, can live which does not encourage and justify the habit of prayer, which does not claim that prayer is heard and answered. In other words, all religion presupposes not only movements of the human spirit towards God, but also a movement of the Divine Spirit towards man. And in every age, and by men of every religious creed, it has been believed—and we cannot doubt that the belief was well founded—that God enters into holy souls and makes known to them His will. In every age and place men have realized His providence, have believed that the Eternal manifests Himself in the world. Now this manifestation may be either *ordinary* or *extraordinary*; by which it is not intended here to suggest any distinction between what is natural and what is supernatural. That distinction may not be tenable, for we do not know all the possibilities of nature, and so do not know what may be above it. But what is meant is that there are two distinct kinds of experience, in which men become assured that God is speaking to them—one the commonplace, everyday routine of life, and the other the experience of rare moments of high spiritual exaltation.

(1) Multitudes of religious men have felt, as they looked back upon the past, that their course was ordered from the beginning by an unseen hand, that a Providence has guided them into the paths which were prepared beforehand for them to walk in, and they have been enabled to perceive in the opportunities of life the calling of a Divine voice. They have felt, moreover, that this is the only intelligible interpretation of life; and that without this revelation—for such it is—of its meaning, life would be chaos, and the secret of the future a dreadful and portentous enigma. The light by which they walk is 'the light which lighteth every man,' and they rejoice in the illumination which it sheds upon their path. Some of the most saintly lives that the world has seen have been lived in the strength of the conviction that the changes and chances, as others call them, of the years are but the unveiling of a Divine face; and that the vision of God becomes brighter when seen through the mists of pain. This is the belief of those men and women among us who have the best right to be heard; their spiritual emotions are not altogether born of their own patient hopes; they are due to the stirring of the Divine Spirit, and the stimulation of the Divine Life; they are a revelation of the unseen.

(2) And to such souls there come rare moments of spiritual ecstasy and exaltation, when they are filled with an overpowering conviction of the presence of God, of His Will for them, of His Will for others. Such a moment it was in the life of St. Peter when he reached the supreme conviction of his life, 'Thou art the Christ, the Son of the living God' (Mt 16^{16}); and we have the highest of all authority for the source of his inspiration: 'Flesh and blood hath not revealed it unto thee, but my Father which is in heaven.' Such a moment came to St. John at Patmos when, being 'in the Spirit on the Lord's day' (Rev 1^{10}, cf. 4^2), he heard the Heavenly voice pronouncing judgment on the Churches, and saw in a vision the Heavenly figure which is always standing unseen in their midst. Such a moment came to St. Paul when the vision of the Christ at the gates of Damascus

changed the whole course of his career; 'is pleased God to reveal his Son in me' (Gal 1^{16}) is his description of the experience. And again and again St. Paul refers the certainty of his convictions to the fact, which is for him indisputable, that they reached him *by revelation*. The 'mystery of Christ,' as he calls it, that the Gentiles are fellow-heirs of the gospel—this was 'made known' to him 'by revelation' (Eph 3^3). The gospel which he preached came to him, he writes to the Galatians, 'not from man, but through revelation of Jesus Christ' (Gal 1^{12}). Such were the revelations of which he wrote, while there were yet others which he counted too intimate, too sacred, to commit to words, as when he says that he 'was caught up into Paradise, and heard unspeakable words which it is not lawful for a man to utter' (2 Co 12^4). It was one of St. Paul's deepest convictions that to him were revealed at times from heaven thoughts greater than his own; so sure is he of this that he is careful on occasion to explain that all his utterances have not the same supreme authority. 'The things which I write, they are the commandment of the Lord' (1 Co 14^{37}). So he says of one subject. Concerning another, 'I have no commandment' (7^{25}) is his prelude, although he concludes, 'I think that I have the Spirit of God' (v.^{40}). But he is sure that the Divine message has been disclosed to him in a fashion which may be sharply distinguished from the ordinary ways in which knowledge is acquired. Human wisdom is not identical with Divine wisdom; so he warns the Corinthians, as he quotes the ancient words, 'Things which eye saw not, and ear heard not, and which entered not into the heart of man, whatsoever things God hath prepared for them that love him'; and declares, 'Unto us God revealed these things'—not the secrets of the future, but the secrets of the present—'these things God revealed through the Spirit' (2$^{9, 10}$).

These and similar passages show beyond doubt that the NT saints, and St. Paul in particular, were quite convinced that God at times reveals His secrets—His mysteries—to a devout and earnest spirit; and that this revelation is consciously recognized by the soul as distinct from the discovery of a Divine purpose in life, or the assurance of Divine guidance, which are reached by patient striving after the highest things. The one is the experience of all good men; the other is the portion of the saints, the elect to whom a fuller disclosure of the Divine will is made. It is the portion of the prophets, the 'seers,' to whom the 'word of the Lord' speaks with an irresistible authority. Yet in both cases—in the ordinary and the extraordinary experiences alike—there is not only a movement of the human soul towards God, but a movement of the Divine love towards man. We generally keep the word 'revelation' for the extraordinary or abnormal experiences; and there is no objection to this restriction, provided we understand that in neither case does man's spirit act without response or without stimulation from heaven. But this it is essential to bear in mind. 'Ye have not chosen me, but I have chosen you' (Jn 15^{16}) are words of universal application.

We have now to interpose with an inevitable question. What is the *test* by which we may assure ourselves that the imaginings of pious souls are not merely of subjective value, that is, that they are anything more than the expression of discontent with the limitations of human knowledge and of human life? What is the test, or is there any test, by which we may 'try the spirits' (1 Jn 4^1), by which we may convince ourselves or others that a true revelation of the Divine will and purpose has been vouchsafed? The theology of the 18th cent. did not hesitate in its answer to this question. The answer was found in the word *miracle*. Miracles were the appropriate credentials of revelation, which could not be guaranteed as objectively valid without them. Paley and Butler and their successors do not delay to prove this; it seems to them beyond dispute. And forty years ago Dr. Mozley put forward the same view in a well-known passage in his Bampton Lectures (*On Miracles*, p. 15) : ' The visible supernatural is the appropriate witness to, the outward sign of, the invisible supernatural — that proof which goes straight to the point; and, a token being wanted of a Divine communication, is that token.' Taking this view of miracles and of revelation, it has been sought to distinguish *natural* from *revealed* religion by the circumstance that miraculous signs are not needed to guarantee the truth of the former, which commends itself at once to man's reason, while they are necessary to confirm our belief in the doctrines of the latter, which are not discoverable by our unassisted faculties, and which may be surprising and even unwelcome to faith.

This is a view which presents many difficulties, clear-cut and definite as it seems. (i.) It is impossible to distinguish sharply *natural* from *revealed* religion, because, in fact, *all* religions have presupposed a revelation, an unveiling of the Unseen Realities. ' Natural religion,' said Guizot (*Méditations*, ii. 237), ' exists only in books.' In all religion there must be a reciprocal communication between man and God ; there must be not only man's aspiration heavenward, but heaven's benediction earthward. And this latter is in its measure a revelation. (ii.) It is true that a revelation of new truths requires to be certified to the intellect as valid, but it is not the *anomalousness* or the *inexplicability* of the circumstances in which it is given that supplies such certificate ; it is their *significance.* A ' sign' need not necessarily be ' miraculous' (see art. ' Sign' in Hastings' *DB*), although it may have this character (see ' Miracle,' *ib.* vol. iii. § 5). The context, so to speak, of revelation helps to disclose its meaning and purpose, and thus enables us to refer it to its true author ; but the significance of the context may depend upon concurrences and combinations, none of which, taken separately, need be abnormal or even unusual. (iii.) The revelation itself may be conveyed by these ' signs' which in fact constitute it. The σημεῖα of the Gospels are vehicles, or media, or instruments of revelation quite as much as evidential adjuncts. Their interpretation leads to new thoughts of God and man, undiscoverable, or at any rate undiscovered, without them ; and thus it is that ' signs' such as the resurrection of Christ (which would be classed as miraculous) or the moral beauty of His life (which some would not regard as necessarily a miracle) form the premises of Christian theology (cf. Westcott, *The Gospel of Life*, p. 80). They unveil the Divine love, and power, and holiness; and they are accepted as true revelations, in part because of the existing testimony to them as historical facts, but in part also because they find a response and a welcome in men's hearts. Such revelations serve to unify the bewildering experiences of life, and provide a means of co-ordinating our thoughts about the highest things. That is to say, in brief, they are accepted as true because they are coherent with our spiritual experience, while at the same time they enlarge its boundaries and illuminate its dark places.

Thus the question, What is the ultimate test of revelation ? is not to be answered merely by pointing to miracle as its guarantee. It is part of a much larger question, What is the ultimate test of ᵗʳuth? And to this there is only one answer : *experience* (cf. Wilson, *l.c.* p. 242), either individual

or general ; that is the one unfailing test of opinion in every department of human life.

(α) First, as to the experience of the individual. That, in the region of the spirit, is not capable of transference from one to another, and—in so far— it can be valid only for him who has had the experience. But for him the sense of ' realized fellowship with the unseen' (cf. Westcott, *l.c.* p. 83) is so vivid and so vital that he cannot call it in question. He is conscious not only of the strivings of his own soul, but of a response from the spiritual world. And if it be urged that, after all, it would be impossible for him to be sure of this, so subtle and deep-seated are the movements of the soul, his only reply can be that he *is* sure of it. He is able to distinguish, he will tell you,—for St. Paul's experience here is not singular or even unusual,—between the convictions which he has reasoned out for himself and those which have presented themselves to him with an irresistible authority from without. And he will point, in justification, to what is an admitted fact of mental life, viz., that our powers of discovery are no true measure of our powers of recognition. We can all recognize as true, and as obviously true, many a principle, or law, or fact, when it is once brought before our notice, which we should have been quite incapable of discovering for ourselves.* And it has been the deep-seated belief of the saints that their most cherished and intimate convictions were such as they could never have reached had they not been guaranteed to them by a message from the spiritual world.

(β) But, it will be said, there can be nothing trustworthy in such merely individual convictions. To claim to be in possession of a revelation from heaven is one of the commonest symptoms of mental disorder ; and those who make such claims most persistently are the most intractable patients in asylums for the insane. There is, unhappily, no doubt of it. The mystical spirit is divorced, in too many cases, from any just sense of the logic of facts ; and incapacity to judge aright of things temporal is often combined with an eager and extravagant judgment upon things eternal. It may be—we do not know—that sometimes a true vision of the spiritual order has proved too much for a brain intellectually feeble, and that the mental powers have been permanently injured by too great an effort being demanded of them. And —conversely—it is undoubtedly true that when the brain fails to do its work, whether from disease, or overstrain, or other causes, the man ceases to be able to distinguish fancies from facts, both in the physical and the spiritual world. But to conclude, therefore, that all alike who have claimed to have had visions of the spiritual order, or who believe that God has answered their prayers directly, are necessarily insane, would be a strangely perverse and illogical inference. Indeed, experience suggests a quite different generalization. Despite these abnormal cases, the men of spiritual insight who see ' visions,' who live near to the boundary of the spiritual order, are the truly ' practical' men, and achieve most of enduring benefit for the race. The truth is that, taken separately, spiritual experiences cannot be verified by any one except the recipient of them ; but they cannot be dismissed as untrustworthy merely because some who claim to have enjoyed them are not very wise.

The spiritual experience of the individual is not transferable—apparently, for it would not be well to dogmatize on such a point—from one to another.

* This is fully admitted by so thoroughgoing a Rationalist as Kant : ' If the Gospel had not taught the universal moral laws in their purity, reason would not yet have attained to so complete a knowledge of them ; although, once they are there, we can be convinced through pure reason of their truth and validity' (Letter to Jacobi in Jacobi's *Werke*, iii. 532).

So far, then, it does not submit itself to any objective test of its trustworthiness. But when we find, as we do find, that in a large number of cases the individual experiences which are reported or recorded are of an identical character as regards the information which they supply of the spiritual order, they present a phenomenon which is within the reach of scientific investigation. That the Eternal guides human lives and does not permit them to drift aimlessly into the paths which lead nowhere, that He answers prayer, that He supplies counsel and strength—these are not specially Christian convictions, they are shared by countless multitudes who would all offer the same proof of their truth, namely, personal experience. This is a solid fact of human nature which demands recognition. And if such convictions are not entirely mistaken, then the Eternal has in so far given a revelation of His power and of His love. He has intervened in human life ; He has given men some insight into His purposes.

The test of truth is experience ; experience must count for something when we are examining the widespread belief of mankind that the Eternal reveals Himself in the life of the individual and in the life of the race alike.

We have seen that the general experience of religious men gives identical testimony as to God's power and willingness to communicate with them in their need. But we saw, too (§ 2), that a certain mental and spiritual capacity must be presupposed in the recipients of any revelation. And, as this grows from age to age in the history of the race, and is by no means equal in all races at the same period, or in all men even of the same race and epoch, it will follow that revelation, if made at all, must be made gradually and progressively, in correspondence not only with the needs but with the capacity of men. We have all learnt the truth of this in regard to the history of the race, and it is unnecessary to dwell upon it. If the minute and careful study of the OT history and literature, which has occupied the best thoughts of so many of our best Christian scholars for 40 years, had taught us nothing but this, we should still have learnt a lesson of the most far-reaching significance—a lesson which is full of hope and inspiration. It is a lesson which is illustrated by the history of every religion in which men have sought to find God ; the measure of His grace is their capacity of receiving it, and not any Divine economy by which there is a jealous hiding of His face. And the same is true of the individual soul. It is in correspondence with the gradual quickening of our spiritual faculty that the Divine secret is gradually disclosed. 'Unto him that hath, to him shall be given' (Mt 13¹²) is not a paradox of the Divine bounty ; it is a law of nature, and therefore of revelation as well. Not all at once can we expect to experience the Beatific Vision, but only in proportion as we grow more and more into the Divine likeness, and learn, through the slow and often disappointing discipline of life, to read the Divine purposes. This is not to evacuate the idea of revelation of its content, and regard our spiritual progress as due entirely to the efforts and strivings of our own souls. These must be present,—there must be a movement on man's part if he is to reach at last his highest,—but the revelation which is given is not his discovery, but a Divine act of unveiling.

It is the consummation of this progress, both for the individual and for the race, which is portrayed in the vision of the prophet as the moment when 'the glory of the Lord shall be revealed, and all flesh shall see it together,'—not as isolated individuals, but as members of the great company of the saints,—'they shall see it together : for the mouth of Jehovah hath spoken it ' (Is 40⁵).

5. The revelation of Christ.—So far, we have been considering the idea of revelation in general —the idea of God revealing His will to man— which appears again and again in Scripture, and which has been abundantly justified by the experience of the saints in every age. But nothing has yet been said which is distinctively Christian, or which touches the belief of Christians that in Christ there is a supreme and sufficient revelation of God. If the doctrine of revelation which has been here set forth exhausted the content of the idea, then there would be no place left for that which is specially characteristic of the Christian religion. What has been said about the possibility and the gradual progress of a revelation would apply to other nations as well as to the Jews, for God has never 'left himself without a witness' (Ac 14¹⁷). And nothing has been said at all about the revelation of God in Christ, which is the centre of the Christian hope. The passages which were quoted from the NT have a general application. We have now, however, to examine passages of a different character.

St. Paul urges, in the Second Epistle to the Corinthians, that if the message of the Christ was not understood by the Jews, it was due to their incapacity, not to its obscurity. 'If our gospel is veiled,' he says, ' it is veiled in them that are perishing' (4³), i.e. the fault lies with the hearers, not with the giver, of the message. That is his way of expressing a great principle which we have already considered, that revelation, to be instructive, presupposes a certain mental capacity, a keenness of spiritual vision, in those to whom it is addressed. In the previous chapter of the same letter, St. Paul had urged that the Jews had never recognized the transitory character of the Law which was their discipline ; 'a veil was upon their heart' (3¹⁵), which prevented them from seeing that the Law was only a stage in the Divine education of Israel. But, he adds, allegorizing the old story of the veil on the face of Moses, 'if they turn to the Lord, the veil is removed ' (v.¹⁶), and an open vision is granted. The consummation to which they should look is that ' the light of the glory of Christ, who is the image of God, should dawn upon them' (4⁴). And, in like manner, he points out elsewhere that ' the law was but a tutor to lead them to Christ' (Gal 3²⁴). ' Christ is the end of the law' (Ro 10⁴), in whom it received a perfect fulfilment. This, indeed, is the burden of the Apostolic preaching, that 'God, who of old time spoke to the fathers by divers portions and in divers manners, hath in these last days spoken to us by his Son' (He 1¹). It is not needful to multiply quotations which illustrate this familiar Christian thought—that highly favoured as the Jewish people had been by revelations of the Divine, yet the complete—the perfect— revelation of God is in Christ.

(1) There is a sense in which it demands no special gift of faith to discern in Christ a revelation such as had not dawned upon the world before. And there are passages in the NT which, taken by themselves, would not go beyond this. He was ' a prophet, like unto Moses' (Ac 3²²), although with a clearer, a more urgent message. For the most part, He is represented in the Synoptics as *the Great Teacher*, strong, wise, and merciful—whose words were powerful to move men towards holiness, and whose teachings shed a new light upon the perplexities of conduct. ' A new teaching,' His hearers said; and they were right. The Fatherhood of God, the dignity and supreme value of the spiritual life, the significance of faith, the Catholic sympathy of love (see

Wendt, *The Idea and the Reality of Revelation*, p. 28)—these are truths of which, indeed, there had been anticipations in the prophets, but they were expounded by Him with a lucidity and an authority which distinguished Him at once from all the great teachers of the past. And even if we could get no further than this, the claim of Jesus Christ to be the spiritual Master of mankind would be a claim which we could not lightly neglect. If the utterances of holy men in every age deserve a reverent attention, as expressing convictions born of a true spiritual experience, the words of Christ demand a deeper reverence of submission, for He was—at the lowest—the greatest Master of the spiritual life.

(2) Not even yet, however, have we touched upon those claims of His which mark Him out as *unique*, those aspects of His life which require us to think of His teaching as differing from other teachings, not only in degree, but in kind. We have not, indeed, to read the Gospels very closely to observe that Jesus Christ claimed to be more than a Teacher, and that His authority was other than that of the greatest of the prophets. He said that He was the Messiah, who was to 'declare all things' (Jn 4[25]). He is the Son beloved of the Father, to whom the Father showed all His works (5[20]). He alone has 'seen the Father' (6[46]); and not only is this vision peculiarly His, but through Him it may be revealed to men: 'He that hath seen me hath seen the Father' (14[9]). These phrases are all taken, it is true, from the Fourth Gospel; but the view of Christ's Person which they present is not peculiar to St. John, for the common tradition of St. Matthew and St. Luke preserves the tremendous assertion, 'No man knoweth the Son, but the Father; neither knoweth any the Father, but the Son, and he to whom the Son willeth to reveal him' (Mt 11[27].= Lk 10[22]). It is clear that Christ is represented in the Gospels as more than a Teacher of Divine wisdom; He is the Revealer of the Divine character. The matter, the content, of the revelation which He offers to mankind transcends the message of prophets and holy men, in this, that it has to do not merely with man's relation to the Supreme, with man's duty and man's destiny, but with the inmost nature of God. Not only is He an ambassador of Heaven; but He has *seen the Father*. No such claim as this is made in the record of the most intimate and sacred spiritual history of the saints.

It is this aspect of Christ as the Revealer of God which is indicated in the profound phrases of the Prologue to the Fourth Gospel. He is the Word, the Eternal Wisdom; He was 'from the beginning with God,' and is God. Revelation is the act of self-manifestation of God to man, and the Word is the eternal expression of Deity, as in Creation at the first, so in the Incarnation when the fulness of time had come. So Athanasius: 'It was the function of the Word, who, by His peculiar providence and ordering of the universe, teaches us concerning the Father, to renew that same teaching' (τοῦ γὰρ διὰ τῆς ἰδίας προνοίας καὶ διακοσμήσεως τῶν ὅλων διδάσκοντος περὶ τοῦ Πατρός, αὐτοῦ ἦν καὶ τὴν αὐτὴν διδασκαλίαν ἀνανεῶσαι, *de Incarn. Verb. Dei*, c. 14). The same idea is in Irenæus. 'Per ipsam conditionem, revelat Verbum conditorem Deum, et per mundum fabricatorem mundi Dominum, et per plasma eum qui plasmaverit artificem, et per Filium eum Patrem qui generaverit Filium' (*c. Hær.* iv. 6). These high speculations are perhaps beyond the modest capacity of human reason, but at all events they are in accordance with the phrases of Scripture, which represent the Word as the Agent of Creation, and as the Expression of the Divine Will. Christ is set before us in the Bible and the Church as the Revealer of the Divine nature and not only as the Revealer of Divine secrets.

It has been urged by some writers that the uniqueness of Christ as Revealer is indicated in the NT by the fact that, while revelation is continually represented as proceeding *from* Him, it is never represented as given *to* Him. He is the exponent, not the recipient, of revelation; and is, in a sense, the Revealer and the Revealed (1 Ti 3[16]), both the subject and the object of revelation. This, however, is to use language that strict exegesis does not justify. 'The revelation of Jesus Christ, which God *gave unto him* to show unto his servants'... (Rev 1[1]), is the view of Christ's office as Revealer which is presented in

the Fourth Gospel as well as in the Apocalypse. Christ describes Himself as 'a man that hath told you the truth which I heard from God' (Jn 8[40]); 'as the Father taught me, I speak these things' (v.[28]); 'the Father which sent me hath given me a commandment, what I should say and what I should speak' (12[49]).

The distinguishing features of the 'revelation of Jesus Christ' are, rather: (*a*) He reveals *the inmost nature of God* (see above). (*b*) The revelation to the Son is not intermittent, but *continuous and perpetual*. 'The Father *showeth* him all things' (Jn 5[20]); 'himself *hath given* (δέδωκεν) me a commandment' (12[49]), the tense marking the continuance of the action of the command (so Westcott).* (*c*) *All* has been revealed to Him. 'The Father showeth him *all* things that himself doeth' (5[20]). The Son sees *all*, while we see *parts* in Him (so Westcott). The revelation which Christ in His own Person gave of the Divine nature is represented as complete; and the task of the Divine Spirit throughout the ages is to assist mankind in the understanding of it (14[26]), and in the application of it to life. It is not to be understood all at once (16[12]), nor will it be perfectly apprehended until the Day of Consummation, when the human race shall have fulfilled its destiny, 'the day when the Son of Man shall be revealed' (Lk 17[3]), the day to which the Apostolic Epistles continually point as the day of 'the revelation of Jesus Christ' (1 Co 1[7], 1 P 1[13]), for which humanity is to wait in patience and hope.

These quotations have been given at length, because it is this claim of Christ to be the Revealer of the Eternal God, as no other was, which is the centre of the Christian religion, and it is this claim which is felt to be difficult to reconcile with the claims of other religions to the possession of revealed truth. But it will bear repetition that it is no article of the Christian faith that God does not reveal His purposes and His will except in Christ, or that those who seek His face without the knowledge of Christ shall be disappointed of their hope. Wherever and whenever the spirit of man has sought communion with the Eternal Spirit, a response—we must believe—has been given; and such response is, in its measure, a revelation of light and life. By whatever avenues of thought men reach new truth about the highest things, the light which makes their journey possible is a light in the heavens. It was a favourite thought of the early Christian apologists that the aspirations of pagan philosophy after God were prompted and encouraged by the Eternal Word speaking to men's hearts. 'Those that have lived with Reason' (οἱ μετὰ λόγου βιώσαντες), writes Justin Martyr, 'are Christians, even though they were counted atheists, such as Socrates and Heraclitus and others among the Greeks, and among the barbarians Abraham and the rest' (*Apol.* i. 46). That there is always the seed of Divine Reason (λόγος σπερματικός) in man is urged by the same writer more than once: τὸ ἔμφυτον παντὶ γένει ἀνθρώπων σπέρμα τοῦ λόγου (*Apol.* ii. 8) is a typical utterance. Whatever we may think of the technical phrases of Christian theology used by these writers, we cannot doubt that their main thought was true. God is *always* revealing Himself to the world. Yet—the question recurs—how then are we to express our belief in a *special* revelation in Christ, a revelation differing not only in degree but in kind from all that went before? We are so much affected, in this age, by the idea of orderly and continuous progress in nature, and by the idea of the gradual quickening of man's spiritual faculty, that we find it unwelcome to be

* Sabatier has observed (*Outlines of a Philosophy of Religion*, p. 41) that a phrase in the Gospel according to the Hebrews brings this out well. At the moment of His baptism, the Holy Spirit says to Jesus: 'Mi Fili, Te exspectabam in omnibus prophetis, ut venires et requiescerem in Te. Tu enim es requies mea.'

presented with the conception of *crisis*, and with any theory of knowledge or life involving a breach of that rule of *continuity* by which we are accustomed to guide our thoughts.

6. Recapitulation.—It will be convenient to approach our final answer by re-stating in our modern ways of speech that view of revelation in general, and of the Christian revelation in particular, which seems to be presented in the NT. It is, at any rate, coherent, and is taught by St. Peter as well as by St. Paul, by the Synoptists as well as by St. John. Nor is it out of harmony with the profoundest teachings of science about nature and about man.

The Christian doctrine of God presupposes that He is a Personal Being who lives and acts eternally. We cannot confine His Personal life by the conditions which limit our own; to use the homely phrase of Wm. Law, perhaps the sanest of English mystics, He is really greater than man; He *transcends* nature, for He is its Author. But He does not stand apart, as it were, from the created life which has issued from Him; He is, as philosophers express it, *immanent* in nature; He is its Life and its Light. The sun enlightens the earth with its beams, and warms into life the beings with which it is peopled; but the Eternal Spirit is the Life and Light of all creation, and communicates this Life and Light consciously and with a purpose of love. In nature and in history God is always present, always active, always compassionate.

But neither in the field of nature nor in the field of history would it be true to say that the purpose of the Supreme is everywhere clearly revealed. On the contrary, it is for the most part veiled from our eyes. We may speak, indeed, of the Creation itself as a revelation of the Eternal. Perhaps it was an exhibition of that Divine law by which love always seeks an object on which to spend itself, that law which in human life at its noblest always demands sacrifice. Perhaps the law that we only secure our highest life by not attempting to save it received here a stupendous illustration. We cannot tell. But, at any rate, throughout creation, as it is, the Divine love is veiled. In the struggles and competitions of created life, pain and death are the inevitable issue for the weak; in nature it is only the strong that survive. It is a perpetual tax upon faith, in the face of nature's cruelty, to believe—as nevertheless we do believe—that God cares for the sparrows, and that the meaner creatures of the earth are not beyond the reach of His compassion.

(1) Where, then, in nature is God most clearly seen? There is only one possible answer. It is in *man*, the highest creature of His that we know; in man, who is unique among the creatures, because he reflects, however dimly, the Divine image in which he was made. Man, indeed, is far removed in fact from that which he was intended to be. *Corruptio optimi pessima.* His capacity for good, by misuse, has become a capacity for evil, to which the humbler animals cannot sink. That is all true. But even in the most degraded man or woman there is that affinity to the Divine which makes redemption possible. In this seed of goodness, which lingers even in the foulest soul, there is always the hope of the future. It is *in* this elect creature—this creature chosen to be the highest because the best fitted for the service of the Creator—that God perpetually reveals Himself, as we perceive that love is, after all, stronger than hate. It is *to* this elect creature—despite his kinship with the beasts, a kinship displayed during every hour of his earthly life—it is *to* this elect creature, and to him alone, that God deigns to reveal His will,—not perpetually, indeed, but at those too rare moments when the spirit is completely master of the flesh. God is always active in nature; He unveils His face only to the elect of creation, and to the elect individuals of the elect race.

(2) The like is true of the Divine revelation in the field of history. Of the destiny of nations, God is the supreme arbiter. Not theologians only, but historians too, will be found to declare that human history is providentially ordered, that 'the Most High ruleth in the kingdom of men' (Dn 4^{32}). And viewing history on a large scale, that *may* be the inevitable conclusion. But we cannot say that it is self-evident, or that perplexities do not present themselves to any one who endeavours to trace an eternal purpose in the decline and fall of empires. In the philosophy of history it is not always easy to find certain tokens of a superintending Providence. In history, as in nature, we see such tokens with greater distinctness when the observation is directed to a particular part of the field. The secrets of the Divine rule are disclosed to us most clearly when we recall the history of the Chosen People, the race elect of the Supreme as His instrument for the education of the world. No history reveals the Divine intention in the same degree as the history of Israel. And thus we rightly look upon the Hebrew literature and history as preserving for us in a special manner the revelation of God's purposes in the education of mankind. This is not to make any arbitrary distinction between sacred history and profane history. All history is sacred, for it is directed and controlled by the Eternal Wisdom. But not in all history alike are we permitted to discern the guidance of God who thus reveals Himself. It is no more anomalous or surprising that the revelation should be explicitly recognized as such only in the history of the elect nation Israel, than that His revelation in nature should be recognized as such only in the character of the elect creature—man. The Divine action is always implicit in nature and in history; both are potential revelations, so to speak, of the Eternal Light and Wisdom, but in neither field does the revelation become actual, save in the chosen organ of the Divine life. Man is not an anomaly among the creatures, nor is Israel an anomaly among the nations; but as man with his reason and power of choice is the best fitted of creatures, and Israel with its genius for religion is the best fitted of the nations, to receive and to impart the revelations of the Divine will, to man and to Israel have they been entrusted in a peculiar degree. The story of *revelation* is always a story of *election* (cf. Martensen, *Christian Dogmatics*, p. 13).

If we can go thus far, we are constrained to go a step farther. For in the Christ is the consummation, the summing up, of humanity. He is the Representative Man. And in the Christ, too, is the fulfilment of Israel's high destiny as the Servant of Jehovah, the Messenger and Ambassador of the Most High. It is not surprising, then, that He should claim to be the Revealer of the Godhead, in a sense and after a manner unexampled elsewhere. He, too, is the *Elect*, the *Beloved*. There is a coherence in the NT account of Christ the Revealer which demands for it a reverent hearing from every thoughtful man, no matter what his belief about historical Christianity may be. We do not assume any breach in the continuity of nature when we hold that a revelation of God may be perceived in man which cannot be perceived in the lower creatures. We do not make history discontinuous if we hold that a revelation of God may be perceived in the record of His dealings with Israel which cannot be perceived in the record of His dealings with Greece, although He is the Supreme Arbiter of the destinies of Israel and Greece alike. To the creature and to the nation uniquely fitted to receive and to reflect a Divine revelation, it has been given, in divers portions and manners, according to the need and the capacity of the recipient. But the Christ stands alone, in nature and in history, the flower of humanity and the culmination of Israel's hope—alone, for God has become man in Him. There can be no interruption or faltering in the communion between the Perfect Man and God, for He is perfect because He shares the Divine nature itself. The revelation is no longer occasional, but permanent; no longer a gradual unveiling, but the full disclosure of the Father's face ; no longer to be conceived as for one race only, for ' this is the revelation of the mystery which was kept secret since the world began, but now is made manifest—made known to all nations for the obedience of faith ' (Ro $16^{25f.}$; cf. 1 Co 2^7).

LITERATURE.—Cremer, *Bib.-Theol. Lex., s.v.* ἀποκάλυψις; Kaftan, *Dogmatik,* §4 ; Martensen, *Chr. Dogm.* p. 5 ff. ; Ewald· *Rev.: Its Nat. and Record* ; Fairbairn, *Christ in Mod. Theol.* p. 493 ff. ; Flint, *Theism,* Lect. x. ; Luthardt, *Fund. Truths f Chty.,* Lect. vii. ; R. H. Hutton, ' Revelation ' in *Theol. Essays;* Newman, *Oxford Univ. Serm.* ii. ; Dale, *Ephesians,* Lect. viii. ; *PRE*[3], art. ' Offenbarung ' ; G. P. Fisher, *Nature and Method of Revelation* ; C. Harris, *Pro Fide,* 274 ; Sabatier, *Outlines of a Phil. of Rel.,* bk. i. ch. 2 ; Bruce, *Apologetics,* 298 ; Christlieb, *Mod. Doubt,* Lect. ii. ; A. J. Balfour, *Foundations of Belief;* W. Sanday, *Inspiration;* Illingworth, *Reason and Revelation;* W. Morgan, ' Faith and Revelation ' in *ExpT* ix. (1898) 485, 537 ; M. Dods, *The Bible, its Origin and Nature.* 61.

J. H. BERNARD.

REVELATION, BOOK OF.—Whatever perplexities may still attend the interpretation of the Apocalypse, there can be no question as to the place which it assigns to Jesus Christ, or the copiousness and variety of the references which the writer makes to His Person and His work. For him the fact of Christ conditions the whole of human history. He is the Lamb slain from the foundation of the world (13^8), and He is the Bridegroom-Judge, whose eagerly expected coming will bring to a close the history of the world that now is. And what is true of the world's history is also true of the book itself ; its whole contents are a ' revelation ' (Apocalypse) of Jesus Christ (1^1), a revelation which proceeds from Him, and is mediated ' by his angel ' to ' his servant John.'

It will be convenient to examine the references and the doctrine which lies behind them in the order of our Lord's experience, beginning with His life on earth. In the first place, it is noteworthy that the human name Jesus, borne by Christ when He was on earth, which is rare in the writings of St. Paul and absent from those of St. Peter, occurs here nine (or ten) times. The martyrs are ' the witnesses of Jesus ' (17^6) ; their witness is ' the testimony of Jesus ' (1^1 etc.) ; and it is by this simple human name that the Divine Speaker describes Himself (22^{16}). In this usage we may see an indication of authorship by one who had ' known Christ after the flesh,' to whom the name He had then borne was both familiar and dear. If authoritative criticism no longer permits us to see direct allusions to either the birth or the ascension of Jesus in the story of the ' man-child ' contained in ch. 12, His death by crucifixion is very pointedly alluded to as an historical fact (11^8), His victory in 3^{21} (' as I also overcame '), and His resurrection in $1^{5.18}$. His twelve Apostles find mention in 21^{14}, and there are echoes of His teaching as recorded in the Gospels in $3^{5.10}$ 7^{17} 21^6 and 21^{23}.

These recollections of Jesus of Nazareth have not been obliterated by the vision of the exalted Christ ; rather are the two elements held together in a singular harmony of conviction. Passing to the second, we find that the richness of the conception of Christ which marks the Apocalypse may be gauged by the variety and significance of the aspects in which He is presented—the Word,

the Lamb, the Shepherd, the Bridegroom, the Judge, the King of kings. Here only outside the Fourth Gospel does Christ receive the deeply significant title of ' the Word of God ' (19^{13}), and the idea of pre-existence which the name carries with it also lies behind the declaration twice repeated, ' I am Alpha and Omega, the beginning and the end ' (1^{17} 21^6). But the commonest and the most characteristic title of Christ in this book is ' the Lamb '—a title which is used by the writer with great freedom, as though it had come to have for him almost the force of a proper name (cf. $21^{9.23.27}$ 22^3). The use of the name is, however, rooted in the conviction of the redemptive efficacy of Christ's sacrifice ; it suggests the aspect of His work which is most prominent to the mind of ' John.' It should be noted that the word itself is not identical with that applied to Jesus in John's Gospel ($1^{29.36}$) ; it is a diminutive and a neuter ; but the meaning is the same, and the sacrificial reference is indubitable. The Lamb stands ' as though it had been slain ' (5^6) ; He is hailed as One who has ' redeemed us to God by his blood ' (5^9) ; the adoring saints in heaven are those ' who have washed their robes, and made them white in the blood of the Lamb ' (7^{14}, cf. 1^5). These latter passages emphasize the ethical consequences of the Atonement, and trace them to the ' blood ' of Christ in the same way as the First Epistle of John. The spiritual principle of the Atonement is suggested by the figure of the Lamb itself, in which are combined the attributes of lamb-like character—meekness, gentleness, and purity—and the sacrificial function historically associated with a lamb. At the same time, ' the Lamb,' originally a figure for Christ in the sacrificial aspect of His work, takes on, besides, attributes which belong to Him in other of His functions, and so we read of ' the wrath of the Lamb ' (6^{16}), of ' the Lamb's book of life ' (21^{27}), of kings making war with the Lamb and being overcome by Him (17^{14}), of ' the marriage of the Lamb ' (19^7), and, finally, of the Lamb as ruler of the heavenly city (22^3), as at once the temple of it and ' the light thereof ' ($21^{23.24}$). Thus, while every aspect of the work of Christ, whether in earth or heaven, finds adoring record here, there is a subtle recognition of the fact that all the forms of His relation to men spring out of the fundamental function of redemption.

The writer of the Apocalypse, therefore, holding firmly to the humanity of the Jesus whom probably he had known in the flesh, yet ascribing to Him as the Lamb functions of redemption, government, and judgment, offers to Him throughout his book the homage which is due only to ' God manifest in the flesh.' This is seen alike in the titles, the functions, and the attributes assigned to Him. Every detail of description serves only to enhance the dignity and the glory of His Person. He is ' the Lord of lords and King of kings ' (17^{14} 19^{16}). To Him is attributed all the honour and authority pertaining to the Messiah and more. Angels who refuse worship offered to themselves (19^{10} 22^8) unite with all creation to worship God and the Lamb (5^{11-13}). His existence reaches back before the beginning of things created. Himself the principle from which all creation issues (3^{14}; cf. Col 1^{15}, Pr 8^{22}), He is the absolutely Living One from whose lips are heard words which can be spoken by God alone : ' I am the first and the last, and the Living One ' (1^{17}, cf. 1^8). He holds the keys of Death and of Hades (1^{18}) — keys which, according to the later Jewish tradition, were held by the hand of the Almighty alone. In the vision of the Son of Man which introduces the Letters to the Seven Churches, the writer takes one after another of those phrases which had been consecrated from old times to the description of the Most High God, those attributes in which He had been apparelled by prophets and psalmists, and lays them simply upon Christ as upon One whose right to bear them was beyond question. The description of 'the Ancient of Days' (Dn 7[9]) is transferred to Him, as well as the power to 'search the heart and the reins,' which is the peculiar attribute of Jehovah (2[23], cf. Ps 7[9]). It is not strange, therefore, that to this Divine Figure is committed the unfolding of the Book of human Destiny (5[5]), the waging of the final conflict with evil, and the holding of the Divine assize.

This complete and unhesitating attribution of Divine rank and authority to Jesus Christ is the more remarkable when we give due weight to the intense Hebraism of the writer. A Jew of the Jews, his mind saturated with Hebrew thought, a true son of the race to which monotheism had become a passion, and the ascription of Divine honour to any other than God a horror and a blasphemy, the author nevertheless sets Jesus side by side with the Almighty. One meaning of the phenomenon is plain. It offers the most striking proof of the impression made by Jesus upon His disciples, one which had been sufficient to revolutionize their most cherished religious belief; for them He had the value of God. And the special aspect of His Person and work which is emphasized, as we have seen, in the Apocalypse, gives the clue to the explanation of this exalted Christology. The kernel of experience from which the process starts is indicated in the declaration: 'He hath loosed (*v.l.* 'washed') us from our sins.' John and those in whose name he wrote had found the sin-barrier between them and God removed, and the sin-dominion over them broken; and this experience they traced to Jesus, to what He had done for them in dying, and in them as living again. And if, along with this their indubitable experience of forgiveness of, and deliverance from, sin, we take the universal conviction of their time, expressed in the question of the Pharisees, 'Who can forgive sins save God only?' we have little difficulty in perceiving the avenue along which the gaze of the Apocalyptist travelled till it beheld the throne of God as a throne which was shared also by 'the Lamb.'

C. ANDERSON SCOTT.

REVENGE.—See VENGEANCE.

REVERENCE.—The sentiment of veneration, a feeling of high regard and admiration. When cherished towards a superior, it is an emotion of respectful awe. When directed towards God, it is an essential factor in Divine worship. This sentiment usually finds expression in acts of courtesy, respect, or adoration, so that the object held in reverential regard receives fitting homage. But it is to be noted that the term θρησκεία, which in Ac 26[5] emphasizes the ritual side of religion, does not occur in the Gospels (cf. Coleridge, *Aids to Reflection*, Introd., Aphor. xxiii.).

The terms which denote reverence towards God come properly under 'worship,' in which reverence is an essential quality; but it may be proper to include in this article passages which involve reverence towards Jesus Christ in the days of His flesh. In the Gospel narratives several terms are used to express the feeling of reverence, but there is no decisive reason to distinguish the usage of these terms as they occur in the Synoptics and in the Fourth Gospel. The term 'reverence,' as the tr. of ἐντρέπεσθαι—'to turn one's self unto'—is found only a few times. It is used in the parable of the Wicked Husbandmen (Mt 21[37], Mk 12[6], Lk 20[13]), where the idea is that even those who had ill-treated the servants might show proper respect and honour to the Son.

(See also the usage of the same word in the parable of the Unjust Judge, who 'feared not God, neither regarded man,' Lk 18[2-4]).

The word τιμή and its derivatives are used to express high reverential regard and profound respect (Mt 13[57] 15[4-6], Mk 7[10], Jn 5[23. 41] 8[49. 54]). Here the regard due to a prophet of God, the affectionate respect of children for their parents, and reverence for the Son, as for the Father, are expressed. The term προσκυνεῖν, which means 'to kiss the hand to,' and then 'to bow down before,' is often used in the Gospels to signify the sentiment of reverential regard, and even of worship (Mt 2[2. 8-11] 4[9] 14[33] 15[25] 20[20] 28[17], Mk 5[6] 15[19]). In these passages we have reference to the adoration of Jesus by the Magi, Herod's desire to do homage to the child at Bethlehem, the request of the devil that Jesus should worship him, the disciples doing homage to their Lord by the sea, the Canaanite woman humbling herself before Jesus, the mother of James and John as she made her bold request for her two sons, the disciples after the resurrection of Christ, the demoniac of Gadara before Jesus, the mock homage paid to Jesus on the Cross. In many of these passages the outward act of bowing down is implied.

In one place (Jn 9[31]) the term θεοσεβής is used to describe a worshipper of God, or one who regards and treats God with reverence. In several places certain physical acts are significant of reverence, such as προσπίπτειν, 'to fall down before' (Mk 3[11] 5[33], Lk 8[28]); γονυπετεῖν, 'to bend the knee' (Mt 17[14], Mk 1[40]); πίπτειν ἐπὶ πρόσωπον, 'to fall upon the face.' These movements of the body are expressive of feelings of reverential regard. In some passages δοξάζειν, 'to glorify,' is used in a rather suggestive way to set forth the idea of giving reverence to (as in Mt 6[2] 9[8], Mk 2[12], Lk 5[25. 26] 7[16], Jn 8[54] 17[1-4]), where hypocrites seeking glory of men, people of different sorts giving glory to God, the Father glorifying the Son, and the Son giving glory to the Father, are alluded to. In the Lord's Prayer, ἁγιάζειν, 'to hallow' or 'hold sacred' (Mt 6[9]) the name of God, implies the sentiment of reverence in its highest form. The terms ἀσπάζειν, 'to salute,' and ἀσπασμός, 'salutation' (Mk 9[15] 15[18], Lk 1[29-41]), are also expressive of reverential regard.

Some additional passages may be merely noted, wherein words and phrases denote reverence in different aspects: Mt 7[29] 8[8] 9[27] 12[23] 16[16] 21[9-15] 22[21] 23[12] 26[12], Mk 17 9[1-10], Lk 2[9-20] 7[16. 44. 45] 8[35-37] 19[35] 23[11], Jn 12[3. 14] 13[13] 21[15-17].

In the Gospel narratives it is evident that the sentiment of reverence has a large place. It is at root a certain psychical state, or temper of the soul. This temper seeks expression in certain outward acts. In religion this state of the soul is fundamental, and its expression in ritual acts is natural.

LITERATURE.— C. F. Kent, *Messages of Israel's Lawgivers* (1902), 247; A. H. M. Sime, *Elements of Religion* [2], 15, *Epic of God* (1902), 53; E. Wordsworth, *Thoughts on the Lord's Prayer* (1898), 63; G. H. Morrison, *Flood-tide* (1901), 103; Newman, *Par. and Plain Serm.* i. 295, v. 13, viii. 1; T. G. Selby, *Lesson of a Dilemma* (1893), 123; Phillips Brooks, *Light of the World* (1891), 253.

FRANCIS R. BEATTIE.

REVILING.—1. Insult was as prominent as cruelty in the tragedy that ended on Calvary. See art. MOCKERY.

2. In Mt 5[11] (‖ Lk 6[22]) Jesus pronounces a blessing upon those who are reviled for His sake (ὀνειδίζω here is the same word as is used in Mk 15[32] of the reproaches of the Cross). That the secret of the blessedness lies in the spirit in which the abuse is borne is shown by the 'Rejoice and be exceeding glad' of the following verse, as well as by St. Paul's 'Being reviled, we bless,' in a passage (1 Co 4[12. 13]) where he evidently has the Eighth Beatitude in mind. St. Peter (1 P 2[23]) says of Jesus that 'being reviled, he reviled not again' (λοιδορούμενος οὐκ

ἀντελοιδόρει). And the author of Hebrews suggests that the best preservative against hasty reprisals and a violent temper is a contemplation of the patient silence of Jesus. 'For consider him that endured such contradiction of sinners against himself, lest ye be wearied and faint in your minds' (He 12³). See also REPROACH.

J. C. LAMBERT.

REWARD.—1. The NT word for this is μισθός, which appears in its more literal sense as 'hire' (Mt 20⁸, Lk 10⁷) or ' wages ' (Jn 4³⁶). Besides μισθός, St. Paul twice uses ἀντιμισθία (Ro 1²⁷, 2 Co 6¹³) ; while Ep. to Heb. uses μισθαποδοσία (2² 10³⁵ 11²⁶). RV prefers, in passages where the Greek has a verb,— ἀποδίδωμι, cf. μισθαποδοσία,—the colourless rendering 'recompense' (Mt 6⁶· ¹⁸). It might be questioned whether in the 17th cent., the Eng. word 'reward' had so definitely as now the sense of a favourable or desirable retribution. Or is there a touch of conscious paradox in the tr. 'reward evil for good' (Ps 35¹²) ? But see Ps 7⁴, He 2². On the other hand, Hooker (*Eccles. Polity*, Books i.-iv., 1592 or 1594) already employs the expression 're- wards *and punishments*,' which stamps a favour- able sense upon the 'rewards' ; cf. also—

' A man, that fortune's buffets and rewards
Hast ta'en with equal thanks.'—*Hamlet*, III. ii. 71.

At Lk 23⁴¹ 'due reward of our deeds,' AV and RV, stands for a periphrasis in the Greek.

2. Christ's teaching is popular, and He has no hesitation in using the conception of 'reward in heaven' as a stimulus to zeal (*e.g.* Mt 5¹² 6²⁰). Reward on earth is also found among His prom- ises, if apparently with a touch of irony (cf. Mk 10³⁰). Yet we cannot conceal from ourselves that reward, like the cognate conception of merit, be- longs to a secondary order of moral categories. ' Merit lives from man to man, and not from man, O Lord, to thee.' In public life the bad citizen is punished, while the good citizen's *reward* is—life as a citizen ! Literal 'rewards' are for the nursery or primary school. There is perhaps more of morality in 'punishment.' Moral protoplasm— potential goodness—may exist in the much decried fear of hell oftener than in the hope of heaven. Punishment emphasizes guilt, calls for repentance, and may prove the door to a new life ; reward im- plies righteousness, and the thought of it may tend to *self*-righteousness. (In order to shut this out, or for some other reason, the 'righteous' (Mt 25³⁷⁻³⁹) are *unconscious* of their claim to reward.) ' Other - worldliness' is a much rarer vice than worldliness, the allurement of such distant prizes being faint and cold. Yet a fanatical greed for the future life is not impossible.

3. In Christ's teaching there is comparatively little which carries us *beyond* the thought of re- ward. Most noticeable is Lk 17¹⁰ ' We are unpro- fitable servants,' or, according to Wellhausen's fine conjecture, ' We are servants ! we have done that which it was our duty to do.' Also there is an approach to the Pauline standpoint in the flavour of irony with which our Lord describes ' the right- eous' in contrast to sinners. He ' came not to call' them (Mt 9¹³ ‖). ' There shall be joy in heaven over one sinner that repenteth, more than over ninety and nine righteous persons which need no repentance ' (Lk 15⁷· ⁽¹⁰· ³²⁾). Lk 7⁴⁷ has the clearest trace of irony. ' Her sins, which are many, are forgiven ; [you can see that it is so] for she ' showed such signs of love. ' But to whom little is forgiven, the same loveth little.' Again, the call to self-sacrifice (Mt 16²⁴ ‖) shuts out any vulgar conception of reward, though, in point of form, the acceptance of *earthly* suffering does not cancel *heavenly* reward.

4. We must recognize, then, that hope of reward is a legitimate motive. It bears the highest *im-*

primatur ; and it keeps a place in the general Christian scheme, even as unfolded by that Apostle who might seem most opposed to it on principle. We need not think to do without it, even while we pass on to higher motives and fuller conceptions of duty. Christian labour and sacrifice are never in vain. The struggle ' availeth ' (A. H. Clough's *Poems*, 'Say not the struggle'). See also art. RETRIBUTION.

LITERATURE.—Studies of the teaching of Christ—*Ecce Homo* (close of ch. xi.), Wendt, Horton ; Huntington, *Chr. Believing and Living*, 209 ; *Expositor*, II. i. [1881] 401 ; Briggs, *Ethical Teaching of Jesus* (1904), 206, 240 ; Manning, *Serm.* (1844) 159 ; Cox, *Expositions*, i. (1885) 68 ; R. Vaughan, *Stones from the Quarry* (1890), 136 ; Liddon, *Serm. on Some Words of Christ* (1892), 19.

ROBERT MACKINTOSH.

RHESA.—A link in our Lord's genealogy (Lk 3²⁷).

RICHES.—See WEALTH.

RIGHT.—In the AV the word 'right' is the equivalent of two distinct Greek words, δίκαιος, 'righteous' (Mt 20⁴· ⁷, Lk 12⁵⁷), and ὀρθῶς, 'cor- rectly' (Lk 7⁴³ 10²⁸ 20²¹). The Eng. word is etymo- logically associated with Lat. *rectus* (from *regere*, 'to rule' ; cf. 'direct' and cognates). It implies that which is *straight, according to rule*. In the Gospels the idea of 'right,' as distinct from the word, runs through the whole of our Lord's revela- tion of God. His teaching is at once a demand for that which is right and the source of all instruction about it.

1. The *standard* of right is always found in the will of God as expressed in His law. Everything is referred to that. Doing the will of God is the simple but exhaustive summary of all true life (Mk 3³⁵).

2. The *extent* of right is to be understood as absolute conformity to the law of God, with no immunity and no reservation. Not only actions and words, but also thoughts, desires, and motives, are always included in its scope (Mt 5²²· ²⁸). Since 'right' means conformity to God's character and will, it necessarily follows that this conformity must be absolute. Our Lord contrasts the right- eousness of the scribes and Pharisees with that which He demanded from His followers (5²⁰). His requirement was higher because of His higher conception of the character, will, and claims of God. To them righteousness was nothing more than a superficial outward conformity to the Divine law as interpreted and altered by their tradition. They measured by means of an im- perfect standard, while our Lord laid down an absolute law (5⁴⁸). See art. RIGHTEOUSNESS.

3. The *motives* to right are variously stated and implied. (*a*) First and foremost is the (always implied) motive based on the truth that right is right and therefore must be done. (*b*) Then obedi- ence to the will of God, because it is God's will, is emphasized (5³³ 7²¹). (*c*) A secondary and yet im- portant motive is found in the spiritual blessings associated with the performance of right (5¹⁻¹¹ 6¹· ⁴· ⁶· ¹⁸). (*d*) Yet again we have the spiritual influences and effects of right as no inconsiderable motive for righteousness of thought, word, and deed (5¹³· ¹⁴).

4. The *encouragements* to right are found in (*a*) the joy of satisfaction in obedience to God ; (*b*) the approving testimony of conscience as the result of righteousness ; (*c*) the blessing of God manifestly resting upon the life (10²⁸⁻³¹) ; (*d*) fellowship with Christ in faithful and true living (10²⁵ 12⁵⁰). These points concerning right are only a bare summary of what is both implicit and expressed in the whole of our Lord's teaching, especially in the five great sections of teaching found in Matthew.

5. The *secret* of right is found in personal union and communion with Christ. There is nothing dry, formal, and abstract in 'right' as conceived of in the NT. It is no question of an impersonal abstract τὸ δίκαιον or τὸ καλόν, but a warm, loving, living, and personal life of right thinking, right speaking, right doing, in union with Him who is pre-eminently ὁ δίκαιος and ὁ καλός. It is this that differentiates Christian ethics from all others. Christianity not only depicts an ideal and insists on its realization; it proclaims and provides the power to realize it, in union with Him who has Himself lived the life and fulfilled the Divine ideal, and whose grace is sufficient for all who receive it. In all that concerns 'right,' the followers of Christ accept and know by experience the truths of two great statements; one of the Master, and the other of one of His Apostles: 'Apart from me ye can do nothing' (Jn 15[5]); 'I can do all things in him who is empowering me' (Ph 4[13]).

W. H. GRIFFITH THOMAS.

RIGHT HAND.—See SESSION.

RIGHTEOUS, RIGHTEOUSNESS. — i. HISTORY OF THE TERMS.—The root notion of the Heb. word צְדָקָה is that which is just, right, and normal; and its exact meaning fluctuates in each epoch according to the standard by which right and wrong are measured. It is true that in the OT this standard is always based on the will of Jehovah; but we observe great changes — chiefly progressive — in the Jewish notion of what He requires. In more primitive times the conception of צְדָקָה is mainly forensic, meaning that which accords with custom as fixed by the Divinely given decisions of the people's judges. But the prophets raised the whole conception of the law of God, and insisted that its moral aspect was infinitely more important than its ceremonial. Indeed, though like all OT writers they dealt with action rather than character, they almost foreshadow in places the NT teaching, that it is a clean heart that makes a righteous deed. Hosea and Jeremiah illumined the conception of man's duty to his neighbour by the preaching of God's loving-kindness to His people. Deutero-Isaiah goes further still, and finds in the thought of God's unfailing righteousness the pledge that He will comfort and redeem His servants. As used of Him, the word צְדָקָה denotes moral consistency and faithfulness to His promises, and in the highest prophetic teaching this was felt to include the love which pardons the penitent, though ever stern to the obdurate.

In the age of formalism, which was marked by the cessation of prophecy, the notion of righteousness became more ceremonial and external. Already in some of the Psalms we have 'the righteous' as a regular party in the land, and the term ultimately became the self-designation of the Pharisees. צְדָקָה was now identified mainly with almsgiving in the sphere of private morals; and, in the judicial sphere, with readiness to help the weak as opposed to the letter of strict judgment.* In the LXX the word is tr. usually by δικαιοσύνη, but also by κρίσις, ἔλεος, and ἐλεημοσύνη; and the adj. צַדִּיק usually by δίκαιος, but also by ἄμεμπτος, καθαρός, πιστός, and εὐσεβής.

The Gr. δικαιοσύνη, like the Heb. צְדָקָה, was generally used in a much broader sense than our word 'justice,' and denoted social virtue as a whole. Aristotle defines it as ἀρετὴ τελεία καὶ οὐχ ἀπλῶς ἀλλὰ πρὸς ἕτερον . . . οὐ μέρος ἀρετῆς, ἀλλὰ ὅλη ἀρετή (*Ethics*, v. 3. 1129c; cf. Plato, *Republic*, 443). The chief difference between the Heb. and Gr. words lies, not in the terms themselves, but in the radical distinction between the religions of the two races,—the former being based on the relation of man to God, the latter on man's duty to himself; thus in Greek ἀδικία is usually distinguished from ἀσέβεια.

* See Dalman, *Die richterliche Gerechtigkeit im AT*, as quoted in art. 'Righteousness (in OT)' in Hastings' *DB* iv. 281.

VOL. II.—34

ii. NT USAGE.—The NT writers inherited the word צְדָקָה with all its religious associations, and used as its equivalent δικαιοσύνη, and as its opposite ἀδικία. The latter word is sometimes contrasted also with ἀλήθεια (e.g. Ro 1[18], 2 Th 2[10]); for 'truth passing into action is righteousness' (Westcott on 1 Jn 1[9]). ἄδικος is also contrasted with πιστός (Lk 16[10, 11]), εὐσεβής (2 P 2[9], cf. Ro 4[5]), ἅγιος (1 Co 6[1]). The first of these three words expresses an idea always present in the word 'righteousness' (namely, consistency); the other two give its basis for man, —devotion to God,—but do not immediately express the notion of duty towards one's neighbour.

Jesus Christ transformed the whole conception of righteousness; for He broke down the externalism of His day by emphasizing character rather than action, and set religion on an entirely new basis by making it a real response of the whole personality to God, and pointing to love as the essence of righteousness. It is significant in this connexion that it was Christianity that created the very conception of personality, and so ultimately the word itself. Jesus Christ tells His followers that their righteousness is to be based on the eternal character of God (Mt 5[44,45]), as uniquely revealed in human life by Himself (11[27] ‖). Accordingly the early Christians seem to have spoken of Christ as 'the righteous one' (see Ac 3[14] 7[52] 22[14], Ja 5[6]). But we must examine in more detail the righteousness taught and exemplified by Him.

1. The Synoptists. — (a) *General usage.* — The Synoptic writers all use δίκαιος and δικαιοσύνη generally, of the man who tries to do his duty in the sight of God, whether Christian or not (Mt 1[19] 5[45], Mk 6[20], Lk 1[6] 2[25]). But St. Matthew also uses the words especially of believers in Christ, to denote the character which He requires in citizens of the Kingdom of heaven (Mt 5[10] 6[1] etc.). St. Luke, indeed, approximates to this in three passages at least (Lk 14[14], Ac 24[15, 25]); but with him it can scarcely be called a well-defined usage. The explanation of this peculiarity of the First Gospel no doubt lies in the fact that its chief aim is to represent Christianity as the consummation of Judaism (cf. Mt 5[17]). But a still more noteworthy fact is that the Synoptic writers do not directly speak of righteousness as a Divine attribute. [Mt 6[33] is no exception, for 'his righteousness' there means the character which God expects of us, though this is implicitly based on the nature of the Father]. Nor is Christ ever directly termed δίκαιος by them, except in the mouth of unbelievers (e.g. Pilate's wife in Mt 27[19]), and in the cases mentioned above from the Acts, where St. Luke represents three different speakers as calling Him ὁ δίκαιος. In this connexion it is significant that in recording the centurion's words at Calvary, St. Luke (23[47]) writes, 'Certainly this was a righteous man'; but St. Matthew (27[54]) and St. Mark (15[39]) give υἱὸς θεοῦ in place of δίκαιος. Now, when we remember that our Lord, in the Synoptic accounts, does not speak of Himself as ὁ υἱὸς τοῦ θεοῦ, though He accepts the title from others, and acknowledges His unique Sonship before the Sanhedrin (Lk 22[70] ‖), we see why He does not call Himself ὁ δίκαιος. He does not put forward His own claims in the Galilæan ministry, but leaves His followers to infer them from His words and acts (cf. Mt 16[15-17]). And when men have drawn the inference, then they call Him ὁ υἱὸς τοῦ θεοῦ rather than ὁ δίκαιος. Similarly, He Himself does not speak of the Father's righteousness, because to His hearers the word would not convey enough. He speaks rather of the Father's love.

(b) *God's righteousness.* — What we have said above leads us on naturally to ask, What is the central idea in Christ's teaching about the Father's righteousness (for though He does not Himself apply the word to God in the Synoptic accounts, the idea is not excluded)? Our Lord bases everything on the truth that God is a loving Father to all men, and they are potentially His sons; by love they may know Him, and so make that potentiality actual. Such is the teaching of the parable of the Prodigal Son (Lk 15[11-32]). In Mt 5[45-48] Christ tells us that God loves both good and evil, both righteous and unrighteous; and His followers are to do the same 'in order that ye may be ($\gamma\acute{\epsilon}\nu\eta\sigma\theta\epsilon=$ 'show yourselves to be'; or else 'become') sons of your Father which is in heaven.' And His summary of the whole matter is, 'Ye therefore shall be perfect (*i.e.* in and through love) as your heavenly Father is perfect.' But this love in God, if it makes Him infinitely merciful to the penitent sinner, makes Him equally stern to the impenitent. Again and again Christ, by means of a series of parables, teaches the future suffering of the wicked. It will suffice to quote one which shows the unity of the Divine love in its two aspects of mercifulness and sternness—the parable of the king that took account of his servants and punished him who showed no mercy to his fellow (Mt 18[23-35]). He is ready to forgive the largest of debts if only the servant proves his love; but he has no mercy for the ungrateful and unloving; 'he delivered him to the tormentors, till he should pay all that was due.'

(c) *Christ's righteousness.* — If we may rightly speak of the absolute righteousness of God in the Synoptic accounts, we have no less reason for speaking of the absolute righteousness of Christ. A close examination of His words may even seem explicitly to sanction this. In Mt 5[10] He pronounces a blessing on those who are persecuted *for righteousness' sake*; and in the next verse He goes on, 'Blessed are ye when men shall . . . persecute you . . . *for my sake.*' We may compare Mk 8[35] 'Whosoever shall lose his life *for my sake and the gospel's* shall save it' (also Mk 10[29]). Throughout his Gospel St. Matthew makes $\delta\iota\kappa\alpha\iota\sigma\acute{\upsilon}\nu\eta$ the character of the citizens of the Kingdom of heaven. But Jesus Christ is the inaugurator of that kingdom (Mt 11[11] 12[28]). It is He, as the Son of Man, who sows the good seed of the Kingdom (13[37]); He, again, who can give 'the keys of the kingdom' (16[19]). He has authority over the angels in *His* kingdom, which is the kingdom of the Father (13[41, 43]). He not only gives to men a unique revelation—the only revelation—of the Father (11[27] ||—a passage which implies His sinlessness), but He is the giver of the Holy Ghost (3[11] ||). This teaching is confirmed by the order of words in Mt 24[36] and Mk 13[32] (men—the angels—the Son—the Father). So He claims to be *the* Son of God (Lk 22[70] ||), and suffers condemnation for blasphemy; as such, He is transfigured, before three of His Apostles, with the Divine glory (Mt 17[1-8] ||). And so again He assents to the statement that He is quite different from one of the prophets (Mt 16[14-16]); they were righteous, but He is *the* righteous Man, and more also. The whole teaching of the Synoptic Gospels is implicitly the same; nowhere does our Lord show any consciousness of sin; again and again He emphasizes the sinfulness of all men and their need of repentance. Therefore He is to be the judge of mankind, in the consummation of God's kingdom (Mt 7[22f.] 13[41] 16[27] 25[31ff.]).

(d) *The contents of righteousness.* — What, in brief, was the ideal of which Christ was the perfect example, and which He sets before His followers? Obviously an adequate answer to this question is far beyond the limits of this article. But we must try to apprehend a few leading principles. This is the easier, because Christ sought to 'educate' His disciples by giving them principles rather than precepts; His service was to be a free development, not a slavish system. St. Matthew has collected for us, in the Sermon on the Mount, much of our Lord's teaching on the Kingdom of heaven and the $\delta\iota\kappa\alpha\iota\sigma\acute{\upsilon}\nu\eta$ which marks its citizens. They are to seek above all else 'the kingdom of God and his righteousness' (Mt 6[33]); they are to 'hunger and thirst' after it (5[6]). The Kingdom only reflects the eternal character of the King (5[45]). Thus $\delta\iota\kappa\alpha\iota\sigma\acute{\upsilon}\nu\eta$, which is very close in meaning to our modern word 'morality,' is throughout based on religion, and treated as inseparable from it. Mt 6 opens with a warning against ostentation in $\delta\iota\kappa\alpha\iota\sigma\acute{\upsilon}\nu\eta$ (if, indeed, that is the right reading); and the examples given are those of almsgiving (v.[2]), prayer (v.[5]), and fasting (v.[16])—the second of which, at least, is often treated by us as outside morality. Now the central principle of God's being is, as we said, represented to be love. Consequently love is the unfailing measure of human $\delta\iota\kappa\alpha\iota\sigma\acute{\upsilon}\nu\eta$. The first commandment is 'Love God'; the second, 'Love thy neighbour as thyself' (Mk 12[29-31] ||); and, according to St. Matthew (22[40]), Christ adds the words, 'on these two commandments hang all the law and the prophets' (words almost repeated in Mt 7[12] and presupposed in Gal 5[14] and Ro 13[8]).

Here, then, is the principle by which we may test all our actions. God judges men by what they are rather than by what they do; we, being human, and unable to read the heart, are to judge by their deeds what men are (Mt 7[16]), though with much caution against rash and censorious judgments (7[1]). But the final judgment is God's, who takes account of motive as well as act. He who nurses wrath against a brother, or treats him with bitter contempt, is guilty before God as well as the man who proceeds to murder (5[21. 22]); and 'every one that looketh on a woman to lust after her hath committed adultery with her already in his heart' (5[28]). It has been well said that 'inwardness' is the guiding principle of the Sermon on the Mount. The hard sayings of Mt 5[39-42] must clearly be interpreted on the same principle of love towards our neighbour, resting on love towards God; they do not forbid all resistance of evil (such as resistance to a thief or one of overbearing temper), but they prohibit resistance which springs from personal resentment; they do not inculcate indiscriminate charity, but command us to do, without thought of self, whatever is best for those in need. On the same principle, Christ tells us that it is quality, not quantity, that matters. In prayer we are not to 'use vain repetitions,' as if we should be heard for our 'much speaking' (Mt 6[7]); yet it is to be observed that Christ Himself sometimes spent the whole or the major part of the night in prayer (Lk 6[12], Mk 6[46-48]). Men may 'cast out devils' and do 'many mighty works' in Christ's name, and yet be no true followers of His (Mt 7[22. 23]). The widow who cast a farthing into the treasury was doing a greater thing than those who brought rich offerings (Mk 12[41-44] ||).

Love to God is the first commandment; love to man is included in it, as the less in the greater. The motive which makes the service of men righteous in the highest sense is that it should be done for Christ's sake (Mk 9[41], Mt 10[42] 18[5]), or, in other words, in order that men 'may glorify your Father which is in heaven' (Mt 5[16]). We must really lose ourselves before we can find our true selves (Mt 16[25] etc.); *i.e.* self-development is included in the end, but it can never come through selfishness. The Christian's paradise is not like the Mohammedan's; the reward of self-denying toil in Christ's service is more toil (Lk 19[17]). The Lord's Prayer opens, not with petition, but with adoration and thanksgiving; and petition must be qualified with the thought, 'nevertheless not my will, but thine, be done' (Lk 22[42]).

Thus one important aspect of love is filial trust, or faith in God. But this faith is certainly not intellectual in essence. Without love it is void and empty (Mt 7[22f.]). It is the faith which seeks God's kingdom and His righteousness *first*, and makes the daily toil for the material necessaries of life subordinate to these, in its calm certitude that God will give sufficient for our needs. But how, it may be asked, are we to win such faith as this? Partly by contemplation of God's love in Nature (Mt 5[45] 6[26-30], Lk 12[24-32]); partly by the evidence of Christ's life, death, and resurrection (Mt 16[8-10] 28[19. 20] etc.); partly by turning into earnest prayer the measure of faith that we have (cf. Mk 9[23. 24]); and partly by loving service of our brother men in all humility (see Lk 17[5-10]).

Again, as love for mankind is incomplete except when based on love for God, so is love for God an idle sentimentality unless it is realized by the service of men. 'Not every one that saith unto me, Lord, Lord, shall enter into the kingdom of heaven; but he that doeth the will of my Father which is in heaven' (Mt 7[21]). This is set forth in detail in the picture of the Last Judgment (Mt 25[31-46]). Here the test of men is whether they gave food, drink, and shelter to strangers and to those who were needy, or sick, or outcast. For the 'Golden Rule,' which sums up 'the Law and the Prophets,' is, 'All things whatsoever ye would that men should do unto you, even so do ye also to them' (Mt 7[12], Lk 6[31]). Nor is any man to be outside the pale of a Christian's love. To the scribe's question, 'Who is my neighbour?,' Christ replies by a parable, in which a Samaritan is represented as doing for one of his traditional enemies, the Jews, what the priest and Levite of the man's own race had left undone (Lk 10[29ff.]). So He abolishes the Jewish belief that 'neighbour' includes only those of one's own race. And His last words on earth lay before His Apostles their duty of teaching *all* nations (Mt 28[19], Lk 24[47], cf. Mk 16[15]). He uses also the term 'brother' in a no less catholic sense, in all probability, though He never explicitly tells His disciples that they are to consider all men as brethren (see Mt 7[3] and 18[15. 21], Lk 17[3. 4]). The teaching of the parable of the Prodigal Son is still more emphatic on this point. It is also true that He uses the word 'brother' in a narrower sense, to denote specially the man, whoever he is, that does the will of God (Mk 3[35] ||). See art. BROTHERHOOD.

It was the simplicity and the 'inwardness' of this supreme test of righteousness by love that were to make Christ's 'yoke easy' (Mt 11[30]), in contrast with the 'heavy burdens' imposed on men's shoulders by the externalism and endless rules of the Pharisees (23[4]). He said, 'Except ye turn and become as little children, ye shall in no wise enter into the kingdom of heaven. Whosoever therefore shall humble himself as this little child, the same is the greatest in the kingdom of heaven' (18[3. 4], cf. Mk 9[35]); and He called the scribes and Pharisees 'children of hell' (Mt 23[15])— a term which He never applies even to the publican or the harlot—because He found in their self-exaltation and censoriousness (cf. Lk 18[11], Mt 23[5-10]) the very antithesis of the meekness and humility which were to Him the essence of righteousness (Mt 11[29] 7[1-5], Lk 17[7-10]). His mission, He says, is not to the self-righteous, but to the man conscious of his sin (Mt 9[13] ||, cf. Lk 15[7]). To the Pharisee ceremonial was everything, the spirit of action nothing (Mt 23[25. 26]); to Him the ceremonial was useless unless carried out in the spirit of love (5[23-25]), and the rule of law must always give way to the rule of love (cf. His treatment of Sabbath-observance, Mk 2[23]-3[5]). Therefore He said, 'Ex-

cept your righteousness shall exceed the righteousness of the scribes and Pharisees, ye shall in no wise enter into the kingdom of heaven' (Mt 5[20]).

This leads us to speak briefly of His treatment of the Mosaic Law. He made a rule of observing it, but never in a literal, slavish manner. In everything He acted on the principle that 'the Son of Man is lord even of the Sabbath' (Mk 2[28]). He yielded to authority (cf. Mk 12[17] ||, Lk 17[14], Mt 17[27]), except when doing so meant the violation of a higher law (see Mt 23[3]). The Law was to Him sound in principle, but not perfect. His work in respect to it was not revolutionary, but evolutionary (5[17-20]). Not 'a jot or tittle' of its underlying principles was to perish; and the man who should 'break' (λύσῃ in v.[19] picks up καταλῦσαι in v.[17]; cf. Jn 7[23]) them would be acting against Christ's command.[*]

On the other hand, He gives new and deeper applications to the laws of Moses, as in the case of the law of murder (Mt 5[21ff.]). He does not hesitate to add new restrictions to it, as in the case of the laws of adultery, false swearing, and retaliation (vv.[27. 33. 38]); and He definitely abrogates a law of Moses when He declares all meats clean (Mk 7[15-19]).

In connexion with the question of Christ's relation to the Law, there is one passage which calls for special mention—Mt 3[15], where, in answer to the Baptist's protest against baptizing Him, He says: 'Suffer it now: for thus it becometh us to fulfil all righteousness.' We are sometimes told that δικαιοσύνη is here equivalent to the ceremonial law; but this cannot be so, inasmuch as there was no ceremonial law about baptism. Nor did baptism mean the same to Him as to most who underwent it. To them the ceremony selected by John brought assurance of forgiveness of sins, but no conscious outpouring of the Holy Spirit (Ac 19[2. 3]); to Him it brought no forgiveness of sins, but a visible descent of the Spirit. For He never, all His life through, raised Himself above the ordinary human dependence on outward act and form, as His use of symbolic action and the institution of the two Sacraments show us. By δικαιοσύνη, then, in this passage, He clearly means the general use of outward religious ritual current at His time, and He makes this the occasion of receiving spiritual power.

(e) *The communication of Christ's righteousness to His followers.*—It would be going beyond the limits of this article to discuss the *method* of Justification and Sanctification (see sep. artt.), as represented in the Synoptic writers; it only remains to show the place they give to the *facts* which these words represent (even though it is impossible entirely to separate method and fact). We have seen that Christ claimed a unique knowledge of the Father and a unique power of revealing Him to man (Mt 11[27] ||),—a revelation which He consistently represented as possible only through love. Nor was this power to fail at His death. As their risen Lord He would always be with His disciples, to pour upon them power from on high (28[18-20], Lk 24[48. 49]). He was now to fulfil the Baptist's prophecy that He should baptize them with the Holy Spirit (Ac 1[4. 5] 2[1-13]). The Holy Spirit, representing the risen Christ (Mt 28[20]), was to give them the righteousness which should, by God's love, fit them for the Kingdom of heaven,— righteousness growing with their growing love and faith, which were to be its essence. Christ distinctly took His stand on the appeal to morality. Works were to be the necessary outcome of true love (Mt 7²¹ etc.). When He says, 'Blessed are they that hunger and thirst after righteousness: for they shall be filled' (5⁶), He does not mean in the next world only, but in this also. Indeed, throughout His teaching, the life to come is treated as an orderly development of this life. He speaks, on the one hand, of the Kingdom of heaven as already come in some measure,—'the kingdom of God is within you' (Lk 17²¹, cf. 6²⁰ 11²⁰), and it is to come with more marked power still within the lifetime of some of His disciples (Mk 9¹ ‖). Yet, on the other hand, its consummation is not for this life, but for the life to come (Mt 25³⁴, Mk 14²⁵ = Lk 22¹⁸ = Mt 26²⁹). So Christ taught His disciples to pray, 'Thy kingdom come,' i.e. in ever more and more fulness until the end (συντέλεια). Meanwhile (as is everywhere implied, and nowhere stated) God sees each member of the Kingdom not as he is, but as he is becoming 'in Christ,' and treats him as a son for his faith and love.

2. St. John.— When we turn to the Johannine writings, we pass into a new atmosphere. We are no longer dealing so much with the outer activities of Christ's life in its earthly setting. St. John had pondered through long years and with deep reverence over the inner meaning of that life. To him Christ was primarily the λόγος, the revelation of the eternal nature of the Father, though it had been given them to touch and see Him in earthly form. Consequently we have a series of sayings unlike anything in the first three Gospels: 'God is Spirit' (4²⁴), 'God is Light' (1 Jn 1⁵), 'God is Love' (1 Jn 4⁸· ¹⁶), 'I am the way, and the truth, and the life' (Jn 14⁶). So the thought of righteousness as a Divine attribute is peculiarly developed in St. John. It is parallel to his favourite use of ἀλήθεια, which he treats almost as a synonym for ἀγιωσύνη, representing the less active side of righteousness (cf. ποιεῖν τὴν ἀλήθειαν in Jn 3²¹ and 1 Jn 1⁶ with ποιεῖν τὴν δικαιοσύνην in 1 Jn 3⁷). So in Jn 8³²⁻³⁴ 'the truth shall make you free . . . but he that doeth sin is a slave.' Again, the conception of the Kingdom becomes in St. John the thought of life eternal; and the latter in Jn., as the former in the Synoptists, is spoken of, now as a present possession (3³⁶), now as that which shall be fully bestowed only in the next life (12²⁵).

Thus the thought of righteousness as a Divine attribute meets us at every turn, and its explicit mention not infrequently. δίκαιος εἶ, cries the angel to the Eternal in the Apocalypse (Rev 16⁵, where the thought is chiefly of His sternness to the wicked [cf. 15³ 16⁷ 19²] in delivering His saints). Πατὴρ δίκαιε are Christ's own words in prayer (Jn 17²⁵), where the thought is primarily of God's gracious mercy and faithfulness in revealing His love to His chosen ones. δίκαιος occurs again in 1 Jn 1⁹ in a similar sense of 'true to his loving nature.' 'If we confess our sins, he is *faithful and righteous* to forgive us our sins, *and to cleanse* us from all unrighteousness.' In exactly the same way righteousness is predicated of Christ throughout as One who is consistent in His mercy to the penitent, and loving in His necessary sternness to the obdurate. 'If any man sin, we have an advocate with the Father, Jesus Christ the righteous' (1 Jn 2¹); 'They that have done good (shall come forth) unto the resurrection of life; and they that have done ill, unto the resurrection of judgment. . . . My judgment is righteous' (Jn 5²⁹ᶠ·). Yet 'I came not to judge the world, but to save the world. He that rejecteth me . . . the word that I spake . . . shall judge him in the last day' (12⁴⁷· ⁴⁸). Christ, that is to say, seeks but to save the wicked, in His love for them; but if they will not have His mercy, they are self-doomed.

The Divine part throughout is that of absolute love: 'God *is* love,'—that sums Him up in a word; and that is the newness of the Christian teaching (13³¹ 15¹²) which transforms the notion of what makes goodness in deed. Our whole duty is to love God, which involves obedience to Him (1 Jn 5³), and is declared to be the only means of knowing Him (4⁷). The love of God necessarily carries with it the love of man (4¹¹· ¹²· ²⁰); it is the love of God, shown by sending His Son to die for the world, which teaches us to love other men (3¹⁶ 4⁹· ¹⁰), and the one love must be as catholic as the other (cf. Jn 12³²). Elsewhere, in emphasizing the inwardness of all true righteousness, Christ shows that it depends on God's nature as Spirit. 'God is Spirit, and they that worship him, must worship in spirit and truth' (4²⁴). And the corollary is that true worship is independent of locality and ceremonial (v.²¹),— though this is not to be taken as implying that all ceremonial may be safely cast aside.

But it is by developing Christ's teaching about the second or spiritual birth that St. John especially marks both the essential inwardness and the continuous growth of righteousness. The *locus classicus* for this is the Lord's discourse given in 3³⁻²¹, where the eternal life given by the second birth is brought into immediate relation with His own pre-existence and resurrection (vv.¹³⁻¹⁶). This chapter is illustrated in the First Epistle, where he writes: 'Every one that loveth is begotten of God' (4⁷). 'Whosoever believeth that Jesus is the Christ is begotten of God' (5¹). 'If ye know that he (probably Christ) is righteous, ye know that everyone also that doeth righteousness is begotten of him' (2²⁹). But here we notice a further point. Christ 'was manifested to take away sins; and in him is no sin. Whosoever abideth in him sinneth not . . .'; the righteous man is 'he that doeth righteousness, . . . even as he is righteous. . . . *Whosoever is begotten of God doeth no sin*, because his seed abideth in him: and he cannot sin, because he is begotten of God' (1 Jn 3⁵⁻⁹). At first sight this seems inconsistent with 1⁸· ⁹, where the Apostle tells us, 'If we say that we have no sin, we deceive ourselves, and the truth is not in us. If we confess our sins, he is faithful and righteous to forgive us our sins . . .' Clearly, in the former passages, sin is thought of as a lasting state of rebellion against God; in the latter, it is treated rather as an act due to weakness. He that is born of God cannot deliberately rebel against God, as long as the new life is in him; cf. Jn 13¹⁰ 'Ye are clean, but not all' (Christ excepts only Judas, v.¹¹); 15³ 'Already ye are clean because of the word which I have spoken unto you'; for, as He goes on to say, this cleanliness of heart comes from the union of Himself with the disciple, effected by love. 'Abide in me and I in you. . . . He that abideth in me and I in him, the same beareth much fruit; for apart from me ye can do nothing' (v. ⁴ᶠ·, cf. 17²¹· ²³). Here we have explicitly stated what is implicit in the Synoptic Gospels, namely, that only by the union of love with the risen Christ (cf. 8³¹· ³² 15¹³⁻¹⁵) can we do righteousness, receiving more and more of 'his fulness . . . and grace for grace' (1¹⁶), having already in us the eternal life which is to be consummated at the last day (cf. 17³ 20³¹). This is the general meaning of 16⁸⁻¹⁰ '(The Holy Spirit), when he is come, will convict the world in respect of . . . righteousness . . . because I go to the Father, and ye behold me no more'; that is to say, the Holy Spirit will not only reveal Christ's righteousness to the world, but will show men the infinite possibilities which are theirs in union with Him, because Christ is henceforth alive for evermore with the Father, having conquered death and sin. All this implies, what St. Paul explains so fully, that God sees us as we are becoming 'in Christ,' rather than as we are; but St. John does not analyze forgiveness as St. Paul does, and throughout he looks rather at the eternal fact than the temporal process.

3. St. Paul.—In St. Paul's Epistles δίκαιος generally bears the same meaning as elsewhere in the NT, and so is associated with ὅσιος and ἅγιος (cf. Tit 1[8], Ro 7[12]). However, once at least he seems to revert almost unconsciously to the Pharisaic idea of the δίκαιος as one who conforms to law; for in Ro 5[7] he apparently differentiates between the 'righteous' and the 'good' (ἀγαθός) man in much the same way as the Gnostics afterwards called the God of the OT 'righteous' (meaning 'just'), and the God of the NT 'good.' This is not his usual custom, however; indeed, in Eph 5[9] he couples ἀγαθωσύνη and δικαιοσύνη; and in Ro 7[12] he puts δικαία between ἁγία and ἀγαθή.

In Ro 14[17] St. Paul tells us that 'the kingdom of God is . . . righteousness and peace and joy in the Holy Ghost,'—words which remind us of St. Matthew. But, unlike the First Gospel, he often speaks of the righteousness of God. In the years which preceded his conversion, he had known all the suffering of a sensitive man who feels that, in spite of all his desire to keep God's law, he is constantly breaking it in act, and generally failing to live up to the spirit of it. The salvation of his life had come to him in the conviction that God takes the will for the deed, and that in union with the risen Christ the human will is kept constantly true. This is the truth that he has to work out intellectually in his Epistles. And he begins by showing that Christ had not lowered the standard of God's righteousness to meet human weakness, but raised it (cf. Ro 3[21-26]). God is and must be true to His righteous nature; He is the righteous judge who will reward those who serve Him and punish those who do not. It is not the fact of God's righteousness that has been abolished by Christianity, but the old standard of service. This comes out very clearly in Ro 10. Israel, he says, were ignorant of God's righteousness (though they knew God's law, v.[3]), for 'Christ is the end of the law unto righteousness unto every one that hath faith' (v.[4]). The Jew had thought that he must 'ascend into heaven' or 'descend into the abyss,' that is, make superhuman efforts to keep the Law. But the righteousness which is of faith saith, '. . . The word is nigh thee, in thy mouth and in thy heart; that is, the word of *faith* which we preach.' 'For with the heart man believeth unto righteousness, and with the mouth confession is made unto salvation' (vv.[6-10]). It is not keeping the Law in act that God demands so much as '*faith working through love*' (Gal 5[6]); 'the end of the charge is love out of . . . faith unfeigned' (1 Ti 1[5]). 'For the whole law is fulfilled in one word, even in this, Thou shalt love thy neighbour as thyself' (Gal 5[14], cf. Ro 13[8]). Without love, the most wonderful of God's other gifts—even faith itself—or the most perfect acts of self-devotion, are vain and empty (1 Co 13[1-3]): love is greater than faith (v.[13]), though it necessarily contains faith (v.[7]). Thus Mosaism is ἡ διακονία τῆς κατακρίσεως, but Christianity ἡ διακονία τῆς δικαιοσύνης (2 Co 3[9]). God, 'the *righteous* judge,' shall give the crown of righteousness (*i.e.* perfect righteousness as a reward; cf. τὸν στέφανον τῆς ζωῆς, Rev 2[10], Ja 1[12]) to all them that have *loved* His appearing (2 Ti 4[8]).

So St. Paul, though he constantly emphasizes the truth that 'faith is counted for righteousness' (Ro 4[5] etc.), never means by faith merely an intellectual belief, but that faith which is part of love, *i.e.* a response of the whole personality to God. Therefore it is obviously quite unfair to represent his

doctrine of justification by faith as entailing a legal fiction. The faith and the love must be actual in the believer, and must issue in action (2[13]), and as they grow, so must action become more perfect; it is not the action, however, that constitutes righteousness in God's sight, but the faith and love. God views us *sub specie æternitatis*: He looks on us as we shall be some day by virtue of our union with Christ. St. Paul puts forward, in different language, the truth which St. John expresses by saying that the man who is begotten of God cannot sin. As the believer beholds through faith 'the glory of the Lord,' he is 'transformed into the same image from glory to glory, even as from the Lord the Spirit' (2 Co 3[18]). Christ is the Second Adam (Ro 5[12-15]); we are, by the mysterious union of love, '*in* Christ Jesus, who was made unto us righteousness and sanctification' (1 Co 1[30]). We may 'become the righteousness of God *in* him' (2 Co 5[21]). 'I can do all things *in* him that strengtheneth me' (Ph 4[13]). Sometimes St. Paul's language touches that of St. John: 'If Christ is *in* you . . . (your) spirit is *life* because of righteousness' (Ro 8[10]; cf. the opposition of θάνατος and δικαιοσύνη in 6[16]; cf. also 'reigning in life,' 5[17], where χάριτος—God's gracious gift—is coupled with δικαιοσύνης).

4. The rest of the NT.—The other books of the NT present few new features which call for notice here. *The Epistle to the Hebrews* emphasizes Christ's absolute righteousness, in order to show Him as the one sufficient Victim and High Priest. He is 'the effulgence of (God's) glory and the very image of his substance' (1[3]). The Psalmist's words apply to Him uniquely, 'Thou hast loved righteousness and hated iniquity' (1[9]). He was 'in all points tempted like as we are, yet without sin' (4[15]). He is the 'king of righteousness' (7[2]). With regard to His work for His followers, the writer of the Epistle usually employs the words ἁγιάζω and τελειόω. He exhorts his readers to have 'experience of the word of righteousness,' that is, 'to press on unto perfection (τελειότης), not laying again a foundation of repentance from dead works, and of faith toward God, of the teaching of baptisms, and of laying on of hands, and of resurrection of the dead, and of eternal judgment' (5[13] and 6[1. 2]). This perfection comes only through Christ (7[11-19]); He is the risen High Priest, who 'ever liveth to make intercession for us' (7[25], cf. 4[16] 5[9] 6[19. 20]). His blood purges us 'from dead works to serve the living God' (9[14]). 'By one offering he hath perfected for ever (*i.e.* potentially) them that are being sanctified' (10[14]). Therefore we must 'follow after the sanctification without which no man shall see the Lord' (12[14]). The Epistle bases our sanctification on love through faith, just as St. Paul does (3[19] with 4[2]). The OT heroes wrought all their great deeds through faith (ch. 11); but faith could not possibly bring them such τελείωσις as it can to the Christian, who is united with his risen Lord (11[40]). The Christian's work rests on a fuller faith; but love is what makes it fruitful,—love to man rooted in love to God (6[10] 10[24]). Our first duty is to offer up loving worship to God; our second, 'to do good and to communicate' (13[15. 16]).

The Epistles of St. Peter touch the subject at several points; but, being practical rather than doctrinal, they do not treat it systematically. The writer of the Second Epistle salutes those 'that have obtained a like precious faith with us in the righteousness' (*i.e.* consistent mercy) 'of our God and (the) Saviour Jesus Christ' (2 P 1[1]). Christ, the righteous, died for us the unrighteous (1 P 3[18]; cf. St. Peter in Ac 3[14]); He is the 'lamb without blemish and without spot' (1[19]). 'He bare our sins in his body upon the tree, that we, having died unto sins, might live unto righteousness' (2^{24}), by the power of the risen Lord (1^3 3^{21}). Our union with Him in love and faith works out the salvation of our souls ($1^{8.\ 9}$). For faith ends in love (2 P $1^{5.\ 7}$). The Christian's duty, therefore, is to love his neighbour 'from the heart fervently' (1 P 1^{22}); 'above all things being fervent in love . . . for love covereth a multitude of sins' (4^8). But the end of all his good works is that men may glorify God (2^{12}). So shall he be saved unto the new heavens and new earth, where this righteousness shall dwell in perfection (2 P 3^{13}).

The Epistle of St. James follows closely the Sermon on the Mount. He speaks once of God's righteousness, meaning the righteousness which God demands of us (1^{20}). And in all probability he refers to Christ as ὁ δίκαιος (5^6). He speaks of love for one's neighbour as 'the royal law' (2^8); and he insists at some length that the faith which was accounted unto Abraham for righteousness was not merely intellectual; it could not be separated from his works, in which it was realized and made perfect ($2^{22.\ 23}$).

LITERATURE.—The subject is treated, in some of its aspects, in so many books that it is hard to select any for special mention. There are chapters on it in almost every work on NT Theology; *e.g.* Beyschlag and Stevens; see also Wendt, *Teaching of Jesus*, vol. i. § iii. ch. iv.; Bruce, *Kingdom of God*, chs. viii. ix. For individual passages in the NT, reference must be made to the standard Commentaries. Probably the fullest analysis of the word is in Cremer's *Bib.-Theol. Lex. of NT Greek.*

C. T. WOOD.

RING.—When the Prodigal Son in the parable returned to his father (Lk 15^{22}), the latter ordered a ring (δακτύλιος) to be placed on his son's finger. This was not only a mark of opulence (Ja 2^2), it is perhaps intended also as a token that he was restored to a place of authority in the house, and allowed to issue orders in his father's name (see Gn 38^{18} 41^{42}, Est 3^{10}). For the allegorical fancies that have clustered round this ring, see the works on the Parables; cf., further, art. SEAL.

C. H. PRICHARD.

RIVER (ποταμός).—'River' (Mk 1^5 etc.), 'flood' (Mt 7^{25}), 'stream' (Lk 6^{48}), and 'waters' (2 Co 11^{26}) stand for the same Greek word ποταμός. 'Stream' in Lk 6^{48} corresponds to 'flood' in Mt 7^{25}.

The Jordan is the one true river in Palestine. The name occurs frequently in the Gospels, but only once connected with 'river' (Mk 1^5). See JORDAN.

The '**stream**' (Lk 6^{48}) or 'flood' (Mt 7^{25}) is evidently the rushing torrent raised by wintry rains. From Rev $12^{15.\ 16}$ we gather that ποταμός may signify any great volume of water rolling over the land. St. Paul's 'perils of rivers' (1 Co 11^{26}) were doubtless such as the Eastern traveller has perpetually to face in fording bridgeless streams in times of rain and melting snow.

To one reared in Palestine, where only water is required to turn the wilderness into a garden, a river, with its beautifying and fertilizing power, might well seem an apt symbol of life (Rev $22^{1.\ 2}$).

W. EWING.

ROADS. — Roads imply a certain amount of civilization. In primitive times it was only near the great centres that regularly built roads were to be found, and even there they were poor and few. In the days of the Empire it was different. The Romans knew the value of good roads, and spared no pains on them. The remains that have come down to us would do credit to modern engineers. They were well bottomed and well laid, and from ten to fourteen feet wide, generally broadest when the cutting was through solid rock. The foundations were of stone, and when allowed to fall into disrepair were rough and slippery, and very trying to the nerves of travellers. In the provinces the roads were under the care of the governors; elsewhere they were under the charge of special officers—frequently of high rank. Along the great military highways were stations, or guard-houses, where the soldiers had not only to see to the preservation of peace and the safety of travellers, but had also to attend to the maintenance of the roads themselves. There the tolls were levied. It was probably at one of these places that Matthew was sitting at the receipt of custom when Jesus called him (Mt 9^9). As the highways between the East and the West passed through the land of the Israelites, making its geographical position unique, it may be well to indicate one or two of these. Cf. map of Palestine in vol. i.

1. The most northerly, and in some respects the most important, was that connecting the Mediterranean Sea and the Euphrates Valley. Starting at Acco (Ptolemais), it ran, according to Ramsay, till it came to Karn Ḥaṭṭin near to Cana, and then almost due east to Tiberias. Skirting the shores of the Sea of Galilee, it crossed the Jordan near Bethsaida, and went over a spur of the Anti-Libanus, and then east by north to Damascus. This road is said to have been a rich source of revenue to the Romans. In the time of the Crusades it was known as the *Via Maris*.

2. From Damascus there came another road, a little to the east of the former, which reached almost to the Sea of Galilee, and then, bending southward on the east side of Jordan, passed beyond the Dead Sea. This was probably the way that the Syrian and Assyrian armies took in their advance on Israel (2 K 8^{28} 9^{14} 10^{32}, 1 Ch 5^{26}).

3. There was also the road along the Mediterranean; and this, both in peace and war, was of the first importance. It ran through Acco, Cæsarea, Joppa, Ashdod, and Gaza into Egypt. Along this road St. Paul was sent to Cæsarea (Ac $23^{23.\ 33}$).

4. From Jerusalem roads branched out to north, south, east, and west. (*a*) There was one through Samaria connecting Judæa and Galilee. Although the direct road from Jerusalem to Galilee, it was seldom used by the devout Jews, on account of the hatred that existed between them and the Samaritans. It was by this road that Jesus journeyed when He spoke to the woman of Samaria (Jn 4^4). (*b*) In ordinary circumstances the Jews preferred to avoid intercourse with the Samaritans, hence in going northward they took the road leading down by Jericho, over the Jordan, and up through Peræa. (*c*) To the west, another road ran from Jerusalem to Jaffa, passing Gibeah, Beth-horon, and Lydda; while (*d*) to the south the road went through Bethlehem to Ḥebron, where it split in two: one going through the wilderness by way of Beersheba, and the other going west to the coast and passing through Gaza. The latter is supposed to be the way taken by Philip (Ac 8^{26}), because tradition has it that the eunuch was baptized in the vicinity of Ḥebron.

These roads played an important part in the diffusion of the gospel. The people who live on the main avenues of traffic are usually of a freer spirit and more open mind than those who dwell in the quiet and cultured towns; and for this reason Jesus got a better hearing in Galilee than in the more polished south. By following the main routes of travel and traffic, St. Paul was led to the chief cities of his day, and found there acceptance for his message, which was carried thence by traders and others into the remote corners of the Empire. The roads were not, even in the days of the Romans, free from danger; witness Lk 10^{30}; but neither brigandage nor violence was common upon them.

LITERATURE.—G. A. Smith, *HGHL*, Index, *s.v.* 'Roads'; artt. by F. Buhl and W. M. Ramsay in Hastings' *DB*, Extra Vol.

pp. 368–402.; Thomson, *LB*; Stanley, *SP*; Conder, *Palestine*; Kinglake, *Eothen*. R. LEGGAT.

ROBBER (λῃστής, Vulg. *latro*) is found in AV only in Jn 10[1. 8] 18[40] (Barabbas). In RV it stands for the same Greek word also in Mt 21[13] = Mk 11[17] = Lk 19[46] ('den of robbers'); Mt 26[55] = Mk 14[48] = Lk 22[52] ('Are ye come out as against a robber?'); Mt 27[38. 44] = Mk 15[27] ('two robbers'); Lk 10[30. 36] ('fell among robbers'). In all these places AV has 'thief,' which elsewhere is the equivalent of κλέπτης. The two Greek words differ precisely as the two English; the λῃστής (robber, brigand, highwayman) takes by force, the κλέπτης (thief) by stealth. Judas was a thief (Jn 12[6]), Barabbas a robber (18[40], cf. Mk 15[7]). But earlier English versions join with AV in ignoring this distinction; 'thief' occurs in them all in the above passages from the Synoptists; in Jn 10[1. 8] when another word was needed, Tind. and Geneva have 'robber,' but Cranmer 'murtherer' (cf. Luther, *Mörder*); in 18[40] Wyc. and Rhem. have 'thief,' Tind. 'robber,' Cran. and Gen. 'murtherer.' But in 16th cent. English, 'thief' was used in a wider sense than now, including all kinds of robbery. Thus Shakespeare calls pirates 'water thieves' (*Merchant of Venice*, I. 3); Latimer (*Sermons*, Parker Soc. 208) calls Robin Hood 'a traitor and a thief,' and (139) applying Is 1[23] says 'He calleth princes thieves. Had they a standing at Shooter's Hill or Standgate Hole, to take a purse?' So Cranmer (*Remains*, Parker Soc. 107), 'Job said not "These wicked thieves have wrought me this woe"; but referred all to God.' See Trench, *NT Synonyms*, §xliv.

Palestine has always, if its government has been weak, been infested by robbers, to whom its rocks and caves afford plentiful cover and shelter (cf. Jg 9[25], Hos 6[9] 7[1]). Herod, when quite young, first made his reputation by ruthlessly executing robbers in Galilee (Josephus, *Ant.* XIV. ix. 2, *BJ* I. x. 5). At a later time he destroyed robbers who lived in inaccessible caverns, by lowering chests full of soldiers from the cliff above (*Ant.* XIV. xv. 4–5, *BJ* I. xvi. 2–4). This reminds us of 'den of robbers' (Jer 7[11], Mt 21[13] ||). Not only had the Temple become a haunt of 'robbers'—the dealers in the Temple market were notorious for their extortion—but it gave them fancied security in their evil-doing. (During the Jewish War the Temple was literally the stronghold of the robbers or Zealots, *BJ* IV. iii. 7, etc.). There was a great outbreak of robbery on the death of Herod (*Ant.* XVII. x., *BJ* II. iv.). We read later of robbers plundering a servant of the Emperor's, near Bethhoron, which was avenged on the neighbouring villagers by Cumanus (*Ant.* XX. v. 4, *BJ* II. xii. 2), and of Fadus, Felix, and Festus destroying large numbers of them (*Ant.* XX. i. 1, viii. 5, 10, *BJ* II. xiii. 2, xiv. 1). Under the later procurators the country swarmed with them. It is probable that some of these 'robbers' were really Zealots, in rebellion against the authority of Rome, so that there was an element of misplaced patriotism and even religion in their proceedings. Trench (*l.c.*) shows how this may throw light on the character of the 'Penitent Robber.' In any case, Josephus at a later date identifies robbers and Zealots (*BJ* IV. iii. 3. 9, etc.).

The road from Jerusalem to Jericho, the scene of the parable of the Good Samaritan, has always had a bad name for robbers. Near it Pompey destroyed two robbers' strongholds (Strabo, xvi. 2); Jerome (on Jer 3[2]) speaks of its dangers, and derives the 'ascent of Adummim' on this road from the blood shed there by robbers (*Loc. Heb. s.v.*). See Stanley, *Sin. and Pal.* 314, 424, and art. SAMARITAN (THE GOOD). HAROLD SMITH.

ROBE.—See DRESS.

ROCK (πέτρα).—**1.** In Mt 7[24] the word stands for a rocky foundation, which would remain solid, notwithstanding the sapping effect of floods; while the sandy foundation means a carelessly chosen site, where the loose formation of the soil would be very easily penetrated by torrents, thus making the building erected on it very insecure. The moral and spiritual parallel is that of two contrasted lives, one durable, the other perishing and worthless. The man who listens to Christ's words but does not carry them out, never allowing them to affect his character, is one who builds upon the sand. He, again, who hears the word and straightway carries it into action, doing the will of God with his might, has chosen the rocky foundation. To him the storms and trials of life act as tests of character, which show it to be securely founded, and make it more firm and durable. Perhaps faith and obedience are the two prominent characteristics of the man who builds his house upon the rock. See art. BUILDING.

2. At Cæsarea Philippi, Christ asked His disciples about the various opinions men were holding regarding Him. St. Peter answered for the Apostles: 'Thou art the Christ, the Son of the living God.' The Saviour was pleased by this answer of faith, which had been revealed to Peter by the Heavenly Father, and commended him by saying (Mt 16[18]), 'Thou art Peter (πέτρος), and on this rock (πέτρα) I will build my Church.' St. Peter thus showed himself to be one who had profited by Christ's teaching, being a doer of the word as well as a hearer. Only the faithful and obedient heart could have given him such a deep knowledge of the truth. As Jerusalem stood on the rocky foundation of Mt. Zion, and was faced by the dark rocks of the valley of Hinnom, a scene of death and corruption; so the new city of God, the ἐκκλησία of Christ, is to be founded on imperishable foundations, so that the opposing gates of Hades (all the power of evil) should never prevail against it. St. Peter, in showing himself a man of faith, is a specimen of the believing ones who shall constitute the strong foundation on which the Church is to rest. As πέτρος is a fragment of πέτρα, so the believing St. Peter is an example of all who should hereafter believe (cf. 1 Ti 1[16]).

It is well to note that the Fathers took the rock to mean either Christ Himself, or the faith or the confession of St. Peter, but never St. Peter as an *individual*. In later days, the text Mt 16[18] was used for polemical purposes, in defence of the Papacy. The Reformers returned to the earlier view of the Fathers, mostly holding that the confession of faith made by St. Peter was the rock. Another view held by Luther, following Augustine, was that Christ, in speaking the words, pointed to Himself as the rock. Perhaps this would best accord with the general teaching of the New Testament. St. Paul calls Christ the foundation (1 Co 3[11]), and again speaks of Apostles and prophets being the foundation, while Christ is the chief corner-stone (Eph 2[20]). Is it not most likely, however, that our Lord looked on St. Peter as the type of converted, believing men, on whom, as a foundation, an unconquerable Church should be built? Origen well says: 'If thou hast Peter's faith, thou art a rock like him. If thou hast Peter's virtues, thou hast Peter's keys.' See also artt. CÆSAREA PHILIPPI and CHURCH.

3. The word 'rock' occurs in Lk 8[6. 13], in the parable of the Sower. It is the equivalent of the 'stony (RV 'rocky') places' of Mt 13[5. 20] (τὰ πετρώδη), and gives at once the right sense, a thin coating of soil covering a hard rocky surface, where there could be no depth of earth. The rock here, in the interpretation, signifies a sinful worldly nature, incapable of being penetrated by the living seed. That which makes a good foundation is not at all fitted to be a good seed-bed. See art. SEED.

4. In Mt 27^{51} we read that the rocks ($\pi\acute{\epsilon}\tau\rho\alpha\iota$) were rent, at the hour of Christ's death on Calvary. There is nothing figurative here; but the earthquake would make it appear to men's minds as if the very earth shuddered at man's wicked deed, so that its hardest elements were broken asunder.

5. Finally, the sepulchre in which our Lord was laid was 'hewn out of a rock' (Mt 27^{60} = Mk 15^{46}). D. M. W. LAIRD.

ROLL ($\beta\iota\beta\lambda\acute{\iota}o\nu$, $\kappa\epsilon\phi\alpha\lambda\acute{\iota}s$). — The word 'roll' is found in NT only in the RV, and in the Gospels only as a marginal reading. In the account in Luke of our Lord's sermon in the synagogue at Nazareth it occurs thrice in the margin ($4^{17\ bis.\ 20}$) as the rendering of $\beta\iota\beta\lambda\acute{\iota}o\nu$, where AV and text of RV give 'book.' In He 10^7 'In the volume of the book it is written of me' RV gives 'roll' for AV 'volume' as the rendering of $\kappa\epsilon\phi\alpha\lambda\acute{\iota}s$. The latter word occurs here only in NT, but it is quoted from the Septuagint (Ps 40^7), and thus its meaning is determined, as it is the translation of the Heb. מְגִלָּה, 'roll,' although in Liddell and Scott $\kappa\epsilon\phi\alpha\lambda\acute{\iota}s$ is given as meaning 'chapter *or* passage.' Why $\kappa\epsilon\phi\alpha\lambda\acute{\iota}s$ is taken to represent מְגִלָּה is uncertain, although it has been held that the reference was to the knobs or rounded heads of the roller about which the manuscript was rolled (see Grimm-Thayer, *Lex. s.v.*). The roll was the form of the book both in Palestine and Egypt, although usually, if not always, the Hebrew rolls were, originally at least, of skins which had gone through some process of tanning (see art. BOOK), while the Egyptian rolls were of papyrus. When papyrus began to be used in Palestine it is difficult to say. The codex form of book is generally held to have been introduced after the invention of parchment, but there is reason to believe that the Egyptians occasionally employed it for papyrus manuscripts, while the roll was the prevailing form.

LITERATURE.—Comm. on the NT; Kenyon's art. 'Writing' in Hastings' *DB*, and his *Textual Criticism of the NT*, p. 19 f.

GEO. C. WATT.

ROME, ROMANS.—Though the name 'Romans' appears only once in the Gospels (Jn 11^{48}), if we except the adverb Ῥωμαιστί (Jn 19^{20}), which is tr. 'in Latin' by AV and RV, Rome and the Romans are a very real presence in the Gospel narratives, forming a sort of background to the action of the leading figures. The influence of the world-power is shown by the references to the Emperor (Mt 22^{17}, Mk 12^{14}, Lk 2^1 3^1 20^{22} 23^2, Jn 19^{12}), the governor Pontius Pilate (see PILATE), the tax-gatherers (Mt 5^{46} etc.), the centurions (Mk 15^{39}, Lk 7^2 etc.), and the soldiers (Mt 27^{27} etc.). The Gospels testify to the ultra-national feeling of those Jews who were antagonistic to the Roman power, and illustrate the hatred and contempt felt for those of their countrymen—the tax-gatherers, for example —who took employment from the government. The more intellectually enlightened among the Jews—the Sadducees, for instance—welcomed the Roman rule as they welcomed the Greek civilization and culture which it brought with it; but the great mass of the people were in a state of unreasoning opposition to it. The disposition of Pilate may be advanced as an excuse for their attitude, but in general it cannot be denied that the Jews did not deserve to retain their former liberty, that they were ungrateful to the Romans for the special privileges conferred on them, and that they forgot the advantages which the powerful protection of Rome and the advancement and security of trade thus accruing brought to them. The student of history will regard the fate which

came upon them in A.D. 70, and which is referred to in Lk $21^{20ff.}$, as deserved. The stiffneckedness of the Jews brought upon them a ruin which other subject-races in the Empire had escaped by a wise submission.

The beginnings of Rome are shrouded in obscurity, but the spade has helped to correct and amplify what we learn from history. The city was situated on the left bank of the Tiber, about eighteen miles from its mouth. The original Rome was built only on the Palatine Hill. When the people of Romulus were united with the Sabines, the Capitoline Hill, the Forum, and perhaps part of the Quirinal, were added. Mons Cœlius was occupied by Etruscan colonists from the other side of the river, and conquest led to the later inclusion of the Aventine, the Viminal, the Esquiline, and Quirinal Hills, on which early settlements had existed. Tradition has it that one of the kings, named Servius Tullius, built a wall to enclose the now largely extended city. This wall, called the *agger*, because it was built specially for purposes of defence, remained the wall of Rome till, late in the Empire, in the time of Aurelian (3rd cent. A.D.), a new and extended line of fortifications was built. Outside the Servian wall there was a trench 100 ft. broad and 30 ft. deep. Within this the wall proper was built of large rectangular blocks, and behind this wall there was an embankment 100 ft. wide and 30 ft. high, pierced by the channels of aqueducts. Portions of the wall have been discovered in thirty-seven different places, and it is possible to trace its entire course. Advantage was taken by the engineers of all the natural features, and where these were lacking, as on the northwest, the above plan was followed. Between the Capitoline and the Aventine the river was thought to afford sufficient protection. The whole circuit of the wall was about 5 miles, and it was pierced by 19 gates. Within there was a large area of vacant spaces, which were gradually built on later, and at the beginning of the Empire the city was not only congested with buildings, but large areas without the wall were also covered with houses. In the year B.C. 10, Augustus divided the city into 14 wards (*regiones*), and these were in their turn subdivided into smaller quarters (*vici*). Some of the principal buildings must be referred to. The Roman Forum, an open space measuring over 300 ft. in length and about 150 ft. in breadth, was the centre of political, legal, and commercial life. At one end was the *rostra* or platform, from which speeches were delivered to the public; at the other end were shops. On one side were the *Curia* or senate-house and the *Basilica Æmilia*, a law-court; along the whole of the other side, with the *Sacra Via* between, stretched the *Basilica Julia*, a very large law-court, surrounded by two rows of square columns. Other important buildings in the immediate neighbourhood were the Temple of Janus, the Temple of Cæsar, the Arch of Augustus, the Temple of Vesta, the Temple of Castor and Pollux, and the Temple of Saturn, where was the treasury, with the *Tabularium* (record-office) behind. On the top of the Capitoline Hill was the *Capitolium* or great temple dedicated to Jupiter, Juno, and Minerva, and on the Palatine Hill the principal residence of the Emperor, and the Temple of Apollo containing public libraries, Greek and Latin. In the Imperial period four additional *fora* were built, devoted entirely to legal, literary, and religious purposes— the *Forum Julium* begun by Julius Cæsar, the *Forum Augustum* built by Augustus, the *Forum Transitorium* completed by Nerva, and the *Forum Trajani* built by Trajan, the most splendid work of Imperial times. Considerations of space will not allow mention of the markets, circuses, theatres, baths, and gardens, which were characteristic features of the city and its life. The great roads which converged at Rome, and the aqueducts, can merely be mentioned. Various estimates of the population of Rome in the time of Christ have been given, ranging from 800,000 to 2,000,000 : the latter seems more likely than the former. All nationalities in the Empire were represented, and the slave population was very large.

Only a very brief sketch of the progress of the Romans can be given. Their history is curiously parallel to our own. They were a mixed race, and passed through the three stages, pastoral and agricultural, commercial, and imperial. The kernel of the race was Latin, but there was an early intermixture with Sabines and Etruscans, the latter, according to tradition, emigrants from Lydia, in Asia Minor. The Romans began as one of the members of the Latin league of which, having become presidents, they eventually became masters. After conquering Latium, they were inevitably brought into conflict with the other races of Italy. They rose again after the Gallic invasion and destruction of their city in 390, and by the time their trade interests brought them into conflict with the Carthaginians, about the middle of the 3rd cent. B.C., they were sovereign over most of Italy. The close of that century saw them possessors of Sicily and Sardinia, as well as conquerors over 'Africa.' About this time they began to interfere in Eastern politics, and the Macedonian wars and the conflicts which grew out of them resulted in the conquest of Macedonia and Greece in the same year as they finally became masters of 'Africa.' Ere this they had become possessed of most of Spain. The extension of Roman territory steadily continued, until in the time of Christ it included, roughly, Europe (except the British Isles, Norway, Sweden, Denmark, Germany, and Russia), the whole of Asia Minor, Syria, Egypt, and the north-west of Africa.

The internal history of the Roman people was no less remarkable. Great dangers from within were successfully surmounted. The conflict between the patricians and the dependent class lasted for hundreds of years. At first the Roman State was ruled by a king, with a body of patrician advisers. On the substitution of a dyarchy for a monarchy— a change effected not without difficulty—the new office, called the consulship, tenable for one year, was open only to the patrician class. Even from the earliest times there appears to have been a popular assembly, which played some part in legislation, but to define its powers or to state their exact relation to the powers of the king and senate is impossible. The consuls were elected by the citizen-army, which assembled in classes according to the property qualification of each citizen-soldier. The whole procedure of this assembly was in the hands of its patrician presidents, so that there was more of the semblance than the reality of power. Further, the plebeian had no appeal against the arbitrary authority of a chief magistrate. At the very beginning of the Republic the famous Valerian law was passed, that no magistrate should put a Roman citizen to death unless the sentence had been confirmed by the assembly of citizen-soldiers. This law was always regarded as the great charter of a Roman's liberties, but at first it was difficult to enforce. The plebeians adopted on more than one occasion the plan of deserting the city for a time, and thus wrung concessions from the unwilling patricians. It was in this way that they succeeded in obtaining magistrates of their own, called tribunes, who were authorized to protect them against the consuls. The development of the powers of this magistracy had more to do with the progress of the Roman democracy than any other factor, and even in the Empire the most

important of the Emperor's statutory powers was his 'tribunician authority.' The tribunes convened assemblies of the plebeians, and carried resolutions of importance to that class. The resolutions of this body, which met by tribes, were later on to become the most powerful force in the State, having at a comparatively early period been declared to have the force of laws (B.C. 287). The first plebeian consul was elected in 367, about a century and a half after the traditional date of the establishment of the Republic, and by the end of the fourth century B.C. every office in the State was open to the plebeian class. The plebeians had won all they sought.

The establishment of the equality of the orders was not the establishment of a real democracy. It was the beginning of a new struggle between the governing class, which was mainly plebeian in origin, and the mass of the people. The rapid expansion of the Roman territory, the necessity for the appointment of new magistrates to govern the new countries, and the establishment of a governing class alone possessed of the experience necessary for coping with foreign affairs, tended more and more to withdraw the real power from the popular assemblies and to concentrate it in the hands of the senate. By the theory of the constitution the popular assemblies had all the power, but in practice, between the middle of the 3rd and the beginning of the 1st cent. B.C., the senate was all-powerful. Circumstances also produced great distress among the people in general. In the absence of the farmer, serving in the army abroad, his farm was neglected, and trouble came upon him and his household. He had to borrow money, which in many cases he was unable to repay. His acres were bought by the rich, who worked them with slave labour, which was cheap owing to the enormous influx of captives seized in war. The small landholder disappeared, to join the hungry proletariat in Rome ; and Italy became a country of large estates, which, in the words of Pliny, wrought her ruin. The attempts made by the Gracchi (B.C. 133–122) to redress this state of matters were rewarded with assassination. Periodically, to the end of the Republic, agrarian laws were brought forward, but were unable to check the evil. Even under the Empire it was only partially checked, and a large part of the Roman population was fed by the Emperors.

A Roman 'province' consisted of the sphere of duty of a magistrate, and the word had not primarily a territorial application. The inhabitants were disarmed and taxed. The main lines under which a province was to be governed were set forth in a special law, generally drawn up by the senate. This law always took account of local conditions, such as the form of government already in existence before annexation, and the favour shown to Rome by particular cities. In some provinces certain States were free, such as Athens in the province of Achaia. It was the custom to send a body of commissioners to start the new constitution on its way. Some of these constitutions were modified as time went on, but others which had been established in Republican times were found still existing in Imperial times. Much was left to governors in the time of the Republic. Cruelty and rapacity were very common, but incompetence was unknown. The provincials could hardly get redress for injuries inflicted on them in Republican times. All the eloquence of a Cicero, engaged to plead the cause of the province of Sicily, availed only to remove Verres, the cause of the evil ; the evil was not healed.

During the last century of the Republic, Rome and Italy were torn by a long succession of ruinous civil wars. It said much for the machinery of the government that foreign enemies did not imperil its very existence. There was a longing among all the better citizens for an era of peace and prosperity, and it had become increasingly clear that this goal could be reached only under an Imperial rule. The need of the time was satisfied by Augustus, who ruled as autocrat under constitutional forms. The appearance of a republic was retained, but the reality was gone, and the appearance itself gradually disappeared also. For the city the Empire was a time of luxury and idleness, but the provinces entered upon an era of progressive prosperity. The Emperor was responsible for the government of all provinces where an army was necessary, and governed these by paid deputies of his own. The older and more settled provinces were governed by officials appointed by the senate, but the Emperor had his financial interests looked after by procurators of his own even in these. The provinces were now much more protected against the rapacity and cruelty of governors. The Emperors themselves stood for just as well as efficient administration, and most of them gave a noble example by strenuous devotion to administrative business.

The resident Romans in any province consisted of (1) the officials connected with the government, who were generally changed annually ; (2) members of the great financial companies, and lesser business men, whose interests kept them there,—the *publicans* of the Gospels were agents of the former ; (3) citizens of *coloniæ* (or military settlements), which were really parts of Rome itself set down in the provinces ; (4) soldiers of the garrison and their officers. These formed the aristocracy of any city in which they lived. A fifth class of Roman citizens might be made out of those natives of the province who, for services rendered to the State, were individually gifted with the citizenship. It was a great honour, which was not conferred on all the inhabitants of the Empire till A.D. 212.

The Romans have left a great legacy to the world. As administrators, lawyers, soldiers, engineers, architects, and builders, they have never been surpassed. In literature they depended mainly on the Greeks, but they claimed that satire was a native product. So with sculpture, music, painting, and medicine. In the arts they never attained more than a respectable standard, by imitating the Greeks, who could turn their hands to anything.

LITERATURE. — For an account of Rome itself, nothing surpasses the various works of R. Lanciani (all published by Macmillan): *Ancient Rome in the Light of Recent Discoveries*, *Pagan and Christian Rome*, *The Ruins and Excavations of Ancient Rome*, *The Destruction of Ancient Rome*, and *New Tales of Old Rome*,—see also his chapters in W. Ramsay, *A Manual of Roman Antiquities* [15] (London, 1894); three excellent Maps, with Key, are in H. Kiepert and Ch. Huelsen, *Formæ Urbis Romæ Antiquæ : accedit nomenclator topographicus* (Berlin, 1896). For the Forum, see Ch. Huelsen, *The Roman Forum : its History and its Monuments* (Rome, 1906). For the general history, Th. Mommsen, *The History of Rome*, 5 vols. (London, Macmillan) [the Republic], *The History of the Roman Provinces*, 2 vols. [one aspect of Imperial history]; H. F. Pelham, *Outlines of Roman History* (London, 1893, 4th edition, 1905), a masterly work ; J. B. Bury, *A History of the Roman Empire from its Foundation to the Death of Marcus Aurelius* (London, 1893, 1896, and later). On the political life, A. H. J. Greenidge, *Roman Public Life* (London, 1901). On the literature, W. S. Teuffel, *History of Roman Literature*, 2 vols. (London, 1891-92); and esp. M. Schanz, *Geschichte der Römischen Litteratur*, four parts (second half of part 4 to complete the work, as yet unpublished), (München ; first three parts in second edition : publication began 1892). The above list constitutes only a small selection of the very best works on what appear to be the more important topics.   ALEX. SOUTER.

ROOF.—See HOUSE in vol. i. p. 753[a].

ROOT (ῥίζα).—The 'root' is that part essential to the life of a plant (Mt 13[6], Mk 4[6]), which penetrates the earth, and draws sap and nourishment from the soil. 'Root' is, therefore, taken to

signify that condition of heart without which religious life is impossible (Mt 13[21], Lk 8[13]). The intelligent and stable Christian is described as 'rooted' in love (Eph 3[17]), and 'rooted' in Christ (Col 2[7]). Utter destruction is signified by plucking up by the root (Mt 13[29], Jude [12]). The Baptist's vivid 'the axe is laid unto the root' (Mt 3[10], Lk 3[9]) points to the complete overthrow he desired for the rampant growth of evils in his day. As applied to Christ (Rev 5[5] 22[16]), the title 'Root' probably means more than 'branch or sucker from an ancient root.' Rather does it point to Him as Himself the 'root' whence David and his tribe sprang, appearing at last to manifest His transcendent power and glory.   W. EWING.

RUE (πήγανον, *Ruta graveolens*) is a low-growing shrubby plant of the natural order Rutaceæ, and is still cultivated in Palestine. It has a strong, unpleasant smell, and is bitter and pungent to the taste. The ancient Romans made use of the leaves of rue for culinary purposes. An essential oil, which is obtained by distillation with water, is used in medicine, chiefly as an antispasmodic. In Lk 11[42], where the only Biblical allusion to rue occurs, it is named along with mint (wh. see) as one of the common garden herbs on which the Pharisees paid tithe.   HUGH DUNCAN.

RUFUS.—See ALEXANDER AND RUFUS.

RULE.—1. (*a*) ἀρχή.—Lk 20[20] παραδοῦναι αὐτὸν τῇ ἀρχῇ καὶ τῇ ἐξουσίᾳ τοῦ ἡγεμόνος, 'to deliver him up to the rule and to the authority of the governor' (RV) — ἀρχή = *principatus*, ἐξουσία = *magistratus* or *munus* (Stephanus, *Thesaurus*, ed. Hase-Dindorf). Here ἀρχή 'relates to Pilate's position and authority [as procurator], ἐξουσία to the executive power connected therewith' (Cremer, *Lex.* 115, 237). Pilate's remitting our Lord to 'Herod's jurisdiction' (Lk 23[7] ἐξουσίας) was intended as an act of civility to a reigning prince ('Jesus of Nazareth' being under Herod's tetrarchate), and perhaps also in order to gain time.

ἀρχή and ἐξουσία are also used together of earthly rulers, Lk 12[11], Tit 3[1] ; of the ranks of the angelic hosts, Eph 3[10], Col 1[16] 2[10] ; of the powers of evil, Eph 6[12], Col 2[15] ; apparently incl. of both heavenly and earthly powers, 1 Co 15[24], Eph 1[21].

(*b*) ἄρχειν.—Mk 10[42] 'Ye know that they which are accounted to rule over the Gentiles (οἱ δοκοῦντες ἄρχειν : in ‖ Mt 20[25] οἱ ἄρχοντες) lord it over them, and their great ones exercise authority over them' (RV). Lk. reports that words of similar import were spoken at the parting meal, 22[25]. οἱ δοκοῦντες ἄρχειν may mean 'they who are supposed to rule,' with the implication that they are not rulers in the true sense of the word.*

Swete (*St. Mark*, 239) renders 'they who are regarded as rulers,' and says that our Lord 'did not admit that the power of such a ruler as Tiberius was a substantial dignity : it rested on a reputation that might be suddenly wrecked, as indeed the later history of the Empire clearly proved.' Cf. Harnack (*What is Christianity ?* 106) and Gould (*Com. on Mk.* 202) for a somewhat similar view.

In Gal 2[2. 6. 9] οἱ δοκοῦντες, Lightfoot thinks (*Com. on Gal.* 107), is 'deprecatory, — not indeed of the Twelve themselves, but of the extravagant and exclusive claims set up for them by the Judaizers.' The Gr. commentators, however, do not find 'any shade of blame or irony in the expression' (see Ellicott, *Gal.* 24[b]). Cf. also Ramsay (*Com. on Gal.* 289, 300), who renders, 'the acknowledged leaders,' and shows that the interpretation 'the so-called leaders,' is opposed to the spirit of the narrative.

The two passages referred to by Winer (*Gram. NT*[8] p. 766) are important : Sus [5] κριτῶν οἳ ἐδόκουν κυβερνᾶν τὸν λαόν, 'judges who were accounted or recognized as governing the people' ; Jos. *Ant.* XIX. vi. 3 οἱ δοκοῦντες αὐτῶν ἐξέχειν, 'they who are recog-

* There are parallels to this idea in Plato : *e.g. Rep.* 336 A, the tyrant is one who μέγα οἴεται δύνασθαι : he and his like have really no power (*Gorg.* 467 A). For the use of δοκοῦντες, cf. *Rep.* 406 C, ἐπὶ δὲ τῶν πλουσίων τε καὶ εὐδαιμόνων δοκούντων εἶναι οὐκ αἰσθανόμεθα, also 420 A, 423 C. Sometimes, however, in classical Greek δοκεῖν does not exclude the reality : *e.g.* Plato, *Rep.* 539 A, and Soph. *OT* 402. [Note by the late Dr. Adam of Cambridge].

nized as outstanding men among them.' In these passages the phrase appears to be used, without any disparagement being implied, in speaking of recognized authorities, or persons of admitted eminence.*

In the words κατακυριεύουσιν and κατεξουσιάζουσιν, —the latter found only here and in ‖ Mt.—an unfavourable judgment is passed upon the manner in which 'the recognized rulers' exercise their authority. 'Civium non servitus sed tutela tradita est.' 'Our Lord spoke at a time when free government all over the world lay crushed beneath the military despotism of Rome' (*EBr* xi. 11). There was present to His mind the fundamental law of His Kingdom, 'My kingdom is not of this world' (Jn 18[36]).

But our Lord's words do not exhibit that 'moral hatred of all the visible power of the world regarded as a vast selfish manifestation and embodiment of evil,' which finds expression in the following passage from one of the letters of Gregory VII. (he is writing to Herman of Metz, one of his partisans): 'Who can be ignorant that kings and nobles took their beginning from those who, not knowing God, by their pride, robberies, perfidy, and murders, in short, by almost every kind of crime, no doubt at the suggestion of the prince of this world, the devil, have in blind ambition and intolerable presumption had a mind to tyrannize over other men who are undoubtedly their equals?' Milman asks, 'Are we reading a journalist of Paris in 1791?' (*Latin Christianity*, iii. 191; cf. Mozley's Sermon on 'The Roman Council,' *Univ. Serm.* p. 1).

Our Lord, it is true, speaks of the exercise of domination and coercion that is characteristic of the rulers of the Gentiles as an example to be avoided by His disciples as members of a Kingdom not of this world : 'so shall it not be among you.' With them, greatness is to come through ministering love (cf. art. MINISTER, 3). At the same time, in His great saying, Mk 12[17],—a saying which reveals that the whole domain of duty lay open before Him,—our Lord teaches that a kingdom of this world, even the principality of a Tiberius, has its own sphere of right, and that when it keeps within it, and exercises its administrative functions,—of which the levying of tribute is a representative instance,—it is to be obeyed without demur. This saying was probably present to the mind of St. Paul when he wrote, under Nero (but in the earlier and better part of his reign), his weighty exposition of the ethics of citizenship (Ro 13[1-7]).

2. ποιμαίνειν.—Mt 2[6] 'And thou Bethlehem, in the land of Juda, art not the least among the princes of Juda : for out of thee shall come a Governor, that shall rule (RV 'be shepherd of') my people Israel' (ὅστις ποιμανεῖ τὸν λαόν μου τὸν Ἰσραήλ). Here three things demand our attention. (i.) *Mic* 5[2] (*5 Heb.*) *and its context.*—Like his older contemporary Isaiah (9. 11), Micah looks forward to the end of the Assyrian invasion as the time when the Messianic hope shall be fulfilled.

'The daughter of Zion must pass through the pangs of labour before her true king is born; she must come forth from the city and dwell in the open field; there, and not within her proud ramparts, Jehovah will grant her deliverance from her enemies. For a time the land shall be given up to the foe, but only for a time. Once more, as in the days of David, guerilla bands gather together to avenge the wrongs of their nation (5[1]). A new David comes forth from little Bethlehem, and the rest of his brethren return to the children of Israel—that is, the kindred Hebrew nations again accept the sway of the new king, who stands and feeds his flock in the strength of Jehovah, in the majesty of the name of Jehovah his God. Then Assyria shall no longer insult Jehovah's land with impunity' (W. R. Smith, *The Prophets of Israel* [1], 291).

This being the meaning of the prophecy, it is evident that it was never literally fulfilled. But when we look at the deeper side of the Messianic hope which it sets forth—the heart-felt longing for a true Kingdom of God, 'the perception that that Kingdom can never be realized without a personal

* This is the usage in class. Gr., *e.g.* Eurip. *Hec.* 295, where οἱ δοκοῦντες is opposed to οἱ ἀδοξοῦντες; Plato, *Euthyd.* 303 C, τῶν σεμνῶν καὶ δοκούντων τι εἶναι, 'the grave and reverend seigniors' (Jowett's tr.).

centre, a representative of God with man and man with God,' who shall attain to true greatness through humility—we see that the purpose which was in the mind of God, when He moved the prophet to write, was fulfilled in the highest sense when He sent His Son into the world, and when Jesus Christ entered, by being born and that in a low condition, on that life of humiliation that led to His exaltation to the place of power, and will finally lead to 'all things being put under His feet.'

(ii.) *The quotation in Mt.*—It is not in verbal agreement with the LXX or with the Heb. text. The most important differences from the latter are the following :—

(α) Instead of צָעִיר לִהְיוֹת, lit. 'little for being' ('a town too small to be reckoned as a canton in Judah,' W. R. Smith, *l.c.*), Mt. has οὐδαμῶς ἐλαχίστη εἶ, 'art in no wise least' (RV). Turpie (*OT in the New*, 190) translates the Heb. 'And art thou, Bethlehem, little for being (=so little as not to be) among the thousands of Juda?'—following Grotius (*Opera*, ii., Amst. 1679), who received the suggestion from Pesh., where the clause is rendered interrogatively. Others conjecture that a לֹא has dropped out of the Heb. text (cf. W. C. Allen in *ExpT* xii. [1901] 283 ; *Com. on Mt.* p. 13). These suggested emendations are unnecessary. Micah says that the ideal king is to come out of Bethlehem, a town held in little estimation ; and Mt., in view of the dignity bestowed on the town by the birth of Christ, says, 'Thou art by no means the least.' They agree in spirit.

(β) The words of Micah, 'he that is to be ruler in Israel,' are expanded by Mt. into 'a ruler who shall be shepherd of my people Israel.' He thus introduces into his quotation the words of the promise to David, 'And thou shalt be shepherd of (תִּרְעֶה) my people Israel' (2 S 5[2] ‖ 1 Ch 11[2]). But in Mic 5[4 (3 Heb.)] the words, 'And he shall stand and be shepherd of' (וְרָעָה), are a reminiscence of the promise to David. The Evangelist simply gives the promise at full length.

To most Biblical scholars these differences will not seem of much account. The quotations in the NT are an important subject of study, but it is not now considered necessary, in the interests of revelation, to make out a verbal correspondence between these quotations and their OT equivalents. See art. QUOTATIONS.

(iii.) *The nature of Christ's rule as set forth by* ποιμαίνειν.—רָעָה is first applied to God by Jacob, Gn 48[15] ('who shepherded me'), 49[24] (prob. 'the shepherd of the stone of Israel,' and ='the God of Bethel' [Driver, *Gen.*[1] Addenda, xvii]). His people are 'the sheep of his pasture' (Ps 95[7] 100[3]) ; He led them and fed them in the wilderness as a shepherd (Ps 77[20] 78[52] 80[1], Hos 13[5] [LXX] ἐποίμαινόν σε ἐν τῇ ἐρήμῳ, Is 63[11], Jer 2[2] 'thou wentest after me'—the shepherd leading) ; He will bring them back from the Dispersion (Ezk 34[12], cf. Ps 147[2]) ; His care for His flock comprehends the most considerate tending of individuals (Ps 23[1-3a], Is 40[11], Ps 119[176] seeking the lost sheep). To David, as His vicegerent, He commits the care of His flock (2 S 5[2], Ps 78[71]), and He will yet set up one shepherd over them, who shall be pre-eminent in those qualities which David in a large measure manifested as a ruler (Mic 5[4], Ezk 34[23] 37[24], Ps 2[9] [LXX, following Pesh., ποιμανεῖς αὐτοὺς ἐν ῥάβδῳ σιδηρᾷ, so quoted Rev 2[27] 12[5] 19[15] ; cf. Briggs, *Com. on Psalms*, i. 22]). To Mt. this shepherd is Jesus Christ, and it is fitting that in this early chapter he should employ this title respecting Him whose life on earth, as set forth in the succeeding chapters of his Gospel, was to illustrate so abundantly His shepherd - rule in its tenderness and strength. Christ is the compassionate Shepherd (Mt 9[36] 15[24]) ; His flock fear no evil, because He is with them (Lk 12[32]) ; He goes after that which is lost till He finds it (Mt 12[11], Lk 15[4-6]) ; He is the noble (καλός) Shepherd, who gives His life for His sheep (Jn 10[2. 11. 16]), who provides for their being fed and tended after His departure to heaven (Jn 21[15-17] ; cf. Ac 20[28], Eph 4[11], 1 P 5[2]), and who still carries on in glory His own work as 'the great shepherd of the sheep' (He 13[20]) and the ἀρχιποίμην (1 P 5[4]—a title combining the two words of our present study) ;—

moreover, their being under His shepherd-rule will be the blessedness and joy of His people to all eternity (Rev 7[17]).

It is well known that ποιμαίνειν is a favourite figure with Greek writers to denote the kingly office. Plato is very fond of the comparison; see *Rep.* 343 A with the note in Adam's ed. (Camb. 1902). In a passage in the *Nicom. Ethics* (viii. 11), Aristotle refers to Homer's well-known words, εὖ γὰρ ποιεῖ τοὺς βασιλευομένους, εἴπερ ἀγαθὸς ὢν ἐπιμελεῖται αὐτῶν, ἵν᾽ εὖ πράττωσιν, ὥσπερ νομεὺς προβάτων· ὅθεν καὶ Ὅμηρος τὸν Ἀγαμέμνονα ποιμένα λαῶν εἶπεν. 'It seems to me desirable,' Dr. Adam observes, 'whenever possible, to quote classical Greek parallels to the figures of the NT, as well as parallels from the Hebrew: the use of figures already familiar to the Greeks cannot but have made the NT writings more acceptable to Greek readers.'

JAMES DONALD.

RULER.—This word is used in AV of the Gospels to tr. six different Greek words, and it is therefore necessary to classify the instances according to the word represented. (1) In Mk 13[9] and Lk 21[12] ἡγεμών (RV 'governor'), for which see art. GOVERNOR. (2) In Mt 24[45 (47)] 25[21 (23)], Lk 12[42 (44)] κύριος, which means an owner of property, especially of slaves. It is hardly too much to say that the word κύριος suggests the word δοῦλος, 'slave.' The one word is correlative to the other. A κύριος is one who possesses slaves; a δοῦλος is one who belongs to and is bound to serve an owner. St. Paul, for example, regarded himself as standing in that relation to Jesus Christ. (3) In one passage, Jn 4[46] (AVm), βασιλικός, a general term, not infrequently found, to indicate any one in the service of a royal person. In this passage a man in the service of Herod, tetrarch of Galilee, is doubtless meant. The word appears to be used only of those in the service of Eastern potentates, and never in connexion with the Roman Emperor. (4) In Jn 2[9] the expression 'ruler of the feast' occurs. This is a tr. of the compound word ἀρχιτρίκλινος, lit. 'ruler of the dining-room' (with three dining-couches). His position at a dinner or banquet corresponded very much to that of a head-waiter at a modern public dinner. He had to see to the arrangement of the dining-couches, the laying of the table, the supply of food and drink; in short, to supervise everything connected with the comfort of the guests and the success of the banquet. (5) In the great bulk of the instances the word 'ruler' represents ἄρχων, a more or less vague term which generally answers to the English (*city*) *magistrate*. In the following passages it indicates a member or officer of the Sanhedrin (wh. see): Lk 23[13. 35] 24[20], Jn 3[1]. In Mt 9[18-23], if we compare the parallel narratives (Mk 5[22], Lk 8[41]), it would appear to mean 'ruler of the synagogue,' as in Jn 12[42], the context of which seems to settle the question. We are probably to understand this implication also in Lk 18[18], Jn 7[26. 48]. (6) The title 'ruler of the synagogue' (ἀρχισυνάγωγος) is explicitly used in Mk 5[22. 35. 36. 38], Lk 8[41. 49] 13[14] (in all the passages except the last it is Jairus that is referred to). The name was applied in Palestine to the chief official of the synagogue as a place of worship. He had, for example, to maintain order in the building, and had to select those who were to take part in the service. Outside Palestine the title was frequently honorary, and carried no duties with it.

A. SOUTER.

RUST (βρῶσις [fr. βιβρώσκω, Lat. *voro*, 'to eat.' Properly the act of eating, and so 'corrosion'], Mt 6[19f.]; also used for 'food,' Jn 4[32] 6[27. 55]).—The corroding influence liable to tarnish treasures or precious metals, which in Eastern countries were often stored in the ground (Mt 13[44]) or on inhabited premises (Lk 15[8]).

C. H. PRICHARD.

RUTH.—Named in our Lord's genealogy (Mt 1[5]), probably for the reason noted in art. RAHAB.

S

SABBATH (Heb. שַׁבָּת, Gr. σάββατον).—**1. Sabbath observance in the time of Christ.**—Although the Mishna dates from *c.* 200 A.D., many of the provisions there recorded were current at a much earlier time; hence we may often use it to illustrate Jewish life in the time of Christ. Two of its treatises, *Shabbath* and *Erubin*, besides portions of others, deal with the observance of the Sabbath. *Shabbath* is concerned with regulations respecting what is lawful or unlawful on that day, and *Erubin* treats of modifications of the laws concerning travelling or moving anything from one place to another on the Sabbath.

In accordance with the Jewish custom (derived from the recurring expression 'the evening and the morning were the . . . day' in Gn 1, see *Erubin*, v. 5), the Sabbath was considered to begin at sunset on the Friday and to end at sunset on the Saturday. The day preceding the Sabbath (or other feast) was called the day of the Preparation, παρασκευή (Lk 23[54], Jn 19[31. 42]), on which all work must be finished, and nothing fresh attempted, unless there was time enough to complete it before sunset. For instance, a tailor must not go out carrying his needle near dusk on the Friday, lest through forgetfulness he should carry it on the Sabbath (*Shabbath*, i. 3); and meat, onions, or eggs must not be fried unless they can be quite done before the sunset at which the Sabbath begins (*ib.* i. 10). This explains the request of the Jews to Pilate that the bodies of Jesus and the two robbers should be taken down (Jn 19[31]), in accordance with Dt 21[23]. It was the custom of the Jews to take down the bodies of those who were condemned and crucified, and to bury them before the going down of the sun (Jos. *BJ* IV. v. 2). It also explains the haste in the entombment of the Saviour. He did not die until the ninth hour, *i.e.* 3 p.m. (Mt 27[45-50]), and Joseph of Arimathæa and his friends had to finish the temporary burial and to return home before sundown when the Sabbath began, leaving the completion of the embalming until the Sabbath was past (Lk 23[56]). They could prepare the spices after sunset on the Saturday, and be ready to go to the tomb very early on the following morning (Lk 24[1]).

Just before sunset the Sabbath lamp was lighted; to neglect this was a transgression (*Shabbath*, 2). As no fire was allowed to be kindled, all meals had to be prepared before the Sabbath began. Three meals were customary (*ib.* xvi. 2), one on the Sabbath eve (Friday after sunset); another on the following morning, called ἄριστον (as Lk 11[38], see Edersheim, *LT*, ii. 205; but in later times the word was applied to 'dinner,' see Grimm-Thayer's *Lex.*); the third meal was towards evening, called δεῖπνον (Jn 12[2]). To preserve the festive character of the day, the provisions were the best obtainable, and the best clothes were worn. Religious exercises were provided by the synagogue services, which were generally two in number, one on the Sabbath eve (Friday night) and the other on the following morning.

The traditional rules of the Mishna, which at least partially existed in the time of Christ, introduced very embarrassing limitations to actions lawful on the Sabbath. The distance which might be travelled was limited to 2000 cubits. This rule was obtained as follows. According to Ex 16²⁹, no man may go out of his place on the Sabbath. The extent of a 'place' was fixed by the Rabbis at the traditional distance of the Tabernacle from the camp of Israel in the wilderness. This was somewhat arbitrarily set down as the same distance as that by which the Ark of the Covenant preceded the people at the crossing of the Jordan (Jos 3⁴). In this way arose the measurement called a 'Sabbath day's journey' (Ac 1¹², see Lumby, ad loc.). This limitation to the distance which might be travelled seems also to illustrate the words of Jesus in Mt 24²⁰ 'neither on the Sabbath day.' (For the way in which this traditional rule might be evaded, see Erubin, iv. and v.). The Mishna names thirty-nine aboth (אָבוֹת) or principal kinds of work unlawful on the Sabbath, and from these it deduces a number of others (called toledoth, תּוֹלְדוֹת), which it pronounces likewise unlawful; and it proceeds by casuistry to define what actions are permissible (see Shabbath; also Edersheim, LT, Append. XVII.). It must here suffice to refer to these rules only in so far as they illustrate passages in the Gospels.

2. Gospel incidents connected with the Sabbath. —(a) Preaching in the Synagogue at Nazareth (Lk 4¹⁶⁻³⁰ ‖ Mk 6¹⁻⁶).—Some regard these passages as referring to two distinct incidents, of which that recorded by Lk. is the earlier (so Edersheim); others think the incident in Mk. is the same as the former, but related out of its chronological order.

(b) Healing of the infirm man at the Pool of Bethesda (Jn 5⁵⁻¹⁸).—It was lawful to carry a sick person on a bed, because the bed was only accessory to the carrying of the person (Shabbath, x. 5), but to carry the bed alone was unlawful, as it was then an ordinary burden. Thus those who carried the man to the Pool of Bethesda escaped censure (although it is difficult to see how they could do this, according to the Mishna, unless the man were in danger of death [see Yoma, viii. 6], but this may be a more stringent rule than was then in force); but when the healed man carried his bed, he was decidedly breaking the Law as interpreted by the Rabbis. Indeed, the healing of the man, unless he were in danger of death, would appear to be regarded as an infraction of the Sabbath law (Mk 3¹⁻⁶). Food or outward applications to the body might be used on the Sabbath only if they were in customary use in health; thus a man who had toothache might not rinse his teeth with vinegar (for that was not a common act in health), but he might wash them as he did every day (Shabbath, xiv. 4). If, however, there were danger of death, the Sabbath law did not apply.

(c) Healing of the man with an unclean spirit at Capernaum (Mk 1²¹⁻²⁷ ‖ Lk 4³³⁻³⁷).

(d) Healing of Peter's wife's mother (Mt 8¹⁴⁻¹⁵ ‖ Mk 1²⁹⁻³², Lk 4³⁸⁻⁴⁰).—The healing of those with divers diseases on the evening of this day took place when the sun set and the Sabbath was past.

(e) Plucking the ears of corn (Mt 12¹⁻⁸ ‖ Mk 2²³⁻²⁸, Lk 6¹⁻⁵).—The action of the disciples was legitimate on week-days, according to Dt 23²⁵; but on the Sabbath it was held unlawful, as involving the two actions of reaping and of threshing. The illustration given by our Lord in His reply (Mt 12⁵)— the Temple service in its relation to the Sabbath— was a difficulty which the Talmud discusses (see Edersheim, LT, ii. 59). In this case the Law

ordained service which apparently broke its own requirements.

Lk. specifies this Sabbath as δευτερόπρωτον (AV 'second Sabbath after the first'; RV omits in text, 'second-first' being placed in the margin as the reading of 'many ancient authorities'). The expression has been variously explained, and no aid is to be derived from the Talmud. The fifty days between Passover and Pentecost were reckoned from the second day of the feast (Nisan 16), on which the wave-sheaf was offered (Lv 23¹¹). Hence the Sabbath indicated has been taken as (i.) the first Sabbath after that second day of the feast (Scaliger, Ewald, de Wette, Edersheim, and others); or (ii.) the second Sabbath after the day (Nisan 16) which was the first in counting the time to Pentecost (Delitzsch). Other explanations are (iii.) the first Sabbath of the second year of the Sabbatical series of seven years (Wieseler); and (iv.) the first Sabbath of the second month. The reading of the text is doubtful; δευτερόπρωτον is omitted in אBL, 1, 33, 69 (see Plummer, 'St. Luke' (ICC), ad loc.; and Edersheim, LT).

(f) Healing of the man with a withered hand (Mt 12⁹⁻¹⁴ ‖ Mk 3¹⁻⁵, Lk 6⁶⁻¹¹).—On the lawfulness of healing on the Sabbath according to the Mishna, see (b) above. The legitimacy of lifting a sheep out of a pit on the Sabbath is discussed in the Talmud (Shabbath, 117a; see Edersheim).

(g) The defence which Jesus made against the charge of Sabbath-breaking (Jn 7²³⁻²⁴).—The Mishna (Shabbath, 19) expressly permits all ceremonies relating to circumcision and all preparation for it to be carried out on the Sabbath.

(h) Opening of the eyes of one born blind (Jn 9¹⁻¹⁶).—This involved the 'making of clay' on the Sabbath for application to the man's eyes, which would be a breach of the Sabbath law, in addition to the general question of the legitimacy of healing discussed in (b) above.

(i) Healing of the woman who had a spirit of infirmity (Lk 13¹⁰⁻¹⁷).—Regulations for the watering of cattle on the Sabbath are found in the Mishna (Erubin, ii.). The Talmud even allows water to be drawn and poured into the trough for the animals to drink.

(k) Healing of the man who had the dropsy (Lk 14¹⁻⁶).

(l) The supper at Bethany (Jn 12¹). — Jesus reached Bethany on Friday, and the supper was the festive meal (δεῖπνον) on the following Sabbath.

(m) The Sabbath between the Crucifixion and the Resurrection (Mt 28¹ ‖ Mk 16¹, Lk 23⁵⁵⁻⁵⁶).

3. Teaching of Jesus respecting the Sabbath.— The observance of the Sabbath was one of the most easily apparent points upon which the teaching of our Lord differed from the punctilious legalism of His time. Mistaken patriotism had employed itself in elaborating the provisions of the Law and raising a fence around it (Aboth, i. 1). The teaching of Jesus was more akin to that of the ancient prophets than to that of the scribes. He preferred spiritual obedience to ceremonial literalism. The traditions of the scribes, which added burdens to the original Law, were regarded by Him as obscuring the underlying truth, and thus hindering true godliness (Mt 15³⁻²⁰ 23¹³⁻³³). This is illustrated in His treatment of the Sabbath.

(1) The practice of Jesus upholds the general use of the institution.—It was 'his custom' to worship in the synagogue (Lk 4¹⁶). He observed the usual requirements of the Law, except in cases where casuistical refinements had brought it into opposition to spiritual service. He seems to have intended this to be the attitude of His Jewish disciples (Mt 24²⁰ possibly supports this), and they certainly understood that this was His will, and they only dropped Jewish ceremonies as the Church outgrew them. The decision recorded in Ac 15²⁴⁻²⁹ did not release Jews who became Christians from obedience to the Law. St. Paul himself kept the Law (Ac 21²⁴⁻²⁶).

(2) Christ asserted that the well-being of man was more important than the rigid observance of

the Sabbath law as interpreted by the scribes.—
This appears in the many instances of miracles of
healing on the Sabbath, and the arguments with
which He met criticism.   He taught that the
Sabbath law is to be subordinated to man's good
(Mk 2²⁷).   This is in accordance with the reason
for the Sabbath in Dt 5¹⁴.   The Sabbath was intended to afford opportunity for religious worship
and the culture of the soul, and we may regard
Jesus as teaching that attention to the physical
well-being of man on the Sabbath was legitimate
in so far as it ministered to spiritual life.   In this
life spiritual exercises are to a certain degree dependent on bodily conditions, just as a sound body
is a condition requisite for a sound mind.   He
taught that physical need supersedes the ceremonial Law, in His illustration from the life of
David (Mt 12³, Mk 2²⁴⁻²⁵), and that God prefers
mercy, exercised by man towards his fellows, and
by Himself towards men, to sacrifices (Mt 12⁷).

(3) *Christ taught that the ceremonial observance
of the Sabbath must give way before any higher
and more spiritual motive.*—Upon this principle
the Temple service to which Christ refers (Mt 12⁵)
was legitimate, and He did not find fault with it.
In this way it is possible to explain the verse
which in Codex Bezæ (D) is inserted after Lk 6⁵
(which may possibly be an instance of a genuine
saying of Christ which is not elsewhere recorded):
'On the same day, seeing one working on the
Sabbath, He said unto him, O man, if indeed thou
knowest what thou doest, thou art blessed ; but if
thou knowest not, thou art accursed and a transgressor of the law.'   That is, the breaking of the
Sabbath in obedience to a higher motive is allowed,
and the man is pronounced 'blessed' as being free
from the trammels of Jewish tradition ; but if his
action lacks such motive, he is guilty of wilful disregard of the command.

**4. The change of day from Saturday to Sunday
in the Christian Church.**—This change took place
very early in the history of the Christian Church,
but its date and reasons are somewhat indefinite.
It scarcely requires any argument in justification,
as (i) it preserves the spirit and purpose of the
older practice ; and (ii) the change occurred so
early that it must have had the sanction of the
immediate disciples of Christ.   Probably the
change arose owing to Sunday being the day of
Christ's resurrection, and the day upon which He
appeared to His disciples (Jn 20¹⁹· ²⁶).   The work of
redemption, being the creation of the new world,
was regarded as superseding in importance the
work of physical creation ; so the *Ep. of Barnabas*
(15) speaks of Sunday as 'the beginning of another
world,' and says : 'Wherefore also we keep the
eighth day for rejoicing, in the which also Jesus
rose from the dead, and, having been manifested,
ascended into the heavens.'   Evidences of the
change are found in the NT in 1 Co 16², and
Ac 20⁷.   The name ἡ κυριακὴ ἡμέρα for Sunday
occurs in Rev 1¹⁰.   In early Christian writings we
find that the change had already taken place
(*Didache*, 14 ; Ignatius, *Magnes.* 9 ; Pliny, *Ep.*
x. 97 ; Justin Martyr, *Apol.* i. 67).   Eusebius
(*HE* iii. 27) says that the Ebionites kept the
Jewish Sabbath and also Sunday (see Lightfoot,
Ignatius, ii. 129 ; Allen, *Christian Institutions*,
p. 467).   See also 'Lord's Day' in art. CALENDAR,
vol. i. p. 251 ff.

LITERATURE. — The Mishna (esp. *Shabbath* and *Erubin*);
Edersheim, *LT*; Geikie, *Life of Christ*; art. 'Sabbath' in
Hastings' *DB*; Farrar, *Life of Christ*, ch. xxxi.; Schürer, *HJP*
II. ii. 96.   For the history of Sunday observance see Hessey,
Sunday (Bampton Lect. 1860).   F. E. ROBINSON.

SABBATH DAY'S JOURNEY. — See preceding
art. and TRAVEL.

SACKCLOTH.—A coarse, dark-coloured cloth,
made of goat's or camel's hair (Gr. σάκκος, Heb. שׂק),
used in ordinary life for sacking, sieves, strainers,
and the like, but in the Gospels twice named in
connexion with prevalent mourning customs
(Mt 11²¹, Lk 10¹³), coupled with 'ashes' (wh. see)
as an expression of penitential grief.   The mourner
wore the sackcloth garment, sometimes next the
skin ; and because of the garment's coarseness it
became a constant reminder of his grief, its irritation being a sort of penance ; sometimes it was
worn as an outer garment as a visible expression
of mourning.   Closely related to this use of sackcloth was the use of it by ascetics and prophets
(cf. later use by pilgrims).   So John the Baptist
wore a garment of camel's hair (Mt 3⁴, Mk 1⁶) as
the expression of a certain austerity of life, and as
a rebuke to the love of ease and luxury which
characterized the age.   E. B. POLLARD.

SACRIFICE.—The saving significance of the
death of Jesus Christ is of necessity the most
important part of any article on the NT idea of
sacrifice ; for it is in the light of the sacrifice of
Christ that all Christian sacrifice must be viewed.
It is now universally admitted that there is development and difference in the doctrinal standpoint of the NT writers.   The old method of
taking texts at haphazard from the various Gospels
and Epistles, and setting them side by side, has
been given up.   The only satisfactory results are
to be obtained by examining in turn the teaching
of each writer ; and this is the method which it is
proposed to adopt in considering the subject of the
sacrifice of Christ.

1. We begin with *the teaching of our Lord as
set forth in the Synoptic Gospels.*   Here there is
nothing to be found in the nature of dogmatic
assertion.   The statements of our Lord as to the
significance of His death are far from numerous,
and in no case can they be looked at wholly by
themselves.   His whole life and teaching are their
context.   To any one carefully reading the Synoptic Gospels it becomes plain that it is only towards
the end of His life on earth that the meaning of
His death begins to occupy anything like a prominent place in the consciousness of Christ.   There
is not a single word regarding it in the Sermon on
the Mount.   There He is the second Moses, the
new Lawgiver, the Revealer of the Father and
His will, the Preacher of that new Kingdom whose
laws should be written upon the hearts of men.
Man is to be transformed inwardly by the renewal
of his mind as leaven works in dough.   All external religious practices are valueless except in so
far as they manifest inward spiritual life.   But it
is already a Father of infinite tenderness and love,
a Father only waiting to be gracious, whom He
reveals, not a God full of wrath against sinful man,
who must be propitiated and reconciled by the
death of His Son before He can pardon.   Forgiveness is already offered to all who will do the
Father's will, to all who in love forgive the trespasses of their brethren.   There is not one word to
suggest that pardon and reconciliation are conditional upon the sacrifice of Himself still to be
offered.   Here Christ is the Teacher of morality,
with an authority greater than that of Moses, it
is true ; but He has not yet revealed Himself as
the Way and the Truth and the Life.   He is implicitly the Saviour in that His Person and work
are alone the guarantee of the will of the Father,
in that He embodies the attractive power of righteousness, in that He is the source of healing grace
to all afflicted ones who come with faith in Him ;
but He has not yet made surrender to Himself the
only way of salvation.   It is only in consequence
of the opposition of His countrymen that He gives

expression to the thought that He is Himself the Mediator of salvation, the only Revealer of God (Mt 11$^{25-30}$). He realizes that it is offence at His humility and lowliness that keeps 'the wise and prudent' from hearing His word, and that it is love to Him that draws the poor and despised and sin-laden to the knowledge of the Father and the doing of His will. From that time the thought that He is the personal Mediator is frequently upon His lips (Mt 10^{40} 12^{30} 18^{20}, Lk 12^{8} etc.). It is opposition, too, that arouses in Him the consciousness of being the Conqueror and Dethroner of Satan and all the powers of darkness (Mt 12^{29}, Mk 3^{27}, Lk 10$^{18. 19}$ 11^{21}). As time goes on, this opposition develops into a bitter hatred which threatens His life. Selfishness and world-love array themselves against Him and His doctrine of world-renunciation. His power is too great to be overlooked. The world-spirit which dominates the bulk of His countrymen demands His death ; and even His most faithful followers are still enslaved by the world's toils—bound to earth by that material glory which, according to their selfish hopes, His Messiahship is to procure for them. While He lives, they will still buoy themselves up with false hopes : they will not understand the pure spirituality of His life and work—that His 'kingdom is not of this world.' The perception of these dangers, then—of that which from the outside threatened His life, of that which from within threatened the purity of His disciples' faith—became to Him a further revelation of the Father's will,—a revelation that His death was decreed, and that by it He should accomplish that for which His whole life had been but the preparation. But we must not expect many explicit statements on the subject. His followers were not yet fit to bear this truth. He was leaving this to be made plain to them by the Holy Spirit after His departure. Yet there are hints enough to lead us to a right understanding. 'I have a baptism to be baptized with,' He says on one occasion, 'and how am I straitened till it be accomplished !' (Lk 12$^{49. 50}$). Manifestly the baptism was the baptism of death (cf. Mt 20$^{22-28}$). In Mt 20^{28} the reason for the necessity of His death is made plain—'to give his life a ransom for many.' The idea clearly is that men are enslaved, and that Christ gives His life to set them free ; but the question still remains as to the nature of the bondage. 'From death, from the guilt of sin and its punishment,' says the old theology, or, as it is sometimes expressed, 'from the wrath of God.' But there is not a single word upon the lips of Christ to justify this interpretation ; and, as we shall see later, wherever in the NT the death of Christ is called a deliverance or a ransom, it is always a being purchased *for* God, a being delivered from the bondage of sin to serve God, that is thought of (Ro 6$^{1-11}$, 1 Co 6^{20} 7^{23}, 1 P 1$^{18ff.}$ etc.). Moreover, the whole mission of our Lord and the whole meaning of His teaching was to deliver man from sin, to make him love, and long for, righteousness. It is impossible to imagine the Preacher of the Sermon on the Mount accounting it the great work of His life merely to deliver men from the consequences of their sins. Can any one believe that such a Moralist would be content with less than the deliverance from sin itself, the worst bondage of all to which man is subject ? The context of the words, too (Mt 20$^{17-29}$), must lead us to the same conclusion. There is no thought of death or even of guilt ; but there is a thought of sin—of the sin of self-seeking, bound up as it was with the expectation of material glory in an earthly kingdom, which had just prompted the request of James and John, and of the selfish indignation of the other disciples who resented that request as an attempt to obtain an unfair advantage over them. That Christ should think of His coming death as certain to break for ever the cords of their worldliness, so that their love for Him might draw them away from the world unto righteousness and God, is perfectly conceivable. His cross, borne for love's sake as the last step in the path of perfect holiness which He was called to tread, must for all time crucify the world unto all who truly believed in Him, and them unto the world. To imagine that Christ in these words represents the Father as requiring a ransom at His hands before He can forgive mankind, is to render His revelation of the Heavenly Father wholly inconsistent, is to give the lie to all His earlier words regarding the mercy and compassion of God. The parable of the Prodigal Son in the light of this later presentation becomes an impossibility.

But let us proceed to the institution of the Lord's Supper, whence the most definite teaching as to the saving import of His death is to be drawn (Mt 26$^{26-28}$, Mk 14$^{22-24}$, Lk 22$^{19-20}$). Here He speaks of the surrender of His life as a thing advantageous to those who believe on Him, and St. Matthew adds the words—'for the remission of sins.' In the Sacrament thus instituted there is a twofold reference to the ritual of the Jews—(1) to the Passover, in the breaking of bread, the symbol of His broken body ; (2) to the sacrifice of the covenant at Sinai, to which the giving of the cup with the words—'This is my blood of the new covenant' clearly alludes. Now the Passover signified exemption from the death of the firstborn which overtook the Egyptians. By the death of the lamb, which the Israelites appropriated to themselves by eating it, forgiveness and life were granted to them. But the Passover meant more than this. It brought them freedom not only from death, but also from bondage. It transformed a multitude of slaves into a free nation ; it made them God's people ; and sent them forth to serve Him. Its aim was the service of God. Our Lord, then, in the institution of the bread expressed the thought that His life given up to death is to be appropriated by His followers, that it may become their life, that it may set them free from the bondage of sin, and make them free servants and sons of God. This, too, must be noted, that it is not the fact of His death in itself that is significant. Had He thought of abiding in death, the whole meaning of the institution would have been taken away. The idea is that He surrenders His physical life for their sakes, that His spiritual life may dwell in and inspire them. In the closing chapters of St. John's Gospel this thought is most clearly expressed. As to the institution of the cup and its reference to the ratification of the Sinaitic covenant, the idea here is that of purification on entering into communion with God. In Ex 24 the sprinkling of the blood is the completion of the covenant already made : it symbolizes the need of purity in those who would obey God. Just as the baptism of John was valueless without change of mind, and could confer no forgiveness without the bringing forth of fruit worthy of repentance, so the sprinkling of the blood expressed the thought that purity and sincerity are necessary for all who would enter into the covenant relationship with God—that there can be no forgiveness except it be followed by sincere obedience. There is further present to the mind of our Lord the prophecy of Jeremiah regarding the New Covenant (or Testament) (Jer 31$^{31-34}$) which should be an inward relationship, a covenant of regeneration—'I will put my law in their inward parts, and write it on their hearts.' In this covenant forgiveness was to be granted in consequence of an internal reformation (v.^{34}). When the power of sin is broken and cast out, when the heart is dead to sin, God is just to pardon. Thus Christ called His blood about to be shed the blood of the New Covenant, in the sense that His death of love would inspire His followers with new life, would be to them in the first place a means of breaking the power of sin in their lives, of recreating them in the love of holiness, and only in consequence of that an assurance of pardon. The saving significance of the death of Christ, then, as it is set forth in the Lord's Supper, is this—to create in the believer a new power of spiritual life which should make sin hateful and so destroy its bondage, and to assure him of pardon by the guarantee of God's perfect love as revealed in the life and death of His Son. Christ's death is a sacrifice in that it removes for ever all doubt of God's forgiving love, and makes man's willing, loving obedience possible; in that it proves the absolute victory of good over evil; and, lifting His life beyond the limits of time and space, makes it a spiritual force communicable to all who accept Him as their Saviour.

2. When we turn to *the Gospel of St. John*, we find at once much to confirm the hints which the Synoptics have already given us. He wrote long after the departure of his Lord, and his experience and spiritual insight had made clear to him the meaning of many words that had been dark to the earlier writers. In the teaching of Jesus as St. John presents it, the thought of His death as setting free a spiritual life-giving principle emerges with much greater distinctness. He is the Bread of Life, the Living Water, that giveth life to men (Jn 6. 7³⁷· ³⁸ 3¹⁰⁻¹⁵); He is the Resurrection and the Life (11²⁵); but that this πνεῦμα ζωοποιοῦν may act with completed power, it must pass through death to larger life. 'Except a corn of wheat fall into the ground and die, it abideth alone,' etc. (12²⁴). 'It is expedient for you that I go away; for if I go not away, the Comforter will not come to you,' etc. (16⁷). But the death itself has a value apart from the resurrection, for in it is revealed the triumph of holy love over the power of evil: it is the means whereby the Father glorifies the Son (12²⁷· ²⁸ 13³¹· ³²). All men are subject to this power save Jesus only; and the power of evil is broken through His meek submission to that death which the evil world forces upon Him (12³¹). The spirit of selfishness no longer rules the earth when its utmost wickedness is outdone by the obedience of perfect love even unto death. This power of overcoming the world and its spirit, He will communicate to those who follow Him. He will draw all men unto Him when He is lifted up (12³², cf. 16³³). The cleansing power of His death, which in the Synoptics is symbolized by the institution of the Supper, here finds its place in the washing of the disciples' feet (13²⁻¹⁷). They were already clean by the word which He had spoken unto them (15³): the death was but the completion, the final cleansing. According to St. John, then, the efficacy of the sacrifice of Christ lay in this—that it was an act of perfect obedience to the will of the righteous Father (14³¹) and of love to the world (10¹¹ 15¹³),—an example, therefore, and an inspiration; but also that it broke the power of sin, and, through the glorified life which of necessity followed it, became a means of spiritual energizing and sanctification to all believers. Once again there is no word to suggest the judicial theory of satisfaction.

3. Proceeding now to *the Acts of the Apostles* and to *the Epistle of James*, we are met by this remarkable fact, that in neither is there a single reference to the saving significance of the death of Christ. The accusation of having put the Holy One to death is brought home most forcibly in the speeches of Peter and Stephen (Ac 2²³ 3¹³⁻¹⁵ 7⁵²); but the Cross is not once spoken of as necessary to salvation. Repentance and conversion are alone mentioned as essential to forgiveness; and even when (Ac 8²⁸ff.) Philip overhears the Ethiopian reading the fifty-third chapter of Isaiah and interprets it for him, though this chapter above all others seems to speak of Messiah's vicarious suffering and death, the all-important passage—'He was wounded for our transgressions, he was bruised for our iniquities,' etc. (v.⁵), is not even quoted. The natural conclusion is that the sacrificial significance of Christ's death, so far from having been a cardinal doctrine of the Church from the outset, had not yet dawned upon the disciples' minds. The glad facts of the Resurrection and Ascension, with all of spiritual quickening that these had brought them, were the all-important things to them. The death, except in so far as it was the passage to this larger life, was still obscure. They had no thought that Christ's sacrifice alone procured their pardon; for if they had, they could not possibly have kept silence regarding it. It was the Resurrection they preached, not the Cross (3¹³⁻¹⁶ 10⁴⁰· ⁴¹).

4. When we turn to *the First Epistle of St. Peter*, we find a marked advance upon this early preaching. The Apostle explains the death of the Lord as an example, as a power of redemption, and as a deliverance from the sense of guilt. But throughout, this development is on the lines of Christ's own teaching. He does not speak a word to which a parallel could not be found in the Gospels. As the Lord told His disciples that the world would treat them as it treated Him, so St. Peter bids his readers follow in the steps of Christ; 'for this is thankworthy,' he says, 'if a man for conscience toward God endure grief, suffering wrongfully.' 'If, when ye do well, and suffer for it, ye take it patiently, this is acceptable with God' (2¹⁹· ²⁰; cf. 3¹⁷ 4¹). Here he inculcates a sacrifice on the part of believers similar to the sacrifice of Christ, and asserts its acceptance in God's sight. Of the redemptive power of Christ's sacrifice he speaks in 1¹⁸⁻²² 2²¹· ²⁴ 3¹⁸; and in each of these it is redemption from sin's bondage that is thought of, with the end in view of service to God. Forgiveness is never thought of by itself as a consequence of the death of the Saviour, but always in connexion with sanctification, its end and aim. Believers are redeemed from their vain conversation by the blood of the Lamb, that they may purify their souls in obeying the truth. He bears their sins that they should live unto righteousness. He suffered for sins to bring them to God. Christ's death is only for those who let it act upon them. It is not a satisfaction of God that removes for ever the guilt of men by bearing their penalty: it is a moral deliverance: it is the impression which it creates upon the hearts of believers that is the delivering power—a power increased and fulfilled by the influence of the quickening Spirit (1²²). In 4¹ St. Peter says, 'He that hath suffered in the flesh hath ceased from sin.' By following Christ's example men are to be delivered. Just as the suffering of a mother for her erring son becomes to that son redemption,—a force to make sin hateful in his eyes,—so the picture of Christ's suffering for us acts upon our hearts; and our imitation of Him, our suffering borne for righteousness' sake, breaks the will of the flesh, so that in St. Paul's words we die to sin and live to God. That Christ 'suffered once for sin, the just for the unjust' (3¹⁸), means simply that human sin brought Him to death, a death which love and righteousness compelled Him to bear for our sakes, and that the spectacle of that Divine transcendent love becomes to all believers a power of regeneration. But, further, it is also a pledge of Divine forgiveness. In 1² he mentions the 'sprinkling of the blood of Christ' along with obedience and sanctification of the

Spirit, and by it he can mean only the remission of sins—the removal of the sense of guilt. Moreover, in 1[18-21] he speaks of the shedding of the blood of the Lamb as having for one object 'that your faith and hope may be in God.' What can this mean but that the love of the Father manifested in the death of His Son is to be to believers a means of breaking down the barrier which the sense of guilt had erected between them and God? It shows the Father ready to forgive and draw men unto Him (3[18]). To get rid of sin and to be assured of pardon are the two essentials to salvation, which by His death Christ has procured, but He has procured them only for those who make Christ their example by suffering Him to write God's law upon their hearts — who appropriate God's life unto themselves.

5. It is in *the writings of St. Paul*, however, that the Cross of Christ attains its pre-eminent position. The whole gospel is to him the preaching of the Cross. 'Christ and him crucified' is the subject of all his teaching. Yet the emphasis he lays on it is never one-sided; for the death of Christ is but the consummation of His holy life of Divine love, and at the same time the prelude to the fuller life of glory beyond; both of which are essential to the meaning and value of the sacrifice. Nor is it that the mind of the Pharisaic Saul has led him to the contemplation of the Cross because of his close study of the OT ritual. It is his own personal experience of salvation that has caused him to understand—the marvellous change wrought in him by the Lord who appeared to him on the road to Damascus, and which he has expressed in the words, 'I am crucified with Christ; nevertheless I live; yet not I, but Christ liveth in me' (Gal 2[20], cf. 6[14]).

It certainly cannot be denied that in many passages the Apostle speaks of the death of Jesus as a means of deliverance from guilt, or of justification (Ro 3[25. 26], 2 Co 5[21], Gal 3[13], Col 2[14] etc.); and in the Epistle to the Romans the first place is certainly given to this doctrine; but justification is always conditioned by faith; Christ is never represented as reconciling God to us, but contrariwise, God through Christ reconciles the world to Himself; even our faith in Christ is useless except Christ be risen (1 Co 15[17]), *i.e.* except He be in us a living power to lead to sanctification; and Christ is never said to die ἀντί, but always ὑπὲρ ἡμῶν; all of which facts are radically opposed to the theory of legal substitution. But, most important of all, guilt is no more than sin's consequence, and we cannot conceive of St. Paul, who above all others understood the meaning of sin's bondage, ascribing to Christ a mere redemption from sin's consequences and not from sin itself. The Apostle, however, speaks for himself. It was, he says, to deliver us from the evil world, it was that we should live together with Him, it was that men should not henceforth serve sin, that Christ died (Gal 1[6], 1 Th 5[10], Ro 6[6]). The whole sixth chapter of Romans is on this theme—death to sin in Christ; and the seventh expresses the same thing in reference to the Law. The death of Christ is in his view, then, the direct cause of our death to sin, the breaking of sin's bondage, the putting off the sensuous selfish nature, the subjugation of its desires and appetites (Col 2[11], Ro 3[24] 6[3. 4] 7[4]); and this is the first step to the energizing of the life-giving Spirit of the glorified Lord within us. The passage in 2 Co 5[14. 15] seems to express St. Paul's view with perfect clearness. Here we are told that it is the love of Christ that constraineth—that makes the death of the One a means of death to sin in all. It is as the Lord of humanity, the spiritual Head, spiritually related to all, that He dies; but He rose again and lives now, so that all who recognize

the relationship are compelled, by the love which His perfect sacrifice excites, to break for ever with sin—sin which slew Him—and to live henceforth His life, the life of love and righteousness (cf. Ro 6[10. 11] 5[19], Gal 2[19. 20]). It is not, however, the love of Christ only that is manifested by His death, but also that of the Father. 'God commendeth his love toward us, in that, while we were yet sinners, Christ died for us' (Ro 5[8. 10]). The attitude of the fleshly mind is enmity against God (Ro 8[7]). Men are rebels towards Him. It is the sense of guilt that keeps them from Him. They cannot even believe it possible that God can pardon. It is this, then, that God seeks to remove by the death of His Son. He gives an infinite pledge of His desire to forgive (2 Co 5[19]). Yet it still remains true that this pledge is not the actual justification of the sinner. He must accept God's offer; he must allow God's love to enter his heart; and that means death to sin, and makes him a new creature (2 Co 5[17]). Sanctification in principle is his from that moment. Thenceforth he lives spiritually—lives to God. In St. Paul, too, we find that aspect of Christ's death as a conquest of evil, an objective breaking of the power of sin, of which we have already spoken. He speaks of Christ coming in the likeness of sinful flesh and condemning sin in the flesh (Ro 8[3]). By this he means that Christ's death was the completion of a life of righteousness, and the final act of triumph over evil. He condemned sin in that He resisted it all His life, and in the end gave His life to that resistance. He submitted to the shameful death of the Cross, because to that the path of Divine righteousness led Him. It is for this reason that there is no condemnation to them that are in Christ Jesus (8[1]). In Him they spiritually delight in the law of God; by their love to Him and life in Him they, too, condemn sin; and 'the law of the Spirit of life in Christ Jesus has made them free from the law of sin and death' (8[2]). It is in the same manner that the Apostle represents the death of Christ as a 'propitiation through faith in his blood' (3[25]). It is not a propitiation to God in the sense that it hides sin from His eyes, but in that Christ's sacrifice contains the power of breaking sin in all who accept Him by faith. God is just in forgiving the sin of the believer, because Christ's victory is the guarantee of ultimate victory to all who live in Him (cf. 2 Co 5[21] and 1 Co 5[7]). Finally, the importance which St. Paul attaches to the resurrection of Christ enforces all that has been said. Without that fact his whole doctrine of the scheme of salvation would fall to pieces (1 Co 15[17]). It is not even the death of Christ, but only the risen Saviour that justifies (Ro 4[25]). It is in Christ—therefore in a Christ who lives—that justification is obtained (2 Co 5[21], Eph 1[7]), and that sanctification is rendered possible (Ro 5[10] 8[34] 14[9], 2 Co 3[17. 18], Gal 2[20]). It is only because the believer is in living union with the holy Lord that God can justify him; for the union and communion are the guarantee that the work of sanctification begun will be carried to completion, that the believer will be conformed in all things to his Redeemer. To have Christ dwell in our hearts by faith, to be rooted and grounded in love, to know the love of Christ, is to be filled with the fulness of God (Eph 3[17-19]). If the old view of legal satisfaction through the sufferings of Christ be accepted, all this becomes absurd.

6. We now come to *the Epistle to the Hebrews*, which, more than any other NT writing, relates the sacrifice of Christ to those of the Mosaic ritual. In this relation the author views the sacrifice of Jesus as the only one that can satisfy the needs of men, the one which alone requires no repetition. Following the example of our Lord Himself in the institution of the Supper, the writer alludes to

the covenant sacrifice of Ex 24 ; and it is perfectly manifest from the way in which he speaks of it that he no more regards Christ's death as having created the New Covenant, than he does the sacrifice at Sinai as having procured the Old. In each case it is but a dedication, a ratification. He also refers to the offering of the great Day of Atonement, and with it he compares the sacrifice of Christ, calling it the great atonement by which the conscience is purged from dead works to serve the living God (9^{14}, cf. 10^{22}). The mention of conscience, of course, suggests deliverance from the sense of guilt ; but the immediately following words—'to serve the living God'—point to something far beyond mere escape from punishment, namely, to sanctification and obedience. Repeatedly he tells us that the sacrifices of the OT could not take away sin ($10^{4. 11}$) ; but if by taking away sin he means merely remission of guilt, his words become meaningless ; for why should not obedience to a Divinely appointed ordinance have procured deliverance from guilt ? Wherein they failed—what made their continual repetition necessary—was not that they could not give the sense of pardon, but that they could not give deliverance from the bondage of sin. It was in this that Christ's sacrifice was superior to all the Mosaic offerings, that it led to the service of the living God, that it put sin away (9^{26}), that it perfected them that are sanctified (10^{14}), that it worked a change in the will of the believer, realizing the covenant which Jeremiah foresaw when God's law should be written on the mind and heart (10^{16}). If holiness is the great essential to salvation (12^{14}), and Christ's sacrifice procured no more than deliverance from guilt, then it did not procure salvation. The old ritual could not make the worshipper 'perfect as pertaining to conscience' ($9^{9} 10^{1}$), because it only pointed to the need of purity : it could not create the power to attain that purity : there was no force in it to break the power of sin and set free the will to attain holiness and communion with God. We are accustomed to think of atonement as meaning that God is made willing to pardon ; but to make Christ's sacrifice an atonement in this sense is to charge it with exactly the same weakness as belonged to the old ritual. Unquestionably Christ's death does, in the writer's view, guarantee forgiveness ; but everywhere this forgiveness is regarded not as an end in itself, but only as the accompaniment of deliverance from the power of sin and the attainment of actual holiness. Indeed, there can be no certainty of pardon to the conscience until it is sensible of sanctification. God forgives not because Christ's death has been accepted in lieu of the punishment of men, but because the perfect holiness and love of Christ's life consummated by a death of shame are a pledge to God for the sanctification of all believers ($10^{9. 10}$). Christ's life and death established perfection as an actual fact in human history, broke the hitherto victorious power of evil ; and by virtue of His resurrection and ascension that power of victory can be communicated to all who believe. It is in this sense that Christ intercedes for men in heaven, in that He is there as a guarantee of the perfectibility of human nature ; and because of His pledge that in those who are His, sin is, and will be, conquered and cast out, God is just to forgive (cf. $7^{25} 8^{1} 9^{12. 14. 24}$ $13^{20} 7^{16} 2^{11} 5^{9}$).

7. We come, finally, to *the Epistles of St. John*, with which we shall conclude our consideration. Here, as was to be expected in the Beloved Disciple, the ultimate explanation of the sacrifice of Christ is love, the love of God (1 Jn 4^{10}). There is nowhere a suspicion of the thought that a change is made in God by the offering of Jesus. It was as the manifestation of the Father's love that the

Son was sent to suffer and die, and it is the influence of this love on us that creates love in us (4^{19}), and renders possible the keeping of God's commandments (5^{3}). To be filled with love is to dwell in God (4^{12}), to be born of God ; and this ensures the victory that overcometh the world, and sin, which is the world - spirit ($5^{4. 5}$). Selfishness and hatred are the signs of unregenerateness, because salvation means love to God, and consequently love to all mankind ($4^{20. 21}$). The death of Christ was the proof of His Divinity, because it showed perfect love. Once more, then, in St. John's view also it is a morally effective sacrifice, a power of renewal, not a substitution. God forgives all in whom sin is broken by the death of Christ, and who are being sanctified by His indwelling life. 'If we confess our sins,' he says, 'he is faithful and just to forgive us our sins' (1^{9}) ; for if we confess, it is plain that the holiness and love of Christ are acting upon us, so that we realize our sinfulness, and hate it (cf. 1^{7}). The belief in Christ, as the whole Epistle shows, to which forgiveness and cleansing are granted, is no mere passive acceptance of deliverance from guilt, no mere belief in substitutionary merit, but the perception of the perfect holiness and love of Jesus Christ, so that sin is revealed in all its hideousness as rebellion against a Father of love, and the man is delivered from its power by his hatred of it, and longing to serve and love God and the brethren. It is the creation in man of a spirit akin to that which fired the life of Jesus, that is man's salvation ; and it is the power in Christ's self-sacrifice to produce this and to perfect it, that is the pledge to God of man's sanctification, and that makes Him just in forgiving sin.

On the whole subject this must be added, that sacrifice is acceptable to God only in virtue of the spirit which lies behind it and which it expresses. It is never the outward value of the offering, never the amount of suffering it entails, that makes it precious in God's sight. The multiplicity and costliness of the sacrifices under the old ritual became hateful in His eyes whenever they became a mere attempt to bribe God's favour, and ceased to be the symbol of dependence and gratitude and obedience in man (cf. Is $1^{13. 14}$). Mercy toward man and love to God must always be the underlying, inspiring spirit of sacrifice, else even the minutest observance of ritual becomes worthless (Mt 23^{23-33} $9^{13} 12^{7}$). Christ's sacrifice, then, was acceptable to God, not because of the amount of suffering or the shame of the death,—the willingness to undergo so much was but the revelation of the greatness of the love,—but because it manifested perfect obedience, perfect holiness, perfect Divine love. It is in the same way—it is in Christ only—that the sacrifices of Christians are a sweet incense unto God. Men no longer need offer sacrifice for sin, but the Father still asks of the believer burnt-offerings of self-dedication (Ro 12^{1}), thank-offerings of grateful love. These are sacrifices which the love of God and the holiness for which the believer longs make it a joy to offer, because they are a revelation of the spirit which inspires his heart and works in his whole life—the spirit of Jesus Christ (Eph 5^{19-21}, He $13^{15. 16}$, Ph $4^{17. 18}$, Mt $5^{23. 24}$). See also next art. and artt. ATONEMENT and PROPITIATION.

LITERATURE.—Art. 'Sacrifice' in Hastings' *DB* and in *Encyc. Bibl.* ; Dorner, *Syst. of Chr. Doct.* iv. 1–124 ; Martensen, *Christian Dogmatics*, 302–315 ; Clarke, *Outline of Christian Theol.* 308–368 ; Bushnell, *Vicarious Sacrifice* and *Christ and His Salvation* ; F. D. Maurice, *Doctrine of Sacrifice* ; Beyschlag, *NT Theol.* ; Weiss, do. ; Cave, *Script. Doct. of Sacrifice* ; Dale, *Atonement* ; Denney, *Death of Christ* ; Fairbairn, *Christ in Mod. Theol.* 479–487 ; Godet, *NT Studies*, 148–200.

W. J. S. MILLER.

SACRIFICES (of OT in relation to Christ).—

Sacrifice is an act of homage resulting in a degree of friendship with God. So long as the creature is not incorporated into the Creator, homage must always be due from man to God. Not even under the gospel have we outgrown the attitude expressed by sacrifice. We have passed away from animal sacrifices, but we have passed into the region of the sacrifice of Christ.

The sacrifices of the OT may be divided into ritual or prescribed, and the spontaneous, primitive usages of which instances occur both before and after the time of Moses, and among heathen as well as in the direct line of revelation (Gn 4³ 8²⁰ 12⁷, Ex 18¹², Nu 23¹, Jg 11³¹, 1 S 7⁹, 1 K 3⁴ 18²³, 2 K 3²⁷). This distinction, however, is not dwelt upon in the NT, and is noteworthy only for the light which the older form of sacrifice throws upon the origin of the Mosaic sacrifices.

1. It is generally agreed that the sacred record represents sacrifice as a practice found already in existence among men, when the special revelation to Israel begins (Gn 4²⁶). A sense of dependence upon God, the need of His friendship, and the duty of rendering homage to Him by gifts, are the universal elements in sacrifice. It is not clear whether the friendship of God was taken to be assured, and the sacrificial meal only expressed it, or whether it was usually felt that there was some amends to be made, and the favour of God obtained, before His friendship could be enjoyed. But this matter was made clearer afterwards in the separate appointment of sin-offerings and peace-offerings in the Mosaic system. Meantime, we have here a universally implanted instinct in human nature that responds to the sovereignty of the Unseen in homage, thankfulness, confidence, or fear. Thus there was in the Mosaic law of sacrifice a language being prepared that would be intelligible to all men, and that was fitted to be the vehicle of a world-wide revelation of God.

It is of importance to notice that the usage of sacrifice is not only adopted and regulated in the OT, but is expressly commanded by prophets of God from Moses to Malachi (Ex 23¹⁵, Mal 1⁷⁻¹⁴). This fact makes the use of sacrificial language in regard to the death of Christ to be of very much greater significance than if sacrifice had merely provided Christ and His Apostles with an illustration that lay to hand. And it is the more to be attended to because so often the sacrifices of the Mosaic law seem to be disparaged by the prophets. What they found fault with was that the people complied with the outward rules of God's worship, and did not lay to heart the high requirements of His law ; for if these sacrifices meant that they were in friendly relations with God, this ought to have carried with it a life and conduct consistent with so high a religious profession (Is 1¹¹⁻¹⁶, Jer 7⁹). Since, therefore, sacrifice was undoubtedly of Divine institution, through the prophets, we may take it that whatever feelings of confidence toward God, or of the consciousness of guilt, were expressed by sacrifice, these were not only Divinely allowed and sanctioned, but were required by God on the part of His people towards Him.

2. The Mosaic ritual was inaugurated by a *covenant* (Ex 24). The sacrifices then offered are called burnt-offerings and peace-offerings (v.⁵). This latter term usually implies that the flesh of the sacrifices was eaten by the worshippers, and accordingly we read that the elders did 'eat and drink' in the presence of God (v.¹¹). The covenant between Jacob and Laban (Gn 31⁵⁴) was of a similar nature. Other covenants are between God and Abraham (Gn 15¹⁸), and in Jer 34¹⁸. It was a feature of these sacrifices that the animals sacrificed were divided, or the blood was divided, so that the parties to the covenant were assumed into a mystic unity of life. It is this particular sacrifice that is adduced in the Epistle to the Hebrews as signalizing the covenant between God and Israel (He 9²⁰). We have then these points to notice—(1) Everything in the subsequent history of the relations between God and Israel depended upon the fact that this covenant had been made. (2) It was a celebration of friendship between God and Israel, involving reverent obedience on their part, and securing to them

the immense privilege of being welcome to draw indefinitely upon the aid of the Almighty. (3) The covenant was sealed by sacrifice, and more particularly by blood. This is insisted on in He 9¹⁸ as giving an element of effective force to what was done. An oath is spoken of in somewhat similar terms (He 6¹⁶). A covenant made by sacrifice was not only dramatic and memorable, but it had a sanctity, as of a visible oath (cf. 1 S 11⁷, Jer 34¹⁸⁻²⁰).

In all this there was no emergence of the question of sin, nor was amends offered to God for sin. There was set forth a tie of friendship between God and His people, to begin with : of the existence of which friendship the whole events of the deliverance from Egypt were incontrovertible proof. At the same time the root-idea of a friendship subsisting between God and His people, and the obtaining of His favour by propitiation, if that should be necessary, are not widely different. A usually friendly attitude on the part of God is the presupposition which underlies the offering of sacrifice to remove His displeasure because of particular sins, or to obtain His favour in any special enterprise (1 S 7⁹). The Creator has bestowed innumerable benefits upon His creatures, and is justly to be regarded by them as their Friend. If Israel limited this to themselves, and had a feeling of their proprietary interest in God, and His in them, there is in that feeling the germ of the doctrine of special providence, and of God's interest in the salvation of individuals ; and all the confidence and intimacy of faithful affection therein contained may be appropriated to the believer's relationship with God. The ignorance of those who thought they alone had a portion in God does not invalidate the truth and beauty of the mutual affection which that very ignorance allowed them to realize.

3. Under the general shelter of this covenant relationship the sacrifices of the Mosaic law were instituted (Gal 3¹⁷· ¹⁹). These consisted of two great classes, Sin-offerings and Peace-offerings. There were sin-offerings for the nation (Lv 4¹³), for the priests (v.³), and for individuals (v.²⁷) : of which the first two were entirely consumed by fire, and the last were eaten only by the priests (v.²⁶). Guilt-offerings, with whatever differences, belonged to the same general class ; and with them may be reckoned the various offerings of purification. All these assumed their most characteristic form in connexion with the yearly Day of Atonement (Lv 16). Peace-offerings, on the other hand, may be taken to include the Passover, and all offerings of first-fruits and tithes and bloodless sacrifices. Thus Christ acknowledged the one class (sin-offering) when He bade the leper 'offer for thy cleansing what Moses commanded' (Mk 1⁴⁴) ; and the other class (peace-offering) when He said, 'Leave there thy gift before the altar' (Mt 5²⁴). As we have seen, the sacrifices offered at the making of the covenant were peace-offerings. These were acts of homage, and seals of a happy relationship between God and His people. Thus Solomon offering sacrifices received a gracious revelation that he might ask what he pleased (1 K 3⁴, cf. Ps. 20³).

Sin-offerings took notice of human unworthiness to approach God. The offences atoned for by sacrifice were sins of ignorance or inadvertence, and also misfortunes such as leprosy (Lv 14¹⁹). For wilful disobedience there was no sacrifice (Nu 15³⁰, 1 S 2²⁵ 3¹⁴, 1 Jn 5¹⁶). Where there was a civil penalty, there was a sacrifice as well. That is to say, the fact of sin against God was taken into account (Lv 6⁵). The holiness of God was the dominating principle of the OT sacrifices for sin. Whatever was unsightly and degrading was to be abhorred : regard to propriety was enforced. By purity and seemliness of outward behaviour everything that tended to pollute the mind was atrophied, and only what was helpful to the higher nature was allowed to influence the future. Constituted as human nature is, physical purity is not only a picture of godliness but a help to it. Thus the OT sacrifices outclassed the customs of the heathen by their blamelessness, and collaborated with the prophets and with God's providences to inculcate a high quality of conduct (Lv 20^{23}, 1 Co 10^{20}).

In the sacrifices which involved the death of animals, a sense of the sacredness of life was expressed by the reverent use of the blood (Lv 17^{11}). Whatever was ratified by the taking of life obtained a sanctity thereby, and the putting away of human sin in making approach to God was so ratified, and the transaction made sacrosanct and secure. So far as we know, the animals sacrificed were put to death with no unnecessary pain; they did not expiate sin by suffering (contrast 1 K 18^{28}): it was the deprivation of life they suffered, and it was the blood representing life which had mysterious significance. No one might eat the blood of sacrifices, or of any animal (contrast Ps 16^4 'drink-offerings of blood'). There was no festive garland placed on the victim, to make believe that it went willingly; but it must be without blemish, partly because only the best should be given to God, and partly, it may be, because the mystery of death is greater in the case of a perfectly healthful life.

In a sense the life of the animal went for the life of the worshipper. This was signified when the offerer laid his hand upon the victim's head (Lv 1^4, etc.). And the same substitution is suggested when a ransom (Mt 20^{28}) was paid for the firstborn, although no animal substitute is mentioned (Ex 13^{13}, cf. Nu 3^{47}). But the vicariousness of the suffering of Christ is anticipated in the OT rather by the priestly feeling of responsibility expressed in Ezr 9^6 and Dn 9^5 (cf. also Is 53) than by anything explicit in the appointment of animal sacrifices. See § 5, below.

4. The prophecy of the New Covenant (Jer 31^{31}) forms the principal link between the sacrifices of the OT and Christ's fulfilment of them. For in that passage the promise of a covenant between God and His people is connected with the forgiveness of sin; and in the NT this conjunction is all-important. The NT is full of allusions to the law of sacrifice: 'Christ died for our sins' (1 Co 15^3); 'Christ our passover is sacrificed for us' (5^7); and the words 'ransom,' 'redemption,' 'propitiation,' 'cleanse,' 'purify,' 'sanctify,'—all occur frequently. But especially this reference is to be found in Christ's words at the institution of the Supper: 'For this is my blood of the covenant, which is shed for many unto remission of sins' (Mt 26^{28}); and in the Epistle to the Hebrews (chs. 8–10). In both these places attention is drawn to the covenant at Sinai. That was the OT sacrifice which especially corresponds in its position and efficacy to the position and efficacy of the death of Christ. By it there was solemnly established a relation of friendship between God and His people, once for all. So for all believers Christ's one sacrifice avails to make them the people and children of God. As the slaying of animals, according to a well-understood language, gave sacredness to the older covenant, so the dying of the Saviour gave greater sacredness to a greater covenant. But these descriptions of the efficacy of Christ's death also refer, as does the prophecy of Jeremiah, to the taking away of sin, to which there was no reference in the Old Covenant. Moreover, the words, 'Take, eat,' 'Drink ye all of it,' taken along with Jn 6$^{53-57}$, introduce in sacrificial language the thought of fellowship with God. Consecration is the other side of reconciliation (Ex 29$^{15. 33}$). 'We have fellowship one with another,

and the blood of Jesus Christ his Son cleanseth us from all sin' (1 Jn 1^7). So in Hebrews, from the words 'Let us come boldly' (4^{16}) to 'Let us draw near' (10^{22}), the whole matter of our salvation is pictured under the form of access into the happy condition of being at peace with God (cf. Ro 5$^{1. 2}$), which was given under the Mosaic law by the covenant sacrifice, and continued by the sacrifices that were commanded; but for us this has been obtained once for all by Christ (He 10^{10}), and remains ours as we abide in Him. It is understood that more had to be done in the fulness of time to assure God's people of His favour than sufficed for that when they came out of Egypt. Now, they had a conscience of sin. This the Law had produced (Gal 3^{19} 4^3). Accordingly, in the New Covenant provision was made for the remission of sin, for redemption, for propitiation (Ro 3$^{24. 25}$, 1 Jn 4^{10}). Even while the Apostles are setting aside the sacrifices of the OT, they can express the work of Christ in no other than sacrificial language. There was something in the sacrifices for sin that could not be set aside. Thus, to meet the displeasure of God witnessed by an accusing conscience (Ro 2^{15}) or by experience of the state of the world (1^{18}), there was need of 'the *redemption* that is in Christ Jesus, whom God set forth to be a *propitiation* by his blood' (3$^{24f.}$).

In the last chapter of Hebrews the fate of the sin-offering is made into a parable of the state of believers (He 13$^{10-16}$). They do not rest in the enjoyment of God's favour in this world, as the Jewish worshippers rejoiced before God and feasted on their peace-offerings. This is not our rest. Here we have no continuing city. We are not of the world, as Christ is not of the world. But the sin-offering was burned 'in a clean place' without the camp (Lv 4^{12}), and it was most holy. The place where it was consumed by fire was made a holy altar by it. So not in a worldly but in a spiritual manner those who go out unto Jesus without the camp have the highest, happiest enjoyment of the friendship of God; Christ Himself by His sacred and faithful life and death is their Temple, and there they 'offer the sacrifice of praise to God continually.'

5. Finally, the sacrifices of the OT do not cover in analogy the whole of the Saviour's work. The Epistle to the Hebrews employs the priesthood of Christ, as well as His sacrifice, to set forth all He is to us. Moses and Joshua and Aaron and Melchizedek were imperfect anticipations of Christ, besides the sacrifices. In Is 53 the prophet is compelled to go beyond his sacrificial parable, and to say, 'By his stripes we are healed,' 'He shall see of the travail of his soul.' The lamb could give its life, but it needs a human representative of the Saviour to show His priestly sympathy and responsibility and sufferings. And this being so, no doubt the decided preference of Scripture and of Christian feeling for dwelling rather on the sacrifices than on the men who were anticipations of Christ, is because it is so supremely important that Christ should be seen to stand alone among men, no one near Him. A prophet may be a man of God, but Christ is the Lamb of God that taketh away the sin of the world,—that to God may be all the glory of man's redemption. See also the preceding article.

LITERATURE.—P. Fairbairn, *Typology*; A. B. Davidson, *Theology of the OT*, and the same writer's Com. on the *Epistle to the Hebrews*; Bp. Westcott, *Hebrews*; Denney, *Death of Christ*; art. 'Sacrifice' in Hastings' *DB* (by W. P. Paterson) and in *Encyc. Brit.*^{9} (by W. R. Smith).

T. GREGORY.

SADDUCEES.—**1. Derivation and use of the name.**—It seems impossible to attain certainty as to the derivation of the name 'Sadducees' (Σαδδουκαῖοι ; םיקדצ). Formerly it was supposed to be connected with the adjective *zaddîk*, 'righteous' ; but this derivation is now generally given up, for philological and other reasons. No explanation can be given of the change from *i* to *u*: and the Sadducees were never regarded, either by themselves or by others, as specially righteous. In more recent times the commonly accepted derivation is from the proper name *Zadok* ; but neither is this without its difficulties. The doubling of the *d* is not well accounted for, and the problem as to which Zadok gave name to the party is one upon which there is considerable difference of opinion. Many hold that it was Zadok the priest, the contemporary of David and Solomon (2 S 8^{17} 15^{24}, 1 K 1^8 2^{35} etc.), whose posterity officiated in the Temple down to the time of the Exile, and even formed the chief element of the post-exilic priesthood ; but Kuenen says this conjecture is 'burdened with insurmountable difficulties' (*Religion of Israel*, iii. p. 122). A Jewish legend states that it was a disciple of Antigonus of Socho, named Zadok ; but this is almost universally admitted to have no historical foundation. To solve the difficulty, Kuenen and Montet postulate a Zadok, 'perhaps a contemporary of Jonathan the Asmonæan' (Kuenen, *l.c.*), from whom the name may have been derived ; but this, again, is purely hypothetical. Yet another suggestion is offered by A. E. Cowley (art. 'Sadducees' in the *EBi*), that the word may have been of Persian origin, connected with *zindîk*, which is used in a general sense for 'infidel.' The suggestion is interesting, but is put forward 'with great diffidence' by its author.

But however uncertain the derivation may be, there is no dubiety about the application of the name 'Sadducees.' It is always used to designate the political party of the Jewish aristocratic priesthood from the time of the Maccabees to the final fall of the Jewish State. The chief authorities for its use are the NT, Josephus, and portions of the Mishna. It is important to note that, while any one, whatever his rank or station, could be a Pharisee, no one could be a Sadducee unless he belonged to one of the high-priestly or aristocratic families. It was not enough to be a priest. There was as great a distance between the higher and lower orders of the priesthood as between the aristocracy and the common people.

2. Outline of history.—From the beginning of the Grecian period of Jewish history, and even before that time, the whole conduct of political affairs was in the hands of the priestly aristocracy. Influenced by Hellenic culture, they sympathized to some extent with the policy of Antiochus Epiphanes which provoked the Maccabæan rebellion ; and although, as a consequence, they fell into the background during the earlier period of Hasmonæan rule, they recovered their position in the time of John Hyrcanus, under whom we find them, now known as Sadducees, in direct antagonism to the Pharisees, or party of the scribes. These for a short time acceded to power under Alexandra, but immediately afterwards the Sadducees came again to the front. In the Roman period their power was considerably diminished, in this respect that while they were able to retain the high offices for themselves, they were compelled to adopt the policy of the Pharisees, who had an overwhelming influence with the people. The high priests at the head of the Sanhedrin were Sadducees, but they were always in a minority ; though essentially a political party, they had apparently no independent existence apart from Jerusalem and its Temple, and with the fall of the Jewish State they disappear entirely from history.

3. Special characteristics.—The chief outstanding feature of the Sadducees was probably their conservatism. They stood by the established position, held by the old points of view, and rejected everything that partook of the nature of novelty. They were priests, but priests of aristocratic family, and, as such, their duties were political as well as religious. Brought into close contact with their Gentile rulers, their political interests tended to thrust the religious into the background. Their aim was the welfare of the State as a secular institution, rather than the purity of the nation as a religious community. As sober, practical statesmen, representative of moderate Jewish opinion, they entertained no extravagant notions of the coming high position or brilliant future of Israel. And being themselves in comfortable circumstances, they were satisfied with the present, and felt no special need of a future rectification in the interests of justice. The intellectual standpoint of the Sadducees seems to have been mainly negative. They were characterized chiefly by their denial of certain doctrines, and had no positive religious or theological system of their own. They stood in most things in direct opposition to the Pharisees, yet in an opposition which involved no fundamental principle, but into which they had been driven by their historical development.

The leading difference between the two parties is to be found in this, that the Sadducees held by the written Law, and rejected the Pharisaic tradition. It is not, however, correct to say that the Sadducees acknowledged only the Pentateuch and rejected the rest of the OT. Kuenen even maintains that they accepted the Oral Tradition, 'in so far as this was already established when they constituted themselves a party' (*Rel. of Israel*, iii. p. 144). Schürer says that they agreed with the Pharisees on some—perhaps many—particulars of the tradition, but 'only denied its obligation, and reserved the right of private opinion' (*HJP* II. ii. 38). A number of minor differences are recorded in Rabbinical literature, of which full accounts will be found in Schürer, or in art. 'Sadducees' in Hastings' *DB*. The Sadducees are stated to have been more severe in penal legislation, adhering more strictly to the letter of the Law ; and in questions of ritual, while admitting the principle of Levitical purification, they ridiculed the Pharisees for the absurdities of their traditional regulations. It has been maintained that the attitude of the Sadducees was largely determined by their desire to magnify the importance of the priesthood ; but Schürer denies that any such motive can be traced. Probably they felt that the Pharisees vitiated the Law by their self-contradictions, and that only by an adherence to what was definite and authentic could the system be conserved according to which alone God could be rightly worshipped.

The distinctive Sadducean doctrines are usually classed under three heads :—(1) They denied the resurrection, personal immortality, and retribution in a future life. So far they merely stood by the old Hebrew position, and from their materialistic and worldly point of view they felt no need of a future life to compensate for the inequalities of the present. In the same spirit they also renounced the entire Messianic hope, at least in the form then current. (2) They denied the existence of angels and spirits. This was scarcely the position of the OT, but their worldly common sense and general culture were bound to prejudice them against the fantastic products of the Pharisaic imagination in the wild extravagances of its angelology and demonology. (3) They denied foreordination and the supremacy of fate, and upheld the freedom of the human will, maintaining 'that good and evil are at the choice of man, who can do the one or the other at his discretion.' This is quite in keeping with the rest of their views. They felt no special need of a Divine Providence to order their life, and claimed that whatever they possessed was due to their own efforts. Generally it may be said that, after the manner of an aristocracy, they resented any attempt to impose on them an excess of legal strictness, and that 'advanced religious views were, on the one hand, superfluous to their worldly-mindedness, and, on the other, inadmissible by their higher culture and enlightenment' (*HJP* II. ii. 41). Yet the distance between them and the Pharisees was not so great as it might appear. Politically at least there was no insuperable barrier. The two could sit together in the Sanhedrin, and could combine to make common cause against Jesus and to plan His destruction.

4. Relations to Jesus.—The Sadducees are not often mentioned by name in the Gospels, but it has to be remembered that, when mention is made of the chief priests, practically the same persons are referred to. Jesus did not come into the same constant antagonism with the Sadducees as with the Pharisees. For the most part they seem to have ignored Him, at least in the early part of His ministry. They joined with the Pharisees in asking Him to show them a sign from heaven (Mt 16[1]), and shortly afterwards He warned His disciples to beware of the leaven of the Pharisees and Sadducees, meaning probably, so far as the Sadducees were concerned, their utterly secular spirit. They resented His action in the cleansing of the Temple, and along with the scribes and elders they demanded His authority (Mk 11[27f.]), and from this time forward sought to destroy Him (v.[18]). They thought to inveigle Him with the Roman power by asking whether it was lawful to give tribute to Cæsar (Lk 20[22]), and they attempted to discredit His teaching by presenting to Him the problem of the woman who had been married to seven brethren, and asking whose wife she should be in the resurrection; but they only brought upon themselves discomfiture, and the reproof that they knew neither the Scriptures nor the power of God (Mt 22[23] ||). They sat in the Sanhedrin which condemned Him, and with the others mocked Him upon the cross. Their opposition to Christian doctrine did not cease with the death of Jesus. There is no record of any Sadducee being admitted into the Christian Church, and before long they were merely a memory, hazy and indistinct.

LITERATURE.—See under PHARISEES and SCRIBES.

JOSEPH MITCHELL.

SADOC.—A link in our Lord's genealogy (Mt 1[14]).

SAINTS.—The word 'saints' (οἱ ἅγιοι) occurs in the Gospels in Mt 27[52] only. Elsewhere in the NT it is never used of any but Christians (*e.g.* Ac 9[13], Ro 12[13], Rev 11[18]). In the LXX (Dn 7[22. 25. 27] 8[24]) ἅγιοι is the equivalent of קַדִּישִׁין 'the holy ones' (*i.e.* angels). The root idea seems to be that of 'separation,' so that a 'saint' is one who is separated, consecrated, one who belongs to God. Its occurrence in Mt 27[52] opens up the entire question of the meaning of the section. The incident is peculiar to the First Gospel, and occurs in the course of the narrative of our Lord's crucifixion and death. It is stated that at the moment of His death there was a supernatural earthquake which caused the tombs to be opened, and that immediately following His resurrection on the first day of the week many *bodies* (σώματα) of dead saints arose from their graves, and the *persons* (ἐξελθόντες, masc.) thus raised from the dead appeared in the city of Jerusalem to many. Several theories have been put forward to account for this remarkable statement.

1. It is said to be an interpolation. In reply, it is argued that the textual evidence of MSS and Versions is exactly the same for this passage as for the rest of the First Gospel. It is also urged that

the incident seems plainly referred to as early as Ignatius (*Ep. ad Magn.* 9).

2. It is said to be a legendary addition. It is thought that the graves were rent by an earthquake which actually occurred, and that then this statement was subsequently added as a spiritual explanation of the natural phenomenon. Bruce (*EGT, in loc.*) says: 'We seem here to be in the region of Christian legend.' Meyer takes the same general view. Those who oppose this view argue that textual considerations give no indication of a later addition, and that the writer of the First Gospel evidently believed in the incident, and wished his readers to do the same.

3. It is accounted for as a wrong explanation of incidents which were in themselves true. Farrar (*Life of Christ*) suggests that these ghostly visitants were the product of the imagination of those who were impressed by the events then taking place. To this it is replied that there is no trace of it in the narrative which now is, and apparently has been from the first, an integral part of this Gospel.

4. It is explained by saying that we have in the incident a striking testimony to the supernatural character and far-reaching power of our Lord's death; that not only did it affect nature (earthquake), the Jewish economy (the rent veil), and human life (centurion), but that its influence penetrated even to the unseen world. The narrative as it stands says that it was at the moment of His death that the tombs were opened, but that the actual rising of the saints did not take place until after the Lord's resurrection. He was 'the first-fruits of them that slept.' The fact that the incident is found in one Gospel only is, it is urged, no necessary argument against its credibility. On this view, the question as to who were the saints would seem to be answered by the narrative itself. The tombs were near Jerusalem, and the fact of recognition implied in the appearance of the risen ones in the city suggests that the saints were some of those who, during their earthly life, had been led to faith in Jesus as the Messiah: godly people of the type of Anna, Simeon, Zacharias, and Elisabeth. Those who accept its genuineness fully recognize that the incident is mysterious, but they point out that the narrative as it stands is a calm, quiet statement, marked by reserve and by the absence of all legendary details. The upholders of the authenticity consider it full of spiritual meaning as to the supernatural character of our Lord's death in relation to the holy dead, holding that it was a manifestation of His power over death and the grave (1) by the resurrection of some from Hades, (2) by the clothing of them with a resurrection body, and (3) by permission to appear to those who knew them. On this theory the narrative is to be accepted as it is, and the exegesis of the passage strictly adhered to without endeavouring to draw conclusions which go beyond the brief record.

LITERATURE.—(1) in favour of historicity: Alford, *Com. in loc.*; Westcott, *Introd. to Gospels*[4], p. 329 f.; *Thinker*, vol. v. (2) in favour of legendary character: Bruce, Meyer, etc.

W. H. GRIFFITH THOMAS.

SALIM.—Mentioned only Jn 3[23] 'Ænon near to Salim,' to fix the place where John was baptizing, 'because there was much water there.' Scrivener's edition of the AV gives as marginal references 'Gn 33[18]? or Jos 15[23]? or 1 S 9[4]?'; other editions only the last passage (where the text has Shalim, or rather Shaalim, in Heb. שַׁעֲלִים), the RV only the first (margin). It is to be noticed that the former view is also that of Jerome, in his *Liber interpret. Heb. Nom.*, when he writes: 'Salim pugilli sive volæ aut ortus aquarum, quod brevius græce dicitur βρύοντα'; *pugilli* and *volæ* = שֹׁעָלִים. And before Jerome, Origen also explained in a similar way (on Jn 10[39], p. 543 of the Berlin ed.):

Αἰνὼν ὀφθαλμὸς βασάνου καὶ Σαλὴμ αὐτὸς ὁ ἀναβαίνων. In the Com. on 3[23] the new edition has in the text Σαλίμ, but thinks in the apparatus that Σαλήμ would perhaps be better. With the view of a plural agrees the fact that most MSS spell the ending -ειμ, and not -ημ, as in the Complutensian Polyglott ; the latter spelling (Σαλήμ) would favour identification with שָׁלֵם. In the article ÆNON (vol. i. p. 35), most of the topographical identifications proposed for these places are discussed. We may add that ΑΙΝΩΝ Η ΕΓΓΥΣ ΤΟΥ ΣΑΛΙ<Μ> is entered already on the mosaic map of Madeba on the left bank of the Jordan, and that the oldest and most explicit discussion of these sites is found in the pilgrimage of the so-called Silvia of Aquitania (or Étheria of Spain), about 385. A special monograph was published in 1903 by C. Mommert (Ænon und Bethania die Taufstätten des Täufers, nebst einer Abhandlung über Salem die Königsstadt des Melchisedech, Leipzig), on which see G. H. Gilbert, AJTh vii. 777 ; cf., further, Κλ. Μ. Κοικυλίδες : ὁ ἐν Ἰορδάνῃ τόπος τῆς βαπτίσεως τοῦ Κυρίου καὶ τὸ μοναστήριον τοῦ ἁγίου Προδρόμου (Jerusalem, 1905) ; also Löhr, 'Wie stellt sich die neuere Palästinaforschung zu den geographischen Angaben des Johannesevangeliums,' Deutsch - Evangelische Blätter, Dec. 1906.

When Silvia had finished Jerusalem, she wished to go 'ad regionem Ausitidem' to see 'memoriam sancti Job.' It took her eight days (mansiones) from Jerusalem to Carneas : 'in quo itinere iens vidi super ripam Jordanis fluminis vallem pulchram satis et amœnam, abundantem vineis et arboribus, quoniam aquæ multæ ibi erant et optimæ satis. Nam in ea valle vicus erat grandis qui appellatur nunc Sedima. In eo ergo vico, qui est in media planitie positus, in medio loco est monticulus non satis grandis, sed factus sicut solent esse tumbæ, sed grandis : ibi ergo in summo ecclesia est.' She inquires after the place, and receives the answer : 'hæc est civitas regis Melchisedech, quæ dicta est ante Salem, unde nunc corrupto sermone, Sedima appellatur ipse vicus.' For further details, amongst which is the statement that when people dig for foundations of new buildings, they find 'aliquoties et de argento et æramento modica frustella,' the reader is referred to Silvia. She then remembered that in the Bible it was written : 'Baptizasse sanctum Johannem in Enon juxta Salim.' Therefore she inquired also after Ænon, and was shown the place 'in ducentis passibus . . . hortum pomarium valde amœnum, ubi ostendit nobis in medio fontem aquæ optimæ satis et puræ, qui a semel integrum fluvium dimittebat. Habebat autem ante se ipse fons lacum, ubi parebat fuisse operatum sanctum Johannem baptistam. Tunc dixit nobis ipse sanctus presbyter : In hodie hic hortus aliter non appellatur græco sermone nisi cepos tu agiu Iohanni, id est quod vos dicitis latine "hortus sancti Johannis"' (for further particulars, see again the text). Going on for some time 'per vallem Jordanis super ripam fluminis ipsius,' the traveller sees after a little the town of the holy prophet Elia, 'id est Thesbe,' where his cave is, and also 'memoria sancti Gethæ,' of whom we read in the Books of the Judges (this is, of course, Jephthah, and not Gad, as has been suggested by Mommert).

This localization of the two places agrees exactly with the statement of Eusebius that Ænon was 8 miles south from Scythopolis (see vol. i. p. 35, and supply from the Berlin ed. p. 152, the reference to Procopius, who helps to fill up the lacuna in the Greek text with Σαλουμίας, just as Jerome reads). But instead of seeking the place west of the Jordan at Sheikh Salim, Mommert now seeks Ænon east of it at 'Ain Djirm ('well of the leprosy'), at the foot of the hill 'Scharabil,' as he spells it, or 'Scharḥabit' as it is spelt on the map

of Fischer-Guthe, opposite to Tell Ridhgah, with which it has been identified hitherto.

We thus get the following identifications : (1) Tell Ridhgah, (2) Sharabil, (3) Salim east of Nâblus, (4) Wady Suleim near Anata, (5) 'Ain Karim, (6) Shilhim in the Negeb. A definite result has not been reached as yet ; the identity of Ænon and Bethany (Jn 1[28] RV) is not improbable.

EB. NESTLE.

SALMON.—A link in our Lord's genealogy (Mt 1[4f.], Lk 3[32] [RVm Sala]).

SALOME (Gr. Σαλώμη, possibly shortened from Heb. שְׁלֹמִיאֵל Shĕlômî'êl, or the name = שָׁלוֹם Shālôm with Gr. termination).—**1.** The daughter of Herodias, mentioned (although not by name) in Mt 14[6-11], Mk 6[22-28]. See HEROD in vol. i. p. 722[a], and HERODIAS.

2. The mother of James and John, and wife of Zebedee (Mk 15[40] 16[1] ; cf. Jn 19[25], Mt 20[20] 27[56]). In St. Matthew's account of the ambitious request of the sons of Zebedee, she is represented as coming with her sons and prostrating herself before Jesus. St. Mark does not mention her in this connexion. She was one of the women who followed our Lord and ministered to Him (ἠκολούθουν αὐτῷ καὶ διηκόνουν αὐτῷ, Mk 15[41], and was present at the Crucifixion. Along with Mary Magdalene and Mary the mother of James the Little, she came after the Sabbath was over, bringing fragrant oils (ἀρώματα, μύρα [Lk 23[56]]) with which to anoint the body of Jesus. In the narrative of St. John there are mentioned as present at the Crucifixion (standing 'by the cross') 'his mother and his mother's sister, Mary of Clopas and Mary Magdalene.' It has been argued by some that three women only are here mentioned, and that the words 'Mary of Clopas' are explanatory of 'his mother's sister.' Most of the more recent commentators, however, notably Westcott ('St. John' in Speaker's NT Commentary, p. 275), hold that four women are meant, and that 'his mother's sister' is Salome. The following considerations seem fairly conclusive in favour of this latter view : (1) it is most unlikely that two sisters in a private family should bear the same name ; (2) the parallelism ('his mother and his mother's sister ; Mary of Clopas and Mary Magdalene') is characteristic of St. John ; (3) 'the circuitous manner of describing his own mother is in character with St. John's manner of describing himself' (W. L. Bevan in Smith's DB, art. 'Salome') ; (4) the Peshiṭta inserts 'and' before Mary of Clopas ; (5) Mary Magdalene, Mary the mother of James the Little (who is certainly the same as Mary of Clopas), and Salome are mentioned by St. Matthew and St. Mark as present. The supposition that Salome='his mother's sister' harmonizes St. John's account with that of St. Matthew and St. Mark.* See also artt. CLOPAS, MARY.

LITERATURE.—Besides the authorities quoted in the article, see Wieseler, SK, 1840, p. 648 ff. ; art. 'Salome' in Hastings' DB (cf. art. 'Herod,' ib.), in Encyc. Bibl., and in Herzog's PRE ; Commentaries of H. A. W. Meyer (Eng. tr. 1880), Alford, and Luthardt (on St. John's Gospel, iii., Eng. tr. 1880, where, against his former view, he identifies Salome with 'his mother's sister').

H. W. FULFORD.

SALT (ἅλας).—Salt has been used from very early times to season and preserve food. In Palestine there was always a plentiful supply. The chief sources were (and are) the great rock - salt cliffs known as the Khasm Usdum to the S.W. of the Dead Sea, and the marshes and pools around its shores. The cliffs are from 30 to 60 feet high, and stretch from 6 to 7 miles along the coast. In the

* Epiphanius (Hær. lxxviii. 8) says that Salome was a daughter of Joseph, and Nicephorus Callistus (HE ii. 3) makes her Joseph's wife. These traditions, at any rate, indicate a belief in some connexion between Salome and the house of Joseph.

Bible this sea is sometimes called the 'salt sea' (Gn 14[3], Dt 3[17]). Three lbs. of its water are said to yield 1 lb. of solid salts.

In addition to its common use as a condiment or preservative of food, salt from early times had religious and social significance. As a fitting emblem of incorruptness, it was habitually offered along with the sacrifices (cf. Lv 2[13]). The preservative qualities of salt probably led to its being regarded as an essential element in the making of any enduring covenant (cf. Lv 2[13], Nu 18[19], 2 Ch 13[5]). As a sacrificial meal was usually celebrated in connexion with the making of a covenant, the salt of the meal naturally became the salt of the covenant. Among Eastern peoples, 'to eat of his salt' is a sign of enduring friendship and peace. The Arabs use the phrase 'there is salt between us' as expressing the fact that a bond of loyalty is in existence (cf. Ezr 4[14]).

In the Gospels, salt is used for the most part metaphorically : (1) As an emblem of preservation from corruption, 'Ye are the salt of the earth' (Mt 5[13]). The new spiritual life of the disciples was to purify and preserve the life of the world. Jesus solemnly warns them against the danger of losing the power which would enable them to fulfil this function, 'for if the salt have lost its savour ('become saltless,' Mk 9[50]), wherewith shall it be salted?' (Mt 5[13] || Lk 14[34]). (2) There is also a suggestion of its significance as a symbol of concord in the counsel, 'Have salt in yourselves, and be at peace one with another' (Mk 9[50]); for it is given in connexion with disputes or discussions as to which of the disciples should be the greatest (Mk 9[33-37]). These disputings may also be regarded as one of the influences which render the salt saltless (ἄναλον). (3) As a symbol of incorruption in connexion with sacrifice. In Mk 9[49] the words πᾶσα θυσία ἁλὶ ἁλισθήσεται are omitted by Tischendorf, WH, and Nestle, following MSS אBLΔ. The words in the text thus adjusted (πᾶς γὰρ πυρὶ ἁλισθήσεται) have been translated 'for every one shall be salted for the fire' (Edersheim, *Life and Times of Jesus the Messiah*, ii. 121), and 'for every one shall be salted with fire' (RV). The latter is almost certainly the right translation, since 'with fire' (πυρὶ) takes the place of 'with salt' (ἁλὶ), as indicating the new spiritual element which was to be present in the sacrificial life of the disciples. In the old economy every sacrifice was to be salted with salt, and would not be accepted without it; so in the new economy, the 'living sacrifice' of the Christian disciple will not be rightly prepared without the 'fire' which alone makes it acceptable. As the old sacrifices were prepared with salt, so the new sacrifices must be prepared with fire. The fire is most probably to be interpreted as the fire of judgment, as in the verse immediately preceding ('where their worm dieth not and their fire is not quenched,' Mk 9[48]). There is a twofold judgment by fire. It may be Divine and penal (Mk 9[48]), or personal and corrective (cf. 'If we would judge ourselves we should not be judged,' 1 Co 11[31]). The previous context interprets the personal, salutary judgment by fire, by which the life is to be prepared as an acceptable sacrifice : 'If thy hand offend thee, cut it off ; it is better for thee to enter into life maimed, than having two hands to go into hell, into the fire that never shall be quenched' (cf. Mk 9[43. 47]). Swete (*St. Mark, ad loc.*) interprets the fire of the Christian life as the Holy Spirit, but fire as a symbol of the Spirit is not found in Mark. It may, however, be said that no self-judgment will be complete, or sufficient, unless it is carried through under the influence of the Holy Spirit.

LITERATURE.—W. R. Smith, art. 'Salt,' *Encyc. Brit.*[9]; E. Hull, art. 'Salt,' Hastings' *DB*.; Beyschlag, *NT Theol.* i. 180 ; Wendt, *Teaching of Jesus*, ii. 62 ff.; Bruce, *Training of the Twelve*, p. 215, notes ; Kelman, *Expos. Times*, xii. [1900] p. 111 ; Shalders, *Expositor*, 1st ser. xi. [1880] p. 79 ff.

JOHN REID.

SALUTATION.—See GREETINGS.

SALVATION.—The Gospel usage of this word is closely connected with that of OT.

The corresponding Heb. words are derivatives of ישׁע and נצל. Of the former, the Niphal and Hiphil are found in the verb ; of noun forms ישׁע or ישׁע, ישׁועה, תשׁועה, תשׁעות and some proper names, of which the most important is יהושׁע, 'Jehovah is salvation.' The root נצל occurs in the Niphal and Hiphil of the verb ; its only noun-derivative is the ἅπαξ λεγόμενον, הצלה, Est 4[14]. The fundamental meaning of ישׁע appears to be 'enlargement,' whence the notion of 'deliverance' naturally springs, the same association of ideas being observed in the use of 'compression,' 'confinement' as figures for 'distress.' So far as the verbal forms of both roots are concerned, the idea of 'saving' is entirely negative, that of deliverance from some evil, no reflexion being passed upon favourable, positive consequences. A negative sense is very clear in such passages as Ps 28[9] 69[35], where the positive results of the saving act are named as something additional. From other words denoting deliverance 'to save' is distinguished by the constant presence of two elements, that of a delivering agent, and that of an active interposition on his part for the removal of actual evil or peril. For mere 'preservation' or mere 'escape' other words are used : 'healing' also is expressed by different terms ; cf. Gn 45[7] 47[25], Ex 1[17], Jer 48[6], Ezk 3[18], Ps 6[5] 41[3], Job 2[6]. The evil from which salvation takes place varies ; in most cases it is the oppression of Israel by its enemies ; sometimes, though not frequently, it appears in the acute form of individual or national death (Ps 68[19. 20]). While the noun-forms frequently have the same negative meaning as the verb, they pass over more readily into the positive sense, so that the act of deliverance becomes the point of departure for the bestowal of favour, blessing, and prosperity. Thus ישׁועה and תשׁעה come to mean 'victory' (1 S 14[45], 2 S 19[2], 2 K 5[1], Is 60[18]). 'Salvation' becomes synonymous with other positive terms like 'righteousness,' 'blessing,' 'light' (Is 45[8] 46[13] 49[6] 61[10] 62[1], Ps 24[5] 106[4]). In the Prophets and the Psalter it obtains an eschatological (Messianic) sense, and stands as one of the terms for the great final deliverance and the final blessedness to follow (Is 12[2f.] 45[17. 22] 49[8] 51[6. 8] 52[7] 56[1], Jer 23[6] 33[16], Mic 7[7], Hab 3[8. 18], Ps 147 354 74[12] 85[8] 98[2. 3] 109[27. 32] 118[15. 21]). The religious importance of the conception in the OT springs not so much from the nature of the evil removed, or from the nature of the blessedness bestowed, as rather from the fact that salvation, of whatever nature, is a work of Jehovah for His people, a Divine prerogative ; hence the frequently recurring statements that salvation belongs to Jehovah, is of Jehovah, that Jehovah is salvation, the Saviour of Israel (1 S 14[39], 2 S 22[3], 2 Ch 20[17], Is 12[2. 3] 33[22], Ps 3[8] 62[2] 118[14. 21]). In so far as salvation is valued not merely from the point of view of its benefits for man, but as a pledge of the Divine favour, the idea becomes spiritualized in principle. Besides, in so far as all national developments in the history of Israel have a religious and moral background, it is felt that every act of salvation must have for its antecedent a change in the people's spiritual condition (Is 33[22. 24]). In a few passages the conception is directly transferred from the national-political to the purely religious sphere, sin being named as the evil from which Israel or the individual is saved (Ezk 36[29], Ps 51[14]).

The LXX renders the Heb. verbs by σώζειν, the nouns by σωτηρία and σωτήριον. These words, however, are likewise used to render Heb. terms of a different shade of meaning, and thus to a large extent the nice distinction of the original between 'salvation' specifically so-called and such more general terms is obscured. Thus σώζειν stands for מלט Niphal, Piel, and Hiphil, frequently in the Passive for mere 'escape,' also for forms of פלט and חיה. On the other hand, σώζειν never bears in the LXX the specific sense of 'healing' (Jer 17[14]).

In the Apocryphal and Pseudepigraphical writings the usage does not vary much from that of the OT ; cf. Sir 51[12] (ἐξ ἀπωλείας), Wis 16[7], Jth 9[11], En 48[7] (of 'the Son of Man' ; 'in his name are they being saved, and he is the God of their life') 50[3] (eschatological - negative, mere salvation without glory) 63[8], 4 Ezr 6[25] 7[131] 9[8] 12[34] 13[26] 45[6] (the righteous shall be satisfied with salvation in connexion with the Messiah), Ps-Sol 6[2] 10[8] 12[6] 18[6], Bar 4[22. 24. 29], Test. Jud. 22, Test. Dan 5, Test. Napht. 8, Jub 23[29], 1 Mac 4[30] 9[9], 4 Mac 11[7] 15[3] ('piety which saves unto eternal life') 15[27]. In most of these passages the conception is eschatological-positive, and in many of them it has reference to the issue of the Last Judgment, wherein lies a transition from the OT to the NT usage. There is also an advance in this, that in a couple of instances the act of salvation is connected with the Messiah.

In the Gospels σώζειν occurs 54 times (not counting Lk 17[33], where ζωογονήσει is better attested than σώσει of the TR, nor Mt 18[11], a verse omitted by the best authorities). The noun σωτηρία occurs 5 times (not counting αἰώνιος σωτηρία in the rejected shorter conclusion of Mk.)—Lk 1[69. 71. 77] 19[9], Jn 4[22].

τὸ σωτήριον is found twice—Lk 2³⁰ 3⁶. Of the instances of this use of the verb 14 relate to the deliverance from disease or demoniacal possession—Mt 9²¹· ²² *bis*, Mk 5²³· ²⁸· ³⁴ 6⁵⁶ 10⁵², Lk 8³⁶· ⁴⁸· ⁵⁰ 17¹⁹ 18⁴², Jn 11¹² ; in 20 instances the reference is to the rescue of physical life from some impending peril or instant death—Mt 8²⁵ 14³⁰ 16²⁵ 27⁴⁰· ⁴² *bis*· ⁴⁹, Mk 3⁴ 8³⁵ 15³⁰· ³¹ *bis*, Lk 6⁹ 9²⁴· ⁵⁶ 23³⁵ *bis*· ³⁷· ³⁹, Jn 12²⁷ ; in the remainder of cases, 20 times, the reference is to religious salvation technically so called—Mt 1²¹ 10²² 19²⁵ 24¹³· ²², Mk 8³⁵ 10²⁶ 13¹³· ²⁰ 16¹⁶, Lk 7⁵⁰ 8¹² 9²⁴ 13²³ 18²⁶ 19¹⁰, Jn 3¹⁷ 5³⁴ 10⁹ 12⁴⁷. The noun σωτηρία is used twice in the OT sense of deliverance from the enemies of Israel—Lk 1⁶⁹· ⁷¹ ; and 3 times in the more specifically religious sense—Lk 1⁷⁷ 19⁹, Jn 4²². τὸ σωτήριον in Lk 2³⁰ has the same distinctly religious associations ; in 3⁶ it stands in a quotation from Is 40⁵, where the meaning is eschatological from the OT point of view.

1. First we examine the passages relating to the *deliverance from diseases or demoniacal possession*. The question is whether the import of σώζειν here is exhausted by the notion of 'healing.' The Greek word has this meaning, being connected with σῶς (σάος), 'whole,' 'sound,' therefore σώζειν = 'to render whole, sound.' The AV accordingly renders in most of these cases 'to make whole' or 'be whole,' in two 'to heal' (Mk 5²³, Lk 8³⁶), in one 'to do well' (Jn 11¹²), and only once 'to save' (Lk 18⁴²). In one instance it offers 'to save' as a marginal reading for 'to make whole' (Mk 10⁵²). RV everywhere follows the rendering of AV except that it makes the two passages where the latter has 'to heal' and the one passage where it has 'to save' uniform with the others ; further, that it renders in Jn 11¹² 'to recover,' and that it offers in all passages except Mk 6⁵⁶ the marginal alternative 'to save.' It should be noticed that on other occasions the Evangelists use, and make Jesus use, different words, whose import is restricted to 'healing' in the medical sense, and that not only where the object is some disease or disability, but also with a personal object ; so θεραπεύειν (Mt 4²³· ²⁴ 8⁷· ¹⁶ 9³⁵ 10¹· ⁸ 12¹⁰· ¹⁵ 14¹⁴ 15³⁰ 17¹⁶· ¹⁸ 19² 21¹⁴, Mk 1³⁴ 3²· ¹⁰· ¹⁵ 6⁵· ¹³, Lk 4²³· ⁴⁰ 5¹⁵ 6⁷· ¹⁸ 7²¹ 8²· ⁴³ 9¹· ⁶ 10⁹ 13¹⁴ 14³, Jn 5¹⁰) and ἰᾶσθαι (Lk 6¹⁹ 9²· ¹¹· ⁴² 14⁴ 22⁵¹, Jn 4⁴⁷). The question is not, of course, whether the element of 'healing' as a connotated idea should be entirely eliminated from σώζειν. Not only would this have been impossible to a Greek speaker or writer in cases where the saving act as a matter of fact consisted in or involved healing, but it is also excluded by the observation that Jesus more than once referred to His saving work as the work of a physician, and in the instruction to His disciples spoke also of it as 'healing' (Mt 9¹² 10¹· ⁸ 13¹⁵, Mk 2¹⁷, Lk 4¹⁸ 5³¹ 9¹· ² 10⁹). The only point at issue is whether the Evangelists are aware of a difference between statements where 'healing' is designated as such, and other statements where 'healing' is implied, but where for a certain purpose it is characterized as 'saving.'

The data above cited show that this last question must be answered in the affirmative. In view of the fact that Aramaic lies behind the Greek form of the words of Jesus or the Evangelists, we shall also have to assume a clearly marked difference between the two sets of cases. The additional element which the use of σώζειν introduces into the situation is that of deliverance from the sphere or power of death. In Mk 3⁴, Lk 6⁹, while speaking of His healing work, our Lord contrasts σώζειν with ἀποκτείνειν, which implies that He regarded it as the opposite of 'killing,' *i.e.* as rescuing from death and restoring to life. According to Mk 5²³, the purpose of 'being saved' is 'to live.' In Lk 7³ διασώζειν, the use of

the preposition marks the process as a transition from death to life. It is true that in some instances the disease or infirmity from which Jesus saves is not fatal in itself, *e.g.* the withered hand (Mk 3⁴), the issue of blood (5²⁸), certainly some of the diseases of 6⁵⁶, blindness (10⁵²). Still even here the act of saving is viewed not from a medical point of view, but from the religious point of view, according to which all disease and infirmity lie on the side of death, so that it belongs to the function of one who delivers from death to work deliverance from these consequences of sin and precursors of death likewise.

This is further confirmed by the general interpretation Jesus puts upon His healing miracles as prophecies and pledges of the approaching Kingdom, in which all sin and death shall be done away with. With regard to the casting out of demons, the correctness of this view is vouched for by the explicit statement (Mt 12²⁸ = Lk 11²⁰). But it applies equally well to the other miracles of healing. Jesus did not look upon these as works of philanthropy merely, or as signs authenticating His mission primarily. While the latter was one of the purposes for which they were intended—and this is brought out prominently in the Fourth Gospel—in the Synoptics, where Jesus' teaching is centred in the Kingdom-idea, the miracles are before all else signs of the actual approach of the Kingdom,—proofs that the saving power of God, which calls the Kingdom into being, is already in motion, and therefore so many instances of σώζειν. Jesus' saving power is simply the Kingdom-power applied to the individual under the influence of sin and death. Thus only can we naturally explain the fact that, where 'salvation' has a direct religious reference, both in our Lord's own and in the later Apostolic teaching, the close connexion between it and the ideas of death and life is unmistakable. If this religious usage is at all dependent on the physical aspect of our Lord's saving activity, it can be only through the common element of victory over sin and death. Jesus Himself has sufficiently indicated the connexion between the two, both in the Synoptical sayings and in the Johannine discourses. In the former the physical evils, which the saving Kingdom-power removes, have a moral and spiritual background. Hence Jesus makes such physical salvation the occasion for suggesting and working the profounder change by which the bonds of sin are loosed, and the rule of God set up in the inner life of man. The external and the internal are significantly placed side by side as co-ordinated halves of an identical work (Mk 2⁹). And in the Fourth Gospel we are explicitly told that the physical acts are intended to point to corresponding spiritual transactions ; the healing of the blind, the raising of the dead, are symbolic of Jesus' saving work in the spiritual sphere (5¹⁴· ¹⁹⁻²⁹ 9³· ³⁹ 12²⁵· ²⁶). On three occasions our Lord has brought out the spiritual significance of the physical salvation by calling special attention to its dependence on the exercise of faith : the woman with the issue of blood (Mk 5³⁴ = Mt 9²² = Lk 8⁴⁸), the blind man near Jericho (Mk 10⁵² = Lk 18⁴²), one of the lepers (Lk 17¹⁹). The words 'thy faith has saved thee' are on these occasions the same as were used in such a case of purely spiritual salvation as is recorded Lk 7⁵⁰. They were intended as a suggestion that faith, which had yielded such results in the physical sphere, could be made equally fruitful in the sphere of spiritual salvation. Thus the external and internal are linked together by the common factor of faith.

That σώζειν has to do with the contrast of life and death becomes plain also from those instances of its natural use where deliverance from evil other than disease or demon-possession is referred to, for here everywhere the evil is that of physical death (Mt 8^{25} 14^{30} 16^{25} 27$^{40.\ 42.\ 49}$, Mk 8^{35} 15$^{30.\ 31}$, Lk 9$^{24.\ 56}$ 23$^{35.\ 37.\ 39}$, Jn 12^{27}).

2. In connexion with the *directly religious use* in the Gospels several questions emerge. (1) Is the saving act, when belonging to the spiritual sphere, still viewed as a translation from death into life, and what is the meaning of death and life as related to salvation in this sphere? (2) Is the deliverance conceived eschatologically, as something to be experienced in the Last Day, or is it treated as an experience already attainable in this present life? (3) Is the conception negative or positive, or both negative and positive, *i.e.* does it express merely the removal of spiritual evil, or also the bestowal of positive spiritual blessings, especially the gift of life in a positive, pregnant sense?

(1) The answer to the first question is that spiritual salvation still revolves around the contrast between life and death, and that in a twofold sense. Both as subjective and as objective states, death and life come under consideration here. In other words: Jesus saves from spiritual death as a condition of the soul, and He saves from eternal death as a punishment awaiting the sinner. As the object of His saving activity, our Lord names τὸ ἀπολωλός 'that which has become lost and now is lost' (Mt 10^6 15^{24} 18$^{12-14}$, Lk 15$^{4.\ 6.\ 8.\ 24}$ 19^{10}). From the figures used it appears that the Gr. ἀπόλλυσθαι has in this connexion the sense 'miss,' 'be missing,' not primarily the sense 'destroy,' 'be destroyed.' The 'lost' are like sheep gone astray upon the mountains, like the coin slipped out of the hand of its owner, like the prodigal who has left the father's home. A lost condition means estrangement from God, a missing of all the religious and moral relations man is designed to sustain towards his Maker. But this lost condition is further identified by Jesus with spiritual death, for of the prodigal the father declares: 'This thy brother was dead and is alive again, and was lost and is found' (Lk 15$^{24.\ 32}$). Elsewhere also the state of sin is described as a state of death (Mt 8^{22}, Lk 20^{38}). Salvation of 'the lost,' therefore, is salvation from spiritual death. As such it includes both forgiveness of sin and moral-religious renewal. To the woman who had anointed Him Jesus said: 'Thy faith hath saved thee; go in peace,' and this obviously repeats in another form the preceding statement, 'Thy sins are forgiven' (Lk 7$^{48.\ 50}$). In the case of Zacchæus also assurance of pardon is undoubtedly implied when Jesus declares 'salvation' to have come to his house (19^9). Here, however, the salvation manifests itself also in the moral transformation of the publican, issuing directly into repentance and good works. The prodigal is pardoned and restored to the privileges of sonship. But salvation is not confined to deliverance from this subjective spiritual death, just as the conception of being 'lost' is not exhausted by estrangement from God. ἀπόλλυσθαι is used in a retributive sense in connexion with the judgment of God to which the sinner is subject; it involves exposure to objective death as a result of condemnation. With reference to this the two senses of the verb, 'to be missing' and 'to be destroyed,' are used side by side. From the point of view of man the judgment may bring a 'losing' or a 'finding,' 'keeping' of the soul or life (Mt 10^{39} 16^{25}, Mk 8^{35}, Lk 9$^{24.\ 25}$ 17^{33}, Jn 12^{25}). From the point of view of God as Judge it may bring 'destruction.' This is the ἀπώλεια, which is spoken of in Mt 5^{30} 7^{13} 10^{28} 18^{14}, Lk 13$^{3.\ 5}$, Jn 3$^{15.\ 16}$ 6^{39} 10^{28} 17^{12} 18^9. The two aspects of ἀπόλλυσθαι — the subjective spiritual 'being lost' and the objective retributive 'being lost' or 'perishing'—are joined together in Mt

18$^{10-14}$, where first the sinning one is compared to a sheep gone astray and to be sought, and then, to give the motive for this search after the subjectively lost, Jesus adds: 'Even so it is not the will of your Father who is in heaven, that one of these little ones should perish' (ἀπόληται); that which is already lost in the one sense must be diligently sought, lest it should be lost in the deeper, absolute sense. And the deliverance from this final ἀπώλεια, as well as the deliverance from the other lost condition, is σώζεσθαι, σωτηρία. Thus in Mk 16^{16} 'to be saved' is the opposite of 'to be condemned'; in Jn 3$^{16.\ 17}$ of 'to be judged' and 'to perish,' in 10$^{9.\ 10}$ of 'to be destroyed,' in 12^{47} of 'to be judged.' This ἀπώλεια, however, not less than the other 'being lost,' is equivalent to death. It is a losing of the *life* (ψυχή, Mt 10^{39} 16^{25}, Mk 8^{35}, Lk 9$^{24.\ 25}$, Jn 12^{25}); its opposite is 'to have eternal life' (Jn 3^{16} 10^{28}), or 'to be raised up at the last day' (6^{39}). Thus it appears that salvation in its specific religious sense is still viewed throughout as a deliverance from death and an introduction into the sphere of life.

(2) The second question was whether 'salvation' is conceived eschatologically or as something experienced already in this present life. It has been answered in principle by the above, for present salvation coincides with deliverance from subjective spiritual death; eschatological salvation coincides with deliverance from objective death in the Judgment. In a number of the passages already considered the reference to the present is very plain. To the woman who anointed Him Jesus addressed the words, 'Thy faith has saved thee.' Of Zacchæus He declared: 'To-day is salvation come to this house'; and in the following statement—'The Son of Man came to seek and to save that which was lost,'—the 'saving' must belong to the same time as the 'seeking,' *i.e.* to the present time of our Lord's earthly ministry. In Jn 12^{47} the saving of the world for which Jesus has come is a present thing as distinct from the judging of the world for which He has not come, but which is reserved for the future. In Mt 1^{21} the sins of the people being the evil from which Jesus saves, the salvation is viewed as a present one. In other passages the eschatological reference is equally obvious. 'He that endures to the end shall be saved' (Mt 10^{22} 24^{13}). Mt 16^{25}, Mk 8^{35}, Lk 9^{24} speak of the finding or saving of life in the future Judgment as conditioned by the willingness to sacrifice one's life here. This is clear from the context (v.^{38} in Mk., v.^{27} in Mt. = v.^{26} in Lk).

The point of the saying is not, as often interpreted, that for one *kind* of life, physical life, given up, another *kind* of life, spiritual life, will be received in return; in which case the future tenses might be purely logical, and no eschatological reference implied. The meaning is that for life, in its general sense, sacrificed by accepting physical death, life in the same general sense will be received in reward through the escape from death, when Jesus comes to judge and to render every man according to his deeds. As Zahn observes, the distinction between two kinds of 'life' or 'soul' is scarcely in harmony with the Hebrew point of view, according to which the 'life' or the 'soul' is frequently called 'the only one' (*Com. on Matthew, in loco*).

Eschatological is also the reference in the question of the disciples recorded in Mt 19^{25}, Mk 10^{26}, Lk 18^{26} 'Then who can be saved?' The question was called forth by Jesus' declaration, that the rich would with great difficulty enter into the Kingdom of God, which was in turn called forth by the question of the rich young man, 'What shall I do, that I may inherit eternal life?' Here 'to be saved' = 'to enter the Kingdom' = 'to inherit eternal life,' and the qualification of life as *eternal*, as well as the further context,—St. Peter's question about future rewards, and our Lord's answer to this,—prove that the whole discussion is eschatological in its scope. Mt 24^{22} ‖ Mk 13^{20} 'Except these days had been shortened, no flesh would have been saved,' is best understood as follows: The temptation in these last times will be so severe, that, if their duration had not been kept within certain limits, all men, even the elect, would have fallen away, and so no flesh would have been ultimately saved in the Day of Judgment.

This interpretation seems to be required by the fact that the shortening of the days is for the sake of the elect. The mere preservation of physical life could have no special bearing upon the destiny of the elect, since, even when killed in the body, they would be sure to inherit the Kingdom; the whole representation concerning the possibility of none being saved, and the elect falling away and the shortening of the days, is, of course, conceived from the human point of view (cf. Zahn, *Com. on Matthew, in loco*).

In the remainder of the passages there are no means of determining whether 'salvation' be future or present. For Mt 18[11] (TR only) the reference to the present is supported by Lk 19[10]. In Lk 8[12] 'that they may not believe and be saved,' the eschatological sense would be quite plausible, but the other view is slightly favoured by the general import of the parables dealing with the present invisible aspect of the Kingdom. In general, the representation of the Kingdom as both present and future creates a presumption in favour of the view that our Lord regarded salvation as both a present and an eschatological experience. The form $\sigma\omega\zeta\delta\mu\epsilon\nu\omega$, 'those who are being saved,' in Lk 13[23], probably reflects the two-sidedness of the process, as belonging to both present and future, and therefore unfinished in this life. In the case of the Johannine sayings (Jn 3[16. 17] 4[22] 5[34] 10[9]) we shall have to assume, in harmony with the generalization of the conception of 'life,' 'eternal life,' in the discourses of this Gospel—which makes out of it a conception indifferent to the distinction between present and future—that the same will be true of the synonymous conception of salvation. The future in 10[9] is purely logical in its force.

(3) The third question concerned what may be gathered from the Gospels in regard to the positive or negative context of the idea of religious salvation. The negative aspect—escape from death—stands in the foreground in Mt 24[22], Mk 13[20]: if the days had not been shortened, not even the elect would have escaped the fate of death in the Judgment; similarly in Mt 16[25], Mk 8[35], Lk 9[24]: he who will sacrifice his life here shall escape the loss of life in the Judgment. Probably Mt 10[22] and 24[13] should be interpreted on the same principle: the enduring now will save from greater calamity in the Last Day. On the other hand, in Mt 19[25], Mk 10[26], Lk 18[26], where 'salvation' is equivalent to entrance of the Kingdom and inheriting of eternal life, the emphasis rests on the positive side. In the Johannine passages the positive content of the idea is very marked. According to Jn 3[16. 17], 'to have eternal life' and 'to be saved' are synonymous. In Jn 5[34] also the preceding context revolves around the idea of life (vv. [21-29]), and in the sequel the same idea is again brought forward (v. [39]). Again, in 10[9. 10] 'salvation' and 'life' appear in close conjunction; 12[47] receives its interpretation from 3[17]. The same difference as is observable with reference to eschatological salvation may be observed where present salvation is spoken of. Sometimes the conception is negative (Mt 1[21], Lk 7[50]), sometimes positive as well as negative (Lk 19[10]); the salvation which came to Zacchæus' house certainly included more than pardon, since it issued in renewal of life. The facts, therefore, do not bear out the contention of B. Weiss, who maintains that $\sigma\omega\zeta\epsilon\sigma\theta\alpha\iota$ has everywhere a purely negative meaning.

In the saying of Lk 19[10] Jesus declares 'saving' to be the highest category under which His Messianic activity is to be subsumed. He *came* to save,

i.e. His entrance into the world was for this specific purpose (cf. Mk 10[45]). The connexion between Him and salvation consists not merely in this, that as a preacher of the gospel He proclaims it. Everywhere the supposition is that salvation is in some way bound to His Person. For the Johannine discourses this needs no proof. But it is no less true for the Synoptics. Because He lodged with Zacchæus, salvation entered the latter's house. The rich young man was not saved, because he refused to follow Jesus. The saving acts in the physical sphere are suspended on faith, and this faith involves trust in Jesus,—in Jesus, to be sure, as the instrument of God, but none the less so that on Jesus' Person together with God the act of faith terminates. It is psychologically inconceivable that in those who were helped by the miracles of Jesus, faith should not have assumed the form of personal trust in Him. Faith in God and faith in Jesus here inevitably coalesce. On the occasion of the storm, Jesus rebukes the disciples for their lack of confidence in His presence with them as a guarantee of absolute safety (Mt 8[26]). Similarly Peter, when walking upon the water, calls upon Jesus to perform the saving act. From the close connexion in which these transactions stand to the specific religious salvation, it may be safely inferred that in the latter also Jesus occupies a necessary place. This is confirmed by Lk 7[50], where the woman's faith, which is declared to have saved her, consists in the attitude of trust she had assumed towards Jesus; the love shown the Lord is here the result of the forgiveness of sins (v.[47]), and inasmuch as this love terminated on Jesus, the faith which conditioned the forgiveness must likewise have had Him for its object. Similarly in the discourse at Cæsarea Philippi, 'salvation' in the Last Day is made dependent on following of Jesus and sacrifice of life for Jesus' sake and the gospel's sake, and the corresponding acknowledgment by Jesus in the Judgment (Mk 8[34. 35. 38] || Mt. and Lk.).

It is not true, as is being frequently asserted of late, that in the gospel preached by Jesus there is no place for His own Person, it being merely a gospel about God. Though not frequently in so many words, yet in acts we find our Lord seeking to cultivate a relationship of faith between the disciple and Himself and, in Himself, with God. If only once in the Synoptics we read explicitly of faith in Jesus (Mt 8[10]), and that in a passage where the authenticity of the words $\epsilon\iota\varsigma$ $\epsilon\mu\epsilon$ is doubtful, this is counterbalanced by the fact that not more than once God Himself is specified as the object of faith (Mk 11[22]). Jesus, conscious of being the Messiah, the Judge at the Last Day, who would finally dispose of the destiny of all mankind, could not help ascribing a central soteriological position to Himself. Such a figure as He was in His own view, could not be kept outside of the saving transaction, which in a certain sense forestalls the Last Judgment. The absence of more direct affirmations of this principle is simply the result of Jesus' method of not directly proclaiming at first His Messianic dignity, but rather allowing it to be gradually inferred from the impression made by His Person and the witness of His works. On the basis of our present Gospels, apart from critical reconstructions of the teaching of Jesus, no other view is possible than that our Lord represented salvation as in some way bound to and wrapped up in His Person. He did not represent salvation as something unconditioned, flowing simply from the love of God, which would overleap every necessity of mediation. The parable of the Prodigal Son, so often quoted to the contrary, furnishes, when rightly read, the clearest demonstration of this, for it was spoken to describe not God's attitude towards sinners in the abstract, but the historic approach of God to lost men in the appearance of His Son Jesus. It was the attitude of *Jesus* towards publicans and sinners that drew forth the parable, and therefore it describes God's attitude towards them as bound to that assumed by Jesus (cf. Ernst Cremer, 'Die Gleichnisse Lukas 15 und das Kreuz' in *Beitr. z. Förder. Christl. Theol.* 1904, Heft 4). The gospel is not a mere announcement of the love of God unpreceded and unattended by any action on His part; it is the glad message of the love of God in action, of what God does in Jesus to give His love effect in actual, substantial salvation. The unfolding of what the Person of Jesus as the bearer and worker of salvation contains could not be fully given by our Lord before His saving work had actually transpired, but had to be left to Apostolic teaching.

3. Humanly considered, *salvation is dependent on faith.* This is not merely explicitly announced

(Mk 16[16], Lk 8[12], Jn 3[16. 17]), it is likewise presupposed or expressed in connexion with the healing acts of Jesus. It is a striking fact that in the Synoptics nearly the whole of our Lord's teaching on faith attaches itself to the performance of miracles. This is because miracles embody that saving aspect of the Kingdom to which faith is the subjective counterpart. The miracles, almost without exception, have two features in common. *Firstly*, they are transactions in which the result depends absolutely on the forth-putting of the Divine supernatural powers, where no human effort could possibly contribute anything towards its accomplishment. And, *secondly*, the miracles are healing miracles, in which the gracious love of God approaches man for his salvation. Faith is the spiritual attitude called for by this twofold element in God's saving work. It is the recognition of the Divine power and grace,—not, of course, in a purely intellectual way, but practically so as to carry with it the movement of the whole inner life. How faith stands related to the saving power of God is most clearly illustrated in the narrative of Mk 9[17-24]. When the disciples could not heal the child with the dumb spirit, Jesus exclaimed, 'O unbelieving generation!' The father says, after describing the severity of the case: 'But if thou canst do anything, have compassion on us and help us.' To this Jesus replies: 'What, *if thou canst!* all things are possible to him that believeth.' Faith is omnipotent. To speak, with reference to it, of an 'if thou canst' is an absurdity. Thus to faith is ascribed what can be affirmed of God alone. And elsewhere also this same principle is emphasized by our Lord (Mt 21[21. 22], Mk 11[22. 23], Lk 17[6]). The explanation lies in this, that faith is nothing else than that act whereby man lays hold of, appropriates, the endless power of God. This line of reasoning, however, is not applicable to the miracles only. The miracles, as has been shown, illustrate the saving work of God in general. All salvation partakes, humanly speaking, of the nature of the impossible : it can be accomplished by God alone (Mt 19[25. 26], Mk 10[26. 27], Lk 18[26. 27]). All genuine saving faith is as profoundly conscious of its utter dependence on God for deliverance from sin and death as the recipients of our Lord's miraculous cures were convinced that God alone could heal their bodies from disease. Faith, however, is more than belief, more than a conviction regarding the necessity and sufficiency of the Divine power. It also involves trust, the reliance upon God's willingness and readiness to save. Jesus never encouraged the exercise of faith as a mere theoretical belief in supernatural power. The performance of a sign from heaven, such as men might have witnessed without trust in God or Himself, He persistently refused. He who truly believes, realizes that God is loving, merciful, forgiving, glad to receive sinners. Faith transfers to God in the matter of salvation what human parents experience in themselves with reference to their own children, the desire to help and supply (Mt 7[7-11]). This reliance of faith is not confined to the critical moments of life ; it is to be the abiding, characteristic disposition of the disciple with reference to his salvation as a whole. Faith, in those on whom the wonderful cures were wrought, may have manifested itself at first as a momentary act, but, as shown above, Jesus frequently called the attention of such people to what faith had done for them, thus suggesting that it was permanently available as an instrument of salvation.

4. In proper names, the conception of 'saving' occurs twice in the Gospels, namely, in the name *Jesus*, and in the exclamation *Hosanna*. A reflexion upon the meaning of the name *Joshua* is found also in Sir 46[1], and in Philo, who explains it

by σωτηρία κυρίου (*de Mut. Nom.* 21). The meaning of Mt 1[21] is not that Jesus will bear this name symbolically in illustration of the fact that 'Jehovah is salvation,' but rather that in Him Jehovah saves, or even, He is Jehovah who saves ; for thus only can we satisfactorily explain the joining together of the two statements, 'Thou shalt call his name Jesus,' and 'for it is he that shall save his people from their sins.' It has been held that in the cry 'Hosanna,' raised by the people at Jesus' entrance into Jerusalem, and by the children in the Temple (Mt 21[9. 15] ||), the original idea of 'saving' inherent in this word as an appeal to God to bestow salvation (Ps 118[25] 'Save now, we beseech thee, Jehovah'), was no longer felt by the Evangelists, and the word meant with them simply a general shout of applause to the Messianic King, equivalent to '*Vivat*' or the German '*Hoch.*' Dalman (*Die Worte Jesu*, i. 180), who takes this view, couples with it the inference that the writer of the First Gospel was not a Hebraist, consequently not the Apostle Matthew, because no Hebraist could have thus misinterpreted a familiar form. He finds the same misunderstanding in Mk. Both Evangelists, according to him, make the people use the shout in the sense which it bore to the early Church, ignorant of the *Hebrew* meaning. Dalman therefore assumes that what the people actually exclaimed was the simple 'Hosanna,' and that both 'to the Son of David' and 'in the highest' are unhistorical embellishments dependent on the Greek misinterpretation of the word. Zahn, on the other hand (Com. on Matthew, *in loco*), takes the view that to the common people of Jesus' time already the old meaning of the Hebrew form may have become obliterated, so that they already used it as a shout of applause for Jesus, in which case the Evangelists would be accurate in their report of the occurrence. But Zahn does not explain what meaning, on this view, the people could have attached to the words ἐν τοῖς ὑψίστοις, which in a shout addressed to Jesus would remain meaningless. In view of this, only two explanations seem possible. Either we may adhere to the older opinion that ὡσαννά is consciously addressed to God, 'save now,' and that τῷ υἱῷ Δαυείδ introduces Jesus as the object of the salvation invoked from God (הוֹשִׁיעָה, as Dalman himself observes, being sometimes construed with ל of the object—Ps 72[4] 116[6]), and that ἐν τοῖς ὑψίστοις designates heaven as the place from which God is called upon to bless the Son of David. That for the expression of the latter idea ἐξ ὑψίστων would have been absolutely necessary can hardly be maintained. Or we may make a distinction between the two hosannas, assuming that the former is addressed to the Son of David, the latter to God, and both not as invocations, but as ascriptions of praise. This is suggested by Lk.'s version (19[38]), which resolves the eschatological into the paraphrase ἐν οὐρανῷ εἰρήνη, καὶ δόξα ἐν ὑψίστοις. This would be a modification of Zahn's view, preferable because it does not leave the ἐν ὑψίστοις unexplained.

5. To the foregoing may be added a rapid survey of the usage of σώζειν and σωτηρία in the remainder of the NT. 'Salvation' in connexion with healing, but at the same time projected into the specific religious sphere, reappears in Ac 4[9. 12] 14[9]. That the idea in the Apostolic teaching largely revolves around the contrast between life and death, is made abundantly plain by the following passages: Ac 3[15] 5[30] 13[46. 47], Ro 1[16. 17], 1 Co 5[5], 2 Co 2[15. 16] 7[10], Ph 3[20], 2 Ti 1[10], Tit 3[5], He 5[7], Ja 5[15. 20], 1 P 3[20. 21]. Where the saving act is referred to a definite point of time, this is most frequently the eschatological future (Ro 13[11], 1 Co 3[15] 5[5], Ph 1[28], 1 Th 5[8], 2 Th 2[13], He 1[14] 2[10] 9[28], Ja 5[20], 1 P 1[5. 9. 10] 4[18]). Instances where salvation is made a matter of the past or present are Eph 2[5. 8], 1 Ti 2[4], 2 Ti 1[9], Tit 3[5], Ja 1[21] (?), 1 P 3[21], Jude 21. In many connexions, however, it is not possible to determine whether the usage is eschatological or not (Ro 1[16] 10[1], 2 Co 7[10], Eph 1[13], He 2[3], Ja 2[16]). For this peculiar indetermination of the idea the following passages are of interest : Ac 2[47], 1 Co 1[18] 15[2], 2 Co 2[15], in all of which the present participle σωζόμενοι, 'those who are being saved,' is found (cf. with the past participle σεσωσμένοι, 'those who have been and are saved,' Eph 2[5]). The negative aspect of the deliverance is on the whole not more prominent than the positive : Ac 2[40] (from this crooked generation, *i.e.* from the judgment which will befall it), Ro 5[9] (from the eschatological wrath of God), Ja 5[20] (from death), Jude 23 (from the fire) ; and, on the other hand, Ac 13[46. 47] (eternal life), 2 Co 2[15] (unto life), Ph 3[20] (Saviour through the resurrection), Tit 3[5] (palingenesia), He 1[4] (inherit salvation), 2[3] (so great a salvation), 5[9] (eternal salvation), 1 P 1[4. 5] (inheritance=salvation), Rev 12[10] (salvation parallel with power and Kingdom), 19[1] (salvation parallel with glory and power). In 2 Ti 1[10] the negative and the positive side are named together : 'our Saviour, who abolished death, and brought life and immortality to light through the gospel.' Salvation from sin specifically appears in Ro 11[26] in a quotation from the LXX of Is 59[20].

6. It ought to be observed that σωτηρία in the NT relates to what is dogmatically called 'the application of redemption' in distinction from 'the impetration of redemption,' or the objective work of Christ. This is the natural result of its original eschatological significance, for what takes place in the end lies on the line of the subjective transformation of the believer.

The view has recently been advocated by Wendland (*ZNTW* v. [1904] 351) that the original background of the conception of σώζεσθαι is the rule and influence of evil spirits, of which death and disease would be only the peripheral manifestations. The facts cited above do not bear out this hypothesis, or even favour it. In the Gospels there is only one passage which applies σώζειν to the casting out of a demon (Lk 8[36]). In all other cases of deliverance from demoniacal possession other expressions are used. It would be far more correct to say that sin and death lie at the centre, demoniacal influence in the periphery of the conception. On the other hand, it creates an equally wrong distribution of the emphasis to conceive of our Lord's σώζειν as in its primary aspect a species of 'healing,' and of Jesus Himself as chiefly a spiritual physician. Against Harnack, who in his work, *Die Mission und Ausbreitung des Christenthums in den ersten drei Jahrhunderten*, goes too far in this direction, Wagner (*ZNTW* vi. [1905] 234, 235) well observes, that the NT writers do not, like the later Church Fathers, who stood under the influence of the Stoic philosophy, view sin as a disease of the soul, but as a species of death, and that Jesus is to them far more than a physician, viz. One who leads from death to life.

LITERATURE.—Cremer, *Lex. svv.* σώζειν and σωτηρία ; the various handbooks on *OT* and *NT Theology* ; Klaiber, *Die NT Lehre von der Sünde und Erlösung*, 1836 ; Titius, *Die NT Lehre von der Seligkeit*, 4 parts, 1895–1900 ; Klöpper, *Der Brief d. Ap. Paul. a. d. Philipper*, on 1[19. 28] (note) and 3[20], *Der Brief a. d. Epheser* on 2[5] and 5[23] ; Anrich, *Das antike Mysterienwesen*, 1894, p. 47 ff. ; Wobbermin, *Religionsgesch. Studien*, 105 ff. ; Harnack, *Reden und Aufsätze*, 1899, 1900, i. pp. 301–311 ; Soltau, *Die Geburtsgesch. Jesu Christi*, 1902 ; Wendland, 'Σωτήρ : Eine religionsgesch. Untersuchung' in *ZNTW* v. [1904] p. 335 ff. ; Wagner, 'Ueber σώζειν und seine Derivata im NT,' *ib.* vi. [1905] p. 205 ff. ; Jeremias, *Babylonisches im NT*, 1905, pp. 27–46.

GEERHARDUS VOS.

SAMARIA, SAMARITANS.— 1. Description.— 'Samaria,' originally the name of the city built by Omri (1 K 16[24]), became in a very short time a common name for the Northern kingdom (Am 3[9], Jer 31[5], 2 Ch 25[13]) ; but during the Greek period it became limited to the province of Samaria, and so in NT times it is the designation of the district that lies between Galilee and Judæa (Jn 4[4]). The limits and extent of the Samaritan territory varied from time to time (Jos. *Ant.* XII. iv. 1 ; 1 Mac 11[34]), and it is impossible to define with absolute certainty the boundaries in Gospel days. These, however, may be known generally. We learn that Ginea—the modern *Jenin*—on the south edge of the plain of Esdraelon, was its northern boundary (*Ant.* XX. vi. 1) ; and this is confirmed by the fact that Caphar Outheni—now *Kefr Adan*—4 miles distant, was in Galilee (M. *Giṭṭin* i. 5). The southern boundary is stated as 'the Acrabbene toparchy' (*BJ* III. iii. 4), and a village named Anuath or Borkeas was on the border (*ib.*). As these have been identified with the modern villages of '*Akrabe* and *Berūkin*, we conclude that this boundary ran westward to the Shephelah along Wady Ish'ār. In that case it would then naturally run eastward to the Jordan down Wady Zamar. There seems, however, good reason to fix it farther north at this point, as Ḳarn Sarṭabeh seems to have been in the hands of the Jews (M. *Rosh.* ii. 4), unless, indeed, it was a border hill accessible alike to Jews and Samaritans. This seems the more likely, as it was the only signalling station in the neighbourhood of Samaritan territory where false lights could be kindled to deceive the Jews on the occasion of the new moons, and this the Samaritans are accused of having done (Bab. *Rosh.* 22*b* and margin). The eastern boundary was, of course, the Jordan, while the hill slopes towards the Shephelah constituted the western—the plain between Caphar Outheni and Antipatris being regarded as a heathen district (Bab. *Giṭṭin* 76*a*). This gives us a territory of about 20 miles from north to south, and 30 from east to west.

The region consists of scattered mountain groups and rounded hills with plains between, the chief of these being Merj el-Mahna, to the east of Nâblus, Merj el-Ghuruḳ or the plain of Sanur (a lake in the winter and spring), and the plain of Dothan, which last opens into the plain of Esdraelon. Samaria presents a striking and beautiful contrast to Judæa with its barren hills. Here they are for the most part covered with fruit trees of every kind, chief among which are the olive, the fig, the mulberry, the orange, the apricot, and the pomegranate. On the Samaritan hills great flocks of sheep and goats find pasture. The whole country is studded with villages, and the fertile plains and valleys produce rich crops of grain. Only to the east, extending along the Jordan boundary, is the country rough and broken, and the mountains, which descend precipitously to the river, naked and barren ; and this they have always been (*BJ* IV. viii. 2). The rest of the country is well watered everywhere, and in many places it is extremely beautiful. In the early centuries the gardens of Samaria (פרדסות, M. *Erakhin* iii. 2) were famous, and to-day the fruit orchards and beautiful gardens of Jenîn are equally well known, while all must agree with Thomson (*LB* ii. 110) when he says : 'One may be excused for becoming somewhat enthusiastic over this pretty vale of Nâblus, sparkling with fountains and streams, verdant with olive groves and fig orchards, interspersed with walnut, apple, apricot, orange, quince, pomegranate, and other trees and shrubs.' But, notwithstanding its superiority in richness and beauty to the south country, the Jews of the 1st cent. were very unwilling to admit that Samaria was part of the Holy Land. When they spoke of it they reckoned only the *three lands*,—Judæa, Galilee, and Peræa (M. *Shebhiith* ix. 2),—always omitting Samaria, as not being Jewish soil. But even the district we have described is not to be regarded as having been at any time fully occupied by the people we call Samaritans. The name was strictly limited to the religious sect, the metropolis of which was Shechem (*Ant.* XI. viii. 6). There, and in many of the towns and villages, they were numerous and strong, but almost everywhere there were also Grecian settlers, and with the city of Samaria itself the Samaritans had little or nothing to do.

2. History of the Samaritans in their relationship to the Jews.—Although the Samaritans claim descent from the patriarchs (Jn 4[12]), and present us with an unbroken history, and although it is to some extent true that they represent the spirit of the tribe of Ephraim (Renan, *Lang. Semit.* p. 230), we must date their characteristic existence as a people only from the time of their conflicts with Ezra and Nehemiah. We regard the Samaritan statement (*el-Tolidoth*), that 300,000 men besides women and children were brought back from captivity in the days of Sanballat, as baseless ; but, on the other hand, when Israel was carried away captive, a remnant must have been left ; and that such was the case we have abundant evidence (2 K 23[17-20], Jer 41[5]). Their appearance as a community dates only from the time of their mingling with the Assyrian colonists settled in the land, and it is from the leading party amongst these that they are frequently designated Cuthæans (2 K 17[24]). There can be no question of the accuracy of the OT narrative of the originally mixed origin of the Samaritans, but repeated accessions from Judaism (Neh 13[28. 29] ; *Ant.* XI. viii. 2 and 6), probably ultimately outnumbering the original colonists, and the manifest reversion to the pure Semitic type, induce us to believe that the existing Samaritan race has but little connexion with the old Turanian colonists, and is probably now of almost as pure Hebrew blood as the modern Jew.

For their rejection from all participation in the rebuilding of the Temple the Samaritans never forgave the Jews (Ezr 4³·⁴, Neh 2²⁰), and for their attempted hindrance of that work the Jews bore the Samaritans no less a grudge. The breach became irrevocable when a rival priesthood and temple were set up on Gerizim. Jewish and Samaritan tradition agree as to the date of this event, which Josephus sets down wrongly in the time of Alexander the Great and Jaddua the high priest (B.C. 332)—one hundred years too late (*Ant.* XI. viii. 2); but, though his account is clearly mixed with fable, there may still be some historical basis for the extra details he gives. About B.C. 200, during the weak rule of the high priest Onias II. (*d.* B.C. 198), the Samaritans, being then in a flourishing condition, are accused of having harassed the Jews and carried away captives to serve as slaves (*Ant.* XII. iv. 1). In his account of Maccabæan times Josephus continually accuses them of denying all kinship with the Jews, when they see them in suffering and difficulties, and of claiming to be Sidonians (*Ant.* XII. v. 5); but, on the contrary, when good fortune befalls the Jews, they claim to belong to that race, and to derive their descent from Joseph (*ib.* IX. xiv. 3, XI. viii. 6, XII. iv. 5). John Hyrcanus (*c.* B.C. 128) made an expedition against Samaria (*Ant.* XIII. x. 2). After repeated successes against their ally and protector Antiochus Cyzicenus, he took Samaria, ravaged the country, subdued the Cuthæans who dwelt about the temple at Gerizim, and destroyed their temple (*Ant.* XIII. ix. 1). During the period of unrest that followed the deposition of Archelaus (A.D. 6), the Samaritans became so aggressive that they came privately into Jerusalem by night, and, when the gates of the Temple were opened just after midnight, they entered and scattered dead men's bodies in the cloisters to defile the Temple (*Ant.* XVIII. ii. 1). Another incident is later recorded, which led to very serious consequences. A number of Galilæan pilgrims were attacked, and many killed, at Ginea (*Jenin*), the first Samaritan village on the way (*Ant.* XX. vi. 1–3). This led to civil war for a time, then to the intervention of the Roman authorities, and ultimately to a decision in favour of the Jews by Claudius himself (A.D. 51). At a still later period we find the Jews excluding the Samaritans, as also Christians and pagans, from Capernaum, Nazareth, and Sepphoris (Epiphanius, *adv. Hær.* i. 11). Nor was it only in Palestine that the jealousies continued to exist. Alexander and Ptolemy Lagi had taken many Jews and Samaritans to Egypt (*Ant.* XI. viii. 6), and there in Alexandria we read of rivalry and disorders between them (*Ant.* XII. i. 1), the disputes being, as usual, regarding the relative merits of Jerusalem and Gerizim.

Jewish literature is full of manifestations of the same spirit. Ben Sira speaks of 'the foolish folk that dwell at Shechem,' and characterizes them as 'no nation' (Sir 50²⁵·²⁶). Josephus invariably calls them 'Cuthæans,' and will not admit—except sometimes for a purpose—that they are of Hebrew blood. The Rabbis, though hesitating to call them 'Gentiles,' use the same name. Regarding their food, we read: 'Let no man eat the bread of the Cuthæans: for he that eateth their bread is as he that eateth swine's flesh' (M. *Shebhiith* viii. 10; *Bab. Kidd.* 76a). In the matter of gifts and offerings to the Temple, including the half-shekel, the Samaritan was put on the same footing as slaves and heathen (M. *Ab. Zar.* i. 5; Jerus. *Ab. Zar.* i. 4). If a Samaritan were witness to a bill of divorce, that in itself made the document invalid (M. *Gittin* i. 5). Rabban Gamaliel, quite in keeping with the liberal spirit he always shows (cf. Ac 5³⁸), was, however, inclined to accept such

testimony, and at a later period we occasionally meet with a less bitter tone; for, while some of the Rabbis, remembering 2 K 17²⁵·²⁸, called them 'proselytes of the lions,' Rabbi 'Aḳiba was ready to recognize them as true proselytes (Bab. *Kidd.* 75b), while others said it was permitted to have dealings with one who became a true proselyte (Jerus. *Shek.* i. 4). Samaritan wine was universally condemned, but 'the victuals of the Cuthæans are permitted if not mixed with wine or vinegar' (Jerus. *Ab. Zar.* v. 4); and the unleavened bread of the Cuthæans is permitted (Bab. *Kidd.* 76a). Although Samaria is not part of Israel, 'the land, the roads, the wells, and the dwellings of the Cuthæans are clean' (Jerus. *Ab. Zar.* v. 4). An Israelite might circumcise a Cuthæan, but the contrary was not permitted, as it might then be done in the name of Gerizim (Jerus. *Jebamoth* vii. 1). It was permitted to add 'Amen' to a blessing asked by a Cuthæan, but only after hearing the whole blessing (M. *Ber.* viii. 8). Meat slaughtered by a Cuthæan is allowed if an Israelite is present, or if the Samaritan himself eats from it (Bab. *Cholin* 3b). Samaritan literature is, on the whole, less aggressive; but that arises from the fact that we have less of it, and the greater necessity the Samaritan had to stand on the defensive. Still, in every proof they bring forward in favour of their sanctuary as the *one* holy place, there is implied or expressed the idea that the Jew is schismatical, if not heretical. They use the designation 'Israelite' for themselves alone, and refuse it to the Jews. Still, they have no objection to be called 'Samaritans,' which they write שומרי תורה or שומרים—'Guardians of the Law.' (See Letter to Ludolf). They have an intense dislike to Jerusalem, and the bitterness of their hate culminates in their play upon its name, when they describe the Jews as ארורי שלם—'accursed to perfection' or 'perfectly cursed' (*el-Tolidoth*). The more moderate attitude of which we have spoken seems to have been, on the whole, later than the days of the Gospels, and may have been caused by the Samaritans having made common cause with the Jews against Vespasian (*BJ* III. vii. 32). At that time they shared in the Dispersion, and their synagogues were then to be found in Egypt and Rome. At the present moment the relationship between the two races is no closer than in the past. Some twenty years ago, the Samaritans, fearing the extinction of their sect, sought to arrange for intermarriage with the Jews, but this was refused.

3. Religion.—The basis of the Samaritan religion is the Pentateuch, as they read and understand it; and to this they have been as loyal as the Jews to their Law. Since long before the Christian era they have been strongly monotheistic. Not only are they the enemies of images and every visible representation of the Deity, but they have ever resented as strongly as do the Jewish Targums every anthropomorphic representation of God; and, so far as we can judge, they have made no concessions to heathenism. They were, indeed, accused by the Rabbis of worshipping a dove on Gerizim (*Cholin* 6a), and also of worshipping the idols Jacob buried (Gn 35⁴) under the oak of Moreh (*Ber. Rab.* § 81); but these were malicious falsehoods. From the Jewish point of view another offence against the Law was that they pronounced the Sacred Name—*Jahweh*—with its own vowels (Jerus. *Sanh.* x. 1; Bab. *Sanh.* 90). Theodoret seems to confirm this, and tells us that their pronunciation was Ἰαβέ (β=v, as in mod. Greek)—a point of interest is that scholars for grammatical reasons pronounce it in the same manner. For some centuries, however, they have been accustomed to pronounce it *Shima* ('the name'), just as the Jews use *hasshem* in conversation (Letter to Ludolf). In the matter of their ritual orthodoxy we have even the testimony of Josephus; for, when he tells of Jewish fugitives accused of ritual irregularities being received by the Samaritans, he adds that they complained of being falsely accused (*Ant.* XI. viii. 7). To this we may add the remarkable confession of Rabban Simeon, the son of Gamaliel, who says: 'Every command which the Cuthæans keep they observe more strictly than the Israelites' (Bab. *Cholin* 4a). They practise circumcision, and keep the Law strictly. They observe all the Mosaic feasts; and, in accordance with their reading of the Law, they go three times a year to Gerizim for the feasts of Passover, Pentecost, and Tabernacles, and at such times practically the whole community lives in the mountain. Only at the Passover season, however, do they offer sacrifices, and, as the arrangements at that time bring before us much more vividly the occasion of the institution of that feast than the calm order of the Jewish ritual, it claims our attention. The usual order is that seven days before the Passover the whole community camps out on the top of Gerizim in the neighbourhood of the sacred rock, which they regard as the site of their ancient temple. On the evening of the 14th Nisan the whole congregation assembles, and the high priest reads the words of institution in Ex 12[1-12]. Precisely at sunset, as he concludes the sixth verse, a sufficient number of lambs for the community is slain by men dressed in white clothing. Each member of the congregation then marks his forehead with the blood. The wool is removed by scalding with boiling water previously made ready. The bodies are now examined, to make sure that there is no blemish, and thereafter they are spitted and roasted in a pit arranged as an oven. An hour or two later, when they are sufficiently cooked, the Samaritans *standing*, eat *in haste* with their *loins girded*, with *shoes on their feet*, and with *staff in hand*. All that remains, together with the right shoulders and hamstrings previously removed, is carefully gathered up and burned in the night. Early on the morning of the fifteenth day they all return to their duties in the town.

In accordance with the Law, the levirate marriage is practised ; but with the difference, that it is not the brother, but the nearest friend that takes his wife. As among the Sephardic Jews also, a second wife is allowed during the life of the first when she has had no children.

Beyond these things their religious ideas are vague. The Pentateuch is their sole canonical book, and beyond its life they never seem to have passed. They were never called upon to go through a stirring national crisis, like the Jews during the Maccabæan times, and so they never rose to the same vigour and intellectual life. The written sources of their dogma are late, but from these and from Jewish sidelights we can learn something. It is discussed in the Talmud as to whether they are to be classed with the Sadducees in belief, and the Jews seem to have had some ground for thinking so, for they are represented as saying that 'no resurrection is recorded in the Law' (Bab. *Sanh.* 90*b*). Still, the modern Samaritan believes in a resurrection, in the distinction between good and evil spirits, in a judgment, and in the creation from nothing. It is to be remarked, however, that Arabic writers in the Middle Ages tell us of Samaritan sects professing the distinctive beliefs of both Pharisees and Sadducees, so that the opinions of both parties must have been held by individuals at an earlier date. In Jn 4[25] we find that the woman of Samaria looked forward to the coming of a prophet whom she, like the Jews, designated 'the Messiah.' That this word should have been used by her has been regarded as peculiar, since it does not occur in the Law, but in the 1st cent. we find Samaritans familiar with and quoting the prophets (*Mid. Debar.* § 3) ; and, besides, we must see that it would be impossible for a faith like theirs, continually under the pressure of a foreign bondage, to survive without absorbing many of the elements of Jewish eschatology ; and of these the Messianic idea was the most widely spread in the 1st cent., so much so that it was hardly possible for even the Samaritans to escape its influence. It was doubtless in connexion with such a hope that the prophet arose, and tumults occurred which were put down by Pilate, causing him finally the loss of his office (*Ant.* XVIII. iv. 1) ; as it also led Simon Magus to give himself out as some great one (Ac 8[9]). When the Messianic idea took final form, they expected the Messiah's coming in the year 6000 A.M., but did not think

that he should be greater than Moses. Whether he should be of the tribe of Joseph does not appear, but they denied the application of Gn 49[10] (where their reading varies from the MT) as proof that he should spring from Judah. From the Jews they adopted the synagogue system ; and, apart from the feast days kept on Gerizim, all their worship is conducted in *Kenîset es-Sâmiré*, the synagogue of the Samaritans, in the S.W. of the town (Nâblus). The high priest, who is said to be of the tribe of Levi, conducts their services, and, according to the Law, he receives tithes from his people.

4. Literature.—The most ancient and important document the Samaritans possess is the (Hebrew-) Samaritan Pentateuch ; and this they seem to have become possessed of at a very early date—indeed, before the Babylonian (אשורי) alphabet had supplanted the older Hebrew, for, like all the later books of this people, it is written in a character that is now peculiar to them, — the Samaritan alphabet,—but which in itself is nothing more or less than a cursive form of the old lapidary script of Hebrew, Phœnician, and Moabite. Another testimony to their early reception of the Torah is that it is not divided into *parāshahs* like the MT, but, on a totally different principle, independent alike of the Rabbis and the Alexandrian critics, into *ketzîn*. These number in all 962, Genesis containing 250, Exodus 200, Leviticus 134, Numbers 218, and Deuteronomy 160. While the language of this recension of the Pentateuch is Hebrew, it supports in the matter of various readings rather the LXX than the MT, the number of agreements being not less than 2000, while in the ages of the patriarchs it differs from both the LXX and the MT. But more to be considered than all these taken together are *certain variations* that have had an important bearing on their religion. The Jews were wont to accuse the Samaritans of having corrupted the Law ; and the charge was well founded. In Dt 27[4] (cf. also v.[7]) we find the substitution of 'Gerizim' for 'Ebal,' and at the close of the Decalogue in both Ex 20[17] and Dt 5[21] a long passage is inserted—

'And it shall be when the Lord thy God shall bring thee into the land of the Canaanite, whither thou goest in to possess it, thou shalt set up for thyself great stones, and thou shalt plaster them with lime, and thou shalt write upon the stones all the words of this law ; and it shall be when ye pass over Jordan, ye shall set up these stones, which I command you this day, on Mount Gerizim, and thou shalt build there an altar to the Lord thy God, and thou shalt offer upon it sacrifices to the Lord thy God, and thou shalt sacrifice peace-offerings, and thou shalt eat there, and rejoice before the Lord thy God. That mountain is beyond Jordan after the way from the rising of the sun, in the land of the Canaanite, who dwelleth in the West, over against Gilgal, near by the oak of Moreh, over against Shechem.'

This, according to the Samaritan division of the Decalogue, was reckoned the *Tenth Commandment*, and, like the others, of perpetual obligation, so that the Samaritans regarded not only the Temple at Jerusalem, but also the tabernacle at Shiloh, though in Ephraim, and the whole Jewish priesthood after the settlement of the land, as schismatical.

Other books of the OT they do not consider canonical. They do, indeed, have a deep veneration for Job and the Psalms, and they read Joshua and Judges, but they are all regarded as apocryphal.

The synagogue system, which among the Jews led to the formation of the Targums, was also the means of producing an Aramaic-Samaritan Pentateuch (תרגום שמרוני), which, however, Nöldeke dates at not earlier than the 4th cent., though it may contain earlier elements ; and in favour of this it is to be noted that in general it agrees with τὸ Σαμαρειτικόν of Origen. It closely represents the Heb.-Sam. Pentateuch, and in language it differs but little from the Palestinian Aramaic.

Their later works consist of material directly connected with their religion and life as a people. They possess over a dozen volumes, mostly unpublished, which they designate *Tarteel* ('chanting'). These are in Hebrew mixed with Aramaic, and contain the services for the various seasons of the year, and they are probably ancient. Another dozen volumes are made up of commentaries on various portions of the Pentateuch text; and, although these also are written in Hebrew, they are usually accompanied by an Arabic translation. The best known Samaritan commentary is that of Markah, which was published in Europe by Heidenheim in 1896. The author probably lived in the 4th century. In addition to these they possess a few historical works:—*Kitab es-Satir*, a history of the period from Adam to Moses; *et-Tabakh*, an account of judgments which befell the Jews; the Book of Joshua (in Arabic, but probably in parts from a Heb. original), which closely follows the canonical Joshua, but has many apocryphal additions and eight concluding chapters, bringing the history down to the time of Alexander Severus; Chronicle of Abul-Fath; *el-Tolidoth*, a short Hebrew history from Adam till the present high priest, accompanied by an Arabic translation.

So far as MSS are concerned, the only one that, on account of its antiquity, merits our consideration is the jealously guarded Pentateuch roll in Nâblus. It is preserved in a covering of crimson satin in a silver case engraved with a plan of the tabernacle. The roll itself is written on parchment much discoloured by age. The Samaritans claim that it was written by Abishua the son of Phineas, thirteen years after the settlement of the land; but this is incredible, though they show an acrostic made by the thickening of certain letters in the roll itself as proof. Socin thinks it may belong to the 6th cent.; but other scholars with whom the present writer has discussed the question, would carry its date back even to a short time before the Christian era, so that there is a bare possibility of its having been in use when Christ passed through the streets of Shechem: like ordinary synagogue rolls, the MS is written in columns. These are 7 in. wide, and contain 70 to 72 lines. The writing is small, and the letters are of the oldest Samaritan type.

Samaritan books are all un-vowelled, and in their pronunciation of both Hebrew and Aramaic this people differs widely from the Jews and Syrians. The gutturals, which the Galilæans confounded with one another, are altogether omitted by the Samaritans. The vowel system also at first sight seems to have nothing in common with the Massoretic pronunciation, so much so that a recent writer on the subject expresses the opinion that 'it follows certain laws of language as yet unknown to us' (Rosenberg's *Lehrbuch*, p. 11). However, when we come to compare the modern Samaritan pronunciation of both Hebrew and Aramaic with that of the Jews and the Syrians, we see that the former in nearly every detail bears to the latter the same relationship as the vulgar Palestinian Arabic dialects bear to the older classical speech. It thus appears that, in the absence of vowels to preserve the memory of the sounds when Arabic supplanted these languages as the colloquial, and in the absence of any formulated grammar till the year 1400, the Samaritan pronunciation was allowed to go through the same processes of decay as the common sister Semitic dialects on the same soil. A careful consideration of these processes enables us to produce the Samaritan as a valuable testimony to the general accuracy of the Massoretic pointing; while, if we read the Samaritan Targum with the pointing of Onkelos, we shall attain to a very close approximation to the speech of Christ with the woman of Samaria and with the people of Sychar.

5. Relationship of Christ to the Samaritans.— To understand even imperfectly the beauty and tenderness of the attitude of Jesus to this despised race, we must remember that His ministry occurred during the period when the separation of Jew and Samaritan was most absolute, and the bitterness of feeling most intense. Yet they were invariably treated with respect and forbearance by Christ, as also by His Apostles after the Resurrection; and just as His gentleness won the affection and gained the gratitude of publicans and sinners, so also did His treatment of the Samaritans. It was the one Samaritan and not the nine Jews who returned to give thanks (Lk 17^{16}), and who was contented to wait for the official verdict, and the freedom it would bring, that he might continue in the company of Jesus; and all that is related of the conversation at the well, and of the relations with the villagers of Sychar, reveals the same attractiveness and consideration. True it is that at the beginning of His ministry, and when sending out the Twelve, He directed them not to enter into 'any city of the Samaritans' (Mt 10^5); but we can well understand the reason for that, when we see that not even the *inner circle* of the Twelve sufficiently understood the nature of the gospel to be entrusted with such a mission (Lk 9^{54}). We must also bear in mind that Samaria was designated by our Lord as the first circuit, beyond Judæa proper, that He meant to receive the gospel message. In the parable of the Good Samaritan, too (10$^{25-37}$), He has taken and ennobled that name which till His time was almost a synonym for devil (Jn 8^{48}), and which no self-respecting Jew would pronounce—even the lawyer evading it (Lk 10^{37}) when forced to confess that he 'showed mercy on him.' In view of such feelings between the two peoples, it would have been, in any mere man, an act of almost unpardonable rashness to have depicted to a Jewish audience the Samaritan as an example of noble generosity and of disinterested neighbourliness; and not only is this what Christ does, but He goes much further. Priest and Levite are put into the balance and outweighed by this wayfaring stranger, and every later point in the picture is incalculably in favour of the Samaritan. He is in the country of the Jews, in a place of bad repute—*Tala'at ed-dam*, the Ascent of Blood,—in danger from the Jewish people—robbers, friends of the man assisted,—even of insult and rejection by the khan-keeper, and of perhaps being taken and treated as the robber himself. He had every reason for excusing himself. He and his provisions, especially the wine, were impure, and there was every prospect that it would be an ungrateful task. What must we think of the Lord Jesus Christ, who, in opposition to every racial prejudice and purely human feeling, depicts with such beauty the hated Cuthæan, and that just after He had been rejected (Lk 9$^{52-54}$) by the Samaritans in such a manner that the hearts of His disciples were filled with bitter indignation? Controlled by circumstances, or a product of the age in which He lived, could He have risen to this?

See also GERIZIM, JACOB'S WELL, SYCHAR.

LITERATURE.—*Samaritan Pentateuch*, London and Paris Polyglotts; Blayney, Oxford, 1790; Petermann-Vollers, *Pentateuchus Samaritanus*, Berlin, 1872–89; *Samaritan Targum*, Brüll, Frankfurt a. M. 1873–76; Nicholl's *Samaritan Grammar*, London, 1858 (pedantic); Petermann, 'Linguæ Samaritanæ Grammatica,' etc., in *Porta Linguarum Orientalium* series; Rosenberg, 'Lehrbuch' in Hartleben's *Bibliothek der Sprachenkunde* (a compilation, but good); Castelli, *Lex. Heptaglotten*, 1669; Gesenius, *De Pentateuchi Samaritani origine, indole, et auctoritate*, Halle, 1824; Grimm, *Die Samaritaner*, München, 1854; Mills, *Nablus and the Modern Samaritans*, 1864; Kohn, *Samaritanische Studien*, Breslau, 1868, also *Zur Sprache, Litteratur u. Dogma der Samaritaner*, Leipzig, 1876; Nutt, *A Sketch of Samaritan History, Literature, and Dogma*, London, 1874; Brüll, *Zur Gesch. u. Lit. der Samaritaner*, Frankfurt, 1876; Herdenheim, *Bibliotheca Samaritana*; Rappoport, *La Liturgie Samaritaine*, 1901; Montgomery, *The Samaritans*, 1907   WM. M. CHRISTIE.

SAMARITAN, THE GOOD (Lk 10$^{25-37}$).—Jesus had bidden His last farewell to Galilee, and was travelling to Jerusalem (Lk 9^{51}). He had passed through Samaria and reached Judæa, and in some town on the route, probably Jericho, He visited the synagogue,* as He was wont (cf. Lk 4[16]), and discoursed to the congregation. It was customary for the hearers, when the preacher had concluded, to ask him questions,[dagger] and so it happened on this occasion. One of those whose business was the interpretation of the sacred Law, rose and asked, 'Teacher, what shall I do to inherit "eternal life"?' He was no anxious inquirer. He thought to display his superior knowledge, and humble Jesus before the congregation; and his question was a foretaste of the dialectical warfare which awaited Jesus in Jerusalem, and which reached its climax in that succession of encounters with the rulers in the Temple court during the Passion week. Nor was Jesus deceived. 'What stands written in the Law?' He asked, 'how readest thou?' Glad to display his theological proficiency, the lawyer glibly replied, 'Thou shalt love the Lord thy God with thy whole heart, and with thy whole soul, and with thy whole strength, and with thy whole mind, and thy neighbour as thyself.' Jesus accepted the answer: 'Thou hast answered rightly. This do, and thou shalt live.' The lawyer was an astute controversialist, and he perceived a new opening for disputation. 'Neighbour' was defined both by the Law and by the Rabbis as a fellow-Israelite, 'a son of thy people,'[double dagger] and he expected that Jesus would give the word a larger significance, thus exposing Himself to a charge of heresy. He clutched at the opportunity. 'And who,' he asked, 'is my "neighbour"?' Jesus answered with a parable.

The road from Jericho to Jerusalem had a very evil reputation. It wound up barren and rugged hills, infested by brigands, who assailed travellers, robbing and sometimes murdering them; and from those deeds of violence it derived a ghastly name —the Ascent of Blood.[section] It was much frequented. It was the highway between the capital and the prosperous City of Palm-trees; and, moreover, since half of the officiating 'course' lodged at Jericho, where provision was abundant,[||] there were continually priests and Levites passing to and fro. Jesus told how a man, travelling down the Ascent of Blood, was set upon by brigands, plundered, maltreated, and left half-dead. Presently a priest came down the road, and, when he spied the wretch, he 'passed by on the other side.' Next came a Levite, and he behaved with like inhumanity. Then came one riding on an ass, a merchant probably, who often passed that way in the prosecution of his business.[¶] Since the holy men had 'passed by on the other side,' it would have been no marvel had he done the like, especially since he was a Samaritan, one of that hated race with which the Jews had no dealings. But he was moved by the piteous spectacle, and, dismounting, he dressed the sufferer's wounds, according to the medical prescription of that day, with oil and wine;[**] then he mounted him on his beast, and conveyed him to an inn and tended him. Those offices of humanity detained him from his journey, and he rose betimes 'toward the morrow' (ἐπὶ τὴν αὔριον), to push forward. But ere he set out he handed the host two *denarii*, and bade him see to

the unfortunate man until he should be fit for the road. Since a *denarius* was a day's wage,* the two would probably suffice; but in case of need he enjoined that no expense be spared, undertaking to settle the account on his return journey.

'Which of these three,' says Jesus, 'seemeth to thee to have proved "neighbour" to the man that fell in with the brigands?' Only one answer was possible. The lawyer should have replied, 'The Samaritan'; but he could not endure to utter the odious name, and he reluctantly faltered out, 'The one that took pity on him.' 'Go thy way,' said Jesus; 'do thou also likewise.' It was a masterpiece of dialectic. He had avoided entanglement in an unprofitable and perilous controversy, and had forced His adversary to pronounce judgment on himself. See also art. NEIGHBOUR.

LITERATURE. — The standard *Comm.*; the works of Trench, Bruce, Dods, and Taylor on the Parables; Edersheim, *Life and Times*, ii. 234 ff.; Vinet, *Vital Christianity*, p. 508 ff.; *Expositor*, I. vi. [1877] 186 ff.   DAVID SMITH.

SANCTIFY, SANCTIFICATION.—Sanctification is the tr. of ἁγιασμός, which is one of the group of words that includes ἅγιος, and ἁγιάζω, and ἁγιωσύνη. The root idea of the group seems to be 'separation' or 'restricted use' (see HOLINESS). ἁγιασμός denotes primarily a process; but in NT it is used also to describe the state resulting from that process. This wider usage is familiar in our language, and therefore we take 'sanctification' to describe both a state and a process. It is the process by which men are made holy, and it is also the state into which men pass as they become holy. Therefore this article must discuss what state is considered by Jesus Christ to deserve the name 'sanctification,' and what is the process whereby He conceives men are sanctified.

The first fact to be noticed about this entire group of words is that it occupies a meagre place in the teaching of Jesus. The number of times when either of them is put into His lips is very small, and none of these few usages refers to man. ἅγιος is used as follows: He addresses God as 'Holy Father' (Jn 17[11]); He speaks of 'the holy angels' (Mk 8[38] ||); He uses the name 'Holy Spirit' (Mt 12[32] || 28[19], Mk 12[36] 13[11], Lk 12[12], Jn 14[26] 20[22]); He warns against giving 'that which is holy' unto the dogs (Mt 7[6]); and He refers to the abomination that stands 'in the holy place' (24[15]). ἁγιάζω is used of 'the temple that sanctifieth the gift' (Mt 23[17. 19]); and there are three very important usages in Jn 10[36] 17[17. 19]. It occurs also in the Lord's Prayer in the sentence, 'Hallowed be thy name' (Mt 6[9]). This petition suggests that both the ceremonial and ethical aspects of the word were present to our Lord's mind. The 'name' of the Father is to be reverenced. It casts awe upon the worshipping soul. But also the name stands for righteousness. It is a name whose ethical splendour must not be smirched. The same double reference can be traced in His usage of ἅγιος. When Jesus employs these words, He seems to give them their true historical sense as implying (1) a state of consecration to the Divine purposes, and (2) a state of ethical holiness.

ἁγιασμός, the NT word for 'sanctification,' does not occur at all in the recorded sayings of Jesus. But He was constantly speaking about the thing itself. Therefore we are constrained to recognize some special significance in the absence of the familiar words from the Lord's teaching. Probably the explanation is found in the state of religious feeling in His day. ἅγιος is the nearest Greek equivalent of the Hebrew קָדוֹשׁ. This term, with its kindred terms, had acquired a distinct con-

---

* The scene was evidently a synagogue, since His hearers were seated (cf. v.[25]).

[dagger] Cf. Lightfoot and Wetstein on Mt 4[23].

[double dagger] Lv 19[18]; Lightfoot on Lk 10[29].

[section] Jos 15[7]. Jerome, *Ep.* xxvii. *ad Eustoch. Virg.*: 'Locum Adomim, quod interpretatur sanguinum, quia multus in eo sanguis crebris latronum fundebatur incursibus'; on Jer 3[2]: 'Arabas, quæ gens latrociniis dedita usque hodie incursat terminos Palæstinæ et descendentibus de Hierusalem in Hiericho obsidet vias.' Hence, probably, the two brigands who were crucified with Jesus. Cf. Lightfoot on Lk 10[30]; G. A. Smith, *HGHL* p. 265.

[||] Lightfoot on Lk 10[30].

[¶] He was known to the innkeeper, and had good credit (cf. v.[35]).

[**] Cf. Wetstein.

* For a vinedresser (Mt 20[1·16]); for a Roman soldier (Tac. *Ann.* i. 17).

notation. It has been pointed out that the idea of holiness in OT is progressively spiritualized, and receives more and more ethical content. But whilst this is true of OT usage, the Greek period in Jewish history had ushered in a time of reaction in the significance of religious terms. The struggle of pious Jews to resist Hellenizing tendencies threw the emphasis of religion upon keeping the Law. Thus arose the Pharisaic interpretation of piety as rigid obedience to the Law. Under this influence holiness was again interpreted ceremonially instead of morally. When Jesus was born, the religious phraseology of the day was legal rather than ethical. Now this conception of sanctification was the subject of unsparing denunciation by Jesus. One long chapter in Matthew's Gospel gathers up scathing rebukes of those who put the emphasis of religion upon what is external (Mt 23$^{1-36}$; cf. Lk 11$^{39-52}$). In the Sermon on the Mount He said: 'Except your righteousness exceed the righteousness of the scribes and Pharisees, ye shall in no wise enter the kingdom of heaven' (Mt 5^{20}). So that, if Jesus had used the current terms, He would have been understood in the current sense. In order to secure new moral contents for the terms, He had to drop them, and to use other phraseology to describe their true meaning.

A further explanation of the absence of the familiar terms is found in Jesus' method of teaching. His teaching was not doctrinal. He did not express His ideals in formulas, but in pictures of what men ought to be. Instead of reiterating familiar maxims, He minted new precepts for men's daily use. Neglecting the outworn dogmas of the scribes, He uttered sharp calls to men as to what they ought to do. His teaching was 'new,' and was 'with authority' (Mk 1$^{22. 27}$). When we turn to the Epistles, we discover that, though the familiar terms reappear, they reappear in a new form. They have no longer the Pharisaic connotation. They have a new Christian connotation, which lifts them above the highest ethical attainment of OT. The NT writers use OT words with the significance that Jesus Christ has given to the idea they represent.

1. Christ's teaching about sanctification.—i. *HIS TEACHING ABOUT THE IDEAL OF SAINTHOOD.*—Jesus Christ's conception of sanctification started from the holiness of God the Father. He found certain attributes in God that are capable of being the ideal for men. These attributes belong to the Fatherhood of God. He summed up many exhortations in the words, 'Be ye therefore perfect, even as your heavenly Father is perfect' (Mt 5^{48}). This command held out a new ideal of perfection. Hitherto men had found their ideal in various human excellences. Jesus fixed attention upon God the Father. There are many Divine attributes that are inaccessible to men. No man can be perfect even as God is perfect. The omnipotence, omniscience, and omnipresence of God are absolutely beyond human reach. But as 'Father,' God displays certain qualities that may be copied by men; and these qualities unite to form the Christian ideal. Such teaching rested upon the underlying belief of Jesus that man has a capacity for sonship of God, and that he reaches his ideal by realizing his sonship. And Jesus could conceive sonship only in the ethical realm. To give men power to become children of God, is to make them resemble their Father ethically (Jn 1^{12}).

The details of the teaching may be summarized conveniently under some of the leading categories of thought used by Jesus:—(1) *His own example.* He claimed to set forth the moral ideal, because He was the Son of God (Jn 14^6). As the Son, He revealed the Father (Mt 11^{27}, Jn 14$^{9. 10}$); therefore the children of God are those who resemble Him

(Mt 11^{29}). The imitation of Christ is the true sanctification.

(2) *Love.* The central and all-pervading glory of the Divine Fatherhood is love (Mt 5^{45}, Jn 14$^{21. 23}$). The Apostolic phrase 'God is love' (1 Jn 4^8) sums up the irresistible testimony of Jesus to the Father (cf. 1 Jn 3^1 4$^{9. 10}$, Jn 3^{16}). Therefore holy people must be loving. The first demand is for love towards God. To 'love the Lord' is the greatest commandment (Mt 22^{37} ||). The character that lacks this devoted love for the heavenly Father is fatally defective. But Jesus bracketed the commandment to 'love thy neighbour as thyself' with this 'first and greatest' (22^{39} ||); and the parable of the Good Samaritan (Lk 10$^{25-37}$) has been interpreted as teaching that 'charity is the true sanctity' (Bruce). Likeness to the heavenly Father is impossible without the cultivation of a loving spirit (Mt 5$^{43-48}$, Lk 15$^{25-32}$). This love must be unselfish (Lk 14$^{13. 14}$). It must forgive freely and unweariedly (Mt 18$^{21. 22}$). It must not judge (7$^{1. 2}$). It must be full of compassion towards all needy ones, and must find a neighbour in any one requiring assistance (Lk 10$^{24-35}$). Jesus also inculcated the supreme importance of love by His rebukes of its opposites: of lack of compassion (Mt 18$^{23-35}$, Lk 10); of selfishness (Lk 16$^{19-31}$); of inhumanity (Mt 25$^{41-45}$). Equally terrible were His denunciations of Pharisaic injustice to the weak (23$^{4. 14}$ ||).

(3) *Righteousness.* The love of the Father is a holy love. God is the 'righteous Father' (Jn 17^{25}). Jesus came into the world from the Father to save from sins (Mt 11^{19}, Lk 15$^{7. 10. 18}$, Mt 26^{28}, Jn 3$^{16. 17}$). Therefore no man can resemble the Father who does not desire supremely to be cleansed from sin. Likeness to the Father involves complete consecration to His holy purpose, and readiness to be separated from every evil thing (Mt 5^6 13^{43} 18^8 ||). The Christian must seek first the righteousness of the Heavenly Father (6^{33}). His goodness must be manifest in deeds as well as words (7^{21}). He must be pure in heart (5^8). His righteousness must be inward and real, not outward and ceremonial (5^{20} 23$^{25-28}$).

(4) *Life.* Jesus came that men might have life (Jn 10^{10}). Moral perfection is conceived as the true self-development (Mt 25^{46}, Mk 10^{30}). God has made us for Himself; unfailing obedience to the will of God leads to fulness of life (Mt 19^{17}, Jn 17^3). Mutilation is urged in preference to the loss of life (Mk 9$^{43. 45}$ ||). But mutilation is only second best. The moral ideal is to find perfect life (8^{35} ||).

(5) *Citizenship in the Kingdom.* Jesus taught that moral perfection cannot be realized by men in isolation. This is the aspect of sanctification brought out by His teaching about the Kingdom of God. His ideal man is a citizen as well as a son. He must live as a member of a Society, showing those qualities that help to build the City of God (cf. Mt 5$^{9. 13-16. 19}$). Such a recognition of other lives will keep men meek (5^5 11^{29}), and will fill their hearts with humility (18$^{1-6}$ ||).

ii. *CHRIST'S TEACHING ABOUT THE PROCESS OF SANCTIFICATION.*—(1) We note that sanctification is *a process having a definite beginning.* It is not another aspect of natural development. Its history is distinct from the record of physiological and psychological growth. We note the striking saying about His forerunner: 'Among them that are born of women there hath not arisen a greater than John the Baptist: yet he that is but little in the kingdom of heaven is greater than he' (Mt 11^{11}). Here two kingdoms are distinguished: the natural kingdom into which men are 'born of women,' and the Kingdom of heaven. The latter kingdom belongs to a higher order than the former, as the animal kingdom is higher than the vegetable, or as the weakest mammal is greater than the strongest reptile. The babe in the higher kingdom of men is greater than the tiger in the kingdom of animals. So the least in the Kingdom of heaven belongs to a higher order, and has larger possibilities of spiritual development, than the greatest among those 'born of women,' *i.e.* produced by natural birth and growth. This implies that entrance into the Kingdom of heaven is secured by a new principle of life. This necessity is further hinted at in the teaching about defilement proceeding from the heart (15[11]). It is not enough to adorn a life with kind actions, to hang bunches of grapes on a thorn bush (7[16]). Good actions must be the fruit that grows on a good tree (Mt 7[16-18], Jn 15[4]). The tree must be made good; the heart must be cleansed; the river of life must be purified at its source. It will not suffice to build a fine house on a wrong foundation. The hidden principle must be made secure if the life is to be saved (Mt 7[24-27]). These hints prepare us for the demand, 'Except ye be converted, and become as little children, ye shall in no wise enter into the kingdom of heaven' (18[3] ||). Sanctification involves the quickening of a new life in men. The maturing of their physical nature cannot suffice; their spiritual nature must pass through the stages of birth and childhood before it can attain maturity. This teaching finds exact expression in the words addressed to Nicodemus : 'Except a man be born anew, he cannot see the kingdom of God' (Jn 3[3]). Man's destiny is not achieved through his physical birth into a physical kingdom. 'That which is born of the flesh is flesh' (3[6]); therefore no number of reincarnations can produce a spiritual result. Before we can be born into a spiritual kingdom, we must have a second kind of birth corresponding to the kingdom; we must be 'born of the Spirit' (3[5-8]).

(2) A second group of passages hints that sanctification may be *a long process before it is completed*. This is suggested in the parable of the Sower (Mt 13[3], Mk 4[3]); the parable of the Seed as growing up—'first the blade, then the ear, then the full corn in the ear' (Mk 4[28]); and in all the figures of fruit-bearing, because fruit-bearing is the late result of a long process (cf. Jn 15[2], Lk 13[8]). Another set of parables represents men as servants of a long-absent Lord, who have to show diligence in trading with the pounds, fidelity in the use of talents, and patience in watching (Mt 25[14], Lk 19[12], Mt 24[42]). Probably this thought is contained also in the identification of true life with the knowledge of God (cf. Jn 17[3], Mt 11[27]). Such knowledge is not merely an intellectual apprehension; it is a spiritual fellowship. It implies ethical likeness through surrender of the whole being to the Divine will. Such likeness can be secured only through long conformity of the heart and mind and will to God. A pure heart is the organ of such a vision of God (Mt 5[8]).

(3) There are definite statements as to *the means* whereby this ethical likeness to the Father is secured. (a) *By prayer*. Jesus was a man of prayer. There are fifteen references to His prayers in the Gospels. It is specially noteworthy that He betook Himself to prayer when any fierce temptation assailed Him (Lk 5[16] 9[28], Jn 12[27], Mt 26[36] ||), when any work of critical importance had to be undertaken (Lk 6[12], Jn 11[41] 17), or when He was exhausted with toil (Mk 1[35], Mt 14[23]); and that it was while He was praying that He was anointed with the Holy Spirit (Lk 3[21]), and that He was transfigured (9[29]). But it is clear also that He was accustomed to pray on all occasions (cf. 10[21] 11[1] 22[32] 23[46]). It is instructive, therefore, that He urged men to pray (Mt 5[44] 6[6] 26[41] ||, Lk 11[2] 18[1] 21[36]). He encouraged prayer by promising large blessing (Mt 7[7-11], Mk 11[24]). He declared that true prayer 'justified' a man (Lk 18[14]) All these references

seem to make it clear that prayer ministers to our sanctification.

(b) *Self-denial*. Jesus had a very definite philosophy of life; but it was clean contrary to worldly wisdom. He summarized it thus : 'Enter ye in by the narrow gate : . . . for narrow is the gate, and straitened the way, that leadeth unto life' (Mt 7[13. 14] ||). 'Whosoever will lose his life for my sake and the gospel's, shall save it' (Mk 8[35] ||). Self-denial is thus taught not for its own sake, but as the only way to reach self-perfection (16[24] ||). (c) *Good works*. We have noticed the emphasis put by Jesus on works of love and mercy. It must be pointed out now that He taught their sanctifying efficacy. The blessed of the Father, who inherit the Kingdom, have qualified by good works (25[31-40]). The young ruler could be perfect if he would keep the commandments (19[21]), and the lawyer could inherit eternal life in the same way (Lk 10[28]). Several times Jesus promised a reward for obedience, fidelity, and diligence (cf. Mt 25[10. 14-30], Lk 19[12-27], Mk 10[29. 30] ||); and if heavenly rewards are granted to those morally fit, as is taught clearly by the parable of the Pounds (Lk 19), these passages imply that sanctification is advanced by a life of obedience to God's will. (d) *Faith in Christ*. There is a large group of passages in all the Gospels, and there are specially important discourses in John, in which Jesus Christ is offered to men as a means of their sanctification.

(α) Sometimes sanctification is promised to those who copy His example. This is done in the gracious invitation (Mt 11[28-30]). Learning of Jesus, we may become meek and lowly in heart; yoked with Him under the yoke which He wears and which He graciously invites us to share, we may bear our burden easily. It is also taught by His claim to be the one Master whom all are to obey (Mt 23[10]).

(β) Sanctification is bound up with obedience to His teaching. The wise man is one who builds on the words of Jesus (Mt 7[24]). He offered His words as the rock of eternal truth on which men may build for eternity, in place of the shifting sand of opinion and hypothesis which will not continue. Eternity will put the strain of judgment upon the characters we are building; and only those characters resting on the rock of His words will stand the strain (vv.[25-27]). The same truth is taught in the impressive words of Mt 10[32. 33]. To confess Him and His words is the same as building upon them; whilst to be ashamed of them is to refuse to make them the foundation for conduct. The same sentiment is expressed in Jn 5[24]. He that 'cometh not into judgment,' because 'he hath passed out of death into life,' is one in whom the signs of sanctification are recognized. This sanctified man is 'he that heareth my word and believeth him that sent me.'

(γ) Sanctification is secured by union with Jesus as the Son of God. It has been pointed out that 'knowledge of the Father' is one of Jesus Christ's descriptions of sanctification. And a very solemn claim made by Jesus is that 'none knoweth the Father save the Son, and he to whomsoever the Son willeth to reveal him' (Mt 11[27]). The Son willeth to reveal the Father to all, for the very next word is, 'Come unto me all ye that labour' : but there is no relaxing of the claim that men must come to Him and learn of Him if they would know the Father; cf. Jn 6[46] 14[6]. Other conceptions of God may be attained by other means. 'The Father' can be revealed only by One who fulfils perfectly the complementary relationship.

(δ) Separate reference may be made to the discourses in John's Gospel, because these amplify the teaching in the Synoptics, though the germs are found there. We may note the claim of Jesus to be the light of the world (Jn 8[12] 9[5] 12[35. 36. 46]; and cf. 14.[5.9] 3[19]); to be the living water (7[37. 38] 4[14]); to be the bread of God come down from heaven to feed the world (6[32-35. 47-58]). These figures imply that men must follow Him if they would walk in the ways of holiness, and must sustain their life by union with Him, if they would have it strong and healthy. This last means of sanctification is described quite definitely in the words, 'He that eateth my flesh and drinketh my blood, dwelleth in me and I in him' (6[56], cf. 15[1-10]). The words have been interpreted sacramentally, as referring solely to the elements offered to the participants in the Lord's Supper. But such an interpretation is entirely opposed to the spirit of Jesus, and would have been inexplicable to the people addressed. And though an allusion to the Lord's Supper as a 'means of grace' need not be denied (cf. Mt 26[26-28] ||), it is plain that our Lord was thinking of a spiritual union between Himself and His followers, maintained by their faith. Another significant passage occurs in 8[31-38]. It has affinity with passages emphasizing the importance of His words (vv.[31. 38]). But it passes on to the statement, 'Ye shall know the truth, and the truth shall make you free.' This is explained to mean freedom from sin (v.[34]); therefore it implies sanctification. And as 'the truth' is changed in v.[36] to 'the Son,' this is another direct claim on the part of Jesus to be our Sanctification (cf. 14[6] 15[3. 4. 10]). It leads us naturally to the very important text 17[17-19]. Jesus prayed for His disciples, 'Sanctify them in the truth : thy word is truth. . . . For their sakes I sanctify myself, that they themselves also may be sanctified in truth.' 'Sanctify' seems to be used here with its full meaning. The idea of consecration is not absent (cf. v.[18] and RVm) ; but vv.[14-16] prove that the ethical significance is prominent. This sanctification is secured 'in truth.' The truth is identified with 'thy word,' which has been given to the disciples by Jesus (v.[14]), partly by His words (14[10]), and partly by His character and example (11[4] 14[9]). The thought seems to be that the disciples are to be sanctified by abiding in this revelation, and by being led farther and farther into it. 'The "truth" . . . is (as it were) the element into which the believer is introduced and by which he is changed. The "truth" is not only a power within him by which he is moved ; it is an atmosphere in which he lives. The end of the truth is not wisdom, which is partial, but holiness, which is universal' (Westcott, *in loco.*). This teaching finds more complete expression throughout chs. 14-16. The disciples must abide in Christ, who is the true Vine, if they would bear much fruit (15[1-8]). When the Master is gone, He will send another Comforter, the Spirit of Truth, who will guide 'into all truth' (14[16. 17. 26] 15[26] 16[13-15]). They are in the truth already ; but they will be guided into its deeper recesses by the Spirit of truth. Thus they will be sanctified, knowing the Father more perfectly as He is revealed in the Son (16[14]), and bearing much fruit through this knowledge (15[5]). All their consecration of themselves to the work to which their Master sent them must move within the sacred sphere of 'the truth.'

(ε) One sentence in this prayer is very valuable for our purpose, 'For their sakes I sanctify myself, that they themselves also may be sanctified' (Jn 17[19]). Jesus Christ's sanctification of Himself is primarily His devotion of Himself to the Father's will. His sanctification was unique in that there never was any refusal of that will as it was made known to Him. But such a refusal was always possible whilst His earthly life lasted. In that sense Jesus had to be progressively sanctified. He had not fulfilled the entire will of His Father until He could say upon the cross, 'It is finished' (19[30]). Therefore He had to continue sanctifying Himself until then. The immediate reference of the words in the prayer seems to be to His death. The prayer is the renewal of His surrender. Again He takes up His cross. He is willing to die, in obedience to the Father's will, that the disciples may be sanctified. Two points must be noticed. (1) This complete surrender to the Father's will, 'obedience even unto the death of the cross,' makes Jesus the absolutely perfect example for our sanctification (Ph 2[5-8]). (2) But also there is a distinct reference to His death as helping to secure the sanctification of His disciples. This hint is not solitary. It gathers other words to itself. 'I, if I be lifted up from the earth, will draw all men unto myself' (Jn 12[32]). This drawing is part of the process of sanctification. 'Except a grain of wheat fall into the earth and die, it abideth by itself alone ; but if it die, it beareth much fruit' (12[24]). By dying Jesus will become a fruitful Personality in the world, producing 'much fruit' in His disciples. 'This is my blood of the covenant, which is shed for many' (Mk 14[24]). The New Covenant is written on men's hearts. It is concerned with a spiritual sanctification as distinguished from one that is merely ceremonial. Jesus connects His death with this New Covenant as a means of securing sanctification 'for many.' The good shepherd giveth his life for the sheep' (Jn 10[11]). This sacrifice by the Shepherd ensures that the lost sheep are found, and being 'found' is one of Jesus Christ's words for at least the beginnings of sanctification (Lk 15[5. 9. 32]). These sayings make it certain that Jesus thought of His death as playing an important part in the process whereby sin's prisoners are delivered, and are set forth upon the road to holiness.

At the same time the reference of Jn 17[19] cannot be confined to His death, if only because His sanctification of Himself in His death was but the perfect flower of a life that was one long sanctification. His death cannot be isolated from His life. He came into the world to save sinners ; and His entire earthly experience ministered to that salvation. At each critical stage He sanctified Himself : the act of the critical moments reflected His daily temper. It is this continued sanctification, culminating in His death, that is the means of the sanctification of His disciples. See, further, on the sanctification of Christ, art. CONSECRATE, CONSECRATION, in vol. i.

(ζ) The passages quoted have led us already to the teaching of Jesus that our sanctification is 'through the Holy Spirit.' Although this teaching is developed in John, it is not absent from the Synoptic tradition. The unpardonable sin is blasphemy against the Holy Spirit—called 'an eternal sin' (Mk 3[29] ∥). Luke's Gospel substitutes 'give the Holy Spirit' for 'give good things' (Lk 11[13], cf. Mt 7[11]). All the Synoptists concur in ascribing to Jesus the promise, 'The Holy Spirit shall teach you what you ought to say' (Lk 12[12], Mt 10[20], Mk 13[11]). Moreover, a large place is given to the Spirit in the sanctification of Jesus. His miraculous birth is ascribed to the Spirit (Mt 1[18], Lk 1[35]). The descent of the Spirit upon Jesus at His baptism was the Father's anointing in response to the Son's consecration (Mk 1[10. 11] ∥). It was the Spirit that drove Him into the wilderness to be tempted (Mk 1[12] ∥). Jesus returned to His work 'in the power of the Spirit' (Lk 4[14]), and He claimed to fulfil the prophecy, 'The Spirit of the Lord is upon me' (4[18]). In answer to the charge that He cast out devils by Beelzebub, He asserted that He cast them out 'by the Spirit of God' (Mt 12[28]). These texts furnish considerable material for a doctrine of sanctification through the Spirit.

But the doctrine is stated very clearly in Jn 14-16. The Holy Spirit is described as the *alter ego* of Jesus : He will do for the disciples, after their Master's departure, what the latter has done for them during His earthly life (Jn 14[16-18]). The Spirit of truth will abide with the disciples and will be in them (14[17]). He will teach them (14[26]), and will guide them into all truth, declaring to them things that are to come (16[13]). He will also convict the world of sin, of righteousness, of judgment (16[8]). The promise of the Spirit is the consolation offered by Jesus in view of His approaching departure (16[7]) ; and His coming will secure their loyalty and their development. Indeed, it may be said that the language of Jesus suggests that the Holy Spirit will be Himself returning in His glorified spiritual nature, and continuing in more complete form the work He has begun in the disciples during His ministry.

2. Christ and sanctification in the NT outside the Gospels.

(1) *The teaching of St. Peter.*—The Petrine conceptions are simple and practical. 1 Peter exhorts to the practice of various virtues that go to make up the Christian character. The starting-point for Christian sanctification is entirely reminiscent of the teaching of Jesus : it is found in the obligation of Christians as children of a holy Father, whose holiness constrains theirs (1 P 1[14. 15. 16]). The attainment of holiness is called 'salvation' (1[5. 9]) ; and 'the two pillars of salvation are the sufferings and death of Christ and the resurrection and exaltation of Christ' (Beyschlag). He is the Son of God whose resurrection 'begat us again' (1[3]). He is the Lamb whose offering has redeemed Christians from their old sins (1[18. 19]). He is 'the chief corner-stone' of that temple of God in which Christians are placed as living stones (2[5. 6]). He is the Example for all who are suffering (2[21]) : especially has He shown us the right attitude to sin by His suffering for sins (2[22-24]). By giving Himself to die for us, He has become the Shepherd and Bishop of our souls (2[25]). He is 'the Lord' who is to be revered in our hearts (3[15]). He is the adorable Saviour whose name is potent enough to secure our devotion (2[13] 4[14]). Finally, He is the coming One, whose appearing will consummate the purposes of God, and will perfect us in salvation (1[7] 5[10]). Thus Jesus Christ focusses all Christian effort and hope and faith upon Himself. The Christ who lived, died, and rose again, and was exalted—the Christ of the Gospels, whom Peter had known (1[3. 8])—is the Divine original for our sanctification, and is the Divine Mediator through whom our deliverance from sin is accomplished.

(2) *The teaching of St. John.*—It is to be noted that St. John makes very slender use of the ἅγιος group of words. In this he is like his Master. In his First Epistle 'sanctify' and 'sanctification' do not occur. 'Holy' is used only once, and then in reference to God (1 Jn 2[20]). In Revelation 'holy' is found frequently. It describes God Almighty (4[8]), Jesus Christ (3[7] 6[10]), the City of God (11[2] 21[2. 10] 22[19]), men (22[11]). Also in Revelation 'saints' is constantly used to describe believers in Jesus Christ. But though the more usual words are absent from the Epistle, it is a passionate plea for sanctification in Christ. John describes sanctification under such phrases as 'walking in light' (1[7] 2[11]), 'not sinning' (2[1] 3[6] 5[18] [the idea of a prevailing habit being prominent]), 'keeping his commandments' (2[3] 3[22. 24] 5[2. 3]), 'overcoming the world' (5[4. 5], cf. 2[13. 14] 4[4], and Rev 2[7. 11. 26] 3[5. 12. 21] 12[11] 21[7]), 'having life' or 'having eternal life' (2[25] 3[14. 15] 5[11. 12. 13. 16. 20], and cf. Rev 2[7. 10] 3[5] 13[8] 17[8] 20[12. 15] 21[6. 27] 22[1. 2. 14. 17. 19]). The core of sanctification is love (4[16-19]), manifested toward God (2[15] 4[20] 5[1. 2]), and towards brethren (2[10] 3[10-18] 4[7-12. 20. 21]). This sanctification is connected intimately with the Person and work of Jesus Christ. He is the propitiation for sins, through whom believers are forgiven, and by whose blood they are cleansed from sin (1[7-22] 4[10]). He is the Advocate upon whom we may rely for help in the struggle with sin (2[1]). He is the Ideal towards whom all Chris-

tian effort must be directed ($3^{3.\ 16}$ 4^{17}). He is the Son of the Father, whose presence in the world manifests the Father's love (3^{16} $4^{9.\ 10.\ 14.\ 16}$), and through whom believers may become possessed of the Father (2^{23} 4^{15}). So He brings to men that eternal life which makes sin impossible (3^9 5^{18}); and He communicates to them that eternal love which is the very essence of goodness because it is the essence of God ($4^{12.\ 16}$). So intimate is this connexion between Christ and sanctification, that the object of His manifestation is declared to be 'to take away sins' (3^5), and 'to destroy the works of the devil,' which are 'sins' (3^{7-10}). It is clear, therefore, that St. John, as well as St. Peter, conceives Christ's redeeming work under the category of sanctification, and also conceives sanctification as possible only through faith in Christ. Both of them view sanctification as a state into which the believer is introduced by an initial act of faith in Christ, through whom he is begotten of God (1 P $1^{3.\ 18.\ 23}$ $2^{3.\ 9}$, 1 Jn 1^9 5^1); but it is also a state which has to be progressively realized by abiding union with Christ (1 P 1^5 2^{11} 5^{10}, 1 Jn 1^7 2^1 3^2).

(3) *The teaching of St. Paul.*—This may be summed up under the chief categories used by St. Paul to describe Jesus Christ's relation to men.

(*a*) *Jesus Christ as the second Adam.*—St. Paul thought of Adam as the pioneer of the race; and he could not escape the responsibility of pioneers. The entire subsequent history of the race is influenced by the course taken by the first man. His sin caused a divergence from the path of rectitude, which grew wider as the race progressed, because the initial direction was wrong. Jesus Christ was introduced into the world as a new pioneer. He was not an ordinary child of the race. He did not inherit the entail of bias to evil. 'The first man is of the earth, earthy' (1 Co 15^{47}). He was the child of an animal ancestry, and was weighted by animal instincts: to him holiness was only a possibility. 'The second man is of heaven.' His antecedents were spiritual. With Him holiness was the instinct, and evil was only a possibility. So He gave a new start in the direction of holiness. He stopped the race's drift from God, and He began a new movement Godward (Ro 5^{12-21}, 1 Co $15^{20-26.\ 45-49}$). Therefore all who become followers of Jesus Christ are rescued from the fatal effects of Adam's sin. They are led into the right road and are under the direct influence of the Spirit of God (Ro 8^{12-17}). Thus they are being sanctified in accordance with the will of God, and will be brought at last to the perfect state He has designed for them (cf. Ro 5^{21} 8^{17}, 1 Co $15^{49.\ 54}$).

(*b*) A corollary from the previous thought is that men may be '*in Christ.*' The second Adam is more than a leader of a redeemed race. He is the Head of a new humanity, which secures its life from Him by vital communion with Him. He brought new spiritual energy into the world: this energy can be communicated to all who are united to Him by faith. The bonds between the first Adam and the race were physical and mechanical; those between the second Adam and the race are spiritual and personal (cf. Jn 5^{21-29}, 1 Co 15^{45}, Eph $1^{6.\ 13}$). This state of union between Christ and the believer is described by St. Paul under the phrase 'in Christ'; and it is mentioned as a condition of sanctification (1 Co 1^2 6^{11}; cf. Ro $1^{6.\ 7}$, Eph $1^{1.\ 4.\ 7.\ 11.\ 13}$ $2^{10.\ 13}$, Ph 1^1, Col 1^2). The idea is the Master's (cf. 'I am the vine, ye are the branches,' Jn 15^5): He connected it with sanctification (15^{4-6}). St. Paul emphasized this message. Thus we are 'complete in him' (Col 2^{10}). Every human being comes into the world as a possibility. A process of involution must go forward, by which the germinal life will absorb from its environment those elements that minister to its development. Our moral possibili-

ties can be realized only when we are 'in Christ.' The soul that lives without Him is stunted, or maimed, or becomes a moral freak. The soul that lives 'in him' becomes 'complete.' All the fulness that can realize our possibilities is gathered into Him (Col 2^9). He is the way in which men must 'walk' who would attain to holiness, the plant in which men must be 'rooted' who would bear much fruit, the plan according to which men's lives must be 'built up' if they are to become temples of God (Col $2^{6.\ 7}$ 1^{23}, and cf. Jn 15^{1-10} 14^6).

(*c*) Another category used by St. Paul is *Jesus Christ's death and resurrection as the source of the believer's renewal.* This thought has affinities with the preceding one. But it shows, from another standpoint, how intimately the Apostle connects our sanctification with Christ. The teaching is developed in Ro 6; it occurs also in Ro 8^{11}, Gal 2^{20}, 2 Co $5^{14.\ 15}$, Col $2^{12.\ 13}$ 3^{1-4}. The believer is associated with the Saviour in His death and resurrection. These crises are not only an ideal for the Christian, but also an experience which in some real spiritual sense he shares with his Lord. By them Jesus Christ became the Conqueror of sin and death. The believer identifies himself with Jesus Christ in the spiritual significance of these tremendous events: then he becomes 'dead unto sin and alive unto God,' though actually he is rather dying than dead to sin, and though the physical process of dissolution has still to be faced—but without its sting. This union with Christ secures the imparting of eternal life, and makes the believer a 'new creature' (2 Co 5^{17}), who is renewed in holiness. Such teaching harmonizes with the demand of Jesus for a new birth (Jn 3^3).

(*d*) A fourth category is *the work of the Spirit using the truth* '*as it is in Jesus*' *as His instrument in sanctification.* This is another of the ideas of Jesus emphasized by St. Paul. The Pauline Epistles connect sanctification with the work of the Holy Spirit (cf. especially Ro 8, 1 Co 2. $3^{16.\ 17}$ 12). 'The Spirit's function is, before all things, to help the Christian to be holy' (Bruce, *St. Paul's Conception of Christianity*, p. 248). The instrument used by the Spirit in sanctifying men is the revelation made in Jesus Christ. This had been foretold by the Master (Jn 16^{14}); St. Paul sees His word fulfilled in all the work of the Spirit. 'The Lord' and 'the Spirit' are identified sometimes (2 Co $3^{17.\ 18}$), and the Spirit dwelling in the heart sanctifies through Christ dwelling in the heart (cf. Eph 3^{17}, Ro $8^{9.\ 10}$, 2 Ti 1^{14}). Man is pictured as a shrine in which the Spirit dwells. This 'temple of the Holy Spirit' must be kept from all defilement, and must ever be made worthier of its Divine guest (1 Co $3^{16.\ 17}$ $6^{19.\ 20}$, 2 Co 6^{16}).

(*e*) *The Church as the Body of Christ* is an important Pauline conception. It bears upon the problem of sanctification, inasmuch as the moral health of each individual member is influenced by the condition of the body (1 Co 12^{12-27}, Eph 1^{23} 4^{16}, Col 2^{19}). The Apostle does not contemplate Christians remaining outside the visible Church, and he always assumes that a Christian's sanctification will be perfected within its fellowship. This does not imply any sacramental conception of sanctification. It rests upon the conviction that the Church is indwelt by the living Christ (Eph 1^{23}, Col 1^{24}). Therefore all believers who remain living members of the Church maintain a vital union with their Lord, through means of His own appointing. This secures their due spiritual development.

(*f*) Finally, we may note St. Paul's thought of *Jesus as 'Lord.'* This name was used by the early Church to express their faith about Jesus. All the NT books reflect the usage, except the Epistles of John. But, owing perhaps to the circumstances of his conversion (Ac 9^5), the designation dominates

St. Paul's thought of Jesus to a remarkable degree. It carries with it an obligation to acknowledge His sovereignty over all our life. Our sanctification is secured by implicit obedience to His commands, and by close imitation of His example.

3. Church History.—It only remains to offer a very brief suggestion as to the historical development of the idea of sanctification in its relation to the Person and work of Jesus Christ. Four outstanding modifications of the idea may be mentioned.

(1) The first is *the monastic idea of sanctification*. It had affinities with tendencies that are native to man; and it gained ground in the 4th cent., when multitudes of semi-converted pagans were pressing into the Church. Although it took its laws from the recorded life and teaching of Jesus Christ, it cannot be recognized as a fruit of vital union with Him. Rather it must be regarded as a product of a restless age of rapid enlargement, reacting upon the longing for reposeful communion with God. During this time the Church's interest in Christ was academic rather than practical, theological rather than religious. Thus men were left to seek holiness by methods of their own devising.

(2) The second idea of sanctification is *the mediæval*. This has many points of union with the monastic; but it shows a much closer relation to Christ. The restlessness had given place to torpor. This drove earnest souls back to Jesus. Many of the monastic evils permeated Europe, and there was very little imitation of Christ amongst the masses of the people. But the mediæval idea of holiness is characterized by a growing devotion to the Lord Jesus, which found expression sometimes in such fervent hymns as those of Bernard, sometimes in such service of the poor as was nobly carried through by Francis of Assisi, and sometimes in such seeking after liberty as has immortalized Wyclif.

(3) The third idea of sanctification is connected with *the Reformation*. That movement placed all the emphasis upon Christ's work for us. One result was the upgrowth of an idea of sanctification as something objective. It was almost identified with 'justification.' Christians are sanctified by receiving the robe of righteousness from Jesus Christ.

(4) The fourth or *modern idea of sanctification* tends to place the emphasis upon Christ's work in us. Sanctification is much more subjective. This is a development which should be welcomed. But care must be taken lest the reaction from a too objective idea of sanctification by Christ leads to a too subjective idea of sanctification in Christ which fails to give the NT emphasis to both aspects of Christ's work.

It may be pointed out that the modern idea of sanctification in Christ has been approached from the standpoint of the work of the Holy Spirit. What is known as the 'Keswick School' has rendered valuable service by calling attention to the Personality of the Holy Spirit, and to His power to sanctify the human soul. But it must be remembered that the Holy Spirit is Christ's *alter ego*, Rightly understood, this modern development leads us to the Pauline position, that 'Christ Jesus is made unto us . . . sanctification' (1 Co 1³⁰).

LITERATURE.—The usage of terms may be studied in artt. 'Holiness' and 'Sanctification' in Hastings' *DB*. For general reference, cf. Beyschlag, *NT Theol.*; Stevens, *The Christian Doctrine of Salvation* and *The Theology of NT*; Harnack, *What is Christianity?*; Forrest, *The Authority of Christ*; the Comm. in the *Internat. Critical Commentary* series. The teaching of Christ is examined by Bruce in *The Kingdom of God* and *The Training of the Twelve*; Wendt, *The Teaching of Jesus*; Du Bose, *The Gospel in the Gospels*; Denney, *The Death of Christ*; and Comm. on the Gospels by Swete, Godet, and Westcott. Bruce discusses the Pauline teaching in *St. Paul's Conception of Christianity*; cf. the Comm. of Lightfoot, Westcott, Delitzsch, and Godet, which are most suggestive; also Haupt on *First Epistle of St. John*. Some of the Sermons in Inge's *Faith and Knowledge* deal with Sanctification in a fresh manner. Valuable discourses on the psychological and physiological aspects are contained in Coe's *Education in Religion and Morais* and *The Spiritual Life*. Amongst modern devotional books, Horton's *The Open Secret* and Gordon's *Quiet Talks on Power* may be highly recommended. The teaching of an influential modern school is contained in 'Addresses on Holiness' (Star Hall Convention, Manchester). Ref. may also be made to C. H. Spurgeon, *The Messiah*, p. 579; H. W. Webb-Peploe, *Calls to Holiness* (1900); W. L. Watkinson, *The Blind Spot* (1899), p. 57; A. J. Gordon, *Yet Speaking* (1897), p. 9.

J. EDWARD ROBERTS.

SAND (ἄμμος).—Sand, which, however closely packed and hard, seems almost to melt at the touch of water, is a foundation on which only a fool would build (Mt 7²⁶). St. Luke in the parallel passage gives ἐπὶ τὴν γῆν, 'on the earth' (6⁴⁹). The surface of the earth, baked hard in the heat, goes swiftly to soft mud when the rains come.

W. EWING.

SANDAL, SHOE.—A covering for the feet was rendered necessary by the burning heat of the ground as well as by the presence of stones and thorns. Such protection was especially required by men on a journey, by shepherds on the hills, and by peasants when cutting wood or collecting thorns for fuel. An Oriental shepherd with bare feet and a crook-headed staff is one of the ignorant traditions of Western sacred art. The sandal consisted of a thick sole of leather attached to the foot by thongs of the same material. The transition to the shoe form was marked by a slipper-like cover and a supporting band behind the heel, which latter, however, the wearer often preferred to press down when walking.

In the East the foot can only be alluded to apologetically, and reference to the shoe is one of the commonest expressions of contempt. To be unworthy to unloose the **latchet** of His shoe was an intense repudiation of all thought of comparison with Christ (Jn 1²⁷). As the shoe was in immediate contact with the common ground, it was removed at the entrance to houses and sacred buildings. As socks are not usually worn in the East, dust is effectively removed either by taking off the shoe and beating it on a stone, or by projecting the foot with the toes bent upwards so that the dust may fall out from the open heel of the shoe (Mt 10¹⁴).

The Roman soldier, like the Eastern shepherd, had nails in the shoe to prevent slipping, and thus the missionary symbolism of Eph 6¹⁵ meant determination as well as direction.

G. M. MACKIE.

SANHEDRIN.—The supreme council and high court of justice in Jerusalem during the Greek and Roman periods.

1. Names and Composition.—(*a*) *Of the whole body*: (α) Greek: (1) συνέδριον, so first, in point of historical reference, in Jos. *Ant.* XIV. ix. 3–5, and thereafter frequent in Josephus and NT. (2) γερουσία, first, in point of reference, in *Ant.* XII. iii. 3; frequent in OT Apocrypha: once in NT, Ac 5²¹ (cf. below). (3) βουλή, fairly frequent in Josephus, especially in the *BJ*, but NT never uses βουλή in this sense, though βουλευτής is used of Joseph of Arimathæa in Mk 15⁴³ and Lk 23⁵⁰. (4) πρεσβυτέριον, Lk 22⁶⁶, Ac 22⁵. (5) Josephus also uses τὸ κοινόν, or κοινὸν τῶν Ἱεροσολυμιτῶν, esp. in the *Vita*, with special reference to the Sanhedrin. (β) Hebrew: (1) In the Talmudic literature the commonest word is סַנְהֶדְרִין, a transliteration of συνέδριον, also written סַנְהֶדְרֵי, and even סַנְדְרִין, from which again plurals were formed, סַנְהֶדְרִיּוֹת, or סַנְהֶדְרָאוֹת (cf. Jastrow, *Dict. of Talmud*, 1005). Variations are סַנְהֶדְרִין גְּדוֹלָה and (2) סַנְהֶדְרִין שֶׁל שִׁבְעִים וְאֶחָד. (3) On Hasmonæan coins חֶבֶר 'collegium,' is associated with the reigning high priest, and presumably designates the Sanhedrin.

These names throw light upon the composition and functions of the court. συνέδριον suggests a court of justice, and so, still more explicitly, does בֵּית דִּין. γερουσία is a term applied only to aristocratic councils, and the Hasmonæan חֶבֶר suggests an aristocratic body associated with the monarch.*

(b) *Of its component parts.* Quite as suggestive are the names of the various classes of members of the court. The principal expressions, ignoring minor variations, are οἱ ἀρχιερεῖς, οἱ ἄρχοντες, οἱ πρεσβύτεροι, οἱ δυνατοί, οἱ πρῶτοι, οἱ γνώριμοι, οἱ γραμματεῖς. Some of these terms are interchangeable, or nearly so, and they fall into three main classes. (1) Most important of all were the ἀρχιερεῖς, the chief priests, the members of the sacerdotal aristocracy. In Josephus and NT they are almost invariably mentioned first when the names of the classes composing the Sanhedrin are given (cf. Mt 27⁴¹; Jos. *BJ* II. xvii. 2, and frequently). Often they are the only class particularly mentioned (cf. Mk 14⁵⁵ οἱ ἀρχιερεῖς καὶ ὅλον τὸ συνέδριον). The high priest was president of the court according to Josephus and NT (cf. Ac 5¹⁷, which testifies not only to the presidency of the high priest, but also to the fact that the priestly party was Sadducee; cf. also Jos. *Ant.* XIV. ix. 3–5, and other passages from both sources). This is in agreement with the general constitution of the post-exilic Jewish community, in which civil as well as religious authority was in the hands of the high priest. The priestly nobility were the leading persons in the community, and they were the most conspicuous members of the Sanhedrin. See CHIEF PRIESTS, HIGH PRIEST. The ἄρχοντες may be roughly identified with the ἀρχιερεῖς as the 'rulers' of the community. Occasionally they are mentioned where one would expect ἀρχιερεῖς: so frequently in Josephus (cf. Ac 4⁵ τοὺς ἄρχοντας καὶ τοὺς πρεσβυτέρους καὶ τοὺς γραμματεῖς, v.⁸ ἄρχοντες τοῦ λαοῦ καὶ πρεσβύτεροι ‖ v.²³ οἱ ἀρχιερεῖς καὶ οἱ πρεσβύτεροι). Very occasionally, however, the ἄρχοντες are mentioned alongside of the ἀρχιερεῖς (cf. Lk 23¹³), showing that the term might be used loosely for 'leaders' or 'rulers.' (2) πρεσβύτεροι = זְקֵנִים, in the first instance a general name for the principal men of the community, and so, apparently, a general designation of members of the Sanhedrin (cf. πρεσβυτέριον). But in actual practice it describes those members who were neither ἀρχιερεῖς nor γραμματεῖς. The πρεσβύτεροι made common cause with the ἀρχιερεῖς against the γραμματεῖς, i.e. they belonged in general to the Sadducee party (cf. Ac 23¹⁻¹⁴). With this class may be identified the δυνατοί, πρῶτοι, or γνώριμοι (unless qualified in some way, as, γνώριμοι τῶν Φαρισαίων). Josephus frequently uses δυνατοί along with ἀρχιερεῖς, evidently as the equivalent of πρεσβύτεροι. They were the secular nobility of Jerusalem, closely allied to the sacerdotal aristocracy. (3) οἱ γραμματεῖς, the scribes, a class which hardly requires description here. In the main they formed the Pharisee element in the Sanhedrin, though individual members of the other classes may have been Pharisees, and many Pharisees, adhering to the scribal party, were not themselves professional scribes. See SCRIBES.

These names indicate with sufficient clearness the general character and composition of the court. It was an aristocratic assembly and high court of justice, in which, alongside of the priestly nobility

---

* Ac 5²¹ presents a certain difficulty in its use of the phrase τὸ συνέδριον καὶ πᾶσαν τὴν γερουσίαν. According to this, the γερουσία would have a wider meaning than συνέδριον, whereas in OT Apocrypha it is the regular word for συνέδριον. The identity of the two terms can hardly be doubted, as there is no evidence of the existence of any other court to which the name γερουσία might be applied. As it is unnatural to take καί in an explanatory sense (=*i.e.*) here, it must be supposed that the author used one of the words loosely, regarding συνέδριον as an inner circle within the general court. Possibly he wished to emphasize the fact that on this occasion not only the necessary quorum but the whole council of 71 members was summoned.

and the noble families outside the priestly circle, representatives of the more numerous Pharisee party found a place, the Sadducee element, however, retaining the weight of influence.

As to the method of appointment to the Sanhedrin, nothing definite can be gathered from the Greek sources. According to the Mishna, new members were appointed by the court itself. At first, membership was confined to the aristocratic families. Subsequently the political rulers of the country seem to have appointed members by their own authority in some cases at least (cf. Salome's introduction of a Pharisee element).

The Greek sources agree in giving one picture of the Sanhedrin, while the Mishnic representation is radically different. That the representations are mutually irreconcilable, and that that of the Greek sources is preferable in all respects, is now generally recognized by scholars, and the point requires to be stated rather than argued here. According to the Greek sources, as appears from the above, the Sanhedrin was composed of chief priests, elders, and scribes, and was presided over by the high priest. The chief priests and elders belonged in general to the Sadducee party, while the scribes formed the Pharisee element, which, however influential among the people, was seldom in the ascendant in the Sanhedrin. The Sanhedrin was thus a political assembly and court of justice, representing in the main the aristocratic elements in the Jewish community. According to the Mishnic literature, on the other hand, it was a court of Rabbis, presided over by the leading Rabbi of the time, in which the priestly element as such does not appear, while the Sadducees are mentioned only as heretics to be refuted. The presiding Rabbi bears the title *Nasi* (otherwise a political title), and another, apparently the vice-president, is called *Ab-beth-din*. It was an ecclesiastical rather than a political assembly. The irreconcilability of the two representations is most marked in the answer they give to the question, Who was the President of the Sanhedrin? We have lists of Rabbis filling the offices of *Nasi* and *Ab-beth-din* during the two centuries preceding the destruction of Jerusalem, whereas the Greek sources furnish explicit evidence that during this period the high priest presided. Where individual names are mentioned in both sources the contradiction is very evident: *e.g.* Gamaliel was president according to the Mishna, but in Ac 5³⁴ he appears simply as Φαρισαῖος ὀνόματι Γαμαλιήλ. The Greek sources are contemporary, while the Mishna is late and was compiled under totally changed conditions. The account given in the Greek sources accords with all that is known of the constitution and history of the Jewish community, from the Maccabæan revolt to the destruction of Jerusalem. Further, the evidence they furnish, while perfectly explicit, is largely incidental, proceeding from no theory, but simply reflecting the actual state of affairs. There is no trace of 'tendency,' and no motive for misrepresentation. On the other hand, the Mishnic account is true only of the reconstituted Sanhedrin which sat at Jamnia after the destruction of Jerusalem and the disappearance of the old aristocratic and Sadducee element. The character of this Sanhedrin, which bore little more resemblance to the older court than the 'Sanhedrin' which Napoleon endeavoured to establish, was transferred to the assembly of which we have accurate descriptions in the contemporary Greek sources. How far the Mishna has preserved reliable traditions on points of detail connected with the Sanhedrin is not easy to determine. Considerable use is often made of it even by those who admit the superiority of the Greek sources (cf. Bacher, art. 'Sanhedrin' in Hastings' *DB*). In view, however, of the chasm which the destruction of Jerusalem made in the constitution and history of Judaism, and the radically false conception of the Sanhedrin which appears in the Mishnic tradition, statements based on the unsupported authority of the Mishna must be regarded as little better than conjectures.

2. History.—The Mishnic tradition connects the Sanhedrin with Moses' seventy elders, then with the alleged Great Synagogue of Ezra's time, then with such names of leading Rabbis as had escaped oblivion (cf. opening sections of *Pirke Aboth*), and so gives the Sanhedrin of Jamnia an appearance of historical continuity with the past. In point of fact, however, the Sanhedrin emerges into authentic history first in the Greek period. It must have existed earlier, but its origin is covered by the darkness which obscures all Jewish history from the time of Nehemiah (and even earlier) till the Maccabæan rising. The post-exilic Jewish community was nominally a theocracy, enjoying a certain measure of independence under foreign rule. At its head was the high priest, who was assisted by a γερουσία consisting chiefly of members of the aristocratic sacerdotal caste. The administration of secular affairs tended to produce in this caste a certain worldliness, a more or less exclusive interest in worldly business and culture, and consequently a readiness to fall under the influence of Hellenism. Passively opposed to them were the *Ḥăsîdîm*, the pious students of the Law and the legal tradition, whose interests and aspirations were exclusively religious and ecclesiastical. When the crisis came under Antiochus Epiphanes, the aristocratic caste, and consequently the γερουσία, or Sanhedrin, was in the main ready to yield completely to the pressure of an enforced Hellenism. The *Ḥăsîdîm* continued to offer steadfast but passive resistance to the persecutor. There arose, however, a third group, consisting of men who, while not specially in sympathy with the *Ḥăsîdîm*, wished to maintain the ancient religion and also the liberties of the people. The Hasmonæan family led them in armed revolt, and under the skilful leadership of Judas Maccabæus and his brothers they not only regained religious liberty, but achieved the political independence of the Jewish State, of which the Hasmonæans and their loyal followers became the rulers. The old aristocracy was practically destroyed, and the remnants of it were forced to acquiesce in the rule of the new dynasty. The *Ḥăsîdîm*, who had supported the Hasmonæans until liberty of religion was secured, drifted away from them as the political aspect of the struggle became more prominent, and resumed towards them the same attitude of passive opposition which had characterized their relation to the older aristocracy. They were especially incensed at the Hasmonæan assumption of the title and functions of the high-priesthood, which they regarded as usurpation and as a secularizing of the theocracy. At the time of John Hyrcanus, therefore, the Sanhedrin consisted of adherents of the Hasmonæan dynasty—the new aristocracy combined with the remnants of the old, representing two of the three elements of the later court, the chief priests and the elders—and was overwhelmingly, if not exclusively, Sadducee. The Pharisees, the representatives of the earlier *Ḥăsîdîm*, stood aloof, and devoted themselves to the cultivation of their moral and religious influence with the people. It became necessary to conciliate them, and Hyrcanus made an effort to do so.* But their terms were too high. They demanded that Hyrcanus should resign the high-priesthood, and thus destroy the constitution and government which his father and uncles had established. His refusal to concede the demand made the opposition of the Pharisees to the ruling party more acute, and under Alexander Jannæus there was open war. The Sanhedrin, composed as it was of the Hasmonæan nobility, supported Jannæus. But the attitude of the people showed that the Pharisees could no longer with safety be left in opposition. Salome reversed the policy of her predecessors, and admitted them to a share in the government—for a time the dominant share—and to the Sanhedrin.

From that time onwards the Sanhedrin consisted of chief priests, elders, and scribes. It was a house divided against itself, and the bitter conflicts of Sadducee and Pharisee contributed in no small degree to the confusion and decay of the century and a half preceding the destruction of Jerusalem. The path of the Romans and of the Herodian house was made smooth by the inability of the Sanhedrin to act in unity and lead a united people. Pompey abrogated the kingship, but left

* Josephus (*Ant.* XIII. x. 5-6) relates a story which tells how Hyrcanus broke with the Pharisees, to whom he had hitherto been attached, and went over to the Sadducees. But a critical examination of the story, and a comparison of its presuppositions with the previous history as related in 1 Mac., show that what took place was not a breach with the Pharisees, but an unsuccessful attempt to conciliate them. There is no evidence that they sat in the Sanhedrin before Salome's change of policy. Cf. Wellhausen, *Pharisäer und Sadducäer*.

the high priest at the head of the people and of the Sanhedrin, as heretofore. Gabinius went further, and established five συνέδρια in place of the single court, thus largely destroying its influence (57-55 B.C.). Some years later, however, the Sanhedrin was restored to its former position, and resumed the exercise of authority over the whole Jewish territory. Herod is stated to have commenced his reign with a massacre of the members of the Sanhedrin (Jos. *Ant.* XIV. ix. 4). According to another account (*ib.* XV. i. 2), he put to death 45 members of the party of Antigonus. His object was to destroy the influence of the Sadducee nobility, his consistent opponents and only possible rivals. With the same object in view, he reduced the dignity and importance of the high-priesthood by making it no longer hereditary and tenable for life, and by frequent changes. Under his rule the Sanhedrin had but little influence,—less probably than at any other time. Herod's death was followed by the dismemberment of his kingdom, and the authority of the Sanhedrin ceased to extend beyond the limits of Judæa.

The government of the Roman procurators was on the whole favourable to the Sanhedrin. They had not the Herodian jealousy of the local nobility, and were content to leave considerable powers of internal control in their hands. Josephus and the NT bear witness to the influence and authority of the Sanhedrin during this period. So long as it retained control of the people, there was a fair measure of peace and good government. Ultimately, however, the people, under the influence of the Zealots, became unmanageable, and, against the advice of the older and more experienced aristocrats, embarked on the fatal revolt against the Roman authority. Even then the Sanhedrin, had it been left to itself, might have saved Jerusalem from total destruction. But the Zealots usurped its authority, rid themselves of those who counselled moderation, and inaugurated a Reign of Terror, which was terminated only by the entry of the Roman troops into the city.

Under the totally new conditions which prevailed after the destruction of Jerusalem, a new court established itself, bearing the name 'Sanhedrin,' but differing in essential features from the older body. The new Sanhedrin had no political authority, and was composed exclusively of Rabbis, whose discussions and decisions were mainly theoretical. It exercised considerable judicial authority over the Jewish people, owing to its moral influence, but was quite without governmental importance. The real Sanhedrin fell with the city.

3. Functions and authority.—The trustworthy sources give only incidental indications of the functions of the Sanhedrin and the extent of its authority. The changes in the constitution, also, from the time of the Maccabæan rising to the fall of the city, were so great and so frequent, that it is difficult to say how much authority was actually vested in the Sanhedrin at any one time. Under the Hasmonæans it must have been considerable, both in administration and jurisdiction, though the stronger kings, like Jannæus, may have ruled very independently. It was much more limited under the Herodian kings, whose authority was quite independent of the Jewish constitution. By the Romans the constitution was as far as possible respected, and the Sanhedrin, though subordinate to the Roman authority, had again considerable powers, perhaps greater than at any other time. The system of short tenure of the high-priestly office would throw more influence into the hands of the permanent body. In these later days, also, its moral authority over the Jewish people was much wider than its actual power. Territorially its actual authority extended under the procurators over Judæa only. On the other hand, its recommendations were regarded by orthodox Jews outside Judæa as possessing the force of commands (cf. Ac 9²). In general, it may be said that under the procurators the Sanhedrin exercised such authority as was not either within the competence of local councils or reserved by the Romans, and that, while it had considerable powers of police administration and in the levying of taxes, and a certain responsibility for the maintenance of order, its main function was that of a supreme judicial tribunal. Except in the case of capital sentences, its authority was absolute, and it had the power to carry its decisions into effect. An effective sentence of death could be pronounced only by the procurator's court. The stoning of Stephen (Ac 7⁵⁷ff.) without the sanction of the procurator was an illegal act, not an execution but a 'lynching.' In the case of one offence, that of profanation of the sanctuary, even Roman citizens might be tried and condemned by the Sanhedrin, subject, of course, to the procurator's revision of the capital sentence. In spite, however, of the constitutional powers conceded to the Sanhedrin, the Roman authority was always absolute, and the procurator or the tribune of the garrison could not only summon the Sanhedrin and direct it to investigate a matter, but could interfere and withdraw a prisoner from its jurisdiction, as was done in the case of St. Paul (Ac 22³⁰ 23²³ff.).

4. Sessions and procedure. — The Sanhedrin could sit on any day except the Sabbath and holy days; and as sentence of death could be pronounced (according to the Mishna) only on the day after a trial on a capital charge, such charges were not heard on the day preceding a Sabbath or holy day. The place of meeting is called by Josephus the βουλή, and was near the Xystus, which appears to be indicated in the Mishnic לשכת הגּזית 'hall of hewn stone' (cf. Schürer, GJV³ ii. 211). It was close to the upper city, but not in it, as it was destroyed by the Romans before they had reduced the upper city (Jos. BJ VI. vi. 3). The references in NT to meetings of the Sanhedrin (cf. Ac 23) show that its proceedings might be enlivened by stirring debates, and by the stormy scenes which occasionally take place even in the most dignified political assemblies. In the case of ordinary trials, the procedure may have resembled that described in the Mishna. According to its account, the proceedings were conducted according to strict rules, and the members gave judgment in regular order. Twenty-three members formed a quorum, and while a bare majority might acquit, a majority of two was necessary to secure condemnation. If a majority of one gave a verdict of guilty, more members were summoned, until either the requisite majority was obtained for a legal verdict, or the full number of seventy-one members was reached, when a majority of one was decisive on either side.

The accounts of the trial of Jesus present considerable difficulty, and it is not easy to accommodate them to the regular procedure of the Sanhedrin. See art. TRIAL OF JESUS CHRIST.

LITERATURE.—This is extensive, comprising all Histories of the Jews during the period B.C. 200–A.D. 70, as well as the relevant articles in all Bible Dictionaries, and some special works. The most useful and accessible comprehensive statement is that of Schürer, GJV³ ii. 188–214 [HJP II. i. 163 ff.]. The most illuminating account of the history and composition of the Sanhedrin is Wellhausen, Pharisäer und Sadducäer. To these may be added Hastings' DB, art. 'Sanhedrin' (Bacher); EBi, artt. 'Synedrium' (Canney), and 'Government' (Benzinger), § 28-31.   C. H. THOMSON.

SAREPTA.—See ZAREPHATH.

SATAN. — 1. The word 'Satan' (שָׂטָן, Σατανᾶς), which in the NT is invariably used as a proper name denoting the arch-enemy of God and man, occurs in the Hebrew of the OT originally as a synonym of the common words for 'adversary,' as the verb שׂטן is used simply in the sense of withstanding, taking the opposite side. In this sense it is used in Nu 22²² even of the angel of the Lord, who is said to go forth to be a Satan to Balaam. In other passages it is applied, with no sinister meaning, to David, who, as the Philistines feared, might desert Achish and turn against them in battle (1 S 29⁴); to Abishai when he opposed David's purpose of clemency towards Shimei (2 S 19²²); and again to a foreign enemy in general (1 K 5⁴); and to Hadad and Rezon in connexion with their revolt against Solomon (1 K 11¹⁴· ²³· ²⁵). Elsewhere, as in the Book of Ps. (109⁶), in the first two chapters of the Book of Job and in Zec 3 it is used in a technical or legal sense as the equivalent of ἀντίδικος, an opponent in law, an advocate, whose function it is to plead for the condemnation of an accused person. In Job 2³ Jehovah taxes 'the Satan' with over-officious zeal in his efforts to test the motives of the righteous man whom he is permitted to accuse; and again in Zec 3² He distinctly rebukes him for pressing his charge against Joshua. But notwithstanding such suggestions that an evil spirit, a malicious accuser, is described (like the Satan, the accuser of the brethren, διάβολος, κατήγορος of the NT), there is no explicit indication that this is the case. The being thus described as 'the Satan' or the Adversary appears in Zechariah as an official accuser, and in the Book of Job he takes his place among 'the sons of God' in the court of heaven as one having a right to be there, and that in connexion with the function attributed to him of 'going to and fro upon the earth,' and 'considering' and reporting upon the conduct of the sons of men. He is recognized as a minister of the Divine justice, although God does tax him with overdoing his part. All that appears to be indicated there is the thought that there is in the Court of God one whose office it is to plead for the condemnation of sinners. Of a malignant enemy of God and His cause, a personal spirit of evil called Satan, there is no express mention in the OT. The temptation of our first parents is ascribed in Genesis to 'the serpent,' and no interpretation is offered of the symbolism of the story. Again, though in one passage in Chronicles (1 Ch 21¹) we read that Satan tempted David to number the people—a presumptuous offence for which the king was severely punished—the parallel passage (2 S 24¹), much the older narrative, attributes David's conduct to trial at the hands of God, not to the temptation of the Evil One. Similarly the deception of the 'lying spirit' who lured Ahab to his destruction (1 K 22¹⁹⁻²³) is said to have had the express sanction of God. Altogether it is one of the most noteworthy features of the theology of the OT, that so little reference is made to Satan as the great adversary of God and His people, or as the malignant tempter and accuser of man. The Satan of the Book of Job and of the prophecies of Zechariah is described in language very different from that in which the arch-enemy is spoken of in the NT.

This fact, together with the circumstance that references to Satan as an accuser of mankind occur only in those books of the OT which belong to a comparatively late period, has been taken as a proof of the theory that the Jewish belief in Satanic agency was introduced into the Hebrew theology from a foreign source. Traces appear elsewhere of early beliefs current among the Hebrews in the existence of demons, satyrs, liliths, and the like, as in the use of the name 'Azazel,' a mysterious being mentioned in the Pentateuch in connexion with the ordinance of the scapegoat (Lv 16).

It has been supposed that upon those popular beliefs of early Semitic religion there was grafted, from Persian sources, the conception of a Prince of Darkness whose agency is similar to that which, in the religion of Zoroaster, is ascribed to the demon-god Ahriman, and that the belief in Satan and his angels as fallen spirits was thus introduced into Hebrew theology. But, as a matter of fact, the connexion between Satan and the Zoroastrian Ahriman is more apparent than real. A simpler explanation of the history of the doctrine of the personality and agency of Satan is that it has been the subject of development under the influence of a progressive revelation. The complete revelation of such a being as the malignant author of evil was reserved for the time when, with the advent of Christ's Kingdom, the minds of God's people were prepared, without risk of idolatry, or of the mischievous dualism of such a religion as that of Zoroaster, to recognize in the serpent of Eden and in the Satan who appeared as the adversary of Job and of Joshua, the great Adversary of God and man, whose power is to be feared and his temptations resolutely resisted, but from whose dark dominion the Son of God had come to deliver mankind.

2. If the OT is remarkable for its reticence on this subject, we find in the NT the doctrine of Satanic agency very fully developed. It meets us on the threshold. It is one of the most conspicuous elements of NT teaching. Jesus and His disciples distinctly assume the reality of Satan and his kingdom as a mighty power for evil, opposed to the Kingdom of God in the world and in the hearts of men. This is nowhere more noticeable than in the Gospels, and there in the direct teaching of our Lord. At the outset of the Gospel narrative Satan appears as the antagonist of Christ. The story of the Temptation, which must have been communicated to the disciples from the lips of Jesus Himself, is related by the three Synoptists. St. Mark (1[13]) informs us that Jesus was forty days tempted of Satan, using that word or title as a proper name. St. Matthew (ch. 4) and St. Luke (ch. 4), who relate the incident with clear circumstantiality of detail, note three distinct temptations, in which they quote the arguments used by the Tempter and the answers returned by Jesus. They describe the Tempter as ὁ διάβολος, 'the devil,' using the recognized word for betrayer or malicious accuser. According to St. Matthew's account, Jesus addresses him as 'Satan.' St. Luke concludes the narrative with the significant words, 'When the devil had ended all the temptation, he departed from him for a season,' as if to indicate that the conflict with Satan was renewed and continued throughout our Lord's ministry. St. Matthew tells us that when the devil left Him, angels came and ministered unto Him. Thus the Synoptic Gospels distinctly describe the source of the temptation as the direct suggestions of a person, and that one who is variously called Satan and 'the devil.'

Again, these same Gospels, as also the Acts of the Apostles, take notice of Christ's works of healing, and especially of those wrought upon persons possessed with demons, as illustrating the nature of His mission, which was to heal 'all that were oppressed of the devil' (Ac 10[38]). St. Luke (22[3]) no less clearly than St. John (13[2]) informs us that Satan entered the heart of Judas and prompted him to betray his Lord.

In the recorded utterances of Jesus, in His express teaching, allusions are clearly made to the power and activity of Satan as a personal being, and the great Adversary of God and man. He attributes the trouble of the woman who had the spirit of infirmity to the malign power of Satan to afflict even the bodies of men (Lk 13[16]). Thus, so far from discouraging the popular belief which ascribed to Satan and his angels power over soul and body, Jesus distinctly acknowledged it. Accused by the Pharisees, representatives of those to whose speculations in angelology and demonology that popular belief has been traced, of casting out demons through Beelzebub the prince of demons, Jesus, so far from controverting or throwing doubt upon the current opinions of the time, repels the charge by the argument that if Satan should cast out Satan, he would only be defeating his own ends and destroying his own work. Then He proceeds to say, 'But if I cast out devils by the Spirit of God, then the kingdom of God is come unto you' (Mt 12[28], cf. Lk 11[20]), illustrating His argument by the similitude of the strong man and the Stronger than he, implying that Satan is the strong man who would enslave mankind, but that Jesus Himself is the Stronger than he, who has appeared for the deliverance of the victims of Satanic power. That Jesus should thus have argued in controversy with the Pharisees has its own significance. We cannot explain it away on the principle of accommodation. Jesus could and did rebuke the spirit of Pharisaic traditionalism which led them to introduce all manner of mischievous subtleties, making void the Law by their unauthorized traditions, but never once did He even cast suspicion upon this part of the doctrine of the Pharisees. He accepted it without question.

Again, when the Seventy expressed their joy at the success of their mission, and exclaimed, 'Lord, even the demons are subject unto us,' Jesus replied, 'I beheld Satan as lightning fall from heaven,' and went on to say, 'Behold, I give you power to tread upon serpents and scorpions, and over all the power of the enemy' (Lk 10[17-19]). Passing over such passages as those in the Sermon on the Mount, 'Whatsoever is more than these cometh of evil' or 'the evil one' (Mt 5[37]); 'Deliver us from evil' or 'the evil one' (6[13]), which have been explained, and even, as in the RV, translated as referring to the personal Author of Evil, we find Jesus in His discourses and in warnings addressed to His disciples making distinct allusion to Satan as the great adversary whom they have cause to fear. In the parables of the Sower and the Tares, the Evil One, variously termed 'the devil,' 'Satan,' 'the enemy,' 'the wicked one,' is described as seeking to frustrate the work of Christ by catching away the good seed sown in the heart (Mt 13[19], Mk 4[15], Lk 8[12]); or by sowing tares among the wheat (Mt 13[38. 39]), the tares denoting the children of 'the wicked one' as the enemy that sowed them is 'the devil.' Here we see clearly illustrated the New Testament doctrine of the irreconcilable antagonism between the Kingdom of Christ and that of Satan.

Again, Jesus warns Peter on one occasion that Satan has asked and obtained the Divine permission to sift the disciples as wheat; and indicates that their only hope lies in the intercession of Christ Himself, who has prayed for Simon that his 'faith fail not' (Lk 22[31]).

Once more, in Christ's discourse on the Last Judgment, it is expressly stated that the everlasting punishment to which the unfaithful are condemned was 'prepared for the devil and his angels' (Mt 25[41]), a passage which well illustrates the manner in which, in the Synoptic Gospels, Jesus is consistently represented as alluding to Satan and his power and kingdom. That is, that the doctrine is not so much set forth by way of dogmatic statement as assumed, taken for granted. Jesus does not enlarge upon it, but quietly accepts it, presupposes it as a matter about which there is no dispute. The belief is there, and Jesus sets upon it the seal of His authority.

To these examples from the Synoptic Gospels must be added the very emphatic testimony of the discourses of Christ according to the Fourth Gospel. The darkness under whose dominion, according to the introductory verses, the world is held, the dead weight, the *vis inertiæ* of human insensibility to the Divine light, is no negative thing, but itself a power, a kingdom in deadly opposition to the Kingdom of Christ, and under the rule of Satan. Jesus directly attributes the opposition of His antagonists to the malice of the devil. So He says to the Jews, ' Ye are of your father the devil, and the lusts of your father ye will do ' (Jn 8⁴⁴). The false accusations of Scribe and Pharisee, and the untiring malignity of their persecuting zeal, show the spirit and are the work of him who was a liar and a murderer from the beginning. Again, He speaks of Satan as the Prince of this world, and represents as the aim and the certain result of His own work, the judgment and the casting out of Satan and his kingdom (12³¹; cf. 14³⁰ 16¹¹).

3. The other portions of the NT confirm but do not materially add to the testimony of the Gospels on the subject of the personality and the power of the Evil One. Thus St. James (4⁷) merely counsels his readers to resist the devil, assuring them that he will flee from them ; while in another passage (2¹⁹) he speaks of ' the demons ' (τὰ δαιμόνια), evidently meaning by the term the subordinate agents of Satanic power, as believing that there is one God— a belief which fills them with terror. St. Peter assures us that Satan, whom he describes as ἀντίδικος (' adversary,' a technical or official word), and compares to a roaring lion, may be successfully resisted by the power of steadfast faith (1 P 5⁸⁻⁹). St. John in his First Epistle repeats the teaching of his Gospel, and in the Apocalypse identifies Satan with the serpent of Eden, and seemingly also with the accuser of Job and of Joshua (Rev 12⁹⁻¹⁰), and foretells his coming doom. St. Paul accepts the current doctrine ; but though in his Epistles to the Ephesians and Colossians he seems to add to the teaching of Christ in the Gospels other elements from the demonology of the Pharisaic schools and from other sources (Eph 2² 6¹¹, Col 2¹⁵), and in his Epistles to the Corinthians and to Timothy (1 Co 5⁵, 1 Ti 1²⁰) ascribes to Satan a certain power of discipline as a minister of Divine judgment, really contributes to this branch of Christian doctrine no essential element additional to that which is furnished in the Gospels. See, further, articles ACCOMMODATION and DEMON.

LITERATURE.—Cremer, *Bibl.-Theol. Lexicon*, *s.v.*; Commentaries of Meyer, Alford, etc.; Cheyne, *The Origin of the Psalter*, pp. 159, 270 ff., 281 ; A. B. Davidson, *The Book of Job* (Cambridge Bible), pp. 7–13, also *Theol. of OT*, p. 300 ff.; Schmid, *Bibl. Theol. of NT*, p. 187 ; Beyschlag, *NT Theol.*⁷ p. 93 ; Reuss, *Christian Theol. of the Apostolic Age*, i. pp. 162, 420 ; Wernle, *The Beginnings of Christianity*, p. 47 ; Gfrörer, *Das Jahrhundert des Heils*, p. 368 ; Wright, *Zechariah and his Prophecies*, p. 46 ff. ; art. ' Satan ' in Hastings' *DB* (Whitehouse), and in the *Encyc. Bibl.* (G. B. Gray and J. Massie) ; art. ' Teufel ' in *PRE*³ (A. Wünsche) ; H. J. Holtzmann, *Lehrb. d. neutest. Theol.* i. pp. 53, 226.   H. H. CURRIE.

SAVIOUR.—' Saviour,' like ' to save ' and ' salvation,' is a word of frequent occurrence in the OT.

It occurs mostly in the form of the ptcpl. Hiph. of עשׁי = משׁיע. For the specific meaning of ' to save ' in distinction from other cognate Heb. verbs, cf. art. SALVATION. Most commonly God is called the Saviour of Israel or individuals. A standing combination is ' God the Saviour ' often with a possessive genitive (1 Ch 16³⁵, Ps 24⁵ 27¹·⁹ 62²·⁶ 65⁵ 79⁹ 95¹, Is 12² 17¹⁰, Mic 7⁷, Hab 31⁸). To be a Saviour is God's exclusive prerogative (Ps 60¹¹ 108¹², Is 43¹¹ 45²²). As instruments of God, however, human deliverers likewise receive the title (Jg 3⁹·¹⁵, Neh 9²⁷). There is no passage in the OT where the Messiah is called ' Saviour.' Wherever the Messiah is connected with the idea of salvation, He is not the subject but the object of it (Ps 28⁸ 144¹⁰, Zec 9⁹). This is different in Apocryphal and Pseudepigraphical literature, for here it is not merely declared that

in the name of the Son of Man the people are saved, and that He is the Goel of their life (En 48⁷), or that the righteous in connexion with Him shall be satisfied with salvation (4 Ezr 45⁶), but also that *Christus liberabit creaturam* (4 Ezr 12³⁴ 13²⁶), and that from Judah and Levi the Lord will raise a Saviour for Israel (Test. Gad ⁸). God, however, here also is more frequently called Saviour (πάντων σωτήρ, Ps-Sol 16⁷ ; αἰώνιος σωτήρ, Bar 4²² ; ἄγιος σωτήρ, 3 Mac 6²⁹ 7¹⁶). Used of God, σωτήρ is synonymous with such terms as גׂאֵל, ὁ ῥύστης, ὁ λυτρούμενος (En 48⁷, 1 Mac 4¹¹, 3 Mac 7²³).

1. In the Gospels σωτήρ occurs but three times— Lk 1⁴⁷ 2¹¹ and Jn 4⁴². In the Song of Mary, the words ' My spirit has rejoiced in God my Saviour ' are a reproduction of the common OT usage. In Lk 2¹¹ σωτήρ is not a formal title, but a descriptive designation of the Messiah, ' a Saviour who is Christ the Lord.' But the word evidently has a deeper meaning to the angels than the noun σωτηρία and the participle ῥυσθέντας have to Zacharias in Lk 1⁷¹·⁷⁴ ; for in the two latter passages the conception moves entirely within the OT limits. The doxology of Lk 2¹⁴ associates Jesus' saving work with the production of peace on earth among mankind as the objects of God's good pleasure. Here σωτήρ undoubtedly covers the Lord's Messianic work in the most universalistic sense. And it will be noticed that σωτήρ is synonymous with χριστὸς κύριος, so that the reference cannot be confined to our Lord's earthly ministry, but extends to His activity as the glorified Messiah. As ' peace ' and ' good pleasure ' indicate, not the giving of life but the bestowal of reconciliation with God stands in the foreground (for the connexion between σωτήρ and εὐδοκία, cf. Ps-Sol 8³⁹). In Jn 4⁴² ὁ σωτήρ τοῦ κόσμου receives its import from the rich and pregnant meaning σώζειν and σωτηρία acquire in the discourses of the Fourth Gospel. As Jesus had represented Himself to the woman not as a mere revealer (vv.¹⁹·²⁶), but as the giver of ' living water,' and ' water unto eternal life ' (vv.¹⁰·¹⁴), so the Samaritans, in acknowledging Him as σωτήρ τοῦ κόσμου, prove to have attained a deeper conception of Messiahship than was commonly current among them, both as to the nature and extent of the Messiah's calling (cf., however, for σωτήρ τοῦ κόσμου, 4 Ezr 13²⁶).

2. The fact has not escaped observation, that St. Luke, who alone of the Synoptists introduces into his record the word σωτήρ, also employs it twice in Acts, where it occurs once in a speech of St. Peter (5³¹), and once in a speech of St. Paul (13²³). In 5³¹ we have the combination ἀρχηγὸς καὶ σωτήρ : Christ was made both by the Resurrection and by the Ascension. ἀρχηγός is found also in Ac 3¹⁵, another speech of St. Peter, and is here combined with ζωή ; the Jews asked for a murderer to be granted them and killed the Prince of Life, whom God raised from the dead. It is plain that the meaning of σωτήρ in 5³¹ is determined by that of ἀρχηγός, and 3¹⁵ proves that ἀρχηγός has specifically to do with Jesus' life-giving power, whence also in both passages the Resurrection is emphasized. Besides Lk., Hebrews is the only NT writing which employs ἀρχηγός (2¹⁰ 12²). The former of these two passages confirms the close connexion already found between σωτήρ and ἀρχηγός, for it calls Jesus ἀρχηγὸς σωτηρίας ; in the other passage He is called ἀρχηγὸς καὶ τελειωτὴς πίστεως, ' the leader and perfecter of faith.' (For a thorough discussion of ἀρχηγός, cf. Bleek, *Der Brief a. d. Hebräer*, ii. pp. 301–303). The use of the word in combination with σωτήρ is interesting, because both are employed in the LXX of the ' judges ' sent by God to deliver Israel (Jg 3⁹⁻¹⁵ 11⁶·¹¹ 12³ [σωτήρ = עישׁׄמ, ἀρχηγός = ןיצק]). In Hebrews, however, the rendering ' captain,' which brings out the idea of military leadership, and the general rendering ' author,' are inadequate ; the word plainly has the connotation of ' model,' ' example,' ' forerunner,' the leader first experiencing in Himself and receiving in Himself that to which he leads others. Thus Jesus is ἀρχηγὸς σωτηρίας in 2[10], because He Himself is conducted to glory by God, and in His attainment to glory draws with Him all the other sons of God. In 12[2] Jesus' career of faith is represented as exemplary for believers; by preceding in the exercise of an ideal faith He enables others to follow in the same ἀγών of faith. He 5[9] proves that where the author does not wish to emphasize this peculiar idea of precession, but merely to express the causal relationship between His work and the salvation of believers, he uses the general term αἴτιος : 'He became author of eternal salvation.' The reference to the Resurrection in both Petrine passages renders it probable that the word ἀρχηγός is here used in the same pregnant sense : Jesus is in virtue of the Resurrection a leader of life, one who has Himself attained unto life, and now makes others partakers of the same. As the murderer in Ac 3[14] inflicts death, so the ἀρχηγὸς τῆς ζωῆς bestows life. σωτήρ, then, is identical with ἀρχηγός so far as the impartation of life is concerned, but leaves the exemplification of the life-content of the σωτηρία in Jesus' own Person unexpressed. In the speech of St. Paul (13[23]) the use of σωτήρ clearly attaches itself to the LXX of the Book of Judges, if the reading ἤγειρε of the TR be followed, for this is the verb by which the LXX in Jg 3[9. 15] renders the Heb. הֵקִים. If, on the other hand, we read with WH ἤγαγε, the more immediate reference seems to be to Zec 3[8] ; but even then the word σωτήρ itself points back to the Book of Judges.

3. In St. Paul's writings, apart from the Pastoral Epistles, σωτήρ is found only twice—Eph 5[23] and Ph 3[20]. The interpretation of the former passage is much disputed. The husband's relation as head to the wife and Christ's relation as Head to the Church are compared, and in this connexion Christ is called σωτὴρ τοῦ σώματος (of the Church). This last statement seems to imply that Christ's headship over the Church is based on His being the Saviour of the Church-body. The question is whether this must be understood in the sense which will likewise be applicable to the relation between husband and wife. In the ordinary sense the husband could hardly be called the saviour of the wife's body. But Wagner (*ZNTW* vi. [1905] p. 220) has called attention to a passage in Clement (*Pæd.* ii. 5) where it is stated that the Creator provides man with meat and drink τοῦ σώζεσθαι χάριν, 'for the sake of keeping alive.' Applying this to our passage, he obtains the very congruous sense : As the husband is σωτήρ of the wife, by supplying the sustenance of her physical life, so Christ is σωτήρ of the Church, inasmuch as He endows her with eternal life ; and for this reason both hold the position of head. This secures for σώζειν the sense of 'endowing with eternal life.' The peculiarity of the passage, thus understood, would lie in this, that the ordinary religious use of σώζειν is illustrated by analogy with a natural use of the verb which seems to be without precedent in earlier Biblical Greek. In Ph 3[20] the word σωτήρ has a specific eschatological reference : Christ is σωτήρ, because at the resurrection He will transform the body of believers into the likeness of His own glorious body. σώζειν therefore here also is equivalent to the bestowal of life.

4. With sudden and remarkable frequency σωτήρ emerges in the Pastoral Epistles (10 times) and in 2 Peter (5 times). In the Pastorals there is further the peculiarity that the name is applied to both God and Christ : to God, in 1 Ti 1[1] 2[3] 4[10], Tit 1[3] 2[10] 3[4] ; to Christ, in 2 Ti 1[10], Tit 1[4] 2[13] 3[6]. In 2 Peter the reference is always to Christ. In Jude also God is once called 'our Saviour through Jesus Christ' (v.[25]). The designation of God as Saviour can appear strange only on the basis of our established custom to reserve this title for Christ ; on the basis of the OT it was a perfectly natural usage, for here always God, never the Messiah, is called מוֹשִׁיעַ, σωτήρ. And in the NT itself the act of saving is, where a subject is indicated, as naturally ascribed to God as to Christ (comparatively few passages reflect on the subject). Except perhaps for the one passage, 1 Ti 4[10], it cannot be said that the meaning of σωτήρ in the Pastorals and 2 Peter differs from its ordinary import, or that of σώζειν in the NT elsewhere. Christ is Saviour, because He abolished death and brought life and immortality to light through the gospel (2 Ti 1[10]) ; as Lord and Saviour, Jesus Christ has an eternal Kingdom into which believers receive entrance (2 P 1[11]). He is called 'the great God and Saviour,' in so far as believers look for the blessed hope and appearing of His glory (Tit 2[13]). The hope of eternal life comes from God our Saviour (Tit 1[2] 2[14]). Eschatological also is the reference in 'the commandment of the Lord and Saviour' (2 P 3[2]). In Tit 2[10] the thought is implied that God is Saviour in the ethical sphere, whence 'the doctrine of God our Saviour' becomes an incentive to holy living. But peculiar is 1 Ti 4[10] where God is called 'the Saviour of all men, especially of them that believe.' Wagner proposes to apply here the same sense given to σωτήρ in Eph 5[23] : God is Saviour of all men, inasmuch as He supplies them with natural life ; Saviour especially of believers, because He supplies these with the higher life of the Spirit (*l.c.* p. 222, where Philo [*de Mundi Opif.* 60 : God=εὐεργέτης καὶ σωτήρ] is quoted). This might seem to be favoured by 1 Ti 6[13] 'God who keepeth all things alive,' or 'who giveth life to all things' (cf. the alternative reading ζωογονήσει for σώσει in Lk 17[33]). But it is less in keeping with Tit 2[11] where a similar universalism of God's σώζειν is affirmed, and yet this is a matter of redemption, not of nature. Wagner is quite correct, however, in urging against von Soden that 'God σωτήρ of all men' cannot mean 'God is *willing* to be σωτήρ of all men' ; and against B. Weiss, that it cannot mean 'God has made salvation objectively possible for all men, while subjectively He realizes it in believers only.' The solution of the difficulty must be sought elsewhere, viz. in connexion with the pronounced universalism of the Pastoral Epistles in general. The emphasis and frequency with which this principle is brought forward render it probable that something specific in the historical situation to which the Pastorals address themselves lies at its basis, and at the basis also of the frequency with which the words σώζειν, σωτηρία, σωτήριος, σωτήρ are employed. There is absolutely no reason to suspect the writer of any intention to weaken or neutralize the doctrine of predestination. Besides involving denial of the Pauline origin of the Epistles, this would leave unexplained why, in other passages, the principle of predestination is enunciated with all desirable distinctness. The only plausible view is that the passages under review contain a warning against the dualistic trend of that incipient Gnosticism to whose early presence in the Apostolic period the Epistles of the First Captivity also bear witness. In a twofold sense it might become of importance to vindicate, over against this theory, the universalism of saving grace : on the one hand, in so far as Gnosticism on principle excluded from salvation those who lacked the pneumatic character ; and, on the other hand, in so far as those belonging to the *pneumatici* might be considered to carry the power of salvation by nature in themselves. In other words, it might become necessary to emphasize that God saves all men, not merely one class of men, and that no man is by his subjective condition either sunk beneath the possibility or raised above the need of salvation. Perhaps also the emphasis upon the fact that God as well as Christ is Saviour, though perfectly natural from the OT point of view, is specially directed against a system which tended to separate between the Creator-God of the old dispensation and the Saviour-God, Christ, of the new. The recent investigations of Friedländer have shown that there existed long before the 2nd cent. of our era a Jewish type of Gnosticism, so that it can no longer be asserted that an anti-Gnostic polemic of this type *per se* militates against the Pauline authorship of the Pastoral Epistles.

In recent times attempts have been made to explain the rise and development of the NT conception of σωτήρ and σωτηρία from extra-Biblical sources. Anrich (*Das antike Mysterienwesen in seinem Einfluss auf das Christenthum*, 1894) pointed out how in the cult of the 'Mysteries' the promise of σωτηρία, in the sense of immortality, plays a large rôle. Similarly Wobbermin (*Religionsgeschichtliche Studien*, 1896), who asserts that especially in the cult of the subterranean gods the word σωτήρ was common as a name for the Deity. In two articles published in the *Christliche Welt* for 1899 and 1900, entitled 'Als die Zeit erfüllt war' and 'Der Heiland,' Harnack calls attention to certain inscriptions discovered in Asia Minor, at Priene and Halicarnassus, dating probably from the year B.C. 9, in which the Emperor Augustus is invested with Divine predicates, and called σωτήρ, the one who has been filled for the good of mankind with gifts, a god whose birthday has brought to the world the evangels connected with his person, the Zeus of the fatherland and the σωτήρ of the human race. Harnack assumes that St. Luke in calling Jesus σωτήρ was influenced by these and similar pagan forms of expression current in the cult of the Emperors, and that the same influence may be seen at work in the frequency with which the Pastoral Epistles and 2 Peter employ the title. He further suggests that St. Paul purposely avoided its use, because of the eudæmonistic, political flavour it had acquired from these pagan associations. St. Luke, in the 'Gospel of the Infancy,' the writer of the Pastorals, the writer of 2 Peter, and the Fourth Evangelist, meant to represent Christ as the true σωτήρ in whom lay the reality of what paganism falsely ascribed to its rulers, dead or living.—Soltau (*Die Geburtsgeschichte Jesu Christi*, 1902) reaches the same conclusions, independently of Harnack, on the basis of the same and other classical material, and also asserts derivation of the story of the virgin birth from the same pagan circle of ideas.—Wendland (*ZNTW* v. [1904], p. 335 ff.) investigates the use of σωτήρ in antiquity with reference to both gods and deified men—a usage dating back from before the production of the LXX. Up to the time of Alexander the Great, σωτήρ was not applied to men, because it was still felt to be a cult-name reserved for the gods. The first trace of its application to men appears in Thucydides, where it is given to Brasidas, and in Polybius, where Philip of Macedon is called σωτήρ. After that, the custom became quite common among the Ptolemies and the Seleucidæ : first the dead, then also the living rulers were honoured with this title. It was also combined with the Oriental idea of the incarnation of the godhead, whence such a term as ἐπιφανής was applied to rulers. A feast celebrated on the day of such a σωτήρ was called σωτήρια. From the Greek dynasties the custom passed over to the representatives of the Roman power, especially to the Emperors. Examples are adduced from Cicero, whose rhetorical exaggerations in speaking of great Romans are believed to have sprung from his knowledge of the Oriental forms of speech. Even a philosopher like Epicurus could be called σωτήρ after a semi-Divine fashion, and that in his lifetime. Finally, in connexion with the recent trend towards explaining Biblical conceptions from Babylonian sources, it has been proposed to find in the NT idea of σωτήρ an embodiment of the Oriental myth of a Saviour-King (*Erlöser-König*) ; cf. A. Jeremias, *Babylonisches im NT* (1905), pp. 27–46.

It is not proposed here to subject the above hypotheses to an exhaustive criticism. To some extent the later forms have effectually criticised the earlier ones. Thus Wendland disposes of much in Anrich, Wobbermin, and Soltau. Wagner (*ZNTW* vi. [1905]) skilfully attacks the position of Wendland. A few remarks must here suffice. The derivation of the whole idea of σωτήρ and σωτηρία from the Oriental expectation of the Saviour-King is impossible, because OT prophecy not at all, and Jewish theology very rarely, applies the name מוֹשִׁיעַ, σωτήρ, to the Messiah, and yet in eschatological Messianism it would be natural to look first of all for the evidence of such Oriental importation. As to the alleged connexion between the Greek mysteries and Christianity, it should be observed that the cult of the mysteries flourished in the 2nd cent. of the Christian era, and that none of the authorities quoted by Anrich in support of his view dates further back than this. The Asian inscriptions, of which Harnack and Soltau make so much, offer at the best some striking analogies to the NT mode of representation ; but a real literary dependence cannot be made out, as even Wendland admits. In his second article, 'Der Heiland,' Harnack expresses himself much more guardedly than in the first, after this fashion : 'On the Jewish and on the Grecian line numerous religious conceptions existed, which covered each other so simply and so simply could pass over into each other.' σωτήρ in the cult of the Emperors has quite a different sense from what it has in the NT ; in Hellenism it never means 'the one who translates from death into life.' It is also exceedingly doubtful whether St. Paul consciously and

purposely avoids the use of σωτήρ with reference to Christ, because of its pagan, idolatrous associations. Why did not St. Paul avoid κύριος for the same reasons? Why not σώζειν and σωτηρία themselves as well as σωτήρ? A far more simple explanation is that the non-use of מוֹשִׁיעַ in the OT with reference to the Messiah continued to exert its influence in the usage of St. Paul. An allusion to the Emperor-cult and the rôle played in it by σωτήρ in Ph 3²⁰ is not impossible, for in the words 'our πολίτευμα is in heaven' the pronoun is emphatic. Where, apart from St. Paul, the conception of σώζειν is first joined to the Person of Christ, this is done in dependence on the Hebrew meaning of the name 'Jesus,' *i.e.* in dependence on the OT (Mt 1²¹). *A priori* there would be no objection to the hypothesis that in Luke and the Pastoral Epistles and 2 Peter and the Fourth Gospel there is a conscious appropriation of, and at the same time a protest against, the pagan use of the word, and that the sudden frequency of its occurrence in the Pastorals and 2 Peter is to be explained from this. As a matter of fact, however, this involves, according to Harnack, the unhistorical character of at least the present form of the *Magnificat* and of the message of the angels to the shepherds (Lk 1⁴⁷ and 2¹¹) ; further, the unhistorical character of at least the present form of the speeches of St. Peter and St. Paul (Ac 5³¹ 13²⁸) ; and, finally, the unhistorical character of at least the form of the discourse of our Lord in Jn 4⁴². It has been shown above, that the Lukan record can be readily explained from the historical situation which it reports. For Jn 4⁴² (and 1 Jn 4¹⁴) σωτήρ τοῦ κόσμου, a comparison with 4 Ezr 13²⁶, where the same phrase occurs, proves that even here we do not necessarily move in Greek trains of thought, but are still in the Jewish sphere. All that remains of Wendland's contention is, that possibly in the Pastoral Epistles there is some adjustment in the use of σωτήρ to the manner of its handling in pagan quarters, for an apologetic purpose. But even here considerable weeding of Wendland's assertions will be necessary. Thus he brings the χάρις, which is named as the motive of the Divine act of σώζειν, into connexion with the *benignitas* and *clementia* of the Roman emperors. But Eph 2⁵⁻⁹ shows how all this can be readily explained without resorting to such far-fetched analogies. Similarly the πρὸ χρόνων αἰωνίων of Tit 1² and 2 Ti 1⁹ is treated by Wendland as an allusion to the eternity of the Roman Emperors, which takes no account of the fact that the latter was an eternity of post- not of pre-existence. In Tit 3⁷, where he would find the same analogy, the eternity is not that of the σωτήρ, but of believers. Most, perhaps, could be said in favour of the Hellenistic association of such terms as ἐπιφάνεια, μέγας θεός, and φιλανθρωπία in their joint use with σωτήρ (cf. Wagner, p. 232). But, taken as a whole, σωτήρ is shown to be a thoroughly OT conception by its dependence on σώζειν and σωτηρία, about whose OT provenience there can be no reasonable doubt.

See also art. SALVATION, and the Literature there cited.   GEERHARDUS VOS.

SAYING AND DOING.—The contrast between 'saying' and 'doing' is based on an axiomatic principle of the moral and spiritual life, which, notwithstanding its simplicity and obviousness, is apt to be overlooked, viz. the importance of character as distinguished from profession, the supreme value of ethical ideals and practice above ritual observance, the vital connexion between creed and conduct. The distinction thus suggested necessarily finds a large place in the teaching of our Lord, who, as the Founder of a religion of inward reality, frequently emphasized the importance of 'doing' rather than 'saying.' 'Not every one that saith unto me, Lord, Lord, shall enter into the kingdom of heaven ; but he that doeth the will of my Father which is in heaven' (Mt 7²¹). Not that Jesus by any means underrated the importance of 'saying' ; He made confession of His name one of the most solemn obligations of discipleship (Mt 10³². ³³, cf. Lk 8³⁸. ³⁹). But a profession must rest upon a solid foundation of character. The recurrence, in various forms, of the phrase 'to do the will of God,' and the prominent place given to this conception, is a marked feature of Christ's teaching ; see Mt 12⁵⁰ ; cf. 7²⁴⁻²⁷ 16²⁷ 25⁴⁰. ⁴⁵, Lk 10³⁰⁻³⁷ 11²⁸ 13⁶⁻⁹ etc. 'Doing' is the testing quality of the Christian life (Mt 5¹⁹. ⁴⁷), and the sure and only way to spiritual enlightenment (Jn 7¹⁷). Of this doing of God's will Jesus Himself set the supreme and inspiring example (Jn 4³⁴ 5³⁰ 6³⁸). In contrast with this ideal of 'doing,' Jesus warned men against the subtle dangers of mere 'saying.' Even when sincerely meant, He checked the impulsiveness of a hasty and ill-considered profession (Mt 8¹⁹. ²⁰ ; cf. 26³³. ³⁴, Lk 14²⁸) ; but His severest rebukes were reserved for those who substituted a hollow and obtrusive pretension for the realities of moral and spiritual character. It was the great sin of the religious leaders of the time that they were so strong in profession and precept, and so neglectful of practical righteousness; 'they say, and do not' (Mt 23[3]); and many too readily followed their example of easy formalism,—'This people honoureth me with their lips' (Mt 15[8]). The same contrast is boldly presented in the parable of the Two Sons (Mt 21[28-32]), with special reference on the one hand to the Pharisees and scribes, and on the other to the outwardly unpromising 'publicans and sinners' who welcomed the message of the Kingdom of heaven. Right action without profession, or even in contradiction to the profession, is better than promises unfulfilled by practice. In this, as in other ways, 'many shall be last that are first; and first that are last' (Mt 19[30]). The 'acted parable' of the withering of the barren fig-tree with its deceptive show of premature leaves, was a solemn warning against the danger and sin of 'saying' without 'doing' (Mt 21[18. 19], Mk 11[12-14]). Better that the 'saying' should follow than outrun the 'doing,' and be inspired by a truthful and humble judgment of even our best efforts and achievements; 'when ye shall have done all the things that are commanded you, say, We are unprofitable servants; we have done that which it was our duty to do' (Lk 17[10]).

LITERATURE.—Dale, *Evangel. Revival*, 104; *ExpT* iii. [1892] 466, viii. [1896] 85; F. W. Robertson, *Serm.* ii. 94.

J. E. M'OUAT.

SAYINGS (UNWRITTEN).—Certain sayings ascribed to Christ, though recorded by early writers, are not found written in the Gospels, and therefore are known as the **Agrapha**, or Unwritten Sayings of Our Lord. They are not as numerous as might, perhaps, have been anticipated, in view of the recorded facts of Christ's ministry, and the comparative brevity of the actual reports of His discourses. The active ministry seems to have lasted for nearly three years. The records convey the impression of preachings and teachings, continued from day to day, with only rare intervals of repose. The audiences were frequently very large; they came from all quarters; the interest was widespread and intense. The words of this Galilæan Rabbi, who attracted some and provoked the wrath of others, but could not be disregarded by any, did not die in their utterance. It was an age when the memory was much cultivated. Christ's hearers would be ready to retain, and repeat at home, and amongst their friends, whatever had impressed them most in the new doctrines. It was a literary age also. Before the Third Gospel was written, many had already composed histories of Christ (Lk 1[1]). The Fourth Evangelist states that he made a selection from available materials (Jn 20[30. 31] 21[25]).

There must once have been a large amount of *Agrapha*—of teachings and sayings which have not reached us in the pages of Holy Writ. While these were for the most part current in Palestine only, a few would spread farther, through the visits of Hellenists, and even Greeks (Jn 12[20]), to Judæa. But the work of converting the world was reserved for the preaching of Christ's Apostles; and the converts' knowledge of Christianity was derived from the traditions which were delivered by the Apostles, and which were subsequently superseded by the texts of the written Gospels. Meanwhile, the Hebrew Church of Palestine, which alone possessed first-hand knowledge of Christ's teachings, faded and ultimately perished with the scattering of the Hebrew race. In these historical conditions we find the reasons why so little of the teaching of the Master has survived beyond the

actual contents of the four canonical records. The entire collection of *Agrapha*, gathered from all sources, is not large. When what is apocryphal, or certainly spurious, has been eliminated, the residuum is found to be small in amount, and not very valuable.

The extra-canonical Sayings are preserved in some MSS of the Gospels, and in those religious romances known as the Apocryphal Gospels, also in the Commentaries of the Fathers; but there are, besides, a few sayings which are *Agrapha* in that they are not included in the written Gospels, but yet possess high attestation as being parts of the text of Acts and 1 Cor. They stand, or fall, with the estimate held of the authenticity of those books. In Ac 20[35] St. Paul quotes the words of the Lord; 'how he said, *It is more blessed to give than to receive.*' This is a specimen of the traditions (2 Th 2[15]) which were delivered by the first preachers of Christianity to their converts. In 1 Co 11[25] St. Paul adds a phrase not found in the Evangelists' accounts of the Institution, '*This do ye, as oft as ye drink it, in remembrance of me*'; but v.[23] may be interpreted to intimate that the Apostle had enjoyed a special revelation ('I have received of the Lord'), independently of any tradition of the words heard by the Twelve. The report of our Lord's last commands to His Apostles (Ac 1[4-8]), though in part a repetition of texts in the Gospels, is distinct in some expressions, and v.[5] has no parallel in the Evangelists. This verse is repeated by St. Peter in Ac 11[16].

The sayings preserved in some MSS of the Gospels are of the nature of textual variations for the most part. A few are absolutely inadmissible on textual grounds; others are accepted only by certain critics. Those which are not universally admitted may yet be authentic traditions, though extra-canonical: relics of the many sayings which were not recorded by the Evangelists. The test of these, and of others which are handed down by the Fathers, is by comparison with the sentiments which are recognized as elements in the character of Christ's teaching. The very ancient MS at Cambridge known as *Codex Bezæ*, which exhibits many remarkable variations from the usual text of the Gospels, has between Mt 20[28] and [29] the following:

'But ye, seek ye from little to increase, and from greater to be less; but also when, having been invited, ye enter in to sup, not to go and sit down in the prominent places, lest a more honourable than thou should come in, and he that invited to the supper should come forward and say to thee, "Withdraw still lower"; and thou shouldest be put to shame. But if thou shouldest go and sit down in the inferior place, and one inferior to thee should come in, he that invited to the supper will say to thee, "Draw together still higher"; and this shall be to thee profitable.'

Between Lk 6[4] and [5] the following occurs:

'On the same day he beheld a certain man working on the Sabbath, and said to him, "Man, if indeed thou knowest what thou art doing, thou art blessed; but if thou knowest not, thou art accursed and a transgressor of the law."'

These paragraphs are not supported by sufficient evidence to warrant their inclusion in the text of the Gospels: whether they are worthy to be considered part of those traditions of Christ's teachings which preceded, and for a time accompanied, the written word, the English reader can judge for himself. Textual criticism has no place outside the region of documents.

The following Sayings, however, are in a different category. The evidence for them is so weighty that all are received into the text by some critics; but to others the evidence is insufficient; yet it will hardly be denied by any that the presence of the words in so many ancient documents stamps them with distinct authority, and demands their recognition as traditions of the Master's teachings. We refer here to the Doxology (Mt 6[13]); the verse Mt 17[21]; the words, 'and every sacrifice shall be

salted with salt' (Mk 9⁴⁹); 'Ye know not what
manner of spirit ye are of. For the Son of Man is
not come to destroy men's lives, but to save them'
(Lk 9⁵⁵·⁵⁶); 'Father, forgive them : for they know
not what they do' (Lk 23³⁴). All these passages
except the last are rejected as parts of the text by
the Revisers, and those of the same school of
criticism ; nor do they accept as undoubtedly
genuine the story of the Adulteress in Jn 8, and
the concluding verses of Mk. ; yet the words attributed to Christ in these two sections, and in the
texts cited above, must certainly commend themselves to unprejudiced ears as authentic reminiscences of the Master's sayings, even if we refuse
them a place in the canonical records.

The Sayings of Christ which have been preserved outside the NT by ecclesiastical writers,
though not actually numerous, are too many for
quotation in this article. The following are specimens ; and, in different ways, of interest and importance.

Clement of Alexandria (*Strom.* vi. 5. 43) quotes
Peter thus :

'The Lord said to the Apostles, "If, then, any one of Israel
wishes to repent and believe through my name on God, his sins
shall be forgiven him. After twelve years go forth into the
world, lest any one say, We did not hear."'

Origen (*in Joan.* ii. 6) has :

'If any one goes to the Gospel according to the Hebrews,
there the Saviour himself saith : "Just now my mother the
Holy Spirit took me by one of my hairs and carried me off to
the great mountain Tabor."'

Jerome quotes from the same Gospel as follows :

(*a*) 'After the resurrection of the Saviour, it records : "But
when the Lord had given the linen cloth to the priest's servant,
he went to James and appeared to him. For James had taken
an oath that he would not eat bread from that hour in which he
had drunk the cup of the Lord, until he should see him rising from
them that sleep." And again, a little farther on, "Bring me,
saith the Lord, a table and bread." And there follows immediately : "He took the bread, and blessed, and brake, and
gave to James the Just, and said to him, 'My brother, eat thy
bread, inasmuch as the Son of Man hath risen from them that
sleep'"' (*de Vir. illust.* ii.).
(*b*) 'There is the following story : "Behold, the Lord's mother
and his brethren were saying to him : 'John the Baptist bap-
tizes unto remission of sins ; let us go and be baptized by
him.' But he said unto them : 'What sin have I done, that I
should go and be baptized by him? unless perchance this very
thing, which I have said, is an ignorance'"' (*adv. Pelag.* iii. 2).
(*c*) 'We read, too, of the Lord saying to the disciples : "And
never rejoice, except when you have looked upon your brother
in love"' (*in Eph.* 5³ᶜ).

The 'Sayings' contained in a fragmentary papyrus of the 3rd cent., discovered at Oxyrhynchus,
are in part equivalent to texts in the Gospels, but
the following have no parallels :

(*a*) 'Except ye fast to the world, ye shall in nowise find the
kingdom of God ; and except ye make the Sabbath a real
Sabbath, ye shall not see the Father.'
(*b*) 'I stood in the midst of the world, and in the flesh was I
seen of them, and I found all men drunken, and none found I
athirst among them ; and my soul grieveth over the sons of men,
because they are blind in their heart, and see not.'
(*c*) 'Wherever there are two, they are not without God ; and
wherever there is one alone, I say, I am with him. Raise the
stone and there shalt thou find me ; cleave the wood and there
am I.' *

The so-called 2nd Ep. of Clement of Rome (c. iv.)
has :

'For this cause, if we do these things, the Lord said, "Though
ye be gathered together with me in my bosom, and do not my
commandments, I will cast you away, and will say unto you,
'Depart from me, I know you not whence ye are, ye workers of
iniquity.'"'

Hippolytus (*Philosph.* v. 7) quotes the Gospel
according to Thomas thus :

'He that seeketh me shall find me in children from seven
years old onwards, for there I am manifested, though hidden in
the fourteenth age.'

---

* Other fragments of MSS containing words ascribed to Christ
have lately been procured from the same place, but the text was
not available when this article was printed. It is not unreasonable to anticipate additions to our store of *Agrapha* by future
discoveries amongst Egyptian ruins.

Many sayings ascribed to Jesus have been collected from Mohammedan sources (cf. art. CHRIST
IN MOHAMMEDAN LITERATURE [in Appendix]).
One such passage is : 'When Jesus was asked,
"How art thou this morning?" he would answer,
"Unable to forestall what I hope, or to put off
what I fear, bound by my works, with all my good
in another's hand. There is no poor man poorer
than I am."' The last sentence agrees in sentiment with a well-known text ; but these Mohammedan traditions of Christ's words are for the most
part of no value.

LITERATURE. — Art. 'Agrapha' in Hastings' *DB*, Extra Vol.
p. 343 ff., where a good bibliography is given. The following
artt. are useful : 'Sayings' from MSS and Fathers — Lock,
Expositor, IV. ix. [1894] 1, 97 ; 'Oxyrhynchus Sayings'—Swete,
ExpT viii. [1897] 544, xv. [1904] 488, Cross and Harnack,
Expositor, v. vi. [1897] 257, 321, 401 ; 'Sayings' from Moham-
medan sources—Margoliouth, *ExpT* v. [1893–94] 59, 107, 177.
　　　　　　　　　　　　　　　　　G. H. GWILLIAM.

SCARLET.—1. Scarlet, as a dye, was obtained
from the body of the female *kermes* insect (*Lec-
anium ilicis*), a native of S.E. Europe, where it
lives upon a species of dwarf oak (*Quercus cocci-
fera*). The insect is of the family Coccidæ, to
which also the cochineal of Mexico belongs. Its
Latin name (derived from its appearance) was
grana ; hence the dye was called 'grain' (cf.
Milton, *Penser.* 33, *Par. Lost*, xi. 242 ; Spenser,
FQ I. vii. 1 ; see Skeat, *Etym. Dict. s.v.*).
2. The *colour* is correctly represented by its
name. Mt 27²⁸ is the only passage in the Gospels
where the word 'scarlet' (κόκκινος) occurs, and it is
there a substitute for the 'purple' of ‖ Mk 15¹⁷·²⁰,
Jn 19²·⁵. It is the latter word that has changed
its meaning (see art. PURPLE).

'The Gr. sense of colour seems to have been so comparatively
dim and uncertain, that it is almost impossible to ascertain what
the real idea was which they attached to any word alluding to
hue' (Ruskin, *Mod. Painters*, iii. 225. Cf. also Gladstone, *Juv.
Mundi*, p. 540).

Yet the ancients, as a rule, carefully distinguished scarlet from purple (Becker, *Gallus*, p.
446). Probably Mt. gives the colour actually used,
Mk. and Jn. the colour intended.
3. The 'scarlet robe' was undoubtedly a military
cloak, either that of a common soldier (*sagum*) or
that of a commanding officer (*paludamentum*).
The latter was longer and of better quality ; both
were regularly of scarlet (Ellicott, *Hist. Lectures*,
p. 348 n.). Westcott (on Jn 19²·⁵) emphasizes, in
the crown and robe, the idea of victory as well as
of royalty : 'this blood-stained robe was the true
dress of a kingly conqueror. . . . So He was
through life the suffering King, the true Soldier.'
　　　　　　　　　　　　　　　　　F. S. RANKEN.

SCHISM.—See UNITY.

SCHOOL.—See BOYHOOD and EDUCATION.

SCIENCE.—1. The word 'science,' in the language
of to-day, refers sometimes to a process and sometimes to the results of that process. The process
itself is the representation in thought of the facts
and events of human experience. The result of
this process is the formulation of statements and
doctrines which are regarded as true. We therefore use the word 'science' generally to embrace
both (1) scientific method and (2) scientific truth.
The object of science is to apply its method to
every field of possible knowledge, and so to include within its doctrine all the facts of human
experience.

I. *STATE OF SCIENCE IN THE CIVILIZATION
IN WHICH CHRIST LIVED.*—1. Relation to Hellenism. — The civilization of Palestine was complex
and syncretic. The two main factors in it were
the ancient Hebrew culture (largely tinctured by
other Oriental elements), which preponderated,

and Hellenism. This latter was a power extending throughout the Græco-Roman world, and tending to influence every department of life; and so, despite the innate conservatism of the Jews, the more external elements of Palestinian culture received a strong Hellenistic tincture. The organism of the State was deeply affected, public institutions were modified, and social relations not untouched. The arts, too, were influenced, but, by the time the science of the Hebrews was reached, the wave of Hellenism had lost much of its vigour. The mind of the Jew was equipped against it. The Greek language was, after all, but slightly known (cf. Ac 21⁴⁰ 22²), and, though Herod surrounded himself with Greek *literati* and many Jews received a Greek education abroad, these facts indicate the limit of the penetration of Greek science into the life of the Jews. This may be illustrated by reference to St. Paul. Though brought up to some extent under Hellenistic influences in Tarsus, his culture was Greek only in its form and in certain of its graces. To the Hebrew mode of thought and Rabbinic logic—inward and characteristic elements of Jewish culture—he tenaciously clung. His writings are all those of a Jew rather than of a Hellenist. It is, then, unnecessary to attend to Hellenistic thought when considering the 'science' that formed the intellectual background of the teaching of Christ. The Aristotelian logic had no nameable influence upon His own thought, or upon the mind of the Synoptists who reported His words, or upon the conceptions of the common people who 'heard him gladly.' The logic of the society in which Christ moved was Rabbinic and not philosophic, and its standard of truth was religious rather than scientific.

2. Hebrew standard of truth.—We recognize that, according to the scientific standard, those propositions are true which accurately and impartially describe observed facts; that is, the test of truth is its logical form as descriptive. This notion of truth was originally foreign to the Hebrews. The words in the OT which are translated 'true,' 'truth,' etc., may be traced to roots which have primarily an ethical meaning and convey 'the notion of constancy, steadfastness, faithfulness' (see art. 'Truth' in Hastings' *DB*). Hence they are more generally applied to a person than a proposition, and attach to a proposition only in a derivative way, the sayings of God being 'faithful' because His character is beneath and behind them, —they are established in the Divine nature, and so cannot be moved. Thus, that a proposition should tally with facts did not stand out with such importance as it does for us moderns: indeed, to the ancient Hebrew, truth was a matter of motive and character rather than of accuracy. Thus in the Decalogue there is no actual and direct condemnation of lying, but the prohibition is directed against the bearing of false witness, the dastardly motive being the thing denounced, rather than the failure accurately to describe facts. This comes out in strong relief in the Jewish notion of history. The aim of the historian was less to give a record of events than to edify. Indeed, by the time of Christ the whole circle of historical ideas had received a fanciful character, because that narrative was deemed to be the best which gave the most laudatory account of the Hebrew heroes.

Truth then, according to the Hebrew mind, was that which edified, and not merely accurate description of fact. Only from this point of view can we understand many NT sayings with reference to truth. Jesus claimed that He Himself *was* the truth. In saying 'I am the way, and the truth, and the life' (Jn 14⁶), He is not referring to what we call scientific truth, but rather edifying and ennobling thought, or, as explained above, religious truth. Pilate, a Roman logician, had quite a different conception of truth. When he said 'What is truth?' (Jn 18³⁸), he was moving in a universe of thought foreign to the Jews.

3. Hebrew method of attaining truth.—The Hebrew idea of truth being so different from our scientific standard, it is to be expected that their way of reaching it would correspondingly differ from our scientific method,—the observation and description of facts. The Hebrew method did not always seek facts, and, when they were at hand, was not content simply to describe them.

(1) Facts were sometimes 'invented.'

This may be illustrated by reference to Talmudic geography. The Talmud answers the question * as to which islands belong to Israel and which do not, by saying that if a straight line be drawn from Amanus (? a mountain in the north) to the River of Egypt, those islands situated within this line belong to the land of Israel, etc. But, of course, no islands ever belonged to the land of Israel at all. Again, it is deliberately asserted that there are seven seas in Palestine. Only six are named, but one of these is named twice in order to make up the number seven, merely so that the holy number may be introduced. And, further, apart from this specific enumeration, the Talmud names only four seas as included in Palestine. These two instances are typical. In the first, islands are said to exist which have never been observed, and in the other the number of actually existing seas is artificially increased in order to bring in the sacred seven.

(2) Metaphysical explanation was sometimes attempted, description in itself being considered inadequate. The introduction of the number seven above is an illustration of this. Ps 24 gives another type, where Jahweh is praised for His power and skill in making the solid and immovable earth to rest upon the fluid and fluctuating sea. The observation is a bad one, but that does not concern us. The point for us to notice is that to the observation that the land is 'founded upon the sea' is added the metaphysical explanation that this is a miraculous exhibition of the power of God. The fact that this is poetry, and could be paralleled with passages taken from modern Western poetry, does not affect the point, for these modern passages are admittedly and obviously poetical in contradiction to scientific statements, whereas in Hebrew literature there is no such distinction. What is said in poetry is equally true to the Hebrew mind when written in prose, as when the idea of the windows of heaven is repeated in such various literary styles as are found in Gn 7¹¹, 2 K 7², Mal 3¹⁰. Hence the indiscriminate Jewish doctrine of inspiration, which made no distinction between styles of literature, ascribing to all passages of the Canon an equal measure of truth.

The Jews did, of course, accumulate, as the Talmud and the OT sufficiently show, a mass of valid technical knowledge. They knew much concerning metals, such as gold; other chemical substances, such as soda; and certain processes of metallurgy. 'The Jews,' says Ernst von Meyer, 'did indeed possess a certain disjointed knowledge of chemical processes acquired accidentally, but these were applied for their practical results alone, and not with the object of deducing any comprehensive scientific explanation from them.' [By 'scientific explanation' here von Meyer means what has been called 'description' above]. They never made experiments. Any conclusions concerning nature at which they arrived were due to haphazard reflexion upon chance occurrences. Accurate description was not their object, nor did they attempt it. The facts of nature, like the incidents of history, were to them properly explained by reference to other things than those which might be observed. Rabbi Joshua, for instance, gives the following account of rain: 'The clouds ascend to the heights of the heavens, then stretch themselves out like a sponge and take up the rain-water; but having holes in them like a sieve, they let the water fall through on to the earth in drops.' That only one drop falls at a time is due to a kindly Providence, for otherwise great harm would be done to the earth (Bergel). The Rabbis explained thunder as the crashing together of clouds, or as the splitting of ice in the clouds when struck by the hot lightning. Earthquakes were variously described as God clapping His hands, or sighing, or treading upon His footstool. Of all scientific efforts the Jewish teachers seem to have been most successful in Astronomy. They described the heavens as a hollow, dome-like, half-ball, spread over the flat earth. The stars they held to be fixed to the inner surface of this dome,

* Tosefta, *Maaser sheni*, ch. 2; *Hallach*, ch. 2; Jerus. *Shebhiith* vi. 2; Bab. *Giṭṭin* 8a.

some of them being firmly fastened and others moving along ways made for them.

To whatever branch of knowledge we turn, we find that *observations* are an insignificant part of the system of teaching about nature, and for the method of mere description we have the method of metaphysical explanation.

4. Defects of Hebrew thought. — The history, political and geographical situation, and religious exclusiveness of the Hebrews assisted in the cultivation of a type of thought as characteristic and powerful as any that the world has seen. It is not enough to say that the Hebrew mind was 'Semitic'; for, while it shares many of the characteristics of the thought of other Semitic peoples, in some respects it stands out from them in bold contrast. Among the fine qualities of the Hebrew mind were : (1) a sanity and sobriety of thought which preserved their religion and literature from all those offensive and extravagant traits which mark the popular religions of Syria, Asia Minor, and Arabia ; (2) an extraordinary gift for the observation of individual incidents and facts, as appears in the inimitable narratives of the historical books of the OT ; the vivid portraiture, satire, and denunciation of the prophets ; and the marvellous, if often trivial, minuteness of Rabbinic discussions ; (3) unparalleled energy of feeling and sense of individuality ; and (4) a strength of will that alone can account for the vitality of a people which has been exposed to a more bitter persecution and more relentless fate than any other race in history. Of these four notable characteristics the third and fourth are obviously not such as tend to the cultivation of the scientific frame of mind. With the first and second it is quite otherwise—sobriety of thought and a keen eye for particulars are necessary to a proper scientific observation. But at the same time they are insufficient for scientific description, which demands certain mental qualities in which the Hebrew mind was notably deficient—breadth of vision, systematic and architectonic power, consistent and persistent thinking. An examination of Hebrew thought discovers, in general, a notable defect, traceable to this failure in breadth of grasp and over-emphasis on the particular and strong development of the emotional and volitional nature. This defect is the absence of the power of logical abstraction, and it shows itself in two ways that are of considerable importance—first, the Hebrew mind could not frame general definitions ; and, secondly, it had no notion of general law.

The Western (Greek) mode of definition *per genus et differentiam* we commonly assume not only to be the only mode possible, but also to be indispensable to thought. While it is indispensable to our modern thought, especially with its highly developed scientific method, it was not indispensable to the Hebrews, for they did without it. The Hebrews defined, not by reference to a class—as when we say 'man is a rational animal'—but by reference to a type, as when it is implied that natural man is Adam, and redeemed man is Christ, the second Adam (Ro 5, 1 Co 15).

In the second place, this inability to think abstractly prevented the Hebrews from arriving at the notion of natural law. The word 'law' in Hebrew literature always meant the arbitrary pronouncement of a ruler (of course a despot) or deity. Law meant nothing general or abstract. The *Torah* was an actual and definite direction given in Jahweh's name by the priest, and was either judicial, ceremonial, or moral. The various synonyms for *torah* have in general the same definite, particular character—'judgment,' 'statute,' 'commandment,' 'testimonies,' and 'precepts'*

* Respectively *mishpāṭ, ḥuḳḳāh, miẓwāh, 'ēdóth, piḳḳūdim.*

(see art. 'Law (in OT)' in Hastings' *DB*). When used in a general sense to indicate a large section of the OT, it is in no way abstract, but only collective.

The nearest approach which Hebrew thought offers to our highly abstract natural laws is to be found in certain proverbial sayings (*e.g.* Jer 31²⁹, Mt 16². ³), and a few rough groupings of empirical facts which we shall notice later on. There is nothing, however, that in any real sense corresponds with the modern idea of law as 'the *résumé* or *brief expression* of the relationships and sequences of' certain groups of' perceptions and conceptions, existing only 'when formulated by man' (Karl Pearson). The same characteristic explains the absence of abstract philosophic terms from Hebrew literature. The doctrine of freewill, *e.g.*, though constantly implied in the OT, is never abstractly stated. 'Instead of saying man is free, Scripture says man can choose ; he can act ; he can do' (Delitzsch, *Syst. of Bibl. Psychol.* p. 192).

5. Hebrew knowledge of Nature.—It follows from what we have seen that the Jews had no sound body of scientific doctrine. They had no very clearly defined conception of the earth and its surroundings, either in early times or at the time of Christ. They regarded the earth as the middle point of the universe. The heavens were a mere material covering or dome (Is 34⁴ 40²², Ps 104², Job 37¹⁸), with doors (Gn 28¹⁷, Ps 78²³) and windows (Gn 7¹¹ 8², 2 K 7². ¹⁹), and the earth rested on the sea (Ps 24²). These are obviously little more than childish reproductions of sense-impressions. The same is true of every department of physical science, including Astronomy. There is no criticism, no classification, no formulation of laws, no definite effort towards a coherent description of phenomena. When we turn to Mathematics, we find traces of very rudimentary knowledge. The square is mentioned (Ex 27¹ 28¹⁶), and the circle (Is 44¹³), the plumb-line and scales were known (Am 7⁷, 2 K 21¹³). The four simple mathematical processes appear also to have been practised : Addition (Nu 1²² 26⁷), Subtraction (Lv 27¹⁸, Ex 16²³), Multiplication (Lv 25⁸, Nu 3⁴⁶), Division (Lv 25²⁷. ⁵⁰).

The only department of thought in which the Hebrews can claim to have elaborated anything at all worthy to be called 'science' is literary criticism. This, however, was pursued, not in a modern spirit of desire for knowledge, but because the disasters which the nation had experienced drove its religious leaders to a more careful analysis and preservation of the Law, in order that, by obeying it, the anger of God might be appeased and the prosperity of the people might return. The scribes 'busied themselves in providing for all conceivable' legal 'cases that might occur, and especially in making a hedge or fence round the Law, *i.e.* in so expanding the compass of legal precept beyond what was laid down in the Pentateuch and in the oldest form of tradition, that it might be impossible for a man, if he observed all their traditional rules, to be even tempted to transgress the Law' (see art. 'Scribes' in Hastings' *DB*). Thus the literary and legal 'science' of the scribes had all the defects of the 'scientific' temper of the Jews—the criterion of truth was not descriptive accuracy, but edification, the method was inventive and metaphysical, there was an absence of generalizing and systematizing power, and an over-emphasis of the particular and concrete.

II. *RELATION OF CHRIST TO THE 'SCIENCE' OF HIS TIME AND RACE.*—We have now to inquire as to the mind of Christ in respect of the various matters discussed above, that is, we have to ask whether His standard of truth was Hebrew or modern ; whether He sought to explain nature by the metaphysical or the descriptive method ; whether He shared the mental characteristics of the Hebrews or not, and whether we are to assume that He held those erroneous views of nature which were common among the Hebrews.

1. Among the most obvious characteristics of the mind of Christ is His sense of the radical opposition between Himself and the life of His own day. This opposition expresses itself at every turn in many ways. The political ambitions of the Herodians, the compromising worldliness of the Sadducees, the formalism and pride of the Pharisees, and the carnal carelessness of the generality, alike met with His denunciation and appeal. The traditions of the scribes He altogether rejected, and even the authority of the Law He subjected to a penetrating criticism. Against all existing systems of thought, all Rabbinical teaching, all conventional observance, He set up one authority—His own consciousness of God, Himself. In a unique way He lived in the realities of things, never compromising, never with double mind. To the great reality of the Father and of the Kingdom was added the great reality of Himself, in simple deep-founded truth.

2. We have seen that the Hebrew notion of truth differed from the modern notion, in that it rather attached to the nature of a person than to the quality of a proposition. A proposition was true, not so much because it tallied with certain facts as because it had its origin in a certain character. In other words, the Jewish idea of truth was religious, while the modern idea is scientific. But the Jewish idea was never purely religious. It was confused with metaphysical and mechanical elements. In the mind of Jesus, however, this Hebrew notion of religious truth is purified of all foreign elements, and ceases all contact with the accidents of experience, making its home in the soul and in God.

It is noteworthy that the Synoptists report no sayings of Jesus from which these conclusions as to the meaning Christ attached to the word 'truth' can be formally drawn, though, when once they have been drawn, it is seen that none of the sayings of Jesus contradicts them. In the Synoptics the word 'truth' is not used by Jesus except in such phrases as 'of a truth,' the Gr. equivalent for 'Amen' (Lk 9²⁷ 12⁴⁴ 21³). When we come to the Fourth Gospel, however (which we assume to be of sufficient historicity to allow us to use the words ascribed to Jesus as representing His thought), we find the words 'true' and 'truth' continually in the mouth of Christ. Now, while the criterion of truth in the mind of Christ does not vary, we must not be surprised if different shades of meaning are expressed from time to time by the same words 'true' and 'truth.' Indeed, Jesus does not use the word 'truth' always with the same *nuance* of meaning. In the first place, it represents a quality in a person (4²³ 18³⁷), then a quality which attaches to actions (3²¹), and, finally, that which may be communicated from God to man in thought so as to affect the life and give the quality referred to above (8³² 14¹⁷ 16¹³ 17¹⁷). The whole conception is summed up in 14⁶, where Jesus says, 'I am the way, and the truth, and the life'—the Personality of Jesus is a revelation that is ethical and vitalizing, and that comes to men to quicken consciences, illumine minds, and arouse affections. There is, indeed, in this thought an element answering to our modern notion of accuracy; it is not, however, explicit, but implicit in the idea of a faithful or reliable character. Thus Jesus carries the Hebrew idea of religious truth to its final expression, and in so doing neither anticipates nor challenges the modern notion of scientific truth. To the modern mind truth is description of phenomena—to Christ it meant spiritual insight: by the modern mind it is reached through demonstration and reasoning—for Christ it was instinctive or inspirational: to the modern mind it is part of a system of thought—with Christ it was an element or moment in life.

'ἀλήθεια,' says Beyschlag, 'is to Him not this or that worldly and finite truth, but the truth of God, the revelation of God as the eternally good, who, as such, is open-hearted to the world . . . it is the sister of χάρις, for every revelation of God is a revelation of holy love' (*NT Theol.* ii. 429). See also TRUTH.

3. But although 'truth,' according to the mind of Christ, was a Hebrew and religious concept and not the modern scientific notion, the thought of Jesus was free from all the extravagances which we have seen to be characteristic of the Jews, though it shared some of their conceptions as to natural phenomena.* If His thought was not scientific, neither was it pseudo-scientific. Neither the *midrash* of the Jewish annalist nor the magical metaphysics of the Rabbis has any place in His teaching. While He was a keen observer of nature (Mt 6²⁶. ²⁸ 13³¹. ³². ³⁶⁻⁴³, Mk 4²⁶⁻²⁹, Lk 13⁶⁻⁹. ²⁰. ²¹), His utterances about nature never attempted explanations beyond the reach of observation; and while His judgment was to an unequalled degree independent, He neither criticised the scientific opinions of His day nor attempted to add to humanity's inadequate store of knowledge. Whether this abstinence from scientific speculation and instruction was intentional (as Wendt suggests), or the natural result of His unwavering and complete concentration of soul upon 'His Father's business,' is not important in this connexion. It is sufficient to notice that He eschewed alike Rabbinical explanations and scientific research, dealing finally only with 'those matters which are naturally the objects of spiritual intuition,' and which, unlike natural phenomena, cannot be adequately investigated by the human understanding.

So far as nature is concerned, then, we may say that the knowledge which Jesus exhibits in His sayings is just such as a free mind with great natural powers of fresh observation might gather from a joyous intercourse with the ordinary aspects of the material world.

4. One matter of considerable controversial importance, however, in this connexion demands brief attention. What was the attitude of Jesus to the literary 'science' of the Rabbis? It was a double attitude. First, He abolished certain precepts of the Law itself (Mt 5³². ³⁸), and added others on His own authority (vv.³². ³⁴. ³⁹); and, secondly, He disparaged and discredited the learned societies of scribes, and, by the weight of His own authority, overthrew their teaching. But this repudiation of the teaching of the schools and criticism of the Law was not conceived in any modern scientific temper, or achieved by means of modern critical apparatus. It was the inevitable outcome of Christ's conception of Divine truth as a living reality within Himself. His utterances concerning the OT were all from this point of view. He judged them according to their spiritual and religious value, not according to any canons of textual criticism, modern or ancient. This is true even in the case of the quotation from Ps 110. 'He did not weigh a truth,' says Bishop Moorhouse, 'in what we should call critical balances . . . the question of the age or authorship of any passage in the OT was never either stated by our Lord Himself or raised by His opponents.'

5. We have next to ask whether we may conclude from His recorded sayings that Jesus shared those logical characteristics which we have seen to be at the foundations of Hebrew 'scientific' thought. We noticed two main marks of the Hebrew mind —its vivid, simple, and temperate apprehension of the details of life and nature, and its inability to take such a wide and comprehensive view of fact and experience as would make the generalizations of modern science possible. The first of these is

---

* Jesus' evident acquiescence in Jewish demonology, at least in its main features, is a case in point.

pre-eminently characteristic of the thought of Jesus. The vivid originality, profound simplicity, and pictorial impressiveness of His speech make every reader of His words agree that ' never man so spake.' His insight into the human soul, His parables so true to life, His startling paradoxes, His telling object-lessons, all show the best traits of Jewish thought carried to their highest power. The concrete, stirring, and simple elements of life are seized and appreciated with the imagination of the poet and the practical sense of the workman. Jesus is never abstract, never modern—but always particular and Hebrew. But, on the other hand, it is impossible to speak of the mind of Jesus as defective in the sense given above. While He always expresses Himself with the simple concreteness characteristic of Hebrew thought, it cannot be said that He is limited by it, for it is the best possible medium or dialectic in which to enunciate *religious* truth. It is scientific truth which demands abstraction, with definitions *per genus et differentiam* and laws. We have seen that Jesus remained always and wholly within the world of religious truth, and always and wholly outside the world of scientific statement. He was not a theologian who theorized about religious truth—He was the Truth. He was not a philosopher who tried to prove the being of God—He declared God. And so the apparatus of scientific description was for Him unnecessary. It would be futile to speculate as to whether He could have used it had He wished. All we need say is that He was a Jew with a Hebrew mind of the highest possible type, and so in the fullest possible sense equipped to utter the highest revelation of God which has been vouchsafed to man.

LITERATURE.—Bergel, *Die Medecin der Talmudister : Studien über die naturwissensch. Kenntnisse der Talmudisten* ; Beyschlag, *NT Theol.* ; Bousset, *Jesu Predigt in ihrem Gegensatz zum Judentum* ; Delitzsch, *System of Biblical Psychology* ; Edersheim, *Life and Times of Jesus* ; Günzburg, *Dogmat.-histor. Beleuchtung des alten Judentums* ; Kopp, *Gesch. der Chemie* ; Lewysohn, *Die Zoologie des Talmuds* ; E. von Meyer, *Hist. of Chemistry* ; Moorhouse, *The Teachings of Jesus* ; A. Neubauer, *Géog. du Talmud* ; W. Nowack, *Lehrb. der Heb. Arch.* ; Karl Pearson, *Grammar of Science* ; Schürer, *HJP, passim* ; Stevens, *Teaching of Jesus* ; Wendt, *Teaching of Jesus.*   NEWTON H. MARSHALL.

SCORN.—Of scorn pure and simple there is remarkably little trace in the recorded words and actions of Jesus Christ. Whereas other teachers of lofty morality have usually treated with some contempt those who made no effort to approach their ideals, Christ's attitude towards the sinner was uniformly one of sympathetic help. He alone recognized the intimate relation which exists between the Creator and the human race, and His knowledge of this relation and of the possibilities of each individual prevented Him from despising man, whom the Father had made in His own image, however much that image might have been defaced. Thus it is that we never find Him using sarcasm, a form of scorn calculated to wound rather than to improve. Even the εἰρωνεία of Socrates, the affected self-depreciation which threw ridicule upon the egotism of others, has no counterpart in the Gospels. When Jesus used scorn, He employed it as a skilled physician, who wounds with the intention of healing. It is thus that He uses it to the Pharisees, whose cloak of self-righteousness needed to be pierced through with some sharp weapon, if they were to be brought to the state of mind in which they might be capable of any improvement.

1. The scorn of contempt.—A single word of unmitigated contempt is recorded by St. Luke as used by Christ. It occurs in His answer to the threat used by certain Pharisees of danger from Herod Antipas (Lk 13³¹· ³²). ' Go ye,' He said,

' and tell that she-fox.' The phrase τῇ ἀλώπεκι ταύτῃ is certainly surprising at first sight, and unlike any other phrase employed by our Lord, not even excepting His comparison of the scribes and Pharisees to ' whited sepulchres,' ' serpents,' and ' offspring of vipers ' (Mt 23²⁷· ³³). The fact of the word ἀλώπεκι being in the feminine gender is perhaps only an accident. The word is found, it is true, in the masculine gender in Ca 2¹⁵, but it is generally found in the feminine, *e.g.* Jg 1³⁵, 1 K 21¹⁰, Mt 8²⁰, Lk 9⁵⁸. The fox was and is a type of knavish craftiness. The particular offence of Herod on this occasion was his crafty endeavour to get rid of an influential preacher of righteousness by uttering a threat by the mouth of others, which he had not the courage himself to carry into effect. He was unwilling to add to the unpopularity caused by his treatment of John the Baptist by a repetition of it in the case of Jesus. No doubt the general character and conduct of Herod helped to suggest the application of the expression,—his unscrupulous nature (Lk 3¹⁹ περὶ πάντων ὧν ἐποίησε πονηρῶν), his tyranny (13³¹), his weakness (Mk 14⁹), his profession of Judaism, combined with his heathen practices, his adultery and incest, and his murder of the prophet John. Such is the character which elicits the one recorded word of contemptuous scorn from the lips of Jesus.

2. The scorn of denunciation.—While remarkably free from any contempt for those people who had ideals and failed to reach them (*e.g.* the young man with great riches and the Apostle Peter), or for those who from lack of any ideal were for the time outcast from society (*e.g.* the despised publicans, Mk 2¹⁵⁻¹⁷), He showed clearly His contempt for all religious professions and practices which were not of the heart. ' The vain practices of devotees,' says Renan, ' the exterior strictness which trusted to formality for salvation, had in Him a mortal enemy . . . He preferred forgiveness to sacrifice. The love of God, charity, and mutual forgiveness were His whole law.' Yet in all His dealings with the systems of the scribes and the teaching of the legal doctors, His words bear little trace of mere contempt, but rather of stern denunciation. His attitude was defined at a comparatively early stage during the ministry in Northern Galilee, when He gave His definition of moral defilement (Mt 15¹¹, Mk 7¹⁵) by saying, ' Not that which goeth into the mouth defileth the man ; but that which proceedeth out of the mouth, this defileth the man.' This attitude culminated in the sublime anti-Pharisaic discourse in which the foibles and vices of a degenerate piety were depicted with prophetic plainness and scornful denunciation (Mt 23 ; cf. also Mk 12³⁸⁻⁴⁰ and Lk 20⁴⁵⁻⁴⁷).

3. The scorn of silence.—Of all the occasions of scorn displayed by Jesus, none are more marked than those when He met mere captious questions and criticism either by a definite refusal to answer, or by absolute silence. Such an instance is recorded (Mt 21²³⁻²⁷) when Jesus met the question of the chief priests and scribes, ' By what authority doest thou these things ? ' with a counter question, and on their refusal to answer declined in turn to reply to their question. Still more impressive was the silent scorn with which He met His accusers at the various stages of His trial, refusing in turn to answer the accusation of false witnesses (Mt 26⁶⁰⁻⁶³, Mk 14⁶¹) and the questions of the chief priests and elders (Mt 27¹², Mk 15³· ⁵), of Herod (Lk 23⁹), and lastly of Pilate himself (Mt 27¹⁴, Jn 19⁹).

In comparing these instances, we find no word used simply for the purpose of causing pain. The contemptuous expression used on the occasion of Herod's threat is, we have seen, amply justified by the character of the man, and destined to hold up to reprobation so paltry a device and so wretched a personality. In the rest His silence is an expression of His own dignity, and of His refusal to give an answer to questions and charges which were not intended to bring the truth to light, but merely to raise unreasonable prejudice ; while His severe attacks on the character of those who were too blinded by their imaginary virtues to try to amend their lives, are wonderful instances of a scorn unmarred by ill-nature and untainted with cynicism.

On scorn of which Christ was the *object*, see artt. DESPISE, MOCKERY, REPROACH.

T. ALLEN MOXON.

SCORPION (σκορπίος).—A real nuisance in hot countries, especially in Bible lands, scarce and comparatively innocuous in Southern Europe, the scorpion is unknown save from hearsay in Central and Northern Europe. It has, however, left its mark in the familiar expression *in cauda venenum*, as well as in astronomical science, where it counts amongst the constellations of the Zodiac.

1. *Zoological description.*—The scorpion is an arthropod, of the class of *Arachnoidæ*, of the subclass of *Arthrogastra*, of the order of *Scorpionidæ*. It has four pairs of legs, and in front one pair of extremely strong claws (*palpi*). Its abdomen consists of 7 anterior segments, broad and intimately connected with the cephalo-thorax, and of 6 posterior segments, which are narrower, and constitute the tail (or post-abdomen). The last of these 6 posterior segments is incurved underneath, and terminates in a pointed hook surrounded by two powerful venomous glands. The scorpion catches its prey with its strong claws, curves its tail towards it above its own back, and inflicts the death sting. The scorpion's sting is very painful even for man ; it may prove fatal when the insect belongs to one of the big tropical species ; and even with minor species life may be imperilled when the throat is concerned ; cf. Tristram (*Nat. Hist. of Bible*[8], p. 303), who has 'known one instance [in Palestine] of a man dying from the effect of the scorpion's sting.'

There occurs in Southern Europe, sometimes even in Switzerland and Southern Germany, a species of scorpion relatively innocuous—the *scorpius Europæus*. In the Mediterranean peninsulæ as well as in the South of France, another more dangerous species is to be found, the *Buthus occitanus*. In the Eastern lands of the Bible there are six, eight, perhaps even twelve different species of scorpions belonging to the genera *Buthus* and *Androctonus*. They reach a length of 5 to 6 inches (in tropical countries 12 inches ; cf. Morris, *Bible Natural History*, Calcutta, 1896, p. 101). Palgrave (*Central and Eastern Arabia*, 1883, p. 28) was stung in Arabia by one of the numerous 'desert scorpions,' which he describes as 'curious little creatures, about a fourth of an inch in length, and apparently all claws and tail, of a deep reddish-brown colour, and very active.' The Talmud of Jerusalem (*Ber.* 9a) says that the scorpion's sting is even more dangerous than that of the snake, because it repeats it. Conder (*Tent Work*[6], 1895, p. 113) tells that he was stung by one scorpion 'in six places along the leg.'

Scorpions are exclusively carnivorous, feeding upon insects and worms. They are useful in destroying mosquitoes. Not infrequently they devour each other. The female scorpion eats up the male after fecundation.

Ancient authors (Aristotle, Pliny) report that scorpions devour their own parents. This assertion is connected with a false etymology of the Heb. word עַקְרָב (true etymology unknown), as if it were derived from עָקַר 'to exterminate,' and אָב 'father.' Thomson (*LB* ii. 480) 'tried the experiment of surrounding a

scorpion with a ring of fire, and when it despaired of escape, it repeatedly struck its own head, and soon died either from the poison or 'ts Satanic rage—I could not be certain which—perhaps from both combined.'

There are differently coloured scorpions : some are black, others brown, reddish, yellowish, grey or white, some are striped. They are frequently found in Palestine under stones, among ruins, in crevices of walls, in dung-heaps, and empty cisterns. Travellers camping in tents or lodging in the houses of natives, as well as archæologists conducting excavations, have to be careful to guard themselves and their men from scorpions ; for even when the sting is not fatal, it is a cause of acute pain, and prevents walking and working.

According to a popular superstition, a man who has eaten a scorpion is immune against the sting of any of these animals, and able to relieve a victim by sucking the wound (Conder, *l.c.*). It is also believed that by applying to the wound a squashed scorpion, or by reading some magic formulæ over the patient, a cure is effected.

2. OT references.—In geography, scorpions gave their name to a place mentioned in the OT—the 'Ascent of Scorpions,' *ma'aleh 'Akrabbim* (Nu 34[4], Jos 15[3], Jg 1[36]), at the limit of the territory of Judah, towards Idumæa, south-west from the Dead Sea ; it is probably the pass now called *Nakb es-Safâ*, leading to Wady-Fikreh, or another pass near the same wady.

This place afterwards gave its name to a toparchy (1 Mac 5[3], Jos. *Ant.* XII. viii. 1), the Idumæan *Akrabattene*, which is not to be confused with another toparchy also called Akrabattene (Jos. *BJ* II. xii. 4, xx. 4, xxii. 2, III. iii. 5, IV. ix. 3, 9), from its chief city, Akrabatta—in the *Onomasticon* Ἀκραββείν (cf. Pliny, *HN* v. 14), in the *Chronicon Samaritanum* Akrabith, in modern times Akrabeh—9 Roman miles (8 English miles) east from Nâblus, on the way to Jericho (Robinson, *BRP* ii. 280, iii. 296 f. ; Guérin, *Samarie*, ii. 3-5 ; *SWP* ii. 386, 389 ; *PEFSt*, 1876, p. 196). There is also near Damascus a village Akraba, which has given its name to the Akrabani, a canal of the Barada (Robinson, *BRP* iii. 447, 459).

Once only in the OT is there mention of scorpions in the proper sense, Dt 8[15], where they are named as one of the plagues of the desert of the wanderings.

In 1 K 12[11. 14] (and v.[24] in LXX, a verse missing in MT) and 2 Ch 10[11. 14] the word 'scorpion' occurs in the threats of King Rehoboam to his subjects. In this case scorpion may be simply a metaphor ; but it is also possible that under this name the Israelites were acquainted with some instrument of torture, either a whip consisting of several thongs loaded with knobs and hooks of metal, or a knotty stick armed with prominent nail heads. The Romans had such an instrument ; cf. Isidorus of Sevilla (*Origines*, 27) : 'Virga nodosa et aculeata.'

In Ezk 2[6] scorpions symbolize (with briars and thorns) the vexations inflicted on the prophet by his companions. In Sir 26[7] the wicked woman is compared with the scorpion ; in 39[30] scorpions are numbered among the plagues God uses for chastising the ungodly. In 4 Mac 11[10] a man fastened in the torture-wheel is compared with a scorpion curving its body. Finally, in 1 Mac 6[51] a kind of machine of war for throwing projectiles is mentioned under the (diminutive) name of σκορπίδια (cf. Cæsar, *BG* vii. 25).

3. NT references.—The Gospels mention scorpions twice. (1) In Lk 11[11. 12] we have three questions concerning a father giving to his son a stone instead of a loaf, a serpent instead of a fish, a scorpion instead of an egg. In the parallel passage (Mt 7[9. 10]) the third question is omitted (and in certain MSS and Versions of Luke the first question) ; hence it has been asserted that the saying of Jesus in its primitive form contained only two questions or perhaps one. But Jesus may have given more than one or two illustrations of His meaning, and we have to remember that bread, fish, and eggs were (and are still) the usual food of the inhabitants of Galilee. It has been frequently asked whether a scorpion bears such a likeness to an egg that a confusion between the two would be natural. But there is no question of likeness or confusion in this third case any more than in the case of the loaf and the stone, the fish and the serpent. It is not at all satisfactory to say with Thomson (*LB* ii. 479), that 'old writers speak of a white scorpion ; and such a one, with its tail folded up . . . would not look unlike a small egg.'

The Greeks had a proverb resembling the text of the Gospels we are discussing—ἀντὶ πέρκης σκορπίον, and they used to interpret it by saying: ἐπὶ τῶν τὰ χείρω αἱρουμένων ἀντὶ τῶν βελτιόνων. The existence of that proverb does not prove that Jesus necessarily associated in one single sentence the fish and the scorpion, and that ᾠόν has to be corrected into ὄψον.

(2) Jesus says (Lk 10[19]) that He has given His disciples τὴν ἐξουσίαν τοῦ πατεῖν ἐπάνω ὄφεων καὶ σκορπίων. There seems to be in these words an allusion to Ps 91[13], where the LXX has (90[13]) ἐπ' ἀσπίδα καὶ βασιλίσκον ἐπιβήσῃ, whereas the MT has 'lion' and 'adder.' The Hebrew and Greek disagreeing, it is not impossible that in another transmission the scorpion has been substituted for one of the terms signifying serpent. It is certainly more natural to combine Lk 10[19] with Ps 91[13], than with Dt 8[15] or with Ezk 2[6] : both these texts are more similar *ad verbum*, not *ad sensum*.

Another question is whether 'serpents and scorpions' means here animals in the proper sense of the word (Mk 16[18] and Ac 28[3-6] might be quoted in support of this interpretation), or if it is a metaphor indicating the powers of evil. This alternative, however, does not correspond to the notions of the ancients, who did not, as we do, make a rigorous distinction between terrestrial and supra-terrestrial beings. Joh. Weiss (*Schriften des NT, ad loc.*) says rightly that an excellent illustration of this passage of the Gospel is given in the famous verse of Luther's hymn : 'Und wenn die Welt voll Teufel wär . . .' Moreover, we have to observe that Rev 9[3, 5, 10] describe supernatural destructive beings similar, at least partially, to scorpions. This has to be brought into conjunction with an antique Babylonian conception. In the epic of Gilgamesh (Table IX. cols. ii.–iv.) we find the mention of two scorpion-men, one male and the other female, terrible giants, keepers of a door (cf. P. Jensen, 'Assyr.-Bab. Mythen und Epen' in *KIB* vi. p. 205 ff., and the same writer's *Das Gilgamesch-Epos in der Weltliteratur*, i. pp. 24–27, 79, 93). A. Jeremias (*Izdubar-Nimrod*, 1891, p. 66 f.) and F. X. Kugler ('Die Sternenfahrt des Gilgamesch,' in *Stimmen aus Maria Laach*, lxvi., 1904, p. 441 ff.) have shown that those two celestial scorpions—reproduced in Babylonian sculptures—were the two zodiacal constellations Scorpio and Sagittarius. We might also see, but less probably, in the second scorpion, the constellation of the Balance, which was called by the ancient Greeks *Chelæ*, i.e. the 'Claws' of the Scorpion (cf. Ideler, *Sternnamen*, pp. 174–178).

In Christian art the scorpion has received a symbolical character, as an emblem of the anti-Christian power. Thus a scorpion is to be seen on the shield of a Roman soldier in B. Luini's celebrated fresco, 'The Crucifixion,' in Santa Maria degli Angeli, Lugano.

LITERATURE.—Bochart, *Hierozoicon*, ii. pp. 632–645 ; Petermann, *Reisen im Orient*[2], 1865, ii. pp. 272, 465 ; Wood, *Bible Animals*, 1869, pp. 640–643 ; *PEFSt*, 1869, p. 148 ; Van-Lennep, *Bible Lands*, 1875, pp. 309–311 ; Tristram, *Nat. Hist. of the Bible*[8], 1889, pp. 301–303 ; Doughty, *Arabia Deserta*, 1888, i. pp. 328, 438 ; R. Hertwig, *Lehrbuch der Zoologie*[4], 1897, p. 441 ff. ; J. H. Fabre, *Souvenirs entomologiques*, ix. pp. 229–343 (extremely patient, accurate, and interesting observations).

LUCIEN GAUTIER.

SCOURGE, SCOURGING.—In the Gospels the vb. 'scourge' is tr. of two Gr. terms, μαστιγόω (fr. μάστιξ, found in Gospels only in a metaphorical sense [EV 'plague,' RVm 'Gr. scourge'], but used in its literal meaning in Ac 22[24], He 11[36]) ; and φραγελλόω (fr. φραγέλλιον, Lat. *flagellum*, which

occurs in Jn 2[15]). φραγέλλιον denotes the scourge proper as an instrument of punishment, while μάστιξ in class. Gr. is often used of an ordinary whip for driving, etc. In NT, however, μαστιγόω is a synonym for φραγελλόω (cf. Mk 10[34] and 15[15], Mt 27[26] and Jn 19[1]). The subject of scourging comes before us in three connexions.

(1) In Jn 2[15] Jesus makes a scourge (φραγέλλιον) of cords (ἐκ σχοινίων) and drives the desecrating crowd of traders, as well as their sheep and oxen, out of the Temple. Farrar and others have represented this scourge of Jesus as nothing more than a whip twisted hastily out of the rushes with which the floor would be littered—a pure symbol of authority, therefore, not a weapon of offence. In this case, however, we should have had σχοίνων, not σχοινίων. σχοινίον is a rope, not a rush, and though originally applied to a rope made from rushes, is used in class. Gr. in a general sense. On the only other occasion of its employment in the NT it means a rope strong enough to tow a ship's boat in a gale (Ac 27[32]). To drive a herd of oxen out of the Temple courts, moreover, something more than a symbol of authority would be required. But we need not suppose that Jesus, even in His indignation, struck the merchants themselves. For them the sign of His authority would be sufficient (cf. Jn 18[6]), and, as Bengel says, 'terrore rem perfecit.'

(2) In Mt 10[17] Jesus forewarns the Apostles of a time when men would scourge them in their synagogues ; and in 23[34] He predicts that the scribes and Pharisees will thus treat those whom He sends unto them. The later history gives ample evidence of the fulfilment of these words (see Ac 5[40] 22[19], 2 Co 6[5] 11[23, 24]).

(3) But, above all, we must think of the scourging endured by Jesus Himself. According to all the Synoptics, Jesus foresaw this as part of the suffering that lay before Him (Mt 20[19], Mk 10[34], Lk 18[33]). It was, indeed, almost inseparable from His vision of the Cross, for scourging formed the ordinary accompaniment of a Roman crucifixion (cf. Jos. *BJ* v. xi. 1). Sometimes it was employed in criminal cases as a means of extracting confession, but regularly as the brutal preliminary to the still more brutal death of the cross. Because of the apparent inconsistency between Mt 27[26], Mk 15[15], on the one hand, and Jn 19[1], on the other, as to the particular stage of the trial at which Jesus was scourged, some have thought that the torture was twice inflicted. A careful comparison of the four Gospels, however, does not support this idea. The statements of Mt. and Mk., though they convey, when taken alone, the impression of a scourging immediately before the crucifixion, do not necessarily bear this meaning, but may quite well be understood retrospectively, and as implying simply that Jesus had to endure the scourge before going to the cross. Probably the key to the difficulty is to be found in Lk.'s narrative, where Pilate says, 'Why, what evil hath this man done? I have found no cause of death in him : I will therefore chastise him and release him' (23[22]). These words show that Pilate meant the scourging to be a compromise between the death which the Jews demanded and the verdict of absolute innocence which was called for by his own sense of justice. And this is confirmed by Jn.'s narrative, which shows Pilate scourging Jesus (19[1]) and holding Him up to mockery (vv.[2, 3]) in the evident hope of satisfying the multitude, still insisting that he found no crime in Him (v.[4]), and yielding at last, only with reluctance, to the demand for His crucifixion (v.[6ff.]). See art. TRIAL OF JESUS CHRIST.

A Roman scourging might be carried out either with rods (*virgæ*, ῥάβδοι)—the weapons of lictors, or with the scourge proper (*flagellum*, φραγέλλιον), in which leather thongs weighted with rough pieces of lead or iron were attached to a stout wooden handle. St. Paul's three Roman scourgings, as distinguished from his five Jewish ones, were inflicted by means of rods (ῥαβδίζω, 2 Co 11[25], Ac 16[22. 23]). But Jerusalem was not a Roman town, like Philippi (Ac 16[12] RV), and Pilate had no lictors. Jesus was scourged by soldiers, and the implement they used, as the vb. φραγελλόω (Mt 27[26], Mk 15[15]) almost implies, would be the dreadful Roman *flagellum*. St. Peter may have witnessed it all ; and what a world of meaning then lies in his words, 'by whose stripes [Gr. 'bruise' or 'weal'] ye were healed' (1 P 2[24], cf. Is 53[5]).

LITERATURE.—The Comm. on the passages quoted, esp. Westcott, *Gosp. of St. John*, and Bruce and Dods in *EGT*; Taylor Innes, *The Trial of Jesus Christ : A Legal Monograph* (1899); Rosadi, *The Trial of Jesus* (1905) ; Farrar, *Christ in Art*, p. 378 ff., *St. Paul*, i. Excurs. xi.   J. C. LAMBERT.

SCRIBES.—The Scribes were a class of learned Jews who devoted themselves to a scientific study of the Law, and made its exposition their professional occupation. The word which we translate 'scribes' is γραμματεῖς, 'the learned,' which corresponds to the Hebrew סוֹפְרִים. This is their usual appellation, but they are also called in the Gospels, especially in Lk., 'lawyers' (νομικοί) and 'doctors of the law' (νομοδιδάσκαλοι). See LAWYER. They are very frequently associated in the Synoptics with the Pharisees, and with the chief priests and elders, but there is no mention of 'scribes' in the Fourth Gospel at all, except in the special passage dealing with the woman taken in adultery (Jn 8[3]).

1. Origin, development, and characteristics.— (1) After the return from the Exile the Jewish community was organized under Ezra and Nehemiah on the basis of the regulations of the so-called Mosaic Law. At a great gathering of the people, of which an account is given in Neh 8–10, the Law was publicly read by Ezra, and a solemn covenant entered into for national obedience to it. Being thus established as the binding rule of both civil and religious life, it became necessary that the Law should be thoroughly studied and interpreted to the people, who otherwise could not reasonably be expected to comprehend fully its principles and their application. This duty at first fell naturally to the priests, who for a time continued the main teachers and guardians of the Law. But gradually there grew up an independent class of men, other than the priests, who devoted themselves to the study of the Law, and made acquaintance with it their profession. These were the Scribes. Possibly at first their chief duty was to make copies of the Law, but the higher function of interpretation was soon added ; and as the supreme importance of the Law came more and more to be recognized, so the profession of a Scribe came to be held in higher estimation than even that of a priest.

(2) During the Grecian period of Jewish history, a strong feeling of opposition was developed between the Scribes and, at least, the higher order of the priests. Even in the time of Ezra a feud had arisen between those who held strictly by the Law—especially in the matter of foreign alliances —and those who, like the aristocratic high-priestly families, had sought to increase their influence by marriage with outsiders. And when, through the influence of Hellenic culture, the priestly aristocracy became infected with heathen ideas, and fell away from the laws and customs of Judaism, the duty of upholding the Law fell mainly upon the Scribes, who from that time forward became the real teachers of the people, and dominated their whole spiritual life. They were still, however, mainly religious students and teachers, and had taken little part in political agitation. Their ideal was not to engage in any political scheme for throwing off the foreign yoke, but to establish the Law of God in their own midst. The attempt of Antiochus Epiphanes to suppress the Jewish religion compelled them to change their character, and drove them into open rebellion. Among the most strenuous opponents of his endeavour to Hellenize the Jews were the Hasidæans, or party of 'the pious,' who may be taken to represent the strictest adherents of the teaching of the Scribes, and who carried their ideas of the sanctity of the Law to the suicidal extent of refusing to defend themselves when attacked on the Sabbath. But it was only the maintenance of the Jewish religion for which they fought, and they had no objections to alien rule, provided they were allowed freedom of faith. This object they regarded as accomplished by the treaty with Lysias, which provided at once for their political subjection and for their religious freedom. When, therefore, it became clear that the Maccabæan party were aiming also at the political independence of the nation, the Hasidæans separated from them, and in the time of John Hyrcanus we find the Pharisees—'the separated' —who practically represented the same party as the Hasidæans, in opposition to the Hasmonæan or Maccabæan dynasty. See PHARISEES.

(3) From this time onward to the time of Christ the influence of the Scribes became more and more predominant. They were given seats in the Sanhedrin, and were held in very high respect by the people. They never, indeed, became the governing class, but in the councils of the nation their influence could always be depended upon to outweigh that of the priestly aristocracy, who held the high appointments. They were usually addressed as 'Rabbi,' *i.e.* 'my master,' an appellation which gradually developed into a title, though not till after the time of Christ. The honour in which they were held by their pupils, and by others, was extraordinary, even exceeding the honour accorded to parents, and they were very particular in exacting it, claiming generally everywhere the first rank. Their scribal labours were understood to be gratuitous, and, if they had no private fortune, they had to provide for their livelihood by combining some secular business with their study of the Law ; but the latter was always regarded as their most important occupation. It is questionable, however, if the theory of gratuitous instruction was always strictly adhered to.

From the earliest period there is evidence to show that they tended to associate themselves in guilds or families — an arrangement which would facilitate the interchange of opinion on difficult points in the study of the Law. Up till the destruction of Jerusalem the main seat of their activity was in Judæa, 'the scribes from Jerusalem' (Mt 15[1], Mk 3[22]) being spoken of as the most important and influential members of the party. But they were to be found elsewhere as well, in Galilee and among the Jews in other lands, wherever the Law and its precepts were held in esteem. As a rule, they may be said to have been Pharisees, although not exclusively. The Pharisees, indeed, were those whose professed object it was to regulate their lives in strict accordance with the Law, written and oral, as that was expounded by its best accredited interpreters. Hence there was a natural affinity between them and the Scribes, whose profession it was to interpret the Law. But it is extremely probable that there were also Scribes who were Sadducees, for the Sadducees also adhered to the written Law, and doubtless had their Scribes to interpret it. Support is lent to this view by the expressions in Mk 2[16] 'the scribes of the Pharisees,' and in Lk 5[30] 'the Pharisees and their scribes,' which seem to indicate that there were other Scribes than those of the Pharisees. In the time of Christ the great mass of the Scribes was divided into two schools, named after the famous leaders, Hillel and Shammai, about whom little is certainly known. The School of Hillel was distinguished for its mildness in the interpretation of the Law, and that of Shammai for its strictness, corresponding to the traditional characters of the respective founders; but the points of difference between them concerned only the trivial minutiæ, and never touched the weightier matters of the Law.

2. Functions.—The functions of the Scribes are well summed up in the traditional saying ascribed to the 'Men of the Great Synagogue.' 'These laid down three rules: Be careful in pronouncing judgment! bring up many pupils! and make a fence about the Law!' The professional employment of the Scribes, therefore, fell under three heads:—(1) The study and development of the Law itself; (2) the teaching of it to their pupils; and (3) its practical administration in the Sanhedrin and other courts; that is to say, they acted as students, teachers, and judges.

(1) *The study and development of the Law.*—The Mosaic Law, as embodied in their sacred records, was definitely recognized by the Jews as the absolute rule of life. To direct his conduct in accordance with it in every minute detail was the ideal of the pious Jew. But there were many subjects upon which the Law, as recorded, gave no precise direction, and much of it, for popular apprehension, required interpretation and exposition. To interpret and expound it, and to fill up what was lacking in the way of casuistic detail, was the business of the Scribes. They devoted themselves to a close and careful study of the Law, to the accumulation of precedents, to the working out of inferences and deductions, and to a general development of legal regulations so as to meet every possible circumstance which might occur in human life, and to keep the Law in harmony with the changing wants of the times. So diligently did they pursue this course, and so extensive and complicated did Jewish Law in consequence become, that only by the assiduous study of a lifetime could a man become an expert in its various branches. The difficulty of doing so was greatly increased by the fact that this mass of accumulated detail was not committed to writing, but was propagated entirely by oral tradition. It was called the Halacha, or Law of Custom, as distinct from the Torah, or Written Law, upon which it was understood to be based. See, further, art. PHARISEES, p. 353 f.

But the Scribes did not confine their labours to the Law. They studied also the historical and didactic portions of Scripture, and elaborated with a very free hand the history and religious instruction contained therein. This elaboration was called the Haggadah. It ran into various extravagant forms — theosophic, eschatological, and Messianic. Imagination was given free play, so long as its products would fit in with the general framework of Jewish thought, and to its influence was largely due the circle of religious ideas existing in New Testament times.

(2) *Teaching of the Law.*—To teach the Law was also the professional business of the Scribes. In order that people should obey the Law, it was necessary that they should know it; and an elaborate system of rules such as was contained in the Jewish tradition could be learned only with the assistance of a teacher. None of these traditional rules having been written down, the teaching was of necessity entirely oral, and round the more famous of the Scribes there gathered large numbers of young men, eager for instruction as to the proper conduct of life. Of these, some in their turn would become Scribes and teachers of the Law. The chief requisite, for both pupil and teacher, was a capacious and accurate memory. The method of teaching was by a constant repetition of the precepts of the Law, as only by this means could its multitude of minute details be at all kept in remembrance. The disputational method was also followed. Concrete cases, real or imaginary, were brought before the pupils, and they were required to pronounce judgment upon them, which judgment the teacher would criticise. The pupils were also allowed to propose questions to the teacher, and to attend disputations amongst teachers over difficult problems. But the two all-important duties were these — first, to keep everything faithfully in memory; and, second, never to teach anything otherwise than it had been taught by the master. Not even the expressions of the teacher were allowed to be changed. Accuracy in the minutest detail was the most commendable achievement.

For purposes of teaching and of disputation there were special places set apart—'houses of teaching,' as they were called—where the teacher sat upon an elevated bench, and the pupils on the ground. In Jerusalem, lectures were delivered in the Temple, somewhere in the outer court. The 'houses of teaching' were distinct from the synagogues; but as it was through the influence of the Scribes that the synagogue service originated, so doubtless they availed themselves of the opportunities which the synagogues gave them of teaching the Law to the common people. The Scripture exposition, which usually formed part of the service, might, indeed, be given by any one qualified to speak; but ordinarily it fell to a Scribe, if any were present, as the one most competent to discharge the duty.

(3) *The Scribes as judges.*—To the Scribes, as specially skilled in knowledge of the Law, it also naturally fell to take a leading part in its practical administration. From the time of the Hasmonæans they had formed a constituent element in the Sanhedrin, being associated in that body with the chief priests and elders, and it was usually the Scribes who exercised the greatest influence in its deliberations. In the local courts they were also naturally looked to for advice and judgment. Any one, indeed, who possessed the confidence of the community might be appointed a local judge, and probably for the most part the small local courts were presided over by unprofessional men. But whenever a Scribe—a skilled lawyer—was available, the choice of the community naturally fell upon him, as, in virtue of his qualifications, he was considered best fitted for the post.

3. Relations of the Scribes to Jesus.—The ministry of Jesus could not but excite interest amongst the Scribes. His first call, like that of the Baptist, was to repentance as a preparation for the Kingdom of God. With this they were bound to sympathize. They held that what the nation needed for its salvation was a stricter obedience to the Law, and they naturally thought that the new Teacher, who was calling to repentance for the past, would be calling also to a new and more rigid obedience for the future. There are not wanting indications that at first they were inclined to regard Him with favour. But they speedily discovered that His teaching was on very different lines from theirs, both in manner and in substance. In the exposition of Scripture their method was to give out a text, and then quote the various comments made on it by recognized authorities. Jesus followed a different plan. He had a message of His own, which He delivered with conviction and enthusiasm, not appealing to authorities, but speaking with the conscious authority of truth. And the substance of His teaching was also very different. He condemned the external, mechanical formalism which they encouraged, and declared that only the inward purity of the heart was of value in the sight of God. See, further, art. PHARISEES, p. 355 f.

4. Later history.—Though it does not properly belong to our subject, it is interesting to note that after the fall of Jerusalem in A.D. 70, the authority of the Scribes increased in importance. Under much discouragement they undertook the difficult task of the reorganization of Judaism. Working on calmly and peacefully, they were able to avoid extremes, and were successful in keeping what was left of the nation faithful to the religion of their fathers, and in stimulating hope for the future. The ordinances of the Oral Law were at last written down, and to their careful preservation by the Scribes we are indebted for the Hebrew Scriptures we now possess.

LITERATURE.—The literature on the subject is very extensive. Every History of the Jews, every Life of Christ, every Commentary on the Gospels, deals to some extent with the Scribes. Schürer's *HJP* may be taken as a standard authority ; Ewald, Kuenen, and Wellhausen are all important ; so are Edersheim's *LT* and W. R. Smith's *OTJC.* A very full bibliography is given in Schürer. See also artt. in Hastings' *DB* and in the *EBi.*
　　　　　　　　　　　　　　　　JOSEPH MITCHELL.

SCRIP.—See WALLET.

SCRIPTURE.—The scope of this article does not permit the discussion in it of the employment of Scripture, or of the estimate put upon Scripture, by either our Lord or the Evangelists. It is strictly limited to the use of the term 'Scripture' in the NT, particularly in the Gospels : and to the immediate implications of that use.

1. The use of this term in the NT was an inheritance, not an invention. The idea of a 'canon' of 'Sacred Scriptures' (and with the idea the thing) was handed down to Christianity from Judaism. The Jews possessed a body of writings, consisting of 'Law, Prophets, and (other) Scriptures (*Kethûbhîm*),' though they were often called, for brevity's sake, merely 'the Law and the Prophets' or simply 'the Law.' These 'Sacred Scriptures,' or this 'Scripture' (הכתיב) as it was frequently called, or these 'Books,' or simply this 'Book' (הספר), they looked upon as originating in Divine inspiration, and as therefore possessed everywhere of Divine authority. Whatever stood written in these Scriptures was a word of God, and was therefore referred to indifferently as something which 'Scripture says' (אמר קרא, or אמר הכתיב, or כתיב קרא), or 'the All-Merciful says' (אמר רחמנא), or even simply 'He says' (ובן הוא אומר or merely ואומר) ; that God is the Speaker in the Scriptural word being too fully understood to require explicit expression. Every precept or dogma was supposed to be grounded in Scriptural teaching, and possessed authority only as buttressed by a Scripture passage, introduced commonly by one or the other of the formulas 'for it is said' (שנאמר) or 'as it is written' (דכתיב or כדכתיב), though, of course, a great variety of more or less frequently occurring formulas of adduction are found. Greek-speaking Jews naturally tended merely to reproduce in their new language the designations and forms of adduction of their sacred books current among their people. This process was no doubt facilitated by the existence among the Greeks of a pregnant legislative use of γράφω, γραφή, γράμμα, by which these terms were freighted with an implication of authority. But it is very easy to make too much of this. In

Josephus, and even more plainly in the LXX, the influence of the Greek usage may be traced ; but in a writer like Philo, Jewish habits of thought appear to be absolutely determinative. The fact of importance is that there was nothing left for Christianity to invent here. It merely took over in their entirety the established usages of the Synagogue, and the NT evinces itself in this matter at least a thoroughly Jewish book. The several terms it employs are made use of, to be sure, with some sensitiveness to their inherent implications as Greek words, and the Greek legislative use of some of them gave them, no doubt, peculiar fitness for the service asked of them. But the application made of them by the NT writers had its roots set in Jewish thought, and from it they derive a fuller and deeper meaning than the most pregnant classical usage could impart to them.

2. To the NT writers, as to other Jews, the sacred books of what was now called by them 'the old covenant' (2 Co 3¹⁴), described according to their contents as 'the Law, the Prophets, and the Psalms' (Lk 24⁴⁴), or more briefly as 'the Law and the Prophets' (Mt 7¹²; Lk 16¹⁶; cf. Ac 28²³, Lk 16²⁹, ³¹), or merely as 'the Law' (Jn 10³⁴, 1 Co 14²¹), or even, perhaps, 'the Prophets' (Mt 2²³ 11¹³ 26⁵⁶, Lk 1⁷⁰ 18³¹ 24²⁵, ²⁷, Ac 3²⁴ 13²⁷, Ro 1² 16²⁶), were, when thought of according to their nature, a body of 'sacred scriptures' (Ro 1², 2 Ti 3¹⁶), or, with the omission of the unnecessary, because well-understood adjective, simply by way of eminence, 'the Scriptures,' 'Scripture.' For employment in this designation either of the substantives γραφή or γράμμα offered itself, although, of course, each brought with it its own suggestions arising from the implication of the form and the general usage of the word. The more usual of the two in this application, in Philo and Josephus, is γράμμα, or more exactly γράμματα ; for, although it is sometimes so employed in the singular (but apparently only late, *e.g.* Callimachus, *Epigr.* xxiv. 4, and the Church Fathers, *passim*), it is in the plural that this form more properly denotes that congeries of alphabetical signs which constitutes a book. In the NT, on the other hand, this form is rare. The complete phrase ἱερὰ γράμματα, found also both in Josephus and in Philo, occurs in 2 Ti 3¹⁵ as the current title of the sacred books, freighted with all its implications as such. Elsewhere in the NT, however, γράμματα is scarcely used as a designation of Scripture (cf. Jn 5⁴⁷ 7¹⁵). Practically, therefore, γραφή, in its varied uses, remains the sole form employed in the NT in the sense of 'Scripture,' 'Scriptures.'

3. This term occurs in the NT about fifty times (Gospels 23, Acts 7, Catholic Epistles 6, Paul 14) ; and in every case it bears that technical sense in which it designates the Scriptures by way of eminence, the Scriptures of the OT. It is true there are a few instances in which passages adduced as γραφή are not easily identified in the OT text ; but there is no reason to doubt that OT passages were intended (cf. Hühn, *Die alttest. Citate*, 270 ; and Mayor on Ja 4⁵, Lightfoot on 1 Co 2⁹, Westcott on Jn 7³⁸, and Godet on Lk 11⁴⁹). We need to note in modification of the broad statement, therefore, only that it is apparent from 2 P 3¹⁶ (cf. 1 Ti 5¹⁸) that the NT writers were well aware that the category 'Scripture,' in the high sense, included also the writings they were producing, as along with the books of the OT constituting the complete 'Scripture' or authoritative Word of God. In 20 out of the 50 instances in which γραφή occurs in the NT, it is the plural form which is used, and in all but two of these cases the article is present—αἱ γραφαί, the well-known Scriptures of the Jewish people ; and the two exceptions are exceptions only in appearance, since adjectival definitions are present (γραφαὶ ἅγιαι, Ro 1[2], here first in extant literature; γραφαὶ προφητικαί, Ro 16[26]). The singular form occurs some 30 times, all but four of which have the article; and here again the exceptions are only apparent, the term being definite in every case (Jn 19[37] 'another Scripture'; 1 P 2[6], 2 P 1[20], 2 Ti 3[16], used as a proper name). The distribution of the singular and plural forms is perhaps worth noting. In Acts the singular (3 times) and plural (4) occur almost equally frequently: the plural prevails in the Synoptics (Mt. plural only; Mk. two to one; Lk. three to one), and the singular in the rest of the NT (John 11 to 1, James 3 to 0, Peter 2 to 1, Paul 2 to 5). In the Gospels the plural form occurs exclusively in Mt., prevailingly in Mk. and Lk., and rarely in Jn., of which the singular is characteristic. No distinction seems to be traceable between the usage of the Evangelists in their own persons and that of our Lord as reported by them. Mt. and Mk. do not on their own account use the term at all; in Lk. and Jn., on the other hand, it occurs not only in reports of our Lord's sayings and of the sayings of others, but also in the narrative itself. To our Lord is ascribed the use indifferently of the plural (Mt 21[42] 22[49] 26[54. 56], Mk 12[24] 14[9], Jn 5[39]) and the singular (Mk 12[10], Lk 4[21], Jn 7[38. 42] 10[35] 13[18] 17[12]).

4. The history of γραφή, γραφαί, as applied to literary documents, does not seem to have been exactly the same as that of its congener γράμμα, γράμματα. The latter appears to have been current first as the appropriate appellation of an alphabetical character, and to have grown gradually upward from that lowly employment to designate documents of less or greater extent, as ultimately made up of alphabetical characters. Although, therefore, the singular τὸ γράμμα is used of any written thing, it is apparently, when applied to 'writings,' most naturally employed of brief pieces like short inscriptions or proverbs, or of the shorter portions of documents such as clauses—though it is also used of those larger sections of works which are more commonly designated as 'books.' It is rather the plural, τὰ γράμματα, which seems to have suggested itself not only for extended treatises, but indeed for documents of all kinds. When so employed, the plural form is not to be pressed. Such a phrase as 'Moses' γράμματα' (Jn 5[47]), for example, probably ascribes to Moses only a single book—what we call the Pentateuch; and such a phrase as ἱερὰ γράμματα (2 Ti 3[15]) does not suggest to us a 'Divine library,' but brings the OT before us as a unitary whole. On the other hand, γραφή, in its application to literary products, seems to have sprung lightly across the intermediate steps to designate which γράμμα is most appropriately used, and to have been carried over at once from the 'writing' in the sense of the script to the 'writing' in the sense of the Scripture. Kindred with γράμμα as it is, its true synonymy in its literary application is rather with such words as βίβλος (βιβλίον) and λόγος, in common with which it most naturally designates a complete literary piece, whether 'treatise' or 'book.' Where thought of from the material point of view as so much paper, so to speak, a literary work was apt to be called a βίβλος (βιβλίον); when thought of as a rational product, thought presented in words, it was apt to be spoken of as a λόγος: intermediate between the two stood γραφή (γράμμα), which was apt to come to the lips when the 'web of words' itself was in mind. In a word, βίβλος (βιβλίον) was the most exact word for the 'book,' γραφή (γράμμα) for the 'document' inscribed in the 'book,' λόγος for the 'treatise' which the 'document' records; while as between γραφή and γράμμα, γράμμα, preserving the stronger material flavour, gravitates

somewhat towards βίβλος (βιβλίον), and γραφή looks upward somewhat toward λόγος. When, in the development of the publisher's trade, the system of making books in great rolls gave way to the 'small-roll system,' and long works came to be broken up into 'books,' each of which was inscribed in a 'volume,' these separate 'books' attached to themselves this whole series of designations, each with its appropriate implication. Smaller sections were properly called περιοχαί, τόποι, χωρία, γράμματα (the last of which is the proper term for 'clauses'), but very seldom, if ever, in classical Greek, γραφαί.

5. The current senses of these several terms are, of course, more or less reflected in their NT use. But we are struck at once with the fact that γραφή occurs in the NT solely in its pregnant technical usage as a designation of the Sacred Scriptures. There seems no intrinsic reason why it should not, like γράμματα, be freely used for non-sacred 'writings.' In point of fact, however, throughout the NT γραφή is ever something 'which the Holy Ghost has spoken through the mouth' of its human authors (Ac 1[16]), and which is therefore of indefectible, because Divine, authority. It is perhaps even more remarkable that even on this high plane of technical reference it never occurs, in accordance with its most natural, and in the classics its most frequent, sense of 'treatise,' as a term to describe the several books of which the OT is composed. It is tempting, no doubt, to seek to give it such a sense in some of the passages where, occurring in the singular, it yet does not seem to designate the Scriptures in their entirety, and Dr. Hort appears for a moment almost inclined to yield to the temptation (on 1 P 2[6], note the 'probable'). It is more tempting still to assume that behind the common use of the plural αἱ γραφαί to designate the Scriptures as a whole, there lies a previous current usage by which each book which enters into the composition of these 'Scriptures' was designated by the singular ἡ γραφή. But in no single passage where ἡ γραφή occurs does it seem possible to give it a reference to the 'treatise' to which the appeal is made; and the common employment in profane Greek of γραφαί (in the plural) for a single document, discourages the assumption that (like τὰ βιβλία) when applied to the Scriptures it has reference to their composite character. The truth seems to be that whether the plural αἱ γραφαί or the singular ἡ γραφή is employed, the application of the term to the OT writings by the writers of the NT is based upon the conception of these OT writings as a unitary whole, and designates this body of writings in their entirety as the one well-known authoritative documentation of the Divine word. This is the fundamental fact with respect to the use of these terms in the NT from which all the other facts of their usage flow.

6. It is true that in one unique passage, 2 P 3[16] (on the meaning of which see Bigg, in loc.), αἱ γραφαί does occur with a plural signification. But the units of which this plural is made up, as the grammatical construction suggests, appear to be not 'treatises' (Huther, Kühl), but 'passages' (de Wette). Peter seems to say that the unlearned and unstable of course wrested the hard sayings of Paul's letters as they were accustomed to wrest τὰς λοιπὰς γραφάς, i.e. the other Scripture statements (cf. Eurip. Hipp. 1311; Philo, de Præm. et Pœn. § 11 near end)—the implication being that no part of Scripture was safe in their hands. This is a sufficiently remarkable use of the plural, no other example of which occurs in the NT; but it is an entirely legitimate one for the NT, and in its context a perfectly natural one. In the Church Fathers the plural αἱ γραφαί is formed freely upon ἡ γραφή both in the sense of 'book' of Scripture and in the sense of 'passage' of Scripture. But in the NT, apart from the present passage, there is in no instance of the use of αἱ γραφαί the slightest hint of a series whether of 'treatises' or of 'passages' underlying it. Even a passage like Lk 24[27] forms no exception ; for if γραφαί is employed in a singular sense of a single document, then πᾶσαι αἱ γραφαί remains just the whole of that document, and is the exact equivalent of πᾶσα ἡ γραφή, or (if γραφή has acquired standing as a *quasi*-proper name) as πᾶσα γραφή (2 Ti 3[16]). Similarly αἱ γραφαὶ τῶν προφητῶν (Mt 26[56]), γραφαὶ προφητικαί (Ro 16[26]) appear to refer not to particular passages deemed prophetic, or to the special section of the OT called 'the Prophets,' but to the entire OT conceived as prophetic in character (cf. 2 P 1[20], Ac 2[30], 2 P 3[16]).

7. In 2 P 3[16], however, we have already been brought face to face with what is probably the most remarkable fact about the usage of γραφή in the NT. This is its occasional employment to refer not merely, as from its form and previous history was to be expected, to the Scripture as a whole, or even, as also would have been only a continuation of its profane usage, to the several treatises which make up that whole, but to the individual passages of Scripture. This employment finds little support from the classics, in which γράμμα rather than γραφή is the current form for the adduction of 'clauses' or fragmentary portions of documents (cf. *e.g.* Plato, *Parmen.* 128 A–D, *Ep.* 3 [317 B] ; Thucyd. v. 29 ; Philo, *de Congr. Erud. Grat.* 12, *Quod Deus immut.* 2). It has been customary, accordingly, to represent it as a peculiarity of NT and Patristic Greek. It seems to be found, however, though rarely, in Philo (*Quis rerum div. hær.* 53, *de Præm. et Pæn.* 11 ; cf. Euripides, *Hipp.* 1311), and is probably an extreme outgrowth of the habit of looking upon the Scriptures as a unitary book of Divine oracles, every portion and passage of which is clothed with the Divine authority which belongs to the whole and is therefore manifested in all its parts. When the entirety of Scripture is 'Scripture' to us, each passage may readily be adduced as 'Scripture,' because 'Scripture' is conceived as speaking through and in each passage. The transition is easy from saying, 'The Scripture says, namely, in this or that passage,' to saying, of this and that passage, severally, 'This Scripture says,' and 'Another Scripture says' ; and a step so inviting was sure sooner or later to be taken. The employment of ἡ γραφή in the NT to denote a particular passage of Scripture does not appear then to be a continuation of a classical usage, but a new development on Jewish or Judæo-Christian ground from the pregnant use of γραφή for the Sacred Scriptures, every clause of which is conceived as clothed with the authority of the whole. So far from throwing in doubt the usage of γραφή pregnantly of Scripture as a whole, therefore, it rather presupposes this usage and is a result of it. So it will not surprise us to find the two usages standing side by side in the NT.

8. It has indeed been called in question whether both these usages do stand side by side in the NT. Possibly a desire to find some well-marked distinction between the usage of the plural and singular forms has not been without influence here. At all events, it has every now and then been suggested that the singular ἡ γραφή bears in the NT the uniform sense of 'passage of Scripture,' while it is the plural αἱ γραφαί alone which in the NT designates Scripture as a whole. The younger Schulthess, for example (*Lucubr. pro divin. discip. ac pers. Jesu*, 1828, p. 36 n.), having occasion to comment briefly on the words πᾶσα γραφὴ θεόπνευστος of 2 Ti 3[16], among other assertions of equal dubiety makes this one : 'γραφή in the singular

never means βίβλος in the NT, much less the entirety of τῶν ἱερῶν γραμμάτων, but some particular passage.' Hitherto it has been thought enough to meet such assertions with a mere expression of dissent : Christiaan Sepp, for example (*De Leer des NT over de HS des OV*, 1849, p. 69), meets this one with equal brevity and point by the simple statement : 'Passages like Jn 10[35] prove the contrary.' Of late, however, under the influence of a comment of Bishop Lightfoot's on Gal 3[22] which has become famous, Schulthess' doctrine has become almost traditional in a justly influential school of British exegesis (cf. Westcott on Jn 2[22] 10[35] ; Hort on 1 P 2[6] ; Swete on Mk 12[10] ; Page on Ac 1[10] ; Knowling on Ac 8[32] ; Plummer on Lk 4[21]). The attempt to carry this doctrine through, however, appears to involve a violence of exegesis which breaks down of itself. Of the 30 instances in which the singular γραφή occurs, about a score seem intractable to the proposed interpretation (Jn 2[22] 7[38. 42] 10[35] 17[12] 19[28] 20[9], Ac 8[32], Ro 4[3] 9[17] 10[11] 11[2], Gal 3[8. 22] 4[30], 1 Ti 5[18], Ja 4[5], 1 P 2[6], 2 P 1[20] [cf Cremer, *sub voc.*, who omits Jn 17[12] 20[9] ; E. Hühn, *Die alttest. Citate*, etc., 1900, p. 276, who adds Jn 13[18] 19[24. 36], Ja 2[8] ; and Vaughan on Ro 4[3], Meyer on Jn 10[35], Weiss on Jn 10[35], Kübel on 2 P 1[20], Abbott on Eph 4[8], Beet on Ro 9[17], Mayor on 2 P 3[16] ; *EBi* 4329 ; Franke, *Das AT bei Johannes*, 48 ; E. Haupt, *Die alttest. Citate in den vier Evang.* 201]). In some of these passages it would seem quite impossible to refer γραφή to a particular passage of Scripture. No particular passage is suggested, for example, in Jn 2[22] or in Gal 3[22], and it is sought and conjecturally supplied by the commentators only under the pressure of the theory. The reference of Jn 20[9] is quite as broad as that of Lk 24[45]. In Jn 10[35] the argument depends on the wide reference to Scripture as a whole, which forms its major premise. The personification of Scripture in such passages as Ja 4[5] and Gal 3[8] carries with it the same implication. And the anarthrous use of γραφή in 1 P 2[6], 2 P 1[20], 2 Ti 3[16], is explicable only on the presupposition that γραφή had acquired the value of a proper name. Perhaps the two passages, 1 P 2[6] and 2 P 1[20], are fairly adapted to stand as the tests of the possibility of carrying through the reference of γραφή in the singular to particular passages : and the artificial explanations which are given of these passages by the advocates of that theory (cf. Zahn, *Einleitung*, etc., ii. 108 ; Hort on 1 P 2[6]) may stand for its sufficient refutation. There seems no reason why we should fail to recognize that the employment of γραφή in the NT so far follows its profane usage, in which it is prevailingly applied to entire documents and carries with it a general implication of completeness, that in its more common reference it designates the OT to which it is applied in its completeness as a unitary whole (cf. Franke, *op. cit.* p. 48). It remains only to add that the same implication is present in the designation of the OT as αἱ γραφαί, which, as has already been pointed out, does not suggest that the OT is a collection of 'treatises,' but is merely a variant of ἡ γραφή in accordance with good Greek usage, employed interchangeably with it at the dictation of nothing more recondite than literary habit. Whether αἱ γραφαί is used, then, or ἡ γραφή, or the anarthrous γραφή, in each case alike the OT is thought of as a single document set over against all other documents by reason of its unique Divinity and indefectible authority, by which it is constituted in every passage and declaration the final arbiter of belief and practice.

9. It is an outgrowth of this conception of the OT that it is habitually adduced for the ordinary purposes of instruction or debate by such simple formulas as 'it is said,' 'it is written,' with the

implication that what is thus said or written is of Divine and final authority. Both of these usages are illustrated in a variety of forms, and with all possible high implications, not only in the NT at large, but also in the Gospels,—and not only in the comments of the Evangelists, but also in the reported sayings of our Lord. We are concerned here only with the formula, 'It is written,' in which the consciousness of the written form—the documentary character—of the authority appealed to finds expression. In its most common form, this formula is the simple γέγραπται, used either absolutely, or, with none of its authoritative implication thereby evacuated, with more or less clear intimation of the place where the cited words are to be found written. By its side occurs also the resolved formula γεγραμμένον ἐστίν (peculiar to Jn. ; cf. Plummer on Lk 4[17]), or some similar formula, with the same implications. These modes of expression have analogies in profane Greek, especially in legislative usages ; but their use with reference to the Divine Scriptures, as it involves the adduction of an authority which rises immeasurably above all legislative authority, is also freighted with a significance to which the profane usage affords no key. In the Gospels, γέγραπται occurs exclusively in Mt. and Mk., and predominately in Lk., but only once in Jn.; most commonly in reports of our Lord's sayings. In the latter part of Lk., on the other hand, the authoritative citation of the OT is accomplished by the use of the participle γεγραμμένον, while in Jn. the place of γέγραπται (8[17] only) is definitely taken by the resolved formula γεγραμμένον ἐστίν. The significance of these formulas is perhaps most manifest where they stand alone as the bare adduction of authority without indication of any kind whence the citation is derived (so γέγραπται, Mt 4[4. 6. 7. 10] [11[10]] 21[13] [26[24]] 26[31], Mk 7[6] 9[12. 13] 11[17] 14[21. 27], Lk 4[4. 8. 10] 7[27] 19[46] 20[17] 22[37] ; γεγραμμένον ἐστίν, Jn 2[17] 6[31] 12[14] [16]). The adjunction of an indication of the place where the citation may be found does not, however, really affect the authoritativeness of its adduction. This adjunction is rare in Mt. and Mk. (Mt 2[5], Mk 1[2] only), more frequent in Lk. (2[23] 3[4] 10[26] 18[31] 24[44. 46]) and Jn. (6[45] 8[17] 10[34] 15[25]) ; and by its infrequency it emphasizes the absence of all necessity for such identification. When a NT writer says, 'It is written,' there can arise no doubt where what he thus adduces as possessing absolute authority over the thought and consciences of men is to be found written. The simple adduction in this solemn and decisive manner of a written authority, carries with it the implication that the appeal is made to the indefectible authority of the Scriptures of God, which in all their parts and in every one of their declarations are clothed with the authority of God Himself.

Literature.—Lightfoot, *Hor. Heb. et Talm.* (ed. Pitman) xi, xii ; Schöttgen, *Hor. Heb. et Talm.* 1732 ; Surenhusius, ‏כפר המשנה‎ *sive βίβλος καταλλαγῆς*, 1713 (pp. 1–36); Döpke, *Hermeneutik d. NT Schriften*, 1829 (i. pp. 60–69) ; Edersheim, *LT* i. 187, n. 2 ; Weber, *Jüd. Theol.*[2] (1897) § 20 ; H. J. Holtzmann, *NT Theol.*, Index ; Weiss, *Theol. of NT*, § 74a, n. 3, § 136b, n. 5, § 152b, n. 4 ; Sepp, *De Leer des NT over de HS des OV*, 1849 ; Tholuck, *Ueber die Citate der AT im NT*[6] ; Turpie, *The NT View of the Old*, 1872 ; Böhl, *Die alttest. Citate in NT*, 1878 ; Toy, *Quotations in NT*, 1884 ; Dittmar, *VT in Novo*, i. 1899 ; Hühn, *Die alttest. Citate im NT*, 1900 ; Anger, *Ratio qua loci VT in Evang. Mat. laudantur*, 1801 ; E. Haupt, *Die alttest. Citate in d. 4 Evangg.* 1871 ; Clemen, *Der Gebrauch d. AT im NT und speciell in den Reden Jesu*, 1891–1893, *Der Gebrauch der AT in den NT Schriften*, 1895 (full literature, p. 19); Massebieau, *Examen des Citations de l'Ancien Test. dans l'Évang. selon S. Matthieu*, 1885 ; Swete, *Gospel acc. to Mark*, pp. lxx–lxxiv ; Franke, *Das AT bei Johannes*, 1885 (pp. 46–88, 225–281); Lechler, ' *Das AT in den Reden Jesu* ' (*TSK*, 1854, 4); Grau, *Das Selbstbewusstsein Jesu*, iv. 1887 ; Barth, *Die Hauptprobleme des Lebens Jesu*, ii. 1899 [2nd ed. 1903]; Kautzsch, *de VT locis in Paulo*, 1809 ; Monnet, *Les citations de S. Paul*, 1874 ; ＊Vollmer, *Die alttest. Citate Paulus*, 1895.

B. B. WARFIELD.

SEA OF GALILEE.—i. Names.—The OT name *Chinnereth* had disappeared, so far as our purpose is concerned, by the time of the Maccabees, and in its place we find a variety of designations. It is then that the familiar name *Gennesaret* first makes its appearance in the τὸ ὕδωρ Γεννησάρ of 1 Mac 11[67]. Josephus uses the forms λίμνη Γεννησάρ (*BJ* III. x. 1), ὕδατα Γεννήσαρα (*Ant.* XIII. v. 7), λίμνη Γεννησαρῖτις (*Ant.* XVIII. ii. 1 ; *Vita*, 65) ; Pliny has *Gennesara* (*HN* v. 15). In the Targums and other Jewish writings the name of the Sea appears as ‏גִּנֵּיסָר‎ or ‏גִּנּוֹסַר‎, these forms supplementing the Heb. *Chinnereth*. But though the word *Gennesaret* was so familiar to contemporary writers, it appears only once in the NT as applied to the Lake, in the ἡ λίμνη Γεννησαρέτ of Lk 5[1]. Following close upon this, however, ἡ λίμνη occurs alone in Lk 5[2] 8[22. 23. 33]. The most popular name in the NT is 'the Sea of Galilee' (ἡ θάλασσα τῆς Γαλιλαίας), which occurs five times (Mt 4[18] 15[29], Mk 1[16] 7[31], Jn 6[1]). The word 'Sea' (θάλασσα) stands alone in Jn 6[17-25], and the form 'Sea of Tiberias' (θάλασσα τῆς Τιβεριάδος) occurs in John 6[1] 21[1]. The modern designation, 'Lake of Tiberias,' does not occur in the NT. It is found for the first time as λίμνη Τιβερίς in Pausanias (v. 7).

Many explanations have been offered of the origin of the word *Gennesaret*. Lightfoot (and others) sought to derive it from the OT *Chinnereth*, which it was supposed to replace. Such an origin, however, seems very improbable, not only on philological grounds, but because the latter name also remains simply transliterated in the LXX as χενέρεθ, and was thus quite familiar to the Hellenistic world. Ritter (*Geog. of Pal.*) suggests that it is derived from ‏גַּן אוֹצָר‎ or ‏גַּן עֹשֶׁר‎ 'garden of treasure,' which term, of course, he refers to the Plain, deriving thence the name of the adjoining Sea. This process is quite natural, and probably correct, but still we may be permitted to doubt his derivation of the name. G. A. Smith (*HGHL* 443 n.) has also noted that the form points to some compound of גַּן 'garden,' or גַּי valley ; and to us this seems indisputable, so that on the whole we must admit that either the explanation given by Caspari (§ 64), גִּנֵּי סַר ('gardens of the [lake] basin '), or that of the older Rabbis (*Ber. Rab* 98), גִּנֵּי שַׂר ('gardens of the prince '), is most satisfactory. The termination in *Gennesaret* might then be regarded as the Aramaic determinative form, and compared with *Nazareth* from Nazara.

With reference to the name 'Galilee,' it has been said that it originally designated only that small tract of land given by Solomon to Hiram (1 K 9[11]), and that the name gradually extended till in the days of the Maccabees it included Zebulun and Naphtali, so that only after this took place could the Sea be known by that name. Furrer (*Wanderungen*) has also drawn attention to the other names. He asserts that *Gennesar* or *Gennesaritis* is characteristic of the 1st cent., being found in Josephus, Pliny, and Strabo, while from the 2nd cent. onwards the official designation became 'Sea of Tiberias'; and as proof of this statement he cites the Palestinian Talmud. He then ventures to infer that Jn 21[1] indicates a later date than the rest of the book demands, and at the same time he suggests that Jn 6[1] has been emended. This reasoning, however, seems inconclusive ; for, apart from the fact that the Palestinian Talmud contains much that is old, it seems impossible, in view of the conservatism of the Rabbis, that such a name as 'Sea of Tiberias' should be found in their writings, unless it had been in common use for a considerable time. For the history of the district surrounding the Lake see art. Galilee.

ii. Description.—The Lake presents 'a beautiful sheet of limpid water in a deeply depressed basin' (*BRP*[2] ii. 380), its average below sea level being 682½ ft. ; but with the season of the year the level may vary to the extent of 10 ft. The rise and fall are dependent on the rainy season on the one hand, and, on the other, on the melting of the snows on Hermon as the spring advances ; and

SEA OF GALILEE

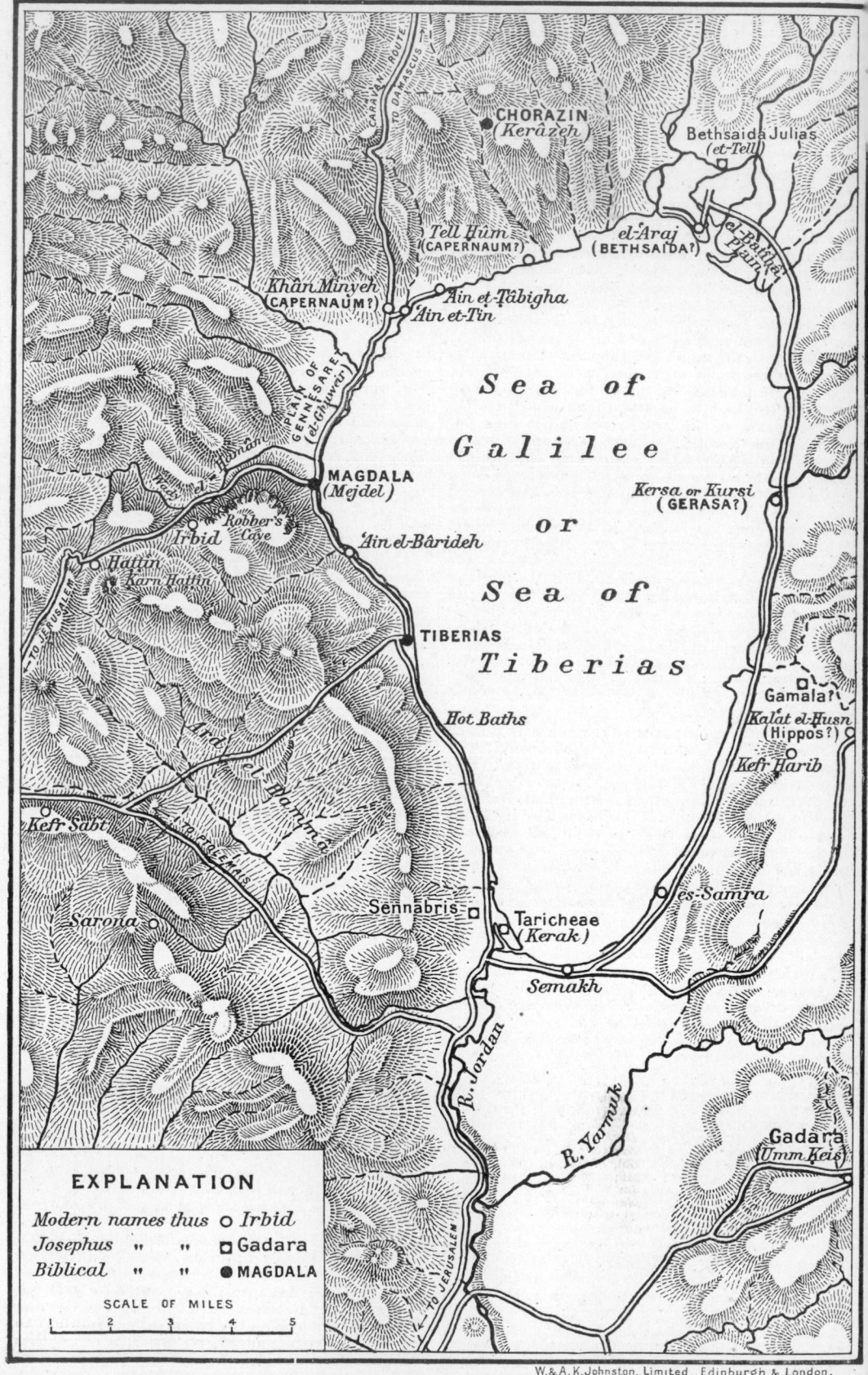

EXPLANATION

Modern names thus	○ Irbid
Josephus " "	▢ Gadara
Biblical " "	● MAGDALA

SCALE OF MILES
1 2 3 4 5

W.& A.K.Johnston, Limited. Edinburgh & London.

it is this latter cause that generally, in conjunction with the later rains, brings about the high level at the time of harvest (Jos 3[15]). But as the heavier rains decrease before the melting of the snow begins, there may have been already a fall of as much as 3 ft. even in March. The Sea is 13 miles long by 7 across at its broadest part—between Mejdel and Kersa; but in the clear Eastern atmosphere it looks much smaller than it really is. From no point on the western shore can it be seen in its whole extent at one time; but from the slopes above Tell Ḥûm, or from almost any point on the eastern shore, it is all visible. It is not quite oval, but rather pear- or harp-shaped (כְּנּוֹר), narrowing to the southern end. The sea level and the configuration of the shores have not changed to any considerable extent during the past nineteen centuries, so that, in so far as hills and valleys, ravines and slopes to the seashore are concerned, their present description gives a very true conception of what they were in Gospel days. On the west the hills are not so high and generally not so steep as on the eastern side; but they approach more closely to the shore, and are more rugged and stony. On the western side, from a short distance above what was once the western outlet of the Lake into the Jordan, and stretching some 3 miles up the Lake-side, the hills—here somewhat rounded and tame, and with but little that is picturesque in their form—slope down to the water's edge. Then to the north of this comes a *strip* (Heb. רקת, which seems to justify the identification of Tiberias with the older Rakkath, Jos 19[35]; *Megilla*, 5b, 6a; G. A. Smith, *HGHL* p. 447) about 2½ miles long and ¼ of a mile broad at its widest part, and at the north end of this is the modern town of Tiberias. Passing it, we have another 3 miles of sloping hills, broken about midway by the *Wady Abu el-Amīs*. At Mejdel we now enter *el-Ghuweir*, the well-known Plain of Gennesaret. Behind the village to the west is *Wady Ḥamâm*, known in the early centuries as בִּקְעַת אַרְבָּאל, and containing in its cliffs the once famous caves of Arbela (*Ant.* XIV. xv. 4). This is certainly the wildest and most impressive gorge around the whole Lake. On its south side it bears some resemblance, though on a far grander scale, to the crags around Arthur's Seat. There is the same perpendicular wall, but here it rises in places to a height of 1500 ft.; and there is also the same mass of broken rocks, making a steep slope to the plain below.

El-Ghuweir curves along the Lake from Mejdel to Khân Minyeh, a distance of 3 miles, and it has a breadth of one mile. In addition to the stream from *Wady Ḥamâm*, it is watered by three others from 'Ain Mudauwarah, Wady Rabadiyeh, and *Wady Leimôn*, and these flow throughout the year. Just behind Khân Minyeh and its fountain 'Ain eṭ-Ṭin at the N.W. corner of the Lake, the rounded hill *Tell Oreime* slopes down to the water's edge, ending in a series of sharp rocks—the only place around the Lake where we find anything like a cliff beside the shore. Around the face of *Tell Oreime* there is a deep rock-cutting now used as a pathway, but in ancient times an aqueduct, as is attested by the discovery of the remains of the old piers of its continuation across the next valley to 'Ain eṭ-Ṭâbigha. Remains of masonry show that the water was led eastward as well as westward from the towers built around the springs of eṭ-Ṭâbigha (Ἑπτάπηγον of Nicephorus), so that there can be little doubt that this is the spring of Capernaum mentioned by Josephus (*BJ* III. x. 8). From this point onward to the Jordan the hills again extend down to the shore, but by gentler slopes than even to the south of Tiberias. Between eṭ-Ṭâbigha and *Tell Ḥûm* the shore forms

a number of semicircular creeks, which, with the sloping embankment at this point, assume the shape of amphitheatres. Studying the subject on the spot, the present author was convinced that one of these must be the place where the sermon from the boat was preached (Mt 13[2] etc.). Something peculiar in the tones of our voices induced us to test the acoustic properties of the place, and we found that a speaker on the boat could be heard far up the slope, while the hum and bustle of a crowd on the shore would not disturb him.

After crossing the Jordan we meet with another plain—*el-Baṭiḥa*—corresponding to the one on the west, but somewhat more extensive. It is covered with green grass (Mk 6[39], Jn 6[10]) at nearly all seasons of the year. With a breadth of 1 to 1½ miles, it extends 3 miles along the coast, and then narrows, extending nearly 3 miles more to Kersa, a short distance to the south of which we meet with the only steep place (Mt 8[32]) on the eastern side of the Lake. At this point there is practically no shore, but immediately the eastern rampart of hills—2000 ft. high, now bleak and bare, but showing streaks of green where the springs trickle out between the white sandstone and the black superimposed lava—begins to recede, leaving a plain ¼ to ½ mile broad, and this to the south of Ḳul at el-Ḥuṣn widens out into the Ghor or Jordan Valley. At the village of Semakh, the southern end of the Lake forms a beautiful circular bay, which is enclosed by earth walls 16 to 32 ft. in height. There is deep water close in to the shore, and the currents manifestly wear away the rich alluvial soil. In so far as physical changes have taken place, we should expect that the land has suffered losses here, while there may have been slight gains by deposits on the shore of the plains of *el-Baṭiḥa* and *el-Ghuweir* (Gennesaret). What used to be the western outlet of the Jordan has also become silted up, for it must be remembered that in former times the Jordan flowed out from the two sides of a triangular island, now occupied by the ruins of Kerak—without doubt the remains of the once famous Taricheæ (*BJ* III. x. 1).

Compared with other lakes, the Sea of Galilee cannot be said to be deep. The maximum depth is from north to south along the course of the Jordan, and here it is 130 to 148 ft. according to the season [greater recorded depths have been proved to be in error], and except along the shores of the Plain of Gennesaret, deep water is reached all round the Lake within a few yards of the shore. The steep place at Kersa slopes down at once to a depth of 49 ft., and a short distance farther out the sounding gives 102 ft. A mile to the southeast of Tell Ḥûm the depth is 78 ft., and midway between Tiberias and Kersa it is 114.

One more notable feature of the Lake valley is to be found in the hot springs with which it abounds. The best known of these are at *Hammam* (cf. Jos. *Vita*, 16), south of Tiberias (132° to 144°), 'Ain Bârideh (80°), 'Ain Mudauwarah (73°), 'Ain eṭ-Ṭin (82°), and 'Ain eṭ-Ṭâbigha (73° to 86°). Others certainly exist in the Lake itself. A brackish taste can be perceived at different places, and especially at a point ⅔ across between Tiberias and Kersa, where in the warmer water great shoals of fish are wont to congregate. It was probably the drinking from a spot of this kind that led Strabo (*Geog.* xvi. 45) to express so bad an opinion of the waters of the Lake (ὕδωρ μοχθηρὸν λιμναῖον). These springs are all more or less sulphurous, and in all the centuries they have been used for medicinal purposes—especially those at Tiberias (*BJ* II. xxi. 6). A reference to these in the Talmud shows us the relationship of the Rabbis to the Sabbath, and throws some light on their attacks on Jesus (Lk 13[14] etc.). The use of the means of healing was forbidden on the Sabbath ; but these baths, though medicinal, were permitted, because in addition they ministered to indulgence in pleasure and luxury, and that was permitted. (*Pesach.* 8*b*).

Complaint has been made by some of the tameness of the scenery around the Lake, and of the want of picturesqueness of the hills ; while, on the other hand, Seetzen (*Reisen, in loc.*) has declared that 'in the whole land of Palestine there is no district whose natural charms could compare with those of this.' There can be no doubt that much depends upon the season of the year when the district is first visited, as well as upon the expectations formed. In the present unwooded state, with its uncultivated fields and barren hills often, as at the north end of the Lake, washed down to the bare rock by the rains of centuries, there may be little to attract, especially when the whole country has been blackened by the summer suns and the burning siroccos. But even now the earliest rains change the whole aspect of nature. The hills and the valleys on both shores become clothed in a luxuriant greenness, while, as the season advances, the fresh bursting buds of the olive, the fig, the vine, and the pomegranate, with here and there a palm tree, add variety and pleasantness to the landscape. Very soon, too, the fields are covered with great patches of anemones of varied colours—white, red, purple, and deep dark-blue, interspersed with various species of the lily family and stretches of the dark green-leaved and yellow-flowered mustard, while the watercourses and shores of the Lake are marked out by the red blooms of the oleander with its dark-green and silvery-backed leaves ; and on the western shore variety is added by the gigantic reeds of the papyrus, topped by their reddish-brown waving plumes ; on the higher grounds, too, every crevice of the rock is shaded by the blossoms of the cyclamen and many another flower of the field. But what must it have been in the year A.D. 27–28 ? It had been passing through, was indeed still in the period of transition after, the desolations of war, famine, and pestilence ; but the worst was now long past, and 20 years of uninterrupted peace and prosperity had made it blossom like the rose. There was nothing in the rule of the tetrarchs Antipas and Philip to discourage perseverance, so that the land was coming more and more under cultivation. It must have been beautiful, indeed, when human industry was developing all its resources and changing the whole scene into a blooming paradise. Nothing can give a better idea of what the whole district was becoming, than the classic passage in which Josephus (*BJ* III. x. 8) describes the Plain of Gennesaret in his own day (see art. GENNESARET [LAND OF] in vol. i.).

With Josephus' glowing description the Rabbis are in fullest harmony. Rish Laqish says : ' If Paradise be in the land of Israel, Beth-Shan is its entrance' (ביתשאן פיתחה). Again we read : 'Seven seas,' spake the Lord God, 'have I created in the land of Israel, but only one have I chosen for myself, that is the sea of Gennesar' (Midr. *Teh.* fol. 4). *Siphrê* on Dt 33²³ explains the fulness of the blessing of the Lord as the Plain of Gennesaret. On the hills around the Lake were ' vines and fruitful fields' (*Meg.* 6*a*). 'It is easier,' saith Rabbi Eliezer ben Simon, ' to nourish a legion of olives in Galilee than to bring up one child in the land of Israel' (*Ber. Rab.* c. 20). The oil of the Galilæan hills was more plentiful than any in Palestine (*Men.* 85*b*), and the wheat of Chorazin is specially commended (*ib.* 86*a*). An illustration of the productiveness of the district, and a parallel to the hundredfold of the parable, may be seen in the enumeration of the products of a single מאה ארבלית 'half bushel of Arbela' (Jerus. *Peah*, vii. 3). The Gentile world also lends its testimony. To the early Fathers the district was τὰ κράτιστα τῆς Γαλιλαίας, 'the crown of Galilee,' while in the 3rd cent. C. Julius Solinus (*Collectanea*, xxxv. 13) says : 'Lacus Tiberiadis omnibus anteponitur ingenuo æstu et ad sanitatem usu efficaci.'

But the district was not yet reduced to the calm beauty of a prosperous agricultural country. There

would still be stretches of woodland remaining, tenanted by birds of brilliant colours and various forms. There would be here and there beautiful oaks, either singly or in groups, that had grown up during the years when the population was small (*Baba Bathra* v. 1). There would be rocky stretches, especially to the north-east of the Lake, covered with brambles, wild mustard, and coarse grass, or dotted with prickly bushes (*nubk*), where the wolf, the jackal, the fox, and the hyæna would make their homes, and where the brown serpent and the silvery - breasted poisonous snake would glide about.

The population would not be so dense nor the land so fully cultivated as in the days when Josephus wrote, so that there would be a more equal mingling of the wild beauties of nature with the advancing and taming conquests of agriculture. The landscape, too, was becoming varied by the presence of many buildings. It has been said that 'the shores of the Lake seem to have borne cities and towns instead of harvests' (Tristram, *Land of Israel*, 444) ; and this, understood in the light of what we have already said, is very true. These would for the most part be constructed of black stone, but varied at times by buildings of white marble, while even the polished granite of Syene helped to break the monotony ; and although, on the whole, the majority of the buildings would be dull and sombre, still, in the midst of waving fields of green and gold, the presence of the humble village, and the beach sparkling with the houses and the palaces, the synagogues and the temples of Jewish and Roman inhabitants, would present a scene of great beauty, so that we can well understand how the wild desolations of the pre-Christian century, and the calm and peaceful years that followed the advent of the Messiah, combined to render the district more beautiful when Christ was a citizen of Capernaum than at any other time during its whole history.

iii. CLIMATE.—The climate of the Jordan Valley is in many ways very peculiar. Its low level—the lowest depression in the world — gives it many characteristics which are all its own. The absence of all frost, and the general warmth throughout the whole year, explain to us fully the peculiar open-air life that we meet with in the Gospels. For the most part Christ speaks out of doors. So did the Rabbis of His time. Ben Azzai taught on the shores of Tiberias (*Erubin*, 29*a*), and Rabbi Jehudah in the open air (*Moed Katon*, 16*a*). In the Gospels the sick are freely carried about (Mt 4²³, Mk 2³), are allowed to wait in the crowd (Lk 8⁴³ᶠ·), and the people are indifferent if the night find them away from home (Mt 15³², Mk 8². ³). The average temperatures of the air (night and day) in January are 37° and 74° respectively, while in June they are 68° and 108° ; but in July the thermometer frequently rises many degrees higher. The present writer has seen it at 106° at 6 a.m., and 139° has been recorded on the shore of the Lake at midday in August ; and even the soil, the rocks, and the pebbles around the Lake side become so intensely heated that the bather must wait till long after sunset if he would enter the water without the risk of burning his feet. In such conditions, under the fiery glow of the sun and with months of drought, we can well understand that all the grass and herbage are burned up, and so in its present state of naked dreariness, visitors at such a season are naturally disappointed ; but in other circumstances, and in days of universal irrigation, the whole scene would be very different (cf. Robinson's *Researches* under 19th June). Another noteworthy point is that the temperature of the body may rise much higher in cases of fever, and without serious results, than would be possible in other climates, *e.g.* a temperature of 110° is not uncommonly recorded. This may explain the expression 'great fever' ($\pi\upsilon\rho\epsilon\tau\hat{\omega}$ $\mu\epsilon\gamma\acute{a}\lambda\omega$) of Lk 4³⁸.

The temperature of the waters of the Lake does not vary so much as might be expected, and is very little lowered even by the melting of the snows on Hermon. This is to be accounted for by the fact that such waters have already passed through Lake Ḥuleh and have also had a considerable course in the upper Jordan. The average to a depth of 30 ft. is 68°, from 30 to 50 ft. it is 62°, and at a greater depth there is a constant temperature of 59° (*PEFQSt*, 1894, pp. 211–220).

Rain.—The average number of rainy days during the year is 60, and the rainfall 22·5 inches. There is no rain during the months of June, July, August, and September. Two-thirds of the rainfall occurs in December, January, and February; the other months having only one to five days on which rain falls, which may mean either now and again, a whole day, or merely slight showers. The degree of humidity is greatest in January, when it stands at 77. It decreases till June, when it is 42; but in August, again, it has risen to 45; while in September it drops as low as 39.

Winds.—From May till October there are often sirocco days. They generally come 3, 7, or 10 at a time, though sometimes the hot wind lasts but one day, and then the day following brings a delightful sensation of coolness, enjoyment, and satisfaction. On the sirocco days the heat on the Lake and in the surrounding region is intensely depressing, but between the visits of the hot wind, westerly breezes blow in summer, and this makes the east side of the Lake pleasant. The western shore, however, south of Mejdel benefits little, as the winds pass over the protecting hills and strike the Sea far out, leaving the air inshore close and stifling. The north end of the Lake does not suffer to the same extent, because to the west of the Plain of Gennesaret the hills are somewhat lower and farther back, and, besides, the wind blows freely down the Valley of Pigeons, and gives the district around Capernaum all that the east side enjoys at such seasons. These westerly winds usually spring up in the afternoon, they become strong as the evening advances, but generally cease about 10 p.m. During the rest of the year the weather is more variable, and the winds blow from different directions. Strong winds sometimes come from the north-east, and when they diverge to the north and come over Hermon the temperature is still more reduced, and a sensation of chill is felt in the atmosphere. This sometimes occurs till well on in May; while, on the other hand, a hot south wind will sometimes blow up the *Ghor* (Jordan Valley) in April, bringing with it clouds of dust which dim the sunlight and darken the hills, giving one a premature sensation of the summer's glow.

Storms.—The rainy season is generally introduced by thunderstorms. In October and November, small clouds, scarcely larger than a man's hand, gather on Tabor, Jebel Jarmuk, and the other hills of Upper Galilee. They grow in size and in threatening aspect, and generally in three days' time a violent thunderstorm with heavy rains bursts over the valley. This is then usually followed by a time of calm with a clear blue sky overhead. Such storms, but not generally so violent, occur from time to time during the winter, and the rainy season may be closed by something of the same nature. In the beginning of May the sky will be clouded, and there will be one or two days' rain with or without thunder. Sometimes, however, when the valley has been enjoying the most peaceful calm, it will be affected by storms that have occurred elsewhere. The hills of Upper Galilee may have been hidden in dense mists for a day or two, but nothing has disturbed the peace of the Lake. There have been rains, however, on the high lands only a few hours distant, and these, forming themselves into mountain torrents, have come down, sweeping all before them (Mt 7²⁷, Lk 6⁴⁹) in their descent, and flooding what but a few minutes earlier had been a dry channel. The present writer has personally watched the *Wady Rabadīyeh* and the *Wady Leimôn*, both of which cross the Plain of Gennesaret, as they became in an incredibly short time changed from little more than dry, stony river-beds to impassable foaming torrents; and, when the hills have been dark with clouds, has heard the warning given to get over these wadys 'before the stream comes down.'

Storms may occur on the Lake at any season, and there are few places where changes come so suddenly. The experience of Lynch is that of every one who has spent any time here: 'While pulling about the Lake, a squall swept down one of the ravines, and gave us a convincing proof of how soon the placid sea could assume an angry look' (p. 164). The storms on the Sea of Galilee are in many ways peculiar, and sometimes the wind seems to blow from various directions at one time, tossing the boat about. This arises from the fact that the winds blow violently down the narrow gorges and strike the Sea at an angle, stirring the waters to a great depth. Many of the storms, too, are quite local in their character. This may be understood by the fact that when a westerly wind is blowing, all may be smooth along the shores to the north and south of Tiberias and for a mile out, but there we may pass in a moment from the region of perfect calm into a gale so violent that the only chance of safety is to run before the wind to the eastern shore. At other times the south end of the Lake may be comparatively peaceful, but, sailing northward, we no sooner reach Mejdel than the wind from *Wady el-Ḥamâm* will seize the sail, and, unless it be instantly lowered, overturn the boat. These winds are from the west, but it is generally the wind from the north-east that raises a general storm over the whole Sea. This wind blows right into the Sea from *el-Baṭiḥa*, and from this direction no part is sheltered. The suddenness, too, with which the storms spring up may be illustrated by a storm which came from this direction, and which the present writer observed. A company of visitors were standing on the shore at Tiberias, and, noting the glassy surface of the water and the smallness of the Lake, they expressed doubts as to the possibility of such storms as those described in the Gospels. Almost immediately the wind sprang up. In 20 minutes the sea was white with foam-crested waves. Great billows broke over the towers at the corners of the city walls, and the visitors were compelled to seek shelter from the blinding spray, though now 200 yards from the Lake side. It is further to be noted that the north end of the Lake, being less sheltered than the rest, is more subject to storms. Indeed, only in peculiar circumstances could it escape having a chief share in any storm.

These facts may now be used to illustrate the two occasions on which Jesus is recorded to have been on the Sea in a storm (Mt 8²³, Mk 4³⁷, Lk 8²³; and Mt 14²⁴, Mk 6⁴⁸, Jn 6¹⁸). On the former of these the journey was from Capernaum to Gergesa, and the wind was from the north-east. Thus the boat was struck on its side, and so 'the waves beat into the ship' and it became 'filled.' On the second occasion they were attempting to pass from Bethsaida Julias to Capernaum. The wind was against them, blowing down the *Wady Ḥamâm* and over the Plain of Gennesaret, so that they were 'toiling in rowing, for the wind was contrary.' It is also made clear to us that, although the wind prevented their getting to Capernaum, it was not such as would prevent boats coming from Tiberias (Jn 6^18-24). Even in the height of the storm they could have, under the shelter of the western hills, proceeded as far as Mejdel, and thus come early upon the scene at any point at the north end of the Lake when once the storm was calmed.

It might be imagined that the cessation of the storms might mean simply the passing from an exposed and stormy to a calmer and protected region, but in both the cases recorded this is impossible. In the first instance, when the wind was from the north-east, the whole Sea would be disturbed; while in the latter case the Sea to the north of Mejdel would be all affected by the storm; and as the passage was between *el-Baṭiḥa* and the Plain of Gennesaret, the boat would not even approach the region of calm.

iv. INDUSTRIES.—During the peaceful years of Christ's ministry the whole Lake-basin was becoming a focus of life and energy. We have already indicated, by references to Josephus and the Rabbis, what the land was in the process of becoming in so far as *agriculture* was concerned. The tilling of the soil must have been a tempting occupation where the land was so fertile, so well watered everywhere, and enjoyed so much of the sunshine. Besides, it could be sown two and even three times in the year. At the present time in the plain of *el-Baṭiḥa* this is the case. After the corn harvest is gathered in, Indian corn may be sown; and when this also has ripened and been cleared off, the land and the season are ready for vegetables and water melons. The peculiar climate, too, ripens the harvest a month earlier than on the higher lands of Galilee and Bashan. The melons and the cucumbers are ready for use fully four weeks before those of Acre and Damascus, so that the prospect of greater gain by being able to anticipate the markets in all the larger towns must have been a powerful incentive to diligence when the means of transport were easier than now. We know that the fruits of Gennesaret were taken to Judæa (M. *Ma'aser Sheni* ii. 3), though it is said that they were not allowed in Jerusalem, lest on account of their goodness they should form an inducement, apart from the spiritual one, for pilgrims to journey thither (*Bab. Pesach.* 8b). With so much activity was this work pursued, that the hiring of day-labourers seems to have been quite common, and they were wont to go from Tiberias to till the lands of Beth-maon (*Kul'at ibn Ma'an*), which lands we believe to have been in the Plain of Gennesaret (Jerus. *Bab. Met.* vii. 1; and cf. Mt 20^1-17). Nor can we overlook the work of the shepherd, so closely bound up with agriculture, and to which there is so frequent reference in the Gospel story; but, just as in modern times, this work would be less pursued by the Lake side than on the neighbouring hills, where we know that even the flocks of Judæa were pastured (*Baba Bathra* v. 1).

Then the Gospels set before us a very great activity in *fishing*. There was a Jewish tradition that the fishing in the Lake was to be free to all, subject to the one condition that stakes were not to be set that might impede the progress of boats; and tradition further said that the freedom had been conferred by Joshua (*Baba Qama*, 80b). Not only the statements of the NT, but the names of the towns and villages, lead us to the knowledge of activity in this direction. Thus we have two towns of the name of *Bethsaida* ('Fisherrow'); a village called *Migdol Nunia* ('Fish-tower'), probably situated at *'Ain Barideh* (*Pesach.* 46a), and the great city of *Tarichea* ('Fish factory') at the south end of the Lake. At *Tarichea*, as the name indicates, the fish were salted and dried, and to-day the salt

can be seen here encrusted on the sand like hoarfrost. So far as the Mosaic law was concerned, the fish in the Sea of Galilee were all clean; but, as one passage in the Gospels draws a distinction between 'good' and 'bad' (Mt 13^47, 48), it may be of interest to note that the Jews of the present day, for some superstitious reason, refuse to eat one kind named *burbūt* (Lynch, p. 165). Josephus (*Vita*, 12) found that the fishers were a strong party in Tiberias also, so we may conclude that the boats that came thence were used for fishing (Jn 6^23).

The chief fishing ground to-day is in the neighbourhood of *el-Baṭiḥa*, and here the work is conducted in boats with drag-nets (σύροντες τὸ δίκτυον, Jn 21^8); but in other places the want of a boat need not prevent a man becoming a fisher. If he simply possess a net and learn to cast it (βάλλοντες ἀμφίβληστρον, Mt 4^18), he may be very successful in places where the water is not deep. Where the warm springs flow into the Lake the fish congregate in great numbers. We have seen shoals at *'Ain Barideh* and *'Ain eṭ-Ṭabigha* so great as to cover an acre of the surface, and so compact together that one could scarcely throw a stone without striking several. In such cases the handnet is thrown out with a whirl. It sinks down in a circle, enclosing a multitude, and these are then gathered in by the hand, while the net lies at the bottom. The hook (ἄγκιστρον, Mt 17^27) is also used in our day, and frequently a large quantity is taken in a short time. In the days of Josephus (A.D. 67) there were very many boats on the Lake,—230 at Tarichea alone (*BJ* II. xxi. 8),— but in the year A.D. 27–28 they must have been still far below the number they reached in later years.

The fishing industry implied many others. Delitzsch (*Handwerkleben zur Zeit Jesu*) tells us that the fish from the Lake were sold in Jerusalem; and when we think of the greater refinement of the Apostle John, his acquaintance with the high priest (Jn 18^15), and his having a house in the Holy City (Jn 19^27), we feel almost compelled to infer with Nonnus that he had acted there as agent. The sale of fish in Jerusalem and elsewhere would mean the employment of a goodly number of muleteers, and in ordinary circumstances the Apostolic band would travel in such caravans, just as Joseph and Mary had previously done (Lk 2^44). We must get away from the idea that they always travelled on foot.

Then on the shore of the Lake itself the fishing industry implied *boat-building and repairing*, and this, amongst other things, may have helped to decide our Lord's settlement in Capernaum, for there, as a carpenter, He could still from time to time exercise His own calling. At any rate, after He had settled here for some time, He was still known as 'the carpenter' (Mk 6^3). That this should be the case was quite in harmony with the practice of the teachers of those days. We find Rabbi Abin also working as a carpenter (*naggār*), while Rabbi Ada and Rabbi Ise are said to have been fishers (*zayyâdīn*). To some extent also the boats may have been used for transport trade; but we are inclined to think that the fact that the two sides of the Lake belonged to two different tetrarchies, each with its own customs and taxation, would militate against this.

The Talmuds and Midrash bring to our notice other occupations carried on beside the Lake, especially at Magdala, a portion of which was named Migdol Zebaya (*Erubin* v. 7) from the *dyeing operations* there conducted. So late as the year 1862, Sepp found this work still in existence, and indigo being grown in the fields of Mejdel. Then we read that there were 80 shops in the same town for the sale of *linen* (*Taan.* iv. 5), and we learn later that the linen of Galilee was *fine* (*Baba Qama*, 119a; *Ber. Rab.* c. 20). But perhaps of more interest than either of these is the fact that Magdala contained 300 shops for the sale of pigeons (Midr. *Echa*, 75*d*), which were used for purifications in the Temple (Lk 2^{24}). These pigeons would be captured among the overhanging rocks of *Wady Ḥamâm*, where they are so plentiful to-day, or trapped in nooses laid out in the adjoining fields (cf. *Baba Qama* vii.). These would be transferred to Jerusalem, where we learn that there were booths on the Mt. of Olives for the sale of such (*Cholin*, 53*a*), as well as in the Temple courts when the sellers had invaded the sacred precincts (Mt 21^{12} etc.). In this connexion it is to be noted that when those who sold doves were driven out of the Temple they could not be ignorant of the personality and power of Him who expelled them. Magdala and the Mt. of Olives being thus connected, another item is cast into the balance in favour of some relationship between Mary of Magdala and the family of Bethany (cf. Baronius, *Annales*, cap. 32). It may also be interesting to note here a still further connexion, for in the year A.D. 67, when the Jewish war broke out, the Jews took occasion to destr y th booths on the Mt. of Olives because the occupants 'established their doings on the Law, and did what was forbidden by the words of the wise' (*Cholin*, 53*a*); and during the same year Magdala and other towns in Galilee were destroyed, and the epithets used in the reasons given seem to indicate that the inhabitants were Christian (Jerus. *Taanith* iv. 5; *Baba Mez.* 88*a*; Midr. *Echa* ii. 2). These industries gave the Lake valley a trade connexion with the outside world; but, apart from those engaged in these occupations, multitudes would be employed in making articles for home use, as well as for the supply of the two courts and the various garrison towns. All trades would be represented, and these we sometimes read of incidentally, as in the case of *tanning* and the manufacture of *earthenware* at Migdol Zebaya.

v. GEOGRAPHY.—This has long been a vexed question, and is likely to remain so till excavating work is undertaken. The sites of Tiberias, Magdala, and Julias seem alone to be undisputed, so far as the Gospel history is concerned. The questions regarding the various sites will be treated each in its own place. The towns with which we are concerned were for the most part Jewish; but there were also Greek cities (πόλεις Ἑλληνίδες) around the Lake. In Tiberias and Julias, built by the tetrarchs, in Gamala, Hippos, Gadara, Tarichеæ, and in Philoteria (Polybius, v. 70), all trace of which has been lost, Greek influence would be paramount, though, of course, there was a Jewish element dwelling among the Gentile population (*Rosh-Hash.* ii. 1). These cities would have their own influence on the people of the surrounding districts. It may seem strange that the Gospels never touch them, and that the fact of their existence is no more than recorded, though they were large and important in comparison with the Jewish towns named. We feel justified in believing that Christ never entered these fashionable Greek cities. We know that the pious Jew specially abhorred Tiberias, and would not enter it, as it had been built on an ancient cemetery (*Shebhiith* ix. 1). We read, indeed, of a circuit through Decapolis (Mk 7^{31}); but in view of Christ's relationship to the nearer towns, and His own statement (Mt 15^{24}), we are constrained to believe that He confined Himself to the country districts as occupied by the Jewish population. In harmony with this is His desire not to have His works proclaimed in these Greek towns (Mk 8^{26}).

Roads.—The Sea of Galilee was in no sense in the 1st cent. what it is now, something of the nature of a retired mountain lake. On the contrary, it was kept in constant touch with the whole world. The western shore was one of the chief meeting-places of the world's highways. The *Via Maris* (the Way of the Sea, Mt 4^{15}), a well-known trade route, along which the wealth of the East passed westward, touched its north-eastern shore. Paved portions of it still remain. Details of the network of highways meeting in this region will be found in their own place (see ROADS); but we have to remark that the Jordan could be passed not only at the usual fords, but, during the spring and summer months, also by wading knee-deep along a kind of bar formed by pebbles and sand, where the river enters the Lake (Mt 14^{13}, Mk 6^{33}). Further, it is to be noted that most if not all of these roads were available not only for mules and camels, as in modern times, but also for vehicles, for we learn that on account of their quantity the contributions were sent from Magdala, Cabul, and Sogane to Jerusalem *in waggons* (*Ta'anith*, iv. 5).

vi. POPULATION.—We can now well understand the various classes of people who dwelt in and around this district. In the Greek towns the population would be chiefly Greek-speaking sojourners of mixed race—the Levantines of those days. The Roman soldiery would be there in considerable numbers as well as scattered through the towns, especially where customs were collected. There would be *courtiers* around the Herods in Tiberias and Julias—'Herodians,' as they were called; and they were, for the most part, *Sadducees*. The *publicans* would have their headquarters in the two capitals, but they would be employed everywhere, and would be specially active at the north end of the Lake, on the great trade routes. There, too, the *Pharisees* and probably also the *Essenes* (*BJ* II. viii. 4) would be chiefly in evidence. It is the population at this north end that chiefly concerns us; for amongst them the Lord dwelt, and there He had His own city (Mt 9^{1}). The people here were essentially Jewish, but there was a world of difference from the Judaism of Judæa. Graetz (ii. 148, Eng. ed.) has well described this when he says: 'Morality was stricter in Galilee, and the laws and customs more rigidly enforced. The slightest infringement was not allowed, and what the Judæans permitted themselves the Galilæans would by no means consent to.' We might almost put it, Judæa had much of the semblance of piety, Galilee more of the reality. Indeed, their piety as Jews had already impressed even the heathen world (Lk 7^{5}). The Talmuds tell us that the Galilæan loved honour more than wealth, and that the contrary was the case in Judæa (Jerus. *Keth.* iv. 14); that the marriages were simpler and more decently conducted (*Keth.* 12*a*, with which cf. Jn 2^{1-11}; Edersheim, *Sketch of Jewish Social Life*, p. 152 ff.), and also that the widow's right of occupancy of her husband's house was fully recognized (Mishna, *Keth.* iv. 12 and Jerus. *Keth.* iv. 14; cf. Mt 8^{14}). The Galilæans, too, were accused by their neighbours of being too talkative with women; and in this connexion the expression סוטה גלילאה 'foolish Galilæan,' came into use (*Erubin*, 53*b*; cf. Jn 4^{27}). Josephus also speaks well of the Galilæans, commending their courage, and adding that they were inured to war from their infancy (*BJ* III. iii. 2). There is another remark in the Talmud regarding their character that is worth noting: אנשי גליל קנטרנין היו 'the men of Galilee were disputatious' (*Nedar.* 48*a*). This has always been a characteristic of the Jew; he has never been able to argue calmly; and when we add to this acknowledged characteristic of the people the circumstances of a fishing and boating life, we must admit the truth of the accusation; and knowing this, we can well understand that many of the scenes around the Lake were much noisier than the calm words of Scripture would lead us to suspect (Mt $9^{24.25}$, Mk 3^{22}, Lk 8^{37} etc.); and we can appreciate the facility with which Peter relapsed into what must have been an old habit (Mk 14^{71}). Then the inhabitants of the district would not be over cleanly in their habits. We can infer nothing from the neglect of hand-washing (נטילת ידים), for it is at best purely ceremonial; but the Jew generally was, in the 1st cent., the butt of the Gentile world on account of his uncleanliness, just as he is to-day (Seneca, *Ep.* 5; Perseus, *Sat.* v.). Apart from the Greek towns, which, like Tiberias and Gamala, were supplied by aqueducts (portions of which still remain), the general water supply was from the Lake; and in consideration of the traffic that existed and the absence of sanitary arrangements, this could not be satisfactory in the neighbourhood of a town like Capernaum. Then every village would have, as at the present time, its own dunghill, a fruitful source of swarms of flies.

Great extremes of wealth and poverty there would not be. We meet, indeed, with a knowledge of wealth (Mt 7⁶ 13⁴⁶ 18²⁴, Lk 12¹⁸. ¹⁹) ; but on the whole the life was of the simplest, as we see from the nature of the household furnishings,—*the* bushel, *the* candlestick (Mt 5¹⁵), there being but one ; and the mention of the food—bread, eggs, fish (Mt 7⁹. ¹⁰, Lk 11¹¹. ¹²).

Then it is to be noted that the people were to a certain extent *bilingual*. Judging from similar conditions in this district and elsewhere at the present day, we should say that the language of the homes and of the Jewish population among themselves was *Aramaic*, but that the men would generally be acquainted colloquially with the *Hellenistic* speech of the larger towns. The native language, too, had its own peculiarities (Mt 26⁷³), the chief of which was a remarkable confusion of the gutturals, which is repeatedly ridiculed in the Talmuds, where a notable example is given of a Galilæan being asked, when shouting on the street, whether he wished to sell ' wool,' ' a sheep,' ' wine,' or ' a donkey' (Bab. *Erubin*, 53*b* ; *Berakhoth*, 32*a*).

To sum up, then, the population of this district was as manly, industrious, independent, moral, pious, and experienced in the world as any in Palestine. It was among men who were *morally right* that our Lord chose to settle. It was such that He made His first disciples, and finally His Apostles. Had these been willing to compromise conscience, they might easily have passed into easier walks of life. In the full strength of early manhood, they might have had a share in the settlement of Tiberias (*Ant.* XVIII. ii. 3), but they had resisted that temptation. It is true that Matthew the publican (Mt 10³) was among them, but it is to be remembered that here he did not serve an alien like the *publicani* in Judæa. The taxes he collected would go to the coffers of Antipas in Tiberias (Titus Livius, 32 F ; Cicero, *in Verr.* ii. 72), and they would be drawn from the tax on goods passing along the highways as well as on the fish from the Lake, as at the present day. This latter fact suggests a peculiar relationship between Matthew and the ' fisher-folk' among the Twelve, and a still more interesting one between him and Simon the Zealot, who had fought against these taxes.

We conclude by observing that, as no land in the world save Palestine could have given us the Bible, no part of the land save this, with its wealth of recent historical association and variety in nature, from the torrid heat of *el-Ghuweir* to the perennial snows of Hermon, could so well have suited the Great Teacher in His appeal to men of every kindred and every clime. In its calm beauty it was in many ways worthy of the presence of the Son of Man, and it presents us with a beautiful picture of many aspects of His life and character. It deserved all that Jew and Gentile said in its praise even in their playing with its names— Tiberias (טבריא) טובה ראייתה, ' beautiful of appearance' ; Capernaum (כפר נעים, χωρίον παρακλήσεως), ' land of pleasantness *or* consolation.' Before the time of the Lord Jesus the Sea of Galilee was to the world an unknown, neglected, and almost unnamed distant inland lake ; but He has changed all this. He has rendered it immortal.

LITERATURE.—Hastings' *DB* and *Encyc. Bibl.* art. ' Galilee, Sea of' ; G. A. Smith, *HGHL*, ch. xxi. ; Merrill, *Galilee in the Time of Christ* ; see also art. GALILEE and the Lit. given there.

WM. M. CHRISTIE.

SEAL.—The only reference in the Gospels to the literal use of a seal is Mt 27⁶⁶,* where we read that the chief priests and Pharisees, after consultation with Pilate, in order to guard against the removal of our Lord's body by the disciples, secured the sepulchre to the best of their power by setting their seal upon the entrance stone (cf. Dn 6¹⁷) as well as by placing soldiers to guard it. The process would be accomplished by stretching a cord across the stone that blocked the entrance, and by sealing the two ends of the cord against the wall of rock. Twice in the Fourth Gospel the act of sealing is used figuratively to describe (*a*) the solemn confirmation by the believer, from his own experience, that God is true (Jn 3³³) ; (*b*) the destination and authentication of the Son by the Father as the bestower of the food which nourishes eternal life (Jn 6²⁷). In all of these three cases it is the verb σφραγίζω that is used, the noun σφραγίς not being found in the Gospels.

C. L. FELTOE.

SEAM.—See COAT.

SEARCHING.—*Searching* (of Latin-French derivation) is a richer word than *seeking* (of Anglo-Saxon origin), because it implies examination as well as looking and asking (cf. 1 P 1¹⁰). Thus while ζητέω and its compounds are always translated ' seek,' the words corresponding to ' search' are ἀνακρίνω (Ac 17¹¹ only), ἐξετάζω, and ἐρευνάω. In Mt 2⁸ ἐξετάζω is appropriately used for the identifying of the child of Messianic promise : ' Search out carefully concerning the young child' (RV ; whereas AV tr. as if it were ἐκζητέω). In Mt 10¹¹ it means ' get to know exactly who is genuinely worthy,' rather than settle down with the first man who is spoken of for his piety. In Jn 21¹² the same word is used to suggest that the disciples did not venture to probe the mystery any further. Reverence held them back,—the sense that faith must at such a moment take the place of criticism.

But the exact equivalent of ' search' is ἐρευνάω. It is used twice in Jn. (5³⁹ 7⁵²) of ' searching the Scriptures.' It may well be believed that it connoted more on the lips of Jesus (5³⁹), who knew how to distinguish the spirit from the letter (Mt 7¹², Lk 7²⁷ 10²⁶ff·, Jn 6⁶³), and to bring forth treasures new as well as old (Mt 13⁵², cf. 5²¹f· ⁴³f· 9¹³ 12⁴⁰ff·), than it did upon the lips of the chief priests and Pharisees (Jn7⁵²).—With Christ it meant to search the Scriptures with a candid mind and reverent spirit to find the will of the holy Father whose name is Love. But there was a ' veil upon the faces' of the Jews (2 Co 3¹⁵), because they did not look behind a private or traditional interpretation. The priests, who were mostly Sadducees, ' searched' for passages that would serve a casual purpose (Mk 12¹⁸ff·), and the Pharisees ' searched' for what would maintain their burdensome traditions (Mk 2⁷· ²⁴, Lk 13¹⁴, Jn 9²⁸), or even enable them to evade a moral issue (Mt 19⁷).

In Jn 5³⁹ ἐρευνᾶτε may be either Imperative (as AV) or Indicative (as RV) [cf. πιστεύετε in Jn 14¹]. The former falls into line with the general tenor of Christ's teaching, that the Jews had only to use the means at their disposal in order to see in Himself the fulfilment of the Law and the Prophets (Mt 5¹⁷, Lk 16³¹ 24²⁷, Jn 7³⁸). But the Indicative seems in best accord with the immediate context (' *because* ye think,' ' *and* these are they,' ' ye will not come to *me*') (cf. Westcott, *in loc.*).

LITERATURE. — Westcott on *John* ; Martineau, *Hours of Thought*, i. 54, 201, ii. 183 f. ; S. A. Tipple, *Sunday Mornings at Norwood*, p. 161 ff. ; Forrest, *Authority of Christ.*

A. NORMAN ROWLAND.

SECOND ADAM.—See DIVINITY OF CHRIST in vol. i. p. 477ᵇ.

---

* A finger-ring (δακτύλιος), in which the seal was usually set, is mentioned in the parable of the Prodigal Son (Lk 15²²).

SECOND COMING.—This is the designation commonly given to the final return of Jesus in glory at the end of the ages, to perfect His Kingdom. The term does not occur in the Gospels, but it has long been adopted in general usage to signify the supreme crisis of the Parousia, the most momentous and decisive of the various future comings which Jesus foreshadowed when He spoke of His death at the hands of men, and the manifestations of His triumphant life and power that would follow it. The subject is dealt with under COMING AGAIN, and more fully, with a note on the Literature, under PAROUSIA.

G. M'HARDY.

SEED.—Excluding the use of this term as equivalent to *progeny*, *offspring*, or *race* (cf. *e.g.* Mk 12[19-24], Lk 1[55], Jn 7[42]), we find it exclusively employed in the parables of Jesus as an apt symbol for Divine influence, or for the expansion of the moral and religious life in communities or individuals.

1. In Mk 4[26-29], a parable peculiar to Mark, Jesus uses the process of sowing and the subsequent conduct of the farmer to illustrate the certain success of His Kingdom upon earth. What He preached about seemed perhaps to the disciples, as well as to outsiders, as weak as a grain of seed flung upon a field. Yet neither is an isolated or foreign thing in the world. On the side of the gospel were certain mysterious powers which would ensure its success, apart from human aid or interference. All it required was time. The order of things was a ripening order, and at the proper moment these favourable conditions would bring about the fruit and result of what at present seemed a very precarious and unpromising movement among men. Such is the general point of the parable. The seed's vital energy and its appointed correspondence with the powers of nature symbolize features in the gospel which enable Jesus to await the future with quiet confidence and an easy mind. Neither is just what it seems to the outward eye. Each sets in action a slow but sure process of growth, upon which the sensible person will count. 'Fruit grows thus,' said Epictetus; 'the seed must be buried for some time, hidden, and then grow slowly if it is to reach perfection.' It is by an extension, or rather a special application, of this usage that the self-sacrifice of man is compared to the burying of the seed in the furrow (Jn 12[23-25]), with special reference to the death of Jesus Himself. The ultimate effects of such self-immolation depend on the thoroughness of the process itself.

The Kingdom is also compared to seed in the parable of the Mustard Seed (Mk 4[30-32] = Mt 13[31. 32] = Lk 13[18. 19]). A small thing to begin with, it ultimately surpasses all other movements which make a greater show at first to the untrained eye. Here the Kingdom is conceived of, not eschatologically, but historically. When it is likened to 'seed,' the thought is mainly of the immense possibilities of growth in it, as compared with its initial size, the correspondence between it and the soul of man, and the pledge, which it contains, of some final and splendid issue.

2. Seed, on the other hand, depends to a certain extent upon soil. While essentially designed to co-operate with the vital forces of nature, it may be rendered wholly or partially barren. And in this further sense it forms a symbol for Jesus of the Divine word and its fortunes in the world of men. Consequently we find that in two other parables the seed represents not the Kingdom, but the word (cf. Mt 13[19]).

The first of these, the parable of the Sower and the Soils (Mk 4[2f.] = Mt 13[3f.] = Lk 8[5f.]), bears on the difficulties and disappointments encountered in the preaching of the word of God. The latter is com-

pared to the vital germ or grain of the plant, which, through no fault of its own or of the sower, may fail to germinate, owing to the unpromising nature of the ground on which it chances to fall. Nevertheless, the work of the sower must proceed. The partial failure of his efforts is not to render his career or calling void. In the parable itself, which is undoubtedly genuine, the original reference is to the experiences of Jesus Himself as a preacher. 'Jesus has to preach; the rest is God's concern' (Wellhausen). But in the subsequent interpretation of the parable, which, like other interpretations, must be held to contain in whole or part reflexions of the Apostolic age and traces of the editor's hand, the scope widens to include the general preaching of Christian evangelists, who are counselled not to let themselves be daunted by finding the unsympathetic and the preoccupied among their hearers. The seed must be sown. The word must be trusted to do its work in congenial hearts. The teaching must be imparted. Such is the supreme lesson for evangelists drawn here by Jesus from the vegetable world.

The other parable is that of the Tares, or darnel (Mt 13[24f.]), which may be an allegorized variation, and in part an expansion, of the ideas contained in Mk 4[26-29]. Certainly, whatever be the original nucleus, the editorial reflexions indicate a rather advanced period in the history of the early Church's mission and discipline. Growth, here too, is a partial feature of the situation. But the seed or word is further exposed to deliberate and widespread corruption and rivalry. Another power of influence is stealthily at work among men. God's message finds no virgin soil, for the growth of the seed is thwarted; and specious, vigorous rivals abound.

Both of the latter parables, in so far as they emphasize the nature of God's word or message as seed, thus touch wisely and earnestly on its mysterious power of growth. The spoken word is essentially fruitful. It is the instrument of the Divine mission. 'We forget too often that language is both a seed-sowing and a revelation,' says Amiel. 'Man is a husbandman; his whole work rightly understood is to develop life, to sow it everywhere.' And the supreme method is the contact of one personality with another, especially through the medium of that spoken intercourse which conveys the truth of God to the soul of man. This, and no external means, is the chosen way of Jesus.

LITERATURE.—In addition to the critical editors on the passages above cited, and writers on the Parables (especially Trench, Bruce, Jülicher, and Godet), cf. T. G. Selby, *Ministry of the Lord Jesus*, p. 157 f. ; Keim, *Jesus of Nazara*, iv. p. 138 f. ; and J. Rendel Harris, *Union with God*, p. 171 f.

J. MOFFATT.

SEEING.—In the Gospels there are three Greek words (βλέπω, θεωρέω, ὁράω) used for 'see,' sometimes rendered in the EV by 'behold,' 'take heed,' 'beware,' 'regard.' The most ordinary significance of the word 'see' is, of course, the natural one—to recognize by the act of vision ordinary external objects, as when the blind are described as seeing (Mt 15[31], Jn 9[7]), or men are promised that they shall see the Son of Man, or when the disciples think they see a vision, or the multitude see the miracles of Jesus (Mk 14[62], Lk 24[23], Jn 6[2]).

The more significant uses of the word are, however, *figurative*. (1) The first usage under this head is where the verb 'to see' is used of the recognition of objects not strictly visible, as, for example, when it is said of Peter that he saw the wind (Mt 14[30]); or when men are told that, if they first cast out the beam out of their own eye, they will then be able to see clearly to cast the mote out of their brother's eye (Mt 7[5]); or, again, when it is said that a man shall see death (Lk 2²⁶, Jn 8⁵¹); or when the Lord speaks of a man as 'seeing the light of this world' (Jn 11⁹), where, of course, it is more strictly the vision of objects made possible through the presence of the light of day.

(2) The second figurative sense is a very ordinary one in the Gospels, where the verb 'to see' is employed in the sense of the spiritual vision of the mind and soul. In the Beatitudes, for example, the blessing of the pure in heart is that they shall see God (Mt 5⁸). The angels also possess the same privilege (Mt 18¹⁰). The disciples are told that in seeing Christ they have already obtained the vision of the Father (Jn 14⁹); while in another passage of the same Gospel the seeing of Christ and believing on Him are the conditions of possessing eternal life (6⁴⁰). In the Lord's great prayer for His disciples He desires that they may see His glory (17²⁴), which implies a participation in the understanding of Divine things of the highest and most intimate character. In this connexion also is to be noted the strange utterance of our Lord in Lk 10¹⁸, where, on the return of the Seventy, He speaks of His beholding Satan 'fallen as lightning from heaven,' which must imply His spiritual prevision of the final overthrow of the powers of evil, and the establishment of His Divine kingdom. Most significant of all this class of passages, however, are those found in Jn 9³⁹, and Mt 13¹⁴⁻¹⁶ with its parallels in Mk 4¹² and Lk 8¹⁰. The passage in Jn. distinctly states that the purpose of Christ's presence in the world was first to bring light to blind eyes, but, secondly, to make blind those who were able to see; and this last statement is further explained in the passage by the answer given to the indignant question of the Pharisees as to whether they also were blind, that their fault consisted in claiming to possess the power of spiritual vision, while their hearts were closed to the real significance of Christ's message; and so their boast of spiritual perception only magnified their sin. On Mt 13¹⁴⁻¹⁶ ‖ see PARABLE, p. 315 f.

(3) A third general significance of the word 'see' is that of an ethical warning in the sense of the English phrase 'take heed.' For example, in Mt 24⁶ we read, 'See that ye be not troubled'; and in Mk 8¹⁵ two words are combined in the warning, 'Take heed (ὁρᾶτε), beware (βλέπετε) of the leaven of the Pharisees, and the leaven of Herod.'

When combined with a preposition (εἰς), the verb βλέπω signifies 'regard,' in the sense of 'pay obsequious attention to,' as in Mt 22¹⁶; and, finally, the word is used of God Himself in His vision of the hearts of men, as in Mt 6⁶, which reads, 'Thy Father which seeth in secret shall recompense thee.'

As a general result of the examination of the above passages, it will be noticed that in Jn. the word 'see' has a special significance. It is, indeed, one of the words that form a leading conception in his writing. Just as the idea of life arises out of the miracle of the feeding of the multitude, so does that of light spring from the miracle of the healing of the man blind from his birth. In Jn.'s spiritual vocabulary, Christ Himself is the light of the world; and the illumination of the souls of men and the blessing of the gospel can be spoken of in terms of light and its enjoyment as suitably as in terms of life and its possession. Thus the miracles of giving sight to the blind become peculiarly significant; but we need not, therefore, assume that, though they are in this way acted parables, the narratives of such miracles are not to be regarded as of any historical value, but as mere pictorial representations of the spiritual truths they are meant to convey.

LITERATURE.—The Comm. on the various passages, esp. the *Expos. Gr. Test.*, and Westcott's *St. John*; Jülicher, *Gleichnis-reden Jesu*, pp. 121–149; Bugge, *Die Haupt-Parabeln Jesu*, vol. i. pp. 1–89; *Expositor*, 6th ser. vol. i. [1900] p. 231 ff.; Fiebig, *Altjüd. Gleichnisse und die Gleichnisse Jesu*; Phillips Brooks, *Mystery of Iniquity* (1893), 208.

G. CURRIE MARTIN.

SELF-ASSERTION.—See CHARACTER OF CHRIST and CLAIMS OF CHRIST in vol. i., and art. RENUNCIATION above.

SELF-CONSCIOUSNESS.—See CONSCIOUSNESS.

SELF-CONTROL.—The Scripture term for self-control is ἐγκράτεια, which with its cognates occurs several times in the NT; but in the Gospels only the privative ἀκρασία is found, with the rendering 'excess' (Mt 23²⁵). The English word is not used in AV, and in RV is confined to the margin, with the single exception of 2 Ti 3³. It denotes (see Chrysostom, *Hom.* Tit 1⁸ τὸν πάθους κρατοῦντα) the exercise of dominion by man over the constituents of character within, as well as over external influences that would tend to baffle or frustrate him. It may be distinguished from self-denial as discipline is from destruction, the one making the self the centre of purpose and effort, the other aiming at its extinction or suppression. The one reduces the self, or certain of its elements, to zero; the other directs and uses it, turning all its powers into the channel of some activity, viewed as advantageous or benign. Mastery within the living organism of man is the principal suggestion of both; but self-denial gives greater prominence to the possible inherence of evil and to the ascetic processes by which it must be purged, whilst self-control implies rather freedom and strenuousness, and involves no depressing view of man or of life (see art. SELF-DENIAL). More particularly, self-control means the control of the temperament, the instincts, emotions, and will, both in themselves and against the various appeals that are made to them in daily life, with a view to the accomplishment of some purpose or the maintenance of some phase of character. In the Gospels it is exhibited in the Man Jesus Christ in a perfect degree, and by Him commended to His disciples, together with the secret of its attainment and retention.

1. Self-control on the part of Christ.—(1) It is rather doubtful whether, in the current, though vague, sense of the word, *temperament* can be predicated of Christ. Strictly the word denotes a certain general characteristic of a man's temper and moods, by which his progress in intelligence and morality is in various ways promoted or hindered. It means the set of the inner life towards some specific expression or action, and implies both a disproportion in the constituents of character and a consequent degree of imperfection and disapproval. From a very early time the typical temperaments have been classed as four—sanguine, sentimental or melancholic, choleric, and phlegmatic; and in each of them is found in varying measure a surplus of some quality which, by reason of its excess, spoils the proportion, and makes self-control under certain conditions specially difficult. As the humanity of Christ is perfect, and in Him all the virtues meet and harmonize, an excess in any direction is out of the question. He had moods of unbounded hope (Jn 12³²), of depression and shrinking (Mt 26³⁸, Jn 12²⁷), of indignant anger (Mt 23¹³⁻³⁶), of equanimity and comparative insensibility to passing impressions (Lk 13³², Jn 19¹¹); but there was no such long-continued pre-eminence of one good quality over another as would allow the placing of Him, in regard to temperament, in any of the ordinary categories. If He is to be placed at all, a new class must be formed, and He may be regarded as the type of the religious temperament (Lk 2⁴⁹, Jn 6³⁸), with the right principles of self-control in action from the beginning. In the same group, though by no means on the same level, may be put all the *animæ naturaliter Christianæ*, amongst whom the obligation of self-control, if rendered easier of discharge by their disposition, should be more quickly and actively met (Mt 13^{12} 25^{29}, Lk $12^{47f.}$).

(2) *Control over instincts and the entire appetitive life*, wherein the ethical rule is indulgence with restraint, is traceable in Christ both in the particulars of His historical manifestation, and as sustained with completeness in times of special temptation. By 'instinct' is meant the impulse and faculty of acting in such a way as to produce certain results, without deliberate or even conscious foresight. Some of these impulses are rooted in the body and aroused into activity by its uneasiness and recurring needs. Christ, for instance, knew weariness and its massive appeals for physical rest, but was so completely master of Himself as to be able to postpone, if not to withhold, the response (Mt 8^{24}, Jn $4^{6ff.}$); and of sluggishness on His part there is no record in the Gospels. During the week of the Passion the nights were spent at Bethany (the village or its neighbourhood: Mt 21^{17}, Mk 11^{11}), in part probably with a view to bodily rest after the busy days. So, too, with hunger and thirst, whose importunity was sometimes clamorous, yet easily silenced or put off (Mt 4^2, Mk 3^{20} 6^{31}, Jn 19^{28}). In regard to the physical nature, Christ neither practised nor enjoined its suppression, but only the maintenance of its proper relation amongst natural promptings and activities. To this rule there were no exceptions, the apparent ones proving on closer examination to be designed each for a special didactic or ethical purpose. The cursing of the fig-tree was not done unthinkingly under the stimulus of a disappointed appetite (Mk $11^{12ff.}$), but in illustration of the doom awaiting Israel, emblem of all who abound in leaves but fail in fruitfulness (cf. Lk 13^{6-9}), and of the power of faith in dealing with evil (Mt $21^{20f.}$). 'A gluttonous man and a winebibber' (Mt 11^{19}, Lk 7^{34}), on account of its very difficulty to some expositors, must not be rejected as an interpolation. It is not meant to indicate Christ's real habit; but it is an almost amused comment by Him on the equal readiness with which certain types of men protest against the severity of one teacher and the graciousness of another. A professed neutrality which is really childish and angry self-will deals of necessity in exaggeration; and in this case its evidence proves no degree of self-indulgence on the part of Christ, but merely magnifies His geniality, and the gentle way in which He moved amongst all innocent forms of human life, into a charge against Him of excess.

Of the mastery exercised by Christ over His emotions the characteristics appear to be a recognition of the legitimacy of emotion, sometimes even of free and unrestrained emotion, with the avoidance of all such qualities and extremes as the world has learned to condemn. Sympathy was full at Bethany (Jn 11^{35}) and on the approach to Jerusalem (Lk 19^{41}), but not allowed to become so sentimental or overwhelming as to interfere with service. The anger of just indignation finds expression and becomes even torrential in Mt 23^{13-36}; but there is nowhere any trace of personal rancour. In Gethsemane the sacred anguish transcends analysis, for the vicarious Passion was begun; but if any influence of fear or regret or intolerable burden (Lk 22^{40}) is to be acknowledged, the shrinking is quickly mastered, and the Saviour goes forth calmly to die (Mt $26^{45f.}$, Mk $14^{41f.}$, He $5^{7ff.}$). Similarly the cry on the cross (Mt 27^{46}, Mk 15^{54}) is no sign of a temporary loss of control, the collapse of the human spirit of Christ in the bitter-

ness of approaching death. It should be connected with His work of atonement rather than with His personal experience, and marks the culmination of the pressure of the world's sin (Gal 3^{13}). For man Christ passes through the deep valley of sin's doom, and at the supreme moment is compassed about by darkness unrelieved; but He did not falter, nor was the ordered unity of His inner life in His oneness of purpose with the Father broken. At the other extreme of emotion are the sense of relief after long strain, with its associated perils of 'letting oneself go,' and such an exultation of joy as is apt to cause a lapse in vigilance. The relief and the joy are traceable in Christ (Mt 11^{25}, Lk 10^{21}, Jn $17^{1.4}$), who on the earlier occasion immediately proceeds, according to the one tradition, to offer rest to the weary, and, according to the other, to pronounce a benediction upon His disciples. Joy that becomes exuberant and beyond control, and wastes itself in moods of sheer ecstasy, is nowhere recorded of Him. He preserves consistently the wise mean, well removed from the ordinary dangers, on either side, of excess and of defect. His self-respect was complete, never degenerating into immodest vanity or giving place to servility (Jn 6^{15} 12^{12-15} $18^{21.37}$). Fear could not be excited in Him by the antagonism of the people or by His apparent powerlessness in the hands of the authorities (Mt $12^{14f.}$, Lk $4^{29f.}$, Jn 18^{23} 19^{11}). He was sociable yet free, interested but not absorbed in nature and in man, subject to every pure emotion but possessed and mastered by none. And the sensitive life of Christ is most correctly viewed as an organized comity of well-graded sentiments and feelings, amongst which due order was maintained without either difficult effort or occasional failure.

(3) To this, the negative side of self-control, the subjection of the various instincts and sensibilities, must be added *the positive introduction of some controlling end or purpose*, without which the main factor in determining the merit of self-control and the moral quality of the life will be absent. Self-control by itself may be simply a tribute to strength of will, neutral in regard to quality, and capable of being turned to bad uses. As exhibited in Christ, it means not only steadiness and freedom from irritability, a calm temper unruffled by influences from without, but the inflexible direction of the spirit and will upon the accomplishment of purposes than which neither ethics nor religion can disclose any worthier. This superiority to disappointment, difficulty, apparent disaster, is shown in many lights; and if there are times when it appears for a moment to be obscured, it is recovered in another moment, and unflinchingly held. The atmosphere in which Jesus lived was often impure, vitiated by the influence of successes that were won by insincerity as well as by the prosperity of many vices; yet by men who are competent to judge, no moral fault or compromise with wrong has ever been charged against Him (Jn 8^{46}). There is no instance of His having been diverted from His purpose by the 'gainsaying of sinners' (He 12^3), the blundering clamour of the people, or their unbelieving disavowal of His mission (Mk 14^{58}); and even widespread alienation amongst His followers was turned into an occasion for deepening the convictions and strengthening the loyalty of the others (Jn 6^{67}). Neither the bitter craft of the religious leaders with their emissaries dogging His footsteps (Mt $22^{15ff.}$, Lk $11^{53f.}$), nor the jealousy or fear of the petty overlords (Lk $13^{31f.}$), could break the inward unity of His spirit or the stability of His will. In the select group of His disciples were dispositions to protest or interfere (Mt 16^{-2}, Lk 9^{54}), sometimes ignorance and unwillingness to learn (Mt $20^{20ff.}$, Lk 17^{20}; cf. Ac 1^6), tempers and views

that were discordant and unseemly, with a traitor lurking in the midst; yet Christ never allowed the strain of His work, or the uncongeniality or impotence of the men who were nearest to Him, to divert His sympathy or to ruffle the settled quiet of His demeanour. Death itself, rendered inconceivably horrible by the concentration upon Him of every man's sin (He 2⁹), was anticipated without alarm, and undergone in all its shame without loss of personal dignity or any weakening of His loving resolution to save. He set His face steadfastly (Lk 9⁵¹) in no sudden bracing of His will in the presence of an unexpected peril; but the perfect self-control, which made it possible for Him to become incarnate, was maintained through all the incidents of the historical manifestation, and even on the cross itself. In the freedom of His contact with nature and man, His heart never more than momentarily failed, and His self-control in times of confusion and danger helped to make Him the most consummate Leader of sinful men, serene and strong, and always confident in God and in the issue.

(4) Beyond the action of Christ's own will, two further causes of His self-control may be distinguished. The one was *His personal trust in God the Father*, and the other *the influence of the Holy Spirit in response*. (*a*) At the beginning of His career the part played both in His practice and in His inner life and thought by the recognition of His Father's claims upon Him, against the attractions that appeal to youth, and the dependence and clinging that earthly parents naturally desire, was indicated in His reply in the Temple (Lk 2⁴⁹), and on later occasions (Jn 4³⁴ 5³⁰ᵇ 6³⁸ 14³¹). A sense of security in the remembrance of the Father's power and purpose is part of the secret of Christ's complete self-possession in the final crisis (Mt 26⁵³). He entered upon His Agony with bitter forebodings, which in solitude became almost unendurable (Lk 22⁴⁴); absolute acceptance of the Father's will (Mk 14³⁶) enabled Him to press down any reluctance to die (He 5⁷ᶠᶠ·)—'made perfect' Himself thereby, and fitted to be 'the author of eternal salvation.' So important was His consciousness of this relationship with the Father, that in it lay for Him the kernel and germ of all truth, and in its revelation to man the sum of all duty and pleasure. (*b*) The action of the Holy Spirit in sustaining the self-control of Jesus against appetites and evil appeals is conspicuous in the records of the Temptation (Mt 4¹, Mk 1¹², Lk 4¹), and referred to by each of the Synoptists (see TEMPTATION). But it also appears elsewhere. From His childhood 'the grace of God was upon him' (Lk 2⁴⁰); and that communicated grace of the Spirit wrought in Him (Lk 2⁵²ᵇ RVm) all that He as a man accomplished or became. The unction or illapse at His baptism was not temporary, but the Spirit permanently abode with Him (Jn 1³²ᶠ·); and if Ac 10³⁸ refers primarily to invigoration for service, St. Luke elsewhere represents Jesus as 'full of the Holy Ghost' (4¹, cf. Jn 3³⁴), and as thereby prepared for personal testing and discipline as well as for His mission of mercy and redemption. For Him, as for His disciples, the soul's thirst for unity and self-mastery is assuaged, and all needed resources are obtained, in the same way and from the same fountain (Jn 7³⁷⁻³⁹).

2. Self-control on the part of man.—For man self-control assumes a double aspect, according as it is a rule of restraint or of activity. On the one hand, it keeps the indulgence of the natural appetites and impulses within the bounds of reason, grading and co-ordinating them all as elements of a coherent rational life. On the other, it concentrates the energies, reversing any original tendency to diffusion, and integrating moral life

under the steady pressure of a master conviction and a master purpose. In other words, since Christianity is not an ideal or a theoretical ethic, but a practicable way of living, and since each man's difficulty does not arise from the impulses generally, but from the predominance of some single group of impulses, self-control as exhibited and required by Christ comes to mean the control of individual temperament, the avoidance of the various evil excesses to which each man is prone, and possibly even the substitution of some form of good for some form of evil as an instinctive besetment. Symmetrical development of each man's spirit may be said to be the object of the Gospels, which are far from silent either as to the method by which it is to be effected, or as to the pains and satisfactions of the process.

Control of the senses and appetites is to be carried, if necessary, to the point of mutilation, for excess must be prevented, whatever the pain or cost (Mt 5²⁹ᶠ· 18⁸ᶠ·, Mk 9⁴³⁻⁴⁸); and not even relationships that are legitimate and pure must be allowed to interfere with the interests of the Kingdom of heaven (Mt 19¹², cf. 1 Co 7³²). Inclinations and impulses are to be distrusted, and the Christian should be their master and not their slave (Mt 5³⁹⁻⁴¹, Lk 6²⁹ᶠ·; cf. Ro 12¹⁷ᵃ). The need of integrating the life by giving supreme sway to some right and rightly conceived purpose at its centre is shown in the conversation with the young ruler (Mt 19²¹, Mk 10²¹, Lk 18²²), where the renunciation of wealth is a necessary preparation for all-absorbing devotion to Christ, the great test of discipleship (as in Jn 10²⁷ 12²⁶), as well as the secret of perfection. The same is the bearing of the sayings as to the 'single' eye (Mt 6²², Lk 11³⁴), the impossibility of serving God and mammon (Mt 6²⁴, Lk 16¹³), the necessity of becoming 'as a little child' (Mk 10¹⁵), as well as the great law of Mt 6³³, the observance of which not only safeguards the spirit from the distressing influence of suspicion and fear, but especially keeps it a well-ordered unity, with quiet strength and readiness to act as its prominent qualities. If the control be threatened from without, it is recovered or retained by recognizing God's superior claims, and counting nothing so important in experience as His good pleasure (Mt 10²⁸, Lk 12⁴ᶠ·). Against opposition and difficulty of every kind the rule is steadiness (Mt 10¹⁶⁻²⁶· ³⁴⁻³⁹), neither purpose nor self-control being shaken, because of the unrivalled constraint of the love of Christ (Mt 24⁹, Jn 15¹⁸⁻²¹ 16²· ²⁰⁻²²). 'For my sake' gives the secret of a self-control that never breaks down; and the love and devotion are continuously fed by the Spirit of the Father (Mt 10²⁰, Jn 16¹⁴). By the forgiveness of sins Christ sets the will free from bondage to past evil, and His Spirit, ruling in the life because in the heart, becomes an unfailing source of strength and peace, reproducing in mortal experience the self-control of Him who never wavered from duty, or yielded to temptation, or allowed the Kingdom within to be disturbed by a breach of will between Himself and the Father. His self-control, in its completeness and in its means, is the measure and guarantee of what is possible to man. See also art. TEMPERANCE.

LITERATURE.—The *Lexx.* of Grimm-Thayer and Liddell and Scott, *s.vv.* ἀκρασία, ἐγκράτεια; Aristotle, *Eth.* bk. vii.; Martensen, *Chr. Eth.* ii. 411; C. E. Searle in *Camb. Serm.* (ed. Bebb), 1893, p. 70; J. Iverach, *The Other Side of Greatness* (1906), 109.

R. W. MOSS.

SELF-DENIAL.—Self-denial is undoubtedly an essential part of the religious life as set before men by Jesus Christ. 'If any man will come after me, let him deny himself' (Mt 16²⁴). The word used (ἀπαρνέομαι) occurs elsewhere only in the parallel passages (Mk 8³⁴, Lk 9²³); in the accounts given by the four Evangelists of St. Peter's denial

(Mt 26[34. 35. 75], Mk 14[30. 31. 72], Lk 22[61], Jn 13[38]) ; and in our Lord's denunciation of apostasy (Lk 12[9]). It is used in the LXX to tr. נֶפֶשׁ. It is a strong word, and its meaning is best understood perhaps by comparing it with the corresponding expression of St. Paul, 'I count as loss' (ἥγημαι ζημίαν, Ph 3[7. 8]). It must be understood to include a conquest of the insistent and unruly demands of the body, denial of the lower self; and a bringing into subjection of the ambitions and emotions of the intellect and spirit, denial of the higher self.

1. The denial of the carnal self. — The practices by which men have sought to accomplish this kind of self-denial pass generally under the name of asceticism. There are five such kinds of discipline recommended or countenanced by our Lord's teaching and example : (1) fasting, (2) celibacy and sexual restraint, (3) almsgiving, (4) vigils, (5) the refusal of luxury in the surroundings of life.

(1) *Fasting* was practised by our Lord Himself (Mt 4[1ff.] ||). It was presupposed as likely to form part of the religious life by His disciples (Mt 6[16ff.], Mk 2[20]). It was practised by the Apostles and the Church in their time (Ac 10[9. 30] 13[3] 14[23], 1 Co 7[5]), and traditions of the severity of their fasting survived into the 2nd cent. (*Clem. Recog.* vii. 6 ; Clem. Alex. *Pædag.* ii. 1 ; *Can. Murat.* i. 11). In the sub-Apostolic age, probably as a result of the example of the Pharisees, fasting on stated days became a common form of self - denial (*Did.* viii. ; Hermas, *Sim.* v. 1 ; Clem. Alex. *Strom.* vii. 12). The Lenten fast grew from an original 14 days (Tertull. *de Jejun.* 15) to 40 days, in imitation of our Lord's fast in the wilderness. The Friday fast, the Lenten fast, and the custom of fasting before receiving the Communion, were very general, if not universal, in the early Catholic and the mediæval Church. See art. FASTING.

(2) *Celibacy* is countenanced by our Lord, but not generally recommended (Mt 19[12], Lk 14[26]). It and temporary sexual restraint are recommended and even deemed specially honourable by the Apostles (1 Co 7[29. 35], Rev 14[3. 4]). In the sub-Apostolic age the idea of the superior sanctity of the virgin state grew rapidly (*Did.* xi. 11 ; Ignat. *Ep. ad Polyc.* v. ; Just. Mart. *Apol.* i. 15 ; Athenag. 33, etc.). See art. CELIBACY.

(3) *Almsgiving*, as a form of self-denial, is distinctly recommended by our Lord (Mt 6[1ff.], Lk 11[41] 12[33], Mk 12[43] ; cf. Lk 6[38], Mt 5[42], Ac 20[35]), and He Himself, though poor, practised it (Jn 13[29]). The Apostles insisted on the duty of almsgiving, at first apparently indiscriminately (Ac 2[44. 45]), afterwards with more caution (Ro 12[8], 2 Co 8[3], Ja 2[14f.], 1 Jn 3[17], He 13[16], Ja 1[27], 2 Co 9[6. 7], Gal 6[9], 1 Co 16[1], 2 Co 9[1], Ro 15[26], Ac 11[27-30] ; cf. 2 Th 3[10]). In the early Church, almsgiving, either weekly or monthly, was a recognized duty (Tertull. *Apol.* 39 ; Cypr. *de Oper. et Eleem.*). See ALMSGIVING.

(4) *Vigils*. — Watching and wakefulness as a form of self-denying service to God were no doubt suggested by our Lord's commands (Mt 24[42] 26[41], Lk 12[37]) as well as by His own practice (Mt 14[23] 26[38]), and in this sense were understood many of the Apostolic exhortations (1 Co 16[13], 1 Th 5[6], Eph 6[18]). Examples of vigil services are to be found in the records of the Apostolic Church (Ac 12[12] 20[7]) and in the practice of St. Paul (2 Co 6[5] 11[27]). The heathen Pliny's description (*Ep.* x. 97) of the Christians as 'meeting before daybreak' probably points to nothing but a desire for privacy and a feeling of the necessity for avoiding public notice, but we have certainly allusions to vigils in the strict sense of the word in the writings of several of the early Fathers (Clem. Alex. *Pædag.* ii. 9 ; Tertull. *ad Ux.* ii. 5 ; Cypr. *de Laps.* **34** ff. ; Lactant. vii. 19 ; August. *Ep. ad*

Januar. 119 ; Socr. i. 37, v. 21 ; Sozom. ii. 29, iii. 6).

(5) *Refusal of luxury.*—Another region in which self-denial might be exercised was found in the surroundings of life, clothes, household arrangements, etc. Our Lord's own example (Mt 8[20]) was appealed to, and certain hints in His teaching were felt to have a bearing on the subject (Mt 10[10] 11[8], Lk 16[19]). The teaching of the Apostles was more detailed and definite (1 Ti 2[9], 1 P 3[3f.]). The question of the amount of luxury permissible to Christians came up in the Montanist controversy (Euseb. v. 18. 4 ; Tertull. *de Coron. Mil.* 5, 10, 11). It occupies a considerable part of the *Pædag.* of Clem. of Alex. (see especially ii. 11, ii. 8–12, iii. 2, etc.), and is discussed by Cyprian (*de Virg. vel.* and *de Cult. fem.*).

2. The denial of the higher intellectual and psychical self.—When we consider the teaching of our Lord Jesus Christ, we are at once struck by His definite and marked departure from the ethics of classical antiquity. For Him there is no such word as ἀρετή (cf. Ἄρης, and the Lat. *vir-tus*) with the sense of elevated manliness. Nor has He anything to correspond with the classical tetrad φρόνησις (or σοφία), ἀνδρεία, σωφροσύνη, δικαιοσύνη. These express the completest development of the higher, better self in man, and proclaim as the ideal the attainment of the truest 'manliness' in the face of an appreciative and admiring world. For our Lord the ideal is a different one. His life fulfils the conception of the prophet. He has no beauty that men should desire Him. He is despised, rejected, a Man of sorrows, acquainted with grief. He is 'meek and lowly of heart' (cf. Zec 9[9], 2 Co 10[1], Ph 2[7]). He is 'one that serveth' (Mt 20[28], Jn 13[13-17]). It is 'the poor in spirit,' 'they that mourn,' 'the meek,' and those that 'are reviled' whom He calls blessed (cf. Mt 18[3. 4] 19[30] 20[14], Mk 10[27ff.], Lk 1[48]). It is quite evident that the ideal here set up is wholly different from that of the classical philosophers. The two are, in fact, in fundamental opposition. The one is the ideal of the development, the other the ideal of the denial of the higher self. The Apostles understood the Master very well and taught as He did (but see the use of ἀρετή in what *may* be its classical sense in Ph 4[8] and in 2 P 1[5]). Indeed, they insisted with even more than His iteration on the denial of self (1 Co 1[28. 29], 2 Co 1[5] 6[10], Ph 2[6-8], 2 Co 10[1], 1 P 2[21], Gal 5[23] 6[1], Eph 4[2], Col 3[12], Ja 1[21] 3[13], 1 P 5[5], 2 Co 12[21]).

LITERATURE.—1. HISTORICAL : Zöckler, *Askese und Mönchtum* (1894), *Die Tugendlehre des Christentums* (1904) ; Mayer, *Die Christl. Askese, ihre Wesen und ihre histor. Entfaltung* (1894) ; A. Ritschl, *Gesch. des Pietismus* (1880–86) ; W. Bright, *Some Aspects of Primitive Church Life* (1898) ; J. O. Hannay, *The Spirit and Origin of Christian Monasticism* (1902) ; Migne, *Dictionnaire d'Ascétisme, Encycl. Théol.* vols. 45, 46 ; Bingham, *Antiquities of the Christian Church.*

THEOLOGICAL AND DEVOTIONAL :—Rothe, *Theol. Ethik*, iii. (1848); Dorner, *Syst. d. chr. Sittenlehre* ; Newman Smyth, *Christian Ethics* (1894) ; Jeremy Taylor, *Holy Living and Holy Dying* ; J. Keble, *Letters of Spiritual Counsel* ; J. H. Newman, *Historical Sketches* ; Bp. Paget, *The Spirit of Discipline* ; J. O. Hannay, *The Wisdom of the Desert* (1904) ; Thomas à Kempis, *The Imitation of Christ* ; Baxter, *Self-Denial.*

J. O. HANNAY.

SELF-EXAMINATION.—'Our conclusion, then, is that the state of mind which is now most naturally expressed by the unspoken questions, Have I been what I should be? Shall I be what I should be, in doing so and so? *is that in which all moral progress originates*' (T. H. Green, *Prolegomena to Ethics*, p. 337).

1. Duty of self-examination.—Every man's conscience bears witness to the reasonableness and necessity of self-examination. It means taking oneself seriously, and applying to the moral and spiritual life methods analogous to those adopted in all other departments of knowledge and skill.

It is the comparison of our motives and actions with the Ideal of what they should be; and all such self-scrutiny, as T. H. Green suggests, has a real identity with the reformer's comparison of what is actual with a social ideal. He who would attain excellence in any difficult work must be constantly testing and examining his results. He must be on the alert to overcome slackness, discover errors, ensure progress. In Christian discipleship, the most arduous, as it is the most noble, of all pursuits, there is the same imperative demand. This duty is enforced (1) *By Holy Scripture.* The mission of the ancient prophet, as distinct from that of the priest, was to apply a constant spur to the consciences of men. Much of his message was expressed in the exhortation, 'Let us search and try our ways, and turn again to the Lord' (La 3[40]). He bade men examine themselves in the light of God's known character and will (Is 1[10-20], Jer 7[1-28], Ezk 18[19-32], Hos 14[1-9] etc.). If Jesus did not in so many words call on men to examine themselves, yet the necessity and duty of such self-criticism were implied in all His ministry and teaching. In the Sermon on the Mount, as in so many of His parables, He was holding up before men the ideal by which they must test their lives. And the same may be said of all the Apostolic Epistles (1 Co 11[28], 2 Co 13[5]).—(2) *By the experience of wise and good men.* The saying, 'Man, know thyself,' was frequently on the lips of Socrates. He made it the text of his life and teaching. But how shall a man know himself unless he brings his thoughts, his passions, his conduct, into strict review, and scrutinizes them in the light of conscience and duty? What a large place, again, did this work of self-examination fill in the lives of serious-minded men and women of earlier and simpler times than ours. Thomas à Kempis, in the *Imitation of Christ*, is much occupied with this duty; and Jeremy Taylor, in *Rules and Exercises of Holy Dying* (chapter ii.), devotes many pages to the reasons and benefits of the habit of the daily examination of our actions. 'He that does not frequently search his conscience,' he remarks, 'is a house without a window.'

2. Difficulties and dangers of self-examination. —(1) There is the danger of a *morbid self-consciousness* hurtful to the spiritual life. An analogy may be drawn with bodily health. A sure way of producing sickness and physical disorder is for a person to be constantly worrying himself about his health, and living, as it were, with his fingers always on his pulse. 'Is this self-consciousness a good thing? Does it not hinder action, destroy energy? Does it not cultivate a habit of mawkishness, an indelicate desire to expose the most secret passages of our souls, even to the public gaze? . . . In how many other ways do men testify that they feel this self-consciousness to be a disease which will destroy them if they cannot be cured of it! What numbers does it bring to the feet of the spiritual director!' (F. D. Maurice). Do we not live our best life when we just go on doing our duty and filling our place, never considering ourselves at all? 'There is a kind of devotion to great objects or to public service which seems to leave a man no leisure and to afford no occasion for the question about himself, whether he has been as good as he should have been, whether a better man would not have acted otherwise than he has done. And again, there is a sense in which to be always fingering one's motives is a sign rather of an unwholesome preoccupation with self than of the eagerness in disinterested service which helps forward mankind' (T. H. Green).—(2) A more serious difficulty is that in this work of self-criticism we occupy *the double position of being both the examiner and the examined*. We are at once the judge, the witness,

and the prisoner at the bar. What scope for self-deception, for evasion, for duping ourselves! Are we not in danger of condemning trifles and overlooking serious faults and vices? How easy to confuse the issues in this complicated process! to lose sight of the due proportion of things! to play tricks with ourselves! Is there any escape from this difficulty?

3. Suggestions for self-examination.—If the dangers mentioned above are to be escaped, this exercise must be conducted (1) *with the most humble dependence upon God and desire for His help and guidance.* Consider specially Ps 139[23, 24]. The Psalmist could not trust himself. He knew how sin eluded him, how it disguised itself, how it hid in secret chambers where his search could not follow it. He needed the aid of One who could accomplish a deeper and more penetrating work than he himself could undertake. Consider also 1 Ch 28[9] 29[17], Ps 26[1, 2] 44[21], Pr 16[1, 2] 20[27], Jer 17[9-10].—(2) The examination must be *very largely objective, i.e.* not merely, or chiefly, a scrutiny of feelings or motives, but an investigation of actual conduct in the light of God's law and of Christian ideals. The desire expressed in the hymn, ''Tis a point I long to know. . . . Do I love the Lord, or no?' may often be best answered by a reference to such words as are found in Jn 14[15, 21] 15[14]. See also Mt 7[21-29], Mk 3[35]. 'Do you notice how many times our Saviour says: "If ye love me, keep my commandments"? It is as if a child should rush passionately to its mother and throw its little arms round her neck, and say convulsively, "O mother! I do love you so!" "Well, my dear child, if you do, why are you not a better child?"' (H. W. Beecher, *Conduct the Index of Feeling*).—(3) Special consideration should be given to 2 Co 13[5] '*Jesus Christ is in you.*' Therein lies the secret by which self-examination may be a reality and not a fiction; therein is found the protection from the dangers already referred to. There is a true Light which lighteth every man; One who dwells with us, near us, in us; One who will save us from self-flattery and self-deception, and from mawkish self-consciousness. In the light of His presence self-examination is safe and fruitful.

LITERATURE.—The most suggestive remarks which the writer has seen on this subject are found in a sermon by F. D. Maurice, *Lincoln's Inn Sermons*, vol. iii. p. 179, 'How Self-Examination is possible.' T. H. Green's *Prolegomena to Ethics*, Bk. iv. 'The Application of Moral Philosophy to the Guidance of Conduct,' chs. i. ii., is worthy of most careful study; cf. Jeremy Taylor, *The Rules and Exercises of Holy Dying*, ch. ii. 'On the Daily Examination of our Actions'; Thomas à Kempis, *Of the Imitation of Christ*, Bk. i. 'Admonitions useful for the Spiritual Life'; W. G. T. Shedd, *Sermons to the Natural Man* (1879), p. 181; W. L. Watkinson, *Studies in Christian Character*, 1st ser. (1901) p. 10; W. S. Wood, *Problems of the NT* (1890), p. 83; T. B. Dover, *Alive unto God* (1888), p. 37.

.ARTHUR JENKINSON.

SELFISHNESS.—The self-sacrifice which Christ demands of all who would be His followers might lead one to imagine that Christianity was a religion of asceticism; that the Gnostic dualism of good and evil, matter and spirit, was the logical outcome of the teaching of Jesus; that God required the renunciation of all earthly things, and even of life, for the sake of the sacrifice itself. But it is a total misconception of the religion of Jesus to suppose that He makes asceticism an end. What we find Him teaching is not that the world is evil, but that the soul of man is good; that the soul is eternal, not of time, and therefore that in God alone, to whom it is akin, can it attain its complete satisfaction (Mt 6[19-21] ‖ Lk 12[33, 34]). He demanded self-renunciation (Lk 14[26, 27, 33]), and at the same time He inculcated the absolute value of the self (Mt 16[26] ‖ Mk 8[36, 37]). He sets moral self-love over against natural selfishness (Mt 16[25] ‖ Mk 8[35]), and He insists that the perfect, the eternal development of the human personality is to be found not in separation and independence, but in union and communion with universal life,—life as it is in God, life as God has put it into the world (cf. Mt 5. 6. 7). To pour out oneself in love, to lose oneself for Christ's sake, to give oneself to God and to the world of men, is 'to find,' 'to save' oneself in Him. To make the law of God, the Creator of the world and the Heavenly Father of each human soul, the fundamental law of one's life, is to render all temporal and corruptible things innocuous. It then becomes possible to employ them, in a way of which the Stoic hardly dreamed, to the end of perfect self-development (Mt 6³³). 'What is a man profited,' Christ asks, 'if he shall gain the whole world and lose his own soul?' To preserve and to save his soul is thus a man's highest profit, his one great task. But to seek to save it in the worldly sense is to lose it in the spiritual and eternal. Natural selfishness is humanity's greatest danger—the great source of sin. It is manifest that our Lord accepts the common division of human nature into its two spheres of flesh and spirit. He has, it is true, no explicit psychology such as St. Paul elaborated; but to Him the natural and the spiritual man are as evidently in continual conflict as to St. Paul. It is the natural self that must be denied, that must be subjected, if the spiritual self is to grow. Each of these Christ calls the 'self,' the 'life'; but it is the latter only—'the soul'—that is of absolute value. The value of the former is but relative; and its good, which has a measure, must always be subordinated to that of the other, which is measureless. Even the gaining of the whole world by the natural self is worthless if it entails spiritual loss; for to lose the true self is to have but the life of time, is to miss that of eternity (cf. the parable of the Rich Fool, Lk 12¹⁶⁻²¹, and the profound statement of the same truth in Christ's Temptation in the Wilderness, Mt 4¹⁻¹¹, Lk 4²⁻¹³). Moral self-love, therefore, consists primarily in love to God; and whenever the good of the natural self conflicts with the dictates of that love, it must be denied as a temptation of Satan (Mt 16²¹⁻²³). To sink the self in the sensuous and finite, to cultivate the lower nature, to lay up abundant goods, and to imagine that the joy of one's soul is to be found therein, is to lose one's soul; and when death comes, the loss of all is immediately manifest (Lk 12¹⁶⁻²¹). It is in the light of eternity that man must view the world. It is the aim of the true self to lay up treasure in heaven, that the heart may dwell continually in the atmosphere of the eternal life.

That the denial of selfish desires is not to be regarded as an end in itself, is made clear by a whole series of parables uttered by our Lord upon the subject of labour. An idle faith, an idle self-sacrifice, did not satisfy Christ. To serve God is the soul's great aim, and at the same time its salvation (cf. parables of the Talents, Mt 25¹⁴⁻³⁰; the Pounds, Lk 19¹¹⁻²⁷; the Servants Watching, Lk 12³⁶⁻⁴⁸; the Ten Virgins, Mt 25¹⁻¹³; the Labourers in the Vineyard, Mt 20¹⁻¹⁵). From all these it is clear that the reward is in no sense proportionate to the work done, but to the zeal and fidelity shown; and, further, that the reward is the labour itself, and grows out of it. It is true that life eternal is the grand reward, but in that life he is already a sharer who makes God's service his aim in this world. The complete perfection of the self comes only when sin has passed away with mortal life; but there will be no gap between this world and the next. To serve God hereafter will be the heavenly joy of the redeemed, just as it is their chief joy on earth. Heaven is not idleness, but holy service rendered in perfect freedom from the constraints of sin. It is thus manifest that there is not the slightest ground for bringing against Christianity the charge of inculcating a higher form of selfishness; for selfishness implies an opposition between the self and the not-self—that the well-being of the former is sought at the cost of the latter, whereas in the religion of Jesus there is no such opposition. The good of the self is itself the good of the world, the fulfilment of the will of God; and even the reward is nothing other than the enlargement of the human powers so that the man becomes capable of yet greater labour for the world's welfare. Selfishness is hurtful alike to self and to mankind. Spiritual self-love is the self's completion, God's glory and the world's joy. By faithfulness in the unrighteous mammon, in that which is another's, we receive that which is our own (Lk 16¹⁰⁻¹²).

LITERATURE.—The Comm. on the NT; standard works on the Parables; Beyschlag's and Weiss' *NT Theology*; Müller, *Christian Doct. of Sin*, i. 94–182; Martensen, *Christian Ethics*, ii. 282 ff.; Newman Smyth, *Christian Ethics*, p. 327 ff.; Laidlaw, *Bib. Doct. of Man*, ch. vi.; Hastings' *DB*, artt. 'Flesh,' 'Psychology'; F. W. Robertson, *Serm.* 4th ser. p. 42; J. Ker, *Serm.* 1st ser. p. 98; R. C. Trench, *Serm. New and Old*, p. 112; J. W. Rowntree, *Palestine Notes* (1906), p. 144.

W. J. S. MILLER.

SELF-RENUNCIATION. — See RENUNCIATION and SELF-DENIAL.

SELF-RESTRAINT.—See SELF-CONTROL.

SELF-SUPPRESSION.—Religion may be thought of as having for its aim either the complete suppression or the development to its highest expression of the individuality of man. In the history of Christianity both these conceptions have been adopted, and each has been regarded as the true interpretation of the spirit of the Lord.

Those Christian teachers whose bent is towards Mysticism have for their ideal the ultimate suppression of self. The elevated expression which their doctrine found in the German mystics of the 14th cent. gives us the clearest view of this tendency. Eckart, and afterwards Tauler, taught that the spiritual life was at its highest when self was annihilated. The complete suppression of self was attempted in a wholly different spirit by certain societies of late origin, notably by the Society of Jesus. In the Jesuit system the individual is completely subordinated to the community, and the suppression of each man's self is of vital necessity for the accomplishment of perfect discipline. The tendency of Protestantism, on the other hand, has been towards the development of individuality. Its teachers have aimed at allowing free play to natural diversities of character, and have even justified the accentuation of the various ways in which men differently constituted have apprehended the gospel message.

Our Lord, in His dealings with men, seems always to have assumed that natural varieties of character and the varied environment of each individual required differences of treatment. His advice changes according to the temperament and circumstances of those to whom it was given. A leper, after his healing, is bidden to 'tell no man' what was done for him (Mt 8⁴). Other lepers are told to go and show themselves to the priests and make the offerings commanded in the Law (Lk 17¹⁴). One who wished to follow Him but desired first to bury his father, receives the stern word—'Let the dead bury their dead' (Mt 8²²). A restored demoniac, anxious 'to be with him,' is told to go home to his friends (Mk 5¹⁹). One rich man is commanded to sell all that he has (Mt 19²¹). Others are allowed to continue in possession of the whole or part of their property (Lk 19⁸, Mt 27⁵⁷). To a certain hard saying the Lord appends the caution, 'He that is able to receive it, let him receive it' (Mt 19[12]). These and other sayings which might be quoted display our Lord's evident desire to develop rather than annihilate individuality. In the training of the Twelve, who were to carry on His work after the Ascension, He aims not at creating a spirit of unquestioning obedience to plain commands, but rather at developing a highly intelligent and spiritually energetic kind of character. We are necessarily ignorant of much that passed between Him and them especially during those forty days when He spoke to them 'of the things pertaining to the kingdom of God' (Ac 1[3]), but we know enough to feel sure that He wished the Twelve to work for His cause with a certain independence and personal responsibility, rather than to suppress in them personal freedom of intellect and will. See also SELF-DENIAL.

LITERATURE.—A. W. Hutton, *The Inner Way*; W. R. Inge, *Light, Life, and Love*, and the same writer's *Christian Mysticism*; R. A. Vaughan, *Hours with the Mystics*; Molinos, *The Spiritual Guide* (Eng. tr. Glasgow, 1885); Zöckler, *Askese und Mönchtum* (pp. 592, etc.); art. 'Jesuitenordnen' in *PRE*[3] vol. viii. 　　　　　　　　　J. O. HANNAY.

SEMEIN.—A link in our Lord's genealogy (Lk 3[26], AV *Semei*).

SEPARATION.—In discourses descriptive of the present condition and future prospects of the Kingdom of God, Christ taught that the Kingdom in its ideal state of purity would not be realized till the end of the world, when the object in view is to be attained by means of a judicial separation between real members and those who are members only in outward appearance or profession (Mt 13[24-30. 36-43. 47-50]). In opposition to prevailing ideas on the subject, Christ plainly indicated that the Kingdom of God, throughout the course of its earthly development, must contain conflicting elements of good and evil, and gravely deprecated any premature attempt at separating them. The intermixture foreshadowed was not a pure kingdom existing amid a corrupt environment, but a kingdom itself invaded and pervaded to some extent by a corrupt element.

Wendt maintains that Christ did not 'contemplate an outward separation of His disciples from the fellowship of the Israelitish nation and religion' (*Teaching*, ii. 351 f.); and that the parables of the Tares and the Drag Net were intended to guard against any attempt in that direction. But the evil element referred to in the parables is not that which has always existed in the world, and must be expected to continue, but that which has entered the Kingdom in the course of, and as the result of, its own operations, which tend to gather within its pale spurious adherents as well as genuine (Mt 13[47]). A separation, moreover, from the Jewish Church, as Christ must have foreseen, was imminent and inevitable, if for no other reason, because the spirit and aims of the society founded by Him were so widely different (Mt 9[16f.]), and it is clearly implied in the announcement of the approaching downfall of the Jewish State (Lk 19[43f.]).

Serious objection must also be taken to the view, which has often been advocated, in the interests of a pure Church, since the Donatist controversy in the beginning of the 5th cent., that the evil element is in the world, the good element in the Kingdom, and the blending of the two merely contiguity or co-existence in space. It is hard to see why our Lord should have been at such pains to point out what must be perfectly obvious to everybody, that the world is evil, and why He should recommend a tolerant attitude toward the evil, instead of making it a reason for earnest evangelistic effort. Such a condition of things had long existed, and was only what might be expected. It could by no possibility give rise to the painful reflexion and inquiry described in the parable (Mt 13[27]), which are in reality due to the circumstance that the sin which exists in the world 'is always forcing its way anew into the circle in which the Kingdom of God is being realized.' The surprise and disappointment expressed by the servants are occasioned by the emergence of a phenomenon wholly unexpected, when the field originally sown with good seed is found *afterwards* to contain tares—an alien and unwelcome addition; and their impatient zeal to begin at once the work of purification is, in the circumstances, extremely natural. It is almost needless to remark that if the Son of Man at the end of the world is to 'gather out of his kingdom all things that offend (πάντα τὰ σκάνδαλα), and them which do iniquity,' they must have existed previously within it (Mt 13[41]).

The contrast is obviously between the mixed state of affairs now prevailing, and the Kingdom as it shall be, when, freed from all admixture, it shines forth in its pure native lustre (Mt 13[43]). Meanwhile the disciples are directed to exercise a wise patience, and to refrain from drastic measures of reform which might result in injuries still more serious to the cause they have at heart (Mt 13[29]). Their attitude of tolerance is by no means to be taken, however, as implying sanction or approval of existing abuses. Christ freely admitted that the presence and conduct of unworthy members were inconsistent with the Divine ideal of the Kingdom, and could not but prove injurious to its best interests (Mt 13[28. 39]). But the possibility of admixture was unavoidable, in view of the fact that the Divine Kingdom welcomed all without distinction, on their professed compliance with the conditions of admission to its membership. The wide and sweeping character of its operations exposed it to the risk of gathering into its bosom some who might do it serious discredit in the eyes of those who had its purity and welfare at heart, as well as of the world at large (Mt 13[47]).

It would be a mistake to suppose that Christ meant to withhold from His disciples authority to exercise discipline in the case of grave offences against the laws of the Kingdom, discipline which they did, in point of fact, afterwards exercise (Ac 8[20-23], 1 Co 5[3-5]), but which had for its object the edification, and not the destruction, of believers (2 Co 10[8]). The infliction of censure or punishment in the case of gross offenders was intended to have a healing effect, and instead of aiming at permanent exclusion from religious fellowship and privileges, had ultimate restoration to these in view. What our Lord deprecates is any attempt to forestall the Final Judgment by the absolute separation of offenders from religious fellowship, a separation issuing only in destruction (Mt 13[40]). Having regard to the imperfections that cleave to human nature while still in a state of probation, it is evidently His intention that lenity rather than severity should characterize the treatment of offenders, lest good and evil be rashly included in one common condemnation, and the remedy prove so violent as to be worse than the disease (Mt 13[29]). Besides, the exercise of a decisive judgment would in many cases require a delicacy of discrimination and an insight into human character possessed only by a Divine person, and it is accordingly reserved for the Son of Man, in His capacity as Judge, at the end of the world. Even strong presumptive proof of moral unworthiness would not, in the case of mere human judgment, afford sufficient guarantee against the risk of mistake (Mt 13[29]). See CHURCH, EXCOMMUNICATION.

While the disciples are enjoined to preserve an attitude of patient endurance toward evil within the Kingdom, Christ held out to them the prospect of a day of final sifting in which it would be completely eliminated (Mt 13[30. 48]). The period of intermingling is at last to come to an end. The great separation to be then effected between the two elements so long opposed, has primarily in view the interest of an ideal purity, for which all earnest ones have anxiously hoped and striven. The burning of the tares does not refer so much to the fate which ultimately overtakes evildoers, as to the fact that they can no longer exert a depressing effect on the fortunes of the Kingdom. Hitherto they have existed as an obscuring medium, but with the removal of the scandals and their authors (v.[41]) the character of the righteous at last appears, without shadow of eclipse, in all its unsullied purity and splendour (v.[43]). The sifting out of unworthy members results in irreparable loss, at the same time leading, as it does, to their permanent exclusion from heavenly privileges (24[50] 25[11f. 30]). The grounds of separation are quite general, consisting in broad fundamental distinctions of moral character, not clearly apparent at the outset, but becoming increasingly manifest as time goes on (13[26]), so that at last a division into two classes, the righteous and the wicked, becomes inevitable (vv.[41. 43. 49]). Elsewhere the twofold classification is made to turn on characteristics of a more specific kind, such as confession or denial of Christ in times of peril (10[32f.]), faithful or unfaithful exercise of stewardship (24[45. 48]), diligence and fidelity in the use of entrusted gifts, or failure to improve them due to unbelief and indolence (25[20. 22. 24f.]). Profession without practice (7[21-23]), selfish ambition (18[1. 3]), an unforgiving disposition (v.[34f.]), mark men out for exclusion from the perfected Kingdom; while childlike humility (v.[3]), lowly acts of service (Lk 22[24-30]), preparedness for all kinds of sacrifice up to that of life itself (Mt 16[25. 27] 19[27-29]), are sure passports to participation in its benefits. See, further, artt. ETERNAL PUNISHMENT, UNIVERSALISM.

LITERATURE.—E. L. Hull, *Serm.* 2nd ser. 191 ; H. Bushnell, *New Life*, 306 ; B. F. Westcott, *Peterborough Serm.* 3 ; T. G. Selby, *Unheeding God*, 24 ; G. Body, *Life of Love*, 27.

W. S. MONTGOMERY.

SEPTUAGINT.—The Version 'according to the Seventy.' **1.** This name for the Greek translation of the OT has its origin in the legend that Ptolemy II. Philadelphus was advised by his librarian Demetrius Phalereus to procure from Jerusalem copies of the Hebrew Scriptures, and men learned in the Hebrew and Greek languages to translate them. Ptolemy accordingly sent ambassadors to Eleazar the high priest, who sent back to Alexandria seventy-two elders, six from each tribe, with magnificent copies of the Hebrew Scriptures. They were treated with the highest honour ; they were assigned a quiet and convenient building on the island of Pharos, removed from the distractions of the city ; and there, in seventy-two days, they translated the Hebrew Bible into Greek, for the enrichment of Ptolemy's library ; and the translation was received with delight by king and people.

This legend is related in a pseudonymous letter purporting to be written by Aristeas (an Alexandrian, and one of Ptolemy's ambassadors to Jerusalem) to his brother Philocrates. The text, edited by St. J. Thackeray, is printed at the end of Swete's *Introduction to the OT in Greek*, and a translation by Mr. Thackeray appeared in the *JQR*, April 1903. Other forms of the tradition are given by the Alexandrian writers Aristobulus and Philo, and by Josephus. And the early Fathers of the Christian Church from the 2nd century onwards received the story without suspicion, and amplified it. What amount of truth underlies the legend it is difficult to decide ; but the following facts are probable : (1) that the translation was begun at Alexandria ; (2) that it was not undertaken officially, by order of the king (though he probably encouraged it), but resulted from the needs of the Alexandrian Jews, who knew no Hebrew and probably little or no Aramaic ; (3) it may be true that Hebrew rolls were brought from Jerusalem ; (4) the translation was, as might be expected, cordially received by Hellenistic Jews, who would be glad to have a Greek account of the origins of the Hebrew people.

The Alexandrian version embraced only the Pentateuch ; and the letter of Aristeas professes no more. Josephus and Jerome recognized this, but Christian writers, generally, failed to notice the limitation. It could not, indeed, have embraced more in the reign of Ptolemy II., for the *Torah* alone was complete by that time, secure in its position as a collection of sacred books and ready for translation (Ryle, *Canon of the OT*, p. 113). But other books would be translated from time to time when they reached Egypt with Palestinian recognition of their canonicity. And before the Christian era Alexandria probably possessed the whole of the Hebrew Bible in a Greek translation, with the possible exception of Ecclesiastes.

2. The importance of the LXX version to the student of Hebrew literature and philology can scarcely be overestimated (see Swete, *Introduction*, Pt. iii. c. 4). And it is hardly less essential to the student of early Christian writings. Patristic writers for the most part accepted it not merely as the best version of the Hebrew OT, but as no less inspired than the original. Even Augustine could say : 'Spiritus qui in prophetis erat quando illa dixerunt, idem ipse erat in LXX viris quando illa interpretati sunt' (*de Civ. Dei*, xviii. 43). Being entirely dependent on it, and unable to appeal to or form comparisons with any other version, 'they adopted without suspicion and with tenacity its least defensible renderings, and pressed them into the service of controversy, dogma, and devotion.' 'It was argued that the errors of the Greek text were due to accidents of transmission, or that they were not actual errors, but Divine adaptations of the original to the use of the future Church' (Swete, Pt. iii. c. 5).

But the present article is concerned with that which is the chiefest importance of the LXX—its relation to (*a*) the beginnings and the growth of Christianity, (*b*) the expression of Christian doctrines and ideas.

(*a*) *The LXX was an important factor in preparing the way for the reception of the Christian religion.* In our Lord's time the Jews were scattered throughout the known world. And though they preserved their religious connexion with Jerusalem by payments of money and by frequent attendance at the three annual festivals (see art. DISPERSION), yet one and all had lost the knowledge of the classical Hebrew of the Scriptures, with the exception of the learned—the priests and Rabbis—of whom the original language of the OT was almost the exclusive property. It may be realized, therefore, what a blessing was conferred upon the Jewish race by Alexandria when she gave them their own Scriptures in the universal language of the day. They were provided with a valuable controversial weapon, whereby they could prove to their heathen neighbours the real importance and the hoary antiquity of the Hebrew nation. An army of apologists was raised up, of whom Josephus and Philo are, for us, the chief, because so much of their work is extant ; but they must have been well-nigh equalled in weight and influence by such writers as the historians Alexander Cornelius ('Polyhistor'), Demetrius, Eupolemus, Artapanus, and Aristeas, the poets Philo, Theodotus, and Ezekiel, the philosopher Aristobulus, and Cleodemus or Malchas, small fragments of whose writings are preserved in Clem. Alex. *Stromateis*, i. 22, 141, 153 ff., and Euseb. *Præp. Evang.* viii. 10, ix. 6, 17–34, 37, 39, xiii. 12.

But though she knew it not, Alexandria provided them with something greater. Christianity, by the power of God and by the coming of Christ, sprang out of Judaism. 'Novum Testamentum in Vetere latet ; Vetus in Novo patet' (Aug.). By enabling Jews and Gentiles to read the OT Scriptures, the Greek version, in spite of all its mistakes and grotesque mistranslations, revealed the guiding providence of God in Hebrew history, and the gradual development of religious ideas of which the OT is the record ; and above all it gave a lasting impetus to the growth of Messianic expectations. A train was laid which only needed the Divine spark to burst into flame. Christ came 'to send fire upon the earth,' and the LXX had been instrumental in supplying fuel.

The quotations from the OT in the NT are seldom mere literary adornments, such as a modern writer might introduce from Shakespeare or other classical authors ; they are for the most part used as a definite foundation for Christian teaching, or at least weighty illustrations of the writers' statements and arguments. Our Lord's teaching struck His hearers with amazement, because it did not blindly follow the footsteps of the scribes. Against the Jews He used their own Scriptures with conclusive force ; and with His loving but fainthearted and ignorant disciples He adopted the same course ; 'beginning at Moses and all the prophets, he expounded unto them in all the scriptures the things concerning himself' (Lk 24²⁷). And His disciples afterwards followed His example both in their speeches and in their writings (Ac 8³⁵).

(*b*) *The LXX played a large part in the moulding of Christian terminology.* It is difficult to gauge the extent to which religious conceptions were affected by the results which ensued from the wedding of the Greek language to Hebrew thought. Their offspring the LXX was the parent of a yet nobler heir. There are few more interesting lines of study than to trace the debt which Christianity owed to the LXX in the matter of words and terms, and to see how the borrowed terminology was consecrated and adapted to higher uses.

3. The LXX must now be studied in two aspects, so far as it affected the four Gospels and the Apostolic conceptions of Christ's Person and work.

A. *Direct quotations.*—It will be convenient to give a list of the direct quotations from the OT in the Gospels, taken from Swete's *Introduction*, pp. 386 ff.

Mt.	Mk.	Lk.	OT
1^{23}			Is 7^{14}*
	?^{23}		Ex 13^{12}
2^{6}			Mic 5^{2}*
15			Hos 11^{1}*
18			Jer 38^{15}
3^{3}	1^{3}	3$^{4-6}$	Is 40$^{3-5}$*
4^{4}		4^{4}	Dt 8^{3}
6		10f.	Ps 90^{11}f.
7		12	Dt 6^{16}
10		13	
15f.			Is 9^{1}f.*
5^{21}			Ex 20^{13}
27			14
31			Dt 24^{1}
33			Nu 30^{3} (cf. Dt 23^{21})
38			Ex 21^{24}
43			Lv 19^{18}
8^{17}			Is 53^{4}*
9^{13} (12^{7})			Hos 6^{6}
11^{10}	1^{2}	7^{27}	Mal 3^{1}*
12^{7}			Hos 6^{6}
18-21			Is 42^{1}*
13^{14}f.			6^{9}f.
35			Ps 77^{2}*
		4^{18}f.	Is 61^{1}ff.+58^{6}*
15^{4}	7^{10}		Ex 20^{12} 21^{17}
8f.	6		Is 29^{13}
	9^{48}		66^{24}
19^{5}f.	10$^{6-8}$		Gn 1^{27}+2^{24}
18f.	19	18^{20}f.	Ex 20$^{12-17}$
21^{5}			Zec 9^{9}+Is 62^{11}*
13	11^{17}	19^{46}	Is 56^{7}+Jer 7^{11}
16			Ps 8^{2}
42	12^{10}	20^{17}	118^{22}f.
22^{24}	19	28	Dt 25^{5} (cf. Gn 38^{8})
32	26	37	Ex 3^{6}
37	29f.	10^{27}a	Dt 6^{4}f.
39	31	27b	Lv 19^{18}
44	36	20^{42}f.	Ps 109^{1}*
32f.			Dt 4^{35}
24^{15}	13^{14}		Dn 12^{11}
		22^{37}	Is 53^{12}*
26^{31}	14^{27}		Zec 13^{7}*
27^{9}f.			11^{13}*
46	15^{34}		Ps 21^{1}*

Jn 1^{23}	Is 40^{3}
2^{17}	Ps 68^{10}*
6^{31}	Ex 16$^{4.\ 15}$ (Ps 77^{24}f.)
45	Is 54^{13}
10^{34}	Ps 81^{6}
12^{15}	Zec 9^{9}*
38	Is 53^{1}*
40	6^{10}
13^{18}	Ps 40 (41)^{10}
15^{25}	34^{19} (68^{5})*
19^{24}	21^{19}*
36	Ex 12^{46} (Nu 9^{12}, Ps 33^{21})*
37	Zec 12^{10}*

(i.) As regards the *matter* and *purpose* of these quotations, it is noticeable that of the 46 in the Synoptic Gospels 17 (marked with *) are 'Messianic,' *i.e.* they are quoted as being predictions of facts connected with the life and work of Christ; and of these, 6 (Mt 21^{42} 22^{44} 26^{31} 27^{46}, Lk 4^{18}f. 22^{37}) are cited by our Lord Himself. With these may be reckoned Mt 22^{32}, quoted as a proof of the resurrection of the dead. 6 (Mt 2^{18} 13^{14}f. 15^{8}f. 21$^{13.\ 16}$ 24^{15}) are quoted as predictions which have found —or, in the last passage, will find—fulfilment in the lives and characters of persons other than Christ, all except the first occurring in His own discourses. 19 of the remainder are quoted by our Lord (except Mk 12^{32}f.), and consist of legal and moral precepts, mostly from the Pentateuch, which should guide men's actions (with the exception of those in Mt 5, which He quotes in order to contrast with them His own higher moral law). 3 which come under none of these heads are Lk 2^{23}, Mt 4^{6} 22^{24}. Of the 13 in the Fourth Gospel, 7 (marked with *) are 'Messianic,' all being quoted by the writer (except 15^{25}, which is by our Lord). In the rest of the NT, 'Messianic' quotations occur chiefly in the Apostolic speeches in the Acts (2$^{17-21.\ 25-28.\ 34}$f. 3^{22}f. (=7^{37})^{25} 4^{25}f. 8^{32}f. 13$^{33.\ 34.\ 35}$), and in Hebrews (1^{5} (=5^{5})$^{6.\ 8}$f. $^{10-12.\ 13}$ 2$^{6-8.\ 12.\ 13}$ 5^{6} (=7$^{17.\ 21}$) 9^{20} 10$^{5-9}$). In the other Epistles see Ro 9^{33} 10^{11} 15^{3}, 1 Co 15^{45}, Gal 3^{13}, Eph 4^{8}, 1 P 2^{6}.

(ii.) As regards the *form* of the quotations, the dependence upon the LXX shown by the NT writers may be seen by the following facts, which are summarized from Swete's *Introduction*, pp. 391–398.

Every part of the NT affords evidence of a knowledge of the LXX, and a great majority of the passages cited from the OT are in general agreement with the Greek version. In the Synoptic Gospels there is a marked contrast between (α) quotations belonging to the common narrative or to the sayings reported by all three or by two of them, and (β) quotations which are peculiar to one of them. (α) The former (with the exception of Mt 15^{8}f. 26^{31}) adhere closely to LXX. (β) Of the 16 in Mt. which are not found in Mk. or Lk., 4 (5^{38} 9^{13} 13^{14}f. 21^{16}) are in the words of the LXX with slight variants; 4 exhibit important variants; and the remaining 7 bear little or no resemblance to the Alexandrian Greek. Neither Mk. nor Lk. has any series of independent quotations; Mk 9^{48} 12^{32} are from the LXX, but show affinities to the text of A; Lk 4^{18}f. differs from the LXX in important particulars.

The causes which have produced variation are manifold: (1) loose citation, (2) the substitution of a gloss for the precise words which the writer professes to quote, (3) a desire to adapt a prophetic context to the circumstances under which it was thought to have been fulfilled, (4) the fusing together of passages from different contexts. Further, (5) some variations are recensional. The Evangelists appear to have employed a recension of the LXX which came nearer to the text of A than to that of our oldest uncial B. In some cases it may be argued that the text of the LXX MSS was influenced by the NT; but this objection is greatly minimized by the fact that Josephus, and to a less extent Philo, show the same tendency. And there are occasional signs that NT writers used a recension to which the version of the later translator Theodotion shows some affinities. (6) Some variations are translational, and imply an independent use of the original, whether by the Evangelist or by the author of some collection of excerpts which he employed. Prof. Swete (pp. 396 ff.) prints in full, and annotates, five of these passages from Mt (2^{6} 4^{15}f. 8^{17} 13^{35} 27^{9}f.), together with the corresponding passages in the LXX; and he comes to the conclusion that while 'the compiler of the First Gospel has more or less distinctly thrown off the yoke of the Alexandrian version, and substituted for it a paraphrase, or an independent rendering of the Hebrew,' 'our evidence does not encourage the belief that the Evangelist used or knew another complete Greek version of the OT or of any particular book.'

The writer of the Fourth Gospel quotes from the LXX, with varying degrees of exactness. The citations in 2^{17} 10^{34} 12^{38} 19$^{24.\ 36}$ are *verbatim* or nearly so; those in 6$^{31.\ 45}$ 13^{18} 15^{25} are freer; in 1^{23} 12$^{15.\ 40}$ he paraphrased loosely, with a general reminiscence of the LXX wording; in 19^{37}, ὄψονται εἰς ὃν ἐξεκέντησαν is a non-Septuagintal rendering of Zec 12^{10}, which was perhaps current in Palestine, since εἰς ὃν ἐξεκέντησαν appears also in Theod. (Aq. ἐξεκέντησαν, cf. Rev 1^{7}; Symm. ἐπεξεκέντησαν).

The quotations in the Acts are exclusively from the LXX, but sometimes they are inclined to be free and paraphrastic.

In St. Paul's quotations the same phenomena

appear : the majority are verbally exact, but many contain important variants ; sometimes the Apostle appears to quote from memory ; in some cases he freely conflates two or more passages. In Hebrews, in which the argument is carried on largely by a catena of quotations from the LXX, 'the text of the quotations agrees in the main with some form of the present text of the LXX' (Westcott, *Hebrews*, p. 476). On 1 P 2[6] see Hort, *St. Peter, in loc.*

In this short summary of Prof. Swete's results enough has been said to show the large extent to which the Alexandrian Greek version influenced the direct quotations made by the NT writers. But direct citation formed only a fraction of the immense use which they made of the LXX. Their writings, and the utterances of our Lord, abound in expressions and phrases from the LXX which are not formal quotations, but which were due to their intimate knowledge of the OT. These are conveniently marked by uncial type in WH's text of the NT. In many cases the force and meaning of the NT passage are multiplied when the OT context is taken into consideration. [N.B.—There are no quotations from the Apocryphal books which were included in the Greek Bible. There are, however, in the Epistles some half-dozen reminiscences ; see Wis 7[26] 9[15] 13[1] 15[7], Sir 5[11] 7[34] 15[11]].

B. *Borrowed terminology.*—It must not be forgotten that the LXX was but a very small part of a large Greek literature whose ideas and vocabulary and grammar differed materially from those of the old classical writers. New philosophical and theological conceptions, changes political and social, developments in the arts of life, increased opportunities of intercourse with foreign nations, all combined to alter the language. The κοινή or Ἑλληνικὴ διάλεκτος ' was based on Attic Greek, but embraced elements drawn from all Hellenic dialects. It was the literary language of the cosmopolitan Hellas created by the genius of Alexander' (Swete, *Intr.* p. 294). ' The language used by the writers of the Greek Diaspora may be regarded as a subsection of an early stage of the κοινή' (*ib.*), and of this subsection the LXX and the NT are the best representatives in Egypt and Palestine respectively. Though a change began to appear as early as Xenophon, the era of the κοινή may be said to have opened in the latter half of the 4th cent. B.C. ; and its golden age extends from c. B.C. 145 (Polybius) to c. A.D. 160 (Pausanias). The NT vocabulary, then, was derived not only from the LXX but from the current language of the day. See the Appendix in Grimm–Thayer's *Gr.-Eng. Lexicon of the NT* (pp. 691–696), in which are collected a large number of non-classical words which find parallels in Greek writings (including LXX) from B.C. 322 to A.D. 100.

For our present purpose, however, a supreme interest attaches to the NT words which, though found in classical Greek, have acquired a new moral or theological meaning. Many words as used in the NT are exclusively Christian, and their special significance is not derived from any literary source (*e.g.* ἀνακεφαλαιοῦμαι, ἀντίτυπον, ἀντίχριστος, δύναμις (miracle), πρωτότοκος, σταυρός —όω, χάρις). But many others have gained, or at least advanced towards, their new meaning by contact with Hebrew thought. The following are among the more important, and will repay careful investigation with the help of Thayer's *Lexicon* and the NT commentaries. The short notes here attached to each word are not intended to be in any way exhaustive of their meanings or applications, but may be helpful in suggesting lines for study. Words which do not occur in classical Greek are marked with *.

ἄγγελος. Classical meaning 'messenger.' Early

Heb. thought conceived of the ' Angel of Jahweh ' as a visible or active manifestation of Himself, Gn 22[11], Ex 3[2], Mt 1[20], Lk 2[9]. But the more developed angelology of later times is reflected in the NT, *e.g.* the names of two great angels appear— Michael (Dn 10[13. 21] 12[1], Jude[9], Rev 12[7]) and Gabriel (Dn 8[16] 9[21], Lk 1[19. 26]). See also Mt 18[10].

ἅγιος. Class. 'sacred (to a god)'; 'holy.' Note two special uses: (*a*) οἱ ἅγιοι, the ideal body of consecrated people, Dn 7[18. 22], 1 Es 8[57 (58)]; freq. in St. Paul's writings of Christians. Not in Gospp., but see Jn 17[14-19]. (*b*) τὰ ἅγια, the holiest part of the Tent ; in NT typical of Heaven where Christ our High Priest intercedes for us, He 9. 10.

ἀδελφός. Class. 'brother'; 'near kinsman.' LXX and NT a member of the same privileged race, Dt 18[15], Ro 9[3]. Hence in NT a fellow-Christian, Mt 23[8] and freq. in Acts and Epistles.

αἷμα. Class. 'blood'; 'bloodshed'; always emphasizes the fact of death. In the Jewish sacrificial system the blood is the *life*, Gn 9[4], Lv 17[11. 14], Dt 12[23]. On the Christian use of this thought see Westcott, Add. note on 1 Jn 1[7] and on He 9[12].

αἰών. Class. 'human life-time'; 'eternity.' (*a*) In LXX freq. in plur., denoting the sum-total of the fixed periods (each being an αἰών) into which eternity is divisible, Ps 77 (76)[8], Lk 1[33]. (*b*) The NT adopts the Rabbinic conception of two 'ages,' ὁ αἰὼν οὖτος (העולם הזה) and ὁ αἰὼν ὁ ἐρχόμενος or ὁ μέλλων (העולם הבא) the age before, and after, the advent of the Messiah, Mt 22[32], Mk 10[30].

ἀνάστασις. Class. ' a rising up' (*e.g.* from a seat) ; 'a making to rise'; 'a removal.' LXX ' resurrection,' 2 Mac 7[14] 12[43] ; cf. Dn 12[2]. Mt 22[23] and freq. (See Æsch. *Eum.* 617 f.).

ἀναφέρω. Class. ' bring up'; 'undertake'; 'refer'; 'restore.' LXX freq. 'offer up' (as a sacrifice)=העלה. He 7[27 bis], 1 P 2[5. 24] *al.*

ἀποκαλύπτειν (*ἀποκάλυψις). Class. 'reveal.' In LXX and NT freq. Divine revelation of things which man of himself could not know.

ἀπολυτρόω (*-τρωσις). Class. 'release on payment of ransom.' In the OT the word is applied (with little or no idea of ransom) to the action of God for His people, in delivering them (גאל or פדה) from trouble or death. This, with the thought of ransom partially restored, appeared in the NT as the Christian ' redemption' from sin. See Westcott, *Hebrews*, pp. 295 ff.

ἄφεσις. Class. ' a setting free' (of a captive); ' discharge' (from the obligations of a bond). In LXX mostly the periodical 'release' of Hebrew slaves. But the Messianic interpretation of such passages as Is 61[1] (cf. Lk 4[18]) was a step towards the NT meaning of 'release from the chain and the guilt of sin.' In Is 22[14] ἀφεθήσεται is used in connexion with ἁμαρτία. See Mt 26[28], Mk 1[4] 3[29], Lk 1[77] 3[3] 24[47].

βαπτίζομαι. Class. metaph. 'to be soaked' (with wine) ; 'to be drowned' (with questions). LXX 2 (4) K 5[14] uses the word in connexion with miraculous cleansing ; Sir 34 (31)[30] with cleansing from ceremonial pollution. Both are partial types of Christian baptism.

βεβαιόω. Class. 'confirm' (a statement); 'secure' (a person in one's own interests). In LXX Ps 41 (40)[13] 119 (118)[28] the word is used of God establishing or strengthening man. Hence in NT of Jesus Christ strengthening the soul and character, 1 Co 1[8].

δαιμόνιον. Class. 'deity'; 'divinity'; also an inferior divine being, ' between divine and mortal ' (Plat. *Symp.*). It needed the OT monotheism to *condemn* the thought of divine beings other than Jehovah, Dt 32[17] Ps 96 (95)[5]. Hence in NT 'evil spirit.' [δαίμων (Mt 8[31]), which is very similar, is not found in the LXX ? Is 65[11]].

διάβολος. Class. of one who accuses maliciously

or slanderously. LXX (= צר or שטן) 'an adversary,' used of a superhuman agent of evil, Job 1⁶· ⁷ ᵉᵗᶜ·, Zec 3¹· ², 1 Ch 21¹. Hence in NT 'the devil,' used by every NT writer except St. Mark.

δίκαιος, δικαιοσύνη, etc. Class. mainly 'just,' 'justice.' See Sanday-Headlam, Add. note on Ro 1¹⁷, 'The word δίκαιος and its compounds.'

δόξα, δοξάζω. Class. 'opinion'; 'credit' or 'renown.' LXX Ex 24¹⁷ al. (= כּבוֹד, New Heb. שְׁכִינָה) the 'glory' of God, the visible manifestation of His presence. Hence in NT (a) the manifestation of God's character, Jn 1¹⁴, (b) the spiritual participation of it by men, Jn 17²². See 2 Co 3⁷⁻¹⁸.

ἔθνος (* ἐθνικός). Class. 'nation.' LXX, NT of nations other than the chosen people; 'Gentiles.'

εἴδωλον. Class. 'phantom'; 'reflected image'; 'fancy.' LXX, NT 'the image of a god'; 'idol.'

ἐκκλησία. Class. 'assembly' of citizens. LXX (= קָהָל) an assembly of Israelites, the chosen people. Hence in NT the body of Christians spiritually called out from the rest of mankind by God; 'the Church.'

ἐκλεκτός. Class. 'selected.' LXX the 'elect' people of God, Is 65⁹· ¹⁵· ²² ⁽²³⁾, 1 Ch 16¹³, Wis 3⁹ 4¹⁵. Hence in NT of Christians, Mt 24³¹ al.

ἐπισκοπέω, -πος (*-πή). Class. vb. 'inspect,' 'examine,' 'visit'; subst. 'overseer,' 'guardian.' The use of the words in the LXX (esp. ἐπισκοπή) of the action of God, either for help or punishment, gave rise to the spiritual force acquired in the NT, Lk 19⁴⁴, 1 P 2¹²· ²⁵.

εὐαγγελίζομαι (*-ζω), **εὐαγγέλιον.** Class. vb. 'bring good tidings'; subst. 'reward for good tidings.' In the OT such Messianic passages as Is 40⁹ al. led to the Christian use of the terms. [Sing. εὐαγγέλιον not in LXX, which always has plur.].

εὐλογέω, -ία. Class. 'praise.' (a) LXX (= בָּרַךְ) 'bless'; and so in NT of the action of either God or man. 'Consecrate with prayer,' 1 S 9¹³, Lk 9¹⁶, 1 Co 10¹⁶. (c) εὐλογία is a concrete blessing or benefit, Dt 11²⁶ al., Eph 1³, He 12¹⁷ al. (not in Gospp.).

ζωή. Class. 'life'; 'existence.' In the LXX (= חַיִּים) it is freq. used of a happy life, blessed by God. Hence in NT of spiritual life (Jn 5²⁴) gained by union with Christ, the source and principle of life (Jn 10¹⁰ 14⁶, 1 Jn 5¹²).

ζωογονέω, ζωοποιέω. Class. 'breed animals, or germs.' LXX 'give life to,' Neh 9⁶; 'preserve alive,' Ex 1¹⁷, Ps 71 (70)²⁰. Hence in NT 'endue with spiritual life,' Jn 6⁶³; 'restore to life,' Jn 5²¹.

ἡμέρα. Class. 'day.' In LXX freq. of the 'Day of Jahweh,' a future time of judgment (Am., Is., Zeph. etc.). Hence in NT of the coming of Christ to judgment, Mt 7²² al. (The thought of 'judgment' was so closely attached to the word that St. Paul could use the expression ἀνθρωπίνη ἡμέρα, 1 Co 4³).

θάνατος. Class. 'death' of the body. From the OT teaching that death is the punishment of sin is derived the NT use of the word for spiritual death, either as a present, unregenerate state (Jn 5²⁴, 1 Jn 3¹⁴), or as a future penalty (Wis 1¹² 2²⁴, Ro 1³²).

θεός. Class. 'a god.' OT monotheism led to the use of ὁ θεός for the One God in LXX and NT. (God's representatives are called θεοί, Ps 82 (81)⁶, quoted in Jn 10³⁴).

ἱλάσκομαι. Class. 'propitiate,' 'appease.' (a) LXX pass. 'be propitiated,' Ps 78 (77)³⁸ 79 (78)⁹. So NT Lk 18¹³. (b) LXX ἐξιλάσκομαι (not in NT) 'make propitiation for,' 'expiate.' So in NT ἱλάσκομαι, He 2¹⁷.

* **ἱλασμός** 'a means of propitiating,' Ezk 44²⁷, 1 Jn 2² 4¹⁰.

* **ἱλαστήριον** 'the place of propitiation,' 'the mercy-seat.' LXX and He 9⁵. [In Ro 3²⁵ masc. adj. of Christ].

κακία. Class. 'badness, depravity'; 'cowardice.' LXX, NT 'evil,' 'trouble,' Am 6³, Mt 6³⁴.

κατάπαυσις. Class. 'a putting to rest'; 'a causing to cease.' LXX (= מְנוּחָה) 'rest,' 'cessation,' Ps 95 (94)¹¹. NT He 3¹¹· ¹⁸ 4¹· ³· ⁵ ᵉᵗᶜ·.

κέρας. Class. 'horn.' LXX, NT symbol of strength, 1 S 2¹⁰, Ps 89 (88)¹⁸, Lk 1⁶⁹.

κληρονομέω, -ία, -ος. Class. 'inherit.' In OT the words are frequently used for the occupation of Canaan by the gift of God. So in NT they are used spiritually for the gaining of the privileges involved in Divine sonship in union with Christ, Mt 5⁵ 25³⁴.

κλῆρος. Class. 'an object used in casting lots.' LXX 'an allotted portion,' a possession or privilege assigned by God to His people, Wis 5⁵. NT in Mt 27³⁵ ||, Ac 26¹⁸, Col 1¹².

κοινόω, -ός. Class. 'to make common,' 'to communicate' (opp. ἴδιος). LXX 'to make unhallowed,' 'profane,' 'defile' (= βεβηλόω, -ος), 4 Mac 7⁶, 1 Mac 1⁴⁷· ⁶². NT Mt 15¹¹· ¹⁸· ²⁰, Mk 7²· ⁵, Ac 10¹⁴· ²⁸.

κόσμος. Class. 'order'; 'ornament'; 'the Universe' (as a system of order). LXX 'the inhabitants of the world,' Wis 2²⁴ 10¹ 14⁶· ¹⁴. NT in Mt 13³⁸ and frequently. Hence in NT 'the ungodly masses of men,' Jn 7⁷ and freq.; also 'things of the world,' 'desires, pleasures,' etc., Mt 16²⁶ and frequently.

κτίζω, κτίσις. Class. vb. 'to found' (city, colony, etc.); subst. 'the act of founding.' LXX vb. 'create' (= בָּרָא), Dt 4³², Ps 51 (50)¹¹, Is 45⁷; subst. 'the sum of created things,' Jth 9¹² 16¹⁴, Wis 5¹⁷ ⁽¹⁸⁾ 16²⁴ al. NT vb. Mk 13¹⁹ al., subst. Mk 10⁶ al.

κύριος. Class. 'lord,' 'master,' 'owner.' LXX passim for יהוה 'Jehovah.' NT both with and without the article (a) for Jehovah, (b) for Christ.

λαός. Class. 'nation,' 'people.' In LXX specially of the chosen people. Hence in NT applied to Christians, Lk 1¹⁷, Ac 15¹⁴, He 4⁹ al.

λειτουργέω, -ία. Class. 'render a service to the state at one's own expense.' LXX (vb. שָׁרַת, subst. עֲבֹדָה), the service of the priests in the Tent and the Temple. So NT Lk 1²³, He 8⁶ 9²¹ 10¹¹. [The classical idea is adopted in 2 Co 9¹², Ph 2³⁰.]

λυτρόω. Class. 'release on payment of ransom'; 'deliver by payment of ransom.' In LXX of the action of God, 'deliverance' from evils, Dt 13⁵, 2 Sam 7²³, Ps 49 (48)⁹ al. So in NT Lk 24²¹ (cf. Ac 7³⁵). **λύτρον** (* **λύτρωσις**). Class. 'the price paid for ransom.' In LXX λύτρον ψυχῆς (= כֹּפֶר 'atonement') Nu 35³¹, Pr 13⁸, and λύτρωσις coupled with λυτρώσεται ἐκ πασῶν τῶν ἀνομιῶν αὐτοῦ, Ps 130 (129)⁷ᶠ·, show that the later writers of the OT were approaching the spiritual use of the words. Hence in NT λυτρόω Tit 2¹⁴, 1 P 1¹⁸, -ρον Mt 20²⁸, Mk 10⁴⁵, -ρωσις He 9¹².

μυστήριον. Class. 'a secret,' a mystery known only to the initiated. LXX 'hidden purpose, or counsel'; of men, To 12⁷· ¹¹, Jth 2²; of God, Wis 2²² 6²². In NT of God's plan of salvation which was not known until revealed to the Apostles, Mt 13¹¹ (= Mk 4¹¹, Lk 8¹⁰), Ro 11²⁵ al.

νόμος. Class. 'usage,' 'custom'; 'law.' LXX 'the Mosaic law.' NT (a) the volume of 'the Law,' Mt 12⁵, or its contents as binding upon Jews, Mt 5¹⁷ᶠ·; (b) a burdensome and ineffectual system of commands and prohibitions from which Christ has freed us, Ro 3²¹ and frequently.

οἰκοδομέω (*-μή). Class. 'build.' LXX metaph. 'grant prosperity to,' Ps 28 (27)⁵, Jer 33 (40)⁷. In NT 'help and prosper spiritually,' 'edify' (this use of the word was rendered easier by the thought of Christians as being the 'building' and 'temple' of God, Ac 20³² al.).

ὄνομα. Class. 'name'; 'fame'; 'pretext.' LXX, all that a person's name implies, his personality and attributes, 1 K 21 (3 K 20)⁸, Ca 1³. Very freq. of the Name of God. So in NT, of men Mt 10⁴¹, Jn 5⁴³ᵇ; of God Mt 6⁹, Jn 12²⁸, and frequently.

οὐρανός. Class. 'heaven,' 'sky.' LXX, a periphrasis used by late Jews for the Divine Name (Dn 4²³ᵃ, 1 Mac 3¹⁸ᶠ· and freq.). NT in Lk 15¹⁸· ²¹ (see Dalman, *The Words of Jesus*, Eng. tr. 217-220, and 91 ff.).

παῖς. Class. 'child'; 'slave.' In LXX the word acquired a special force as representing a 'servant of Jehovah'; of men, Ps 113 (112)¹, Wis 2¹³ *al.*; of the Messianic Figure in Is 41. 42 etc. So in NT of men who devoutly serve God, Lk 1⁵⁴· ⁶⁹; of the Messiah, Mt 12¹⁸, Ac 3¹³· ²⁶ 4²⁷· ³⁰.

παράδεισος. Class. 'park,' 'pleasure-garden.' From the story of the garden of Eden (Gn 2. 3) the word came to be used figuratively in the OT for Divinely given peace and prosperity, Ezk 28¹³. In Jewish apocryphal writings it acquired the meaning of an upper region in the 'third heaven'; cf. 2 Co 12²· ⁴. Hence it was used of the abode of the pious after death, Lk 23⁴³, Rev 2⁷.

πειράζω (*-ασμός). Class. 'test,' 'try.' LXX (=נִסָּה) (a) of men trying God, Ex 17², Dt 6¹⁶, Is 7¹²; (b) of God testing men, Gn 22¹. So in NT (a) Mt 4⁷, Ac 15¹⁰; (b) 1 Co 10⁹. Hence freq. of 'temptation' by the Devil.

περί. The LXX use of περί [τῆς] ἁμαρτίας to express חַטָּאת or חַטָּאָה 'a sin-offering,' Lv 6¹⁸ ⁽²⁵⁾ 14¹⁹ *al.*, Ps 40 (39)⁷, led to the use of περί in the NT with a sacrificial force, 'to expiate or atone for (sins)' (He 10⁶), Ro 8³, He 5³ 10¹⁸· ²⁶ *al.*

περιτέμνειν (*-τομή). Class. 'cut round'; 'curtail'; 'intercept.' LXX freq. 'circumcise,' NT (a) 'circumcise' (physically); (b) 'separate from lust and spiritual impurity,' Col 2¹¹, Ro 2²⁹ (cf. Ex 6¹²· ³⁰, Lv 26⁴¹, Ezk 44⁷, Ac 7⁵¹).

πιστεύειν, πίστις. The broad distinction between the classical and the Biblical use is that in the former 'belief' is intellectual, in the latter it is spiritual. (See Hatch, *Hibbert Lectures* 1888, Lect. xi., and *Essays in Biblical Greek*, pp. 83–87; Sanday-Headlam on Ro 1¹⁷, 'The meaning of Faith').

πνεῦμα. Class. 'wind,' 'air'; 'spirit,' the life principle of all created things; also 'inspiration,' 'afflatus'; later 'the all-pervading Soul' of the Stoics. In the OT a moral force is added to the word, a power derived from God, Ps 51 (50)¹²· ¹³, Job 32⁸, Is 48¹⁶ 61¹. Hence in NT (a) the 'spirit' of man, the highest part of his trichotomy; (b) the Holy Spirit.

πορνεύω, -νεία, -νή. Class. 'commit fornication.' LXX metaph. of the worshipping of idols by Israel, God's bride, Hos 1² 9¹, Ps 73 (72)²⁷, Jer 3⁶ *al.* Hence freq. in Apoc., and at least with the underlying thought in Jn 8⁴¹.

προφήτης, -τεύω (*-τεία). Class. 'interpret an oracle,' 'foretell.' In LXX and NT the words gain a higher meaning than that of interpreting the frenzied utterances of a μάντις. A 'prophet' is one inspired with a Divine intuition to declare God's will both in historical events and in things spiritual.

σάρξ. Class. 'flesh' (physical). LXX and NT (a) 'physical origin,' 'relationship,' Gn 37²⁷, Jg 9², 2 S 5¹ 19¹³, Jn 3⁶, Ro 1³ 11¹⁴, Gal 4²³· ²⁹; (b) 'man,' considered as weak and mortal, Ps 56 (55)⁵ 78 (77)³⁹ *al.*, Jn 1¹⁴, Mt 16¹⁷, Jn 8¹⁵, 1 P 1²⁴. Hence in NT (c) the lowest part of human nature (opp. πνεῦμα) with its tendency to sin, Mt 26⁴¹, 1 Jn 2¹⁶; and (d) an unspiritual, unregenerate state, only in St. Paul, Ro 8⁴⁻¹³ *al.*

σκότος (* σκοτία). Class. 'darkness,' 'obscurity.' LXX attaches to it a moral significance, Job 30²⁶,

Ps 112 (111)⁴, Is 5²⁰ 9². So in NT, Mt 6²³, Lk 1⁷⁹ 11³⁵, Jn 1⁵ 3¹⁹ 12³⁵ *al.*

σώζω, σωτήρ, -τηρία, -τήριον. Class. 'save' (from injury, death, etc.). LXX to deliver from the penalties of the Messianic judgment, Jl 2³² (3⁵), Is 45¹⁷ 49⁸ *al.* Hence in NT 'save from sin,' Mt 1²¹, Lk 2¹¹ 1⁶⁹ 2³⁰ and frequently.

φῶς, φωτίζω (*-τισμός). Class. subst. 'light'; vb. 'shine,' 'give light.' In LXX the subst. acquires a moral force (opp. σκότος), Ps 27 (26)¹ 119 (118)¹⁰⁵, Is 5²⁰ and freq.; and the vb. is used transitively 'to teach,' Ps 119 (118)¹³⁰, Sir 45¹⁷. Hence both in NT freq. of spiritual enlightenment and freedom.

χάρις. Class. 'kind feeling'; 'a kindness done'; 'gratitude' and 'thanks'; 'enjoyment.' In LXX (=חֵן) freq. in the expression 'find favour before God.' In NT this kindness of God becomes a twofold theological conception: (a) the undeserved kindness by which man is saved from sin, (b) the state of heart kept alive by the Holy Spirit in one who has received God's grace.

χριστός. Class. 'to be rubbed on,' 'used as ointment.' LXX 'a person who is anointed'— king, priest, or prophet—for מָשִׁיחַ. Hence the Messianic conception which gave rise to the NT title ὁ χριστός.

LITERATURE.—Swete, *Introd. to the OT in Greek*; art. 'Septuagint' (Nestle) in Hastings' *DB*; *Speaker's Commentary*, 'Apocrypha,' vol. i. pp. xi.–xxiii.; art. 'Apocrypha' (Ryle) in Smith's *DB²*; Toy, *New Testament Quotations*; Hawkins, *Horæ Synopticæ*; Hatch, *Essays in Biblical Greek*; Grimm-Thayer, *Greek-Eng. Lexicon of the NT*; H. A. A. Kennedy, *Sources of NT Greek*; Dittmar, *Vet. Test. in Novo*; Hühn, *AT Citate u. Reminisc. im NT*; Commentaries on the NT. A very full Bibliography will be found at the end of Nestle's art. 'Bibelübersetzungen (Griechische)' in *PRE³*.

A. H. M'NEILE.

SEPULCHRE. — See TOMB; and for 'Holy Sepulchre' see GOLGOTHA.

SERMON ON THE MOUNT.—Professor Votaw's learned and exhaustive article in the Extra Vol. of Hastings' *DB* is a mine of information and critical study, to which the reader is referred for a full treatment of questions concerning the Sermon on the Mount that must here be treated more briefly.

1. Sources.—The contents of Mt 5. 6. 7 are commonly regarded as constituting one discourse, with the title 'The Sermon on the Mount,' on account of the introductory statement in 5¹. Some portions of the contents of these chapters reappear, with more or less difference of form, introduced in a somewhat similar way, in Lk 6. Other sayings of Jesus contained in the three chapters of Mt. are found scattered over the narrative in Lk., and a few are in Mk.; two are duplicated in Mt., and one is duplicated in Lk. The following is the Synoptic distribution of the Sermon:

Matthew.	Mark.	Luke.
5¹		6¹⁷· ²⁰ᵃ
5³· ⁴· ⁶		6²⁰ᵇ· ²¹
5¹¹· ¹²		6²²· ²³
5¹³	9⁵⁰	14³⁴· ³⁵
5¹⁵	4²¹	(1) 8¹⁶, (2) 11³³
5¹⁸		16¹⁷
5²⁵· ²⁶		12⁵⁸· ⁵⁹
(1) 5²⁹· ³⁰, (2) 18⁷· ⁸	9⁴⁷· ⁴⁸· ⁴³· ⁴⁵	
(1) 5³², (2) 19⁹	10¹¹· ¹²	16¹⁸
5³⁹⁻⁴⁸		6²⁹⁻³⁶
6⁹⁻¹³		11²⁻⁴
6²⁰⁻²¹		12³³⁻³⁶
6²⁴		16¹³
6²⁵⁻³⁴		12²²⁻³⁴
7¹⁻⁵		6³⁷⁻⁴²
7⁷⁻¹²		11⁹⁻¹³
7¹³· ¹⁴		13²²⁻²⁴
7¹⁶⁻²⁷		6⁴⁴⁻⁴⁹

A comparison of these columns will bring out certain clear results, viz.:

(1) Mk. is not the source of any of these sayings. Only four verses or paragraphs of them are in that Gospel at all. Of these four, three are also in Lk,

A comparison between the several forms of the three shows (*a*) that Lk. and Mt. are nearer to one another than either of them is to Mk., and (*b*) that in the two cases of duplicates in Mt., Mk. is nearer to Mt.'s second renderings of the sayings than to his earlier renderings, which are those of the Sermon on the Mount, showing that if Mt. is dependent on Mk. in either case, it is in the later passages where the sayings are given in another connexion, not in the Sermon. We may account for the duplicates in this way. The first appearance of them is due to the non-Markan source ; the second is perhaps derived from Mk.

(2) It is now generally conceded that the main sources of the common elements in the Synoptic Gospels are Mk., and the collection of *Logia* which Papias says Matthew compiled and wrote in Hebrew, or Aramaic. Further, it is agreed that the *Logia* must have been translated into Greek, and that it was in a Gr. form that our Evangelists used it. More recently the differences between Mt. and Lk. in their renderings of the same sayings, as well as various other phenomena connected with them, have led scholars to the conclusion that (*a*) there were two or more versions of Matthew's *Logia*, or (*b*) that there were other collections of sayings of Jesus besides that made by Matthew (Wendt, Jülicher, Wernle, J. Weiss, Feine, Hawkins, Votaw, Bacon). Probably both of these suggestions must be admitted. Nevertheless, even after admitting this, we may still recognize the probability that the Sermon, as we have it in our First Gospel, is derived from Matthew's *Logia* ; for (*a*) that Gospel—apart from its opening and closing sections—consists virtually of Mk., split at 5 places, or as some reckon at 7 places, with blocks of *Logia* wedged in at these openings, the Sermon being the first such insertion ; and (*β*) since our chief collection of the sayings of Jesus is that contained in Mt., since Papias ascribed to the Apostle Matthew the only collection of *Logia* he is reported to have mentioned, and since the Gospel containing it bears the name of that Apostle in all Patristic references to its origin, there is a strong presumption that the *Logia* it contains are from Matthew's collection, although this does not forbid us to conclude that the collection may have been used by the Evangelist in a revised form. Nor, of course, does it exclude the suggestions of interpolations, glosses, etc., which can only be considered in detail as they arise in the course of the study of the text. The general conclusion is that as a whole our Sermon on the Mount is derived from Matthew's *Logia* in a Greek version.

2. Integrity.—The question of the integrity of the Sermon must be considered quite apart from that of its genuineness. We may be convinced that the three chapters of Mt. contain only true *Logia* of Jesus, and yet see reason to think that these *Logia* were not all spoken on one and the same occasion, in fact, that they do not actually constitute a sermon. (*a*) The first difficulty arises from the wealth and multiplicity of the utterances. We have here a concise concentration of many most pregnant sayings of Jesus. It is not to be supposed that a popular audience could take in so much at one hearing. But Jesus was welcomed everywhere by simple peasants and the people generally much more than by trained thinkers and the educated classes. Since 'the common people heard him gladly,' His style must have been adjusted to slow-moving minds ; but no popular preacher would pack so much into one sermon as we have in Mt.'s three chapters.

(*b*) The variety of topics treated in the three chapters is inconsistent with the unity of a single discourse. Thus the encouragements to prayer and the warnings against anxiety are alien to the main topic in which the principles of the new order are contrasted with the old laws and customs.

(*c*) A more important consideration arises from a comparison of the portions of these chapters which reappear in Lk. with the circumstances in connexion with which they are there introduced. *A priori* it is improbable that any Evangelist would break up a discourse of Christ and scatter its sentences among his narratives, fitting them into the incidents gratuitously. But a study of the circumstances under which these sentences are met with in Lk. inclines us to think that they are in their right place. It will be observed that the Gospel's most full and consecutive rendering of sayings found in St. Matthew 5–7 is in St. Luke 6. Provisionally we may regard this chapter as giving St. Luke's version of the Sermon on the Mount. Let us turn to those sayings of the Mt. chapters that are in other parts of Lk. First we have Mt 5^{13} reappearing in Lk $14^{34. 35}$. This is a warning against degenerating and becoming as salt that has lost its savour. In Mt. it has no evident connexion with the Beatitudes that it follows ; in Lk., however, it occurs in connexion with warnings of the danger of abandoning the following of Christ after having commenced, and serves to clinch those warnings with a final illustration. Moreover, this saying is also in Mk. (9^{50}), where it seems to have been introduced by association with another reference to salt in the previous verse. Therefore it would seem to have been a floating *logion*, which naturally found its way into Mt.'s collection. In Mt. the saying about salt losing its savour is followed by that of the lamp under the bushel—a *logion* which appears in Mk. (4^{21}) and twice in Lk. (8^{16} 11^{33}). None of these passages evinces much connexion with its context. It is to be observed that the second appearance in Lk. is nearer to Mt. than the first, since it has 'the bushel' as the covering article, as also Mk. has, while the first of Lk.'s renderings of it has 'a vessel.' Here again it would appear we have another floating *logion*. The solemn assurance that the Law cannot fail is not more intelligible in Lk. ($16^{17. 18}$) than in Mt 5^{18} ; this, therefore, is rather exceptional.—The next of the Third Evangelist's departures from the order of the Sermon on the Mount in Mt. is Lk $12^{58. 59}$ which corresponds to Mt $5^{25. 26}$. This is the advice to agree quickly with an adversary lest it be too late, and a serious judicial sentence have to be submitted to. In Mt. this follows advice to be reconciled with a brother on grounds of the higher principles of Christ's teaching, which forbid the quarrelsome temper. In Lk. it follows the warnings of the approach of a day of reckoning. In neither place is it inappropriate. Perhaps it was spoken on two occasions. We must always allow for that possibility.—The next three cases are more convincing. Mt. has the Lord's Prayer following warnings against hypocrisy in prayer, which are associated with other cases of hypocrisy (Mt 6^{1-18}). The subject of this whole paragraph is unostentatious sincerity, as opposed to pretentious hypocrisy. In Lk. (11^{1-4}) the Lord's Prayer is introduced after Christ's disciples have asked Him to teach them to pray, as John had taught his disciples to pray. Thus it comes appropriately as a model prayer, while in Mt. no form of prayer is immediately required when the subject is privacy in prayer as against public display. Next, the warning against worldly anxiety (Mt 6^{19-34}) has no direct connexion with the rest of the Sermon on the Mount. In Lk 12^{22-34} it follows the warning against covetousness and the parable of the Rich Fool, which were occasioned by one of the multitude appealing to Jesus to decide a question of inheritance between himself and his brother. — Lastly, the saying about the narrow gate (Mt 7[13, 14]) appears in Lk. in reply to the question whether they are few that be saved (Lk 13[22-24]).

For such reasons it is now generally admitted that the three chapters in Mt. contain sayings of Jesus which were not parts of the original Sermon. This fact, however, does not justify the assertion that Matthew's Sermon on the Mount 'is a composition rather than an actual address' (Moffatt, *EBi*, vol. iv. col. 4377). While Bacon rules out the matter which is not in Lk 6, and is scattered over other parts of Lk., he allows that the Sermon, apart from such interpolations of alien sayings of Jesus, is a connected discourse (*The Sermon on the Mount: Its Literary Structure*, etc.). Votaw, while admitting some interpolations, vindicates the greater part of Mt.'s rendering of it (*loc. cit.* pp. 7-9). The fact that we have a block of *Logia* here inserted in the narrative of Mt. is no proof that much, if not all of it, may not belong to a single discourse. Moreover, the descriptive introduction (4[23]-5[1]) indicates an important discourse given on a specific occasion. It is the same with the parallel in Lk 6[17-20]. Then there is a clearly marked unity in those parts of the Sermon in Mt. that remain after the apparently alien matter has been removed, and this is the case with the whole of Lk.'s shorter version. Nor need we cut down the Sermon to the limits of what is contained in Lk., for there was an evident reason for the Third Evangelist's omission of the references to the Pharisees and to Jewish customs which Mt. has preserved, since the former was writing for Gentiles who would not be interested in these matters; while, on the other hand, they are evidently integral to the discourse as this is given in Mt., because they help to bring out the ethical principles of the new order that Christ was introducing by contrast with the old order that He was superseding.

3. Original form.—A comparison of Mt 5-7 with the parallel passages in Lk. (especially with the discourse in Lk 6) raises the question as to which of these two versions of our Lord's utterances is the more original. For, while it has been maintained (by Auger, Greswell, Osiander, Patricius, Plumptre, Sadler, etc.) that we have here reports of sermons given on two occasions, this view is not widely accepted by scholars at the present day.* It is not to be denied that Jesus may have repeated the same discourse on more than one occasion. But, in the present case, it is to be observed: (*a*) Each Evangelist has only one report, neither betraying any knowledge that the Sermon was preached twice. (*b*) Both Evangelists describe the same circumstances in introducing the Sermon— *i.e.* the gathering of the multitude, the collecting of disciples, and the connexion of the scene with a mountain (for though in Mt. the Sermon is on the mountain and in Lk. on a level place after Jesus had come down, this is only one of the small discrepancies invariably met with in separate accounts of the same event, and, in fact, it does not involve a direct contradiction even in the details referred to). (*c*) The character of the Sermon and its position in the life and work of Christ give it a unique value as the presentation of fundamental principles for the guidance of Christ's disciples in their conduct among men. But if we grant that we have here two reports of one and the same discourse, the striking differences between them lead us to ask, In what form was this discourse actually given? In the first place, it cannot be that either

* See Paul Feine, 'Ueber das gegenseit. Verhältniss d. Texte der Bergpredigt bei Mat. und Luk.' (*Jahrb. f. prot. Theol.* xi. 1); also Plummer, 'St. Luke' (*ICC*), pp. 176-179.

of the two Evangelists simply used and altered materials that he had derived from the other, for on wider grounds it seems to be demonstrated that neither drew upon the other in any case; the probability is that while both knew Mk., neither the First nor the Third Evangelist knew the other (see Wernle, *Die Synopt. Frage*, p. 20). Nor can so violent a dealing with his materials be charged against either Evangelist. For a similar reason, we cannot suppose that they were both dependent on the same version of Matthew's *Logia*; because, if so, one or both of them must have treated its venerated contents — consisting of reports of the sayings of Jesus—in the same unscrupulous way. They must have been working on two different collections of *Logia*, though perhaps both originally based on Matthew's Hebrew collection; and the divergence must have taken place earlier— among irresponsible transcribers—by more gradual stages. But if this be the case, the task of determining between the two reports is exceedingly difficult. Probably neither can be preferred in all respects to the other. In some cases Mt. appears to be the more correct, but in other cases the probability is with Luke.

In this connexion the most important question is that of the original form of the Beatitudes, in regard to which the following points claim our attention: (1) In Mt. there are 7 (or perhaps 8) Beatitudes; in Lk. there are 4 Beatitudes, followed by 4 Woes which do not appear in Mt. (2) The Beatitudes in Mt. are (all but the last) in the 3rd person: those in Lk. are in the 2nd person. (3) The Mt. Beatitudes describe character and its corresponding rewards; those in Lk. describe only social conditions and the future reversal of them. Now, in favour of the originality of Mt., it may be urged that the greater spiritual value of its version of the Beatitudes points to their originality, for we cannot believe that it was given to copyists and catechists to greatly enrich their Master's teachings. On the other hand, the following points should be noted: (*a*) It is not denied that the four Beatitudes not found in Lk. are genuine and characteristic sayings of Jesus. Assuredly the blessing on the pure in heart, which is among them, fell from His lips. But we may admit the genuineness of the sayings and yet deny them a place in the original Sermon on the Mount; for it has been shown above that Mt.'s three chapters contain insertions of sayings of Jesus spoken on various occasions. (*b*) The First Evangelist — or St. Matthew himself, the author of the *Logia*—elsewhere makes collections of sevens. Thus he gives 7 clauses in the Lord's Prayer (6[9-13]), 7 parables (ch. 13), 7 woes (ch. 23). The genealogy consists of a triad of fourteens (1[1-16]). [See Hawkins, *Hor. Synopt.* pp. 133, 134]. We know that Jesus uttered beatitudes on other occasions (*e.g.* 11[6] 13[16] 16[17] 24[46]). (*c*) It is difficult to think that if our Lord gave the sayings originally with their ethical and spiritual characterization, this could have dropped out accidentally, or have been deliberately eliminated so as to confine them to social relations. To attribute the alteration to St. Luke's 'Ebionism' is to accuse the Third Evangelist of an offence in flat contradiction to his honest, declared purpose (κἀμοὶ παρηκολουθηκότι ἄνωθεν πᾶσιν ἀκριβῶς, Lk 1[3]). (*d*) If, however, Jesus gave the Beatitudes as in Lk., His disciples may have discerned in them a deeper meaning, knowing that He was accustomed to speak in parables; or He Himself may have explained them, for we must remember that in the Gospels we have excerpts from the teachings of Jesus, pregnant sayings, parables, and aphorisms that stuck in the memory, while the fuller exposition which must often have followed is rarely given, perhaps never completely. (*e*) It is more likely that Jesus, when addressing His own disciples, would have used the 2nd person than that a later hand would have turned the 3rd person style of speech into the 2nd. The direct address is the more original in form ; it would be natural for catechists to generalize this, rather than the reverse. We cannot say that it was according to St. Luke's style for the 2nd person to be substituted for the 3rd, for the reverse is the case ; almost every other ascription of blessedness in Lk. is in the 3rd person (*i.e.* 1^{45} 7^{23} 10^{23} $11^{27.\ 28}$ $12^{37.\ 38.\ 43}$ 14^{15} 23^{29}),* while in Mt. we have benedictions in the 2nd person (*i.e.* 13^{16} 16^{17}, although 11^{6} 24^{46} are in the 3rd person). Mt. even concludes the Sermon on the Mount Beatitudes with one thrown into the 2nd person style (5^{11}). (*f*) It must be admitted that the Woes upon the rich seem out of place in an address to Christ's disciples. These, like the Beatitudes in Lk., are in the 2nd person ; they must be taken as apostrophizing the absent. Still, it was our Lord's method on other occasions to speak antithetically (*e.g.* Mt $6^{19.\ 20}$ $7^{13.\ 14.\ 24-27}$ $8^{11.\ 12}$). On the whole, these considerations point to Lk.'s as the original version of the Beatitudes.

In the teaching on divorce, Lk.'s absolute statement (16^{18}) must be preferred to Mt.'s more qualified form of the saying (5^{32}), containing the clause παρεκτὸς λόγου πορνείας, although that recurs in Mt 19^{9} (so Holtzmann, *Hand-Com.* ; but Swete, *St. Mark*, accepts the clause as original), because (*a*) it is not found in the more primitive version of the saying in Mk $10^{11.\ 12}$, and (*b*) the softening of an apparently harsh saying by a gloss was in accordance with the tendency of scribes.

The case of the Lord's Prayer is more difficult. We saw above that the way in which it is introduced in Lk. points to the conclusion that the original setting of it was in the incident there recorded rather than in the Sermon on the Mount. Jesus may well have given the Prayer more than once (so Bernard in Hastings' *DB*, vol. iv. p. 43ᵃ), but in Lk. it certainly appears as something new for the benefit of the disciples in answer to their request, and this is later than the version in the Sermon.

The two versions are as follows :

Mt 6^{9-13} RV.	Lk 11^{2-4} RV.
Our Father which art in heaven,	Father,
Hallowed be thy name.	Hallowed be thy name.
Thy kingdom come.	Thy kingdom come.
Thy will be done, as in heaven, so on earth.	
Give us this day our daily (ἐπιούσιον) bread.	Give us day by day our daily (ἐπιούσιον) bread.
And forgive us our debts, as we also have forgiven our debtors.	And forgive us our sins : for we ourselves also forgive every one that is indebted to us.
And bring us not into temptation, but deliver us from the evil one.	And bring us not into temptation.

AV of Lk. had all the clauses in Mt., but there is ample justification for the omissions seen in RV (see art. LORD'S PRAYER, p. 57ᵇ). They could easily have come in through assimilation to Mt. The enrichment of the Invocation would be a natural growth. Elsewhere Mt. shows a *penchant* for the use of the word 'heaven.' Thus he, and he alone, has the expression 'the kingdom of heaven,' elsewhere invariably 'the kingdom of God.' In Ro 8^{15} we have 'Abba, Father,' as the Christian invocation ; cf. Mk 14^{36} (see Wellhausen, *Einleit. in die drei ersten Evangelien*, p. 38). The clause 'Thy will be done,' etc. (which is better attested than the other omitted words, since it is in א), may be regarded as an expansion of the clause which precedes it—'Thy kingdom come'—founded on words of Jesus spoken on another occasion (Mt 26^{39}, Mk

* Lk 14^{14} is in the 2nd person ; but this takes the form of a promise, not that of benediction ; similarly Lk 1^{22}.

14^{36}, Lk 22^{42}). The final clause in Mt. may be taken as the antithesis and completion of the clause 'and bring us not into temptation.' These points seem to be in favour of the originality of Lk. Nevertheless, it was the Mt. fuller form of the Prayer that was adopted in the Church, as far as we have evidence, from the earliest time, for this is the form in the *Didache* (viii.). Both forms must be traced to a common Greek tr. of the Aram. original, since they both contain the rare and difficult word ἐπιούσιον. Dr. Chase considers that they both exhibit the Prayer as changed for liturgical purposes.* Dr. Plummer considers that Mt.'s form of the Prayer is the nearer to the original (Hastings' *DB* iii. 141 f.). Thus he points out that the δὸς ἡμῖν σήμερον of Mt 6^{11} is more likely to be genuine than the δίδου ἡμῖν τὸ καθ' ἡμέραν of Lk 11^{3}, because (*a*) καθ' ἡμέραν occurs in NT in St. Luke's writings only (Lk 19^{47}, Ac 17^{11}), and (*b*) the present form of the verb (δίδου), which this involves, is an exception to the forms in the other clauses, which have aorists, as Mt. has here (δός).

It is not so easy to account for the omission of whole clauses by Lk. Accordingly, Dr. Plummer holds that Christ gave the Prayer originally on two different occasions in two different forms. But it has been pointed out that Lk.'s occasion requires us to view it as the first introduction of the Prayer, and yet this is later than the Sermon on the Mount. Besides, we must compare the briefer form of the Prayer with the briefer form of the Beatitudes. In both cases it is likely that the explanation is the same. Either Lk. abbreviates in both cases, or Mt. expands in both cases. With the Beatitudes we saw that the latter is the probability. Moreover, viewing Mt. as a whole, we see in it a fulness of expression not found in the other Gospels, due possibly to a catechetical use of the sayings of Christ. Thus we have the sign of Jonah explained in Mt 12^{40} with a reference to the whale, while it is left indefinite in Lk 11^{30} ; in Mt 16^{16} 'the Son of the living God' added to St. Peter's confession in Mk 8^{29} 'Thou art the Christ,' where Lk 9^{20} has 'the Christ of God' ; in Mt 16^{28} 'the Son of Man coming in his kingdom,' while Mk 9^{1} and Lk 9^{27} have only 'the kingdom of God,' etc. ; at Mt 26^{28} 'unto remission of sins' with reference to the blood of the covenant at the Lord's Supper, a clause not found in Mk 14^{24}, Lk 22^{20}, 1 Co 11^{25}. Still Lk. has characteristic additions, such as in the verse, 'I am not come to call the righteous, but sinners *to repentance*' (5^{32}), where the last two words appear to be a didactic gloss, since they are not found in Mt 9^{13}, Mk 2^{17}, and are not required by the context, but are congenial to Lk., the penitents' Gospel. Lk. has also characteristic alterations ; for instance, for 'good things' in Mt 7^{11}, Lk 11^{13} has 'the Holy Spirit,' in accordance with that Gospel's peculiarly frequent references to the Spirit of God—leaving the probability of originality with Mt. in this case. Therefore we cannot make an invariable rule of giving Lk. the preference. While, however, we cannot be positive in deciding the question, the reasons stated above seem, on the whole, to point to Lk.'s version of the Lord's Prayer as the more original. While admitting this, we may hold it probable that Mt.'s additional clauses are echoes of teachings of Jesus given on other occasions, or of His own explanations of the Prayer, analogously to the case of Mt.'s Beatitudes compared with Lk.'s. See, further, art. LORD'S PRAYER.

In other parts of the Sermon on the Mount the question of priority and superiority of authority is of less importance, since the divergences between

* *TS*, vol. i. No. 3 ; this is cited by Dr. Plummer in *ICC* on 'St. Luke.'

Mt. and Lk. are less significant (see Wellhausen, *Einleitung*, pp. 67–73).

4. Scene and circumstances.—A Latin tradition, that cannot be traced back earlier than the 13th cent. and is not found in the Eastern Church, gives *Ḳarn Ḥaṭṭin*, a two-peaked hill a little south-west of the plain of Gennesaret, as the locality of the delivery of the Sermon. All that can be said in its favour is that this mountain would be a very suitable spot; but there is no means of confirming so late a tradition. There is a discrepancy between Mt. and Lk., the one stating that Jesus gave the Sermon when He was on the mountain, the other that it was on a level place after He had come down from the mountain. It has been suggested by the harmonists that the level place might be somewhere among the hollows and shoulders of the mountain, so that, while Jesus had to descend to it, it was still in some degree on the mountain. But while this may be allowed as a possibility, the discrepancy is only one of many that are scattered over the Gospels, most of which may be regarded as too trivial to affect the question of historicity.

The circumstances under which the Sermon on the Mount was delivered justify the exceptional importance that has always been attached to it. It was given early in our Lord's ministry, though not at the commencement. It belongs to the first year, before the disfavour of the authorities had arisen, or at all events before it had become serious; but it is sufficiently late for the popularity of the new Teacher to have reached a climax. The primitive stage of the Galilæan mission consisted of a round of preaching in the synagogues; the second stage, still in the first year, is characterized more by open-air preaching, necessitated by the vast growth of the crowds who pressed to hear the popular Teacher, and by their insistence on hearing Him in season and out of season without waiting for the set times of the synagogue services. Internally the teaching of Jesus has undergone development. At the primitive stage it followed closely the lines laid down by John the Baptist, and could be summarized under the formula, 'Repent: for the kingdom of heaven is at hand,' that is to say, it was an announcement of the coming Kingdom. But at the more advanced stages, to which the great Sermon belongs, Jesus had passed on from 'preaching' (κήρυγμα) to teaching (διδασκαλία), and was now expounding the nature of the Kingdom, its character, principles, processes. The Sermon on the Mount comes into this category. It is teaching, rather than preaching. Further, as a consequence, it was originally designed for disciples, for those who seriously desired to learn. This is made evident by the introductions of both Evangelists. In Mt. we read, 'And seeing the *multitudes* (τοὺς ὄχλους), he went up into the mountain: and when he had sat down, his *disciples* (οἱ μαθηταὶ αὐτοῦ) came unto him: and he opened his mouth, and taught them (αὐτούς),' *i.e.* the disciples (Mt 5[1.2]). Here the distinction between the crowd and the learners is very marked. It was to avoid the crowd that Jesus retreated to the mountain—a common habit, referred to on several occasions. Then the eager inquirers followed; and finding Him there, led Him to speak to them, or, as seems more likely, they came at His own invitation. The situation is not so clear in Lk., where the coming of the crowd to Christ follows His visit to the mountain, which He had ascended for prayer (Lk 6[12]), and where He had chosen the Twelve Apostles (v.[13]); and whence He had come down with them, after which He 'stood on a level place' (v.[17]). Still Lk. preserves the distinction between the disciples and the crowd by saying, 'And a great multitude of his *disciples*,

and a great number of the *people* from all Judæa,' etc. (v.[17]). Having described the cures, which in Mt. preceded the ascent of the mountain, he says, 'And he lifted up his eyes on his *disciples*, and said,' etc.—here commencing his version of the great Sermon. Thus in Lk. this is delivered to the first of the two groups, the disciples in distinction from the crowd, as in Mt. Moreover, the use of the 2nd person in the Lukan version of the Beatitudes evidently indicates disciples—a fact which the apostrophe of the absent rich does not nullify; because in each case a specific class, not the mixed multitude, is contemplated. As we proceed with the Sermon, this fact repeatedly emerges. It is only to His own disciples that Jesus could say, 'Ye are the salt of the earth' . . . 'Ye are the light of the world' (Mt 5[13.14]). It is no objection that towards the end of the discourse Jesus says, 'Not every one that saith unto me, Lord, Lord, shall enter into the kingdom of heaven,' etc. (7[21]), and concludes with the parable of the Two Foundations, because these warnings might well be needed by many disciples. There was a traitor even among the Twelve. We are not to conclude, however, that these disciples consisted only of the Apostles. St. Luke had expressly said that 'there was a great multitude of his *disciples*' (Lk 6[17]) present on this occasion.

In Lk. (6[13]) the Sermon follows the choosing and appointment of the Apostles; and this fact has led some to regard it as 'the charge to the Twelve.' But in Mt. there is no description of the choice of the Apostles, and they are not especially associated with the Sermon. In both Gospels the introduction of the Sermon introduces a much larger audience. All the genuine 'hearers of the word,' all who expressly sought out Jesus and set themselves to learn of Him, are included in the comprehensive group of 'disciples.' Still the audience was virtually confined to this group. The Sermon was for disciples, not for the world at large. It may be pointed out, on the other hand, that while the introduction to the Sermon in both Gospels has this indication, the comments which follow it in each case seem to point to the general public. Thus in Mt 7[28] it is said, 'And it came to pass, when Jesus ended these words, the *multitudes* were astonished at his teaching,' etc., and in Lk 7[1] 'After he had ended all his sayings in the ears of the *people*.' The language, however, is indefinite in both cases and perhaps not specially considered, for no emphasis is here laid on the nature of the hearers, as was the case in the introductory descriptions.

5. Purpose and character.—The purpose of the Sermon on the Mount can be understood only when account is taken of the audience to which it was addressed. Since this audience consisted of disciples and not the public, we must read the discourse as an ethical directory for Christians. Therefore the question as to whether its precepts can be embodied in the laws of the State is irrelevant. A group of Galilæan peasants in a province of the Roman Empire had nothing whatever to do with the business of legislation; and even in contemplation of the future spread of Christianity it could not have been the intention of Christ that principles which He desired to see working outward from the heart should be imposed upon a community by force with the external authority of the magistrate. But while it is a mistake to regard the Sermon on the Mount as a model for civil and criminal law, on the other hand it would be an error to abandon its ideal in favour of a lower code of ethics even in the police courts. The disciple of Christ will always desire to see His will carried out; but this does not mean that he is at liberty to force his Master's precepts on a society that is reluctant to obey them because it has not submitted to the authority from which they emanated. If we can look forward to a condition in which the State is effectually Christianized, then we shall have a society in which the magistrate is not needed ; that is to say, the removal of the conditions which now prevent the Sermon on the Mount being applied in the police court will abolish the police court itself as an anachronism. Therefore we must view the Sermon on the Mount as primarily aiming at the direction of the conduct of Christians in their personal behaviour as individuals and members of a brotherhood. It has relations to the outside world in so far as Christian men and women have such relations. For instance, commands about love to enemies and kindness to persecutors are especially concerned with the conduct of Christians towards people who are not of their own fellowship. Still, it is the conduct of Christians only that is considered. These considerations should safeguard the interpreter against two other misapprehensions : (1) It is an error to regard the Sermon on the Mount as the sum and substance of Christianity, and to condemn later developments as not of the essence of Christianity (Hatch, Harnack). We have no evidence that Jesus Christ intended to put His whole message into this one discourse. He is here discussing the ethics of the Kingdom of heaven. Elsewhere He treats of other features of the Kingdom. (2) Since this discourse lays down principles of conduct for discipleship, the discipleship must have been previously established in other ways (e.g. denying self, taking up the cross, following Christ, turning and becoming as little children, etc., as elsewhere indicated by Jesus Christ).

In the main, the Sermon on the Mount indicates the character of life and conduct that Jesus Christ commends to His disciples as the rule of life. Commencing with the Beatitudes, He points out the way to true happiness. This is more apparent in Mt. than in Lk. ; but if the Beatitudes in the former Gospel may be taken as at least a true exposition of the deeper meaning of the simpler felicitations in the latter Gospel, it is safe to say that Jesus here teaches that blessedness is associated with character. The conduct commended throughout the Sermon is set forth by Christ as a fulfilment of the Law and the Prophets (Mt 5¹⁷). It completes what was imperfect in the earlier religion by realizing its essential principles and developing them to perfection. The consequence is that external precepts of the more primitive condition are abrogated — not universally, but wherever they conflict with a later ethical development. This applies to the Sacred Torah as well as to traditions of the scribes, as in the examples of hatred, divorce, swearing, and revenge, formerly permitted under certain conditions, though regulated and restrained by the Law, but now absolutely forbidden by Christ. In the next place, conduct condoned or even honoured hitherto is condemned as unworthy of the higher standard set up by Christ. In particular, ostentation in almsgiving, in public praying, and in fasting is reprobated, and the habit of judging others is reproved. The Sermon closes with warnings against false prophets, and insists forcibly that mere discipleship in hearing the teaching is vain ; the end of all is energetic conduct in obedience to this instruction. The principal interpolations consist of (1) two passages encouraging prayer (Mt 6⁹⁻¹⁵ 7⁷⁻¹¹), and (2) one long passage discouraging worldly anxiety (6¹⁹⁻³⁴). They rest their exhortations equally on the Fatherly goodness of God. They are among the choicest and most beautiful of our Lord's teachings, plainly vindicating their right to places in the *Logia* by their character as of the

inner essence of His message, even if their inconsistency with the flow of the argument in the Sermon, supported by the fact that they are placed in other parts of His narrative by Lk., leads us to regard them as out of place when inserted in this particular discourse.

See also such articles as AUTHORITY OF CHRIST, LAW, TEACHING OF CHRIST, etc. etc.

LITERATURE.—This is given exhaustively at the end of Votaw's art. 'Sermon on the Mount' in the Ext. Vol. of Hastings' *DB*. The following selection may be found useful : Tholuck, *Bergrede Christi* [Eng. tr. from 4th ed., Edin. 1860] ; Achelis, *Die Bergpredigt*, 1875 ; B. W. Bacon, *Sermon on the Mount*, 1902 ; J. B. Bousset, *Le Sermon sur la Montagne*, 1900 ; C. Gore, *The Sermon on the Mount*, 1896 ; W. B. Carpenter, *The Great Charter of Christ*, 1895 ; J. Oswald Dykes, *The Manifesto of the King*, 1881 ; the Comm. of B. Weiss, H. Holtzmann, Morison, Bruce, Plummer, etc. W. F. ADENEY.

SERPENT.—The prevalence of serpents in ancient Palestine is illustrated by the fact that no fewer than 11 Heb. words are rendered 'serpent' in OT. Tristram (*Nat. Hist. of Bible*) states that 33 different species of serpent are still found in Syria. Of 18 varieties which he himself secured, 13 were innocuous and 4 deadly, including cobras and vipers. Naturally there are numerous references, in the OT, in the NT, and in Rabbinical literature, to serpents as well-known but generally disagreeable inhabitants of the country. So unpleasantly common were they, that it was regarded as one of the perpetual miracles of Jerusalem that no one was ever bitten by a serpent there. The references in the Gospels may conveniently be grouped under three heads.

1. In Mt 10¹⁶ our Lord charges His disciples, ' Be ye wise as serpents' (φρόνιμοι ὡς οἱ ὄφεις). There may be here a reference to Gn 3¹ ' the serpent was more subtil (עָרוּם) than any beast of the field.' The Heb. word means 'shrewd,' and is used also in a good sense (cf. Pr 12¹⁶· ²³), although the parallel root in Arabic suggests only a bad sense. It is probable, however, that our Lord refers to the well-known habits of the serpent, its ability to conceal itself in unexpected places, and to escape swiftly and silently in time of danger (cf. נָחָשׁ בָּרִחַ ' the *swift* serpent' RV, Job 26¹³, Is 27¹).

2. But the phrase which follows in Mt 10¹⁶ ' and harmless (ἀκέραιοι) as doves,' suggests that there was also in the mind of Jesus the equally well-known reputation of the serpent as a dangerous reptile ; and this is borne out by other passages in the Gospels. Almost parallel are Mk 16¹⁸ ' they shall take up serpents,' and Lk 10¹⁹ ' I give you power over serpents' ; while the noxious and repulsive nature of the serpent is referred to in Mt 7¹⁰, Lk 11¹¹ ' if he ask a fish, will he give him a serpent ? '

In all the above passages, ὄφις, the generic name for a serpent, is used. But in Mt 3⁷ 12³⁴ 23³³, Lk 3⁷ we find ἐχιδνα, which probably means a *poisonous* serpent, and is rendered 'viper' both in AV and RV. In Mt 23³³ Jesus employs both words to describe the Pharisees—ὄφεις, γεννήματα ἐχιδνῶν, 'serpents, offspring [see GENERATION] of vipers' (cf. Mic 7¹⁷).

3. Very different is the passage Jn 3¹⁴ ' and as Moses lifted up the serpent (τὸν ὄφιν) in the wilderness, so must the Son of Man be lifted up,' where the reference is to the plague of serpents among the Israelites in the wilderness and the miraculous cure, as recorded in Nu 21⁶⁻⁹. Full consideration of this passage, and of its relation to 2 K 18⁴, does not fall within the scope of this article (see art. ' Nehushtan' in Hastings' *DB* iii. 510ᵇ). It is interesting, however, to note, in connexion with Jn 3¹⁴, that both passages in the OT have been regarded as pointing to serpent-worship in some form among the early Hebrews.

LITERATURE.—On the symbolism of the serpent : Baudissin, *Studien zur Semit. Religiongesch.* i. 257-292 ; Nöldeke, ' Die Schlange nach arab. Volksglauben' in *Ztschr. f. Völkerpsycho-*

logie. On natural history : Tristram, *Nat. Hist. of the Bible* ; O. Günther, *Die Reptilien und Amphibien von Syrien* ; Doughty, *Arabia Deserta.* See also Schultz, *OT Theol.* (Eng. tr.) ii. 272 ; Sayce, *Religions of Ancient Egypt and Babylonia*, pp. 208–214 ; Hastings' *DB* iv. 459.   **G. GORDON STOTT.**

SERUG.—A link in our Lord's genealogy (Lk 3³⁵, AV *Saruch*).

SERVANT.—See artt. SERVICE, SLAVE ; and for 'Servant of the Lord' see PROPHET, p. 432ᵃ.

SERVICE.—There are 5 words which with their derivatives are used to convey the idea of 'service' in the NT : λειτουργεῖν, λατρεύειν, ὑπηρέτης, διάκονος, and δοῦλος. Of these λειτουργεῖν (λεῖτος = δημόσιος and ἔργον) is used to denote service rendered to the State. It indicates the unreckoned generosity, the uncalculating devotion of patriotic service of city or country. This idea is fully indicated in such passages as Ro 15¹⁶, Ph 2¹⁷, and in connexion with διακονία in 2 Co 9¹². The word was early used in the Christian Church to indicate the service of God in special offices and ministries. Thus in the one passage in which it appears in the Gospels (Lk 1²³) it is used of the priest Zacharias, as it is afterwards used of the great High Priest in He 8¹ᶠᶠ. Very much the same may be said of the second word λατρεύειν. In classical Greek it was used of the service of the gods, and in the NT it is used of the service rendered to Jehovah by the whole tribe of Israel (Ac 26⁷ and Ro 9⁴). Thus Augustine says : 'λατρεία . . . aut semper aut tam frequenter ut fere semper, ea dicitur servitus quæ pertinet ad colendum Deum' (*c. Faust.* 20, 21). This distinct use of the word appears in all those passages in which it is used in the Gospels : Mt 4¹⁰, Lk 1⁷⁴ 2³⁷. Though these words are full of significance as used in the NT, we need not in this article examine further into their use, inasmuch as they do not appear in the Gospels in connexion with that form of service which Christ either illustrated in Himself or explicitly taught. It is in the remaining words that we must find whatever teaching is suggested by the terminology of the Evangelists.

διάκονος is used in what was doubtless the original meaning of the word, *i.e.* 'one who waits at table,' in Jn 2⁵·⁹ (see also Mt 22¹³ and Jn 12²). It represents the servant in his activity rather than in any relation to his Lord. The διάκονος executes the commands of his master. Thus, while in Mt 22²⁻¹⁴ the δοῦλος invites the guests to the feast, it is the διάκονος who expels the unworthy guest. Another word closely allied in use to διάκονος is ὑπηρέτης, 'the rower,' then the subordinate official, and then the performer of any hard labour (Mt 5²⁵, Lk 4²⁰). The difference between the two words is to be sought in the direction of the official relation of the ὑπηρέτης to his master.

By far the most commonly used word in this connexion is δοῦλος, 'the bondservant.' It is used almost as an equivalent to διάκονος to indicate the lowliness of the service rendered. Where the two words are brought into juxtaposition, the difference between them seems to lie in this, that while διάκονος indicates the activity of the servant, δοῦλος indicates rather the completeness of his subordination. Thus, in speaking of Christ, St. Paul calls Him the διάκονος of the circumcision (Ro 15⁸), while he says that He took upon Him the μορφὴν δούλου (Ph 2⁷). So also in Lk 12³⁷ watchfulness is the token of the activity of the servant. The humility of service, therefore, while not lacking entirely from the word διάκονος, belongs more particularly to δοῦλος. It is on the lines of this distinction that the words of Christ as recorded in Mt 20²⁶· ²⁸ may be explained. There it will be seen that, while διάκονος is the antithesis of μέγας, the antithesis of

δοῦλος is found in πρῶτος ; as though Christ would teach that true greatness lies in the doing of service, while the highest position in His Kingdom belongs to him who will accept the lowly position of the slave.

In this last passage and again in Lk 22²⁶ Christ lays down service as the law of His Kingdom. The position of a minister was that which He accepted for Himself ; 'He came not to be ministered unto, but to minister' (Mt 20²⁸), and He looked to those who would follow Him to accept a similar rule of life for themselves (Lk 22²⁶, Jn 13¹⁶, cf. 12¹⁶). This idea of service as the law of the Kingdom of God was no new one in Jewish thought. Many years before, the author of Is 40–56 had spoken of both the deliverer and the delivered as 'the servant of Jehovah.' Both He who through suffering should redeem the people, and the people themselves, idealized as they were in the vision of the seer, were to serve. The one was to be 'despised and rejected of men,' and the other, blind, deaf, plundered, and despised, was to be exalted by the very service in which he proved his submission and obedience. Each was to be Jehovah's δοῦλος.

Throughout the parabolic teaching of Jesus the use of this word is sufficiently frequent to be significant ; but if He had given no other teaching in this connexion, His mind would have been sufficiently expressed in His acted parable on the occasion when He Himself stooped to the most menial of all menial service, and washed the feet of His disciples. When at length His self-imposed task was complete, 'He said unto them, A servant is not greater than his Lord ; . . . I have given you an example that ye also should do as I have done unto you' (Jn 13¹⁻¹⁷). In this service, which Christ enjoins as well as accepts, there are one or two notes which are peculiarly His own. The first of these is, that it is a service which is not imposed upon the individual from outside, but is a spontaneous act of submission. It was in this way that He Himself had entered upon that service μορφὴν δούλου λαβών (Ph 2⁷), and it is in this way that He calls upon His disciples to serve (Mt 20²⁶). Indeed, it was only thus that service could be of any moral value to the servant. The compelled service is barren of aught but the spirit of rebellion, and it finds no place in Christ's scheme. The service that is grudged or unwilling is not to be discovered in His example. As St. Paul afterwards taught, there is a recognition of the freedom of the individual in this, that he is allowed to 'yield himself a servant unto obedience,' and the bond which he thus casts upon himself grows closer with every subsequent act of obedience (Ro 6¹⁶). The second note is that of completeness. This service is complete in its self-dedication and exclusive in its object. Christ acknowledged from the beginning a sense of constraint when He said that He must be in His Father's house (Lk 2⁴⁹). His surrender to that compelling force was full ; He found it His 'meat to do the will' of His Father, and to accomplish His work (Jn 4³⁴). Equally full was the devotion which He realized, for He 'did always the things that pleased him' (Jn 8²⁹).

These with the other passages already cited sufficiently indicate the character of the service which belongs to the Kingdom of God. It has a definite and undivided purpose. It is not qualified either in its sanction or in its claim to occupy and dominate the whole life of the Christian. Equally marked is its measure or intensity. Both in the terms that are used and in the examples afforded, it is taught that sacrifice, even that ultimate form of sacrifice which for mortals is realized in death, is the one condition of service.

LITERATURE.—Fairbairn, *Religion in History and in the Life of To-day* ; Church, *The Gifts of Civilization* ; Westcott, *Lessons from Work* ; Wendt, *The Teaching of Jesus*, i. p. 325 ff. ; Bruce, *The Kingdom of God*, p. 220 ; Peabody, *Jesus Christ and the Social Question* ; Ely, *Social Aspects of Christianity* ; Lyman Abbott, *Christianity and Social Problems* ; S. D. Gordon, *Quiet Talks on Service* ; J. H. Thom, *Laws of Life*, 2nd ser. 347 ; Phillips Brooks, *Addresses*, 1 ; A. Smellie, *Service and Inspiration* (1904).

W. W. HOLDSWORTH.

SESSION.—In the exaltation of Jesus Christ which followed His death upon the Cross, three distinct stages are indicated, viz. the Resurrection, the Ascension, and the Session, which means the *sitting* or the *state of being seated*. Harnack indeed thinks that in some of the oldest accounts the resurrection and the sitting at the right hand of God are taken as parts of the same act, without mention of any ascension. But take one of these accounts : in Ro 8³⁴ St. Paul writes : Χριστὸς Ἰησοῦς ὁ ἀποθανὼν μᾶλλον δὲ ἐγερθεὶς ἐκ νεκρῶν, ὅς ἐστιν ἐν δεξιᾷ τοῦ θεοῦ, ὃς καὶ ἐντυγχάνει ὑπὲρ ἡμῶν. 'Here,' writes Swete (*Apostles' Creed*, p. 67 f.), 'are four well-marked links in a chain of facts—our Lord's Death, Resurrection, Session, Intercession. It is difficult to see why the second and the third, the Resurrection and the Session, should be taken as parts of the same act, when the first is clearly distinct. If the Ascension is not mentioned, it is implied in the Session, for it is contrary to the usage of the NT to interpret ἐγείρεσθαι of any exaltation beyond the mere recall from death. In other passages the ellipsis is equally easy to supply. Thus St. Peter's words in Ac 2³² (τὸν Ἰησοῦν ἀνέστησεν ὁ θεός . . . τῇ δεξιᾷ οὖν τοῦ θεοῦ ὑψωθείς) are interpreted by 1 P 3²¹· ²² (δι' ἀναστάσεως Ἰησοῦ Χριστοῦ, ὅς ἐστιν ἐν δεξιᾷ τοῦ θεοῦ, πορευθεὶς εἰς οὐρανόν). It would go against the whole tenor of the NT to regard them as merely different names for the same event ; the Session is the glorified state into which the Ascension was the solemn entrance.

The Session is related as a fact of history only in Mk 16¹⁹ : He 'sat down at the right hand of God,' which belongs at latest to the earlier sub-Apostolic age. Yet this is not so remarkable when we remember that St. Matthew and St. John do not carry their accounts beyond the Resurrection. Its truth, however, is amply established by the fact that it was expressly foretold by Christ Himself (Mt 19²⁸ 25³¹ 26⁶⁴ ‖). It was the fulfilment of prophecy ; cf. Ps 110¹, to which reference was made by the Lord (Mt 22⁴²ᶠ·), which was quoted by St. Peter (Ac 2³⁴) and the author of Hebrews (1¹³), and enlarged upon in Eph 1²⁰ᶠ· ; cf. also Ps 2⁶ 45⁹, Is 16⁵, Lk 1³². And it found a prominent place in the doctrinal system of the NT writers (Eph 1²⁰, Col 3¹, He 1³· ¹³ 8¹ 10¹², Ro 8³⁴, 2 Co 5¹⁰ (βῆμα τοῦ Χριστοῦ), 1 P 3²², Rev 3²¹).

That Ps 110¹ was taken in the Messianic sense by the Jews of the time of our Lord is evident from Mt 22⁴²ᶠ·, where His opponents did not deny that the writer was speaking of the Christ ; and in many of their older exegetical writings this interpretation was adopted. Jennings and Lowe (*The Psalms*) quote the following passage which occurs in the Midrash *Tillim* on Ps 18³⁶ : 'R. Yoden said in the name of R. Chama, In the time to come the Holy One, Blessed be He, causes the King Messiah to sit at His right hand, according as it is said, "The utterance of Jehovah to my Lord, Sit Thou on My right hand," and Abraham on His left. And the face of Abraham grows pale, and he says, "The son of my son sits on the right hand, but I on the left" ; and the Holy One, Blessed be He, appeases him, and says, "The son of thy son is at My right hand, but I am at thy right hand" : and this is implied by (ביכל), "Jehovah upon thy right hand."' Later Jewish writers sought to explain the words as referring to Abraham (Rashi), David (Aben Ezra, Mendelssohn), Hezekiah, or Zerubbabel, with regard to which interpretations see Jennings and Lowe, *op. cit.*; Pearson, *On the Creed*, Art. vi.; and Edersheim, *Life and Times of Jesus the Messiah*, ii. 405. Kautzsch in his art. 'Religion of Israel' (Hastings' *DB*, Extra Vol. p. 727), thinks the primary reference was to a Maccabæan priest-prince, possibly Simon, who in the year 141 B.C. became by a popular resolution hereditary high priest and prince of the people. Delitzsch considers this Psalm the only one which is directly Messianic, in the sense that it contains

prophecy immediately pointing to the person of a coming Anointed One, who was fully to set up God's Kingdom on earth. On the whole question of interpretation consult Davison's art. 'Psalms' in Hastings' *DB*, vol. iv. p. 160.

Accordingly the Session forms a distinct article ('ascendit in cœlos, sedet ad dexteram Patris') in the old Roman Creed as represented in the Greek confession of Marcellus and in the Latin of Rufinus, of which Harnack writes : 'We may regard it as an assured result of research that the old Roman Creed . . . came into existence about or shortly before the middle of the second century.' It is found also in a form of creed given by Tertullian (*de Præscr. Hæret.* c. 13), 'in cœlos ereptum sedisse ad dexteram Patris,' and in another (*de Virg. Vel.* 1), 'receptum in cœlis sedentem nunc ad dexteram Patris.' Its importance is equally marked in the formulæ of the Eastern Church, καθίσαντα ἐκ δεξιῶν τοῦ Πατρός (early Creed of Jerusalem collected from Cyril), καθεσθέντα ἐν δεξιᾷ τοῦ Πατρός (Creed of the *Apostolic Constitutions*, vii. 41), καθεζόμενον ἐκ δεξιῶν τοῦ Πατρός (Creed of Constantinople).

In NT the reference is sometimes to the act of taking a position ; cf. He 1³ 'sat down (ἐκάθισεν) on the right hand of the Majesty on high,' which describes the solemn assumption of the seat of authority, which rightly belongs to One whose dignity is expressed in such unique terms as are used in the preceding clauses ; and 'throughout the Epistle to the Hebrews (except 1¹³, κάθου from LXX) the reference is uniformly to the act of taking the royal seat' (Westcott on 10¹², cf. also Rev 3²¹) ; in 12² the Perfect (κεκάθικεν), found in the best MSS, denotes the entrance on a permanent state. In Mt 19²⁸ 25³¹ the reference is to taking the throne of His glory for judgment. The verb is twice used transitively to describe the action of the Father in raising Christ from the dead and making Him to sit at His right hand (Eph 1²⁰ and Ac 2³⁰ RV). Elsewhere the Session is described rather as a state ; cf. Mt 26⁶⁴, Lk 22⁶⁹ (RV 'shall be seated,' Vulg. 'erit sedens'), Col 3¹ (οὗ ὁ Χριστός ἐστιν . . . καθήμενος, 'where Christ is seated,' RV), and Ro 8³⁴, 1 P 3²² where ὅς ἐστιν ἐν δεξιᾷ τοῦ θεοῦ has the same meaning ; in Ps 110¹ κάθου (LXX) also marks continuous session as distinct from assumption of place.

The Session is spoken of as 'at the right hand of God' (Mk 16¹⁹, Col 3¹ *et al.*; cf. Eph 1²⁰ and Ac 2³³ RVm), elsewhere variously, 'at the right hand of power' (Mt 26⁶⁴), 'of the power of God' (Lk 22⁶⁹), 'of the Majesty on high' (He 1³), 'of the throne of the Majesty in the heavens' (8¹), 'of the throne of God' (12²). The Greek is either ἐκ δεξιῶν, which is the uniform phrase in the Synoptics and in quotation of Ps 110¹ (Ac 2³⁴, He 1¹³), or ἐν δεξιᾷ, which is used in the Epistles (Ro 8³⁴, Eph 1²⁰ *et al.*; cf. Ac 2³³ τῇ δεξιᾷ, 'at the right hand,' RVm). It is difficult to determine what is the exact force of the expression. God is Spirit, He has no body, and He is omnipresent, consequently the right hand of God is everywhere (*dextera Dei ubique est*). Therefore its use as referring to the Father is to be taken as a necessary accommodation to our limited minds, which can think only in terms of time and space, and which can have no conception of pure spirit. Among men, to be set on one's right hand has a well-defined meaning : it signifies to be in the highest place of honour, to be recognized as a sharer in rule ; cf. 1 K 2¹⁹, Ps 45⁹, Mt 20²¹ ; Jos. *Ant.* VI. xi. 9 (παρακαθεσθέντων αὐτῷ, τοῦ μὲν παιδὸς Ἰωνάθου [1 S 20²⁵] ἐκ δεξιῶν). Thus 'Hiempsal . . . dextra Adherbalem adsedit . . . quod apud Numidas honori ducitur' (Sallust, *Jugurtha*, xi. 3). See art. 'Symbol' in Hastings' *DB*, Extra Vol. p. 172. This is the sense in which the Fathers interpret the words ; as Westcott points out in his notes on

He 8[1], they carefully avoided all puerile anthropomorphism in their treatment of 'the right hand of God'; for example, 'plenitudinem majestatis summamque gloriam beatitudinis et prosperitatis debemus per dexteram intelligere in qua filius sedet'. (Primas.); οὐχ ὅτι τόπῳ περικλείεται ὁ θεὸς, ἀλλ' ἵνα τὸ ὁμότιμον αὐτοῦ δειχθῇ τὸ πρὸς τὸν πατέρα (Theophylact).

As regards Jesus Christ, however, it is not so clear that the expression is entirely figurative. He ascended with His human body, which was indeed glorified and freed from many of its previous limitations; but it belongs to the very essence of the idea of a body that it should occupy a certain definite space. Since, then, His body cannot be ubiquitous, it seems necessary to think of it as raised at the Ascension to some distinct place. 'He went into the place of all places in the universe of things, in situation most eminent, in quality most holy, in dignity most excellent, in glory most illustrious, the inmost sanctuary of God's temple above' (Barrow, *Sermon on the Ascension*). Thus Stier holds fast 'the certain ποῦ of heaven, yea, of the throne of God in it.' And Meyer (on Mk 16[19], Eph 1[20]) says the expression is not to be transferred into a vague conception of a *status cælestis*, of a higher relation to the world and the like, but is to be left as a specification of place; for Christ is with His glorified body, as σύνθρονος of the Father, on the seat where Divine Majesty is enthroned (cf. Mt 6[9]), from which hereafter He will return to judgment; meantime He is patiently waiting at the centre of all worship and power (He 10[12. 13]): cf. also Ellicott on Eph 1[20]. This view agrees with the tenor of the Holy Scriptures, which seem to imply that while God is everywhere, yet there is a place (described as ἐν ὑψηλοῖς, ἐν οὐρανοῖς) where He specially manifests Himself in peculiar glory to heavenly beings (cf. Is 6[1] 66[1], Ps 2[4] 102[19], 1 Ti 6[16]), whence the Holy Spirit and the voice of God came (Mt 3[16. 17], Jn 12[28]). Yet, on the other hand, Milligan (*The Ascension of Our Lord*, Lect. I.) points out that heaven in the NT 'is contrasted with earth less as one *place* than as one *state* is contrasted with another,' comparing Jn 3[13] 'No man hath ascended into heaven, but he that descended out of heaven, even the Son of Man which. is in heaven' [but אBL do not give ὁ ὢν ἐν τῷ οὐρανῷ], and quoting Westcott (on He 1[3]), 'all local association must be excluded,' the reference being to dignity and honour, not locality; cf. also Jn 1[18], Eph 4[10]. And Grimm-Thayer says 'that these expressions are to be understood in this figurative sense and not of a fixed and definite place in the highest heavens, will be questioned by no one who carefully considers Rev 3[21].' See also Abbott, 'Ephesians' (*ad* 1[20]), in the *ICC*.

Sitting at the right hand of God is the compendious description of the present life of Christ in glory. It is evident from those passages which speak of it as a continuous state, that the expression cannot be taken literally, otherwise they would convey the idea that the attitude of sitting is perpetual. Besides, we find simply 'is at the right hand' in Ro 8[34], 1 P 3[22]; in other places He is represented in a different attitude, as standing (Ac 7[56]), walking (Rev 2[1] 3[4] 14[4]); and John (Rev 1[13]) saw Him 'girt about at the breasts with a golden girdle' (which was 'worn in this manner by priests when they were engaged in active service' [Milligan]).

In the vision of St. Stephen a beautiful explanation of the 'standing' has long been given, viz. that he saw Jesus as risen from His throne and in the act of coming to help His suffering servant and faithful martyr. So Meyer, Trench, Conybeare and Howson, *et al.*, following Chrysostom, τί οὖν ἑστῶτα καὶ οὐχὶ καθήμενον; ἵνα δείξῃ τὴν ἀντίληψιν τὴν εἰς τὸν μάρτυρα· καὶ γὰρ περὶ τοῦ πατρὸς λέγεται 'ἀνάστα ὁ θεός,' and Gregory the Great, 'Stephanus in labore certaminis positus

stantem vidit quem adjutorem habuit.' See the Collect for St. Stephen's Day, and Alford's note on Ac 7[55], where he inclines to a different interpretation.

The Session of Christ is connected with His work as King, Priest, Intercessor, and Judge. (1) It expresses His *sovereignty and majesty*; thereby He entered on the full and permanent participation in the Divine glory, not merely resuming the glory which He had resigned at the Incarnation (Jn 17[5]), but receiving the added glory won by His obedience even unto the death of the Cross (Ph 2[8f.], He 2[9]); thereby the promises made to David concerning his son were fulfilled (cf. Ps 2[6] 24[9], 1 Co 15[25], Eph 1[20f.]). All power is given unto Him in heaven and in earth (Mt 28[18]), God 'hath put all things in subjection under his feet' (1 Co 15[27]). (2) It betokens *an accomplished work* (He 10[12f.]); His earthly life completed, the suffering and the humiliation ended; *yet not inactivity*, for Jn 5[17] still holds true of the exalted Christ; such perfect rest as 'answers to the being of God "who worketh hitherto" without effort and without failure' (Westcott, *The Historic Faith*, Art. vi.), and is consistent with His readiness to sympathize with His people on earth, and to help them in time of need; cf. He 2[18] 4[15f.]. (3) It signifies His *unique dignity and honour*. In God's presence the angels stand, or fall on their faces (Is 6[2], 1 K 22[19]); the priests stood in the Temple when ministering (He 10[11]). He alone is said to sit on God's right hand. τὸ ἑστάναι τοῦ λειτουργεῖν ἐστι σημεῖον, οὐκοῦν τὸ καθῆσθαι τοῦ λειτουργεῖσθαι, and τοῦτο οὐχὶ τοῦ ἱερέως ἀλλὰ τούτου ᾧ ἱερᾶσθαι ἐκεῖνον χρή (Chrys.). Θεὸν ἔχομεν ἀρχιερέα. τὸ γὰρ καθῆσθαι οὐδενὸς ἄλλου ἢ θεοῦ (Theophylact). (4) It expresses His *dignity as Priest-King*. Westcott remarks (Add. Note on He 8[1]) that in this Epistle to the Hebrews His Session is always (except in 1[13]) connected with the fulfilment of priestly work, of which it marks two different aspects. Before He sat down He fulfilled the type of Aaron, offering the sacrifice of Himself and passing into heaven, into the presence of God. Since that time He fulfils the royal priesthood of Melchizedek; He intercedes for men as their representative (Ro 8[34], He 7[25], 1 Jn 2[1]), presenting their petitions and praises (He 13[15], Ro 16[27], 1 P 2[5]), securing access for His people now to 'the holy place' where He Himself is, by His blood (He 4[16] 10[19f.]), and acting as a minister (λειτουργός) of the sanctuary and of the true tabernacle (8[2] where see Westcott's note): He also rules and guides His Church, being with His people always, even unto the end of the world (Mt 28[20]), and in the midst where two or three are gathered together in His name (18[20]). (5) It implies His work as *Judge*, which is the aspect chiefly presented in the Gospels (Mt 19[28] 25[31], Mk 14[62]; cf. Is 16[5] and 2 Co 5[10] 'the judgment-seat of Christ'). Thus we are to understand by the Session that Christ, having accomplished on earth the work of redemption, now occupies the place of highest honour, most exalted majesty, and perfect bliss, and that God has conferred upon Him all pre-eminence of dignity, power, favour, and felicity. With regard to the particular form in which this is expressed, Sanday (in his art. 'Jesus Christ' in Hastings' *DB* ii. p. 642[b]) well says: 'We speak of these things κατὰ ἄνθρωπον; or rather, we are content to echo in regard to them the language of the Apostles and of the first Christians, who themselves spoke κατὰ ἄνθρωπον. The reality lies behind the veil.' See also art. ASCENSION.

LITERATURE. — Denney, art. 'Ascension' in Hastings' *DB*, vol. i.; Sanday, 'Jesus Christ,' *ib.* vol. ii. p. 642; Swete, *The Apostles' Creed*; Westcott, *The Historic Faith* and *Epistle to Hebrews*; Milligan, *The Ascension of Our Lord*; Trench, *Exposition of the Sermon on the Mount*, ch. vi.; Pearson, *Exposition of the Creed*, Art. vi. The relation of the Session of Christ to His presence among His people and to the Lutheran doctrine of

His ubiquity is discussed at length in Martensen's *Christian Dogmatics*, §§ 174–180.　　　W. H. DUNDAS.

SETH.—The patriarch, mentioned as a link in our Lord's genealogy (Lk 3[38]).

SEVEN, SEVENTY.—See NUMBER.

SEVEN WORDS, THE.—These words, spoken by our Lord from the cross, are recorded by the different Evangelists, one by St. Matthew and St. Mark conjointly, three by St. Luke, and three by St. John. The progressive stages by which they are characterized may be taken to show a gradual unfolding of the will and purpose of God for the redemption of mankind. They seem to sum up in themselves the whole of the gospel. The first three words, 'Father, forgive them; for they know not what they do' (Lk 23[34]), 'Verily I say unto thee, To-day shalt thou be with me in paradise' (Lk 23[43]), and 'Woman, behold thy son . . . behold thy mother' (Jn 19[26. 27]), were spoken between the third and the sixth hour, and they reveal to us the great High Priest, in His life of ministry, interceding for the transgressors, proclaiming pardon to the penitent, and blessing His own. The two next words, 'My God, my God, why hast thou forsaken me?' (Mt 27[46], Mk 15[34]), and 'I thirst' (Jn 19[28]), were spoken in the darkness; nature is wrapped in gloom as the God-man, bearing the burden and the curse of sin that is not His own, reveals to us something of the mystery of suffering. The two last words, 'It is finished' (Jn 19[30]), and 'Father, into thy hands I commend my spirit' (Lk 23[46]), were spoken in the restored light. They reveal to us the victory, the completed work, and the entering into rest. All seven words are words of love It was love that animated Him from the time when 'for us men and for our salvation He came down from heaven, and was incarnate by the Holy Ghost of the Virgin Mary, and was made Man' (Nicene Creed). It was love that entered into the whole of His life on earth, but that love shines with its brightest lustre in the cross. His ministry of intercession, of reconciliation, of blessing, His suffering, His thirsting, His triumph, all reach their climax in the cross. They are the outcome of the great love wherewith He so loved us that He gave Himself for us.

1. 'Father, forgive them; for they know not what they do.'—This first word was probably spoken when the soldiers were driving the nails into His hands and feet, and were about to lift up the cross with its sacred burden and plant it in the ground. From His hard bed, the cross, while suffering untold agony, He intercedes for them, and adds to His intercession an excuse for their deed, 'They know not what they do.' In one sense they did know, they must have known, even those rough Roman soldiers, that they were perpetrating an act of gross cruelty; but familiarity with suffering had made them callous. It was part of their work; they were paid to do it, and they did it. But they did not know all, they did not know that they were crucifying the Lord of glory, they were but unconscious instruments doing what they were bidden; and so the Saviour prayed for them and made excuse for them, and not for them only, but for all who had taken part in that deed of violence, for all who, during all the ages that have since elapsed, have been crucifying the Son of God afresh.

2. 'To-day shalt thou be with me in paradise.'—Having interceded for the transgressors, Christ from His cross proclaims pardon to the penitent robber on his cross. This man had been one of a band of robbers, perhaps the same band to which Barabbas belonged, a band of men living wild and reckless lives; and now both he and his fellow, having fallen victims to the power against which they have been in revolt, are suffering the extreme penalty of the law. Crucified with them, in the same condemnation, is the pure and holy Jesus, who did no sin, neither was guile found in His mouth. He was numbered with the transgressors. He descended to the lowest depth of human degradation that He might lift humanity to the height of holiness and heaven. From His cross He will exert a world-wide attraction: 'I, if I be lifted up from the earth, will draw all men unto me' (Jn 12[32]); and now this attraction is beginning. Both these robbers had at first reviled the Holy Sufferer; one remained hardened and impenitent to the end, but the other was brought to a better mind. Perhaps this was not the first time that this man had seen the Christ; he may have been among those who listened to His words on some previous occasion, he may have seen some of His miracles; now, however, he is brought face to face with the power of His love, conviction dawns within him, he sees himself in his true light; turning to his fellow, he says, 'Dost not thou fear God, seeing thou art in the same condemnation? And we indeed justly, for we receive the due reward of our deeds; but this man hath done nothing amiss' (Lk 23[40. 41]). He confesses his sins, and not only is there a confession of sins but a wonderful faith, and this faith is manifested, not when Christ is at the height of His popularity, but in the depth of His humiliation. He sees in the cross a throne, and in the thorn-crowned sufferer a king seated upon it, and he prefers his request, 'Lord, remember me, when thou comest in thy kingdom.' And Jesus turns to this penitent robber and proclaims the gospel of forgiveness, 'To-day shalt thou be with me in paradise.'

3. 'Woman, behold thy son . . . behold thy mother.'—Christ from His cross has interceded for the sinful world, He has proclaimed the gospel of forgiveness to the penitent robber; but He has yet, in the progressive stages of His ministry of love, another blessing to bestow. In this word our Lord comes near His own. His first word was for His enemies; His second for one who had been His enemy, but was no longer one; His third was for those who had never been His enemies—for His mother and the disciple whom He loved. 'There stood by the cross of Jesus his mother' (Jn 19[25]). For this the aged Simeon had prepared her, when, taking the infant Jesus in his arms, he had told her that a sword should pierce through her own soul (Lk 2[35]); and now these words were being fulfilled. Jesus from His cross beholds His mother, and is mindful of the years which He had spent under her tender care in the quiet home of Nazareth. He had told her, both when she found Him in the Temple and also at the marriage feast in Cana (Lk 2[49], Jn 2[4]), that there was a higher duty than that which He owed to her, a higher relationship than that between mother and son,—He was not only her son, He was also her Lord,—yet the earthly relationship is not forgotten. He will not depart before He has provided a home for her; with His parting breath He commits her to the care of the disciple whom He loved: 'Woman, behold thy son . . . behold thy mother.'

4. 'My God, my God, why hast thou forsaken me?'—A long space of time intervenes between the third and fourth words. 'From the sixth hour there was darkness over all the land unto the ninth hour' (Mt 27[45]). The first three words were spoken before the darkness, but now a change has come—darkness reigns on Calvary, as if God had drawn a veil over the scene. Three hours of silence and darkness. It is the climax of the sufferings of our Lord, the hour and power of darkness; what takes place we know not; He trod the winepress alone (Is 63³). He is alone in His conflict with the powers of evil, dark without, dark within,—how dark we may gather from the awful cry that escaped from His lips at the end of those long hours, 'My God, my God, why hast thou forsaken me?'

What did it mean? It did not mean that He was forsaken by His Father. Had not the Father said, 'This is my beloved son in whom I am well pleased' (Mt 3¹⁷)? Had not He Himself said, 'Behold the hour cometh, yea, is now come, that ye shall be scattered, every man to his own, and shall leave me alone: and yet I am not alone, because the Father is with me' (Jn 16³²)? But there was a connexion between the death of Christ and sin; it was an atonement for sin: 'The Lord hath laid on him the iniquity of us all' (Is 53⁶). And the misery of sin is that it hides the face of God. It is the loss of God's presence; and Christ, as our representative, in bearing our sins, entered into our condition, involving the consciousness of the loss of God's presence. He felt as though God had hidden His face. He descended with us into the depth of our degradation, made like unto us in all things, yet without sin. But the mystery of this bitter cry we, with our finite understandings, can never fathom: 'I and the Father are one,' and yet 'My God, my God, why hast thou forsaken me?' This the early Christians fully realized, for in their oft-repeated litanies they used to say, 'By Thy sufferings known and unknown, good Lord deliver us.' See also art. DERELICTION.

5. 'I thirst.'—'The last word,' it has been said, 'was the cry of the human soul in separation; this is the cry of the human body in its weakness.' The darkness is now passing away, and as, at the Temptation, He suffered hunger when the crisis was over, so now He gives expression to the thirst that is parching Him. Intense thirst was usually the most intolerable part of the suffering of those who were crucified, and He had been hanging there for six long hours, His open wounds scorched by the blazing sun. Two draughts were offered to our Lord: the one He refused, the other He accepted; the one which He refused was the 'vinegar mingled with gall' (Mt 27³⁴) or the 'wine mingled with myrrh' (Mk 15²³). It was a cup of wine drugged with bitter herbs of a narcotic tendency, and it was given in kindness to condemned malefactors to deaden pain. Our Lord refused the soporific; He would not meet death with His senses stupefied; but the undrugged wine which was offered to Him when He said 'I thirst,' He accepted. He would not add to His sufferings by refusing the cooling draught.

6. 'It is finished.'—The conflict is over and the victory won. Christ from His cross announces to the world that all is finished. Τετέλεσται. In one word He sums up the whole of man's redemption. Finished was all that prophecy had foretold and type foreshadowed. Finished was the work which His Father had given Him to do. He looks back on His life from the time when He said, 'Lo, I come to do thy will, O God' (He 10⁹), and is able to say with regard to every jot and tittle of His life's work, 'It is finished.' He has made a full, perfect, and sufficient sacrifice, oblation, and satisfaction for the sins of the whole world. We enter into no theory of the Atonement, we accept it as a fact; we know that the chasm between God and man, formed by the sin of man, has been bridged over, and that the way to the Father is open, for 'when He had overcome the sharpness of death, He opened the Kingdom of heaven to all believers' (Te Deum).

7. 'Father, into thy hands I commend my spirit.'—The two last words were spoken in rapid succession. The word of victory is followed by the word of rest—rest after the burden and heat of the day. It is a word of calm, beautiful trust, of perfect sympathy between the Father and Son, revealing to us what death was to Christ and what it is to all those who are united to Christ by a living faith; that it is not a leap in the dark, not a plunge into an unknown void, but a going home. 'Man goeth forth unto his work and to his labour until the evening' (Ps 104²³), and then cometh rest—rest with 'Christ in Paradise. Death is the summing up of the life; repeated acts form habits, habits form character, and character is the sum-total of the life, which we carry with us into the unseen world. To live the forgiven life, the life that is being formed and fashioned after the life of Christ, by the power of the Holy Ghost—this is the true preparation for death. This alone can rob death of its sting; one with Christ in our life, we shall be one with Him in our death. 'To me to live is Christ, and to die is gain' (Ph 1²¹). 'Father, into thy hands I commend my spirit.'

LITERATURE.—The *Lives* of Christ, esp. Edersheim, *Life and Times*, ii. 593–610; Stier, *Words of the Lord Jesus, in loc.*; Tholuck, *Light from the Cross*; Stalker, *Trial and Death of Jesus Christ*; F. W. Robertson, *Sermons*, iv. 307; Fairbairn, *Studies in the Life of Christ*, 324; C. Stanford, *Voices from Calvary* (1893); W. R. Nicoll, *Seven Words from the Cross* (1895); M. Creighton, *Lessons from the Cross* (1898), 75–132; W. Lowrie, *Gaudium Crucis* (1905).   ROWLAND ELLIS.

SEVENTY.—The mission of the Seventy,* recorded in Lk 10, belongs to the third year of our Lord's public ministry. They were sent forth some time after the Transfiguration (10¹), when the Galilæan ministry of Jesus had closed, and when He had 'set his face to go to Jerusalem' (9⁵¹). The mission of the Twelve had taken place in the previous year (9¹· ¹⁰).† Seventy was regarded by the Jews as a complete number of persons for any important work.‡ Our Lord may have had specially in view (1) the seventy elders under Moses, who was a type of Himself; (2) the Hebrew tradition that the nations scattered at Babel were seventy in number (pseud.-Jon. Targ. on Gn 11⁸),§ just as the appointment of the Twelve may have been suggested by the number of the tribes of Israel.

1. *The office and mission of the Seventy resemble those of the Twelve.*—(1) A twofold commission is given in each case to preach and to heal, Mt 10⁷· ⁸, Lk 10⁹. (2) Instruction is given to both (*a*) to go in pairs, two and two, Mk 6⁷, Lk 10¹, in order to strengthen their testimony and to give mutual help and sympathy; (*b*) to take with them neither purse (for the labourer is worthy of his entertainment), nor wallet (for needless encumbrance was to be avoided), nor shoes, *i.e.* in addition to the sandals which they wore (for sandals befitted the poor, shoes the well-to-do), Mt 10⁹· ¹⁰, Mk 6⁹, Lk 10⁴. ‖ (3) In each case the burden of the message was 'Peace' and the 'Kingdom of God.' Peace was and still is the favourite Eastern salutation;

---

* Some very ancient MSS (BDMR) read Seventy-two (ἑβδομήκοντα δύο); but ℵACLΞ, etc., omit δύο.

† Although only Luke mentions the Seventy, indications of Jesus having a wider circle of 'disciples' than the Twelve are found elsewhere, as in Jn 6⁶⁶, Ac 1¹⁵, 1 Co 15⁶.

‡ The descendants of Jacob who entered Goshen were seventy (Gn 46²⁷). Seventy elders assisted Moses in the work of judgment and instruction (Ex 18²⁵ 24⁹, Nu 11¹⁶· ²⁵). The Sanhedrin consisted of seventy besides the president (Hastings, *DB* iv. 399). The LXX is so called from the tradition (first told in a literary fiction usually ascribed to about B.C. 200) that seventy or, more exactly, seventy-two elders executed the version (Hastings' *DB* iv. 438). Josephus appointed seventy rulers of Galilee (*BJ* ii. xx. 5).

§ Seventy-two, according to *Clem. Recogn.* ii. 42. See Driver, *Dt.* p. 355 f.

‖ A somewhat similar prohibition existed (no staff, shoes, scrip, or purse) for those about to enter the Temple: so that this particular instruction to the Seventy may suggest that those sent forth were to perform their service in the spirit of worshippers (Edersheim, *The Temple*, etc. p. 42).

the Kingdom of God was the Jews' highest aspiration. The Seventy, however, like the Twelve, would use these words, doubtless, with a fresh significance. Peace would include peace with God as well as with men, peace of conscience, the peace of discipleship to a perfect Master (Mt 11[28-30]) : the Kingdom of God would be, not a mere external, but an internal theocracy, the reign of God within as well as over men (Mt 12[28], Mk 4[26, 27]) ; and this Empire of God was Peace. (4) In both instructions the warning is added that they would be as sheep or lambs amid wolves, Mt 10[16], Lk 10[3]. The Seventy, like the Twelve, were to be prepared for persecution and tribulation. Even in Christ's lifetime there are indications of His followers being persecuted (Jn 9[34] 12[10]) ; and some of the Seventy at least were destined to suffer for Christ's sake.

2. On the other hand, there are *important differences in the two commissions.* (1) The mission of the Twelve was permanent ; they were pre-eminently Christ's Apostles : that of the Seventy was temporary ; they disappear, as a body, from view, like the Seven of Ac 6, although the office of evangelist, without Apostolic status, continues (Ac 21[8], Eph 4[11]). (2) The Twelve were not only to minister, but to administer—to exercise discipline and government (Jn 20[23], Ac 1[20-26]). To the Seventy no such functions were committed : they were simply preachers and healers. (3) The commission to the Twelve was expressly limited to 'the lost sheep of the house of Israel.' 'Go not into the way of the Gentiles, and into any city of the Samaritans enter ye not' (Mt 10[5, 6]). It was expedient at first to postpone the obtrusive extension of the privileges of the Kingdom beyond the Jews, lest these should be prejudiced against the gospel. By the time, however, that the Seventy were sent forth, Christ Himself had gone into 'the borders of Tyre and Sidon' (in addition to His earlier visit to Samaria), and had healed the Syrophœnician's daughter (Mk 7[24]). His disciples had thus been educated so far into realization that the Kingdom was intended to embrace others than Jews. The restriction, accordingly, is omitted in the commission to the Seventy, although there is no positive evidence that any of them preached, at this time, to Gentiles. (4) The commission to the Twelve included not only healing, but raising from death : that to the Seventy omits the latter. It is notable that only Apostles in the special sense are ever represented in the NT as raising the dead (Ac 9[40] 20[9, 10]). (5) A definite itinerary was arranged for the Seventy : they were to go 'into every city and place where Jesus himself intended to come' (Lk 10[1]), so as to prepare the way for Him. Their mission field thus included the country east of the Jordan, which was visited by our Lord during this closing year of His ministry. (6) A special feature of the directions to the Seventy was the injunction to 'salute no man by the way.' The 'time when he should be received up' was at hand : there were many places still to be visited ; delay in preparing the way must be avoided ; the profuse and elaborate salutations, customary on a journey, must be forgone.*

3. *Return of the Seventy* (Lk 10[17-20]). (1) Their return collectively is related ; but we need not infer, what the nature of the case must have prevented, that they all returned simultaneously. As Christ approached some town or district in the itinerary, some pair out of the Seventy would report the outcome of their particular mission. (2) The Seventy return with exultation. Their

* Geikie (*The Holy Land and the Bible*, i. pp. 328–329) describes graphically the salutation of two Orientals in Palestine even at the present day. On meeting, each lays his right hand on his heart, then raises it to his brow or mouth. Thereafter they take hold each of the other's hand, and a series of particular inquiries follows, taking up considerable time.

satisfaction culminated in this : 'Even demons are subject to us in thy name.' There was something commendable, and something defective in their joy. It was right to rejoice in the power of exorcism, but there was a higher joy of which, apparently, they thought little, the joy of enrolment among the servants of God. Accordingly (3) the Lord (*a*) manifests His sympathy, 'I was beholding Satan fall like lightning from heaven' ; as if He had been following the Seventy in spirit during the progress of their mission. (*b*) He assures them of security against real harm from the powers of evil. Although they were among 'serpents and scorpions,' 'nothing shall in any wise hurt you' ; a special providence would be their privilege. (*c*) He raises their aspirations to a higher level. Even to die in such a service would be 'gain' ; their 'names are written in heaven' (cf. Is 4[3], Dn 12[1]). They were fellow-workers with the King, whose cause, even should they suffer tribulation, must prevail.

4. *The credibility of the mission of the Seventy* has been doubted by Strauss, Baur, de Wette,* and others, owing to (1) the silence of the other Gospels regarding it ; (2) the lack of later authentic trace of the Seventy ; the close resemblance between the mission of the Seventy and that of the Twelve, being suggestive, it is argued, of confusion.

(1) The argument from silence is not strong ; because, owing to the temporary character, so far as appears, of the commission, there was nothing in the organization of the Church, as it existed when the three Gospels were written, such as would constrain an Evangelist to relate the history of the Seventy ; whereas the position and work of the Twelve made it natural, if not necessary, to give some account of the origin of the Apostolate. (2) The fact that Luke relates also the mission of the Twelve, and the notable differences (chronological and circumstantial) between the accounts of the two missions, render it highly improbable that the two narratives refer to a single event. (3) It is inaccurate to say that there is no authentic trace of the Seventy in later times. Philip 'the evangelist' was probably, from this designation (Ac 21[8]), one of them. Clement of Alexandria, writing in the latter part of the 2nd cent., names Barnabas, Matthias, and Cephas, who 'had the same name with the Apostle,' as others of the Seventy.† The historian Eusebius, without giving his authority, states that the Barsabbas of Acts and the Sosthenes mentioned in 1 Co 1[1] are said to have been of the same company.‡ The early disappearance of the Seventy as an organization is readily accounted for. They had no authority as rulers such as would make the appointment of successors requisite. One, as we have seen, became an Apostle ; Philip became one of the 'Seven' of Ac 6 ; a considerable number were probably included in one or other of the orders of evangelists, prophets, pastors, and teachers (Eph 4[11]). The individuals thus, for the most part, doubtless survived, and occupied more or less influential positions ; although the office itself, like that of the 'Seven,' disappeared.§

* Strauss, *Life of Jesus*, ii. 94–96 ; Baur, *Evangelien*, pp. 435, 498 ; de Wette, *Erklärung Luc.* p. 79 : Köstlin, *Com.* p. 267.
† *Strom.* ii. 20, *Hypotyposeis*, v., as quoted by Eus. i. 12.
‡ Eus. i. 12.
§ A professedly complete catalogue of the Seventy is given by pseudo-Dorotheos (6th cent.) as follows :—James (brother of the Lord), Timothy, Titus, Barnabas, Ananias, Stephen, Philip, Prochorus, Nicanor, Simon, Nicolas, Parmenas, Cleopas, Silas, Silvanus, Crescens, Epenetus, Andronicus, Amplias, Urbanus, Stachys, Apelles, Aristobulus, Narcissus, Herodion, Rufus, Asyncritus, Phlegon, Hermes, Hermas, Patrobas, Rhodion, Jason, Agabus, Linus, Gaius, Philologus, Olympas, Sosipater, Lucius, Tertius, Erastus, Phygellus, Hermogenes, Dermas, Quartus, Apollos, Cephas, Sosthenes, Epaphroditus, Cæsar, Marcus, Joseph Barsabbas, Artemas, Clemens, Onesiphorus,

5. *The appointment of the Seventy* for a definite ministry, yet without ecclesiastical authority such as was conferred on the Twelve, is significant and instructive. Our Lord does not appear to have instituted any definite and detailed form of Church government, but to have left such outward arrangements to the Apostles as His chosen disciples, and through them eventually to the Church itself, under the guidance of the Holy Spirit. Yet the appointment of the Seventy clearly indicates the principle that Christian ministry, including preaching, is neither to be confined to those who bear rule, nor regarded as entitling those who exercise such ministry to receive office as rulers. On the one hand, some who are able to give valuable service to the Church as evangelists or teachers may not be suitable, or even if suitable may not be required at the time, for rulership. On the other hand, those who bear rule in the Church are not, in the spirit of hierarchical exclusiveness, to discourage brethren who (without having the faculty or opportunity of government) possess some useful gift, from exercising it under due supervision, for the good of the Church and of the community at large.

LITERATURE.—Trench, *Studies in the Gospels*, 231–242; Plummer, 'St. Luke' in *ICC*; A. B. Bruce, 'Synoptic Gospels' in *EGT* i. pp. 538–542; Meyer, *Com. in loc.*; Edersheim, *Life and Times*, ii. pp. 37–43; *ExpT* xv. [1903] 14.

HENRY COWAN.

SHAME.—**1.** *Objectively* = dishonouring treatment, that which causes shame; usually ἀτιμία, ἀτιμάζειν (Mk 12⁴, Lk 20¹¹). Shame is mentioned in several passages of the OT which are usually applied to Christ's sufferings (Ps 44¹⁵ 69⁷· ¹⁹ 89⁴⁵, Is 50⁶); but the word is, curiously enough, never so used in the Gospels. He 12² speaks of the shame (αἰσχύνη) of the cross, 13¹³ of Christ's reproach (ὀνειδισμός), and in 6⁶ those who fall from grace are said to crucify Him afresh and put Him to an open shame (παραδειγματίζειν). In Jn 8⁴⁹ the unbelieving Jews dishonour (ἀτιμάζειν) Him, and in Ac 5⁴¹ the Apostles rejoice at suffering shame (ἀτιμασθῆναι) for His name.

The shame which Christ in fact bore is seen specially in such incidents of the Passion as the night arrest as of a thief or robber, the spitting, the scourging and the mockings, the public procession through the streets of Jerusalem, the taunts, the stripping naked of His body, and the hanging side by side with criminals. But above all, it is seen in the manner of His death, the cross being peculiarly the death of shame.* In the passages in the Gospels which speak of crucifixion and taking up the cross (Mt 20¹⁹, Mk 8³⁴ etc.), though the prominent thought is that of suffering, the idea of shame and ignominy is undoubtedly present as well. This shame must be willingly borne both by Christ and by His followers.

2. *Subjectively* = the feeling of shame; usually αἰσχύνη and cognate words.† It is interesting to note that the typically Greek and almost untranslatable αἰδώς has practically dropped out of Biblical Greek. In the LXX it occurs twice in Mac.; in NT only in 1 Ti 2⁹ μετὰ αἰδοῦς κ. υωφροσύνης ('with shamefastness and sobriety,' RV; 'shamefacedness,' AV*), and in TR of He 12²⁸ (AV 'reverence'), where edd. read δέους. It may be that, like such words as ἀρετή and φιλία, it was avoided as having a technical and unsuitable sense. In Homer and Hesiod it ranks high, being coupled with νέμεσις, and personified; it is the sense of what is due to oneself and others. Aristotle,† however, regards it not as a virtue, but an emotion (πάθος), which he does not consider very valuable to ethics. It is the fear of ἀδοξία, the loss of reputation, and, while proper to the νέος, it is out of place in the πρεσβύτερος or ἐπιεικής (the good man). They ought never to do, or wish to do, things that might evoke the feeling of shame.

Shame is not, then, a motive which we shall expect to find prominent in Christian ethics. Its essential idea being φόβος ἀδοξίας, it looks only to the varying standard of public opinion, to what people would say, or might be conceived of as saying if they knew. And its source is not the moral sense of right and wrong, but at best the feeling of propriety and decency. At its highest it is a neutral word. If it may sometimes deter from a wrong action, regarded as disgraceful, it is even more likely to deter from a right action, as unpopular.

It is in this sense that it is most prominent in the Gospels. It may keep a man from honest work (Lk 16³). Christ warns those who are ashamed of Him and of His words, that He too will be ashamed of them (Mk 8³⁸, Lk 9²⁶; cf. Jn 12⁴³). It is this false shame that is emphatically repudiated by the Apostles (Ro 1¹⁶, 2 Ti 1⁸· ¹², 1 P 4¹⁶).

Shame may also follow an action; and here too the idea is not the conviction of sin, but the confusion which comes from discovery, though this may be an element in a future awakening of conscience. It is the fate of one who unduly exalts himself (Lk 14¹⁰). Christ's enemies are put to shame (13¹⁷), *i.e.* they are enraged at being exposed before the people. Though the word is not mentioned, it is presumably the feeling of the man who hid his talent or pound, when brought face to face with his master (Mt 25²⁴, Lk 19²⁰); and it is certainly implied in Jn 8⁹, whether the words 'convicted by their conscience' are genuine or not. The Pharisees are ashamed of being found exploiting a sin for their own ends.

It is possible that in the passage last quoted (the episode of the woman taken in adultery) we have an instance of shame in another aspect, the sympathetic shame evoked by sin in others. Christ was face to face with the type of sin which particularly rouses that feeling, and with a callous attempt on the part of His enemies to use that sin for their own advantage. He blushed for those who did not blush for themselves.

'He was seized with an intolerable sense of shame. He could not meet the eye of the crowd, or of the accusers, and perhaps at that moment least of all of the woman. . . . In his burning embarrassment and confusion he stooped down so as to hide his face, and began writing with his finger on the ground' (Seeley, *Ecce Homo*, ch. ix.).

We may note that the word is far rarer in the NT, and particularly in the Gospels, than in the OT. The typically Hebraic use of בּוֹשׁ = *to be disappointed of a hope*, is not found in the Gospels; it occurs in Ro 5⁵ 9³³ 10¹¹, 1 P 2⁶. In each case a quotation is implied or expressed, though, curiously enough, from a passage (Is 28¹⁶) where בּוֹשׁ does not occur in the Hebrew. The shame or reproach of childlessness, which is so prominent in the OT, is referred to in Lk 1²⁵.

Tychicus, Carpus, Euodius, Philemon, Zenas, Aquila, Priscas, Junias, Marcus (2), Aristarchus, Pudens, Trophimus, Lucas the Eunuch, Lazarus. The list is manifestly untrustworthy. With some probability, indeed, are included all the seven 'deacons' (so called), along with some others (as Barnabas, Barsabbas, Marcus, Cleopas, Silas, Agabus, and Ananias), who were primitive disciples resident in or near Palestine. But many others, including such Gentile Christians as Titus, Tychicus, Trophimus, and brethren like Timothy and Apollos, who became converts long after our Lord's Ascension, are obviously the outcome of indiscriminating conjecture.

* See the well-known passage in Cic. *in Verr.* v. 66: 'Quid dicam in crucem tolli? Verbo satis digno tam nefaria res appellari nullo modo potest.'

† For distinction between αἰσχύνη and αἰδώς, see Trench, *NT Syn.* §§ 19, 20. The latter is the better word; 'αἰδώς would always restrain a good man from an unworthy act, while αἰσχύνη would sometimes restrain a bad one.'

* See Hastings' *DB*, s.v.
† See *Eth.* iv. 9; *Rhet.* ii. 6.

LITERATURE. — Hastings' *DB*, art. 'Shame'; Trench, *NT Synonyms*; G. Salmon, *Gnosticism and Agnosticism* (1887), 164; R. W. Church, *Village Serm.*, 3rd ser. (1897), 236.

C. W. EMMET.

SHEALTIEL.—A link in our Lord's genealogy (Mt 1¹², Lk 3²⁷, AV both times *Salathiel*).

SHECHEM.—See SYCHAR.

SHEEP, SHEPHERD.—

ἀμνός, 'lamb': Jn 1²⁹·³⁶, Ac 8³², 1 P 1¹⁹; with the classical acc. plur. ἄρνας, Lk 10³ (where Cod. A reads πρόβατα), and the diminutive from the same stem, ἀρνίον, in Jn 21¹⁵ (אABC²) and (of Christ) Rev. *passim* (5⁶–22³). All three words are used only figuratively in NT.

πρόβατον, 'sheep': Mt 9³⁶ 12¹¹·¹² 18¹², Lk 15⁴·⁶, Jn 2¹⁴·¹⁵ 10, Rev 18¹³, and (figuratively) Mt 7¹⁵ 10⁶·¹⁶ 15²⁴ 25³²ᶠ· 26³¹, Mk 6³⁴ 14²⁷, Jn 10. 21 (15·C*D)¹⁶·¹⁷, Ac 8³², He 13²⁰, 1 P 2²⁵; its diminutive προβάτιον in Jn 21¹⁶·¹⁷ (B, C, Tisch., WH).

ποίμνη, 'flock': Lk 2⁸, 1 Co 9⁷, and (fig.) Mt 26³¹, Jn 10¹⁶; its diminutive ποίμνιον, always figurative, in Lk 12³², Ac 20²⁸·²⁹, 1 P 5²·³.

ποιμήν, 'shepherd': Mt 9³⁶ 25³², Mk 6³⁴, Lk 2⁸·¹⁵·¹⁸·²⁰, Jn 10²·¹², and (fig.) Mt 26³¹, Mk 14²⁷, Jn 10¹¹·¹⁴·¹⁶, Eph 4¹¹, He 13²⁰, 1 P 2²⁵.

ἀρχιποίμην, 'chief shepherd' (fig.), 1 P 5⁴.

ποιμαίνω, 'shepherd,' 'tend,' a flock: Lk 17⁷, 1 Co 9⁷, and (fig.) Mt 2⁶, Jn 21¹⁶, Ac 20²⁸, 1 P 5², Jude ¹², Rev 22⁷ 7¹⁷ 12⁵ 19¹⁵.

βόσκω, 'feed a flock': Mt 8³⁰, Mk 5¹¹, Lk 8³² 15¹⁵; οἱ βόσκοντες, Mt 8³³, Mk 5¹⁴, Lk 8³⁴. βόσκω is fig. only in Jn 21¹⁵·¹⁷.

1. The sheep of Palestine are still the broad-tailed breed of Biblical times (Ex 29²², Lv 3⁹·¹¹ RV 'fat tail'). The tail is from 5 to 15 inches wide, and weighs from 10 to 15 lb., sometimes even as much as 30 lb., supplying 10 lb. and upwards of pure fat, which is packed for winter use. The sheep are white, though some have brown faces: only the rams have horns. They 'find pasture' (Jn 10⁹) in the lower lands in winter and on the mountains in summer, the best pastures being in S. Palestine (the Negeb and Gerar) and on the plain to the E. of the Jordan; but even 'the pastures of the wilderness' (Ps 65¹², Jl 2²²) are welcome in spring, when grass and flowers have grown which are burnt up in summer. The shepherd leads his sheep (Jn 10⁴) during the day in the cool months, but in the hotter part of the year from sunset to early morning, when he brings them back to the fold (vv.¹·¹⁶) or leaves them to lie under a prepared shelter in the bushes (Ca 1⁷). The **fold** (αὐλή) is a low flat shed or series of sheds, with a yard surrounded by a wall (Jn 10¹; cf. Nu 32¹⁶, Jg 5¹⁶, Zeph 2⁶); on cold nights the flocks are shut in the buildings. The wall is surmounted by a fence of sharp thorns to keep out the wolves (Jn 10¹²) and other wild beasts (Is 31⁴, 1 S 17³⁴); jackals and hyænas prey almost up to the walls of Jerusalem, while leopards and panthers often leap over the high fence of the fold, and the shepherd is still at times known 'to lay down his life for the sheep' (Jn 10¹¹). Robbers are as great a source of danger; a lamb or a kid is sometimes carried off by a bird of prey, and there are deadly snakes in the limestone rocks. The Gospel parable does not exaggerate the rejoicing of the shepherd when he has recovered a sheep that has gone astray 'upon the mountains' (Mt 18¹²·¹³, Lk 15⁴).

The shepherd keeps watch by night in the open air (Lk 2⁸, cf. Nah 3¹⁸), sometimes using a temporary shelter or a shepherd's tent (Ca 1⁸, Is 38¹²), which recalls the nomad habits of the early Israelites and their Semitic ancestors (He 11⁹, Gn 4²⁰). On the march he carries a bag or wallet (Mt 10¹⁰), a staff (Mt 10⁸, Ps 23⁴), and a sling (1 S 17⁴⁰). At the watering-places (Ps 23²) the sheep answer to the shepherd's call (Jn 10³·⁴), and, when they have drunk, move on at his word to make room for another flock. A shepherd is sometimes followed by several flocks, but each comes or goes at a separate call, and he often knows each sheep by a name (Jn 10³). Sheep-dogs (Job 30¹) are not mentioned in the NT, but they must have been used,

as they are still, to protect the flock and keep the sheep together.

2. Sheep were used for food (Rev 18¹³), and their milk for drink (1 Co 9⁷, Dt 32¹⁴); their skins were used for tents and for a baggy kind of coat (μηλωτή, He 11³⁷). The importance of sheep to a pastoral people like the Israelites is emphasized by one of their favourite names, *Rachel*, which means 'ewe' (W. R. Smith, *Rel. Sem.*² 311), and by the choice of a lamb for the Paschal Supper in their most sacred festival. Every morning, also, and every evening, they had to offer in sacrifice 'a he-lamb without blemish for a continual burnt-offering' (Nu 28³⁻⁶), with two he-lambs in addition every Sabbath day (v.⁹). Seven he-lambs and one ram were required at every new moon, on every day of the Passover, and at the Feast of Weeks (vv.¹⁶⁻³¹), at the Feast of Trumpets, and on the Day of Atonement (29¹⁻¹¹). At the Feast of Tabernacles (vv.¹²⁻³⁸) this offering was included on the eighth day, but was doubled on each of the first seven days, with varying numbers of bullocks. Goats were generally used for sin-offerings, but a leper in the day of his cleansing (Lv 17¹⁴) had to bring a he-lamb for a guilt-offering, besides a he-lamb for a burnt-offering and a ewe-lamb, the two latter being commuted for a pair of turtle-doves in the case of the poor (Lv 14¹⁰⁻²²). Any of the common people, also, might substitute for the male goat of the ordinary sin-offering a female lamb without blemish (Lv 4²⁷⁻³²). This piacular offering of sheep was a Semitic practice which is found also in ancient Cyprus, and was adopted by Epimenides at Athens when he was summoned from Crete to purify the city from the Alcmæonid pollution (W. R. Smith, *Rel. Sem.*² note G).

3. The interest of these sacrificial requirements centres in the NT round the representation of Christ as 'the **Lamb**' (Rev 5⁶ 22³). To some extent, of course, the figure is suggested by 'the meekness and gentleness of Christ' (2 Co 10¹, Mt 11²⁹), the perfect realization in Him of the spirit of beautiful confidence and loving obedience which we associate with Ps 23 (cf. *Ecce Homo*, chs. i. and ii. pp. 5, 6, 10, 12). But where the figure is explained, it is always in a sacrificial sense: 'He was led as a sheep to the slaughter' (Ac 8³²); 're-deemed . . . with precious blood, as of a lamb without blemish and without spot, (even the blood) of Christ' (1 P 1¹⁸·¹⁹); 'a Lamb standing as though it had been slain'; 'worthy is the Lamb that hath been slain' (Rev 5⁶·¹²); 'the book of life of the Lamb that hath been slain from the foundation of the world' (Rev 13⁸). In the same way John the Baptist hailed Jesus of Nazareth as 'the Lamb of God which taketh away the sin of the world' (Jn 1²⁹). It is superfluous to say (with Alford) that the reference is not to the Paschal lamb, 'which did not suggest atonement for sin'; on every day of the feast, as we have seen, lambs were offered as a burnt-offering; and if it was not Passover-time when John spoke, his hearers would readily understand his meaning from the sin-offering of the poor, or the morning and evening sacrifice of every day. These kept before the eyes of all Israelites the principle of substitution, the surrender of another life for the human life that was forfeited or consecrated (He 11⁴ 10¹⁰). John may have uttered his prophecy at the time of the regular evening sacrifice, the time at which the prophecy was afterwards to be fulfilled (Mt 27⁴⁵); but the language of Is 53⁷⁻¹² would of itself explain the meaning of his words. The correspondence of Christ's death with a sin-offering is distinctly assumed in He 13¹⁰⁻¹³, and St. Paul also sees in the occurrence of that death at Passover-time the true Passover sacrifice of the Lamb (1 Co 5⁷). We need not be concerned to limit to any one ceremony the thought in the mind of the Baptist: the Lamb, in his words, was the atoning Lamb. Christ (as M. Dods suggests in *Expos. Gr. Test.*) may have revealed the truth to him after the return from the Temptation in the wilderness: He Himself three times foretold His coming death (Mt 16[21] 17[22. 23] 20[18. 19]) before He repeated the substance of John's prophecy as His own (Mt 20[28]).

4. Christ is also '**the Good Shepherd**' (Jn 10[11. 14]), 'the Shepherd and Bishop (overseer, guardian) of souls' (1 P 2[25]), 'the chief Shepherd' (1 P 5[4]). His people are His flock (Jn 10[16], Lk 12[32]), as the chosen people of old were the flock of God (Ps 77[20] 79[13] 80[1] 95[7] 100[3]). As God undertook by the voice of His prophets to feed His flock (Is 40[11], Ezk 34[14. 15]), so Christ pledges Himself 'to give unto them eternal life' (Jn 10[28], cf.6[48-58]), to 'guide them unto fountains of waters of life' (Rev 7[17]). He requires of His sheep (Jn 10[14. 27]) the life of unquestioning obedience and trust which the Psalmist accepts with such happy contentment (Ps 23): He promises that no one shall snatch them out of His hand if they hear His voice and follow Him, if they make themselves familiar with Him (γιγνώσκουσι, v.[14]) as He makes it His concern to know them and to know the Father. When He speaks of 'the fold' in which they will find protection, He calls Himself 'the door' (Jn 10[7-10]) through which one must enter in to be made safe: He becomes the shepherd (vv.[11-16]) as He passes from the thought of the fold to describe the flock. So later (Jn 14[6]) He says, 'I am the way,' before He calls Himself 'the truth and the life.' No one 'fold' can include all His sheep (Jn 10[16]): the flock is greater than the fold, the shepherd more essential than the door: and the one necessary condition of the Christian life is the personal devotion and obedience to the living Shepherd. Where that condition is observed, there may be many folds, 'other sheep'; but He will know His own (v.[14]), and in the eyes of all at last 'they shall become one flock, one shepherd' (v.[16]).

In His more active ministry Christ found the appropriate figure for His disciples in the patient hard-working cattle which ploughed the earth to prepare it for men's food, or carried the burdens of their daily life (Mt 11[29. 30]): work under His guidance with the meek and lowly spirit is the secret of rest. It was as the shadows of the end fell upon Him that He returned to the OT figure of the sheep of God's pasture: 'Fear not, little flock' (Lk 12[32]), resumes the 'Be not afraid' of v.[4] at the close of the perilous scene when the crowded courtyard was His refuge from the hatred of His enemies (Lk 11[37-54]). So the beautiful pictures and promises of Jn 10 belong to the time of danger (v.[39]) in the closing winter (v.[22]) of His life, when He was being forced into the retirement (v.[40]) from which He came out at the risk of death to restore Lazarus to his sisters. The Shepherd's care of His sheep is the gospel first for the sorrowful and helpless: 'the whole portraiture of the Good Shepherd is a commentary on Is 53' (Westcott).

5. One other NT analogy is derived from the same figure. As rulers who 'observe dooms from Zeus' are called in the *Iliad* (i. 263, ii. 243, etc.) ποιμένες λαῶν (cf. Mic 5[4], Mt 2[6]), and he that receives authority over the nations 'shall shepherd them with a staff of iron' (Rev 2[27] 12[5] 19[15]), so the Church receives ποιμένας καὶ διδασκάλους among the gifts of its glorified Lord (Eph 4[11]). Their duty is to 'tend the flock of God' (1 P 5[2]), 'the flock in the which the Holy Ghost hath made you overseers' (Ac 20[28]): it is the false shepherds who 'without fear feed themselves' (Jude [12]). In 'tending' the flock, the first and last duty is to 'feed' it: βόσκε τὰ ἀρνία μου, ποίμαινε τὰ προβάτιά μου, βόσκε τὰ προβάτιά μου (Jn 21[15-17]). The shepherd's ways with

the sheep may be most winning and his music of the sweetest; but if he does not minister to them 'the bread of life,' other shepherds will have to be found who will 'feed them' (Jer 23[4]). As the shepherds themselves belong to the flock of Christ, they are also to be 'examples to the flock,' 'and when the chief Shepherd shall be manifested, ye shall receive the crown of glory that fadeth not away' (1 P 5[3. 4]).

LITERATURE.—For the sheep and shepherds of Palestine see Thomson, *The Land and the Book*, pp. 201-205; Geikie, *The Holy Land and the Bible*, pp. 13, 81-84; Post in Hastings' *DB* iv. 487; Shipley and Cook in *Encyc. Bibl.* iii. 4441 (cf. *ib.* i. 711). There are expository sermons in F. W. Robertson, *Serm.* 2nd ser. (1875) 251; H. Alford, *Eastertide Serm.* (1866), 32, 62; B. F. Westcott, *Revelation of the Father* (1884), 77; A. F. W. Ingram, *Good Shepherds* (1898); A. G. Mortimer, *Studies in Holy Scripture* (1901), 161; also W. Lock on 'the Sheep and the Goats' in *The Bible and Chr. Life* (1905), 162. For connected subjects see Literature under ATONEMENT, CHURCH, REDEEM, RULE (p. 539), SACRIFICE.   FRANK RICHARDS.

SHEKEL.—See MONEY.

SHEKINAH (Heb. שְׁכִינָה 'that which dwells' or 'resides,' the 'dwelling').—This term, together with 'the Glory' (יְקָרָא) and 'the Word' or 'Memra' (מֵימַר, מֵימְרָא), is used in the Targums as an indirect expression in place of 'God.' It denotes God's visible presence or glorious manifestation which 'dwells' among men: the localized presence of the Deity. See art. 'Shekinah' in Hastings' *DB*. In the NT the term Shekinah appears in more than one Greek form. The invisible Shekinah is also alluded to, as well as the visible. The visible Shekinah, though distinct from 'the glory,' was associated in the closest way with the Divine 'glory.' It was conceived of as the centre and source from which the glory radiated. In the NT this 'Shekinah-glory' is several times denoted by δόξα. The classical passage is Ro 9[4], where St. Paul, enumerating the list of Israel's privileges, says: 'whose is the adoption, *and the glory*,' *i.e.* the Shekinah-glory, 'the visible presence of God among His people' (cf. also Ac 7[2] where St. Stephen speaks of 'the God of glory,' *i.e.* the God whose visible presence, manifested in the Shekinah, had sanctified Jerusalem and the Temple). In the Gospels this 'glory' is referred to in Lk 2[9] 'the glory of the Lord (δόξα κυρίου) shone round about them.' There is also an obvious allusion to the Shekinah in the description of the theophanic cloud of the transfiguration-narrative (Mt 17[5] 'a bright cloud overshadowed them, and behold a voice out of the cloud, saying,' etc.; cf. Mk 9[7], Lk 9[34f.]). Here the same verb (ἐπισκιάζω) is used as in the LXX of Ex 40[34. 35] of the cloud which rested on the Tabernacle when it was filled with the 'glory of the Lord,' which in the Targum (pseudo-Jonathan) becomes the 'glory of the Shekinah of the Lord.' The 'voice out of the cloud' is also, doubtless, the voice of the Shekinah; cf. 2 P 1[17] where, in reference to the transfiguration, a 'voice' uttered by 'the excellent glory' (*i.e.* the Shekinah-glory) is spoken of.[*] In He 9[5] 'the cherubim of glory' must be explained in the same way, as meaning the cherubim on which the Shekinah was enthroned.

In three NT passages (all having reference to Christ)[†] an allusion to the Shekinah is probable, though disputed, viz. (a) Ro 6[4] 'Christ was raised from the dead by means of (διὰ) the glory of the Father.' Here 'glory' prob.=the Shekinah-glory rather than 'glorious power' (cf. the *Midrash Rabbe* to Gn 44[8], in which the Shekinah is said to release the bound in Sheol); [‡]

---

[*] Similarly in the Jerus. Targum to Gn 28[13] the *glory* of J″ says, 'I am the God of Abraham' (Marshall in Hastings' *DB*, *loc. cit.*).

[†] See Marshall, *ib.*

[‡] A similar idea may be implied in the words ascribed to our Lord in Jn 11[40], where, with reference to the release of Lazarus from the grave, Jesus says to Martha: 'Said I not unto thee, that, if thou believedst, thou shouldest see *the glory of God*?'

(b) 1 P 4¹⁴ 'the (Spirit) of glory and the Spirit of God' (τὸ τῆς δόξης καὶ τὸ τοῦ θεοῦ πνεῦμα). Here 'glory' may = Shekinah, which is identified with Christ. This identification may be seen more clearly, perhaps, in (c) Ja 2¹ τὴν πίστιν τοῦ κυρίου ἡμῶν Ἰησοῦ Χριστοῦ τῆς δόξης, which not improbably = 'the faith of our Lord Jesus Christ, the Shekinah' (Mayor). For further doubtful reff. in the NT, see below.

There can be no doubt that the word σκηνή, 'tabernacle' (and its verb σκηνοῦν, 'to tabernacle'), has been chosen for use in Jn 1¹⁴ and Rev 21³ from its likeness both in sound and meaning to the word Shekinah, and conveys a direct allusion to the latter. The Revelation passage runs : 'Behold the *tabernacle* (σκηνή) of God is with men, and he will *tabernacle* (σκηνώσει) with them.' In Jn 1¹⁴ 'The *Word* (Logos) . . . *tabernacled* (ἐσκήνωσεν) among us, and we beheld his *glory*,' etc., all the three Hebrew terms, *Memra* (מֵימְרָא = ὁ λόγος), *Shekinah*, and *Yeḳara* (δόξα = קְרָא) are represented. 'All the three entities became incarnate in Jesus.'*

The identification of Jesus with the Shekinah has already been referred to above in connexion with 1 P 4¹⁴ and Ja 2¹. Another example where the same idea may be implicit is Mt 18²⁰ 'Where two or three are gathered together in my name, there am I in the midst of them'; compare with this *Pirke Aboth* iii. 5 : 'Two that sit together and are occupied with words of Torah, have the Shekinah among them.' Cf. also 2 Co 4⁶ 'God that said, Out of darkness light shall shine, is he who shone in our hearts for the illumination of the knowledge of *the glory of God in the face of Jesus Christ*.' The last phrase may = the glory of God made manifest in the presence of Jesus Christ, i.e. Jesus is the Shekinah of God. Shekinah in these connexions is practically = Immanuel ('God with us').

Other passages worth examination in this connexion are Eph 1¹⁷ (the remarkable phrase 'the Father of the glory' [ὁ πατὴρ τῆς δόξης] = ? 'the father of the Shekinah (incarnate in Jesus)'), Lk 2³² ('the glory of thy people Israel'). Cf. also 1 Co 2⁸ (Jesus 'Lord of glory'). The representation of man as a temple in which God dwells (cf. 2 Co 6¹⁶ 'we are a temple of the living God,' Jn 14²³ 'we will come . . . and make our abode with him') was probably suggested by the Shekinah-idea, which may also have influenced the language applied to Christ in Col 2⁹ ('for in him dwelleth all the fulness of the Godhead bodily').

In the identification of the Shekinah and cognate conceptions with the incarnate Christ, 'a use is made of these ideas,' as Dalman says, 'which is at variance with their primary application.' It marks a specifically Christian development, though the way had certainly been prepared by hypostatizing tendencies.

LITERATURE.—Weber, *Jüd. Theol.*² esp. pp. 185–190 ; Gfrörer, *Das Jahrhundert des Heils*, i. esp. p. 301 ff. ; Langen, *Judenthum zur Zeit Christi*, 201 ff. ; art. 'Shekinah' in Hastings' *DB* and in *JE* ; the Lexicons, s.v. שכינה (Buxtorf, Levy, Jastrow, Kohut) ; Taylor, *Sayings of the Jewish Fathers*², p. 43 ; the Comm. on Ep. of St. James by Mayor and Knowling (on Ja 2¹).

G. H. BOX.

SHELAH.—A Judahite ancestor of our Lord (Lk 3³⁵).

SHEM.—The patriarch, mentioned as a link in our Lord's genealogy (Lk 3³⁶).

SHEWBREAD, 'bread of the face *or* presence' (*leḥem pānîm*), was placed on a special table in the Holy Place, in the presence of God. This was a very ancient custom in Israel, and is found also among other Semitic peoples. The bread was originally designed for the god to eat, but, of course, this early notion did not persist ; the bread, however, was still held to imply the presence of God, and His acceptance of the worship rendered to Him.

Shewbread is mentioned in the Gospels on only one occasion, Mt 12⁴ ∥ Mk 2²⁶ and Lk 6⁴. Jesus and His disciples, passing through the cultivated fields on the Sabbath, were plucking the ears of grain, rubbing out the kernels, and eating them. They were challenged by the Pharisees for doing what was unlawful on the Sabbath. The plucking of grain without instrument, while walking through another's field, was expressly permitted by the Jewish law, but the manual labour involved was interpreted as harvesting and threshing, which

* Dalman, *Words of Jesus*, p. 231. To these should be added the great passage in He 1³, where the Son is said to be the 'effulgence of *the glory*,' i.e. of the Shekinah-glory as 'the manifested Deity.'

were forbidden on the Sabbath. Jesus replied to the Pharisees by citing two illustrations (according to Mt.), one of which was an act of David as recorded in 1 S 21¹⁻⁶. In David's flight from Saul he had come to Nob, to Ahimelech the priest. He was hungry, and asked for food for himself and his men. There was no bread at hand except the shewbread, which, after lying on the table for the week, had been replaced by fresh bread. The bread is described as 'holy.' There is no hint in the passage that David did an unlawful thing in eating the bread. He did not do it without due deliberation, for the question of the legality was expressly raised by the priest. Before giving the men the bread, he asked if they were 'clean.' This was his one concern, and, being satisfied on this point, he readily gave it to them. If it had been unlawful for any to eat except the priests, that surely would have been stated, and the 'cleanness' would have been of no moment. In case the parley is considered, as it may be, to have been the effort of later tradition to clear the king from the charge of irregularity in the matter, the state of the case is not altered. The passage seems to show that no law was knowingly broken in the transaction.

Jesus, however, says that it was unlawful. The statement is in accord with the Jewish law of His day, which can be traced back to a provision of the Priests' Code from post-exilic times (Lv 24⁹), which says that the shewbread was for the priests, and must be eaten by them in the Holy Place. Such an act as David's was illegal in the time of Christ ; it was not illegal in the time of David. The real issue between Jesus and the Pharisees in Mt 12 was the extent to which such laws as that of the Sabbath were binding. The Jews held that the law was eternal, unchangeable, supreme. Jesus held that it was 'for man,' and the Son of Man was lord of it. More recently the argument of Jesus has been vastly strengthened by the recognition of the gradual development of the OT legislation. According to the Jews, their great king had violated the Law, and the only justification was the stress of his hunger ; but to use this argument to justify David was in effect to acknowledge the very principle upon which Jesus acted in allowing His disciples to pluck the grain.

LITERATURE.—Stade, *Bibl. Theol. des AT*, p. 168 ; art. 'Shewbread' in Hastings' *DB* and in the *JE*.   O. H. GATES.

SHILLING.—See MONEY.

SHIP.—See BOAT.

SHOE.—See SANDAL.

SHORE.—See BEACH.

SICK, SICKNESS.—See DISEASE.

SICKLE (δρέπανον).—The crops in Palestine are, to this day, reaped almost entirely with the sickle (Mk 4²⁹). The scythe is seldom seen save in the hands of a foreigner, and the whirr of the reaping machine is still unknown. δρέπανον is the LXX equivalent of two Heb. words חֶרְמֵשׁ and מַגָּל which seem to have been two names for the same thing. The Palestinian sickle is a little longer than our common shearing-hook ; the blade describes a somewhat wider curve, and the point, instead of terminating sharply, is slightly turned backward. Sometimes the edge is toothed like a saw, but oftener it is plain and sharp like our own hook. The total length of handle and blade is from 18 to 24 inches.   W. EWING.

SIDON (for much of common reference, see TYRE).

—A narrow, rocky district as well as a once famous city in Phœnicia, the city being 30 miles S. of Beirût and 26 miles slightly N. by E. of Tyre, and 60 miles N. of Capernaum. Like nearly all settlements on the east coast of the Mediterranean, Sidon owed its location to certain prominent rocks in the sea, which at first served as a breakwater, and then, through gradual connexion with the land, produced a northern and a southern harbour, the latter now filled with sand.

Sidon is so ancient that all certainty as to the origin of its name has vanished. Some have deemed it 'fishing'-town, others the seat of the worship of a deity Sid. Sidon and the Sidonians are heard of earlier and more influentially than Tyre, which finally distanced its northern rival. All the Phœnician cities seem to have known little but rivalry down to the appearance of such world-powers as Assyria, Babylonia, Persia, Greece, and Rome, which made them all, sooner or later, subject and abject. Each had its 'king,' its 'god,' its colonies, its coinage. Each sent its trading vessels seaward to the Mediterranean world; landward, each was in touch with the markets of Damascus and the East by means of those caravans of 'ships of the desert'; each sat as queen over a semicircular domain with a radius of some 15 to 20 miles. Through faction in the 8th cent. B.C. Sidon lost many of her merchants, chiefly to Tyre. At length her limited territory, her merely commercial aim, her being sapped by colonization and dissension, her final surrender of leadership to Tyre, combined with her conquests by the world-powers, left her under the Romans in the days of Christ a merely provincial capital, richer in the vices of ancient paganism than in its virtues. Some from Sidon were in the multitude that thronged Jesus at the Sea of Galilee (Mk 3⁸), and Sidon was pronounced more excusable in the day of judgment than the more favoured cities of Jesus' own country and race (Mt 11²¹ᶠ·). The present *Saida* has about 10,000 inhabitants, and is surrounded by delightful orange groves, beneath which lie archæological treasures. Beirût, with its Damascus railway and improved harbour, has robbed Sidon of its last vestiges of commerce.

In a sense Sidon was, and in another sense was not, within the limits of the Holy Land. In the ideal distribution of Canaan recorded in Joshua the lot of Asher would seem to have included about all of Phœnicia, extending 'even unto great Sidon' (Jos 19²⁸). The coast cities and their daughter villages, however, remained utterly unconscious of their assignment, while Asher became so assimilated thereto as to retain in Israelitish history little more than a name.

The RV declares that Jesus 'came through Sidon,' a distinct and exact statement unknown to the AV; and thereon depends our conception whether or not Jesus Himself, from choice, ever went into the way of the Gentiles. Many points as to the primariness, structure, and transmission of the Gospels are illustrated by this case.

Mt 15²¹ᶠᶠ· AV	Mk 7²⁴ᶠᶠ· AV
v.²¹ Then Jesus went thence, and departed into the coasts of Tyre and Sidon. v.²² And, behold, a woman of Canaan came out of the same coasts, etc.	v.²⁴ And from thence he arose, and went into the borders of Tyre and Sidon, and entered into an house, and would have no man know *it*: but he could not be hid. For a *certain* woman, etc. [A Greek].
v.²⁹ And Jesus departed from thence, and came nigh unto the sea of Galilee; and went up into a mountain, and sat down there.	v.³¹ And again, departing from the coasts of Tyre and Sidon, he came unto the sea of Galilee, through the midst of the coasts of Decapolis. [East of the Jordan].

After the Revisers' most conscientious work, with their better evidence, this is the form in which we read the same:

And Jesus went out thence, and withdrew into the parts of Tyre and Sidon. And, behold, a Canaanitish woman came out from those borders, etc.	And from thence he arose, and went away into the borders of Tyre and Sidon. And he entered into an house, and would have no man know it: and he could not be hid. But straightway a woman, etc. [A Greek].
	Marg. 'Some ancient authorities omit *and Sidon.*'
And Jesus departed thence, and came nigh unto the sea of Galilee; and he went up into the mountain, and sat there.	And again he went out from the borders of Tyre, and came through Sidon unto the sea of Galilee, through the midst of the borders of Decapolis.

B. Weiss sides completely with the 'some ancient authorities' of RVm, and reads: Jesus 'went away into the borders of Tyre. . . . And again he went out from the borders of Tyre, and came through Sidon unto the sea of Galilee,' etc. Thus the primary Gospel of Mark, the more ancient Sinaitic and Vatican MSS, Professor Weiss, and the Revisers do not hesitate to depict Jesus as entering Gentile territory (twice), entering a (probably) heathen house, and dispensing blessings upon a pagan woman, going then yet farther 'through Sidon' and Decapolis. The more theological First Evangelist, however, and the judicious transcribers disliked so to state the case. So Edersheim: the 'house in which Jesus sought shelter and privacy would, of course, be a Jewish home'; and 'by "through Sidon" I do not understand the town of that name, which would have been quite outside the Saviour's route, but the territory of Sidon' (*Life and Times*, ii. 38, 44).

Anything like a direct 'route' from the Israelitish borders of Tyre, or of Tyre and Sidon,—for Edersheim emphasizes Matthew's indication that the woman came from her territory to that of Jesus, —would take one in a south-easterly direction, and therefore away from Sidon. Accordingly, Jesus' choice to go in a northerly direction, 'through Sidon,' shows that He was not taking any near and direct and usual 'route,' but for a reason was seeking travel into heathen territory. Mk.'s connexion indicates that Jesus journeyed into the Gentile land with His disciples, on the occasion of the abolition of the Levitical distinctions as to the ceremonially clean and unclean, so as to give to His followers an example and object lesson as to the same. Sidon on the far north was for this reason included, as was the hog-herding Decapolis. It was at Cæsarea, a similar Gentile city almost 100 miles nearer Jerusalem, that St. Peter received his fuller lesson on the same subject.

WILBUR FLETCHER STEELE.

SIFTING.—The vb. 'sift' (Gr. σινιάζω, fr. σινίον, a late word for a sieve) occurs only in Lk 22³¹. Two varieties of sieve were used for separating the finer particles of substances from the grosser (see art. AGRICULTURE). Scripture refers to the sieve and the process of sifting only rarely (Is 30²⁸, Am 9⁹, Lk 22³¹), but is full of the idea of sifting. In this process the methods of different industries join to give force to the metaphor which they supply. Of these farming is the chief, with its floors, fans, etc. (Mt 3¹², Lk 3¹⁷). The preparation of wine also enters in with its emptying from vessel to vessel (Jer 48¹¹). The refining of metals (Is 1²⁵, Mal 3²ᶠ·), too, contributes to the contents of the idea of sifting. All these moralize it. It concentrates on character. St. Peter and his fellow-disciples [plur. ὑμᾶς] are sifted; Pharisees strain out gnats (Mt 23²⁴); evil work avoids the sifting of the light (Jn 3²⁰). The ministries of John, Jesus, and the Holy Spirit (Jn 16⁸), all have this trait— they sift men. Yet Jesus is Himself sifted by Satan, whose 'findings' are *nil* (Jn 14³⁰), while, also, the disciples are not above the Master. 'As the wheat in the sieve is shaken backwards and forwards, and thus the refuse separates itself from the grain, and falls out; so Satan wishes to trouble you and toss you about (by vexations, terrors, dangers, afflictions) in order to bring your faithfulness to me to decay' (Meyer's *Luke* 22[31]).* The case of St. Peter is not singular. St. Paul underwent the process (Ph 3[7], 2 Co 6[4ff.]). The sifting is a law of life. All the Father's chastenings are with a view to sift His children as wheat. It is of the essence of the ways of God with men alike in providence and grace. Its place in that economy is among the final, not initial, processes. Readier and rougher means of grace have their earlier day; this is a delicate, even final, means of dealing with the finest of the wheat.

LITERATURE.—*Ecce Homo*, ch. vi.; Bushnell's *New Life*, sermon on 'Spiritual Dislodgements'; Longfellow's *The Sifting of Peter*.
J. R. LEGGE.

SIGHING.—The expression of trouble by means of involuntary respiration. This expression is used in connexion with our Lord twice, both times in St. Mark's Gospel. It is expressed in 7[34] by the word στενάζω—in the LXX the equivalent of אנח—and in 8[12] by the compound ἀναστενάζω. In both instances the words appear in this Gospel alone, and only in these passages. The expression is evidently meant to convey the fact of the Lord's sympathy with men. In the first, the healing of the deaf and dumb man, our Lord felt the burden of the disease which He was about to cure. And here the expression is associated with prayer on His part: 'And, looking up to heaven, he sighed.' In the second, where a stronger expression is used through the compound, the Pharisees are asking for a sign, and He 'sighed in his spirit,' evidently thinking of the speedy appearance of the sign for which they asked, and mourning over the terrible nature which it would bear. On the 'groaning' of Jn 11[33, 38] see ANGER in vol. i. p. 62[b].
W. H. RANKINE.

SIGHT. — Christ rejoiced in His power of restoring sight to the physically blind (see below), and points to it as a most fitting exercise for One sent of God (Mt 11[5], Lk 7[21-22]; see also art. SIGN). When He speaks of Himself as Deliverer, in terms borrowed from the prophets (combining Is 61[1] and 42[6-7]), one of the chief features of the commission He announces is the recovering of sight to the blind (Lk 4[18-19]). At that rapt moment of high spiritual experience it is certain that, while bodily sight may be referred to, the emphasis lies on the higher vision He had come to impart. The need of man for true inward sight, for the knowledge of God and of self, was ever central to Jesus. That men should see Him and thus see the Father was the one burning passion of His life (Jn 14[9], cf. 16[12-13, 16] 17[3, 6, 25-26]). That men should have the capacity of vision and yet be blind to the true significance of Himself and His work, was a sincere embarrassment to Him (Mk 8[18]).

In Mt 6[22] and Lk 11[34-36] He employs bodily sight with its commanding relation to the whole of human activities as an image of inward vision. The eye was the means of guidance and surety and power to the whole body—the lamp (λύχνος) of the body. If the eye be unperverted ('single,' or, literally, 'simple,' ἁπλοῦς), the whole body is lighted for all the work it has to do. If 'evil' (πονηρός), the whole body is darkened, and every part of the complex activity is rendered inefficient if not impossible. So of the inward, mental and spiritual eye. The power of vision is central. If that

* Note that the point of the comparison lies in the *shaking*. Satan aims at destruction; Jesus is thinking of purification as the real result. Christ comes with His fan to get rid of chaff (Mt 3[12]); Satan sifts in order to get rid of wheat. For, as Thomas Fuller says somewhere, when Satan comes with his sieve, he desires to find the chaff and not the wheat.

capacity to see things as they are be unimpaired, the man can be and do that for which God created him. But the man who has lost his power of inward sight is enveloped in the deepest and most hopeless gloom. If the light in a man be darkness, how great is that darkness! On Mt 13[13ff.] see PARABLE, p. 315 f.; and on Jn 19[30ff.] see SEEING.

In our Lord's healing of the multitude which the Gospels on several occasions record, cases of blindness were found, loss of sight being then as now common in Syria. The common cause of loss of sight was and is ophthalmia, which varied in severity from a minor form causing redness of the lids and loss of the eyelashes, to an extreme form affecting the whole eyeball, lachrymal ducts, the glands, eyelids and lashes, and resulting in the total destruction of sight and the eyeball. The disease is still prevalent in the East, and especially in Syria, being traceable to the intensity of light and heat, and to the strong winds bearing sand and other injurious matter. The matter secreted from the inflamed glands is also transferred to other persons, making the disease highly contagious. Ophthalmia might also give rise to blindness from birth, by causing permanent opacity of the cornea.

Other affections of the parts connected with the organ of vision might produce blindness, *e.g.*, affection of the nerves. Mt 12[22] was a case of this kind, being probably also complicated with nervous disorder. The blindness, deafness, and dumbness point to some serious defect or disease in the nervous tissue which controls the organs of vision, hearing, and speech; and the mental disorder is organically connected with the cerebral disorganization.

As a rule, the cases of loss of sight are not sufficiently described to enable us to know what particular cause produces the blindness. Mt 9[27-31] is a case in point, the interest of the narrative being the quick faith of the blind and the sympathetic response of Jesus. The case of the man blind from his birth may have been due to any of the causes above mentioned, or to cataract (Jn 9). The feature of our Lord's cure of the blind is narrated in the above instances — His touching of the eyes. The blind man of Bethsaida (Mk 8[22-26]) was treated similarly. Twice Jesus laid His hands upon the blind eyes. Also He spit upon his eyes—having previously gently led him by the hand out of the village. He spoke to him also of the healing which they both desired, and called forth the energy of the man in response to His own power: 'Seest thou aught?' In this instance a process was observable in the recovery, or possibly there is indicated the difficulty in one who had never seen of being able to interpret to himself new sensations. In Jn 9 we note that Jesus speaks concerning the cure to be wrought. His words in Jn 9[3-5] would be spoken in the hearing of the one to be healed, and would have a salutary effect in restoring hopefulness to one who might not unnaturally have given up all hope of restoration. The eyes are anointed with clay and saliva, and the man sent in the obedience of a strong faith to a distant pool.

These two instances in which our Lord uses saliva recall the familiar folk-lore of curing sore eyes. The use of saliva, especially of fasting saliva, for bleared eyes, still persists. The Talmud ascribes special efficacy to the saliva of an eldest son. Royal saliva was greatly in request for healing purposes, and an instance is recorded of Vespasian using his saliva with excellent effect, after having first inquired of the physician if the malady were curable (Tacitus, *Hist.* iv. 2; Suetonius, *Vespasian*, 7). Our Lord's use of saliva, or of saliva and clay, had no connexion with these as physical remedies, but may have been designed to encourage the mind of the patients, who were familiar with the remedy. And it is significant that all the action of Jesus was upon the psychical side. The means taken were exactly adapted to call out the response of the patient, and to evoke a real co-operation between Healer and healed. Cf. the means used in Mk 8$^{22-26}$, and for the deaf mute in Mk 7$^{31-35}$, the signs employed being evidently meant for the one to be restored.

We may note (1) that both Jn. and Mk. in the last two cases, give substantially the same account of the methods employed by Jesus. Considering the wide difference in the standpoint of the two writers, this is most significant, and indicates clearly that both descriptions are drawn from life, and that the actual method of Jesus was remembered and so far understood as to be regarded as memorable. (2) The suggestive likeness between the action of Jesus and modern therapeutic methods. Not that these deeds of Jesus are explained by the latter, but that the Divine life manifested in Him did not work on totally different lines, although His method completely overpassed and overwhelmed them in essential power. See also BLINDNESS, and SEEING.

LITERATURE.—Martineau, *End. after the Christian Life*, p. 463; Phillips Brooks, *Candle of the Lord*, p. 74; N. Smyth, *Reality of Faith* (1888), 1; B. Wilberforce, *Speaking Good of His Name* (1904), 137; Macmillan, *Ministry of Nature*, ch. xii.; Hastings' *DB*, art. 'Medicine'; *Comm.* on passages referred to; Trench and W. M. Taylor on *Miracles*.

T. H. WRIGHT.

SIGN (σημεῖον, *signum*).—The Gospels contain many references to signs in connexion with the anticipations of Messiah's advent and with the life and work of Jesus Christ. But the various shades and degrees of significance attached to the word 'sign' by speakers, writers, and the people generally, must be carefully discriminated by a close regard to the particular occasion on which it is employed. Most of all must distinction be made between the value placed upon the word by the people of our Lord's time and by our Lord Himself.

1. The fixed expectation of the generation into which Jesus was born, that signs would be associated with every true prophet and reformer and supremely with the Messiah, that marvellous events, largely of a material character, would occur in connexion with every authoritative teacher, and with every manifestation of the will of God, was part of the mental fabric of the Jewish people. The depth to which this expectation penetrated into the general consciousness may be judged by the traces of it in the Apostolic writers and in those trained under their influence. The Apostles generally did not easily throw aside Jewish prepossessions in regard to the kind of phenomena which might be expected to accompany a Messianic advent or a Divine revelation. Although they lay the main emphasis on the ethical and spiritual elements of Christian authority, the lower conceptions persist, and often no clear distinction is made between the σημεῖον and the τέρας (cf. Mt 24$^{29f.}$, Mk 13$^{24f.}$, Lk 21$^{11. 25}$, Ac 2^{22}, He 2^4, 2 Co 12^{12}, Rev 12^1 13^{13} 15^1 16^{14} 19^{20}, 2 Th 2$^{8f.}$).

It is abundantly clear that the general assumption was made that credentials of a striking and material character must be demanded of the Messiah as a proof of the authority of His teaching and Person. Repeatedly the Jews, and especially the scribes, Pharisees, and Sadducees (see below), pressed this demand upon Jesus. They wanted a clear convincing proof of His authority. The signs they had seen were possible by collusion with the powers that rule the lower world, by a compact with Beelzebub (Mk 3^{22}). Only a sign in the heavens would satisfy them. Clearly what they

sought was of the nature of a prodigy, properly to be classed with the τέρατα, with which our Lord stedfastly refused to have any part or lot. Similarly, Herod's desire to see Jesus was animated by his wish to see a miracle (σημεῖον) performed by Him. We can be sure that what Herod desired had more relation to prodigies, as most in harmony with his nature and suited to his capacity, and the word used is due to the Evangelist, who himself drew no clear line between the σημεῖον and the τέρας (Lk 23^8).

2. *Our Lord's attitude towards signs.*—Indications are given that the common expectation of signs on the part of His generation was not without its solicitation to Jesus. One temptation in the wilderness was an urgent pressure on the noblest side of His nature to give a sign of this character with the view of gaining a more speedy influence over the people (Mt 4$^{5-7}$, Lk 4$^{9-12}$). The temptation was resisted and overcome. Our Lord would put no trust in external and magical signs for the furtherance of His work or the emphasizing and enforcing of His teaching. He knew their futility for the purpose of bringing real conviction to men (Lk 16^{31}). And the strenuous effort of His life was to resist these unspiritual conceptions of truth and reality.

The request for a sign in confirmation of His teaching He uniformly refused. The apparent response in Jn 2^{18} is no exception. The sign He would give would be granted only in its due place as His career was consummated by His own resurrection. Jn 6^{26} contains an apparent commendation of those who accepted Him because of His wonder-working, but it was only a relative commendation in comparison with the far lower spirit which was unconcerned about any spiritual authority so long as their physical wants were easily and bountifully provided. Lk 7$^{21-22}$ on the surface appears to be a sign given for the sake of convincing John the Baptist, and if ever our Lord could have departed from His habitual way, it was to help that lone prisoner, suffering mental and spiritual anguish because the work Messiah was doing was so unlike what he had expected—deeds of quiet beneficence instead of sharp vengeance against iniquity. But the action sprang out of the Divine impulse as our Lord, deeply moved by John's doubt, realized afresh that to bless and heal men was the truest mark of One sent of God.

Jesus resolutely and persistently refused to give any external sign for the sake of evidencing His claims, and only in the most chary manner spoke of His miracles as signs. He chose rather to call them ἔργα ('works') arising out of the need of man and prompted by His own inner life in response to that need (see art. MIRACLES). His works were 'signs' because they were part of His whole revelation of God, and elsewhere He regards opportunities for His miracles as occasions for the manifestation of the works of God (Jn 9^3), or for the glorifying of Himself (11^4). Self-manifestation and Divine revelation were identical in the mind of Jesus (14^{13}). Clearly our Lord only refrained from applying the word σημεῖα to His miracles because of the general associations of the word. To Him they were vital parts of the revelation of Divine power which He came to give.

A very particular and urgently-pressed demand for a sign 'in the heavens' is recorded in Mt 12$^{38-41}$ 16$^{1-4}$, Mk 8$^{11-12}$, and Lk 11$^{16. 29-32}$. The various accounts give a full idea of the occasion, or occasions. Mk. records the astonishment and bewilderment of Jesus at such a claim made by those who professed to be religious leaders. In an age which was full of signs, in which He Himself had been the most signal manifestation of the Divine presence and power, these religious teachers were still asking for signs. 'Why doth this generation seek after a sign? No sign shall be given.' Mt. and Lk. record our Lord's answer that no sign should be given but that of Jonah. Lk. gives the explanation of that sign to the Ninevites as consisting in the man and his message, not in his deliverance from the sea-monster, which they could only have believed on the strength of their faith in the man himself. Mt 16[1-4] gives the same interpretation, as also does Mt 12[38-39. 41], which forms a consistent whole and regards Jonah's preaching as the sign. Mt 12[40], with its parallel to the Resurrection of Jesus, must be regarded as an afterthought incorporated incongruously into the narrative. And the chief point is that our Lord declares that the one Divine sign to that generation was Himself, the Son of Man, His Person and His teaching. Simeon, under the exaltation of the Spirit, gives expression to the same essential truth (Lk 2[34]). Jesus entirely severs Himself from the common conception of a sign. A mere sign was the prodigy desired by an evil generation; His 'works' were signs in the truer and higher sense of having in them a spiritual and Divine significance, and as pointing to greater possibilities of soul and higher regions of reality. They were signs of the Divine power and life which dwelt in Himself.

Jn 10[41], declaring the embarrassment felt by those who were conscious of the truth of the Baptist's message regarding Christ, together with the fact that he 'wrought no sign,' is witness that more spiritual conceptions were breaking through the ancient crust of superstition. And the Fourth Gospel is evidence that one Evangelist was able to disentangle the spiritual and ethical from the material and catastrophic. The conceptions of Christ's power set forth in this Gospel are of a distinctly more spiritual order. The word used by the writer is invariably σημεῖον (Jn 2[11] 3[2] 4[54], etc.), and there are plain indications that the truer and higher significance was attached to it. The value of the sign is seen to be its revealing quality. The miracle of the Cana-marriage is described as the beginning of His signs, in which He manifested forth His glory (ἐφανέρωσε τὴν δόξαν αὑτοῦ), showing that the disciple had truly apprehended the Master's teaching.

T. H. WRIGHT.

SILENCE. — 'Speech is of time, Silence is of Eternity. Thought will not work except in Silence; neither will Virtue work except in Secrecy.' Carlyle's words (*Sart.* 151) are well known and profoundly true. The silences of great men are often more significant and self-revealing than their words. Silence has an eloquence that speech cannot rival. It is in silence that souls meet and strong emotions pass from one to the other. This is peculiarly true of Jesus, whose character can never be fathomed without a special study of His silences. The sayings of Jesus are limpid gems of ethical thought, flawless in their purity, enunciating principles of universal applicability. His deeds are the perfect expression of His sinless nature. But His silences are as essentially significant of the impression He made upon the world, for they reveal the spiritual atmosphere in which He lived and which determined His attitude to human life and to the problems of human nature.

1. For thirty years after His advent, Jesus was silent as to His mission. He allowed Himself ample time for the natural development of all His powers and faculties. He passed through the ordinary phases of childhood, boyhood, youth, and attained the maturity of manhood before He took up the burden of His brief career. It is the lesson of self-repression, of concentrated preparation for

a great work. Jesus took no step He was obliged on maturer consideration to retract.

2. And before He took up His lifework there is a still deeper and more significant silence, the silence of the Temptation (Mt 4[1-11], Mk 1[12. 13], Lk 4[1-13]). Acts are but symbols, the true human drama is the drama of the soul. All epoch-making events have been lived through in some human soul before they emerged upon the arena of history. It was in the monastery of Erfurt that the Reformation was wrought out. It was in the cave of Manresa its victorious progress was stayed. And it was in the wilderness that Jesus lived His life, fought His tremendous battle with evil, faced every possible contingency of temptation, and came out victorious. In the silence of His own great soul was the campaign finished and the adversary baffled.

3. After the ordeal in the wilderness, Jesus began His active career, which was merely the symbol and seal of the victory already gained. The Synoptists are uniform in asserting that during the greater part of His ministry He was silent as to His Messiahship and His supernatural origin. His teaching, of which the Sermon on the Mount is a summary, is purely ethical. The first indication of any recognition of His true nature is to be found in the striking incident near Cæsarea Philippi, and it is significant that it is the spontaneous acclamation of His own disciples. It is Peter who gives expression to the general feeling in the historic words, 'Thou art the Christ, the Son of the living God.' Peter's confession draws forth the immediate injunction to the disciples that they tell no man that He was Jesus the Christ (Mt 16[20]). This silence of Jesus as to His Messiahship was not merely, or mainly, from motives of prudence. It was because the only homage He valued was the homage that sprang from a real perception of the inherent *Divineness* of His character. He sought to draw out of men a recognition of His Divine nature by the sheer force of His Personality. It was the tribute of the heart, the spontaneous uprising of the spiritual instinct in response to His Godhood, that alone had ethical worth. The mere tribute of the lips, the result of convention or authority, was meaningless to Him. Jesus was silent in order that those who knew and loved Him, and in whose soul the Divine energy was working, might testify of Him.

4. The silence of Jesus regarding His miracles is significant of His own attitude towards them (Mk 3[12], Lk 5[14]). Silence here cannot have been from prudential considerations, for miracles must undoubtedly have enhanced His reputation among the people, and it was His refusal to work miracles to gratify the Pharisees that formed the ground of their offence against Him (Mt 16[1ff.]). But Jesus knew how little miracles really proved. He knew that the faith given to Him merely on account of the physical marvels He did was on a distinctly lower level than the soul's spontaneous recognition of His spiritual transcendence (Jn 14[11]). He was afraid that the unhealthy craving of a superstitious people would dull their perception of ethical truth.

5. Very striking is the silence of Jesus to direct questions asked. He never ignores a question sincerely put, or even when it is put as a challenge, but He rarely gives it a categorical answer (Mt 11[3] 16[1] 21[23] 22[16. 34], Mk 10[17], Lk 13[13]). He generally rises above the individual case and settles the general principle of which it is an instance. Jesus knew what was in men. He answers their thought rather than their words. Soul meets soul with no interposing medium of physical utterance. The sincere seeker after truth gets a truth deeper than he dreamt of, while the insincere casuist is put to silence.

6. There are various striking silences of Jesus to individuals which have each its own peculiar meaning. (1) *The silence of probation* (Mt 15²³). When the Syrophœnician woman pleads with Jesus to cure her daughter, He answers her not a word. When she persists in her pleading, in spite of all dissuasion, He speaks, but the ethical position of the two is strangely inverted. The words of Jesus breathe the narrowness of Judaism. Those of the woman reflect the universality of the gospel. This silence of Jesus to her pitiful entreaty is the silence of probation. He recognizes her faith ; and because He sees it will stand the strain, He tests it to the uttermost. See SYRO-PHŒNICIAN WOMAN.

(2) *The silence of horror* (Mt 14¹³). When Jesus heard of the death of John the Baptist, He said no word, but departed into a desert place to calm the tumult of His spirit in silence. The iniquity of the world He had come to redeem swept over the pure spirit of Jesus with such overwhelming force that utterance was choked, and His human nature had to seek, in silence, communion with the Father in order to regain its equanimity. It is a silence more eloquent than words of vehement denunciation would have been. It is the instinctive shrinking of a high nature from the grossness and baseness of sin.

(3) *The silence of shame* (Jn 8⁶). *The Pericope Adulteræ*, though not in the original Gospel of St. John, must have belonged to a very early tradition. It is the birth of the Christian grace of modesty. When confronted with the woman, Jesus is silent, stoops down, and writes upon the ground. He averts His face from the shameful spectacle. He is filled with pity and sorrow for the woman who has lost the virgin glory of her womanhood, and with indignation against the men whose shameless indelicacy in exposing her fault shows that they utterly fail to realize in what the true gravamen of her offence consists. To the pure soul of Jesus the sin of the one is greater than the sin of the other. Hence His words, ' He that is without sin among you, let him first cast a stone at her.' The rebuke strikes home, the sense of shame flushes their cheeks, and the woman's accusers silently steal away.

(4) *The silence of indignation* (Mt 26⁶³, Mk 14⁶¹). Jesus, after His apprehension, was first led before Caiaphas, the high priest. Caiaphas sought to incriminate Him by bringing against Him witnesses who made garbled and irrelevant statements of words they had heard Him utter. The high priest urged Him to say something in His defence, but Jesus held His peace. It was the silence of indignation against the utter mockery of His trial and the attitude of the time-serving president of the Court.

(5) *The silence of contempt* (Lk 23⁹). Herod was a different type. He is the representative of superstitious profligacy. Herod was a weak man, with a conscience certainly, but a conscience that could be touched only by his superstitious fears. He liked to have a saint under his patronage, provided the saint would be pliable enough to leave his patron's vices unrebuked. He had tried John the Baptist, but that experiment had failed, and now he would try Jesus. And so he questioned Him in many words, but Jesus answered him nothing. Here is apparently a seeker after truth to whom Jesus has nothing to say. It is not so. The gospel refuses the patronage of the vicious. Jesus has nothing to say to craven superstition seeking to condone its own vices by taking religion under its protection.

(6) *The silence of self-containment* (Jn 19⁹). Pilate, again, represents another and a higher type. To him Jesus opened Himself more fully than to any of His judges. He recognized in him one whose instincts were those of a capable and genuine ruler, and He sympathized with the dilemma in which Pilate was placed. Though the final decision rested with Pilate, he was the least guilty of all who were responsible for the tragedy of Calvary (Jn 19¹¹). In Pilate's soul a great struggle was going on. He was looking for a way of escape from a difficult situation, but he dared not take the only way that true magnanimity required. He dared not be true to his own high function of asserting the impartial justice of Imperial Rome, and the result was moral ruin. It is always so with Jesus. To the soul that once recognizes His claims no half measures are possible. It is all or nothing— absolute loyalty or a treason that leads downwards to the pit. And Jesus had a clear perception of the character of the Roman ruler, who alone had insight enough to recognize the essential greatness of his prisoner. One imperial soul met another. On the plane on which they met there was no difficulty of intercommunication. Jesus has no hesitation in asserting His royalty and His claim to be the Revealer of eternal truth. Pilate has culture enough at least to understand what He means, and his scepticism is the scepticism of sadness and perplexity rather than of scorn. But when Pilate, struck with the largeness of soul displayed by Jesus, touches on the higher mysteries, He is silent. To the question, ' Whence art thou ? ' Jesus has nothing to say. It is not that He fears to commit Himself. It is simply that He cannot give an answer that would be intelligible to Pilate.

(7) *The silence of self-absorption.* There have been many commentaries on the seven words of Jesus on the cross, but His silence there is as striking as His speech. Jesus has nothing to say to the jeers and mockery of the infuriated people, or to the taunts of priests and Pharisees. He is self-absorbed. For the self-hood of Jesus is His mission, His purpose, the idea of His life. And even in the agony of the cruelest death the malignity of man has ever devised, He is not shaken out of this self-absorption. His words have all reference to the central idea which constitutes His earthly existence. Pity for sinning humanity, love for those whose hearts are His, His attitude to the Father with whom all along He has realized His oneness,—these are the emotions that dominate His soul. There is not even the faintest trace of anger against those who have wreaked their vengeance upon Him. There is scarcely even a consciousness of their presence.

7. It is instructive to note the different valuation put upon speech and silence by Jesus and those who surrounded Him. Jesus silenced the Sadducees when they propounded to Him knotty points of theology (Mt 22³⁴), and suffered not the demons to speak (Mk 1³⁴). But when the multitude rebuked the blind men who cried importunately to Him at the gate of Jericho, Jesus listened to their appeal (Mt 20³¹) ; and when the disciples sought to silence the mothers who brought their children to be blessed, Jesus encouraged them with one of His most striking and characteristic sayings (Mt 19¹³, Mk 10¹³, Lk 18¹⁵). And, further, He who in the earlier part of His career carefully concealed His Messiahship from the people, on the critical occasion when He made His triumphant entry into Jerusalem gave an emphatic refusal to silence the acclamations with which He was hailed by the people.

LITERATURE.—Carlyle, *Sartor Resartus* ; Maeterlinck, *Treasure of the Humble* ; E. A. Abbott, *Philochristus* ; Seeley, *Ecce Homo* ; the various Lives of Christ ; W. M. Taylor, *The Silence of Jesus* (1894), p. 105 ; H. P. Liddon, *Passiontide Sermons* (1891), p. 153 ; W. W. Sidey, *The Silent Christ* (1903) ; A. Maclaren, *The Holy of Holies* (1890), p. 255 ; Phillips Brooks, *The Light of the World* (1891), p. 124.   A. MILLER.

SILOAM.—Josephus (*BJ* v. iv. 1) places the spring at the mouth of the Tyropœon Valley. This, and references of later writers, point to *Birket Silwān*, on the slope S. of the Temple area. A larger pool, *Birket el-Ḥamra*, now almost filled up, lies lower in the valley. *Birket Silwān* is built within the rock-hewn space occupied by the original pool, 75 ft. × 71 ft. The water was approached by steps cut in the rock. In NT times a covered arcade within the pool, 22½ ft. high and 12 ft. wide, ran round the four sides. From '*Ain Sitti Maryam*, the Fountain of the Virgin, on the slope below the eastern battlements, a conduit led the water to the pool; but, probably in Hezekiah's time, a tunnel was cut through the rock, and the fountain apparently covered over, as Josephus does not seem to have known it apart from Siloam. An inscription in ancient Heb. characters was found on the wall of the tunnel in 1880, which gives an account of the cutting. The tunnel is about ⅓ of a mile in length. It is bent as if to avoid obstructions. Two shafts to the surface, at important points, would afford guidance as to direction. The spring is intermittent. During the rains it may flow twice a day, but in the late summer, once in two days. Such springs are held in superstitious reverence, and credited with power to heal many diseases. Josephus pronounces the water good and plentiful, and says that this and other fountains flowed more copiously after falling into the hands of Titus.

The phrase 'tower in Siloam' (Lk 13⁴) perhaps indicates that this part of the city was called Siloam, 'the tower' being part of the adjoining wall.

A church was built above the pool in the 5th cent., and later was altered by Justinian. Ruins, possibly of this building, block a great part of the pool.

On the last day of the Feast of Tabernacles, water from this fountain was poured on the altar (Neubauer, *Géog. du Talm.* 145). In the 10th cent. the water was 'good' (Muḳaddasi); it is good no longer, percolating, as it does, through vast accumulations of refuse. The village of Siloam, *Kefr Silwān*, on the E. slope of the valley, over against the pool, dates from post-Arab times. Its handful of poor inhabitants still use the impure water for domestic purposes.   W. EWING.

SILVER.—See MONEY.

SIMEON (Συμεών) is a transliteration into Greek of the common Heb. name שִׁמְעוֹן, which is first met with as that of the second son of Jacob and Leah in Gn 29³³, where a derivation from שָׁמַע, 'hear,' is suggested.

1. An aged saint (Lk 2²⁵ff.), who took the infant Jesus in his arms at the Presentation in the Temple on the completion of the mother's period of purification, and broke out into an exultant song of praise. Afterwards he foretold to Mary the varied results that would attend the mission of her son.

He has been identified with a Rabbi of the same name, who is described as the son of Hillel and father of Gamaliel I.; but the original author (*Shabbath*, 15*a*) merely mentions him as intermediate between Hillel and Gamaliel as *Nasi* of the Sanhedrin. Beyond that statement, which is not in the Mishna, nothing is known of him; and the Lukan phrase, 'a man in Jerusalem whose name was Simeon,' is too modest to allow of identification with one who was at once the son of Hillel and the leading authority on jurisprudence in the nation. Another legend is preserved in the *Gospel of Nicodemus*, to the effect that Charinus and Leucius, two sons of Simeon, had been raised from the dead, and had been summoned to describe before the Sanhedrin the occurrences they had witnessed in the underworld at the death of Jesus. Their narrative is said to have been afterwards reported to Pilate, who ordered its incorporation in the official *Acts* of his procuratorate. This Apocryphal Gospel is not only of a late date (4th or even 5th cent.), but was evidently composed in the interest of apologetics, with a view particularly to represent the resurrection of Jesus as attested by evidence which even His enemies regarded as irrefutable. Until the period of uncritical search for legends in the 13th cent., little historical value was ascribed to the story, which may be confidently regarded as destitute of any.

Of the lineage or descendants of Simeon no contemporary evidence has survived; and for the man himself St. Luke is our only authority.

Simeon is described as (1) 'righteous and devout,' or conscientious in regard to God and His law (cf. Ac 22¹²); (2) as looking for the Messiah; and (3) as moved by the Holy Spirit (not merely the spirit of prophecy) to believe that he would not die before he had seen the Messiah. Guided by the Spirit to the courts of the Temple, he no sooner saw Jesus there than the words of the famous *Nunc Dimittis* (wh. see) rose to his lips. Whilst Mary was wondering at the meaning of such words, Simeon turned to her and foretold the diverse results of the mission of Jesus. A stumbling-block and an offence to some, it would be the inspiration of a new life to others; and with her own blessedness would mingle anguish unspeakable. In the issue the deepest needs of many souls would be excited and met, and men's hearts would be probed, enriched, and satisfied. After this brief appearance in history, Simeon passes again into obscurity, leaving only a few imperishable words behind him.

2. An ancestor, otherwise unknown, of Joseph, the husband of Mary (Lk 3³⁰). In this case, with some inconsistency, RV turns the name into '**Symeon**' (as in Ac 13¹ 15¹⁴), which is the more normal vocalization of the Greek, though not of the Hebrew.   R. W. MOSS.

SIMON.—The form *Simon* is not a transcription of שִׁמְעוֹן, but is either a contraction for *Simeon* or an independent Greek name. The latter view is much the more probable. In the NT the name is frequent. The Gospels mention—**1.** Simon the brother of our Lord (Mt 13⁵⁵, Mk 6³). **2.** Simon the Zealot (see CANANÆAN), one of the twelve Apostles (Mk 3¹⁸ ∥). **3.** Simon of Cyrene, who was impressed to bear our Lord's cross (Mt 27³² ∥). **4.** Simon 'the leper,' in whose house the anointing of our Lord by Mary of Bethany took place (Mt 26⁶, Mk 14³). **5.** Simon the Pharisee, in whose house the penitent woman anointed our Lord's head and feet (Lk 7³⁶ff.). See ANOINTING. **6.** Simon the father of Judas Iscariot (Jn 6⁷¹ 13². ²⁶). **7.** Simon Peter. See PETER.   W. PATRICK.

SIMPLE, SIMPLICITY (ἁπλοῦς, ἁπλότης; the latter does not occur in the Gospels; the former only in Mt 6²² and Lk 11³⁴).

The words ἁπλοῦς, 'simple,' and 'single' spring from the one root (Giles, *Man. of Comp. Philol.* p. 156). It appears in Greek in ἵν (= σμεν), ἅμα, and as ἁ in ἅπαξ and ἁπλοῦς; in Lat. in *semel*, *simul*, *simplex*, and *similis*; in Eng. in *same*, *simple*, and *single*. The basal meaning, therefore, is *oneness*, *sameness* (cf. 'one and the same'); the fundamental contrast is between one and more than one; and only in *similis* and its derivatives does it branch out into the idea of *likeness*. In medicines it yields the antithesis: simple or pure *v.* mixed or adulterated; in other realms, that of single or double—as of a road, the sole of a shoe, etc. The former, transferred to the moral sphere, gives the idea of *purity*, *genuineness*; the latter, that of *singleness*, *openness*, *frankness*, *straightforwardness*, *simplicity*, *candour*, *artlessness*. The antithesis in the former is *impurity*, *adulteration*; in the latter, *double-mindedness*, *duplicity*, *hypocrisy*, etc. The two conceptions really flow together in *guilelessness*, *sincerity*.

These meanings are found throughout the classical and NT periods. A third appears in Isoc. and Arist., where the word sometimes descends to *silliness* or *folly*, as in English. But this is never so in LXX or NT (see Liddell and Scott, Cremer, and Hastings' *DB*, *s.v.*). Of the meanings given above, 'singleness' almost exhausts the thought of simplicity in the Gospels. But 'guilelessness' is so close to it that it must also be briefly treated. Other Eng. senses of the word, as well as the idea of purity above, do not properly come under this head in the Gospels.

1. The leading passage is Mt 6²². In that chapter Jesus expounds the first great commandment touching our duty to God, as in 7¹⁻¹² He enforces the second, which concerns our duty to man (cf. Mk 12[29-31]). The form of the teaching was determined by Pharisaism, which serves as a dark foil for the truth. Outwardly religious, the Pharisees were essentially worldly. Professing ostentatiously to be servants of God and shepherds of the people, they were oppressors of the people and servants of their own selfish ambitions. Thus they lived a double life, loving the praise of men more than the praise of God. Over against their worldliness, with its doubleness and hypocrisy, Jesus sets before us the obligation to obey and please God in everything as our supreme duty (vv.[1-18]), while in vv.[19-32] He meets our unbelieving fear that such a course would bring loss and bankruptcy, by assuring us that we may well trust our Heavenly Father's care. It is all summed up in v.[33f.] in the command to seek first God's Kingdom and righteousness, and in the promise that He will give all needful earthly good, so that we need not worry. That this singleness of aim is the main thought, is clear from the illustration He employs in v.[22]. The 'single' eye is that which looks at one object alone, and sees that clearly ; as contrasted with it, the 'evil' eye is that which (not 'sees double,' but) endeavours to look at two objects at the same time (and the context suggests two in opposite directions), and therefore sees neither clearly. The natural antithesis to ἁπλοῦς would have been διπλοῦς, instead of which πονηρός is used, both to turn attention sharply from the physical to the moral which it was meant to illustrate, and, by avoiding the thought of 'seeing double,' which διπλοῦς in itself would naturally suggest, to make it easier to think of the unusual attempt to see things in opposite directions, and so pass to the common moral experience of cherishing, as objects of ambition, things that are diametrically opposed. Accordingly, πονηρός must be interpreted as 'evil' in this particular sense. For the double aim to serve God and mammon is evil, both in its very nature, as being really a rejection of the sole sovereignty of God, and in its results, as leading inevitably to the double life with its darkness and doom. Such a life is only apparently possible. Really it is impossible ; a choice must be made. We cannot serve God and mammon. Pharisees could not believe, because they sought glory from one another rather than the glory that comes from God (Jn 5[44] ; cf. Jn 12[42f.]). Life becomes simple when we accept God's will as our law and His Kingdom as the object of our endeavour. And that life leads to the blessings here mentioned. It floods the whole being with light. It means, as surely as God cares for birds and flowers (v.[22]), that He will care for our temporal needs better than any man can care for himself, though he be rich, cultured, and powerful as King Solomon (vv.[25-32]). Moreover, it ensures imperishable treasures in heaven (v.[19]).

2. The passage in Lk. (11[34-36]) is to the same effect. That wicked generation forms the background (v.[29]). Some of them had charged Jesus with being in league with Beelzebub (v.[15] ; Mt. calls them 'Pharisees,' 12[24] ; Mk. 'scribes,' 3[32]). In refuting that charge, He declares that it is by the finger of God He casts out demons, and that therefore in Him the Kingdom of God has come near to them (v.[20]). The man who is not with Him is against Him (v.[23]), and therefore against God. None such can be blessed, but only those who hear God's word and keep it (v.[28]). Then to the thronging multitudes He points out the sin of that generation (v.[29]). He is a sign to them, as Jonah was to Nineveh. But inasmuch as He is superior to Jonah and all who have gone before Him (vv.[31, 32]), and His light has not been hidden, but conspicuous (v.[33]), He has, with unparalleled clearness, presented to men God's claim upon themselves. Then, with a swift turn to personal warning and appeal (shown

in the singular pronoun), He declares to each of them that, if he strives to lead the double life, he will inevitably be guilty of refusing God's claim, and so will sink into darkness and condemnation ; but if, with single-eyed devotion, he heeds God's message and claim, he shall be filled with light and blessedness.

3. Very similar to this is the thought in Mt 11[16-30], though the word ἁπλοῦς is not employed. The upbraided cities, with much formal religion, were yet devoted to mammon and had no real heart for God. Hence their darkened judgment, as shown by their inability to understand John or Jesus, and hence their inevitable doom. Over against these worldly 'wise and understanding' people Jesus sets the 'babes'—those who, less wise in their generation than the children of the world (cf. Lk 16[8]), cry out in their need and helplessness not for the world's prizes, but for the One they must have, even the Father. Their cry the Father answers ; to all such the Son gives rest. The same idea is expressed pointedly in Lk 10[20] ('rather rejoice that your names are written in heaven') and Lk 10[42], where the one thing needful is to listen to Him. This passage (Mt 11[16-30]) shows how easily the transition is made from 'singleness of aim' to 'childlike guilelessness.' In the eyes of the world this may seem foolishness, but in Jesus' thought it is wisdom (11[19]). It is a mark of those in His Kingdom (Mt 18[3ff.], Mk 10[15], Lk 18[15-17]). Apart from these, there are only two or three passages that properly belong here. One is Mt 10[16]. The Eng. 'harmless,' based on a false derivation of ἀκέραιος, is unfortunate. It should be 'guileless' or 'simple' as in the Lat. and many Eng. versions. Prudence alone may lead to trickery ; simplicity alone, to silliness. The Apostles are to be both prudent and guileless. Nathanael is already an illustration of it—it constitutes the true spiritual Israelite (Jn 1[48]).

Such is the gospel conception of the simple life—a life of trustful obedience to the will of God. It will manifest itself in various ways :—in unequivocal speech (Mt 5[37]) ; in healthy independence of the opinion of men (Mt 6[1, 5 etc.], Jn 5[41]) ; in judgments based on principle and reality rather than on appearance or custom—as about the Sabbath (Mk 2[23]-3[6]) and the two anointings (Lk 7[36-50], Mk 14[3-9]) ; in righteousness (Mt 6[33]), calm (Mt 12[19] 11[29]), courage (Mt 14[4]), etc. It is indeed the very root of all virtue, the very heart of the Christian life. It underlies all Christ's teachings. To exhaust it in all its implications would be to exhaust the Gospels.

Jesus Himself is in this, as in all other matters, the incarnation, the living illustration, of His own teachings. His first recorded utterance strikes that note (Lk 2[49] AV) ; it reappears on the threshold of His public career (Mt 3[15]), repeatedly in the course of His ministry in conversations with disciples or controversies with opponents (Jn 4[34] 6[38] 8[29, 42-47] 9[4]), and even in His prayer to the Father toward its close (17[4]). And, as we study His conduct and character as He moves in the midst of friends and foes, we can see how unfailingly that life of single-hearted devotion to God is marked by insight and wisdom ; courage and calm ; stedfastness and consistency ; beauty and strength ; loyalty, patience, and heroism ; righteousness, truth, and love ; grace, majesty, and blessedness. It cuts a straight path through all the shams and sophistries of men, and rises victorious over all weakness and worry, all waywardness and wickedness.

LITERATURE.—Of the Comm. those of Broadus and J. A. Alexander on Matthew give the best exposition. Bengel on Mt 6[22] shows his usual insight, though he has tripped on 10[16]. See also Hastings' DB, artt. 'Simple,' 'Simplicity.' We may add, for the benefit of any who are interested in modern discussion of 'the Simple Life': Wagner, *The Simple Life*; W. J. Dawson, *The Quest of the Simple Life*; M'Leod, *The Culture of Simplicity*; and *Letters on the Simple Life*, republished from the *Daily Graphic*. Some of these are as instructive by their contrasts to, as in their agreements with, the NT conception. See also R. F. Horton, *The Commandments of Jesus* (1898), 63; Phillips Brooks, *New Starts in Life* (1896), 158; S. A. Brooke, *The Gospel of Joy* (1898), 161; G. H. Morrison, *Sunrise* (1901), 124.

J. H. FARMER.

SIN.—Sin is personal hostility to the will of God. Christian teaching with regard to it is relative to the facts of the gospel, being necessarily implied by the death of Christ considered as a work of redemption. It is the Christian interpretation of facts of experience, which are independent of any explanation of life, whether offered by theology, philosophy, or scientific theory. Its value is irrespective of the view which historical criticism may suggest of the literature of the OT. Neither is it affected by theories of the organic development of the world or human life derived from modern biological thought. Philosophic systems, monistic or otherwise, cannot be allowed to govern or modify a doctrine which in the first instance can be tested only by relation to beliefs grounded not upon metaphysic, but experience. The Christian will rather hold that a philosophic theory inadequate to the facts of the gospel has been too hastily identified with reality.

1. *The gospel* never rises above the limits of its first publication as the Kingdom of God (Mk 1[14. 15]). No doubt the terms are deepened and spiritualized, as well by the subsequent teaching of Jesus (Lk 17[20] 19[11], Ac 1[7. 8]) as by the accomplishment of His atoning work (Lk 24[44-49]). But though what might have remained an external and almost physical conception became the manifestation of one eternal life (Jn 3[15. 16], 1 Jn 1[1-3]), nevertheless the Church of the living God (1 Ti 3[15]), the relation of a people of possession to their rightful Lord, King, and Father (Tit 2[14]) is constant. Allegiance, faith, sonship are the marks of those who share the membership of this Kingdom. What Jesus the Messiah found was disobedience and disloyalty. Human life, as He was called upon to deal with it, involved subjection to another prince (Jn 14[30]), bondage to another master (8[34]), 'sonship' to another 'father' (8[44]). To the consciousness of Jesus, Satan was present, not as a convenient personification of evil that became actual only in the individual wills of men, but as the author of sin, the person in whom evil has its spring, even as God is the fount of life. Jesus' sense of dependence upon the Father did not carry with it a monism which saw God in all and all in God. For Him, as for St. John, the whole world lay in the Evil One (1 Jn 5[19], cf. Lk 4[5. 6]). His own conflict was with the prince of this world (Jn 14[30]). To be delivered from the Evil One was the converse of being brought into temptation (Mt 6[13]: the insertion of ἀλλά in Mt., and the absence of the clause in the best MSS of Lk 11[4] suggest that it is correlative to the preceding clause, representing the same act differently). He had seen Satan fallen as lightning from heaven (Lk 10[18]). Over against the Kingdom of God was the kingdom of Satan (Mt 12[26-28] 16[27] 25[41], cf. Rev 16[10]). The drama of human life was accomplished in presence of this already existing dualism. Christ assumes the current Hebrew conception of a world of spiritual personalities under the leadership of Beelzebub (Lk 11[14-26]). The stampede of the swine at Gerasa witnesses to their control, within the limits of Divine permission, over natural forces (Mk 5[13]). Physical disease results from Satan's bondage (Lk 13[16]). Possession by demons is an abnormal case of its influence over human beings (*e.g.* Mk 9[20-22]). And all opposition to the purpose of God is inspired by Satan (Jn 8[42-47]). The Jews were of their father the devil, so that the works wrought by them were antithetic to the works of God manifested in Jesus (v.[44]). Even the chosen Twelve Satan had asked to have, that he might sift them as wheat (Lk 22[31]). So the Passion was a continuation of the Temptation, a direct agony and death-struggle wherein the prince of this world was cast out (Jn 12[31] 16[11]), the strong man spoiled (Lk 11[21]).

From the first the proclamation of the good news, accompanied as it was with the curing of diseases and the casting out of demons (Mt 10[7. 8], Lk 9[1. 2]), witnessed to the real character of Christ's work as redemption, ransom, and salvation. For the true unification between the normal and universal purpose of the gospel—the forgiveness of sins—and the occasional and particular accessories of it—exorcism and healing—lay not so much in the analogy between bodily disease and spiritual wickedness, as in the fact that both are the exercise of the one Satanic power within the usurped kingdom of evil. No doubt there is a certain suggestiveness in the parallel between disease and sin, which Jesus Himself recognized. But there is nothing in His teaching to suggest the later ideas of taint, infection, vitiated nature. It is trespasses which the Heavenly Father must do away, and that by forgiveness (Mt 6[15]); salvation from sins (1[21]), *i.e.* actions involving guilt, is implied by the name *Jesus* (see art. GUILT). The bringing forth of the people from Pharaoh's bondage to serve Jehovah is the ancient experience which is before the mind of devout men under the old covenant as the pattern of the deliverance which Messiah was to accomplish (Mt 2[15], cf. Hos 11[1]). Salvation is therefore not the restoration of spiritual health, but the liberation of God's people from an evil service. The ministry of the Son of Man consists in giving His life a ransom (Mk 10[45], Mt 20[28]; cf. 1 Ti 2[6]). And the Fourth Evangelist only interprets the mind of the Master when he speaks of Jesus as dying for the nation, and destined to gather together into one the scattered children of God (Jn 11[51. 52]). He was the shepherd bringing home the lost sheep dispersed upon the mountains (10[16]); or, somewhat to vary the idea, the Redeemer coming into the world, not to judge it along with its prince, but to save it from the Evil One (3[17. 18] 12[31. 47] 17[15]), and casting out the indwelling Satan by the finger or Spirit of God (Lk 11[20]). The acceptable year of the Lord is a year of release (4[18. 19]).

2. From the implications of the Gospel narrative we pass to *the theology of the Epistles*. In order to gain a clear view of St. Paul's doctrine of sin in its completeness, it is necessary to go behind the Epistle to the Romans. We must bear in mind, first of all, the essentially Jewish basis of his thought. To him salvation, or redemption, carried all the associations which had gathered round it in Hebrew history. The Kingdom of Messiah was a vivid reality, and the earlier Epistles show that at first he was not without the common anticipation of its immediate establishment in manifested power. Satan was a concrete fact. If at one time it was the Spirit of Jesus that suffered him not (Ac 16[7]), at another Satan hindered him (1 Th 2[18]). The thorn in the flesh was a messenger of Satan (2 Co 12[7]). The Christian is armed in order to ward off the fiery darts of the Evil One (Eph 6[16]). Principalities and powers were the unseen antagonists of Christ's servants (Eph 6[12], cf. Lk 22[53]), the enemies over whom Christ triumphed in the Cross (Col 2[15]). If Messiah was to be manifested at the Parousia, Satan was also destined to be manifested in the Man of Sin (2 Th 2[3-11]). A remarkable parallel to the conception of 'the Evil One,' which appears both in the Synoptics and in the Fourth Gospel, is found in 'the prince of the power of the air' (Eph 2²). The same passage describes those who become sons of God as by nature children of wrath (2³), dead not in sin but through trespasses (v.⁵), sons of disobedience because inwrought by this evil spirit (v.²). Demons are as much part of St. Paul's world as of that which appears in the Synoptists. He identifies them with the heathen gods (1 Co 10²⁰. ²¹). Belial is the antithesis of Christ (2 Co 6¹⁵). To lapse from Christian conduct is to turn aside after Satan (1 Ti 5¹⁵); to be separated from Christian fellowship is to be delivered to Satan (1 Co 5⁵, 1 Ti 1²⁰). And that redemption meant primarily for St. Paul translation from the kingdom of Satan to the Kingdom of God (Col 1¹³), is attested by the form in which he narrates before Agrippa the story of his commission as Apostle of the Gentiles (Ac 26¹⁸). All this is in close correspondence with the mind of Jesus, and must be brought with us to a closer examination of the Pauline doctrine of sin.

That sin is essentially disloyalty to God is the substance of the *locus classicus* on the nature of sin, Ro 1¹⁸⁻³² 'Knowing God, they glorified him not as God, neither gave thanks' (v.²¹). It will be observed, first, that the Apostle here speaks of sin in its widest signification, including such distinctions as are involved in the theological conceptions of original and actual. We have here, therefore, a definition of sin which must govern all subsequent uses of the term. All the elements which enter into particular sins, or transgressions of known law, are represented—knowledge of God and dependence upon Him (v.²⁰), wilful and therefore inexcusable refusal of due homage (v.²¹), the incurring of guilt and consequently of God's wrath (v.¹⁸). Further, it is noticeable that the plural 'men,' not the collective 'man,' is used throughout the passage. There is nothing abstract in this general view of sin, even though it be universal (cf. 'all sinned,' Ro 5¹²; 'all died,' 2 Co 5¹⁴). Another point is, that St. Paul is led to disclose this 'vision of sin' as the necessary postulate of the gospel (Ro 1¹⁶⁻¹⁸), in which is revealed a righteousness of God' (v.¹⁷ 3²¹). Lastly, there is no confusion, as in the popular mind, between those physical excesses which are called vice, and the inward refusal 'to have God in their knowledge' (v.²⁸), whether it applies to the sensuous or the spiritual nature of men, which alone is sin. 'God gave them up unto a reprobate mind' (v.²⁸), with all its consequences to the complex personality of man. This is of great significance. St. Paul's appeal is not to the equivocal testimony of external facts, which considered in themselves are non-moral, but to facts as interpreted by conscience. Fundamentally this is the appeal to personal experience, and it is clear from the Epistle to the Romans, as from the whole Pauline theology, that the Apostle is universalizing his own experience, as he saw himself in the light of the vision of Jesus of Nazareth (Gal 1¹¹⁻¹⁷, Ro 7⁷⁻²⁵).

Now St. Paul expresses his relation to sin in the phrase 'sin dwelleth in me' (Ro 7¹⁷). He is describing the common experience of an inward struggle, when neither good nor evil is finally in the ascendant. The complete sinful condition would be one of consent (Ro 1³², 2 Th 2¹²), in which 'the law of sin' was unchecked by 'the law of the mind' (Ro 7²³, Gal 5¹⁷). The terms must not be misunderstood in view of the modern conception of scientific law. 'Law' in St. Paul's theology involves the personality of the lawgiver, so that to find this 'law in the members' (Ro 7²³) to be inwrought by sin, seems to point to an indwelling spiritual presence. Is this a mere figure? St. Paul reverts to it in a still more significant form. Christians are not to let sin reign in their mortal bodies (Ro 6¹²). Compliance with evil involves an obedience (v.¹⁶), a slavery (v.¹⁷). There is a close parallel

between those who, as alive in Christ Jesus, are servants of God, and those who being dead in trespasses serve sin (vv.¹⁵⁻²³). Two hostile kingdoms, two rival loyalties, make their claim upon a man's allegiance. So, when under the form of 'Adam's transgression,' sin is considered in its universal aspect (Ro 5¹⁴), a personal sovereignty is again suggested—'death,' *i.e.* sin in its consequent development, 'reigned through the one' (v.¹⁷). The effect of Adam's transgression is represented as the establishment of an authority (cf. 1 Co 15²⁴, Eph 2² 6¹², Col 1¹³) over his descendants rather than as a corruption of their nature, carrying with it therefore condemnation (Ro 5¹⁶; see art. GUILT) as the due sentence of God upon those who reject His law. This personal embodiment of hostility to the Divine law and government, in view of St. Paul's general outlook on the spiritual world, can be none other than Satan, exercising, as captain of 'spiritual hosts of wickedness in the heavenly places' (Eph 6¹²), not an external compulsion but an inward influence, not therefore impairing the responsible personalities that are indwelt. Thus St. Paul can say, 'Death passed unto all men, for that all sinned' (Ro 5¹²). Sin is always a personal attitude, never a pathological condition. Death is its consequence (v.¹²), but the physical analogy of St. James (1¹⁵) has no parallel in St. Paul. It is always the sentence, punishment, or wages (6²³; see art. GUILT), the sequel to the righteous judgment of God (2⁵). So, too, salvation is not a remedy for mortal disease, but a personal act of kindness and mercy on the part of an offended but loving God (Eph 1⁵⁻¹⁰ 2⁷, Tit 3⁴⁻⁶). Looking to the state from which men are rescued, it is redemption (Gal 3¹³ 4⁵); looking to that into which they are brought, it is reconciliation (Ro 5¹⁰. ¹¹ 11¹⁵, 2 Co 5¹⁸. ¹⁹). Both involve the personal action of the Father's loving will, whereby He chooses to forgive the past and bring back His children into fellowship with Himself (Ro 5⁶⁻⁸, Col 1¹⁹⁻²²; cf. 1 P 3¹⁸). As applied to the individual, this is justification (Ro 3²⁴ 4²⁵ 5⁹ *al.*), which represents not a process of renewal, but an amnesty extended to the sinner. What Christ slew by the Cross was the enmity (Eph 2¹⁵. ¹⁶). Its effect, therefore, is not an infused righteousness, but a free pardon whereby sins are no longer reckoned (Ro 4⁷⁻⁸, 2 Co 5¹⁹).

3. The rest of the NT is in general agreement with St. Paul. *St. James*, though he speaks of sin as the intermediate stage between lust and death (Ja 1¹⁵), yet by the very figure used to describe their relationship, clearly recognizes that all three are essentially the same in kind. Lust is not animal impulse but undeveloped sin. The sinner is one who has committed sins (5¹⁵), which may be covered by repentance (v.²⁰) and forgiven in answer to prayer (v.¹⁵). Sins, therefore, are personal transgressions against God, which, if unremitted, involve judgment (v.¹²), a personal condemnation and sentence on the part of the Judge (4¹² 5⁹). Lust is not even a pathological condition of the will. It has the nature of sin, being not a result of ignorance, but essentially a personal determination of will. This is more clearly brought out by the assertion that lust, not God, is the tempter (1¹³. ¹⁴), which suggests the presence of an evil will, the source of that friendship of the world which is enmity against God (4⁴), taking occasion of the natural passions and desires of men to influence spiritually the human personality. The wisdom which cometh down from above is set over against a wisdom which is devilish (3¹⁵. ¹⁶. ¹⁷).

St. Peter, while he speaks of fleshly lusts that war against the soul (1 P 2¹¹), is even more emphatic than St. James in his recognition of the personality of evil. Sin is part of a man's activity, a vain manner of life from which we are redeemed by the blood of Him who bore our sins, *i.e.* our actual transgressions, that He might bring us to God ($1^{18.\ 19}\ 2^{24}\ 3^{18}$). For the redeemed Christian it still exists in the person of God's enemy, who is now the adversary of God's people also, seeking once more to draw them away from their allegiance (5^8).

St. John, with his profounder insight, gives to the doctrine of sin what is perhaps the widest and most comprehensive sweep in the NT. 'Sin is lawlessness' (1 Jn 3^4). This sentence, with its co-extensive subject and predicate, is all but a definition. It recognizes no distinction in kind between 'sin' and 'sins,' which are practically interchangeable in the Johannine writings. If the Lamb of God 'taketh away the sin of the world' (Jn 1^{29}, Vulg. *peccata mundi*), the Son is manifested 'to take away sins' (1 Jn 3^5). If the blood cleanseth from all sin (1^7), Jesus Christ is the propitiation for our sins (2^2). The cleansing is sacrificial ($\iota\lambda\alpha\sigma\mu\delta s$), implying personal dealings with God. It is therefore forgiveness of sins which those for whom it is prevalent receive (1^9 2^{12}). St John does not speak of sin as a state. Doing sin is opposed to doing righteousness ($3^{4.\ 7.\ 8}$). 'In him is no sin' (3^5) is equivalent to 'Which of you convicteth me of sin?' (Jn 8^{46}, cf. 1 P 2^{22}),—a clear record rather than a perfect state. That which abides in him who believes in the name of Jesus (1 Jn 3^{23}) is the love of the Father, a personal relation having been established which is opposed to the love of the world ($2^{15.\ 16}$). Here, however, is no condemnation of the natural impulses or of matter. That Jesus Christ is come in the flesh to save the world is St. John's cardinal doctrine (4^2, 2 Jn 7). But, as with St. James and St. Peter, it is lust, and the corruption that is in the world through lust, which constitute the bondage from which men need deliverance (1 Jn $2^{16}\ 5^{4.\ 5}$). What then is lust? That is the point at which St John's whole view opens out before us. The Fourth Gospel has recorded the prayer of Christ for His disciples, not that they should be taken from the world, but that they might be kept from the Evil One (Jn 17^{15}); and also His condemnation of the Jews because, continuing in the bondage of sin, it was their will to do the lusts not of their body, but of their father the devil (Jn 8^{44}). And the Apocalypse unfolds the mystery of iniquity in language fully accordant with the view of sin implied in the Gospel. The old serpent the devil (Rev $12^9\ 20^2$) deceives the whole world ($12^9\ 20^{2.\ 10}$), having power ($\delta\dot{v}\nu\alpha\mu\iota s$, 13^2) and even authority ($\dot{\epsilon}\xi o\upsilon\sigma\acute{\iota}a$, 13^4; cf. Lk 4^6) over the nations, manifesting his rule in the mystic Babylon ($16^{19}\ 17^{1-6}$), and the kingdom of the beast (13 *passim*), until He who is the Alpha and Omega, having by His angel sealed the servants of God ($7^{2.\ 3}$), brings in the final salvation, the Kingdom of God and the authority of His Christ (12^{10}). St. John's last word is written in the First Epistle. Behind human history is the devil, 'who sinneth from the beginning' (1 Jn 3^8). The explanation of human sin, therefore, is the relation of the world to this spirit. 'The whole world lieth in the evil one' (5^{19}). To be begotten of God (3^9), who is light (1^5), truth (5^{20}), and love (4^8), is a reversal of those relations described as being 'of the devil' (3^8), who is a murderer and liar (Jn 8^{44}), and the power of darkness (1 Jn 2^{11}; cf. Lk 22^{53}, Ac 26^{18}). Philosophically, there can be little doubt that St. John is content with a dualism, which he is not concerned to resolve, starting as he does from the facts of experience (1 Jn 1^1 4^{14}; cf. Jn 19^{35}). Though evil is antithetic to good, it is not in a Platonic sense as non-being ($\tau\dot{o}\ \mu\dot{\eta}\ \acute{o}\nu$). The problem is approached from the positive and concrete standpoint of personality. Though God is indeed the beginning and the end (Rev $1^8\ 21^6\ 22^{13}$), yet a similar phrase is used in speaking of the author of evil as in describing the Word (1 Jn $3^8\ 1^1$): both are 'from the beginning.' The final triumph, though complete, is represented symbolically as the imprisonment (Rev $20^{2.\ 3.\ 7.\ 10}$), not the annihilation, of Satan. The Hebrew mind, which, in spite of mystical affinities with Platonism and, possibly, of direct influence from Greek sources, is dominant in St. John, did not feel the necessity of a metaphysical monism, being content to respond to the revelation of a supreme spiritual Person, the fear of whom was the beginning of wisdom and man's chief end (Job 28^{28}, Ps 111^{10}, Ec 12^{13}). It is enough to know that they who 'abide in him that is true' have by a transference of allegiance overcome the Evil One (1 Jn 2^{13}).

The *Epistle of Jude*, with which *2 Peter* must be closely associated, clearly exhibits that apocalyptic view of the spiritual issues behind the facts of human life and experience of which there are abundant traces in the NT outside the Book of Revelation, and which indicate a 'war in heaven' (Rev 12^7) as the ultimate explanation of sin (Jude $6.\ 9.\ 14$, 2 P $2^4\ 3^{7.\ 12}$). To the Jewish mind this language is not what Western thought would understand by mere symbol. It is rather the symbolic representation of real existence, the Hebrew equivalent of Greek mysteries. It is a mistake, therefore, to neglect either the Apocalypse or the apocalyptic passages of other writings in the interpretation of the NT, or to fail to perceive that their characteristic ideas underlie the theology of the Apostolic age, as the Platonic mould of thought governs the religious philosophy of the 4th cent., the biological that of the 19th. The contempt of millenarianism, while it banished much that was fantastic in Christian teaching, had the correspondingly unfortunate result of obliging interpreters of the NT to arrange its statements against a background not contemplated by the writers themselves. The result in the case of sin has been the assigning of inadequate and shifting values to the term, and the misapplication of physical or other analogies. For Apostolic Christianity the background is always God with His Kingdom of angels and men on the one hand, and on the other the devil with his angels, extending his usurped authority over those human servants whom he holds captive. Sin is active hostility to God.

4. The whole question of **original sin** is removed from the atmosphere in which it is usually discussed, when it is realized that the difference between sin and righteousness is not one of infused or implanted characters, but of relationship to God. It need not be either affirmed or denied that moral and spiritual tendencies are, like the physical organism, capable of transmission. Still more irrelevant is the discussion whether acquired characters descend by inheritance. These are questions for psychological research, and may be left for decision upon scientific grounds. No doubt theories of transmission, from the crudest Augustinian notions of sexual propagation to the subtlest doctrine of heredity, have been advanced by religious philosophers to account for the universal need of salvation. So inveterate has this type of thought become, that it adheres to the phrases, *e.g.* 'depravity,' 'corruption of nature,' and the like, in which theology has endeavoured to express the Scripture teaching. Though the confessional formulas that employ such phrases are not committed to interpretations of the NT which imply a theory, opponents of what is supposed to be the traditional doctrine have in consequence been allowed to attack it in the interests of a more scientific psychology, on the assumption that original sin is held to be a predisposing cause of actual sin. Mr. F. R. Tennant, for example, in his *Hulsean Lectures*, starting from the premiss that ethical attributes are not rightly applied to anything but the activities of a will that knows the moral law, has no difficulty in proving that appetites and passions are the raw material of morality, belonging to the environment of the will, not an 'universal and hereditarily transmitted disturbance of man's nature.' The consequence follows that sin, which must involve guilt, applies properly only to the individual, while 'original sin' is little more than a name for the solidarity in nature and environment of the race of actual sinners. Whatever may be said of the background of Augustinian thought or the atmosphere in which the confessions of the 16th cent. were drawn, there can be no doubt that they only reasserted the language of the NT in ascribing the wrath of God to the race no less than to the individual. Terms like 'abnormal humanity,' 'taint of nature,' 'infirmity of will,' may be useful practical analogies, but, like all analogies, they defeat their end if rigorously pressed. For what Scripture means is, not that individual responsibility is conditioned by racial defect, but that the guilt attaching to individuals belongs, in the first instance, to the community (see art. GUILT).

5. The controversies that have arisen about the question whether sin is a *privation* or a *depravation of nature*, would have lost much of their force if theological thought had adhered more closely to the Scripture mode of regarding sin. The later mediæval view, stereotyped by the standards of Trent, represented man as deprived of a gift which raised him above nature (*supernaturale donum*). The unsophisticated experience of human nature leads us to regard it as not in its chief outlines evil, and so far as it denies an inherent corruption in the actual content of manhood the Tridentine position is sufficiently justified. But the Reformers were right in their main contention, which was that sin involved a positive departure from the Divine purpose. If sin in its essence is neither the loss nor the disturbance of personal endowments, but simply disloyalty to God, then to be outside the Kingdom and to own allegiance to the Evil One means that positive hostility to the law of God which is to be 'very far gone from original righteousness.' For sin disturbs nature only in the sense in which all personal action disturbs, by directing towards spiritual ends the material which nature supplies. Again, we have to emphasize the truth that sin enters only when spiritual relations have been established.

6. This consideration will also show the irrelevance of inquiring into *the origin of sin*, in so far as this means an empirical investigation of human history. For if sin postulates responsibility, we are no nearer a solution of the problem by a knowledge of the rudimentary forms of what, in its final development, we call conscience. Only if emotions and passions be regarded as sinful, can it be of use to note that impulses, the ultimate restraint of which becomes imperative, are at certain stages necessary for the preservation of the individual or the propagation of the race. There need be no desire on the part of any Christian theologian to question the premises on which the scientific evolutionist pursues his investigations into the origin of the human species. We may grant, for example, that no chasm separates the appearance of man upon the earth from the development of other and lower forms of life. It is hazardous, and quite unnecessary, to contend for organic and moral life as new departures. Taking a merely external view of man, we may say that the conditions under which sin not only becomes possible but actually takes place, are 'the perfectly normal result of a process of development through which the race

has passed previously to the acquisition of full moral personality' (F. R. Tennant, *Hulsean Lect.* p. 81). But then sin is a determination of the 'full moral personality.' Even if we accept the story of man's first disobedience as historically a fact, it is no more explicable as a necessary stage in human evolution than the latest instance of wrong done by one man against another. That all men are the enemies of God until reconciled by the mediation of Christ, is a question of personal relationship unaffected by scientific research. The observer can do no more than register, so far as he can discover them, the conditions under which activities have resulted which, in view of the will of God, assumed to be known, are recognized as disloyalty and therefore as sin. No doctrine of sin is possible except on the assumption of a personal experience involving the recognition of God. The universality of the need which it expresses is attested, not by any demonstrative proof, but by the conviction of sin through which each individual has passed to the freedom of the Christian life. Of such Christian experience the witness of the Church is the summary, and its missionary labours are the measure of its faith that redemption is applicable to all. With this alone is Christianity as such concerned. It does not go behind the activity of a self-determining being, judged by conscience. Its doctrine of the 'Fall,' therefore, is not a pseudo-scientific account of the strength of passion or of the 'survival of habits and tendencies incidental to an earlier stage in development,' which is refuted by the discovery that the story of mankind is that of a continuous progression. It has nothing to do with the material of actual sin, which, though environment may have been vastly modified by corrupt action, cannot rightly be spoken of as 'polluted.' But it is the expression, in the only manner of which language admits, of the postulate of guilt and slavery involved in preaching the gospel, God's message of free salvation, to every creature.

The story of the Fall, recorded in Gn 3, though it shaped the form in which St. Paul stated the universality of sin, does not vitally affect a teaching which, in its absence, would have sought another method of expression. Indeed, its essential features are all present in the Epistle to the Romans before it is stated in terms of Adam's transgression. To say that the doctrine is merely illustrated by the story, would be to attribute to the Hebrew Christian mind of the 1st cent. an attitude towards the OT possible only in a critical age. Nor will the use of 'Adam' as a category for summing up the human race in 1 Co 15²¹· warrant us in believing that St. Paul was led to his characteristic idea of human solidarity otherwise than along the lines natural to a Jewish interpreter of the OT in Apostolic times (see Sanday-Headlam, *Romans*, p. 136, 'Effects of Adam's Fall,' etc.). But it is equally certain that St. Paul's use of the OT is far removed from a hard Western literalism, its narratives being the authoritative forms under which spiritual truths are apprehended rather than the material of historical science (see Sanday-Headlam, *ib.* p. 302, 'St. Paul's use of the OT'). The canons of interpretation applied to the early narratives of Genesis cannot affect their doctrinal use in the NT. If the first truth which concerns the moral life of man be the Divine origin, and therefore the essential goodness, *i.e.* conformity to the Divine intention, of the material world and of his own personality, the second is that nevertheless he is an alien from God. This interpretation of the facts of life, which escapes the negation of a true morality involved alike in Oriental dualism and philosophic monism, is entirely independent of the Genesis stories, and separable from them in the NT. It is, however, remarkable that even in these early narratives the religious truth is presented with a completeness conspicuously absent from many later theologies. The three personalities of God, Man, and the Evil One,—disobedience, guilt, exclusion from the Kingdom, the need of liberation from an external tyranny typified in the promised bruising of the serpent's head,—all are essential to the reality of sin. It is difficult to understand how this could be better represented than by attributing an act of disobedience against God and of compliance with 'the voice of a stranger' to a common ancestor of all living. The situation thus expressed is briefly summarized by St. Paul, 'All have sinned, and (therefore) fall short of the glory of God' (Ro 3²³).

Confusion is often caused by the tendency to revert to a materialistic conception of sin on the part of those who would explain its presence in terms of the evolution hypothesis. It is sufficient, so the argument runs, to observe the difficulty that each must encounter ' of enforcing his inherited organic nature to obey a moral law' (Tennant, *Hulsean Lectures*, p. 81). But, apart from the fact that what needs explanation is the self-arraignment which the process entails, it is contrary to experience, no less than to Scripture, thus to place the 'organic nature' in an essential relation to sin, which is made to consist in the failure to 'moralize' it. The publicans and harlots go into the Kingdom of heaven before those with whose wilful rejection of God the physical and emotional nature has least to do. Even popular Christianity places 'the devil' at the climax of temptation; nor are 'youthful lusts,' though they may constitute the earliest and most obvious material of transgression, the deadliest and most intimate occasion of sin. The impulse to make stones bread, or appropriate the kingdoms of the world, masks a temptation to independence of Divine authority which is the essential element in guilt. St. Paul's doctrine of the Flesh with its passions and lusts (Ro 7⁵ 8⁸, Gal 5²⁴ etc.) cannot be set against this. It has been abundantly shown that the Pauline anthropology, to use the words of Lipsius, 'rests entirely on an OT base.' The 'old man' (ὁ παλαιὸς ἡμῶν ἄνθρωπος, Ro 6⁶ etc.) is, therefore, the body, not as uncontrolled by spirit, but as inwrought by the Evil One (see above). According to Christian teaching, sin 'takes occasion' by any commandment or recognized purpose of God, whether related to the physical nature or not; nor would the theologian of any age be a whit less emphatic than the modern theorist in placing it, not in the impulse, but in the 'deliberate refusal to reject the impulse.' All men are born in sin, not as inheriting insatiable and abnormal appetites, which, however strong, are still outside their personal responsibility, but as subject to influences which, 'felt within us as ourselves' (Tennyson, *Locksley Hall Sixty Years After*), well up in personalities hostile to the Kingdom of God.

It will be urged that influences such as these are still external to the individual, of whom, therefore, sin cannot be predicated anterior to positive acts of transgression. But, in the first place, this separation between actions and character does not correspond with experience. The man as distinct from his activities is an abstraction. The 'psychological infant' is an ideal construction (see Martineau, *Types of Ethical Theory*, bk. ii. c. 2). No one has any knowledge of himself except in action. It is empirically true that 'concupiscence hath of itself the nature of sin' (*Thirty-nine Articles*, 9), because in experience the line between suggestion and acquiescence is imaginary, and 'he that looketh on a woman to lust' knows that he has already committed adultery. And this is not inconsistent with the complementary truth that

temptation is not sin. But, secondly, while it may be admitted that sin on this view is metaphysically not free from difficulty, it must be observed that no peculiar problem is created by it. It is not exposed to the objection which naturally arises if it is explained in terms of a theory of heredity. Such theories are necessarily tentative and provisional, and it is the vice of all explanations based upon the current hypotheses of scientific investigation, that they tend to outrun assured results, and to involve religious truth in the imperfections of systems always in process of becoming antiquated. As soon, however, as it is perceived that the supposed analogy of an 'acquired character' transmitted by propagation to descendants does not accurately represent the teaching of Scripture, objections raised on this score from the point of view of advancing science lose their force. The problem involved in the exercise of personal influence acting through the self-determining will of another personality, remains just where it is, whether sin be a reality or not; St. Paul's 'I, yet not I' stands for an experience which is constant, whether the inspiring influence be 'the grace of God' or 'sin that dwelleth in me.' Whatever may be true of hypnotic suggestion or of abnormal conditions like demoniacal possession, the normal course of personal influence, even of one man upon another, is not to paralyze the individual, so that the resultant action is not his but another's. That sharp separation of personalities which makes one human being wholly external to another may to some extent be due to the illusion of physical limitations. But at any rate, in dealing with 'spiritual wickedness,' we reach a sphere where these conditions are left behind, and the distinctions which they involve are inapplicable. That spirit should thus act upon spirit involves no new difficulty, because its possibility is involved in the creation of free, responsible personalities, capable of love and therefore of enmity, of responding to a spirit of evil no less than to the Spirit of God. This may involve a race, just as the Holy Spirit indwells the Kingdom of heaven and each member of it. Sin is the antithesis, not of freewill, but of grace. The true analogy of redemption is rather the exorcism which leaves the subject 'clothed and in his right mind,' than the remedy which repairs the ravages of disease. Salvation is not the process by which the sinner is gradually transformed into the saint, but the justifying act whereby the unrighteous is transferred to the Kingdom of grace. No doubt the evil spirit may return to the house from which it went out, and we are not, therefore, compelled to reject facts of experience, and deny the gradual nature of self-conquest. But to think of sin as an inherited or acquired character which is being gradually reduced, is to introduce a distinction between original and actual sin which removes the former altogether from the category of guilt. Satan 'entered into Judas' (Lk 22³, Jn 13²⁷); and our Lord's statement—'He that is bathed needeth not save to wash his feet' (Jn 13¹⁰)—seems to imply liability to incur fresh guilt rather than a redemption as yet incomplete. That sin remains even in the regenerate is sufficiently accurate as an expression of the observed fact of the imperfect lives of Christians. But the deeper view of St. John is that disciples, being still in the world, have constant need to be kept from the Evil One in whom it lies, and to receive afresh propitiation and forgiveness for sins actually committed in consequence of this spiritual contact.

7. The Biblical doctrine of sin, as here outlined, enables us to interpret *the Incarnation* in harmony with the best modern psychology. It is no longer possible to think of human nature apart from personality as a bundle of facilities, among which, as we have experience of it, is the faculty of sin. Sin therefore is not an ingredient in ordinary humanity, which must be regarded as absent from the pure humanity assumed by the Son of God. To inquire whether the manhood in Christ was capable of sin is irrelevant, when it is perceived that impersonal natures are abstractions of thought with no existence in fact. Sin is hostility to what Jesus Christ is, the living God. The house of a personality, human or Divine, or, as in the case of Christ, both, cannot be divided against itself. The truth expressed in the old theological conception of the impersonal humanity of our Lord is simply this, that He received by inheritance from the human race whatsoever is capable of transmission, the structural fabric with which biology is concerned, the material within which conscious personality expresses itself. Thus He is in all points like to His brethren, who inherit from their ancestry what in itself is morally neither good nor bad. He was identified with human sin, not only representatively but vitally (Ro 5$^{12-20}$, Ps 2^{24})—a truth which so far eludes statement as almost inevitably to involve in heresy those who, like Edward Irving, seek to express it. But the Word became flesh, and that without sin, not because the virus was omitted in the act of conception, but because, being God, He cannot deny Himself, the terms 'sin' and 'God' being mutually exclusive. God became man under those conditions which sin had created, viz. the environment of Satan's kingdom together with the guilt and penalty of death. He did not therefore redeem by becoming man, but by surrendering Himself to the entire consequences, reversing the sentence of condemnation, by death overcoming death, and opening the new environment of the Kingdom of heaven to all believers. The fact of the Atonement witnesses against the view that the Incarnation was the destruction of an evil heredity through union with the Divine nature. Its principle is the indwelling of the Personal Spirit of holiness first in Jesus Christ (Ro 1^4) and thereafter in the free personalities of the children of God (8^{11}), expelling by His presence and power 'the spirit that now worketh in the sons of disobedience' (Eph 2^2).

LITERATURE.—J. Müller, *The Christian Doctrine of Sin*, Eng. tr. 2 vols.; J. Tulloch, *The Christian Doctrine of Sin*; A. Moore, *Some Aspects of Sin*; C. Gore, Appendix II. on 'Sin' in *Lux Mundi*[10]; O. Pfleiderer, *Philosophy of Religion*, § 'Sin'; Clemen, *Die Christl. Lehre v. der Sünde*; F. R. Tennant, *The Origin and Propagation of Sin* (Hulsean Lectures), also *Sources of the Doctrine of the Fall and Original Sin* (valuable on account of its historical survey of the development of Christian theory); Professor James Orr, *God's Image in Man*, etc.; *The Child and Religion* (a volume of essays by various authors; Hastings' *DB*, artt. 'Sin,' 'Fall, and 'Heredity.' In addition to these, most of the standard works on Systematic Theology may be usefully consulted; also Sanday-Headlam's *Commentary on the Epistle to the Romans*. For science, G. Romanes, *Exam. of Weismannism*; Haeckel, *The Last Link*; P. N. Waggett, *Religion and Science*. For the Ritschlian theory see A. Ritschl, *Justification and Reconciliation*, Eng. tr. ch. 5; also A. E. Garvie, *The Ritschlian Theology*, ch. 10.

J. G. SIMPSON.

SINCERITY.—

The term.—In the English of 1611 'sincere' was an apt tr. of ἄδολος applied to γάλα—'the sincere milk of the word' (1 P 2^2). It has no longer, however, the sense of 'unadulterated' other than in an ethical sense, so that the RV goes back to the older version of Wyclif—'without gile.' 'Sincerity' must, however, always bear the association of that which is *unmixed*. In origin and in meaning it is akin to 'simplicity' and 'singleness' (ἁπλοῦς); in meaning to 'purity' (καθαρός, ἁγνός); but it is most often used in the RV to tr. εἰλικρινής. In so far as this word differs from others of like meaning, it contemplates character as 'the purged, the winnowed, the unmingled.' If 'purity' (καθαρός) speaks of freedom from the defilements of the world as soiling the soul, 'sincerity' speaks of freedom from its falsehoods as from a foreign admixture (Trench, *Synonyms*, § lxxxv.). The word is used also to tr. ἄγνος and γνήσιον; but in every case it implies the absence of all that is false and that makes life double (Lightfoot on Ph 1^{10}).

It follows from the usage of the word that it may be applied to mind, or to act, or to speech; but everywhere it carries the sense of unadulterated or unmingled, so that, while the word is not used in the Gospels, it is plain that these set forth in Christ the pattern of sincerity. It is also clear that Christ demanded of men sincerity, if they were to enter and to abide in the Kingdom of God. It is at once the presupposition of a Christian experience, and the bond of the Christian society.

1. The sincerity of Jesus.—The character of Jesus sets the standard of perfect sincerity; 'guile was not found in his mouth' (1 P 2^{22}); He is 'the true one' (ὁ ἀληθινός, 1 Jn 5^{20}), opposed by that title to all that is counterfeit. To know Him is to know the Truth and the Life (Jn 17^3). The perfectly sincere man must be one (*a*) whose mind is perfectly responsive to the truth. It is not enough that he should speak and act from conviction. The conviction must be *sincerely formed*, without doublemindedness, without any falsehood of heart (Mt 5^8, 2 P 3^1). All that Jesus said and did must be the manifestation of an inner life; but the believer needs also the assurance that there was nothing in the mind of Jesus to distort the truth. It is not enough to believe that He means what He says; we must believe that He is able to receive without loss or deflexion the rays of the truth. In the Fourth Gospel much is said of the truth of Christ; this is more than His veracity (cf. Robertson's *Sermons*, vol. i. 'The Kingdom of the Truth'). He is the Way because He is the Truth (Jn 14^6); He is the Light of the world (8^{12}), and His light is the light of life. He is full of grace and truth (1^{17}). His Kingdom is of the truth (18^{37}). He is set over against all that is unreal and partial and transitory. In Him there is an unbroken course for the revelation of the light and life of God (17$^{6.\ 10.\ 21}$ etc.). Sincerity implies the single heart and eye, which alone can receive the vision of God. The sincerity of Jesus is more than the consistency of His action and speech with His thought; it involves His trustworthiness as a mediator of the truth. (*b*) But sincerity, in the more common usage of the word, implies that between the inner self and the expression, nothing intervenes to confuse or to distort. In the Gospels there is a picture of a life in which there is nothing to conceal; Jesus speaks and acts in such a way as to convince men that He is revealing His conviction. The Gospels manifest a life of perfect harmony. The manifestation is varied, but the motive is single. His gentleness and His sternness are alike the expression of His holy love, and never spring from idle sentiment, or personal feeling, or those cross-motives which break the peace of other lives.

At the outset of His ministry there comes the temptation to accept a compromise in the pursuit of His aims: He answers, 'Thou shalt worship the Lord thy God, and him only shalt thou serve' (Lk 4^8); no tampering with the mission in its means or its ends could be tolerated. 'His means are pure and spotless as his ends' (Wordsworth). He is early contrasted with the scribes because of His authority (Mk 1^{27}); this impression could have been made only by One acknowledged to be sincere. He wins from the first group of disciples the confidence accorded only to a manifest conviction. Even the scribes come to shrink from His clear gaze (11^{18}). The accepted opinion is that Jesus speaks truly (Lk 20^{21}). Many think Him mistaken, or beside Himself (Mk 3^{21}), or blasphemous (14$^{63.\ 64}$), but none treat Him as a conscious deceiver. Jesus proves His sincerity by His stedfastness in His calling; dark as the way becomes, He never wavers (Mt 16$^{22.\ 23}$). It is possible that the Pharisees would not have been unwilling to compromise with Jesus, but He would keep back nothing of the truth.

In his *Life of Jesus*, Renan makes allowance for a lower standard of sincerity in the East than that to which the Western nations conform. 'To the deeply earnest races of the West, conviction means sincerity to one's self. But sincerity to one's self has not much meaning to Oriental peoples, little accustomed to the subtleties of a critical spirit. . . . The literal truth has little value for the Oriental ; he sees everything through the medium of his ideas, his interests, and his passions. History is impossible if we do not fully admit that there are many standards of sincerity' (ch. 16). By such means Renan seeks to explain the attitude of Jesus to popular illusions, and the willingness which he finds in Jesus to take advantage of them in the interest of His enthusiastic purpose.

A truer criticism would rather attribute the story of such accommodation, if it were discerned, to the imperfect understanding of the disciples. There is, however, no need to resort to such explanations ; the narratives make it sufficiently plain that Jesus deliberately refused to work upon popular illusions. Nor can it be forgotten that the standard of sincerity, of which Renan speaks, has been set by Christian faith. Nowhere is there a more stern demand for truth and sincerity than in the Apostolic writings, which owe their inspiration to 'the mind of Christ.' It is impossible to regard as one among many phases of Oriental religion a faith which in its preparatory history declared that God demanded truth in the inward parts, and in its fulfilment manifested to the world One who was known as 'the Truth.'

2. Teaching of Jesus. — Everywhere Jesus demands reality. It is the pure in heart who see God (Mt 5[8]). It is the condition of spiritual vision. If the eye be single, the whole body shall be full of light (6[22]). Jesus calls for truth of heart. 'There is a truth which lies behind the recognition of particular truths. It is the basis of all right beliefs.' 'Sincerum est nisi vas quodcunque infundis acescit' (Horace, *Ep.* i. 2. 54). Those who receive the revelation which Jesus brings are likened to babes ($\nu\eta\pi\iota\iota\iota\iota\varsigma$) (Mt 11[25]). Only those who become as little children can enter into the Kingdom (18[3]). It is the singleness of the child, his truth of heart, and freedom from ulterior motives, that are praised. In the life that is in the Kingdom there must be no confusion of ends ; it must be perfect ($\tau\acute{\epsilon}\lambda\epsilon\iota\varsigma$), as the Father is perfect (5[48]). It is the unpurged mind that misses the vision. If the soul is divided, the profession of the lips will be of no avail (7[22]). Words must not be idle (12[36]) ($\acute{\alpha}\rho\gamma\acute{o}\nu$), without any correspondence in inward thought and outward action. Words must be the 'incarnation of thought.' Nothing must intervene between the mind of the speaker and his word. Oaths are condemned as likely to take from the severe demands of truthful speech. The yea must be yea, the nay, nay (5[37]). An oath lowers the value of normal speech. In all other departments of life there must be the same absence of duplicity. There cannot be two masters (6[24]). The disciple must seek first the Kingdom (6[33]), and must not be over-anxious for food and raiment. He must not only be wise as a serpent, but sincere, simple ($\acute{\alpha}\kappa\acute{\epsilon}\rho\alpha\iota\varsigma$) (10[16]) as a dove (cf. Ph 2[15]). He must worship in spirit and in truth (Jn 4[24]). It was this simplicity that Jesus found in the disciples whom He chose ; like Nathanael, they were Israelites *without guile* (1[47]), $\acute{\epsilon}\nu$ $\acute{\phi}$ $\delta\acute{o}\lambda\sigma\varsigma$ $\acute{o}\nu\kappa$ $\acute{\epsilon}\sigma\tau\iota$.

LITERATURE. — W. Bright, *Morality in Doctrine*, 220 ; G. Matheson, *Leaves for Quiet Hours*, 10 ; W. G. Rutherford, *Key of Knowledge*, 40 ; G. H. Morrison, *Flood-Tide*, 22 ; R. M. Pope, *Poetry of the Upward Way*, 29.

E. SHILLITO.

SINGING.—See MUSIC.

SINLESSNESS.—'The sinlessness of Jesus' is a phrase which only imperfectly indicates the ground it is intended to cover. It is too negative. 'The sinless perfection of Jesus' would be a more adequate phrase. But 'the sinlessness of Jesus' has an attractive sound ; it is the title of a book—that of Ullmann cited below — which may be called classical ; and it would be unwise to displace it from the position of honour it occupies, although we must use it with the understanding that it means more than it says. It is not to be confounded with the errorlessness of Jesus. Indeed, the very latest writer on the subject (Max Meyer, *op. cit. infr.*) refers with the utmost frankness, if we ought not rather to say thoughtlessness, to the mistakes of Jesus (p. 9), while vigorously defending His sinlessness. But on this subject see the much more profoundly considered judgments of Dorner (*Glaubenslehre*, ii. p. 472 ff.) and Tholuck (*Das AT im NT*, p. 24 ff.).

An argument for the sinlessness of Jesus has been elaborated by Ullmann from the prevalence of holiness in Christendom.

Wherever Christianity exists—thus the argument proceeds—there holiness also is to be seen. While exceptionally advanced holiness may be of rare occurrence in any society, there is not a country, or even a town or village, in which Christianity is established but there will be found in it numbers of persons striving after a holy life. In every Christian congregation there are at least a few specimens of character so striking that even those who are themselves destitute of religious aspiration acknowledge them to be no earthly products, but to have a heavenly origin ; while more sympathetic observers will say that to them the sight of one such holy person has been a more convincing argument for the reality and the blessedness of religious experience than all the verbal arguments they have ever listened to. For this phenomenon is specifically Christian. It is true that heathenism has its so-called holy men—that is, persons separated from the world and devoted to God—but it requires little discrimination to perceive the difference between an Indian fakir and a Christian saint. The classical nations produced many a splendid specimen of human nature ; but the best of them were essentially different from those whom Christendom would recognize as holy. Even Socrates, as every one must know who has read the *Memorabilia* of Xenophon, was not holy in the Christian sense, but, at certain points, very much the reverse. In what precisely the difference consists it may not be easy to say, but it is quite easy to feel, holiness being, like beauty and some more of the finest things, in the last resort indescribable. But whatever may be its exact definition, holiness is, at all events, essentially Christian. Those who are possessed of it would acknowledge that they owe it to Christ, their communion with God being based on the sense of reconciliation through Christ, and their benevolence towards men due to their adoption of His views as to the dignity and destiny of human nature. They are imitators of Him, yet they always know Him to be infinitely above them. Here, then, is the argument : 'If Christ is the source of holiness in others, and if He stands far above the holiest of those who derive it from Him, it is a reasonable inference that He must Himself be sinless' (*op. cit.* pt. ii. ch. 2, § 3).

On different minds such an argument will make different impressions ; but we are certainly going upon more solid ground when we turn to the testimony of Scripture.

1. Here the first thing to be noted is **the impression which He made in the days of His flesh on both friends and foes.** Thus, when He presented Himself for baptism among the multitude at the Jordan, the Baptist forbade Him, saying, 'I have need to be baptized of thee, and comest thou to me?' (Mt 3[14]). Whether this sense of inferiority and unworthiness on the part of the Baptist is ascribed to a long acquaintance with Jesus beforehand, or to the rapt dignity in the expression of Jesus at the moment, it is equally remarkable. Even more pronounced was the sense of the same contrast expressed by St. Peter, when, after the miracle wrought before his eyes in his own boat, he shrank away, exclaiming, 'Depart from me ; for I am a sinful man, O Lord !' (Lk 5[8]). This was the spontaneous effect on a sensitive conscience of the proximity of the Divine ; it was the terror of sin at the manifestation of sinlessness. These were testimonies of friends ; but His enemies, in their involuntary tributes, were no less explicit. Thus, the centurion who presided over the crucifixion exclaimed, as he saw Him expire : 'Certainly this was a righteous man' (23[47]). The wife of Pilate made use of almost the identical expression when she sent to her husband the message : 'Have thou nothing to do with this just man' (Mt 27[19]). Pilate himself said : 'I find no fault in him' (Jn 19[6]). And even Judas Iscariot, though he had known Him long, and had, at the moment when he spoke, a strong interest in recalling anything with which he could have found fault as an excuse for his own conduct, acknowledged that he had betrayed 'innocent blood' (Mt 27⁴).

2. Of more theological importance are **the statements in what may be called the authoritative parts of the NT.** St. John says: 'Ye know that he was manifested to take away sins; and in him is no sin' (1 Jn 3⁵). Such was the total impression carried away by this disciple from the years of intimacy with his Master. Elsewhere he expresses the same sentiment more positively, as for instance in the prologue to his Gospel; but this statement of the negative may here suffice. Next to St. John in intimacy was St. Peter; and he summed up his experiences, very soon after these had been received, when, in his great speech on the Day of Pentecost, he referred to Jesus as 'the Holy and Righteous One' (Ac 3¹⁴); and that, with the process of time, his convictions on this point had not changed is proved by the declaration in one of his Epistles: 'Christ also suffered for sins, the righteous for the unrighteous, that he might bring us to God' (1 P 3¹⁸). St. Paul echoes the same sentiment when he states: 'Him who knew no sin he made to be sin on our behalf, that we might become the righteousness of God in him' (2 Co 5²¹). No other NT writer has, however, set down statements on this theme so striking and beautiful as those of the author of the Epistle to the Hebrews, who calls Jesus 'holy, guileless, undefiled, separated from sinners' (7²⁶); and, in another passage, declares: 'We have not an high priest that cannot be touched with the feeling of our infirmities, but one that hath been in all points tempted like as we are, yet without sin' (4¹⁵). These quotations are not exhaustive; but they are so directly to the point that it is useless to add to them. If there be any virtue in proof-texts, the sinlessness of Jesus is proved beyond contradiction.

3. Of all the testimonies of the NT, however, the one to which we turn with the keenest curiosity is **the testimony of Jesus Himself**; and we have to see whether He committed Himself on this subject. The result of such an investigation is perhaps less satisfying than might have been hoped. On one occasion, indeed, He said to His opponents: 'Which of you convicteth me of sin?' (Jn 8⁴⁶); and if, as appears to be the case, this was a general challenge in reference to His whole life and conduct, and not a denial of a particular sin, it would hardly have been possible to make a more distinct claim to sinlessness. On the same occasion He said: 'He that sent me is with me: he hath not left me alone; for I do always the things that are pleasing to him' (v.²⁹). Very similar was His declaration on another occasion: 'My meat is to do the will of him that sent me, and to accomplish his work' (4³⁴). To the Apostles, at the Last Supper, He said: 'I will no more speak much with you; for the prince of this world cometh, and he hath nothing in me' (14³⁰), which seems to be a denial that in Him there was any point of contact where the Evil One might bring his accusations or fasten his temptations. It will be observed that all these citations are from the Gospel of St. John; and there are none of equal force in the other Gospels.

But if the things about Himself which He says in this connexion are less striking than might have been expected, all the more impressive are the things about Himself which He does not say. He never makes any confession of personal sin. This is one of the cardinal facts of the Gospels. It is not as if He had been one of those religious teachers who, whether deliberately or inadvertently, pass by the subject of sin. Not only did He spend a great deal of His activity in the denunciation of sin, but He taught His own intimate disciples to pray habitually for deliverance from it; no fewer

than three of the petitions of the Lord's Prayer being to this effect. Yet what He advised others to do He never, as far as we can learn, did Himself. Of His intimate life of prayer we possess pretty ample records; but in none of these are there any confessions of sin. This omission is all the more remarkable when the practice of other conspicuous figures in Holy Writ is noticed. The most prominent names of the OT are all remarkable for their frequent and ample confessions of personal guilt. Thus the Psalmist says: 'Behold, I was shapen in iniquity, and in sin did my mother conceive me' (Ps 51⁵); Isaiah says: 'Woe is me; for I am undone; for I am a man a man of unclean lips' (6⁵); Job groans: 'I abhor myself, and repent in dust and ashes' (42⁶); Ezra prays: 'O my God, I am ashamed and blush to lift up my face to thee, my God: for our iniquities are increased over our heads, and our guiltiness is grown up unto the heavens' (9⁶). With the corresponding figures of the NT it is not different. Thus, St. Paul cries: 'O wretched man that I am! who shall deliver me out of the body of this death?' (Ro 7²⁴); and even the saintly St. John confesses: 'If we say that we have no sin, we deceive ourselves, and the truth is not in us' (1 Jn 1⁸). Thus, both the worthies of the OT, from whom Jesus learned, and the worthies of the NT, who learned from Him, speak on this subject with one consent; and it may be added that the more of religious genius any of them had, the more poignant were their cries for pardon. Jesus, however, differs in this respect radically from them all, and science must assign a reason for the contrast. If it was a defect, it was a serious one. If He sinned, like the other children of Adam, but failed to be humbled and to confess His fault, this brings Him down beneath the religious heroes of the race; for what feature of religious genius is more essential than humility? But if it was no defect, what other explanation of it can there be but sinlessness?

4. Objections. — Ever since the time of Celsus there have been objections raised to the sinlessness of Jesus, and exceptions, more or less specific, taken to His moral character. During the greater portion of Christian history, however, it has been taken for granted that He was without sin; this being the very least that has been spontaneously conceded by any affecting to believe on Him in any sense. Even the early Socinians were ardent defenders of this doctrine. It was not till the age of Deism and Rationalism that to express doubts on this subject became a common characteristic of unbelief. The revival of evangelical faith in the nineteenth century raised up a host of defenders, not only those in the full current of the revival being on this side, as a matter of course, but many distinguished scholars who stood somewhat aside, such as Schleiermacher, Schweizer, Hase, Keim and Weizsäcker being forward in the same cause. On the contrary, Strauss, in his books on the Life of Jesus, advanced further and further in the direction of denial; and Pécaut in *Le Christ et la Conscience*, 1859, displayed a zeal worthy of a better cause in heaping up every conceivable objection to the Saviour's conduct. On the whole, the great series of Lives of Christ, which have formed a leading feature of the theology of the last two generations, have been loyal to the conviction and testimony of Christendom; but, in the very latest productions which have appeared in this field, an uncertain sound is heard (see, *e.g.*, O. Holtzmann, *Leben Jesu*, esp. p. 34; Weinel, *Jesus im neunzehnten Jahrhundert*, esp. pp. 61 ff. and 274 ff.), so that it is quite within the bounds of possibility, or even probability, that this belief may have to be earnestly contended for in the not distant future.

The objections alleged are either (*a*) of a more

general and philosophical order, or (*b*) relate to actions of Jesus in the Gospels which are considered inconsistent with a perfect character.

(*a*) In the days of the Old Rationalism the commonest objection was that sinless perfection is inconsistent with moral development : man has to raise himself from matter to spirit, and from imperfection to perfection. Kant held that virtue consists solely of moral conflict ; and many, appealing to him, concluded that Jesus could not be a genuine man unless He began in imperfection and fought His way up to sinlessness. Similar to this is the well-known position of Strauss, that it is not the way of the idea, in fulfilling itself in actuality, to pour all its fulness into one specimen, which is thereby enabled to boast itself over all the rest ; but that, on the contrary, it likes to display its riches in a multiplicity of specimens, which mutually supplement and complete one another. Such objections formed part and parcel of the intellectual world in which they were excogitated ; and, as that world has long ago passed away, it is hardly necessary now to attempt the refutation of them.

Far more persistent has been the impression that sinlessness is inconsistent with genuine temptation ; and as it is certain that Jesus was tempted, it may be argued that He cannot have been sinless.

Under the stress of this consideration, Schleiermacher, who made the sinlessness of Jesus the very basis of his speculative system, practically denied the reality of the temptations of Jesus. Edward Irving, on the other hand, appealing to such texts of Scripture as Ro 8^2 and Col 1^{22}, taught that the human nature of Jesus had in itself the principle of sin and error, and not only was capable of erring and falling, but was disposed to all evil ; although, by the energy of the Holy Ghost within Him and the energy of His holy will, He overcame every temptation as it arose.

What Irving and others who have agreed with him or adopted kindred notions have felt has been that, without such imperfection in the human nature of Christ as they postulate, there can have been no real conflict with evil, and that so the accounts of our Lord's temptation, which are intended to be so priceless to His tempted disciples, lose their virtue, the conflict being reduced to a sham fight. To this it has been replied, by Dorner and others, that the presence in the human nature of our Lord of the contrast between knowing and willing makes real conflict possible ; for the knowledge is antecedent, and then the will has to be brought up to the level of knowledge. Further, the contrast between body and spirit makes conflict possible, because the body may, without sin, feel strongly all the instincts of life ; yet the spirit may discern the necessity for overcoming these and accepting, as Jesus did, suffering and death in loyalty to a peculiar vocation. As a faultless man, Jesus had a right to all the rewards and pleasures which ought, in the nature of things, to ensue upon well-doing ; and it could not be without conflict that He resigned His rights and embraced a lot so contrary to His deserts. In the little work of Meyer, mentioned below, the greater part of the space is devoted to the solution of these riddles.

However the enigma is to be solved, certain it is that Jesus was tempted. The scenes in the Wilderness, in Gethsemane, and on the Cross, when He is represented as in conflict with the powers of evil, were not less severe than the similar experiences of ordinary mortals, but far more so. His purity made the inrush of temptation more painful. His humanity had not the stolid calm of a lethargic temperament, but was sensitive at every pore ; He felt not less but more than others the condemnation of unjust authority, the desertion of friends, and the apparent frustration of Providence. Even if the attempt to reconcile the two should be beyond the reach of human wisdom, we will not surrender either member of the great assertion, that He was tempted 'like as we are, yet without sin' (He 4^{15}).

(*b*) The other kind of objection relates to specific statements of the Gospel history which are held to be inconsistent with sinlessness. Thus, it is contended that His staying behind at Jerusalem, when He was twelve years of age, and His answer to Joseph and Mary, were not worthy of an obedient child ; and objection is, in like manner, taken to His sharp reply to His mother when she tried to turn Him back from the fulfilment of His vocation. In cleansing the Temple, He is charged with displaying undue vehemence, and it is held that He exhibited an arrogance unbecoming His youth and His position in His attacks on the scribes and Pharisees. In cursing the fig-tree, it is claimed, He gave way to temper ; and, in the casting of the demons out of the possessed man of Gadara and giving them permission to enter the swine, with the result that two thousand of these were lost to their owners, He displayed a lack of respect for the rights of property. Most of such charges are venerable with age and have been answered so often that it may be scarcely necessary to attempt to answer them again ; but there are two more, of which something may require to be said.

It has been held that the action of Jesus in presenting Himself before John to receive 'the baptism of repentance for the remission of sins,' betrayed a consciousness of guilt. This objection has been recently revived by O. Holtzmann, who quotes from the *Gospel to the Hebrews* — a document to which he attaches great importance—a statement to the effect that, when solicited by His mother and His brethren to accompany them to the Jordan, Jesus demanded wherefore He should go, as He had no sin to wash away, but immediately checked Himself by adding, 'Unless, indeed, this is uttered in ignorance' ; and the author adds that, unless Jesus had said this, no writer of a Gospel would have invented it. Much more, however, than is known of the *Gospel to the Hebrews* would require to be ascertained before this could be asserted ; it may have been the organ of an Ebionite tendency in the early Church, to which such an invention would have been congenial (cf. Euseb. *HE* iii. 27). The movement of John had a positive as well as a negative side : it was not only a 'baptism of repentance,' but a great new consecration to God and country, in which Jesus was bound to take the lead ; and many may have believed that, even at this stage, He so identified Himself with His people that He felt their sin to be His own, and in the act of baptism symbolized that washing of it away which was to be accomplished through His death.

The other objection to which importance attaches is the answer of Jesus to one who addressed Him as 'Good Master'—'Why callest thou me good ? there is none good but one, that is, God' (Mk 10^{18}). It is not obvious why Jesus should have objected to be called 'Good Master,' such a mode of address being, one would suppose, a form of courtesy in which there was no harm ; and this suggests the probability that the humour or irony of Jesus may have been at play ; so that it is dangerous to interpret Him too literally. What was it that He wished to turn the inquirer's attention to ? Stier's dilemma ought not to be forgotten : 'Either, There is none good but God ; Christ is good ; therefore Christ is God : or, There is none good but God ; Christ is not God ; therefore Christ is not good.' The reading in Mt. (19^{17}), where the point under discussion is the Good in the sense of the *Summum Bonum*, renders it dubious what was the real topic of the conversation. But if it really was about whether or not Jesus was good, then it is possible to say that Jesus was not 'good' in the same sense as God ; because His goodness, being that of a human being, was only in process of becoming, and had to realize itself on every step of a long ascent. The comment of Dr. A. B. Bruce in *EGT* may be subjoined : 'The question means not "The epithet is not applicable to Me, but to God only," but "Do not make ascriptions of goodness a matter of mere courtesy and politeness." The case is parallel to the unwillingness of Jesus to be called Christ indiscriminately.' Weinel complains that this objection is usually answered with too much levity ; and it cannot be denied that there is a body of objections worthy of candid and careful investigation. Not only will they bear pondering, but they will reward it ; for if they do not cause the student to stumble, they will have the opposite effect of leading him further into the mystery of the Person of Christ.

5. The relation of the sinlessness of our Lord to other elements of the Christian system.

(1) It has an obvious bearing on *the Virgin-birth.* Had Jesus been an ordinary link in the chain of humanity, He could not have been sinless ; for ' there is none righteous, no, not one ' : in all who have descended from Adam by ordinary generation, there is a ' law in the members warring against the law of the mind.' It has been said, indeed, that immunity from this sad inheritance could not have been secured in the way suggested, because the motherhood of Mary, unless she also had been sinless, would have transmitted the tainted nature. We know, however, too little of the way in which the soul is transmitted to be sure of this. And if it must be allowed, on the other hand, that we know too little to have scientific assurance of the contrary, yet the providential arrangement seems intended to suggest this end. It may, indeed, be said that it suggests it too obviously, and that the story of the miraculous birth was an afterthought, to confirm the sinlessness. But the theory of the Gospel history which presents one part as fitted to another with miraculous cleverness, so as to make one idea account for another, is not consistent with the simplicity of the character of the authors or the straightforwardness of their narration. There is a logic in facts as well as in ideas ; and this seems to be an instance of fact answering to fact in the Divine intention, the human mind only discerning the fitness as it looks back on the accomplished history.

(2) It has a bearing on the doctrine of *the Divinity of Christ.* Some have, indeed, held it directly to prove His Divinity ; because, they have argued, the moral force of mere manhood would not have been equal to the task of maintaining a life of sinlessness in a sinful world. If even Adam, in an empty and sinless world, fell, what chance was there of another, standing in a world so corrupt and a society so perverted as that in which Jesus lived, moved and had His being? To bring the Divine nature, however, into play, to account for the sinlessness, would obscure the reality of the temptation of Jesus ; and it obscures the vital truth that His sinlessness was not only a gift but an attainment, which He had to secure afresh on every step of a human development, and which rendered Him supremely well-pleasing to His Father in heaven. God gave the Spirit without measure unto Him (Jn 3[34]) ; and, by constantly receiving this Divine communication and giving it free play within Him, He garrisoned His human nature against the advances of sin. This is enough to account for His constant victory over temptation. Although, however, His sinlessness does not directly prove His Divinity, it is not without a bearing on it of an important kind : it lends weight to all His statements, and especially to His statements about Himself. A sinless being could not make statements which were false, extravagant, or overweening. Now, Jesus made statements about Himself that either were visionary and unbecoming, or proved Him to be greater than the children of men ; and if His character supplies strong reason for accepting these as words of truth and soberness, the bearing of this fact on our beliefs about Him cannot be ignored.

(3) It has a bearing on the doctrine of *the death of Christ.* The Apostles of Jesus did not expect Him to die ; and the reason of this was that they knew Him to be without sin. Death is for sinners ; but why should one die who is sinless? This was the puzzle with which the followers of Jesus were perplexed when He was lying in the grave, and it seemed as if His cause had perished in this unanswerable enigma. It is well known what came, through the illumination of the Resurrection and the outpouring of the Holy Spirit, to be the Apostolic solution of this mystery. The Apostles believed and taught that He had, indeed, died on account of sin, yet not on account of sin of His own, but for the sins of others. Jesus Himself had declared in the days of His flesh that He would give His life a ransom for many (Mt 20[28]). Had He been one of the sinful sons of Adam, He could have done nothing of the kind ; for ' none of them can redeem his brother or offer to God a ransom for him ' (Ps 49[7]). Had Jesus been a sinner like the rest, He would have had to die like the rest for His own sin.

There are probably other elements of the Christian faith on which this subject could be shown to have a bearing ; but these will suffice. Since Ullmann's celebrated exposition this argument has proved one of the handiest and most effective of apologetic weapons. Persons who have grown up in a Christian atmosphere readily yield to its truth ; and then they can be shown how much more it involves. In those times of inward storm, due to many causes, to which young minds are subject, it is sometimes of the greatest advantage to find a spot of shelter in which to cast anchor, till the onset of doubt has subsided a little ; and for this purpose the sinlessness of Jesus is without a rival. It is not a place to rest in, but a stage on the way.

LITERATURE.—Ullmann, *Die Sündlosigkeit Jesu* [first sketch appeared in 1828 in *SK*, seven editions in author's lifetime, Eng. tr., T. &. T. Clark]; Dorner, *Jesu sündlose Vollkommenheit* [appeared in 1862 in *JDTh*], see also chs. 105 to 107 in the same author's *Glaubenslehre* [Eng. tr., T. & T. Clark]; Schaff, *The Person of Christ* [12], 1882 [with bibliography]; Liddon, *BL*, Lect. iv. ; Forrest, *Christ of Hist. and of Experience*, Lect. i., and *Authority of Christ*, 10. The latest publication is Meyer's ' Jesu Sündlosigkeit ' in *Zeit- und Streitfragen*.

JAMES STALKER.

SINNERS.—In order that we may understand what the word means in the Gospels, it is necessary to consider for a moment the peculiar viewpoint of the Law, by which the teaching of Christ and that of the Rabbis are utterly differentiated. To the latter the Law came with the inexorable demand for absolute and complete obedience, as something to be dreaded, therefore. Thus the mass of the people, who were ignorant of the endless Rabbinical precepts, were held to be ' accursed ' (Jn 7[49]). Christ, on the contrary, saw in the Law a moral ideal, something to be befriended and loved. He bade men strive after attaining this ideal, which was the embodiment of love, and He sought to set them free from the Rabbinical interpretation of the Law. A mere outward violation of the letter of the Law did not necessarily constitute an offence. Thus He exculpated His disciples, who had plucked ears of corn on the Sabbath day, by citing the example of David (Mt 12[1-4]). He excused the healing of the impotent man (Jn 5[1-9]) by citing the custom of circumcising on the eighth day, though it fell on the Sabbath (7[23]). With Christ a higher principle always set aside the letter of the Law. This viewpoint fully explains His attitude to sin and to the sinner. And yet these peculiar views of the Law are associated with the profoundest reverence for it (Mt 5[17f.] 7[12] 22[40], Lk 16[17] etc.).

1. Christ's relation to sinners.—Here His mission shone resplendent in all its fulness. For them He came to this world, to them He had a special message. (*a*) *He freely mingled with them,* and that without fear of contamination, Mt 9[10. 11] 11[19], Mk 2[15. 16], Lk 5[30] 15[2] 19[7]. The Samaritan woman is a clear case in point, Jn 4. (*b*) *He had compassion on them,* Lk 7[47]. (*c*) *He irresistibly drew them,* Lk 15[1] etc. (*d*) *He specially called them,* Mt 9[13] || Mk 2[17] and Lk 5[32]. (*e*) *He rejoiced in their salvation,* Lk 15[7. 10] 18[13. 14].

2. Use of the word ' sinners ' in the Gospels.—The word ἁμαρτωλός from ἁμαρτία, ' sin ' or ' error,' is used in several senses. (*a*) *The national sense.* Thus it indicates the distinction between Jew and Gentile from the ethnico-religious standpoint. St. Paul thus later used the word, Gal 2[15] 'We who are Jews by nature and not sinners of the Gentiles.' Thus it is used Mt 26[45], Mk 14[41], Lk 24[7]. See also Lk 6[32f.], where ἁμαρτωλοί replaces τελῶναι and ἐθνικοί in the parallel passage Mt 5[46. 47], which would seem to indicate that St. Luke also uses it here in the national rather than in the ethical sense. (*b*) *The social sense.* Thus it seems to indicate the distinction between the righteousness of the Law-burdened Jew and his more ignorant brethren, who, not knowing the Law and therefore continually trespassing its commandments, were deemed 'accursed.' Here the word seems to have a negative rather than a positive meaning, pointing to the absence of legal righteousness rather than to actual transgression. Thus 'publicans' and 'sinners' are always associated in the Gospels. In this connexion the latter term does not qualify the moral status of the publican, but rather points to the forced association of the ignorant and ostracized elements of Jewish society with the hated minions of Rome. (*c*) *The purely ethical sense.* In this sense conscious or unconscious moral guilt is associated with the word. Thus Peter in Lk 5[8]; 'sinners' and 'righteous' people are placed in antithesis in Mt 9[13], Mk 2[17], Lk 5[32]; in Mk 8[38] the word is associated with μοιχαλίς; so also in the story of the sinful woman, Lk 7[37]; so in the great parables of Lk 15, and esp. in the story of the healing of the man born blind, in Jn 9, where it repeatedly occurs in a manifest ethical sense. See, further, art. SIN. HENRY E. DOSKER.

SIR (κύριε).—The title is employed as a term of courtesy or reverence in various relationships. It is the salutation of servants (slaves) to their masters ('Sir, didst thou not sow good seed?' Mt 13[27]); of a son to a father ('I go, sir,' Mt 21[30]); of the priests and Pharisees to Pilate ('Sir, we remember that that deceiver said,' Mt 27[63]); of the Greeks to Philip ('Sir, we would see Jesus,' Jn 12[21]). In the English versions 'lord' (κύριε) is frequently used in the same sense ('Lord, thou deliveredst unto me five talents,' Mt 25[20. 22. 24]; 'Lord, let it alone this year also,' Lk 13[8. 14[22] 19[16. 18. 20]). It is also a term frequently employed in addressing Jesus, both by disciples and others ('Lord, if thou wilt thou canst make me clean,' Mt 8[2], Jn 11[12]); so the woman of Samaria says to Jesus, 'Sir, thou hast nothing to draw with' (Jn 4[11]). See art. LORD. JOHN REID.

SISTERS.—1. Nothing is known positively of these *female relatives of Jesus.* There is but one incidental reference to their existence (Mk 6[3] = Mt 13[56] αἱ ἀδελφαὶ αὐτοῦ) by His fellow-townsmen of Nazareth, who were astonished and offended by His assumed claims to be their religious Teacher. The knowledge which they possessed of His family affairs was too intimate to allow them to examine without prejudice the words and deeds of Jesus. The question as to the precise family relationship which His 'brothers' and 'sisters' bore to Jesus is one which has occupied the attention of scholars and writers in every age of the Christian Church (see art. BRETHREN OF THE LORD). It is, perhaps, significant of the estimation in which women were held, that although the names of Jesus' 'brothers' are given in detail, we are nowhere in the canonical Gospels told either the names or the number of His 'sisters.' That there were more than two seems to follow from the Matthæan addition (πᾶσαι) to the Markan question, 'Are not his sisters here with us?' It is true that tradition ascribed two daughters to Joseph, though one uncanonical Gospel at least describes Joseph as acknowledging sons, but denying the presence of daughters in his household.

This interpretation of the words ἀλλ' οἴδασιν πάντες οἱ υἱοὶ Ἰσραὴλ ὅτι οὐκ ἔστι μου θυγάτηρ (*Protev. Jacobi*, c. xvii., in Tischendorf's *Evang. Apocr.*) seems to the present writer to be warranted by the context, though doubtless the words have a primary reference to the Virgin Mary (see Lightfoot's 'The Brethren of the Lord' in *Dissert. on the Apostolic Age*, p. 28). The daughters of Joseph are almost universally said to be two in number ('Genuit quoque sibi . . . duas filias,' *Hist. Jos. Fabri Lignarii*, cap. ii.; 'Ambæ pariter nupserunt filiæ,' *ib.* cap. xi., cf. also pseudo-Matt. cap. 42), while there seems to be no agreement in these documents, nor, indeed, among Church writers generally, as to their names ('nomina duarum filiarum [erant] Assia et Lydia,' *Hist. Jos. Fabri Lignarii*, cap. ii.; cf. the Bohairic Version of the same writing, which changes their names to Lysia and Lydia). Other writers give their names very variously as Mary and Salome, Anna and Salome, Esther and Thamar; while Theophylact curiously enough names three as the daughters of Joseph—Esther, Thamar, and Salome (see Donehoo's *Apocryphal and Legendary Life of Christ*, p. 27 n.[4]).

These Apocryphal additions can, however, have but little claim on our sympathy, and one Church Father at least betrays his sense of the inadequacy of the sources of his information by appealing to Scripture as his authority for the names Mary and Salome (Epiphanius, *Hæres.* p. 1041, ed. Petav. referred to and quoted by Lightfoot [*op. cit.* p. 40]), which he chooses as the names of Jesus' 'sisters.'

If Jesus had sisters, as the writers of the first two Gospels evidently believed, it is easy to understand what was the source of His general attitude towards women which drew them to Him in humble and loving service (cf. Lk 7[37f.] 8[1-3], Mk 14[3-9] = Mt 26[6-13], Jn 12[1-8] 47[ff.] 8[10]), outlasting in its loyalty the devotion of the majority of His disciples, and stretching beyond the cross and the grave (Mk 15[40f.] 16[1], Mt 27[55f.] 28[1], Lk 23[49. 55] 24[1-10], Jn 19[25] 20[1f. 11. 18]). Traces, moreover, of His keen appreciation of the beauty and happiness attaching to the home life of the human family may be seen in His reference to the highest act of self-abnegation demanded from His followers; where the pointed reference to 'sisters' (ἀδελφάς) alongside 'brethren' (ἀδελφούς) marks this characteristic feature of Jesus' teaching (see Mk 10[29f.] = Mt 19[29], Lk 14[26]).

2. On *the sisters of Bethany* see artt. MARTHA, and MARY § 3.

3. Amongst the witnesses of the Crucifixion mentioned by all four Evangelists were, according to St. John, two sisters—Mary the mother of Jesus, and His mother's sister. Though it has been argued that Mary the (wife) of Clopas (Μαρία ἡ τοῦ Κλωπᾶ) was the sister of the Virgin, it is now generally agreed that the interpretation of Pesh. (Jn 19[25]), which inserts the conjunction 'and' between the words 'His mother's sister' and 'Mary of Clopas,' is correct (cf., on the other hand, *pseudo-Matt.* c. 42: '. . . Jesus et Maria mater ejus cum sorore sua Maria Cleophæ,' where the reason given why two sisters should have the same name is that the first having been devoted to the service of the Lord, the second too was called Mary for the consolation of her parents). From a comparison of the names of the women who witnessed the Crucifixion, given by the first, second, and fourth Evangelists, the most likely conjecture would seem to be that by 'the sister of his mother' St. John meant his own mother Salome (see, however, Schmiedel's art. 'Mary' in *EBi* iii. 2969, which denies her identity either with 'Mary of Clopas' or with Salome; cf. also Edersheim, *LT* ii. 602, and Westcott, *Gospel of St. John, ad loc.*). If the identification by Hegesippus of Clopas with the brother of Joseph be correct, we have the interesting fact that this Mary, thus referred to by St. John, was closely connected with Jesus by the ties of family relationship (see Euseb. iii. 11, iv. 22). J. R. WILLIS.

SKINS.—See BOTTLE and WINE.

SKULL, PLACE OF.—See Golgotha.

SKY.—In the two places (Mt 16², Lk 12⁵⁶) where this word occurs in the AV of the Gospels, the term 'heaven' is substituted in RV. There is no doubt that this tends towards consistency of rendering, as heaven is the translation of the Greek word (οὐρανός) elsewhere (see Redness of Sky). Where 'sky' is referred to in the Gospels it is the usual sense of cloud region or aerial expanse that is intended. This was the primary sense, indeed, of οὐρανός—the firmament, the vault above the earth. There is nothing in the two passages above to differentiate the 'sky' from the 'heaven' of Mt 24³¹. The word is the representative of the Hebrew שָׁמַיִם the upper regions. It reflects the old supposition that the firmament was an actual canopy above the earth. Still the figurative use of the term is indispensable even in scientific treatises (like, for instance, Tyndall's *Fragments of Science*). In both passages the immediate reference is to the meteorological interpretations of the colour of the sky.   W. S. Kerr.

SLAVE, SLAVERY.—While δοῦλος is the general term for 'a slave,' οἰκέτης (Lk 16¹³; cf. Ac 10⁷, Ro 14⁴, 1 P 2¹⁸) denotes specifically one employed in household service or in immediate attendance upon the master or δεσπότης. Except in the latter form the institution did not flourish amongst the Jews in NT times. Field-work was done generally by hired labourers (μίσθιος, Lk 15¹⁷; or less technically ἐργάτης, Mt 10¹⁰ 20¹, cf. Ja 5⁴). In large houses, especially of a Gentile (Lk 7²) or foreign type, there would be slaves, generally of non-Jewish or mixed blood, as also in the great establishments of the Sadducæan and priestly aristocracy. In Palestine the institution was familiar enough in experience as well as tradition to supply popular illustrations and give point to practical religious teaching; but features met with in Greek and especially in Roman usage must not be transferred without modification to the Jewish practice. Not only were the dimensions different, but the prevalent oppression and fear in the one case were replaced in the other by a general spirit of kindliness and content.

1. Jewish slaves abroad.—On several occasions before the Fall of Jerusalem, large numbers of Jews had been deported and sold into captivity. Such incidents were frequent during the wars of the Seleucids and Ptolemies (cf. 1 Mac 3⁴¹, 2 Mac 8²¹), and recur during the period of the Roman over-rule (Jos. *BJ* VI. ix. 3). Herod ordained that thieves should be sold to foreigners; but the enactment aroused such a degree of animosity as rendered its enforcement impracticable (Jos. *Ant.* XVI. i. 1). The supply of Jewish slaves was kept up almost entirely from among prisoners taken in the numerous campaigns, and the children of those who were already in captivity, with a few who lost their freedom under the laws of the foreign country or city in which they resided. Their treatment, like that of other slaves, was as a rule cruel to the degree of barbarity. Exceptions are met with, where courtesy to slaves is commended, as by Seneca (*Ep.* xlvii.). But the great mass of evidence is on the other side. Pallas, a brother of Felix (Ac 23²⁴), considered his slaves too abject to be spoken to, and would signify his pleasure to them only by a gesture or nod (Tac. *Ann.* xiii. 23). The slave was merely property, and could be transferred like any other property. He was incapable of contracting a legal marriage, and was not regarded as invested with any rights. On the ground of expediency, he was gradually protected against excessive cruelty. By the Lex Petronia, which may have been first enacted in the time of Augustus, a slave could not be punished by con-

demnation to fight with gladiators or wild beasts; and the master's power of life and death was threatened, if not actually restricted, by Claudius. In such hesitating improvements of their condition Jewish slaves abroad would share.

The redemption of Jewish slaves was regarded in theory as a sacred duty (cf. Neh 5⁸); but there is no evidence of any general attempt during our period to acquire the merit of such service. The wealth of the country was chiefly in the hands of those sections of the people in whom racial feeling was not strong; and the majority were at once too poor and too much hindered by political conditions to be able to act in other than rare individual cases. The price of a slave, or of his redemption, varied with his qualities, and with the state of the market. Exact particulars for the 1st cent. are not available. Ptolemy Philadelphus redeemed Jewish captives in Egypt at the price of 120 drachmæ, or about £4 each (Jos. *Ant.* XII. ii. 3). And Nicanor endeavoured to raise the Roman tribute of 2000 talents by the sale of Jews at the rate of ninety per talent (2 Mac 8¹⁰ᶠ·).

2. Slaves in Palestine.—Nehemiah's influence had made it a fundamental rule in Jewish practice that no Jew should be held as a slave by another Jew (cf. Neh 5⁸); and as the rule obtained also in Talmudical times (cf. Winter, *Die Stellung der Sklaven*, 10 ff.), it is almost certain to have been observed in the intermediate period. Even thieves were not to be reduced to a state of permanent slavery; and while the disorganization of trade due to a strict observance of the Sabbatic law of Dt 15¹⁻¹¹ was prevented by Hillel's statute of *Prosbol*, which made registered debts always recoverable, other means were adopted of freeing poor Jews from the burden of their mortgages than that of their reduction to actual servitude. Work was accepted and required as a substitute for repayment, but as far as possible the personal freedom of the debtor was respected. In regard to females, the Talmud decides that a wife can never be sold into slavery, but that a daughter under marriageable age can; with the apparent proviso that, if she be sold again, the purchaser must not be a foreigner. Amongst the Essenes, the holding of slaves was unknown and not allowed (Philo, ed. Mang. ii. 457, 482; Jos. *Ant.* XVIII. i. 5). In a few of the great houses of alien officials there would be the retinue usual in other lands; but even then the slaves would be chiefly of Canaanitish or mixed blood. In Jewish houses free service was the rule for men, whilst some of the girls might be servile in status, though comparatively unrestrained. By law, and even more effectually by usage and public sentiment, they were protected from many cruelties customarily practised upon their class elsewhere.

3. Treatment of slaves.—Discipline without undue laxity was recognized as the right treatment of slaves (cf. Sir 33²⁴ᶠᶠ·, where the two prominent features are the severity to which the discipline might legally be carried, viz., 'yoke and thong' and even 'racks and tortures,' and the kindliness that was the customary rule). So in NT times the master could legally imprison or chastise a slave (Mt 25³⁰, Lk 12⁴⁶ with the alternative rendering 'severely scourge'), though the power of life and death was withheld, as also any punishment that led to the loss of a limb. An early tradition recounts a controversy between Pharisees and Sadducees, assumed to have taken place in or about our period, as to the incidence of the responsibility for an injury done by a slave (*Yadayim*, iv. 7). The solution of the Pharisees was that the slave himself, and not the master, must be held responsible, as the slave was capable of reasoning, and not to be classed with beasts of burden. Another regulation (*Babâ ḳammâ*, viii. 4) required the slave to make compensation on his release, and thus has clearly in view a case of temporary servitude amongst Jews, akin to those met with in the OT.

At a time when Pharisaism was predominant, such slaves as were found in a Jewish household, whether Hebrews or aliens by birth, had on religious grounds to be treated humanely. They shared the family worship, and in regard to obligations were classed with the women and children as bound to observe all religious ritual in the home, except the repetition of the *Shema* and the wearing of phylacteries. Laws of an earlier date required the circumcision of slaves (Gn 17¹²) and their participation in feast and sacrifice (Dt 12¹⁸ 16¹¹). Such regulations could not have fallen into desuetude without involving the ceremonial pollution from which it was one of the first objects of the legalists of the first century to escape. The knitting together of master and slave in religious bonds supplied a strong motive for kindness and forbearance. And in later literature the life of the Jewish home is represented as united and happy, master and slave partaking of the same food, exchanging words of respect and tenderness, and mourning over the separation effected by death (*Berakhôth* 16b, *Kethubôth* 61). Altogether the condition of slavery, as far as it existed, was much less oppressive than in Greece or Rome, and was already being superseded by the freer relationships of voluntary service, which alone are in complete accord with the genius of Christianity.

4. Teaching of the Gospels.—The institution of slavery was not directly condemned by Christ, but its continuance was undermined by the new principles of social life which He emphasized. Supreme praise is passed upon service marked by absolute submission (Mk 10⁴⁴). The title of slave is appropriated to the highest usage (Mt 21³⁴, Mk 12². ⁴, Lk 20¹⁰ᶠ·), and sanction is thus given to the practice which had applied it to Moses (cf. Jos 14⁷, Ps 105²⁶), and made it the formal style of a prophet (cf. Jer 7²⁵, Zec 1⁶, and the Pauline usage of the term). Redemptive love recognizes no distinctions of sex or status, but makes men of all social ranks equally responsible for their attitude towards God ; and thus society becomes an organism of free men, amongst whom the only authority that is strictly imperial or beyond questioning is that of Christ. The bond-servant of Jesus Christ can be bound to no other master ; and in their equal dependence upon Him disciples cease to be able to maintain artificial distinctions of grade or privilege.

LITERATURE.—Articles in the handbooks of Jewish Archæology, and in such Cyclopædias as those of Hamburger, Riehm, and Herzog-Hauck ; Winter, *Die Stellung der Sklaven bei den Juden . . . nach talm. Quellen* ; Grünfeld, *Die Stellung . . . nach bibl. und talm. Quellen* ; Brace, *Gesta Christi*, ch. v. For the conditions in non-Jewish districts see Mommsen, and Smith's *Dict. of Gr. and Rom. Ant.*   R. W. MOSS.

SLEEP (ὕπνος, καθεύδω, ἀφυπνόω, κοιμάομαι).—The mention of sleep is frequent in the Gospels, both in its literal and in its figurative meanings.

1. *Literally, e.g.* 'Joseph being raised out of sleep' (Mt 1²⁴) ; 'Peter and they that were with him were heavy with sleep' (Lk 9³²) ; (Jesus) 'findeth them asleep' (Mt 26⁴⁰⁻⁴³) ; 'Simon, sleepest thou ?' (Mk 14³⁷). Jesus, as is noted by all the Synoptists, fell asleep in the boat as He and His disciples were crossing to the other side of the Sea of Galilee (Mt 8²⁴ ‖ Mk 4³⁸ ‖ Lk 8²³). Mk. adds the detail that He slept 'on the pillow' (ἐπὶ τὸ προσκεφάλαιον), probably a boat cushion, or a headrest made of wool. Lk. indicates that He was fast asleep (ἀφυπνόω), which accords with the fact that

the severe storm which had burst forth while they were crossing did not awake Him.

2. *Figuratively* : (i.) As a metaphor for death, 'The maid is not dead, but sleepeth' (καθεύδει, Mt 9²⁴ ‖ Mk 5³⁹ ‖ Lk 8⁵²) ; 'Our friend Lazarus sleepeth' (is fallen asleep, κεκοίμηται, Jn 11¹¹). No distinction is to be made between the verbs καθεύδω and κοιμάομαι, for the disciples reply, 'Lord, if he sleep (κεκοίμηται), he shall do well' (v.¹²) ; cf. also Mt 27⁵² with Mt 28¹³ ‖ Lk 22⁴⁵, and Ac 7⁶⁰ 13³⁶ with Ac 12⁶. St. Paul frequently uses κοιμάομαι to describe the dead (1 Co 15¹⁸. ²⁰ ‖ 1 Th 4¹³⁻¹⁵), and to express the fact of death (1 Co 7³⁹ 11³⁰ 15⁶. ⁵¹ ; cf. also 2 P 3⁴). The metaphor is very ancient. It is found in the OT, 'Since thou art laid down' (in the LXX 'fallen asleep' [κεκοίμησαι], Is 14⁸ ; cf. Is 43¹⁷ ‖ 1 K 11⁴³) ; and in classical literature (Hom. *Il.* xi. 241 ; Soph. *Elect.* 509). (ii.) As symbolizing the lack of watchfulness : 'while men slept his enemy came' (Mt 13²⁵) ; 'lest coming suddenly he find you sleeping' (Mk 13³⁶). (iii.) The interpretation of the sleep of the virgins ('while the bridegroom tarried, they all slumbered [νυστάζω, 'nodded'] and slept,' Mt 25⁵) is uncertain. Many of the ancient interpreters take it as the sleep of death which comes to all. By some modern writers it has been interpreted as the sleep of ignorance, symbolizing that the day of the coming of the bridegroom, *i.e.* of Christ, is unknown, or as a hint that that day is not immediately at hand. Others take it as the sleep of security, indicating that the wise and the foolish virgins, having made such preparation as they thought necessary, awaited the coming of the bridegroom with such calmness of mind that they fell asleep. Probably the best interpretation is that which regards the sleep as the natural and innocent unconsciousness or obliviousness of the future and the eternal, and especially of the coming of Christ, which inevitably creeps over the wise and the foolish alike. This forgetfulness, however, is full of danger to those who do not keep themselves in such a condition of readiness for any event that they are prepared for it when it comes. We are not to be always thinking of the Lord's coming, but are to live so that that event will not come upon us in a state of unreadiness. 'The tension of the mind may innocently and must naturally vary. It is enough that its intention is ever the same—that we live under the power of the future and the eternal even when not thinking of it' (Bruce).

LITERATURE.—Trench, *Parables* ; Bruce, *Parabolic Teaching of Christ* ; Winterbotham in *Expos.*, 1st ser. ix. [1879] p. 76 ff. ; Jülicher, *Die Gleichnisreden Jesu* ; Goebel, *Parables* (T. & T. Clark) ; Wendt, *Teaching of Jesus* (T. & T. Clark), vol. i. p. 136 ; R. Rainy, *Sojourning with God* (1902), 95.

JOHN REID.

SLOTHFULNESS.—1. *Gospel usage.*—The noun 'sloth' is not found ; the adj. 'slothful' (ὀκνηρός) occurs only once (Mt 25²⁶). The wicked, slothful, and unprofitable servant is silhouetted once, for all men and time. The words, 'Thou wicked and slothful servant,' 'were in the Gospel well coupled' ; and the first epithet was grounded on the second, he being therefore wicked, because he had been slothful' (Barrow). It is the man of one talent, and he who has buried the same, that is guilty of the sin of sloth. That is true psychology. But let every man give heed unto himself. Genius has yielded to this sin as well as mediocrity. Stewardship of five talents has been neglected, and equally in that case the 'precipitate' of character has been sloth.

2. *The life of Jesus a rebuke to slothfulness.*—The Saviour was in all respects a complete opposite to 'the slothful servant.' The zeal of the Lord ate Him up (Jn 2¹⁷). Early and late He wearied not in well-doing, but accomplished what was given Him to do. 'Our great example, the life of our blessed Lord Himself, what was it but one continual exercise of labour? His mind did ever stand bent in careful attention, studying to do good. His body was ever moving in wearisome travel to the same Divine intent' (Barrow). His practice stimulates to diligence, His preaching warns to avoid sloth. The Apostle Paul was built on the same model. When he bids men be 'not slothful in business' (Ro 12[11] AV), these are the words of a man who was in labours most abundant (2 Co 11[23]).

LITERATURE.—Bruce, *Parabolic Teaching of Christ*, 'The Talents'; Horton, *Proverbs*, 'Idleness'; Barrow, *Sermons*, on 'Industry'; Drummond, *Natural Law in the Spiritual World*, 'Degeneration'; Stalker, *Seven Deadly Sins* (1901), 115.

JOHN R. LEGGE.

SLOWNESS OF HEART.—A disposition which our Lord discerned in His disciples, especially in relation to His Person and work (Lk 24[25] βραδεῖς τῇ καρδίᾳ). He connects it with 'emptiness of mind' (ἀνόητος, cf. Bengel, who paraphrases, 'void of mind and slow of heart') as the joint cause of their failure to understand and believe the testimony of the prophets concerning Himself. This dual disposition is characteristic of the disciples' attitude toward the whole of Christ's teaching (cf. Mt 15[15-17] 16[8-12], Jn 14[9]); and the order in which the epithets are employed in Lk 24[25] suggests that slowness of heart is the root from which dulness of mind concerning spiritual truth springs. The disciples believed, but slowly, and with a heavy heart. There was an element of reluctance in their faith. Jesus was not the sort of Messiah they expected, and His teaching was not the kind of teaching they desired. He and His words, in consequence, encountered in their hearts an unwillingness to believe which generated, in its turn, failure to understand. Slowness of heart thus reveals a moral fault. The free action of faith is hindered by prejudice of one kind or another. The will is biassed in a different direction (cf. Jn 7[17]). As Godet says, 'If they had embraced the living God with more fervent faith, the fact of the resurrection would not have been so strange to their hopes' (Com. on *St. Luke's Gospel*, vol. ii. p. 354). Slowness of heart is the opposite extreme to that over-quickness of faith which our Lord stigmatized in the parable of the Sower under the figure of the rocky ground. Between these extremes there is a quickness of heart which is ready to believe whatever bears the sufficient warrant of the Word of God. Of this quickness Nathanael is a striking instance (Jn 1[45-49]). Thomas, on the other hand, illustrates slowness of heart, while Christ's treatment of him shows us how He deals with such slow believers and quickens their faith into great confessions (20[24-29]).

JAMES MURSELL.

SMOKING FLAX (λίνον τυφόμενον, Mt 12[20]).—The little earthenware lamp is largely replaced to-day, even in the houses of the *fellahin* in Palestine, by lamps made by travelling tinsmiths from the tins in which petroleum is imported. But the old-fashioned lamp, resembling those dug out of ancient graves, is still to be seen. Olive oil is poured into the bowl of the lamp, and for wick a few strands of flaxen fibre or cotton thread twisted together are inserted. As the oil is consumed the flame sinks, and the wick fills the house with peculiarly disagreeable smoke. The lamp must be replenished with oil, and the wick trimmed, or, as more frequently happens when the smoking stage is reached, the flax is 'quenched' and cast out.   W. EWING.

SNARE (παγίς, βρόχος).—παγίς (Lk 21[31], Ro 11[9], etc.) is primarily a trap, then a trick or snare. βρόχος (1 Co 7[35]) is a noose or slip-knot for hanging

or strangling, then a snare for birds, or the mesh of a net. We can hardly take παγίς in Lk 21[35], with Godet (Com. *in loc.*), as a net enclosing a flock of unsuspecting birds. The idea in both words is simply that of taking unawares, as the bird in the fowler's trap—the *fakhkh*, in the use of which Arab boys are so expert—or the hare in the noose cunningly spread in its path.

W. EWING.

SNOW.—See AGRICULTURE in vol. i. p. 40[a].

SOCIABILITY.—See CHARACTER OF CHRIST in vol. i. p. 289 ff.

SOCIALISM.—1. Definition, etc.—'The watchword of the Socialist is *Co-operation*; the watchword of the anti-Socialist is *Competition*. Any one who recognizes the principle of Co-operation as a stronger and truer principle than that of Competition, has a right to the honour or the disgrace of being called a Socialist.' This definition was written by Frederic Denison Maurice in the first of a series of Tracts on Christian Socialism, which was published in 1849. Maurice, Kingsley, and T. Hughes deliberately adopted the word 'Socialist' for the movement which they founded, and incurred, as Hughes has testified, much 'anger and bitterness' as a result; but, since then, the Socialist idea has had a secure place in the speculations and activities of modern Christianity. It is evident, however, that Socialism so defined is a much broader thing than the State Socialism of economic theory, or than that of the Social Democratic parties of contemporary politics. Fifty years ago, indeed, many men did regard competition as a stronger and truer principle than co-operation; and Socialism (in Maurice's sense) has had an easy victory over the *laissez-faire* Individualism which was dominant in the political economy of his day; in this sense the famous saying is true that 'We are all Socialists now.' But a man may be against Individualism or Anarchism, and to that extent a Socialist, and yet may be opposed to the current conceptions both of economic and political Socialism; he may possibly regard the growth of municipal undertakings with alarm, and he may even look, as Thomas Carlyle did, to the 'strong man,' and not to the democracy, for deliverance from the evils of insufficiently restricted competition.

Yet general principles are of more importance than economic theories which must necessarily shift with changing conditions of life; and Socialism, defined as the principle of fellowship, may safely claim to be an integral part of Christianity, working itself out in one age through feudalism and canon law, in another through representative government and factory legislation, and tending, through the improvement of individual character, to the ideal state. That ideal state might prove to be either socialist or anarchist, or to be (as society now is) somewhere between these two extremes; for, indeed, if men were perfect, the machinery of society would be a matter of indifference. It is because men are imperfect that the economic and political machinery is a matter of urgent importance. Here 'Socialism,' as an active Christian principle, comes in; for though Christians must always claim the supreme importance of personal regeneration, as against those who think that society can be made perfect by the mere operation of the State, it must also be admitted that a religion which attempts to deal only with the individual, and leaves society to its own devices and the laws of supply and demand, is untrue to itself, and is doomed to failure. Individual character cannot be regenerated while it is being destroyed by bad housing, or by intemperance, or by commercial selfishness and dishonesty, or while multitudes are 'submerged' and 'sweated.' Such things as these are therefore the immediate concern of the Christian; and far more so the great causes—economic, political, ethical—which lie behind them. Now it is undeniable that, for a considerable period before Maurice wrote, the 'religious world' as a whole had ignored this truth, and had neglected its social duty to the weak and oppressed,—a neglect of which the results are still painfully evident to-day. There had indeed always existed a better tradition: the Quakers* had been a powerful leaven of commercial morality; Wilberforce and his friends had, after a protracted battle of 20 years, conquered Individualism in the interests of the black slaves; Shaftesbury (a Conservative in politics) had already won a signal victory over the even more horrible 'white slavery' that went on in English factories. Both these men were devoted religious leaders: but they were not the 'religious world'; hence the protest of the Christian Socialists,—a protest which has really changed the face of British Christendom.

The Maurician definition of Socialism is thus a very real one, and is practical as well as fundamental. The Christian men who opposed Shaftesbury were Individualists; they left society to the laws of supply and demand—in other words, to competition; they regarded the aim of Christianity as the salvation of individuals—or perhaps of a small minority of the elect, for Calvinism was in truth the theological parent of this Individualism. If Socialism be regarded broadly as the antithesis of Individualism, as a theory of life and not only of economics, then it is true that the Christian Socialists won the day and now hold the field. It will clear the ground if we give here a definition of Bishop Westcott in which Maurice's words are repeated and expanded:

'The term Socialism has been discredited by its connexion with many extravagant and revolutionary schemes, but it is a term which needs to be claimed for nobler uses. It has no necessary affinity with any forms of violence, or confiscation, or class selfishness, or financial arrangement. I shall therefore venture to employ it apart from its historical associations as describing a theory of life, and not only a theory of economics. In this sense Socialism is the opposite of Individualism, and it is by contrast with Individualism that the true character of Socialism can best be discerned. Individualism and Socialism correspond with opposite views of humanity. Individualism regards humanity as made up of disconnected or warring atoms; Socialism regards it as an organic whole, a vital unity formed by the combination of contributory members mutually interdependent.

It follows that Socialism differs from Individualism both in method and in aim. The method of Socialism is co-operation, the method of Individualism is competition. The one regards man as working with man for a common end, the other regards man as working against man for private gain. The aim of Socialism is the fulfilment of service, the aim of Individualism is the attainment of some personal advantage—riches, or place, or fame. Socialism seeks such an organization of life as shall secure for every one the most complete development of his powers; Individualism seeks primarily the satisfaction of the particular wants of each one, in the hope that the pursuit of private interest will in the end secure public welfare' (Westcott, Socialism, pp. 3, 4).

If the social principle, the principle of brotherhood, had been forgotten, it certainly came to its own again in the 19th cent., though it may be at present rather overwhelmed by the problems which had grown up during its abeyance. Its rapid revival in the Churches was due to the fact that the men who proclaimed it were able to point to half-forgotten Scripture ideas—as with other objects men had gone back to the teaching of Scripture at the Reformation. It was easy for the pioneers of the social revival to show that the Gospels and Epistles were full of social teaching, and gave no support to the doctrine of 'the devil take the

* A good example of 18th cent. Quakerism is John Woolman. See the Bibliography in the Fabian Society's edition of his tract, *A Word of Remembrance and Caution to the Rich.*

hindmost,' or (in more subdued language) of non-interference. The following extract from a pronouncement of the entire episcopate of the Anglican Churches throughout the world (Lambeth Conference, 1887) shows, on the one hand, how completely the principle was accepted within 40 years of the first Christian Socialistic movement, and, on the other, how entirely its justification was felt to lie in the NT. Such utterances seem commonplace now, only because the Christian Churches have changed. They are not to be found in the official documents of the preceding era:

'The Christian Church is bound, following the teaching of her Master, to aid every wise endeavour which has for its object the material and the moral welfare of the poor. Her Master taught her that all men are brethren, not because they share the same blood, but because they have a common heavenly Father. He further taught her that if any members of this spiritual family were greater, richer, or better than the rest, they were bound to use their special means or ability in the service of the whole. . . . It will contribute no little to draw together the various classes of society, if the clergy endeavour in sermons and lectures to set forth the true principle of society, showing how Property is a trust to be administered for the good of Humanity, and how much of what is good and true in Socialism is to be found in the precepts of Christ.' *

2. The Gospels.—The Gospels are certainly full of those ideas which inspire the Christian Socialist. The Incarnation itself proclaims as the root principle of religion the unity and solidarity of the human race (this is worked out in Westcott, *The Incarnation, a Revelation of Human Duties* (S.P.C.K.)); and the manner of Christ's coming— His lowly birth, His humble companions, His hard life, His death at the hands of the Law—can well be claimed as democratic. He declared, indeed, at the outset, according to St. Luke (4^{18}), that He had come to preach good tidings to the poor; to His mother His coming meant the exaltation of them of low degree (1^{52}); to His forerunner also it meant a certain levelling of existing conditions (3^5), and indeed John the Baptist himself advocated that *voluntary* communism which is an undisputed characteristic of all early Christian teaching ('He that hath two coats, let him impart to him that hath none,' etc., 3^{11}). There is in all this a definite proclamation of *brotherhood*. When we turn to the teaching of our Lord, we find quite clearly that He concerned Himself with secular things, and did not give any justification for that 'other-worldliness' which would ignore physical evils. His miracles were in the main works of mercy, designed to reduce the misery, or, as at Cana, to increase the happiness, of everyday life. His parables teach social principles of the most far-reaching importance. The parables, *e.g.*, of the Kingdom explain the nature of the Christian fellowship, its inclusiveness (*e.g.* Mt $13^{24\text{-}30}$), its ultimate world-wide extension (*e.g.* $13^{31\text{-}33}$). The condemnation of riches could hardly be more strongly expressed than in the parables of Dives and Lazarus (Lk 16), and of the Rich Fool (ch. 12), and in the warning about the needle's eye (Mk 10^{25}). The parable of the Good Samaritan (Lk 10) gives a new meaning to the word 'neighbour,' and teaches the obligation of what nowadays is called

* This extract is given because it emanated at a comparatively early date from a body which had for long been specially associated with conservative opinions. Its sentiments can be paralleled from the statements of the Lambeth Conference of ten years later, and from the official utterances of most other religious bodies in recent years. The Church of England, the Church of Scotland, and some other Churches have now large 'Christian Social' societies. Nor must it be supposed that the movement which it illustrates is confined to Great Britain. It is equally strong both among Protestants and Roman Catholics on the Continent of Europe and in America; indeed, it is numerically far stronger on the Continent than in Great Britain. The subject may be studied in Professor Nitti's *Catholic Socialism*, Laveleye's *Socialism of To-Day*, the Preface to Ensor's *Modern Socialism*, and other works mentioned at the end of this article. The most recent English work on the subject is Woodworth's *Christian Socialism in England.*

social service ; and this lesson is even more strongly
expressed in the most important parable of all—
that of the Judgment (Mt 25³¹⁻⁴⁶)—where we are
told that salvation will depend on whether we
have succoured the poor and outcast, with whom
Christ identifies Himself.

The Sermon on the Mount in this aspect may be
called a simple manual of social teaching. It is
sufficient to allude to the Beatitudes, and to point
out how much of the teaching in the rest of the
Sermon is still regarded as Utopian, as that about
love of enemies (Lk 6²⁷), oaths, non-resistance,
litigation and property, free giving (Mt 5³³⁻⁴⁸),
lending without interest (Lk 6³⁴·³⁵), money-making
(Mt 6¹⁹), worrying about the future (vv.²⁴⁻³⁴). The
Christian Socialist may agree with the 'Socialist
of the Chair' that Collectivism would make these
principles less difficult of application than they
are to-day ; but he would add the warning that
the secular regeneration of the world can only be
accomplished by spiritual means. One sentence
of the Sermon sums up the whole truth, when,
after picturing in a vivid image material well-
being (vv.²⁶⁻²⁹), our Lord says, 'Seek ye first the
kingdom of God, and his righteousness ; and all
these things shall be added unto you' (v.³³).

If we turn to another central part of Christ's
teaching, the Lord's Prayer, we find again the
social side interwoven with the spiritual. It was
given as a private prayer (v.⁶), yet it begins, 'Our
Father,' and is throughout a prayer for the human
brotherhood. It asks for the hallowing of God's
name, the coming of His Kingdom, and the doing
of His will upon earth,—in other words, it teaches
the Christian to pray for Utopia, and it makes
incumbent upon him the duty of considering all
social and political schemes with a view to the
perfecting of society in this world. The prayer
for daily bread asks that all may have the necessities of material life, and this again involves far-
reaching social considerations. The prayer for forgiveness is accompanied by a special clause guarding it against an individualist interpretation. As
for the prayer against temptation, the temperance
movement alone shows that British Christianity has
appreciated the social significance of that clause ;
and in other matters it is clear that, if the worship
of Mammon be the antithesis of the worship of
God, a society based upon commercial competition
is constantly leading its members into the gravest
temptation of all.

Christ then teaches that man has a double duty
—to love God and love his neighbour. He must
love his neighbour not less than himself, and must
do to others as he would have them do to him.
Christ condemns the rich and blesses the poor ;
He teaches brotherhood, social service, and the
abnegation of private possessions ; He teaches
that men are to strive to bring about a Divine
Kingdom of justice on the earth, and that they
will finally be judged by their works of mercy to
those whom the world despises. And, binding it
all together is the gospel of Love which St. John
has preserved most fully—'This is my commandment, that ye love one another' (Jn 15¹²).

3. The Apostles.—The rest of the NT contains
abundant evidence that this social gospel was
understood. Indeed, in the first flush of their enthusiasm the Christians of Jerusalem established
a *voluntary* communism, and 'had all things common' (Ac 4³²⁻³⁵). It was voluntary, and did not
deny the right of a man to possess his own property, as St. Peter said to Ananias (5⁴), but it
shows that almsgiving had a very thorough meaning to the first Christians. The doctrine of equality
and brotherhood was also strongly felt. St. Paul
more than once had to remind slaves that though
in the sight of God there was no respect of per-

sons (Col 3²⁵, cf. Ja 2⁹), yet slaves must not turn
against their masters : this balance between the
brotherhood of master and slave on the one hand,
and the duty of slave to master on the other, are
very beautifully expressed in Philemon (cf. 1 Co
7²⁰⁻²⁴, Eph 6⁵⁻⁹). This is characteristic of the early
Fathers also (see below, 'Patristic Teaching') ; the
conditions of society were to be accepted, and
men were to do their duty in them, although the
Christian fellowship was working out towards a
higher ideal (e.g. 1 Ti 6¹⁻², cf. 1 P 2¹³⁻¹⁷). But
St. James (whose Epistle contains passages which
are often quoted on democratic platforms at the
present day) is very definite as to the levelling
power of the gospel, e.g. 'But let the brother of
low degree glory in his high estate : and the rich,
in that he is made low : because as the flower of
the grass he shall pass away' (1⁹·¹⁰, cf. 2⁵⁻¹⁰). St.
Paul is as strong as St. James as to the danger of
riches (e.g. 1 Ti 6¹⁰), and the evil of covetousness
(e.g. Col 3⁵), and the duty of mutual service (e.g.
Ph 2⁴), and of mutual love (1 Co 13). But his
most valuable contribution to the social aspect of
Christianity is his teaching about the solidarity of
mankind ; the social principle in its very essence
is in the declaration that 'There can be neither
Jew nor Greek, there can be neither bond nor free,
there can be no male and female : for ye are all
one man in Christ Jesus' (Gal 3²⁸ ; cf. Col 3¹¹, 1 Co
12¹³) ; nor could it be better taught than by the
illustration of the body and its members in 1 Co
12, and the great description of the unity of the
Christian body in Eph 4. The fundamental doctrine of brotherhood and love is the theme of the
First Ep. of St. John, in which it is definitely
stated that without loving his brother whom he
hath seen, a man cannot love God (1 Jn 4²⁰) ; that
the children of God are distinguished from the
children of the devil by their righteousness and
love of their brethren (3¹⁰) ; that to dwell in love
is to dwell in God (4¹⁶), and that 'every one that
loveth is born of God and knoweth God,' while
'he that loveth not, knoweth not God' (vv.⁷·⁸).
This is indeed the evidence of salvation—'We
know that we have passed out of death into life,
because we love the brethren' (3¹⁴). It is clear,
then, that from the beginning it was taught that
Christianity had an intensely strong and real
practical side in secular matters, that this side—
the duty to the neighbour—was equally incumbent
on the believer with the duty to God, and that it
is bound up with the 'social' ideas of brotherhood, solidarity, unity, mutual love, co-operation,
voluntary equalization of condition by giving up
of possessions—in some cases, as in that of the
Rich Young Man (Mk 10²¹), of all possessions ;
while there is throughout strong condemnation
of riches, of luxury, pride, and the clinging to
class distinctions.

4. Patristic Teaching.—There is not space to do more than
allude to the teaching of the Christian Fathers. Authorities
on the subject are given at the end of this article : some of their
more salient sayings will be found in Nitti's *Catholic Socialism*,
where their socialist character is exaggerated, and in Carlyle's
Mediæval Political Economy, vol. i., where this side is perhaps
underestimated. The Patristic writings are, indeed, extremely
difficult to estimate, because of the distinction between what was
ideally right as belonging to God's plan (*Jus naturale*) and what
was right under present conditions (*Jus gentium*)—a distinction
which is characteristic of Cicero and Seneca as well as of the
Christian writers of a later date. Thus the Fathers held that
all men were naturally equal, but at the same time they
accepted slavery, though indeed the manumission of slaves was
a recognized Christian virtue. It was the same with private
property. Extracts can be gathered from the Fathers which
are as strong as anything in the writings of modern socialists ;
for instance, Proudhon's famous saying, 'La propriété, c'est le
vol,' is almost exactly paralleled by St. Ambrose's 'Natura igitur
jus commune generavit, usurpatio jus fecit privatum' (*de Off.*
i. 28). But St. Ambrose does not mean that property is unlawful, only that it is not a 'natural' institution—it belongs to
the *jus gentium*. In the same way he does not advocate land-
nationalization when he says, 'Deus noster terram hanc posses-

sionem ominum hominum voluerit esse communem, et fructus omnibus ministrare : sed avaritia possessionum jure distribuit' (*In Ps.* cxviii. 8, 22) ; but goes on to say that for this reason the poor have a *just* claim on the rich to give them a share of what was meant for all. This may be taken as typical also of the earlier Christian writers. They assume the existence of private property as an institution, and that it is not evil if rightly used ; but they do not consider it as belonging to the state of innocence —like slavery it is due to the fall into sin ; ' their whole thought,' Mr. Carlyle says, ' is dominated by the sense of the claims of the brotherhood,' and the Christian man is bound to use his property to relieve the wants of his fellow-man. This is almsgiving, but, unlike modern almsgiving, it is based on a definite principle of justice. An early example of this is in the *Didache* (iv. 8), ' Thou shalt not turn away from him that hath need, but shalt share all things with thy brother, *and shalt not say that aught is thine own* : for if ye are partners in the immortal, how much more are ye partners in the perishable ?' Here the reference to the community of goods in Ac 4³² is obvious. Compare with it the ' All is common with us, except women,' of Tertullian (*Apol.* xxxix.), or St. Justin's declaration, ' We bring all we possess into a common stock, and share everything with the poor' (*Apol.* i. 14). There are many passages in other Fathers, such as Chrysostom and Basil, Augustine, Jerome, and Gregory the Great, which have a strong socialist character, and they all used language about the selfishness of the rich which would cause some offence if uttered from the pulpits of the present day. The fact that Clement of Alexandria took a different view in his *Quis Dives salvetur* considerably increases the significance of the rest of the Patristic literature : he explains the command to the Rich Young Man in Mk 10²¹ in a purely allegorical sense, and protests that there is no advantage in poverty except when it is incurred for a special object, and that riches are serviceable if rightly used, and are not to be thrown away. That he should stand almost alone even in this much qualified defence of property is a remarkable fact.

If we turn from theory to practice, there is no doubt that the Church produced a profound social change in the Roman Empire, and was recognized from the first as based upon the principle of fraternity. In this connexion it is noteworthy that Lucian was struck as much by the social as by the theological aspect of the new religion—' Their original lawgiver,' he remarks, ' had taught them that they were all brethren one of another.' Membership in the Church meant the admission into a fellowship in which the rich man became poorer and the poor man richer ; in which the stranger, the outcast, and the slave were welcomed and loved as brothers. Harnack, in his *Expansion of Christianity* (i. bk. ii. c. iii.), describes this change, pointing out, amongst other things, that the principle of *Labour* was consistently put into practice. Following St. Paul's maxim (2 Th 3¹⁰), the Church insisted, (1) that it was the duty of every Christian man to work, (2) that it was the duty of the Christian Society to see that there was work for all its members, and (3) that it was the duty of Christians to make provision for those who were not able to work. This fails to be pure State Socialism only because the Church was not yet coterminous with the State.

5. Later Developments.— It is impossible here even to sketch the developments of Christian social theory and practice in subsequent history. The subject can be conveniently studied in Ashley's *Economic History and Theory.* But it is necessary to point out two main facts : first, that the principle of voluntary communism was preserved as a living fact by the Monastic orders, and was pressed further by St. Francis and the early Friars ; and, secondly, that the Church taught certain social doctrines which were accepted and practised by the whole community. The two leading doctrines were that concerning the *justum pretium,* and that concerning usury : these were enforced not only in the pulpit but also in the ecclesiastical courts. The first doctrine was aimed against free competition : a man was not to ask what he could get for an article, but the ' just price,' what it was worth, that is, what would enable him to earn by his work a decent living according to a definite standard. The second doctrine was aimed against usury (because of Lk 6³⁴·³⁵), and usury meant all receiving of interest on capital. In other words, the system upon which modern manufacture and commerce and indeed the whole of modern society is based, was forbidden by the Church up till the Renaissance and Reformation ; and not only this, but the prohibition was accepted and carried out in ordinary business affairs. Here again the modern social-democrat touches hands with Christian principles that were practised throughout the Middle Ages and summed up by St. Thomas Aquinas ; just as the modern trade unionist finds that the great Christian trade gilds were carrying out his principles of fellowship even among the peasantry before the modern era began. The gilds were destroyed in the sixteenth century, and the whole mediæval system crumbled away to make room for a new order. Of that system Professor Ashley says : ' No such sustained and far-reaching attempt is being now made, either from the side of theology, or from that of ethics, to impress upon the public mind principles immediately applicable to practical life' (*Econ. Hist.* i. 388). The modern era has brought many reforms, notably in connexion with liberty and the democratic idea ; but as the humanitarianism of its later phase has begun to work in the realms of sociology and economics, it has but joined hands with the great tradition of Christian fraternity,—a tradition that has always been at work in society since the foundations of brotherly love were laid by our Lord and His Apostles. The success of the Christian principle has always been partial and its application incomplete, because its perfect realization is dependent on

the regeneration of mankind. Whether we call it Socialism will depend upon our conception of what Socialism is ; but those to whom Socialism is an ethical ideal will not cease to find their inspiration in Christianity ; and those who take Christ in thoroughness and simplicity as their Guide in secular affairs will increasingly remember that He who said ' One is your Master,' said also ' and all ye are brethren.' From St. John to St. Francis of Assisi, from Latimer to Maurice, what is now called Christian Socialism has had many prophets. At the present day it is a great and growing force in all Christian countries.

LITERATURE.—The mass of Literature on Christian Socialism in general is very large. A list of 140 books and pamphlets bearing specially on the movement in England was compiled by the present writer in 1897, and may be mentioned because it can be obtained for a penny (Appendix to *Socialism and the Teaching of Christ,* by [J. Clifford, Fabian Society, Clement's Inn, W.C.). A better and more recent bibliography is in A. V. Woodworth, *Christian Socialism in England.* Tracts containing statements of the position can be obtained from the Hon. Sec., Christian Social Union, Pusey House, Oxford. This Union has also produced several volumes of Sermons, *Lombard Street in Lent, The Church and New Century Problems, Preachers from the Pew* (lay sermons on social questions), etc. For the social teaching of the Fathers, see A. J. Carlyle, *History of Mediæval Political Theory in the West,* vol. i. (1903), with its bibliography ; F. S. Nitti, *Catholic Socialism* (1895) ; Laveleye, *Le Socialisme Contemporain* (*Socialism of To-day*) (1890) ; Feugueray, *Essais sur les doctrines politiques de Saint Thomas d'Aquin* (1857) (ch. on ' Démocratie des Pères de l'église ') ; F. Villegardelle, *Histoire des Idées Sociales* (1846) ; L. Brentano, *Die Arbeiterversicherung gemäss der heutigen Wirthschaftsordnung* (1879). The mediæval history of the subject can be studied in W. J. Ashley's *Economic History,* where a list of authorities is given at the head of each chapter. Kirkup's *History of Socialism* is an admirable summary. An excellent short history is H. de B. Gibbins' *Industrial History of England.* Perhaps also it may be worth while to allude to the various Lives of the Saints, and to the literature of St. Francis, *e.g.* the *Fioretti* ; to T. Carlyle's *Past and Present,* W. Morris' *Dream of John Ball,* Thorold Rogers' *Six Centuries of Work and Wages,* Hyndman's *The Hist. Basis of Socialism in England* ; to Ruskin's works in general, and especially *Unto this Last* ; and to such classics of English literature as *Piers Plowman,* Latimer's *Sermons,* and More's *Utopia.* For the history of modern Christian Socialism, see L. Brentano, *Die Christliche Sociale Bewegung in England* (1883), and cf. B. Webb, *The Co-operative Movement,* and S. and B. Webb, *History of Trades Unionism.* See also Kingsley's *Letters and Life* (1877) ; Ensor, *Modern Socialism* ; M. Kaufmann, *Christian Socialism* (1888) and *Charles Kingsley* (1892) ; E. de Laveleye, *The Socialism of To-day* ; F. Maurice, *Life of F. D. Maurice* (1884) ; F. S. Nitti, *Catholic Socialism* (1895) ; J. Rae, *Contemporary Socialism* (1901) ; G. von Schulze-Gävernitz, *Zum Socialen Frieden*—tr. ' Social Peace' (1893). See also the files of *The Christian Socialist, Journal of Association, Politics for the People, The Church Reformer, The Economic Review, The Commonwealth,* the last two being still in existence. See also the writings of T. Hughes, Charles Kingsley, F. D. Maurice, E. V. Neale among the early Christian Socialists, and the following among the later, J. G. Adderley, Prof. R. T. Ely, Bishop C. Gore, T. Hancock, Stewart D. Headlam, H. Scott Holland, Bishop C. W. Stubbs, and Bishop B. F. Westcott. Among these may be specially mentioned Kingsley, *Sermons, Alton Locke,* and *Yeast* ; Maurice, *The Kingdom of God* ; Ely, *Social Aspects of Christianity* ; Gore, *The Social Doctrine of the Sermon on the Mount* ; Hancock, *Christ and the People* ; Headlam, *The Laws of Eternal Life* ; Holland, *Sermons* ; Stubbs, *Christ and Economics,* and *A Creed for Christian Socialists* ; Westcott, *The Incarnation, a Revelation of Human Duties,* and especially *Social Aspects of Christianity.* The name of Tolstoi should also be mentioned, since, though his writings cannot be classed with the above, they have a far-reaching influence over European and American thought.

PERCY DEARMER.

SOCIAL LIFE.—1. State of society in the time of Christ.—(1) A sympathetic reconsideration of the materials at our disposal has gone far to prove that the society of the Roman world at the beginning of the Christian era was not in the absolutely rotten state apparently pictured by contemporary satirists and moralists. Their animadversions and strictures cannot be regarded as applying to more than a proportion of the population. The vigour and earnestness of their denunciations are proofs in themselves of a spirit to which the prevalent immoralities were odious. That age is not wholly bad which has grace in some of its members to be ashamed. Juvenal denounces the inhumanity with which slaves were so often treated, and gives vivid and pungent utterance to an indignant tenderness and pity which would no longer submit to be stifled. From other sources of information it appears that there were middle-class circles, particularly in the provinces, which maintained a laudable level of life, keeping themselves free at least from the polluting and demoralizing vices of the capital and its urban imitators. Of them the worst that could be said was that they pursued empty lives devoted to frivolous aims and bubble ambitions, whose vanity was accentuated by their unconsciousness of it. The age was not without its high ideals and earnest idealists. But aspiration was crippled through lack of clearness as to the ideals it would realize. There are abundant manifest indications that a deep, strong, spiritual movement which made for better things had begun. Springing from a profound realization of the evils current, it yet had no clear understanding of their origin and causes, and blindly groped after ways of cure.

(2) It would seem as if the coming of Jesus opened the channels for the inflow of fresh Divine influences which voicelessly and mysteriously began to permeate human hearts and quicken a new and healthy life. The vague ideal which hung in solution in so many minds began to take shape and form. The Divine Spirit gave content and direction to the semi-conscious aspirations and half-blind desires moving restlessly in the deeps of the human heart, reinforced the spirit of reaction which had set in, imparting to its champions a new passion for the righteous, the pure, and the true.

2. Influence and methods of Jesus.—(1) Into the society in which this new life was stirring came Jesus, and very soon the influence of His teaching and spirit began to make itself felt. It would be an error, however, to attribute to that alone the social reformation which gradually evidenced itself as in progress. Other factors were already operating. The rebellion of misery against cruel economic conditions, a mutinous sense of the unjust and unjustifiable inequalities of life, the strong infusion of democratic sympathies into the governing circles, through the increasing number of those whose native ability had secured them wealth and position, the mixing of different races whose blood was strongly impregnated with inherited qualities often anti-toxic and mutually corrective,—these were factors which contributed to bring about radical changes in outlook and conduct. The social teaching of Jesus was not entirely new. Much of it had already been the staple propaganda of eloquent and earnest advocates. But Jesus made the body of principles He inculcated vitalizing forces in the shaping of human society, determining and dominating factors in its evolution, after an unprecedented fashion. He made them the accepted and controlling commonplaces of reform and reconstruction. He enunciated laws for the regulation of communal life which tended to eliminate the disorderly element of mere personal caprice and whim. In a word, He created a social conscience.

(2) In any consideration of Christ's influence upon social life, it must be clearly recognized that it operated not only, and perhaps not so much, through the propagation of His teaching as through the infusion of His spirit into society. The work of His Holy Spirit in awakening men to the evils amidst which they lived, and impelling them to energetic suppressive and alterative measures, must be assigned its due place and value. The changes wrought upon society in the course of generations are the product of men educated upon the principles of Jesus, but freely using their personal judgment under the guidance and inspiration of the Holy Spirit.

(3) Nor must it be left out of account that the fact of the Incarnation, theologically conceived and estimated, with its pregnant suggestions of the worth and destiny of man and the Divine hopes and aims regarding him, provided for thoughtful and responsive minds a purified impulse towards a new humanitarianism.

(4) Profound as the influence of Jesus upon social life has been, it was by no means His primary function to procure its reformation. The social rectifications which unquestionably trace their original impulse to Him are of the nature of by-products of His work. He came to reveal God to man and to bring man to God. Nevertheless, He had an ulterior purpose, to which this was in a sense a preliminary step, in the founding of an ideal community, designated the Kingdom of God, composed of individuals whose mutual relations were determined by the implications of their proper relationship to God. The immediate implication of the doctrine of the Fatherhood of God is the brotherhood of man. These two doctrines are basal to, and determinative of, Christ's whole ethical system. The ultimate aim of Jesus, then, may be said to have been social, inasmuch as the final end of His mission would be achieved only in the realization of a regenerate society.

(5) Jesus consistently set an ideal of perfection before men. Himself sinless, He would have all men sinless as well (Jn 5^{14} 8^{11} 'Sin no more'; Mt 5^{48} 'Be ye perfect, even as your Father in heaven is perfect'). But this perfection was not merely a negative condition, a state of freedom from every evil spot or stain. The context of Mt 5^{48} clearly indicates the connotation the word τέλειος is intended to have. It meant such perfection as that of His Father in heaven, which, on the positive side, was determined by the gracious activities and loving ministries of which men were the objects and beneficiaries. Human perfection was then to be attained only through a life of similar beneficent activity. It cannot be achieved in isolation. Christ never contemplates human life so situated. He regards man as essentially a social being, whose full self-realization can only be attained in vital relationship with his fellows. No man may go apart by himself and live a truly godly or saintly life (Jn $17^{11.\ 15}$). The ideal character, according to Jesus, is to be realized only through the proper discharge of the social responsibilities entailed by communal life (Mt 19^{21}). Sin with Him, and sin of the most blameworthy kind, is largely neglect or failure to fulfil social duties and obligations (Mt $25^{42f.}$). The virtues, on the other hand, which distinguish the good man after the mind of Christ are those which emerge in a life of vigilant and incessant beneficence and self-sacrificing love (Mt $25^{35ff.}$, Jn 15^{14}). The whole spirit of Christ's teaching condemns the hermit existence as one which gravely imperils a man's title to be considered a citizen of the Kingdom of God. The root of the world's evil is selfish individualism.

(6) Jesus, then, was not properly a social reformer; He was an inspirer of social reform. He enunciated principles in the light of which the evil of prevalent conditions, practices, and accepted institutions became increasingly apparent. He changed things by first changing men. He made many things impossible by making them intolerable to the sensitized conscience and Christianized heart.

3. Attitude of Jesus to existing social relationships.—(1) All this is borne out by the consideration of Christ's attitude to the society of His own day. Upon its constituent elements He passed no strictures suggestive of an attitude of protest or condemnation. He accepted its inequalities of position and possessions without demur; nor did He range Himself with that species of socialism which anticipates an epoch when the relationships of master and servant, rich and poor, employer and employed, capital and labour, shall cease to exist (Mt 10^{24}, Lk 17^{7-9}, Mk 14^7). These characterize the normal and stable state of society, which He seemed to regard as fittingly ordered to provide the opportunities or agencies for the evolution of the type of character which most conformed to the image of God, and the realization of the type of life which best expressed His spirit.

(2) If, then, the essential features of society as presently constituted undergo 'a sea-change into something rich and strange,' it will not be because Jesus deliberately legislated to that end, but because the spirit He infused into men, educated on His principles, demanded different conditions for its fuller and more perfect expression. His sympathies were inferentially on the side of an industrial and economic order wherein individual talents, capabilities, and fidelities would have ample scope to prove and exercise themselves, and would meet with such suitable and proportionate reward as would stimulate and foster healthy aspiration, honest ambition, and those qualities of industry, integrity, and disinterested fidelity which go to form the ideal character (cf. Lk 12$^{42ff.}$ 19$^{12ff.}$).

(3) Jesus did not forbid the accumulation of *private property*. Rather He accepted it as a fundamental right of every man to possess in security whatever property honestly belonged to him (Mt 20^{15} 25$^{20f.\ 29}$ 13$^{44-46}$). That is the underlying assumption of those maxims which inculcate giving, and of those utterances which approve a saintly charity (Lk 6$^{30.\ 35.\ 38}$). He had no word of censure for the many persons of means whom He numbered amongst His friends. His disciples continued to own property (Jn 21$^{3ff.}$, Lk 19$^{2-9}$), and His little company subsisted on a common, if meagre, purse (Jn 12^6 13^{29}). Poor Himself, He inflamed no envy of the rich, nor fostered any class feeling. Money He accepted as an effective instrument for the furtherance of the Kingdom of God. He recognized that, while for one it might be a snare and therefore should be foregone (Lk 18$^{22.\ 24}$), for another it provided means towards the better doing of God's will. He was urgent in His warnings regarding the spiritual dangers which attended its ampler possession. He magnified its subtle power to enthral the affections and divorce the heart from God by winning that trust for itself which should be reposed in Him alone (Mk 10^{24}, Mt 13^{22}). He vividly portrayed how it dried up the spirit of unselfish sympathies and tended to render men indifferent and callous to human need (Lk 16$^{19ff.}$). He understood how its successful acquisition developed an unquenchable thirst for more, and therefore He admonished all to beware of covetousness, the greedy spirit which wants more than it can profitably or enjoyably use (Lk 12$^{15ff.}$). In various ways He impressed upon men that money was not the true wealth, and could not of itself procure true blessedness (Lk 18$^{18-23}$ 12^{21} 16^{11}). See, further, art. WEALTH.

(4) It is evident that Jesus held the institution of *the family* in profound reverence. He expounded His theology in terms of its relationships. He displayed a peculiarly anxious concern in dealing with questions that affected its integrity. The state of things in His day urgently called for outspoken protest and warning. There was an increasing laxity of view and practice with regard to marriage. Divorce (which see) was common, and resorted to upon meagre enough grounds. The school of Hillel sanctioned it for no better reason than that a wife had spoilt her husband's dinner, this opinion being founded upon a liberal interpretation of Dt 24^1. There is no subject on which Jesus spoke more uncompromisingly and unequivocally. He recognized that the stability and wholesomeness of social life depend largely on the health and purity of domestic life. While recognizing its physical basis, Jesus conceived of marriage as an essentially spiritual union. He regarded it as a Divine insti-

tution and ordinance, which involved the parties entering into it in the most solemn and sacred mutual obligations. In the highest, and to Him the only legitimate view of it, it was a consummation of mutual love mediated by God Himself (Mt 19^6). That was therefore no true marriage which was entered into for the gratification of sensual passion or on the score of worldly considerations. It was not within the province of man to sunder those whom God had joined, *i.e.* to cancel their vows and annul the relationship that had bound them to one another. No human lawcourt has the right to undo the tie made and sealed by God Himself. See, further, artt. ADULTERY, DIVORCE, EUNUCH, FAMILY, MARRIAGE.

(5) Jesus, then, acquiesced in the indefinite continuance of the ordinary relationships of life then obtaining, as constituting the normal state of society. He gave *no countenance to anarchism*. He Himself offered an example of law-abiding citizenship, consistently demanding that due respect be paid to the requirements and enactments of the civil power legislating within its own proper sphere. He rebuked the spirit of revolt which demurred to the right of government to levy taxes, He himself submitting to be taxed, even when He might have claimed exemption (Mt 17$^{27ff.}$). He consistently acquiesced in the right of properly constituted authorities to act in accordance with their legal powers; He would permit of no resistance to the emissaries of the Sanhedrin sent to arrest Him. The case against Him founded on charges of law-breaking collapsed. Pilate, with the best will, could find no fault in Him (Lk 23^{14}).

4. Jesus nevertheless did not fail to denounce with vehemence current injustices and abuses. His recognition of the prevalence of oppression, extortion, corrupt practices, and the pinched poverty due to them, not only finds explicit and scathing utterance (Lk 20^{47}), but is reflected in many of His parables and implied in many of His sayings. Yet He does not speak as if the emergence of these were the inevitable outcome of established social conditions. The blame is always laid upon individuals who guiltily abused their powers and opportunities. He allowed no word to escape His lips which might countenance the methods of violent revolution. He started no popular agitation to secure social reconstruction. No forcible alteration in the mere externalities of life would ensure the disappearance of prevalent evils. Jesus plainly taught that social amelioration must be brought about by the gradual assimilation of the mass to the ideal type, and the infusion of the principles of His gospel into all the veins of the body politic (Mt 13^{33}). By evolution, not by revolution, lay the path to the realization of the Kingdom of heaven. Jesus did not share the prophetic enthusiasm of impatient expectation to which the Day of the Lord seemed already at the doors. From the beginning He impressed it upon His disciples that it was indefinitely far off (Mk 4$^{26ff.}$, Mt 24^{14}). He had a profound appreciation of the protracted manner in which a regenerate state of society of a stable kind may only be attained, through the working of healthy spiritual forces in individual hearts (Mt 5^{13}). In this He stood alone. His doctrine surprised and perplexed His disciples. It was out of harmony with the traditional beliefs and hopes on which they had been nurtured (Mk 13$^{3ff.}$).

Nevertheless, Jesus did not anticipate that the Kingdom would come by a peaceful and progressive process of evolution, without the shocks of revolution. He foresaw that the forces of reform would rouse the strenuous hostility of antagonistic spiritual elements in society, with the consequent outbreak of anarchic convulsions (Mt 24$^{3ff.}$). Indeed, He anticipated that the ideal society would never be attained as the result of pure evolution. The forces of evil would refuse to be ousted, and would prove too strong to be suppressed. Successive Divine interferences would be required, culminating in a final catastrophic one, to secure their suppression and the realization of the Kingdom of heaven on earth in stable and universal sway (Mt 10²¹ 11¹² 13⁴¹· ⁴⁹).

5. Fundamental principles of Christ's social teaching, and their outcome.—(1) Jesus laid the foundation of the social structure of the future by His doctrine of *the equal essential worth of the individual*. This had already been preached with conviction and power, but with little practical outcome. Rigid lines of demarcation continued to separate the various classes in Roman society (cf. Dill, *Roman Society*, p. 270 ff.). It was through Jesus that the doctrine ceased to be little more than an academic proposition, and became a vitalizing element in civilization, and a regulative principle in the development of the new social organism. He laid the foundations of a pure, universal democracy—a democracy based, not on equality of personal possessions, but on equality of individual rights. He awakened a new sense of the essential dignity of human nature, and gave a meaning and a value to the most obscure life. He invested the common people with a new self-respect which elevated and fortified, and with a sense of personal responsibility which steadied and deepened, while eliminating the dangerous sense of purposelessness and insignificance. Every human being was a storehouse of Divine potentialities; His whole ministry consistently enforced and illustrated this pregnant truth. Though consenting to social inequalities, He did not allow these to be regarded as the sign or token of any differences in the intrinsic worth of the human soul. In His intercourse with all sorts and conditions He manifested a lofty indifference to rank and position, practically ignoring the artificial distinctions of society (Lk 7³⁶ᶠᶠ·). There was no human being beneath respectful regard or outside the radius of brotherly love. This He drove home by incarnating God's concern for the outcasts and the fallen, the pariahs of society. The express purpose of His mission was to seek and save that which was lost. By His self-sacrifice on the Cross, necessitated to procure redemption, approved and accepted by the Father, He made plain that the worth of the individual soul was, in God's regard, beyond calculation. Thus was a new sense of the sacredness of personality impressed upon the mind and heart of the world. From the acceptance of this doctrine flowed many and far-reaching consequences. Life might no longer be held cheap. Every human being, whatever his position, had certain rights which must be respected.

(a) *Slavery* could not and did not long persist as a normal institution of society. It speedily came under the ban of healthy Christian sentiment (Philem ¹⁶). Such a condition was not consonant with the essential dignity of human nature as hall-marked by Christ. It became impossible to regard human beings as mere goods and chattels, to be bought and sold as household furniture. Nor might they be treated with the callous brutalities of an inhumanity which made no distinction between slaves and beasts. The slave was also a man, and entitled at least to the regard proper to one possessed of an immortal and priceless soul.

(b) *Woman* also came into her kingdom. Generally speaking, she had been treated as an inferior being, who had duties but no rights, except what man chose to grant her. Her nature was 'cribb'd, cabin'd, and confin'd.' There were indeed many and brilliant exceptions in women who dignified the sex and won the warmest admiration. But the common contempt in which woman was held inevitably reacted on her nature, and, by lowering her self-respect, made of her what went to confirm the general opinion regarding her. Jesus changed all that. He emancipated her from her position of sex-inferiority. He did this by Himself treating her as an equal, in no wise of less essential worth than man (Lk 10³⁸ᶠᶠ·, Jn 11⁵). He gave her peculiar honour. Some of the most significant incidents in His life are associated with women (Jn 4⁹ᶠᶠ· 11³²ᶠᶠ·). He overturned the estimates of the past and revoked its unquestioned judgments. See, further, art. WOMAN.

(c) Jesus was the Saviour of the *child*. He put an end to the inhumanities with which unwelcome infants were treated (Mt 18⁶· ¹⁰· ¹⁴, Lk 17²). He gave the child an importance which resulted in increasing attention being paid to its well-being. The Early Church led the way in interpreting and applying the mind of the Master. Wherever His spirit has been most active, there has the child been the object of the most thoughtful and solicitous care. One of the fruits of the Reformation was the new interest taken in the education of the young. The modern deep and earnest study of child life, the many and varied institutions for promoting the physical and moral welfare of the young, are the outcome of a deepening and more sympathetic appreciation of the worth Jesus gave to the child (Mk 9³³⁻³⁷, Mt 18⁵). See, further, art. CHILDREN.

(2) Jesus preached *the brotherhood of men*, based on their common relationship to the Father-God, to whom all alike owe their being. Thus He linked the whole human race in a common kinship. The Stoics had ineffectively taught this doctrine. Jesus made it a substantial fact. Through Him it became a principle profoundly influential in determining the nature of the relations between man and man. It operated towards the obliteration of the artificial distinctions between class and class which obtained in a society ordered according to pagan ideas and ideals, distinctions which almost implied the tacit assumption of a gradual differentiation of nature. The Early Church gave practical illustration of the necessary outcome of Christ's teaching in their gatherings for worship, where rich and poor, master and slave, employer and employed, mingled indiscriminately, with the freedom and mutual regard based on the cordial recognition of their common brotherhood.

(a) Through the inculcation of this doctrine Jesus generated a social conscience, the sense of individual responsibility for the corporate well-being. He sowed the seed of the fruitful idea of the solidarity of the race. He gave a new meaning to the word 'neighbour,' and exalted neighbourliness to the rank of a supreme Christian virtue (Lk 10²⁹ᶠᶠ·). He widened the area of duty till it embraced the whole of mankind (Ac 1⁸). There is no horizon to the sphere of personal obligation. It reaches to the circumference of human need.

(b) Jesus thus evoked a new sense of humanity. He gave it a comprehensiveness, an outlook, and an insight, which it never possessed before. The Mosaic Code contains many enactments relative to the treatment of strangers and foreigners, but these rested on no broad human basis. They were instructed and qualified by considerations of nationality, antecedents, and prudential policy. Jesus refused to allow barriers of race to restrict the outflow of the spirit of beneficent love (Mk 7²⁶, Jn 4⁹· ⁴⁰). He taught it to reach out to the uttermost, as well as to reach down to the lowermost. His Church was to make the brotherhood of man a visible reality, environing within it people of all nations and tongues (Lk 13²⁹, Jn 12²⁰ᶠᶠ·). The duty of preaching the gospel to every creature involves the obligation of treating all alike in the spirit of the gospel. The sympathetic appreciation of the Heavenly Father's attitude to the erring and the wretched, as pictured in the parables, and as reflected in His own life, set men of whatever race or condition in a new light. The outcast, the fallen, the depraved, all those whose moral and spiritual condition classed them amongst the lost, became the objects of a compassion which yearned for their restoration. Their recovery became the serious concern of every soul bent upon the imitation of God. Christ infused the Saviour-spirit into the world, to which all need is a summons to help, and in whose eyes every sinner is a possible saint (Mt 12²⁰, Lk 23⁴³). There was no bondage to sin from which emancipation was not possible, no far country from which there was no return. Despair was a word foreign to Christ's vocabulary (Lk 6³⁵). He instituted the method of redemption by pity and love, whose intelligent application is gradually operating to effect what He proved in individual instances it was actually fitted to achieve (Jn 8¹¹, Lk 19¹ᶠᶠ). He discredited the method of spiritual cure which relies upon threats and penalties alone.

(c) He inaugurated the day of specifically Christian charity. Charity had been exercised before, but it was largely a matter of expediency, or the outflow of a mere pitifulness for misery and want. Jesus gave it a new heart and a new will, a new sight and a new insight. It was not to be left henceforth to a few munificent gentlemen like Pliny to dispense. Its exercise became the duty of all alike, according to their ability and opportunity. The organization of charity has been justly characterized as the finest achievement of the Early Christians (v. Dobschütz). Jesus erected charity into a supreme Christian virtue. He regarded its absence as a convicting proof of the absence of that spirit which qualified for entrance into the Kingdom of God. That was a sure indication of a soul out of fellowship with God (Mt 25⁴¹ᶠᶠ, Lk 12²⁰ᶠ 16²⁰ᶠᶠ). Jesus enjoined as a primary duty the prompt and ungrudging use of one's means in the relief of necessity of whatever kind. The priest and the Levite who passed by on the other side were transgressing the first and last law of love. Jesus would allow of no limit to the sacrifices one must be prepared to make in obedience to its legitimate demands (Lk 12³³). Charity must not be of the nature of unwilling acquiescence in a begging request. It must be the fruit of that spirit which is ready to give more than is asked, and will err on the side of generosity rather than of meanness (Lk 6³⁰). Yet the exercise of charity must not be indiscriminate or unregulated. It must always tend to promote the ends of the law of Christian love. It must be regulated by regard to the Golden Rule, interpreted in the light of the Heavenly Father's example. It must be well considered, ever keeping in view the highest welfare of those who invite its aid. Each case must be taken on its own merits. Charity is legitimate, only when it subserves the spiritual interests of the individual assisted,—when it makes him not only better off, but a better man. It is forbidden to give after such wise as will only encourage or confirm evil habits. To do so were to keep the lower law while breaking the higher,— the law of Christian love, which forbids the infliction of the ultimate moral injury that inevitably eventuates from indiscriminate and heedless giving. We must always do the studiously loving thing. True charity finds its exemplar in the Heavenly Father, who will not give what is harmful or useless, but only good things (Mt 7¹¹, Lk 11¹³); and it seeks with wise concern to foster the virtues of self-reliance, self-help, manly independence, and industry, whose exercise reduces the occasions of charity.

(3) Jesus preached *life as a stewardship*, and its powers, means, opportunities as a trust from God for the proper use of which each man was answerable. Talents must be regarded as gifts, to be used, not for the possessor's selfish purposes, but for the ends of an altruistic love. The teaching of Jesus uncompromisingly condemns the life which is spent in the pursuit of wealth for what it may yield of selfish pleasure, and the expenditure of means on purely personal gratification (Lk 12¹⁶ᶠᶠ). We are given that we may give. 'A man does not own his wealth; he owes it.' From the highest point of view, there is no such thing as private means. All possessions are a public trust. Jesus was urgent in His demand for the generous openhandedness of a large-hearted benevolence whose instinct was always to consent or comply rather than to refuse or withhold (Mt 5⁴²). To those who exercised it He made the most lavish promises (Lk 6³⁸ 18²⁸ᶠᶠ). The only saying preserved in the Canon outside the Gospels is an incitement to unselfish liberality on the ground of the blessedness it procures (Ac 20³⁵). Jesus bestows as strong condemnation upon the indifferent spirit which fails to use its means for the right ends, as upon those who wantonly abuse them for the wrong ones (Mt 25²⁶ᶠᶠ, Lk 16¹⁹ᶠᶠ). Means must always be regarded as a means. Their exploitation for selfish or sinister purposes invites and incurs penalties of the direst kind (Mt 24⁵¹). The same duties and responsibilities are laid upon small means as upon large,— upon the man of one talent as upon the man of ten (Lk 16¹¹ 19¹³⁻²⁷).

LITERATURE.—Brace, *Gesta Christi*; Dill, *Roman Society from Nero to Marcus Aurelius*; v. Dobschütz, *Primitive Life in the Primitive Church*; Lecky, *History of European Morals*; Peabody, *Jesus Christ and the Social Question*; Sanday, art. 'Jesus Christ' in Hastings' *DB*; Wendt, *Teaching of Jesus*; Westcott, *Social Aspects of Christianity*; Seeley, *Ecce Homo*; Harnack, *What is Christianity?* Forrest, *Authority of Christ*.

A. M. HUNTER.

SODOM.—The overthrow of the 'cities of the plain' was, according to Hebrew traditions, a Divinely-sent catastrophe, second only to that of the Deluge. The sinfulness of Sodom (often with the addition of 'Gomorrah') is frequently referred to as typical of terrible *wickedness* (e.g. Dt 32³², Is 1¹⁰ 3⁹, Jer 23¹⁴, La 4⁶, Ezk 16⁴⁶⁻⁴⁹, Wis 10⁶⁻⁸); and even more frequently is the devastation of the guilty cities typical of Divine *punishment*. And similarly in the NT:

1. Mt 10¹⁵ ‖ Lk 10¹². In St. Matthew the words occur in the course of our Lord's charge to the Twelve. If they came to any place in which their words were not received, they were to shake off the dust of their feet; 'Verily I say unto you, it shall be more tolerable for the land of Sodom and Gomorrah in the day of judgment than for that city.' In St. Luke, on the other hand, the words form part of the charge to the Seventy; he has 'Sodom' for 'the land of Sodom,' 'Gomorrah' is omitted, and instead of St. Matthew's favourite expression ἐν ἡμέρᾳ κρίσεως ('in the day of judgment'), is used ἐν τῇ ἡμέρᾳ ἐκείνῃ ('in that day') [D ἐν τῇ βασιλείᾳ τοῦ θεοῦ, so Syrr.]. In Mk 6¹¹ the whole phrase from St. Matthew (exc. Σοδόμοις ἢ Γομόρροις for γῇ Σοδόμων καὶ Γομόρρων) is inserted in A and some Latin MSS. Hence it found its way, through the TR, into the AV.

Our Lord here implies the great fact, which in the passage dealt with in the following section He states more clearly, that since privileges bring responsibilities, their neglect brings punishment. And therewith He further implies the mysterious truth that at 'the day of judgment' the punishments awarded to men will vary. 'It shall be more tolerable—more bearable' cannot be a mere figure of speech. The same truth is taught in Lk 12⁴⁷ᶠ·, and its converse in Lk 19¹⁶⁻¹⁹.

2. Mt 11²³· ²⁴. Our Lord uttered Woes against three Galilæan cities which refused to accept His mighty works and repent (v.²⁰). These denunciations were a practical carrying out of the figurative injunctions which He gave to His disciples in 10¹⁴. The three cities named are Chorazin, Bethsaida, and Capernaum. The two former He compares with Tyre and Sidon; and to the latter He uses somewhat similar language in referring to Sodom: 'for if in Sodom had been done the mighty works (δυνάμεις) which are being done in thee [the city], it would be remaining until to-day. However, I say unto you [the people] that for the land of Sodom it shall be more tolerable in the day of judgment than for thee [the city].' St. Luke has not preserved this reference to Sodom, though he gives the denunciation against Capernaum (10¹⁵). With regard to Mt 11²⁴ Wright (*Synopsis*², p. 216) says that the author 'appends a sentence which reminds us of [Mt] 10¹⁵. These refrains are very effective for Church reading, but they often seem to be editorial.'

The typical use of 'Sodom' as an example of sin reaches its height in Rev 11⁸, where Jerusalem is described as 'the great city, which spiritually is called Sodom and Egypt.'

3. Lk 17²⁹. This passage, like the two preceding, is absent from the Markan tradition. Sodom is here not so much a type of sin as of sudden and fearful destruction. Our Lord uttered many *logia* concerning the coming of the Son of Man. In one of these (Mt 24³⁷⁻³⁹, Lk 17²⁶ᶠ·) He likened the 'parousia' (Mt.)—the 'days' (Lk.)—of the Son of Man to the Deluge in the days of Noah. St. Luke alone adds, ' In like manner as it came to pass in the days of Lot; they were eating, drinking, buying, selling, planting, building; but in the day that Lot went out from Sodom, he rained [Gn 19²⁴ κύριος ἔβρεξεν] fire and brimstone from heaven and destroyed (them) all. Likewise shall it be in the day that the Son of Man is revealed.' The destruction of Sodom and Gomorrah is also coupled with the Deluge in 2 P 2⁵⁻⁷ as an example of punishment. See also Jude ⁷, Ro 9²⁹ = Is 1⁹.

A. H. M'NEILE.

SOLDIERS.—Throughout the Roman Empire, and especially in a prætorian province like Syria, of which the various divisions of Palestine practically formed part, soldiers were a common sight, and took a prominent share in the administration of affairs. The references to them, however, in the Gospels, except, as is natural, in connexion with our Lord's trial and crucifixion, are not numerous.

1. In Lk 3¹⁴ we read of soldiers who came to John the Baptist and asked him what they were to do. The word here is στρατευόμενοι (not στρατιῶται) and implies that they were on active service at the time. They can hardly have been Roman legionaries, but may have been members of Herod Antipas' army engaged in some local expedition, of which we know nothing, or even, as Ewald supposes, only a kind of police or gendarmes employed in custom-house duties. The Baptist's answer to their inquiry shows what the temptations of such folk were in those days. They must be careful, he says, henceforth not to do violence or extort money by false accusations, and to be content with their pay.

2. In Mt 8⁹ and Lk 7⁸ the centurion (no doubt a proselyte, though a Roman officer; cf. Ac 10¹) who desired to have his servant healed, speaks of the soldiers who were under his command, and, in contrast to (**1**) above, his remarks bring out forcibly the idea of discipline and organization, which was to be found in a Roman legion.

3. The armies (στρατόπεδα) that would encircle

Jerusalem in the fatal siege of Titus (A.D. 70) are referred to in Lk 21²⁰ (cf. 19⁴³).

4. In the parable of the Marriage of the King's Son (Mt 22¹ᶠᶠ·) we read of the armies (στρατεύματα) which the king sent to avenge the murder of his servants.

5. After the trial before Pilate, when our Lord had been scourged and condemned to be crucified, Pilate's soldiers on duty took Him into their own quarters, and, gathering the whole band together, proceeded to treat Him with the grossest insults and mockery (Mt 27²⁷, Mk 15¹⁶, Jn 19²). And during the long hours of crucifixion He had to endure similar maltreatment from the soldiers who were in charge (Lk 23³⁶; cf. Mt 27⁴⁸, Jn 19²⁹). It is recorded also (Jn 19²³· ²⁴) how they parted His garments among them (see COAT and QUATERNION); and further that, when the end had come, finding He was already dead, they refrained from breaking His legs, as Pilate had ordered, before taking Him down; but 'one of them with a spear pierced his side, and forthwith there came out blood and water' (Jn 19³²· ³⁴).

6. Lastly, soldiers were keeping guard at the sepulchre when the Resurrection took place (Mt 27⁶⁵ᶠ· 28¹¹⁻¹³; see WATCH). C. L. FELTOE.

SOLITUDE.—We may infer from the phrase used in Lk 5¹⁶ (ἦν ὑποχωρῶν, see Bengel's note, *ad loc.*) that our Lord frequently sought solitude during the period of His ministry. Sometimes He retired from the multitude, but did not seclude Himself from His disciples (*e.g.* Mt 14¹³ 17¹). At other times His solitude was absolute, and He only returned to His disciples or was rejoined by them after an interval (*e.g.* Mt 14²³, Mk 1³⁵, Lk 5¹⁶ 6¹²). It is this latter complete solitude that is of importance to the student of our Lord's Person and work.

1. We observe that He sought solitude, or, if the phrase is permissible, was forced into solitude, at certain critical times of special trial. The battle of the Temptation (Mt 4¹ᶠᶠ·, Mk 1¹²ᶠᶠ·, Lk 4¹ᶠᶠ·) was fought out in solitude. No human being was within call, and only after the victory was won did angels come to minister to Him. The final struggle against the weakness inherent in the flesh took place in solitude (Mt 26⁴¹, Lk 22³⁹). Although He yearned for human sympathy, He deliberately withdrew Himself from the companionship of His disciples. The account of the supreme crisis of His work of redemption witnesses to a solitude too complete and awful for our understanding (Mt 27⁴⁶). We ought perhaps to class the solitude which He sought after the feeding of the five thousand (Mt 14²³, Mk 6⁴⁶, Jn 6¹⁵) with the three instances just mentioned. The people wished to make Him a king, and may well have suggested a temptation similar to that recorded in Mt 4⁸.

2. Our Lord sought solitude in order to obtain spiritual help for specially important work (Lk 6¹²), and spiritual refreshment after periods of exhausting labour (Mk 1³⁵· ⁴⁵, cf. Lk 5¹⁶). We may suppose that on these occasions, as on another, 'virtue had gone out of him,' and that in a literal sense 'Himself took our infirmities and bare our sicknesses' (Mt 8¹⁷), thereby coming to feel the need for fresh intercourse with the Father unvexed with human companionship.

A very curious and suggestive commentary on this twofold use of solitude in our Lord's life is afforded by the experience of the earliest monks, those Egyptian recluses whom we shall not be wrong in regarding as specialists in the spiritual life. They believed that in solitude a man is exposed to the full fury of the powers of evil, that temptation is not completely conquered because not met in its utmost strength except by him who ventures to meet it alone (Cass. *Coll.* vii. 23; Athanas. *Vita Anton.* xiii.). Their thought would explain our Lord's 'being led up of the Spirit into the wilderness, to be tempted of the devil' (Mt 4¹). It was, no doubt, necessary (cf. the general conception of Milton's *Paradise Regained*) that He should be exposed to the utmost strength of the Tempter.　Therefore He faced the Evil One in solitude.

The hermits also believed that spiritual communion with God and the graces which flow from it are attainable best in solitude. The abbot Allois sums up their teaching in his deeply suggestive word, 'Except a man say in his heart, "I and God are alone in the world," he cannot have peace' (*Verba Seniorum*, *ap.* Rosweyd, *Interpr. Pelagio*, x. 5 ; see also Cass. *Coll.* xix. 5, xxiv. 4). In this respect their experience fits in with our Lord's retirements in search of refreshment and strength.

The literature of early Western monasticism and much of the teaching of the later Mystics on the subject of solitude fall into line with the recorded experience of the Egyptians, and form a further commentary on the recorded facts of our Lord's solitude.　On the one hand, there is an evident dread of the extreme temptations of solitude, and a feeling that they ought not to be faced except by those far advanced in the spiritual life. On the other hand, there is a recognition of the possibilities of spiritual advancement which solitude affords (see, besides books cited below, Cass. *Inst.* v. 4 ; Basil, *Reg. Fus. Tract.*; *Reg. Brev. Tract.* ; Bened. *Reg.* i. ; Joann. Clim. *Grad.* iv. etc.; Basil, *Epp.* ii., xxiii., xlii. ; Bened. *Reg.* iv., xlviii. etc.).

LITERATURE.—Works quoted ; Martin Crugott, *Der Christ in der Einsamkeit* (1761); I. G. Zimmermann, *Die Einsamkeit* (1784); R. W. Emerson, *Society and Solitude* (1862); P. Zingerle, *Reden des hl. Ephraem über Selbstverleugnung und einsame Lebensweise, aus dem. Syr. übersetzt.* (1871); H. D. Thoreau, *Walden* (repr. 1886); T. T. Lynch, *Letters to the Scattered*, 522 ; F. W. Robertson, *Serm.* i. 220 ; Martineau, *Endeavours*, 159 ; Rendel Harris, *Memor. Sacra*, 135.　　J. O. HANNAY.

SOLOMON. — Jesus makes two references to Solomon, speaking on one occasion of his 'glory,' and on another of his 'wisdom.'　In Mt 6²⁹=Lk 12²⁷ He places the pure natural beauty of the lilies above the consummate type of artificial splendour, and uses the contrast to point the lesson of trustful dependence upon God, the Giver of all that is necessary for the body as well as for the spirit.　In Mt 12⁴²=Lk 11³¹ the eagerness of Solomon's contemporaries to hear his words of worldly wisdom is contrasted with the indifference and spiritual blindness of the men of Jesus' own day, who failed to understand and appreciate the truer wisdom of a greater teacher.

For 'Solomon's Porch' see TEMPLE.

C. H. THOMSON.

SON, SONSHIP.—

υἱός, which definitely='son,' is of commonest occurrence in the Gospels, though the more indefinite τέκνον is also frequently used interchangeably with υἱός.　The use of τέκνον in the vocative as an affectionate form of address ('child,' 'my child') is specially noticeable (see, *e.g.*, Mk 2⁵, Lk 2⁴⁸ 15³¹, Mt 21²⁸). The latter term is several times rendered 'son' in EV without discrimination.　RV, indeed, usually indicates 'child' in mg. as the exact equivalent, but this is not always the case (see Mt 21²⁸ τέκνα).

1. The duties and privileges of the filial relation find frequent incidental illustration in the Gospels. The son has a natural claim on parental bounty (Mt 7⁹) ; he is the object of deep parental love and solicitude (Mt 10³⁷ 20²⁰ᶠ·).　(A peculiar appeal to such solicitude is made in Lk 14⁵, if we are to follow the best attested reading (see RVm) ; though the collocation of υἱός and βοῦς is so odd that it is a temptation to defy the canons of textual criticism, and, following rather the analogy of kindred passages (13¹⁵, Mt 12¹¹), still read ὄνος).　By consequence, strife between father and son is a most painful form of estrangement (Lk 12⁵³), whilst the restoration of a happy relationship between those who have been so estranged calls for the highest rejoicing (Lk 15²²⁻²⁴).　The natural heirship of the son appears in Mk 12⁶ (and parallels) and in Lk 15¹², where the technical term (τὸ ἐπιβάλλον μέρος) for the heir's portion occurs (see Deissmann, *Bible Studies*, Eng. tr. p. 230).　In the former instance—. the parable of the Wicked Husbandmen — the position of an only son as carrying with it sole heirship is emphasized.　The ὁ υἱὸς ὁ ἀγαπητός of Lk 20¹³, in this connexion, appears to be tantamount to ὁ υἱὸς ὁ μονογενής (Jn 3¹⁶), as denoting an only son (cf. also Mt 3¹⁷ 17⁵ etc.).　In the latter case (Lk 15¹²) we have a son claiming and obtaining his inheritance during his father's lifetime.　This

serves the purpose of the parable ; but it may be doubted whether such an occurrence was common in actual life.　The counsels of ancient Jewish prudence (Sir 33¹⁹ᶠᶠ·) were, at any rate, dead against it.　The more usual course is exemplified in the case of the elder son, whose share in the patrimony was still in his father's hands (Lk 15³¹), but was fully assured to him in spite of his complaint in v.³⁰ (ὁ καταφαγών σου τὸν βίον).　A special instance of a son's privilege is made use of in Mt 17²⁵ᶠ· ; the sons of 'the kings of the earth' are exempt (ἐλεύθεροι) from the tribute exacted from their subjects.

On the other hand, the duty of sons to render obedience, service and help to parents similarly appears.　The parable of the Two Sons (Mt 21²⁸ᶠᶠ·) thus illustrates filial dutifulness and undutifulness. The significance of our Lord's words, 'Behold thy son,' in Jn 19²⁶, is at once understood as securing loving care and provision for His mother (v.²⁷). Christ's interpretation of the Fifth Commandment as involving the duty of helping and supporting parents in case of need, is accompanied by a biting denunciation of the Pharisaic ruling that such duty could be nullified by a vow (Mk 7¹⁰ᶠᶠ· *Corban*).

It is clear that Jesus found in sonship an instrument of prime importance for the illustration and enforcement of His teaching.　It is certain His exemplification of the filial relationship in His own life was perfect.　The scanty hints of Lk 2⁴⁰⁻⁵² (in such striking contrast to the volubility of the Apocryphal narratives) may be accepted as witnessing to such a fulfilment of filial duties during the long years of silence as makes Him the very 'flower and pattern' of all good sons.　Mary's surprised expostulation in v.⁴⁸ suggests the perfect dutifulness of His childhood's years ; and we may be sure the child was 'father of the man,' as to what He was in the after-time as (probably) the mainstay and head of the home at Nazareth on the death of Joseph.　Yet the day also came when He illustrated in His own experience His own exacting demand (Mt 10³⁷), and showed how filial regard must yield to higher claims, summing all up in the impressive *logion* of Mk 3³⁴ᶠ· (= Mt 12⁴⁹ᶠ·, cf. Lk 8²¹).　Lk 11²⁸ embodies a similar sentiment.

2. Arising out of the notion of the filial relation in its natural sense, we have the idiomatic use of the phrase 'son of' as a familiar characteristic of the Gospel phraseology.　A poetic feeling underlies the description of a wise man as a 'son of wisdom,' and at the same time its appropriateness is self-evident.　υἱός and τέκνον both occur in this connexion, and instances of the use of the idiom found in the Gospels may be grouped as follows : (*a*)=*belonging to, connected with,* or *destined for*.　Persons are described as sons 'of the kingdom' (Mt 8¹² 13³⁸) ; 'of this world' (age) (Lk 16⁸ 20³⁴) ; 'of the bridechamber' (Mk 2¹⁹ ‖) ; 'of Jerusalem' (=inhabitants) (Mt 23³⁷) ; 'of the Pharisees' (followers, adherents, Mt 12²⁷=Lk 11¹⁹) : 'of the evil one' (Mt 13³⁸ ; *Twentieth Cent. NT* renders simply 'the wicked,' evading a personal significance in τοῦ πονηροῦ) ; 'of Gehenna' (Mt 23¹⁵) ; 'of perdition' (Jn 17¹²) ; 'of the resurrection' (Lk 20³⁶).　(*b*)= *characterized by certain qualities* : 'sons of thunder' (Mk 3¹⁷) ; 'of peace' (Lk 10⁶) ; 'of light' (Jn 12³⁶) ; 'of wisdom' (τέκνα, Mt 11¹⁹=Lk 7³⁵) ; as similarly 'of consolation' in Ac 4³⁶ (this without reference to the correctness of the etymology indicated).　(*c*)=*descendants* : 'sons of them that slew the prophets' (Mt 23³¹) ; 'of Israel' (Mt 27⁹, Lk 1¹⁶) ; 'of Abraham' (τέκνα, Jn 8³⁹ ; υἱός, Lk 19⁹, cf. 13¹⁶).

Deissmann (*Bible Studies*, pp. 161–166) labours to modify the common explanation of such circumlocutory forms as Hebraisms and due to 'the Oriental spirit of language' (Buttmann, quoted in *loc. cit.*).　As features of NT diction he is willing to see in them a 'Hebraism of translation' (due to Semitic originals rather than to a Hebraistic style or habit in the writers themselves), but is eager to maintain that such constructions are not foreign to the genius of Greek. He is not, however, entirely successful. Of course, the use of the phrase 'sons of' as = inhabitants or descendants, may be widely paralleled in various languages (as, *e.g.*, the Homeric υἷες Ἀχαιῶν = 'Αχαιοί); but in manifold other uses, especially as in (*b*) above, the case is different. The expression υἱὸς τύχης (in Horace, *filius fortunœ*) is noteworthy, but 'one swallow does not make a summer'; and, moreover, Plato's use of ἔκγονος, specially adduced by Deissmann, hardly affords a true parallel. In *Phœdr.* 275 D, *e.g.*, τὰ ζωγραφίας ἔκγονα, denoting the *productions* of art, a painter's *works*, falls short of such uses as are indicated in (*b*), whereby personal qualities are described. The expression is, on the other hand, so characteristic of Semitic speech as to amount to an idiom, and the OT writings abound in it. Its occurrence in the NT is best explained in this connexion: and it is difficult to think that it might have occurred in exactly the same way had the writers been writing in an independent Greek style.

3. An arresting feature in the teaching of Jesus is His description of men as the sons (υἱοί, τέκνα) of God. The most conspicuous name that He uses for God in His relation to men is that of 'Father,' usually with the Jewish addition of 'in heaven' or 'heavenly.' Some of His most noticeable parables and illustrative sayings are based on the relation of father and son as best representing the relation between God and man (see, *e.g.*, Lk 15^{11ff.}, Mt 7^{9ff.}). See artt. CHILDREN OF GOD, SON OF GOD.

Notice may be taken of the curious phrasing of Lk 20^{36} υἱοί εἰσιν θεοῦ τῆς ἀναστάσεως υἱοὶ ὄντες. This *per se* seems to limit the description 'sons of God' to those who are accounted worthy to attain the resurrection life (v.^{35}). They 'are sons of God *through* being sons of the Resurrection' (Weymouth). Or perhaps we may equally well interpret by saying that the fact of their having risen *shows* that they are God's sons. It has to be pointed out, however, that this is part of an expansion of our Lord's reply to the Sadducees quite peculiar to Lk., presenting a striking divergence from the Synoptic parallels. It seems to be merely an amplification of the term ἰσάγγελοι, itself a Lukan ἅπαξ λεγ. for the simpler ὡς ἄγγελοι of Mt. and Mk. At any rate, it cannot be pressed so as to conflict with the general representation of men as being all God's sons in one way and another, found so often in the Gospels. A connexion with Ro 8^{19} may be suggested (cf also phrasing in Ro 1^4).

4. The term 'son' is used of Jesus Himself in various ways. (*a*) In the ordinary sense of the word He is described as 'the son of Joseph' and 'the son of Mary.' See Mk 6^3 = Mt 13^{55} = Lk 4^{22}. Jn 6^{42} (cf. 1^{45}) is also in close agreement with Lk 4^{22}, with the interesting addition, 'whose father and mother we know.' (This is one of the smaller points in which the Johannine Gospel stands on a basis of common tradition with the Synoptics). The expression in Mt 13^{55} ὁ τοῦ τέκτονος υἱός, may possibly have originally meant no more than ὁ τέκτων in Mk 6^3. Cheyne's conjecture, that 'Jesus the son of Joseph' may mean 'Jesus a member of the house of Joseph' (*EBi* ii. 2598), may be ingenious, but is an unnecessary departure from tradition. We cannot arbitrarily push aside the plain suggestions of the Birth-narratives and the genealogies as to the personality of Joseph in this connexion.

It is to be pointed out that it is only in the account of the visit to Nazareth, as above, that the Synoptists explicitly indicate such a designation of Jesus. (The Johannine instances are in quite different connexions). Corresponding references to His parentage are found, however, in such passages as Lk 2^{22-51} ('his father and his mother,' 'his parents,' 'thy father and I') and Mk 3^{31ff.} with its parallels. τέκνον as applied to Jesus occurs just once, in Lk 2^{48}. The dominant presentment of our Lord in the Gospels transcends the interest attaching to simple human relations. See also the following three articles.   J. S. CLEMENS.

SON OF DAVID.—The phrase is used in the NT as a title of the Messiah, except in Mt 1^{1. 20} (cf. Lk 1^{27}), where it has the ordinary genealogical force. For the general discussion of the Messiahship of Jesus, and of the Messiah as king, see MESSIAH; the present article concerns only the use of this particular title.

1. The Messianic value of the title comes out forcibly in the puzzling question put by Jesus to the Pharisees (Mt 22^{42f.}, Mk 12^{35}, Lk 20^{41})—a question that they were unable to answer : 'The scribes say that the Christ is (to be) the Son of David ; but David calls him Lord ; how then is he his son ?' The passage is not to be interpreted as a repudiation of the title on the part of Jesus. Of such a repudiation there is no evidence either in His own teaching, or in other parts of the NT. On the contrary, the relationship is specifically taught by St. Paul (Ro 1^3, 2 Ti 2^8), seemingly as of some importance, and it is assumed of the Messiah in the Apocalypse (Rev 5^5 22^{16}). The passage is a repudiation of the notion of the Jews—implied in their use of the title—that it fully expresses the functions of the Messiah. The Messiah does not owe His dignity to His Davidic descent. His work far surpasses that of the great king of Israel. The proper answer to Jesus' question would have involved an entire reconstruction of the ideas of the Jews concerning the Messiah, of which they were, of course, utterly incapable. If Jesus did not expect this result to follow from His question, He could at least show by it the logical absurdity of the emphasis they put upon the Davidic sonship. The connexion of the Messiah with the royal house and city was deemed so essential, that Jesus, of Galilæan extraction, was declared by some to be ineligible to the high office.

2. The particular phase of Messiahship which the title properly expresses is, of course, the royal estate and function. Such was the case when it was applied to Jesus on the occasion of His triumphal entry into Jerusalem (Mt 21^{9. 15}). It was so understood, and the anger of the priests and scribes was aroused in consequence. Compare also the Annunciation (Lk 1^{32}), where it is said that Jesus shall be given the throne of His father David.

3. There is, however, no reason to suppose that, as used in NT times, the title alluded to military prowess, or to a career of conquest on the part of the Messiah. Indeed, the Hosannas of the people were in praise of very different qualities. Such a conception of the force of the phrase is entirely inconsistent with the cry of the blind men (Mt 20^{30f.} [= Mk 10^{47f.}, Lk 18^{38f.}] and 9^{27}) and of the Canaanitish woman (Mt 15^{22}), 'Son of David, have mercy.' The title came naturally to the lips of those who sought Jesus' aid in their great distress. Likewise the works of healing which He had wrought called forth—so characteristic were they of the Messiah who was expected—the query whether this might not be the Son of David (Mt 12^{23}).

4. These NT applications of the title are in close harmony with the OT description of the Messiah. David was the founder of the kingdom of Israel. Whenever in later centuries the nation and its welfare were in the mind, the thought naturally turned to David. When the house of David no longer ruled, and the kingdom was shattered, prophets and singers lamented the misfortunes that had overtaken David and his house. When their hopefulness and faith in God expressed itself in visions of a bright future, they naturally spoke of a second David, a branch of his house, who should restore the nation to its former prosperity. As the past, and especially David's rule, grew fairer by contrast with the dismal present, so the new kingdom of David in the future was pictured in extravagant colours. The Kingdom should extend over the whole earth, irresistibly, triumphantly. But this conquest was not conquest for conquest's sake. It was a process without which the longed-for prosperity could, in their imagination, not be realized. It was but an incident in the larger blessedness of the future. To the

Jew of the later pre-Christian centuries, David stood for much else besides military prowess and political prestige. If this element had been predominant, it would have been incongruous to ascribe to him so large a part of the Psalms as bear his name. If we seek for the cause of this change of emphasis, it is doubtless to be found in the very distress that they suffered. That distress was personal, individual. Character became the condition of enjoying the benefits of the new Kingdom, and in turn the new Kingdom—Messianic, ideal—was to exist for the sake of the individual, to save him from his woes, and to lead him to righteousness. Ps 72, in spite of its warlike sentiments, is the utterance of one to whom, after all, the welfare of the people, the oppressed and the defenceless, is paramount. These are the poor and the blind to whom Jesus gave salvation, by such ministry proving, even to His contemporaries, that He was worthy to be called the Son of David.

See also art. NAMES AND TITLES OF CHRIST.

LITERATURE. — Briggs, *Messianic Prophecy*, pp. 492–496; Wendt, *Lehre Jesu*, ii. 434 ff.; Schürer, *HJP* II. ii. § 29.

O. H. GATES.

SON OF GOD.—As the word 'Christ,' which was at first a title, has come to be a proper name, this change being, indeed, accomplished even in the NT, so the title 'Son of God' is now appropriated to the Second Person of the Trinity; and the ordinary reader of the Bible assumes this to be the meaning wherever he finds the phrase. He has only, however, to read with a little attention to perceive that this is an assumption which ought not to be made without inquiry, because in Scripture there are many 'sons of God.' (1) The angels are thus designated, as when in the Book of Job (38[7]) it is mentioned that at the dawn of creation 'the morning stars sang together, and all the sons of God shouted for joy.' (2) The term is applied to the first man, when, in Lk 3, the genealogy of the Saviour is traced back to Adam, 'who,' it is added (v.[38]), 'was the son of God.' And, if the general scope of Scripture may leave it questionable whether the same high title can be applied to all the first man's descendants, the authority of our Lord may be claimed, on the ground of the parable of the Prodigal Son, as deciding the question in the affirmative. (3) The Hebrew nation collectively is frequently thus designated, as when, in the land of Midian, Jehovah sent Moses to Pharaoh with the message: 'Thus saith the Lord, Israel is my son, even my firstborn, and I say unto thee, Let my son go' (Ex 4[22f.]). Whether, according to Scripture usage, it was applicable to individual Israelites, is not so clear, but probably it was; for not only did the Jews, in speaking to Jesus, claim, 'We have one Father, even God' (Jn 8[41]), but Jesus Himself said, 'Let the children first be filled' (Mk 7[27]). (4) It was a title of the kings of Israel. Thus, in Ps 89[26f.], an ancient oracle is quoted in which Jehovah says of King David, 'He shall cry unto me, Thou art my Father, my God, and the rock of my salvation; also I will make him my firstborn, higher than the kings of the earth.' Similarly Jehovah says of King Solomon (2 S 7[14]), 'I will be his Father, and he shall be to me a son.' (5) In the NT the title is conferred on all who believe in the Saviour. Thus, in the Prologue to the Gospel of St. John, it is said, 'But as many as received him, to them gave he power to become the sons of God, even to them that believe on his name' (Jn 1[12]); and, in his First Epistle, the Evangelist exclaims, 'Behold what manner of love the Father hath bestowed upon us, that we should be called the sons of God' (1 Jn 3[1]).

It would require some investigation to determine what is the reason for the bestowal of this lofty title in each of these cases, and in all probability the reasons might be different in the different cases. In the case of the angels, the relation suggested may be that of the Creator to His creatures; and this notion may cover also the application to man in general, who were made in 'the image of God.' The application to the nation of Israel refers undoubtedly to the choice which the grace of God made of the Hebrew people from among all the nations of the earth; and in the Jewish kings this grace reached its climax. In the case of Christians, the reasons are obvious in the texts quoted in reference to them. It is usual to lay all the emphasis on the sentiments entertained by God towards those honoured with this title, as if it expressed solely His choice of them; but Nösgen (*op. cit. infr.*) contends that in all cases at least some reason for the designation must lie in the qualities or history of the person designated; and this is a contention which seems to have common sense on its side.

It will thus be seen that 'the son of God' was a phrase much in use in the world before it was attached to our Lord; and the question naturally arises, from which of its anterior uses was that its transference to Him took place. In all probability it was from the fourth mentioned above—that is, its application to the Jewish kings. If the application to the nation culminated in that to the kings, so the application to the kings culminated in Him who was to be the fulfilment of the regal idea in Israel. That is to say, the term is, in the first place, politico-Messianic. But it does not follow, as is too often assumed, that this is its only sense. On the contrary, in all the deeper passages where it occurs, whether in the Synoptics or in Jn., it points strongly to the personal qualities of Him who bears it, and to an intimate relationship with Him whose Son He is said to be. The political title rests upon personal qualities and experiences; He is not the Son of God because He is the Messiah, but, on the contrary, He is the Messiah because He is the Son of God. That is to say, the term is ethico-religious. But it does not follow, as is often assumed, that because it is official-Messianic and ethico-religious it is not also physical or metaphysical. On the contrary, the closeness of the ethico-religious relation may be such as to demand a metaphysical relationship of an intimate and peculiar kind between Father and Son. It seems to be strangely forgotten in many quarters that ethical intimacy is, in all cases, limited by the closeness of metaphysical relationship; the limitation of the intimacy between a dog and a man, for example, is due to the lack of metaphysical unity between them, whereas the closeness of sympathy and intimacy possible between a woman and a man is due to their metaphysical oneness. There is no reason whatever why all the three kinds of relationship indicated above should not be united; in point of fact, they often are. The kingship of a king, for example, may be, first, official, he being actually the reigning monarch; secondly, personal, he possessing the ethical qualities which become and secure his position; thirdly, physical or metaphysical, because he is of the blood royal, and has in his composition the hereditary instincts of long descent. In like manner the Messiahship of Jesus may rest on a spiritual and ethical relationship to God; but this may be of so intimate a kind as to demand a peculiar relationship to the Father physically or metaphysically; and in all the Gospels there is reference, more or less, to all the three.

1. The Synoptics.—In the Synoptics Jesus does not, of His own motion, call Himself in so many words 'the Son of God.' But the title is applied to Him in about twelve passages in Mt. and fully half that number each in Mk. and Lk., and in several of these cases He treats this application in such a way as to show that He adopts it. On several occasions (six times in Mt., once in Mk., thrice in Lk.) He denominates Himself 'the Son' in such a way as to prove unmistakably that He regards Himself as 'the Son of God'; and many times in all three Gospels (over a score of times in Mt., thrice in Mk., nine times in Lk.) He in the same way refers to God as His Father. (The quotations in detail will be found on p. 86 of Stalker's *Christology of Jesus*, mentioned below in the List of Literature).

(1) Beyschlag observes (*NT Theol.* i. 68) that *the occurrence of the term in the mouths of others* shows that it has its roots in the OT and was already current in Israel, and therefore, that for the sense in which Jesus applied it to Himself we must go back to the OT. It is also usual to state that it is employed in the pseudepigraphic literature of the period between the OT and the NT as a synonym for the Messiah. If, however, the only two passages of this sort supplied by Dalman (*op. cit. infr.*) be referred to, it will be found that this notion rests on a very slender basis. If the TR of Mk 1¹ be correct,—'the beginning of the gospel of Jesus Christ, the Son of God,'—it would be rash to limit the Evangelist's intention to the Messiahship; but the reading is suspected. In Lk 1³⁵ the reason why Jesus is to be called 'the Son of God' is supplied in the memorable statement to Mary, 'The Holy Ghost shall come upon thee, and the power of the Highest shall overshadow thee.' This is a physical explanation of the term, which it is rather surprising never to find elsewhere. The nearest approach to it in the Gospels would be the exclamation of the centurion at the Cross, 'Truly this was the Son of God' (Mk 15³⁹); but it is dubious what a heathen may have meant by such an observation.

Still more dubious, one would suppose, must it remain what the demoniacs intended by calling Jesus by this title, though it is usually taken for granted that they must have used it in the Messianic sense, because they also sometimes acknowledged Him as the Messiah. When Satan, in the Temptation, played with the title, he was obviously referring back to the voice which, at the Jordan during the Baptism, recognized Jesus as 'the Son of God'; but how much that voice intended, or how much the Tempter understood of what it meant, might require considerable discussion.

When 'they that were in the ship' on the occasion when Jesus stilled the tempest and rescued St. Peter from the sea, 'came and worshipped him,' saying, 'Of a truth thou art the Son of God' (Mt 14³³), the most natural interpretation may be that they were acknowledging Him as the Messiah. If they were, they anticipated, in a remarkable manner, the subsequent confession at Cæsarea Philippi; and this raises a doubt which may incline us to understand their language rather as an involuntary recognition of the Divine in Jesus, occasioned by the sight of a remarkable miracle.

Undoubtedly the most convincing case for the identity of meaning in the terms 'the Messiah' and 'the Son of God' is the confession of the Twelve, through the lips of St. Peter, at Cæsarea Philippi; because, whereas St. Matthew reports them as confessing, 'Thou art the Christ, the Son of the living God' (16¹⁶), the other two Evangelists omit the second phrase (Mk 8²⁹, Lk 9²⁰). Now, it is argued, they could not have omitted this, had it contained a momentous addition to the acknowledgment of the Messiahship; against which the only *caveat* that can be hinted is that there are many examples to prove that it is perilous to rest much on the silence of one or more of the Gospels.

Another passage which is confidently appealed to as demonstrating the identity of meaning between the two terms, is the demand addressed by the high priest to Jesus, on His trial, to say whether He were 'the Christ, the Son of God.' Yet, in reporting this incident, St. Luke excites doubt as to the identity, because he represents Him as being asked first simply if He were 'the Christ'; but when He wound up His reply with the imposing words,

'Hereafter shall the Son of Man sit on the right hand of the power of God,' they proceeded, 'Art thou, then, the Son of God?' and the affirmative answer to this second question seems to have shocked and irritated them far more than the answer to the first, occasioning a tempest of rage and insult in all present, with a unanimous agreement that He had been guilty of blasphemy (Lk 22⁶⁹). H. J. Holtzmann, who writes with extraordinary feeling on this subject, recently, in a review in the *Theologische Literaturzeitung*, declaring it to be a shame that Protestant scholars should even doubt the identity, affirms that 'the blasphemy can only have been found in the fact that a man belonging to the lower classes, one openly forsaken of God and going forward to a shameful death, should have dared to represent himself as the object and fulfilment of all the Divine promises given to the nation'; but the blasphemy is far more obvious if the claim to be 'the Son of God' was understood to mean more than even Messiahship.

From the foregoing examination of the passages in the Gospels where the phrase is used of Jesus by others than Himself, it will be perceived that there is considerable variety of meaning and application; it certainly is Messianic, but it is not uniformly or exclusively so.

(2) When we turn to *the passages in which Jesus speaks of Himself as 'the Son,' or calls God His Father*, the official-Messianic element is almost entirely absent, the language being that of intimacy and confidence. Here and there, indeed, there may be Messianic associations involved, as when Jesus promises to the Twelve that, in the day of the full manifestation of the Kingdom, they shall sit on thrones judging the twelve tribes of Israel (Mt 19²⁸), or when He predicts that on the judgment-day He will appear in the glory of His Father and of the holy angels (Mk 8³⁸); but, as a rule, one might read the greater number of these sayings without being reminded that they proceeded from the lips of one claiming to be the Messiah. The consciousness to which they give expression is that of a personal relationship, as when, in Gethsemane, He prays, 'O my Father, if it be possible, let this cup pass from me; nevertheless, not as I will, but as thou wilt'; and, farther on, 'O my Father, if this cup may not pass away from me, except I drink it, thy will be done' (Mt 26³⁹·⁴²); or when, on the cross, He cries, 'Father, forgive them: for they know not what they do'; and, farther on, 'Father, into thy hands I commend my spirit' (Lk 23³⁴·⁴⁶).

The climax of this ethico-religious sentiment is reached in the great saying of Mt 11²⁷ ‖ Lk 10²² 'All things are delivered unto me of my Father; and no man knoweth the Son but the Father, neither knoweth any man the Father save the Son, and he to whomsoever the Son will reveal him.' In recent times this passage has attracted great attention, not a few looking upon it as the profoundest utterance of Jesus in the Synoptics. Holtzmann, indeed, hesitates between such a decision and a suggestion of Brandt's that it is a cento, put into the mouth of Jesus, of words borrowed partly from other Scripture and partly from the Apocrypha; but by Keim it has been reverentially interpreted, and scholarship has, on the whole, knelt before it as expressing the innermost mystery of the consciousness of Jesus. The words were spoken at a crisis, when He was roused out of deep depression at the apparent failure of His mission, by the return of the Seventy, bringing a joyful account of the results of their labours. 'In that hour Jesus rejoiced in spirit, and said, I thank thee, O Father, Lord of heaven and earth, because thou hast hid these things from the wise and prudent, and hast revealed them unto babes; even so, Father, for so it seemed good in thy sight' (Mt 11[25f.]). Then followed the words already quoted. The first of them, 'All things are delivered unto me of my Father,' may be best understood, as is suggested by Lütgert (*op. cit. infr.*), of the Messianic dominion in its widest extent, as it had been promised in prophecy from of old; while the next words, 'For no man knoweth the Son but the Father,' etc., express the consciousness of His own right and ability to fill this position, because He has all the resources of the Divine nature to dispense to those who come to Him. This is why He proceeds immediately to say, 'Come unto me, all ye that labour and are heavy laden, and I will give you rest' (v.[28]). The mood in which He was consisted of a joyful uprising within Himself of the consciousness of all He was able to do for those who trusted Him; and this was due to His intimate and perfect union with Deity.

Most scholars, however, hasten to add that this sonship was purely ethical, and was not different from that to which He was prepared to introduce His disciples. He showed, it is remarked, the true pathway to this position, and the one by which He had reached it Himself, in such sayings as the following: 'Love your enemies, and pray for them that persecute you; that ye may be sons of your Father which is in heaven; for he maketh his sun to rise on the evil and on the good, and sendeth rain on the just and the unjust' (Mt 5[44f.]). Certainly this sonship of Jesus is ethico-religious, and this indicates the pathway by which the disciples of Jesus may participate in His sonship; but that His sonship and theirs are in all respects identical is contradicted by the unfailing usage of Jesus in speaking of God as 'my Father' and 'your Father,' but never as 'our Father.' Of this difference Holtzmann makes light in the same way in which he lays down the wholly unsupported assumption that Jesus prayed the Lord's Prayer with the disciples, including the fifth petition; but the fact is a radical one; and the conclusion to which it points is not without other confirmation.

Thus, in the parable of the Wicked Husbandmen, the owner of the vineyard, after sending servant after servant to negotiate with the labourers, sends his own son, Mk. adding 'his well-beloved,' by whom Jesus obviously intends Himself. Of course, it may be said that the Messiah was different from all the prophets, and that this difference may be indicated by the difference between a son and a servant; but the analogy would be closer if a more intimate and personal relationship were assumed.

One of the most striking passages pointing in the same direction is one that, at first sight, seems to point the opposite way. In Mk 13[32], speaking of a date in the future, Jesus says, 'But of that day and that hour knoweth no man, no, not the angels which are in heaven, neither the Son, but the Father.' Naturally this has been often quoted as a conclusive disproof of the orthodox doctrine of the Sonship of our Lord, and it has been one of the chief occasions for the invention of the kenotic theories, as they are called, of His Person; but, on the other hand, it is one of the clearest indications of a consciousness superior to mere humanity, for it places the speaker above both men and angels so obviously, that even Holtzmann, in an unwonted outburst of concession, exclaims: 'This is the single passage in which the Son, while opposed along with the angels to the Father, appears to become a metaphysical magnitude' (*NT Theol.* i. 268).

The inference appearing to follow from the passage just quoted is that Jesus was a Being above both men and angels, but inferior to God. But a more profound and true knowledge is supplied by the most impressive passage of all on this subject in the Synoptics—the words of Jesus with which the First Gospel concludes: 'All power is given unto me in heaven and in earth. Go ye, therefore, and teach all nations, baptizing them in the name of the Father, and of the Son, and of the Holy Ghost: teaching them to observe all things whatsoever I have commanded you: and, lo, I am with you alway, even unto the end of the world' (28[19f.]). The close resemblance will be noted between the opening words of this statement and the opening words of the saying in Mt 11[27], already commented on. The promise, 'Lo, I am with you alway,' has likewise a parallel in Mt 18[20] 'Where two or three are gathered together in my name, there am I in the midst of them.' But the association of 'the Son' with the Father and the Holy Ghost is the most remarkable expression in the Synoptics of the self-consciousness of Jesus. How much it implies is a problem for dogmatic theology; but it is enough to remark here that it undoubtedly runs up into the ontological or metaphysical. Of course, its authenticity as a saying actually proceeding from Jesus has been fiercely disputed, and in certain quarters the air is affected of treating it as beyond dispute an addition to the actual words of Christ; but its place in the ordinance of baptism connects it closely with the Author of that rite; and there is no reason for rejecting it which would not, at the same time, imply the rejection of the whole section of the life of our Lord which follows His death on the cross.

2. The Fourth Gospel.—When we turn from the Synoptics to the Fourth Gospel, we are immediately conscious of being in a different atmosphere and at a different altitude, and the effect is at first bewildering. Instead of a studied reticence on the subject of who and whence He was, such as we encounter in the previous Gospels, Jesus places this subject in the foreground, and instead of letting His higher claims escape only at rare intervals and in the society of His chosen friends, He proclaims them to all and sundry, and, as one might say, from the housetops. This raises many questions as to the origin and purpose of this Gospel, which cannot be fully discussed in this place; but it may be said that, if both representations are to be accepted as historical, we must conceive the words of Christ as having ranged over a wider area than is usually assumed. If in His mind there were circles of thought as diverse as those of the Synoptics and the Fourth Gospel, there must have been ample spaces round both circles, in which the outer elements of both might touch and blend. There is a tendency, due to the preoccupation of study, to narrow the life of Christ down to what has been actually recorded; but this is in many ways misleading, and it is mistaken. It is certain that the acts recorded of Him are only a few stray flowers thrown over the wall of an ample garden; and it is not unreasonable to infer that the same is true of His words.

As, however, we grow accustomed to the new environment in the Gospel of St. John, we begin to perceive that the figure which stands in the midst is not so different as it appears at first sight from the one we have just been studying. He is still 'the Son of Man' as well as 'the Son of God,' though the proportion in which these names occur is reversed. The way in which He here calls Himself 'the Son' and God His Father is exactly similar to the usage in the Synoptics, only He has these terms far more frequently on His lips. Not a few of the most astonishing statements He makes about Himself are substantially anticipated in the verse of an earlier Gospel so frequently referred to, Mt 11[27]. He does not hesitate, even in

Jn., to say 'my Father is greater than I' (14²⁸), or to speak of God as 'my God' (20¹⁷). We have here the same three elements in the sonship as formerly—the theocratic - Messianic, the ethico-religious, and the physical or metaphysical—only they may be mingled in somewhat different proportions. The Messianic we see in its most unmistakable form in the testimonies of the Baptist (1³⁴), of Nathanael (1⁴⁹), of Martha (11²⁷), and of others; but the boundaries of the other two will require more careful investigation.

Two things are new—the description of the Son as 'only begotten' (1¹⁴. ¹⁸ 3¹⁶. ¹⁸), and the claim to pre-existence on the part of Jesus.

(1) The adjective μονογενής describes the unique Sonship of Jesus. St. John is not unaware that there are other sons of God. So far from it, his Gospel opens with the great statement, already quoted, 'But as many as received him, to them gave he power to become the sons of God, even to them that believe on his name' (Jn 1¹²); and in his First Epistle he exclaims, 'Beloved, now are we the sons of God, and it doth not yet appear what we shall be: but we know that, when he shall appear, we shall be like him; for we shall see him as he is' (1 Jn 3²); but such are not sons of God in the same sense in which Jesus is 'the Son of God.' Wherein, then, does the uniqueness consist? It cannot lie in the ethico - spiritual region; for it is there that in this respect Jesus and those who receive Him are one, except in degree of intimacy with the Father. Most assume that it lies in Messiahship; and, no doubt, in being the Messiah, Jesus is unique. Even Weiss takes it for granted that this is where it lies, contending again and again that nothing metaphysical is suggested. This, however, is a mere piece of dogmatism; for the uniqueness might quite as well lie in this quarter. In fact, the verbal idea in the adjective rather suggests it; and it is very significant that St. John treats the claim of Jesus to Sonship as involving equality with God. In 5¹⁸ we read, 'Therefore the Jews sought the more to kill him, because he not only had broken the Sabbath, but said that God was his Father, making himself equal with God'; and in 10³³ 'The Jews answered him, saying, For a good work we stone thee not, but because that thou, being a man, makest thyself God,' this being because He had stated, 'I and my Father are one' (v.³⁰).

The force of this is turned aside by Wendt with the assumption that these notes are from the pen of a redactor, who, both here and elsewhere, has wrought confusion in the record emanating from the disciple whom Jesus loved. Beyschlag takes the bull more boldly by the horns with the suggestion that these remarks of the Jews are quoted as evidences of their perversity and stupidity, the sayings of Jesus on which they were comments not having implied at all what they supposed. But it may be left to everyone to say whether or not this is a natural manner of reading St. John's narrative. At all events, as a historical statement, it is of the utmost importance that by the contemporaries of Jesus His claim to be the Son of God, put forward as it was by Him, was interpreted in this way.

(2) The passages in which Jesus claims pre-existence are four—6⁶² 'What and if ye shall see the Son of Man ascend up where he was before?'; 8⁵⁸ 'Verily I say unto you, Before Abraham was, I am'; 17⁴. ⁵ 'I have glorified thee on the earth, I have finished the work which thou gavest me to do; and now, O Father, glorify thou me with thine own self, with the glory which I had with thee before the world was'; and especially, 17²⁴ 'Father, I will that they also whom thou hast given me be with me, that they may behold my glory, which thou hast given me; for thou lovedst me before the foundation of the world'; to which may be added 16²⁸ 'I came forth from the Father, and am come into the world; again, I leave the world, and go to the Father.' In all these cases, not excepting the last, the leaving of the world—

surely a real, historical event—is put in the plainest terms in opposition to His entry into the world, which must, therefore, be equally a real, historical event.

Beyschlag attacks the pre-existence with vigour, and displays remarkable ingenuity in explaining it of an ideal existence in the mind and purpose of God. Thus, before God thought of Abraham, He was thinking of Jesus, who was anterior and superior in the Divine plan. But, after the laborious analysis is over, these great sayings draw themselves together again and stare the reader in the face as a united and coherent aspect of the self-consciousness of Jesus. Wendt applies to these texts his favourite device of showing that what is said of Jesus, and is supposed to imply something superhuman, is also applied to others of whom nothing superhuman can be predicated. Thus, if Jesus (8³⁸) says to the Jews, 'I speak that which I have seen with my Father,' He adds, 'And ye do that which ye have seen with your father,' explaining, further on, 'Ye are of your father the devil, and the lusts of your father ye will do' (v.⁴⁴); and the argument is, that if this implies that Jesus pre-existed with God, it must imply also that the Jews with whom He was contending had pre-existed with the devil. But how futile this kind of argumentation may sometimes be, is shown when the statement of St. Paul, that 'the saints shall judge the world' (1 Co 6²), is used to take all the greatness and solemnity out of the statements of Jesus as to the position which He is to occupy at the Last Day as the Judge of the quick and the dead. Wendt habitually reduces the great sayings of Jesus to the lowest possible terms, and then assumes that this must be the meaning in every case. But the reader wearies of such a process: he feels that surely Jesus cannot have put the minimum of significance into His words on all occasions; or, if so, how is He to escape the charge of employing big language to express small ideas, or confusing His hearers with enigmas which might easily have been cleared up, had He only uttered a few plain words of explanation? Holtzmann gives up the attempt to read a commonplace meaning into words like these. Such sayings, according to him, are not genuine words of Jesus: they are utterances of Christianity rather than of Christ, and of Christianity after it had passed through the mind of St. Paul (op. cit. infr. ii. p. 433). But the situation is in all probability the reverse: the deep resemblance between the Christology of St. John and that of St. Paul, which undoubtedly exists in spite of superficial unlikeness, is due rather to what St. Paul learned from the older Apostle either directly or through the knowledge and ideas of the beloved disciple being diffused in the atmosphere of that age; while the consent on this great subject, not only of these two but of the primitive Church as a whole, may be traced back without hesitation to the tradition of our Lord's own testimony to Himself.

The witness of Jesus to His own pre-existence is not confined to the texts just quoted, remarkable as these are, but pervades the whole mass of His words in the Fourth Gospel, and forms the presupposition of all the rest of His utterances about Himself. It is by commencing at this starting-point and following this clue that the student finds everything expanding before him as he goes on, and all the various ideas arranging themselves in their places on the right hand and on the left.

Whether there be any analogy to the consciousness of Jesus at this point in what some of the ancients believed about this life being a reminiscence of a life preceding, or in what some of the modern poets have hinted about human beings trailing clouds of glory from an antecedent home, may be left to everyone's own judgment; but Jesus habitually spoke as if He were conscious of having had an anterior existence, where He had seen and heard what He repeated during His earthly life, and had received commandment how He should afterwards act. Thus to Nicodemus He says (3¹¹⁻¹³), 'Verily, verily, I say unto thee, We speak that we do know, and testify that we have seen; and ye receive not our witness. If I have told you earthly things, and ye believe not, how shall ye believe, if I tell you of heavenly things? And no man hath ascended up to heaven, but he that came down from heaven, even the Son of Man which is in heaven.' In the great intercessory prayer He says to His Father (17⁸), 'I have given unto them the words which thou gavest me; and they have received them, and have known surely that I came out from thee, and they have believed that thou didst send me.' Cf. also 6⁴⁶. ⁶² 7²⁸. ²⁹ 8²³. ²⁶. ²⁷. ³⁸ 12⁴⁹ 14³¹ 15¹⁵ 17⁸.

Out of this pre-existent state Jesus was conscious of having been 'sent' into the world. This recalls the mission of the prophets of the OT, who, though not haunted by any reminiscence of a previous state of existence, yet were all profoundly conscious that they had been chosen and ordained to do a particular work at a particular time ; some, like Jeremiah, being told that even from the womb they had been destined to their peculiar vocation. With this prophetic consciousness that of Jesus was in close analogy ; yet the references to it suggest a deeper mystery. Corresponding with this sending on God's part is a 'coming' on the part of Jesus Himself ; and in some of the passages in which He says, 'I am come,' there is the same suggestion of something weighty and more than usually significant. Not infrequently both conceptions are blended, as in 6^{38} 'I came down from heaven, not to do mine own will, but the will of him that sent me'; or $7^{28.\ 29}$ 'Ye both know me, and ye know whence I am ; and I am not come of myself, but he that sent me is true, whom ye know not ; but I know him ; for I am from him, and he hath sent me'; or 8^{42} 'If God were your Father, ye would love me ; for I proceeded forth and came from God ; neither came I of myself, but he sent me.' Cf. $5^{23.\ 24.\ 36.\ 37.\ 38}$ 6^{44} $7^{16.\ 33}$ $8^{16.\ 18.\ 26.\ 29.\ 42}$ 9^4 10^{36} 11^{42} $12^{44.\ 49}$ 14^{27} 15^{21} 16^5 $17^{8.\ 18.\ 23}$ 20^{21} ; also $6^{33.\ 38}$ 7^{14} 9^{39} 10^{10} $16^{27.\ 28}$.

The object or purpose for which He was thus 'sent' and 'came' into the world is expressed in a great variety of forms, all of which, however, are more or less suggestive of the dignity and uniqueness of Him of whom they are predicated, though of course some make this impression more than others. Thus He comes to reveal the truth and to glorify God thereby. So He said to Pilate, 'To this end was I born, and for this cause came I into the world, that I should bear witness unto the truth' (18^{37}). In His great High-Priestly prayer He says to the Father, 'I have glorified thee on the earth, I have finished the work which thou gavest me to do'; again, 'I have manifested thy name unto the men which thou gavest me out of the world'; and again, 'I have declared unto them thy name, and will declare it ; that the love wherewith thou hast loved me may be in them, and I in them' ($17^{4.\ 6.\ 26}$). So illuminating and comprehensive is this revelation, that He calls Himself 'the light of the world' (see 8^{12} 9^5 $12^{36.\ 46}$). Sometimes He comes to judge. He even goes so far as to say, 'The Father judgeth no man, but hath committed all judgment unto the Son' (5^{22}). Sometimes He comes to 'save,' as in 10^9 'I am the door : by me if any man enter in, he shall be saved, and shall go in and out, and find pasture'; or 12^{47} 'I came not to judge the world, but to save the world.' But oftenest His mission is to give life, this being expressed in a great variety of forms. Thus, in 10^{10}, He says, 'I am come that they might have life, and that they might have it more abundantly.' Sometimes the opposite alternative is tragically suggested, as in the well known 3^{16}, where 'to perish' stands in contrast with 'life'; or in 8^{51} 'Verily, verily, I say unto you, If a man keep my saying, he shall never see death,' where death awaits those who do not receive 'life' from Christ. Frequently the adjective 'eternal' is joined with life. It is a peculiarity of the Fourth Gospel to conceive of eternal life as capable of being enjoyed even in the present world ; but it also comprehends the future, and this is sometimes the ruling idea. The intimate connexion of Jesus Himself with the bestowal of this life is extremely significant. Thus, in 5^{26}, He claims, 'As the Father hath life in himself, so hath he given to the Son to have life in himself.' At the grave of Lazarus He exclaimed, 'I am the resurrection and the life ; he that believeth in me, though he were dead,

yet shall he live ; and whosoever liveth and believeth in me shall never die.' The communication of natural life is interchanged with that of spiritual life ; in 5^{21}, for example, He says, 'As the Father raiseth up the dead, and quickeneth them, even so the Son quickeneth whom he will'; and farther on, at 5^{25}, it is added, 'Verily, verily, I say unto you, The hour is coming, and now is, when the dead shall hear the voice of the Son of God, and they that hear shall live.' The personal share of Jesus in all this is further indicated in His claim to be the bread of life ($6^{27.\ 32.\ 33.\ 47.\ 51}$), and to give the water of life ($4^{10.\ 14}$ $7^{37.\ 38}$). In view of such sublime statements, the term 'Messianic' is frequently used in a way that is a delusion and a snare. What explanation of such pretensions is it to say that He who made them differed from other men and prophets by being the Messiah? The possession of no office whatever is able to make a mortal capable of such functions : there must be something far above the competency of mere man in any one who can be the subject of such predicates. In *Cur Deus Homo* Anselm develops the argument that, the Person being such as He was, the work must be Divine ; but the logic tells equally in the opposite direction : the work being such, the Person must be Divine.

Some of these works are, however, invisible, because spiritual, and some belong to the distant future. Hence Jesus could not show Himself in the act of doing them. But He did works, which all could see, that were signs and guarantees of these. He healed the blind, in order to prove that He was the organ of revelation ; He raised the dead, in order to prove that He would be the Lord of the resurrection at the Last Day. So He Himself interpreted His miracles ; and He appealed confidently to their evidential power, 'If I do not the works of my Father, believe me not ; but, if I do, though ye believe not me, believe the works ; that ye may know and believe that the Father is in me and I in him' ($10^{37.\ 38}$; see also 1^{48} 4^{18} 8^{18} 10^{25} $11^{4.\ 15}$ 14^{11} $17^{23.\ 24.\ 26}$).

All the time, however, whilst doing His works on earth, He was in uninterrupted communion with His Father in heaven, actually speaking of Himself once (3^{13}) as 'in heaven,' if the reading can be trusted. Such expressions have been used to break down the testimonies to His pre-existence, as if none of these might mean any more than such an ideal presence elsewhere. But this is a distinct aspect of His testimony to Himself, and there is no inconsistency between the two. His doctrine, His words, His works He knew to be all the Father's (7^{16} 8^{26} $14^{10.\ 24}$ $5^{19.\ 20}$). He could say, 'He that sent me is with me ; the Father hath not left me alone ; for I do always those things that please Him' (8^{29}). With the most touching *naïveté* He spoke of the Father's love to Him and His own love to the Father (10^{17} $17^{23.\ 24.\ 26}$). He strives for language strong enough to express the unity between His Father and Himself (6^{36} 10^{38} 14^{10} 17^{21}). At last the climax is reached in the utterance which brought down on His head the charge of blasphemy, 'I and the Father are one' (10^{30}).

Though, however, thus united with God on earth, He longs for return to the other world, which is His true home. To this He often refers, not infrequently connecting the thought of going thither with that of having come from the same place ; and what could be more natural? Thus, in 8^{14} He says, 'Though I bear record of myself, yet my record is true ; for I know whence I came and whither I go ; but ye cannot tell whence I come and whither I go': and in 16^{28} 'I came forth from the Father, and am come into the world ; again, I leave the world, and go to the Father.'

See also 6^{62} $7^{33.\ 34}$ 8^{21} 13^{33} $14^{2.\ 12.\ 28}$ $16^{5.\ 7.\ 10.\ 16}$ $17^{11.\ 13}$ 20^{17}.

Such is a slight sketch of the Christology of Jesus as presented by St. John. Not every statement is expressly connected with 'the Son of God' in so many words; but this is the phrase that embodies all these various elements. The summits of the testimony are such verses as $5^{23.\ 26}$ 8^{58} $10^{15.\ 30}$ $11^{4.\ 25}$ 12^{45} $13^{31.\ 32}$ $14^{6.\ 7.\ 9.\ 13.\ 14}$. Longer passages specially worthy of consideration are 3^{10-21} 5^{19-47} 6^{35-40} 8^{42-47} 15. 17. In one passage He deals directly and deliberately with the charge that, in calling Himself 'the Son of God,' He was making Himself equal with God. Here was an opportunity of disclaiming anything of the kind, and explaining, as many are now forward to do for Him, that the question was only of function and character, not of nature. He did, indeed, refer to some who, in the OT, were called 'gods' on account of function alone; but He set His own claim above theirs as supported by a far higher reason: 'If he called them gods unto whom the word of God came, and the Scripture cannot be broken, say ye of him whom the Father hath sanctified and sent into the world, Thou blasphemest, because I said, I am the Son of God?' ($10^{35f.}$). And He goes on to affirm, 'The Father is in me and I in him' ($v.^{38}$). It is true that it is arguable whether in these words only function is referred to, but the point is that something deeper is not only not excluded but suggested. Those who believe that all such expressions have reference to superiority of function and character, but not of nature, have no difficulty in finding words by which this distinction can be made perfectly intelligible. Why then did Jesus, when thus directly challenged, not find such words? The numerous sayings quoted in the foregoing paragraphs amply prove that, in speaking of His own origin and the source of His authority, He habitually used language of dazzling splendour and magnificence. Was this an exaggerative manner of expressing what was ordinary, or was it an effort to body forth in human speech what was too glorious to be expressed? The halo round the head of 'the Son of God' is not an invention of primitive Christianity or ecclesiastical councils—for whatever excesses of superstition or dogmatism these may be answerable—but is due to the consciousness and the testimony of Jesus Himself; and by the character of Him who was 'meek and lowly in heart,' as well as by the conviction of His power to save wrought by centuries of experience into the mind of Christendom, the acknowledgment is demanded that it is not an exhalation from beneath, but an emanation from the eternal throne.

LITERATURE.—The relevant portions of the works on NT Theology by Weiss, Beyschlag, H. J. Holtzmann, Stevens, Bovon; also of Wendt's *Teaching of Jesus*, Dalman's *Words of Jesus*, Nösgen's *Gesch. Jesu Christi*, and Beyschlag's *Christologie des NT*. See also Grau, *Das Selbstbewusstsein Jesu*; Nösgen, *Der Menschen- und Gottessohn*; Gore, *Bampton Lectures and Dissertations*; Stevens, *The Johannine Theology*; Weiss, *Der Johanneische Lehrbegriff*; Lütgert, *Die Johanneische Christologie* (1899) and *Gottes Sohn und Gottes Geist* (1905); Stalker, Cunningham Lectures, *The Christology of Jesus*[2] (1900); F. W. Robertson, *Serm.* ii. 136, 235; P. Brooks, *Law of Growth*, 346.   JAMES STALKER.

SON OF MAN.—1. Occurrences of the expression in the NT.—

(a) *In the Gospels* it is found in the following passages— eighty-one in all: Mt 8^{20} 9^6 10^{23} 11^{19} $12^{8.\ 32.\ 40}$ $13^{37.\ 41}$ $16^{13.\ 27.\ 28}$ $17^{9.\ 12.\ 22}$ 19^{28} $20^{18.\ 28}$ $24^{27.\ 30\ bis.\ 37.\ 39.\ 44}$ 25^{31} $26^{2.\ 24\ bis.\ 45.\ 64}$—[30 times]; Mk $2^{10.\ 28}$ $8^{31.\ 38}$ $9^{9.\ 12.\ 31}$ $10^{33.\ 45}$ 13^{26} $14^{21\ bis.\ 41.\ 62}$—[14 times]; Lk 5^{24} 6^5 7^{34} $9^{22.\ 26.\ 44.\ 58}$ 11^{30} $12^{8.\ 10.\ 40}$ $17^{22.\ 24.\ 26.\ 30}$ $18^{8.\ 31}$ 19^{10} $21^{27.\ 36}$ $22^{22.\ 48.\ 69}$ 24^7—[25 times]; Jn 1^{51} $3^{13.\ 14}$ $6^{27.\ 53.\ 62}$ 8^{28} 9^{35} RVm $12^{23.\ 34\ bis.}$ 13^{31}—[12 times]. It is obvious to remark that these eighty-one passages do not by any means represent as many different occasions on which the phrase is reported to have been used. Thus of the thirty passages cited from Mt. it will be found on examination that nine have direct parallels in both Mk. and Lk.; that four have parallels in Mk. only, and

eight in Luke only; while the remaining nine are peculiar to Matthew (see the tables provided by Driver in Hastings' *DB* iv. 579, Schmidt, *EBi* iv. 4713, and by J. A. Robinson in *The Study of the Gospels*, p. 58 f.). To the parallel passages in the Synoptics, which exhibit diversity in regard to this particular expression, attention will be directed later.

(b) *Apart from the Gospels* 'the Son of Man' is found only in Ac 7^{56} (cf. Lk 22^{69}). In Rev 1^{13} and 14^{14} the expression used, though akin, is not the same: it is 'one [sitting] like unto a son of man,' which is a precise reproduction of the phrase in Dn 7^{13}.

With but one exception the name as found in the Gospels is used only by our Lord Himself. The exception is Jn 12^{34}, and even there it is presupposed that Jesus had spoken of Himself as 'the Son of Man.' 'The multitude therefore answered him, We have heard out of the law that the Christ abideth for ever; and how sayest thou, The Son of Man must be lifted up? Who is this Son of Man?' The multitude are familiar with the title 'the Son of Man'; to them it is a designation of the Messiah; their difficulty is to reconcile Messiahship with exaltation through death. The impression derived from this passage, that the title under discussion was by no means new upon the lips of our Lord,—however great the access of content it received from His employment of it,—is confirmed by the significant fact that throughout the Gospel narratives there is not a trace that disciples, or the wider public, were in any wise perplexed by the designation. This fact, it may be remarked in passing, has not been allowed its due weight by those who, like Westcott (*Gospel of St. John*, p. 33 ff., 'It was essentially a new title'), regard the designation as originating with our Lord; or who, like B. Weiss (*NT Theol.* i. 73), explain the employment of it by Jesus on the supposition that, if not new, it was not one of the current Messianic titles. If new, or unfamiliar, the frequent use of such a self-designation must have occasioned remark, and called for explanation, which would surely have found record in one or other of the Evangelic narratives. If then the Gospels, both by what they say and by what they leave unsaid, favour the view that 'Son of Man' was already known, prior to the ministry of Jesus, as a Messianic title, it becomes needful to trace, in so far as we may, its history. Next, we must try to ascertain at what period in His ministry this title was assumed by our Lord, and why He used it with such marked preference; and, finally, we must seek an explanation of the absence of the name in NT writings other than the Gospels.

2. Source of the title.—Baldensperger, writing in 1900 (*Theol. Rundschau*, p. 201 ff.), regards it as one of the 'fixed points' gained in the course of recent discussion, that the origin of the NT phrase, and in large part its explanation, are to be sought in the OT, and especially in Dn 7^{13}. Previous discussion had been limited too exclusively to the Gr. expression ὁ υἱὸς τοῦ ἀνθρώπου; and, owing to such limitation, results were obtained (such as that our Lord reiterated 'His mere humanity,' or that He was 'the ideal man,' or that 'nothing human was alien to Him') which stood in no obvious relation to passages in which the title is predominantly used —passages bearing on our Lord's Passion and Parousia. The appropriateness of the use of the title in sayings of the latter class was at once apparent when it was viewed in the light of Dn 7^{13}. Not that the title itself is to be found there. The writer of Daniel describes a vision in which four great beasts come up from the sea—a lion, a bear, a leopard, a beast with ten horns. They are judged by the 'Ancient of Days,' and their dominion is taken from them. Thereupon the prophet proceeds:

'I saw in the night visions, and, behold, there came with the clouds of heaven one like unto a son of man, and he came even to the ancient of days, and they brought him near before him. And there was given to him dominion, and glory, and a kingdom, that all the peoples, nations, and languages should serve him : his dominion is an everlasting dominion, which shall not pass away, and his kingdom that which shall not be destroyed.'

It will be noted that in this more accurate rendering (that of the RV) the phrase which is of most moment in the subject now under discussion is quite indefinite : 'one like unto *a* son of man,'— *i.e.* one with human attributes in contrast to the ferocity of 'the beasts.' The question at once arises, Whom are we to understand by the 'one like unto a son of man'? The answer most commonly given has been—the Messiah ; and there is much to be said for that answer yet, in spite of the dissent of a large number of more recent exegetes. They point to the fact that when Daniel receives the interpretation of his vision (7[17-27]), not a word is said about the 'one like unto a son of man,' but with threefold iteration (vv. [18. 22. 27]) it is asserted that after judgment upon the beasts, dominion will be given to 'the saints of the Most High.' Hence it is said that on the testimony of the text of Daniel itself, the 'one like unto a son of man' does not denote a person, but 'the glorified and ideal people of Israel' (see, *e.g.*, Driver, *Com. on Daniel*, p. 102 ; Drummond, *Jewish Messiah*, p. 229). So strongly indeed has this view impressed itself upon the minds of some, that they apply the impersonal interpretation of the phrase in Dn 7[13] as a test to the passages in which our Lord is represented by the Evangelists as using the words 'the Son of Man.' Thus J. Estlin Carpenter (*The Synoptic Gospels*, pp. 372, 388), regarding the phrase in Daniel as 'emblematic and collective,' and maintaining that Jesus used it in its original meaning, arrives at the conclusion that 'wherever . . . the term is individualized and used Messianically, we have evidence of the later influence of the Church. Jesus never used it to designate Himself.' It is obvious that the application of such a canon would have far-reaching results. But is the interpretation upon which it is based quite sure ? The writer of Daniel does not regard 'the saints of the Most High' as coming down from heaven. They are already upon the earth, suffering the oppression of the tyrant symbolized by the 'little horn,' and awaiting deliverance and reversal of condition, which come when the Most High sits for judgment. It would surely be somewhat incongruous to symbolize the saints passing from the depths of misery to exaltation by one who descends from heaven to earth. On the other hand, it accords entirely with the conception which dominates Dn 7 of a complete change of conditions, if by 'one like a son of man' we understand a Divinely empowered Ruler sent from on high to reign where the 'four kings,' the 'great beasts,' whose origin had been of the earth (v.[17]), had borne sway.

If it be urged that had the writer of Dn 7 intended the Messiah in v.[13], he could not have omitted mention of Him when he goes on to interpret the vision, and could not have spoken so unreservedly of the bestowal of 'kingdom and dominion' upon the saints of the Most High, it may be replied that it is quite in harmony with what may be discerned in other prophetic writings, if the thought of the author of Daniel is found to dwell more on the glories of the Kingdom of the latter days and the felicity of those who have part in it, than upon the Messianic King. Large sections of prophecy, so far as they seek to portray the better future, omit all direct reference to the Messiah. There is no warrant, therefore, as Driver (who, however, holds that 'the title . . . does not in Daniel directly denote the Messiah,' *op. cit.* p. 104) points out, for saying that 'the Kingdom is not to be thought of without its King.' And there is also no sufficient warrant to assume that if in the recital of a vision there is mention of the Messianic King, He, rather than His subjects, must have mention when the vision is interpreted. It is through failure to make allowance for this that N. Schmidt (*EBi* iv. 4710) complains that the Messianic interpretation of Dn 7[13] 'fails to explain how the Messiah, once introduced, can have dropped so completely out of the author's thought, not only in the explanation of the vision, where He is unceremoniously ignored, but also in the future deliverance, with which Michael has much to do but the Messiah nothing.' Hence Schmidt suggests that the 'one like unto a son of man' is no other than Michael him-

self, the guardian angel of Israel ('Michael your prince,' Dn 10[21]) —a belated expedient, affording no real assistance. The absence of any mention of the guardian angel in the interpretation of the vision is not more easy of explanation than the absence therefrom of the mention of the Messiah. Indeed, of the two conceptions, that of the gift of everlasting dominion over all peoples to the guardian angel Michael, being the more unfamiliar, would urgently demand some explicit word of explanation.

In order to discover how Jewish readers of the Book of Daniel in the time shortly preceding and shortly following our Lord's ministry interpreted that figure, which was presented so suddenly, to be so speedily withdrawn, we turn to the evidence of the *Similitudes* of the Book of Enoch and of 2 Esdras. Both books are quite certainly of Jewish origin, and both afford unmistakable testimony as to the deep impression made by the apocalyptic teaching of Daniel, which would carry with it familiarity with the concept of 'one like a son of man.' The date of the Book of Esdras is undisputed ; it belongs to the closing decades of the first century of our era, approximately to A.D. 81. The date of the *Similitudes*—a later portion of the Book of Enoch—is more open to doubt. R. H. Charles (*Book of Enoch*, p. 29) holds them to have been written between B.C. 94–79, or B.C. 70–64. Schürer (*HJP* II. iii. 68) places them somewhat later : 'at the very soonest, in the time of Herod,' *i.e.* between B.C. 37–4. Thus, according to both these authorities, the *Similitudes* are pre-Christian. Whether they have been subjected to interpolations at Christian hands has been much debated. The plea that such interpolations, had they taken place, must have gone further, appears conclusive. Schürer (*l.c.*) claims, with reason, that 'this much at least ought to be admitted, that the view of the Messiah presented in the part of the book at present under consideration [the *Similitudes*] is perfectly explicable on Jewish grounds, and that to account for such view it is not necessary to assume that it was due to Christian influences. Nothing of a specifically Christian character is to be met with in any of this section.' We are concerned here with the Messianic teaching of the *Similitudes* only so far as they adopt and develop the concept derived from Daniel of a heavenly 'Son of Man.' The following extracts (cited from Charles' tr.) may suffice :

In ch. 46, Enoch is represented as saying, when relating his vision of the Judgment : 'And there I saw One who had a Head of Days, and His head was white like wool, and with Him was another being whose countenance had the appearance . . . like one of the holy angels. And I asked the angel who went with me and showed me all the hidden things, concerning that Son of Man, who he was, and whence he was, and why he went with the Head of Days? And he answered and said unto me, This is the Son of Man who hath righteousness, with whom dwelleth righteousness, and who reveals all the treasures of that which is hidden, because the Lord of Spirits hath chosen him, and his lot before the Lord of Spirits hath surpassed everything in uprightness for ever. And this Son of Man whom thou hast seen will arouse the kings and the mighty ones from their couches, and the strong from their thrones, and will loosen the reins of the strong and grind to powder the teeth of the sinners. And he will put down the kings from their thrones and kingdoms, because they do not extol and praise him, nor thankfully acknowledge whence the kingdom was bestowed upon them.' In ch. 62 we read : 'And thus the Lord commanded the kings and the mighty and the exalted, and those who dwell on the earth, and said, Open your eyes and lift up your horns if ye are able to recognize the Elect One. And the Lord of Spirits seated him (*i.e.* the Messiah) on the throne of His glory, and the spirit of righteousness was poured out upon him, and the word of his mouth slew all the sinners, and all the unrighteous were destroyed before his face. And there will stand up in that day all the kings, and the exalted, and those who hold the earth, and they will see and recognize him how he sits on the throne of his glory, and righteousness is judged before him, and no lying word is spoken before him. . . . And one portion of them will look on the other, and they will be terrified and their countenance will fall, and pain will seize them when they see that Son of Man sitting on the throne of his glory. And the kings . . . will glorify and bless and extol him who rules over all, who was hidden. For the Son of Man was hidden before Him, and the Most High preserved him in the presence of His might, and revealed him to the elect.' See also 69[27] 'And he sat on the throne of his glory, and the sum of judgment was committed unto him, the Son of Man, and he caused the sinners and those who have led the world astray to pass away and be destroyed from off the face of the earth.' These passages leave no room to question how the author of the *Similitudes* interpreted Daniel's 'one like unto a son of man.' To him the phrase characterized no symbolic figure, but a celestial person, Divinely endowed with world-wide dominion, and appointed to be the judge of all men. The descriptive expression is in process of becoming a title ; passing through demonstrative stages—' *this* Son of Man,' ' *that* Son of Man,'—it emerges as ' *the* Son of Man.'

In 2 Es 13 there is no such development of the phrase, 'one like unto a son of man,' as we find in the *Similitudes*, but the dependence upon Daniel and the Messianic interpretation of Dn 7¹³ is not less clear. Esdras is represented as recounting a dream, in which he saw coming ' up from the midst of the sea as it were the likeness of a man ; and I beheld [he proceeds], and, lo, that man flew with the clouds of heaven : and when he turned his countenance to look, all things trembled that were seen under him. . . . And after this, I beheld, and, lo, there was gathered together a multitude of men, out of number, from the four winds of heaven, to make war against the man that had come out of the sea.' This multitude he destroys by the mere breath of his mouth, and then he is seen to ' call unto him another multitude which was peaceable.' When Esdras seeks the interpretation of the dream, he is told : 'Whereas thou sawest a man coming up from the midst of the sea, the same is he whom the Most High' hath kept a great season, which by his own self shall deliver his creatures : and he shall order them that are left behind. . . . Behold, the days come when the Most High will begin to deliver them that are upon the earth. . . . and it shall be when these things shall come to pass, and the signs shall happen that I showed thee before, then shall my Son be revealed, whom thou sawest as a man ascending. . . . And this my Son shall rebuke the nations which are come for their wickedness. . . . And he shall destroy them without labour by the law, which is likened unto fire.' The ' peaceable multitude' is further explained to be Israel, of whom this ' son' of the Most High is not the symbol, but the Saviour.

The writings of Enoch and Esdras are, it is reasonable to assume, only the survivors of other Apocalypses of the same period, which in like manner founded themselves on the vision of Daniel, and sought to supply in their own way what the prophet had left untold concerning ' one like unto a son of man.' If so, that phrase would also inevitably turn in the popular mind into a definite Messianic title, calling for no question when it was heard from the lips of Jesus, unless it were as to His right to appropriate it. It is suggestive to find that later on a more subordinate expression in Dn 7¹³ was adopted in similar fashion, and that נפלי=בר ' son of cloud,' or ' cloud-man,' became a Rabbinic title for the Messiah (see Levy, *NHWB*, s.v. נפל).

At this point it is needful to pause to consider how our Lord's use of the expression ' the Son of Man' is affected by the fact that He spoke Aramaic. If ὁ υἱὸς τοῦ ἀνθρώπου is turned into Aramaic, does it give an expression which could be employed as a title ? Or, to put it otherwise, is perhaps ὁ υἱὸς τ. ἀνθρώπου a mistranslation of the words actually uttered by Jesus, or an expression of later growth imported into His sayings by Greek-speaking Christians ? Within the last decade, more especially, these questions have been keenly discussed. Wellhausen gave stimulus to the debate by a footnote in his *IJG*[2] (1895, p. 346), in which he said : 'Since Jesus spoke Aramaic He did not call Himself ὁ υἱὸς τοῦ ἀνθρώπου, but *barnascha* ; that, however, means ' the Man,' and nothing else, the Aramæans having no other expression for the notion. The earliest Christians did not understand that Jesus called Himself simply the Man. They held Him to be the Messiah, made accordingly a designation of the Messiah out of *barnascha*, and translated it not by ὁ ἄνθρωπος, as they should, but quite erroneously by ὁ υἱὸς τοῦ ἀνθρώπου.' Wellhausen further lays stress on the fact that St. Paul makes no use of the expression ' Son of Man,' and refuses to admit any evidence which might be cited from Enoch, on the arbitrary plea that ' the Son of man in the Book of Enoch must be left out of account, so long as it is not established that the relative portion of the book was known, or could be known, to Jesus.'

In 1896, H. Lietzmann published a brochure—*Der Menschensohn*—in which, after a review of previous opinions, he enters into a discussion of ' Son of Man' in Aramaic, with the result that he declares the expression to have been in Galilæan Aramaic, 'the most colourless and indeterminate designation of a human individual'—one that might be used as an indefinite pronoun (p. 38). The use of בר in the compound phrase is described as a 'genuine Semitic pleonasm,' and it is maintained that no intelligible distinction existed between אנש and בר נש. To say with Wellhausen that where the Gospels have ὁ υἱὸς τ. ἀνθ. the translation should have been ὁ ἄνθρωπος will not do, according to Lietzmann, since that could be no distinctive designation, and the Evangelists do most certainly intend the phrase they use as a definite title ; but ' Jesus has never used the title " Son of Man" of Himself, since in Aramaic it does not exist, and for linguistic reasons cannot exist' (*op. cit.* p. 85). The formula is to be regarded as a *terminus technicus* of Hellenistic theology, which, originating in Christian Apocalypses, was applied first to passages relating to our Lord's Return, then to His Passion, and finally to other sections of the narratives.

In 1899, Wellhausen returned to this subject (*Skizzen und Vorarbeiten*, Sechstes Heft), and in the main declared his adoption of Lietzmann's conclusion that Jesus, speaking Aramaic, could not make the difference which is made in Greek between ὁ ἄνθρωπος and ὁ υἱὸς τ. ἀνθ. :—that so far as this difference is made in the Gospels it is not authentic, but is derived from interpreters and editors. Wellhausen withdraws from the position he had formerly advocated, that Jesus did adopt ' the Man' as a title, meaning thereby that He fulfilled the ideal of humanity. He now declares that to impute such a meaning to our Lord is not warrantable, and that in the absence of that meaning the supposed title would be wholly meaningless, and therefore it was not employed. The use of ὁ υἱὸς τ. ἀνθ. in the Gospels is explained as due to the fact that the expressions of Dn 7¹³ are put into the mouth of Jesus in Mk 13²⁶, that thereafter it became the custom in all passages which refer to the Return of Jesus to avoid the *pronoun*, and to place instead ' the Son of Man.' Then followed the same usage in other than eschatological passages (*op. cit.* p. 210). Wellhausen again adduces in confirmation of the position that this self-designation of Jesus is not authentic, the *argumentum ex silentio*—the entire absence of the expression in other NT writings than the Gospels.

On the other hand, Dalman (*Die Worte Jesu*, 1898 [Eng. tr. 1902]) and Schmiedel (*Protestant. Monatshefte*, 1898, Hefte 7 and 8) called in question the linguistic premises of Lietzmann and Wellhausen, and contested their conclusions. They both maintain that Jesus did certainly call Himself ' the Son of Man,' using the title in a Messianic sense, and with direct reference to Dn 7¹³, though both hold the primary sense of ' a son of man,' in that verse, to be collective, and not personal. Dalman adduces evidence to show that ' the Jewish Palestinian Aramaio of the earlier period possessed the term אנש for a human being, while to indicate a number of human beings it employed occasionally בני אנשא. The singular number בר אנש was not in use ; its appearance being due to imitation of the Hebrew text, where [apart from Ezekiel] בן אדם is confined to poetry, and, moreover, uncommon in it. The case in Dn 7¹³, where the person coming from heaven is described as כבר אנש, ' one like unto a son of man,' is just as uncongenial to the style of prose as the designation of God in the same verse as עתיק יומיא ' the advanced in days' (*op. cit.* p. 237). Moreover, just as in Hebrew בן אדם is never made definite, so is the definite expression בר אנשא ' quite unheard of in the older Jewish Aramaic literature.' The common use of בר אנש = ' man' in Jewish Galilæan and Christian Palestinian literature is to be regarded as a later innovation. That this later usage was not already in vogue in the dialect spoken by our Lord (of which no written specimen from His time is in evidence) is demonstrated by His words as reported in the Gospels. ' " Man," both in the singular and in the plural, is frequently enough the subject of remark. How is it that υἱὸς ἀνθρώπου never occurs for ' man,' and οἱ υἱοὶ τῶν ἀνθρώπων only in Mk 3²⁸? Can the Hellenistic reporters—apart from the self-appellation of Jesus—have designedly avoided it, although Jesus had on all occasions said nothing but " son of man" for " man"? That cannot be considered likely. Hence, against Lietzmann and Wellhausen, Dalman holds both that ' Son of man' was a possible expression in the Aramaic of our Lord's day, and that by its singularity it was adapted for use as a title. ' To the Jews it would be purely a Biblical word.' To the same effect Schmiedel, who sums up his view of the linguistic part of the controversy thus : the Aramaic Lexicon ' must not say *barnascha* means " man," and nothing more, but it must run thus : *barnascha*, (1) man, (2) abbreviated designation of the form " like a son of man" (*i.e.* " like a man ") in Dn 7¹³, which, although, according to vv.18. 22. 27, signifying the saints of the Most High, was held to be the Messiah. We, on our part, declare that second meaning to be extant, and to have been so already before the time of Jesus' (*l.c.* 264). Reference is made below (§ 5) to the replies of Dalman and Schmiedel to the argument *ex silentio*, by which, as already stated, it has been sought to lend support to the theory that ' the Son of Man' in the Gospels is no genuine utterance of Jesus.

In 1901, P. Fiebig published the result of a fresh and very thorough examination of the linguistic evidence on the matter at issue. The main contribution in his dissertation (*Der Menschensohn*) is a demonstration that אנש and אנשא were, in spite of their formal indefiniteness and definiteness, completely interchangeable; and that similarly the compound expressions בר נש and בר נשא were alike employed to express either of the three meanings—(1) the man, (2) a man, (3) some one. Hence, either expression might be rendered by ὁ υἱὸς τ. ἀνθ., or by υἱὸς ἀνθ., or—since, according to Fiebig, the use of the compound expression as the precise equivalent of אנש without בר was no relatively late introduction from the Syriac—by ἄνθρωπος (p. 56). That in the Gospels a distinction is maintained by using ὁ υἱὸς τ. ἀνθ., and not ὁ ἄνθρωπος alone, is due to the desire to bring out that the fuller phrase is used with direct reference to בר אנש in Dn 7¹³. But whether in all cases the distinction has been accurately made by the translators is matter for investigation, having regard to the ambiguity of the Aramaic expression. Further, Fiebig holds, on the evidence of Enoch and Esdras, and of the Synoptics themselves, that 'the Son of Man,' or rather 'the Man,' was in our Lord's day a current title for the Messiah.

The above linguistic discussion has demonstrated considerable diversity of opinion, as could hardly fail to be the case in the absence of any contemporary example of the dialect spoken in Galilee at the time of our Lord's earthly ministry. In their estimate of probabilities afforded by cognate dialects, or by later usage, scholars are sure to differ somewhat. Nevertheless, the whole investigation has been fruitful in suggestion to the NT critic. But the attempt made in connexion with it to account for the presence in the Gospels of 'the Son of Man' on some other grounds than that it represents a self-designation employed by our Lord, can only be characterized as an elaborate failure. Wellhausen's invocation of hypothetical Apocalypses to explain the presence in the records of Jesus, and in those records not in the apocalyptic passages alone, of a title which (*ex hypoth.*) He did not use, removes no difficulty, but only calls aloud itself for explanation how such a thing could be. The belief that the title is the genuine utterance of Jesus is left unshaken.

3. When did our Lord adopt the title 'Son of Man'?—There can be but one answer, if we are justified in assuming that 'the Son of Man' was already a Messianic title before our Lord employed it. He can have adopted it only subsequently to St. Peter's confession of His Messiahship at Cæsarea Philippi. But do the Gospels lend colour to any such limitation? Turning to the earliest of the Synoptics,—and we may confine our attention just now to the Synoptics,—we are met by the significant fact that St. Mark has the phrase only twice (2¹⁰. ²⁸) prior to the Cæsarean incident; St. Luke has it four times (5²⁴ 6⁵. ²² 7³⁴), and St. Matthew nine times (8²⁰ 9⁶ 10²³ 11¹⁹ 12⁸. ³². ⁴⁰ 13³⁷. ⁴¹). Thus, in by far the greatest number of cases the title occurs subsequent to Peter's confession. What, then, is to be said as to its occurrence in such cases as are prior to that confession? No one answer will suffice. Certainly it will not do to resort to the expedient of saying that the title was but little known, and that its Messianic application might be missed until our Lord Himself, late in His ministry, brought it into direct relation to Daniel's prophecy; or to adopt the alternative offered by Holtzmann (*NT Theol.* vol. i. p. 264) of saying that 'the son of man' or 'man' was used by Jesus at first in its ordinary significance, and then, by reason of the stress He laid on it, came to be to the disciples an enigmatic word, which brought them to see that their Master was a man not as others, but with a unique calling, and at length to find in Him the Messiah. Either supposition would leave unexplained how the adoption of the title, whether unfamiliar or familiar, could have passed unchallenged, and not have called forth questions as to the sense in which Jesus was using the words. As little is help to be found in Fiebig's suggestion that one reason why our Lord chose this title ('the Man,' according to Fiebig), was that men would find in it *a* meaning, though they might fail to apprehend *the* meaning with

which Jesus employed it (*op. cit.* p. 120). Here, again, allowance is not made for the extreme difficulty of supposing that a speaker could apply a title to himself unless it were with an obvious purpose, which his hearers would certainly discern. There is not the least ground for supposing that it was a more usual thing in Aramaic than it is in our own language for any one to speak of himself in the third person. Such a form of speech might lend itself to more definite self-revelation, but clearly it was in no wise calculated to secure self-concealment. Wrede, in a note in *ZNTW* (1904, Heft 4), urges that in recent discussions about the 'Son of Man' too little attention has been given to the really astonishing fact that Jesus is represented in the Gospels as quite habitually speaking of Himself as of a third person, and yet, so far as the Gospels show, no one thought it strange. Wrede is justified in saying that only our early familiarity with the language of the Gospels makes us insensible to the difficulty created by the frequency of the recurrence of the title; but he surely greatly exaggerates the difficulty when he finds in it a most convincing argument to deny that Jesus used this self-designation at all. Certainly it was an unusual and striking form of speech to adopt. But that constitutes no sufficient reason for assuming that our Lord did not adopt it, even because it was more calculated to arrest attention when He desired to lay stress on His Messianic claims, and on special aspects of them. The real difficulty lies in the supposition that an unwonted form of speech, most calculated to provoke inquiry concerning the speaker, was adopted by Jesus at a time when, according to the testimony of the Synoptics, He studiously avoided making His identity known, when He had not even affirmed His Messiahship to the inner circle of the Twelve. It is needful, therefore, to look in detail at the passages cited above, in which the title is found prior to the declaration of our Lord's Messiahship. For that declaration, see Mt 16¹⁶, Mk 8²⁹, Lk 9²⁰.

Taking first the passages in St. Mark, with their parallels in the other Synoptics, and turning to Mk 2¹⁰ (cf. Lk 5²⁴, Mt 9⁶), we are confronted at once with the representation that quite early in His ministry, when in the presence of hostile scribes, Jesus definitely identifies Himself with the 'Son of Man.' '. . . that ye may know that the Son of Man hath power on earth to forgive sins . . . I say unto thee, Arise.' It is, of course, possible that the incident is not here in its due chronological position—that it properly belongs to a much later time in the Evangelical narrative. But there is no reason, unless it be the presence of the phrase now in question, to think so. More likely is it that in this case the ambiguity of the Aramaic is accountable for the presence of the title in the Greek rendering. The scribes were charging Jesus with blasphemy because He assumed to pronounce the forgiveness of sins, that being, as they held, in the power of God only, and not in that of any man. Jesus responds by undertaking to afford a convincing sign that even 'a man [meaning Himself] hath authority,' etc. Such a reconstruction of the passage finds support in Mt 9⁸, where we read that the multitudes who stood by 'glorified God, which had given such authority unto *men*'—the multitudes understanding our Lord to have employed no title, and taking the expression He used in its collective sense.

In Mk 2²⁸ (cf Lk 6⁵, Mt 12⁸) our Lord's argument in regard to the observance of the Sabbath seems to demand that 'man' should be substituted where we now read 'the Son of Man.' He is vindicating the action of His disciples, and asserting for all others the same freedom in regard to the use of the Sabbath as they had exercised. Jesus is not concerned to assert His own personal rights, but those of His followers, and of all who suffered from restrictions which threatened to turn that which was given for man's benefit into a bondage. 'The Sabbath was made for man . . . so that man is lord [or rather "owner"—κύριος answering here to a familiar sense of the Hebrew בעל—Swete, *Com. on St. Mark*] even of the Sabbath.'

Taking next the two remaining pre-Cæsarean occurrences of 'the Son of Man' in St. Luke, the earlier of the two, Lk 6²², presents little difficulty. It is an obvious case of an editorial insertion of the title. Where St. Luke has 'for the Son of Man's sake,' Mt 5¹¹ has, 'for my sake'—the latter being clearly the earlier form of the saying. Lk 7³⁴ (cf. Mt 11¹⁹) is quite conceivably another case of the reverent substitution by tradition of the title in place of a pronoun. Our Lord is contrasting His action with that of the Baptist. What more likely than that He should say, 'John the Baptist is come . . . I am come'? The title can be deemed here in no wise essential.

It remains to glance at six passages in the First Gospel besides those already mentioned, in which 'the Son of Man' is found prior to Peter's confession. Taking these cases in order of their occurrence in the Gospel, it is sufficient as to the first, Mt 8²⁰, to note that its parallel is Lk 9⁵⁸—*i.e.* according to St. Luke the incident of the scribe who volunteered to follow Jesus was subsequent to Peter's confession. There is no reason to suspect here any misconception of our Lord's words on the part of His translators. He cannot have said that in contrast to beasts and birds 'man' hath not where to lay his head. The contrast drawn is between such creatures and Himself, the Messianic 'Son of Man.' If even He had no resting-place, His followers might know thereby what hardship they must be prepared to undergo. Mt 10²³ is quite clearly not in its true chronological order; it belongs to a later time than the first mission of the Twelve, and to a connexion in which a larger work was contemplated than that with which they were then entrusted. But the Evangelist, following his preference for topical arrangement, has linked these later words to the instructions given to the Twelve when they were about to set out on their earliest missionary expedition.

Mt 12³², when compared with Lk 12¹⁰ and with Mk 3²⁸, is found to be a combination of two different reports of our Lord's saying as to blasphemy against the Holy Spirit. Mk 3²⁸ has no mention of 'the Son of Man,' but it has the expression, quite unique in the Gospels, 'the sons of men.' It runs thus: 'All their sins shall be forgiven unto the sons of men, and their blasphemies . . . but whosoever shall blaspheme against the Holy Spirit. . . .' In the parallel in St. Luke, the unwonted phrase 'the sons of men' disappears, and its place is taken by the familiar expression 'the Son of Man,' and the entire saying is modified in accordance therewith. That St. Mark has the utterance in its genuine form is unquestionable. Whether it properly belongs to the period before the incident at Cæsarea, or, as St. Luke suggests, was later than it, it did not contain the title 'the Son of Man.'

Mt 12⁴⁰ (cf. Lk 11³⁰). It is sufficient to point out that St. Luke places this saying in order of time considerably later than does St. Matthew, and as before, preference must be given to St. Luke in a matter of chronological order.

Finally, the parable of the Tares, in the explanation of which the title appears twice (Mt 13³⁷·⁴¹), may, with good reason, be said to belong to a late period in our Lord's ministry. It owes its present position to St. Matthew's desire to bring it into the collection of parables comprised in his 13th chapter.

Thus, of the instances in which our Lord's self-designation appears in the Synoptic Gospels prior to their recital of Peter's confession at Cæsarea Philippi, there is not one which can, on examination, be held to afford proof that this Messianic title was used by Him before His follower had declared Him to be the Messiah, or to invalidate the assumption that the use of the title by our Lord began at the time of that declaration, not earlier.

In St. Matthew's account of the incident at Cæsarea there are remarkable additions, both to our Lord's question and to Peter's answer. In Mt 16¹³ we read : 'Who do men say that the Son of Man is?' The answer is given : 'Thou art the Christ, the Son of the living God.' In Mk 8²⁷ the question is: 'Who do men say that I am?' The answer is simply : 'Thou art the Christ.' St. Luke (9¹⁸·²⁰) agrees, with but slight variations, with St. Mark. He has : 'Who do the multitudes say that I am? . . . The Christ of God.' We have here another case—the most notable of all such cases—in which the title has been substituted for the pronoun which our Lord employed. It is possible that in this case the additional clause was first appended to Peter's answer, and that the substitution in our Lord's question was occasioned by it—a substitution which represents the desired answer as already provided in the statement of the question. Holtzmann may be right in suggesting that doctrinal interests are answerable for such a result. He says (*op. cit.* vol. i. p. 258) that 'the First Evangelist appears as the theologian, who sees in the "Son of Man" the obverse of the "Son of God," and so prepares the way for the doctrine of the two natures.' Whether the clauses in question are to be ascribed to St. Matthew himself, or whether they may be due to the theological tendency of a later hand, may be regarded as an open question.

For other instances than those already cited of this variation—the title appearing in one Gospel, but not in the parallel passage in another, or in the other two—see Lk 12⁸ as compared with Mt 10³²; Mt 16²⁸, cf. Mk 9¹ and Lk 9²⁷; Mk 10⁴⁵ and Mt 20²⁸, cf. Lk 22²⁷; Mk 8³¹ and Lk 9²², cf. Mt 16²¹.

As to the occurrence of 'the Son of Man' in the earlier chapters of the Fourth Gospel, it need here only be pointed out that such occurrence is in entire accord with the representation of St. John, that from their earliest association with Him our Lord's followers knew that He was the Divine Christ. The declaration of Messiahship and the use of the title are concurrent in the Fourth Gospel as in the Synoptics. This agreement is to be emphasized here : the reconciliation of the view, which represents our Lord's Messiahship as declared from the outset of His ministry, with the threefold testimony that such declaration followed only when disciples had received prolonged training in the course of that ministry, does not come within the scope of our present purpose. The first occurrence of the self-designation in St. John's Gospel affords a striking parallel to our Lord's use of it in response to Peter's confession (Mk 8²⁹·³¹). Nathanael declares Jesus to be 'the Son of God . . . king of Israel,' and to that confession Jesus responds with the promise : 'Ye shall see the heaven opened and the angels of God ascending and descending upon the Son of Man' (Jn 1⁵¹). Similarly in 3¹³, it is when Jesus has declared to Nicodemus that He has Himself descended from heaven and can therefore tell of heavenly things, that He goes on to designate Himself 'the Son of Man,' and to foretell His suffering on behalf of man. Here it may be noted that in the Fourth Gospel, precisely as in the Synoptics, not a hint is given that the title was unfamiliar and one that called for explanation. Nicodemus was not indisposed to ask questions; but St. John leaves us to infer that as to this designation he found no difficulty. Three times in ch. 6 (vv.²⁷·⁵³·⁶²), in connexion with the discourse in which Jesus speaks of Himself as 'the bread which came down out of heaven,' the title occurs, accompanying and used to emphasize an open declaration of our Lord's claims as to His Person and Work.

The later occurrences of the title in the Fourth Gospel all, with the exception of 9³⁵ (if ἀνθρώπου be the right reading there), are found—as is the case with most of its later occurrences in the Synoptics—in passages relating to our Lord's Passion, or to the glory which would follow thereon. This fact suggests, at least in part, the answer to a further inquiry which must now be made.

4. Why did our Lord adopt this in preference to any other Messianic title?—Nowhere does He tell us in precise terms; but His usage leaves no room to doubt that its attraction lay in its freedom from the limitations which beset other Messianic names.

(*a*) First and foremost, *it permitted the blending of the conception of the Suffering Servant with that of the Messianic King.* That was the great enlargement which Jesus gave, in His use of it, to the title He adopted. True, there was nothing in Daniel's delineation of 'one like unto a son of man' to suggest such a blending, but there was also nothing to preclude it. Whether the coming of the heavenly Son of Man in glory, and for universal dominion, was to be preceded by a coming in humiliation and a reascension through suffering, the writer of Daniel did not tell. But what the prophet failed to disclose, Jesus revealed. He was indeed the son of man, whom Daniel beheld, but passing through a phase of existence anterior to that of which the seer had a glimpse, and a phase which none were anticipating. Jesus was indeed the Messiah; but the expectations which gathered about that name made no allowance for that which was foremost in the purpose for which He came to earth. Hence, no sooner did His disciple exclaim 'Thou art the Christ,' than 'he began to teach them [the disciples] that the Son of Man must suffer many things, and be rejected by the elders and the chief priests and the scribes, and be killed, and after three days rise again.' Put even so,—as a fresh disclosure concerning the Son of Man,—the teaching was not easy of reception, as Peter's remonstrance showed; but to have said at that juncture that the 'Son of David,' or 'the Christ,' must suffer and be killed, had been to make the teaching yet harder of reception.

As Dalman says (*op. cit.* p. 265): 'The name Messiah denoted the Lord of the Messianic age in His capacity as Ruler; in reality it was applicable only when His enthronement had taken place, not before it. Suffering and death for the actual possessor of the Messianic dignity are, in fact, unimaginable according to the testimony of the prophets. When Jesus attached to the Messianic confession of Peter the first intimation of His violent death, He did so in order to make it clear that the entrance upon His sovereignty was still far distant. . . . But the "one like unto a son of man" of Dn 7¹³ has still to receive the sovereignty. It was *possible* that he should also be one who had undergone suffering and death.'

Hence, in reiterated statements to the disciples concerning the death toward which He moved, the invariable self-designation on the lips of our Lord is 'the Son of Man.' See Mk 9⁹·¹²·³¹ 10³³ 14²¹·⁴¹, and the parallels in St. Matthew and St. Luke. Only when the Crucifixion and the Resurrection were accomplished facts, in the light of which His disciples might discern how false and misleading had been their narrow conception of what Messiahship could be, does Jesus speak to them of Himself in other terms: 'Behoved it not the *Christ* to suffer these things?' and again: 'Thus it is written that the *Christ* should suffer' (Lk 24²⁶·⁴⁶).

(*b*) If 'the Son of Man' was a title capable of being associated with suffering and death, it was *a title already associated with the glorious coming of One who should have everlasting rule over a world in which the powers of evil should no more have sway.* That was the form of expectation present to the mind of Jesus as He passed on His way to the baptism of suffering, and that was the form of Messianic hope which He sought to strengthen in His followers as He spoke to them, with growing frequency, of the coming of 'the Son of Man.' The

utterances concerning the return of 'the Son of Man' in glory, and the predictions that 'the Son of Man' must suffer and die, are in strict correlation (see Bousset, *Jesus*, p. 92 ff.). It is this coming from heaven, this realization of the Kingdom of heaven upon earth, to which Jesus looks forward. Wholly unlike the anticipations entertained by men around Him concerning the Davidic Messiah, the vision of Daniel is that which Jesus again and again calls to mind. He will come 'in the glory of the Father with the holy angels' (Mk 8³⁸); 'They shall see the Son of Man coming in clouds with great power and glory' (Mk 13²⁶; see also 14⁶²); 'When the Son of Man shall come in his glory and all the angels with him, then shall he sit on the throne of his glory: and before him shall be gathered all the nations: and he shall separate them one from another . . .' (Mt 25³¹ᶠᶠ·). This function of separation, of judgment, is not in the Danielic sketch of 'the son of man'; it is a feature added by our Lord. In Daniel the judgment is effected by the Most High. It is significant of much, that Jesus, while adopting and citing that prophecy, does not hesitate to modify it in this important particular, and to declare that it is *He* who will come to be our Judge (cf. Jn 5²⁷).

(*c*) If 'the Son of Man,' telling of descent from heaven, spoke of a closer association with God than did any other current Messianic title, so did it speak also of *closer association with man—with the race*. All narrow particularism falls away. He who bears this title is no mere 'Son of David,' or 'King of Israel.' Especially when regard is had to the idiomatic use of בר in Aramaic, as of בן in Hebrew, such a title expresses in the strongest possible way that He who is called by it has the nature and the qualities of mankind, and that He who calls Himself by it claims thereby relationship with man everywhere.

It is in such reasons as these that we may find the true clue to our Lord's adoption of this name—not in its supposed unfamiliarity, nor in an ambiguity enabling the speaker to use it in one sense, while He could confidently anticipate that it would be understood in another by His hearers.

5. Why did our Lord's followers, with the exception of Stephen, not apply this title to Him?—The fact that a designation which meets us so frequently in the Gospels is, with the single exception of Ac 7⁵⁶, wholly absent from the rest of the NT, is remarkable and significant. But of what? Wellhausen and Lietzmann answer, of this: that it was unknown to St. Paul and the other writers of the Epistles and to the author of the Apocalypse that such a title was employed by Jesus, and that the presumption is that only after their day was it introduced into the Gospels. But how this could be done, and how such an important modification of the most cherished records of the Church could be carried out with such enduring success, there is nothing to show. Certainly it is not safe to conclude that St. Paul and other NT writers did not know that this was our Lord's self-designation because they make no direct reference to it. Schmiedel (*l.c.* p. 260 f.) points to He 2⁶ᶠᶠ· as affording evidence that the name was not unknown to the writer of that Epistle. Similarly, he holds that St. Paul in 1 Co 15²⁷ makes his reference to Ps 8 because of the presence in that psalm of the terms which he associated with his Lord—'the Son of Man.' Schmiedel is on firmer ground when he goes on to rebut the contention, that had St. Paul known of the title he must have cited it in such a verse as 1 Co 15⁴⁷. He urges that it should be borne in mind that St. Paul wrote for Greeks, who would not, like the Jews, understand by 'the son of man' simply 'man,' but would take 'son' quite literally. To this may be added that, apart from the suggestion of a purely human parentage, which Gentiles might receive from the title, its use would for them lay an undue, and therefore a misleading, stress on our Lord's humanity. To the Jew 'the Son of Man' suggested the Lord from heaven ; not so to the Gentile. Where the association of the name with heavenly origin and majesty could not be assumed, there the Apostles and early exponents of Christianity adopted other terms as they spoke or wrote of their risen and ascended Lord, and proclaimed Him as 'the Christ, the Son of God' (Jn 20[31]). To use the words of Dalman (*op. cit.* p. 266), 'the Church was quite justified in refusing, on its part, to give currency to the title ; for in the meantime "the Son of Man" had been set upon the throne of God, and was, in fact, no longer merely a man, but a Ruler over heaven and earth, "the Lord," as St. Paul in the Epistles to the Thessalonians, and the *Teaching of the Apostles* in its apocalyptic statement, rightly designate Him who comes with the clouds of heaven.'

In short, the absence of the title 'the Son of Man' from other early Christian records than the Gospels, is significant of the widening range of the Church's appeal beyond the confines of Judaism ; its retention in the Gospels is no less significant of the fidelity with which the words of Jesus were preserved by His followers.

LITERATURE. — For a summary of various interpretations of 'the Son of Man,' see articles by Driver in Hastings' *DB* ; N. Schmidt in *EBi* ; and Baldensperger in *Theol. Rundschau*, 1900, Hefte 6 und 7. Many of the more important modern contributions have already been indicated. Of those not directly cited may be mentioned : Appel, *Die Selbstbezeichnung Jesu* ; Bruce, *Kingdom of God* ; Sanday, *Expositor*, Jan. 1891 ; Bartlet, *ib.* Dec. 1892 ; Stanton, *The Jewish and the Christian Messiah* ; Wendt, *The Teaching of Jesus* ; Keim, *Jesus of Nazara* ; Weiss, *Life of Christ*.   GEORGE P. GOULD.

SON OF PERDITION. — See JUDAS ISCARIOT, ii. (*g*).

SON OF THE LAW. — See BOYHOOD and EDUCATION.

SONS OF THUNDER. — See BOANERGES.

SOP. — 1. *The meaning of the word.* — 'Sop' occurs in EV only in Jn 13[26 bis. 27. 30] (AVm 'morsel'). It is akin in derivation to 'sup' and 'soup,' and denotes food soaked in liquid before being eaten. The Gr. word in each case is ψωμίον, dim. of ψωμός, 'a morsel.' ψωμίον does not occur in LXX, but ψωμός is found in Ru 2[14], Job 31[17], and in EV is rendered 'morsel.' Its use in Ruth — 'Dip thy morsel (ψωμόν) in the vinegar' — is exactly analogous to that of ψωμίον in John.

2. *The nature of the sop given to Judas.* — Edersheim (*LT* ii. 506) and others, on the ground especially of the definite art. (τὸ ψωμίον). Edersheim says, 'Mark the definite article — *not* "a sop"'), hold that it was a specific sop, used at the Passover supper in the time of Christ, which consisted of a piece of the flesh of the Paschal lamb, a piece of unleavened bread, and some bitter herbs, all wrapped together and dipped in the *harôseth* — a sauce made of raisins, dates, and other fruits, mixed with vinegar — and then passed round to the company by the host. Jesus, as the host at the Last Supper, would hand this sop, first of all, to Judas, who is supposed to have occupied the place of chief honour at the table (see art. PASSOVER [I.], p. 326[b], and UPPER ROOM). It is not enough to brush this view aside, as Meyer does, on the ground that, according to John, the Last Supper was not a Passover meal ; for, even though it was not the regular Passover of the Jews, it may have been a Supper of a similar kind (see art. PASSOVER [II.], p. 327[b]). On the other hand, Edersheim's argument from the definite art. is precarious, since its use in v. [26b] is doubtful

(see WH) ; and, in any case, the Evangelist, writing long afterwards and with a profound sense of the momentous character of the incident, probably wrote 'the sop,' meaning thereby 'the tragic sop,' 'that fatal sop' — which sealed the traitor's doom. It seems much more probable, then, that this sop was not the specific Paschal sop passed round to the company by the host, but a particular sop that Jesus offered to Judas on purely personal grounds. At an Oriental feast the host sometimes presented a guest with a special tit-bit from the food on the table, as a distinguishing mark of his favour. And it was not by any accident of Judas' position at the table, but because of a deep purpose in the heart of Jesus, that this sop was given.

3. *Its significance.* — This offering of the sop to Judas, which is not mentioned by the Synoptists (though Mt. and Mk. make Jesus say that the betrayer should be the one who dipped his hand with Him in the dish [Mt 26[23], Mk 14[20]]), comes before us with a double significance. (*a*) It was a sign given to the beloved disciple, in response to his question, 'Lord, who is it ?' that Judas was the one of the company who was about to betray his Master (vv.[25. 26]). (*b*) But it was much more than this. There was nothing hypocritical on Christ's part in the action. He did not make a show of friendliness to Judas merely for the sake of giving John a private sign. What was commonly understood to be a token of hospitable goodwill was, without doubt, meant in this case to be the expression of a feeling deeper than any ordinary human affection, and at the same time to be a last appeal to the better nature of this erring disciple, with a note of warning underlying the appeal (cf. vv.[18. 21]). A whole world of blessed possibility lay for Judas in that proffered sop ; Divine love was in it, and free forgiveness, and full restoration — if only he would repent of his meditated crime. And just because of the immensity of meaning that lay in Christ's gift was the awfulness of its result. Judas 'received the sop' (v.[30]), and doubtless ate it. He understood what Jesus wished him to understand — the mingled love and warning and promise and appeal that lay in His act. But at this crisis of his fate he closed his ears to Christ's offers and his heart to Christ's grace. And immediately the light that still lingered in him was turned into darkness. For 'after the sop, then [τότε — at that very moment] Satan entered into him.' 'The violent effort he made to close his heart to the heavenly power opened it to the powers of evil' (Godet). Jesus knew that all was over. 'That thou doest,' He said, 'do quickly' (v.[27]). And so Judas, 'having received the sop' [note the significant repetition of the ominous word], 'went out straightway : and it was night.'

LITERATURE. — The Lexx. *s.vv.* ψωμίον, ψωμός ; Hastings' *DB*, art. 'Sop' ; the Comm. of Meyer, Godet, Westcott, Dods, *in loc.* ; Edersheim, *LT* ii. 505 ff. ; *ExpT* iii. [1891] 107 ; Martin, *Winning the Soul*, 17.   J. C. LAMBERT.

SORROW, MAN OF SORROWS. — We shall find in the Gospels no theory of sorrow, or abstract discussion of the problem of pain and suffering. The problem is taken for granted, and a solution is given. The solution is experimental, and centres round the life of Christ. If we ask why sorrow comes, the answer is not speculative, but practical ; we are simply pointed to His experience (He 12). Accordingly, the method of this article will be to deal first with Christ as the Man of Sorrows, and afterwards with the meaning of sorrow in human life generally, and particularly in the life of the Christian.

1. **The 'Man of Sorrows.'** — The phrase comes from Is 53[3] (אִישׁ מַכְאֹבוֹת ; LXX, ἄνθρωπος ἐν πληγῇ ὤν ; Vulg. *virum dolorum*).

Objection has been taken (*e.g.* by Cheyne, G. A. Smith, Skinner, Workman) to the rendering 'sorrows,' 'pains' being preferred in this verse and the next as a nearer parallel to חֹלִי ('sickness' rather than ' grief'). But the *Oxford Heb. Lex.* gives many instances of both the vb. and noun as referring to *mental pain*, and classes this passage under that head. While allowing that the picture in Isaiah is primarily of physical suffering, we may without hesitation retain the familiar rendering of AV and RV.

The title is never applied to Christ in the NT. It belongs, in fact, to popular rather than to technical phraseology, expressing in picturesque form what the theologian means by speaking of Christ as the 'Suffering Servant of Jehovah.' Either phrase implies equally that the prophecy of Is 53 was in a true sense fulfilled in Him. Whatever may have been the primary historical bearing of that passage, it is generally admitted that in the time of Christ there was no expectation of a suffering Messiah. The indications of the Gospels and Acts agree completely with the evidence of pre-Christian Jewish literature. 'The idea of the Messiah's sufferings is not found in any Jewish document up to the close of the first century' (Stanton, *Jewish and Christian Messiah*, p. 123). 'Man of Sorrows' would have been the last title to have caught the popular imagination of that age. 'Son of David' expressed the contemporary hopes of what the Messiah was to be. That the one title has been entirely displaced by the other is significant. The one is national, more or less materialistic, pointing to an earthly kingdom. The other expresses the universal attraction of Christ, His spiritual empire over the hearts of men, and the means by which His influence has been won. See, further, art. MESSIAH.

2. The nature of the sorrows of Christ.— Though, as noted above, the phrase 'Man of Sorrows' may be retained as the translation of Is 53[3], there can be little doubt that the general picture of the passage in its literal sense is of one visited with the extreme of physical suffering, a Job; many see in it the description of a leper, as in Ps 88. If the view is correct that it was never intended to apply to an individual, but was typical of the nation, or of part of it, it will none the less remain true that the figure the writer has chosen is that of bodily sickness. The sorrows of Christ were not of this nature, nor was His appearance unattractive, still less repulsive, as of one suffering from a loathsome disease. In the Gospels but little stress is laid on the physical sufferings even of the last days. He Himself expressly deprecates so doing (Lk 23[28]). He once refers to the privations of His life (Lk 9[58]) in order to check one who had not counted the cost of discipleship. A single word from the Cross (Jn 19[28]) has to do with His bodily needs. Where the thought of His own sufferings comes to His mind, the impression we have is of spiritual sorrow (Mk 10[32] 14[34] 15[34], Lk 12[50], Jn 12[27]), and commentators of all schools have connected this sorrow with His contact and conflict with sin. He sighs at the presence of the deaf and dumb man (Mk 7[34]). When face to face with death, He is moved with sympathetic compassion (Lk 7[13]) ; He groans in spirit, is troubled, and weeps (Jn 11[33]). The underlying thought in these passages seems to be His sense of what lies behind human suffering. So it is different degrees of sin at which His sorrow is implied or expressed :—dulness, unbelief, or hardness of heart in the disciples (Mt 16[8], Mk 8[21] 9[19] 10[14] 14[27. 37], Lk 22[38], Jn 14[9]) ;—the wilful blindness and opposition of His countrymen (Mk 3[5] 6[6] 8[12], Lk 13[15]). Specially significant are the laments over Jerusalem (Mt 23[37], Lk 19[41]). He is grieved at ingratitude (Lk 17[17]), at lack of hospitality (Lk 7[44]), at the profanation of the Temple (Mt 21[12]), above all, at the treachery of Judas (Mt 26[20], Jn 13[21]). He feels sorrowful compassion over the multitude

without a shepherd (Mt 9[36], Mk 6[34]). On the other hand, His joy is specially mentioned at the conquest or removal of sin (Mt 18[13], Lk 10[21] 15[5]). A study of these passages will show the sense in which He was a Man of Sorrows. On the one hand, He was brought into a relation to sin from which His nature shrank, and which even seemed at its climax to lead to a separation from God (Mk 15[34]). On the other hand, in His conflict against sin He was spiritually alone. He knew more clearly than any the nature of sin and its results. He saw what man might be if he chose, and what in fact he was. He realized every hour the tragic irony of the situation, that He had come to His own and they would not receive Him. The horror of His rejection by His countrymen lay not so much in the suffering it implied for Himself, as in their own loss of opportunity. Is 53 was profoundly true. Men did not perceive or desire the beauty of His holiness. They despised and rejected His message ; they hid their face from Him because they could not bear to look on the splendour of the goodness and love He came to reveal.*

3. The necessity of sorrow in the life of Christ came from the spiritual character of His work. From the point of view of the disciples, and the popular conception of the Messiah, a certain amount of conflict and hardship could readily be allowed for. The Roman could not be expected to yield without a blow ; and as it became clear that opposition from within His own nation was to be expected, temporary disappointments and misunderstandings would fall within the disciples' scheme of the future. They were ready for the hardships of an earthly struggle, *i.e.* to drink His cup as they understood it. They were not prepared for the Cross, because they had not a deep enough conception of His work. Not Roman or Sadducee, but sin, was the enemy ; His end was the establishment of a spiritual and universal empire. The national mission of the Son of David had passed into the world-wide mission of the Servant of Jehovah,† and the means which might have sufficed for the one would no longer serve the other. His work moved on a higher plane, and the weapons of His warfare must be more mysterious and spiritual than any outward miracle. These weapons were the attractive and atoning power of service, and sorrow. Mk 10[45] shows this clearly. The Cross, the life of service, and all it implied of sorrow and suffering, were necessary because He had come to give His life a ransom for many (cf. Jn 12[32]).

The fuller discussion of the redemptive value of Christ's sufferings belongs to other articles (see art. ATONEMENT). It must suffice here to insist on what all theories admit, that only as Sufferer could He be Saviour. He had come to serve God as man ; therefore suffering was necessary to the perfection of His obedience (He 2[10] 5[8]). It is a fact of history that as the Sufferer He has conquered and drawn men unto Him. The title 'Man of Sorrows' expresses, more perhaps than any other, His attractive power ; it has been the inspiration of Christian art and music. The thought underlying it is not primarily any logical theory of Atonement, but the all-embracing sympathy of the God-man. His 'Come unto me' (Mt 11[28]) is a comfortable word, because it is spoken by One 'who, in that he himself suffered being tempted,

---

* From this point of view the nearest parallel to Christ is Jeremiah, the 'man of sorrows' of the OT. There, too, we have the one standing in moral solitude over against the whole nation, in bitterness of soul because he knows that none will listen to his message. If, as is often thought, his experience had some share in moulding the conception of Is 53, that chapter forms a close link between him and Christ, pointing back to the one and forward to the other (cf. G. A. Smith, *Isaiah*, vol. ii. ch. 2, etc.).

† See Workman, *The Servant of Jehovah*, ch. vii.

is able to succour them that are tempted' (He 2[18] 3[15], cf. Mt 8[17]).

4. The Christian conception of sorrow.—Sorrow is, properly speaking, a psychological term, being a description of a state of mind. It should be distinguished from the suffering, mental or physical, which may be its occasion. We may define it as the sense of discord, the consciousness that things are not as they should be, in ourselves, or in the world. It is an experience peculiar to man, and can be attributed to animals only by an effort of personification.* In the fact of its being a privilege peculiar to man we may begin to see something of its purpose.

'The inherent necessity in man of sorrow . . . testifies that his essential constitution and nature, as man, is something which all this world's life and the conditions of it—by the very fact that they are what they are—cannot match and cannot satisfy. The very constitution of his being and the necessary conditions of his life are out of harmony together. They do not and cannot fit ; the one is too small to satisfy the other. Set man, being what man is, in this world, as the conditions of this world are, and the necessary result is, sooner or later, sorrow' (Moberly, *Sorrow, Sin, and Beauty*, p. 7).

To a creature made in the image of God, sorrow is the necessary condition of the struggle against sin in an imperfect world. Given the fact of sin, suffering ceases to be a problem. Only in a perfect state could it be desirable that sorrow and sighing should flee away.

Hence if sorrow is a privilege of man as a spiritual being, we shall expect to find that it is in a special sense the privilege of the Christian. The second Beatitude (Mt 5[4]) speaks absolutely of its blessedness. The underlying thought seems to be that dissatisfaction with things as they are will lead to the effort to right them. Discord within the soul, *i.e.* sin, is specially in view. Mourning is the evidence of the break-up of the self-complacency which is the chief obstacle to the Kingdom of God. Sorrow, indeed, is of no value unless it leads to the striving after higher things. There is no blessedness attached to vain regret for the past (Mt 25[11] 27[3], Mk 10[22]), or to the sorrow which finds its vent in weary sleep instead of in prayer (Lk 22[45]). The bearing of pain, voluntary or otherwise, is in itself neutral ; it is effective only when it is the means of rooting out from the self a cause of offence (Mt 5[29], etc.). The sorrow which is fruitful is the travail which issues in the birth of a new life (Jn 12[24] 16[21]). The one object of the purging is that the branch may bring forth more fruit (Jn 15[2]).

If sorrow is a necessary accompaniment of the attempt to right things in oneself, it will also accompany the attempt to right things in the world. It was Christ's experience, and it will be the experience of His followers (Jn 15[20] etc.) as they share His work. The traditional saying of Christ that 'he who is near me is near the fire' (Orig. *Hom. in Jer.* xx. 3) is at least authentic in spirit. The disciples must bear the cross He bears (Mk 8[34]), drink His cup, and be baptized with His baptism (Mk 10[38]), carry His yoke (Mt 11[29]). The sword must pierce the Virgin's heart because of her nearness to Him (Lk 2[35]) ; even the Innocents suffer unconsciously on account of their connexion with Him (Mt 2[16]). The *via dolorosa* is the only road to union with Him.†

In Jn 16 the sorrow of the disciples is contrasted with the transient joy of the world. The world rejoices (16[20]) 'as having been freed from one who was a dangerous innovator as well as a condemner of its ways' (Westcott, *ad loc.*) ; *i.e.* it is satisfied to have no Christ, even to have removed Him, and is content with things as they are. The sorrow of the disciples is connected with the departure of Christ. The primary reference is to the immediate crisis, but in all ages His disciples will have sorrow in all that hinders their full vision of Him, the complete establishment of His Kingdom, and His return in glory. Though He has overcome the world, they must have tribulation in it, till the victory won ideally is realized in fact (16[33]). Sorrow cannot be completely turned into joy till what is, is identical with what should be, till He returns again and we see Him as He is (1 Jn 3[2]). As we said before, we find no abstract discussion of the nature and meaning of sorrow. The solution of the problem is found in the experience of Christ, which is the experience of the Christian.* Sorrow is bound up with every attempt to combat sin in the self and in the world. It is the reaction against sin, and those who feel this most keenly must drink most deeply of the cup. The consolation lies in the fact that the disciple is sharing the lot of His master here, and will share His joy hereafter (Mt 19[28], Ro 8[17], 2 Ti 2[11]).

5. Sorrow and happiness.—It would be an inadequate treatment of the teaching of Christ to conceive of sorrow merely as the condition of future happiness. Christianity is a religion of present happiness. An exultant joy is the note of the songs which hailed Christ's birth. Joy is a present fruit of the Spirit (Gal 5[22]) ; the Kingdom of God is now joy and peace (Ro 14[17]). The promises of the New Heaven and the New Earth are not purely eschatological ; they belong, ideally at least, to our life now. One of the characteristic paradoxes of Christianity is that its sorrow and happiness coexist. Again we turn first to the experience of Christ. He is the Man of Sorrows, yet we cannot think of Him for a moment as an unhappy man. He rather gives us the picture of serene and unclouded happiness. Beneath not merely the outward suffering, but the profound sorrow of heart, there is deeper still a continual joy, derived from the realized presence of His Father, and the consciousness that He is doing His work. Unless this is remembered, the idea of the Man of Sorrows is sentimentalized and exaggerated. And again the disciple shares the experience of His master. Neither Christ nor the true Christian can for a moment wish, like a Job or a Jeremiah, that he had never been born. The Beatitudes express His own humanly discovered secret of happiness ; He has Himself known the blessedness of mourning, though never, of course, over His own sin, and He imparts the secret to His follower. And though the promises of Jn 16 can be completely realized only when the Christian departs to be with Christ (Ph 1[23]), yet even now His joy is in him and is fulfilled (Jn 15[11]) ; even now, in prayer and in communion with Him, he knows the joy which no man can take from him (Jn 16[20. 22. 24]). 'Sorrowful, yet always rejoicing' (2 Co 6[10]), is the paradox of the gospel, and each side of the paradox is needed to counteract an unbalanced view of life. On the one hand, sorrow is no figment of the imagination, to be thought away. It is a fact of life, and a necessary fact, necessary to the perfection of the sinless One, much more to our own ; the condition of all progress and of all true work for God. This is the truth ignored by the 'sky-blue' optimism, which strives to live ever in the sunshine and blinds itself to sin.† On the other hand, sorrow is not the last word of life. The world is a κόσμος, a creation of order and beauty. We find in Christ's teaching

---

* See the remarkable passage in Ro 8[22], where Nature is represented as sharing in the imperfection and hopes of man. Cf. Sanday-Headlam, *ad loc.*

† It need hardly be added that this thought dominates the rest of the NT (*e.g.* Ph 3[10], Col 1[24], 1 P 4[13]).

* 'The real Christian looks at sorrow not from without, but from within, and does not approach its speculative difficulty till he is aware by experience of its practical power' (*Lux Mundi*[15], p. 89).

† See James, *Varieties of Religious Experience*, p. 80 ff.

nothing of the sentimental attitude, which looks on suffering with complacency, as though it were good in itself. To Him evil is evil, and suffering is suffering; He came as the Saviour to destroy them.* Here Christianity is in strong contrast to Buddhism, and to all forms of morbid asceticism. Bacon's aphorism that 'prosperity is the blessing of the OT, adversity the blessing of the NT,' is true only when it is understood that beneath the adversity, and the sorrow of heart which it brings, there is even here and now the peace which passeth understanding, the joy which comes of union with Christ, of sympathy with man, and of work for God.

LITERATURE.—Davidson, *OT Prophecy* (ch. 22); Stanton, *Jewish and Christian Messiah*; G. A. Smith, *Isaiah*, vol. ii.; Moberly, *Sorrow, Sin, and Beauty*; Du Bose, *Gospel in the Gospels*; *Lux Mundi*, 'The Problem of Pain'; Workman, *The Servant of Jehovah*.　　　　　　　　　　**C. W. EMMET.**

SOUL.—In every act of thinking, a distinction exists between the thinker and his thought, or, as it is otherwise expressed, between the self and the not-self, the ego and the non-ego, the thinking subject and the object of thought. This ego, self, or thinking subject, is denominated *the soul* (ψυχή, נֶפֶשׁ, נְשָׁמָה), or *spirit* (πνεῦμα, רוּחַ; see SPIRIT); often also, both in the OT and NT, *the heart* (καρδία, לֵב, לֵבָב; see HEART). In the OT the soul is sometimes confused with the blood or with some important physical organ, but in the NT it is clearly distinguished from the body as an immaterial principle, the seat of conscious personality, and essentially immortal (Mt 10²⁸ etc.; see IMMORTALITY). There was much speculation in our Lord's time, and had been for some two centuries, on the mysterious questions of the soul's origin and destiny. Some, following Plato and Philo, believed in its eternal pre-existence (cf. Wis 8¹⁹ RV); others (mainly orthodox Rabbis) in its creation at the creation of the world (cf. 2 Es 4³⁵ff.); others in its premundane creation (Slavonic Enoch 23⁵); others (perhaps the majority) in its concreation with the body, which is apparently the doctrine of the OT (Is 44²· ²⁴ 49¹· ⁵, Job 31¹⁵). A few supported the Platonic speculation of metempsychosis (so apparently Josephus; see *BJ* III. viii. 5). The disciples of Jesus were aware of these discussions, and on one occasion asked Him whether a certain man had been born blind as a penalty for sins committed by him in a previous state of existence. It is a significant illustration of the economy of revelation that Jesus avoided entering upon the discussion (Jn 9²).†

1. The use of ψυχή in the Gospels.—In the Pauline Epistles, as is well known, there is frequently a decided difference of meaning between ψυχή and πνεῦμα. There ψυχή is used for the principle of life of the natural man, while πνεῦμα is the principle of supernatural life which manifests itself in the regenerate Christian. Hence the derivative ψυχικός (literally 'soulish') comes to be used in a depreciatory, and even in a bad sense (1 Co 12¹⁴ 15⁴⁴, Ja 3¹⁵, Jude ¹⁹). But in the Gospels there is no such distinction of usage. As applied to the human soul, ψυχή and πνεῦμα are synonyms throughout the range of their meaning. Thus in the sense of *natural life*, we have Mk 3⁴, cf. Jn 13³⁷ (ψυχή); and Mt 27⁵⁰, cf. Lk 23⁴⁶, Jn 19³⁰ (πνεῦμα). (For the lower sense of πνεῦμα, cf. also Mk 8¹², Lk 8⁵⁵ 24³⁷· ³⁹, Jn 11³³ 13²¹). ψυχή, as well as πνεῦμα, is used quite normally for the soul in its highest religious activities (see, *e.g.*, Lk 1⁴⁶, where

* So Harnack most admirably, in *What is Christianity?* ch. vi.
† The Creationist view of the soul's origin was held by all Jews in our Lord's time. The Traducianist hypothesis first appears in Tertullian (A.D. 200).

the identity of ψυχή and πνεῦμα is especially apparent; Mt 11²⁹ 22³⁷ ‖; cf. 1 P 2¹¹· ²⁵ 4¹⁹, 2 P 2⁸ etc.; and even in the Pauline Epp. see 2 Co 1²³, Eph 6⁶, Ph 1²⁷; cf. He 6¹⁹ 13¹⁷). In one passage (Jn 10²⁴) ψυχή seems even to stand for the rational or deliberating faculty (λόγος, νοῦς). There is, however, between ψυχή and πνεῦμα, as used in the Gospels, one slight distinction. ψυχή emphasizes more strongly than πνεῦμα the idea of individual personality. Hence ψυχαί (not πνεύματα) is used for 'individuals' or 'persons' (Ac 27³⁷, 1 P 3²⁰); and it is usual to speak of the salvation or loss of the ψυχή rather than of the πνεῦμα (Mt 6²⁵ 10³⁹ 16²⁵· ²⁶, Mk 8³⁵, Lk 9²⁴ 17³³ 21¹⁹, Jn 12²⁵, He 10³⁹, Ja 1²¹ 5²⁰, 1 P 1⁹). Yet the salvation of the πνεῦμα is alluded to (1 Co 5⁵, 1 Th 5²³). πνεῦμα, however, is not by any means a strictly impersonal term (see Mt 5¹⁶, He 1¹⁴). It is used like ψυχή to denote a disembodied soul (Lk 24³⁷· ³⁹, He 12²³, 1 P 3¹⁸, Rev 6⁹ 20⁴). In Mt 12¹⁸ (a quotation from Is 42¹) God is said to possess a ψυχή. In Jn 4²⁴ He is said to be spirit (πνεῦμα).

The following particular statements about the soul (ψυχή) are made in the Gospels. As the principle of physical life it is sustained by food (Mt 6²⁵); as the organ of spiritual life it 'magnifies the Lord' (Lk 1⁴⁶). It is capable of physical and sensuous pleasure (12¹⁹), also of spiritual rest and refreshment (Mt 11²⁹). It can suffer acute sorrow (Lk 2³⁵) and anxiety (Jn 10²⁴). It can grieve (Mt 26³⁸) and love (22³⁷). It can be lost and saved (10³⁹ etc.). At death it is yielded up (Jn 10¹¹· ¹⁵ 12²⁴), but survives as a personal self-conscious being (Mt 10³⁹ etc.).* See, further, SPIRIT.

2. Christ's teaching about the soul.—According to Jesus, the soul, being a man's inmost self, the seat of his self-conscious personality, and inherently immortal (Mt 10²⁸), is precious beyond all price. Nothing can be accepted in exchange for it, and the gain of the whole world will not compensate for its loss (16²⁶). Jesus drives home this truth in the parable of the Rich Fool, who said to his soul, 'Soul, thou hast much goods laid up for many years; take thine ease, eat, drink, and be merry'; and whom God rebuked with the awful words, 'Thou fool, this night *they* (*i.e.* the ministers of my vengeance) require of thee thy soul' (Lk 12¹⁶⁻²¹). Much is said in the Gospels about the gain or loss of the soul, generally with a play upon the double meaning of ψυχή ('life' or 'soul'). Most of these passages take the form of exhortations to martyrdom, as, for instance, Mt 10³⁹ 'He that findeth his soul (*i.e.* he that saves his life by denying me in time of persecution) shall lose it (by eternal punishment in Gehenna); and he that loseth his soul for my sake (*i.e.* he who confesses me in time of persecution, and suffers a martyr's death), shall find it (in heaven)'; (see also 16²⁵, Lk 17³³, Jn 12³⁵). All these passages refer primarily to martyrdom, but in their secondary applications teach that even lesser sufferings and trials endured patiently for Christ's sake have as their reward the salvation of the soul (Mt 10³⁸). The same idea is expressed in Lk 14²⁶, where the strange phrase 'to hate the soul' is a rhetorical expression for willingness to suffer martyrdom or any lesser inconvenience for Jesus' sake (cf. also Jn 12²⁵). The gain or salvation of the soul means certainly its eternal happiness in heaven, and the loss or destruction of the soul, as certainly, not its annihilation, but its eternal punishment in Gehenna. The endlessness of the soul's final retribution is not simply an inference from the soul's immortality,

* It follows from this, that in the view of Jesus and the Twelve, the ψυχή and πνεῦμα of man are not distinct principles or entities, as, according to some, St. Paul affirms in 1 Th 5²³; cf. He 4¹². The language of the Gospels makes decisively for the *unity* of the soul, and for a *dichotomy* of man (body and soul), not for a trichotomy (body, soul, and spirit).

but is exegetically established from Mt 25⁴⁶ etc. According to the conceptions represented in the parable of Dives and Lazarus, retribution does not wait till the Last Day, but begins as soon as the soul leaves the body. At death the disembodied soul passes to a 'middle state' (Hades), where, if righteous, it experiences rest and refreshment in 'Abraham's bosom,' or 'Paradise'; or, if unrighteous, expiatory punishment (symbolized as a tormenting flame) in a *limbus* or 'prison,' which is separated by an impassable barrier from the abodes of the righteous. The disembodied souls are represented as conscious and intelligent, able to converse with one another, and interested in the welfare of their friends upon earth (Lk 16¹⁹ 23⁴³, 1 P 3¹⁸, Rev 6⁹).

The most important question about the intermediate state is whether spiritual change is possible in it. The point has been keenly debated, but the affirmative opinion seems to have the better exegetical support. For (1) the NT represents not death, but the Second Advent, as the time when the soul will render its final account to God. Presumably, therefore, the middle state is included in the period of probation. (2) Christ appears to the present writer to teach that some sins may be forgiven after death (Mt 12³²; and at least to hint that even grievous sinners may be released from torments, after adequately expiating their crimes (5²⁶). (3) The torments of Dives seem to have been remedial in effect, causing him for the first time to interest himself in the spiritual welfare of others (Lk 16²⁷). (4) The descent of Christ into Hades, and His preaching to the disobedient spirits there (1 P 3¹⁸), plainly presuppose the possibility of repentance after death.'*

At the Last Day, according to Jesus, there will be a bodily resurrection of all men, followed by a final judgment, and a final settlement of the destiny of each soul (Mt 25³¹⁻⁴⁶). The resurrection of the wicked is clearly taught in Mt 10²⁸, Jn 5²⁹. See, further, RESURRECTION OF THE DEAD, ESCHATOLOGY, ABRAHAM (§ '**Abraham's bosom**'), PARADISE, HELL [DESCENT INTO].

Jesus claimed to stand in the same relation to human souls as God Himself; and as the Lord of souls issued the universal invitation, 'Come unto me, all ye that labour and are heavy laden . . . and ye shall find rest unto your souls' (Mt 11²⁸⁻²⁹). He also declared that His special object in coming into the world was to save souls (Lk 9⁵⁶) by laying down His own soul as a ransom (Jn 10¹¹·¹⁵ 17³).

3. The soul of Jesus.—If Jesus was perfect man, it follows that He must have possessed not only a human body, but also a human soul and a human spirit; and this is, in fact, the doctrine of the Gospels and of the NT generally. Thus He came to give His soul (ψυχήν) a ransom for many (Mt 20²⁸ ‖). After the interview with the Greeks (Jn 12²⁷), His soul (ψυχή) was troubled, and He doubted what to say. In Gethsemane His soul was exceeding sorrowful (περίλυπός ἐστιν ἡ ψυχή μου, Mt 26³⁸ ‖). There are similar references to His human spirit. He groaned (or was angry) in spirit (ἐνεβριμήσατο τῷ πνεύματι, Jn 11³³); and was troubled in spirit (ἐταράχθη τῷ πνεύματι, 13²¹). On the cross He commended His spirit to God (παρατίθεμαι τὸ πνεῦμά μου, Lk 23⁴⁶), and yielded up His spirit (ἀφῆκε τὸ πνεῦμα, Mt 27⁵⁰; παρέδωκε τὸ πνεῦμα, Jn 19³⁰). After death, His Divine Personality, still in hypostatic (*i.e.* personal) union with His disembodied human spirit, descended to Hades, and there preached to the disobedient spirits in prison (1 P 3¹⁸, cf. Eph 4⁹); visiting also, we infer from Lk 23⁴³, that compartment of Hades which is

reserved for the spirits of the just. It is obvious from these and other passages, that the view of Apollinaris that Christ did not possess a human soul,* but that the Divine Logos took its place, is not Scriptural. The soul and spirit of Jesus were subject to human weakness and infirmity, and were therefore human, not Divine.

But the rejection of Apollinarism, and the adoption of the view that Christ possessed a perfect human soul, involves a great psychological difficulty. A perfect human soul is *personal*, and therefore, if Christ was perfect God and perfect man, it seems to follow that He must have been *two persons*, as Nestorius thought, or was supposed to think. This difficulty has never yet received a full solution. The solution of the ancient Church was that the human nature of the incarnate Christ was *impersonal*. The human ψυχή of Christ, which, under normal conditions, would have developed independent personality, was prevented, owing to its hypostatic union with the Logos, from doing so. It attained personality, not in itself, but in the Divine Logos with which it was united; and hence, though Christ possessed a true human ψυχή, His personality was single, being seated entirely in the Divine Nature. The Patristic view is open to criticism on several grounds, but it still holds the field as the best attempt to reconcile the two apparently conflicting principles of Scripture, that Christ is perfect God and perfect man, and yet only one Person.†

4. The human will of Jesus.—Jesus, as possessing a human soul, possessed also a human will, for volition is one of the most characteristic activities of the soul. The Gospels regard Jesus as endowed with a human will, which, though in the end always conforming itself to the Divine will, yet did so sometimes at the cost of an inward struggle. Thus in the Agony in the Garden, Jesus prays (Lk 22⁴²), 'Father, if thou be willing, remove this cup from me; nevertheless not my will, but thine be done' (πλὴν μὴ τὸ θέλημά μου, ἀλλὰ τὸ σὸν γινέσθω). The distinction of wills is evident also in Jn 5³⁰ (cf. 6³⁸) 'I seek not mine own will, but the will of him that sent me.' It is thus the teaching of Scripture that there are two wills in Christ, a Divine and a human, and that these two wills are united in one Person. The reconciliation of the two different points of view (duality of will, and unity of Person) is not easy. According to modern ideas, the faculty of willing is so essentially a function of personality, that it seems necessary to postulate two egos where there are two wills. The ancients, however, did not connect willing with personality so closely as we do; and, moreover, 'will' is too strong a term to translate their θέλημα (*voluntas*). θέλημα, it is true, in its stronger sense, approaches the meaning of 'will,' but more often it bears the weaker sense of 'wish,' 'liking,' 'inclination,' 'propension.' The true Greek term for will in our sense is γνώμη, or more definitely προαίρεσις, or still more definitely αὐτεξουσιότης, or αὐτεξούσιον (self-determination). It is clearly in the weaker sense of 'inclination' that θέλημα is used in the Gospels, and it is probably in the same sense that Dyothelitism was declared by the Sixth General Council (A.D. 680) to be the doctrine of the Church.‡

---

* Cf. the striking words of Clement of Alexandria: 'The Apostles, following the Lord, preached the gospel to those in Hades. . . . [God's] punishments [in Hades] *are saving and disciplinary, leading to conversion, and choosing rather the repentance than the death of a sinner.* . . . Did not the same dispensation obtain in Hades, so that even there, all the souls, on hearing the preaching, might either exhibit repentance, or confess that their punishment was just because they believed not?' (*Strom.* vi. 6). See also the *Shepherd* of Hermas, *Simil.* ix. 16: 'These Apostles and teachers, having fallen asleep, preached also to those who had fallen asleep before them, and themselves gave the seal of their preaching.'

* Apollinaris admitted that Jesus possessed the lower or animal soul (ψυχὴ ἄλογος), but denied to Him the distinctively human or rational soul (ψυχὴ λογική).

† The details of the question are in the highest degree intricate, and cannot be entered upon here. The reader may consult Dorner, *Person of Christ*, II. i. 116 ff., 152 ff., 201 ff., 266 ff., for an acute criticism of the Patristic view. See also Ottley, *Incarnation*, pt. vii. 1. 4, 2. 2.

‡ On the Monothelite and Dyothelite question see Dorner, *op. cit.* II. i. 155 ff. The last word (even from the strictly orthodox point of view) has not yet been said upon this difficult subject.

See also art. INCARNATION in vol. i., esp. p. 812 f.

LITERATURE.—M. F. Roos, *Fundamenta Psychologiæ ex sacra Scriptura collecta* (brief, but valuable) ; J. T. Beck, *Umriss der bibl. Seelenlehre* [Eng. tr. 1877] ; Böttcher, *de Inferis* (a storehouse of Biblical and Rabbinical material) ; Olshausen, *de Nat. Human. Trichotomia* (in *Opusc. Theol.*) ; von Rudloff, *Die Lehre vom Menschen* ; Franz Delitzsch, *Syst. d. bibl. Psychol.* [Eng. tr. 1867] (learned, but fanciful) ; J. Laidlaw, *The Bible Doctrine of Man* ; J. B. Heard, *The Tripartite Nature of Man* ; W. P. Dickson, *St. Paul's Use of Flesh and Spirit* (contains short bibliography) ; Ellicott, 'The Threefold Nature of Man,' in *The Destiny of the Creature* ; W. R. Alger, *Destiny of the Soul* (contains exhaustive bibliography by Ezra Abbot) ; R. H. Charles, *A Critical History of the Doctrine of a Future Life* ; Salmond, *Christian Doctrine of Immortality* ; F. W. H. Myers, *Human Personality and its Survival of Bodily Death* ; Piat, *Destinée de l'homme* ; Welldon, *The Hope of Immortality* ; Martineau, *Study of Religion*, bk. 4 ; Mason, *Purgatory* ; Plumptre, *Spirits in Prison* ; Luckock, *After Death* ; Pusey, *What is of faith as to Everlasting Punishment?* ; C. Harris, *pro Fide*, c. xv. ; A. Westphal, *Chair et Esprit* ; Lüdemann, *Die Anthropologie des Ap. Paulus* ; art. 'Psychology' in Hastings' *DB* ; art. 'Geist' in *PRE³* ; artt. 'Soul,' 'Eschatology,' 'Immortality of the Soul' in *JE* ; art. 'Eschatology' in *EBi.*; consult also OT Theologies of Schultz, Smend, Oehler ; and the NT Theologies of Schmid, van Oosterzee, B. Weiss, Holtzmann.   C. HARRIS.

SOUTH (νότος).—**1.** *The locality indicated.*—The southern direction was called by the Hebrews *Têman* (Jer 49²⁰), that is, the country 'on the right side' to one facing eastwards in Palestine. In the same way their kinsmen and successors, the Moslem Arabs, called the southern part of their empire *Yemen*, the 'right hand' country, and designated Syria and Palestine to the North as *al-Shâm*, the 'left' region. The queen of Sheba was referred to as the queen of the South (Mt 12⁴²). In a more limited and special sense the Hebrews gave the name 'South Country' to the wilderness of Judæa and the region lying beyond it (Jos 12⁸, Ac 8²⁶).

2. *Character of south wind.*—Passing over an area with little or no vegetation, it was both hot (Lk 12⁵⁵) and lacking in vitalizing power. The rarefaction produced by the sun's rays on the bare desert gave rise to whirlwinds, which gathered up the dust in tall swaying columns that moved like evil genii over the land until they suddenly broke and dispersed (Job 37⁹, Zec 9¹⁴). It was essentially a transition current, being the dry east wind shifting round towards the humid west. It thus partook of the nature of both, and resembled the close steamy air of a palm-house. The allusion in Job 37¹⁷ is either to the lethargy induced by its enervating influence, or to the cool refreshment of the showers that usually follow it.

             G. M. MACKIE.

SOWING.—For 'sowing' as a metaphorical expression of the activity and influence of Christ and His Apostles, see under SEED. The Gospels further contain, however, three semi-proverbial uses of the term which merit notice.

1. One is in connexion with the counsel against worldly anxiety (Mt 6²⁶ = Lk 12²⁴ birds neither sow nor reap), where sowing denotes one of the ordinary operations and occupations of men in order to secure a livelihood. Jesus is here quoting a familiar proverb of the ancient world, which was current in several forms (*e.g.* 'aves sine patrimonio vivunt et in diem pascuntur').

2. In Mt 25²⁴· ²⁶ = Lk 19²¹· ²², a grasping, unscrupulous character is defined as one that reaps where it has not sown, *i.e.* enriches itself at the expense of other people. Several ancient parallels, both from Jewish (cf. Taylor's *Sayings of the Jewish Fathers*, 1897, p. 143) and from pagan (*e.g.* Ælian, *Var. Hist.* iii. 46 and iv. 1 ; and Plato, *Leges*, xi. 913 C) sources, are quoted for the second clause of the verse, which is probably to be taken as an expansion of the first.

3. Finally, two semi-proverbial (cf. *e.g.* Mic 6¹⁵, Ps 126⁵· ⁶) sayings upon sowing, in a figurative sense, are preserved in Jn 4³⁶· ³⁷. Taken as part of the story of Jesus at Sychar, the passage starts from the responsiveness of the Samaritans to the gospel (their full-grown faith being contrasted with the indifference and unbelief of Judaism upon the whole). The sight of the Samaritans streaming out of the city suggests to Jesus that a rich harvest of souls is to be reaped here, and reaped apparently without the usual delay and interval. Samaria is ripe already for the gospel. 'Four months more, then harvest,' may be the time in Nature ; but here, in the order of the Spirit, sowing is hardly done ere reaping begins.   J. MOFFATT.

SPARROW.—See ANIMALS in vol. i. p. 66ᵃ.

SPEAR.—This word occurs in NT only in Jn 19³⁴ 'one of the soldiers pierced Jesus' side with a spear' (λόγχη). A comparison, however, of Mt 27⁴⁸ 'put [the sponge] on a reed' (περιθεὶς καλάμῳ), makes it probable that in Jn 19²⁹ for ὑσσώπῳ περιθέντες, 'put it upon hyssop,' ὑσσῷ π. should be read. ὑσσός is the Roman *pilum* (Polybius, i. 40. 12, etc.). The head of this spear is said to have been buried within the principal church of Antioch, where, under direction of Peter of Amiens, it was discovered by the besieged Crusaders, and proved their salvation from the onslaught of the prince of Mosul in 1098.

             T. H. WEIR.

SPICES (Lat. *species*).—The word denotes primarily the kind of a thing, a sample or specimen of anything. Then it means a certain touch or taste of something. More definitely, it denotes any aromatic or pungent substance. In general, spices are aromatic condiments used for seasoning food, or fragrant ointments used as perfumes. In the NT the term is used in both of these senses ; and, in a few cases, it has a somewhat wider meaning.

In the Gospels there are several words used to describe various kinds of spices. It is scarcely possible to classify them. See artt. MYRRH, FRANKINCENSE, NARD, SPIKENARD, MINT, ANISE, CUMMIN, RUE.

Spices (Gr. ἀρώματα, Lat. *aromata*) are mentioned in Mk 16¹, Lk 23⁵⁶ 24¹, Jn 19⁴⁰. We have here probably a general term to denote the mixed spices used in embalming the bodies of the dead.

             FRANCIS R. BEATTIE.

SPIES (ἐγκάθετοι, best derived from ἐγκαθίημι, 'to send down in (secret)' [Grimm-Thayer], 'men suborned to lie in wait' ; Vulg. *insidiatores*).— Though the word occurs only once in the Gospels (Lk 20²⁰ ; cf. Job 19¹² 31⁹, Sir 8¹¹), there is abundant evidence of a regular system of espionage directed against Jesus from the time when He first attracted the notice of the ruling classes. Emissaries were sent from Jerusalem for this purpose (Mk 7¹ and Mt 15¹ RV), and in the latter portion of His public ministry He could hardly speak in any synagogue or other public place without seeing some of these spies in His audience. Their action is variously described : (1) 'They watched him' (παρατηρεῖν, παρατηρεῖσθαι, 'to watch insidiously, in a furtive manner'—'ex obliquo et occulto,' Bengel) ; cf. Mk 3²=Lk 6⁷ 14¹ 20²⁰, where EV add 'him,' though the verb is probably used generally of watching for an opportunity. (2) 'They began to press upon him vehemently, and to provoke him to speak of many things (ἀποστοματίζειν αὐτόν), laying wait for him to catch something out of his mouth' (ἐνεδρεύοντες αὐτὸν θηρεῦσαί τι ἐκ τοῦ στόματος αὐτοῦ, Lk 11⁵⁴), where ἀποστοματίζειν is explained by Euthym. Zig. as ἀπαιτεῖν αὐτοσχεδίους καὶ ἀνεπισκέπτους ἀποκρίσεις ἐρωτημάτων δολερῶν (the Vulg. gives *os ejus opprimere*, as if from a reading ἐπιστομίζειν). So Lk 20²⁰ tells how the chief priests and scribes watched and 'sent forth spies, which feigned themselves to be righteous, that they might take hold of his speech, so as to deliver him up to the rule and to the authority of the governor.' The putting of the question about the tribute money, which immediately follows, was a cunning plot, in which the Pharisees and the Herodians, two mutually hostile parties, joined (cf. for a similar union in Galilee, Mk 3⁶). The Pharisees sent their disciples (Mt 22¹⁶), young men apparently, fresh, earnest, zealous, and anxious to do right, hoping thus to avoid exciting suspicion of their designs. St. Mark (12¹³) describes their object as 'that they might catch him in talk' (ἵνα αὐτὸν ἀγρεύσωσι λόγῳ) ; St. Matthew (22¹⁵) says they took counsel 'how they might ensnare him in his talk' (παγιδεύσωσιν ἐν λόγῳ), the verb used being from παγίς, 'a trap or snare,' into which if He fell He would be held fast with a view to further proceedings. Compare also Mt 19³, Jn 11⁴⁶, and Lk 19³⁹ where some Pharisees mingled with the rejoicing multitude, no doubt for a similar purpose. The murmuring in favour of Jesus mentioned in Jn 7³² was possibly reported to the Pharisees by spies. Christ was always conscious of the presence of such men, and on these occasions seemed to court publicity for His actions ; cf. the direction to the man with the withered hand, 'Stand forth' (Mk 3³). The futility of the system of espionage as directed against Him was shown at the trial, where all their efforts resulted in inability to bring forward anything as a charge except His words about the Temple.

The use of spies for a different purpose, viz. to facilitate His arrest, is implied in Mk 14¹, where His enemies sought how they might take Him with subtilty (ἐν δόλῳ), and in Jn 11⁵⁷ by the command that if any man knew where He was he should give information (μηνύσῃ), that they might take Him. Such a measure was necessary because of His popularity with the multitude. In this sense Judas was the great spy, being in close touch with Jesus, and familiar with all His movements,—a fact which explains the roundabout directions given to the two Apostles as to where they should prepare the Passover meal. It was essential that Judas should not know the place beforehand, in order that the solemn proceedings and Christ's last discourse might not be interrupted by the coming of the band from the priests to effect His arrest.

W. H. DUNDAS.

SPIKENARD (='spiked nard').—The AV and RV rendering of νάρδος πιστική in Mk 14³, Jn 12³, or rather of the Vulg. nardi spicati (in Jn. nardi pistici). The word 'spikanard' (sic) appears first in Wyclif's version, the Anglo-Saxon having merely 'deorwyrðes' (='precious'). Tindale has 'pure.' These various translations indicate the doubt as to the meaning of the Greek, which was felt from very early times, and is reflected in the Versions generally. The oldest Syriac version and some Old Latin texts simply transliterate, while the Peshiṭta renders by rishâyâ (='choicest'). Of the various explanations of the word πιστική, the most generally accepted are: (1) 'Genuine,' as though it were connected with πίστις (Meyer, Weiss, etc.). The word πιστικός does actually occur in Artemidorus (Oneir. 2. 32) in the sense of 'faithful' (γυνὴ πιστικὴ καὶ οἰκουρός) ; and we learn from Pliny (HN xii. 26) that adulterations of nard were frequent.* (2) 'Liquid,' as though it was connected with πίνω. Ovid (Ars. Am. iii. 443) uses the epithet liquida with nardus ; and Clement of Alexandria (Pæd. II. viii. 64) distinguishes between μύρα ὑγρά and μύρα ξηρά. (3) 'Drinkable.' Athenæus tells us that some unguents were drunk (689 C). But the Greek word for drinkable is ποτός, not πιστικός.† Some have suspected a 'primitive error'

* Cf. Theophylact, τὴν ἄδολον νάρδον καὶ μετὰ πίστεως κατασκευασθεῖσαν (Com. on St. Mark, Migne, Pat. Gr. cxxix.).
† Scaliger derived the word from πτίσσειν, 'to pound.' But this does not give a satisfactory sense.

in the text here, and have proposed various emendations. It has been suggested that the true reading is Ἰνδικῆς. All our authorities agree in stating that the genuine nard came from India, while inferior sorts came from other countries. Others would read σπικάτης (=Vulg. spicati), a word found in Galen, vi. 178 C, 182 C, E. Naber (Mnemosyne, 1902, pp. 1–15) conjectures an original form, σπειστικῆς (='liquid'), which, being a ἅπαξ λεγόμενον, might have been corrupted into πιστικῆς. Prof. E. N. Bennett (Classical Review, 1890, p. 319) suggests that the true form may be πιστάκης, and points out that the resin of the Pistacia terebinthus was anciently mixed with the oil of nard, and that it was a very valuable scent (Dioscorides, i. 91). All these emendations, however, ingenious and interesting as they are, are rendered improbable by the fact that neither in St. Mark nor in St. John is there any variation in the MSS.

It is difficult to say with anything like certainty what the meaning of the word was. It may be a local name, as RVm suggests.* Possibly it is the Greek equivalent of Pisitá, one of the Skr. names for Nardostachys jatamansi (Dymock, Pharmacographia Indica, ii. p. 233). But most likely it is a technical term denoting some specially valuable kind of nard.† Modern experience goes to show how easily the exact meaning of similar technical or 'fancy' names can be lost. Such has probably been the case with the word we are discussing. See also artt. NARD, OINTMENT.

LITERATURE.—See the authorities cited at end of art. NARD. The question is discussed by C. F. A. Fritzsche (Com. on St. Mark, Leipzig, 1830) at great length, and very fully by Morison (Com. on Mk., in loc.).   H. W. FULFORD.

SPINNING.—From very early times in Palestine, spinning of wool and flax by means of hand-spindles was one of the common occupations, especially of women. Jesus referred to spinning (νήθειν) in teaching God's providential care, even of the lilies of the field, which are richly clothed though they neither toil nor spin (Mt 6²⁸, Lk 12²⁷).

E. B. POLLARD.

SPIRIT (πνεῦμα).—This word occupies a very important place in the writings of the Evangelists, covers a wide area of thought, and is not always clearly defined as to the particular use it is put to in a given context. The prominent place thus assigned to the word may be considered as indicative of the position which the principal idea embodied by it fills in the general scheme of constructive Christian psychology. In this respect we have a good example of the almost instinctively creative power of Jewish, and especially of Christian-Jewish, religious thought. In classical writings πνεῦμα is found largely employed in a physiological sense (cf. τῷ πνεύματι τοῦ στόματος αὐτοῦ, 2 Th 2⁸ ; and for a similar use see Jn 3⁸, He 1⁷), but in them it never appears as a psychological term, as it does so often in Biblical writings both of the OT and the NT (see Cremer's Bibl.-Theol. Lex. s.v.).

The determining factor in the employment of this word by NT writers is the profound belief, inherited from the prophets and teachers of the OT, that there existed from the very beginning a unique fellowship between God and man (cf. πνοὴν ζωῆς, Gn 2⁷ [LXX]). In spite of much and repeated unfaithfulness on man's part (cf. the difficult, though, for our present purpose, the sufficiently significant passage, 'My spirit shall not remain [καταμείνῃ] for ever in man,' Gn 6³), this fellowship continued to be realized more and more intensely as one gene-

* Ὁπιστικῆς (from Opis, near Babylon), Ψιττακικῆς (from Psittake on the Tigris), and Πιστης (from the (?) Persian town Pisteira) have been suggested as possible readings. But none of these is an Indian town.
† This idea is found as early as Theophylact (c. 1077 A.D.), who says that the word may denote εἶδος νάρδου οὕτω λεγόμενον.

ration succeeded another, and warriors and poets, prophets and priests, all found their inspiration in the firm belief that the Spirit of God was the living motive power animating their words and deeds.

There can be no doubt that the Incarnation formed the culminating point, as well as the final guarantee of the truth, of this historic realization. Henceforth there was established in the human consciousness a relationship between God and man which can be conveyed only in terms expressive of the closest mutual intimacy and communion. Not only can it be asserted that God's Spirit 'dwells in' man, but the counterpart of that truth consists in the resultant abiding of man 'in the Spirit' (ἐν πνεύματι, Ro 8⁹). The consequence of the Divine Spirit's activity in this sphere is the co-operative activity of man's spirit attesting the reality of the relationship and working towards 'the righteousness of God' (Ro 10³, 2 Co 5²¹; cf. Ro 8¹⁰⁻¹⁶). The Pauline identification of 'the Spirit of Christ' and 'the Spirit of God' is for us ultimately justified in the twofold story of the birth of Jesus, narrated, as we must think, from two distinct points of view. The Spirit of God was the operative agency by which the Incarnation was accomplished (Mt 1¹⁸· ²⁰; cf. the interchangeable terms πνεῦμα ἅγιον and δύναμις Ὑψίστου, Lk 1³⁵). The revelation of the Sonship of Jesus followed immediately upon His anointing (ἔχρισεν, Ac 10³⁸) with the Holy Spirit, and the twofold connexion established by the Synoptists between this revelation and His Temptation seems to establish beyond doubt that, in their opinion, the consciousness of Jesus became then for the first time fully alive to the wondrous position which He occupied, and to the character of the work He was destined to undertake (cf. the burden of the heavenly message ὁ υἱός μου ὁ ἀγαπητός, and the implied doubt repeated in the Temptation εἰ υἱὸς εἶ τοῦ θεοῦ, as well as the part played by the Spirit in each of these incidents, Mt 3¹⁶ 4¹ff·, Mk 1¹¹f·, Lk 3²² 4¹ff·, also Jn 1³²f·; see Plummer, 'St. Luke,' in ICC, ad loc.).

The realization of the abiding presence of the Spirit continued to be for Jesus the dominating feature in His ministry of power (see Mt 12²⁸; cf. the corresponding expression ἐν δακτύλῳ θεοῦ, Lk 11²⁰), and gives terrible force and point to His solemn warning against that continued deliberate opposition to His claims which springs from love of darkness and obedience to the spirit of evil. Here, too, lay the secret of that absolute conviction of the truth of His message to the world, resulting as it did in the astonished recognition of its inherent authority by those who heard it (cf. Jn 6⁶³ 7³⁹· ⁴⁶, Mt 7²⁸f· 13⁵⁴ 22³³, Mk 1²² 6² 11¹⁸, Lk 4³²). Nor would Jesus confine this conviction to Himself. The descriptive title 'the Spirit of truth,' three times reiterated in the Johannine discourses, emphasized that side of His teaching which laid particular stress on the identity of the guiding principle of His life and work with that moulding the activity of His disciples. At the same time it guaranteed the continuity of the context of His message and theirs to the world (Jn 14¹⁷ 15²⁶ 16¹³, cf. the actual bequest in which His promises were, partly at least, fulfilled, Jn 20²²; see also 7³⁹). That they might entertain no doubt as to the authoritative position they were to occupy in carrying out the work begun by Him, Jesus spoke of His own permanent return to them as practically identical with the continual abiding of the Holy Spirit in and with them (cf. the phrase ἔρχομαι πρὸς ὑμᾶς, Jn 14¹⁸). 'Christ is in fact from the moment of His Resurrection ever coming to the world and to the Church, and to men as the Risen Lord' (Westcott, Gospel of St. John, on 14³). In fact the work of 'the Spirit of truth' is mainly the glorification of Jesus by gradually making Him known

to the world as to His Person and work (ἐκεῖνος ἐμὲ δοξάσει, ὅτι ἐκ τοῦ ἐμοῦ λήμψεται καὶ ἀναγγελεῖ ὑμῖν· πάντα ὅσα ἔχει ὁ πατὴρ ἐμά ἐστιν, κ.τ.λ., Jn 16¹⁴f·; cf. ἐκεῖνος μαρτυρήσει περὶ ἐμοῦ, Jn 15²⁶).

The profound oneness of Jesus and His followers is nowhere more insistently dwelt on than in these passages, and that not alone in the character of the aims which He and they have in view, but also in the motive power helping and the underlying principle guiding them, which are identified by Him as the forces at work in His own life and Person. By an argument a fortiori He gives them an assurance that He will bestow the Holy Spirit on those who recognize their need of His guidance (Lk 11¹³). To such the gift will always be proportionate to their immediate needs (12¹²). We must not forget that the peculiar Lukan phrase πνεύματος ἁγίου ἐπλήσθη (1¹⁵· ⁴¹· ⁶⁷) is used in connexion with the spiritual experiences of three people whose work lay in the preparatory stage of the coming Kingdom of the Incarnation.

Notwithstanding the transcendent relationship in which Jesus stood to the Holy Spirit, we are not left without witness that even in this sphere of His life He was like us in all things (see Westcott, Gospel of St. John, on Jn 11³³). It is this word (τὸ πνεῦμα) that is used to describe the death on the cross by three of the Evangelists (cf. Mt 27⁵⁰, Lk 23⁴⁶, Jn 19³⁰), although in other places we find ψυχή employed in a sense very similar (see Jn 10¹⁵· ¹⁷, cf. 15³ 10¹¹). It is possible, however, to see in the use of the former word a wider range of thought, as if it was intended to include the latter in its scope. It is as if Jesus desired to commend to His Father's keeping not only the spirit, the principle of His highest and Divinest life, but also the soul, the seat of His personal earthly life (cf. Hastings' DB, vol. iv. 612ᵃ).

That ψυχή is, nevertheless, sometimes found to denote more than this is evident from references by Jesus Himself to its indestructibility and its incomparable value as the goal of all human progress, where we should have expected either πνεῦμα or πνεῦμα and ψυχή to convey His full meaning (cf. Mt 10²⁸· ³⁹, Lk 17³³, Mk 8³⁵, Jn 12²⁵). The distinction and confusion, however, in these two words are in accordance with OT usage, where rûaḥ (NT πνεῦμα) denotes the Divinely imparted principle of life, and nephesh (NT ψυχή) the result of the impartation (see 1 Co 15⁴⁵; cf. Gn 2⁷, where nephesh ḥayyāh occurs, an expression which is also used of the lower life of the animal creation, Gn 1²⁰). The indiscriminate use of these two words to denote the same idea is found, e.g., in Is 26⁹ (LXX), a parallel to which we have in the Song of the Virgin Mary (Lk 14⁶f·). See SOUL.

In other places where this word is used in connexion with the Personality of Jesus, we find it employed somewhat vaguely and in loose contrast with the outward or physical senses. He is said to have perceived the gist of the murmured reasonings of His critics 'in his spirit' (ἐπιγνοὺς τῷ πνεύματι αὐτοῦ, κ.τ.λ., Mk 2⁸; cf. Gould, 'St. Mark' in ICC, ad loc.). There is here an evident contrast implied between that intuitive knowledge gained by inference and deduction, and that acquired by direct hearing with the ears. Again, He is spoken of as sighing inwardly, as distinct from audibly (ἀναστενάξας τῷ πνεύματι αὐτοῦ, Mk 8¹²), and being indignant 'within himself' or 'in his spirit,' without expressing His feelings in words (cf. ἐνεβριμήσατο τῷ πνεύματι, Jn 11³⁸, and ἐν ἑαυτῷ, 11³⁸). An interesting example of a subtle psychological distinction between πνεῦμα and ψυχή is found in the personal experiences of Jesus with two distinct sources of trouble and sorrow. As the cross drew near, His 'soul' (ἡ ψυχή μου τετάρακται, Jn 12²⁷) revolted from the horrors of the vision; while we, as we read the narrative of self-revelation, perceive the origin and cause of His sympathy with 'the feeling of our infirmities' (He 4¹⁵). On the other hand, and in close connexion with His approaching death, there was the dark treachery of Judas; and when we remember the profound joy and holy satisfaction with which Jesus reviewed the success of His work in keeping near Him those committed to His charge (see Jn 17[12]), we can understand the grief caused by the loss of 'the son of perdition.' With reference to this fact, St. John notices that Jesus 'was troubled in spirit' ('Ιησοῦς ἐταράχθη τῷ πνεύματι, 13[21]), as though he would wish us to infer that He was stirred to the very depths of His being by the sight of a soul hurrying to its doom.

Instances are not wanting in the Gospels of contrasts, simple and definite, in which this word plays a part, though we have no example of the antitheses so familiar to students of the Pauline Christology. Perhaps the nearest to the latter is the reference by Jesus to the contrast between the strength and perseverance of the spirit and the weakness of the flesh (τὸ πνεῦμα πρόθυμον . . . ἡ σὰρξ ἀσθενής, Mk 14[39] = Mt 26[41]). When, in His conversation with Nicodemus, Jesus refers to fleshly (ἐκ τῆς σαρκός) birth and spiritual (ἐκ τοῦ πνεύματος) birth, He is not contrasting the limitations of the one with the inherent independence, as to time, space, etc., with their consequent imperfections, of the other. He has in His mind simply the two spheres of being to which man, quâ man, stands related. By his σάρξ he is in fellowship, spiritual, mental, and physical, with the whole visible creation. By his πνεῦμα he touches and enters the sphere of spiritual life in the entirety of his complete nature. Both orders of existence have their characteristic principles, and it is man's unique privilege to unite the two in his complete life and experience. The perfect synthesis is accomplished only in the Incarnation, and it is only by keeping steadily in view the two great constituent elements in Jesus' Person that we shall succeed in truly interpreting His language in His discourses at Capernaum, which were so vitally misunderstood. Neither the spirit alone nor the flesh alone can apprehend and appropriate the Christ, the Son of Man. 'The flesh' is of no avail (ἡ σὰρξ οὐκ ὠφελεῖ οὐδέν, Jn 6[63]), 'the spirit' alone has the power of conveying life (τὸ πνεῦμά ἐστιν τὸ ζωοποιοῦν). At the same time, in order to a genuine participation, the life-giving message must be clothed in language which may be heard and, in part at least, understood (τὰ ῥήματα . . . πνεῦμά ἐστιν καὶ ζωή). The historic fact of the Incarnation was necessary to meet the needs of man both on his spiritual and fleshly side, and so we understand the force of the words of the writer of the Epistle to the Hebrews (οὐ γὰρ δή που ἀγγέλων ἐπιλαμβάνεται, He 2[16]). And while it would be going beyond the strict limits of certainty to say that Jesus on this occasion is making specific reference to the rite which He afterwards instituted in words of similar import, it will scarcely be disputed that in His Last Supper He embodied the principles referred to above. In it, too, 'the flesh profiteth nothing,' it is the spirit that giveth life; but the invisible, intangible spirit is clothed with a visible, tangible body, while man, working through and by the latter, reaches upwards and partakes of the former (cf. Westcott, Gospel of St. John, ad loc.).

When Jesus, in His conversation with the woman of Samaria, identifies Spirit with the Being of God (πνεῦμα ὁ θεός, Jn 4[24]), He at once proceeds to foreshadow the abiding result, as well as the condition of man's approach to Him. The arena, so to speak, upon which the activity of the Divine Spirit displays His manifold and world-wide character, is the human spirit. If we are to offer to God a spiritual (ἐν πνεύματι) worship, and apprehend clearly the methods by which He quickens human life, the first and last requisite is that we shall be in the Spirit (Jn 4[24]; cf. Ro 8[15f.], Eph 2[18] etc.). It is not enough, though it is perfectly true, to say that 'the spirit in man responds to the Spirit of God' (Westcott, Gospel of St. John, on 4[23]). The spirit in man becomes the spirit of man (τῷ πνεύματι ἡμῶν, Ro 8[16]), and acting, as it does, in harmony with the Spirit of God, is guided into all the truth (cf. the sequence τὸ πνεῦμα τῆς ἀληθείας . . . εἰς τὴν ἀλήθειαν πᾶσαν, Jn 16[13]). Henceforth man's spiritual home is within the region of that absolute truth which the Person and the work of Jesus were destined to disclose and make real.

Just as we are led to believe in and hope for this co-operative activity of the Holy Spirit, so the Evangelists are insistent in the belief that the spirits of evil are ever watchful to make their home within us. In words of solemn warning Jesus implies that our need of spiritual guidance is so profound that we stand in constant danger of harbouring these active enemies (note εἰς τὸν οἶκόν μου, Lk 11[24]), and that the only way of successfully guarding against their presence is to admit the Holy Spirit as the supreme and only Guest (cf. Plummer, 'St. Luke,' in ICC, on 11[25]). So close is the analogy between these conceptions that St. Mark does not hesitate to denote the presence and the relation of the evil spirits to the possessed by using the same preposition (ἐν) which he employs when speaking of the guiding influence of the Holy Ghost (Mk 1[24] 3[22] 5[2]; cf. 12[36], Lk 2[27]). The diseases which these spirits were supposed to convey to their victims were often spoken of as belonging to them inherently (Mk 9[17. 25] etc. See art. DEMON).

We shall not be surprised, after these considerations, to learn that when men have the same ends in view, pursue them by similar methods of work, and betray the same general characteristics in their mental and spiritual outlook, they are said to have the same spirit. John the Baptist and Elijah, though separated by centuries of time, were believed to be so far identified that the former lived and acted 'in spirit and in power' (ἐν πνεύματι καὶ δυνάμει, Lk 1[17]), i.e. under the shadow and guidance of the latter (cf. Jesus' method of interpreting the popular belief in the pre-Messianic return of Elijah, Mt 11[14]). At the same time, the historian is careful to note that the Baptist's childhood was marked by a gradual development and strengthening in spirit side by side with his bodily growth (Lk 1[80]). See, further, artt. FLESH, HOLY SPIRIT, SOUL.

LITERATURE.—In addition to the Lexx. and Dictionary artt. and the Lit. at SOUL, see Laidlaw, Bible Doct. of Man, esp. 131 ff.; Weiss, Bibl. Theol. of NT, § 27; W. H. Hodge, 'Bibl. Usage of Soul and Spirit' in Præs. Ref. Rev. viii. (1897), 251; F. E. Brightman, 'Soul, Body, Spirit' in JThSt ii. (1900) 273; W. H. Schoemaker, 'Use of Pneuma in NT' in JBL xxiii. (1904) 13.   J. R. WILLIS.

SPIRITUALITY.—See CHARACTER OF CHRIST in vol. i. p. 286 f., and art. SPIRIT.

SPIRITUALIZING OF THE PARABLES.—'The legs of the lame,' says a Hebrew proverb, 'hang loose; so is a parable in the mouth of fools' (Pr 26[7]); but it is possible to err in the opposite direction by pressing a parable too far, and, if the expression may be allowed, riding it to death. Such was the manner of the ancient interpreters, and it has been imitated by not a few in modern times. The error lies in forgetting that a parable is designed to teach one broad lesson, and insisting on discovering some significance in every detail. A glaring instance is Theophilus of Antioch's exposition, quoted approvingly by St. Jerome,* of the parable of the Steward (Lk 16[1-12]), which inculcates simply the duty of being as shrewd in spiritual matters as men are wont to be in worldly affairs. The rich man, according to Theophilus, is Almighty God; the steward, St. Paul; the debtor who owed 100 baths of oil, the Gentiles, 'qui

* ad Algas. Quæst. vi.

magna indigebant misericordia Dei'; the debtor who owed 100 *cors* of wheat, the Jewish people, 'which had been nourished by the wheat of God's commandments.' Euthymius Zigabenus, whose interpretation of 'the fatted calf' (Lk 15²³) as 'the holy body of Christ' is saved from being blasphemous only by the good monk's simple piety, makes out that the rich man is God (τὸν φιλάνθρωπον καὶ ἀνενδεῆ θεόν); the steward, every possessor of riches, such being 'not lords but stewards'; the steward's dismissal, death. Some modern interpreters have gone quite as far in extravagance. Schleiermacher makes the rich man represent the Romans, the steward the tax-gatherers, the debtors the Jewish people. According to Olshausen, the rich man is ἄρχων τοῦ κόσμου, while the steward is the man who applies earthly riches to spiritual uses.

Origen's exposition of the parable of the Good Samaritan (Lk 10³⁰⁻³⁷) is a masterpiece of ill-applied ingenuity. The traveller is Adam; Jerusalem is Paradise; Jericho is the world; the robbers are hostile demons; the Priest is the Law; the Levite is the Prophets; the Samaritan is Christ; the wounds are disobedience; the beast is the Lord's body; the inn is the Church; the two *denarii* are the Father and the Son (the New and the Old Covenant, says Euthymius Zigabenus); the inn-keeper is the Bishop.*

The parable of the Ten Virgins (Mt 25¹⁻¹³) has furnished another fruitful field to spiritualizing interpreters. According to St. Chrysostom the lamps are the grace of virginity (τὸ τῆς παρθενίας χάρισμα); the oil is philanthropy, alms (τὴν φιλανθρωπίαν, τὴν ἐλεημοσύνην); the sellers are the poor, who afford the opportunity for alms-giving; the sleep of the virgins is death; the cry at midnight (cf. 1 Th 4¹⁶) shows that the Resurrection will take place by night. The lesson of the parable is that virginity without philanthropy is darkness. According to Origen and St. Jerome, the five virgins are the five senses. According to the latter, the oil is good works; according to the former, it is teaching, the vessels being the souls of the learners. There is much shrewd sense in Calvin's caustic remark : 'Some greatly torment themselves about the lamps, about the vessels, about the oil; but the simple and real gist is that eager zeal for a brief space does not suffice, unless unwearied constancy be added thereto.' See, further, artt. PARABLE and CIRCUMSTANTIALITY IN THE PARABLES.

DAVID SMITH.

SPITTING, SPITTLE (πτύω, πτύσμα, ἐμπτύω).— References to spitting occur in the NT in the Gospels only, and there always in connexion with Christ.

1. Spitting was a common mark of derision and contempt. Christ foretold it among the insults which He as Messiah would endure (Mk 10³⁴, Lk 18³²); and during His Passion He was spit upon both by Jews (Mt 26⁶⁷, Mk 14⁶⁵) and by Gentile soldiers (Mt 27³⁰, Mk 15¹⁹). Allusions to the custom with this injurious meaning are found in the OT (Nu 12¹⁴, Dt 25⁹, Is 50⁶). Variant forms, still customary among Orientals, are spitting upon the ground before any one, or even at the mention of a despised and hated name.

2. Three occasions are recorded on which Christ made use of His spittle in the work of healing : with a deaf and dumb man in the Decapolis (Mk 7³³), when He touched the tongue of the afflicted with moisture from His own mouth; with a blind man at Bethsaida (Mk 8²³), when He 'spat upon his eyes'; and with one born blind, at Jerusalem (Jn 9⁶·⁷), when He made clay of the

---

* In *Luc. Hom.* xxxiv. St. Augustine (*Quæst. Ev.* ii. § 19) gives a similar interpretation, but with still greater luxuriance of fancy.

spittle and anointed the eyes of the blind. In the two former instances Christ is stated first to have taken the man apart, and Meyer suggests that this secrecy was due to His use of the spittle; but no reason for secrecy suggests itself, and the third act of healing appears to have been performed publicly. Trench (*Miracles*, on Jn 9) adduces Pliny (*HN* xxviii. 7), Suetonius (*Vespas.* 7), Tacitus (*Hist.* iv. 8), to witness to the prevalence of an ancient belief in the medicinal value of human saliva, especially for eye troubles. See BLINDNESS.

JOHN MUIR.

SPONGE.—See ANIMALS in vol. i. p. 67ᵃ, and VINEGAR.

STAFF.—Two different words occurring in the Gospels are rendered 'staff' in EV.—(1) ῥάβδος, (2) ξύλον.

1. Only once is ῥάβδος found in the Gospels, viz. in the Synoptic account of the instructions given by Jesus to the Twelve as He sent them on their mission (Mk 6⁸=Mt 10¹⁰=Lk 9³). It denotes, of course, the ordinary walking-staff of the traveller, which, as used in the East, is somewhat longer than the walking-stick we know, and is simply a long, slightly-tapering rod, serviceable for support and for defence.

The main interest of the reference to the staff in the connexion above mentioned lies in the textual difference exhibited by the parallel passages. The instruction as given in Mk 6⁸ was that the Twelve were to take nothing with them, 'except a staff only' (εἰ μὴ ῥάβδον μόνον); whereas, according to Mt. (μηδὲ ῥάβδον) and Lk. (μήτε ῥάβδον), they were to take nothing at all, not even a staff. Wright cites this in suppport of a suggestion that Mt. and Lk. were 'affected by the tendency to expect exceptional severity in the case of religious teachers' (*Synopsis*, p. 57). But perhaps it is adequately explained as due at first to a mere copyist's assimilation to the other negative items that occur. In both Mt. and Lk., again, there is a *v.l.* in some MSS which gives the plural ῥάβδους, 'neither staves.' This variant is not necessarily to be ascribed to a set purpose to afford a loop-hole for harmonizing the accounts. The AV, however, reading 'staves' in both cases, lies open to suspicion on this point; for in Mt 10¹⁰ it gives 'nor yet staves,' with the extraordinary marginal note 'Gr. *a staff*,' showing that their text actually read ῥάβδον. So the way is left open for the puerile suggestion that the accounts are consistent, inasmuch as Jesus meant that His disciples were not to take more than one staff each! Yet Wyclif's earlier version (following the Vulg.) had rendered 'nether a yerde' in Mt 10¹⁰ (similarly Lk 9³), careless of the discrepancy with Mk 6⁸ ('but a yerde oneli'). Cf. Tindale in Mt 10¹⁰ 'nor yet a rodde.' The superiority of Mk.'s account is self-evident : there is a touch of perfect naturalness about it.

2. The ξύλον mentioned in Mk 14⁴³ (‖ Mt 26⁴⁷, and see Lk 22⁵²), like the sword, is distinctly a weapon. Jn 18³ uses the general expression ὅπλα. The ξύλα (EV 'staves') were the wooden truncheons or clubs of the Jewish police (ὑπηρέται). Josephus (*BJ* II. ix. 4) mentions them as weapons used by Pilate's soldiers in attacking a crowd of Jews at Jerusalem.

J. S. CLEMENS.

STALL.—See MANGER.

STAR.—1. Introductory.—Occasional reference is made in the NT to a star or stars, and, in most cases, an extraordinary significance of some kind is associated with the mention of such.

Two Greek words are employed, viz. ἀστήρ and ἄστρον. The latter also bears a collective meaning (=a group of stars, a constellation), but not in the NT. ἀστήρ is often applied metaphorically (see below). ἄστρον occurs in Lk 21²⁵, Ac 7⁴³ 'the star of the god Rephan' (a quotation from Am 5²⁵f.), 27²⁰, He 11¹². Elsewhere (exc. 2 P 1¹⁹, where φωσφόρος, 'day-star,' occurs) ἀστήρ is used.

Sometimes these references are without any special significance (*e.g.* Ac 27²⁰, He 11¹² 'as the stars of heaven in multitude'), but more often some definite symbolical application is apparent, as, for example, when a period of calamity marking a Divine visitation is described as a time when the light of the sun and the moon is withdrawn and 'the stars fall from heaven' (Mt 24²⁹ ‖ Rev 6¹³ 8¹⁰·¹¹; cf. Ezk 32⁷). In Rev 9¹ the image of the 'fallen star' has a personal reference, Satan apparently being denoted by it (cf. Lk 10[18] 'I beheld Satan fallen as lightning from heaven'); on the other hand, by the figure of 'the seven stars' which Christ holds in His right hand (Rev 1[16] 2[1] 3[1]) are signified the angels of the seven churches under the direction of Christ; cf. 1[20] (Grimm-Thayer). In Rev 12[1] the 'crown of twelve stars' may be intended to symbolize the twelve tribes (or the twelve Apostles 'regarded as the crowning ornament of the Jewish Church'). A mythological allusion is apparent in Rev 12[4] ('a woman arrayed with the sun, and the moon under her feet, and upon her head a crown of twelve stars'). One passage (22[16]) identifies Christ with 'the bright, the morning star' (ὁ ἀστὴρ ὁ λαμπρός, ὁ πρωινός), in accordance with which also 2[28] ('I will give him the morning star') and 2 P 1[19] ('until the *day-star* [φωσφόρος] arise in your hearts') are probably to be interpreted (see, further, below).

2. The star of the Magi (Mt 2[1-12]).—In its main outlines the story of the visit of the Magi to Jerusalem and Bethlehem is probably based upon what the compiler of the First Gospel believed to be facts. It rests upon a historical basis. The widespread expectation of the coming of a World-Redeemer, about the time of the beginning of the Christian era, and the interest of Eastern astrologers in His advent in the West are well attested, and may well have led to some such visit as is described in Mt.* (See, further, art. MAGI). It must be remembered, however, that Mt.'s narrative is governed by an apologetic purpose. It was written for the special object of meeting the needs and objections of Jewish readers. One influential motive at work in Mt 2 seems to be a desire on the part of the Evangelist to suggest a likeness between the Divinely guided career of Moses, the instrument of Israel's redemption from Egypt, and the Messianic Redeemer who saves His people from their sins. 'Thus the story of the Magi and the star has a striking parallel in the *Midrash Rabbā* to Exodus in the section which deals with the birth of Moses. There we are told that Pharaoh's astrologers (האסטרולוגין) perceived that the mother of the future redeemer of Israel [*i.e.* Moses] was with child, and that this redeemer was destined to suffer punishment through water. Not knowing whether the redeemer was to be an Israelite or an Egyptian, and being desirous to prevent the redemption of Israel, Pharaoh ordered that all children born henceforth should be drowned.'† But perhaps the leading motive in Mt.'s narrative in this section of it is to suggest the homage of the Gentile world, and the selection of the gifts (gold, frankincense, and myrrh) may have been influenced by passages from OT Messianic prophecy which predict the allegiance of the nations (Is 60[1f. 5], Ps 72[11. 12. 15]).‡ A contrast may also be intended to be suggested between the spiritual Kingship of the Messiah, and the earthly kingship of secular rulers (like Herod) who are instinctively hostile to the new force that has entered the world.

It is noticeable, however, that Mt. here does not cite any proof-passages from the OT (in vv.[5. 6] the quotation from Micah is placed in the mouth of the Sanhedrin). If the compiler had in mind the passage in Nu 24[17] ('There shall come forth a star out of Jacob,' etc.), as has been sometimes supposed,§ his failure to cite it would indeed be sur-

prising. But it is to be observed that in Numbers the star is identified *with* the Messiah, and would hardly be applicable in this story. (See, further, below).

It may be, as Zahn* suggests, that Mt. regards the episode of the visit of the Magi to render homage to the newborn King not so much in the light of a fulfilment of ancient prophecy, as a *new* prophecy 'which indicates that the Messiah Jesus, who has been born to save His own people from their sins (1[21]), will be sought out and honoured by heathen, while the leading representatives of the religious thought and worship of Israel ask no questions concerning Him, and leave it to the tyrant, who enslaves them, to concern himself about the true King of the Jews, and then only with the object of compassing His destruction.' On this view the star and the astrologers—the Magi—become significant as proof that God uses even such imperfect means as astrology for bringing the heathen to the knowledge of the truth.

The 'star' of the narrative doubtless refers to some particular star, or to some unique astral phenomenon which the Magi were led to connect with the birth of the World-Redeemer in the West. The detail about the star 'which they saw at its rising' going 'before them, until it came and stood still above (the place) where the child was,' is, doubtless, not intended to be understood literally. It is merely a poetical description of the illusion which makes it appear that a luminous heavenly body keeps pace and maintains its relative position with the movement of the observer.

Various attempts have been made to identify the 'star' of this narrative with some exceptional heavenly phenomenon, and to fix its occurrence by means of astronomical calculation. The most famous of these is that of Kepler (1605), who thought of a close conjunction of the planets Jupiter and Saturn in the constellation Pisces,—a rare combination which takes place only once in 800 years, and which occurred no less than three times in the year 747 A.U.C. (=B.C. 7). See Edersheim, *LT* i. p. 212 f. But the data are too indefinite to allow of any certain conclusion in the matter. Moreover, the ignorance displayed by Herod and 'all Jerusalem' as to the nature of the star hardly suggests that its appearance would strike any but practised astrologers.

The association of the birth of great men with such phenomena was a common feature in the ancient world where astrology was held in high esteem. Thus, *e.g.*, 'on the birth-night of Alexander, Magi prophesied from a brilliant constellation that the destroyer of Asia was born' (cf. Cic. *de Divinatione*, i. 47, cited by Allen, *op. cit.* p. 12). On Jewish ground we have already seen the same idea at work in connexion with the birth of Moses in the Midrash passage cited above. Edersheim (*op. cit.* i. p. 211 f.) also cites some late Midrashic passages which connect the coming of Messiah with the appearance of a star. But these are of very uncertain value.

3. The star of the Messiah.—Sometimes the Messiah Himself is metaphorically referred to as a Star,† a description which is based, apparently, on Nu 24[17]:

'There shall come forth a star out of Jacob,
And a sceptre shall rise out of Israel';

In the Targum Onkelos this is rendered:

'When a king shall arise out of Jacob,
And the Messiah shall be anointed from Israel';

And in pseudo-Jonathan:

'When the mighty King of Jacob's House shall reign,
And the Messiah, the Power - sceptre of Israel, shall be anointed.'

Here, it will be noticed, the Star is expressly identified with the Messianic King. A similar Messianic application of this passage meets us in the *Testaments of the Twelve Patriarchs*, where (Judah, 24 [Greek text]) the following occurs:

'Over you a star shall proceed out of Jacob,
And a man shall arise from my seed like the sun of right eousness' (cf. Mal 4[2]). Cf. also Test. Levi 18.

In the first part of the 3rd Messiah-Apocalypse embodied in

---

* See esp. the admirable discussion in W. C. Allen's 'St. Matthew' (*ICC*), pp. 11–15.
† See an art. by the present writer in *The Interpreter* (Jan. 1906) on 'The Gospel Narratives of the Nativity and the alleged influence of heathen ideas.'
‡ Notice esp. Is 60[3] 'And the Gentiles shall come to thy light.'
§ *E.g.* by Wünsche, *Neue Beiträge zur Erläuterung der Evangelien*, p. 12.

* *Das Evangelium des Matthäus* (1903), p. 101.
† The same word is used metaph. in Arabic for a ruler.

The Apocalypse of Baruch (ch. 53), the seer beholds the Messiah appear like lightning ' on the summit of the cloud '; and this lightning 'shone exceedingly so as to illuminate the whole earth' (cf. Mt 24²⁷ 'For as the lightning cometh forth from the east, and is seen even unto the west, so shall be the coming of the Son of Man'; Lk 17²⁴ and the other NT passages cited below; cf Volz, *Jüd. Eschatologie*, p. 221).

It was apparently from Nu 24¹⁷, Messianically interpreted, that the false Messiah Simeon derived his designation *Bar Cochba* (*i.e.* 'Son of the Star'). When Rabbi Aḳiba acknowledged him as the Messiah, he expressly cited this Scripture passage (Bab. *Sanh.* 97*b*) as applicable to Simeon, though this opinion was not generally shared by the learned among the Jews of the time. Bar Cochba seems to have been invested with a Messianic character by the irresistible force of popular public opinion. After the disastrous issue of his revolt it became necessary to apologize for Aḳiba's mistake, and one such explanation seems to be reflected in some of the minor *Midrashim* which make the reference apply to Messiah ben Joseph, who was destined to be killed in battle before Messiah ben David could appear.* There is thus good evidence that in the time of Christ the 'Star' of Nu 24¹⁷ was popularly identified with the Messianic King.†

This idea may have influenced those NT passages where Jesus is represented as the 'Morning Star' (Rev 22¹⁶ 2²⁸), though it must be remembered that the angels are described symbolically in the Bk. of Enoch (lxxxvi. 1, 3) as 'stars'—a metaphor which helps to explain the symbolism by which Jesus is here described as 'the Morning Star.' 'Among the stars of the spiritual firmament,' Jesus is 'the brightest in the whole galaxy' (Swete, *Apocalypse*, p. 306). A similar conception meets us in 2 P 1¹⁹ ('Take heed unto the lamp of prophecy until the day dawn, and the day-star [φωσφόρος] arise in your hearts'), and, in fact, the essential idea is present in all those passages of the NT which speak of the spiritual illumination that accompanies the revelation of the Messiah (cf. the fragment of an old Christian hymn in Eph 5¹⁴ 'Awake, thou that sleepest . . . and Christ shall *shine* upon thee'; cf. Jn 1⁹ Christ 'the *Light* which lightens every man coming into the world,' etc.). There is also the remarkable description of the Messiah as the 'Day-spring from on high' (ἀνατολὴ ἐξ ὕψους) in the Song of Zacharias (Lk 1⁷⁸), which may possibly have been associated in thought with the Messianic Star.‡

The association of the idea of light with the Messiah and the Messianic age was well established in Jewish Literature. This idea is founded on— or, at any rate, finds classical expression in—Is 60¹ᶠ. ('Arise, shine; for thy light is come'). The Midrash (*Yalkut Shim.*) on this passage is instructive. It comments thus:

'What is asserted by the words of the Psalm, "In thy light shall we see light" (Ps 36¹⁰)? It is *the light of the Messiah* that is meant. For when it is said, "God saw the light that it was good" (Gn 1⁴), it is thereby taught that the Holy One (Blessed be He) contemplated the generation of the Messiah and his works, before the world had been created, and that He concealed the light for the Messiah and his generation beneath His throne of glory. Then spake Satan before the Holy One (Blessed be He): "Lord of the World, for whom is the light hidden beneath Thy throne of glory destined?" [Answer] "For him who in the time to come will subdue thee and bring thee to shame."'

The Midrash then goes on to relate that at his request Satan was allowed to see the Messiah, and at the sight of him trembled and sank to the ground, crying out: 'Truly this is the Messiah,

who will deliver me and all heathen kings over to Gehenna.' *

Gressmann (*Der Ursprung der isr.-jüd. Eschatologie*, p. 307 f.) traces the association of light in connexion with the Servant of Jahweh, who is represented as the Light of the World in Deutero-Isaiah (Is 49⁶ 51⁴), to the mythical representation of the World-Ruler as a solar hero in the old Saga.

In fact, under the figure of light the salvation and felicity of the Messianic age are constantly depicted (see esp. Volz, *Jüd. Eschatologie*, pp. 328–331). The heavenly Jerusalem of the Apocalypse is a city filled with celestial light (Rev 21²³⋅ ²⁵ 22⁵). The long drawn out contrast between light and darkness that pervades the Fourth Gospel is also significant in this connexion.   G. H. Box.

STATE AFTER DEATH.—See Dead and Eschatology, I. (A.) § 5 (*c*).

STATER.—See Money.

STATURE.—See Age.

STEWARD, STEWARDSHIP.—

The former word is a tr. of ἐπίτροπος in Mt 20⁸, Lk 8³, and of οἰκονόμος in Lk 12⁴² 16¹⋅ ³⋅ ⁸; the latter, of οἰκονομία in Lk 16²⋅ ³⋅ ⁴. In v.² the verb οἰκονομεῖν occurs. The distinction between ἐπίτροπος and οἰκονόμος has been variously stated. Horne treats them as synonyms; Meyer says the former is a more general term; Schleusner, that the ἐπ. is appointed by law or a magistrate, the οἰκ. by will; Elliott and Lightfoot agree in thinking that ἐπ., like our 'guardian,' has special reference to 'persons'; οἰκ., like 'steward,' to property (see their notes on Gal 4² and references there cited, and Smith's *Dict. of Gr. and Rom. Ant.*, *s.v.* ἐπίτροπος). The last view is probably the right one. But the exact duties of each of them doubtless varied in different cases and under different masters, and often the two are used interchangeably (so Meyer on Mt 20⁸). Meyer's view is probably true of the Gospels, although if Chuza as ἐπίτροπος (Lk 8³) had special charge of the education of the royal children, it might lend further colour to Sanday's theory of Joanna's relation to the authorship of Lk 1. 2. In Mt 24⁴⁵ δοῦλος is used of one whose position is evidently that of the steward, as may be seen by comparison with Lk 12⁴². Usually, indeed, the steward is a slave or freedman, corresponding to Lat. *dispensator* or *villicus* (as in Lk 12, Mt 24); occasionally he is a freeman, Lat. *procurator* (Lk 16). See Plummer in *ICC* on Lk 12⁴² 16¹, and Hatch, *Bibl. Greek*, p. 62.

The primary passages are Mt 20¹⁻²⁰ (Labourers in Vineyard), 24⁴⁵⁻⁵¹, Lk 8³ 12⁴²⁻⁴⁸ 16¹⁻²¹ (the Unjust Steward). Some would add the parables of the Prodigal and of Dives as illustrations of wealth wrongly used. The secondary are Mt 21³³⁻⁴⁶ (Wicked Husbandmen) 25¹⁴⁻³⁰ (Talents), Lk 19¹²⁻²⁷ (Minæ), Mt 10²⁴ᶠ· 18²³⁻³⁵, Mk 13³⁴, Jn 15¹⁴⁻³⁰, Lk 17¹⁰. Of these Lk 8³ yields no teaching.

The facts and teachings of the others may be thus summarized:

1. The steward's position.—He was entrusted with the oversight of part or all of his master's estate, including persons and property. He had the 'management of his affairs, the care of receipts and expenditures, and the duty of dealing out the proper portion to every servant and even to the children' (Grimm-Thayer). The education of the children as well as their maintenance was under his charge. His control was more or less absolute according as the master was absent or present. Christ teaches that we are all God's stewards. The trust covers (*a*) ourselves (for we are His); (*b*) others whom we can influence; (*c*) our time, means, opportunities, etc. For everything we rightfully have is from God (cf. Mt 5⁴⁵). What one has wrongfully seized is no part of his trust.

2. The steward's duty was to manage everything with most watchful fidelity and utmost efficiency, and to do it in the interest of his master. So with us. We should therefore (*a*) discipline ourselves—body, soul, and spirit, so as

---

* Cf. the *Pesiḳta Zutarta* (ed. Wilna, 1880, p. 129*b*) and Jellinek's *Beth ha midrasch*, iii. p. 141, etc.

† For an early Christian application of Nu 24¹⁷ to Christ, cf. Justin Martyr, *Apol.* i. 32: 'Isaiah, another prophet, prophesying the same things by other expressions, thus spake: "There shall rise a star out of Jacob, and a blossom shall ascend from the root of Jesse,"' etc.

‡ See an art. by the present writer in *ZNTW*, vol. vi. p. 96 f. (Feb. 1905), where this point is specially discussed.

---

* See the whole passage in Weber, *Jüd. Theol.*² p. 397 f. Edersheim, *LT* ii. p. 728 (Appendix IX.).

to realize God's ideal for us and be most efficient for service—a duty demanding care of the body, training of the mind, culture of the affections, discipline of the will, etc.; (*b*) pursue our calling, whatever it may be, in the interest of God's Kingdom, whether our work be that of the labourer, the farmer, the merchant, the lawyer, physician, statesman, teacher, preacher, or any other ; (*c*) utilize time, influence, opportunities, money, in the wisest way ; (*d*) urge and help others to do the same. One must plan one's probable life as a whole that it may subserve God's purposes in the largest measure possible.

3. The master's duty was (*a*) to assign to the steward only just and honourable work, and (*b*) to provide for his needs. The righteous God can be trusted to do both (Mt 6³³). This leads to the topic that is commonly uppermost when Christian stewardship is thought of ; only it approaches the matter from a rather different, but the true, standpoint.

The arrangements between master and steward varied. Is it so in our relation to God? or is there any definite arrangement or understanding? Some have held that tithing represents it. Yet a regulation like that does not seem fully in harmony with the spirit of the new dispensation (cf. Jer 31³³), which deals in principles rather than rules, just because God is more careful to develop character than to get men's gains. Perhaps the best way of stating the case, however, would be this : God wills that His stewards should spend on themselves such a proportion of the income as is necessary to their highest working efficiency. This will vary with different persons according to conditions. Each must determine honestly for himself. 'To his own Master he stands or falls.' In general, it will mean less than is commonly supposed. It must be determined not by love of ease or pleasure, not by selfishness or pride, not by custom or fashion (where these are wrong), nor even by what would be reasonable and allowable in a normal world of sinlessness and blessedness, but wholly by the spirit of Divine love in view of the pressing needs of this abnormal world with its appalling sin, ignorance, and wretchedness.

4. Rewards and penalties. All rewards are of grace (Lk 17¹⁰). These begin now, but their fulness is hereafter. Through faithful service there comes the perfecting of character, the richer development of the personality, and the final winning of our souls (21¹⁹). We are now stewards holding all on trust. We shall then receive as our own the inheritance prepared from the foundation of the world (Lk 16¹², Mt 25³⁴). We shall be welcomed into eternal tabernacles (Lk 16⁹) and be entrusted with the rule and authority for which we have become fitted (Lk 12⁴⁴, Mt 24⁴⁷ 25²⁰⁻²³). The unfaithful shall be beaten, or stripped of what they had, cut asunder as hypocrites, and cast into outer darkness with the unbelieving (Lk 12⁴⁶, Mt 24⁵¹ 25²⁸⁻³⁰).

Literature.—Commentaries : works on the Parables ; Stirling, *Stewardship of Life* ; Hartman, *The Business Aspect of Christian Stewardship*; F. W. Robertson, *Serm.* iv. 239 ; C. H. Spurgeon, *An All-round Ministry*, 260 ; A. L. Moore, *God is Love*, 52 ; W. Houghton, *Secret of Power*, 80 ; the best treatment is that of C. A. Cook, *Stewardship* (Am. Bapt. Publ. Soc.).

J. H. FARMER.

STIGMATA (στίγματα, EV 'marks').—The word occurs only in Gal 6¹⁷ 'From henceforth let no man trouble me : for I bear branded on my body the marks of Jesus' (RV). The subject of the 'stigmata (*or* marks) of Jesus' comes before us in two ways : we have to consider (1) the meaning of the word *stigmata* as used by St. Paul ; (2) the special sense in which it has come to be employed from the time of St. Francis of Assisi and onwards, esp. in the Roman Catholic Church.

1. St. Paul's use of the word. — (1) By the 'stigmata of Jesus' Bonaventura and many others have supposed the Apostle to refer to bodily marks resembling the nail-prints and other insignia of the Saviour's Passion—thus making him affirm an experience, in his own person, of the phenomena of 'stigmatization' (see 2). But the technical sense in which the word *stigmata* was used in the time of St. Paul—viz. as denoting marks of ownership (either brands made with hot irons, or cuts which, as they healed, were prevented from closing, and so became broad scars), as well as the meaning of the whole verse when considered in the light of the context and its analogies in other parts of the Apostle's writings (esp. 2 Co 11²³ff.)—shows that 'Ἰησοῦ must be taken as the gen. of possession, and that the reference is not at all to the wounds on the Lord's body, but solely to certain marks on St. Paul's own body that stamped him as belonging to Jesus Christ.

(2) A few commentators, following Augustine (*Com. on Gal., in loc.*), have transformed St. Paul's *stigmata* into his manifestation of the fruits of the Spirit, with special reference to his Christian asceticism (cf. 1 Co 9²⁷). But the technical signification of *stigmata*, as well as the expression 'on my body,' seems to put such an interpretation altogether out of the question.

(3) Assuming, then, that the *stigmata* were marks of ownership, what is the particular figure that St. Paul means to suggest? (*a*) Soldiers, in honour of an adored commander, sometimes branded on their bodies the initial letter of his name. But though the idea of the Christian life as a military service is a familiar one in the Pauline writings (1 Co 9⁷, 2 Co 10⁴, 1 Ti 6¹², 2 Ti 4⁷), it is not in keeping with the present context, which brings Jesus before us as Lord (vv.¹⁴⁻¹⁷), not as Captain. (*b*) Slaves attached to the service of a heathen temple (ἱερόδουλοι) were branded with the names of the deities to whom they ministered ; and Lightfoot (*Com. on Gal., in loc.*) and others (*e.g.* Westcott in *Expos.* vi. [1887] 241) have thought that the metaphor is most appropriately understood in the light of this fact. But, as Meyer pointed out (*Com. in loc.*), the references to the branding of ἱερόδουλοι found in Herod., Plut., Lucian, etc., bear upon the usage of other nations, and we have no evidence for Galatia itself. Even if we had, a reference to the branding of the slaves in heathen temples would be needlessly recondite, in view of the much more familiar practice of branding domestic slaves. And, above all, as the ἱερόδουλοι were very frequently women attached to a temple for immoral purposes, it seems unlikely that the Apostle would have in his mind a term that carried associations so degrading. (*c*) It is most likely, therefore, that St. Paul is alluding to an ordinary domestic custom. In the East (not in Rome, where branding was the mark of a runaway slave, and so a badge of disgrace) slaves were regularly branded by their owners, and Artemidorus Daldianus bears witness to the practice in Galatia (*Oneirocritica*, i. 8. The verb he uses is στίζω, from which στίγμα comes. See W. M. Ramsay, *Hist. Com. on Gal.* pp. 84, 472, who tells us that this ancient custom is familiar even yet to the observant traveller in Turkey). St. Paul never calls himself a ἱερόδουλος, but the thought that he was the δοῦλος of Jesus Christ was one of his ruling ideas (Ro 1¹, 1 Co 7²², 2 Co 4⁵, Gal 1¹⁰, Ph 1¹). And when he says, 'I bear branded on my body the marks of Jesus,' he means certain marks that bore witness to the fact that Jesus was his Master and he was Jesus' slave.

(4) But what were these marks that St. Paul bore branded on his body? Without doubt, he meant the scars he had earned in the service of Christ — perhaps the general signature upon his face and whole person of all his toils and trials,

but, at all events, the laceration and disfigurement produced by Jewish scourges and lictors' rods and the cruel stones of the multitude (Ac 14¹⁹ 16²³, 2 Co 11²⁴· ²⁵). These marks of his servitude to his Lord the Apostle looked upon not only as a badge of honour, but (and this is his reason for referring to them here) as seals set upon his claim to be the Apostle and minister of Jesus Christ (cf. 2 Co 11²³ᶠᶠ·), and so as tokens of his right to speak with authority. (For the idea of authority as springing out of complete subjection to a greater, cf. the centurion's 'I also am a man under authority,' Mt 8⁹, Lk 7⁸). The verse thus falls into line with the whole Epistle as an intensely personal message of remonstrance and appeal. Once more, at the end as at the beginning (cf. 1¹), St. Paul exalts his Apostleship. And what he says here is, 'Let no man trouble me after this, by challenging my right to declare the truth of the gospel ; for I bear branded on my body the marks which testify that I am the slave of Jesus —that He is my Master and my Lord.'

2. The ecclesiastical use of the word.—According to the earliest biographers of St. Francis of Assisi (Thomas of Celano, the 'Tres Socii,' and Bonaventura, whose 'Vitæ' are all included in the *Acta Sanctorum*), the saint, while meditating in his cell on the sufferings of Jesus, fell into a trance, and had a vision of the Crucified Himself in the form of a seraph. When he awoke he found that he was marked in hands and feet and side with the wounds of the Lord—wounds which remained till the time of his death, that in the side bleeding occasionally. Numerous witnesses testify to having seen these marks in the body of Francis, both during his life and after he was dead. Bonaventura (*op. cit.* xiii. 4) addresses the saint in the following words : 'Jam enim propter stigmata Domini Jesu quæ in corpore tuo portas, nemo debet tibi esse molestus.' This is an appropriation to the case of Francis of the Vulg. version of St. Paul's language in Gal 6¹⁷ : from which the inference is natural that the biographer, by a mistaken interpretation of the text, conceived the *stigmata* of Francis and those of the Apostle to be of a like kind.

From the first the stigmatization of St. Francis was generally accepted in the Catholic Church, not only as a fact, but as a miraculous evidence of the Divine favour ; though the Dominicans objected, and attributed the alleged miracle to Franciscan deceit. In the next century, however, similar marks were affirmed to have shown themselves on the person of the well-known Dominican nun, St. Catherine of Siena ; and thereafter down to modern times (the last well-authenticated instance was in 1868) the phenomena of stigmatization have repeatedly been vouched for, the subjects, in the great majority of cases, being women. That some of the alleged instances were pure frauds is practically certain, while in other cases the *stigmata* appear to have been nothing more than wounds self-inflicted by persons in a state of epileptic hysteria. On the other hand, in a number of cases, and notably in that of St. Francis, the positive evidence is too strong to be rejected on either of the above grounds (see esp. the biography of St. Francis by P. Sabatier, mentioned below). And now modern investigations, esp. in the region of psycho-physics, have furnished evidence that goes to support the historical testimony, by assuring us that there is a 'scientific background' to the phenomenon of stigmatization. It is certain that, in sensitive subjects, the influence of the mind in modifying bodily states and producing new conditions is exceedingly great ; and stigmatization is now commonly placed by competent students among the peculiar phenomena attributed to hypnotic auto-suggestion. It is accepted as a fact that *stigmata* have actually appeared on the bodies of persons whose nervous susceptibility was abnormal, when, under the excitement of strong feeling, they have fixed their minds steadily upon the thought of the sufferings of Jesus, and especially on the *insignia Passionis* (see *EBr* xxii. 550, xxxii. 53 ; Otto, *Naturalism and Religion* (1907) 351–52). But while modern science leads us to accept stigmatization as a pathological certainty, it also teaches us to regard it not as a mark of the Divine favour, but as an evidence rather of the presence of hysterical neurasthenia. And modern criticism, again, assures us that the view that it is identical with St. Paul's 'stigmata of Jesus' must be relegated, in Sir W. M. Ramsay's words (*op. cit.* p. 472), to the 'Dark Ages' of scholarship.

LITERATURE. — For **1** : the Comm. of Lightfoot, Alford, and Meyer, *in loc.* ; Ramsay, *Hist. Com. on Gal.* 472 ; Phillips Brooks, *Candle of the Lord*, 355. For **2** : artt. 'Stigmatization' in *EBr* (by Prof. Macalister of Cambridge) and *PRE*³, 'Stigmata' in *Prot. Dict.*, 'Franz von Assisi' in *PRE*³ ; the Lives of St. Francis by Thomas of Celano and Bonaventura in *Acta Sanctorum* ; P. Sabatier, *Vie de S. François d'Assise* (1894—Eng. tr. same year), ch. xvii., and 'Étude critique sur les stigmata' in the Appendix ; W. J. Dawson, *The Reproach of Christ*, p. 167 ; Hastings' *DB*, Ext. Vol. Index, *s.v.* 'Stigmata'.

J. C. LAMBERT.

STONE.—**1. The Greek terms.**—Apart from the vb. 'to stone' (for wh. see STONING), there are 5 Gr. words tr. 'stone' in the NT which call for notice in the present article. (1) λίθος (LXX for אֶבֶן) is the general term. It occurs very frequently in the Gospels, and is the word with which in this art. we are chiefly concerned. λίθος is distinguished from πέτρα as in Eng. 'stone' is distinguished from 'rock.' (2) λίθινος (fr. λίθος), 'made of stone' ; found in the Gospels only in Jn 2⁶ λίθιναι ὑδρίαι, 'waterpots of stone.' (3) πέτρος is rendered 'stone' only in AV of Jn 1⁴² 'Cephas, which is, by interpretation, a stone.' AVm gives 'Peter,' while RV has 'Peter' in the text and 'rock or stone' in the margin. 'Rock' is certainly more adequate than 'stone,' for πέτρος properly denotes a mass of detached rock, as πέτρα does a living or solid rock. (So πετρώδης in the parable of the Sower [Mt 13⁵· ²⁰, Mk 4⁵· ¹⁶] does not mean 'stony' [AV] but 'rocky' [RV]—not ground full of loose stones, but a thin soil with shelves of rock lying underneath). Probably, however, the sense is best conveyed by the proper name 'Peter' —the meaning of 'Peter' being, of course, understood (cf. Mt 16¹⁸). (4) λαξευτός, 'hewn in stone' (fr. λᾶς 'stone' and ξέω 'scrape' or 'carve'), applied in Lk 23⁵³ to the tomb in which Jesus was laid. Mt. (27⁶⁰) and Mk. (15⁴⁶), however, describe it as hewn out of rock (πέτρα). (5) ψῆφος, 'pebble,' represents 'stone' in the 'white stone' which in the Ep. to the Church in Pergamum Christ promises to him that overcometh (Rev 2¹⁷).

2. Stones crying out.—The stones of Christ and the Gospels form a suggestive subject. There are sermons in these stones, we might say, for they have lessons to impart to us regarding Christ's history, His teaching, and His Person as the Messiah.

(1) *His history.*—(*a*) Whether or not we accept the ancient tradition that Jesus was born in one of the limestone caves of Bethlehem, it is very likely that His manger would be a manger of stone— built with stones and mortar if not hollowed out of the solid rock (see Thomson, *LB* [ed. 1878] p. 413). If so, the first bed on which the Lord was laid, like the last one to which He was carried by Nicodemus and Joseph of Arimathæa (Jn 19³⁸ᶠᶠ·), was a bed of stone.

(*b*) In Christ's spiritual struggles on the very threshold of His public life, He had to do with the stones. It is a curious fact that they play a part in two out of the three acts that make up the drama of the Temptation in the Wilderness. In the one case, Jesus is tempted to use His miraculous powers to turn the stones that lie about Him on the rough mountain-side into loaves of bread wherewith to satisfy His hunger (Mt 4²⁻⁴, Lk 4²⁻⁴). In the other, He is tempted to leap from a pinnacle of the Temple by the reminder that it is written (Ps 91¹¹· ¹²) that God's child shall be upheld by angels, and so preserved from dashing his foot against a stone (Mt 4⁵⁻⁷, Lk 4⁹⁻¹²). In the one case, the stones were to nourish His life ; but contrary to God's law of sowing and reaping. In the other, they were to refuse to dash Him to death ; but contrary to the Divinely fixed law of gravitation. Satan meant the stones to be stones of stumbling to Jesus, on that difficult path of obedience and self-renunciation to which in His baptism He had just consecrated Himself. But Jesus by His faith and patience turned them into stepping-stones to higher things.

(*c*) At Cana of Galilee Jesus 'manifested his glory' ; and there, we might say, He was again beholden to the stones ; for the six waterpots by whose aid He wrought His first miracle were waterpots of stone (Jn 2⁶).

(*d*) But not always were the stones His servants and ministers. Twice in Jn.'s Gospel (8⁵⁹ 10³¹, cf. 11⁸) we read how the enemies of Jesus took up stones to cast them at° Him, because He claimed that He was the Son of God.

(e) Against the cave which was Lazarus' tomb there lay a stone (Jn 11³⁸)—rolled there to shut in the dead during the awful process of decay (v.³⁹), as well as to shut out the ravening wild beasts. 'Take ye away the stone,' Jesus said (v.³⁹); and when they had done so, another word of command turned that gravestone at Bethany into a parable to all the ages of the rolling away from human hearts of the crushing bondage of death (He 2¹⁴·) by Him who is the Resurrection and the Life (Jn 11²⁵).

(f) It was not long after, when the Lord's own body was carried to another tomb 'hewn in stone' (Lk 23⁵³), and laid on one of the stone shelves prepared for such a purpose. Against the door of His sepulchre also 'a great stone' was rolled (Mt 27⁶⁰ ||), and a seal was set upon the guardian stone. And that great stone, which the Jewish rulers would fain have made the incontrovertible proof that the world had seen the last of Jesus of Nazareth (v.⁶²ᶠᶠ·), has become the shining and perennial monument of His victory over death—proclaiming, in St. Peter's words, that 'it was not possible that he should be holden of it' (Ac 2²⁴). For whenever Christian men think of the Lord's sepulchre, they always see that great stone rolled back from the door, and the angel of the Resurrection sitting upon it (Mt 28² ||).

(2) *His teaching.*—One of the most self-evident proofs that Jesus ever gave of the Heavenly Father's love and the reality of prayer, lay in the question, 'What man is there of you, who, if his son shall ask him for a loaf, will give him a stone?' (Mt 7⁹). One of the most memorable examples of His heart-searching irony was when He said to the accusers of a sinful woman, 'He that is without sin among you, let him first cast a stone at her' (Jn 8[7]). One of the most striking assertions of His claim to Messianic dignity lay in His answer to the Pharisees when they appealed to Him to rebuke the enthusiastic shouts of His disciples: 'I tell you that if these shall hold their peace, the stones will cry out' (Lk 19⁴⁰). One of His clearest and most emphatic predictions of the coming fate of Jerusalem was when He said of the Temple, adorned with goodly stones, 'There shall not be left here one stone upon another, that shall not be thrown down (Mk 13² ||).

In the Ep. to the Church in Pergamum the author of the Apocalypse represents Jesus Christ as promising a 'white stone' to the victor in the good fight of faith (Rev 2¹⁷). Numerous explanations of this white stone have been suggested, but the one that seems best to satisfy all the requirements is that which takes it to be the *tessara gladiatoria*, bestowed on the victorious young gladiator when he exchanged the name of *tiro* for that of *spectatus* (see *ExpT* i. [1889] p. 2, viii. [1897] p. 291; Hastings' *DB* iv. 618ᵇ).

The 5th of the Oxyrhynchus (1897) 'Sayings of Jesus' contains the striking words, 'Jesus saith . . . Raise the stone and there shalt thou find me; cleave the wood and there am I.' The words have lent themselves to various ingenious explanations; but the most probable interpretation is the one which also most readily suggests itself—that we have here an affirmation of the immanence of Christ in natural things. The saying may be understood in a sense that is perfectly in keeping with teaching that is found in the NT (*e.g.* Jn 1³, Col 1¹⁶ᶠ·), but was more probably written with a leaning to a kind of Gnostic Pantheism. It is generally agreed that, in their present form at least, these 'Sayings of Jesus' were not spoken by the Lord Himself, and do not even belong to the earliest age (see Lock and Sanday, *Two Lectures*

on the '*Sayings of Jesus*' (1897); cf. *ExpT* ix. [1898] p. 194 ff.).

(3) *His Person.*—On one occasion (Lk 20¹⁷ = Mt 21⁴²) Jesus took a stone (λίθος; cf. His symbolic use of 'rock' (πέτρα) in Mt 7²⁴ᶠ· ||, 16¹⁸, and St. Paul's 'spiritual rock,' 'that rock was Christ,' 1 Co 10⁴) as a symbol of His own Person. He had just spoken the parable of the Wicked Husbandmen, and after announcing their doom, He quoted epexegetically Ps 118²² 'The stone which the builders refused is become the head stone of the corner.' Thus He identified the rejected 'Son' of the parable with the rejected stone of the Psalm, and the wicked husbandmen with the scribes and Pharisees as the 'builders' of Israel's theocratic edifice; but at the same time intimated to the latter that they must not think that by rejecting Him and putting Him to death they would be done with Him for ever. So far from that, He went on to say, 'Every one that falleth on that stone shall be broken to pieces; but on whomsoever it shall fall, it will scatter him as dust' (Lk 20¹⁸ = Mt 21⁴⁴).

In Ac 4¹¹ we find St. Peter taking up Christ's symbol, and boldly declaring to the Sanhedrin that Jesus Christ of Nazareth was the stone set at naught by them the builders, but made by God the head of the corner. And in his Epistle he returns to this parable of the stone as a symbol of Christ's Person, and dwells upon it with much greater fulness (1 P 2⁴⁻⁸). He describes the Lord now, with evident reference to His Resurrection (cf. Ac 4¹⁰ with v.¹¹), as a 'living stone,' rejected indeed by men, but to God chosen and precious, upon whom His people are built up into a spiritual house. The allusion to the verse in Ps 118 is unmistakable; but in what he proceeds to say the Apostle makes use further of two passages in Isaiah. First he quotes Is 28¹⁶ 'Behold I lay in Zion a chief corner stone,' etc., and next the words of 8¹⁴ about the 'stone of stumbling and the rock of offence.' And it seems clear that his reminiscence of the latter passage has been inspired by his recollection of the Lord's own words as to those who fall upon the Stone which is Himself, and those upon whom that Stone shall fall (cf. vv.⁷· ⁸ with Lk 20¹⁷· ¹⁸ = Mt 21⁴²· ⁴⁴). See, further, art. ROCK.

LITERATURE.—The Lexx. on the various Gr. words, and the Comm. on the passages quoted.   J. C. LAMBERT.

STONING.—There are three Greek verbs in the NT which mean 'to stone'—λιθοβολέω, λιθάζω, and καταλιθάζω. These, again, are the equivalents of the two Heb. synonyms סקל and רגם, each of which may denote either the mere throwing of stones by a mob at any person who has incurred their ill-will (Ex 17⁴, Nu 14¹⁰), or the legal execution of a criminal by letting fall one or more large pieces of stone upon his body. Mere stone-throwing is mentioned in the Gospels in the following passages: The priests fear that the people may stone them (Lk 20⁶); the prophets were so treated (Mt 23³⁷, Lk 13³⁴); the husbandmen in the parable beat or stone the messengers (Mt 21³⁵, Mk 12⁴ AV); and in St. John's Gospel the Jews so threaten Jesus (8⁵⁹ 10³¹⁻³³ 11⁸).

The Jewish Senate (*Bêth Dîn*) recognized four forms of capital punishment,—stoning, burning, beheading, and strangling (*Sanh.* vii. 1). In the case of stoning, the two witnesses took their stand on an elevation of about twice the height of a man. The convict was laid on his back beneath, and one of the witnesses dropped a stone upon his heart. If this did not prove fatal, the second witness cast one; and if the victim still survived, then all Israel (Dt 17⁷). The bodies of all stoned persons were crucified according to one account; according to another, only those of blasphemers and idolators, a man being hung with his face to the people, a woman with hers to the tree. According to another account, women were not crucified (*ib.* vi. 4). A person who had been stoned was not buried in the sepulchre of his fathers (vii. 1).

In the Law and in practice capital punishment was inflicted for offences against any of the first seven ordinances of the Decalogue—that is, upon persons guilty of apostasy (Dt 13¹⁰), idolatry (17⁵), blasphemy (Lv 24¹⁶, 1 K 21¹³), Sabbath-breaking (Nu 15³⁵), disobedience to parents (Dt 21²¹), murder (Lv 24²¹), unchastity (Dt 22²¹· ²⁴), as well as for practising sorcery (Lv 20²⁷), for kidnapping (Ex 21¹⁶), and for special offences (Jos 7). An ox which gored a man in the course of a bull-fight was not stoned (*Baba kamma*, iv. 4 ; Ex 21²⁸). In each of the above cases the penalty takes the form of stoning, though this is not explicitly mentioned in the case of murder, of kidnapping, or of unchastity on the part of a married woman (Dt 22²²). Stoning was thus the regular means of executing criminals among the Hebrews, as strangling was with the later Jews. Both processes avoided the shedding of blood, and reduced the risk of vengeance on the part of the relatives.

In the narrative Jn 8¹⁻¹¹, which is generally regarded as spurious, not being part of the text of the best MSS, the scribes were therefore justified in stating that 'Moses in the law commanded us that such should be stoned,' the reference being to Dt 22²³· ²⁴. This would imply that the woman was betrothed merely, but not married, the mode of execution in the case of a married woman not being specified (Dt 22²²), and being, in fact, at the time strangling (*Sanh.* 51*b* : 'A daughter of Israel who is married, by strangling, who is betrothed, by stoning').

                          T. H. WEIR.

STORM.—See SEA OF GALILEE, p. 591.

STRANGER.—The AV has only the one rendering—'stranger'—for five different words in the Greek. It is the natural translation of the term which has the most general signification — ξένος (Mt 25³⁵· ⁴³ 27⁷ etc.) ; and there is no other word in English to express the exact force of ἀλλότριος (Mt 17²⁵· ²⁶, Jn 10⁵ ; cf. 10¹²—the ἀλλότριος is the one 'whose own the sheep are not'). For ἀλλογενής the proper equivalent is 'alien,' as in Lk 17¹⁸ (RVm). For πάροικος and παρεπίδημος RV rightly uses 'sojourner' (Ac 7²⁹, 1 P 2¹¹ ; cf. Lk 24¹⁸, 1 P 1¹, He 11¹³). These words indicate a sentiment which is (1) racial or national (Mt 17²⁵· ²⁶ the kings of the earth take tribute from 'strangers,' not from sons), (2) humanitarian (Mt 25³⁵ 'I was a stranger, and ye took me in'), and (3) religious (1 P 2¹¹ 'I beseech you as sojourners and pilgrims to abstain,' etc.).

Generally, however, it may be said that the connexion in which the words occur in NT is illustrative of the difference between the current Jewish conception of the stranger in the time of Christ, and that which is suggested by the Gospel. Jesus found His countrymen steeped in the idea that all foreigners were 'dogs,' that 'the peoples' was a term almost synonymous with 'the heathen,' and that only under rigid conditions and upon sufferance might a non-Jew obtain any of the privileges considered to be the Divine right of a Jew. He left His followers possessed of the thought, however unconscious they might be of all that it involved, that to Him the Samaritan and the Gentile, the man outside the pale and the man of no caste, were as much the objects of His mission as the favoured son of Abraham. 'Stranger,' to the average Jew, was the name for one with whom he might have commercial dealings and certain social or political relations, but with whom religious affinity or fellowship was practically impossible ; to Jesus it meant one who had a special claim upon Him and His (Mt 25³⁵ff·). The impression which He created was not merely that Christianity meant a deepening and extending of that sense of the sacred duty of hospitality and kindness which already existed in the Jewish mind, as it does throughout the East (Ex 23⁹ 22²¹, Lk 19³³, Dt 10¹⁸· ¹⁹, Jer 7⁶ etc. ; cf. the practice existing among the Essenes, Jos. *BJ* II. viii. 4, 5), but that it involved a complete change of the attitude which assumed that a different treatment was to be meted out to the stranger from that which was naturally shown to one's own kith and kin (Mt 5⁴³⁻⁴⁸ etc.). See, further, artt. COSMOPOLITANISM, HOSPITALITY, GENTILES, UNIVERSALISM.

It is further to be noticed that Christianity gave a new signification to the word 'stranger.' The way had been prepared by the use of the Hebrew word 'Ger' (LXX. πάροικος, see artt. 'Ger' in *DB* and 'Stranger' in *Encyc. Bibl.*), which designated the sojourner who dwelt within the gates of Israel, and who, while having a certain status there and a temporary home, belonged to another country. The fact also that the Jews themselves had from the time of Abraham so often been sojourners in a land not their own (Ac 7⁶· ²⁹, He 11⁹), and the lessons taught by the dispersion in post-exilic times, led to that metaphorical use of the term which has entered so largely into religious speech and poetry. The follower of Christ saw in it a description of himself as of one who was absent from his proper country, and whose citizenship was in heaven (Ph 3²⁰). When St. Peter writes to the 'sojourners of the Dispersion' (1 P 1¹), and beseeches them 'as sojourners and pilgrims' to abstain from fleshly lusts (2¹¹), he is diverting the term from a geographical to a spiritual sense (cf. 1¹⁷). The writer of the Epistle to the Hebrews has the same thought, 'For we have not here an abiding city, but we seek after the city which is to come' (13¹⁴, 11¹³⁻¹⁶).

LITERATURE. — Uhlhorn, *Chr. Charity in the Ancient Ch.* ; Brace, *Gesta Christi*, ch. xvi. ; Seeley, *Ecce Homo*, chs. xiv. xvii.

                       J. ROSS MURRAY.

STREAM.—See RIVER.

STREET.—In place of 'street' in Mk 6⁵⁶ we should read with RV 'market-place,' the open space or square (ἀγορά) where goods are brought for disposal to the merchants from the bazaars, and where people at leisure gather for conversation. πλατεῖα stands for 'street' in the ordinary sense. In Lk 14²¹ it is apparently distinguished from ῥύμη, as 'street' from 'alley' or 'lane.' But the distinction is ignored elsewhere ; and certainly the 'street' (ῥύμη) called 'Straight' in Damascus (Ac 9¹¹) is no 'alley.' In the East it would be difficult to maintain the distinction. Even the main streets in cities like Jerusalem and Cairo are often narrow and crooked, more like 'alleys' than 'streets' in our sense. The footway is made narrow, the upper storeys frequently overhanging the road, for protection against the heat of the sun. Seclusion is a main object aimed at in building Eastern houses : the wall to the street is seldom pierced by windows ; the door usually leads through a passage into a court, round which the rooms are arranged. All sorts of filth are cast into the streets (Rev 11⁸). In spite of the scavengering of dogs, their condition is often not only loathsome, but a source of danger to health.

                       W. EWING.

STRUGGLES OF SOUL.—The Gospels use varied language in describing the conflicting emotions of Jesus. At the grave of Lazarus He *groaned* in the spirit or in Himself (Jn 11³³· ³⁸, Gr. ἐνεβριμήσατο and ἐμβριμώμενος, from ἐμβριμάομαι *to snort in, to be very angry, to be moved with indignation*, Mk 14⁵; *sternly to charge*, Mt 9³⁰, Mk 1⁴³); He was disturbed inwardly by pity for the mourners, by grief at their hopeless view of death, and by disappointment at their lack of trust in Him. His feeling found expression in tears (v.³⁵). When restoring hearing and speech by the unusual means of putting His hands in the ears and touching the tongue, prayer, and the word 'Ephphatha,' He *sighed* (ἐστέναξεν, Mk 7³⁴). Unbelief either in the sufferer or in the multitude seems to have been felt by Jesus as a hindrance to the cure, to which His pity moved Him (cf. Mt 13⁵⁸). Soon after, when asked for a sign, He '*sighed* deeply in spirit' (ἀναστενάξας τῷ πνεύματι, Mk 8¹²), distracted by His desire to win the nation and His purpose not to use any illegitimate means (cf. the second temptation, Mt 4⁶). When the Greeks sought an interview with Him, He confessed, 'Now is my soul *troubled*' (τετάρακται, Jn 12²⁷); the possibility of finding faith among the Gentiles, and the necessity of His sacrifice on account of Jewish unbelief, were probably the thoughts that so distressed Him. The knowledge that Judas would betray Him *troubled* Him *in spirit* (ἐταράχθη τῷ πνεύματι, Jn 13²¹), love, grief, disappointment, indignation struggling together. His emotions in Gethsemane are described in varied phrases by the Evangelists (see AGONY). There, as Bengel comments on Jn 12²⁷, 'concurrebat horror mortis et ardor obedientiæ.'

Besides these descriptions of the Evangelists, we have other indications of the struggles of soul of Jesus. His *prayers* on other occasions than Gethsemane were probably strenuous efforts to discover and to submit to the Father's will. He withdrew for prayer after the first Sabbath of healing in Capernaum (Mk 1³⁵), after the cleansing of the leper (Lk 5¹⁶), and after dismissing the multitude which He had fed (Mk 6⁴⁶). He was prepared by prayer for the choice of the Twelve (Lk 6¹²), and for His willing acceptance of death (Lk 9²⁸). But inward conflict arose also from *temptation* (see TEMPTATION), for 'he was in all points tempted even as we are' (He 4¹⁵). This experience was not confined to one occasion, for, as Luke (4¹³) states, the tempter 'departed from him for a season,' and it is not improbable even that the narratives of the Temptation (Mt 4¹⁻¹¹, Mk 1¹². ¹³. Lk 4¹⁻¹³) bring together a series of trials, separated by intervals of time. The language He used shows that He felt as temptations to turn from His Divinely appointed path, His mother's appeal at Cana (Jn 2⁴), and Peter's remonstrance at Cæsarea Philippi (Mt 16²³); and even the request of the Greeks for an interview (Jn 12²⁷). Gethsemane must also be regarded as a time of temptation (Mt 26⁴¹, Mk 14³⁸; cf. Lk 22⁴⁰. ⁴⁶). His dread of encouraging curiosity or wrong belief by His miracles (Jn 4⁴⁸) came in conflict with His desire to help and comfort; and when the Evangelists call attention to *compassion* as the motive of His performing a miracle, we may conclude that there had been such a struggle of soul (Mt 14¹⁴ 15³² 20³⁴, Mk 1⁴¹, Lk 7¹³). So also this feeling of sympathy came in conflict with His desire for rest and privacy (Mt 9³⁰, Mk 1⁴⁴ 6³¹). His conflict with the scribes and Pharisees regarding Sabbath observance, fasting, ceremonial washing, and intercourse with sinners must have distressed His spirit; for He too would need to face the issue—would He follow custom or conscience? We have more distinct evidence of the inward strain felt by Him, because His regard for Jewish prejudice and exclusiveness in relation to the Gentiles, in order that He might not estrange His countrymen, compelled Him to assume an attitude of aloofness to the Gentiles (the Roman centurion,

Mt 8¹⁰; the Syrophœnician mother, Mt 15²⁶; the Greeks, Jn 12²³).

What struggles of soul must have resulted from the thwarting of His love and grace by the misunderstanding or unbelief of His relatives (Mk 3³¹⁻³⁵), His disciples (Mt 15¹⁷ 16⁹ 26³¹, Mk 14²⁷), His fellow-townsmen (Mk 6⁶), and the Jerusalem which He so loved that He wept over it (Lk 13³⁴ 19⁴¹)! He strove to turn Judas from his betrayal (Jn 6⁷⁰, Mt 17²² 26²³, Jn 13²⁷, Lk 22⁴⁸), and to save Peter from his denial (Lk 22³²). His struggle of soul culminated, severe and grievous as it had often been, in the agony and desolation of the Cross, when the beloved Son of God was so made sin (2 Co 5²¹) and a curse (Gal 3¹³) for mankind, that in His darkness and loneliness He felt Himself forsaken of God (Mt 27⁴⁶).

ALFRED E. GARVIE.

STUMBLE, STUMBLING-BLOCK.—See HINDRANCE.

SUFFERING.—Suffering was not a mere accident in the career of Christ. Neither is it so in the life of any of His true followers. It came to Him in the fulfilment of His Divine mission. Just so must it come to all those who are co-workers with Him in the Kingdom of God. Therefore in the NT the sombre background of physical and spiritual suffering is never absent from the thought of the writers. St. Peter, perhaps more than any other, dwells upon it in its doctrinal and practical aspect, but all were profoundly impressed by the significance of Christ's sufferings, and endeavoured to interpret the tribulations of His followers in the light of His own varied experiences.

1. Concerning the distressing events in the Master's life, the NT gives us warrant for holding to several conclusions. We misinterpret the meaning of Christ's entrance into humanity, if we limit His tribulations merely to the agony of the Passion. The bitter experiences of His last week were typical of the harsh events of His life as a whole. His emptying of Himself (Ph 2⁷) to become the humble partner of humanity in its struggle against sin and for holiness, was itself the acme of suffering. The Agony in the Garden and the terrors of the death on the Cross were but the last scenes in the drama of His humiliation. Nor must the intensity of His physical sufferings blind us to the reality of the woes of His spirit. With His Divine sensitiveness to selfishness and disobedience and hard-heartedness and unresponsiveness and sin, how poignant must have been the griefs which His sinless soul endured! For this 'man of sorrows, acquainted with grief' (Is 53⁸), every day must have been one of crucifixion. Against Him who came to destroy sin was displayed all the violence of which evil was capable. That He must needs suffer in His effort to accomplish His mission was the inevitable consequence of His Messiahship (Ac 26²³, Lk 24²⁶). But not by His mere sufferings did He redeem humanity. These, in themselves, were not necessary to His office as the 'anointed One,' but were the certain results of the lifework upon which He had entered. Only as He was willing to endure whatever human experiences might come to Him could He reveal the Father and help to turn men to righteousness, by showing them the enormity of sin (He 13¹²). Against Him were displayed the fearful extremes to which sin would go in its effort to overcome good. But by this high discipline was His own spirit cultured (5⁸); and through His heroic, victorious endurance of sin-imposed suffering did He become our High Priest, able to succour those who are tempted (2¹⁷. ¹⁸ 4¹⁵). In this noble sense are the sufferings of Christ central to His gospel, so that St. Peter can justly call himself a witness of the sufferings of Christ (1 P 5[1]).

2. Nor are the followers of Christ to escape the experiences that came to Him (Jn 15[20]). See art. SORROW.   CHARLES W. RISHELL.

SUMMER ($\theta\acute{\epsilon}\rho o\varsigma$, Mt 24[32], Mk 13[28], Lk 21[30]).— This term stands in the Gospels for the time of heat as distinguished from $\chi\epsilon\iota\mu\acute{\omega}\nu$, the season of cold and rain-storms. These terms indicate the great division of the year in the East. Scripture has no special words for 'spring' and 'autumn'; and while the Arab speaks of er-rabî'a, 'the time of fresh pasture,' and el-kharîf, 'the time of gathering' of grapes and other fruits, they are hardly regarded as distinct seasons. Ṣaif wa shitta', 'summer and winter,' sum up the year for him. When, in the less frequent showers of early April, the fig-leaves burst out and cover the immature fruit on the twigs, the days of cloudless sunshine are 'at hand.' These last from April, through the harvest in the end of May, the threshing and winnowing that follow, and the gathering of the fruits in August and September, until the clouds of October herald the coming of rains and cold.

W. EWING.

SUN.—The rising of the sun marks the morning (Mk 16[2]), and its setting the evening (Mk 1[32], Lk 4[40]). Its light is one of the gifts which the Creator bestows on all men without distinction (Mt 5[45]). By 'signs in the sun' (Lk 21[25]) we are to understand the phenomena of eclipse, as described more clearly in the parallel passages, Mt 24[29], Mk 13[24]. The statement in Lk 23[45] as to 'the sun being darkened' (AV) or 'the sun's light failing' (RV) at the time of the Crucifixion, cannot be explained in this way, since an eclipse of the sun can happen only at new moon, whereas the Crucifixion took place at a Passover, when the moon was full. The sun's scorching heat, so destructive to vegetation, is an emblem of tribulation or persecution (Mt 13[6. 21], Mk 4[6. 17]). The appearance of the face of Christ at the Transfiguration (Mt 17[2]) and in the opening vision of the Apocalypse (Rev 1[16]) is compared to the brightness of the sun. The same thing is said of the glory in which the righteous shall appear after the final judgment (Mt 13[43]).

JAMES PATRICK.

SUPERNATURAL.—It is generally recognized that this word is difficult to define, and its definitions are difficult to defend. The reason of this is simple. It is not a scientific but a popular term, and is therefore liable to the ambiguity and vagueness besetting words which really involve metaphysical considerations, but which have grown into use without any proper discussion of the metaphysical questions involved. The word means that which is *beyond* or *above nature*; but the word 'nature' is ambiguous, and it is therefore uncertain what, if anything, corresponds to the word 'supernatural.' In ordinary speech, 'supernatural' would appear to mean anything outside the ordinary course of the phenomenal world. Everything connected with ghosts, for instance, is described as supernatural, and such things as telepathy are said to border on the supernatural. But even in such cases as this the idea attached to the word is not clear. A ghost, let us say, raps on a table, or makes the sound of a carriage driving up to the door. These are perfectly natural and ordinary sounds: they are called 'supernatural' only in the sense that they are produced in an extraordinary way. And by this is apparently meant that the spiritual or volitional cause of the sounds is in an unusual relation to the material world. A chairman rapping on the table at a meeting, or a cabman driving up to the door, is a spiritual or volitional cause of the sounds produced,

but he is in the ordinary relation to matter. So the phenomena of telepathy are said to border on the supernatural, because in them effects are produced in a way which the popular mind regards as peculiarly mysterious.

Those who hold that the world was made and is ruled by God, have to imagine to themselves in some shape the mode in which God exercises His sway. For ordinary purposes it suffices to treat the world as an independent organization, carried on by laws which are regarded as invariable, and it is unnecessary to refer continually to the Primary Cause of all. This view of the world is harmless enough, but it has the disadvantage of developing an inveterate tendency or habit of thought, by which the world is set up over against God, as equivalent to 'nature' or the 'natural order'; while all action on the part of God is treated as having the character of disturbance or interference in an order which possesses independent rights, or as being supernatural, in virtue of the fact that it does interfere or disturb. From this habit of mind come all those phrases by which miracles are described as 'suspensions of the order of nature,' and the like. If a person under the influence of this habit of thought meets with the suggestion that miracles are themselves orderly, and illustrate a higher law than that of ordinary experience, he is disquieted, because he thinks that in losing the character of disturbance, miracles lose their 'supernatural' character.

Two things are clear in regard to this difficulty: (1) that the source of it lies in the (unverified) dualism between God and the world; (2) that there is a real point involved in the distress of the plain man at what he thinks is an attenuation of the meaning of miracle. We will consider the second point first. It is manifest that if the law which governs miracle differed from that governing ordinary experience, merely in complexity, the distinction of natural and supernatural would disappear; so far the plain man is right. A conjurer does not profess to use any but the most ordinary laws: yet a savage might look upon the common trick of bringing live pigeons out of a hat as a real, creative 'supernatural' act. Some of the language used by critics of miracles and the term 'supernatural' have a tendency to bring these events down to the level of tricks or deceptions. It is said, for instance, that a fuller knowledge of natural processes would lead us to see in the miracle at the wedding-feast at Cana merely an acceleration of such processes, which would quite surrender itself to ordinary methods of interpretation. If this were true, the miracle would cease to be in any sense 'supernatural'; it would be merely a special, imperfectly analyzed case of an ordinary occurrence. This is a real attenuation of the meaning of the word, and the plain man is right in objecting to it. But he is wrong if he objects to it on the ground, expressed or implied, that Divine action is necessarily explosive or disruptive; for this would mean that Divine action is irrational, and that a miracle must be as great a marvel to God as to man. Whatever the appearance of the supernatural to us, to God it must appear rational and orderly. God is the author of nature and its laws. Their uniformity represents His normal action and will for the world. But nature and its laws have no independent validity or rights as against God. They are entirely at His disposal and under His control. If, for whatever reason, He diverges from what is normal, it will be for sufficient cause. He will act in a new way upon the old material, reminding man of the dependence of all upon Him. And the difference between the normal and the abnormal action does not consist in the nature of the laws employed, as if the usual operation of natural law were broken or suspended by some intrusive and alien force; but in the fact that the action of God upon the order of created being is in one case what we expect, in the other widely different. There is no reason why the word 'supernatural,' which will certainly not be driven out of our vocabulary, should not be used as a label for certain characteristic groups of actions and events. It appears necessary to vindicate the freedom of God to take such action: otherwise we subject Him to the tyranny of His own laws. But there is no reason to associate the word with a variety of half-conscious dualistic assumptions, which cannot be defended in theory. See also art. MIRACLES.   THOMAS B. STRONG.

SUPERSCRIPTION.—See TITLE ON CROSS.

SUPPER (δεῖπνον).—The term applied in the time of Christ to the principal meal usually partaken of in the evening, and also to more elaborate collations for the entertainment of guests (weddings, birthdays, arrival and departure of friends or distinguished persons, sheep-shearing, completion of wine-making, funerals, etc.). Invitations were conveyed by slaves (Mt 22³ff.). Guests were welcomed by the host with a kiss (Lk 7⁴⁵); their feet were washed by slaves (7⁴⁴); their hair, beards, and sometimes their clothes and feet were anointed with perfumed oil (Lk 7³⁸, Jn 12³); and garlands of flowers were sometimes provided for the decoration of their heads (Wis 2⁷f.; Jos. Ant. XIX. ix. 1). On formal occasions the guests were arranged at the table by the master of the feast (ἀρχιτρίκλινος), usually a friend of the family, according to his conception of their relative social rank, nearness to the host being the mark of honour. Guests commonly reclined on benches (sometimes elaborate and luxurious), three or five to the bench, the feet of each extending behind, and the back of the head of each reaching to the bosom of his neighbour on the left (Jn 13²³ 21²⁰). The tables were usually three in number, arranged to form three sides of a square. The guests reclined upon the outside, and the servants ministered from the inside. The left elbow was used for support, while the right hand and arm were free for conveying food. A somewhat formal giving of thanks preceded each meal (εὐλογία, εὐχαριστία). This practice was carefully observed by Jesus and His disciples (Mt 14¹⁹ 15³⁶ 26²⁶, Lk 9¹⁶, Jn 6¹¹). At suppers of the more formal or festive type the host served the guests with equal portions as far as was practicable, where no special honour was to be done to special guests. In the latter case, a double, triple, or even quintuple, or a particularly choice portion was bestowed upon the guest of honour. At less formal suppers the food was cut into small pieces and put into large dishes, from which the guests took them with their fingers and conveyed them to flat cakes of bread which served as plates, where they pulled them to pieces before conveying them to their mouths. Pieces of the bread were used as spoons for dipping gravy from the common dish. Individual knives, forks, and spoons were not used even by the wealthy until long after NT times. The practice of hand-washing immediately before the meal had thus its special appropriateness. When women were admitted to suppers of the more formal kind (which was probably unusual), they seem to have sat rather than reclined. Wine was drunk during the meal and after the eating (Mishna, Berakhoth vi. 5 f., cf. viii. 8). Thanksgiving and hand-washing closed the meal.

The ordinary suppers of the well-to-do classes were far less formal. The suppers of the poor were no doubt partaken of without tables or seats, the family sitting, or squatting on the ground, around a skin or mat, and partaking of the plain food (flesh being rarely used) out of common vessels with the fingers. See also artt. FOOD, MEALS, and LAST SUPPER.

LITERATURE.—Artt. in the Bible Dictionaries of Smith, Kitto Hastings, Schenkel, Riehm, the EBi, Winer's RWB, Herzog-Hauck, PRE³; Wetzer u. Welte, Kirchen-Lexikon; Lightfoot, Hor. Heb.; E. Robinson, BRP; Buxtorf, de Conviviis Ebræorum; and Ugolini's Thesaurus, vol. xxx.
         ALBERT HENRY NEWMAN.

SUPREMACY.—Few things are more remarkable in the Gospels than the absolute supremacy over nature and man which Christ is represented as both claiming and exercising. In this respect the Synoptics bear, if anything, a more striking witness than the Fourth Gospel. Christ appears from first to last as exercising lordship over matter and natural forces. He heals incurable diseases, stills the storm by a word, multiplies food, withers the barren fig-tree. And, beyond these things, He appears also as supreme over the world of spirits. He calls back the human soul to the body after they have been separated by death. He is acknowledged as lord by the unwilling and undesired testimony of the demons (Mk 1³⁴, Lk 4³³⁻³⁵ etc.). Such a supremacy He appears, in the Gospel narrative, to exert without laying any special claim upon it. He accepts, indeed, with praise the confession of the centurion (Mt 8⁵⁻¹³), that such authority belongs naturally to Him; yet He does not represent these wonders as being the chief purpose of His ministry. He appeals at times to their evidence; but His most characteristic claim is something even greater and more fundamental.

Christ plainly claims supremacy over the moral nature of man, over human conscience and human destiny—a supremacy extending through all time, and without limitation. His association with or subordination to the Father is not referred to as limiting, but rather as justifying His own claim (Mt 16²⁷, Jn 5¹⁹⁻²⁷). On His own sole word He reverses human standards of judgment (Mt 5³⁻¹⁰ 19³⁰, Lk 6²⁰⁻²⁶). He expands, modifies, or abolishes by His own 'I say unto you,' laws or institutions which were admittedly Divine in their origin (Mt 5. 19³⁻⁹; cf. 7²⁸. ²⁹). Yet at the same time He refuses to enter into competition with temporal rulers, or to give decisions, as even a prophet might have done, on human matters of dispute (Jn 6¹⁵, Lk 12¹³. ¹⁴). His supremacy is too great and too comprehensive for Him to involve Himself in such controversies, which men will learn to settle when they have learned the greater lesson. His words, He asserts, are more lasting than heaven and earth (Mt 24³⁵). He proclaims Himself King and Judge of the Kingdom which He is founding. The members of it are His servants, and responsible to Him alone (Mt 24. 25, Mk 13³⁴⁻³⁷, Lk 12³⁵⁻⁴⁸). But His supremacy extends beyond the limits of His own Kingdom. He claims to be the final Judge of all the nations, to allot the eternal punishment or reward of every individual soul (Mt 16²⁷ 25³¹⁻⁴⁶; cf. Mk 13²⁶. ²⁷, Lk 21²⁷. ³⁶). And this universal dominion over both matter and spirit is expressed finally in the tremendous closing verses of Mt., 'All authority hath been given (ἐδόθη, the aorist of an eternal fact) unto me in heaven and in earth.' It is indeed in this Gospel that the claim of Christ to be King and Judge of all men is stated in the most detailed and vivid manner. But there is no inconsistency with the other Gospels. A similar claim is implied in all; cf. esp. Lk 19¹¹⁻²⁷.

In the Acts, Christ is preached by the Apostles as 'Lord' (2³⁶), as 'prince (ἀρχηγός) of life' (3¹⁵), as universal Judge of men (10⁴² 17³¹). St. Paul from the moment of his conversion speaks of Jesus as his absolute Master, whose 'slave' he is (Ro 1¹), whose 'marks' he bears branded upon his body

(Gal 6[17]). The descriptions of the nature and office of Christ in the Epistles of the First Imprisonment state and justify this supremacy in the most startling and comprehensive manner. 'In the name of Jesus' all creation must bow; all creation must confess His Lordship (Ph 2[10, 11]). All things have been created through Him and unto Him : creation not only starts from Him, but converges in Him (Col 1[16-18]). Christ is the 'head of all principality and power' (2[10]). All things are 'in subjection under his feet' (Eph 1[21. 22]).

This supremacy of Christ is again the most characteristic feature of the teaching of the Epistle to the Hebrews. Everywhere the eye of the believer is directed to Him (2[9] 3[1] 4[14] 8[1] 12[2. 3] 13[8. 20]). His figure dominates the whole of man's life ; and the writer plainly implies that this supremacy is essential and indefeasible.

The same teaching appears in a more pictorial form in the changing scenery of the Apocalypse. Christ receives the homage of all creation (Rev 5[9-14]), He is associated with God the Father in the possession of 'the kingdom of the world' (11[15]), He Himself is 'King of kings and Lord of lords' (19[11-16]).

Christian worship, Christian art, Christian sufferings are full of the same testimony. Christ is worshipped personally as Lord and God. He is portrayed as universal ruler, bearing the insignia of empire over all the thoughts and needs and works of men. The martyrs incurred the reproach of disloyalty to temporal rulers, nay, even of being enemies to human society, by their unswerving allegiance to Christ as supreme over all human laws and customs. Polycarp, confronted with death, confesses Him as 'Saviour and King.' The narrative of his martyrdom contrasts the brief authority of Jewish and Roman officials with 'the reign of the eternal King, Jesus Christ' (*Letter of the Smyrnæans*, 21).

The Christ of the Gospels, the Christ of Christian experience, must be supreme or nothing at all. The idea of a limited or temporary supremacy is self-contradictory. The Christian conscience, however laggard the will, cannot but confess the justice of the Master's question : 'Why call ye me Lord, Lord, and do not the things which I say ?' (Lk 6[46]). See also artt. AUTHORITY OF CHRIST, DIVINITY OF CHRIST, KING, LORD.

LITERATURE.—Liddon, *Divinity of our Lord* (Bampton Lectures, 1866); Gore, *Incarnation of the Son of God* (do. 1891); Seeley, *Ecce Homo*, 1866 ; Edersheim, *Life and Times of Jesus the Messiah*, 1883 ; Père Didon, *Jésus Christ*, 1891 ; Sanday, art. 'Jesus Christ' in Hastings' *DB* ; Westcott, *Christus Consummator*, 1887 ; Ellicott, *Christus Comprobator*, 1891 ; Stubbs, *Christus Imperator*, 1894.   A. R. WHITHAM.

SURPRISE.—The word has an objective as well as a subjective reference : it means both 'the act of taking unawares' and 'the emotion caused by anything sudden.' The emotion is closely akin to *wonder*, 'the state of mind produced by something new, unexpected, or extraordinary' ; but sudden emergence is its distinctive characteristic. It may enter in as an element in *disappointment*, when hopes are defeated, purposes miscarry, or efforts are frustrated suddenly. When the nature of an object is inexplicable, unintelligible, when the occurrence of an event is unexpected, uncalculated, *surprise* is felt. It necessarily implies limitation of knowledge, an incapacity of the subject knowing to completely possess and command in thought the object known. In the objective reference, some instances of surprise, or at least the attempt to surprise, are found in the Gospels. The enemies of Jesus tried to 'catch Him in talk' (Mk 12[13], Lk 11[54]) by the questions they put to Him. They 'watched Him whether He would heal on the Sabbath day, that they might find an accusation

against him' (Lk 6[7]). He had to be constantly on His guard against their malignity. By the treachery of Judas they were able to surprise Him, unprotected by the multitude, in Gethsemane. Peter's denial was in some measure due to his being taken by surprise, even although Jesus had forewarned him. It is in the subjective reference of the term that we are specially interested in reading the Gospels—the surprise Jesus felt and the surprise He caused. So different was Jesus in character, purpose, spirit, from His environment, that He could not always understand it, still less could it understand Him. During His earthly ministry the secrets of all hearts were not laid bare to Him, although He occasionally displayed an extraordinary insight into the thoughts and wishes of others ; nor was the veil of the future altogether withdrawn, even although He did, in regard to His own death and resurrection, and the doom of the city which rejected Him, show an exceptional knowledge. But supernatural as in these respects His knowledge was, it was not a Divine omniscience—for which *surprise* is impossible, as for it there is neither the inexplicable nor the unexpected. The subject of the limitation of Jesus' knowledge is more fully dealt with in the art. KENOSIS. Jesus was *surprised* by the anxiety felt and the search made for Him by His parents, when He remained behind in the Temple. 'How is it that ye sought me ?' (Lk 2[49]) ; He 'marvelled because of their unbelief' in Nazareth (Mk 6[6]) ; He was disappointed at the dulness of understanding of His disciples (Mt 15[17] 16[9. 11]), and of His hearers in Jerusalem (Jn 8[43]), and at the unbelief of His generation (Mk 8[12]). But, on the other hand, the faith of the centurion (Mt 8[10]) and of the Syrophœnician woman (Mt 15[28]), brought Him glad surprise. The storm on the Sea of Galilee (Mt 8[24]) was a surprise to Him even as to His disciples, although His faith was not disturbed as theirs was ; so also He knew not that He was sending His disciples into any danger when He dismissed them after the feeding of the five thousand (Mt 14[22] ; see the discussion of these two incidents in Adamson's *The Mind in Christ*, pp. 5–10). He was disappointed in His desire for rest with His disciples (Mk 6[31. 34]), and for secrecy (Mk 7[24. 25]). He expected to find fruit on the barren fig-tree (Mk 11[13]). Although the growing estrangement of Judas was, from its beginnings, perceived by Him (Jn 6[64] ; see Dods' comment *in loco* in *Expositor's Gr. Test.* i. p. 759), yet when He called him He did not anticipate his treachery. His state in Gethsemane was one of *amazement* (Mk 14[33]) ; there was an element in the doom He looked forward to that He could not understand, and had not looked for. His amazement is expressed in the cry of desolation on the Cross (Mt 27[46]). What He then experienced was worse than He had anticipated. As man's sin had ever been a surprise to Him, so was its worst consequence when it fell on Him.

Jesus Himself so transcended the world in which He lived, taught, and wrought, that He was constantly a surprise to men. This He Himself expected (Jn 3[7] 5[20. 28] 7[21]). The marvel began with Joseph and Mary in the Temple at Simeon's prophecy, and at Jesus' own words (Lk 2[33. 50]). The multitudes marvelled at His teaching, His healing, His forgiveness of sins, His wisdom in answering the questions of His opponents, and His grace in preaching the gospel (Mk 1[22. 27], Mt 7[28. 29], Mk 2[12] 5[20. 42], Mt 9[8. 33] 12[23], Lk 9[43] 7[49], Mt 22[22], Lk 20[26] 4[22]). His disciples were astonished at His command over the storm (Mk 6[51]), His teaching regarding the rich (Mt 19[25]), and the curse on the fig-tree (Mt 21[20]). His disregard of the current customs caused surprise (Lk 11[38], Jn 4[27]), as did the freedom from these He allowed to His disciples (Mk 2[18] 7[5]). The world's surprise at Jesus is its tribute to His unique perfection ; His surprise at man's sin and unbelief the evidence of its need of the grace and truth of the Son of God. See, further, AMAZEMENT.

LITERATURE.—A. J. Mason, *Conditions of Our Lord's Life on Earth*, 135–138 ; T. Adamson, *Studies of the Mind in Christ*, 5–12, 167 ; Gore, *BL* 147 f.   ALFRED E. GARVIE.

SUSANNA (Σουσάννα fr. שׁוֹשַׁנָּה, fem. of שׁוֹשָׁן, which denotes a lily or any lily-like flower).—All that is known of her is that she was one of the women who ministered to Jesus (Lk 8[3]). The mention of her name without further particulars implies that she was well known. This may have been due to her special devotion, in which case reference to her on other occasions would have been expected, or to her social rank, which view may derive support from the succession of her name to that of Joanna (wh. see).   R. W. MOSS.

SWADDLING CLOTHES.—The custom of wrapping the newborn infant in bands of cloth (σπαργανόω) has long prevailed, and still exists in the East. This treatment was supposed to make for the strengthening and proper growth of the back and limbs, as well as being convenient for carrying the child. The infant Jesus was not neglected in this particular, though laid in the manger (Lk 2[7. 12]) ; the absence of swaddling bands being regarded as a sign of extreme poverty or of neglect (cf. Ezk 16[4]).   E. B. POLLARD.

SWEARING.—See OATHS.

SWEAT.—The word 'sweat' occurs only in one passage in the NT, namely Lk 22[44], in the narrative of our Lord's agony in Gethsemane, where we read : ' His sweat became, as it were, great drops of blood falling down upon the ground.' In approaching the discussion of the passage there are three matters to be considered : (1) the textual problem, (2) the interpretation of the words 'became, as it were,' and (3) the possibility of the phenomenon known as 'bloody sweat' (*hæmadrosis*).

1. In turning first to the textual question, we find that vv. [43. 44] are omitted in many of the best authorities for the text of the NT (the great uncials ℵ[a]ABRT). A number of other uncials (ESVΓΔΠ) mark the passage as doubtful ; and in the case of Codex ℵ the hand of one corrector has apparently inserted it, while that of another has deleted it. The Church Fathers, Hilary, Jerome, and others bear witness that there were many MSS known to them which did not contain these two verses ; and certain MSS insert them in the parallel passage in Mt.'s Gospel, namely after Mt 26[39]. Of the Versions, one MS of the Old Latin omits them, as do also the best of the Egyptian, Armenian, and the oldest Syriac versions. Cyril of Alexandria omits the verses in his *Homilies* on Lk.'s Gospel, while the silence of such writers as Clement of Alexandria and Origen cannot be without significance. One cursive MS (124) omits them, while No. 13 has them inserted by a corrector. In the Greek Lectionaries the verses are generally omitted from the lesson in which they would naturally appear, but are inserted in the Mt. passage, a custom that seems to have influenced Chrysostom in his reference to the passage, though, as WH admit, ' a mere comparison of the parallel narratives of the Evangelists would suffice to suggest to him the reference.' On the other hand, the MSS that include the verses as they stand in Lk. are the following : uncials ℵ*DFGHKLM QUXΛ, and nearly all cursives. While A omits

the passage, as we have seen, it has the reference section-number in the margin, showing that its presence in other MSS must have been known to the scribe. The verses are contained also in the majority of the MSS of the Old Latin, some few Egyptian, the Syr-Pesh. and Syr-Hier. They are known also to Justin Martyr (who quotes them in his *Dialogue with Trypho*, 103), Iren., Jerome, and Augustine. The verses gave rise to much discussion among early writers, some of whom held that they had been wilfully cut out by some who were afraid of their employment by unorthodox writers ; though, on the other hand, they constituted a strong weapon of proof against those who denied the reality of our Lord's humanity.

The conclusion to be drawn from this evidence is that the main witness to the presence of the verses is of a Western order ; but this need not mean more than that, as is the habit of the Western text of Lk. in particular, many elements of tradition that would otherwise have been lost are contained in it. This is the conclusion to which WH come. Their words are : ' These verses can only be a fragment from the traditions, written or oral, which were, for a while at least, locally current beside the canonical Gospels, and which doubtless included matter of every degree of authenticity and intrinsic value. These verses and the first sentence of 23[34] may be safely called the most precious among the remains of this Evangelic tradition which were rescued from oblivion by the scribes of the 2nd century.' Neither do these editors think that there is any evidence of the omission of the verses for doctrinal reasons. It would appear, therefore, as if they stood very much in the same position as does the *Pericope Adulteræ* ; that is, as an early story of the Evangelic tradition that had not found its way into all the copies of the canonical Gospels.

2. The next point to consider is the interpretation of the words 'as it were great drops of blood.' Here again there is a secondary question of reading, because certain manuscripts and versions (ℵVX, Vulg. Boh.) read the genitive of the word rendered ' falling down,' agreeing with the word for ' blood,' and not the nominative in agreement with the word for ' drops,' as do the majority of the authorities. The Greek word θρόμβος, either with or without αἵματος, can itself bear the meaning 'a drop of blood,' and is so used in classical Greek writers (see Æsch. *Eum.* 184 ; Plato, *Crit.* 120 A). Tatian in his *Diatessaron* renders in an exaggerated form, ' like a stream of blood,' which Bernard supposes would be visible in the moonlight.

When Justin quotes the verse he also omits 'of blood' ; but this may be because he regarded the word θρόμβοι as bearing that signification. Even when all is said, however, the expression may not mean more than that there was a resemblance between the falling of the heavy drops of perspiration and the plashing of blood-gouts from a wound, so that the verse does not absolutely and necessarily assert that blood flowed from our Lord's body in the moment of His extreme anguish.

In a special discussion of the subject by Harnack, that writer maintains that the stamp of Lk. is clearly manifest on the verses in question, and it is to be remembered that it is a very remarkable thing that the only record of this event should occur in the Gospel attributed to the man whom tradition asserts to have been a physician, and whose own language supports the statement. This remarkable phenomenon is the very thing we should expect a physician to take special pains carefully to record. Harnack in the same discussion draws attention to the passage in Jn 12[27-30], which he regards as that Evangelist's account of the same incident. It is remarkable that while the passage in Lk. speaks of an angel succouring Jesus, the passage in the Fourth Gospel tells of a voice from heaven that answered His prayer, which voice was regarded by some of the people as that of an angel. In Harnack's opinion the Fourth Gospel draws its material for the Passion narrative from the Synoptics, and here he thinks we have another version of the story contained in Luke. Harnack also reminds us that there are two points in the Lukan story that would offend orthodox readers, first, the mention of an angel as strengthening our Lord, which might be a strong support to those who exaggerated the importance of angel ministry ; and, second, the fact that the agony was the result of an inward struggle, which might be taken as pointing to too great human weakness in our Lord's Person to be consonant with the full maintenance of His Divine nature.

3. There has been much discussion as to whether such a thing as a bloody sweat is a possibility, and here we come into the realm of medical evidence. Much has been written on the matter, both in older days and up to the present time; a great deal of it, one must admit, being irrelevant. The less critical medical writers of an earlier time were content to quote Galen as their authority for the statement that sometimes ' the pores are so vastly dilated by a copious and fervent spirit, that even blood issues through them and constitutes a bloody sweat' (see R. Mead, *Medical Works*, 1762, ch. 13). The most recent medical conclusion on the subject seems to be that it is physically possible for blood to exude through the sweat glands, as the contiguity of the blood vessels and these glands is so close and oftentimes the walls that divide them are so extremely thin.* It may thus be granted that such an event as the ordinary text describes was a possibility, though nothing very closely allied to it has ever been observed, and one would naturally manifest great caution in accepting the historicity of it, in view of all that has already been said about the passage.

Some writers have understood the phrase 'drops of blood' as a purely figurative one, being simply expressive of the intense agony undergone by the sufferer, and not in any sense to be taken either literally or as even suggesting that the perspiration was itself so heavy as to suggest the dripping of blood.

There remains one interesting instance of the use of the verb 'sweat' in a passage of the early Christian writing known as the *Didache*, where in ch. 1 we read, 'Let thine alms sweat into thine hands until thou shalt have learned to whom to give.' The words, indeed, are not actually quoted as Christ's, but there can be little question that the author regarded them as a traditional saying of the Lord.

LITERATURE.—The Comm. on the passage, esp. Plummer, *ad loc.*, and the additional note on p. 544 ; Holtzmann in the *Hdcom.* ; the *Expos. Gr. Test.* ; WH, 'Notes on Select Readings,' pp. 64–67 ; Hastings' *DB*, art. ' Medicine' ; *Encyc. Bibl.*, art. ' Sweat(Bloody),' col. 4824, also ' Cross,' par. 5, col. 959; Harnack's discussion in *Sitzungsber. der Berl. Akad. der Wissensch.* 1901 ; Quain's *Dict. of Medicine* (ed. 1902, Murray), 'Sudoriparous Glands (Diseases of)' ; R. Mead, *Medical Works*, 1762, p. 630 ; W. Stroud, *A Treatise on the Physical Cause of the Death of Christ*, 1847 ; *Allgemeine Ztschr. für Psychiatrie*, 1863, xx. 51 ; on the case of Louise Lateau see *Macmillan's Mag.* 1871, and *Lancet*, 1871, 1, 543 ; Gould and Pyle, *Anomalies and Curiosities of Medicine*, 1897, ix. 388 ff. ; T. M. Anderson, *Contributions to Clinical Medicine*, 1898, p. 43 ; Besnier et Jacquet, *La pratique dermatologique*, vol. iv. 1904, pp. 420–424 ; Hobart, *Medical Language of St. Luke*, 79 ff. ; Harnack, *Luke the Physician* [Eng. tr.], 194 n.   G. CURRIE MARTIN.

SWINE.—See ANIMALS in vol. i. p. 64[b].

SWORD.—In Lk 2[35] and in some passages in the Apocalypse the word for 'sword' is ῥομφαία ; elsewhere in the NT it is μάχαιρα. The former denoted a weapon used by barbarous nations, especially the Thracians (Livy, xxxi. 39 : 'Thracas quoque romphææ ingentis et ipsæ longitudinis, inter objectos undique ramos impediebant'). It thus appears to have been rather a lance or javelin than a sword, and so may reflect the Hebrew *rōmah*. In the Syr. of Lk 2[35] the word used is *romha*, and the phrase is probably a reminiscence of Ps 37[15] (LXX). The word μάχαιρα may denote nothing

*In the case of hæmophilic persons it seems not only possible but probable. Again, however, the relevancy is not very apparent.

more than a knife or dagger, as in the LXX of Jos 5[2, 3] of flint knives, but also a sword. The people who came to arrest Jesus were armed with swords and clubs : Jesus' followers also had two swords, which Jesus declared to be enough ; and one of them (Peter) drew his sword and wounded a servant of the high priest (Mt 26[47-55], Mk 14[43-48], Lk 22[36-52], Jn 18[10. 11]).

Metaphorically the sword stands as a symbol for war (to 'fall by the edge of the sword' means to die in war), or for a divided state of society (Mt 10[34] 'I came not to send peace, but a sword' [in Lk 12[51] 'division ']). In Mt 26[52] 'They that take the sword shall perish with the sword,' the sword probably denotes the use of physical force generally, although we have also the belief that a tyrant is despatched with the very weapon which he employs against the victims of his tyranny. The expression in Lk 2[35] 'A sword shall pierce through thy own soul,' was sometimes interpreted as a prediction of martyrdom (Epiphanius, *Hær.* 78).
                 T. H. WEIR.

SYCAMINE.—The sycamine-tree (συκάμινος) is mentioned in the Gospels only once, viz. in Lk 17[6]. The Heb. םיִמְקִשׁ, from which the Gr. name seems to be derived, denotes the **sycomore,** but the sycamine is by general consent identified with the black mulberry (*Morus nigra*). In his Hebrew NT, Delitzsch renders by חות, which is the name given to the mulberry in the Mishna (cf. Arab. *tût*). Two species are common in modern Palestine, the black mulberry and the white (*M. alba*). The latter, however, which is cultivated for purposes of sericulture, and whose fruit, owing to its insipidity, was little eaten, was hardly likely to be known in our Lord's time. The black mulberry, on the other hand, yields a compound fruit which, eaten fresh, is of fine flavour, and is a great favourite in the East. This tree, which is deciduous, has a dense foliage, and affords a most welcome shade during the heat of summer.

Thomson (*LB* pp. 23, 24) would identify the sycamine with the sycomore. In support of this view he appeals to the common Hebrew origin of the two names ; but his main argument is that

' the mulberry is more easily plucked up by the roots than any other tree of the same size in the country, and the thing is oftener done. Hundreds of them are plucked up every year in this vicinity, and brought to the city for firewood. It is not to be supposed,' he adds, ' that He who spake as man never spoke would select this tree, with its short, feeble roots, to illustrate the irresistible power of faith.'

The argument is plausible, but not conclusive. On the contrary, what weight it has must be laid in the scale against this theory rather than in its support. The rooting up of the mulberry tree was a common practice. Granted ; but was it not from the commonest doings and happenings that our Lord habitually drew His illustrations ? When He would find some fit emblem of the Kingdom of God, He appealed not to the unusual but to the familiar, not to the heroic but to the homely. One of the marked charms of His teaching is the gift He had of making the commonplaces of earth speak the language of heaven. When, therefore, He would figure forth ' the irresistible power of faith,' it need not surprise us that He selected the mulberry tree, the uprooting of which was quite familiar to His hearers. True, it was more easily plucked up than any other tree of the size. But that fact does not impair the force of the figure. The law of gravitation is as clearly manifested in the fall of the leaf as in the majestic order of the planets, and the power of faith is as vividly illustrated in the figure of uprooting a mulberry tree by the word of command, as in that of uprooting a sycomore, or even of moving a mountain.
                 HUGH DUNCAN.

SYCHAR (Συχάρ) is mentioned in connexion with

the journey of Jesus from Judæa to Galilee recorded in Jn 4[4f.]. We learn from v.[5f.] that He came 'to a city of Samaria called Sychar, near to the parcel of ground that Jacob gave to his son Joseph: and Jacob's well (πηγή) was there'; v.[11] adds the information that 'the well (φρέαρ)' was 'deep.' Jacob's fountain, referred to here, is one of the undisputed sites of the Gospels. It lies in the mouth of the valley running up between Mts. Ebal and Gerizim to Shechem, 1½ miles E. of the city and about 1100 yds. from the traditional site of Joseph's Tomb (Jos 24[32]). The source of its water is still uncertain. Probably rainfall and percolation contributed most to the supply. According to Sanday (*Sacred Sites of the Gospels*, 32), 'it is possible that the special sacredness and real excellence of the water (on a hot day it is beautifully soft and refreshing) had something to do with' the presence of the woman from Sychar, though it has been suggested that she was fetching water for workmen employed on the adjacent cornlands and not for her own household. Now Sychar lay 'near' Jacob's ground and well, and the problem is whether it should be (1) identified with **Shechem**, or (2) located at the little hamlet of '*Askar*, near the foot of Ebal, about a mile N. of the well and 1¾ miles E.N.E. of Nâblus. The balance of expert opinion seems to be in favour of the latter identification.

In support of (1), several considerations have been adduced. (*a*) Shechem could certainly be roughly described as 'near' Jacob's ground, and the disciples who went to 'the city' to buy bread were away during the whole of the conversation, that is, for some considerable time. Cheyne (*Encyc. Bibl.* iv. 4831) considers it unlikely that 'the city' which fills such a prominent place in the narrative of Jn 4 should be any other than Shechem. Then (*b*) Jerome (*Ep.* 86 and *Quæst. Heb. in Gen.* 48. 22) states that Sichem and Sichar are one and the same place, and that Συχάρ is a copyist's error for Συχέμ. Cheyne defends Jerome's hypothesis, holding that modern criticism has *not* disproved its possibility. It has also been urged (*c*) that the Jews called Shechem *Shikor* (='drunken') and *Sheḳer* (='false')—hence the transition from Shechem to Sychar. It can be added (*d*) that, for centuries after Jerome's time, his view was adopted by 'pilgrim' writers, among whom may be mentioned Arculf (A.D. 700), Saewulf (*c.* 1102), Theoderich (1172), Maundeville (1322), and Tuchem of Nurnberg (1480).

But strong objection has been taken to most of these contentions, in favour of (2). (*a*) Over against Cheyne's expression of opinion as to the likelihood of identification with Shechem may be set the view of G. A. Smith (*HGHL* 368), that the Evangelist, who had such a good acquaintance with the OT, could not, in face of Gn 33[19] and Jos 24[32], have substituted (in error) *Sychar* for *Sychem*, and that if he possessed only such knowledge of the locality as the OT gave him, he would have used the name Συχέμ (like Stephen in Ac 7[16]). Then (*b*) Jerome offers no evidence for his identification, and Συχάρ has now been generally adopted as the correct reading. Also Jerome translates Eusebius' note, which *separates* Sychar from Neapolis (or Shechem), without comment or correction (in *Onom. s.v.* 'Sychar'). (*c*) There is no proof whatever that the nicknames 'Shikor' and 'Sheḳer' were ever given to Shechem (*HGHL* 369, and *Encyc. Bibl.* iv. 4830). And (*d*) in spite of the pilgrims' belief in Jerome, there is clear evidence for Sychar as a separate town, from the 4th cent. onwards.

The evidence just referred to is briefly as follows. Eusebius (*Onom. s.v.* Συχάρ) writes to the effect that Sychar lay 'before Neapolis, near the

piece of ground which Jacob gave to his son Joseph, where Christ, according to John, held discourse with the Samaritan woman, by the fountain: it is shown to this day.' Jerome simply translates this, adding in place of the last sentence, 'ubi nunc ecclesia fabricata est.' [But see Eusebius' *Onom. s.v.* Συχέμ and Βάλανος Σικιμῶν, where *Shechem* is distinguished from Neapolis]. The Bordeaux Pilgrim (*c.* 330 A.D.) mentions a Sychar distinct from Shechem, and about a Roman mile away— to which testimony must be added that of the *Itinerary of Jerusalem* (A.D. 333), and later on of the Abbot Daniel (A.D. 1106), of Fetellus (1130), and of John of Würzburg (*c.* 1165). In the *Samaritan Chronicle* (not later than the 14th cent.) a town spelt '*Ischar* (with initial Aleph) is referred to, 'apparently near Shechem' and the same as Sychar. Finally, the traveller Berggren found the name '*Askar* or '*Asgar* (with Ayin) given both to a spring and to the whole plain. This name still attaches to the modern village at the foot of Ebal. G. A. Smith (*HGHL* 371) and Cheyne (*Encyc. Bibl.* iv. 4831) agree that '*Askar* may well have grown out of *Suchar*—the intermediary form being '*Ischar*. There is a parallel in the case of 'Ashḳelon, mod. '*Askalan*. To this evidence for separating Shechem and Sychar must be added references in the Talmud (noted by Lightfoot) to a place called *Suchar* or *Sichar*, a 'fountain of Suchar' and 'a plain of en-Suchar.' The spring and the plain just mentioned can hardly be other than those referred to by Berggren (*Reise*, ii. 267).

These references and opinions seem to justify the conclusion that St. John's Sychar is the modern '*Askar*, with its ruins and fine spring.

LITERATURE.—Hastings' *DB* iv. 635; *Encyc. Bibl.* iv. 4828 f.; Robinson, *BRP* iii. 133; Stanley, *SP* 240 f., 223 (note); Thomson, *Land and Book*, ch. 31; Buhl, *GAP* 203; Sanday, *Sacred Sites*, 31–33, 91; Baedeker-Socin, *Pal.* pp. 328, 337; G. A. Smith, *HGHL* 367 f.; Ewald, *Gesch.* iv. 284; Neubauer, *Géoa. du Talm.* 169; Raumer, *Pal.* p. 163.   A. W. COOKE.

SYCOMORE. — The sycomore tree (συκομορέα, Lk 19[4] only), of which mention is made in the story of Zacchæus, is the *Ficus sycomorus*. The Gr. name means literally a 'fig-mulberry,' and was bestowed upon it because it yielded a fruit akin to the fig, while its leaves, which are heart-shaped, bore some resemblance to those of the mulberry. In the OT it is called *shiḳmîm* (1 K 10[27] etc.), from which is probably derived the Gr. συκάμινος, though that denotes a quite different tree (see SYCAMINE). The sycomore, which must not be confounded with the British sycamore (*Acer pseudo-Platanus*), flourishes best in districts having a warm, equable climate. In Palestine it is found principally along the coast and in the low-lying plains around Jericho, and is often planted by the roadside. In the extreme north of Syria it is not met with, as it is not hardy enough to withstand the occasional frosts (Ps 78[47]). It attains a great size, and its principal branches being long and wide-spreading, and its foliage plentiful, it yields a most delightful shade. It is deciduous, but the old leaves do not fall off till the new ones come out. Its fruit resembles that of the common fig (*Ficus carica*), but is much smaller, and very much inferior in flavour. It is eaten only by the poorer classes of the population. The 'figs,' of which there are several crops each year, grow on short, leafless stems which spring from the trunk and from the larger branches. The process of ripening is hastened by cutting off the apex of the fruit or making an incision in it (cf. Am 7[14] where the prophet describes himself as בּוֹלֵס שִׁקְמִים, a 'nipper of sycomore-figs'). The tree is very easily climbed, and its lower branches are a favourite perch for children.   HUGH DUNCAN.

SYMEON.—See SIMEON, No. **2.**

SYMPATHY.—The subject of sympathy, considered in its relation to Jesus Christ, is so large as to be almost co-extensive with His whole life and work. The Incarnation and the Atonement, whatever be the exact theological meaning of the two words, are undoubtedly exhibitions of the intense sympathy which resulted not only in the human ministry of Christ, but in the redemption of the world. It is therefore impossible here to treat fully of the sympathy of Christ in its broader aspect. The scope of the present article will be limited to the consideration how far the sympathy of Christ which made the redemption of the world possible was manifested in His dealings as the Son of Man with His fellow-men.

1. The miracles as expressive of sympathy.—(*a*) *Miracles of healing.*—The miracles of healing are truer expressions of the sympathy of Christ to us to-day than they were in the earlier days when miracles were regarded more as a proof of His Divinity than an incident connected with it. The tendency of Biblical critics of late years has been to modify very considerably the scepticism of a generation ago. Especially in reference to cures of disorders of a nervous character, men of science have no hesitation in admitting the power of such a Personality as that of Jesus Christ in dealing with these complaints. Yet this way of regarding the miracles adds greatly to the significance they possess as expressive of human sympathy. The power to perform such acts of healing presupposes a combination of the tenderest sympathy with commanding authority, and it is interesting to consider that some, at least, of these miracles are instances of *sympathy* according to its etymological meaning (σύν, παθεῖν), and that Christ Himself shared the suffering in the act of relieving it. This idea is suggested by His remark with regard to the healing of certain demoniacs (Mk 9²⁹), that the performance of the miracle must be preceded by prayer, and is illustrated in the healing of the woman with the issue of blood (Mk 5³⁰), when Christ perceived 'that virtue had gone out of him.' According to this view, the healing ministry is not to be regarded as a proof of His Divinity so much as an outcome of it; and in this context it is especially important to notice that He never appears as a mere worker of marvels, but in a larger and grander way as the friend of sufferers, relieving their physical suffering, no less than their sorrows and their sins, by human sympathy.

(*b*) *Nature miracles.*—The sympathy of Christ, as revealed in His miracles, was not confined to the relief of physical sufferings occasioned by disease. The feeding of the 5000 (Mk 6³⁵ etc.) shows sympathy for the ordinary needs of the body; the raising of Jairus' daughter, of the widow's son at Nain, and of Lazarus at Bethany, illustrates His sympathetic interest in family life with all its joys and sorrows. The stilling of the storm (Mk 4³⁷) shows His willingness to allay the fears of His disciples in the time of personal danger. Standing in a class by itself among the miracles is the turning of the water into wine (Jn 2), and yet this is an act of especial interest as revealing an aspect of the sympathy of Christ which must be borne in mind. It reminds us that His sympathy extended to a wider range than the mere relief of distress. He who watched the games of the children in the market-place, as they played at weddings and funerals (Mt 11¹⁷, Lk 7³²), and used their games as illustrations in His discourses, entered no less readily into the social pleasures of their elders. The sympathy of Christ was broad enough to cause Him to desire actively

to promote social happiness, and to supply not merely the necessaries of life, but the means of enjoying its luxuries.

2. Christ's teaching as expressive of sympathy.—What Christ showed by His own deeds and actions to be the rightful attitude in dealing with others, He also enunciated clearly in His teaching, which may be regarded as the ethical counterpart of His sympathy. The central feature of Christ's teaching dealt with the 'Kingdom of God,' and the subjects and members of this Kingdom in their relation to one another no less than in their relation to God. The Sermon on the Mount is full of His teaching on this subject. The 'Reign of God' would witness the transmission of the Divine love and sympathy into the various subjects of the Kingdom. The clearest enunciation of the principle is in His 'Golden Rule,' which bids us place ourselves in the position of others in order that we may be guided as to the effect of our actions upon them (Mt 7¹²). Combined with this are His various injunctions to be merciful (Mt 5⁷, Lk 6³⁶), forgiving (Mt 6¹⁴, Lk 17³), pitiful (Mt 18³³), and to show these qualities to enemies as well as to friends (Mt 5⁴⁴). In all these cases the Divine example is adduced as the chief motive. God makes His rain to fall on the evil and on the good, on the just and on the unjust; and His children must be ready to follow His example, to reconcile an offended brother, and to forgive an enemy. The teaching is further illustrated in several of the parables. The unmerciful servant (Mt 18²³⁻³⁵) forfeited his claim on God's mercy. Every act of love and kindliness would be revealed in the final separation on the Judgment Day as done to Himself (Mt 25³¹⁻⁴⁶). The parable of the Good Samaritan (Lk 10³⁰) taught the universal brotherhood of man, apart from the artificial distinctions of creed and country; that of the Prodigal Son (Lk 15²⁰) shows the Great Father as bestowing the same mercy and forbearance as He would have us display. The parable of Dives and Lazarus (Lk 16¹⁹⁻³¹), again, inculcates the duty of mercy, while that of the Pharisee and the Publican (Lk 18⁹) was directed against certain who 'despised others.' Such teaching as this is thoroughly in keeping with the life of One whose chief occupation was to go about doing good, and who on the cross prayed for His murderers.

3. Christ's relation to others as expressive of sympathy.—(*a*) *Christ's relation to sinners.*—By His friendly attitude towards 'publicans and sinners' He gave a practical expression of His doctrine of mankind, and of the power of human sympathy to reclaim. The great social gathering of outcasts in Capernaum (Mk 2¹⁵⁻¹⁷), brought together by Levi or Matthew, was a concrete statement of the great truth that a man at his worst is still a man, and a bearer of the Divine image, however that image may have been defaced by faults of character and actual sin. It was this attitude towards the individual—an attitude so different from the conventional attitude of the religious world of the day—that gave Him power over such a soul as Mary Magdalene. Two classical instances of this power may be quoted, and both from St. Luke's Gospel. One is the feast in the house of Simon the Pharisee (Lk 7³⁶ff.). The contrast is pointed between the self-righteous host and the sinful woman who loved much because she had been forgiven much. Christ had come to call not the righteous, but sinners to repentance, and so His work lay with the publican, with the harlot, and the poor. The other instance is that of Zacchæus (Lk 19¹⁻¹⁰). The reclaiming of Zacchæus is an illustration of the fact that a man will tend to assimilate his character to the opinions which others entertain of him. Zacchæus was an outcast only so long as he was treated as an outcast. Jesus reclaimed him not by condoling with his trials, not by talking to him about his soul or by preaching to him about his sins, but simply by treating him as a friend and an equal. His simple words, 'I will abide at thy house,' seemed to identify Him with the publican, and to acknowledge a brother.

(b) *Christ's relation to various people.*—His sympathy was not confined to publicans and sinners. He was sorry for the young man whose riches stood between him and life. He could deal with the unbelief of Thomas and the fall of Peter. His heart went out particularly to those who were in any spiritual need, and the conversation with the woman of Samaria shows how the 'doctrine of mankind' rose superior to the superficial cleavages of race, descent, occupation, or even character, and pronounced them all of small account in comparison with that which is common to all humanity —a soul. Indeed, as His whole mission was one of self-sacrifice and compassion for the race, it is fitting that the rare instances recorded of His weeping should be for the sorrows of others—at the grave of Lazarus—and for the sufferings of Jerusalem, rather than in the Garden of Gethsemane or for His own sufferings; and that in His death-pangs His thoughts should be on the daughters of Jerusalem, on His mother, on the dying robber, and on His murderers, rather than on Himself. It is left to the writer of the Epistle to the Hebrews (4[15f.]) to state plainly the continuing nature of the Divine compassion of the Son of Man : 'We have not an high priest which cannot be touched with the feeling of our infirmities ; but was in all points tempted like as we are, yet without sin. Let us therefore come boldly,' etc.

4. Characteristics of Christ's sympathy.—(a) *It was universal.*—It was not evoked by any one need, but by every need of which the human nature is capable. He could rejoice with them that did rejoice, and weep with them that wept. His presence at festivities of various kinds caused the Pharisees to bestow on Him the title of 'glutton and wine-bibber.' He appears at other times as the patron of family life, sharing alike in its joys and sorrows. Yet amid all this there stands out conspicuously the claim of the outcast, which He expressed Himself by saying that 'the Son of Man was come to seek and to save that which was lost' (Lk 19[10]). The call of pain, whether bodily, mental, or spiritual, was especially strong.

(b) *It was individual.*—There is a vague way of speaking of the work of Christ in the Atonement which does not realize the tender, affectionate, and personal love by which that constant reconciliation is effected. The sympathy of Christ was not merely love of men in masses. He loved the masses, but He loved them because they were made up of individuals. 'He calleth his own sheep by name' (Jn 10[3]). Christ held the master-key to the being of each one. In the Garden He uttered the one word 'Mary' (Jn 20[16]). Many had called her by that name before, but none with the same revealing and interpreting inflexion. It is true that 'he had compassion on the multitude,' but He had also discriminating, special tenderness for erring Peter and Thomas. He felt for the despised and lonely Zacchæus in the sycomore tree. He had compassion on the discomfort of His disciples. He added His tears to those of others by the grave of Lazarus. He called the abashed children to His side. He detected the individual touch of faith : 'Master, the multitude throngs thee, and sayest thou, Who touched me? . . . Someone hath touched me' (Lk 8[45f.]).

(c) *It was loving and judicious.*—Sympathy is not always welcomed by those on whom it is bestowed. When it savours of superiority, it is resented more than scorn. Yet this was never the case with Christ's sympathy. 'He knew what was in man' (Jn 2[25]), and was capable of sympathizing in the full meaning of the word,—of entering into the state of the individual for the time being, and of identifying Himself with it. An interesting question arises on account of the persistent mention of the need for faith on the part of the recipient of His acts of compassion, and it has been asked whether mutual sympathy was the medium of the miraculous cures. Suffice it to say here that the sympathy of Christ was so tactful and so judicious as to inspire confidence, and with it the faith that was needful on the part of the sufferer to co-operate in the work of relief.

(d) *It was practical.* — Christ did not openly sympathize with the sinner as such on account of the supposed beauty inherent in the sinner's nature, as has been suggested by a recent writer of the æsthetic school (Oscar Wilde, *De Profundis*, pp. 113–116). He sympathized only with the sinner in whom the germ, at any rate, of repentance was present. Compassion would have been wasted upon the Pharisees ; stern treatment was necessary there. They were in the position of a man who suffers from a hidden disease, and must have it revealed to himself before he will co-operate in effecting a cure. Divine sympathy is a remedy which can operate only when the wound is open.

(e) *It was free from mere sentiment.*—The sympathy of Christ has nothing in common with a type of modern humanitarian sentiment, which is but a parody of the Divine compassion. There is a tendency to prize feeling *qua* feeling, and to praise and admire its possessor. There is a kind of sympathy which exists only to palliate sin,—to excuse it on grounds of environment, antecedents, and other causes. Such sympathy rarely does good, and generally leaves the sinner where it finds him. Christ's sympathy was no such exotic, beautiful to look at, too delicate to use. With Him feeling led to this : 'He went about doing good' (Ac 10[38]). With Him sympathy expressed itself in this : 'grace to help in time of need' (He 4[16]).

(f) *It was consistent with sinlessness.*—There is an idea that it is necessary to have experienced a state of mind to be able to enter into it with proper sympathy, and that it is necessary for us to obtain experimental proof of the power of sin in order to sympathize with those who are under its sway. This was not so with Christ. He could sympathize with the sinner, because He knew what it was to be tempted. He had all the natural appetites of mind and body. 'He *suffered* being tempted' (He 2[18]). Yet He exhibited a sinless nature by a perfect subjugation of the desire to sin to the will to do right. And the sympathy of Christ is valuable in disproving the fallacy that only the guilty can sympathize with the guilty. 'We have not an high priest which cannot be touched with the feeling of our infirmities ; but was in all points tempted like as we are, *yet without sin*' (He 4[15]). See, further, art. PITY.

LITERATURE.—F. W. Robertson, *Serm.* i. 99 ; A. B. Bruce, *Gal. Gospel*, 128 ; R. W. Dale, *Jew. Temple and Chr. Church*, 88, *Laws of Christ for Common Life*, 123 ; Seeley, *Ecce Homo*, chs. xix. xx. ; B. Jowett, *College Serm.* 148 ; *ExpT* v. (1894) 156, x. (1899) 360.   T. ALLEN MOXON.

SYNAGOGUE.—1. The name.—συναγωγή is the Gr. equivalent for the Heb. נְסֶת, derived from the rare verb כָּנַס, of which the radical meaning is 'to gather.' The term means primarily a gathering together of any objects or persons for any purpose, in Scripture an assembly of the members of a local community either for the purpose of worship or for joint action under professedly religious sanctions (Lk 12[11] 21[12]). Thence the word was applied to the building in which such a meeting was held, and in that sense is of frequent occurrence in the NT. For a time the term was current amongst Christians as the designation of their meetings or places of meeting ; cf. Ja 2², He 10²⁵ (Gr.), and such Patristic notices as Epiphanius, *Hær.* xxx. 18, συναγωγὴν δὲ οὗτοι καλοῦσι τὴν ἑαυτῶν ἐκκλησίαν καὶ οὐχὶ ἐκκλησίαν. This usage lingered amongst the Ebionites and longer still amongst the Marcionites, but in other quarters a distinction early appeared. Either because of the growing divergence between the two faiths, or because ἐκκλησία was regarded as a better expression of the genius of Christianity with its preference for other than ethnic or racial ideals, the terms 'church' and 'synagogue' ceased to be interchangeable. The two senses of each were retained, as an assembly and a place of assembly ; but a strictly Christian or Jewish association was definitely attached to each.

2. Origin and history.—In NT times the institution of the synagogue was popular and widespread, and was believed to date back 'from generations of old' (Ac 15²¹) ; but few materials are available for assistance in the attempt to trace its actual history, and its origin can only be conjectured. Later traditions (*e.g.* Pal. *Targ.* on Ex 18²⁰, a Midrash in *Pesiḳta*, ed. Buber, 129*b*) connect it with the primitive times after the settlement in Canaan. During the exile in Babylon, worship at the Temple necessarily ceased, and the conditions of the Captivity have consequently been regarded as a favourite soil for the germs of the institution (Wellhausen, *IJG*³ 193). But the purposes served by the synagogue make it indispensable that some such institution should have been in existence centuries earlier. The synagogue was a school and a court of local government before it became pre-eminently a place of worship. In ancient times the scattered peoples might go up to the Temple at the festivals, and in the intervals avail themselves of the local sanctuaries ; but as business connexions multiplied (cf. § 7), the father could no longer be relied upon for the regular instruction of his sons, whilst a centre would have to be found in every village or group of villages for the administration of justice, and for the transaction of the affairs of the community, in subordination to the recognized authority, whether regal or priestly. Hence the germs of the institution are to be sought far back in the exigencies that arose as civilization became more complex ; and the Exile marks not the first stage in the origin of the synagogue, but an important modification of its functions, worship becoming thenceforward the principal though far from the sole occupation, and the administrative functions falling for a time into abeyance. After the Temple was rebuilt, popular usage may well be conceived as temporarily reverting to the previous practice ; hence the silence of the later part of the OT, Ps 74⁸ (though Briggs *in loc.* substitutes 'festivals' for 'synagogues,' whilst retaining the latter term in his lexicon, cf. *Oxf. Heb. Lex. s.v.* מוֹעֵד) containing the only explicit reference. In the OT Apocr. the silence is even more complete ; and the post-Maccabæan revival of the strong accentuation upon the religious side of the functions of the synagogue was contemporaneous with the revival of interest in the study of the Law at the close of the bitter struggle for national independence.

3. A feature of normal Jewish life.—In the 1st cent. A.D. synagogues abounded wherever a Jewish population was found. In Jerusalem itself the number is variously given as 394 (Bab. *Kethub.* 105*a*) or 480 (Jer. *Megilla*, 73*d*). The figures are, of course, exaggerated, but are an indication of the degree to which the institution had extended.

In addition, there was a synagogue within the Temple itself, with others for the communities of foreign Jews settled in the city (Ac 6⁹, cf. 9²⁹). Galilee was studded with synagogues, as the thickness of its population would lead one to expect. Mention is made in the Gospels of those at Nazareth (Mt 13⁵⁴, Mk 6², Lk 4¹⁶) and at Capernaum (Mk 1²¹, Lk 7⁵, Jn 6⁵⁹). It is not improbable that the last-named should be identified with the ruins recently discovered at Tell Ḥûm—one of eleven groups of ruined synagogues found in Northern Galilee and dating in part from the 1st cent. (*SWP* i. 231 f., 252, 397 ff., 401). Agrippa I. built a synagogue at Dora (Jos. *Ant.* xix. vi. 3), in imitation of his grandfather's practice elsewhere. The same state of things obtained outside Palestine. In Asia Minor and Greece, St. Paul found synagogues everywhere. Philo speaks of 'thousands of houses of instruction' opened on the Sabbath day (Mangey, ii. 282). And in our Lord's time the synagogue was as common a feature of Jewish life as places of worship are of conventional life in our own country to-day.

4. Site, architecture, equipment.—Two rules as to the building of synagogues require that they should stand on an elevated site, and, like the Temple, be entered from the east. The Galilæan ruins show that these rules were not followed in the 1st cent. in Palestine ; for the ruins do not occupy prominent positions, and in every instance except one the entrance is from the south. In different countries the local style of architecture was adopted, and there never was any style peculiar to synagogues. In Palestine, as the ruins indicate, Græco-Roman influences can be traced, with an over-elaboration of ornament that was rather Oriental in its character. The building proper consisted of a quadrilateral, divided into three or five aisles by means of two or four rows of pillars. Admission was gained through three doors, in front of which was sometimes a highly decorated portico. Of the equipment the most important item was the press or *ark* containing the sacred writings. Above it was a canopy, and in front a curtain ; and each of the rolls was wrapped in an embroidered cloth. In small synagogues, near the ark, which stood probably against the wall opposite the entrance, was a raised *tribune*, furnished with a lectern for the reader and a chair for the speaker (Lk 4²⁰). In larger buildings this platform was brought forward nearly to the centre. The *chief seats* (Mt 23⁶, Mk 12³⁹, Lk 11⁴³ 20⁴⁶) were in front of the platform and ark, or in larger synagogues at the further end of the building, opposite the doors, and in either case faced the congregation, who generally sat on chairs or mats arranged across the building, sometimes lengthways, with an open space between the first ranks on either side. *Lamps* were a regular part of the furniture, and were probably in use in our period, since two early traditions refer to the oil that was burnt and to the custom of keeping the lamps lighted through the Day of Atonement (*Terumoth*, xi. 10; *Pesachim*, iv. 4). The adoption of a screened gallery or even of *separate seats for women* was a late arrangement, and not the custom in our period. No such rule occurs in the Talmud or other ancient source, whilst the evidence points to the actual participation of women in the synagogal service (cf. *JBL*, 1898, 111 ff. ; and Abrahams, *Jew. Life in Mid. Ages*, 25 f.), and their qualification to serve in the Diaspora even as ἀρχισυνάγωγος (*REJ* vii. 161 ff.), which should not be resolved into a mere title of honour.

5. Officials.—In a large synagogue a numerous staff might be employed, the principal officials being duplicated, and a variety of teachers and interpreters added. But no synagogue would be without two officers. The duty of *the ruler of the synagogue* was not to conduct the service himself, but to choose and invite competent persons for the purpose (cf. Ac 13[15]), and to check any indecorum or disorder (Lk 13[14]). In all probability he was responsible also for the maintenance of the synagogue in good repair, and for the safe keeping of its property. He might or might not be, but probably generally was, one of the elders, who occupied with him the chief seats, and formed together the governing body of the community. The other indispensable official was *the attendant* (*ḥazzan* or ὑπηρέτης, Lk 4[20]), whose duties were varied and, whenever possible, distributed. He had to prepare the building for the public services, and to announce with a thrice repeated trumpet-blast from the roof the advent of the Sabbaths and other festivals. In the course of the services he presented the sacred roll to the reader, and in due course replaced it ceremoniously in the ark. In small congregations he had to read the lesson himself (Bab. *Meg.* 25*b* gives an instance at the beginning of the 2nd cent.), and to lead the prayers (Jer. *Berakh.* 12*d*). Besides all this, he had to teach the children, and to scourge such culprits as the synagogue, when acting as a court of law, condemned to that punishment. For the faithful discharge of these manifold duties he was treated with special respect (*ib.* 6*a*), and classed in rank with one of the grades of scribes. Other officials, where the synagogue was large enough to need them, comprised the administrators and collectors of alms, and the translators of the Scripture lessons from Hebrew into the vernacular of the congregation. In our Saviour's time these offices, where they existed, were honorary, as was probably always the case with the controllers of the charities.

6. The synagogue as a place of worship.—Before the destruction of the Temple the ordinary services were simpler than they afterwards became ; but the order followed generally the rule prescribed at a later date in the Mishna (*Meg.* iv. 3). Of the four principal parts (*a*) the first was the *Shema'* (so called from the opening word of Dt 6[4], which should read 'Hear, O Israel ; the Lord our God, the Lord is one,' as cited in Mk 12[29]), with introductory and closing benedictions. It is true that this verse is cited in the NT without any mention of its liturgical use ; but other evidences point to a contrary conclusion. The *Shema'* comprised altogether Dt 6[4-9] 11[13-21] and Nu 15[37-41], in which the wearing of frontlets and fringes is prescribed as a symbolic reminder of legal obligations. That these injunctions were interpreted literally by the zealous legalists of our Saviour's time is shown by His references to the wearing of phylacteries (Mt 23[5]). This practice is difficult to explain except on the assumption that the passages quoted in justification were supposed to be invested with special sanctity. Both customs may be confidently referred to the period of the ascendency of the *Ḥasidim*, a century and more before the birth of Christ ; and the recitation of the *Shema'* with its accompanying ritual was a confession, both of faith in the unity of God and of the imperative obligation to keep His Law. (*b*) What prayers originally followed the recitation of the *Shema'*, it is impossible at present to say. Those adopted at a later time would be inappropriate before the destruction of the Temple, the memory of which colours several of the phrases. From the example of the Baptist in teaching his disciples to pray, and from the request for similar instruction addressed to Jesus (Lk 11[1]), it may be inferred that forms of prayer were not yet familiar to the Jews, and possibly that a disposition towards the adoption of such forms was now arising. Psalms or selections may have been used ; but the time had apparently not

yet come for anything more. (*c*) The reading of extracts from the Law and the Prophets was the central part of the synagogal worship on the Sabbath day. That this was customary in NT times appears from many passages (*e.g.* Lk 4[17], cf. Ac 13[15] 15[21], 2 Co 3[15]). The sections of the Law were apportioned among several members of the congregation, any male who was acquainted with Hebrew being eligible. Next a passage was read from the Prophets by any one upon whom the choice of the ruler of the synagogue fell. Eventually an official lectionary was adopted, so arranged that the reading of the Pentateuch was completed in a year, the section from the Prophets being selected as far as possible with a view to enforce the lesson of that from the Law, but in the time of Christ the reader of the Prophetic section seems to have been at liberty to select whatever part he liked (Lk 4[17]). (*d*) With the reading of the Scripture the service proper terminated. Gradually, as Hebrew ceased to be a spoken language, it was found necessary to translate the lessons into Aramaic or Greek or whatever might be the vernacular of the congregation. For this purpose an interpreter (*methurgeman*) was employed, or the schoolmaster or any competent man amongst the audience acted in his stead. The lesson from the Law was paraphrased verse by verse, that from the Prophets by three verses at a time (*Meg* iv. 4). These paraphrases were not literal translations, but rather condensed interpretations, of a passage, and mark an important stage in the history of preaching. The next development was an extended exposition, which was the usage in NT times (Mt 4[23], Mk 1[21] 6[2], Lk 6[6], Jn 18[20]) The instruction was didactic rather than rhetorical, as may be inferred from the sitting posture (Lk 4[20], cf. Mt 5[1] 26[55], Jn 8[2]) ; and though naturally the Rabbis were looked to for such service, they had not yet become a class of professional preachers, but any distinguished stranger (cf. Ac 13[15]), or even any ordinary member of the community, might be invited to give an address.

7. The synagogue school.—The OT ideal makes parents responsible for the education of their children, and draws an idyllic picture of the father and the son turning every opportunity to profit for instruction in religion and in duty (Dt 6[7]) Such an arrangement was suitable only to primitive times (cf. § 2) ; and as trade extended, and the father's absence from home became necessary and frequent, the need of public elementary schools made itself felt. The main idea of the synagogue service was originally instruction rather than worship, for which in its associated forms the Temple was provided, and in its intimate forms privacy could be secured. Not only does the NT make teaching the chief function, but Philo in one place (Mangey, ii. 168) almost protests against synagogues being regarded as other than schools. The adults in their regular services educated themselves in the Law, and strengthened the social as well as the private sense of obligation The children were gathered regularly for instruction of a similar kind in the synagogue itself or an adjoining room, under the care of the *ḥazzan*, or, in larger centres of population, of a professional teacher. For advanced studies and for technical Jewish training, provision was made in some of the towns or near the residence of some distinguished Rabbi ; but everywhere the elementary school was an inseparable adjunct of the synagogue. See artt. BOYHOOD (JEWISH), and EDUCATION.

8. The synagogue as a court.—Under the strict conception of a theocracy there can be no distinction between things ecclesiastical and things civil. Hence, in places where the population was preponderantly Jewish, local administration was in the hands of a court, which took cognizance of all the Jewish interests of the neighbourhood, and of which the Roman over-rule was apt to avail itself for both executive and minor judicial business. Where the Jews were outclassed in numbers or influence, the synagogal authority was proportionately reduced, though without any loss of respect within the Jewish community. If there were several synagogues in a Jewish town, all were knit together into some kind of organization, under a controlling council which regulated also all the civil affairs of the community. The case of a town with but a single synagogue was simpler, but not radically distinct. Here the council, or local Sanhedrin (Mt 5[22] 10[17], Mk 13[9]), met in the synagogue, where their plans were matured, their decisions taken, and often their penalties exacted. The court proper consisted of twenty-three members where the population was considerable, elsewhere of seven; and this college of elders (Lk 7[3]) or rulers (Mt 9[18. 23], Lk 8[41]) exercised a wide jurisdiction. For minor offences (*Makkoth* iii. 1) the penalty was scourging (Mt 10[17] 23[34], cf. Ac 22[19]; not to be confused with the Roman penalty of scourging of Mt 20[19] and Jn 19[1]), limited to forty stripes save one (cf. 2 Co 11[24]), and administered in the synagogue by the *hazzan*. Excommunication was the punishment of offences that were thought to imperil the stability of the Jewish community (Lk 6[22], Jn 9[22] 12[42] 16[2]). See art. EXCOMMUNICATION in vol. i. p. 559[a].

9. Other uses of the synagogue. — There are indications in early Jewish literature, belonging some of them to the 1st cent., that the synagogue served also the purposes of a public hall or general meeting-place, and regulations for its reverent treatment were gradually adopted. Notices respecting the interests of the community at large, or even of private members, were given there (*Baba mezia*, 28b). It was the place for funeral orations over the death of men of distinction, and at a later period could be used for some of the ceremonies of private mourning (*ib.*). Josephus says (*Vita*, 54) that political meetings were held in the synagogues at the time of the war against Rome. They became increasingly a common meeting-ground for the Jews of the neighbourhood, where their affairs might be discussed informally or in a summoned assembly, and a variety of matters might be conveniently settled. Thus a secularizing—or, from a Jewish point of view, a communal—tendency developed, such as had already shown itself in the case of the courts of the Temple (Mt 21[12], Mk 11[15], Jn 2[14ff.]); and arrangements had eventually to be made in the interest of decorum. People were forbidden to discuss trifles on the premises of a synagogue, or to walk aimlessly about, to shelter there from the heat or rain, to come in with soiled shoes or garments, or to make a thoroughfare of the courts. Some of these regulations are of a later date than the Gospels, but their necessity arose from habits that were already becoming fixed. The synagogue was not only a place of authoritative instruction in the Law, but the centre of the Jewish life of a district, and, as such, its purposes were determined by both social and racial needs.

10. Financial administration. — Most of the officials of the synagogue were honorary; but the schoolmaster and the attendant would require at least partial support, whilst the cost of erection, with that of repairs and maintenance, must have been considerable, to say nothing of the fees paid at a later period to 'ten unemployed men' as the minimum of a congregation. It is a problem, for the settlement of which sufficient materials are not at present available, how these expenses were met. In some cases a wealthy man, Jew or Gentile, wishing to ingratiate himself with the people or out of pure kindness, may have provided a syna-gogue (cf. Lk 7[5]; Jos. *Ant.* XIX. vi. 3). In other cases, though the authorities are not explicit, the synagogue must have been erected by means of a general levy upon the community, and the revenue for its maintenance provided in the same way. The Mishna invests the whole property, including buildings and equipment, in the civic community (*Meg.* iii. 1; *Nedarim*, v. 5), and classes it thus with the baths and roads of the neighbourhood. But as to the principle on which the necessary moneys were raised, and the means by which payment was enforced, very little is at present known. A set of synagogue accounts from the early part of the 1st cent. would be a discovery of much value.

LITERATURE.—Of the works cited in Hastings' *DB*, Schürer is still the most important. The German edition is the best; the reference to the Eng. tr. is II. ii. 52–89. Add Dalman's art. 'Synagogaler Gottesdienst' in *PRE*[3] vii. 7–19; Nowack, *Heb. Arch.* ii. 83 ff.; Dembitz, *Jewish Services in Syn. and Home.* Any of the technical Cyclopædias may be consulted; but care should be taken, especially in the case of Hamburger, by checking the dates of the original authorities, to distinguish the periods for which they stand. R. W. MOSS.

SYNOPTICS, SYNOPTISTS. — The term 'Synoptics' is, according to the universal practice of modern NT scholars, applied to the Gospels of St. Matthew, St. Mark, and St. Luke, as distinguished from the Gospel of St. John, and these three Evangelists are known as the 'Synoptists.' It is so used because these Gospels are so constructed that, together, they present a *synopsis* or conspectus of the leading features of the work and teaching of our Lord. From Tatian, in the 2nd cent., to our own day, frequent attempts have been made to exhibit the Canonical Gospels in the form of a Harmony. Such a Harmony usually took the form of a compilation of these accounts of the life of Jesus, arranged in parallel columns, so as to present a complete Gospel, constructed out of the materials supplied by each Evangelist. The title of Tatian's lost work, the *Diatessaron* (τὸ διὰ τεσσάρων, 'the one by means of four'), illustrates the principle adopted in such Harmonies. In the early Church, and indeed until the time when the modern view of the mutual relations of the Gospels was first stated by Griesbach in 1774, the example of Tatian was followed, and the Synopsis was made to embrace all four Gospels; some, like Irenæus, being led by various reasons, more or less fanciful, to lay stress upon the fourfold nature of the Gospel. Modern scholars, however, observed that the Fourth Gospel differed from the others in so many important points as to call for separate treatment. It has been noted, for instance, that while St. Matthew, St. Mark, and St. Luke, except in their accounts of the closing scenes, relate almost exclusively the Galilæan ministry of Jesus, St. John confines himself mainly to His work in Judæa. It may be observed, in particular, that the first three Gospels 'proceed in the main upon a common outline . . . variously filled up and variously interrupted, but' which 'can be easily traced as running through the middle and largest section of each of their Gospels.' These Gospels form, in fact, a group altogether unique, in which, while each member has its own distinctive peculiarities, all three are of a common type. See, further, art. GOSPELS, and the artt. on each of the Gospels. HUGH H. CURRIE.

SYROPHŒNICIAN WOMAN.—So designated in Mk 7[26].[*] She is described further (1) in the same passage as a Greek ('Ελληνίς), *i.e.*, according to Heb. usage, one who spoke Greek as her ordinary language;[†] and (2) in Mt 15[22] as a Canaanite

* The readings are various. אAKL and other MSS have Συροφοινίκισσα; EFGH, etc., Σύρα Φοινίκισσα. For the Συροφοίνισσα of the TR there is little authority.
† The word "Ελλην is, indeed, often used in the NT in a yet wider sense, as the equivalent of Gentile (Ac 19[10], Ro 1[16. 29],

(Χαναναία), equivalent here to Phœnician, in conformity with the LXX, which renders *Canaan* by Φοινίκη. The woman was apparently a Greek as regards language and culture, a Phœnician by descent, and a Syrian by provincial connexion.* Her name is mentioned in the *Clementine Homilies* (ii. 19, iii. 73) as Justa, and that of her daughter as Bernice.

1. *The woman's approach to Christ* on her daughter's behalf is remarkable, for (1) Jesus belonged to a race which hated or despised her countrymen, and were hated and despised by them. (2) He had healed none of her people, and had come into her district not for ministry, but for retirement and rest. (3) She had evidently received no encouragement from the disciples. Yet she comes to Him and addresses Him not as a general philanthropist, but as Son of David. She had heard about Christ, probably, from some of 'those about Tyre and Sidon' who had waited early on His ministry before the appointment of the Twelve (Mk 3⁸). Her national prejudice against Jesus and a Jewish Messiah had been broken down, her faith in His healing and exorcizing power was complete. The incentive to her faith and appeal is maternal love along with sore need. She is in great trouble, and one who has helped others in trial is at hand. She loves her stricken daughter, and warm affection surmounts all barriers.

2. Still more remarkable is *our Lord's triple apparent repulse.* (1) His silence at first and seeming indifference: 'He answered her never a word' (Mt 15²³). (2) His apparent refusal on account of lack of authority: 'I am not sent but unto the lost sheep of the house of Israel.' (3) His seemingly scornful reproach: 'It is not meet to take the children's bread and to cast it to the dogs' (Mt 15²⁶, Mk 7²⁷). For this repeated repulse, however, there was a triple reason. (1) Consideration for Jews. It was part of God's providential plan to use the Jews for the education and conversion of the world; therefore they must not be needlessly and prematurely alienated from a Christ who was to be a Messiah equally for Jews and for Gentiles. The alienation was destined to come eventually for the nation as a whole, but it must not be hastened and intensified through any sudden process; the extension of the Kingdom must be shown to be natural and inevitable — the proper recompense of a faith in Jehovah which constituted Gentiles genuine sons and daughters of Abraham. (2) Education of disciples who shared more or less in the national prejudice and exclusiveness. The Twelve were to become Apostles to the world, and Christ wished their eventual mission not to be merely imposed by authority, but to be the outcome of inward prompting. Accordingly He excites (*a*) their pity, so as to cause them to become, even if selfishly, intercessors for the woman;† and (*b*) their admiration, by the manifestation in her of a faith which exceeded that of their own countrymen. (3) Development of the woman's faith and love. He who 'knew what was in man' saw the

strength of the Syrophœnician's faith, and He desired to perfect it (Ja 1³) through such trials as, to His discerning insight, she appeared able to bear. He sought to deepen within her that humility which is the condition of exaltation, and to render yet warmer that motherly love which had opened her eyes to love Divine. Doubtless, had her faith been less strong, her humility less deep, her love less self-forgetful, He would have dealt more tenderly with her, so as not to 'break the bruised reed'; but these qualities being already well developed, He braced her character with the cold yet wholesome wind of seeming discouragement.

3. *The woman's triumph and reward.* — Over Christ's silent apathy, as it appeared (Mt 15²²), she triumphs with renewed supplication; over His seemingly narrow refusal of ministry to an alien she triumphs with lowly worship of Him as Son of David,—such worship as was withheld by His own countrymen, as a whole; His outwardly harsh description of her as a heathen dog, to whom it was not meet to give the children's bread, she overcomes with the apt rejoinder that the little dogs (κυνάρια) under the table eat of the children's crumbs.* Her victory is signal. Her faith, like that of the centurion in Mt 8, is attested as great (Mt 15²⁸), and the more than willing surrender of Christ is graciously ascribed by Him to herself. 'For this saying go thy way' (Mk 7²⁹). The reward is complete and immediate: 'Be it unto thee even as thou wilt'; 'her daughter was made whole from that very hour' (Mt 15²⁸).

4. *The main lessons* of this incident are obvious. (1) What the Christian preacher or teacher is tempted to regard as the least promising soil — individuals or communities outside the Church's pale—is sometimes that from which the richest harvest is reaped. (2) What men most fear in their life's experience—suffering, adversity, trouble —often serves as a straight path to God, often reveals itself as a husk of evil enclosing and concealing a kernel of spiritual blessing. While sorrow does not always sanctify, but sometimes breeds moroseness or scepticism, still it is Divinely fitted to move us to go to Him who can sympathize and relieve. (3) Warm love towards those near and dear to us, although sometimes leading the heart away from the Creator to idolatry of the creature, is intended and fitted to open the eyes of the soul to the Fatherly mercy of God, to the brotherly sympathy and saving grace of Christ. Love within us discerns, believes in, realizes love outside of us in God, in Christ, and in fellow-men. (4) What *men* dislike most in a request is among the things that please God best — importunity. This lesson taught us by the record of the miracle is also impressed on us by two of Christ's parables — those of the Midnight Guest (Lk 11⁵) and of the Importunate Widow (18¹). It is the same lesson that was inculcated long before by the suggestive story of Jacob's wrestling, when the patriarch cried, 'I will not let thee go, except thou bless me' (Gn 32²⁶).

Col 3¹¹); cf. the Oriental use of the word 'Frank' as equivalent to 'West European.'

* In the reign of Hadrian, Syria was subdivided into (1) Syria proper, (2) Syro-Phœnicia, (3) Syria-Palestinia (Lucian, *de Con. Deor.* 4). The political division, then officially made, probably followed an already existing popular nomenclature, so that a Syrophœnician may mean simply a Syrian resident in Phœnicia proper (Hastings' *DB* iv. 652). There is no distinct authority for the possible interpretation, half - Syrian, half - Phœnician; although Juv. (viii. 159) is regarded by some as such, and there is an analogy in the use of *Libyphœnix* to denote a mongrel person (Livy, xxi. 22).

† Mt 15²³· ²⁴, where Christ's reply indicates that He understood the disciples to mean, 'Send her away with her entreaty granted.'

LITERATURE.—Trench, *Miracles*, pp. 359-369; Edersheim, *Life and Times*, ii. 37-43; E. P. Gould, 'St. Mark' in *ICC* pp. 133-137; A. B. Bruce, 'Synoptic Gospels' in *EGT* p. 390 f.; Chadwick, 'Gospel of St. Mark' in *Expositor's Bible*, pp. 195-200; Luckock, *Footprints of the Son of Man*, pp. 156-161; Sam. Rutherford, *Trial and Triumph of Faith* (Twenty-seven sermons on the Syrophœnician Woman); Ker, *Serm.* ii. 200; Lynch, *Serm. for my Curates*, 317; Bruce, *Kingdom of God*, 103, *Galilean Gosp.* 154; *ExpT* iv. [1892] 80, xii. [1901] 319; Dale in *Expositor*, v. v. [1897] 365.

                                 HENRY COWAN.

---

* Christ Himself had suggested this response by His use of the diminutive κυναρίοις, which was applicable not to the roaming dogs of a city, but to the pet dogs of a home.

T

TABERNACLES, FEAST OF.

TABERNACLES, FEAST OF. — The Feast of Tabernacles is mentioned in Jn 7[2. 37]. It was the third and the most important of the Jewish festivals, requiring the presence of all males at Jerusalem. It began on the 15th of the seventh month, the month Tishri, and in the time of Christ continued for eight days.

In early times it was called the Feast of Ingathering (Ex 23[16] 34[22]), a name that testifies to its agricultural origin and character. In the time of the Judges it appears as a Canaanitish festival at Shechem (Jg 9[27]), and as an Israelitish festival at Shiloh (21[19], 1 S 1). It was the occasion that Solomon chose on which to dedicate his Temple (1 K 8[2]). The date given in this chapter, viz. the seventh month, does not correspond with the date of the completion of the Temple as given in 1 K 6[38], and may be a later insertion giving the date of the Feast as fixed later. From the original character of the Festival, it is obvious that no precise date could be fixed at first. The early legislation in Exodus requires its observance, but does not give its date or duration.

The Deuteronomic Code calls it the Feast of Tabernacles, and requires it to be kept seven days, but does not fix a date. It describes it as a day of joy for all, including servant, stranger, and widow (Dt 16[13ff.]). In accordance with the sweeping centralization of worship of Deuteronomy, it must be kept at Jerusalem, and we may be sure that this change involved very radical alterations in its character.

The Book of Ezekiel significantly assigns it an exact date (45[25]).

The Priests' Code requires (Lv 23[33-43]) the people celebrating it to dwell in booths to commemorate the fact that their fathers did likewise of necessity as they came out of Egypt. Sacrifices are prescribed (Nu 29[12-38]), and an eighth day is added. At the time of the promulgation of the Code as the law of the land in post-exilic times, the Feast was kept with the greatest enthusiasm (Neh 8[14ff.]), and as an examination of the Law showed that the dwelling in booths was required, this was done, as an innovation. The early practice had doubtless died out as incongruous with the centralized observance from the time of Deut., but was now restored with a special significance attached to it.

Later Jewish laws added to the regulations, and the Feast was kept at Jerusalem until the destruction of the Temple. Since then it has remained one of the great feasts of the Jews, although then the mode of its observance has suffered changes to accord with modified conditions.

One rite which was observed in NT times was the drawing of water from Siloam, and the pouring of it out as a libation in the presence of the people. This Feast was regarded as the appropriate time for special prayer to ensure a plentiful harvest for the ensuing year. Many hold that this rite and custom furnished our Lord the occasion for using the figure of water for the thirsty, in His invitation on the great day of the Feast (Jn 7[37. 38]). This may have been the case, even though that particular rite was regularly omitted on the eighth day; but the teaching of Jesus seems to be very different, at least from the original thought of the rite on the Feast of Ingathering. It may be only a natural coincidence that an important part of Solomon's prayer at the dedication of the Temple on the occasion of this Feast was for answer to prayers for rain, as they should be made statedly thereafter.

LITERATURE.—Art. 'Tabernacles [Feast of]' in Hastings' *DB*, and in *EBi* and *JE*; Edersheim, *LT* i. 145 ff.; cf. Benzinger, *Heb. Arch. passim*; and the Comm. *ad loc.*

O. H. GATES.

TABLE, TABLET (Lk 1[63] πινακίδιον, 2 Co 3[3] and He 9[4] πλάξ).—The word πινακίδιον, not wholly unknown in classical Greek, although it is not commonly used, occurs but once in the NT and not at all in the Septuagint. When it is used in Lk 1[63] it denotes, in all probability, a wax-covered wooden writing-tablet. The ordinary LXX word for 'tablet' or 'table' is the word πλάξ, which is found also, as mentioned above, in the NT in two pass-

ages. In Is 30[8] we find πυξίον (ἐπὶ πυξίον), which is a writing-tablet of box-wood, and in Jer 17[1] we have στῆθος (ἐπὶ τοῦ στήθους τῆς καρδίας), 'breast,' 'surface.' Both πυξίον and στῆθος, however, stand for the Heb. לוח, which is the ordinary word for 'tablet' or 'table,' and is used, *e.g.* in Ex 31[18], in reference to the tables of the Law. גליון (Is 8[1]), rendered in the AV 'roll,' is in the RV more suitably rendered 'tablet.' Tablets were in almost universal use in the ancient world alike for purposes of correspondence and for literary purposes in general, and were formed of various materials, such as stone, clay, and wood, the wood being sometimes whitewashed, sometimes covered with wax. Bronze also was employed for tablets, at least in some of the countries about the Mediterranean, but seemingly only for such tablets as contained inscriptions of an official nature.

LITERATURE.—The Commentaries; artt. in Hastings' *DB* and *Encyc. Bibl.*; works on Assyria, Babylon, and Egypt in general; allusions in Ramsay's *Letters to the Seven Churches*.

GEO. C. WATT.

TABOR, MOUNT.—A notable landmark, of rare beauty and symmetry, six miles east of Nazareth, on the north-east arm of the plain of Esdraelon. In the works of Josephus and the Septuagint its designation is *Itabyrion*; in Polybius, *Atabyrion*; elsewhere, *Thabor*. The modern Arabic name—identical with the name of the Mount of Olives—is *Jebel et-Ṭur*. Mount Tabor stands apart, clear and distinct, from the rugged elevations grouped around it, except on its western side, where a low narrow ridge connects it with the hills of Galilee. Its apparent isolation, and its noble domelike contour, rising directly from the level of the Plain, make it the most conspicuous mountain in Lower Galilee. Its outline varies somewhat when viewed from different positions. As seen from the south and south-west, it resembles the segment of a sphere; from the north-west a truncated cone. Its true figure, according to W. M. Thomson, is an 'elongated oval, the longitudinal diameter running nearly east and west.' Its flattened summit, not easily distinguishable from the levels near its base, is 1400 feet above the average elevation of the plain, and almost 1900 above sea level. Like the hills south and west of it, Tabor is a mass of cretaceous limestone, and the soil on its summit and sides is deep and rich. It is conspicuous among the mountains of this section for its wooded slopes and leafy glades, as well as for its regular form and graceful outline, and yet it is not 'densely wooded,' as some have described it. There are dense clumps of undergrowth in places, but the trees, which for the most part are scrub and evergreen oaks, resemble the growth of an orchard or park rather than of a forest. The summit of the mountain is a flattened platform, oval in outline, and thickly strewn along its outer edges with ruined walls and massive substructions of different periods and styles of architecture.

A tradition as old as the 4th cent. locates the scene of the Transfiguration on Mount Tabor, and until the middle of the 19th cent. this was the generally accepted place of pilgrimage and devotion in commemoration of this event. The earliest references in this connexion are by Cyril of Jerusalem, Jerome, and others (*Cat.* xii. 16; *Epp.* 44 and 86). In the 6th cent., three churches, corresponding to the three tabernacles of Peter

(Mk 9⁵), were built on its summit. Saewulf speaks of three monasteries (c. A.D. 1103), which, with later reconstructions by the Crusaders, were destroyed in the 13th century. There is no mention of Mount Tabor in the NT, and no intimation which in any way connects it with the scene of the great Epiphany. It is an unquestioned fact, based upon the statement given above, that Tabor at the date of this occurrence was not a suitable place for a quiet retreat, such as is implied in the narrative of the Evangelists. Apart from this objection, not in itself decisive, all the events immediately associated with it unquestionably took place on or about the southern slope of Mount Hermon (Mt 16¹⁷⁻²⁸, Mk 8²⁷⁻³⁸, Lk 9¹⁸⁻³⁷). Of the six days which followed the prophetic declaration of Jesus concerning His approaching sufferings and death, there is no record, but it is in keeping with the entire narrative to assume that they were spent in retirement and prayer. There is no intimation that He passed the momentous hours of this transition period in travel, or that He sought another place in the most densely populated part of Galilee for this crowning manifestation of His Divinity and Messiahship. On the contrary, it is asserted in Mk 9³⁰ that Jesus 'passed through Galilee' after He had healed the spirit-possessed child at the foot of the mountain. While, for the reasons given, the time-honoured tradition which connects this 'strange and beautiful mountain' with the Transfiguration has been almost universally abandoned, it is nevertheless true that it was one of the most prominent objects of vision from the outskirts of the early home of Jesus, and its graceful outlines were often before Him, as He journeyed to and fro during the greater part of His public ministry.

LITERATURE.—Thomson, *Land and Book*, ii. 136 ; Schaff, *Through Bible Lands*, 330–336 ; Baedeker-Socin, *Pal.* 364 ; Stanley, *SP* 419 ; Merrill, *Galilee*, 54 ; Robinson, *BRP* ii. 353, and iii. 221 ; Ritter, *Erdkunde*, xvi. 391 ; Andrews, *Life of our Lord*, 357, 358 ; *PEF Mem.* i. 388–391 ; de Vogüé, *Églises de la Terre Sainte*, 353 ; G. A. Smith, *HGHL* 394, 408, 417 ; C. W. Wilson in Hastings' *DB* iv. 671 f. ; Buhl, *GAP* 107 f., 216 f.

R. L. STEWART.

TALENT.—See MONEY.

TALENTS (PARABLE OF).—In Mt 25¹⁴⁻³⁰ we have the story of a man who went away on a journey into a far country, and entrusted to one of his slaves five talents, to another two, and to another one. The story resembles so closely the parable of the Pounds in Lk 19¹¹⁻²⁷ that many scholars have considered them to be different versions of the same parable.

1. It is therefore necessary to begin with an investigation of *the relations between the two parables*. (*a*) In the parable of the Talents we have three slaves mentioned, who seem from the expression chosen—'his *own* slaves'—to stand in a relation of peculiar intimacy to their master. He is, therefore, already familiar with their capacity, and allots the talents he distributes to them in harmony with his knowledge. To the most capable he gives five talents, to one not so capable he entrusts two, and to a third with less ability than either he entrusts one. He does not give them any instructions, since they ought to understand that such large sums of money are not intended to lie idle, but should be used in increasing their master's possessions. As soon as his master has departed, the first servant goes at once and trades with his lord's money. The master is absent for a long time, so that by legitimate trading the servant doubles the capital he has received. The second servant, although of less capacity, exhibits an equal devotion to his lord's interests, and while his capital is smaller, he also succeeds in doubling it. The third servant, however, while he does not

squander the money entrusted to him, buries it in the earth, and keeps it safe for his master's return. After a long period has elapsed, the master comes back and reckons with his servants. The first two slaves bring the capital they have originally received and that which they have made by trading. In each case they use the same formula ; each receives precisely the same commendation and reward. The third servant is conscious that he must find some excuse for his failure, and he throws the responsibility for it on the character of his master. He is a driving, avaricious man, determined to enrich himself even at the cost of dishonest reaping where others have sown. He was therefore afraid to trade with the money lest misfortune should overtake him, and he lose some or all of the capital entrusted to him. The master, without deigning to justify himself from the harsh character thus given to him, points out that were the slave right in his estimate, he ought at least to have taken the trouble to see that the money was entrusted to the bankers. Lazy as he was, he ought not to have grudged the trouble involved in taking the talent and flinging it down at the banker's, so that the capital might at least have accumulated interest. He is accordingly deprived of his talent, and it is given to him who has ten. And, of course, he cannot enter into the joy of his lord, but from the brilliantly lit banqueting-hall where the feast is held is thrust into the homeless darkness outside the mansion. He has proved himself a useless servant, and the penalty of uselessness is that his master has no further use for him.

(*b*) The parable of the Pounds (see art. POUND) has many significant points of contrast with that of the Talents, and the contrasts harmonize with the difference of the situation presupposed. It is in this case not a merchant, but a nobleman, and his object in going to a far country is to receive a kingdom. It is, in fact, held by many that in the parable of the Pounds we have two parables blended together, one of which described how a nobleman was opposed in his efforts to obtain a kingdom by his fellow-citizens, and how, having received the kingdom, he executed vengeance upon them. The other parable went on similar lines to the parable of the Talents, the differences being due either to a difference in the lesson Jesus intended to teach, or to variations of the story that grew up as it was told and retold in the Christian Church. It is, however, important in this connexion to observe that the whole parable is dominated by the idea that it is of a prince that the story speaks. In other words, the situation from which the story of the nobleman starts out is reflected in the details of the story of the servants, some of which, indeed, become intelligible only in the light of it. It is probable that the parable rests on a historical incident, and the view of most interpreters is that it is the journey of Archelaus to Rome to secure his kingdom and the embassy of the Jews to thwart him to which Jesus here alludes. The internal harmony of the story speaks strongly for its unity. In this case the nobleman calls his ten servants and gives each of them a pound. It would, of course, be possible to suppose that, while nobly born, he is in indigent circumstances, and has little money to spare ; but this is probably not the real reason why the sum entrusted is so small. In the parable of the Talents we have apparently to do with a merchant whose object is to make money. He therefore entrusts his servants with a large capital in order that they may have ample opportunity for gaining large sums of money. Moreover, he has already tested their capacity in precisely this kind of work. That accounts for the difference in distribution, and for the absence of any command that they should trade with the money. They know their master and his objects too well to doubt what he means them to do. But naturally a nobleman is not a merchant, hence his servants are quite unpractised in commercial enterprise. If, however, he is to receive a kingdom, it will be necessary for him to have men who are skilled in financial administration. He therefore employs the interval of his absence in testing the business capacity of his slaves, in order that he may know whom to appoint to the various offices of State when he comes into his kingdom. Accordingly he assigns to each an equal sum of money, that all may have equal advantages and be differentiated according to their zeal and capacity. And inasmuch as his object is not to make money, for he will have ample opportunities of doing that when he receives his kingdom, he does not entrust them with a large but with a slender capital. Fidelity and ability can be tested by the use of slender as well as of large resources. When the servants come back, three of them are specially singled out for mention. There is no need to suppose that this is an incongruity in the parable. Ten slaves are, it is true, selected, because there are several offices in the State to be filled, whereas in the case of the merchant only three are chosen, because the capital is more profitably distributed into few than into many hands if the purpose is to make money. It would have been tedious, however, to mention each slave individually in the parable of the Pounds, hence three only are introduced as specimens of the rest. Besides, the parable is subordinated to the aim of teaching its lesson, and attention would have been distracted by the multiplicity of detail, even if ten different lessons could have been drawn from the different conduct of the ten slaves. The vital thing was to bring out the main lessons, and not confuse the broad issues by minute differentiations. The first slave tells the prince that his pound had won ten pounds. His zeal and enterprise win the prince's warm approval, and, since he has been faithful in a very little, he receives authority over ten cities. The second has been less successful, his pound has made only five. He receives a reward proportionate to that of the other; that is, he is set over five cities; but apparently the prince suspects that his relative failure is due not simply to his slighter capacity, but to his feebler devotion to his master's interests. Accordingly he meets with a chill reception, and there is no word of approval, but simply the curt indication of the office he is to fill in the government. When we compare the treatment of the two servants in the parable of the Talents, the difference becomes significant. In that parable the two slaves have unequal capacity, but they have exhibited the same zeal for their master, and achieved a similar result; that is, each has doubled his capital: accordingly they receive the same reward with the same warmth of praise. In the parable of the Pounds the slaves start from an equal position, but achieve an unequal result. They therefore receive an unequal reward, and the commendation given in the one case is withheld in the other. The case of the third servant is substantially the same in both, though with verbal and other differences. It is, of course, obvious that the slave who has received a pound will treat it otherwise than the slave who has received a talent: the large sum is naturally buried in the earth, the smaller one is carefully put by in a napkin. He, too, is deprived of his pound, and it is given, in spite of the protests of the bystanders, to the one who has ten. The parable concludes with the genuinely Oriental trait of the execution of the malcontents who sought to keep the prince out of his kingdom.

It will be clear, then, from this comparison, that the two parables presuppose different situations, each of which is harmoniously worked out in detail, and that each has different lessons to teach. There is, therefore, no substantial reason for assuming that the same original parable has been developed into these two very different stories. It is difficult to believe that, had this been the case, the internal consistency of each should have been what it is.

The above conclusion is due to no harmonistic prejudices, for it may be freely granted that different versions of the same sayings were current in the Church, and have been incorporated in our Gospels. But it is a mere prejudice, on the other side, to imagine that similarities are always to be accounted for as variants of the same original, and we may well hold that Jesus deliberately developed a similar story along these two different lines, just because He thus brought out significantly different lessons. It is by the comparison of the two that the full meaning of each becomes clear. At most, it might be admitted that the two stories exercised a mutual influence on each other. Possibly the words, 'I will set thee over many things,' are an intrusion in the story of the Talents. Apparently the main portion of the master's capital has already been entrusted to his slaves (v.^{14}), so that there is an incongruity when the five talents are called 'few things,' and that over which the slave is to be set is called 'many things.' And the incongruity is even greater when the same promise is repeated to the second slave. The total amount is in each case merely a doubling of the original capital, and the contrast between half and the whole is exaggerated if it is described as a contrast between few and many. Acordingly, it is not impossible that here the parable of the Pounds has influenced the report. There the contrast between the one pound and the ten cities might well be described in the terms employed in the parable of the Talents. It is, however, possible that here the application determined the form of the story, and that Jesus, or possibly His reporter, is thinking of the contrast between earthly opportunities and the heavenly reward. In that case the contrast between the many and the few is quite appropriate. The passage, however, reminds us strongly of Mt 24$^{45-47}$ = Lk 12$^{42-44}$ on the faithful servant whom his lord set over his household in his absence, and whom on his return he will set over all that he has. In the parable of the Pounds the description of the sum entrusted as very little is entirely appropriate.

The significance attached to the parts relating to the first two servants has already been pointed out in the course of the comparison. In the parable of the Talents the lesson is, that difference in endowment or opportunity involves no difference in the reward. It is assumed that such differences exist; all that is demanded is that the opportunities afforded should be faithfully employed. Where like faithfulness has been shown, like reward will be given, in spite of the disparity of opportunity and of result. The significance in the parable of the Pounds is different: each starts from the same level, but they reach a very different result. To what the difference is due is not stated, but to a certain extent, at any rate, it seems to be to the comparative slackness of the second servant. The lesson again is that devotion to the master's interests is what counts in the final reward. Another lesson, common to both parables, is that reward for work is more work, but work on a larger scale with ampler opportunities. In the case of the third servant, some of the lessons are quite clear. Slothfulness in the service of the king is the unpardonable sin. The failure to use opportunity is punished by the withdrawal of opportunity and dismissal from the master's service. What further lessons can be drawn out depends on the view we take of the servant's excuse. If it really represented his belief, it suggests that unjust thoughts of God may paralyze a man's action. The servant had constructed a caricature of his master, and feared that his grasping avarice might be disappointed if he lost part of the capital in trade; and therefore he felt that his duty was done if he returned it to his master as he received it. But the words of the master, 'Out of thine own mouth will I judge thee,' suggest rather that the fault did not lie with the wrong estimate that he had formed of his master's character, but with the laziness of his disposition. If he was unwilling to trade with it himself, he might at least have taken it to those who would have traded with it and returned it with interest. And, in any case, the slave had his orders, tacitly, it is true, in the parable of the Talents, but explicitly in the parable of the Pounds. The responsibility for misfortune was therefore removed from his shoulders; his duty was to obey orders.

2. The question remains as to *the relation between these two parables and the Second Coming.* Lk. introduces the parable of the Pounds with the statement that it was occasioned by the approach of Jesus to Jerusalem, and the expectation entertained by His followers that the Messianic Kingdom was immediately to be established. The parable of the Pounds fits that situation in so far as it indicates that the master is going on a distant journey and will be away for a long time, and that the kingdom is to be established only upon his return. The opposition of the Jews to the Messianic claims of Jesus, and the vengeance that is to come upon them at the Parousia, are also suggested. The eschatological colour is not so deep in the parable of the Talents, still it is present. It is, however, noteworthy that the main point of both parables is not the explanation of the delay in the Second Coming. This comes out more clearly in Mt 24[48-51]. There the unfaithful servant abuses his trust precisely because his lord delays his coming, and there are other closely related sayings and parables which bear on the need for watchfulness and on the suddenness of the Second Coming. There is no need to suppose that the parables of the Pounds and the Talents are a development of Mk 13[34-37], or to think that the experience of delay in the early Church created the parables. Even if it be true that Jesus expected to return within a generation, the evidence that He warned His disciples that His absence might be protracted is very strong. Lk. may have accurately stated the occasion of the parable of the Pounds, though there are other parables that would suit better the particular situation.

LITERATURE.—Commentaries on Matthew and Luke. Discussions in works on New Testament Theology, Teaching of Jesus, and Lives of Christ, and especially the works on the Parables by Trench, Bruce, Dods, Jülicher, and Bugge.
ARTHUR S. PEAKE.

TALITHA CUMI (for Greek ταλιθὰ κούμι, which, in turn, is a transliteration of the Aram. טְלִיתָא קוּמִי 'Maiden, arise').—The words occur in Mk 5[41], and were uttered by our Saviour over the daughter of the Jewish ruler, Jairus. The Aram. noun is טְלִי ='lamb.' This has its emphatic form, masc. טַלְיָא, fem. טַלְיְתָא; or, according to the analogy of Edessene Aram. preserved in the Peshiṭta, טְלִיתָא. It is interesting to note that in Palestinian Aram. the word טְלִי passes from meaning 'lamb' to being a term of endearment for a 'child.' We thus reproduce the words of Jesus accurately, if we render them, 'Lambkin, arise.' In the Gr. of Mk 5[41] the Aram. words are translated τὸ κοράσιον, ἔγειρε. The 'articular nominative' is in NT used sixty times for the vocative case (Moulton, *Gram. of NT Gr.* p. 70). In Lk 8[54] we have ἡ παῖς, ἔγειρε.

The Gr. codices אBC read κούμ for κούμι. The latter is more accurate for Galilæan Aramaic. The former is due to the fact that in some Aram. dialects the final letter, though written, was not pronounced. J. T. MARSHALL.

TAMAR.—An ancestress of Jesus (Mt 1[5]). Cf. art. RAHAB.

TARES (ζιζάνια, Mt 13[25ff.]; only in this passage in NT and only in Gr. and Lat. authors influenced by the NT; Arab. *zawân* ['nausea']; Syr. *zizna*; Lat. and scientific name, *Lolium temulentum* ['drunken']).—The bearded darnel, a weed much resembling wheat in its earlier stages, and growing mostly in grain fields. Its area of distribution is wide, embracing Europe, Western Asia, North Africa, India, and Japan. The kernel is black, bitter, and smaller than wheat. As a matter of fact it is poisonous, producing dizziness, sleepiness, nausea, diarrhœa, convulsions, gangrene, and sometimes death; this is due, however, not to the darnel itself, but to the ergot which usually infests it. It does not harm poultry, for which it is raised and sold in Oriental markets. Though very closely resembling wheat till the grain is headed out, afterwards 'even a child knows the difference' (Thomson). See Tristram (*Nat. Hist. of the Bible,* p. 486), and Thomson (*LB,* vol. ii. pp. 395–397) esp. for an explanation of the common Oriental but unscientific idea that darnel is degenerate wheat.

The parable of the Tares and its explanation are found only in Mt 13[24-30. 36-43]. Our interpretation of it is affected by a few exegetical details. In v.[24] the aorist ὡμοιώθη is significant (as also the aorists in 18[23] and 22[2], and the future in 25[1]) if the use of this tense means that the Kingdom of heaven has 'been made like,' etc., by the course of events, that in the progress of the history it has become like. This ties the parable to the historical situation in which it was spoken, forbidding an exclusive reference to the future; while the fact that it is the Son of Man (=Messiah) who has sown the good seed (cf. v.[37]) excludes all reference to the origin of evil in the world. The time of the parable is the time of the question of the servants (v.[27]), when the tares had been already recognized as such (ἐφάνη, v.[26]). As to v.[25], it is not at all necessary to think that this was a common method of revenge in Jesus' day and country. Thomson did not find a person in Palestine who had ever heard of sowing darnel maliciously. If new to Jesus' hearers, it would emphasize this quite possible malice as extraordinary, unheard-of, and outrageous. In v.[26] χόρτος means the grassy crop, including all that grew in the field, and was chosen just in order to embrace both tares and wheat. 'Made fruit' does not mean 'produced fruit,' but refers to the period of the formation of the kernel. 'Then, and not till then, appeared also the tares as tares. V.[27] and the following verse show that the idea of wheat degenerating into darnel is foreign to the parable; the servants think of mixed seed, the master of an independent sowing of darnel. Still less is there any idea in the parable that darnel may become wheat (B. Weiss). Weeding wheat (vv.[28. 29]) is common to-day in Palestine as in America, and has been observed there by Stanley, Thomson, and Robertson Smith; but it must be done either before the milk stage of the wheat, *i.e.* before it is headed out (impossible in this case on account of the similarity between wheat and darnel in the earlier growth), or later when the kernel has hardened. The reason for this is that any disturbance of the wheat when 'in the milk' is especially harmful to it. So the master will not allow the weeding then, lest the servants pull out and so disturb the roots of the wheat, interlaced as they are with the roots of the darnel. There is no question here of pulling up wheat for darnel by mistake. The darnel has already appeared as darnel, and just on that account comes the servants' question (v.[27]). The question of the servants is then, from the point of view of the Galilæan agriculturists addressed, an intrinsically foolish one. No one who knew anything about farming would think of removing the darnel at that juncture. The master's reply does not seem strange to the crowd. It is reinforced by their knowledge and common sense. So Jesus gains the approval of the common man to back His teaching. The harvesters of v.[30] (cf. v.[39]) are different from the servants, although this is merely implied here, and is first made perfectly clear only in the explanation. It is absolutely necessary to avoid the mingling of the kernels of the darnel and the wheat, lest the bread be poisoned. This may be effected (a) by weeding, (b) by carefully picking out the stalks of darnel one by one from the cut grain, probably the former here (cf. vv.[30. 28] συλλέξατε, συλλέξωμεν), or (c) by sifting (after threshing) with a sieve so constructed as to allow the smaller darnel seeds to fall through, while retaining the larger wheat. All three methods are used in Palestine to-day. The weeding would trample down the grain, to be sure; but, as to-day in America, it would rise again enough to be cut by the sickle, always used in Palestine; cf. Dt 16[9] 23[25], Mk 4[29], Rev 14[14-19]. It is probable that τὰ σκάνδαλα in v.[41] is to be taken personally as in 16[23]. The πάντα, not repeated before τοὺς ποιοῦντας, seems to include both under one vinculum; up to this time all, both tares and wheat, have been interpreted as persons (v.[38]); and, finally, only persons are subject to the final judgment (v.[42]).

The correct interpretation of this parable flows directly from its historical setting. It is a stage in the development of the Kingdom which allows itself to be described (ὡμοιώθη, v.[24]) by the story of the Tares. The men addressed, whether the Twelve or the multitudes, were Jews, with the common Jewish ideas of the Messianic Kingdom, and these ideas Jesus was engaged in modifying and spiritualizing. The Sower had been a parable of disillusionment, disclosing that the success of the Messianic Kingdom would not be so universal or immediate as they had fondly imagined, that its method was to be preaching and not cataclysm, that it depended for its spread on its reception in human hearts. The Tares is equally a parable of disillusionment. John the Baptist had at least, publicly and prevailingly, described the Messiah as coming for judgment (Mt 3[10-12]), and this was in perfect accord with the popular anticipation that the Messianic reign would begin with a judgment (Schürer, *HJP* II. ii. 163–168, 181). But Jesus had not shown any indication of being such a judge, nay He had taken quite another course (Mt 12[15-21]), so that doubt came into the mind even of John the Baptist (11[2ff.]). For the inauguration of the Messianic reign with a judgment the disciples were eagerly looking. 'On that day' (13[1]) of the parables, or at least a short time before it, the Pharisees had shown their true colours by charging that Jesus cast out demons by Beelzebub, the prince of the demons (12[22-32]). Jesus *had* indeed given them a solemn warning (v.[32]), but no lightning stroke had destroyed them, and the disciples were disappointed. Their spirit, described in the question of v.[28], was later expressed by James and John (Lk 9[54f.]), 'Lord, wilt thou that we bid fire to come down from heaven and consume them?' In this parable Jesus teaches them that *the judgment which they momentarily expected, the separation of the sons of the Kingdom and the sons of the Evil One, shall surely come, not now, but at the end of the age, and that meantime the wicked shall continually spring up among the righteous. This is to be expected, and is to be borne with patience.* The parable therefore discloses the fact that, instead of being victorious at one stroke, the progress of the Kingdom is to be continually hindered and hampered (cf. τὰ σκάνδαλα, v.[41]), till the consummation of the age.

This interpretation leaves unanswered those questions about Church discipline which have made the parable an ecclesiastical battle-ground for centuries, because *the parable has nothing to do with such controversies.* (1) The field is not the Church, but the world of men (v.[38]), the Messiah's world which He is sowing, just as it is in the Sower, the Mustard Seed, and the Leaven. (2) The Kingdom is not the Church, but the Messianic Kingdom of Jewish expectation. It is extremely doubtful if the Kingdom ever = the Church, certainly never the visible, organized Church. (3) There was no background for the idea of 'Church,' much less of Church discipline, in the disciples' minds at this time. It is only at Cæsarea Philippi (16[18]) and afterwards (only 18[17]), that Jesus begins to introduce that idea in a very rudimentary way, by what Aramaic word we know not. (4) If the parable refers to Church discipline, it forbids it *in toto*, while the parable of the Net on a similar interpretation makes it impossible. It is idle to say that it prohibits only the exclusion of masses, and permits that of the very bad, or inculcates a general attitude of mind towards Church discipline. (5) All men are to appear at the Judgment, not merely professing Christians (25[31. 32]). (6) The Apostles did not so understand the parable, for they insisted on Church discipline (1 Co 5[2. 13], 2 Co 2[5-11], 2 Th 3[6. 13], Rev 2[14-16. 20-23]; cf. Mt 18[15-20]). The history of the interpretation of the parable shows that such a use of it was first made by Cyprian during his bishopric (248–258), in support of his theories of the Church. Tertullian, a half century earlier, may have held it. Origen (b. 182, d. 250) knew of this interpretation, but rejected it. Irenæus knew nothing of it. (7) Last and most important, such an interpretation ignores the historical situation, would have been a riddle to the disciples (cf. Bruce, *Parabolic Teaching*, p. 43), a prophecy with no root in the present; it takes no account of the emphasis in Christ's interpretation, and of His omission of the servants' question and the master's answer therein (cf. vv.[28b-30a] with vv.[37-43]).

Two objections to the interpretation of the parable proposed in this article deserve attention. (1) In v.[41], Jesus says that the angels shall gather *out of His Kingdom* all offences and them that do iniquity, whence it is inferred that the tares were in the Kingdom and not in the world. It is admitted that the word 'Kingdom' is used in this parable in a very loose sense. But this is the universal fact throughout the Synoptics, in proof of which the long controversies in the theological world about its meaning are conclusive (cf. Sanday in Hastings' *DB* ii. 619 f.). The Kingdom of v.[24], which the course of events has already made like the field of the following narrative, is a most intangible and indefinable entity, a congeries of truths and principles characteristic of the coming age, which take shape in the world as they embody themselves in the lives of men. In the process of taking shape, the parable tells us, opposition has risen in the world of men which these truths and principles claim as their rightful sphere, and which men expect them to occupy. The sons of the Kingdom (v.[38]) are those who receive these truths and embody them in their lives and conduct. These are sown in the wide field of the world of men, which the Messiah claims as rightfully His—His Kingdom (v.[41]), or, if preferred, which He calls His Kingdom at His coming to claim it as such (cf. Mt 16[28], 2 Ti 4[1], Rev 11[15]; cf. Mt 13[49]). Finally, the Kingdom of their Father (v.[43], cf. Mt 26[29] 25[34. 46]) is the consummated Kingdom of glory. (2) The related parable of the Net (13[47-50]) is supposed to refer to the discipline of the Church. This is, however, a mistake. (a) The Kingdom is not like the Net; but its principles and history, here especially its consummation, are illustrated by the following story (cf. Mk 4[26]). (b) The explanation of vv.[49. 50] lays not the slightest emphasis on anything except the consummation.

(c) Those who draw the net and those who separate the good and the bad are the very same persons (v.[48]), i.e. the angels (v.[49]). (d) The parable, if it relates to Church discipline, makes that absolutely impossible. (e) Its position at the end of the sermon of Mt 13, whether due to Jesus or Mt. or an editor, is an additional proof that its teaching is the same as that of the Tares : i.e. at the end of the age, and only then, shall the good and the bad be separated.

The historical criticism of the Gospels gives no assured results here. Holtzmann and Pfleiderer think that the Evangelist has worked over and added new traits to Mk 4[26ff.]. B. Weiss says that Mt. and Mk. have worked over the same original parable, Mt., however, adding only vv.[25. 27. 28a]. The explanation, as also that of the Sower, is from the Evangelist's hand. Jülicher acknowledges an unrecognizable parable-kernel here, which lies at the bottom of both Mt. and Mk. The parable, as it stands in Mt., is, however, the result of a working over of Mk.'s parable and the original parable, the companion of the Net, while the explanation is from the same editor's hand. Hilgenfeld and Holsten look on Mk.'s parable as a weakened form of the Tares, or a substitute for it. J. Weiss thinks that the idea of gradual development is not in this or its sister parables.

LITERATURE.—Broadus, Com. on Mt. ; Jülicher, Die Gleichnisreden Jesu, ii. 546–569 ; also B. Weiss, Zahn, Goebel, Trench, and Bruce (Parabolic Teaching), cf. his remarks in Expos. Gr. Test., in loc. ; Arnot (Parables) may be compared as a pioneer of the correct interpretation. See also R. Flint, Christ's Kingdom upon Earth (1865), 122 ; H. S. Holland, God's City (1894), 181 ; R. J. Campbell, The Song of Ages (1905), 77. The controversy of the Donatists with Augustine first brought out the arguments on both sides.

FREDERICK L. ANDERSON.

TAX (ἀπογράφω, RV 'enrol '), **TAXING** (ἀπογραφή, RV 'enrolment '), occur in the Gospels only in Lk 2[1-5]. The words refer to the registration of the inhabitants of Palestine, with a view to levying taxation upon them for Imperial purposes. In the present instance this appears to have been done, not by the usual Roman method of enrolling persons under their place of residence, but by the Jewish method of enumerating them according to the cities and towns with which their families were originally connected. For the enrolment is mentioned in order to explain why Joseph and Mary came from Nazareth to Bethlehem at the time when Jesus was born. The passage would need no further comment, were it not for the historical difficulty that has been raised in connexion with the statement of v.[2] about Quirinius. There was a well-known enrolment (Ac 5[37]) which took place in Judæa under his supervision, after the deposition of Archelaus in A.D. 6 (Jos. Ant. XVII. xiii. 5, XVIII. i. 1) ; but it has been seriously questioned whether he held an earlier governorship of Syria before the death of Herod the Great, and whether such an enrolment as St. Luke describes really took place at that time. With regard to the first point, it is now admitted that Quirinius probably held a post of responsibility in Syria before the governorship which began in A.D. 6 (see Schürer, HJP I. i. 353 ff., and art. QUIRINIUS). With regard to the second point, it has been shown by Sir Wm. Ramsay (Was Christ born at Bethlehem?) that, in Egypt at least, enrolments took place every fourteen years, that traces of the same arrangement have been found in other parts of the Empire, and that it may have extended to Palestine. The dates, when traced backwards, would include A.D. 20, A.D. 6, and B.C. 8. If an enrolment were actually due in Palestine in the last-named year, its completion may have been somewhat delayed by the disturbed state of Herod's kingdom, and may have fallen as late as B.C. 6, which is the probable date of the birth of Jesus. JAMES PATRICK.

TEACHER.—διδάσκαλος, though strictly meaning 'teacher,' is tr. 'master' by AV throughout the Gospels except in Jn 3[2]. In two other passages besides this, viz. Mt 23[8] and Jn 3[10], RV gives the correct translation ; and in every case where both

AV and RV translate 'master,' RVm gives 'teacher' as an alternative reading. In Lk 2[46] διδάσκαλος is rendered 'doctor,' and in Jn 1[38] it is stated to be equivalent in meaning to 'Rabbi' (see artt. RABBI and MASTER).

This was the word by which our Lord was always addressed. Even His enemies admitted His claim to be a teacher. And not only was He recognized as a teacher, but the supremacy of His teaching was, and is, universally acknowledged. His contemporaries felt His superiority and could not withstand the influence of His teaching, 'for he taught them as one having authority, and not as the scribes ' (Mt 7[29]), and 'never man so spake' (Jn 7[46]). In modern times, too, even those who cannot assent to some of the cardinal doctrines of His religion bow before the majesty of His speech, and proclaim Him the greatest moral and religious teacher the world has ever seen. See SUPREMACY.

Christ's great bequest to the world as a teacher is His revelation of the Fatherhood of God and the brotherhood of man. This twofold message is peculiar to His gospel, and forms the keynote of His teaching. Christ the Teacher is indeed Christ the Revealer. He reveals the truths concerning man's true nature and destiny, and his relationship to God ; and sheds an ineffable light upon all the dark and perplexing problems of life, death, and immortality.

But Christ was more than a mere teacher. His teaching is not only instructive : it is also creative. His words do not come with power to the intellect alone : they also appeal to the heart and influence the will. 'They are spirit and they are life' (Jn 6[63]). They pass into the soul of man and there quicken and create new life. The discourse with Nicodemus (Jn 3) was intended to emphasize this very fact, that Jesus was not only a Teacher but a Saviour, and that the passport into the Kingdom of God was not mere knowledge, but a new life which demands new birth. Christ is not merely the truth : He is also the life. His truth liberates and saves ; and those who receive it into their hearts and minds are thereby raised to a higher and a nobler life of righteousness and holiness, and are endued with power to become 'sons of God' (Jn 1[12]). His teaching still exercises this cleansing and life-giving power ; and everywhere men in quest of God and salvation re-echo the assertion of St. Peter, 'Lord, to whom shall we go? Thou hast the words of eternal life' (Jn 6[68]).

DUGALD CLARK.

TEACHING OF JESUS.—The place and meaning of knowledge in the Christian religion constitute a question of supreme importance. It has been answered in differing ways in different times and places, and with far-reaching effects, often of the saddest character. Yet the answers have usually been of the nature of instinctive assumptions rather than results of deliberate investigation into the grave problem involved ; indeed, it has seldom been realized that a problem existed. In our own day, however, the spread of the mode of thought known as Agnosticism—a term coined in protest against a too confident attitude of gnosis or full knowledge—has helped to bring home the fact and something of the nature of the problem underlying the various bodies of 'doctrine' claiming the authority of Christ. In so stating the case, our thoughts travel back to the final form of the question,* which must control all others, viz., What sort of '**knowledge**' did Jesus Himself offer to men, and how is it related to human knowledge in general and to man's religious consciousness as such? Some suggestions towards a true answer may be gained from a study of the terms found in

* In this connexion Latham's Pastor Pastorum, chs. i. and iii., offers certain regulative ideas of high value.

our Gospels as used in this connexion, such as 'know,' 'knowledge,' 'teach,' 'teaching,' 'teacher,' 'mystery,' in the light of their originals, Aramaic and Greek. Here, on the whole, it seems needless to distinguish between Christ's own usage and that of the Evangelists themselves, for these coincide generally. The few exceptions in the Synoptics can be noted incidentally, while the special Johannine usage is treated by itself.

The characteristic Greek term γνῶσις occurs in our Gospels only in Lk 1[77] 'knowledge of salvation,' and 11[52] 'the key of knowledge' (see below); and the intellectual interest connoted by it, as also by 'wisdom' (σοφία) and 'the Wise man,' among the Greeks, is here quite absent (ἐπιστήμη does not occur at all). All this points to the concrete, personal, or experimental nature of the knowledge implied in the religion of the Gospels, as of the OT,—a fact which comes out also in the contexts in which 'know' occurs.

'The OT everywhere assumes that there is such a thing as the knowledge of God, but it is never speculative, and it is never achieved by man. God is known because He makes Himself known, and He makes Himself known in His character. Hence the knowledge of God in the OT = true religion; and as it is of God's grace that He appears from the beginning speaking, commanding, active, so as to be known for what He is, so the reception of the knowledge of God is ethically conditioned. . . . It is in this sense of an experimental acquaintance with God's character, and a life determined by it, that a universal knowledge of God is made the chief blessing of the Messianic age. . . . Side by side with this practical knowledge of God, the OT makes room for any degree of speculative agnosticism. This is especially brought out in the Book of Job' (Hastings' DB iii. 8 f.).

The distinction between gradual experimental recognition (γινώσκειν, ἐπιγινώσκειν) and the actual possession of knowledge (εἰδέναι) is well preserved; e.g. in Jn 14[7] 'If ye had come to recognize me (in my true character), ye would have had knowledge of my Father also.' Corresponding to the ethical quality of the knowledge acquired by growing personal receptivity, is the nature of the 'teaching' * (διδαχή), as defined by the contexts in which this term and its verb stand; e.g. Mt 7[28] 'The crowds were exceedingly astonished at his teaching; for he was teaching them as having authority, and not as their scribes' (after Sermon on the Mount). Finally, the fact that Jesus was habitually addressed as 'Rabbi,' and so treated, suggests that He dealt with the same subject-matter as the official 'teachers' of the Jewish Law (Tôrah), viz. the sort of conduct pleasing to the God of Israel (cf. Mt 5[17-20]), though He differed in going behind the act to the motive, and in setting this in the light of the Father's character. There was, we may be sure, a certain fitness in the plausible compliment, as coming even from Pharisaic lips, 'Rabbi, . . . of a truth thou teachest the way of God' (Mk 12[14]||, cf. 12[32]). We do well, then, to approach the meaning of 'knowledge' and 'teaching' in the Gospels through the senses which these terms bore in contemporary Judaism. Philo describes Jews as 'taught . . ., even long before the sacred laws and also the unwritten usages, to recognize as one God the Father and Creator of the world' (Legatio ad Gaium, 16). Here we have a starting-point for consideration of the knowledge Jesus offered to impart, as regards its substance.

i. THE SYNOPTIC GOSPELS.—Jesus' own knowledge was rooted in the essential teaching of the OT, interpreted by a unique religious experience, which even in childhood enabled Him to make marvellous use of its contents (Lk 2[46f.]), and which developed as a 'wisdom' that matured with His years (v.[52]). The determinative element in it was a consciousness of the God of Israel as His Father

* This didache consisted of didaskaliæ or definite 'instructions' as to conduct, cf. Mk 7[7], Mt 15[9] 'teaching for instructions human injunctions' (διδάσκοντες διδασκαλίας ἐντάλματα ἀνθρώπων, after Is 29[13]).

in a peculiarly intimate personal sense. Through this the OT revelation, as written and as currently taught, was gradually filtered, until only those elements and interpretations remained effective in His mind and speech which were valid in the light of the idea of the Holy Father and His practical relations with men. Thus the 'sacred laws' of Mosaism were transmuted into 'the teaching' of Jesus, the Messiah, with its new spirit and fresh emphasis. But the lines of the new were continuous with the old as regards the primarily practical reference of the new teaching, which superseded that of the scribes of the Pharisaic school, then dominant (Mk 1[22. 27] 2[16. 18]). Thus the 'knowledge' which Jesus aimed at imparting in His 'teaching' was analogous in scope to that recognized as such in current Palestinian Judaism, and bore essentially on true piety conceived as doing 'the will of God' (Mk 3[35]). But the form of its presentation, and much of its resulting spirit, were largely determined by two features peculiar to Jesus as a teacher: (a) a note of fresh, personal authority, in contrast to the derivative authority claimed by the scribes (Mk 1[22]); (b) constant reference to 'the kingdom of heaven,' the true Theocracy for which Israel had long been waiting and watching, in connexion with Messiah, its Divinely commissioned Inaugurator. John the Baptist had spoken of such a Theocracy as imminent. Yet so little had he realized the spiritual experience proper to it in its fulness, that Jesus, even in the act of recognizing John's supremacy in the order of prophets, can declare that 'He that is but little in the kingdom of heaven is greater than he' (Mt 11[11], Lk 7[28]). The Messianic Kingdom, then, is bound up in a unique manner with Jesus Himself as its Announcer (κηρύσσων) and Legislator (διδάσκων)—the two aspects in which He conveys 'knowledge' of it, and so of religion as it is known to the Gospels.

Wellhausen, indeed, roundly denies this (Einleitung in die drei ersten Evangelien, 1905, 106 ff.): 'From the Kingdom as present, Jesus as already constituted (dagewesener) and present Messiah is inseparable; accordingly He cannot Himself have spoken of it. . . . In Mark He speaks only of the future Kingdom; but He does not say that He is to bring it. . . . It is thought that the declaration of this future Kingdom was actually the proper content of His preaching. Far from this, it recedes completely into the background in Mark. In the Galilæan period He does not as a rule preach at all, but He teaches: and indeed not about the Kingdom of God (which does not occur at all, save in the addition 4[30-32]), but, in unconstrained succession, touching this and that matter which comes in His way; obvious truths, with reference to the needs of a general public, which is misled by its spiritual leaders' (p. 106). As regards the Kingdom of God, the idea of which He could assume as present to His hearers' minds, 'He emphasized in any case warning more than promise. . . . He began not with allusions to blessings (Glückwünschen und Seligpreisungen), but with the preaching of penitence: The Kingdom of God is at hand, repent! Like Amos before Him, and like John the Baptist, He thereby protested against the illusion of the Jews, as though to them the Judgment were bound to bring the fulfilment of their wishes' (107 f.). Wellhausen goes on to question whether the phrase 'the gospel' was ever found on Jesus' own lips, since even in Mark 'the gospel is tantamount to Christianity,' i.e. what the Church came to understand as the purport of its Master's life and death. Here Wellh. seems to take 'gospel' in too rigid and uniform a sense, rather than as 'good tidings' which may vary in connotation. In any case, it is one thing to argue that the Evangelists have made Jesus use a phrase proper to their age, not His (yet Is 61[1], in view of Mt 11[5], Lk 7[22], cf. 4[18], makes His use of the verb 'preach good news' [εὐαγγελίζεσθαι]—as in Lk., who never uses the substantive [εὐαγγέλιον]—far from unlikely): it is quite another to have disproved the historic truth of the idea thereby conveyed, viz. that Jesus' own announcement of the Kingdom as imminent was in a different key from John the Baptist's. Both, no doubt, urged repentance as befitting such an expectation; but how differently this may be done, how different the motives suggested—in a word, how different the spirit of the two messages! (see Mk 2[18f.] ||, Mt 11[16-19], Lk 7[31-35]). In the one the note of severity was uppermost, in the other that of gladness. Surely the very point of the striking saying in Mt 11[11], Lk 7[28] is that the spirit of John's message was defective, as we feel it to be, in its negative and threatening tone, as compared with the positive and winning note of benediction and hope added by Jesus, in the light of God's true attitude to men—a revelation which by no means took from the force of the summons to repentance for sins, now seen more clearly in the purer light. So we read in Mk 6[12], even after much of the Galilæan teaching was already given, that the Apostles 'went out and preached that men should repent' (Wellh. *l.c.* p. 112, questions even whether there were any 'apostles' during Jesus' lifetime). The spirit of the above distinction is finely given by Longfellow's lines (cited in Sir A. F. Hort's Com. on Mk 1[15]):

> 'A voice by Jordan's shore,
>   A summons stern and clear:
> Repent! be just, and sin no more!
>   God's judgment draweth near!
>
> A voice by Galilee,
>   A holier voice I hear:
> Love God, thy neighbour love! for see
>   God's mercy draweth near.'

The idea of the Kingdom necessarily determines the sense and emphasis given to 'repentance' in relation to it; and as 'righteousness' meant to Jesus something very different from what it did on John's lips, so with their respective teaching as to 'the Kingdom.'

As to the 'future' and 'present' Kingdom, surely on Jesus' idea of the essentially spiritual nature of the Kingdom this distinction loses its full force; where the righteousness of the Kingdom is, there is the Kingdom already in a real sense.

As 'preaching' the Kingdom, He declares the fact of its near advent, so 'giving knowledge of salvation' as yet nearer than John's preaching was able to announce (Lk 1[77]). Reception of such knowledge meant repentance for sins as unfitting the sinner for membership in the Kingdom soon to 'appear,' and confidence in the forgiveness which was part of the expected Messianic blessings. Then as 'teaching,' He gave knowledge of the laws and principles of the coming era of the Father's realized sovereignty. Relying on this teaching and obeying its precepts, the man who accepted the 'preaching' of the Kingdom as at hand was assured of participation therein when it arrived. Of such 'teaching' the Sermon on the Mount is the summarized expression (Mt 7[28f.]). It represents 'the key of knowledge' touching God's will, as it should be done in the true Theocracy or Kingdom, which the official guardians of the Law had removed out of men's reach by their traditions (Lk 11[52]). But the same knowledge was also given less fully and formally, in occasional and piecemeal fashion, in the 'teaching' Jesus was wont in His earlier ministry to give at the Sabbath services in synagogues of Galilee, in close connexion with the reading of the Law and its regular exposition (Mk 1[21] 6[2], Lk 4[15]; cf. v.[43] for 'preaching' also), as well as on other and less formal occasions. Its main subject 'would seem to have been the nature of the Kingdom and the character required in its members' (Sanday), treated in the light of the Fatherhood of God.

At first, moreover, His own Person formed no part of His explicit teaching. Apparently the practical recognition of His plenary authority as Revealer of the Kingdom and the truths constitutive of it, enforced by the object-lesson of His deeds (Lk 10[23. 24]) of beneficent authority in the healing of the body and soul (see Mk 2[5-12]), was what Jesus had most at heart in the earlier stage of His ministry at least. What went beyond this was allusive and suggestive rather than dogmatic, being contained in the title by which, in preference to all others, He chose from first to last to refer to Himself and His ways—'the Son of 'Man.' The sense which He gave to it, as distinct from the associations currently attaching to it in various circles of Judaism, seems to be chiefly 'brotherhood with toiling and struggling humanity, which He who most thoroughly accepted its conditions was fittest also to save' (Sanday). It was only as criticism and challenge forced Him to fall back upon His ultimate and inner credentials, that He referred explicitly to His mysteriously unique experience of Sonship to the Father as the ground of the revelation He imparted in His teaching— particularly as to the Divine Fatherhood which lay

at the heart of that teaching (Mt 11[25ff.], Lk 20[21-24]).

In this we get some insight into one of the most significant features of Christ's teaching, viz. His pedagogic method, which implied that religious knowledge is not to be thought of or taught as if it were all on one level, or as if it were of little moment how it is imparted and acquired. In other words, nothing is more characteristic of 'truth as it is in Jesus' than the psychological conditions under which it should be learned, by progressive assimilation, as the learner is able to bear it. His was the experimental method of religious knowledge, to a degree surpassing all other teachers. This fact comes out in several connexions,[*] of which His use of **parables** deserves special notice.

As regards Jesus' use of the parable proper, as distinct from mere figurative maxims or illustrations, it is often strangely overlooked that the Gospels do not represent it as a form of communicating religious knowledge employed by Jesus from the first. In fact it emerges relatively late in His ministry, when already He had proved the general unreceptiveness of His hearers and the positive hostility of their official teachers. This appears not only from the first occasion on which, in the relatively historical order preserved in Mk., Jesus is said to have 'taught in parables' (Mk 4[2], Mt 13[3]; Mk 3[23], Lk 5[36] 6[39] do not prove the contrary), but also from the fact that His disciples ask Him as to the meaning of the first recorded parable, plain as its meaning is to us (Mk 4[10. 13]). Further, that meaning is one which implies a disappointing experience of various types of hearer,—the good being in the minority,—such as suits a comparatively prolonged period of experiment, during which Jesus had proved how unprepared the majority of His countrymen were to embrace the Kingdom as He meant it. In fact the psychological moment at which He began His full parabolic method on principle, was just that depicted in Mark's narrative (cf. Latham, *op. cit.* p. 324). Already the Scribes, both local (2[6. 16]) and from the religious centre in Jerusalem (3[22]), the Pharisees generally (2[18. 24] 3[6]), and even the disciples of John,—presumably a specially prepared class,—had indicated pretty clearly that their attitude was likely to be unreceptive. Thus we read in Mk 3[7] of His withdrawing from before Pharisaic hostility—which already felt that He must be got rid of at any cost (v.[6])— with His circle of disciples, from the synagogue and the city, where friction was likely, to the seashore, there to continue His effort to win the unsophisticated hearts of the common people. Then follows the selection of the Twelve from the larger body of disciples habitually about Him, with a view to their acting as 'apostles' or missionaries, to assist in what was opening out before Him as a longer and more arduous ministry than had, perhaps, at first seemed needful. That in itself is significant; and its significance is enhanced by the scene which precedes the first parables, when He dwells on the spiritual ties binding Him to the disciples, in contrast even to His own blood relations. All this implies that Jesus fell back, as it were, upon the parabolic teaching which we regard as so beautifully characteristic of Him, largely under the necessity of adjusting the form of His teaching, for deep spiritual reasons, to the disappointing unreceptivity of His hearers generally. Nor was the state of His disciples much better in point of intelligence, though their practical self-committal to Him as their trusted authority and teacher implied a moral affinity of great latent

---

* Among these we can only allude to the stages in Jesus' teaching of His disciples in the latter part of His ministry, which dates from the decisive confession at Cæsarea Philippi.

possibility for future insight and knowledge. This comes out most clearly in Mark's narrative, which, throughout the chapter on the beginnings of parabolic teaching, preserves the original historic atmosphere to a degree far surpassing what the other Evangelists, owing to their later perspective, particularly as regards the intelligence at that time of Christ's personal disciples (see Mk 4[13], omitted by Mt. and Lk.), have been able to achieve.

Observe the following, compared with the parallel passages in Mt. and Lk.: 'He proceeded to teach them in parables many things, and to say to them in his teaching, Listen (Mk 4[2]) . . . He who has ears to listen, let him listen (v.[9]). . . . And he went on to say to them * (that the light of the lamp is meant to be seen, and so), there is nothing hidden except with a view to its being ultimately made manifest. . . . If any one hath ears to listen, let him listen (vv.[21-23]). And he went on to say to them, See to it what ye hear (=understand, cf. Lk 8[18] 'how ye hear'). According to the capacity of the measure ye use, it shall be meted out to you, and with interest ($\pi\rho\sigma\tau\epsilon\theta\acute{\eta}\sigma\epsilon\tau\alpha\iota$ $\acute{\nu}\mu\hat{\iota}\nu$, cf. Mt 13[12] 25[29] $\varkappa\alpha\grave{\iota}$ $\pi\epsilon\rho\iota\sigma\sigma\upsilon\theta\acute{\eta}\sigma\epsilon\tau\alpha\iota$, after the next clause); for he who hath (i.e. by receptiveness), there shall be given to him, and he who hath not (by unreceptiveness), even that which he hath (through his ears merely, cf. Lk 8[18] 'what he supposes he hath') shall be taken from him' (Mk 4[24-25]). Then, after two more parables,[†] we read : 'And with such parables, and many of them, he used to speak to them the word just as they were able to listen ; but without parable used he not to speak to them, whilst privately to his own disciples he used to resolve (the meaning of) all things' (v.[33f.]).

Running throughout the whole account in Mk. is a single coherent conception of the function of parable as a vehicle of religious knowledge, viz. that it is a sort of veil spread over the face of truth, in order that only those who are morally ready to act aright in regard to it shall perceive its Divine lineaments. This implies (a) that it is bad for a man to see the truth in the wrong, i.e. unsympathetic, mood, and (b) that it is the special nature of spiritual or religious knowledge to be morally conditioned in its communication. Accordingly it can be received, in the sense alone valued by Jesus, only gradually, by successive acts of use or vital obedience. But the teacher's ulterior object in parable, as in plainer modes of speech (as the context of the simile of casting pearls before swine helps to make clear, Mt 7[6ff.]), was that as many, not as few, as possible of the average hearers addressed might, by seeking and its discipline, come to find aright, instead of resting in imaginary possession of a knowledge that was really error.[‡] The treasure of knowledge touching the Kingdom could not be had without real spiritual quest ; it was a 'secret,' to be shared in only by awakened curiosity and desire. What is received too easily is held loosely ; or rather, in the case of spiritual truth, it is not received at all, when taken passively and not by the activity that is also self-committal ; or, again, it is received in so crude a sense—what comes from without being overlaid or distorted by what already exists within —that it had better not be received at all in this fashion. The remedy is that the reception should be gradual, through a process of piecemeal and even painful adjustment of the mind and will of the hearer to the essential form of the truth enshrined in the message or teaching. Then, what is so won becomes the basis of fresh discoveries of the same kind. In this beneficent yet deeply serious sense Jesus 'was wont to speak the word' to men 'just as they were able to listen to it.'

Such seems the philosophy of Christ's parabolic teaching, when we regard the trend of this fundamental section and the general effect of His teach-

ing in the Gospels. But what are we to make of the motive assigned fo it in Mk 4[12] 'That seeing they may see, and not perceive ; and hearing they may hear, and not understand ; lest haply they should turn again and it should be forgiven them'? Can we believe that in these words—if read in the sense of a 'judicial blinding'—we have a quotation from Jesus' lips uncoloured by the tradition lying between Him and the Gospel records? Hardly. The saying is an isolated one in the Synoptics. But a like use of the passage in Isaiah (6[9f.]) here drawn upon, occurs in Ac 28[25-27], in an address to leading Roman Jews, and in Jn 12[39, 40], which contains the reflexions of the Evangelist himself. Here we seem to have the clue to the 'paradox' as some would call it, 'incompatibility' as it will seem to others. That is, Jesus' own use of Isaiah's language underwent development in the Church's tradition, being first reapplied to specific Jewish unbelief (as in Acts), and then hardened in its spirit * (as in Jn.). The conclusive thing appears to be this. Not only are the words virtually quoted from Is 6[9f.], but they are not given uniformly in the other Synoptics. Then it is only in the anti-Judaic reflexions in Jn. that the sense of judicial blindness is given to them at all, by a deliberate change of form, which attributes the blinding and dulling of hearing to direct Divine action. It seems natural, then, to assume that Jesus simply made an allusive use of the phraseology of Is 6[9], so far as it lent itself to His purpose ; and that in the Church's tradition this reference was taken up, fully applied, and even, as in Jn 12[40], emphasized in an anti-Jewish direction. Here Mk. shows us the first stage in the tradition, at which the regret with which Jesus contemplates the inevitable effect of the law that unreceptiveness tends to become a fixed habit, is apparent in the quick transition to 'lest haply they should turn back and forgiveness should be theirs' ($\acute{\alpha}\phi\epsilon\theta\hat{\eta}$ $\alpha\acute{\nu}\tau o\hat{\iota}\varsigma$, an adaptation of Isaiah's $\acute{\iota}\acute{\alpha}\sigma o\mu\alpha\iota$ $\alpha\acute{\nu}\tau o\acute{\nu}\varsigma$ on Jahweh's behalf). Against this the telic 'with a view to' ($\acute{\iota}\nu\alpha$) cannot weigh decisively, since its exact degree of purposiveness is not always the same. Here it may well be no more than a recognition of the providential nature of the law of moral continuity, as well as of those inevitable effects which Jesus knew to be involved in His deliberate resort to parabolic teaching,[†] in place of plainer proclamation, touching the Kingdom—its inner and gradual operation, and its fortunes, especially in the near future. Further, the less severe reading seems required by what follows in Mk 4[21-23], viz. that the object of the light's coming is to be seen ; and any temporary 'covering' or 'hiding' is all meant to be subservient to this. All is simply adjusted to existing ability to hear (Mk 4[33]).

Why then, it may be asked, resort to this obscurer form of instruction? Because He was now passing on to a new side or aspect of His teaching. Henceforth the more unambiguous form of declaration would have met immediately with a summary rejection [‡] so decisive as to jeopard-

---

* i.e. to the disciples, to whom He is explaining His new method.

† Probably not spoken on the same occasion, but added by the Evangelist (in keeping with catechetical tradition), by affinity of theme ; and this addition leads up naturally to the use of 'to hear' in v.[33] = to the people.

‡ Cf. A. B. Bruce, The Parabolic Teaching of Christ, pp. 18-23, and Latham, Pastor Pastorum, ch. x. ('To those who have, is given '), in support of this and much of what follows.

* Surely Dr. Sanday (Hastings' DB ii. 618) does not allow enough for the change of spirit between Jesus' own reference to the law of continued insensibility involved in Isaiah, and the less sympathetic use of the words in John. Hence he speaks of their 'strange severity' in Mark's context, 'which would be mitigated if they could be put later in the ministry, where they occur in St. John.' We have argued that even in Mk. they do belong to a relatively late stage in the ministry ; but we would give them a gentler sense on Jesus' own lips, viz. one of sadness, not of severity.

† Which is, as Matthew Henry puts it, a 'shell that keeps good fruit for the diligent, but keeps it from the slothful'; cf. also Bruce, l.c. pp. 21 23.

‡ The lessons as to the slow and gradual progress of the Kingdom, as bound up with its spirituality, 'were so strange to the Jews . . . that He had to adopt a method of instruction that might conciliate and provoke reflection, and gradually make a way to their minds for new truth' (Salmond on Mk 4[1] in Century Bible).

ize the very completion of His own ministry and cut short the training of His disciples, the actual nucleus of the coming Kingdom, on whom its future realization depended. The popular receptivity towards such a Kingdom as Jesus had in mind, one radically spiritual,—as distinct from national and hedonistic,—had already been tested by clear enunciation of its ethical nature and requirements ; and but few had definitely responded. That was the daunting experience which had been His for some months at least, months of such ethical intensity for all within range of His influence as to mean more than as many years of the ordinary testing of life. Already He saw that His lot was to be akin to that of the prophets of old, who achieved their mission only after and through a period of general rejection, during which disciples learned their message vitally, and then helped in the conversion of Israel. But while this was the case on the whole, there were still individuals to be gained over one by one to the 'little flock' of His disciples, if only they had time to ponder the new ideal of the Kingdom—as coming only *gradually*, from *a very small nucleus* (Mk 4$^{26-32}$). Elect souls could do so most profitably under the very stimulus of curiosity aroused by the parabolic or suggestive method, regarded on its positive side ; while for the impatient mass it had only its negative function, veiling the full truth from the profane gaze of those insensible as swine to the real charm of pearls—and apt, when disappointed, to turn like swine and rend the bearer of jewels. Hence Jesus spoke His parables publicly, to call such prepared or preparing souls, as well as to instruct His own inner circle in the deeper or more trying aspects of the Kingdom they had already in principle and at heart received. For this seems the point of Mark's 'To you the secret * (mystery) hath been given, touching the kingdom of God' (v.^{11}). Disciples as such had the qualifying 'secret' in their souls, the key to further understanding in the detailed knowledge of the Kingdom It is rather this latter that Mt. and Lk have in mind in writing (according to the form of the saying most familiar to them), 'to you it hath been given to recognize the secrets (mysteries) of the kingdom.' This probably represents a later turn given to the original thought as found in Mk., the truth of which is borne out by what follows at once in Mt 13^{12} 'he that hath, to him shall be given,' etc. Here the possession that is the basis for further additions, must be primarily the recognition of the Kingdom in principle. When this fundamental issue, as conditioned by the original historic situation, faded more and more into the background, and various detailed aspects of the Kingdom came practically to the front in the Church's experience, it was natural that the saying should be coloured thereby and its shade of meaning changed. Further, we can see how the later form would lend itself to the growing reflective tendency which showed itself in Gnosticism, a mode of thought alike unbiblical and un-Jewish in spirit, but akin to Greek intellectualism or one-sided reliance on 'knowledge' (*gnosis*) as such. Yet rightly understood, *i.e.* in relation to the whole genius of Christ's 'teaching' in the Synoptic Gospels at least,† not even the

later form warrants the idea that 'Gnostic' or metaphysical doctrines are here meant in any degree. The 'secrets' in question are just those detailed aspects of the Kingdom and its development, as parts of the Divine counsels, which form the essence of the parables which follow in this connexion and elsewhere. They are of the nature of moral principles such as verify themselves in the experience of the loyal life, rather than remain 'mysteries of faith' in the later sense of these words.

This is not the place for full discussion of the limits of knowledge, even religious knowledge in a sense, attaching to the gospel in the mind of Jesus Himself. Such limits clearly exist as regards 'the times and seasons' of the Kingdom's temporal development. This is manifest in the saying in Mk 13^{32} ‖ ' But of that day or that hour knoweth no one, not even the angels in heaven, neither the Son, but the Father' (alone). It is also implied in the parable of the Seed Growing Unobserved (Mk 4$^{26-29}$), if the Sower who 'himself knows not *how*' the seed grows, be none other than Christ, as seems to be the case,—a fact which at once explains the omission of the parable by Mt. and Luke. Such ignorance only confirms our general view as to the strictly spiritual character of the 'knowledge' conveyed by Jesus in His 'teaching,'—a statement which applies even to the knowledge referred to in the high utterance in Mt 11$^{25-27}$, Lk 10$^{21f.}$, touching Jesus' unique knowledge of the Father and His corresponding 'revelation' of Him to receptive souls. See, further, art. KENOSIS.

ii. THE FOURTH GOSPEL.—So far we have had in view 'knowledge' and the 'teaching' of it in the Synoptic Gospels only. But like results hold good in essence of the Fourth Gospel also, though with characteristic differences as to form. There, while the special word for 'knowledge' (γνῶσις) does not occur, the corresponding verb, with its suggestions of progressive insight gained by moral affinity, is very frequent (*e.g.* 10^{38} 'recognize and go on recognizing,' 13^7 'thou dost not know now, but thou shalt come to recognize hereafter,' cf. 14^7). The knowledge in view is still such as can be verified by spiritual experience, and not such as must necessarily remain mere objective theory or 'dogma' in the later sense.

A typical passage is 3$^{1-21}$, where, however, it is impossible to say exactly how much is due, in form at least, to the Evangelist, and how much to Him of whom he writes. At v.^{16} even the form ceases to be historic, and passes into reflexion on the principles involved in what precedes. But what underlies the whole is the idea of religious experience as conditioning insight into such knowledge as the new Rabbi had to convey (3$^{2ff.}$). Its subject-matter is the 'Kingdom of God,' the nature of which dawns on a man's inner eye like the light of a fresh world of experience, into which he comes as by a new birth. This correlation of 'light' and 'life' implies that the knowledge in question is not abstract or impersonal, but vital and personal, such as can best be learned from and through a person, as it animates and gives him his specific character and attitude to life. Thus the 'life' in Jesus Himself was the 'light' He bore about in His personal walk among men. This is why 'belief in' Jesus as a person and recognition of the 'light' of His message are so closely related, indeed practically identified, in the Fourth Gospel in particular. Both attitudes of soul are conditioned by a man's will, and this again by his underlying character—so far as developed—and the sympathetic affinities proper thereto. 'For everyone that doeth ill hateth the light, and cometh not to the light, lest his works should be reproved. But he that doeth the truth cometh to the light, that his works may be made manifest, that they have been wrought in God' (3$^{20f.}$). Here we get the

---

* The 'secret' consisted of the true nature of the Kingdom itself, as being such as Jesus revealed it in Himself and His ministry of deed and word (corresponding to 'seeing and 'hearing' in the next verse). This fundamental 'secret' made its possessor a 'disciple' (cf. Mt 13^{52} 'every scribe made a disciple to [or 'by'] the kingdom of heaven' μαθητευθεὶς τῇ βασιλείᾳ τ. οὐρανῶν), corresponding to the 'initiated' in the Greek and other Mysteries. Those who shared it not were 'those outside,' who move wholly in the sphere of 'parable,' the outer simile never opening and revealing the inner truth or reality thus kept 'secret.'

† Confirmed also by the character of 'the Teaching of the

Lord through the Twelve Apostles' as it was understood in the circle represented by the *Didache*,—a fact the more striking if, as seems probable, this compilation of traditional matter represents in the main Syrian Christianity (*c.* 75–100 A.D.), the source also of our Synoptic tradition.

Johannine terms in their most essential meaning, as defined by the context. Christ's manifestation of the knowledge of God (on which the Kingdom depends) as His essential life, is the 'truth' about God and man in their mutual relations,—a truth, therefore, practical in its scope,—and so the 'light' of men as regards their special concern, the art of life. 'He that followeth me shall not walk in darkness, but shall have the light of life' (8[12]). 'My teaching is not mine, but his that sent me. If any man willeth to do his will, he shall know of the teaching, whether it be of God, or whether I speak from myself' (7[16f.]).

This agrees essentially with the Synoptic teaching as to 'righteousness' and its conditions;* it even coincides in form as regards the metaphor of 'light' for man's footsteps in the journey of life (Mt 6[23], Lk 11[33f.], Jn 8[12]), and the vision or blindness of men as determined by their prior moral affinities (Mt 15[14] 23[16-26], Lk 4[18] 6[39]). What is peculiar to the Johannine presentation is the use of 'truth' where the Synoptic word is 'righteousness.' But OT usage † helps us to see their equivalence in idea, and that 'truth' is here at bottom no more speculative or dogmatic than 'righteousness.' It means 'the way of God in truth' (Mt 22[16], Lk 20[21], cf. 16[11]); and the Fourth Evangelist's choice of the more intellectual synonym is probably due to a habit which he had adopted in bringing the message home to men of Greek rather than Jewish training. But the practical and vital sense in which the term is used appears, for instance, in the central saying: 'I am the way, the truth, and the life. No man cometh to the Father but by me' (Jn 14[6]). When, too, Jesus goes on with, 'If you had come to recognize me (for what I am), of my Father also you would have had knowledge' (εἰ ἐγνώκειτε . . . ἂν ἤδειτε), He does not pass into another sphere than that of spiritual quality and power, experimentally perceived: 'He that hath seen me, hath seen the Father.' The very fact that this is said in surprised reply to Philip's request, 'Show us the Father,' proves that distinct and explicit teaching as to the Father in Himself had formed no part of 'the teaching'; it had all been implicit in the authoritative yet dependent or filial mien with which the Son had spoken and acted for God.‡ How far any sayings recorded in the great discourse and prayer which follow, go beyond such manifested spiritual unity, into the realm of metaphysics, is still an open question among scholars. Yet it should be remembered that the thought moves ever on the devotional rather than the dogmatic level of thought, especially in the prayer in ch. 17; and that to all believers is open a like oneness to that between Jesus and His Father (ἵνα ὦσιν ἐν καθὼς ἡμεῖς ἕν, 17[22]), though this comes to others through relation to Himself (ἐγὼ ἐν αὐτοῖς καὶ σὺ ἐν ἐμοί, v.[23]). In any case the unity is that of Love made perfect (vv.[23. 26]), and rests on recognition of the Father's name, gained by recognition of Jesus as sent of the Father (v.[25f.]).

In confirmation of this view, namely, that Jesus' teaching, even in the Johannine Gospel, moved essentially in the region of knowledge accessible to spiritual perception acting on kindred facts of experience, analogously to ordinary sense perception, we have the idea of Jesus as 'the true and faithful witness' (Rev 1[5] 3[14]). Jesus 'witnesses' to His message in various aspects (Jn 3[11] 5[31] 7[7] 8[13f.] 18[37]), in such words and deeds as make failure to recognize its truth a self-judgment passed by each man upon the state of his own conscience or spiritual faculty, as determined by past conduct and motive (Jn 3[17-21] 15[22. 24], cf. Mk 4[21-25] ||). Thus 'the witness' of Jesus constituted a 'manifestation' (2[11] 7[4] 17[6]) within the reach of men independently of intellectual capacity, on the sole basis of moral perceptivity and receptivity (see 7[16f.], quoted above, cf. 5[30]), in which the common folk excelled the learned (Mt 11[25]). The real object of such perception by nascent moral affinity, the specific revelation in Christ, was the total effect of Jesus' teaching, what we should style its 'spirit.' To resist this impression by practically judging it evil in nature and origin, was sin against 'the Holy Spirit' at work in the conscience—the most fatal, because the most radical of all sins (Mk 3[28-30], Mt 12[31]). The ultimate source, then, of insight into the message witnessed and the character of the Messenger as sent of God, especially in the full and perfect sense constituting Him the Messiah (Mk 8[27-30] ||), was the revealing action of the Father Himself (Mt 16[17], Jn 5[32] 6[44] 8[18], cf. Mt 11[27]), as distinct from all mere human conditions of knowing (cf. Latham, op. cit. 337 f.). The Father Himself was the ultimate witness. Not only were Jesus' works manifestly God's works (Jn 5[36] 17[10]); His 'voice' gave the final silent confirmation within the conscience; His 'immanent word' answered to the word uttered without by His witness; the vaguely dim outline of His character or Name was but fulfilled in clearer form in the Name given by and in His witness (Jn 5[37f.]). And so the 'light' from within met and recognized the light from without, and rose to the triumphant faith that the Light promised to Israel had indeed risen upon it.

iii. GENERAL RESULTS.—In all this there seems essential harmony between the Synoptics and the Fourth Gospel, though in the latter the emphasis on the inner conditions of insight, and upon the Person of Jesus as summing up the spirit of His own teaching by word and deed, is more marked. In both types of Gospel the educative method * of Jesus appears, even if, from its different scope, the Fourth Gospel does not bring this out concretely and progressively, as does the Synoptic narrative by its very nature as a narrative largely concerned with the gradual 'training of the Twelve' through actual intercourse with their Master. Perhaps we may say that the immediate influence of the Personality of Jesus, through eye and ear, is more apparent in the Synoptic account; while in the Johannine, the universal significance of His 'Person' as Messianic and Divine is set in relief —as it would be in later Christian experience. But in neither does the knowledge go beyond the scope of the Kingdom of God, the true Sovereignty of the Righteous Father—first its principles, and then its future developments—in close connexion with the destiny of its Founder and Lord, the Messiah, seen in His true character as unique Son of God. It is continuous with the Covenant idea of personal relations between God and His chosen people, and with the Divine name or character revealed in concreto through those relations.† The

---

* Cf. Wendt, The Teaching of Jesus, i. 256 ff., as well as his general conception of the relation between the Synoptic and the Johannine representations of Jesus' teaching.

† Cf. Hastings' DB iii. p. 9[a]: 'The conception of true religion as the knowledge of God is probably the true antecedent and parent of some NT expressions for which affinities have been sought in the phenomena of Gnosticism. John (6[45]) quotes Is 54[13]' ('All thy children shall be taught of the Lord').

‡ Latham, op. cit. p. 17, observes that Jesus 'trusts to men's believing that the Father is in Him, not because He has declared it in set dogmas, but because He has been "so long with them."' This is part of His chosen method of teaching, to the most religious effect, in view of the nature of man as a being whose spiritual faculties are to be evoked and trained freely and ethically.

* The wonderfully original and quickening nature of this is analyzed in Latham's Pastor Pastorum as nowhere else, perhaps, not excepting Ecce Homo.

† Cf. Ps 25[14] RV, 'The secret (counsel) of the Lord is with them that fear him; and his covenant, to make them know it' (τοῦ δηλῶσαι αὐτοῖς). Here the LXX inserts reference to 'the name of the Lord' between the parallel clauses, as a third synonym.

'secret' or mystery revealed is the more spiritual and less national nature of the Kingdom ; and its essential contents form the New Covenant, which, towards the end of His private teaching to the inner circle of disciples, Jesus declared was destined to be consecrated or sealed in His own life-blood. The emphasis on the connexion between the message and the Messenger, the Messianic Kingdom and His own Person as Messianic Son of God, increased with the growing opposition encountered ; so that confidence in Himself became the very sheet-anchor of the cause to which He was from the first consecrated. Thus the perspective of the 'teaching' changes somewhat. The side at first implicit, becomes more and more explicit, especially in the intimate intercourse of Jesus and His inner circle. But there is essential continuity of spirit throughout. Nor is there any esoteric knowledge, in the strict sense, different in kind from the public teaching. The inner side was simply the darker side of difficulty and rejection, that most apt to repel the hearer until his confidence in the Master was well grounded. These were 'the mysteries'* of the Kingdom, if Jesus ever used such an expression (Mt 13[11], Lk 8[10], where Mk. has 'the mystery,' and above, p. 702). There was no new 'theology' in the abstract and Greek sense, as distinct from that of personal relations with man. Accordingly there is in the teaching of Christ no real warrant for the Gnostic developments which began once the Gospel passed from Jewish to Greek soil. It is significant that religious knowledge was not taken in a Gnostic sense among Palestinian Christians (as distinct from the mixed Samaritan type). This implies that Christ's teaching was felt to move within the circle of general Hebrew metaphysics, and not to have any direct knowledge here to convey.

Such a judgment is confirmed, positively, by the so-called 'Teaching of the Twelve Apostles,' which in its present form is probably of Palestinian or Syrian origin, and understands 'the teaching (διδαχή) of the Lord' to have differed from Judaism only ethically, in the deeper knowledge of God's will, fuller spiritual life, and firmer grasp on immortality (γνῶσις καὶ πίστις, ζωή, ἀθανασία, ix. 3, x. 2), which it bestowed. Its negative confirmation lies in the very fact that Gnosticizing versions of Christ's teaching early arose in the centres where the Hellenic spirit was strongest. Such 'apocryphal' Gospels, professing, as a rule, to supply from a secret line of tradition the words of 'deeper wisdom' which it was assumed must have fallen from the lips of the great Revealer of the spiritual world (here regarded cosmically rather than ethically), only show what the speculative spirit missed in our Gospels, with their concrete, practical teaching, often in terms of an individual case. Most probably Christian Gnostics felt some encouragement and justification afforded them by the less Hebraic tone of the Fourth Gospel, even though it is mystical rather than metaphysical in its distinctive elements, and is tinged with Christian experience rather than cosmical philosophy. Probably also their first efforts at Gospel-writing were more ethical than metaphysical in scope and interest. This was certainly the case in some circles, notably that represented by the Gospel to which belong the Oxyrhynchus 'Sayings of Jesus' (published in 1898, 1904), in which the non-original element is largely inspired by the 'Wisdom' literature of Hellenistic Judaism, and takes the form mainly of glossing certain actual sayings of Jesus with developments and expansions in terms of the deeper moral philosophy of the day, e.g. of the

maxim, 'Know thyself,' and the Platonic doctrine of Wonder as the mother of Wisdom. Once this process of free development was started, however, and sanctioned among Christians imbued with Hellenic and Oriental notions, both philosophical and mythological,—for the age was one of syncretism or the blending and fusion of ideas of very diverse origin,—it was bound to go ever further and further away from the attitude and horizon of historic Gospels. If the remains of 2nd cent. Gospels known to us were not so scanty, we should be able to see the stages by which the later types, in which the historic element of Jesus' teaching in word and deed is at a minimum, evolved gradually, rather than sprang full-blown to life. Thus the uncanonical Gospel drawn on by the preacher whose homily is known traditionally as '2 Clement,' whether it be the *Gospel according to the Egyptians* or not, represented the next stage of idealization to that marked by the Oxyrhynchus Gospel ; but it still contained much matter found in (and probably borrowed from) our Synoptic Gospels.* Quite the opposite kind of development, though one which also carries us away from the historic teaching of Jesus, is seen in the Judaizing *Gospel according to the Hebrews*, in its two forms or stages, in which the reactionary reading of Jesus' message, the tendency to make it Judaic in letter and spirit, becomes more and more manifest.

Midway between these two opposed tendencies— the Judaic or legal, and the Gnostic or esoteric, mysterious, metaphysical—lie our historic Gospels. They are full of the spirit of Hebraic teaching as to knowledge of Divine things ; but raise it to a new power and universality by contact with the Personality and spirit of Jesus, Himself the heart of the Gospel within the Gospels, the prime source of their perennial vitality and authority. Nor must we overlook the fact that the very form of these Gospels fits them, in a wonderful way, to be the vehicles of religious teaching after the mind of Jesus Himself, through ' being narrative instead of didactic, and coming from the Evangelists instead of from Christ' Himself direct. 'If our Lord,' says Latham (p. 13), 'had left writings of His own, every letter of them would have been invested with such sanctity that there could have been no independent investigation of truth. Its place would have been taken by commentatorial works on the delivered word,' on the lines of the scribes and Rabbis. The letter of Jesus' teaching would have been so revered, that its 'spirit and life' would have had less chance of reproducing itself through personal effort freely to find its meaning by inner moral quest. So would the very end of that teaching have been frustrated. For 'in all His sayings and doings, our Lord was most careful to leave the individual room to grow.' 'He cherishes and respects personality.' And so 'He gave *seed thoughts* which should lie in men's hearts, and germinate when fit occasion came' (*ib.* pp. 5, 10, 12). All this is permanently secured by the simple narrative form of the Gospels, especially the Synoptics. Herein the outer form of the NT—its Epistles hardly less than its Gospels —is as characteristic of the religion it enshrines as the Koran is of Islam. It is a notable fact that the Apocryphal Gospels steadily moved away from the narrative to the didactic manner, many of them transposing their key from the third to the first person, by the device of making their teaching ostensibly post-resurrectional (even the Oxyrhynchus Gospel does this), with a view to make it more dogmatically impressive. In so doing they came nearer the Koran and most other sacred

---

* True to the OT usage='secret counsels'; cf. Rev 10[7] 'then is finished the mystery of God, according to the good tidings which he declared to his servants the prophets.'

* See *The New Testament in the Apostolic Fathers*, Oxford, 1905.

books representing founders of religions ; but they receded further from the earlier type of Christian written Gospel, of which the four in the Church's canon are the most perfect samples.

See also artt. DISCOURSE, ILLUSTRATIONS, ORIGINALITY, PARABLE, etc.

LITERATURE.—As bearing on the form of Jesus' teaching and its leading terms, so far as determined by their original Aramaic character, Dalman's *Die Worte Jesu* is invaluable [Eng. tr. of first part=*The Words of Jesus*, Edinburgh, T. & T. Clark, 1902]. Equally fundamental for the meaning of Jesus' teaching in the Synoptics, compared also with that in the Fourth Gospel, is Wendt, *Die Lehre Jesu* [Eng. tr. *The Teaching of Jesus*, 2 vols., Edinburgh, T. & T. Clark, 1892]; cf. A. B. Bruce, *The Kingdom of God*, Edinburgh, 1890, *The Parabolic Teaching of Christ*, London, 1889. Perhaps the best book in English on the whole subject is Latham's *Pastor Pastorum* (Cambridge, 1890), which gives special attention to 'the way in which our Lord taught His disciples, both in what He did and in what He refrained from doing' and saying. Incidental help is also afforded by the larger *Lives of Christ* ; while the articles on 'Knowledge' and 'Teaching' in Bible Dictionaries and Encyclopædias often contain a section on our special subject.

VERNON BARTLET.

TEARS.—The only two passages in EV of the Gospels where tears are mentioned are Mk 9²⁴, where the father of the epileptic lad is said in AV to have cried out with tears, 'Lord, I believe, help thou mine unbelief' [RV, however, following decidedly the best MSS, omits the words 'with tears']; and Lk 7³⁸⁻⁴⁴, where, in Simon the Pharisee's house, the penitent harlot washed with her tears the Saviour's feet. If, however, we enlarge our article by references to weeping, we have several instances of sorrow calling forth those tears which are its frequent, but by no means invariable, expression. Mary of Magdala wept when on the third day after the crucifixion she found that the body of her beloved Lord was no longer in Joseph's sepulchre (Jn 20¹¹⁻¹⁶). Peter wept tears of bitter shame when the sound of the cock-crowing brought home to him his sin in denying the Master on the night of betrayal (Mk 14⁷² and parallels). In each of these cases it may be useful to notice that tears were turned into joy ; for to the penitent woman Christ said, 'Go in peace'; Mary's grief was changed to adoring rapture when the risen Saviour pronounced her name ; and to Peter, by a special revelation of grace, He granted the blessedness of the man whose transgression is forgiven and whose sin is covered. In no case was the lamentation vain remorse, like that of Esau, who found no place of repentance, though he sought the blessing of his father diligently with tears (He 12¹⁷).

Most important of all are the passages where Jesus Himself is reported to have wept. They are three. (1) On the day when He rode into Jerusalem on the ass's colt, while the multitudes were rejoicing with shouts of Hosanna, His heart was not in tune with their mirth. Lk 19⁴¹ says that when He was come nigh, He saw the city, and wept over it. There was good reason for His wails. [The word ἔκλαυσεν does not actually express tears so much as loud cries]. The sins which that city had committed in killing the prophets and stoning them that were sent unto her—sins which were to culminate in a few days when He Himself was to be the victim of their malice—lay sore on the heart of Him who would gladly have gathered her children together, even as a hen gathereth her chickens under her wings, and who saw His salvation rejected. The dishonour done to His Father and the degradation of His Father's house filled Him with a grief which not only made rivers of waters run down His eyes, but drew words of indignation from His lips. The sorrows which were about to swamp Jerusalem in a flood of woe wrung from His heart the agonizing cry, 'If thou hadst known in this day, even thou, the things which belong unto peace ! but now they are hid from thine eyes' (Lk

19⁴²). It was not for Himself that He lamented, nor for Himself that He would allow tears to be shed by others. Even while He was ready to faint under the load of the cross that was to be His anguish and shame, He said, 'Daughters of Jerusalem, weep not for me.' If they had tears, let them prepare to shed them now for themselves and for their children, because of the fearful tragedies that were to be enacted in their city ere a few years had passed (Lk 23²⁷⁻³¹). The Man of sorrows and acquainted with grief (Is 53³) was in His characteristic attitude of agonizing for others when the load of their sins lay heavily upon Him that day, and He was like the prophet (Jer 9¹) who wished that his head were waters and his eyes a fountain of tears, that he might weep day and night for the slain of the daughter of his people.

(2) Jn 11³⁵ 'Jesus wept.' The word here is ἐδάκρυσεν, 'shed tears.' This was at the grave of Lazarus when He was about to raise him from the dead. There is something here to surprise us, though much that was very natural in the tears of the Saviour. To the widow of Nain who was following the bier of her only son He said, 'Weep not' (Lk 7¹³), as He had said to those who lamented the daughter of Jairus, 'Why make ye this ado, and weep?' (Mk 5³⁸⁻³⁹). He was about to dry their tears and silence their wails by restoring their dead to life. Yet here (Jn 11³⁵⁻³⁵) it is recorded that He Himself groaned in spirit, and wept as He joined the company of those who were weeping with the bereaved sisters. The tears of Jesus on this occasion have been a source of much consolation to those who mourn their dead. One is reminded of the lines of Erasmus Darwin—

'No radiant pearl which crested Fortune wears,
　No gem that, twinkling, hangs from Beauty's ears,
　Not the bright stars which Night's blue arch adorn,
　Nor rising stars that gild the vernal morn,
　Shine with such lustre as the tear that flows
　Down Virtue's manly cheek for others' woes.'

They prove to us the perfect humanity of the Redeemer. He who with Divine authority was about to call the dead to life yet had the human weakness to shed tears. 'The possession of a body enabled Him to weary ; the possession of a soul enabled Him to weep' (F. W. Robertson). They also show His thorough sympathy with those who have to endure grief, especially bereavement, how in all their afflictions He is afflicted. Perhaps they may also be evidence of the anguish He felt at the woe which was caused in the world by that sin in the train of which misery and death came into the world. Further, the tears may have been drawn forth as He thought of the anguish that would be caused to His mother and His friends when He Himself should be laid within such a sepulchre as that before His eyes. And no doubt while on this occasion in Bethany He was about to turn sorrow to joy and heaviness to mirth, yet He was aware that there were multitudes who would have to sorrow without hope, and bewailed that he who had the power of death must claim so many victims ere he was himself destroyed.

(3) He 5⁷⁻⁸. In this interesting passage, which, while it does not occur in the Gospels, refers to Christ, we are reminded how, in the days of His flesh, He offered up prayers with strong crying and tears unto Him who was able to save Him from death. The allusion is chiefly to the agony of Gethsemane, though possibly to other occasions of Christ praying to the Father. It is hardly within the scope of this article to discuss the question of what it was for which our Lord then prayed. It can hardly have been merely such a prayer as that of Hezekiah when he turned his face to the wall and wept sore on being told that his sickness was

mortal (2 K 20[1-3]), or that of the Psalmist who, as he mingled his drink with weeping, said : 'O my God, take me not away in the midst of my days' (Ps 102[9. 24]).   For a discussion of the subject see Westcott, *Hebrews* ; Schauffler in *Sunday School Times*, of America, 1895 ; *Expository Times*, vi. 1894–95, pp. 433, 522.   It is evident that the writer's thought is to a large extent linked with the mediatorial office of Christ in the perfect obedience of His humanity which was learned through suffering.   Death to Him, as well as to all Christians, had an awful meaning ; and however willing the spirit of Christ might be to meet it, yet the flesh was weak, and tears might well gush forth in prospect of its bitterness.   Here, again, from the tears of the Saviour, we learn the thorough sympathy of Christ with men, even the identification of the Son of Man with those for whom He was to die.

LITERATURE.—Lives of Christ and Commentaries on Gospels and on Hebrews ; numerous published sermons, among which there stand out as noteworthy : Donne (vol. i.) ; Henry Melvill, 'Fifty Sermons' ; F. W. Robertson, 'The Human Race.'

ARTHUR POLLOK SYM.

TEMPERANCE.—In the Sermon on the Mount Christ dwells on the restraint under which not only our actions and our words must be held, but also our thoughts.   He sees in the angry thought the germ of murder, in the impure thought the germ of adultery, and so He goes to the root of the matter.   It is of no use to try to cleanse the stream at a certain point in its course, if the fountain from which it flows is impure ; if the stream is to be kept pure the fountain must be kept pure ; and if the words and actions are to be under control, the thoughts of the heart must be under control.   It is from within, out of the heart, that all kinds of irregularities proceed, therefore 'keep thy heart with all diligence,' or, as in the marginal note, 'above all that thou guardest, for out of it are the issues of life' (Pr 4[23]).

In the parable of the Prodigal Son we see the depth of degradation into which a man is brought when he breaks away from his God.   In the case of the prodigal, the initial step was taken when the undisciplined thought was harboured in the heart.   His mind fretted and rebelled against the restraints of his father's house, he wished to go out into the world and to see life, he wanted to be free from all control.   The next step was the undisciplined word, 'Give me the portion of thy substance that falleth to me.'   And the final step was the undisciplined act, 'He took his journey into a far country, and there he wasted his substance with riotous living.'   Here the thought first ran riot, and the rest followed.

Christianity, therefore, is a religion not merely for a part of our being, but for the whole man ; it touches him in every relationship of life and in every aspect of that relationship.   It teaches him to 'live soberly, righteously, and godly in this present world' (Tit 2[12]).   While righteousness represents his attitude towards his fellow-men and godliness his attitude towards God, soberness represents his attitude towards himself.   Soberness ($\sigma\omega\phi\rho\sigma\sigma\acute{\upsilon}\nu\eta$) is a right balance in all things ; it is the bringing of the lower part of the nature into subjection to the higher, the flesh into subjection to the spirit ; it means the spirit of man, guided by the Holy Spirit of God, governing the soul or intellect ; then the soul or intellect, thus sanctified, governing the flesh ; and the whole man, body, soul, and spirit, kept under control, held in hand, just as a spirited horse is held in hand by an experienced rider ; moving on, not torn asunder by conflicting interests, but advancing steadily in one direction upwards and heavenwards.

A temperate man is one who rules himself, who lets every act that he performs have its own proper place, who gives everything its own due proportion, who does not eat too much, drink too much, sleep too much, talk too much, or do anything in excess.   We live in days when there is an inordinate craving for amusement : amusements have their place, and, within limits, are not only necessary but good for us ; but when they absorb so large a portion of our life that its more serious duties have to give place to them, then they become extremely hurtful.   They should be regarded as sidings off the main line of our life, opportunities for recruiting our tired and weary energies, so that we may return to our work with renewed vigour ; and when thus used they are very helpful. A temperate man will exercise self-control with regard to these as well as in all other matters.

But while temperance is an all-round virtue, the term has come to be used very largely with reference to self-control in a particular direction, viz. in the matter of strong drink.   When we speak of 'the Temperance cause' or 'Temperance work,' we generally mean the efforts that are being made to suppress intemperance in the use of alcohol. Our Temperance Societies are directed towards this object, and so the word 'temperance' has come to be used almost exclusively in this connexion ; and it cannot be denied that there is some justification for it, because the effects of the abuse of strong drink are so patent and so terrible that they attract attention in a way that few other sins do.   Temperance is not necessarily total abstinence ; it is the use, as distinct from the abuse, of strong drink.   Total abstinence may be necessary ; for the inveterate drunkard it *is* necessary ; for him the only remedy, under God, is to abstain altogether from that which he cannot use in strict moderation (cf. Jesus' words in Mt 5[29. 30]).   Again it may be necessary for others besides drunkards, viz., for those who are to rescue the victims of strong drink, for we all know that example is far more powerful than precept ; we are far more likely to be able to help those who have fallen into this abyss by saying to them, 'Do as we do,' than by saying, 'Do as we tell you.'

But while total abstinence may be necessary for some, especially for those of us who are working in the slums of our large towns, it is not enjoined upon all ; the strictly moderate use of alcohol cannot be said to be a sin ; and to speak of it as though it were a sin, as has sometimes been done, is only to weaken the cause that we have at heart ; it is the abuse of it that is a sin, and therefore, while abstinence is not enjoined upon all, temperance is enjoined upon every Christian man and woman.

Our Lord tells us what is the end and aim of our fallen but redeemed and regenerate humanity, 'Ye therefore shall be perfect, as your heavenly Father is perfect' (Mt 5[48]).   This is the goal set before us ; and to reach this goal our attitude must be that of the spiritual athlete, straining every nerve and exerting every muscle, keeping under the body and bringing it into subjection, running the race set before us, 'looking unto Jesus' (He 12[2]), looking unto Him as our example, looking unto Him for strength, pressing onward from stage to stage, from strength to strength, from one degree of perfection unto another, 'unto a full-grown man, unto the measure of the stature of the fulness of Christ' (Eph 4[13]).

And here our Lord stands before us as our Ideal. The Jesus of the Gospels presents to us a life which is the very embodiment of temperance, a life of perfect self-restraint, of complete self-mastery ; a life free from excess on the one hand and defect on the other, well-balanced, well-proportioned, without flaw, without spot, perfect in all its parts; a life which had for its object the glory of God, from the time when He came into the world, saying, 'Lo, I come to do thy will, O my God' (He 10[7]), to the time when, having finished all, He exclaimed with the voice of a conqueror, 'I have finished the work which thou gavest me to do' (Jn 17[4]). To copy this perfect Ideal and to reach this goal we, by a life lived in union with Him and by the power of the Holy Ghost, must strive to be temperate in all things. See, further, art. SELF-CONTROL.

ROWLAND ELLIS.

TEMPEST.—See SEA OF GALILEE, p. 591.

TEMPLE.—i. *USE OF TERMS.*—**1.** The word which is most frequently used in the Gospels for the temple is τὸ ἱερόν (בֵּית הַמִּקְדָּשׁ); it occurs nearly 50 times. Under this term is included, generally speaking, the whole of the temple area, *i.e.* the Court of the Gentiles, the Court of the Women, the Court of the Israelites, the Priests' Court, and the Holy Place, together with the Holy of Holies. In this wide sense it is used in Mt 12[6] 24[1. 2], Mk 11[11] 13[1. 3] 14[49], Lk 19[47] 21[37. 38] 22[52] 24[53]; but in a number of passages it is used in a more restricted sense, viz. : in reference to the *Court of the Gentiles*, Mt 21[12-16. 23], Mk 11[15-18. 27], Lk 19[45] 22[53], Jn 2[14. 15] 5[14] 8[59]; in reference to the *Court of the Women*, Mk 12[41], Lk 2[27. 37] 21[1]; in reference to the *Court of the Israelites*, Mt 26[55], Mk 12[35], Lk 2[46] 18[10] 20[1], Jn 7[14. 28] 11[56] 18[20]. The particular part of the temple referred to cannot always be ascertained with certainty, especially in the case of the *Men's Court* (Court of the Israelites), but presumably the mention of 'teaching in the temple' would usually refer to Christ teaching the Jews (in view of such passages as 'I am not sent save unto the lost sheep of the house of Israel,' Mt 15[24]), in which case the women, according to Jewish custom, would not be present. In a few instances ἱερόν is used of some particular part of the temple, viz. of the actual sanctuary, Lk 21[5], Jn 8[20]; in this passage the treasury is spoken of loosely, as being in the temple (ἱερόν), strictly speaking it was in the Sanctuary (ναός). The same applies to the mention of Solomon's Porch in Jn 10[23]. In reference to the wing or pinnacle of the temple (Mt 4[5], Lk 4[9]) πτερύγιον τοῦ ἱεροῦ is used; as to where this spot was precisely scholars differ. See PINNACLE. Once the phrase τὸ ἱερὸν τοῦ θεοῦ is used (Mt 21[12]), but the addition of τοῦ θεοῦ is not well attested.

2. The word ναός[*] (הֵיכָל) denotes the *Sanctuary*, *i.e.* that part of the temple which was holy, and to which, therefore, none but the priests had access; it included the Holy Place and the Holy of Holies (see Lk 1[21. 22]). The ναός was built of white marble, overlaid in part with gold sheeting; this costliness is referred to in Mt 23[16. 17]. Other references to the Sanctuary are : 23[18. 19. 35], which speak of the altar; 27[5. 6], the treasury (but see below); Lk 1[9], the altar of incense (here the phrase ὁ ναὸς τοῦ κυρίου occurs for the only time); Mt 27[51], the heavy veil between the Holy of Holies and the Holy Place (see also Mk 15[38], Lk 23[45]). Finally, Christ speaks of His body as symbolizing the Sanctuary in Jn 2[19-21], cf. Mt 26[61] (where the only occurrence of the phrase ὁ ναὸς τοῦ θεοῦ is found) 27[40], Mk 14[58] 15[29]. In Jn 2[20] ὁ ναός is inaccurately used in the words 'Forty and six years was this temple in building' (*i.e.* has this temple been in building up till now), for it was the whole temple area with all included in it that had so far been

worked at for forty-six years; it was not finished until shortly before its final destruction by Titus in A.D. 70-71.

3. A few other expressions used for the temple may be briefly referred to : ὁ οἶκός μου,[*] Mt 21[13], Mk 11[17], Lk 19[46], Jn 2[17]; οἶκος προσευχῆς, Mt 21[13], Mk 11[17], Lk 19[46]; ὁ οἶκος τοῦ πατρός μου, Jn 2[16]. All these expressions are used in the larger sense of τὸ ἱερον. The 'Holy Place' is specifically referred to in Mt 23[35] 'between the sanctuary (ναός) and the altar,' *i.e.* the space between the outer veil (see below) and the altar for burnt-offerings; in 24[15] ἑστὸς ἐν τόπῳ ἁγίῳ, but in the parallel passage (Mk 13[14]) the reading is ἑστηκότα ὅπου οὐ δεῖ.[†] Lastly, the expression ὁ οἶκος ὑμῶν, Mt 23[38] ('*Your* house is left unto you desolate'),[‡] apparently also refers to the temple, for it is in the temple that these words were spoken, and it is to the temple that the disciples point when admiring the beauty of the building, in reply to which Christ says : 'There shall not be left here one stone upon another, which shall not be thrown down'; thus 'your house' evidently means the temple building in its external form, in contradistinction to the 'house of God,' the spiritual building not made with hands.

ii. *HEROD'S TEMPLE.* — There are several admirable descriptions of Herod's temple published and easily available; [§] all are based on the main sources, viz. Jos. *Ant.* XV. xi., *BJ* v. v., *c. Ap.* i. 22, and the Mishnic tractate *Middoth.*[‖] It will, therefore, not be necessary to give a detailed account here, but a general outline to illustrate the Gospel references is necessary. Herod the Great commenced rebuilding the temple ¶ in the year B.C. 20 (the eighteenth year of his reign), on the site of the second temple; but the available space was insufficient for the much larger building which he intended to erect. He therefore constructed immense vaulted chambers [**] on the south side of the hill on which the earlier temple stood; by this means the area at his disposal was doubled. A general idea of the whole will be best gained by indicating its main divisions :

1. The Outer Court. — This large space (two *stadia* [††] in length, one in breadth, the perimeter being six *stadia*), which surrounded the temple proper, was enclosed by a battlemented wall. The main entrances to this enclosure were on the west, leading from the city; here there were four gates, the remains of one of which have been discovered.[‡‡]

---

[*] It was that part in which God 'dwelt' (ναίω), and corresponded to what was originally also the most sacred part, *i.e.* *bêth-'El* (cf. the Hebrew name for the temple as a whole, בַּיִת 'house'), the 'house of God'; the early conception of a temple was that of being essentially a 'dwelling-place' for God (cf. 2 S 7[5-7]).

[*] ὁ οἶκος τοῦ θεοῦ (Mt 12[4], Mk 2[26], Lk 6[4]) is used in reference to the sanctuary at Nob, 1 S 21[4-6].

[†] On this passage see Swete, *in loc.*

[‡] ἔρημος is read by אCD OL, but omitted by all other authorities.

[§] The most useful are those in Riehm's *HBA* ii. pp. 1636-1645; the section 'Tempel des Herodes' in Nowack's *Heb. Arch.* ii. pp. 74-83; the account in Guthe's *Kurzes Bibel-Wörterbuch*, pp. 653-658. The best, however, is that in Hastings' *DB*; it is very full, and the excellent illustrations enable one to form a definite picture of what the temple looked like in the time of Christ; the art. in the *Encyc. Bibl.* is very useful; there is also an interesting art. in vol. xii. of the *Jewish Encyclopedia*. See, further, the literature at the end of this article.

[‖] ed. Surenhusius, see also Hildersheim's description in *Jahresbericht des Rabbiner-Seminars für das orthodoxe Judenthum* (Berlin, 1876-1877). *Middoth* belongs to the 2nd cent. A.D., but its account of the temple is evidently based on reliable data. The original sources are not always in agreement, but taking them together a sufficiently accurate picture of Herod's temple is obtainable.

[¶] It was not completed until the procuratorship of Albinus (A.D. 62-64). Its site is to-day occupied by the Ḥaram es-Sherif, though this includes also part of the site formerly covered by the Tower of Antonia, which stood at the north-west of the temple area.

[**] Called by the Arabs 'Solomon's Stables'; opinions differ as to whether they belong to an earlier period, and were only renovated by Herod, or whether Herod constructed them himself, or whether they belong to a later date altogether.

[††] A *stadium* = 606⅔ English feet.

[‡‡] Known, after the name of the discoverer, as Wilson's Arch (see Warren and Conder's *Survey of Western Palestine*, 'Jerusalem,' p. 196).

On the south side were the two 'Huldah' gates, remains of which have also been discovered. On the south-west corner there was a bridge which led from the city into the temple area; a huge arch which formed part of this bridge was discovered by Robinson, and is called after him. There was one gate on the east, which has been walled up; this was called the 'Golden Gate,' which tradition identifies with the 'Beautiful Gate' mentioned in Ac 3[2].* On the north there was likewise one gate, called in *Middoth* the 'Tadi Gate.'† All these gates led directly into the great temple area, or outer court; around the whole area, within the walls, were ranged porticoes with double rows of pillars; but the finest was that on the south side; here there were four rows of Corinthian columns made of white marble. All these porticoes were covered with a roof of wood. The eastern portico was called **Solomon's Porch** (Jn 10[23], cf. Ac 3[11] 5[12]); it belonged to an earlier building which tradition ascribed to Solomon. On the north-west two sets of steps led up to the **Tower of Antonia;** the Roman garrison stationed here kept constant watch during the feasts and other occasions of great gatherings, in case of tumult (cf. Ac 21[35. 40]). This temple area was called the 'Court of the Gentiles'; it was not part of the temple proper, and therefore not sacred soil, consequently any one might enter it. It is to this outer court that reference is made in Mt 21[12-16], Mk 11[15ff.], Lk 19[45. 46], Jn 2[13-17]; the money-changers‡ and those who sold animals for the temple sacrifices had free access here.

2. The Court of the Israelites.—This inner court was raised fifteen cubits§ above the outer one just referred to; it was surrounded by a terrace (*ḥêl*), ten cubits in breadth, which was approached from the outer court by ascending fourteen steps; these steps ran round the whole terrace, and at the bottom of them there was a low wall or breastwork (*ṣôrêg*) which was the limit to which non-Israelites might approach; along it were placed, at intervals, inscriptions warning Gentiles not to pass beyond, on pain of death; they were written in Latin and Greek; one of the latter has been discovered by Clermont-Ganneau.‖ On entering this inner court, 'holy' ground was reached, which accounted for the prohibition just referred to; only the seed of Abraham might enter here, hence its name. It was divided into two portions:

(*a*) *The Women's Court.*—This was the smaller division; it occupied the eastern part. The court received its name from the fact that it formed the limit to which women might advance towards the sanctuary, not because it was reserved for the use of women.¶ It was on a lower level than the Men's Court, which was entered through six of the nine gates belonging to the Women's Court. Of these gates, three deserve special mention, viz. that presented by Alexander of Alexandria; it was one of the largest, and was covered with gold and silver; secondly, the Eastern gate, which was covered with Corinthian bronze; and, above all, the gate

of Nicanor;* this was called the 'Great Gate'; it was fifty cubits high and forty broad; fifteen steps, semicircular in form, led up to it from the Women's Court. Whether the 'Beautiful Gate' mentioned in Ac 3[2] referred to this or to the Eastern gate of the Outer Court (see above) is quite uncertain.

(*b*) But the *Court of the Israelites* proper was the western and larger court, called also the *Men's Court*, and to this only men had access. It ran round the whole of the Sanctuary itself, in which was included the Priests' Court (see below). In the Men's Court were (according to Josephus) the treasury-chambers, where all the more valuable temple belongings were kept. The 'treasury' spoken of in Mk 12[41. 43], Lk 21[1] was clearly entered by women; the discrepancy may, however, be explained by supposing that one of the trumpet-shaped receptacles into which offerings were cast, and which usually stood in the Men's Court, was at certain times placed in the eastern portion of the court, so that every one, including the women, might have the opportunity of making the offerings; on such occasions the Women's Court was, for the time being, a treasury. On the other hand, the treasury mentioned in Jn 8[20] would appear, from the context,† to refer to that in the Men's Court, the word being used here in the strict sense (see, too, Mt 27[5. 6]).

3. The Court of the Priests.—Before entering the most sacred parts of the Sanctuary, the Priests' Court had to be traversed. In this court there stood, in the centre, the great altar for burnt-sacrifices, and close to it the brazen laver for the priestly ablutions. On the right of these, on entering, was the place for slaughtering the animals brought for sacrifice. On either side of the court were the priests' chambers; it is probable that one of these was the *Lishkath parhedrin*, 'the Hall of the πρόεδροι ('assessors'), in which the members of the Sanhedrin met in a *quasi*-private character before they met officially in the *Lishkath ha-gazith*,‡ 'the Hall of hewn stone.' Where this latter was precisely, it is impossible to say, owing to the conflicting evidence of the authorities; the only thing that seems tolerably certain is that, while it was within the enclosure of the temple proper, it was not within the Priests' Court; this is certain from the fact that none but priests might enter the court called after them; the only exception to this was that which permitted the entrance of those who brought offerings, for they had to lay their hands upon the sacrifice, in accordance with the prescribed ritual.

4. The Holy Place (*hêkhāl*).—This was separated from the Priests' Court by a high porch (*'ûlām*, see above, i. **1**), running north and south; it was a hundred cubits in height (the highest part of the whole temple) and breadth, but only eleven in depth. The Holy Place stood on a higher level than the surrounding court, from which twelve steps led up to it. Its furniture consisted of the altar of incense (see Lk 1[9]), the table of the shew-bread, and the seven-branched candlestick.

---

* Possibly to be identified with the 'Shushan Gate' mentioned in *Middoth.*

† The 'private' gate, used only by mourners and those who were ceremonially unclean.

‡ The temple tribute was half a shekel annually; as this had to be paid in the form of the ancient coin, the money-changers who exchanged them for current coin had an opportunity, which they did not neglect, of making considerable profits on commission.

§ A cubit = 1 ft. 5½ in. or 1 ft. 8½ in., according to the shorter or longer measurement; see Hastings' *DB* ana *Encyc. Bibl.* art. 'Weights and Measures.'

‖ It runs: 'No Gentile may enter within the balustrade and wall encircling the temple. Whosoever is caught (doing so) will have to blame himself for the consequence,—the death penalty' (cf. Ac 21[26ff.]): see *PEFSt*, 1871, p. 132; cf. Jos. *Ant.* xv. xi. 5.

¶ In modern Jewish places of worship a special gallery is reserved for the women.

* An interesting reference to the gate of Nicanor is to be found on a recently discovered bilingual inscription, in Greek and Hebrew, in the neighbourhood of Jerusalem; it was found inscribed on an ossuary from a sepulchral cave, and runs : Ὀστᾶ τῶν τοῦ Νεικάνορος Ἀλεξανδρέως ποιήσαντος τὰς θύρας. נקנר אלכסא ('The bones of [the children of ?] Nicanor, the Alexandrian, who made the doors. Nicanor Aleksa.'). Prof. Clermont-Ganneau says that this inscription 'can scarcely refer to any other than the family or descendants of Nicanor,' and that the 'doors' must be understood as referring to 'the famous door of the temple of Herod, known as the Gate of Nicanor, after the rich individual who had presented it to the Sanctuary'; see *PEFSt*, 1903, pp. 125–131.

† ταῦτα τὰ ῥήματα ἐλάλησεν ἐν τῷ γαζοφυλακίῳ διδάσκων ἐν τῷ ἱερῷ. It was teaching which, according to Jewish ideas, concerned men.

‡ The tribunal was called בֵּית דִּין הַגָּדוֹל ('The great house of judgment').

5. The Holy of Holies (*dĕbîr*).—No human foot might enter here, with the one exception of the high priest, who entered once a year, on the Day of Atonement, for the purpose of presenting sacrifice and incense before God. It was properly the place wherein the ark should have rested; but nothing is heard of the ark after the Captivity, and the Holy of Holies was, therefore, quite empty. The 'foundation stone' (אֶבֶן שְׁתִיָּה) upon which, in the first temple, the ark had stood, was nearly in the centre of the Holy of Holies; in the second temple it was exposed to the extent of about six inches;* there is no mention of this anywhere in reference to Herod's temple, but, as this was built on the site of the earlier temple, it is difficult to believe that it was not there. There was no means whereby any light could enter the Holy of Holies; it was, therefore, always in total darkness, excepting when artificially lighted. It was separated from the Holy Place by means of two veils, with the space of a cubit between them; in Mt 27⁵¹, Mk 15³⁸ Lk 23⁴⁵ (cf. He 6¹⁹ 9³ 10²⁰, though it is not Herod's temple that is referred to in these passages) only one veil† is spoken of; but as the two were so close together, they were probably regarded as two parts of one whole.

iii. *CHRIST AND THE TEMPLE.*—**1.** The earliest mention of the temple in connexion with Christ is on the occasion of His being brought there for 'presentation' and 'redemption' thirty-one days after His birth, in accordance with Jewish law (Lk 2²²⁻³⁹, cf. Ex 13¹⁻¹⁶). This ceremony took place in the Court of the Women, as the presence of Mary and Anna shows; it was a simple one,‡ consisting only of the formal presentation of the child to the priest, who offered up two 'benedictions,' or thanksgiving prayers, one on behalf of the child for the law of redemption, the other on behalf of the mother for the gift of the firstborn son.

From Lk 2⁴¹ it may be assumed that Christ was brought annually to Jerusalem for the Passover celebration in the temple; there was no need for Him to be left behind,§ and the presence of children in the temple was evidently of common occurrence (Mt 21¹⁵); the visit, therefore, recorded in Lk 2⁴² was not the first time that Christ was present at the yearly Passover feast in the temple.‖

One other reference, prior to the time of Christ's public ministry, but on the threshold of it, is contained in the parable of His Temptation, whose second scene (in Lk. the third) is represented as having taken place on the pinnacle of the temple.

2. By far the most important part of Christ's connexion with the temple is His teaching given within its precincts. On a number of occasions we read of the representatives of different classes coming to Him in the temple, often, no doubt, with the genuine object of profiting by His teaching, but frequently also for a more sinister purpose (*e.g.* Mt 16¹ 22¹⁵). The most elaborate account of such teaching is probably that contained in the long passage Mt 21²³–23³⁹; the whole of this discourse, addressed, as opportunity offered, to a variety of hearers, would appear to have been spoken in the large outer court (ii. **1**). The many-sided character of Christ's teaching in the temple is well illustrated by this section; the first who

* *Jewish. Encyc.* xii. 92.
† This must not be confounded with the 'Babylonian' veil, which hung before the Holy Place, and which is not referred to in the Gospels. See Warren and Conder, 'Jerusalem,' pp. 340–341.
‡ Probably more simple even than among modern Jews; see FIRSTBORN.
§ Josephus tells us that the provincial towns of Judæa were empty and deserted on the occasions of the annual feasts,—though there is an obvious exaggeration when he says that at the Passover in the year 63 there were no fewer than 2,700,000 Jewish people present in Jerusalem (*Ant.* XIV. xiii. 4, *BJ* VI. ix. 3).
‖ Against Edersheim, *Life and Times*, ii. 242. See also art BOYHOOD, vol. i. p. 225ᵇ.

are here mentioned as coming to Him were the chief priests and elders of the people, who asked Him by what authority He taught; the series of parables which constituted His reply to their question concluded with an appeal to Scripture : 'Did ye never read in the Scriptures, The stone which the builders rejected, the same is become the head of the corner?' (Ps 118²²); there was peculiar aptitude in the quotation being given in the temple, for 'stone' was a figurative expression for the leader of the people, which must have been familiar to His hearers (cf. Is 19¹³, Jg 20², 1 S 14³³, Zec 10⁴); a family, and also a nation, were conceived of as a building (cf. 1 P 2⁵), the head of which was regarded as the most prominent feature—the part of the spiritual building which stood out most conspicuously. There is ample evidence to show that the Jews regarded the temple as, in a real sense, a symbol of their nation. When Christ spoke of Himself as the 'corner-stone,' He was claiming for Himself the leadership of the people, *i.e.* He was, in effect, declaring Himself to be the Messiah.* Christ's teaching was next addressed in turn to the Pharisees, the Herodians, the Sadducees, the lawyers, and, lastly, to the surrounding people; the whole section gives a vivid picture of the use He made of the temple for His teaching of all sorts and conditions of men. Other references to His teaching in the temple are Lk 19⁴⁷·⁴⁸, from which it is clear, on the one hand, how exasperated the chief priests and scribes were, and, on the other hand, how the people flocked into the temple to hear Him (Mt 26⁵⁵, Mk 14⁴⁹, Lk 21³⁷·³⁸ 22⁵³, Jn 18²⁰).

But perhaps the most impressive teaching of Christ in the temple was during the great festivals, when immense numbers of people from all parts of the country came up to Jerusalem. It is in the Fourth Gospel that the details of this teaching are, for the most part, preserved; thus in Jn 7¹⁰ff. we read that during the Feast of Tabernacles, Jesus went into the temple and taught, so that the people marvelled at His teaching; and that on the last day of this feast a climax was reached; for, while on the one hand He was declared to be the Messiah, on the other this claim was disputed; and that the chief priests and Pharisees, believing that their opportunity had come, attempted to take Him, but in vain, for the majority of the people sided with Christ. The method of Christ's public teaching in the temple, together with the way in which the learned Jews sought to combat it, is graphically described in such passages as Jn 7. 8; the whole of the episode dealt with in these chapters took place in the outer Court of the Gentiles, where the largest number of people congregated : this is clear from the fact that some of the people took up stones† to cast at Christ (8⁵⁹). Again, at the Feast of Dedication, Christ was once more in the temple, teaching, with the like result, that the people threatened to stone Him : in this case we are definitely told (Jn 10²²⁻⁴²) that it took place in 'Solomon's Porch,' which was in the Court of the Gentiles (see above, ii. **1**). Lastly, that Christ was again present in the temple, and teaching, during the other great feast, the Passover, seems tolerably clear from Jn 12¹²⁻³⁶.

It is certain, therefore, that Christ made every use of the opportunities afforded of pressing home

* The 'corner-stone,' as implied above, has nothing to do with the foundation of a building; this is quite clear from the Heb. רֹאשׁ פִּנָּה and from the Syr ܪܝܫ and Pesh. ‫ܪܝܫ ܙܘܝܬܐ‬; the root-idea of ‫ܪܝܫ‬ is that of 'excrescence' (see Brockelmann, *Syr. Lex. s.v.*). Literally, the phrase might be rendered, 'the top of the highest point'; and the spot indicated would probably be the same as that referred to in the narrative of the Temptation.
† The other courts were paved.

His teaching in the temple;[*] no other spot offered the same favourable conditions, viz. it was the most convenient centre for the gathering together of the multitude ; the frequent presence of priests, Pharisees, scribes, and lawyers enabled Christ, in the hearing of the multitude, to contrast His teaching with theirs ; there was also the fact that teaching in the temple naturally appealed to the multitude more than if given anywhere else, as the temple was the officially recognized place for instruction.

3. It is extraordinary that no instance of a miracle of healing by Christ is recorded in the Gospels as having been performed in the temple ; but in view of such passages as Ac 3[1-12] 5[12] we cannot doubt that such did take place, especially as the Outer Court of the temple would be a natural spot for the lame and crippled to congregate for the purpose of arousing the pity of those going up to worship.

Only once is the temple the scene in a parable, namely, in that of the Pharisee and the Publican (Lk 18[10-14]) ; while in one other, the Good Samaritan (Lk 10[30-36]), temple officers are referred to.

4. There are, in the next place, a certain number of passages in the Gospels in which there are direct references to the temple, or something connected with it, though it is not mentioned by name. The temple and its furniture would have been so well known to the people that Christ could use both symbolically without actually mentioning them, and yet His hearers would perfectly understand the reference. The most striking instance of this is where the sanctuary is used as a symbol of Christ's risen body (Jn 2[19-21] ; cf. Mt 26[61] 27[40], Mk 14[58] 15[29]). But, as a rule, these references are not so obvious to modern ears as to those who heard them. The significance of these examples is enhanced in the case of those which were spoken in the temple itself ; among them are : Jn 8[12] 'I am the light of the world' ; one may reasonably infer that there was a reference here to the seven-branched lampstand in the Holy Place ;[†] but for this artificial light it was altogether in darkness ; the context ('he that followeth me shall not walk in darkness') receives emphasis when one remembers this. Christ is drawing out the contrast between the Jewish teaching, according to which the close approach to God in the Holy of Holies meant darkness, and His own, according to which the nearer one approached to Him, the Son of God, the greater the light. Again, there is a reference to the temple service of praise when Christ quotes Ps 8[2] (LXX) : 'Out of the mouths of babes and sucklings thou has perfected praise' (Mt 21[16]) ; here again was an implied contrast between the formalism of the temple-worship and the whole-hearted praise of the children crying, 'Hosanna to the Son of David.' A further and more direct reference to the worship of the temple is to be found in Mk 12[29], where Christ quotes the *Shema* : 'Hear, O Israel, the Lord our God, the Lord is One' ; the *Shema* (Dt 6[4]) was one of the earliest portions of the temple liturgy,[‡] and was recited every morning and evening.[§] In the same section occurs a reference to the daily sacrifices in the temple, viz. that to love God and one's neighbour is 'more than whole burnt-offerings and sacrifices' (Mk 12[33]). Other references of this kind are in Mt 5[22], where Christ speaks of the Sanhedrin ('Council') ; Mt 5[23. 24], where the offering on the altar in the Court of the Priests (see above, ii. **3**) is mentioned ; Mt 23[16ff.], which contains the pro-

[*] Cf. also the activity of Jeremiah in this respect.
[†] But cf. Westcott, *in loc.*
[‡] See Box in *Encyc. Bibl.* iv. cols. 4953, 4954.
[§] Queen Helen of Adiabene fixed a golden candelabrum in the front of the temple, which reflected the first rays of the sun, and thus indicated the time of reciting the *Shema* (*Yoma*, 37b, quoted in *Jewish Encyc.* xi. 266).

hibition of swearing by the temple or the altar ; Mk 7[11], where Christ speaks against an abuse which was clearly of frequent occurrence ;[*] the word *ḳorban* (see CORBAN) was a technical term used in making vows, and meant that a gift was made to God ; the abuse arose when a man would say to another (who as a relative or the like had a claim upon him) : 'My property is *ḳorban* to thee,' for by this means he could prevent his relative from deriving any benefit from his possessions. *Ḳorban* means lit. 'offering' ; it was used also of the sacred treasury in which gifts for the temple were kept ; it is used in this sense in Mt 27[6].[†] In Mt 23[2] Christ speaks of 'Moses' seat,' *i.e.* the Rabbinic college, the official deliberations of which took place in the temple. Not all of these references were spoken in the temple itself, but it cannot be doubted that Christ had the temple, or something connected with it, in His mind when He spoke. Lastly, there are other passages which record sayings or actions of Christ in which a connexion of some kind with the temple is to be discerned, *e.g.* Jn 15[1] 'I am the true vine' ; golden vines, with immense bunches of grapes, were carved on the door leading into the Holy Place (*Hêkhāl*) ;[‡] it is permissible to assume that Christ based His teaching here, as so often elsewhere,[§] on what was familiar to His hearers. Again, at the washing of the disciples' feet, Jn 13[5ff.] recalls to mind the priestly ablutions at the brazen laver near the great altar in the Priests' Court,[||] preparatory to their undertaking the duties of the priestly office ; it must be remembered that Christ, in the episode referred to, was about to perform an act appertaining to His high-priestly office, and the disciples were being consecrated in a special manner to their future work.

One has but to bear in mind the part that the temple and its worship played among the Jews, not only of Palestine but also of the Diaspora, to realize that the references indicated above are not fanciful.

iv. *CHRIST'S ATTITUDE TOWARDS THE TEMPLE WORSHIP.*—The Gospels present to us two elements in Christ's attitude towards the temple and its system of worship which appear, at first sight, to be contradictory ; but they can, nevertheless, be satisfactorily accounted for.

On the one hand, Christ evinces a great love and reverence for the temple ; His frequent appearance there cannot have been only for the purpose of teaching the people, for, while it is true that the Gospels never directly record an instance of His offering sacrifice, there can be no reasonable doubt that He fulfilled the duties incumbent upon every true Israelite ; this the following considerations will bear out :

The keynote of Christ's subsequent observance of the Law (cf. Mt 5[18]) was already sounded at His presentation in the temple (Lk 2[22-24]) ; from boyhood He was taught to observe the Passover (Lk 2[41. 42]), and it is inconceivable that He should, later on, have omitted what was a sacred duty in the eyes of every Jew, viz. taking His share in the family sacrifice in the temple at the Passover feast.[¶]

[*] See Ec 5[2-5].
[†] Cf. Jos. *BJ* ii. ix. 4, where it is spoken of as the 'sacred treasure.'
[‡] Cf. Westcott, *ad loc.* Jos. (*BJ* v. v. 4, cf. *Ant.* xiv. iii. 1) and Tacitus (*Ann.* v. 5) refer to this ; the vine was the symbol of the Jewish nation, and is found as such on Maccabæan coins.
[§] *e.g.* in Mt 4[19] 22[19] etc.
[||] See above, ii. **3**.
[¶] Although the Passover was celebrated in the home in our Lord's time as well as at the present day among Jews, yet the Paschal lamb might be killed only in the temple, the central sanctuary. At the Passover even laymen were permitted to kill the sacrificial animals, on account of the immense number that were offered. But, in any case, every Jew had to take part in the offering, by means of the consecrating act of laying the hand upon the victim on the altar.

Moreover, all Jews took a direct share in the ordinary services and worship of the temple ; a crowd of worshippers was always present at the daily morning and evening sacrifice which was offered up on behalf of the congregation ; they waited either in meditation or in prayer while the high priest entered into the Holy Place to present the incense-offering, and when he came forth they received, with bowed head, the priestly benediction ; they listened to the chant of the Levites, and at the conclusion of each section, when the priests sounded their silver trumpets, the whole multitude prostrated themselves.[*] That Christ, furthermore, observed the Jewish feasts has already been shown, and His own words as to the celebration of the Passover (Lk 22$^{7ff.}$) clearly show His attitude towards the sacrificial system generally. Then, again, several occasions are recorded of His distinctly enjoining the fulfilment of the law of sacrifice : Mt 8^4 (cf. Mk 1^{44}, Lk 5^{14}) 5$^{23.24}$ 23^2, Lk 17^{14} (cf. Jn 5^{46} 7^{23}) ; and His reference to the shewbread in Mk 2^{26}, Lk 6^4 is also to the point. Indeed one has but to recall His instinctive desire to be 'in his Father's house' (Lk 2^{49}), His zeal for the 'house of prayer' (Lk 19$^{45.46}$), His sense of the holy character of the sanctuary (Mt 23^{17}), His insistence on the need of paying the temple tax (Mt 17$^{24f.}$), to realize how fully He acquiesced in the contemporary conceptions regarding the temple and its worship.

But, on the other hand, there are references, equally decisive, though fewer in number, in which both the temple and its worship are regarded as of quite subordinate importance. Thus in Mt 12^6, where Christ speaks of Himself as 'greater than the temple,' He was uttering words which, at all events to Jews, must have implied a depreciation of the temple ; in the same passage the quotation from Hos 6^6 'I will have mercy and not sacrifice' (repeated in Mt 9^{13}) pointed distinctly to the relative unimportance of sacrifice. Again, the parable of the Good Samaritan illustrates what Christ thought of the priesthood (Lk 10^{31}) ; and most striking is His reply to those who lavished praise on the beauty of the temple : 'Verily, I say unto you, There shall not be left one stone upon another, that shall not be thrown down' (Mt 24^2, Mk 13$^{1-3}$, Lk 21$^{5.6}$), in connexion with which must be taken Jn 4^{21} 'Neither in this mountain nor in Jerusalem shall ye worship the Father.'[†]

This twofold, and apparently contradictory, attitude of Christ towards the temple and its worship has also a twofold explanation. There can be little doubt, in the first place, that Christ's realization of the relatively minor importance of the temple and its worship stood in the closest relation to His second coming (παρουσία) and the doctrine of the last things. This is very distinctly seen in that it is immediately after the prediction of the destruction of the temple (Mt 24^2, Mk 13^1, Lk 21^6)[‡] that He recounts the signs which shall precede His second coming (see esp. Mt 25$^{31ff.}$, cf. 2 Th 2$^{1-12}$) ; the near approach of the end (Mt 24^{14}) emphasized the temporary character of the temple and all that pertained to it.[§] In the second place, it is to be

[*] See Bousset, *Religion des Judentums*, p. 94.
[†] This attitude of Christ towards the temple and its worship receives corroboration in an exceedingly interesting fragment of a lost Gospel, discovered at Oxyrhynchus, which contains an account of a visit of Christ and His disciples to the temple ; they meet there a Pharisee who reproaches them with neglecting to perform the usual purification ceremony before entering the 'holy place' (presumably the Court of the Israelites is meant). Christ, in reply, emphasizes the need of inward purity, compared with which the outward ceremonial is as nothing (cf. Mt 23$^{25.26}$, Lk 11$^{37-40}$).
[‡] On the 'Abomination of Desolation' see Cheyne in *Encyc. Bibl.* i. cols. 21–23.
[§] This was in direct contradiction to the Jewish belief in the inviolability of the temple, see Jos. *BJ* vi. v. 2 ; cf. Bousset, *op. cit.* p. 97 ; cf. Ac 7$^{48f.}$

explained by the ever-widening conceptions which Christ experienced regarding His Person and work. In the early part of His ministry the influence of Jewish up-bringing and environment was strongly marked ; but as the realization of His own Divine Personality and the world-embracing character of His work grew more and more clear, all that was distinctively Jewish and of local colour receded into comparative insignificance. The evolution of Christ's Divine consciousness brought with it a new perspective, which revealed Him to Himself not merely as King of the Jews, but also as the Divine Saviour of the world (cf. Mt 24^{14}).

Cleansing of the temple.—This episode, together with the triumphal entry into Jerusalem, is one of the few events (apart from the story of the Passion) recorded by all four Evangelists ; this is significant, for its importance can scarcely be exaggerated. There are slight variations in the four accounts, but the substantial fact is identical in each (Mt 21$^{12-17}$, Mk 11$^{15-18}$, Lk 19$^{45.46}$, Jn 2$^{14-21}$). It is necessary to realize clearly that this act of 'cleansing' (the expression is quite misleading) belonged to a definite course of action marked out by Christ for Himself, and that it formed the last great act [the narrative in Jn. being misplaced] of His public ministry prior to the Passion. It is therefore important to connect it with the leading events of the few months preceding it.

According to Mk., which may be regarded as offering the earliest and most strictly historical account, that which definitely and irrevocably marked the final breach between Christ and the ecclesiastical authorities was the question of Sabbath observance (cf. Burkitt, *The Gospel History and its Transmission*, p. 68 ff.) ; the controversy on this subject culminated in the healing of the man with the withered hand on the Sabbath (Mk 3$^{1ff.}$). This occurred in the country under the jurisdiction of Herod Antipas, *i.e.* during the Galilæan ministry, which had as one of its most notable results the adhesion to Christ of the masses. It was on account of this popular support that the religious authorities deemed it advisable to get help from the secular arm, if this movement, so dangerous from their point of view, was to be checked. For this reason they appealed to the Herodians (Mk 3^6) ; their appeal was evidently successful, for Christ found it necessary to leave Galilee, and to remain in such parts of the country as were outside the jurisdiction of Herod Antipas ; thus freeing Himself from the molestations of the Herodians. During this time the multitudes flocked to Him ; but His main purpose consisted in preparing His disciples for what was to come. This preparation went on for some months. Then Christ determined to go up to Jerusalem for the Passover and appear publicly once more,[*] though He knew what the result must be, and did not hide it from His disciples (10$^{32-34}$). He thereupon entered Jerusalem publicly, accompanied by His followers (11$^{7ff.}$), and the next day the 'cleansing' of the temple took place. That is to say, in the cycle of events just referred to, the 'cleansing' formed the climax. Now, the essence of *practical* Judaism, according to the ideas of the religious official classes, consisted, above all things, in the strict *observance of the Sabbath*, and the due and regular carrying out of the *sacrificial system*. Christ had dealt with the former of these, as referred to above ; and, in making it a real blessing, had of necessity run directly counter to the traditional rules of observance ; that is to say, while holding firmly to the spirit of the Law, He abrogated the Sabbath in the old Jewish sense of the word. The 'cleansing' of the temple denotes His intention of doing the same

[*] As Judæa was not under the jurisdiction of Herod Antipas, Christ would be more unfettered in His action there.

with the other prime mark of practical Judaism, viz. the sacrificial system. That this is really the inner meaning of the 'cleansing' of the temple, the following considerations will show :

(i.) Excepting on this supposition, there was no meaning in Christ's action ; the *Outer Court*, or 'Court of the Gentiles,' where the 'cleansing' took place (see above, ii. 1), was not 'sacred' soil ; it cannot, therefore, have been on account of profanation of the temple that Christ acted as He did. The sheep and oxen, doves, and money-changers, were all absolutely essential for the carrying on of the sacrificial system of the time ; Christ's action was too significant to be misunderstood.—(ii.) The stress laid in each of the three Synoptics on the temple being a 'house of prayer,' seems to point in the same direction. There is some significance, too, in the dialogue which took place very shortly after between our Lord and one of the scribes (Mt 12[28]), when the latter says : ' . . . and to love his neighbour as himself, is much more than whole burnt-offerings and sacrifices,'—words which Christ describes as 'discreet.'—(iii.) The event took place just before the Feast of the Passover, *i.e.* at a time when the sacrificial animals would be crowding in as they did at no other time of the year. This made Christ's action all the more significant.—(iv.) The whole belief and attitude of both hierarchy and people regarding the sacrifices were such that the abrogation of these latter was an indispensable necessity if Christ's teaching was to have practical and permanent results. Vast as the number of public, official sacrifices were, those of private individuals were of an infinitely greater number ; it was these latter that formed one of the characteristic marks of the worship at Jerusalem.

'Here, day after day, whole crowds of victims were slaughtered and whole masses of flesh burnt ; and when any of the high festivals came round, there was such a host of sacrifices to dispose of that it was scarcely possible to attend to them all, notwithstanding the fact that there were thousands of priests officiating on the occasion. But the people of Israel saw, in the punctilious observance of this worship, the principal means of securing for themselves the favour of their God' (Schürer, *HJP* II. i. 298).

These considerations seem to show that the 'cleansing' of the temple really did connote an intention in the mind of Christ to abrogate entirely the Jewish sacrificial system ; if this is not what it meant, it is difficult to see any point in it at all. In how far Christ intended to mark Himself out as Him in whom was hereafter to be centred a purified, spiritual 'sacrificial system,'—or, in other words, what the relations were between the 'cleansing' of the temple and the words spoken in the upper chamber, 'This is my body,' 'This is my blood,'—is a question which cannot be dealt with here.

If the meaning of the Cleansing of the Temple here advocated be correct, it will at once be seen that few actions of our Lord possessed greater significance.

Literature.—Besides the various works referred to above, the following selection of books is recommended : Fergusson, *The Temples of the Jews*, London, 1878 ; Warren and Conder, *Survey of Western Palestine* : 'Jerusalem,' pp. 117–341, London, 1884 ; Stade, *GVI* ii. p. 491 ff., Berlin, 1888 ; Benzinger, *Heb. Arch.* pp. 402–404, Leipzig, 1894 ; Clermont-Ganneau, *Archæological Researches in Palestine*, chs. iv.–vii., London, 1899 ; Box in *Encyc. Bibl.* iv. 4948–4956 (for the services of the temple), London, 1903 ; Sanday, *Sacred Sites of the Gospels*, pp. 106–117, Oxford, 1903 ; Babelon, *Manual of Oriental Antiquities*, ch. vii., London, 1906. **W. O. E. OESTERLEY.**

TEMPTATION.—The word πειράζω (noun πειρασμός, Lk 4[13] 8[13] 22[28], Mt 6[13] 26[41] ; intensive form ἐκπειράζω, Lk 10[25], Mt 4[7]) has a neutral, a good, and a bad sense. It may mean simply 'to try,' 'make trial of,' 'test,' for the purpose of ascertaining the quality of a man, what he thinks, or how he will behave himself ; but usually there is

either a good (Jn 6[6], perhaps also Mt 22[35]) or a bad intent. In the latter case it means *to solicit to sin*, *to tempt*. That the word may be used in the wider sense, even when rendered 'tempt,' must not be forgotten. In Ja 1[12] 'temptation' is used of *trial* generally, the issue of which is intended to be the crown of life ; but in v.[13] 'tempted' is used in the sense of *solicited to sin* ; and the writer very emphatically asserts, 'God cannot be tempted (ἀπείραστος) with evil, and he himself tempteth no man.' This statement seems to be contradicted by Jesus' quotation from Dt 6[16] in His answer to the second temptation in Mt 4[7], as well as by the sixth petition of the Lord's Prayer (Mt 6[13]) ; but tempting God does not mean soliciting Him to sin, but trying His justice and patience, challenging Him to give proof of His perfection to such a degree as to incur His displeasure, and to expose oneself to His judgment ; and the temptations into which God is asked not to lead us, are the circumstances or the states of mind which, though to the strong they might prove the opportunities of winning 'the crown of life' (Ja 1[12]), to weakness may be the occasions of failure and transgression. This weakness of His disciples, while admitting their good intentions, Jesus recognizes in His warning in Gethsemane (Mt 26[41]), and commends their fidelity to Him in the trying experiences they had shared with Him (Lk 22[28]). To the enthusiastic but shallow hearers of His words He affirmed that trials (persecution, etc.) would prove morally fatal (Lk 8[13]). The cares and riches and pleasures of this life (v.[14]) He regarded as hindrances to the higher life. Noteworthy is the emphasis He lays on the peril of wealth (Mt 19[23. 24]). That Jesus discovered the moral peril in which Judas was placed from the very first indications of distrust and disloyalty to Himself, is suggested by Jn 6[70. 71], which shows also the danger He feared for the other disciples. His repeated references to His coming betrayal (Mt 17[22] 20[18] 26[2]), His plain allusion to the presence of the traitor at the Last Supper (Lk 22[21]), His giving the sop to Judas (Jn 13[26]), may all be regarded as loving endeavours to strengthen him against temptation ; and even when all these efforts had proved vain, what good was still in him was appealed to in the pathetic reproach, 'Betrayest thou the Son of Man with a kiss ?' (Lk 22[48]). Peter, too, was warned against the temptation that threatened him (Lk 22[31. 32]) ; and Jesus, who feared his fall through his self-confident weakness, hoped for his recovery, and the help he could be to others after his recovery, because He believed in the power of His own intercessory prayer.

Jesus Himself was both tried and tempted. He seems to confess His own liability to temptation when He refuses the epithet 'good' (Lk 18[19]), although He never confesses to have fallen before temptation ; and the attitude He assumes to sinners implies His own sinlessness. The writer of the Epistle to the Hebrews (4[15]) states His moral position in the words, ' in all points tempted like as we are, yet without sin' ; and St. Paul seems to indicate this liability to temptation without the actuality of sin in the phrase 'in the likeness of sinful flesh' (Ro 8[3]). St. Luke's statement that the tempter 'departed from him for a season' (4[13]), and Jesus' own reference to the temptations (Lk 22[28]) which His disciples had endured with Him, show that the experience in the wilderness was not solitary. It is not improbable even that the narratives of the Temptation (Mt 4[1-11], Mk 1[12. 13], Lk 4[1-13]) are a summary of a succession of moral trials through which Jesus in the course of His ministry passed, or at least that this record of an early experience has been coloured by reminiscences of later experiences. Be this as it may, we can find in the Gospels indications of similar trials of His fidelity to God. The desire of the people for healing (Jn 4[48]) and bread (6[26]), the demand of His enemies for a sign (Mt 16[1]), the attempt to make Him a king (Jn 6[15]), may be regarded as illustrations of the three kinds of temptation recorded. A careful study of the record of the early ministry (in Jn 2-4) warrants the assumption that Jesus was tempted by His *enthusiasm* (which see) to force the issue between Him and His enemies prematurely, and that the reserve in language and restraint in action He displayed as soon as He had discovered this peril, are to be regarded as a conquest over temptation. His 'escapes,' as Bruce calls them (*With Open Face*, ch. vii.), were intended, in the later part of His Galilæan ministry at least, not only to secure quiet for the training of the Twelve, but to withdraw Him from the danger threatened by His enemies. Had He run risks before His hour, He would have fallen before what seems to be indicated by the Second Temptation (Mt 4[5. 6]). His own family were a source of moral peril to Him. His words to His mother in Cana (Jn 2[4]) are explicable only if in her request He found a suggestion of evil, that He should use His miraculous power at the bidding of His natural affection instead of at God's command alone. The completeness of His repudiation of the claims of His mother and brethren upon Him in relation to His public ministry indicates how intensely He felt this peril (Mt 12[48. 49]). The attempt to influence Him was nevertheless renewed by His brethren, when they advised Him to go up to the feast and so manifest Himself to the world (Jn 7[3. 4]). Peter was rebuked as the Tempter (Mt 16[23]) almost immediately after being commended as the Confessor, because he sought to turn Jesus from His sacrifice. May His refusal of the request of the Syrophœnician woman (Mt 15[24-27]) not have been due to the fear lest a ministry of healing among the Gentiles might divert Him from the path of sacrifice to which He knew that His Father called Him? The request of the Greeks also (Jn 12[21]) stirred so deep emotion, because it seemed to suggest the possibility of an escape from the Cross, which had to be rejected as a temptation. The same temptation in its most acute form presents itself in the Agony (which see) in Gethsemane.

Tests or trials which were not felt by Jesus as temptations, but which were intended by His enemies either to discredit Him with the multitude or to obtain some ground of accusation against Him, were the questions addressed to Him about the tribute to Cæsar, the resurrection, and the greatest commandment (Mt 22[15-40]), and divorce (19[3]). The man with the withered hand in the synogogue (Lk 6[6. 7]) was a trap set for Him, to involve Him in the guilt of Sabbath-breaking; so also was the woman taken in adultery (Jn 8[6]), that He might either by His severity estrange the people, or by His laxity be shown to be in opposition to the Mosaic law. The sufferings and sorrows Jesus passed through were Divinely appointed trials that He might learn obedience, and so be made perfect (He 5[8] 2[10]); but it is not necessary here to illustrate this discipline in detail (see STRUGGLES OF SOUL). To the data from the Gospels here presented, a few observations may be added regarding the possibility, the necessity, and the nature of temptation in Jesus' life.

As God cannot be tempted, the liability of Jesus to temptation proves that there was a Divine *Kenosis* (which see) involved in the incarnation of the Son of God. Jesus could be tempted, because He was limited in knowledge, subject to emotion, and undergoing a moral development. Omniscience has an insight into the moral character of all conduct, and a foresight into the moral issues of all choice, which exclude even the possibility of temptation; omnipotence has such a command over all its moral resources that its moral efforts can never involve any moral strain, such as is experienced in temptation; omniscience and omnipotence, therefore, cannot know the disturbance of feeling which is possible to limited knowledge and power. To ascribe these Divine attributes to the incarnate Son of God is to deny His liability to temptation, and to make His moral development a semblance and not a reality. Liability to temptation, necessary to moral development, does not, however, imply any necessity to sin. There may be growth unto perfection, with a constant choice of good. Temptation does not arise only in a sinful nature. Natural instincts and appetites, which are morally neutral, become sinful only when seen to be in conflict with the will of God as revealed in conscience. The opinions, sentiments, and desires of sinful men may become the occasions of temptation to a sinless nature. Temptation is not sin, involves no necessity of sin, although it brings the possibility of sin.

It was necessary for the fulfilment of Christ's vocation as the Saviour of men that He should be tempted without sin. His moral teaching gains force from His moral example, and He can be a moral example to us only because He passed through a human moral development. His own moral struggles enable Him to feel with us in ours (He 4[15]). To condemn the sin of mankind (Ro 8[3]) it was needful for Him not only to suffer for sin, but also to overcome sin by withstanding its assaults.

The nature of His temptation was determined by His unique vocation. The lower passions and appetites seem never to have assailed Him. He was tempted to abuse His miraculous power, His privileged position, His supreme authority as Son of God, to fulfil the popular expectations instead of His own ideal of the Messiahship, to shrink from the agony and desolation of the Cross. His temptations transcended the common experience as much as He Himself did; but, though possible to Him alone, they were as real for Him as are the lower temptations for other men. See, further, the following article.

LITERATURE.—Butler, *Anal.* ch. v.; Dods, *The Prayer that Teaches to Pray*, 143 ff.; Liddon, *BL*[3] 512; Ullmann, *Sinlessness of Jesus*, 123 ff., 264 ff.; W. C. E. Newbolt, *Gospel of Experience*, 98; J. D. Jones, *Elims of Life*, 92; D. Fairweather, *Bound in the Spirit*, 33; W. H. M. H. Aitken, *Temptation and Toil*, 1-205; G. A. Smith, *Forgiveness of Sins*, 51; J. Stalker, *The Four Men*, 29.　　ALFRED E. GARVIE.

TEMPTATION (in the Wilderness). —[On the general subject of temptation see preced. article]. The continuousness and variety of our Lord's temptations have probably been obscured by the circumstance that attention has been concentrated upon one episode in His life which is distinctively known as '*The* Temptation.' This very significant incident is fully related in Mt. (4[1-11]) and Lk. (4[1-13]), mentioned in Mk. (1[12. 13]), and omitted from the Fourth Gospel. St. Mark's account is of the briefest: 'And straightway the Spirit urges him forth into the desert. And he was in the desert forty days, tempted by Satan; and he was with the wild beasts; and the angels ministered to him.'* The mention of 'wild beasts,' which is peculiar to Mark, is usually supposed to be introduced for the purpose of accentuating the solitariness of Jesus, and His remoteness from all human aid. But Professor Bevan (*Trans. of Soc. of Hist. Theol.* 1901-2) finds in this mention the key to

---

* The 'desert' is possibly that known as Quarantania, from the *forty* days, and since the 12th cent. traditionally accepted as the same, a few miles from Jericho; or it may have been, as Conder thinks, some miles farther south—the dreary desert which extends between the Dead Sea and the Hebron mountains. See his picturesque description, pp. 213 to 214 of his *Handbook.*

the whole incident. It seems that in the East, or at any rate in Persia, there is a traditional custom, called 'the subjugation of the *jinn*.' In order to achieve this victory the candidate retires to a desert place, fasts for forty days, and when the jinns appear in the forms of a lion, a tiger, and a dragon, he must hold his ground fearlessly. Doing so, power over the demons is attained. 'The conclusion,' says Professor Bevan, 'which we may draw from these facts is that the story of the Temptation, in its original form, was a description of a practice by means of which it was believed that man could acquire the power of controlling the demons.' The analogy is interesting. Our Lord in this critical conflict with Satan did 'bind the strong man,' and secured that in all future encounters He would conquer. But is there any evidence at all that the Persian custom prevailed among the Jews? Is there any ground for supposing either that our Lord would follow such a custom, or, on the other hand, that there is no foundation for the story of the Temptation in the facts of His career? And is not the simple expression, ἦν μετὰ τῶν θηρίων, inadequate to suggest such a conflict as is supposed ?*

Order of Temptations.—In Mt. and Lk. the order of the second and third temptations is inverted, while the substance of them remains identical. The order followed by Mt. is generally accepted as correct. There seems to be an ascending scale in the temptations as recorded in the First Gospel, though Plummer (Lk 4⁵) says : 'The reasons given for preferring one order to the other are subjective and unconvincing. Perhaps neither Evangelist professes to give any chronological order.'

Source of the story.—As, according to all the accounts, Jesus was not accompanied by anyone during His temptation, the question naturally arises, How did the knowledge of what took place become public property? To this there can be but one answer : Our Lord informed His disciples of what had taken place. That He should have done so is probable. At first, perhaps, they might not be prepared to understand the incident ; but after they had acknowledged Him as Messiah many questions as to His procedure must have arisen in their minds, and to these questions an account of His initial temptations was the best answer.

Character of the incident.—The more clearly the reality of the Temptation is grasped, the less need does there seem for supposing that the tempter took a visible shape, or that any bodily transport to 'the high mountain' or 'the wing of the temple' took place. It is more difficult to determine whether such bodily transport was thought of by the Evangelists or is implied in their words. In Lk. the 'high mountain' is omitted except in so far as reference may be found to it in the word ἀναγαγών. In the *Gospel of the Hebrews* there occurs a characteristic apocryphal embellishment : 'Forthwith my Mother the Holy Spirit took me by one of the hairs of my head and carried me away to the high mountain of Tabor.'

Its connexion.—In all the Synoptic Gospels and in the development of our Lord's life, the Temptation follows upon the Baptism. In His Baptism He had been proclaimed Messiah, called out of private into public life, summoned to take among men a place which could be filled by Himself alone. He was called from the carpenter's shop to redeem a world. The village youth was to represent in His person the wisdom, the holiness, the love, the authority of the Highest. How could He face this task? By what hitherto untried methods accomplish it? He had no counsellor, example, or guide. None had as yet attempted or even adequately conceived the part He was to play.

Its necessity.—The burden and glory, the hazard and intricacy and responsibility of His vocation must have stirred in His soul a ferment of emotions. O. Holtzmann may overstate the risk when he says (*Life of Jesus*, Eng. tr. 141) : 'There was a grave danger of His personal life being disturbed by so august a revelation, of its causing Him to plunge headlong into fantastic dreams of the future, and into acts of violence, with the object of realizing His dreams.' Our Lord was not unprepared for the great vocation ; He must often have considered how He could best bring light and life to His fellow-countrymen, but now that He was actually launched on the work, all past thoughts must have seemed insufficient, and He felt that still His decisions were to be made. Solitude was necessary. The Spirit that came upon Him in Baptism compelled Him to contemplate action, and in order that He might finally choose His path and His methods He must turn away from the expectant gaze and eager inquiries of John's disciples and seek the solitude of the desert.

Its conditions.—The intensity of our Lord's emotion and the difficulty of decision are conveyed by the Evangelists' statement that for forty days (*i.e.* for an unusually long period, 'forty' being used as a round number indicative of magnitude) * He forgot to eat. This gives us the measure of His absorption in thought. The temptations indeed are spoken of as if they occurred at the close of the forty days' fast ; naturally, because then only out of the turmoil of thought did these three possible lines of conduct become disengaged and present themselves as now finally rejected. To one who adequately conceives the stupendous task awaiting our Lord and the various methods of accomplishing it which He had often heard discussed, no statement of His absorption in thought or of the strife of contending pleas will seem exaggerated.

Lines on which the Temptation proceeded.—The key to the Temptation is found in the necessity laid upon Jesus of definitely determining the principles and methods of the great work that awaited Him. There were necessarily present to His mind as possible courses the various expectations current among the people. Eventually these presented themselves in three great questions : Am I as Messiah lifted above human needs and trials? What means may I legitimately use to convince the people of my claims? What kind of Messianic kingdom and Messianic King am I to represent? To each of these questions there was an answer present to the mind of the Lord, cherished by most of the people He was now to influence, and with much which superficially commended it, but which He recognized as Satanic.

The absence of the article before υἱός has given rise to the idea that the temptations were not Messianic. Against this it has been pointed out that the predicate is regularly anarthrous. But Middleton (*Gr. Article*, p. 62) shows that 'we sometimes find that the predicate of the εἰμί has the Article, where the subject is a personal pronoun or demonstrative, ἐγώ, σύ, οὗτος,' etc. This rule is borne out by NT usage : see Mt 16¹⁶ 26⁶³ 27¹¹, Mk 3¹¹ etc. For this and other reasons we should expect the Article here, if the meaning were, 'If thou art the Son of God,

---

* Besides, as O. Holtzmann (*Life of Jesus*, 143) says : 'In old Israelitish times lions still inhabited the thickets beside the Jordan (Jer 49¹⁹) ; in the age of Jesus the chief beast of prey in Palestine was, as it still is, the jackal. But Mark's sole object in making this addition would appear to have been the desire to bring into greater relief Jesus' complete severance from human society, with the idea of imparting more body to his description.' Dr. Abbott's *Clue*, p. 115, is suggestive in this connexion.

* 'It is only by travelling that one becomes aware how universal is the application of the number 40 to the features of Oriental architecture. If there is a famous building with something over a score of columns, or a town with a like number of minarets, it will be styled the hall of 40 columns or the city of 40 towers' (Arthur Arnold in *Academy*, 12 March 1881). ' "Forty" means "many" ' (Angus, *Bible Handbook*).

or, the Christ.' The meaning rather is, ' If thou art God's Son ' [the emphatic place being given to υἱός, εἰ υἱός εἶ τ. θεοῦ], if this relationship to God be the determining element in your life. But this by no means excludes reference to His Messianic dignity, it rather implies it. It was as God's Son He had been hailed at His baptism proclaiming His Messianic vocation, and fitly, because Divine Sonship was that out of which the Messiahship sprang, and which underlay the whole vocation of Jesus as the Christ.

First temptation.—The first temptation was to use for His own comfort and preservation the powers committed to Him as Messiah. The circumstances in which He found Himself lent immense force to the appeal. He found Himself faint and ready to perish. What a fiasco would His Messianic calling seem if He died here in the wilderness, and how easy apparently the means of relief : ' Say the word.' ' How oft the sight of means to do ill deeds makes ill deeds done !' Once only in His life can He have suffered more acutely from this same temptation : only when He knew He could command twelve legions of angels to His aid, only when He was taunted, ' He saved others, himself he cannot save.' The use He might legitimately make of His powers as God's Son must once for all be settled : and He settles it by recognizing that having taken human nature He must accept human conditions, and elevate human life not by facing life's temptations on wholly different terms from the normal, but by accepting the whole human conflict : ' Man lives—and I, being man, therefore live—not by bread only, but by every word that proceedeth out of the mouth of God.' He accepted absolutely the human condition with its entire dependence on God. Duty was more than food. His life was to be ruled by intimations of God's will, not by fear of death by starvation. He, like all other men, was in God's hand.

Second temptation.—The second temptation was to establish the Messianic claim by the performance of some astounding feat, such as leaping from the roof of the wing of the temple into the crowded courts below. Once for all our Lord had to settle by what methods His claim could be made good. That which the people so frequently demanded, ' a sign,' must have suggested itself as a possible means of convincing them. And it was an easy means, for was it not written in the book He had pondered as His best guide : ' He shall give his angels charge concerning thee, and in their hands they shall bear thee up, lest haply thou dash thy foot against a stone' (Ps 91[11f.]) ? Were these words not prepared for this Messianic manifestation ? Could the people, ever craving for signs, be in any other way led to accept Him as God's messenger ? Might not His whole mission fail, might He not miss the accomplishment of God's purpose, if He did not condescend to the weakness of His countrymen and grant them a sign ? But now, as always, He saw the incongruity and insufficiency of such signs : ' an evil and adulterous generation seeketh a sign, and *no* sign shall be given to it' (Mt 12[39] ||). But that which settles the matter in His own mind is the consideration that to attempt the performance of any such feat would be a tempting of God. He rebuts the temptation with the words, ' Thou shalt not tempt the Lord thy God.' He perceived that He had no right to expect the protection of God in any course but the highest, in any course which His own conscience told Him was a short cut to His end. To abandon the region of man's actual needs and work wonders not for their relief and as the revelation of God's love, but for mere display, was, He felt, to trespass the Father's intentions. He could not count upon the Father's countenance and help if He departed in the slightest degree from His own highest ideal. Spiritual ends must be attained by spiritual means, however slow and uncertain these seem.

Third temptation.—The third question which had now once for all to be settled was, What kind of kingdom must the Messiah establish ? Shall it be a kingdom of this world, such as many expected and would promptly aid Him to secure ? The glory of the kingdoms of the earth had a present lustre all its own. There was in their power and opportunity an appeal to beneficent ambition not easily resisted. What might not be accomplished for the down-trodden, the heavily-taxed, the outcast, the despairing ? He had Himself groaned with the rest of His countrymen under the unrighteous exactions of fraudulent publicans ; why not win for His people the blessings of freedom ? More than once this temptation returned in the attempts of the multitude to make Him a king. But our Lord recognized that for Him to depart from the idea of founding a spiritual kingdom in which God should be acknowledged would be to serve Satan. The craving for earthly dominion was inextricably mixed up with worldly ambitions, and could only be gratified by the use of means alien to the Divine Spirit. He felt such a kingdom to be incompatible with the sole and exclusive service of God—not that all earthly kingdoms are necessarily Satanic, but His calling was to introduce the true reign of God among men. He saw that in order to win earthly dominion He would require to appeal to evil passions and use such means as the sword—in a word, to avail Himself of the aid of evil. This was impossible.

LITERATURE.—The various Commentaries on the Gospels, and the Lives of Christ ; Liddon, *Bamp. Lect.*[8] p. 512 f.; *Expos. Times,* iii. [1891] 118 ff., xiv. [1903] 389 ff. ; *Expositor,* i. iii. [1876] 321 ff.; Trench, *Studies in the Gospels,* 1 ; W. H. Brookfield, *Serm.* 252, 262, 275 ; T. Christlieb, *Memoir with Serm.* 219, 238, 255 ; A. B. Davidson, *Waiting upon God,* 107 ; H. Wace, *Some Central Points of our Lord's Ministry,* 59–132 ; Th. Zahn, *Bread and Salt from the Word of God* (1905), 1.

MARCUS DODS.

TENT (σκηνή).—The light shelter of the nomad, here to-day and away to-morrow, is an apt symbol of what is fleeting and transitory. This lends the suggestion of irony to our Lord's phrase (Lk 16[9]) ' eternal *tents.*' The notion of transiency is uppermost also in 2 Co 5[1. 4] (σκῆνος).

The ordinary Eastern tent is made of black goats'-hair cloth, spun and woven by the women with very primitive implements. The women pitch the tents, and on removing they strike and pack them for the journey. The roof is supported by three rows of three upright posts, from 6 feet to 8 feet in height, the middle row being highest. It is stretched by cords fastened to the edges, and attached to pegs driven firmly into the ground. The ' walls' are hung like curtains round the eaves, and a breadth of cloth across the tent cuts off the women's compartment from that open to the public. It is an effective shelter from the sun. When wet, the cloth shrinks and becomes quite waterproof. σκηνή may also mean a hut, booth, or other temporary structure, like those made by the Arabs of *el-Ḥuleh* from the reeds that abound in the marshes close by the base of Hermon. Peter was doubtless familiar with these rude peasant structures, the leafy shelters erected on the roofs for cool retreat in summer, and the booths for the Feast of Tabernacles (Mt 17[4] etc.).   W. EWING.

TERAH.—Father of Abraham ; named as a link in our Lord's genealogy (Lk 3[34]).

TESTAMENT. — 1. The Gr. word διαθήκη, tr. ' covenant' Lk 1[72] AV, ' testament' Mt 26[28] || Mk 14[24], Lk 22[20] AV and RVm, is in RV, *ll. cc.,* uniformly ' covenant.' The last of these passages is bracketed by WH as a ' very early interpolation.' The word does not occur elsewhere in the Gospels. The rendering 'covenant' (wh. see) is unquestionably right: 'testament' has come from the Lat. Versions.

2. In classical literature διαθήκη denoted a will, and apparently nothing else (Ar. *Av.* 440, if an exception, is unique). A Greek will, however, was a settlement or trust-deed rather than a will in the Roman (*i.e.* the modern) sense. In it the conditions of inheritance were, indeed, in the first place at the sole discretion of the testator, but it was publicly and solemnly executed, and thereupon at once became absolute, irrevocable, and unalterable.

3. The LXX translators adopted the word as the equivalent of the Heb. בְּרִית. The following considerations are supposed to have influenced their choice :—(*a*) διαθήκη represented essentially a 'one-sided covenant,' συνθήκη (the ordinary word) a mutual one ; (*b*) διαθήκη was charged with religious ideas, inasmuch as the Greek will conveyed the religious institutions as well as the property of the family (cf. the similar case of the Hebrew 'birthright'). It may possibly also have been used, in the popular spoken dialect, in a wider sense than that of a will (cf. διατίθεσθαι).

4. (*a*) The special reference in Lk 1⁷² [= Ps 105⁸ᶠ·?] is to the covenant with Abraham (Gn 15. 17). (*b*) The words of Mt 26²⁸, Mk 14²⁴ [Lk 22²⁰] are plainly drawn from Ex 24⁸. The addition of 'new' (AV, RVm) in Mt. and Mk., *ll.cc.*, has small MS authority, and is rejected in RV text : it is due to 1 Co 11²⁵. Yet the idea of a 'new covenant' had been the theme of OT prophets (cf. Jer 31³¹ᶠᶠ· etc.), and its application to the Christian covenant was in current use among the Apostles : the 'old' covenant in the implied contrast was the Mosaic not the Abrahamic (2 Co 3⁶, He 9¹⁵ etc.), and the allusion to Ex 24⁸ seems tacitly to suggest the same contrast here.

LITERATURE.—Ramsay, *Hist. Com. on Galatians*, p. 349 ff.; Westcott, *Hebrews*, p. 298 ff.; Hastings' *DB*, artt. 'Covenant,' 'Testament.'   F. S. RANKEN.

TETRARCH (τετράρχης is the classical form, but in NT the MS evidence is strongly in favour of τετραάρχης [Tisch., WH, and Nestle]).—The title is used in the Gospels of Antipas (Mt 14¹, Lk 3¹· ¹⁹ 9⁷), and of Philip and Lysanias (Lk 3¹). Originally it denoted the ruler of a fourth part of a country or province. Euripides (*Alc.* 1154) is the earliest writer to use the term τετραρχία, and applies it to Thessaly, which in primitive times was divided for civil administration into four districts. This arrangement was restored in the constitution given by Philip of Macedon (Demos. *Philipp.* iii. 26, where the word is clearly technical and free from the doubt in which Euripides leaves it). A similar system was met with in Galatia, where each of the three tribes had its four tetrarchs (Strabo, 430, 566 f.). Pompey afterwards reduced the number to three, one for each tribe, but retained the original title (Appian, *Mithridat.* 46). Thenceforward, if not at an even earlier date, the name lost its etymological meaning, and could be applied to any petty dependent prince, subordinate in rank to kings but enjoying some of the prerogatives of sovereignty (Cic. *pro Milone*, xxviii. 76 ; Hor. *Sat.* I. iii. 12 ; Tac. *Ann.* xv. 25 ; *et al.*). Such tetrarchs seem to have been numerous, especially in Syria. Antony conferred the title upon both Herod and his brother Phasael (Jos. *Ant.* XIV. xiii. 1, *BJ* I. xii. 5) ; but the rank was almost purely titular, and left them inferior in dignity to the high priest, Hyrcanus II. In B.C. 30 another brother, Pheroras, was made tetrarch of Peræa (Jos. *Ant.* XV. x. 3), the nominal honour being maintained on an income granted by Herod himself. In the Gospels the etymological signification of the term has evaporated. For, though Herod divided his kingdom into four parts, the one assigned to Salome consisted merely of a palace with the revenue of certain so-called free towns, and was in no sense a tetrarchy. With this exception, his kingdom was divided into three parts, and the title of 'tetrarch' was conferred by the will of Rome upon Antipas and Philip, whilst that of 'ethnarch,' or recognized head of a nation, was similarly bestowed upon Archelaus. On two occasions Antipas is styled 'king' (Mt 14⁹, cf. 14¹, Mk 6¹⁴· ²²· ²⁶ᶠ·) ; and the obvious explanation is that his subjects were encouraged, and some of them perhaps disposed, to speak of him by the higher title, for which Rome had substituted a lower, without any allusion to its strict meaning. Similarly in the case of Lysanias. He was ruler of the district of Abila in the Lebanon, which had been severed from the kingdom of Ituræa on the execution of Lysanias I. in B.C. 36. That kingdom was in the course of time broken up into three parts, of which Abilene formed one, with another Lysanias as its tetrarch (Jos. *Ant.* XVIII. vi. 10, XIX. v. 1 ; *CIG* 4521, 4523). The term may have been selected because of the smallness of the district in comparison with the earlier kingdom, but it preserves no record of the division of a country or association of tribes into four parts. In the Gospels the tetrarch is merely a petty prince, dependent upon Rome for the retention of his few emblems of sovereignty, whilst encouraged to self-repression and loyal service by an occasional promotion to a higher dignity.   R. W. MOSS.

TEXT OF THE GOSPELS.—1. The problem.— All true criticism must begin by taking cognizance of, and as far as possible accounting for, existing facts. The leading facts in regard to the text of the Gospels may be briefly stated as follows :

(i.) A Greek text substantially the same as the text underlying the AV has been almost universally accepted by Christendom as the authentic Greek text from about the year A.D. 350 till the development in modern times of the critical study of the text of the NT. This text is found in the great mass of existing Greek MSS, and was used by almost all ecclesiastical writers from Chrysostom onwards. Translated into Syriac, under the name of the *Peshitta* version, it was used by most of the Syriac-speaking Churches from at least the 4th cent. onwards. It was the only Greek text printed on the revival of learning in the West, and received the name of *Textus Receptus* (TR) from an expression used in the preface to the second Elzevir edition, 1633 : 'textum ergo habes nunc ab omnibus receptum, in quo nihil immutatum aut corruptum damus.'

(ii.) Against this general unanimity in regard to the Greek text must be set the fact that the Churches of the West read the Gospels in the Latin translation of Jerome (A.D. 384), according to a text substantially different from the TR. Moreover, existing MSS and Patristic quotations of the earlier Latin versions differed from the TR even more fundamentally, and similar types of text are found to have been very widely spread, speaking in a geographical sense, and occur in some important MSS, in many ancient Versions, and in the quotations of many Christian writers, especially in the earliest times. This text (or, more correctly speaking, texts of this type) has been named 'Western' ; and, although it has long been well known that the term is not exclusively applicable in a geographical sense (indeed, it is quite possible that at least some members of this family may have had their rise in the East), yet for the sake of convenience it must for the present be employed.

(iii.) But a few of our earliest Greek MSS, supported by the quotations of the most scholarly Fathers of the earlier centuries, and by a few Versions, present a different text, which has commended itself on its intrinsic merits, as well as on account of its proved antiquity, to most modern critical scholars : it forms the base of practically all the modern critical editions, and of our English RV.

2. The Received Text.—A text substantially the same as the TR has been called by Dean Burgon and his school the 'Traditional Text'; by Dr. Hort (in the Introduction * to Westcott and Hort's *The New Testament in the Original Greek*) the 'Syrian' Text. Hort also suggests the name 'Antiochian,' which is preferable, because it avoids any chance of confusion with the totally distinct Syriac versions. For reasons that will be explained later on in this article, Hort considers that the Antiochian text affords practically no evidence for the reconstruction of the original Greek of the NT, and he may therefore be considered as the most extreme opponent of the TR. In his opinion (*Introduction*, § 185) the Antiochian text 'must be the result of a recension in the proper sense of the word, a work of attempted criticism, performed deliberately by editors and not merely by scribes.' He further distinguishes two stages in the revision, and thinks (§ 190) that the final process was completed by 350 or thereabouts, and that the first process took place at some date between 250 and 350. According to Burgon and his close follower Miller, these recensions are purely imaginary creations; they believe the Church of Antioch (in company, no doubt, with practically all the Greek-speaking Churches) to have preserved the pure text from the first. It is at any rate certain that Chrysostom used this text : he was born at Antioch about the middle of the 4th cent., and lived in that city till 398, when he became bishop of Constantinople. We have seen above that even the main opponents of this text allow that it took its final shape probably about the time of Chrysostom's birth. From that time onwards it held practically undisputed sway, and the main mass of later MSS contain it. When at length, some time after the introduction of printing, the first New Testaments in Greek were published, they naturally rested on the MSS in ordinary ecclesiastical use, and thus the Antiochian text became the 'Received' Greek text of modern Christendom, from which our own AV was made.

As has been shown above, the history of the printed text in the 16th cent. is part of the history of the Antiochian text; although of no critical importance, it is a subject very full of interest. [A good short account of the early printed editions will be found in Scrivener's *Plain Introduction* (ed. Miller, 1894), vol. ii. ch. vii. Cf. also Tregelles, *Account of the Printed Text of the Greek NT*, 1854]. The NT was first printed in Greek as vol. v. of the Complutensian Polyglott Bible. This magnificent work was prepared at the cost of Francis Ximenes de Cisneros, Cardinal-Archbishop of Toledo, and was printed at Alcalá (*Complutum*), where he had founded a university. The OT was given in Hebrew, Latin, and Greek; the Apocrypha and NT in Greek and Latin. The volume containing the NT (which was the first to be printed) was completed on 10th Jan. 1514; but owing to the death of the truly great Cardinal, the publication of the whole work was delayed, the Pope's license not being granted till 22nd March 1520. Meanwhile, in order to forestall the Spanish edition, John Froben, the celebrated publisher at Basle, employed Erasmus to prepare an edition of the NT in Greek, accompanied by a revised Latin version: this was hurried through the press, and published in 1516. Erasmus published other editions in 1519, 1522, 1527, and 1535. Other important editions are those of Robert Stephen (especially the folio of 1550, which is regarded by many as the standard text), Theodore de Bèze (Beza), and the brothers Elzevir. All printed editions, even those prepared by the great founders of textual criticism, were based upon the TR until 1831, when Lachmann published a text constructed directly from the ancient documents.

* This Introduction was written by Dr. Hort, and will in this article be cited under his name, though the two editors accept joint responsibility for it.

Whatever may be the ultimate verdict of textual criticism, the TR must always remain a monument worthy of deep veneration and of close study. It is an essential factor in the history of the development of Christianity. Through it the Spirit of God has, during the greater part of the existence of the Church of Christ, spoken to the greater number of her members. It has controlled the doctrine and the life of Christians, and by its means we have been freed, in part at least, from the heavy yoke of mediæval sacerdotalism and superstition. Those who translated it into modern languages have left us in their work something of their own life and spirit. If extent of influence for good is to be our criterion, then surely, whatever its origin, the TR and the translations made from it bear the impress of the seal of God's Spirit, and have an unsurpassed and almost unsurpassable claim to the veneration and gratitude of mankind.

This much every thinking Christian will surely grant. But it is a different thing to go on to say : 'therefore this text must be the original authentic text.' It would be as logical to argue that because the gospel was given to the world in the Greek language, therefore Jesus must have spoken in the same language. It is quite in accordance with our experience of God's methods of working that He should employ an instrument fashioned and conditioned not only by the circumstances under which it took its rise, but also by those through which it has passed in the course of its history.

It is an unfortunate thing that Burgon and Miller's writings seem to imply (we believe, indeed, that the Dean stated it in so many words) that of necessity God must have provided for the accurate preservation of the text of the book which He had given to man. It appears to have been inconceivable to Burgon that the true text should be any other than that commonly accepted by the Church : to him the Church was the guardian of Holy Writ in the same sense as some people believe her to be the guardian of doctrine. If this view, even though not expressly stated, is felt to underlie the student's conclusions, then those conclusions are removed from the domain of matters with which the critic can deal. They may, as in the case of views as to the authority of the Church in matters of faith, or of theories as to the inspiration of the Bible, conceivably rest on a true spiritual perception, but they do not rest on evidence, with which alone the critic is competent to deal. We have pointed out above that a large, and the most enlightened, portion of the Christian Church read the Scriptures in the Vulgate, or Latin translation of Jerome, and regarded it as the only authoritative exponent of the true text and sense of the original. There never has been a unanimous tradition as to the text of Scripture : only for the three centuries that followed the first printing of the Greek NT has there been even an appearance of such unanimity. But though the writings of Burgon and Miller force one to the conclusion that for them personally their theory rested on *a priori* grounds, yet they have with great labour, assiduity, and learning collected a vast amount of evidence in support of the 'Traditional Text.' Unfortunately, Burgon wrote in such a contemptuous manner of the leading textual critics and of the most ancient MSS of the NT that most of his work has the appearance of an *ex parte* statement rather than of a solid contribution to the investigation of a difficult problem. Miller, who edited and completed many of Burgon's papers after his death, adopted a more temperate tone ; but so much of Burgon's language is incorporated, that the subject is still treated rather after the fashion of a polemical controversy than of a critical investigation. Moreover, Burgon's contention was that the 'Traditional Text' is the only one that has any claim to be regarded as the true text; all documents that differ from it are treated as of practically no value. Hort, on the other hand, considered the 'Traditional' or 'Antiochian' text to be valueless as evidence. Thus the subject has been treated at its extreme points, and neither side has taken sufficient trouble to discover how much truth is contained in the views of the other side. We lay a good deal of stress on this matter, because we think there has been a strong disposition to regard the 'Traditional Text' as a hobby of Burgon's, and to treat his defence of it with the same contempt that he poured so freely on others.

3. Hort's 'Syrian' or 'Antiochian' Text. — In part iii. of Hort's *Introduction,* chapter ii. bears the heading, 'Results of Genealogical Evidence proper,' Section i. (§§ 130–168) is devoted to proving the posteriority of Antiochian to other known types of readings. We hope to show later on that the evidence here adduced is not entitled to be called 'genealogical' in a strict sense, but with this we are not for the moment concerned. Hort begins (§ 130) by stating the incontrovertible fact that all great variations of text were prior to the 5th cent., since the text of Chrysostom and other Syrian Fathers of the 4th cent. is substantially identical with the common late text; and (§ 131) the text of every other considerable group of documents is shown by analogous evidence of Fathers and Versions to be of equal or greater antiquity. If we were living in the age of Chrysostom, the problem to be solved would in all essential points be the same as it is now. Hort then adduces three lines of evidence to prove the posteriority of Antiochian readings : (i.) by analysis of conflate readings (§§ 132–151), (ii.) by Ante-Nicene Patristic evidence (§§ 152–162), (iii.) by internal evidence of Syrian (*i.e.* Antiochian) readings (§§ 163–168). We must deal with each of these divisions separately.

(i.) When one reading is found in one group of documents, another in a second group, and the two different readings are found combined in a third group, this reading is said to be 'conflate.' Of course it has to be assumed that the first two readings are prior to the conflate reading, or else it is not a conflate reading at all. Thus the argument goes in a circle, unless *either* it can be proved that the two separate readings existed at a time when it can be shown that the conflate reading did not, *or* the conflate reading is so obviously wrong that it cannot conceivably be the original reading. If neither of these conditions is fulfilled, then conclusions based on the so-called conflate readings are matters of judgment, not of evidence. Hort adduces and examines eight cases of readings which he believes to be conflate : in each case, according to his view, the Antiochian text has combined two separate readings found in earlier texts. Obviously eight examples, taken four from Mark and four from Luke, afford but a slender foundation on which to build : it may be, and has been, urged that these eight examples are only specimens taken from a large number available, but until further examples are collected and published the case must be judged by the eight given.

For the sake of illustration, we give here the main readings in the instance selected for special discussion by Hort. In Mk 6³³ (following *and the people saw them going, and many knew them, and they ran there together on foot from all the cities*) we find the following readings :

καὶ προῆλθον αὐτούς (*and outwent them*), אB lect 49 Lat. vg Boh Arm and (with προσῆλθον for προῆλθον) LΔ 13 lect 39 ; Syr. vg has καὶ προῆλθον αὐτῶν ἐκεῖ.

καὶ συνῆλθον αὐτοῦ (*and came together there*), Dᵍʳ 28; 604 b (2ᵖᵉ *d ff i r* have καὶ ἦλθον αὐτοῦ, a simply *et venerunt,* Syr. sin and *when they came* : these documents might be taken to support either of the shorter readings).

καὶ προῆλθον αὐτοὺς καὶ συνῆλθον πρὸς αὐτόν (*and outwent them,*

and came together unto him), all known uncials, except the five named above, all cursives except eight, *f q* Syr. hcl Æth.

In this case it will be noticed that there is no evidence to show that καὶ συνῆλθον πρὸς αὐτόν alone was ever read ; moreover, the evidence for καὶ συνῆλθον αὐτοῦ is very slender, and quite possibly later than the supposed conflation. Mill suggested with much probability that D omitted the words *and outwent them* because they contradicted Mt 14¹³ and Lk 9¹¹ 'the crowds *followed* him.' Swete, *ad loc.,* quotes 33 as reading συνέδραμον προς αὐτοὺς καὶ συνῆλθον πρὸς αὐτόν : this appears to have been another way of getting rid of the words objected to. The reading of the mass of MSS gives such good sense that Hort himself says (§ 136), 'There is nothing in the sense that would tempt to alteration : all runs easily and smoothly, and there is neither contradiction nor manifest tautology'; and again (§ 138), 'Had it been the only extant reading, it would have roused no suspicion.' He does, indeed, argue that the fresh point made by *and came together unto him* 'simply spoils the point of ἐξελθών in v.³⁴ ; the multitude "followed" (Mt., Luke) the Lord to the desert region (ἐκεῖ), but the actual arrival at His presence was due to His act, not theirs, for He "came out" of His retirement in some sequestered nook to meet them.' But Swete, *ad loc.,* far more naturally takes the ἐξελθών to mean 'having landed,' and thus the only objection that Hort could find to the language of the fuller reading falls to the ground : the crowd were the first to reach the spot whither Jesus and His disciples were going, they ran together on the beach to meet Him ; and as He landed He saw them, and realized that He could not secure the quiet He sought. It is therefore quite possible that the reading of אBLΔ is due to the accidental omission of a clause.

In none of the eight cases can it be proved that the two parts of the longer reading both existed separately at a time when the combined reading did not exist, and it is a matter of opinion whether the readings in which the two separate ones are combined are likely to be right or not.

Dr. Salmon (*Some Thoughts on the Textual Criticism of the NT,* p. 68) says that 'Canon Cook elaborately discussed Hort's eight cases, contending that in every one of them the conflation hypothesis gives the less probable account of the facts.' He adds : 'In each of these cases I did not myself follow Hort altogether without misgivings.' Miller also discusses the supposed conflations in Appendix ii. of his 'Causes of Corruption,' and makes out a fairly good case for the originality of the supposed conflate readings.

(ii.) Hort's next argument to prove the posteriority of Antiochian readings is founded on Ante-Nicene Patristic evidence.

It will be convenient to follow Hort's example in giving at this point some general considerations in regard to the character and the use of Patristic evidence. We will speak first of the disadvantages and difficulties experienced in using it. To begin with, the material is necessarily very fragmentary in more senses than one. Each writer quotes but a limited number of passages, so that it is only in the case of a few specially prominent passages that we can get together a really representative collection of Patristic quotations. It follows that any kind of Patristic apparatus is more or less deceptive. It may be, for instance, that Origen has a reading which agrees with MSS most approved by critical writers, but that the passage in which it occurs is not quoted by Clement of Alexandria. Here we are placed in a difficulty, because Clement and Origen did not by any means always agree, and, if a quotation had been preserved in which Clement used a different reading, it would be probable that Origen's reading did not belong to the text traditionally current at Alexandria, but that he had obtained it from some other source ; his evidence, therefore, would be simply of a personal character. It is necessary, therefore, in weighing Patristic evidence to deal with the author's quotations as a whole, in order to form a judgment of the character of the text he used. When Clement's and Origen's quotations are thus dealt with, it is found that Origen in part agrees with the text most favoured by critical editors, but that his predecessor Clement used a substantially different text of a 'Western' type ; Origen too, in part, followed 'Western' texts : the conclusions to which these phenomena lead will be discussed later on. The important point to note at this stage is that the whole mass of a writer's quotations must be treated as one whole, and that, while we can discover the type of text he used, our knowledge of it is only fragmentary, and necessarily confined as far as details are concerned to the passages explicitly quoted.

A moment's reflexion on the way in which the Bible is quoted in extempore sermons or in conversation will be sufficient to show that a writer's quotations may not always reproduce the text that he considered the best, supposing him to have formed a critical judgment on the subject. Natural looseness of quotation from memory, familiarity with more than one text, and confusion between parallel passages in the Gospels, will account for many deviations that cannot be considered genuine variant readings. A knowledge of the proneness of the human brain to repeat a mistake once made, will render us cautious even when a writer quotes a passage more than once in the same unusual form. Even with great care and wide experience it is difficult for a student to feel sure that a quotation gives the reading which the writer, in answer to a direct question, would have deliberately stated to be the right one.

Moreover, we often feel great doubt whether the quotation stands in our printed editions in its original form. The works of many Greek Fathers have been notoriously badly edited, and it is only when we have had personal experience of the editor's methods that we can feel any security that full advantage has been taken of the MSS and other evidence available. Dr. Nestle (in his *Introduction to the Textual Criticism of the Greek NT*, Eng. tr. 1901, p. 145) refers to an extreme instance of supineness and ignorance on the part of even a fairly recent editor : he gave in his MS the first and last words of quotations, and left the printer to fill them up from a printed copy of the NT.

And when we go behind the editions, we often find that only comparatively late MSS are now extant, and we have to allow for the natural tendency of scribes to substitute, both consciously and unconsciously, familiar for unfamiliar readings. Sometimes the comments that follow the quotation enable the student to detect the substitution, but such alterations must have been made by scribes in numberless passages in which there are no means of discovering them.

The case of Fathers writing in a language other than Greek presents further difficulties, because it is often impossible to say how far the form of the quotation is due to a knowledge of the original Greek, and how far to familiarity with the version in their own language. Analogous difficulties arise in the case of works which are preserved only in translations, because the translator was likely to introduce readings familiar to him in the vernacular.

We have enlarged somewhat on this matter in order to show how much care is needed in forming a judgment on the Patristic evidence in regard to individual readings. But, on the other hand, we desire to emphasize as strongly as possible the immense importance of Patristic evidence when employed with due precautions for its proper purpose, namely, the dating and localizing of special types of text.

But, again, we must remember that the remains of Ante-Nicene Christian literature that have come down to us are very fragmentary. 'The only period for which we have anything like a sufficiency of representative evidence consists roughly of three-quarters of a century, from about 175 to 250' (Hort, § 158). Besides Clement and Origen, Hort names Irenæus, Hippolytus, Tertullian, Cyprian, and Novatian, belonging to the period named ; Methodius towards the close of the 3rd cent. ; and Eusebius of Cæsarea in the first third of the 4th century. 'The text used,' writes Hort (§ 159), 'by all those Ante-Nicene Greek writers, not being connected with Alexandria, who have left considerable remains, is substantially Western.'

We are now in a position to consider the value of the argument for the posteriority of Antiochian readings which Hort bases on Ante-Nicene Patristic evidence : it is an *e silentio* argument—that no extant writer before Chrysostom used the Antiochian text. The force of this argument is considerably lessened if we reflect that, had the writings of Origen perished, we should have had practically no Ante-Nicene Patristic evidence for the type of text contained in the RV.

Miller (*The Traditional Text*, p. 94 ff.) has attempted to prove the antiquity of the Traditional or Antiochian text by a wide appeal to Patristic evidence. In a sense he fails, because if a reading is shown to be older than the supposed revision which produced the Antiochian text, it is said by the school of Hort to be not distinctively Antiochian, but a 'Western' reading adopted by the revisers. To one who does not adopt an extreme view on either side, this will probably appear very like a fight over empty names. The Antiochian text confessedly contained an ancient element, and the real question is whether critical editors have paid sufficient attention to the evidence afforded by it. Call the text by what name you will, but let it be judged on the intrinsic value of its readings, not in accordance with uncertain theories. Its very existence forms evidence in favour of certain types of the Western text, which must go back to the 2nd cent., as is shown by Miller ; and the real question at issue is, What weight is to be attached to the evidence of these texts ?

(iii.) The judgment of such a scholar as Dr. Hort on the intrinsic value of the Antiochian readings must carry the greatest weight. It will be most satisfactory to quote his own words. 'Another step is gained by a close examination of all readings distinctively Syrian (Antiochian) in the sense explained above, comparing them on grounds of Internal Evidence, Transcriptional and Intrinsic, with the other readings of the same passages. The result is entirely unfavourable to the hypothesis which was mentioned as not excluded by the phenomena of the conflate readings, namely that in other cases, where the Syrian text differs from all other extant ancient texts, its authors may have copied some other equally ancient and perhaps purer text now otherwise lost' (§ 163). This decision may be regarded either as an expression of subjective judgment, in which case its value will vary according to the estimate formed of its author's ability as a critic ; or else it can be regarded as the result of certain lines of argument, in which case it is the business of other critics to examine those arguments.

The conclusions which Hort reached in regard to the conflate readings discussed above rest on, and indeed may be fairly considered to assume the truth of, his views as to the genealogical relations of the different families into which he divides all extant NT documents. His whole text is indeed based on those views ; and therefore, if we are to discuss the problem before us intelligently, it is essential to have correct knowledge of the exact nature of genealogical evidence, and of how far it is available for the criticism of the NT text.

It is an obvious truth that, if the original of a document exists, no number of copies will possess any value for settling its text, which can be ascertained by reference to the document itself. This is the simple ground on which all genealogical evidence rests. If three independent copies have been made of a document which has itself perished, it may fairly be assumed that where all three agree they correctly represent the original ; and further, in cases where two of the copies agree against the third, we shall confidently judge that these two preserve the right text, and that the third is in error. Now suppose that fifty copies have been made of this third original copy, and that it has itself perished, then it is clear that the evidence of the two extant primary copies outweighs the evidence of the fifty secondary ones. In this example it is assumed that the exact parentage of every copy is known. This is, of course, seldom the case with the MSS of ancient authors ; but when the parentage of every MS concerned can be ascertained, then genealogical evidence gives results from which there can be no appeal.

This matter is of such importance that it is worth while to illustrate further what we have said, by reference to an actual instance. A fair number of MSS exist of the *Pædagogue* of Clement of Alexandria. In one family of these, consisting of eight or more members, a passage of considerable length is left out. Now two leaves have been lost from a MS preserved at Florence (called F), which contained exactly this passage ; it is therefore beyond doubt that the MSS referred to were copied from F after the loss of these leaves, and they are therefore of no value as evidence. There exists also at Paris another MS (P), considerably older than F. At one time there was some little doubt about the relation existing between these two MSS ; but after a time it was pointed out by a German scholar, Dr. Stählin, that certain notes that were written in P by different people and at different times, are written in F in the hand of the original scribe ; this makes it certain that F was copied, directly or indirectly, from P, and it can therefore also be put aside. Further researches showed that every known MS of the work was derived from P, which consequently forms our only authority for the text. It is very seldom that such certain results as these can be reached in actual practice. It is generally possible to group MSS to some extent by observing their agreement in obvious errors, because it is not likely that different scribes would make the same mistakes independently in several different places. It is obvious that the confidence with which we can employ genealogical evidence is proportionate to the certainty with which the relations of the MSS have been ascertained. In the case of certain cursive MSS of the Gospels strictly genealogical evidence is forthcoming, and it has been shown that the cursives 13, 69, 124, 346, and certain others, are derived from one common ancestor ; but, except for this one important and interesting case, the genealogical relations of Gospel MSS are matters of deduction, if not of guesswork.

It appears, then, that it is impossible to acquiesce in Hort's unqualified condemnation of the

Antiochian text, so far as that condemnation rests on (i.) the analysis of conflate readings, which presupposes certain genealogical relations to exist between certain groups of MSS, and involves an argument in a vicious circle, because those relations cannot be independently shown to exist; and (ii.) so far as it rests on Patristic evidence, this being precarious from its fragmentary character, while at the same time it does prove that the Antiochian text contains a very ancient element. It remains, therefore, to judge this text on its intrinsic merits.

4. The generally accepted Critical Text.—Once again, it is with Hort's views that we must principally concern ourselves, because WH's text is the only one published which can be regarded as in any way self-consistent. No textual student would place much confidence in Tischendorf's judgment, which is embodied in his *editio octava critica major*; the Greek text underlying the RV does not appear to have been formed in accordance with any ascertainable principles; and Weymouth's 'Resultant Text,' and similar editions, founded on the consensus of critical editors, from their nature have no independent critical value. We have, therefore, to consider the principles on which WH founded their text. We have already shown how the great mass of documents, containing an Antiochian text, were set on one side. The pre-Antiochian texts Hort divided into three families, and, on what appear to many students insufficient grounds, assumed that they stood in certain genealogical relations to one another. One of these families consists of the group of texts commonly called 'Western'; after setting these aside as obvious corruptions of the original text, only a small body of MSS, Versions, and Fathers remains. This small residuum, however, Hort proceeds to again divide into 'Neutral' and 'Alexandrian' documents. It is now, we think we may say, generally acknowledged that this distinction cannot be maintained (cf. Salmon, *Some Thoughts on the Textual Criticism of the NT*, p. 50 ff.). Practically, he classes as 'Alexandrian' the readings of documents which usually agree with Codex B, when they differ from B and are not supported by much Western evidence. We shall therefore treat these documents as forming one group, and distinguish the readings, as Salmon suggests, as early and later Alexandrian. Hort frankly admitted the close relation existing between his Neutral and Alexandrian readings, since he conceived both sets of readings to be derived from a common non-Western ancestor; this led him, in the case of an important set of readings, which he called 'Western non-interpolations,' to prefer the testimony of a small group of Western documents to the practically unanimous evidence of all other documents.

It will be convenient here to give a list of the main documents with which criticism has to deal. We begin with those which more or less regularly support the Alexandrian readings. See also art. MANUSCRIPTS.

B, the famous Codex Vaticanus, assigned to the 4th cent., is by far the most interesting; according to Hort, it contains a purely 'Neutral' text in the Gospels.

א, Codex Sinaiticus, discovered by Tischendorf on Mt. Sinai, and probably to be assigned to the 4th century. This MS is thought by Hort to be free from Antiochian readings, but to contain a 'mixed' text, that is, one in which Western, Neutral, and Alexandrian elements are all found, though in the Gospels he looks on it as largely Neutral; this is equivalent to saying that its agreements with B are very numerous.

C, Codex Ephræmi Rescriptus, a palimpsest preserved at Paris, and belonging probably to the 5th century. The text of this MS is undoubtedly of great importance. Miller (*Plain Intr.*4 vol. i. p. 123) well describes its text as 'standing nearly midway between A and B, somewhat inclining to the latter.' Hort considers C to contain an Antiochian and also a Western element.

L, Codex Regius, preserved at Paris, belonging to the 8th century. This MS is especially remarkable for the number

of readings it has in common with B. According to Hort (§ 209), 'The foundation of the text is Non-Western Pre-Syrian.' But he adds: 'The fundamental text has been largely mixed with late Western and with Syrian elements.'

T. Under this symbol are placed several fragments of MSS containing a Greek text and a translation in the dialect of Upper Egypt (Sahidic or Thebaic). They range in date from the 5th to the 7th century.

X, Codex Monacensis, preserved at Munich, of the 9th or 10th cent., has a fundamentally Antiochian text, but is of interest because it often joins with CL in giving readings which may be regarded as late Alexandrian.

Z, Codex Dublinensis Rescriptus, perhaps to be assigned to the 4th cent., contains 295 verses of Mt. in 22 fragments. The text is apparently pre-Antiochian, and agrees more closely with א than with B.

Δ, Codex Sangallensis, of the 9th or 10th cent., has an ordinary Antiochian text, except in Mk., in which Gospel it has many readings in common with CL.

Ξ, Codex Xacynthius, a palimpsest, probably of the 8th cent., belonging to the British and Foreign Bible Society in London. This MS contains 342 verses of Lk., giving an apparently pre-Antiochian text, in which both Western and Alexandrian elements are found.

1, A minuscule, preserved at Basle, assigned to the 10th, 12th, or 13th cent., often agrees with אB and BL.

33, A minuscule of the 10th cent., preserved at Paris, has been called 'the queen of cursives.' It has a very interesting text, containing many ancient elements, but agreeing now with one, now with another type of readings.

The ancient Egyptian Versions, as might be expected, to some extent support the Alexandrian text; but there is so much uncertainty in regard to these Versions that it is not easy to reckon with them as an element in the critical problem presented to us. Forbes Robinson, in his art. 'Egyptian Versions' in Hastings' *DB*, declines to follow Lightfoot and Hort in assigning one, if not both, of the principal Egyptian Versions (*i.e.* the Bohairic and the Sahidic), or at least parts of them, to the close of the 2nd century. He gives good reasons for thinking that the Sahidic Version, which was current in Upper Egypt, was the earlier of the two; and it must be regarded as fundamentally Western rather than Alexandrian. The Bohairic (misleadingly called Coptic, and also Memphitic) Version, current in Lower Egypt, confessedly agrees in general with B, and perhaps even more closely with the text used by Cyril of Alexandria. If it has to be assigned to a date as late as the middle of the 3rd cent., it is evident that it may be the result of the type of text then current in Alexandria, and cannot be used as evidence for the greater antiquity of that text. The remains of the Bashmuric Versions—those current in Middle Egypt—are so scanty that they offer little help at present.

It would be easy to extend this list by including documents which occasionally support the Alexandrian text, but it will be found that the nucleus of the attestation for most of Hort's readings lies practically in the group אBCLX 33, often supported by the Egyptian versions.

At the same time, it is most necessary to bear in mind that the greater part of the attestation for Hort's readings is often afforded by documents which he classes as Western, and whose evidence he would put on one side were it not supported by some member or members of the Alexandrian group. We proceed, therefore, to give a list of the main Western documents, which have not already been mentioned as containing an Alexandrian element.

D. Codex Bezæ Cantabrigiensis, of the 6th century. This is in many ways the most interesting MS of the Gospels extant: its text is, to a great extent, unique, and gains in interest and importance from the support which it often receives from the most ancient versions known, the Old Latin and the Old Syriac. All evidence tends to show that it preserves for us a text which was widely read in the 2nd cent., and the questions connected with this text are likely to increase rather than to decrease both in importance and in practical interest.

P and Q. Two palimpsests preserved at Wolfenbüttel, assigned respectively to the 6th and 5th centuries. P contains 31 fragments, consisting of 518 verses from all four Gospels; Q 12 fragments of 247 verses from Lk. and John. The ancient element in these MSS is partly Western and partly Alexandrian.

R. Codex Nitriensis, a palimpsest of the 6th cent., in the British Museum, contains 25 fragments of Lk., consisting of about 516 verses. The pre-Antiochian readings are mostly Western.

Two groups of minuscules are of importance. 1–118–131–209 are fairly closely related, and offer some interesting readings; but far more important are the minuscules of the Ferrar group, mentioned above, 13–69–124–346–543–(788)–826. This group preserves the readings of a lost MS containing a peculiar Western text, different from that of D, but in a manner parallel to it. Another important minuscule, of the 9th or 10th cent., is preserved at St. Petersburg, and is named by Miller-Scrivener 473 (565 of Gregory, 81 of Hort, 2ᵖᵉ of Tischendorf).

The evidence of the Versions is of great importance in regard to the Western text, for it shows how widespread this text was in the earliest times, and teaches us that the name 'Western' cannot properly be applied to it in a geographical sense. From East and West and from the south of Egypt we get evidence of the prevalence of distinctively Western types of readings.

The Old Latin (*i.e.* the pre-Vulgate Latin) is found in different forms, which have been distinguished as African, European, and Italic; the last of these, however, approaches so nearly to the Vulgate text, that we shall now leave it on one side. The most important MS of the *African* Latin is *k* (Codex Bobbiensis), of the 5th or 6th cent., preserved at Turin. Unfortunately, it contains only portions of Mt. and Mark. The close agreement of its readings with the quotations of Cyprian proves that it contains a text used in Africa in early times; *e* (Codex Palatinus), of the 4th or 5th cent., preserved at Vienna, contains a version of a similar type, though by no means so homogeneous as that of *k*. Of the *European* Latin there are several MSS: *a*, *b*, *ff* (Mt. only), *h* (part of Mt.), *i* (part of Mk. and Lk.), *m* (not a MS, but a collection of passages [*testimonia*] from the OT and NT, known as the 'Speculum'); this type is also found to some extent in *c*, *f*, and *q*, and in many fragments of MSS.

The text of the Latin Vulgate is preserved in very numerous MSS. It is fundamentally Western in character, as being a descendant of the Old Latin, but has been much modified, especially in the Gospels, by the influence of Greek MSS of the Antiochian type.

In Syriac, the Peshiṭta Version holds a place analogous to St. Jerome's Vulgate in Latin, and supports the Antiochian text. Another Version, called by the followers of Hort the 'Old Syriac,' is preserved in two MSS; one in the British Museum, the text of which was published by Cureton, is called after him the 'Curetonian Syriac' (Syr cur); the other was discovered by Mrs. Lewis and Mrs. Gibson in the Library of the Convent on Mount Sinai, and is known as the 'Sinaitic Syriac' (Syr sin). These Versions, allied, but by no means identical, have an essentially Western text. Another factor in the Syriac problem is the *Diatessaron* of Tatian (flourished A.D. 160), the text of which has to a great extent been recovered from an Arabic translation, from an Armenian translation of the Syriac commentary of Ephraem Syrus, and from the quotations of the Syrian writer Aphraates. The *Diatessaron* was a harmony of the four Gospels, which was widely used in Syriac-speaking countries in preference to the separate Gospels; and in compiling it Tatian used a Western text, similar in character to the Old Syriac. The mutual relations of these documents are still in dispute, but the most probable view is that the Old Syriac stands to the Peshiṭta as the Old Latin does to Jerome's Vulgate. Two later versions must be mentioned; one is the Harkleian revision of the Philoxenian Syriac, made by Thomas of Harkel about the year 616, the text of which is based on the Peshiṭta, but important readings from Greek MSS of a Western type are given in the margin; the other is an Evangelistarium, or Church-lesson book, of the 11th cent., known as the 'Jerusalem Syriac,' which sometimes offers very interesting readings of the Alexandrian type. It has already been stated that the Sahidic version of Upper Egypt is fundamentally Western.

In order to complete this brief survey of the most important documents, we must here mention A—the important Codex Alexandrinus of the 5th cent., preserved in the British Museum; it contains a pure form of the Antiochian text, and it is quite possible that critics will learn to allow more weight to its evidence than is at present the case. The main mass of uncials that have not been here mentioned, and of the minuscules, may be regarded as simply supplementing the evidence of A, because the importance to be attached to them depends upon the estimate formed of the value of the text of A.

We have now to consider in more detail the use which Hort makes of the Alexandrian group of documents. We have already tried to show how precarious any argument is which rests on genealogical considerations, owing to the lack of sufficiently full evidence; at the best, genealogical evidence affords us no help in judging between the Western and the Alexandrian texts, because they are confessedly parallel to each other, and have equal claims to consideration on genealogical grounds. But if it can be shown that the Alexandrian group consistently supports readings intrinsically better than those of the Western documents, this will afford good reason for following it. In other words, the question comes to this: Is the text of WH, which all critics admit to be substantially a text used at Alexandria early in the 3rd cent., *on the whole* preferable to the TR, and to such a text as would be formed by following exclusively Western documents? The answer of critics at the present time to this question would undoubtedly be in the affirmative. But, in the great majority of cases in which it differs from the TR, WH's text has the support of the best Western as well as of the Alexandrian documents; it is

possible, therefore, to argue that its general excellence is due to the pure form of the Western element which it contains, and to look upon the distinctively Alexandrian readings as blemishes. On what grounds does Hort prefer these distinctively Alexandrian readings? His main argument is the internal evidence of groups; all the readings supported by a group such as אB or אD are examined, and judgment is passed on them collectively, and also on the text common to the MSS forming the group. Now, the text common to א and D is, according to Hort's classification, Western, and in his opinion gives inferior readings (of course, when unsupported by other primary documents); whereas the agreement of א and B almost invariably gives readings which he considers intrinsically excellent. This method of forming a judgment on a wide consideration of the general readings of a group, to a great extent does away with the personal element which is so great a danger when individual readings are considered each on its intrinsic merits, but it still leaves plenty of room for the personal equation, since a general judgment is based on a special individual judgment in a number of separate cases; thus Hort's system is far less impersonal than it appears to be at first sight. It is obviously impossible to enter into all this minute research unless one is able to devote many years of close work to the subject; yet, without doing so, it appears presumptuous to dispute Hort's conclusions.

But judgment in this matter really rests on a wider question. If it can be shown to be probable that the Alexandrian text is the result of a revision, then the greater part of Hort's work has been expended in restoring the original text of that revision, and is only a step, though an important one, in getting back to the readings of the original autographs. Now, recent investigations seem to tend to render two facts probable: (1) that all documents giving an Alexandrian text are connected with Egypt, and (2) that the text current in Egypt prior to the time of Origen was fundamentally Western, not Alexandrian. If a strong probability can be made out for these two views, then it will be a reasonable conclusion that the Alexandrian text had its rise in Egypt during the early part of the 3rd cent., and it will have to be treated as parallel to, though earlier and more important than, the Antiochian text. Egypt was the home of scholars, and if such a recension was made there, it is natural that the conclusions of early scholars should commend themselves on their intrinsic merits to men of similar training even at a much later date; we have also to remember that it is quite probable that those early scholars, with more evidence before them than we now have, did select the best readings, and may have preserved to us many true readings which would otherwise have perished. The dislike with which the later students of Antioch regarded the opinions of the earlier Alexandrian Fathers, and the taint of heresy which attached to them, easily account for the text they preferred not having continued in general use, if indeed it was ever widely current. Hort has declared that there are no grounds at all for believing in this Alexandrian revision, but we are not aware that he has gone beyond assertion on this point. In the same way, Burgon and Miller declared that Hort's Antiochian revisions were the creations of Hort's imagination. But the fact remains that the Alexandrian text cannot be traced earlier than the first quarter of the 3rd century. Clement of Alexandria used a distinctively Western text; it is true that he sometimes has what are commonly regarded as Alexandrian readings, but it is manifestly impossible to prove that these may not have been part of the Western text, current in

Alexandria, and naturally taken up by the revisers. If it is the case that the Sahidic version is earlier than the Bohairic, again we find the Western type preceding the Alexandrian ; and if Robinson is further right in assigning the Bohairic to the 3rd, and not the 2nd cent., then it may very possibly have been made from MSS with the revised Alexandrian text, and its character is thus accounted for.

The great importance which Hort assigns to the agreement of ℵ and B depends on his contention that the two MSS are independent of each other ; but there are really strong reasons for doubting this. Hort (§ 288) admits the truth of the fact pointed out by Tischendorf, 'that six leaves of the NT in ℵ, together with the opening verses of the Apocalypse, besides corrections, headings, and in two cases subscriptions, to other parts, are from the hand of the same scribe that wrote the NT in B.' He adopts the obvious conclusion that the scribe of B was the corrector of ℵ, and adds that it shows that the two MSS were written in the same generation, probably in the same place. He argues, however, that the evidence of the text, supported by differences in the order of the books and other externals, creates a strong presumption that they were copied from independent exemplars. But where so much depends on the absolute independence of two witnesses, this close local connexion must cause the most serious doubts. Have we any means of saying where it is likely that the two MSS were written ? Both MSS contain a peculiar system of chapter numbers in the Acts, in each case in a very early hand, and with such differences that in neither case can the numeration have been copied from the other MS, but must have come from a common original. Dean Armitage Robinson, in his 'Euthaliana' (*TS* iii. 3), gives reasons for believing that this chapter-numeration is the same as that connected with the name of Euthalius, and points out (p. 35) that a Euthalian codex claims to have been collated with the accurate copies in the library at Cæsarea of Eusebius Pamphyli. The connexion of Origen with this great library is well known, and suggests (though it can hardly be called more than a suggestion) that the same library may have been the birthplace of these two great MSS which, when in agreement, support the text which Origen mostly used, and with the rise of which he may well have been connected. It is impossible to speak with any confidence until a great deal more work has been done, but it does seem as if the evidence in favour of an Alexandrian revision is growing (cf., further, Burkitt, *TS* v. 5).

We are able to judge of Hort's work only by the results, and to some extent our judgment must be based on a consideration of extreme instances, that is, we must judge the theory by cases in which he has pushed it to its furthest limits. No one denies that the greater part of his text, right or wrong, is of extreme antiquity, being based on the agreement of Alexandrian and Western documents ; the question is whether his theory has led to the inclusion of readings that cannot be shown to be earlier than Origen, and may therefore be due to an Alexandrian revision, or may be errors that had crept into the Western text current at Alexandria on which that revision was based. We propose to examine a few examples which throw light on the methods he employed.

One of the most important, instructive, and truly typical examples occurs in Jn 1¹⁸. The passage has been exhaustively discussed by Hort in the first of his *Two Dissertations* (1876). The verse runs in the Alexandrian MSS : θεὸν οὐδεὶς ἑώρακεν πώποτε· μονογενὴς θεὸς ὁ ὢν εἰς τὸν κόλπον τοῦ πατρὸς ἐκεῖνος ἐξηγήσατο. For μονογενὴς θεὸς the vast majority of documents give ὁ μονογενὴς υἱός : Hort's reading is supported by a small, and nearly homo-

geneous, group of documents, ℵBC*L 33, the Pesh. Syriac, the margin of the Hark. Syriac, and the Bohairic. The Sahidic and Gothic Versions and the Sinaitic Syriac are not extant here, and the evidence of the Æthiopic is divided. So far, this would appear to be an exclusively Alexandrian group, were it not for the support of the Pesh., which can hardly be suspected of complicity with BC*L, and seems to show that the reading must be older than the alleged Alexandrian revision. The Patristic evidence is as usual confused and doubtful, but there can be little doubt that Clement of Alexandria's usual reading was ὁ μονογενὴς θεός (the article is found with θεός also in ℵᶜ 33 Bohairic), but he was acquainted with the reading υἱός which comes once in an allusion of his own, once in the *Excerpta ex Theodoto*. Irenæus seems to have known the reading θεός, which is also found in several later Fathers, including Origen. But the important point is that we have good evidence for the existence of this reading prior to the time of Origen. We may therefore regard it as an old reading current in Alexandria. On the other hand, the evidence of the great majority of MSS and Versions, supported by a good array of Fathers, shows that the rival reading was widely spread at an equally early period. Hort had no doubt how to decide on the evidence, impressed as he was with the general excellence of the Alexandrian group, and he argued so well that internal evidence supports μονογενὴς θεός that it is hard to read his words without feeling convinced that he is in the right. Yet it is at least doubtful whether such a phrase as μονογενὴς θεός could have been used before Greek philosophy obtained a commanding influence over Christian theology. Godet, who was second to none in the exegesis of St. John's Gospel, and was singularly unbiased in matters of textual criticism, deals with the rival readings in a few words (*Com. ad loc.*): 'La leçon des Alexandrins : *le Dieu fils unique*, malgré l'autorité du *Vatic.*, n'a été admise à peu près par aucun des éditeurs modernes, et l'appui du *Sinaït.* ne lui procurera pas à l'avenir un meilleur accueil. Elle a trop la saveur de la dogmatique postérieure. Le fait qu'elle se trouve chez Clément d'Alexandrie et chez Origène, est un indice de son lieu d'origine.' It does, indeed, seem impossible to believe that the writer of the Gospel, immediately after saying 'God, no one has ever seen,' should continue, 'the only-begotten God . . . has declared him.' In fact, the word θεός can apparently be in place here only if used in the secondary sense assigned to it by Origen, as distinguished from ὁ θεός, a term which he thought could not properly be used of the Logos. Hort thinks that the reading cannot have arisen from an accidental confusion of θς and υς, because of the omission of the article in most MSS reading θεός ; but the testimony of Clement suggests that ὁ μονογενὴς θεός may have arisen accidentally ; the reading would be welcomed by the school of Origen, but the article would naturally be omitted.

We next select an instance which exemplifies a particular excellence of the Alexandrian text—freedom from readings introduced to make one Gospel harmonize with the parallel passage in another. In Mt 1²⁵ ℵBZ 1, 33 read ἕως οὗ (B omits) ἔτεκεν υἱόν, and they have the support of important MSS of the Old Latin (aᵛⁱᵈ *b c g¹ k*), of the Egyptian versions, and the Curetonian Syriac. The mass of MSS and Versions bring Mt. into harmony with Lk. by reading ἕως οὗ ἔτεκεν τον.υἱὸν αὐτῆς τὸν πρωτότοκον.

A very similar group (with the addition of D, but without the Curetonian Syriac) omits the doxology to the Lord's Prayer in Mt 6¹³.

In Mt 7¹³ we have one of the instances in which WH desert B, omitting the words ἡ πύλη with ℵ* and the Old Latin, supported by strong Patristic evidence. But the Patristic evidence is discounted by the fact that the extreme familiarity of expressions referring to the 'Two Ways' (cf. *e.g. Didache*, § 1) might easily result in no reference being made to the 'Gate.' Most people who are not professed textual critics would prefer to follow the main mass of MSS.

Mt 16²ᵇ·³ is omitted by ℵB, supported by 3 uncials (including X), 14 minuscules, the Curetonian Syriac, one MS of the Bohairic, and apparently Origen. Jerome says that the passage was omitted in most MSS. Hort says : 'Both documentary evidence and the impossibility of accounting for omission prove these words to be no part of the text of Mt. They can hardly have been an altered repetition of the parallel Lk 12⁵⁴·⁵⁵, but were apparently derived from an extraneous source, written or oral, and inserted in the Western Text at a very early time.' This example brings us face to face with an important problem : the natural tendency of scribes was to make their MS as full as possible, and it is usually impossible (except in cases of homœoteleuton) to account for omission. B and its allies frequently omit phrases or passages found in the majority of documents. Is this a proof of the superiority of their text? It is hard to resist the conclusion that it is. Yet it is unsatisfactory, and indeed uncritical, to adopt a sweeping theory that all omissions are right, for they may have arisen from accidental causes which we cannot know of.

A far more interesting and important case is the omission of Mk 16⁹·²⁰. It is impossible here to go into the evidence fully. The internal evidence of these verses renders it most probable (personally we think it almost conclusively proves) that they did not belong to the original Gospel. But textual criticism has to answer only the question, Were they in the copy from which our MSS are derived? They are omitted by ℵB : let us deal first with the evidence of these two MSS. Are they independent witnesses? The question is well discussed by Dr.

Salmon, *Histor. Introd. to the Study of the Books of the NT*, in a note at the end of ch. ix. The leaf containing the conclusion of Mk. in ℵ is admitted to have been written by the scribe who wrote B: apparently as corrector of the former MS he cancelled and rewrote the leaf. Lk. begins as usual on a new leaf, and there would be room on the last leaf of Mk. for the disputed verses. It is an obvious conjecture that the scribe of ℵ copied the verses from his archetype, and that the corrector deliberately removed them. We have seen that there is some reason for connecting ℵ and B with the great library of Cæsarea: Eusebius was no doubt a great authority on points of Biblical criticism there, and we know that his opinion was against these verses (Mai, *Script. Vett. Nov. Collect.* i. p. 1). They were not reckoned in the Ammonian Sections or the Eusebian Canons. His 'testimony is to the effect that some of the copies in his time contained the verses, and some did not; but that those which omitted them were then the more numerous, and, in his opinion, the more trustworthy.' It is quite possible that the evidence we have so far considered comes to no more than this —'MSS preferred by Eusebius.' If he rejected these verses on internal grounds, we believe he was right in doing so, but we must take care that subjective evidence is not treated as objective textual evidence. It is probable that the scholia found in various minuscules, to the same effect as the testimony of Eusebius quoted above, are derived from him, and have no independent value. But a shorter ending to the Gospel was also current, which was undoubtedly spurious, and this affords indirect, but definite, evidence for the omission of vv.9-20, because it could arise only through the Gospel ending abruptly at v.8. This shorter ending is found in the Old Latin MS *k*, 247 *margin*, Hark. Syriac *margin*, one codex of the Bohairic *margin*, and in the Æthiopic Version. Both endings, the shorter coming first, are found in L ₁12 Ρ·Ψ. It is obvious that the strictly textual evidence against vv.9-20 is very inconclusive: apparently they were omitted (either on internal evidence, or through a strange coincidence by accidental damage to a papyrus roll) in an early group of MSS; and the omission commended itself to Eusebius, as it does to most scholars at the present day.

In Mk 6²² nearly all documents read καὶ εἰσελθούσης τῆς θυγατρὸς αὐτῆς τῆς Ἡρωδιάδος : WH follow ℵBDLΔ 2ᵖᵉ (238) in substituting αὐτοῦ for αὐτῆς τῆς, making the dancer a daughter of Herod bearing the same name as her mother Herodias. This is quite impossible, and we have to understand τῆς θυγατρὸς αὐτοῦ to mean step-daughter ; but even so an unknown character is introduced, for the daughter of Herodias, according to Josephus, was named Salome. Clearly B and its allies, in spite of the support of D, must be wrong here.

In Mt 27⁴⁹ ℵBCL, with some late support, add (after σώσων αὐτόν) the words ἄλλος δὲ λαβὼν λόγχην ἔνυξεν αὐτοῦ τὴν πλευράν, καὶ ἐξῆλθεν ὕδωρ καὶ αἷμα. WH suspend judgment by placing the words in the text within double brackets ; but they are fairly obviously an interpolation, put in at the wrong place, from Jn 19³⁴.

In Mk 6²⁰ WH read, with ℵBL Boh., ἠπόρει for ἐποίει. Both readings make excellent sense, but many people will think the simpler one the more likely.

In Lk 4⁴⁴ WH read Ἰουδαίας instead of Γαλιλαίας. It is difficult to understand how any one can accept Ἰουδαίας as even a possible reading in view of the context (but see Hastings' *DB* i. 406 f.). In the RVm we read that 'very many ancient authorities read *Judæa.*' It is interesting to observe the authorities which agree in this obvious error : they are ℵBCLQR 1-131-209, 22, 157, and 11 other minuscules, 6 lectionaries, the Bohairic, and the text of the Hark. Syriac—an unusually wide and very representative Alexandrian group. Soon after (Lk 6¹), a similar though smaller group (ℵBL 1-118-209, 22, 69, 33, 157, with the Bohairic and some Latin and Syriac documents) omits the difficult word δευτεροπρώτῳ. WH and the RV accept the evidence of this group.

The excellence of the Alexandrian group is well seen in Lk 11²-⁴ ; there can be little doubt that the short form of the Lord's Prayer is right in Lk., as Godet unhesitatingly declared. The constant element in the attestation for the three omissions consists of BL 1, 22, 130, Latin Vulgate ; ℵ and 57 join in two of the three places.

The number of Patristic references to the omission in MSS of Lk 22⁴³, ⁴⁴ (the ministering angel, the bloody sweat) renders it almost certain that they do not form part of the true text ; they are omitted by ℵᵃ ABRT 13ˣ-69-124 *f*, Hark. Syriac *margin*, and some MSS of the Egyptian Versions ; they are marked as probably spurious in many later documents.

The variants in Jn 7³⁹ are of peculiar interest, because there can be little doubt about the right reading, οὔπω γὰρ ἦν πνεῦμα without addition. The difficulty of this statement is so obvious, that it is a wonder more attempts were not made to soften it down. We do not think any passage bears more conclusive testimony to the excellence of the text of the NT as transmitted to us. The words are found without addition in ℵTKΠ 42, 91, some MSS of the Latin Vulgate, the Curetonian Syriac, the Bohairic, and the Armenian. The great majority of documents add ἅγιον—a natural insertion which does not affect the main point. Most Latin documents support the insertion of δεδομένον after πνεῦμα. It is very remarkable that B (254) (with *e q*, Jerusalem and Hark. Syriac) has the fullest reading, πνεῦμα ἅγιον

δεδομένον. D (with *f* go) gets over the difficulty in a different way by reading τὸ πνεῦμα ἅγιον ἐπ' αὐτοῖς.

It is not an easy thing to convey a fair impression by a selection of readings, but we hope the above passages are sufficient to show two things, the undoubted excellence of the Alexandrian tradition, and the inadvisability of following it against internal evidence of readings. If Hort's views of the genealogical relations of the main texts are, as we believe, unproved, then the Alexandrian group must stand on its merits alone, and we must bear in mind that its readings may be due to a definite revision ;* in any case, however, whether there was an Alexandrian revision or not, the text preserved by this group of documents is the purest and the most important now known to us. We believe that the following passage from Dr. Salmon (*Introd. to the NT*⁴, p. 164, note) well expresses what will be the ultimate verdict in regard to the work of the two great Cambridge critics :

'It seems to me that textual critics are not entitled to feel absolute confidence in their results, if they venture within range of the obscurity that hangs over the history of the first publication of the Gospels. Such a task as Bentley and Lachmann proposed to themselves, viz., to recover a good fourth-century text, was perfectly feasible, and has, in fact, been accomplished by Westcott and Hort with triumphant success. I suppose that if a MS containing their text could have been put into the hands of Eusebius, he would have found only one thing in it which would have been quite strange to him, namely, the short conclusion on the last page of St. Mark, and that he would have pronounced the MS to be an extremely good and accurate one. But these editors aim at nothing less than going back to the original documents ; and, in order to do this, it is in some cases necessary to choose between two forms of text, each of which is attested by authorities older than any extant MS. Now, a choice which must be made on subjective grounds only cannot be made with the same confidence as when there is on either side a clear preponderance of historical testimony. And, further, there is the possibility that the Evangelist might have himself published a second edition of his Gospel, so that two forms of text might both be entitled to claim his authority.'

In his treatment of this difficult subject, the present writer has tried to set out main principles rather than to go into minute details : he has also tried to show how a judgment must be formed rather than to express his own opinions. But it is almost impossible to move in textual criticism without having a working hypothesis. Supporters either of the Traditional Text or of WH's views have the advantage of starting from a clearly defined position, and attack or defend definite theories. The present writer has found it necessary to intimate, as a working hypothesis, what his own views are, and has attempted to show the reasons why he holds them. We can reconstruct a text which was current at Antioch by the middle of the 4th cent., and which won its way to practically universal acceptance in countries which used the Greek language ; this would not differ in any material respects from the Textus Receptus. We can also reconstruct a text current in Alexandria probably as early as the first quarter of the 3rd cent. ; this would be almost the same as Westcott and Hort's text, if we except those passages where they give the preference to Western documents. What are we to do with the documents of very divergent types, which are loosely classified as Western ? This is really the main problem which textual critics now have to face. We may perhaps roughly distinguish the following groups of documents as attesting different types of readings, but it is necessary to remember that there is continual cross-attestation : (*a*) D supported by the old Latin ; (*b*) groups in which ℵ sides with Western documents against distinctively Alexandrian readings ; (*c*) the ancient text underlying the Antiochian revision, which is often very difficult to distin-

* Hort looked upon what he called the Alexandrian text (as distinguished from the Neutral) as the result of a revision ; according to the view of the present writer, ℵ and B were not unaffected by the revision.

guish; (d) the Ferrar group of minuscules; (e) the Old Syriac; we also know of a certain number of readings which were evidently widely spread in early times, but which have left little or no trace of their existence in extant MSS and versions.

It is impossible within the limits of this article to enter on this very wide question; nor is it possible at the present stage of criticism to say that any really definite results have been reached. Whatever may be the history of the origin of the Western texts, and however strongly certain isolated readings may commend themselves to the judgment of a few students, it is not likely that any known type of Western text in its entirety will ever command the respect of a considerable body of students of textual criticism and of exegesis; and it must be borne in mind that the final decision must rest on exegesis, unless textual evidence at present not even guessed at should be brought to light. The truth appears to be that the Antiochian text adopted much of what was best in the various Western texts; but at the same time the agreement of Western and Alexandrian documents in many readings that are almost undoubtedly right warns us that right readings may lurk in the most divergent texts, though it is improbable that much of value escaped both the Alexandrian and the Antiochian revisers.

But the existence of these early divergent types of text, in regard to which textual criticism can give no definite verdict, has a very distinct practical lesson to teach, and one which is greatly needed at this critical period in the history of Christianity; it is impossible to recover at present the *ipsissima verba* of the NT writers. Of course the limits of doubt are very narrow, and the possible variants are few and for the most part unimportant; but the fact of doubt remains, and is a standing protest against all mechanical theories of inspiration, for however slight the discrepancies the question must arise, ' Which text or reading is inspired ? ' We must build on the general sense, not on the mere letter of Scripture; this is the practical lesson which textual criticism teaches us at this moment. And what result can be happier than if the study of the letter, by its inconclusiveness, leads us to a firmer grasp of the general sense, in which is the ' spirit that maketh alive ' ?

LITERATURE.—Art. 'Textual Criticism (of NT)' in Hastings' *DB*, Ext. Vol. p. 208 ff.; Scrivener, *Introd. to Criticism of NT*[4], 1894; Gregory, *Textkritik des NT*, 1900, *Prolegomena* to Tischendorf, 1884–94, *Canon and Text of NT*, 1907; von Soden, *Die Schriften des NT*, 1902 ff.; E. Miller, *Guide to the Textual Criticism of the NT*, 1886, *The Oxford Debate*, 1897, *The Present State of the Textual Controversy*, 1899, *The Textual Controversy and the Twentieth Century*, 1901, *The Traditional Text of the Holy Gospels*, 1896 [jointly with Burgon], *Causes of the Corruption of the Traditional Text*, 1896; Hort, Introduction to WH's *NT in Greek*[3], 1896; Nestle, *Introd. to Text. Crit. of Gr. NT*, 1901; Salmon, *Some Criticism of the Text of the NT*, 1897; K. Lake, *The Text of the NT*, 1900; Kenyon, *Handbook to the Text. Crit. of NT*, 1901; Hammond, *Outlines of Textual Criticism applied to the NT*, 1902.   **P. M. BARNARD.**

THADDÆUS occurs only Mk 3[18] and Mt 10[3]; in the latter place in the AV in the form : ' Lebbæus, whose surname was Thaddæus.' On the textual questions, see artt. JUDAS (vol. i. p. 906), LEBBÆUS (above, p. 22), and ' Thaddæus' (*DB* iv. 741). In the Western Church neither 'Lebbæus' nor 'Thaddæus' became common, their place being taken by 'Judas,' occurring in Lk.'s Gospel and Acts as *Judas Jacobi*, and found in Mt. as *Judas Zelotes* in the oldest Latin witnesses, and as *Judas son of James* in Syr-Sin; his day falling with that of Simon on the 28th October.* But even under the name of Jude

* In the Calendar of Cordova for 961 the entry runs : ' festum Simonis Cananei et Tadei apostolorum'; see M. Férotin, *Le liber ordinum en usage dans l'église Wisigothique et Mozarabe d'Espagne*, Paris, 1904 (= *Monumenta ecclesiæ liturgica*, ed. Cabrol-Leclerq, vol. v.).

this Apostle never became very popular. The *Calendar of the English Church, Illustrated* (Oxford and London, 1851), knows only of *two old* churches in England dedicated in the joint names of Simon and Jude, and of several instances in *modern* churches of their names being honoured separately, as in Liverpool, Manchester, Bethnal Green, West Derby; ' but this is quite against the mediæval custom.' Neither was ' Thaddæus' frequent as a proper name; cf., however, for instance, the Italian painter Taddeo Gaddi. In the Greek Church the 19th June is kept as μνήμη τοῦ ἁγίου καὶ ἐνδόξου ἀποστόλου 'Ιούδα, who by Luke, in the Gospel and Acts, is called 'Ιούδας; by Matthew and Mark, Θαδδαῖος καὶ Λεββαῖος, ἀδελφὸς κατὰ σάρκα χρηματίζων τοῦ κυρίου ἡμῶν 'Ιησοῦ Χριστοῦ ὡς υἱὸς 'Ιωσὴφ τοῦ μνήστορος, ἀδελφὸς δὲ γνήσιος 'Ιακώβου τοῦ ἀδελφοθέου, ὁ καὶ τὴν φωτιστικὴν καὶ δογμάτων ἔμπλεον τοῦ Πνεύματος ἀνθρώποις ἅπασιν ἐπιστείλας ἐπιστολήν. It is then told that he was sent by Christ Himself ὡς ἀδελφὸς καὶ μυσταγωγός to Mesopotamia, came to Edessa, healed Abgar, and was shot with arrows by the infidels in the town Ararat. On 30th June, the day of all Apostles, he is numbered 12th; the place where he died in one MS being called ἐν 'Αράτῳ τῇ πόλει. On the 21st August the Greek Church celebrates μνήμη τοῦ ἁγίου ἀποστόλου Θαδδαίου τοῦ καὶ Λεββαίου ἑνὸς τῶν ἑβδομήκοντα. He is said to have been from Edessa, a Hebrew by birth, who came to Jerusalem in the days of John the Baptist, was baptized, and afterwards followed Jesus till His Passion. Then he returned to his home, healed Abgar of the ' black' leprosy, came to Syria, and died in Βήρυτος; cf. the *Acta Apostolorum Apocr.*, ed. Tischendorf.

On the identity of Lebbæus-Thaddæus-Judas Jacobi with the author of the Epistle and the brother of Jesus, see Mayor, 'Brethren of the Lord' (*DB* i. 320); Dom J. Chapman (*JThSt* vii. 412–433); Th. Zahn, *Forschungen*, vi. [1900] 225–363. For evidence that the Epistle of Jude is quoted occasionally under the name of Thaddæus, see *ZNTW* iii. [1902] 251. In the Syrian Churches, Jude is identified with Thomas, and sometimes regarded as twin brother of Jesus; see J. R. Harris, *Dioscuri in the Christian Legends*, and *The Cult of the Heavenly Twins* (1906), p. 105. In the *Onomastica sacra* the name 'Thaddæus' is explained by αἰνετός (ed. Lagarde, 202. 83). The same etymology is followed in the Talmud, *Sanh.* 43*a*, where the last of the five disciples of Jesus is called *Thoda*, and Ps 100[1] 50[23] are applied to him.

On monuments of Christian art the name does not seem to occur frequently (see Mrs. Arthur Bell, *The Saints in Christian Art* (1901), vol. i. ch. viii. 'The Twelve Apostles'; ch. xvi. 'St. Simon, St. Jude, and St. Matthias'). In the mosaic of S. Paolo fuori le Mura, Thaddæus is the last of the Apostles; on its bronze doors, cast at Constantinople in 1070, he is left out altogether along with James the Less and Matthias. The Romanic *frontale aureum* of the altar of the church at Comburg (Würtemberg), representing the Salvator Mundi in the midst of the Twelve Apostles, gives him under the name *S. Tatheus*. When the Creed is apportioned among the Twelve, 'Thaddæus dixit: *carnis resurrectionem*.' In the Hexameters ascribed to Bernard of Clairvaux, ' *Restituit carnem Judas*'; with Firminius: ' Judas Jacobi dixit: *sanctorum communionem, remissionem peccatorum*' (Hahn, *Bibliothek der Symbole*[3], pp. 52–54, 97, 104).

In the *Const. Apost.* the ordinances about widows are ascribed to Thaddæus (viii. 25).

Very complicated is the question about the relation of the Apostle Thaddæus to Θαδδαῖος, who is said by Eusebius to have been one of the Seventy, and to have been sent after the Ascension, by Thomas, to Edessa to heal King Abgar. Jerome, on

Mt 10⁴, tells the same about the Apostle Thaddæus, while in the Syrian legend the messenger to Edessa is called *Addai* (on the form *Haddai* in one of the MSS of the Syriac Version of the *HE* of Eusebius, see *DB*, *s.v.* 'Thaddæus'). Zahn thinks that Eusebius is guilty of the confusion of Addai with Thaddaios. On the Syriac *Doctrine of Addai*, see Lagarde, *Reliquiæ juris eccles. antiqu. syr.* p. 32 = Gr. p. 89; Cureton, *Ancient Syriac Documents*; G. Phillips, *The Doctrine of Addai* (1876).

As the place of his burial there is mentioned, besides Beirut in Phœnicia, the town Ostracine in Egypt (see *Const. Apost.*, ed. Lagarde, p. 283), where Θαδδαῖος ὁ Λεβαῖος καὶ Ἰούδας is distinguished from Judas Jacobi; the latter, after preaching throughout the whole of Mesopotamia, was stoned by the Jews, and lies at Edessa; the former preached to the Edessenes, was crucified, and buried in 'Ostracine,' the town of Egypt.

The most probable etymology of the name 'Thaddæus' seems to be that proposed by Dalman, who sees in it the Heb. abbreviation of a Greek name beginning with Theo-, as in *Theudas*. The 'Gospel of Thaddæus' mentioned in some MSS and editions of the *Decretum Gelasii* is due to a clerical error. On the legends connected with Thaddæus see Lipsius, *Die apokr. Apostelgeschichten*, ii. pp. 142–200 (1884).

LITERATURE.—Artt. JUDAS 1 and LEBBÆUS in the present work; 'Judas' in *DB* ii. 798ᵃ; 'Lebbæus,' *ib.* iii. 92; 'Thaddæus,' *ib.* iv. 741; 'Judas,' 'Lebbæus,' 'Thaddæus,' in *EBi*; Zahn, *Forschungen*, vi. 293, 321, 344; Dom Chapman, 'The Brethren of the Lord' in *JThSt* vii. 412 ff.   EB. NESTLE.

THANKSGIVING (εὐχαριστία, εὐχαριστέω) is an important Christian virtue, and in pre-Christian Greek the word is rare. Used chiefly of man's attitude to God, it implies a recollection of Him, a recognition of His actions in the past (cf. ὁμολογεῖν and cognates, He 13¹⁵, Mt 11²⁵ etc.), quite apart from any thought of petition for the future. Meaning originally *to do a good turn to a man* (cf. ἔχειν χάριν, 1 Ti 1¹²), εὐχαριστία acquires the meaning of repaying a favour, and hence of showing gratitude. Philo uses it in the technical sense of thank-offering. Outside the Gospels and Apocalypse it occurs in the NT only in the writings of St. Paul.

1. Usage in the Gospels.—The word εὐχαριστέω (εὐχαριστία does not occur in the Gospels), though found in other connexions (Jn 11⁴¹, Lk 17¹⁶), occurs principally in relation to grace before meat, especially at the miracles of the loaves, and the institution of the Lord's Supper (Mt 15³⁶ 26²⁷, Mk 8⁶ 14²³, Lk 22¹⁷· ¹⁹ [before the breaking of the bread we have in the ‖ Mt 26²⁶, Mk 14²² εὐλογήσας (EV 'blessed') for εὐχαριστήσας in Lk.], Jn 6¹¹· ²³). From this fact, in later times, though not in the NT itself, the word *Eucharist* became a recognized term for the Holy Communion, and is found in the *Teaching of the Twelve Apostles* (9¹) and other sub-Apostolic literature (Ign. *Smyr.* 7, Just. Mart. *Apol.* 1, 65), as well as in later writings. See, further, artt. BENEDICTION and BLESSING.

Besides εὐχαριστέω we find in the Gospels, as terms denoting the giving of thanks, (1) ἐξομολογέομαι (Mt 11²⁵ ‖ Lk 10²¹, RVm 'praise'); (2) ἀνθομολογέομαι (Lk 2³⁸); and (3) ἔχω χάριν (Lk 17⁹, cf. 6³²ff.). In (1) Jesus Himself thanks His Father for revealing to babes what is hidden from the wise and understanding. In (2) Anna the prophetess gives thanks to God for the vision of the infant Jesus. In (3) Jesus sets aside the idea that a servant should be thanked for doing the things which were commanded him.

2. Christ's lessons regarding thanksgiving.—(1) *His own example is a lesson.* He gives thanks to His Father for daily bread (Mt 15³⁶ ‖ Mk 8⁶, Jn 6¹¹· ²³; cf. Lk 24³⁰); for the revelation to babes of the secrets of the heavenly Kingdom (Mt 11²⁵ ‖ Lk 10²¹); for the Divine hearing of His prayer (Jn 11⁴¹); for the bread and wine of the Holy Supper, and all the

spiritual blessings which they connote (Mt 26²⁶ff·, Mk 14²²f·, Lk 22¹⁷· ¹⁹, 1 Co 11²⁴f·). (2) *His words convey lessons.* We have no claim to be regarded as profitable servants, deserving to be thanked, if we have merely done our duty (Lk 17⁹f·). There is a kind of thanksgiving to God which is only a form of hypocrisy, being really a flattery of ourselves (Lk 18¹¹). The truly thankful heart is rare (Lk 17¹⁶ff·); it recognizes God's hand in the gifts of human benefactors (v.¹⁸); it is inspired by faith, and wins great blessings (v.¹⁹).

It is worth noting that it is to St. Luke alone that we owe the story of the Ten Lepers and the Grateful Samaritan, which is typical of the Christian grace of gratitude that finds expression in thanksgiving; while it is to St. Luke's beloved friend and teacher, St. Paul, as to no other, that we owe the repeated and characteristic Christian utterance of thanks to God for His unspeakable gift (2 Co 9¹⁵, and the Pauline Epistles, *passim*).

LITERATURE.—Cremer, *Lexicon*, *s.vv.* εὐχαριστία, εὐλογέω; Swete, *JThSt*, Jan. 1902, p. 163; Trench, *Miracles*, 357 ff.; Mozley, *University Serm.* 253; Rashdall, *Christus in Ecclesia*, 179.   H. C. LEES AND J. C. LAMBERT.

THEOPHILUS.—The name of an early Christian to whom a couple of NT documents, the Third (canonical) Gospel and its sequel, the Acts of the Apostles, are addressed (Lk 1³, Ac 1¹). This does not, of course, imply that the writer had no wider audience in view. The two books in question are far too carefully composed to be mere private communications. In modern parlance they are 'dedicated' rather than addressed to Theophilus; that is, if we suppose the name to be a genuine proper name. On this point, however, there has been some difference of opinion. Conceivably *Theophilus* (= OT *Jedidiah*, 'God's friend') might be no more than a conventional title for the average Christian reader, an imaginary *nom de guerre* for the typical catechumen. This symbolic sense of the word was conjectured by Origen. At the same time, instances of *Theophilus* as a proper name are not uncommon, and it seems simpler, on the whole, to regard it as such in the NT. A modification of the above theory has also been proposed (*e.g.* by Ramsay and Bartlet), which would make Theophilus a baptismal name given to a Roman official, and employed here for the sake of safety. This is possible, but rather unlikely.

The name, then, is to be taken as denoting some contemporary of Luke (or of whoever wrote the Third Gospel and Acts). Otherwise he is unknown to history. Later tradition naturally busied itself with fanciful conjectures upon his personality, turning him eventually into the bishop of Antioch or of Cæsarea (cf. Zahn's *Einleitung*, § 58. 5). But this is the region of guesswork, though modern critics have often been tempted to stray back into it. As, for example, Beck, who, in his *Prolog des Lk.-Evangeliums* (1900), deduces from ἐν ἡμῖν (1³) the fact that the author was one of the two Emmaus disciples, while Theophilus must have been a wealthy Antiochene tax-collector, an acquaintance of Chuza and Herod, who accompanied Herod and Bernice to Cæsarea, where he fell in with St. Paul and St. Luke. Godet opines that Luke was a freedman of Theophilus. The latter, at any rate, may have been the *patronus libri*, expected to be responsible for the publication and circulation of the Gospel and its sequel. Whether he was of Greek extraction or a Roman, possibly of equestrian rank, it is impossible to say; but one may cheerfully set aside the theories which identify him with Philo or Seneca.

We are thus reduced to an examination of the internal evidence for any knowledge of the position and character of the man. (1) Plainly, to begin with, he was a Christian when the Third Gospel was composed. He had been 'instructed' in the faith by some Christian teachers as a catechumen. But either he or his friend, the author, felt that some fuller acquaintance with the historic basis of the Christian religion (not of the Pauline gospel, as Hilgenfeld argues in *Ztschr. für Wiss. Theologie*, 1901, pp. 1–11) was advisable, and it was with this end in view that the Third Gospel and its sequel were addressed to him, in order to remove uncertainties caused by diversity, inexactness, lack of thoroughness, and absence of order, in the current accounts of Christ's life on earth. Some critics still hold that Theophilus was simply a pagan interested in Christianity. But the term κατηχήθης (Lk 1[4], cf. Ac 18[25] 21[21]), especially in the light of its context, seems to preclude this hypothesis. St. Luke's preface implies that he was more than merely an interested inquirer. It suggests, as Wright says (*Composition of the Four Gospels*, p. 55), that 'busy men like Theophilus had been catechized in their youth, but later occupations had driven out many of the lessons, and unless a man could secure the same catechist whom he had attended as a boy, the frequent discrepancies in the ever-changing tradition would jar on the precision of youthful memory, and produce a general sense of disappointment and uncertainty.' Oral tradition had its merits. It was vital and free from any danger of codifying the Christian spirit. But among its defects were liability to discrepancies (cf. Jos. *c. Apion.* i. 2) and absence of uniformity. Furthermore, if there is no other instance of one Christian hailing another by a secular title in the NT, on the other hand there is no case of a Christian writing for the benefit of any save fellow-Christians. Besides, such a title need not have been incongruous with Christianity. If Theophilus was of high rank, the faith which bade Christians honour all men would not preclude a Christian author from employing such a title once in a semiformal prologue to his work. (2) That Theophilus was a man of rank is suggested by the term κράτιστε = 'most excellent' or 'your excellency' (Ac 23[26] 24[3] 26[25]), which may be almost semitechnical, and in any case implies respect for exalted position and high authority, though the idea of intimacy and affection need not be excluded (cf. Jos. *Ant.* vi. 8, etc.). He may have been on the proconsular staff, or an official of some kind in the Imperial service. And this would tally with the special emphasis laid by St. Luke upon the relation of the Church to the Empire, and the repeated connexions which he suggests between the political affairs of the age and the progress of Christianity (cf. *e.g.* Ramsay, *Was Christ born at Bethlehem?* ch. iii.), especially in Acts. His social position is further suggested by the internal evidence of the Third Gospel, which, as has been often pointed out (cf. *e.g. Encyc. Bibl.* 1792), is specially concerned with the hindrances thrown up by money and rank in the path of a consistent Christian character. 'Lk. seems to see, as the main obstacles to the Faith, not hypocrisies, nor Jewish backsliding, but the temptations of wealth and social position acting upon half-hearted converts; and his sayings about building the tower, putting the hand to the plough, renouncing all one's possessions, and hating father and mother, are pathetic indications of what must have been going on in the divided household of many a young Theophilus.' In the case of Theophilus, however, wealth and dignity did not form an obstacle to faith. It says something for this well-to-do Christian that he was willing to be instructed, and evidently keen to learn the historic principles of his faith. To his open-mindedness we owe, in one sense, two of the most important historical documents in early Chris-

tian literature. For it is plain that this man's need stirred his friend to write. Behind Theophilus he probably saw many a likeminded inquirer. This catechumen's case was in some ways typical and characteristic, and thus St. Luke was led to write his Gospel narrative, an instance of the 'first and noblest use' of the human imagination, 'that is to say, of the power of perceiving things which cannot be perceived by the senses,' viz. 'to call up the scenes and facts in which we are commanded to believe, and be present, as if in the body, at every recorded event of the history of the Redeemer' (Ruskin, *Frondes Agrestes*, § 9). The writer's aim was personal, as well as modest and religious. Early Christian literature sprang from no literary ambition. Even in its historic form it was practical and didactic. But in this case the writer, like Burke, who originally drew up his *Reflections on the French Revolution* for the benefit of a puzzled young friend, has gained a wider reach and range for his pen's products than perhaps he contemplated when he began.

The omission of the semi-formal adjective κράτιστε in Ac 1[1] is not unnatural. It is needless to see anything subtle or significant in the change from Lk 1[3]. No doubt the excessive use of the term was one feature of ancient servility (Theophrastus, *Char.* 5). But St. Luke might well have used it twice in two volumes without any fear of incurring the charge of obsequiousness, and we cannot suppose he dropped the adjective lest he should be guilty of bad taste. Still less probable is the conjecture that the absence of the title in Ac 1[1] denotes the conversion of Theophilus to Christianity since Lk 1[3] had been written. For this there is no evidence whatsoever, and we have already seen that there was no necessary incongruity in applying such a title of honour, pagan though it was, to a fellow-Christian.

LITERATURE.—In addition to the articles in Bible Dictionaries *s.v.*, and to the critical editors on Lk 1[1-4], see the monographs on that passage already referred to, and add Blass, *Philology of Gospels*, pp. 7–20, with Zahn's *Einleitung in das NT*, § 60.

J. MOFFATT.

THIEF (κλέπτης).—Thieves are mentioned in the following passages of the Gospels, besides several others where RV substitutes 'robber' as the equivalent of λῃστής. See ROBBER. **1.** Mt 6[19. 20] = Lk 12[33]. Christ's disciples should have their treasure where thieves do not break (lit. 'dig') through and steal. Eastern houses, being commonly of mud or sun-dried brick, are easily broken into; cf. Ex 22[2], Job 24[16], Ezk 12[5. 7]. **2.** Mt 24[43] = Lk 12[39]. The unexpectedness of Christ's coming is compared to that of a thief's entry. This figure seems to have greatly impressed the Apostles; it is echoed several times in the NT (1 Th 5[2(4)], 2 P 3[10], Rev 3[3] 16[15]). **3.** Jn 10[1. 8. 10]. False and self-seeking teachers—whether false Christs, or, more probably, Pharisees—are compared to thieves and robbers. **4.** Jn 12[6]. Judas 'was a thief, and having the bag' (lit. 'box') 'took away what was put therein' (RV).

HAROLD SMITH.

THIRST.—The occasions on which the physical suffering arising from thirst is noted by the Evangelists are connected in every instance with the personal experiences of Jesus. Early in His public ministry, as He was journeying back from Judæa to Galilee, leaving the former country as a result of Pharisaic hostility, the writer of the Fourth Gospel notices that Jesus suffered the pangs of thirst, and records His request for a drink of water from the Samaritan woman as she came to draw water from 'Jacob's spring' (πηγὴ τοῦ Ἰακώβ, Jn 4[6]). It is remarkable that this author mentions this fact, as well as the weariness felt by Jesus in His journey, side by side with the title (ὁ κύριος, 4[1]) which betrays the writer's attitude towards His claims over human life and conduct.

The other instance of Jesus' suffering in this respect is also mentioned by this writer, who records His cry 'I thirst' ($\delta\iota\psi\hat{\omega}$, 19[28]) from the cross. And although he seems to connect the expression with the fulfilment of Messianic prophecy (cf. Ps 69[21]), there can be no doubt as to the reality of the feeling which prompted the utterance of the Sufferer. The intensity of His suffering is attested by the unwonted interference of one of the soldier-guards, who, out of compassion for the Crucified, attempted to allay His anguish. One result of these and such like incidents in the course of His life is to be seen in the vivid portraiture by Jesus of the great Day of final judgment. The common physical wants of struggling humanity afford opportunities of service in the sacred cause outlined by the two great commandments of the Law (Mt 22[36ff.]). Nor must we omit to notice the basis upon which Jesus has placed the service of man by men, and the grounds upon which He distributes the final awards. To every believer in the cosmic significance of the Incarnation the use of the first person ($\dot{\epsilon}\delta\dot{\iota}\psi\eta\sigma\alpha$, etc.) by the Judge-King (Mt 25[34]) who is 'the Son of Man' (v.[31]), reveals the nature and character of His sympathy with our weaknesses ($\sigma\upsilon\nu\pi\alpha\theta\hat{\eta}\sigma\alpha\iota$ $\tau\alpha\hat{\iota}s$ $\dot{\alpha}\sigma\theta\epsilon\nu\epsilon\dot{\iota}\alpha\iota s$ $\dot{\eta}\mu\hat{\omega}\nu$, He 4[15]), and guarantees the truth of the assertion that 'it was necessary that he should in all things become like his brethren' ($\dot{\omega}\phi\epsilon\iota\lambda\epsilon\nu$ $\kappa\alpha\tau\dot{\alpha}$ $\pi\dot{\alpha}\nu\tau\alpha$ $\tau\hat{o}\hat{\iota}s$ $\dot{\alpha}\delta\epsilon\lambda\phi\hat{o}\hat{\iota}s$ $\dot{o}\mu o\iota-\omega\theta\hat{\eta}\nu\alpha\iota$, He 2[17]).

Following the example of OT thinkers, Jesus employed the idea embodied in the word 'thirst' to express the conscious needs of the human soul for something higher and more satisfying than it could discover in its earthly experiences (cf. Is 55[1], Ps 42[2] etc.). Just as man in the vigour of physical health revolts against physical deprivation in the shape of thirst, so in proportion to his spiritual health and energy he reaches out and cries for spiritual satisfaction, and cannot rest as long as his wants are unsupplied. In this restlessness Jesus sees a source of men's ultimate happiness, and those He accounts blessed ($\mu\alpha\kappa\dot{\alpha}\rho\iota o\iota$) who thirst for righteousness ($\delta\iota\psi\hat{\omega}\nu\tau\epsilon s$ $\tau\dot{\eta}\nu$ $\delta\iota\kappa\alpha\iota o\sigma\dot{\upsilon}\nu\eta\nu$, Mt 5[6]). As might perhaps be expected, the Johannine writer makes the most frequent reference to this feature of Jesus' teaching. Belief in Himself, Jesus asserts to be the means by which spiritual thirst is assuaged (cf. Jn 6[35] 7[37]); and if we compare this statement with its expansion and elaboration, we will observe that by belief He means the spiritual appropriation of His entire Manhood ($\dot{\eta}$ $\sigma\dot{\alpha}\rho\xi$ $\mu o\upsilon$ . . . $\tau\dot{o}$ $\alpha\hat{\iota}\mu\dot{\alpha}$ $\mu o\upsilon$ $\dot{\alpha}\lambda\eta\theta\dot{\eta}s$ $\dot{\epsilon}\sigma\tau\iota$ $\pi\dot{o}\sigma\iota s$, 6[56]).

On two distinct occasions Jesus makes incidental, though didactic, reference to the profound union, between Himself and those who believe on Him, hinted at above. In His conversation with the woman of Samaria He characteristically emphasizes His teaching by the details in her drawing of the water from the fountain. For her the well was a source of the satisfaction of personal need, and at the same time a means of supplying the needs of others dependent on her. In a manner analogous to this, if she had drunk of the living water which He was ready to supply, Jesus promised her a part in His glorious work of sharing with others out of the fulness she had received (cf. 1[16]). In her the living water would become 'a fountain springing unto eternal life' ($\dot{\epsilon}\nu$ $\alpha\dot{\upsilon}\tau\hat{\omega}$ $\pi\eta\gamma\dot{\eta}$ $\ddot{\upsilon}\delta\alpha\tau os$ $\dot{\alpha}\lambda\lambda o\mu\dot{\epsilon}\nu o\upsilon$ $\epsilon\dot{\iota}s$ $\zeta\omega\dot{\eta}\nu$ $\alpha\dot{\iota}\dot{\omega}\nu\iota o\nu$, 4[14]). This thought is more definitely and directly stated by Jesus during the Feast of Tabernacles which He attended in Jerusalem. His invitation to all who thirsted ($\dot{\epsilon}\dot{\alpha}\nu$ $\tau\iota s$ $\delta\iota\psi\hat{\alpha}$, 7[37]) to come to Him and drink was followed by the promise, founded on the phraseology and thought of the OT (Is 12[3] 58[11], etc.),

that they who accepted would themselves become sources of blessing and satisfaction to their fellow-men ($\pi o\tau\alpha\mu o\dot{\iota}$ $\dot{\epsilon}\kappa$ $\tau\hat{\eta}s$ $\kappa o\iota\lambda\dot{\iota}\alpha s$, $\kappa.\tau.\lambda.$, 7[38]). 'He who drinks of the Spiritual Rock becomes in turn himself a rock from within which the waters flow to slake the thirst of others' (Westcott, Gospel of St. John, ad loc.). It is impossible not to see in this living relationship between Jesus and believers the foundation upon which must ultimately rest all human activities, as they display themselves in the service of the race.   J. R. WILLIS.

THISTLES.—In the NT thistles ($\tau\rho\dot{\iota}\beta o\lambda o\iota$) are mentioned twice (Mt 7[16], He 6[8] RV). The term, however, is loosely employed, and probably embraces several genera of spinous plants, in which Palestine is peculiarly rich. In Hebrew there is a very extensive and varied nomenclature, about twenty terms being employed which denote prickly shrubs or weeds; but in many instances the precise meaning is unknown, while in many others the words are used in the most general way. Tristram, who goes very fully into the matter (Nat. Hist. of Bible, 423–432), identifies Heb. ḥôaḥ with the common thistle (Carduus) and dardar with knapweed (Centaurea). Of the former there are many species, the most common among them being: (1) Notabasis syriaca, a tall thistle with pink flowers; (2) the yellow spotted thistle (Scolymus maculatus); and (3) Carthamus oxycanthus, which has a yellow flower. Of the latter there are also many species, notably the star-thistle (Centaurea calcitrapa). These plants were exceedingly troublesome to the farmer, the corn-fields often being overrun with them.

The only reference to thistles which occurs in the Gospels is in our Lord's question, 'Do men gather . . . figs of thistles?' (Mt 7[16]).
                                        HUGH DUNCAN.
THOMAS.—One of the twelve Apostles. (For the name see DIDYMUS). In the lists of the Twelve his name is always in the second group of four. In Mk 3[18], where the names are not in pairs, he is eighth; so in Lk 6[15], where he is coupled with Matthew. In Mt 10[3] he is seventh, coming before Matthew. In Acts 1[13] he is sixth, and is coupled with Philip. No incident is recorded of him in the Synoptics or in Acts; but he comes into some prominence in the later scenes in the Fourth Gospel. When Jesus is about to return to Judæa because of the death of Lazarus, and the disciples are afraid of Jewish hostility, Thomas says, 'Let us also go, that we may die with him' (Jn 11[16]). In the conversation after the Supper, Thomas interjects the remark, 'Lord, we know not whither thou goest; and how can we know the way?' (14[5]); and thereby elicits the great saying, 'I am the way, the truth, and the life' (14[6]). When Jesus appeared to the disciples on the evening of the Resurrection day, Thomas was absent, and was unable afterwards to accept the testimony, 'We have seen the Lord.' He must himself not only see the Master, but touch His body before he could believe (20[24. 25]). A week later Thomas is present when Jesus again appears; and then his doubts vanish, and he rises to the completest confession of faith recorded in the Gospels, 'My Lord and my God' (20[26-29]). Thomas is mentioned also in 21[2] as one of the group to whom Jesus appeared on the morning by the Lake-side.

Later traditions of Thomas, obviously of little value, are mentioned in Eusebius and in the Apocryphal Acts of Thomas. He is spoken of as a missionary to Parthia, or to India. Some traditions assign to him the honour of martyrdom; and his supposed grave was shown at Edessa in the 4th century.

The personality of Thomas has a clear and consistent expression in the incidents which the Fourth Gospel records. He belongs to the quiet, reflective group of the Apostolic company; and his temperament is that of a man who finds the best things too good to be true, and who usually imagines that the worst foreseen possibility will be realized. He requires direct personal evidence, and will not hastily accept the testimony even of his friends. Yet he is not lacking in devotion and love to his Lord. He will die with Him rather than desert His cause; and in his gloomiest days of unbelief he does not separate himself from the Apostolic company. Though not persuaded of the reality of the Resurrection, he keeps his old loyalty and love; and when the Master's presence is utterly sure, he gladly accepts the highest that the revelation of Christ implies. His unbelief was never a failure to respond to the spiritual truth and love brought to him by his Master; at most it was an inability to accept unexpected and marvellous external manifestations of that truth. 'In Thomas we have a man incredulous but tenacious; despondent but true; with little hope but much courage; sincere in love though perplexed in faith; neither rushing to the right conclusion as Peter might have done, nor rushing away from it into danger and dishonour as Peter did' (T. T. Lynch).

The scepticism of Thomas has a real apologetic value. It goes to disprove the contention that the Apostles were credulous persons easily misled by their hopes, and so deluded into a mistaken belief that their dead Master had spoken to them. Thomas believed because the fact which was too good to hope for became too certain to reject.

LITERATURE.—Among expository sermons on Thomas may be named F. W. Robertson, *Serm.* ii. 268; T. T. Lynch, *Serm. for my Curates*, 33; H. M. Butler, *Univ. and other Serm.* 43; A. B. Davidson, *The Called of God*, 317.

E. H. TITCHMARSH.

THORNS.—Palestine is unusually rich in acanthous plants. As many as 50 genera and 200 species occur in Palestine and Syria, 'besides a multitude clothed with scabrous, strigose, or stinging hairs, and another multitude with prickly fruits' (Post in Hastings' *DB* iv. 753). In the OT references to thorns are numerous, and many different words are used to express them. But the vocabulary, though full, is very indefinite, many of the terms employed being as vague and general as our own English word 'thorns.' We have the reflex of this uncertain terminology in EV, which renders almost indiscriminately by 'thistle,' 'thorn,' or 'bramble,' a single Hebrew word. In the NT three terms occur, viz. ἄκανθα, τρίβολος, and σκόλοψ. The last-named is found only in 2 Co 12⁷ 'There was given to me a thorn (σκόλοψ) in the flesh,' but in this instance the rendering should rather be 'stake' or 'pale.' The second (τρίβολος) has already been explained (see THISTLES). It remains that we should consider ἄκανθα (Mt 7¹⁶ 13⁷· ²², Mk 4⁷· ¹⁸, Lk 6⁴⁴ 8⁷· ¹⁴, Jn 19², He 6⁸), which is invariably translated 'thorns.' Strictly speaking, this term denotes *Acanthus spinosus*, a showy perennial with deeply indented and spiny leaves, and bearing white flowers tinged with pink. In the NT, however, it is a quite general term for all thorny or prickly plants, and is applied to bushes and weeds alike. Among the most common are thorny Astragali, which abound in the higher mountainous regions, and many species of Acacia, Eryngium, Rhamnus, Rubus, Solanum, etc. Some of them, such as *Poterium spinosum* and *Rhamnus punctata*, are found in all parts of the country. In our Third Gospel mention is made of the bramble (βάτος, Lk 6⁴⁴). This may quite possibly be the common bramble (*Rubus fruticosus*), which is found in many parts of Palestine. It is noteworthy, however, that, except in this one passage, βάτος is always rendered 'bush,' and is used only of the 'burning bush' of Moses (Mk 12²⁶, Lk 20³⁷

etc.). The corresponding Heb. word (סנה) is similarly restricted in its use. As the bramble is not found on Horeb (Sinai), it has been thought by some that the 'bush' was a kind of acacia. For the crown of thorns which was set in mockery on the head of Christ (Jn 19²), see CROWN OF THORNS.

Much might easily be said regarding the symbolism of thorns in the Scriptures. But it may be sufficient merely to note that they were regarded as the direct consequence of human sin, and so became the natural symbols of sin and the sufferings in which it issues (Gn 3¹⁸, Nu 33⁵⁵, Pr 22⁵ etc.). In the light of this symbolism there is an apt pathos and beauty in the fact that Christ was crowned with thorns (see Cox, *An Expositor's Note Book*, 349 ff.; and Earl Lytton, *Fables in Song*, i.).

HUGH DUNCAN.

THREE.—See NUMBER.

THRESHING - FLOOR. — See AGRICULTURE in vol. i. p. 40ᵃ.

THRONE (θρόνος) is a term applied, first of all, to the royal seat of a king; and, secondly, to the official seat of a judge or subordinate ruler. In the former sense it is employed of heaven as the throne of God (Mt 5³⁴ 23²²). The Messianic reign of Jesus is foretold by Zacharias in the words, 'The Lord God shall give unto him the throne of his father David' (Lk 1³²). Jesus speaks of His own exaltation as the time 'when the Son of Man shall sit on the throne of his glory' (Mt 19²⁸ 25³¹). The universal dominion which He is to share with His Father is suggested by 'the Lamb in the midst of the throne' (Rev 5⁶ 7¹⁷), and by 'the throne of God and of the Lamb' (22³). So in He 8¹ 12² Christ is seated 'on the right hand of the throne' of God. The promise given to the Twelve, of sitting on thrones of judgment (Mt 19²⁸ ‖ Lk 22³⁰), is practically given to all who overcome in the battle with evil (Rev 3²¹). In Col 1¹⁶ 'thrones' are among the subordinate powers of the universe which owe their creation to Christ.

JAMES PATRICK.

THUNDER (βροντή) is but twice mentioned in the Gospels (Mk 3¹⁷, Jn 12²⁹). In mountainous Palestine, with the long deep gorge of the Jordan, it is perhaps the most awe-inspiring of natural phenomena. It seldom occurs save in the winter half of the year, and is almost invariably accompanied by rain. For the old Israelites thunder was the voice of God, with a meaning which persons specially gifted might understand. 'It seems probable that the "voice out of heaven" (Jn 12²⁸· ²⁹) was a thunder-peal, as indeed most of those present thought, and that its significance was recognized and interpreted by Jesus alone' (Hastings' *DB* iv. 757ᵇ). The surname 'sons of thunder' given to James and John (Mk 3¹⁷) disappears at once and finally from the records. On the available data no sure opinion can be formed as to why it was applied to them. As men in the East are called 'sons' of that which is most characteristic of them, there was doubtless something 'thundery' about them,—a tendency, *e.g.*, to wrathful resentment of slight or injury (Lk 9⁵⁴). See BOANERGES.

W. EWING.

TIBERIAS (Τιβεριάς).—A city situated on the W. shore of the Sea of Galilee, founded by Herod Antipas, and named by him in honour of the Emperor Tiberius. The original inhabitants were foreigners, whom Herod either forced to reside in the new city or to whom he gave special inducements if they would. Our Lord, so far as is known, never visited Tiberias, it being His custom to avoid Gentile cities. The only reference to the city in the NT is Jn 6²³, in which it is stated that 'there came boats from Tiberias unto the place where they ate the bread after the Lord had given thanks' (cf. Jn $6^1 21^1$).

1. Location.—The ancient city was situated directly on the shore of the Sea of Galilee, and therefore approximately 682 feet below the level of the Mediterranean, at the north end of a narrow rectangular plain about two miles long, which was bounded by a rather steep ridge of hills rising abruptly to the west. From the ruins still to be found in the vicinity it is probable that the ancient city extended considerably farther south of the modern town. Josephus (*Ant.* XVIII. ii. 3; cf. *BJ* IV. i. 3) says that there were 'warm baths a little distance from it in a village called Emmaus' (Hammath?). According to the Talmud (Jerus. *Megilla*, i. 1), the city was built upon the ancient site of Rakkath of Naphtali; and it is further stated (*Sanhed.* 12a) that in the 4th cent. the Jews had actually dropped the name Tiberias and reverted to the ancient name Rakkath. On the other hand, in the Bab. Talmud, Tiberias is sometimes identified with Rakkath, sometimes with Hammath, and sometimes with Chinnereth (cf. Jos 19^{35}). Jerome (*Onom.* 112. 28 ff.) identifies it with Chinnereth.

2. History.—Herod Antipas is supposed to have completed the building of Tiberias about A.D. 22. Ancient sepulchres were removed to make room for the new foundations, and accordingly the Jews regarded the new city as legally unclean (cf. Nu $19^{11ff.}$). Nevertheless the town grew with great rapidity, and, before the downfall of Jerusalem had become one of the chief cities of Palestine. Herod had made it the capital of Galilee, removing the seat of government from Sepphoris, the former capital. The city was fortified by Josephus when commander-in-chief of Galilee (c. A.D. 66). During the struggle of the Jews with Rome, its inhabitants remained loyal to the national cause. When, however, Vespasian appeared before its walls with three legions, the citizens yielded without resistance. Vespasian restored it to Herod Agrippa II., who stripped it of its political prestige by transferring the capital again to Sepphoris. When Agrippa died (A.D. 100), it fell directly under Roman rule. Shortly after the destruction of Jerusalem (A.D. 70), Tiberias became the chief seat of the Jews and of Jewish learning. According to Epiphanius, it was not long before the city was inhabited exclusively by Jews. In the 2nd cent. the Sanhedrin, which had been shifted from Jerusalem to Jamnia and then to Sepphoris, was established at Tiberias under the presidency of the celebrated Rabbi Judah the Holy.

3. Present condition.—The modern town is called by the Arabs *Ṭâbarîyeh*. Traces still remain of the ancient city along the Lake, especially to the south of the present town. Heaps of stones, columns of grey granite, foundations of buildings, and of a thick wall which extended almost to the famous baths, all confirm the supposition that the ancient city extended at one time farther south. The present town is defended on the land side by a wall furnished with towers. There are the ruins of a once imposing castle at the N.W. corner. But castle, walls, and houses were seriously damaged by the earthquakes of 30th Oct. 1759 and of 1st Jan. 1837. Among the famous tombs of Tiberias are those of Maimonides, and Rabbis 'Aḳiba and Jochanan. To-day Tiberias has a population of approximately 4000 souls, of whom about two-thirds are Jews and the other third Mohammedans and Christians of different sects. The Protestants have a well-equipped hospital, and are doing a good religious work under the United Free Church of Scotland. The Jews occupy a squalid quarter in the middle of the town, adjacent to the Lake. The city as a whole is 'a

picture of disgusting filth and frightful wretchedness.' Of late, however, the place is improving somewhat, having become the seat of a Turkish *ḳaimaḳan*, or governor.

Tiberias is hot and fever-haunted. The breezes from the Mediterranean are prevented from striking the city by the hills which bound the plain on the west. The winters are mild, snow being very rarely known. The Lake furnishes the only supply of water. The view from the city embraces the whole extent of the Sea of Galilee except the S.W. extremity. Schürer speaks of Tiberias as 'the most beautiful spot in Galilee,' which, however, is an exaggeration. At present it is one of the four sacred cities of the Jews in Palestine, the others being Jerusalem, Hebron, and Safed. The study of the Talmud still flourishes in Tiberias.

LITERATURE.—Robinson, *BRP* iii. 254 ff.; Baedeker-Socin, *Pal.* 286 ff.; Guérin, *Galilée*, i. 250 ff.; Neubauer, *Géog. du Talm.* 208 ff.; Merrill, art. 'Tiberias' in Hastings' *DB*; Buhl, *GAP* 226 f.; Reland, *Pal.* ii. 1036; G. A. Smith, *HGHL* 447 ff.; Burckhardt, *Travels*, 320 ff.; Murray, *Syria-Pal.* 251; Schürer, *HJP* II. i. 143 ff.; Wilson, *Lands of the Bible*, ii. 116 ff.; Ritter, *Geog. of Pal.* ii. 256 ff.; art. 'Tiberias' in *EBi* iv.

GEORGE L. ROBINSON.

TIBERIUS.—In Lk $3^{1f.}$ it is stated that a word of God came upon John the Baptist, in the 15th year of the rule of Tiberius Cæsar. It is by no means certain what year is indicated by this date. The sole rule of Tiberius began in A.D. 14; the 15th year of this sole rule would be A.D. 28. But it is more probable that we ought to count from the time at which Tiberius received power equal with that of Augustus over the provinces of the Empire, that is, from the end of A.D. 11; this brings us to A.D. 25–26 (Ramsay, *Was Christ Born at Bethlehem?* p. 199 ff.).

Tiberius Claudius Nero, named after his adoption Tiberius Julius Cæsar, on the monuments bears the name Tiberius Cæsar Augustus. He was the son of Tiberius Claudius Nero (a Roman noble) and Livia (whom Augustus took to wife while her husband was still alive), and was born in B.C. 42. Constitutionally, the principate died with each Emperor, and the Emperor could not appoint a successor. Augustus got over this difficulty by appointing a partner or co-regent in the Empire: it was practically impossible to pass over such in electing to the principate. The Imperial powers were gradually conferred on this consort. M. Vipsanius Agrippa first held this position (died B.C. 12). Marcellus (who died B.C. 23) and Gaius and Lucius Cæsar were marked out as successors. In their youth they were entrusted to the care of Tiberius, who was forced to divorce his wife and marry Augustus' daughter Julia (B.C. 11). By this time Tiberius had proved himself an able soldier, and in B.C. 9 was raised to the position which Agrippa had occupied. Augustus had a dislike to Tiberius, and did not desire his succession. This obvious desire to use Tiberius selfishly, for his own ends, embittered the life of the latter, and in B.C. 6 he retired to Rhodes, and remained there eight years in solitude, while his young stepsons received advancement in the State. But they died—Lucius in A.D. 2, and Gaius in A.D. 4. In this latter year Tiberius was adopted by Augustus, and was at the same time compelled to adopt his own nephew Germanicus. In A.D. 11 he was raised practically to a position of equality with Augustus. On the death of the latter, in A.D. 14, his sole reign began. He was a thoroughly competent Emperor; but a naturally reserved temperament, influenced by early disappointments and outraged feelings, resulted in weakness and cruelty. His fear of conspiracy made him encourage informers, and many supposed rivals were put to death. In the second half of his reign he was much under the influence of one Sejanus, an accomplished schemer, whose duplicity and crime he realized only after much evil had been wrought by him. By this time he had retired to spend the closing years of his life in the island of Capri, where he died on 16th March A.D. 37. His principate thus covers all the period of the Gospel history.

LITERATURE.—J. B. Bury, *A History of the Roman Empire* (London, 1893 and later); J. Bergmans, *Die Quellen der Vita Tiberii des Cassius Dio* (Amsterdam, 1903); R. Cagnat, *Cours d'Epigraphie Latine* [3] (Paris, 1898), p. 179 ff. etc. It is generally admitted that the ancient authorities take too severe a view, based on the memoirs of Agrippina, the enemy of Tiberius: these ancient authorities are, Tacitus, *Annals*; Suetonius, *Life of Tiberius*; and Dio Cassius.   ALEX. SOUTER.

TILES.—The man sick of the palsy was let down 'through the tiles' (AV 'tiling'). See art. HOUSE in vol. i. p. 753[a].

TIMÆUS.—See BARTIMÆUS.

TIME.—**1.** The word 'time' is used in the Gospels in a variety of phrases more or less indefinite. Probably the most definite expression is ἐν στιγμῇ χρόνου, 'in a moment of time' (Lk 4[5]). χρόνος is used of time in general (Lk 1[57] 8[27], Mk 9[21], Jn 5[6]), passing or having passed. In a similar sense we find ὥρα (Mk 6[35]) rendered 'day' in RV (see DAY). More definite is ἀπὸ τότε, 'from that time' (Mt 4[17] 16[21], Lk 16[16]), and ἕως τοῦ νῦν, 'until now' (Mt 24[21] RV, Mk 13[19]). The most important word, however, is καιρός, used invariably of a definite period or occasion. Three uses in this sense are noteworthy. (1) It is used to indicate the time of certain events in the ministry of Jesus (Mt 11[25] 12[1] 14[1]). (2) In a special sense we have the remarkable passage Jn 7[6, 8] 'My time is not yet come, but your time is always ready,' where the contrast is used apparently to emphasize the peculiar character of Jesus' mission and the hostility which it aroused in Jerusalem. (3) Most important is the use of καιρός to indicate the dawn of a new epoch—πεπλήρωται ὁ καιρός, 'the time is fulfilled' (cf. 13[33], Lk 12[56], Mt 16[3])—which the ministry of Jesus had inaugurated. This new era is contrasted with the past (Mk 1[15]) and with the future (Mk 10[30], Lk 18[30]; see artt. DAY [THAT], GENERATION). In a similar sense of world-period or era we have καιροὶ ἐθνῶν, 'the times of the Gentiles' (Lk 21[24]; but cf. עֵת גּוֹיִם, i.e. judgment-day, Ezk 30[3]). καιρός is also used of a season of the year (Mk 11[13], Mt 13[30]; cf. Lk 12[42]).

2. Various methods of reckoning time were in existence at the beginning of the Christian era, and this fact makes it extremely difficult to locate events with any certainty. The time of day was reckoned at the outset mainly by physical considerations, temperature, etc. (Gn 3[8] 18[1], 1 S 11[9], Job 24[15]), or by the sun's movements (Gn 19[15] 32[24]); the night in early Jewish history was reckoned by watches (see artt. DAY, HOUR, NIGHT, WATCH). The days of the week were numbered, not named.

The division of time into **weeks** was probably of Babylonian origin, and would be suggested by the moon's phases, although there is no trace of this influence either in OT or NT. The word for 'week' in the Gospels is σάββατον (Lk 18[12]). The use of the plural (Mt 28[1], Mk 16[2], Lk 24[1]) may have arisen from the Aram. *Sabbĕthā*, 'the Sabbath' (Heb. *Shabbāth*), which at an early date gave its name to the whole week.

Of the larger divisions of time, the **month**, so familiar in OT times, is hardly mentioned in the NT (Lk 1[26, 36], Jn 4[25]). The Jewish month was lunar. Hence the usual Hebrew name for 'month' (חֹדֶשׁ) is properly the 'new moon.' Three methods were employed to distinguish the month: (1) old Canaanite names, of which only four now survive; (2) numerals (Gn 7[11], Ex 19[1] etc.); (3) Babylonian names (see Hastings' *DB* iv. 765).

The Jewish **year**, like the month, was originally lunar, consisting of 354 days. But as this fell so far short of the full solar year, difficulty would naturally arise in celebrating feasts at the same time in each year. To avoid this, it became necessary to add an extra month at least once in three years. This was done by adding a second Adar (the Bab. name for the twelfth month), February-March, so contrived that the Passover, celebrated on the 14th Nisan (the first month), should always fall *after* the spring equinox. The exact method of doing this is somewhat obscure. But as a month in three years was hardly sufficient, a cycle of eight years was observed in which three months were intercalated, based on general observation of the seasons. This continued until some time after the Christian era, when a more perfect system, a cycle of nineteen years with seven months intercalated—the invention of an astronomer of Athens named Meton—was adopted. It seems unlikely that the Jews had any fixed chronological calendar in the time of Christ, but this is disputed (see Wieseler, *Chronol. Synopsis of the Four Gospels*, p. 401, etc.).

The *method of reckoning years* is a complicated and difficult subject. In accordance with Eastern ideas, that precision in reckoning events to which we moderns are accustomed was unknown. It was not considered necessary (cf. *e.g.* the loose phrases 'in the days of Herod the king,' Mt 2[1]; and 'Herod being tetrarch of Galilee,' Lk 3[1]); nor was it easily attainable. For it was possible for a writer in NT times to employ various systems of reckoning, and it was also possible to employ any one system in various ways. In addition to the various eras in which it was common to reckon, viz. the Olympiad era beginning B.C. 776; the Seleucid, used in the Books of the Maccabees, beginning B.C. 312; the Actian beginning B.C. 31; there was also the Roman method of reckoning by consuls or emperors (Lk 3[1]), and the Jewish by high priests. Further, the year began at a different time in different countries, *e.g.* the Roman year began on Jan. 1, but in a few cases the emperors dated their years from the date of their election as tribunes of the people on Dec. 10. The Jewish *sacred* year began about the vernal equinox, as did also, in all probability, the years of the Seleucid era. But in Asia Minor a year beginning in autumn was also observed in ordinary use. These and other considerations render it almost impossible to give the precise date of any event even in NT times (see art. DATES). The one date given with any apparent precision is in Lk 3[1] 'in the fifteenth year of the reign of Tiberius Cæsar.' This seems tolerably accurate, but the actual date intended depends on how St. Luke reckoned. He may have dated from the death of Augustus, Aug. 19, A.D. 14, counting that year as the first of Tiberius' reign, or from the beginning of A.D. 15, which was also a method of reckoning. Or he may have reckoned from Dec. 10, A.D. 15, when Tiberius assumed tribunician authority. Or, as the tribunician authority was interrupted in the reign of Tiberius, St. Luke may have dated his reign from the time when he assumed tribunician power the second time. In addition, there is the question whether St. Luke would reckon according to the Roman year from Jan. 1, or, according to local methods prevalent in Syria, from the autumn equinox.

LITERATURE.—Kaestner, *de Aeris*; Bilfinger, *Die antiken Stundenangaben*; Schwarz, *Der Jüd. Kalender*; Lewin, *Fasti Sacri*; Wieseler, *Chron. Synopsis of the Four Gospels*; Ideler, *Handbuch der Chronologie*; Schürer, *HJP* i. 37, ii. App. iii. and iv.; W. M. Ramsay, *Was Christ born at Bethlehem?* v.–xi.; Hastings' *DB* iv. pp. 762[b]–766[b], also specially Ext. Vol. 473[b]–484.
                                          G. GORDON STOTT.

TITHE.—On the tithe as a Jewish institution, see art. 'Tithe' in Hastings' *DB*.

Our Lord makes but three references to the tithes, and they are all of the observance of them by the Pharisees (Mt 23²³, Lk 11⁴² 18¹²). In the first two passages He contrasts the minute exactness with which the Pharisees observe their less important and external laws of tithe with their careless disregard of the inner and more important virtues of justice, mercy, faith, and the love of God. In Lk 18¹² He illustrates how compliance with external requirements, especially when these are exceeded, as in the case of the Pharisees, and dissociated from the corresponding state of heart, breeds a culpable and overweening self-righteousness. Our Lord in these references, as also in Mt 5¹⁹, recognizes degrees of importance in the Law's demands. Minute observance of the less important does not excuse from attending to the greater, but neither does compliance with the greater absolve from the obligation to observe the lesser. 'This ought ye to have done, and not to leave the other undone.' Our Lord evidently thought the tithe, as well as the other OT institutions, of Divine origin, and binding upon the Jews of His day. At the same time, He foresaw a period when outward observances should give place to the more purely inward, as men should worship the Father in spirit and in truth (Jn 4²¹⁻²⁴). See also artt. ANISE and RUE.   G. GOODSPEED.

TITLE ON THE CROSS.— The technical word τίτλος is found only in Jn 19¹⁹; Mt 27³⁷ has αἰτία, Lk 23³⁸ ἐπιγραφή, and Mk 15²⁶ ἡ ἐπιγραφὴ τῆς αἰτίας. Again, as regards the wording of the *titulus*, no two Gospels agree exactly. Mt. has οὗτός ἐστιν Ἰησοῦς ὁ βασιλεὺς τῶν Ἰουδαίων; Mk. ὁ βασιλεὺς τῶν Ἰουδαίων; Lk. ὁ βασιλεὺς τῶν Ἰουδαίων οὗτος; and Jn. Ἰησοῦς ὁ Ναζωραῖος ὁ βασιλεὺς τῶν Ἰουδαίων.

The only important variation is in the case of Lk., where the TR reads οὗτός ἐστιν ὁ β. τ. 'I., probably from assimilation to the form given by Mt. The form above given (Lk 23³⁸) is found in אBL, and is supported by the Latin of D: *rex Judæorum hic est*. The so-called Gospel of Peter, taking the words as an insult to Jesus on the part of the Jews, reads: οὗτός ἐστιν ὁ β. τοῦ Ἰσραήλ.

It was customary at Roman executions, at least in the case of remarkable prisoners, for the charge under which the prisoner was suffering to be written briefly on a tablet (σανίς) covered with gypsum (γύψῳ ἀληλιμμένος, Suidas; cf. *titulus qui causam pœnæ indicavit* [Suet. *Cal.* 32], and μετὰ γραμμάτων τὴν αἰτίαν τῆς θανατώσεως αὐτοῦ δηλούντων [Dio Cassius, liv. 3]). This was usually hung round the neck of the criminal, or carried before him to the place of execution (*præcedente titulo* [Suet. *Cal.* 32]). It was afterwards hung from, or fixed to, the top of the cross.

Other words for this tablet are πίναξ and λεύκωμα. The letter of the Churches of Vienne and Lyons, preserved by Eusebius (*HE* v. 1), gives an instance of such a *titulus* in the case of one of the martyrs. The words are: πίνακος αὐτὸν προάγοντος, ἐν ᾧ ἐγίγραπτο Ῥωμαϊστί, οὗτός ἐστιν Ἄτταλος ὁ χριστιανός. This agrees exactly with the form of the title as given by Mt.

The Synoptists merely mention the fact that such a title was placed over the cross of Jesus. St. John, who writes as an eye-witness, adds some interesting particulars—(1) that Pilate wrote the title ; (2) that it was written Ἑβραϊστί, Ῥωμαϊστί, Ἑλληνιστί (the similar words in the TR of Lk. are merely an interpolation from Jn.); (3) that Pilate, in spite of the expostulation of the chief priests, scornfully refused to alter the form of what he had written. With reference to (1) Westcott (on Jn 19¹⁹) remarks: 'The Roman governor found expression to the last for the bitterness which had been called out in him by the opposition of the Jews . . . the heathen governor completed the unwilling testimony of the Jewish priest' (Jn 11⁴⁹ᶠ.). The three languages of the τίτλος—Hebrew (*i.e.* Aramaic), Latin, and Greek —represent, as Westcott remarks, the national, the official, and the common dialects respectively. The true reading, therefore, preserves the more natural order.

Bilingual and trilingual inscriptions such as this were naturally common in the East under the Roman Empire. Grotius (on Mt 27³⁷) mentions the case of the inscription on the tomb of the Emperor Gordian, which was written in no fewer than five languages ; the five being the three above mentioned, together with Persian and Egyptian.

The wording of the title differs in all the four Gospels, as above remarked, and many attempts have been made to harmonize or explain the variations. Wordsworth (on Jn 19¹⁹) has even supposed that the title really ran thus : 'This is Jesus of Nazareth, the King of the Jews.' Such an attempt at harmonizing the variations is absolutely unnecessary. All four Gospels agree in giving the important words which were offensive to the chief priests, viz. 'the King of the Jews.' Others have supposed the variations to be due to slight differences in the form of the title in the three languages. This, as a general idea, is possible, even probable ; but, as regards detail, agreement seems to be nearly hopeless. The uncertainty appears greatest as to the Latin form, which Edersheim finds in Mt., Cook (*Speaker's Com.*) in Mk., Farrar in Lk., Grotius and Swete in John. In the case of the other two languages the more general consensus of opinion finds the Greek in Mk. and the Hebrew, or rather Aramaic, in John. It can be said with some confidence that it is more natural that ὁ Ναζωραῖος should represent the word of the Aramaic inscription, as this method of description would have little point for those who would read the Greek or the Latin (cf. Sadler on Jn 19¹⁹). We have seen above that the form given by Mt. agrees with that of the Latin *titulus* mentioned in the letter of the Churches of Gaul. Assuming, then, that Jn. gives the Aramaic form and Mt. the Latin, the Greek must be looked for in Mk., as Lk. agrees with Mt. in retaining the word οὗτος. We may suppose, then, that the various forms were somewhat as follows :

Aramaic : יֵשׁוּ הַנּוֹצְרִי מַלְכָּא דִיהוּדָאֵי
Latin : Hic est Jesus Rex Judæorum.
Greek : ὁ βασιλεὺς τῶν Ἰουδαίων.

This view agrees with Edersheim (*Life and Times*, ii. 591 n.), except as regards the order. He supposes the Latin to have been at the top and the Aramaic last ; but this is contrary to the only evidence we have. He is certainly right in his attempt to give the Aramaic form of the inscription in words which are really Aramaic. It is strange to explain Hebrew to mean Aramaic and then to give the words in their Hebrew form (cf. Geikie, quoted in Hastings' *DB* iv. 781, and Farrar's *St. Luke*).

It may be, as Alford writes, 'hardly worth while' to comment on, and endeavour to explain, 'the variations in the Gospels with regard to the Title on the Cross ; but one can hardly forbear to remark, what has been so often noticed before, how the three great languages of the world of the time bear witness to the Saviour of Mankind.' ' The three representative languages of the world at that time,' says Plummer (on Jn 19¹⁹) —'the languages of religion, of empire, of intellect—were employed. Thus did they tell it out among the heathen that the Lord is king (or reigned from the tree. Ps 96¹⁰ LXX).' These three languages, Westcott writes, 'gathered up the results of the religious, the social, and the intellectual preparation for Christ, and in each, witness was given to His office.' These modern writers expand slightly the more expressive words of Grotius: ' Ille enim erat cui cedere debebat religio judaica, eruditio græca, robur latinum' (cf. also some little known words of Priscillian [Tract. i. p. 30] : ' In omni littera sive hebræa sive latina sive græca in omni quod videtur aut dicitur, rex regum et dominorum dominus est, in quibus linguis etsi titulus crucis ponitur, divinum tamen deo testimonium litteratur'). 'Thus the three languages represent not only three races, but their qualities and tendencies. Wherever these exist—where there is an eye to read, a hand to write, a tongue to speak—the cross has a message and the King a kingdom. The "Title" is, in St. John's view, the witness of language to the King of the Jews, who is also the King of humanity' (Alexander, *Leading Ideas of the Gospels*, pp. 277, 278).

Literature.—The Comm., esp. Swete on Mk 15²⁶, Plummer and Farrar on Lk 23²⁸, Grotius on Mt 27³⁷ ; art. on same subject in Hastings' *DB*, vol. iv.; and Edersheim, *LT* ii. pp. 590–591.

J. M. HARDEN.

TITTLE (Gr. κεραία [WH κερέα ; see vol. ii. App. p. 151]).—Both the Gr. and the Eng. words occur in NT only in Mt 5¹⁸, Lk 16¹⁷. κεραία ('little horn,' dim. of κέρας) was used by Hesychius and other grammarians of the accents and diacritical marks in Gr., and the slight points and bends by which in Heb. such letters as ב and כ, ד and ר, ה and ח are distinguished from each other. 'Tittle,' which is just 'title' in another form of spelling (the shorter form is used in all the Eng. VSS, except the Rhemish, up to and including the AV of 1611), comes from *titulus*, which was used in late Lat. to denote any mark or stroke whereby one letter was distinguished from another. It was adopted by Wyclif and Tindale to render κεραία—Luther similarly employing *Tüttel* (*Titel* in modernized Germ. spelling). Great importance was attached by the Rabbis to the little marks by which certain Heb. letters are distinguished from others that they closely resemble, and there are several Jewish sayings which declare that any one who is guilty of interchanging such letters in certain passages of the OT will thereby destroy the whole world (see Edersheim, *LT* i. 537 f. ; cf. Lightfoot, *Hor. Heb.* xi. 99).

On the lips of Jesus the saying, 'One jot or one tittle shall in no wise pass away from the law till all be fulfilled' (Mt 5¹⁸), is startling ; and a number of modern critical scholars are inclined to meet the exegetical difficulty by denying the genuineness of the *logion*—regarding it as an answer of the Evangelist himself to the Pauline anti-legalism, or even as a later Jewish-Christian insertion. Certainly, if the saying stood by itself, unqualified and uninterpreted in any way, there might be some warrant for such criticism, even although on textual grounds there is nothing to be said against the verse, which, moreover, reappears in Luke, though in a shorter form. But the very fact that our Lord proceeds in what follows to repeal the old Law at various points, and to substitute for its enactments precepts of His own (vv.³¹ᶠ· ³³ᶠᶠ· ³⁸ᶠᶠ·), suggests that v.¹⁸, so far from being likely on His lips to mislead His hearers utterly, would be understood easily enough as nothing more than an emphatic affirmation, in the Master's own characteristic style, of the rounded perfection of the ideal law. The objection that the reference to the jot and the tittle implies the written Law, and not the ideal law, has little force. One might as well say that when Jesus, in vv.²⁹· ³⁰, bids His disciples pluck out their right eyes or cut off their right hands, He is urging them to a literal self-mutilation, inasmuch as hands and eyes are physical realities, not ideal things.

When we remember that Jesus was constantly charged by His enemies with being a law-breaker (Mk 2¹⁶· ¹⁸· ²⁴ etc.), we may see in the saying an utterance that has its polemical bearing. Immediately after (v.²⁰) we find Him declaring, 'Except your righteousness shall exceed the righteousness of the scribes and Pharisees, ye shall in no wise enter into the kingdom of heaven.' And elsewhere He affirms that the Pharisaic and Rabbinic legalism led to a positive dishonouring of the Divine law in the interests of a human tradition (Mk 7⁸· ⁹· ¹³). There were thus two reasons why on polemical grounds Jesus should assert the claims of the OT Law in the strongest possible way : (1) Because His enemies themselves continually dishonoured it : (2) because they falsely accused Him of being indifferent to it. And apart from polemics altogether, there was this positive reason why He should 'magnify the law and make it honourable'—He knew (v.¹⁷) that the very purpose of His coming was, not to destroy it, but to fulfil. And so in the striking language of paradox and even of hyperbole that He was wont to use when He felt strongly and desired to speak strongly, He exclaimed, 'For verily I say unto you, Till heaven and earth pass away, one jot or one tittle shall in no wise pass away from the law, till all be fulfilled.'

The point of the saying clearly lies in the word 'fulfilled.' Christ comes, not to lower the standards of righteousness, as His enemies said, but to exalt them (cf. v.²⁰). He comes, indeed, to repeal much in the old Law. The jots and tittles, be it observed, *are* to pass away when the Law is fulfilled. But He is to repeal the old by supplying the power for its true fulfilment, and by showing how the letter is transcended by the spirit. Regarded in this way, the saying is nothing more than an arresting utterance of the familiar Christian truth of the relation in spiritual things between the kernel and the husk, the calyx and the flower. Every fibre of the husk is precious—until the time comes for the living germ to be released. Each tiny, pointed sepal of the enfolding calyx must be preserved in its integrity—until the hour arrives for the bursting of the perfect corolla. Thus Jesus comes, not to destroy the least commandment (v.¹⁹), but to fulfil it. His 'royal law,' as St. James calls it (Ja 2⁸), the law of liberty and love, is an abrogation of the Divine Law that went before only in the sense in which the blossom abrogates the bud and the flower the blossom. See, further, art. LAW, § **6.**

Literature.—Hastings' *DB*, art. 'Tittle,' and Ext. Vol. p. 24 f. ; Weiss, *NT Theol.* i. 108 ; Beyschlag, *NT Theol.* i. 40 ; Wendt, *Teach. of Jesus*, ii. 7 ff.; Bruce, *Kingdom of God*, p. 64, and *EGT*, Mt. *in loc.*; Dods in *Expositor*, iv. ix. [1894] 70 ff.

J. C. LAMBERT.

TOLERATION, TOLERANCE.—The Lord Jesus Christ exemplified the highest forms of toleration and encouraged the virtue in His disciples (Mk 9³⁸⁻⁴⁰). The Jews had no dealings with the Samaritans (Jn 4⁹), yet Jesus laboured in Samaria (Jn 4 , Lk 9⁵²), healed and praised a Samaritan leper (Lk 17¹⁵⁻¹⁹), and chose a Samaritan, in preference to a Levite and a priest, to exhibit the meaning of the term 'neighbour' (10³⁰⁻³⁷). When His enemies asked, 'Say we not well that thou art a Samaritan, and hast a demon?' He passed over the former and limited His reply to a denial of the latter charge (Jn 8⁴⁸ᶠ·). While by example and teaching He sought to build a bridge of kindly consideration from the side of Judaism, He built also from the other side, and declared in Samaria that the Jews were to be respected as the possessors of the means of salvation (Jn 4²²; cf. Ro 3¹· ² 10² 11²⁵⁻³¹). There are other kinds of tolerance manifested by the Lord. Persons of diverse views, habits, temperaments, were attracted to Him, so that Petrine and Johannine minds, the tax-gatherer Matthew and the tax-hater Simon, Nicodemus and Zacchæus, Martha and Mary, found in Him what they needed. His gracious comprehensiveness shielded the good in all. The ascetic Baptist (Mt 11¹⁸), who drew men into the wilderness (11⁷⁻⁹), received the highest commendation (Lk 7²⁶⁻²⁸) from Him whose scene of ministry was the street and the synagogue, and who honoured with His presence bridal and other feasts (Mt 9¹⁰⁻¹², Jn 2¹⁻¹¹ 12²). The Samaritan villagers (Lk 9⁵²⁻⁵⁶), whose intolerance James and John would have avenged, were left alone ; thus were they punished, whereas they might have made their place glorious, as he did who lent the Lord the room in which the Holy Supper was instituted (22⁷⁻²⁰). In this case we see the intolerance of the Samaritans borne with, and (as in 9⁴⁹· ⁵⁰) the intolerance of the disciples rebuked.

Again, though the Lord Jesus was frequently

compelled to attack the Pharisees on account of their doctrines and practices, He showed them consideration by accepting their hospitality (Lk 7[36] 11[37]) ; and He reminded His disciples, on an occasion when His enemies criticised His conduct (5[30-33]), that those who preferred old ways were to be judged leniently (5[39]). The great parables of Lk 15, besides being a rebuke of the leaders in religion for neglecting to minister to publicans and sinners, are a gracious appeal to share in the delight of seeing men saved,—an appeal to the benevolence latent in the hearts of Christ's unscrupulous critics. He was tolerant to the intolerant. There is, moreover, a striking proof of the existence, in the minds of the Pharisees, of a strong belief in our Lord's toleration. No matter how vehemently He denounced their hypocrisy, they were convinced that He was free from animosity. Always they counted upon His forbearance. Of the reality of His power they entertained no doubt, though they could assign it to a Satanic origin (11[15], Mt 9[34] 12[24]) ; and yet so confident were they of impunity, that they never anticipated injury at His hands, and they ridiculed Him openly (Lk 16[14]). They were aware that His graciousness alone spared them, and they knew that that graciousness would not fail.

W. J. HENDERSON.

TOLL.—See PUBLICAN, and RECEIPT OF CUSTOM.

TOMB, GRAVE, SEPULCHRE.—

The terms 'tomb' and 'sepulchre' are used in AV indifferently to tr. μνημεῖον, μνῆμα, and τάφος. 'Grave' is used 8 times (Mt 27[52. 53], Lk 11[44], Jn 5[28] 11[17. 31. 38] 12[17]) as rendering of μνημεῖον. This last is by far the most frequent Greek word, μνῆμα occurring only in Mk 5[3. 5] 15[46], Lk 8[27] 23[53] 24[1]. The usage of the RV is as follows. 'Sepulchre' is reserved as tr. of τάφος (lit. 'burying-place') : Mt 23[27. 29] 27[61. 64. 66] 28[1] [all the Gospel occurrences of τάφος]. In all the other passages 'tomb' is substituted for 'sepulchre,' or retained where AV already has it, as tr. either of μνημεῖον or μνῆμα. 'Grave' thus disappears entirely in RV.

The forms of sepulture that a people adopts depend partly upon religious belief, partly upon climate, partly upon the geological structure of the country. Among the Hebrews, while the conception of a personal resurrection arose only after the return from the Exile, the belief in Sheol as a place where the soul after death remained in some sort of connexion with the body did much to determine the disposal of the corpse and the nature of the tomb. Early in Hebrew history the burial customs became stereotyped. Between the days of Abraham and Jesus they underwent no essential modification.

1. Religious belief demanded (*a*) that the body should be buried (see BURIAL). The soul of the unburied person was supposed to have no rest, and even in Sheol the souls of such lurked in the corners (Is 14[15], Ezk 32[23]). Any one, therefore, who discovered a dead body was under a sacred obligation to bury it. The soul of the body left unburied was regarded as almost under a curse (1 K 14[11] 16[4] 21[24]). (*b*) That members of the same family should be buried, if possible, in the same tomb (Gn 47[29. 30] 49[29-31], 2 S 19[37], 1 K 14[31], Neh 2[5]). For this reason the family tomb was often situated upon the family property. It was this dread of being buried apart from one's kith and kin that was one of the elements of the Hebrew's hatred of the sea (Rev 21[1]). (*c*) That, except under very exceptional circumstances, the family sepulchre should be reserved for the burial of members of the one family. There are no Hebrew monumental inscriptions ; but from Aramæan inscriptions calling down curses on any who should intrude their dead upon the dead already lying there, we can measure the intensity of feeling on this point. To allow a stranger to be buried in the family tomb was a sign of the very greatest magnanimity

and love (Mt 27[60], Gn 23[6]). (*d*) That no body should be *burned* except as part of the punishment of the most odious of crimes (Lv 20[14] 21[9], Jos 7[25]). To burn the body of a foe was to do something that passed all the rights of belligerents (Am 2[1]).

2. Climate demanded that interment should take place as soon as possible after death (Mt 9[23], Ac 5[6. 10] 8[2]).

3. The geological character of the country conditioned to a large extent the particular form of sepulture. The country is one long limestone ridge, and almost everywhere the hills are naturally terraced, while the soft rock is easily worked. But the simplicity of the Hebrew burial customs should be noticed. It is not a little remarkable that a people living between two such civilizations as those of Babylonia and Egypt, in which the cult of the dead played so large a part, should have remained uninfluenced by such ornate and imposing ceremonial. The Jews did not embalm their dead. They raised no elaborate sepulchres over them ; indeed, the building of a sepulchral chamber was an innovation based on the practices of Greece. While this may have been due in some degree to the lack of artistic capacity in the Hebrew, it was due also to spiritual views of death, and to the dread of idolatry that had always characterized the Semitic race. Wherever, in Syria or Arabia, Greek or Roman civilization has left some representation of the human body, the traveller finds that the face at least has been disfigured by the nomads.

The forms of sepulture were these :—(*a*) The simplest, though not the commonest, form was an excavation in the rock surface, roughly corresponding to the shape of the human body, and covered with a slab of stone countersunk till it was level with the ground. All over Syria these primitive graves are to be met with. The Jews were most careful to keep the stone whitewashed, lest any should unwittingly walk over the grave and so incur ceremonial defilement. This kind of burial is referred to in Lk 11[44] 'Woe unto you, scribes and Pharisees, hypocrites, for ye are as graves which appear not, and the men that walk over them are not aware of them.' (*b*) A chamber was excavated in the limestone rock-face, and long narrow recesses, perhaps six feet by two, were cut into the rock at right angles to the face. The bodies, covered with the simplest of grave-clothes (Mt 27[59], Jn 11[44]), were thrust into these. The recesses were known as *kokim*, and were frequently made of double width, intended for the reception of two bodies. Sometimes, but very rarely, a chamber would have only one recess ; generally it had several. It might, as in the case of the Tombs of the Kings and the Tombs of the Prophets, have one chamber opening off another, each chamber having many *kokim*. Three other forms of sepulture are in reality only modifications or combinations of these two main modes already mentioned. (*c*) Shelf tombs. Inside the chamber the recess for the body, instead of running in at right angles to the wall, was simply cut parallel with the wall, and formed a shelf on which the body was laid. The notable thing about many of these shelves is their narrowness. (*d*) The shelf was sometimes excavated so as to form a trough in which the body was laid. (*e*) In the floor of the chamber itself, or in the passage leading from one chamber to another, a grave might be cut, as in (*a*), and covered with a slab.

It was in one of those chamber-tombs that our Lord was laid (Mt 27[60], Mk 15[46], Lk 23[53]) ; and disused tombs of this kind were used as places of abode by the outcast and the homeless (Mk 5[2]). To prevent desecration by wild beasts, the tombs were often cut in almost inaccessible places ; and ancient tombs in the Ḳidron Valley and in the face of Mount Quarantania are used even now as cells by anchorites, who may be seen climbing by ladders to and from their abodes. This form of sepulture in chambers was used also by the tribes of the desert. Doughty found such tombs at Medain Salih.

'The mural *loculi* in the low hewn walls of these rudely four-square rooms are made as shallow shelves, in length as they might have been measured to the human body, from the child to the grown person. . . . In the rock floors are seen grave-pits, sunken side by side, full of men's bones, and bones are strewed upon the sanded floors. . . . In another of these monuments I saw the sand floor full of rotten clouts, shivering in every wind, and taking them up, I found them to be those dry bones' grave-clothes' (*Arabia Deserta*, i. 108).

In the time of Christ the protection of the tombs was comparatively easily secured. The door of the sepulchre was made intentionally small, and was closed by a great stone, sometimes circular, that ran in grooves in the rock. Ceremonial defilement was guarded against by whitewashing the stone at the door of the sepulchre every spring (Mt 23²⁷). In Lebanon the present writer saw a tomb which had been excavated in the rock-face from a point below the normal level of the soil. After a body had been interred, the stone was replaced in the entrance, the earth was tossed back against the door, and all trace of the tomb was obliterated. This special precaution may have been peculiar to a district where wild animals were common. A tomb was never opened save for a fresh interment. It is this that gives point to St. Paul's saying (Ro 3¹³, cf. Ps 5⁹) : 'Their throat is an open sepulchre' (τάφος), *i.e.* at every opening of their mouth they bury, by slander and detraction, some one's fair fame. On the Holy Sepulchre see GOLGOTHA.

LITERATURE.—Artt. 'Burial' and 'Sepulchre' in Hastings' *DB*, 'Tombs' in *Encyc. Bibl.*, 'Begräbnis bei den Hebräern' in *PRE*³, 'Beerdigung' in Hamburger's *RE* ; Nowack, *Heb. Arch.* i. 8 f., 187 ff. ; Benzinger, *Heb. Arch.* 163 ff., 224 ff. ; Bliss, *Excavations at Jerusalem* ; *PEFSt, passim* ; *ZDPV, passim* ; Tobler, *Topogr.* ii. 227 ff. ; Sepp, *Jerus. und das heilige Land*, ii. 273 ff. ; *Revue Biblique, passim.*

R. BRUCE TAYLOR.

TONGUE (γλῶσσα).—**1.** *The organ of speech* (Mk 7³³· ³⁵). Its power for good or evil is indicated in Scripture by the figures of a sword (Ps 57⁴ 64³), a serpent (140³), an arrow (Jer 9⁸), fire (Is 30²⁷, Ja 3⁶), a beast of prey (Ja 3⁸). It is referred to as a personality with independent will and the power of devising and executing plans (Ps 50¹⁹ 52², Pr 18²¹). It walks (Ps 73⁹), it rises in rebellion (Is 54¹⁷), it has ethical and emotional qualities (Ps 120²· ³ 126²), it performs acts of worship (Is 45²³, Ro 14¹¹, Ph 2¹¹).

2. *Language* (Mk 16¹⁷, Ac 2⁸).—In this sense it forms a counterpart to deed and actuality (Mt 7²¹, 1 Jn 3¹⁸). In RV of Ac 1¹⁹ 2⁸ 21⁴⁰ 22² 26¹⁴ 'language' is substituted for AV 'tongue' as tr. of διάλεκτος, local and provincial speech. Language formed one of the first antipathies that the preaching of the Kingdom encountered, and one of its earliest triumphs was in the discovery and declaration that in the new citizenship there was neither Greek nor barbarian (Ro 1¹⁴, Col 3¹¹).

3. *Index of nationality*, Rev 5⁹ 14⁶, being thus equivalent to 'race,' 'people,' 'humanity.'

In keeping with the important influence attached to language, Christ charged His disciples to avoid unloving, untruthful, and irreverent speech (Mt 5²²· ³³⁻³⁷). He trusted the defence of Himself and His teaching to the power of right words (Lk 12¹¹· ¹²), and the future extension of His Kingdom to the proclamation of a definite message (Mt 10²⁷ 28¹⁹).
G. M. MACKIE.

TOOTH (ὀδούς).—**1.** *In legal compensation.*—The tooth was the least important of the particulars enumerated as exemplifying the exaction of like for like (Ex 21²⁴, Lv 24²⁰, Dt 19²¹). Under primitive conditions of social life, this law acted mercifully in repressing wanton disregard of life and limb in the relationship of master and slave, and of the strong towards the weak generally. It also inculcated respect for the body by the compensation awarded when any mutilation had been inflicted or disability incurred. Although the item of loss was in itself insignificant, the claim connected with it lay within the area and application of a great principle, which by its recognized standard of liability protected both parties, and prevented private abuse. It thus in due time formed part of the boundary line of an outgrown ideal, the transcending of which led at once and definitely into the Kingdom of the Beatitudes (Mt 5³⁸· ³⁹).

2. *In emotional expression.*—Gnashing of the teeth, with weeping and wailing (Mt 8¹² 13⁴²· ⁵⁰ 22¹³ etc.), is the physical expression of regret over remembered advantages and opportunities lost. It was also a sign of evil possession (Mk 9¹⁸), and a manifestation of malignant hatred (Ac 7⁵⁴). Among the modern inhabitants of Palestine, on account of the similarity in physical accompaniment, the same Arabic word is used to indicate both violent indignation and the sorrow of bereavement. When a forgotten promise or matter of neglected duty is suddenly recollected, or it is discovered that a grave mistake has been committed, Orientals indicate their feeling of annoyance and regret by slapping the hand on the thigh (Jer 31¹⁹, Ezk 21¹²), and by thrusting the knuckle of the forefinger into the mouth, as if instinctively seeking something on which to press and clench the teeth.
G. M. MACKIE.

TORCH.—In the six passages in which the word 'torch' occurs in the Gospels (AV and RV), once in the text (Jn 18³) and five times as an alternative rendering in the margin (Mt 25¹· ³ᶠ· ⁷ᶠ·), it answers to the Greek λάμπας, which in the LXX represents the Hebrew *lappîd* in Gn 15¹⁷, Ex 20¹⁸, Jg 7¹⁶· ²⁰ 15⁴ᶠ·, Job 41¹⁹, Is 62¹, Ezk 1¹³, Dn 10⁶, Nah 2⁴, Zec 12⁶. Now the regular meaning of *lappîd* is 'torch,' by which it is mostly rendered in the OT either in the text or in the margin. This meaning fits in very well with the context in Jn 18³, but seems unsuitable in the other passages, where a light fed with oil is required. Probably we are to think in them of a lamp borne on a pole, and therefore bearing some resemblance to a torch, or of a torch fed with oil in some way from time to time. The use of the former is attested for Arabs in the Middle Ages by a statement to which Lightfoot called attention (*Works*, ed. 1684, vol. ii. p. 247), found in the mediæval lexicon 'Aruch, and, on the authority of Rabbi Solomon, in a gloss on the reference to *lappîd* in *Kelim*, ii. 8. It has been often cited or referred to, but a literal translation from the gloss may be of interest :

It is a custom in the land of Ishmael for the bride to be conducted from the house of her father to the house of her husband in the night before she goes into the *ḥuppah* (cf. Ps 19⁴), and for ten poles to be borne before her, on the top of each of which is a sort of saucer of brass containing pieces of garments and oil and pitch—these are kindled, and give light before her.

The other custom, the use of torches fed with oil, is said by the German writer, Ludwig Schneller, who was born in Jerusalem, and was for a time a minister in Bethlehem, to be in force in the Holy Land at the present day. These torches consist of long poles, round the upper end of which are wrapped rags saturated with olive oil. Unless fed with fresh oil, they burn down in less than a quarter of an hour (*Evangelienfahrten*, p. 460). The maidens of Bethlehem, says the same writer (*ib.* p. 459), assemble at sunset on the occasion of a marriage, and move with dance and song through the street to the house of the marriage festival bearing torches in their hands. Bauer also (*Volksleben im Lande der Bibel*, p. 94) mentions the use of oily torches by the women who go out to meet the bridegroom. On the other hand, Robinson Lees (*Village Life in Palestine*[2], p. 87 f.) affirms that small earthenware lamps are still carried in villages by the virgins who go to meet the bridegroom, together with little jars containing an additional supply of oil. He admits, however, that torches are used in the cities. With our present slender knowledge of the marriage customs of the Jews in the time of our Lord, it is impossible to determine exactly the nature of the torches or lamps of the parable, but the balance of probability seems to incline to some kind of lamp-torch lifted high into the air. See LAMP.

LITERATURE.—Besides the authorities cited above, see Wetstein and Zahn on Mt 25[1]; Edersheim, *LT* ii. 455.

W. TAYLOR SMITH.

TORMENT.—The literal and figurative references to suffering in the Gospels are to be distinguished. **1.** In *the natural sense* of pain caused by disease the words βάσανος and βασανίζειν are used (Mt 4[24] 8[6]); also, of evil spirits anticipating Christ's displeasure (Mt 8[29] ‖). Similarly, the use of the word 'tormentors' (βασανισταί) by Christ (Mt 18[34]) must be taken as a reflexion of well-known severities of the time; cf. 'cut him asunder' (with scourging) in Mt 24[51]. It has not been an infrequent occurrence that cruelties have been inflicted on prisoners with a view to inducing their friends to raise the sum of money demanded for their release. **2.** The one example of *the figurative use* of the word in the Gospels is in the parable of Dives and Lazarus (Lk 16[23-28] βάσανος, 'torment'; ὀδυνᾶσθαι, 'to be tormented'). Christ addressed the startling language of this parable to men who were hurting their souls by covetousness. To pierce the hard crust of complacency born of wealth He used the heaviest strokes of threatening; and, choosing language that was most fitted to cause a smart to the softness of their luxury, He spoke of torture, agony, and fire. Ethical truth has always to be expressed in terms of physical sensibility, and these were things His hearers could understand. Christ read off to them in vivid words what their vision was too dull to see,—the penalties attached to their sin by the law that 'Justice founded and eternal Love.'

T. GREGORY.

TOUCH.—The word 'touch' is always associated in the Gospels with Christ Himself, except in one instance. The exception is Lk 11[46] 'Ye yourselves touch not the burdens with one of your fingers,' a passage requiring no exposition.

I. *CHRIST'S TOUCH.*—**1. Christ's touch of healing.**—Christ habitually established outward contact with the sick as a sign and means of healing. Besides the word ἅπτεσθαι, 'touch,' there are used such phrases as ἐπιτιθέναι τὴν χεῖρα, 'to lay the hand upon,' and κρατεῖν τῆς χειρός, 'to take by the hand.' It might at first be supposed that there was a slightly more mediatorial significance about the latter phrases, as though our Lord were rather acting as the delegate of another than on His own authority, but it will be found, on examination of parallel passages, that this distinction cannot be observed. The wide extent of Christ's contact by touch with human malady is seen as soon as the passages recording this act are enumerated. By a touch only, recorded in its simplest form (ἅπτεσθαι), Christ healed a leper (Mt 8[3]), fever (v.[15] where Mk 1[31] has κρατήσας τῆς χειρός), blind people (*e.g.* Mt 9[29]), the ear of Malchus (Lk 22[51]). By a touch, recorded in its stronger form of grasp or imposition of hands, He healed one deaf and dumb (Mk 7[33]), the blind man at Bethsaida (8[22-26]), a woman with

a spirit of infirmity (Lk 13[13]), the epileptic lad (Mk 9[27]), many divers diseases (6[5]), and the dead daughter of Jairus (Mt 9[25]).

2. Christ's touch, other than of healing.—Here four instances are to be noted: the *arresting* touch laid upon the bier of the widow of Nain's son (Lk 7[14] ἥψατο τῆς σοροῦ); the *upholding* touch or grasp offered to Simon Peter upon the sea (Mt 14[31] ἐκτείνας τὴν χεῖρα ἐπελάβετο αὐτοῦ); the *encouraging* touch laid upon the disciples after the Transfiguration, when 'he touched them, and said, Arise, and be not afraid' (Mt 17[7] ἥψατο αὐτῶν; cf. Rev 1[17] 'He laid his right hand [ἔθηκε τὴν δεξιάν] upon me, saying, Fear not'); the touch of *blessing* vouchsafed to the children brought by their mothers (Mt 19[15] ἐπιθεὶς αὐτοῖς τὰς χεῖρας.

The Incarnation itself has been truly described in one of its aspects as God's coming into touch with men, or God's putting Himself where men can touch Him. St. Paul says that men 'seek the Lord, if haply they may feel after [lit. 'handle'] him' (ψηλαφήσειαν, Ac 17[27]); and one purpose of the Incarnation is that in Christ this desire may be satisfied. And, accordingly, to recognize something symbolic about the 'touches' of Christ mentioned in the Gospels, is no mere exercise of fancy.

(1) In the instances recorded above we are, as a first step, permitted to see the broad fact of Divine love seeking friendly *contact* with those for whom it cares. Our Lord is not ashamed to call men brethren. He lays His hand upon the bier; takes children in His arms; holds up a sinking disciple; encourages by touch as well as by word those who otherwise are overwhelmed by fear. Thus we see already an acted parable of how in the Incarnation our Lord ' *taketh hold of* the seed of Abraham' (He 2[16] ἐπιλαμβάνεται, the word already quoted of Jesus 'catching' Peter on the waves to hold him up). In Christ, 'God put on the garment of humanity, and drew near in person, that we might clasp Him as a kinsman in our arms' (Ker, *Sermons*, 1st ser. 191). Instead of the spoken 'word' of the OT prophets, addressed only to the hearing, there is now the living 'Word,' meeting the lives of men in warm and friendly contact.

(2) But a further and deeper truth suggests itself when we pass to the many records of Christ's touch of healing. There we see what might be called the victorious *vitality* of the Incarnate Saviour, whose touch represents not only a sign of friendliness, but the opening of a channel of life-imparting power. If it be true that the 'fundamental meaning of the symbol' of laying on of hands in the OT—on an offering, a criminal, a young disciple, etc.—was 'identification by contact' (Swete in Hastings' *DB* iii. 85[a]), then even to the self-consciousness of Jesus there must have been something deeply significant about the deliberate touch or imposition of hands on others. It meant that He identified Himself with them in their weakness; and that He identified them with Himself in His superabounding life. 'He touched nothing which He did not'—*heal*. Christ said to men, 'Because I live, ye shall live also' (Jn 14[19]). He revealed this Divine power amid immense variety of malady, and amid the human helplessness of many of the cases.

(3) Still another step is offered to us when we observe that Christ healed by touch such a disease as *leprosy*, where contact with the polluting ailment was distinctly forbidden by the Levitical law (Lv 13[46]). For here we see a vivid representation of Christ's identification with mankind, not only in weakness but in *defilement*. To touch the blind or deaf was the act of a Divine physician; but to touch the leper was more than this—it was the act of One who could triumph over pollution, who could

come in contact with defilement and yet not be defiled. 'Another would have defiled *himself* by touching the leper : but He, Himself remaining undefiled, cleansed him whom He touched ; for in Him health overcame sickness, and purity defilement, and life death' (Trench, *Miracles*, 233). Thus the life revealed in the Incarnation not only sustains and heals, but delivers from the guilt which it is not afraid to meet in closest contact.

(4) Finally, in many of the instances we can discern in Christ's touch an admirable means of suggesting the presence of a Healer, and so of *challenging faith*. 'Then touched he their eyes, saying, According to your faith be it unto you' (Mt 9²⁹). The touch of our Lord must often have been of the nature of a challenge. It provoked attention, proffered help, and awaited response.

II. *TOUCHING CHRIST.*—The occasions on which men are recorded in the Gospels to have touched, or sought to touch, our Lord may be arranged as follows. The principle guiding the arrangement will be referred to when the instances have been collected.

1. The touch of desire or faith (the verb in this first group is ἅπτεσθαι).—'As many as had plagues pressed upon him, that they might touch him' (Mk 3¹⁰). 'They besought him that they might touch if it were but the border of his garment' (Mk 6⁵⁶ ‖). 'A woman . . . came in the crowd behind and touched his garment. For she said, If I touch but his garment, I shall be whole' (5²⁷· ²⁸ ‖). With these may be associated the act of the woman in Simon's house, who washed Christ's feet with tears, and anointed them with ointment, and of whom the Pharisee said later, 'This man, if he were a prophet, would have perceived who and what manner of woman this is which toucheth him' (Lk 7³⁹).

2. The touch of curiosity or indifference.—The most vivid instance of this is in the story above referred to of the woman with an issue of blood, where, in the different Gospels, no less than four Greek words are used to depict the thronging of the multitude, so finely distinguished from the significant touch of faith which brought healing to the sufferer. Mk.'s word is συνθλίβειν, 'throng' (Mk 5³¹). Lk. uses no fewer than three words : συμπνίγειν, lit. 'choke' ; συνέχειν, 'press' ; ἀποθλίβειν, 'crush' (Lk 8⁴²· ⁴⁵). 'Out of that thronging multitude one only touched with the touch of faith. Others crowded upon Him, but did not touch Him, did not so touch that virtue went forth from Him on them' (Trench).

3. The hostile hold of restraint or enmity.—Since, in dealing with the touch of Christ, we included instances of His 'laying hands' on others, so in pathetic contrast the following instances must be included here. 'And when his friends heard it, they went out to lay hold on him' (κρατῆσαι αὐτόν, the word often used of Christ's more kindly activity) (Mk 3²¹). 'No man laid hands on him (ἐπέβαλεν τὴν χεῖρα), for his hour was not yet come' (Jn 7³⁰). Though the connexion be not one of verbal identity, such references to a false or hostile touch of Christ suggest themselves as the betraying kiss of Judas (Mk 14⁴⁵), and the smiting in the high priest's palace (v.⁶⁵).

4. It is better to class separately the very interesting references to **the touching of our Lord after the Resurrection.** These are as follows : 'They came and took hold of his feet (ἐκράτησαν αὐτοῦ τοὺς πόδας), and worshipped him' (Mt 28⁹)—the *permitted grasp* of recognition and adoration. 'Handle me (ψηλαφήσατέ με), and see' (Lk 24³⁹) ; 'Reach hither thy hand (φέρε τὴν χεῖρά σου), and put it into my side' (Jn 20²⁷)—the *solicited touch* of reverent experiment. 'Touch me not (μή μου ἅπτου), for I am not yet ascended unto the Father' (Jn 20¹⁷)

—the *forbidden handling* of selfish and premature rapture.

When God and man were brought near in the Incarnation, it was natural that the Divine hand should be seen stretched out manwards in healing and help (see above) ; but natural also that human hands should be seen groping Godwards, seeking closer contact. An American missionary bishop tells of an Indian who knocked one day at his door, and said : 'I have often gone out into the woods, and tried to talk to a Great Spirit of whom my father told me. But I could never find Him. Perhaps you don't know what I mean. You never stood in the dark, and reached out your hand, and *could not take hold* of anything.' The idea is precisely that of St. Paul ; men 'seek the Lord, if haply they may *handle* him' (ψηλαφήσειαν αὐτόν, Ac 17²⁷). Now it is this identical word, strangely enough, that our Lord uses in the gracious invitation to His disciples : 'Why are ye troubled ? See my hands and my feet, that it is I myself ; *handle* me and see.' In the Incarnation this longing has been responded to. So that, when St. John sets forth the main purpose of his First Epistle, he uses this same word again, and with what Westcott declares to be a 'distinct reference' to the passage in Luke, he states that purpose to be the disclosure to others of 'that which we beheld, and our hands *handled*, concerning the Word of life' (1 Jn 1¹).

In the Incarnation, then, God has put Himself where men might touch Him ; and in the various instances of touching Christ, grouped above, we see how men responded to this opportunity. There were those who sought with all their hearts for closer contact, impelled by the sense of need, or by the impulse of adoring love ; 'the history of all God's dealings with man is the record of an approach nearer still, and nearer . . . until faith puts its fingers into the print of the nails, its hand into the wounded side, and constrains us to cry, My Lord, and my God' (Ker, *l.c.*). There were those who merely jostled and thronged our Lord, but obtained no blessing, because enlightened by no deep desire. And there were those whose only impulse towards God manifest in the flesh was one of repudiation and dislike.

Only one passage of those quoted above seems at first sight to put itself outside the general symbolism. This is the record of our Lord's saying to Mary Magdalene : 'Touch me *not*, for I am not yet ascended unto the Father,'—a passage of which the interpretations are nearly as numerous as the commentators. But is not the explanation to be found in the present tense of the injunction, combined with the contrasted command, 'But *go*,' etc.—as though our Lord were saying, 'Keep not on touching me, making sure of me in a selfish rapture, for the duty of the moment calls thee to be a witness to others ; handle me not, but *go* to my brethren, and say unto them' ? And if it be objected, as by Godet, that on that view the following words, 'I am not yet ascended,' present 'absolutely no sense,' the answer is that the hour was coming later, when, after the gift of the Spirit, close and intimate communion with Christ could be given *along with* the work of witness and service,—when it would be possible for a soul to be both in contact with the living Lord and also a messenger for Him,—when (in other words) the disciple could be in 'touch' with Christ by His Spirit and also 'go' on His errands.

R. STEVENSON.

TOWEL.—'Towel' in the two passages in which it occurs in the Gospels (Jn 13⁴ᶠ·) represents λέντιον, which is clearly the Latin *linteum*, a word meaning, in the first instance, 'linen cloth,' and then 'napkin' or 'apron' worn by slaves or servants, and especially 'bath-towel.' Under the Empire this Latin word made its way not only into Greek, but also into late Hebrew in the form *'aluntith*. It is found in the Mishna (*Shabbath* xxii. 5) of the bath-towels used at the hot baths of Tiberias and elsewhere. That slaves or attendants wore the *linteum* is more than once referred to in the classics. The best known passage is in Phæd. *Fab.* II. v. 11 ff., where an officious attendant of Tiberius, who was snubbed for his pains, is described as—

> 'Ex alticinctis unus atriensibus
> Cui tunica ab humeris linteo Pelusio
> Erat destricta.'

Less known, but even more interesting, as at the same time supplying parallel and contrast, is the anecdote given by Suetonius (*Calig.* 26) of the humbling of distinguished senators by the mad Cæsar Caligula, by allowing them to stand at his couch or his feet, girt with towels (*succinctos linteo*). This is evidently recorded as a grave indignity to which the haughty Romans submitted with the greatest reluctance.

LITERATURE.—Wetstein on Jn 13[5]; Becker's *Gallus* (Eng. tr.), 1849, p. 395; Fürst, *Glossarium Græco-Hebræum*, 1890, p. 51[a].

W. TAYLOR SMITH.

TOWER.—'Tower' (πύργος) is mentioned three times in the Lord's teaching: in the parable of the Wicked Husbandmen (Mt 21[33], Mk 12[1]), in the allusion to an accident in Siloam which led to the loss of eighteen lives (Lk 13[4]), and in the illustration of the builder who was unable to complete his undertaking (Lk 14[28]). Two, if not three, kinds of tower may be referred to in these passages:— (1) The builder who exposed himself to ridicule by beginning what he could not finish (Lk 14[28]) may be thought of as building a house. The larger houses in the Holy Land are sometimes provided at one end with a tower-like annex. A good representation of one in the neighbourhood of Sidon is given in the *Polychrome Bible* ('Judges,' p. 59). The *'aliyyah* or upper storey, seen from a little distance, must suggest a tower rather than a dwelling-house (see also *Land and Book*, ed. 1874, p. 160). (2) The tower in Siloam (ἐν τῷ Σιλωάμ, Lk 13[4]) may have been connected with some fortifications. The walls of ancient Oriental cities were generally provided with towers at frequent intervals. Many illustrations could be given from Assyrian sculptures, and the old wall in the Jerusalem of the 1st cent. A.D. had sixty towers (Jos. *BJ* v. iv. 3), two of which, Hippicus and Phasaelus, are probably represented to some extent by two of the towers of the modern citadel, the latter being partly preserved in the so-called David's Tower (*Picturesque Palestine*, i. pp. 1, 5, 7–11). Edersheim (*Life of Jesus the Messiah*, ii. 222) suggests that the tower may have been connected with the building of the aqueduct constructed by Pilate with money taken from the temple treasury (Jos. *Ant.* XVIII. iii. 2; *BJ* II. ix. 4); but that is unsupported conjecture. If the Tower was situated literally in Siloam, the nature of the ground may help to explain the accident. The village of *Silwân*, which represents the ancient Siloam, 'is built on a steep escarpment of rock, on which a building with good foundations would stand for ever; ill-laid foundations would drop their superstructure to the very bottom of the valley' (Hastings' *DB*, art. 'Tower'). For the Tower of Antonia see art. JERUSALEM. (3) The vineyard tower referred to in the two other passages (Mt 21[33], Mk 12[1]; cf. Is 5[2]) can be illustrated from ancient ruins and modern practice. Tristram remarks (*Eastern Customs in Bible Lands*, p. 139 f.) that 'in many cases we still find the remains of the solidly-built tower which commanded a view of the whole enclosure, and was probably the permanent residence of the keeper through the summer and autumn.' Dr. W. Wright observes that every vineyard and garden in Syria

has its tower (*Palmyra and Zenobia*, p. 332 f.). A representation is given in that work (p. 279) of a stone tower in the Hauran constructed of black basalt, with a stone loft at the height of 14 feet, reached by a spiral staircase (see also Porter, *Jerusalem, Bethlehem, and Bethany*, p. 18; Stanley, *Sinai and Palestine*, 421).

LITERATURE.—Besides the authorities cited above, see Heber-Percy, *Bashan and Argob*, p. 123 ff.; Swete on Mk 12.

W. TAYLOR SMITH.

TRACHONITIS.—A Roman province of Eastern Palestine over which Herod Philip held rule when John the Baptist entered upon his public ministry (Lk 3[1]). The Greek word τραχωνῖτις or τράχων signifies a 'rough or stony place,' and its identification with the wild and rugged volcanic region within the limits of ancient Bashan, which the Arabs designate *el-Lejā* ('the refuge'), is unquestioned. This was the heart, as well as the most notable portion, of the province, and gave to it its distinctive name. The phrase τραχωνίτιδος χώρας ('the Trachonite region,' Lk 3[1]) implies an extent of territory beyond the limits of the Trachon, or lava-bed section. The name does not occur elsewhere in the NT, but the boundaries of the province can be approximately defined, from statements concerning it in the works of Josephus, Ptolemy, Strabo, and other writers. Josephus informs us that its N.W. limit extended to the districts of Ulatha and Paneas, at the southern base of Mount Hermon; and also that it bordered on Auranitis (*en-Nukra*) and Batanæa (*Ant.* XV. x. 3, XVII. ii. 1; *BJ* I. xx. 4). The line of the western border is not definitely given, but probably extended to the eastern limit of Gaulanitis (Jaulan), which is frequently alluded to as a separate district of Herod Philip's dominion.

LITERATURE.—Burckhardt, *Travels in Syria*, 110 ff.; Wetzstein, *Reisebericht über Hauran*, etc., 110 ff.; de Vogüé, *Syrie Centrale*, 89 ff.; Schumacher, *Across the Jordan*; Porter, *Damascus*, ii. 268–272, *Giant Cities of Bashan*, 24–97; Graham in *Jour. Royal Geog. Soc.* 1858, p. 256 ff.; Ewing in *PEFSt*, pp. 41 ff., 60 ff., 131 ff., etc.; Merrill, *East of the Jordan*; Stewart, *Land of Israel*; G. A. Smith, *HGHL*; Tristram, *Topog. of the Holy Land*; Baedeker's *Pal.*[5] pp. 193–194; Hastings' *DB*, articles 'Argob' and 'Trachonitis.'

R. L. STEWART.

TRADE AND COMMERCE.—**1. The terms.**—The terms used in the NT in its allusions to mercantile transactions give but little indication of the remarkable developments which had taken place in the trade and commerce of Palestine since OT times.

Schürer (*GJV*[3] ii. 50–61) gives a considerable list of trading terms which had been borrowed from the Greek, and were in ordinary use among Palestinian Jews, but few of these appear in the NT. The only term, *e.g.*, for '**merchant**' is ἔμπορος (Mt 13[45], Rev 18[3. 11. 15. 23]), this being the equivalent etymologically of the two terms which are common in OT—סֹחֵר and רֹכֵל—both of which seem to have the root-idea of *travel*, whether by land or sea. What is, however, significant is the frequency of the words ἀγορά and ἀγοράζω (Mt 20[3] 23[7], Mk 6[56] 7[4]; Mt 21[12] 14[15], Mk 14[5] 15[46], Lk 14[19], Jn 4[8] etc.), which, when it is remembered that in the OT, with the exception of Is 23[3],* there is no mention of markets properly so called, shows that the old conception of the merchant, as one who travels with his goods, is giving place to a more settled and organized system of trade. But the NT indications of a busy and complex commercial life are mostly indirect and general, *e.g.*, in such terms as ἐργάζομαι, Mt 25[27]; πραγματεύομαι, Lk 19[13] (see context in both places); τραπεζίτης and τόκος, Mt 25[27]; cf. the apocryphal saying of Jesus, 'Show yourselves tried bankers' (τραπεζῖται, see Westcott, *Introd to Gospels*, p. 458). Though general references of this kind are fairly numerous, technical names for traders, such as πορφυρόπωλις (Acts 16[14]), are very rare. Even in the graphic description of the trade of the Roman Empire in Rev 18[11–20] there is no word more specific than ἔμπορος, the various trades of the merchants being described simply by mentioning the article in which they deal.

2. The status of the trader.—There is considerable evidence that in Herodian times the occupa-

---

* In Ezk 27[12–25] the words translated (AV) 'fairs' and 'market' will not bear that meaning; see RV.

tion of a merchant was held in more repute than had formerly been the case among the Jews. Such a statement as that of Josephus—'We have no taste for commerce or for the relations with strangers which it establishes' (*c. Apion*, i. 12), must not be taken too literally (cf. Herzfeld, *Handelsgesch. der Juden*, p. 80). Josephus himself makes numerous references to the widespread trade carried on by Alexandrian Jews, without any implication that they incurred disparagement thereby ; he mentions the 'Upper Market-place' of Jerusalem ; the Valley of the Cheesemongers (*BJ* v. iv. 1), the wool-merchants, the cloth-mart (v. viii. 1), the timber-market (II. xix. 4) ; he tells us of the exportation of corn from Judæa to Arabia (*Ant*. XIV. v. 1), and through Joppa to Phœnicia (XIV. x. 6) ; he mentions the influence which a Jewish trader, Ananias, exercised at the court of Adiabene (xx. ii. 3, 4) ; he relates how John of Giscala made himself rich by obtaining the monopoly of exporting oil from Galilee (*BJ* II. xxi. 2) ; and in various places indicates the growing prosperity and affluence of the Jews (*e g. Ant*. XII. iv. 10, *Vit*. 26, etc.). In no case do we discover any indication that the fact of engaging in trade was a reflexion upon a true Jew, so long as he took care not to defile himself by such contact as the Law forbade (cf. Mk 7[4] 'when they come from the market-place, except they wash themselves they eat not'). There can be little doubt that the encouragement which high priests like John Hyrcanus gave to trade, and the fact that Herodian princes themselves engaged in it, tended to raise the status of the Jewish trader. Priests were sometimes themselves traders. Josephus describes the high priest Ananias as a keen money-lender (*Ant*. XX. ix. 2) There were, of course, different grades of traders recognized. Sirach (26[29]) distinguishes between a merchant and a huckster. Between the merchant-prince and the mere pedlar there was a vast variety of persons who found no difficulty in reconciling their commerce with their religion, and perhaps we may infer from the following that even the humblest trade was not despised : 'Rabbi Jehudah the Nasi called Elazar b. Azariah a huckster's basket, and compared him to a huckster who, taking his basket, goes about the country, and the people come flocking around him, inquiring for various articles, and find he has everything' (*Aboth*, 2). In the Gospels the allusions to persons engaged in trade take it for granted that merchants have a responsible and even an honourable place in the national economy. In the parable of the Pounds (Lk 19[12-27]), a man of noble birth carries on trade through the agency of his servants, and there seems to be no sufficient reason for A. B. Bruce's supposition (*Parabolic Teaching of Christ*, p. 219) that such a transaction was 'a most unusual one for a nobleman.' In the East, indeed, royalty from early times had associated itself closely with the development of trade.* The teaching of Jesus is 'full of appreciation of the bigness of the methods of trade and of the brave tempers required in it.' †

The gradual change by which the Jews, from being an agricultural people, became a people devoted to commerce, is illustrated by many Talmudic passages : *e.g.* 'Rabbi Eleazar said, There is no worse trade than agriculture ; and Rabbi Rab added, Commerce is worth all the harvests of the world' (*Jebamoth*, 63. 1). This change, however, took place only very slowly ; the time of Christ was the transition period, and while there were many pious Jews who did not hesitate to

engage in foreign trade, there were others who viewed it with suspicion and dislike, and some who would have nothing to do with it. The Essenes abjured trade, apparently, at least among themselves (*BJ* II. viii. 4). The two things which laid a stigma upon it were (1) the extensive contact with foreigners which it involved, and the consequent risk of ceremonial pollution ; and (2) the moral deterioration which it seemed to bring.

The fact that Sirach has several passages emphasizing the latter danger indicates the prevalent fear that, with the growth of Hellenistic influences, there was coming in a relaxation of Hebrew strictness and integrity : *e.g.* 'A merchant shall hardly keep himself from doing wrong, and a huckster shall not be acquitted of sin' (Sir 26[29]) ; 'Sin will thrust itself in between buying and selling' (27[2]) ; 'Take not counsel with a merchant about exchange nor with a buyer about selling' (37[11]).

Delitzsch, indeed, thinks that it was not until about 500 years after Christ that the Jewish people began to show any special preference for those branches of trade which deal in work furnished by others (*Jewish Artisan Life in the time of Christ*, p. 19), but the passages which he quotes appear to be not so much indicative of the Jew's aversion from trade, as such, as instances of the feeling that a commercial occupation is hardly compatible with a devout life : *e.g.* 'Wisdom, says Rabbi Jochanan, in reference to Dt 30[12], is not in heaven,—that is to say, not to be found among the proud ; nor beyond the sea—that is to say, you will not find it among traders and travelling merchants' (*ib.* and *Erubin*, 55a).

In the NT there is no disparagement of trade as such. A passage like Ja 4[13] 'Go to now, ye that say, To-day or to-morrow we will go into this city and spend a year there and trade (ἐμπορεύομαι)' is not directed against trading, but only against that commercial spirit which leaves God out of account. The passage Rev 18[11ff.] (based on Ezk 27) suggests, not the prevalence of an anti-trade spirit in the early Christian community, but a Puritanic protest against the excessive luxury of a materialistic society.* Whatever the obscure passage Rev 13[16] 'that no man should be able to buy or to sell save he that hath the mark, even the name of the beast or the number of his name,' may mean, the writer can hardly be taken to mean more than that the habits of trade were so mixed up with pagan practices that it was difficult for a Christian to be a trader without becoming stamped with the 'mark of the beast.' In this connexion it may be noted that Deissmann (*Bible Studies*, p. 241 ff.) finds a reference to seals, bearing the name of the Roman emperor, which seem to have been necessary in documents of a commercial nature. We may, at any rate, set over against Delitzsch's assertion that 'in the whole Talmud there is scarcely a word in honour of trade,' the statement that in the NT there is no word in its dishonour.

3. Commercial morality. — From some of the passages already quoted it might be inferred that trade in the Roman Empire in the 1st cent. was particularly corrupt. Was this actually so ? It is, of course, not difficult to put together a number of instances in which the trader appears as a person of smirched reputation. Autolycus had his parallel in Palestine. The merchants of Lydda seem to have been notorious for dishonesty (according to *Pesachim*, 62b). Sirach (29[1-7]) dwells upon the difficulty of getting loans repaid, and upon the ready excuse of 'bad times.' Zacchæus (Lk 19[1-10]), who probably farmed the revenues from the famous balsam-gardens of Jericho (see Jos. *BJ* IV. viii. 3, *Ant*. XIV. iv. 1 ; cf. G. A. Smith, *HGHL* p. 267, note), was, according to the generally received interpretation, given to unscrupulous exaction. In the parable of the Unjust Steward (Lk 16[1-9]) we have a graphic picture of a factor whose dealings are a tissue of knavery. It is probable, too, that the publicans, who appear in the Gospels with so poor a reputation, owed this partly to a shady connexion with the traffic which passed through their hands. But it is obviously unfair to assume from such data as these that there was any more dishonesty among Jewish than among other traders. Herzfeld justly claims (p. 276 f.) that, though the reproach of usury attached to the Jews of the Middle Ages, it appears that among the Jews of earlier times the rate of interest was lower than among other peoples engaged in trade. The enemies of the

---

* See art. 'Trade and Commerce' in *EBi* p. 5192a.

† *Ib.*; cf. also To 1[13], where a Jew is the honoured purveyor (ἀγοραστής) of a foreign monarch, and his nephew is steward and accountant (1[22]).

* For a description of the demands of society for which the trade of the day catered, see Friedländer, *Darstellungen aus der Sittengesch. Roms*, iii. 'Der Luxus.'

Jews in Roman times did not scruple to bring against them the most ridiculous charges, but precisely this charge of dishonesty in business relations is not found. In the Talmud usurers are regarded as in the same category with gamblers (*Rosh ha-shana*, i. 8). Surely, too, the close connexion between business and religion, which is so often emphasized in the Bible (*e.g.* Lv 19³⁵. ³⁶ 25³⁶. ³⁷, Dt 15² 23²⁰, Pr 11¹ 16¹¹ 20¹⁰ 23⁴ᶠ. 28²², Am 8⁵, Mic 6¹⁰. ¹¹, cf. Sir 42⁴), and of which the Talmudic writers have so much to say (cf. Herzfeld, p. 162 f.), was not without its effect upon mercantile morality. That trade was directly recognized as having the sanction of religion would appear from an allusion (*Joma*, v. 3) to a prayer offered by the high priest on the Day of Atonement for ' a year of trade and traffic.' The indignation of Jesus when He ejected the traders and money-changers from the Temple courts (Mt 21¹². ¹³, Mk 11¹⁵⁻¹⁸, Lk 19⁴⁵⁻⁴⁷, Jn 2¹⁴⁻¹⁶) must no doubt have been prompted partly by a knowledge of the dishonesty of their dealings (' a den of robbers '); but His denunciation is a quotation from Jeremiah (7¹¹), and must not be pressed. What stirred His wrath was the conjunction of unscrupulousness with high religious pretensions. It was because their practice was not in harmony with their principles that He drove them forth. That they suffered it with so little resistance seems to show a tacit admission on their part that they were departing from the strictness of Jewish law. Jesus never singles out the trader, as such, as an example of covetousness or fraud ; when He inveighs against corrupt practices, it is rather the Pharisees ' who devour widows' houses ' (Mk 12⁴⁰), and who are ' full from extortion ' (Mt 23²⁵) that are selected for castigation. If, as is not improbable, the Good Samaritan of Lk 10³⁰⁻³⁷ was suggested by the merchants who travelled regularly on the trade-route that led through Jericho (cf. v.³⁵), we have an instance of the way in which Jesus contrasted the humanity often characterizing men of the world with the inhumanity which professors of religion may be capable of showing.

4. Relations of Jesus with the mercantile community.—It has been said * that the trade of Palestine is often reflected in the parables of Jesus spoken as He passed along the busy trade-routes of Galilee and Judæa. Typical of these is the parable of the Merchant seeking Goodly Pearls (Mt 13⁴⁵. ⁴⁶). Jesus would be sure to meet traders on His frequent journeys. Merchandise was still carried, for the most part probably, on pack-animals—asses, mules, or camels (cf. Jos. *Vit.* 26 f.) ; for, though under Imperial Rome there had been a great development of the means of transit, and a fast service of conveyances had been established on the great trunk roads of the Empire, this would hardly be 'the case in Palestine in the time of Jesus. But conditions had arisen more favourable to commerce : the roads were safer ; brigandage was put down with a strong hand (Jos. *Ant.* XIV. ix. 2, xv. 4) ; in addition to the usual town-markets, which in the time of the Maccabees seem to have been held monthly, and to which the country people came in (1 Mac 1⁵⁸, cf. Herzfeld, p. 75 f.), there was a good deal of trade done at the regular stopping-places of the caravans, and at the inns ; periodical fairs also sprang up at certain places, *e.g.* Gaza, Acco, and Tyre (Herzfeld, p. 134). In the towns, at any rate the larger towns, merchants would have their recognized exchange for corn, wool, etc., and their bazaars for manufactured articles. They had their trade guilds, capable sometimes of exercising a considerable influence (cf. Ac 19²³ᶠᶠ.), and their trade leagues between neighbouring towns, *e.g.* those

* *EBi*, art. ' Trade and Commerce,' 5191*a*.

of Decapolis (Herzfeld, p. 148 ; *HGHL* p. 595) ; there were trading corporations, which had their representatives in the important centres. Thus, there were Antiochian Jews settled in Jerusalem presumably for purposes of trade (2 Mac 4⁹. ¹⁹), and there is little doubt that at the times of the great feasts, many who came up to Jerusalem combined business with religion, and used the opportunity to establish trade relations with their fellow-countrymen coming from other parts of the Empire. The sea, now cleared of pirates, no longer offered obstruction to the spread of commerce ; the Jews had at last ports of their own ; Philo (*in Flaccum*, 8) refers to Jewish shipmasters at Alexandria ; Josephus (*Ant.* XVIII. ix.) and the Talmud refer to the wealth of Babylonian Jews. Through Galilee ran some of the most frequented trade-routes ; and in this province, more than elsewhere, the influence of the enterprising Greek was in evidence.

Jesus was in close contact, then, with the busy traffic of His day, and the allusions to it in the Gospels are many ; *e.g.* the trade in oil (Mt 25⁹), in spices (Mk 16¹ 14⁵, Jn 19³⁹ ; an indication of the extent of this traffic may be gathered from the statement made by Josephus, that at Herod's funeral there were 500 spice-bearers [*Ant.* XVII. viii. 3]), in clothes (Mk 15⁴⁶, Lk 22³⁶), in cattle (Lk 14¹⁹), in weapons (Lk 22³⁶). It is a little remarkable that there is no special reference to what must have been the trade best known to Christ's disciples, that in dried fish, for which Taricheæ on the Lake of Galilee was a famous centre (Strabo, XVI. ii. 45 ; *BJ* III. x. 6 ; *HGHL* p. 455). Absorption in trade is hinted at in the case of the man who neglects the king's invitation, that he may go to his merchandise (Mt 22⁵), and in Mt 18²⁵ we get a glimpse into a trade the dimensions and importance of which must have been much greater than is indicated by anything in the NT,—the slave-trade. This, however, would be wholly in the hands of foreigners, its chief centre being at Delos (Strabo, XIV. v. 2), where as many as 10,000 slaves might be found at one time. Phœnician merchants seem to have been the usual intermediaries in this traffic (1 Mac 3⁴¹, 2 Mac 8¹¹, *Ant.* XII. vii. 3) ; and, while the only direct allusion to the slave-merchant in the NT is Rev 18¹³, this personage must have been a too familiar figure on the roads of Galilee.

LITERATURE.—Herzfeld, *Handelsgesch. der Juden des Alterthums* ; art. ' Trade and Commerce ' in Hastings' *DB* and in *EBi* ; on the general subject of the relation between commerce and religion see G. A. Smith's *Isaiah*, vol. i. ch. 18.

J. ROSS MURRAY.

TRADES.—It had long been a custom, which almost had the force of law, among the Jews, that every youth, of whatever station, must have a trade. The Rabbis insisted upon it. Of the distinguished teachers in the days of Herod the Great, Hillel and Shammai learned and wrought the trade of mechanics. So with Gamaliel, a contemporary of our Lord. It was quite usual, though by no means universal, for a son to follow the trade of his father, as Jesus did that of Joseph, who was a carpenter (Mt 13⁵⁵, Mk 6³). Tradition says Jesus made ploughs, ox-yokes, chairs, and the like. The most common trades of Christ's day were those of the smith, the carpenter, the stone-mason, the baker, the tanner, the sandal-maker, the weaver, the spinner, the wool-comber, the tailor, the tent-maker, the potter, the perfumer, the jeweller, the fuller. These occupations are seldom directly mentioned in the Gospels, but the implements or wares connected with many of them are referred to, or are used as illustrations in parables of our Lord : ploughs and yokes, work of the carpenter, Lk 9⁶² Mt 11²⁹ ; of the mason, Lk 23⁵³, Mt 21⁴² ; of the weaver, Mt 3⁴. Jn 19²³; of t'ie tailor, Mk 2²¹; the fuller, Mk 9³; of digging, Lk 16³; of spinning, Mt 6²⁸.

While mechanical labour was regarded with honour among the Jews, all the trades were not looked upon with equal respect. The tanner, probably because of the unclean nature of his work, the donkey-driver, the butcher, and the followers of a few other occupations, were more or less discredited. Sewing, weaving (Jn 19²³), spinning (Lk 12²⁷), grinding (Mt 24⁴¹), baking (Mt 13³³), and the like, were largely occupations of women. The industry of catching and curing fish (see art. FISH) was a most important one, more particularly about the Sea of Galilee; Jesus called several of His disciples from this occupation, Mt 4¹⁸, Mk¹⁶. See separate articles on several of the trades above mentioned.   E. B. POLLARD.

TRADITION.—In its simplest and most primitive form, the conception of tradition involves what is contained in the English word *delivery*. Tradition is the act of transmitting the story of an event or the teaching of a master. From being thus first of all the act of transmission, it becomes in the next place the thing transmitted, and finally a whole body of narratives or teachings passed from generation to generation. In the history of all religions, traditions play a very important part. The times of Jesus and the Gospels were not exceptional in this regard. Explicit mention of tradition is made in Mt 15². ³. ⁶, Mk 7³. ⁵. ⁸. ⁹. ¹³. Both of these passages refer to the same transaction, and therefore represent the same condition of affairs in the environment and the same attitude on the part of Jesus towards the subject.

The environment was as thoroughly pervaded by the recognition of the authority of tradition as any other that we know of, either in ancient or in modern times. In fact, it stands pre-eminent in this particular (Mt 15², Mk 7³). The Sadducees took exception to the prevalent state of mind (Jos. *Ant.* XIII. x. 6); but the attitude of the Pharisees was the very opposite, and exerted a dominant influence in the matter. In the Talmud it was written that 'Moses received the oral Law from Sinai and delivered it to Joshua, and Joshua delivered it to the elders, and the elders to the prophets, and the prophets to the men of the Great Synagogue. They said three things: Be deliberate in judgment, raise up many disciples, and make a fence for the Law' (*Aboth* i.). The Rabbis interpreted Ex 20¹ as involving the idea that all that was to guide the Israelite into the knowledge of the nature and the law of God had been given to Moses on Mount Sinai. More expressly, they found the different parts of the complex rule of faith advocated in the phraseology of Ex 24¹². The expression used in this passage is, 'I will give thee the tables of stone, and the law, and the commandments, which I have written, that thou mayest keep them.' The 'tables of stone' were understood to mean the Ten Commandments; 'the law,' the written prescriptions of the Pentateuch; 'the commandments,' the Mishna; 'which I have written,' the prophets and Hagiographa; 'that thou mayest teach them,' the Talmud (*Berakh. 5a*, lines 11–16). A place was thus made for a large body of precepts which do not appear in the OT Scriptures; and all this was of at least equal authority with the written Law, because given at the same time and through the same person, Moses. To the question why it was not written down at the same time as the written Law, the answer was that Moses did indeed desire to reduce it to writing, but was forbidden by God, because in the days to come Israel would be scattered among the Gentiles, and the written Law would be taken from them; the oral Law would then be the distinctive badge of the Israelite.*

By some it was held that the oral or traditional Law was even superior to the written, because the latter was dependent for its authority upon the oral testimony of Moses. In other words, the oral precedes and underlies the written. The covenant was founded not on the written, but on the oral word of God; for it is said, 'after the tenor of these words I have made a covenant with thee and with Israel' (Ex 34²⁷).

From the nature of the case, tradition was not a clearly defined body. A large portion of it was simply a repetition of the written Law, with elaborations of detail and embellishments. Another portion consisted of distinct additions, a third of provisions looking to the strict observance of the Torah. As far as this tradition was prescriptive or legal, it was called *Hălākhā (-khôth)*, *i.e.* decision (or decisions) having the force of statutes. As far as it was narrative, it was called *Haggādā* (that which is related). As a reiteration of the Mosaic Law, it was called *Mishna* (repetition). As a series of questionings into or investigations of the meaning of the Law, it was called *Midrāsh* (*Midrāshîm*). As a means of teaching, or the body of what was to be taught, it was the *Talmud*. The whole body of tradition together with the Prophets and Hagiographa, in fact the whole rule of faith with the exception of the Pentateuch, was called *Kabbālāh*, that which is received. A doctrine of *paralepsis* was thus developed, to correlate with the doctrine of *paradosis*, 'tradition.'

The administration or practical use of such a body of tradition was not an easy matter. In fact, for the average layman it was an impossibility; hence the rise of a class of men who devoted themselves to the work of studying it, and informing inquirers about it (see SCRIBES, LAWYERS). But this method raised the interpreters of the Law to a place of authority. Interpretations of the Law were accepted as binding, because they said so, not because the Law was seen to involve them. The Law was obeyed not because its Divine origin was perceived, but upon the authority of men. Tradition thus came to be doubly the enthronement of human authority. On the one side, it massed together man-made rules and representations of God's thought; on the other side, it wrought out man-made interpretations of the Law which truly came from God. For the former a direct Divine authority was claimed in the teaching that they were actually delivered to Moses on Sinai; some corroboration for each separate precept thus brought down was sought for in the written Law. For the latter not even this semblance of connexion with the known revelation of God could be adduced. In neither case could the stream rise higher than its source. The teachings of men came to take the place which belonged to those of God. It could not go further back than the elders (Fathers), and those who were called upon to accept it must do so upon the authority of human statements. Tradition thus canonized the media of communication, and lost sight of the value and validity of the things communicated on one side, and of the authority of Him from whom the communication came on the other. Whatever the claim for the Divine origin of the Mishna might be, the practical result of its acceptance was the exaltation of the means through which it came to the supreme place of authority.

Jesus' attitude towards tradition relates itself decidedly to this aspect of it. He saw in it a means of transgressing the commandments of God. He denied first of all the Pharisaic teaching that

---

* Hence the name Oral Law has prevailed in modern Jewish usage. (Cf. *JE*, art. 'Oral Law').

tradition was of equal weight with the Law. He did not, however, definitely affiliate Himself with the Sadducaic teachings on the subject. As against the Pharisees, He taught that the Law of God could not come in conflict with itself, whereas between the traditions current and the Law there were conflicts. In many cases traditional prescriptions did stand in the way of the right observance of the Law (Mk 7[11ff.]). As contrasted with the Divine Law, He calls the tradition 'your tradition.' Finally, He classes all tradition with matters of form or lip-service. He relegates the application of it into the sphere of the non-ethical. So far as such traditions could be made serviceable in the promotion of ethical or spiritual ends, they might be unobjectionable, but they must in no case stand in the way of the clearly revealed will of God (Mt 15[2-20], Mk 7[2-23]. See also art. CORBAN).

LITERATURE.—Barclay, *The Talmud*, 1878; Eisenmenger, *Entdecktes Judenthum*, 1711; Zunz, *Die Gottesdienstl. Vorträge d. Juden*[2], 1892; J. H. Weiss, *Dor* [1876], i. 1–93; Edersheim, *LT*[3] [1886], ii. 205–211; Friedländer, *The Jewish Religion*, 1891, pp. 136–139.   A. C. ZENOS.

TRAITOR.—See JUDAS ISCARIOT, ii. (*e*).

TRANSFIGURATION.—The name given to that event in the course of Christ's ministry in which He was visibly glorified in the presence of three selected disciples. Difficulty has always attached to any attempt to explain it. That it represents a singular enhancement of His Person and a singular attestation of His message was seen from the beginning (2 P 1[16-18]). As such it took its natural place among the evidences of His Divinity. To that position its significance has been very generally limited, and there conceived for the most part in a purely external manner. The paucity of essential ideas associated with it has diverted attention to its details, which have lent themselves to much conjectural and picturesque description, too realistic in character to be serviceable to knowledge. In recent NT scholarship a new interest in the event has sprung up, directed by the modern analytical study of Christ's self-consciousness, and discerning in the experience it embodies a moment of profound import in His self-development.

1. Narratives of the event.—(1) The *evidence* for the Transfiguration is remarkably strong. It is recorded by all three Synoptics in its incidents, and by the Fourth Gospel in its inner mood (Mt 17[1-9], Mk 9[2-10], Lk 9[28-36], Jn 12[23-41]). In the first three Gospels both the precision of detail and the agreement are striking, including the following facts: the occasion—six days after the preceding incidents just narrated; the place—a high mountain apart; the chosen three—Peter, James, John; the supernatural light; the heavenly visitants and their speech; the suggestion of Peter; the overshadowing cloud and the Divine voice from its midst; the awe, yet joy, of the disciples; the return of Christ to ordinary conditions of human life; the charge of silence. Additional features of importance are given by Lk. (9[28f.]): the motive of the ascent, viz. prayer, during which the unearthly lustre appeared; the subject of discourse, viz. the decease which He should accomplish at Jerusalem (v.[31]); the physical state of the disciples, viz. 'heavy with sleep, and, having kept themselves awake, they saw his glory' (v.[32]); together with two points of time, viz. 'about eight days' (v.[28]), and the descent from the hill 'the next day' (v.[37]). Touches, less important, peculiar to the others, are Christ's allaying the fear of the disciples (Mt 17[7]), and Peter's embarrassment and agitation (Mk 9[6]). The silence of Jn. has been specially commented on as weakening the authority of the Synoptic witness (cf. Strauss, *Leben Jesu*, pt. ii.

c. 10). But when we recognize the totally different *animus narrandi* in his case from that which we discover in the Synoptics, we may be reassured. The Fourth Gospel separates itself from the others in making prominent the fact that the *motif* and explanation of Christ's words and acts are to be found, not in the circumstances and persons around Him, but in a higher necessity incumbent on Him in virtue of His nature or His office or His work or the will of God, *i.e.* a higher law at work. Accordingly we may expect in the Fourth Gospel, less the outward incidents * and more the interior mood corresponding to them, to be emphasized. There can be little doubt that the Johannine counterpart of the Synoptic narration is to be found in Jn 12[23-41], the passage which stands between the record of Christ's public ministry and the ensuing scenes of His glorifying through death, resurrection, and ascension — a position identical with that occupied by the Transfiguration event in the Synoptics.

The details of the Transfiguration are seldom referred to throughout the rest of the NT. Explicit allusion is made only once, viz. in 2 P 1[16-18], a writing whose authenticity is seriously doubted.† The effort (Jannaris, *ExpT* xiv. [1903] 462) to find in the Prologue to the Fourth Gospel a direct reference to the Transfiguration is of interest, but unconvincing. Better material may be found in such passages as 1 Jn 1[1-4], Rev 1[13-17], He 1[3. 4] 3[3. 6. 7], 2 Co 4[6], in which we have statements obviously coloured from immediate conviction of Christ's visible glorification; even here, however, we have only indirect testimony. The extra-Synoptic reticence is not to be denied. It is quite explicable. It is as to details only a reticence: the *idea* of the Transfiguration story is so manifestly accepted that he who runs may read. In the Epistles the aim of the writers is not historical statement, but doctrinal elucidation and practical edification—an aim which calls for but slight advertence to the outward facts of Christ's earthly life. There is, too, the clear belief in the minds of the writers that all those facts pale in impressiveness and meaning before that of the Resurrection, the event which is not simply analogous to them, but that in which they find their rationale and explanation. By that fact more than by any other the glory of Christ's Person was revealed, and the Divine purpose and message in Him realized. In the light of it, the Transfiguration appeared but its pledge and forecast (cf. Mt 17[9], Mk 9[9]). It is probably true to affirm that the central idea of the event lay in its significance for Christ Himself rather than for His disciples, who are brought in more as spectators of its marvel than as participants in its meaning.

(2) The *place* of the Transfiguration is not definitely located in the Gospels. The phrases are in Mt. and Mk. 'unto an high mountain apart,' and in Lk. 'into a mountain.' Earlier tradition almost ‡ unanimously fixed on Mt. Tabor—a tradition which has enshrined itself in the calendar of the Eastern Church, where the Festival of the Transfiguration is celebrated on 6th Aug. as τὸ Θαβώριον. Modern opinion almost as unanimously regards as more likely Mt. Hermon, either one of its spurs or even its summit (Conder, *Tent-Work in Palestine*). The argument relies mainly on the fact of the distance of Mt. Tabor, lying near Nazareth, far to the south from Cæsarea Philippi in the N.W., in whose neighbourhood the immediately preceding incidents took place. The departure of Christ and His company from Cæsarea is not mentioned till later (Mt

---

* Cf. the omission of the Temptation narrative.
† Cf. Moffatt, *Historical New Testament*, pp. 596–598; *per contra*, Swete, *Epistles of St. Peter*.
‡ There appears to have been another, identifying the site with the Mt. of Olives.

17²², Mk 9³⁰). There is, perhaps, a certain fitness in the Transfiguration scene having occurred in the vicinity of its intimate antecedents, and in the intense atmosphere charged with their novel and perplexing intimations. It is perhaps, too, not a mere fancy that Hermon's glittering cone of snow suggested Mk.'s expression, λευκὰ λίαν ὡς χιών, if the last words are to be admitted into the text.*

(3) There is a little more definiteness about the *occasion*. Each of the three narrators connects it by time with what goes before : 'six days,' 'eight days'; the latter (Lk.) evidently, according to the common Jewish reckoning, inclusive. The note of time is not without a purpose. The link is intentional between the new wonder and the surprising revelations recounted. Those were three in number : (*a*) the great confession by Peter of Christ's Messianic dignity (Mt 16¹³⁻²⁰, Mk 8²⁷⁻³⁰, Lk 9¹⁸⁻²¹); (*b*) our Lord's solemn announcement of His near suffering (Mt 16²¹⁻²⁶, Mk 8³¹⁻³⁷, Lk 9²²⁻²⁶); and (*c*) the definite prediction of His coming in His Kingdom (Mt 16²⁷·²⁸, Mk 8³⁸ 9¹, Lk 9²⁶·²⁷). Compare with these the statements concerning His mind in (*a*) Jn 11²⁷, (*b*) 11⁴⁷⁻⁵² 12⁷, and (*c*) 12¹²⁻²⁶.

(4) As for the *time* of the day when the occurrence took place, the favoured view is that it was by night. For (*a*) night was generally the time of His retirement for prayer (cf. Lk 6¹² with 9²⁸); (*b*) the disciples were 'heavy with sleep,' and had to 'keep themselves awake';† and (*c*) they descended the mountain 'the next day,' *i.e.* after spending the night on its summit.

On the high land,‡ then, close by Cæsarea, possibly in the early dawn, withdrawn a stone's cast from the disciples (cf. Lk 22⁴¹), communing face to face with the Father, Christ yielded His heart, wholly preoccupied with self-discovery and tragic anticipation, to the experience of the hour, and received the illumination and strength for which He was ripe. To the disciples it seemed as if a Divine splendour beamed around Him, lighting up the departing darkness, imparting its brightness to His raiment, and suffusing His features with a wondrous lustre, so that He appeared to be transformed.§ And with it, from within the veil, came, standing forth as men (Lk 9³⁰), the greatest of OT men of God, Moses and Elijah, to talk with Him of His decease (ἔξοδος), and to manifest the absorbing interest of the spirit-world in His work (cf. 1 P 1¹²). Then, to the overwhelming awe of the three, there drew near a still Greater Presence, for the cloud which now cast its shadow over them all was the cloud of God Himself, and the voice heard was His, proclaiming the Son's high state and attesting His heavenly call.

2. Reality of the occurrence.—The narratives throw upon the mind of the reader the most powerful sense of the reality of the event. Their primary impression is of the outward actuality of the scene. The structure defies dissection,‖ the substance invention. The simple naturalness of the one, the stupendous magnitude of the other, betray no indications of artificiality, while the story as a whole is as inextricably embedded in the surrounding records as the supernatural element in the historical setting of the Gospel itself. It presents accordingly a problem to faith and unfaith alike. For the former its substance is too thin,

* For a fuller discussion on the site, consult Keim, *Jesus of Nazara*, iv. 306, n.; Edersheim, *LT*; Farrar, *Life of Christ*. For an interesting note against Hermon's claims, see *ExpT* xviii. [1907] p. 333. The facts are too few for anything beyond conjecture.

† διαγρηγορήσαντες = 'having kept themselves awake throughout.'

‡ τὸ ὄρος ὑψηλόν may mean simply 'the high land.'

§ μεταμορφώθη : μετά change of, μορφή 'the abiding form.'

‖ Of its textual construction, criticism has, so far, failed to give any clear account. Cf. the divergent theories of, *e.g.*, Strauss, Keim, Bacon, Schmiedel.

for the latter its form too full; both are often in danger of missing its inner force.

With the external details of the Transfiguration of Christ primitive opinion concerned itself but slightly. It dwells on the fact they served to portray—'his majesty,' with the assured conviction of which the whole attitude of the early Church was animated. Patristic and mediæval expositors connect the event with the prediction preceding, defining it as the inauguration of His Kingdom, not indeed in its actual working, but in that personal condition of their Lord which should be the cause and signal of its commencement. Doubt of the objective reality of the glorification of Christ does not occur, and only rarely even any doubt of the literal realism of its accompanying details.*

In the modern period the historical credibility of the Transfiguration has been ably contested by rationalistic criticism, and unwisely defended by spiritualistic theory. The prepossession of naturalistic thought against the supernatural has pushed it to a variety of shifts. There is the hypothesis of *fraud*, according to which Jesus had arranged a secret meeting on the hill, when a peculiar play of light and of clouds, perhaps also a thunderstorm, caused the disciples to suppose they had perceived the transfiguration of Jesus, and helped them to mistake the two confederates † in the plot for Moses and Elijah (Paulus, Schleiermacher)—an unfounded conjecture, which has justly lost all repute. There is the hypothesis of *myth*. Here the incident is taken in connexion with the subsequent Elijah conversation (Mt 17¹⁰⁻¹³, Mk 9¹¹⁻¹³) as its duplicate, and regarded as originating at a later date, when it was not held sufficient that in the Messianic time of Jesus, Elijah should only have appeared figuratively in the person of the Baptist—when it was thought fitting that he should also have shown himself personally. The legend was constructed skilfully from OT figures and analogies (especially from the parallel illumination of Moses' countenance on Sinai), and from the prophecies as to the appearance of the Messiah and His forerunner (Mal 4⁵) Elijah. The aim of the story was to glorify Christ over Moses, and to exhibit His message as the fulfilment of the Law and the Prophets (Strauss). With inconsiderable modifications, the foregoing view is maintained by Keim and others. The mythical hypothesis has the merit of directing attention to the probable sources from which the descriptive details were drawn, and to the natural character of their application in the picture of the event. There is the hypothesis of *allegory*, which finds in the incident a symbolization of the disciples' intoxicated perception of the destiny of Jesus and His relation to the OT. The high mountain symbolizes the height of knowledge which the disciples then attained; the metamorphosis of the form of Jesus and the splendour of His clothes are an image of their intuition of the Messianic idea; the cloud which overshadowed the appearances signifies the dimness and indefiniteness in which the new knowledge faded away, from the inability of the disciples to retain it; the proposal of Peter to build tabernacles is the attempt of this Apostle to fix at once in dogmatic form the sublime intuition (Weisse)—an absurd suggestion of ill-fitting symbols. There is the hypothesis of *dream-vision*. During or after prayer offered by Jesus or by themselves, in which mention was made of Moses and Elias, and their advent as Messianic forerunners desired, the three disciples slept, and dreamed that Moses and Elijah were present, and that Jesus conversed with them—an illusion which continued during the first confused moments after waking (Neander and others) —a most superficial perception of the situation.

The latest attempts have more interest, as discovering a certain measure of independent fact in the event. One finds the substratum of real history embodied in it in the confession of Peter made previously, which was elaborated by idealizing tendency into a vision and attributed to the disciples (Bacon, *AJTh*, 1902, pp. 236-265). A second regards as the reality underlying the occurrence an inner revelation made to Jesus alone, a short time before Peter's confession and in his presence; Peter had discernment enough to recognize its effect on the Master's mind and intuitively grasped its meaning (Réville, *Jésus de Nazareth*, ii. 204-206). A third holds that the story reflects the crisis when Jesus became convinced that He was the chosen heir of God. The event admits very easily of being regarded as having taken place in the inner consciousness of Jesus; probably in the company of the three, who, after awaking from sleep perhaps, received a powerful impression of the wondrous majesty with which Jesus came to meet them after He had heard the heavenly voice, the terms of which He afterwards made known to them (Schmiedel, *EBi* 4571). A fourth sees in the scene a report by men who were confessedly in great agitation when they witnessed it, who yet were well aware that what they saw was not reality but vision. It is to be regarded as symbolic, and consequent on the determination of Jesus to go to Jerusalem and possibly encounter a fate which, to the ordinary Jewish mind, would entirely destroy His claim to be the Messiah, or in any way a chosen instrument of Deity. It is at this moment that He puts on, to the eyes of His most intimate friends, heavenly radiance, and appears as One whose true nature is not to be judged by His human mien or His outward fortunes. It is then that His figure becomes framed to His friends' eyes in the same picture with the principal figures of the sacred history of Israel : Elijah, because of his prominence in Messianic thought, and Moses, the founder of the Old Covenant : their presence indicating that He is not to destroy their work, but

* Tertullian is the most outstanding exception.

† One writer, Venturini, identifies them with Joseph of Arimathæa and Joseph father of Jesus.

to carry it further. The Transfiguration is the enthronement of the Apostolic Christology (Menzies, *Earliest Gospel*, p. 174). Akin in one respect to the foregoing is the theory of Wimmer and Holtzmann, that we have here *Dichtung*, truth in a picture. The glorified conception of Christ reached by His followers after His death is transferred to the time of His ministry, and in this picture represented as foretold then. The attractive aspect of these efforts is that they seek to identify the Transfiguration of Christ with a fresh increase of His self-realization. The event centres in His Person, and for it marks a period. All the foregoing hypotheses prove inadequate in failing to recognize the super-terrestrial powers which are represented as appearing, and as communicating a sense of their presence, to the disciples.

The lacuna is filled by Spiritualism, which finds a congenial theme in the very facts which rationalism would dissipate. The super-terrestrial is its special delight. It sets forth principles which are alleged to account for the unaccountable features of the light, the visitants, the voice. The existence of a 'spiritual body' is asserted, by means of which man may pass out of his ordinary mode of being, of sight and of hearing, into the spirit-sphere or unseen world which is everywhere around him, and there be and see and hear, in the unusual conditions subsisting in that sphere, what he never can in this. The notion seems to be that in each man there is a 'spirit,' made of a sort of thin matter, existing within the outward body, but having a purer existence.

> 'Deep within,
> Some say, the spirit has another frame,
> Invisible, magnetic, beauteous, thin,
> And fine as any ether, scent, or flame.'
>   (J. C. EARLE, *Light leading unto Light*).

In the Transfiguration the 'spiritual body' in Christ shone forth in its native might and splendour, overpowering the dimness of the flesh which He had assumed. And by the 'spirit-body' in them, the disciples were enabled to contemplate His and those of Moses and Elijah.

Scarcely so materialistic, yet quite in the same plane of thought, are the ideas of the spiritualization and subtilizing of the bodily frame until it became luminous by some inherent law connecting the physical radiance with the ripened image of God in man * (cf. *e.g.* George Macdonald, *Miracles of our Lord*, xii.). The error of such theorizing springs from imagining the two as existences of the same kind, and from not realizing the conception of spirit as mind or self-consciousness, which is the only way of conceiving its actual presence in our world. Spirit exists in the medium of consciousness, not in a peculiar kind of matter. The spiritualization of the natural body is not to be looked for in an astral or angel-body, but in the gesture, dignity, and noble mien that make the body of the civilized man the outward image of his soul. When we leave this track we land in vulgar mysticism,—and 'that way madness lies.'

The reality of the Transfiguration may be reasonably maintained on the basis of such considerations as these :—(*a*) that it primarily displays the state of the inner consciousness of Christ at its height ; (*b*) that it was the direct resultant of the preceding events ; and (*c*) that in the description, on the face of it, there is much that is symbolical. The Transfiguration is the transcript of an exalted spiritual experience, and only in the form of symbol can such be portrayed. To the writers it was the natural mode where their Master was concerned (cf. the Temptation and Christophanies). They were but following illustrious models on which their faith had been nurtured—of Abraham (Gn 15), of Jacob (28[10-22]), of Elijah (1 K 19), of Isaiah (ch. 6), of Jeremiah (1[4-10] 20), and above all of Moses (Ex 34[1-10. 27-35]), of Daniel (ch. 10), and of later Jewish Apocalyptic. The story is written in one mould ; it is not manufactured ; it tells its truth in words and images that come easily for the purpose, and wed themselves to the truth so freely that it is not possible to divorce them. Material fact and impalpable vision shoot through each other and cannot be dissevered. But this at least is plain, the body † shared in the experiences.

---

* Olshausen has a theory that all through the earthly life Christ's body was being etherealized, and that here we have a glimpse into the process.

† It is a just instinct which relates the lustre to the inner life. No satisfactory explanation has yet been given of it. For hints, but only hints, cf. Dean Church's sermon on 'Sense of Beauty a witness to Immortality' in his *Cathedral and University*

There is no attempt to picture more than has been seen, but it is implied that what has been seen is nothing in comparison with what has been felt.* It is the picture of an exalted emotion quickened by the sense of contact with a fact so vast that the spectators are absorbed in contemplation of it. The thought of it cannot be recaptured or recounted, because it is so unexpected, so surprising, so new, so unlike all else. Everything is swallowed up in awe and in joy, the joy of feeling face to face with a tremendous experience, an adventure beside which all the glory of the world sinks into insignificance.† Accordingly we find two unique characteristics, the absence of imagination, and the sober insistence on circumstance. Both testify to reality. The fact to which the narrators point transcends experience, and imagination can create nothing which transcends experience. Then, odd as it may seem, the mind in recovering from transcendent wonder and retailing it, continues to regard as impressive details which are really immaterial, but without whose aid the wonder itself would remain hid. Here, then, we have no dream of a fevered twilight, but the fit expression of a mystery, beyond thought and observation, of insight and vision,‡ where the soul is like a dreamer, enthralled by sleep, and struggling with all his might to make some familiar motion.

3. Significance of the Transfiguration. — The inner meaning of the Transfiguration is best brought out by considering it in relation to Christ's Person and Ministry. In relation to His Person it denotes (*a*) *a sublime self-discovery*, and (*b*) *a supreme self - dedication*. In relation to His Ministry it initiates *important departures in the purpose, method, and sphere of His activity*.

The event was naturally led up to. We can distinguish the several moments of its development. There was, to begin with, Jesus' gradual enlargement of the Messiah-ideal. Neither Moses nor the prophets satisfied Him. This is one of the most certain results of contemporary NT learning. Jesus claimed to be the Messiah of prophecy, but declined the current expectations of what the Messiah should be. His own thought immensely enriched both the prophetic and the popular forecasts. The Temptation implies that consciousness. The interval between the Temptation and Transfiguration, *i.e.* His public ministry in Galilee, reveals it partly in acts, partly in hints, partly in explicit reserves. At the beginning we see the clear - cut decision ; throughout its course the deepening realization of what the decision involved : *there* He is neither simply working, nor simply instructing, He is also 'manifesting' Himself. In the life of that *Self* the lines are complex and interwoven. They include, but are not circumscribed by, those specifically appropriate to the Messianic Hope. His *Self* is greater. That at the Baptism and the Temptation Christ saw the plenitude of its greatness and the multiplicity of its interior self-relationships is not to be believed. It revealed itself in the living process of His mental and practical powers which it excited to constant energy, and which all radiate from and converge again into it. It is a Self which has its definite stages of progression, whose outward signs are traceable,§ but which finds within the veil of

---

Sermons. Cf. also Browning's fine passage in *Easter Day*, in which he suggests the thought of Michael Angelo painting in heaven.

* Cf. the disciples' awe.

† Cf. Mt 17[2], Mk 9[3].

‡ The name used by Christ Himself (Mt 17[9])—τὸ ὅραμα = 'vision,' not in the sense of dream, but 'that which has been seen.' For the closing reflexion, cf. Tennyson, *The Higher Pantheism.*

§ Cf. His expressions : His 'time not come,' His 'hour,' His being 'straitened to accomplish,' He 'must work the works of

outward seeming its proper home, living there a concurrent life on a higher plane, with peculiar relations to an unseen world, holding power over it, and bringing power from it ; and in such wise that men, observing His external attitudes, grew in wonder, debate, belief, or unbelief. His *Self* grew. Day by day it enlarged its domain, and took on an extraordinary presence of which He was conscious, a secretly luminous life known to Himself, only glimpses of which He could bring within the ken of the disciples.

Nor was this whole process secret from the disciples. We have to note in them a growing perception of the mystery of His life. They began their following of Him with their own mental prepossessions. These He was daily disturbing. Their attention He was continually arresting. The particulars of His life they were driven to scan eagerly from their various points of view, curious concerning it, questioning regarding it, taking sides about it, some slowly rising towards a clear knowledge of the reality, others hardening into the exact reverse. A calm and unimpassioned looking at the material outside manifestation of His Life without any reference to the inward reality of it, was precisely the one thing that did not happen. That it was more than human they divined, but what, how, to what extent the 'more' came in, they could not explain; they were earnestly inquiring. And thus they reached the stage when they could acknowledge His Messianic proportions : the confession at Cæsarea. That great avowal precipitated the crisis. It was bound to be followed by a further revelation of His purposes. Then came the startling announcement of the Death, opening before their eyes a dark foreground of repudiation and suffering, of whose features Christ Himself, it is probable, could at the moment furnish no clear picture : an announcement whose effect was not mitigated by the further revelation of Resurrection and the coming of the Kingdom. It was a memorable week that followed. The silence of the narrative tells of the intensity of the time. They were on the summits where life absorbs the soul. Thither the juncture of events had brought them. The Master must be lucid.

But first to Himself. A necessary hour is upon Him. Knowing it, He, according to His wont, restrains not the inevitable, but seeks solitude and God. He spends the night in prayer. In the light of His people's destiny, in the face of His prophetic forerunners, conscious of a deeper need and a more desperate struggle than theirs, He presses His life closer to God's reaching out after completer sympathy and perfect understanding of His purposes and of His own part in fulfilling them, and receives in return that wonderful and beautiful inflow of life which stirs to unfathomable springs of purity within, and transmutes even His face and form. It was as when in the sunlight, peering into the heart of a gem, we see depth opening beyond depth until it looks as if there were no end to the chambers of splendour that are shut up in the little stone ; flake after flake of luminous colour floating up out of the unseen fountain which lies somewhere in its heart. In that high hour Christ knew Himself.

He likewise learned His task. In the same self-revealing hour the issue of His life was registering itself in the sight of God, who 'seeth the end in the beginning,' and with His approval. The issue was inevitable. For Christ to know God's will was to do it. There was neither doubt nor debate, but immediate decision. He had no instinctive unwillingness like Jeremiah. Rather He resembled Isaiah, who, when he had seen the Majesty of

God,' His raising Lazarus 'for the glory of God,' His cure of the blind man 'that the works of God be made manifest,' etc. etc.

Jehovah, came forth from His presence with an awe upon him that never left him, and a force of conviction that never deserted him, and with the feeling of an imperative necessity lying on him to speak His word to men which he could not resist. So Christ. He had seen His own glory and felt its power in Him, and was uplifted with a radiant energy before which, as it seemed, no wickedness could stand, and which inspired with a joy deep and strong and solemn. The sweet and awful gladness of His consecration fills His heart and shines out in His face. The Transfiguration was the Divine defiance of the coming darkness (cf. 2 Co 4[6]).*

The Transfiguration event transformed His mind : it transformed also His ministry. Its fascination was upon Him, impelling Him to make it manifest with a certain eager wistfulness. The motive is not : Death is before Me, the sooner it is over the better ; but, The beauty of the Father's face has risen upon Me, let it shine out into the hearts of men, and draw all men unto it.

The endeavour to bring this home to the disciples now dominates His thought and directs His activity, dividing both from His Galilæan teaching and work by the clearest line of demarcation. Themes original to the Law and the Prophets yield to the 'excellent glory' of the Cross, and the nature of the Kingdom His death would introduce. Miracles† and parables cease as an integral part of His ministry. Public addresses, which hitherto had been the rule, are now limited, so far as we read, to the Temple courts and the Sanhedrin ; their place is taken by more private converse. There is a less obvious calling of attention to Himself, in view of a keener anxiety to concentrate *attention on the Spirit that animates Himself and the Father*, and is needful for that higher form of fellowship of men with God than Israel had known, which He Himself enjoyed, and which He promises will glorify them as it had glorified Him.‡ From this last consideration we deduce the significance of the event for us. It is the same as for Christ and His disciples. 'We shall be like him,' says the disciple who had felt most effectually the power of His personal presence (1 Jn 3[2]).

That points to an organic change that will take place in us at His coming. It has to be taken in conjunction with this other, 'Christ in you the hope of glory' (Col 1[27]). The moral transformation is the root and beginning of the organic. Christ not only so acts upon us as to conform us to His holy and exalted pattern now ; when He comes again, it shall be to reflect His glory into the persons of His believing followers. The Church of the redeemed will mirror His surpassing loveliness and majesty, 'He shall come to be glorified in his saints, and to be marvelled at in all them that believe' (2 Th 1[10]).

LITERATURE.—The literature of the Transfiguration is not large, and is found chiefly in sermons, for a bibliography of which see *ExpT* xviii. [1907] p. 313, adding, Ruskin, *Frondes Agrestes*, 178 ; Rendel Harris, *Memoranda Sacra*, 87. For critical discussion consult Strauss, *Leben Jesu*, pt. ii. c. 10 ; Keim, *Jesus of Nazara*, vol. iv. ; *JThSt*, Jan. 1903, July 1903, Jan. 1904 ; *AJTh*, 1902. For expository articles see *ExpT* xvii.

* Dr. Matheson (*Studies in the Portrait of Christ*, vol. ii.) interprets the Transfiguration as designed solely to inspire and comfort Christ in prospect of His approaching Sufferings by providing an anticipation of the glory of the Resurrection ['decease' = exodus by resurrection and ascension]. Dr. Mason (*Faith of the Gospel*, p. 194) thinks the Transfiguration an opening of the door of heaven for a splendid departure, His earthly probation being now ended. An ingenious writer in the *Church Quarterly Review* (July 1901, 'A Study of our Lord') draws out these parallels :—transfiguration of body in face of maltreatment of body, appearance of Elijah and Moses in face of rejection by rulers and people, the cloud and voice in face of the hiding of the Father's face. Such exegesis is exaggeration and misses proportion.

† Miracles are now rare—and enter exceptionally

‡ Cf. Jn 16 17.

[1906] p. 372 ff., xiv. [1903] p. 442 ff. ; Trench, *Studies in the Gospels*, Essay 8 ; Hastings' *DB*, art. 'Transfiguration'; the Lives of Christ, specially those by Farrar, Edersheim, and Matheson.

A. S. MARTIN.

TRANSMIGRATION.—The idea of the pre-existence of the human soul seems to be assumed in the question which the disciples put to Jesus with reference to the man born blind (Jn 9²). The pre-existence hinted at is presumably and at first glance an incarnated one, for it is possible to sin in it. But if this exegesis of the passage be correct, then, at least in the minds of the disciples who propounded the question, there was a doctrine of transmigration. In order to ascertain the correctness of the exegesis, it is necessary to look into the antecedents and broad setting of the thought.

The doctrine of transmigration, *i.e.* the idea that when the soul leaves the body at death it passes into another body, was held widely among the Egyptians, the Hindus, and the Greeks. Each one of these peoples, however, developed it in a peculiar form of its own. Through the long history represented by their combined life, it assumed a large variety of aspects. Broadly speaking, these may be reduced to two, the cruder and the more refined metempsychosis.

(*a*) In the crudest form, belief in transmigration was simply the belief that the moving principle of a living being, either immediately upon the death of that being or after a more or less prolonged interval, takes upon itself another organism. In this form of it, the doctrine does not distinguish between human bodies and bodies of other living beings ; or, to be more precise, of other material forms reputed to be living. The soul is supposed to pass into another organism of the same class, or of a higher or a lower class. A man might be reborn as a brute, or as a tree or stream, or even as a star. The ethical idea associated with this form of metempsychosis is in the belief that the kind of body taken by the soul depends on its realizing or failing to realize ethical ideals. Of this form of the doctrine, it is quite safe to say, there is not the slightest trace either in the NT or in the whole range of Hebrew literature, with its sequel of Jewish Rabbinical teaching of the earlier period. If it appear at all in Jewish thought, it does so as an importation in a much later stage than the Biblical.

(*b*) The more refined form of the doctrine of transmigration limits the sphere of movement to the human race. The human soul or personality is, according to this conception, capable of reappearing and taking part in the world. In the strictest sense of the word this is, of course, not transmigration, but reincarnation. But whatever it may be called, there are a number of expressions in the Gospels which point to the existence of the belief in the time of Jesus. Chief and foremost among these are the passages which refer to John the Baptist (Mt 11⁴ 17¹²·¹³, Mk 9¹³). Here the disciples are puzzled by the apparent inconsistency between the fact that Jesus is the Messiah and the fact that Elijah has not appeared, as, in accordance with an authoritative interpretation of the prophecy of Malachi (4⁵), he was expected, to precede and prepare the way for the Messiah. The disciples evidently accepted the teaching of the scribes. This belief, however, does not put it beyond doubt that the doctrine of transmigration or even reincarnation was current. Elijah had not died and been divested of his first body. His reappearance could only be conceived of as involving his descent from heaven with the same body which he took there at the time of his ascension. The difficulty in believing that John the Baptist was Elijah consisted, at least in part, in the fact that he was known to have had a natural birth ; whereas the return of Elijah would necessarily exclude such birth. Jesus' answer to the disciples simply removes the case from the physical into the spiritual sphere, and thus makes the question before their minds an irrelevant one. The prophecy had been fulfilled, but its fulfilment involved neither the reincarnation of Elijah nor his descent from heaven with his first body.

Another instance of belief which might be mistaken for transmigration is that suggested in Herod's words (Mt 14¹ᶠ·) identifying Jesus with John the Baptist. But here, too, the words scarcely point to belief in transmigration. All that is necessary to assume is that the remorse-stricken Herod saw in the miracles reported of Jesus that John the Baptist had risen from the dead. It is belief in resurrection rather than in rebirth.

Still another case is that in which the disciples, in answer to the question of Jesus, report that some believed Him to be Elijah, others Jeremiah, and others one of the prophets (Mt 16¹⁴, Mk 6¹⁴⁻¹⁷). The idea of transmigration is more natural in this passage, but even here it is not clearly set forth. As far as Jesus is concerned, it is certainly not only not held or encouraged by Him, but quite definitely set aside. At most, it can be only an idea entertained by the common people.

Outside of the Gospels, the traces that a belief in metempsychosis was held in Palestine at the time of Jesus are very scanty. It appears that among the Essenes it was held that the soul was immortal, and its life upon earth due to its being drawn from its native ether and entangled in the body as in a prison cell (Jos. *BJ* II. viii. 11). The affinity of this belief with the Platonic teaching regarding the nature and origin of the soul suggests that the Platonic idea of transmigration, as its inevitable logical corollary, was held also by the Essenes.

In general, there was nothing in the nature of Jewish thought to prevent the adoption of the idea of transmigration as soon as the distinction between soul and body supplanted the older idea of the unitary character of the human being. On the contrary, there was very much to make the thought welcome in the Rabbinical system. The doctrine of pre-existence (of the Messiah, of the Torah, of the Tabernacle) would easily lend itself as a basis for the idea of the pre-existence in some form or other of human souls. Further, belief in the possession of the body by more than one spiritual being (demoniac possession) would tend to prepare the way for the belief in the return of disembodied spirits into human bodies. Finally, the idea of resurrection from the dead furnished an analogue to reincarnation. It is not to be wondered at, therefore, if the notion should appear more or less clearly in the later Rabbinical theology (cf. Epiphanius Wilson, *The Talmud*, Preface). The question of its existence in the days of Jesus Christ must be left open while the question of its being entertained by Him or taught in the Gospels must be answered in the negative.

LITERATURE.—On the general subject of metempsychosis, cf. Alger, *Hist. of the Doctrine of the Future Life*, 14, Boston, 1889, pt. v. ii. ; ed. D. Walker, *Incarnation : A Study of Forgotten Truth*, Boston, 1888. On the allied doctrines of pre-existence of souls in Jewish thought, cf. Weber, *Jüd. Theol.*² pp. 212, 225 ff. ; Drummond, *Phi Judæus*, i. 336 ; Siegfried, *Philo v. Alexandria*, p. 242 ff. On the idea of transmigration in the NT, Pryse, *Reincarnation in the NT*, N.Y. 1900. [This last work, however, is scientifically of very little value].

A. C. ZENOS.

TRAVEL.—Travelling for pleasure was almost, if not altogether, unknown in the ancient world. This is to be accounted for by lack of roads, lack of conveyances, and peril by the way. Travellers had usually some definite object in view ; Abraham seeking for a home at the command of Jehovah (Gn 12$^{1\text{ff.}}$); Jacob fleeing from his brother (Gn 28^{10}); the Israelites going up to their sacred places, and later to the Temple at Jerusalem. As the sea had special terrors, travelling was chiefly by land, and not till well on in history did men launch boldly out into the deep. In the days of the Empire, sailing was confined to certain well defined tracks, and to certain seasons. On land, travel was done for the most part on foot; hence the custom of washing the feet (Gn 18^4, Jg 19^{21} etc.) was almost a necessity as a token of hospitality. Horses were used for war, and camels for the desert. Persons of rank rode on mules (2 S 13^{29}, 1 K 1^{33}), while the ass was more usually kept as a beast of burden. Wheeled waggons were not in general use, and, on the rare occasions on which they were employed, were heavy, cumbersome, and without springs. Joseph sent waggons for his father (Gn 45$^{19.\ 21}$); the kings of Israel had their chariots (1 K 22^{35}); and the Ethiopian eunuch made his journey to Jerusalem in a chariot (Ac 8^{28}); but wheeled vehicles of any kind were rare. Long journeys were generally undertaken in the summer, when the roads were good and firm. In the winter the roads were soft, and other conditions unfavourable. In Mt 24^{20} Jesus says, 'Pray that your flight be not in the winter time,' which means the rainy season, when roads are practically impassable, and food difficult to obtain *en route*. This accounts for St. Paul's desire to have Timothy with him before the winter set in (2 Ti 4^{21}). In the morning the traveller started on his journey, and continued it till noon-day, when he took refuge for an hour or two under some kindly shade from the scorching rays of the sun, and then resumed his course (Ca 1^7). To refuse hospitality to a traveller was a breach of good manners, if not, indeed, an insult to God. This state of affairs continues largely in Palestine to-day, though on the tourist routes the people have fallen in with the spirit of the age.

The ordinary way of reckoning the length of a journey was not by miles, but by time (Gn 30^{36} יָמִים דֶּרֶךְ, Jon 3^4 יוֹם מַהֲלַךְ, Lk 2^{44} ἡμέρας ὁδός), and this makes it difficult to determine accurately the distances covered. Moses asked that the children of Israel should be permitted to go into the wilderness a three days' journey (Ex 5^3), and in Gn 31^{23} it is said that Laban pursued after Jacob a seven days' journey. There would be a great difference between the speed of these two companies, and consequently in the ground traversed. In hilly districts the progress would be less than in the flat country, and a small company or a single individual would go faster than a caravan. An ordinary day's journey might be put down at about 20 miles, but it would require an extraordinary stretch of imagination to make that fit in with Nu 11^{31}. In Lk 2^{44} it probably meant not more than 6 miles, for these festal caravans, with their crowds, moved at a leisurely pace; and tradition has it that the halting-place was Beeroth, which is 6 miles north of Jerusalem.

The longer the journey the slower the pace, for provision for man and beast and equipment for the way had to be carried. 'Take victuals with you for the journey' (Jos 9^{11}) was the rule and not the exception. This led Christ to say to the Twelve, when He sent them out, 'Provide neither gold nor silver for your journey' (Mt 10$^{9.\ 10}$ ‖), so that they might not be hampered by these things, and that they might receive a much-needed lesson in faith.

Reference is made in Ac 1^{12} to a **Sabbath day's journey** (σαββάτου ὁδός). This is the only place where the phrase occurs. Olivet is said to be a Sabbath day's journey from Jerusalem. The expression is very indefinite. Josephus in one place (*Ant.* xx. viii. 6) gives the distance from Jerusalem to the Mount of Olives as 5 furlongs, and in another as 6 (*BJ* v. ii. 3). Schleusner makes it 7½ stadia or furlongs. The difference seems to lie in the varying length of the cubit, which in the older Hebrew measurement was longer than in the later. The result is the same—2000 cubits, which would bring it into conformity with Rabbinical law, 'Let no man go walking from his place beyond 2000 ells on the seventh day' (Jerus. Targ. on Ex 16^{29}). A Sabbath day's journey was by common consent 2000 cubits or ells, though some Rabbis allowed a kind of sliding scale, and spoke of the greater journey (2800), the medium (2000), and the smaller (1800). This was purely Rabbinical, and deduced from (1) Ex 16^{29} 'Abide ye every man in his place, let no man go out of his place on the seventh day'; (2) from the distance between the Ark and the people on the march (Jos 3^4); and (3) from the conditions laid down as to the cities of refuge (Nu 35^5). In Ex 16^{29} the 'place' by a process of Rabbinical reasoning became the city where a man dwelt; and it was argued that 'if one who committed murder accidentally was allowed to take this journey of 2000 ells on the Sabbath day without violating the sanctity of the day, innocent people might do the same.' By a little ingenuity a Sabbath day's journey could be considerably extended. If a person desired to do so, he had simply to carry to some point within the Sabbatical limit two meals before the Sabbath began, one of which he had to eat and the other to bury; and that place became for him his dwelling-place. It is even alleged that by fixing his eye upon a tree or wall within the prescribed limit, and uttering certain words, he could make that his starting-point.

In NT times it was customary, as indeed it is to-day, to accompany a departing guest on a part of his way (Ro 15^{24}, Ac 15^3, 1 Co 16^6) as a token of goodwill and affection.

LITERATURE.—Thomson, *LB*; G. A. Smith, *HGHL*; W. M. Ramsay, *The Letters to the Seven Churches*; Conder, *Palestine*; *PEFSt*; *RP*; artt. in Hastings' *DB*, Extra Vol. pp. 368–402.

R. LEGGAT.

TREASURE. — The word 'treasure' upon the lips of a Hebrew signifies a store of anything that constitutes wealth—of corn and wine and oil, as well as of gold and silver and precious stones (Mt 13^{52}). Hence spiritually the word suggests an apt figure of the true eternal riches. Just as on earth the worldly-wise may lay up stores of wealth, so in the heavens the man who seeks after spiritual things may lay up for himself an eternal treasure. It has been imagined by some commentators that by 'treasure in heaven' our Lord means merely the reward which shall be given hereafter to all who suffer loss for His sake on earth. 'Go and sell that thou hast, and give to the poor, and thou shalt have treasure in heaven' (Mt 19^{21}, Mk 10^{21}, Lk 18^{22}), they take to mean merely, 'Give away thine earthly wealth, and God shall give thee instead heavenly blessedness'; but so to interpret the words is to miss by far the most valuable part of their teaching. It was this interpretation that formed the chief justification for the monkish asceticism of the Middle Ages. It gave rise to a false spiritualism, to the fatal and irreconcilable dualism of sacred and secular. In addressing the words to the rich young man, our Lord was treating a particular case, the case of one whose spiritual aspirations were crushed beneath the burden of his wealth. The treasure in heaven which Christ told him he should have was not to be gained by the simple process of denuding himself of his worldly possessions — God would not step in to supply in the next world what he had voluntarily sacrificed in this. Such teaching would have been an appeal to selfish prudence merely, would justify, if it were correct, all that unbelievers have said about the selfishness of Christianity. It was not to the man's selfishness that Christ addressed Himself, but to the earnest longing after righteousness which He perceived in him. ' What lack I yet ? ' the man had said, even after asserting that he had kept the commandments from his youth up. Christ therefore bade him cast aside the temptation which bound him down, that his aspirations might at last have free play ; that, untrammelled by earthly cares, he might take to himself the treasure of righteousness and truth which he had always longed to make his own.

That spiritual treasure is regarded by our Lord as a personal thing, not as a mere reward assigned from without, is rendered even more plain by what He says regarding the ' treasure of the heart ' (Mt 12³⁵ ‖ Lk 6⁴⁵). This treasure of the heart is manifestly the accumulated tendencies which we call character, the habits which a man makes, the qualities which he acquires, by the repeated choices of his life. He who strives continuously to follow the dictates of righteousness and love, makes for himself a righteous and loving character. His past deeds become a store from which he can continually draw anew. The more good deeds he does the richer grows his heart in goodness, and the greater will his joy become in doing what is right. His heart will of itself bear fruit of goodness. But the same is true also of the evil man. The second lie is proverbially easier than the first. The more evil he does, the more evil grows his heart, until it is well-nigh impossible for it to produce what is good. His heart becomes callous and hard, so that he can no longer take delight in goodness. Thus, again, it is true that ' where the treasure is, there will the heart be also.' The heart of the good man brings down heaven to earth, while that of the evil man could find no bliss in heaven itself.

When in Col 2³ St. Paul tells his readers that in Christ are hid all the treasures of wisdom and knowledge, he is but following out the same figure. ἐν Χριστῷ expresses one of the two great principles of the Pauline theology. To win the true treasure a man must be in Christ ; for He is the universal Man, the ideal of manhood, the only perfectly loving and wise and true of all mankind. In Him only was the heavenly treasure revealed in perfect fulness. He who would share it must therefore be in Christ, must be inspired by His spirit.

The true treasure of the human heart is the Kingdom of heaven. To have the Kingdom of God within one, is to be spiritually rich indeed. In setting forth the manner in which the Kingdom is received into different kinds of hearts, our Lord once again uses the figure of treasure, in the parable of the Treasure hid in a field (Mt 13⁴⁴). Here He refers to an experience not uncommon in the East, where the uncertain tenure of property led men often to hide their wealth, and where the equal uncertainty of life caused it often to remain unclaimed. This and the parable of the Pearl of Great Price (another kind of treasure), which follows it, describe the two ways in which the truth of the gospel is received by men. There is the finder who has never sought at all, and who comes upon his find by accident ; and there is the finder who has spent his life in seeking. In this, however, they are like, that when the treasure is discovered each is willing to part with all he has for its possession. Indeed, this willingness is the test of the true finder ; but it is also the essential mark of the true treasure. It is of such a nature that it cannot be possessed for less than all that a man is and has. It lays hold upon the true finder's

heart ; for in it he recognizes the satisfaction of all his longings : it is the completion of his being, the source of his life to all eternity.

LITERATURE.—The Comm. on the NT ; standard works on the Parables ; Beyschlag's and Weiss' *NT Theol.*; Flint, *Christ's Kingdom upon Earth* (1865), 196 ; H. Scott Holland, *God's City* (1894), 161 ; W. G. Tarrant in *Serm. by Unitarian Ministers*, i. (1905), 25.

W. J. S. MILLER.

TREASURY.—Two words are trᵈ· ' treasury ' in the Gospels. **1.** γαζοφυλάκιον (fr. γάζα, a word of Persian origin = θησαυρός, ' treasure,' and φυλακή, ' guard '), ' a place for keeping treasure,' *i.e.* either a treasure-chest or a treasure-chamber (Mk 12⁴¹· ⁴³ ‖ Lk 21¹, Jn 8²⁰). (1) In the two Synoptic passages it is used, in connexion with the incident of the poor widow who gave her two mites, to denote a treasure-chest, or receptacle into which offerings were cast by worshippers coming into the Temple —a sense in which the word is found also in Josephus (*Ant.* XIX. vi. 1, where Agrippa hangs his chain of gold ὑπὲρ τὸ γαζοφυλάκιον). According to the Talmud (*Sheqalim*, vi. 5), there stood in the court of the women, the most frequented part of the sacred enclosure, 13 brazen chests, into which were dropped the contributions made for the service of the Temple, the support of the poor, and other pious purposes. These chests were of a peculiar shape—bulging out beneath so as to be of considerable capacity, but tapering upwards to a narrow mouth, into which the offerings were put—and, because of their resemblance to inverted trumpets, were known as *shôphārôth* (שׁוֹפָרוֹת, ' trumpets '). It was into one of these *shôphārôth* that the widow would cast her all. (2) In the EV rendering of Jn 8²⁰ Jesus is said to have spoken ' in the treasury ' (ἐν τῷ γαζοφυλακίῳ), as He taught in the Temple. This rendering would imply that the γαζοφυλάκιον in question was not a treasure-chest merely, but a part of the Temple itself in which treasure was kept. Now, we know that there were special treasure-chambers within the inner court, in which not only the precious vessels of the sacrificial service and the costly garments of the priests, but vast sums of money and various other valuables were kept, and that these treasure-chambers, which were under the charge of officers known as γαζοφύλακες, were called γαζοφυλάκια (Neh 10³⁷ LXX; Jos. *BJ* vᵢ. v. 2). That Jesus would be found teaching in one of these inner treasure-chambers is, however, exceedingly improbable. And when we put such a supposition aside, two views may be taken of the meaning of ἐν τῷ γαζοφυλακίῳ. (*a*) We may take γαζοφυλάκιον to denote, as in the Synoptics, nothing more than a treasure-chest, and understand ἐν to be used in the sense of proximity merely (so Meyer ; cf. ἐν δεξιᾷ θεοῦ [Ro 8³⁴ and frequently], ' at the right hand of God '), so that the phrase would signify ' at or near the treasury.' (*b*) We may take ἐν in its strict local sense (so Winer, *Gram. of NT Gr.* 481), and then understand γαζοφυλάκιον to denote that part of the Women's Court in which the treasure-chests were kept. But in either case the general meaning will be the same. Jesus was not in some closely guarded chamber of the inner Temple, but sitting ' near the *shôphārôth*,' or ' in the colonnade where the *shôphārôth* stood.'

2. κορβανᾶς (fr. κορβᾶν ; see CORBAN) occurs in NT only in Mt 27⁶, where it denotes the sacred treasury of the Temple. Into this treasury the chief priests would not put Judas' thirty pieces of silver, ' because it is the price of blood.' In Josephus (*BJ* II. ix. 4) the word is used not of the Temple treasury, but of the treasures it contained. Herod is said to have created a disturbance in Jerusalem by expending upon aqueducts ' that sacred treasure which is called *corbanas* ' (τὸν ἱερὸν θησαυρόν, καλεῖται δὲ κορβανᾶς).

It may be added that, although in EV θησαυρός is invariably rendered 'treasure,' it is occasionally used in a sense that corresponds to 'treasury' or the place where treasure is kept. In Mt 12³⁵ ‖ Lk 6⁴⁵ it denotes the treasury of the heart; in Mt 13⁵² that of the well-provided householder, to whom Jesus likens the 'scribe who hath been made a disciple to the kingdom of heaven.'

LITERATURE.—The Lexx. and Comm.; Lightfoot, *Hor. Heb.* p. 536 ff.; Buxtorf, *Lex. Talm.* p. 2506; Keim, *Jesus of Nazara*, v. 192 ff.; Edersheim, *LT* ii. 164 f., 387; Schürer, *HJP* I. ii. 260 ff.

J. C. LAMBERT.

TREE (ξύλον, Lat. *lignum, arbor*).—A poetic name for the Cross (Ac 5³⁰ 10³⁹ 13²⁹, 1 P 2²⁴; cf. Gal 3¹³; nowhere in Gospels). The name no doubt originated in the practice (cf. Jos 10²⁶) of employing a tree in case of haste for the purpose of crucifixion * (cf. *gallows-tree*), but in mediæval times it was explained by a quaint legend. As he lay a dying, it was said, Adam sent his son Seth to the angel that guarded Paradise, to crave a bough from the tree of life. The angel gave it, and Seth carried it to his father, but found him dead. He planted the bough upon his grave. In course of time, when Solomon was building the Temple, the tree was cut down, but it refused to be fitted into any part of the Temple, and was placed over a stream to serve as a bridge. By and by the queen of Sheba came with her gifts and offerings. Seeing the tree she would not walk over it, since she recognized that the Redeemer of the world would suffer on it. Long afterwards, the Jews took it and cast it into a stagnant pool, which derived a miraculous virtue from its presence: an angel descended from time to time and troubled the water, and the first that stepped in after the troubling was healed (cf. [Jn] 5⁴). There it remained until the time of our Lord's Passion, when it was taken out of the pool and fashioned into the Cross on which He suffered.†

Much devout fancy was inspired by the term. It suggested a reference to the Cross in Ca 2³·⁵, which runs thus in the Vulgate: 'Sicut malus inter ligna silvarum, sic dilectus meus inter filios. Sub umbra illius, quem desideraveram, sedi: et fructus ejus dulcis gutturi meo. Fulcite me floribus, stipate me malis: quia amore langueo.' The hymn-writers extolled the 'arbor salutifera' which bore such sweet and precious fruit. One says: ‡

'Fertilitate potens, O dulce et nobile lignum,
Quando tuis ramis tam nova poma geris.'

And in his exquisite *Laudismus de S. Cruce* St. Bonaventura says: §

'Crux est arbor decorata,
Christi sanguine sacrata,
  Cunctis plena fructibus;
Quibus animæ eruuntur,
Cum supernis nutriuntur
  Cibis in cœlestibus.'

The Fathers loved to contrast the first tree whose fruit brought death into the world, and the second tree whose 'leaves are for the healing of the nations' (Rev 22²). Cf. St. Jerome on Mk 15²³ 'Hic figitur salus in ligno, ligno primo infixa est mors. Lignum primum lignum scientiæ boni et mali est. Et secundum lignum boni tantum nobis et vitæ lignum est.' In *Evangel. Nicodem.* xxiii., after the 'harrying of hell' Hades says to Satan: 'All that thou gainedst by the tree of knowledge (διὰ τοῦ ξύλου τῆς γνώσεως), by the tree of the Cross (διὰ τοῦ ξύλου τοῦ σταυροῦ) thou hast lost.' See also art. CROSS.

LITERATURE—Reference may be made to 'The Legend of the Cross' in Baring-Gould's *Curious Myths of the Middle Ages*, and to Farrar's *Christ in Art*, p. 276.   DAVID SMITH.

---

* Lips. *de Cruc.* II. v. Though ξύλον is rarely applied to *live* wood in classical Greek (see Liddell and Scott, *s.v.*), it is frequently so used in later and Biblical Greek; cf. Jg 9⁸⁻¹⁵, Ps 96 (95)¹² 104 (103)¹⁶, Lk 23³¹, Rev 27 22².

† Daniel, *Thes. Hymnol.* I. c. n.

‡ *Ib.* I. cxli.   § *Ib.* II. cxxii.

TRIAL OF JESUS.—The narratives of what may be termed, for the sake of convenience, the two-fold trial of Jesus yield a record of the proceedings which is fairly intelligible and substantially authentic, but which is bound up with a triple set of problems. Some of these are topographical or archæological; some are legal, connected with the jurisprudence of the trial; while others are historical, arising from the literary criticism of the Evangelic traditions. The fragmentariness of these traditions * and the lack of any outside testimony occasionally prevent criticism from throwing a steady ray of light upon the exact course of affairs, and this is particularly the case with regard to the first two classes of the trial-problems.

1. The topographical problem.—This includes the question of Pilate's Prætorium (see vol. i. p. 859, and PRÆTORIUM), the precise meaning of Gabbatha (Jn 19¹³, cf. GABBATHA and PAVEMENT), the problem whether Annas and Caiaphas had separate residences or stayed together in an official house, and the site of the meeting-place of the Sanhedrin (in the house of Caiaphas or elsewhere). These details are discussed elsewhere in this Dictionary, and it is unnecessary to examine them afresh, particularly as the decisive evidence, such as it is, has to be drawn as a rule from considerations which lie outside the words of the Gospels. The same remark applies, though in a less degree, to

2. The legal problem.—The question whether Jesus was legally condemned to death starts an interesting problem in historical jurisprudence, but it was not present to the minds of the Evangelists or of the original reporters of the Passion; and this, combined with the condensed, fragmentary, and even discrepant character of their traditions, renders it extremely difficult to answer the question with any confidence in the affirmative or the negative. If the Talmudic law was in force in Palestine during the lifetime of Jesus, there would be no course open but to agree with some savants of last century that the Sanhedrin acted illegally.† But the Talmud represents a much later phase of Jewish jurisprudence, and it is probable that, viewed in the light of contemporary practice, the Council were careful on the whole to observe the letter, though not the spirit, of justice, and to practise most of the forms of legality.‡ Thus it is far from certain that they met formally at night, though it seems as if they passed their resolution before daybreak; and the main counts against them are the neglect to warn the witnesses solemnly before giving evidence, the judicial use of the prisoner's confession, and the undue haste with which the proceedings were rushed through. They were kept within judicial limits only so far as it was necessary to save appearances.

The proceedings before Pilate are less obscure. It was necessary for the Jewish authorities to obtain the governor's sanction for the execution of the death sentence, and this involved a fresh trial of the accused. Pilate seems to have acquitted

---

* The relevant passages are Mk 14⁵³⁻¹⁵²⁰, Mt 26⁵⁷⁻²⁷³¹, Lk 22⁵⁴⁻²³²⁵, Jn 18¹²⁻¹⁹¹⁶.

† Thus the ablest of recent jurists who have discussed the problem, Mr. A. Taylor Innes, sums up his inquiry in the words: 'A process, begun, continued, and apparently finished in the course of one night, commencing with witnesses against the accused who were sought for by the judges, but whose evidence was not sustained even by them;' continuing by interrogations which Hebrew law does not sanction; and ending with a demand for confession which its doctors expressly forbid; all followed, twenty-four hours too soon, by a sentence which described a claim to be the fulfiller of the hopes of Israel as blasphemy—such a process had neither the form nor the fairness of a judicial trial.' This needs to be qualified, but substantially it seems accurate.

‡ Contrast, on this point, the juristic colouring of the *Acta Pilati* (cf. von Dobschütz, *ZNTW*, 1902, 89–114, and Mommsen, *ib.* 198 f.).

Jesus of the *majestas* or high treason which the Council first brought forward against Him, but there is some doubt as to whether the acquittal was formally pronounced in accordance with law. In the Markan tradition, followed by Matthew, Pilate never pronounces Jesus to be innocent, although it is plain that he did not believe Him to be guilty. His reason for allowing Him to be crucified is a desire to curry favour with the people. When he discovers that they prefer Barabbas to Jesus, and that the latter is not after all a popular infatuated leader, he has little or no scruples about handing Him over to the tender mercies of His compatriots. His blood be on their heads !

The Lukan tradition, followed substantially in the Fourth Gospel, raises the problem of jurisprudence definitely by affirming that Pilate thrice pronounced Jesus innocent ($23^{4. \ 14. \ 22}$). If so, the first acquittal makes the reference of Jesus to Herod illegal. But, as we shall see, it is probable that this formal verdict is at least antedated, and that Jesus was not finally acquitted, if He was acquitted at all, until He had been sent back from Herod. Thereafter the proceedings are destitute of justice ; Pilate is concerned not with his legal duty, but with the interests of his personal safety and popularity, which were endangered by his conscientious desire to release the prisoner.

Only a critical analysis and comparison of these early Christian traditions can yield evidence for estimating aright the problems of the jurisprudence of the trials ; and even the results of such an inquiry are not final, especially in the case of the Jewish trial. It is with a preliminary caution of this kind that we enter on the third and most important stage of our discussion.

3. The historical problem.—The confusing and even conflicting features in the narratives of the trial of Jesus, which followed His arrest (cf. ARREST and BETRAYAL), are due to the fact that no uniform or complete account of it was ever circulated among the early Christians. The Gospels betray different currents of tradition, and these currents do not always flow in the same channel. Here and there, in different circles, different phases or reminiscences of the trial were preserved ; but not even in the Markan narrative, with its Petrine basis, does an exhaustive, accurate record of the proceedings lie embedded. The later Gospels treat the account in their own way, omitting, adapting, and adding, to suit their own religious interests ; and one of the tasks of criticism is to determine how far these may preserve some authentic traits, for it is as erroneous to presuppose that all later additions to the Markan outline are unhistorical as to assume that the details of the four canonical stories can be harmonized into a protocol of the actual proceedings.

In compiling the later Acts of the Martyrs, Christians were better off. For one thing, these subsequent trials were usually deliberate ; occasionally they were expected for some time, so that the Church was not taken by surprise, and in any case attention was piously paid to the last words and experiences of the saint. By the 4th cent. the shorthand reports of the trials became also accessible to the martyrologist ; he was thereby enabled to write dialogues which had the merit of expressing not only what the accused and the accusers should have said, but sometimes what they did say.* The trial of Jesus found His adherents quite unprovided for any such record of what happened. 'The sudden Roman faces and the noise,' the circumstances of horror and surprise which attended the arrest of their Master, the haste of the proceedings, and the shock of fear which overtook them, were enough to prevent the disciples from realizing what was going on. All was over before they could steady their minds to anything except the general fact of the Master's arrest and execution. Afterwards, they were able to piece together, from their own observation and from the information of councillors like Nicodemus and Joseph of Arimathæa, or of sympathizers in the crowd, or of some of the women, several of the words and experiences

of their Lord before the Council and the procurator. The exigencies of controversy with the Jews and the natural desire to remember as vividly and completely as possible the details of the scene, would foster this movement towards a recollection of the trial. The extant records show how comparatively scanty was the harvest of memory. But their very scantiness proves that the instinct for embroidering the facts with unhistorical fancies did not operate to any serious extent within the primitive Christian traditions, while their tone of moderation tells in favour of the essential historicity of the method in which they record actions of the Jews and Romans which must have outraged and shocked the later Christian conscience. There is neither reprobation of the accusers and judges, nor any effusive sympathy shown with the Sufferer. The Evangelic narratives do not burn emotional incense before the figure of Jesus. Nor are they tinged with serious and direct censure. Thus St. Luke, *e.g.*, is content to record the painful story without pointing a moral or adorning the tale ; he does not stop or step aside to blacken Judas or Herod, as Thucydides has exposed Cleon and Hyperbolus, or as many subsequent writers in Christianity have treated the Jewish and Roman actors in the Passion-story. Against the sentimental, unhistorical rhetoric of the latter class, John Stuart Mill's protest may stand. In the second chapter of his essay *On Liberty*, he remarks: ' The man who left on the memory of those who witnessed his life and conversation, such an impression of his moral grandeur, that eighteen subsequent centuries have done homage to him as the Almighty in person, was ignominiously put to death, as what? as a blasphemer. Men did not merely mistake their benefactor ; they mistook him for the exact contrary of what he was, and treated him as that prodigy of impiety, which they themselves are now held to be, for their treatment of him.' These men, he proceeds to argue, ' were, to all appearance, not bad men—not worse than men commonly are, but rather the contrary ; men who possessed in a full, or somewhat more than a full measure, the religious, moral, and patriotic feelings of their time and people ; the very kind of men who, in all times, our own included, have every chance of passing through life blameless and respected. The high priest who rent his garments when the words were pronounced which, according to all the ideas of his country, constituted the blackest guilt, was in all probability quite as sincere in his horror and indignation as the generality of respectable and pious men now are in the religious and moral sentiments they profess.' This estimate is, of course, too roseate to stand the scrutiny of historical research. Even a Jewish authority like Jost admits the illegality of the verdict against Jesus. Mill forgets, too, that some of the blackest crimes of history have been connived at, if not started, by men of quite respectable character. Sincerity is no essential proof of innocence, even if it could be shown that Caiaphas and the other priests were open-minded people who acted in good faith when they misunderstood their prisoner. But the spirit which Mill properly desiderates in an estimate of such men is wonderfully preserved in the Gospels. Their records have no trace of the outraged partisan, any more than of a pious desire to cast some adventitious halo round Jesus ; and when one considers how numerous were the temptations to make capital against the Jews out of this Passion-story, or to decorate it with trivial and extravagant circumstances (as is the case in most of the relevant Apocryphal Gospels), one can better appreciate the sober and wonderfully restrained character of the Evangelic traditions.

To receive the due religious impression of the Evangelic narratives, it is generally enough to read each by itself. But while devout feeling is seldom perturbed by any discrepancies, such differences do exist both in conception and in detail, and the juxtaposition of the four Gospels in the canon obliges faith to look at the variety of the records and make some attempt at a historical estimate of their relative contents. The main business is to appreciate their religious interests. Yet, whilst these are both obvious and independent of critical research, a comparative inquiry into the different traditions is imperative. ' Investigations of this kind, which attempt to weigh the merits of conflicting or parallel accounts, have always a somewhat cold-blooded and judicial spirit in them, a spirit which cannot but be out of harmony with that in which we can study the Passion of our Lord to our soul's profit. Yet these historical questions must be faced, if our estimate of the gospel is to be lifted out of the region of mere inherited sentiment.' * Fortunately, verbal accuracy is not equivalent to inner veracity. The occasional divergences of the records do not affect seriously either the religious truth or the historical value of the traditions as a whole.

The primary fact which emerges from such a study is that when Jesus was brought before the

---

* Cf. F. C. Conybeare, *The Apology and Acts of Apollonius*, pp. 6–7.

* Professor Burkitt, *The Gospel History and its Transmission* (p. 139).

Jewish authorities,* He was judged worthy of death, and thereupon remitted to Pilate. But was He really tried? and if so, before what authorities? and of what specific charge was He found guilty? These questions cannot be answered off-hand. Still less can any one Gospel be assumed to be the standard by which the others are to be measured. An examination of all four is necessary, if the problems are even to be stated, much less solved.

(a) *Jesus before the Jewish authorities* (Mk 14[53-65] = Mt 26[57-68] = Lk 22[54-71]).—The arrest of Jesus, all the Gospels agree, was at once followed by His removal to the palace of the high priest in custody of the guard. What occurred between this and the crucifixion on the following day is usually described as the trial of Jesus, but a glance at the order of affairs will soon show that it is extremely doubtful if Jesus really was ever tried, in the strict sense of the term. Pilate made an attempt to try Him, yet we cannot be sure if it was carried out adequately. He gave his general impressions of the prisoner, asked a few questions of Him and His accusers, and strove to avoid a decision. A rough and honest informality marked the opening stages, at least, of the intercourse between the Roman governor and the Galilæan prisoner. Latterly, Pilate failed to recognize any rights on the part of Jesus. When he gave Him up to be crucified, it was against his better judgment, and in ratification of a previous sentence pronounced by the Jewish Council. Even here, as we shall see, it is questionable if all the legal forms were observed.†

According to one tradition, the Jewish trial took place at once in the house of Caiaphas, where the Sanhedrin had gathered, despite the lateness of the hour. Not a moment was lost. The arrest was followed by the examination. Then, after being found guilty of blasphemy, Jesus was kept waiting till morning, and exposed meanwhile to the coarse mockery and rough play of the company (probably, for the most part, the servants of the high priest and the rest of the underlings). At daybreak an adjourned meeting was held, at which He was formally bound (the sentence perhaps being ratified) and handed over to Pilate's jurisdiction.

The Lukan tradition defers the examination till the morning. After His arrest, Jesus was detained in custody in the house of the high priest, and, in the absence of the judicial authorities, suffered violence at the hands of His captors. Then, at daybreak, the Sanhedrin was hastily convened. An abbreviated account of its proceedings is given, in which all reference to false witnesses and the charge about the Temple is omitted, but the end is the same. Jesus is found guilty, and taken away to Pilate.

The latter tradition is more true to the regular practice of the Sanhedrin, which met by day; for

only then were its decisions valid (cf. SANHEDRIN). But this does not necessarily prove that it is more original, for St. Luke may have been smoothing out what appeared to him an irregularity in the previous tradition. Upon the other hand, the difficulties involved by the Markan view are serious. Once Jesus was in their hands, the authorities had nothing to gain by rushing through the trial before morning. It would be in their own interests to preserve most of the forms of legal process; and it is difficult to think of the Council, or even a quorum of twenty-three members, being already summoned hurriedly to await the nocturnal arrest of Jesus, when nothing decisive could be done for hours.

The probability is, therefore, that while, no doubt, Caiaphas, Annas, and some others were on the spot, the Council was not formally convened until the early morning, about 6 a.m., and that Jesus spent the night in custody. Even the Markan tradition includes a morning examination (Mk 15[1] = Mt 27[1], a full and formal meeting of the court), which, after the nocturnal one, would be no more than a closing deliberation or a hasty ratification of the sentence already passed. The colourless and brief mention of this second examination shows that the Petrine tradition had no exact knowledge of its proceedings. In reality, it had no room for it, and its preservation is due simply to the fact that the morning trial, which St. Luke has described, was too firmly established in the primitive record to be entirely ignored even when it was deprived of its proper point. As to the reasons which led the Markan tradition to dilate on a nocturnal trial, the clue is probably to be found in the fact that there really was such a hasty preliminary cross-questioning of Jesus; only, it was not before Caiaphas, but before Annas (see ANNAS), the influential ex-high priest, who had been at the bottom of the whole movement to arrest Jesus. The prisoner was taken illegally and informally before him, questioned about His disciples and His teaching,* and then removed to the house of Caiaphas, where the proceedings eventually took place which are recorded by Mark and Matthew.

The fact that this preliminary examination or ἀνάκρισις before Annas is recorded only in the Fourth Gospel (18[12-14. 19-24]) has excited, not unnaturally, strong suspicion of its authenticity, and efforts, more or less plausible (cf. Keim, vi. 36 f.), have been made to show that the author has wrongly inferred from Lk 3[2], Ac 4[6] 5[17], the high authority of Annas; and that the latter is brought in for the sake of novelty or variety. These efforts are quite unconvincing. Historical criticism cannot be put off nowadays with the assumption that the Markan tradition is so exhaustive and infallible as to prove a standard for judging the later Gospels. Certain data in the tradition even of the Fourth Gospel (e.g. the date of the Crucifixion, cf. vol. i. 413 f., 882 f., with Kattenbusch in *Die Christliche Welt*, 1895, pp. 317 f., 331 f.) are winning more and more credence from critics of all schools, and the insuperable difficulty about eliminating the Annas trial is the impossibility of detecting any adequate motive for its invention and introduction. The various theories which explain its growth from a misconception of the Synoptists will not hold water. The details of it are also uncoloured by any specific Johannine interest.† It is not shot through, as is the later trial before

---

* St. Paul sometimes makes the whole nation (1 Th 2[14. 15]), sometimes the rulers especially (cf. Ac 13[27. 28]), responsible for the crime, and once he ascribes it to demonic impulse (1 Co 2[8]). St. Peter, in Ac 3[13ff.], also blames the Jerusalemites, rather than Pilate, whom from the first the Evangelic tradition rightly regarded as less culpable. But even within the circle of the canonical Gospels it is possible to trace the beginnings of that tendency to compare Pilate favourably with the Jews, which afterwards went to quite extravagant lengths.

† Chwolson, in the appendix to his *Das letzte Passamahl Christi*, argues that the illegal haste of the proceedings was due to the fact that the Sadducees, who were adherents of the Roman government, were in power at the time. Their antipathy to one whose teaching threatened their class privileges in the Temple and the political *status quo* of the nation, led them to breaches of the law which would have been less probable in the case of the Pharisees. Derenbourg in his *Essai sur L'Histoire et la Géographie de la Palestine* (1867), p. 201, had already urged this view. He explained the precipitate conduct of the proceedings as impossible for Pharisees, and due to the well-known severity of the Boethusians. Rabbi Ziegler (in *Der Kampf zwischen Judentum und Christentum*, 1907, p. 34 f.) fixes the blame upon the Herodians.

* Jesus ignores the query with regard to the disciples (which involved an insinuation of sedition and conspiracy), and asserts that His teaching was open and above-board, no esoteric doctrine. The well-known parallel is the remark of Socrates in the *Apologia* (xxi.): 'If any one says he ever learnt or heard from me in private what all other people did not hear, be sure he is not speaking the truth.' Twice only, here and in Mk 14[48], does He expostulate with the priestly authorities for their unfair treatment of Him. Evidently He saw that they were determined to have their way, and no further protest fell from His lips (see vol. i. 756-757). The blow of Jn 18[22] is illustrated by that of Ac 23[2]. It is arbitrary to take the latter as the prototype of the former.

† The historical basis of the report is recognized not merely by Ewald, Renan, and Hausrath, but by so thoroughgoing a critic as A. Réville (*Jésus de Nazareth*, ii. 378 f.). The likelihood is that it forms, as Oscar Holtzmann admits of Jn 18[28] (*Life of Jesus*, Eng. tr. p. 480), 'a fragment of the good tradition preserved in the Johannine Gospel.' The idea of Christ's publicity (18[20]) is, of course, a genuinely Johannine trait (cf. 7[14f.]), but this does not explain why the author should have invented the Annas trial for it.

Pilate, by Johannine conceptions. The Fourth Gospel, it is true, ignores the details of the trial before Caiaphas; but this difficulty is not more serious than that of the Synoptic silence upon the Annas trial, for the latter might well appear too insignificant or private to be retained beside the Caiaphas trial, or even to be accurately distinguished from it. As the ex-high priest had no power to pronounce sentence, the tendency of tradition would naturally be towards the decisive proceedings before Caiaphas.

The traditional order of the text in Jn 18, however, does not appear to represent the original. Some distortion has taken place, as the Sinaitic Syriac version shows, and efforts have been made to restore the true sequence (see Moffatt, *The Historical New Test.* pp. 528 f., 693 f.), perhaps the most plausible proposal being that of Professor G. G. Findlay, who would read vv.[19-24] between v.[14] and v.[15]. Some such rearrangement is necessary, at any rate, in order to give a coherent sense to the passage, the denial of Peter taking place, as in the Synoptic account, at the house of Caiaphas (18[15-18. 25-27]). On Wellhausen's recent attempt to excise all the allusions to Caiaphas, see the present writer's paper in the *Expositor* (July 1907, pp. 55–69).

It does not necessarily follow from Lk 3[2] that St. Luke assumed the high priest of 22[54f.] was Annas. But if he did, he (or his source at this point) tacitly corrects the Markan tradition. On the other hand, St. Luke ignores Caiaphas entirely. When the Council meet, they act unanimously and simultaneously (22[66f.]); there is no need of any mouthpiece or spokesman.

These efforts of the high priest and the Council to secure evidence against Jesus proved at first a failure. Many witnesses came forward, but nothing tangible or crucial could be made out of their statements.* At last some people appeared with a garbled version of one saying which seemed relevant and final. As given by the three writers who record it, it runs thus :

MARK (14[58]).	MATTHEW (26[61]).	JOHN (2[19]).
I will destroy ($\kappa\alpha\tau\alpha\lambda\acute{\upsilon}\sigma\omega$) this temple made with hands, and after three days 'I will build another not made with hands.	I am able to destroy the temple of God, and after three days to build it.	Destroy ($\lambda\acute{\upsilon}\sigma\alpha\tau\epsilon$) this temple, and in three days I will raise it.

The saying bears on its face the stamp of authenticity,† but it is impossible to ascertain its original place or significance. The Synoptic omission of its utterance by Jesus is all the more striking, since it would fit in excellently with the Synoptic account of the cleansing of the Temple, which preceded and determined the arrest of Jesus. The Fourth Evangelist, who misplaces this incident, actually cites it in this very connexion (Jn 2[19]), but characteristically he gives it a double meaning. Jesus, he declares, was speaking of His resurrection, the temple being the body—according to the familiar symbolism of the age. The Jews, however, took Him literally. In all probability the saying was 'one of those mystic pregnant words which imply more than they explicitly state, or than any one thought of when they were first uttered' (cf. Bruce, *Kingdom of God*, pp. 306–310). The original meaning may have been that Jesus, who claimed to be greater than the Temple (Mt 12[6]), would raise His community, even though the Jewish system of worship was shattered. His cause was not bound up with the Temple. If He came to associate His own death with the ruin of the sanctuary, it was inevitable that the conception of His personal resurrection should further colour the saying. But in any case the later Christian reflexion would read it in the light of the resurrection, whether with or without any historical justification. The Fourth Evangelist, who makes Jesus not only fully conscious of His Messianic dignity and approaching death from the first, but outspoken on the subject, has naturally no difficulty in placing the statement at the threshold of His ministry, and it has been argued that this length of time between the saying and its quotation at the trial is historically neces-

* The term ἴσαι (Mk 14[56], cf. v.[59]) refers to harmony of statement. Had the Evangelist meant 'adequate,' 'equal to the occasion,' he would have used ἱκαναί or some equivalent.
† Compare the discussion of Strauss (*Life of Jesus*, Eng. tr. by George Eliot, § 114), who upholds its historicity against the suspicions of Bretschneider.

sary in order to explain 'that hesitation and contradiction about the evidence of the "false witnesses," and the extreme difficulty in procuring it, which both St. Matthew's and St. Mark's accounts of the trial of Christ distinctly attest' (R. H. Hutton, *Theological Essays*, p. 228). The contention is unconvincing. Such a saying, if uttered even a day or two before to an excited crowd, would readily be caught up and twisted according to the sympathies or the antipathies of people. Words such as those of Mk 13[2] would inevitably colour it, and the passion of these utterances indicates that the mind of Jesus must have been concerned with the Temple and its future in relation to His message more deeply than our extant records happen to disclose. In any case, popular *animus* needed but a few days to distort an enigmatic saying of this kind. Many versions of it would be afloat on the bubbling tide of gossip in the Jerusalem streets, and some of these were uttered by hostile lips to hostile ears before the Council.

St. Mark bluntly calls this information a piece of false evidence, false because it misrepresented the real meaning of Jesus by attributing to Him a revolutionary design of which He was innocent. It failed, owing to the disagreement of the witnesses. For some reason, which the Evangelist leaves unexplained, their testimonies did not tally ; no coherent and decisive proof could be picked out of their conflicting reports. St. Matthew, on the other hand, will not go this length. Not merely is he silent upon the disagreement of the witnesses (contrast Mk 14[56. 59]), but he refuses to call them *false* witnesses outright, although this may be implied in 26[59-60]. To the Evangelist any witness against Jesus probably counted as false witness. He lays stress upon the original desire of the authorities to find false witness, implying that they would stick at nothing to secure the conviction of Jesus, and that they eventually managed to secure evidence which, being in itself blasphemous, and being legally corroborated by two witnesses (26[60-61]), enabled them to proceed with their design. St. Mark, who admits that the authorities were bent on compassing the death of Jesus, does not accuse them of deliberately searching for false witness from the first, though he points out that even the evidence they secured was inadequate from a legal standpoint (cf. vol. i. 575–576).

Both agree, however, that Jesus, on being challenged by the high priest, refused to answer the charge. He kept a dignified silence,* probably for the reason given in the words put by Luke into His mouth (22[67. 68]). It was idle to argue with those who had already made up their minds to find Him guilty. His stern, calm silence was a judgment of His so-called judges. Their malevolent prejudice deprived them of the right to demand information about His mission. The high priest, who spoke in their name, was eager, not to elicit the truth, but to make the prisoner incriminate Himself as a *mezith* or sacrilegious foe of Judaism, by giving some explanation of the alleged saying. The silence of Jesus baffled and irritated him. It threw him out in his calculations. There were probably some in the Council who were not particularly favourable to the designs of Annas and Caiaphas; the failure to attack Jesus for cleansing the Temple may indicate, perhaps, that several members † rather approved of

* Cf. Bushnell's *Nature and the Supernatural* (ch. x.).
† They reasoned, or might have reasoned, that the cleansing of the Temple would be a very unlikely act on the part of a reformer who designed its destruction. But in any case, that action was not seriously and instantly challenged by the authorities (Mk 11[27]), and its sequel proves that no exception was taken to it by the religious people of the city or even by the Romans.

the act ; and it was a matter of moment to bring the whole Council into line against Jesus, to rouse every interest, sacerdotal (cf. vol. i. pp. 297–298) and official, in order that a unanimous verdict might be carried to Pilate. Furthermore, there was the people to consider. Jesus had sympathizers whose number was unascertained. If He was to be got rid of, it must be on some broad, serious charge which might command a wave of overwhelming popular enthusiasm and indignation. Sacerdotal diplomacy is generally a past master in the art of playing upon such prejudices and organizing popular feeling in aid of its own ends, and the next move of the high priest showed no inconsiderable skill. He chose his new ground admirably. But it is not clear why he shifted his position so suddenly. Was he aware of the Messianic claims of Jesus and astute enough to use them, as a last resource, for the purpose of forcing some incriminating answer ? Or was the ground really shifted ? Might it be inferred from the primitive Evangelic tradition, as reproduced by Mk. and Mt. alike, that the saying about the Temple (Mk 14^{58} = Mt 26^{61}) was held to imply a sort of Messianic claim * upon the part of Jesus ? In that event, the high priest's next question would be simply a further move on the line already taken. The former hypothesis is, upon the whole, the more likely of the two. But in any case the point is plain. Foiled by the silence of Jesus in his attempt to make capital out of the witnesses' report, Caiaphas proceeds to put the straight and final question, '*Art thou the Christ?*' (Mk 14^{61} = Mt 26^{63}, cf. Lk 22^{66} ; Mk.'s addition, '*the Son of the Blessed,*' is probably more original than Mt.'s generalized '*the Son of God*').[†] It was a categorical and crucial query. Matters were now brought to an issue which Jesus could not and would not evade.

His answer is variously reported : '*I am* (ἐγώ εἰμι): *and you will see the Son of Man seated on the right hand of the Power, and coming with the clouds of heaven*' (Mk 14^{62}) ; '*It is as thou sayest* (σὺ εἶπας). Yet I tell you, in future you will see the Son of Man seated on the right hand of the Power, and coming on the clouds of heaven*' (Mt 26^{64}) ; '*You will not believe if I tell you, nor will you answer if I question you. But from henceforth the Son of Man shall be seated on the right hand of the Power of God*' (Lk $22^{67\text{-}69}$). Primarily, the saying is a reminiscence and application of the Messianic passage in Dn 7^{13}, though the Speaker has also the opening of Ps 110 in His mind—a psalm which in those days was more than once upon His lips (cf. Mk 12^{36}). So much is clear. But the details of the answer are not always quite intelligible. Thus St. Luke[‡] divides the question into two, and, in reply to the query, '*Art thou the Son of God?*' makes Jesus reply : ὑμεῖς λέγετε, ὅτι ἐγώ εἰμι (22^{70}). On the other hand, the Markan answer is perfectly explicit (cf. Menzies, *The Earliest Gospel*, p. 267). Jesus replies, '*I am.*' St. Matthew, again, gives an evasive or ambiguous turn to the words by the phrase σὺ εἶπας, which here, as in 26^{25}, is commonly understood to mean a qualified affirmative. The person addressed replies in the sense of the questioner. 'You say so. I will not contradict you.' 'I answer you out of your own lips.' Recently, however, Chwolson, followed by Merx, N. Schmidt (*The Prophet of Nazareth*, p. 287), and others, has

challenged the interpretation of the phrase as a Rabbinic form of affirmation ; instead of being equivalent to the Latin *dixisti*, it is held to be really a denial. This is most unlikely, to judge from the context ; and even linguistically, as Dalman has shown (*Words of Jesus*, p. 309 f.), it is unnecessary.[*]

But, minor discrepancies apart, the answer reveals three cardinal traits of Jesus : His courage in confessing the Messianic vocation, when death was the inevitable consequence ; His serene confidence in the success of His cause upon earth ; and His admission that only the future could unfold the real meaning of His Person.[†] The last point is to be noted specially. The high priest's question was so contrived as to make any answer fatal, whether negative or affirmative. In the one case, Jesus would lose all His influence and authority ; in the other, He would be liable to judgment as a pretender. But Jesus realized that even a bare affirmative would be misleading, since His Messianic vocation was widely different from what the ordinary expectation imagined. Hence the fuller statement, wrung from the tension and passionate faith of His soul. The words seized on by the Council were those referring to His claim to sit at the right hand of the Power, but it must not be inferred[‡] from this that the charge of constructive blasphemy for which Jesus was condemned was dissociated from His Messianic claims. The contention that such claims were not blasphemous in themselves all depends on the character of the person who made them. The Council considered themselves, rightly or wrongly, absolved from entering into any minute examination of the conduct and aims of Jesus.[§] On that their minds were already made up, as His arrest shows. The attitude of Jesus to the Law and the Temple and the cherished religious traditions of Judaism left no doubt in their minds that He was a dangerous person, in whom it would be superfluous to look for any Messianic criteria. His presumption in claiming Messianic honour was in itself blasphemy of a capital order, as it involved a supersession of the Mosaic Law, and His words now corroborated the impression already made by His actions that He was a discredited pretender to Divine rank, and a false and disloyal prophet. In short, the verdict of the historian, as Holtzmann puts it, must be : 'Jesus confessed Himself to be Messiah, was condemned as a false Messiah, and executed as a pretender.'[||]

Caiaphas had now gained his point. He had induced Jesus to convict Himself out of His own mouth, and with a pious gesture of horror (cf. 2 K 22^{11}, 1 Mac 11^{71}, Is 37^{1} etc.) he professes himself at once shocked by the blasphemy of the Galilæan, and satisfied with the result of his interrogation. He appeals theatrically to the Council if this is not enough evidence, and they obsequiously agree.

The condensed and cursory nature of the report makes it impossible for us to be sure whether this verdict was as premature and illegal as it appears to be, and whether the irregularities were held to

---

* The reconstruction of the Temple in the new age was one work of the Messiah, according to some circles of pre-Christian Judaism (cf. Enoch 90^{28} etc.; Bousset, *Religion des Judentums*, 226 f.).

† The avoidance of God's name, in accordance with Jewish usage, is, as O. Holtzmann points out (*Life of Jesus*, pp. 164, 475), 'a strong point in favour of the soundness of our tradition.'

† '*The Power*' of Mk. and Mt. is more original than Lk.'s explanatory phrase.

---

* Cf. H. Holtzmann, *Das messianische Bewusstsein Jesu* (1907), pp. 29–31, as against Wrede's idea (*Das Messiasgeheimnis*, 74 f.) that the phrase 'Son of God' must be taken in a metaphysical, not in a theocratic sense.

† Bengel, on Mt 26^{64}, has one of his fine comments : '*In adversissimis quibusque rebus summos fines exitusque intueri, maxime juvat filios dei.*'

‡ As by Wellhausen, who omits Mk $14^{61. 62}$ in order to support this reading of the incident. But 14^{63} does not follow the silence of Jesus very aptly ; the blasphemy is more naturally connected with the straightforward utterance of Jesus than with the divergent reports of the witnesses, and Lk.'s ἀπὸ τοῦ στόματος αὐτοῦ is probably a correct gloss.

§ Cf. Mk 27.

|| *Das Messianische Bewusstsein Jesu* (1907), pp. 35–36, where the various views of recent critics on this point are adequately summarized. For the punishment of a false prophet, see Dt $13^{1\text{-}5}$ $18^{20\text{-}22}$.

be justified by the emergency which had transpired. The Evangelic tradition was naturally more concerned with the result than with the precise processes of the trial. In any case, however, it is unmistakable that the priests had now got what they wanted. They had secured from Jesus a confession which was nominally equivalent to a blasphemous claim (on this see vol. i. pp. 209–210), derogatory to the Divine Being. But we are in the dark as to how far the ordinary forms of jurisprudence were observed, whether the witnesses were cautioned before giving evidence, whether the case for the defence was first of all opened, and so forth. The outstanding point is that Jesus was condemned primarily for blasphemy. To convict Him of claiming to be Messiah, and charge Him with that, would not have appealed to the Sadducees. More was needed, and this was supplied by the fact of Jesus, a Galilæan peasant, with revolutionary views upon the cultus, daring to claim for Himself Messianic honours, and thus threatening to supersede the sacrosanct legal system of Judaism.

(*b*) *Jesus before Pilate* (Mk 15$^{1-20}$ = Mt 27$^{1-31}$ = Lk 23$^{1-25}$ = Jn 18^{28}–19^{16}).—If the proceedings before the Jewish Council strained even the letter of justice, those before the Roman authorities show little or no attempt whatsoever to try the prisoner judicially. Jesus does not appear to have been legally tried before Pilate. The Roman governor, after the first turn in the case, seems to have been principally anxious to discover the most politic course of action, as well as to thwart the authorities. His sense of justice was overborne by considerations of personal advantage and civil prudence. But he was not driven to this end without reluctance, and the record of the proceedings, which took place in the open-air in front of his palace or tribunal, is of considerable psychological interest.

The first phase of the trial before Pilate is the procurator's dismissal of the grave charge of *majestas* brought against Jesus by His accusers,* who naturally fixed upon the political rather than the religious side of the Messianic claim as the more likely to carry weight with the governor.

According to one tradition,† Pilate takes the initiative by asking Jesus if He is really the king of the Jews. The question breathes pity and contempt and wonder. This forlorn Galilæan peasant (σύ emphatic) a claimant of royalty! The quiet reply is, σὺ λέγεις (cf. vol. i. 931^b). To the subsequent outburst of accusation from the Jewish leaders, Jesus vouchsafes no reply; nor will He even deign to interpret His silence to the astonished procurator. Plainly, this is a very abridged version of the actual facts, and we turn for fuller details to Luke. According to his account, the Jewish authorities push forward with their accusation before Pilate has time to speak, and the charge is threefold: He is accused of being a seditious agitator, of forbidding the payment of tribute to the Roman emperor, and of claiming to be 'Christ, a king.' A political charge is thus cleverly foisted into the religious complaint, and the procurator, who would have nothing to do with a vague accusation, naturally fixes on the third point, asking Jesus (as in the other tradition) if He is really the

king of the Jews. Luke's account certainly gives a better sense here than the other, for it explains how Pilate came to put his question; whereas, in the evidence of Mk 15^2 = Mt 27^{11}, there is nothing to account for the governor seizing this point at all. That the charge of the Jews was astute but unjust needs no proof (cf. vol. i. p. 246^a). The Gospels show how scrupulously Jesus kept clear of abetting the fanatical hatred of Rome felt by many of His fellow-countrymen, and probably it was this refusal to side with them which secretly instigated their plan of attack. At any rate, as Renan observes, 'Conservative religious bodies do not generally shrink from calumny.' To refute the charge was superfluous in the eyes of Jesus. His silence did all that was necessary; it repudiated the accusation.

The silence of Jesus before Pilate was due to moral reasons. Dr. Salmon, in his posthumous work, *The Human Element in the Gospels* (1907, p. 512), prefers, indeed, to attribute it to physical fatigue. 'The only way that occurs to one of accounting for His silence is that, after the strain of the work of the previous day, of the sleepless night, and the brutal insults of His tormentors, His physical frame was incapable of conducting a discussion. And we could sufficiently account for Pilate's unwillingness to condemn, if he perceived that the man against whom so much accusation was brought was quite unable to say a word in His own defence. In this choice between Jesus and Barabbas, might he not feel that the more dangerous enemy to Cæsar was the man in vigorous health who had already taken part in an insurrection in which many lives had been lost, and not the so-called prophet, who seemed unable to speak, much less to act. And if he had no trust in the loyalty of the Jewish advisers, might he not have even suspected that they were willing to sacrifice one whom they regarded as useless, in order to save the life of one who would be really dangerous?' Whatever may be thought of the psychological suggestions in the latter part of this paragraph, the opening sentence does not seem adequate to the facts. Even when wearied (46^f.), Jesus would not allow fatigue to prevent Him from speaking, if utterance were necessary. If He was silent, it was because He was unwilling, not because He felt unable. Besides, the impression left by the record of the last two days of the life of Jesus is that His physical strength must have been considerable. Upon the whole, then, it is needless to attribute His silence before Pilate to any other reason than a belief that protestations of innocence were useless, coupled, as that belief was, with a calm consciousness of truth which left no room for even a vestige of anxiety about the ultimate success of His cause.

The impression made by Jesus upon Pilate started a series of attempts upon the part of the procurator to extricate himself and his prisoner from the situation created by the rancour of the Jewish authorities. Three separate movements were made by him in this direction. The first was to change the venue of the trial; for Herod as a Galilæan might be expected to judge this Galilæan peasant more fairly than the Jerusalem authorities. After this device had failed, Pilate tried to get behind the priests, and appeal to the better feelings of the people when unbiassed by sacerdotal and ecclesiastical intrigues; surely a Messiah would be popular, he argued, recollecting the hot patriotism of the nation. But, to his disgust and dismay, Barabbas was preferred to Jesus. Finally, as a last resource, he tried to work on their pity, now that their patriotism was out of the question; he presented Jesus to them, with the bloody marks of scourging upon Him, as an object to excite compassion (Jn 19^{1f}.). This again proved of no avail, and with its collapse Pilate saw the disappearance of the last chance of rescuing the prisoner. Such is, in rough outline, the scheme of events which we can recover from a careful scrutiny of the extant records.

St. Luke, indeed, makes Pilate at once pronounce Jesus innocent (23^4). But this is far too abrupt. The probability is that (Mk 15$^{3-5}$ = Mt 27$^{12-14}$) the priests and elders continued to heap fresh accusations upon Him, and that His silence under the strain of calumny roused Pilate's astonishment. The procurator was evidently puzzled to know what to do with this prisoner. For though silence may have been equivalent, in Roman law, to a

* Their ritualistic scruple about entering the Prætorium is noted by the Fourth Evangelist (18^{28}) with deliberate meaning. In the light of the Christian interpretation, it acquired a sinister significance. 'Polluting their souls with blood, they dare not pollute their bodies by breach of outer etiquette. . . . Men must have some scrap of conscience left to hide them from themselves. Inward defilement, unprincipled action, are atoned for by outer decorum' (Reith, *Gospel of John*, ii. 135).

† The Fourth Evangelist (18^{33}), like St. Matthew (27^{11}), here follows the condensed Markan tradition (15^2), leaving it unexplained how Pilate had come to hear of the accusation of royalty, but implying that Jesus had not heard the priests laying this information before the governor.

confession of guilt, he was unwilling to pronounce sentence in this case without some further evidence, and the invectives of the Jewish authorities did not point to any conclusive or reliable ground for arriving at a judgment. The very silence of Jesus, as Keim properly observes, impressed the procurator more than the eager, noisy vehemence of His opponents. 'He did not infer guilt or obstinacy from the silence, as the official and imperious consciousness even of a mild Pliny the Younger was apt so quickly to do: an evidence this of Pilate's intelligence, and still more of the impression produced by the Lord even when He uttered no words.' In the midst of this perplexity the word 'Galilee,' flung up on the torrent of invective, caught his ear. He seemed to see a chance of relieving himself, and perhaps of helping Jesus. For if Jesus had been guilty of crime within the borders of Galilee, plainly Herod Antipas was the man to deal with Him; he might be more impartial, too, than the local priests and scribes. Besides, it was a politic attention to Antipas. So the procurator gladly dismissed his prisoner to the Galilæan tetrarch, only too relieved to be quit, as he hoped, of this inconvenient responsibility. But this change of venue was futile. It was not exactly illegal, for, as has been observed, the words of Lk 23[4] are probably introduced too early; the other Gospels know nothing of such an acquittal at this point. But it did not help Pilate. The crafty Herod was shy of touching any charge of *majestas*. As Mr. Taylor Innes puts it, 'the Idumean fox dreaded the lion's paw, while very willing to exchange courtesies with the lion's deputy.'

The transference of Jesus to Herod (cf. vol. i. 722) is one of St. Luke's special contributions to the story of the Passion (23[6-16], cf. Ac 4[27]). Whether taken from oral tradition (cf. Justin Martyr, *Dial.* 103) or from the Jewish Christian source (note the technical Jewish χριστὸν βασιλέα=king Messiah, 23[2]) which some critics trace below his narrative, it goes back to the memories of the Christians who belonged to the Herodian *entourage* (cf. 8[3] 9[4]), and ought never to have been suspected by a sane criticism. No satisfactory motive for its invention can be adduced.* St. Luke (13[1]) was perfectly aware that, when it suited his purpose, Pilate had no hesitation in killing Galilæans. The author rightly hints at other motives for his action now. The presence of the high priests and scribes at the interview (v.[10]) is, at first sight, certainly a difficulty; it might suggest that here, as perhaps at 22[52] (cf. 22[66]), the historian has gone too far in emphasizing the activity of the Jewish authorities. But it is just possible that they feared to let the prisoner out of their sight. Herod was not to be relied on. He might take it into his head to release Jesus out of spite or caprice, as Pilate had threatened to do, and with relentless† vigour some of the authorities may have kept on the track of their victim. The omission of 23[10-12] in the Sinaitic Syriac version is probably due to harmonizing tendencies. Certainly 23[15] affords no adequate ground for excising it (so Wellhausen‡) as a later gloss, for even if the inferior reading, '*I sent him (Jesus) to him (Herod)*,' be adopted, it does not necessarily imply that the authorities were not present at Herod's examination. Pilate is not giving them fresh information. He is simply rehearsing the facts of the case in a semi-formal fashion.

St. Luke does not exaggerate the share of Herod in Christ's death, as does the later Gospel of Peter, which makes Antipas sentence the prisoner formally. The historian simply brings out the idle curiosity of the tetrarch.§ The mockery of Jesus, in which he is said even to have participated himself, was probably due to irritation at his failure to elicit any answer from the prisoner. Herod's wounded dignity and baffled curiosity were up in arms to take a petty vengeance (cf. vol. i. 454a), and both he and Pilate were consoled for their trouble and annoyance by getting their feud

* The ordinary theory that Herod is made the representative of Judaism, to exculpate paganism (Pilate), contradicts 23[15].

† There is a dramatic contrast between the two uses of this Lukan term εὐτόνως here and in Ac 18[28].

‡ He deserts here his favourite D (ἀνέπεμψα γὰρ ὑμᾶς πρὸς αὐτόν). Compare, against him, Blass in *The Philology of the Gospels*, pp. 183–184.

§ Bengel's caustic comment on v.[8] is: '*Potentes minus obvium habuere Jesum: et illi solent esse ultimi in cognoscendis rebus regni dei.*'

patched up and their mutual jurisdiction recognized. Their treatment of Jesus gave each the opportunity of a politic and inexpensive generosity.

Pilate then, according to Luke, proposes a weak compromise (23[13-16]). To appease the Jews he will scourge this harmless fanatic, Jesus, before releasing Him; for release Him he must, as His guilt has not been proven. The innocence of Jesus seems to be formally pronounced. Herod's refusal to convict Him gives Pilate the tardy courage to acquit the prisoner before His accusers, but it does not lend him courage to carry out the strict legal consequences of the decision. Utilitarian motives come into play.* The governor realizes that he must try to conciliate the infuriated Jews. Since his offer to scourge Jesus is ignominiously rejected, some other compromise must be devised.

Here all the Gospels come into line, with an account of Pilate's next attempt to save Jesus, this time at the expense of Barabbas (see BARABBAS and INSURRECTION), though St. Luke less happily omits all reference to the custom of releasing a prisoner, and makes the idea of Barabbas originate with the Jews (23[18]), not with Pilate, while St. Matthew inserts a piece of very secondary tradition about Pilate's wife (27[19], cf. vol. i. p. 495) in order to explain the governor's hesitation, as well as to throw the malice of the Jews into relief. A further addition † of St. Matthew is the dramatic incident of Pilate washing his hands before the people, and proclaiming his innocence of the judicial crime which they were bent on perpetrating (27[24. 25]).‡ The incident may be St. Matthew's anecdotal way of depicting the idea of the Jews' real responsibility for the death of Jesus. In any case, once the people deliberately prefer Barabbas, Pilate plainly throws off all responsibility for all that follows. Probably the revelation of Christ's unpopularity § removed the last scruple of conscience which he felt. Why should he endanger his position and risk a tumult among the people for the sake of a Galilæan dreamer who had not a single adherent to stand by Him? Pilate could afford to thwart the priests, perhaps, but it was another matter when the people asserted their wishes.

In response to his half-perplexed, half-ironical inquiry as to what, then, is to be done with Jesus the so-called Christ, the reply (unanimous, according to Mt 27[22]) is, '*Crucify him.*' Carlyle, in the sixth of his *Latter-day Pamphlets*, takes this to be an illustration of the absurdity of universal suffrage. 'Can it be proved that since the beginning of the world there was ever given a universal vote in favour of the worthiest man or thing? I have always understood that true worth in any department was difficult to recognize; that the worthiest, if he appealed to universal suffrage, would have but a poor chance. . . . Alas, Jesus Christ asking the Jews what He deserved, was not the answer, Death on the gallows!' But the point of the incident is not quite this. The Markan tradition, followed by Matthew (27[20] = Mk 15[11]), indicates the responsibility of the priests rather than of the people. The latter were in-

* Compare the defence of the governor's action in Sir James Stephen's *Liberty, Equality, Fraternity*, p. 88 f. It is not a bench on which historical criticism will be content to rest for long. See Zimmermann's *Histor. Wert der ältesten Ueberl.* (1905) p. 184 f.

† Besides the account of Judas (27[3ff.]; cf. vol. i. 911); on these fragments of Palestinian Jewish tradition see W. C. Allen's 'St. Matthew' (*ICC*), p. 315. 'When truth is in danger,' said Dr. John Ker, 'the conduct of many is to wash their hands in Pilate's basin of weak neutrality; but they only soil the water, and do not cleanse their hands.'

‡ Note the intentional repetition of ὑμεῖς ὄψεσθε from 27[4].

§ The opposition of the people to Pilate's suggestion may have been due in part to his own unpopularity. The Jews would readily take any opportunity of thwarting a proposal from one who had so repeatedly defied their prejudices and religious tastes.

stigated by the sacerdotal authorities, who were afraid of Pilate's appeal, and jealous* of the possible popularity which Jesus might win among the crowd. Accordingly they worked — how, we are not told—upon the passions of the mob, religious and political. The result was a wild outcry for the release of Barabbas, which at once showed Pilate that Jesus was not a favourite of the people, but merely a discredited provincial.

The general outline of the closing scene, despite variations in detail, is fairly distinct. Pilate allows himself to be overborne by the popular clamour. Finding that his attempts to expostulate with the mob are fruitless, he at last lets them have their own way, pronouncing the fatal words ἐξελευσῇ εἰς σταυρόν (*ibis ad crucem*).

Before ordering the prisoner off to the death which, in Roman law, must immediately follow the capital sentence, he bids the lictor, *I, lictor, conliga manus, flagellis verberetur*; Jesus is then subjected to the scourging which preceded, in Roman usage,† the last act of the death punishment. Such at least, according to one tradition (Mk 15¹⁵ = Mt 27²⁶), was the significance of the scourging; it was a mere accessory to the crucifixion. In Luke, it occupies an earlier and a different position, as we have seen, whilst ‡ in the Fourth Gospel (19¹ᶠ·) it forms part of the mockery, and issues in Pilate's presentation of Jesus to the people in order to excite a pity or a contempt which might allay their malice. This is probably correct. In closely associating the scourging with the mockery, though not in placing them prior to the formal condemnation, the Fourth Evangelist is following the Markan tradition. He rightly brings out the third and last appeal of Pilate, before the final sentence is pronounced. But for the details of this bloody punishment we must look outside the Gospels. All four eschew any harrowing pictures of the scene. The simple and sober mention of the fact is all that the tradition has preserved.

(c) *The mocking of Jesus* (see CROWN OF THORNS, MOCKERY, REED, THORNS).—That Jesus was insulted and ill-treated during the course of His trial is a fixed part of the Evangelic tradition,§ but it is uncertain when and where the cruel sport took place. According to one tradition (Mk 14⁶⁵ = Mt 26⁶⁷· ⁶⁸) it followed the condemnation by the Sanhedrin; either the bystanders ‖ or the servants of the high priest or the councillors (Mt.) blindfolded Him, spat in His face, and rained blows upon Him,* asking Him with jeers to prophesy who struck Him. St. Luke (22⁶³⁻⁶⁵) more accurately places this horseplay during the nocturnal interval between His arrest and the assembling of the Council in the morning, when no responsible parties were present to prevent vulgar indignities being heaped on the defenceless prisoner. St. Luke also narrates (23¹¹) that Herod and his troops treated their prisoner with rough ridicule as a *soi-disant* king; and, when the incident of the Herod interview is accepted as historical, there is no reason to doubt that such violence may have been inflicted, unless Luke is held to have transferred to Herod the mockery which the earlier tradition (Mk 15¹⁶⁻²⁰, Mt 27²⁷⁻³¹) ascribes to Pilate.

This second mockery consisted in the troops arraying Jesus in a scarlet military mantle, spitting on Him (in caricature of the kiss of homage), crowning Him with thorns, putting a reed in His hand, and paying mock deference to Him.† Then, beating Him unmercifully, they stripped Him of this finery, and reclothed Him in His own garments. 'In our time, when a man has been sentenced to death, we do not think it right to add to his sufferings by preliminary torture; but it was not so in former days; if bystanders, in their indignation, added to what had been sentenced by the judge, all this was looked upon as no more than giving the criminal his deserts; and this volunteered addition to the judge's sentence was no doubt the severest part of the penalty.' ‡ The rough treatment of Jesus, however, by the soldiers of Pilate took place within the barracks. As it was aimed at the nation through the person of Jesus, it was not politic to conduct it in the open air.

The mockery of Jesus was thus twofold. That inflicted by the Jews was meant for Jesus the prophet; that of the Roman soldiers, as of Herod's Syrian troops, was occasioned by His pretensions to be a king. He was ill-treated, as He was condemned and crucified, for being a royal pretender. There is no reason to suppose that the second mockery is an unhistorical echo of the former, or that even the former is (Brandt, *Evangel. gesch.* p. 69 f.) constructed elaborately out of Old Testament suggestions. But a more real problem has been raised, in recent years, with regard to the meaning of the mockery. Several scholars § have attempted to find, in the details of this incident, allusions to the mock coronation which preceded the grotesque Saturnalia of the Sacæan festival in ancient Babylonia,—celebrated throughout Asia

---

* This ill-will (Mk 15¹⁰ = Mt 27¹⁸) towards one who had challenged their vested interests and ecclesiastical authority was patent to Pilate (cf. vol. i. 521 f., and Lidgett's *Spiritual Principle of the Atonement*, p. 11 f.). As we know from the record of his previous conflict with the Jews, he took an insolent delight in humiliating them, which had thrice led to an even more humiliating surrender upon his own part. The trial of Jesus gave him another chance of thwarting the authorities. But he had learned prudence by this time. He would use Jesus as far as possible to exasperate the Jews, but he would have little hesitation in sacrificing his prisoner to safeguard his own credit and popularity, particularly when he found that the Galilæan was unpopular Himself.

† Thus the Jews caught outside Jerusalem during the siege by Titus 'were first scourged, then tormented with all kinds of torture before they died, and were crucified opposite the walls of the city' (Jos. *BJ* v. xi. 1).

‡ Perhaps founding on the hint of Lk 23²², where it is part of Pilate's suggested compromise. The position of the scourging, with the subsequent *Ecce Homo* incident (Jn 19¹⁻³· ⁴ᶠ·), is rightly assigned by the Fourth Evangelist.

§ How far the tradition has been affected by the natural desire (cf. Ac 13²⁷· ²⁸) to conform the sufferings of Jesus to such OT prophecies as Is 50⁶ᶠ· (cf. Mic 5¹), it is impossible to determine. Even Matthew, with his predilection for discovering fulfilment of prophecy, does not refer to such passages. The likelihood is, as Strauss admits (§ 128), that while Jesus was actually maltreated as the Evangelists record, 'their descriptions are modelled on prophecies which, when once Jesus appeared as a sufferer and maltreated person, were applied to Him.'

‖ Apparently including even some of the councillors themselves — a trait of Oriental passion which, in view of Jos. *BJ* vi. v. 3, is not to be taken as a touch of the Evangelic tradition inconsistent with the dignity of the authorities. Wellhausen thinks Mt.'s version (= high priests) is original.

* Professor Burkitt (*The Gospel History and its Transmission*, pp. 51–53) holds that τίς ἐστιν ὁ παίσας σε (Mt 26⁶⁸) is a secondary addition of the Evangelist, and that the real meaning of Mk 14⁶⁵ is that the face of Jesus was covered because He was formally condemned (Est 7⁸). But, in this event, the blindfolding would immediately follow the condemnation, whereas the spitting intervenes, showing that horseplay had begun. Besides, Luke's version corroborates the Markan view as reproduced in Matthew, and probably is one of his harmonizing touches, which smooth out details in Mark and Matthew into a graphic and intelligible picture. Wellhausen omits the blindfolding in Mk 14⁶⁵ (with D and Syrˢⁱⁿ), which, in his view of the context (see above), implies that the prophesying of Jesus was to be about the destruction of the Temple.

† A similar grim jest was practised by the Mediterranean pirates upon any Roman citizen whom they captured. Plutarch (*Vita Pomp.* xxiv.) describes how they affected to be struck with terror, dropped on their knees before him, threw a toga round him, and finally made away with him.

‡ Salmon, *The Human Element in the Gospels* (p. 506). The soldiers were probably seizing the opportunity to vent their contempt for the Jews, quite as much as to express personal animosity towards Jesus.

§ J. G. Frazer, *Golden Bough²*, ii. 24 f., 253 f., iii. 150 f. Wendland, in his paper on Jesus as a Saturnalian king (*Hermes*, 1898, pp. 175–179), thinks that the Roman troops ridiculed Him in the farcical garb of Saturn; but the late *Acta* of Dasius the martyr are too unreliable to serve as evidence for this period, even had the Romans been tolerant of human sacrifices.

Minor in connexion with the worship of the Persian goddess Anaitis,—where, in the course of other orgies, 'a condemned prisoner was arrayed in royal attire, only in the end to be stript of his borrowed finery, scourged, and hanged or crucified.' Another theory (advocated by Reich in his essay on *Der König mit der Dornerkrone*, 1905) casts back to the popular buffoonery which accompanied the mimes, *e.g.* at Alexandria (cf. Philo, *in Flacc.* 5–6, quoted by Grotius in this connexion), while Mr. W. R. Paton (in *ZNTW*, 1901, 339–341) further points out that the trait of a triple crucifixion reflects the Persian custom of crucifying a pretender or usurper upon three crosses. It is, of course, quite possible that two robbers were crucified with Jesus simply because no more happened to be in prison at the moment ; but, in view of this custom, it seems not unlikely that the number of victims, like the mock homage paid previously to one of them, may have been determined by some hazy notion of imitating a pagan bit of ritual. The un-Jewish character of these accompaniments of the crucifixion would certainly lend additional relish to the soldiers' contemptuous pleasure in crucifying a caricature of a Jewish monarch.* But, while the possibility of this may be granted, it is impossible to regard the Gospel accounts as legendary products of any such pagan custom. For one thing, Jesus was not crucified on three crosses, nor was His death taken as an offering. Again, Dr. Frazer's identification of Purim with Sacæa is too precarious† to support firmly the inference that Jesus perished as a Haman at this Jewish festival ; nor did it require any coarse pagan rite to stimulate military horseplay among soldiers, even although they may have been, like Herod's Syrian troops, familiar with such customs, or had been, like Pilate's Roman legions, stationed at one time on the Euphrates where the rites in question may have survived. It is extremely unlikely that such a confusion of Sacæa with the Jewish festivals should have arisen, or that any reminiscence of the Alexandrian outburst should have prompted the records of the horseplay at Jerusalem.‡ See, further, art. MOCKERY.

ῥάπισμα (Mk 14⁶⁵, Jn 18²²) is a blow inflicted with the open hand (cf. Field's *Notes on the Transl. of the NT*, p. 105). This is the most probable meaning, on the whole, though the dubiety of the reading in the former passage (ἐβαλλον or ἐβαλον, ἐλάμβανον or ἐλαβον) introduces a slight element of uncertainty as to the sense.

4. Special points in the NT narratives.—Most of the characteristic features in the various reports of the trial have already been noted, but it remains for us to glance briefly at the Evangelic records one by one. The Petrine tradition in Mk. (cf. Bennett in *Expositor*, Dec. 1906, p. 545 f.) is substantially reproduced in Mt., most of whose additions are of secondary historical importance. St. Luke, again, appears to have access to a special source for this part of his narrative, while the Fourth Gospel presents a problem of peculiar intricacy, since its record of the Passion contains not merely elements which in form and content are plainly due to the writer's underlying religious aims, but also one or two passages which are either modelled upon the Lukan tradition or due to a good source which may have been known, at an earlier period, independently to St. Luke himself. St. Mt.'s omission of the blindfolding of Jesus (26⁶⁶· ⁶⁷) is certainly remarkable, but it merely gives another view of the scene. We see Jesus pulled hither and thither by a crowd of exasperated

* Cf. the present writer's remarks in the *Hibbert Journal* (1903), p. 775 f.
† Cf. Andrew Lang's criticism in *Magic and Religion*, pp. 76 f., 200 f.
‡ This is well put by Dr. J. Geffcken in *Hermes* (1906), p. 220 f., and by Vollmer in *ZNTW* (1905) 194–198, criticising Reich.

fanatics, twisted from side to side, knocked about, struck behind His back, and jeeringly invited to guess who struck Him. The blindfolding makes the picture more dramatic, but not more intelligible. On the other hand, the introduction of οἱ πρεσβύτεροι in 27¹²· ²⁰ (cf. 27⁴¹), and of τὸν λεγόμενον Χριστόν (27²²), is probably due to the author's characteristic desire to accentuate the Jewish details, while changes such as the omission of Mark's favourite ἤρξαντο (26⁶⁷· ⁷¹ 27²⁹), or the substitution of aorists for imperfects (26⁶⁰· ⁶⁷· ⁷²· ⁷⁵ 27¹⁸· ³⁴), are simply literary and stylistic, adding nothing to the real sense of the narrative. Evidently the author or editor of Matthew had not access to any wider channel of authentic information than he found in the Markan tradition. At one point it is possible that the canonical text of Mark has even been enriched from Matthew, for the words ὅ ἐστιν πραιτώριον (Mk 15¹⁶), as Prof. Menzies (*The Earliest Gospel*, p. 276) after Brandt observes, do nothing 'to make Mark's narrative clearer, but rather the opposite, and may have crept in first as a gloss on the margin from Matthew, where the statement appears to be that the soldiers took Jesus off to another building, viz. to the prætorium, and collected there the whole cohort.' See Blass in *ExpT* x. [1899] 185 f.

A much more significant and complex character belongs to the Lukan narrative. Thus the freedom with which the historian has treated the Markan narrative* may be gathered from the fact that his order, in the opening scenes of the trial (denials of Peter, mockery of Jesus, examination of Jesus), exactly reverses that of the earlier Gospels. He also forgets to mention that any evidence† was laid against Jesus (cf. 22⁶⁶), or that Jesus was ever bound—a point on which the Fourth Evangelist is more correct (Jn 18¹²). Furthermore, he omits all reference to the saying about the destruction of the Temple, though it was plainly known to him (cf. Ac 6¹⁴). Possibly an 'apologetic' motive underlay this alteration. If Luke, writing after the destruction of the Temple, viewed it as a Divine judgment upon Israel, 'which might be regarded as inflicted by Jesus Himself, he might wish to avoid saying that the testimony' of the witnesses 'was false,' and so left out the entire inquiry before the Council (*EBi* 1772). The attempt to trace an 'apologetic' element in 23¹², as though this meant the pact of Judaism and paganism against Christianity (cf. Ac 4²⁷), is rather beside the mark, however. Herod considered Jesus quite beneath his notice, no danger was to be apprehended from Him ; He was beneath hatred, though not below contempt. Nor did Pilate regard the prisoner with enmity. It is indubitable, on the other hand, that St. Luke views the conduct of the people at this point in a more severe light than the other Gospels. He omits the sacerdotal device (cf. 23¹⁸ with Mk 15¹¹ and Mt 27²⁰), writing as though the people of their own accord demanded Barabbas (cf. also 22⁶⁶ 23¹· ²· ¹³), at one in this with the high priests and the rulers, though possibly, in view of passages like 18⁴³ 19⁴⁸ 21³⁸, we are to take the people here as supporters of the priests.‡ The Fourth Evangelist, again, takes a slightly milder view of the people (cf. the omission in 19⁶), and this leads us to notice the idiosyncrasies of the trial-story in that Gospel.

Here Peter (cf. vol. i. 444–445) is not the only

* Compare Sir John C. Hawkins in *Expository Times*, xv. [1903] 124 f. On Luke's omissions see *EBi*, col. 1793 f.
† The condensed nature of his account here lends too precipitate a character to the proceedings. Possibly the search for witnesses was loosely begun during the night ; but even so Luke's narrative is defective on this point. That he knew the Markan tradition of the false evidence is plain from the retention of ἔτι in 22⁷¹. On his own scheme the word is superfluous, since no word of any previous witnesses occurs in the narrative.
‡ So B. Weiss in *Die Quellen des Lukasevangeliums* (1907), 225–226.

disciple who follows Jesus into the place of trial ; another disciple, who is probably to be identified with the ' beloved disciple,' enters the high priest's palace, and, in virtue of his position there ('he was known to the high priest'), is able to introduce Peter. The estimate of this assertion depends upon the general view taken of the relation between the historical and the religious element in the Gospel ; either (a) the anonymous disciple is the author, John (see vol. i. 880 f.), or (b) the authority to which the author refers, or (c) a purely ideal figure (cf. E. F. Scott, *The Fourth Gospel*, 1907, pp. 57, 144, etc., and, from the opposite side, Lepin's *L'Origine du Quatrième Évangile*, 341–398).

While the Synoptic Gospels make the entire proceedings before Pilate take place in the open air, the Fourth Evangelist makes Pilate repeatedly go between the Jews outside and Jesus inside the palace.* The attempts of the governor to save his prisoner are dramatically sharpened, if not multiplied ; Jesus speaks far more than in the earlier accounts ; and a certain superstitious fear is even attributed to Pilate as one result of these interviews (19[8]).

The two private conversations between Pilate and Jesus (18[33-38] 19[8-11]) bring out the Evangelist's conception of Christ's Kingdom as a reign of truth, not of political or military force. In dramatic juxtaposition, Pilate and Jesus, the representatives of world-power and heavenly power, are confronted, and Jesus meets the Roman governor with undaunted calmness, actually putting questions to him as One possessed of independent authority. He judges His judge, in fact.† The Evangelist uses his favourite form of dialogue in order to bring out this conception of the meaning of the crisis. Pilate, to him, is less culpable than the Jews. He is first impatient, but soon impressed by Jesus, and finally convinced of His innocence. The insolence and rancour of the Jews form a foil to his anxiety to release the prisoner, and the dramatic conversations between the governor and the accusers bring out the contempt felt by the former for the latter's intriguing spirit, but also the weakness of character upon which the Jews were clever enough to play. Threatening Pilate with high treason to the emperor Tiberius (cf. vol. i. 246[a]) if he acquits Jesus, they force his hand, until angry, like any weak man who is publicly forced to be disloyal to his convictions, he hands over the prisoner to be crucified.‡

It is plausible to read, between the lines of this scene, the author's plea for the political innocence of Christians at the opening of the 2nd cent. (as in Luke's Gospel and Acts), and to this apologetic element may be added an emphasis on the malevolent instigation of persecution by the Jews (as at Polycarp's martyrdom in Smyrna), and a corresponding emphasis on the greater hopefulness of the Gentile mission. The Jesus of the Fourth Gospel's trial recognizes no duty of confession towards Judaism. While in the Synoptic Gospels He confesses His Messiahship to the Sanhedrin, and is silent on it before Pilate, the reverse is the

case in the Fourth Gospel (cf. 1 Ti 6[13]). But even in describing and defending His mission before the governor, Jesus appeals not to him but to the world of sincere, elect souls, who are ' of the truth ' (cf. 12[20f.]), Greeks or Jews, the latter having no precedence whatsoever. It is in this light, as Loisy points out, that Pilate's famous question, *What is truth?* must be read, not as the word of an inquirer, nor of melancholy regret, but as a reflexion of the half-contemptuous scepticism felt by some Roman authorities for the inconvenient enthusiasm of Christians, who persisted in taking seriously what no man of the world would allow to disturb his own conscience (cf. TRUTH).* The idea of a man letting himself suffer for the sake of ' truth,' a chimera of the schools ! As for the dramatic confession of the Jews, *We have no king but Cæsar* (19[16]), with its affectation of patriotism in order to get rid of the King of truth, what the author means to bring out, especially in the light of the crisis of 70 A.D., when Cæsar destroyed the Jewish State, is the abnegation by Judaism of its proper mission. That mission was spiritual. ' Judaism was the sheath to a seed : if it ceased to enfold transcendent hope, it lost all meaning. What found its expression in the rejection of Christ was that renegade Judaism in alliance with the world which we know as Pharisaism. For Judaism to ally itself with Rome, with Herod, with any earthly dominion, is for a race called on to uphold trust in God, to confess that in any real stress of need the recourse must be to material springs of power' (Julia Wedgwood, *The Message of Israel*, p. 302).

Three further points in the Johannine narrative demand a final word of notice. (a) Are the famous words *Ecce homo* (19[5], cf. vol. i. 507) meant to represent Pilate, like Caiaphas (11[49-52]), as an involuntary prophet ? This would be likely if ὁ ἄνθρωπος were taken (with Nestle, *Einführung in das Griech. NT*, 237 f.) in the sense of the Son of Man (cf. 15[1] 3[14]), an interpretation favoured by Grill (*Untersuchungen über die Entstehung des vierten Evangeliums*, pp. 49–50). We should then have a play upon words which literally meant, ' Behold the fellow ! ' or, ' Look at this poor wretch ! '

(b) To whom does Jesus refer in the words (19[11]), ' He that delivered me to thee has the greater sin ' ? To Satan, to Judas, or to Caiaphas ? Most probably it is the high priest who is in the author's mind. The previous words of the verse (cf. Coleridge's *Table Talk*, May 20, 1830) emphasize one cardinal idea of the Gospel, viz. that the fate of Jesus was due to the Divine will alone ; the latter part of the verse reiterates the other conception of the Jews as more culpable than the Roman authorities (cf. A. R. Eagar in *Expositor*, July 1905, p. 33 f.).

(c) Is ἐκάθισεν (19[13]) intransitive or transitive ? Did Pilate seat himself or Jesus on the tribunal ? The latter rendering, supported by a tradition voiced in the Gospel of Peter and Justin Martyr (see vol. i. 678[a]), would give a good sense, Jesus being symbolically enthroned as the King of truth, and Pilate's irony really indicating the true position of his prisoner (so Loisy, after Professor Roberts, *Expositor*, 1893, 296 f., and others) ; but unfortunately the grammatical and psychological probabilities tell seriously against it.†

LITERATURE.—Besides the references already cited, the literature under CAIAPHAS, JUDAS, PETER, and PILATE, and the relevant sections in the various editions of the Gospels and the biographies of Jesus (notably those by Strauss, B. Weiss, Neander, Farrar, Beyschlag, Keim, A. Réville, Edersheim, O. Holtzmann), there are special studies of the subject by Brandt, *Die evangel. Gesch. und der Ursprung des Christenthums*, 1893, pp. 53–68, who gives the most searching and sceptical view of the details, and, on conservative lines, by S. J. Andrews, *The Life of our Lord* (1892), pp. 505–544 ; Ewald, *History of Israel*, vi. 429–437 ; F. L. Steinmeyer, *The History of the Passion and Resurrection of our Lord, in the light of Modern Criticism* (Edinburgh) ; Prof. Stalker, *The Trial and Death of Jesus Christ* (London, 1894) ; Dr. John Watson, *The Life of the Master* (pp. 363–382) ; and Auguste Wabnitz, *Hist. de la Vie de Jésus—La Passion, la Mort, et la Résurrection de Jésus* (Montauban, 1904), pp. 175–273 ; see also H. B. Workman, *Persecution in the Early Church* (1906), pp. 10–20 ; and, from a different standpoint, the tenth chapter of E. Clodd's *Jesus of Nazareth*. On the legal aspects the standard monograph in English is Mr. Taylor Innes's *The Trial of Jesus Christ : A Legal Monograph* (1899), a

---

* Jn 18[31, 32] is the early Christian interpretation of what was necessary for several ordinary reasons. The Jews could not stone their false prophet to death with impunity. They preferred to make the Romans responsible for the death of Jesus, as well as to make that death more infamous in the eyes of the people. Besides, they had no witnesses to cast the first stones, after the breakdown of the evidence about the Temple saying. Compare Nestle's *Einführung in das Griechische NT*, p. 213.

† In v.[37] Jesus appeals to a higher court than that of Pilate As the Evangelist suggests, the verdict passed on Jesus had been subsequently reversed.

‡ ' That a Roman administrator capable of taking this sensible view of a case so dishonestly got up should nevertheless suffer his sense of justice to be overborne by the outcry of a threatening priesthood and a noisy populace, is indeed deplorable, but only too credible in that age of decay of the civil virtues' (Martineau, *Seat of Authority in Religion*, bk. v. ch. ii.).

* As usual in the Fourth Gospel (cf. 12[34]), Jesus is made to utter a deep, enigmatic saying which is misunderstood by the literal mind of His opponent. See, further, Matheson's *Landmarks of NT Morality*, p. 244 f.

† Cf. Abbott's *Johannine Grammar*, 2537, and Zahn's *Einleitung in das NT* (§ 69, note 12).

dignified and subtle study, to which the relevant pages of Signor G. Rosadi's *The Trial of Jesus* (Eng. tr. of 3rd Italian ed. 1905) add little or nothing ; see, further, Dalman in *Sunday School Times* (May 6th, 1899); H. M. Cheever, 'The legal aspects of the trial of Jesus,' *Bibl. Sacra* (1903), 495–509 ; and the popular descriptions in two works by S. Buss, viz. *Roman Law and History in the NT* (1901), pp. 174–239, and *The Trial of Jesus : Illustrated from Talmud and Roman Law* (1906). In addition to these studies, the preacher will find excellent material in W. F. Besser, *Leidengeschichte* (1855) ; H. Müller, *Der leidende Jesus*(Halle, 1856) ; A. Nebe, *Die Leidengesch. Jesu* (Stuttgart, 1881) ; Süskind, *Dispositionen zur heil. Passion* (Berlin, 1887) ; M. J. Ollivier, *La Passion* (Paris, 1902) ; H. Werner, *Christi Leidensgesch. das Meisterwerk des göttliches Vorsehung* (1902) ; J. L. Meagher, *The Tragedy of Calvary, or The Minute Details of Christ's Life from Palm-Sunday morning till the Resurrection and Ascension* (New York, 1905) ; together with A. M. Fairbairn's *Studies in the Life of Christ* (ch. xvi.) ; W. R. Nicoll's *The Incarnate Saviour* (ch. xviii.) ; Parker's *The Inner Life of Christ*, iii. 232 f. ; Joseph Hall's invaluable *Contemplations* (vol. iii. ch. xxx.–xxxi.) ; W. M. Clow's volume, *In the Day of the Cross* (1899) ; Dr. William Hanna's *The Passion Week* ; Gerhard's *Erklärung der Historie des Leidens und Sterbens unseres Herrn Jesu Christi* (Berlin) ; and Hengstenberg's devout volume of *Vorlesungen über die Leidengeschichte* (Leipzig, 1875). There are notable sermons on Mk 15[15-20] ('Crowned Suffering') by H. W. Beecher, on Mt 27[12-14, 20-23] by Prof. G. A. Smith (*The Forgiveness of Sins*, 1904), on Mt 27[22] ('What will you do with Christ ?') by H. W. Beecher, on Jn[18][31, 38] ('The Postponement of Pilate') by S. A. Brooke (*Sermons*, second series, p. 294 f.), and F. W. Robertson (*Sermons*, first series, xix.–xx.), on Jn 18[36] by Mozley (*University Sermons*, No. 1), and on Jn 19[10, 11] by Liddon (*University Sermons*, second series, p. 236 f.). Compare also Steele's paper in the *Spectator* (No. 356) for April 18, 1712, Mr. Wratislaw on 'The Scapegoat—Barabbas' (*ExpT* iii. [1892] 400–403), and, on Jn 18[37, 38], Phillips Brooks' *The Influence of Jesus* (ch. iv.) ; with R. J. Campbell (*City Temple Sermons*, p. 50 f.) on Jn 19[5].   JAMES MOFFATT.

TRIBE (φυλή) is used mostly in the special OT sense of an Israelitish tribe, composed of the descendants of one of the sons of Jacob. The prophetess Anna belonged to the tribe of Asher (Lk 2[36]). The Messianic claims of Jesus were strengthened by the fact that He sprang from the royal tribe of Judah (He 7[14]). Galilee comprised the territories allotted in OT times to the tribes of Zebulun and Naphtali (Mt 4[13, 15]). The promise to the Twelve Apostles that they should judge the twelve tribes of Israel (Mt 19[28] ‖ Lk 22[30]) may be regarded as an instance of the way in which Jesus sometimes expressed His teaching in the language of popular apocalyptic conceptions of the Kingdom of God (cf. Rev 7[4ff.]). Less probable is the explanation of Weiss, that 'their judging the twelve tribes is only the reverse side of their being sent to the twelve tribes, which are exposed to judgment just because the offer of salvation was made to them through the Apostles' (*NT Theol.*, Eng. tr. i. 154). In Mt 24[30] (quoted from Zec 12[12]) 'tribe' has the wider sense of a branch of the human race.
                                            JAMES PATRICK.

TRIBULATION.—The Gr. word θλίψις (which means literally 'a pressing,' 'a pressing together,' 'pressure') is translated in the AV by the words 'tribulation,' 'affliction,' and 'anguish.' In every instance of its occurrence save one, viz. Jn 16[21], where the AV tr. 'anguish' is retained, the RV uniformly employs the term 'tribulation.' The verb θλίβω occurs twice in the Gospels : in Mk 3[9], where it describes the action of the crowd in 'thronging' Jesus ; and Mt 7[14], where it represents 'the way that leadeth unto life' as being 'straitened' (τεθλιμμένη). In his *Study of Words*, Trench gives a very interesting account of the history of the Eng. word 'tribulation.' Derived from Lat. *tribulum*, the threshing instrument or harrow by means of which the corn was separated from the husks, *tribulatio*, the term applied to the process of separation, came to be used for the disciplinary ordeal of distress and adversity. The following grouping of passages indicates the various usages of the word in the Gospels :—
1. In the Apocalyptic discourse 'tribulation' is declared to be in store for the Jewish nation (Mt 24[29], cf. Mk 13[19]). The necessity of this

tribulation is emphasized (Mt 24[6], Mk 13[7], Lk 21[9]), and the circumstances attending it are described in terrible and pathetic detail.
2. 'Tribulation' is announced by Jesus as the outward lot that awaits His disciples. (*a*) In the confusion and conflict that would sweep the nation on to the final catastrophe, the disciples were to be involved (Mt 24[9]). They would draw this relentless hostility on themselves in consequence of their testimony and activity as disciples. It behoved them to endure (ὑπομένειν, v.[13]) and prove themselves 'brethren and partakers in the tribulation, and kingdom, and patience (ὑπομονή) which are in Jesus' (Rev 1[9] RV, cf. Ro 5[3]). (*b*) Similarly, but without reference to any particular ordeal, the disciples are warned about the treatment they must expect to meet with 'in the world' (Jn 16[2, 33]). On account of their relation to Jesus, they would be subjected to this treatment. But their attitude ought to be one of 'good cheer' (θαρσεῖτε). 'The way that leadeth unto life' was, therefore, in the case of the disciples to prove 'straitened' (τεθλιμμένη).
3. 'Tribulation' and persecution (διωγμός) 'because of the word' are mentioned in the parable of the Sower as the conditions which cause those 'to stumble straightway' that 'hear the word, and straightway with joy receive it, and have no root in themselves' (Mt 13[21], Mk 4[17]). A mind only emotionally interested in the 'word,' that is to say, as distinct from one intellectually and morally interested (Mt 13[23], Mk 4[20]), is incapable of withstanding the emotional shock occasioned by tribulation and persecution. With his feelings sustained and refreshed by no continuous and immediate experience in relation to the 'word,' such a person cannot resist the assault upon them of actual harassing events. See also SORROW, SUFFERING.

LITERATURE.—Trench, *Study of Words* ; Bushnell, *The New Life* ; Maclaren, *The Unchanging Christ* ; W. Archer Butler, *Serm.* 2nd ser. (1866) 78 ; T. Arnold, *Christian Life* (1878), 217 ; Moulton-Geden, *Gr. Concordance* ; Grimm-Thayer, *Gr. Lex. s.vv.* and Comm. on passages.   A. B. MACAULAY.

TRIBUTE is used in the Gospels in two distinct senses. 1. The *tribute-money* (δίδραχμον, Mt 17[24ff.]) was the Temple-tax levied on all male Israelites of twenty and upwards, to meet the cost of the daily burnt-offering and the other sacrifices offered in the name of the people, and for other objects of a public character. In the days of Nehemiah the amount was a third of a shekel (Neh 10[32, 33]), but in NT times it was half a shekel (Jos. *Ant.* XVIII. xix. 1), which was also the sum fixed in Ex 30[11-13]. It was collected in the month Adar, and was paid in money of the early Hebrew standard. The 'piece of money' (στατήρ) of Mt 17[27] was equal to a shekel (about 2s. 9d.), and so was sufficient to meet the Temple-tax for two persons. 2. *The tribute to Cæsar* (φόρος, φόροι, κῆνσος) denoted the taxes payable by the Jews, as Roman subjects, into the Imperial treasury (*fiscus*). These included taxes on land and property (*tributum soli*), and the poll-tax (*tributum capitis*), from which only children and old men were exempt. The Roman authorities made use of the Jewish courts in collecting their revenue from these sources (Jos. *BJ* II. xvii. 1). It was the lawfulness of paying such taxes about which Jesus was questioned by His enemies (Mt 22[17] ‖ Mk 12[14] ‖ Lk 20[22]). His reply gave no ground for the charge of forbidding their payment, which was afterwards brought against Him (Lk 23[2]).

LITERATURE.—Schürer, *HJP* I. i. 65, ii. 107 f., II. i. 250 ff., ii. 162, and the authorities there cited.   JAMES PATRICK.

TRINITY.—Our subject is the doctrine of the Holy Trinity in relation to Christ and the Gospels.

We have to consider how far that great conception of God's being and nature is revealed or implied in the fact of Christ as presented in the Gospels and in the teaching of our Lord Himself.

I. The witness of our Lord's consciousness as revealed in the Gospels.—(i.) *AS REGARDS HIMSELF.*—It was not our Lord's custom to take to Himself the names and titles to which He knew He had a right. The passage which exhibits this fact most clearly is that in which we find Him questioning His disciples, first as to the popular opinion, and then as to their own belief (Mt 16[13ff.], Mk 8[27ff.], Lk 9[18ff.].). After St. Peter had made his great confession, our Lord charged the disciples to keep the truth which had just emerged, to themselves. No doubt He desired to avoid the mistakes arising from the popular conceptions of the Messiah. He wished also to train the minds of the disciples, to lead them gently from truth to truth, so that spiritual experience might keep pace with knowledge. And yet our Lord's thoughts about Himself were loftier far than could be imagined from the mere names and titles which He acknowledged. When the passages which contain His statements about His own relation to God and man are collected and viewed as a whole, they are found to imply claims which are far in advance of the first and more obvious meanings of the titles.

It is being more and more fully recognized by critical students of the life of Jesus that He certainly regarded Himself as the Messiah, and that the names and titles by which He described Himself and permitted others to describe Him are Messianic in their significance. But when this has been granted to the full, there remains a very large proportion of His self-revelation unaccounted for. Bousset considers that the reserve of our Lord on the subject of His Messiahship was due to His deep sense of the inadequacy of the Messianic title for that which He felt Himself to be (*Jesus*, p. 175 ff., Eng. tr.). And certain it is that, among all the conceptions which clustered round the Jewish anticipation of the Messiah, none is great enough, none deep enough, to correspond with the revelation of Himself which our Lord makes in the Gospels. (See art. 'Development of Doctrine' in Hastings' *DB*, Ext. Vol. ; Charles, 'Enoch' and 'Eschatology' in vol. i. ; also Briggs, *The Messiah of the Gospels*). True, we have the great OT conceptions of the later Isaiah and of the Book of Daniel, and we have the latter repeated, and in some respects enlarged, in the *Similitudes of Enoch*. In this probably pre-Christian work there is a wonderful picture of the *Son of Man*, which corresponds remarkably with certain passages in the Gospels. He is, as it seems, regarded as pre-existent, was named in the presence of God before creation, and takes part in judgment. But there is no anticipation of that extraordinary union of earthly humiliation with transcendent relationship to God the Father which is the principal deliverance of our Lord's consciousness concerning Himself. The truth is that the difficulty of representing that consciousness by means of the understood and recognized terms of the religion and theology of the day was almost inconceivably great.

It was this very inadequacy of all existing conceptions to convey the truth of our Lord's Person in His relation to God and man which rendered necessary that careful and patient handling of the faith of the disciples which we find everywhere in His dealing with them. A spiritual experience of a new kind had to be created before the new language could be learned. The new wine needed new bottles. The first danger to be guarded against was a premature precision, a hasty definition. The one title which our Lord constantly used of Himself, 'the Son of Man,' most skilfully avoided anything of the nature of definition. Messianic in its associations, it was yet not so distinctively Messianic as to constitute a claim, and it was capable of infinite suggestion, according to its application and context. It was a continual challenge to reflexion. See art. SON OF MAN above and in Hastings' *DB*.

These reflexions will help us to discern the true nature of the problem which is presented by our Lord's revelation of Himself. The facts of that problem may be summarized as follows, the Synoptic evidence and that of the Fourth Gospel being exhibited separately.

(1) *Direct statements or claims to a position or authority more than human.*—The strongest passage in the Synoptics is the solemn declaration recorded by Mt. (11[27]) and Lk. (10[22]), 'All things have been delivered unto me of my Father : and no one knoweth who the Son is, save the Father ; and who the Father is, save the Son, and he to whomsoever the Son willeth to reveal him.'

These words form the most striking connecting link between the Christology of the Synoptics and that of the Fourth Gospel. But they do not, as some critics would have us believe, stand alone. On the contrary, they but sum up teaching which may be found everywhere, expressed or implied. In many places our Lord speaks of His mission from God in a manner which sets Him above and apart from men (Mt 20[28], Mk 9[37] 10[45], Lk 9[48], Mt 28[18] etc.). He is King in a superhuman sense of the term (Mt 24[30ff.] 25[34. 40], Mk 15[2], Lk 19[38-40] 22[29] 23[2. 3]). He is Judge of all and Lord of the future (Mt 25[31ff.] 16[27] 19[28] 26[64], Mk 8[38] 13[26. 27] 14[62], Lk 9[26] 12[8. 9. 40ff.] 13[25ff.] 17[30] 21[36] 22[69] etc.). He is David's Lord (Mt 22[43-45], Mk 12[35ff.], Lk 20[44]). He is higher than the angels (Mk 13[32]). He demands the most complete devotion as His right, and the most extreme self-sacrifice (Mt 8[22] 10[32. 33. 37-39] 11[29] 16[24-26] 26[10ff.], Mk 8[34ff.] 10[29], Lk 9[23ff.] 14[26ff.] 21[12ff.] etc.). These passages express the Divine claim upon the loyalty of mankind in terms which could not be surpassed. So it is that our Lord declares Himself greater than the Temple (Mt 12[6]), Lord of the Sabbath (Mt 12[8], Mk 2[28]), greater than Solomon (Mt 12[42]).

In the Fourth Gospel this great claim of Christ occupies a much larger space, and is more explicit and more fully stated, but it is a mistake to suppose that it is more strongly expressed. Such a passage as Jn 5[22. 23] 'He hath given all judgment unto the Son ; that all may honour the Son even as they honour the Father,' is very definite, but it is only putting into general terms the teaching of Mt 10[37] 25[31ff.], Mk 8[34-38], Lk 14[26]. The tremendous statement in Jn 10[30] 'I and the Father are one,' summing up as it does the teaching of the whole Gospel, finds perhaps its most perfect explication in Mt 11[27], Lk 10[22]. The great section, Jn 14–17, is but the further development of the same doctrine, introducing, as was necessary, the promise of the Holy Spirit and certain fundamental instruction concerning His function and work.

(2) When from direct statements made by our Lord Himself we pass to the revelation of His consciousness of His unique relation to God which is to be found implied in *His life and methods*, we are able to note the following :

(*a*) *The unvarying tone of authority* which characterizes all His actions and utterances—authority as regards the greatest subjects which have ever engaged the mind of man. See, further, artt. AUTHORITY OF CHRIST and CLAIMS OF CHRIST.

(*b*) *The serene certainty of His judgments upon the greatest questions of morality and religion.* This characteristic is most noticeable in the Sermon on the Mount, and in all those parts of His teaching which deal with His own relation to God, and God's love to man. All the highest and greatest things are to Him easy and familiar. He walks upon the mountain peaks of vision with unhesitating confidence. He speaks as One who sees clearly into the heart of God. Examples will be found in the following passages :

Mt 5[43ff.] 6[25-34] 7[7-12] 11[20-30] 12[30-37] 17[20] 18[7-14] 22[19-21. 29-33] 23[37], Mk 2[18-22. 27] 9[33-50] 10[42-45] 14[3-9], Lk 2[49] 4[21] 7[22. 23. 47-50] 10[24. 25-37] 15 17[4. 10. 20. 21] 18[9-14], Jn 3[3] 4[24] 5[17] 14[2] etc.

(*c*) *He never prays with His disciples.* He teaches them to pray, He prays for them, but not with them. (See Chadwick, *Christ bearing witness to Himself*, pp. 104, 105 ; and Forrest, *The Christ of History and of Experience*, p. 22 ff., and Appendix to 5th ed.). We read of solitary prayers (Mk 6[45-48], Jn 6[15]).

(*d*) *The harmonious combination of opposite qualities in His character.*—Characteristics which would be incompatible in any one else unite freely and with perfect consistency in Him. Here is perhaps the strongest proof of the absolute truth of the portrait presented in the Gospels. Nothing but the strength and reality of the Personality which inspired the various accounts could have made such a result possible. See, further, artt. CHARACTER OF CHRIST, DIVINITY OF CHRIST, MENTAL CHARACTERISTICS.

(ii.) *HIS RELATION TO THE FATHER.*—(1) Our Lord asserts and implies that He stands in a relation of *unique intimacy with God the Father.* The great passage already quoted (Mt 11[27], Lk 10[22]) is the fullest statement in the Synoptics. The language here associates the Son with the Father in a manner which exalts Him above all creation. It corresponds with certain characteristic phrases and mental habits of our Lord. For example, He calls God 'my Father' in a manner which sets the relation indicated by the words far apart from that Fatherhood which He attributes to God in relation to men, whether disciples or not : see Mt 7[21] 10[32. 33] 11[27] 15[13] 18[10] 20[23] etc., Mk 8[38], Lk 2[49] 22[29] 24[49], Jn 5[17] 10[29. 30] 14[20] 20[17] etc. These passages but supply the correlative to the announcement at the Baptism and the Transfiguration (Mk 1[11] 9[7]). They also interpret for us the title 'Son of God' attributed to Him and accepted by Him (Mt 4[3. 6] 8[29] 14[33] 27[40. 43. 54], Mk 3[11] 12[6-8] 15[39], Lk 4[41] 22[70], Jn 1[34. 49] 9[35] 11[27] etc.).

In connexion with this we observe the cloudless serenity of His relation to God. It has been remarked that the absence of any note of repentance is the strongest proof of our Lord's perfect sinlessness. But we have in His life the marks of a moral state which is very much more than mere sinlessness. The value of the negative is entirely relative to the corresponding positive. The perfect innocence of a soul which possessed but small moral capacity would, so far as we can see, be of but little value as a moral factor in the universe. But, in the case of our Lord, we find a moral capacity which is absolutely without parallel in human experience, and we find the moral Being who possesses this capacity not merely conscious of innocence, but living a life which is wittingly and willingly all that God would have it be (see Forrest, *op. cit.*, Lect. I.).

(2) *Unity with the Father.* — The revelation which our Lord gives us of His relation to the Father amounts to much more than a manifestation of a peculiar intimacy between Himself and God. He claims distinctly certain Divine attributes and privileges. He is King and Judge of all. He is to be the object of the most absolute trust, the utmost devotion. No sacrifice is too great to be made for His sake (see above). To reject Him or His messengers is to reject God and to incur the severest judgment (Mt 10[15. 40] 11[22. 24], Mk 12[9], Lk 10[13. 14. 16] 13[34. 35] etc.). The right of the Almighty to supremacy over the hearts and lives of men could not be expressed in stronger terms than those in which Jesus claims human allegiance. The only possible explanation of His attitude is that given by His own words, 'All things have been delivered unto me of my Father' (Mt 11[27], Lk 10[22]).

When we turn to the Fourth Gospel, we find this teaching expressed with a fulness and clearness of statement which ought not to appear extraordinary. There must surely have been an inner side to such a life as we find portrayed from the outside in the Synoptics. If the external accounts give so many indications of a unique relation to God, the revelation of the inner life of the wonderful Personality must display that relation with special clearness. What is truly extraordinary is that the inner history, as we have it in St. John's Gospel, does not reveal any essential element which cannot be found, expressed or implied, in the external histories (see above). And this is the more remarkable when we consider that the method and style of the Fourth Gospel contrast so strongly with those of the others.

From St. John we learn then to think of our Lord : (1) As One who came from God, with whom He was before, on a mission of mercy to mankind, Jn 3[11-14. 16. 17. 31ff.] 5[24. 30. 43] 6[29. 32. 33ff.] 6[2] 7[16. 28] etc. 8[23. 42] etc. 16[28ff.]. (2) As One whose relation to the Father is essential and unique, 3[13. 18. 34] 5[17. 18. 23. 26] 6[57] 8[16] 10[15. 38] 14[7. 11]. (3) As the only-begotten Son of God, 3[16. 18], and see 1[14. 18] (in v.[18] the stronger μονογενὴς θεὸς seems the better reading). (4) As with the Father from all eternity. This may be gathered from 8[58] 'Before Abraham was, I am,' and 17[5. 24] 'the glory which I had with thee before the world was,' 'Thou lovedst me before the foundation of the world.' These passages justify the extraordinary language of the Prologue (1[1. 2]), 'the Word was with God,' 'the same was in the beginning with God' (πρὸς τὸν θεόν). The ἐγὼ εἰμι of 8[58] certainly implies more than mere pre-existence. (5) As one with the Father : 'I and the Father are one' (10[30]) ; 'All things whatsoever the Father hath are mine' (16[15]) ; 'All things that are mine are thine, and thine are mine' (17[10]), etc. The ἕν (one) in 10[30] is very remarkable. It signifies *essence*, as distinguished from person, which would be εἷς. The force of it is greatly strengthened by its relation to the context. Our Lord is declaring His power to keep His people. He appeals to the Almighty power of God (v.[29]), identifying His own power with it and adding the explanation, 'I and the Father are one.' See also 5[17] 12[45] 14[7-10] etc.

This classification of passages enables us to pass along an ascending plane of thought to that great doctrine which is so comprehensively and yet so briefly expressed in the Prologue to the Gospel. We learn that the Evangelist intended us to gather that the conception of the Logos which is there presented is the true and necessary implication of our Lord's consciousness of Himself and His work in relation to God and the world.

II. The revelation of God in the Gospels.—

(i.) *THE FATHER.*—We must never forget that Christianity was built upon the foundation of Jewish monotheism. A long providential discipline had secured to the Jewish people their splendid heritage of faith in the One and Only God. 'Hear, O Israel, Jehovah our God is one Jehovah : and thou shalt love Jehovah thy God with all thine heart, and with all thy soul, and with all thy might' (Dt 6[4f.]). This was the corner-stone of the religion of Israel. These were perhaps the most familiar of all sacred words to the ears of the pious Jew. They were recited continually. Our Lord Himself had them frequently in His mind (Mt 22[37], Mk 12[29. 30], Lk 10[27]). That He thought of God always as the Supreme One is unquestionable. Indeed the very idea of Fatherhood, which, with our Lord, is the characteristic conception, and which is capable of being presented in a way which might weaken or injure a true monotheism, becomes in His teaching absolutely monotheistic because absolutely universal (see Mt 5[45. 48] 7[11] 8[11] 10[29], Lk 6[35] 13[29. 30] 15). To the Jewish mind, the sovereignty of God was the natural and characteristic thought. In our Lord's teaching the Divine Fatherhood overshadows and also transforms the Divine sovereignty, but never threatens to dissolve the pure and splendid monotheism of the original doctrine.

There are three degrees of the Divine Fatherhood presented in the teaching of our Lord : God is the universal Father (see reff. given above) ; He is, in a very intimate and special way, the Father of the disciples of Jesus (Mt 5[16] 6[1. 8. 9ff.] 7[11], Lk 12[32] etc.) ; He is, in the highest, and unique, sense, the Father of our Lord Jesus Christ (see above).

It is evident that our Lord makes a very clear distinction between His own Sonship and the relationship in which others, even the most faithful of disciples, stand towards God. Yet, in thus setting Himself apart as the Son of God, He was in truth providing that very element which was required to form a connecting link between the Divine and the human. The great danger of monotheism is its tendency towards a *transcendence* which removes man to an infinite distance : God and man seem to stand apart from one another in hopeless opposition. Such was the tendency of the Jewish conception in the time of our Lord. (See art. 'God (in NT)' by Dr. Sanday in Hastings' *DB*).

We find, then, that the teaching of our Lord and of the Gospels concerning God is the union of a true and unwavering monotheism with a great doctrine of mediation, according to which God and man enter into very close relationship in the Person of Jesus Christ, the Son of God.

(ii.) *THE SON.*—(1) *The Son is a distinct Person*

from the Father.—It is easy to complicate this question by a discussion of the meaning of the word 'personality.' The Latin word *persona* was chosen to represent the Greek ὑπόστασις, but neither the original nor its translation was adequate. To endeavour to minimize the difficulty of the traditional doctrine by recalling the primitive meaning of *persona* is surely vain. The truth is that the conception of personality, as we now understand it, did not enter into the thoughts of the ancients at all. They used the language which attached itself most easily to the new distinctions which the rise of Christian theology forced upon their attention, and, in doing so, laid the foundations of our modern philosophical and theological terminology. But the true force of their technical terms may be more accurately gauged by considering the meanings to which they tended, than by going back to meanings which they forsook. It is much better to interpret the Trinitarian doctrine with the help of the modern conception of personality than by means of the Latin word *persona* ; for if the connotation of the term has altered, its denotation is, in this case, the same, and the change of meaning was simply the inevitable development.

The truth of this will become evident when we turn from abstract doctrines and *a priori* arguments to the facts of the life of Christ as we have them in the Gospels. If any result has emerged from our examination it is this : the Personality of our Lord is the most distinct and the most concrete of which we have any knowledge. If His consciousness included elements which are outside the range of our experience, if His character combined qualities which do not coexist under ordinary human conditions, if there was an unexampled completeness about His moral and spiritual being, then all these great spiritual possessions belonged to His Ego, and therefore that Ego had a distinctness and concreteness surpassing any other human being who ever lived. To confuse the boundaries which give the Ego its distinctness, for the sake of making an abstract doctrine appear more intelligible, is surely a dangerous error. Our Lord was very man, and His Ego had all the self-possession and self-consciousness which give to every human soul its personal distinctness. While we find, in His self-revelation, that He constantly entered into a communion with God which is quite without parallel in human experience, and that He knew the heart of God from within, we also find Him ever distinguishing Himself as a Person from the Father. There is no trace anywhere of the breaking down of the boundaries of personal life. The Hebrew prophet was frequently impelled to speak as the mouthpiece of Jehovah, his personality seemed to dissolve, and the voice of Deity seemed to speak through his lips. So with the mystic, the individual being seems to vanish in the moment of insight, the human drop seems to blend with the ocean of Divinity. In the records of the inner life of our Lord will be found no sign of such experiences. His utterances reveal no displacement of the centre of personal life. He is always self-contained, even in Gethsemane.

This personal distinctness may be seen clearly in the following passages. They are among our Lord's greatest utterances : 'All things have been delivered unto me of my Father, and no one knoweth the Son save the Father,' etc. (Mt 11²⁷, Lk 10²²) ; 'The Son of Man shall come in the glory of his Father with his angels' (Mt 16²⁷) ; 'Whosoever shall be ashamed of me and of my words in this adulterous and sinful generation, the Son of Man also shall be ashamed of him, when he cometh in the glory of his Father with the holy angels' (Mk 8³⁸) ; 'Not what I will, but what thou wilt' (Mk 14³⁶) ; 'Father, into thy hands I commend my spirit' (Lk 23⁴⁶) ; 'My God, my God, why hast thou forsaken me?' (Mk 15³⁴) ; 'My Father worketh hitherto and I work' (Jn 5¹⁷) ; 'I and the Father are one' (10³⁰) ; 'I am the way, and the truth, and the life : no one cometh unto the Father but by me' (14⁶), etc. These examples are selected out of a great number. The Fourth Gospel is especially rich in such passages, and this fact is the more remarkable because it is the Gospel of Christian mysticism. In it we are taught to think of the great unities which are realized in Christ : 'Thou, Father, art in me, and I in thee, that they also may be one in us' ; 'I in them and thou in me, that they may be perfected into one' (17²¹·²³), etc. Yet St. John is very clear as to the distinctness of the Persons : 'The Logos was with God,' 'The same was in the beginning with God' (1¹·²). The phrase is remarkable, πρὸς τὸν θεόν. It signifies personal distinctness with active relationship. (Cf. 1 Jn 1² πρὸς τὸν πατέρα). We have already seen how emphatic this Evangelist is as to the humanity of our Lord. We now find him equally emphatic as to the true Personality. Yet he is our clearest teacher about the Divinity. Surely we must recognize, as the source of this extraordinary combination, the reality of the life and consciousness to which he testifies, the fact of Christ.

(2) *Organic relation of the Son to the Father.*— (*a*) *The subordination of the Son.*—This truth is presented everywhere in the teaching of our Lord. Though He speaks ever as One who enjoys a unique relation of intimacy with the Father, though He claims God as His own Father, yet it is clear that He was filled with reverence towards the Eternal Source of all things from whom His own being is derived.

Certain passages express this very distinctly : Mk 13³² 'Of that day and that hour knoweth no one, not even the angels in heaven, neither the Son, but the Father.' These words are usually considered in connexion with the doctrine of the *kenosis* (wh. see). But they are quite as important as a testimony to our Lord's consciousness of His own Divine Sonship. Here we find Him placing Himself above the angels in heaven, next to the Eternal Father, and the fact of His ignorance of the great secret noted as extraordinary. The truth is that the implications of this passage involve a Christology which agrees perfectly with the teaching of St. John. There is, however, the clear assertion of the subordination of the Son ; and even if His ignorance of the great day be-regarded as temporary, part of the limitation involved in His humiliation while on earth, none the less the assertion remains.

Secondly, especial mention may be made of Jn 14²⁸ 'The Father is greater than I.' As Coleridge observes (see *Table Talk*, 1st May 1823), these words, which have been used to supply an argument against the orthodox creed, contain, in truth, a very strong implication of our Lord's Divinity. For a mere man to say, 'God is greater than I,' would be monstrous or absurd. Comparison is possible only between things of the same nature. While, therefore, the assertion implies the Divinity, it is a direct statement of the filial subordination of the Son. It is remarkable that, in this statement, our Lord uses the emphatic 'I,' as in 8⁵⁸ (πρὶν Ἀβραὰμ γενέσθαι ἐγὼ εἰμί) and 10³⁰ (ἐγὼ καὶ ὁ πατήρ ἓν ἐσμεν). He does not say, 'the Son,' or, 'the Son of Man.' It is inadmissible, as Westcott points out, to suppose that He is speaking here otherwise than 'in the fulness of His indivisible Personality.' We cannot think that the statement refers merely to the human life of Christ on earth. 'The superior greatness of the Father must therefore be interpreted in regard to the absolute relations of the Father and the Son without violation of the one equal Godhead.' (See Westcott, *loc. cit.*, and Additional Note on 14²⁸).

(*b*) *The derivative nature of the Son's Divinity.*— We are left in no doubt as to what is the essential nature of this subordination. The Son derives His being, His knowledge, His power, His active life, at every moment, from the Father. For the detailed proof of this we are mainly dependent upon the Fourth Gospel. But here the range of passages which may be adduced is extraordinary.

'The Son can do nothing of himself' (Jn 5¹⁹) ; 'As the Father hath life in himself, even so gave he to the Son also to have life in himself' (v.²⁶) ; 'I can of myself do nothing' (v.³⁰) ; 'I am come down from heaven, not to do mine own will, but the will of him that sent me' (6³⁸) ; 'I do nothing of myself' (8²⁸) ; 'I spoke not from myself ; but the Father which sent me, he hath given me a commandment, what I should say and what I should speak' (12⁴⁹) ; 'The Father abiding in me doeth his works' (14¹⁰) ; 'Thou, Father, art in me, and I in thee' (17²¹).

(*c*) *The kenosis.*—It is this derivative nature of the Son's Divinity which helps us to realize that the limitations to which He submitted during His life on earth involved no breach of His Divine identity. Our ordinary experience teaches us that the limitation of our powers does not destroy our identity. If we shut our eyes, we impose upon ourselves voluntarily a limitation which, while it lasts, diminishes very considerably our hold upon reality ; yet we continue to be the same identical persons that we were before, and that we shall be again when the voluntary limitation has come to an end. But it is hard to imagine anything similar in the case of the Eternal Source of all being. All that is depends on Him, and any reduction or limitation of His power is inconceivable. Certainly that would seem to be the case, when we think of the Eternal Father. But surely it is different with the Eternal Son. His Divinity is derivative, dependent from moment to moment upon the Father : and therefore there is no difficulty in accepting what seems to be a necessary inference from the facts of the Gospel history, that, during our Lord's life on earth, there took place a limitation of the Divine effluence. Nor is it necessary to suppose that this limitation was always the same in extent or degree. Here may be the explanation of the awful cry, ' My God, my God, why hast thou forsaken me?' Such a view is not inconsistent with the declaration of St. Paul that 'it was the good pleasure of the Father that in him should all fulness dwell,' the whole $\pi\lambda\dot\eta\rho\omega\mu\alpha$ of the Deity (Col 1^{19}).

(d) *The Logos.*—For the use of this term in Christian theology we are indebted to St. John. It is a mark of the inner truth of the Fourth Gospel that nowhere is our Lord represented as using it ; for it is not in His manner, nor does it arise naturally out of the thought of the first age of Christian experience (but see Rev 19^{13}). It belongs essentially to the age of reflexion and philosophic construction. Yet the term was familiar to the minds of thinkers of various schools at the time. It was the means of drawing together the religious thought of Palestine and the philosophy of Alexandria. In the former, the *Memra* or Word of Jehovah was regarded as a *quasi*-personal Divine agency by which the Most High effects His purposes in the world. In the latter, the Logos is a personified abstraction, and must be connected with the Immanent Reason of Greek speculation, though sometimes conceived more concretely (by Philo) as executive power. (See Harnack, *Hist. of Dogma*, ch. ii. § 5, etc., and throughout, for further development of the Logos conception). See, further, art. LOGOS.

Both speculatively and historically the Incarnation is the starting-point for that course of thought which leads inevitably to the doctrine of the Blessed Trinity. As soon as Christian thinkers came to realize that the Christ is the Son of God as being the Incarnate Divine Logos, their thought was launched upon that vast speculation as to the nature of God, and especially as to the relation of the Son to the Father, which occupied the minds of theologians during the earlier centuries of Church history.

(iii.) *THE HOLY GHOST.*—For a general statement of the doctrine of the Holy Spirit the reader may be referred to art. HOLY SPIRIT in vol. i. and the corresponding art. in Hastings' *DB*. Here a briefer and more limited treatment must suffice.

(1) *The evidence of the Synoptic Gospels.* —The Gospels record a renewed activity of prophetic inspiration in connexion with the Advent of Christ. Of John the Baptist it was foretold, ' He shall be filled with the Holy Ghost, even from his mother's womb' (Lk 1^{15}). So we read (vv.$^{41.\,67}$) of Elisabeth and Zacharias, that, filled with the Spirit, they uttered prophetic language. See also Lk $2^{25.\,26.\,27.\,36}$. Again, the miraculous conception is ascribed to the operation of the Spirit (Lk 1^{35}, Mt $1^{18.\,20}$). Equally clear is the statement of the agency of the Holy Spirit at the Baptism of our Lord (Mk 1^{10}, Mt 3^{16}, Lk 3^{22}). As He entered upon His ministry, the Evangelists tell us that our Lord was guided by the Holy Spirit (Mk 1^{12}, Mt 4^1, Lk $4^{1.\,2.\,14.\,18}$). His miracles are performed in the Spirit (Mt 12^{28}). In His hour of most profound concentration upon the mystery of His own Person and work we are told, ' He rejoiced in the Holy Spirit' (Lk 10^{21}).

Our Lord's own teaching on this subject, as given in the Synoptics, recognizes the inspiration of the OT (Mk 12^{36}, Mt 22^{43}), and connects His own miraculous works (Mt 12^{28}) and His mission (Lk 4^{18}) with the agency of the Holy Spirit. Certain of His promises to His disciples can be fully understood only in the light of the teaching which we find in the Fourth Gospel. See Mt 10^{20}, Lk 11^{13} 12^{12} 24^{49}, Ac $1^{4.\,5.\,8}$. Perhaps, however, the strongest passage of all is that in which our Lord warns against the awful sin against the Holy Ghost (Mk 3^{29}, Mt 12^{32}, Lk 12^{10}). The intensity of our Lord's language here certainly points to the Deity of the Spirit. See, further, art. UNPARDONABLE SIN.

(2) *The evidence of the Fourth Gospel.*—Here the work of the Holy Spirit is frequently mentioned. He is the agent in the new birth (3^{5-8}); the living water (4^{14} 7^{39}) ; the Paraclete (14^{16}) ; the Spirit of truth (14^{17} 15^{26} 16^{13}), etc. In these and other passages the relation of the Holy Spirit to the Father and to the Son, and His agency in connexion with the work of God in the Church and the world, are presented with extraordinary impressiveness.

(3) *The Personality of the Holy Ghost.*—It is inevitable, owing to the very use of the ambiguous word $\pi\nu\epsilon\hat\upsilon\mu\alpha$, that in many cases it is impossible to be certain, from the mere language of the passages in which the word occurs or from their context, as to the nature of the agency to which reference is made. It is also necessary to remember that the personification of abstractions may be carried to great lengths when the conception of personality is indefinite, as it certainly was among the ancients, at least to a far greater degree than at present. It would, therefore, be a mistake to infer the Personality of the Holy Spirit from the mere use of language concerning Him which seems to imply it. Such language must be understood in relation to the whole Christian revelation and its interpretation in terms of thought. Yet the language is very strong and very definite. ' I will pray the Father, and he shall give you another Paraclete, that he may be with you for ever ; even the Spirit of truth' ($14^{16.\,17}$). The Spirit is here indicated as 'another,' One who is to take the place of our Lord Himself as His substitute. Also He is ὁ παράκλητος, τὸ πνεῦμα τὸ ἅγιον (v.^{26}). The masculine form of the word is certainly used to impress upon the disciples the truth that the Presence which is to take the place of that to which they had been accustomed is no less a Personal Presence than the other. And this view is strengthened by the repeated and emphatic ἐκεῖνος : ' he shall teach you' (v.^{26}) ; ' he shall bear witness' (15^{26}) ; ' he, when he is come, will convict . . .' (16^8) ; ' he shall guide you . . .' (v.^{13}) ; ' he shall glorify me' (v.^{14}). Not merely the language, strong and emphatic as it undoubtedly is, but the whole argument demands the doctrine of the Personality of the Spirit.

This group of passages also shows very clearly that we are here taught to think of the Spirit as not only personal, but as distinct from the Father and the Son. This appears remarkably in 14^{26} ' The Paraclete, the Holy Spirit, whom the Father will send in my name, he shall teach you all things, and bring to your remembrance all that I said unto you.' Again in 15^{26} ' Whom I will send unto you from the Father, even the Spirit of truth which proceedeth from the Father, he shall bear witness of me.' Language could not make the distinctness of the Persons clearer. Yet strong and clear as this teaching is, we find its strength and clearness greatly increased by the fact that it fits into the scheme of Christian thought as we find that scheme developing in the Epistles of St. Paul and taking more rounded dogmatic form in the later ages of Christian reflexion.

(4) The Divinity of the Holy Ghost.—We can have no doubt on this subject when we have reached the point at which we attain the conviction that, in His great discourse, our Lord teaches us unmistakably the Personality of the Spirit as distinct from that of the Father and of the Son. The Three Persons are here viewed upon a plane of being which is above that of all created things.

In Jn 14¹⁶⁻¹⁸· ²⁶ 15²⁶ 16¹⁴· ¹⁵ the inter-relationship of the Divine Three is expressed and implied. The dependence of both the Son and the Holy Ghost upon the Father appears : 'I will pray the Father, and he shall give you another Paraclete.' The Spirit 'proceeds' from the Father and is sent by the Son (15²⁶ 16⁷). His presence is equivalent to the presence of the Son, for with reference to His coming, our Lord declares (14¹⁸), 'I will not leave you desolate : I come unto you.' In His relation to the Son, the Spirit is to bring all our Lord's words to the remembrance of the disciples (v.²⁶); He is to bear witness of our Lord (15²⁶), to glorify Him (16¹⁴), etc. So important is the work of the Spirit in its connexion with that of the Son, that our Lord solemnly declares the expediency of His own departure in order that the period of the Spirit's activity may begin. And to this teaching we must add such statements as the following : 'He that hath seen me hath seen the Father' (14⁹); 'I am in the Father, and the Father in me' (v.¹⁰); 'If a man love me, he will keep my word : and my Father will love him, and we will come unto him, and make our abode with him' (v.²³); 'All things whatsoever the Father hath are mine, therefore said I, that he (i.e. the Spirit) taketh of mine and shall declare it unto you' (16¹⁵). All these refer to the nature and effects of that dispensation of the Spirit concerning which our Lord is instructing His disciples in this great discourse.

Such teaching certainly implies both the Divinity and the Unity of the Three Persons, which throughout are at once distinguished, regarded as inseparably united, and placed upon a plane of being far above all created existence.

III. Summary.—(i.) *THE BAPTISMAL FORMULA.*—We have omitted from our consideration one great passage of first-rate importance on every branch of our subject. It has been kept to the last because it is the nearest thing to a comprehensive and formal statement of the doctrine of the Trinity to be found in Holy Scripture. In Mt 28¹⁸⁻²⁰ there is, as the last word of that Gospel, a solemn charge which it is stated our Lord gave to His disciples when they met Him, by His special command, after His resurrection. The charge includes : (1) a declaration of *His universal authority*, 'All authority hath been given unto me in heaven and in earth,' containing a very strong implication of His Divinity and agreeing with Mt 11²⁷ and Lk 10²² as well as with the teaching of the Fourth Gospel. (2) *A great commission*, 'Go ye therefore and make disciples of all the nations, baptizing them into the name of the Father and of the Son and of the Holy Ghost ; teaching them to observe all things whatsoever I have commanded you,'— words which are at once the greatest command, the greatest prophecy, and the greatest dogmatic statement ever given. (3) *A promise*, 'Lo, I am with you alway, even unto the end of the world,' which has been a source of power and inspiration to the Church ever since.

It is true that this passage belongs to a part of St. Matthew's Gospel which has been assailed with great persistence, and, on internal grounds, with some apparent reason. It is often argued that the First Gospel contains many additions to the Evangelic narrative which arose from the habits of thought and practice, as well as from explanatory teaching, current in the primitive Church. The account of baptism given here would then be a reflexion of the teaching of a later time. Against this, we have to note that there is no textual evidence against the passage, that 2 Co 13¹⁴ contains the threefold Divine name in a way which shows that the combination was familiar to the mind of the Christian Church at a time which was certainly less than thirty years after the Ascension, and that there is a continuous stream of testimony from the earliest times as to baptism into the threefold name, the *Didache* providing the connecting link between the Apostolic age and Justin Martyr. But stronger than all these is the fact that this passage merely sums up the teachings concerning God which, as we have seen in detail, may be found scattered throughout the four Gospels. It is surely somewhat hard to suppose that the Christian doctrine of God could have so rapidly assumed the form in which we find it in St. Paul's Epistles, if our Lord Himself had not brought together the various strands of His teaching ; and when was

this so likely to happen as when He manifested Himself to His disciples after His resurrection? The truth is that this passage in Mt. supplies exactly the clue we need in order to understand the rapid development of doctrine and the continuity of custom in the early Church. (See Sanday in art. 'God' in Hastings' *DB* ii. p. 213, and his *Criticism of the Fourth Gospel*, p. 218 ; also Scott in art. 'Trinity' in *DB*, Ext. Vol. p. 313). But there is this further proof of genuineness, that the language here possesses all the power, concentration, and authority which are everywhere the marks of the true sayings of Jesus. There is not a word in this utterance, from ἰδοὺ, to αἰῶνος, which has not been, in all ages, a source of life to the Church. Here the meaning of the life, death, and teaching of the Son of God is translated into a language which appeals to the minds and hearts of all ages of human history, and this in the most Jewish of the Gospels. Moreover, the prophecy here contained is on too large a scale to have arisen naturally out of the life of the Christian community of the 1st century. Not even to St. Paul was granted so wide an outlook upon the history of mankind. This great vision of a world-wide Christianity belongs to the mind of Him who spoke of the Grain of Mustard Seed and the Draw-Net, and taught His disciples to pray, 'Thy kingdom come.'

We may, unless our judgments are obscured by critical prejudices, turn to this passage as supplying the needful summary of all those thoughts about God which we have gleaned from the teaching of Christ and the Gospels. The expression εἰς τὸ ὄνομα is important : Christian Baptism is to be 'into the name.' The phrase recalls the language of the OT in which the 'Name' of God stood for Himself as revealed or brought into relation to men. So the name *Jehovah* was the sign or mark of the old covenant. Can we fail to gather that the name which marks the new covenant is that of Father, Son, and Holy Ghost? In this name is contained the revelation of God which Christ brought to man. It must also be observed that the word is singular, τὸ ὄνομα, suggesting the unity of the Godhead. The name is threefold, yet it is *one*.

The doctrine of the Trinity is, then, the summing up of the teaching concerning God which is contained or implied in the Christian revelation. It is not a philosophic construction. It is not the outcome of abstract discussion upon the Being and attributes of God. In its origin it had nothing to do with logical or dialectical methods, nor did it arise out of the efforts of the understanding. Its source is simply the fact of Christ Himself. That amazing and, to the merely scientific intelligence, most mysterious fact, which still, after so many centuries, presents to mankind the old question, 'Who say ye that I am?' is the revelation of the Trinity. Jesus Christ manifests God as Father, Son, and Holy Ghost.

(ii.) *THE ILLUMINATING POWER OF THE DOCTRINE.*—When from the position which has now been attained we look back over the life and teaching of our Lord, we find that sudden light is thrown upon much that otherwise seems obscure. It is this reflex illumination of Christian experience which constitutes the verification of the doctrine— a verification which may be traced throughout the whole history of the Church, and which to this day may be discerned in the vitality of orthodox Christianity and its continued value for the religious consciousness of mankind in contrast with Deism in all its forms. Here we confine our brief survey to the Gospels, and note the following. At the Annunciation the angel replies to the Virgin's question (Lk 1³⁵) : 'The Holy Ghost shall come upon thee, and the power of the Most High shall overshadow thee : wherefore also that which is to be born shall be called holy, the Son of God.' At the Baptism the three Divine Persons are represented : 'He saw the heavens rent asunder and the Spirit as a dove descending upon him ; and a voice came out of the heavens, Thou art my beloved Son, in thee I am well pleased' (Mk 1¹⁰· ¹¹, also Mt 3¹⁶· ¹⁷, Lk 3²¹· ²²). At the Transfiguration the glory of the Son and His relation to the Father are manifested (Mk 9⁷, Mt 17⁵, Lk 9³⁵).

But more profound even than such indications as these is the truth that the doctrine of the Trinity underlies the whole movement of Divine providence for the redemption and elevation of man as we have it presented in the NT. Here it is sufficient to note that everywhere in the Gospels, while God the Father is regarded as the ultimate source of all things, both in creation and in redemption, certain special functions are declared to belong to the Son and the Spirit, and yet there is no separation or opposition between the Divine Persons. God the Father is the Creator, yet all things were made by (διά) the Logos, καὶ χωρὶς αὐτοῦ ἐγένετο οὐδὲ ἓν ὃ γέγονεν (Jn 1³). Redemption is the work of the Son : 'The Son of Man came to seek and to save that which was lost' (Lk 19¹⁰). He came 'to give his life a ransom for many' (Mk 10⁴⁵, Mt 20²⁸). He is the Shepherd seeking the lost sheep (Lk 15³⁻⁷). But the love which surrounds the sinner from his birth, which remains constant throughout his life of sin, and which receives him into a perfect reconciliation on his repentance, is the love of the Father (Lk 15¹¹ff.). Further, the salvation which is the result of the death of Christ is everywhere presented as the work of God Himself. Thus is the love of God revealed in Christ, and assurance as regards God's mind and will towards us attained. The unity of the Divine Persons is the underlying truth of the Atonement. So again, the works of Christ are 'in the Spirit' (Mt 12²⁸), and the Spirit is called by Christ 'the Spirit of your Father' (Mt 10²⁰). The Son is the means of communication between man and the Father (Mt 11²⁷, Lk 10²², Jn 14⁶ etc.), yet the Spirit is the source of the life which makes this communication possible (Jn 3³⁻⁸). Further, the Spirit is the gift of the Father (Lk 11¹³), and none can come to the Son unless the Father draw him (Jn 6⁴⁴). It is sufficient to point out, finally, how closely interrelated are the functions of the Three Persons as described in Jn 14–16. The coming of the Paraclete is identified with a coming of the Son (14¹⁸), and the coming of the Son with a coming of the Father (vv.⁹,²³). His office is to carry on the work of the Son, which is the work of the Father (16¹⁴,¹⁵), in the Church (14¹⁷ff. etc.) and in the world (16⁸) after the departure of the Son. It is commonly said that the characteristic work of the Father is creation, of the Son redemption, of the Holy Ghost sanctification. The distinction is certainly Scriptural, and yet there is no one of these works in which each of the Divine Persons has not a share. The Trinity in Unity is, to use the old-fashioned language, both ontological and economical.

And all this has its counterpart in the Christian experience of our own time, for Christianity is, for the Church and for the individual, the revelation of the Fatherhood of God through and in that Christ who presents Himself afresh to every age as the manifestation of the love of God, and whose personal influence, in some mysterious manner, survives every shock of revolution as well as the slow movement of the ages.

(iii.) *THE PHILOSOPHICAL ASPECT.* — This is not the place to consider the great question as to how far the doctrine of the Trinity can commend itself to, or be justified by, the philosophical reason of mankind. The problem is as old as Christian theology, and is latent in all discussions which touch the life of the Christian creed. If it has not been greatly canvassed, at least directly, in recent times, it is because all the resources of Christian thought have been devoted to a work which has been in truth more pressing, the endeavour to grasp more firmly and to realize more perfectly the facts to which the Scriptures testify, the elements of the great revelation upon which the doctrine depends. When the time for full discussion comes, there is at least a probability that the general mind will be prepared. The old objection that the doctrine is apparently contradictory, that it cannot be made logically consistent, is certainly losing its plausibility. All the lines of thought which have guided so many in the direction of Agnosticism have converged upon this : that there must be an element of mystery in the nature of God. The old Deistic conception of a solitary Sovereign in the skies, standing above and apart from creation, is now impossible for the instructed. The doctrine of the Trinity stands in truth midway between Agnosticism and Deism. With the former it recognizes the impossibility of presenting to our minds the inmost nature of the Supreme One, with the latter it insists upon the absolute necessity of thinking of the Deity in terms of personality. But it keeps closer than either to the facts of the religious consciousness and the needs of humanity, because it builds upon actual experience, the experience which stands central in the history of the race, and it interprets this experience by means of the only perfect Personality known to man.

In addition to this general consideration, there are tendencies in recent thought which seem to promise new light on the old doctrine. Philosophy and psychology have both been dealing with the question of personality, and have been revealing the existence of problems of extraordinary complexity and suggestiveness in connexion with it. For both, human personality appears, from one point of view, as a self-sufficing unity, and, from another, as an illuminated portion of a vast world of spiritual existence. It is both inclusive and exclusive, both universal and limited, according to the way in which it is regarded, and no principle has yet come to light by means of which these oppositions can be shown to be overcome.

The more usual way of approaching the application of the principle of personality to the doctrine of the Trinity is to follow the line indicated by Lotze (*Microcosmos*, bk. ix. ch. iv.) and regard personality as it exists in man as incomplete, perfect personality belonging to God only. If this conception be justifiable, we may well expect to be able to apply an ancient method and find that distinctions which we know to exist in man's personality may be correctly regarded as corresponding to distinctions of a much profounder degree in the Divine Being. The best modern exposition of this view is Illingworth's *Personality, Human and Divine*, a work which may justly be regarded as representing for our time the classic point of view, that of St. Augustine in his *de Trinitate*.

The difficulty which is inherent in this method was, however, clearly seen by Augustine himself, and it cannot be said that modern philosophers have been able to surmount it successfully. Regarding the distinctions in the Godhead as corresponding to the three, 'memory, understanding, love,' which we know of in ourselves, he yet perceives that 'Tria ista . . . mea sunt, non sua ; nec sibi sed mihi agunt quod agunt, nec ego per illa,' and again, 'Ego per omnia illa tria memini, ego intelligo, ego diligo, qui nec memoria sum, nec intelligentia, nec dilectio, sed hæc habeo. Ista ergo dici possunt ab una persona quæ habet hæc tria, non ipsa est hæc tria' (*de Trinitate*, bk. xv. ch. xxii. § 42). Nor can it be said that Augustine or any of his successors in this great adventure, not even Hegel in his *Philosophy of Religion*, has been able to show how what in us is only the attribute, faculty, or thought of a *persona*, can become a *Persona* in the Deity.

There is, however, another line of thought in recent philosophy, which seems to the writer to promise much better results for the Christian thinker. Out of the Hegelian school have arisen some who, feeling the force of certain considerations relied on by Agnostic reasoners, hold that the nature of the Ultimate Reality is beyond us, our highest categories and our most concrete experiences being inadequate alike to express or to present it. In addition to this, there has been slowly gaining recognition the importance of the conception of *degrees of reality*. Bradley in his *Appearance and Reality* has done more than any other writer to call attention to this principle. Foe to theology, as he professes to be, he may prove its most useful ally. The work of Pringle-Pattison points in the same direction. Personality may be, for human thought, the highest of all categories ; but the existence of certain fundamental antinomies and oppositions, speculative and practical, proves clearly that it is not the ultimate form of being. There is a degree of Reality, a final Unity, higher, more concrete, than Personality. There must be, because a person is, after all, essentially one among many. A person is what he is, not merely because he is inclusive as regards his own experience, but because he is exclusive as regards his neighbours' experience. Personality cannot therefore be a full definition of the Divine nature. God is personal and something more. In His final Unity He is super-personal, and this super-personal unity is the ultimate Reality, concrete and universal. Here is exactly the condition demanded by the Christian doctrine of the Trinity. The most complete monotheism is compatible with the recognition of a personal multiplicity in the Godhead.

LITERATURE. — Bull, *Defensio Fidei Nicœnœ* ; Waterland, *Vindication of Christ's Divinity*, and other works ; Dorner, *Syst. of Christ. Doctrine*, and *Hist. of the Development of the Doctrine of the Person of Christ* ; Pearson, *On the Creed* ; H. Browne, *Exposition of the Articles* ; Swete, *The Apostles' Creed* ; Martensen, *Dogmatik* ; Works on *NT Theology* by Schmid, Weiss, Oosterzee, and Beyschlag ; Liddon, *Divinity of our Lord* ; Gore, *The Incarnation, and Dissertations* ; Scott, art. 'Trinity' in Hastings' *DB* (Ext. Vol.) ; Sanday, art. 'God (in NT),' *ib.* (vol. ii.) ; art. 'Trinität' in *PRE* ; Chadwick, *Christ bearing witness to Himself* ; Forrest, *The Christ of History and of Experience* ; R. H. Hutton, *Theol. Essays*, Essay on 'The Incarnation and Principles of Evidence' ; Knight and Martineau, *Inter Amicos* ; Armstrong, *The Trinity and the Incarnation* (from the Unitarian point of view ; see also Martineau, *Seat of Authority in Religion*). On the philosophical side, Hegel, *Philosophy of Religion*, must not be forgotten. Among recent books, Illingworth's *Personality Human and Divine*, Rashdall's *Doctrine and Development*, and the present writer's *Idealism and Theology*, endeavour to deal with aspects of the question. The subject has not been treated systematically by recent writers. CHARLES F. D'ARCY.

TRUMPET.—The sole mention of the trumpet in the Gospels occurs in Mt.'s version of the small apocalypse which has been incorporated in the eschatological discourse of Jesus. There (Mt 24[31]) we read that when the Son of Man comes in the clouds for the final judgment, He despatches His angels 'with a loud trumpet' to gather His elect from the four corners of the earth. The context, especially in Mt., is a Jewish-Christian application of the older Messianic tradition (cf. *e.g.* Is 27[13], Zec 2[10] [LXX]) which depicted the scattered members of Israel being summoned together by a trumpet-blast at the Messiah's advent. The figure was natural, for the trumpet-blast denoted the approach of majesty. 'Power, whether spiritual or physical, is the meaning of the trumpet : and so, well used by Handel in his approaches to the Deity' (Fitzgerald's *Letters*, i. 92). It was a favourite figure of John Knox, too, as Stevenson has noted (in *Men and Books*). But it is rather as a rallying summons than as a herald of royalty or even an awakener of sleepers, that the trumpet is employed as a pictorial detail in the passage before us. The writer does not develop the sketch. We are not told who blows the trumpet, though possibly the angels were meant. St. Paul seems to reflect, in 1 Th 4[16], the tradition which connected it with the archangel Michael, but Mt. merely inserts the realistic trait, owing to his characteristic love of Hebrew Messianic prophecy.*

* Wellhausen argues that as 'the trumpet is singular, it cannot be connected with the angels, but must be posited as a separate unit.' This seems prosaic. 'Trumpet' may have been

LITERATURE.—See Huhn's *Messianischen Weissagungen* (§ 45). Volz's *Jüdische Eschatologie* (1903, § 45*b*) ; Bousset's *Antichrist* (Eng. tr. pp. 247, 248), and the same author's *Die Religion des Judentums* (1903, p. 224 f.) ; also Haupt's *Die eschatolog. Aussagen Jesu* (1895, pp. 116 f., 128 f.).

JAMES MOFFATT.

TRUST.—That personal trust is the innermost essence of the faith that God requires, is almost universally recognized by Protestant theologians. Only in rare instances may one still meet with the pronounced intellectualistic view which regards faith as the assent to a sum of doctrines. On the other hand, one may note here and there a tendency towards the opposite extreme—to ascribe a value to faith as a subjective state without special regard to the reality of its ground and content. But the one view is as un-Evangelical and un-Biblical as the other.

When Bellarmin (*de Justif.* i. 4) declares : 'hæretici fidem *fiduciam* esse definiunt ; Catholici fidem *in intellectu* sedem habere volunt,' he states accurately enough the fundamental distinction between the Catholic and the Evangelical conception of faith, and yet in his discussion he betrays a fatal misapprehension concerning the latter. Protestants do define faith as *fiducia* (trust) ; but this is not a bare and empty trust —the *inanis hæreticorum fiducia* against which the Council of Trent impertinently protested. A trust that is merely subjective is indeed groundless and empty, and therefore worse than worthless (cf. 1 Co 15[2. 17-20]). Faith has no value *per se* ; its value lies solely in its object. If the object is unreal, the faith is vanity. Or if the object, though real, is not strong enough to bear up him that trusts himself to it, his confidence can bring him only loss. It is not enough that a man believes ; the vital question is, *whom* he believes. We may not divide men into the two classes : those who believe and those who do not. For in varying degrees of confidence all men believe (trust). He who doubts God, believes men or the spirit of this world. Confidence in any object other than God, who alone has power over sin and death, could not in any case have saving value. And even so our faith would not be 'saving,' unless God freely purposed to save. And man, though free in the act of faith, is utterly unable to produce it of himself. Only the revelation of His grace can call forth and ground faith in God. Any possible confidence toward God not grounded in the revelation of His purpose is not faith, but presumption.

When it is said that Christian faith is personal trust in God in and through Jesus Christ, one need not conclude that 'faith' and 'trust' are exactly equivalent terms. The thought is only that the deepest essence of faith is trust, and that there is no Christian faith that is not personal trust in God. An examination, however, of the passages in the NT in which these words occur will clearly show that even here—to say nothing of later ecclesiastical usage—faith, *formally regarded*, is the more comprehensive term.

'Two factors (*Momente*) are to be distinguished in faith, one relating to the object, the knowledge of God mediated through Christ, the other relating to the state of the subject, the trust in salvation resting upon Christ. But the two cannot be separated from each other, since the Christian knowledge of God arises only in and with the trust in salvation. To the distinction between these two sides of faith correspond the two formulæ *fides quæ creditur* = the content of faith, and *fides qua creditur* = the attitude of faith. Only it should be kept in mind that the content of faith consists primarily not in a theologically formulated doctrine, but in the immediate beholding and understanding of the saving revelation itself' (Kirn, art. 'Glaube' in *PRE* [3]).

It is accordingly unwarrantable to speak of 'a purely intellectual faith in God.' The mere holding a doctrine to be true is not faith at all. Earlier dogmaticians divided the function of faith into three acts : *notitia*, knowledge, instruction in the facts and doctrines of Christianity ; *assensus*, assent to the teaching ; *fiducia*, personal trust. This view, however, is misleading ; for faith, however many aspects it may have, is yet an integral thing, not formed by the synthesis of several acts. And

'*notitia* and *assensus* have nothing to do with religious faith except as they are included in the *fiducia*. That saving trust

meant to denote 'trumpet-blast,' as indeed the gloss φωνῆς suggests. We should rather conjecture that μετὰ σάλπιγγος μεγάλης, preceded by καί, originally stood after δόξης πολλῆς, which would give a better order.

does not arise without the hearing of the message of salvation ($\dot{\alpha}\varkappa o \acute{\eta}$, Ro 10[17]) is self-evident and undisputed. On the other hand, the *assensus*, as the sure persuasion of the power of Christ as Redeemer and of the reality of the God who is above the world, is brought about only in and with the *fiducia*. . . . Only this one thing must remain unobscured, that the right and proper answer of man to the saving revelation that comes to him is the *fiducia*, and that out of it grows all certainty and knowledge of God and Divine things' (Kirn).

Some, again, have attempted to draw a positive distinction between faith and trust, regarding faith as the receiving from God, and trust as the yielding of self to God. The essential characteristic of faith is indeed receptivity ; but it is a mistake to suppose that the trustful yielding of self to God is anything more or other than the opening of the heart and life to His influence and control through the overmastering revelation of the grace of Christ. In other words, even the trustful devotion of self to God remains at bottom a receiving from God.

The attempt has been made (cf. esp. E. W. Mayer, *Das christliche Gottvertrauen und der Glaube an Christus*, 1899) to show that while Christ, according to the NT, is the object of 'faith,' only God is the object of the full 'trust' of the Christian. As Jesus, the Christ, revealing in word and deed the Father's holy love, bears the offer of salvation to men, so through their faith in His revelation He brings men to the Father in trust. Trust in God is the consequence of faith in Christ. But can this view be consistently maintained ? Faith in Christ—not as Prophet merely, but as the Bearer of salvation—is justified only as we have ground for the assurance that in Him God is dealing with us. So then faith in Christ *is* trust in the Father, and trust in the Father as revealed in Christ is also trust in the Son, the Bearer of salvation (Jn 14[1ff.]). Certain it is that the writers of the NT saw in Christ more than Teacher and Example. Even as their exalted Lord He continued to be a personal Helper.

So long as the revelation of God's grace was not yet complete in the sending forth of His Son and then of the Spirit of His Son (Gal 4[4. 6]), faith could not rise to its full measure. Before Christ the full conception of faith could not be reached. The word 'trust' occurs frequently in the Psalms and not seldom in certain other OT books. It does not, however, signify the perfect fellowship of the child of God, but only a reliance upon God's faithfulness. The predominant idea in the trust of the OT was *hope*. There were heroes of faith before Christ, but their faith could not be perfect, for they had not received the object of their hope (He 11[39. 40]). In Christ the filial disposition is established (cf. *e.g.* 1[1ff.]). And so fundamental and all-comprehensive was His work as Mediator of the New Covenant that He could be truly called 'the author and perfecter of faith' (12[2]). Only as men know God in Christ can they know what faith in its full sense is. The life of faith is communion with God in and through Christ, and the nerve of that communion is personal trust. Christian trust is reliance upon God, but not upon 'God out of Christ.' Neither can it be reliance upon Jesus except as the essential revelation of the Father.

Not unknown in Church history is a view of the redemptorial work of Christ which would make it consist in appeasing an angry God. According to this view Christ and not the Father is the Reconciler, God and not the world is reconciled. In such a case perfect childlike trust is not to be thought of. There would be no firm ground for it. If God has once changed His purpose, why should He not do so again ? Only where God is manifest in Christ as the Reconciler of the world (2 Co 5[19]) can there be perfect security for time and eternity. Where Christ is thought of as having wrought a change in the will of God, men will with wavering hope implore Him to intercede with God on their behalf, and will perhaps also invoke the aid of many saints. Perfect assurance is not to be reached by this road.

Only as we have the Son do we have the Father

(Jn 14[6ff.], 1 Jn 2[23. 24]), but we have the Son only because of the Father's love (Jn 3[16]). Jesus knows the Father, and He teaches us to know Him. His life is the glorious example of trust in the Father's love. But it is not through the contagious example of the 'inner life' of Jesus that men are led into perfect filial trust. He promised His disciples a perfect joy, which no one should take away (16[20-24]), but this was to come only after He should have been glorified. God's boundless love for sinners must first be manifested in the cross of Christ (Ro 5[8] 8[32]). Yet even Christ's dying and rising again on our behalf (2 Co 5[15]) is not the final proof of God's love. God has also sent forth the Spirit of His Son into our hearts (Gal 4[6], Ro 8[14ff.]). The gift of the Spirit means the reality of communion in prayer, and the Spirit's work in us is the pledge of our complete salvation at last (cf. *e.g.* Ro 8[26], 2 Co 5[5]). To be rooted and grounded in the love of God, that one may be strengthened to know that love which passeth knowledge (Eph 3[17ff.]) ; to know and have believed the love which God hath in us (1 Jn 4[16]) ; and to keep ourselves in the love of God (Jude v.[21])—this is the meaning of Christian trust.

Since the sovereign grace of God manifested in Jesus Christ is the only ground of our assurance, we must place no confidence in the flesh (Ph 3[3ff.]). The seed of Abraham or of Israel may not trust in this relation (Mt 3[9], Jn 8[33ff.], Ro 2[28. 29], Gal 3[28. 29]). Nor may we trust in works of righteousness (*e.g.* Ro 3[19ff.], Eph 2[9], Tit 3[5]), or in our good purpose, effort, or zeal (*e.g.* Ro 9[16] 10[6ff.], Ph 3[6]). Even the confession of Christ and the profession of faith will avail nothing without the vital union with Him in the faith that works by love (Mt 7[21ff.], Ja 2[14ff.], 1 Co 10[1-13], Rev 3[1]). Moreover, not even what men call a good conscience can give security (1 Co 4[3. 4], 1 Jn 1[8ff.]). The wondrous fact of fellowship in the love of God is indeed a token of the life of God in us. And whereinsoever our heart condemn us, we shall obtain assurance in the way of sincere obedience to the Spirit of love. God is greater than our heart.—He can pardon and heal. And when by His grace our heart is set free from self-condemnation, our communion with God may be unbroken.

Upon the immovable foundation of the reconciliation of the world in Christ (2 Co 5[14ff.]) the individual appropriates to himself the promise by faith. Thereby he experiences a present grace and rejoices in the sure hope of the glory of God (Ro 5[1. 2]). Because he has the earnest of the Spirit—because God's love has been shed abroad in his heart—he can even glory in tribulations (5[3-5], cf. 12[12]). Even bearing the cross and being crucified with Christ are his joy and glory (Gal 2[20] 6[14], Ph 3[8ff.]). Out of the richness of the grace of this fellowship he can know that all things work together for his good, that is, for his salvation, and he is persuaded that nothing can separate him from the love of God which is in Christ. There is no power that can gainsay the loving will of the eternal God (Ro 8[18-39]). In every condition he proves the sufficiency of Christ's grace (*e.g.* 2 Co 12[9]), and by prayer and supplication finds that God's peace, far surpassing all understanding of men, keeps guard over his heart and thoughts in Christ Jesus (Ph 4[6. 7]). Through faith he is kept in a hope sure and steadfast unto the final salvation which awaits him (*e.g.* 1 P 1[3ff.]). But the sureness of the hope does not work carelessness. 'Every one that hath this hope set on him purifieth himself even as he is pure' (1 Jn 3[3]). The true believer is 'careful without care.' Moreover, the grace of our fellowship works zeal in service (1 Co 15[10]). Only the Christian can enjoy perfect freedom from anxious care in order that he may devote himself fully to the work which God has given him. The past is under the blood and the future is secure in the promises of God (Tholuck). And because he sees in Christ the grand purpose of God in the redemption of the world and the security for the final accomplishment of that purpose, he cannot despair of the world any more than he can despair of himself. Because he knows the grace of Christ he can gladly accept his own lot in life, and 'in the patience of hope and the labour of love' serve and wait and watch (Lk 12[35. 36], 2 Co 5[9. 10]).

Christian trust is a state of heart; yet it has seemed better to lay stress upon its ground and essential significance than upon its psychological aspects. Christian joy and peace are effects of a power beyond ourselves. Only God can give them. It is our part to make sure of our union with Christ, and then to see that we receive not the grace of God in vain (2 Co 6[1]). The full realization of the meaning of Christ's promise of peace is not to be had at once. It is the goal of the path of trust. But if there is established the relation of such confidence in God that all our weaknesses, doubts, fears, and sins drive us to our sure Helper, the goal of perfect peace will surely be reached at last (cf. Mt 11[28-30], He 4[16]).

LITERATURE.—The art. FAITH is presupposed throughout, and also that of Dr. Warfield in Hastings' *DB.* See also Drummond, *Pax Vobiscum*; Herrmann, *Faith and Morals*, and *The Communion of the Christian with God*; Kähler, *Zur Lehre von der Versöhnung*, and *Der Lebendige Gott*; J. G. Tasker, 'Trust in God and Faith in Christ' in *ExpT* xi. [1900] 490.

J. R. VAN PELT.

TRUTH.—Apart from the adverbial phrases 'of a truth' (Mk 12[32], Lk 4[25]) and 'truly' (*e.g.* Mk 14[70], Lk 9[27] 12[44]), which are used in their ordinary colloquial sense (cf. Dalman, *Words of Jesus*, p. 227), the only occurrence of this term in the Synoptic Gospels is in the hypocritical address of the Pharisees and Herodians to Jesus (Mt 22[16], Mk 12[14], Lk 20[21]), where these *soi-disant* inquirers compliment Him on His sincerity as a teacher. Here loyalty to the truth is opposed to the disingenuous spirit that allows itself to be swayed by fear or flattery. The impression made by Jesus on His opponents was one of fearless honesty and candour; He was no casuist or time-server, and it was His recognized character of religious frankness and veracity which suggested their trap. For all His sympathies, they knew He would be straightforward. They could count upon His telling dangerous and unpleasant truths, no matter what His word might cost Him. He had the courage without which truthfulness is impossible, and these Jews were cunning enough to trade upon His very virtues.

In the Fourth Gospel, however, 'truth' is used in a special, pregnant sense, characteristic of the writer and of his age. It is one of the leading categories or themes of the book, and its proportions, as well as its perspective, are entirely different from anything in the Synoptics. Occasionally, no doubt, the ordinary sense of the term occurs, as in the phrases about true witness (5[31. 32] 21[24]), or credible statements (8[14]); here, as elsewhere, the word means no more than veracity, and its adjective represents 'trustworthy' (cf. 10[41] with 7[18] 8[16f. 40. 46] and 16[7]). In Pilate's remark, 'Truth! what is truth?' (18[38]), however, we are on the way to a more definite conception. There is, no doubt, in this scene the implied censure of a false attitude to truth, as Cowper has pointed out.—

' But what is truth? 'Twas Pilate's question put
To Truth itself, that deigned him no reply.
And wherefore? will not God impart His light
To them that ask it?—Freely—'tis His joy,
His glory and His nature, to impart.
But to the proud, uncandid, insincere,
Or negligent inquirer, not a spark.'

(*Task*, bk. iii. l. 270).

Truth, in this passage, however, has the further connotation of speculative or abstract knowledge, and the majority of the references throughout the Gospel are tinged by such associations. They converge on the principle that the spiritual is the real, and that the truth of human life is attainable only in relation to Christ, who is at once the true Life of God and the true means whereby men appropriate that Divine and absolute nature.

Two small linguistic problems lie at the threshold of any attempt to investigate the meaning of 'truth' in the Fourth Gospel. (*a*) Attempts have been made, notably by Wendt (*e.g.* in *SK*, 1883, p. 511 f., and *Teaching of Jesus*, i. p. 259 f.), to read ἀλήθεια as equivalent to 'faithfulness' or 'rectitude,' on the analogy of the LXX rendering (ἔλεος καὶ ἀλήθεια) for the Hebrew original of 'grace and truth.' Certainly, in 1[14. 17], the OT antithesis is unmistakable. But, apart from the fact that χάρις is substituted for ἔλεος, the author is evidently using 'truth' here in a deeper and special meaning of his own. The general usage of the term throughout the Gospel, whether as applied to God or man, cannot be explained by 'faithfulness' or 'righteous conduct,' any more than by mere 'veracity.' Even where the OT form of expression is retained, the content and the substance of the thought are extended and intensified. (*b*) A cognate difficulty is occasioned by the use of two adjectives, ἀληθής and ἀληθινός, in connexion with ἀλήθεια (see *ExpT* xv. [1904] 505, xvi. 42-43). No rigid distinction can be drawn between them in the Gospel (note the variant in 8[16]), as if they were equivalent precisely to *verax* and *verus*. The latter may be translated 'true,' in the sense of *real*, as opposed to what is counterfeit (1[51]) or transient and inadequate (1[9] 6[32. 51]); but often what is *true*, in the sense of veracious and sincere, is thereby substantial, the sole reality amid the shadows of falsehood, just as God, who is *true* (cf. Field, *ON* iii. p. 104), as opposed to deceptive and disappointing idols, is also *real*, in the sense of being living and lasting. Hence ἀληθής (8[26]) and ἀληθινός (7[28]) are applied equally to God (cf. 3[33]), as the Father who has sent the Son, while the former adjective is used (*e.g.* in 6[55]) where the latter, in the sense of *real* or genuine, would have been equally appropriate (cf. 6[32] 1[9]).

Truth, in this specific sense, forms one of the *nuclei* of the Fourth Gospel. It is equivalent either to the knowledge of God's being and will, or to the Divine being and will itself; in other words, it represents the higher and heavenly reality of things, transcendent and absolute, and corresponds generally to light (cf. 1[8] and 5[33]) in its sphere and functions. Like the light, however, the truth is not an abstract entity, much less an intellectual system, to the author, but this Divine reality as manifested in the incarnate Logos, as revealed in the Son. He is the Truth (14[6]); He and it are identified (cf. 8[32. 36]). All else is transitory and unsubstantial. Whatever appears to compete with this truth is either counterfeit or merely relative. Jesus, as the perfect Son of God, is the final and adequate embodiment of God's saving will; and the common term for that heavenly nature, in relation to man's errors and ignorance, is *the truth*. But the errors and ignorance against which it has to struggle are moral rather than intellectual. It is truth to be *done* (3[21]), not speculation to be understood. The prerequisite for coming to the light of the Logos is a sound moral disposition, faithfulness to the light of conscience, and genuine sincerity of thought and deed. Such is the point pressed by the author of this Gospel. He was surrounded by a world which included earnest seekers for the truth (cf. 12[20ff.]) and so-called 'philosophers' or religious theorists, in Judaism and paganism, who refused to accept the Christian estimate of Jesus, and probably preferred Gnostic presentations of communion with God. To meet both of these contemporary currents, he states his conception of Christ as the Truth. With that Christ all truly sincere souls have an affinity, which, if allowed to develop naturally, will bring them into touch with Him. On the other hand, the objections to Christ, often paraded on intellectual grounds, are run back to moral defects, and failure to see the reality of God in Christ is attributed to some unreality of human character.

The roots of this unique conception may partly be found in Philo, but ultimately they run back to

Platonism and the later Stoicism (cf. Grill, p. 204f.), while even Egyptian theology had crowned the god Thoth with the attribute αἰὲν ἀληθής of the Logos (cf. Reitzenstein, *Zwei religionsgesch. Fragen*, pp. 56, 80 f.). But the distinctive usage of the Fourth Gospel lies in its correlation of this conception with the historic personality of Jesus Christ. The Asiatic-Greek audience for which the book was immediately composed, learnt that He was a king of truth (18[36]), instead of being king of some realm whose Jewish Messianic associations failed to impress Hellenic readers. This was a timely presentation of the Gospel. It was a reading of Christ's personality which could not fail to commend itself to those for whom the more local and national associations of Judaism, or of Jewish Christianity, had lost much, if not all, of their interest and appeal. Hence the emphasis on the two realms of truth and falsehood, or of reality and unreality, which, like the cognate antithesis of light and darkness, helps to body forth the moral dualism of the Gospel. The opposition of men to Christ as the Logos is referred to their connexion with the realm of the devil (8[40f.]), whose hereditary policy is hatred of the Divine truth. The author does not speculate on any fall of the devil, nor does he discuss the origin of this cosmic feud; he is content to trace it through history, in the practical experience of mankind. Truth and falsehood, reality and unreality, light and darkness, are set in juxtaposition. His Christ is a King of Truth. 'He reigns as Himself holy and true, by the power of the truth which He reveals —truth in the conscience, truth in the heart, and truth in the mind—and over those who, through His grace and spirit, have become fundamentally true; who stand in the eternal, abiding relationship of peace and love and holiness towards God' (Reith, *The Gospel of John*, ii. p. 138). The contrast between this and the realm of falsehood and unreality is moral, rather than metaphysical, for the writer, though the metaphysical basis is plain.

Hence there is a distinction between the witness borne to the truth by John the Baptist (5[33]) and that borne by Christ (8[40] 18[37]). The former passage (where 'the truth' is meant to cover more than its ordinary sense, although the language of the latter is employed) is in the line of 1[7f. 19f.]. But when Jesus is said to bear witness to the truth, or to tell the truth, it is in the sense that He bears witness to Himself (8[14]) as the Truth. His whole Person and work are an adequate revelation of the Father's inner being. To see Him is to see the Father. His witness, therefore, consists in what may be termed His loyalty to Himself, and His devotion to that vocation of being true to God's will for which He became incarnate, and from which no fear of death could deter Him (cf. Lidgett, *The Spiritual Principle of the Atonement*, p. 24 f.). A further line of witness to the truth of God is afforded by those who accept the revelation of Christ (3[33]). Their adhesion to the truth affords to the world fresh evidence of the truth's power; they, as it were, accredit the transcendent purpose of God by their obedience to it as the moral ideal of their life. This is indicated already in the Prologue by the words 'we beheld . . . we have all received.' Finally, there is the living witness of the Spirit of Truth (see below) in the Church, which, unlike the so-called Gnostic revelations of fresh knowledge, is ever loyal to the historical personality of Christ, and aims consistently at glorifying, instead of obscuring or diminishing, the vital significance of His life for the human soul.

This note is struck loudly and clearly at the very outset, in the Prologue: 'And the Logos became flesh and dwelt among us. And we beheld his glory, glory as of the only begotten from the

Father, full of grace and truth. . . . For of his fulness we have all received, even grace upon grace. For the law was given through Moses: grace and truth came through Jesus Christ' (Jn 1[14. 16. 17]). Here, just as the conception of the Truth is subordinated to that of the Way in 14[5. 6], the aspect of grace controls that of truth. Religion, in this definition, is not the arduous aspiration of man's soul, stretching up wistfully to communion with God, but the gracious revelation of God to men through the Person of Jesus Christ; the initiative is on God's side; and the Divine nature, in its absolute reality, is mediated for the soul by Christ alone, not by any number of theosophic æons. All that either the OT economy or contemporary Gnosticism could offer the soul was a partial disclosure of God's inner being. Time-honoured and plausible as rival methods might be, they were at best imperfect. The full revelation was in Christ as the Logos or Son of God *par excellence*, the Truth of God, and therefore of man, amid shadows and appearances. He is the revealer, or rather the revelation Himself. His personality is the sum and substance of that Divine essence which He alone can communicate in all its fulness to believing men, and through which men realize themselves fully. He is the true way to life. The author emphasizes this central and primary conception on two lines. Not only does he change the 'mercy' of the Gr. OT into 'grace,'—a change which is all the more significant that this great Pauline term never recurs in the Gospel,—but the companion idea of *truth* (cf. Ex 34[6]) is expanded from faithfulness or veracity to what a modern might describe as the absolute character of the Divine Being, an inner, heavenly reality, or rather the Reality, which Christ alone (1[18]) could disclose. The 'truth' of God is thus neither information to be gained, nor dogmas to be supernaturally revealed, but is at once personal and full of initiative. It is God Himself manifesting His essential life to the faith and need of man. As Maurice once put it, 'Truth must be a person seeking us, if we are to seek him.'

While this mission and ministry of the truth have reached their climax in the brief earthly life of Jesus, the latter phase was only its final, not its first manifestation. Like the Light, the Truth has been in the world prior to its absolute revelation and embodiment in Christ the Logos (3[20. 21]). In all ages, and from all quarters (cf. 18[37]), Christ draws to Himself those who *practise the truth*. In the OT and elsewhere (Jos 2[14] [LXX], Ps-Sol 17[17] with ἔλεος, cf. Ps 83[12]) this phrase means simply to deal truly or to act sincerely, according to the context. The author of this Gospel, however, follows his usual method of putting into such phrases a deeper and specific content, so that here it denotes rather the active exercise and practical manifestation by good people of what corresponds to God's real character. To *practise the truth* is a synonym for doing works *in God* (3[21]). This is independent of nationality. It is also evidently intended to cover the pre-Christian era; or rather, according to this Gospel, the history of humanity, prior to the coming of Christ, was not wholly out of touch with the true Spirit and Life of God (1[5. 9]). The present passage, taken along with a remark like that of 18[37] ('every one that is of the truth heareth my voice'), suggests a view of paganism similar to that of Ro 2[12f.] Furthermore, it implies that men grasp this 'truth' of God by the exercise of their entire moral nature. The reality of God, as Spirit and as Personal Life, cannot be known except by real men, by those whose character is real to the core. The conditions of that personal knowledge are singleness of mind, purity of conscience, and openness of heart. It is the exercise of these that brings a man into permanent touch with the reality of the Divine nature as manifested in Christ. The *locus classicus* for this profound conception is 7^{17}; although the term 'truth' does not occur there, the identification of disinterestedness and candour with the genuine spirit of truth (cf. 7^{18}) shows that the idea was in the writer's mind.

This inwardness, with its corollary of freedom from national or local cults, is brought out with especial clearness in the well-known definition of Christian worship ($4^{23.\ 24}$), where *truth* is associated with spirit. In contrast to external and ritual worship, the genuine worshipper must approach God inwardly; it is like to like, as in 3^{21}. The spiritual is the inward, the real. As God's nature is such, His worshippers must correspond to Him; and if worship is offered *in the spirit*, it is thereby genuine. A similar antithesis to the symbolic and unsubstantial worship of the OT underlies 17^{17-19}, where *truth*, in a certain abstract sense, denotes the eternal reality of the Divine nature as revealed to men, the ideal or truth of life realized in Christ, and, through Him, in His people. By His consecration or devotion of Himself to the fulfilment of this purpose of revelation, Christ makes it possible for His disciples to be consecrated to God's service—a consecration which, as the double meaning of the term allows, implies personal purification from sin. Negatively, the vocation is equivalent to a deliverance from the stains and illusions of the transient world, which is superior to the OT ritual. Positively, it denotes an adherence to the cause of God. His name and His truth are the same. They represent the reality of the Divine revelation in Christ, with the twofold antithesis, running through the entire Gospel, between this final revelation and the inadequate OT religion on the one hand, and contemporary philosophic or theosophic speculations about truth on the other.

A further application of this freedom, inherent in the absolute and inward character of the Christian revelation, occurs in the debate (cf. Peyton, *Memorabilia of Jesus*, p. 446 f.) between Jesus and the Jews in $8^{31f.}$—a passage which reproduces the great Pauline ideas of Gal 3^7–5^{13}, although redemption as usual is included under the aspect of revelation, rather than *vice versa*. The effects of truth, when received by men, are here described summarily as *freedom* ($8^{32f.}$). The argument is this. As the Father seeks true worshippers, whose note is spirituality, so the Son seeks true disciples, whose characteristic is loyal adherence to His teaching, *i.e.* to Himself (cf. $8^{32.\ 36}$) as the revelation of the Father. Adherence or obedience of this kind yields a knowledge of God's real nature; it initiates men into the true purpose and mind of the Father, and invests them with the Divine nature itself (17^3). Their knowledge, that is to say, is not a process of abstract learning. There is no intellectualism about it. It is not a mastery of theosophic principles or subtle theories, but participation in a personal Life. And contact with this brings a verve and independence into life, a simplicity and a reality, a freedom from bondage and legalism, which can be attained only by a nature whose capacities are set free to realize themselves fully. In another aspect, freedom may be considered as deliverance from sin; although such a reference is not excluded even in 8^{32}, it is definitely suggested in 17^{19}, where participation in the Divine life is made to involve personal purification, through the death of Christ. 'What men needed was to be sanctified, that is, to be consecrated to God. It was not in their power—surely no reason can be conceived for this, but that which lies in their sin —to consecrate themselves, and what they were not able to do for themselves Christ did for them

in His own person. He consecrated Himself to God in His death' (Denney, *The Death of Christ*, p. 269).

A third aspect of this inward and absolute knowledge of God in Christ is presented in the conception of the Spirit or Paraclete throughout the closing chapters (14–17). Considered under the category of a liberating power, these references to the function of the Spirit of Truth (which, it is curious to recollect, were applied to Mohammed by Mohammedan divines) may be defined as a presentation of the liberating effect of the truth, as opposed to traditional and antiquarian views of Jesus which, even within the Church, might restrict the full appreciation of His Person. The author had to meet a twofold danger, and he chose to state his new conception of Christ and Christianity in the form of a Gospel, not of a treatise or an Epistle. One reason for this, as he suggests in the sayings reproduced in 15^{26} and 16^{13}, is his heartfelt conviction that the Person of Christ is the sum and substance of the Divine revelation, and that no fresh statements or progressive views, such as those promulgated by Cerinthus and other Gnostics, are authoritative unless they represent elements already present by implication in the words and works of the incarnate Logos. The deeper interpretation of Christ, with which he came forward to meet the requirement of a later age, is none other than a fresh discovery of latent truths in Christ. The influence of the Spirit on the consciousness of the Church is not directed to the manufacture of independent oracles or to the task of striking out original additions to the revelation of Christ, which would render the latter, in any sense, superfluous or inferior. The test of all such new interpretations is their loyalty to the historic manifestation of the Logos. The *Spirit of Truth*, bestowed by Christ upon His Church ($14^{16f.}$), recalls to the mind of all true disciples the bearing and meaning of Christ's own teachings; 'he shall bear witness of me . . . he shall guide you into all the truth (for a different reading in Jerome, etc., cf. Nestle's *Einführung* [2], p. 98), for he shall not speak from himself . . . he shall glorify me, for he shall take of mine, and shall declare it unto you' (cf. Bruce, *The Training of the Twelve*, pp. 376 f., 418 f.). This great definition of the right and limitations of true freedom of movement within the Christian consciousness, safeguards it alike against the abuses of Gnostic speculation and the disinclination to advance beyond the Jewish-Christian, or rigidly Messianic, interpretation of Christ's Person which had been promulgated by the first generation of the disciples. To *know Christ after the flesh* was far from exhausting the significance of His Person. His Spirit, *i.e.* His living presence in the Christian Church and consciousness, had still more to unfold of truth and grace. Hence one privilege of being in contact with this 'Truth,' as embodied in Christ, is that disciples, no longer in touch with the earthly Jesus, are fitted to adapt it to varying conditions, to see it in ever fresh bearings, and to apply it with inexhaustible power, while at the same time they preserve its essential meaning. Their training in it, so far from involving any disloyalty to it, is a part of their fidelity to its principles.

'They who follow the Spirit's guidance will not receive an illumination enabling them to dispense with truth, but the enablement to lay hold of truth. . . . On the one hand, the Truth given in Christ will need from age to age His expounding to unlock its stores; and, on the other hand, the faith in Him and His office in the present shall never loosen men from the Gospel given once for all, or draw them away from the eternal Father, by enabling any voice born only of the present to seem wholly Divine. Standing fast in the unchanging Truth, and an endless progress in taking knowledge of it shall be indissolubly united' (Hort, *The Way, the Truth, and the Life*, p. 58 f.).

Thus, while the author carefully and stringently safeguards the future revelations of religious truth by limiting them to the sphere of the historical Logos, he contemplates fresh advances in the apprehension of Christ (16¹³), just as he does in the practical extension of the Church (17²⁰). Revelations in the future, and of the future, fall within the scope of the Spirit of Truth. The latter is not fettered by the past. This prophetic function of the Spirit may seem rather one-sided (so Beyschlag, *NT Theol.* i. 282) as compared with its ethical presentation in Paul. But it is in line with the Synoptic tradition, where the Spirit is primarily, if not entirely, a spirit of witness ; while the other, more ethical aspect, is at least suggested in the context (cf. 14¹⁶. ¹⁷). The *truth* or reality of the Divine life, at any rate, includes the future (cf. Ps 25⁵ [LXX]) ; as indeed it must, if God's purpose is a developing plan throughout history and experience, and if this truth or reality is personal. For as a personality is *ex hypothesi* full of resources and surprises, the richer is its life. Its spirit must be a perennial self-expression, conditioned only by the receptive powers of men. Consequently the aim of the Fourth Gospel, in these allusions to the progressive witness of the Spirit of Truth, in the future and of the future, is to prevent loyalty to the historic essence of Christianity from degenerating into stagnant adherence to an institution or a creed. What Jesus said, as Cyprian used to insist, was : ' I am *the Truth*,' not, ' I am *Tradition*.' Christ is God's last Word to the world. But, as the writer strikingly implies in the phrase, ' The Spirit shall guide you into all the truth,' the full interpretation of that Word was not attained by the primitive generation of the disciples. They had no monopoly of it. ' Most friends of truth,' said Vinet, ' love it as Frederick the Great loved music. It used to be said of him that, strictly speaking, he was not fond of music but of the flute, and not indeed fond of the flute but of his flute.' It is to prevent any religious aberration of this kind that such words of the Fourth Gospel are put forward. They express the spirit of Christ's revelation, which cannot be held by a trivial or narrow life, any more than it can be selfishly grasped or adequately weighed by the most advanced age of Christendom.

LITERATURE.—The conception of truth in the Fourth Gospel is handled by all the editors, notably by Westcott and Oscar Holtzmann. Besides the special essays of Wendt (see above) and Rüling (*NKZ*, 1895, 625 f.), see Schrenck's *Die johann. Anschauung vom Leben* (1898), p. 86 f. ; J. Grill, *Untersuchungen über die Entstehung des vierten Evang.* (1902) pp. 201–206 ; E. A. Abbott, *Johannine Vocabulary* (1703, 1727) ; V. H. Stanton in Hastings' *DB* iv. 816–820 ; Cheyne in *EBi* 5217–5219 ; Weiss, *NT Theol.* (Eng. tr.) ii. § 147 ; H. J. Holtzmann, *NT Theol.* ii. p. 375 f. ; Hort, *The Way, the Truth, and the Life* (1894), p. 41 f. ; Du Bose, *Soteriology of NT*, pp. 291 f., 297 f. ; R. H. Hutton, *Theological Essays* (p. 18 f.) ; Phillips Brooks, *The Influence of Jesus* (p. 142 f.) ; E. F. Scott, *The Fourth Gospel*, 253 ff.

JAMES MOFFATT.

TURNING. — 1. The Gospel terms. — In EV of the Gospels the vbs. ' turn,' ' convert ' represent no fewer than 8 different Gr. words. The ordinary terms, and the ones we have almost exclusively to do with in the following article, are στρέφω and ἐπιστρέφω (whence ἐπιστροφή, ' conversion,' in Ac 15³). In addition to these we find (each, however, used only once in the Gospels) ἀποστρέφω (Mt 5⁴²), ὑποστρέφω (Lk 2⁴⁵), ἀναχωρέω (Mt 2²²), ἀνακάμπτω (Lk 10⁶), ἀποβαίνω (21¹³), γίνομαι (Jn 16²⁰)—all associated with the idea of turning, and rendered by ' turn ' either in AV or RV.

(1) *Literal turning.*—Both στρέφω and ἐπιστρέφω are used in this sense. Once στρέφω occurs transitively, where Jesus bids His disciples, when smitten on the right cheek, turn the other to the smiter (Mt 5³⁹). Both vbs. frequently occur in the passive form, but with a reflexive or middle meaning, to denote the turning of oneself round. Usually it is Jesus Himself who thus turns round (στραφείς,

ἐπιστραφείς), to look for someone (*e.g.* Mk 5³⁰, Lk 22⁶¹), or to address some pointed word to those who follow (*e.g.* Mt 16²³, Lk 9⁵⁵).

(2) *Figurative or spiritual turning.*—In this sense both στρέφω and ἐπιστρέφω are employed, but the former only once (Mt 18³). The noun ἐπιστροφή, corresponding to ἐπιστρέφω in its spiritual sense, does not occur in the Gospels, and is found only in Ac 15³. Both in the Gospels and elsewhere in the NT the AV frequently renders these vbs., when they denote a spiritual turning, by ' **convert,**' and in Ac 15³ it renders ἐπιστροφή by ' **conversion.**' RV retains ' conversion ' in the last-mentioned passage, and ' convert ' in Ja 5¹⁹. ²⁰ (where the vb. is active and transitive—' convert a sinner ') ; but otherwise it has substituted ' turn ' for ' convert '— a wise course, in view of the fact that in modern religious speech ' conversion ' has come to be used in a conventional sense that does not always correspond to the meaning of the original. In another important respect the RV has corrected a wrong impression produced by the AV renderings. The latter, through the influence of the Vulg. (*convertor*), not only uses the vb. ' convert,' but renders the reflexive στρέφεσθαι, ἐπιστρέφεσθαι as if they were genuine passives, and instead of ' turn ' has ' be converted.' A still more glaring mistranslation appears in the quotation from Is 6¹⁰ [LXX] given in Mt 13¹⁵, Jn 12⁴⁰, Ac 28²⁷ (cf. Mk 4¹²). In Is 6¹⁰ AV, correctly enough, has ' lest they convert '— ' convert ' in the time of King James being used intransitively. But in the NT passages, though the Gr. vb., except in Jn 12⁴⁰, is in the active form, just as in the LXX, the ' convert ' of Isaiah is changed into ' be converted.' Both in the last-mentioned passages and in those cases in which, in accordance with the ordinary usage, the vbs. though passive in form are certainly reflexive in meaning, RV has changed the ' be converted ' of AV into ' turn ' (see Mt 13¹⁵ 18³, Mk 4¹², Lk 22³², Jn 12⁴⁰, Ac 3¹⁹ 28²⁷). It is with this spiritual turning or ' conversion ' that we shall be occupied in the remainder of the article.

2. The NT facts.—(1) So far as *the term* ' turn ' or ' convert ' is concerned, the Gospels can hardly be said to afford sufficient data for a doctrine of conversion in the modern sense of the word. In Mt 13¹⁵, Mk 4¹², Jn 12⁴⁰ an OT prophecy (Is 6¹⁰) is referred to ; but both in its original use and its NT application it is a national rather than an individual turning that is meant. Again, the notable passage, Mt 18³ ' Except ye turn, and become as little children,' etc., though often taken as a fundamental utterance of our Lord on the subject of conversion, can hardly be used for this purpose when read in the light of the context. For it was addressed directly to the Twelve at a time long subsequent to their call to the Apostolate ; and, with the exception of Judas, who will venture to say that the Apostles at this period were ' unconverted ' men ? Moreover, the turning which Jesus demanded of them was not that absolute turning from sin in order to follow Himself which the word ' conversion ' is used to denote, but a turning from those foolish, unworthy ambitions which had just prompted the question, ' Who is the greatest in the kingdom of heaven ? ' (v.¹), and a recognition of the truth that in God's Kingdom humility is the real badge of greatness. Similarly, when our Lord says to Peter, ' When once thou hast turned again (AV ' When thou art converted '), stablish thy brethren ' (Lk 22³²), it seems evident that the Apostle did not lack conversion in the technical meaning of the word, but that he was being summoned beforehand to a fresh and more devoted return to his Master's service after his fall.

When we pass to Acts, however, we do find ἐπιστρέφω and ἐπιστροφή in a sense that corresponds to the familiar use of the term 'conversion.' When St. Peter, preaching to the multitude in Solomon's Porch, says, 'Repent ye therefore, and turn again, that your sins may be blotted out' (Ac 3[19]), the turning he demands is unquestionably the kind of turning that conversion implies. When it is said of the inhabitants of Lydda that they 'turned to the Lord' (9[35]), it is their conversion that is referred to. So likewise at Antioch, when 'a great number that believed turned unto the Lord' (11[21]); and when Paul and Barnabas preached to the people of Lystra that they should 'turn from these vain things unto the living God' (14[15]); and again when the same Apostles passed through Phœnicia and Samaria 'declaring the conversion of the Gentiles,' and causing great joy unto all the brethren (15[3]; see, further, v.[19] 26[18. 20]).

In the Epistles the use of the figure of turning to denote the great spiritual change that constitutes a man a Christian is infrequent; but we have it in 2 Co 3[16], and notably in 1 Th 1[9] 'How ye turned unto God from idols, to serve a living and true God.' And this use of the word 'turn,' we must remember, was not only a natural figure to denote a great spiritual transformation, but one that was especially familiar to every pious Jew. The prophetic writings are full of it. And nowhere, whether in the OT or the NT, is there a finer expression of the idea than in the words of Deutero-Isaiah : 'Let the wicked forsake his way, and the unrighteous man his thoughts : and let him return unto the Lord, and he will have mercy upon him ; and to our God, for he will abundantly pardon' (Is 55[7]; cf. 6[10], Ps 51[13], Jer 3[14], Ezk 33[11], Hos 12[6], Jl 2[12f.], Zec 1[3f.]).

(2) But we are not confined to the terms for 'turning' in the NT, in seeking there for the fact of conversion. *The reality itself* is constantly in evidence. In the ministry of our Lord Himself we have manifest cases of conversion in the sinful woman in the house of Simon the Pharisee (Lk 7[47ff.]), in Zacchæus the publican of Jericho (19[8ff.]), in the penitent robber on the cross (23[42. 43]). The parable of the Prodigal Son (15[11ff.]), who 'came to himself' and then returned to his father, is a parable of conversion. And what are those great appeals that Jesus constantly makes—for a taking up of the cross in order to follow Him (Mt 16[24] ||), for a willingness to lose one's life in order to find it (10[39] 16[25] 18[8. 9]), for a 'hating' of one's dearest friends in order to be His disciple (Lk 14[26])—but a demand for conversion, even though the figure of turning is not employed?

In the story of the Apostolic Church, again, we have constant illustrations of the great spiritual change—the 3000 souls brought into the Church on the day of Pentecost (Ac 2[41]), and those who thereafter were added to them day by day (v.[47]); the results that everywhere followed the preaching of the word, whether by the lips of evangelists (8[5. 6. 12] 11[21. 24]) or Apostles (9[35] 10[44] 14[1] etc.); the striking individual cases of the Ethiopian eunuch (8[37]), Cornelius (10[44ff.] 11[18]), Lydia of Thyatira (16[14f.]), and the jailer of Philippi (v.[30ff.]). Above all, we have the case of St. Paul himself—the most typical and remarkable example the world has ever seen of that complete and conscious turning of the soul which we name conversion (9[3ff.] 22[6ff.] 26[12ff.]).

(3) Once more, the fact of conversion is brought before us in *the teaching of the Epistles*, and above all in the Pauline Epistles, by the employment of other figures than that of turning. For it is evidently conversion that is described by the putting off of the old man and the putting on of the new (Col 3[9]), by the transition from a world of darkness to a kingdom of light (Ro 13[12], Eph 5[8], Col 1[13], 1 Jn 1[7] 2[8]), by the ideas of a crucifixion of the old

self (Ro 6[6]), an awaking out of sleep (Eph 5[14]), and even a rising from the dead with a view to walking in newness of life (*ib.*, Ro 6[4]). This last figure of a rising from the dead reminds us how near conversion as a forthputting of the human will approaches to regeneration as an act of the Divine Spirit, and so brings us to consider the subject in its larger doctrinal relations.

3. The Christian doctrine.—Properly speaking, conversion as we use the word is a modern and popular rather than a Scriptural or theological term ; but, while its inexactness leads sometimes to its being misapplied, it is nevertheless a convenient word to denote the conscious side of that great change by which a man becomes a Christian. In dwelling further on it we may think (1) of its essential nature ; (2) of its particular contents ; and (3) of its types or modes.

(1) *The essential nature of conversion.*—There is a very frequent misconception, according to which conversion is thought of as a passive experience rather than an active energizing of the human will. We have often heard it said, for example, that someone 'has got converted.' Most, if not all, of the blame for this incorrect use of the word must be laid at the door of the AV, with its ' be converted' instead of 'turn.' The Greek lends no support to the idea of a passive conversion. If we except Ja 5[19. 20] (where the reference is to the action, not of the Divine power, but of the human preacher or teacher who mediates the message of salvation), there is not a single case in the NT where the word for turning or conversion is so employed as to suggest that something is wrought upon a man from without. Always it is an act of the man himself that is so described ; the turning is a self-turning, a human and moral, not a supernatural and metaphysical change.

This, of course, is not to deny that there are other figures in the NT which represent the process of becoming a Christian as something that is carried through by the operation of a Divine power. The new birth (Jn 3[3ff.]), the new creation (2 Co 5[17], Gal 6[15]), the washing of regeneration and renewing of the Holy Ghost (Tit 3[5]), all point to another side of the matter. But what we have to notice here is that, as distinguished from regeneration, conversion at all events is always represented as a work and a duty the full responsibility for which is laid upon man.

When we come to consider the precise relations between conversion and regeneration, we pass into a difficult region where questions are raised which, as Professor Laidlaw has said, it has been the habit of theologians to avoid. 'Reformed theology presents no reasoned connexion between regeneration in the stricter sense and conversion with its fruits' (*Bib. Doct. of Man*, 266). And for lack of a reasoned and definite theory, or even of a careful study of the NT teaching, the figure of regeneration has very commonly been overworked, while the moral side of the change involved in becoming a Christian has been neglected. But, while it is Scriptural to say that when a man becomes a Christian a mysterious Divine work has been effected within him, it is equally Scriptural to say (and Scripture says it much oftener) that we become Christians by our own free choice, and that the power of deciding whether we are to be Christ's disciples or not rests with ourselves. Thus we are brought face to face with the larger problem of the relation between human freedom and the Divine will, and can only say here that in the NT regeneration and conversion come before us as one and the same process, looked at from the Divine and the human side respectively, but looked at as essentially a moral rather than a metaphysical change. Men are born of the Spirit, but they must turn if they are to enter into the Kingdom of God. 'This my son was dead, and is alive again,' exclaimed the father of the Prodigal, for he recognized a miracle of Divine grace in his son's return. But that heavenly mystery had its human counterpart, that miracle of grace its moral coefficient; for the Prodigal had turned away from the swine-trough, 'and he arose and came to his father.' See, further, art. RE-GENERATION.

(2) *The particular elements of conversion.*—When we analyze conversion, two elements show themselves; for two moments are involved in every act of turning: there is a turning *from* and a turning *to.* Christian conversion is a turning from self, the world, and sin; and a turning to God in Christ. But these are just the two moral acts which in the NT are commonly designated by the names 'repentance' and 'faith.' And so it seems proper to say that repentance and faith are the elements that go to make up conversion. And this is confirmed when we find that in the record of the Apostolic preaching conversion or turning is associated with repentance on the one hand and faith on the other. 'Repent ye therefore, and turn again' is the point to which St. Peter brings his sermon in Solomon's Porch (Ac 3[19]); and St. Paul's claim, as he stands before King Agrippa, is that he has declared alike to Jew and Gentile 'that they should repent and turn to God' (26[20]). On the other hand, we read of the Greeks of Antioch that 'a great number that believed turned unto the Lord' (11[21]). Corresponding again with this separate presentation of the two sides of conversion, is the fact that St. Paul combines the two when he says to the elders of the Ephesian Church, as he sums up his ministry among them, that both to Jews and Greeks his testimony has been this: 'repentance toward God, and faith toward our Lord Jesus Christ' (Ac 20[21]). Much has been written on the question whether in conversion repentance comes before faith, or faith before repentance. From the point of view of theory it is a somewhat barren discussion; and when we come to practice, the fact appears to be that in the conscious experience of the soul faith rises into more immediate prominence in some cases and repentance in others. But what is of importance is to note that in conversion both are inextricably joined together in the unity of a complex but single moral act.

(3) *The modes or types of conversion.*—(*a*) Two strongly contrasted types meet us in the NT and in the whole history of Christian experience. The one is marked by deep contrition for sin—contrition that amounts in some cases to a positive agony of mental distress. From the other the element of pain and contrition is almost wholly absent; it consists in a joyful and unclouded acceptance of the love of God as revealed in the face of Jesus Christ. St. Paul and the jailer of Philippi are representatives of the *violent and painful* type of conversion—reproduced in the later history of the Church in the experience of such men as Augustine and Bunyan. Cornelius, the Ethiopian eunuch, and Lydia 'the seller of purple,' may stand, perhaps, for the *gentler and simply trustful* type—forerunners of multitudes like them in every subsequent age. Theologically the difference between these two types might be accounted for by saying that as repentance and faith are the two elements that go to make up conversion, in the one case repentance is more prominent, and in the other faith. For while it is true that repentance is primarily a change of mind, and is not to be confounded with the mere feeling of sorrow on account of sin, yet repentance is at all events that side of conversion which represents the soul's backward and downward look, just as faith is the aspect of it in which the soul looks forward and upward. And so contrition for the sorrowful past, even while it must be distinguished from true repentance, is yet in certain cases its very natural accompaniment. The full explanation, however, of the differences between these two types of conversion must be sought from psychology rather than theology, in the field of experience and not in that of doctrinal theory. They are due for the most part to diversities in natural temperament, in personal history, in religious education, and especially in the prevailing atmosphere of religious thought and belief. Professor Henry Drummond, remarking on the fact that in his wide experience as an evangelist he had never met with conversions of the agonizing type so common in an earlier generation, once raised the question whether the Holy Spirit may not in these days have changed His *modus operandi.* The question is startling; but considered in the light of Jn 16[13] it may have the kernel of truth in it. For the Holy Spirit has led the Church of our time into new and larger views regarding the revelation of God in Christ; and the comparative infrequency of a once familiar type of conversion is probably due to the fact that, without surrendering their belief in the reality and heinousness of sin, both the Christian evangelist and his hearers have gained a better understanding of all that is involved in the Fatherhood of God and the grace of our Lord Jesus Christ.

(*b*) Two other well-known and strongly contrasted types are those of *sudden* and *gradual* or, as it is sometimes called, *nurtural* conversion. Of the former the NT affords numerous examples; indeed, nearly all the NT conversions are evidently sudden in their mode. It does not follow, however, that we should take this to be the ordinary, much less the only legitimate type. In NT times it lay in the nature of the case that conversion should be sudden. The gospel made its appeal at first to those who had grown up in a world ruled by principles the very opposite of those of the Divine Kingdom, and the transition from either Judaism or paganism to Christianity was bound to be of the nature of an absolute and sudden break. And such conversions, of course, are common still, in Christian lands as well as in the mission field,—in the case of those who find themselves standing face to face at last with the Christ of whom they have never heard before, or of whom they have never rightly thought, or whose grace, though long familiar enough, they have hitherto deliberately resisted. Then constantly there takes place, as Henry Drummond said, 'an experience which words are not allowed to utter—a something like the sudden snapping of a chain, the waking from a dream' (*Nat. Law in the Spir. World,* 94).

It is different in the case of those who from infancy have been brought up under the nurturing care of the Christian Church and a Christian home, and who have almost unconsciously been responding to this nurtural treatment. Timothy suggests to us an example in NT times of gradual or nurtural conversion (Ac 16[1], 1 Ti 1[5]); though it was through St. Paul's teaching, no doubt, that his early training blossomed into the flower of a rich personal faith (1 Co 4[17]). In later times nurtural conversions become common; and under ideal conditions of Christian education they may be regarded as the normal type. When one has been born in a Christian home, dedicated to Christ in infancy, surrounded continually by a Christian atmosphere, and so has learned 'from a child' to know and love and follow Jesus, a sudden and startling conversion is not to be looked for. Christians with such a history can seldom tell the day and hour of their conversion. And yet the name of 'conversion' is not to be withheld from certain experiences that have usually come into such lives. For the unconscious Christianity of childhood needs to be transformed into the conscious Christianity of developed character. There may be no day and hour that can be named, but there is generally a pretty well-defined period when the first instinctive love and faith and obedience pass into the deliberate attitude of the surrendered will.

Modern students of the psychology of religious experience have proved to how large an extent what we call 'conversion' is associated with those physiological and psychological changes that belong to the transition from childhood to dawning manhood or womanhood. This transition is not a sudden process, not a thing of a day or an hour. It covers a considerable period, but in that period a momentous work is going on. And in those days there comes to every young soul that has been well nurtured a new feeling of the beauty and mystery of life, and a fresh sense also of the possibilities that life offers of good as well as of evil. The old Greek stories about the parting of the ways and the choice of youth are not only perennially true, but have a special Christian application. Even those who have learned from their earliest childhood to love and honour Christ as their Saviour and Lord do not escape the need for a critical decision. When the time comes for taking up the free development of character, Jesus Christ stands at the parting of the ways ; and though He knows of very many that they have been following Him hitherto, He asks whether they are going to forsake Him now or follow Him still. When a young heart replies, like Simon Peter of old (Jn 6[67f.]), 'Lord, to whom shall we go? thou hast the words of eternal life,' that heart has turned consciously and deliberately to Christ. Of such conversions there are multitudes ; for in order to conversion a soul does not need to be violently plucked up by the roots and transplanted to another soil. It is enough if, knowing what it does, it turns joyfully to Christ, as the flower turns to follow the pathway of the sun.

(c) The question is sometimes raised whether it is possible for a man to be converted more than once ; and point is given to the inquiry by the fact that in the night in which He was betrayed the Lord said to Peter, 'When once thou has turned again (AV 'when thou art converted'), stablish thy brethren' (Lk 22[32]). It is impossible, however, to suppose that that process of conversion which is the full equivalent on the human side for the Divine act of regeneration is an experience that can be repeated. And in the case of St. Peter, it is evident from the Gospels that the definite yielding of his will to Christ took place at the beginning of the Lord's ministry, and not after the ministry was ended. But these words of Jesus to His Apostle suggest that while conversion in the express and primary sense can be experienced only once, there are *secondary conversions*, of one kind or another, that may fall within the compass of a true Christian life. One such is when a Christian man, as in Peter's case, has fallen into grievous sin, but repents and turns to Christ again, not only 'with grief and hatred of his sin,' but with a fuller purpose of new obedience than he ever cherished before. This is that repentance of a Christian man which St. Paul describes in 2 Co 7[11]—a repentance which may work in him such indignation against himself, such vehement desire to make amends for his backsliding, and as it were to be 'avenged' upon it, that he may become in many respects a stronger Christian than he was before, and thus better able to stablish and strengthen his brethren. Another type of secondary conversion is when a man, without the quickening spur of repentance for some great backsliding, comes to a fuller realization of Christ's claim upon him for the

costliest and best he has to give, and so makes a fresh and higher departure in the Christian life, a departure that is deliberate and definite, and thus may properly be described as a turning. In ways like these there may be several conversions or spiritual turning-points in a Christian's history— zigzags, so to speak, on the steep ascending path upon which he made his definite entrance when he first turned to Christ, with full consciousness, as the Lord and Master of his life.

LITERATURE.—The *Lexx.* of Cremer and Grimm-Thayer, *s. vv.* στρέφω, ἐπιστρέφω; Hastings' *DB*, art. 'Conversion'; Field, *Notes on the Translation of NT* (1899), 246 ; *ExpT* vii. [1896] 396, xi. [1899–1900] 4, 244, 289, xv. [1904] 337. On the doctrine of conversion see Augustine's *Confessions* ; Bunyan's *Grace Abounding* ; Charnock, *Works* (Nichol's ed.), iii. 88 ; Laidlaw, *Bib. Doct. of Man*, 263 ; W. N. Clarke, *Outline of Chr. Theol.* 401 ; Stevens, *Chr. Doct. of Salvation*, 483 ; Stearns, *Evid. of Chr. Experience*, 126 ; Drummond, *Nat. Law in the Spir. World* ; 'The Psych. of Conv.' in *Ch. Quart. Rev.* lvi. (1903) 17 ; A. R. Whately, 'Conv. and Mod. Thought' in *Churchman*, xx. (1906) 413 ; A. J. Mason, *The Ministry of Conversion* (1902) ; W. Adams Brown, *Chr. Theology in Outline* (1907), 408; and more fully, for the psychology of the subject, J. B. Pratt, *Psych. of Rel. Belief* (1907), with the literature on p. 312 f.

J. C. LAMBERT.

TURTLEDOVE.—See ANIMALS in vol. i. p. 65[b].

TWELVE. — See artt. APOSTLES, DISCIPLE, SEVENTY.

TYRE (for many common features, see SIDON). —The most noted district and city of Phœnicia, the city being 40 miles N.W. of Capernaum in Galilee. Its name is simply the 'Rock,' from two rocks in the sea—a larger and a smaller—a mile distant from the shore, lying parallel therewith, about 3000 feet in length, and containing some 150 acres. This 'Rock,' as a breakwater, early invited mariners, and ultimately furnished the elements of two harbours,—the Sidonian, north ; and to the south the Egyptian, now long filled with sand. It served also as a fortress, as well as a treasure-house for the merchandise that there was stored for transshipment between East and West. Old Tyre was the residential portion, extending at times for 5 miles along the shore.

As early as the monuments of Egypt and the Amarna tablets, Tyre is mentioned with Sidon as a locality of note. Its daring sailors had mastered the art of sailing the open sea by the stars, thus outdoing rivals who as yet had to steer by sight of land, and anchor at night. In the height of their power Tyrian merchantmen frequented every Mediterranean port, sailing the Atlantic to the tin mines of Britain, and even perhaps circumnavigating Africa.

In the middle of the 7th cent. B.C. Ashurbanipal laid siege to Tyre and practically destroyed the land city. Alexander the Great besieged Tyre for seven months, at the end of which he completely subdued it. Under the Romans it was in a state of decay, morally as well as otherwise. To-day it clings to the rock, a community of some 4000, a stagnant Arab village of fisher-folk.

As the conflict between the authorities and Jesus waxed to the murder-point, the masses of the people flocked to Him all the more. St. Mark (3[8]) paints the mixed throng on the banks of Gennesaret as coming from all points of the compass, including a curious Gentile multitude from 'about Tyre and Sidon.' St. Luke's specification (6[17]) is not so extensive, but, true to his breadth of interest, portrays 'a great multitude of the people from . . . the seacoast of Tyre and Sidon,' while St. Matthew (4[25]) is oblivious to such. Compared with the disbelief of Jesus' hearers and kin in Galilee, Tyre should stand immeasurably above those of greater light and opportunities, but of less susceptibility and response to the same (Mt 11[21f.]). Guilt and condemnation are relative. When Jesus had had to break with the carnally-minded populace that desired only an insurrectionary leader and temporal king, He retired for intensive instruction of the Twelve to the parts of Tyre (15²¹ ‖); and there it

was that there was found and shown to them a rudimentary, but for all that a potent, faith in an apparently pagan heart. See SYROPHŒNICIAN WOMAN. WILBUR FLETCHER STEELE.

U

UBIQUITY.—See OMNIPRESENCE.

UNBELIEF.—The withholding of belief, incredulity. In respect to Divine things the term implies absence of faith, credence refused to religious tenets. *Infidelity*, in its sense of want of faith or belief, is a synonym; not, however, *scepticism*, for the latter word is more properly used of the indecision of the reflective mind. Nor is *disbelief* an exact equivalent: *unbelief* suggests rather the failure to admit; *disbelief* implies deliberate and positive rejection. The *unbeliever* is open to conviction; the one who *disbelieves* is convinced (at all events for the time being) of the inadequacy of proofs submitted, of the improbability or impossibility of that which is proposed for acceptance. In the one case the explanation may point to want of knowledge; in the other the exercise of the reasoning faculty presupposes acquaintance, if imperfect, with the questions at issue.

Illustrations in the Gospels.—The term rendered 'unbelief' is the noun ἀπιστία (occurring 5 times: Mt 13⁵⁸ 17²⁰, Mk 6⁶ 9²⁴ 16¹⁴), with a range of meaning between distrust and disbelief. There is the use of the verb πιστεύω with the objective (οὐ) or subjective (μή) negative; occasionally the intensitive (οὐ μή) is met with: here again varying shades of significance are observable. Four times (Mk 16¹¹·¹⁶, Lk 24¹¹·⁴¹) the verb ἀπιστέω occurs; and in each case the 'disbelieve' of RV suggests that it is used absolutely. It may be remarked generally that the questions at issue differ, and that there are differences in regard to mental attitude.

(*a*) *In the Synoptics.*—Jesus is on a visit to 'his own country.' If Lk 4¹⁶ refers to a previous visit (which is unlikely), He will seek once more to win His fellow-townsmen when (Mt 13⁵³·⁵⁴, Mk 6¹·²) He takes His stand in the synagogue at Nazareth. They are, indeed, astonished at His wisdom: the reports of mighty works done by Him have filled them with amazement; but they are little disposed to give a patient and sympathetic hearing to one of whom they themselves have known so much, and withal nothing that has augured greatness. His claims scandalize them. They reject His teaching and Himself. 'And he marvelled,' διὰ τὴν ἀπιστίαν αὐτῶν (Mk 6⁶); it became evident that 'a Divine "cannot" answers to a Divine "must"' (Westcott). If the unbelief manifested on that occasion amounted to a positive disbelief, it was certainly not consequent on prolonged and serious reflexion. Adverse opinions were precipitated by bias; those who were swayed by prejudice were quick to disallow. And this unbelief of prejudice is again met with in the case of elders and chief priests and scribes as they question Jesus in their council (Lk 22⁶⁶⁻⁶⁸). The reply which comes from Him is significant: 'If I tell you, ye will not believe' (οὐ μὴ πιστεύσητε); in the face of hostile and preconceived opinion further speaking would be to no purpose.

A group of passages may be taken next where the unbelief illustrated is, generally speaking, that of incredulity. But the incredulity is diverse: its explanations point to reasonable distrust, want of receptiveness, power of discernment overcome for the time being by various emotions, knowledge limited, inability to apprehend that which is outside the sphere of previous experience. Thus Lk 24¹¹ (καὶ ἠπίστουν αὐταῖς): where reports brought by the women are discredited as idle tales by disciples unable to grasp the idea of a life lived under new conditions. Their doubt becomes assurance; but the sudden gladness told of in Lk 24⁴¹ (ἀπιστούντων αὐτῶν ἀπὸ τῆς χαρᾶς) renders it impossible to rise to a full apprehension of what is still the inexplicable. Despondency lies in the background of the unbelief referred to in the appendix to the Second Gospel (Mk 16¹¹·¹³); a despondency which, because yielded to, has sunk into a settled disinclination to be convinced. The thought here is of that stolid unbelief in which the heart is hardened and the mind unreceptive of spiritual truth (Mk 16¹⁴). And this incredulity of apathetic minds is perhaps noticeable in the attitude which 'the priests and the scribes and the elders' had adopted in the case of John the Baptist (cf. Mt 21²³⁻²⁷, Mk 11²⁷⁻³³).

If, on the one hand, there is an incredulity which Jesus reproves (Mk 16¹⁴), so, on the other hand, there is an incredulity which He not merely sanctions but enjoins. He makes large demands for faith, trust, belief; what He will not have is that mere credulity which bespeaks the inert mind, that superficiality which is ready to assent to anything. There is surely a depth and width of meaning in the μὴ πιστεύσητε addressed to the disciples in His recorded predictions (Mt 24²³, Mk 13²¹); and the warning against false Messiahs may be equally a warning against perverted notions of Deity, false conceptions of religion. By implication, a demand is made that tests be applied, discrimination exercised. The reality of faith will then manifest itself in the deliberate rejection (disbelief) of whatever does not bear the hall-mark of eternal truth. 'Religion is belief—surely it requires little thought to see that religion is, or should be, belief in what is true' (A. T. Lyttelton).

There is an unbelief which is indicative of a want of knowledge. But along with it there is the desire to know, to rise to a fuller apprehension of that whereof already there is the dim perception. Faith shines out in it; faith which, up to a certain point, is strong, and which can even declare itself openly; at the same time there is a profound consciousness of infirmity and limitations. And this is strikingly exemplified in the father of the demoniac boy (Mk 9¹⁴⁻²⁹); the unbelief which, realized by himself, he will not conceal from Jesus, has not deprived him of the capacity to trust. That he can, and does, trust is evident from his pathetic utterance (Mk 9²⁴ πιστεύω, βοήθει μου τῇ ἀπιστίᾳ). Pleading the compassion of Jesus instead of his own faith, he unconsciously shows a genuine faith (Gould, *St. Mark*).

(*b*) *In the Fourth Gospel.*—A characteristic feature should be duly noted, the enhanced demand for belief in the Son of God ('statt der Sache überall nur die Person' is the distinction drawn by Wernle [*Quellen des Lebens Jesu*, 18]). Passages bearing on the subject will, however, be discussed as they stand, and without raising questions dealt with elsewhere (see JOHN [GOSPEL OF]).

There is the conversation with Nicodemus. The unbelief referred to by Jesus (Jn 3^{12} καὶ οὐ πιστεύετε) is the failure to apprehend, which involves spiritual unreceptiveness. No credence has been given to things which lie within the range of human experience; how then shall there be perception of truths which have their sphere in a higher order? A few verses further on there come the reflexions of the Evangelist, and here thought is directed to that from which such unbelief springs. Sharp is the contrast between the ὁ μὴ πιστεύων of v.[18] and the ὁ πιστεύων εἰς αὐτόν of its opening words; in the former case full adherence to the Son of God has been deliberately refused; that refusal has meant a rejection of the highest manifestation of God, which is ultimately traceable to an evil disposition, evil works. Of similar import are the comments of the Evangelist in $12^{37\text{-}40}$; the miracles wrought by Jesus had not indeed been denied, at the same time they had made but a transient impression, and had sometimes been attributed to the powers of darkness; of unreserved confidence in and full acceptance of Himself there had been none whatever. That it should be otherwise was, after all, impossible where perceptive faculties had been dulled and moral sense blunted. The unbelief manifested was but the effect produced by the abuse of religious privileges and failure to profit by a progressive revelation. To look back to 5^{44} is to find precisely the same thought expressed by Jesus Himself. The long-continued education in Divine things had been all in vain for those Jews who had studied 'Moses' and yet remained blind to the progressive teaching of the OT. How then should they have ready acceptance for the One in whom another, and a higher, revelation had been given?

The attitude of the rulers referred to in $12^{42.\ 43}$ demands consideration. It would seem that conviction had come to them; closer examination shows that it was a conviction of the intellect only; that, because of unworthy fears, it went no further, it found no outward expression in the life. 'This complete intellectual faith (so to speak) is really the climax of unbelief' (Westcott); and yet it may be capable of transformation, of passing into that larger faith which dominates the whole man. Possibly the case of Nicodemus may serve as illustration. It was an intellectual conviction that brought him to Jesus in the first instance ($3^{1.\ 2}$); if he shrank then from publicity, he appears later on as one who has felt his way to an avowal of discipleship; the τὸ πρῶτον of 19^{39} is at least suggestive of repeated interviews and faith in process of development. Where there was the secrecy of the earliest visit there is at length the act of reverence done openly at the Cross.

It has become customary to speak of the 'doubt' of Thomas. 'Unbelief' would be the better word; for the attitude ascribed to him is rather suggestive of emphatic if tentative denial than of perplexity and hesitation. And yet it is not incompatible with an allegiance deep and strong to which all the stories told of him (in Fourth Gospel only) bear ample testimony. He is pictured as ready to go with Jesus to death (11^{16}); the thought of separation from his Master (14^{5}) has sorely distressed him; the crucifixion has dashed his hopes, but he will not sever himself from the company of the disciples (20^{26}) although for him the assurance is wanting which has come to others (20^{25}). For want of conclusive proof their glad tidings leave him unconvinced, and so there comes that round disclaimer (ἐὰν μὴ ἴδω . . . οὐ μὴ πιστεύσω) which reveals his unbelief. And this attitude of his, how is it to be explained? Is it really the case that he is to be regarded as the 'rationalist among the

Apostles'; that with him the reflective powers are stronger than the susceptive (see Robertson's sermon on *The Doubt of Thomas*, ii. 268); that he is one who will not be satisfied until all his grounds are established; that, ready to believe when he can, he is healthily averse from the belief of mere credulity; that his soul desires 'not a refuge but a resting-place' (Toynbee), and that he knows no security as long as there is one possibility of delusion left? The explanation is an attractive one, but it is doubtful whether it can be sustained in the face of the narratives above alluded to. They are scarcely suggestive of the highly speculative turn of mind. What they do betray is a gloomy temperament, a tendency to pessimism. Thomas is so constituted that he will always take the darker view of things. He simply cannot shake off the 'desponds and slavish fears' (*Pilgrim's Progress*) which weigh down his soul. Of himself he is incapable of gladsome belief; and yet, when assurance comes, he can rise to the great confession (20^{28}). As the light breaks in upon him he can say his 'Farewell night, welcome day' with a full heart.

It is difficult, then, to see in Thomas one who will painfully think out truth in order that when once found it may be the more firmly grasped. Not, therefore, is he to be classed with those referred to in 4^{48} (ἐὰν μὴ σημεῖα καὶ τέρατα ἴδητε, οὐ μὴ πιστεύσητε). They stand on a far lower level. For with all his defects of character, Thomas has nothing shallow about him; nothing to suggest the undeveloped intellect. The Galilæans, on the other hand, would seem to be characterized by childishness. Like the emissaries of Vladimir, who reported in favour of Greek Christianity because the grand services at Constantinople had appealed to their imagination, they are to be reached only by that which strikes the eye. The faith to which they can rise is, at best, a feeble faith. And yet, with one of them, it is strong enough to secure a blessing ($4^{49.\ 50}$). There is a 'complete spiritual parallel' (Westcott) between the nobleman of Capernaum and the father of the demoniac boy (Mk 9^{24}).

See also artt. BELIEF, DOUBT, FAITH.

LITERATURE. — Flint, *Agnosticism*, 381; Christlieb, *Modern Doubt and Christian Belief*, 325 and *passim*; Newman, *Oxford Univ. Serm.* 230; Ker, *Sermons*, ii. 1, 83; Martineau, *Endeavours after the Christian Life*, 343.   H. L. JACKSON.

UNCLEANNESS.—See PURIFICATION.

UNCLEAN SPIRIT.—See DEMON.

UNCONSCIOUS FAITH.—Faith is a venture of the soul. In the highest instances the soul stakes its all, and if the faith proves vain, is then of all most pitiable; but if the venture be justified, discovers that it has lost itself only to find itself as never before, and so in its endurance the soul is won. Can faith thus understood be unconscious? Assuredly it can. On the one hand, ignorance may conceal the fact that any venture is involved; and, on the other hand, where the actual stake is known, it may be welcomed through sheer exuberance of spiritual vitality without any such reflexion on the risk as to make it a conscious venture. An investor may put his capital into some undertaking without knowing that it is a speculation, or he may do so because his native enterprise prompts him to seize an opportunity without reflecting that the best opportunities are connected with larger risks. And the soul which ventures faith may do so without consciousness of what it is doing, either because its knowledge of life is restricted, or because it acts from instinct rather than consideration. But usage gives to the expression 'unconscious faith' a wider scope than this its strictest meaning. A faith conscious of its own activity may yet be unconscious of the person or fact on which it is actually set. The soul's venture may be made on the ground of an object of faith which is either unrecognized or unperceived, and which is yet, in point of fact, the ground of such a venture being made at all. Where the real object of faith does not come into consciousness, there is still warrant for calling this 'unconscious faith,' even though verbal exactitude might stickle at such phraseology. But when this degree of latitude is conceded, it ought not to be forgotten that the definition of 'unconscious faith' is made more difficult, not only in respect of its connotation, but of its denotation also. For the cases in which there is no consciousness of the true object on which faith rests, pass by imperceptible gradation into those in which there is some consciousness of the object, but no true perception of its real nature, and even into those in which the perception of this is markedly imperfect. But, of course, there are few cases of faith where this perception is anything like perfect; for not only is our knowledge usually very far from complete in matters spiritual, but where it is most nearly co-extensive with the truth, least occasion is left, as a rule, for faith. Bearing all these limitations in mind, however, 'unconscious faith' stands for an experience by no means rare in human life, and of very great importance in the Kingdom of God. Our object must be to understand its nature, and to realize the place it holds, and has held, in the relations of mankind to Christ.

1. At the outset we must recognize fully *Jesus Christ's constant requirement of faith* from all who sought or needed His help, and His refusal to give help where this requirement was not met (Mt 13[58], Lk 23[8. 9]). Only so shall we appreciate the welcome He always showed for every sign of unconscious faith. 'He that is not against us is for us' (Mk 9[40]) is a principle which recognizes what may be far short not only of full avowal, but also of conscious faith. It is obvious that in saying, 'I know that Messias cometh' (Jn 4[25]), the woman of Samaria had little consciousness of the real meaning of her words, yet her imperfect faith drew the disclosure, 'I that speak unto thee am he.' Similarly the faith of the Syrophœnician woman, who won the help she sought, can hardly have been conscious of what she was pleading for when she urged that 'even the dogs under the table eat of the children's crumbs' (Mk 7[28]). A more striking instance is that of the cripple who was cured of his infirmity on Christ's order to rise, of whom it is recorded that 'he that was healed wist not who it was' that had healed him (Jn 5[13]). And to this the case of the blind man who received sight in Jerusalem is somewhat similar; for when the Lord afterwards confronted him with the question, 'Dost thou believe on the Son of God?' he was only able to reply, 'Who is he, Lord, that I may believe on him?' (9[35]). An instructive passage as to Christ's estimate of faith which is unconscious is Lk 11[29-32]. He was condemning the contemporary generation in Galilee for its want of faith shown in the repeated demand for a 'sign.' In contrast with this He set two instances of greater faith recorded in much earlier days where less might have been looked for. The first is that of the men of Nineveh, whose repentance on Jonah's appearance among them is told in the Book of Jonah; the second is that of the Queen of the South, whose visit to Solomon's court is picturesquely narrated in the Book of Kings. In the one case it is written, 'The people of Nineveh believed God, and they proclaimed a fast' (Jon 3[5]); in the other the queen says: 'I believed not the words until I came . . . and, behold, the half was not told me' (1 K 10[7]). The credit given to the prophet's message, and to the fame of Solomon's wisdom, is taken as evidencing a deeper and unconscious faith in the righteous God who was judging the iniquity of the great city, and in the all-wise God whose inspiration was the source of the king's wonderful ability. And this unconscious faith of heathens is deemed worthy to shame and condemn the faithlessness of the generation which demurred to Christ's claims, and demanded signs.

2. There were times when the Lord Jesus put this point of view into express teaching with more of generality. Perhaps the words, 'If ye have faith as a grain of mustard seed . . .' (Mt 17[20], Lk 17[6]), were not intended solely to suggest the diminutive size of the seed, but also the inert grain in which the life lies latent for the present, though hereafter it will become active and develop. At all events when 'he called to him a little child and set him in the midst' (Mt 18[2]), bidding His disciples 'become as little children,' no characteristic of childhood can have counted for so much in His mind as the spontaneous readiness to trust without limit where love is, which at the same time makes a child so wonderfully teachable, and gives it charm too apt to be robbed by increasing years. A child is the very personification of eager instinctive faith unconscious of itself. There were times too when Christ's gaze ranged wider, and He welcomed the unconscious faith in Himself of those who had never known an opportunity of trusting Him. Such was the case when the Greeks who were introduced by Andrew and Philip seemed to Him the first-fruits only of a far greater harvest, and He looked on to the time when, 'being lifted up,' He 'would draw all men unto himself' (Jn 12[32]). It is impossible to limit this forecast to cover those only who in time to come should consciously become His disciples. He has drawn, and is now drawing, many to Himself who are unconscious of the power which is attracting them. And there seems to be a similar recognition of a widespread unconscious faith which needs to be made conscious that it may be perfect, in the saying, 'Other sheep I have, which are not of this fold; them also I must lead, and they shall hear my voice' (Jn 10[16]). A still more remarkable recognition of an unconscious faith in Himself, in days long anterior to His manifestation in the world, is to be found in the saying, 'Your father Abraham rejoiced to see my day, and he saw it, and was glad' (Jn 8[56]).

The instance last cited opens out a view of the propædeutic character of the whole life history of Israel, as it has been well called. Not Abraham alone, but all the prophets in Israel, and even all 'they that feared the Lord, and thought upon his name,' rejoiced to see Christ's day, and saw it with joy; for all of them are included in the Divine saying, 'They shall be mine in the day which I do make, even a peculiar treasure' (Mal 3[16. 17]). For whatever of Divine truth, of spiritual life, was discerned in those earlier ages, was just so much of the revelation of God made in Jesus Christ His Son. He 'was the light of men,' and those who saw His light saw Him, and rejoiced to see Him. This, of course, was the real nature of prophecy. It was not its function to be predictive of historical detail before the event, but to discern and disclose the unseen and eternal in the things that were seen and temporal. Inasmuch as the eternal belongs to no one epoch more than another, the teaching of the prophets was bound to find its realization in after times so far as it concerned itself with the real principles and laws of spiritual life; and to this extent it was predictive in what concerned 'the deep things of God.' But the special power of prophecy was insight, not foresight. This, however, was of necessity both preparatory and anticipatory, since the revelation of God was an evolution in time. So the prophets are accurately described by St. Peter as 'searching for what, or what manner of season, the spirit of Christ which was in them was disclosing, protesting beforehand of the sufferings destined for Christ (τὰ εἰς Χριστὸν) and the glories that should follow them' (1 P 1[11]). The faith of the prophets was thus an unconscious faith in Christ no less truly than it was a conscious faith in God. And this view is explicitly taught both in His own words and in the NT Epistles. To the professed students of Scripture round Him He said: 'Ye search the Scriptures, because ye think that in them ye have eternal life: and these are they which bear witness of me; and ye will not come to me that ye may have life' (Jn 5[39. 40]). And among His own disciples, 'beginning from Moses and from all the prophets, he interpreted to them in all the Scriptures the things concerning himself' (Lk 24[27], cf. 24[44-47]).

There are two sections of the NT in which this idea of unconscious faith is developed at some length, and given the emphasis which its importance deserves. The more obvious is in the Epistle to the Hebrews, in the great roll-call of those sons of faith in many ages who were 'looking unto the Pioneer and Perfecter of faith, even Jesus' (He 12[2]). Of these it is written that they 'all died in faith, not having received the promises, but having seen and greeted them from afar, and having confessed that they were strangers and sojourners on the earth' (11[13], cf. vv.[39. 40]). The faith by which they lived and in which they died was no doubt a more or less distinctly conscious faith in God and in the unseen world; but the writer of the Epistle is not content to view it so. To his eyes it was also an unconscious faith in Jesus Christ, who alone embodies faith in its conscious perfection, and is Himself the ultimate ground of its reality in all.—The other, and the deeper treatment, is in St. Paul's later Epistles. In his earlier writings there are occasional passages in which the same thought is expressed, e.g. 'They drank of a spiritual Rock that followed them, and the Rock was the Christ' (1 Co 10[4]); but it is only in the Epistles to the Colossians and Ephesians that St. Paul discloses his whole mind. In these he dwells with enthusiasm on 'the mystery which hath been hid from all ages and generations . . . which is Christ in you (Gentiles), the hope of glory' (Col 1[26. 27], cf. Eph 3[1-12]). St. Paul is not so deeply moved by the thought of a secret kept out of sight in the Divine counsels, while for ages men were being destroyed for lack of knowledge, and only disclosed at the last. God's purpose, he felt, was an eternal purpose; and if salvation through faith in Christ—in whom He 'purposed to sum up all things' (Eph 1[10])—remained for long a hidden mystery, it was not for the interval ineffectual. All through the long time of waiting, here was a secret hope for all men, though theirs might be an unconscious faith as yet. And 'in the fulness of the times' this hope was revealed through Apostles and prophets and saints in the Church (Eph 3[5], Col 1[24]), that the faith which had been unconscious and incomplete might become conscious and resolute and full of glory, working in power in all (ἐνεργουμένη ἐν δυνάμει). It is a truly magnificent view of life which is here unfolded to sight. It brings all time before Christ's earthly manifestation, and all races which have not known Him, and—we may fairly add—all souls which love and revere the holiness which they see in Him, though they do not feel able to confess His Name as the Saviour, or the Son of God, within the reach of healing and help in virtue of their unconscious faith. This is not, indeed, universalism, for it does not anticipate the ultimate judgment of God; but it does teach that it is God's will 'that all men should be saved and come to a knowledge of truth'; and it teaches that this is through faith—conscious or unconscious—in 'one mediator between God and men, himself man, Christ Jesus, who gave himself a ransom on behalf of all, the testimony being appointed for its proper seasons' (1 Ti 2[4-6]).

E. P. BOYS-SMITH.

UNDERSTANDING.— 1. συν-ιέναι, -εσις, adj. ετός (priv. ἀσύνετος), to bring one thing alongside of another : (1) for combat ; (2) metaph., for critical comparison, 'to bring the outward object into connexion with the inward sense' (Liddell and Scott), 'to put the perception with the thing perceived' (Grimm-Thayer), to 'apprehend the bearings of things' (Lightfoot, Col.). The typical passage is Mt 13[19. 23], where the exact significance is distinctly brought out. The hearer 'by the wayside' differs from 'him that was sown upon good ground' in this, that the former 'understandeth not' while the latter 'understandeth'—the former does not apprehend the bearing of what he hears on practical conduct, the latter sees the bearing and acts accordingly. The former 'does not recognize himself as standing in any relation to the word which he hears or to the kingdom of grace which that word proclaims' (Trench, Parables, in loc.), while the latter does so recognize. In v.[51], concluding the series of parables, Jesus asks His disciples if they have apprehended the meaning of all that He has said. In the same sense (Mt 17[13]) the disciples have, by the exercise of their critical faculty, recognized that in speaking of Elias, Jesus was in fact referring to the Baptist. Hence the contrast between συν. and other words—ἀκούειν, Mt 13[13. 14. 15. 23], Mk 7[14], Lk 8[10], the sound of the word spoken falling on the ear contrasted with the exercise of such criticism as leads to the apprehending of its personal bearing : νοεῖν, Mk 8[17], perceiving contrasted with earnest reflexion. A comparison of Mt 16[12] with || Mk 8[21] is interesting, Mt. representing the

disciples as having recognized on further consideration, while Mk. gives 'a stimulating question which leaves the Twelve to think out for themselves' the comparison of leaven with teaching (Swete, in loc.). Similarly, Mk 6[52] (RV, 'considered' AV) of the miracle of the loaves and the walking on the sea ; 'debuerant a pane ad mare concludere' (Bengel). Lk. employs the word less frequently than Mt. or Mk. In 2[50] 18[34] 24[45], where it occurs in the narrative, the meaning of apprehending the significance of the word spoken, recognizing its bearing on the circumstances (the mission of Jesus, the crucifixion, and the sufferings), is apparent. He does not use the special thought in his account of the exposition of the parable of the Sower.

The privative adj. ἀσύνετος 'without understanding,' exhibits the precise meaning of the verb, Mt 15[16] || Mk 7[18]. 'The ἀσύν. is the man who lacks the discernment which comes from the due use of the illuminated intelligence' (Swete). The positive adj. συνετός (Mt 11[25] || Lk 10[21]), AV 'prudent,' RV 'understanding,' preserves the idea of critical comparison, in contrast with the more general intelligence denoted by σοφός ; but the reference is to material not spiritual things : 'the "wisdom of the world" which is "foolishness with God" [contrasted with] the "foolishness of the world" which is "wisdom with God," on which St. Paul was so fond of dwelling' (Farrar).

The noun σύνεσις occurs only in Lk 2[47], where the precise idea is implied of the growth of Jesus in the development of His faculty of recognizing truth in every aspect along with His growth in stature ; and Mk 12[33], where, however, the reading is more than doubtful.

St. Paul's usage of the word cannot be overlooked. It is in strict harmony with that of the Gospels. See especially Col 1[9], where he combines 'understanding' with 'wisdom' in his prayer, and Eph 3[4] of 'the mystery of Christ,' 5[17] of 'the will of God' (Eph 1[18] διανοίας is a disputed reading). See Lightfoot, Col., where Aristotle's definition is expounded.

2. νοεῖν, Mt 15[17] || Mk 7[18], Mt 16[9] || Mk 8[17], Mt 16[11] RV 'perceive,' Mt 24[15] || Mk 13[14] (AV and RV), Jn 12[40] (from Is 6[9]) RV 'perceive': to perceive (1) with the senses, (2) with the mind. As distinguished from συν. it occupies a middle place between bodily sensation and critical apprehension. The first step is the sensuous perception (ἀκούειν, ἰδεῖν, etc.), then the mental act of attention to what is thus presented (νοεῖν), which in turn precedes the derivative critical act (συνιέναι), by which one is enabled to form a judgment on it. The process of digestion, the multiplication of the loaves, the passage read, the word heard, are objects first of sensation, then of attention, and lastly of reflexion, in order that their true bearing may be apprehended. Cf. 2 Ti 2[7] and Ellicott's note.

3. γιγνώσκειν is rendered by 'understand' (AV) in Mt 26[10], Jn 8[27. 43] 10[6] 12[16] (cf. rendering of its privative ἀγνοεῖν in Mk 9[32] = Lk 9[45]). In other cases γ. is rendered by 'know,' and it is difficult to find a reason for not adhering to that rendering in these verses. γ. differs from συν. in so far that while συν. generally marks an antithesis to sense-perception, γ. marks an advance upon it. Preoccupation with lower thoughts, self-complacency excluding apprehension of spiritual truths, present circumstances obscuring the full significance and necessitating a further enlightenment by new circumstances and prolonged pondering, hinder this advance. Only when these difficulties are removed can one come to know the higher aspects of the reality. (For the thought, compare Jn 2[22] 13[7] 14[26]). ἀγ. (Gospels only Mk 9[32] || Lk 9[45]) preserves this idea of advance, 'there was a Divine purpose in their temporary ignorance' (Swete). The disciples were unwilling to admit the idea of suffering

and death, and the rebuke administered to Peter made them afraid to ask questions; thus they remained ignorant for a time.

Literature.—The Lexicons and Commentaries, all of which refer to Lightfoot's *Colossians*, 1⁹; R. W. Dale, *Week-Day Sermons* (1867), p. 10.   R. MACPHERSON.

UNDRESSED CLOTH.—1. Ingredients in dressing.—The principal cleansing agents were two kinds of crude alkali salt.—(*a*) *Mineral.* This consisted of the natural deposits, chiefly in Egypt, of potassium or sodium carbonates. It was the Heb. *nether*, Arab. *natrûn*, EV (incorrectly) 'nitre,' RV 'lye' (Jer 2²²). White clay was also used, chiefly as a detergent or scrubbing agent.—(*b*) *Vegetable.* This was obtained chiefly from the soap plant called in Arabic *ishnân*, growing on the desert plains of Syria. When burnt, it yields a crude substance named *ḳali* in Arabic, corresponding to the Heb. *borith*, 'soap' (Mal 3²).

2. Process of dressing.—(*a*) *For cotton and linen.* The cleansing of these was carried out after the cloth had been woven. The present custom in Syria is to dip the cloth in water, and lay it out on a flat surface of rock. It is then sprinkled with *natrûn* (lye) or *ḳali* (soap), and beaten with rods or clubs, and is finally rinsed in fresh water and spread out under the sun to dry.

(*b*) *For wool.* On account of the presence of natural oil and many accretions and impurities in the fleece, the cleansing had to be done before the cloth was woven. For this the chief ingredient was urine collected and kept till it formed ammonium carbonate during putrefaction. Because of the offensive odours of such cleansing agents, as well as on account of the free space needed for drying purposes, the fullers' establishments were placed near or outside the city walls. The wool was further purified in several changes of water containing the lye or soap already mentioned, and was finally rinsed in running water.

(*c*) *For silk.* This also had to be treated before being woven, in order to remove from the thread the gluey substance called sericin (fr. σηρικόν, Rev 18¹²), which not only gave off an offensive odour, but, if allowed to remain, would make the cloth hard and lustreless. To remove this, the silk fibre had to be kept for several hours in a bath of hot water containing soap made of olive oil and alkali salt. This process tested the skill of the fuller; for if the soaking were insufficient, some of the sericin still adhered to the silk fibre, and if prolonged beyond a certain point it imparted an indelible yellow stain. The raw silk was then transferred for a short time to a bath of water in which dog or pigeon dung had been mixed, and, as in the case of the other materials, the last stage was a thorough washing in pure water.

The eye-witnesses of our Lord's majesty in the Mount (Mk 9²⁻⁸) testified that on that occasion the white radiance of His garments was beyond the art of any fuller on earth.

3. Christ's parabolic use of undressed cloth.—In Mt 9¹⁶ ‖ Mk 2²¹ Christ, in reply to the question of the disciples of John the Baptist as to why His disciples did not fast, employs the figure of a piece of undressed cloth (ῥάκος ἄγναφος) sewed on an old garment, to show the incongruity between fasting according to rule and the new spirit of Christianity. ῥάκος (fr. ῥήγνυμι, 'to break') is properly a piece of cloth torn off, cf. Eng. 'rag'; ἄγναφος (fr. α privative and γνάπτω, 'to full *or* dress cloth' [whence γναφεύς, 'a fuller,' Mk 9³]) = 'unfulled,' 'undressed.' Neither of the Gr. words occurs elsewhere in NT. In the parallel passage Lk 5³⁶, where, however, a somewhat different turn is given to the saying, ἱμάτιον καινόν ('new garment') occurs instead of ῥάκος ἄγναφος. By the rendering 'undressed

cloth' RV brings out the point of the original, which is quite lost in the colourless 'new cloth' of AV, though suggested by the 'raw *or* unwrought' of AVm. A piece of cloth that is undressed or unfulled is certain to shrink with a wetting, and so to strain and tear away the old garment to which it is sewed. Thus, as Christ said, it 'taketh from the garment, and a worse rent is made.' For the religious significance of the saying see esp. Bruce, *Parabolic Teaching of Christ*, p. 302 ff. Cf. also artt. BOTTLE in vol. i., and LAW, above, p. 12ᵇ.

         G. M. MACKIE AND J. C. LAMBERT.

UNION.—1. Union of the world with God.—In a sense the creation is always closely related to the Creator, and has no separate, independent existence: 'thy heavens' (Ps 8³), 'in him we live, and move, and have our being' (Ac 17²⁸). Yet it is in a relative independence of the creation that all things happen. Hence we read in Eph 1¹⁰ and Col 1²⁰ that God will gather together all things in Christ, and will reconcile all things unto Himself. This is spoken in reference to the human spirit and its salvation. By the redemption of man, God will perfect the relationship of the creation to Himself. All things are so linked together that God's approach to the human race, and His causing of the human race to approach to Him in Christ, is also a drawing of the whole world into a more perfect union with God.

2. Union between God and the human race.—It is only from the human side, and as matter of history, that we can study the union into which God has progressively entered with the spirit of man. It is the effect of any religious exercise that is matter of observation. Thus we are made aware of the dawning consciousness of God in the human spirit; 'then began men to call upon the name of the Lord' (Gn 4²⁶). Those who were receptive above their fellows of the Divine influence were prophets (Dt 18¹⁵, 1 S 9⁹). This being the case, we are led to postulate and believe in a corresponding communication on the part of God towards men, and to observe its development (see REVELATION). The history of Israel was so shaped by providences, and spiritual progress was so determined by prophecy, that Christ was prepared for, and came (Gal 4⁴), and in Him the union of God with our race was perfected (Is 7¹⁴ 8¹⁰).

In regard to the union of God with man in Christ, the emphasis in Scripture is not laid upon the manner of that union so much as upon the fact of it. If Creeds and Catechisms seem to do otherwise, it is still to be remembered that their chief concern is to establish the fact that God was in Christ. In Ph 2⁵⁻¹¹ St. Paul says nothing of the manner of the union of the Divine and human natures in Christ, but accepts as assuredly true that He was God with us, and that the same Person who emptied Himself and took the form of a servant, also humbled Himself and became obedient even unto death, yea the death of the cross.

When we turn to the narrative of Christ's words in the Gospels, we find that His attitude towards God was ethically perfect, as of a Son to a Father, in obedience, sympathy, comprehension, honour, love, trust (Mt 11²⁵⁻²⁷, Jn 5¹⁹·³⁰ 6⁵⁷ 10³⁰ 11⁴¹, Lk 23⁴⁶, and many other passages). This is what we are permitted to see of the relationship between God and Christ. But the Son who so manifested His oneness with the Father did so in our human nature. Here therefore is humanity in the person of its Head seen to be in union with God. So far as every OT saint was able to anticipate and prefigure Christ, so far this union between God and man was a process which was progressively unfolded and perfected. And so far as believers by fellowship with Christ enter into His relationship with God, the union between God and our race is still being realized ; and it must always take the form perfectly set forth by Christ (1 Jn 4¹⁷).

3. Union between believers and Christ.—It is necessary that individual souls should be united by faith to Christ, if the union of mankind with God is to be general (Jn 10¹⁶ 12³²). The Gospels record how in process of events men became disciples of Christ (Jn 1³⁷, Mk 1¹⁸). That which was so effected was afterwards in many ways confirmed (Jn 6⁶⁸ 20²²), and is described in the parable of the Vine and its Branches (ch. 15). Again, those who believed when the Apostles preached, and to whom the Spirit was given, without being personally attached to Christ in His earthly life, nevertheless became partakers of spiritual union with Him (Ac 11¹⁷. See also He 3¹⁴, 1 Co 1⁹, 1 Jn 1³). This union of the believer with Christ is more than the tie between a disciple and a teacher, and is expressed by the words 'in Christ,' 'in the Lord,' 'in him,' which occur more than 150 times in the NT, notably in 2 Co 5¹⁷ (RVm) and Ro 16⁷. As this union is entered into by trust and obedience and full consent, so it consists of identity of interests and companionship in everything. In the region of the *conscience*, union with Christ gives peace (Ro 8¹) ; in that of the *will*, regeneration (Gal 2²⁰) ; in regard to our *activity*, 'we are labourers together with God' (1 Co 3⁹, 2 Co 6¹) ; and in regard to all *events*, we are sharers with Christ in suffering and in glory (Ro 8¹⁷, 2 Ti 2¹² ; see also Jn 17²⁰⁻²⁴).

4. Union of believers with one another.—The Lord's Supper is the simplest and most perfect outward expression of the union of Christians with one another, because of their common attachment to Christ, and deriving of benefit from Him. Thus in Ac 2⁴² 20⁷, 1 Co 10¹⁶. ¹⁷ it is assumed that heart-union with Christ and with one another went along with the outward expression of that union, in their partaking of the same significant bread. The obedience of the soul to Christ which alone constitutes any one a disciple may or may not coincide with participation in this or any other outward observance. Yet, like the kernel and the containing shell of a nut, they as a matter of fact appeared and developed together. Union with Christ produces an attachment of loyalty to Him, and to everything that belongs to Him ; besides also the fruits of Christ-like character, which are in their nature unifying : 'The glory thou gavest me I have given them, that they may be one' (Jn 17²²). Should this unity be broken, the remedy is that all parties should renew their allegiance to Christ (1 Co 1–3, 2 Co 10⁷).

Union among believers is compared to the organic unity of a body (Ro 12⁴, 1 Co 12¹², Eph 4⁴). This has not the effect of ignoring the differences between believers ; on the contrary, the fullest provision is made for differences of gift. So far from the eye ceasing to be specifically an eye, because the body has hands and feet, there is the more need of the eye, and it has more work to do. Individuality is to be conserved and strengthened, and not destroyed or weakened. The case taken for comparison is not that of the failure of the eye to see, when the hand would do its best to aid the eye, and do its work ; but such a healthy state of things as would allow every sense to do its own work. At the same time, all are under the law of love to Christ and to one another, and are sensitive to each other's suffering or success, and their life is wholly directed to mutual helpfulness. The result is that each is exercised in the use of whatever gift he has, and the whole society is maintained in spiritual vigour and growth (Eph 4¹², Phil 6). See also ONENESS, UNITY.

LITERATURE.—Westcott, *Gospel of St. John* ; Sanday, *Jesus Christ* (reprinted from art. in Hastings' *DB*) ; A. B. Davidson, *Theol. of OT* ; Rendel Harris, *Union with God* ; A. Maclaren, *Holy of Holies* ; Illingworth, *Divine Immanence*.

T. GREGORY.

UNIQUENESS.—Beyond dispute Christ appears on the theatre of human history as a unique Personality. In however large a sense He may be revealed as sharing the lot and the nature of men, He stands forth as the possessor of traits which have never been duplicated. Let a parallel be drawn between Him and any other who has won renown in human annals, and it will be found that the points of unlikeness more than match the points of likeness.

1. In several respects the self-consciousness which the Gospels show to have been resident in Christ was of a unique kind. (1) We look in vain throughout their records for any indication that He recognizes the common call to repentance as applying to Himself. No utterance that is put into His mouth conveys a hint that the slightest shadow of condemnation ever rested upon His spirit. He speaks as if He felt Himself to be the channel rather than the needy recipient of grace, as if, in truth, His inner life was as stainless as it was assumed to have been in Apostolic thought. (2) Again, the self-consciousness of Christ appears to have been of a unique type as including a perfectly clear and marvellously potent sense of sonship towards God. So rounded is the filial ideal which He presents that it is impossible to find a point at which it admits of supplement. Who can imagine a more complete expression of filial trust than that which is contained in His precepts on putting away every anxious care about the stores which the morrow may bring (Mt 6²⁵⁻³⁴ ∥)? Who can conceive of filial devotion ascending to a higher stage than was made manifest in the words, 'Not my will, but thine be done' (Lk 22⁴² ∥), spoken in the presence of the most bitter cup of shame and suffering? Who can think of filial intimacy more close and constant than is attested by the whole body of Christ's words and deeds? In truth, it is impossible to review the record without being struck with the aptness of the Evangelical description which speaks of Him as the 'beloved Son' (Mt 3¹⁷ ∥) and as dwelling 'in the bosom of the Father' (Jn 1¹⁸). (3) Still further, a unique order of self-consciousness is disclosed in the pronounced sense of an extraordinary mediatorial vocation which was characteristic of Christ. 'No man cometh unto the Father but by me' (Jn 14⁶)—that is the strong declaration which the Fourth Gospel places upon His lips ; and a full equivalent is supplied by the other Gospels in such sentences as these : 'The Son of Man came not to be ministered unto, but to minister, and to give his life a ransom for many' (Mt 20²⁸ ∥). 'All things have been delivered unto me of my Father ; and no one knoweth the Son save the Father ; neither doth any know the Father, save the Son, and he to whomsoever the Son willeth to reveal him' (Mt 11²⁷ ∥). To what prophet or leader of the race beside have we any warrant for imputing such a conception of personal vocation? Surely it must be admitted that in His sense of the prerogative and the burden of mediation Christ makes a class by Himself ; He has no peer or companion. (4) Once more, the unique character of Christ's self-consciousness is seen in His extraordinary sense of authority or rightful lordship. While He came not to be ministered unto, He still made it evident that in the depths of His spirit there was an unhesitating affirmation of a pre-eminent royalty. He spoke as one who needed not to accommodate His words precisely to the instructions of Moses or to any other ancestral standard. He claimed an allegiance so unqualified as to reduce to a secondary place the most imperative obligations enforced by earthly ties. In words which match the significance of the Pauline declaration that in His name every knee shall bow and every tongue confess His lordship (Ph 2[10f.]), He pictured the gathering of all nations before His throne of judgment, to receive from His lips the merited sentence (Mt 25[31ff.]). Thus in various ways Christ gave expression to a transcendent and marvellous self-consciousness.

2. Almost rivalling the impression which comes from a consideration of the exceptional self-consciousness in Christ is that which is properly derived from a contemplation of the union and reconciliation in Him of strongly contrasted traits. (1) He was unique in His combination of meekness with the fullest energy and force of character. With quietness of mind He accepted the yoke of parental and national requirements. He submitted to a consecration rite at the hands of one who declared that he was not worthy to unloose the latchet of His shoe (Jn 1[27] ||). In all His conduct there was no trace of aristocratic superiority ; among all His mighty works no deed that savoured of ostentation. But while He was meek and lowly of heart, He was masterful and commanding, inflexible in purpose, remote from weak conciliation, perfectly resolute to march against a perverse generation, to confront its frown, its mockery, and its homicidal hatred. (2) Again, Christ exemplified the union of tender compassion for the sinner with sharp intolerance for sin. He was neither moved by the depth of His compassion to make unguarded allowances for the transgressor, nor incited by His intense repulsion against sin to lose the brother in the censor. In dealing with erring souls that had any longing for better things He fulfilled the prophetic picture of one who should not break the bruised reed or quench the smoking flax (Is 42[3], cf. Mt 12[20]). At the same time, He showed Himself the absolutely uncompromising enemy of unrighteousness, insisting that it must be excluded from the thoughts as well as from the deeds, and requiring that the offending right hand should be cut off and the offending right eye be plucked out (Mt 5[29f.]). Tender as the dew where there was any place for a healing ministry, He was yet sharp and unsparing as the lightning against every form of iniquity. (3) In another respect also Christ exhibited a unique ability for reconciling diverse traits. We see in Him a remarkable union of spirituality with kindly contact with the world. He knew how to be unworldly without being ascetic ; how to throw the weight of emphasis upon the treasure laid up in heaven without patronizing any eccentric form of self-denial. He ministered to bodily needs as well as to the needs of the spirit. Herald as He was of the Kingdom of heaven, He yet stood in sympathetic relation with the sensible world, treated it as the workmanship of His Father's hands, and used it as a book of divinity from which to read to His hearers most beautiful and comforting messages of truth.

3. Corresponding to this extraordinary balance of the various traits of ideal character, Christ showed a unique competency as a teacher to bring into a unity the diverse orders and interests of truth. In the standard of life which He set before His disciples He reconciled loftiness with simplicity. The standard is undoubtedly very high. It towers above the average level of human living like an Alpine summit. But with all its loftiness it is peculiarly free from the strained and the unnatural. Its attainment involves no sacrifice of manhood or swamping of the true self, but rather just the achievement of manhood and the realization of the true self. Rebuking nothing

that is purely and truly human, it requires only that the human should come to its best by standing in the transfiguring light of intimate association with the Divine. A great reconciling function is also fulfilled by Christ's teaching in the just tribute which it pays at once to morality and to religion, and in the indissoluble union which it assumes to subsist between them. From the standpoint of that teaching no man is a fit subject to bring a gift to God's altar until he has done his utmost to establish right relations with his fellows (Mt 5[23f.]). No man is an acceptable petitioner for the Divine clemency until he is willing to forgive the one who has trespassed against himself (Mt 6[14f.]). Ceremonial scrupulosity and ecclesiastical performances count for nothing apart from the intention and the habit of righteous dealing. They are no better than a counterfeit appearance, a whitewash upon the sepulchre (Mt 23[27]). Religion divorced from morality is a delusion and a pretence. But, on the other hand, the teaching of Christ is vastly remote from contentment with a bare morality or discharge of the common duties of man to man. The presence of the Heavenly Father lay about Him like a radiant atmosphere. To do the will of that Father He regarded as the prime necessity of His life, His very meat (Jn 4[34]). In the assurance of the Father's complacent love He found the unfailing spring of consolation and rejoicing, and the return of His heart in fervent love to the all-perfect One He counted the most obvious and the sweetest of all conceivable obligations. Accordingly, it could not but come about that His teaching should be thoroughly transfused with a religious element, with the thought of Divine relationships. From beginning to end it is beautified and illumined by lofty and intense religious convictions. In short, stress upon the ethical factor is not permitted in the least degree to diminish the emphasis rendered to the religious factor in man's life. The harmonious combination of the two makes one of the fairest and most fruitful ideals that has been brought to the attention of the race.

LITERATURE.—Carl Ullmann, *The Sinlessness of Jesus* ; G. A. Gordon, *The Christ of To-day* ; A. B. Bruce, *With Open Face* ; Hastings Rashdall, *Doctrine and Development*, 77 ff. ; Lives of Christ by Edersheim, Geikie, Farrar, Rhees, Sanday, and Keim ; Works on NT Theology by Weiss, Holtzmann, Beyschlag, Stevens, and Adeney. HENRY C. SHELDON.

UNITY. In the NT the term 'unity,' like its Gr. equivalent ἑνότης, occurs only in Eph 4[3. 13]— both times with reference to the unity of the Christian Church (v.[3] 'the unity of the Spirit,' v.[13] 'the unity of the faith'). But the idea of the unity of the Church as the 'body of Christ' is one that constantly meets us both in positive and in negative forms—in connexion, *i.e.*, alike with exhortations to Christian unity and with the deprecation and rebuke of **schism** or of the divisive spirit.

St. Paul in 1 Cor. (1[13] 11[18] 12[25]) is the first to use 'schism' (σχίσμα) with an approach to its present technical meaning. The σχίσματα, however, which he condemns are parties only in the Church, not sects ; 'strifes,' but not separations. There is no suggestion that those who called themselves 'of Paul' had ceased to communicate with those who called themselves 'of Apollos' (1[12]). The 'divisions' apparent in their meetings for worship (11[18-21]) were of class, of richer and poorer (v.[22]), and did not prevent the common meeting. The 'schism' deprecated in his parable of body and members (12[25]) amounts only to carelessness of mutual interest ; solution of continuity in the body of Christ is not contemplated. The word αἵρεσις (EV. 'sect,' 'heresy') comes nearer in NT use to the idea of 'sect,' though it does not reach it. It still denotes any party or faction within a single communion, as of the Sadducees (Ac 5[17]), of the Pharisees (15[5] 26[5]), or of Christians considered as a school of Judaism (24[5. 14] 28[22]). It goes no farther in Gal 5[20], where αἱρέσεις are counted among works of the flesh, as the natural sequence of ἐριθίαι and διχοστασίαι. In 2 P 2[1] they are the secret work of pseudo-prophets, and are αἱρ. ἀπωλείας ; but there is no suggestion that they amounted to separations: they work 'among you.' The strongest expression used on the subject is that of St. Jude (v.[19]), who speaks of some as ἀποδιορίζοντες, 'marking themselves off' from their fellows ; but apparently only in tone and conduct —there was no interruption of formal fellowship : the murmurers still 'feasted' with the Church, and were present at its ἀγάπαι. The Nicolaitans (Rev 2[6. 15]) were a party within the Church, not a separation from it. The idea of communions severally arranged upon differing bases of opinion or order does not exist within the NT thought. What is conceived as possible, only to be reprobated, is the tendency to faction, or the spirit of party, or the 'divisive course' : as for actual schism—μὴ γένοιτο.

1. *Our Lord's personal teaching* on the subject is positive, not negative ; He inculcates unity rather than forbids division. It is to be gathered (1) from His example, (2) from His recorded sayings.

(1) The condition of religion in the Jewish commonwealth of His time was profoundly unsatisfactory to Him. It called forth His sharp rebuke. Its teachers, their doctrine and their practice, incurred His denunciation. The Temple demanded cleansing at His hands ; the synagogues were in possession of those scribes and lawyers and Pharisees on whom He cried 'Woe,' as hypocrites. Nevertheless, He bade His disciples respect their authority and obey their ordinances—always without imitating their conduct. They 'sit in Moses' seat' (Mt 23[2]) ; a seat self-assumed,—their office had no recognition in the Law,—but in a sense they represented the prophetic succession, and *de facto* stood for constituted order. Christ neither separated Himself, nor allowed others to separate, on the ground of their corruption, error, or abuse of power ; though He recognized that all these existed, and protested against them. His custom was to go up to the synagogue on the Sabbath days. He observed the Feasts of the Temple, that of the Dedication (which had only customary sanction) as well as those prescribed. His example suggests no extremity of circumstance under which separation from the Divine Society becomes the course of duty.

(2) His express teaching is as emphatic as the circumstances permit us to expect. He establishes a Kingdom which in time and place is to be represented by the Ecclesia which He will build upon the confession of Himself (Mt 16[18]). The essential unity of the Kingdom necessarily reflects itself in the unity of the representative society. Unity is involved in the fact that its bond is a relation to Himself : the one Shepherd implies the one flock, the one door implies the one fold (Jn 11[9. 16]). It is presented under similes which convey the idea of unity : it is one building on one foundation (Mt 16[18]), one enclosed vineyard (20[1-11]), one shoal taken in a single net (13[47. 48]), one company of watchers (25[1-13]), or of guests at one feast (Lk 14[7-24]) ; it is a perfect century of sheep, a complete sum of money, and the breaking of its completeness is intolerable (15[4. 8]).

Its unity is primarily theological, necessitated by its causation in the unity which is in God (Jn 17[11. 21]), and objectively effected by the indwelling in its constituents of the one Christ (17[23]). The subjective unity in mutual affection of which Christians are conscious is a result of this objective unity, and is evidential of their common relation to Christ (Jn 13[35], cf. 1 Jn 3[14. 19]) ; but that sense of unity does not constitute the bond which unites Christians ; the bond is antecedent to the sense of it, and stands in the life of Christ transfused through the discipleship. This transfusion of life is effected by the mission of the Paraclete, the Holy Ghost mediated by Christ in His heavenly intercession (Jn 14[16-19]), and results in a vital unity of Christ with the recipients of the Paraclete ; which is comparable to that of a single organism (the True Vine, 15[1-8]) in which the individual inheres by the fact of his inherence in Christ (15[6. 7]). So much our Lord declares of His own operation ; for the rest, He implies that He is in

measure, in this as in all, dependent for the realization of His purpose on our apprehension of it and co-operative obedience. Undoubtedly He desires that the vital and spiritual unity which He effects should have a concrete expression—such expression as is apprehensible, not only to the spiritual man discerning spiritual things (1 Co 2[11-16]), but to the world, which cannot receive the Spirit (Jn 14[17]), and is aware of that only which with eyes of flesh it sees. He commands us, as a condition of the world's recognition of our discipleship, to love one another 'as I have loved you' (13[34]). He prays the Father that we may be one in such fashion that the world, seeing it, may believe in His mission : and defines this unity as comparable to His own unity with the Father. Beyond question He demands a unity manifested in terms of the common understanding of the man of this world. He prays, not that believers may be 'at one' (in harmony of faith or temper—or as Abraham and Lot were at one in agreeing to part peaceably), but that they may be 'one thing,' ἵνα ὦσιν ἕν (17[11. 21. 22]) ; 'completed into one thing' (17[23]). It is difficult to avoid the conclusion that this 'one thing' is, spiritually, the Kingdom which His Incarnation brings among us (Lk 17[21]) ; representatively, the Society which He builds (Mt 16[18]), to which by His institution the one Baptism (Eph 4[5]) admits, and which the one Bread (1 Co 10[17]) shows. Every kingdom, He says, divided against itself (the Kingdom of heaven is included in the argument) is brought to desolation ; every city or house (the City of God, the House built of living stones, is included) divided against itself shall not stand (Mt 12[25], Mk 3[24. 25]). The unity which our Lord teaches appears, then, to be a visible and organic unity, based upon a vital unity in the Holy Ghost, and necessary both for evidence and for stability. His verdict upon schism, as the interruption of such unity, must be inferred—it is nowhere stated [*] —from the sanctions assigned to unity, and from the intensity of His supplication that it may be realized in the experience of His Church.

2. In this sense *the Apostolic writers* have understood Christ. It is noted that the disciples were 'all with one accord in one place' to receive the Spirit (Ac 2[1]) ; that, as the result of Pentecost, they 'were together, and had all things common' (2[44]) ; 'the multitude of them that believed were of one heart and of one soul' (4[32]). The assumption of the Epistles is that 'the saints' anywhere are 'the church of God' which is there (Ro 1[7], 1 P 1[1] etc.). If they are 'churches,' they are not less one fellowship in the unity of Christ (Gal 1[1], Rev 1[4]).

St. Paul is copious on the subject. The unity on which he insists is not only of spirit ; it is also embodied unity. Many as we are, we are one loaf and one body, being partakers of the one sacramental food (1 Co 10[17] ; cf. *Did.* ix. 4). The one Spirit makes us one body, and members one of another (1 Co 12[4-27]), 'that there should be no schism in the body.' The unity of the Spirit is to be guarded in the bond of peace—'one body, one Spirit,' as there is unity in every basis of our life (Eph 3[4-6]). This body is the Body of Christ, and requires for its attainment to completion the harmonious interworking of every member and group, as constituting a single organism in which

---

[*] The possible exception is where (Mt 24[51], Lk 12[46]) Christ threatens the evil servant who smites his fellow-servants and eats and drinks with the drunken, that He 'will come and cut him asunder (διχοτομήσει αὐτόν).' The RV translators and others suggest for this remarkable phrase (ἅπ. λεγ. in NT) 'will scourge him severely'—which is as if one were to say in our speech 'will flay him alive,' and is an expression which one has difficulty in hearing with that sense from those lips. Ruskin somewhere interprets it of the judicial aspect of schism, as 'God's revenge' upon worldly and oppressive priesthoods—an interpretation which the history of schism may seem to commend.

all inhere (Eph 4^{13-16}). The Church is a Body, of which Christ is Head (Col $1^{18.\ 24}$ 2^{19}). It is 'the mystery of Christ' that the Gentiles should be of the same body with Israel (Eph 3^6). Baptism is into a unity to which neither race nor status nor sex is a barrier (Gal $3^{27.\ 28}$). It is against first principles to assume the name of any leader as a party distinction (1 Co 1^{13}); to do so is 'carnal' ($3^{3.\ 4}$). God is to be glorified with one mouth, as well as with one mind (Ro $15^{5.\ 6}$). The Churches of God have no custom of love of controversy (1 Co 11^{16}); God is not the author of confusion but of peace; and so it is in all the Churches (14^{33}). The contentious earn indignation and wrath (Ro 2^8); those who cause divisions are to be noted and discouraged (16^{17}); a partisan after repeated admonition is to be rejected (Tit 3^{10}). A Church is commended which follows other Churches already in Christ (1 Th 2^{14}). Doubtful disputations are to be avoided; the weak to be borne with; uniformity of opinion on ceremonial or ritual points is not to be insisted upon; to insist on uniformity may be 'to destroy the work of God' (Ro 14–15^3). It becomes the gospel of love that men should stand fast in one spirit with one mind (Ph 1^{27}): nothing is to be done through strife or vainglory—the guard of unity is humility (2^3); we are to do all things without murmurings or disputings, as children of God ($2^{14f.}$).

St. Peter assumes the same general conception; diffused as the Church is (1 P 1^1), it is one building, one priesthood, one nation ($2^{5.\ 9}$). *St. John* conceives of the Church as a fellowship with Apostles who have fellowship with God (1 Jn 1^3), united in love, which is to be in deed and truth, not in phrase (3^{18}). The Epp. to the Churches of Asia deal with conditions of corruption, moral and doctrinal; but there is no thought of self-segregation as the duty of the faithful, even where deeds that Christ hates are tolerated (Rev 2^6); He lays no other burden on His servants but to hold fast ($2^{24.\ 25}$).

The teaching of the NT, in fact, is positive. It shows *a threefold unity* of the Church:—(1) *An objective unity* of origin and of vital relation of its constituent elements, which (like the racial unity of blood) is constituted by the Divine act and exists antecedently to any action, for it or against it, of ours; to which we may do violence, but which we cannot abrogate; and which is the Church's spiritual oneness. (2) *A social unity*, the result and therefore the manifestation of this common Divine life, which is related to the life communicated in the Holy Spirit as the physical organism of the individual is to the personal life which co-ordinates that of its component cells, one body for one spirit; which (being body) may be wounded, but only with suffering and to its hurt and weakening. (3) *A unity of temper and intention, of consent in belief and thought*, which it rests with us to supply; which is the co-operation with the Divine action that is required of us,—obedience to the law of the nature of the Body of Christ in which we find ourselves — the bond of peace in which we are to observe ($\tau\eta\rho\epsilon\hat{\iota}\nu$) the unity of the Spirit (Eph 4^3). The existence of a state of schism is not contemplated in the NT, nor is any direction given for conduct in such a case. Party spirit and divisive courses are condemned, but there is 'no precept for the regulation of the relations of one sect to another.' The Apostolic doctrine as to schism can be inferred only from these facts.

letters of their respective chief pastors, and later by common Conciliar action. It was jealously a unity in the faith, but not necessarily in identity of expression of the faith; the Creed, as repeated in different Churches, was not in all verbally the same. It was a unity in moral obedience, but not a uniformity in ceremony or custom: each Church ordered its own liturgy, and determined its own ritual and usage; wide differences might exist in practices, *e.g.* of fast and festival (Eus. v. 24—Polycarp and Anicetus, Irenæus and Victor). Such differences were held only to demonstrate identity in the faith: 'in una fide nihil officit sanctæ ecclesiæ consuetudo diversa' (Greg. *ad Leandr.*, quoted by Bingham; see also his letter to Aug. of Cant. in Bede, *Hist.*). For the sojourner or incomer to scruple at local custom in things indifferent, or to abstain from the common worship on account of unfamiliar details, was in itself a schismatic act (Aug. *ad Januar.*, *ib.*).

In the earlier stages of the Church's life, government by bishops and presbyters in one local community could coexist with government by college of presbyters in another, without offence to either; Antioch, Ephesus, Smyrna communicated with Rome and Corinth. Ignatius addresses the collegiate Church at Rome as cordially as he does the monepiscopal elsewhere. Clement has no criticism for the absence of a bishop at Corinth, but only for insubordination to its presbyters. Churches autocephalous (externally independent of each other) might exercise large discretion in internal arrangement, yet recognize each other's sacraments and discipline. The centre of unity was in heaven, not on earth. It was a unity as that of Hellas, rather than as that of the Empire. Local Churches were 'as bays of the one sea.' Unity was essentially maintained when intercommunion was maintained. Schism was the interruption of communion: 'schismaticos facit, non diversa fides, sed disrupta communionis societas' (Aug., quoted by Sprott, *Macleod Lect.* 'Schism,' p. 2).

As for local unity, the safeguard of that was the recognized principle that only one valid ecclesiastical authority could exist in the same community; latterly, that only one bishop could validly occupy one seat, that presbyters could not act validly without him, and that the flock should communicate with him in sacraments and prayer. The worst form of schism was held to be the violation of this rule, as it produced sect within the same area, and led to the setting up of 'altar against altar'—a greater evil than interruption of communion between one local Church and another, as civil war is a greater evil than war between State and State. The converse responsibility was equally recognized: that no uncatholic or heretical term of communion should be locally imposed or required between Church and Church. In the case of that being done, the schism was held to be on the part of the authority imposing such terms, or of the Church requiring them. Thus Firmilian writes (with reference to the excommunication by Stephen of Rome of those who disallowed the baptism of heretics): 'While thou thinkest that all may be excommunicated by thee, thou hast excommunicated thyself alone from all' (*Epp. of Cyprian*, lxxv., Oxf. tr. p. 284).

4. It was to this latter principle that the *Reformers* generally appealed, as justifying in Catholic order their action in reclaiming the autonomy of national Churches, and in continuing their administration independently of the Roman See; which they regarded as a 'tyranny,' under which impossible terms of communion were schismatically demanded. As to schism generally, the Reformers maintained the traditional doctrine, and Calvin's view may be taken as typical: 'Such is the value which the Lord sets on the communion of His Church, that all who contumaciously alienate themselves from any Christian society in which the true ministry of His word and Sacraments is maintained, He regards as deserters of religion' (*Inst.* iv.).

5. The modern tendency is to recognize that responsibility for divisions has generally been a diffused responsibility, and that a distinction is to be drawn between that of the authors of separation and of the inheritors of positions of confusion which personally they have not created; to accept the essential validity of the conceptions of unity which guided the Church in its inception, while recognizing the difficulty of return to their practice; and to welcome the efforts of those who desire to be called 'repairers of the breach, restorers of paths for men to dwell in.' See, further, artt. CHURCH, COMMUNION, ONENESS.

LITERATURE. — Augustine, *de unitate Ecclesiæ*; Ambrose, *Epistles*; Calvin, *Institutes*, iv.; Bacon, *Essays*, 'Of Unity in Religion'; Barrow, *Of the Unity of the Church*; Bingham, *Ant.* xvi.; Archp. Wake, *Letters*; Walker, *Scot. Theol.*; Durham, on 'Scandal,' 1659, *Com. on Revelation*, 1660; Boston, Serm. on 'Schism'; Wood of St. Andrews, *Works*, 1664; Ferguson, 'Sermon before the Synod of Fife,' 1653; Rutherford, 'Due right of Presbyteries,' 1644; Bp. A. P. Forbes, *Nicene Creed*; Sprott, *Macleod Lecture*, 1902; Lightfoot, *Apostolic Fathers*; Gore, *Body of Christ*; Dale, 'The Idea of the Church' in *Essays and Addresses*, and 'The Unity of the Church' (Lect. xv.) in *Ephesians*; Fairbairn, *Christ in Modern Theology*, 513 ff.; Denney, *Stud. in Theol.* 186 ff.; Lindsay, *Church and Ministry*, 10 ff.   H. J. WOTHERSPOON.

UNIVERSALISM.—Three different, though connected, problems are raised by this word: (1) The universality of Christianity as a gospel for all races (as against the early Ebionism (wh. see) which confined Christianity to the circumcised); (2) the universal purpose of Christ's death—for 'all men'

---

3. According to the conception of *the Church of the first centuries*, unity was locally constituted by association in acts of communion with God (especially in the Eucharistic *synaxis*), and by recognition of the authority representing the discipline of the Church; œcumenically, it was constituted by intercommunion, evidenced by reception on the part of each local community of the *formatæ* (commendatory letters) of the rest, by homologation of each other's discipline, by the encyclical

(as against the Augustinian and Calvinistic doctrine of Christ's death on behalf of those elected out of the mass of sinful mankind) ; (3) the ultimate salvation of *all* souls (as against the eternal suffering of the wicked ; or, their destruction ; or perhaps as against uncertainty—subjective uncertainty, due to our ignorance, or objective uncertainty, due to the *indefiniteness* of the sentence of the Great Day ; see below).—A study of Christ and the Gospels is very specially concerned with the first problem.

I. *UNIVERSALITY OF CHRISTIANITY.*—**1.** There are two ways in which religions qualify as 'universal.' They may reveal the missionary impulse (Zoroastrianism? see Jackson, *Zoroaster the Prophet of Ancient Iran*, 1899, p. 92 ; Modern Hinduism, sucking up hill-tribes into its fellowship?). Or *in addition* they may simplify very greatly—in contrast with the legal or national character of developed systems of religion in the ancient world.

Buddhism went furthest in the way of simplifying. From the first, apparently, a proselyte might have the benefits of Buddhism without renouncing the practices of his former faith ; and at this hour many of the population of China are said to practise concurrently the three religions—Confucianism, Taoism, Buddhism. Muhammadanism is missionary and is simple, but it institutes a new legalism in the strictest sense. Pre-Christian Judaism, in its proselytizing, revealed the missionary impulse ; but simplification of ritual—a simplified *creed* was hardly needed—could not be granted, unless to the σεβόμενοι ('devout persons') ; and their position was theoretically very insecure.

2. The Apostolic Church had the missionary impulse, but practised the OT law as inherited custom ; was it also sacred duty? The question threatened to rend the new fellowship. Should the missionary impulse be given free scope? And should life be simplified—in the first instance, for those of Gentile birth—by abrogation of OT law? Or should the missionary impulse be slowly throttled by Jewish laws and customs? Both parties were pushed back, and led to define their principles more sharply. The Judaizers claim that the Law is necessary to salvation (Ac 15¹), or at least to full salvation (Gal 3³). St. Paul justifies his attitude of antagonism by declaring that the Gentile Christian, who accepts circumcision and the Law, renounces Christ (Gal 5²⁻⁴). On both sides, law is treated, not as customary, but as religious in value — good religion to the Judaizers, bad religion to St. Paul (though in mere custom he himself ' became a Jew to win Jews,' 1 Co 9²⁰). In the end the various sections of Christian Jews all died out, or merged themselves in the rival camps—the Synagogue and the Catholic Church. It may seem as if universalism failed. Christianity has been known to history as a Gentile and non-Jewish institution—a strange state of matters, were we not blinded by familiarity. And in other ways, too, success has been very partial. No religion, not even the Christian, has ever attained the destiny of universal sway to which all the higher prophetic religions aspire. Yet Christianity persists in claiming that it is truly universal. It excludes none. The Jewish people excludes itself. (Individual Jews, of course, are entangled in hereditary custom, and can break away only by self-will or moral heroism).

3. The simplifying of religion, which was carried through in controversy by St. Paul, begins uncontroversially in the teaching of Jesus. He brings the Law to a principle (Mt 7¹²) or to a pair of principles, drawn from different parts of the OT (Dt 6⁵, Lv 19¹⁸), and recognized by the Master as connected by an inward likeness (Mt 22³⁷⁻⁴⁰ ||). All these principles, of course, are moral and indifferent to ceremonial. So, too, the religious life is brought to a single principle by the name which Jesus steadily uses for God. If God is our Father, religion is sonship. This is a simplifying of the highest order—a simplifying which is also a deepen-

ing, an ennobling, a perfecting of the religious life. Thus Christ's teaching is universalist at the core. If religion consists in the belief of God's Fatherhood and in love to man, there is no reason why a Jew should be preferred to a Gentile. Nor do corollaries from these principles fail to appear in the teaching of Christ. He rejects, as lacking Divine authority, that tradition (15³⁻⁹ ||) by means of which the Pharisees, morally the most earnest among the Jews, safeguarded the OT law and applied it to new details, at the cost of making it ever more and more a burden. He hints repeatedly that ceremonies, even those taught by the OT, are of inferior moment in comparison with moral duty (9¹⁶. ¹⁷ 12⁷, cf. 17²⁶ 22²¹ ||). He speaks of sin and pardon (Mt 9⁶||, Lk 7⁴⁸), and of His own approaching death (Mt 20²⁸||, 26²⁸ ||), in words which send us back to the prediction of a 'new covenant' (Jer 31³¹). And thus He connects the new body of principles contained in His teaching with His own Person and destiny.

4. On the other hand, the universalist corollary itself seems strangely absent. For Christ conceives His calling upon earth as confined to Israel (Mt 15²⁴ ||). His intercourse with Gentiles (8⁵ᶠᶠ.), or even with the half-heathen Samaritans (Jn 4⁹, Lk 9⁵² 17¹⁶), was but casual. He bids His disciples, at their first going out, confine themselves to Jews (Mt 10⁶). All this, as we can see, was involved in His recognition that God called Him to be Messiah —Israel's king. If 'anointed' to 'preach' (Is 61¹, Lk 4¹⁸), He must direct His prophetic message to Israel. The shaping out of His royalty depends, under God, on the attitude of Israel in response to His appeal. These things are plain to us ; still, there was room for doubt under the historic conditions of the early disciples. It was plausible for Jewish Christians to hold that the Master's example sanctioned particularism rather than universalism. Very possibly Mt 10—as borrowed by the author of our Gospel from an older document (the *Logia*? one version of the *Logia*?, see LOGIA)—was originally a gathering together in a single context of sayings that might throw light on the *permanent* duties of an evangelist ; if so, the original draft of the chapter confines the itinerant preacher to an audience of Jews. (We must not expect that Evangelists should write like critical historians, with exact notes of time and circumstance). On the other hand, our Gospel of Mt., as a whole, certainly presents a different outlook. Yet it is only after the Resurrection—and, in all the Synoptics, with a very definite contrast to the past—that we have the record of a positive command to preach to all men. Not that the mind of our Master is really uncertain on this point. OT prophecy had extended hope to Gentiles (Is 2², *e.g.*) ; and Jesus stands higher, not lower, than His prophetic forerunners. Could He—speaking in the light of such promises ; or could He *at all*—preach a gospel universalism from its centre outwards, and not know what He was doing? He knew it well. And so the principles of His teaching come to their rights through the witness of St. Paul, who—in forms of his own, or, at any rate, in forms which owed to him their full and sharp development—vindicates the universal religion which has succeeded to the Old Covenant through the atoning death for sin. See also artt. COSMOPOLITANISM, EXCLUSIVENESS, GENTILES, MISSIONS.

LITERATURE. — The present writer's *Christ and the Jewish Law*, 1886, quotes older literature. Interesting recent statements, from a position of some theological latitude, in Harnack's *What is Christianity?* ; Wernle's *Beginnings of Christianity*, and Weinel's *Jesus Christus im 19ten Jahrhundert* [the last not yet translated].

II. *UNIVERSAL PURPOSE OF CHRIST'S DEATH.* —**1.** Granted that Christ is the Saviour of all races, did He die for all men in all races, or only for such as actually reap the benefits of His sacrifice? The question may seem somewhat academic. It is admitted on both sides of the controversy that the merits of Christ suffice to redeem all men; and it is [or was; but see III. below] admitted on both sides that only a certain number of souls are advantaged by the Christian salvation. Still, it seemed—e.g. to Wesley—a new and ugly particularism to affirm that, by Divine decree, the salvation, professedly offered to all, was confined to some, chosen arbitrarily or upon unknown grounds.

2. In our Lord's Synoptic teaching, or in the very simple theology of the first three Evangelists, the point now before us is hardly touched on. Christ is to give His life a ransom for 'many' (Mt 20^{28} ||); and so, too, His covenant blood is shed for 'many' (26^{28} ||). The contrast in view is between the One suffering and the many saved. In Jn. the phenomena are more various. The shepherd gives His life for the sheep (Jn 10^{11}). Christ loves His own (13^1). He prays for them and not for the world (17^9). On the other hand, the ulterior aim is 'that the world may believe' ($17^{21\,(20)}$). Lifted up, He is to draw 'all men' (12^{32}). And, when we turn from the Johannine teaching of Christ to other parts of the Fourth Gospel, we find strong emphasis laid on the fact that Christ is the Saviour of the whole world (1^{29} 3^{17} 4^{42}). A Gospel so penetrated with the thought of universalism (I.) was not likely to lend itself to a new particularism as against universalism (II.).

3. It is to St. Paul that the Augustinians and Calvinists look back as their explicit master. All that happens, happens by God's will. All that fails to happen, fails just because it was no part of God's purpose. Salvation, especially, is efficacious; grace is 'irresistible.' Predestinated — called — justified—glorified—the stately sequence moves on without pause or uncertainty (Ro 8^{30}). (We omit the initial term 'foreknown' as somewhat difficult—difficult perhaps to both schools of theology). What God plans, He accomplishes. The necessary obverse of this doctrine — unless transformed by universalism (III.); so Hastie, *Theology of the Reformed Church*, 1894 — is that neither God nor Christ meant any blessing for those who are in the issue unsaved. Christ died for some, not for all. But the NT writes differently. Even St. Paul joins in the common confession — 'He died for all' (2 Co 5^{15}). Language which in later theology is found characteristic only of transition Calvinism—i.e. of Calvinism in a state of decay, like Amyraldism—is the natural expression of the faith of St. Paul and of all the NT writers. True, A. Ritschl (*Justification*, vol. iii., tr. H. R. Mackintosh and A. B. Macaulay, ch. ii. § 22) contends that this form of expression is of inferior scientific value to the other set of expressions—noted by us in the Johannine teaching, and in Ro 8—according to which grace is destined to the Church. Ritschl's peculiar doctrine—the Elect=the Church and not =a body of individuals—has found few supporters, and probably will find fewer in the future. His preference for Calvinism is noteworthy, though he was no genuine Calvinist.[*] Yet we feel bound to hold that it is deeper spiritual vision and not simply lowered logical acumen that makes the NT writers—conceivably, sometimes, at the cost of systematic coherence—hail Christ as Saviour of all men. Otherwise, Universalism (I.) seems emptied of moral meaning. In point of fact, the Calvinistic limitation is little heard of now in Great Britain, except among some of the Evangelicals in the Church of England and some of the Baptists. And few would now rank it as a burning question.

[*] Universalism (III.), Ritschl dismissed as 'sentimental.' His own inclination was towards a doctrine of conditional immortality, but he left his eschatology somewhat in the dark.

The controversy has gone to sleep. Or judgment in the cause goes by default.

LITERATURE.—Besides Ritschl and Hastie, referred to above, the attentive reader will find fossil marks of the controversy in some of the hymns of the Evangelical Revival, both Calvinistic and Wesleyan.

III. *UNIVERSAL ULTIMATE SALVATION.*—**1.** At the present day, 'Universalism' most naturally suggests to the reader the doctrine of the final restitution of all souls (there are Universalist churches in America in this sense). The doctrine is not, indeed, a novelty. It is found, qualified by his extraordinary insistence upon individual free-will, in Origen's closely-knit speculative system; also in Gregory of Nyssa, and others. And Ritschl (*Gesch. des Pietismus*) notes, with scorn, among the symptoms of post-Reformation 'pietism,' that, ever and anon, hope is expressed even on behalf of condemned and lost souls. The most earnest and ardent supporters in Great Britain of the universalist doctrine have been Thomas Erskine of Linlathen (in his later years; d. 1870), Samuel Cox (*Salvator Mundi*, 1877), and Caleb Scott of Manchester. But Tennyson's *In Memoriam* (1849) has perhaps done more than any formal theological work to move opinion in this direction; and there has been a great break-up of the old unhesitating belief in literally unending punishment. Some have taught conditional immortality (E. White, *Life in Christ*, 1875; Petavel [French-Swiss], *The Problem of Immortality*, 2 vols. 1890–91 (Eng. tr. in one vol. 1892); W. D. Maclaren), others a mitigated punishment (F. W. Farrar, *Eternal Hope*, 1878, *Mercy and Judgment*, 1881; hinted also in J. R. Illingworth's *Reason and Revelation*, 1902, ch. xii.). Others plead for uncertainty (E. H. Plumptre, *Spirits in Prison*, 1884, with full and interesting references; Plumptre's brother-in-law, F. D. Maurice (*Theological Essays*, 1853), had stated philosophic doubts as to the meaning of 'eternal.' Present writer's *Essays Towards a New Theology*, 1889). An original and very curious suggestion is found in A. M. Fairbairn's *Christ in Modern Theology*, 1893, p. 467. Deity 'cannot' annihilate, but the sentence of condemnation is *indeterminate* rather than eternal (like sentences of committal to Elmira reformatory prison, N.Y.). Repentance *always* remains possible. If or when the damned repent, they shall emerge. Besides all these changes or innovations in belief, the growing reticence, and one may say reluctance, among those who maintain full traditional orthodoxy is even more significant. Few would now write as Charles Reade did (1856) in his brilliant novel, *Never Too Late to Mend* (ch. 21), as if the last moments of life on this side the veil were necessarily the last moments of hope for the soul ('Never' too late?).

2. Much of what we have just mentioned concerns us only in so far as it represents a great swaying of opinion towards universalism (in the fullest sense). The three senses of the word which we have been studying form a climax—Christ for all races, Christ for all souls, Christ actually redeeming and winning all. In the theological discussion just noted—Fairbairn is an exception—the question is generally argued as one of NT interpretation. The present writer does not think that hopeful. He sees no ground for challenging the old doctrine on exegetical lines. Words often applied to the universalist hope—*Apokatastasis*, 'restitution of all things,' Ac 3^{21} (cf. Mt 17^{11} ||, Ac 1^6)—do not really bear the meaning supposed. One passage teaches probation after death (1 P 3^{19}), but it hardly falls within the limits of this article. Eternal punishment had come to be the doctrine of the synagogue, and it passed into the NT with perhaps even sharper definition, as a witness to the unspeakable evil of sin. True, the doctrine was not rigorously formulated, and it is a question among interpreters whether St. Paul's teaching *is* eternal punishment or rather a certain type of conditional-immortality doctrine. But generally the NT is clear, even the language used by Christ; although we note that what is freshest and most personal in our Lord's words (Lk 12⁴⁷· ⁴⁸) goes to modify the dreadful wholesale dogma, and fore-shadows, at however remote a time, the ultimate challenging of the *letter* of this article of the theological creed. Again, as a matter of exegesis, we cannot claim either the Johannine teaching of our Lord (Jn 12³²), or the culminating point in St. Paul's great argument (Ro 11³²), as asserting universal salvation. Other plainer passages are decisive. There is a 'son of perdition' (Jn 17¹²), and St. Paul denounces 'eternal destruction' on sinners (2 Th 1⁹). Still, the question recurs here, too, whether the spirit and inner drift of such words—words spoken on the mountain-tops of spiritual vision—can be satisfied by anything less than their full meaning.

3. Recent change in theological opinion is largely a matter of moral recoil. We may sum up the moral postulate by saying that, as long as there is hope of rescuing the soul, any severity is a holy and even—though one trembles at the words—a gracious thing. But if character sets permanently in the ways of evil, can we credit long-drawn-out suffering? Our generation, from a sense of duty, puts even the cruellest of murderers to a painless death. We, who dare not torture, cannot conceive that God's administration includes endless torment.

4. Passing from simpler moral considerations to a religious speculation, we note that optimism enters into every theistic creed. In some sense—in the deepest sense—what happens in God's world is the best. It is best that evil should be per-mitted, should show what is in itself, should be conquered. Above all, when God's providence and grace have reached their goal in history, we must be able to say, 'It is best.' Again, God is omnipo-tent. He cannot, of course, do anything formally impossible or inherently absurd; nor can He 'deny Himself.' But any lawful desire of His children He can and will supply. All that He has is ours, for we are 'heirs of God.' He acts in His own way, according to His own will; yet He grants what we desire, *or something better.* This is the key which unlocks the riddles of our private lives. Its grandest and most public application is found in redemption. God could not, or would not, ignore the world's sin. He did what was far better, when He sent Jesus Christ. Now, here it seems incomparably the divinest issue of history that redemption should prove universal, and God all in all, not through slaughter of His enemies ('Order reigns in Warsaw'), still less through chaining them in hopeless misery and hatred, but through winning in every heart that victory which, in some of the hardest and darkest of hearts, Christ has won already.

> 'His blood can make the foulest clean;
> His blood availed for me.'

Again, God is our Father. Men have said in the writer's hearing,—some lightly, some with the profoundest gravity and tenderness,—'I could leave no child of mine to endless misery. Can God do that?' We, being evil, cannot but raise this ques-tion. Our Maker must answer it.

5. On the other hand, we cannot banish from our minds the tendency of character to set, for good or for evil. As we know it, this tendency remains incomplete. None are perfect, nor may we regard any as beyond rescue. But even a child learns how repetition facilitates either evil or good, and how a delayed reform grows harder and less likely to be achieved. It is no skirmish or sham fight for which we are enlisted. As right differs from wrong by the whole diameter of being, so the issues of the life that has been won for righteous-ness and love must differ from those of the life that has willingly preferred sin. Measured and limited ill-consequence is in no sort of proportion to the infinite evil of wilful wickedness; and the rhetoric of universalism in the minds of those who 'eddy round and round' is the lazy and lying assurance, 'It will come to the same thing in the end.' God cannot brook this. He must needs threaten sin with its wages; and we have no right to affirm that the most awful of all threats is but an empty or ideal possibility. So, longing with full hearts for a universal restitution of lost souls, we must leave this theme of mystery and terror upon the steps of the Redeemer's throne of grace.

LITERATURE.—Besides the works cited in the art., cf. Salmond, *Chr. Doct. of Immortality*, 628; J. A. Beet, *Last Things*, 203; Newman Smyth, *Orthodox Theol. of To-day*, 55; Alcott, 'Uni-versalism a Progressive Faith' in *New World*, iii. (1894), 38.

ROBERT MACKINTOSH.

UNLEAVENED BREAD.—See PASSOVER.

UNPARDONABLE SIN.—The expression is not a Scriptural one, but rests partly upon a saying of Jesus reported in different forms by all the Synop-tists, and partly upon two analogous passages in Hebrews and one in 1 John. It is only with the saying in the Gospels that we are directly con-cerned, but the passages in the Epistles must be glanced at as bearing upon our interpretation of Christ's words, and something must be said also as to the place of the subject in Christian experience.

1. In the Gospels.—It is the solemn declaration of Jesus that blasphemy against the Holy Spirit shall never be forgiven which forms our funda-mental authority. In an examination of these words, several points have to be considered. (1) *The occasion of the utterance.*—Both Mt. and Mk. connect the saying with calumnious charges of the scribes and Pharisees, based upon our Lord's action in curing demoniacs (Mt 12²²ᶠᶠ·, Mk 3¹¹· ²²ᶠᶠ·). Lk. gives it a different setting (12⁸ᶠᶠ·; cf. 11¹⁴ᶠᶠ·); but while it is possible that Jesus used the words on separate occasions, there can be little question that, if He spoke them only once, it is from Mt. and Mk. that we get the proper historical con-nexions. His work in delivering demoniacs from the power of evil spirits had deeply impressed the multitude, who, according to Mt. (12²³), began to ask, 'Is this the Son of David?' But when the Pharisees heard it, they said, 'This man doth not cast out devils but by Beelzebub, the prince of the devils' (v.²⁴, Mk 3²²; cf. Lk 11¹⁵). Jesus showed the absurdity of such a charge, considered from the point of view of mere reason and common sense (Mt 12²⁵ᶠᶠ·, Mk 3²³ᶠᶠ·, Lk 11¹⁷ᶠᶠ·). And then, suddenly changing His tone as He passed from the logical weakness of His adversaries to lay His finger on their moral and spiritual fault, He uttered those memorable words in which He declared that while all other sins and blasphemies, even blasphemy against Himself, shall be forgiven, whosoever shall blaspheme against the Holy Spirit shall never be forgiven (Mt 12³¹· ³², Mk 3²⁸· ²⁹; cf. Lk 12¹⁰).

(2) *The nature of the sin.*—In seeking for this, the occasion of the utterance serves as a guide. A study of the context in Mt. and Mk. at once disposes of some of the views that have been enter-tained as to the nature of the sin against the Holy Spirit—all those, *e.g.*, that are associated with the idea that only Christians can be guilty of it. Jesus was speaking to Pharisees, and it is by thinking, in the first place, of the Pharisees and their attitude to Him and His teaching that we get on the right line for arriving at the meaning of His words. He had cast out demons; and the

Pharisees said that He did this by the help of Beelzebub. He had delivered men and women from unclean spirits (Mk 1²³ff., Mt 10¹, Lk 4³³ff. and *passim*) ; and they said of Himself, ' He hath an unclean spirit' (Mk 3³⁰). Now, such language regarding Jesus strikes us, first of all, as blasphemy against the Son of Man Himself—and this it undoubtedly was. But this was not the aspect of the sin upon which Jesus fastened. On the contrary, He declared that all blasphemy against the Son of Man shall be forgiven. It was possible for men to insult Him personally, through want of thought or ignorance as to His real character. Of all such offenders He was ready to say, as He said at last of those who nailed Him to the cross or reviled Him hanging there, ' Father, forgive them ; for they know not what they do' (Lk 23³⁴). But apart from all questions of His personal dignity, Jesus came revealing in His words and deeds the Divine spirit of holiness and love. The works He did testified to the manner of spirit He was of. But in the presence of the Divine goodness that shone from His beneficent activities, the Pharisees only gnashed their teeth and declared that the spirit of Jesus was the spirit of Satan. This was blasphemy, not against Jesus only, but against the Divine Spirit that was manifested in Him. And such blasphemy, we must remember, the Pharisees were guilty of, not once, but constantly. Jesus might have affirmed of them, as Stephen afterwards affirmed in the face of the Sanhedrin, ' Ye do always resist the Holy Ghost' (Ac 7⁵¹). John the Baptist had come ' in the way of righteousness' (Mt 21³²) ; and they said of him, ' He hath a devil' (Mt 11¹⁸, Lk 7³³). Jesus came in the way, not only of righteousness, but of love ; and of this incarnation of the Divine grace they said again and again, ' He hath a devil' (Mt 9³⁴ 12²⁴, Mk 3²², Lk 11¹⁵, Jn 7²⁰ 8⁴⁸· ⁵² 10²⁰). They said this, moreover, not rashly or carelessly, but deliberately and malignantly ; not because they were blind to the tokens of God's presence with Jesus, but because they hated Him for having crossed them in their paths of selfishness and pride, and revealed both to themselves and others the utter emptiness of their religious life. Their blasphemy thus was not the hasty utterance of a moment, but a vice of their indwelling thoughts and character (Mt 12²⁵) ; not a single act, but a habitual attitude. The light that came into the world shone round about them ; but they loved the darkness rather than the light, because their deeds were evil. And at last they came not only to prefer the darkness, but to hate the light so bitterly that nothing would serve them but to declare to others and try to persuade themselves that it came not from God, but from the devil.

(3) *Its unpardonable character.*—The unpardonableness of such blasphemy as this, Jesus affirms in language that can hardly be mistaken. In Lk. once (12¹⁰) and in Mt. twice (12³¹· ³²) He declares, ' It shall not be forgiven'—adding in Mt. (v.³²) the ominous words, ' neither in this age (αἰών), nor in that which is to come.' The attempt is sometimes made to soften down the force of the last expression. The present age, it is said, was simply the Mosaic age or dispensation under which the Jews were living ; while ' the age to come' was the Messianic age or Christian dispensation. Our Lord's words thus mean only that, whether men live under the Law or the Gospel, blasphemy against the Holy Spirit is unpardonable They have no reference to the future life ; they tell us nothing about a state of doom after death ; they do not carry us on to any final issues (so Cox, *Expositor*, II. iii. [1882] 322). But while it is true that the Jews of our Lord's time used the phrases ' this age' and ' the coming age' to denote the

period before and the period after the advent of the expected Messiah (cf., however, Schürer, *HJP* II. ii. 177), it is clear from the Gospels that Jesus Himself habitually employed them to indicate the age before and the age after His own Parousia (see Mt 13³⁹· ⁴⁰· ⁴⁹ 24³ 28²⁰, Mk 10³⁰, Lk 18³⁰ 20³⁵), thereby throwing ' the age to come' into that future world which lies beyond His Second Advent and the resurrection of the dead (see Salmond, *Chr. Doct. of Immort.* 381). And if Mt.'s language left us in any doubt as to the absoluteness of His meaning, the doubt would disappear when we turn to Mk. For there we find Him saying of the man who blasphemes against the Holy Spirit that he ' hath never forgiveness, but is guilty of an eternal sin' (3²⁹ RV). Even if it stood by itself, ' hath never forgiveness' would carry a sound of finality with it. And when there is added, ἀλλὰ ἔνοχός ἐστιν αἰωνίου ἁμαρτήματος, it seems hardly possible to escape from the conclusion that blasphemy against the Holy Spirit is here described as a sin for which there is no remedy. The words in the original are exceedingly striking. ἔνοχος (= ἐνεχόμενος, fr. ἐν and ἔχω) means ' held in the grip of' (see Morison, *Matthew, in loc.*). And if we give to αἰώνιος the meaning it regularly has on the lips of Jesus, ' an eternal sin' appears to mean a sin that eternally persists, a sin that has so engrained itself in the character as to become fixed in the form of destiny. See, further, ETERNAL SIN.

(4) *The reason for its unpardonableness.*—This does not lie in any limitation of the grace of Christ or of the forgiving mercy of God. It lies in the very nature of the sin as just described. The sin is unpardonable because the sinner has no desire for pardon ; it ' hath never forgiveness' because it is not repented of. For when men for selfish reasons hate the light, and persistently shut their eyes against it and blaspheme it, they gradually put their eyes out. God's ' sov'reign vital lamp' still shines about them, but they can no more see it, since they have extinguished their own power of seeing. Eternal darkness is the necessary consequence of eternal sin. It is quite true that ἁμάρτημα generally stands for an act, not a state But from the point of view of exegesis, little can be built upon this. For an act may be the revelation of a state ; and when the Pharisees said of Jesus, ' He hath an unclean spirit,' this particular piece of blasphemy, as we have seen, was really the expression of a settled attitude of mind.

2. In the Epistles.—There are two passages in Hebrews that bear upon the subject. In 6⁴⁻⁸ the writer describes the impossibility of a renewal unto repentance for Christians who have fallen away from Christ after having once ' tasted of the heavenly gift' and become ' partakers of the Holy Ghost.' In 10²⁶⁻³¹ he declares that there is no more sacrifice for sins in the case of those who sin wilfully and persistently after they have received the knowledge of the truth. It is impossible to suppose that he means that a Christian cannot be forgiven if he falls into sin, however grievous, or that Jesus is unable to save men to the uttermost (cf. 2¹⁷ 4¹⁶ 10¹⁹ff.). In the second passage certainly and presumably in the first also, he is speaking of a deliberate repudiation of Christ on the part of those who have tasted His blessings. Once they were enlightened, but they too loved the darkness rather than the light, and so shut the light out of their hearts, and trampled under foot the Son of God, and did despite unto the Spirit of grace. Thus we have here again, though now in the case, not of Pharisees, but of members of the Christian Church, a manifestation of the same kind of sin as before.* In 1 Jn 5¹⁶ the writer distinguishes be-

* The case of Esau (He 12¹⁶· ¹⁷), though often quoted in connexion with this sin, has no real bearing upon it. The repent-

tween 'a sin unto death' and 'a sin that is not unto death'; and while urging Christians to pray for one another with respect to the latter, says that he does not bid them make request to God concerning the former. It seems evident that there is a reference here to our Lord's language in Mt 12³¹f·||, but in itself the passage adds nothing to our knowledge of unpardonable sin.

3. In Christian experience.—The subject is of importance, not only exegetically and theologically, but because of its practical bearings, and that in two different directions. (1) Bunyan at a certain period of his religious history (see *Grace Abounding*, §§ 96–230) is a type of multitudes who have suffered agonies of spiritual torture through the fear that they have committed a sin for which there is no forgiveness. But if the view taken above is the right one, there is no specific act of blasphemy in word or deed, standing by itself, that we are entitled to think of as '*the* unpardonable sin.' The phrase, in fact, is as erroneous as it is unscriptural, though the common use of it has helped to load thousands of sensitive souls with a burden of intolerable pain. There is no mysterious transgression which is sufficient of itself to put a man beyond the power of repentance, and so outside the pale of forgiveness. Blasphemy against the Holy Spirit may find expression and come to its culmination in some specific way; but essentially it is a settled attitude of mind and heart. It is a deliberate extinguishing of that inner light which God Himself has kindled within us, and which ought to respond to His clear shining from without. Such compunctions as Bunyan had are the very best proof that a man has not committed any unpardonable sin, for they are the experiences of one who, though he has not yet realized the all-sufficiency of Christ's grace, is possessed at least of that contrite spirit which trembles at God's word, and so may rest upon the prophet's assurance that unto him the Lord will look (Is 66²). 'Sell Him! sell Him! sell Him!' was the urgent persuasion of the Tempter in Bunyan's ear. But though at last in his distraction he felt the thought, 'Let Him go if He will,' pass through his mind, the true intention of his heart was always, 'No, no! not for thousands, thousands, thousands!' (*op. cit.* § 139). (2) But if anxious and fearful souls need to be reminded that blasphemy against the Holy Spirit is not some mysterious sin into which a man may fall against all the promptings of his better nature, the case of the Pharisees and Jesus conveys to all a message of serious warning. No one can stumble suddenly into irremediable sin; but men may drift into it after the fashion of the Pharisees. Selfishness and pride, and not least religious selfishness and pride, may slowly harden the heart and sear the conscience and seal the eyes, until men come to call good evil and light darkness, and are ready at last to say, even of one who manifests the Spirit of God and of Christ, 'He hath a devil.' The special monition of the incident in the Gospels is against that loss of vision which comes from the hardening power of sin, that continual resistance of the Spirit which leads at last to hatred of the Spirit. Poor Francis Spiera, whose case seemed to Bunyan so like his own (*op. cit.* § 163), may not himself have been guilty of unpardonable sin (cf. Martensen, *Chr. Eth.* ii. 128); but there is deep significance for all in his solemn sentence, 'Man knows the beginning of sin, but who bounds the issues thereof?' See, further, artt. BLASPHEMY, FORGIVENESS.

LITERATURE.—Schaff, *Die Sünde wider d. heil Geist*; Müller, *Chr. Doct. of Sin*, ii. 418; Gloag, *Exeget. Stud.* i.; Salmond,

Chr. Doct. of Immort. 379; Stevens, *Theol. of NT*, 102; Butler, *Serm.* x. 'Upon Self-Deceit'; Mozley, *Univ. Serm.* ii. 'The Pharisees'; Bunyan, *Grace Abounding*; *ExpT* iii. [1891–1892] 49, 215, 240, 555, xi. [1899] 1, 49; *Expositor*, II. iii. [1882] 321.

J. C. LAMBERT.

UPPER ROOM.—**1. The words 'guest-chamber' and 'upper room.'**—(1) *Guest-chamber* (κατάλυμα). In the LXX κατάλυμα denotes (*a*) an inn or lodging-place: Ex 4²⁴, Sir 14²⁵, Jer 14⁸; (*b*) a dwelling-place in general: Ex 15¹³, Jer 32²⁴ (=25³⁸) 40¹² (=33¹²), Ezk 23²¹, 1 Mac 3⁴⁵; (*c*) a chamber connected with a sanctuary or the Temple: 1 K (=1 S) 1¹⁸ 9²², 1 Ch 28¹³, being in one case the room where the sacrificial meal was eaten, 1 K (= 1 S) 9²²; (*d*) a tent: 2 K (=2 S) 7⁶; (*e*) the tabernacle: 1 Ch 17⁵ (not B). In the NT κατάλυμα occurs only in Lk 2⁷ (inn, or possibly guest-chamber) and Mk 14¹⁴, Lk 22¹¹ (apparently guest-chamber). The best MSS of Vulg. have *diversorio* in Lk 2⁷; *refectio mea* (also in *bfi*) in Mk 14¹⁴, *diversorium* in Lk 22¹¹. Of other Lat. MSS (besides differences of spelling,—*divor.*, *dever.*), in Lk 2⁷ *e* has *stabu.*; in Mk 14¹⁴ X* *q* have *diversorium meum*, Z has *diversorium meum refectio mea*, B H Θ Mt O have *diversorium meum et refectio mea*, *ff₂* has *refectorium*, *k* has *hospitium*; in Lk 22¹¹ *efr* have *hospitium*, *a* has *refectio*, *l* has *locus.**

(2) *Upper room* (ἀνάγαιον in best MSS: other MSS have ἀνόγαιον, ἀνωγέων, ἀνωγέως, ἀνώγαιον, ἀνώγεον).

In the LXX ἀνάγαιον does not occur in any form, ὑπερῷον occurs twenty-three times, apparently always in the sense of upper room. In the NT ἀνάγαιον (TR ἀνώγεον) occurs only in Mk 14¹⁵, Lk 22¹², ὑπερῷον occurs only in Ac 1¹³ 9³⁷· ³⁹ 20⁸, both words in the sense of upper room. The best MSS of Vulg. have *cenaculum* for both words in all places. Of other Lat. MSS (besides differences of spelling,—*caen.*, *coen.*, *cin.*, *cenn.*), in Mk 14¹⁵ *k* has *sub 'pedaneum' sterranæum* (having apparently first written *subpedaneum*, and then tried to alter it to *sterranæum*), *q* has *locum stratum*, *ff₂* has *stratum*; in Lk 22¹² *a* has *mædianum*, *b* has *pede plano locum*, *d* has *superiorem domum*, *q* has *superiorem locum*, *c ff₂ i r* have in *superioribus locum*, *l* has in *superioribus*; in Acts 1¹³ *d e gig* MSS used by St. Augustine (*Adv. Fel. Man.* i. 4; *De unit. eccl.* 27) have *superiora*, Grec Θ *p²* *tepl* have *cum introissent in cenaculum ascenderunt in superiora* (combining *cenaculum* with *superiora*: see Wordsworth and White's note on Ac 1¹³ in their edition of Vulg.); in Ac 9³⁷ *m* has *superiori cœnaculo*, *p* has *superioribus*; in 9³⁹ *m* has *superiora cœnaculi*, *e p* have *superioribus*; in 20⁸ *d* has *superioribus*.

2. Events in the upper room.—(1) The Last Supper (wh. see): Mk 14¹⁷, Mt 26²⁰, Lk 22¹⁴; (2) the washing of the Apostles' feet and subsequent discourse: Jn 13²⁻²⁰; (3) the prophecy of the betrayal of our Lord by Judas: Mk 14¹⁸⁻²¹, Mt 26²¹⁻²⁵, Lk 22²¹⁻²³, Jn 13²¹⁻³⁵; (4) the Institution of the Eucharist: 1 Co 11²³⁻²⁵, Mk 14²²⁻²⁵, Mt 26²⁶⁻²⁹, Lk 22¹⁹· ²⁰ (see LORD'S SUPPER); (5) the prophecy of the denial of our Lord by St. Peter and subsequent discourse: Lk 22³¹⁻³⁸, Jn 13³⁶⁻³⁸; cf. Mk 14²⁷⁻³¹, Mt 26³¹⁻³⁵, where such a prophecy—either that here recorded or a repetition of it—is placed after the departure from the upper room; (6) discourse: Jn 14; (7) the departure from the upper room: Mk 14²⁶, Mt 26³⁰, Lk 22³⁹, Jn 14²¹.

It is possible that the room in an unspecified house in Jerusalem where the disciples met after the Resurrection (Mk 16¹⁴, Lk 24³³· ³⁶, Jn 20¹⁹· ²⁶), and 'the upper chamber (ὑπερῷον) where they were abiding' after the Ascension (Ac 1¹³), were the same as the 'upper room' (ἀνάγαιον) in which the

ance which he sought was a change of mind on his father's part, not on his own. But Isaac had already bestowed the blessing, and the past could not be undone..

* The signs here used are those adopted in Wordsworth and White's edition of the Vulgate, and *Old Latin Biblical Texts.* See also Hastings' *DB* iii. 47–62, iv. 873–890.

above events took place; and that this, again, was in 'the house of Mary the mother of John whose surname was Mark' (Ac 12¹²). 'The combinations are quite legitimate, and only give unity and compactness to the history, if we suppose that the house of Mary and her son was the one central meeting-place of the Church of Jerusalem throughout the Apostolic age' (Sanday, *Sacred Sites*, p. 83). At the same time, there is no positive evidence in the NT for identifying the ἀνάγαιον of Mk 14¹⁵, Lk 22¹² with the ὑπερῷον of Ac 1¹³, or for placing it in the house of Mary the mother of John.

3. Places at table in the upper room.—There is some probability in the suggestion (Edersheim, *LT* ii. 494–95) that our Lord occupied the place of the host, that St. John was on His right hand, Judas in the place of honour on His left hand, and St. Peter in the least honourable place opposite St. John, as shown in the accompanying diagram.

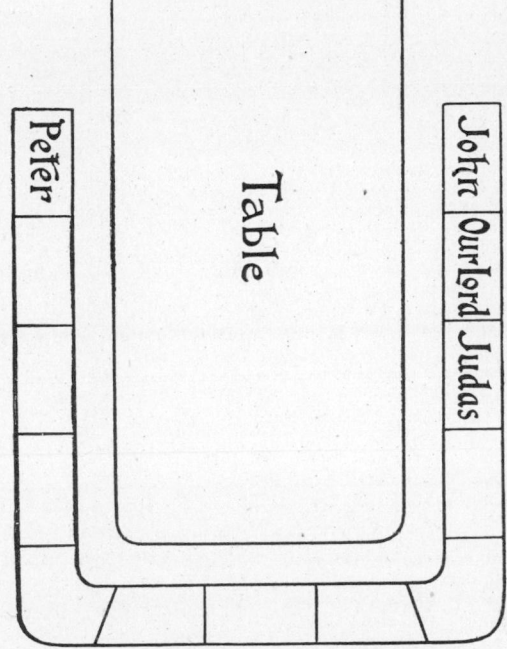

Such an arrangement would account for (1) our Lord telling St. John by what sign to know the traitor without the rest hearing, Jn 13²⁶; (2) the giving of the 'sop' first to Judas, Jn 13²⁶, Mk 14²⁰, Mt 26²³; (3) the inquiry of Judas whether he was the traitor, and our Lord's reply without the rest hearing the latter, Mt 26²⁵, Jn 13²⁷⁻³⁰; (4) the beckoning of St. Peter to St. John, and St. Peter's request that St. John should ask our Lord who was the traitor, Jn 13²³·²⁴; (5) the possibility that in the 'contention' among the Apostles (Lk 22²⁴), if this took place in connexion with the Supper and before it, Judas claimed and obtained the chief place; (6) the possibility that after our Lord's rebuke of the 'contention' (Lk 22²⁵⁻³⁰), St. Peter eagerly seized on the lowest place.

4. The identification of the site.—It is thought by many good judges that the traditional site of the *cenaculum* (the present building dates from the 14th cent.) is probably the place where the upper room stood. Dr. Sanday (p. 77) writes, 'I believe that of all the most sacred sites it is the one that has the strongest evidence in its favour. Indeed, the evidence for it appears to me so strong that, for my own part, I think that I should be prepared

to give it an unqualified adhesion.' The most interesting testimonies in the tradition are the following:

St. Cyril of Jerusalem, *Cat.* (A.D. 348) xvi. 4: 'The Holy Ghost, who spake in the prophets and on the Day of Pentecost, came down on the Apostles in the form of fiery tongues here in Jerusalem, in the upper church of the Apostles; for with us are the most valuable privileges of all. Here Christ came down from heaven. Here the Holy Ghost came down from heaven. And truly it is most fitting that, as we speak of Christ and Golgotha here in Golgotha, so also we should speak of the Holy Ghost in the upper church. But, since He who came down there shares in the glory of Him who was crucified here, we speak here of Him who came down there, for the worship of Them is indivisible.'

Silvia (or Etheria), *Peregrinatio* (c. 385 A.D.), 39–43: At Easter 'all the people conduct the bishop with hymns to Sion. When they have come there, suitable hymns for the day and place are said, prayer is made, and that passage from the Gospel is read in which, on the same day, in the same place where the church itself in Sion now is, the Lord came in to the disciples when the doors were shut, that is, when one of the disciples, namely, Thomas, was not there.' On the octave of the Resurrection 'all the people conduct the bishop with hymns to Sion. When they have come there, suitable hymns for the place and day are said, and that passage from the Gospel is read in which, eight days after the Resurrection, the Lord came in where the disciples were, and rebuked Thomas for his want of belief.' At Pentecost 'all the people conduct the bishop with hymns to Sion, so that they may be in Sion at the third hour. When they have come there, that passage from the Acts of the Apostles is read in which the Spirit descends. . . . In Sion is the very place, though there is a new church, where of old after the passion of the Lord the multitude was gathered together with the Apostles.'

Epiphanius, *de Mens. et Pond.* (A.D. 392) 14: 'Hadrian' 'found the whole city [Jerusalem] razed to the ground, and the temple of God trodden under foot, except for a few buildings and the little church of God. It was there that the disciples, on their return when the Saviour had ascended from the Mount of Olives, went up into the upper chamber (τὸ ὑπερῷον); for on that site had it been built.' (If Epiphanius possessed accurate information, this statement carries back the tradition about the site to the reign of Hadrian, A.D. 117–138).

Lucian of Caphargamala, near Jerusalem, *Ep. de revel. corp. Steph.* 8, after describing the discovery of the relics of St. Stephen (A.D. 415): 'Then, with psalms and hymns, they carried the relics of the most blessed Stephen to the holy church of Sion, where also the Archdeacon had been ordained.' Cf. *Breviarium Romanum*, lect. v. for August 3; *Breviarium Ambrosianum*, lect. iii. for August 3.

Theodosius, *De situ terræ sanctæ* (A.D. 530), 7: 'Sion, which is the mother of all churches, which our Lord Christ founded with the Apostles. It was the house of holy Mark the Evangelist.'

Liturgy of St. James (Brightman, *Liturgies Eastern and Western*, i. 53, 54): 'Thy all-holy Spirit,' 'who came down on Thy holy Apostles in the form of fiery tongues in the upper chamber (ἐν τῷ ὑπερῷῳ) of the holy and glorious Sion on the Day of the holy Pentecost.' 'We offer unto Thee, O Lord, also for Thy holy places, which Thou didst glorify with the manifestation of Thy Christ and the descent of Thy all-holy Spirit, especially for the holy and glorious Sion, the mother of all churches.'

Hippolytus of Thebes, *Chronicle* (usually assigned to 10th cent., but perhaps of 7th cent.): 'This is John, whom the Lord loved, the virgin and evangelist, who remained at Jerusalem, the mother of the churches, at his own house, to which the Apostles fled in fear of the Jews. There also was prepared the Passover. There also the first mystery was consecrated for the disciples. There also the Lord appeared to them after the resurrection. There also He showed the prints of the nails to Thomas. There the Apostles ordained as first bishop the son of Joseph, the brother of the Lord. . . . He [John] received the all-holy Mother of God (Θεοτόκον) in his house until her assumption (μέχρι τῆς ἀναστάσεως αὐτῆς).'

See also the plan, identifying the place of the Last Supper, of the descent of the Holy Ghost, and of the death of the Blessed Virgin, left by Bishop Arculf, who visited Jerusalem in A.D. 685, with Adamnan at Iona, and reproduced in Adamnan, *De locis sanctis*, of which reproduction there is a facsimile in vol. xxxviii. of the Vienna *Corpus Script. Eccl. Lat.* p. 244.

LITERATURE.—Edersheim, *Life and Times of Jesus the Messiah*, ii. 482–519; Le Camus in Vigouroux, *Dict. de la Bible*, ii. 399–403; Zahn, 'Die Dormitio Sanctæ Virginis und das Haus des Johannes Markus' in *NKZ*, vol. x.; Mommert, *Die Dormitio und das deutsche Grundstück auf dem traditionellen Zion*; Sanday, *Sacred Sites of the Gospels*, pp. 77–88; J. Watson. *The Upper Room* (1895); J. Telford, *The Story of the Upper Room* (1905); D. M. M'Intyre, *The Upper Room Company* (1906).

DARWELL STONE.

URIAH.—The Hittite (Mt 1⁶).

USURY.—See INTEREST.

UZZIAH.—A king of Judah, named as a link in our Lord's genealogy (Mt 1⁸).

V

VAIN.—**1.** 'In vain': Mk 7⁷ (‖ Mt 15⁹) μάτην δὲ σέβονταί με διδάσκοντες διδασκαλίας ἐντάλματα ἀνθρώπων. This is the only place in NT where the adverb μάτην is found (orig. accus. from μάτη, 'a folly'). The Vulg. has *in vanum* in Mk., *sine causa* (= 'without reason,' Cic.) in Mt. Both senses are perhaps included: their worship was 'meaningless' and 'to no purpose' (cf. Ja 1²⁶ μάταιος θρησκεία, with Mayor's [*Com. on James*, 71] apt quotation from Isocrates, *ad Nicoclen* 18 E, ἡγοῦ θῦμα τοῦτο κάλλιστον εἶναι καὶ θεραπείαν μεγίστην ἐὰν ὡς βέλτιστον καὶ δικαιότατον σαυτὸν παρέχῃς).—Our Lord quotes here from Is 29¹³, where LXX reads μάτην δὲ σέβονταί με διδάσκοντες ἐντάλματα ἀνθρώπων καὶ διδασκαλίας. The clause in the Heb. text may be literally rendered, 'And their fearing me is become (וַתְּהִי) a statute of men which they have learned.' How to account for μάτην in the Gr. text is a question still unsolved. Grotius (*Opera*, ed. Amsterdam, 1679, ii. 155) thought it evident that the LXX read וְתֹהוּ (= μάτην, cf. Is 49⁴) and not וַתְּהִי in the Heb. text, so that the clause would then have meant, 'And their fearing me *is vain*—a statute of men which they have learned!' This brilliant emendation of the text is adopted by Turpie (*OT in the New* (1868), 196) and Nestle (*Expos. Times*, xi. 330). It is quite possible that our Lord 'read וְתֹהוּ in His Hebrew scroll of Isaiah,' and that this was the received reading at the time that the Gospels were written. Such a solution of the difficulty would indeed be completely satisfying, but we must remember that the proposed reading is merely a conjectural one, and that no external evidence in its favour has been found. Other suggested explanations of the μάτην in the Gospels are, that our Lord used the LXX and quoted from it, or that in reporting His answer to the Pharisees the writer or writers quoted *memoriter* from the LXX (it will be observed that the order of the last words is not the same in the LXX and in the Gospels). The latter explanation is the one generally preferred by expositors, some of whom assign reasons still more unsatisfying for the presence of μάτην. But seeing that it cannot be proved that our Lord did not use an Aramaic word corresponding to μάτην in quoting the passage from Isaiah, we feel it best to accept the μάτην as stamped with His authority.—Our Lord by this citation authenticates and carries forward the teaching of the prophets of the OT as to the vanity of that worship which merely conformed to human traditions, and by which it was thought possible to gain the favour of God without moral obedience (cf. W. R. Smith, *OTJC* 293–295; Driver, *Is.* 57; Wendt, *Teaching of Jesus*, i. 282).

2. 'To use vain repetitions': Mt 6⁷ προσευχόμενοι δὲ μὴ βαττολογήσητε ὥσπερ οἱ ἐθνικοί. Mrs. A. S. Lewis (*Expos. Times*, xii. 60) approves of the derivation of βαττολογέω from the Arabic *b'ṭal*, 'vain,' 'useless,' recently suggested by Blass. 'It is one of those hybrid compounds which come into existence in countries where two or more languages are spoken.' But it is more probable that the word is onomatopoetic (like βατταρίζω, see Stephanus, *Thesaurus*, *s.v.*), and is derived from the sound made by the repetition of the same syllable in stammering or stuttering. Our Lord gives the interpretation of the word in the clause following, 'For they think that they shall be heard for their πολυλογία' (cf. Meyer, Holtzmann, *in loc.*). What He here condemns is the heathenish idea that a reluctant and ungracious Deity is to be worked upon by our saying the same thing over and over again (cf. 1 K 18²⁶), or by repeating His honours and titles (cf. Ac 19³⁴). In the words ὥσπερ οἱ ἐθνικοί He calls up a picture of those whom His hearers have no desire to resemble (*Expositor*, 1900 (i.), 239). 'Pestering the gods with entreaties,' 'dinning into the ears of the gods,' were Roman phrases: thus Tacitus speaks of Galba 'wearying with entreaties the gods of an empire no longer his' (*Hist.* i. 29); cf. Statius, *Thebais*, 2. 224, 'Superos in vota fatigant Inachidæ'; Ter. *Heaut.* v. 1. 6, 'Desiste, inquam, deos obtundere.' Such expressions set forth the contrast between Jesus' teaching of the Divine Fatherhood and the low conceptions about God on which the prayers of the heathen were founded, and give point to the precept, 'Be not ye therefore like unto them: for your Father knoweth what things ye have need of before ye ask him' (Mt 6⁸).

That our Lord's prohibition of βαττολογία is not meant to exclude such prolonged and repeated prayers as are genuine utterances of love and desire, the impassioned pressing-in of the devout spirit into communion with God, is evident from His enjoining increasing earnestness (Mt 7⁷⁻¹¹, Lk 11⁹⁻¹³) and persevering importunity (Lk 11⁵ff· 18¹ff·) in prayer, as well as from His own example, when He sought relief from the weight and pressure of His work and 'continued all night in prayer to God' (6¹²), or when He 'offered up prayers and supplications with strong crying and tears unto him that was able to save him from death' (He 5⁷), satisfying the fervour of His feeling of Sonship with the cry, 'Abba, Father,' and returning to His oratory in the depth of the Garden to offer the same prayer as before (Mk 14³⁹ (Mt 26⁴⁴) τὸν αὐτὸν λόγον εἰπών, 'the same petition,' rather than 'the same words'; cf. Swete, 327). Our Lord's prayers were the beginning of His ever-continuing intercession (Ro 8³⁴, He 7²⁵), and in the one instance reported of a prayer of considerable length which He offered as His disciples stood around Him (Jn 17) there is a repetition of the same expressions. With respect to the perfect form of words which He taught us in the Lord's Prayer (wh. see), it is by our repeating it often that we come to understand its real depth, and how all our requests are to be brought under one or other of its petitions; and when we have not said it well, we should try to say it better a second or a third time. The true sense of our Lord's saying is set forth in one of Bp. Wilson's 'Maxims of Piety': 'The eloquence of prayer consists in our proposing our wants to God in a plain manner' (*Maxims*, 132), and still better by Hooker in the words, 'The thing which God doth regard is how virtuous our minds are, and not how copious our tongues in prayer; how well we think, and not how long we talk, when we come to present our supplications before Him' (*Eccles. Pol.* v. 32. 1); cf. Augustine's letter to Proba, quoted by Trench (*Ser. on the Mount*, 255).

LITERATURE.—Grotius, *Com. on the Gospels*; *Expos. Times*, xi, xii, *ut sup.*; Hatch and Redpath, *Concordance to the LXX*.

JAMES DONALD.

VEIL.—'The veil of the temple was rent in twain from the top to the bottom' when Jesus died (Mt 27⁵¹, Mk 15³⁸, Lk 23⁴⁵). The Temple is, of course, the Temple of Herod, and the veil is, the 'second veil' (He 9³) which divided the הֵיכָל or Holy Place from the דְּבִיר or Holy of Holies. This is the only reference to the veil of the Temple in the NT, that in Hebrews being to the veil of the Tabernacle. The Greek words are τὸ καταπέτασμα τοῦ ναοῦ. In the LXX ναός = דְּבִיר in Ps 28 (27)[2] and κατ. = (1) מָסָךְ, the curtain before the door of the Holy Place and before the gate of the fore-court in the Tabernacle; and (2) פָּרֹכֶת, the curtain between the Holy Place and the Holy of Holies (similarly Philo, *Vita Moysis*, iii. 5). The Gospel according to the Hebrews, as quoted by Jerome, had in the above passage 'lintel' instead of 'veil' ('superliminare templi infinitæ magnitudinæ fractum esse atque divisum'). It is asserted that in the Temple of Solomon there was no veil, since it is mentioned only in 2 Ch 3[14]; but Thenius' emendation of 1 K 6[21] 'drew the veil across with golden chains' is good. In the Mishna the veil of the sanctuary is presupposed, *e.g.* in *Yoma* v. 1, where the mention of the ark shows that the writer is thinking of the Temple of Solomon. Josephus (*BJ* v. v. 4) mentions a gorgeously embroidered veil before the הֵיכָל, and a second veil, which he does not describe, in front of the דְּבִיר of the Temple as he knew it.

A difficulty is occasioned by the fact that there appear to have been in Herod's Temple not one but two veils between the Holy Place and the Holy of Holies, each representing a surface of the wall one cubit thick, which in Solomon's Temple separated the two places. In *Yoma* v. 1 the high priest on the Day of Atonement leaves the Holy Place by the south end of the outer veil, walks northwards down the cubit space between the two veils, and enters the sanctuary by the north end of the inner veil. This cubit space is in *Middoth* iv. 7 called טְרַקְסִין, that is, τάραξις, because in the first Temple it was filled with the wall, and the builders of the second did not know whether to reckon the space as belonging to the Holy Place or to the Holy of Holies. According to another account, there was only a single veil. In any case *the* veil would mean the outer one, which alone was visible to any except the priests. The Kaabah in Mecca has also a veil over its door.

The rending of the veil of the Temple would indicate the end of its sanctity, just as the tearing of a woman's veil means dishonouring her (Hamasa, *Freytag*, i. 141).

It is a curious fact that Jewish tradition also records the occurrence of certain prodigies about this time. Josephus (*BJ* VI. v. 3) enumerates several portents which presaged the destruction of the Temple: a sword appeared suspended over the city, a heifer about to be sacrificed brought forth a lamb, and the brazen gate opened of its own accord. Lightfoot (*Prospect of the Temple*, xx. 1 [Pitman's ed. ix. 329]) says: 'There are three remarkable things, which the Jews do date from forty years before the destruction of the Temple—namely this of the Temple-doors' opening of themselves, and the Sanhedrin's flitting from the room Gazith, and the scarlet list on the scapegoat's head not turning white.' Compare Plutarch's account of the prodigies which foreshadowed the murder of Cæsar.

In He 10[20] the veil of the Tabernacle is interpreted as symbolizing the corporeal nature of Christ, and in later mysticism phenomenal existence is termed 'the veil.' In 2 Co 3[12ff.] the veil (κάλυμμα) which Moses put on (Ex 34[33] מַסְוֶה, LXX κάλυμμα) becomes the spiritual blindness of the Jewish nation, probably without any reference to Is 25[7], where the words are different. The veil on Israel's heart is 'done away in Christ' (ἐν Χριστῷ καταργεῖται).

LITERATURE.—Grimm-Thayer, *Lex. s.v.* καταπέτασμα; Hastings' *DB*, art. 'Veil'; Edersheim, *LT* ii. 610 ff.

T. H. WEIR.

VENGEANCE.—The word 'vengeance' (ἐκδίκησις) occurs in EV of the Gospels only in Lk 21[22], where it refers to God's providential punishment of sin. ἐκδίκησις occurs also in the phrase ποιεῖν ἐκδίκησιν (EV 'avenge') in the parable of the Unjust Judge (Lk 18[7. 8]), and the corresponding verb ἐκδικέω (also rendered 'avenge'; cf. RVm 'do me justice of') is found in the same parable (vv.[3. 5]). Outside the Gospels these words and the cognate ἔκδικος occur exactly a dozen times. Some of the passages will call for reference in the course of this article. We are not left, however, to the very rare use of

this small group of words for our Lord's teaching on vengeance. We gather it from several passages of direct instruction, from His continual insistence on an unrevengeful, a forgiving, loving spirit, and from His own conduct throughout His ministry, but especially at its close.

Our word 'vengeance' is closely related to two others,—'avenge' and 'revenge,'—between which, at least in modern usage, an important distinction is made. Both have to do with the redress of wrong. In 'avenge' the idea of the justice of the redress or punishment is prominent. In 'revenge,' on the other hand, the predominant thought is that of the infliction of punishment or pain, not necessarily unjust, for the gratification of resentful or malicious feelings (note, *e.g.*, in Jer 15[15] the substitution in RV of 'avenge' for AV 'revenge,' and on the other hand the retention of 'avenge' in Ro 12[19]). 'Vengeance' leans, now to the one, now to the other of these meanings. It may be just, it may be malicious; even when it is just, the motive may be wrong.

1. The aim of Christ was to create in His disciples a new attitude towards those who had wronged them. Evidently He was preparing them, at least in part, for injuries that must come to them as His followers (Mt 5[10ff.]); but His teaching has, of course, a much wider application. The permission, even encouragement, of retaliation by the OT, and still more the interpretations, exaggerations, limitations of the scribes and Pharisees, Christ swept away with an authority which astounded His hearers. He denounced the attitude of retaliation and hatred, and commanded His disciples to accept the sufferings which fell to their lot. But this was more than a demand for a new attitude. It was the exorcizing of an evil spirit, and the opening of the doors of the heart to a new spirit. An attitude may be merely external and mechanical. Christ wants more. The negative must have a corresponding positive or be morally worthless. Forgiveness and benevolence must take the place of vengeance; love, not hatred, must be the motive of thought and act. 'Enemy' must be blotted out of the vocabulary of the follower of Christ, at least as a category in which any of his fellow-men may be included. Others may hate and persecute him; he must love and pray for them, and do them good. It is this new spirit that is the supreme moral difficulty; it is here that all questions of interpretation and application must find their solution. We must remember, not only Christ's 'resist not,' but also His 'pray for,' and His 'love.'

This teaching of Christ is found constantly throughout the Gospels. He pronounced 'blessed' the meek, the merciful, the peacemakers, the persecuted (Mt 5[5. 7. 9. 10ff.]). He rebuked James and John when they would have called down fire from heaven on the Samaritan village that would not receive Him (Lk 9[51ff.]). He taught His disciples to forgive a sinning but penitent brother, not with a niggard, but with a generous and inexhaustible forgiveness (Lk 17[3f.], cf. Mt 18[21ff.]). He even makes God's forgiveness of a man depend on the man's forgiveness of his fellow (Mt 6[14] 18[35], Mk 11[25f.]). He taught His disciples to pray that they might be forgiven as they forgave others (Mt 6[12], Lk 11[4]). He warned the Twelve, as He sent them out on their mission (Mt 10), that they would suffer hatred, persecution, even death, for His sake; and charged them to be, in the midst of wolves, 'wise as serpents and harmless as doves' (v.[16]), in the endurance of their sufferings to have no fear, but to rely on God.

2. His own conduct during His ministry is the best commentary on His teaching. It is true that there is much denunciation of evil (*e.g.* Mt 23), that He upbraided for their unbelief the cities where He had wrought His great miracles (Mt 11[20ff.] ||), that He swept the Temple clear of those who had robbed it of its sanctity (Jn 2[14ff.], Mt 21[12ff.] ||). But these are echoes of the Divine wrath; they are not in any single instance the expression of personal anger, of retaliation, of hatred. On the other hand, we have His patient endurance of all manner of personal abuse, His heart-broken lament over Jerusalem (Mt 23[37] ||), His bearing during and after His trial (Mt 26. 27), and above all, His prayer on the cross: 'Father, forgive them: for they know not what they do' (Lk 23[34]).

3. This teaching of Christ, forbidding vengeance, requiring forgiveness and love, is built on a firm religious basis. His aim as a religious Teacher, as the Sent of God, was to renew the sin-broken fellowship between men and God, to make men sons of God; but the indispensable condition of sonship is unity of nature. The essence of the Divine nature is love, and the highest manifestation of the Divine love is forgiveness and benevolence. The spirit of malevolence, of retaliation, of vindictive dealing with men, is alien to the spirit of God. Therefore it must be banned out of the heart of those who would be sons of God, and replaced by the spirit of forgiveness, of ungrudging love. It is this conception of the essential love of God issuing in forgiveness, in love, that is the basis of the high demands of Christ, and the inspiration and possibility of our response (Mt 5[43-45. 48] 18[23-35], Lk 6[35]. Note, also, how Christ links the Second Commandment to the First as 'like unto it,' Mt 22[39] ||).

4. If the teaching of Christ seem at first sight impracticable, destructive of moral order, and delivering wrong-doers from the fear of punishment, the answer to these objections is not far to seek. In the first place, liberation from the spirit of vengeance is a moral triumph for the sufferer of wrong. Revenge is evil. It belongs at best to a lower stage of morality and of the knowledge of God. It cannot justify itself to those who have seen God in the face of Jesus Christ. The sons of God must be like the Son of God, like God Himself, who loves and forgives without limit. Further, love is the most potent moral force that the world has ever known. To meet wrong with revenge may be a satisfaction, and may seem a right thing to the natural man. Vengeance may accomplish its object, may fully punish and even crush the wrong-doer. But it does not conquer him, it does not crush the wrong out of his heart, it does not make him ashamed of his sin, it does not win him to good and to God. Love does—not always indeed, but often—and nothing else can. Love is a heaping of coals of fire on an enemy's head (Ro 12[20]), the kindling of a burning shame in his heart, the overcoming of evil with good, the triumph of God. See art. RETALIATION.

5. There is a further and a very solemn strain in the teaching of Christ, in which we find the final answer to the fear that moral anarchy may arise from the exorcism of the spirit of vengeance. The clearest expression of it is found outside the Gospels (Ro 12[19]): 'Avenge not yourselves, beloved, but give place unto wrath [τῇ ὀργῇ, *the* wrath, the wrath of God]: for it is written, Vengeance belongeth unto me; I will recompense, saith the Lord.' To avenge ourselves is to assume the prerogative of God. So Christ teaches, *e.g.*, in the parable of the Unjust Judge: 'Shall not God avenge his own elect? . . . I say unto you, that he will avenge them speedily' (Lk 18[7f.]). It is in this light that we must read all Christ's words of denunciation, His parables of Judgment, His judicial acts (such as the cleansing of the Temple), His lament over impenitent Jerusalem. 'It shall be more tolerable . . . *in the day of judgment*' (Mt 10[15]; cf. 10[33] 11[20ff.] 12[36f.] 16[3f.], Jn 8[44]). The moral order of the world will be vindicated by Him whose right alone it is to mete out vengeance to evil-doers, who alone has adequate knowledge and wisdom to do justice to sin.

It would, of course, be easy to hold this teaching of Christ in a wrong spirit, to cherish a sense of satisfaction that, even if we may not avenge ourselves, yet vengeance is certainly in store for wrong-doers. This would be entirely contrary to the spirit of Christ. It would be the old evil spirit of vengeance in a new form, a more subtle and therefore a worse form. It would mean an utter absence of the love which Christ inculcates, which desires and prays for the good of the enemy. It would be the conquest of ourselves by evil, not of the evil in others by good. But, on the other hand, the moral sense which God has implanted in us, and which He has strengthened by His revelation of Himself, could not rest satisfied unless it were assured that evil shall not go unpunished, that unrepented wrong shall receive its due reward from an all-wise and, let us add, an all-loving God.

LITERATURE.—Grimm-Thayer, *Lex. s.vv.*; *EGT, ad locc. cit.*; Maclaren, *Expositions of Holy Scripture*, 'Matthew'; Tholuck, *Com. on Sermon on the Mount*; Goebel, *Parables*; Sanday-Headlam, *Romans*; Moule, *Romans*; Stevens, *Teaching of Jesus*; Wendt, *Teaching of Jesus*; Hastings' *DB*, artt. 'Anger (Wrath) of God,' 'Avenge,' 'Ethics,' 'Forgiveness,' 'Goel'; *JE*, artt. 'Forgiveness,' 'Goel,' 'Retaliation.'

CHARLES S. MACALPINE.

VERILY.—A formula of asseveration or corroboration.

The Hebrew is אָמֵן, and, while it is translated in the OT by the LXX into γένοιτο (cf. Ps 72[19]) or ἀληθῶς (cf. Jer 28[35][6]), and by Aquila into πεπιστωμένος, it is simply transliterated by the NT writers, except St. Luke, who, in deference to his Gentile readers, gives ἀληθῶς in three instances where the parallels have ἀμήν (Lk 9[27] = Mt 16[28] = Mk 9[1]; Lk 12[44] = Mt 24[47]; Lk 21[3] = Mk 12[43]).

According to R. Judah ben Sima, the formula had three uses: (1) in swearing (cf. Nu 5[22]), (2) in accepting (cf. Dt 27[15]), and (3) in expressing confidence (cf. 1 K 1[36]).[*] When a Rabbi would add impressiveness to a doctrine, he prefaced it with *Amen*, 'Verily,' signifying that it was a tradition received by Moses on Sinai.[†] The congregation responded *Amen* to the prayers in the synagogue, a usage which passed into the Christian *ecclesia*;[‡] and the Talmud warns against 'an orphan *Amen*,' meaning one uttered without consideration, or in ignorance whereto the response is being made.[§]

It is somewhat unfortunate that, where it is an asseverative preface, our versions have translated ἀμήν by 'verily,' and, where it is a liturgical response, have simply transliterated it. Let it be understood that the word is the same in both cases. See art. AMEN.

Jesus, like the Rabbis, was accustomed, by way of bespeaking His hearers' attention, to preface important declarations with *Amen*, 'Verily.'[||] All our Evangelists represent Him as doing so; but whereas the Synoptists put on His lips a single 'Verily,' St. John makes Him in every instance reduplicate the formula, saying 'Verily, verily.' What is the explanation of this divergence? It is out of the question to suppose that, since the Johannine and the Synoptic *logia* are in no case identical, Jesus may have spoken after both fashions, employing now the single, now the double 'Verily.' It does not appear that the latter was in use among the Jews, and it may be assumed that Jesus always spoke according to the Synoptic representation. Lightfoot makes a shrewd and far-reaching comment on Mk 5[41]. *Talitha, kûm* means merely "Maiden, arise!" And this is all that Jesus actually said; 'but in His pronunciation and utterance of these words there flashed forth such authority and commanding energy, that they sounded no less than if He

[*] Wetstein on Mt 6[13].
[†] Lightfoot on Mt 5[18].
[‡] 1 Co 14[16]; Aug. *de Catech. Rud.* § 13.
[§] Lightfoot on 1 Co 14[16].
[||] Aug. *in Joan. Ev.* Tract. xli. § 3 : 'Multum commendat quod ita pronuntiat; quodammodo, si dici fas est, juratio ejus est, *Amen, amen dico vobis.*'

had said : "Maiden, I tell thee, arise."' (Cf. Mt 9⁶ with Mk 2¹¹ = Lk 5²⁴). May not this be the explanation of St. John's reduplicated 'Verily'? Jesus actually used the single formula ; but such was the authority of His tone that St. John, reproducing not merely His language but His spirit, reiterated the asseveration, very much as a modern writer might underline the word, or as the Hebrew idiom expressed *plurality* or *magnitude* by repetition ; *e.g.* Gn 14¹⁰ 'full of pits of asphalt,' literally 'pits, pits of asphalt.' The beloved disciple held every tone, look, and gesture of the Master in reverent remembrance ; and when he limned His picture, he was in nowise careful to reproduce details with slavish and pedantic accuracy, but, with the artist's instinct, sought to catch those subtle and elusive expressions which reveal the true personality. When he reduplicated 'Verily,' he designed to make his readers realize the majesty wherewith the Lord spoke and the authority which His words carried.*

LITERATURE.—Bruder, *Concord.*, and Grimm-Thayer, *Lex. s.v.* ἀμήν ; Hastings, *DB*, art. 'Amen'; *ExpT* viii. [1896] 100 ff., 190 f., xiii. [1902] 563 ff. ; Dalman, *Words of Jesus*, 226 ff.

DAVID SMITH.

VICARIOUS SACRIFICE.—The word 'vicarious' (*vicarius* from *vicis*, 'change,' 'alteration') means acting, or suffering, for another, or in the place of another. The idea of change, transfer, or substitution pertains to the term. It has the same root as 'vice' in 'vicegerent,' 'viceroy' or 'vicar,' and other words which signify that one person has assumed the place, position, or office of another. It may mean 'instead of' (ἀντί), or 'in behalf of' (ὑπέρ). The word 'sacrifice' (from *sacer*, 'sacred,' 'holy,' and *facere*, 'to make') means something devoted, or offered at a cost ; and in the stricter religious sense means something consecrated, or offered to a divinity as an acknowledgment of benefits received, or as a propitiation for favours to be extended. Sacrifice (wh. see) is a somewhat different act in different cults and in different stages of religious development, but has in it the idea of a means of approach to Deity through a material oblation for the purpose of securing His favour. When the service is voluntarily undertaken, or when it is assumed at a cost to the individual and for the sake of another, no personal benefit being expected in return, we have sacrifice which is vicarious. Vicarious sacrifice, therefore, has been appropriately defined as 'voluntarily assuming the place and entering into the condition of some one for his benefit.' The two words, 'vicarious' and 'sacrifice,' add to each other, and together well define a phenomenon which we find occurring in the more advanced religions, and especially in the religion of Christ.

'Vicarious sacrifice' is not a Scripture expression, but is used by theologians to represent the meaning of a large number of passages found in the NT, in which the substitutionary character of Jesus' sufferings are referred to, as, *e.g.*, the one in which Jesus describes the end of His coming as a λύτρον ἀντὶ πολλῶν, a ransom for many (Mk 10⁴⁵). These passages have generally been held to teach vicarious sacrifice ; but just how the words are to be understood, in what sense the sufferings of Jesus were vicarious, whether we are to consider the terms to mean 'in behalf of,' or 'in the place of,' whether the vicarious sacrifice was made in the interests of God (Satisfaction theories), or of men (Moral and Sympathy theories), or both (Mediation theories)— these questions have constituted some of the most disputed problems of theology, and have been the

ground on which have been developed diverse conceptions which for hundreds of years have agitated the Church. As far as the words 'Vicarious sacrifice' are concerned, they can be used in either sense, for Christ's sacrifice would be vicarious if it were made to propitiate the offended dignity of God, or uphold His justice, or maintain His law, or satisfy the demands of His ethical life, or reveal the content of His ethical nature in a supreme manifestation of saving love. To determine in which sense the words are to be understood, that they may reveal to us the true teachings of Scripture, it is necessary to make a careful study of those passages which they are used to sum up or represent.

In doing this we meet with the following serious difficulties. (1) The lack of unity in the Biblical mode of representation, the view-point of Christ's work and sufferings being diverse and manifold. (2) The fact that Christ's work is set forth both by Himself and the Apostles in metaphors and symbols which cannot be given a close logical interpretation. It has been well said, ' We make a mistake if we take their symbols of thought as equivalents of spiritual realities, or if we treat their sentences as propositions from which we may deduce the uttermost corollaries. Their figures are illustrations, not definitions ; their expressions were forced on them by their past thought and experience, and are flung out towards truth as their best means of approximating to it' (Lewis). (3) While some of the figures are rooted in popular conceptions of religious service and are drawn from the Jewish sacrificial system, others are bold strokes of the imagination, and are capable of various meanings. (4) The different views held of the Jewish sacrificial system from which the NT figures and expressions are drawn constitute a difficulty. Some regard them as close types and symbols of Christ's work, and give them expiatory value (P. Fairbairn) ; while others affirm that 'they disclose no trace of the idea of vicarious substitution, nor of propitiation' (Westcott). (5) Some texts used singly seem to teach what other texts contradict, showing that they are loose statements, not to be taken with logical exactness ; or that they represent phases of a doctrine and not the whole of it, or that they are metaphorical. (6) The fact that there are two ideas of sacrifice in the OT—one of the priests and the other of the prophets ; and that Hebrews and Jn. seem to have worked out their ideas on the basis of the Levitical standpoint, while Jesus and St. Paul represent more the ideas of the prophets. (7) The difficulty of freeing ourselves of *a priori* ideas in our interpretations of Scripture, dogmatic conceptions having been planted in our minds in childhood, and become a part of the religious atmosphere in which we move. (8) Finally, the difficulty of getting at the meaning attached to terms among the Palestine Jews of Jesus' time, such terms, for example, as 'ransom,' 'redemption,' 'propitiation,' and certain legal expressions. In studying the Scriptures, therefore, to ascertain in what sense we are to understand Christ's vicarious sacrifice, we are to note the individualism of the expressions, their figurative character, their lack of logical exactness and definition, their relation to their time, and the fact that their authors are concerned with stating facts and results rather than developing theories. We are to interpret the passages in a free and vital rather than in an exact and literal way, note the general impression they make, the essential truth they reveal, and the conception of their meaning which will best harmonize the variant and diverse statements into a consistent unity.

1. The teachings of Jesus in the Synoptics.—Our first source of information concerning the way we are to understand the vicarious sacrifice of Jesus must be His own teachings. Too many have overlooked this and started with the conceptions of St. Paul, as if the human teacher were a clearer witness than He who was Himself the revelation. If there is any squaring to do, St. Paul must be squared with Jesus, not Jesus with St. Paul, for the Master did not preach a partial gospel. As we study His sayings concerning His sacrifice, we note that He regards it as necessary, voluntary, vicarious, and redemptive, and that He relates it (1) to the establishment of the Kingdom, (2) to the remission of sins, (3) to the ratifying of the covenant. (1) Jesus considers His vicarious sacrifice as necessarily involved in His work of establishing His Kingdom. He opened His ministry with the announcement, 'The time is fulfilled, and the kingdom of God is at hand' (Mk 1¹⁵, cf. Mt 4¹⁷). The Kingdom of God was not the 'politico-ethical commonwealth' (Pfleiderer) which Jewish prophecy had described, but a spiritual society, established by the grace of God, of righteous men having fellowship with one another and with a common Father. To the

* Cf. Just. M. *Dial. c. Tryph.*, ed. Sylburg, p. 225 C : δέος γὰρ τι ἔχουσιν ἐν ἑαυτοῖς, καὶ ἱκανοὶ δυσωπῆσαι τοὺς ἐκτρεπομένους τῆς ὀρθῆς ὁδοῦ, ἀνάπαυσίς τε ἡδίστη γίνεται τοῖς ἐκμελετῶσιν αὐτούς.

founding of His Kingdom He devoted Himself with singleness of heart, understanding well the hazard it involved ; for He realized the traditionalism of the age, its formalism, its lack of spiritual vision, its worldly lust and ambition, and He knew full well the opposition He would stimulate and the conflicts He must encounter. The history of the prophets was before Him, and the blood of the martyrs cried to Him from the ground. Even Plato was able to perceive 'that one perfectly just could not appear among the senseless and wicked without provoking a murderous hatred.' The law of righteousness, fundamental in His Kingdom, would, He knew, cut across the self-interests of men, as well as the conservatism of the Rabbinical teachers of the day. Consequently He compares Himself to the good shepherd who lays down his life for the sheep, and states the terms of His discipleship as follows : 'If any man will come after me, let him deny himself and take up his cross and follow me' (Lk 9²³). Nor did He mistake the facts, for early in His career the antagonism developed which increased in intensity until it culminated in the Crucifixion. Only by a denial of His vocation in establishing the Kingdom of God could He have saved His life ; only by what was impossible with Him—the forgetting of the will of God and the ceasing to love men. Thus we see that vicarious sacrifice was necessarily involved in His work of establishing His Kingdom, and in this sense was not singular or exceptional, but came under the general law of service. 'Whatever more is to be said as to the significance of Christ's death, this at least is certain, that he died as a faithful martyr for truth and love' (Bruce).

(2) There seems, however, to be something deeper in Jesus' consciousness than the mere fact that His work of founding His Kingdom will so cross the world-spirit of selfishness and sin that He will develop an antagonism which will end in His vicarious death. He clearly relates it to the fact of *remission of sins*. In Lk 22³⁷ there is a deeper thought than Hollmann has in mind when he says : 'He is only thinking of the dreary fact that His countrymen are going to treat Him as a criminal instead of as the Holy One of God,' for this passage was associated in the minds of His hearers with a Messianic work of the greatest significance. Stronger statements are found in Mk 10³²· ³³ff. Jesus is going with His disciples to Jerusalem, and on the way seeks to impress them with what He has stated very earnestly before, that in Jerusalem He will be delivered to mockery and death, but in three days will rise again. This announcement is followed by the ambitious request of James and John for chief seats in His Kingdom. With His mind filled with the thought of His coming passion, He replies to them, 'Ye know not what ye ask. Are ye able to drink the cup which I drink, or be baptized with the baptism with which I am baptized ?' Then follows in an address to the disciples, who are indignant at James' and John's request, the notable words, 'For the Son of Man also came not to be ministered to, but to minister, and to give his life a ransom for many.' The correct interpretation of this passage is most important, for it is much emphasized by those who seek to find in Jesus' teaching an expiatory reference.

Dr. Baur and others have questioned its integrity, affirming that there is nothing like it in the Synoptics except Mt 20²⁸, which Baur also casts under suspicion, that it is introduced so abruptly as to be questionable, and that it has a Pauline flavour, and if genuine, would not have been omitted by Luke. The criticism, however, seems scarcely valid, for in speaking to the disciples about the nature of greatness—that its value lies in service—it was natural that Jesus should allude to His expected death of which He had previously spoken, using it as an illustration of the point He was enforcing.

The passage has had various interpretations.

Usually much weight has been attached to the word λύτρον, 'ransom,' and its Heb. equivalents, these being assumed to fix its meaning ; but this is unsatisfactory, for the LXX has employed λύτρον to translate four different Heb. terms, and besides, since Jesus spoke Aramaic, it is not certain that λύτρον, in the way the LXX uses it, exactly represents what Jesus said. If an exact interpretation were required, we should have to know the Aramaic word of which λύτρον is the translation. Hollmann has discussed this term cogently and ably, showing that Jesus probably did not use the Aram. cognate of *kōpher*, but the equivalent of a Heb. word derived either from פָּדָה 'to ransom,' נָּאַל 'to deliver,' or פָּרַק 'to set free.' Thus λύτρον would mean a purchase price, or a means of setting free. In this case ἀντί, of which much is made, would not signify 'in place of' and establish a thought of substitution, but 'for,' and the passage would mean that Jesus would give His life for the freeing or saving of many—an interpretation which would fit in with the context much better than if λύτρον is taken as the equivalent of *kōpher*. The idea would then be that men of the world find greatness in assuming superiority over others, whereas Jesus finds it in serving others. But if we assume that λύτρον means in this passage what it means in the LXX tr. of Leviticus, where the main idea of the ransom is that of substituting one thing for another, and if we hold that ἀντί means 'in place of,' the most that we can make out of the passage is that Jesus gives His life as a ransom price to liberate many who are in bondage. But what is the bondage ? Taking Jesus' other teachings into account, we cannot doubt that it is bondage to selfishness and sin, such selfishness and world-spirit as James and John had just shown. This would accord with the use of λυτρόω found in 1 P 1¹⁸ and Tit 2¹⁴. But even if this is the meaning, the passage does not state the *process* or *manner* of the ransom. The thought that because the word is taken from the old sacrificial system we must find there the meaning that is to be attached to it, is not warranted by sound principles of exegesis. That the thought of a vicarious satisfaction offered to God is not intended, is rendered clear by the fact that such an interpretation would contradict the whole tendency of the teachings of Jesus, who constantly emphasized the free grace of God as ready to forgive every repentant sinner. Jesus does not conceive of His work as an offering to God, or for the sake of God, but as performed solely in behalf of men. We conclude, then, that this important passage simply means that Jesus vicariously sacrificed His life in order to save men from the selfishness of sin. How He thought His death would accomplish this is not stated, and is a matter of inference. If anything is implied, it is that a complete surrender to the good of men is such a break with the world-spirit which has just revealed itself, even in such good men as the sons of Zebedee, that if men will accept this serving spirit and act from the motive of self-denying love, they will thereby win an inner, moral victory over the world, and thus be freed from its bondage and evil.

Another passage in the Synoptics which has been made to do service in attempts to explain the nature of Jesus' vicarious sacrifice and its relation to the remission of sins, is His utterance upon the cross. The depth of agony there expressed in the cry, 'My God, my God, why hast thou forsaken me ?' is said to indicate that in this dark experience Christ as a substitute was suffering in its fulness the wrath of God against sin ; that He was exiled from the joys of God's presence (Dale), because He was vicariously bearing the consequences of the transgressions of the race. There has been a tendency since asceticism invaded the Church, and the body was made the seat of sin,—and to crucify it was considered a way to please God,—to magnify the importance of the physical sufferings of Christ and make them the supreme sacrifice through which remission of sins has come. This was not the thought of the Apostolic age, which was impressed with His grace rather than by His physical sufferings. Christ's death had long been before His contemplation, and from it He never shrank. He spoke of it with calmness and dignity, and sometimes with apparent rapture : ' the Son of Man should be glorified ' (Jn 12^{23}). But when He refers to its modes and agents, He assumes another tone. It is the *form* not the *fact* of death from which He appears to shrink. He is overcome by the thought that the agents of His suffering are the religious leaders of His time, and that from His own company has arisen a traitor. Evil is using the occasion of His voluntary, vicarious death as an opportunity for more violent manifestation, and the men He is trying to save are at work to put Him to death. The highest revelation of His grace is the occasion for the highest manifestation of wickedness. Being in the midst of it, not thinking about it, but experiencing it, this fact of evil comes upon Him with an overwhelming reality, and for a moment His sensitive soul is clouded, and He lays hold of a sentence found in Ps 22^1 and utters it as the most suitable words at hand by which to express His agony. The psalm does not mean abandonment by God, but abandonment to suffering, for later it increasingly expresses the confidence of the sufferer that he will be heard and delivered by God, so that he shall yet come to praise Him ; nor does Jesus mean that He is abandoned by God and, substitutionally, under the crushing load of His displeasure, for He stays Himself on the fact that in His agony God is His God. As has been said : ' He who wrestles with death with such pious longing upon His lips has not fully lost His God, but rather presupposes a still abiding relationship with Him ' (Wendt). We cannot, therefore, believe that the words on the cross are in any sense a consciousness of God's displeasure.

(3) But not only do the Synoptics relate Christ's vicarious sacrifice to the remission of sins, they also connect it with *the ratification of the New Covenant*, especially by the words spoken at the Last Supper. The account is found in all the Synoptics and in 1 Co 11. There has been a good deal of criticism concerning the true text, some holding that εἰς ἄφεσιν ἁμαρτιῶν and περὶ πολλῶν, ὑπὲρ ὑμῶν are later additions. Some also affirm that ἡ καινὴ διαθήκη of Lk. are words due to the influence of St. Paul. Some of the reasons suggested for this criticism seem to have weight, but nothing that has been said is at all decisive, so that it is best to let the text stand. To interpret its meaning we must remember the occasion with which it is connected—the celebration of the Passover. This feast was regarded as a memorial of the delivery from bondage, and was at the time of Jesus a joyful festival. In the discourse of the Last Supper the symbolism used is not drawn from the Paschal lamb, but rather from Ex 24, where the sacrifice established to celebrate the new covenant between Jahweh and Israel at Mount Sinai is described. The victim was slain, divided into two parts, and the contracting parties passing between these parts were sprinkled with blood. Thus the covenant was solemnized, and the partaking of the flesh in common indicated communion. As the offering at Sinai sealed the Old Covenant, so Jesus, when about to die, looked upon Himself as the victim whose blood would seal the New Covenant which He had established in inaugurating the Kingdom of God. Says Stevens (*Chr. Doct. of Salv.* 50) :

' The Supper is, then, the symbolic ratification of the New Covenant, analogous to the solemn rite by which the ancient covenant was confirmed by an offering denoting the establishment of communion with God and participation in the blessings of His grace. If regard be had solely to the language of our Lord at the institution of the Supper, it must be admitted, I think, that it is adapted to carry our thoughts not in the direction of the current Jewish ideas of propitiation by sacrifice, but rather toward the conception of a new relation of fellowship with God and obedience to Him constituted by Jesus' death.'

We conclude, therefore, that we do not find in the Synoptics any teaching which warrants the theological deduction often made, that the vicarious sacrifice of Christ is an offering made to satisfy the justice of God, propitiate Him in the sense of removing His displeasure, or secure the remission of sins by removing objective obstacles to the free movement of God's grace.

2. Vicarious sacrifice in the writings attributed to St. John.—The writings which are ascribed to St. John present the vicarious sacrifice of Christ in a somewhat different light from the Synoptics. There is much use, in these writings, of the thought that men become free through light, or that salvation is by revelation. If one walks in the light, that is, holds fellowship with God in righteousness and love, he is saved.

It is not necessary here to go into the critical questions concerning authorship and other special difficulties which these writings present. We believe the balance of argument is in favour of their authenticity. One cannot fail, however, to note that the historic reality which characterizes the Synoptic accounts is here invaded by the subjective, mystic type of thought of the author. The parable gives way to the doctrinal discussions. The doctrine of the Kingdom is supplanted by discourses about eternal life. There is also clear evidence that the discourses of Jesus found in Jn. were not delivered in the form there presented, but have been worked over in the contemplations of the Apostle. St. John's religious consciousness, however, has been developed under the influence of Jesus, and his statements and discourses are built up on the basis of the real sayings of the Master. They are therefore of the highest value.

(*a*) The Prologue to the *Gospel* especially draws out the above conception, and makes the object of Christ's vicarious sacrifice the revelation of the Father. By illuminating the world, Jesus saves the world. He shines in on the darkness of human society and thus gives life. ' This is life eternal, that they should know thee, the only true God, and Jesus Christ whom thou hast sent ' (Jn 17^3).

But along with this conception of redemption through revelation, there is another line of passages which refer to the sufferings and death of Christ, and which relate these to His saving office. St. John seems to have clearly recognized that sin is a power which excludes the coming in of light, and that therefore it needs in some special sense to be overcome. The first of these passages is the announcement of John the Baptist : ' Behold the Lamb of God, which taketh away the sin of the world ' (Jn 1^{29}). Many have questioned the genuineness of a statement so different from those with which the Synoptics begin the ministry of Christ ; but admitting it to be authentic, we have the following facts to note concerning it : (1) It is suggested by Is 13^7. (2) The phrase ὁ αἴρων means ' who removes,' as the LXX uses other terms for bearing sin. (3) While the words ' the Lamb of God ' go back to the Jewish sacrificial system, as here used they are connected with the conception of prophecy and not of ritual. (4) There is certainly nothing clearly to join this passage to the idea of bearing the consequences, or punishment of sin. Jn 3$^{14-16}$ is a passage which seems to represent a sentiment of Jesus, probably enlarged and given in the words of the Apostle. It contains the following teaching : (1) That the vicarious sacrifice of Christ originated in the love of God. (2) That acceptance of it by faith secures eternal life. (3) That the lifting up on the cross is an exaltation before men. (4) That it is necessary (δεῖ) in order that men should not perish, but have eternal life.

There is no expiatory idea suggested in the passage, but the thought seems to be that the voluntary death of Christ on the cross 'is the mode in which the love of God asserted itself and became effectual for the salvation of the world' (Terry).

The vicarious sacrifice of Jesus is taught also in other passages; as Jn $6^{50.\ 51}$ $10^{11.\ 15}$ 12^{24} 15^{13}, and in the High-Priestly prayer in ch. 17. Jn $6^{50.\ 51}$ is not an allusion to the Lord's Supper, but is connected with the miracle of the loaves, the feeding of the multitude suggesting the idea of spiritual feeding, of Jesus' mission to bring to men spiritual manna by the partaking of which they would have life. It does not refer to atonement, but to something present and available.

The dominating idea is that of ethical appropriation, which Lightfoot describes as follows: 'To partake of the Messiah truly is to partake of Himself, His pure nature, His righteousness, His spirit.' Jn $10^{11.\ 15}$ does not speak of an expiatory offering for sin, but rather 'of an exposure to loss of life consequent upon faithful care of the sheep' (Terry). Jn 12^{24} states only the general law that to effect results in the moral world one must sacrifice himself, a principle of which the life of Jesus is the supreme illustration. Jn 15^{13} is an important passage, as some have made τιθέναι τὴν ψυχὴν ὑπέρ point to a substitutionary death of judicial significance; but there is no reason to see in it more than a complete consecration of life to the good of others, that witholds not even when it leads to death. The Johannine use of τιθέναι favours this interpretation, as does the relation of this passage to the counsel how men should give themselves to one another's good. Nor does the word ἁγιάζειν (17^{19}) necessitate a sacrificial or expiatory giving of Himself; for in other passages in Jn. the word is not used in this sense. Moreover, the disciples could not sanctify themselves in this manner. The passage simply means the complete consecration of His life to His work with all that it involved, but it does not give any special interpretation of His death.

(b) In the *Epistles* of St. John we come upon passages which seem more dogmatic, notably 1 Jn 1^7 $2^{1f.}$ 3^{15} 4^{10}. In these passages, as in the Fourth Gospel, we have clearly set forth the fact that the work of Christ originates in the love of God, and is 'a move on His part to provide a covering of sins.' The word ἱλασμός, which is tr. 'propitiation,' means covering or blotting out. Westcott says: 'It contains the notion not of appeasing one often in anger, but of altering the character of that which interposes an inevitable obstacle to fellowship. The propitiation, when it is applied to the sinner, neutralizes the sin.' Deissmann shows that its strict classical meaning is lost in the NT, and that it is applied to any sacrificial offering. The context in 1 Jn. also is against giving the term a relation to the righteousness of God, since it is deduced from the Divine love (4^{10}). Consequently we must see in this word a covering of sin in the sense of cleansing from it, or *propitiation*. That which separates from the fellowship of God is not any exigency of the Divine government, or any offence to the Divine nature, but it is the fact that man has chosen to walk in darkness, has participated in the works of the devil. His sin must be put away, and this the blood of Jesus is able to accomplish. If we are asked how, we know no better reply than that of Beyschlag in the following passage (*NT Theol.* ii. 448):

'Now what can "cover" the sin of the world in the eyes of God? Only a personality and a deed which contain the power of actually delivering the world from sin. For the sin which allows itself to be broken, and to disappear—that only can God forgive and consider extinct. This is the general view of the OT and the NT. Christ in His death has gained a power to thus deliver the world from sin. By His union with God and His love to God and the brethren in the conflict, even to blood and death, with the spirit of the world, He has overcome the spirit of selfishness and evil which rules the world, and in consequence of that He is able to overcome it in every heart into which He finds entrance. He has thus become to the Father the Surety for the purification of humanity, and for His sake the Father can offer forgiveness, if men will receive and obey Him.'

(c) The ideas found in the *Apocalypse* are practically the same as those found in the Fourth Gospel and the Johannine Epistles. They have been summarized as follows: '(1) That death is regarded as a great demonstration of love (1^5). (2) It is a death which once for all has achieved something. There is a finished work in it (1^5). (3) It is a death which has an abiding power (v.[6]). (4) This abiding power is exercised in this, that it enables men to be faithful to Christ under persecution, to suffer with Him rather than sin, finally, rather to die than to sin (12^{11}). (5) Hence the blood of Christ both does something once for all, in breaking the bond which sin holds us by, and bringing us into such a relation to God that we are a people of priests; and does something progressively, in assuring our gradual assimilation to Jesus Christ the faithful witness' (Denney, *Death of Christ*, p. 250).

3. The doctrine of vicarious sacrifice in the writings of St. Paul.—St. Paul's doctrine of vicarious sacrifice is very difficult to interpret, although strongly emphasized; and consequently opinions have varied more concerning his meaning than concerning the thought of any other Biblical writer.

The reasons for this are: (1) The unsystematic form in which he often presents his ideas. (2) The use of diverse figures. (3) His considering the subject from different standpoints. (4) His frequent use of abstract and ideal rather than historic conceptions. (5) The failure to realize that St. Paul is controlled by a practical rather than a theoretical motive, that he is not consciously developing a systematic statement, but is writing out of his experience, and trying to adjust his own religious conceptions. (6) His large use of Pharisaical phrases and forms of thought in describing his new experiences, making it difficult to decide how literally they are to be taken. (7) His evident desire to find a harmony between certain incongruities between his old beliefs and his present conceptions and experience. (8) His rhetorical temper, leading to extravagant emphasis in the midst of logical discussion. (9) The necessity he felt of dwelling on some conceptions, as the sufferings and death of Christ, because they were so contrary to current thoughts and expectations. (10) The confusing way in which the doctrinal and the historical are sometimes mixed, and his taking Adam and the Fall as literal historic facts. (11) The little use he makes of the Christian tradition, seldom referring to the life or teachings of Jesus—'I neither received it from man, neither was I taught it' (Gal 1^{12}). (12) The fact that Christ with him is the Christ of his spiritual intuition rather than of historic knowledge and observation.

Because of these characteristics, we are, in interpreting St. Paul, to observe the following principles: (1) Not to be too literal or exact in method, or to crowd his figures. (2) To understand that we have to do not simply with the revelation of Christ, but with the reflexion of a man of deep religious feeling, 'fiery fancy,' and extraordinary logical power, who is developing facts into doctrines. (3) That he is doing this for practical purposes rather than to give the Church a theology, and aims to meet needs and special points of view characteristic of his day. (4) That the inner religious experience of the man, out of which he wrote, is not fully dissociated from Rabbinical dialectics and Pharisaical conceptions, which had been well wrought into the framework of his religious thinking. He had to express himself by means of 'the ideas and association of ideas lying ready in his consciousness,' which bore a decided Jewish stamp. (5) That he is sufficiently tinctured with Alexandrian methods of interpreting Scripture to use Biblical citations in accommodated senses. (6) That the Alexandrian ideas about the opposition of flesh and spirit, the earthly man and the heavenly man, have determined the direction of some of his reflexions. (7) That the Pharisaical theology had much to do in determining the form of his presentation of the doctrine of vicarious sacrifice. This theology construed the relations between man and God from the legal standpoint. Men who do not fulfil the Law are responsible and involved in guilt. This guilt must be recompensed, or punishment must be visited on the offender. Good deeds, meritorious performances, voluntary mortifications are availing, but with most men the guilt of misdoing is so great that such compensations are not sufficient to balance accounts and avert deserved punishment. Hence it is necessary to look to the superfluous merits of some eminently just or holy person to be imputed to sinners for the covering of their deficiencies. (8) While the husk of St. Paul's thought is at times Jewish, there is in him a kernel of his own, a spiritual and inner side which we must grasp to understand his real teachings. Most of the theories of vicarious sacrifice which do not accord with our modern ethical spirit and with the principles of our modern thought, arise from making too much of the 'earthen vessels' into which Paul's real beliefs are cast, and it is clear that we must get rid of these to find the 'heavenly treasures.'

Most interpreters see in St. Paul a twofold representation of Christ's vicarious sacrifice, a juridical, based on his Pharisaical conceptions, and an ethico-mystical, a product of his vital religious experience. A. B. Bruce thinks they indicate different stages of the development of the doctrine of reconciliation in the Apostle's thinking, but one can scarcely consider them as 'two doctrines,' for (1) They are wrought out in the same Epistles; (2) They interpenetrate. Pfleiderer explains them psychologically, making them the expression of 'two souls which always struggled with each other in the breast of the Pharisee and the Apostle Paul, namely, the legal Jewish soul and the evangelical Christian soul.' As the juridical conception arises in his discussion with the Jews and has reference to Jewish ideas only, it may be that the juridical element is adopted as a form of argument which will be most convincing to a special class, and that it is not intended for a universal form in which to put the doctrine. We shall, therefore, not depend so much on the form as on the reality which seems to lie behind it—the spiritual idea—in trying to set forth Paul's view. The main positions of the Apostle which bear on his conception of Jesus' vicarious sacrifice can be stated under the following heads:

(1) *Man is separated from God by the fact of sin.* —This is due (*a*) to the attitude of God toward sin. The wrath of God is revealed from heaven against all ungodliness and unrighteousness of men, who, light having been given them, are without excuse and are treasuring up for themselves wrath in the day of wrath (Ro 1[18ff.], Eph 5[6], Col 3[6]). (*b*) Man because of sin is at enmity with God, minding the things of the flesh and not the things of the spirit, nor being subject to the law of God (Ro 8[6-9]). For men to be brought back to God they must be led to renounce sin, for God can never allow it or harmonize with it.

(2) *God wants to save men from sin and reconcile them to Himself.*—(*a*) The work of reconciliation, St. Paul says, is begun by God, who was in Christ reconciling the world unto Himself (2 Co 5[18. 19]), who sent Him forth (Ro 3[25], Gal 4[4]) to redeem them which were under the Law; and since He 'spared not his own Son, but delivered him up for us all, how shall he not also with him freely give us all things?' (Ro 8[32]). In view of these explicit statements, there is no place for the idea that Jesus' vicarious sacrifice was to reconcile God to us. The word καταλλάσσω, 'reconcile,' is used three times in 2 Co 5[18-20], and in each case the reconciliation is to God, and not of God to the world. The noun καταλλαγή is twice used in this passage to indicate something given to us, and reinforces the affirmation of the verb. The peace the sinner receives through this reconciliation is a peace πρὸς τὸν θεόν, *toward God*, and not a peace of God toward men. Christ, therefore, in seeking the salvation of man, is the expression of God; it is God's action, God's kindness, God's sacrifice. Whatever Christ meant in His life and work God meant. (*b*) This idea is further enforced by the passages which speak of Christ's work as one of grace (Ro 3[24]): those who would be justified by the Law are fallen away from grace (Gal 5[4]), for salvation is the gift of God (Eph 2[7. 8]).

(3) *There are certain obstacles to God's free forgiving grace which must be overcome.*—(*a*) Such an obstacle is not the ethical nature of God, or His justice, which demands a propitiatory offering or substitute in punishment to make it possible for Him consistently to forgive. This idea is entirely out of harmony with the passages just referred to, which make God originate the vicarious sacrifice of Christ, and which make Christ's act God's own. If God is Himself acting in Christ, St. Paul cannot anywhere mean that Jesus is seeking in His sacrifice to obtain something from God which He is not willing to give. It has been well said, 'since God was working in Christ there was nothing in God to overcome' (Clarke). Certain passages, however, are said to teach a theory of expiation which has objective reference, and show the necessity of removing obstacles to forgiveness in the nature of God. Some of these are Ro 3[26], 2 Co 5[21], Gal 3[13], and Col 2[14]. St. Paul, it is held, in these passages teaches that sin is an offence to the righteousness of God, and this righteousness must be vindicated and compensated before forgiveness is possible. Bearing in His death the punishment due to us, Christ has satisfied the Divine righteousness, so that God can consistently exercise His grace toward sinners. This makes Christ's vicarious sacrifice penal.

The interpretation is objectionable for the following reasons :—(*a*) Judicial punishment and forgiveness are incompatible, for forgiveness means the withdrawal and not the infliction of such punishment. The disapproval of God is the soul of the punishment of sin, but this is withdrawn when forgiveness is extended. If it is the purpose of God to reconcile man to Himself, and if He is in the world in Christ seeking to bring this about, the attitude of disapproval of the sinner which makes the penalty of the sin has been cancelled by His own act, and there can be no moral necessity in God which demands a judicial rather than an ethical vindication of His righteousness. (*β*) Punishment is non-transferable, and any infliction of it on a substitute is not punishment but something else. (*γ*) When St. Paul speaks of Christ's sacrifice in relation to us, he always uses ὑπὲρ ἡμῶν 'in our behalf,' not ἀντὶ ἡμῶν, 'instead of us.' (*δ*) St. Paul's conception of the righteousness of God is not judicial but ethical, and it is not satisfied by something offered to it, but by such an expression of it as destroys sin in man. (*ε*) It is difficult to see how, if our sins have been atoned for by a substitutionary sacrifice, faith in Christ is necessary to salvation. When a debt is paid the obligation is released. (*ζ*) The idea does not do full justice to God's antagonism to sin, as the extinction of it is more to be desired than the punishment of it.

The statement in Ro 3[25] that God sent forth Christ to be a propitiation through faith in His blood, to show His righteousness, cannot mean that Christ's vicarious sacrifice is intended to *make it* righteous for God to forgive sin. εἰς ἔνδειξιν means to show, or demonstrate. Now, as Tymms has said: 'Before the righteousness of an act can be shown, or proved, or demonstrated, it must actually be righteous in itself. To say that a demonstration of a thing or a quality can produce a thing, or confer the quality demonstrated, is absurd.' If God is in Christ, this whole line of interpretation must be cut out. The passage is contradictory and incapable of being understood, if with Sanday ('Romans' in *ICC*) we reply to the question, Who is propitiated ?, 'the answer can only be "God."' The word ἱλαστήριον has been given four interpretations, of which we prefer the tr. 'mercy-seat,' since this is its accredited meaning in Biblical Greek, and since the symbolic significance of the mercy-seat made it a fitting figure for the Apostle to use. This interpretation also best explains the phrase '*in his blood,*' and the middle voice employed in the Gr. verb προέθετο, 'set forth for himself.' The thought, therefore, is that God sent forth His Son 'as the reality and fulfilment of all that was symbolized in the mercy-seat.' God will no longer look upon sin, or consider it, in the case of those who by faith in the blood of Christ accept His provision. Thus God's righteousness will be revealed in His grace.

(b) Nor is the obstacle to God's forgiveness 'the Law,' of which St. Paul makes so much, considered as a judicial principle, having rights which must be met. It is often said that Christ suffered vicariously to satisfy the claims of the Law, and sometimes this idea of law is developed into a system of moral government which must be vindicated. Gal 3[13] says, 'Christ redeemed us from the curse of the law.' 'The law' here is manifestly the Mosaic law, and the 'us' cannot mean those who never lived under this law, but must refer to Hebrew Christians. The Jews who were under this discipline were freed from it when they believed in Christ, for He established a new covenant. St. Paul's language must not here be made universal, for it applies only to a limited class of people. St. Paul clearly tells us that we are justified, not by anything done to or for law, but 'apart from law,' as a pure act of grace. All thought of justification on the principle of law is in Ro 3[20] ruled out. As has been said, Christ's gospel is not a 'veiled legalism,' and He did not work out for men a 'law-righteousness which they could not have obtained for themselves.' Says W. N. Clarke (Outline of Theol. p. 336): 'If grace comes simple and whole-hearted into the world, it does not come to satisfy legal demands or win law-righteousness. . . . God does not deal with men through Christ in the character of lawgiver, or judge, or in any special character, but in His real character as God, His own very self, in personal relations with His creatures as their very selves.' Indeed, what is the Law in any true sense but God revealing to men His nature as righteous? It is not an abstract thing apart from God that has rights, or can make demands, or needs vindication. Our relations are with a person and not with a system.

There is, however, according to St. Paul, one thing necessary in order to make it possible for God to forgive, and that is, His opposition to sin must be shown. He must be Himself revealed as One who wants men to leave off sinning and become righteous. God could not be satisfied without providing some adequate revelation of this fact, and He has provided it in Christ.

(4) *The reconciliation which God desires to effect is accomplished by the vicarious sacrifice of Christ*; for this Christ was sent into the world; for this He lived, suffered, and died. St. Paul makes much of the cross. It is the heart of his theology, because it is God's supreme self-expression in sacrifice to sinful man. In 2 Co 5[15] we read: 'He died for all, that they which live should no longer live unto themselves, but unto him who for their sakes died and rose again.' No clearer passage is needed to show that God's forgiving grace is mediated through the vicarious sacrifice of Christ, and that His inmost heart is thus made manifest. Christ became man's Saviour (a) by His absolute obedience. 'For as by one man's disobedience many were made sinners, so by the obedience of one shall many be made righteous' (Ro 5[19]). Christ has resisted sin unto suffering, sacrificed the creature will to the will of God, become obedient unto death, even the death of the cross (Ph 2[8]), and so has conquered sin by breaking through its general dominion. To those who join themselves to Him, He imparts the same power through the influence of the Spirit. (b) He has also vicariously borne our sins. St. Paul does not say that He has borne the consequences of them, or the punishment of them, but He has taken our sins on Himself in such a way that they have been a burden to His heart and caused Him to suffer. He has borne them in the sense that He has borne with them. To God incarnate in Christ, sin, as the despoiler of those whom He loves and wishes good, must be offensive, must be an affliction, a source of suffering and pain. God's sympathy is always being taxed by the evil of the world, His holiness is always being offended, and His heart is ever being grieved. In a real and vital way this is sin-bearing—this enduring it in patience, this carrying it upon the heart. Another way in which Christ bears our sins is in labouring to overcome them. Sin puts on God a great task, that of suffering and labouring to save the world. This sin-bearing is what St. Paul refers to when he says, 'Him who knew not sin he made sin on our behalf, that we might become the righteousness of God in him' (2 Co 5[21]). This does not mean that He made Him a sinner, for God was in Christ; but in His work of expressing God's love for men, Christ so identifies Himself with humanity that He feels its sin as a personal burden. It is an utter mistake to interpret this passage, as many have done, to mean that Christ was made to suffer the punishment of sin, or that guilt was imputed, or transferred to Him, which is an ethical impossibility. The bold figure simply refers to such an identification with men as to make their burden of sin Christ's own. The much quoted passage in Gal. (3[13]), 'Christ redeemed us from the curse of the law, having become a curse for us; for it is written, Cursed is every one that hangeth on a tree,' is to be explained in a similar manner. This is a strong expression based on Dt 21[22. 23]. Christ's death on the cross had the outward appearance of His being an accursed criminal, and by metonymy expresses the humiliation and sin-bearing of Christ in 'His vicarious identification with man under the curse of the law.' Says Terry: 'He entered into the depths of human suffering, and felt most keenly the bitter exposure of sinful man to the curse of violated law; and, being Himself personally without sin and without any condemnation from law, He was the more capable of becoming "greatly amazed and sore troubled" over the desperate situation of sin-cursed humanity under the curse of holy law' (c) In bearing sin, Christ condemns it and establishes God's righteousness, establishes it by manifesting it. The punishment of sin is not the strongest way of expressing one's condemnation of it; a stronger way is to be willing to endure sacrifice to save one from it. It must be an awful thing, if God will go to such lengths of suffering to rescue men from its evil (Jn 3[16]). Men risk their lives only to save their fellows from calamitous dangers. God suffers in Christ, only because He looks at sin as an awful, destructive fact. Nowhere is the righteousness of God, as over against sin, seen so clearly as in the death of Jesus. (d) The vicarious sacrifice of Christ also expresses God's willingness to save. 'God commendeth his own love toward us, in that, while we were yet sinners, Christ died for us' (Ro 5[8-11]). It is a voluntary expression of interest in us that withholds not at the greatest possible cost; and wins gratitude and response if anything can awaken them. Love can go no farther. In such a work God does His utmost to bring men to Himself. The vicarious element in Christ's life satisfies God, for it is God's highest effort for man's recovery; and it satisfies man, for it shows Jesus as his personal Saviour.

(5) *The vicarious sacrifice of Christ becomes available through faith.*—Men cannot maintain a passive relation to Christ and be saved from sin; they must join themselves to Him by a living faith.

They must die with Him on the cross, and rise with Him to newness of life. They must be one with Him in the fellowship of His sufferings. Christ must be in them their hope of glory. 'I live no longer,' cries the Apostle, 'but Christ liveth in me; and the life I now live, I live by faith in the Son of God' (Gal 2²⁰). By fellowship with Christ the old man is put off and dies. The Christ living in us becomes the power by which we break absolutely with the sin of the world, and win a victory over it. This is being saved—being delivered from sin and brought to righteousness. A man who in the obedience of faith—faith being not the intellectual principle of belief, but the act of trust—joins himself to Christ, brings himself thereby into fellowship and moral unity with Him, and becomes possessed of the mind of Christ—the mind of hostility to sin and love of the good (Gal 3²⁶). Christ who has ascended in the Resurrection, descends into the heart of the believer in order to assist and complete the freeing, saving work. It is because of this that St. Paul lays such emphasis on the Resurrection in connexion with his doctrine of salvation. He 'was delivered up for our trespasses, and was raised for our justification' (Ro 4²⁵). Having been reconciled to God, the believer lives the new life of righteousness by faith, which becomes a continuous experience, and will be consummated in an eternal salvation.

(6) St. Paul also has a doctrine of *a new humanity obtained through Christ's vicarious sacrifice*, which grows out of the importance he attaches to human solidarity. Salvation is not only individual, but also social. This feature of St. Paul's thought has recently been worked out in an interesting way by Dr. Olin A. Curtis in *The Christian Faith* (pp. 317–337). The end of God in redemption is 'to obtain a race of holy men.' 'God wanted an entangled race.' While Christ is the source of help and strength, the social solidarity of men makes it essential that the social organism be redeemed, for men must help to complete one another. The new humanity built up in Christ becomes a body of which He is the living head, and for which He ever makes intercession.

4. The doctrine of vicarious sacrifice in Hebrews.—The doctrine of vicarious sacrifice as set forth in Hebrews, although elaborate, need not be especially considered here, as this Epistle gives us no new information of importance. The subject is extensively discussed with special reference to the symbolism of the OT, the doctrine being set forth largely in terms of sacrifice. We do not hear anything about 'the law,' or about satisfaction to it or to God's righteousness. Here Christ is a pure offering in sacrifice to God, but His death is not received as a substitutionary expiation. The absence of this idea is the more remarkable that the author so closely approximates it. Had he shared this conception, it is not easy to see why he did not bring it forward in connexion with such assertions as that Christ made propitiation (ἱλάσκεσθαι) for the sins of the people (2¹⁷), tasted death for every man (2⁹), and was offered to bear away the sins of many (9²⁸).

'Not the satisfaction of the law, the removal of the curse, the endurance of the penalty of sin, but a Divine fitness, or decorum, is assigned as the reason why the Author of salvation should be made perfect through sufferings (2¹⁰). Elsewhere he deduces the necessity of Jesus' death from the very fact that He is a priest. It is the calling of a priest to offer sacrifice, hence "this high priest must also have somewhat to offer" (8³), and that "somewhat" can only be His own life. In another place this necessity is derived from the import of the word διαθήκη. This word has two meanings—"covenant" and "testament." Our author passes from one meaning to the other in the elaboration of his argument. The first *covenant* was sealed by a death; in fact, wherever a *testament* or will goes into effect, it does so in consequence of a death: therefore it was needful that the establishment of the *New Covenant* should be ratified by a death, that is, by the death of Christ' (Stevens, *op. cit.* 76 f.).

One interesting fact concerning this Epistle is the ethical meaning the author attaches to the whole conception of sacrifice, making it, as applied to Christ, an entirely different thing from what it is in the Levitical ritual and ceremonies.

The Epistles of St. Peter will not be considered, for they shed no new light on the problem under discussion.

5. Summary of results.—In concluding our investigation of vicarious sacrifice in the NT, we summarize our results as follows : (1) The doctrine of vicarious sacrifice is the very heart of the Scriptures. It is the harmonious note of all the Biblical writers, finding expression in the OT sacrifices, in the life and teachings of Jesus, and in the writings of the Apostles. God is seeking to develop a righteous people, a holy race, and the process or method is by vicarious sacrifice.

(2) In the Scriptures the doctrine is largely expressed in figures, and symbols, and current conceptions which make its interpretation difficult, and have led to much misunderstanding. Many theories have been built up on what close analysis shows to be only a metaphor, or Jewish sacrificial term. We must not strain popular language to give exact scientific statement.

(3) While Biblical writers assert their individuality in stating the fact of vicarious sacrifice, setting it forth in different ways, they all agree in what it is and what it does—that it is a method of God to save men from sin and bring them into fellowship with Himself.

(4) The Scriptures discuss the doctrine of vicarious sacrifice from different standpoints and in different relations, and do not give us what may be called a theory of the subject. It is proper for us to attempt to construct one from what is revealed, but we must have in mind the significance of the Scripture presentation.

(5) St. Paul differs from other writers in having a theology, and in having worked over the facts of Christ's vicarious life and death in the crucible of his own thinking. In doing this he has had in mind a special class of hearers, the Jewish law under which they and he have lived, and the relation of Christ's work to it; and he has expressed his thought in terms of the Pharisaic theology in which he has been trained, and has used certain conceptions from Palestinian and Alexandrian sources which we must take into account in interpreting him. While he has developed his conceptions in legal forms, he has saved himself from legalism by exhibiting the ethical content of Christ's work and vitally relating it to life.

(6) The doctrine of vicarious sacrifice is grounded not in a judicial or rectoral relation of God, but in a deeply personal fact and expression. (*a*) It is founded by God in His personal interest in and love for men. It is the unfolding of God's heart to sinners, and God is in Christ reconciling the world to Himself. (*b*) It seeks a personal end, namely, the salvation of sinners and their restoration to the personal relation of fellowship with God. (*c*) All theories, therefore, which make it effect a change in God are un-Scriptural. The fact that Christ is the Logos effectually routs such conceptions.

(7) Christ's vicarious atonement, because grounded in personal relations, is to be explained not as a judicial, but as a deeply ethical and spiritual fact. It embodies and represents not God's rectoral or judicial relations, but His moral nature. It is a transaction in the realm of spirit, expressing in an empirical event a spiritual principle. We can interpret it only by rising above the abstract fictions of logic into the realm of the realities of the moral life, seeing in it not forensic transactions, but the living action of spiritual laws. Therefore, it is not (*a*) a compensation to law, as if law had an

objective reality, and rights apart from the Being whose expression it is; or (*b*) a compensation to justice, as if justice and grace were in antagonism in the Divine nature, and His attributes were more than diverse reflexions of the action of His harmonious being, or as if a mechanical device, of which God is Himself the author, can compensate His justice. 'Divine justice seeks the triumph of good over evil, and hence identifies itself with love.' (*c*) It is, therefore, in no sense penal. It really impeaches the moral government of God to introduce an expedient, in order to render it possible for a moral Being who has created men, and taken upon Himself responsibilities in so doing, to be able to forgive His erring creatures. All these and other theories are developed out of the old idea of God's transcendence, considering Him as a Being above, ruling from without, a King on His throne, a Judge on His judicial bench, at least a Being separate, outward, remote, when the true conception is that of His immanence, as One who acts in the world, tabernacles with men, entangles Himself with our life. This is the Scriptural idea : 'In him we live and move and have our being.'

(8) Vicarious sacrifice is an expression and revelation of God. This the Scriptures abundantly teach. It manifests God's feelings about sin, the intense opposition with which He regards it; and it reveals God's love for the sinner, the depth and power and sacrificial character of it, leading even to suffering and death.

(9) The work of Jesus in salvation is closely related to the Kingdom of God. The teachings of Jesus centre about this Kingdom. He dwells on it, and puts it forth as the thing He is come to establish on the earth. But men can enter this Kingdom only by availing themselves of the benefits of the vicarious sacrifice of Christ. They must thus come to know God, and live in that spiritual fellowship with Him which constitutes the social bond of His Kingdom.

(10) The mediation of Christ's sacrifice is rendered available through faith. Not all receive its benefits as they would if it were a penal satisfaction rendered to law or Divine majesty. It must be changed from an outer to an inner fact, to an experience of life, and this is possible only through a living faith which unites men to God in obedience and fellowship. By the personal participation in Christ's vicarious work for us, we become 'partakers of the divine nature' (2 P 1[4]), and Christ comes to 'live within us,' 'our hope of glory' (Gal 2[20], Col 1[27]). God's method of salvation, therefore, is by faith, bringing the soul into constant and living contact with One who embodies the higher spiritual life. We are not saved by example, but by touch.

(11) Salvation through the appropriation of Christ's vicarious sacrifice is a continuous process, and not a finished work. His life and death are historic facts, but they are perpetuated in their meaning in this, that Christ has passed into the heavens, where He abides as our perpetual Mediator. He was 'raised for our justification'; but, more than that, He has come to us invisibly in the person of His Spirit, who continues His work by taking on Himself the burden of trying to influence us to accept the benefits of Christ's sacrifice and God's forgiving grace. 'The eternal Spirit and God and Christ are all one in this ministry of reconciliation, and the Lord Christ has no more finished His work of mediation than has the Holy Father or the Holy Spirit finished yearning for mankind' (Terry).

(12) Christ's vicarious sacrifice has constituted a new humanity, for it is not simply an individual, but a racial fact, seeking to produce a redeemed human family, that shall constitute the very 'body of Christ.' There is a profound meaning in the intercessory prayer of Jesus that we may be *one*, as He and the Father are one,—'I in them and they in me,'—and to the effect that we may be 'sanctified by the truth' and 'perfected in one,' and finally be with Him where He is, participating in the glory which He had with the Father before the world was (Jn 17[19-24]). St. Paul has this end in mind in Eph 2[6], where he speaks about being raised up with Christ, and coming to sit with Him in the heavenlies. The discipline of life is to help in completing our work of preparation, and in enabling us to realize the great consummation of our salvation in Christ.

For the history of the doctrine see art. REDEMPTION.

See also artt. ATONEMENT, DEATH OF CHRIST, PROPITIATION, RANSOM, REDEMPTION, SACRIFICE, ETC.

LITERATURE.—Schultz, *OT Theol.* ; Smend, *Alttest. Religionsgesch.* ; G. F. Moore, art. 'Sacrifice' in *EBi* ; A. B. Davidson, *Theol. of OT* ; Trumbull, *The Blood Covenant* ; Hollmann, *Die Bedeutung des Todes Jesu* ; Hoffmann, *Der Tod Christi in seiner Bedeutung für die Erlösung* ; Denney, *Death of Christ* ; Ritschl, *Justification and Reconciliation* ; Beyschlag, *NT Theol.* ; Wendt, *Teaching of Jesus* ; Weiss, *NT Theol.* ; Babut, *La Pensée de Jésus sur sa Mort d'après les Évangiles Synoptiques* ; Stevens, *Christian Doctrine of Salvation* ; Weber, *Jüd. Theol.*[2] ; Bousset, *Religion des Judentums* ; Pfleiderer, *Paulinismus* ; Feine, *Jesus Christus und Paulus* ; Cone, *Paul, the Man* ; Cremer, *Die Paulin. Rechtfertigungslehre* ; Ménégoz, *Le Péché et la Rédemption d'après St. Paul* ; Everett, *The Gospel of Paul* ; Ménégoz, *La Théologie de l'Épître aux Hébreux* ; Bushnell, *Vicarious Sacrifice* ; Tymms, *The Christian Idea of Atonement*.

SAMUEL PLANTZ.

VICTORY (νîκος, Mt 12[20], 1 Co 15[55, 57] ; νίκη, 1 Jn 5[4] ; תְּשׁוּעָה 1 S 19[5], Pr 21[31]).—Mt 12[20] is a quotation from Is 42[3] ; but in the latter the word used is אֱמֶת 'truth,' and not 'victory.' It is the same word, νενίκηκα (fr. νικάω), which is used by our Lord in Jn 16[33] 'I have overcome the world,' and in many other passages throughout the NT, to express the idea of 'overcoming.' To the mind of Jesus there is only one kind of victory. It is not the triumph over social and financial difficulties which issues in worldly success, but that mastery over our lower nature and the powers of evil within and around us which issues in self-control, and the subjection of the whole life to the will of God. This is the one real victory, without which any other is but a fleeting phantom. It was the victory which He Himself gained, and which His true disciples are enabled to achieve through His aid and guidance. This victory brings with it such blessings as forgiveness, deliverance from the dominion of sin and from the fear of death, a deep sense of the moral order of the world, peace with God, and life everlasting.

DUGALD CLARK.

VINE, VINEYARD (ἀμπελών).—Vine-culture was one of the oldest industries in Palestine. This is attested by the presence of rock-hewn wine-presses and traces of ancient vine terraces where all is wilderness to-day. Work in the vineyard furnished occupation to many (Mt 20[1ff.] 21[28]). Landowners planted vineyards, and let them to husbandmen (Mt 21[33ff.] etc.). The vineyard requires much care and attention. It is surrounded by a dry-stone wall, a bank of thorns, or fence of prickly pear. If it be on a slope, the terraces must be kept in good repair, lest the soil be washed away by winter rains. The ground is well worked with the hoe, and thoroughly cleansed of alien roots. Pruning is done in Dec. or Jan. ; the blossom is out in April and May ; the vintage is general in Sept., but somewhat earlier in the Jordan Valley. The 'tower' (Mt 21[33] etc.) is the shelter for the watchman who guards the crop against injury from man and beast.

The familiar form of the vine, with its abundant and luxuriant branches, would lend itself all the more readily to the allegorical use of Jesus, inasmuch as 'in the OT, and partially in Jewish thought, the vine was the symbol of Israel, not in their national, but in their Church capacity' (Edersheim, *LT* ii. 520; cf. Jn 15). See next article.

The fig and the vine are often closely associated (Lk 13[6]). The mod. Arab. *karm* stands for both vineyard and fig-orchard. From the Mishna we gather that 200 years after Christ vine-culture was still a flourishing industry in Palestine. With the coming of the Arabs, vineyards almost entirely disappeared. During the last cent. the industry has in some measure revived under the influence of the German and Jewish colonists in Palestine, and the French in the Lebanon. Both E. and W. of Jordan the vine is now largely cultivated. The grapes of Eshcol are in high repute.   W. EWING.

VINE, ALLEGORY OF THE.—In the allegory of the vine (Jn 15[1-10]) Christ describes the close relation which exists between the disciples and Himself, and impresses on them the necessity of the continuance of this intimate union as the indispensable condition of fruitfulness on their part. The figurative side of the allegory is not developed first and then followed by the interpretation, but figure and interpretation are woven together throughout the passage. When we separate them we find that the figurative material is comparatively slight. It presents to us the picture of a vine tended by a husbandman who takes away the unfruitful branches and cleanses the fruitful, *i.e.* cuts off from them all useless shoots, that they may become more productive. Attention is also directed to the fact that the unfailing condition of fruit-bearing is that the branch abide in the vine. If by any chance it is separated from the parent stock, it is of no more use, but is cast forth from the vineyard and withers away, and is fit only for firewood.

In the interpretation Christ Himself is the vine ('the true vine' is the phrase used, of which we shall discuss the significance presently); His Father is the husbandman, believers, especially the disciples, are the branches. As there are unfruitful branches in the natural vine, so there may be some who, in spite of their communion with Christ, yet prove unproductive. The fate which overtakes them is similar to that of the unfruitful branches of the natural vine. The Heavenly Husbandman severs the connexion between them and Christ (v.[2a]). Wherein fruitfulness consists Christ does not say. Some take it as the keeping of His commandments (v.[10]), and the practice of that righteousness whereby the soundness of the tree is proved (Mt 7[16. 20-21]), while others think specially of that Apostolic work which is to fall to the disciples (so Bruce, *Training of the Twelve*, p. 402). By the cleansing of the branches (v.[2b]) we must understand such Divine dealings as tend to greater fruitfulness in the life of the believer. The process of cleansing in the natural vine suggests to us the chastening discipline to which the Father subjects believers (so de Wette). But in proceeding to speak of the disciples, to whom He now directly refers as the branches, Christ gives a more general interpretation of the figure of cleansing. They are already clean, He says (v.[3]), on account of the word which He has spoken to them, *i.e.* the revelation He has given them has had a purifying influence upon their life. The vital matter for them is to continue in such close relationship to Christ, whose word has had this cleansing influence upon them, that they may ever remain clean. Therefore He proceeds to insist upon the necessity of their abiding in Him, *i.e.* making Him the source from which they derive all their strength and

nourishment (v.[4]). This is the indispensable condition of fruitfulness in the spiritual life (vv.[4. 5]).

Before proceeding to describe with greater fulness the blessed results that follow from such close adherence to Him, Christ pauses to indicate the fate of those who sever their connexion with Him (v.[6]). They are like the branches that have been broken off from the vine, which are cast out of the vineyard and wither away, and are gathered together and burned. Some would find an exact equivalent to all the details in this description. The casting forth corresponds to their exclusion from the Church, the withering to their loss of spiritual life, the gathering to the work of the angels (Mt 13[30. 39]), and the fire to Gehenna. In any case the language indicates the certainty of the destruction that awaits all who break away from their adherence to Christ. In contrast to this, Christ proceeds to describe the condition of those who abide in Him. United to Him in close communion, they will obtain whatsoever they ask (v.[7]). The result will be abundant fruitfulness to the glory of the Father, whereby they will become true disciples of Christ (v.[8]). The exhortation to abide in Him is finally strengthened by an appeal to the example of God and Christ in their relation to one another. Christ's love to the disciples is like the love of the Father to the Son. As Christ abides in the love of the Father by keeping His commandments, so will the disciples abide in the love of the Son if they keep His commandments (vv.[9. 10]).

Such is the course of the allegory. The following points in connexion with it may be briefly discussed:

1. What is meant by the *true* (ἀληθινή) vine? It is often taken as suggesting that the natural vine only imperfectly represents the idea of the communion of Christ with believers. But why should the vine be selected rather than any other plant? And in what respect is the organic relationship suggested by the figure only imperfectly represented by the natural vine? H. Holtzmann understands the phrase as meaning that Christ is the vine which belongs to the higher world and has been planted by God in the midst of mankind; and he finds here another instance of the Platonic tendency of the Fourth Gospel to regard sensible things as imperfect copies of archetypes which exist in the world above (*Handcom. ad loc.* and p. 35). Calvin takes the phrase as equivalent to 'Ego vere sum vitis'; and van Koetsveld (*De Gelijkenissen van den Zaligmaker*, ii. 199 f.), on the analogy of the true light (1[9]), and the true bread (6[32-35]), understands it as meaning the vine which may be called so in truth, and does not merely bear the name and appearance of such. But in the case of the true light and the true bread we can understand the force of the adjective in this sense, as light and bread are metaphors which we are in the habit of employing in a spiritual reference, and it is proper to emphasize the fact that, for the illumination and nourishment of the spiritual life, a higher light and bread than the natural are necessary. But before we can understand the force of the adjective as applied to the vine, we must recognize in what sense it is appropriate to introduce the vine metaphorically in a religious reference. The Old Testament supplies the connexion. The vine was a familiar metaphor as applied to Israel (Jer 2[21], Ezk 15[1ff.] 19[10ff.], Ps 80[8ff.], cf. Is 5[1ff.]). But Israel had proved unfaithful to her calling. She had 'turned into the degenerate plant of a strange vine' (Jer 2[21]). Delitzsch has further pointed out that the vine is used as a symbol of the Messiah (*Iris*, Eng. tr. pp. 184–186). It is with reference to this familiar metaphor that Christ calls Himself the *true* vine.

The idea that was held before Israel in the prophetic application to her of the figure of the vine is realized in Him and His disciples.

2. What is the relationship between Christ and the disciples indicated by *the mutual abiding in one another*? Viewed from the side of the disciples, this relation is presented as an injunction, 'Abide in me'; from the side of Christ as a promise, 'and I in you,' *i.e.* and I will abide in you (v.[4]). This is the usual interpretation of the verse, though Bengel makes the injunction embrace the whole: 'Facite ut maneatis in me et ut ego maneam in vobis.' In the following verses more particular statements occur, which seem to define more clearly the relationship thus indicated. But the difficulty is to determine to which of the sides of the relationship the statements in question apply. Thus in v.[7] we have the phrase, 'If ye abide in me and my words abide in you.' Does the latter clause take the place of the 'and I in you' of v.[4], or is it a fuller description of the clause immediately preceding it, thus corresponding to the 'abide in me' of v.[4]? Either view may be adopted with some show of reason. In support of the first, it may be pointed out that, on this interpretation, the phrase exactly corresponds to the 'He that abideth in me and I in him' of v.[5]. On the other hand, when it is remembered that the 'and I in you' of v.[4] contains a promise, and that in v.[7] the two clauses together embrace the condition upon which the promise which immediately follows ('ask what ye will, and it shall be done unto you') depends, there seems good ground for taking the clause 'and my words abide in you' as a more definite statement of what is involved in our abiding in Christ; while the promise which immediately succeeds may be regarded as presenting under a new aspect what is meant by Christ's abiding in us.

Again, in v.[9] we have another aspect of abiding presented, 'Abide ye in my love,' *i.e.* continue to be the objects of my love. Here again the question arises, To which of the two abidings does the phrase apply? To our abiding in Christ, or to Christ's abiding in us? The parallelism of the phrase to the 'abide in me' of v.[4] favours the first alternative. On the other hand, it may be pointed out that while the phrase occurs in v.[9] as an injunction, it is repeated in v.[10] as a promise, conditional on our keeping Christ's commandments. Now, in the interpretation of v.[7] suggested above, to have Christ's words abiding in us, *i.e.* to keep His commandments, corresponds to the 'abide in me' of v.[4]. Here, therefore, the promise which is held forth to those who keep the commandments, *i.e.* to those who abide in Christ, will correspond to the promise of v.[4], and to abide in Christ's love will represent under a new aspect what is meant by Christ's abiding in us.

Each of the ways of regarding the verses in question yields a view of the relationship of the believer and Christ to one another which seems to be true in fact, and to harmonize with the general Johannine conception of that relationship. To have Christ's words abiding in us is a phrase which, in view of the importance assigned in this Gospel to the word, may well represent what is meant by abiding in Christ. It is in the word that Christ reveals Himself, and that only is the true relationship to His Person which involves trustful acceptance of, and obedience to, His word (8[31] 14[15. 21]). On the other hand, just because of the importance thus assigned to the word as that through which Christ reveals Himself, the phrase may likewise denote the manner in which Christ abides in the believer. The sanctifying power of the word has already been referred to in the passage (v.[3]). The words which Christ speaks, they are spirit

and they are life (6[63]), and to have them abiding in us is already to have everlasting life (5[24]). In like manner, to abide in Christ's love is a phrase which may equally well describe either our abiding in Him or His abiding in us. Our abiding in Christ may in v.[4] be the condition upon which the promise of Christ's abiding in us is given. But in the spiritual life it is difficult to draw a hard and fast line between conditions and consequences. The conditions upon which promises of blessing are fulfilled become an integral part of the blessedness bestowed. To abide in Christ's love is at once the condition and the constituent of spiritual blessedness. It is at once our abiding in Christ and Christ's abiding in us. These two abidings seem to be the same relation regarded from different sides. On the one side we have the subjective aspect of the relation presented, on the other the objective (Weiss, *Die johan. Grundbegriffe*, p. 71); on the one side the attitude of faith towards the Saviour, on the other the response of the Saviour to the faith which unites the believer to Him. See also art. ABIDING.

3. Can we accept the allegory as *authentic in its present form*? It has been felt by some that that form is far from satisfactory. Illustration and interpretation are mixed together throughout. No clear and connected picture, of which the details are in due course interpreted, is brought before the mind; but the figure of the vine is used as the foundation upon which is based a series of metaphors, loosely strung together, describing the relation of Christ and the believer to one another. When we compare it with the parables and similitudes of the Synoptic Gospels, we realize at once what a vast difference there is between them. It has been suggested that the allegory of the vine may have been originally a parable which John has worked up into its present form. B. Weiss believes he can find the original elements in vv.[2. 4. 6], and thinks that it had taught that, as the husbandman does all in his power to make the vine productive, but if his efforts are in vain casts forth the worthless branches and burns them up, so God's purpose in the planting of the Kingdom of God in Israel had been to increase the fruitfulness of its members, and if that purpose is not fulfilled the only result will be the exclusion of Israel from the Kingdom. The main point in the parable could not have been that the increasing fruitfulness of the branches depended upon their abiding in the vine, but that this abiding might be forfeited by continued unfruitfulness. But the Evangelist, who ever puts the personal relation to Christ in the foreground, made this abiding in Christ as the condition of fruitfulness in the religious life the central thought, though in vv.[2. 6] the original tendency of the parable is still apparent (in Meyer's *Kommentar*, 1893, *ad loc.*, and *Leben Jesu* ii. 334 ff.). Jülicher thinks that Weiss is influenced by a desire to make John approach as closely as possible to the Synoptists; and while he does not believe the allegory as preserved by John to be genuine, confesses himself unable to conjecture what its original form was, supposing it to be based upon authentic reminiscences (*Die Gleichnisreden Jesu*, 1888, pp. 120, 196).

4. Is the *present place* of the allegory in the Gospel the *correct* one? Sanday (*Fourth Gospel*, p. 231) thinks that it belongs to an earlier and more didactic period in the life of Christ, and that it is out of place in the present speech, of which the object is to comfort the disciples in view of their Lord's departure. De Wette and B. Weiss bring forward the same objection. The latter thinks that the allegory in its original parabolic form, of which the main point was a warning against unfruitfulness, belongs to the period of crisis in the

life of Christ, when the multitudes who had been attracted to Him fell away, and He foresaw that even one of the Twelve was to prove unfaithful. The Evangelist has brought together in these farewell speeches all that seemed to deal with the self-revelation of Christ to believers ; and as the interpretation which he put upon the allegory, by making the central point of it an exhortation to abide in Christ, led him to include it in this category, he has inserted it here (*Leben Jesu*, ii. 334). Bruce meets the objection that the allegory is out of place in the farewell discourse, by showing that Christ's object in that discourse is not merely to comfort the disciples in view of His departure, but to prepare them for the continuance of His work. When we realize that this is the purpose of the speech in which it occurs, the aptness of the allegory cannot, he thinks, be questioned (*Training of the Twelve*, p. 401).

LITERATURE.—The various commentaries and works on NT theology ; Wendt, *Lehre Jesu*, ii. 497 f.; Weiss, *Die johan. Grundbegriffe*, § 8 ; van Koetsveld, *De Gelijkenissen van den Zaligmaker*, ii. 194–204. For homiletical treatment see Maclaren, *Holy of Holies*, 168 ff. ; Macmillan, *Bible Teachings in Nature*, 174 ; A. Whyte, *Walk, Conversation, and Character of Jesus Christ*, ch. xxxiv. ; A. Murray, *Abide in Christ, passim* ; Westcott, *Revelation of the Father*, 119 ; P. J. Maclagan, *Gospel View of Things*, 146 ; *ExpT* ix. [1898] 211.

G. WAUCHOPE STEWART.

VINEGAR (ὄξος, *acetum*) was credited with manifold efficacy by the ancient physicians.[*] Nor was the medicinal its sole use. It served as the drink of the lower orders, especially slaves ;[†] and it was the only refreshment allowed to soldiers while engaged in active service. 'The vigilant humanity of Julian,' says Gibbon, [‡] 'had embarked a very large magazine of vinegar and biscuit for the use of the soldiers, but he prohibited the indulgence of wine.'

It is twice mentioned in the story of the Crucifixion. The quaternion of soldiers (cf. Jn 19[23]) charged with the execution had with them a jar of their *posca*, as it was termed ; and, when they had accomplished their laborious task, they refreshed themselves from it. The bystanders, led by the exultant priests, were meanwhile mocking the meek Sufferer and deriding His Messianic claim. 'He is King of Israel,' they cried : 'let him come down now from the cross, and we will believe on him.' The soldiers heard the taunt and joined in (Lk 23[35-43] = Mt 27[39-44] = Mk 15[29-32]).

Again, after He had uttered His cry of desolation : *Eli, Eli, lama 'azabhtāni* (see DERELICTION), Jesus moaned, 'I thirst' ; and one of the bystanders, probably a Roman soldier,[§] moved by pity, took a sponge and, dipping it in the *posca*, put it on the end of a hyssop reed. His comrades interfered. Ignorant of Hebrew, they took *Eli* for the name *Elias*, and supposed that Jesus was invoking the help of one of that name. 'Hold !'[‖] they cried. 'Let us see if Elias is coming to save him.' But the man persisted in his humane purpose, and held up the sponge to the parched lips (Mt 27[45-50] = Mk 15[33-37] = Jn 19[28-30]).

St. Mark's account is much confused. It represents the offering of the vinegar as an act of mockery, in opposition to both St. Matthew and St. John, and the cry, 'Hold,' etc., as uttered, without any apparent provocation, by the man with the reed. There is here an example of the style of modification which the Evangelic tradition—in this instance correctly reproduced by St. Matthew—suffered in the process of oral transmission : (1) The interference of the bystanders was omitted ;

[*] Plin. *HN* xxiii. 27 ff.
[†] Plaut. *Mil. Glor.* iii. 2. 23.
[‡] *Decl. and Fall*, ch. xxiv. See Wetstein on Mt 27[34].
[§] So Jerome, Euth. Zig., on the ground that Jews would have understood the Hebrew *Eli.*
[‖] Mt.'s ἄφες may be the Hellenistic sign of Imperat. (modern Gr. ἄς): cf. Mt 7[4]=Lk 6[42] ; but its construction as an independent Imperat. is equally permissible (cf. Epict. IV. i. 79) and yields a better sense, besides being favoured by Mk.'s ἄφετε.

and (2) ἄφες, suitable when addressed to one man, was altered to fit the new conception of the situation into ἄφετε.

It is nothing strange that Jesus accepted the *posca* after refusing the 'myrrhed wine' (Mk 15[23] = Mt 27[34]). He refused the narcotic (see CRUCIFIXION), He accepted the refreshment.

DAVID SMITH.

VIOLENCE.—In Lk 3[14] part of the advice given by John the Baptist to the soldiers was, 'Do violence to no man' (μηδένα διασείσητε), the verb meaning, 'like *concutio* in juridical Latin, to extort from one by intimidation money or other property' (Grimm-Thayer). The word occurs again in Mt 11[12], where the adjective 'violent' is also found in AV. The adverb 'violently' appears in Lk 8[33] AV, 'the herd ran violently (ὥρμησεν) down a steep place,' and in Lk 16[16] RV, 'every man entereth violently into it' (βιάζεται). Interest centres chiefly on the two passages Mt 11[12] and Lk 16[16], which are so much alike, though in different contexts, that they are obviously two versions of the same saying. We place them side by side in order that they may be more easily compared.

Mt 11[12. 13.]	Lk 16[16].
(*a*) πάντες γὰρ οἱ προφῆται καὶ ὁ νόμος ἕως Ἰωάννου προεφήτευσαν (v.[13]).	(α) ὁ νόμος καὶ οἱ προφῆται μέχρι Ἰωάννου.
(*b*) ἀπὸ δὲ τῶν ἡμερῶν Ἰωάννου τοῦ βαπτιστοῦ ἕως ἄρτι.	(β) ἀπὸ τότε.
(*c*) ἡ βασιλεία τῶν οὐρανῶν βιάζεται.	(γ) ἡ βασιλεία τοῦ θεοῦ εὐαγγελίζεται.
(*d*) καὶ βιασταὶ ἁρπάζουσιν αὐτήν.	(δ) καὶ πᾶς εἰς αὐτὴν βιάζεται.

It is evident that *a, b, d* closely correspond to α, β, δ ; why, then, should not *c* be taken to convey the same idea as γ ? This is the view of Melanchthon, Stier, Banks, and others, who hold that βιάζεται in Mt. is the Middle voice, as it undoubtedly is in the last clause of Luke. The translation will then be, 'the kingdom of heaven advanceth violently,' it forcibly introduces itself, coming with urgency and beating down all obstacles, 'sese vi quasi obtrudit' (Bengel, who adds 'sæpe LXX βιάζομαι ponunt, vim adhibeo'). This is quite in keeping with the context, where Christ is extolling the work which John the Baptist had done as a pioneer and forerunner (cf. Mt 3[5f], Mk 1[5], Lk 7[29]). It may be illustrated by the parables of the Mustard Seed and the Leaven (Mt 13[31-33]), and it has the great advantage of conveying the same sense as the parallel clause in Lk. 'the kingdom of God is preached.' The only serious objection urged against such a rendering by Meyer, Alford, and Bruce (in *Expos. Gr. Test.*) is that it would be inconsistent with the words following—'the violent take it by force.' Is there necessarily any inconsistency, however ? May we not have here one of those passages where by a slight change in the expression, by a turning of the coin, as it were, a new and complementary truth is conveyed ? Would there be any inconsistency if one were to say 'the train is advancing quickly, and those who are quick succeed in entering it' ? On the other hand, the translation of the EV is open to the charge of being tautological.

βιάζεται is, however, usually taken as Passive in Mt 11[12] ('suffereth violence,' AV and RV ; 'is gotten by force,' AVm ; *vim patitur*, Vulg.; βιαίως κρατεῖται, Hesychius). The image may be taken from the storming of a city or from forcing an entrance through an opposing army : the word is used in Thucyd. *Hist.* vii. 70, 72, of the Athenian fleet forcing its way out of Syracuse (βιάζεσθαι τὸν ἔκπλουν), and in Xen. *Hell.* v. ii. 23, of cities forced into a union (πόλεις τὰς βεβιασμένας).

The further question now arises, From whom does the violence proceed ? and three answers are possible : (1) from true disciples, (2) from other aspirants, (3) from enemies, *e.g.* the scribes and

Pharisees. If the last be adopted, the meaning will then be, 'the kingdom of heaven is violently resisted, is crushed, and violent men tear it to pieces.' So Dalman explains the passage (see below), and similarly Hilgenfeld in Mt. ('is violently crushed'), but he would render in Lk. 'every man is constrained by the gospel,' taking βιάζεται as Passive). This, however, is partly an anachronism, for the imprisonment of John hardly justifies such strong language, and is partly forbidden by the connexion with v.[13] and with what goes before (see Meyer's note). 'Non est h. l. querela de vi mala, nam querela incipit versu 16' (Bengel). 'The subject is not the resistance made to the kingdom of heaven, but the difference between a prophesied and a present kingdom of heaven' (Alford). The second answer is based on the supposition that Jesus here meant to rebuke a wrong method, not to commend a right one, and expressed disapproval of the violence of those who, misled by the free invitations of the gospel, were inclined to force an entrance, disregarding the requirements of the Law. In its favour it may be urged that this explanation admirably suits the difficult context of Lk 16[16] and the use of πᾶς, 'every man entereth violently into it.' Jesus shows in v.[17f.] that 'the same orderly methods were to obtain in the Kingdom as under the Law; so much so that the Law itself might be said to be maintained in every detail. The Gospel was not a release from, but a deepening and widening and spiritualizing of the Law's requirements' (Canon Bindley, who advocates this view in a paper entitled 'The Method of the Christ,' *Expos. Times*, Feb. 1905).

The first answer, however, is preferred by most commentators, viz. that the βιασταί are the disciples who seek a share in the Heavenly Kingdom with ardent zeal and intensest exertions, 'who strive to obtain its privileges with the utmost eagerness and effort' (Grimm - Thayer), 'men of violence' (RV; there is no art. in the Greek), 'violent men' (Wycl.), 'they that go to it with violence' (Tind.), 'the violent' (AV, Cran., Gen., Rhem.), πάντες οἱ μετὰ σπουδῆς προσιόντες (Chrys.). Like the publicans and sinners, like Zacchæus, they take the Kingdom by force, they drag it to themselves (ἁρπάζουσι, cf. Jn 6[15]), they clutch at it like spoils and make it their own, 'ut raptim, celerrima vi, perruptis obstaculis, ad se redigant bonum in medio positum' (Bengel). This explanation agrees best with Pindar's use of the similar word βιατάς, which has always a good sense (Meyer), 'mighty, strong,' and closely corresponds to Luke's πᾶς εἰς αὐτὴν βιάζεται, 'entereth violently into it' (RV), 'vi ingruit pia' (Bengel); 'presseth into it' (AV) is too weak. The hindrances are like a hostile army round a city which must be broken through with force; the same strenuous effort is required which is commanded in such passages as 'strive (ἀγωνίζεσθε) to enter in by the narrow door' (Lk 13[24]), 'ask, seek, and knock' (Mt 7[7]), 'fight the good fight of the faith' (ἀγωνίζου, 1 Ti 6[12]), 'so run that ye may attain' (1 Co 9[24]), 'contend earnestly for the faith' (ἐπαγωνίζεσθαι, Jude [3]). 'Every man' (πᾶς) is perhaps emphatic, showing that the Pharisees and the scribes must no longer look on the Kingdom as the exclusive possession of their nation or class; it was open to all nations, and might be entered by even the lowest men, though it would appear from the warning of the following verses that not all would seek it in the right spirit. 'Jesus uses this strong figurative expression of violence and seizure, which in their peculiar meaning were applied to the unjust, forcible appropriation of others' goods, not because He finds the point of analogy in the injustice and violence, as if men could appropriate a share in the Kingdom of God in opposition to the Divine will, but because He

sought to lay stress upon the necessity of urgent energetic laying hold of a good to which they can make no claim. It is of no avail in regard to the Kingdom of God to wait idly, as in other cases men may take a waiting attitude in regard to a gift; nor does it avail to seek laboriously to earn it: but it does avail energetically to lay hold of and to retain it. It is ready as a gift of God for men, but men must direct their desire and will towards it' (Wendt, *The Teaching of Jesus*, ii. 49, Eng. tr.). It is possible, however, to take the words as a description rather than as a commendation of the disciples, and to find in them a reference to those earthly ideas of the Messianic Kingdom which even the Apostles held until the day of the Ascension (cf. Ac 1[6]).

Dalman (*The Words of Jesus*, pp. 139–143, Eng. tr.) in an important section, the substance of which is here transcribed, seeks to find the probable Aramaic antecedent of βιάζεται. A. Meyer suggests חָסַן, cf. Dn 7[18. 22]; but this would mean merely 'to take possession of,' and would hardly cause one writing in Greek to use βιάζειν. He finds a better equivalent in תָּקַף, which means in Peal 'to be strong,' in Aphel 'to hold fast'; in Dt 22[25], Onḳelos has וְיַתְקֵף for Heb. וְהֶחֱזִיק, while the LXX renders by βιασάμενος. It is important to remember that תְּקַף has no Passive; from this it would follow that the Passive βιάζεται is not derived immediately from an Aramaic prototype. A solution more in conformity with the Greek may be arrived at provided אֲנַס be made the starting-point, for it can mean 'to use force' and 'to rob.' The text (Mt 11[12]) thus refers to that period of the theocracy (*i.e.* the Kingdom of God) which was introduced by the imprisonment of John the Baptist; it is its peculiarity that the theocracy suffers violence, not, of course, from believers, but from those in authority. The words ἁρπάζουσιν αὐτήν (אָנְסָהּ) are not intended to suggest that the violent seize the theocracy, but merely that they maltreat it in the persons of its representatives. The utterance occurs in St. Luke in an entirely different connexion. According to him, it is applied in opposition to the Pharisees, who despised the admonition as to the right use of money. Jesus declared to them that the proclamation of the theocracy since the time of John made it possible for any one to intrude himself violently into it; nevertheless it was not their own estimate, but the judgment of God that decided who was worthy of entrance. The context, however, in Lk. may be pronounced peculiarly Greek. Neither the Passive εὐαγγελίζεται nor εἰς αὐτὴν βιάζεται is capable of being directly rendered into Aramaic, especially if אֲנַס is used.

If it be supposed, adds Dalman, that by using (vv.[15-18]) sayings of our Lord which originally had quite a different association, Lk. obtains the transition to a new parable, it may be surmised that he has given to v.[16] its present form to accommodate it to the context. The saying which Mt. and Lk. found in their sources made mention only of the violent treatment of the theocracy since the time of John. St. Luke thought of attempted entrance into it, and thus found it natural to insert it here. St. Matthew, with greater reason, understood it to refer to the violent treatment of the preachers of the theocracy, and therefore connected it with the answer of Jesus to John. Neither by Jesus nor by the Evangelists is it suggested that any one could actually appropriate the theocracy by force. Unless absolutely driven to it, we ought not to try to discover beneath these words an idea so distinctly at variance with the whole style of our Lord's teaching.

LITERATURE.—In addition to the works cited above, a good article in *Expos. Times*, 1892–93, p. 510, by J. S. Banks, will be found useful. See also *Expositor*, I. iii. [1876] 252, v. [1877] 197, IV. vii. [1893] 224.   W. H. DUNDAS.

VIPER.—See ANIMALS in vol. i. p. 66[b].

VIRGIN BIRTH.—*Introductory.*—A cursory examination of the Gospel narratives is sufficient to reveal certain apparent inconsistencies of statement and implication regarding the parentage of Jesus. He is popularly regarded and spoken of as the son of Joseph (cf. Mt 13[55] 'Is not this the carpenter's son?' Lk 4[22], Jn 1[45] 6[42]); and even in the Nativity narrative of the Third Gospel, Mary and Joseph are several times referred to as 'his parents' (γονεῖς, Lk 2[27. 41. 43]),* while once the mother of Jesus herself is made to say, 'Thy father [*i.e.* Joseph] and I sought thee sorrowing' (2[48]). It is quite clear that Jesus was popularly looked upon by His contemporaries as Joseph's son by natural generation. On the other hand, both the First and the Third Gospels contain special sections dealing with the circumstances of the birth of Jesus in detail, and, though obviously independent, the two traditions embodied in the Nativity narratives agree in stating unequivocally that Jesus was born of a virgin mother without the intervention of a human father (Mt 1[18f.], Lk 1[34. 35]).

No real inconsistency is, however, necessarily involved in the narratives as they stand. The secret of Jesus' birth may have been for long jealously guarded within the narrow circle among whom it was originally known. It apparently formed no part of the early Apostolic teaching and preaching, and was not included in the common form of the Synoptic Gospel-tradition (note that the Second Gospel begins with the Baptism). In preserving, therefore, the popular references to Jesus as Joseph's son, the First and Third Gospels conform to psychological and historic truth. In one part of the narrative, popular opinion is accurately reflected and expressed; in the other, knowledge of a special character derived from private sources.

That no inconsistency was felt to exist in this double use of description appears from the fact that it occurs even in the Apocryphal Gospels, where the virginity of the mother of Jesus is often insisted upon with unnecessary stress. Thus in the *Gospel of pseudo-Matthew* (ch. 27) the following, *e.g.*, occurs : 'And some went away to the chief priests, and to the chiefs of the Pharisees, and told them that Jesus the son of Joseph had done great signs,' etc. A few pages further on (ch. 30) Jesus is made to say : 'But I am an alien in your courts, because I have no carnal parent.' On the other hand, if such references as those cited above from the Gospels had exhibited a mechanical consistency in describing Jesus as the Son of Mary (to the entire exclusion of Joseph), the representation would have justly been impugned as violating the canons of historical and psychological truth.

In social life and as a member of the Jewish nation, Jesus, during His earthly life, would necessarily be regarded as Joseph's son. As Dalman has pointed out, 'If no other fatherhood was alleged, then the child must have been regarded as bestowed by God upon the house of Joseph'; and while Joseph was alive, Mary and her son were undoubtedly under his legal protection. This consideration will help to explain the fact that both genealogies trace the Davidic descent of Jesus through Joseph (not through Mary). On any view Jesus belonged to the family of Joseph; and if any formal and official birth-register ever had any independent existence in the Temple or elsewhere, Jesus would naturally appear therein as Joseph's son.

The genealogy in Mt 1 in anything like its present form can hardly have formed part of such a document. Special didactic features are too pronounced in it.† Regarding the text of Mt 1[16] see esp. Sanday, art. 'Jesus Christ' in Hastings' *DB* (ii. 644 f.). On the other hand, the genealogy in the Third Gospel (Lk 3[23-38]) has a greater appearance of independence, and may have been incorporated by the Evangelist from a written source (cf. Sanday, *op. cit.* 645).

It would be strange, indeed, if the writer of the Fourth Gospel possessed no knowledge of the tradition of the virgin birth of Jesus as embodied in Mt 1-2 and Lk 1-2. Silence in this case would presumably imply not ignorance, but tacit acceptance. Unless the tradition were contradicted either explicitly or tacitly, the presumption in such a case is that it was accepted. It is certainly significant that the Prologue to the Fourth Gospel, which occupies a similar place to that of the gene-

* Once 'his father and his mother' (2[33]).
† Cf. for this point a discussion in *ZNTW* by the present writer (1905, Heft 1, p. 85).

alogy in the First Gospel, traces the origin of the Logos, which became incarnate in Christ, to the inner life of God. What the genealogies attempted to do partially is here carried out fundamentally and finally. The question arises, Is the Prologue intended to be a tacit correction of the Matthæan and Lukan Nativity traditions ? Or are these—at any rate as regards their central feature — the virgin birth—silently accepted and supplemented by the statement of fuller and deeper truth ? The latter alternative accords with the characteristic manner and method of the Fourth Evangelist. So far from excluding the possibility of the virgin birth, it may be argued that the Prologue presupposes it. In view of the fact that the tradition of the virgin birth must already have been current in certain Christian circles, and can hardly have been unknown to the writer of the Johannine Prologue, this conclusion becomes at least highly probable. If the writer had conceived of the method of the Incarnation of the pre-existent Logos as being otherwise, we should at least have expected to find some hint or suggestion to that effect. In the only verse, however, in the Prologue where any allusion to birth occurs (Jn 1[13]), the reference is certainly not incompatible with the tradition of the virgin birth, but may be regarded as lending it, if anything, some presumptive support.

This conclusion is reinforced if the contention of Carr (*ExpT* xviii. [1907] 522) is accepted, that μονογενοῦς (Jn 1[14]), 'from its position in the Prologue, and from its form as a composite of γίγνεσθαι, must refer not to the eternal generation of the Son of God, but to the human birth of the Son of Man' (cf. also Allen, *Interpreter*, Oct. 1905, p. 52 f.). There is also the remarkable reading, known to Justin, Irenæus, Tertullian, and perhaps Hippolytus, according to which v.[13] directly refers to Christ's supernatural birth : '*who* (sing.) *was* born not of blood, nor of the will of the flesh, nor of the will of man, but of God.' Here natural generation by a human father is denied and excluded in the most categorical manner. Even if this reading be not accepted, it is a pertinent question to ask : 'Why the elaboration of the theme, above all why the θελήματος ἀνδρός, unless he [the writer of the Prologue] has in mind the supernatural birth of the Logos as a kind of pattern or model of the birth of the children of God? As He was born into the world by supernatural conception, not through the process of human generation, so they were born out of the world into the higher life by a spiritual process, symbolized indeed by generation, but transcending it' (W. C. Allen, *ib.* p. 57 f. ; see, further, the whole of his admirable discussion).

With regard to the alleged silence of St. Paul, it is by no means clear that silence in this case any more than in that of the Johannine writings is to be taken as implying ignorance. Nor is it certain that indirect allusions to the virgin birth are entirely absent in the Pauline Epistles (cf. Gal 4[4] 'born of a woman,' 1 Ti 2[15]). The most that can be urged is that in the Pauline Christology no emphasis was laid on the dogma of the virgin birth.

1. The Gospel sources. — The question really narrows itself down to one concerning the amount of credibility that is to be attached to the Gospel narratives of the Nativity contained in Mt 1-2 and Lk 1-2. This is not the place to enter into a full discussion of these narratives as a whole, or to repeat what has already been said on the subject in the art. BIRTH OF CHRIST in this work. But one or two points of special significance in this connexion may be dealt with. Recent critical discussion has largely been concerned with these narratives, around which the critical battle has fiercely raged. In the result it may be said with confidence (*a*) that the Palestinian character and origin of the narratives have been firmly established, and (*b*) that the attempt to disintegrate the Lukan account has not been attended with signal success.

(*a*) *The establishment of the Palestinian origin and character of the two Birth narratives* carries with it important consequences. The narratives have been shown to be Jewish-Christian through and through. It follows that the tradition of the virgin birth gained currency among Christian circles in Palestine at a relatively early date, probably by the middle of the 1st century.* A further inference is that we must look for the *origin* of this tradition 'on Palestinian soil at sufficiently early a date to account for its presence in two quite independent forms in the First and Third Gospels. That being so, the view that they are based upon actual facts and came ultimately from the family of Christ Himself, is infinitely probable.'†

(b) *Critical objections have been raised to the integrity of the Lukan Birth narrative.* In Lk 2, it is urged, the view of the narrative is that Mary was Joseph's wife, and that he was the father of Jesus (cf. 2³³ 'his father and his mother,' v.⁴¹ 'his parents,' v.⁴⁸ 'thy father and I'); the Davidic pedigree of Jesus is traced through Joseph, with the harmonistic explanation 'as was supposed' (3²³); 'and with this agrees the early reading apparently preserved in the Sinaitic-Syriac, 2⁵, "with Mary his wife."'‡ The narrative in ch. 1 could be harmonized with that in ch. 2 if vv.³⁴·³⁵ —which contain 'the only reference to the virgin birth in the Third Gospel'—could be removed as an interpolation. This procedure—which has the support of such scholars (among others) as Harnack, Holtzmann, Pfleiderer, Schmiedel, and Usener—is justified on the following grounds:

The reference to Elisabeth in v.³⁶ certainly seems to follow better on v.³³. In that passage, moreover, the child whose birth is announced is already designated Messianically as 'Son of the Most High'; but the title 'Son of God' in v.³⁵ has a quite different signification; it denotes not official adoption, but actual origin : v.³⁵ is thus a doublet of vv.³¹·³² on another plane. Moreover, the incredulity of Mary concerning the possibility of motherhood (v.³⁴) seems inexplicable in one already betrothed; yet it does not (like that of Zacharias, vv.¹⁸⁻²⁰) expose her to rebuke or penalty; the doubt seems introduced only to give occasion for the explanation in v.³⁵. The real reply of Mary to the original announcement in vv.³⁰·³², ³⁶·³⁷ follows in v.³⁸ 'Be it unto me according to thy word,' and her submission to the heavenly will wins the blessing of Elisabeth (v.⁴²).§

A closer examination of the suspected verses does not, however, lend any support to the theory of interpolation. Their phraseology is unmistakably Hebraistic in character, the language being suggested by and derived from the OT. In fact, as Professor Briggs has pointed out, 'the Annunciation represents the conception of Jesus as due to a theophany.'‖ The verses are of the same character as the rest of the narrative, and must be the work of a Jewish writer; and there is every reason to believe, with Gunkel, that they are translated from a Hebrew original. This consideration will help to elucidate the meaning of the announcement in v.³¹ more closely. The Hebrew original of συλλήψῃ there would be a participle,¶ and the exact rendering would be, 'Behold, thou art conceiving now.' An immediate conception is meant, not one that would naturally follow after Joseph had in due course taken her to wife; and this immediate conception is implied by the words 'with haste' in v.³⁹. Besides, v.³⁶ ('And behold, Elisabeth, thy kinswoman, she *also* hath conceived a son in her old age') implies that a conception of an extraordinary character has been mentioned in the previous verses in reference to Mary; and the words suggest that a not unnatural doubt and surprise on her part are being set at rest (cf. esp. v.³⁷ 'for no word of God shall be impossible'). There would be nothing extraordinary in Mary's conceiving a son as Joseph's wife.

Again, the Lukan genealogy, far from discrediting, seems to the present writer to offer a positive argument for the authenticity of the suspected verses. Jewish genealogies usually have

some edifying purpose in view, and the list in Lk 3²³⁻³⁸ seems to be no exception to the rule. The striking feature about it is that it traces the descent of Jesus right up to Adam (*the son*) of *God.* Evidently, in linking Adam to Christ, the editor or compiler intends to suggest that Christ is the Second Adam, the re-founder of the human race; and that just as the first Adam was *son of God* by a direct creative act, so also was the Second (by the power of the Holy Spirit). For genealogical purposes it was necessary to link Jesus to previous generations through His foster-father Joseph. But the suggestion is that the Second Adam, like the first, owes His human existence to a direct creative act on the part of God. Lk 3³⁸ thus supports the genuineness of 1³⁵ (υἱὸς θεοῦ), and the whole genealogy, viewed in the light of its edifying purpose, guarantees the original character of the alleged interpolation.

The fact that υἱὸς θεοῦ in the genealogy involves the occurrence of υἱός in the physical sense of origin exactly as in 1³⁵, has an important bearing on the objection noted above, viz. that while in v.³² ('Son of the Most High') 'son' denotes official adoption, in v.³⁵ it describes actual origin.* But the two ideas are not mutually exclusive. At the same time, it is difficult to see what can have suggested such an otherwise un-Jewish application of the term 'son' in such a context, and amid language so Hebraistic, except the actual occurrence of the fact narrated.

But the theory of interpolation is confronted with a further radical difficulty. It is not enough to remove the suspected verses to make the narrative congruous with a non-miraculous birth. The significant fact still remains that the figure of Joseph is quite subordinated in the Lukan account, while that of Mary is proportionately enhanced in lonely importance. This feature dominates the whole structure of Luke's first two chapters; and in this particular a sharp (and obviously designed) contrast is suggested between the nativity of John the Baptist and that of Jesus. While in the case of the Baptist's birth the annunciation is made to the father (1¹³ᶠ·), in that of Jesus it is made to the mother (1²⁸); and while the Baptist's birth is represented as the occasion of such profound joy on the part of Zacharias that the latter's dumbness is overcome, and he bursts into the strains of the *Benedictus* (1⁶⁸⁻⁷⁹), no such rôle is assigned to Joseph. What reason can be adduced for this deliberate minimizing of the part assigned to Joseph—a feature that characterizes the Lukan narrative throughout — except it be that the fundamental fact, dominating and forming the climax of the whole, is the miraculous birth of Jesus of a virgin mother?† [Cf. also the criticism of this theory of interpolation in the art. BIRTH OF CHRIST, vol. i. p. 203].

(c) *The Matthæan account of the virgin birth* (Mt 1¹⁸⁻²⁵) has already been discussed in the art. cited above (vol. i. p. 206). Here it will be necessary to emphasize only one or two special points. The intensely Jewish character of the narrative, its sobriety and delicacy, have been justly insisted upon. It is difficult to trace in so restrained a narrative the 'pagan substratum' of which Usener speaks. The full-blown myth has certainly been divested of all its bloom. In fact, the points of difference far outnumber the resemblances with the ancient myth, as even Cheyne admits (*Bible Problems*, p. 89 f.). In this connexion the difficult problem arises as to the real significance of the quotation in Mt. of Is 7¹⁴ (LXX): '*Behold, the virgin* (ἡ παρθένος) *shall conceive and bear a son, and they shall call his name Immanuel.*' Two points are clear: (1) No trace exists in Jewish (as distinct from Christian) literature known to us of any Messianic application of this

* See W. C. Allen, *Interpreter*, Feb. 1905, p. 115.
† W. C. Allen, *ib.* p. 122.
‡ J. Estlin Carpenter, *The Bible in the XIXth Century*, p. 486.
§ J. Estlin Carpenter, *ib.* p. 487 f.
‖ *The Messiah of the Gospels*, p. 50.
¶ Cf. the translations in the Hebrew New Testaments.

* The former is a characteristic Hebrew usage.
† Cf. the article (cited above) by the present writer in *ZNTW* p. 93.

text; nor is it possible to adduce any indubitable evidence from Jewish sources that the belief in the Messiah's being born of a virgin was ever current among the Jews. (2) It is generally agreed among critical scholars that the narrative of Mt. could not have been suggested by the quotation (Is 7[14]), but that the quotation was, in accordance with his usual method, added by the narrator as a proof-passage from Scripture in support of the story.

It is, however, difficult to account for the LXX rendering (παρθένος). It may, perhaps, have been adopted under the influence of 'current mythological ideas' in order to enhance the mysteriousness of the future Deliverer's origin, or it may be due simply to the fact that the translators regarded παρθένος as being the true Greek equivalent of הָעַלְמָה, without consciously giving it any definite reference to the Messiah. If, as Gunkel supposes, Messiah's birth of a virgin had become a fixed element in Jewish Christological belief before the birth of Jesus, which was afterwards transferred in Jewish-Christian legend to our Lord's nativity, how is it that no trace of such a belief has survived in Jewish literature? Why the reluctance and reserve manifested in proclaiming the alleged fact, if such a birth had come to be regarded as one of the distinguishing marks of the true Messiah? But so far from its being a popular or even familiar belief among the Jews, it may be inferred with practical certainty from Mt.'s narrative that the story of the virgin birth was to Jewish readers a stumbling-block, which it required special apologetic efforts to overcome. Not improbably Jewish calumny regarding Jesus' birth had already made itself felt before Mt.'s narrative was published. The reference of Is 7[14] to the circumstances of Jesus' birth can, therefore, only have been suggested by the event, or, at least, by what the narrator looked upon as the actual facts. Consequently the Messianic application is purely Jewish-Christian. In Justin Martyr (*Dial. c. Tryph.* lxiii.) there is a curiously interesting collection of proof-passages from Scripture in support of the virgin birth: viz. besides Is 7[14], also 53[8] ('Who shall declare his generation?'), Gn 49[11], Ps 110[3] ('In the beauties of thy saints, from the womb have I begotten thee before the morning star': so LXX). In the last passage the LXX clearly interprets of the pre-existent Messiah; [*] the application to the virgin birth of Messiah would seem to be Jewish-Christian. Ps 110 was undoubtedly understood Messianically in the ancient synagogue. Cf. also the passages quoted in Raymundus Martini, *Pugio Fidei* (ed. Carpzov, p. 154 f.) on the authority of R. Moses ha-Darshan (which cannot now be verified): '*Redemptor quem suscitabo e vobis non habebit patrem*'; cf. Zec 6[12], Is 53[2] ('a root out of a dry ground'), Ps 110[3] and 2[7].

The obviously mythological figure in Rev 12 of the woman 'arrayed with the sun' who 'was delivered of a son,' if it is derived from an earlier Jewish source, shows that the Babylonian myth was not unfamiliar among apocalyptic circles within Judaism. It can hardly, however, have influenced or suggested the Jewish-Christian tradition of the virgin birth. 'But,' to use Mr. Allen's words, 'it is worth while raising the question whether the author of the book [of Revelation] did not incorporate this section with direct reference to the tradition of the supernatural birth of Christ, with which he must therefore have been acquainted' (*Interp.*, Feb. 1905, p. 123). It is possible, of course, that in Is 7[14] the prophet makes use of current eschatological ideas, and by the 'young woman' means the mother of the coming Deliverer (whom he expected to appear at the same time as the Assyrian invasion). 'The wonderful child of whom you all know, of whom the ancient prophecy speaks, whose name is Immanuel, is already on the way to being born.' The prophet is not thinking so much of the circumstances of the birth as the time. What was generally regarded as a vague possibility of the unknown future is announced by the prophet to be a present reality. No stress, it will be noticed, is laid upon the virginity of the mother. The point does not arise. And this remark applies to the later Jewish transformations of the idea (the origin of the Messiah is often pictured as mysterious and obscure); and the 'woman' of Rev 12 is no exception.

It is important to remember that the Nativity narrative of the First Gospel is governed by an apologetic and (partly) polemical purpose. The compiler is meeting Jewish objections and (probably) Jewish calumny, which finds its explanation in a distorted version of the virgin birth. The prominence of Joseph is also noticeable. This may also, perhaps, be due to the compiler's desire to meet Jewish calumny. It was important to show what exactly Joseph's relations were to his espoused wife, to make clear that Mary and her child enjoyed his protection, in order to meet Jewish slander. Another motive, too, may have been at work. The Jews were at no time disposed to exalt the unmarried state above the married. The story of the Virgin, with Joseph

* Cf. for traces of this idea in the LXX, Bousset, *Relig. d. Judent.*[2] 303 f.

completely subordinated, might easily lead to such a result, which, from the strict Jewish point of view, it was important to avoid.

2. The sources of the two Nativity narratives. —The present writer's conclusion, arrived at independently, closely approximates to that of Professor Briggs, who points out that the material of which the 'Gospel of the Infancy' is composed is in the form of poetry embedded in prose narrative. This poetry is of the same kind as the poetry of the Old Testament. It was translated from Hebrew originals,[*] and in its Greek form embodied by St. Luke in his opening chapters. 'It is probable that the prose which encompasses this poetry comes from the authors of the Gospels, the poetry from other and probably several different authors. Therefore we are not to look for an earlier written Gospel of the Infancy of Jesus, but are to think of a number of early Christian poems with reference to that infancy from which the author of our Gospel [St. Luke] made a selection. . . . These songs which have been selected for use in the Gospel of Luke doubtless represent reflexion upon these events by Christian poets who put in the mouths of the angels, the mothers and the fathers, the poems which they composed. But the inspired author of the Gospel vouches for their propriety and for their essential conformity to truth and fact.'[†] In the Matthæan narrative the annunciation to Joseph (Mt 1[20, 21]) is probably a citation from one of these Hebrew hymns, which has been translated into Greek. All the hymns were, perhaps, composed for liturgical use, and were so used in the early Jewish-Christian community in Palestine. As we have seen, they will probably have been in existence at least as early as the middle of the 1st cent. A.D. Their whole tone—so intensely Jewish and Messianic, but yet so spiritual—and their primitive Christology suggest early conditions. Their authority must therefore rank exceedingly high. It has often been remarked that the narrative in the First Gospel is written from the standpoint of Joseph, that in the Third from the point of view of Mary. The delicacy of feeling, the exquisite reserve, the intimate touches which mark each narrative, well accord with this conclusion. Sanday's conjecture, that the Lukan material is based upon a tradition derived from the mother of Jesus through one of the women mentioned in Lk 8[3] 24[10], is a suggestive and valuable one.

3. Heathen analogies.—As early as the time of Justin Martyr (*Dial. c. Tryph.* lxvii.), the mythological tales of virgin birth were cited to discredit the Christian doctrine. 'Amongst the Grecian fables,' says Trypho, 'it is asserted that Perseus was born of the virgin Danae; Jupiter, as they call him, coming down upon her in a shower of gold.' Such tales are widespread. 'We can no longer ignore the fact,' says Mr. Estlin Carpenter, 'that the idea of a wondrous birth without human fatherhood appears in a multitude of tales which can be traced literally round the world "from China to Peru." '[‡] A large collection of these has been made in Hartland's *Legend of Perseus*. But for purposes of comparison here the great majority of them can be dismissed. The Greek fables, which impute the physical origin of great men (heroes and benefactors) to the gods (not only to Zeus, but to Apollo, Mars, Mercury), doubtless are the expression of popular feeling which finds in splendid endowments and achievements something marvellous and inexplicable on natural grounds. The

* The poetical pieces are not confined to the 'Canticles' usually recognized, but include the words of the Annunciation (Lk 1[28, 30-33, 35-37]) as well as other pieces.
† Briggs, *Messiah of the Gospels*, p. 42 ff.
‡ *Op. cit.* p. 490.

soil for such beliefs in the popular feeling and consciousness was a fertile one. But this was not the case among the Jews. Such feeling assumed quite a different form among them, at any rate within historical times. It is difficult to see how ideas of the kind prevalent in the pagan popular consciousness regarding the sons of the gods could have found an entrance into primitive Christian circles—least of all *Jewish*-Christian circles. To borrow Dr. Weiss' words, 'The shameless glorifying of sensual desire in these myths could only provoke in the primitive Christian consciousness the deepest abhorrence; every endeavour to refer any such idea to Jesus must have appeared a profanation of what was most holy, by thus dragging it through the mire of sensuality.'* Cheyne, indeed, following Gunkel, has made out a stronger case for the introduction of mythical material regarding the mother of the Messiah from Babylonian sources (cf. *Bible Problems*, p. 76 f.). As has already been pointed out, the 'woman clothed with the sun' of Rev 12 is clearly mythological. And she was regarded by the author of the chapter as being the mother of the Messiah.

Now it is undoubtedly true that the Jewish Messianic idea bears traces of the influence of the universal myth of the World Redeemer. It is indeed, when analyzed critically, found to be largely a transformed and refined edition of the old material. The universal craving which found varying expression in the world-myth of the coming Deliverer assumed its highest and most spiritual phase in some forms of Jewish Messianic belief. One feature of the myth was the representation of the mother of the coming Deliverer. The mother plays an important rôle, but no father is mentioned. Here in all probability we must see a survival of the idea of the goddess-mother as distinct from the later one of the goddess-wife.† In Is 7¹⁴ the goddess-mother has been transferred to earth, and has become simply the Israelitish woman who is to bear the wonderful child.

In Rabbinical literature this idea seems to have survived in the various forms in which the conception of the Messiah's earthly pre-existence comes to expression.

(1) He is represented as leading a hidden life and then suddenly manifests himself (cf. Mt 24²⁷·⁴³·⁴⁴). In the Midrash *Ex. Rabba*, i., it is said that as Moses, the first deliverer, was reared at the court of Pharaoh, so the future Deliverer will grow up in the Roman capital. Another Midrash says that the Messiah will suddenly be revealed to Israel in Rome.

(2) The Messiah is represented as born, but not yet revealed.‡ Cf. the well-known passage *Sanh.* 98b, where R. Joshua b. Levi is quoted as saying that the Messiah is already born and is living in concealment at the gates of Rome. According to the Targ. (Jerus.) on Mic. 4⁸, the Messiah is on the earth, but is still in concealment because of the sins of the people.

(3) The Messiah is represented as having been born at some time in the past (according to one account, born at Bethlehem on the day the Temple was destroyed; according to another, born in the days of king David and now dwelling at Rome).§

In the curious story of the Messiah's birth quoted by Lightfoot (*Horæ*, on Mt 2¹), the birth of the Messiah (whose name is Menahem, son of Hezekiah) is connected with Bethlehem and the destruction of the Temple. His mother's name is not given, she being described simply as 'the mother of Menahem.' At Bethlehem she is found with her infant son by the Jew who has been mysteriously apprised of Messiah's birth. The Jew leaves, and 'after some days returns to that city, and says to her, "How does the little infant?" And she said: "From the time you saw me last spirits and tempests came, and snatched him away out of my hands."'

In all these forms of the myth it is to be observed that the mother of the Redeemer is nowhere called a 'virgin.' Where the mention of a father does not occur, this feature may be due to the prominence of the mother in an earlier social stage, surviving in

the form of the goddess-mother; an idea which later assumed the form of the Messiah's being concealed and unknown, and manifesting Himself suddenly. It is also to be observed that in Rev 12 the woman is a heavenly being: in other words, the conception in this passage is nearer the primitive myth than it is in Is 7¹⁴. It is difficult to imagine how the representation in Rev 12 can have suggested the idea of the *virgin* birth, though it is easy to see that the prominence assigned to the virgin mother of Jesus in the Christian story may have influenced the author of Revelation in selecting so crude a piece of mythological material for the purposes of his book. In other words, it was the Gospel story that suggested the selection of the mythical representation in Rev 12. It would be easier to suppose that the LXX of Is 7¹⁴ had given rise to the story of the virgin birth than the mythical figure in Revelation.

In order to overcome this difficulty, Professor Cheyne is driven to conjecture 'that in some of the early Jewish versions of the Oriental myth of the Divine Redeemer (which has not, so far as we know as yet, been preserved) the mother of the Holy Child was called a "virgin"' (*Bible Problems*, p. 81). And, further, it is necessary to suppose that παρθένος ('virgin'), which in its original application (*e.g.* to the great mother-goddess of Asia Minor) meant one who was not bound by the marriage tie (and therefore connoted anything but the virginity of Lk 1³⁴), in the process of transition to the *conjectured* Jewish version of the myth, lost its original connotation, and was interpreted in the strict sense; 'for nothing is easier than for Divine titles to pass from one religion to another, and for their original meaning to be forgotten' (*ib.*). This, however, is hardly a plausible explanation of the idea of virgin birth in its various heathen forms. Some at least of these inherently possessed a high religious value (cf. the Egyptian examples cited by J. Estlin Carpenter, *op. cit.* p. 491 f.). On the whole question, some weighty words of Professor Sanday may well be pondered. 'If we believe that the course of human ideas, however mixed in their character—as all human things are mixed— is yet part of a single development, and that development presided over by a Providence which at once imparts to it unity and prescribes its goal, —those who believe this may well see in the fantastic outgrowth of myth and legend something not wholly undesigned or wholly unconnected with the Great Event which was to be, but rather a dim unconscious preparation for that Event, a groping towards it of the human spirit, a prophetic instinct gradually moulding the forms of thought in which it was to find expression' (*op. cit.* p. 647).

It is, however, all-important to remember that the Gospel narratives belong to the sphere of history, and were produced under the limitations that condition the record of historic facts. The creations of the mythopœic fancy flourish in a different atmosphere. 'They are part of a common stock of imaginative material reproduced without purpose or authority from age to age and land to land, destitute of historic significance.'*

4. Results of the discussion.—Is the Gospel story of the virgin birth a legend? If so, it must have grown up within the Jewish-Christian community of Palestine, and must represent a primitive Christological dogma expressing the idea of the perfect moral and spiritual purity of Jesus as Son of God. The Christian consciousness, it might be urged, working on such a passage as '*Thou art my Son, this day I have begotten thee*' (Ps 2⁷), together with the Scripture promise of the fulness of the Spirit that should rest upon the Messiah (Is 11²), may have been led to transfer these ideas to the

---

* Quoted by Knowling, *Our Lord's Virgin Birth*, p. 42 f.

† Cf. Barton, *A Sketch of Semitic Origins*, ch. iii.

‡ Cf. Justin Martyr (*Dial. c. Tryph.* viii.): 'But Christ, if He is come, and is anywhere, is unknown; nor does He know Himself, nor can He be endued with any power till Elijah shall come and anoint Him, and make Him manifest to all men'; cf. also xlix.

§ Cf. *JE* viii. 511, where the above details are given.

* J. Estlin Carpenter, *ib.* 490.

physical beginnings of Jesus' life.[*] But in the absence of any analogous developments in the Christian consciousness elsewhere, this is hard to believe. Why did the Christological process assume just this form, and in this (*a priori* most unlikely) quarter? The impulse must have been given from without. But the hypothesis that it was imported from heathen sources into so strictly Jewish a circle is incredible; consequently it must have grown out of a conviction, cherished originally within a limited Palestinian circle of believers, that the traditional belief among them was based upon facts, of which some members of that community had been the original depositaries and witnesses.

When subjected to the criteria properly applicable to it, such a tradition would seem to possess high claims to historical credibility. The restrained character of both narratives of the virgin birth, the verisimilitude of small details, the reserve that characterizes them, their very inconsistencies, argue against the hypothesis of invention or of their being mere mythical figments. And these characteristics distinguish them as much from the apocryphal Christian versions as from heathen myths. Everything, indeed, suggests their 'essential conformity to truth and fact.' The essential truth embodied in the Christian tradition has been admirably stated by Professor Briggs : [†]

'The virgin conception of Jesus . . . is not to be interpreted as if it were a miracle in violation of the laws of nature, but rather as brought about by God Himself present in theophany. The conception of Jesus in the womb of the Virgin Mary differs from all other conceptions of children by their mothers, in that there was no human father. The place of the human father was taken by God Himself; not that God appeared in theophany in human form to beget the child, after the analogy of the mythologies of the ethnic religions, but that God in a theophany in an extraordinary way, unrevealed to us, and without violation of the laws of maternity, impregnates the Virgin Mary with the holy seed. The words of the angel imply a theophanic presence; for though it might be urged that the coming of the Spirit upon her was an invisible coming, after the analogy of many passages of the Old Testament, yet the parallel statement that the Divine power overshadowed her cannot be so interpreted. For it not only in itself represents that the Divine power covered her with a shadow, but this is to be thought of, after the uniform usage of Scripture, as a bright cloud of glory, hovering over her, resting upon her, or enveloping her with a halo of Divinity, in the moment when the Divine energy enabled her to conceive the child Jesus.'

The evidence suggests that the secret of Jesus' birth was not at first generally made known. 'The doctrine of the Virgin Birth was not generally revealed in the earlier part of the Apostolic Age.' Mr. Arthur Wright (*Synopsis*[2], p. xlii) believes it 'to have been kept back until conflict with heresy brought it forward.' This is not improbable. It has already been pointed out above that in all probability one strong motive at work in the Matthæan account was to meet Jewish calumny regarding Jesus' birth. If this view is correct, the Matthæan narrative must have been composed later than the Lukan, which shows no such strong interest, and contains more original material.

5. Meaning of the virgin birth.—If we assume, then, that the virgin birth is a fact, in accordance with the conclusions reached above, we have further to ask, What is the meaning of the fact? In the Lukan account the birth is already invested with a Christological significance. Jesus is Son of God, because He is begotten in the womb of the Virgin by the Divine energy. This represents an

[*] This is substantially the position taken up by Lobstein in his Essay on *The Virgin Birth of Christ* (Eng. tr., Williams & Norgate, 1903). Lobstein contends that 'the conception of the miraculous birth of Christ is the fruit of religious feeling, the echo of Christian experience, the poetic and popular expression of an affirmation of faith' (p. 96). He also denies pagan influence, and maintains that the conception 'has its roots deep down in Israel's religion transformed by the new faith' (p. 75, cf. p. 69 f.).

[†] *Op. cit.* p. 49 f.

early stage in Christological development. In St. Mark the Divine Sonship of Jesus is connected with the Baptism (1[11]); in St. Luke (1[34. 35]), with the supernatural birth; in St. Paul, with the Resurrection; in St. John (Prologue to the Fourth Gospel), with the essential and eternal relationship subsisting between the Father and the Son.

But the central and abiding significance of the fact consists in the expression it affords of the perfect moral and spiritual purity of Jesus. It proclaims the entrance into the world of a sinless manhood, in which 'the sinful entail' has been broken. 'It involves the introduction of a new factor, to which the taint of sin does not attach. If like produces like, the element of unlikeness must come from that to which it has itself affinity. Our names for the process do but largely cover our ignorance, but we may be sure that there is essential truth contained in the scriptural phrase, "The Holy Ghost shall come upon thee, and the power of the Most High shall overshadow thee; wherefore also that which is to be born shall be called holy, the Son of God." ' [*]

LITERATURE.—To the literature already cited in the body of the art. and in the art. BIRTH OF CHRIST, add W. C. Allen, 'St. Matthew' (*ICC*) on chs. 1-2; an art. by Briggs in the *North American Review* (June 1906) on 'Criticism and the Dogma of the Virgin Birth'; a series of Lectures on 'The Virgin Birth of Christ,' by Dr. J. Orr (1907).   G. H. BOX.

VIRTUE.—AV tr. in Mk 5[30], Lk 6[19] 8[46] of δύναμις (RV 'power'), referring to the healing influence that went out from Jesus. On the early English use of the term see art. 'Virtue' in Hastings' *DB*.

VISION.—See DREAM.

VISITATION.—**1.** The ecclesiastical term applied to the visit of the Virgin Mary to Elisabeth three months before the birth of the Baptist (Lk 1[39-56]), commemorated in Western Church Calendars on 2nd July.

2. ἐπισκοπή (Lk 19[44]). Occurs only once in the Gospels, but is found also in Ac 1[20], where it = 'charge,' 'office,' 'bishopric' (AV); cf. 1 Ti 3[1], where it = 'oversight,' 'office of a bishop' (AV). It occurs in a sense more nearly approaching that of Lk 19[44] in 1 P 2[12], where, however, 'the day of visitation' (ἡμέρα ἐπισκοπῆς) seems to imply trial and affliction, whereas in Lk 19[44] 'the time of visitation' (ὁ καιρὸς τῆς ἐπισκοπῆς) is suggestive rather of the special care and mercy of God, and the opportunity thereby afforded.

In classical Greek ἐπισκοπή is found only in Lucian, ἐπίσκεψις being the usual form. In LXX פָּקַד, פְּקֻדָּה are rendered by ἐπισκέπτομαι, ἐπισκοπή (Gn 50[24. 25], Ex 3[16] 13[19], Is 10[3] [ἡ ἡμέρα τῆς ἐπισκοπῆς, as in 1 P 2[12]], Jer 10[15] [καιρὸς ἐπισκοπῆς, as in Lk 19[44]], Ps 88[4]). In the Apocrypha the word is used in the sense of inspection or examination, though in Wis 14[11] there is an implication of Divine wrath, derived, however, mainly from the context. In NT ἐπισκέπτομαι is used to signify visitation in sympathy or compassion (Mt 25[36. 43], Ja 1[27]); God's gracious regard (Lk 1[68. 78] 7[16], Ac 15[14], He 2[6]); in the sense of 'going and seeing' (Ac 7[23]); and to imply enquiry for the purpose of selection (Ac 6[3]).

To the general use of ἐπισκέπτομαι, ἐπισκοπή, we may find a parallel in the use of the English word 'regard,' which, in addition to the sense of 'observation,' may imply also a kindly or gracious purpose. ἐπισκοπή may be said generally to signify critical inspection (by God), in which due regard is had to the good and bad features in the characters of the persons inspected. ἐπισκέπτομαι implies also a Divine purpose of blessing. [The technical use of ἐπισκοπή, indicated above, to denote the office of a bishop, is of course secondary]. Thus in Lk 19[44] we may understand the 'time of visitation' as being either the time during which Jerusalem

[*] Sanday (*ut cit. supra*).

was being critically regarded by God, and neglected, through ignorance of this inspection, to display those features of national character which would have redeemed it in God's eyes; or the time of spiritual opportunity, afforded by the presence of 'God manifest in the flesh,' in which it might have known and sought 'the things which belonged unto its peace.' In the latter sense, the 'time of visitation' would be equivalent to 'this thy day' in v.⁴².

S. J. RAMSAY SIBBALD.

VOICE.—**1. Introductory.**—The Gr. word of which 'voice' is a rendering in the NT is φωνή. In the AV other renderings are sometimes given: as 'sound' (Jn 3⁸) and 'noise' (Rev 6¹) [but cf. RV where this inconsistency is generally removed *]. The Gr. word is sometimes used of inarticulate utterance (='sound'), e.g. of trumpet, Mt 24³¹, 1 Co 14⁷ ('things without life, giving a voice, whether pipe or harp,' etc., AV 'sound' here), Rev 14² ('voice of many waters,' AV and RV), Jn 3⁸ of the wind ('thou hearest the voice thereof,' RV), etc.; sometimes of articulate utterance, ascribed to God (Mt 3¹⁷ etc.), and, naturally, to men (Mt 3³ e.g.).

φωνή is often used in such combinations as τὴν φωνὴν αἴρειν (ἐπαίρειν)='to lift up the voice' (e.g. Lk 17¹³ 11²⁷), with the general meaning 'to cry out,' 'call'; φωνῇ μεγάλῃ, 'with a great (loud) voice,' is often added to verbs; see the Lexx. and cf. art. CRY.

The 'voice' of God and the 'voice' of Christ are referred to in various connexions (some eschatological). Jesus compares the call which He makes to that of the shepherd to his sheep (Jn 10³⁻⁵ 'the sheep hear his voice'; cf. 10¹⁶· ²⁷ 18³⁷); in an eschatological connexion, Rev 3²⁰ ('Behold, I stand at the door and knock: if any man hear my voice and open the door, I will come in to him and sup with him, and he with me'); of the resurrection cry, 1 Th 4¹⁶ (the voice of the archangel awakening the dead; cf. Jn 5²⁵· ²⁸, the voice of Christ awakening the spiritually dead). The voice of God is spoken of as admonishing in the OT Scriptures (Jn 5³⁷, He 3⁷· ¹⁵ 4⁷), and as 'shaking the earth' (He 12²⁶).

An antithesis is drawn by Gr. writers (esp. Plutarch) between φωνή and λόγος, and this was afterwards transferred by the Fathers (Origen, Augustine) to John the Baptist and Christ, 'the first claiming for himself no more than to be "the voice of one crying in the wilderness" (Jn 1²³), the other emphatically declared to be the Word which was with God and was God (Jn 1¹).' See, further, Trench, NT Synonyms, § lxxxix., where Augustine's interesting disquisition on this contrast is summarized.

2. The Voice from Heaven.—(a) In the NT.—A 'voice from heaven' is mentioned in the Synoptics in Mt 3¹⁷ ‖ (φωνὴ ἐκ τῶν οὐρανῶν), in the narrative of the Baptism ('And lo, a voice out of the heavens, saying, This is my beloved Son in whom I am well pleased'), and again in Mt 17⁵ ‖ in the narrative of the Transfiguration a 'voice out of the cloud' is spoken of ('And behold, a voice out of the cloud, saying,' etc.). In both cases, as Dalman (Words of Jesus, p. 204) has pointed out, the mention of the heavens and the cloud is derived from the context, and both representations are due 'to the Evangelic narrative and not to the words of Jesus.' In the Fourth Gospel one reference occurs, viz. in Jn 12²⁸ 'There came therefore a voice out of heaven, saying,' etc.; and it is mentioned several times in the Apocalypse (Rev 10⁴· ⁸ 14² 18⁴ etc.) —in all these passages introducing a heavenly revelation.

(b) In Rabbinical literature.—The 'Heavenly Voice' is frequently met with in Rabbinical literature under the designation Bath Ḳol ('daughter-voice'). Here also it often introduces a Divine revelation. The Bath Ḳol was one of the means used by God for imparting a revelation. It was heard all through Biblical times, and, in fact, oftenest during the classical period of Israel's history before prophecy was extinguished, and while the Holy Spirit was abiding in its fulness among the people (symbolized by the Temple). Thus at the death of Moses a Bath Ḳol was heard saying: 'Fear thou not, Moses! I myself will care for thy burial' (Deut. R. on xxxiv.). But it also survived beyond the

Biblical period, and was regarded as the only means of Divine revelation then operative (Bab. Sota, 48b; Yoma, 9b). In time, however, it fell into disrepute, owing, perhaps, to the assiduous way in which it came to be looked for and appealed to by certain teachers as a means of further revelations; and by the Rabbis of the 2nd cent. it was decided that 'no attention is to be paid to it when arrogating to decide against the moral conviction of the majority. The Torah is not in heaven. Its interpretation is left to the conscience of catholic Israel.' *

A distinction must be drawn between the true Bath Ḳol—the Heavenly Voice which proceeded really and miraculously from God Himself directly—and the secondary Bath Ḳol, which was merely 'a human utterance heard by some chance, to which was attributed the significance of a Divine intimation' (Dalman). In the former of these senses the expression is used to denote audible speech, appealing to the faculty of hearing, uttered by God Himself. Only, the Rabbis shrank from saying baldly, 'God said so and so,' and made use of the phrase 'A Bath Ḳol came (or was given)' instead. The phrase, like many others, is merely precautionary, nor has it any hypostatic significance.

One striking feature about the revelations conveyed by the Bath Ḳol is that these were usually expressed not in original words, but in some verse or sentence taken from the Hebrew OT or (in some cases) from the Apocryphal books. Thus it is said that when the Rabbinical authorities proposed to include King Solomon among the finally lost, a Bath Ḳol was heard saying in the words of Job 34³³ 'Shall his recompense be as thou wilt, that thou refusest it?' †

(c) Significance of the Heavenly Voice in the NT. —Parallel with the true Bath Ḳol, which was regarded as one of the organs of Divine revelation, is the Heavenly Voice, heard at the Baptism of Jesus (Mt 3¹⁷, Mk 1¹¹, Lk 3²²), at the Transfiguration (Mt 17⁵, Mk 9⁷, Lk 9³⁵), at the Passion (Jn 12²⁸), as well as that heard by St. Peter and again by St. Paul (Ac 9⁴, cf. 22⁷ and 26¹⁴; 10¹³· ¹⁵). It is to be noticed that the Voice at the Baptism and the Transfiguration combines two sentences of Scripture (Ps 2⁷ and Is 41¹) quite in the manner of the Bath Ḳol spoken of in Rabbinical literature. An audible voice solemnly affirming or introducing a Divine revelation seems to be intended in every case.

The NT formula ἦλθεν οὖν φωνὴ ἐκ τοῦ οὐρανοῦ (Jn 12²⁸, cf. Rev 10⁴· ⁸ 18⁴ etc.) is the equivalent of the Rabbinical Hebrew יצאה בת קול מן השמים and the Aram. נפקת ברת קלא מן שמיא. In later Rabbinical literature the expression was abbreviated ('from heaven' being omitted), but its significance remained unaltered. For parallels in the extra-canonical literature of the OT, cf. Jub 17¹⁵, Bk. of Enoch lxv. 4, 2 (4) Es 6¹³ᶠ. 'God's Voice,' i.e. the Heavenly Voice, is, of course, the correlative of 'God's Word' or 'Speech' (the Memra of J". (דִּבּוּרָא, מֵימְרָא דַיָי). Cf. Bousset, Rel. d. Jud.² p. 362 f.

The attempt of Edersheim (LT i. p. 285 f.) to discredit 'any real analogy' between the Bath Ḳol and the Voice from Heaven mentioned in the Gospels is unwarranted. His contention that the Bath Ḳol could not be represented as accompanying the descent of the Holy Spirit is shown by the facts adduced above to be baseless. On the contrary, it would only be natural to represent the revival of prophecy and the return in full power of the Holy Spirit as including also the mode of revelation expressed by the 'Daughter-Voice.' Only so would the scale of revelation be complete.

LITERATURE.—The Lexx. s.v. φωνή, esp. Grimm-Thayer and Schleusner. To the important literature on Bath Ḳol already cited in the body of the article, add art. 'Bath Ḳol' in JE (with the literature cited at end) and in PRE³ ii. 443 f. (by Dalman); Weber, Jüd. Theol.² (reff. in Index). The passages relating to בת קול have been collected by Pinner in his ed. of Berakhoth (Berlin, 1842), pp. 22–24; an elaborate presentment of the data with full discussion is given by E. A. Abbott in From Letter to Spirit (1903), pp. 139–460; add also Lightfoot, Hor. Heb. on Mt 3¹⁷.

G. H. BOX.

VOWS.—A vow (votum, εὐχή) is a promise made to God ('promissio Deo facta,' Thom. Aquin. II. ii. Q. 88). It is a perfectly natural, and indeed inevitable, expression of religious feeling wherever there is a conception of a personal God with whom men come into any kind of relationship. Thus vows form part of the great pre-Christian and non-Christian religious systems. They are of two kinds: (1) vows made in hope of receiving some desired good, or of delivery from some special danger; and (2) vows of devotion made in expectation of attaining closer relationship with God. In

---

* Cf., however, Mt 24³¹ ('sound' both in AV and RV).

* Schechter, 'Rabbinic Parallels to the NT,' JQR xii. 426 (April 1900).
† Cited by Schechter (op. cit. ib.). There are many other instances.

the OT we have examples of (1) in Gn 28²⁰· ²², Jg 11³⁰, 1 S 1¹¹. Such vows may involve the dedication to God of a person, an animal, a field, a house or other property. Accurate laws were made for the regulating of such vows and the defining of persons competent to make them (Lv 27, Nu 30¹ff·). Of (2) the Nazirite vow taken for life (Jg 16¹⁷) or for a fixed period (Nu 6¹³) is an example.

In our Lord's teaching there is only one mention of vows (Mt 15⁴ff· ‖ Mk 7¹⁰ff·). Here He rebukes in the severest manner the making of vows which interfere with the simple and obvious duties of man to man, and, as may be gathered from the Rabbinical teaching on Corban, hypocritical vows which were not meant to be kept. He says nothing about the making and keeping of justifiable and proper vows. It is therefore in accordance with a natural religious instinct and with the assumption of the rightness of making vows which underlies our Lord's rebuke of the Pharisaical abuse of them, that the Church subsequently imposed vows upon candidates for baptism. The baptismal vow is in reality a dedication of the whole person to God, and is in harmony with the general spirit of the gospel as well as with the Apostolic teaching (Ro 5¹¹ 12¹· ², 1 Co 7¹⁶· ¹⁷). The various monastic vows were supposed to be analogous to the OT Nazirite vow, and were regarded as means of attaining specially close communion with God.

LITERATURE.—Robertson Smith, *RS* ², 1894 ; Rothe, *Theol. Ethik*, vol. iii. [1848] ; Zöckler, *Krit. Gesch. der Askese* ; Daab, *Die Zulässigkeit der Gelübden*, 1896 ; Ramsay, 'Greek of Early Church and Pagan Ritual' in *ExpT* x. (1899) 13.

J. O. HANNAY.

VULTURES.—RVm for 'eagles' in Mt 24²⁸ and Lk 17³². See ANIMALS in vol. i. p. 65ᵇ.

W

WAGES.—1. ὀψώνιον is the technical term for a soldier's pay, and occurs only in Lk 3¹⁴. 'From a root πεπ we get ἕψω, ὄψον, "cooked" meat, fish, etc., as contrasted with bread. Hence the compound ὀψώνιον (ὠνέομαι, "to buy")=(1) provision money, ration money, or the rations in kind given to troops. (2) In a more general sense, "wages"' (Sanday–Headlam on Ro 6²³). In the time of Julius Cæsar, a foot soldier received ⅔ of a denarius a day. This was increased by Augustus. John the Baptist bids the soldiers (probably those engaged in police duty connected with the customs) abstain from adding to their wages by extortion through violence, threats, or false accusations.

2. μισθός is the ordinary term for wages, and is translated indifferently throughout the Gospels as 'wages,' 'reward,' 'hire.' The labourers in the parable hire themselves for a denarius a day (Mt 20⁸). That was a fairly generous rate for such work (cf. 5¹⁴). The denarius was equivalent in money value to 9½d., and in purchasing value to about 2s. (see artt. 'Money,' § 8, and [in Ext. Vol.] 'Wages' in Hastings' *DB*).

The analogy of service and wages is freely used by Jesus in His teaching ; but it is not so much the receipt of wages that rules the thought as the quarter whence they come. The labourer is always worthy of his hire, but what that will be depends upon whether he is serving the world or God. The Pharisee is really the world's hireling, and receives his wages from it, viz. honour, consideration, power, wealth, and not from God, whom nominally he serves (Mt 6². ⁵· ¹⁶). But those persecuted for righteousness' sake (Mt 5¹¹), those whose religious obedience is unobtrusive and self-forgetting (6⁴· ⁶· ¹⁸), those who help any of God's servants and do them a kindness for His sake (10⁴¹· ⁴², Mk 9⁴¹), those who go beyond the world's self-regarding way, and love their enemies, and do good and lend, hoping for nothing again (Lk 6³⁵, Mt 5⁴⁵· ⁴⁶), are servants of the unseen Father. Their wages are not counted out to them in the world's coin ; they receive the Father's open acknowledgment and gather fruit unto life eternal (Mt 6⁴· ⁶· ¹⁸, Jn 4³⁶).

Jesus' remark that the labourer is worthy of his hire, or of his meat (Lk 10⁷, cf. Mt 10¹⁰), probably a quotation of a common proverb, is of a different order. It is an encouragement to His disciples to accept hospitality, in their missionary journeys, from those to whom they have ministered in spiritual enlightenment.

LITERATURE.—The vols. on the Parables, esp. Bruce, *Parabolic Teaching*, 178 ; Phillips Brooks, *New Starts in Life*, p. 1 ; Griffith Jones, *The Economics of Jesus* (1905) ; *Expos.* I. iii. (1876) 81, 427 ; *ExpT* v. (1894) 549.

RICHARD GLAISTER.

WAGGING.—See GESTURES in vol. i. p. 646ᵇ.

WAILING.—The expression of sorrow by loud cries is several times alluded to in the Gospels : Mt 2¹⁸ 'In Rama was there a voice heard' ; Mt 11¹⁷ 'We have mourned unto you' (cf. Lk 23²⁷, Jn 16²⁰). The Jewish custom is abundantly evidenced from the OT (see esp. Jer 9¹⁰· ¹⁷) ; in the Gospels only two instances are detailed, one at the death of Jairus' daughter, and the other at Christ's death. On both of these occasions mourning with loud cries is indicated (Mt 9²³ 'flute-players,' 'tumult' ; Mk 5³⁸ 'wailing' ; Lk 23²⁷ 'lamented,' ἐθρήνουν). The word used in Mk *l.c.* is ἀλαλάζειν (cf. Ja 5¹ ὀλολύζειν, 'howl'). In most other places the word tr. 'wail' or 'bewail' is κόπτεσθαι, literally, *to beat upon the breast*, so that any outcry is inferred only. The phrase ὁ κλαυθμὸς καὶ ὁ βρυγμὸς τῶν ὀδόντων was formerly tr. 'wailing and gnashing of teeth' only in Mt 13⁴²· ⁵⁰ ; but now the RV has brought these passages into line with the others where the same words occur, and correctly renders 'weeping.' See also MOURNING.

T. GREGORY.

WALK.—1. περιπατεῖν. The passages in the Gospels where this word occurs may be classified as follows : (1) 'To move along leisurely on foot without halting.' It is used in this literal sense of our Lord's walking by the Lake (Mt 4¹⁸ περιπατῶν δέ),—the words following show that the subject of His thoughts as He walked was the analogy between Peter and Andrew's present occupation and the work to which He was about to call them, that of 'fishers of men,'—Mk 1¹⁶ has the more vivid παράγων παρά, 'passing along by' (RV, cf. LXX Ps 128 (129)⁸) ; of His walking near Jordan, when His mien as He passed riveted John's gaze (Jn 1³⁶) ; of His walking on the sea (Mk 6⁴⁸· ⁴⁹, Mt 14²⁵· ²⁶, Jn 6¹⁹—ἐπὶ τῆς θαλάσσης in Mk. and Jn., ἐπὶ τὴν θάλασσαν in Mt.).

'The genitive points to the apparent solidity of the water under His feet (cf. Mk 6⁴⁷ ἐπὶ τῆς γῆς), the accusative to the progress implied in περιπατῶν' (Swete, *St. Mark*, 130). Cf. LXX Job 9⁸ περιπατῶν ὡς ἐπ' ἐδάφους ἐπὶ θαλάσσης, 38¹⁶ ἦλθες δὲ ἐπὶ πηγὴν θαλάσσης, ἐν δὲ ἴχνεσιν ἀβύσσου περιεπάτησας, Sir 24⁵ ἐν βάθει ἀβύσσου περιεπάτησα. Particular OT events also form suggestive parallels : Ex 14²² (cf. Ps 77¹⁹· ²⁰, Hab 3¹⁵), Jos 3¹⁶, 2 K 28· ¹⁴.

Our Lord's walking on the sea reveals Him as making material nature an instrument through which His interest in us is shown (Illingworth, *Div. Immanence*[1], 124), as coming to our aid across the troubled waters in which our conflict lies (Westcott, *Characteristics of Gosp. Mir.*[1] 15, 19), and so leading us to the confidence expressed in Ro 8²⁸·³⁵. The same word is used also of Peter's walking on the sea (Mt 14²⁹ περιεπάτησεν ἐπὶ τὰ ὕδατα), so that it is incorrect to say that Peter merely 'attempted' to walk on the water: the words imply that he made some progress in going to Jesus. By the invitation 'Come!' Jesus expressed His warm sympathy with Peter in his desire for closer fellowship with Him, and gave a pledge that He would support him in the enterprise of his faith. The cause of his temporary failure was his betaking himself again to his own resources after having committed himself to a course that involved full dependence on Christ's strength. Then, after the grasp of our Lord's hand had revived his faith, he was really enabled to carry through what he had undertaken, probably walking on the sea with Jesus in returning to the boat (cf. A. B. Davidson, *Waiting upon God*, 241, 250). Two texts, Jn 15⁵ and Ph 4¹³, show how we should apply this narrative to ourselves. περιπατεῖν is also used: of men's gait, whereby the blind man who was being gradually restored to sight recognized the true nature of the objects which he would otherwise have taken for trees (Mk 8²⁴ βλέπω τοὺς ἀνθρώπους ὅτι ὡς δένδρα ὁρῶ περιπατοῦντας, 'I see men; for I perceive objects like trees, walking'; cf. Jg 9³⁶; Swete, *in loc.*); of people's walking over hidden graves (Lk 11⁴⁴: see WOE); of the scribes, τῶν θελόντων περιπατεῖν ἐν στολαῖς (Lk 20⁴⁶ ‖ Mk 12³⁸ 'love to go in long clothing,' AV; see DRESS); and in the question with which the Risen Lord began the conversation with His two disciples whom He joined on the road to Emmaus (Lk 24¹⁷ τίνες οἱ λόγοι . . . οὓς ἀντιβάλλετε . . . περιπατοῦντες; cf. Mk 16¹²).

(2) Of those to whom Jesus miraculously restored the power of walking: the paralytic (Mk 2⁹ ‖ Mt 9⁵, Lk 5²³). No passage in the Gospels is more significant of the character, or more persuasive of the credibility, of our Lord's miracles of healing than this. He says to the paralytic, 'Son, thy sins be forgiven thee'; and in order that those who cavil at this saying 'may know that the Son of Man hath power on earth to forgive sins,' He commands him, 'Arise, take up thy bed, and walk,' which was, from their point of view, a harder thing for Him to say, because it could at once be proved whether His words had any effect. The miracle is thus an outward and visible sign of something greater than bodily healing; it points to an inward and spiritual power, destructive of evil, now present among men. It is implied that disease is the physical effect of sin (cf. Jn 5¹⁴), and by healing the one our Lord gives an evidence of His power to destroy the other (cf. 1 Jn 3⁸). He teaches that the perfect idea of redemption is realized in 'a redeemed soul in a redeemed body,' and that He is come to deliver the entire personality of man, soul and body, from the dominion of evil (cf. Illingworth, *l.c.* 97). Man forgiven is enabled to 'walk and not faint' (Is 40³¹), and this looks forward to the time when 'the inhabitant of Zion shall not say, I am sick; the people that dwell therein shall be forgiven their iniquity' (Is 33²⁴, cf. Rev 7¹⁴⁻¹⁷). So of the impotent man at Bethesda (Jn 5⁸·⁹·¹¹·¹² —a Sabbath miracle: the others being Mk 1²³·³¹ 3¹ and ‖, Lk 13¹⁴ 14³, Jn 9¹⁴); the lame who walk (Mt 11⁵ 15³¹, Lk 7²²; cf. LXX Is 35³ ἰσχύσατε . . . γόνατα παραλελυμένα, also v.⁶; Ac 3⁶ 14⁸); also of the daughter of Jairus whom our Lord raised from the dead (Mk 5⁴² περιεπάτει, 'she began walking about').

In all His raisings from the dead there was an immediate restoration of the bodily powers (Lk 7¹⁵, Jn 11⁴⁴).

(3) It is also used in a special sense of our Lord's life of movement and unwearied activity. This use of περιπατεῖν is peculiar to St. John. In Jn 11⁹·¹⁰ Jesus speaks in parabolic fashion, first of His having a full working day (cf. 9⁴) of twelve hours, during which He walks in the light of life without fear of danger in the path of His heavenly Father's will, and then of the coming on of the night of death, when walking, as regulated by present conditions, will be ended for Him; because it is His enemies' 'hour,' coinciding with that permitted to 'the power of darkness' (Lk 22⁵³; cf Jn 13³⁰; Plummer, *St. Luke*, 513; Camb. Bib. *St. John*, 230). Jn 6⁶⁶ 'many went back,' καὶ οὐκέτι μετ' αὐτοῦ περιεπάτουν; the last words picture His journeyings to and fro, in which they had been in the habit of accompanying Him on foot, and hearing His teaching. In the same sense: Jn 7¹ 'walked in Galilee, for he would not walk in Jewry'; 10²³ walking in the Temple ('ut in sua domo,' Beng.; cf. Mk 11²⁷); 11⁵⁴ 'walked no more openly among the Jews.' This use of περιπατεῖν is also found in Rev 2¹ of our Lord's life of activity in His exalted state: 'walketh in the midst of the seven golden candlesticks,' as if journeying forth by the circular route which, after traversing all the Churches mentioned, returns to Ephesus (Ramsay, *Letters to the Seven Churches*, 'Letter to the Church in Ephesus,' Introduction). It is likewise used by our Lord of Peter's working life (Jn 21¹⁸ περιεπάτεις ὅπου ἤθελες, as when he had said to his fellow-disciples, 'I go a fishing,' v.³), and of the life of the redeemed (Rev 3⁴ περιπατήσουσι μετ' ἐμοῦ ἐν λευκοῖς; cf. Zec 3⁴·⁷), which is thus suggestively represented as a life of action conjoined with purity (cf. 1 Jn 3²·³).

(4) 'To act and behave in any particular manner,' 'to pursue a particular course of life': Mk 7⁵ (the only passage in the Synoptic Gospels where περιπατεῖν is used in this sense—'why walk not thy disciples κατὰ τὴν παράδοσιν τῶν πρεσβυτέρων', κατὰ indicating conformity with a standard [as in Ro 8⁴ 14¹⁵, 2 Co 10²·³, Eph 2²; Win.-Moult. 500]. הֲלָכָה in Rabbinical language is 'the rule by which men must walk' [הָלַךְ]; cf. Swete, *in loc.*; see TRADITION), Jn 8¹², where the condition of 'not walking in darkness' (= ignorance and self-deception, narrowness, joylessness, and death) is stated to be our 'following the Light of the world,' Jesus our Sun (cf. 11⁹, Ps 27¹, Is 9² 42⁶ 60¹⁹·²⁰, Mal 4²), whose rising is the signal to awake and work (Eph 5¹⁴, He 3¹³), and whose movement as He mounts to attain His perfect day is a call to progress in righteousness and love (Ps 19⁵, Pr 4¹⁸, Ph 3¹⁴). St. Paul developed this figure: he who follows the Light of the world becomes himself 'light in the Lord' (Eph 5⁸·⁹, 1 Th 5⁵). Cf. Jn 12³⁵ ('fides non est deses sed agilis in luce,' Bengel. So also is love, 1 Jn 2⁹⁻¹¹).

περιπατεῖν is used of the conduct of life; Aquila, Gn 5²² (Enoch) περιεπάτει σὺν τῷ θεῷ, where LXX has εὐηρέστησεν (cf. He 11⁵); LXX 2 K 20³, Ps 11⁹ (12⁸), Pr 8²⁰, Ec 11⁹. St. Paul uses περιπατεῖν in the ethical sense thirty times, and it is found in this sense in all his Epistles except Philem. and the Pastorals. He has also another word for 'to walk' which is not found in the Gospels (στοιχεῖν, 'to march in file'). This word 'may imply a more studied following of a prescribed course than περιπατεῖν' (Ellic. on *Gal.* 122). Compare with the passages in St. John's Gospel, 1 Jn 1⁶·⁷ 2⁶·¹¹, 2 Jn 4, 3 Jn 3·⁴.

2. πορεύεσθαι is used in the same sense as περιπατεῖν (3) in Lk 13³³ 'I must walk to-day, and to-morrow, and the day following'; 'I must go on my way,' RV. 'The duration of my course is ordained by God, and no power on earth can shorten it' (cf. Jn 11⁹ᶠ·; Burkitt, *Gosp. Hist. and its Transmission*, 95). It is used in the same sense as περιπατεῖν (4) in Lk 1⁶ ('walking in all the commandments and ordinances of the Lord blameless ') ; cf. LXX Pr 10⁹ (with Barrow's Sermon) 14², Mic 6⁸ πορεύεσθαι μετὰ κυρίου θεοῦ σου, '.to walk humbly with thy God,' AV and RV.

3. διέρχεσθαι, 'to pass through' : Mt 12⁴³ (‖ Lk 11²⁴) 'walketh through dry places,' 'passeth through,' RV (cf. Ps 106 (107)³⁵). 'Apart from humanity, evil powers have only an empty, unproductive existence ; and accordingly they lie in wait continually for the opportunity to return to the world of men, and to set up their abode there' (Martensen, *Dogmatics*, 196).

LITERATURE.—Swete, *Com. on St. Mark*; A. B. Davidson, *Waiting upon God*; J. H. Jowett, *Thirsting for the Springs*, 167 ; Illingworth, *Div. Immanence*; Westcott, *Characteristics of the Gospel Miracles*; Hatch and Redpath, *Concordance to the LXX*.   JAMES DONALD.

WALLET (RV tr. of πήρα, Mt 10¹⁰ etc. ; AV 'scrip').—This corresponds to the kĕlī hārō‘īm, or yalḳūṭ, of 1 S 17⁴⁰ (see, however, H. P. Smith, *Samuel, in loc.*). It is a bag made of partially tanned kid-skin, bound by a strap round the waist, or slung from the shoulder. In it the shepherd carries his supply of provisions when going with the flock to distant pasture. The coarse loaves of the country, olives, and dried fruit form the staple diet, with an occasional lump of cheese. The wallet, however, serves the purpose of the boy's pocket among ourselves, and often contains a curious assortment of articles. The AV 'scrip' appears in our literature with the same meaning. Milton (*Comus*, line 626) speaks of the shepherd's 'leathern scrip' in which are carried 'simples of a thousand names' (cf. Shakespeare, *As You Like It*, Act iii. sc. 2). Setting out on a journey, the Syrian peasant carries a wallet well furnished, which he opens for refreshment as he rests by the way, or in the shelter of the khān at nightfall. Christ's Apostles were to go unencumbered on their special mission (Mt 10¹⁰, Mk 6⁸, Lk 9³ 10⁴), trusting to hospitality, and the providing care of their Master.* But, as an ordinary rule, provident forethought is to be commended (Lk 22³⁶).

                  W. EWING.

WAR (πόλεμος).—As the Gospels record the story of Christ, whose mission was to bring 'peace on earth and goodwill to men,' the references to war are not numerous. But St. Luke has three references well worthy of attention.—**1.** In Lk 3¹⁴ 'the soldiers' (στρατευόμενοι, RVm 'soldiers on service') consult John the Baptist. It is not possible to say who the soldiers were, or in what expedition they were engaged, but they were not Roman soldiers, or any part of the force of Herod Antipas against his father-in-law Aretas, since the quarrel between Herod Antipas and Aretas had not developed then.—**2.** In Lk 14³¹ (where He is enforcing the general lesson that we should not undertake what we have neither the strength nor the will to achieve, or enter upon His service unless we are prepared, if necessary, to sacrifice life itself) our Lord draws attention to the action of a king in calling a council of war. Possibly there is here a historical allusion to the war between Herod Antipas and Aretas (Jos. *Ant.* XVIII. v. 3).—**3.** In

* Edersheim compares certain Rabbinical ordinances which laid down that no man might go on the Temple Mount with his staff or with shoes, or with his scrip, or with money tied to him in his purse. Whatever he might wish to contribute must be carried in his hand, possibly to indicate that the money about him was exclusively for an immediate sacred purpose. He suggests that, for similar reasons, Jesus transferred these very ordinances to the disciples when engaged in the service of the *real* Temple, and says the direction of Mt 10⁹ᶠ· will then mean : 'Go out in the same spirit and manner as you would to the Temple services, and fear not,—"for the workman is worthy of his meat." In other words : Let this new Temple service be your only thought, undertaking, and care' (*The Temple*, etc. p. 42).

Lk 19⁴³ our Lord shows His familiarity with the history of warfare when He prophesies that the enemy will cast up a bank (χάραξ) or a trench round Jerusalem. This prophecy was literally fulfilled forty years afterwards, when Titus surrounded Jerusalem with a palisaded mound and wall of masonry (*agger* and *vallum*).

Jesus seems to have recognized war as rising from the nature of man and the constitution of society ; but as His teaching lays hold upon nations, the methods of war become less barbarous, and we have good cause to anticipate a time, and to work for it, when 'nation shall not lift up sword against nation, neither shall they learn war any more.' While, therefore, Jesus Christ did not condemn war in the abstract, the whole spirit of Christianity is against it (see Hastings' *DB*, art. 'War').

              COLL. A. MACDONALD.

WASTE.—The idea of waste is presented in the Gospels in two figures. (1) The first of these appears in the word διασκορπίζω, which indicates the scattering of one's possessions. It is the act of the man who, like the Prodigal, makes 'ducks and drakes' of his goods (Lk 15¹³), or, like the Unfaithful Steward, squanders his master's property (Lk 16¹).

(2) The second word is ἀπώλεια, which denotes the doing to death of that which should have remained to enrich and beautify life. Judas thought that the pouring forth of the ointment upon the head of Christ was ἀπώλεια (Mt 26⁸ ‖). In his opinion it was waste, because the price of it might have been added to his bag, and might have remained to enrich himself (Jn 12⁶). It was put to a use which did not commend itself to him, and this seemed to the man in whose heart the love of a once accepted Master had now been usurped by the money with which he had been entrusted, a loss of something like 'three hundred pence' (Mk 14⁵). It is very significant that Christ used the word, which Judas had applied to Mary, of Judas himself. So far wrong was he that Mary had rendered an ever memorable act of devotion. The true 'waste' was in himself ; he was the 'son of waste' (ὁ υἱὸς τῆς ἀπωλείας, Jn 17¹²). See art. JUDAS ISCARIOT in vol. i. p. 909ᵇ.   W. W. HOLDSWORTH.

WATCH.—**1.** The *noun* 'watch' in the Gospels represents (1) κουστωδία (Lat. *custodia*) in Mt 27⁶⁵· ⁶⁶ 28¹¹ AV ('guard' RV). This word, which is said to have been the technical term for a company of 60 men, is used here to describe either the Roman soldiers, whom the chief priests and Pharisees obtained from Pilate, or the Temple guard, which he reminded them they already had and could employ to protect the sepulchre from being rifled. (2) φυλακή, where it denotes the divisions of the night either into 3 (Jewish and Greek ; cf. Lk 12³⁸ (?)*) or 4 (Roman ; cf. Mk 13³⁵) parts. The word in this sense occurs (*a*) in the account of our Lord's walking upon the Lake of Galilee, which was 'at the fourth watch,' *i.e.* just before dawn (Mt 14²⁵, Mk 6⁴⁸) ; (*b*) in His remarks upon the uncertainty and unexpectedness of the Presence (παρουσία) of the Son of Man (Mt 24⁴³, Lk 12³⁸). (3) φυλακή in an active sense, denoting a watching or keeping watch (Lk 2⁸).

2. 'Watch' as a *verb*.—The duty of constant watchfulness (γρηγορεῖν) and vigilance (ἀγρυπνεῖν) is insisted upon by our Lord in two main connexions : (*a*) in regard to the particular, immediate need for it on the night of the Betrayal (Mt 26³⁸· ⁴⁰· ⁴¹, Mk 14³⁴· ³⁸), and (*b*) in regard to the general attitude of disciples who await their Lord's Return (Mt 24⁴²· ⁴³, Mk 13³³· ³⁴· ³⁷, Lk 12³⁷· ³⁹ 21³⁶).

* It is not unlikely that in this case the fourth watch is not named, simply because the return is not likely to be so long delayed. So Meyer, Alford, Bruce, etc.

As to the general attitude or frame of mind in which the Church is bidden by her Lord to look for His coming, the burden of His teaching is that ours must be the steadfast, active readiness of dutiful, trusty servants, who are not afraid of being caught idle or in mischief, when the Master appears and reveals His welcome, though awful presence.

C. L. FELTOE.

WATER (ὕδωρ).—For an Eastern country, Palestine (except in the Negeb and the districts which are desert) has a fairly abundant supply of water. It is described as 'a land of brooks (torrent-valleys), of fountains and depths, that spring out of the valleys and hills' (Dt 8[7]). It is a matter of dispute whether the climate has changed since OT times. The rainy season is in winter, from November to March, when the rains are generally heavy. At other times there are only occasional showers. 'The former rain and the latter rain' (Dt 11[14]) come about the autumn and spring equinox respectively. The rainfall on an average is from 25 to 30 inches in ordinary seasons (the average rainfall in England is less than 30 inches), but there are times of drought which cause great loss and suffering. In Galilee the water supply is much greater than in Judæa. The storage of water is much more imperfect than in former times. In many places the ruins of artificial tanks, pools, and aqueducts are visible. The chief waters which are referred to in the Gospels are those of the Sea of Galilee and the river Jordan.

Water is frequently mentioned in the Gospels (most instances are found in Jn.), both in its literal and figurative meanings. **1.** *Literally : e.g.* 'Jesus went up straightway out of the water' (Mt 3[16] ‖ Mk 1[10]) ; 'Send Lazarus, that he may dip the tip of his finger in water' (Lk 16[24]) ; 'John was baptizing in Ænon, near to Salim, because there was much water there' (Jn 3[23]). The water of the pool of Bethesda (Jn 5[1-7]) was supposed to have curative powers. Part of v.[3] ('waiting for the moving of the waters') and the whole of v.[4] are now rejected by critical editors. The moving of the water was a natural phenomenon, the flow of the spring being intermittent. The disciples who were sent to prepare for the observance of the Passover were instructed to look for 'a man bearing a pitcher of water' (Mk 14[13] ‖ Lk 22[10]). As water is usually carried by women in the East, the man bearing the pitcher would easily be distinguished. It was perhaps a token arranged beforehand, so that the place of observance should not be known till the last moment. See also art. PITCHER. In Jn 19[34] it is recorded that at the crucifixion of Jesus one of the soldiers pierced His side with a spear, and forthwith there came out blood and water ; see art. BLOOD AND WATER.

2. The *figurative* use of water in the Gospels is varied. It is a symbol (i.) of the moral cleansing of life in repentance, 'I baptize you with water unto repentance' (Mt 3[11], Mk 1[8], Lk 3[16], Jn 1[23-26]) ; (ii.) its symbolical reference in connexion with the new birth is admitted, but its significance is uncertain, 'Except a man be born of water and spirit (ἐξ ὕδατος καὶ πνεύματος), he cannot enter into the kingdom of God' (Jn 3[5]). The phrase 'water and spirit' has been regarded as an instance of hendiadys, and interpreted as 'spiritual water' (Neil, *Figurative Language in the Bible*). Others take it as referring to the baptism of John, and as indicating that repentance is an essential factor in the new birth (*Expos. Times*, vol. iii. p. 318). It has also been interpreted as referring to the sacrament of baptism. This is the most ancient and general view. Wendt and others, however, regard the words ὕδατος καί as a post-Apostolic interpolation (*Gospel according to St. John, ad loc.*). This is the most probable conclusion, unless the words are interpreted as referring to the baptism of John unto repentance ; see *Expos. Times*, vol. xv. p. 413. (iii.) Water is also used as a symbol of innocence : 'Pilate took water, and washed his hands before the multitude, saying, I am innocent of the blood of this just person' (Mt 27[24]). (iv.) As a sign of hospitality or respect (see Gn 24[32] 43[24]). Jesus said to Simon the Pharisee, 'I entered into thy house, thou gavest me no water for my feet' (Lk 7[44]). (v.) At the supper in the upper room (Jn 13[1-17]) the water for the feet had not been provided. The disciples had not noticed the omission, or they were each unwilling to undertake the servile duty. Then 'Jesus riseth from supper, and laid aside his garments ; and took a towel, and girded himself. After that, he poureth water into a bason, and began to wash the disciples' feet' (Jn 13[4. 5]). The ordered detail of the narrative is an indication of the profound impression which the action of Jesus had made upon the Evangelist. The act was full of significance. It was a symbolic service. It taught the disciples the duty of humility, and the need of daily cleansing from the daily defilement of sin. (vi.) In His conversation with the woman of Samaria, Jesus linked the water which she sought at the well with the living water which He alone could give. He uses it as a symbol of eternal life, the blessings of the gospel in their satisfying and permanent power of good (Jn 4[11-15]). (vii.) On the last day of the feast Jesus stood in the Temple and cried, 'If any man thirst, let him come unto me and drink. He that believeth in me, as the scripture saith, out of his belly shall flow rivers of living water' (Jn 7[37f.]). The Evangelist interprets the symbol : 'This spake he of the Spirit, which they which believed on him should receive : for the Holy Spirit was not yet given ; because Jesus was not yet glorified' (v.[39]). The accuracy of the interpretation has been doubted (Wendt, *Teaching of Jesus*, vol. i. p. 256 n.). (viii.) It is also used as a symbol of the smallest service : 'Whosoever shall give unto one of these little ones a cup of cold water only in the name of a disciple, verily I say unto you he shall in no wise lose his reward' (Mt 10[42] ‖ Mk 9[41]). It is possible to punctuate the sentence so that it reads 'a cup of cold water only' or 'only in the name of a disciple.' But the first is greatly to be preferred.

LITERATURE.—Conder, *Palestine*, pp. 25–29 ; Robinson, *BRP* i. 342 f.; Smith, *Expositor*, 6th ser. vii. [1903] 212 ff.; art. 'Water' in Hastings' *DB* ; Thomson, *LB* p. 459 ; Neil, *Figurative Language in the Bible* ; *Expos. Times*, vol. iii. [1892] p. 318, vol. vi. [1895] p. 389, vol. xv. [1904] p. 413.

JOHN REID.

WATERPOT (ὑδρία, freq. in LXX for כַּד Gn 24[14], Jg 7[16], 1 K 17[12] 18[33], Ec 12[6]).—**1.** Jn 2[6. 7] λίθιναι ὑδρίαι ἓξ κείμεναι . . . γεμίσατε τὰς ὑδρίας ὕδατος. The stone waterpots (כְּלֵי אֲבָנִים in Rabbinic writings) were placed outside the reception-room, for the washing of the hands before and after eating, as well as of the vessels used (cf. Mk 7[2-4], Mt 15[2], Lk 11[38]). 'For such an occasion the family would produce or borrow the largest and handsomest stone vessels that could be procured' (Edersheim, *LT* i. 357).

The view of Westcott, first put forth in 1859 in a note to his *Characteristics of the Gosp. Mir.* (p. 14), and afterwards stated more fully in his *Com. on St. John* (37, 38), that it was not the water in those vessels that was changed into wine, but the water which the servants drew from the source after having filled the vessels, has commended itself to many students of the Gospels. But it has not superseded the traditional view, which must be acknowledged to have in its favour the first impression produced on the minds of readers of the narrative in all ages,—a fact of great weight. Readers in general have understood that the number and capacity of the vessels were stated immediately before the command to fill them, in order to convey the idea that their entire contents were changed into wine (Dods, *Expos. Gr. NT* i. 704), and also that the clause 'they filled them up to the brim' was added in order to exclude all possible suspicion of collusion (Trench, *Mir.* 104, after Chrys.). Such are the principal objections to Westcott's view, which, however, must not be hastily pronounced to be inadmissible, or even improbable. When the arguments in its favour are carefully weighed, the balance seems to lie almost equal between it and the ordinary view.

(i.) 'It is unlikely that water taken from vessels of purification should have been employed for the purpose of the miracle.' This argument holds good even supposing that the vessels had already been partially or wholly emptied by pouring water on the hands of the guests (Plummer, *in loc.*). (ii.) The words 'Draw out *now*,' etc., are perhaps most naturally understood to mean that the same action of drawing water from the source was to be carried on as before, but that the water so drawn was now to have a different destination. In like manner v.⁹ seems to imply that the servants who had drawn the water had borne it, in obedience to Jesus' word, straight from the source to the ruler of the feast. It may, however, be argued that the νῦν may equally well mean, 'Now that the vessels are quite full, bear from them to the ruler of the feast' (in pitchers out of which he would fill the cups of the guests, Meyer, *in loc.*). (iii.) Though it would be hazardous to say that the words οἱ ἠντληκότες τὸ ὕδωρ in v.⁹ render it probable that ὕδωρ (also from the source) is to be understood after ἀντλήσατε in v.⁸, it may yet be stated that ἀντλεῖν is frequently used of the drawing of water (cf. Gn 24¹³, Ex 2¹⁶, Is 12³, Jn 4⁷·¹⁵), but rarely of the drawing of wine, so that on the whole the use of the word is in favour of Westcott's view.* (iv.) It is suggested that this view is most in keeping with the symbolical and spiritual character of the miracle. The turning of the water into wine was a σημεῖον by which Jesus manifested His glory. The filling of the vessels with water was part of the 'sign,' and pointed to the fulfilling of the Law (cf. Mt 5¹⁷). At the command of Jesus 'they filled them up to the brim.' This may have been designed to show that the preparation of the Law was now complete. It had reached its high-water mark, if we may so speak. The number and capacity of the vessels, and their being utilized for 'the purifying of the Jews,' may thus be regarded as providentially ordered circumstances, designed to bring out the significance of Jesus' act in its relation to the Law. The vessels were filled and then left as they stood, while the water which the servants, in obedience to Jesus' word, drew from the source was carried past them and delivered to the ruler of the feast, who on tasting it said to the bridegroom, 'Thou hast kept the good wine until now.' Full justice, it may be argued, is thus done to the spiritual import of the miracle, which was intended to represent that what the Law with its elaborate ceremonial could not do, Jesus could now do for those unto whom He had come—impart to them the true joy of salvation (cf. Ps 104¹⁵, Mk 2²² and parallels). The views set forth in the *Encyc. Bibl.* ii. 1796, 1800, 2539; Wendt, *St. John's Gospel*, 83, 240, may be compared with the foregoing statement.—'The symbolical interpretation of Scripture must not be hastily set aside because it has been often disfigured by unlicensed fancies' (Westcott, *Char. Gosp. Mir.* xii.). A symbolical interpretation may also be quite consistently held by those who maintain the traditional view. But apart from symbolism altogether, the miracle taken by itself is comforting and edifying in the highest degree, as a proof that Christ's hallowing presence is with us in our common interests and enjoyments, and that He blesses all life's relationships.—It may be added that if it was the entire contents of the vessels that became wine, the magnitude of the gift is an example of our Lord's abundant mercies, with which we may compare the miracle of the loaves and the twelve baskets of fragments that were left.

2. Jn 4²⁸ ἀφῆκεν οὖν τὴν ὑδρίαν αὐτῆς ἡ γυνή. The waterpot of the woman of Samaria was one of those jars of sun-dried clay which are still in use in the East, and which are carried upon the head or on the shoulder (*Encyc. Bibl.* i. 887, iii. 3818; *Land and Book*, 576; Lane, *Mod. Egyptians*⁵, i. 187–188, who calls attention to the word *garrah* or *jarrah* for a water-pitcher, from which our word

* Dr. Giles of Emmanuel College, Cambridge, has favoured the writer with the following note on the use of ἀντλεῖν. 'I do not know of any example in Attic Greek of ἀντλεῖν in the sense of 'draw wine' (for which ἀρύτω or ἀφύσσω (in poetry) would be expected) except the following from a fragment of Pherecrates, the comic poet, κόραι . . . πλήρεις χύλικας οἴνου μέλανος ἀνθοσμίου ἤντλουν διὰ χώνης τοῖσι βουλομένοις πιεῖν (Meineke, *Frag.* ii. 300). Though the comic poets have so much to say of wine, this, apparently, is the sole instance. It was possibly slang, and the verb is certainly used by the Alexandrian writers as a slang word, as in the recently discovered Herodas, iv. 14, οὐ γάρ τι πολλὴν οὐδ' ἕτοιμον ἀντλοῦμεν (like our 'raking in the shekels'). The use for wine had also continued, because in Theocritus x. 13 occurs the proverb ἐκ πίθου ἀντλεῖς (like our 'going it '). Something nearer NT times would be useful, but I cannot discover that it occurs in the Papyri.'

'jar' is derived). Her leaving her waterpot was not, as some say, because her faith in Christ made her forget the purpose for which she had originally come, but because it impelled her to announce her discovery of Him to others without delay; and in her haste to return to Sychar with the news, she did not choose to be encumbered with her heavy waterpot, which could be fetched at any time.

LITERATURE.—Westcott, *Characteristics of the Gosp. Miracles*, and *Com. on St. John*; Edersheim, *LT*; Dods, *EGT*; Dictionaries of the Bible; Lane, *Modern Egyptians*.

JAMES DONALD.

WAY.—The term 'way' is used in the OT and NT in a great variety of senses, physical (see art. ROADS) and moral. Any good concordance will show the frequency of the word and the range of its application. Jesus calls Himself 'the Way.' 'I am the way, the truth, and the life; no man cometh unto the Father, but by me' (Jn 14⁶). In the remarkable interview in which this passage occurs, the subject of conversation was the goal of life, the ultimate destiny of the little company. 'I go to prepare a place for you.' The declaration was an enigma. Thomas and Philip gave expression to the perplexity of the rest. 'We know not whither thou goest, and how can we know the way?' The *whither* is (1) union with God, (2) the Father's home, and as a corollary, (3) holiness. But the way to the end what is it? 'I am the way.' As if He said, 'Through me, through what I have done, through what I have been teaching, through what I am about to do.' They had forgotten, or not understood, that He was the Incarnate Word, that He and the Father were one, and that He was laying down His life for them; but when they did understand these things then they would know the way. In He 10¹⁹·²⁰ the blood of Christ seems to be the way: 'Having therefore, brethren, boldness to enter into the holiest by the blood of Jesus, by a new and living way which He hath consecrated for us.' Those who believe in Christ are 'of the Way' (Ac 9² 19⁹ 22⁴). Saul 'desired of the high priest letters to Damascus to the synagogues, that if he found any that were of the Way, he might bring them bound unto Jerusalem.' The name served as a convenient term by which to describe the disciples in the early Church. Among the orthodox Jews it was a term of contempt; among the disciples of honour: for had not Jesus claimed to be the Way? A way leads to somewhere. Christ the new and living way leads to holiness, and heaven, and God.

LITERATURE.—The *Lexicons* of Cremer and Grimm-Thayer, *s.v.* ὁδός; *Expositor*, IV. x. [1894] 450 ff.; Paget, *Christ the Way* (1902).

R. LEGGAT.

WAYSIDE.—Two blind men sat by the wayside begging, as Jesus left Jericho on His way to Jerusalem (Mt 20³⁰). They had probably taken their station at a spot near the city where several paths met, and which may have been planted with trees. Again, in the parable of the Sower, some of the seed fell 'by the wayside' (Mt 13⁴), *i.e.* along the road (παρὰ τὴν ὁδόν), where the ground was so hard as to be impenetrable by it. Jesus gave His own interpretation of the parable. (1) Owing to their hardness of heart men do not understand the word. They hear but do not heed. It falls like seed on a drumhead; and then (2) the fowls of the air come and devour it. Hearts worn hard by selfishness and worldliness do not give entrance to the Divine truth, and the truth lying there is either trampled and destroyed by cares and anxieties, or snatched away by the host of passing thoughts.

R. LEGGAT.

WEALTH.—1. The Gospels differ from each

other very considerably in their contributions to the subject of wealth. The Gospel of Jn. contributes scarcely anything. Such words as πλούσιος, πλοῦτος, πλουτεῖν, θησαυρός, θησαυρίζειν do not occur in it; and πτωχός is found only in $12^{5.\ 6.\ 8}$ and 13^{29}. Mk. contributes little—only 4^{19} and a few characteristic touches in the narrative of the Rich Young Ruler and the discourse following upon it, as for instance 10^{24}. It is to Mt. and Lk. that we are indebted for practically all the teaching in the Gospels on this subject. And the material supplied by them is specially rich. But it is not uniform. There is a contrast between the teaching on wealth in Lk. and that in Mt. Lk. has preserved a series of utterances of our Lord, which on the face of them seem hostile to wealth and partial to poverty. These consist partly of sayings peculiar to Lk. and partly of sayings common to Lk. and Mt., but having in Lk.'s version a sense apparently less favourable to wealth. The following sayings regarding wealth are peculiar to Lk. : 1^{53} 3^{11} 4^{18} $6^{24.\ 25}$ 12^{13-21} $14^{12-14.\ 33}$ $16^{1-13.\ 19-31}$. The following are illustrations of sayings common to Mt. and Lk., but with an apparent bias against wealth in Lk.'s version of them : Mt 5^3, cf. Lk 6^{20}; Mt 6^{19-21}, cf. Lk 12^{33}; Mt 5^{42}, cf. Lk 6^{30}; Mt 19^{21}, cf. Lk 18^{22}; in the parable of the Marriage Feast (Mt 22^{1-14}) it is the 'good and bad' who are gathered in from the highways, in the parable of the Great Supper (Lk 14^{16-24}) it is the 'poor and maimed and blind and lame.'

Because of these differences the Gospel of Lk. has been charged with Ebionism (wh. see). It has been said that it preaches the sinfulness of wealth and the merit of poverty. By some this characteristic is taken to be a faithful reproduction of the spirit and teaching of Jesus; by others it is attributed to Lk. or to his sources, or to the influence of the sub-Apostolic period to which, by them, this Gospel is assigned. But before the Gospel of Lk. is credited with a bias against wealth and in favour of poverty, certain facts, pointing to a different conclusion, have to be taken account of. In the first place, what might be construed as proofs of Ebionism are to be found in some of the other Gospels also. The strongest saying of Jesus against wealth, 'It is easier for a camel to go through a needle's eye than for a rich man to enter into the kingdom of God,' is recorded by Mt. (19^{24}) and Mk. (10^{25}) as well as by Lk. (18^{25}). So also are the incidents of Peter and Andrew, of James and John, and of Matthew or Levi leaving all to follow Jesus (Mt 4^{18-22} 9^9, Mk 1^{16-20} 2^{14}, Lk $5^{11.\ 27.\ 28}$). Mt. and Mk. tell of the Baptist's ascetic manner of life (Mt 3^4, Mk 1^6). It is to Mt. that we are indebted for the record of the sayings, 'Lay not up for yourselves treasures upon the earth' (6^{19}), and 'The poor have good tidings preached to them' (11^5). In Mt 13^{22} and Mk 4^{19} Jesus is represented as using the phrase 'the deceitfulness of riches,'—words not recorded by Lk.; and it is Mt. and Mk., not Lk., who have preserved the saying of our Lord in which He speaks of the blessedness of leaving lands (ἀγρούς) for His sake (Mt 19^{29}, Mk 10^{29}). On the other hand, Lk. reports incidents and sayings the reverse of Ebionitic. In the parable of the Rich Man and Lazarus recorded by him alone (16^{19-31}), rich Abraham is in bliss as well as poor Lazarus. It is Lk. who tells of the women of position who ministered to Jesus of their substance ($8^{2.\ 3}$). He alone records Jesus' injunction to His disciples, 'He that hath a purse, let him take it' (22^{36}). To him we owe the story of Zacchæus, a rich man who won Jesus' commendation even though he still retained half his wealth (19^{1-10}). And he, in common with the other Evangelists, speaks in terms of approval of another rich man, Joseph of Arimathæa (23^{50-53}). At the same time it can scarcely be doubted that the prominence accorded in Lk. to the contrast between poverty and wealth, and to sayings of our Lord which seem to favour the poor, indicates a deep interest on the part of the writer in the problem of wealth and poverty. See POOR and POVERTY.

2. What, then, is the view of wealth presented in the Gospels? What, in particular, is Jesus' view of wealth? (1) He assumes, though He nowhere explicitly declares, *the lawfulness of the possession of wealth*. This is implied in such parables as those of the Talents (Mt 25^{14-30}), the Pounds (Lk 19^{12-27}), and the Unjust Steward (Lk 16^{1-8}), all of which deal with the uses of money, without any disapprobation of its possession being indicated. It is implied in His parting injunctions to His disciples (Lk $22^{35.\ 36}$), and in the saying, 'Make to yourselves friends by means of the mammon of unrighteousness' (Lk 16^9), which also involve the possession and use of money. It is implied even in the demand which He made of the Rich Young Ruler and others to part with wealth (Mt 19^{21}, Lk 18^{22} 12^{33} 14^{33}), and in the exhortation, 'Lay not up for yourselves treasures upon the earth' (Mt 6^{19}). In each of these cases Jesus appealed to men to forego what He did not deny was their right. 'He was pressing on them a moral choice, not establishing an economic law' (Speer). The woes pronounced upon the rich and prosperous (Lk 6^{24-26}) have parallels in the OT (Is 10^2, Am $2^{6.\ 7}$ 8^6), and are to be explained on the ground of the moral dangers of wealth as well as on the ground of the oppression of the pious poor by the rich. Nor is the fate of Dives (Lk 16^{19-31}) any proof that Jesus condemned the possession of wealth as such. See DIVES.

(2) Jesus implies that *wealth is the gift of God*. This is the view of the OT (Ps 89^{11} $50^{10-12.\ 14}$ etc.). And it is accepted by Jesus and illustrated in the parables of the Talents (Mt 25^{14-30}), the Pounds (Lk 19^{12-27}), and the Foolish Rich Man (Lk 12^{16-21}). In all these, gifts and possessions, including wealth, are represented as bestowed on men by God. And this is made specially clear with regard to wealth in the parable of the Foolish Rich Man. The Rich Man's wealth came to him through the medium which is most evidently at God's discretion, namely, through his ground bringing forth plentifully. The same truth is implied in the petition, 'Give us this day our daily bread' (Mt 6^{11}, Lk 11^3), and in the sayings : 'If God so clothe the grass of the field, which to-day is and to-morrow is cast into the oven, shall he not much more clothe you, O ye of little faith?' (Mt 6^{30}, Lk 12^{28}); 'Your heavenly Father knoweth that ye have need of all these things. . . . All these things shall be added unto you' (Mt $6^{32.\ 33}$, Lk $12^{30.\ 31}$). And the description of wealth as τὸ ἀλλότριον (Lk 16^{12}) seems to carry with it the idea that wealth belongs really to God, and is only lent or entrusted by Him to men.

(3) Wealth, according to Jesus, is essentially *a subordinate good*. It is characterized by Him as ἐλάχιστον (Lk 16^{10}) compared with spiritual interests. It is too uncertain to be the goal of life (Mt $6^{19.\ 20}$). Inasmuch as it is something outside man and apart from him, the possession of it does not necessarily contribute to riches of character, but may, on the contrary, coexist with poverty of soul (Lk 12^{16-21} $14^{18.\ 19}$, Mt $22^{5.\ 6}$). Nor will the possession of wealth compensate for the loss of the true life (Mt 16^{26}, Mk $8^{36.\ 37}$; Lk 9^{25}). Life, in fact, in the highest sense of the term, is a larger and richer thing than mere possession of wealth (Lk $12^{15.\ 23}$, Mt $6^{20.\ 25.\ 33}$); and it is, to a considerable degree, independent of wealth (Mt $6^{25.\ 33.\ 34}$, Lk $12^{22.\ 23.\ 29-34}$).

(4) Wealth is *a means, not an end*. It is subordinate to the great moral issues of life, and it is of value only in so far as it promotes the true purpose of life. It is a test and discipline of char-

acter. The getting, possessing, and spending of wealth develop qualities which survive death, and are fraught with important consequences in the world to come. This view of wealth is presented in the parables of the Talents (Mt 25[14-30]), the Pounds (Lk 19[12-27]), the Foolish Rich Man (Lk 12[16-21]), the Unjust Steward and Christ's comments on it (Lk 16[1-13]), Dives and Lazarus (Lk 16[19-31]), and in the picture of the Judgment of Men (Mt 25[31-46]). In these passages wealth is regarded as a trust committed by God to man, demanding in the possessor of it fidelity, watchfulness, and foresight. Faithfulness in the administration of the unrighteous mammon prepares for greater and more serious responsibilities in the world to come, and contributes to our well-being there (Lk 16[1-13]); but failure to use wealth aright entails loss and condemnation (Lk 12[16-21] 16[10-13. 19-31]). On the other hand, we are taught in the parable of the Unrighteous Steward that as the Steward employed his lord's wealth in securing for himself friends who would support him after he was deprived of his office, so we should administer the wealth committed to us in such a way that it will contribute to our well-being in the world to come.

As to how exactly this is to be done Jesus lays down no detailed rules, trusting rather to the impulses of the regenerate heart issuing in right action. Where love to God and love to man rule the life, wealth will be wisely administered. 'The cross of Christ is the solution of the social problem' (Kambli). At the same time, we are not left without hints and indications as to how one inspired by the enthusiasm of Christianity will deal with wealth. In acquiring wealth he will have regard to the rights and claims of his fellow-men as much as to his own (Mt 22[39] 7[12], Mk 12[31], Lk 6[31]). He will be sparing in his own personal expenditure, and will aim at simplicity of life (Lk 10[41. 42] RVm). He will be mindful of the claims of relatives (Mk 7[10-13]). He will contribute liberally in gifts and personal service for the advancement of God's Kingdom, even at much sacrifice and inconvenience (Lk 21[1-4] 8[1-3] 23[50-56]). Nor need the gift necessarily be justifiable on purely utilitarian grounds: it may be artistically expressive of devotion and gratitude (Mt 26[6-13], Mk 14[3-9], Jn 12[2-8], Lk 7[36-50]). Such a one will also relieve the needs of his fellow-men, either by almsgiving or by personal ministration, or in some other way suggested by circumstances (Mt 6[2-4] 19[21] 25[31-46], Mk 10[21], Lk 6[30] 10[30-37] 12[33] 14[12-14] 19[8], Jn 13[29]), care, however, always being taken that ostentation or other wrong motives mar not the value of the gift or service (Mt 6[2-4]). And Jesus, by His commendation of Mary for her gift of costly spikenard (Mt 26[6-13], Mk 14[3-9], Jn 12[3-8]), and of the woman who was a sinner for a similar act (Lk 7[36-50]), as well as by His presence at the marriage at Cana of Galilee (Jn 2[1-11]), and at feasts, and by His appreciation of nature, seems to sanction expenditure of wealth in ministering not merely to the necessities of men, but also to their happiness through the gratification of their social instincts and their love of beauty.

(5) But whilst Jesus implies the lawfulness of private possessions and gives guidance as to the right use of them, He is at the same time keenly alive to *the perils attached to wealth*; and His recorded utterances contain many warnings with reference to them. This is the explanation of those sayings of His which seem on the first reading of them to condemn wealth and the possession of it. He characterizes money as 'the mammon of unrighteousness' and 'the unrighteous mammon' (Lk 16[9. 11]), not because money is evil in itself, but because the getting and possessing and spending of it are so apt to lead to unrighteousness. Again,

He pronounces woe upon the rich and prosperous (Lk 6[24. 25]), not only because they were too often guilty of oppressing the pious poor, but also because their wealth exposed them to grave spiritual perils. And He indicates what some of these perils are. Wealth tends to delude a man as to his real worth, and to invest him with a factitious importance (Lk 12[16-21]). It tends to become a man's god, and to oust the true God from His supremacy in the heart (Mt 6[24], Lk 16[13] 12[16-21]). The rich man is apt to trust in his riches, not in God, and to think that the possession of them insures him against adversity (Lk 12[16-21]). Wealth is also apt to make him forgetful of his indebtedness to God, and to lead him to regard God's gifts to him as his own absolute possessions to do with as he pleases (Lk 12[16-21]). Further, wealth has the tendency to deaden the possessor's sense of spiritual need and his aspirations after spiritual good (Mt 13[22], Lk 12[16-21] 16[19-31], Mt 22[5], Lk 14[18-20]). It tends also to limit the possessor's thoughts to this present world and its interests, to the exclusion of higher things (Mt 6[19-34], Lk 12[16-21] 16[19-31]). It is apt to come into conflict with the demands of the Kingdom of God and to indispose to the acceptance of them (Mt 19[16-26], Mk 10[17-27], Lk 18[18-27] 9[57-62] 14[18-20], Mt 22[5]). There is the danger, too, of producing alienation of sympathy from our fellow-men and selfish ignoring of their needs and claims (Lk 12[16-21] 16[19-31]). And, lastly, there is the danger of covetousness (Lk 12[15], Mt 13[22]), wealth tending to breed the desire for more wealth (Lk 12[16-21]), though this sin may beset those also who do not possess (Lk 12[13-15]).

(6) These dangers, vividly realized by Jesus and greatly dreaded by Him, led Him to make use occasionally of *language which, interpreted literally, would seem to teach the incompatibility of the possession of wealth with membership in the Kingdom of God*. Such are the Woes pronounced on the rich and prosperous (Lk 6[24. 25]), the conversation following the incident of the Rich Young Ruler (Mt 19[23. 24], Mk 10[23-25], Lk 18[24. 25]), and the demand that whosoever would be His disciple must renounce all that he hath (Lk 14[33]). These utterances are to be explained partly by the circumstances of the age in which they were spoken. Jesus foresaw trouble and affliction for His followers. In the world they would have tribulation: they would be hated of all men for His name's sake. Hence, if they were to endure unto the end, it was necessary that they should hold property and friends and life cheap, always ready to part with them for the sake of Christ (Mt 10[34-39], Lk 14[26]). And this was specially incumbent on those who were to be the preachers and missionaries of the gospel (Lk 9[57-62], Mt 8[18-22]). Hence Jesus' demand that those who would be His disciples should renounce all that they had. And hence also the severe things He says regarding the rich. But these utterances are to be interpreted also in accordance with Jesus' practice of embodying His teaching in bold, striking, picturesque utterances designed and fitted to arrest attention. He expresses Himself thus strongly in order to impress men in all ages with the extreme peril of wealth, and to admonish the rich that they should hold their wealth lightly, and be ready to sacrifice it if duty demands.

But Jesus went further, and in one case at least demanded of an aspirant for eternal life that he sell all and give to the poor if he would have treasure in heaven (Mt 19[16-22], Mk 10[17-22], Lk 18[18-23]). This demand may have been made to make clear to the Young Man the inadequacy of his observance of the Divine law, and especially the shallowness of his love for his neighbour. But more probably it was made in accordance with the principle, laid down elsewhere by Jesus, that whatever interests or relationships conflict with a man's spiritual well-being and with the claims of God's Kingdom should be sacrificed, even though in themselves legitimate (Mt 5[29. 30] 19[10-12], Mk 9[43. 45. 47], Lk 14[26]). It was probably perceived by Jesus that the Young Ruler's wealth was interfering with his realization of the highest good, and would render loyal and enthusiastic discipleship impossible for him. Hence Jesus called upon him to part with it. Though this is the only case of the kind recorded in the Gospels, it may well be that there were others similar. But even though it stand alone, it is sufficient to establish the principle that the influence of wealth on the possessor may be so injurious to his highest interests that he must renounce it if he is to enter into life. See also PROPERTY.

LITERATURE.—Rogge, *Der irdische Besitz im NT*, 1897; Jacoby, *Jesus Christus und die irdischen Güter*, 1875; Holtzmann, 'Die ersten Christen und die sociale Frage,' and Kambli, 'Das Eigenthum im Licht des Evangeliums,' both in *Wissenschaftliche Vorträge über religiöse Fragen*, 1882; Wendt, 'Das Eigentum nach christlicher Beurteilung' in *ZThK*, 1898; Naumann, *Jesus als Volksmann*, 1894; Peabody, *Jesus Christ and the Social Question*, 1900; Orello Cone, *Rich and Poor in the NT*, 1902; Harnack, *Das Wesen des Christentums*, 1901; Heuver, *The Teachings of Jesus concerning Wealth*, 1903; Speer, *The Principles of Jesus*, 1902; Dickie, *The Christian Ethics of Social Life*, 1903; Stubbs, *Christ and Economics*, 1894; Abbott, *Christianity and Social Problems*, 1896; Denney, 'Christ's Teaching on Money' in *Union Magazine*, September 1901; Ottley, 'Ethics of Property' in *Lombard Street in Lent*; James, *Varieties of Religious Experience*, 1902; Feine, *Eine vorkanonische Ueberlieferung des Lukas*, 1891; Campbell, *Critical Studies on Luke*, 1891; Milligan, 'A Group of Parables,' *Expos.*, Sept. 1892; Hicks, 'The Communistic Experiment of Acts ii. and iv.,' *Expos.*, Jan. 1906; also Lives of Jesus by Strauss, Renan, Keim, Weiss, Beyschlag, etc.; B. Weiss, *NT Theol.* 1880; Beyschlag, *NT Theol.* [Eng: tr. 1895]; Wendt, *Teaching of Jesus*, 1892; various works on the Parables; commentaries on Mt. and Lk., esp. Plummer's 'St. Luke' in *ICC*; artt. 'Matthew,' 'Luke,' and 'Gospels' in Hastings' *DB*.

J. W. SLATER.

WEARINESS.—The one reference to the weariness of our Lord which we find in the Gospels occurs in the account of His journey from Judæa into Galilee. We read that on His way, beaten down by heavy toil (κεκοπιακώς), He sat upon the well near to the village of Sychar (Jn 4[6]). The allusion is an eloquent testimony to the fact that He who is touched by the feeling of our infirmity shared that infirmity in its commonest effect of physical exhaustion. See HUMANITY OF CHRIST.

W. W. HOLDSWORTH.

WEAVING.—In our Lord's day weaving was done by hand-looms, as still in the East generally. The loom, with its 'beam' and 'shuttle,' which furnished to OT poet and prophet figures of life's swiftness and brevity (cf. Job 7[6], Is 38[12]), is not directly mentioned in the Gospels. While in the earlier days in Palestine weaving was done mostly by men, later it fell more and more into the hands of women. The Rabbis did not give it a high place among the crafts. Among the materials used in weaving were flax, wool, camel's hair and goat's hair. Flax and wool made 'soft clothing' for the royal and the rich (Mt 11[8], Lk 16[19]), the rest were wrought into the coarser garments of the more austere, like John the Baptist (Mt 3[4]), into the sackcloth of the mourner (Mt 11[21], Lk 10[13]), or into tents or sails. Jesus wore a seamless garment (χιτὼν ἄρραφος, Jn 19[23]), woven in one piece, from the top throughout, made probably by faithful, ministering women (Lk 8[2f.], Mt 27[55]); and when He was buried, the cloth in which His body was wrapped was of linen (Mk 15[46], Mt 27[59], Lk 24[12], Jn 19[40]).

E. B. POLLARD.

WEDDING GARMENT.—The parable in which the incident of the wedding garment occurs is recorded in Mt 22[1ff.]. As there is good reason to believe that the similar story told in Lk 14[16ff.] is not a different version of the same parable, but another teaching given on a different occasion, there will be no attempt made to find what light Lk.'s parable of the Great Supper throws on it. The wedding garment fits in as naturally with Mt.'s story as it would be out of place in Lk.'s.

Questions have been discussed with much learning as to whether the wedding garment means the righteousness of Christ or the righteousness of good works, whether it be something that we must do for ourselves or something that is done for us. The story, however, makes it quite plain that

it is nothing we can do for ourselves. Those gathered from the highways and lanes had certainly no opportunity for making themselves garments that would be fit for the royal presence. There is no occasion to search for illustrations showing that in the East it was not uncommon at high festivals to provide guests with suitable garments, because whether that was the case or not historically, it is certainly the case parabolically. The attitude of the king throughout the story is represented as so generous that it is inconceivable that he should fling one of his guests into a dungeon because he was unable to find for himself a suitable marriage garment. The man is punished for his impudence in supposing that he could come into the king's presence just as he was. If, then, we inquire what the truth is that our Lord wishes to express, it is plainly this, which we find again and again in Scripture, that no one is clean in God's sight. And when this sinful condition is contrasted with God's absolute holiness, no conclusion can be drawn but that man as he is cannot stand in God's presence.

The wedding garment means, then, something that God supplies, enabling the sinner to stand in His presence. Now there is nothing in the spiritual world that properly answers to a cloak or garment. Here, dress may effect a deception, may make a man appear to be what he is not, but there all is real, and the character is seen through and through. Commentators have therefore rightly felt that the wedding garment must denote an element in character. It is not, on the one hand, what is popularly known as good works, because they may have no root in the character; nor is it some fictitious imputation of what does not really belong to us; nor is it, as Archer Butler suggests, a spirit of sympathetic joy with the wedding festivities. It is something the lack of which deserves searching judgment, the presence of which is absolutely necessary. What is it? Is it not that definite relationship with Christ which is so clearly expressed in the hymn—

'Rock of Ages cleft for me,
Let me hide myself in thee,'

a relationship implying the closest possible union!? It is not something fictitious or unreal, but something which the fact of sin demands. For just as the spirit of independence is a ridiculous assumption for the creature in the presence of his Creator, so that of dependence on a perfect character carries with it a definite moral quality.

It may be said that this interpretation explains the substantive but not the adjective, that we have a meaning for 'garment' but not for 'wedding garment.' The wedding of the parable stands for the union of God with humanity—the Incarnation, as we call it. The indifference to that fact is the heaviest condemnation the world can receive. That was the blunder of the commercial people of our Lord's time, who were so engrossed with their own business as to pay no attention to the presence of Christ in the world, and who, when it seemed as though it would interfere with their concerns, did their best to destroy it. The blunder of the outcast is to suppose that this wonderful condescension was not necessary. It is this that is depicted in the incident of the wedding garment.

G. H. S. WALPOLE.

WEEK.—See TIME.

WEEPING.—See TEARS.

WEIGHTS AND MEASURES.—The specific object for which the Gospels were composed did not call for anything like a full detailed use of metrical data. Within their limited compass there are only incidental allusions to a system, or rather systems, of weights and measures. These are naturally scanty and obscure. The most that can be done with them is to identify them as nearly as possible with equivalents in modern systems, and to ascertain their places in those that were current in the Palestine of NT times. At this last point a difficulty at once emerges, due partly to the absence of regard for accuracy and precision in such matters prevalent at the time and place, and partly to the mixture of standards derived from successive and widely differing populations coming in with successive waves of conquest and invasion. The situation was not unlike that of modern Syria, with its bewildering confusion of coinage and other standards of value, brought in and grafted on the native system by French, German, and English merchants.

It is generally agreed by expert metrologists that the basis and fountainhead of all systems of measurement is to be traced to Babylonia. But in passing into Western countries, the Babylonian system was naturally subjected to as many modifications as it entered regions, and gave rise to quite as many secondary or derivative systems. These, during the course of the interrelations of the peoples using them, mutually affected one another ; and the result was a variety of values called by the same name, or by names derived from the same original. On account of this fact, etymological processes of reasoning are in this field of little value, if not altogether valueless and misleading. Moreover, throughout the whole history of metrology there is a tendency noticeable towards the shrinkage or reduction of primitive values, making it essential to distinguish with great care between the values current under the same name in different periods of history. In the attempt to reach the exact facts as far as the 1st cent. A.D. is concerned, it will be best to bear in mind that in Palestine during the OT period three main systems of metrology came into use more or less extensively, the Babylonian, the Egyptian, and the Phœnician, and that to these, just before the times of Jesus, the Roman conquest added a fourth as a disturbing element.

I. WEIGHTS.—The primitive unit of weight was the **shekel.** This developed into two forms, the heavy and the light (cf. Kennedy in Hastings' *DB*, art. 'Weights and Measures'). The heavy shekel weighed 252·5 grs., and the light just one-half of that. Perhaps while the shekel was still being used in these forms, a third value was attached to it by the introduction of the Syrian shekel of 320 grs., and a fourth value later, viz. the Phœnician of 224·4 grs. In Roman times the *denarius* was introduced. This was equivalent to the Attic drachm. But Josephus (*Ant.* III. viii. 2) represents the Hebrew shekel (σίκλος) as equal to a tetradrachm (4 drs.), and a drachm-denarius was fixed by Nero at 52·62 grs. At least approximately, therefore, for the 1st cent. A.D., three units in the scale of weights may be determined, as follows : the drachm-denarius=52·5 grs., the light shekel= 105 grs., and the heavy shekel=210 grs. Of the higher units the *mina* is equated with 100 drs., and the **talent** with 60 *minœ*, hence the scale :

	Dr.-Den.	Shek.	Tetr.	Min.	Talent.	
Drachm-Denar.	1					52·5+grs.
Shek. (light) .	2	1				105+ ,,
Shek. (heavy)	4	2	1			210+ ,,
Tetradrachm						
Mina . .	100	50	25	1		5250+ ,,
Talent . .	6000	3000	1500	60	1	315000+ ,,

In the Gospels the words δίδραχμον (light shekel, Mt 17²⁴) and τάλαντον * (talent, Mt 18²⁴ 25¹⁵⁻²⁸) occur, but not as the names of weights ; they are the designations of coins (see MONEY). The only term

* ταλαντιαῖος in Rev 16²¹ (cf. also Jos. *BJ* v. vi. 3) can in the nature of the case be only an approximation. The *PEFSt*, 1892, 289 f., records the discovery of a large stone weighing 64600 grs. (41900 grammes), used as a heavy talent weight.

purely designating a weight is λίτρα (**pound**, Jn 12³ 19³⁹).* This was identified with the *mina* of the above scale as its approximate equivalent. Its exact weight in the Roman scale of weights is given as 5050 grs., or 11 oz. avoirdupois.

II. MEASURES.—**1.** *Measures of Length.*—The unit of linear measurement in earlier Biblical times was the **cubit** (אַמָּה). This was obtained by the adoption of the length of the forearm from the elbow to the tip of the middle finger as the standard. There are evidences that such a standard was early averaged, conventionalized, and made the legal unit among the Israelites, being introduced like other standards of the kind from Babylonia. The cubit did not, however, remain a fixed unit throughout. From Ezk 40⁵ (cf. 43¹³) we learn that two standards of measurement called cubits had come into use, and were employed in the prophet's day, and that these differed by one hand's breadth. The common cubit was six handbreadths in length, the sacred cubit, seven. The question of the absolute length of either is, therefore, resolved into the value of the handbreadth. It would be useless to discuss in detail the various processes through which the solution of the problem has been attempted. The results of these processes show a divergence of over nine inches. Conder (*Handbook of the Bible*) finds the cubit to be 16 in. in length. Petrie (*Ency. Brit.*⁹ xxiv. 484) finds it to be 25·2. Between these extremes are the following : A. R. S. Kennedy (Hastings' *DB*, art. ' Weights and Measures '), 17·5 in. ; Watson (*PEFSt*, 1897, 203 ff.), 17·7 ; Beswick (*ib.* 1879, 182 ff.), 17·72 ; Warren (*ib.* 1899, 229 ff.), 17·75 in.; Smith's *DB*, based on Thenius, 19·5 in. ; and Petrie (*PEFSt*, 1892, 31), 22·6. If we set aside the extremes by Conder and Petrie and Smith's *DB*, the divergence in the remainder is reduced to a margin not larger than ·25 inch. Accordingly, the consensus of the most recent investigation may be safely taken to fix the value of the cubit in inches at between 17·50 and 17·75. Therefore the symbol, 17·5+ may be accepted as the approximate value of the common cubit among the Israelites. Upon this basis the longer cubit of Ezk 40⁵ was 20·6 in. This result coincides with the Egyptian metrological system, and it appears probable that, being introduced from Egypt as the equivalent of the royal Egyptian measure of the name, the cubit was gradually reduced until in Ezekiel's day the shorter form of it had been definitely fixed. This, then, persisted up to NT times, and was identified with the Roman *cubitus* of a little less than 17·5 in. (cf. Smith, *Dict. of Antiq.* p. 1227).†

The subdivisions of the cubit were the **span**, equalling half a cubit ; the **palm** or *hand-breadth*, one-sixth of a cubit; and the **digit** or **finger-breadth**, one twenty-fourth of a cubit. The multiples in common use were the **fathom**, consisting of four cubits, and the **reed**, of six cubits. Hence the table :

	Digit.	Palm.	Span.	Cubit.	Fathom.	Reed.	
Digit (Finger-breadth)	1						·73 in
Palm (Hand-breadth)	4	1					3· ,,
Span . .	12	3	1				8·75 ,,
Cubit . .	24	6	2	1			17·52 ,,
Fathom .	96	24	8	4	1		70·+ ,,
Reed . .	144	36	12	6	1·5	1	105·5 ,,

* In this place, according to Hultsch, the λίτρα is not the same as in Jn 19³⁹. He understands the term to be the name of a translucent horn vessel with measuring lines on the outside, used by apothecaries in dealing out medicines. Such a measuring instrument was used ; but that it served for carrying ointment is improbable, and the identification of the λίτρα here with Jn 19³⁹ seems more natural.

† In Egypt, too, there was a longer cubit and a shorter, and these two were related to one another as 7 to 6, their values in inches being respectively 19·43 and 16·66.

In the Gospels the cubit is mentioned in Mt 6²⁷, Lk 12²⁵, and Jn 21⁸. In all these passages it appears as an approximation, and neither requires nor admits of precise determination. Lengths less than that of the cubit are not alluded to. Of greater lengths the following occur, being outside the usual scale as given above. The *stadium* or **furlong** (Lk 24¹³, Jn 6¹⁹ 11¹⁸). The term is borrowed from the Greek scale, and appears there as the equivalent of 600 ft. (more precisely 600 ft. 9 in.), or 400 cubits. The **mile** (Mt 5⁴¹) was also borrowed, but is taken from the Roman scale, and was equal to 7·5 Greek stadia (furlongs), or 3000 cubits (1700 yds.). The **day's journey** (Lk 2⁴⁴), which is a common Oriental way of reckoning distances of considerable length at the present day, seems to have been used in ancient times also. It is not, however, reducible to any definite equivalent, and was no doubt a very elastic term. See on this and on 'Sabbath day's journey,' art. JOURNEY.

2. *Measures of Surface.*—Of measures of area no mention is made in the Gospels or in the NT anywhere. Occasional allusions to the purchase of land (Mt 13⁴⁴ 27⁷, Lk 14¹⁸; cf. Ac 1¹⁸) are not of such a character as to include the measurement used in these and similar transactions.

3. *Measures of Capacity.*—These naturally fall into liquid and dry measures. Primitively the most common word for measure of volume in Bible lands was perhaps the *seah* (σάτον, μέτρον, cf. Mt 13³³, which is also the usage of the LXX). This was the '**measure**' *par excellence*. This, however, became differentiated at least as early as before the NT age into a unit of dry measure, and the *hin*, with twice the capacity of the *seah*, took its place in the corresponding liquid scale. Nevertheless, in ascertaining the values of both liquid and dry standards of measurement, the most convenient starting-point is the *seah*. This, on the one hand, is easily traceable in its equivalents in the Græco-Roman metrology, and, on the other, as the unit on which the ephah-bath is based, furnishes a key to the Palestinian metrology of both dry and liquid varieties.

As to the equivalency of the *seah* in the classical Græco-Roman system, the following data give testimony: Josephus (*Ant.* IX. iv. 5) says, 'A *seah* is equal to one and one-half Italian *modii.*' An anonymous writer, cited by Hultsch (*Metr. Script.* i. 81. 6), speaks to the same effect; so also Jerome (on Mt 13³³), who, however, probably simply reproduces this representation. On the other hand, according to Epiphanius (*Metr. Script.* i. 82. 8), the *seah* was equal to one and one-quarter *modii* (20 *sextarii*); but that this is not a precise statement appears from the same writer's equating the *seah* with 22 *sextarii* elsewhere (*Metr. Script.* i. 82. 9). Indirectly from the identification of the *bath*, the *cor*, and the *hin* by Josephus, with their corresponding Roman equivalents (cf. *Ant.* VIII. ii. 9, XV. ix. 2, III. viii. 3), the value of the *seah* is computed at 22 *sextarii*; and as this agrees with the equation of the Babylonian *ephah-bath* with 66 *sextarii* (Hultsch, *Griech. and Rom. Metr.* ii. p. 412), it may be taken as correct.

This gives us the value of the *seah* in Roman *sextarii*. The reduction of the *sextarii* to present-day English standards may be made either upon the basis of the calculations of Hultsch (*Metrol.* p. 453), which yield a *sextarius* of ·96 pt. (cf. Smith, *Dict. of Ant.*, followed by Harper's *Dict. of Class. Lit. and Ant.*, ed. H. T. Peck), and a *seah* of 21+ pts. (2 gals. 2 qts. and 1+ pts.); or this reduction may be made upon the basis of the use of the Farnese *congius* (=6 *sextarii*) in the Dresden Museum, which yields a *sextarius* of ·99 pts. The difference in results between these methods amounts to no more than ·03 pt. in the Roman *sextarius*.

Neither of the two methods positively excludes the possibility of error, but the latter appears upon the whole more trustworthy. Thus in the reconstruction of a table we have the equation to start with: *sextarius* = ·99 pt. The *seah* (22 *sext.* =2 gal. 2 qts. 1·78 pts.) is, then, approximately 23+ pts.

This yields for the dry measure the scale as follows:

	Log.	Kab.	Omer.	Seah.	Ephah.	Cor.		
Log	1						= 1	pt.
Kab	4	1					= 4	pts.
Omer	7·5	1·8	1				= 7½	,,
Seah	24	6	3·6	1			= 23·75	,,
Ephah	72	18	10	3	1		= 71·28	,,
Cor (Homer)	720	180	100	30	10	1	=712·8	,,

And for the liquid the scale as follows:

	Log.	Hin.	Seah.	Bath.	Cor.		
Log	1					= 1	pt.
Hin	12	1				= 11·9	pts.
Seah	24	2	1			= 23·8	,,
Bath	72	6	3	1		= 71·28	,,
Cor	720	60	30	10	1	=712·8	,,

These two scales represent the values of measures of capacity of the later days of Judaism. For OT times the value of the *seah* would have to be made larger, and the table correspondingly increased. For practical purposes the *log* = *sextarius* = pt. equation may be deemed sufficient.

In the Gospels the following allusions to the scales occur. The *seah* (Mt 13³³, Lk 13²¹) is the equivalent of one-third of an *ephah*, and so is meant to designate generally as large a quantity as was usually handled in household necessities. Three *seahs* are equal to 35½ qts. or 1 bushel. The *cor* (Lk 16⁷) appears under the name of '**measure**,' the expression being naturally a general and inexact one. The total quantity intended to be indicated is 100 *cors* or 1110 bushels.

Measures not included in the above scales occur as follows. The *xestes* (ξέστης, translated '**cup**,' Mk 7⁴ ⁽⁸⁾) was probably a small and handy household vessel, with the capacity of a pint measure, and used as such. The *modius* (μόδιος, Mt 5¹⁵, Mk 4²¹, Lk 11³³, tr. in all the English versions '**bushel**') is not the English bushel, but the Hebrew *seah*. The name is borrowed from the Græco-Roman usage. The measure itself was, like the *xestes*, a useful household utensil. The *metretes* (μετρητής, Jn 2⁶, tr. '**firkin**') is evidently the *bath* of the Hebrew scale, containing approximately 9 gallons.

LITERATURE.—Hultsch, *Griech. u. Röm. Metrologie*, ii. (1882), also his Collection of Greek and Roman Sources, under the title of *Metrologicorum Scriptorum Reliquiæ*, 2 vols. (1864–1866); Lehmann, 'Altbab. Mass u. Gewicht' (in *Verhandl. d. Berliner Gesellschaft f. Anthropol.* 1889); Zuckermann, *Das Jüdische Masssystem* (1867); Nowack, *Heb. Arch.* i. 198 ff.; Benzinger, *Heb. Arch.* 178 ff.   A. C. ZENOS.

WELL (πηγή, φρέαρ, Jn 4⁶. ¹¹).—The one well mentioned in the Gospels is that of Jacob, near ancient Shechem, under the northern cliffs of Gerizim. There is no reasonable doubt that this is the well pointed out to this day as *Bîr Ya'ḳûb* in the eastern opening of the pass of Nâblus. Samaritan, Jewish, Christian, and Moslem traditions support this identification with absolute unanimity. See JACOB'S WELL.

There is a law of the well in the East, which, although unwritten, receives well-nigh universal homage. Drawing water from the cisterns or wells that abound in Palestine occupies much of the women's time. The stones round the mouth of many a well are scored deeply by friction of the ropes to which the bucket or leather *daluw* is attached. Few experiences are more trying than to pass one of these 'wells' in the heat, seeing the water in the cool depths but having 'nothing to draw with.' The appeal of the thirsty to one drawing, 'Give me to drink,' is never refused.

While surprised that a Jew, even when urged by thirst, should thus accost a Samaritan, the woman did not deny the Saviour's request. Even a *Metâwileh*, one of the most fanatical of all Oriental sects, will give water to the thirsty, if appealed to, although to avoid the possibility of pollution he must destroy the vessel from which the infidel has drunk.   W. EWING.

WEST (δυσμή).—In Palestine the direction of the setting sun is also that of the sea, and the West is therefore the source from which rain is generally expected (1 K 18⁴⁴, Lk 12⁵⁴). The observed connexion between western clouds and rain led Christ to remark on the strange inattention to the spiritual trend of the times (Lk 12⁵⁶). He attributed such disregard and misrepresentation to self-delusion resulting from insincerity. He recognized that the final stage of imperviousness and impotence had been reached, and that the Kingdom of Heaven required the removal of both teachers and teaching and a re-baptism of religious vision and thought (Mt 23³⁶⁻³⁹, Mk 8¹², Jn 4²¹).

The reference to North, South, East, and West as the equal sources from which the Kingdom of Heaven was to draw its membership, indicated the universal scope of His own relationship to the world. The same truth is suggested in the vision of the New Jerusalem as the city with an equal number of open gates on its four sides (Rev 21¹³). Hence to-day, in the statesmanship of that Kingdom, it is unwise and wasteful to transport to the East the controversies and cleavages of Western Christianity. Only the universal truths of the gospel should be presented to the universal mission field.   G. M. MACKIE.

WHALE.—See JONAH, NINEVITES, SIGN.

WHEAT.—Of all the cereals, wheat is at once the most valuable and the most widely distributed. It has been cultivated from very early times, as is proved by the finding of wheat grains in some of the oldest Egyptian tombs. In what land it had its origin is unknown, but de Candolle assigns the honour to Mesopotamia. In Palestine its cultivation dates back to a time prior to the Hebrew conquest (Dt 8⁸). How long before cannot be said, but it was probably a considerable time. In the OT the most common name for it is חִטָּה, which the LXX renders in most instances by πυρός (Gn 30¹⁴, Ex 9³² etc.) but sometimes by σῖτος (Jg 6¹¹, Ezk 27¹⁷), and the Vulg. by *triticum* and, in a few cases, *frumentum*. On the other hand, σῖτος is used also to render בַּר (Jer 23²⁸, Jl 2²⁴), דָּגָן (Nu 18¹², Jer 31¹²), עָבוּר (Jos 5¹¹), and שֶׁבֶר (Gn 42²·³). In the NT this is the term invariably employed (Mt 3¹², Lk 16⁷ etc.), and in EV it is nearly always translated 'wheat.' Like the Heb. דָּגָן, however, σῖτος is really a general term for the cereals. But we can readily understand how, just as in Scotland the word 'corn' has become practically the equivalent of oats, so in Palestine σῖτος should come to mean wheat. For it was the most common and the most valued of the staple products of the country, and was, as it still is, its principal breadstuff. Several varieties of wheat are grown in Palestine. Tristram (*Nat. Hist. of Bible*, 492) mentions specially three of them: *Triticum compositum*, *T. spelta* (which is the most common of all), and *T. hybernum*.

Wheat is sown about November, shortly after the first rains have softened the soil and rendered it fit for ploughing. It is ripe in May or June, but the time of harvest varies for the different districts, being earliest in the low-lying Jordan Valley, and latest in the Lebanons. The processes of reaping, threshing, winnowing, and sifting have already been described (see AGRICULTURE). The return yielded by wheat varies greatly. Thirty-fold is, according to Tristram, reckoned a good return (*op. cit.* 489). But that applies to Palestine as it is now. The sixty-fold or hundred-fold of the parable (Mt 13⁸ ‖) might well have been obtained in the days of its former prosperity. Wheat was an article of export from very early days (Ezk 27¹⁷, cf. Ac 12²⁰), and even to this day considerable quantities are exported by way of Haifa and Beirut. It is obtained mainly from the Ḥaurān.   HUGH DUNCAN.

WICKED.—Wickedness (πονηρία) is sin contemplated, not in the light of judicial guilt, or even of moral badness, but of the active mischief which it works.

Four Greek words in NT are translated 'wicked' in EV.
(1) ἄθεσμος (only in 2 P 2⁷ 3¹⁷). This describes the man who will not walk according to the lines laid down (τίθεσθαι) for him by others; the man who gratifies his own desires and whims, in defiance of public opinion, or even of Divine regulation.
(2) ἄνομος (Ac 2²³, and nine other times; ἀνομία, sixteen times). This word originally has to do by derivation with the sheep that will not stay in its own pasture (νομός), or the man who breaks through limits (νόμοι) assigned, and hence signifies a lawless man. The thought is similar to that in (1).
(3) κακός. Meaning originally 'unpleasant' (cf. Lk 16⁵, Ac 28⁵, Rev 16²), and then 'failing to answer expectation or fulfil the apparent reason for existence,' the word comes to mean 'morally bad' as opposed to ἀγαθός, morally good (Mt 21⁴¹ 24⁴⁸, Col 3⁵ etc.).
(4) πονηρός. This is the usual NT word; and it occurs very frequently, being usually rendered 'wicked' or 'evil.' It is connected by derivation with toil (πόνος). J. J. Schmidt suggests that, like the word 'villainy,' it has drifted from meaning 'labouring' and hence 'lower class' to 'degraded' and thence 'vicious.' But it seems more probable that the root thought in πονηρός is 'causing trouble,' 'mischievous,' and thence 'actively wicked' in contrast to χρηστός, 'actively good.' A vivid picture of the thought involved is found in Mt 13²⁴⁻³⁰. ³⁶⁻⁴³, where the tares are the fruit of the 'wicked one,' ὁ πονηρός. The bad man (κακός) may be content to sin alone, the wicked man (πονηρός) seeks to draw away others also.

1. *The causes of wickedness.*—(*a*) The wicked one (Mt 13¹⁹. ³⁸, Eph 6¹⁶, 1 Jn 2¹³. ¹⁴ 3¹², perh. Mt 6¹³, etc.). The first great source of evil is apparently the devil. He is the great mischief-maker who disarranges God's orderly world (κόσμος, Mt 4⁸ 13³⁵, etc.), and is ever found in antagonism to Christ's dominion (Mt 13³⁷. ³⁹, 1 Jn 5¹⁸⁻²⁰ RV). (*b*) Wicked spirits. Scripture reveals to us not only a general, but also an army of wicked spirits who are ever ready to do his work (see Mt 12⁴⁵, Ac 19¹². ¹³, etc.). (*c*) Fallen human nature. Suggestions from without are reinforced by willingness from within. Depraved human nature (cf. Mt 7¹¹) is traitor to Christ (Mt 15¹⁹, Mk 7²², Lk 11³⁹, Ro 1²⁹). This is the permanent condition of the world apart from Christ (1 Jn 5¹⁹, Gal 1⁴).

2. *Manifestations of wickedness.*—The tree of wickedness has many kinds of fruit, by which we detect its character (Mt 7¹⁷. ¹⁸): *e.g.* violence (Mt 5³⁹, Ac 17⁵, 2 Th 3²), hypocrisy (Mt 22¹⁸), an unforgiving spirit (Mt 18³²), idleness (Mt 25²⁶), unbelief (He 3¹²), self-sufficiency (Ja 4¹⁶), spite (3 Jn¹⁰); everything, in fact, that is unlike Christ, flourishes in the devil's Eden—the lost world.

3. *The consequences of wickedness.*—The 'children of the wicked one,' if unredeemed from his service, will share his doom (Mt 13⁴⁹. ⁵⁰ 25²⁶. ³⁰, Ro 1²⁹. ³²; cf. Eph 2². ³).

4. *The remedy for wickedness.*—God's attitude towards the wicked man is not one of implacable anger, but of winning kindness (Lk 6³⁵). Reconciled through the cross of Christ (Col 1²⁰. ²¹), the wicked man may find complete pardon for the past. Nay more, he may be so renewed in nature as to have no taste for his former way of life (Ro 12⁹, Ac 3²⁶, 1 Co 5⁸, 1 Th 5²²). And further, he may not only be completely ransomed from the slavery in which he was formerly held (Mt 6¹³, Jn 17¹⁵, 2 Th 3³, 1 Jn 5¹⁸ RV), but may become actually victorious, through the imparted power of Christ, over the evil one, who is now bitterly antagonistic to his former subject (1 Jn 2¹³· ¹⁴, Eph 6¹¹⁻¹³).

LITERATURE.—Trench, *Synonyms*; Grimm-Thayer and Cremer, *Lexx. s.vv.* κακός, πονηρός. H. C. LEES.

WIDOW (χήρα).—Four widows are referred to in the Gospels.

1. Anna of the tribe of Asher (Lk 2³⁶⁻³⁸), a devout woman described as a prophetess, who had been a widow eighty-four years, and who constantly frequented the Temple, passing her time in fastings and prayers, and who, coming up at the moment of the presentation of the infant Saviour, moved by the spirit of prophecy, spake of Him to those present who were expecting the redemption of Jerusalem. The Lewis MS of the Syriac Gospels says that Anna lived only seven days with her husband, an alteration not improbably made by some scribe with the object of reducing Anna's age to a less unusual limit. See also art. ANNA.

2. The widow of Sarepta or Zarephath, referred to by our Lord in the synagogue at Nazareth (Lk 4²⁵· ²⁶) as an instance of a Gentile who had entertained Elijah, and had received a blessing by his means. It has been suggested by A. Meyer (*Jesu Muttersprache*, iv. 8) that the word 'widow' here may have been 'Gentile' in some Aramaic original, ܐܪܡܝܬܐ (*armaitha*), the feminine of 'Gentile' or 'Syrian' having been confused with ܐܪܡܠܬܐ (*armalta*), 'a widow.' If this were so, then our Lord's reference to Naaman the *Syrian* would be balanced by a reference to 'a woman who was a Syrian' or 'Gentile.'

3. The widow of Nain (Lk 7¹¹⁻¹⁷), a little town situated a few miles to the south of Mount Tabor in Galilee, to whom our Lord uttered His compassionate 'Weep not' just before restoring her only son to life. The people who witnessed the miracle exclaimed that a great prophet had risen up among them, probably with reference to Elijah or Elisha, the former of whom, like Christ, had raised a widow's son.

4. The poor widow who cast her two mites into the treasury (Mk 12⁴¹⁻⁴⁴, Lk 21¹⁻⁴), whom Christ commended. It should not be forgotten in practical applications of this incident and of our Lord's praise of the widow, that she cast in 'all her living,' that is to say, her day's entire income, or 'all that she had to live upon until more should be earned' (Swete), and that consequently the phrase 'widow's mite' is incorrectly applied to small sums deducted, and more or less easily spared, from a daily income.

In addition to these four widows, who were actual persons, a widow is a character in one of our Lord's parables (Lk 18¹⁻⁸), who, having no power to enforce the justice she claims, obtains it at length by her importunity ; and from this our Lord draws His *a fortiori* conclusion that God will hear and answer those who cry day and night unto Him. Further, widows are referred to by Christ (Mt 23¹⁴ [omitted by RV], Mk 12⁴⁰, Lk 20⁴⁷) as being often cruelly oppressed and defrauded by the Pharisees of His day.

It may be regarded as certain that our Lord's mother was a widow during the time of His ministry, hence His recommendation of her, just before His death, to the beloved disciple (Jn 19²⁶ᶠ·).

The honourable and important position which widows occupied in the early Church is entirely in harmony with the respectful and sympathetic tone in which they are referred to in the above places of the Gospels.

In the Lewis MS of the Syriac Gospels the Syrophœnician woman (Mk 7²⁶) is described as a widow. This may be another instance of the possible confusion of 'widow' and 'Gentile' alluded to above. ALBERT BONUS.

WIFE (γυνή).—For the general subject see FAMILY, MARRIAGE, WOMAN.

Our Lord places the claims of a wife above those of a father or mother, and emphasizes in the most striking way the spiritual and bodily unity, indissoluble except for one cause, of the two who have been joined together in marriage (Mt 19³ᶠ·, Mk 10²ᶠ·). And precisely because of His exalted conception of a wife's place in her husband's heart, He teaches the absoluteness of His own claims on the loyalty and obedience of His disciples, by setting them clearly in a man's eyes over against those of the wife of his bosom. It was on the same occasion on which He pronounced what might be called the *Magna Charta* of married womanhood that He uttered those solemn words about the need of forsaking a wife for His sake and the gospel's (Mt 19²⁹, Mk 10²⁹; cf. Lk 18²⁹). And in the parable of the Great Supper, among the rejected excuses of those who do not accept the gracious invitation, is that of the man who said, 'I have married a wife, and therefore I cannot come' (Lk 14¹⁹). J. C. LAMBERT.

WILD BEASTS.—See ANIMALS in vol. i. p. 64ᵇ f.

WILDERNESS.—The word or words (more or less synonymous) which the EV tr. by 'wilderness' or 'desert' afford a striking example of the difficulties which translators, and after them the ordinary readers of Holy Scripture, have to contend with, because that word does not convey to our mind the idea of something we know : in our western European countries there is not, properly speaking, any desert or wilderness, in the Biblical sense of the word. Thus, unable to consult our own experience, we have to fall back upon books we have read, and upon notions obtained in that way. Immediately there rises in our memory the view of a desert of sand, stretching itself out of sight in a complete solitude, and giving to the caravans of travellers scarcely any other choice but death from thirst, or burial under the moving soil blown up by some terrible windstorm. Such is the classical representation of a desert or wilderness, and it is a constant source of errors for the understanding of numerous passages of the Bible where that word occurs. There is no 'desert of sand' either in Palestine or in the neighbouring countries. In fact, the Hebrew word which is usually tr. 'desert' or 'wilderness' (*midbār*) does not in the least convey the idea of solitude or desolation ; on the contrary, it belongs to a root which means 'to pasture,' and therefore, etymologically, 'feeding-ground' or 'pasture-land' would seem to be the most exact translation. But if we should adopt it, another ambiguity would be created, and a false notion suggested. Indeed, for a European reader, a pasture is a meadow with abundant grass, which is not at all true of the Palestinian *midbār*.

For a correct understanding of the meaning of the word 'wilderness' in the Bible, one has to remember that there were—and are still—nomads in Bible lands. Those people are not addicted to agricultural life, but to the breeding of cattle ; they live on the borders of cultivated lands, between these and other regions which are either uninhabitable or practically uninhabited. The territories held by those nomads—called Bedawîn in modern times—are not without water and grass ; but these indispensable resources, required for the herds, are both scarce, and the tribes of shepherds are compelled to remove their camps from one place to another for feeding and watering their cattle. The *midbār* is therefore essentially the ground occupied by nomad tribes ; it forms around agricultural districts a zone variable in extension or breadth; sometimes culture wins over uncultivated lands, sometimes these regain spaces formerly tilled and sown. At the boundary itself of those two tracts of land live some populations which hold a sort of intermediate position in the progress of civilization: they are half-sedentary, half-shepherds (half-*Fellaḥin*, half-*Bedawîn*), and, dwelling still under tents, they cultivate the ground, plough, sow, and reap (cf. Max von Oppenheim, *Vom Mittelmeer zum Persischen Golf*, 1900, ii. pp. 78–84). Even in the interior of cultivated districts, where villages and towns exist, there are frequently patches of land where the soil remains abandoned to itself, without culture, and they offer, therefore, the same character as the exterior zone inhabited by nomads. Those spaces are generally used as pasture-grounds for the cattle, and have also been called *midbār*. They are found even near towns; thus the OT mentions the wildernesses of Gibeon, of Teḳoa, of Damascus, of Riblah (MT *Diblah*, Ezk 6¹⁴). Besides those local denominations, others occur which apply to peripheric regions: wildernesses of Shur, of Sin, of Sinai, of Paran, of Zin, of Ḳadesh, of Ethan (or Yam-Suph), of Maon, of Ziph, of Beersheba, of Engedi, of Jeruel, of Beth-aven, of Edom, of Moab, of Ḳedemoth. Several of these wildernesses, as their names show, cover vast spaces; others, on the contrary, represent quite limited places.

One of the most important deserts is the **Wilderness of Judah,** twenty hours in length and five in breadth, which constitutes, with the Mountain (*Har*), the South (*Negeb*), and the Low-Country (*Shephelah*), the four parts of the territory of that tribe. The Wilderness of Judah is the region situated east of the watershed, between this high line and the western shore of the Dead Sea. The wildernesses of Ziph and of Maon are portions of it in the south, as well as those of Engedi and Teḳoa in the middle; and finally also, in the north, the rough, barren, and uninhabited district where the road runs from Jerusalem to Jericho (cf. Lk 10³⁰ᶠᶠ·). That wilderness is an uneven, undulating table-land, where conical hills and rocky hillocks arise, where deep ravines are cut between steep walls of rocks; it falls down towards the east— here in gradual declivities, there in sudden and abrupt slopes—in the direction of the Dead Sea, situated 1500 or 2000 feet below. No river or rivulet, no trees, no villages; a soil without vegetation, either sandy or stony, here and there with scarce and meagre grass, which is avidly sought for by small flocks of sheep and goats, belonging to a few miserable camps of black or brown tents. That wilderness was the refuge of David when persecuted by Saul (1 S 22–26); he knew it from the time of his youth, having, when a boy, followed there the herds of his father (16¹¹ 17¹⁵· ³⁴). Later on the same region sheltered Judas Maccabæus and his companions (1 Mac 9³³).

The wildernesses mentioned in the Bible are not all as inclement and inhospitable as the Wilderness of Judah. They are sometimes inhabited; they contain wells and cisterns, towns (Jos 15⁶¹ᶠ·, 1 K 9¹⁸, 2 Ch 8⁴) and houses (1 K 2³⁴), herds of sheep (1 S 17²⁸), and pastures (Ps 65¹³ᶠ·).

The Gospel of John alludes twice to the sojourn of Israel in the wilderness (3¹⁴ Moses lifting the serpent, and 6³¹· ⁴⁹ the manna). The Synoptics do not mention it; but it is spoken of in the Book of Acts, specially in Stephen's discourse (7³⁶⁻⁴⁴) and in 13¹⁸, and in 1 Co 10⁵ and He 3⁸ (quoting Ps 95⁸) and 3¹⁷.

The Wilderness of Judah is named several times in connexion with John the Baptist. His youth, according to Lk 1⁸⁰, was spent 'in the deserts'; that is, certainly, with the keepers of herds, away from towns or villages, in solitude and contempla-

tion. In that respect, as well as in others, John is like Amos, the shepherd of Teḳoa. According to the Gospels, 'the deserts' included also the country near Jordan—beyond, that is, east of, the river— where John began his ministry, preaching and baptizing (Mt 3¹, Mk 1⁴, Lk 3²; cf. Mt 11⁷, Lk 7²⁴; see artt. BETHABARA, JOHN THE BAPTIST, JORDAN), and the four Gospels apply to that event the prophecy of Is 40³ (Mt 3³, Mk 1³, Lk 3⁴, Jn 1²³).

Ecclesiastical tradition has not been content with the indications given in the Gospels which connect John the Baptist's life and work with the wilderness: it has connected also his birth with it. The place where Zacharias and Elisabeth dwelt being only vaguely named in Lk 1³⁹, it has been identified by the Christians of the Holy Land and the pilgrims, since the time of the Crusades, with a village situated about 4 miles west from Jerusalem; the Arabs call it '*Ain-Karim*, but it is known in the language of the Churches as 'St. John in the Desert' or 'St. John in the Mountain.' That place is not in the Wilderness of Judah; its neighbourhood is cultivated and fertile, at least in the sense in which one can use that word when speaking of Judæa. Even if we should suppose that such was the birthplace of John, it would be unjustified to consider it as being 'in the wilderness' (cf. *ZDPV* xxii. pp. 81–93).

It is also in the wilderness that the Gospel narratives place the scene of the Temptation of our Lord (Mt 4¹, Mk 1¹², Lk 4¹). Since the time of the Crusades, ecclesiastical tradition has contrived to localize that event in a particular, well-defined spot, and has chosen for it the wild and desolate mountain which arises almost vertically above the Fountain of Elisha, west from the oasis of Jericho. A Greek convent, continuation of a very old laura, which was, if not founded, at least developed by Elpidius (*ZDPV* iii. p. 13), is suspended on the side of that mountain, which has received the name of Mount of the **Quarantania** (*Jebel Ḳarantul*), on account of Jesus fasting 40 days. It is, of course, equally impossible to prove or to disprove that this place is the one mentioned in the narratives of the Temptation.

Galilee, and particularly the shores of the Lake of Gennesaret, was at the time of our Lord relatively well peopled: this is proved by the Gospels, and still more explicitly by the testimony of Josephus. There were, however, spaces of land without human habitations, and probably left to the shepherds and their cattle. According to the narratives of the Gospels, several scenes of the Galilæan ministry of Jesus, and some of His teachings, were connected with places of that sort, designated now as 'a desert' or 'a wilderness' (ἔρημος or ἐρημία), now as 'a desert place' (ἔρημος τόπος). We have to mention here (*a*) the multiplication of loaves (Mt 14¹³⁻²¹, Mk 6³⁰⁻⁴⁴, Lk 9¹⁰⁻¹⁷, Mt 15³²⁻³⁸, Mk 8¹⁻¹⁰); (*b*) Jesus withdrawing for prayer (Mk 1³⁵, Lk 5¹⁶), or to avoid the crowd (Mk 1⁴⁵, Lk 4⁴², Jn 11⁵⁴); (*c*) the demoniac of Gadara (Lk 8²⁹); (*d*) the parable of the Lost Sheep (Lk 15³⁻⁷), where the 99 sheep remain 'in the wilderness,' whereas the shepherd goes after that which is lost until he finds it.

LITERATURE.—*PEFSt*, 1871, pp. 3–80; E. H. Palmer, *The Desert of the Exodus*, 2 vols., 1871; Furrer, art. 'Wüste' in Schenkel, *Bib. Lex.* v. pp. 680–685; G. A. Smith, *HGHL*, pp. 312–317; Buhl, *GAP*, pp. 96–99; Lagrange in *RB*, 1896, pp. 618–643, 1897, pp. 107–130, 605–625, 1900, pp. 63–86; B. Baentsch, *Die Wüste, ihre Namen und ihre bildliche Anwendung in den Alttest. Schriften*, 1883; Pierre Loti, *Le Désert* ⁶, 1895 [descriptive], and other [more scientific] books of travels in the Sinai-Peninsula; Bönhoff, 'Die Wanderung Israels in der Wüste' in *SK*, 1907, pp. 159–217. LUCIEN GAUTIER.

WILL.—'Every man,' says Thomas Reid (*Works*, 1863 ed., p. 530), 'is conscious of a power to determine, in things which he conceives to depend upon his determination. To this power we give the name of *Will*; and, as it is usual, in the operations of the mind, to give the same name to the power and to the act of that power, the term "Will" is often put to signify the act of determining, which more properly is called *volition*.' On the question of the freedom of the will see FREE WILL and LIBERTY; and on the human will of Jesus see SOUL, 668[b]. Our Lord Jesus Christ has given us a perfect example of how our great possession of freedom should be used, has shown us by His own perfect subordination of His will to the will of His Father, that the goal at which we should aim is to have our wills in perfect accord with the will of God, whether it be His will as to our enduring or His will as to our doing. 'O my Father, if it be possible, let this cup pass from me; nevertheless not as I will, but as thou wilt' Mt (26[39]); 'I came down from heaven, not to do mine own will, but the will of him that sent me' (Jn 6[38]). It is our part to seek to have the mind of Christ, and to obey where God would have us to obey, and endure where He would have us to endure.

'Our wills are ours to make them thine.'

LITERATURE.—NT Commentaries; Hastings' *DB*; the works of Thomas Reid; R. A. Thompson, *Christian Theism*; Hill, *Lectures in Divinity*; A. M. Fairbairn, *The Philosophy of the Christian Religion*; Ritschl, *Justification and Reconciliation*; and Philosophical and Theological works in general.

GEORGE C. WATT.

WIND (ἄνεμος; πνεῦμα only in Jn 3[8]).—'The four winds' (Mt 24[31], Mk 13[27]) is an expression standing for 'north, south, east, and west,' the winds in Palestine coming mainly from these directions. These winds retain their character, varied only in degree, throughout the year. The north wind is cold; the west, from the sea, moist; the south, warm; and the east, from the desert, dry. This last is very pleasant in the winter months; but in spring and autumn, when it is prevalent, it is exceedingly oppressive, a few hours often causing every living thing to droop. The popular belief that the most violent winds are from the east is not confirmed by the writer's experience of over five years in Galilee. The most memorable storm in that period was from the west. See, further, SEA OF GALILEE, p. 591. W. EWING.

WINE (οἶνος; once, Ac 2[13], γλεῦκος).—The climate and soil of Palestine are excellently adapted to the production of grapes, and from very early times wine has been a common beverage in the country. In the OT it is praised as a source of good cheer to the heavy of heart, as a stimulant for the faint, and as a token of a full, happy, and prosperous life (Pr 31[6], Ps 104[15]). The dangers of excessive indulgence are indeed clearly indicated. The priest while on duty, and the Nazirite during the currency of his vow, might not touch it (Lv 10[9], Nu 6[3]). The sin of drunkenness is presented in revolting colours (Pr 23[29ff.], Is 28[7f.]). The Rechabite abstinence from wine, however, arose probably from the nomadic view of the vine as the symbol of the settled life, not from any objection to the use of wine in itself (W. R. Smith, *Prophets*, 84, 389). In the Gospels wine appears with bread as representing ordinary fare (Lk 7[33]); it is drunk on festive occasions (Jn 2[3]), and at religious feasts (Mt 26[29] etc.). Mingled with oil, it is applied to wounds as a healing agent (Lk 10[34]); mingled with myrrh, it is used as a narcotic (Mk 15[23]).

The ancient methods of wine-making persist to the present day. Commonly the grapes are placed in a large shallow trough, cut in the surface of the rock. The juice is there trodden out, and conducted by a channel to a deeper trough at a lower level. The time of the vintage and wine-treading is one of great joyfulness among the people, their labours being enlivened by the singing of songs, and rhythmic clapping of the hands. Fermentation sets in quickly. The first, or what the Jews called the 'tumultuous' stage, might be passed in four days, during which the wine remained in the trough, or vat, if possible. It was then put into

earthenware jars which had been lined with pitch, or, if it were to be sent to a distance, into 'bottles,' where the process was completed. In about three months the wine was fit for use.

Where the soil was deep, a **press** was 'digged' in the earth (Mt 21[33] etc.). This, built round with masonry, and carefully cemented, received the juice expressed in a wooden structure set on the surface.

The '**bottles**' are partially tanned goat-skins. The apertures where legs and tail have been severed are sewn up, leaving only that at the neck, which is firmly tied when the skin is filled. The wine in the first stage of fermentation, if tied in the skins, would, by reason of the gas generated, burst them. When the 'tumultuous' stage is passed, the new 'bottle' yields sufficiently to permit completion of the process. 'Bottles' once stretched in this way had no further powers of distention, and if used again for the same purpose would, of course, burst (Mt 9[17] etc.).

Different qualities of wine were distinguished (Jn 2[10]), probably indicated, as they are still, by the localities where they are produced. The 'new wine' of Ac 2[13] (lit. 'sweet wine') was probably 'the wine made from the drip of the grapes before the clusters are trodden in the wine-press—stronger than the thin sour wines used as daily beverages' (Lindsay, *Acts, in loc.*). The modern 'sweet wine' is made from the white or green grapes, the juice being slightly boiled.

There is nothing known in the East of anything called 'wine' which is unfermented. Pharaoh's butler pressed grapes into his master's cup (Gn 40[11]). 'In a text found at Edfu, it is said that grapes squeezed into water formed a refreshing beverage which was drunk by the king' (Driver, *Genesis, in loc.*). This possibly corresponds to the Spanish drink made by squeezing grapes not quite ripe into water. But it is never called 'wine.' The γλεῦκος of Ac 2[13] was certainly fermented. Apart from the fact that the vintage was eight months passed, which put the keeping of unfermented grape juice out of the question, it was alleged as the cause of drunkenness by those who must have known its character. The wine used by the Jews in Palestine —people most conservative in their religious customs—at the Passover, is of the ordinary kind. And there is no trace of any tradition among them of a change having been introduced. Their attitude towards the drinker of unfermented grape juice may be gathered from the saying in *Pirke Aboth* (iv. 28), 'He who learns from the young, to what is he like? to one that eats unripe grapes, and drinks *wine from his vat*.'

While in the NT wine is plainly regarded as good, and its medicinal value is recognized (1 Ti 5[23]), there is no blindness to the danger attached to its abuse (see, *e.g.*, Eph 5[18], 1 Ti 3[8], Tit 2[3]). The question of total abstinence, like that of slavery, had not yet been raised. No argument for total abstinence can be built on the significance of terms used for 'wine' in Scripture. But 'the Apostle Paul has stated the case for total abstinence in Ro 14 in a way that does not need the treacherous aid of doubtful exegesis for its support' (*DB*, *s.v.* 'Food'). See, further, Hastings' *DB* ii. 31 ff.; Mackie, *Bible Manners and Customs*, 43 ff.; Benzinger, *Heb. Arch.* (Index); Fowler, *The Wine of the Bible*. W. EWING.

WINTER (χειμών, Mt 24[20], Mk 13[18], Jn 10[22]).—This is the time of cold and rain-storms. The modern Arab. name, *esh-shitta'*, means literally 'the rain.' It is the season in which the rain supply of the year falls; it lasts roughly for seven months, from October till April inclusive, thus including the part of the year which we call spring (see SUMMER).

While in the deeper parts of the Jordan Valley it is never very cold, the raw air breeds many discomforts in the rainy season. On the higher lands, however, the cold is often intense, snow lying at times—e.g. in Jerusalem—to a depth of some inches. The rain moistens the soil, hard baked by the summer sun. In a land where the science of road-making is practically unknown, the paths go swiftly to mud, so that travel in winter is always toilsome, and not seldom perilous.   W. EWING.

WISDOM.—

i. Use of the conception in Biblical history and literature.
   A. As applied to a school of thought.
     1. The 'wise men.'
     2. Their writings.
   B. As applied to the Spirit of God.
     1. Jewish hypostatization.
     2. Christological development.
A. ii. NT use of the word σοφία.
     1. In the Gospels.
     2. In the Pauline Epistles.
     3. In the Ep. of James and elsewhere.
iii. Use of word and concept in the discourses of Jesus.
     1. In comparisons of His message with the Baptist's.
     2. To rebuke blasphemy against His work.
iv. Matthæan connexions of the two groups of sayings.
     1. Wisdom sayings of Mt 11.
     2. Wisdom sayings of Mt 12.
v. Lukan connexions of the two groups.
     1. Lk 11⁴⁹⁻⁵¹ a Wisdom utterance.
     2. Relation to context of Lk 7 = Mt 11.
     3. Connected discourse-elements of Lk.-Acts.
       (a) Lk 12¹³⁻³⁴.
       (b) Lk 16. 18⁹⁻¹⁴.
       (c) Lk 11¹⁻¹³ 18¹⁻⁸.
vi. The Wisdom utterances represent a special type of Gospel tradition.
     1. Independent of Matthæan Logia.
     2. Inseparable from narrative.
     3. Employed in common Greek form by Mt. and Luke.
     4. More fully and authentically present in Luke.
vii. Relation of this to narrative-elements of Synoptic tradition.
     1. Dependence of Mark.
     2. Relation to peculiar narrative-element of Luke.
viii. Conclusions as to proto-Lukan source.
B. ix. Wisdom speculation in the development of Christology.
     1. The Wisdom doctrine of St. Paul as related—
       (a) to (Jewish) Stoicism.
       (b) to Apocalyptics.
       (c) to Mystery-religion.
     2. The Johannine and Patristic Christology.
       (a) Substitution of Greek terminology (Logos for Wisdom).
       (b) Standpoint of the Fourth Evangelist.
       (c) The Wisdom utterance Mt 11²⁵⁻³⁰ the link between Synoptic and Johannine Christology.
       Literature.

i. THE BIBLICAL CONCEPTION.—In Biblical language the term 'wisdom' (OT חָכְמָה ḥokhmāh, LXX and NT σοφία, rarely φρόνησις (Lk 1¹⁷, Eph 1⁸), or σύνεσις (Lk 2⁴⁷, Eph 3⁴)), is applied (A) to a human, (B) to a Divine attribute.

A. Under the former head is included.—1. The type of thought illustrated in the school of religio-philosophical thinkers contemporary with and later than the prophets, rivalled and ultimately displaced by the scribes. Thus the designation of Mt 23³⁴, 'prophets and wise men and scribes,' is seen to be historically correct, as against the modified form of Lk 11⁴⁹ ('prophets and apostles'; cf. 1 Th 2¹⁵, Eph 2²⁰ etc.), the representatives of these schools of Jewish thought being regarded as commissioned by and endowed with the Divine Spirit. 2. In a derived sense the writings of these inspired men (ἡ πανάρετος σοφία, applied by Hegesippus and Palestinian writers generally to the group Pr.-Wisd. of Sol.; see Eus. HE IV. xxii. 8, 'Nicene and post-Nicene Fathers' [ed. Schaff-Wace], with note by McGiffert), regarded as utterances of the Spirit of God: 'the Wisdom of God saith' (Lk 11⁴⁹) = 'the Holy Ghost saith' (He 3⁷) = 'the Spirit (of apocalyptic prophecy) saith' (1 Ti 4¹, perhaps referring to Jannes and Jambres, 2 Ti 3⁸).

B. The designation 'Wisdom of God,' or simply 'Wisdom,' is sometimes applied to the Spirit of God as manifest in creation and redemption, in the illumination of the mind and regeneration of the soul.

1. In the Ḥokhmāh, or Wisdom literature, this is the habitual designation of the Divine Spirit, especially conceived as manifesting the redeeming love of God, which goes forth to seek and save the erring (Wis 1⁶ 7²²⁻²⁸). Personification of Wisdom (Job 28, Pr 8), under the later speculative influence of Stoic metaphysics, passes imperceptibly into hypostatization and a Logos-doctrine, cosmological as well as soteriological (Wisdom = the Metathron, Wis 9⁴·¹⁰; cf. Sir 24, Wis 7²⁴ᶠ·). In Philo the terms 'Wisdom' and 'Logos' are practically equivalent, the Stoic term naturally tending among Greek readers to displace the Hebrew. Contemporaneously, under the mythologizing influence exerted through apocalyptic literature, the redemptive mission of Wisdom (Wis 9¹⁷ᶠ·) develops into an unmistakable avatar doctrine, wherein Wisdom becomes incarnate, and dwells among men (Bar 3³⁷, cf. Oxyrh. Frgts. Log. iii.), or even descends to the underworld to 'visit all that sleep, and shine upon all that hope in the Lord' (Sir 24³² Lat.; cf. pseudo-Isaiah, ap. Iren. Hær. III. xx. 4, and Eph 5¹⁴). Rejected by men, she ascends again to her seat in heaven (Enoch xlii. 1),[*] whence she returns to be poured out upon the elect in the Messianic age (xlix. 1). The mythologizing tendency was strongly reacted against by the scribes, especially in the period of Aḳiba, during the rivalry of Synagogue and Church in Palestine (A.D. 70–135). On the Jewish side, from this time forward, all personifications of the Divine Wisdom were rigidly restricted in their application to the Mosaic Torah (Sir 24²³⁻²⁷, Bar 4¹, Pirke Aboth, iii. 14, vi. 10). We even find later readings in Jewish texts altering ḥokhmāh to tôrāh (σοφία to νόμος). In general, after the schism of the Nazarenes, speculative thought (doctrine of the Merkabah) is rigorously suppressed.

2. On the Christian side Wisdom speculation continued to develop in both the cosmological and the soteriological directions, with the Pauline Epistles as a basis. In the Johannine literature the Greek term 'Logos' is adopted, though the Wisdom doctrine itself continues Hebrew; but in the 2nd cent. Fathers, as in Philo, 'Wisdom' and 'Logos' are interchangeable and equivalent. Both designate the Spirit of God incarnate in Christ. The influence of mystery myths, already traceable in pre-Christian apocalypse, becomes more pronounced, Gnostic speculations becoming completely mythological. In these Wisdom (ἡ Σοφία, or Achamoth = ḥokhmāh) is the feminine or passive principle in the scheme of redemption, Σωτήρ the active. The present discussion will confine itself to the NT use of the two conceptions of wisdom: (A) as the inspired message of God through the 'wise men' (ḥăkhāmîm); (B) as the Divine Spirit itself, resident in Jesus, and manifested in His life as well as in His teaching. For the history of Wisdom as the Hebrew philosophy, and as a hypostasis equivalent to the Stoic Logos, the reader is

[*] The note of R. H. Charles on this passage of Enoch is too significant to be omitted: 'The praise of wisdom was a favourite theme. Wisdom was regarded as having her dwelling-place in heaven (lxxxiv. 3, Job 28¹²⁻¹⁴·²⁰⁻²⁴, Bar 3²⁹, Ecclus 24⁴), and as coming to earth and desiring to make her abode with men Pr. 1²⁰ᶠᶠ· 8ᶠᶠ· 9¹⁻¹⁰, Ecclus 24⁷; but as men refused to receive her (cf. xciv. 5), she returned to heaven. But in the Messianic times she will return, and will be poured out as water in abundance, xlix. 1, and the thirsty will drink to the full of wisdom, xlvii. 1; she will be bestowed on the elect, v. 8, xci. 10; cf. Apoc. Bar. xliv. 14, 4 Ezra viii. 52; and the spirit of wisdom will abide in the Messiah, the Elect One, xlix. 3.' What is here said of the outpouring of the spirit of wisdom is parallel to Ac 2¹⁶ᶠᶠ· of the spirit of prophecy (cf. Nu 11²⁹) and to the agraphon: 'Et factum est cum ascendisset dominus de aqua, descendit fons omnis Spiritus Sancti, et requievit super eum,' etc.

referred to the artt. 'Wisdom,' 'Wisdom Literature,' 'Wisdom, Book of,' in Hastings' *DB* and in the *Encyc. Biblica.*

ii. NT USE.—**1.** A study of the use of the word σοφία, and its cognates in the Gospels, shows it to be, in some sense, distinctive of the Lukan writings, in which Jesus' teaching is presented primarily under this aspect of 'wisdom of God,' many examples having the characteristic forms of the *Ḥokhmāh* (Wisdom) literature (see Briggs, *Expos. Times*, viii., ix. [1897–98] four articles on 'The Wisdom of Jesus the Messiah'). The characteristic strophic form is apparent also in some discourse-material found only in Mt. (*e.g.* 5[21f. 27f. 31f. 33f. 38f.], 6[2-6. 16-18]), but is disarranged by additions in the canonical form of this Gospel. The word σοφία occurs but once in Mk. (6[2] = Mt 13[54]), and is applied, as in Lk 2[40. 52] and the series cited below, to Jesus' endowment with the Spirit. It occurs twice in Mt. (11[19] 12[42]), both occurrences being in passages verbally identical with Lk., and in a less original form. In Lk.-Acts it occurs 10 times; but the Lukan use is specially noteworthy, because endowment with the Spirit of God is here habitually spoken of, whether in the case of Jesus, of His forerunners, or of His successors, as the χάρισμα of 'wisdom.' So of Jesus (Lk 2[40. 52], cf. 2[47] σύνεσις and 4[22] λόγοι χάριτος), of the endowment of the Twelve with the Spirit (21[15]), of the Seven (Ac 6[3]), of Stephen (6[10]), of Joseph (7[10]), of Moses (7[22]). In the Fourth Gospel the conception of the endowment of Jesus with the spirit of wisdom is supplanted by that of an incarnation of the Logos. The word σοφία and its cognates are wholly wanting.

2. With this Gospel use should be compared that of the NT elsewhere. In the Pauline Epistles the word occurs 16 times in the passage 1 Co 1[17-319], wherein St. Paul contrasts 'the wisdom of God,' which endows those who 'have the mind of Christ' with 'the wisdom of this world'; and 9 times in the twin Epistles (Eph.-Col.), written to oppose a 'philosophy and vain deceit' (Eph 4[14] 'wiles of error') by means of the Divine gift of 'a spirit of wisdom and understanding in the mystery of the Divine will.' It is used by St. Paul in but three other instances, two of which (1 Co 12[8], 2 Co 1[12]) are directly related to the group first mentioned, while the third occurs in the doxology Ro 11[33]. The χάρισμα of wisdom claimed by St. Paul (1 Co 1[17-216], Eph 3[3-11], cf. 1 Co 12[8]) is conceded to his letters in 2 P 3[15].

3. The only other NT employments of the word, or of the connected group of ideas, are in James and the Apocalypse. In Ja 1[5] 3[13. 15. 17] 'wisdom' is more exclusively practical and ethical, but is emphatically a Divine endowment. The conception of 'the wisdom which cometh from above' (*i.e.* the Divine Spirit, given to all that ask, Ja 1[5]), manifested in works of love, is contrasted with wisdom of the tongue in Ja 3. The former is the fundamental characteristic of the just or righteous man (ὁ δίκαιος), a use which agrees closely with that of Sirach and the OT Wisdom literature. Cf. Lk 1[17] φρόνησις δικαίων, and 16[8] φρονιμώτεροι . . . φρονιμώτεροι. In the Apocalypse 'wisdom' is an attribute of God in the doxologies 5[12] 7[12] (cf. Ro 11[33]); otherwise it is referred to only as an endowment like that 'of Joseph (Gn 41[38f.]) and Daniel (Dn 5[14]), requisite to solve riddles (Rev 13[18] 17[9]). The usage and conception of the Third Evangelist appear thus to stand midway between that of St. James and of St. Paul, with traces of the same use in certain parts of Mt. and Mark.

iii. USE IN THE DISCOURSES OF JESUS.—The discourses of Jesus furnish a meagre but trustworthy starting-point for a history of the term in its Christological development. Among these discourses we cannot venture to reckon the saying Lk 21[15] (= 12[11] = Mt 10[19f.] = Mk 13[11] = Jn 15[26f.]), since the parallels make it probable that στόμα καὶ σοφία (cf. Lk 2[47] *prudentiam et os*, cod. e.) is only the characteristic Lukan mode of expressing the promise of the Paraclete. All other occurrences of the word or connected idea in the discourses stand more or less closely related with one of two incidents : (1) Jesus' denunciation of the faithless generation which rejected for opposite reasons both the Baptist's mission and His own (Mt 11), or (2) His denunciation of the scribes who blasphemed the Spirit of God whereby He wrought, demanding a sign from heaven (Mt 12[22-45]). These discourses are variously distributed in our First

and Third Gospels (Mt 11[2-30] 12[22-45] 21[28-32] 23[34-39] and Lk 7[18-35] 10[13-15. 21f.] 11[24-26. 29-32. 49-51]), but have in common a close connexion in thought and a resemblance of language in exceptional degree as between the two canonical reporters. In these two groups of discourses, therefore, must be found, if anywhere, the basis in Jesus' own utterances for the subsequent application in Christology of the conception of the Divine Wisdom.

iv. MATTHÆAN CONNEXIONS OF THE TWO GROUPS OF SAYINGS.—**1.** The Matthæan context of group (1) starts from the question of John's disciples. This is made the occasion by Jesus of a comparison of unrepentant Israel to children who are pleased with neither the mournful nor the gay melodies of their playmates. His hearers had been displeased at the asceticism of John, and are equally so with the genial life of the 'Friend of publicans and sinners.' As against this rejection by the self-righteous of the message of repentance and forgiveness, 'Wisdom's children' (here those who had repented at the preaching of John, cf. 21[31f.], Lk 7[29f.]) afford the justification of her methods (Mt 11[2-19]). In Mt. the discourse continues with the denunciation of 'the cities wherein most of his mighty works were done,' a paragraph which is perhaps accountable for the reading ἔργα in some MSS for τέκνα in v.[19]. These verses (Mt 11[20-24]) are otherwise placed by Lk. ; but those which follow (Mt 11[25-27] = Lk 10[21f.]) again relate to the wisdom of Jesus which is delivered to Him (παρεδόθη μοι) by His Father (in contrast with the παράδοσις of the scribes, Mk 7[13]), and, though hid from the wise, is revealed to the 'little ones.' This in turn introduces in Mt 11[28-30] an invitation closely resembling those placed in the mouth of the Divine Wisdom in the literature of this class (cf. Sir 51[26ff.] 6[28] and *Oxyrhynchus Log.* iii. [iv.]). This closes the chapter and the discourse.

2. In Mt 12[38-45] substantially the same subject is resumed, but it is now *à propos* of the blasphemy of the scribes against the Holy Spirit in ascribing Jesus' exorcisms to Beelzebub (12[22-37]), the intervening material (12[1-21]) comprising the two Sabbath incidents of Mk 2[23]–3[6]. In this further denunciation, not of the scribes but still of 'this evil and adulterous generation,' Jesus declares that it will fare worse than the Ninevites ; for, while these repented at the warning of Jonah, this generation has rejected a greater warning (*i.e.* the Baptist's ; cf. 11[11-14] and Bacon, *Sermon on the Mount*, App. C. iv. v. pp. 216–231). It is condemned also by the Queen of the South, because she came to hear 'the wisdom of Solomon,' whereas this generation has rejected a more gracious appeal (πλεῖον = 'a greater matter,' *i.e.* Jesus' message of forgiveness conceived as the 'wisdom' of God). A concluding parable (Mt 12[43-45] = Lk 11[24-26]) likens 'this evil generation,' with its Pharisaic *mania purifica*, to 'a house swept and garnished' which becomes the abode of demons, because inhospitable to the Spirit of God. It is highly noteworthy that in both groups the condemnation is uttered by Jesus for rejection of the Spirit of God, which in the case of the discourse anent the Baptist is assumed to be manifest in Jesus' *message* of forgiveness, in the case of the blasphemy of the scribes in His healing *power*. The significance of the use of the term 'wisdom' in both cases (Mt 11[19] 12[42]) for the gracious and winning appeal of God's redeeming, forgiving love, is made more apparent by the contrast in both instances with the Baptist's harsher message of warning against 'the wrath to come.' This is manifest from the figures of wailing *versus* piping, mourning *versus* dancing, fasting *versus* feasting, preaching of Jonah *versus* wisdom of Solomon.

v. LUKAN CONNEXIONS OF THE TWO GROUPS.—

A further discourse, correctly connected in Lk $11^{49\text{-}51}$ with group (2) (in Mt $23^{34\text{ff.}}$ incorrectly attached to Mk $12^{38\text{-}40}$ = Mt $23^{1\text{-}12}$) carries to its logical conclusion the denunciation of the scribes who had blasphemed the Holy Spirit. Speaking now directly in the name of 'the wisdom of God' (Lk 11^{49}), Jesus predicts their impending fate, and in the Matthæan form (which properly includes the pathetic appeal to Jerusalem, separated from it in Lk. [Mt $23^{37\text{-}39}$ = Lk $13^{34\text{f.}}$]), the forsaking of 'your house' by God's Spirit. Not only have we throughout this context the characteristic forms and modes of expression of the Wisdom literature, but the final warning is expressly introduced as an utterance of 'the wisdom of God' ($\dot{\eta}$ σοφία τοῦ θεοῦ), by which should be understood not the specific title of an individual writing of this literary category, but the entire canon of 'Wisdom' writings, inclusive of the lost work from which the extract is made. The following considerations will make this clear :—

1. The continuation of the previous line of thought is apparent from the allusion to the fate of God's messengers (with Mt 23 $^{34\text{-}37}$=Lk 11$^{49\text{-}51}$ 13$^{34\text{f.}}$ cf. Mt 12$^{39\text{ff.}}$=Lk 11$^{29\text{ff.}}$), to the vain plea of the Spirit [Wisdom] (with Mt 23$^{37\text{-}39}$=Lk 13$^{34\text{f.}}$ cf. Mt 12$^{38\text{-}42}$=Lk 11$^{29\text{-}32}$), and to the house left desolate (with Mt 23$^{38\text{f.}}$ =Lk 13^{35} cf. Mt 12$^{43\text{-}45}$=Lk 11$^{24\text{-}36}$). Many considerations, on the other hand, make it probable that Mt 23$^{34\text{-}39}$ (=Lk 11$^{49\text{-}51}$ 13$^{34\text{f.}}$), if not more, is really drawn from some lost 'Wisdom' writing. (a) The sending of 'prophets and wise men and scribes' (ḥăkhāmîm and ṣôphĕrîm) is something which cannot be ascribed to Jesus (Mt.) but only to the Divine Spirit (Wisdom). (b) The adoption of the figure of Ps 36^7 91^4, Is 31^5, Dt 32^{11} is appropriate only to the Divine Spirit, which broods over Jerusalem ; it is actually so applied in 2 Es 1^{30}. It will appear to many inappropriate if made an utterance of Jesus personally. The same may be said in less degree of the threat of the forsaking of the house (cf. Jer 12^7 22^5. Josephus preserves a kindred legend of voices in the Temple saying, ' Let us remove hence,' BJ vi. v. 3). (c) The whole context Mt 23$^{34\text{-}39}$ reappears in paraphrase in 2 Es 1$^{28\text{-}37}$, which, though late and Christianized, preserves the material in the form of an utterance of 'the Lord Almighty.' (d) Mt 23^{35} contains, as some think, an anachronistic reference to the murder of Zechariah the son of Baruch, shortly before the siege of Jerusalem (Jos. BJ iv. v. 4). This consideration, however, may be disregarded, as the reference may also be explained as a confusion of Zechariah the son of Jehoiada (2 Ch 24$^{20\text{-}22}$) with the prophet Zechariah son of Berechiah (Zec 1^1).

2. Lk 7$^{1\text{-}83}$ presents a context interconnected by the thought fundamental to the saying Mt 11$^{16\text{-}19}$—the Friend of publicans and sinners—the narrative-material with the exception of 7$^{1\text{-}10}$ = Mt 8$^{5\text{-}10, 13}$ being peculiar to Luke. The discourse and narrative-material have the same bearing, and the former includes the nucleus of the 'wisdom' sayings of Mt 11.

It thus appears that in the two groups of discourse-material principally represented in Mt 11 and 12 and Lk 7 and 11 we have inextricably intermingled (1) sayings of Jesus wherein His own gracious mission was set over against the harsher warning of the Baptist as the message of the Divine Wisdom ; and (2) extracts in defence of His beneficent works, from the actual Wisdom literature, these extracts having been embodied along with His words of denunciation of the scribes, either by Himself or in the subsequent development of Evangelic tradition. To draw the line with precision between authentic utterances of Jesus, and material subsequently adapted from the Wisdom literature because pronounced by 'the wisdom of God' (Mt 11$^{28\text{-}30}$?) surpasses the powers of criticism ; but the endeavour is the more needless because the really significant fact is that Jesus' actual teaching, at least in the form given it by the source here employed in common by Mt. and Lk., was so closely allied to the ideas of this Wisdom literature as to permit of intermingling at an extremely early date. A later example of the process of adaptation is furnished by the Oxyrhynchus papyrus which puts in the mouth of Jesus the characteristic Wisdom utterance : 'I stood in the midst of the world, and in the flesh was I seen of them (cf. Bar 3^{38}), and I found all men drunken, and none found I athirst among them, and my soul grieveth over the sons of men because they are blind in their heart' (Oxyrh. Log. III.).

3. Other elements of discourse-material from the Third Gospel and Acts may be clearly traced to a source of the same Wisdom type, if not the same composition. (a) In particular, the wisdom of Solomon, especially as exhibited in the hedonistic Epicureanism of Ecclesiastes, is pointedly contrasted with a higher wisdom in the great discourse on the true riches of Lk 12$^{13\text{-}34}$, part of which is taken up in Mt 6$^{19\text{-}34}$. The polemic against Ec 2 in 12$^{13\text{-}21}$ becomes tenfold more pointed as the discourse proceeds to compare the beauty of the lilies and the provision of the ravens 'which have neither store-chamber nor barn' (cf. v.^{18}) with 'Solomon in all his glory' (cf. Ec 1$^{12\text{-}18}$ 2$^{1\text{-}25}$). The subject of the discourse ('wherein life consists,' vv.$^{15.}$ $^{22\text{f.}}$) is as distinctive of Hebrew Wisdom literature as the form and phraseology.

(b) To the same original context must be reckoned the greater part of Lk 16, the material of which is peculiar to Luke. The 'wisdom' of the unrighteous steward in the use of 'the mammon of unrighteousness' is a subject manifestly in close relation to the use of riches commended in 12$^{13\text{-}34}$, the affinity extending even to the phraseology (with 16^9 'riches that fail' cf. 12^{33} 'treasure that faileth not'). The combination of the two, therefore, in Mt 6$^{19\text{-}34}$, à propos of the heavenly recompense (Mt 6$^{1. 4. 18}$), probably reflects a real connexion of Lk 12$^{13\text{-}34}$ with 16$^{1\text{-}13}$ in the source. Similar reasoning, based partly on the phraseology (cf. 16^{15} with 18^{14}) partly on the subject-matter, connects the rest of Lk 16 (exc. v.$^{17. 18}$) with 18$^{9\text{-}14}$ (19$^{11\text{-}27}$?). The two companion parables 16$^{19\text{-}25}$ (vv.$^{26\text{-}31}$ seem to be a later addendum) and 18$^{9\text{-}14}$ exemplify the principle laid down in 16^{15}, while 16^{16}=Mt 11$^{12\text{-}14}$ links the whole with Lk 7$^{29\text{f.}}$. The whole group of teachings and parables on worldly conditions is thus seen to have a common occasion and bearing, a common spirit, and a common point of view not elsewhere shown in the Gospels, but closely resembling the social teaching of James (cf. 1$^{9\text{-}11}$ 2$^{1\text{-}9}$ 4$^{2\text{f.} 6. 10. 13\text{f.}}$ 5$^{1\text{-}6}$).

(c) A kindred subject having a similar development in Lk., but otherwise only scantily represented in the Gospels, is that of dependence on the Divine bounty in answer to prayer (Lk 11$^{1\text{-}13}$), which can hardly be dissociated from the companion parables (11$^{5\text{-}8}$ and 18$^{1\text{-}8}$). The bare and wholly disconnected fragment taken up in Mt 7$^{7\text{-}11}$ is as inadequate to represent this exquisite group as is Mt 6$^{19\text{-}34}$ if bereft of the parables on the Foolish Rich Man and the Shrewd Steward. Once more, it is the Ep. of James that supplies an echo of the same spirit (cf. 1$^{5\text{-}8. 17}$ 4$^{2\text{f.}}$ 5$^{13\text{-}18}$).

It is clear that the method here applied may be extended to much of the special discourse-material of Lk., including perhaps some elements of Acts (on Solomon in Ac 7$^{44\text{-}50}$ see Yale Bicentennial Contributions, 1901, p. 271 f.). It is sufficent for the present to indicate that a large element of our Third Gospel is thus characterized.

vi. WISDOM UTTERANCES REPRESENT A SPECIAL TYPE OF GOSPEL TRADITIONS.—The question of the relation of the Wisdom discourses to the recognized Gospel sources is one which inevitably suggests itself as soon as the fact is recognized that they are characterized by a peculiar and distinctive point of view. It becomes our duty, accordingly, to trace at least the outline of an answer.

1. The discourse-material of Mt 11–12 falls outside the pentad characterized by the colophon καὶ ἐγένετο ὅτε ἐτέλεσεν κ.τ.λ. already discussed in art. LOGIA.

2. Besides being separated by narrative-material from these groups, Mt 11–12 differ from them in the fact of their relation to the narrative, from which

they are inseparable, and in the degree of similarity in their language to the Lukan parallels. As against the groups of *logia* which have not, and from their character do not require, a narrative setting, the discourse of Mt 11 not only relates the coming of the Baptist's disciples, but presupposes an account of Jesus' works of healing, and even requires us to suppose the reader somewhere informed of what had given rise to the taunt 'Behold a gluttonous man and a wine-bibber, a friend of publicans and sinners.' The same applies to the discourse in defence of Jesus' exorcism 'by the Spirit of God.' This indispensable narrative-element is always supplied more fully and in better connexion by Lk., in some cases by Lk. alone (Lk 11$^{1ff.}$ 12$^{13-21}$).

3. The similarity of language to the Lukan parallels is here very exceptional, reaching the degree of verbal identity for whole sentences, and positively requiring the use of the same written *Greek* source.

4. This marked difference in the degree of resemblance serves to connect other non-Markan elements of Mt., such as 3^{1}-4^{11} 8$^{5-13.\ 18-22}$, which are again found to fall outside the Matthæan pentad, to differ in content and point of view from the *Logian* source, and to be at once more complete and for the most part more authentic in detail in Luke than in Matthew. Linguistic peculiarities in several instances prove the dependence of Mt. in these portions. Thus Ἰερουσαλήμ is used by Lk. 68 times against 3 (5 ?) employments of Ἰεροσόλυμα. The latter form on the contrary is invariably employed in Mt., Mk., and Jn., *except* thrice in Mt 23^{37} = Lk 13^{34}. βασιλεία τοῦ θεοῦ is systematically changed by Mt. to τῶν οὐρανῶν. There are but four exceptions: Mt 19^{24} (= Mk 10^{25}) and 12^{28} 21$^{31.\ 43}$ (cf. Lk 7^{29} 11^{20}).

vii. RELATION TO NARRATIVE-ELEMENTS OF SYNOPTIC TRADITION.—Although our First and to a less extent our Third Evangelist both derive the main framework of their narrative from our Second, this Second itself is not wanting in evidences of dependence on the source to which we have traced the Wisdom chapters of Mt. and Luke.

1. This relation appears in the description of the Baptist as Elias (Mk 1$^{2.\ 5.\ 6}$; * cf. Lk 7$^{24f.\ 33}$, Mt 11^{14}, 2 K 1^{8}); of the Temptation (Mk 1^{13}, the ἄγγελοι and θηρία coming from Ps 91$^{11-13}$ quoted in Lk 4$^{10f.}$); of Jesus as 'eating and drinking' while the disciples of the Baptist were fasting, and as 'a friend of publicans and sinners' (Mk 2$^{18-22.\ 13-17}$; cf. Lk 7$^{33f.}$); of the blasphemy of the scribes (Mk 3$^{22-35}$; cf. Lk 11$^{14-28}$), and perhaps of the Transfiguration (Mk 9$^{2-13}$; cf. Lk 9$^{28-36}$). In all these passages of Mk. and in other loosely connected material (9$^{38-40}$ = Lk 9$^{49f.}$ 12$^{41-44}$ = Lk 21$^{1-4}$) the context of Lk. gives more or less conclusive evidence of priority. It is but reasonable to suppose that other Markan narratives such as 6$^{1-6}$ may also have been derived hence, though the present Lukan form has been affected by it.

2. Of the connexion of the narrative-elements peculiar to Lk. with the source thus characterized it is hardly needful to speak. The common point of view of this material, presenting Jesus as the friend and champion of the lowly, from His childhood in the manger, welcomed by shepherds, to His acceptance by the thief on the cross, is well known. Nor can such narratives as that of the repentant harlot (Lk 7$^{36-50}$) be separated without violence from the discourse context. It is only in Mt. and Mk. that Lk 7$^{1-10}$ and 21$^{1-4}$ find themselves on a foreign soil.

* Note especially the rare form ἔσθω found only in Lk 7$^{33.\ 34}$ 10^{7} and 22^{30}. In all the other 55 occurrences of the verb in the NT, including 10 in Mark and 9 of Lk.'s own, the regular form ἐσθίω is used.

viii. CONCLUSIONS AS TO PROTO-LUKAN SOURCE.—Admitting the precarious character of all attempts at extricating the Synoptic sources, and the probable development of the Antiochian (?) tradition between the period of its employment by Mk. and Mt. and its ultimate incorporation by Lk., enough remains to justify the following inference. A type of Gospel-tradition grew up (at Antioch ?) intermediate between those to which tradition attaches the names respectively of 'Matthew' and 'John,' and containing the ἢ λεχθέντα ἢ πραχθέντα traditionally ascribed to the preaching of Peter. The Matthæan tradition is especially connected both by the unanimous testimony of antiquity and by internal evidence with Jerusalem. It takes as its method the agglutination of the *logia* of Jesus into a five-fold new *Torah*, as 'commandments given by the Lord to the faith.' This agrees with the legalistic tendencies of the Palestinian Church and the methods of the Synagogue as illustrated, *e.g.*, in the *Pirke Aboth* (cf. the Oxyrhynchus *Logia*). Besides the *halachic* type of Gospel tradition the earliest testimony recognizes a *haggadic*, of which Peter is the authoritative source. It seems to have had two branches, the earlier (Mk.) connected by tradition and internal evidences with Rome, the later (Jn.) with Ephesus, both almost as wholly preoccupied with the doctrine of the Person of Christ as the Pauline Epistles, and appealing to the drama of the Ministry and Passion for proof of the Divine sonship of Jesus. In the earlier (Mk.), connexion with the Petrine tradition is still close. In the later (Jn.), Pauline Logos-doctrine wholly dominates. Midway between these two types of Gospel tradition, the Hebrew and the Græco-Roman, is developed that which tradition credibly associates with the name of Luke at Antioch. Combining both sayings and doings (ἤρξατο ποιεῖν τε καὶ διδάσκειν, Ac 1^{1}) in juster proportion than Mk., it finds in the *history*, as exhibited in both elements, a manifestation of the Spirit of God in terms of the Jewish Wisdom-doctrine. As our First canonical Evangelist presents as the opening scene of the ministry the new Lawgiver on the Mount of Beatitudes, so our Third presents the scene in the synagogue of Nazareth where the 'words of grace' uttered by the bearer of 'the Spirit of the Lord God' are rejected by His own people, the tragedy of the Divine Wisdom. The theme is constant, but is developed alike in message of grace and deed of mercy. The whole career of Jesus is a manifestation of 'the power of God and the wisdom of God.' Analysis of the sources of canonical Lk.-Acts reveals no difference in this fundamental point of view. From the beginning, as in the 5th cent., the Antioch school is historical, and its historical sources admittedly include, in Acts, if not in the Gospel, the oldest narrative of the NT. By the standard of internal evidence its tradition is more markedly Petrine than Mk.; its Christology roots itself, like the Pauline, but with less of the Hellenic speculative development, in that broadest, most humanitarian, most tolerant school of Hebrew thought, the followers and exponents of 'all-virtuous Wisdom.'

ix. WISDOM SPECULATION IN THE DEVELOPMENT OF CHRISTOLOGY.—The conception of Wisdom as affecting Synoptic tradition involves such literary analysis of the source as the foregoing. As affecting the doctrine of the Person of Christ it involves at least a passing glance at the Pauline Christology, the link between Synoptic and Johannine doctrine.

1. The Wisdom-doctrine of *St. Paul* stands in unmistakably close relation, as regards its antecedents, with the Wisdom literature; and, as respects its subsequent development, with the Johannine Logos-doctrine. St. Paul's indebtedness to

Stoic philosophy and ethics is set forth by no less a master than Lightfoot ('St. Paul and Seneca' in *Com. on Phil.*). Recent demonstrations of his much more extensive and direct dependence on the Wisdom literature, especially the Book of Wisdom (*Internat. Crit. Com. on Romans*, by Sanday and Headlam, p. 51; cf. Grafe, 'Das Verhältniss der paulinischen Schriften zur Sapientia Salomonis' in *Th. Abh. C. v. Weizsäcker gewidmet*), should by now have made it plain that Stoicism comes to St. Paul mainly through Jewish channels. Again, since it is certain that St. Paul both by temperament and by experience was more apocalyptist than scribe, it should not have been overlooked that he has advanced, however briefly, his own decision on the moot point, whether the complete manifestation of the Divine Wisdom is simply the Torah of Moses (so the scribes on the basis of Dt 4[6-8]), or whether it is the living Spirit of God sent forth in human form. Ro 10[4-8] and Bar 3[9]-4[1] (especially 3[29f.]) contain contemporary and rival interpretations of Dt 30[12. 13]. By St. Paul's interpretation 'the word' (of revelation) is nothing more or less than 'Christ' as pre-existent spirit, the same Wisdom which, 'because she was the artificer of all things,' passing into the soul of Solomon gave him 'an unerring knowledge of the things that are, to know the constitution of the world,' etc. (Wis 7[17-22]), the same 'mind of Christ' by possession of which Christians have similar knowledge of the purposes of the Creator, just as a man's own consciousness gives him knowledge of his private designs (1 Co 2[6-16]; see MYSTERY). Definite identification is thus made by St. Paul in this and many other passages between the Divine Spirit of Wisdom, through which, according to 'Wisdom,' God created the world, and the pre-existent Christ. Even the avatar doctrine of the descent and ascent of Wisdom (see references above, i. 1) is unmistakably adopted by St. Paul partly in opposition to, partly in rivalry with, the widespread conceptions of mystery religion (see MYSTERY). But just as a study of the Pauline ethics will show that its Stoic elements have been subsumed under the Christian principle of altruistic service (Eph 5[1f.], Ph 2[1-13]), so it should be recognized that the Pauline Logos-doctrine, while clearly incorporating in Eph 4[4-16] a *quasi*-mythological interpretation of Ps 68[18], rests upon an authentic teaching of Jesus. According to St. Paul, Ps 68 sets forth the descent, conflict with the hostile powers, triumph and ascent of the Divine Spirit (cf. Col 2[15], 1 P 3[19]) after releasing the captives of Death (cf. 1 Co 15[26f.]). But Eph 4[8-10], when compared with the earlier and later related passages concerning the avatar of Wisdom (Bacon, *Story of St. Paul*, p. 316 ff.), will be seen in some sense to rest upon the parable of Jesus concerning the 'spoiling' of the Strong Man armed, by the Stronger than he (*i.e.* the Spirit of God operative in Jesus, Mt 12[28]). We find it, in fact, habitually applied in this sense by the Fathers (Apollinaris, frag. 2 in *Pasch. Chron.*; *Heads against Caius*, vii.; cf. Huydekoper, *Works*, vol. ii., 'Christ's Mission to the Underworld'). Thus the Pauline Wisdom- or Logos-doctrine of a pre-existent, spiritual Christ is firmly rooted in the authentic teaching of Jesus Himself. To Jesus also 'the power of God and the wisdom of God,' were exhibited in His own mighty works and God-given teaching, and were a 'sign' to His generation (Mt 11[2-24] 12[38-42]; cf. 1 Co 1[17-2][16]).

2. *Johannine and Patristic Christology.*—(*a*) It matters little that after St. Paul the Wisdom-doctrine should have been rebaptized by the Greek title of Logos, perhaps under the influence of Philo, perhaps as a concession to a Greek-speaking Church. Even in the Fourth Gospel the basic conception remains Hebrew and Pauline. Sanday as a student of Johannine thought, Sabatier as a student of Pauline, concur in admitting the identity of doctrine under the diverse terminology.

(*b*) In the Fourth Gospel the standpoint of the Evangelist is purely and simply the theological. He depicts the self-manifestation of the Divine Wisdom or Logos as incarnate in Jesus by word and deed. Her 'dwelling among men' (1[10-14]; cf. Enoch 42[2]), rejection and apotheosis (20[17]) is his theme. It is characteristic that here, as in the Wisdom literature in general, Wisdom is made to 'praise herself' (Sir 24[1]). The incarnate Logos preaches Himself; His seven parables are seven 'I am's,' His seven mighty works manifest His own glory (Jn 2[11]). In Jn 7[38] Jesus even quotes again an unknown 'scripture' which by all analogy is drawn from the Wisdom literature (cf. Sir 24[30f.] [applied in vv.[23-29], by analogy with *five* rivers, to the five books of the Torah], Enoch 48[1] 49[1], and for Rabbinic interpretation in the scribal sense, *Emek Hammelech*, 196[a], on Is 12[3], 'The waters are nothing else than the Torah, and the waters of salvation nothing else than the Torah of Messiah,' Weber, *Lehre d. Talm.* p. 360 f.; cf. also 1 Co 10[4] and *Oxyrh. Log.* III.).

(*c*) The Wisdom utterance Mt 11[25ff.] may be regarded as marking the transition-point between the Synoptic and Johannine representations of Jesus' teaching. Not its doctrine alone, nor its mysticism, paralleling 1 Co 2 (see MYSTERY), but the very form of its utterance is thus seen to be characteristic; for the Wisdom of God habitually speaks in the first person. Herein the discourses of the Fourth Gospel are as close to the spirit of the Wisdom literature as its Logos-doctrine is close to the Wisdom-doctrine of St. Paul. In the development of Gospel literature the presentation of Jesus' career and teaching as the manifestation of the Divine Wisdom takes a place analogous to that of the Wisdom-doctrine of St. Paul in the development of Christology.

LITERATURE.—On the Wisdom hypostasis see, in addition to the works cited above, Bousset, *Religion des Judenthums*[2], p. 394 ff.; Brandt, *Evangelische Geschichte*, pp. 537, 561 f., 576; J. Drummond, *Philo Judæus*, ii. p. 201 ff.; Aall, *Gesch. d. Logosidee*, i. p. 204 f. On Hebrew Wisdom literature: Cheyne, *Job and Solomon, or the Wisdom of the OT*, 1887. On the literary forms: Norden, *Antike Kunstprosa*; Wilke, *Die neutest. Rhetorik*; Moffatt, *Historical New Test.*[2] pp. xx, 704. On the influence of the *Hokhmah* literature on the gospel: F. C. Porter, *Messages of the Apocalyptic Writers*, 1905, p. 19. On the discourses of the Third Gospel: Bacon, *The Sermon on the Mount*, 1900, Appendix C. On Mt 23[34-39], D. F. Strauss, 'Jesu Weheruf über Jerusalem und die σοφία τοῦ θεοῦ' in *Ztschr. wiss. Theol.* vi. (1863), pp. 84-93; Loman, *Th. Tijdschr.* i. pp. 550-560.

B. W. BACON.

WISDOM OF CHRIST.—1. Christ, being God and man, possessed naturally two distinct kinds of wisdom—*Divine wisdom* and *human wisdom*. The former, as part of the totality of the Divine attributes (τὸ πλήρωμα τῆς θεότητος), He necessarily possessed from eternity, and, according to Pauline teaching, He continued to possess it, in spite of His κένωσις, or self-emptying (Ph 2[7]), even after His Incarnation (Col 1[19] 2[9], cf. 2[3]). The continued possession by the Incarnate Logos of the fulness of the Divine wisdom is no isolated doctrine, but is necessarily involved in the Logos-Christology of St. Paul and St. John, according to which the Father does not create and sustain the world directly, but mediately through the Logos, who is the Creator (Jn 1[3. 10], Eph 3[9], Col 1[16], He 1[2]), the Life (Jn 1[4]), and the Light (v.[9]) of the world, the cause of its rational order, and the principle of its coherence and subsistence (Col 1[17]). Cosmical functions of such a kind as this, assigned to the Logos in accordance with His essential nature and position in the Godhead, cannot be supposed to have been laid aside at the Incarnation, and therefore the limitations of Christ's knowledge, which the Synoptic Gospels recognize, either must be attributed to His manhood, or else it must be supposed that in the historical Christ were *two* centres of Divine consciousness—an unlimited one, in which He knew all things, and a limited one, in which He condescended to be ignorant of certain things. The latter view, which is based on an ultra-literal interpretation of Mk 13[32], postulates three different kinds of wisdom in Christ—an *unlimited* Divine wisdom, a *limited* Divine wisdom, and a *human* wisdom. This scheme appears to us unnecessarily complicated. The 'ignorance' of Mk 13[32], although ascribed to *the Son*, can quite naturally, on the principle of *communicatio idiomatum*, be attributed to Christ's human nature (οὐκ ἀγνοῶν ὁ Λόγος, ᾗ Λόγος ἐστίν, ἔλεγεν, Οὐκ οἶδα, οἶδε γάρ, ἀλλὰ τὸ ἀνθρώπινον δεικνύς, ὅτι τῶν ἀνθρώπων ἴδιόν ἐστι τὸ ἀγνοεῖν, Athan. *c. Arian.* iii. 45); and consequently there is no need to recognize in Christ more than *two* wisdoms, a human and a Divine (see, further, KENOSIS).

(1) In virtue of His Divine wisdom, Christ is *omniscient*, i.e. He knows all actual and possible things, present, past and future, including the future contingent actions of beings possessed of free-will. The nature of this last kind of knowledge (sometimes called *scientia media*) is altogether inscrutable to us ; but it is expressly ascribed to God in many passages of both Testaments (1 S 23[1-13], Is 41[22. 23], Jer 38[15ff.], He 4[13] etc.), and is frequently claimed by Jesus (Mt 11[20-23] 26[21], Jn 6[70] etc.), who is represented as able to read the heart of man (Jn 1[47-51] 2[24. 25] etc.).

(2) With regard to Christ's *human wisdom*, believers in a real Incarnation (ἐνανθρώπησις), as distinguished from ·a mere assumption of a body (ἐνσάρκωσις, ἐνσωμάτωσις), are bound to recognize both its *finite character* and its *gradual development*. The gradual development of Christ's wisdom is twice noticed by St. Luke (2[40] πληρούμενον σοφίᾳ [σοφίας], 2[52] προέκοπτε σοφίᾳ καὶ ἡλικίᾳ), and once by the author of Hebrews (5[8] καίπερ ὢν υἱός, ἔμαθεν ἀφ' ὧν ἔπαθε τὴν ὑπακοήν, καὶ τελειωθεὶς ἐγένετο, etc.). To understand the growth in wisdom here spoken of as merely *exhibitive*—Christ being supposed, as He grew in age, to manifest more and more of the hidden wisdom which He possessed entire from the first (so John of Damascus and most of the later Fathers; also Aquinas and the Scholastics)—is not only bad exegesis, but is virtual Apollinarism. Apollinaris denied to Christ a real human soul; but Aquinas virtually does the same when he asserts that the soul of Christ was created *mature*, in the full enjoyment of free-will and of the Beatific Vision, and possessed of wisdom and knowledge practically coextensive with the Divine.*

Far different is the representation of the Gospels. In them Christ undergoes not simply a bodily, but a normal psychical development. He is true infant, true boy, true youth, in mind as well as in body. As Irenæus beautifully says : ' He came to save all by means of Himself—all, I say, who through Him are born again to God—infants, and children, and boys, and youths, and old men. He therefore passed through every age, becoming an infant for infants, thus sanctifying infants ; a child for children, thus sanctifying those who are of this age, being at the same time made to them an example of piety, righteousness, and submission ; a youth for youths, becoming an example to youths, and thus sanctifying them for the Lord' (*Against Heresies*, ii. 22–24). *The Incarnation of Christ thus restored the norm of human development.* In the growth of the child Jesus, God saw

for the first time human nature expanding and perfecting itself according to its original ideal and plan, unhindered and undistorted by sin ; and upon the gracious spectacle God and man looked with approval (Lk 2[40. 52]).

(3) By the human wisdom (σοφία) of Christ is meant His quick understanding in the things of God (cf. Ja 1[5]) ; His knowledge of the Scriptures, and His power of interpreting them (cf. Ac 6[3. 10]) ; His deep moral insight, gained by actual experience of temptation and suffering (He 5[8]) ; His capacity for learning His lessons at the synagogue school (cf. Ac 7[22]) ; His skill as a carpenter (cf. Ex 31[2f.]) ; the power of asking and answering hard questions (cf. Rev 13[18] 17[9]) which He displayed even as a boy (Lk 4[6]), and which stood Him in good stead on so many occasions during His ministry ·(Mt 22[15. 23. 34] etc.) ; His skill in constructing parables, allegories, and sententious sayings, like those of the wise men of old (cf. Mt 12[4]) ; His persuasiveness as a teacher and eloquence as a preacher (see Mt 13[54], cf. 1 Co 1[17] 2[1. 4]) ; His common sense and practical ability (cf. Col 4[5]) ; probably also His power of working miracles (Mk 6[2], cf. Ac 7[10]), and His prophetic gift (2 P 3[15]), which were in Him, partly at any rate, *human* endowments, as in other prophets (see Mk 13[32]).

(4) It is implied in Scripture that Christ's human knowledge received *a great extension at His Resurrection and Ascension.* At the Resurrection He received all authority (πᾶσα ἐξουσία) in heaven and on earth (Mt 28[18]), and this authority He exercises *as man*, and not simply as God (Ph 2[10], Rev 5[6-14] etc.). His human knowledge, therefore, must now be coextensive with His human authority ; that is, it must embrace all cosmical facts—past, present, and future. It is an error, however, to suppose that His human knowledge is even now infinite. Human nature is essentially *finite*, and therefore the human soul of Christ, though glorified, can never completely know the Infinite Essence of God. See, further, CONSCIOUSNESS.

2. On Christ as the Wisdom of God, see preceding article.

LITERATURE.—Dorner, *Person of Christ* ; Baldensperger, *Das Selbstbewusstsein Jesu* ; Liddon, *BL* ; Gifford, *The Incarnation* ; Gore, *Dissertations* ; Bruce, *Humiliation of Christ* ; Hall, *Kenotic Theory* ; Mason, *Conditions of our Lord's Life on Earth* ; Powell, *Principle of the Incarnation* ; *Expositor*, IV. iv. [1891] p. 1 ff.
C. HARRIS.

WISE MEN.—See MAGI.

WITNESS.—The idea of witness as related to Christ and His gospel plays an essential and highly important part in the NT writings and in the Christian faith and life universally. Not only in the primitive preaching, but also in all effectual preaching throughout the history of the Church, the gospel is conceived not as a speculative system, but as a *witness to Jesus the Christ* as being Himself *God's Witness* to the world.

Among the NT writers none appears to have so definitely and fondly reflected upon the idea of witness as St. John. It is one of his 'leading ideas.' In his Gospel (cf. Westcott, *Speaker's Com.* on 'St. John,' Introd.) he mentions a sevenfold witness to Christ: the witness (1) of the Father (5[34. 37]), (2) of the Son (8[14] 18[37]), (3) of His works (10[25] 5[36]), (4) of the Scriptures (5[39-46]), (5) of the forerunner (1[7] 5[35]), (6) of the disciples (15[27] 19[35]), (7) of the Spirit (15[26] 16[14]). In view, however, of the unique significance of the Person of Christ, and in harmony with the method of the NT preaching, it will be most appropriate to consider our subject under these two heads :—I. The witness of Jesus Christ the Son, supported by the witness of the Father and of the Spirit. II. The witness of the disciples to Jesus Christ the Son

---

* The Scholastic doctrine is that from the moment of conception Christ's soul knew *all actual events and things, past, present, and future*. Only abstract possibilities, which were never to be realized, were hidden from Him.

of God, supported by the witness of the Holy Spirit.

I. *THE WITNESS OF JESUS, SUPPORTED BY THE WITNESS OF THE FATHER AND OF THE SPIRIT.* — **1. Jesus' personal witness.** — His first disciples Jesus gathered about Himself through the power of the truth which He spoke and of His own Personality, so marvellously at one with His word. He did not begin with declarations about Himself. He came to make the Father known. He came fulfilling, in word and deed, the Law and the Prophets. He preached repentance and inward righteousness. With a wealth of light He set forth the nature of the Kingdom of God. But in all this Jesus spoke as *witness.* He was conscious of an immediate, intimate, and unique fellowship with the Father, and out of this consciousness He spoke (Mt 11[27], Jn 3[11] 10[15] 14[10] 17[21. 25]; see also art. CONSCIOUSNESS). The tone and manner of spiritual authority permeated all that He said and did from His earliest teaching to His sublime declaration before Pilate, and even to His words upon the cross (cf. esp. Mt 5–7, Jn 18[37] 19[30], Lk 11[43. 46]). But this consciousness of speaking as witness finds also distinct and emphatic expression in His word (cf. esp. Jn 8[12ff.]).

While Jesus' witness was primarily concerning the Father,—He even denied in a certain sense that He bore witness of Himself (Jn 5[31]),—it is yet certain that He also bore witness of Himself (cf. esp. Jn 8[14] 18[37] 14[6]). Jesus testifies of Himself as *the Way.* This testimony is unmistakable and unqualified. And yet the method of this witness was chiefly indirect or by way of necessary implication. He appealed to the Father's testimony concerning Him, or else silently waited till it should be brought to light. And when the revelation from the Father produced in the disciples a believing confession of His Son, Jesus clearly accepted and sanctioned that confession (*e.g.* Mt 16[16-20]).

2. The witness of the Father to Jesus includes both the personal, inward testimony to Jesus Himself, which resulted in His full consciousness as Messiah and Son (see art. CONSCIOUSNESS), and all the works of God preparatory to and accompanying the life of Jesus Christ on earth designed to lead men to the certainty of faith in Him as Redeemer and Lord. Under this head we note : (1) The *witness of the Scriptures* (cf. esp. Jn 5[39], Lk 24[27], Ac 10[43]). This must be taken in the most real sense and yet not narrowly. The OT is full of the Messianic hope, and that hope was inspired by God. Jesus was steeped in the Scriptures, and He understood the things in them concerning Himself. We have no longer reason to insist upon a scheme of minute prediction and fulfilment, and yet we still affirm that Jesus is not to be understood otherwise than as the Fulfiller of the Law and the Prophets. (For a fuller discussion of this point see art. FULFILMENT. Cf. also Valeton, *Christus und das AT* ; and Kähler, *Jesus und das AT*).

(2) The *witness of John* as a prophet of God (cf. esp. Jn 1[7. 8. 15. 19ff.] 5[36]) is manifestly closely related to that of the Scriptures ; but John is, of course, more specific than the earlier prophets could be. John's witness Jesus accepts as having a very real significance, for He regards it not as the witness of man merely, but as inspired of God.

(3) The *witness of the works* (cf. esp. Jn 5[30. 36] 10[37. 38] 14[10. 11], Ac 2[22-24]). The works are a testimony from the Father ; for Jesus declares : 'The Father abiding in me doeth his works.' It would, doubtless, be a grave mistake to regard Christ's word, 'The works which the Father hath given me to accomplish, the very works that I do, bear witness of me, that the Father hath sent me,' as meaning *only* His miracles. The testimony of the works issues from His whole life and ministry. His whole life-

work was a manifestation of God, and as such was, in the larger sense, truly a miracle. See, further, artt. MIRACLES, RESURRECTION OF CHRIST, and SIGN.

3. The witness of the Spirit to Jesus the Son.— The witness of God concerning His Son calls for faith in the Son (1 Jn 5[6ff.]). This witness is borne to us primarily in objective facts (1 Jn 1[1ff.] 5[8. 10]), but it is borne in upon our consciousness only by the Spirit of God. 'It is the Spirit that beareth witness, because the Spirit is the truth' (1 Jn 5[7] ; cf. also Mt 16[17]). It cannot be too strongly emphasized that the Person and work of Jesus Christ are the object of this testimony. The Paraclete, the Spirit of truth (Christ says), '*shall bear witness of me*' (Jn 15[26]). The witness of the Spirit, according to the NT, is a much larger thing than the assurance of personal sonship through Christ (Ro 8[16] ; cf. art. ASSURANCE). Personal assurance is an essential and unspeakably important part—in a sense the climax—of the Spirit's witness. But it is un-Biblical to speak of this unqualifiedly as *the* witness of the Spirit. The Spirit's testimony is *coextensive with the objective testimony.* The manifestation of the truth of God in objective facts becomes to us an inward illumination only through the inward witness of the Spirit. Without the *testimonium Spiritus sancti internum* the objective witness is unable to produce full assurance. On the other hand, an inward persuasion that is not firmly grounded in objective reality is miserably insecure. The climax of the inward testimony is personal assurance ; but the inward witness is inseparable from the outward. They are not two separate and independent testimonies. God would make us certain of His wonderful love and grace. To this end He reveals Christ *for us,* and He also reveals Him *in us.* The outward manifestation is the indispensable means to the inward revelation. The fact of the fellowship with God through the Spirit (*e.g.* Ro 8[14ff.]) is not a thing by itself, it is the demonstration of the truth of the promise by an initial and progressive realization of the same. The actual fellowship of the Spirit is the Spirit's own witness. See, further, art. HOLY SPIRIT.

II. *THE WITNESS OF THE DISCIPLES, SUPPORTED BY THE WITNESS OF THE HOLY SPIRIT.* —Nothing could be clearer than that the primitive Christian preaching was not only the most direct and specific witness to Jesus the crucified and risen Lord, but also a witness irrepressibly spontaneous and full of the unconquerable assurance of an overpowering certainty (Ac 4[20], 1 Co 9[16], 2 Co 4[13]).

What constitutes, according to the NT, the equipment and competence of a witness of Jesus Christ ? Were His original disciples the only genuine witnesses ? Are not those also 'who have not seen and yet have believed' (Jn 20[29]) competent witnesses ? In the first place, then, let us inquire how the original witnesses were prepared for their office. Early in His public ministry Jesus chose from out the larger number of His disciples 'twelve that they might be with him, and that he might send them forth to preach' (Mk 3[14]). These He trained to be heralds of His gospel (see art. APOSTLES ; and Bruce, *The Training of the Twelve*), and declared that, when the Paraclete should have come to them, they should *bear witness* of Him (Jn 15[26. 27]). After His Passion and Resurrection He expressly commissioned them to go forth as His witnesses (Lk 24[48], Ac 1[8]). They could, of course, have had no vital conception of Jesus and His mission without the illumination of the Holy Spirit. But was there something in their experience which constituted them the only real witnesses ? Some have so held ; but this is a view unwarranted by Scripture and out of harmony with the principles of evangelical Christianity. The original disciples, it is true, were the only eye- and ear-witnesses. Yet what they literally saw and heard was not the revelation itself, but only the means thereto. In Jesus the flesh was, so to speak, 'a transparency for the Word.' Nevertheless multitudes 'saw and heard' Jesus and understood not. None of the rulers of this world recognized in Him the Lord of glory (1 Co 2[8]). The original heralds of Christ did indeed lay a certain stress upon their being eye- and ear-witnesses. But they prized their experience of sensible intercourse with the Lord not for its own sake, but because it was to them the means of entering into an inward personal fellowship with Him. In the days of His flesh this personal fellowship with Him was necessarily mediated through the senses, though the fellowship itself was not sensuous but spiritual. Even for these original disciples the time must come when their fellowship with their Lord should be wholly independent of the senses. Through the Paraclete the Lord would renew and continue His fellowship with His disciples (cf. esp. Jn 14 and 16 and 17[26]). But He would be no longer manifest through the senses (Jn 20[17]; cf. the fine sermon of H. Hoffmann, *Eins ist not*, p. 153). It is clear from the NT that after Pentecost the original disciples were immovable in their persuasion that they possessed and had fellowship with their exalted Lord.

From all this it is clear that the visible manifestation of the Lord was designed to be superseded by a manifestation through the word of His witnesses. But can the word really take the place of the sensuous contact with the Lord's Person? For answer let it be remembered in the first place that Christ foretold that it should be sufficient (*e.g.* Jn 17[20ff.], Mt 28[20]). What the original witnesses enjoyed, others should enjoy too—the same immediate fellowship, the same certainty. As the men of Sychar believed at last not for the woman's speaking, but because they had heard for themselves (Jn 4[42]), so through the word of the Apostles others are brought into actual saving relation with the same Lord Christ. Alike for those who saw Him, and for those who saw Him not, the outward facts must be inwardly apprehended and inwardly tested. And as was the design, so also is the actual experience under the gospel: where the word is truly preached the Spirit does energize and seal it, and those who believe receive the same certainty as the original disciples possessed. The whole NT preaching manifestly rests upon the full persuasion that this is and must be so (*e.g.* 1 P 1[8], He 13[8], 2 P 1[1], esp. Ac 11[15. 16]). Faith *does* come by hearing (Ro 10[17])—the *fact* of the vital union with Christ is proof of the adequacy of the word of testimony. Such is the argument of that wonderful passage, 1 Jn 1[1-4]. Those who through their association with Christ in the flesh had apprehended the life manifested, bear witness to others, *that these also may enter into the same fellowship with them*—the glorious fellowship with the Father and with His Son Jesus Christ. In the days of His flesh, Jesus was (according to an expression of Beyschlag in his *Leben Jesu*) 'His own prophet.' After His resurrection this office is committed to faithful witnesses. And it is thus that they conceive their office. The ministry of reconciliation is committed to them. As ambassadors of Christ they stand in Christ's stead (2 Co 5[19. 20]). To bear witness to Christ is their one aim as heralds (1 Jn 4[14]). And their word is effectual. He who believes through their word is not then 'a Christian of a secondary order'; his knowledge of Christ is indeed mediated and yet immediate (cf. the vigorous discussion of E. Haupt, *Die Bedeutung der heiligen Schrift für den evangelischen Christen*).

The same holds good throughout all time. The word stands firm; it never passes away (He 2[1. 2], Mk 13[31]). Wherever the word of Christ is preached with the certainty of faith, it can bring the hearer into 'the like precious faith' (2 P 1[1]).

But the effectiveness of the word of testimony is absolutely conditioned upon the operation of the Holy Spirit. The essence of the word is the promise of fellowship, grace, eternal life through Jesus Christ. Unless the preacher has the inward consciousness of the reality of the life with Christ through the Spirit, his word is no witness. And unless the hearer is aided by the Spirit to apprehend and to prove the testimony, the word concerning peace, fellowship, freedom, and the power of an endless life would be but empty sound. When, however, the word is spoken in the Spirit, it is quick, powerful, convincing, saving (He 4[12], Jn 16[8], Ja 1[21]).

Have, then, the original witnesses no peculiar privilege and authority? So far as personal certainty is concerned, they have no advantage over true believers of any age. Nevertheless, in the *economy* of the gospel dispensation, the word of the original witnesses is manifestly of cardinal importance. The mere fact that they were the *first* witnesses is of itself sufficient to give to their testimony a peculiar importance and to make it for evangelical Christians the last resort. Even those believing critics who go farthest in the sifting of Apostolic tradition, agree that the saving knowledge of God in Christ is mediated to us through the primitive Christian preaching. Either we must gain our knowledge of Christ by this means, or else we must give up the inquiry, for no other way is open to us (cf. art. BACK TO CHRIST). The primitive witnesses, however, were more than merely the first, as though there by chance. They had been *chosen beforehand and specially trained* for the work of bearing witness. Either our Lord succeeded in giving to His chosen Apostles such an understanding of His mission and work as to enable them to bear competent witness, or else He failed. If He failed, there could be no certainty for them and no gospel to us through them. The soundness and sufficiency of their witness are established by the demonstration of the Spirit and of power, and this accompanies the same witness in every succeeding age.

For the sake of their testimony many of Christ's servants have been called upon to suffer death. Such were called in a special ethical sense μάρτυρες Ἰησοῦ (Ac 22[20], Rev 2[13] 17[6]). 'This is not to be understood, as in ecclesiastical Greek, in the sense that death was the form of their testimony, but in reference to their testimony of Jesus as having occasioned their death' (Cremer, *Lex.*; cf. also Rev 20[4]). An approach to the analogous use of μαρτυρέω is probably to be found in 1 Ti 6[13] 'Jesus Christ, who before Pontius Pilate witnessed the good confession.'

LITERATURE.—Besides reff. in the art., see Dale, *Living Christ and Four Gospels*; Hare, *Mission of the Comforter*; Stearns, *Evid. of Chr. Exper.*; Smeaton, *Doct. of Holy Spirit*; Forrest, *Christ of Hist. and of Exper.*; Brace, *Gesta Christi*; R. J. Knowling, *The Witness of the Epistles*, and *The Witness of St. Paul to Christ*; Herrmann, *Warum bedarf unser Glaube geschichtl. Thatsachen?*; H. Scott Holland, *Creed and Character*, 1, 19; C. Wordsworth, *Primary Witness to the Truth of the Gospel*; Th. Zahn, *Bread and Salt from the Word of God*, 185; T. H. Green, *The Witness of God*; *Bapt. Rev. and Expos.* i. [1904] 321; Kähler, *Zur Bibelfrage* (1907).

J. R. VAN PELT.

WOE.—The word οὐαί (in LXX for the most part the tr. of אוֹי and הוֹי) was spoken by our Lord in virtue of His prophetic office. He was 'the prophet that cometh into the world' (Jn 6[14]), the decisive exponent of God's will (Dt 18[15f.], Ac 3[22f.], He 1[1. 2]). As in the mouth of the OT prophets, so in His, 'the word of Yahwè must of necessity be a word of woe to a sinful people' (*Encyc. Bibl.* iii. 3875). Like them, He was 'full of power by the spirit of the Lord, and of judgment, and of might, to declare unto Jacob his transgression, and to Israel his sin' (Mic 3[8]). Two characters He specially abhorred — those of the seducer and the hypocrite. His language respecting the Jewish leaders is 'part of the judicial language of the first Advent' (Mozley, *University Serm.* 29). Other Woes He utters with a sob of pity ; but His indictment of the scribes and Pharisees is spoken with the wrath of love (cf. Rev 6[16]). His 'prophetic plainness' is a trait that must not be left out of view in studying 'the mind of Christ,' and in contemplating His work as Priest and King. 'As well as meekness there was anger, and besides tenderness there was strength' (Hall Caine, *Illus. Lond. News*, 7th Mar. 1891 ; cf. Tennyson, *Memoir by his Son*, i. 326 ; *Ecce Homo*[1], 272, 276).—St. Mark reports only two instances of our Lord's using the word οὐαί. It does not occur in St. John. But St. John reports many stern utterances respecting those who sinned against light.

The Woe of Mk 13[17] (‖ Mt 24[19], Lk 21[23]) was spoken by Christ with deep commiseration ; at the same time the passage in which it occurs is a prophetic one relating to the doom of Jerusalem which had rejected Him (cf. Lk 23[28.29]). Eusebius (*HE* iii. 5) and Epiphanius (*de Mens.* 15) mention the flight of the Christians. Mt 11[21] (‖ Lk 10[13])—where the mention of Chorazin shows how much of our Lord's work is left unrecorded (Plummer)—is part of a farewell lamentation over the three cities by the Lake which had seen His manifestations of Divine power but had not repented, and agrees with other forewarnings that judgment will be most woeful for those who have thrown away the highest opportunities (Mt 12[41.42] ‖ Lk 11[31.32] ; cf. Lk 12[47.48]).— In Mt 18[7] (‖ Lk 17[1], cf. Mk 9[42]), the first Woe is spoken in pity, but the second in wrath. As is shown by the ἀνάγκη γάρ and the corresponding words in Lk., as well as by the context, οὐαὶ τῷ κόσμῳ is a lamentation over the ills brought on mankind by ambitious and selfish passions. The egotist and ambitionist (to use a word of Carlyle's) becomes the oppressor of the weak, and he also becomes their seducer,—a character for which Christ had such a loathing that He said 'it were better for him [who bears it] that a millstone were hanged about his neck, and that he were drowned in the depth of the sea.' The second Woe, introduced by πλήν (on which word see Plummer, *St. Luke*, 182), is directed against a man of this sort ⟨τῷ ἀνθρώπῳ ἐκείνῳ, the latter word putting him outside the pale of sympathy and respect), who, in our Lord's view, has committed the most heinous crime against the law of love (cf. Bruce, *Expos. Gr. Test.* 237 ; Wendt, *Teaching of Jesus*, i. 344 ; Carr, *Expositor*, 1898 (ii.), 348 ; Hastings' *DB* iii. 586[a]).

Of the two passages in which our Lord pronounces woe against the contemporary leaders of Judaism, the one in Lk 11 is an early utterance, and was spoken in the house of a Pharisee who had asked Him to dine with him (v.[37]), while the other in Mt 23 is a late and public denunciation of them in Jerusalem on the eve of His death. It was spoken when they were present, and for the purpose of warning the multitudes and His disciples to beware of them : hence, the real parallel to Mt 23 in Mk. and Lk. is to be found in the brief sayings reported in Mk 12[38-40] and Lk 20[45-47].

In Lk 11[42.43.44.46.47.52] there are two indictments containing three Woes apiece, and addressed to Pharisees and lawyers (wh. see) respectively. Sentence is first pronounced upon the Pharisees for being so punctilious about matters of a subordinate nature, which should be kept in their

proper place, while they neglected those moral obligations, which were of far higher moment, 'judgment and the love of God' (v.[42]) ; for putting themselves forward into the first seats in the face of the congregation, and their fondness for having reverence done to them in public (v.[43]) ; and for being a secret source of defilement to others who were not aware of the evil tendency of their principles (v.[44], cf. 12[1]). The second of these charges occurs, but without a Woe in Mt 23[6.7] ; while the other two are repeated in a more severe form in Mt 23[23.27].

The lawyers are then condemned for amplifying the written Law with their intolerably burdensome enactments, which they contrive to evade themselves, while so rigorous in exacting obedience to them from others (Lk 11[46]) ; for their zeal in the erection and adornment of the tombs of the prophets, which, in bitter irony, is pronounced to be a sign of their continuing the work of the murderers of the prophets (vv.[47.48] ; Wendt, i. 281 ; *Ecce Homo*[1], 267) ; and for taking away 'the key of knowledge' (see KEYS) by their traditional interpretations, which rendered the people incapable of recognizing the living truth (v.[52]). The first of these charges is found in Mt 23[4] without a Woe ; the others are repeated in Mt 23[13. 29ff.].

This later denunciation (Mt 23[13. (14)* 15. 16. 23. 25. 27. 29] ; cf. Is 5[8. 11. 18. 20-22], Hab 2[6. 9. 12. 15. 19]) is still more impressive on account of its epic strain ('octies vae ; Mt 5[3-11] octies beati,' Bengel). It shows how intense is the heat of our Lord's wrath when it is kindled (Ps 2[12]), as no other continuous passage in the Gospels does. In it, our Lord pronounces woe against the scribes and Pharisees for their 'hypocrisy' or their dishonesty and love of stage-effect in religion, which was to Him the most hateful impiety ; also for shutting the doors of the Kingdom of God which He had opened by His preaching, and so preventing people from entering (v.[13], cf. Rev 3[8]) ; for plundering (prob. wealthy and devout) widows (Plummer cites examples from the Talmud), and deceiving simple-minded people (Theophylact) by the long prayers they make (v.[14]) ; for carrying on a most laborious propaganda for the purpose of gaining proselytes (cf. Jos. *Ant.* xx. ii. 4), and then making them more full of spiritual pride than themselves (v.[15], cf. the Judaistic proselytizers who so relentlessly dogged St. Paul's footsteps, Hastings' *DB* iv. 136[b]) ; for pretending to guide others in the doing of God's will when they showed that they were so wanting in moral perception themselves (cf. Mt 15[14] ‖ Lk 6[39]) ; as, for example, when they subverted truth and justice by the sophistical distinctions they made in regard to the binding nature of different kinds of oaths (vv.[16-22], cf. Mk 7[6-13]). He then condemned them for omitting 'the weightier matters of the law, judgment, mercy, and fidelity,' while they were so exact in tithing their smaller garden herbs, thus 'straining out a gnat and swallowing a camel' (vv.[23.24]) ; and for so carefully observing, 'in preparing their food, the ceremonial rules for preserving their Levitical purity,' while they were not careful 'to avoid the moral defilement caused by the unlawful acquisition of that food, and by using it to minister to intemperance' (vv.[25.26], Wendt, i. 327). He compared the fair show of goodness they made with the artificial whiteness imparted to sepulchres by washing them with lime in spring (vv.[27.28], cf. Holtzmann, Meyer, *in loc.* ; *Encyc. Bibl.* iv. 5138). The final Woe was pronounced with a stinging reference to the honours they were paying to the

---

* V.[14] is probably an interpolation from Mk 12[40]. It[s] omission or transposition in the MSS may, however, be due to the fact that several sentences in succession begin with the same words (Scrivener, *Introd.*[4] i. 9).

prophets whom their fathers killed (vv.[29-31]); and, the cup of His indignation brimming over at the thought of His own impending death at their hands, He said, 'Fill ye up then the measure of (the sins of) your fathers' (v.[32]).

'Tremendous' (Mozley) as this language is, we are not to think that it was meant to apply to all the Pharisees indiscriminately. Nicodemus was a Pharisee (Jn 3[1]), and there were, doubtless, many others (cf. Ac 5[34]) with respect to whom the charge of hypocrisy was inadmissible. Paul, as a Pharisee, was no hypocrite (Ph 3[5, 6]); his Pharisaic upbringing was an important part of his providential training for his Christian Apostleship, and 'from Pharisaism in so far as it meant zeal for the highest objects of Jewish faith he never departed, and never could depart' (Ac 26[5, 22]; Hort, *Judaistic Christianity*, 108 ff.). In this very chapter, our Lord admits their authority as that of those who 'sit in Moses' seat,' and even gives His sanction to some of their minor observances (Mt 23[2, 23]; cf. Hort, 31–32). A well-known passage in the Talmud, distinguishing the various classes of Pharisees from each other, says that the real and only Pharisee is 'he who does the will of his Father in heaven because he loves Him' (Levy, *NHWB* 4. 143).

In his famous article on the Talmud (*Qu. Review*, Oct. 1867), the late Emanuel Deutsch pronounced a warm panegyric on 'the chiefly Pharisaic masters of the Mishnic period' for their 'wisdom, piety, kindness, and high and noble courage' (*Literary Remains*, 29). C. G. Montefiore (*Hibbert Journal*, Jan. 1903) has called attention to the 'new and large material, so interesting, so counter to current conceptions and verdicts,' produced by Schechter, 'the foremost Rabbinic scholar of his age,' in his articles in the *JQR* (1894–1900). But 'Schechter confesses that the view he has to give of Rabbinic religion *presents a blank at the important period*'—the time of Christ. 'We are driven back, therefore, on the Gospels.* . . . The evidence they afford appears irresistible . . . and an appeal to the principles of the religion as set forth in the OT and in the Mishnah cannot prevail to discredit the facts there recorded' (Menzies, *Hibbert Journal*, July, 1903). There is thus no reasonable ground for doubt that during our Lord's life on earth the scribes and Pharisees were immersed in that externalism and religious affectation which He so vividly depicted; and it was their implacable hostility to His spiritual teaching, begun at a very early period in His ministry (Mk 3[6]), that in the end brought about His crucifixion.

Mk 14[21] (|| Mt 26[24], Lk 22[22]) οὐαὶ δὲ τῷ ἀνθρώπῳ ἐκείνῳ δι' οὗ ὁ υἱὸς τοῦ ἀνθρώπου παραδίδοται; Lk. has πλὴν οὐαί, bringing out with emphasis the responsibility of Judas, who was free to act, notwithstanding the τὸ ὡρισμένον. This, which is perhaps the saddest sentence in the Gospels, was spoken without vindictiveness, although it undoubtedly reveals that our Lord was wounded to the quick by the treachery of Judas. The ἐκείνῳ seems to set him finally outside the circle of the disciples (cf. Westcott on Jn 13[27]). But this Woe is not an imprecation like Ps 109. It is not the devoting of Judas to destruction. Similarly the words which follow, καλὸν αὐτῷ εἰ οὐκ ἐγεννήθη ὁ ἄνθρωπος ἐκεῖνος, are 'not to be pressed with logical rigour' (Meyer), but are to be understood as meaning, 'Better not to have lived at all than to have lived to betray the Son of Man.' The whole saying witnesses to the anguish that our Lord felt on account of the perfidy of this false friend (cf. Ps 41[9], Jn 13[18]); and we can sympathize with Keim when he says (*Jesus of Nazara*, v. 286) that we should have to greet it as the removal of a hundred-pound weight from the heart of Christendom if the treachery of Judas could be proved to have had no existence. But this is as impossible as to remove the burden, 'Tiberio imperitante, supplicio adfectus erat,' from the heart of mankind.

There still remain the four Woes which in Lk 6[24-26] are set over against the four Beatitudes in

* Ch. 7 of the *Assumption of Moses* (not later than A.D. 30), which has been supposed to refer to the Pharisees (Hastings' *DB*, Extra Vol. 53[a]), is more probably a description of the Sadducees (Charles, *Encyc. Bibl.* i. 236).

vv.[20-23]. Their authenticity, as well as that of the Beatitudes in their Lukan form, is called in question by many distinguished scholars (Hastings' *DB*, Ext. Vol. 16; *Encyc. Bibl.* iv. 4383), but on grounds that are very far from convincing. The objection taken to the Woes from their being omitted in Mt. is not of much weight. The data for determining the precise relation between the sermons in Mt. and Lk. are wanting. Each of the writers may have had before him a different report of the same Sermon; or there may have been two similar but different Sermons, reported in two distinct documents, of which the one was used by Mt. and the other by Luke. In either case, the omission of the Woes in Mt. would be sufficiently accounted for (cf. Sanday, *Expositor*, 1891 (i.), 311 ff.; Loisy, *Le Discours sur la Montagne*, quoted in *Expositor*, 1904 (ii.), 103). The external form in which the Woes (and also the Beatitudes) are set forth illustrates our Lord's method of teaching 'by aiming at the greatest clearness in the briefest compass' (Wendt, *Teaching*, i. 130, 134; cf. ii. 68); the characteristics stated were comprehensive and significant enough to enable His hearers to understand who were the persons intended. When He began by saying, 'Blessed are ye poor: for yours is the kingdom of God,' He gave His hearers the key to the meaning of the other utterances which followed. For 'the poor' (the *ăniyyīm*) was a term that had long had an ethical and spiritual connotation (cf. Driver, art. 'Poor' in Hastings' *DB* iv. 19, 20; Harnack, *What is Christianity?* 92); and this would prevent our Lord's utterances from being interpreted in a materialistic sense. See artt. EBIONISM, POOR, POVERTY, WEALTH.

In our opinion it is more probable that the Woes are authentic than that they are inferences from our Lord's teaching (Bruce, *Kingdom of God*, 10), or that they 'arose in consequence of the affliction of the persecuted Christians' (Meyer, *Com. on Lk.*, p. 55), or that they 'were constructed for the purpose of strengthening and interpreting the Beatitudes, after the model of Dt 27[15ff.], Is 5[8ff.]' (Holtzmann, *Hand-Commentar*, 104). In view of the social conditions that exist at the present day, can it be said that their admonition is unneeded, or that they are not still living utterances? See also artt. BEATITUDE and SERMON ON THE MOUNT; and cf. Moulton, art. 'Synoptic Studies' in *Expositor* for August 1906.

JAMES DONALD.

WOLF.—See ANIMALS in vol. i. p. 65[a].

WOMAN.—The relation of Christ to woman is one of the most interesting and one of the most difficult topics in the Gospels. In order to estimate it aright it will be necessary to say something of the position of woman at the time when our Lord was born. In the East generally, the penal code of Babylon well describes her abject humiliation: 'If a husband say unto his wife, Thou art not my wife, he shall pay half a mina and be free. But if a woman repudiate her husband, she shall be drowned in the river.' And her position was not much better in Judæa, where any, even the most frivolous, pretext could be given for divorce. 'The Jewish Law unquestionably allowed divorce on almost any ground' (Edersheim, *Life and Times*, ii. 333). The school of Hillel declared it a sufficient ground for divorce if a woman had spoiled her husband's dinner. In Greece the dignity of married life was very inadequately appreciated; even Socrates invites the courtesan Aspasia to talk with him 'as to how she might ply her occupation with most profit.' In Rome there were signs of better things. There was always a halo over the old Roman matron, and though time dissipated this, and divorce was so common that Seneca tells us that ladies reckoned their ages not by the consuls, but by the number of their husbands,* yet women were gradually acquiring more and more influence and being more widely educated. In parts of the Roman Empire, especially in Macedonia, 'her social position was higher than in most parts of the civilized world. At Philippi, at Thessalonica and Bercea, the women—in some cases certainly, in all probably, ladies of birth and rank—take an active part with the Apostle (Paul). . . . The extant Macedonian inscriptions seem to assign to the sex a higher social influence than is common among the civilized nations of antiquity.'† But however this position might vary in different parts of the Empire, it was clearly exceptional for the relation of woman to man to be other than a degrading one. The many exceptions only draw attention to the prevailing feeling.

This relation was necessarily profoundly modified by our Lord's birth of the Virgin Mother. This fact, though it could have been known to only a very few during His lifetime, had nevertheless its own particular bearing. It brought Mary into a prominence which otherwise would have been unaccountable. It is true that Joseph may have died when our Lord was a child or before He began His ministry, but even this does not fully account for the position the mother occupies in the Gospels. It is not much we learn, for we know it was her habit to ponder over and keep to herself the secrets connected with His early life (Lk 2$^{19. 51}$), but that one scene at the village wedding (Jn 2) is sufficient to give us a clear conception of her importance. She alone knew how great He was, and how wonderful the destiny that was promised Him. And yet she was not so overwhelmed by its greatness as to lose her own personality. The ordinary Oriental mother would not have presumed to guide or direct the life of one so mysteriously born and whose future was so infinitely great. But she has so long been accustomed to suggest, if not to direct, that it is natural for her, when she sees an opportunity for the display of His power and the satisfaction of a need, to point it out. The reply, seemingly so harsh to us, only marks out her position the more clearly. The words, 'Woman, what have I to do with thee? mine hour is not yet come,' could not have been said to one who had occupied but a subservient position in the home; on the contrary, they suggest that for many years she had been accustomed to speak freely as to her wishes for Him, and that this time was now over. From this it may be inferred that our Lord rejoiced in the true development of womanhood, was glad that the mother should not be a mere drudge or slave, but one occupying a definite position with definite duties and responsibilities. Further, it is clear from her question that He had not checked her interest in the wider events of the world and the Kingdom of God. A veil will always rest over the frequent communings between the Mother and the Son, but it is quite clear from the use of the expression 'mine hour,' that she had been led to think of and desire that time of manifestation when His Personality should be revealed. From the beginning, even before His birth, her mind had often been occupied with that revelation from the spiritual world in which the angel had spoken of a 'throne' and a 'kingdom' (Lk 1$^{32. 33}$). Her mind, then, was not to be confined to the limited sphere of the household duties of the peasant's home. At the same time, it is clear that the natural desire, even in one so humble and lowly as she was, to have some share in the events which would lead to the bringing in of the Kingdom, was not to be

gratified. Her part lay in the careful training, educating, and helping of that great Life which was entrusted to her.

It is singular, and some have thought that it was designed with a view to checking the Mariolatry which in the years to come was to dominate a large section of the Church, that Jesus refuses to allow the unique distinction which Mary certainly had in being the mother of the world's Redeemer to weigh against the worth of religious character. It was natural that one who recognized the beauty of His character and the power of His words should say, 'Blessed be the womb that bare thee, and the breasts that thou didst suck' (Lk 11^{27}); but the answer, whilst admitting the blessing, pointed to a higher one within the reach of all. 'Yea rather, blessed are they that hear the word of God and keep it' (v.^{28}). This teaching is akin to that He gave when some one directed His attention to the fact that His mother and brethren were waiting to see Him. 'Who is my mother, and who are my brethren?'—He cried—and then stretching forth His hand towards His disciples, He said, 'Behold my mother and my brethren! For whosoever shall do the will of my Father which is in heaven, he is my brother, and sister, and mother' (Mt 12$^{47ff.}$). From this it is clear that whilst He gave her, who was blessed indeed amongst women in being His mother, full opportunities for the development of her mind and spirit, never checking during those thirty years those natural desires to know all that He would tell her of the Kingdom of which the angel had spoken to her, yet He chiefly valued in her the growth of those spiritual graces which had led to her being selected for the high position she held. And nothing is more remarkable than the response she gave. During those three years she almost disappears from sight; and when at the very last she is seen beside the cross, her attitude expresses that dignity, reserve, and self-control which she had learned of Him. When the great tragedy is being enacted, and the greatest possible excitement prevails, she, like her Divine Son, maintains an attitude of quiet self-restraint. The Oriental, even the Jewish, mother would have been prostrate, with dishevelled hair and garments; Mary is found 'standing' (Jn 19^{25}). There is no mention of words, not even of tears. Silently and quietly at the direction of her Son she leaves the cross, though we know that a sword was at the time piercing her through and through.

We have given much time to the study of the Virgin Mother because she was the only woman really educated by Christ, in the sense that St. John and St. Peter were, and we see in the little that is told of her what a true woman ought to be. The relation of Christ to the other women of the Gospels is just what we should expect from our knowledge of His relation to His mother. There is a freedom which surprises even His disciples (Jn 4^{27}), and a readiness to help which laid His character open to misconception (Lk 7^{39}). There is also the most delicate sensitiveness to the inner consciousness of shame in the sinner which at once wins confidence. His hatred of the sin never dominates over His love of the sinner. Simon was right in feeling that a prophet who knew the character of the woman who had intruded into his house would never have allowed her such close fellowship as the Saviour allowed. None but He, the sinless, could have done so. Again, none but He would have shown such patience as was seen in His treatment of the woman of Samaria (Jn 4). When He makes it plain that He knows her sin, and she changes the subject, He does not refuse to follow her, but makes the very controversy she introduces a means of spiritual help. It was this combination of strength and tenderness, of respect

* Dill, *Roman Society from Nero to Marcus Aurelius*, pp. 77–80.
† Lightfoot, *Ep. to the Philippians*, pp. 55–56.

for the individuality of the soul and yet desire to disentangle it from its sins, that gave Him just that same pre-eminent place amongst the women as amongst the men of His day. They were glad to be of what assistance they could to His work, and ministered of their substance (Lk 8³). It is characteristic that whilst they show a courage which surpasses that of the Twelve, they also show a wealth of devotion which is unintelligible to them. The presence of some near the cross, where they would be exposed to insults and rudeness, is as remarkable as St. Mary's gift of the alabaster cruse of ointment in the last week of His life. They respond more readily and easily to the power of His words and Personality. From Martha our Lord obtains a confession, even fuller and more far-reaching than that of St. Peter (Jn 11²⁴⁻²⁷). And from the heathen Canaanitish woman He received one of the most remarkable illustrations of faith, the woman's insight penetrating beyond the words to the love which lay underneath them (Mt 15²²ff·, Mk 7²⁵ff·).

The great respect in which Jesus held the position of woman, the high dignity He attached to it, is shown not only by His actions and words, but by the new sanctity which He gave to marriage. The words, 'The twain shall become one flesh' (Mt 19⁵=Mk 10³), placed the wife at once on a level with the husband, and made the divorces that were so common impossible. Directly this teaching was received, it was impossible that woman should be deprived of her right as wife on the flimsiest excuse, or without any excuse at all. The revolution such a declaration made is realized only when we hear the comment of the spiritually minded disciples, 'If the case of the man is so with his wife, it is not expedient to marry' (Mt 19¹⁰). That woman had a position in life of equal importance with that of man is made plain by the whole story of the Gospels : Anna, Elisabeth, the Virgin Mary, Martha, Mary, and Mary Magdalene rivalling in their own spheres St. Peter, St. John, St. James, St. Andrew. Without the part played by woman, that story would have been altogether incomplete.

One other suggestion as to the influence of woman which St. Matthew gives us is as interesting as it is unexpected. The dream of Pilate's wife is an evidence of the power that Christ's life and teaching exercised beyond the narrow circle of Jewish thought. Pilate, governor though he is, neither hears nor sees anything, and even when face to face with Christ is only puzzled not convinced. His wife, on the other hand, is deeply interested in all that she hears. Her mind is full of the doings of the Prophet of Nazareth. Her sleep is disturbed. She wakes frightened, and so convinced of the greatness of the issue her husband is trying, that she dares to interfere, though without success (Mt 27¹⁹). Not too much can be made of this ; but it is an indication, which the Gospel narrative emphasizes, that women are more susceptible to religious impressions than men, and are ready to make larger sacrifices. As women ministered at the Birth, the Presentation in the Temple, and during those early years when His mother was His chief teacher, so they ministered at the Entombment, when they anointed His body ; at the Resurrection, when they carried the news to the frightened disciples ; and at the Ascension, when they with the Apostles and the rest of His disciples received His blessing. Cf. next article.

LITERATURE. — Edersheim, *LT* ; Dill, *Roman Society from Nero to Marcus Aurelius* ; *PRE*³, art. 'Familie und Ehe' ; Brace, *Gesta Christi* ; Church, *Pascal, and other Serm.* 264 ; Moore, *God is Love*, 184 ; Lightfoot, *Serm. on Special Occasions*, 220 ; Gunsaulus, *Paths to the City of God*, 232.

G. H. S. WALPOLE.

WOMANLINESS.—Christianity is distinguished for the honour it assigns, the liberty it allows to woman. 'Christianity raises woman from the slavish position which she held, both in Judaism and in heathendom, to her true moral dignity and importance, makes her an heir of the same salvation with man, and opens to her a field for the noblest and loveliest virtue' (Schaff's *Apostolic Christianity*, p. 441 f.). The duties of husbands are, according to St. Peter (1 P 3⁷), to be regulated by a recognition of the principle that their wives are 'also joint heirs of the grace of life.' In the Christian society 'the conventional distinctions of religious caste or of social rank, even the natural distinction of sex, are banished,' for 'there can be neither Jew nor Greek, there can be neither bond nor free, there can be no male and female ; for ye are all one man in Christ Jesus' (Gal 3²⁸). Lightfoot *in loco* quotes a saying of Jesus from the Apocryphal Gospel of the Egyptians, which may be founded on this verse—'Being asked by Salome when His kingdom should come, He is reported to have answered, "When the two shall be one, and the male with the female, neither male nor female."' This mystical saying has its fulfilment in the character of Jesus. For the characteristic of Jesus Christ, and so the regulative principle of Christian morality, is completeness, symmetry, harmony, balance. Other men are known and loved for this or that excellence ; but of Jesus Christ, with respect to His personal perfection, we can say what was said of Shakspeare with regard to his artistic pre-eminence, 'His speciality is everything.' Manhood in its wholeness and fulness is found in Him, alike wide in its range and lofty in its reach. Hence Jesus Christ is not a pattern merely for one sex, or one age, or one time, or one temperament, or one class. In this sense, too, there is in Him neither male nor female, bond nor free, Jew nor Greek, learned nor unlearned.

The sphere of woman is the home, not the world. Man lives in effort and conflict. 'But woman is at home in the region of feeling and affection, and she finds her highest vocation in the cultivation of those loves and sympathies that make home the dearest spot on earth.' Man, being thus active and even combative, develops 'pertinacity and self-assertion ; whereas the receptive nature of woman manifests itself rather in patient endurance and tender devotion to the service of loved ones. Her emotions dominate her intellect ; her judgment to a certain extent is biassed by her feelings. On the other hand, where moral as well as intellectual considerations come into view, woman's judgment is likely to be as just as that of man, whose decisions are frequently based on grounds of reason alone' (Bruce, *The Formation of Christian Character*, p. 57 f.). May we find any such signs of womanliness in the character or teaching of Jesus?

Jesus assigned great importance to marriage and family, the sanctity and unity of the home. Although His vocation required His abandonment of home (Jn 2⁴, Mk 3³³· ³⁴), and He required of His disciples also the same renunciation (Lk 14²⁶), yet He missed the shelter and peace of home (Mt 8²⁰), and recognized the greatness of the sacrifice involved (Mt 19²⁹). His denunciation of the lax traditions of the elders regarding divorce (Mt 19³⁻⁹) and the duty of children to their parents (Mk 7⁹⁻¹³ was in defence of the home. It is supremely significant that love, the grace of the home, and not justice, the virtue of the State, is made the first and greatest commandment (Mk 12²⁹⁻³¹). The child is nearer, means more, to the mother than to the father ; and Jesus understood and cared for children (Mt 11¹⁶ 18²⁻³ 19¹³⁻¹⁵). Does not the modesty of the woman appear in His reference to the lustful glance (Mt 5[28]), and His stooping to write upon the ground when the woman taken in her sin stood before Him (Jn 8[6])? Jesus understood the heart of a woman in penitence (Lk 7[47]) and in gratitude (Jn 12[7, 8]). His defence of the offering of love shows not only His active but also His receptive affectionateness, His yearning for, as well as bestowal of, the generosities of the heart. He was not only intensely emotional, but quick in expressing His emotions (Jn 11[33, 38], Mk 7[34] 8[12], Jn 11[35], Lk 13[34] 19[41], Mt 23[37]). His tenderness, gentleness, patience, and forbearance are more distinctively feminine than masculine graces. In His resignation and obedience to His Father's will (Mt 11[26, 29]) is there not a womanly rather than a manly submissiveness? The prominence He gives in the Beatitudes to the passive graces of endurance rather than the active virtues of endeavour (Mt 5[3-10]) vindicates the distinctive excellence of womanhood. His teaching about non-resistance (Mt 5[38-42]), so much misunderstood and neglected, can be better appreciated by women than by men, for such patience under wrong has entered into their life more than into that of men. The mind of Jesus was intuitive rather than ratiocinative; His moral judgment was swift and sure; His spiritual discernment direct; and these are characteristic of women rather than of men.

Doubtless it was this *womanliness* in Jesus that attracted and attached so many women to Him during His earthly ministry: and they received from Him a loving welcome such as they did not find in any other religious teacher of the age. His disciples were astonished that He was speaking to the woman of Samaria (Jn 4[27]), and doubtless the prejudices of many were offended by His action regarding women. His defence of the sinful woman and of Mary has been already noted. 'We have a lovely group of female disciples and friends around the Lord: Mary, the wife of Clopas; Salome, the mother of James and John; Mary of Bethany, who sat at Jesus' feet; her busy and hospitable sister Martha; Mary of Magdala, whom the Lord healed of a demoniacal possession; the sinner, who washed His feet with her tears of penitence and wiped them with her hair; and all the noble women who ministered to the Son of Man in His earthly poverty with the gifts of their love (Lk 8[3], Mt 27[55], Mk 15[41]), lingered last around His Cross (Jn 19[25]), and were first at His open sepulchre on the morning of the resurrection (Mt 28[1], Jn 20[1])' [Schaff, *op. cit.* p. 442]). The reverence that the mother of Jesus has properly inspired has given to womanhood a glory, and to woman a position and influence in the Christian Church, never before and nowhere else recognized. To the instances given above of the relation of Jesus to women we may add His compassion for the widow of Nain (Lk 7[13]), and His commendation of the widow's mites (Mk 12[43, 44]). His treatment of a woman on three occasions appears harsh, but a consideration of the circumstances in each case removes this impression. His rebuke to His mother at Cana (Jn 2[4]) expresses His dread of any human interference with His fulfilment of His Divine vocation (cf. the rebuke of Peter, Mt 16[23]); His repulse of the Syrophœnician mother (Mk 7[27]) was His own indignant protest against Jewish exclusiveness; His requirement that the woman healed by touching His garment should confess her deed was no violence done to her sense of modesty, but was intended to replace the uncertainty of a cure snatched unawares by the assurance of healing willingly bestowed (Mk 5[34]). What Christ has been to and done for women throughout the history of Christendom, and what women have suffered and accomplished for His Church and Kingdom on earth, afford abundant and conclusive evidence of the *womanliness* of Jesus in presenting in His character all womanly grace as well as manly virtue, and offering in His salvation what meets the deepest needs, and fulfils the loftiest hopes of womanhood in all lands and ages. See also WOMAN.

ALFRED E. GARVIE.

WONDERS.—The two terms 'signs' and 'wonders' are frequently joined in the OT, and this usage is carried over into the NT. The word τέρας, 'wonder,' never occurs in the NT except in connexion with σημεῖον, 'sign' (wh. see). The Heb. correlatives were מופת and את. Jesus used the conjoined terms twice in His recorded sayings—once when He foretold that false prophets would come and 'show great signs and wonders' (Mk 13[22], Mt 24[24]), and once when He complained that the people demanded such things of Him before they would have faith in Him—'Except ye see signs and wonders, ye will in no wise believe' (Jn 4[48]). The word τέρας occurs nowhere else in the Gospels. Elsewhere in the NT it is found once in a quotation from Joel to represent the marvels wrought by Jehovah in the heaven (Ac 2[19]), and twelve times in reference to miracles wrought by Moses (7[36]), by Jesus (2[22]), by the man of sin (2 Th 2[9]), and by the Apostles and early missionaries (Ac 2[43] 4[30] 5[12] 6[8] 14[3] 15[12], Ro 15[19], 2 Co 12[12], He 2[4]). From the use of the word made by Jesus we might conclude that He did not esteem signs and wonders very highly, and that He freely granted that they were possible to false prophets as well as to Himself. In Origen (*c. Celsum*) we find practically the same attitude of thought. Origen is disposed to concede that signs and wonders are wrought among the heathen.

'Now, in order to grant that there did exist a healing spirit named Æsculapius, who used to cure the bodies of men, I would say to those who are astonished at such an occurrence, that since the cure of bodies is a thing indifferent, *and a matter within the reach not merely of the good, but also of the bad*, you must show that they who practise healing are in no respect wicked' (iii. 25 [Migne, vol. xi. col. 948]).

On the other hand, Celsus is willing to acknowledge that signs and wonders were wrought by Jesus, but he thinks the inference from these is unwarranted. They are to him no proof of Deity. He compares them to—

'the feats performed by those who have been taught by Egyptians, who in the middle of the market-place, in return for a few obols, will impart the knowledge of their most venerated arts, and will expel demons from men, and dispel diseases, and invoke the souls of heroes, and exhibit expensive banquets and tables and dishes and dainties having no real existence, and who will put in motion, as if alive, what are not really living animals, but which have only the appearance of life. Then he asks: "Since, then, these persons can perform such feats, shall we of necessity conclude that they are sons of God, or must we admit that they are the proceedings of wicked men under the influence of an evil spirit?"' (i. 68).

It was easy for Origen to answer that Jesus never wrought His signs and wonders only for show, as magicians did, and that His constant aim was the reformation of character, as that of the magicians most evidently was not. Then he adds:

'How should not He, who by the miracles which He did induced those who beheld the excellent results to undertake the reformation of their characters, manifest Himself not only to His genuine disciples, but also to others, as a pattern of most virtuous life, in order that His disciples might devote themselves to the work of instructing men in the will of God, and that the others, after being *more fully instructed by His word and character than by His miracles* as to how they were to direct their lives, might in all their conduct have a constant reference to the good pleasure of the universal God?' (i. 68 [Migne, vol. xi. col. 788]).

Origen seems to have caught the very mind of the Master at this point. Jesus made use of signs and wonders to authenticate His mission, but His chief emphasis was always upon His 'word and character' rather than upon His miracles. Both Origen and Celsus, however, as these passages show, are willing to grant that signs and wonders were wrought by Jesus and by false prophets alike. Origen calls attention to the fact that Jesus, as indeed the entire NT, never calls miracles by the name τέρατα alone, but always joins this to some other term suggesting higher things (*in Joan.* xviii. 60 [Migne, vol. xiv. col. 521]). The τέρας was to the heathen merely a portent or prodigy, something unusual and extraordinary, something strange and abnormal, or, as Augustine put it, 'quidquid arduum aut insolitum supra spem vel facultatem mirantis apparet,' and more closely, 'quædam sunt quæ solam faciunt admirationem' (*de Utilitate credendi*, cap. xvi. [Migne, vol. xlii. col. 90]). Jesus could not be content to allow this name to stand alone for any of His miracles. It had to do merely with the outward effect or the temporary impression caused by the marvel, and some other term was added to show that the marvel was an exhibition of Divine power and a sign of a Divine presence among men. The wonder caught the attention and impressed the memory, and was subservient to the interests of the Kingdom in attracting men to listen and investigate, to hear and be saved. Jesus used it for an immediate individual benefit, but always with an eye to a further spiritual end. For the discussion of the nature and credibility of miracles in general, see art. MIRACLES.

D. A. HAYES.

WORD.—(λόγος, ῥῆμα) is employed in the Gospels in a large variety of senses : (1) articulate utterance of any kind ; (2) the inspired word of Scripture (cf. Mk 7[13]—'making the word of God of none effect through your traditions'); (3) a Divine message generally (Lk 3[2] 'The word of God came to John in the wilderness,' so Lk 4[4] 8[11] 11[28]) ; (4) the 'word of the kingdom,' *i.e.* the gospel message (Mt 13[19ff.], Mk 16[20], Lk 5[1]) ; (5) Christ's word of authority (Lk 4[36] 'What a word is this, that even the winds and the sea obey him'); (6) in the Prologue to the Fourth Gospel, Christ Himself is the 'Word made flesh' (see LOGOS).

The peculiar significance attached to the spoken 'word' is to be explained in the light of Hebrew usage. In the OT, as in all primitive thought, a word is something more than an articulate sound with a given import. It is endowed with a certain power and reality. It carries with it some portion of the life and personality of the speaker. This is true more especially of a word spoken by God. Such a word is instinct with the Divine will, and effects by its own inherent power the thing which it indicates. 'As the rain cometh down and the snow from heaven, so shall my word be that goeth forth out of my mouth ; it shall not return unto me void, but it shall accomplish that which I please' (Is 55[10f.]). The 'word' delivered to the prophets is here conceived as an active power, which will bring about its own fulfilment. So in His creation and government of the world, God effects His purpose by His 'word' (Gn 1, Ps 33[6.9] 107[20]). It is regarded not simply as a commandment, but as a vital energy which is sent forth from God and realizes His will.

The references in the Gospels are coloured throughout by this Hebrew conception. Even where Divine utterance is not in question, a value is ascribed to 'words' which does not belong to them according to our modern modes of thought. 'For every idle word that a man speaks, he shall give account in the judgment ;—for by thy words thou shalt be justified, and by thy words thou shalt be condemned' (Mt 12[36f.]). Jesus regards the most casual word as more than wasted breath. It is a spiritual force, and the man who sets it free is responsible for the good or evil which it produces. A similar estimate of the value of words underlies the many injunctions against profane, or foolish, or thoughtless, or unkind speech (Mt 5[22. 34-37], Lk 12[10], Mt 12[34]). Such 'words' have all the significance of wicked actions. Coming 'from within a

man,' they express his mind and character even more truly than deeds, and will bear witness of him in the Judgment.

The influence of the OT conception appears more clearly, however, in the allusions to Christ's own 'word.' It is the vehicle of His wonder-working power. It has virtue in it to heal diseases and to quiet the winds and the sea. In several passages the 'word' is explained as one of kingly authority, which had might over the spiritual agencies at work in nature (cf. Lk 4[36], Mt 8[16]). But the radical idea is undoubtedly that of a 'word with power' (Lk 4[32]) analogous to the Divine word. To give effect to His will, Jesus had only to utter it ; the word that went out from Him was itself 'quick and powerful,' and acted in His stead. In this sense also we must interpret the references to the message of Jesus as 'the word.' As thus described, the gospel is something more than the Christian teaching or the proclamation of the Messianic Kingdom. The idea is suggested that a new power had entered the world through Jesus, and communicated itself in His spoken message. Thus in the parable of the Sower, the word is compared to seed which contains in itself wonderful potentialities. All that is required of men is the right disposition of heart ; the message, once received into the 'good ground,' will henceforth work of itself, with a living and ever-increasing power.

In the Fourth Gospel, more especially, the allusions to the words of Jesus have everywhere a pregnant meaning. 'The words that I speak unto you are spirit and life' (Jn 6[63]) ; 'Now ye are clean through the word which I have spoken unto you' (15[3]) ; 'He that heareth my word hath everlasting life' (5[24]) ;—in such sayings and many others the idea of whole-hearted assimilation of the teaching of Jesus is certainly present, but it is by no means the only, or the central, idea. It is indeed characteristic of the Fourth Gospel that Jesus says little by way of positive teaching. He Himself, in His own Person, is the revelation, and the words ascribed to Him have reference mainly to His supreme worth as the Light of the world— the Way, the Truth, and the Life. Because they thus give expression to His Divine claim, they in a manner represent Himself. To accept the words is to receive Jesus, in His life-giving power, into one's heart (cf. 15[7] 'If ye abide in me and my words abide in you').

It has often been suggested that the peculiar emphasis on the words of Jesus in the Fourth Gospel is intended to illustrate the thesis of the Prologue that He was Himself the Word made flesh. The absence of the Logos theory from the body of the Gospel would thus be counterbalanced by the many references to the 'words.' Against this view, however, it may be urged : (1) that no consistent rule is traceable in the use of λόγος and ῥῆμα, as might have been expected if the writer were working out some definite idea ; (2) that λόγος in the Prologue bears a twofold significance ('word' and 'reason') which can nowhere be discerned in the later references. The more probable conclusion is that the value assigned to the words of Jesus is connected, not so much with the specific Logos doctrine, as with the general conception that Jesus was one in nature with God. His words were therefore of the same quality as the Divine creative word. They were 'spirit and life' (6[63]).

LITERATURE.—Smend, *Alttest. Theol.* p. 87 f. (1893); Wendt, *Die Lehre Jesu* (1901) ; H. Holtzmann, *Neutest. Theol.* ii. 396 f. (1897); Titius, *Die Johann. Ans-hauung der Seligkeit*, 70 f. (1900) ; J. Ker, *Serm.* i. 1 ; J. H. Newman, *Parochial and Plain Serm.* v. 29 ; F. W. Robertson, *Serm.* iv. 145 ; R. W. Church, *Pascal, and other Serm.* 255.

E. F. SCOTT.

WORK.—See ACTIVITY, LABOUR.

WORLD (κόσμος).—**1.** The underlying significance of the term κόσμος is that of *order*. Its probable derivation is from a root κομιδ, which appears in Lat. *comptus* and in our 'comb.' This order, regularity, neatness receives the widest illustration in classical usage. Thus κόσμος includes the idea of decency of behaviour (Æsch. *Ag.* 521, cf. Soph. *Aj.* 293), of constitutional government (Thuc. iv. 76), of elegance of attire (Hdt. iii. 123), and so, by just transference, of the world or universe (Plat. *Tim.* 27 A, cf. Arist. *Cœl.* i. 10), as exhibiting perfection of arrangement, and standing in eternal contrast with chaos. In this, its widest application, it became employed by all writers on natural philosophy, though the meaning oscillates, with some uncertainty, between the earth and the universe generally (see Liddell and Scott, *s.v.*, from which the quotations are taken). It is interesting to observe that *ordo* in Latin does not, as might have been expected, stand as an equivalent for κόσμος. Its equivalent in Latin is *mundus* (cf. Sanskr. *mund*), the root idea of which again is cleanliness, neatness, or order. Thus both the Latin and the Greek pass through, with a singular exactness of analogy, the same transferences of meaning, so that Cicero (*Univ.* 10) identifies κόσμος and *mundus* in that widest application of the term above referred to (see Lewis and Short's *Dict. s.v.* 'Mundus'). There is, however, a further transference of meaning in a use of *mundus* by classical writers not found in the corresponding use of κόσμος. It is employed (Hor. *Sat.* i. 3. 112, cf. Luc. *Pharsal.* v. 469), but somewhat rarely, in a social sense to signify mankind, whereas this application is not given to κόσμος except in so-called Alexandrine Greek. In a word, the conception of order covers every departmental application of the Greek κόσμος and its Latin equivalent.

2. If proof on such an issue were needed by students, the use of the word κόσμος would strikingly show the original way in which NT writers handle and apply such terms. Certainly, to the ancients, with the word κόσμος the vision of the figure of order would be manifest in thought. Generally speaking, in the NT the ancient conception falls so far into the background as sometimes to vanish. But what the word has lost in one way it has gained in other ways, as will be seen upon a brief examination of its employment generally in NT literature.

It is interesting, however, to note that, in the transferred applications of the word, this literature follows the lines of classical usage. Thus κόσμος is used of women's attire (1 P 3³), of the universe (Ro 1²⁰), of the earth (Mt 4⁸ [cf. Lk 4⁵ τῆς οἰκουμένης] 16²⁶), and of human society (Jn 12⁹). In such illustrations we do not part company with the radical idea of 'order,' but it is only faintly made apparent.

In the Synoptics the term is rarely employed, and the student of the AV must be put on his guard against supposing that, in all cases where the tr. 'world' is used, it stands for κόσμος in the original. In some six cases it stands for αἰών, and in two for ἡ γῆ οἰκουμένη. But, as any confusion is sufficiently checked by RVm, the point need not be pursued here. The use of the word, rare as it is in the Synoptics, is largely free from Johannine or Pauline sentiment on the idea. It is difficult to find a passage in them in which the term is used absolutely *in malam partem*, as it is found not only in the writings of St. John and St. Paul, but also in those of St. Peter and St. James. In the parable of the Wheat and the Tares (Mt 13²⁴⁻⁴³) the 'world' appears in no dark or ominous colouring. It is not its cares, but the cares of the age (αἰών, Mk 4¹⁹), that choke the word so as to render it unfruitful. When our Lord in the Sermon on the Mount speaks of His disciples as the light of the world (Mk 5¹⁴), we find the figure interpreted by the parallel expression which precedes it : 'Ye are the salt of the earth' (Mt 5¹³). To declare that the world needs purification and illumination is not a wholesale condemnation of the world. There is in the Synoptics no violence of contrast between it and the Divine society. In its rare occurrences in the Synoptics the world is a sphere in which Christ's disciples live and move and have their being. For them it has its pitfalls (Mt 18⁷), its characteristic dangers, but nowhere does it appear as wholly or inherently evil.

3. When one turns from the Synoptics to St. John's writings, for here it is impossible to separate his Gospel from his letters, the contrast appears startling. Instead of a rare appearance of the term, we find that it occurs some eighty times in the Gospel, and twenty-two times in the First Epistle (A. Plummer, Com. on the Gospel in *Cambridge Bible*). And with this frequently comes a change in meaning, a change, however, which in the Gospel appears gradual and climactic. For in the Prologue of the Fourth Gospel the term appears with the same lack of colour in which it is painted in the Synoptic Gospels.

The world is indeed seen to be beset by the grave fault of indifference to its own darkness. The light came, but it was not recognized. Yet in this lack of welcome His own were involved (Jn 1¹¹, cf. 8¹²). The testimony of the Baptist advances the issue a step farther. His recognition of Jesus as the Lamb of God (1²⁹·³⁶) implies his recognition of the purpose of His mission as the world's Saviour from its sin. Later, our Lord's testimony to Nicodemus informs him of the gracious fact of His love towards the world. His deliberate intention in regard to the world was not its condemnation but its salvation. Life, not death, through Him was the Father's eternal purpose (3¹⁶·¹³, cf. 4⁴² 12⁴⁷). Through the type of the manna, our Lord brings Himself, if it may be so expressed, into still closer touch with the world. He is the Bread of heaven which gives life to the world (6³³). Later, with more awful explicitness, the bread is identified with His flesh, and its offering is on the world's behalf (v.⁵¹).

So gracious, indeed, are the Lord's utterances in regard to the world, that twice the group of the disciples appeared unable to distinguish themselves from it. They could not understand in the earlier stage of their discipleship why any manifestation of Jesus should not be made on equal terms to the world as to themselves (7⁴, cf. 14²²). They omitted to see that a manifestation of Himself could be made only through the medium of love. A difference, therefore, not only in point of time but also in degree of training, explains any seeming inconsistency in our Lord's teaching in respect of the attitude of the world towards His own. At an earlier stage He declared that the world could not hate His followers,—there was nothing then to excite hostility either by way of their belief or their love (7⁷). At a later stage the parting of the ways had come. His own had made their final choice. With the choice came the world's hatred. The persecution which He endured was to be theirs also (15¹⁷⁻²⁰). All turned upon the identity of themselves with Him. This once established, His own exhibited love and obedience. The world was seen as penetrated by hatred and disobedience. In this awful contrast and conflict, victory was assured for His own, and with victory would come its fruit. He was their surety. Peace and triumph were their lot through Him (16³³).

But Johannine teaching on the subject of the world cannot be regarded as complete if the First Epistle be ignored. The scope, however, of this Dictionary must limit the inquiry to general references. The doctrinal differences here are explicable, as Bp. Westcott has pointed out (*Gospel of St. John*, Introd. lxxviii), because the Gospel is related to the Epistle, as history to its comment or application; the former is throughout presupposed in the latter. 'The Lord's words in the Gospel have been moulded into aphorisms in the First Epistle'; and in the latter document the Apostle writes, conscious that the Church must be in dire conflict with the characteristic dangers and heresies of the age. It would seem reasonable to regard the teaching of the First Epistle on the world as a commentary, in particular, on our Lord's pregnant utterances on the 'convictions' of the world (Jn 16[8-11]; see Westcott, *in loco*.). In that passage, the world appears as separate from God, 'yet not past hope.' Our Lord declares there, not that He will convict the world simply as sinful, etc., but that He will show that it lacks the knowledge of what sin, righteousness, and judgment really are.

We conclude that the general teaching of St. John's Gospel on the subject of the world is that it is an order or sphere touching man's life, affecting man's life considered as apart from God; but that in the First Epistle the world is seen more darkly and ominously still: it is not merely regarded as apart from God, but as alien to Him, in direct opposition to His eternal and gracious purposes. St. John would teach us that if it is to be overcome, it must be by powers which lift us above it, and those are the twin powers of love and faith (Liddon, *Easter Sermons*, No. xxii.).

LITERATURE.—In addition to the Lexx. and Comm., J. H. Newman, *Par. and Plain Serm.* vii. (1868) p. 27; F. W. Robertson, *Serm.*, 4th ser. (1874) p. 145; A. Maclaren, *A Year's Ministry*, 1st ser. (1884) p. 83; B. F. Westcott, *The Gospel of Life* (1892), p. 20; C. J. Vaughan, *Doncaster Serm.* (1891) p. 225; R. W. Church, *Village Serm.*, 2nd ser. (1894) p. 326; Stopford A. Brooke, *The Ship of the Soul* (1898), p. 31; R. Flint, *Serm. and Addresses* (1899), p. 145. B. WHITEFOORD.

WORLDLINESS.

WORLDLINESS.—The teaching of Christianity concerning worldliness forms one of the most important parts of its practical message to mankind. And yet, more or less strongly marked at different periods, a tendency to serious misconception of this doctrine has probably existed in every generation since the days of Christ. The error into which it has led man is that of regarding the material world and whatever strictly pertains to it, as inherently evil and anti-spiritual. Such a misconception, it is true, did not originate in Christian times, but was taken over by Christianity from earlier systems of religious thought. The source from which it sprang, however, does not affect the gravity of its persistent survival; and inasmuch as the attitude of any faith to the present world must always deeply influence men's estimate of its claims, a clear apprehension of Christ's own teaching on the subject becomes of more than ordinary importance.

I. To reveal the basis of our Lord's doctrine of worldliness, we must review briefly one or two broad outlines of His message.

1. Christ's teaching concerning the existence of a spiritual realm.—Man has contact with two worlds. (*a*) Of his communion with the material universe and of the various relationships involved therein, he has by nature a vivid consciousness. This temporal world forms a realm of which, by his birth, he himself has become a part. It has for his possession a special form of life adapted to it. It reveals relationships of its own, as laying their obligation upon him—relationships to a properly constituted authority to be obeyed, and to relatives and friends to be loved. It provides also certain standards of judgment by which the various experiences of its inhabitants are deemed happy or sad, prosperous or unsuccessful. (*b*) But man has contact also with another world— the spiritual. Of his communion with this world

he has, by nature, but dim and uncertain comprehension. It was to reveal the truth concerning it that Christ came to earth. Its existence and claims form one of the principal themes of His teaching. Of this realm also it is by a birth that a man becomes a part (Jn 3[3-6]). This realm also has, adapted to it, a special form of life (6[33] 17[3]) which becomes his upon his entrance into it, and which receives its own spiritual sustenance (4[14. 32. 34] 6[35. 48-51] 7[37]). This realm also imposes certain relationships upon him; for it, no less than the other, has its sanctions of authority (Mk 11[9], Jn 12[13] 18[33-37]) and ties of kinship, both of man with God (Jn 1[12], 1 Jn 3[2]) and of man with men (Mk 3[34. 35] ∥ 10[29. 30], Jn 19[26. 27]). Moreover, this realm also possesses standards of its own by means of which its citizens estimate the events and experiences of their lives (Mt 5[3ff.]: for the contrast offered to the standards of the temporal realm, see Mt 5[10-12], and consider the force of δοξασθῆναι in Jn 13[31]). The sphere in which these spiritual relationships are acknowledged and their obligations become operative, was named by Christ the Kingdom of God (or, of Heaven), and it formed the theme even of His earliest teaching (*e.g.* Mk 1[15]). This invisible world is as real as the visible. It is clearly marked and self-contained (Jn 3[6]). Its citizens possess definite characteristics (Mk 10[15], Lk 18[16. 17]), and, as it is essentially spiritual in character (Lk 17[20. 21], Jn 4[23]), a certain fitness is necessary to those who would belong to it (Lk 9[62]). Hence it has to be definitely entered (Mt 7[13. 14], Mk 10[15] 12[34], Jn 3[3. 5]).

2. His teaching concerning communion with this spiritual world.—Now, just as man has communion with the temporal world and its life, so he may have communion with this spiritual world and its life. (*a*) Christ Himself, as man, constantly enjoyed such fellowship. The Gospel narratives reveal Him as holding converse with the Father (Mk 1[35] *et passim*; see art. COMMUNION), with angels (Mk 1[13], cf. Mt 26[53]), and with departed spirits of holy men (Mk 9[2ff.]). Indeed, this realization of His communion with the unseen realm formed the basis of His sense of mission (Lk 2[49], Jn 7[16] 8[16b. 29] 16[32]) and the source from which He derived His strength in suffering (Jn 18[11]). (*b*) And the fellowship with the spiritual realm which Christ thus exemplified in His own life upon earth, He enjoined upon His followers also (Jn 15[4ff.], cf. 6[53-55] *et passim*). While they must live before men their outward life in contact with the visible universe and its affairs, they possess also an inner life which must be lived 'in secret'—in contact with the unseen (Mt 6[1-18] 10[19. 20]).

3. The twofold communion.—Man, therefore, belongs to two worlds, and may have communion with both. But just as, possessing a twofold nature, carnal and spiritual, he knows that the spiritual is the higher, so, enjoying a twofold communion, he is to learn that the spiritual fellowship must take precedence, its realization being his supreme duty and the end of his creation. Yet, as in the freedom of his will he is able to cultivate the carnal in him at the expense of the spiritual, so too he is free, as the whole appeal of Christ's teaching presupposes, to choose for himself with which realm, the temporal or the spiritual, his fellowship shall be the more real and intense.

II. *CHRIST'S TEACHING UPON WORLDLINESS.* —**1. Christ encouraged no indifference to the claims of the temporal world.**—There is an unworldliness which so emphasizes spiritual realities as to undervalue the material universe and its lawful concerns. This attitude, which, as we have hinted, has found frequent and varied expression among His followers, derives no support from the life or teaching of Christ Himself. The beauty and charm of the visible world appealed to Him

(Mt 6[26. 28]). Its incidents furnished illustrations for His sermons (Mk 4[3], Mt 25[14]). He participated in its festivals (Jn 2[1ff.]), and contrasted Himself with one whose asceticism disparaged its good cheer (Mt 11[18. 19]). Again, the claims of this world's lawful authorities always received His ready acknowledgment. Respect for them was scrupulously evinced alike in His advice (Mk 12[17]) and in His example (Mt 17[27]). Further, in His thought, the welfare of men is by no means a merely spiritual matter. On the contrary, the social obligations imposed by His religion form one of His most constant themes. Love towards others is the very test by which His true disciples can be identified (Mt 5[43-48], cf. 1 Jn 2[9-11] 4[20] etc.), and that love is to find expression not in vapid sentiment, but in whole-hearted service (Mk 10[42ff.], Mt 22[36-39], Lk 10[30ff.]). Indeed, Christ teaches that this love and service to man are the criterion of love and service to God (Mt 25[40. 45]), while in several suggestive passages He even hints that the earthly life forms in some sense an interpretation of the spiritual life (see Mk 2[5. 10. 11], Mt 18[10]). Christ therefore calls His followers not to neglect the temporal world, much less to despise it, but to recognize that they have a function to fulfil in it by permeating every part of its life with beauty and truth (Mt 5[13-16] 13[33], Jn 17[15]). So far, indeed, is He from any underestimation of the present life, that we know of no teacher in any age whose principles, carried into effect, would so ameliorate the material condition of mankind in all its individual aspects and social relationships.

2. Christ uttered no condemnation of worldly possessions.—See art. WEALTH.

3. A false antithesis.—It is clear, therefore, that in our study of the Christian doctrine of worldliness we must eliminate what is now seen to be a false antithesis. In view of the unfortunate ambiguity in meaning both of the Greek and of the English word, it is necessary to define closely the sense in which Christianity sets the 'world' in opposition to its own life and principles. The Christian teacher has to distinguish two forms of contrast. There is the contrast of *difference* or *distinction*, and there is the contrast of *opposition*. It is in the former sense alone, as our Lord's own life and words declare, that the material is set by Christianity over against the spiritual. The contrast of *opposition* established by Christianity is never between the spiritual and the material, but always between the spiritual and the anti-spiritual. The material, it is true, may be made the instrument of the anti-spiritual; but the two are essentially distinct, and confusion between them, signally absent from the Gospel teaching, must never be condoned in its exponents. It is of the utmost significance in this connexion that our Lord deliberately refused to recognize a contrast of opposition between the powers of the heavenly and those of the earthly realm (Mk 12[13-17] ‖ Jn 6[15], cf. Ro 13[7]): the antithesis He accepted was that of the Heavenly King and 'the prince of this world' (Jn 12[31] 14[30] 16[11] in each case ὁ ἄρχων τοῦ κόσμου or ὁ τοῦ κόσμου ἄρχων). The 'world' He condemned is not the material world, in which He Himself took delight, or its claims, which He loyally acknowledged, or (in themselves) its possessions, of which He spoke with guarded moderation, but a certain spirit of the world fundamentally antagonistic to man's highest life, and the men in whom that spirit has established its abode (cf. the careful definition in 1 Jn 2[16] and that implicit in Jn 12[31]). It is between Christ's Kingdom and the 'world' in *this* sense that there is opposition, and in this case the opposition is final and complete (Jn 15[18. 19] 16[33]—note the terms of the contrast, ἐν τῷ κόσμῳ and ἐν ἐμοί—17[14], 1 Jn 2[15] 3[13] 4[4-6]).

4. The consequent meaning of worldliness.—The accurate recognition of Christ's attitude to the temporal world at once yields the accurate conception of worldliness. Worldliness will clearly consist in devotion to 'the world,' not in *any* sense of that ambiguous term, but in the particular sense in which Christ revealed it to be evil. Inasmuch, therefore, as 'the world,' in the only signification in which He condemned it, is the spirit of antagonism (whether expressed as a principle or personified in individuals) to His spiritual kingdom, worldliness must be the possession of this spirit, and the practice of worldliness must be its manifestation. In view of persistent misconception of the teaching of Christianity on this subject, clearness at this point, even at the risk of repetition, is of the utmost importance. Worldliness does not consist in a love of the temporal world and its concerns, for between the Kingdom and 'the world' in this sense Christ acknowledges no necessary opposition, and a man may so use both realms as to fulfil the rightful claims of each without setting them in any inevitable antithesis. Nor does worldliness lie in the performance or non-performance of any particular actions (Mk 2[18. 24] 3[4] 7[5. 8. 15. 21], Lk 11[39-41], Jn 5[10] 7[23. 24] *et passim*); for, since it is the possession of a certain spirit, the most scrupulous punctiliousness in outward conduct may coexist with the deepest unspirituality (Mt 27[6], Jn 12[5. 6] 18[28] 19[31]; cf. the significant pronouncement in Mt 21[28-31]), and the truest unworldliness with apparent indifference to its formal expression (11[18. 19]). It is quite true that a love of the temporal world and indulgence in particular actions closely associated with it, may constitute manifestations of worldliness. A realm not evil in itself may easily become the medium of evil, and so, owing to an undue emphasis, man's fellowship with the temporal world may, both by its positive and by its negative influence, prove injurious to his fellowship with the spiritual. Such a misuse of the two realms inevitably turns the contrast of distinction between them into one of opposition. This result, however, is reached not because of any anti-spiritual quality intrinsic in the material realm itself, but through the employment of that realm as a vehicle of the anti-spiritual. The essence of worldliness lies deeper than any particular form in which it may be expressed, and, according to the Christian teaching, its essence is found in the mind—in *whatever* form embodied—which leads a man to identify himself with that 'world' which is anti-spiritual in its nature and influence.

5. The manifestation of worldliness.—Such a self-identification is revealed in practice by the point at which a man lays the chief emphasis of his life. As our review of Christ's teaching has shown, man has communion with two worlds—the temporal and the spiritual. Right and lawful, however, as the first communion may be, there come frequent crises in which its interests are found to be in rivalry to those of the higher fellowship. To cling in such crises to the lower communion, in other words, to sacrifice the spiritual to the temporal, this is to be worldly, for this is to make the temporal world, innocent and good in itself, a vehicle of the anti-spiritual. It is unnecessary, and, in the strict sense, even impossible, to identify particular actions as in themselves involving the anti-spiritual; for, as we have seen, worldliness in practice is the possession of a certain spirit, and there is no action which must necessarily embody that spirit nor any which cannot be made a medium for it. The whole question of worldliness in action is ultimately one of arrangement and precedence. The things of the temporal world are right in their right place, but that is the second place in a man's life. What Christ teaches is that they must never be allowed the first place, for that belongs to God (see Mt 6[33], where both elements are recognized and the true order is laid down ; and for a striking illustration in OT, 1 K 3[4-15]). The practice of worldliness, therefore, consists in such an arrangement of these two elements in life as, from the standpoint of God, is false. It is the laying of a disproportionate emphasis upon the temporal, to the impoverishment of the spiritual, elements in life. In some cases this may be recognized by the entire exclusion of the spiritual (Lk 12[15-21]) ; in others by its subjection to the temporal (Mt 8[21] 10[37. 38], Mk 5[17], Lk 14[15-24], Jn 3[19]). The error, however, always lies not in the cultivation of communion with the temporal world, but in the untrue emphasis laid upon it ; in the failure to see that, while many things appear desirable, only one thing is needful (Lk 10[41. 42], cf. Mt 13[44-46]) ; in the self-identification with that 'world' which is the direct antithesis of the Kingdom of heaven.

6. The Christian's true relation to the temporal world. — Our Lord's example and teaching, thus briefly reviewed, enable us to infer the Christian's true relation to the temporal world. (a) Like his Master, he will be fully cognizant of its charms and fully responsive to its lawful claims. Christianity is a religion calculated to make true lovers of Nature, and to produce good fathers, good husbands, good rulers, good servants, good men of business and men of public spirit. Those who have truly learnt the mind of Christ will never shrink from their obligations to the full-orbed life of the world in which He has set them. On the contrary, it is their simple duty to see that every sphere of human life, public and private, individual and social, shall be permeated by His spirit (Mt 5[13. 14] 13[33]). (b) Yet, while the claims of the temporal world will receive their due acknowledgment, the main stress of the Christian's life will lie elsewhere. He is in the world ; but, like his Master (Jn 8[23]), he is not of it (17[14-18]). He will mix freely even in its darker scenes, but without sharing their spirit (Mk 2[16]). For he is no longer a slave to that spirit : he has acquired the independence of real freedom (Jn 8[31-36]). Indeed, his whole attitude to the temporal world has been changed. He no longer regards himself as a permanent holder, but as a temporary steward, ever awaiting the return of an unseen Lord (Mk 13[35-37]). He thus maintains his fellowship with the two realms to which he belongs, but there is no division in his mind (μὴ μετεωρίζεσθε in Lk 12[29] according to interpretation of AV and RV : cf. the supreme submission of Mk 14[36]) as to their comparative claims. His real world is the spiritual world. Whether he is giving alms, praying, fasting, or whatever he is doing, his true life is a life lived 'in secret' away from the gaze of men (Mt 6[1-18]). (c) And it is the claim of this unseen life that dictates his policy in all his earthly concerns. If it require that he sacrifice his own temporal fame (cf. Jn 3[29. 30]) or temporal possessions (Mt 9[9]), he does so with joy. If, on the contrary, it require that he retain these and employ them for the advancement of the Kingdom, he is equally, but no more, ready to obey While some men make a temporal use of eternal conditions (21[12ff.] and ||), he makes an eternal use of temporal conditions (Mt 25[40], Lk 16[9-11]). While some interpret spiritual facts by the material (Mt 16[23], Jn 6[42. 52]), he seeks the key to material facts in the spiritual. Like his Lord, he never condemns as inherently evil the things which are temporal and material, but throughout his life he subjects them to what is spiritual and eternal (cf. 2 Co 4[18]). And herein he has found life's true interpretation (cf. Jn 6[63]).

LITERATURE.—Cremer, *Lex. s.v. κόσμος* ; Weiss, *NT Theol.*, Index ; Beyschlag, *NT Theol.* ii. 250, 435, 471 ; F. W. Robert-

son, *Serm.*, 2nd ser. xiii ; Dale, *Laws of Christ*, 217 ; *ExpT* v. [1894] 201 ; J. Watson, *The Inspiration of our Faith*, 122 ; J. H. Jowett, *Apostolic Optimism*, 47 ; E. Grubb in *Present-Day Papers*, i. (1898) 7 ; J. Rickaby, *Oxf. and Camb. Conferences*, 2nd ser. (1900–1) p. 25.　　　　　　　　　　H. BISSEKER.

WORM.—See ANIMALS in vol. i. p. 67[a].

WORMWOOD.—See GALL.

WORSHIP.—See PRAISE, PRAYER, SYNAGOGUE, TEMPLE.

WRATH.—See ANGER.

WRITING.—The allusions to writing in the Gospels may be classified under four headings, none of which requires any elaborate discussion.

1. In one series of passages ('Moses wrote,' or 'it is written') the reference is to the OT Scriptures, whose letter was held to be authoritative on matters of faith and morals. This view of Scripture was due mainly to the influence of the earlier Rabbis, and naturally it dominated more or less the thinking of the primitive Church, whose one sacred book was the OT. But the formula 'as it is written' had already acquired a juristic sense, as may be seen from numerous inscriptions and papyri (Deissmann, *Bible Studies*, pp. 112–114, 249, 250), so that the LXX translators were not striking out a new line in rendering *Torah* often by νόμος. 'A religion of documents—considered even historically —is a religion of law.' It is in this legal or semi-technical sense that Pilate is said to have written the charge against Jesus (Jn 19[19] etc.), while another metaphorical application occurs in Lk 10[20] 'rejoice that your names are written (or enrolled) in heaven.' The latter passage alludes to the well-known Rabbinic and apocalyptical conception of the heavenly books or registers, a figure employed to denote the indelible mercy of God and the certainty of the believer's relation to Himself, as a citizen of the heavenly state. To have one's name written in the heavenly archives, or inscribed on the Divine roll of citizens, was equivalent to the enjoyment of a safe and sure lot with God. On the general use of γραφή in the Gospels and Epistles, see art. SCRIPTURE, and *ExpT* xiv. [1903] 475–478.

2. Twice the phrase is used of the composition of the Gospels (Lk 1[3], Jn 20[30. 31] and 21[24. 25]), the object of the undertaking in both cases being carefully explained as practical, not literary. To confirm faith, if not to awaken it, is the aim of a written Gospel. Thus an implicit divergence from the above-mentioned sense of γραφή emerges here. No writer of the Gospel claims a juristic authority for his statements. There is nothing legal or formal about their contents (cf. Moffatt, *Historical New Testament*[2], pp. 42 f., 258, 259, 537, 538), nor, as the very persistence of oral tradition suggests, was there any notion of setting them up as infallible tests. Faith sprang from hearing rather than from reading in those days of primitive Christianity. The rise of written records was late, and even their growing prominence did not as yet shift the centre of gravity and influence from living intercourse to scholastic or doctrinal prepossessions. The living voice, the fellowship of the Christian Church, the witness of Apostles—these prevented anything like degeneration into a book religion. The *litera scripta* had its place and merits. But it was produced in and for the Church. And not until it became isolated from the Church did its abuse begin. 'For the general principles of any study you may learn by books at home ; but the detail, the colour, the tone, the air, the life which makes it live in us, you must catch all these from those in whom it lives already' (Newman). Thus the rise

of written records in Christianity introduced a real problem, which is soluble only upon a proper view of the mutual relations between living intercourse, such as the Church provides, and literary standards and sources (cf. Tolstoi's *Essays*, 170 f.).

3. The ordinary use of writing is twice mentioned, in connexion with domestic (Lk 1⁶³) and business (16⁶·⁷) affairs. The three R's were taught in Jewish schools, so that writing would be a fairly common accomplishment, indispensable, of course, to the higher branches of trade and culture (cf. Edersheim's *Sketches of Jewish Social Life*, p. 130 f.). See art. EDUCATION.

4. Jesus Himself is only once said to have writ-ten — and that upon the dust (Jn 8⁶·⁸), stooping and scrawling with His finger on the ground to conceal His embarrassment and to avoid answering the brazen questions of the woman's accusers (cf. *Ecce Homo*, ch. ix.). It is idle to suppose that He wrote any sentence, or to conjecture what that sentence was, whether the sins of His interrogators or some text like Mt 5³ or Ps 50¹⁶. It is the action and nothing else that is significant. Jesus stooped to write, in short, by one of those natural gestures which a pure-minded man, seated on the ground, would employ to hide his confusion and put by a question which should never have been asked.

J. MOFFATT.

Y

YEAR.—See TIME.

YOKE.—The yoke (ζυγός, Mt 11²⁹ᶠ·) supplied Jesus with one of His agricultural metaphors (cf. Mt 13³⁸, Lk 12¹⁷ 15¹⁴, Jn 15¹). It was 'a bar which connects two of a kind usually—as the ox-*yoke*—fastened by bows on the necks of a pair of oxen and by thongs to the horns or the foreheads of the oxen. It consists generally of a piece of timber hollowed or made curving near each end, and fitted with bows for receiving the necks of the oxen, by which means two are connected for drawing. From a ring or hook in the bow a chain extends to the thing to be drawn' (Lloyd's *Ency. Dict.*). Another use of the word is found in Lk 14¹⁹ (ζεῦγος, tr. 'pair' in 2²⁴), where it means a pair of draught-oxen. Now, while the facts of farm-life supplied the form for this metaphor of Jesus, it was not there alone that He found the idea of the metaphor. When from the fields His eye turned to the Scriptures to survey the story of His people, on many a page the yoke met His vision. There it is, in prose, poetry, and prophecy; about it have gathered the country's glory and grief. To itself it has harnessed the people's experiences. Ideas of opposing character—joy and woe, freedom and slavery, peace and war, plenty and poverty—are symbolized by it (Dt 28⁴⁸, Job 1³ 42¹², Jer 2²⁰, Is 58⁶, 1 K 12⁴, La 3²⁷). Moreover, it is in His treatment of those bitter-sweet memories and realities of life that the teaching of Jesus, *under this figure of speech*, touches and keeps a lonely sublimity. Only once (Mt 11²⁹ᶠ·) He uses the metaphor. Now it is in everyday use. For He 'touched nothing that He did not adorn.' And He so adorned the *yoke* as to draw after it the whole gospel.

When Jesus turned His gaze from the fields of industrial life, and from the book of remembrance of the past to the book of the life of His own generation, He discovered a nation under the yoke, a race under the harrow. He hit the mark when He spoke of yokes. His audience was made up of those who were wearing yokes of all sorts and sizes, but no man with his own yoke harnessed on exactly as his neighbour's. On the other hand, that audience was suffering under an intolerable strain. Three yokes were galling and killing them —(1) the yoke of the Law, (2) of Rome, (3) of sin. Their leaders (Mt 23⁴) bound grievous burdens on the people's shoulders; nor would they remove them. Of some it was the constant temptation to throw off the yoke of the foreigner. The Zealots (Lk 6¹⁵) were most restive under Rome. They were the political Nationalists of the day. Again, who of them all was not 'sold under sin' (Ro 7¹⁴)?

These were the yokes of the people. The yoke of Jesus was the will of the Father. He wore it always, never worked without it; never against it, always *with* it (Jn 8²⁹). Once He asked thrice if He might take it off (Mt 26³⁹ᶠ·) for the road was steep. The yoke of Jesus was the welfare of man. He came to serve (Mk 10⁴⁵). To be Saviour was at once the lowliest, loftiest, and loneliest way of working out the welfare of man. And this yoke was tied with cords of love (Jn 13¹) unto the end. The humanity of Jesus was His yoke. He was, not the angel (He 2⁹·¹⁶), but the man Christ Jesus (1 Ti 2⁵); and He did the perfect will of the Father under this yoke, frail but firm—the body of His humiliation.

LITERATURE.—Bishop Thorold's *The Yoke of Christ*; *Expositor*, i. vi. [1877] 142, vii. [1878] 348, xi. [1880] 101; *Exp. Times*, iii. [1892] 512, vi. [1895] 176; Henry Drummond, *Pax Vobiscum*, 41; W. A. Butler, *Sermons*, ii 320; G. A. Chadwick, *Pilate's Gift*, 62; G. Macdonald, *Hope of the Gospel*, 152.

JOHN R. LEGGE.

YOUNG MAN.—In the Gospels we have on four occasions incidents of importance described, in which 'a young man' (νεανίσκος, not νεανίας [as in Ac 7⁵¹ of Saul, 20⁹ of Eutychus, 23¹⁷ of St. Paul's nephew]) is one of the figures.

1. St. Matthew (19²⁰·²²; cf. Mk 10¹⁷, Lk 18¹⁸) describes by this name the 'ruler' who asked our Lord what he must do to inherit eternal life. It adds to the pathos of the scene to know that this man, who 'went away sorrowful' because he could not give up his great possessions in the quest for life, was still so youthful as to be called νεανίσκος. He had not reached the prime of life,* when the love of money had cankered his heart and soul.

2. The widow's only son at Nain, who was being carried out to burial when our Lord touched the bier and raised him to life, was comparatively young: our Lord called him νεανίσκε when He bade him arise (Lk 7¹⁴). An additional touch is given to the beauty of the miracle if we may infer the mother's early widowhood and the youth's career of promise cut short, for which the Saviour's gift of life restored (ἔδωκεν αὐτόν, v.¹⁵) made ample and unexpected compensation.

3. St. Mark (14⁵¹·⁵²) records a brief and somewhat mysterious incident, which occurred on the way from Gethsemane to the high priest's palace on the night of the Betrayal. When 'all the disciples forsook him and fled' there 'followed with him' still 'a certain young man' who had 'a linen cloth cast about him, over his naked body.' Perhaps he had been roused from sleep that night, and

---

* The word νεανίσκος stands for any age from boyhood up to 40 years. See Liddell and Scott, *s.v.*, and cf. Swete's note on Mk 10¹⁷

so had nothing but his bed-robe on as he rushed from the house to see what was taking place at the garden. And when some of the 'multitude with swords and staves' who arrested Christ tried to lay hold on him also, he escaped, but left the linen cloth behind him in their grasp. Evidently the slight event had some special association for St. Mark with the memories of that night, and it has been conjectured that the νεανίσκος is, in fact, the Evangelist himself; and, further, that he was a member of the household where the Last Supper had just been eaten, perhaps the son of the οἰκοδεσπότης (v.[14]). Others, with less probability, have wished to identify him with St. John or with St. James the Lord's brother (see Swete's notes, *in loc.*). In art he is sometimes represented as the keeper of the garden (*l'ortolano* : see Mrs. Jameson's *Hist. of our Lord in Art*, vol. ii. p. 43). Bengel's inference (*locuples igitur erat*, Mt 11[8]) tallies well with the idea that he was John Mark (see Ac 12[12]).

4. According to Mk 16[5], he who appeared to the women at the sepulchre on the morning of the Resurrection was 'a young man sitting on the right side, arrayed in a white robe.' In St. Matthew's account he is described as 'an angel of the Lord' (28[2]), while St. Luke tells us of 'two men in shining garments' who spoke to them (24[4]: but in v.[23] 'a vision of angels'). In apt illustration of St. Mark's version Swete quotes 2 Mac 3[26. 33] δύο ἐφάνησαν αὐτῷ νεανίαι . . . διαπρεπεῖς τὴν περιβολήν . . . οἱ αὐτοὶ νεανίαι πάλιν ἐφάνησαν τῷ Ἡλιοδώρῳ ἐν ταῖς αὐταῖς ἐσθήσεσι ἐστολισμένοι ; and Jos. *Ant.* V. viii. 2, where the angel who appears to Manoah's wife is φάντασμα . . . νεανίᾳ καλῷ παραπλήσιον μεγάλῳ. Cf. also *Evang. Petr.* §§ 9, 11, and 13.

LITERATURE.—For homiletical treatment of these four incidents referring to νεανίσκοι, the following may be consulted :—**1.** Lynch, *Sermons for my Curates*, p. 175 ff. ; Martineau, *End. after the Christian Life*, p. 265 ff. ; *Expositor*, I. vi. [1877] p. 229 ff. **2.** Trench, *Notes on the Miracles* ; W. M. Taylor, *Miracles of Our Lord.* **3.** *Expositor*, I. i. [1875] p. 436 ff. See art. MARK. **4.** Maclaren, *Sermons preached in Manchester*, 2nd ser. p. 190 ff.

C. L. FELTOE.

Z

ZACCHÆUS (Ζακχαῖος ; Heb. זכי 'pure').—The graphic narrative of Lk 19[1-10] tells us all that we know of Zacchæus, and his name does not occur elsewhere in the NT. The importance of Jericho as a trade centre, the abundance and value of whose products called forth the enthusiastic approbation of Josephus (*BJ* IV. viii. 2, 3), required the employment of a considerable number of tax-collectors, and these were under the general direction of Zacchæus (cf. ἀρχιτελώνης, v.[2]), who may, in point of fact, have been himself the fortunate leaseholder of the customs of that particular district. In other words, he may have purchased from the authorities the right to be as exacting as he pleased in his demands upon the people, provided he knew enough of the law to avoid the risk of exposure. There is no reason to believe that Zacchæus was a notoriously bad representative of his class ; but, on the other hand, having regard to that remorseful cry of his which seems to have been the product of an awakened conscience (v.[8]), it does not appear that his methods were always strictly equitable. He was, so far as one may gather, a *publicanus* (see art. PUBLICAN) of more than average respectability, yet not above some of the questionable ways associated with his profession. To paint his character in lurid colours, as distinguished by unusual heartlessness and selfishness, is not in accordance with the impression conveyed by the narrative.

One is never quite safe in venturing upon a pronouncement with regard to motives — they are generally so curiously mixed ; and possibly a variety of motives contributed to the impulse which brought Zacchæus into contact with Jesus that day. But while it might be too much to say that higher motives were entirely absent, it is quite obvious that the part played by a naturally lively curiosity was not inconsiderable. In this connexion, the contrast between Matthew *sitting* at the receipt of custom and Zacchæus leaving all thoughts of business behind and *climbing a tree* with eager speed, is sufficiently great to indicate a vital difference in character between the two men.

More interesting than the attitude of Zacchæus towards Jesus is the attitude of Jesus towards him. If we look for an explanation of the wonderful transformation, implicated in the resolve in which Zacchæus gave expression to his feelings, we find it, undoubtedly, in the delightful frankness of Christ's first salutation, and in His courageous brushing aside of popular prejudice. In no other way could He have so completely gained, first, the attention, and then the heart of one whom society united in passing by. Nothing, surely, could be more remarkable than the delicate insight which led Jesus to choose Zacchæus as His host. It was an irresistible touch, and, mingled with the other happy recollections of that day, it would abide in the mind of the publican as a peculiarly grateful memory.

LITERATURE.—In addition to the various Comm., see A. B. Davidson, *Called of God*, 275 ; Matheson, *Representative Men of the NT*, 205 ; F. W. Robertson, *Serm.* I. v., II. xvi. ; Lynch, *Serm. for my Curates*, 71 ; A. Maclaren, *Paul's Prayers*, etc. 88 ; Seeley, *Ecce Homo*, xx. ; C. S. Horne, *Rock of Ages*, 281 ; artt. 'Jericho' and 'Publican' in Hastings' *DB*.

A. G. CAMPBELL.

ZACHARIAH.—See BARACHIAH.

ZACHARIAS (Ζαχαρίας). — Father of John the Baptist (Lk 1[5-25. 57-80]) ; a Jewish priest, who was an old man at the close of the reign of Herod the Great (B.C. 4). 'The strawberry grows underneath the nettle,' and, even in that evil time of wickedness in high places in Church and State, there lived in Palestine no inconsiderable number of just and devout persons both among priests and people. Of such was Zacharias. A Jewish priest, a member of the family of Abijah, Zacharias had been so careful to observe the law regarding the marriage of priests (Lv 21[7-14]), that he chose for wife one of the sacerdotal house, a daughter of Aaron (v.[5]), named after Aaron's wife (Ex 6[23]), Elisabeth, who was as pious as himself. They were righteous not only in the sight of men but of God, and blameless in their care to observe all His commandments and ordinances ; but notwithstanding this, and the promise of God by Jeremiah (Jer 33[18]), and their eager desire, and Zacharias' lifelong prayer (v.[13]), their union was not blessed with offspring. It was due to Elisabeth's barrenness (v.[7]) ; and she keenly felt the reproach which it occasioned (v.[25]), for it was a common opinion among the Jews that childlessness was God's punishment for guilt. They had both reached old age when the miraculous event occurred which surpassed all they could have looked for.

Zacharias had left his home in the hill-country

of Judah to fulfil in the Temple at Jerusalem his week of service; and it fell to his lot to perform the very special duty of burning incense in the Holy Place, separated only by the veil from the Holy of Holies. It was a very notable occasion in a priest's life, which did not come at all to many a priest (it is said there were 20,000 of them altogether about this period), and it was not likely the lot would ever fall on him again to offer it. The offering of incense was symbolical of prayer (Rev 5[8]); the people worshipping in the courts outside were praying while the smoke was rising from his censer within (v.[10]); it was impossible that he should not be praying too, and if only by the force of long habit, the old petition rose once more to his lips. Suddenly there stood in front of him, on the right side of the altar of incense (v.[11]), where no mortal man should be, an angel of the Lord. In the presence of the supernatural, Zacharias feared and trembled; but the angel reassured him, told him that his prayer was heard, that his wife Elisabeth should bear him a son, whom he should live to see, and name John (= 'the grace of Jehovah'), which would be no barren title, but describe his character and mission: 'he shall be great in the sight of the Lord' (cf. Mt 11[11], Lk 7[28]). This son must be brought up as a Nazirite in the highest form of Levitical devotion (Nu 6[4], Jg 13[4], La 4[7], Am 2[12]); he should, like another Elijah (1 K 18[37]), turn many of the children of Israel unto the Lord, and be the forerunner, as foretold by Malachi, to Messiah Himself (vv.[15-17]).

Zacharias had not the faith of Abraham, who staggered not through unbelief (Ro 4[19]) at a promise of God exactly similar, 'involving human generation, but prophetically announced and supernatural' (Alford). He asked for a sign ($\kappa\alpha\tau\grave{\alpha}\ \tau\acute{\iota}$;), and pointed out the difficulties in the way. Some (e.g. Bruce) have expressed surprise that 'so natural a hesitation' should be treated, and punished, as a sin'; but to whom much is given, of him much shall be required. Others have asked why Zacharias should be censured here, and not the Virgin Mary (vv.[34. 35]), not observing that hers was not a question of doubt, 'Whereby shall I know?' but a request for direction ($\pi\hat{\omega}\varsigma\ \xi\sigma\tau\alpha\iota\ \tau o\hat{\upsilon}\tau o$;), 'How is it to be brought about?'—a question implying faith as to the event itself. She got a sign too, though she had not asked one; but hers was joyful, Zacharias' punitive, yet merciful. 'Thou shalt be dumb,' not only as one stupefied with wonder, but also 'unable to speak'; yet for a season merely, till, at the proper time, the promise has its fulfilment. Thus, on the threshold of the Gospel, at the very outset of its great series of miracles, is unbelief chastised. The soul that will not believe shall not be allowed to speak (cf. 2 Co 4[13]).

It was not, the Talmudists inform us, the custom of the priests, when officiating inside the Holy Place, to make their own devotions long, lest the people outside should be anxious; but Zacharias' interview with Gabriel, and perhaps the feelings it awakened, caused him to delay. The worshippers in the Temple courts marvelled why he tarried so long; the thought likely to occur to them was that God had slain the priest as unworthy (Bruce); and when at last he did make his appearance, he could neither explain the reason for his delay, nor give them the Aaronic benediction (Nu 6[22-24]), which was pronounced after every morning and evening sacrifice by the priest with uplifted hands, the people responding to it with a loud Amen (Keil, Bibl. Archœol.). Like the dying St. Columba before the altar at Iona, though for a different reason, Zacharias signed with his hand the blessing which he could not speak (v.[22]). As soon as the days of his ministration were accomplished, he returned to his home; the tokens of his wife's pregnancy soon

added a sign of joy to the sign of punishment which he bore about with him. The promised child was born, but the chastisement was not taken off till the hour arrived when he had his predicted function to fulfil, by calling the infant by his appointed name.

Godet remarks on the pleasant picture of family life presented by the scene of the Baptist's circumcision. It had been a custom since the birth of Isaac (who received his name at his circumcision) to give a child his name on the same day in which he was signed as one of God's people: for a similar reason, Christian children are named on the occasion of their entrance by baptism into the Church. A difficulty which some have felt, that Zacharias was dumb only and not deaf, yet is treated by the company as if unable to hear, is met by Olshausen by the remark that these two afflictions go so frequently together, that men easily accustom themselves to treat dumb persons as deaf.

The heart of Zacharias had been gathering thoughts to itself through all those months of silence, and no sooner was his mouth opened than he poured forth to God the hymn of priestly thanksgiving which we call, from its first word in the Latin version, Benedictus (wh. see). Here we need only note in it an evident allusion to his own name (signifying 'Remembered by Jehovah') and his wife's (Elisabeth = Eli-sheba = 'the oath of God')—'to remember his holy covenant; the oath which he sware to our father Abraham' (Lk 1[72. 73]).

Nothing is said of Zacharias after this. The statement of several of the Fathers (Origen, Greg. Nyss., Cyr., and Pet. Alex.), though accepted by Baronius, that this Zacharias was slain by Herod between the Temple and the brazen altar, has no historical basis; it is a mere guess to explain the difficulty, that whereas many of the prophets were martyred at a later date than Zechariah the son of Jehoiada (2 Ch 24[20]), yet our Lord, summing up the list of such murders, begins with Abel and ends with Zechariah (Mt 23[35]). See BARACHIAH. Zacharias having been by this mistake made a martyr, his relics were forthcoming, and Cornelius a Lapide speaks of seeing and venerating his head in the Lateran basilica at Rome.

JAMES COOPER.

ZAREPHATH (AV **Sarepta**). — A town of the narrow rocky Phœnician coast, 9 miles S.W. of Sidon, 17 miles N. of Tyre, and 60 miles directly N. of Nazareth, whence NT reference is made to it. Perched 500 feet high on a steep hillside a mile from the coast road, the modern shrunken hamlet looks down upon the traveller riding through a mile of the ruins of the ancient Zarephath, which once as a populous city extended to the sea, was provided with walls, and had a commodious harbour, now filled with sand and ruins.

While, in the theoretical division of the Holy Land among the twelve tribes by Joshua, Zarephath fell into the lot of Asher, going down, as that did, 'even unto great Sidon,' 'and to the fortified city of Tyre' (Jos 19[28f.]), it, together with the most of Asher's territory, remained almost wholly Phœnician and Gentile. St. Luke's report of Christ's sermon at Nazareth distinctly connects Zarephath with Sidon, as do the LXX and MT in the account of Elijah's sustenance by the widow there. This Evangelist—apparently the only Gentile-Christian NT writer—seizes as does no other upon the thought that the boundless grace of God has been extended in certain typical cases to remote Gentiles, even to the superseding and exclusion of those who were of the stock of Abraham and dwelt within the Holy Land. The choice, among all others, of the widow of pagan Phœnician Zarephath, and of Naaman the leper of heathen Syrian Damascus, to receive the favours of the prophets Elijah and Elisha, filled the crabbed synagogue hearers of Nazareth with wrath and murder (Lk 4[25ff.]).

WILBUR FLETCHER STEELE.

ZEAL.—It is not easy to distinguish zeal (Gr. $\zeta\hat{\eta}\lambda o\varsigma$ from $\zeta\acute{\epsilon}\omega$ 'to boil') from enthusiasm (which see); but, as regards the derivation, the former indicates the character, the latter the source of the inward state; and, as regards the meaning, the former lays stress on the volitional, the latter on the emotional aspect of the complex condition of soul. As 'ardour in embracing, pursuing, or defending' an object, it is ascribed to Phinehas (Nu 25[11. 13]), Elijah (1 Mac 2[58]), the Jewish people (Ac 21[20], Ro 10[2]). St. Paul claims it for himself (Ac 22[3], 2 Co 11[2], Gal 1[14], Ph 3[6]), and commends it in the Corinthians (2 Co 7[7. 11] 9[2]) and Epaphras (Col 4[13], variant reading for *labour*). The same Greek word is used in the bad sense of *jealousy*, which is condemned in the Apostolic writings (1 Co 3[3], 2 Co 12[20], Gal 5[20], Ja 3[14. 16]). A quotation from the Psalms (69[9]) is applied to Jesus to describe the impression made on the disciples by the first cleansing of the Temple (Jn 2[17]). This may throw some light on the problem of the repetition of the act at the close of the ministry (Mt 21[12-17], Mk 11[15-18], Lk 19[45. 46]), as the first may have been due to His fresh enthusiasm for His vocation, the second may have been a more deliberate assertion of His Messianic claim. As *zeal* in the fulfilment of His purpose is ascribed to God (2 K 19[31], Is 9[7] 37[32] 59[17] 63[15], Ezk 5[13]), the mood itself as well as the occasion of it was worthy of Jesus as the Son of God.

From this term is derived the name of one of the Jewish parties, the *Zealots* (which see), to which, as his surname indicates, Simon the disciple (Lk 6[15], Ac 1[13]) had belonged. The zeal of Jesus for the Temple may have been what drew Simon to Him.   ALFRED E. GARVIE.

ZEALOT (Gr. ζηλωτής) occurs in Lk 6[15] and Ac 1[13] as the designation of Simon, one of the Twelve. In the lists given by Mt. and Mk. the equivalent 'Cananæan' (Καναναῖος) is used. The Zealots were the rigorous Nationalists, the party of violent opposition to Roman domination. Josephus (*Ant.* XVIII. i. 6) calls them a 'fourth sect of Jewish philosophy,' and says that 'Judas the Galilæan was the founder.' He adds : 'These men agree in all things with the Pharisaic notions ; but they have an inviolable attachment to liberty, and say that God is to be their only Ruler and Lord' ; he speaks of their 'immovable resolution' and their indifference to suffering and death. These qualities were all abundantly illustrated in the final struggle at Jerusalem and at Masada. Edersheim (*LT* i. 237 ff.) dates the rise of the party from the accession of Herod the Great, and the activity of guerilla bands in Galilee under the leadership of one Ezechias. 'It was in fact a revival of the Maccabean movement, perhaps more fully in its national than in its religious aspect.' Plummer ('St. Luke' in *ICC*) attaches more importance to the religious aspect of the movement :—'The Zealots date from the time of the Maccabees as a class who attempted to force upon others their own rigorous interpretations of the Law.' In the later stages of the Jewish history the party grew more violent. Its ringleaders were known as the *Sicarii*, and their overthrow of all moderating leadership sealed the doom of Jerusalem. There is no special difficulty in believing that a member of this party might be attracted to Jesus and become one of His chosen disciples. Galilee was the home of the party, and it naturally included in it men of very different types, from the religious fanatic to the partisan of revolution. Simon's zealotry, purified by the knowledge of Jesus, might readily become true loyalty to the Kingdom of God. Edersheim gives us the additional explanation that, at the period when the ministry of Jesus began, 'A brief calm had fallen upon the land. There was nothing to provoke active resistance, and the party of the Zealots, although existing, and striking deeper root in the hearts of the people, was, for the time, rather what Josephus called it, "the philosophical party"—their minds busy with an ideal, which their hands were not yet preparing to make a reality' (*op. cit.* p. 243). We should, however, take note of the alternative possibility (see Plummer, *loc. cit.*)

that Simon may have been called ζηλωτής 'because of his personal character either before or after his call,' as St. Paul (Gal 1[14]) styles himself περισσοτέρως ζηλωτής . . . τῶν . . . παραδόσεων. See also CANANÆAN.   E. H. TITCHMARSH.

ZEBEDEE (Ζεβεδαῖος) is mentioned several times in the Gospels, but always as the father of James and John. Like his sons, he was a fisherman, and he and they were partners with Simon (Lk 5[10]). He was with James and John in a boat when they were summoned by Jesus (Mt 4[21]), and their call as disciples left him with the hired servants (Mk 1[20]), and broke up the partnership with Simon. There is no record of any direct association of Zebedee with Jesus.   JOHN HERKLESS.

ZEBULUN. — **1. Description.** — Our knowledge of the limits of Zebulun are even more indefinite than in the case of Naphtali (wh. see), and for the same reasons. It was bounded on the east by that tribe, while on the south it seems to have touched the northern edge of the plain of Esdraelon, and to have included a portion of it towards the Kishon at the foot of Carmel. On the west the slopes towards the plain of Acre, and on the north the plain of Suchnīn, seem to have been the boundaries. Josephus, indeed, tells us (*Ant.* v. i. 22) that 'the tribe of Zebulun's lot included the land that lay as far as Gennesaret, and that which belonged to Carmel and the sea.' The latter portion seems to have been implied in the promises of Gn 49[13] and Dt 33[18], but it is excluded in Joshua's (Jos 19[10-16]) division of the land. The seeming contradiction may perhaps be explained by supposing that Zebulun possessed a detached portion in Haifa (חֵיפָא), for the emphasis in the repetition of חוֹף אֳנִיּֽת and חוֹף יַמִּים (Gn 49[13]) clearly assigns that port to this tribe. This would agree also with the statement of the Rabbis : 'Zebulun was going out to the seas,' 'Zebulun was diligent in business (פרקמטיא),' 'Zebulun was bringing in merchandise in ships' (*Ber. Rab.* §§ 72, 99 ; *Waikra Rab.* § 25 ; *Yalkut Shimeoni*, § 161 ; *Mid. Tanh.* ; *Pesikta Zutarta* and *Zohar* on Gn 49[13]). Still the main body of Zebulun touched no sea. Apart from the southwest portion in the plain of Esdraelon, the tribal lands consist of undulating hills and narrow valleys, which, however, widen out at places into small but extremely fertile plains, the chief of which are the plain of Toran in the east, the plain of Suchnīn in the north, and *el-Baṭṭauf* or the plain of Asochis in the centre. Zebulun is not so wild in scenery as Naphtali, nor has it the same variety of climate, being wholly situated in Lower Galilee (M. *Shebiith*, ix. 2). It varies in elevation from 365 feet in the plain to 1780 feet at *Tell Jefāt*. It possesses no perennial stream of any size, and has no lake of any kind except that from the beginning of the rainy season *el-Baṭṭauf* is flooded. It remains in this condition all winter, and often contains a large quantity of water till June or July. This must always have been, and still is, in itself a fruitful source of malaria, as also through the springs it feeds in the direction of Gennesaret. Elsewhere Zebulun is well supplied with springs. The rock of the district is the same soft white limestone we meet with in Naphtali. Of this there are great barren ridges especially to the north of the plain of Toran and west of *el-Baṭṭauf* ; but, as we have observed in Naphtali, they might easily be transformed into orchard land. The other hills, which for the most part run east and west, are covered with low prickly oak. There is nothing of the nature of forests now except in the west and south-west—beside *Shefā-'Amr* and *el-Ḥāriṭīye*, still there is abundant evidence to show that in the 1st cent. other places, especially in the north, were well wooded (*BJ* III. iii. 2 and vii. 8). The chief business of the population is now and must always have been *agriculture*. At the present time good crops are reaped in the plains and valleys and on the hill sides. Everywhere we meet with fruits of all kinds, olive trees in the valleys, and around all the villages, orchards and vineyards, with an abundance of figs and pomegranates. On the hills, flocks of sheep and goats are pastured. But, fruitful as the land now is, it was formerly more so. We are told that in the early centuries 'the land for sixteen miles around Sepphoris flowed with milk and honey' {Jerus. *Biccur.* i. 8), and that means the whole tribe of Zebulun. Olive oil was plentiful around Jotapata —*Tell Jefât* (*BJ* III. vii. 28) ; Araba in the north was a great grain market ; while Suchnīn, close by, produced the best wine, and Shikmona in the south was famous for its pomegranates, just as Kefr Kenna is renowned to-day for the size and quality of those it produces. Antoninus Martyr (6th cent.) draws a most enchanting picture of the regions around Nazareth, and he compares the district to Paradise (*Itiner.* §5). He was doubtless controlled to a great extent by sentiment, but it must be admitted that even at the present day many of the valleys, especially to the west of Nazareth, and above all that of *Seffurieh*, justify his description, with their profusion of flowers, fruits, and greenness so pleasing to the eye in contrast to the white rocks.

2. People and historical associations.—As in the rest of Galilee, the Jewish population here had come in during the later days of the Maccabees and the reign of Herod. During the century preceding our Lord's Advent, Zebulun had passed through more stirring times than any other tribe of Israel. Its chief town, Sepphoris (Dio-Cæsarea), —the traditional home of the parents of Mary,— had been repeatedly taken, and immediately after the death of Herod, when the young child Jesus was safe in Egypt, it had been twice besieged and captured, once by Judas the son of Hezekiah (*BJ* II. iv. 1 ; *Ant.* XVII. x. 5), and then by the troops of Varus assisted by a detachment of Arabs (*BJ* II. v. 1 ; *Ant.* XVII. x. 9). On the latter occasion the city was burned, and many of the inhabitants were sold into slavery. Such an event would be long impressed on the minds of the people, especially those of Nazareth, who from *three miles distant* would view the scene from the hill tops around their city. They would lament many a friend and brother there, and during the years to come they would be making efforts to redeem their relatives from slavery. When the boy Jesus was ten years old, the land was again to pass through the horrors of war, when Judas and his Zealots held out till overcome by Gessius Florus (*Ant.* XVIII. i. 6 ; cf. *BJ* II. vii. 1). Thenceforward for many years there was peace, industry, and progress. The people of Zebulun are not to be thought of as poor. We learn that the inhabitants of Sepphoris had ample means. It was one of the cities rebuilt and fortified by Herod, who made it again the capital of Galilee (*Ant.* XVIII. ii. 1) ; and amongst its inhabitants were senators and citizens (Jerus. *Horaioth* iii. 5). We read also of a city named Zebulun in this district. It is described as πόλις ἀνδρῶν, and was said to have houses like those of Tyre, Sidon, and Berytus, and to possess all sorts of good things (*BJ* II. xviii. 9). But whatever may have been the extent of Zebulun's trade on the sea, the people would be familiar with, and at least engage in the *carrying* trade on land, for the great *Via Maris* of ancient and modern times passes along the plains of *Toran* and *el-Battauf* westward to the sea, so that, whatever wealth the people may have become possessed of, they would at least be familiar with the sight of earth's treasures.

Not only would the memories of the events, through which the newly settled Zebulun had passed, influence its people, but their thoughts would also be moulded by the scenes around, which were rich in old historical associations. The tribe had given two judges to Israel, Ibzan of Bethlehem (Jg 12⁸) and Elon (12¹¹), while 3 miles from Nazareth was Gath-hepher, the birthplace of Jonah, the first prophet to the Gentiles, and his tomb is still shown there. Then to the young Israelite of the 1st cent. no scene in the whole land could be more inspiring than the view from the hills of Zebulun. To the south the plain of Esdraelon, the battle-ground of Israel, lies stretched out—a glorious panorama. Every crisis in the nation's history had a memory there. Close at hand, by Tabor and Kishon, the men of Zebulun had 'jeoparded their lives to the death' (Jg 5¹⁸). Little Hermon—the Hill of Moreh —and Gideon's fountain (7¹) would recall the 'day of Midian' ; while Gilboa would bring thoughts of Israel's darker days, and Jezreel memories of sad declension in the time of Ahab. Shunem, Endor, and Bethshean could also be seen, and Megiddo too, —the scene of Josiah's heroic fight ; while nearer still on the shoulder of Carmel was 'the place of burning,'—the site of Elijah's sacrifice, and of Baal's inglorious defeat before the God of Israel. More distant were Mt. Ebal, with its memories of blessing and cursing, and Pisgah's peak in the distant haze ; while westward there would be a glimpse of the 'great sea.' All these and many more historical sites are to be seen, and thoughts of them rise and stir the heart of him who views the scene ; and if so to the passing stranger, what must they have been to the young Zebulunite, whose daily food they were, and who, in virtue of His blood, was the heir of all their most glorious memories?

The relationship of this people to the Gentile world is also worthy of note. Josephus (*BJ* I. iv. 3) tells us of the innate enmity of the Syrian to the Jew ; but here such feelings would be less intense. We are repeatedly told of bonds of union between Zebulun and Issachar, and that this latter tribe busied itself with the Torah and made many proselytes (*Ber. Rab.* § 98) ; and before such was possible mutual jealousies must have ceased. At the same time the people would become familiar with the ceremonials of admission to Judaism, including that of baptism (Bab. *Jeb.* 46 *a, b*). It is further to be remarked that, though the text seems doubtful, the town of Nazareth in this tribe is named in the songs of Eliezer Ha-kalīr as one of the meeting-places of the priests, when they assembled to go up into serve in the Temple.

3. Christ in Zebulun.—Although our Lord's teaching was for the most part given in the tribe of Naphtali, the land of Zebulun takes precedence not only in the prophecy (Mt 4¹⁵), but also in historical sequence, and it is equally important for a knowledge of the Gospels. If Naphtali experienced most of the brilliancy of the noonday of the Sun of Righteousness, it was in Zebulun that the dawn appeared and shone more and more unto the perfect day. In a city of this tribe the Lord Jesus was brought up (Lk 4¹⁶). As He increased in wisdom and stature, its associations aided in the moulding of His human character. During a period of well nigh 30 years His life was passed in one of its valleys, broken into only by visits to the Holy City. His earlier years were spent in the midst of its fierce politics, He knew the various party watchwords ; He knew what was meant by 'wars and rumours of wars' ; He had come into contact with soldiers from Tabor and Sepphoris, and early learned the terrors associated with the word 'legion' ; He had met returned slaves— redeemed, freed, or fugitive ; He had wrought in the villages of this tribe, and we can even think of

Joseph taking the young Jesus to work with him at Sepphoris during the busy days of its rebuilding —for there was not the same objection to entering it as the polluted Tiberias. The flowers of Nazareth had fostered His love of Nature, the operations in its fields and the products of its gardens were to be used to teach lessons for eternity. Nathanael, and perhaps other disciples, were from Cana in Zebulun (Jn 21^2). It was in it too that Christ publicly declared His office in the gracious words He spoke (Lk 4^{21}), that He performed His first miracle, and 'manifested forth his glory' so that 'his disciples believed on him' (Jn 2^{11}). But when we have studied the power of all these influences, and considered to what they should lead, we only convince ourselves the more 'that what He was and what He became for the world cannot be explained or grasped by the help of contemporary history or social conditions' (Delitzsch, *Handwerkleben*, § 1).

As in the case of Naphtali, the Rabbis have something to say of Zebulun. They discuss the question as to what Jacob saw in vision, in that he blessed Zebulun immediately after Judah (Gn 49$^{10\text{-}14}$), and the usual answer they give is that he foresaw the glories of Rabbinism in the presence of the Sanhedrin at Sepphoris before it was removed to Tiberias (*Yalkut. Shimeoni*, i. § 161). It is, however, also recognized that 'The Holy One, blessed be He, should cause His Shekinah to dwell in Zebulun' (*Shem. Rab.* § 1).

LITERATURE.—See under NAPHTALI.

WM. M. CHRISTIE.

ZERAH.—A link in our Lord's genealogy (Mt 1^2).

ZERUBBABEL.—Mentioned in both Mt.'s (1$^{12\text{f.}}$) and Lk.'s (3^{27}) genealogy of Jesus.

ZION.—See JERUSALEM, vol. i. p. 850^b f.

APPENDIX

———◆———

CHRIST IN THE EARLY CHURCH.—To treat this subject exhaustively, it would be almost necessary to write a complete history (if such a thing were possible) of the early Christian Church. Christ fills the field of vision. Christian life and Christian thought centre round His Person. It is obvious that in an article of limited length, only salient points can be touched upon, a few typical quotations given, and lines of thought suggested rather than developed.

The first Christians happily knew little of the distinction between the theological and the practical. Belief and life were one. Still, for clearness' sake, it is proposed in this article to discuss separately, as far as possible, (1) the beliefs of the early Church concerning the Person of Christ; (2) the feeling of the early Church as expressed in practice and devotion, with regard to the living Christ and His present relationship to mankind.

The term 'early Church' is, of course, an elastic one. It can scarcely, from a theological point of view, be limited to a shorter period than that which is closed by the Sixth Œcumenical Council (A.D. 681). But within these limits a very special interest attaches to the pre-Nicene period, both from its comparative nearness to the time of Christ, and from the extreme value and interest of its records, scanty though they are. It is with this period (from the closing years of the 1st cent. to A.D. 325) that this article will chiefly deal.

i. BELIEFS OF THE EARLY CHURCH AS TO THE PERSON OF CHRIST.—**1.** (*a*) The earliest Christian writing extant outside the limits of the NT, and one which was for long on the verge of admission into the Canon, is the *Epistle to the Corinthians*, usually assigned to **Clement,** bishop of Rome. It was written probably about A.D. 95, to exhort a disordered church to unity and charity. Its interest is therefore chiefly practical, but it should be noted that at least once a doxology is addressed directly to Christ as to a Divine Person (20); that His unique dignity and pre-existence are evidently assumed in such a phrase as 'the sceptre of the majesty of God, even our Lord Jesus Christ, came not in the pomp of arrogance, or of pride, though He might have done so' (16); and that Christ is spoken of as shedding His blood for the salvation of the whole world (7).

(*b*) The so-called *Second Epistle of Clement* dates probably within the first half of the 2nd cent., and is a sermon rather than a letter, the earliest Christian sermon extant after the NT. Here Christ is definitely spoken of as 'God' (1), as pre-existent (14); and His Incarnation is described in the remarkable words, 'the Lord who saved us, being first spirit, then became flesh' (9).

(*c*) The seven genuine *Epistles of* **Ignatius** of Antioch are in some respects the most notable writings of the 2nd century. They were written by him while he was on his way to martyrdom at Rome, probably in the year A.D. 107, and are addressed to the Churches of Ephesus, Magnesia, Tralles, Rome, Philadelphia, Smyrna, and to Polycarp of Smyrna. With Ignatius, Jesus Christ is 'our God' (*Eph.* 1. 18, and elsewhere). His blood is 'the blood of God' (*ib.* 1). He is 'the only Son of God' (*Rom.* 1); 'the unerring mouth in whom the Father hath spoken' (*ib.* 8). Ignatius speaks in significant language of the Incarnation, of the human life, sufferings, resurrection, and continued existence of Christ; and of His double nature; 'There is one only physician, of flesh and of spirit, born and unborn, God in man, true life in death, Son of Mary and Son of God, first passible and then impassible, Jesus Christ our Lord' (*Eph.* 7; cf. also *ib.* 18. 19. 20; *Trall.* 9; *Smyrn.* 1–3). The Virgin Birth of Christ is also distinctly alluded to in *Eph.* 18. 19.

(*d*) Another writing usually classed among the 'Apostolic Fathers,' is the so-called *Epistle of* **Barnabas,** of which the probable limits of date are between A.D. 70 and 132 (Lightfoot). The writer speaks of Christ as 'Lord of the whole world, unto whom God said from the foundation of the world, "Let us make man after our image and likeness"' (5).

(*e*) A mystical work which enjoyed considerable popularity in the early Church, the *Shepherd,* attributed in the Muratorian Canon to that **Hermas** who was brother of Pope Pius I. (A.D. 140–155), contains incidental statements about Christ which point generally in the same direction as those quoted above. The Son of God existed before all creation, and was God's fellow-counsellor in the work of creation (*Simil.* ix. 12). He supports all creation (*ib.* 14). At the same time the language of Hermas about the Incarnation is vague, almost as if the Son of God and the Holy Spirit were identical (*Simil.* v. 6). It is scarcely fair, however, to interpret this as if it were a careful theological statement. Hermas evidently was not a man of deep thought or originality. His aim is practical rather than doctrinal. Probably such expressions are to be understood in the same sense as 1 Co 15[45].

2. A very interesting feature of the first half of the 2nd cent. is the rise of *the Apologists,* men of learning who had exchanged heathenism for Christianity, and who addressed heathen readers in justification or explanation of their new faith. (*a*) **Aristides** the philosopher (about A.D. 125), addressing the emperor Hadrian, speaks of Jesus Christ as 'God' who 'came down from heaven, and from a Hebrew virgin took and clad Himself with flesh ; and in a daughter of man there dwelt the Son of God.'

(b) **Justin Martyr,** in his *Dialogue with Trypho the Jew*, traces not only prophecies of Christ in the OT, but identifies Him with the God, or the 'angel of the LORD,' who appeared in the OT theophanies, and with the Divine Wisdom of Pr 7, etc. Justin practically anticipates the Nicene formula ὁμοούσιος τῷ Πατρί (128), though, as in the case of Hermas, some of his statements are vague, and, if pressed verbally, might appear inconsistent with later definitions. There can be no question, however, that he teaches the pre-existence and the Divinity of Christ, and that his writings were deeply influenced by the Logos doctrine of St. John.

(c) One of the most beautiful as well as most intellectual productions of the early Church is the anonymous *Epistle to Diognetus*. Here Christ is spoken of as 'the very Artificer and Creator of the Universe'; and the Father sent Him into the world, 'as sending God,' 'as a king might send his son who is a king' (7).

3. It was, however, the necessity of meeting both outside attacks on Christianity, and misconceptions of it from within, that gradually forced Christian writers to define more clearly and exactly the nature of Christ. This process of theological definition, which began towards the end of the 2nd cent., culminated in the decisions of the great Councils. Early in the 2nd cent. had begun to appear the curious half-heathen travesties of Christianity which are classed under the general name of *Gnosticism*. These may be described as attempts to combine Christian ideas and phraseology with ideas drawn from Greek and Oriental religions. The Gnostic systems really differed from Christianity on first principles, as they were generally dualistic, and assumed the essential evil of matter. They denied in consequence the perfect humanity of Christ (a tendency alluded to in the later writings of the NT ; cf. 1 Jn 4²ᵗ·), and the true union of human nature with the Divine nature in one Person. The Gnostic Christ was not really born of Mary, nor did He truly suffer.

(a) The first and chief opponent of Gnosticism, one of the most extensive writers of the early Church, was **Irenæus,** bishop of Lyons from 177–202(?). He meets the Gnostic systems by stating what was definitely believed about Christ in the Christian Church, which is the repository of truth, —truth inherited from the Apostles, preserved by the Church, and the same in all parts of the Church (i. 10, iii. 1, 4, 24). Irenæus states this faith of the Church in language very similar to that of the later Creeds. The Church, he says, believes in 'one Christ Jesus, the Son of God, who became incarnate for our salvation ; . . . and the ascension into heaven in the flesh of the beloved Christ Jesus, our Lord, and His future manifestation from heaven in the glory of the Father to gather all things in one, and to raise up anew all flesh of the whole human race, in order that to Christ Jesus, our Lord and God and Saviour and King, every knee should bow,' etc. (i. 10). Irenæus clearly teaches the pre-existence of Christ, that He was begotten and not created (iii. 18) ; that His humanity is perfect, sinless, yet absolutely real and not Docetic (*ib.*) ; and that He is God and man in one Person (iii. 16). Perhaps the most remarkable contribution of Irenæus to Christology is his teaching that all mankind is gathered together and summed up in the Incarnation ('in seipso recapitulavit,' iii. 18, etc.).

(b) In the East, Gnosticism was met by the great writers of the School of Alexandria, **Clement** and **Origen,** who further developed the conception of Christ as the Logos who is immanent in the Universe. Origen was in some respects a thinker in advance of his age, and his teaching was undoubtedly misunderstood by his successors. Whether his doctrine of Christ was altogether in harmony with the later definitions of the Councils has often been questioned. That it was really so has been maintained strongly by Bishop Bull in his *Defence of the Nicene Creed*, and by Bishop Westcott. Origen certainly taught the eternal generation of the Son of God (*de Princ.* i. 2), which doctrine supplies the basis of the reply to the Arian quibbles about the posteriority of the Son to the Father ; the reality of the Incarnation (*de Princ.* ii. 6) ; and he spoke of Christ as the God-man (θεάνθρωπος).

4. The 3rd cent. is marked by a series of heresies which from different points of view attacked the doctrine which, as we have seen, had been consistently held in the Church, though at times vaguely stated, of the unique relationship of the Son to the Father, in other words, of the Divinity of the historic Christ. How, it was asked, could the Divinity and the eternal pre-existence of Christ be reconciled with the *unity* of God? There were two principal heretical answers to this problem, and they may be called 'heretical' in a sense that Gnosticism was not, because they arose within the Church itself, and claimed to be the original doctrine.

(a) The *Adoptianists*, who seem to have been the doctrinal successors of the early Judaic-Christian sect of the Ebionites, and whose chief teachers at Rome were Theodotus and Artemon, all taught a subordination, to a greater or less degree, of the Son to the Father, even making Christ nothing more than a highly exalted man, who was 'adopted' to His Sonship by the Father. This last point was reached by the teaching of the brilliant Paul of Samosata (260–270), who was condemned by a series of Councils at Antioch, and finally deposed in 270.

(b) On the other hand, the *Monarchians* or *Patripassians*, represented by Praxeas, Noetus, and Sabellius, so merged the personality of the Son and the Holy Spirit in the unity of the Father, that it practically followed from their teaching that the historic Christ was actually the Father Himself who was incarnate, and suffered on the cross, so that, in the spiteful epigram of Tertullian, Praxeas 'put to flight the Comforter and crucified the Father.'

The most important opponents of these heresies were **Hippolytus,** bishop of Portus (d. 258?), and **Dionysius,** bishop of Rome (d. 269). Only a fragment remains of the writings of the latter ; and those of the former, as well as the exact nature of his teaching, are wrapped in considerable obscurity.

The controversies of the 3rd cent. obviously still waited for a final solution. It is quite evident that the general conscience of the Church revolted against both Adoptianism and Patripassianism, though the uncertainty of theological terms, the absence of a fixed theological vocabulary, and the difficulty of arriving at common action owing to the stress of frequent persecutions, rendered it difficult for the Church as a whole to come to close quarters with these different forms of error. This slight sketch of pre-Nicene theology should, however, be sufficient to show that, despite the absence of any statement of faith common to the whole Church, there is an overwhelming consensus of Church belief from the first to the effect (1) that the historic Jesus Christ was truly God, pre-existent with the Father ; (2) that He was also truly man ; (3) that in Him are permanently united God and man in one Person.

5. The Edict of Milan (312) introduces a new

era of Church history. Persecution ceased, Christianity tended at once to become the recognized religion of the Empire. This sudden outburst of popularity brought into the Church an influx of ill-instructed converts, who were naturally eager to assimilate Christianity as far as possible to their old heathenism.

(a) The teaching of *Arius,* a parish priest of Alexandria, who had, however, previously studied at Antioch, brought swiftly the crisis when the Church must definitely and clearly state her belief as to the Person of Christ. We thus enter upon the era of the great Councils, called 'Œcumenical,' as involving an appeal to the universal conscience and witness of the Christian Church throughout the world.

Arius seems to have taught a form of Adoptianism : Christ was the Son of God, and prior to all other created things, and yet Himself a creature. To pay Divine honours to a creature, however exalted, was, of course, really idolatry ; but for this very reason Arianism was popular with those nominal converts who had never in their heart relinquished their old polytheism. To the teaching of Arius, the Church at the Council of Nicæa (325), mainly through the exertions of the great **Athanasius,** opposed the key-word of the Nicene Creed. Christ, the Son of God, is 'of one substance' (ὁμοούσιος) with the Father, *i.e.* He is, and was from all eternity, of the same Godhead as the Father. Strife and controversy raged round this celebrated phrase during most of the 4th century. It was defended consistently by Athanasius, Basil, and the two Gregorys (of Nyssa and Nazianzus). Ultimately all attempts to substitute for it some vaguer expression failed, and the Council of Constantinople (381) definitely re-affirmed the Nicene statement. The absolute Deity of Christ in the fullest sense of the term was thus finally vindicated. Other problems, however, remained.

(b) *Apollinarism,* a reaction against Arianism, ascribed to Christ an imperfect *human* nature, in which the Divine nature took the place of the human 'spirit' (πνεῦμα), the highest part of man's rational nature. This error was condemned at Constantinople (381) ; and it seems that at some later date other clauses were added to the original Nicene Creed, derived apparently from a Jerusalem baptismal creed, which emphasized the true and perfect humanity of Christ.

(c) The Council of Ephesus (431) dealt with a further problem, the 'Hypostatic Union,' *i.e.* the union of two whole and perfect natures, Divine and human, in the one Person of Christ. (a) The teaching of *Nestorius,* in which there are distinct traces of Gnosticism, practically made two persons of Christ, by denying that the infant child of Mary could properly be called 'God' ; and by asserting apparently that at some time after the birth of Jesus, the Divine Logos united Itself with Him. The key-word which the Church adopted to refute Nestorius was the title *Theotokos,* 'mother of God,' applied to the Virgin Mary. (β) A reaction in an opposite direction led *Eutyches* a few years later to exalt the Divinity of Christ at the expense of His humanity, by teaching that the humanity was in some way swallowed up in the Divinity. The famous 'Tome' of Pope Leo I. stated the balance of faith clearly and antithetically, and the fourth Council (Chalcedon, 451), in condemning Eutyches, laid down that the two natures of Christ are to be acknowledged ἀσυγχύτως ('without confusion'), ἀτρέπτως ('without change'), ἀδιαιρέτως ('without division'), ἀχωρίστως ('without separation'). The same truths were stated in a Latin dress, for liturgic use, about this time, in the so-called 'Athanasian' Creed.

(d) Eutychianism, however, with its disproportionate reverence for the Divinity of Christ, proved too fascinating for the Eastern mind to be disposed of by the Council of Chalcedon. Political as well as religious causes entered into the long 'Monophysite' controversy. The fifth Œcumenical Council (Constantinople, 553) again condemned those who were unwilling to admit the full and perfect humanity existing in the one Person of Christ. The sixth Council (Constantinople, 681) marks the last phase of the long debate. *Monothelitism,* the last stronghold of Monophysitism, was overthrown by the statement of two wills in Christ, human and Divine, the former perfectly subject to the latter.

The steps by which the halting theology of the pre-Nicene period led finally to the full statement of the Catholic faith, were a legitimate and, indeed, a necessary development. It is not one of the least evidences to a Divine power working in the Christian Church, that, in an age of cosmopolitan superstition and intellectual unrest, all attempts to assimilate Christianity to heathenism were rejected, and a clearly defined and balanced statement of truth emerged and gained almost entire possession of the field. With all its mystery, the Catholic faith of Nicæa and Chalcedon was felt by the common Christian conscience alone to satisfy all the different sides of truth as they are contained in Scripture, and to do justice to all that Christians from the first had believed concerning their Master. To-day there is practically no alternative left between the Nicene Creed and humanitarianism. If the latter is true, the appearance of Christ and its subsequent effect on the world must remain an insoluble enigma,—a miracle even more difficult of credence than the stupendous statement of the Nicene formula.

ii. DEVOTION OF THE EARLY CHURCH TO CHRIST. —Whatever uncertainties or faulty definitions may be detected in the statements of pre-Nicene theology, there is no uncertainty as to the attitude of the early Church towards the personal Christ. *Lex supplicandi, lex credendi.* In the devotion which made men and women and little children live and die for Christ, we shall find even a surer guide than in the attempts of Christian writers to explain their belief. From the very first Jesus Christ stands out in all the records of the early Church as the personal, living Master, not merely the Shepherd and High Priest of His faithful ones, but the true Lord and King of the Universe. He is the object of passionate love, obedience, prayer, and worship.

1. (a) To Clement of Rome, Christ is 'the high priest of our offerings, the guardian and helper of our weakness' (36). Through Him the Father 'instructed us, sanctified us, honoured us' (59).

(b) The unknown author of the *Second Epistle of Clement* opens his sermon with a burst of enthusiastic gratitude : 'What recompense then shall we give to Him (Jesus Christ)? or what fruit worthy of His own gift to us? And how many mercies do we owe Him ! For He bestowed the light on us ; He spake to us, as a father to his sons ; He saved us when we were perishing — He called us when we were not, and from not being He willed us to be.'

(c) The epigrammatic sentences of Ignatius glow with passionate love to Christ. 'Jesus Christ' is 'our inseparable life' (*Eph.* 3); true Christians are 'arrayed from head to foot in the commandments of Jesus Christ' (*ib.* 9) ; faith and love in Jesus Christ are 'the beginning and the end of life' (*ib.* 14). 'He that possesseth the word of Jesus is able to hearken to His silence' (*ib.* 15),—a remarkable and pregnant phrase. Ignatius desires suffering and martyrdom that he 'may attain Christ,' and 'rise free in Him' (*Rom.* 4. 5. 6). The blood of Jesus Christ is 'eternal and abiding joy' (*Phil.* 1). Those who 'speak not concerning Jesus Christ' he looks on as 'tombstones and graves of the dead, on which are inscribed only the names of men' (*ib.* 6).

(*d*) The *Epistle to Diognetus* speaks of 'the Word, who was from the beginning, who appeared as new and yet was proved to be old, and is engendered always young in the hearts of saints,—through whom the Church is enriched and grace is unfolded and multiplied among the saints, grace which confers understanding and reveals mysteries' (11).

(*e*) Justin Martyr describes how, after searching vainly for truth and satisfaction among the Stoics, the Peripatetics, the Pythagoreans, and the Platonists, he at last was led by the advice of a certain aged man whom he met on the seashore to study the Scriptures, and to conceive a love of Christ. 'Straightway,' he says, 'a flame was kindled in my soul' (*Trypho*, 8).

2. Not only was Christ loved, He was also *obeyed*. His commandment must take precedence of every other claim. To Hermas, divorce and remarriage after divorce are as absolutely forbidden as unchastity (*Command.* iv. 1). Justin Martyr similarly regards as absolute the teaching of Christ respecting divorce, forgiveness, charity, endurance of injuries, swearing, and civil obedience (1 *Apol.* 15–17).

3. That the personal Christ was *worshipped* by the early Church as Lord and God is indisputable. Prayer and thanksgiving were addressed directly to Him.

(*a*) The famous letter of Pliny to Trajan (A.D. 113?) speaks of having elicited from Christians, who had been examined, that it was their custom on a fixed day to assemble before daylight and sing alternately 'a hymn to Christ as God.'

(*b*) A remarkable hymn attributed to Clement of Alexandria, intended apparently to be sung by Christian children, in which Christ is addressed throughout and praised as Ruler, Shepherd, and King, is found in his *Pædagogus* (iii. 12). Of a slightly later date are such hymns as the *Gloria in excelsis* and the *Hail gladdening Light*. Indeed, it seemed to the Church, when confronted by the Arian problem, one of the most convincing proofs of the error of the teaching of Arius, that Christ had always received Divine honours in the Church.

(*c*) The personal nearness of Christ to the believer during Christian worship was especially associated with the Eucharist. To Ignatius, 'the Eucharist is the flesh of Jesus Christ,' though the false teachers deny it (*Smyr.* 6). 'There is one flesh of our Lord Jesus Christ, and one cup unto union with His blood' (*Phil.* 4). To Justin Martyr, the Eucharist, the conditions of receiving which are belief, baptism, and a life according to the commandments of Christ, is not common bread and common drink, but the flesh and blood of the incarnate Jesus, by which our blood and flesh are nourished (1 *Apol.* 66). To Irenæus and the Christian Fathers generally, participation in the Eucharist is the actual means whereby Christians share in the life and resurrection of Christ.

(*d*) The testimonies of the Christian martyrs are most suggestive. Ignatius, brought before the emperor Trajan, calls himself *Theophorus*, 'Bearer of God,' saying that he bears the Crucified within his breast. Polycarp of Smyrna, when called upon by the pro-consul to revile Christ, confessed in memorable words, 'Fourscore and six years have I served Him, and He hath done me no wrong. How then can I blaspheme my King and Saviour!' And the apparently contemporary record of the martyrdom of Polycarp closes with the significant words: 'The blessed Polycarp was apprehended by Herodes, when Philip of Tralles was high priest, in the proconsulship of Statius Quadratus, *but in the reign of the Eternal King, Jesus Christ.*' The martyrs of Lyons and Vienne (177) are spoken of in the contemporary letter which describes their sufferings (Eus. *Hist. Eccl.* v. 1) as 'hastening to Christ'; 'through them Christ showed that things which appear mean and obscure and contemptible to men are with God of great glory.' One of them, St. Blandina, 'was clothed with Christ, the mighty and conquering Athlete.' Their patience manifested 'the measureless mercy of Christ.' And with one and all who suffered, the simple confession of the name of Christ seems to have been the strength which sustained them. St. Perpetua, the African martyr (early in the 3rd cent.), was comforted before her sufferings by a vision of Christ as an aged man, a shepherd, sitting in the midst of a spacious garden, who said to her, 'Thou hast done well, my child, in coming.' St. Maximus, who suffered under Decius, declared, 'These are not torments, but anointings which are laid upon us for the name of our Lord Jesus Christ' (Ruinart, *Acta Martyrum*, p. 204). Phileas of Thmuis, put to death in Diocletian's persecution, said in his last words: 'Now we begin to be disciples of our Lord Jesus Christ. Beloved, attend to the commandments of the Lord.—Let us call upon Him, the spotless, the infinite One, who sitteth upon the Cherubim, the Maker of all things, who is the Beginning and the End, to whom be glory for ever and ever. Amen' (*ib.* p. 521).

4. Interesting light on early Christian feeling is thrown by the funeral inscriptions and symbols of *the Catacombs*. As a rule, the inscriptions are of extreme brevity. Their leading thought is that dead Christians are with Christ in a continued existence of peace and joy. The aspirations and prayers of their friends on earth go with them, and the departed in turn remember the living in prayer to Christ, *e.g.* 'Vivas'; 'Vivas in Deo Christo'; 'In pace'; 'Deus refrigeret spiritum tuum'; 'Quam stabile tibi hæc vita est' (*i.e.* the life beyond the grave); 'Spiritus tuus in pace et in Christo'; μνήσκεσθε δὲ καὶ ἡμῶν ἐν ταῖς ἁγίαις ὑμῶν πρεύχας (προσεύχαις).

5. Most of the early Christian pictures of Christ are merely symbolical, the Lamb and the Fish being the most common. But the earliest personal representation is suggestive; it is the figure of the Good Shepherd, sometimes bearing the lost sheep on His shoulders, sometimes surrounded by His flock. This tender personal relationship between the soul and the Saviour, or between the Church and her Lord, which stands in such striking contrast to the trials and sufferings that surrounded the daily life of the Christian in a hostile world, was evidently the aspect which appealed most deeply to the heart of the early believer.

6. The relation of Christ both to His Church and to the world was also set forth impressively in the so-called 'majesties,' with which from the 4th cent. onwards the Christian art began to adorn the churches. In these pictures Christ is represented as reigning now in glory, bearing the symbols of His royal, prophetic, and priestly offices. It was not merely to an historic Christ that Christians looked back, or a future coming to judgment that they anticipated, though both these conceptions were vividly present in the mind of the early Church. It was a Christ actually in possession of His Kingdom, even now ruling over the nations, and surrounded by His worshipping saints (who even in this present time shared His throne), that dominated the thought of the early centuries. So in the great mosaics in the Church of St. Cosmas and St. Damian at Rome (6th cent.), the colossal figure of Christ stands in the apse, fronting the worshippers, portrayed on a dark-blue ground amid golden-edged clouds of sunset; His right hand is raised in blessing, His left holds a written scroll. The figures of St. Peter and St. Paul, with palm-trees of Paradise and the phœnix (the emblem of the Resurrection), stand on each side of the Christ, and beneath His feet flows the river Jordan. Below this again is the representation of the Lamb, with the four rivers of Paradise and twelve sheep on either side.

The representations of the suffering and dying Christ, which became the favourites of a later age, have, of course, an independent value. Nevertheless there is a peculiar beauty and significance in the mingled majesty and tenderness of those earlier pictures of the living Christ, which expressed the love of those whose faith in Him had literally overcome the world. See CHRIST IN ART.

7. The two strands of theology and devotion which we have endeavoured to trace in the early Church seem fittingly to meet in the most remarkable man after St. Paul whom the Church has seen, the great Athanasius. It was largely due, as we have seen, to him that the traditional belief of the Church, at the greatest crisis of Church history, took its clear and definite and accurately reasoned shape in the Catholic creeds. And it is interesting to note that the secret of Athanasius' defence of the *Homoousion* was seen by his contemporaries to lie in his own personal devotion from childhood onwards to the Person of the Redeemer. 'Athanase était enflammé, dès sa jeunesse, de la passion qui fait les saints, l'amour de Jésus Christ' (De Broglie, *L'Église et l'Empire*, i. 372). 'His maintenance of dogma was a lifelong act of devotion' (Bright, *Church Hist.* p. 149). The great treatise *On the Incarnation of the Word*, which marks an epoch in theological writings, is no mere dogmatic statement, but glows with the pure passion of belief. It is the work of one who profoundly and from the heart believes in Christ as a living Person, in His present power, and His absolute claim upon mankind. The power of the Cross of Christ and His Resurrection from the dead are to Athanasius the greatest of facts, unparalleled in history, illimitable in their future consequences. 'The achievements of the Saviour,' he says, 'resulting from His becoming man, are of such a kind and number that if one should wish to enumerate them, he may be compared to men who gaze at the expanse of the sea and wish to count its waves . . .; to sum the matter up, behold how the Saviour's doctrine is everywhere increasing, while all idolatry and everything opposed to the faith of Christ is daily dwindling and losing power and falling; and thus beholding, worship the Saviour, who is above all and mighty, even God the Word' (54, 55).

8. Not only on the highways of Church history does the figure of the living Christ stand out as the central object of Christian love and loyalty. Such a wonderful production as the Hymn of St. Patrick, with a quotation from which we will close this brief survey, illustrates the impression which the preaching of Christ produced upon the infant nations just emerging from barbarism. It belongs to the 5th or 6th cent., a time when the civilization and empire of Rome were failing, and men were clinging to Christ as the one power which could guide and set free their lives:

'Christ with me, Christ before me,
  Christ behind me, Christ within me,
  Christ beneath me, Christ above me,
  Christ on my right, Christ on my left,
  Christ in the fort,
  Christ in the chariot-seat,
  Christ on the poop.

Christ in the heart of every man who thinks of me,
  Christ in the mouth of every man who speaks to me,
  Christ in every eye that sees me,
  Christ in every ear that hears me.'

LITERATURE.—*The Apostolic Fathers*, one volume edition, containing text, translations, etc., by Lightfoot and Harmer (Macmillan & Co., 1891); 'The Apology of Aristides,' *Texts and Studies*, Cambridge, 1891; *The Ante-Nicene Christian Library* (T. & T. Clark); Smith-Wace, *Dictionary of Christian Biography* (Murray, 1877–1887 [the articles on 'Athanasius,' 'Origenes,' and 'Christology' are especially useful]); Smith-Cheetham, *Dictionary of Christian Antiquities* (1875–1880); Wace-Schaff, *Select Library of Nicene and Post-Nicene Fathers* (Oxford and New York, 1890–1900), especially the volumes 'Eusebius,' 'Athanasius,' and 'The Seven Œcumenical Councils'; Schaff, *History of the Christian Church* (T. & T. Clark); Bright, *History of the Church*, 313–451 (Parker & Co., 1888); Ruinart, *Acta Martyrum* (Ratisbon, 1859); Newman, *Arians of the Fourth Century* (Longmans & Co.); Bull, *Works* (edited by Burton, Oxford, 1846); Burn, *Introd. to the Creeds* (1899).

A. R. WHITHAM.

CHRIST IN THE MIDDLE AGES.—The Christology of the Middle Ages was, of course, the outgrowth of that of the earlier time, and each mediæval type can readily be traced to its source. The main lines of influence are: that of Augustine, working directly through the continued use of his writings, and indirectly through the personality and writings of Gregory the Great, Anselm of Canterbury, Bernard of Clairvaux, Abelard, Peter Lombard, Thomas Aquinas, etc.; that of the Neo-Platonic pseudo-Dionysius the Areopagite, working directly through the continued use of his writings, and indirectly through the propagation of his modes of thought by Maximus the Confessor, Scotus Erigena, the German Mystics, etc.; Adoptianism, which flourished in the immediately post-Apostolic (if not in the Apostolic) times, was vigorously propagated in Armenia, and perpetuated there by the Paulicians even down to the present time, had a vigorous development in Spain during the 8th and 9th cents., and affected much of the dissenting evangelical thought of the mediæval time; and the Gnostic-Manichæan modes of thought, perpetuated from the early time, and reappearing in the Catharistic sects. For the Greek Church the Christology of John of Damascus, who in the 8th cent. reduced to system the net results of the Christological controversies of the three preceding centuries, continued to be normative during the Middle Ages, and little independent theorizing seems to have found place.

1. Beyond almost any other Christian thinker, **Augustine** magnified Christ. This name, drunk in piously and deeply, even with his mother's milk (*Conf.* iii. 8), never lost its power over him even during his years of wandering. Having become emancipated from Manichæan dualism through the study of Neo-Platonic writings (Plotinus, Amelius, *et al.*) he found himself unable with satisfaction to fix his gaze upon the glories of the invisible and unchangeable God until he had embraced that 'Mediator between God and man, himself man, Christ Jesus,' 'who is over all, God blessed for ever,' 'the way, the truth, and the life.' Yet he did not at once grasp the mystery of the Incarnation, and he failed for a time to attain to anything higher than Adoptianism. He thought of Christ 'as of a man of excellent wisdom,' virginborn and surpassing other men, an example to us of 'contemning temporal things for the obtaining of immortality.' Fully assured of the unchangeableness of the Divine Word, he was unable to believe that He ate, drank, slept, walked, rejoiced, was sad, and discoursed; and so felt compelled (against Arians and Apollinarians) to insist upon a complete humanity in Christ to which such actions and experiences would be appropriate (*Conf.* vii. 24, 25). Though strongly influenced by Neo-Platonism, which generally made for Monophysitism, Augustine was a Dyophysite of the most pronounced type. Yet one would search in vain in his writings for any accurate definition of the relations of the Divine and the human in the Person of Christ, or of the manner in which the Divine Logos and the man Jesus were united in a single personality. He guarded carefully against any admission of a blending of Deity and humanity, as well as against the supposition that Christ's humanity is converted into Deity. He calls the humanity of Christ 'garment,' 'temple,' 'vehicle,' 'instrument.' By virtue of its association with Deity, the soul of Christ possessed perfect knowledge from the very beginning; and His disclaiming of knowledge about this or that was for the sake of His disciples. Yet Augustine denied freedom of choice to the humanity of Christ, which he made subject to predestination. He regarded the Incarnation of the Logos as necessary in order that our souls might become His members, and that the devil might be vanquished by the same nature that he had seduced. The Incarnation was the work of the entire Trinity, and the Word stood in no nearer relation to the Son than did the entire Trinity (cf. Harnack, *Dogmengesch.* iii. 116 [Eng. tr. v. 226]). The following sentence is highly significant:

'God assumed (*suscepit*) our nature, *i.e.* the rational soul and flesh of the man Christ, by an assumption singularly wonderful and wonderfully singular, that, no merits of his own righteousness having preceded, he should thus become Son of God from the beginning in which he began to be man, that he himself (the man Christ) and the Word might be one person' (*de Correptione et Gratia*, 30).

Augustine seems never to have reached a thoroughly wrought-out and self-consistent Christology. He was uncertain whether the Incarnation was necessary to man's redemption, conceiving it possible that God might have chosen another way. The body of Christ he regarded as a part of the Adamic mass, which was constituted a body by the act of assumption, conceived by Mary not by carnal concupiscence, but by spiritual faith (Dorner, *Pers. of Christ*, II. i. 398). By the Incarnation our souls become Christ's members, and the devil is vanquished by the same nature that he seduced. As in accordance with the Divine plan of redemption Christ must needs purchase sin-cursed men with His own death, He assumed a human body with all human affections and infirmities, including mortality, yet without concupiscence. In assuming human nature He cleansed it. 'He became man in order that He might make us gods.' Yet He did not renounce the 'form of God,' but continued with the Father in heaven, while Jesus was sojourning upon earth. His emptying was merely an occultation. Like St. Paul, Augustine laid the utmost stress on the humiliation involved in the Incarnation, the human life, and the obedience even unto death; and yet he insisted that the Divine nature as being absolutely immutable could only join sympathetically with the human in psychical and physical suffering. The atoning work of Christ he thought of as redemption from the power of the devil—who had taken up his abode in human souls deserted by God because of sin, and who was conceived of as having a sort of vested right in them—quite as much as reconciliation to God. By receiving the penalty of sin, and not taking upon Himself the fault (*culpa*), He blotted out both penalty and fault for us. Christ's death possessed atoning power because of His virgin birth, spotless righteousness, and voluntary obedience to God. The temporal death of Christ frees believers from eternal death.

Side by side with Augustine's magnifying of Christ went his disposition to exalt the Church and its sacraments. He supposed that the benefits wrought for man through the Incarnation and sufferings of Christ become available for man only through the medium of the sacraments of which the Church is the sole dispenser.

2. Gregory the Great was not an original thinker on Christological questions. He went far beyond Augustine in his ecclesiasticism and sacramentalism, and while professing to be a devout follower of Augustine, greatly enervated his doctrines in reproducing them. In his teaching regarding the atoning work of Christ he laid more stress than did Augustine on the rightful power of the devil over mankind, and the ransom paid him by Christ in His death. The God-man, virgin-born and without concupiscence, he regarded as both a mediator between God and man, and an example for us. The atoning work of Christ does not avail for human salvation unless man fills up by a life of humility and suffering that which remained of the sufferings of Christ. 'He who strives to be redeemed and to rule with Him must be crucified.'

'Without intermission the Redeemer offers up a burnt-offering for us, in that without ceasing He shows to the Father His incarnation on our behalf; since His incarnation is an oblation for our cleansing: and when He showed Himself as man, by intervening, He washed away the faults of man. And by the mystery of His humanity He perennially offers sacrifice, because these faults also which He cleanses away are eternal' (*Moral.* i. 24).

He laid much stress upon the constant intercession of Christ; but this was supposed to be mediated by angels, saints, alms, masses, and by other forms of meritorious works. In fact, he was so overmastered by the efficacy of sacramental forms and the continuous sacrifice, that he regarded the death of Christ as not absolutely necessary for man's redemption. God who created us might have delivered us from the consequences of sin without the death of Christ. He thought of the death of Christ as an exhibition of the Divine love, and as an example wherewith to teach us not to fear the misfortunes and sufferings of this world, but rather to avoid earthly good fortune. His sacrificial view of the Lord's Supper, with its sacerdotal accompaniments, greatly enervated his conception of the Person of Christ and its historical significance. In this rite the suffering of Christ is repeated continuously for our reconciliation, 'the whole Christ being in each portion' of the consecrated elements. In the words of Harnack:

'Christ as a person is forgotten. He is a great title in dogmatics . . . ; but the fundamental questions of salvation are not answered in relation to him, and in life the baptized person has to avail himself of "means" which exist partly side by side with him (Christ), partly without him, or only bear his badge' (*Dogmengesch.* iii. 241 f. [Eng. tr. v. 271]).

Fear and hope take the place of faith and love; fear of punishment takes the place of repentance for sin. Thus the mediæval type of ascetical piety was fully established (cf. Harnack, *l.c.*).

3. A vigorously led Adoptianist movement in Spain during the later years of the 8th century, probably influenced by Saracen thought, led **Alcuin,** supported by Charlemagne and the Council of Frankfort (794), to set forth as the Christological teaching of the Frankish Church, in opposition to the Nestorian doctrine, alleged to be involved in the Adoptianism of bishops Elipandus of Toledo and Felix of Urgel, a doctrine scarcely distinguishable from Eutychianism. Alcuin insisted that Christ is not 'man,' but the 'God-man'; that He is not 'in everything like us apart from sin,' but 'in many things.' He taught that in the union of the Divine and the human the human personality was blotted out (*deleri*) or consumed (*consumi*) by the Divine, and that the Divine personality took the place of the destroyed human personality. 'In the assumption of flesh by God the person of man perished, not the nature' (*adv. Felicem*, 2. 12). Thus Adoptianism provoked a reaction in the Western Church against an extreme as well as against the natural and proper interpretation of the Chalcedonian Symbol; and while it did not lead to the general acceptance of pure Eutychianism, it came perilously near eliminating from Western Christology the conception of the real and complete humanity of Christ.

It has been pointed out by Dorner, with admirable insight (II. i. 270 ff.), that while Christ continued to be regarded by the Greek Church as the revealed wisdom of God, and stress was laid upon His prophetic office employed in the diffusion of enlightenment as embodied in the 'orthodox faith,' in the Latin Church He was regarded during the mediæval time as first and foremost a King, Christianity was regarded as a means of securing power, and the hierarchy was supposed to have been appointed by Christ to occupy His place, rule in His stead, virtually to supersede Him in personal government, and to abolish any direct intercourse between Him and believers. No longer was personal fellowship of the believer with Christ thought of as the supreme good or even as a possibility. Having founded the Church and endowed it with plenary powers, Christ was no longer needed as a personal presence, and was deistically regarded. If a personal and highly sympathetic supernatural was desiderated, this was to be found in the Virgin Mary, who had already been exalted to almost Divine proportions. The Church came to be regarded as the present living incarnation of Christ.

4. Next to that of Augustine, the most potent influence on mediæval Christology in the West was that of the unknown writer (probably active during the later years of the 6th cent.) whose *Ecclesiastical Hierarchy*, *Heavenly Hierarchy*, *Divine Names*, and *Mystical Theology* were credited to **Dionysius the Areopagite**, converted by St. Paul on the occasion of his visit to Athens. The writer was thoroughly imbued with the Neo-Platonic thought of Plotinus, Proclus, Jamblicus, etc., and wrought out a magnificent and highly impressive scheme of Christian theosophy on a Neo-Platonic basis. The credit of these works was greatly enhanced by the supposition that they constituted the esoteric teachings of the Apostle Paul, which were too spiritual and exalted for the people of his time. In *The Divine Names* (ii. 10):

'The Son is all in all and the head of all things . . . , for He is the fulness and cohesiveness of all things, and He conserves and firmly binds the parts by the wholeness, and He is neither part nor whole for He is above these, but both part and whole as having embraced all things; for He is exalted above nature, and is antecedent to causation; and He is the perfect among us imperfect, and imperfect among the perfect angels as being superperfect and anteperfect, and having no point of comparison with them as regards perfection; and He is the formative principle in things lacking form as the creator and originator of all form, and without form with respect to things that have received form as being above form.'

Much more is said by way of emphasizing the absolute transcendence and the relative immanence of the Son.

This view of Christ and the world would seem to preclude belief in a specific Incarnation; but the devotion of pseudo-Dionysius to the creed of the Church and his sense of the reality of historical Christianity held him back in some measure from sheer Docetism. He maintained, therefore, that the Deity of Jesus in its exceeding goodness came even to our nature and truly assumed the substance of our flesh, so that the Most High God could be called man, the super-essential essence thus shining forth out of humanity. He communicated Himself to us without mixture or change, suffering no harm from His unspeakable humiliation. He was supernatural in our natural, super-essential in what belongs to our essence, and He possessed in a unique manner all that is ours, of us, and above us. True to his pantheistic conception that God can be named with the names of all His creatures, pseudo-Dionysius asserts that He who is the author of

man was truly man as to His entire nature. Yet He was not merely man, and not merely super-essential in relation to man; but He is actually man above men and according to men, or, in other words, He is the archetypal man of whom all individual men are the unreal copies. In a superhuman manner He performed human acts. He was a man humanly born, but man above man; and inasmuch as in Him God had become man, He developed a Divine-human energy (*Ep. ad Caium*, iv.). The pseudo-Dionysius found it practically impossible to find any place in the Universe for the God-man Jesus Christ, thus vaguely and Docetically conceived (Dorner). To assign Him a place in the earthly sphere would be degrading; to place Him in the heavenly order would involve Docetism. Without being quite willing to do so, he virtually relinquished the historical Christ, retaining only the eternal. These writings figured largely in the Christological controversies in the East during the 7th and 8th centuries.

5. Maximus the Confessor (d. 662), though a staunch advocate of Dyothelitism, taught a form of mysticism derived largely from the pseudo-Dionysius. Banished by the Eastern Emperor because of his uncompromising opposition to Monothelitism, he made Carthage the scene of his later activities, and from this vantage ground diffused throughout the Western Church the pseudo-Dionysian mysticism. He regarded the pseudo-Dionysius as the holy revealer of Divine mysteries, as the 'all-holy,' the 'great saint,' the 'God-revealer,' and he had no doubt as to his identity with St. Paul's Athenian convert. Almost equally with the Areopagite, Maximus falls into pantheistic and Docetic conceptions.

The fulness of the Godhead which was in Christ by nature is in Christians by grace, as far as their nature is capable of receiving it. Man on account of his love to God becomes God for God; on account of his love to man he becomes man for man. Christ is continually and if His own will mystically born, for He is made flesh in and through the redeemed. The Logos became the Son of Man in order that He might make men gods and sons of God.

The Incarnation can hardly be said to have been regarded by Maximus as more than a theophany, and it was by no means limited to Jesus. If the latter participates in the Divine more fully than other men, it is only because His nature laid hold of it more fully (cf. Dorner, II. i. 228 ff.). The heterogeneous mixture of pseudo-Dionysian Neo-Platonic mysticism and mystagogy with Dyothelitism in Maximus opened wide the door in the West as well as in the East for the influence of the former.

6. That the influence of the Areopagite and of Maximus was brought mightily to bear upon the orthodoxy of the East is manifest in the *Fountain of Knowledge* of **John of Damascus** (d. about 754), who yet uncompromisingly maintained the persistence of two wills in the Person of Christ (Christ unitedly willing in correspondence with each of the two natures), and the freedom of His human will. The pseudo-Dionysian formula, 'Divine-human energy,' he understood to imply a Divine and a human activity each permanently differentiated from the other; yet he was at great pains to show the unity of the two natures (cf. Dorner, II. i. 210). The permeation of the human nature by the Divine involved in his conception the deification of the human. He illustrates the relation of the Divine and the human in Christ by the permeation of iron by heat. The human intellect of Christ, by virtue of this permeation, participated in the all-comprehending Divine knowledge from the beginning. He takes a Docetic view of the NT representation that Jesus grew in wisdom and favour. So also he regards Docetically the prayers of Christ. God constituting the personality in Christ, there was no occasion for prayer except to furnish an example to us and to do honour to God. Yet he was very far from accepting the Eutychian idea that Divine attributes were communicated to the human nature. While the flesh became the flesh of the Word, and the soul of Jesus the soul of the Word, the human nature remained unaltered in essence. Solely on the ground of the fellowship of the Divine and the human was the flesh of the Lord enriched by the Divine activities. It is evident that this great thinker, whose *Fountain of Knowledge* is still normative in the Greek Church, failed to gain a perfectly consistent view of the relations of the Divine and the human in the Person of Christ.

7. The views of the pseudo-Dionysius and Maximus reappeared among the monks of Mount Athos about the middle of the 14th cent. (**Hesychasts, Quietists**), and occasioned the Hesychastic controversy, the chief opponents being the leaders of the party that was promoting union with the Latin Church. The cause of the Hesychasts was ably defended by Nicolaus Cabasilas, bishop of Thessalonica, and by Marcus Eugenicus, archbishop of Ephesus. The Christology of Cabasilas is highly transcendental. He regarded Christ as the resting-place of those human yearnings that are directed towards the highest good, as the luxuriant pasture of the thoughts, as the eternal good incorporated with time. Although he held fast to the Chalcedonian doctrine of two natures and two wills, he yet regarded the Word as superessential even in the Incarnation, and the humanity of Christ as superhuman and deified though of like substance with us. The sacraments of the Church he regarded as the channels through which life streams forth from Christ to us. Baptism represents the generation in us of the new Christ-life. Everything pertaining to man's salvation was accomplished by the death and resurrection of Christ. Baptism simply transfers the saving efficacy to the individual. The purification of human nature accomplished in the Incarnation in Christ is accomplished in the individual Christian by his partaking of the Divine-human nature present in the Eucharist. Appropriating Christ in this feast, we enter into a blood-relationship with God and Christ; and as Christ's humanity became deified in the Incarnation, so do believers by partaking of Him.

8. In the West, **John Scotus Erigena** (d. about 880) translated, under the patronage of Charles the Bald, the pseudo-Dionysian writings, by which, as well as by the writings of Maximus, he had been profoundly influenced. Through him the Neo-Platonic mysticism was transplanted to the West, and came to exert a marked influence on later Christological thought. His teachings were even more openly pantheistic than those of his Oriental masters, and his denial of the reality of derived existence and his thoroughgoing Docetism make it extremely difficult to interpret much of the language in which he strives to give a certain value to the historical facts of redemption. While asserting that Christ took upon Him the form of a servant and human nature in its entirety, he shows at once how little his language accords with common-sense usage by saying that the human nature that the Word assumed contains in itself the entire visible and invisible creation. Christ's mission was to call back effects into causes, and thus to prevent causality itself from perishing. Thus in assuming and renovating human nature He renovated the whole of the creation visible and invisible. In assuming and renovating human nature thus with its universal contents, Christ raised it in Himself above all that is visible, and converted it into His Deity. He saved the entire human nature which He entirely assumed entirely in itself and entirely in the entire race. Entire humanity is exalted in Him and sits at the right hand of God, having become God in Him. It is manifest that such conceptions of incarnation leave no place for evangelical views of sin or redemption. By his seeming recognition of the historical life of Christ he can have meant only to set forth belief in a theophany which had the effect of furthering and facilitating the rise of men above theophanies to the archetypal (cf. Dorner, II. ii. 294 ff.).

9. A far more evangelical type of mystical Christology is found in the writings of **Hugo of St. Victor** (d. 1114) and **Richard of St. Victor** (d. 1173). In them the theosophy of Erigena was transformed into ecstatic enjoyment of God Himself. They were unable to find satisfaction in the Church doctrine of the transubstantiation of the bread and the wine into the body and the blood of Christ as the form in which Christ may be enjoyed, but yearned for a spiritual union with Christ, the transubstantiation of the believer by an ecstatic exaltation into a mystical union with Christ. The Christology of Hugo and Richard was clearly that of the pseudo-Dionysius and of Erigena; but with them the Incarnation was conceived of more distinctly as a historical fact, and the ecstatic union of the believer with Christ did not so clearly involve loss of individual consciousness and virtual absorption.

10. The pantheistic features of the teaching of Erigena found their most extreme development in **Amalric of Bena** (d. 1204), who identified God with the world and with man. Yet he did not wholly ignore the historical, and maintained that God revealed Himself as Father in Abraham, as Son in Mary, and as Holy Spirit daily in us. He declared that we are the natural members of Christ, because the identical soul of Christ dwells in all good men. Spiritual exaltation from Christ dwelling in us emancipates us from all moral obligation, and makes sins of the flesh a matter of indifference.

11. More profoundly philosophical but scarcely less destructive to the Christology of the NT and to true religion was the mysticism of **Master Eckhart** (d. *c.* 1327). He refused to recognize any distinction between man and God, in nature or in persons. All creatures he regarded as a 'pure nothing.' Every believer is God's only-begotten son in the same sense in which this is true of Christ. 'Whatever God the Father has given to His only-begotten Son in human nature, He has given wholly to me. Here I except nothing, neither union nor sanctity.' 'Whatever the Sacred Scripture says concerning Christ is also absolutely true of every good man.' Eternal generation applies to every good man as fully as to Christ. In fact, man as well as God may be said to have created the heaven and the earth, and to have generated the eternal Word.

12. In **John Tauler** (d. 1361) we have a highly Neo-Platonic mode of thought combined with the most devout and heartfelt recognition of the Incarnation and the propitiatory sufferings of Christ as absolutely necessary for our salvation. Christ's being is cause, essence, and beginning in relation to all things. He is the life of the living, the resurrection of the dead, the restorer of the deformed and disordered who have corrupted and spoiled themselves by sin, the beginning of all light, the illumination of all those who are illuminated, the revealer of obscurity according to what it is proper for us to know, and the beginning of all beginning. His being is inconceivable and unspeakable, and without names. In becoming flesh and making atonement for the guilt of humanity He is its Redeemer. The Holy Spirit took of the most pure blood of the virginal heart of Mary, which was glowing with the powerful flame of love, and created of it a perfectly pure little body with all its members, and a pure clean soul, and united these together. This soul and body, the Person of the Son of God, who is the eternal Word and the reflexion of the Father's glory, from genuine love and mercy, for the sake of our blessedness, took upon Himself and united with Himself into the unity of the Person. Thus the Word became flesh and dwelt with us. The humanity of Christ he regarded as even in the humiliation permeated by the Divine, and sharing in the possession and use of the Divine attributes. The same was true even when He suffered and died on the cross. According to its lower powers Christ's soul was subject to needs. From this point of view he could say that not a drop of His Deity came for one moment to the help of His poor agonizing humanity in all its needs and in its unspeakable sufferings. Tauler is never weary of emphasizing the importance of the death of Christ. He speaks of the whole human race as fallen into eternal death and the eternal wrath of God, with the loss of the Holy Spirit, the Comforter. Christ broke the bands of eternal death in His death on the cross, and made a complete peace and reconciliation between man and the Heavenly Father. This reconciliation is confirmed by the gift of the Holy Spirit. The sufferings and death of Christ he regarded as an equivalent for man's guilt, as a fulfilling of the Law which we were under obligation to fulfil, in that He suffered in our place and on our behalf. Tauler dwelt with great persistence and with remarkable pathos on the details of the sufferings of Christ and His infinite love for the souls of men. It will not be practicable to give here any further phases of mystical Christological thought.

13. *Scholastic Christology* next demands attention. **Anselm of Canterbury** (d. 1109), in some respects the most important of the mediæval theologians, wrought out no new theory of the Person of Christ; but his satisfaction theory of the Atonement, involving the abandonment of the supposition that the death of Christ was a ransom paid to the devil, and basing the necessity of the death of the God-man on the infinite weight of sin and its infinite offence to the honour of God, was an important contribution to soteriology. Satisfaction to the Divine majesty could not be made by man, seeing that he is finite, or by the Son of God alone, seeing that He owed no satisfaction; but it must be made by the God-man. While perpetuating the Augustinian modes of thought as they had been modified by Gregory the Great, Alcuin, etc., Anselm was also greatly influenced by the Neo-Platonic semi-pantheism of Erigena. In opposition to the tritheism of Roscellinus, which seemed to him to require the Incarnation of Father, Son, and Spirit, and not of the Son alone, as the means of man's redemption, he insisted that it was impossible for Father and Spirit to become man. The Incarnation merely accomplished the union of the Divine and human personalities, and not the union of the Divine and human natures. The Divine Person became man and formed one Person with the humanity assumed, but not the nature. There was no transformation of Deity into humanity or of humanity into Deity. Not the Divine nature but the Person of the Son became man. If the Divine Person alone and not the Divine nature took part in the Incarnation, it is plain that we cannot speak of the three Persons having become man in Christ, unless we hold that several persons could become one person (Dorner, II. i. p. 442 ff.). Anselm as a Realist insisted that in the Incarnation the Logos united Himself not with an individual man, but with impersonal humanity, in this opposing the Nominalists, who insisted that the humanity of Christ was individual and personal.

14. Abelard (d. 1142) was essentially Sabellian in his doctrine of the Trinity, and insisted that, being unchangeable, God could not have become something which He was not eternally. He rejected such expressions as 'God is man,' 'Man became God.' He affirmed 'God did not become anything in and through the Incarnation.' He preferred to say in effect, 'in the man Jesus, God worked'; that 'in Jesus the wisdom of God revealed itself, in order to lead men to salvation by doctrine and example' (*Theologia Christiana*, iv. 13). This thought he is never weary of iterating and enforcing, that whatever our Lord did in the flesh was for our instruction by way of example. This includes His walk, His death, and His resurrection. He regarded Incarnation in the proper sense of the term as unthinkable and impossible, because of his conception of the omnipresence and the unchangeableness of God.

15. Peter Lombard (d. 1160), in his *Sentences*, which became the text-book of mediæval scholasticism and thus exerted a moulding influence upon later scholastic thought, asked and sought to answer nearly every conceivable question respecting Christ. His great master was John of Damascus; but he was well acquainted with Augustinian thought, and no doubt with the works of Anselm and Abelard. He was also somewhat familiar with Neo-Platonic modes of thought without being overmastered by them. He sees no reason why Father or Holy Spirit might not have become incarnate, but finds especial appropriateness in the fact that He who created the world should deliver it, that He who proceeded from another rather than He who is self-existent should be sent on the mission of redemption. It would have been less fitting for Him who is Father in heaven to become Son in the sphere of revelation. The human nature that the Son assumed comprised body and soul, the substance of humanity. This humanity, which was impersonal, was free from any stain of sin; yet, because He so willed, the liability to punishment which clung to humanity in general remained. Though as regards His flesh He descended from Adam and Abraham, He did not sin in Adam, there being no concupiscence in His conception. The question then arises, whether the Personality or the nature of the Son assumed humanity. As he felt the necessity of maintaining that the Son, as distinguished from the Father and the Spirit, became incarnate, and as nature is what the Persons of the Godhead have in common, while personality connotes the distinctions in the Godhead, he could only answer that the Personality and not the nature of the Son assumed humanity (against Augustine). But he seems to have held that in and through the Son the Divine nature as such united itself with, and appropriated to itself, humanity. Yet, in agreement with John of Damascus and the Antiochene theologians of the 4th cent., he thought it advisable to avoid the expression 'the Divine nature became flesh.' In further discussing the significance of the Incarnation, he rejects the Eutychian and the Nestorian views of the union of Divine and human in the Person of Christ. He denies that out of the two natures was formed a single compound nature. The Word of God, on the contrary, was simply clothed with body and soul as with a garment, in order that He might appear in a form accommodated to human vision. Thus he virtually denied the reality of the union, and reduced to a mere theophany the Incarnation of the Son. The humanity being regarded as a non-essential, accidental feature of the Son of God, its end and aim was solely that of manifestation, and

God might for this purpose have used some other means for helping man than that of Incarnation. He regarded Christ's mediatorial work as accomplished by His humanity alone, the Divine nature remaining apart by itself. We are reconciled with the Son as with the Father and the Spirit. The entire Trinity blots out our sins through the mediation of the humanity of Christ. The work of atonement is accomplished chiefly, if not exclusively, by Christ in His humanity setting forth by His sufferings the fact of God's reconciliation, and by thus awakening in men love for God and a desire to follow Christ's example of love to God and self-sacrifice for men. In some passages he seems virtually to deny that God became objectively a man in Christ, and to maintain that the humanity of God was a purely subjective conception of the human mind. Moreover, reconciliation was not really effected by Christ, but God intended that His life and death should be regarded as propitiatory. His denial of personality to the humanity of Christ necessitated his denial of the growth of Christ in grace and wisdom. Peter Lombard's denial that God became anything through the Incarnation which He was not before, involves the doctrine more fully wrought out by his successors and known in the history of doctrines as Nihilianism. This conclusion had already been reached by Abelard (see above) ; but the general orthodoxy of Peter Lombard gave it increased importance.

16. Gerhoh of Reichersberg (d. 1169) protested most earnestly against the Nestorianism or Nihilianism involved in the teachings of Abelard and Peter Lombard, and maintained that 'the man born of the virgin mother is in truth also to be called the Most High, not only in the nature of the Word always most high, but also in His human nature that has been exalted even to the point of sitting with God the Father.' He claimed for the humanity of Christ 'the same glory, omnipotence, omnisapience, omnivirtue, omnimajesty, which belong to the Most High Father,' and held that 'the man in Christ is to be adored with worship' in the highest sense. 'Christ who is everywhere, according as He wills, cannot be shut up in a place, however beautiful or desirable.' The body of Christ 'so grew, became so dilated, that it filled the whole world.' Again he speaks of Christ's body as 'a spiritual body that has overstepped every limitation of time and space.' Thus we see in this German theologian a strong reaction against French Nominalism towards the Realism of Eutychianism and Neo-Platonism, which was to go to the utmost extreme in German Mysticism (see above) and to be perpetuated in Lutheranism.

17. Thomas Aquinas (d. 1274) built upon the foundations of his Scholastic predecessors, and was much influenced in his Christology by the works of John of Damascus and the pseudo-Dionysius. Like most of the mediæval theologians, he denied the necessity of Incarnation apart from human sin ; yet he guarded carefully against representing it as a mere accident as regards God, a mere assumption of flesh by God as a garment. He insisted upon a personal union of God with humanity ; and yet denied that 'the Divine Person so assumed one human nature that it could not assume another.' 'That which is uncreated cannot be comprehended by a created thing.' While he opposed the Nihilianism of Abelard and Peter Lombard, he yet minimized the part taken by the Divine essence in the Incarnation. Like most of his mediæval predecessors, he denied the personality of Christ's humanity in Christ. Personality it found in the Logos as a distinction Divinely conferred. Like Peter Lombard also, he maintained that not the Divine nature (which would involve Father and Spirit as well as Son), but only the Divine Person of the Son, became in any sense united with humanity in the Incarnation. This union bestowed upon humanity nothing of the Divine nature, but only such created graces as humanity was able to appropriate. 'The soul of Christ is a creature, having finite capacity.' This creaturely grace was bestowed in perfection at the moment of incarnation in such measure that its increase is inconceivable. Christ's knowledge did not embrace the Divine knowledge, it being 'impossible for any creature to comprehend the Divine essence.' Whatever has been, is, or will be, was within the sphere of the comprehension of Christ's soul in the Word ; but not the knowledge of the possible, involving a knowledge of the Divine essence. Thus even the time of the Divine judgment which Christ professed not to know He really knew, but was ignorant of only in relation to others. Thomas also denied omnipotence to the soul of Christ on the same ground. Only as the instrument of Deity could the human soul exert superhuman influence. He maintained that in Christ there were two wills, a Divine, which was the active cause of all He did, and a human, which was purely instrumental. In the human will he distinguished between the sensuous (*sensitiva*) will and the rational will, the former sometimes willing things other than God willed, but not contrary things ; the latter co-operating and harmonizing perfectly with the will of the Word. Yet, while His human will was free, Christ did not have the power to decide for Himself, but was determined by God. Like Peter Lombard, Thomas ascribed Christ's mediatorial function to His humanity and not to His Deity. He agreed with most of his predecessors in denying the necessity of the Incarnation and suffering of the Son for man's salvation, maintaining that without injustice God might have freely pardoned human sin. Yet he recognized the propriety of the plan of redemption actually adopted. The very least degree of suffering on the part of the God-man would have sufficed. He finds difficulty in reconciling Christ's sufferings with His blessed fruition, and reaches the conclusion that the higher aspect (the essence) of His soul continued in perfect fruition while the lower suffered. It is evident that this great thinker, while rejecting Eutychianism, Nestorianism, and Adoptianism, failed to reach a self-consistent view of the relation of the Divine and the human in the Person of Christ.

18. We must conclude our survey of Scholastic Christology with some account of the contribution of **John Duns Scotus** (d. 1308). Although Scotus differed in many respects from Thomas, and gave his name to a party antagonistic to the latter (Scotists *versus* Thomists), in Christology he was content for the most part to follow in the path that had been so well beaten by Thomas and his predecessors. Like these, he maintained that the union of the Divine and the human was only a relation so far as the Divine was concerned, and that for the Divine to become anything that was not eternal is inconceivable. More than Thomas he laid stress on the relative independence and separateness of the human in Christ. Independence he regarded as indispensable to personality. He supposed that the human nature of Christ was such that it would have attained to personality apart from the Word ; yet a personality dependent on God, and not, like the Divine, incommunicable. More than Thomas also he kept clear of Adoptianism, and guarded against representing Christ's humanity as a selfless husk (Dorner). He regards Christ's humanity by virtue of Divine predestination and grace as exalted to a dignity not possessed by nature. Scotus had an exalted idea of human nature as such, and attributed to it a capacity for the Divine that enabled it through the Word to gain an intuitive view of creation that may be said to be infinite in its scope. In the Incarnation the infinite ethical susceptibility of the human soul was filled by the infinite God. He did not regard the humanity as merely passive and instrumental. In joining itself with the will of the Son that was seeking union with humanity, the human will of Jesus was not passive, but being wrought upon by the Divine it determined itself to increasing susceptibility to the Divine. He attributes to the humanity of Christ growth in knowledge and volition, and suffering of soul and body. He regards as miraculous and inexplicable the fact that the Divine nature did not swallow up the human so as practically to annihilate it, but rather caused it to retain its true humanity. The necessity of supposing the humanity of Christ active in the Incarnation, doubtless had to do with the stress that Scotus laid on the immaculate conception of Mary in whom this activity could be assumed. In some respects Scotus advanced beyond any of the Scholastic theologians in his efforts to solve the mysteries of the Incarnation.

19. The Christology of the Evangelical sects of the mediæval time (Petrobrusians, Henricians, Arnoldists, Waldenses, Taborites, Lollards, and Bohemian Brethren) may be characterized in general as naïvely Biblical, and accordant with that of the orthodox teachers of the 2nd and 3rd centuries. Much of the mediæval Evangelical Christology, as well as much of the Anabaptist Christology that was its outgrowth, savoured strongly of Adoptianism. This was no doubt due in part to the widespread influence of the Paulicians, who were transported in large numbers from Armenia to Bulgaria by the Eastern Empire during the early Middle Ages. All the Evangelical sects of that era laid the utmost stress upon obedience to the precepts of Christ, especially the Sermon on the Mount, and on following the example of Christ. While they kept the humanity of Christ constantly before them, they worshipped Him as God, repudiating utterly all Mariolatry, and all worship of images, holy places, saints, martyrs, etc. They seem not to have concerned themselves at all about the relations of the Divine and the human in the Person of Christ, but to have been content with the NT representations accepted in a devout and simple-minded way. It is probable that nearly all of them would have accepted without hesitation the so-called Apostles' Creed, but would have hesitated to accept the so-called Athanasian Creed. The inquisitors frequently charge the Waldenses and related parties with denying the true Deity of Christ, although they had the profoundest reverence for Him and gladly gave their lives for Him. The Catharistic sects, following the Gnostics and Manichæans of the earlier time, denied the true Deity of Christ (regarding Him as one of many angelic beings or emanations), and the reality of His Incarnation and suffering.

Chiliastic views were widely prevalent among the heretical offshoots of the Franciscans, Joachimites, Olivists (followers of Peter Olivi), Taborites, etc.

20. The idolatrous disposition of the Greek and Roman Catholic Churches in the mediæval times created an insatiable demand for holy objects connected with the Person and the life of Christ (articles of clothing, fragments of the cross, etc.), and especially for portraits and statuettes produced from life by contemporaries or miraculously formed. In the East the ikons, as they existed at the beginning of the Middle Ages (close of the Iconoclastic Controversy), which had long before become conventionalized, furnished the models for all later productions, and little scope was given to the imagination of the artist or the exploitation of fraudulent antiquities. In the West unlimited license was given to both. The Abgar picture (see ABGAR), whether what purported in the 4th cent. to be a contemporary portrait had been preserved or not, was sure under the circumstances to reappear in the mediæval West, and it could hardly have been expected that one church would be allowed to enjoy a monopoly of an object at once so desirable and so easily made. There is no sufficient foundation for the story that the handkerchief-portrait remained in Edessa till 944, whence it was taken to Constantinople by Imperial order, and thence went to Italy in the 14th cent., presumably in connexion with the Crusades. It is not likely that so perishable an article would have lasted for six centuries, to say nothing of the thousand years that have elapsed since its supposed removal from Edessa, and the ecclesiastics of the mediæval time were so unscrupulous in providing themselves with revenue-producing holy objects that no dependence can be placed on their accounts of their sources. It may safely be assumed that neither the Roman, the Genoese, nor the Parisian handkerchief-portrait is that which long abode in Edessa, and that all alike are of mediæval or later origin, though the Genoese enjoys the honour of having been pronounced genuine by Pius IX. Even more manifestly spurious and lacking in antiquity is the so-called Veronica portrait, said to have been transferred by Boniface VIII., in 1297, from the Hospital of the Holy Spirit to St. Peter's in Rome. Those who have been vouchsafed a glimpse of the sacred object represent it as almost completely faded out. The legend is that a pious woman (according to some the woman cured of the issue of blood), moved with compassion for Jesus, as, bleeding and sweating, He was going to the cross, gave Him her head-cloth to wipe His face with, and that Jesus imprinted His features upon it and returned it to her as a token of love. The name Veronica was by some supposed to be the Latin equivalent of the name of the woman; but by others it is taken to mean 'true image,' as etymologically it might. The Roman Church has canonized this purely mythical woman as St. Veronica. The picture, according to copies made before it faded out, represents an oval bearded face with thin hair reaching to the temples, eyes closed, and a somewhat agonized expression. This inartistic picture became a model for Correggio and other artists of the later Middle Ages. The stories about the sweat-cloth image, and probably pictures purporting to be the original, may have found place as early as the 7th or 8th cent.; but those exhibited in the mediæval and later times were probably of purely mediæval origin, and were no doubt freely produced as they were needed. Rome was not allowed to monopolize the 'original' Veronica portrait, Milan and Jaen having put forth rival claims. Many other pictures, equally lacking in authenticity and with similar claims to antiquity, were produced and exhibited during the Middle Ages, portraits of the earlier time (4th cent. onward) being for the most part taken as models. The symbolical representation of Christ as a fish was perpetuated from the earlier time. Christ as the Good Shepherd, with the face of a beardless youth, was a common form of representation during the Middle Ages, as earlier. It is the opinion of many that the artists of the Renaissance, while influenced to some extent by the older portraits, drew freely on pagan materials, using especially the earlier representations of Æsculapius to aid their imaginations in depicting the ideal Christ. Crucifixes with agonized face and bleeding wounds were freely used during the Middle Ages. It needs scarcely be said that the Evangelical and Catharistic parties utterly repudiated the use of pictures of Christ and crucifixes as idolatrous.—See CHRIST IN ART.

LITERATURE.—Writings of the theologians whose opinions are presented : works on the History of Doctrines by Harnack (German and English), Baur, Seeberg, Thomasius (ed. Seeberg), and Loofs ; Bach, *Dogmengesch. d. M.A.*, 1873–5 ; Schwane, *Dogmengesch. d. mittleren Zeit*, 1882 ; Reuter, *Gesch. d. Aufklärung im M.A.*, 1875–7 ; Dorner, *Entwickelungsgesch. d. Lehre v. d. Person Christi*, 1853 (also Eng. tr.) ; works on Church History by K. Müller, Möller, Gieseler, Neander, Schaff, and Hase ; art. on 'Christologie,' 'Christusbilder,' and on theologians and systems concerned in *PRE*[3], and in Hastings' *Encyclopædia of Religion and Ethics* ; Gottschick, 'Studien zur Versöhnungslehre d. M.A.' in *Zeitschr. f. Kirchengesch.* xxii., xxiii., and xxiv.; Döllinger, *Beiträge zur Sektengesch. d. M.A.*, 1890 ; Denifle, *Archiv f. Lit.- u. Kirchengesch. d. M.A.*, 1885, and onward.   ALBERT HENRY NEWMAN.

CHRIST IN REFORMATION THEOLOGY.—It is commonly said that the whole Christian Church has taken its doctrine of the Person of Christ from the Eastern Church, and simply adopted the definitions formulated at the Councils of Nicæa, Constantinople, and Chalcedon ; and further, that at the Reformation the Reformers contented themselves with brushing away the meaningless refinements of the Scholastic divines of the Middle Ages, and accepted without change the conclusions come to in the Councils of the undivided Church. Neither of these statements is strictly accurate. They have this basis of truth that both East and West accepted the same forms of sound words, and professed the Creeds and verbal definitions sanctioned by the Œcumenical Councils down to that of Chalcedon, but they do not take into account the fact that verbal statements may cover a great deal of divergence in intellectual views— a divergence which in the present case was not merely in intellectual conception, but represented fundamentally distinct types of Christian piety.

The Western Church owed very little to the Eastern, and had a Christology of its own with a clearly marked history, from Tertullian to Augustine ; and its intellectual definitions corresponded to a definite type of Christian piety. Athanasius and Augustine alike dwell on the mystery lying in the union of the Divine and the human in the Person of Christ the God-man, and can express their thought in the same language ; but for Athanasius the mystery lies in the union of two natures, while for Augustine the mystery lies in the Person. 'My Saviour,' says Athanasius, 'must be the great God who made heaven and earth ; and He must unite the human and Divine natures which He possesses, in a union which for me is a mystery to be believed, but which my intelligence can never explain or penetrate.' The Greek type of piety fed itself on the mysterious union of natures ; the Incarnation was the central thought in Christianity, and salvation appeared to the Eastern Church as a species of diffusion of the Incarnation : men were saved when they were absorbed in the Divine. Augustine felt as strongly the need for a Saviour who was both God and man ; and, inheriting the theology tradition of the West, first established by Tertullian and confirmed by Ambrose of Milan, he found a clue to a statement of the Person of Christ in the NT phrases, 'the *form of God*,' and 'the *form of a servant*,' and held that these two forms coexisted in the unity of the Person (see above, p. 854[a]). There was no mystery in the natures. They did not coalesce or blend or unite so far as the natures themselves were concerned. The Person possesses both these forms simultaneously ; the one and the same Person was at one and the same time in the *form of God* and in the *form of a servant* ; and in this unity of the Person lay the mystery. 'Filius

Dei semper, filius hominis ex tempore, tamen unus Christus ex unitate personæ. In cœlo erat quando in terra loquebatur. Sic erat filius hominis in cœlo, quomodo filius Dei erat in terra ; filius Dei in terra in suscepta carne, filius hominis in cœlo in unitate personæ.' All believers feel this unity so very strongly that they instinctively create this unity of the Person for themselves. The unity exists in the heart of every Christian. The common Christian thought is that there is a Man in whom God dwells, and who is God. This is the mystery of the Person. 'Proprium illius hominis sacramentum est.'

It is evident that the piety which dwells on the mystery of the Person as opposed to the mystery of the union of the natures has its attention directed to the personal saving acts rather than to the passive condition of incarnation, and sees its salvation worked out for it in the life, death, and rising again of the Divine Person, rather than in the diffusion of the Incarnation. Thus two types of Christian piety correspond to the two differing intellectual conceptions of where the mystery lies in the Person of Christ, and each can accept the same verbal definitions.

Luther and all the Reformers held the Western conception of the Person of Christ. For Luther and for Calvin the most venerated creed was the Western symbol which is called the Apostles' Creed, which in its old Roman form can be traced back to the first half of the 2nd century. Luther and Calvin both placed it in their catechisms for children. Calvin declares that the whole of his *Institutio* is its exposition, and Luther always understood the Nicene and the Athanasian Creeds to be explanations of the Apostles' Creed. For Luther, as for Augustine, Jesus is a Man in whom God dwells, and who is God.

Luther always declared that he accepted the doctrine, and nothing but the doctrine, of the ancient Church on the Person of Christ. 'No one can deny,' he says, 'that we hold, believe, sing, and confess all things in correspondence with the Apostles' Creed, that we make nothing new therein, nor add anything thereto, and in this way we belong to the old Church, and are one with it.' The Schmalkald Articles and the Augsburg Confession begin with stating over again the doctrines of the Old Catholic Church, founding on the Nicene Creed, and quoting Ambrose and Augustine ; and Luther's contention always was that, if the sophistry of the Schoolmen could be cleared away, the old doctrines of the ancient Church would stand forth in their original purity. When he spoke of the Scholastic Theology as sophistry, he attached a definite meaning to the word. He meant not merely that the Schoolmen played with the outsides of doctrines, and asked and solved innumerable trivial questions, but also that the imposing edifice they erected was hollow within, and had nothing to do with the God and Father of our Lord Jesus Christ. He maintained that in the heart of the system there was, instead of the God whom Jesus had revealed, the abstract entity of pagan philosophy, an unknown deity—for God could never be revealed by metaphysics. All this sophistry he swept away, and then declared that he stood on the ground occupied by the theologians of the ancient Church, whose faith was rooted in the triune God, and in belief in Jesus Christ the Revealer of God. The old theology had nothing to do with Mariolatry or with saint-worship ; it revered the triune God and Jesus Christ, His Son, the Saviour of mankind. Moreover, Luther believed, and rightly believed, that for the Fathers of the ancient Church, the theological doctrines in which they expressed their conceptions about God and the Person of Christ were no dead formulas, but were the expression of a living Christian experience. Luther took the old dogmas, and made them live again in an age in which it seemed as if they had lost all their vitality and had degenerated into mere dead doctrines on which the intellect could sharpen itself, but which were out of all relation to the practical religious life of men. That is to say, in other words, Luther gave to theology a religious interest, and this was a recovery of something which had been lost. Mediæval theology had little sense of religion. Religious phenomena, like the appearance of St. Francis and the existence of the 'Brethren,' were not taken into serious consideration by theologians. The *Summa* of Thomas Aquinas gives little insight into the deep and genuine religious experience of the writer, and gets no inspiration there. The efforts of the Schoolmen were directed solely to the exposition of the philosophical implications of traditional doctrines ; they ignored the relation to actual religious life in the Church, apart from which theology becomes unreal. Probably it requires a succession of religious geniuses to maintain the right connexion between theology and contemporary religious experience, and it is the opinion of Ad. Harnack that the Church had no genius between Augustine and Luther. No one realized that a supreme utterance of faith like St. Bernard's hymn—

'Jesus, our only joy be Thou,
    As Thou our prize wilt be ;
Jesus, be Thou our glory now,
    And through eternity'—

and such experience as finds expression there, formed any part of the material of theology. And so theology missed its opportunities of serving the Church. Had theology undertaken the task of understanding and interpreting words like these, it would have cleared the path to new truth, and set pious souls free. As it was, for want of its proper food, theology languished, and simple saints, though at times soaring on the wings of faith, still carried their crutches lovingly about with them. They still believed in an exclusive priesthood, in magical sacramental grace, in prayers to saints, and works of merit and Papal dispensations. Even the ' Brethren' who, all through the Middle Ages, pointedly ignored the ecclesiastical system and obstinately put to all who tried to force doctrines upon them the question, ' Where did Christ teach that ?' were strangely without any impulse to state a theology of their own. For centuries the breath of pure devotion to Christ never fertilized the learning of the schools, and no genius arose—no great churchman in whom personal religion was the inspiration of a mind at once critical and constructive. Not till Staupitz, on his visit to Luther's convent, recommended the old German theology of Tauler to the youthful scholar-monk, did the secret of Christian piety once more find lodgment in the soul of a religious genius, who saw how to make the thoughts of faith supreme throughout the whole sphere of religion—in church life, in ritual and theology, as well as in the lonely heart. Through Luther came the rediscovery that there was theological material in the living experience of Christian souls. And since in the Christian soul Christ is always enthroned, this amounted to a rediscovery of the place of Christ in theology. Directing itself thus to experience, theology realized that its important task is not to give the metaphysical assurances about Christ's Person with which the Schoolmen laboriously occupied themselves, but to explain the nature of His saving work which makes believers hail Him as Lord.

But if Luther accepted the old formulas describing the nature of God and the Person of Christ, he did so in a thoroughly characteristic way. He desired to state them in plain German, so that they could appeal to the ' common man.' Neither he nor any of the Reformers believed that theology, which for them was, or ought to be, the most practical of all disciplines, was a secret science for experts, described in a language which must be unintelligible to the multitude. He confessed with some impatience that technical theological terms were sometimes necessary, but he did not like them, and he used them as little as possible.

' Quodsi odit anima mea vocem *homoousion*, et nolim ea uti, non hæreticus ero, quis enim me coget uti, modo rem teneam, quæ in concilio per scripturas definita est' (Erlangen ed. Lat. xxxvi. 506). Like Athanasius, he preferred the word *oneness* to express the relation between the Persons in the Trinity. He even disliked the term *Trinity* or its German equivalents *Dreifaltigkeit, Dreiheit*. ' Dreifaltigkeit ist ein recht böse Deutsch, denn in der Gottheit ist die höchste Einigkeit. Etliche nennen es Dreiheit ; aber das lautet allzuspöttisch . . . darum lautet es auch kalt, und viel besser spräch man Gott denn die Dreifaltigkeit' (Erlangen², xii. 408). He called the technical terms used in the old creeds *vocabula mathematica*, and did not use any of them in his Small or Large Catechisms.

In framing his conception of what was meant by the Person of Christ, Luther, like all the Reformers, started from the saving work of the Redeemer. He approached the Person of Christ from our Lord's mediatorial work, and not from any metaphysical way of thinking what Godhead must be, and what manhood must be, and how Godhead and manhood can be united. He rises from the office to the Person, and does not descend from the Person to the office.

' Christ is not called Christ because He has two natures. What does that matter to me? He bears this glorious and comforting name because of His office and work which He has undertaken' (*ib*. xii. 244).
It is a true appreciation of His work that leads to a real knowledge of His Person. ' He who, with Peter, has a true view of the office which Christ must exercise in the world, and effect with us, must conclude with Peter that Christ must be God in like omnipotence' (*ib*. vi. 286). ' To remove from us the burden of sin, death, hell, and the devil, and to vanquish their power, and to bring again righteousness, life, and salvation, are the works neither of men nor of angels, but only of the One, Eternal, Divine Majesty, the Creator of heaven and earth.

Therefore must this seed of Abraham be true, everlasting, Almighty God, equal to the Father from all eternity' (*ib*. xix. 18). He who accomplished an effectual redemption for fallen and enslaved humanity must needs be Divine. The idea of a redeemer of man, Himself no more than man, or rather, Himself less than the one eternal God, was to Luther an absurdity. Redemption and Godhead were inseparably bound together.

So, like Athanasius, Luther found in his salvation the proof of the Divinity of the Saviour. Beneath all the reasonings of the great Alexandrian there lay his fundamental Christian experience that the Saviour who redeemed him must be the great God who made heaven and earth. It was the same with Luther.

In the second article on the Creed in his Catechism, he says, ' This means that I believe that Jesus Christ, true God . . . is my Lord who has redeemed me,' and again : ' We must have a Saviour who is more than a saint or an angel ; for if He were no better and greater than these, there were no helping us. But if He be God, then the treasure is so ponderous that it outweighs and lifts away sin and death ; and not only so, but also gives eternal life. This is our Christian faith, and therefore we rightly confess : "I believe in Jesus Christ His only Son, our Lord, who was born of Mary, suffered and died." By this faith hold fast, and though heathen and heretic are ever so wise, thou shalt be blessed' (Erlangen ed. xlvii. 3, 4).

Jesus Christ was for Luther *the mirror of the fatherly heart of God*, and therefore was God ; God Himself was the only Comforter who could bring rest to the human soul burdened by sin and grief ; and the Holy Spirit was God. The old creeds confessed One God, Father, Son, and Holy Ghost, and the confession contented him, whatever words were used. Besides, he rejoiced to place himself side by side with the Christians of the ancient days, who were free from the sophistries of the Schoolmen, and to feel that he also belonged to the ancient Church, the communion of the saints.

But although Luther and the other Reformers accepted the theology of the ancient Church and introduced its creeds into the reformed services of public worship, they put a richer meaning into the doctrine of the Person of Christ than had ever been done before their day ; and the thought of the Divinity of Christ meant more to them than it had done to their early predecessors. Jesus, the Saviour, seemed to be God in a more intimate way to them than to the earlier divines. The old theology had stated the doctrine of the Two Natures in the Person of Christ, in such a way as to suggest that the only function of the Divine nature was to give to the human work of the Saviour such an importance as to make it effective. This is seen in Augustine, in Anselm, and in the Reformed Scholastics of the 17th century. Luther and his fellow-Reformers always refused to take this limited way of regarding the Divinity of Christ. They did not refuse the expression ' Two Natures in One Person,' but Luther makes it plain that the words suggested an idea which he believed to be wrong, and which had to be guarded against. He declares frequently that we must beware of thinking that the Deity and the humanity of Christ are united in such an external fashion that we may look at the one apart from the other. When we see Jesus, we perceive God and man really and intimately united.

' This is the first principle and most excellent article, how Christ is the Father : that we are not to doubt that whatsoever the man says and does is reckoned, and must be reckoned, as said and done in heaven for all angels ; and in the world for all rulers ; in hell for all devils ; in the heart for every evil conscience and all secret thoughts. For if we are certain of this : that when Jesus thinks, speaks, wills, the Father also wills, then I defy all that may fight against me. For here in Christ have I the Father's heart and will' (Erlangen ed. xlix. 183, 184).

Luther's sense of the rich and full Divinity of Christ is not won at the expense or neglect of His humanity. On the contrary, he believed that the reason why the Schoolmen had made so many mistakes was that they had practically omitted the humanity of Christ altogether. They had obscured His humanity by a multitude of conceptions and fancies which Luther could not abide. The legends of meaningless miracles and supernatural claims attributed to the infant Jesus, he characterizes as 'pure foolishness.' For it widened the gulf between Him and us. Where a mediæval preacher delighted in recounting marvels taken from apocryphal sources, emphasizing all that tended to put Christ in a different order of being from us, Luther dwelt continually on all His characteristically human traits, on all that made Him one with us.

'The deeper we can bring Christ into our humanity, the better it is,' he says in one of his sermons (Erlangen ed. vi. 155). So his frequent pictures of the boyhood of Jesus are full of touches from the family life of the home at Wittenberg. The boy Jesus lived just like other boys, was protected, like them, by the dear angels, was suckled at His mother's breast, learned to walk, ate and drank like other children, was subject to His parents, ran errands for His mother, brought her water from the well, and firewood from the heap in the yard, and finally, when He grew up and became stronger, began to ply the axe to help His father (*passim*). And this, Luther asserted against those who had erected it into an article of faith that Christ from the first moment of His life was so full of wisdom that there was nothing left for Him to learn. He will have nothing to do with those who ascribe to Christ only a mutilated humanity. 'By humanity I mean body and soul. And this I wish to emphasize because some, like Photinus and Apollinaris, have taught that Christ was a man without a human soul, and that the Godhead dwelt in Him in place of the soul' (Erlangen ed. x. 131).

As with every other article of his creed, Luther had a practical religious interest in holding so firmly to the humanity of Christ. The human life of Jesus glorified humanity, and was a pledge of the final glory of all redeemed humanity.

'It is,' he says in his exposition of Jn 1¹⁴, 'the most precious treasure and highest comfort that we Christians have, that the Word, the true natural Son of God, became man, having flesh and blood, like any other man, and became man for our sakes, that we might come to the great glory: thereby our flesh and blood, skin and hair, hands and feet, belly and back, sit in heaven above, equal to God, so that we can boldly bid defiance to the devil and all else that harasses us. We are thus made certain, too, that they belong to heaven and are heirs of the heavenly Kingdom' (Erlangen ed. xlvi. 12 f.). It was no mere semblance of a man who was now exalted at the Father's right hand, but one who was bone of our bone, and flesh of our flesh, to whom no human experience, save sin, was foreign,—a boy who enjoyed his play and helped in little household duties, a man who shared the common lot of toil and weariness and temptation, a real man living a true human life under conditions not so far removed from our own. Having life—a true human life—He understands us fully, and we can know Him, and God through Him. Through Him alone can we come to know God. 'Outside of this Christ no other will of God is to be sought. . . . Those who speculate about God and His will without Christ, lose God completely' (Walch's ed. vol. v. p. 198).

With the Reformers, therefore, the historical life of Jesus is of the utmost importance, far exceeding all metaphysical dissertations upon the nature of a God-man. We can all have naturally a human sympathy with that marvellous life; but faith, the gift of God, is needed to see the Divine meaning in that life and death. The meaning, put in its briefest form, is that in Jesus we see God appearing in history and addressing man. Hence the Person of Christ was something more than a mere doctrine for them—an intellectual something outside us. It must be part of that blessed experience which is called Justification by Faith. It is inseparably connected with the recognition that we are not saved by the good deeds we are really able to do, but solely by the work of Christ. It is what makes us cease to trust all work-righteousness, and to confide ourselves to God alone, as He has revealed Himself in Jesus Christ. When we know and feel that it is God who is working on our behalf, then we instinctively cease trying to think that we can work out our own salvation (Erlangen ed. xii. 244). Hence the Person of Christ must always be something more than a mere doctrine for the true Christian. It is something which we carry about with us, as part of our lives.

'To know Jesus in the true way means to know that He died for us, that He piled our sins upon Himself, so that we hold all our own affairs as nothing, and let them all go and cling only to the faith that Christ has given Himself for us, and that His sufferings and piety and virtues are all mine. When I know this, I must hold Him dear in return, for I cannot help loving such a man.'

Here we reach the kernel of the Reformation thought about Christ Jesus, and the master-thought which distinguishes its theology from all previous teaching about God and the Person of Christ.

Luther lets us see, over and over again, that he believed that the only thing worth considering in theology was the Divine work of Christ and the experience we have of it through faith. He did not believe that there was any real knowledge of God without these limits. Luther, as Ad. Harnack says, 'in his relation to God, only thought of God at all as he knew Him in Christ.' Beyond them there is the unknown God of philosophical paganism, the God whom Jews, Turks, and pagans ignorantly worship. No one can really know God save through the Christ of history. Hence, with Luther, Christ fills the whole sphere of God: 'He that hath seen me hath seen the Father,' and conversely, 'He that hath not seen me hath not seen the Father.' The historical Jesus Christ is for Luther the revealer, and the only revealer, of the Father. The revelation is given in the marvellous experience of faith in which Jesus compels us to see God in Him—the whole of God, who has kept back nothing which He could have given us. This is the distinctive mark of the way in which the Reformers regarded Christ; all theology is Christology; they knew no other God than the God who had manifested Himself in the historical Christ, and made us see in the miracle of faith that He is our salvation.

'There is only one article and rule in theology. He who has not a full and clear grasp of it is no theologian; namely, true faith and trust in Christ. Into this article all the others flow, and without this they are nothing' (Erlangen ed. vol. lviii. 398). 'In my heart there rules alone, and shall rule, this one article, namely, faith on my dear Lord Christ, which is, of all my thoughts on things spiritual and Divine, the only beginning, middle, and end' (*ib.* lviii. 63).

The early Christians had said of Jesus that He must be conceived of as belonging to the sphere of God (2 Clement, i. : ἀδελφοί, οὕτως δεῖ ἡμᾶς φρονεῖν περὶ Ἰησοῦ Χριστοῦ, ὡς περὶ θεοῦ). The Reformers added: and that He fills the whole sphere of God, so that there is room for no other vision of God than that which Christ gives us. This master-thought of Reformation theology simplified Christian doctrine in a wonderful way. It justified Luther's rejection of the complicated discussions of the Schoolmen, and his accusation that what they called their 'sophistry' was partly pagan; and it also showed clearly that Christian worship ought to be simplified too.

The reader of the second part of the second book of the *Summa Theologiæ* of Thomas Aquinas cannot help seeing that the really evangelical aspirations of the great Schoolmen are everywhere thwarted and finally slain outright because the theologian has to start with the thought that God has been first defined as either the *Absolute*, or the *Primum Movens*, or the *Causa efficiens prima*, or the *Intelligens a quo omnes res naturales ordinantur in finem*—conceptions which can never imprison, without destroying, the vision of the Father who has revealed Himself to us in Jesus Christ. What have Christians to do, the Reformers asked, with a great Eternal Something, which is not the world, when they have the Father? It would have been well had their followers in after generations realized this principle, and the Church might have been spared the 17th cent. Scholasticism, where God was defined as the *Principium essendi et cognoscendi*, where His purpose in salvation became a Divine decree, taking the place of the category of substance, and where theology, borrowing as much from Aristotle as from the Scriptures, became a second-rate metaphysic.

The older theology had never grasped the thought that Jesus Christ filled the whole sphere of God. It limited the work of Christ to the procuring of forgiveness of sins, and left room outside Christ for many operations of Divine grace which were supposed to begin when the work of forgiveness was ended. So there grew up the complex system of expiations and satisfactions, of magical sacraments and saints' intercessions, which made the mediæval Christian life so full of superstitions, and, to all seeming, so empty of Christ. To the mediæval theologian all these could be justified, because they came from that portion of the sphere of God which was, as it were, beyond Christ. The influence of Christ was exhausted, they thought, when bare forgiveness had been won; and the grace needed for all holy living came from operations of the grace of God which did not necessarily come through Jesus Christ. But when the Reformers thought of God, they thought of Christ and of Christ alone. The grace of God was always to them the grace of Christ; the Holy Spirit was the Spirit of Christ; the presence of God was the presence of Christ, and the possession of God was the possession of Christ. They could not, therefore, regard grace as a mysterious something, different from the soul and outside it, and at the same time different from Christ and outside Him also. Grace became simply the possession of, and the presence of, Christ, who is the whole God. This simplified the Christian life, and swept away at once the whole complex system which had bred so much superstition.

This characteristic of Reformation thought and of Reformation piety, that Christ fills the whole sphere of God, appears everywhere in the writings of the Reformers and in the rites and worship of the Reformed Churches, and may be illustrated, if not exhaustively described, in the following instances of its application.

1. The Reformers swept away every contemplation of intercessors who were supposed to share with our Lord the procuring of pardon and salvation, and they declared against all attempts to distinguish between various kinds of worship, which could only lead pious souls astray from the one worship due to God in Christ. The Romish Church said that saints did not receive actual worship, and that images were reverenced only in the same sense as copies of the Scriptures. Calvin has no difficulty in showing that these distinctions were not popularly grasped.

'Such subtle distinctions,' he says, 'as *latria, doulia, hyperdoulia*, are neither known nor present to the minds of those who prostrate themselves before images until the world has become full of idolatry as crude and plain as that of the ancient Egyptians, which all the prophets continuously denounced; they can only mislead, and ought to be discarded. They actually suggest to worshippers to pass by Jesus Christ the only Mediator, and betake themselves to some patron who has struck their fancy. They bring it about that the Divine offices are distributed among the saints as if they had been appointed colleagues to our Lord Jesus Christ; and they are made to do His work, while He Himself is kept in the background like some ordinary person in a crowd. They are responsible for the fact that hymns are sung in public worship in which the saints are lauded with every blessing just as if they were colleagues of God.' In this connexion he quotes the 'impious stanza heard in many churches': 'Ask the Father, command the Son,' addressed, of course, to the Virgin; and the invocation of St. Claud as 'the life and resurrection of the dead.' *

In the same way he inveighs against the doctrine of works of supererogation as derogatory to the merits of Christ, and says that 'in making up the treasury of the Church, the merits of Christ and of the martyrs are thrown together in the slump,' 'mixing up the blood of Christ with the blood of martyrs, and forming out of them a heterogeneous mass of merits or satisfactions.' †

In conformity with these thoughts, the Confessions of the Reformation all agree in repudiating prayers to the saints. The Augsburg Confession says:

'The Scripture teacheth not to invoke saints, nor to ask the help of saints, because it propoundeth to us one Christ: the Mediator, Propitiatory, High Priest, and Intercessor. This Christ is to be invocated, and He hath promised that He will hear our prayers, and liketh this worship, to wit, that He be invocated in all afflictions: " If any man sin, we have an advocate with God, Jesus Christ the righteous " ' (1 Jn 2¹). The Second Helvetic Confession in its fifth chapter lays down the rule that prayer is to be through Christ alone, and saints and relics are not to be worshipped. And all prayer-books and liturgies in every branch of the Reformed Church, even when taking over, with little alteration, old forms of prayer, carefully exclude addresses to the Virgin or to any of the saints.

In any case, the theoretic distinctions between reverence and worship never applied to the adoration of the consecrated host. This even in theory was absolute worship, and was felt to be abhorrent and profane by the Reformers, who had experienced

spiritual communion with the living Christ. Calvin calls it a 'theatrical exhibition.'

2. The Reformers insist on the necessity of Christ, and Christ alone, for all believers. Their confessions abound in expressions which are meant to magnify the Person and work of Christ, and to show that He fills the whole field of believing thought and worship; and, as Reformation theology was based on experience rather than on philosophy, and aimed at expounding the faith of the pious believer rather than at unfolding metaphysical mysteries, we find a constant reference to the various names and offices of Christ and to the manifold aspects of His work.

The brief Netherlands Confession of 1566 has no fewer than three separate sections: on 'Christ, the only Mediator and Reconciler,' on 'Christ, the only Teacher,' and on 'Christ, the only High Priest and Sacrifice.' The Heidelberg or Palatine Catechism, calls Christ 'my faithful Saviour,' and says that we can call ourselves Christians, 'because by faith we are members of Jesus Christ and partakers of His anointing, so that we both confess His Holy Name and present ourselves unto Him a lively offering of thanksgiving, and in this life may, with free conscience, fight against sin and Satan, and afterwards possess, with Christ, an everlasting kingdom over all creatures.' The Scots Confession abounds in phrases intended to honour our Lord Jesus Christ. It calls Him, 'Messiah,' 'Eternal Wisdom,' 'Emmanuel,' 'our Head,' 'our Brother,' 'our Pastor and great Bishop of our Souls,' 'Author of Life,' 'Lamb of God,' 'Advocate and Mediator,' 'the onlie Hie Priest.' The English Prayer-book, while for the most part reflecting the stereotyped conclusion of the breviary *per dominum*, in the endings of the Collects introduces new forms, such as, 'for the honour of our Advocate and Mediator, Jesus Christ,' and 'through the merits of Jesus Christ our Saviour.' All the Confessions and Liturgies of the Churches of the Reformation abound in the same or similar expressions.

3. The Reformers declare that Christ is the *only* revealer of God.

'We would never recognize the Father's grace and mercy,' says Luther in his Large Catechism, 'were it not for our Lord Jesus Christ, Who is the mirror of the Father's heart.' 'We are not affrayed to cal God our Father,' says the Scots Confession, 'not sa meikle because He has created us, quhilk we have in common with the reprobate, as for that He has given us His onely Son.' The instructions issued by the Synod which met at Bern in 1532 are very emphatic upon this thought, as may be seen from the headings of the various articles: (Art. 2) 'That the whole doctrine is the unique Christ' (*Das die gantze leer der eynig Christus sye*); (Art. 3) 'That God is revealed to the people in Christ alone'; (Art. 5) 'That the gracious God is perceived through Christ alone, without any other mediation'; (Art. 6) 'A Christian sermon is entirely about and from Christ.' It is said under the third article, 'His Son, in whom we see the Work of God and His Fatherly heart toward us . . . which is not the case where the preacher talks much about God in the heathen manner, and does not exhibit the same God in the face of Christ.'

The means of this revelation are the Spirit, which all the Confessions unite in declaring to be the gift of Christ, and the Holy Scriptures. The claim of the mediæval Church to be the sole trustworthy exponent of the Scriptures had barred the way to Christ through the Word, and had driven men to seek contact with Him in the sacraments, a region where they were more at the mercy of ecclesiastical assumption. The Church itself had used the Bible chiefly as a quarry for proof-texts of ecclesiastical dogmas. But for the Reformers the Scriptures are the plain man's guide to Christ. In them Christ Himself speaks to each soul.

In the Formula of Concord it is said that Christ 'offers Himself in the Word as Redeemer.' The Thirty-nine Articles of the Church of England say: 'Both in the OT and in the NT everlasting life is offered to mankind *by Christ*.' The Scots Confession says: 'We believe and confess the Scriptures of God sufficient to instruct and make perfect the man of God. So do we avow the authority of the same to be of God, and neither to depend on man or angels.' In the decrees of the Bern Synod (1532) Scripture is called 'a witness to, a means of access to, and a remembrancer of Christ.' And again it is said that 'the Scripture leads us to Christ and teaches (Him) as the Saviour.'

We thus see clearly that the Reformers' conception of Christ as the revealer of God at once restored the Scriptures to their rightful place in popular religion, and gave to the Bible a new unity. To the mediæval Church it had been a

* Calvin, *Opera Omnia* (Amsterdam, 1667), viii. 38, 39.
† Calvin, *Necessity of Reforming the Church*.

difficult collection of isolated doctrinal texts; to the Reformers it formed a complete book with one centre, the Person of the Redeemer.

4. The conception that Christ filled the whole sphere of God, which was for the Reformers a fundamental and experimental fact, enabled them to construct a spiritual doctrine of the sacraments, which they opposed to that of the mediæval Church. It would be unfair to ignore the germ of an evangelical idea even in the materialistic Romish doctrine of transubstantiation. While the way to Christ through the Scripture was barred by the refusal of the Church to place the Bible in the hands of the people, here was one way in which the common man might suppose he got into direct contact with his Redeemer. We see this religious use of this doctrine in its crudest form in the hymn of St. Francis:

> 'Oh, how pure and worthy should be the priest
> Who touches the living, glorified Jesus.
> Let the whole earth tremble,
> Let the heavens thrill with joy,
> When Christ the Son of God descends upon the altar.'

What made the sacrament holy to Francis was the personal presence of Christ. Nevertheless, the ordinary attitude to the sacraments was grossly superstitious. The doctrine of transubstantiation, interpreting the presence of Christ in a material sense, practically annulled the reference to Christ altogether, and made the sacrament an exhibition of the magic powers of the priesthood. The sacraments were looked upon as magical channels of Divine grace. The accepted doctrine was, in the words of the decrees of the Council of Florence, that 'while these others (the sacraments of the OT) do not convey grace but only figure the grace given by the Passion of Christ, these sacraments of ours both contain grace and confer it upon the worthy receiver.' Thus in theory, as in practice, the sacraments usurped the place of Christ. Now, although it was the various theories about the sacraments that caused the chief differences among the Reformers themselves,—Luther, with his mediæval philosophy, insisting that, by virtue of Divine omnipresence, the words, 'This is my body,' might be literally and physically true; Calvin, with his more spiritual doctrine, insisting that the presence of Jesus is in spiritual power; Zwingli, casting overboard the whole question of the real presence and dwelling only on the memorial aspect of the feast,—still, with all their varying ideas, the Reformers united on the thoughts that the efficacy of the sacraments depended entirely on the promises of Christ contained in His word, and that the virtue in the sacraments consisted in the presence of Christ to the believing communicant. What was received in the sacrament was not a vague, mysterious, not to say magical, grace, but Christ Jesus Himself. He gave Himself in the sacraments, in whatever way His presence might be explained. The efficacy of the sacrament depends on Christ, not on any magical powers of priests; and what is received in the sacraments is not any mysterious grace, but Christ Himself.

All the Reformers taught that the efficacy of the sacraments depends on the promise of Christ contained in their institution, and they insisted that word and sacrament must always be taken together.

Thus Luther points out in the *Babylonish Captivity of the Church*, that one objection to the Romish practice is that the recipients 'never hear the words of the promise which are secretly mumbled by the priest,' and exhorts his readers never to lose sight of the all-important connexion between the word of promise and the sacraments; and in his Large Catechism he declares that the sacraments include the word. 'I exhort you,' he says, 'never to sunder the Word and the water, or to separate them. For where the Word is withheld we have only

such water as the maid uses to cook with.' The Augsburg Confession says, 'The sacraments are effectual by reason of the institution and commandment of Christ.' Non-Lutheran Confessions are equally decided on the necessity of connecting the promise and the words of Christ with the sacraments. The Second Helvetic Confession says, 'There remains efficacious in the Church of God, Christ's primal institution and consecration of the sacraments, so that those who celebrate the sacrament, not otherwise than the Lord instituted it at the beginning, enjoy even now that primal most glorious consecration of all. And therefore, in the celebration of the sacraments the very words of Christ are recited.' The Thirty-nine Articles declare that the sacraments are effectual because of 'Christ's institution and promise.' The Heidelberg or Palatine Catechism of 1563 says that the sacraments 'are holy and visible signs ordained of God to the end that He might thereby the more fully declare and seal unto us the *promise* of the Holy Gospel.'

Further, against the Roman doctrine of sacramental grace we have these Reformation statements. In the articles of the Bern Synod (1532) we are told that the sacraments are mysteries of God, 'through which, from without, Christ is proffered to believers.' The First Helvetic Confession (1536) says, concerning the Holy Supper, 'We hold that in the same the Lord truly offers His Body and His Blood, that is, Himself, to His own.' The Second Helvetic Confession (1562) declares that 'the Body of Christ is in heaven at the right hand of the Father,' and enjoins communicants 'to lift up their hearts and not to direct them downwards to the bread. For as the sun, though absent from us in the heaven, is none the less efficaciously present . . . so much more the Sun of righteousness, absent from us in the heavens in His Body, is present to us not indeed corporeally, but spiritually by a life-giving activity.' The French Confession of 1557 says that the sacraments are pledges and seals, and adds, 'Yet we hold that their substance and truth is in Jesus Christ.' So the Scots Confession of 1560 declares that 'we assuredlie beleeve that be Baptisme we ar ingrafted in Christ Jesus to be made partakers of His justice, be quhilk our sinnes ar covered and remitted. And alswa, that in the Supper richtlie used, Christ Jesus is so joined with us, that Hee be cummis very nurishment and fude of our saules.' In the *Manner of the Administration of the Lord's Supper* the Scottish Reformation Church directed the minister in his exhortation to say to the people: 'The end of our coming to the Lord's Table . . . is to seek our life and perfection in Jesus Christ, acknowledging ourselves at the same time to be children of wrath and condemnation. Let us consider then that this sacrament is a singular medicine for all poor sick creatures, a comfortable help to weak souls, and that our Lord requireth no other worthiness on our part, but that we un-feignedly acknowledge our naughtiness and imperfection.'

The Reformation was a revolt from a system which removed God far from the common man's understanding by means of metaphysical speculations, and brought Him near only in super-stitious and materialistic ways, through sacraments and priests. It was seen again that in Christ God had come close to the ordinary believer, and the appeal to religious experience proved that alike in prayer, in worship, and in teaching, Christ filled the whole sphere of God. Jesus was God appearing in history and addressing man.

LITERATURE.—Luther, *Opera*, 2nd Erlangen ed.; Calvin, *Opera Omnia* (*Corpus Reformatorum*), 1893 ff.; John Knox, *Works*, ed. D. Laing, 1846–64; Lindsay, *History of the Reformation*, vol. i. 1906, vol. ii. 1907; E. Doumergue, *Jean Calvin*, 1899 ff.; Th. Harnack, *Luther's Theologie*, vol. i. 1862, vol. ii. 1886; Köstlin, *Luther's Theologie*, 2nd ed. 1901; Müller, *Die Bekenntnisschriften der reformirten Kirche*, 1903; Schaff, *History of the Creeds of Christendom*, 1877; and the standard works on the History of Dogma and on Christology.

THOMAS M. LINDSAY.

CHRIST IN THE SEVENTEENTH CENTURY. —The 17th cent. is the age of Protestant scholasticism. A strong Catholic reaction had set in, which weighed on the minds of the defenders of the Protestant faith, and shackled the freedom of theological thought. In their treatment of the Christological problem, both Lutheran and Reformed theologians clung fervently to the traditions of the past, and to the Confessional theology of the previous century. The main results were regarded as finally attained; and while the religious motive was not wanting, the genial spirit that had guided Luther in his most surprising paradoxes was now weighed down by the love of system and scholastic disputation. Instead of reconsidering the first principles involved, the orthodox theologians wasted their ingenuity in inventing distinctions to conceal the most obvious doctrinal inconsistencies.

1. The **Lutheran Church** led the way in this scholastic development, by its endeavours to set in clearer light the unity of the God-manhood of Christ. The Formula of Concord (1577, published in the *Book of Concord*, 1580) struck a compromise between the divergent views of the Brenzian and the Chemnitzian doctrine. It held that the two natures of Christ had direct and real communion with each other; and it condemned as Nestorian the view that rested the unity of Christ upon the unity of the *Person*, as if the natures were combined in an external way, like two boards glued together. There was a real passing over of the properties of the Divine nature to the human nature; not in the sense that the human nature was essentially altered thereby, or made the Divine properties its own by a 'physical communication' or 'essential transfusion,' but in the sense of a real and permanent communication, such that Christ 'performed all the works of His omnipotence in, through, and with His human nature.' It was admitted that this majesty communicated to the human nature was hidden or withheld during Christ's earthly life; He did not always manifest it, but only when it pleased Him to do so; or (as it is elsewhere expressed) He 'divested Himself of His Divine majesty in the state of His humiliation,' though retaining it through the personal union. By the resurrection this occultation of the Divine majesty came to an end, and He was placed in the plenary use, revelation, and manifestation of all Divine powers, so that 'now not only as God but also as man He knows all things, is able to do all things, and exercises an omnipresent dominion.'

This Formula of Concord proved in reality a formula of discord to the Lutheran divines; it was variously interpreted, and not even universally accepted. The theologians of Helmstädt, who followed the more moderate Chemnitzian view, were all the more opposed to the Formula that it was interpreted by the Swabian theologians in a sense that restored the Brenzian tradition. The Swabians presented the doctrine of the *Communicatio idiomatum* in the most uncompromising form; and, in the most incautious and absolute terms, they attributed the Divine attributes of eternity, omnipresence, omnipotence, and omniscience to the earthly human Christ. For a time the Swabian views prevailed; but something had still to be done to harmonize them with the historical facts of Christ's earthly life. A new controversy arose, in which the differences between Chemnitz and Brenz reappeared in an acuter form, as to what was involved in the state of humiliation, or the extent to which the human Christ had divested Himself of the Divine powers. The controversy raged chiefly between the theologians of Giessen and Tübingen. The theologians of Giessen, following the line of thought of Chemnitz and the divines of Helmstädt, endeavoured to reconcile theory with fact by distinguishing between the *possession* of Divine powers and their *use*. Looking to the facts of weakness, ignorance, and growing development in the life of the earthly Christ, they maintained that, while possessing all Divine properties, Christ did not make use of them in the state of humiliation, but entered on the full exercise of His powers at His exaltation. Only occasionally (miracles, transfiguration) did rays from the Divine majesty shine through; in general the Logos remained quiescent, and the human nature, though Divinely endowed, did not advance to the actuality of exercise (κένωσις τῆς χρήσεως). This doctrine was contested by the theologians of Tübingen, who regarded the distinction as futile and involving a betrayal of the Lutheran position. They insisted that there would be no real communication of

Divine attributes to the humanity unless the human Christ both possessed and used them. They would admit only that the earthly Christ hid His majesty for the time, and usually made a veiled use of His Divinely communicated powers (κρύψις). This theory was apparently more logical than that of the Giessen theologians; but neither could be harmonized with the facts of Christ's earthly life, and the Tübingen theory brought the inconsistency into more startling evidence. The Giessen distinction between use and possession of Divine powers might be applied with some meaning to the property of omnipotence; but it had no conceivable meaning as applied to omniscience or omnipresence. But it fared even worse with the Tübingen view when brought face to face with the facts. For how could a Christ who possessed and used the property of omnipresence in His humanity be at the same time and in the same nature circumscribed in time and space? How could a growing intelligence be at the same time endowed with absolute omniscience? Or how could the weak, human, suffering Christ be also in the full exercise of His omnipotence? The Tübingen theologians did their best to solve these startling contradictions by making small concessions, and minute distinctions that concealed these concessions. Thus they maintained that the earthly human Christ exercised His omnipresence not *actu naturæ* but *actu personæ*; or, in other words, that the Person exercised it while the human nature remained under limitations—a verbal distinction which left the difficulty where it was. In regard to the omniscience of Christ, which seemed to clash with the fact of His gradual growth in knowledge, they submitted that omniscience was not incompatible with growth in a perfected human nature; and they suspected Mk 13[32], where Christ confesses His own ignorance, of being an interpolation. Or, again, when pressed with the facts of Christ's suffering and weakness as being inconsistent with a full energizing omnipotence, they admitted that Christ, for the sake of His redemptive work, 'retracted' somewhat of His Divine majesty. They made a distinction between the 'reflex' and the 'direct' use of omnipotence, declaring that Christ, *qua Sacerdos*, withdrew the reflex use of His majesty with reference to His own body, while He still, *qua Rex*, exercised the direct use of it in reference to creation.

These explanations of an intelligence that writhed under its own obvious inconsistencies, served only to bring in doubt the reality of Christ's human life, and more moderate views at length prevailed. The *Saxon Decision* of 1624 expressed a view favourable to the Giessen theology: 'We constantly affirm that He used His royal majesty most freely when, how, and where He would; but we deny that Christ as a man, immediately from His incarnation, always, fully, and universally exerted His Divine majesty of omnipotence and omnipresence, . . . since Christ could not have been taken, crucified, and put to death had He willed to use fully and universally His omnipotence and omnipresence.' The Tübingen theologians adhered to their views till nearly the end of the century, but they became more and more isolated in their opinion. The common Lutheran view was that represented by Quenstedt, the Lutheran Aquinas, who completely systematized the Lutheran doctrine. He held that, from the first moment of the Incarnation, Christ was, even in His human nature, in possession of the Divine majesty, and did exercise it occasionally when His work made it expedient to do so; but He abdicated its plenary use. The human Christ on earth emptied Himself by giving up for the time the glory of the μορφὴ θεοῦ, *i.e.* the 'divinæ majestatis plenarius, universalis, et non interruptus sive indesinens usus.' He thus reduced the possession by the human Christ of omnipotence, omnipresence, and omniscience to a mere potentiality. Christ was omnipresent while on earth, but not *actu*; He was everywhere present in fact, but not in act. He was omnipotent, but He preferred usually to act according to His natural powers. He had the *primum actum* of omniscience, but not the *secundum actum*; He had the potentiality of absolutely Divine knowledge, but ordinarily He willed not to use it.

On the whole it must be admitted that the Lutheran theologians had little success in their efforts to unify the God-manhood of Christ. Their well-meant endeavour to supplement the defects of the two-natures theory by a doctrine of intercommunication brought only more prominently into relief the contradictions involved. The further development of doctrine in this century shows that the Lutherans themselves were becoming less sure of their own principles. The old axiom that the human was susceptible of the Divine (*finitum capax infiniti*) was still maintained in its non-ethical sense, but it was surrounded with more definite cautions and limitations. Thus, in order to meet the charge made against them by G. Calixtus, and still more forcibly by the Reformed and the Roman Catholic Churches, that by their doctrine of *Communicatio idiomatum* they overthrew the distinction between the human and the Divine, they distinguished more carefully than hitherto between a *personal* and an *essential* communication of properties. It was insisted that the Divine properties communicated did not become the essential properties of the human nature, but were only personally possessed and exercised. Or, as it was otherwise expressed, the human nature of Christ possessed the Divine powers, not by absolute appropriation (μέθεξις), but by conjunction (κατὰ συνδιασμόν, *per unionem et conjunctionem*, Meisner, Hollaz, Buddeus). Still further, it was held that the principle *finitum capax infiniti* was applicable in the case of Christ alone. It was admitted that human nature was naturally and in general incapable of receiving the Divine powers, and that the human nature of Christ had been endowed with this capacity by a special act of the Divine power. When the principle of the *Communicatio idiomatum* is thus narrowed down on this side and on that, the old dualism reappears, and the Lutheran doctrine of the thorough union of the Divine and the human is in a state of collapse. Later attempts to rescue the *Communicatio idiomatum* from oblivion by removing it from its basis, the doctrine of the two natures (Dorner, and still more elaborately H. Schultz, *Lehre von der Gottheit Christi*), only repeat the mistake of pouring new wine into old bottles; for, as Baur says, when once the duality of natures is abandoned, there can be no further talk of a *Communicatio idiomatum*. Schultz tries to revitalize the doctrine in its triple form by an infusion of new ideas which have little historical connexion with it, and which could be better expressed in less scholastic forms.

The different kinds of *Communicatio* as given by Quenstedt may be here tabulated :—

I. Genus *idiomaticum*, where the qualities of either nature are attributed to the person : (*a*) when the person is the subject : Christ is eternal : Christ has died ; (*b*) when the concrete human nature is subject : the Son of Man is from heaven ; (*c*) when the concrete Divine nature is subject : God has suffered.

II. Genus *apotelesmaticum*, marking some activity in the redemptive work in which both natures concur : God is redeemer (*i.e.* God incarnate) : the Son of Man is redeemer (*i.e.* He who is Son of Man and Son of God) : the blood of Christ cleanses (*i.e.* the blood of Him who is both God and man).

III. Genus *majestaticum*, the attribution of Divine properties to the human nature : (*a*) *Divina nomina* ; (*b*) *Opera divina* ; (*c*) *Cultus divinus* ; (*d*) *Essentialia Dei attributa* : *e.g.* omnipotence, omnipresence, omniscience. The main controversy raged around this last genus.

2. The **Reformed Church** took a different path. Its theologians held fast to the principle of the Middle Ages, that finite human nature is not *capax infiniti*; but they applied it, as the Middle Ages had failed to do, to set in stronger relief the reality of Christ's human life. They considered the unity of Christ to be sufficiently safeguarded by the fact of the personal unity and the correspondence of the two natures, and emphasized the distinctness of the natures to the point of being charged with Nestorianism by their Lutheran opponents. Instead of such a communication between the natures as the Lutherans maintained, they were content to think of the human nature of Christ as working in harmony with the Divine through the anointing and activity of the Holy Spirit. Through this Holy Spirit, coming by way of the Logos, the human nature of Christ received certain Divine charisms ; but it did not receive the absolute Divine attributes, or any other powers than such as a human nature, remaining human, could receive. Thus they claimed for the human Christ sinlessness, infallibility in His teaching, and abiding fellowship with God the Father ; but they were earnest also in maintaining a true growth in Christ of positive knowledge, holiness, and power. Not even did the risen and exalted Christ surpass the limits of the human, or arrive in His humanity at complete coincidence with the Divine. On the other hand, they balanced this doctrine of a truly human development by the position that the personality of Christ lay in the Logos, who, in assuming this human nature, and appearing on earth in lowly guise, at the same time also remained outside of the human Christ, clothed with all the attributes of heavenly glory. (The Logos was *totus in carne*, but also *totus extra carnem*). Their theory results practically in the doctrine of a *double life*, the eternal life of the Son of God, the pure Logos *ex carne*, who remains unchanged in heavenly dominion and glory ; and the life in time of the man Christ Jesus, the Logos Incarnate, the God-man in lowly form. (This is the interpretation given by Bruce, *Humiliation of Christ*, 163 ff., Schultz, *Gottheit Christi*, 180, and others). It may be mentioned, as indicating the growing importance attached to the humanity of Christ, that the idea of Christ's *pre-existent humanity* gained ground during this century as well among the Reformed as the Lutheran divines. It recommended itself to the Lutheran theologian as exalting the human nature, and affording some support to his doctrine that the whole earthly life of Christ rested on the voluntary self-humiliation of the God-man ; while to some of the Reformed side it seemed to explain the position of Christ as the type and instrument of creation, and the medium of revelation prior to the Incarnation.

Comparing the views of the Reformed and Lutheran Churches, we may say that while both adhered to the ancient formula of Chalcedon, the Lutheran Church emphasized the Divinity of Christ, and the Reformed Church the humanity. In the Lutheran field of vision stands the figure of the Divine, omnipotent, omniscient, omnipresent Christ, upon which the humanity hangs like a thin transparent garment ; while, for the Reformed Church, the human Jesus of Nazareth stands in the foreground, and the Divinity lies in the background of faith, constituting a union with the human Jesus that is beyond comprehension. It cannot be said that either Church solved the problem of Christ's Person, for indeed no solution is possible on these terms. So long as the Divine and the human are defined by categories that are absolutely inconsistent—omnipotence and weakness, omniscience and ignorance, the infinitude of omnipresence and local bodily finitude—the union of these in one person is inconceivable. It is only when we read the glory of God in the face of Christ, and realize that the central and essential attributes of God are love, grace, compassion for human frailty and need, that we can recognize the Divine and the human as one, and acknowledge in Christ the revelation of the Divine, the Word of God Incarnate.

3. Outside of the orthodox theology a freer development of thought took place, under the influences derived from the anti-Trinitarianism of the 16th cent., and the growth of modern philosophy. **Socinianism** was a growing power, and the influence of its criticisms passed into every land. The Socinians made a clean sweep of the old Trinitarian and Christological dogmas, and so cut the knot of the intellectual difficulties involved. In their view it was irrational and unscriptural to speak of God as being three. It was equally irrational to think of God generating a Son after the manner of corruptible animals, or to speak of two natures, each complete in itself, coming together and forming one person. The rational and Scriptural doctrine was that Christ was *verus homo*. Yet, having once made this fundamental position clear, the Socinians made many concessions in favour of Christ's uniqueness in respect of Divine supernatural endowment. He was born supernaturally of a virgin. He was equipped for His work on earth by ascending into heaven, and receiving there all needful supernatural knowledge. He also exercised supernatural powers on earth; and after His ascension He was exalted to the right hand of God, and was endowed with new Divine powers for the guidance of His Church. As thus exalted He might be called God, and Socinus himself went so far as to justify the adoration of Christ. This Socinian doctrine rests on the same presupposition as the orthodoxy of the day, viz. that the supreme and essential characters of Deity are omnipotence, omniscience, unchangeableness; but by applying this conception logically to the Person of Christ, Socinians emptied their Christology of all religious value. For union with God is the need of the human heart; and the doctrine of the God-man, contradictory as it was, held a truth for which Socinianism found no expression.

4. The **Arminian** doctrine was a *via media* between the Socinian and the orthodox doctrine. The Arminian theologians adhered to the doctrine of the Trinity, but maintained that the Son, as begotten of the Father, was essentially subordinate, though still a Person within the Deity. They also maintained the full humanity of Jesus. Though one with the Son or Logos, He lived a truly human life; He had a human body and a human soul, and, according to Curcellæus, a human personality. The union with the Logos appeared in the communication to Jesus of Divine spiritual powers, but only of such as were possible to a creature. While they held His actual sinlessness, they denied His impeccability. Had they carried out their conception logically, they could scarcely have halted short of Socinianism.

Before the close of the century the Arminian Christology had multitudes of adherents, not only in Holland but also in Switzerland and England. In the latter country Deism had already begun to undermine the Trinitarian and Christological doctrines, and Arminian and even Arian views were widely spread within the Church. The whole tendency of the period was towards a more frankly humanitarian view of Christ's Person; and leading representatives of thought, like Milton, Locke, and Newton, whose sympathies were with the Christian faith, were estranged from the orthodox rendering of the Christian verities. The great variety of view, prevailing both in the Churches and beyond them, indicated the approaching dis-solution of the old dogma, while as yet the rationalism of the age had little to set in its place.

5. In this as in other centuries, **Mysticism** pursued its own path, and afforded to some minds relief from the high and dry dogmatism of orthodoxy. Starting from the true thought of the affinity of God and man, the Mystics tended either to lose sight of the historical Jesus entirely, or to see in Him but one manifestation of the eternal Word. Jacob Böhme may be taken as their noblest representative. Böhme stood too near to the Christian faith to sublimate Christ, and see in Him nothing more than the type of a universal incarnation; but history and dogma are but the material of his all-mastering speculation. The Trinity represents for Böhme the thought that God has life and movement, that He is no abstract, changeless entity apart from the world, but a living God, working in and through all, the source and goal and spirit of all, the unity in which all contradictions are resolved. He interprets the dogma in a variety of ways. The Father is the abyss; the Son is the first forthgoing of desire in the form of will; the Spirit is the eternal out-breathing of that will. Or, the Father is the originating will, the Son is the power of love which the will generates in determining itself, and the Spirit is the will's eternal outgoing. Or again, the Father is the source of all powers, Himself the one all-inclusive power; the Son is the heart and kernel of all powers; and the Spirit is their living movement. But Böhme sees the Trinity everywhere: in the soul of man (power, light, and the spirit of understanding), in plants (power, sap, peculiar virtue), nay, in all things that conceivably exist—even in the burning candle with its heat, light, and ascending air. In similar ways Böhme descants on the Person of Christ,—His double birth, in time and in eternity; His double body, the heavenly and the mortal. In spite of their incoherence, one may gather from Böhme's writings a suggestion here and there, but so far as definite ordered thought goes, his vagaries resemble the play of shadows on a wall. His meaning may be profoundly spiritual, but his language is a perverse interweaving of physics and chemistry with ethics and theology.

In no century was the *rabies theologica* more pronounced. The scholastic extravagance of the orthodox doctrine did not fail to work injuriously and sometimes disastrously on the religious life, while the intellectualism of the more critical circles did not directly serve the growth of religious piety. For the evidence of true and sincere devotion to Christ in this age we must look rather to the obscure and humble in the Churches, who found sustenance for their souls in a faith that surpassed all formulas, and which no scholasticism or criticism could rob of its transcendent power.

LITERATURE.—Planck, *Gesch. der prot. Theologie von der Concordienformel bis in die Mitte des achtz. Jht.*; Schneckenburger, *Vergleichende Darstellung des Luther. u. Reform. Lehrbegriffs*; Dorner, *Doctrine of the Person of Christ*, div. ii. vol. ii.; Schultz, *Gottheit Christi*; A. Réville, *The Deity of Jesus Christ*; G. Bonet-Maury, *Des origines du Christianisme unitaire*; A. B. Bruce, *The Humiliation of Christ*; artt. in *PRE*[3] on 'Kenosis,' 'Communicatio Idiomatum,' and on the various theologians referred to.   J. DICK FLEMING.

CHRIST IN MODERN THOUGHT. — **1. The modern spirit.** — (1) *Its genesis.* — The modern spirit manifests its characteristic modes of thought by contrast with the mediæval age. It carries to their ultimate result the tendencies that produced the Reformation and the Revival of Letters. It has revealed itself in positive and distinctive form only in our own day and after a long process. A brief general statement of the course that process took will serve to indicate at once its legitimacy and the extent to which it was likely to affect ideas of Christ.

In essence and at the outset the gospel appeared as a revolutionary idealism, inverting the old standards of excellence and the old criteria of truth, yet not outwardly revolutionary in its immediate aims. Continuous with this instinct grew up the mediæval mind. It is a mind which sees its ideals with the vividness of reality and in the same instant confesses the no less insistent reality of the actual, and the impossibility of transforming it as yet by the ideal. It is a mind therefore of compromises and contrasts. Familiar as a summary of the mediæval spirit at its maturity are these : (*a*) the contrast between this world and the other world ; (*b*) the contrast between faith and reason, philosophy and theology ; (*c*) the contrast between the secular and the sacred—which three are all aspects of one fundamental antagonism, that, viz., between the natural and the supernatural. The practical consequences of these postulates everywhere penetrated the common life and thought. The 16th cent. awoke to the keenest consciousness of their baleful influence. What characterized that age was its fresh sense of the reality of this life and of nature, and of the interests of both. Baptized anew in mental and spiritual experience, its loftier minds were enabled to initiate those departures from the mediæval system which were destined to determine the most powerful currents of the modern spirit and which still rule modern thought. Modern thinkers frankly abandon the idea of irreconcilable difference between nature and the supernatural. They acknowledge no revealed thought that is beyond their judgment, and believe in nothing which is in its nature inexplicable or irrational. They work in a spirit of rational freedom led by the conviction that there are not two worlds but one ; that it is one mind that lives in both ; that not the spiritual *and* the natural, but the spiritual *in* the natural, is the formula alone adequate to represent the truth. The modern spirit differentiates itself from the mediæval by conceiving the distinction between nature and spirit as one not of separation but of unity. To *spiritualize the natural* by force of insight into its deeper meaning is the ruling motive, the starting-point being experience—the experience in one life of both realms.

(2) *Its characteristic impulses.*—Only by a slow and gradual logic has clear self-consciousness of aim been reached. Among the contributory causes four are of special importance : the rise of speculative philosophy ; the scientific movement and the application of scientific method in historical and critical research ; the growth of socialistic theory ; revived interest in the psychological processes that enter into the construction of knowledge.

In *speculative thought* the new point of view formulates itself in theoretic form under the name of the 'absolute' standpoint. Absolute here means that the universe is wholly knowable. The term does not exclude relativity ; it only excludes an unknowable relativity divorced from all the phenomena of being and action. It points to two facts that must never be lost sight of, viz. that the Ultimate Reality is not abstract but the highest concrete, and that it can be reached by confidence in the power of Reason. The idealistic systems of Germany, in spite of their excesses, did magnificent service by their imperishable vindication of both truths. The *scientific spirit* observes patiently that it may define accurately. It is the spirit which takes nothing on trust, and seeks a reason for everything. It ranges knowledge in diverse spheres according as the facts it studies fall within the perceptions of sense, or manifest themselves in history, or are known in personal emotion and insight. Each science rests on its own proper principles, obtained from a study of its own facts, without reference to ideas drawn from other departments. Only thus is it possible to bring into clear relief the specialities and differentiæ of the various kinds of knowledge, and so establish the contribution of each to final truth. The scientific spirit has given birth to modern *History* and *Criticism*. *Social theory* embraces innumerable divergences of opinion, all of which have been influential in directing attention to the social situation and its effects on character. The Socialistic controversy has enormously deepened the feeling of human solidarity. Liberty, we are learning, does not depend on the absence of social pressure. Social power is the organ of personal character. The new *psychology* is the latest conspicuous intellectual movement of the time. It is the peculiar product of modern philosophy. Kant's achievement was to reassert against Hume's scepticism the claims of reason ; but also to limit their range ; to show that there are elements in the mind which underlie the very possibility of experience, and therefore cannot be derived from it : which elements are beyond the reach of Reason. In effect Kant showed that life is more than knowledge. That persuasion rules the modern world. The key to all problems lies in man ; and the key to the nature of man lies not solely in his thought, but mainly in his will. The whole man is seen in man active. There is an enhanced idea of personality. That idea carries with it two others whose significance for religious reconstruction we cannot overestimate. There is (*a*) the *ethical* character of man's experience ; his life is the fulfilment of relations with others ; (*b*) the

revealing power of his experience ; to the whole man in action and passion the inner meaning of things comes nearest.

Under the above mentioned impulses the modern mind has passed through the realms of nature, history, personal experience to a more complete mastery of knowledge. The effort has brought great gain to theology.

(3) *Its influence on theological method.* — Contemporary theological aims illustrate the direct effect of the foregoing forces in at least four directions : (*a*) towards a more scientific system of theology ; (*b*) towards a better appreciation of the nature of religious experience ; (*c*) towards insistence on moral personality as the determining principle in theological construction ; (*d*) towards recognition of the 'social consciousness' as contributory to theological truth.

'Scientific' applied to theology signifies a new method. The motive here is to vindicate for theology a sphere of knowledge of its own, precisely as for any other science ; and to assert and defend the right of theology to employ a method peculiar to its own facts, appropriate to its own sphere. The vindication successful, it follows at once that both theology and natural science may pursue each its own independent path, limited only by its own law, yet both moving in real harmony. The antagonism between science and theology vanishes. The vulgar conception of the supernatural, indeed, vanishes too ; but simply because the richer idea has taken its place of an inherent Divine Spirit in nature and in man, both of which are moments within the Spirit of the Divine Being. The facts alluded to in the *ethical* and *social* constituents of theological truth reveal the partial character of the sources from which in the past doctrinal construction has drawn. They were chiefly two, the intellect of Greece, the polity of Rome. Greek philosophy and Roman jurisprudence, working on the Christian facts, yielded the orthodox formulas. The genius of Northern Europe had later to enter in and infect the conscience of the Church with its own deep feeling. The temper of the present age is its fruit. It offers a wide contrast to the earlier age. It is an age less of intellect than of feeling ; it is less objective, precise, actual, but more inward, refined, wistful. Ultimate explanations take with us a touch of what is subjective and personal. Personality is one of the dominant categories of the hour. It is just what may be looked for that theology should seek to interpret its problems in terms of personality. The new method is a radical departure from the old. It begins with religion as actually experienced in personal life, and from that reaches, so far as it can, the thought of God and the nature of Christ ; whereas the dogmatic method begins with the thought of God authoritatively given and passes on from that to religion. The new method can never reach belief in any attribute of the Divine Nature which is not involved in religious experience. Merely metaphysical conceptions of Divine truth in terms of 'substance' or 'essence,' as these are commonly taught, fail to satisfy. A sufficient self-revelation of God can be given only in a full personal life. Fresh grace is discovered in the conscience. What the higher nature of man, his Moral Reason, witnesses to, that is the sure guide to the apprehension of Divine reality and the true foundation of religious feeling. For in that nature man is at his best ; there relation to God finds place, His revelation is received and His life shared. With the ethical goes *pari passu* the social. Society arises where the mutual intercourse of moral spirits is possible. The conviction has grown, in a degree unknown to earlier times, that such intercourse, realized in a true brotherhood of mutual service, may minister untold blessing to men. The 'social consciousness' is simply the growing sense of the power, the worth, the obligations of our intercourse with one another. From the intercourse of man with man, the communion of God with man is known. Growth in religious knowledge follows the laws of a deepening friendship.

The working motive here is worthy of special remark. It is that man has discovered *within himself* the starting-point and the test of religious verity. His deepest assurance comes to him as the outcome of his experience in life, as a person, active and patient, growing stronger as faculty springs up within him at life's stern challenge. Finite human experience, imperfect though it be, affords real if limited knowledge of the Infinite. And this knowledge is to be gained, not by putting ourselves outside of experience and by way of contrast constructing a Being with qualities diametrically opposed to the human, but rather by seeking to understand experience, and to determine which alone of the qualities and purposes it contains have permanent meaning and worth. The religious transition of the last four centuries has been a slow but continuous passage from the Aristotelian principle, that there is no 'proportio' between the finite and the infinite, to the principle first adopted by the Lutheran divines, that the finite is *capax infiniti.*

2. Modern conceptions of Christ.—Modern conceptions of Christ vary according as one or another of the characteristic forces of the modern spirit predominates. We may range them in a threefold order : (1) the Christ of Speculation or the Ideal Christ, (2) the Christ of Experience or the Ethical Christ, (3) the Jesus of History or the Historical Christ.

(1) *The Christ of Speculation.* — Each of the transcendental philosophies involved a speculative Christology. The first phase appears in **Kant** (1724–1804). The work of Kant in religious theory is the work of a pioneer. His equipment was not rich enough in mind or heart for more. Hume, as he tells us, 'awaked him out of his dogmatic slumber,' but only in philosophy. In religion he stood in line with the previous age. He shared the unhistorical views of the 18th cent. and its 'rational' religion. What of personal religion he knew, he knew intensely, as the class to which he belonged, the poorer citizen class, knows it; but, like that class also, with narrowness. It was a Christianity of heart and will, as practised among the common people, which was real to him. He stood quite outside Christianity in its ecclesiastical or mystical forms. Religious experience of any independent type, except as a department of moral life, he was unconscious of. He had no consciousness of God distinct from the dictates of conscience. Hence, when he came to rationalize his religious experience, the outcome, as was natural, was the simple translation into forms of reflexion of an imperious moral sense. The Kantian position is usually termed Ethical Deism. The extreme deistic view is, that creation is left to itself save for occasional Divine interferences. Kant's central doctrine is in harmony — asserting 'the absolute value of the ethical life.' God having originally created man and endowed him with reason and free will, nothing further is necessary on the Divine side for moral advance or redemption. Each man, as a moral personality, rests entirely on himself, on his own reason and freedom, and may make moral progress quite independently. His moral consciousness is conceived as so absolutely self-sufficient as to have no need of outward aid, whether from Nature, or Society, or God. On this general idea he constructs his conception of Christianity and Christ in his treatise, *Religion within the Bounds of mere Reason* (1793).

He starts with the perception of conscience of a *radical evil* dwelling in human nature as an indubitable fact of experience. The return to good prescribed by the moral law can be accomplished only by a thorough revolution of the entire mode of thought which establishes a new character, one susceptible of good, on the basis of which progressive moral improvement is made possible. The means by which this change in man is brought about is that the idea of moral perfection, for which we are destined from the first, is brought to a new life in his consciousness. But in no way can the ideal of a humanity well-pleasing to God be brought home to us more vividly than under the image of a man, who not only himself promotes the good by word and deed, but is also ready for the benefit of the world to endure all sorrows, since we measure the greatness of moral strength by the hindrances to be overcome. In the historical figure of Jesus this ideal appears. Not as though the idea of a humanity well pleasing to God were first invested with power and obligation by means of an example furnished by experience; rather has the idea its reality in itself, since it is founded on our moral reason. Only as an *historical exemplar* of this eternally true idea can such a figure as that of Jesus be presented to us. In Him the ideal of the good appeared in bodily form. When we believe in Him as the Son of God, the object of our saving faith is this eternal ideal of God-pleasing humanity, *not the historical man*; the ideal of which the historical man is but the highest representation. Incarnation is the 'personalization of the Moral Ideal.' Jesus first declared the moral to be the only saving, and afforded in His life and death an example of it. This exhausts the significance of His Person.

Opposition to Kant's interpretation of religion as mere ethics and of Christ as a Moral Example, impelled more genial minds like Hamann, Herder, Jacobi, and others to reactionary insistence on the immediacy of the religious consciousness and the speciality of the Christian revelation; but with neither critical nor philosophical depth. The direct succession from Kant appears in **Fichte** (1762 – 1814), who was impressed with Kant's results, started from them as a disciple, and later carried them to further consistency, and in so doing advanced decisively beyond them.

With Fichte, Christ was the first to apprehend the Divine, the first to recognize clearly and embrace freely the Divine will, and hence is the first-begotten of God. The manner of His apprehending was peculiar to Himself. The immediate unity of God and man in the spirit in which religion consists, came to Christ not by speculative philosophy or tradition as it does to us, but simply through His existence. This knowledge was to Him the primary and absolute thing, immediately identical with His self-consciousness. In Him, therefore, it may be said that God became incarnate. Fichte labours under the delusion of conceiving personality as a *limit* of the Divine nature. That God in becoming man might not annihilate but enhance personality and raise it to its true infinite capacity, had to be discerned. The attempt came with **Schelling** (1775 – 1854), whose philosophy is a philosophy of the Incarnation. His problem is determined for him by the conclusions of Fichte. According to the latter, the relation of the subject and object, human and Divine, is a unity of simple identity. But such an identity, it is to be noted, ignores the characteristic *differentia* of the human, *i.e.* that in the essence of the human which it is necessary to safeguard in its union with the Divine. The unity with which Christology is particularly concerned, cannot be understood if the two members of the antagonism are not thought out purely by themselves according to their idea. The unity is not a true unity if the members of the antagonism are not united by that which distinguishes and opposes them. Those two considerations, the essential unity of the subject and object, and their unity in the midst of their differences, form Schelling's contribution to this high debate. Together they yield his doctrine of the Absolute.

Whatever is, nature and spirit, is within the Absolute. It embraces all reality. It is the meeting point, — the neutrum, the 'indifference point,' — of subject and object, preserving the opposite alongside the negation for each *per se*. Moreover, it is living, concrete, being by ceaseless self-birth a mobile, willing, creative unity, and on that very ground necessarily a growth or historical process (*Werden*). In history the Absolute realizes itself. It could not become manifest in itself; to manifest itself it submits to limitations. The manifestation is not in any one form of finite limitation, but in the whole field of history. The finite or the historical is that in which the Absolute has its life: the form in which the Absolute reveals itself. It is thus not merely finite, it contains the Infinite within it; the human holds the Divine. The domain of history is the birthplace of spirit; history itself is the incarnation of God. Everything is explainable by this idea; God in His growth (*Werden*) or the Son of God. Nature points to Him, and has in Him its final causes; history unfolds the aspects of His life; religion experiences Him as personal freedom from personal evil.

The same idea is the essence of the Christian religion. Christ, in His historical individuality, is not the Son of God: the eternal Son of God is collective humanity, and what is true of collective humanity is not to be limited to Him. The Incarnation is falsely received when received as an isolated fact in time — it was from all eternity, and is not to be interpreted in an empirical way. Christ, however, is in a sense the beginning of this incarnation; since without Him it could not have come to be or be known. In Him God first becomes truly objective. As such He is the archetypal Man, the universal ideal Man. None before Him revealed God in such a manner, and from Him all men since have learned. But He is not the God-man. Of peculiar significance is the description Schelling gives of the manner in which Christ objectifies the ideal or Divine principle immanent in history. At one period he teaches that the Divine can manifest itself only in an endless series of finite forms, in the totality of which its inner essence is to be known. Here there are two points which reveal how far short of the truth of the ancient Creeds such theories fall. In the first place, the finite forms are a mere series of fugitive appearances of the Infinite, into no one of which the Divine veritably enters to abide: they can only signify the Divine. And secondly, so long as it is so the finite forms are essentially equal to each other: they represent a uniform series. On this line of thought the difficulty of appreciating Christ aright is insuperable. In the last and highest form of his philosophy, Schelling set forth a more fruitful estimate of the finite forms which reveal the Divine. He gives them more substance and concrete content. He arranges and organizes them, not in a monotonous series, but in ascending scale according to the measure in which the Divine spirit rises victorious in each. He is thus enabled to point to the uniqueness of Christ, and to place Him at the head of the series. From another direction deepening experience led him to a richer appreciation of Christ's Person. The power of evil, he came to see, was too vast to be overcome by man alone ; the redemption of the personal spirit is necessarily the work of God, and can be effected only by the immediate presence of God in human consciousness and knowledge. The more mightily evil had come forth in personal form, the more necessary was it that spirit should appear in human form as mediator—for ' only the personal can heal the personal.' God must become man. In Christ He did thus become man. In the Personality of Christ the Divine spirit is not simply signified, it is actualized. In Him the single personality is regarded as capable of taking up the perfect will of God into itself, and thereby of attaining absolute worth and becoming a true representative instead of a transitory husk of the Divine life. *The infinite significance* of personality is declared.

In **Hegel** (1770–1831) speculation reaches its culmination. Possessed of an imperial intellect, he succeeds in constructing a system (Absolute Idealism), with extraordinary skill and infinite detail, which co-ordinates and harmonizes into organic unity the various principles of his predecessors. His indebtedness to Kant and Schelling is real, and to the latter special. In the working out of the Hegelian scheme, logical considerations are determining. The process of human knowledge, with its alternate analysis and synthesis, is the type of the larger process of the universe. All progress is through distinction, and moves through the three steps of thesis, antithesis, and synthesis. A simple truth, once discovered, is affirmed as if it were the whole. Presently a larger experience forces man to the recognition of its apparent opposite, only to be succeeded later by the reconciliation of both in a higher unity. Given this simple formula, Hegel will build you the universe.

Hegel admits with Schelling the absolute unity of all things and the identity of the subject and object. But while Schelling, in order to explain how everything is derived from this unity, takes his point of departure in the Absolute, Hegel starts from the Idea (German, *Idee*), and professes by the force of dialectic alone to make all things spring from the Idea. The Idea includes the Absolute (which is the pure idea considered in itself and in an abstract manner), Nature (which is the idea manifested and become object), and Spirit (which is the idea turning back on itself and beholding itself as soul, as society, as God). The whole course of history is the coming to consciousness of the Absolute as Spirit, an august process which culminates in religion. The world of concrete finite experience is not outside of God, but is a moment in His consciousness. History is not un-Divine, but is the manifestation of God, a process within His infinite Spirit. Religion is the function of the human spirit through which the Absolute comes to full self-consciousness, and as such is the synthesis of finite and Infinite. Its highest form is the Christian religion.

In the eternal Idea there is but one Son, who exists in the first place simply for the 'thinking speculative consciousness,' but who, in order to be universally accessible, must also exist for the 'sensuous representative consciousness,' must be seen to sensible intuition as an historical event. The Idea must realize itself in fact if all men are to be made conscious of it and the unity of Divine and human it stands for. 'It must become an object in the world. It must *appear*, and that in the sensuous form appropriate to Spirit, which is the human' (*Phil. of Religion*, Eng. tr. p. 336). This is what has happened in Christianity. 'Christ has appeared ; a Man who is God ; God who is Man.' Christianity centres in the historic Christ. 'The manifestation of God in the flesh took place at a determinate time and in this particular individual.' In consequence of the Incarnation of God in Christ, man has learned the universal truth that it is eternally and essentially characteristic of God to be and to become man, that God's true existence is in humanity which is termed His Church, and that man is essentially one with God.

It is unquestionable that the broad effect of such speculation was to evaporate the facts of Christianity, and to substitute a 'somewhat else' (ἕτερον εὐαγγέλιον) for the firm truths of a revealed religion. A God personal only in man, such as the Absolute, clearly implies that God is not personal. An ideal relation without personality has been likened to a painted horse which you cannot ride ; and when the abstraction of the metaphysician interwoven in the universe is offered to us as the object of Christian belief, one who feels anything of the burdens and problems of life will turn away like Jacobi, little caring to know of a God who made the eye but sees not, the understanding but neither

knows nor wills. An Incarnation which maintains a continuous manifestation of God, of which all men are the bearers, which is never complete, and which dismisses Christ's pre-existence, sinless birth, resurrection, Divine authority and sole mediation, is not only irreconcilable with Scripture statements, but wholly inadequate to the requirements of the Christian consciousness.

But whatever view be taken of the speculative movement as a whole, certain outstanding services to Christological theory cannot be denied it. It has revolutionized the study of Christ's Person, and in so doing reacted on the whole theological field. By constructing a theory in which the Infinite and the finite, the Divine and the human, are not exclusive of each other, it demonstrated the *rationality* of the Incarnation. By its discovery of the spiritual principle in Nature, History, Man, as the truth which gives them all their reality and unity, and by the identification of this principle with Incarnation, it showed the *naturalness* of Christ's Incarnation. By its insistence on the truth that the organon of religion is not different in kind from that of philosophy, it has, so to speak, rehabilitated the validity of religious facts, the treatment of which with the contemptuous indifference characteristic of the previous age becomes hereafter an unphilosophical dogmatism. It has vastly widened the range and deepened the bases of belief in the Incarnation, and made possible a fresh and thorough investigation, in the way of criticism and understanding, into the data which support that belief.

(2) *The Christ of Experience.* — The Christian facts and the Christian consciousness assert themselves in the experiential theology initiated by **Schleiermacher** (1768–1834). As Kant inherited the sturdy conscience of the Lutheran Reform in his 'categorical imperative,' so Schleiermacher embodies its religious fervour in his 'feeling of dependence,' or *experience of God.* When Kant describes the essence of religion as the recognition of all our duties as the commands of God, he says the same thing in balder language, in language less mystically attractive, than that of Schleiermacher when he asserts that the essence of the religious life is the sense of utter and all-round dependence on God. From his training among the devout brethren of Herrnhut, and by a natural temperament of warm susceptibility, Schleiermacher was more akin to Schelling than to Kant, who reiterates the essentiality of duty as Kant does, but of duty inspired by something higher than Kant dreamed of. What is this something higher? Schelling had termed it 'faith,' 'fidelity to yourself and God.'

'By religiosity—the inner power and spirit of religion—I understand not an instinct groping towards the Divine, and not mere emotional devoutness ; for God, if He be God, must be the very heart of life, of all thinking and all action, and not a mere object of devout passion or of belief. That is no real knowledge of God where He is merely object ; either God is not known at all, or He is at once subject and object of knowledge. He must be at once our very self, our heart of hearts, yet comprehending all other hearts.' 'Faith is to be understood in its original sense of a trust and confidence in the Divine.' Fundamentally this is Schleiermacher's view, when he bases his thought on 'experience' (*Reden über die Religion*).

Religion is the *element of life* whose influence penetrates all other parts of life. Religion is not a knowing ; nor an action : it is a *feeling*. It is not as science, the knowledge of finite things in relation to each other. It is not as philosophy, the knowledge of the nature of the Supreme Cause. It is not as morals, which is rather the full exercise of its impulses in action. It contemplates the universe indeed, but not to discover the relations of its parts ; rather to watch it reverently in the representations and acts characteristic of it, and to let itself be seized and filled in childlike passivity by its immediate influences. It is the immediate consciousness of the universal being. 'Thus to see and find in all that lives and moves, in all becoming and change, in all action and suffering, thus to have and know life itself only in immediate feeling as this being, this is religion.' Its seat is in the soul. The central quality of the soul or self-consciousness is a certain emotion engendered by the contact of the objective world with the individual; an emotion which is prior to both thought and action, and animates both. It is this emotion which, as the centre of existence and the meeting-point of the individual and the universe, constitutes the religious sphere of man. It is thus not the mystical sense of absorption in the Infinite. Mysticism has always supposed that the experience of God can be reached only by means which are independent of the world and the ordinary experiences of life; it takes the whole world of sensible objects and human interests to be a barrier between the soul and God; the way of perfection consists in escaping from all these until the impassioned soul in its upward flight loses itself in the formless and viewless light of God. Schleiermacher, on the contrary, teaches that the experience of God's real existence is not something apart from all the human interests of life. It can come through these interests only by deepening them. The roots that join man to God are the same as those that join men to one another and to Nature, only they go deeper. The religious experience, again, is marked by spontaneity. It is in every man with the original impress which his individuality gives it. Its range and variety are infinite. It may be known to us, shining, as it were, through the beauty and glory of the world in which we live. Sometimes in sorrow and suffering it comes as 'a deeper voice across the storm.' So, too, it may arise when the presence of something true or beautiful or good uplifts us above ourselves. In short, everything visible and invisible, every part and event of experience, may become an appearance of God, and be a means of grace. Every experience may be a religious experience. A strong current of individuality is characteristic of religion. There is no such thing as an absolute religion. And there is no man without religion. Hence, too, the relation of the founder or teacher of any historic religion to that religion is intimate and necessary; the study of his character indispensable to the true understanding of it and its after growths.

On the basis of these ideas Schleiermacher constructs his view of Christ and the Christian religion (*Reden*, and *Der Christl. Glaube*). Here the point of departure is Christian experience and the historic Jesus. For Schleiermacher there is not religion, but simply religions; the historical relationships of the religions he does not know. Every new religion rests upon a new intuition of the universe. Jesus of Nazareth had such an intuition. What was it? The idea of Christianity is stated, in the fifth *Rede*, to be that the ruin of the finite in its alienation from God is removed: 'ruin and redemption are in this mode of feeling inseparably bound up with each other, and form the fundamental relations by which its form is determined.' Christianity makes 'religion itself the matter of religion.' Christ discerned in all things the Divine element. He discerned at the same time an irreligious principle everywhere. And the clearness with which He saw the need and the means of overcoming the unspiritual by the spiritual constitutes what is specific to Him and His faith. What is Divine in Him is not His purity or originality of character; but the 'splendid clearness with which the idea He had come to represent shaped itself in His soul, the idea that all that is finite needs the help of something higher to be connected with the Deity; and that for the man who is entangled in the finite and particular, salvation is to be sought only in redemption.' 'This consciousness of the uniqueness of His knowledge of God and being in God, and of its power to communicate itself and stir up religion, this was the consciousness of His mediatorship and Divinity.' To those who come to know Christ it does communicate itself with salutary energy, so that they become new creatures: He is the cause of the new life. In this relation He is the ideal type of humanity, and possessed a unique perfection. The proof lies in the existence of the Church, on the one hand, and the inexplicability of His religious consciousness by natural forces. He is perfect in what concerns His religious consciousness; here He was what He was by a primitive communication from God, in virtue of which also He was sinless. Otherwise He was truly man and subject in all respects to the laws of human growth. Divine in a sense, He was not veritably God; had no pre-temporal being, or miraculous birth, or bodily resurrection. He is

Divine simply in the unique and perfect satisfaction He supplies to the needs of the believing conscience; and in the unique and perfect manner in which He Himself realized this satisfaction in His Person.

The culminating point of Schleiermacher's theory is the affirmation of the supernatural consciousness of Christ and the absolute value of His Person. In this regard his influence on subsequent theology has been of rare fruitfulness. From a multitude who own his inspiration, two may be selected as having, in an original manner, corrected and enlarged his principles: Rothe and Ritschl.

Rothe (1799–1867) was probably the most eminent divine of the middle of last century. He maintained throughout his career, amid the strong intellectual and critical currents of that time, in all of which he shared, a personal faith of extreme warmth and tenderness in Christ's Person. 'Bear with you the living certainty of the reality of the historical fact Christ, and simply live your human life in the light of that certainty,' was the ruling motive of his inner life and also of his whole theological work (*Theol. Ethik* and *Dogmatik*).

Rothe takes his start with Schleiermacher in the consciousness, the feeling of God which is found therein. In the presonality of man, this, the Divine principle, is at war with the lower or material principle, its contrary spirit. Not until the lower is vanquished is man free or truly himself. Its conquest is the moral task of mankind. The task can be discharged only in a moral progress of two stages, in which the whole nature of the material principle shall make itself felt and be transformed, and in which the whole nature of the spiritual principle shall display itself. The first stage involves the passage of man through sin. In the second, man will reach complete unity with God. The race of Adam is humanity in the first stage; Christ crowns it. In completing its task, He brings with Him a new power, a miraculous force, which serves as the point of departure for a new development of the race. Here the moral evolution is at the same time religious, since the more subordinate the insistence of sin, the more direct the emergence of the spirit of holiness of the new power, the more perfect, *i.e.*, the assimilation to God. The appearance of Christ is due to a creative act. For although the world and man are made by God in an organic oneness, they are not so made that He cannot enter in. In Christ He does thus enter. In Christ He posits a new commencement of humanity; and in order to prepare for it Rothe admits a special revelation in miracle and inspiration. The new power, the advent of Christ, are by supernatural conception. The ministry of Christ was a continuous spiritualization and growing deification; in actualizing the constant conquest of sin, He at the same time unfolds the wealth of the life of God. The living substance of God comes forth in Him. The historical growth of Jesus is the divinization of man at the same time as it is the Incarnation of the Logos; its course is uninterrupted from His birth to the sacrifice of Calvary which marks its last step and its triumphant close. Triumphant, for the Redeemer could not die; face to face with Him, the Holy of God, death had no power. When then His spiritualization is achieved, Jesus lets fall His earthly envelope; and from that hour is truly God. Not that He is to be identified with God the Father. God-man on earth, He remains such in the heavens, liberated from His physical organism, and invested with a body corresponding to His celestial estate. But no material barrier now restrains His power, His Spirit acts without hindrance on the world. The glorified Lord reveals Himself as 'central individuality,' *i.e.* the secret of the increasing triumph of the spiritual principle from age to age. When the totality of His disciples are gathered, the Incarnation will be complete and the creation of the universe closed. At this stage God will live no longer in man only, but in the organism of renewed humanity ('Auf diesem Punkt ist das Menschsein Gottes zu seinem Menschheitsein,' *Dogm.* ii. 179).

Rothe's is a grandiose conception of *Moral Incarnation* exhibited with incomparable vigour of thought. Christ is no incarnation of the mythical sort, as in the imagination of India. Nor is He as one of the Heroic age, such as most primitive peoples magnify. He is man truly, yet less individual man than man generic, while at the same time God, the potency that rules the whole world-process. In its cosmical significance the Christian interpretation of Christ has never before received so impressive a statement.

Less original than Schleiermacher or Rothe, **Ritschl** (1822–1889), taking impulse from both, elaborates a system less speculative, more positive and Scriptural. His, like theirs, is a doctrine of redemption, and rests on experience. He construes his material, however, by a widely divergent method. The critical results of Tübingen had affrighted him with their divorce of the facts of Christ's life from the idea of His Person. The metaphysical and emotional elements in the idea of Christ's Person current in the schools around him. Ritschl had a singularly self-conscious and self-reliant character, and at the bar of the rich ethical experience yielded by the inner secrets of conscience his sense of the insufficiency of contemporary tendencies deepened. Injustice was done, he felt, to the historical and social and practical aspects of Christian truth. From that standpoint he directs a pungent criticism against the theological methods in vogue. They sought to construe Christianity by reference to the conception of God reached by a consideration of His relations to the finite world and human history and experience. Ritschl seeks the meaning of God as it is disclosed in the workings of the soul of Christ and in the activities of His earthly life. It was in that soul and in His earthly experience that the work of Christ in the salvation of men was achieved. Not in the heavens by transactions on man's behalf within the Trinity, as the orthodox schools taught; nor by His immanent operations in cosmic and human progress, as speculation dreamed; but in the moral personality and acts of the Redeemer. The process of redemption is not metaphysical or evolutionary, it is psychological. It was not to provide the prior conditions which should release the mercy of God, on the one hand; or, on the other, to overthrow an enemy encamped in man. Yet it was more than the announcement as by a prophet that God had forgiven or was ready to forgive. Both Anselm and Socinus failed Ritschl. According to his view, what is meant by God in Christ reconciling the world to Himself is that when God took human nature in Christ He actualized the forgiving presence of God. God in Him was in human nature, not on a visit, not arranging the conditions on which it could be redeemed, but actually redeeming and appropriating it. Christ revealed the Father not by holding Him up to be seen, but by bearing Him in upon us, leavening us with Him practically and consciously. The field of Christ's work lay therefore in His own spiritual history, and among the conditions of spiritual human nature (cf. Forsyth, *Religion in Recent Art*, Lect. 7). This is Ritschl's first important deflexion from Schleiermacher's procedure. The Christian consciousness or experience to which he appeals is found in the contemplation of the historic Jesus, as made known in the Gospel records. It is not to be regarded in isolated individualism, as was the case with Schleiermacher's appeal to the inner consciousness. It has in consequence an objective character alien from his method and from the subjectivism and sentimental piety often accompanying it. There is a second deflexion of not less importance. The Christian experience to which Ritschl appeals is realized socially and practically in the Kingdom of God.

'There must be added [to Schleiermacher's theory] the pregnant truth that this religion, like all religions and all spiritual activities, can only be rightly set forth in the fellowship which, on the presupposition of the redeeming work of the Founder, exists as the sharing and spreading of this redeeming activity. Redemption, the Redeemer, and the Redeemed Community stand for theological knowledge in an inseparable relation' (*Just. and Recon.* i. p. 495 f.).

Ritschl's doctrine of the Kingdom is specially worthy of study. The Kingdom of God in his view is at once (*a*) a moral ideal, (*b*) a social organization, (*c*) a religious good. The Kingdom and not the individual man is the object of the Divine electing love. To the Kingdom, the Fellowship of Faith, belongs redemption, which is appropriated by the

believer only as a member of it. And he shares in it in the measure in which he discharges his obligations towards it; it is as he loves and serves his neighbour that he is justified of God. The reciprocal action and reaction of the community of believers engenders experience of Christ, by which men learn His worth for them. As the value of each is determined by his service to the whole, so is Christ's *worth* (equivalent in Ritschl's phrase to His nature in so far as it can be known to us) to be estimated by His work.

Ons uch principles, what, then, is the worth of Christ? Christ has the worth of God. He is a prophet sent from God, yet more than all the preceding prophets of the OT. He makes Himself known as, and is, the Son of God.

In the moral world all personal authority is conditioned upon the nature of one's vocation and upon the connexion between one's fitness for his special calling and his faithful exercise of it. Accordingly the permanent significance of Jesus Christ for His community is based, first, on the fact that He was the only one qualified for His special calling, the introduction of the Kingdom of God; that He devoted Himself to the exercise of this highest conceivable calling in the preaching of the truth and in loving action without break or deviation; and that, in particular, as a proof of His fidelity, He freely accepted in willing patience the wrongs which the leaders of the Israelitish nation and the fickleness of the people brought upon Him, and which were so many temptations to draw Him back from His calling. Second, the work of Jesus Christ in His calling or the final purpose of His life, viz., the Kingdom of God, is the very purpose of God in the world, and is thus recognized by Christ Himself. The solidaric unity between Christ and God, which Jesus accordingly claims for Himself, has reference to the whole extent of His activity in His calling, and consists in the reciprocal relation between the love of God and the obedience of Jesus in His calling. Now Jesus, being the first to realize in His own personal life the final purpose of the Kingdom of God, is therefore alone of His kind; for should any other fulfil the same task so perfectly as He, yet he would be unlike Him because dependent upon Him. Therefore, as the original type of humanity to be united into the Kingdom of God, He is the original object of the love of God, so that the love of God for the members of His Kingdom also is mediated only through Him. When, therefore, this Person, active in His peculiar calling, whose constant motive is recognizable as unselfish love to man, is valued at His whole worth, then we see in Jesus the whole revelation of God as love, grace, and faithfulness' (*Unterricht*, pt. i. §§ 21–22). There is a third consideration (§ 23), Christ's lordship over the world and resurrection. 'These relations which are necessary to the full appreciation of Jesus and are apparent in the account of His life, are referred to in the confession of the Godhood of Christ which the Christian community has made from the beginning' (§ 24).

In sum, Christ's Divinity is confessed when it is seen that His will was in perfect identification with the Divine purpose in things or the will of God; and that He displayed in the moral sphere the highest Divine attributes. He is the Son of God by His perfect knowledge of the Father's will and by His perfect obedience to it. After this manner He fully revealed the essence of God; and that in the activities of a human life; and in a sinless human life. The Divinity of Christ is thus not based, as is usually done, on the supernatural facts of pre-existence, virgin birth, miraculous works, and resurrection. These, however, are not denied; only, Ritschl would contend, the right appreciation of their truth comes after the moral witness, from reflexion on believing experience.

Ritschlian principles and results have been the subject of violent polemic. It is with their broad effect only that we are here concerned. What that is, is obvious. Ritschl has brought back men's thought to Christ as the centre of Christianity, to Christ's character as moral power, and to religion as the builder up of spiritual life by enlightening the conscience and educating the will. Religious truth can be verified by the moral sense. It is a question of fact; inner fact, no doubt, and not scientific, but truer than what is outward. But when the theological reasoner abandons the ground of fact and the safe circle of practical reason for the shifting mirages of speculation, then he uses words without meaning. Christian verity rests primarily on internal experience, and answers to the most urgent necessities of the moral life. It has, indeed, other relations and aspects that transcend experience and, consequently, our understanding. All that can be said there is, *Exit in mysteria*. Ritschlian modesty is often misunderstood. But it has served to clear the ground within the range of spiritual experience, and floods this ground with light. There is no true doctrine that can contradict this light, or shelter itself from its penetration.

The influence of Ritschl is the predominant theological force of the hour. It is felt wherever the attraction of religious problems is felt. He is best interpreted, not as the propounder of a 'theology without metaphysics,' or a 'religion without mysticism' (for he propounds neither), but as an exponent of the 'Christian consciousness' of Schleiermacher. He closes so far the movement begun by the latter. That movement is familiar to religious thinkers in this country in the more sober theology of Coleridge, of Maurice, and of Erskine of Linlathen, who may justly be termed the guides of the higher religious thinking in England in the first half of last century. **Coleridge** (1772–1834), adopting Kant's forms of thought and imbibing Schleiermacher's spirit, introduced the fruits of their teachings into England, where thought was dominated by Locke in philosophy and Paley in theology. The 'Reason' of Coleridge is the 'Practical Reason' of Kant, which grasps the higher principles. Like Schleiermacher, he falls back on experience as the test of sacred truth. He believes Christian truth because it 'finds' him. Coleridge shared in all the characteristics of the German school from whom he borrowed. He was no metaphysician. He was a great interpreter of spiritual facts, a student of spiritual life, a subject of spiritual experience. He saw in Christianity the true explanation of the facts of our spiritual being. He brought human nature near again to Christianity. He changed the conception of Christianity from being a traditional creed till it became a living expression of spiritual consciousness. 'After him,' says Mark Pattison, 'the evidence makers ceased as beneath the spell of some magician.' The line of thought marked out by the disjointed reflexions of Coleridge was continued by **F. D. Maurice** (1805–1872), who had been influenced also by Erskine, and still more by his own inner conflicts. His best energies were absorbed in the interpretation of religious thought from the standpoint of the Incarnation. By it alone, according to his view, could our nature be sufficient for perfect life. Quite in the style of the later Ritschl, he rests faith on historic fact, and finds the essential ground of human life in the Personality of Christ as the Revealer of the Divine will and character. Akin, in like manner, is his insight into the social aspects of Christian truth, the spring of his abounding personal philanthropy, and the inspiration of that movement which had for its chief tenet the social utilization of religion, the movement of Christian Socialism. More apart and less orthodox stood **Thomas Erskine**, who recalls his friend Fichte in not a few touches of nature and conviction. He was no student as Coleridge, nor of practical bent as Maurice. Meditative and introspective, he sought the truth by patient thoughtfulness and deduction from his own experience—deeper thought, not larger knowledge. He brings out an aspect of the 'theology of consciousness' not emphasized hitherto, viz. that religious experience is a growing and endlessly growing inner perception.

The experiential movement has a second phase, which calls for some mention in its bearing on present-day ideas of Christ. It is a phase outside the Churches, although not always, or necessarily, hostile to them. It shows itself in the rise of *ethical societies* in America, France, Germany, Holland, and this country. Its aims are familiar to us in Britain from the writings of **Matthew Arnold** (1822–1888). Much theological liberalism moves in the same direction.

In the last forty years a succession of writers has maintained that while the moral and practical elements of Christianity are entirely commendable and necessary, its theology is discredited, and must be abandoned. The aspirations of such writers are not to be confounded with those of writers still more radical, who denounce not only the theology, but the ethics as well, of the Christian Church,—writers including men so widely parted from each other as Nietzsche the Darwinian and Maeterlinck the mystic. Of these societies it is relevant to our purpose to say that they cannot be viewed as within the line of progress. The Ethical Theology, and in particular the school of Ritschl, is sometimes set side by side with them. But without warrant. These societies, often divergent from one another, have a certain unity, and it is precisely by the principle of that unity that they separate themselves from the ethical movement in theology as well as from orthodox Christianity. The Person of Christ is all in all to these last. It is nothing to those schools. They are inimical not only to historical Christianity, but to the historical Christ. They combine in identifying all, in historical Christianity and in the historical Christ, that is not purely moral and spiritual, with the mere swathing-bands which the spirit is to outgrow. Nurtured on the modern conscience, they have not drunk its deepest draught, that inner power of Divine mystery which awakens conscience and deepens it as nothing else. The spiritual side of the Christian conscience, in its sense of sin and revelation of Divine pity and forgiveness, is unfelt. It is here, too, that so much 'Broad' or 'Liberal' religious thought fails. There is a liberalism which is only the rich and complex manifestation of the magnificent capacities of the Christian Faith claiming all life for Christ; and there is a liberalism which, when extracted from the haze which its upholders cast around it, is found to be, in its underlying postulates, totally inconsistent with the historic faith. It seeks a purely spiritual Christ. And when it has found Him, He is neither truly human nor Divine; He is at once a non-historical and a non-mysterious Being. Undogmatic Christianity is simply abstract theism. Against its empty abstraction of the Divine Spirit, and its anæmic conception of Christ's Person, the experience-theology is a passionate protest.

(3) *The Christ of History.*—Concurrently with the foregoing movements has gone another, simpler indeed, and, since there are no truths which more readily gain assent or are more firmly retained than those of an historical order, more within the grasp of the popular mind, but also for that very reason more nearly touching the instincts of the popular faith—the historical and literary criticism of the Scriptures. It finds its sources and growth both within and without the ecclesiastical sphere. It is part of the general movement of science, the application of the methods of science, observation, hypothesis, and induction, to the facts of Hebrew and Christian history. It was not likely that the universal spirit of investigation and discovery should feel itself free to range over the whole field of secular history, and be restrained from operating in the departments of sacred. And so the Scriptures have been taken, as scholarship had already been taking the classical books of the ancient world, as a literature of many fragments and times, and of varying authority. Their commands and teaching and records, all alike have been judged according to the occasion and circumstances in which they were given forth. In other words, they have been interpreted, not absolutely, but relatively. The Bible, as to its text, structure, the authorship of its several parts, and its literary and didactic form, is read and understood like all other ancient literature. Then, too, from the theological fluctuations of the 18th and 19th centuries, special impulses entered. Religion, as Coleridge reminds us, consists of ideas and facts both; the Christian religion blends together inseparably the historical and the spiritual. The variations in religious and philosophical theory in consequence closely affect the character of historical study, and in an instance such as that of the Christian history, where the historical substance is large, with effects of the gravest kind. Further, the emergence of the hypothesis of evolution in scientific circles in the middle of last century, and

its rapid acceptance and application to all kinds of knowledge, created a temper of naturalism, which reacted on Biblical criticism and Christological doctrines. Especially in the forms of Positivism (Comte) and of Agnosticism (Huxley and Spencer), this temper rejects every form of theism which asserts the personality of the Divine Being and the beneficent character of His relation to the world of men and things ; and, professing itself ignorant of anything better, has lost all belief in any wisdom or love but that which springs from the brains and hearts of men. It is a theory which limits knowledge to experience, and experience to the physical senses—the sensations produced in us by the external world. It has its own view of history, and of Christian history, as a natural evolution. The new historical sense, combined with the new interpretation of Christianity, in terms of the facts of man's existence and human experience, incited to a re-reading of the Biblical records and a resetting of their material data, which has to an extraordinary degree stimulated the interest of the general mind, and most powerfully influenced the growth of a purely *humanitarian* conception of the Person of Christ. 'History,' says Mommsen, 'has a nemesis for every sin.' For seventeen centuries the facts of Christ's life had been carelessly or impatiently treated : they were now to take emphatic revenge.

The process begins with **D. F. Strauss** (1808–1874). Strauss runs his theory through the Gospels like a ploughshare through a field of daisies. His interest is of a purely negative character. He disintegrates the narratives and dissolves the facts in a series of writings, in which, with frankness and lucidity, he expounds what it has become common to call the point of view of modern science as to Christ's Person. His object throughout was polemical. It was to find a way out of supernaturalism. Whatever system furnished him with the means of attaining his object he eagerly embraced. In his first book he employs, on the basis of the well-known Hegelian distinction between the idea and the fact, the notional and the historical, his mythical theory as a means of exit ; in his last, Darwin and natural science come to his aid.

It is by his 'mythical theory' that Strauss is best known. 'Myth,' he says, 'is the creation of fact out of an idea.' The miraculous is a foreign element in the Gospel narratives of Christ which defies all historical treatment, and the conception of the myth is the means which we shall use in order to eliminate this element from our subject. The mythical principle is well expressed by de Wette : ' When any record relates inconceivable things in good faith, it is to be considered, not as historical, but as mythical.' Strauss lays it down as an absolute principle that miracles are impossible, so that every narrative which is in disaccordance with the laws of nature is pronounced to be mythical. The narratives connected with the birth of John the Baptist are poetical myths. That prophet having afterwards played a great part, and having been found in relation with Jesus, the Church judged it appropriate to glorify him in this way. The two genealogies of Jesus have nothing historical about them : they are the work of Judaizing Christians, who believed that the Messiah must necessarily descend from David. The history of the birth, baptism, and temptation of Jesus are myths designed to establish His supernatural origin. Jesus was a disciple of John the Baptist, whose work at the outset He undoubtedly wished only to continue ; but by degrees He came to believe Himself the Messiah, and hoped to found a political kingdom by supernatural means. Putting the moral laws above the Mosaic, He abolished the latter. He made missionary journeys. He did not perform miracles ; but could heal demoniacs, and on that account all sorts of marvellous facts have been attributed to Him. He did not foretell His death or resurrection. He did not institute the Lord's Supper. The disciples, convinced that the Messiah could not remain in the tomb, had visions and hallucinations which showed Him to them risen again. Life did not exist in Christ in a perfect manner ; He is not the ideal of humanity. The traditional faith is entirely without historical foundation.

The work of Strauss was continued with modifications peculiar to themselves by Bruno Bauer and others, and suggested the more serious labours of the Tübingen School, headed by **F. C. Baur** (1792–1860). The all-important problem was now the historical reality of Jesus. Baur, differing in this from Strauss, seeks a solution through St. Paul, and a critical investigation of the sources of Christianity. His theory shows the influence of the Hegelian category of thesis and antithesis.

In four Epistles—in Romans, 1 and 2 Corinthians, and Galatians—we have, according to Baur, authentic Apostolic documents, genuine Epistles of Paul. They are our best authorities on every question touching the origin, nature, and principles of primitive Christianity. They reveal antitheses of thought, a Petrine and a Pauline party in the Church. The Petrine was the primitive Christian, made up of men who, while believing in Jesus as the Messiah, did not cease to be Jews. The Pauline was a reformed and Gentile Christianity, which aimed at universalizing the faith in Jesus by freeing it from the Jewish law and traditions. The universalism of Christianity, and therefore its historical importance and achievements, are thus really the work of the Apostle Paul. His work he accomplished in the face of, and in spite of, the opposition of the older Apostles. The men who had been with Jesus did not understand Him ; Paul did by natural ability. Not the unity but the differences and antagonisms of the Apostolic Age are the key to all its problems, the point on which the constructive historian must stand if he would do his work. The memorials of the struggle and of the compromises by which it was ended lie in the canonical literature of primitive Christianity. They are best understood as *Tendenz-schriften*.

It is not easy to affirm what position Baur assigns to Christ. He is preoccupied with Paul. In a study on the meaning of the expression ' Son of Man,' he strives to reconstruct, by means of the historical data which the Gospels furnish us, the consciousness which Jesus had of Himself and His Messianic character, but the results at which he arrives are vague and contradictory. Sometimes he admits that the historian finds in Jesus certain characteristics which indicate that He possessed qualities unknown to other men ; sometimes he affirms that it is less the original Person of Christ than faith in His Person that has been the basis of the historical development of Christianity.

Baur's picture of the early Church and of Christ is now everywhere recognized as utterly incorrect in its chief and essential features. Why is this ? Simply because he was under the domination of a rigid philosophical system which narrowed his outlook, and prevented him from seeing a multitude of historical facts of a different character from those upon which he based his reconstruction. The scholars who have done most to secure recognition for those new facts are Ritschl and Renan. The essence of the advance made by Ritschl lies simply in the denial that the evolution of early Christianity was a purely immanent process, and in the recognition of certain outside forces as determinative factors in the development. The cardinal factor assumed by him was the spirit of the Graeco-Roman world. According to his view, the rise of the Catholic Church, which means the substitution of institutionalism, ecclesiasticism, and sacerdotalism for the spiritual individualism of the earliest period, was due primarily to the influence of the Graeco-Roman spirit which came into the Church with the conversion of the Gentiles in the 1st cent., and which was thenceforth a controlling influence in its development. Essentially in his spirit a group of younger historians have sought for still other outside factors, and greatly enlarged the historian's outlook.

E. Renan (1823–1892), trained for the Romanist priesthood, which he renounced, and attracted for a time by German Idealism without settling in it, encountered influences which were to enlighten the obscurity that his Catholic education and German initiation had left in his thought. His special work was done in the Semitic domain.

A visit to Palestine in 1860 offered the occasion for a *Life of Jesus*. In reading the Gospel in Galilee, he tells us, the personality of this great Founder had forcibly appealed to him ; and the first sketch of the book was traced amidst the scenes of the Gospel history. It is no common book, the *Vie de Jésus*. It sketches a life of Christ which has won wide attention and acceptance. Jesus of Nazareth was a simple, contemplative, innocent, rustic saint, with a villager's childlike ideas of the kingdoms of the world and the glories of a court. These ideas He expresses in His parables about kings, says Renan, with the most delightful naïveté and want of *connaissance des choses*— but with a religious fire of love burning in His heart, a profound apprehension of God as His Father, and that ardour to bring others to the same love of Him which gives force and breadth to the least experienced wisdom. His whole nature revolted against the hard and false sanctimony of the Pharisees. With regard to the Law, He had eagerly accepted the teaching, then widely disseminated among the Jews, of the school of Hillel. But it would not be for even the widest interpreters of the Law, says Renan, that Christ could have felt any great fascination. The Psalms, Isaiah, and more recent Messianic literature had for many reasons a greater imaginative charm for His genius. From the Book of Daniel He drew the Messianic title 'Son of Man,' which, with a fine appreciation of His own exquisitely human genius, He reserved specially for Himself. Moreover, the attempt in these books to sketch the future course of history was the origin of Christ's own millennial dreams, and the source of much of His imaginative power over His countrymen. Then there was the freedom of His life in Galilee. 'That mountain summit of Nazareth where no man of modern days can sit without a troubled feeling about his destiny, there Jesus sat twenty years without a doubt. Delivered from self-seeking, the source of our troubles, which makes us seek bitterly for some interest in virtue beyond the tomb, He thought only of His work, of His nation, of the human race. Those mountains, that sea, that azure heaven, those high tablelands on the horizon, were for Him not the melancholy vision of a soul which interrogates nature about its lot, but the certain symbol, the transparent shadow, of an invisible world and a new heaven.' Thus love of His spiritual Father, Hebrew poetry, the living spirit of the Law, the visions of a Messianic age that should include the whole race of man, His ignorance of science and belief in the plenary force of Divine volition, the political freedom of His time which scarcely interfered with individual action, the beauty of nature about Him, and His wonderful power of inspiring love in the simple men who came to Him—all tended to raise to the highest intensity a character of marvellous breadth and force. Jesus did not come 'stainless out of the struggle of life.' It was the instinct of genius for acting upon the world that led Him into the Messianic groove of thought. It was that that soiled His purity, though without it He never could have founded a lasting Church. If He had any original defect of nature, it was the universal Eastern fault of a want of sincerity with Himself. The growing fascination of His spiritual and Messianic ideas gave Him impatience of the appetite for miracle on the part of the people. The demand for miracle He had to meet, and was not above getting up fictitious miracles as a sort of 'pious fraud,' e.g. the resurrection of Lazarus. The same necessity led Him into fanaticism, which eventually urged Him to death; 'the tone which He had taken could not be sustained; it was time for death to come and unloose the knot of a situation of the extremest tension.'

Renan's *Life of Jesus* is penetrated by a profound feeling of His human personality, its charm, its potence, its pre-eminence, its capability to create a faith. It has been shown to be inaccurate in details, and meagre and uncertain in its knowledge, especially of the Jewish environment in which Jesus grew up. It displays an excess of precision in the psychology of illusion, a too ready emotion, and a want of *gravitas*. Yet withal the book did this service, that it introduced into the reading of Christ's life on its human side a greater sense of reality than modern criticism had hitherto attained. For the action of ideas, as in Strauss and Baur, Renan substitutes the play of individual passion and character. The arid logic of the Germans is absent, and something of the wonder and beauty of the NT story is not wholly lost. It is here that the arrears in the 'scientific' or 'historical' Christ have most to be made up. The Apostolic conception of the Saviour, however uncritical and untrustworthy in details at the bar of modern history, embodies in that very supernaturalism which is the *bête noire* of the scientific mind, a spirit so potent as to seem to those who gave the record the most striking reality in His life. To reproduce that spirit in natural terms calls for a depth of feeling and width of experience which the critical movement so far has shown no signs of possessing. There hangs about its Christological creations such a rawness as to tempt one to the statement that it has not yet found the equipment adequate to its task. Christ must be interpreted *from within*. The interest of His life is in large measure independent of its historical framework, as the orthodox construction has rightly seen, and as criticism itself acknowledges when it starts from the teaching of Christ in preference to the events of His career. Higher instincts, therefore, than the merely intellectualist

instincts of 'science' or 'history,' instincts akin to the poet's when he grasps the very spirit of poetry, or the artist's when his unique sensibility unveils a new revelation of beauty, are requisite if the mystery of Christ is not to be profaned. Hostility to the supernatural is an unscientific dogmatism. Equally unscientific is the explanation of it as 'myth' or 'vision.' The supernatural in Christ took such a hold on the minds of those who gave themselves to Him, as to render them readier than otherwise to reduce His human nature in its interests. The supernatural in Christ is that in Him to which the Church has at all times clung as the sustainer of her intensest faith and hope. It has enriched and not weakened the life of the spirit. What is the secret? How explain the tenacity with which the supernatural in Christ has fastened on the conscience of Christendom? Is it not that it has shown at all times power to embody men's highest religious hopes and aspirations, and has satisfied them? And should this not strengthen rather than lessen belief in its reality? Science has here a problem not to be evaded. In reaching a solution, the *psychological* trend science has recently taken cannot fail to furnish important data. A true 'philosophy of the unconscious' is a desideratum. Already we have learned many facts having an intimate bearing on the old Christological problems. What they suggest is that within the depths of a single personality there may coexist parallel states of spirit-life; a consideration which, if vindicated, will make us pause before repeating the dogmas of negation which were framed with regard to simpler and narrower facts.

A sense of such necessity is apparent in the most recent phase of 'scientific' reconstruction of the Life of Christ. The articles of **P. W. Schmiedel** and others in the *Encyclopædia Biblica*, the *Jesus* of **W. Bousset** of Göttingen (tr. Williams & Norgate), and the *Jesus* of **Arno Neumann** (tr. A. & C. Black), based on essentially rationalist principles, manifest an advance on the old rationalism. They seek the secret of Jesus in a *psychological uniqueness*. They are indeed in line with previous radical tradition in rejecting the integrity of the Gospels as a reliable source of information, and in reducing to a minimum the available historical material at their basis, in regarding the major portion of the written record as artificial and adapted, of the nature of pious legend and idealizing poetry, and in asserting the impossibility of considering the claims Christ made for Himself an adequate foundation for such a superstructure as the Church reared in the dogma of His Divinity; yet they are confident where earlier effort was often in doubt; they are also more reverent, genial, and expectant. A firm historical foundation is acknowledged, and that both in facts regarding His Person and particularly in His words and teaching. They are facts, too, which point to a 'sovereign self-consciousness,' worth to men more than kings and prophets had been, potent over present powers and offering promise of constant conquest (Bousset, *Jesus*, p. 96). 'He bound His disciples to His Person as never again one man has bound men.' His uniqueness is not to be confounded with singularity, but denotes unequalled excellence in goodness and greatness. He constrains not physically but psychically; He overpowers us inwardly by His spirituality, His purity, truthfulness, and love. He is the Master of the inner life. 'We may also speak of Him as "the Redeemer."' Not in the sense that His death was a propitiatory sacrifice without which the God of love would not have been able to forgive us our sins. Not in this sense: yet it was indeed His special work to redeem by guiding us from the letter to the spirit, from the feeling of a slave to the love of a child, from self-seeking to brotherly love, from the dominion of the visible to that of the invisible ; and His death showed that He was ready and determined to offer in order to procure these benefits, not His labour only but also His life (Neumann, *Jesus*, c. 19). Not Divine, He is none the less not to be denied worship. The interest of the situation here created is vast. It is not only the new facts and the finer appreciation of them, but the plane in which they stand and the wide range of it. Scientific criticism has tapped a new source. Discussion of the philosophical implications involved in the wider range of facts discernible will lead thought to a *new Idealism* which, analyzing the 'transcendental' element in man more clearly, will the better and the more convincingly interpret the Divine in Christ.

In close association with the larger view of history and science in influencing religious ideas is the great democratic movement of the modern world. Our sense of growth in knowledge has reacted upon our anticipations and hopes for the *social state* of men. It is only natural that the relation of Christ to the social problem should have come to occupy a foremost place, and that the traditional Christian ideas should be greatly affected by it. Almost every variety of socialist aspiration has made its appeal to Christ. It is remembered that He pronounced a special Beatitude on the poor, called to Himself the weary and heavy laden, offered a personal friendship to the publican and sinner, commanded His followers to be helpers of men's material needs ; that He was Himself of the poor, and denounced in unmistakable terms, if not the rich and capitalism, then their closest neighbour, Mammon. The situation in itself is of the deepest interest, but its Christological import is but slight. Christ's supernatural dignity is ignored. He is looked upon as nothing more than man, and even then as nothing more than a 'Social Reformer,' the 'people's man,' 'Jesus the demagogue,' an unmysterious human leader of the poor, claimed now for this school and now for that, according to the partial and prejudiced predilections of His sponsors. To the great majority the Christ of the Creeds is an object of complete indifference, if not of dislike, while the Christ of the Churches, of worship, and of believing experience, is unknown or scorned. The transcendency of the Divine Life depicted in the Gospels finds no echo in their hearts.

It remains merely to remind ourselves that these three movements of Christological conception are all needful. They are not to be separated or considered antagonistic. They are complementary, helping each other to the new and richer belief in Christ. That belief will exhibit the ideal content of Christ's Person as the sum of all experience and all existence, seeing Him in all Nature, in all the forms of Nature, in all human life, in the whole range of life's experience, as that in which they all alike find at once their living energy and their goal, the ground and the final end of the successively emerging and developing phenomena that we behold as Nature, History, Experience. It will not be like the older faith, a strange hybrid, compounded part of philosophy, part of history, part of moral effort ; it will be the apprehension of a Person behind the facts and processes of all three, reached through the study of His working in them and the sense of kinship with and nearness to Him ; who thus known will not be found to be summed up in them but rather sums them up in Himself, whose History no history has yet exhausted, whose Life not all the lives of men have outgrown.

LITERATURE. — *GENERAL* : Indispensable books in German dealing with the whole subject for the whole period are Pfleiderer, *Religionsphilosophie auf geschichtl. Grundlage* (*Philosophy of Religion on the basis of its history*, 4 vols., Williams & Norgate); Pünjer, *Gesch. der christl. Religionsphilosophie*, 2 vols. (vol. i. tr., T. & T. Clark); Dorner, *Entwickelungsgesch. der Lehre der Person Christi* (tr., 5 vols., T. & T. Clark). The best writings in English relevant to the article are Principal Fairbairn's *Christ in Modern Theology*, *Philosophy of the Christian Religion*, *Studies in the Life of Christ*. On the specific characteristics of the modern spirit there are suggestive chapters in George Brandes' *Main Currents in XIXth cent. Literature*, vol. i. ; Royce, *Spirit of Modern Philosophy* ; Merz, *Hist. of European Thought in XIXth century* ; cf. also Ziegler, *Die geistigen und socialen Strömungen des 19ten Jahrhunderts*, Berlin ; and Flint's *Hist. of the Philosophy of History*, vol. i.

SPECIAL : On the Idealistic movement ; for Kant, *Religion innerhalb der Grenzen der blossen Vernunft* (tr. by Semple) ; for Schelling, *Die Methode der academ. Studiums*, and *Philos. Untersuchungen* (not translated) ; for Hegel, *Philosophie der Religion* (tr. by Speirs and Sanderson) ; for Lamennais, *Essai sur l'Indifference*, and *Esquisse d'une Philosophie* ; for Coleridge, *Aids to Reflection*, *Confessions of an Inquiring Spirit* ; for F. D. Maurice, *Kingdom of Christ*, *Essays* ; for T. H. Green, *Prolegomena to Ethics*, *Two Sermons*, etc.; for the Cairds, Ed. Caird, *Evolution of Theology*, *Critical Philosophy of Kant* ; John Caird, *Fundamental Ideas of Religion*, *Philosophy of Religion*. For sketch of later developments in Germany see Frank, *Gesch. und Kritik der neueren Theologie.*

On the Experience movement there is an extensive literature associated with Schleiermacher, his theology and his influence on theology ; and with Ritschl and his school (chiefly in German), cf. in English, Pfleiderer, *Development of Theology in Germany and in Great Britain in 19th century* ; Adams Brown, *Essence of Christianity* ; Oman, translation of Schleiermacher's *Reden*, Introduction ; Garvie, *The Ritschlian Theology* ; M. Arnold, *Literature and Dogma*, *Last Essays on Church and Religion* ; Seeley, *Ecce Homo.*

On the Historico-critical movement noteworthy are the following : Gardner, *A Historic View of the NT* ; Moffatt, *Historical NT*, Prolegomena and General Notes ; O. Cone, *Gospel Criticism and Historical Christianity* ; Schweitzer, *Von Reimarus zu Wrede* ; Otto Schmiedel, *Die Hauptprobleme der Leben-Jesu-Forschung* ; the works of Strauss, Renan, Keim, etc., to be found in translations.

On the Social and Psychological influences consult C. C Everett's *Psychological Elements of Religious Faith* ; Valli, *Il fondamento psicologico della Religione* ; Naumann, *Das soziale Programm der evangelischen Kirche*, *Jesus als Volksmann* ; James, *Varieties of Religious Experience* ; Hyde, *Outlines of Social Theology* ; King, *Theology of the Social Consciousness* ; Dole, *Theology of Civilization* ; Nash, *Genesis of the Social Consciousness* ; Peabody, *Jesus Christ and the Social Question*, *Jesus Christ and the Christian Character* ; Weinel, *Jesus im XIXten Jahrhundert* ; Du Bose, *The Gospel in the Gospels.*

Minor books worth study are Kaftan, *Kant der Philosoph des Protestantismus* ; Bergmann, *Ethik als Kulturphilosophie* ; Goguel, *Wilhelm Herrmann et le problème religieux actuel* ; Mellone, *Converging Lines of Religious Thought*, *Leaders of Religious Thought* ; Mallock, *Reconstruction of Belief* ; King, *Reconstruction in Theology* ; Gordon, *The Christ of To-day* ; Van Dyke, *The Gospel for an Age of Doubt* ; Macdonnell, *Christ* ; Sheldon, *An Ethical Movement* ; Dole, *The Coming People* ; Coe, *Religion of a Mature Mind* ; F. W. Newman, *The Hebrew Jesus* ; Hughes, *Ethical Christianity* ; Blatchford, *God and My Neighbour* ; J. M. Robertson, *Pagan Christs* ; Cairns, 'Christianity in the Modern World' (*Contemp. Rev.* 1903-1904). The works of Nietzsche and Tolstoi may be had in excellent translations.

On Christ in modern English literature cf. Armstrong, *Faith and Doubt in the Century's Poets* ; Wilson, *Theology of Modern Literature* ; Lyttelton, *Modern Poets of Faith, Doubt, Paganism* ; Stubbs, *The Christ of English Poetry* ; Stopford Brooke, *Theology in the English Poets.* A. S. MARTIN.

CHRIST IN JEWISH LITERATURE.

In spite of the fact that Jewish literature covers the whole period from the time of Christ to the present day, and that the relations between Jews and Christians during that period have usually been far from friendly, the references to Christ in the writings of Jews are, comparatively speaking, few and unimportant. What there are do not add anything to our knowledge of the history of the life of Christ. Such interest as they possess is due to their significance as indications of the way in which Jews were wont to think and speak amongst themselves of the Founder of Christianity. And it is safe to assert that in general they did not often occupy their thoughts with Him. Whatever may have been the reason, they very seldom mentioned Him ; and they seem to have neither received any direct impression, nor inherited any tradition of His spiritual greatness. The few allusions to Him contained in the Talmud and the contemporary literature are, for the most part, contemptuous references to one who deceived Israel, and who owed his birth to the unfaithfulness of his mother. But they are a mere drop in the ocean of the Talmud, and do not warrant the assertion of a general and bitter hatred on the part of the Rabbis towards Him. In the mediæval literature the scattered hints of the Talmud were developed into the book called the *Tôl'dôth Jêshū*, which is a mere lampoon, and in some parts a very disgusting one. But there is good ground for saying that this book was not countenanced by the best representatives of the Jewish religion, and did not express their opinion. It is on a level with such misrepresentations of the Roman Catholic and Protestant religions as find favour with the ignorant and bigoted of the opposite party, but are repudiated by the responsible leaders on either side. Instances are to be found in which leaders of Jewish thought in the Middle Ages have made reference to Christ in the language of civil courtesy, or even of appreciation. It is true that such allusions are mostly contained in speeches addressed to Christians on the occasion of public debates, and were, perhaps, influenced by the thought of the danger incurred by plain speaking. But there is evidence to show that in writings intended only for Jews the writers could refer to Jesus without bitterness, and point out what they deemed to be His mistakes without blackening His character. In modern literature the chief Jewish historians write of Jesus as of a great historical personage; and though they, naturally, do not see in Him as much as Christians see, they honestly try to present historical truth and to avoid traditional prejudice. It is only in modern literature that there is to be found a serious and deliberate Jewish opinion about Jesus, a real contribution to the study of His life and character. The earlier references illustrate chiefly the effect of persecution and mutual hatred upon the Jewish mind.

In accordance with the brief sketch just given, it will be convenient to treat the subject chronologically under the three heads of (i.) the Talmudic Literature, (ii.) the Mediæval Literature, (iii.) Modern Literature.

i. CHRIST IN THE TALMUDIC LITERATURE.—The period included under this head extends from the time of Christ Himself to the closing of the Babylonian Talmud, *i.e.* about five centuries. The literature comprises several works besides the Talmud, and falls chronologically into two main groups. The first group is that whose chief representative is the *Mishna*, the code of the Traditional Law completed by R. Judah the Holy, about A.D. 220. To this group also belong the *Tosefta*, a collection of traditions partly coinciding with the Mishna, and the Midrashim known as *Siphrē*, *Siphra*, and *Mechilta*. The second group contains the *Gemārās*, *i.e.* the commentaries on the Mishna made in the schools of Palestine and Babylonia respectively, and forming, together with the Mishna, the Jerusalem Talmud and the Babylonian Talmud. The Gemaras contain many traditions not included in the Mishna but contemporaneous with it; such a tradition is called a *Baraitha*. To this same group belong the earlier parts of the *Midrash Rabbah*, *Pesikta*, and *Tanhuma*, though the date of compilation of these is much later. The Rabbis whose works form the first group are called *Tannaim*, those of the second *Amoraim*; and it is usual to distinguish the two periods before and after the closing of the Mishna, as the Tannaite and the Amoraite periods respectively.

The question has often been raised whether there is any mention at all, in the Talmud, of the historical Jesus of Nazareth. Until recently, Jewish writers have usually answered this in the negative. They have pointed out that the person supposed to be Jesus is described as a contemporary either of R. Joshua b. Perahiah or of R. Akiba, thus either a century before or a century after the beginning of the Christian era. This is true, but it only shows the anachronism of the tradition. For the person so indicated is called variously Ben Stada, Ben Pandira, Jeshu, Jêshū ha-Nōtzri (*i.e.* the Nazarene), Jêshū b. Pandira; and what is said of this person makes it impossible to doubt that the reference is to the historical Jesus. The following passages decide the question:

Bab. *Sanh.* 107b, 'Jêshū ha-Nōtzri practised magic, and deceived and led astray Israel.'
Bab. *Sanh.* 43a, 'Jêshū (ha-Nōtzri) had five disciples.'
Tos. *Hull.* ii. 22, 23, 'There came in Jacob, a man of Chephar Sechanja, to cure him in the name of Jêshū b. Pandira.'
Bab. *Sanh.* 43a, 'On the eve of Passover they hung Jêshū ha-Nōtzri.'

It is not likely that there should have been a second Jesus the Nazarene, otherwise wholly unknown, who 'deceived and led astray Israel,' who was executed for doing so, who had disciples, and in whose name those disciples sought to heal the sick. It is now generally admitted by Jewish writers that the reference is to the historical Jesus. At the same time it is possible that the name Ben Stada did not originally refer to Jesus, although in the later tradition the two are identified.

The present writer has suggested elsewhere (*Christianity in Talmud and Midrash*, 345 n.) that Ben Stada denotes 'that Egyptian' who is mentioned in Ac 21³⁸; Jos. *Ant.* xx. viii. 6, *BJ* II. xiii. 5. As to the meaning of the two names, Ben Stada and Ben Pandira, various explanations have been proposed; but none has, in either case, been generally accepted. The Talmud (Bab. *Shabb.* 104b) explains *Stada* as equivalent to *Stāth dā*, 'such a one has been unfaithful,' and refers it to the alleged illegitimate birth of Jesus. But this is certainly not the original meaning of the epithet. That *Stada* is made up of the Latin words 'sta' 'da,' and denotes a Roman soldier, is a mere guess, with nothing in its favour. *Pandira* has been explained as πενθερός, or πάνθηρ, or παρθένος; but beyond some likeness of sound there is nothing to recommend these suggested equivalents. The riddle is as yet unsolved.

The following summary contains all that the Talmudic literature has to say about Jesus. The passages referred to will be found in full and translated in the present writer's work already mentioned.

Jesus, called *ha-Nōtzri*, B. Stada, or B. Pandira, was born out of wedlock (M. *Jeb.* iv. 13, cf. Bab. *Shabb.* 104b). His mother was called Miriam, and was a dresser of women's hair (Bab. *Shab.* ib. where 'Miriam megaddelah nashaia' is a play on 'Miriam Magdalaah,' *i.e.* Mary Magdalene). Her husband was Pappus b. Judah, and her paramour Pandira. She is said to have been the descendant of princes and rulers, and to have played the harlot with a carpenter (Bab. *Sanh.* 106a). Jesus had been in Egypt, and had brought magic thence. He was a magician, and deceived and led astray Israel. He sinned and caused the multitude to sin (Bab. *Sanh.* 107b). He mocked at the words of the wise, and was excommunicated (*ib.*). He was tainted with heresy (*ib.* 103a). [He] called himself God, also the Son of Man, and said that he would go up to heaven (Jerus. *Taan.* 65b; Jesus is not mentioned by name, but there is no doubt that He is meant). He made himself live by the name of God (Bab. *Sanh.* 106a, also anonymous). He was tried in Lydda (Lūd) as a deceiver and as a teacher of apostasy (Tos. *Sanh.* x. 11; Jerus. *Sanh.* 25c, d). Witnesses were concealed so as to hear his statements, and a lamp was lighted over him that his face might be seen (*ib.*). He was executed in Lydda, on the eve of Passover, which was also the eve of Sabbath; he was stoned, and hung, or crucified (*ib.* and Tos. *Sanh.* ix. 7). A herald proclaimed, during forty days, that he was to be stoned, and invited evidence in his favour; but none was given (Bab. *Sanh.* 43a). He (under the name of Balaam) was put to death by Pinhas the Robber (Pontius Pilatus), and at the time was thirty-three years old (Bab. *Sanh.* 106*b*). He was punished in Gehenna by means of boiling filth (Bab. *Giṭṭ.* 56*b*, 57*a*). He was 'near to the kingdom' (Bab. *Sanh.* 43*a*). He had five disciples (*ib.*). Under the name of Balaam he was excluded from the world to come (M. *Sanh.* x. 2).

The several items of the foregoing tradition about Jesus are of various date. The Mishna does not contain the names Jeshu, B. Stada, or B. Pandira; so that it is not absolutely certain that Jesus is referred to in the Mishna at all. The Tosefta contains all three names, but not Jēshū ha-Nōtzri. Neither *Siphrē*, *Siphra*, nor *Mechilta* contains any allusion to Jesus. The main authorities, therefore, for such allusions in the Tannaite period, are Tosefta and the *Baraithas* embedded in the Gemaras. The *Baraithas* contain the statements that Jesus brought magic from Egypt, that he deceived and led astray Israel, that He was tried at Lydda and hung on the eve of Passover which was also the eve of Sabbath, that a herald proclaimed the approaching execution and invited evidence in his favour, and that he had five disciples. The statements contained in Tosefta have been noted above.

The tradition concerning Jesus appears to have started with R. Eliezer b. Horkenos; at least it cannot be traced earlier. R. Eliezer was the chief disciple of R. Joḥanan b. Zaccai, who died about A.D. 80, and was living in Jerusalem at the time when Jesus was crucified. R. Eliezer was an old man in A.D. 109, and died probably in A.D. 117. Both he and his brother-in-law R. Gamaliel (grandson of the Gamaliel of Acts) had dealings with Christians. The tradition passed from R. Eliezer to R. Aḳiba and from him to R. Meir, in each case from teacher to disciple. The tradition represented by R. Gamaliel passed to his grandson R. Judah the Holy, who gathered in also the tradition of R. Aḳiba and R. Meir. This completes the Tannaite period.

In the Amoraite period the tradition is twofold, Palestinian and Babylonian. The former contains very little that is new. R. Joḥanan was a disciple of R. Judah before mentioned, and his disciple R. Abahu uttered the famous dictum: 'If a man say to thee "I am God," he is a liar,' etc. On the whole, the Palestinian Rabbis took very little interest in the tradition about Jesus.

The Babylonian tradition starts with Rab, who was a disciple of R. Judah; and though Rab himself did not add anything concerning Jesus, his disciple R. Ḥisda gave the explanation of the relation of Jesus to Stada and Pandira. It was he also who quoted the saying that 'Jēshū ha-Nōtzri burned his food in public,' *i.e.* was tainted with heresy. A contemporary of R. Ḥisda and, like him, a disciple of Rab, R. Judah. b. Ezekiel handed on the tradition to R. Joseph, who corrected the explanation of the name *Stada*, and mentions 'Miriam Megaddelah,' evidently supposing that Mary of Magdala was the mother of Jesus. R. Papa, disciple of Abaji, who received the tradition from R. Joseph, added the remark about 'her who was descended from princes,' etc. A few of the statements concerning Jesus in the Gemaras are anonymous, notably the story of His excommunication by His teacher R. Joshua b. Peraḥiah, and His punishment in Gehenna.

The Talmudic references to Jesus afford no ground for correcting the narrative of the Gospels. There is sufficient likeness between the general outlines of the Jewish and the Christian traditions to show that the same person is referred to; but it is very doubtful if the Jewish tradition rests upon a knowledge of the Gospels. It is hardly more than a careless memory, retained in unfriendly or indifferent minds. There is also no warrant for

arguing, from the Talmudic allusions, that Jesus actually lived a hundred years before the time usually accepted as the date of His birth. An equally good case might be made out for placing Him a century after that date. Rabbinical chronology is to be used only with great caution; and the statement that Jesus was the disciple of R. Joshua b. Peraḥiah (who did live about 100 B.C.), is made in the Talmud without the support of any authority. Moreover, the story, as referring to Jesus, appears only in the Babylonian Gemara; the Palestinian version does not give the name of the disciple who was excommunicated. There is nothing to show how Jesus came to be associated, in the tradition, with the famous Rabbi of a century before His time.

It is from the Talmudic allusions to Jesus that the mediæval caricature of Him was elaborated, which will be described in the following section. It is therefore important to note that the chief points in the Talmudic tradition which furnished the base for that caricature were His alleged illegitimate birth, and His character as a magician and a deceiver. The former is a coarse interpretation of the Christian assertion that Jesus was not the son of Joseph, while the latter is due to His reputation as a worker of miracles, and to the undoubted fact that He had created a serious dissension amongst the adherents of the Jewish religion.

LITERATURE.—Herford, *Christianity in Talmud and Midrash*, 1904; Laible-Dalman, *Jesus Christus im Talmud* [Eng. tr. by Streane]; also, Mead, *Did Jesus live 100 years B.C.?*

ii. CHRIST IN MEDIÆVAL JEWISH LITERATURE. —There are to be distinguished a popular and a serious treatment of the subject by Jewish writers in the Middle Ages. On the one hand, there is the book called the *Tōl'dōth Jēshū*, which relates the story of Jesus as of a vulgar impostor; on the other hand, there are references to Jesus by Jews of repute which are dignified and respectful in tone, and show a real desire to be fair towards the Founder of that Christian religion whose adherents had inflicted such injuries on Jews.

(*a*) *The Tōl'dōth Jēshū.*—In the printed editions this is a small book of some 24 pages, in which is told the story of the birth, public career, and death of Jesus, and the origin of the Christian Church. It makes no pretension to be a serious history, though it certainly does not deserve the torrent of abuse which its Christian editors have poured out upon it. It is merely a rather stupid and silly tale intended to tickle the ears of ignorant Jews, and to satisfy their contempt and hatred of the Christian religion by mockery of its Founder. To Christian readers it is, of course, highly offensive. But it should be remembered that the book was not written for Christians, and also that Christian treatment of Jews made such retaliation only natural.

What the origin of the book was is not certainly known. Traces of statements contained in it are found in the writings of Tertullian and Eusebius; but the first evidence of the existence of a distinct book of this character appears only in the 9th century. In the work *de Judaicis superstitionibus*, written about A.D. 830 by Agobard of Lyons, there is an extract from a written Life of Jesus, which has considerable likeness to the *Tōl'dōth*; and a similar writing, perhaps the same, is mentioned by Rabanus Maurus in 847. The *Pugio Fidei* of Raymundus Martinus (13th cent.) contains the whole of the *Tōl'dōth* as known to him. From this time onwards the *Tōl'dōth* has never wholly disappeared; but it was, naturally, never published by Jews, or even acknowledged by them. Christian writers who succeeded in finding a copy speak of it as being jealously secreted by Jews, and to be obtained only by bribery. Buxtorf in 1696 (*Bibliotheca Rabbinica*, p. 148) says: 'We procured a copy from a friend who bought it from "verpo quodam" for some Hungarian gold pieces.' The copies so obtained were written in Hebrew, but it would seem that the original language was German, or at all events the vernacular of the country where the book first appeared. The translation into Hebrew was presumably made in order to render the book accessible to all Jews.

In the case of a work which existed only in manuscript, it is inevitable that there should be considerable differences in different copies. S. Krauss, who is the chief authority on the subject, enumerates 22 complete MSS and 6 fragments of the *Tōl'dōth*, which he arranges in five groups, according to their points of resemblance. It seems likely that these were not all derived from a single original, but rather that the story, founded on the scanty notices in the Talmud, was told and circulated orally, and in course of time written down by several hands in different countries. With the exception of the fragments, no existing MS of the *Tōl'dōth* appears to be older than the 16th century. There are five printed editions, the best known being those of Wagenseil (in *Tela Ignea Satanæ*, 1681) and Huldreich, 1705.

A short summary may suffice to indicate the contents of the book; and for this purpose the Wagenseil edition will be followed. Joḥanan, a pious youth in Jerusalem, is betrothed to Miriam, the daughter of a widow. Joseph Pandira, of the tribe of Judah, forms a plan to seduce Miriam, and effects his purpose on a Sabbath eve. Three months afterwards, Joḥanan, learning the condition of Miriam, consults R. Simeon b. Sheṭaḥ, and accuses Joseph Pandira. Having, however, no proof, Joḥanan deserted Miriam and went to Babylonia. In course of time Miriam bears a son, who is Jesus. The boy is placed under the tuition of R. Elḥanan, and by his conduct causes the Rabbis to suspect his birth. R. Simeon b. Sheṭaḥ reveals the story, and Jesus is expelled from the community. He first went to Upper Galilee, and thence to Jerusalem, where he contrived to learn the secret of the Ineffable Name (of God). By the help of this he worked miracles, and proclaimed himself the Son of God, born of a virgin. The queen of Jerusalem, Helena, believed in him, by reason of the miracles. The leaders of the Jews, becoming alarmed, set up Judas, one of themselves, as an antagonist to Jesus. They allowed him to learn the Name, and arranged a trial of strength between him and Jesus. The latter was defeated, and condemned to death, but made his escape. Judas followed him, disguised as one of his disciples, and contrived to steal from him the Divine Name, which Jesus kept written on parchment and hidden in an incision in his flesh. Jesus, in order to obtain possession of it again, went once more to Jerusalem. There Judas betrayed him to the rulers. He was captured, scourged, stoned, and hung—upon the stalk of a cabbage, because no tree would consent to bear him. After he was dead, Judas stole the corpse and flung it in the ditch of his garden. The disciples, not finding the body, said that Jesus had risen from the dead. The queen believed this, and the Jews were again alarmed. The corpse, however, was discovered, and dragged before the queen at the tail of a horse. The Christians were furious against the Jews. One of the latter, Simon Kepha, undertook to solve the problem by completely separating the Christians from the Jews. He learned the Name, worked miracles; and, having thus gained the confidence of the followers of Jesus, proclaimed to them, in his name, new laws of religion. They accepted his teaching. Thereupon he withdrew into a town, built especially for him, where he remained, sitting upon a stone, until his death. After his death another Christian teacher arose in Rome, who annulled the laws given by Simon Kepha, and gave new ones, instituting baptism instead of circumcision, and the Sunday in place of the Sabbath. The new teacher, however, in trying to perform a miracle, was killed by a stone falling upon his head. 'So let all thine enemies perish, O Lord.'

The other editions follow, more or less closely, the line sketched out above, though in detail there is considerable variety. All of them describe the seduction of Miriam by Joseph Pandira, some with a disgusting relish of obscenity. The remainder of the story is variously embellished with wonder-working and low comedy, and that word-play in which Jewish wit delighted. There is not the faintest ray of genius, or the least sign of literary skill in any of the versions, or the slightest indication that He of whom the story was told was a great or a good man. If, as Krauss is bold to affirm, the *Tōl'dōth* was intended seriously as a history of Jesus, it says little for the intelligence of its author and its readers. It is rather the wretched device by which ignorant and persecuted Jews revenged themselves, and found a pitiful amusement in mocking the Christ of their persecutors. It remains, an unseemly relic of evil days, but still claiming a place in mediæval literature; and if it bears witness against those who wrote it, it does so no less against those whose cruelty drove them to write it (see Krauss, *Das Leben Jesu nach jüd. Quellen*, 1902, for an exhaustive treatment of the whole subject).

(b) *Polemical references to Christ.*—We pass to a pleasanter region of literature, one where mention is made of Jesus in terms which, if not such as Christians would use, are very different from those of the *Tōl'dōth*.

The references to Jesus in the mediæval Jewish literature, apart from the *Tōl'dōth*, are not numerous. The reasons for this seem to be two: (1) that in controversy with Christians the Jews were not disposed to say more than they could help upon a subject where every word was likely to give offence and draw down persecution upon themselves; and (2) that the Jews were well aware of the difference between the Founder of Christianity and His followers. Their main quarrel was with the latter; and in their theological arguments they defended the unity of God, and denied the Trinity, upon Scripture grounds, with hardly any reference to the actual Jesus. To the Jews He was, of course, only a man. To the Christians He was God; and there was no common ground between them, or any occasion for debate as to His personal character and the events of His life. The controversy between Jews and Christians was fought in regard to principles, not persons, and was further embittered by mutual hatred. The Jews, if left to themselves, would never have mentioned Jesus at all, though armed at all points against Christians. Even in their own writings intended for Jewish readers, they say extremely little about Jesus, and in what they do say there is no attempt to estimate His character. For them He is simply 'that man,' or 'he who is known.'

The foregoing may be taken to represent the general attitude of the mediæval Rabbis towards Jesus; indeed, it is found in much later times. It may be described in the phrase 'cold neutrality'; and it remained unaltered until the great Jewish historians of the last century made a serious study of Jesus as a figure in their national history. The attitude of Jews towards Christians began to change much earlier; but that does not come within the scope of this article.

The mediæval Jewish references to Jesus may be illustrated from the report of a disputation, held at Paris on June 25, 1240, between R. Jehiel and a certain Nicolaus Donin (fragment published by Wagenseil in his *Tela Ignea Satanæ*, 1681). The Christian, who was a converted Jew, quoted the passages from the Talmud (described in § i. of this article) as evidence of Jewish blasphemy. The Jewish champion denied that these referred to the Jesus whom Christians worshipped:

'In truth, we have not spoken thus against the God of the Gentiles (*i.e.* Christ), but only against another Jesus, who mocked at the words of the wise, and did not believe in their words, but only in the written Law, as thou dost. And thou mayst know that this is true; for behold, it is not written "Jesus the Nazarene," but "Jesus Gereda." Moreover, if it had been he (*i.e.* Jesus the Nazarene), he not only did this, but also deceived and led astray Israel, and made himself God, and denied the essence (of religion). But, clearly, it was another man, who did not deny the written Law, but only the oral, and is called a *min* (heretic)' (p. 16 in Wagenseil). R. Jehiel also lays stress on the fact that the man of whom the Talmud speaks was a contemporary of R. Joshua b. Peraḥiah, while the Jesus of the Christians lived a century later (p. 21). He says that it is quite possible that both were called Jesus, 'just as there are many boys in France called Louis, who are not on that account kings of France.' Being solemnly adjured to declare his real thought on the matter, he says : 'As I live, and hope to return home in safety, we have not thought of him (*i.e.* Christ) that he should be " condemned to filth " (according to the Talmudic assertion), nor have we said these things concerning him' (p. 24).

A further illustration is found in the book entitled *Juḥasin*, by R. Abraham Zacuth (b. 1504). This is a sort of dictionary of biography for the period of the Talmud, but containing also references to other periods. On p. 15 (ed. Filippowski, London, 1857) is the following notice of Jesus :

And the truth (is this) that the Nazarene was born in the fourth year of the reign of Jannai II., *i.e.* Alexander (Jannæus); this is the year 263 from the building of the Temple, and the 51st year of the Hasmonæans, and the year 3675 from the Creation (B.C. 85). Although the Nazarenes say that he was born in the time of Herod, the slave of the Hasmonæans, in the year 3760 (from the Creation), and that he was hung 35 years before the destruction (of the Temple), being 32 years old, to our shame and to declare to us that at once, speedily, 40 years in advance, the Temple was destroyed for the guilt of what we did to him. But this is not so ; for his birth was 89 years before the birth which they affirm. And the truth is that he was born in the year 3675, and in the year 299 (of the Temple) he was arrested (*i.e.* B.C. 49), and he was 36 years old in the third year of Aristobulus, the son of Jannai. And for this reason the sages of Israel, in the controversy which they have had with the Nazarenes, have written that in the Talmud there is no mention of the Nazarene whom they mean. Moreover, in the chronicles of the Nazarenes there is a dispute amongst them as to the year in which he was born.' There is a further reference in the same book, p. 86, where the writer deals with the assertion that Jesus was the contemporary of R. Akiba, his mother having been the wife of Pappus b. Jehudah (see above, in § 1). The writer decides against this, and says : 'According to the knowledge of the Nazarenes, the man who is known was in the time of R. Eliezer ; and thus it appears in ch. i. of *Aboda Zara* that R. Eliezer talked with Jacob, a disciple of Jeshu the Nazarene.' A few lines farther down he quotes from Rashi the words, 'Ben Stada is the man who is known, the Nazarene ' ; but they are not found in the passage to which he refers, nor are they mentioned by Rabbinowicz.

It will be observed that the above passages deal only with the chronology of Jesus, and this is, with a few exceptions, the sole point on which the mediæval Rabbis enlarge in their references to Him. The reason is, of course, their desire to ward off the charge made by the Christians, that the Talmud contains blasphemous allusions to Jesus. The following references, which all deal with chronology, may serve to illustrate this side of the subject :

R. Abraham b. David in the *Sepher ha-Kabbalah*, 1195 (Neubauer, *Med. Jew. Chron.* ii. 53), R. Jehudah ha-Levi (*Cusari*, ed. Buxtorf, p. 240), R. David Gans in *Zemaḥ David*, 1592 (edition of 1785, pt. ii. p. 12ᵇ). The last comes nearer to the Christian date. He says : 'Jesus the Nazarene was born in Bethlehem, a "parsah" and a half from Jerusalem, in the year 3761 from the Creation, *i.e.* the year 42 of Augustus Cæsar. Abarbanel (*Maj. Jeshua*, p. 67ᵃ, cited by Eisenmenger, *Entd. Judenthum*, i. 239) maintains strongly the Talmudic date, and ends thus : 'And the wise men of that time bore witness concerning him, his friends and companions' [*i.e.* the friends of R. Joshua b. Peraḥiah whose disciple Jesus was said to have been], 'and how shall we believe the substitution of [another for] him, from the mouth of men who did not know him, and were not there ? . . . And we will not depart from the truth and tradition of our fathers, who did not tamper with the fact, and who related the facts as they took place without addition or omission ; and all this shows that this [the Christian] theory is untrue.'

The fullest and most elaborate statements of the chronological argument, from the Jewish side, are those of R. Salman Zebi (cited in Eisenmenger, i. 231) and R. Abraham Perizzol (contained in the same work, pp. 250-253).

There are, however, one or two mediæval Jewish works which deal with more than the chronological question. Wagenseil (in *Tela Ignea Satanæ*) published the *Nizzaḥon* (which he distinguishes as *N. Vetus*), composed by a writer in the 12th cent., as he supposes. Buxtorf, misled by the name,

attributed the work to R. Lipman in the 15th cent., the author of another book bearing the same title, and also published by Wagenseil. The author of the older work was acquainted with the Gospels, and he ranged over the whole field of Jewish Christian controversy, refuting the Christians out of their own Scriptures. His arguments all tend to show that Jesus was not God ; but it is worthy of note that he very seldom speaks disrespectfully of Jesus Himself. His quarrel is with the Christians, not with their Master.

Another work of a similar character is the *Ḥizzuk Emunah* (*Munimen Fidei*) of R. Isaac Troki, a Karaite, written about 1575 (printed by Wagenseil in the *Tela Ignea Satanæ*). The author shows an even wider acquaintance with the NT than the writer of the *Nizzaḥon* possessed ; and he mentions the fact that he read the NT in the translation made by Budnæus in 1572. He lays stress on the fact that Jesus stood much nearer to Judaism than His followers did ; that He never claimed the title of God ; that He said, 'I am not come to destroy the law and the prophets' ; that He enjoined the keeping of the Commandments on one who would obtain eternal life ; that He gave many precepts which His followers disregarded. He does not hesitate to admit a saying of Jesus as true, though he immediately turns it against the Christians. All through the book his arguments are directed against what Christians asserted about Jesus, hardly at all against what Jesus said of Himself. And he may perhaps be claimed as a forerunner of the later Jewish historians who have really tried to be fair in writing of Jesus, who have at least abandoned the attitude of cold neutrality, and have scorned the wretched mockery of the *Tōl'dōth*.

It will have been observed that nothing has been said of the opinion of Maimonides about Jesus. In such of his works as the present writer has been able to consult he has found no allusion whatever. Dr. M. Friedländer, in his work on *The Jewish Religion*, p. 227, quotes from Maimonides, but without giving the exact reference, the following : 'Also Jesus the Nazarene, who imagined he would be the Messiah, and was killed through the court of Law, is alluded to in the Book of Daniel, as it is said, "And the sons of the transgressors among thy people will rise in order to establish a vision, and will stumble." Can there be a greater stumbling than this ?' This is interesting as being more than a mere chronological note.

On the whole, the attitude of the mediæval Rabbis towards Jesus was one of indifference. Apart from the necessity of controversy or the exposition of their own tenets, they had little inclination or occasion to mention Him. In Him, as a man, they had no interest. Their tradition taught them that He was one who had 'deceived and led astray Israel,' and they would not be at the pains to show that, although not God, He was still a good man. Controversy with Christians turned mainly on the questions of His Deity and His Messiahship, and the Rabbis fought the battle with texts, while they left the personality alone. It is probable that the great majority of the mediæval Rabbis were utterly ignorant of what Jesus had said and done ; they were concerned to defend themselves against the charge of blasphemy based on the Talmud, and for that purpose worked out the chronological argument. But only one or two seem to have had the courage to read the NT ; and in studying their works, the present writer is inclined to believe that these Jewish controversialists had not altogether failed to perceive that Jesus was a great man. This may be a mistaken impression ; it is at least a charitable one. We shall find in the modern historians a welcome change from the mediæval attitude towards Jesus ; and to the consideration of those modern writers we must now proceed.

LITERATURE.—' Disputatio R. Jehielis,' ' Nizzaḥon Vetus,' and ' R. Isaaci Hizzuk Emunah ' in Wagenseil, *Tela Ignea Satanæ* ;

Liber Juhasin, ed. Filippowski, London, 1857; also, Eisenmenger, *Entdecktes Judenthum*, and incidental references as given above, where they occur.

iii. CHRIST IN MODERN JEWISH LITERATURE.—So far as the modern Jewish attitude towards Jesus differs from that of the mediæval writers, it is to be found in the works of the great historical scholars of the last century, and in a few utterances by liberal Jews at the present day. Apart from these, the influence of which, however, must tend to promote a truer view of Jesus amongst Jews, the mediæval attitude towards Him still widely prevails. New editions of the *Tōl'dōth* are still published, and find readers among the uneducated, in Russian Poland. And, as regards the educated, there is still the same cautious reserve which so far as possible avoids mention of Jesus. The late Professor Theodores of Manchester, in a lecture on the Talmud, delivered in 1874, took elaborate pains to show that Jesus was not referred to at all in that work. And later still, Dr. M. Friedländer, in his book on *The Jewish Religion*, makes only the slightest reference to Jesus, and, so far as the present writer has observed, does not offer any opinion of his own upon the subject.

The first Jewish writer who fairly broke away from the traditional attitude towards Jesus was Grätz, in his *Gesch. der Juden* (vol. iii. 1856). He boldly declared (p. 224 n.) that in estimating Christianity the historian must take his stand on the historical, *i.e.* the critical, method. He made no apology for the shock which he must have given to the majority of Jews by his new departure. And he was not afraid to express high admiration for the character of Jesus as a man. He formed his views upon the subject mainly under the influence of Strauss and Baur, by whose help he was enabled to put aside as unhistorical most of the non-Jewish elements in the Gospel representations of Jesus, and to emphasize the strong affinity between His teaching and Judaism. Grätz claims that Jesus was, in the main, an Essene, as the Baptist also had been; that His whole purpose was that of a moral reformer, and that He had no intention of attacking Judaism, even the Pharisaic Judaism, as such, but only the depravity of those who professed it. The objections to this view are obvious; but the fact that Grätz presented a portrait of Jesus in which the Jewish lines were overdrawn and the rest nearly obliterated, does not lessen his merit as the first Jew who gave a real portrait of Jesus at all. Later Jewish writers have, on the whole, followed the lead of Grätz; some of the exaggerations of his work have been toned down, and more recognition has been given to the originality of Jesus; but the general outline of his work is still maintained, according to which Jesus was a high-minded and saintly Rabbi, whose fate it was to be maligned and persecuted, and whose enemies were His own professed followers quite as much as His Jewish contemporaries.

The work of Jost (*Gesch. d. Judenthums u. s. Sekten*, 1863) shows less of exaggeration than that of Grätz, and perhaps even more of personal veneration towards Jesus. Jost's chief contribution is his indignation against the 'judicial murder' of Jesus. There was no regular trial, such as Jewish law required. There was only a high-handed act of violence on the part of the chief priests.

He says: 'We hold it to be historical honesty, without regard to misinterpretation, to give to the fact its right name, in order to throw the responsibility upon those fanatics who did such a deed by their own power. It was not the Jews who crucified Jesus. Thousands of them revered in Jesus their teacher and friend. . . . It is time at last to judge without prejudice the authentic records of the Evangelists, who relate the course of events in simple words, albeit according to traditions of very

unequal worth. Only the most blinded partisan can wish to justify the crucifixion of Jesus as it was effected, or to burden afresh the whole nation, or its law-abiding posterity, with the hateful deed of Caiaphas and his associates.'

J. H. Weiss (*Gesch. d. jüd. Tradition*, 1871, Hebrew) is interesting chiefly as showing how the radical influence of Grätz and Jost reacted upon the more conservative Jew. Weiss asserts the Essenism of Jesus (i. p. 232), and remarks that His deplorable fate was due not to His teaching, which was not new, but to the means which He took to promote it.

'For he claimed to be a prophet, and drew away many in Israel to believe in his Divine work and his miracles. And he said, before the multitude and even before his judges, that he was the Son of God. These three claims were the reason for all that was done against him.'

Weiss, beyond question, here puts his finger on the real Jewish grievance against Jesus—'He spake as one having authority, and not as their scribes.' Grätz and Jost had made it impossible for a Jewish historian to revert to the mediæval attitude towards Jesus; but one seems to hear, in Weiss, the echo of the ancient condemnation, 'He was a magician, and deceived and led astray Israel.'

The *Jewish Encyclopedia* may be taken as the authorized exponent of Jewish opinion, and in its 7th volume it contains a careful and critical article upon 'Jesus.' It is the work of three writers, Jacobs, Kohler, and Krauss; and is written with a full knowledge of recent Christian as well as Jewish scholarship. It is admitted that, while the teaching and practice of Jesus were in many respects Jewish and even Essene, He yet departed widely in other respects from Essenism, particularly in His association with publicans and sinners. His attitude towards the Law, insisting on the spirit rather than on the Halachic development of it, is represented as not necessarily or essentially un-Jewish. He was, in fact, the representative of the *Am-ha-aretz*, the 'people that knoweth not the Law'—a rather acute remark. Weiss was right in pointing to His assumption of power and authority as the reason 'of much modern antipathy to Jesus, so far as it exists.' He did not, at least publicly, claim to be the Messiah; and His trial and execution were quite irregular. But, after all, it is freely admitted that 'a great historic movement, of the character and importance of Christianity, cannot have arisen without a great personality to call it into existence and give it shape and direction. Jesus of Nazareth had a mission from God; and he must have had the spiritual power and fitness to be chosen for it.' That is finely said, and it is with one exception the fullest Jewish recognition of the greatness of Jesus that is known to us. That exception is contained in an article by C. G. Montefiore (*JQR*, 1894, p. 381 ff.). He there speaks of Jesus as 'the most important Jew who ever lived, one who exercised a greater influence upon mankind and civilization than any other person, whether within the Jewish race or without it.' . . . 'A Jew whose life and character have been regarded by almost all the best and wisest people who have heard or read of his actions and his words, as the greatest religious exemplar for every age.' . . . 'It may be asked, "Was Jesus an original teacher, and on what grounds does his originality depend?" Now there is no *a priori* reason why Jesus should not have been original. Jewish authors sometimes write as if there were an antecedent improbability in his having made any big religious or moral step in advance.' . . . 'A religious teacher might, I suppose, be called original who combined and collected together the best elements of religion existing in his time, emphasized those most important and fruitful, developed them, drew out their implications, and rejected or ignored other elements which either did not harmonize with the first, or which, though he and his contemporaries may have been unaware of it, belonged in reality to a lower level and an outgrown age. I am inclined to believe that herein to a great extent lay the originality of Jesus.' Mr. Montefiore's article shows how it is possible for a Jew to remain a whole-hearted Jew, while yet he feels a frank admiration and reverence towards Jesus. With his full recognition of the spiritual grandeur of Jesus, the fullest that would seem to be possible without crossing the frontier of Judaism, we will close this study of Christ in the Jewish literature. (See, further, the histories of Grätz, Jost, and Weiss; *Jewish Encyc.* vol. vii., and *JQR,* 1894).　　　　R. TRAVERS HERFORD.

CHRIST IN MOHAMMEDAN LITERATURE.—
i. **In the Koran.*** — The earliest mention of Jesus Christ in the Koran is in ch. 19, the *Suratu Maryam,* which was delivered in Mecca. It refers to His birth—

'Make mention in the Book, of Mary, when she went apart from her family eastward, and took a veil to shroud herself from them, and we sent our spirit to her, and he took before her the form of a perfect man. She said: " I fly for refuge from thee to the God of Mercy: if thou fearest Him." He said: "I am only a messenger of thy Lord, that I may bestow on thee a holy son." She said: "How shall I have a son, when man hath never touched me? and I am not unchaste?" He said: "So shall it be. Thy Lord hath said, Easy is this with me, and we will make him a sign to mankind and a mercy from me; for it is a thing decreed." And she conceived him and retired with him to a far-off place. And the throes came upon her by the trunk of a palm. She said: "Oh, would that I had died ere this, and been a thing forgotten, forgotten quite." And one cried to her from below her, "Grieve not thou." Then came she with the babe to her people, bearing him. They said: "O Mary, now hast thou done a strange thing, O sister of Aaron; Thy father was not a man of wickedness, nor unchaste thy mother." And she made a sign to them, pointing towards the babe. They said: "How shall we speak with him who is in the cradle, an infant?" It said: "Verily, I am the servant of God; He hath given me the Book, and He hath made me a Prophet"' (vv. 16-24, 28-32).

The child is represented as miraculously speaking in defence of His mother. He claimed to be the servant of God to whom a revelation—the Book— was made. It is said that this refers to the Injil, or Gospel, revealed to Him whilst yet in His mother's womb. The idea of speaking in the cradle is taken from the apocryphal Gospel of the Infancy. The idea of the palm tree is taken from a story in the History of the Nativity of Mary, when she rests under it on the way to Egypt.

In *Suratu'z Zukhruf* (ch. 43), also a Meccan *Sura,* we read—

'And when the son of Mary was set forth as an instance of Divine power, lo! thy people cried out for joy thereat. And they said: "Are our gods or is he the better?" . . . Jesus is no more than a servant whom we favoured and proposed as an instance of Divine power to the children of Israel. And he shall be a sign of the last hour' (vv. 57-61).

The idolaters of Mecca put the question recorded in the second of the above verses to Mohammed, when he condemned their gods. The Christians worship as a God, Jesus whom you praise: do you, therefore, condemn Him as you do our gods? We are quite willing to let our gods be treated as you

* The form in which the name 'Jesus' appears in the Koran is *'Isā* (عيسى), which appears to represent 'Esau' rather than 'Ieshua.' A similar variety is said to be found in Mandaic documents (Brandt, *Die Mandäische Religion,* 1889, p. 141); but this, like their *Yaḥyā* for 'John,' may be due to Moslem influence. It seems unlikely, though not wholly impossible, that Mohammed may have confused the personalities of Esau and Christ; it is more probable that the Koranic form is due either to intentional alteration or to mishearing. Fränkel (*WZKM* iv. 336) suggested that the initial ﻉ instead of the final ﻉ was due to mishearing on Mohammed's part, whereas the other alterations were due to his desire to make the word rhyme with *Mūsā* (Moses); and this accounts for the facts (cf. Sycz, *Biblische Eigennamen im Koran,* 1903, p. 62). It is, however, equally likely that the alteration was due to Mohammed's informant, who may have been moved by some superstitious consideration.

treat Him. This seems to be their line of argument, and it led to the emphatic declaration that whatever the Christians might think of Him, in the opinion of Mohammed He was 'no more than a servant.'

All the other references to Jesus Christ occur in Medina *Suras.* We give the principal ones in their historical order.

In *Suratu'l Baqarah* (ch. 2) we read—

'And to Jesus, son of Mary, gave we clear proofs of his Mission, and strengthened him with the Holy Spirit'* (v.81).
'To Jesus, the son of Mary, we gave manifest signs, and strengthened him with the Holy Spirit' (v.254).

In the *Suratu Ali Imran* (ch. 3) there are several references—

'Remember when the Angel said: "O Mary, Verily, God announceth to thee the Word from Him. His name shall be Messiah, the son of Mary, illustrious in this world and in the next, and one of those who have near access to God. And he shall speak to men alike when in the cradle and when grown up, and he shall be one of the just." She said: "How, O Lord! shall I have a son, when man hath not touched me?" He said: "Thus will God create what He will. When He decreeth a thing, He only saith Be, and it is." And He will teach him the Book and the Wisdom and the Law and the Evangel, and he shall be an apostle to the people of Israel' (vv.40-43).

It is said that Mary was thirteen or fifteen years old when the announcement was made to her. The commentators say that Jesus was specially set apart to speak in the cradle, and later on to the Jews.

The phrase 'son of Mary' had become so fixed in Mohammed's mind that he puts it into the mouth of the Angel, even when he is addressing Mary herself. There are several interpretations of the words 'teach him the Book.' The most generally received one is that it refers to the Divine books of previous prophets other than the Law of Moses. There is a curious saying of Imam Mohammed bin Ali Baqir—

'Jesus was so intelligent that, when nine months old, his mother sent him to school. The master said the Bismillah— "In the name of God, the Merciful, the Compassionate"— which the child at once repeated after him. The Master then gave a number of words to be read, of which the first was *abjad.* Jesus wished to know why he should do this, upon which the master became angry and struck him. The child said: "If you know, explain; if you do not, listen. In *abjad,* a stands for Allah la ilah ('there is no God but God'), b for Bahjat Ullah ('grace of God'), j for Jalal Ullah ('glory of God'), d for Din Ullah ('religion of God')."'

Mohammed says that Jesus was sent as an apostle to the Jews, in order to show that his Mission was limited, whilst that of Mohammed was for all people. In Medina, the idea of a Mission far beyond the confines of Arabia had now taken hold of Mohammed's mind, and he thus suggests by the reference to the limited Mission of Jesus his own superiority.

In v.43 of the above ch. 3 a miracle is also referred to—

'"How have I come," he will say, " to you with a sign from your Lord; out of clay will I make for you, as it were, the figure of a bird; and I will breathe into it, and it shall become, by God's leave, a bird. And I will heal the blind and the leper, and, by God's leave, I will quicken the dead."'

It is said that the bird was a bat which flew away whilst they looked at it, and, when out of sight, fell down dead. Traditions also state that he cured fifty thousand people in one day, and raised not only Lazarus, but also Shem, the son of Noah, from the dead. The story of the bird was evidently suggested to Mohammed by the account of the creation of twelve sparrows from mud, recorded in the apocryphal Gospel of Thomas the Israelite.

In the same *Sura* the death of Jesus is referred to—

'O Jesus! verily I will cause thee to die. I will take thee up to myself and deliver thee from those who believe not' (v.48).

The commentary Ma'alim says that he died for three hours and then went up to heaven: others

* By 'Holy Spirit' Mohammed means Gabriel.

say it was seven hours. Jalalain says that God took him away in a trance. Others interpret it in the sense of protection from adversaries, or the destruction of evil which would hinder the ascent to the world of spirits. The difficulty the commentators feel over this verse is that it clearly contradicts *Sura* 4[155] which distinctly denies that Jesus was put to death. In v.[52] Jesus is compared to Adam, that is, neither had a human father.

The next reference is in *Suratu's Saff* (ch. 61), and is intended to show that Jesus had foretold the advent of Mohammed—

'Remember when Jesus the son of Mary said, "O children of Israel! of a truth I am God's apostle to you to confirm the Law which was given before me, and to announce an apostle that shall come after me whose name shall be Ahmad "' (v.7).

Mohammed here confounds the term 'Parakletos,' the Comforter promised by Jesus to His disciples, with the word 'Periklytos,' which has somewhat the same meaning as *Ahmad*, from the root of which his own name Mohammed ('praised') also is derived.

The next reference is in *Suratu'l Hadid* (ch. 57)—

'We gave him the Evangel,* and we put into the hearts of those who followed him kindness and compassion.'

The next reference is in *Suratu'n Nisa* (ch. 4). It is a denial of the crucifixion of Jesus. The Jews are reproached for speaking against Mary, and—

'for their saying, "Verily we have slain the Messiah, Jesus the son of Mary, an apostle of God." But they slew him not, and they crucified him not, but they had only his likeness . . . they did not really slay him, but God took him up to Himself' (v.156).

Mohammed here adopts the view of Basilides, an early heretic, who affirmed that the spirit who constituted Jesus the Son of God left Him before the crucifixion. He did it to prove that Jesus was not really a man, but only the semblance of one; and this is opposed to the Koran as well as to the Gospel. Mohammed apparently did not see the inconsistency of adopting the views of Basilides. Another verse denies the Divinity of Christ.

'The Messiah, Jesus son of Mary, is only an apostle of God, and His word which He conveyed into Mary, and a Spirit from Him. Believe, therefore, in God and His apostles, and say not "Three" (*i.e.* there is a Trinity). Forbear! it will be better for you. God is only one God. Far be it from His glory that He should have a son' (v.169).

In a later *Sura, Suratu'l Maida* (ch. 5), we read—

'Infidels now are they who say, "God is the Messiah, son of Mary"' (v.76). 'When God shall say, "O Jesus, son of Mary, hast thou said unto mankind—Take me and my mother as two gods besides God?," he shall say, "Glory be unto thee, it is not for me to say that which I know to be not the truth "' (v.116).

Mohammed represents Christians as worshipping a Trinity consisting of the Father, the Son, and the Virgin Mary. The undue veneration paid to the Virgin Mary may have misled him in his earlier days, but he had opportunities of correcting his error; and yet in this the latest of the *Suras* he makes the charge. By this time his breach with the Christians was complete, he had no hope of winning them, nothing to gain from them, and so he either seeks to misrepresent their chief dogma, or, at least, takes no pains to ascertain what it really was.

In the same *Sura* we have a passage which has given rise to many traditions—

'Remember when the apostles said, "O Jesus, son of Mary, is thy Lord able to send down a furnished table to us out of heaven?"' (v.112). 'Jesus, son of Mary, said : "O God our Lord! send down a table to us out of heaven, that it may become a recurring festival to us "' (v.114).

---

* By 'the Evangel' Mohammed evidently meant the revelation which he supposed Jesus received in the same mechanical way as he received the Koran.

Mohammed may have had some idea of the Lord's Supper when he recited these words, or of the love-feasts which were 'recurring festivals'; but the commentators do not so interpret it. Some say it was a parable, and that a table did not actually come down; but most consider that a real table descended. Jesus made the ceremonial ablutions, recited the names of God, and then said the prescribed prayers. After this he uncovered the table and found, according to one account, many kinds of food; according to another, a fish ready cooked, without scales or prickly fins, dropping with fat, well seasoned, surrounded with all kinds of herbs, and leaves on which were olives, honey, cheese, and so on. Jesus restored the fish to life, then caused it to die again, and fed one thousand three hundred persons with it. Still the fish remained whole. The table then flew up into heaven. The miracle was repeated for forty days.

ii. The following traditions referring to Jesus Christ are found in the *Qisasu'l Anbiya* or **Tales of the Prophets.**

One day Mary in the house of her husband had arranged a *purdah* behind which she intended to bathe. Then Gabriel in the form of a beautiful young man appeared. Mary feared, and said : 'I seek protection of God from thee, if thou fearest.' Gabriel said : 'I am sent to thee from thy Lord that a beautiful child may be given to thee.' Mary said : 'Whence shall a child come to me, for no man has touched me, I am not an evil-doer.' Then Gabriel came near to Mary and breathed on her. Some say on her sleeve, others on her neck, some on her womb. Some say that this breath was a sneeze made by Adam and preserved by Gabriel.

Mary spoke of her conception to her cousin Joseph, who was to come into the house. He in sorrow expressed his doubts about her, and, on being told to speak his mind freely, said, 'There is no cultivation without seed, and no seed without a tree.' Mary said : 'If you say God at first made the trees, then they were produced without seed : if first He made seed, then seed came without a tree.' Joseph said : 'Is a child born without a father?' Mary said : 'Yes, without parents, just as Adam and Eve were.' Joseph assented, and expressed regret for the doubts he had entertained. Then Mary told him about the good news Gabriel had brought.

They say that Jesus in the womb spoke with his mother and said the *Tasbih: Subhana' llah*—'I extol the holiness of God.' When the days of her confinement drew near, Mary was told to go to Bethlehem, lest her people should injure the child. Mary and Joseph went, under the guidance of Gabriel. The pangs of child-birth coming on, she got off her riding animal and rested under a date tree. Then Christ was born. Immediately a spring appeared and angels bathed the child. It is said that Jesus said then to his mother, 'Do not sorrow, God has provided this fountain.' Then ripe dates fell at her feet, and she said : 'O Lord, Thou hast granted me sustenance.' The reply came, 'O Mary, thy heart turned to me, love for Jesus has come into it; be tranquil, sustenance will be provided, eat and drink and have joy in the Messiah.'

Then Mary said to Gabriel : 'If people ask how the child was born, what shall I reply?' He said : 'Say, "I have seen no man, I am fasting; I speak with none about it."' It is said that when the Jews found her and the child under the tree, they began to make a tumult and reproached her, saying, 'Neither thy father nor mother were evil-doers.' She replied : 'I am fasting to-day, whatever you want to know, ask the child.' They became very angry, and said : 'How shall we speak to the infant?' However, they asked him the circumstances of his birth. He said : 'I am the slave of God, appointed to be a prophet and a blessing in whatever place I may be, and He has ordered me to keep the fast and almsgiving as long as I live. I am not appointed a tyrant, but the peace of God is upon me from the day of my birth to the day of my death and resurrection to life again.' Having said this, he did not speak again till the natural time for an infant to speak arrived. Having witnessed the miracle, the Jews gave up their suspicion and reproach, and said that this was the prophet of whose birth the preceding prophets had spoken.

Then Mary went to Jerusalem, where, seeing the miracles done by the child, people sought to destroy him. Then, by the order of God, Mary took him to Egypt. Some say she went with Joseph and the child to Damascus, to the house of a rich man, who protected and provided for them. He nourished many lame and blind persons. At this time a very valuable article of his was stolen, and no trace of the thief could be found. Jesus said : 'Such a lame and such a blind man stole the thing.' When accused, the blind man said : 'How could I see to steal?,' and the lame man, 'How could I walk to do so?' Jesus said : 'The blind man carried the lame man, who then from a shelf took the goods and divided the booty.' So the theft was found out.

Then Jesus, having received from God the gift of prophecy, returned to Jerusalem and invited the Jews to embrace the strong religion ; but they were displeased, and only his apostles followed him.

It is said that the term *hawari*,* 'apostle,' comes from a word meaning 'to whiten,' and that the apostles were so called because they were fullers by trade. Jesus said to them : 'Just as you make clothes clean, so by faith in God cleanse your hearts from the dust of sin.' Then they asked for a miracle. Jesus took various clothes and filled a jar with them. Some time after he took them out, when they were all of one colour. These twelve men then believed in him. God told Jesus to tell people first, that 'God is one without a partner,' then to tell them of the coming of Mohammed as a prophet, and say : 'A prophet will come after me, Ahmad by name.' Then Jesus, wearing a woollen cloth, with staff in hand went here and there. At night he used a stone for a pillow and lay on the ground. His food was barley bread and greens. He cared nothing for worldly wealth. He never desired the society and friendship of women. His life was one of great simplicity. Seeing his fatigue in walking, his disciples brought him an animal to ride ; but after using it once he returned it to them, for the anxiety of providing it with fodder was more than he could bear. They then wished to procure him a house ; he declined it on the ground that if he lived long it would go to ruin ; if he soon died, some one else would get it.

One day he saw an old man sitting by the grave of his son. Jesus, after two prostrations in prayer, said : 'O certain one, rise by the order of God.' The grave opened, and the corpse came forth and said : 'O Lord, why didst thou call me?' The Jews said : 'We have never seen such a sorcerer.'

It is related that God ordered Jesus to go to the king of Nasibin, a proud and infidel ruler. Jesus went with his twelve disciples, and on arriving near the place said : 'Who of you will go and announce to the people of this place my arrival?' James and Thomas and Simon Peter went. When near the place, Simon told the other two to go on and give the news, and he would wait ; so that if evil

* Really the Ethiopic for 'messenger,' 'apostle.'

should fall on one of them he might make some plan. Then James and Thomas entered the city, and cried out, 'Jesus the Prophet of God and the Spirit of God has come to the city.' The people seized Thomas and took him to the king, who said : 'Who has spoken here of a prophet, and God, and the Spirit of God? if he does not repent, I will kill him.' Thomas said : 'I will not repent. Let the king do as he wills.' Then by the order of the king the people cut off the hands and feet of Thomas, and left him in an unclean place. Simon then came and sought the audience of the king, and begged to be allowed to interrogate Thomas. He then asked him how he supported the statement he had made. Thomas replied that Jesus worked miracles, for the blind and lame and sick were healed. Simon said : 'Doctors do this ; what other proof have you?' 'Jesus knows what people eat, and drink, and say in their houses.' Simon said : 'This too can be done by intelligence and hearing : give another proof.' 'He makes birds of mud, and makes them fly.' Simon said : 'This is simply magic : give another proof.' Thomas said : 'He raises by the order of God the dead to life.' Simon then said to the king : 'If this is so, it is advisable that your honour should send for Jesus, and see whether what Thomas says is right : if he raises the dead he is a true prophet.' The king approved, and sent for Jesus, to whom Simon told all that had passed. Jesus asked what miracles were called for. Simon said to heal the hands and feet of Thomas ; then to state what each one in the assembly had eaten, and what stores he had ; then to make mud birds fly. Jesus did all these things. Salman al-Farisi says that when all the sick in Nasibin were healed, the people asked Jesus to raise the dead. Jesus said he would do so. They came to the grave of Shem, son of Noah, and said, 'Revive him.' Jesus made two prostrations in prayer and prayed to God. Then by order of God the earth opened, and a person with white hair and beard came forth from the grave, and, having saluted Jesus, said to the people : 'Certainly, Jesus is a prophet of God. All of you should believe in him and obey him.' Then Jesus said to Shem : 'In your lifetime no one had white hair ; how is it yours is white?' He replied : 'When I heard your voice, I thought the day of judgment had come, and my hair turned white with fear.' Jesus said : 'How long have you been dead?' He replied : 'Four thousand years.' Jesus wished to pray for his life, but Shem said : 'Again I must die, I have no wish to live on, if you will ask God to have mercy on me.'

One day when a crowd was following Jesus, they said they were hungry. The Apostles urged him to relieve them. This relief came in the form of a tray of God from heaven. When Jesus and the Apostles saw it, they offered thanks to God. Then Jesus said : 'Let the most pious one amongst you lift up the cover of the tray.' The Apostles requested him to do it. He did so, and then they saw on the tray a fish without bones from which oil was flowing, and round it were all kinds of vegetables, but there was no garlic or leeks. Near the head of the fish was some vinegar, and near the tail some salt. Round it were placed five loaves, and on each loaf were a few olives, five pomegranates, and five dates. Simon, on seeing this, said : 'This is heavenly food.' Then Jesus told the people to eat. The Apostles said : 'You eat and then we will.' Jesus said : 'I do not eat. Let the people for whom I obtained it eat.' Then the people ate. The sick, after eating this food, were restored to health. Multitudes ate, but the food was not less. It is said that for forty days this tray came down each morning and remained till mid-day. Then the word came to Jesus : 'Only the poor, the orphans, and the sick should eat.' The rich murmured, and God threatened them with punishment. Some said : 'Make the fish alive again, and we will believe.' Jesus did so ; but they believed not, and seventy men perished.

A man came to Mary one day, and said : 'The king has said that a ryot each day is to make a feast for him and his army. To-day it is my turn, and I have not the means to do it.' Mary turned for aid to Jesus, who hesitated ; but Mary said that aid would be a great favour to the ryot. Jesus then sent for the master of the house, and said : 'Get ready jars and pots, and fill up with water,' which Jesus changed into pure wine. In other pots cooked meat was found, and newly baked bread on trays appeared. The king wished to know where the wine came from. The man replied, From such and such a place. The king, knowing the wine of that place, said : 'Why dost thou lie ? no such wine is to be found there.' Then the man confessed that a neighbour had by his prayers provided all. The king then called for Jesus, and said : 'The heir to my throne died a little while ago, restore him to life.' Jesus said that his return to life meant many evils to the country. The king said : 'Let the country be ruined if I only get one glimpse of him.' Jesus said : 'If I raise him, will you let me go in peace ?' The king agreed ; so the prince came to life, and Jesus went away. But the prince was a tyrant, and the people killed both father and son.

One day Jesus met a Jew with two loaves. The Jew agreed to share food ; but when he saw Jesus had only one loaf, he hid one of his, and next morning appeared with one only, and denied that he had more. Then Jesus, when going on the way, asked a shepherd to feed him, who said : 'Tell one of my men to slay a sheep that it may be cooked.' Jesus from the skin and bones revived the sheep. 'Who art thou ?' said the shepherd. 'Jesus, son of Mary.' Then Jesus asked the Jew where the two loaves were. He swore he had only one. Jesus remained quiet. At the next stage he had a calf killed, and they all ate of it, and again he restored the calf to life and gave it back to its owner, and again asked the Jew where the two loaves were. He again denied that he had two. They then come to a city where the king was sick and at the point of death. Then the Jew told the nobles that he could cure all diseases and even raise the dead. They said : 'Cure the king and we will give you much money.' He began to beat the king with his staff, and the king died. The nobles ordered that he should be hanged. Jesus, seeing this, said : 'If I raise your king, will you forgive my friend ?' Jesus raised the king and released the Jew. The Jew was profuse in his thanks. Jesus said : 'Where is the second loaf ?' The Jew said he had only one.

Jesus went one day to an infidel king like Pharaoh, and called upon him to embrace Islam. The king, being annoyed, determined to kill him. Jesus hid in a mountain cave, and after a few days told his disciples that this revelation had come : 'Truly I will raise thee up and bring thee back to myself.' The Apostles wept at the idea of separation from him. He said : 'You weep now, when the enemy comes you will forsake me.' They declared that they would allow no enemy to come near him, and would protect him. They also said : 'Will another prophet come after thee ?' He said : 'Yes, of the Quraish tribe, an unlettered prophet, Mohammed, superior to me, will come. Tell the generations to come to follow him.' He then added : 'Now I make Simon my Khalifa (successor), all of you obey him.' They agreed. He

said : 'After my death trays full of light will come, and by the blessing of that light you will know the languages of all tribes.'

Some say that the Jews, by the advice of that bad king, and by means of an old Apostle, seized Jesus and imprisoned him all night, and in the morning prepared a cross on which to crucify him. Then great darkness fell, and angels released Jesus from prison and carried him up on high, and took the old man prisoner. The Jews, thinking he was Jesus, quickly killed him, and he was crucified, though he protested that he was not Jesus, but the man who had betrayed him. The Jews did not believe it. All historians say Mary was then alive. Others say the Jews watched and guarded the cave where Jesus was, but Jesus at night was taken up under cover of darkness. In the morning the Jews sent a man to find Jesus, but he returned and said that no one was there. Then the Jews said : 'Thou art Jesus,' and crucified him.

Others say the Jews imprisoned him with eighteen men in a house. Jesus said : 'If one of you will assume my appearance, God will reward you in Paradise.' One agreed. Jesus ascended on high. In the morning the Jews said, 'There were eighteen men with Jesus ; one is short.' The prisoners said Jesus had gone on high ; but the Jews saw one like Jesus and crucified him. After a few days Jesus returned to the Apostles ; then he died, but God restored him to life and made him like an angel.

It is said that at the last day, when Dajjal the cursed, with Imam Mahdi, collects the people at morning prayers, Jesus will appear on the Mosque at Jerusalem, and will descend to join Imam Mahdi, and kill Dajjal. He will engage in *Jihad*, or wars of religion, and bring people to Islam. Such will be his justice that the lion and the sheep will dwell together, and children will play with serpents. When Jesus dies again, the burial prayers (*namaz-i-Janazah*) will be said over him, and he will be buried in the tomb of Mohammed at Medina.

LITERATURE.—The Christology of the Koran is the subject of a considerable literature, which is best represented in recent times by Ed. Sayous, *Jésus-Christ d'après Mahomet*, Paris, 1880. Somewhat earlier are Gerock, *Versuch einer Darstellung der Christologie des Korans*, Hamburg and Gotha, 1839 ; and Manneval, *La Christologie du Koran*, Toulouse, 1867. See also H. Preserved Smith, *The Bible and Islam*, New York, 1897 ; and the missionary tract 'Islam and Christianity,' American Tract Society, 1891.

In the post-Koranic literature of Islam three classes of writers are occupied with the Person of Christ, for different purposes.

1. *The theologians.*—These persons, so far as they argue with Christians, are compelled to discredit the Christian Gospels, against which they urge objections often identical with those popularized in recent times by Strauss. The remarkable treatise by Ibn Ḥazm (d. 1063 A.D.), published in Cairo, 1903-4, represents the extreme of negative criticism. The author refuses to trust the Gospels even for the names of the Apostles ; nothing whatever, he holds, is known about 'Isā beyond the statements of the Koran. For the mode in which his arguments can be met we may refer to St. Clair Tisdall, *Muhammadan Objections to Christianity*, 1904. Ibn Ḥazm's view is not generally popular among Moslems ; and some, such as Fakhr al-din al-Razi (d. 1209), a commentator of high repute, even use the Gospels to illustrate the Koran. This practice is imitated by the Egyptian mufti, Mohammed Abdo, from whom Islam expected so much, in the commentaries which are published in the Cairene bi-monthly *Manār*. It is not unusual to find illustrations of the Koran from the Gospels in commentaries by authors who would not consult them ; in such cases they are given after a chain of authorities going back to one of the companions of the Prophet.

2. *The preachers.*—The Moslem sermon ordinarily consists largely of anecdotes or maxims connected with persons of eminence. These include prophets ; Greek, Roman, and Persian sages ; companions of the Prophet ; and Moslem saints. In the works of these writers the name of 'Isā figures very frequently, the sayings and doings assigned to Him being sometimes traceable to the Gospels, but often assigned in different works to a variety of persons. A great quantity bearing the name 'Isā are to be found in the great homiletic encyclopædia called 'Revival of the Religious Sciences,' by al-Ghazzali (*ob.* 1126 A.D.), whence they were collected and translated in the

Expository Times (Nov. and Dec. 1903, and Jan. 1904) by D. S. Margoliouth.

3. *The story-tellers.*—The profession of these persons does not differ technically from that of the preachers ; but, as their purpose is only to entertain, they may be distinguished from those who aim at reforming. The work by Tha'libi (d. 1036) cited above, called 'Tales of the Prophets,' emanates from this class, whom the more serious preachers reproach for their mendacity (*Luzumiyyat* of Abu 'l-'Alā of Ma'arrah, ii. 77, Cairo, 1895). The stories told by them are often purely the product of their fancy, though at times they go back to some apocryphal Gospel, or some passage of the Old Testament. The character of Christ, as it appears in Moslem fabrications, is modelled on that of the *Sufi* saint, who is a benevolent ascetic. Ibn 'Arabi (d. 1240 A.D.), the chief mystical writer of Islam, accounts for the mild, philanthropic, and non-resistent character of Christianity by the fact that its founder was fatherless. That Christ will return to judge the world *according to the law of Mohammed* is a text on which his 'Meccan Revelations' contain many a homily. The Christian doctrine of the 'Son of God' was attributed by ingenious Moslems to a *misreading* of Ps 27 'Thou art my Son,' in Arabic *bunayya*, which should have been read *nabiyyun*, 'a prophet,' two words which, in the ordinary Arabic writing, are barely distinguishable (*al-Bhaith al-Musajjam*). In the anecdotes told by the preachers, the Apostles are ordinarily made to address him as 'O Spirit of God' or 'O Word of God,' for both of which there is authority in the Koran. As has been pointed out above, the third Person of the Trinity was supposed by the Moslems to be the Virgin.

E. SELL and D. S. MARGOLIOUTH.

PAUL.—It is fortunate that our subject is limited for us at the outset. We are not called upon to consider the life and theology of St. Paul *per se* and in all their bearings, but only in that particular relation which belongs to a Dictionary of 'Christ and the Gospels.' That aspect alone is momentous enough. The figure of St. Paul looms so large and fills so much of the NT that he may well seem to stand between Jesus Christ and the history of the Christian Church. ' *The* Apostle' was the name given in the early Church to the *corpus* of thirteen (or fourteen) Epistles called after him. And in the NT at least he does throw the other Apostles—or all but one—into the shade. The Epistle to the Hebrews, if not actually his, is allied to him in spirit. Even 1 Peter is impregnated with his teaching, however this has come about. If we are to believe many modern critics, we should have to number among his disciples the author of the Fourth Gospel and the three Johannine Epistles. The only two really independent books are James and the Apocalypse.

It is indeed well to remind ourselves that this state of things is in part appearance. We are always at the mercy of our evidence, *i.e.* of such evidence as survives. And while St. Paul has ample justice done to him, the Judæan Apostles and the Judæan Church have not. Still even this is a testimony to the energy and widespread influence of the Apostle of the Gentiles.

The fact remains that the dilated figure of St. Paul seems to bar the way between the subsequent history of Christianity and its Founder. And we are compelled to ask ourselves whether that history may not have undergone a certain amount of deflexion. In other words, Christianity in its first stage appears to have passed through a powerful medium ; and the question is, whether that medium left it substantially unchanged, whether it still is what its Founder intended it to be. Two things strike us at once. One is, that the teaching of St. Paul, as compared with that of his Master, is highly theological. The apparent simplicity of the Gospels has given place to elaborate arguments and statements of doctrine. We shall consider the significance of this fact shortly ; but in the meantime it rather forces itself upon our attention. And the second point is, that this Apostle whose influence has been so great was not one of the original Twelve, and was not himself a personal companion of Christ.

These considerations are enough to make the question before us one of some urgency. We shall need to examine with all the closeness in our power the nature of the relation between St. Paul and Christ, or—what almost amounts to the same thing—between the Epistles (as represented by their central group) and the Gospels, as the two main divisions of the Christian half of the Bible. To do this methodically, we will break up our inquiry into the following heads :

I. General character of St. Paul's teaching. —1. *St. Paul the first Christian theologian on a larger scale.*—It is true broadly to say that St. Paul is the first Christian theologian in the more technical sense of the word. He is the first to formulate doctrine on any considerable scale. The first Christians had their simple formulations : such as that 'Jesus is Lord' (1 Co 12³), 'Jesus is the Christ' (Ac 5⁴² 17³), 'Jesus is the Son of God' (Ac 9²⁰), 'He died for our sins according to the scriptures' (1 Co 15³), 'Christ rose from the dead the third day' (1 Co 15⁴), 'The Lord is at hand' (Ja 5⁸, 1 P 4⁷). Many of these occur in Pauline contexts, but in such a way as to show that St. Paul took them over from the common stock of Christian teaching. He no doubt added to and expanded these simple formulæ. In his hands they became a theology—not exactly a system, in the sense in which (*e.g.*) Aristotle's *Ethics* or Calvin's *Institutes* are systems ; for such coherent logical construction is alien to the Semitic mind, and St. Paul was thoroughly Semitic—but yet, at least, a body of reasoned and elaborated doctrines. In other words, the teaching of St. Paul is a great constructive effort of thought.

2. *Place of theology in religion.*—Now it is also true that at the present day, in certain wide circles, theology in this technical sense has a bad name. It is regarded as something hard, cold, and formal, possessing, perhaps, a certain relative truth for the age to which it belongs, but hardly beyond this, and in our own age only a stumbling-block and hindrance to religion.

But this is just one of those *idola tribûs* that exaggerate a certain element of truth so far as to make it untrue. Theology is a necessity of life—for the few, consciously ; for the many, unconsciously. It is like philosophy. Every man really has his philosophy, expressed or implied. It is inevitable that thought should play upon subjects of such supreme interest ; inevitable that it should try to formulate its beliefs, and to bring them into relation with one another. And if it does not do this upon right lines, it will do it upon wrong ones.

It is therefore a mistake to place theology, as religious thought, in contrast with religious feeling, and to call the one warm and living and the other cold and dead. It is the nature of feeling to be warm, and the nature of an intellectual process to be by comparison cold. But the two things should not be opposed to each other ; they rather supplement and complete each other. They appeal to different faculties ; the one supplies material for the other. Each without the other is wanting ; and it is together that they become an activity of the whole man.

3. *In the teaching of St. Paul there is no divorce between theology and religion.*—In the teaching of St. Paul there is certainly no lack of religious emotion. And it is not fair to concentrate attention upon one side of his teaching and to ignore the other. What can be more intense or more elevated than the feeling of Ro 8³¹⁻³⁹, or more exquisitely delicate than that of 1 Co 13? And passages like the first of these and Ro 11³³⁻³⁶ are striking examples of the way in which theological thought supplies the ground for, and passes into, religious emotion. The controversial argument of Gal. is not the most attractive part of the Apostle's writings; but how lovely are the pictures of Gal 5²²· ²³ 6¹· ²! And yet these pictures are in closest contact with his theology. Indeed, the sustained enthusiasm which is so characteristic of the Apostle is kindled directly by his convictions (2 Co 5¹⁴, Ro 5¹⁻¹¹).

II. Data of St. Paul's theology.—St. Paul's theology, then, was an effort of intellectual construction. And the first question that meets us is, What had he to build with?

1. *Old Testament.*—Like his Master, St. Paul had behind him the OT as an authoritative volume, a sacred book. He was himself to bear a part in laying the foundation of another sacred book; but this, after all, was but a second volume in continuation of the first, and which in course of time came to be placed upon the same level with it. The OT was the religious authority from which all Christians alike started. And yet new conditions had to be met in new ways. The Master boldly laid down a new law: 'Ye have heard that it was said to them of old time . . . but I say unto you' (Mt 5²¹ᶠ· etc.). The disciple could not do this; but when, at a critical stage in his career, he found himself in collision with the letter of the older Scriptures, he showed great skill in turning the edge of the arguments directed against him, by the use of current methods of interpretation.

2. *Contemporary Judaism, Rabbinical and Apocalyptic.* — Generally speaking, the Apostle was in regard to the interpretation of the OT at the common level of his time. But he rose above this through his superior insight and strong grasp of religious principle. The OT really was a revelation from God and the work of inspired men; and by virtue of his essential kinship with these St. Paul was able to elicit from it deeper truth than his contemporaries. His methods are not exactly those which the Christian exegete of to-day cannot help adopting; but, as he had the heart of the matter, and the OT writers also had in their measure the heart of the matter, his interpretations are really in harmony with all that was best in them. We might take as an example his treatment of Abraham's faith. There are in the OT the two elements of Law and Faith; and their ultimate relation to each other in the counsels of God is not really different from that which St. Paul made it to be.

It was not, however, purely a question of interpretation. On the common basis of the OT, the contemporaries of St. Paul had developed a number of inferences and ideas which the Apostle began by sharing with them. We may distinguish—not sharply, and as though they were mutually exclusive, but rather as at one time in alliance and at another in opposition—two main streams, the Rabbinical and the Apocalyptic. From the second century of our era onwards the former became more and more dominant, while the latter dropped into the background. And, even in the time of St. Paul, the official classes inclined strongly to Rabbinism; it was chiefly the freer speculation of the time that took the shape which is found in the Apocalypses. On both sides, along with much that was arid or fantastic, there was also not a little that was penetrating and beautiful: witness the *Pirke Aboth* on the one hand, and 4 Ezra and Apoc. Baruch on the other. St. Paul had at his command all this accumulated material, and he used it as it suited him. But he was not in bondage to it, and he applied it in connexion with root ideas that were peculiarly his own.

3. *The teaching and life of Christ.*—The touchstone that St. Paul applied to the current ideas of his day and generation was their bearing upon his own intense faith in Christ. Those which proved capable of assimilation to this he retained and worked into his own teaching; those which were not capable of assimilation he simply let drop.

We have spoken of faith in Christ; it is a further question how far this faith is related to detailed knowledge of Christ's life and teaching. We shall have to estimate the extent of this presently. For the moment we need only note that, whether in greater or less degree, St. Paul must have had some such knowledge, and that knowledge must have played some part in the construction of his theology.

4. *Palestinian traditions.*—Nearly all his knowledge of Christ must have come to St. Paul mediately, and not immediately. It seems a natural inference from 2 Co 5¹⁶ that the Apostle had at least had sight of Jesus during His lifetime; but it can hardly have been more than this, or his self-accusations would have been even more bitter than they were. We are coming very soon to the question of the information about Christ which St. Paul derived from others. But, besides this, there must have been in any case those simple formulæ to which we have already referred, in which the first disciples summed up their fundamental beliefs. We shall see later how St. Paul dealt with these; but they must at least have formed the starting-point of his own more adventurous and developed thinking.

III. Genesis of St. Paul's theology.—We have seen what were the materials that St. Paul had to work upon. The other leading factor that gave shape to his thoughts was the subjective habit and attitude that he brought to bear upon these materials. On this head, too, there are some remarks to be made.

1. *St. Paul not an immediate disciple of Christ.* —No doubt it is an important fact, and from one point of view a defect and loss, that St. Paul had not been a personal companion of Christ. And yet, when we look a little further, we can see a certain appropriateness that he should have come upon the stage as he did, and at the point where he did. Christianity consists not only in a particular body of teaching, but also in the working of great spiritual forces that flow from the incarnation of Jesus Christ. That is to say, it includes not only the teaching of Christ, but an estimate, or apprehension, of His Person and work.

From this side it was not altogether a disqualification that the Apostle's outlook should be directed forwards rather than backwards. The principle of Tennyson's well-known lines holds good, that the past does not present itself in a complete and rounded form to those who are actually moving in it. So we may well believe that the first disciples were for a time immersed in the details of their own recollections, and that their grasp on the whole as a whole was weaker in consequence. In proportion as St. Paul was less involved in such concrete details, his grasp on the central idea of his faith seems to have been all the stronger. This may seem at first sight paradoxical; but there are paradoxes in the use which God makes of His instruments. There was a sense in which the knowledge of Christ after the flesh hindered rather than helped the apprehension of Him according to the spirit.

2. *His temperament and training.*—St. Paul was not one of those who need for their mental sustenance a great wealth of concrete details. He had the gift of religious imagination, to fill out an idea or an impression and convert it into a powerful motive. So the vision on the road to Damascus held his fascinated gaze throughout his career. It worked ceaselessly within, and dominated all his thinking.

And then we have to remember that according to the standards of his time St. Paul was highly educated. His bent was intellectual, and it was encouraged by his training. When he sat at the feet of Gamaliel, he must have heard problems discussed like the faith of Abraham, to which we have already referred, or the origin of evil desire in connexion with the Fall of man. These active discussions took with him the place that books do with us. St. Paul was learned as his age counted learning, and he could not help treating the questions that arose after the manner of the learned.

3. *Spiritual experience.*—But a deeper influence than learning was his own spiritual experience. Continually we see this living experience reflected in what comes to us as doctrine. St. Paul taught what he had first felt, and he verified his teaching by experience. We shall naturally illustrate this when we come to speak of his theology more in detail.

4. *The teaching of history.*—At the same time St. Paul was not a mere student, but an active missionary, who soon came to be burdened with 'the care of all the churches.' He had something else to do besides following the logic of his own thought. The controversy with the Judaizers was one important episode in his life: and this had a great influence upon the form which his teaching took while it was going on.

Later on, when the victory was won, when the free admission of the Gentiles was secured and Jewish churches and Gentile churches stood over against each other on an equal footing, the Apostle is able to see the Divine purpose running through the alternate acceptance and rejection, and to map out the periods of history as the balance swayed now to one side and now to the other. The letters of St. Paul all bear traces, more or less distinct, of the occasions which called them forth. If, as we believe, the Pastoral Epistles are his, their different tone and style can only be accounted for by the special object with which they were written.

For the sake of clearness we have tried to distinguish the particular causes that contributed to make the theology of St. Paul what it is. But because we have singled out these causes, we of course do not suppose that only one was at work at a time. Very often two or more were at work together, subtly blended and passing into each other. The abstract distinctions that the mind creates always have about them something artificial; and yet history becomes clearer when the process of analysis precedes that of synthesis.

IV. St. Paul's knowledge of Christ.—We now come to the direct question, What means had St. Paul of knowing about Jesus, and what did he know? We will take the latter half of this question first, as being the less speculative, and as helping us to answer the first.

1. *Extent of his knowledge.*—We are speaking now of the historical Jesus, and not of the glorified Christ. And here we are met at the outset by exaggerated statements, that St. Paul had little or no interest in the historical Jesus, and knew little or nothing about Him. It is coming to be seen that these statements are exaggerated, and in recent years allowance is being made for knowledge on a considerably larger scale than used to be the case (see, for instance, the opinions

mentioned by Knowling, *The Testimony of St. Paul to Christ,* pp. 201–204, 503–518). There are, however, certain points that we are obliged to leave undecided.

(i.) The most important of these has reference to the two well-known passages in which St. Paul appears to show detailed knowledge—1 Co 11[23-25] (the institution of the Lord's Supper) and 15[3-8] (the appearances after the Resurrection). Are these passages to be treated as just samples of St. Paul's ordinary knowledge—so that he might, if he had pleased, have described other incidents in the Lord's life with equal fulness and precision? Or are we to take these two specimens of detailed information as something altogether exceptional and abnormal? For ourselves, we believe that the first alternative is far nearer the truth than the second. The very precision with which the Apostle writes looks as if he were drawing from a well furnished store. On the other hand, the paucity of the references proves hardly anything. There is frequently something that will seem to be capricious in our experience of such matters—the proportion in which a writer quotes what he might have quoted. We have to remember that, if this one Epistle had chanced not to survive, we should have had no evidence that St. Paul possessed detailed knowledge of this kind at all. This, then, is our own belief; but at the same time, if it is questioned, we cannot profess to make it good to demonstration.

(ii.) We note further that there are express appeals to 'words of the Lord' in 1 Co 7[10] and 9[14]. Besides these, there are coincidences of expression so striking as almost to amount to quotation in Ro 12[14], 1 Co 4[12. 13] 6[5] 12[2. 3].

(iii.) Again, St. Paul shows a marked insight into the character of Jesus as it is described in the Gospels. He singles out exactly those traits ('the meekness and gentleness of Christ,' 2 Co 10[1]) which the Jesus of the Gospels took as characteristic of Himself ('Take my yoke upon you, and learn of me; for I am meek and lowly in heart,' Mt 11[29]). Other allusions point in the same direction (*e.g.* Ph 2[5-8]).

(iv.) Really this insight into the character of Christ is part of a phenomenon that strikes us on a larger scale. The hortatory passages of St. Paul's Epistles show that he understood to a nicety the new religious ideal introduced by Christ. The ideal was really a new one. The nearest approach to it was that of 'the poor' in the Psalter, 'the poor in spirit' of the Gospel (Mt 5[3]). But even these were not free from vindictiveness; they were not prepared to say, 'Love your enemies, and pray for them that persecute you,' or 'If thine enemy hunger, feed him; if he thirst, give him to drink' (Mt 5[44], Ro 12[20]). It is not merely a question of verbal parallelism; the whole conception is really the same. It could not be more perfectly delineated than it is in 1 Co 13. When it is contended (as it is, *e.g.*, by Wrede, *Paulus,* p. 91) that St. Paul is thinking mainly of those who are brethren in the faith, that is really not the case; his exhortations are in no way confined to the relations of the brethren to one another.

2. *Sources of this knowledge.*—That there is a real connexion, and a close connexion, between the ideal laid down by Christ and that inculcated by St. Paul cannot be denied; it is really one and the same. How did St. Paul acquire the knowledge of it? He must have done so in no merely transient manner; he must have had the ideal so completely set before him that it sank deep into his soul.

(i.) In spite of the independence which he claims for himself, we know that St. Paul had long and familiar intercourse with disciples, like Barnabas and Mark, and with others in the church at Antioch (Ac 13^1), who could not fail to instruct him as to what was new and distinctive in the teaching of Christ. In Gal 1^{18} he speaks of himself as paying a visit to Peter at Jerusalem and spending a fortnight in his company. Both there and in Gal 2^2 a considerable comparing of notes seems to be implied. There are sufficient indications of oral intercourse between St. Paul and the older disciples to explain the knowledge which he evidently possessed.

(ii.) Had he, in addition to this, anything in writing that he could refer to? He cannot have had access to our present Gospels; but is it not possible that he may have had in his hands one or other of the documents out of which our present Gospels are composed? The Mark-Gospel is excluded by its date; but not so the second main document, often called *Logia*, and now generally known by the symbol Q. There is nothing, so far as we can see, in this document to make it impossible for St. Paul to have had the opportunity of consulting it. If we are right in forming our conception of it from the passages common to St. Matthew and St. Luke that are not found in St. Mark, it would be a work of precisely such a character as would bring out clearly the new moral ideal taught by Christ. We may well believe that this was really the object with which it was composed — that it was a manual for Christian missionaries to put into the hands of their converts as supplying them with a rule of life. The principal argument against this view is that, if it was early enough to be used by St. Paul, it is difficult to see why it should not have been used by St. Mark. Some scholars think that it was used by him, but we should not like to commit ourselves to that alternative. The question must be left open.

On the other hand, the markedly individual character of the two chief specimens of the Pauline tradition, as compared with the Gospels, would go to show that the sources from which he drew were distinct from those used by our present Evangelists.

V. Outlines of the Pauline theology.—As we have already implied, the great and central event in St. Paul's career was his conversion. It is this that really gives the key to his theology. It determined for him at once his conception of Christ, and the nature of his own response to the appeal which Christ made to him.

1. *The glorified Christ.*—The vision that he saw was of Christ glorified. In other words, Christ appeared to him as Spirit; and it is this spiritual Christ that henceforth controlled his experience. And yet, not that alone. The glorified Christ was none the less identical with the crucified Jesus of Nazareth. It is in this double aspect that the exalted Form that he saw made such an intense impression upon the Apostle.

2. *Christ within.*—The vision was for *him*; it appealed personally and directly to him; and he responded with all the ardour of his being. It was as if he clasped to his heart the image of Christ that he saw, and it entered into him and possessed him. Or, conversely, it might be said that the extended arms of the Christ whom he saw embraced and enfolded himself. These two ways of speaking St. Paul always treats as equivalent—to say that he clasped Christ or that Christ clasped him, that he was 'in Christ' or that Christ was 'in him,' meant the same thing. The same act had a Divine side and a human; and the one corresponded to the other. The process of which the Apostle was conscious in himself had to be repeated in his converts (Gal 4^{19}). It is all a way of expressing the closest appropriation, assimilation, and union.

3. *Faith.*—In another connexion St. Paul calls the act by which he entered into this relation 'faith.' This act of faith could be expressed intellectually as assent to the proposition that 'Jesus is the Christ,' or that 'Jesus is Lord.' But any such process of the intellect was swallowed up at once in the warmer emotion of loyalty, gratitude, and adoring love. We must think of it always as love for One who is in heaven and not on earth, and therefore as at one and the same time love and adoration. It is this which gives its peculiar quality and value to 'faith,' as St. Paul conceived it. The impression that the Apostle received was so overpowering, that it seemed to make his whole life a different thing; 'a new creation,' he called it himself (Gal 6^{15}); 'the life which I now live in the flesh, I live by the faith of the Son of God, who loved me, and gave himself for me' (2^{20}).

4. *The death of Christ.*—We go back to the Damascus vision. It was proof that Jesus of Nazareth, whose followers the Apostle in his blindness had persecuted, was no mere ambitious pretender, but all that His disciples believed Him to be—both Lord and Christ. But if that was so, the apparently shameful death that He died could not be really shameful: whatever appearance it wore in the eyes of men, there must really be in it a Divine virtue—a virtue infinite, because Divine.

Already in the infant Church, following, as we believe, hints of the Lord Himself, there was a tendency to explain the death of the Crucified by means of principles inherent in the OT, by the idea of sacrifice and by the idea of vicarious suffering; on the one hand, by the analogy of the Levitical sacrifices, and, on the other hand, by the description of the Servant of Jahweh in Deutero-Isaiah. St. Paul took up these ideas, and worked them out in his own manner: the sacrificial idea, especially in Ro 3^{25} 5^9, 1 Co 5^7 (cf. He 9^{22}); the vicarious idea, esp. in 2 Co 5^{21}. St. Paul also added a new explanation of his own in Gal 3^{13}. This last might be described as somewhat Rabbinical; but the same cannot be said of the other two. The principles of sacrifice and of vicariousness are deeply impressed upon God's world; and that they should culminate in a supreme act of self-devotion has in it nothing incredible.

5. *Justification and reconciliation.*—The death of Christ established a new relation between God and man. It established it, as it were, objectively and ideally. For it to take full effect, man had to do his part; he had to realize the new relation in a reformed and regenerate life. But the Christian was allowed to anticipate this. He had not to wait for the Divine forgiveness, which was vouchsafed to him at once as soon as he became a Christian and was launched upon that career of amendment and advance to which as a Christian he was pledged. St. Paul uses a judicial term, and describes the convert from the first as 'justified,' *i.e.* 'declared righteous' or 'acquitted.' This is the Divine answer to the faith by which he makes his profession and has it sealed by baptism. By this decisive act the Christian enters at once into the circle of the Divine favour; he is received as a son reconciled to his Heavenly Father, as a prodigal returned. Henceforth his course is not one of weary effort and failure, but the way is smoothed for him and brightened by the Father's love.

This was one way of describing the process. Another way turned round St. Paul's characteristic manner of conceiving the relation of the Christian to Christ of which we have spoken. We have said that in St. Paul's own experience the vision of the exalted Christ was, as it were, clasped to his heart. The act was so intense and so absorbing that it amounted to a kind of identification: 'No longer I, but Christ liveth in me.' And yet this ideal

Christ still wears the features of the historical Christ. It is the Christ who died and rose again. The Christian who is identified with such a Christ must himself also die and rise again—in such sense as he can, *i.e.* in a moral and religious sense; he must die to sin, and rise again to newness of life (Ro 6[1-11]); he must emerge from the imprisonment in which he is held by sin into the free and spacious life of the Spirit (see below).

6. *Law and grace.*—In his earlier experience, religion for St. Paul, as for the rest of his countrymen, meant primarily obedience to law; to be righteous was to keep the Law. But that was really an impossible task. The Law might command, but it could not secure performance. Human nature was too weak to keep up obedience to its rigorous behests. In the multitude of rules and precepts there were always some that were neglected. And to break the Law in any degree was to break it, and to forfeit the reward of well-doing.

It was otherwise with the service of Christ. Here the motive was personal loyalty and devotion, carried out under the conditions which have just been described, with the assurance of forgiveness, of Divine favour and Divine aid. Thus, whatever might be its outward conditions, the life of the Christian was one of inward joy and peace.

An incidental consequence of this new experience was that in his controversy with the Judaizers St. Paul was able to take his stand upon a broad ground of principle. He was able to contrast Christianity with Judaism as a higher type of religion, as a reign of Grace over against a reign of Law.

7. *Developed Christology.*—At this point we may turn to consider St. Paul's contribution to the Christian doctrine of God. So far as Christianity brought a change in this doctrine, it all arose from the recognition of the Divine nature and mission of Christ, and from the further consequences which that recognition brought with it. Jesus Himself had certainly come as the promised Messiah, though during His life on earth the full supernatural attributes of the Messiah were veiled and restrained. The Resurrection was the decisive proof that they were really there; and from that time onwards the little band of believers proclaimed openly the central article of its faith. It did so especially under the double title of Messiah and Son of God. St. Paul took over these titles in the full depth of their meaning. We have seen that for him the Messiah was especially the glorified Messiah. That was, indeed, since the Resurrection, essentially the case with all Christians, but St. Paul grasped his belief with peculiar intensity and concentration. Whereas, too, the title 'Son of God,' though literally and strictly meant, was used by the first disciples in a way that was naïve and unreflective, St. Paul evidently dwelt upon it, and pressed its full metaphysical meaning. He had clearly satisfied himself that the manifestations of Christ's Divine Sonship required nothing short of this. And then, as we might expect, he went on to make use of other terms that his speculative training naturally suggested, to illustrate and carry home the same fundamental idea.

8. *God the Father.*—There are three ways in which St. Paul adds to the doctrine of God the Father: (i.) By discriminating and correlating the spheres of Him whom we call God the Father and of Him whom we call God the Son. The designations were already current, and the tendency to discriminate or define all grew out of the Incarnation. There is not much set teaching, but there are many side allusions which testify to considerable activity of thought on the subject.—(ii.) By calling attention to the work of the Son as revealing the character of the Father. The whole scheme (so to speak) of the Incarnation proceeds from the Father, and therefore itself bears witness, more direct and more unmistakable than any other, to the love which underlies the dealings of God with man—to the love not only of the Son who becomes incarnate and who suffers for human sin, but also to that of the Father who sent Him (Ro 5[8], 2 Co 5[13. 14. 17. 18], Col 1[19. 20]).—(iii.) By marking out in a sort of broad chronology the periods of the world's history (Ro 9–11, 1 Co 15[20-28]). It is, no doubt, possible to press particular expressions (such as Ro 9[17. 18]) in such a way as to make them conflict both with the free will of man and with the justice of God. That was not at all the Apostle's intention, but only to enforce that strong sense of a providential ordering of successive events which must be felt by every religious mind.

9. *The Holy Spirit.*—The belief in the Holy Spirit was just shared by St. Paul with his fellow-Christians. The remarkable phenomena which they saw around them—prophecy, speaking with tongues, exorcisms, and the like—were all in the language of the time naturally referred to His activity. St. Paul did but adopt this language, and then perhaps extend it, more than his neighbours were in the habit of doing, to phenomena that were less extraordinary but more deeply related to the moral and religious life (we remember that 1 Co 13 comes in the midst of a long passage dealing with gifts of the Spirit). It is noticeable that he—not alone, but in company (*e.g.*) with Lk. in Ac 16[7] (RV)—expressly associates the Spirit, not only with God, but with Christ (Ro 8[9]).

10. *The Church and the Sacraments.* —It was obvious and natural that the blessings brought by Christ must hold good in the first instance for those who rallied to the cause of Christ, and ratified their adhesion to Him by confession and baptism. The society so formed could not but start with a position of privilege analogous to that of the Jewish Church under the old dispensation. But neither under the one dispensation nor under the other was that position of privilege given only to be selfishly enjoyed. For the OT see Is 2[2-4] 11[10] 19[18-25] 42[1-7] 49[6], Mic 4[1-3] etc. It was just an instance of 'the purpose of God according to selection.' The recipients of it were to be missionaries who were to carry the gospel to the end of the world.

This was always the ulterior object with which Christians were to use and enjoy their privileges (Ro 11[28] 10[12-15]). They might enjoy them, but they were bound to do what in them lay to spread them. Therefore, when St. Paul enlarges upon the felicity of being a Christian (*e.g.* in Ro 5[1-11]), it is in no spirit of narrowness or exclusiveness, but rather the contrary (as appears from ch. 11). The exhortations to the Church to organize itself as efficiently as possible, and to prosecute the Christian life to the uttermost, must all be taken with this tacit condition.

The two Sacraments belong to the internal organization of the Church. They are neither of them due to the initiation of St. Paul. He found them in existence, and he fully accepted them, and from time to time he dwells upon them in such a way as to show that he was well aware of their significance and value. St. Paul distinctly recognizes them as means of grace essential to the life of Christians. We cannot at all accept the view that he was the first to introduce repeated acts of communion; 1 Co 11[25. 26] implies that he found it a regular practice.

11. *The Last Things.*—The Epp. supply an important part of the evidence that the element of eschatology in the teaching of Christ, and in His own conception of Himself, was as large as we find it in the Gospels. In proportion as we go back in time to the earliest Epp., this element is seen at its greatest. In 1 and 2 Thess. it is the main topic, and in 1 Cor. it is very prominent. It became less so as time went on, but even in the latest period it does not wholly disappear (Ph 4⁵).

The Pauline Epp. are even more important still from the part that they play in covering the transition from a form of Christianity in which eschatology is prominent, to one in which it has fallen into the background. In the later Epp. the basis of Christianity has been silently shifted; its foundations have been 'underpinned' by doctrines of more permanent applicability—esp. by the stress that is laid upon the working of the glorified Christ or the Spirit of Christ.

VI. Comparison with the teaching of Christ.—We are now in a better position to take a *coup d'œil* of the relation of St. Paul's mission and teaching as a whole to that of his Master. It has been rightly observed by more than one of those who have treated of the subject (see Knowling, *Testimony of St. Paul to Christ*, p. 514), that the Gospel of St. Paul begins where the earthly life of Jesus ends. The *dictum* needs some qualification (as we have seen); but it is in the main true. It means that the elaborate Pauline theology is of the nature of a development, so that what we have to consider is how and in what sense it is a development.

1. *The teaching of Jesus presupposed.*—That this was the case, we may see (i.) from the easy and natural allusions to the character of Christ and the Christian ideal (§§ IV. 1. (iii.) (iv.) above); (ii.) from the general position in the earlier Epp. on the subject of eschatology, which directly continues the attitude described in the Gospels; (iii.) and, in particular, from the conception of the 'Kingdom of God.' This last point is so important that we must give it a section to itself.

2. *The Kingdom of God in St. Paul.*—There is no exposition of the idea of the Kingdom; it is taken for granted as well known. There are several examples in Epp. of all dates in which the phrase is used in its ordinary future sense: *e.g.* Gal 5²¹, 1 Co 6⁹ᶠ·, Eph 5⁵. Similar to these is the use in 1 Th 2¹². But by the side of these are other passages in which the Kingdom is evidently present. Such would be: 1 Co 4²⁰ 'the kingdom of God is not in word, but in power'; in Col 1¹³· ¹⁴ it is the sphere of present forgiveness into which the Christian is translated; in Col 4¹¹ it has reference to the work of missions. But most significant of all is Ro 14¹⁷ 'the kingdom of God is not eating and drinking, but righteousness and peace and joy in the Holy Ghost.' Here the Kingdom is entirely a present idea, and it seems to cover the whole range of the gospel. Nothing could better mark the transition spoken of above.

3. *Pauline developments.*—So far, the teaching of St. Paul has been just a continuation of the teaching of Christ. But in the outlines of his theology which have been sketched above it will have been seen that there is much which goes beyond this. This developed teaching has reference primarily and especially to the conception of the Person of Christ. Another new element is the elaborate psychological analysis of the process of belief, and generally of the Christian habit of mind. And lastly, as we have seen, there is certain special teaching that has grown out of the circumstances of the time.

4. *Origin of the developments.*—It would be an utter mistake to suppose that St. Paul's teaching as to the Person of Christ was a new invention of his own. We have seen that it was really nothing more than a further analysis of the meaning contained in the simple doctrinal formulæ of the primitive Church: such as that 'Jesus is Lord,' 'Jesus is the Christ,' 'Jesus is the Son of God.' It would be equally an utter mistake to imagine that the primitive Church was going against the will of Jesus Himself. There are indications enough that it was in no sense doing this. The only thing that has given any colour to such an idea is the great reticence and reserve that our Lord showed in putting forward His claims. There is something of a problem in this. But that Jesus knew Himself to be both Messiah and Son, we may regard as quite certain.

It is true that St. Paul reflected upon these titles, and true that in all his teaching his own experience entered as a shaping force; but it is just that fact which gives to his teaching such depth of reality.

VII. Legitimacy of the Pauline construction.—It may be said, not without truth, by way of discounting these Pauline developments: (i.) that the methods of argument by which they are supported, especially the exegetical methods, are not always what we should consider valid; (ii.) that the personal experience on which they rest is exceptional and peculiar; and (iii.) that, in like manner, the conditions of early Christian history by which they were shaped necessarily had about them something relative and transient.

But, on the other hand: (i.) few propositions are more true than the proverbial one, that conclusions are often more right than the explicit reasoning that leads up to them. Methods of proof are often of the nature of a scaffolding the real purpose of which is to set up a construction in presentable shape, when it verifies itself after the fact by its own inherent properties in the experimental field of life.

(ii.) It is not to be denied that the personal experience of St. Paul has in it much that is exceptional and peculiar. But that is far more because of its penetrating intensity along lines that are common to lesser men, than because there is in it anything eccentric that disqualifies his experience from representing theirs. In other words, St. Paul was a religious genius of the highest order that human nature has ever produced—in the same category with the writer whom we call Second Isaiah, with Jeremiah, with many of the Psalmists, with St. John, and at a later date with that astonishing genius, St. Augustine. We believe that men like these were specially raised up by God, and endowed by His Spirit with many marvellous gifts, for the express purpose of pointing out the way in which the crowd of religious people may follow, of setting before them an ideal after the heights and depths of which they may strive. We have only to think of the consummate beauty of the chapter on Charity, which, after all, is but the culmination of other passages that are strewn thick over the hortatory portions of the Epistles; and to remember, along with this, that such passages do but translate the theoretic side of theology into the activities of daily life.

(iii.) It might be said of each of the foregoing heads, and it may be said specially of that which turns upon the relativity of the teaching that emerges from history, that at most the objection does but amount to this, that the theology of St. Paul, so far as it rests on the grounds enumerated, is subject to the conditions of all things human. All things human are relative, and relative, in particular, to the age to which they belong. But in this class at least of things human, while there is the perishable envelope which is inevitably stripped off by time, there is no less something permanent as well, a permanent residuum or deposit —not always definable in words, but very real and very precious—which passes on into all the ages that follow. This we believe to be true pre-eminently of the first age of Christianity, and true, in particular, in a very high degree of the teaching of St. Paul. The world since his day—and not the Christian world alone—has drawn sustenance from it to an extent of which it is probable that, with all its eulogies of the Apostle, it has never been fully aware. There is a large ingredient of Pauline teaching in the very life-blood that courses in a Christian's veins.

LITERATURE.—The subject of St. Paul in his relation to Christ has been much discussed in recent years, and that on critical and modern lines. The larger works are : Feine, *Jesus Christus und Paulus* (1902) ; Goguel, *L'Apôtre Paul et Jésus-Christ* (1904) ; and in English, Knowling, *Witness of the Epistles* (1892), and *The Testimony of St. Paul to Christ* (1905). Dr. Knowling's two books are written with exhaustive knowledge, and with his invariable lucidity and accuracy of statement and admirable temper ; they cover a wide extent of surface, and all that can be said on the other side is that, perhaps owing to some defect of construction, they may seem to be more upon the surface than they really are. There is a crowd of smaller tracts and articles, for the most part dating from the last two or three years. Among these may be mentioned : H. J. Holtzmann, 'Jesus und Paulus' in *Prot. Monatschrift* (1900) ; Kölbing, *Die gtistige Einwirkung der Person Jesus auf Paulus* (1906) ; Wrede, *Paulus* [2] (1907) Jülicher, *Paulus und Jesus* (1907) [both in the series of *Religions-geschichtliche Volksbücher*] ; Julius Kaftan, *Jesus und Paulus* (1906) ; and Arnold Meyer, *Wer hat das Christenthum begründet ; Jesus oder Paulus?* (1907). Of these, the writer thinks that he has derived most from the two tracts of Wrede and Jülicher—from Wrede in a negative sense, and from Jülicher in a positive. Wrede has constituted himself a sort of *advocatus diaboli* in the case of St. Paul : his writings are all marked by very great sincerity ; and his sincerity takes the form of bringing all the objections that the natural man of the twentieth century might be moved to bring. Wrede's striking career was cut short somewhat abruptly on 23rd Nov. 1906. Jülicher's pamphlet the writer believes to be one of the very best productions of its author ; when allowance is made for the point of view, it is full of sympathy and insight. Kaftan is also very good, but not quite so good in the second part of his little treatise as in the first. The anon. work, *The Fifth Gospel: being the Pauline Interpretation of the Christ* (1907), and Du Bose, *The Gosp. acc. to St. Paul* (1907), may also be recommended.

W. SANDAY.

INDEXES

I. INDEX OF SUBJECTS

II. INDEX OF GREEK TERMS

———◆———

ἀγαλλιᾶν, i. 903[a].
ἀγαπητός, i. 188[b].
ἄγγελος, ii. 605[a].
ἁγιάζειν, i. 366[a, b], 700[b].
ἁγιασμός, ii. 561[b].
ἅγιος, i. 728[a] ff., 730[b]; ii. 550[a], 605[b].
ἁγνός, ἁγνίζω, i. 728[b]; ii. 459[a].
ἀγρός, i. 591[a].
ἀγωνία, i. 36[b].
ἀδελφός, ii. 605[b].
ἄδολος, ii. 635[a].
ἄθεσμος, ii. 821[b].
ἀθετεῖν, i. 453[b].
αἰγιαλός, i. 176[a].
αἰδώς, ii. 619[a].
αἷμα, ii. 605[b].
αἰνεῖν, i. 211[a].
αἰσχύνη, ii. 618[a].
αἰών, αἰώνιος, i. 540[a], 787[a]; ii. 376[a], 605[b], 839[a].
ἀλάβαστρος, -ον, i. 41[b].
ἀλήθεια, -ής, -ινός, i. 570[b], 892[b]; ii. 768[b], 801[b].
ἁμάρτημα, i. 788[a].
ἁμαρτωλός, ii. 639[b] f.
ἀμνός, ii. 620[a].
ἀμφίβληστρον, ii. 241[b].
ἀνάγαιον, ii. 788[b].
ἀνάθεμα, i. 404[b].
ἀναίδεια, i. 793[a].
ἀνάμνησις, ii. 74[a].
ἀνάπαυσις, ii. 500[a].
ἀνάστασις, ii. 605[b].
ἀνατολή, i. 425[a].
ἀναφέρω, ii. 605[b].
ἄνοια, ii. 96[a].
ἄνομος, ii. 821[b].
ἀντλεῖν, ii. 815[a].
ἀπαρνέομαι, ii. 598[b].
ἀπαύγασμα, i. 97[b].
ἀπιστία, -έω, ii. 775[a].
ἁπλοῦς, -ότης, i. 589[a]; ii. 628[b].
ἀποθνήσκειν, i. 791[b].
ἀποκαλύπτειν, -ψις, i. 79[b]; ii. 605[b].
ἀπόλλυμι, i. 791[a]; ii. 76[a], 554[a].
ἀπολυτρόω, -ύτρωσις, ii. 605[b].
ἀπορέω, i. 491[a].

ἀπόστολος, i. 105[b].
ἀπώλεια, i. 455[a], 791[b], 909[b]; ii. 813[b].
ἀργύριον, ii. 198[a].
ἀρετή, ii. 599[b].
ἀρχή, ii. 538[b].
ἀρχηγός, i. 271[a]; ii. 20[b], 419[a], 571[b].
ἄρχειν, ii. 538[b].
ἀρχιερεῖς, i. 297[b].
ἄρχων, ii. 419[a].
ἀστήρ, ἄστρον, ii. 674[b].
ἀσσάριον, ii. 200[b].
ἀσύνετος, ii. 778[b].
ἀσφαλής, i. 276[b].
ἀτιμία, ii. 619[a].
αὐξάνω, i. 693[a].
ἄφεσις, i. 437[b] f.; ii. 605[b].

βαπτίζω, i. 169[a]; ii. 605[b].
βάπτισμα, -μός, i. 168[b].
βάρος, i. 241[a].
βαστάζω, i. 908[b].
βάτος, i. 242[b] f.; ii. 729[a].
βαττα[-ο-]λογέω, ii. 499[b], 790[a].
βδέλυγμα τῆς ἐρημώσεως, i. 6[b].
βεβαιόω, i. 626[a]; ii. 605[b].
βέβηλος, -όω, ii. 422[b].
βιάζεται, ii. 803[b].
βίος, ii. 39[a].
βλασφημία, ii. 423[b].
βλέπω, i. 446[b]; ii. 596[a].
βόθυνος, ii. 367[b].
βόσκω, ii. 620[a].
βρέφος, i. 161[a], 823[a].

γαζοφυλάκιον, ii. 748[b].
γελάω, ii. 9[b].
γενεά, i. 639[b].
γενέσια, i. 208[b].
γεννάω, i. 182[b].
γίγνεσθαι, ii. 281[a].
γιγνώσκειν, ii. 778[b].
γλωσσόκομον, i. 167[b].
γογγύζω, ii. 211[a].
γράμματα, i. 202[a]; ii. 584[b] f.
γραφή, ii. 584[b] f.

δαιμόνιον, ii. 605[b].

δακρύειν, ii. 706[b].
δειλός, i. 381[a].
δευηύτης, ii. 55[a].
δευτερόπρωτον, i. 411[b]; ii. 541[b], 724[a].
δηνάριον, ii. 199[b].
διάβολος, ii. 605[b].
διαγογγύζω, ii. 211[a].
διαθήκη, i. 374[a]; ii. 717[a].
διάκονος, -εῖν, ii. 182[b], 613[a].
διακρίνεσθαι, i. 491[b].
διδασκαλία, i. 485[a].
διδαχή, i. 485[a].
δίκαιος, δικαιοσύνη, i. 915[b]; ii. 529[a], 606[a].
δικαίωμα, ii. 283[a].
δίκτυον, ii. 241[b].
διστάζειν, i. 491[a].
δοκός, i. 176[a].
δόξα, -άζω, i. 648[b], 892[b]; ii. 606[a], 621[b].
δοῦλος, i. 221[a]; ii. 613[a].
δραχμή, δίδραχμον, ii. 200[a].
δυνάμεις, ii. 188[a].
δύναμις, i. 607[a].
δυνάστης, ii. 419[a].
δωρεάν, i. 647[a].

ἐθνικός, ii. 606[a].
ἔθνος, ii. 229[a], 606[a].
εἴδωλον, ii. 606[a].
εἰλικρινής, ii. 635[a].
εἰρήνη, ii. 330[b].
εἰς, i. 795[b].
ἐκκλησία, i. 329[b], 560[a]; ii. 606[a].
ἐκλέγειν, i. 307[b].
ἐκλεκτός, i. 308[a], 511[a]; ii. 606[a].
ἐκπλήσσομαι, i. 48[a], 131[b].
ἔλεος, i. 687[b].
Ἕλλην, Ἑλληνιστής, i. 691[a, b].
ἐμβριμᾶσθαι, i. 62[b].
ἐμφανίζω, ii. 112[b].
ἐν, i. 794[b].
ἐν τοῖς τοῦ πατρός μου, i. 228[a, b], 243[a, b].
ἐν Χριστῷ, i. 795[a]; ii. 403[a, b], 411[b], 565[a], 748[a].
ἐνέργεια, i. 607[a].

905

III. INDEX OF SCRIPTURE TEXTS